MACKENZIE, SELBY & HARRIS
HUNTER CHASERS &
POINT-TO-POINTERS
2005

FORTY-SIXTH EDITION

WEATHERBYS
CHASE

Every effort is made to ensure that the information contained in this book is as accurate as possible. Nevertheless, some errors are certain to occur and a few of the opinions expressed about the horses will prove to be incorrect (it would be foolish for anyone to expect otherwise).

A book of this nature that made no conclusions would be valueless, one that was invariably correct miraculous.

The conclusions are those of the writers only (mostly of Iain Mackenzie and Martin Harris), and our team of correspondents play no part in the preparation of the horse commentaries beyond supplying their excellent race comments.

ISBN 1-872437-27-3

Published by Weatherbys Chase Ltd
Stour House
Grove Road
Wimborne
Dorset BH21 1BW
Tel: Wimborne (01202) 888200
Fax: Wimborne (01202) 886090

Typeset by
Weatherbys Printing Services
Wellingborough, Northants

Printed and Bound by
Polestar Wheatons Limited, Exeter

Cover picture by
David Trundley

MACKENZIE, SELBY & HARRIS
HUNTER CHASERS & POINT-TO-POINTERS 2005

Editors

IAIN MACKENZIE
TERRY SELBY
MARTIN HARRIS

Contents

Acknowledgements . . . 7
Review of 2004
David Turner . . . 11
East Anglia . . . 13
Sandhurst . . . 17
Wessex . . . 18
Devon & Cornwall . . . 22
South Midlands . . . 26
Midlands . . . 27
West Midlands . . . 31
Welsh Borders . . . 33
South & West Wales . . . 35
North Western . . . 38
Northern . . . 39
Yorkshire . . . 41
South East . . . 44
The Top Horses of 2004 . . . 47
The Handicap 2004 . . . 47
Results of 2004 . . . 65
Runners in 2004 . . . 559
Point-to-Point Owners & Riders Association . . . 1065
Point-to-Point Secretaries Association . . . 1067
Point-to-Point Secretaries 2005 . . . 1069
Important Races - Hunter Chases . . . 1077
Important Races - Point-to-Point . . . 1083
Point-to-Point Courses . . . 1089
Quiz . . . 1120
Top Young Horses of 2004 . . . 1125
Champion Hunter Racing Sires . . . 1128
Leading Point-to-Point & Hunter Chase Sires 2004 . . . 1128
Sires of Point-to-Point & Hunter Chase Winners in 2004 . . . 1132
Most Prolific Winners 2004 . . . 1135
Leading Post-War Point-to-Point Riders . . . 1136
Champion Point-to-Point Riders . . . 1137
Leading Point-to-Point Riders 2004 . . . 1138
Winning and Placed Point-to-Point Riders 2004 . . . 1140
Winning and Placed Hunter Chase Riders 2004 . . . 1154
The Busiest Riders of 2004 . . . 1157
Leading Point-to-Point Owners 2004 . . . 1158
Horse & Hound Leading Horse . . . 1159
Top of the Handicap . . . 1160
Performance of the Handicap in 2004 Hunter Chases . . . 1161
Sales 2004 . . . 1162
Point-to-Point Race Statistics . . . 1165
Point-to-Point Runner Analysis . . . 1170
Index to Advertisers . . . 1170
Annual Statistical Summary . . . 1171
Analysis of Point-to-Point Winners by Sex & Age . . . 1172
Index to Point-to-Point Fixtures in 2005 . . . 1174
Point-to-Point Fixtures in 2005 . . . 1176
Jockey Club Enquiries 2004 . . . 1181
Index to Photographs . . . 1183

RACING POST
The paper for winners
Your best bet - every day

Acknowledgements

Together the writers of this book personally attended over 40 per cent of the 203 meetings held in 2004, but we relied on our nationwide team of correspondents to report the others.

The meetings they reported or areas covered were as follows:

Bob Bracher: South & West
Scott Brinded: ubiquitous, South East
David Coulton: North West
James Crispe (East Anglia)
Catriona Edwards: South & West Wales
David Gadian: Devon & Cornwall
Mark Johnson: Sandhurst
Peter Mansell (Andoversford),
John Milburn: Yorkshire
Lee & Myles McNulty: Northern
Jonathan Neesom: ubiquitous
Steve Payne: ubiquitous
John Rowden: South East
Granville Taylor: Somerset, Devon & Cornwall

We are very grateful to them all, and to **Edward Dingle** (United), and **Darren Owen** (Vale of Lune), and to the many others who covered meetings exclusively for *Racing Post* or *Talking Point*.

Especial thanks to our dear friends, **Hugh Condry** for most efficiently and professionally compiling the Review of 2004 and co-ordinating the weekly *Racing Post Weekender* reports, **Bob Bracher** for compiling the course details, doing the bulk of the proof-reading and providing our soon-to-close office in Wimborne, **David Trundley** for once again painting the dust jacket, **Jeanette Dawson** and **Keren** of the PPORA for being so careful of us and the sport, **Alex** for her skill and good humour (which will be even more important in 2005), and **Maurice Smith** for his unwavering support. Thank you to **Brian Armstrong** for sorting the photographs; to **Fraser**, **Vicky** and most welcome returnee, **Lucy** at Portman Square; to the Point-to-Point Secretaries and **Area PROs**, and to the staff at Wellingborough, particularly **Justyn**, **Sarah**, **Maggie** and **Anita** with our best wishes for the busy coming season. A most sad *au revoir* to **Gazza**, **Mo** and **Hel** of Gazelle Design with our grateful thanks for their total loyalty and dedication; and finally thank you to two very special people, **Marian** and **John Selby**, who are to losing their places in the new Norhants-based Weatherbys Chase operation; they have enormous experience and will not easily be replaced.

We gratefully acknowledge **Raceform**, Compton, Newbury RG20 6NL (01635 578101) and **Mike Barrett of Formcard**, Carrigtwohill Co Cork (00 353 21 613251) for allowng us to use their copyright material where necessary in the horse essays.

PHOTOGRAPHERS Please support our photographers, all will be happy to supply copies of their work reproduced herein, and many have large portfolios of other racing pictures:

Brian Armstrong, Pantiles, Penselwood, Wincanton, Somerset BA9 8NF (Tel/Fax: 01747-841059);
Baths Photographic, 11 Allhalland Street, Bideford, Devon EX39 2JD (Tel: 01237-479331);
Christopher Beasley c/o John Beasley, 30 Thistlebarrow Rd, Bournemouth, Dorset BH7 7AL (Tel/Fax:01202-309489);
Linda Charles, 16 Fulmar Drive, Hythe, Southampton SO45 3FZ (Tel: 02380 844948);
Tim Holt, 21 Tarratt Rd, Yeovil, Somerset BA20 2LJ (Tel: 01935-478982);
Liz Howard; **Carrie Janaway**, Bury Hill, Didmarton, Badminton, Avon GL9 1DX (Tel: 01454 238565);
Nick Jay, 1 Merriotsfield, Merriott, Crewkerne, Somerset TA16 5NH (Tel: 01460 78037);
David Jones, 47 Brynglas Avenue, Pontllanfraith, Blackwood, Gwent NP12 2DB (Tel: 01495 221246);
Adrian Long, TTL Video Productions, Bramble Cottage, Bremhill, nr Calne, Wilts SN11 9LD (Tel: 01249 814869);
Dr Alan Mitchell, 102 Redford Loan, Colinton, Edinburgh EH13 0AT (Tel: 01314-416711);
John & Kathleen Mullen, Aintree, 67 Chartist Way, Blackwood, Gwent NP2 1WH (Tel: 01495-227864);
Roy Parker, The Old Byre, Dale End, Hutton Buscel, Scarborough, Yorks YO13 9LR (Tel/Fax: 01273-862094).

David Turner

DAVID TURNER, who during 29 years in the racing saddle partnered more Point-to-Point winners than any other rider and was National Champion eight times, died 13 days before the start of the 2004 season. He was 59 and had finally lost a courageous battle with cancer lasting two and a half years.

In the 1970s and early '80s he was part of a team — together with his father, the inimitable Joe, and sister, Josie (now Mrs Sheppard) — which from its Ampton Hall base in Suffolk dominated East Anglian sport as well as the National Championships. Since his retirement, success has continued for the family — though on a lesser scale — using other riders, among them David and Rose's daughter Zoe, who won the PPORA's Wilkinson Sword as the leading under-21 Novice in her first season, 1992, and, after breaking her neck in a fall at Charing in 1996, returned to sweep up more East Anglian Ladies Championships, most recently in 2004.

Her father rode his first winner wearing the so-familiar navy blue and white colours on 33-1 outsider The Babe II at the Norwich Staghounds meeting in 1961. By the time he notched a final success, on even money favourite Pusharda at the Essex Farmers and Union in May 1989, he had accumulated no fewer than 345 victories. This figure (the 343 total accepted for the last 25 years was found to be incorrect after a recount) is a record which stands to this day. It might have been even more. He had been intending to ride for a 30th season in 1990 but retirement was forced when he sustained a broken pelvis in a training fall.

Turner's first National Championship was secured in 1970 and, after finishing third and then twice second in the ensuing three seasons, he went on to equal David Tatlow's achievement by winning the title in four consecutive years from 1974-77 (his sister took the equivalent Ladies award in the same seasons). Second again in 1978, he came back to be champion once more in 1979 and to share the top spot with Ian McKie the following year. Then, in 1984, his name was inscribed on the *Daily Telegraph* Cup for an eighth time.

His best season was 1977, when he rode 29 winners, and his 345 career tally came from 89 horses, all but nine of them family-owned. He helped Ampton to take the season's Leading Horse prize for five years in succession, with Master Vesuvius, Boy Bumble, Even Harmony and Hardcastle (twice). Numerically his biggest scorers were Culford Cottage (28 wins), Even Harmony (25), Hill Point (20) and Hardcastle (18). Apart from the notoriously lazy Hill Point, who always needed his special driving, these horses also won numerous races for his sister, while Even Harmony spent his last four seasons winning for new owner Andrew Berry, to reach an incredible 58 wins before he collapsed and died after contesting his 98th race.

Of Turner's 35 Hunter Chase victories, 23 were gained locally at Fakenham and another 10 at Folkestone. Most favoured Point-to-Point courses were near-to-home Marks Tey and Higham, where he landed 70 and 69 wins respectively, followed by Ampton and Horseheath with 40 apiece.

But if the championship was at stake the Turner box was always ready to roll. The 1980 title was shared with Ian McKie only after journeys on the last three Saturdays of the season (no Sundays in those days) to win five races at Llantwit Major, Bratton Down and Umberleigh, while it was a victory on Swarm at Umberleigh's finale meeting that took Turner one ahead of Peter Greenall in 1984 — the year of the mysterious 'Woodford walkover'.

At Woodford, a few weeks before Umberleigh, Turner had been declared to ride Laurel Hill at the Point-to-Point Owners Club meeting against a solitary opponent, Harringworth, when Laurel Hill's declaration was withdrawn (quite legally) and he replaced Caroline Saunders (now Bailey) on Harringworth to benefit from the resulting walkover.

Before his days of Point-to-Point fame Turner had gained no little success in the show jumping arena, graduating to horses after starting out on ponies and competing as far up the scale as the Horse of the Year Show. Following his retirement he continued to train the Ampton runners with his father and filled a steward's role at several of his local NH courses. He was elected to the Jockey Club in 2000.

Always hard to beat but always first to congratulate a successful rival, Turner's near-30 seasons in the racing saddle earned him a unique place in Point-to-Point history and the universal respect of his peers.

HC

REVIEW of 2004

by Hugh Condry

THE outstanding feature of what might otherwise have been a relatively run-of-the-mill season was the battle that raged from January to June for the Men Riders Championship between Ashley Farrant and the title-holder Richard Burton, during which both smashed the existing seasonal record of 43 wins set by Julian Pritchard five years earlier and both achieved their half-centuries.

That their absorbing contest should finally end in victory for Farrant, by 54 wins to 50, was begrudged by no-one, not even the most ardent Burton supporter, since this was to be Farrant's final season in the racing saddle after a career that had so often seen his title hopes dashed by injuries. He now intends to expand his training operation on the family farm near Bampton in Devon and goes into retirement from race-riding having accumulated 156 Point-to-Point winners since opening his account at the South Pool meeting in 1992 — when he was pupil-assistant to John Edwards and had already won 19 races under Rules.

His table-topping performance could never have been achieved without backing from the powerful stable of David Pipe, who, coincidentaly, has also announced that he is quitting the Point-to-Point scene. He provided no fewer than 42 of Farrant's winners, whereas Burton's successes were drawn from 17 different stables, top of the list being that of Sheila Crow, for whom he won a dozen races.

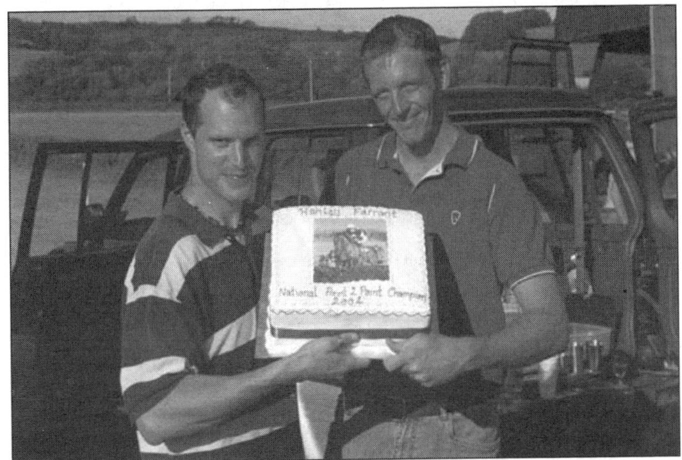

PLATE 1 Champion Rider, Ashley Farrant, left, and leading Trainer, David Pipe say it with icing
PHOTO: Brian Armstrong

Burton has also previously lost a championship chance through injury. In 2002 he was going strong up with leaders on 23 wins when a shoulder dislocated in a fall at the end of April effectively ended his campaign. His career tally now stands at 179 after 11 seasons and for him there will surely be further opportunities to regain the crown.

Both Farrant and Burton were at Cottenham for Hunt racing's earliest-ever start on January 4, though neither was among the winners as the Cambridgeshire Harriers Hunt Club staged the first meeting in the **EAST ANGLIAN** Area, which had suffered a double blow before the season's curtain went up. David Turner's death in December is recorded elsewhere but two months before that, as mentioned briefly in last year's annual, his brother-in-law Gurney Sheppard, for so long a leading figure in Point-to-Pointing and National Hunt racing, had died. Whether any lasting memorial to either or both men will be instituted remains to be seen, but the faithfully-observed silences at Cottenham on the first day and later at Ampton provided ample testimony to the esteem in which both were held.

Though Turner's death left a tragic gap in the family team, his father Joe, Master of Ampton Hall, again cantered away with the Leading Owner titles locally and nationally, winning 19 races with 10 horses, plus a Hunter Chase with one of them, Celtic Duke, while stable jockeys Jamie Owen and David's daughter Zoe retained the local points awards.

In February Zoe steered home the stable's first winner, Celtic Duke at Marks Tey — the course on which her father gained his greatest number of victories — and thereafter business continued much as usual for the Ampton horses, with a treble at the Granta Harriers, plus doubles at the Suffolk, the Essex and, for the third year running, at the Essex and Suffolk on Easter Saturday.

Zoe achieved a personal best of 11 wins, to which The Wiley Kalmuck and Spring Gale each contributed four, but perhaps the palm should go to Celtic Duke, whose three victories included a third consecutive success in in the Essex's Warwick Vase Ladies race and a repeat performance in the Eldred Wilson Hunter Chase at Fakenham in May.

This was the 16th time Joe Turner had won the Essandem Trophy presented for this Fakenham race, the successes having begun with Convoys in 1968 and 69. Culford Cottage (hat-trick), Hardcastle, Swarm, Barstick, Skygrange (twice), Dromin Leader (twice), Spring Gale and Corston Joker were others to precede Celtic Duke. Indeed, the family connection goes back even before Convoys, since David won the 1967 race on Dick Stennett's Prepotent.

Appropriately East Anglia's final race of 2004 — a Marks Tey Maiden — went to the Ampton seven-year-old On The Day, under Jamie Owen, who won again in Sussex the following week with Persian Hero before the Turner season ended at the annual PPORA Stratford lunch when Joe appeared almost reduced to tears when he was presented with the Weatherbys Chase Jim Mahon Industry Award for services to the sport.

Another lady rider to enjoy her best-ever campaign was Alex Embiricos, whose six successes included two Ladies Opens on the ex-Nicky Henderson-trained 10-year-old Placid Man. Last seen winning a Fontwell Beginners Chase in January 2003 — after appearing only once in the previous two years — Placid Man scored with almost contemptuous ease before winning a Fontwell Hunter Chase. Nick Moore then rode him to win another Hunter Chase at Warwick before being unseated two out when holding every chance in the Intrum Justitia Championship at Stratford.

Other winners for Embiricos included Highland Rose, who won three races at Cottenham — two of them Ladies Opens — Filou Du Bois, Conquistador and five-year-old Mr Hawkeye. The last-named, partnered by Moore, slaughtered a field of maidens on his only run at Higham on Easter Saturday before making 17,000 guineas at Doncaster the following month.

Yet another personal best riding performance was achieved by David Kemp, whose 13 wins equalled the score of Area Points Champion Jamie Owen. Kemp has taken up the training reins from his father, Malcolm, and principal contributors to his total were Bard Of Drumcoo (five wins) and Madmidge (four), but the stable star was Cantarinho. Though unable to cope with the Crow hotpot Fane Counsel at Horseheath, Cantarinho won his other two Point-to-Points and took Hunter Chases at Fakenham and Huntingdon before ending his season with a fine victory in the Weatherbys Chase John Corbet Novice Championship. The only disappointment with Cantarinho came in the rain-softened ground at Cheltenham's Hunter Chase evening, but connections must be anticipating a return to the Gloucestershire course for the 2005 Foxhunters with considerable enthusiasm.

Of other established yards the Sporborgs took the Area's Weatherbys Chase Young Horse Award thanks to three-time winner Mister Ringa (bred in Dorset by Mrs Susan Woodhouse out of her good mare Panda Pops), but otherwise had little to offer once The Red Boy showed he had his own ideas after a couple of minor wins in January (Andrew Braithwaite appeared harshly treated when fined for 'not riding his mount out' at Cottenham), while the Howland Jackson horses seemed out of sorts throughout.

But the Area's senior rider, George Cooper, had another successful time with horses trained in partnership with Cherie Cunningham. Even one of Cooper's experience could not hold tearaway Another Leader, but there were wins for the faithful if quirky Endeavour, Rip Kerby and three five-year-olds, Eurogaedal (seen just once, at the Suffolk), Magic Lodge and Monarch Ruler, on whom Rupert Stearn took a share of the riding honours. Rip Kerby was sold for 7000 guineas in August at Doncaster, where Magic Lodge failed to reach his reserve after a final bid of 14,500 guineas.

National Novice achievement in the Harley Racing Points Championship (confined to Novice Rider races) came to the Area from, with all due respect, an unlikely quarter: Paul Chinery, who qualified for both Novice and Veteran events, being aged 44. He did not come to racing until his mid-thirties, but over the last three seasons, operating on a shoestring budget, he has struck up a happy relationship with now 11-year-old Royal Action, with whom he won three Novice Rider races to keep clear of Harry Fry and Daryl Jacob, neither of whom are even half his age. In no previous season had Chinery won more than once, but now he also took the Suffolk Land Rover qualifier on Royal Action and was successful in non-Novice races with Baron Bernard and Ginger Bug.

Chinery was the Area's Leading Male Novice, the Ladies equivalent going to one at the other end of the age scale, Lucinda Barrett-Nobbs, which represented quite an achievement since she was seriously underhorsed, both in quality and quantity. After an initial win on Lambrini King in the Waveney Members race and another aboard Tartar Sabre in a Fitzwilliam Maiden, she had few further opportunities to progress.

Other first-time winners included 18-year-old George Greenock, with his first ride on Homme De Fer in the Essex and Suffolk Open (Nibby Bloom, his mentor, had earlier warmed up the horse with a North Norfolk Open win), Matt Cobbald, 27, who managed the tricky task of completing a Marks Tey Members race solo on Rip Kerby after both his rivals had been eliminated by the third fence, and Claire Bartlett, 29, who broke her duck out of the Area in a Godstone Maiden in May on Julia Shaw's Mr Know What.

On the training front, after many a try Martin Ward finally produced a first winner with Polo Ridge at Northaw, while the 'come-backs' included Simon Marriage, whose 15-year wait for another Marks Tey success ended when he legged up Nicky Barnes to win on the ex-Turner horse Pampered Gale.

The experiment which required entries for all four Cottenham meetings to be made to Weatherbys seemed to work smoothly — at least five additional meetings are to use the service in 2005 — and weather interventions were few. Principal meteorological problems had come the previous autumn, when a shortage of rain resulted in a lack of grass growth, noticeable in the spring at Cottenham, Higham and High Easter. No such problems arose at Marks Tey or Ampton, the latter course going from strength to strength, with the Dunston Harriers in January putting on what was arguably the Area's best fixture.

A late February freeze forced a week's postponement of the Thurlow, while two other fixtures only survived thanks to the laudable efforts of stewards and officials. At the beginning of February the North Norfolk's tentage at Higham was wrecked by gales on the meeting's eve, but, with the employment of horseboxes for changing rooms, declarations, etc, the organisers were able to carry off a marathon nine-race card. Then at the end of the season the stewards of the Cambridgeshire and Enfield Chace fixture showed commendable resolve when navigating through monsoon-like conditions which, by the end of the afternoon, had reduced the Northaw course for the Maiden race to 10 fences on a day when Noah — the Biblical character not Ray York's horse — would have felt more at home than the bedraggled Bank Holiday crowd.

The season's most bizarre note was struck by the appearance of 16-year-old Algan, who had won a King George VI Chase at Kempton for France when trained by Francois Doumen in 1994 but now, qualified with the Cambridge University Draghounds, was entered as the property of Miss Riikaa Heikkola, a Finnish nurse, and trained by JJ Ryan, an ex-jockey from Ireland and reportedly a sometime worker on the London underground railway. Ridden by Phillip York, the veteran won Confined races at Horseheath and Cottenham before the novelty of Point-to-Pointing began to pall.

Another former top Doumen-trained chaser, the three years younger Djeddah, was fielded by the same owner-trainer combination, but sadly he collapsed and died on his Hunt racing debut in the Land Rover qualifier at the Hursley Hambledon. This meeting was the second put on by the **SANDHURST** Area, which staged seven fixtures in 2004, one more than the previous year, in consequence of the return, for the first time since 2000, of the Thames Valley Combined Hunts Club, whose races were, confusingly, held on a South Midlands Area track at Kingston Blount.

Tit for tat, as it were, the Sandhurst Area's Tweseldown course was venue for the South Midlands Area Club meeting, which had been cancelled the previous year when its organisers were unable to agree terms over a planned new home at Towcester after deciding to quit Mollington.

Improvements continue in vogue at Tweseldown. This once busy centre disappeared from the list completely in 2002 but returned under the energetic management of Brynley Powell and his team with a single meeting last year and in 2004 was used three times, taking one of the three Vale of Aylesbury with Garth and South Berks fixtures in addition to that of the Thames Valley Racing Club.

The former was a bit of a disaster for runners and included a Men's Open walkover, but the latter meeting, though unfortunately permitted to clash with a Larkhill fixture on the season's first Sunday, January 11, still managed the Area's best turnout, though only a relatively sparse 59 in six races. From then on things went downhill and the Area's final runners-per-race average of below six is hardly something to be shouted from the roof tops.

The Karen Lawther-trained Tanager, who benefited from the walkover mentioned above, later showed himself capabale of winning 'real' Open races, scoring twice for Ben King at Kimble and Kingston Blount. Likwise Dancing Fosenby, from the Penny Lownds yard, needed little exertion to take the Confined immediately preceding the walkover, but later won the South Midlands Area feature race at Lockinge on Easter Monday and gave Mick Holdforth a first Hunter Chase success at Folkestone.

Since the retirement of Philip Scouller, the Effingham, Surrey, establishments of the Yorks — Phillip and his father Ray — have been dominant in these parts. York jnr is much in demand as a rider, too — particularly on inexperienced horses — and in 2004, apart from bringing up his career century, he achieved a personal best 26 wins which earned him third spot — his highest placing yet — in the Men's Championship behind the big two, Farrant and Burton.

Ten of his successes came on eight horses from his own yard, while victories for his father, who holds a professional licence, included Morph and the Petoski six-year-old Charango Star, for whom York snr stepped up to receive the Area Young Horse Award at the PPORA Stratford lunch.

Those that Phillip won on from his own stable included two five-year-olds, Drumdowney Lad and Jacob's Choice, the mare Kayleigh, who made £5200 at Ascot in June, and Star Glow, who appeared only once, in early January, comfortably accounting for subsequent Turner winner Fine And Dandy at Higham. Probably just about best of the string was Eastern Point, whose four victories included a Maiden Hunter Chase at Leicester. The horse also won the Area's feature race, the Vine and Craven Mixed Open, with a walkover — further evidence that prize money is not of first importance to owners.

Needless to say York took the Area's two senior riding awards, while the Novice prize went to Frank Buckett, 37, a builder who was successful with his first-ever ride when he partnered the former undistinguished novice chaser Sharp Seal in a Maiden at the Tweseldown Racing Club meeting, which drew many leading riders. Reigning champion Richard Burton got off the mark for the new season on the Cheshire-qualified Lambrini Mist in one of the Maidens, there were victories for former champions Julian Pritchard and Evan Williams and the opening of what was to be a best-ever season for one of the sport's most respected seniors, Godfrey

Maundrell, who at Stratford in May received the Dick Woodhouse Memorial Trophy as the Leading Owner-Rider of 2004.

PLATE 2 The man and his horses: Godfrey Maundrell (left) and Paul Thompson with L to R, Bally Wirral, Quickswood, Rhythm King and Headwrecker *PHOTO: Carrie Janaway*

Helped by a new private trainer in Paul Thompson, Maundrell, who has been racing for about 35 seasons (missing one year in the mid-1990s when he was otherwise engaged surviving major cancer surgery), won 12 races, 11 of them on four of his own horses, including the five times successful Rhythm King and Bally Wirral, who won three. The animals are qualified with the Avon Vale and Royal Artillery, which moves this review into the **WESSEX** Area, which is second only in its number of meetings to the Devon and Cornwall. This time there were 24, no fewer than seven of them on the country's busiest course, Larkhill, which was also used by the Staff College from the adjoining Sandhurst region.

Though rain was in moderately short supply from March onwards, resulting in firmish ground at some meetings, this does not entirely explain the marked dip in the number of runners noted within Wessex. This was particularly in evidence at the mid-season fixtures at Larkhill, where one, the New Forest, gained the unenviable distinction of having the lowest turnout at any meeting nationwide — just 20 horses contesting six races. On the same course a fortnight earlier seven races had drawn 21 runners. Overall the average-per-race figure only just topped seven, compared with a national average of 8.1. In 2003, when drought conditions were much worse, the average for the 152 races at 22 Wessex meetings was 8.2.

There was, however, no shortage of runners or excitement when the Army began the season on the Salisbury Plain course on Sunday, January 11, clashing with Tweseldown but featuring the first 2004 Land Rover qualifier, won by Always On The Line from Aberfoyle Park. The winner, who had helped Alex Merriam to the Wilkinson Sword in 2003 when trained by the Blooms in East Anglia and had been switched to Richard Barber's Dorset stable as Merriam is now studying at Bristol University, failed to shine therafter. Aberfoyle Park easily turned the tables on him at the next Larkhill meeting and he made little mark in subsequent Hunter Chases.

The highly-rated Aberfoyle Park, who again failed to see out the season, was one of the enormously successful string controlled by Sally Alner. She saddled eight horses to win 17 Point-to-Points and won six Hunter Chases with three of them. Top of the bunch was the six-year-old Free Gift, whose only previous racecourse experience had been in a couple of Newbury bumpers.

He now remained unbeaten after a seven-race campaign, staring in a Larkhill Maiden and culminating in an impressive victory in a Novice Hunter Chase at Folkestone.

Free Gift gave Irishman Daryl Jacob the lion's share of the 10 winners which left him heading the National Novice table. Jacob would also have walked away with the PPORA's Wilkinson Sword for under-21s had he not, about three weeks before the season's start, rendered himself ineligible by winning his first race in an Amateur Hurdle at Exeter. His tally would also have been greater but for being grounded for more than a month after breaking a collarbone when Aberfoyle Park fell heavily three from home in the the United Services' Coronation Cup, of which more later.

PLATE 3 Honouring a great friend of this book: Daryl Jacob, the leading Novice Rider at Badbury Rings, receives the Eric Dymott Memorial Trophy from his widow, Brenda PHOTO: Linda Charles

Mrs Alner, joint-top Hunter Chase trainer with Paul Nicholls, had another young Irishman riding for her, the latest to bear a famous racing name. This was 20-year-old Tom Dreaper, son of Jim and grandson of Tom. He won only one Point-to-Point but scored four times in Hunter Chases for the stable aboard eight-year-old Kingston-Banker and won another at Fontwell for Wiltshire trainer Sally Mullins.

Dido Harding, a long-time owner-rider patron of the Alners, won two Point-to-Points and a Hunter Chase aboard her Unlimited Free, and another multiple scorer for the yard was Miss O'Grady. Michael Miller, who partnered this mare to win three races, achieved his career century during the season and ended on a total of 107, still 71 behind the tally achieved by his twice champion father Richard.

At the successful United Services meeting, the Coronation Cup Mixed Open — one of four 'national classics' — was a thrilling affair, though only seven starters were attracted by the double prize money. Tales Of Bounty held on by the narrowest margin from County Derry, who stormed up to gain nearly 10 lengths on the flat after Aberfoyle Park crashed at the final ditch three from home — and stayed down for some time.

Tales Of Bounty was one of 16 horses saddled to win 25 races by Richard Barber, again the Area's top trainer, and was ridden by his stable jockey Nick Williams, the season's leading rider in Hunter Chases. He rode six horses to win nine races in this latter sphere, including, for Barber, Mouseski and Garruth, and, for Nicholls, Torduff Express and Silence Reigns. Riding Torduff

Express, Garruth and Mouseski, Williams became the first rider ever to complete a treble at the Cheltenham Hunter Chase meeting.

In the Aintree Fox Hunters, Torduff Express had never looked likely to repeat his 2002 triumph, but he followed his success at the rain-ravaged Cheltenham evening meeting with an Intrum Justitia victory at Stratford — once Right To Reply had fallen at the final fence when almost alongside and in the process brought down the rapidly-closing Earthmover. Tragically Right To Reply collapsed and died after scrambling to his feet and cantering loose to the post.

There was no immediate rest for Torduff Express. Five weeks after Stratford he finished a well-beaten fifth in the £75,000 English Summer National over four miles at Uttoxeter. Bright Approach, who had been a 15-length third to him at Stratford, also contested this Uttoxeter marathon, taking third place again, this time 10 lengths ahead of Torduff Express.

Mouseski, owner-bred by Michael Dare by Petoski from his good Point-to-Point mare Worth Matravers, won three consecutive Hunter Chases, while Garruth triumphed in the Land Rover final after Williams had skilfully overcome the handicap of a slipping saddle. At Wincanton in February a similar slip had cost Garruth his weight-cloth and second place.

Barber sent out five five-year-old winners, of which the best was probably the Mister Lord gelding Noble Action, who, after taking a Maiden and Restricted, failed narrowly to account for three-time winner Father Mansfield in an Axe Vale Intermediate and can be excused his run-out in the lead at Bratton Down, also the consequence of a slipping saddle. Five-year-old Lord Anner — another Mister Lord — won unchallenged at Bishop's Court and impressed again when taking a Berkeley Restricted, with Ashley Farrant substituting for an absent Williams.

Six-year-olds Combat Drinker and Spot The Difference, who were each confined to a single appearance, looked useful recruits when winning on their respective debuts. The former was led out unsold after being bid up to 24,000 guineas at Doncaster in August. One of the busiest of the Barber string, Lord Of The Mist (Mister Lord again), who did not lose his maiden certificate until a nine-year-old last year, won five of his seven starts between the flags and was second in the other two before graduating to hunter chasing. He looked a mite unlucky to stumble into a rival at the first fence at Newton Abbot but then, with Polly Gundry up, he beat all but comfortable winner Colquhoun in the Ladies race at Stratford's Intrum Justitia meeting.

PLATE 4 543 Christie's Foxhunters HC, Cheltenham: Following Earthmover's triumph, a radiant Rilly Goschen hopes the horse's owner's company will be along to pick up the trophy PHOTO: Tim Holt

The afore-mentioned Earthmover, winner of the Foxhunters when trained by Barber in 1998, repeated the performance magnificently at the age of 13, saddled by Paul Nicholls, for whom he had been an honest servant in handicaps since his first Cheltenham victory. Still owned by Roger Penny, the gallant veteran drew away up the final climb from the Irish top-rated Never Compromise. Rilly Goschen had formed a successful partnership with Earthmover when Nicholls brought the horse back to hunter chasing in 2003, and the Somerset rider had every reason to be pleased with herself at the end of the season, finishing second in the Hunter Chase table with six wins, and also second — with 15 wins on 13 horses — to Polly Gundry in the Ladies Point-to-Point Championship. She rode seven of the 10 winners saddled during the season by John Dufosee and two of her Hunter Chase victories came on one she trains herself, Chasing The Bride.

Nicholls owned two of obvious Hunter Chase potential in Ask The Natives and Mister Benjamin, each trained and ridden by Chloe Roddick to win both their starts in Ladies Opens, but then both suffered pelvic injuries and neither was seen out after February.

Springford, who had been off with a minor tendon problem since winning his only start of 2003, was another worthy hunter chasing representative for Wessex, dividing Torduff Express and Bright Approach in the Intrum Justitia and beating Garruth at Wincanton, after winning three Point-to-Points from Caroline Keevil's Mendip stable. He was a regular mount for Dominic Alers-Hankey, who, after missing all 2003 as a result of a leg broken in a hunting fall, rode a double on his first day back at the Army meeting in January.

Six weeks later he was briefly sidelined again with a damaged shoulder after a fall at the South Dorset. The fences at Milborne St Andrew that day caused no little havoc: a third of the 57 starters either fell, unseated or refused. During Alers-Hankey's latest absence Jamie Snowden proved an able deputy on such as Gunner Welburn in the RA Gold Cup and Springford's useful stablemate Out The Black, before the latter gave his regular partner a second winning return when landing an impressive fourth victory of the season in the Wilton Open. In October, by that time transferred to Philip Hobbs, but still owned by James Drummond, Out The Black made a promising Rules debut in a Beginners Chase at Exeter, beating a better-fancied stable-companion by a dozen lengths.

Wessex had one new meeting in 2004, the Taunton Vale Harriers, whose fixture since the mid-1970s had been amalgamated with the Taunton Vale Foxhounds and staged on Easter Monday. In 2004 the Harriers shared the same course at Kingston St Mary and for this first year the Foxhounds continued on the Bank Holiday while the Harriers tried a mid-week evening meeting in mid-May, the idea being that they will alternate in future. All the season's mid-week evening racing (three meetings) is in Wessex, but unfortunately for the Harriers, by the time of their fixture (and the one at Larkhill seven days later), the absence of rain was having a marked effect, so only 29 runners were declared all evening, with Ashley Farrant winning the first three races on David Pipe-trained animals, all at long odds-on.

Nearly half of Pipe's winning horses earned their certificates with the Taunton Vale Harriers but most of his successes — and Farrant's — were gained in the **DEVON & CORNWALL** Area, though their first victory of the year came at the PPORA meeting at Barbury Castle, when Lord Atterbury, the 2002 Irish Maiden winner who had surged up the ratings following five 2003 English victories, was in devastating form in the Land Rover qualifier. From then on he headed the market for the Foxhunters at Cheltenham, where he had won over four miles the previous April, but his trainer was unable to give him a second preliminary run before the big race, in which he proved a major disappointment, eventually being pulled up. However, transferred to Pipe's father Martin, he turned in an heroic performance under a featherweight and Mark Bradburne to finish a close third in the Grand National, before reverting to Hunter Chases and Farrant for a trailing fourth place behind Torduff Express in the Intrum Justitia at Stratford.

Farrant, whose 54 victories were gained on 25 horses, led the championship table by early February and, apart from the first weekend in May, when Burton nipped momentarily in front, he stayed there to the end. En route to his title he rode four-timers at three meetings — the East Cornwall, the Western and the Dulverton West — and trebles at four others, to say nothing of 11 doubles. Numerically his top winner for Pipe was David Johnson's East Devon-qualified five-year-old Vivid Imagination, whose only defeat in seven races came when he unshipped his rider at the second ditch when apparently cruising easily with the leaders in the Berkeley Open race. A declared starter for the Weatherbys Chase John Corbet Cup — and likely favourite — he was withdrawn because the ground was thought unsuitable, but earlier that day his trainer had stepped up to receive the Area Young Horse Award on behalf of Johnson at the PPORA's Stratford lunch.

Two others from Pipe's string, the prolific hurdle and chasing winner Polar Champ and Ballysicyos, both carried Farrant to five successes, and he scored four times each on Cimmaroon, I Am Said I and Oneminutetofive. The last-named, who had taken a Black Forest Lodge Maiden on his only outing of 2003, began with a second to the useful Teme Valley horse Fertile Valley on the opening day at Cottenham and then won all his following starts between the flags (he may have been fortunate to get a dead-heat with Springford in the Eggesford Open) and was best of three stable runners in the Cheltenham Foxhunters, finishing a reasonably close fourth. But hopes of a bright future under Rules were dashed when he fell and broke a shoulder on his first outing for Martin Pipe at Stratford in October.

I Am Said I was one of a five-strong team which returned empty-handed after travelling from Devon to the Middleton meeting in Yorkshire on the first Sunday in April. All five were owned by Pipe patron P.J. Finn, who hunts his horses with the Middleton, but the nearest any came to collecting was a second by dual winner Canterbury Jack — who a month later was to break a leg at the Modbury meeting — and a third from Euwiluwil, who won his two other starts in Devon. I Am Said I — subsequently successful in summer jumping and knocked down for 24,000 guineas at Doncaster in August — found the Grimthorpe Cup's four miles beyond him.

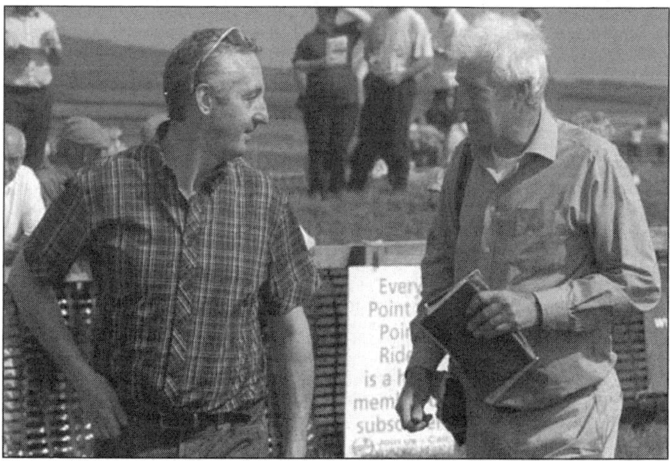

PLATE 5 1557 Tiverton Staghounds Confined: The elusive Mr P.J. Finn has been cornered by ace local reporter, Granville Taylor (with the Loose-Leaf to the fore) PHOTO: Brian Armstrong

Pipe and Farrant did well for owner Brian Kilpatrick with five-year-old Cimmaroon and Colquhoun. Farrant scored three times on Colquhoun before the trainer's head-girl Ollie Jackson (who will be in charge of the Point-to-Pointers in 2005) took over to triumph in the Ladies Hunter Chase at Stratford, after stablemate Polar Champ had unseated Lucy Bridges when four lengths up at the last.

So the season ended better than it had begun for Mrs Jackson, who at the PPORA meeting in January had come to grief two from home with Ballysicyos when still leading the Ladies Open field. Nothing much went right for her after that — until she presaged her Stratford victory with success on Epicure at Kingston St Mary in May — and she failed twice more on Ballysicos. But

Pipe never lost faith in this horse and, after that third failure, wagered owner Pam Deal and his mother £100 that the nine-year-old would win six races before the season's end — and he nearly won his bet. Teamed up with Farrant, Ballysicyos won five of his next six starts, giving best only to Tigger Barnes and Kingston Venture at the Axe Vale, before the busy programme began to take its toll and he was beaten in the Exmoor Open when Colin Heard took him on from the start aboard Friar Waddon.

The latter was never worse than fourth in eight runs, winning four — including the Beaufort Mixed Open, the West Midlands Area feature race — and was the best horse trained by Keith Cumings, who also sent out five-year-old Touch Of Flame, a first foal of that grand race mare Flame O'Frensi, for a promising debut win over two-and-a-half miles at Great Trethew. Judgement must be reserved on this youngster, who next appeared at Bratton Down almost three months later only to fall at the first fence.

Farrant now plans to expand his own training operation. In 2004 he won a couple of minor races with a mare from his small establishment, Just Sally, and another on Baldara. Probably best of his outside rides was Red Native, on which he was legged up to win two Open races by Richard Barber, who also gave him the winning ride in the Berkeley Restricted on the promising five-year-old Lord Anner.

Despite the domination of Pipe and Farrant there were plenty of opportunities for others during an uninterrupted season in this biggest of all Areas, with its 27 meetings on 16 courses. Field sizes thinned from mid-April on, producing a final average-per-race of 7.8, slightly down on the previous year, but the East Devon's fixture on Oliver Carter's excellent course at Bishop's Court on the last Saturday in February — a day when all others had fallen victims to frost — was the country's busiest, with 146 runners in the 12 races. That dozen might have become 14 had not balloting-out been ordered for the last two Maiden divisions because of failing light. Indeed, it was getting decidedly murky by the time the 17 runners in the final event were flagged away.

A fairly distant runner-up to Farrant for D&C's Male Rider points award was Richard Woollacott, while Exeter trainer-rider Lucy Gardner (whose five-year-old winner Ask Again made 23,000 guineas at Doncaster in May) just beat Wessex-based Tabitha Cave for the Ladies equivalent. The region's Leading Horse was Sandy Duff, trained by Nicky Frost to win five races and principal contributor to the several awards gained by barrister Mary McCarthy, not least the Lady Riders National Novice title. Sandy Duff was the big winner for the Frost yard, which won 13 races with seven horses, which meant a career-best six for Jimmy Frost's head-lad Derek McKenna.

Woollacott won 13 races, seven of them on three horses trained for the first time by his partner, Emely Thompson, on the family farm near South Molton. Best of this trio was Sir William, successful twice in Open company at Cothelstone, on the second occasion beating Hylters Chance, whose rider, Cornishman Colin Heard, had allegedly been involved in a first-fence incident in the race when Richard Burton's mount Jemaro crashed through the wing. The local stewards found Heard guilty of dangerous riding and fined him £140. He immediately found another £250 as the deposit to accompany his speedy appeal to the Jockey Club, where, more than three months later, he was exonerated and the fine quashed when the Disciplinary Panel, which took evidence from Heard, Burton and others, besides viewing video recordings, found that there was 'insufficient evidence' that interference had taken place.

The ill-fated Right To Reply, a comfortable conqueror of Monty's Lass at Buckfastleigh in February before unseating Neil Harris in the lead at Bishop's Court, deserved his high rating among hunter chasers after a victory at Newbury. He was trained near Brompton Regis by Jeremy Scott, as is County Derry, who was never worse than fourth in five Hunter Chases, winning two and finishing third to Earthmover in the Foxhunters after beating him the previous month at Fontwell.

Colin Blank's seven-year-old Bengal Bullet, who had ended the previous season winning four Point-to-Points in a row, did well on graduation to the larger obstacles, scoring at Newton Abbot and Exeter for Tabitha Cave before unseating her at halfway in the Weatherbys Chase John Corbet. Mike Biddick's Kestick also went well for Miss Cave, scoring twice at Taunton and winning two Point-to-Points, the first at a storm-lashed Wadebridge on the last Saturday in January. Biddick's 17-year-old son Will received D&C's Male Novice award, thanks to two wins on Let's Fly, in the second of which — at Bratton Down in June — he upset the odds on Ashley Farrant and Colquhoun. Let's Fly had been warmed up for Biddick by Mandy Hand, who had won

twice on him earlier and achieved her ambition of taking the Area's Veteran Rider prize. She turned 40 before the season's start and has accumulated 125 firsts between the flags since gaining her first success over 20 years ago.

Hobbycyr, ridden by Polly Gundry for Richard Kelvin-Hughes, stopped the winning run of the Richard Barber hotpot Ease the Pressure when the Dart Vale put on the region's feature race in March and the horse was not disgraced later when third to County Derry over four miles at Cheltenham. Another trainer who can look back on a successful season is Buckfastleigh-based Gordon Chambers, who won eight races with six horses, among them Province, successful in the four-miler at the Dartmoor meeting.

In her Cullompton stable Ollie Bush kept a useful string, mostly partnered by Polly Gundry. Five-year-old Flash Point won his only start for a syndicate of three and the same trio thrilled to the performances of the mare What A Mover, successful in three of her four outings. In just three tries seven-year-old stablemate Vinnie Boy registered a Maiden, Restricted and Intermediate sequence, carrying the colours of John Burbidge, owner of the stable star, fast ground specialist Bright Approach, who was ridden by Tom Malone to beat Macgeorge, Earthmover and County Derry at Cheltenham in April.

In January the Bush box made a successful raid on the **SOUTH MIDLANDS** Area when What A Mover (Gundry) and Bright Approach (Julian Pritchard) landed an Open race double at the Heythrop meeting. The men's event, over four miles and a furlong and one of the four national classics, is for the prized Lord Ashton of Hyde's Cup and Bright Approach was scoring for the second successive year.

A week earlier the South Midlands programme had received a flying start from the Point-to-Point Owners and Riders Club at Barbury Castle, where the eight races drew 111 runners. The Men's Open success of Lord Atterbury has been mentioned in the Devon & Cornwall survey; the Ladies equivalent brought a first win of 2004 for the eventual Champion Mare and Leading Horse, Upton Adventure — after the penultimate fence fall of the front-running Ballysicyos. Upton Adventure qualified with the Ledbury (there will be more about her in the West Midlands review) and indeed horses from South Midlands Hunts were conspicuously absent from the PPORC winner's enclosure, the best they could manage all afternoon being a couple of third places.

No other meeting in the Area could match the PPORC's turnout. The Bicester with Whaddon Chase's February fixture at Mollington was next best with 97 in nine races — the Hunt's April meeting on the same course drew only 37 in six — and the organisers of the South Midlands Club could congratulate themselves on their decision to quit Towcester and move beyond the region's boundaries to Tweseldown, where eight races drew 87 declarations. Fields inevitably fell away in the second half of the season, but the Area did not seem so much affected as some others by firm ground and produced a fairly healthy average-per-race figure of 8.6. Two meetings were lost, frost and snow forcing the abandonment of the Farmers Bloodhounds Dunthrop races at the end of February, while the VWH's Siddington fixture fell victim to the March gales.

Another meeting to leave Towcester (after a stopgap year there) was the Oakley. The loss of the excellent line at Newton Bromswold is still mourned but the Hunt has found a satisfactory new venue at Brafield-on-the-Green, where racing took place after overnight rain had dissolved the snow which had covered the course the day before. Being on part of an old airfield and therefore flat, viewing is not of the finest but riders thoroughly approved. Sadly George Weaving, the popular Hon. Secretary at Newton Bromswold for nearly 30 years, did not see the successful renewal, having died the previous month. A minute's silence was observed in his memory before the first race.

Once again local horses did not get much of a look in. Richard Burton rode two of the winners and Rowan Cope three, but one of the latter's was the impressive six-year-old maiden Born To Dream, qualified with the VWH and trained by the new man at the Goess Saurau's Barbury Castle establishment, James Richardson. Later in the season Richardson sent out a Gildoran five-year-old called Lord Of The Road, bred by his parents and owned by his grandfather, to win his only start in sparkling style at the Berkeley. The following month Lord Of The Road made 50,000 guineas at Doncaster. His handler ended his first season with five winners of six races to his name.

Another newcomer to the training ranks, the Towcester-based Anna Brooks, who had the riding services of the accomplished James Diment, also gained six successes — though all outside the

Area. Her first winner, Esendi in a Higham Maiden on the second Sunday of the season, failed to build on that bright start, but stablemate Wincy Spider won his only two races — both in East Anglia — and their trainer later took the Area's Young Horse prize with the six-year-old Franco. Qualified like the others with the Grafton, Franco's three victories from five starts were all at Garthorpe and culminated in the Melton's Marie Curie Novice Championship.

Most successful of the established yards was that of Lawney Hill at Aston Rowant, from where six horses won nine races. One of them, the former highly-rated Mr Snowman, who was making a welcome return after a two-year absence, also won a Hunter Chase at Towcester, while another, Gray Knight, did likewise at Folkestone. James Tudor did most of the riding, achieving a career best tally of 11 and finishing runner-up in the Area's Men's Points table to Rowan Cope, who also took the Midlands award. That elder statesmen among South Midlands riders, Jimmy Tarry, was restricted to just one success (Lah Di Dah Lad in a Grafton Maiden) and so remains two short of his double century.

The region's top lady was Heather Irving, whose eight victories included four Ladies Opens om Killerine, a nine-year-old she owns with her partner, Tony Kemp, and trains at Culworth, near Banbury. Killerine shared the Leading Horse Points prize with one from Fred Hutsby's Warwickshire stable, Ryans Star, who was never worse than third in six starts under Joanna Parris, winning twice. Hutsby also saddled Campden Kitty to win three times out of the Area and rode Prate Box himself to win two races, including the last Men's Open of the season at the Torrington Farmers.

Simon Bloss, stud groom to John Phillips at Bibury, Glos, did well for his employer with four VWH-qualified horses, the rides being shared by their owner's sons, Nick and George. Of the three horses which won twice each, the best was probably Camden Carrig, who, after successive victories, completed his hat-trick very easily in a Novice Hunter Chase at Chepstow. The stable's home-bred five-year-old Leachbrook Lady did not appear again after being gifted a Maiden on her February debut at Mollington, when the two in front both came to grief at the final fence.

Rosemary Gasson, another owner-trainer based near Banbury, who qualifies her horses with the Farmers Bloodhounds, had lost her useful performer Romany Chat the previous November when he broke a leg out in his field. She did not have to wait long for a change of fortune, sending out Viscount Bankes to win a Cottenham Maiden on the season's opening day. The six-year-old failed to follow up, but his stablemate Freedom Fighter won three times and then added a Towcester Hunter Chase, while Abitofahike won a Maiden when taken down to the evening meeting at Kingston St Mary in May. Mrs Gasson's jockey, farrier Andy Martin, also won on his own mares It's Missy Imp and Lady Baronette.

Top string in the adjoining **MIDLANDS** Area was, as usual, that of Caroline Bailey. She saddled 13 horses to win 21 races and took a Hunter Chase with one of them, Find Me Another, who stayed in the yard after being sold by owner Charles Dixey seven days prior to the horse recovering winning form in the Pytchley Ladies Open under Amy Stennett. She was his pilot when he went on to beat a big field at Huntingdon at the end of May.

Mrs Bailey could not give the retiring Chairman of the PPORA, Richard Russell, what would have been an appropriate winner at the PPORC meeting, when his Agua Ardente finished second for a sixth time in seven runs, this time by just a neck to the useful Out The Black, but at the SMAC's Tweseldown races three weeks later the seven-year-old finally made the number one spot that had eluded him for so long. This was the stable's first victory of 2004 and a first win as an owner for Russell (whose successful career in the saddle had been ended by his crash from Teaplanter in the 1995 Foxhunters) since Avostar had won a Towcester Hunter Chase five years before. Agua Ardente began to creep up the ratings after winning twice more before the end of the season to ensure that his owner (now succeeded after a very successful four years as PPORA Chairman by Cheltenham Clerk of the Course Simon Claisse) received the Area's Young Horse Award at the PPORA lunch, over which he presided at Stratford in May.

Age seemed to have caught up with the Bailey stable stalwart Red Rebel, whose only success from seven outings came in the Oakley Men's Open, but the year older Shanavogh scored three times in Open class for owner-rider Richard Hunnisett before meeting a tragic end at the third last fence at the Melton meeting. Hunnisett also managed one victory in Confined company on his Springlea Tower and saw his colours twice carried to success by Rowan Cope aboard seven-year-old Choral Dream.

Cope, whose sucesses for Mrs Bailey included two in succession on the smart five-year-old Killard Point, finished on a career-best tally of 19, but many of his wins for his home stable and others were gained outside the Area so it was only at the concluding meeting, the Blankney, that he snatched the local Men's title by a couple of points from Joe Docker, after he had won the Restricted with a useful seven-year-old from the Bailey yard, the Melton Maiden winner Tom Tobacco.

Docker's principal mount was the much-improved Nautical Lad. The nine-year-old's three previous wins had been spread over as many seasons but now, trained as before by the rider's father, John, he collected five firsts in a row, the last three of them in Men's Opens, and took the Area Leading Horse prize for his syndicate of owners. Nautical Lad made no show in the Land Rover final on the night the rains came at Cheltenham and may still have been feeling the effects of that run when he was held at bay by Bill Warner's charge Blue Royal in the Melton Open.

Docker finished on a tally of 11, one fewer than his career best achieved the previous season. He looked unlucky to be denied a treble at the South Notts Easter Monday races, when his mount Moscow Tradition, apparently the half-length winner of the Restricted, was placed second to Dante's Banker. This must have been a harrowing race for the judge. He originally named as first Near And Phar, but this mare had continued after an earlier run-out, missing all fences until her rider failed to prevent her jumping the last. Further confusion came with the revised result announcement. Apart from awarding first place to the horse most thought had been beaten, this also gave as third the horse who had clearly finished fourth, about 25 lengths behind the third, who was not mentioned. Following protests from the rider of the third horse — the real one — he received the consolation of fourth place!

The one in part responsible for the confusion, Near And Phar's rider, was subsequently fined £75 but no fine was announced for the judge. Near And Phar, who had earlier done well to win a Mares Maiden in Yorkshire, featured in another stewards inquiry in her next race, the Fernie Restricted, after which her trainer and rider were each fined £125 for 'not allowing the horse to achieve the best possible placing.'

Best of trainer Antonia Bealby's winners was King's Hero, who was successful at Dingley and Garthorpe but proved no match for the best of Bill Warner's, six-year-old Coolefind, at the Huntingdon Hunter Chase meeting in May. Coolefind was completing a four-timer, following victories in minor company at Garthorpe, Guilsborough and Ashorne. He was ridden in all his races by Warner's jockey Stuart Morris, who had also partnered King's Hero to his pointing victories. Morris equalled Cope in the number of winners ridden, but finished third to him and Docker in the Area Championship.

The 16 Midlands meetings (the Brocklesby was abandoned to snow at the end of February) drew generally good fields, and could boast a race average only a whisker below nine. The Cottesmore did best on the first Sunday in March, the eventual 10-race card being contested by 108 runners, with, for the first time ever, a Land Rover qualifier divided on the day. The Cottesmore's was the first of five meetings at Garthorpe, a course established in 1955 by the Belvoir, which Hunt celebrated 50 years of racing there at the end of March. The following month the Atherstone drew a tremendous crowd for its 50th meeting at Clifton-on-Dunsmore, where the Men's Open race trophy commemorates the name of its first winner, Mythical Ray. Shanavogh won it for Richard Hunnisett, just holding off the Grafton horse Longville Lad after they had battled in front from the fifth fence.

Guilsborough, home of the Pytchley fixture, which in 2004 staged the Area's feature Open race (won by Nautical Lad) goes back a little further than Garthorpe or Clifton, to 1951 in fact, but in the longevity stakes none of these three can hold a candle to Dingley, first used for a Point-to-Point in 1931. It is now home to the Woodland Pytchley, the Fernie and the Harborough Race Club, which, for some unannounced reason, is the new title of the former Harborough *Hunts* Club. At the Harborough fixture that long-time supporter of hunting and Point-to-Pointing, Joan Tice, achieved a double in the first and last races with two of her numerous home-breds, Teeton Priceless and her five-year-old maiden half-brother Teeton Prince.

The region's newest course, set in the superb parkland surrounding Welbeck Abbey, was used for a second time by the Grove & Rufford. Gales the previous day had flattened much of the tentage but all went off successfully (eight races and 75 runners) after horseboxes had been pressed into service for changing rooms, declarations, etc. Nokimover, who was to score again at the Melton,

took the Ladies Open comfortably, but in the Men's equivalent trainer-rider Nick Kent and Ramirez had to be at their best to resist Mashwe, a mare having her first run since 2002, in which year she won four of her last five races. Unfortunately this was to be her only start. Six-year-old Ramirez, who was never out of the first three in four outings, had given Kent his first training success at the region's curtain-raiser, the Lincolnshire UHC fixture at Market Rasen in January. Newgate Wells made it an extra-special day for Kent later when winning one of the Maidens there, but sadly did not survive a subsequent outing at the next Market Rasen meeting, the Burton. Before this unhappy time, Kent had legged up Rachel Clark to win the Ladies race on another from his yard, Supreme Silence, and then ridden the South Notts seven-year-old Oh Highly Likely to success in the Land Rover qualifier in what was to be the seven-year-old's only run.

Gemma Hutchinson finished well clear in the region's Ladies Championship, thanks to two victories on the aforementioned Nokimover and Ladies race successes with two other family horses, Free and Linlathen. Another Hutchinson horse, Fami, had looked good when winning his last two races of 2003, but failed to follow up, ejecting his rider three from home when in with every chance in the Melton Ladies Open.

The Melton meeting featured the final of the Mares race series — for which a new sponsor, Panacur, had joined the TBA — but the £1000 prize money on offer (four times that of an Open race) failed to attract a decent entry or field, the nine nominations reducing to five declarations on the day. Neither of the local runners played much part and the prize went to one from the **WEST MIDLANDS**, Sovereign Gale, from Theresa McCurrich's stable hard by the Chaddesley Corbett course. Sovereign Gale had won her two previous starts, the most recent at Chaddesley on Dudley Cup day when her trainer had also won with Carthago, both of them ridden by Micky Harris.

Another mare to win at Chaddesley that afternoon was Upton Adventure, whose performances have brought local and national recognition to her owner-breeder, Peter Corbett, her trainer, Nicky Sheppard, and her rider, Emma James. Few mares possess such a consistent record as Upton Adventure. She has won 21 of her 39 starts and been in the frame in all bar her five non-completions — and her eight wins in 2004 won the *Horse & Hound* Trophy as the season's leading winner, the first West Midlands horse to be top since Pensham in 1972. Besides this, and the rest of the silverware her owner has collected through 2004 and preceding seasons, Corbett also had to find room for the newly-instituted TBA Champion Mare prize.

Thanks to Upton Adventure, Emma James finished on a career-best 13 wins, fourth-best nationally. She runs her own yard at Stoke Bliss, near Bromyard, from where she won races with three mares, Certain Surprise, Dorset Fern and Franco Lady.

Most of the credit for Upton Adventure's success must go to Mrs Sheppard, who kept her in race-winning condition during a four-month campaign. Only once was luck on her side — on her seasonal debut when Ballysicyos fell in front two out at Barbury Castle in January — and connections offered no excuses for her two defeats, behind Whether The Storm and Find Me Another at Thorpe in February and by De Chelly at Ystradowen in April. She would have surely been good enough to win under Rules but Point-to-Pointing is her owner's first love.

One of her stablemates, Allez Toujours, who had struggled to make the grade in Novice Hurdles, hit the bull's eye on his first pointing run at Maisemore Park and has potential for more, though his subsequent absence gives cause for concern. Another from the yard, five-year-old Penny Blue, caught the eye with a Brampton Bryan debut third. Favourite on her next run in a Dudley day Maiden, she travelled no farther than the first fence, but gained consolation at Upper Sapey a week later thanks to a superb display by Geoff Barfoot-Saunt, who overcame the handicap of a slipping saddle to claim a well-deserved victory.

Another West Midlands horse to capture the public's imagination with a winning run was Caught At Dawn, who had gained minor successes in several previous seasons but made significant improvement as a 10-year-old, ridden by Hindlip owner-trainer Martin Weston's 17-year-old schoolboy son Tom. After a warm-up outing at Weston Park, he scored at Whitwick, Brampton Bryan, Andoversford and Upton-on-Severn before being allowed to take his chance in the 'classic' Lady Dudley Cup, to which challenge he responded as he had to all the others, powering to victory over the final two fences.

Some doubted his ability to cope at higher level, but 11 days after his Dudley win he jumped the testing Cheltenham fences well and gained a narrow verdict over the Polly Gundry-ridden Balinova after a battle up the final hill — to give his young rider a win on his first attempt under Rules. A second Hunter Chase appearance in the Weatherbys Chase John Corbet at Stratford was eagerly awaited, but he had to be withdrawn on the morning of the race after sustaining a slight cut.

Dick Baimbridge's enthusiasm for the sport remains undimmed by the passing years and his 2004 campaign was a carbon copy of those that have gone before, with a steady flow of winners emanating from his Hill Farm stables in Gloucestershire. His forte is to succeed with horses that have defied the efforts of others, and this time it was April Treasure who provided the example. The mare is a confirmed front-runner whose attempts under Rules always petered out after two-and-a-half miles and that set the pattern for her early efforts between the flags until, at Andoversford in April, after Geoff Barfoot-Saunt managed to restrain her headstrong tendencies for the first circuit, she scooted clear once given her head.

Baimbridge runners are always well-schooled so it was a surprise when Father Tom twice paid the penalty for careless fencing — at Whitwick and Maisemore. A change of tactics provided the key, with Julian Pritchard bringing the 10-year-old ex-Irish pointer from well off the pace to run up a four-win sequence. Stablemate Titus Bramble's form tailed off after two early wins in Tweseldown Opens (the second a dead-heat) and the veterans Well Ted and Teme Willow also each contributed a couple to the stable's total.

Alison Dare and Dick Baimbridge were a formidable combination during the last two decades; now the six-time Champion Lady rider has joined the training ranks and landed her first success with the Machalini in the Beaufort Members race at Didmarton, scene of many of her former triumphs. Ridden by owner Andrew Marley, the ex-chaser scored again in a Novice Riders event at a Cothelstone evening meeting, while the error-prone Babs Wheal gave the trainer another success at the Croome in April, when, thanks to a fine ride from Adrian Wintle, she stayed on her feet to catch tiring rivals on the run-in.

Diana Williams's Enville, Staffs, stable suffered an early loss when Hoodwinker broke a leg when raiding East Anglia in February. The owner-trainer's daughter Jane is a fast-emerging talent and finished third in the Ladies National table, with 14 wins, but, though her mother's yard is packed with class, she will need more outside opportunites if she is to mount a challenge for the title. One who might have helped in 2004 was Dusk Duel, who disposed of a quality field on the opening day at Cottenham only to suffer a fatal injury after the third last when apparently about to tackle Ballysicyos at Barbury Castle a fortnight later.

The much-travelled Supreme Citizen continued his winning ways for the Williams yard, taking his first three Ladies Opens, but then inexplicably, when 2-7 to make it four in a row at Brampton Bryan in late April, he tried to run out in the lead at the final fence, knocking his rider out of the saddle. The always-sweating Sapega went from strength to strength, winning all his three starts, while Step And Run also landed a hat-trick for the Williams team before fading into third at the Worcestershire, where he was backed to beat Upton Adventure.

Mrs Williams also saddled Lord Kilpatrick to give owner Tim Edwards his first win for 10 years at Barbury Castle in January. Her seven-year-old Phase Three, winner of an Irish Maiden in January, figured prominently under Edwards in two visits to Wales and should make his mark in 2005.

Tim Stephenson, riding with a North Ledbury certificate, was always well to the fore on horses from his Castlemorton stable, winning on four or five maidens, among them eight-year-old Wind On The Common, owned and bred by the rider's father, Mike, a familiar figure in the winner's enclosure supporting his son. His Wind On The Common followed an initial success at the Croome by winning the Wheatland Restricted the next month and could be going places. Sadly his owner-breeder will not be there to follow his fortunes, having died shortly after the end of the season.

The North Western Area's Wheatland Hunt had switched course allegiance to Chaddesley Corbett the previous season and the presence of Wheatland-qualified horses was another factor helping to raise the region's standard of racing. Not least among them were those owned by Jane Thornton and her daughter, Hannah Hinckley, such as Hot Toddy (unbeaten in three starts), Paddy For Paddy, Minella Silver and Special Friend, who all made contributions to the title-chasing efforts of Richard Burton, though they were, in fact, all trained by Guy Landau in Somerset.

The useful Roselier 11-year-old Minella Silver, who was returning to Point-to-Points after a season under Rules, scored in his only two starts. Burton rode him the first time, at the High Peak in April, but on the second occasion, in the Wheatland Open, Burton elected to partner instead another of his regular mounts, the Sheila Crow-trained Fane Counsel, who started at 2-5 but was beaten into third place as Adrian Wintle romped home on Minella Silver. Wintle returned the favour later, stepping down from Snowtre, owned and trained by Jim Callow and his daughter Helen Needham, to allow Burton an end-of-season hat-trick on this seven-year-old. Another of Wintle's rides, Snowtre's 10-year-old brother Philtre, was regularly in the frame without quite recapturing his winning form of 2003.

Ledbury-based Julian Pritchard had enjoyed a remarkably injury-free career while accumulating 300-plus winners since 1985, but fate turned against him last season. He had to spend a month on the sidelines after breaking a collarbone at Chaddesley Corbett on February 21, then aggravated the injury on March 28 when Father Tom hit the deck at Maisemore Park and so it was not until April 10 that he made a winning return on the same horse. In the circumstances he did well to finish on a score of 18, which lifted his career total to 326, closing in on the 345 of all-time leader David Turner. Pritchard has enjoyed a fruitful association with Jelly Nolan's Naunton yard, which, by its high standards, suffered a decline in 2004, though the youngsters Fergal's Find and Gregory Peckory give hope for the future.

The profile of Martin and Belinda Keighly's Condicote stable was raised in 2003 by the Sandown Hunter Chase success of Bosuns Mate. He failed to build on that but stablemate Prince Dundee impressed when beating Down at Garthorpe, though he disappointed next time behind Caldamus at Andoversford. Hijacked provided Alan Hollingsworth with two early wins, but another of his home-breds, five-year-old Blackanblue, by Alflora, is the apple of the Feckenham trainer's eye and duly came up trumps under a patient ride from Gary Hanmer at Woodford.

Despite The Campdonian's best efforts he ended the season with just a solitary success, but Lucy King campaigned her horse exclusively in the West Midlands and seven seconds and a third earned sufficient points for the region's Leading Horse prize. The Campdonian also helped jockey Ed Walker to his first Leading Man award, with the Ladies National Champion Polly Gundry taking the female equivalent. Six-year-old maiden Che Guevara was top Novice Horse after finishing second in all his four runs, though the best young animal was probably the Andrew Dalton's Wheatland-qualified seven-year-old Jackson, whose success on his debut run in the Area was followed by two more outside its confines.

Giles Smyly is reported to be trying his luck under Rules in 2005 so wife Kim will have sole charge of the pointers in the Broadway stable. Parahandy was best of them in 2004. Jon Rudge has already tried the senior game, without making much mark, but his runners between the flags have landed some spectacular gambles. However, one on ex-hurdler Is Wonderful at Kingston Blount in May went wrong when the six-year-old, who started 2-1 favourite after opening at 33-1, had to be pulled up lame soon after halfway.

Ben Tulloch teamed up with Clive Bennett in his Dymock stable, from which most of the horses qualify in the West Midlands — Balinova (Ledbury) struck a rich vein of form — but a notable exception was Fertile Valley, who raced with a Teme Valley certificate and was a leading contender among **WELSH BORDER COUNTIES** horses, though his two wins from two starts under Polly Gundry were both gained outside the Area. Successful in an Irish Maiden last year, he was given his first run in this country at Cottenham on the opening day, accounting for the David Pipe-trained favourite Oneminutetofive in the Restricted, and followed up seven weeks later at the Harkaway, on both occasions setting the fastest time for the standard distance races.

Meetings in the Welsh Borders are always well-supported — three of the eight drew over 100 runners and the race average was 9.5 starters — but quality fails to match quantity and it is fair to say that horses in the top flight could be counted on the fingers of one hand. Apart from Fertile Valley, probably only Beauchamp Oracle, Guignol De Cochet and Just Cliquot deserve a place in this category.

Just Cliquot, trained by Corinne Swarbrick for Ken Hamer, provided the perfect mount for Gary Hanmer to demonstrate the waiting tactics which he executes so well. The mare's three Point-to-Point wins, the first after travelling north to Witton Castle, were gained with the utmost ease, while Hanmer was at his brilliant best when bringing her to catch Coole Venture in the final strides of a Bangor Hunter Chase. Unfortunately she lost her season's unbeaten record when she unseated him at Cartmel.

Beauchamp Oracle and Guignol De Cochet were both stabled at Shobdon, near Leominster, with the region's most successful trainer, Steve Flook, who has successfully made the transition from harness racing, where he achieved much. He sent out the winners of eight Point-to-Points and four Hunter Chases. Like Dick Baimbridge, Flook possesses the knack of improving relatively inexpensive horses and best of his string was the former undistinguished chaser Guignol De Cochet, who won the Brightwells Challenge — presented by the auctioneers for the best Point-to-Pointer sold through an Ascot Sale in 2003. Flook bought the gelding there for £6000 and the prize was worth £4000 to him and £3000 to the vendor, Lydia Richards.

Heavily-backed (16-1 to 9-2) on his seasonal debut at Barbury Castle, where he led three out before weakening into fifth, he recovered losses (7-1 to 3-1) in a Novice Riders race at Thorpe Lodge next time out, handled by his part-owner, 41-year-old Kington butcher Glyn Slade-Jones, also well-known on the harness racing circuit. Guignol De Cochet was thereafter campaigned exclusively in Hunter Chases and during a purple patch towards the end of the season won three of his last four starts ridden by three different jockeys, by Dave Mansell at Ludlow, by Thomas Greenall in the £10,205-to-the-winner One and Only Handicap Hunter Chase at Newton Abbot and at Stratford in the miserably-supported Dodson & Horrell Final by Slade-Jones, whose over-exuberant celebration of his first success under Rules nearly cost him the race on the run-in.

Flook ran up a hat-trick of wins in Maiden to Confined class with Beauchamp Oracle, whose form on his Hunter Chase debut at Uttoxeter in May was made to look all the better when his conqueror by a neck, the Yorkshire-trained Scottish Roots, won again on his next outing. Five-year-old former hurdler Enitsnag won a Novice Hunter Chase at Fakenham for the stable and Mister Falcon took two Welsh Open races.

Lady Sue Brooke, Clive Davies, Penny Grainger and Geoff Evans are trainers who can usually be relied upon to supply winners but they all had a fairly dismal time. Ann Price, a staunch supporter of Point-to-Points in this part of the world for over 40 years, also suffered a success shortage in her Presteigne yard, but still managed to secure the Leading Owner and Trainer prize, thanks largely to Genereux (who later made £3700 at Ascot's end-of-season sale) and Huntersway. 'Lad of the Year' Angie Murphy works in the Price yard and Rob Hodges, who rode both horses to win, was the Area's Leading Man Rider.

Hodges, a care worker from Hope-under-Dinmore, near Leominster, enjoyed his most successful season in the saddle and his never-say-die attitude was never better demonstrated than when he took over Genereux on Steve Blackwell's retirement. This horse has always needed plenty of driving and cajoling and, though on several occasions all efforts proved fruitless, everything clicked into place at the Radnor and West Herefordshire meeting at Cold Harbour in May when Genereux came from well off the pace to land the four-mile Crudwell Cup.

Another Shobdon-based trainer, Steve Isaac, is making steady progress. He took the Area's Leading Horse Award thanks to Shemardi, the first racehorse owned by another Shobdon resident, Barbara Gibbons. Isaac also had for the same owner Magicien, who proved an in-and-out performer but managed to get his head in front when ridden by Rachel Reynolds in a Chaddesley Restricted.

Caroline Walker, also based in the Welsh Marches, raced a useful sort in seven-year-old Jimmy Cricket, whose second fence fall at Barbury Castle in January preceded a Restricted and Confined double in his other outings. At Weston Park, those who had backed him from 14-1 to 6-1 never had a moment's anxiety as Nick Oliver brought him home 25 lengths clear of subsequent winner Sutton Courtenay.

Lancastrian Jet was the highest-rated horse in the Welsh Borders thanks to four Hunter Chase wins under Marc Barber. It might have been five had Barber not been knocked out of the saddle by a loose horse when odds-on at Towcester. The 13- year-old was trained professionally by Henry Daly.

Several runners from Jo Priest's stable raced with Teme Valley certificates and the Eyton-on-Severn course proved a happy hunting ground for them. Stretching won two Ladies Opens there under Jane Williams and was third in another, while William Hill won a Restricted on the subsequently disappointing six-year-old Heavy Weather.

Two first-time winning jockeys will remember Welsh Border meetings with affection. John Taylor, 37, opened his account on Clive Hitchings's Better Future at Garnons, where the veteran has scored seven of his 15 victories, while at the Golden Valley's Bredwardine fixture 20-year-old

Patrick Crozier. a grandson of the Golden Valley's founder-Master Vivian Bishop, scored his first success on his mother's Highbridge.

Billie Brown sent out a couple of winners at Cold Harbour in May. Percy Priday's modest performer Persona Pride followed six failures by winning for Julian Pritchard, while Ben Shaw finally managed to get Lou Biarnes home for owner Michael Ings, who also won at the meeting with another of his numerous home-breds from the Dunsmore Lass line, the improving mare Withybrook Lass. Her dam, Broadbrook Lass, won twice between the flags in 2002 prior to scoring under Rules for Heather Dalton, whose husband Andrew legged up Richard Burton to score on the six-year-old in a Mares Maiden.

The fact that well-maintained courses, where sufficient effort has been expended to provide the best possible racing ground, will always attract good fields was exemplified at Cold Harbour and even more at the mid-May Bredwardine fixture, which drew 117 runners. Its attractions were not lost on owners in Wales, who supplied nearly 25 per cent of the starters and won two of the Maiden divisions, thanks to Blakeney Hill and five-year-old Neminos, both qualified with packs in the **SOUTH WALES & MONMOUTHSHIRE** Area.

Sunday racing is still resisted in these parts. Only two of the 11 meetings were staged on the seventh day — and one of those, the second Curre & Llangibby, only after an enforced waterlogging postponement from its original Saturday (the first Curre & Llangibby was also put back, but found another Saturday slot). It was similar in **WEST WALES**, where the Carmarthenshire was the sole Sunday meeting. Was it just coincidence that its fixture, despite watering at Lydstep, had the region's poorest turnout? Runners tailed off sharply after the first two meetings in West Wales — the Banwen Miners had two walkovers, including one in the featured four-mile West Wales Grand National — resulting in a race average of only 6.5, against the 8.3 recorded for South Wales.

The South Wales feature race was also a four-miler — the Welsh Point-to-Point Grand National at the Pentyrch meeting — and attracted a better field of 10, but none of the local hopes could offer any resistance over this trip to the Warwickshire 13-year-old Down, who completed a hat-trick of victories in this stayers test.

Before the start of the season Welsh followers had mourned the loss of three stalwarts who had given so much to the advancement of Point-to-Pointing in the Principality: former senior steward John Cory, Jockey Club course inspector Wyndham James and Brian Jenkins, who, like James, had been a notable rider in his younger days.

The season's start was twice delayed, first by a week when the Vale of Clettwr fixture had to be postponed when the Erw Lon track was waterlogged — and then by another 90 minutes when the paramedic team was late turning up on the revised date! This meant a fair rush to get through before the daylight departed. The holding ground presented something of a test, too, and in fact only 23 of the afternoon's 69 starters completed the course. Former Novice Hurdler Cannon Bridge was an exception and positively loved the mud, opening his account on his first run over fences. Trained for Keith Pritchard by Nikki Hughes, who had given birth to a baby girl on the meeting's original date, the six-year-old won his only two following starts, ridden by Dai Jones, who ended Welsh Champion for the third time, partnering 16 winners in all to reach a career total of 159.

One of Jones's regular mounts, Sohapara, who the previous year had travelled to Garthorpe to win the Marsh Mares final at the Melton meeting, was again in form, her four successes including a Hereford Hunter Chase and a Bonvilston Open race walkover. Following the walkover she was saddled again an hour or so later and had another victory booked until slipping up on rain-soaked grass as she rounded the bend before the final fence in a comfortable lead.

Evan Williams made an early start, travelling to Tweseldown in January to win on Paul Morgan's Mensch, but the former National Champion (who in April was temporarily laid low by chickenpox) is successfully developing his licensed stable and so left the Point-to-Pointers to his wife Cath, who sent out five horses to win 10 races. Best of them was Pat Tollit's home-bred Bright Beacon, who cantered away with Open races at Erw Lon and Garnons before tragically breaking a leg when going well in a Chepstow Hunter Chase. Six-year-old Rag Week and seven-year-old Like The Buzz each won three times for the yard and the former was among numerous successes landed by Williams when he made hay during summer jumping.

Bridgend trainer John Moore had a couple who more than paid for their keep in Red Neck and Aljoash. The latter, who failed to make her reserve at Doncaster in August, won three races, while Red Neck's four victories included both Men's Opens at Lydstep. The pair were the mounts of Tim Vaughan, whose trainer girlfriend, Abbi Johns, provided him with a couple of seven-year-old Maiden winners, Clear Away and Roboastar. He also rode another from the stable, Doc Ryan's, before handing over to Charlotte Owen to bring off a surprise Ladies' Open victory when the Pembrokeshire brought the Welsh season to a close at Trecoed.

Before that Mrs Owen had caused an even greater surprise in the Glamorgan's Ladies race, when she and De Chelly were responsible for the first of only two defeats suffered all year by the season's Leading Horse Upton Adventure, who started 1-4 favourite. Upton Adventure gained ample revenge when the pair met at Bredwardine later in the season, but De Chelly followed her Glamorgan victory by catching the useful Ashfield Orchestra on the run-in at the South Pembrokeshire on Easter Monday. This was Ashfield Orchestra's third consecutive runner-up spot (the first was to Upton Adventure) after she had started her campaign with a good Ladies' race victory at Howick in March.

Detroit Davy, from Phil Williams's Tonyrefail stable, just accounted for Ashfield Orchestra on his seasonal debut in the Monmouthshire Ladies race but failed to gain further distinction. His rider, physical education teacher Fiona Wilson, finished top of the ladies list in South Wales, collecting a career best nine wins. She was in demand by several trainers, not least David Brace, for whom she won two Ladies Opens with Dawn's Cognac and a Maiden and a Restricted with Rostock. Dawn's Cognac's form went downhill after his fall in the Chepstow Hunter Chase sponsored by Brace's company, but Rostock, something of a wild thing, won twice more at Bonvilston meetings with male riders up before the end of the season.

The Chepstow race referred to — the Dunraven Bowl Hunter Chase — went for the third time to Evan Williams, who was riding the previous year's winner Cherry Gold. Unbeaten in an Open and two Hunter Chases in 2003, he slipped down the ratings a little in 2004, finishing a long way behind in Caught At Dawn's Cheltenham race, for which he started favourite. Other Welsh Hunter Chase winners included Monks Error and Longstone Boy. The former, an ex-Irish chaser, appeared only twice, in May, finishing a fair third at Folkestone and then, with Nick Williams up, beating Macgeorge at Uttoxeter. Williams also rode Longstone Boy when he won at Leicester after giving a first Point-to-Point win, in a Ladies Open in Somerset, to Jodie Hughes, who had ridden a Hunter Chase winner in 2003.

Rider Lee Stephens recorded his best season since he started winning when working for the Sheila Crow stable six years ago. He rode 11 winners, eight of them for Pontypridd-based Robert Rowsell, the region's most successful trainer. Rowsell's first success was not gained until mid-April but he finished the season on a tally of 10 wins, gained by five horses. Stephens owned part of his success to the absence of the trainer's wife, Lucy Rowsell, who was kept out of the saddle for maternal reasons.

In less health-and-safety-conscious days — 1991 in fact — the then star East Anglian lady rider Lucy Gibbon returned to ride a winner 26 days after the birth of her second son, but Mrs Rowsell's efforts to persuade the Jockey Club's Doctor, Michael Turner, that she was fit to resume race-riding following the birth of a daughter, Holly Beth, in late March, were not successful until just before the Tredegar Farmers meeting on May 23 at Rhydygwern, where, eight weeks and two days after Holly Beth's arrival, she rode Khatani to win the Ladies Open. She triumphed again aboard the same horse at the Torrington Farmers grand finale meeting in June.

Stephens had earlier won a Men's Open at Laleston with Khatani and he also landed a hat-trick for the stable with seven-year-old Chancy Guy — from three starts, Maiden to Open — and on eight-year-old Wellheseemedsoslow twice from two late-season outings — Maiden and Restricted. Best of Stephens's rides other than for Rowsell was the aforementioned Rostock, who gave him the third leg of a treble at the Gelligaer Farmers meeting.

Mrs Rowsell was not the only lady rider to achieve newsworthy post-natal success in 2004. Carrie Ford made the headlines in April when, ten-and-a-half weeks after the birth of her daughter, Hannah, she triumphed over the Grand National fences in the Martell Fox Hunters, riding Forest Gunner, a horse trained by her husband, Richard, who had won the big Aintree test on Rolling Ball eight years before.

PLATE 6 1483 Tredegar Farmers Ladies Open: A jubilant Lucy Rowsell is led back after winning on Khatana just 10 weeks after the birth of her daughter *PHOTO: David Jones*

Mrs Ford, who had 'retired' the previous season with over 50 Point-to-Point winners to her name, had shown that she was fit for the task when winning a hurdle race at Huntingdon on the Sunday before the Fox Hunters, while Forest Gunner, who had been fired after finishing sore at Fakenham in December, 2002, had confirmed his well-being when third behind County Derry and Earthmover on his comeback run at Fontwell in February. Three weeks after Aintree he finished fifth in a Perth handicap, having made several mistakes, but his rider gained successes in her trainer's role, saddling Palisander to win the Cheshire Forest Ladies Open under Caroline Hurley over a Tabley course which had been lengthened this year and now demands 20 jumps. Palisander, a 10-year-old modest performer under Rules for Richard Ford, proved an admirable 'recruit' in Hunt racing, winning his only other start in the Pendle Forest's Ladies Open.

Mrs Ford has frequently won the Ladies Championship in the **NORTH WESTERN** Area but in 2004 that honour went to Tessa Clark, a sister of event rider Polly Stockton. She had missed much of the previous season because of a bad collarbone break but now achieved a career-best tally of five wins, two of them in Ladies Opens on Richard Francis's veteran Wandering Light, who in his younger days had taken the NH Chase at Cheltenham in the colours of Anne Duchess of Westminster. Runner-up was Sue Sharratt, whose only successes within the Area were gained in Maiden races on Richard Froggatt's home-bred half-brothers Ridware Pride and Ridware George.

Top man, needless to say, was the 2003 National Champion and 2004 runner-up Richard Burton, who, despite numerous triumphs elsewhere, comfortably outpointed Gary Hanmer. Burton posed a constant threat to Ashley Farrant in the race for the *Daily Telegraph* Cup, briefly heading the West Countryman after the May Day Bank Holiday weekend had yielded him seven wins, including a four-timer at the South Shropshire, and not conceding defeat until the final day. His 50 winners (37 had been sufficient to win him the title the previous year) were spread wide, being provided by no fewer than 17 stables, with Sheila Crow's Shropshire yard the biggest contributor with 12 winners, followed by that of Caroline Robinson (eight) and Guy Landau (six).

The latter's useful team have been mentioned in the West Midlands review, while best of Mrs Crow's string ridden by Burton was Clive Hitchings's six-year-old Irish import Fane Counsel, who first caught the eye when winning on his English debut in a Restricted at Horseheath in February. He returned to that Hertfordshire course the following month to set a very fast time in an Intermediate but, though his other starts were nearer home, local supporters didn't see the best of him. He cocked his jaw and ran out on a bend before halfway when 1-3 favourite at Brampton Bryan and then, as mentioned in the West Midlands review, weakened into third when 2-5 for the Wheatland Open, in which Burton chose to ride him rather than the Landau representative Minella Silver, who won.

Mrs Crow's Coole Venture was ridden to win Opens by Burton at Brampton Bryan and Sandon, though overall this one failed to recapture his form of 2003, when he had run Sheriff's Friend to a neck in the Weatherbys Chase John Corbet. Burton also steered five-year-old debutant Best Accolade to win his only starts in a Maiden and a Restricted for the stable and scored four firsts and two seconds from six outings aboard Pristeen Spy. This Teenoso seven-year-old had done little since winning his Maiden two years before but now collected the Area's Young Horse prize for owner-breeder David Heys.

Before leaving Mrs Crow's stable it must be recorded that her son Alastair, the National Champion with 30 winners in 1995, reached his career double century (194 Point-to-Points, six Hunter Chases, starting in 1985) when six-year-old Along The Lawn was left clear in a Tanatside Maiden after Bless Yourself ejected Gary Hanmer at the final fence.

Burton's successes for the Caroline Robinson stable included three Opens on Jemaro and an Eyton Maiden with five-year-old Reflected Glory. This first-season youngster, who was having his second outing (runner-up in the first), very nearly threw the race away when jumping violently right two from home and was not seen again until May at the Doncaster Sales, where he was knocked down for 33,000 guineas.

Pamela Sykes had a quieter time than usual from her stable at Bishop's Castle, but provided Burton with three young horses to win on — six-year-olds Pot Shot and King's Reply and seven-year-old Cousin George. All three victories were gained outside the Area, as were the two wins from two runs (Maiden and Restricted) achieved by Burton on the promising Mark Williamson-trained six-year-old Lambrini Mist.

Numerically second to Mrs Crow in the Area training statistics was Gary Hanmer, who sent out nine horses to win 10 races. He rode eight of them himself, including the two wins of veteran

Analystic, who broke down fatally at the Fernie in May, and a victory on his sole run with five-year-old newcomer Border Fusion at Eaton Hall in late March. He won an Eaton Hall Open with ex-Venetia Williams chaser Soundtrack, who later made 6000 guineas at Doncaster, and just about best of the eight winners he rode for others were Ken Hamer's Just Cliquot, whose four wins have been mentioned in the Welsh Border review, and the Paul Jones-trained six-year-old Thyne Man, on whom he replaced tbe injured William Hill to land an impressive Restricted win at Eyton-on-Severn.

Thyne Man was partnered by Paul Cowley when he ran second to Althrey Dandy in the North Western Area P-t-P Championship Hunter Chase at Bangor in May as Hanmer was aboard Soundtrack, who finished a well-beaten third ahead of Coole Venture. The Meynell-qualified Althrey Dandy, trained by Carly Goodall, rose rapidly up the ratings after winning all his three starts under Lennie Hicks. Nothing could get near him in a Maiden and a Restricted and the only surprise about his Bangor victory was that he started at 10-1.

The Holcombe meeting, which had to be called off when furious gales struck the Whittington course, was the Area's sole loss, the only other weather interruption coming when the Tanatside fixture had to be put back a fortnight because of waterlogging at Eyton-on-Severn. The remaining 14 fixtures drew a reasonable 835 runners, producing a race-average of 8.2, fractionally above the national norm. This was nearly matched in the **NORTHERN** Area, though here the figure — precisely 8.06 — was greeted with some concern, since it indicated continuation of a downward spiral; the 960 runners at the 17 fixtures was the lowest total since 1991. The hunting ban in Scotland is held to blame by some, though in this context it is good to hear that the Dumfriesshire meeting, absent for four years, is due back in 2005 following the Hunt's renaissance, though not on the famed Lockerbie course but at a new venue just over the Border at Netherby in Cumbria.

All 17 meetings went ahead on their appointed dates bar the Jedforest, which was delayed for six days because of drifting snow on parts of the Friars Haugh course. Attendance was poor on the revised date, as it was at the other two Kelso fixtures, all three suffering from inclement weather.

Lambourn-based property agent Ranald Morgan, 28, clinched the Area Men's Championship for the first time, thanks to a purple patch at the last four meetings, when he chalked up five of his eight wins to finish nine points ahead of Andrew Richardson. Pauline Robson took the Ladies' title for the 12th time in the last 13 years, besides landing her 150th Point-to-Point win and also saddling five winners over jumps in her first season as a licensed trainer.

Her partner, David Parker, now trains the Point-to-Pointers in their Capheaton livery yard and achieved a remarkable strike rate, sending out 14 runners between the flags to win 11 races and finish second in three others. That was from six horses, King Barry, Rainha, Hallrule, Lordberniebouffant, Mytimie and Benbeoch.

Five-year-old King Barry looks to possess a touch of class. He picked up a Maiden and a Restricted in his only starts, as did the Alflora mare Rainha, though her Restricted victory at the Percy was officially a dead-heat. Peppernick, who shared the prize with Rainha, was coming back after a two-year lay-off but did not appear again. He is ridden out every day by his spritely owner-breeder, Bobby Brewis, 78, who won the Cheltenham Foxhunters with Whinstone Hill in 1958 and 1960.

Hallrule, off the track since 2000, failed to finish in three Chases from another yard in the early summer of 2003 but seemed rejuvenated, winning a Maiden and Restricted before switching to the Robson string to capture two Handicap Chases in April. Hallrule's form was boosted when Steve Marshall's home-bred Miss Mattie Ross, a close second to him on her seasonal debut at Alnwick, then rattled off a hat-trick of Hunter Chase victories at Kelso under Michael McAlister, who is attached to Len Lungo's stable.

Lordberniebouffant, just touched off by Parade Racer in the Tynedale Ladies Open, twice came up trumps for Parker in May when dropped in class, while former chaser Mytimie won two Ladies Opens before disappointing in Hunter Chases, after which he made 14,000 guineas at Doncaster May Sales. Miss Robson partnered all these winners, while Kevin Anderson gave Benbeoch a peach of a ride when the five-year-old made a winning debut in the Border Maiden on his only appearance.

Busiest livery stable in the Area was that of ex-NH jockey Tim Reed, who ran no fewer than 15 horses, of which seven won to give Reed his best-ever figures of 11 wins, three of them — Lord

Edwards Army, Blyth Brook and Commanche Law — in Hunter Chases. Alison Hamilton, an Edinburgh investment manager, brings out the best in Commanche Law, producing the 11-year-old with perfectly-timed challenges to win the Morpeth Ladies' Open and the Gerrard Hunter Chase Final at Huntingdon. Blyth Brook made a winning seasonal debut in a Musselburgh Hunter Chase under Ran Morgan, who also rode Lord Edwards Army to upset the odds-on Sad Mad Bad at Ayr in April.

Reed's stable star, Three Spires, picked up for only 1500 guineas at Doncaster the year before with no form to speak of — though he is a son of dual *Horse & Hound* Cup winner Mystic Music — was superbly handled by Andrew Richardson to win a Maiden, Restricted and Intermediate and be placed in his other three starts. A Reed non-winner, seven-year-old Uncle Neil, was runner-up three times before being bought for 20,000 guineas at Doncaster by Edward Crow. Another northerner to make good money here was six-year-old Capybara, who fulfilled 2003 promise by winning a Friars Haugh Maiden in very testing conditions before being put away for the sale, where he was knocked down for 21,000 guineas to trainer Henry Hogarth. He looks a decent chasing prospect.

Nicola Stirling, runner-up again in the Area Ladies Championship, equalled her best seasonal score of nine. Her mother Pat's ultra-consistent Pharmistice added another four Ladies Opens to his career tally, Clifford Bay completed a hat-trick in his last three races and the promising six-year-old Ofcoursehekhan overcame a slipping saddle to land a Lauderdale Maiden. He looks to have scope to progress in 2005, when his owner will be riding as Nicola Neill following her marriage in July.

The local Novice Championship was lifted by Newcastle-upon-Tyne stockbroker Adam Waugh, a first-season rider thus confirming that life begins at 40. He looked as if he had been at it all his life when partnering his own Just Barney Boy to a memorable debut win in the College Valley Open. Another accomplished performance brought him victory in the Buccleuch Open and he and his seven-year-old failed by a mere neck to peg back Red Gauntlet in the Border Open. Chris Gillon, winner of the National Novice title in 2003 when he worked in George White's Rennington yard, gave up race-riding before Easter to be a fencing contractor, his decision perhaps prompted by the miserable season suffered by White's virus-hit stable, while the previous year's Area Champion, Tom Oates, had his season curtailed after a nasty fall early in March.

But for Victor Thompson, who trains on the Northumberland coast at Low Newton-by-the-Sea, 2004 brought a marked change of fortune. Following a decade in which he had saddled only a handful of winners, he recorded best-ever figures, with seven successes from Falcon's Flame, The Cincinatti Kid and Decent Bond. The last-named was his top winner, scoring four times and taking the Area's Young Horse Award. All three were ridden by Chatton farmer Roger Green and Thompson deserves credit for producing each one spot on to score first time out. He is certainly not resting on his laurels and prepared for 2005 by going on something of a buying spree at Doncaster in August, laying out over 65,000 guineas for six five-year-olds.

Rhona Elliot endured a blank season with her licence but her husband, Peter, and Morag Neill did well with the pointers in the Hownam yard. Their principal owner is Duncan Davidson, the Persimmon Homes chairman, whose horses are ridden by his daughter, Rose, who commutes north each weekend from Lambourn. Davidson's company supported the Area's first-ever feature race, the four-mile Mixed Open at the Percy, and appropriately his Passing Danger went ahead on the flat to lift the £350 first prize. This progressive nine-year-old won three other races and was second or third four times from his eight starts.

Stable-companion Dere Street landed the West Percy Members on his reappearance and was second or third in five Ladies Opens, while five-year-old Eighty Days, bought by Davidson from Yorkshire owner Maxine Stirk following his Maiden win at the West of Yore, landed a Buccleuch Restricted in testing conditions and looks an exciting prospect for 2005, when Miss Davidson, who led the National Novice table until overhauled by the West Country's Mary McCarthy in the closing weeks, may also partner former Henrietta Knight chaser Kick For Touch, a 34,000-guinea purchase at Doncaster last May.

Jimmy Walton is as enthusiastic now as when he first started race-riding in 1964 and enjoyed three wins on the progressive More Flair. His Posh Stick struggled to stay the three miles but opened her account in a two-and-a-half-mile Cumberland Farmers' Maiden.

Things were quieter than usual in Clive Storey's Yetholm yard. He rode three young Maiden winners himself, Sharp Fountain, General Jake and River Alder, and also saddled Harden Glen to make all in the College Valley Ladies Open under owner Jenny Riding. A week later the 13-year-old dropped dead on the gallops, but subsequently Miss Riding won two Kelso Hunter Chases aboard the Maxine Bremner-trained Nisbet. He won again at Perth for Jane Hollands, who enjoyed some cracking rides on Royalecko, trained by her mother, Joan, and twice a winner in minor company before finishing a good second to Clifford Bay in his first attempt at a Ladies Open, in which sphere he could go well in 2005.

River Alder, who carried the colours of rider-turned-commentator Michael Dun — whose Lord Lane was ridden to win a Maiden by Nicola Stirling — romped home in a two-and-a-half-mile Novice Hurdle under Mark Bradburne after being switched to Sandy Forster's pro yard.

After enduring a near-12-month blank spell, Cumberland Joint-Master and permit-holder John Brockbank sent out four winners over a 25-day period in May. Trivial set the ball rolling in the Lauderdale Men's Open less than 24hrs after unseating at the third fence at Hexham and towards the end of the month the mare followed up by taking a Cartmel Hunter Chase. She was partnered by Luke Morgan, whose brother Ranald helped the Brockbank fortunes by winning a Members and a Restricted on Distracting.

The Morgan brothers clashed in the Haydon Open at Hexham, with Luke on Starbuck (already twice a winner for him) narrowly resisting Ran and Hoh Tel after a blazing finish in which both incurred the wrath of the stewards over their whip use, Luke being fined £60 and Ran £100.

The Area's prestigious Heart of All England Maiden Hunter Chase at Hexham went to Mid Summer Lark, trained by Ian McMath, a glazier based at Cumwhinton, near Carlisle. Confident that the eight-year-old — a maiden between the flags — would benefit from stronger handling, McMath engaged Miles Seston for a preliminary Hunter Chase at Carlisle. The partnership clicked straight away and, after finishing second to Black Smoke that day, the eight-year-old kept up a relentless gallop in front at Hexham, jumping boldly when the chips were down.

Following the previous year's debacle at Ayr Racecourse, the Eglinton/Lanarks & Renfrew fixture at Overton Farm, Crossford, was a resounding success, attracting a bumper crowd to reward all the hard work of landowner Willie Young and his team in creating a new course, though, the terrain being flat, viewing was far from ideal. In contrast, the Northern Association's Club fixture at Musselburgh Racecourse has proved costly to stage and has swiftly lost its popularity after drawing a massive attendance for the inaugural meeting in 2002. It is no surprise to see it missing from the 2005 list.

Balisteros, that wonderful veteran from the Berwickshire who took the Leading Horse award for owner Billie Thomson four years ago, clocked up another 12 appearances and won three more Ladies races at the age of 15 to raise his career tally to 33, including four Hunter Chases, from 94 outings. He finally went into retirement after being pulled up in the Handicap Chase named after him at Kelso on May 20. His first two victories, in 1995, came when he was in the Dorset stable of Richard Barber, but all the rest were for Mrs Thomson, who rode him herself to score three times in 1998. Jill Wormall won 10 races on Balisteros, but his most successful partner, with 13, was Pauline Robson, who was in the saddle when he landed his first two wins of 2004, both at meetings in the **YORKSHIRE** Area.

He earned the biggest cheer of the day from the generous Yorkshire crowd — it lasted all the way to the winner's enclosure — after making virtually every yard at the Sinnington. The following weekend at the West of Yore (where the stewards gamble that the overnight snow would melt away was justified), Balisteros fought back gamely to snatch a half-length verdict from another of advancing years, Silver Groom, who three weeks before, in the Ladies race at the Area's first meeting, the Old Raby, had given Jacqueline Coward her initial success. On Silver Groom she later twice chased home Texas Ranger (see next paragraph) and these performances, plus a win with Clonshire Paddy, ensured that she took the local Leading Lady Novice award ahead of Rachel Clark, three of whose four wins with Supreme Silence and Claire's Nomad were gained outside the Area.

Silver Groom was trained by Miss Coward's uncle, David Easterby, and in 2003 had won four Ladies Opens in five weeks to help gain the Area Ladies Championship for Jo Foster, who in 2004 took the senior title for a third year running — by a couple of points from Serena Brotherton — this time mainly thanks to one from her own yard, Texas Ranger, a horse she bought for new owner Richard Chew. The six-year-old landed a comfortable Ladies Open hat-trick at the

Holderness, Hurworth and Bedale before travelling north to Hexham to stop Pharmistice's winning run at the Border meeting. Texas Ranger, successful in four successive races over hurdles when with Charlie Mann two seasons earlier, won the PPORA's Young Horse Award for Yorkshire but had to settle for second place in the Area's Open Horse prize. Though he went into the final meeting at Heslaker holding a two-point lead over Hadeqa, he was easily beaten there by that horse, who had arrived just in time for declaration after being re-routed from his intended target in the Stratford Ladies Hunter Chase when owner Michael Brown did not fancy the going there.

Hadeqa had been a revelation since being switched to Ladies races under Serena Brotherton in the second half of the season and at last began to reward his owner's faith. After finishing second to Texas Ranger at the Bedale, the eight-year-old, so often a disappointment since his victories on the flat and over hurdles in 1999, gained revenge at the York and Ainsty (where Texas Ranger fell at the last when only fourth) and then, after being outpaced by Supercharmer at Witton Castle, scooped up the last two Ladies races in the Area at Mordon and Heslaker fairly comfortably. Miss Brotherton also scored twice each in non-Open company with Emperor's Son and Mister Bromley.

The Men's riding title went to the reigning champion, Nigel Tutty, who nearly did a Kieren Fallon on Journey at the York and Ainsty. Coasting up the run-in in the Confined without a care in the world after landing over the last 20 lengths clear, he suddenly came under assault from Michael Morley on Glendamah and held on by only a neck. At the Bilsdale in early May Tutty took a slender lead over Guy Brewer when riding seven-year-old Silogue to win the Maiden and then he stormed clear with a treble at the following week's South Durham, where he won in his own colours aboard Silogue and Sarak, both trained by his wife, Karen, and on the Sarah Dent-trained Dumadic in the Men's Open.

Tutty also took the Area's Leading Owner award, while the owner of the best home-bred was Charmaine Raw with her six-year-old Nought To Ninety, who, after being a tailed-off last at the Middleton, came from miles behind to win his Maiden at the Staintondale and turned in a like performance in the York and Ainsty Restricted, ridden each time by Lee Bates.

In Men's Open races the out-and-out stayer Mr Mahdlo holds claims for top spot, though only because he remained unbeaten in his two runs between the flags; three outings in Hunter Chases found him wanting and he did not jump the bigger fences with any zest. Ridden by the 2003 Area Novice Champion Ben Woodhouse, he brought off a 33-1 surprise against most of the Area's leading Open horses in the Sinnington's Land Rover qualifier in February and a fortnight later won a high-class Mixed Open at the Derwent. Behind him there Texas Ranger was a well-beaten third, the pair being divided by Mr Pendleberry who, after an initial second in sticky ground at Thorpe Lodge on February 1, just caught San Francisco in the following week's feature event at the Old Raby. Ridden by Nicky Tinkler and trained by his mother, the consistent Mr Pendleberry went on to take two more races, including a head victory over Nordic Crest in the Staintondale Goathland's Mixed Open, and was never worse than fourth in his eight runs.

Following that narrow defeat by Mr Pendleberry, Nordic Crest cantered away with Men's Opens at both Easingwold meetings, ridden by Mark Walford for Cherry Coward, whose charge Clonshire Paddy showed his liking for a distance of ground when making a successful raid on Dingley in May for the Fernie's four-mile Men's Open, where he was ridden by Thomas Greenall.

Greenall rode winners for David Easterby, whose string at Sheriff Hutton included the unrelated High Peak and High Fields, who ended up respectively first and second in the region's Novice Horse points table. Seven-year-old High Peak's debut over fences at the Old Raby was anything but promising when the former undistinguished hurdler fell at the first. However, sent to the Burton meeting a fortnight later, he strolled home in a Maiden and then won all his following three starts, a Restricted and two Opens. Greenall was the rider in all but High Peak's last outing at the Bedale, when he was away winning a Hurdle at Carlisle. So Richard Wakeham was called in as substitute — and was seen at his coolest when bringing High Peak through to score, never off the bridle. Wakeham was pretty cool later in the year, too, when he was one of the protesters 'invading' the House of Commons during the passage of the anti-hunting Bill. Another of his mounts, the seven-year-old Duchess Account, could be one to keep an eye on next year. A fair third at the Middleton, she later ran away with a York and Ainsty Maiden.

Five-year-old High Fields won a Maiden and Restricted for Greenall before having to give best in the Middleton Members race to another Easterby-trained horse, Scottish Roots, who was a first winner for Greenall's 17-year-old Shrewsbury schoolboy brother Oliver. Scottish Roots was otherwise kept to Hunter Chases ridden by the elder brother — who had also chalked up his first success in the Middleton Members race two years before — and, after finishing third in the Heart of All England, won sub-three mile events at Uttoxeter and Hexham.

Easterby had another good Hunter Chase winner in Sikander A Azam, owned by Greenall's father, Lord Daresbury. Successful in his only two starts between the flags in 2003, he began with a comfortable victory over two miles, three-and-a-half furlongs at Ascot, then ran second to Forest Gunner in the Martell Fox Hunters at Aintree and also second — to the formidable East Anglian Placid Man — at Warwick. Greenall also won Hunter Chases at Newton Abbot on Guignol De Cochet (Steve Flook's Brightwells Challenge winner mentioned in the West Midlands review) and for Mick Easterby at Perth on Hermes III, a late defector from the Grand National.

Torn Silk was another dual Men's Open winner, scoring at both the Heslaker meetings under Clive Mulhall, while seven-year-old Dumadic, just headed on the line by Torn Silk at the first Heslaker, reversed placings with his conqueror at the South Durham a fortnight later and then went to Doncaster Sales, where he was led out unsold after being bid up to 24,000 guineas. At the South Durham Dumadic had been the middle leg of Nigel Tutty's treble which sent him clear of Guy Brewer in the Area's Men's Championship.

Brewer's winning total — 11 — was three ahead of Tutty's, but more of them were outside the Area boundaries. He collected nine of his victories on horses trained by Mary Sowersby, most of them maidens, and was also the rider when the owner of the former Midlands-trained Upham Lord, winner of the *Horse & Hound* Leading Horse Trophy in 2002-03, responded to allegations of pot-hunting by sending him to Peter Beaumont to be qualified with the Middleton for Hunter Chases. The venture was not a success. Though Upham Lord won first time out at Fakenham in February, he could never stage a repeat and in fact finished on the floor in three of his last four outings.

Grant Tuer, who had carried all before him in 2003, enjoyed another good year, winning three Hunter Chases with Golden Chimes, Sad Mad Bad and Son Of Anshaan. He had taken the Middleton's 'classic' Grimthorpe Cup the previous year with the last-named and now, after first steering Golden Chimes home in the meeting's Confined race, won this coveted prize again when Sad Mad Bad triumphed in a highly-competitive field of 17, of which at least half a dozen were still in with a chance in the final two furlongs. A short-priced favourite following his Sedgefield victory, Sad Mad Bad was held up at the rear until making headway with five to jump, to take over from long-time leader Dorans Magic at the penultimate and quicken clear. Tuer had acquired Sad Mad Bad the previous summer from the then BHB chairman Peter Savill, for whom the 10-year-old won over hurdles and fences when trained by Mary Reveley.

Joss Saville, who trains in stables formerly occupied by Harvey and Sue Smith at Bingley and retains a close connection with them, was Yorkshire's leading trainer and made an early strike when sending Mrs Smith's Omni Cosmo Touch south to win the Men's Open at the second Cottenham meeting. The eight-year-old followed up three weeks later with a comfortable success in a Novice Hunter Chase at Sedgefield, but after the race the horse tested positive to a banned painkiller and suffered inevitable disqualification, with Mrs Smith fined £600. Her horse ran disappointingly in the Cheltenham Foxhunters, but sluiced up later in the Belvoir Men's Open, still trained by Saville but by then sold to Alan Potts.

The trainer's younger brother Niall was in the saddle on all the stable's winners — apart from when he arrived too late for the Belvoir Open, when Andrew Sansome was the winning substitute — and other useful performers he rode included two more of Mrs Smith's, Ten Bob and Cross River, who both won Maiden divisions at the Old Raby. Six-year-old Ten Bob followed up in a very hot Restricted in Brocklesby Park before disappointing at the Middleton fixture, while Cross River also took a Restricted. He then showed very little in a couple of Hunter Chases before landing quite a coup for connections in the final such event of the season, at Cartmel on May 31. The Saville brothers had also scored in the season's first Hunter Chase, at Wetherby on February 7, with the promising seven-year-old Star Of Raven, while another of the same age in the yard to catch the eye was Sizer. He gave his rider a hair-raising time on his February debut at Witton Castle, where he started favourite, but recovered losses impressively in a Grove and Rufford Maiden the following month.

Niall Saville also won twice in succession on Willie Bethell's Dolphin Square and the 11-year-old completed a hat-trick in the Vale of Lune's Intermediate when giving a first-ride win to the owner's 17-year-old schoolgirl daughter Harriet.

Gill Walford commenced operations even earlier than the Savilles, sending Guilsborough Gorse south to win the Men's Open at Cottenham under her son Mark on the season's opening day. Three weeks later this consistent gelding routed all opposition in the PPORA race at the Lincolnshire Club meeting — where Mark Walford was the star of the day, completing a treble on stable-companions Henry Murphy and Golden Rivet in the two Maiden divisions. Guilsborough Gorse remained unbeaten after his only other run in a Musselburgh Hunter Chase, while Golden Rivet (sold for 5000 guineas at Doncaster in August) also won his only other start, at Charm Park in March, but the major prospect in the Walford yard was five-year-old Black Collar. She had just two runs in March, winning a Maiden and a Restricted in effortless style, and, after shaping well in a two-mile bumper at Market Rasen, was snapped up for 41,000 guineas at Doncaster in May by Kim Bailey.

In addition to Yorkshire hunter chasers already mentioned, The Butterwick Kid won at Newcastle and Dorans Magic took the Area's own event at Wetherby, while after Peter Atkinson's owner-ridden Go Nomadic had triumphed in the Tynedale's three-mile-five-furlong Land Rover qualifier, he was second or third in each of five subsequent outings over the bigger fences. But the star in Yorkshire was surely Peter Armitage's six-year-old Bohemian Spirit, who won at Ayr, Cheltenham and Aintree under Steve Charlton and at Fakenham for Serena Brotherton. He started favourite for the Weatherbys Chase John Corbet only for a blunder at the 16th to put paid to his chance. He failed to make his reserve at Doncaster (closing bid 52,000 guineas) but was later sold privately to go racing under Rules.

John Wade tried an interesting experiment for the South Durham fixture in mid-May on his land at Howe Hills Farm, Mordon, going all out for sponsorship — everything from fences and winning post to starter and commentator — upping racecards (also sponsored) to £3, but allowing free admission for all. It worked, with attendance on a beautiful sunny day reckoned to be about three times normal. Next year the Badsworth and Bramham Moor, which, because of the non-availability of Wetherby, found a temporary home a long way out of the Hunt's country on the Pendle's Heslaker course, will stage an Easter Saturday meeting at Mordon.

The weather was generally kind to Yorkshire meetings. The Cleveland's mid-April fixture was lost due to waterlogging at Stainton (seven days later a massive York & Ainsty crowd, bathed in sunshine, watched the Area's biggest turnout of 98 contest nine races at Easingwold) while at Hutton Rudby in March high winds forced abandonment of the second half of the Hurworth's card due to concerns for the safety of riders and spectators. Otherwise, apart from soft conditions at the Middleton, most racing took place on decent ground (watering, when it was needed, was carried out to a very high standard, thanks to a lot of hard work by many volunteers), producing an excellent starters-per-race average of just over nine. Racing was ultra-competitive and only five meetings, all in May, had undivided Maiden races.

From the going point of view it was a somewhat similar story in the **SOUTH EAST** Area, where the word 'good' — admittedly usually with a qualification — appeared in the ground description for every meeting. Ironically it was 'good to firm' only at the first two meetings, both at Charing in February and March. But turnouts were generally poor, the maximum being 62 in seven races at the second Charing, and overall the 13 meetings (the Chiddingfold, Leconfield and Cowdray was frozen off at Parham in late February) produced a total of only 574 runners for a race average of 6.67.

Happily rain tended to miss race-days and it was only the two West Street Tickham fixtures — at Detling in mid-March and Aldington on May Day — which really suffered. Detling was hit by high winds, too, so that many spectators were heading for home after the Kent Grand National and only four bookies stood their ground until the concluding Maiden.

The customary late start to the season — exacerbated by the Parham abandonment — resulted as usual in numerous south-easterners travelling in search of early success. Pippa Hall aboard Tom Cobbler — later to win Ladies Opens on successive weekends at Godstone and Parham — won at Tweseldown on the second Sunday of the season, when Stuart Robinson was scoring with Great Jubilee at the Waveney Harriers. At the end of January there was an Open race double for the South East at the Dunston Harriers, thanks to Kincora (Lisa Stock) and Pendle Hill (James Owen deputising for Andrew Hickman), while Chris Gordon won the Restricted with Teach Altra. A couple of weeks later no fewer than five of the North Norfolk prizes went to challengers from south of the Thames, including all four Maiden divisions with Asthefellowsaid, Greybrook Lad, Charango Star and Morph. Greybrook Lad did not appear again while Charango Star and Morph, qualified with the Staff College from Ray York's Surrey stable, have been mentioned in the

Sandhurst Area notes, but seven-year-old Asthefellowsaid's claim to be the Area's best maiden was challenged only by another of the same age, Toujours, who opened his account very easily at Charing in early March.

Both these two remained unbeaten in three outings, Asthefellowsaid, trained by Sara Hickman and ridden by husband Andrew, following a comfortable Restricted success at Detling with a gutsy victory in the Crawley and Horsham Confined. He may be Maurice Smith's best hope for 2005 since Splash And Dash ran below expectations and was sent to Doncaster Sales in May — where he failed to make his reserve after a final bid of 12,500 guineas. Asthefellowsaid also went to Doncaster — and came home again when 27,000 guineas failed to secure him at the August auction.

Toujours was one of the Simon Tindall horses trained by Jenny Gordon, who was again the Area's top lady rider, while her husband, Chris, took the Men's Championship for a sixth consecutive season. Mrs Gordon, who has now retired from the racing saddle, once more achieved a remarkable training strike rate, sending out 34 runners and winning 15 races with six horses. Sheriff's Friend, the previous year's Weatherbys Chase John Corbet winner, is undoubtedly the stable star, but his trainer deserves congratulation for her expert placing of Lively Lord, whose score of 11 wins from 21 outings in the last three seasons includes three Novice Riders races. It was Lively Lord who provided Mrs Gordon with her last winning mount at the Southdown and Eridge meeting in May.

Sheriff's Friend and Struggles Glory were the only horses to win more than one Men's Open in the South East. The two met on the first day of the Area season at the Mid-Surrey meeting, where they had dead-heated in the equivalent race of 2003. Now Sheriff's Friend was untroubled to land his tenth consecutive victory. He ended his campaign with another three successes on the bounce, but in between had been among the non-finishers in the Cheltenham Foxhunters and had fallen four from home when jumping upsides eventual winner Satchmo in the South East Club's Land Rover qualifier. Satchmo, trained by Di Grissell and ridden by Philip Hall — and later a creditable fourth in the Martell Fox Hunters despite almost losing Hall at the fourth last — was making his second appearance in an English Point-to-Point. His first — he has been chasing since — was back in 2000 at Charimg when he beat another leading Tindall/Gordon horse, the well-remembered Seod Rioga.

Stuart Robinson took over from his father, David, aboard Struggles Glory for the veteran's first three races and, after two Charing seconds, scored decisively from Little Farmer at the Southdown and Eridge March fixture. Robinson senior recovered the saddle for his horse's final two runs, ending their season together (and maybe their careers) with an Ashford Valley Men's Open victory after the downhill fourth-last, which had caught out Sheriff's Friend against Satchmo, again proved decisive when the challenging Belvento was outjumped by the winner and unshipped Mick Sheridan.

It was a generally poor year for Area representatives in Hunter Chases. The only two scorers were King Of The Dawn, who, after losing to Sheriff's Friend at the second Penshurst, came up in a two-miler in bottomless ground at Towcester under Jody Sole, and Cape Stormer, successful earlier at Leicester for Marcus Gorman.

The local Leading Horse award went to 12-year-old Dick McCarthy, a model of consistency for Sarah Ashby with three firsts, three seconds and a third. But his place at the top was only confirmed at the closing meeting at Godstone, when seven-year-old Cedar Chief, who might have shared the prize had he won, was beaten by the Turner horse Spring Gale in the Ladies Open. A week earlier Cedar Chief had won an Open at Kingston Blount under Chris Gordon (his fourth winning rider of 2004), and, with four wins and three second places, he outpointed all the other young horses in the country so that owner Kevin Tork received the Weatherbys Chase Championship award at the Stratford PPORA lunch. Tork's horse next appeared at the Doncaster August Sale but was led out unsold after a final bid of 30,000 guineas.

Apart from the previously-mentioned Toujours, Jenny Gordon had two other Maiden winners in Little Mickey and Granny Smith. The latter also took a Restricted but Little Mickey, a six-year-old, was not seen out again after a success on his fencing debut at the Mid-Surrey's opening meeting and so remains an unknown quantity. Another locally-trained maiden who went into many notebooks for 2005 was David and Heather Silk's five-year-old Hever Road, out of their good True Song mare The Little Bag. Fourth after a race full of promise on his debut at Garthorpe and subsequently just touched off by Ministerial at Parham, Hever Road looked looked sure to open his account on his return to Garthorpe in April until unshipping Stuart Morris when leading over the second last. He looks a certain future winner provided he proves easier to train than his half-brothers.

Ministerial was one of three seven-year-old maidens to carry the colours of Nigel Benstead, all of whom won with other riders while he was recovering from injuries sustained when one of them, Lord Of The North, was looking to have the beating of Little Mickey at the Mid-Surrey until crashing out at the penultimate. On his next run Lord Of The North won at the Ashford Valley under Chris Gordon, who rode Ministerial to win at Parham, while Jay Pemberton steered Midnight Lord home at the Old Surrey. None of the trio followed up in a Restricted, though Phil York had Ministerial 10 lengths clear when he crumpled on landing over the penultimate at Aldington in May. Five days later he went down by a head to Sutton Courtenay at Kingston Blount after surviving several mistakes.

Stuart Robinson also did well with his three new ones, all six-year-olds. Two have been mentioned, the Irish import Greybrook Lad and Great Jubilee. The latter, who won a Maiden in Cornwall when trained by David Pipe the previous season, followed his Waveney Restricted success by easily accounting for Algan at Parham to give Robinson the second leg of a double initiated in the Restricted by another former Irish pointer, Magnus Veritas. So the three, trained by Gina Weare, notched up four wins from six runs and should collect more in 2005.

For many years the Southdown and Eridge have vied for runners with the East Kent on Easter Monday but in 2004 there was at last a change of heart, with the S and E moving instead to an end-of-season date (next year it will be the curtain-raiser) at Godstone in mid-May and offering £40 travel allowances to horses from outside the Area. The move proved an enormous success, though East Anglian raiders 'got their own back' for their North Norfolk rout in February by winning five of the six races for which they were eligible. Local pride was salvaged by Paul Blagg, who scored his first-ever double aboard the maiden Private Percival and in the Confined on Kenny Davis. Local hopes were also extinguished four days later at the Folkestone United Hunts meeting at Folkestone, where Jenny Gordon had her final rides.

Another notable retirement was that of the mud-loving Real Value, a worthy south-eastern representative ever since he won his Maiden at Heathfield in 1998. He came agonisingly close to Cheltenham Foxhunters glory when caught by Cavalero two years later and, though clearly on the decline in 2004, managed a hard-fought victory over Pendle Hill at Aldington on Easter Monday — to take his final tally to 13 Point-to-Points, two Hunter Chases and one success under Rules. Sadly he could not go out on a winning note in his final race over the same course three weeks later.

PLATE 7 'It can get crowded round the paddock and we advise bringing something stout to stand on'
PHOTO: Brian Armstrong

The Top Horses of 2004

Horse	Rating
Torduff Express (IRE)	11-10
Earthmover (IRE)	11-9
Never Compromise (IRE)	11-8
Springford (IRE)	11-8
Forest Gunner	11-7
Lord Atterbury (IRE)	11-6
Right To Reply (IRE)	11-6
Placid Man (IRE)	11-5
Bright Approach (IRE)	11-4
Ask The Natives (IRE)	11-3
Macgeorge (IRE)	11-3
Sikander A Azam	11-3
Gun'n Roses II (FR)	11-2
Mister Benjamin (IRE)	11-2
Balinova (IRE)	11-1
Lindsay (FR)	11-1
Monks Error (IRE)	11-1
Mouseski	11-1
Oneminutetofive	11-1
Satchmo (IRE)	11-1
Aberfoyle Park (IRE)	11-0
County Derry	11-0§
Delgany Royal (IRE)	11-0
Dusk Duel (USA)	11-0
Fane Counsel (IRE)	11-0
Galapiat Du Mesnil (FR)	11-0
Philson Run (IRE)	11-0
Bengal Bullet	10-13
Kingston Venture	10-13
Vivid Imagination (IRE)	10-13
Cantarinho	10-12
Caught At Dawn (IRE)	10-12
Chasing The Bride	10-12
Crevamoy (IRE)	10-12
Hermes III (FR)	10-12
J-Okay (IRE)	10-12
Kingston-Banker	10-12
Lancastrian Jet (IRE)	10-12
Paddy For Paddy (IRE)	10-12
Sheriff's Friend (IRE)	10-12
Silence Reigns	10-12
What A Mover	10-12

The Handicap 2004

Horse	Rating
Ababou (FR)	10-4
Abbey Days (IRE)	8-9
Abbeyknock Boy (IRE)	10-1
Aberfoyle Park (IRE)	11-0
Abinger	9-7§
Abitofahike (IRE)	9-9
Able Bob (IRE)	7-0
Abseal	9-5
Absolutely Hopeful	9-6
Abu Dancer (IRE)	9-0
Across The Card	9-5
Act In Time (IRE)	10-3
Advice Taken (IRE)	9-3
Aficionado (IRE)	8-0§
A Fine Story	9-11
African Dawn	9-5
Aftermeyourfirst	7-0
Agent	9-0
Agent Provocateur (NZ)	9-0
Agile King	10-4
Agua Ardente	10-7
Aircon (IRE)	10-3§
Air Leader (IRE)	7-8
Airoski	10-5
Albamart Wood	9-9
Alexander Nevsky	9-3
Alex In Action	8-9
Alex Thuscombe	9-12
Alfie Moon (IRE)	8-9
Alfies Rocket	9-0
Algan (FR)	10-1
Alheri	9-12
Alice Reigns	9-8§
Alice's Old Rose	7-2
Alittlebitopower	10-4
Aljoash (IRE)	9-13
All Alight (IRE)	7-12
Aller Coombe	9-4§
All Eyez On Me (IRE)	9-4
Alleywell	9-4
Allez Toujours (IRE)	9-12
All For Jake (IRE)	9-11
Allied Imperial	9-0
Allotrope (IRE)	7-7§
Alltime Dancer (IRE)	9-1§
Almazard	8-8§
Along The Lawn (IRE)	9-4
Alpenstock (FR)	9-5
Alpha Romana (IRE)	10-9
Alpine Fugue (IRE)	9-5§
Alska (FR)	10-1
Althrey Dandy (IRE)	10-9
Alvero (FR)	9-12
Always Good (IRE)	8-0§
Always On The Line (IRE)	10-5
Aly Daley (IRE)	9-0
Analan	8-0
Analystic (IRE)	10-6
An Capall Dubh (IRE)	10-5
Andre Laval (IRE)	9-8
Andsuephi (IRE)	10-2
Andy's Lad (IRE)	9-7
Angus Airways (IRE)	9-0§
Anneka Louise	9-8
Annie Fleetwood	8-12
Anniejo	9-5§
Another Bit	9-4
Another Bula (IRE)	9-4
Another Half	9-6
Anotherhandyman	9-0§
Another Leader (IRE)	9-5
Any Other Business	-
Apatura Joe	9-0
Approaching Land (IRE)	9-13
April Treasure	9-5

A Proper Charlie 8-11
Araminta. 10-11
Archbishop 9-12
Arctic Burner (IRE) . . . .9-10§
Arctic Grey (IRE). 9-2
Arctic King . . . . .10-2§
Arctic Penguin 9-12
Arctic Snip 9-4
Arctic Summer (IRE). 9-1
Arctic Sun (IRE) . . . . . . .9-4§
Arctic Times (IRE). 10-9
Ardkilly Warrior (IRE) . . . . . -
Ardmayle (IRE) 10-1
Ardnut 9-2
Ardross Gem (IRE) 10-3
Arewetoolate. 8-7
Arkay 6-0
Arlequin De Sou (FR) 9-9
A Romp Too Far (IRE). . . .9-3
Artic Ground (IRE) . . . . .8-8§
Ascoolasice. 7-0
As De La Garenne (FR). 8-12
Ashbury Star (NZ). 10-0
Ashfield Orchestra (IRE) 10-1
Ashgan (IRE) 10-5
Ashgreen. 10-4
Ashwell Boy (IRE). 10-1
Ashwicke Gambler 7-12
Ask Again 9-3
Askers Jack. 9-12
Ask The Natives (IRE). . 11-3
Aslapoftheeuro (IRE). . . 8-12
Asthefellasays (IRE) . . . 9-13
Asthefellowsaid (IRE) . . 10-6
Astley Gold (IRE) 10-1
Atavistic (IRE). 10-2
Atlantic Drift (IRE) 9-2
Aughmor River (IRE). . . 9-10
Aunt Gladys (IRE) 9-7
Auntie Kathleen 9-9
Autcaesar Autnihil (IRE) . .9-9
Autumn Flame (IRE). . . 8-10
Avalon Buck (IRE). 9-6
Avec Plaisir (IRE) 9-3
Avondale Illusion (IRE) .8-13§
Aztec Rule (IRE) . . . . . . .9-9§
Babs Wheal 9-4
Baby John (IRE) 9-6
Bacarese. 8-9
Backsheesh (IRE) 10-8
Badger Beer 10-4
Bak On Board. 10-0
Balau 9-7
Baldara (IRE) 9-8
Baldhu Jack 9-8
Baldhu Jay Arr 9-9
Balinova (IRE) 11-1
Balisteros (FR) 10-2
Ballad (IRE) . . . . .9-11§
Ballad Minstrel (IRE) . . 9-13
Ballet Red. 9-2
Ballingale Dawn (IRE). . 10-0
Ball In The Net. 9-9
Ballinure Boy (IRE). . . . 10-7
Ballyalbert 9-13
Ballyblack (IRE) 8-11
Bally Blue. 9-9
Ballyhannon (IRE). 7-0
Ballyknock Rose (IRE) . 9-12
Bally Leader (IRE). 7-13
Ballylesson (IRE). 8-11
Bally Lir Lady 8-12
Ballysicyos (FR) 10-7
Bally Wirral (IRE) 10-6
Balmoral Spring (IRE). .9-10§
Banana Ridge 9-13
Bankersdraft 8-12
Bankit. 9-8
Bank On Lady. 8-9
Bansha House 9-8
Barbed Broach (IRE). 8-4
Bard Of Drumcoo (IRE). 10-4
Barneys Gold (IRE) 9-11
Baron Bernard 8-13
Baron Ridge 9-6
Barron Bay (USA) 8-0
Barry Lydon (IRE) 9-1
Barrys Lord (IRE) 9-8
Barton Dream (IRE) . . . 10-2
Barton Rose . . . . .9-9§
Barton Saint (NZ) 9-11
Barty Boy (IRE). 9-2
Batchworth Lock. 9-5
Bathtime Boys 9-10
Batoutoftheblue . . . . . .9-10§
Battle Honours 9-6
Bay Island (IRE) 10-9
Bay Mouse 8-4
Bay Of Dreams 9-5
B B Boy 6-8
Be A Better Boy 9-8
Beachcomber 9-11
Beachtime . . . . .9-0§
Beacon White 8-12
Beadnell Bay 10-3
Beaford Princess. 8-0
Beasley. 9-4
Beat The Retreat. 9-6
Beauchamp Oracle 10-5
Beau Jake (IRE) 8-6
Bebe Bleu (IRE) 9-0
Be Bop Bentley. . . . . . . .7-6§
Bedtime Boys 10-3
Beehawk. 9-11
Beehive Lad 8-10
Beet De Bob (IRE) 10-3
Belarus (IRE) . . . . .9-13§
Belle Moss 9-8
Bell Rock 9-9
Belvento (IRE) 10-10
Be My Dream (IRE) . . .10-0§
Benbeoch 9-8
Benbow . . . . .9-12§
Ben Buckley 9-0
Benetton (U). 4-12
Ben From Ketton. 10-5
Bengal Boy 9-11
Bengal Bullet 10-13
Benson (IRE) 9-12
Bering Gifts (IRE) . . . . .9-13§
Berkeley Frontier (IRE) . . .9-7
Bermuda Blue. 9-12
Bessie Bunter 9-7
Best Accolade. 9-11
Bethin. . . . . .8-7§
Better Future (IRE) . . . .9-12§
Beyond The Stars 10-0
Biddy 8-1
Big Brendan (IRE). 9-8
Big Mossy. 8-8
Bilingual 9-12
Bill Haze. . . . . .9-11§
Bill Me Up (IRE). 10-4
Billy Coleman (IRE) . . . 8-12
Billy Whitelies (IRE) 9-5
Bilton's Nap 9-9
Birkwood 9-5
Bishop's Blade 10-9
Bitofamixup (IRE) 10-6
Black A Brook (IRE) . . . .8-9§
Blackanblue 9-13
Blackberry Way. . . . . . .10-5§
Blackchurch Lass (IRE). . .8-2
Black Collar 10-8
Blackhill Princess 7-10
Black Hope (IRE) 8-10
Black Leopard (IRE) . . . 9-10
Black Optimist (IRE). . .10-2§
Black Rainbow (IRE). 9-5
Black Smoke (IRE) 10-9
Blackwater Brave (IRE). 9-11
Blakeney Hill 9-0
Blakes Road (IRE) 8-13
Blank Cheque 10-1
Blazing Pride 7-11

Horse	Handicap
Bless Yourself (IRE)	8-12§
Blin (CZE)	9-4
Bloomfield Storm (IRE)	10-3
Blue Bud	9-0§
Blue Jar	7-8
Blue Royal (FR)	10-9
Blyth Brook	10-8
Bobby Buttons	9-1
Bobtail (IRE)	9-6
Boddidley (IRE)	10-0
Bohemian Spirit (IRE)	10-11
Bold Classic (IRE)	10-0
Bold King (FR)	9-12§
Bold Statement	9-9
Bold Tactics (IRE)	10-2
Bolide Du Aunay (FR)	9-5
Boogy Woogy	9-10§
Border Burn	9-4
Border Farmer (IRE)	9-7
Border Fusion	9-12
Borderline Breeze (IRE)	9-7
Border Run	10-1
Borleagh Pilot (IRE)	9-3
Born To Dream (IRE)	10-9
Born Winner	8-13
Borrow Mine (IRE)	9-7
Bosuns Mate	10-0
Boulta (IRE)	10-3
Boyne Banks (IRE)	10-9
Braceys Girl (IRE)	10-2
Brackenheath (IRE)	10-1§
Bradford Bridge	8-12
Brandnewplan (IRE)	7-6
Brass Razoo	9-10
Brave Albert (IRE)	9-2§
Brendas Nightmare	8-12
Brer Bear	9-13
Breteche (FR)	10-3
Briary Boy (IRE)	9-9
Briery Fox (IRE)	9-7
Briery Hill	10-5§
Bright Approach (IRE)	11-4
Bright Beacon	10-8
Bright Dawn (IRE)	9-5§
Bright Flash (IRE)	9-3
Broad Edge (IRE)	9-5§
Broadspeed	9-2
Brockbuster	9-12
Brombil Lady	8-0
Bronllys Skyvor (U)	9-6
Brook Bee	10-2§
Brookfield Bass	9-4
Browjoshy (IRE)	9-11§
Brown Chieftain (IRE)	9-8
Brown Esquire	9-11
Brownies Tale (IRE)	8-3
Brown's Beck	7-11
Brown Seal	9-12
Bruan (IRE)	8-8§
Brummel (U)	5-0
Bruthuinne (IRE)	9-7
Bucket Awl (IRE)	9-0
Buckland Bobby	9-4
Buckland Boy	9-12§
Buckland Lad (IRE)	10-2
Buckley's Chance (IRE)	9-2
Buddy Girie	10-1
Budghill	9-0
Budle Bay	9-6
Bullfinch	10-1
Bunratty's Sole (IRE)	10-5
Burley Don Carlos	10-2
Bush Hill Bandit (IRE)	10-5
Butleigh Rose	8-10
Butler Didit	9-2
Butterwick King (IRE)	9-7
Button Boy	9-9
By My Side (IRE)	9-6
Cabille (FR)	9-4
Cabin Boy	8-5
Cadougold (FR)	9-7
Cadravel	8-9
Cadrillon (FR)	9-7
Cage Aux Folles (IRE)	9-1
Caher Society (IRE)	10-2
Caipiroska	10-1
Calamint	7-6
Caldamus	10-3
Calfstown Lord	9-0
Calhoun (FR)	9-2
Calleva Star (IRE)	8-12
Calling Home (IRE)	8-13
Callitwatulike	8-7
Call Me Again	8-3
Call Me Sonic	9-9
Camair Commander (IRE)	8-13
Camden Bus (IRE)	9-7
Camden Caramel (IRE)	9-9
Camden Carrig (IRE)	10-9
Camden Fellow (IRE)	9-5
Camden Loch (IRE)	9-9
Camitrov (FR)	7-5
Campbellhill (IRE)	8-0§
Campden Kitty	10-6
Cannon Bridge (IRE)	10-1
Cantarinho	10-12
Can't Catch Me (IRE)	7-0
Canterbury Jack (IRE)	10-0§
Can You Talk	7-8
Capacoostic	9-4
Cape Stormer (IRE)	10-4
Cappa Hill (IRE)	9-0
Capriole (U)	5-10
Captain Random	9-7
Captain's Log	8-7
Captive (IRE)	9-12
Capybara (IRE)	9-6
Caraiyni (IRE)	9-9
Carat	10-0
Carbonado	10-2
Carefree Love (IRE)	9-4§
Carew Lad	9-12
Cargo Flight	9-1
Carling Elect	9-2
Carl's Boy	9-0§
Carlton Brae	9-10
Carnage (IRE)	9-0
Carnalway (IRE)	9-0
Carrigafoyle	9-0
Carrington House	9-4
Carthago (IRE)	10-6
Carvilla (IRE)	8-8§
Cascum Lad (IRE)	10-1
Cashari (IRE)	9-7
Cashew Cache (IRE)	9-7
Cash 'n Carrots	9-7
Caspers Case	10-5
Castle Arrow (IRE)	9-2§
Castlediva	9-10
Castle Lodge	8-8§
Castle Road (IRE)	8-2§
Catchatan (IRE)	8-11
Catch On (IRE)	9-12
Catchphrase	9-8§
Catch The Bus (IRE)	9-6
Catechist (IRE)	10-4
Catherine's Way (IRE)	8-7
Cath's Lass	6-3§
Cathy Come Home (IRE)	8-0
Catosphere (IRE)	9-0
Caught At Dawn (IRE)	10-12
Caundle Chase	10-0
Cawkwell Princess	9-8
Ceasers Reign (IRE)	9-7
Cedar Chief	10-3
Celtic Duke	10-8
Celtic Season	8-11
Cento (IRE)	10-3§
Centurian (U)	1-0
Certain Surprise	9-13
Chadswell (IRE)	9-7§
Challis Choice (IRE)	8-9
Champagne (U)	4-11
Chancy Guy	10-6
Change	9-7

Changing Fashion (IRE) . . 7-6
Channel's Brook 8-5
Chaos Theory 10-2
Chaparro Amargoso (IRE) . 8-7
Chapners Cross. 9-7
Charango Star. 10-0
Charlestown Lass 9-9
Charlieadams (IRE). 9-6
Charlie Hawes (IRE) 6-7
Charlie's Angel 9-13
Charlie Strong (IRE) . . . 10-9
Charminsky. 9-0
Chase The Moon. 7-0
Chasing Buttercups. . . . . 7-2§
Chasing The Bride . . . 10-12
Chatabit 9-6
Chateau Burf 9-4
Chaucers Miller. 9-13
Che Guevara 9-7
Chelsea King (IRE) . . . . . 9-5§
Cheltenham (U) 4-6
Cherokee Boy 9-1
Cherokee Run (IRE) . . . 10-2
Cherry Gold 10-11
Chesnut Wood 9-11
Chicago City (IRE) 10-2
Chicago's Padre 8-0
Chief Of Justice 9-10
Chief Predator (USA). . . 9-10§
Chief Seattle (IRE) 9-4
Chief Suspect (IRE). . . . 8-11§
China Lal 9-7
Chism (IRE) . . . . 9-8§
Choc. 9-13
Choice Cut (IRE). 8-6
Cho Polu (IRE) 9-13
Choral Dream (IRE) . . . 10-3
Christy Beamish (IRE). . 10-9
Chunito. 8-3
Churchill (U). 3-13
Cider Man. 10-8
Cimarrone Cove (IRE) . . 10-8§
Cimmaroon (IRE) 10-4
City Gent 9-13
Civil Gent (IRE). 10-4
Claire's Nomad 10-5
Clarice Starling 9-7
Clarky's Choice (IRE) 9-6
Classic Fable (IRE) 9-0
Class Of Ninetytwo (IRE). 10-3
C L B Jemilla 9-0
Clear Away (IRE) 9-11
Cleopatra (U) 5-6
Clever Dickie. 8-12
Clever Fella. 9-11

Clifford Bay (IRE) 10-7
Clodagh Valley (IRE). . . 9-11
Clonshire Paddy (IRE). . 10-4§
Cloudy Bay Boy 9-12
Cloudy Creek (IRE) 10-2
Coal Queen. 7-5
Coastal Flight 8-8
Coastal Safari 8-9
Coddington George 7-12
Coddington Girl. 9-8
Codys Castle. 8-0
Coffee Morning (IRE) . . 8-12
Coldabri (IRE). 10-0
Collier. 9-7
Colombian Green (IRE). 9-13
Colonel Blazer. . . . . 9-7§
Colonel Carats. . . . . 9-10§
Colonel Conca. 10-1
Colonel Ludlow (IRE) 9-0
Colonel North (IRE). . . . 9-12
Colquhoun 10-8
Columna. 7-9
Combat Drinker (IRE) . . 9-11
Come On Boy 8-2
Comfortably Numb (FR) . . 9-7
Commanche Fox (IRE) . . . 9-5
Commanche Law (IRE). 10-7
Commanche Spirit (IRE) . . 7-7
Commanche Summer 9-9
Commander Cully (IRE) . . 9-0
Commasarris. 9-6
Conquistador (IRE) 9-11
Contingency . . . . 9-12§
Contra Charge. 9-3
Coolarne Leader (IRE). . . 7-7§
Coole Chief. 9-2
Cooleen Strong (IRE). . . 9-11
Coolefind (IRE) 10-10
Coole Glen (IRE). 10-1
Coole'sabbot (IRE) . . . . 9-11§
Coole Venture (IRE). . . . 10-9§
Coolteen Hero (IRE) . . . 9-11
Cool Wager. 9-11
Coomakista. 10-3
Coombe Quest 9-8
Coombs Spinney. 9-0
Copper Grove (IRE). . . . 9-13
Copybook 8-11
Coquet Gold 8-7
Coralinga 9-9
Corky Browne 10-0
Corrie Mor (IRE) 9-13
Corston Joker . . . . 9-11§
Cosmic Sky. 9-11
Cotton On. 9-9

Countess Kiri 9-2
Count Keni 9-9
Countryside Counts. 8-7
Countryside March 8-0
County Derry. . . . . 11-0§
Courage Under Fire. . . . 10-4
Courseman (IRE). 8-12
Court Adjourn 10-5
Court Alert 10-2
Cousin George. . . . . 9-2§
Cowanstown Prince. . . . 9-12
Crackrattle (IRE) 9-10
Craiova Comet (IRE) 9-5
Cresswell Gold 9-2
Crested Manor 10-2
Crevamoy (IRE). 10-12
Croesy Pennant. 8-5
Croft Court . . . . 9-12§
Cromaboo Count. . . . . . . 7-3§
Cross River 10-8
Crown And Cushion . . . 9-13
Crown Rule (IRE) . . . . . . 9-0§
Crystal Brook 8-1
Crystal Soldier 9-2
Currow Kate 8-1
Cutina. 9-10
Dainty Man (IRE) 9-10
Daisy Duke. 8-8
Daisy Fay 10-2
Daisy's Choice 8-0
Daktari (U) 2-0
Dale Creek (IRE). 8-13
Damiens Pride (IRE) . . . 10-0§
Dammitu 7-7
Dam The Breeze. 10-9
Dancetillyoudrop (IRE) . 10-4
Dancing Dasi (IRE) 9-3
Dancing Fosenby 10-6
Dannicus 9-0
Dans Blarney (IRE) . . . . . 8-0§
Dante's Banker (IRE) 9-7
Dante's Promise (IRE). . 9-12§
Dantie Boy (IRE). 10-6
Danzante (IRE) . . . . 9-8§
Darak (IRE). 10-0
Darcey Mae 9-8
Darcy Jones 9-7
Dare 10-3
Darkarrow (IRE) . . . . . . 9-10§
Dark Challenger (IRE) . . 10-0
Dark Comedy 8-5
Darrell Boy (IRE). . . . . . . 9-4§
Dat My Horse (IRE) . . . 10-10
Daydreamer (USA) 9-10
Dean Deifir (IRE) 9-8

Horse	Rating
Dear As Saffron	9-0
Decent Bond (IRE)	10-5
De Chelly	10-3
Deep Dale	9-11
Deep Design (IRE)	7-7
Defendtherealm	9-12
Definite Flash (IRE)	8-2
Delaware (FR)	9-9§
Delgany Royal (IRE)	11-0
Dellone	9-6
Deltic Arrow	8-0
Denvale (IRE)	10-5
Deputy Leader (IRE)	9-5
Dere Street	9-12
Detroit Davy (IRE)	9-10
Devil's Perk (IRE)	10-0
Devonshire (IRE)	9-10
Dexter Gordon (IRE)	10-0§
Diamond Stone (IRE)	9-4
Dick McCarthy (IRE)	10-3
Dinan (IRE)	8-0§
Dinsey Finnegan (IRE)	10-3§
Distinct (IRE)	9-6§
Distracting	9-12
Divine Mist (IRE)	9-1§
Dixon Varner (IRE)	10-0
Doc Ryan's	10-5§
Doctor Dunklin (USA)	8-8§
Do It Once (IRE)	10-0
Dolitanlad	7-0
Dolphin Square (IRE)	10-1
Donallach Mor (IRE)	9-8
Donnegale (IRE)	9-13§
Donrico (IRE)	9-7
Don Rio (IRE)	9-3
Don Royal	10-6
Dons Delight (IRE)	10-1
Don'ttellthetaxman (IRE)	9-8
Dook's Delight (IRE)	9-4§
Dorans Magic	10-8
Dorset Fern (IRE)	9-0
Dos Desperados (IRE)	7-10
Double Rich	10-0
Doublet	10-2
Double Thatch (IRE)	9-8
Down (FR)	10-5
Dragon Lord	9-13§
Dr Deductible	9-12
Dreamie Battle	9-8
Dream Of My Life (USA)	10-0
Dream On Then	8-13
Drom Island	9-6
Drovers Road	8-10
Druid's Brook	9-0
Drum Battle	9-10
Drumdowney Lad (IRE)	9-6
Drumhorc (IRE)	9-11
Drumlin (IRE)	9-10§
Duchess Account	9-2
Dukestown (IRE)	7-0§
Dumadic	10-4
Dun Distinctly (IRE)	10-0
Dunmanus Sound (IRE)	8-9
Dunmanus Supreme (IRE)	8-6
Dunrig (IRE)	9-7§
Dun Rose	10-5
Dun Victory	10-2
Dursey Island (IRE)	9-0
Dusk Duel (USA)	11-0
Earl Of Buckingham	9-8
Earl's Toy (IRE)	9-7
Earl Token	8-10§
Early Morning Call (IRE)	9-7§
Earthmover (IRE)	11-9
Ease The Pressure (IRE)	10-5
Eastern Apple	9-1§
Eastern Point	10-7§
Eastern Royal	9-9
Ebony Jack (IRE)	9-10
Echo Blu (IRE)	9-0
Eco Warrior (IRE)	9-9
Edmond (FR)	9-12§
Edstone (IRE)	8-7§
Effessbee	8-10
Eighty Days (IRE)	10-5
Ela Agapi Mou (USA)	9-10§
Elegant Light	10-2
Ellemford	8-0§
Ellofamonkey	10-3
Emali	9-10
Emerald Mist (IRE)	9-6
Emperor Roscoe	10-5
Emperor's Castle	7-11
Emperor's Magic (IRE)	10-5
Emperor's Son	10-5
Endeavour (FR)	10-4
Energy Man	9-10§
Enitsag (FR)	10-4
Epicure (FR)	10-3§
Epsilo De La Ronce (FR)	9-9§
Ercon (IRE)	7-12
Erzadjan (IRE)	9-12
Esendi	10-0
Eskimo Gold	9-1
Esprit De Cotte (FR)	10-4§
Esterelle (USA)	9-10
Et Light (FR)	10-4
Euro Alert (IRE)	10-6
Euro Bob (IRE)	10-4
Eurogaedel (IRE)	9-9
Euwiluwil (IRE)	10-1
Evanly Miss	9-0§
Evans The Coal	8-7§
Exact (FR)	9-7§
Execute (IRE)	8-7
Extra Jack (FR)	10-7
Extra Stout (IRE)	9-10
Fables Green	8-12
Faircatcher	8-0
Fair Charmeur (IRE)	9-12
Fair Exchange	10-5
Fair Kiowa (IRE)	9-12
Fair Wind (IRE)	10-11
Falcon's Flame (USA)	10-0
Fami (FR)	10-2
Fane Counsel (IRE)	11-0
Fanion De Nourry (FR)	9-9§
Far Glen (IRE)	10-7
Farnando (IRE)	9-8
Far Too Crowded (IRE)	10-2
Fassan (IRE)	9-0§
Faster Sweep (IRE)	9-10
Fast Lane Harry (IRE)	9-5
Father Andy (IRE)	10-3
Father Jim	9-12§
Father Mansfield (IRE)	10-6
Father Tom (IRE)	10-8
Fawsley Lake	7-0
Fayalie (IRE)	9-0
Federal Case (FR)	9-3
Feeling Grand (IRE)	8-10
Feels Like Rain	9-3
Felix Randal (IRE)	9-7
Felloo (IRE)	9-7
Fencethegap (IRE)	8-9
Fergal's Find (IRE)	9-3
Fern Leader (IRE)	9-0
Ferryhill (IRE)	9-1
Fertile Valley (IRE)	10-9
Festival Time	9-8
Fiesty Frosty (IRE)	9-0
Filou Du Bois (FR)	9-12
Filscot	10-0§
Final Chorus	8-12
Final Escapade	8-0
Finbar (IRE)	9-0
Finder Keeps (USA)	10-0
Find Me Another (IRE)	10-7
Fine And Dandy (IRE)	10-3
Finest Of Men	9-7
Fine Times	9-8
Finne Gaoithe (IRE)	9-9
Fiolino (FR)	6-0
Fisherman Jack	10-3
Five Minutes	8-12

Horse	Weight
Flash Point (IRE)	9-13
Flat Stanley	10-2
Flat Top	10-0§
Flaxley Abbey	9-4
Flockmaster (IRE)	9-13
Flo Keen	9-4
Floodgate	8-9
Floorex Carpetman	8-10§
Flora Macdonald	9-9§
Fluted Edge	8-6
Fly For Paddy	9-6
Flying Past	9-11
Flying Pennant (IRE)	9-4
Foggy Hill (IRE)	8-11
Folliday (FR)	8-5§
Folly Road (IRE)	10-3§
For A Pagan Song	8-3
Force Ten	7-10
Foreign Field (FR)	7-12
Forest Fortress (IRE)	9-0
Forest Gunner	11-7
Forest Jump (IRE)	9-4
Forglori	8-10§
Fornaught Alliance (IRE)	9-7§
Fort Apache (IRE)	7-13
Forty Shakes (IRE)	9-0
Fortysixallout (IRE)	9-10
Fossy Bear	10-3
Foston Second (IRE)	9-8
Fou Doux (FR)	9-8
Four In Hand	9-7
Four Of A Kind	9-7
Four Opinions	9-0
Fours Are Wild (IRE)	10-0
Fourspice Allspice (IRE)	9-5
Foxy Royale	9-0
Franco (IRE)	10-11
Franco Lady (IRE)	9-2
Frank Byrne	9-12
Frankly Fear	9-2
Freddie Muck	10-1
Free	10-7
Freedom Fighter	10-6
Free Gift	10-10
Freeway	8-11
French Cedar	10-3
French Venture	9-5
Friar Waddon	10-6
Frileux Royal (FR)	10-5§
Frosty Fella	8-7
Fuero Real (FR)	6-6
Gabaka De Thaix (FR)	9-0
Gaetano (IRE)	8-5
Galapiat Du Mesnil (FR)	11-0
Galaxy Girl	9-6
Galaxy Minstrel (IRE)	9-10
Galeaway (IRE)	9-9
Gale Damage (IRE)	8-10
Gale On The Lake (IRE)	8-4
Galeshan (IRE)	9-11
Galevanter (IRE)	9-0
Gallant Glen (IRE)	10-10
Gallion's Reach (IRE)	10-2
Game Endeavour (IRE)	8-13
Game Gunner	10-11
Gangster	9-4§
Gardor (FR)	8-7
Garethson (IRE)	10-2
Garolo (FR)	10-5§
Garrison Friendly (IRE)	9-5§
Garruth (IRE)	10-7§
Gatchou Mans (FR)	10-3
Gatsby (IRE)	10-11
Gaultier Gale (IRE)	9-12§
Gavroche Collonges (FR)	5-0
Gawngadinn (IRE)	9-5§
Gay Baratineur (FR)	9-13
Gayble	8-13
Gaynor's Gamble (IRE)	9-9
Geal Farraige (IRE)	9-6
Gee A Two (IRE)	7-6
General Claremont (IRE)	10-8
General Craig	8-12§
General Jake (IRE)	9-11
General Wolfe	9-12
Genereux	9-12§
Gentleman Charles (IRE)	9-7
Gentlemans Relish	9-4
Geordies Express	10-7
Georges Pleasure	9-6
Germany Park (IRE)	9-8
Ghutah	9-11
Gigi Beach (IRE)	9-2§
Gillie's Nephew	9-12
Gillone	10-1
Gilly Weet	8-7
Gilzine	10-2
Ginger Bug	9-5
Ginmini (IRE)	8-4
Gin N Ice (IRE)	8-11§
Gipsy Cricketer	10-1
Gipsy Girl	10-7
Gipsy Wood	9-2
Give Him A Chance (IRE)	9-4
Given Grace (IRE)	6-7
Glacial Boy	9-7
Glacial Dancer (IRE)	9-9
Glacial Pearl (IRE)	9-12
Glacial Sygnet (IRE)	9-11
Glad All Over	7-12
Gladiatorial (IRE)	10-4
Glemot (IRE)	8-5
Glenahary Rose (IRE)	8-13
Glenalla Braes (IRE)	8-11
Glen Amber (IRE)	9-1
Glendamah (IRE)	10-2
Glen Mist (IRE)	9-6
Glenmont (IRE)	9-7
Glensan (IRE)	9-13
Glory Trail (IRE)	9-9
Go Boy	8-7
God Of War	8-5
Go Go Gallant (IRE)	9-0
Golden Chimes (USA)	10-7
Golden Dawn	8-7
Golden Jack (FR)	9-12
Golden Pride	8-6
Golden Rivet	10-7
Golden Shred	9-6§
Golden Spirit	8-10
Gold Kriek	10-2
Golf Land (IRE)	9-6
Gollinger	9-6
Gone On (IRE)	9-0
Go Nomadic	10-2
Good Boy (FR)	10-8
Good Gracious	7-4
Good Heart (IRE)	9-12
Good Morning	9-2
Good Thyne Murphy (IRE)	8-11
Good Time Melody (IRE)	10-9
Go Positive	9-6
Gortroe Guy (IRE)	9-1§
Got Alot On (USA)	8-5
Gotha (FR)	9-11§
Got News For You	10-7
Grand Ambition (USA)	9-5§
Grand Canyon (IRE)	9-6§
Grand Gousier (FR)	9-0
Grandmere	9-5
Granny Dick	8-9§
Granny Smith (IRE)	9-12
Grantie Boy (IRE)	7-0
Graphic Designer (IRE)	8-3
Gratomi (IRE)	9-9
Gray Knight (IRE)	9-12
Great Jubilee (IRE)	10-2
Grecian Star	10-2
Greenkeys (AUS)	9-11
Greensleeves	9-7
Greet You Well	10-0
Greybrook Lad (IRE)	10-0
Grey Fandango (IRE)	9-8
Grizzly Golfwear (IRE)	10-4

Horse	Handicap
Guard A Dream (IRE)	9-0
Gudasmum	10-0
Guest Alliance (IRE)	8-7
Guignol Du Cochet (FR)	10-6
Guilsborough Gorse	10-4
Gumlayloy	9-0
Gunnaballright	9-12
Gunnerbe Posh	9-3
Gunner Be True	8-12§
Gunner Sid	10-0
Gunners Mistake	9-3§
Gun'n Roses II (FR)	11-2
Gunville	9-0
Guru Rinpoche	10-1
Gus Berry (IRE)	9-7
Gutsy Dalton (IRE)	9-5
Hadaway Lad	9-9
Hadeqa	10-6§
Hail Stone (IRE)	9-12§
Hailstorm (IRE)	9-10
Half A Story	9-3
Hallrule (IRE)	10-1
Handstand	9-11
Handy Boy	9-11
Handy Hill	9-4
Hanisia	8-12
Happy Team	9-7
Hapthor	9-9
Harden Glen	10-2
Harding	9-12
Harjach	9-5
Harnage (IRE)	10-2
Harppy (FR)	8-11§
Harry Hotspur (IRE)	5-0§
Harry Jay	6-12
Harry's Mare (IRE)	8-0
Has She Bucked Yet	9-4
Hasten Bak	10-3
Haste Ye Back (IRE)	10-3
Hatch Gate	10-0§
Hattie	9-8
Have A Chat	9-7
Hawkers Hill	9-9
Hay Dance	9-8
Haydn James (USA)	10-5
Hayling Star	8-6§
Head Gardener (IRE)	9-3§
Headwrecker (IRE)	9-10
Heather Lad	9-6
Heathyards Element	9-1§
Heavy Weather (IRE)	9-11
Hedzamarley (IRE)	9-9
Heidi III (FR)	10-7
Heidi Moo (U)	5-0
Heisamodel (IRE)	9-12
Hellodock (IRE)	10-0
Hello Roscrea (IRE)	10-0
Henbury Dancer	9-0
Hendrix	9-0
Henry Bruce	9-10§
Henry Henbit	9-0§
Henry Murphy	9-13
Henwyn	9-3§
Here Comes Choosey (IRE)	8-9
Here's To Lucy	9-5
Hermano (IRE)	7-4
Hermes III (FR)	10-12
Herswell Castle	9-6
Hervey Bay	9-10
Hessac (FR)	9-6§
Hever Road (IRE)	9-7
Hidden Pearl (IRE)	8-13
Highbridge (IRE)	9-8§
Highcroft Boy	9-6
High Fields	9-10
Highfield's Clover	8-11
Highland Brig	9-9
Highland Dancer (IRE)	9-2
Highland Rose (IRE)	10-6
Highland Wonder	7-11
High Mood	9-11
High Peak	10-5
Highway Oak	10-1
Hijacked	9-13
Hilarity	8-12
Hillcrest Manor (IRE)	8-0
Hill Of Kilfeacle (IRE)	8-10
Hill Top Flyer (IRE)	7-0
Hill Trail	10-1
Himalayan Heights	8-7
Hi Rudolf	10-2
Hi Tech Man (IRE)	9-7
Hi Up Brenkley	8-12
Hobbycyr (FR)	10-6
Hobo	7-12
Hoh Tel (IRE)	10-0§
Hokey Wokey	8-10
Holdimclose	9-12
Holding The Fort (IRE)	10-3
Hold On Harry	10-1
Hollyhock	8-7
Holly Park	3-0
Holy Moses (IRE)	9-9§
Home Again (IRE)	10-2
Homeleigh Meadow	8-0
Home Tor	9-0§
Homme De Fer	10-7
Honiton (U)	4-7
Hoodwinker (IRE)	10-6
Hooray Henry	9-5
Hope Value	8-7
Hoplite	9-8
Horrified	9-2§
Hors Concours (NZ)	7-0
Horton-Cum-Peel (IRE)	9-6
Hostetler	9-1
Hot Bricks	5-5
Hoteliers' Dream	8-9§
Hot Plunge	10-4§
Hotters (IRE)	9-12
Hot Toddy (IRE)	10-3
Hougham George	9-6
House Colours	8-13
Houselope Beck	9-6§
How Burn	9-9
How To Run (IRE)	9-8
Howya Matey (IRE)	9-6
Hug The Bend	9-3
Hunca Munca (IRE)	10-6
Hunter Gold (FR)	9-11
Huntersway (IRE)	10-2
Hurricane Lamp	10-4
Hydemilla	8-12§
Hylters Chance (IRE)	10-0
Iadora	9-7
I Am Said I (IRE)	10-5
Ian's Boy	9-4
Ical (IRE)	9-0
Iconic	8-7
Idiot's Star	9-7
Igam Ogam	5-0
Igloux Royal (FR)	8-5
Ile Distinct (IRE)	8-3§
Imago II (FR)	9-11
I'm Dreaming (IRE)	9-9
I'm No Fairy	8-0
Impatient Lady	10-1
Imperial Line (IRE)	9-9
Imperial Prince	9-0
Imps Way	10-0
Imustgeton	9-5
I'm Willie's Girl	9-0
Inagh Road (IRE)	9-8
Inching Brook	7-0
Incroyable Mais Vrai (FR)	10-2§
In Demand	9-5
Indiana John (FR)	9-6
Indian Raider (IRE)	9-5
Indian Renegade (IRE)	8-8
Indian Rope Trick	9-6
Indian Trix (IRE)	7-8
Indian Wings (IRE)	10-1
Indien Du Boulay (FR)	10-1
Infamelia	9-10§

Inglemotte Miss 8-6§
Inis Cara (IRE) 9-11
Inis Eile (IRE) 9-2§
Inner State 8-2§
Inspector Blake 9-6
Inter Rock (FR) 9-13
Interrogator 9-3
In The Van 9-0
Involved (IRE) 10-3
Iorana (FR) 8-6
Irbee 10-7§
Irilut (FR) 9-10
Irish Paddy (IRE) 9-8
Irish Sea (USA) 9-12
Ironbridge 8-13
Iron N Gold 9-10
Iron Trooper (IRE) 8-8
Isefoul De Bellevue (FR) 8-7
Italian Clover 8-5
Itchen Mill 9-10
Its A Handfull 8-2§
Itsallupintheair 9-9
Itsdigitalis 9-0
Itsforu 9-0
It's Missy Imp 9-12
Itsmyturnnow (IRE) 10-0
It'snotsimple (IRE) 10-4
Its-On-The-Cards (IRE) 10-0
Itsthebrass 7-7
Itworked 10-1
Ivans Dream 9-5
Ivory Cross 8-0
I Will Survive (IRE) 9-6
Izzuthefox (IRE) 8-13
Jabiru (IRE) 10-11§
Jack Hackett (IRE) 9-9§
Jackie Jarvis (IRE) 10-6§
Jackofalltrades (IRE) 8-3
Jack Of Kilcash (IRE) 9-0
Jackson (FR) 10-6
Jackson Hill 9-8
Jack's The Boy (IRE) 7-13
Jack The Bear (IRE) 9-7
Jacob's Choice 9-8
Jag 8-0
Jakes Progress (IRE) 7-7
Jalcanto 10-0
James Victor (IRE) 9-7
Jamie Browne (IRE) 8-13
Jaunty Janner 8-11
Jazz Night 10-4
Jd Trout 8-5
Jelali (IRE) 9-1
Jemannette 9-2
Jemaro (IRE) 10-9
Jenko (FR) 9-6
Jenny's Charmer 9-6
Jentar Equilibra (IRE) 9-13
Jerome Jerome 9-2§
Jerroboam (FR) 9-2
Je Suis (IRE) 8-3
Jethro Tull (IRE) 9-6
Jeune Premier (FR) 9-10
Jewel Song 8-13
Jimmy Cricket 10-4
Jimmy Jumbo (IRE) 9-12
Jims Belief (IRE) 9-8
Jim's Gift (IRE) 9-13
Jinful Du Grand Val (FR) 9-10
Jobee Jack 8-8
Joe Lively (IRE) 7-5
John Foley (IRE) 9-13
Johnny Ross (IRE) 8-4
Johnnys Gone (IRE) 10-4§
Johnsair (IRE) 9-12
Johns Legacy 10-11
Johnston's Ville (IRE) 8-10
J-Okay (IRE) 10-12
Jolejoker 9-10
Joli Christmas 9-3
Jolie Roslin 9-7
Jolitan 10-5§
Jolly Jake 9-8§
Jolly Minster 10-0
Jona Holley 4-13§
Jonno 8-2
Jorodama King 9-11
Josanjamic 9-9
Josh's Choice (IRE) 8-0§
Journey 10-3
Joves Shadow 8-12
Jovian Pond 8-9
Joyce Bel (FR) 9-5
Joy For Life (IRE) 10-0
Joyful Jade (FR) 8-10
Jubileeman (IRE) 9-13
Judy's Lad 8-8§
Jump For Paddy 8-11
Jumping Jack 9-3
Jupiter George 9-6§
Jupiter Jay 7-12
Jupiter Jo 9-11
Jupiter's Fancy 9-11
Jurist 9-6
Justadream 9-10
Just A Lady 8-8
Just A Man 6-11
Just Aretha 7-7§
Just Barney Boy 10-7
Just Bert (IRE) 9-10
Just Caramel 8-2
Just Champ 7-0
Just Cliquot 10-8
Justenough 9-2
Just Fable 8-13
Just Fluster 9-11
Just For Now (IRE) 8-0
Justin Mac (IRE) 10-0§
Justjim 9-10
Just Jove 9-13
Just Lark 9-6
Just Lute 9-5
Just Sally 10-0
Just The Job Too (IRE) 10-4§
Just Whiskey (IRE) 9-13
J W (U) 4-12
Kalahari Ferrari 8-7
Kalypso De Laugere (FR) 9-5
Kandy Four (NZ) 9-5
Kanturk Star (IRE) 9-0
Karadin (FR) 10-1
Karinga Lane 9-7
Karinga Leap 9-11
Karzhang 9-13
Kasilia (FR) 10-1
Katinka 10-2
Kayleigh (IRE) 9-11
Keegan Bearnais (FR) 9-9
Keep The Day Job 8-5
Keitho (IRE) 9-8
Keltic Lord 10-5
Kenny Davis (IRE) 10-0
Kentford Bracken 8-11
Kentford Busy B 9-12
Kepi Royal (FR) 10-1
Kerres Noires (FR) 10-0
Kerry Zulu Warrior 9-11
Kerstino Two 10-5
Kestick 10-10
Kestle Mill (IRE) 9-10
Khatani (IRE) 10-8
Khayal (USA) 9-12
Kilcaskin Gold (IRE) 9-12
Kildysart Lady (IRE) 9-10
Killard Point (IRE) 10-3
Killerine (FR) 10-4
Killiney Bay (IRE) 10-1
Killough Hill (IRE) 8-8
Kilvoydan (IRE) 10-4§
Kincora (IRE) 10-2
Kindle A Flame 8-12
King Barry (FR) 10-4
Kingfisher Star 8-7§
King Freddy 9-0
King Of Swing (IRE) 8-11

King Of The Dawn 10-3
King Of The Sea (IRE). . . .6-5
Kingsbridge (IRE) . . . . .9-11§
Kings Command 9-2
King's Hero (IRE) 10-9
Kings Minstral (IRE) . . . 9-11
King's Reply 9-3
Kingston-Banker 10-12
Kingston Venture. 10-13
Kirkfield (IRE). 9-7
Kirkharle (IRE) 9-7
Kissed By Moonlite 8-3
Knickers 8-4
Knight Of Kilcash (IRE). . .9-5
Knight Of Passion 10-3
Knight Ofthe North 7-7
Knighton Star 9-7
Kniveniven (IRE). 8-0
Knockaun Wood (IRE). . . .9-1
Knockholt 10-1
Knock It Back (IRE) 9-8
Knock Star (IRE). 9-11
Kotori (IRE). 8-0
Kovach (IRE) 10-0
Krac De Mirande (FR). . . .9-3
Krystal Tip 9-11
Kupto (FR) 9-4
Kustom Kit Grizzly (IRE) . 9-13§
Kuwait Millennium 9-11
Kyalami (FR). 9-12
La Colina (IRE). 9-12
Lady Baronette 9-13
Lady Blackthorn 5-7
Lady Dot (IRE) . . . . .9-4§
Ladygal (IRE) 8-10
Lady Misprint 10-11
Lady Mordaunt (IRE) 8-1
Lady Of Jazz. 8-2
Lady Palamon (IRE) 9-3
Lady Widd (IRE). 9-7
Laganside (IRE) 9-13
Lah Di Dah Lad 9-12
Lakeland Prince 8-5
La Maestra (FR) 9-3
Lambrini King (IRE) . . . 8-10
Lambrini Mist. 10-8
Lamerton Quest 5-0
Lancastrian Island. 7-11
Lancastrian Jet (IRE) . 10-12
Lance Feather (IRE) 8-0
Landford Lad (IRE) 9-5
Lansdowne Park 9-12
Lateen 4-7
Laura Lugs (IRE). . . . . -
Laurelgirl (IRE) 8-3
Lava 9-11
Lazy Lemon 9-7
Leachbrook Lady. 8-13
Leading Case 9-10
Lead Story (IRE). 10-5
Leatherback (IRE). . . . .9-10§
Le Cure. 10-3
Ledgendry Line 10-2
Legal Storm (IRE). 9-13
Legend Of Light (IRE) . . 9-10
Le Millenaire (FR). 9-12
Leon Garcia (IRE) 10-0
Le Prince 10-3
Lethem Air 9-10
Let's Fly (FR) 10-7
Letsgeton 8-6
Let's Rock. 8-5
Liberty Livelihood 9-10
Libido. 8-9
L'idefix (IRE) 10-0
Life Of A River (IRE) . . . 9-10
Life's Work . . . . .9-10§
Lightning Fork (IRE) 9-5
Lightning Rebel. 6-7
Lights On 9-9
Light The River (IRE) . . 10-1
Light The Sky 9-10
Like The Buzz (IRE) . . . 10-2
Lilabet 8-7
Lily Brown 9-2
Lily Lane. . . . . .8-6§
Lima Bravo 10-2
Lindron 9-5
Lindsay (FR). 11-1
Lingering Fog (IRE). . . . 9-13
Lingham Lady. 9-10
Link Copper . . . . .8-10§
Linlathen 10-3
Lirkimalong. 9-8
Lirsleftover 10-0
Liscombe 8-0
Listen To Us (IRE). 8-12
Little Apple Bay 8-6
Little Dish. 9-7
Little Farmer 10-5
Little John . . . . .9-3§
Little Lord Lewis 6-6
Little Mickey. 9-2
Little Native (IRE). 10-3
Little Rosie . . . . .7-10§
Little Santa (IRE) 9-12
Littleton Zeus (IRE). 8-2
Little Word 8-9
Little Worsall (IRE) 9-12
Lively Dessert (IRE) . . .9-10§
Lively Lord (IRE). 10-3
Live Wire (IRE). 9-10
Lolloping Lad 8-6
Londolozi Lad (IRE) . . . 9-13
Lone Star (IRE). . . . . . .8-10§
Longstone Boy (IRE). . . 10-4
Longstone Lad 10-0
Longstone Lady (IRE) 9-6
Longville Lad 10-6
Looking Deadly. . . . . . . .5-7§
Looking Magic (IRE) 7-9
Loose Cannon (IRE) 8-5
Lord Alpha (IRE). 9-8
Lord Anner (IRE). 10-5
Lord Atterbury (IRE) . . . 11-6
Lord Beau (IRE) 8-13
Lordberniebouffant (IRE) 10-4
Lord Castle (IRE) 9-12
Lord Dorcet (IRE) 9-10
Lord Edwards Army (IRE) . 10-4
Lord Esker (IRE) 9-2
Lord Euro (IRE). 9-11
Lord George 9-3
Lord Jurado (IRE) 6-13
Lord Ken (IRE) . . . . . . .10-3§
Lord Kilpatrick (IRE). . . 10-5
Lord Lane 9-7
Lord Montagu (IRE) 9-1
Lord Nick 9-8
Lord Of Heaven (USA) . . .9-1
Lord Of The Chase (IRE). .8-0
Lord Of The Flies (IRE). .9-3§
Lord Of The Mist (IRE) . 10-9
Lord Of The North (IRE) 9-10
Lord Of The Road 9-9
Lord Of The West (IRE). . .9-9
Lord Oscar (IRE). 10-4
Lord Scroop (IRE) . . . . . .9-0§
Lord Stroller 7-10
Lord Valnic (IRE) 10-8
Lord Woodyard . . . . . . .8-13§
Lothian Rising. 9-7
Lottery Lil 9-10
Lottie The Lotus 9-10
Lottie (U) 7-7
Lou Biarnes (FR). 8-12
Love At Dawn 10-0
Luck In Run'in 8-9
Lucky Brush (IRE). . . . .10-0§
Lucky Master (IRE). . . . 10-0
Lucky Wyn 9-13
Lugs Brannigan (IRE) . . 10-1
Lutteur Bleu (FR) 9-11
Lydford Castle. . . . . .9-7§
Lydia's Echo 8-4

Lynwood Legend 7-0
Lyphard's Fable (USA) . . 9-2§
Lyrical Seal 9-2
Macaroni Beach 9-11
Macfin (IRE) 10-2
Macgeorge (IRE) 11-3
Macgyver (NZ) 10-1
Machalini 10-8
Mackoy (IRE) 9-6
Macrobert's Reply (IRE) 7-10
Macy (IRE) . . . . 8-7§
Madam Attorney 8-3
Madame Cholet 7-8
Mademist Sam . . . . 10-3§
Mademist Sparky 9-0
Mad Jack 9-5
Madmidge 10-5
Maggies Brother 10-7
Magical Approach (IRE) . . 9-9
Magical Fun (IRE) 9-8
Magicien (FR) 9-13
Magic Lodge 10-1
Magic Performer 9-13
Magic Route (IRE) 9-5
Magnatism 8-0
Magnemite (IRE) . . . . . . 9-10§
Magnus Maximus 9-5
Magnus Veritas (IRE) . . 10-3
Maharajah (IRE) 9-8
Maidstone Monument (IRE) 10-11
Mainlier 9-4
Mai Point 9-12
Maitre De Musique (FR) 10-1
Majestic Approach (IRE) 9-12
Major Adams 10-0
Major Reno (IRE) 9-2
Makhpiya Patahn (IRE) . . 9-4§
Maloney (IRE) 8-12
Maltby Son 9-8
Man At The Top . . . . 9-0§
Mandagus (IRE) 8-6
Mandate Man (IRE) 9-7
Manhatton Storm (IRE) . . . 9-2
Maquilleux 10-2
Marciano . . . . 9-3§
Marcus William (IRE) . . 9-13
Margery's Opera 9-5
Market Springer (IRE) . . 9-10
Market Value (IRE) . . . . . 8-5§
Marlmont Lad (IRE) . . . 7-11
Marquis Max 9-9
Marsden 8-4
Marston Moses 10-5
Martby 9-9
Marteeny . . . . 9-11§
Martha Jane 8-9
Martha's Boy (IRE) 10-8
Martin Ossie 9-9
Marty's Lamp 7-11
Masalarian (IRE) 10-10
Mashwe (IRE) 10-6
Masitat 9-2
Master Adam (IRE) 8-9
Master Chief (IRE) . . . . . 8-7§
Master Club Royal . . . . . 9-7§
Master Cruise 8-7
Master Grass 9-8
Master Jock 10-4
Master Wood 10-4
Maybe A Double 9-5
Mayday Girl . . . . 8-9§
Mazury (USA) 9-7
Meadows Prince (IRE) . . 8-0§
Meander (IRE) 10-3
Mecca Prince (IRE) . . . . 9-12§
Meentagh Loch 9-7
Mel In Blue (FR) 10-10
Memsahib Ki Behan 8-6
Menantol 9-8
Mensch (IRE) 10-6
Merlin Meg 8-12
Merlins Bay (IRE) 9-0
Merry Christmas 9-9
Merry Melody 9-3
Merry Minstrel (IRE) 9-0
Merry Shot (IRE) 9-6
Mervsintrouble . . . . 9-1§
Miaheyyun 8-11
Mickthecutaway (IRE) . . 10-0
Micky Mansions (IRE) . . 9-12
Midnight Coup . . . . 9-11§
Midnight Cowboy 9-3
Midnight Lord (IRE) 9-8
Midnight Moon 9-0
Midnight Reiver 7-2
Mid Summer Lark (IRE) 10-7
Midy's Risk (FR) 9-0
Mighty Mack (IRE) 8-5
Mighty Willing 10-5
Milamoss 8-8
Milbrig 8-11
Militaire (FR) 10-5
Milla's Man (IRE) 10-0
Milldalus (IRE) 9-6
Millenium Run (IRE) . . . . 9-1§
Millenium Way (IRE) . . . 10-2§
Millennium Gold 9-11
Milliners Guide 8-11
Mill Lord (IRE) 9-9
Millyhenry 9-10
Millys Filly . . . . 8-1§
Milnstorm (IRE) 9-8
Mind The Gate 10-1
Minella Hotel (IRE) 10-0
Minella Silver (IRE) . . . 10-10
Minella Storm (IRE) . . . 10-3
Mini Cruise 9-8
Minino (IRE) . . . . 10-2§
Ministerial (IRE) 9-13
Minster Belle 9-3
Minster Echo . . . . 8-11§
Minster Sunshine 10-0
Miorbhail 9-11
Miss Biddy 9-3
Miss Chloe (IRE) 8-3
Miss Danbys . . . . 8-0§
Miss Flinders 9-6
Miss Foley 9-8
Miss Hoity Toity . . . . . . 10-0§
Missilebrook Lass . . . . . . 7-0§
Miss Illustrious 9-9
Miss Karingaroo . . . . 9-4§
Miss Man 9-2
Miss Mattie Ross 10-10
Miss Moss 9-12
Miss O'Grady (IRE) 10-6
Miss Portcello 9-12
Miss Royello 10-1
Miss Zarnni . . . . 9-12§
Miss Ziggerson 9-8
Mister Audi (IRE) . . . . . . 9-6§
Mister Benjamin (IRE) . 11-2
Mister Bromley 9-7
Mister Cone 9-9
Mister Falcon (FR) . . . . . 9-8§
Mister Moss (IRE) 9-13
Mister Pepper (IRE) . . . 10-3§
Mister Rf (IRE) 9-2
Mister Ringa 10-0
Mister Rose (IRE) 8-7
Mister Swallow . . . . . . 10-3§
Mistrio 8-7
Misty Ramble (IRE) . . . 10-0
Modesty Forbids 8-12
Mollycarrs Gambul 9-8
Monarch Ruler 9-13
Money Magic 9-5
Monks Error (IRE) 11-1
Monnaie Forte (IRE) . . . 10-3
Mon Performer 8-7
Monsukh (IRE) . . . . 7-11§
Montenegro 9-12
Monty's Lass (IRE) 10-8
Moon Tiger 10-5

Horse	Rating
Moorepark Joy (IRE)	7-6
Moorfoot Blaze	8-10
Moorland Rose	9-6
Moraira (IRE)	8-13
More Flair	10-3
Morph	9-11
Morris Piper	10-0§
Moscow's Return (IRE)	9-3§
Moscow Tradition (IRE)	9-11
Mo's O Friendly	8-12
Mosscroft Jack	9-4
Mother's Ruin	9-1
Mountain Lily	9-0
Mountain Trooper	9-8
Mounthenry Star (IRE)	10-2
Mountsorrel (IRE)	9-10
Mouse Bird (IRE)	9-12§
Mouseski	11-1
Mozielaw	9-4
Mr Baldwin (IRE)	7-8
Mr Baloo	8-12§
Mr Ben Gunn	9-12
Mr Buckle (IRE)	8-12
Mr Hawkeye (USA)	10-8
Mr Kermit	9-11
Mr Know What (IRE)	9-3
Mr Mackenzie (IRE)	9-12
Mr Magget (IRE)	9-0
Mr Mahdlo	10-7§
Mr Max (IRE)	9-13
Mr McDuck (IRE)	10-0§
Mr McDuff (IRE)	9-1
Mr Naborro (IRE)	9-5§
Mr Pendleberry	10-1
Mrs Be (IRE)	10-11§
Mrs Goldfarb	9-2
Mr Smudge	10-1
Mr Snowman	10-0
Mrs Peggoty	9-0§
Mr Splodge	10-5
Mrs Sherman	9-2
Mucky Man (IRE)	9-10
Mullarts Lad (IRE)	9-9
Mullensgrove	10-11
Mullover	8-7
Multi Franchise	9-8
Murphy's Magic (IRE)	9-11
Muscadin	8-6
Musical Hit	8-13§
Musical Sleuth	9-4
Musical Socks	9-2
Mussel Buoy (IRE)	10-6
Mustang Molly	9-0
My Best Buddy	10-5
My Brother Jack	9-5
Mydante (IRE)	9-5
My Jess	9-5
My Little Lady	9-1
My Moondancer (FR)	9-6
My Native Knight (IRE)	10-2
My Native Land (IRE)	8-11
Mystical Spot	8-4
Mystic Isle (IRE)	10-4
Mystic Warrior (USA)	10-0
Mytimie (IRE)	10-3
My Whisper (IRE)	9-10
Nailed On	9-8
Namron (IRE)	9-12
Naomh Padraig (IRE)	9-5§
Nashville Star (USA)	9-0§
National Debt	7-12
Native Alibi (IRE)	9-10
Native Christy (IRE)	9-2§
Native Daisy (IRE)	9-13
Native Isle (IRE)	9-0
Native King (IRE)	10-4§
Native Man (IRE)	10-3
Native Spin (IRE)	9-5§
Native Thunder (IRE)	9-11
Naughty Dandy (IRE)	9-9
Naughty Noah	8-5
Nautical Lad	10-8
Nditlir	8-7
Nealie Mac (IRE)	9-2
Near And Phar (IRE)	9-10
Nearly A Mildred	9-4
Nearly Dark	7-4
Nearly Gold	9-3
Nearly Noble (IRE)	10-0
Needsmoretime (IRE)	7-11§
Needwood Neptune	7-0§
Nelsun	9-11
Neminos (IRE)	9-9
Nessarc (IRE)	8-9
Never Compromise (IRE)	11-8
Never In Debt	9-0§
Never Sayaarr (IRE)	6-13
Newby End (IRE)	9-8§
Newgate Wells (IRE)	9-6§
New Lodge Express (IRE)	9-11
Newmarket Magic (IRE)	8-5
New Ross (IRE)	9-10§
News Flash (IRE)	10-10
New World Comet	8-7
Nice Approach (IRE)	8-12§
Nicholls Cross (IRE)	9-11
Nickit (IRE)	9-8§
Nicky The Kip (IRE)	8-7
Nicodemus	9-0
Niloufer	9-4
Nimbus Stratus	9-0§
Nip On	10-0
Nisbet	10-8
Noaff (IRE)	10-2
Noble Action	10-6
Noble Affair	10-0
Noble Colours	8-10
Noble Hymn	10-0
Nocash (IRE)	9-8
Nodform Returns	9-0
No Dramas (IRE)	9-10
Noel's Pride	9-13
No Fiddling (IRE)	10-1§
Noggler	8-7
No Info (IRE)	8-8
No Keep (IRE)	9-2
Nokimover	10-10
Nomadic Blaze	9-10
Nomadic Star	10-0
No Nay Never (IRE)	8-7
Nonplussed	8-7§
No Penalty	9-12
No Pressure (IRE)	9-5
Norbert (IRE)	7-13
Nordic Crest (IRE)	10-8
Nordic Spree (IRE)	9-1§
No Remorse	9-8
No Reward (IRE)	9-8
Norlandic (NZ)	10-0
Normania (NZ)	9-10
Norman Way	9-2§
Norse	8-1
Norski Lad	10-6
Northall Lad	8-5
Northern Breeze	8-9
Northern Castle (IRE)	8-10
Northern Prince	9-3
Northern Thatch	8-10
North Pass	7-12§
Northsprite	9-10
Norton Wood (IRE)	7-0
Notable Exception	9-2
Not For Parrot (IRE)	9-5
Notsotiny	9-0
Not Yet Decent (IRE)	9-5
Nought To Ninety	9-12
Nousayri (IRE)	9-11
Nowornever (IRE)	9-10
Now Young Man (IRE)	8-10
Nubro (IRE)	9-12§
Oaklands Billy	7-7
Oaklands Luis	9-8
Oaklands Ted	8-4
Ocki	9-6
Octagonal (IRE)	9-2

Octane Booster (IRE) 8-5
O'ech 10-0
Ofcoursehekhan (IRE) . . 9-10
Office Hours 9-6
Officer Cadet (IRE) 9-7
Off Piste 9-1
Offshore (IRE). 9-9
Offspringer 9-3
Off The Hook (IRE). 9-5
O'flaherty's (IRE). 8-0
Oh Highly Likely (IRE) . 10-0
O J Selym (IRE) 9-3
Ole Gunnar (IRE) . . . . . .9-9§
Olly May. 9-4
Omni Cosmo Touch (USA) 10-11
On A Full Wager 8-3
Oneanthreequarters (IRE)8-11
One For Olly (IRE) 8-10
Oneforthefrog (IRE). . . . .9-7§
Oneminutetofive 11-1
One Of The Natives (IRE) .9-0
On His Toes 10-0
On The Day (IRE) . . . . .9-11§
On The Mend (IRE). . . . 9-10
Onward Bound . . . . .9-4§
Opal'lou (FR) 10-1
Oranbay (IRE). 9-8
Orchestra's Boy (IRE) . . 9-12
Orinoco's Flight (IRE) 9-8
Orleans (IRE) . . . . .9-13§
Orphan Spa (IRE) 8-4
Oscar Wilde 9-11
O So Bossy. 9-11
Oswald 6-2
Our Weddingpresent (USA) 8-13
Out The Black (IRE) . . 10-10
Over The Beck (IRE). . . 9-13
Over The Master (IRE) . 10-0
Over The Rhee (IRE). 9-1
Owenabue Valley (IRE) . . .9-7
Owen's Pet (IRE). 10-1
Owl Vulgan (IRE) 9-8
Oxendale. . . . . .9-10§
Pacon (GER). 9-13
Paddies Boy (IRE). 9-10
Paddy Bettalot 9-9
Paddy For Paddy (IRE) 10-12
Paddy's Dream (IRE) . . 9-13
Pagermar (IRE). 9-13
Palisander (IRE) 10-9
Pampered Gale (IRE) . .10-0§
Pams Oak. . . . . .9-4§
Pandeli . . . . .8-9§

Panhandle. 9-13
Panooras Lord (IRE) 9-6
Panto 8-6
Panto Pixie 9-7
Pa Pierre (IRE) 10-4
Parade Racer . . . . .10-0§
Paradisio (FR). 10-4
Parahandy (IRE) 10-5
Parsifal 9-11
Parte Prima. 10-5
Passing Danger (FR) . . . 10-4
Past Forte 7-9
Pauls Legacy. 7-12
Peaceful Bow (IRE). 9-3
Peats Ridge (IRE) 8-9
Pekan Polly. 8-6
Pendils Charm . . . . .9-1§
Pendle Hill 10-4
Pendragon 9-13
Penlet Too. 8-7
Pennyahei. 10-9
Penny Blue 8-11
Penny Native (IRE) 10-4
Penny Poor (IRE) 9-2
Peppernick 10-0
Perchancer (IRE). 10-6
Perching (IRE) 9-12
Perfect Bear 8-5
Perfect Finisher. 9-5
Perkys Pride (IRE). 10-7
Perky's Wish (IRE) 7-10
Pernickety King. 7-2
Perryman (IRE). 9-10
Persian Dawn 7-0
Persian Hero (IRE) 10-2
Persona Pride . . . . .9-7§
Pete The Painter (IRE) . 9-12
Petrie 8-7
Petrouge . . . . .9-11§
Phar Afield (IRE). 9-0
Pharailde 9-13
Phar From Chance 10-2
Pharlindo (IRE). . . . . . . .9-7§
Pharmistice (IRE) 10-2
Pharshu (IRE). 9-4
Phar To Comfy (IRE). 9-2
Phase Three (IRE). 9-11
Philson Run (IRE). 11-0
Philtre (IRE) 10-6
Phoenix Phlyer 10-3
Phyllis 9-11
Picket Piece 9-11
Pillager 9-6
Pilot's Harbour 9-0
Pinmoor Hill 9-11

Piper's Rock (IRE) 10-1
Pistol Knight 9-4
Pitchfork Pete 9-9
Place Above (IRE). . . . .9-12§
Placid Man (IRE) 11-5
Plain Chant. 9-7
Planet Ireland (IRE) 9-2
Play Alone (IRE) 9-3
Plenty Inn Hand . . . . . . .7-7§
Poacher's Pride. 6-8
Polar Bright (IRE) 9-5
Polar Champ. 10-10
Polar Flight. 10-8
Polar King (IRE) . . . . . .10-0§
Polka 10-2
Polly Come Back. 8-13
Polly Flinders 9-8
Polo Pony (IRE) . . . . . .9-11§
Polo Ridge (IRE) . . . . . .10-0§
Poppers 8-7
Poppet 10-1
Poppy Maroon 10-5
Porlock Hill. 10-1
Porto (IRE) 10-0
Port Valenska (IRE). . . .6-10§
Posh Stick 9-10
Pot Shot 10-3
Prah Sands . . . . .8-7§
Prate Box (IRE). 10-4
Preacher Boy 9-12
Preferred (IRE) 9-4
Present Moment (IRE). . . .9-9
Preston Brook 9-5
Pretoria Dancer. . . . . . .10-2§
Pride Of Kashmir 10-0
Priestthorn (IRE). 9-11
Prime Course (IRE) 10-2
Primero (IRE) 9-0
Primitive Rites 9-10
Primitive Satin 10-1
Primitive Son 9-8
Primitive Way 10-3
Prince Dundee (FR) . . . 10-5
Prince Mouse 8-6
Prince Of Beal. 9-4
Princess Derry 9-7
Princess Hatie. 8-0
Prioritisation (IRE). 9-0
Pristeen Spy 10-3
Private Percival 8-7
Private Pete 9-12
Proby Lady (IRE) 9-10
Procol's Boy 9-8
Prologue (IRE) 9-5
Prominent. . . . . .9-13§

Horse	Weight
Proper Primitive	9-10
Province	10-1
Pudding And Pie	8-10
Pulham Downe	9-12
Pure Steel (IRE)	10-1
Purevalue (IRE)	9-5
Purple Jean	10-0
Purslet	9-0
Pusey Sance	8-0
Puzzleman	10-1
Quango	10-0
Queenies Girl	8-11§
Queen Of Araghty	9-2
Queens House	7-10
Quel Regal (FR)	9-0
Questionaire	10-1
Questionit	9-3
Quetal (IRE)	10-5
Quick Response (IRE)	9-12
Quickswood (IRE)	10-4
Quizzal	9-8
Raconteur (IRE)	9-13
Radbrook Hall	9-4
Raffles Rooster	9-7§
Raging Torrent	9-13
Rag Week (IRE)	10-3
Rainbow Ranch (IRE)	9-12
Rain Delay	10-0
Rainha	10-1
Rainton	9-13
Raiseapearl	9-11
Rakaposhi Raid	9-5
Ramirez (IRE)	10-3
Ramon Allones (IRE)	8-9
Random Trix	8-0
Raregem	9-12
Rash Moment (FR)	8-7
Rathbarry Lad (IRE)	9-10
Rathbawn Prince (IRE)	10-11
Rathgibbon (IRE)	9-9§
Rathnally Park	9-13
Ravenscar	9-10
Ravensworth	9-6
Raymond James	9-8§
Real Value (IRE)	9-12
Rectory Garden (IRE)	9-10
Red Brook Lad	10-10
Red Channel (IRE)	7-13
Red Gauntlet	10-8
Redhouse Chevalier	9-8
Red Jupiter	9-2
Red Native (IRE)	10-5
Red Neck	10-2
Red Rebel	9-12§
Red Ringa	8-10
Red Rose Dixie	7-10
Red Salmon Dancer	9-0
Red September	9-6
Red Spark	9-0
Red Square Knight (IRE)	8-10
Red Square Prince (IRE)	9-5
Red Tyrant	7-4
Reeker Pike	8-0
Reflected Glory (IRE)	10-2
Regal Bride	9-4
Rescindo (IRE)	9-8§
Retorrick Rose	8-8
Return The Call (IRE)	9-9
Rhythm King	10-3
Rian Bo Padraig (IRE)	9-5
Ribble Assembly	9-6
Rice Point	9-11
Rich Song (IRE)	8-13
Ricky B	10-0
Ridgeway (IRE)	10-3§
Ridware George	9-5
Ridware Pride	9-7
Ridware Rose	9-0
Rifton Bramble	5-10
Rigadoon (IRE)	9-13
Right To Reply (IRE)	11-6
Rightun	9-6
Rimpton Boy	10-3
Ringside View (IRE)	9-5
Rings Of Power (IRE)	9-12
Rio Pops	9-5
Rio's Lord (IRE)	10-7
Rip Kirby	9-10§
Rising Talisker	9-2§
Risk Advisory (IRE)	8-2
River Alder	10-4
River Bailiff (IRE)	10-0§
River Dante (IRE)	9-12§
River Lossie	10-3
River Ness	10-6
River Treasure (IRE)	9-7
Robbie's Adventure	10-0
Robert The Rascal	10-0§
Robins Pride (IRE)	9-8
Roboastar (USA)	9-2§
Rocastle Lad (IRE)	9-10
Rockfield Lane (IRE)	7-12
Rockford (IRE)	8-12
Rock Rose	10-2
Rocky Fountain	9-6
Rodney Trotter	10-7
Rody (IRE)	9-9§
Roebucks Way	8-2
Rolling Maul (IRE)	9-7
Romabit Tom	7-0
Romanybaan	8-10
Romany Move	9-10
Romany Pearl	9-12
Romanys Chance	7-2
Rommel	9-7
Ronans Choice (IRE)	10-6
Ron Miel (IRE)	8-12
Rooster	10-1
Rosalee Royale	9-9
Roscoe Burn	10-1
Roseacre (IRE)	8-3§
Rosegrove Rooster	9-2§
Rosehill Doorbell	9-2
Rosemead Tye	9-5
Rose Of The Hill (IRE)	9-12
Roseta (IRE)	9-10
Rosetta	9-6
Rosie Stroud (IRE)	9-2§
Ross Poldark	9-10
Rostock (IRE)	10-6
Rough Tiger (IRE)	8-11§
Round The Bend	10-0
Round The Isles	8-12
Route One (IRE)	10-5
Route Two (IRE)	9-3
Roxtons	8-12
Royal Action	10-0
Royal Arctic (IRE)	8-9§
Royal Barge	10-3
Royal Crimson	10-1§
Royal Cruise (IRE)	8-13
Royal Czarina	9-11
Royal Dew (IRE)	8-12§
Royalecko	10-5
Royal Snoopy (IRE)	10-8
Royal Squeeze (IRE)	8-11
Royaltino (IRE)	10-6
Royrace	9-0§
Rubian Princess	9-3
Rubon Prince (IRE)	8-7
Ruby Dante (IRE)	9-8
Ruling The Roast	9-0
Rumour Has It (IRE)	9-0
Rundetto (IRE)	8-5
Run For Hannah	8-6
Run Monty (IRE)	9-9
Running Hot	9-12§
Running On Red	8-7
Running Times (USA)	10-0
Runningwiththemoon	9-10
Rushing Again	10-5
Rush Job	8-0
Rusnetto (IRE)	9-10
Russian Connection (IRE)	9-1
Russian Friend	10-1

Rusty Fellow . . . . 9-9§
Rutherford 9-10
Ruth's Boy (IRE) 9-13
Ryans Star 9-13
Ryders Hill 8-10
Sabena Canyon 9-13
Sadler's Realm 10-5
Sad Mad Bad (USA) . . . 10-7§
Safawi 9-3
Saffron Hill (IRE) 9-4
Saffron Moss 9-6
Sailors Folly (IRE) 10-2
Saint-Declan (IRE) 9-13
Sales Dodger (IRE) . . . . . 9-6§
Sally Scally 10-0
Sams Sister 8-8
Sams Way 9-7
San Antonio (U) 5-0
Sandy Duff 10-8
Sandy Lark 9-13
San Francisco 10-4
Sapega (IRE) 10-10
Satanas (FR) 5-9
Satchmo (IRE) 11-1
Satco Prince (IRE) 8-11
Satcotino (IRE) . . . . 9-8§
Saucy Arethusa 10-0
Sawbridge 8-11
Saxon Gold 10-0
Saxon Victory (USA) . . . 9-11§
S B S By Jove . . . . 9-12§
Scalby Croft 8-0
Scallybuck (IRE) 9-10
Scallyweld 8-7
Scarlet Boy 8-11
Scarlet Glory 9-9
Scenic Storm (IRE) 9-7
Schoolhouse Walk 10-5
Scotch Bob (IRE) 9-0
Scotsbrook Lass 8-7
Scottish Roots 10-9
Scowlin Brig 9-9
Seabrook Lad . . . . 10-2§
Sean's Minstrel (IRE) . . . 9-8§
Search Party (FR) 9-5
Seasmith 9-4
Sea Snipe 9-11
Sea Tarth 9-8
Secrete Contract 9-12
See More Fun 8-11
Sefton Clover 8-8
Selectric (IRE) 4-0
Senior Moment 8-0
Senor Cid 9-2
September Harvest (USA) . 9-10
Serves You Right 8-2
Sett Aside 8-12
Sevensider (IRE) 9-7
Severn Magic 10-0
Sex Kitten 8-5
Seymour Of Me 7-10
Shadar (IRE) 9-2
Shady Affair (IRE) 9-1
Shafts Chance (IRE) 9-5
Shaking Chief (IRE) 9-8
Shalabibubbly 9-6
Shallee Term (IRE) 8-6
Shallow River (IRE) 9-2
Shambob 8-3
Shanavogh 10-8
Shanavoher (IRE) 9-7
Shankly 10-4
Sharlom (IRE) 9-12
Sharpaman . . . . 9-10§
Sharp Embrace 9-0
Sharp Fountain 9-2
Sharp Sarah 8-4
Sharp Seal 10-5
Sheila McKenzie 9-12
Shekels (IRE) 8-12
Shemardi 10-0
Sherbourne Guest (IRE) . . 9-4
Sheriff's Friend (IRE) . 10-12
Sheskinqueen (IRE) . . . 10-0
Shillelah Law . . . . 9-5§
Shining Light (IRE) 8-13
Shiny Bay (IRE) 10-5
Shirostran 8-10
Shobrooke Mill 10-2
Shock's Pride (IRE) . . . . . 9-6§
Shortcut Shorty 9-10
Shot Of Jollop (IRE) . . . . 8-9§
Shraden Edition 10-7
Shu Gaa (IRE) 10-4
Shy Lizzie 9-10
Shylock (IRE) 8-13
Shy Paddy (IRE) 9-10
Sijujama (IRE) 8-9
Sikander A Azam 11-3
Silence Reigns 10-12
Silent Action (USA) 9-0
Silent Keys (SWE) 8-0
Silk St Bridget 9-3
Silk Vestments . . . . 9-10§
Silly Boy 9-0
Silogue (IRE) 9-10
Silver Baron 8-11
Silver Buzzard (USA) . . 10-2
Silver Castle 10-3
Silverdalesureshot 10-5
Silver Groom (IRE) 10-4
Silver Image 7-10
Silver Lake (IRE) 9-10
Silver Man 9-6
Silver Orchid 9-3
Silver Pot Black . . . . 9-6§
Silver Styx 9-0
Silver Tray (IRE) 8-5
Simber Hill (IRE) . . . . . 9-12§
Simply A Star (IRE) . . . . . 8-2§
Simply Bruno 8-11
Simply Sam 10-2
Simply The One (IRE) . . 10-3
Sing High 9-7
Single Man (IRE) 8-12
Siobhans Quinner (IRE) . . 9-0
Sip Of Brandy (IRE) . . . 9-12
Sir Alf 9-12
Sir Dante (IRE) 10-3
Sir D'Orton (FR) 10-5
Sir Lancelot 10-0
Sir William 10-6
Sir Williamwallace (IRE) . 9-6§
Sissinghurst Star (IRE) . . 9-9§
Sister Ali (IRE) 8-0
Six Clerks (IRE) . . . . 9-5§
Sixties Melody 9-0
Sizer (IRE) 9-12
Ski Pass 9-8
Skip 'n' Tune (IRE) 10-6
Slaney Lass 10-4
Slaney Native (IRE) 9-7
Slave's Adventure 9-7
Sledmere (IRE) . . . . 8-7§
Sliabh Foy (IRE) 9-13
Sliema (IRE) 9-9
Slingsby Lady 8-5
Slip The Ring 10-4
Slytherin Falls 9-2
Small-Lir 8-10
Smart Cavalier 9-7
Smarty (IRE) 10-6
Smile Pleeze (IRE) . . . . 10-0§
Smokey Joe (IRE) 9-8
Smokey Robot (IRE) . . . 7-13
Snitton Salvo . . . . 9-3§
Snitton West . . . . 9-2§
Snizort (USA) 9-8
Snooty Eskimo (IRE) . . . 10-0§
Snow Nymph 8-9
Snowtre (IRE) . . . . 10-3§
Society Scandal (IRE) 8-7
Socute 9-10
Sohapara 10-6
Sol Music 10-6

Solo Gent	9-5§
Solsgirth	9-9§
Solvang (IRE)	9-13
Some Go West (IRE)	9-6
Some Tool	8-2
Some Tourist (IRE)	8-0
Songino (IRE)	9-3
Sonnant (FR)	9-11
Son Of Anshan	10-9§
Son Of Sam	9-10
Sootsir	8-11
So Peaceful	10-1
Soul King (IRE)	10-2
Sound Sense	9-7
Soundtrack (IRE)	10-7
Southern Cross	9-12§
Southern Ha'i	8-12
Sovereign Dove	9-5
Sovereign Gale (IRE)	10-1
Spanish Dolphin (IRE)	10-0
Sparkle (U)	8-7
Sparkling Cascade (IRE)	9-9
Sparkling Missile	8-12
Special Friend (IRE)	9-9
Speed Board (IRE)	10-2
Spencive	7-0
Spicey Case	8-7
Spiers Peace (IRE)	8-12
Spikey Passage	6-4
Spinning Silver	8-2
Spinosa	7-12
Spizzichino	9-6
Splash And Dash (IRE)	10-5
Sporting Chance	10-7
Sporty Spice (IRE)	9-6
Spot The Business	9-9
Spot Thedifference (IRE)	10-11
Spot The Native (IRE)	9-1
Spring Double (IRE)	10-3
Springford (IRE)	11-8
Spring Gale (IRE)	10-6§
Springlea Tower	9-8
Spring Marathon (USA)	9-2§
Springwood White	9-13
Spruce Goose (IRE)	8-2
Spy Boy (IRE)	9-4
Squaddie	9-12
Stag Party (IRE)	10-5
Stalbridge Rose	9-10
Stand On	9-4
Stanley Island	4-2
Stantons Church	8-11
Stanwick Gypsy	9-5
Staple Sound	8-0
Starbuck	10-1
Star Changes	10-0
Star Glow	10-6
Star Of Kilcash (IRE)	9-4
Star Of Raven	10-8
Star Of William (IRE)	8-11
Starpath (NZ)	9-12
Start It Up	7-0
Stately Progress (IRE)	7-10
State Medlar	9-11
Stay Lucky (NZ)	9-5§
St Bee	9-4
Steady Lass (IRE)	6-0§
Steel Gem (IRE)	9-0
Steel Rigg (IRE)	8-4
Stennikov (IRE)	10-1
Step And Run (IRE)	10-5
Stepasideboy	10-2
Step In Line (IRE)	9-3
Step On Eyre (IRE)	10-0§
Steponthebandit	8-0
Steve Ford	8-9
Stevie Dee	9-6
Stick Or Bust	9-3
Stockton Wolf	9-2
Stonesby (IRE)	9-13
Stone Valley	9-12
Stoney River (IRE)	9-12§
Storm Ahead (IRE)	9-0
Stormalong (IRE)	9-5
Storm Castle (IRE)	10-4
Storm Forecast (IRE)	9-4
Stormy Pass	10-1
Stormy Session	9-8
Stormy Sunrise (IRE)	9-6
St Palais	8-12
Straight Baron	8-4§
Street Smart (IRE)	9-3
Stretching (IRE)	10-7
Stride To Glory (IRE)	9-3§
Strong Chairman (IRE)	9-0
Strong Finish	8-11
Strong King (IRE)	9-4
Strong Tartan (IRE)	10-6
Strong Tea (IRE)	10-3
Strong Weld	8-7
Struggles Glory (IRE)	10-8
Stylish Dave (NZ)	9-4
Sugar Toi	8-6
Sulalah Sunrise	7-12
Sula Queen	8-6
Sumerian Lad	9-9
Summer Snow	8-12
Sunburnt	10-4
Sunczech (IRE)	9-6
Sunleys Quest	8-7
Suny Henry	8-10
Supercharmer	10-4
Super Dolphin	9-2
Superior Footwork	7-7
Superior Weapon (IRE)	10-1
Superstar Express (IRE)	9-9
Sup Of Tea (IRE)	8-7
Supreme Citizen (IRE)	10-10
Supreme Silence (IRE)	10-2
Supreme Storm (IRE)	9-12
Sure How Bad (IRE)	9-0
Susies Melody (IRE)	10-0
Sutton Courtenay (IRE)	10-0
Sutton Lighter	8-7
Sweeping Storm (IRE)	10-0
Sweet Chestnut	8-13
Sweet Kari (IRE)	9-3
Sweet Reward	9-4
Swingingbridge	8-4
Switchback (IRE)	9-7
Sword Fighter	8-10§
Sydney Hobart	9-3
Sylcanny	9-0
Sylvias Dream	7-8
Tabernacle	9-5
Table For Four	9-7§
Take The Brush (IRE)	9-0
Taleban	9-7
Tale Bridge (IRE)	9-8§
Tales Of Bounty (IRE)	10-8
Tallaburn	9-1
Tall Hat (IRE)	9-4
Tanager	10-8§
Tap Dance	9-5§
Tarpon Tale (IRE)	9-0§
Tartan Rising	5-0
Tartar Sabre	9-8
Tea Box (IRE)	10-3
Teach Altra (IRE)	9-13
Tea Time (IRE)	7-13
Teeton Diamond	9-7
Teeton Fizz	9-13
Teeton Glaive	9-1
Teeton Priceless	10-3
Teeton Prince	9-7
Teeton Toast	6-12
Tejaque	9-3§
Tellaporky	9-0
Teller Of Tales	10-4
Tell Tale (IRE)	10-7
Tell The Nipper (IRE)	10-0
Teme Willow (IRE)	10-3
Templebreedy (IRE)	10-0§
Temple Glen	8-13
Templenoe Hare (IRE)	9-5

Tenacious Melody 9-13
Ten Bob (IRE) 10-3
Tender Tangle 9-12
Teninarow (IRE) 10-1
Terimon's Dream 9-10
Terino 9-4
Texas Ranger 10-8
Thanks Jim (IRE) 10-5
Thatsforeel 10-0
That's My Boy (IRE) 9-8
The Archdeacon (IRE). . . .9-6
Theatreland (USA) . . . . . .9-4§
The Bounder. 9-8
The Broken Man 9-10
The Brooklet 9-11
The Butterwick Kid 10-7
The Campdonian (IRE) . 10-6
The Cincinnati Kid 9-9
The Cooling Agent. 8-12
The Earth Moved (IRE) . . .9-8
The Flying Dragon. 8-7
The Footsy 7-11
The Gambling Lady. 9-0
The Glen Road (IRE). 9-6
The Graduate 10-4
The Granby (IRE) 10-3
The Grandson (IRE) . . . 8-12
The Green Goblin (NZ) . . .9-6
The Grey Baron. 9-2
The Grey Shadow 9-0
The Hearty Joker (IRE) . 10-0
The Kings Fling. 10-2
The Lord Roberts (IRE). . .9-8
The Lords Cross (IRE). . . .8-5
The Luddite 8-7
Themaster's Choice (IRE) . 8-12
The Melting Pot (IRE) . . .8-9§
The Milecastle (IRE) 8-5
The Minister (IRE) 10-2
The Murphy Meister (IRE). 9-3§
The Nelson Touch. 9-0
The Nobleman (USA) . . . .9-6§
The Noble Roman. 8-11
The Only Option (IRE). . 10-1
The Panjshir 8-2
The Pickled Duke (IRE). 8-11
The Preacher Man (IRE) 9-12
Therealbat (IRE) 9-12
The Real Murphy (IRE). . .8-9
Theridamas (IRE) 9-5
The Sea Club (IRE). 9-3
The Singing Nun (IRE) . . .9-8
The Sky Is Blue 9-4
The Sycophant (IRE). 9-2
The Vintage Dancer (IRE) . 10-1
The Wee General (IRE) . . .9-0
The Well Lad (IRE) 8-6
The Wiley Kalmuck (IRE) . 10-4
The Writer (IRE) 10-1
Think Commercial (IRE) 9-10
This One Is A Boy (IRE) . .9-3
Thixendale . . . . .8-5§
Thorsgill 9-0
Three Of Clubs (IRE). . . 8-12
Three Saints (IRE). 9-0
Three Spires 10-2
Throwaparty 9-6
Thunderpoint (IRE) 7-11
Thunder Thighs. . . . . . . .10-0§
Thurles Pickpocket (IRE) 8-12
Thyne Express (IRE) 8-6
Thyne Man (IRE) 10-7
Thyny Glen (IRE) 8-0
Tictac (FR) 10-4
Tidal Beach 9-0
Tidal Reef (IRE) . . . . . . .7-0§
Tiger Rag 7-7
Tiger Talk . . . . .9-9§
Tiger Ted. 8-10
Tight Fisted Benny (IRE). .9-5
Timberley 10-2
Time Can Tell . . . . .9-5§
Times Two 9-5
Timpani (IRE). . . . . .9-11§
Tinarana Lord (IRE) . . . .9-7§
Tinder-Box 9-8
Tiraldo (FR) 9-11
Tirley Gale 9-6
Tisallover (IRE) 9-5
Titus Bramble. 10-6
T'nightsthenight 9-12
Tod's Brother 10-3
Toffee Lady 9-2
Tom Brown (IRE) 10-0
Tomcappagh (IRE) 8-2
Tom Cobbler (IRE) 10-5
Tom De Savoie (IRE). . .10-2§
Tommy Hotspur (IRE) . . .9-6§
Tom Putt. . . . . .9-10§
Tom's Man 9-9
Tom Tobacco. 9-12
Tonrin . . . . .9-5§
Tooley Park . . . . .9-5§
Toon Society (IRE) 9-3
Too Phar To Touch 7-0
Toorak (USA) 9-11
Top Boots (IRE) 7-7
Topical Tip (IRE). 9-9
Top Light 9-3
Top Of The Charts. . . . . .9-3§
Top Weld 9-0
Torduff Express (IRE) . 11-10
Tor Head. 10-5
Torn Silk 10-3
Tortugas (FR) 9-4
Toscanini (GER) . . . . . .8-12§
To The Top 9-6
Touchez Du Bois (IRE) . . .9-2
Touching Down (IRE) 9-3
Touch Of Flame 9-9
Tough Terms (IRE) 10-0
Toujours (IRE). 9-12
Touring-Turtle (IRE) 9-4
Traditional (IRE) . . . . . .10-0§
Travelling Jack . . . . . . .10-0§
Treasulier (IRE). 9-2
Treasure Dome (IRE). . . .9-0§
Treble Trouble 8-5
Trevveethan (IRE) 8-10
Trial Trip 9-6
Tricky Trevor (IRE) 10-5
Trigger Again. 9-10
Trigger Castle . . . . .7-10§
Trinity Buoy (IRE) 9-8
Trivial (IRE). 10-4
Troedrhiwdalar 9-9
Trooper Collins (IRE). . .10-2§
Trouble Loves Me (IRE). . .8-5
Troubleshooter . . . . .9-0§
Trouvaille (IRE) . . . . .9-4§
True Chimes 9-8
Truicear. 9-1
Trumper 9-13
Trust Fund (IRE) 10-0
Try A Bluff (IRE) 9-11
Try Me And See 9-6
Tubber Roads (IRE). . . .9-10§
Tuck Tin 9-4
Tuftex King 7-0
Tullineaskey Kitty (IRE). . .6-7
Tupelov (IRE) 9-0
Tursal (IRE). 9-9
Twilight Dancer (IRE) . . 10-1
Twinkle Toe Titch (IRE). . .7-3
Two Hoots 9-6
Two Of Diamonds . . . . . .7-9§
Tycoon Ted 9-6
Uncle Ada (IRE) . . . . . .9-11§
Uncle Den 8-2
Uncle Neil (IRE) 9-13
Under Milk Wood 9-2
Unlimited Free (IRE). . . 10-8
Upham Lord (IRE) . . . 10-10
Up The Pub (IRE). 10-2
Upton Adventure. 10-11

Up To The Minute. 9-4
Urban Hunter (IRE). 9-9
Valjean (IRE). 9-6
Valley Erne (IRE). 9-13
Valley Garden 8-11
Vansell 9-12
Velvet Dove. 9-10
Velvet Victory (IRE). 8-1
Vercheny. . . . . .9-7§
Veredarius (FR). 6-0
Vicars Chalet (IRE) 9-12
Vic's Brush (IRE) 9-5
Vics Fane (IRE). 8-11
Victim (IRE) 8-12
Victoria's Boy (IRE). . . . 10-6
View Hollo 9-0
Viking Lily (IRE) 9-11
Village Copper 9-10
Village Queen (IRE). . . . 8-12
Vinnie Boy (IRE) 10-4
Virgos Bambino (IRE) . . 9-11
Virtuoso 9-12
Viscount Bankes 9-13
Vital Issue (IRE) . . . . . . .8-6§
Vitinsel 9-3
Vivaldi Rose (IRE). 8-12
Vivid Imagination (IRE) 10-13
Waddon Hill 7-10
Waders (IRE) 10-0
Wag The Brush. 10-0
Wandering Light (IRE). . 10-0
Wandering Wild 9-0
Wanna Be Bay 7-12
War Bride 9-3
Warkswoodman 6-0
Warner For Players (IRE). .9-8
Warren Hill 9-12
Watchyourback (NZ). . .10-4§
Waterliner. 8-12
Waterloo Leader (IRE). . 9-10
Wayward Spree. 9-10
Weallwayswillbeone (IRE) . 9-4§
Weavers Choice . . . . . . .9-7§
Welburn Boy. 9-8
Welcome News. 10-1
Wellheseemedsolow (IRE) 10-0
Well Said Sam 9-8
Well Ted (IRE) 10-8
Welsh March (IRE) 9-13
Welsh Warrior. 9-4
Wend's Day (IRE) 10-6
Wensley Blue (IRE). 9-5
Westar Lad (IRE) 8-1
Westcoast. 9-12
Western Frontier (IRE). . 9-10
Westerton (IRE) 10-6
Westfield John 10-2
Westie 9-9
Westington 9-0
West Pal (IRE) . . . . .9-7§
Whatafellow (IRE). . . . .9-10§
Whatamonkey. 9-9
What A Mover 10-12
What A Night 8-4
What Next (IRE). 8-7
Whats Up Jake. . . . . .8-9§
Whats Up Maid 8-8
What Will Be (IRE). 9-0
Whether The Storm (IRE)10-7
Which Pocket (IRE). 9-4
Whitebarn Vixen (IRE) . . .8-0
Whitegates Willie 9-13
Whitleygrange Girl 7-6
Who Dares Wins. 10-5
Who's Eddie (IRE) 9-9
Wibbley Wobbley 10-0
Wicked Imp 9-2
Wild Blade (IRE). . . . . . .8-9§
Wild Chimes (IRE) 9-12
Wild Edgar (IRE). 10-5
Wild Edric. . . . . .9-7§
Wilfie Wild 9-6
William Lionheart 10-7
Willie The Kid. 9-1
Willoughby Flyer. 9-9
Willow Ryde (IRE) 9-2
Will Shakespeare 9-3
Will You Come On (IRE) 7-12
Wilton Bridge (IRE). . . . 9-12
Wincy Spider 10-0
Wind On The Common . 10-0
Wink And Whisper 10-2
Winners Enclosure (IRE) 10-0
Winnick (IRE) 8-12
Winnie The Pooh 9-3
Winning Leader (IRE) 9-7
Winning Town. . . . . .9-4§
Winsley Spirit . . . . .8-7§
Winter Gale (IRE) 10-3
Win The Toss 9-13
Winward. . . . . .8-0§
Wise Advice (IRE). 8-4
Wishful Thinker 9-3
Wiston Wizo . . . . .8-3§
Withybrook Lass 9-1
Withycombe 9-8
Wonderful Remark 9-3
Woodlands Beau (IRE) .9-12§
Woodyouever (IRE) 8-3
Worth A Shot (IRE). 8-2
Wraparound You (IRE) . . .8-3
Wychnor King (IRE) 9-6
Wynford Eagle 9-4
Wynyard Dancer . . . . . . .9-9§
Yer 'umble (IRE) 9-0
Yorkshire Edition (IRE) . 9-12
You Can Call Me Al. 9-1
Young General. . . . . .9-5§
Young Manny . . . . .9-4§
Young Tomo (IRE). . . . .9-10§
Youwoudhavethat (IRE). . .8-9
Zabadi (IRE). . . . . .8-7§
Zafan (IRE). 9-3
Zakley. 9-12
Zamhareer (USA) 9-12
Zingibar . . . . .7-12§
Zola (IRE). . . . . .9-11§

Results

Point-to-Point Meetings
Hunter Chases 2004

A chronological numbered list of all British hunter racing results in 2004 with comments-in-running

Meetings are arranged alphabetically for each day with Hunter Chases first.

The figure to the left of the horse's name is the number of the race in which it last appeared, and the superscript character its fate in that race.

In Hunter Chase results the weights shown are those actually carried.

In Point-to-Point results any penalty, allowance or overweight is shown alongside the horse's name, this is followed by the Starting Price.

Figures to the left of the finishing position are our correspondent's estimate of how far the horse was beaten.

All Tote returns are to a £1 stake unless stated.

These results include changes made after Jockey Club enquiries of which there is a full list near the back of this volume.

UNDER JOCKEY CLUB REGULATIONS

Index to Point-to-Point Fixtures in 2004

Albrighton *(Weston Park)* 91
Albrighton Woodland *(Chaddesley Corbett)* 1527
Aldenham Harriers *(Cottenham)* 995
Army *(Larkhill)* 9
Ashford Valley *(Charing)* 802
Atherstone *(Clifton-on-Dunsmore)* . . . 1118
Avon Vale *(Larkhill)* 632
Axe Vale *(Stafford Cross)* 1126
Badsworth & Bramham Moor *(Heslaker)* 1455
Banwen Miners *(Pentreclwydau)* 1234
Bedale *(Hornby Castle)* 808
Belvoir *(Garthorpe)* 680
Berkeley *(Woodford)* 1069
Berks & Bucks Draghounds *(Kingston Blount)* 1513
Berwickshire *(Friars Haugh)* 281
Bicester with Whaddon Chase *(Mollington)* 288,1030
Bilsdale *(Easingwold)* 1300
Blackmore & Sparkford Vale *(Charlton Horethorne)* 350
Blankney *(Garthorpe)* 1500
Border *(Hexham)* 1418
Braes of Derwent *(Corbridge)* 1036
Brecon & Talybont *(Llanfrynach)* 446
Burton *(Market Rasen)* 297
Cambridgeshire Harriers Hunt Club *(Cottenham)* 1
Cambridgeshire with Enfield Chace *(Horseheath)* 123
Cambridgeshire with Enfield Chace *(Northaw)* 1241
Cambridge University Draghounds *(Cottenham)* 98
Carmarthenshire *(Lydstep)* 1519
Cattistock *(Littlewindsor)* 687
Cheshire *(Alpraham)* 1043
Cheshire Forest *(Tabley)* 748
Clifton-on-Teme *(Upper Sapey)* 1135
College Valley & North Northumberland *(Alnwick)* 210
Cotley *(Cotley Farm)* 1247
Cotswold *(Andoversford)* 755
Cotswold Vale Farmers *(Andoversford)* . 815
Cottesmore *(Garthorpe)* 378
Countryside Alliance Club *(Bonvilston)* . . 1533
Crawley & Horsham *(Parham)* 638
Croome & West Warwickshire *(Upton-on-Severn)* 976
Cumberland *(Aspatria)* 1306
Cumberland Farmers *(Dalston)* 761
Curre & Llangibby *(Howick)* 356,694
Dartmoor *(Flete Park)* 1001
Dart Vale & Haldon Harriers *(Buckfastleigh)* 491
Derwent *(Charm Park)* 388
Devon & Somerset Staghounds *(Holnicote)* 1180
Duke of Beaufort's *(Didmarton)* 364
Duke of Buccleuch's *(Friars Haugh)* . . . 547
Dulverton Farmers *(Mounsey Hill Gate)* . 1461
Dulverton West *(Bratton Down)* 1378
Dunston Harriers *(Ampton)* 38
East Cornwall *(Great Trethew)* 305
East Cornwall *(Great Trethew)* 701
East Devon *(Bishops Court)* 318
East Essex *(Marks Tey)* 243
East Kent *(Aldington)* 895
Easton Harriers *(High Easter)* 217
East Sussex & Romney Marsh *(Catsfield)* 1050
Eggesford *(Lifton)* 821
Essex *(High Easter)* 646
Essex & Suffolk *(Higham)* 828
Essex Farmers & Union *(Marks Tey)* . 901,1312
Exmoor *(Bratton Down)* 1506
Fernie *(Dingley)* 1213
Fife *(Balcormo Mains)* 1076
Fitzwilliam *(Cottenham)* 555
Flint & Denbigh *(Eaton Hall)* 708
Four Burrow *(Trebudannon)* 907
14 Regiment Royal Artillery *(Larkhill)* . . . 1491
Gelligaer Farmers *(Bonvilston)* 1318
Glamorgan *(Ystradowen)* 735
Golden Valley *(Bredwardine)* 1387
Grafton *(Mollington)* 582
Granta Harriers *(Higham)* 396
Grove & Rufford *(Welbeck)* 590
Hampshire *(Hackwood Park)* 716
Harborough Race Club *(Dingley)* 1468
Harkaway Club *(Chaddesley Corbett)* . . 251
Haydon *(Hexham)* 1474
Heythrop *(Dunthrop)* 46
High Peak *(Flagg Moor)* 984
Holderness *(Dalton Park)* 499
Hursley Hambledon *(Badbury Rings)* . . 260
Hurworth *(Hutton Rudby)* 562
Jedforest *(Friars Haugh)* 131
Lamerton *(Kilworthy)* 566
Lanarkshire & Renfrewshire and Eglinton *(Overton)* 653
Lauderdale *(Mosshouses)* 1219
Ledbury *(Maisemore Park)* 722
Lincolnshire United Hunts Club *(Market Rasen)* 54
Llangeinor *(Laleston)* 1187
Ludlow *(Bitterley)* 834
Melton Hunt Club *(Garthorpe)* 1396
Mendip Farmers *(Ston Easton)* 598
Meynell & South Staffordshire *(Weston Park)* 225

Mid Devon *(Black Forest Lodge)* 144
Middleton *(Whitwell-on-the-Hill)* 769
Midlands Area Club *(Thorpe Lodge)* . . . 106
Mid Surrey Farmers Draghounds *(Charing)* 180
Minehead Harriers & West Somerset *(Holnicote)* 1325
Modbury Harriers *(Flete Park)* 1194
Monmouthshire *(Llanvapley)* 841
Morpeth *(Tranwell)* 914
New Forest *(Larkhill)* 455
North Cornwall *(Wadebridge)* 76
North Cotswold *(Paxford)* 921
Northern Point-to-Point Area Club *(Musselburgh)* 506
North Herefordshire *(Whitwick Manor)* . 512
North Ledbury *(Maisemore Park)* 1253
North Norfolk Harriers *(Higham)* 151
North Shropshire *(Eyton-on-Severn)* . . . 928
North Staffordshire *(Sandon)* 847
North West Point-to-Point Club *(Tabley)* . 1424
Oakley *(Brafield-on-the-Green)* 461
Old Berkshire *(Lockinge)* 935
Old Raby Hunt Club *(Witton Castle)* . . 160
Old Surrey, Burstow & West Kent *(Penshurst)* 777,1083
Oxford University Hunt Club *(Kingston Blount)* 187
Pembrokeshire *(Trecoed)* 1547
Pendle Forest & Craven *(Heslaker)* . . 1201
Pentyrch *(Bonvilston)* 1089
Percy *(Alnwick)* 854
Point-to-Point Owners & Riders Club *(Barbury Racecourse)* 30
Portman *(Badbury Rings)* 860
Puckeridge *(Horseheath)* 741
Pytchley *(Guilsborough)* 783
Quantock Staghounds *(Cothelstone)* . . 468
Quorn *(Garthorpe)* 1056
Radnor & West Herefordshire *(Cold Harbour)* 1226
Ross Harriers *(Garnons)* 402
Royal Artillery *(Larkhill)* 84
Seavington *(Littlewindsor)* 1007
Silverton *(Black Forest Lodge)* 61
Sinnington *(Duncombe Park)* 266
Sir W.W. Wynn's *(Eaton Hall)* 1142
South & West Wilts *(Larkhill)* 1097
South Cornwall *(Trebudannon)* 1431
South Devon *(Black Forest Lodge)* 411
South Dorset *(Milborne St Andrew)* . . . 232
Southdown & Eridge *(Godstone)* . 605,1404
South Durham *(Mordon)* 1412
South East Hunts Club *(Charing)* 418
South Herefordshire *(Garnons)* 612
South Midlands Area Club *(Tweseldown)* . . 168
South Notts *(Thorpe Lodge)* 941
South Pembrokeshire *(Lydstep)* 947
South Pool Harriers *(Buckfastleigh)* . . . 193
South Shropshire *(Eyton-on-Severn)* . 1260
South Tetcott *(Lifton)* 1540
South Wold *(Brocklesby Park)* 476
Spooners & West Dartmoor *(Cherrybrook)* 790
Staff College & R.M.A. Sandhurst Draghounds *(Larkhill)* 331
Staintondale Goathland *(Charm Park)* . 954
Stevenstone *(Vauterhill)* 1267
Suffolk *(Ampton)* 520
Surrey Union *(Peper Harow)* 1207
Tanatside *(Eyton-on-Severn)* 526
Taunton Vale *(Kingston St Mary)* 961
Taunton Vale Harriers *(Kingston St Mary)* 1445
Tedworth *(Barbury Racecourse)* 1062
Teme Valley *(Brampton Bryan)* 660
Tetcott *(Lifton)* 1348
Thames Valley Combined Hunts Club *(Kingston Blount)* 1103
Thurlow *(Horseheath)* 371
Tiverton *(Chipley Park)* 114
Tiverton Staghounds *(Bratton Down)* . 1554
Tivyside *(Cilwendeg)* 669
Torrington Farmers *(Umberleigh)* 1560
Tredegar Farmers *(Rhydygwern)* 1481
Tweseldown Racing Club *(Tweseldown)* . 16
Tynedale *(Corbridge)* 425
United Pack *(Brampton Bryan)* 1109
United Services *(Larkhill)* 138
Vale of Aylesbury with Garth & South Berks *(Kimble)* 866
Vale of Aylesbury with Garth & South Berks *(Kingston Blount)* 1332
Vale of Aylesbury with Garth & South Berks *(Tweseldown)* 622
Vale of Clettwr *(Erw Lon)* 201
Vale of Lune *(Whittington)* 872
Vine & Craven *(Hackwood Park)* 968
Warwickshire *(Ashorne)* 1273
Waveney Harriers *(Higham)* 22
Western *(Wadebridge)* 483
West Norfolk *(Fakenham)* 1150
West of Yore *(Hornby Castle)* 338
Weston & Banwell Harriers *(Cothelstone)* . 1364
West Percy *(Alnwick)* 69
West Somerset & Minehead Harriers *(Holnicote)* 273
West Somerset Vale *(Cothelstone)* 878
West Street Tickham *(Aldington)* 1280
West Street Tickham *(Detling)* 534
Wheatland *(Chaddesley Corbett)* 1339
Wilton *(Badbury Rings)* 574
Woodland Pytchley *(Dingley)* 885
Worcestershire *(Chaddesley Corbett)* . 1014
York & Ainsty *(Easingwold)* 1157
Ystrad Taf Fechan *(Ystradowen)* 1021
Zetland *(Witton Castle)* 1286

Abandoned Meetings

Six meetings were abandoned totally:

Brocklesby (*Brocklesby Park*, Feb 28th - snow); **Chiddingfold, Leconfield & Cowdray** (*Parham*, Feb 28th - frost); **Farmers Bloodhounds** (*Dunthrop*, Feb 29th - frost); **Holcombe** (*Hutton Rudby*, Mar 20th - high winds); **V.W.H** (*Siddington*, Mar 20th - high winds); and **Cleveland** (*Stainton*, Apr 18th - waterlogging).

Postponed Meetings

Seven meetings originally postponed went ahead within 15 days with entries standing. They were:

Jedforest (*Friars Haugh*, Feb 7th, after postponing on Feb 1st - snow); **Vale of Clettwr** (*Erw Lon*, Feb 14th, after postponing on Feb 7th - waterlogging); **Curre & Llangibby** (*Howick*, Mar 6th, after postponing on Feb 29th - waterlogging); **Thurlow** (*Horseheath*, Mar 6th, after postponing on Feb 28th - frost); **North Hereford** (*Whitwick Manor*, Mar 14th, after postponing on Feb 28th - waterlogging); **Tanatside** (*Eyton-on-Severn*, Mar 14th, after postponing on Feb 29th - waterlogging); and **Curre & Llangibby** (*Howick*, Mar 28th, after postponing on Mar 20th - waterlogging).

Index to Hunter Chases in 2004

Aintree . . . 732,1374
Ascot . . . 545
Ayr . . . 439,992
Bangor . . . 435,1176,1375
Bangor . . . 994
Carlisle . . . 1028
Cartmel . . . 1490
Cartmel . . . 1526
Catterick . . . 436
Cheltenham . . . 543,974,991,1168,1169,1170, 1171,1172,1173
Chepstow . . . 1294
Exeter . . . 629,799,975,1293,1363
Fakenham . . . 242,544,892,893,1295
Folkestone . . . 239,345,1438,1439,1440,1441, 1442,1443
Fontwell . . . 280,581,800
Haydock . . . 179
Hereford . . . 209,434,628,734,1175,1358
Hexham . . . 1178,1179,1499
Huntingdon . . . 177,1359,1360,1361,1362, 1497
Kelso . . . 349,678,797,798,1174,1296,1444
Leicester . . . 440,441,442,443,444
Ludlow . . . 176,317,346,630,801,1117,1372
Market Rasen . . . 377,679,1347
Musselburgh . . . 240,330
Newbury . . . 348,631
Newcastle . . . 546
Newton Abbot . . . 1166,1167,1437,1498
Perth . . . 1068,1373
Sandown . . . 241,445
Sedgefield . . . 316,542,894,1177,1489
Stratford . . . 541,1029,1451,1452,1453,1454
Taunton . . . 347,733,993
Towcester . . . 437,891,1354,1355,1356,1357
Uttoxeter . . . 1376,1377,1512
Warwick . . . 490,1299
Wetherby . . . 122,1297
Wincanton . . . 178,747,438,1298

132 Hunter Chases were scheduled in 2004, 126 were actually run, the races lost were:

Bangor-on-Dee (Feb 13th - waterlogged); **Doncaster** (Feb 25th - frost); **Huntingdon** (Feb 26th - frost); **Warwick** (Feb 27th - frost); **Chepstow** (Feb 28th - frost); and **Hexham** (Apr 19th - waterlogged).

Abbreviations used in Results Section

5a . . . . . 5lb allowance
7a . . . . . 7lb allowance
12a . . . 12lb allowance
a . . . . always
ab . . . . about
advant . . . . advantage
aft . . . . after
agn . . . . again
ahd . . . . ahead
a.p . always prominent
app . . . . . approaching

(b4) bandaged all round
bbv . broke blood vessel
bckwd . . . . . backward
bd . . . . . brought down
(bf) . . . bandaged front
bef . . . . before
bet . . . . between
(bh) . . bandaged behind
bhnd . . . . behind
(bl) . . . . blinkers
blkd . . . . baulked
blun . . . . . . blundered
(bnf) bandaged near-fore
(bnh) bandaged near-hind
(bof) bandaged off-fore
(boh) bandaged off-hind
btn . . . . beaten
btr . . . . better

cert . . . . certain
cf . . . . compare
CF . . . . . . co-favourite
ch . . . . chance
chall . . . . . challenged
chsd . . . . chased
chse . . . . chase
chsng . . . . chasing
circ . . . . circuit
cl . . . . close
clsd . . . . closed
clsr . . . . closer
clr(d) . . . . . . clear(ed)
clsng . . . . closing
comf . . . . comfortably
comm . . . . command
confid . . . . confidently
cont . . . . continued
(cp) . . . . . cheekpieces

dang . . . . danger
dd-ht . . . . . dead-heat
delib . . . . deliberately
def . . . . definite
dem . . . . demoted
desp . . . . despite
detach . . . . . detached
d ht . . . . . . dead-heat
diff . . . . different
disapp . . disappointing
disg . . . . disgraced
dism . . . . dismounted
disp . . . . disput(e)(ing)
disq . . . . . disqualified

dist . . . . distant
div . . . . division
drpd . . . . dropped
drvn . . . . driven
drvng . . . . driving

eff . . . . effort
esp . . . . especially
ev . . . . every
event . . . . . eventually
exhaust . . . exhausted
ex . . . . extra

F . . . . favourite
fdd . . . . faded
fdng . . . . fading
fin . . . . finish(ed)
flatt . . . . flattered
fncs . . . . fences
fnd . . . . found
f.o . . . . fell off
frm . . . . from
fs . . . . fences

gd . . . . good
gng . . . . going
grad . . . . gradually
gvn . . . . given

(h) . . . . hood
hd . . . . head
hdd . . . . headed
hdstrng . . . headstrong
hdwy . . . . . . headway
hld . . . . held
hldng . . . . holding
hmpd . . . . . hampered
hrd . . . . hard
hvly . . . . heavily
hvy . . . . heavy

imm . . . . immediately
imp . . . . . . impression
impd . . . . . . improved
inj . . . . injured
ins . . . . inside

j(s) . . . . jump(s)
jb . . . . . . jumped badly
JF . . . . . joint-favourite
jw . . . . . . jumped well
jn . . . . join
jnd . . . . joined

kpt . . . . kept

l . . . . length(s)
ld . . . . lead/led
ldng . . . . leading
ldr(s) . . . . leader(s)
lft . . . . left
lkd . . . . looked
lkng . . . . looking
lsng . . . . losing
lw . . . . looked well
lvw . . . looked very well

m . . . . mile
(martin) . . . martingale
mid-div . . . mid-division
min . . . . minute(s)
mist(s) . . . . mistake(s)
mod . . . . moderate

nd . . . never dangerous
nk . . . . neck
nr . . . . near
nrly . . . . nearly
nrr . . . . nearer
nrst . . . . nearest
nt . . . . not
nvr . . . . never

obj . . . . objection
oht . . . on his(her) toes
one-pcd . . . one-paced
(orb) over-reach boot(s)
ord . . . . order
out . fences from finish
outj . . . . . . outjumped
outpcd . . . . . outpaced
outrdn . . . . . outridden
overj . . . . overjumped
ow . . pounds overweight

padd . . . . paddock
pce . . . . pace
pckd . . . . pecked
pckng . . . . pecking
plcd . . . . placed
plce . . . . place
posn(s) . . . . position(s)
pr . . . . pair
press . . . . pressure
prob . . . . probable
prog . . . . progress
prom . . . . . . prominent
prox . . . . proximity
prsd . . . . pressed
prsng . . . . pressing
pu . . . . pulled up

qck . . . . quick
qckly . . . . quickly
qckn(d) . . quicken(ed)
qckng . . . . . quickening
qv . . . . which see

rap . . . . rapid(ly)
rcd . . . . raced
rch(d) . . . . . reach(ed)
rdly . . . . readily
rdn . . . . ridden
rdng . . . . riding
rdr . . . . rider
rec . . . . recover(y)
ref . . . . refused
releg . . . . . . relegated
reluct . . . . . . reluctant
rem . . . . remote
resp . . . . response
rfo . . . . . . rider fell off
rgn(d) . . . . regain(ed)

rjnd . . . . rejoined
rmdr(s) . . . reminder(s)
rmtd . . . . . . remounted
rn . . . . ran
rnwd . . . . renewed
r.o . . . . ran/run on
rr . . . . rear
rstrnd . . . . . . restrained
rt . . . . right
rtrcd . . . . retraced

sa . . . . . . slowly away
sev . . . . several
s hd . . . . . . short head
shkn . . . . shaken
sis . . . slowly into stride
slpd . . . . slipped
slt(ly) . . . . . . slight(ly)
snsoon
spd . . . . speed
ss . . . . . started slowly
stdd . . . . steaded
stdly . . . . steadily
stdy . . . . steady
stpd . . . . stopped
str . . . . strong(ly)
strugg . . . . . struggling
sust . . . . sustained
svs . started very slowly
swtng . . . . sweating

tch . . . . touch
tde . . taken down early
thro . . . . through
til . . . . until
tk . . . . took
tkn . . . . taken
t.o . . . . tailed off
trbld . . . . troubled
trckd . . . . tracked
trckng . . . . tracking
(tt) . . . . tongue tied

u.p . . . under pressure
unchall . . unchallenged
und . . . . under
unprom . . unprominent
ur . . . . . unseated rider

v . . . . very
(vis) . . . . visor
virt . . . . virtually

w . . . . with
wknd . . . . . weakened
wkng . . . . . weakening
wl . . . . well
wnr . . . . winner
wrs whipped round start
ww . . . . . waited with

x . . . . lbs extra

(xnb) . . cross-noseband
yds . . . . yards

Cambridgeshire Harriers Hunt Club

Cottenham (RH 9F,19J)

Sun, 4 Jan (GOOD to FIRM)

1 Cambridgeshire Harriers Hunt Club Members, 12st — 8 ran

THE RED BOY (IRE) 9-2 **A Braithwaite** *Jw; a.p; went 2nd 5; ld 10; drew 7l clr aft 2 out; idled flat; rdly* 1

The Kings Fling (3x) 6-4F **Miss P Gundry** *(xnb) Nt fluent; hld up; 3½l 5th ½way; went 2nd 14; rdn & no imp 2 out; stayed on flat* 2½ 2

Pendle Hill 6-1 **A Hickman** *Ld 2; blun 9; hdd 10; 6l 3rd 16; no ex 2 out* . 7 3

Colonel Conca 5-2 C Ward-Thomas *(xnb) 7s-5/2; nt fluent & rdr waving; chsd ldrs; 3l 4th ½way; went 2nd 12 til app 14; wknd & 10l 4th nxt; t.o & pu last* P

High Mood 20-1 M Howells *Mist & rdr lost iron 3; 5th when rfo 6* . . . . U

Merry Minstrel (IRE) 10-1 A Sansome *Ld to 2; mist 9; 2nd/3rd to 13; wknd 14; 17l 5th when fell 16*. . . . F

Noble Colours 33-1 N Pearce *Hld up; 5l 6th ½way; wkng when pu 13* . . . P

Pacon (GER) 20-1 Miss H Kinsey *Last til mist & rfo 10*. . . . U

OFFICIAL DISTANCES: 3*l*, 5*l* **TIME:** 5min 54.7s **TOTE:** £4.80 **DF:**£3.80

PLATE 8 1 Cambridgeshire Harriers Hunt Club Members: L to R at the first of the first: Pendle Hill, Colonel Conca and Merry Minstrel, lead The Kings Fling and High Mood PHOTO: Tim Holt

2 Restricted — 14 ran

FERTILE VALLEY (IRE) 7-1 **Miss P Gundry** *(xnb) Opened 14s; tde; tk keen hld & rcd wide; ld to 2; 2nd/3rd til ld 14; r.o wl* 1

Oneminutetofive 4-6F **A Farrant** *(xnb) Hld up; 11l 6th ½way; hdwy 14; went 2nd aft 16; 2l down when mist 2 out; sn rdn & no imp* 3½ 2

Jims Belief (IRE) 14-1 **G Cooper** *(xnb) Ld 2-14; 8l 3rd & wkng when hit 3 out* 30 3

Hessac (FR) 33-1 N Tinkler *2nd/3rd to 8; 6l 4th ½way; 11l 5th 16; wknd 3 out* 1½ 4

Teeton Fizz (5a) 14-1 A Sansome *Hld up; lost tch & 17l 8th ½way; wl bhnd 13; t.o 15; stayed on* 15 5

Donrico (IRE) 12-1 R Cooper *Nd; jmpd slow 4; pckd 9; lost tch & 20l 10th ½way; t.o 15; stayed on* 1 6

Give Him A Chance (IRE) 10-1 N Moore *Chsd ldrs; 7l 5th ½way; went 10l 4th 16; wknd 3 out; t.o*. . . . 1 7

Imperial Prince 14-1 Miss K Smith *Bckwd; nd; 13l 7th ½way; lost tch 13; t.o* 1½ 8
Teach Altra (IRE) 14-1 C Gordon *Hld up; hdwy 7; 4l 3rd ½way; went 2nd 12 til app 14; wknd & 12l 6th 16; t.o* . . . 3 9
Magnus Veritas (IRE) 8-1 Stuart Robinson *Hld up; lost tch & 18l 9th ½way; wl bhnd 13; t.o* . . . hd 10
Templenoe Hare (IRE) 20-1 G Barfoot-Saunt *A wl bhnd; 32l last ½way; t.o 12* 25 11
Ginger Bug (5a) 33-1 P Chinery *A wl bhnd; 28l 11th ½way; t.o 12* . . . 6 12
Run Monty (IRE) 7-1 T Lane *(xnb,bf) Lw; chsd ldrs; 5th when blun bad & reins broke 8; pu 9* . . . P
Zafan (IRE) 25-1 H Fowler *Ur 2* . . . U

OFFICIAL DISTANCES: 4*l*, dist **TIME:** 5min 54.3s **TOTE:** £6.10 **DF:**£3.40

3 Mens Open, 12st — 13 ran

GUILSBOROUGH GORSE (7x) 5-1 **M Walford** *8s-5s; ww; 10th ½way; stdy hdwy & 4l 6th 14; went 2l 3rd 3 out; ld on inner app last; rdn clr flat* . . 1
Cape Stormer (IRE) (7x) 3-1 **M Gorman** *Hld up; mist 9; 8th ½way; hdwy 12; 2l 4th 14; went 2nd 16; ev ch when mist 2 out; sn rdn & nt qckn* 4 2
Hotters (IRE) 14-1 **W Hill** *Hld up & bhnd; last ½way; 7l 10th 14; stayed on frm 3 out; mist 2 out; nt rch ldrs* . . . 2½ 3
Silver Lake (IRE) 8-1 P Cowley *W ldrs; 5th ½way; disp 4l 6th 14 & 2½l 4th 3 out; one pce* . . . 2½ 4
Marcus William (IRE) (7x) 10-1 R Stearn *Hld up; hdwy & 4th ½way; ld aft 12 til hdd & wknd app last* . . . ¾ 5
Grand Gousier (FR) 6-1 R Burton *8s-6s; 2nd til ld 3; hdd 5; ld 10 til aft 12; lost plce 16; no ch aft* . . . 5 6
Little Worsall (IRE) (7x, 5ow) 5-1 F Marshall *Hld up & rcd wide; last til hdwy 10; 5l 8th 14; wknd app 3 out; t.o* . . . 25 7
Gallant Glen (IRE) (4x) 7-2 M Mackley *Prom; ld 5 til carried out by loose horse bend aft 9* . . . C
Glemot (IRE) (7x) 20-1 N Pearce *Bckwd; ld to 3; 2nd/4th til wknd 10; t.o & pu 14* . . . P
La Colina (IRE) (7x) 12-1 James Tudor *(xnb) Prom; mist 3; went 2nd 6; hit 8; lft in ld aft 9-10; 1½l 3rd 14; wknd qckly 3 out; wl bhnd when pu last*. P
Real Value (IRE) (7x) 5-2F A Hickman *Hld up; 7th ½way; 6l 9th 14; no hdwy when fell 16* . . . F
Sheila McKenzie (5a) 10-1 B King *Oht; tde; hld up; 9th when mist & ur 7* . U
Shiny Bay (IRE) 20-1 A Sansome *Hld up; hdwy & 2nd 10-12; 3l 5th 14; wkng when blun 2 out; pu last* . . . P

OFFICIAL DISTANCES: 2*l*, 2*l* **TIME:** 6min 02.4s **TOTE:** £24.90 **DF:**£10.10 (1st+any)

4 Countryside Alliance Club Members (Nov Rdrs) — 8 ran

TICTAC (FR) 11-10F **T Eades** *(xnb) Made virt all; lft clr brief 9; drew 10l clr 3 out; easy* . . . 1
Aughmor River (IRE) 7-2 **R Stearn** *Chsd ldrs; 10l 4th ½way; went 2nd aft 10; rdn 16; plodded on* . . . 15 2
Storm Forecast (IRE) 8-1 **P Andrew** *Prom; lft 7l 2nd 9-10; 9l 4th 14; wknd 16; lft dist 3rd at last* . . . 25 3
Crackrattle (IRE)(tt) 4-1 A Brown *A.p; rdr nrly f.o & lost iron 1; 8l 3rd ½way; no hdwy 14; disp 15l 2nd 2 out; 18l 3rd & wkng when mist & rfo last* . . U
Mosscroft Jack 20-1 D Greenway *(xnb) Bckwd; climbed fncs & sn wl bhnd; t.o & pu 6; clueless* . . . P
Mr Lowry 25-1 M Howells *Bckwd; chsd ldrs; went 2nd 6 til fell 9; broke nk; dead* . . . F
Pampered Gale (IRE) 11-2 Miss N Barnes *Lost tch aft 7; t.o 11; pu 13* . . . P
Red Channel (IRE) 33-1 D Brightling *Nd; 13l 5th ½way; lost tch 11; pu 13* P

OFFICIAL DISTANCES: 15*l*, dist **TIME:** 6min 03.6s **TOTE:** £2.40 **DF:**£3.80

5 Ladies Open — 13 ran

DUSK DUEL (USA) 6-4F **Miss J Williams** *5/2-6/4; lw; hld up; stdy hdwy & 3l 6th ½way; went 2nd 14; ld 3 out; qcknd clr flat*. . . 1
Winter Gale (IRE) (2ow) 16-1 **Miss L Eddery** *Hld up; 4l 7th ½way; hdwy to ld 11; hdd aft 12; ld 14-3 out; rdn 2 out; no ex flat*. . . 7 2
Garolo (FR)(bl) 3-1 **Miss S Samworth** *A.p; mist 2; 2½l 5th ½way; lft 2nd 11; ld aft 12-14; 6l 3rd 16; one pce 3 out* . . . 8 3

Buckland Lad (IRE) 12-1 Miss H Grissell *Hld up; disp 12l 9th ½way; 12l 7th 14; went 14l 4th 16; nvr able to chall.* 3 4
Sea Tarth (5a)(cp) 8-1 Miss H Kinsey *(xnb) Hld up; 12l 9th ½way; disp 12l 7th 14; 20l 7th 3 out; nvr on terms* 2½ 5
Village Copper 14-1 Miss A Stennett *(xnb) Lost plce 6; 9l 8th ½way; rallied & 8l 5th 14; wknd 16* 1½ 6
Balisteros (FR) 5-1 Miss P Robson *Nvr gng wl; last & rdn 8; 18l 11th 14; sn wl bhnd.* 1½ 7
Dellone 33-1 Miss T Clark *Last to 8; 15l 12th ½way; 15l 9th 14; wl bhnd 16* 2 8
Solo Gent 16-1 Miss K Jones *A bhnd; 14l 11th ½way; last 11; t.o 15* 15 9
China Lal (5a) 20-1 Mrs K Diggle *Ld to 8; 1l 3rd ½way; ld 10-11; wknd 12; 17l 10th 14; t.o.* 7 10
Colquhoun 5-1 Mrs O Jackson *(xnb) Prom; 1l 2nd ½way; w ldr when fell 11* F
Polar Flight 3-1 Miss P Gundry *(xnb) Prom; went 2nd 3-8; 2l 4th ½way; 6l 4th 14; sn wknd; wl bhnd when pu 2 out.* P
Step In Line (IRE) 16-1 Mrs S Hodge *Sn prom; ld 8-10; wknd & 9l 6th 14; wl bhnd when pu 3 out; gurgled* P

OFFICIAL DISTANCES: 5*l*, 8*l* **TIME:** 5min 56.2s **TOTE:** £5.10 **DF:**£119.10

6 Open Maiden 8yo&up, 12st — 16 ran

MINSTER SUNSHINE 6-1 **N Tinkler** *Ld 2; 5l clr 15; rdn aft 2 out; edged lft & hld on wl flat; fin lame* 1
Morph 5-1 **P York** *Ww; stdy hdwy 6; 7l 4th ½way; went 5l 2nd 15; rdn app last; nt qckn flat.* 1½ 2
Jolly Jake 7-1 **E Walker** *(xnb) 2 handlers; hld up; 11l 9th ½way; hdwy & 7l 6th 14; went 17l 4th 3 out & poor 3rd nr fin* 25 3
Beat The Retreat 6-1 E Andrewes *2nd til aft 14; 8l 3rd 16; wkng when mist 2 out* hd 4
Ski Pass(cp) 4-1F T Lane *Hld up; mist 9; 10l 8th ½way; mist & rmdrs 11; 9l 8th 14; wl bhnd 16* 7 5
Greenkeys (AUS) 10-1 T Stephenson *Bckwd; hld up; mist 7; 12l 10th ½way; hdwy & 6l 5th 14; wknd 16* 5 6
My Native Land (IRE) 6-1 G Barfoot-Saunt *Ld til mist 1; lost plce & 9l 7th ½way; lost tch 12; 20l 11th 14; t.o* 6 7
Manhatton Storm (IRE) 16-1 N Bloom *Oht; lw; prom; 6l 3rd ½way; mist 11; wknd & 11l 9th 14; t.o* 3 8
Going Primitive 12-1 A Merriam *(xnb) Bckwd; hld up; hdwy & 8½l 6th ½way; 8l 7th 14; wknd 16; t.o.* 2 9
Coddington George 6-1 Julian Pritchard *A bhnd; 15l 11th ½way; mist 12; 12l 10th 14; t.o 16* 20 10
Arctic Snip 7-1 N Moore *2 handlers; bckwd; chsd ldrs til lost plce 8; 13th ½way; t.o 12; pu 16.* P
House Colours 10-1 N Saville *(xnb) Bckwd; a wl bhnd; t.o 12; pu 3 out.* P
Igloux Royal (FR) 7-1 S Morris *(xnb) Mist 5; bhnd til fell 9* F
Society Scandal (IRE) 16-1 P Millington *A bhnd; 12th ½way; t.o when mist 13; pu 16.* P
Spring Promise(vis) 12-1 A Charles-Jones *Lw; chsd ldrs; 7½l 5th ½way; mist 11; went 6l 3rd 15; wknd 16; 6th & no ch when ref 3 out.* r
Street Smart (IRE) 14-1 Miss B Donnelly *14th when rfo 2* U

OFFICIAL DISTANCES: ¾*l*, dist **TIME:** 6min 00.6s **TOTE:** £6.10 **DF:**£15.40

7 Open Maiden 56&7yo (Div 1), 2m4f, 12st — 11 ran

GRAY KNIGHT (IRE) 4-1 **James Tudor** *A.p; 1l 3rd ½way; ld 9-10 & 12-3 out; ld agn nxt; lft clr last* 1
Tooley Park 12-1 **A Sansome** *(orbs) Hld up; 3l 5th ½way; lost plce & 8l 6th 12; stayed on one pce frm 3 out; lft 3rd & hmpd last; went 2nd nr fin.* 10 2
Krac De Mirande (FR) 11-4 **S Waley-Cohen** *(xnb) 2nd til ld 6; jb lft & hdd 8; ld 10-12 & 3 out-nxt; sn wknd* 1 3
Cousin George 2-1F R Burton *Ld to 6; lft in ld 8-9; 4l 3rd 12; drpd out tame* 5 4
Beacon White(tt) 20-1 P Hall *Bckwd; w ldrs; 2l 4th ½way; 5l 4th 12; wknd 2 out* 4 5
Lakeland Prince (7a) 12-1 A Braithwaite *(xnb) A bhnd; 13l 8th ½way; t.o; easy rn* 25 6
Lance Feather (IRE) 12-1 M Keel *A bhnd; jmpd slow 2; 14l last ½way; t.o.* 20 7

Cash 'n Carrots (7a) 20-1 A Martin *(xnb) Lw; 2 handlers; hld up; hit 7; 4l 6th ½way; 6l 5th 12; went 4l 3rd aft 3 out; 2l 2nd & clsng when fell last* . . F
Donnini (IRE) 16-1 P Millington *Fell 3*. . . . . F
Groovejet (7a) 14-1 Miss K Smith *(xnb) Ss; nt jw; sn wl bhnd; rn out 3* . . . R
Rash Moment (FR) (7a) 5-1 C Ward-Thomas *Oht; hld up; 8l 7th ½way; rdn 9; no hdwy when fell 10* . . . . F

OFFICIAL DISTANCES: 10l, 1½l **TIME:** 4min 40.7s **TOTE:** £5.10 **DF:**£102.10

8 Open Maiden 56&7yo (Div 2), 2m4f, 12st — 11 ran

VISCOUNT BANKES 20-1 **A Martin** *(xnb) Mist 5; 2nd & clr of rest til ld aft 9; drew clr app last; unchall* 1
Big Brendan (IRE) 7-2 **A Charles-Jones** *Hld up; 13l 5th ½way; went 10l 4th 10 & 9l 3rd 2 out; stayed on to tk 2nd flat; no ch w wnr* 12 2
Drumdowney Lad (IRE) (7a) 4-1 **P York** *Oht when mounted; lw; a.p; mist 1; 8l 3rd ½way; went 4l 2nd 11; rdn & wknd app last; hung lft & dem flat* . . 2½ 3
Cimmaroon (IRE) (7a, 3ow) 3-1 A Farrant *Hld up; 15l 7th ½way; 12l 6th 12; went 9l 3rd 3 out; wknd 2 out* 5 4
One For Olly (IRE) 12-1 B King *A bhnd; jmpd slow 2; t.o 7* . . . . runin 5
Mister Ringa 2-1F A Braithwaite *(xnb,orbs) Hld up; 14l 6th ½way; 11l 5th when mist & ur 12* . . . . U
Moratti (IRE) 12-1 G Maundrell *Mists; sn wl bhnd; t.o & pu aft 5* . . . . P
Potter's Wheel (7a) 10-1 R Burton *Ss; a bhnd; t.o 7; pu 12*. . . . . P
San Malo (IRE) 7-1 C Gordon *Hld up; 11l 4th ½way; wknd 11; 22l 5th 3 out; pu 2 out* . . . . P
Shallee Term (IRE) 16-1 P Millington *Sn wl bhnd; t.o 7; mist 9; pu 2 out*. . P
Terimon's Dream 20-1 Julian Pritchard *2 handlers; charged into ld & up to 8l clr to ½way; hdd aft 9; 7l 3rd 12; stpd to nil & 25l 6th nxt; t.o & pu last* P

OFFICIAL DISTANCES: 15l, 3l **TIME:** 4min 36.1s **TOTE:** £29.00 **DF:**£9.60

Army

Larkhill (RH 13F,18J)

Sun, 11 Jan (GOOD)

9 Army Saddle Club Members, 12st — 6 ran

STRONG TEA (IRE) 5-4JF **D Alers-Hankey** *Tchd 6/4; mounted on course & tde; 2nd/3rd til 5l 4th ½way; rdn 11; lost tch 13; went 12l 3rd aft 15; str rn to ld 2 out; sn clr* 1
Puzzleman 7-1 **S Wheeler** *Ld; mist 3; hdd 12; ev ch 14; sn outpcd; stayed on frm 3 out; 7l 4th nxt; lkd to tk 2nd nr fin* . . . . 15 2†
Norski Lad(bl,tt) 5-4JF **J Snowden** *(xnb) Jmpd rt; hld up; went 2l 3rd ½way; jnd ldr & jmpd slow 13; ld app 15-2 out; sn wknd; lkd to fin 3rd* . . . . . ½ 2†
Mollycarrs Gambul (12a, 1ow) 20-1 A Michael *Went 2nd 5; ld 12 til app 15; ev ch when mist 2 out; sn wknd* 6 4
Alltime Dancer (IRE) 20-1 C Lambert *A bhnd; 13l last ½way; t.o 12*. 30 5
Folly Road (IRE) (7x) 5-1 Miss L Horner *7s-5s; lost plce 4; 6½l 5th when mist & ur 8; rdr broke jaw*. . . . . U

OFFICIAL DISTANCES: 12l, d ht **TIME:** 6min 16.1s **TOTE:** £2.30

10 Ladies Open — 16 ran

RIMPTON BOY 2-1 **Miss R Green** *Hld up; hdwy & 8l 6th ½way; jnd ldrs 13; ld 15; qcknd 4l clr 2 out; just hld on; wl rdn* 1
Mrs Be (IRE) (5a) 11-8F **Miss P Gundry** *Tchd 11/4; hld up; 12l 10th ½way; stdy hdwy & 5l 6th 14; outpcd nxt; went 5l 3rd 2 out; chsd wnr app last; r.o wl flat; just failed* . . . . hd 2
Bosuns Mate 14-1 **Mrs B Keighley** *W ldrs; 7l 5th ½way; went 3rd 12; ld 14-15; 4l 2nd 2 out; sn wknd*. 12 3
Sir D'Orton (FR) 10-1 Miss C Tizzard *Tchd 12s; a.p; 6l 4th ½way; 3l 5th 14; ev ch 15; wknd & 6l 4th 2 out*. 4 4
Alska (FR) (5a) 33-1 Miss W Southcombe *Nvr on terms; 15l 11th ½way; 10l 9th 14; stayed on*. 20 5
Rock Rose (5a) 33-1 Miss E Tory *(xnb) Hld up & bhnd; 11l 9th ½way; hdwy & 6l 7th 14; wknd app 2 out*. . . . . ½ 6
Polo Pony (IRE) 50-1 Mrs G Harvey *Nd; 8½l 7th ½way; 11l 10th 14; t.o* . 25 7

Dawn's Cognac (IRE) 20-1 Miss F Wilson *2 handlers; prom; went 2nd 5; lft in ld 10-12; wknd & 9l 8th 14; t.o* . . . 2½ 8
Ariann Sound (IRE) 33-1 Miss C Jones *Jmpd lft; a wl bhnd; 32l last ½way; t.o 11; pu 15* . . . P
Caldamus 7-1 Miss A Goschen *Prom; 4l 3rd ½way; lft 2nd 10; ld 12-14; wknd 15; wl bhnd when pu 2 out* . . . P
Garethson (IRE) 50-1 Mrs S Heath *Hld up; mist 6; 10l 8th ½way; hdwy 11; went 2nd aft nxt; ev ch 14; 8l 5th & wkng 2 out; mist & ur last* . . . U
Gigi Beach (IRE) 50-1 Mrs S Reynoldson *9th when rn out 4; jmpd 7; rdr unable to pu* . . . R
Hi Rudolf 20-1 Miss E Jones *6th when mist & ur 5* . . . U
Moorlands Again 9-1 Miss S Samworth *(xnb) Ld til rn out 10* . . . R
Northern Bluff 50-1 Miss V Sturgis *Lost tch 8; 28l 13th ½way; t.o & pu 11* P
Western Chief (IRE)(tt) 33-1 Miss V Flood *Ss; a bhnd; 20l 12th ½way; 15l 11th 14; t.o & pu 2 out* . . . P

OFFICIAL DISTANCES: hd, 8*l* **TIME:** 6min 02.6s **TOTE:** £4.20

11 Land Rover Mens Open, 12st 15 ran

ALWAYS ON THE LINE (IRE) 6-1 **A Merriam** *10s-6s; jw; 2nd til ld app 13; rdn clr flat* . . . 1
Red Brook Lad (7x) 11-10F **N Mitchell** *Opened 6/4; hld up & bhnd; 15l 9th ½way; hdwy 12; lft 5l 2nd nxt; poised to chall frm 15; rdn 2 out; nt qckn* 5 2
Aberfoyle Park (IRE) 6-1 **T Dreaper** *10s-6s; hld up; 12l 7th ½way; went 12l 3rd aft 14; nvr able to chall; btr for rce* . . . 8 3
Don Royal 14-1 N Harris *Nvr nr ldrs; 20l 10th ½way; 21l 6th 14; poor 4th frm 3 out* . . . 20 4
Oscar Wilde 5-1 D Drake *Jmpd delib & sn wl bhnd; t.o 6; last til aft 12; some hdwy 15; nvr on terms* . . . 2 5
Spring Marathon (USA) 50-1 D Green *1st ride; a bhnd; 26l 13th ½way; t.o 13* runin 6
Arlequin De Sou (FR) (7x)(bl) 16-1 C Heard *Ld 2 til hdd & fell 13* . . . F
Bargin Boy 33-1 J Snowden *(xnb) Lw; ld to 1; 5th when blun bad 4; lost plce 6; 22l 11th ½way; mist 11; sn t.o; pu 13* . . . P
Carbonado(tt) 20-1 G Barfoot-Saunt *(xnb) Bckwd; lost plce 5; 13l 8th ½way; lost tch & 19l 5th 14; t.o when mist & ur last* . . . U
Chaucers Miller 100-1 D I Turner *Prom; 5l 3rd ½way; lft 13l 3rd 13; sn wknd; t.o & pu 2 out* . . . P
Chism (IRE) 66-1 W King *Bckwd; 10th when ur 5* . . . U
Katarino (FR) (7x) 5-2 S Waley-Cohen *(xnb) Tchd 3s; hld up; hdwy 8; 7l 4th ½way; went 3rd 11; ev ch when bd 13* . . . B
Kingston Venture 16-1 J Barnes *(xnb) Chsd ldrs; 10l 6th ½way; wknd qckly 12; t.o & pu 14* . . . P
Mustang Molly (5a) 66-1 A Martin *(xnb) W ldrs; 8l 5th ½way; wknd 12; 25l 7th 14; pu 15* . . . P
Running Times (USA) (7x) 100-1 A Charles-Jones *Bckwd; a bhnd; 25l 12th ½way; t.o & pu 14* . . . P

OFFICIAL DISTANCES: 4*l*, 8*l* **TIME:** 6min 05.3s **TOTE:** £4.60

12 Open Maiden 567&8yo (Div 1), 12st 11 ran

FREE GIFT 9-1 **D Jacob** *(xnb) Lw; 2 handlers; a.p; mist 5; 5l 3rd ½way; went 5l 2nd 14; ld aft 15; drew clr 2 out; pckd last; easily* . . . 1
Preacher Boy (7a) 7-2 **Miss P Gundry** *Opened 4s; 2 handlers; hld up & bhnd; mist 2; 20l 7th ½way; hdwy & 17l 4th 12; lft 10l 3rd 14; jnd ldrs nxt; 4l 3rd & wkng when mist 2 out* . . . 25 2†
Up The Pub (IRE) 7-4F **T Dreaper** *(xnb) Hld up & bhnd; 18l 6th ½way; hdwy & 12l 5th 13; jnd ldrs 15; went 2½l 2nd 3 out; wknd aft nxt; eased when btn flat* . . . d ht 2†
Sonnant (FR) (7a) 5-1 P Cowley *(b4) 10s-5s; ld; 10l clr 6; mist 15; sn hdd & wknd* . . . 15 4
Let's Rock 20-1 M Green *A wl bhnd; jmpd slow 3; 22l last ½way; t.o 12* . . 20 5
Has She Bucked Yet (5a) 14-1 C Wadland *Nd; mist 6; 17l 5th ½way; wl bhnd 12; t.o* . . . 1½ 6
Bally Blue 9-2 L Jefford *(xnb) 6s-9/2; hld up; hdwy 7; 15l 4th ½way; wknd & 15l 6th 13; wl bhnd when pu 3 out* . . . P
Jd Trout (12a) 14-1 Miss L Gardner *Bckwd; ur gng down; hld up; lost tch & 21l 8th ½way; wl bhnd when blun & ur 11* . . . U

Jupiter Jay 16-1 A Sansome *Chsd ldrs; 15l 5th when fell 7* . . . . F
Princess Hatie (12a) 16-1 M Sweetland *8th when blun & ur 5* . . . . U
Spanish Dolphin (IRE) (7a) 7-2 N Williams *(xnb) Tchd 4s; sn prom; mist 5; went 3l 2nd 8; dem & fell 14*. . . . . F

OFFICIAL DISTANCES: 20*l*, d ht **TIME:** 6min 08.4s **TOTE:** £9.50

The rider of Up The Pub was cautioned by the stewards for failing to ride his mount out to the finish

13 Open Maiden 567&8yo (Div 2), 12st - 17J 10 ran

SPIERS PEACE (IRE) (7a) 8-1 **Miss A Goschen** *2 handlers; hld up; jmpd slow 3; mist 8; 26l last 1/2way; wl bhnd til hdwy & 15l 4th 13; went 8l 2nd aft 3 out; stayed on to ld bef omitted last; sn clr*. 1
Roseacre (IRE) 20-1 **Miss P Gundry** *Hld up; rmdrs 6; lost tch & 20l 6th 1/2way; eff 12; 17l 5th & rdn 14; stayed on frm 3 out; went 12l 3rd nxt & 2nd flat; nvr nr to chall*. 10 2
Kings Command 11-4 **D Alers-Hankey** *Opened 3s; lw; ld; went 10l clr 13; wkng when lft 8l clr 3 out; hit nxt; hdd bef omitted last; fin tired* 6 3
As De La Garenne (FR) (7a) 3-1 S Waley-Cohen *(xnb) 7s-3s; hld up; hmpd 5; 10l 4th 1/2way; hdwy & 5l 2nd 11; dem 14; 7l 3rd when mist nxt; wkng when lft 8l 2nd 3 out; sn dem; fin 36l 4th; disq - nt weigh-in* 4d
Dart View Lass (5a) 20-1 A Charles-Jones *Broke loose padd; ur when mounted; drpd rdr sev times at start inc in false start & galloped off; withdrawn und orders* . . . . W
Leader Du Turf (FR) (7a) 4-1 T Dreaper *2nd/3rd til wknd qckly 12; pu 13* . P
Rostock (IRE) 14-1 Miss F Wilson *(xnb) Tchd 16s; carted rdr to post; reluct to line up; tk off in opposite direction in false start & pu & dism nr 11; withdrawn und orders* . . . . W
Roxtons 11-1 D I Turner *2 handlers; swtng; 4th when fell 5; broke hind leg; dead*. . . . . F
Wild Chimes (IRE) (7a) 2-1F N Williams *Opened 3s; ss; hld up & bhnd; 14l 5th 1/2way; hdwy 11; went 10l 2nd 14; 2l down & clsng when fell 3 out.* F
Worthy Man 12-1 L Jefford *(xnb) Prom; 2nd when blun 6 & 7; 6l 3rd 1/2way; wknd aft 12; wl bhnd when pu 14* . . . . P

OFFICIAL DISTANCES: 10*l*, 8*l* **TIME:** 6min 26.9s **TOTE:** £4.20

As De La Garenne finished fourth but was disqualified when the rider failed to weigh-in; he was fined £40; fence 18 was omitted - fallen horse

14 Restricted (Div 1), 12st 8 ran

KERSTINO TWO 2-1 **D Alers-Hankey** *Tchd 5/2; a.p; 3rd when mist 6; ld 8; 5l clr 12; drew rt away aft 3 out; unchall*. 1
Frankly Fear(tt) 10-1 **N Heath** *(xnb) 2 handlers; chsd ldr to 8; mist 9; went 2nd 10; wknd app 2 out* 30 2
Little Native (IRE) 2-1 **Miss P Gundry** *Opened 3s; hld up; hit 5; 10l 6th 1/2way; mist 12; 14l 5th 14; sn wl bhnd; went poor 3rd flat* 4 3
Horrified 4-1 D Edwards *Opened 5s; 2 handlers; hld up; last to 6; 12l 7th 1/2way; went 11l 4th 13; wknd 3 out*. . . . . $2^1/2$ 4
Hawkers Hill 4-1 Miss A Goschen *Swtng; hld up; lost plce 5; 20l last 1/2way; 22l 7th 14; t.o & pu 3 out*. . . . . P
Magnemite (IRE) 6-4F J White *Hld up; 5l 4th 1/2way; went 8l 3rd 11; disp 6l 2nd & rdn 3 out; 13l 3rd & wkng when blun nxt; pu last* . . . . P
Twilight Dancer (IRE) (5a) 6-1 M Barber *Swtng; ld; mist 5; hdd 8; 2nd/3rd til wknd 11; t.o & pu 14* . . . . P
Withycombe(cp) 12-1 J Snowden *Chsd ldrs; 6l 5th 1/2way; wknd 13; 20l 6th nxt; t.o & pu 2 out* . . . . P

OFFICIAL DISTANCES: 25*l*, 6*l* **TIME:** 6min 12.9s **TOTE:** £8.50

15 Restricted (Div 2), 12st 7 ran

CHOC 4-1 **E Kenney-Herbert** *2nd til ld 5; made rest; clr 2 out; r.o wl* 1
Love At Dawn 9-1 **P Mason** *Mists; hld up; 10l 6th 1/2way; went 15l 4th 14 & 8l 3rd 3 out; went 5l 2nd aft nxt; no imp flat*. 3 2
Chief Suspect (IRE) 9-1 **R Bliss** *Hld up; 7l 5th 1/2way; went 8l 3rd 13-3 out; no imp* 15 3

Not Yet Decent (IRE) 6-4F A Puddy *2nd ride - aft gap of 7 yrs; tchd 7/4; w ldrs; went 2nd 10; clr w wnr 13 til wknd app 2 out; poor eff* 2½ 4
Eskimo Gold (5a) 3-1 M Sweetland *(xnb) 10s-3s; sn prom; 3l 4th ½way; wknd qckly aft 12; pu 13* . . . . P
Gami (FR)(vis) 5-2 Miss A Goschen *4s-5/2; nt jw; tk no interest & sn wl bhnd in last; t.o 6; blun 8; pu 11* . . . . P
I Will Survive (IRE) 10-1 M Wilesmith *Swtng; ld to 5; 2nd to 10; wknd 13; t.o & pu 3 out* . . . . P

OFFICIAL DISTANCES: 1½l, 10l **TIME:** 6min 21.7s **TOTE:** £7.60

Tweseldown Racing Club

Tweseldown (RH 9F,19J)

Sun, 11 Jan (GOOD)

16 Tweseldown Racing Club (Vet & Nov Rdrs) & City of London P-t-P Club Members 8yo&up, 12st — 10 ran

QUICKSWOOD (IRE) (8x) 4-1 **G Maundrell** *Prsd ldr to 11; prsd new ldr aft; rdn & btr j to ld last; hld on wl; all out* 1
Tell The Nipper (IRE) 10-1 **M Gorman** *Wl in tch; disp 3rd but outpcd 12; clsd agn 16; prsd ldrs 3 out; stayed on to tk 2nd & clsng on wnr nr fin* . . . . . ½ 2
Kustom Kit Grizzly (IRE) 2-1F **A Barlow** *(xnb) Wl in tch; prog to ld 11; nt fluent nxt & 14; hrd prsd frm 3 out; hdd & outj last; kpt on flat; outrdn* . nk 3
Tanager 5-2 J Docker *4s-5/2; hld up; prog 11; outpcd nxt; clsd grad on ldrs frm 16; r.o flat; just too much to do* . . . . ¾ 4
Quick Response (IRE) 10-1 Miss B Donnelly *(xnb) Made most to 11; outpcd by ldng pr nxt; rallying when jmpd slow 16; cl up 3 out; no ex flat* . . . . ½ 5
Sissinghurst Star (IRE) 20-1 P Mann *(xnb) 1st ride; chsd ldrs; lost plce 10; outpcd 12; nd aft; wl bhnd 2 out* 25 6
One Of The Natives (IRE) 16-1 Miss J Jenner *(xnb) Tchd 33s; rdr unstdy & waving; in tch to 12; sn outpcd & bhnd* 2½ 7
Always Good (IRE) 25-1 P Needham *(xnb) In tch in rr; outpcd frm 12; nd aft; t.o & pu last* . . . . P
Brown Chieftain (IRE) 33-1 Miss C Haydon *Prom to 9; sn lost plce; bhnd frm 12; poor 9th when ur 16* . . . . U
Grand Canyon (IRE) (3x) 10-1 N Docker *Mists 3, 5 & 6 & drpd to last; a strugg aft; lost tch 12; t.o & pu last* . . . . P

OFFICIAL DISTANCES: ½l, 1l, ½l **TIME:** 6min 26.2s

17 Mens Open, 12st — 7 ran

TITUS BRAMBLE(bl,tt) 11-8F **Julian Pritchard** *Lw; jmpd fast & low; prsd ldr; ld 10; drew 5l clr frm 16; shkn up app last; stayed on str & drew further clr flat; impressive* 1
Find Me Another (IRE) 11-4 **R Cope** *4s-11/4; lw; made most to 10; chsd wnr aft & clr of rest frm 13; 5l down 16; rdn 2 out; no imp aft; lost further ground flat* 12 2
Travelling Jack 12-1 **J Young** *Chsd ldng pr to 11; sn outpcd; 27l 4th 16; went rem 3rd 2 out; strugg on* . . . . runin 3
Good Boy (FR) (7x) 9-4 A Barlow *Chsd ldrs; went 3rd 11; outpcd by ldng pr frm 13 but clr of rest; jmpd slow 16; tired & lost 3rd 2 out; plugged on* . ¾ 4
Picket Piece 20-1 M Goldstein *Jmpd lft; chsd ldrs but nvr on terms; wl outpcd frm 12; plodded on frm 2 out* . . . . ½ 5
Toscanini (GER) (7x) 25-1 M Legge *Jmpd slow 3 & bhnd; jnd chsng group 9; outpcd 12; cont wl in rr* 8 6
Life's Work 12-1 M Gorman *2 handlers; a last pr; t.o 7; pu 13* . . . . P

OFFICIAL DISTANCES: 15l, dist, ½l **TIME:** 6min 17.4s

18 Ladies Open — 6 ran

TOM COBBLER (IRE) 13-2 **Mrs P Hall** *Tchd 8s; hld up; jmpd slow 4; trckd ldng pr 10; jnd ldr 13; ld 3 out; forged clr aft 2 out; bumped along flat* . 1
Killerine (FR) (7x) 4-1 **Miss H Irving** *8s-4s; trckd ldrs; jnd ldr 8-13; 5l 3rd & hanging 16; no imp aft til kpt on to snatch 2nd nr fin* 5 2

Bitofamixup (IRE) (7x)(tt) 4-7F **Mrs J Gordon** *Ld 2-3; ld 5; rchd for 7 & rdr waving; jnd 8; nvr gng as wl as rivals aft but ld agn 14; hdd 3 out; one pce app last; dem nr fin* . . . 3/4 3
Celtic Season 9-1 Miss T Cave *(xnb) Ld to 2; disp 4th & wl in tch when mist & ur 9* . . . U
Perfect Finisher 33-1 Miss R Lobley *1st ride; ld 3-5; wknd rap 9; t.o & pu aft 10; bbv* . . . P
Robbie's Adventure 33-1 Miss E James *In tch til wknd 12; t.o & pu 15* . . . P

OFFICIAL DISTANCES: 10*l*, 1/2*l* **TIME:** 6min 24.0s

19 Tweseldown Racing Club Members Moderate, 12st 15 ran

MENSCH (IRE) (5x)(cp) 6-1 **E Williams** *(xnb) Midfield; prog to trck ldrs 12; mist 13; ld nxt; rdn 2 out; kpt on* . . . 1
Denvale (IRE) 3-1F **R Cope** *Trckd ldrs; went prom 13; chsd wnr 16; rdn & kpt on frm 2 out; a hld* . . . 2 1/2 2
Buckland Boy (5x) 10-1 **T Vaughan** *W ldr til blun 12; rallied 15; kpt on to chall for 2nd flat; one pce nr fin* . . . 1 3
3U Sheila McKenzie (5a, 5x) 12-1 B King *Tde; midfield; prog to trck ldrs 11; chall 14; chsd wnr 15-16; wknd rap 2 out* . . . 25 4
The Vintage Dancer (IRE) (5x) 10-1 B Pollock *Prom til outpcd frm 13; nd frm 16* . . . 3/4 5
Dante's Promise (IRE) (5x) 7-1 M Walters *Lw; tde; reluct to post; rcd in midfield; outpcd 14; wknd frm nxt* . . . 12 6
Acuteangle (IRE) (5a, 5x) 33-1 Miss H Grissell *Bckwd; a towards rr; hopelessly t.o last when pu 12* . . . P
Bally Wirral (IRE) (5x) 7-2 G Maundrell *Made most to 14; still prom when hmpd & rn out thro wing nxt* . . . R
Dragon Lord(vis) 10-1 C Gordon *(xnb) Bit bckwd; hld up wl in rr; prog to trck ldrs 11; wl on terms when ur 15* . . . U
Jack Hackett (IRE) (5x) 33-1 P Bull *Chsd ldrs to 6; sn strugg; lsng tch 11; t.o & pu 16* . . . P
Live Wire (IRE) (5x) 12-1 Miss C Benstead *Last 7; bhnd aft; t.o & pu 16* . . . P
Makhpiya Patahn (IRE) (5x)(cp) 25-1 R Woollacott *(xnb) Chsd ldrs; rdn & reluct 10; sn wl bhnd; t.o & pu 15* . . . P
Mr Naborro (IRE) (5x)(cp) 8-1 A Wintle *Midfield; wl in tch 12; wknd 14; pu 3 out* . . . P
Phar Afield (IRE) 14-1 D Brightling *Mist 6; wl in rr aft; miles bhnd when pu 15* P
Wild Blade (IRE) 33-1 R Jenkins *(xnb) A rr; wl bhnd frm 12; t.o & pu 16* . P

OFFICIAL DISTANCES: 4*l*, 1/2*l*, dist **TIME:** 6min 27.3s

20 Open Maiden (Div 1), 12st 12 ran

LAMBRINI MIST 10-1 **R Burton** *20s-10s; bit bckwd; settled in tch; prog 11; ld 13; clr 15; sn in comm; crossing line as surviving rivals ref last* . . . 1
Be Bop Bentley 33-1 A Maskill *(xnb) W ldr til aft 11; sn wknd; poor 4th 16; lft 3rd 2 out; exhaust when inherited rem 2nd & ref last* . . . r
Bloowit 33-1 M Legge *(xnb) Rr when blun & ur 2* . . . U
Dolitanlad 16-1 P Millington *Rdr tried to mount without leg-up & failed; event mounted out of sight bhnd hedge; blun 2; chsd ldrs til wknd 12; t.o when pu 3 out (but nt as tired as some in front)* . . . P
Gloves Off (IRE) 7-1 Miss H Irving *T.o frm 3; pu 12* . . . P
Keegan Bearnais (FR) 12-1 T Mann *Ld to 13; chsd wnr aft; 15l down when mist 2 out & rdr event ur* . . . U
Milamoss 5-1 T Vaughan *14s-5s; bit bckwd; keen; cl up til slpd up bend aft 5* S
On A Full Wager 6-1 J Docker *Trckd ldrs; went 3rd & wl in tch when blun & nrly fell 13; nt rec; pu nxt* . . . P
Run For Hannah 14-1 J Trice-Rolph *(xnb) Keen; trckd ldrs; outpcd 12; pu 14; inj* . . . P
8P San Malo (IRE) 10-1 C Gordon *Late to padd; wl in tch til outpcd 13; bhnd & pu 16* . . . P
Silver Baron 4-1 M Wall *Nt jw in rr; prog to chse ldng pr 14; jmpd slow nxt; no imp aft; lft rem 2nd 2 out; v tired when hmpd by loose horse & ref last* . r
Two Oceans (IRE) 2-1F R Cope *3s-2s; in rr & lost tch 8; t.o & pu aft 12* . . P

OFFICIAL DISTANCE: Finished alone **TIME:** 6min 38.4s

21 Open Maiden (Div 2), 12st — 9 ran

SHARP SEAL 8-1 **F Buckettt** *1st ride; pulled hrd early; in tch til outpcd 12; disp 25l 4th nxt; lft prom 16; r.o to ld 2 out; hrd prsd & gd j last; kpt on und unstylish rdr* . . . 1

Cho Polu (IRE) evensF **Julian Pritchard** *Hld up wl off pce; disp 25l 4th 13; lft disp 3rd & in tch 16; chsd wnr 2 out; chall & outj last; nt qckn flat* . . . 1½ 2

Just Jove 3-1 **R Cope** *Prom in chsng group; chsd clr ldr 14; lft in ld 16; hdd & wknd 2 out* . . . 15 3

Lord Of The North (IRE) 12-1 N Benstead *Jmpd slow early; in tch to 11; sn wl bhnd; plodded on frm 16* . . . 15 4

Tall Hat (IRE) 7-1 B Pollock *Ld to 5; chsd ldr to 14; wknd rap app 2 out; fin v tired* . . . 20 5

7F Donnini (IRE) 20-1 P Millington *Rdr late to padd; sn in rr; in tch to 12; t.o aft; last when pu 16* . . . P

Hidden Exit (5a) 14-1 M Wall *(xnb) Prom; mist 10 & rmdr; wknd 12; t.o 7th when pu 3 out* . . . P

Huic Holloa (IRE) 10-1 T Vaughan *Mostly last; wknd 12; t.o 8th when pu 16; school* . . . P

Rhythm King 8-1 G Maundrell *(xnb) Bit bckwd; ld 5; sn clr; 12l up 12; 15l ahd & still galloping when mist & ur 16* . . . U

OFFICIAL DISTANCES: 2*l*, 15*l*, ½*l* **TIME:** 6min 28.2s

Brownies Tale (state of the ground - owner fined £155) and Rockfield Lane (declared rider no longer available) were both withdrawn not under orders

Waveney Harriers

Higham (LH 8F,19J)

Sun, 11 Jan (GOOD to FIRM)

22 Hunt Members, 12st — 5 ran

LAMBRINI KING (IRE) 10-1 **Miss L Barrett-Nobbs** *(xnb) Bckwd; wl in tch; mist 11; 3l 3rd 16; went 2nd aft 2 out; gd j to ld last; sn clr; rdr's 1st wnr* . . . 1

Treasure Dome (IRE) (7x) 6-4F **H Fowler** *5/2-6/4; trckd ldrs; went 2nd 10; rdn to ld 2 out; outj & hdd last; no ex* . . . 4 2

No Nay Never (IRE) 11-2 **Miss A Bowles** *Ld at stdy pce til hdd 2 out; sn btn* 8 3

Border Burn (7x) 7-4 M Valdes-Scott *Bckwd; a last pr but wl in tch; 5l last 16; outpcd nxt* . . . 3 4

Musical Hit (7x) 7-1 J Bevan *Prom; disp ld 12-13; 4l 4th 16; wknd nxt* . . 4 5

OFFICIAL DISTANCES: 4*l*, 6*l* **TIME:** 6min 24.0s **TOTE:** £7.80 **DF:**£27.00

23 Confined, 12st — 5 ran

1¹ **THE RED BOY (IRE)** (3x) 4-5F **A Braithwaite** *2 handlers; ld to 2 & agn 7; qcknd clr app 12; unchall aft; v easily* . . . 1

Royal Action 6-1 **P Chinery** *In tch; mist 10; went 2nd 12; bumped along 14; no imp on wnr; dem 3rd agn app 16; lft mod 2nd at last* . . . 30 2

4P **Pampered Gale (IRE)** 8-1 **Miss N Barnes** *Ld 3-6; last frm 8; lost tch app 12; t.o; lft poor 3rd at last* . . . runin 3

Endeavour (FR) (6x) 6-4 G Cooper *Ld 2-3; chsd ldrs; 5l 2nd when blun 12; sn strugg; went 2nd agn app 16; wl hld when blun & ur last* . . . U

Highland Rose (IRE) (5a) 6-1 Ms A Embiricos *(xnb) Tk keen hld; hld up in last; 4th & in tch 12; wknd qckly 15; t.o & pu 2 out* . . . P

OFFICIAL DISTANCES: dist, dist **TIME:** 6min 04.0s **TOTE:** £2.40 **DF:**£5.50

24 Mens Open — 7 ran

3C **GALLANT GLEN (IRE)** 7-4 **M Mackley** *Mid-div til lft in ld 7; made rest; drew clr frm 13; nt extended* . . . 1

Win The Toss 33-1 **Richard Green** *Bhnd; mist 4; jmpd slow nxt; lft 7l 3rd 7; outpcd 13; stayed on flat; went 2nd nr fin* . . . 15 2

Gatchou Mans (FR) 12-1 **C Ward-Thomas** *(xnb) Chsd ldrs til lft 2nd 7; outpcd by wnr frm 14; lost 2nd nr fin* . . . nk 3

Fatalistic (IRE) 14-1 H Fowler *(xnb) Mist 2; drvn along nxt; lft 4th 7; 8l 3rd & u.p when mist 12; outpcd frm nxt; t.o when jb rt 3 out; pu nxt* . . . P

Galeaway (IRE) 20-1 J Barnard *Chsd ldr 3 til bd 7* . . . B

Hatch Gate 7-2 P York *Reluct to line up desp man flapping coat at him; ref to rce* . . . . r
Shanavogh 5-4F R Hunnisett *Ld; clr 3; 2l up when fell 7*. . . . F

OFFICIAL DISTANCES: 15*l*, hd **TIME:** 6min 05.0s **TOTE:** £2.20 **DF:**£103.00

25 Ladies Open — 6 ran

PLACID MAN (IRE) 4-5F **Ms A Embiricos** *Made virt all; blun & nrly ur 1; jmpd bold aft & gained lengths at fncs; stdd & hdd brief aft 3; 8l clr 12; unchall aft; eased flat; impressive* 1
Fair Kiowa (IRE) 6-1 **Mrs S Hodge** *Mists; chsd ldrs; prog to 2nd aft 11; 8l down when mists 12 & 13; sn drvn along; lost ground ev fnce but clsd inbetween; kpt on flat; nt rch wnr* 6 2
Pride Of Kashmir 3-1 **Miss S Phizacklea** *Bhnd; rdn 11; went mod 3rd 15; nd* 8 3
The Wiley Kalmuck (IRE) 3-1 Miss Gemma Hutchinson *Bckwd; chsd ldrs til 4th & outpcd 15; no ch aft* 2 4
Attack 10-1 Miss A Stennett *(xnb) Chsd ldr til aft 11; 9l 3rd nxt; wknd qckly 14; t.o & pu 3 out* . . . . P
Hay Dance 12-1 Miss L Barrett-Nobbs *A bhnd; lost tch 12; t.o & pu 15* . . P

OFFICIAL DISTANCES: 5*l*, 6*l* **TIME:** 6min 11.0s **TOTE:** £2.40 **DF:**£6.50

Ical (got loose gng to padd & galloped off) was withdrawn not under orders; Rule 4 deduction 5p in pound on bets struck before withdrawal

26 Open Maiden (Div 1) — 8 ran

ESENDI 7-4F **J Diment** *(xnb) 2 handlers; chsd ldrs; mist 4; ld app 9; drew clr frm 15; v easily* 1
What Next (IRE) 7-2 **A Hickman** *Ww; lft 4th 8; some prog to 12l 3rd 16; chsd wnr app 3 out; no imp*. . . . 30 2
Golden Shred (5a) 3-1 **S Morris** *(xnb) Mid-div; lft 3rd 8; mist 11; 12l 4th & u.p 14; sn lost tch; lft poor 3rd 2 out* 25 3
Sister Ali (IRE) (5a) 6-1 S Gordon-Watson *A bhnd; t.o frm 12*. . . . 20 4
Battle Honours 8-1 F Wheeler *Lw; ld to 3; cl 3rd when fell hvly 8* . . . . F
Castlediva (5a) 4-1 N Pearce *Bhnd; some prog to 11l 4th aft 11; no hdwy aft; 5th & no ch when fell 15*. . . . F
Hailes Gate (7a) 5-1 P York *Last when mist 1; 12l last when fell 5* . . . . F
Mistrio 10-1 M Mackley *Tk keen hld; ld 3; mist 6; hdd 9; chsd wnr til wknd qckly aft 16; 3rd & exhaust when tried to ref & fell 2 out*. . . . F

OFFICIAL DISTANCES: dist, dist **TIME:** 6min 17.0s **TOTE:** £3.00 **DF:**£2.40

27 Open Maiden (Div 2) — 8 ran

JACOB'S CHOICE (7a) 5-1 **P York** *Hld up; mist 2; stdy prog to trck ldrs 12; ld & pckd 14; 2l clr 16; in comm frm nxt; easily* 1
Brookfield Bass 7-1 **A Braithwaite** *(xnb) Chsd ldrs; prog to 2nd 11-12; 5l 4th & hrd rdn 16; rallied to chse wnr app 2 out; btn when hit last* 10 2
Another Leader (IRE) 6-1 **G Cooper** *(xnb) Jmpd rt; keen; ld app 4; mists 6, 8 & 9; 6l clr app 12; hdd 14; 4l 3rd 16; wknd nxt*. . . . 15 3
Abbey Days (IRE) 7-2 J Owen *(xnb) Ww in mid-div; prog 10 to 2nd 12-14 & agn brief 16; btn nxt; fin tired* 10 4
6[4] Beat The Retreat 7-4F E Andrewes *3rd when blun 3 & imm pu; dead* . . . . P
Charlotte Russe (5a) 7-1 S Morris *Wl bhnd when jmpd slow 4, 5 & 6; t.o when fell nxt* . . . . F
Sharp Sarah (5a) 8-1 P Chinery *Oht; bckwd; chsd ldrs; went 2nd 10; blun & lost plce nxt; sn outpcd; t.o & pu 16*. . . . P
Victory Salute (5a) 16-1 S Gordon-Watson *Jb rt; ld til app 4; blun & lost plce 10; sn bhnd; pu 12* . . . . P

OFFICIAL DISTANCES: 10*l*, 15*l* **TIME:** 6min 20.0s **TOTE:** £10.00 **DF:**£19.50 (1+any finisher)

28 Intermediate, 12st — 5 ran

STAR GLOW (5x) 4-9F **P York** *Made all; drew clr frm 15; nt extended*. . . . 1
Fine And Dandy (IRE) (5x) 11-4 **J Owen** *Ww in tch; went 2l 2nd app 12; outpcd frm 15* 15 2
Tartar Sabre 16-1 **Miss L Barrett-Nobbs** *Bckwd; in tch til 3rd frm 12; lost tch 14; t.o* 25 3

Ballylesson (IRE) 12-1 N Moore *Bckwd; tk keen hld; hld up til prog to chse wnr 6; wknd rap app 12; sn t.o; pu 16* . . . . P

Galaxy Minstrel (IRE)(tt) 10-1 J Newbold *Chsd ldr til mist & ur 4* . . . . U

OFFICIAL DISTANCES: 15*l*, dist **TIME:** 6min 09.0s **TOTE:** £1.20 **DF:**£1.20

29 Restricted, 12st 7 ran

GREAT JUBILEE (IRE) evensF **Stuart Robinson** *6/4-evens; ld to 4 & 11-15; ld agn app 3 out; rdn & r.o wl app last* 1

Paddy's Dream (IRE) 8-1 **N Moore** *Ww in tch; prog to trck ldrs 11; 2nd nxt; ld 15-3 out; one pce u.p* 5 2

General Confusion (IRE) 5-1 **S Morris** *In tch; 6l 5th app 12; prog nxt; 1l 3rd 16; btn app 2 out; nt pushed aft* 10 3

2^{U} Zafan (IRE) 20-1 H Fowler *Chsd ldrs to 4; 7l 5th when blun 12; outpcd frm nxt; nd aft* 10 4

Bebe Bleu (IRE) (5a, 1ow) 20-1 C Ward-Thomas *(xnb) Hld up; 12l last & blun 13; outpcd when hit 15; mod 4th 2 out; dem nr fin* . . . . nk 5

2^{P} Run Monty (IRE) 2-1 T Lane *(xnb) Chsd ldrs; mists 5 & 6; blun & rmdrs 8; hrd rdn 14; wknd nxt* 6 6

Josh's Choice (IRE)(bl) 4-1 A Braithwaite *8s-4s; cl up; ld 4; mist 10; hdd nxt; chsd ldrs til wknd 15; t.o last when ref last* . . . . r

OFFICIAL DISTANCES: 3*l*, 15*l* **TIME:** 6min 11.0s **TOTE:** £2.00 **DF:**£22.50

Point-to-Point Owners & Riders Club

Barbury Racecourse (LH 8F,18J)

Sun, 18 Jan (GOOD, GOOD to FIRM in places)

30 PPORA Club Members Maiden 6&7yo (Horses & Geldings), 12st 12 ran

OUT THE BLACK (IRE) 2-1F **D Alers-Hankey** *7/2-2s; trckd ldrs; went 2nd 12; til mist 14; rallied to 2nd aft 3 out; chall nxt; hrd rdn to ld last; all out* . 1

Agua Ardente 4-1 **R Cope** *Tchd 5s; lw; ld; hit 2; jmpd rt frm 10; rdn & mist 2 out; hdd u.p last; fnd nil* . . . . nk 2

Killough Hill (IRE) 10-1 **Miss P Gundry** *Prom; went 2nd 9-12 & 14 til wknd app 2 out; fin tired* 15 3

Bay Mouse 20-1 Miss A Goschen *Bhnd; lost tch 6; 15l 7th when mist 10; cont t.o* . . . . runin 4

Cotton On 5-1 M Wilesmith *(xnb) Bckwd; bhnd; hdwy 12; 6l 4th 14; wknd qckly & nt pushed; pu 2 out* . . . . P

Kalypso De Laugere (FR) 20-1 H Fowler *2nd to 9; prsd ldrs til wknd 13; t.o & pu 2 out* . . . . P

No Pressure (IRE) 12-1 D Harvey *Rcd wide; prom to 8; sn bhnd; t.o & pu 13* P

Off Piste 5-1 A Farrant *(xnb) Collapsed in box park; hld up towards rr; 7th & strugg when pckd bad 10 & lost tch; pu 12* . . . . P

8^{5} One For Olly (IRE) 33-1 B King *Hmpd & ur 1* . . . . U

On The Deck 25-1 P Millington *Terrible mist 3; rr aft; jmpd slow 4; lost tch 10; t.o & pu 14* . . . . P

See More Fun 14-1 A Charles-Jones *Tchd 16s; bckwd; jmpd crooked & fell 1; rdr broke nose* . . . . F

Shaking Chief (IRE) (4ow) 16-1 A Wintle *Settled midfield; outpcd 12; 6l 4th 13; lkng outpcd when ducked into wing & ur 15; rdr inj* . . . . R

OFFICIAL DISTANCES: nk, 15*l* **TIME:** 6min 26.5s

31 Dodson & Horrell PPORA Club Members 6yo&up (Nov Rdrs), (Div 1) 12 ran

LORD KILPATRICK (IRE) 6-4F **T Edwards** *3s-6/4; 3rd til 2nd 8; ld 10; forged clr frm 2 out* 1

Topical Tip (IRE) 8-1 **Mrs E Chugg** *Made most to 9; prsd wnr til tired frm 2 out* 8 2

Holdimclose 4-1 **Miss V Tremlett** *Tchd 5s; chsng group but nd; 30l 4th 10; went 3rd 13 & kpt on same pce* 25 3

Forest Jump (IRE) 8-1 R Lee *Tchd 9s; jmpd wild 2 & lost tch; rem 10th 10; still poor 7th 3 out; fin str past btn horses* 12 4

16^{7} One Of The Natives (IRE) 20-1 Miss J Jenner *(xnb) Rdr v novicey; cl 2nd to 8; 10l 3rd 10; releg 4th 13 & no ch aft* 7 5

Ferryhill (IRE) 20-1 N McDiarmid *(xnb) Sn bhnd; mist 9; 43l 7th 10; cont t.o; rem 5th 3 out* 8 6

Magical Approach (IRE) 20-1 T Phillips *(xnb) A towards rr; 50l 8th 10; mist 11; plodded on*. 1½ 7

Mind The Gate 14-1 Miss A Dudley *Sn bhnd; 62; 9th 10; furlongs bhnd frm 14* 30 8

Buadhach (IRE) (7x) 25-1 D Cook *(bf) 15l 4th 4; disp 40l 5th & wkng 10; t.o when pu 12; lame* . . . . . . P

Henry Bruce(cp) 25-1 Miss S Davies *Reluct in last; wl t.o 4; pu 2 out*. . . . P

Nelsun 9-1 A Corbett *(xnb) Tchd 9s; rfo 1 & pulled horse over* . . . . . . U

Sydney Hobart 7-2 A Vaughan-Jones *Rdr v unenterprising; midfield; nrly f.o 3; disp 40l 5th 10; rem 6th 3 out; pu last; over-reached* . . . . . . P

OFFICIAL DISTANCES: 10*l*, 30*l* **TIME:** 6min 29.5s

PLATE 9 31 PPORA Club Members 6yo&up (Nov Rdrs) (Div 1): R to L: Mind The Gate, Sydney Hobart, Buadhach and Forest Jump take the1st ahead of Ferryhill and Nelsun PHOTO: Tim Holt

32 Dodson & Horrell PPORA Club Members 6yo&up (Nov Rdrs), (Div 2) 13 ran

MICKTHECUTAWAY (IRE) (7x) 11-2 **D Skelton** *1st ride; hit 1; hld up midfield; 20l 6th 10; clsd str 12; rdn to chall 3 out; sn ld; pckd last & hdd; rallied to ld agn nr fin* 1

Boyne Banks (IRE) 12-1 **G Disney** *Tchd 16s; mist 11; 2nd/3rd til ld 3 out; rdn & hdd aft nxt; lft in ld last; r.o; hdd nr line*. . . . . . hd 2

Legal Storm (IRE) 33-1 **Richard Green** *Ld to 12; 2nd/3rd & ev ch til 2 out; one pce aft* 4 3

Silverdalesureshot 6-1 W Kinsey *Bit bckwd; prom; mist 2; cl 4th; 10; ev ch til wknd app 3 out; btr for rce* 8 4

Guignol Du Cochet (FR) 9-2 G Slade-Jones *16s-9/2; hld up; stdy prog 8; 6l 5th 10; ld aft 12 til hdd 3 out; lost plce qckly & eased* 15 5

Frank Byrne (4x) 7-2 N McDiarmid *V late to padd; mist 3; sn lost tch; 7th & t.o 12*. 20 6

Tale Bridge (IRE) 12-1 J Russell *Tchd 14s; 1st ride; imm lost tch; 20l last 4; cont t.o*. . . . . . runin 7

Lyphard's Fable (USA)(bl) 50-1 D England *(xnb) Midfield & nvr gng keen; 20l 7th 10; t.o 12* 6 8

6F Igloux Royal (FR) 33-1 M Briggs *Mists & rn free; prom to 8; wkng in 8th 10; pu 12*. . . . . . P

Mouse Bird (IRE) 25-1 C Smyth *A wl bhnd; 10th & t.o when pu 14; subsq destroyed.* . . . . P
Newby End (IRE)(vis) 25-1 Miss C Cowe *Nt fluent; midfield & off pce; tlng off when ur 10* . . . . U
18^{P} Perfect Finisher 33-1 Miss R Lobley *Sn lost tch; 9th & t.o 12; ur 15.* . . . . . U
4^{1} Tictac (FR) evensF T Eades *(xnb) Opened 8s in plce; prom; 2nd 8-11; 5th & wkng 13; t.o & pu last.* . . . . P

OFFICIAL DISTANCES: hd, 4*l* **TIME:** 6min 27.8s

33 Ladies Open - 17J — 18 ran

UPTON ADVENTURE (5a) 5-1 **Miss E James** *Tchd 6s; prom; 3rd 10; 9l 4th & outpcd 15; lft 2nd aft 3 out; lft in clr ld nxt; fin tired* 1
Chasing The Bride(tt) 14-1 **Miss A Goschen** *Hld up & wl bhnd; poor 12th 10; still rem 8th 15; stayed on wl aft; inherited rem 2nd at last* 15 2
10^{3} **Bosuns Mate** 7-1 **Mrs B Keighley** *Tchd 8s; outpcd; 35l 10th 10; still 9th & t.o 15; fin str; btr for rce* 3 3
The Bounder 10-1 Miss C Tizzard *Cl up; 7th 10; wknd 12; t.o 3 out.* 27 5
Sailors Folly (IRE) 7-1 Miss P Gundry *(xnb) Sn prom; 4th 10; wknd qckly 12; 35l 6th 15; blun bad last; fin 33l 4th; disq - nt weigh-in.* 4d
Ballysicyos (FR) 7-1 Mrs O Jackson *(xnb) 10s-7s; set v fast pce & ab 6l clr mostly; prsd frm 15 but lft 5l clr app 2 out; lkd wnr when fell 2 out* . . . F
Blackberry Way (5a) 33-1 Miss S Phizacklea *(xnb,bf) Hld up; 5th & prog 10; went 2nd 12 til releg 3rd 15; lft tired 2nd 2 out; exhaust but still 2nd when ref last* . . . . r
Craven Hill (IRE) 66-1 Miss A Wells *(xnb) A wl bhnd; 15th & t.o 10; pu 2 out* P
5^{1} Dusk Duel (USA) 10-11F Miss J Williams *Hld up; 6th & prog 10; went 2nd gng str 13; ev ch 3 out; pu rap 2 out; destroyed* . . . . P
Nearly Gold 25-1 Miss T Cave *Sn bhnd; 13th & t.o 10; pu 13* . . . . P
Optimistic Thinker 50-1 Mrs K Baimbridge *2nd when hit 2 & ur* . . . . U
Priestthorn (IRE) 33-1 Miss W Southcombe *Prom til mist 1 & rdr lost iron; drpd to rr 4; sn t.o; pu 2 out* . . . . P
Sadler's Realm 20-1 Miss E Jones *Lft 2nd 2-10; stpd to nil 12; pu 13* . . . P
Shamel 50-1 Miss S Sharratt *(xnb) Jmpd rt 1; mist 3; impd qckly to 3rd 6 but 14th & stpng to nil 10; pu 11* . . . . P
Soul King (IRE) 66-1 Miss S West *(xnb) Midfield; poor 9th 10; t.o & pu 15* P
Sunshine Leader (IRE) (5a) 14-1 Miss S Samworth *25s-14s; prsd ldrs til mist & ur 6; rdr broke collar-bone* . . . . U
Tiraldo (FR)(cp) 25-1 Miss S Carter *Opened 50s; a wl bhnd; 11th 10; t.o 12; pu 2 out* . . . . P
Wink And Whisper (5a, 3ow) 25-1 Miss E Tory *Midfield; 20l 8th & outpcd 10; no ch aft; poor 6th 15; pu 2 out.* . . . . P

OFFICIAL DISTANCES: 15*l*, 2*l* **TIME:** 6min 21.6s

Fence 14 omitted - fallen rider; Sailors Folly finished 4th but was disqualified when the rider failed to weigh-in; she was fined £40

34 Land Rover Mens Open, 12st — 20 ran

LORD ATTERBURY (IRE) (7x) 1-2F **A Farrant** *(kineton) Lw; hld up; smooth prog to 3rd 10; ld 12 & 15l clr nxt; nt fluent 14 & 15; rdn 2 out; unchall* 1
Garruth (IRE) (7x) 6-1 **N Williams** *Tchd 8s; chsd ldrs; 8th 10; eff 12; drvn into 2nd nxt; mist 3 out; fnd nil u.p aft but clr of rest* 12 2
Ashgreen 16-1 **D Jones** *Tchd 20s; bckwd; rcd keen; ld 3-11; wknd 15 but plugged on game; btr for rce* 12 3
Father Andy (IRE)(tt) 25-1 S Morris *Fat; chsd ldrs; 6th 10; 5th & outpcd 13; plugged on in rem 4th frm 3 out.* 8 4
Poppet (5a, 7x) 14-1 H Fowler *Prom; 2nd 10; wknd aft 3 out & sn v tired.* 2½ 5
Choral Dream (IRE) 5-1 R Cope *Midfield & nvr on terms; blun 6; hmpd 7; t.o 8; poor 12th 10; stayed on flat.* 4 6
Tubber Roads (IRE) (7x) 20-1 J Jenkins *Prom early; drpd back 10th & rdn 10; no ch aft; plugging on at fin.* 4 7
Benson (IRE) (7x) 25-1 R Webb-Bowen *(xnb) A wl bhnd; t.o 8; 15th 10* . . 12 8
Drum Battle (7x) 10-1 T Messenger *(xnb) Prom til wknd & mist 9; t.o 15.* . 12 9
Dons Delight (IRE) 25-1 G Kerr *(xnb) Handy early; 11th & strugg 10; pu 14* P
Involved (IRE) 7-1 R Burton *Hld up; 13th 10; no ch aft; pu 14* . . . . P
Le Cure 20-1 J Barnes *(xnb) Chsd ldrs; hit 5; 7th when mist & ur 11; rdr broke collar-bone* . . . . U

Manavite (IRE) 25-1 T Lane *Bit bckwd; prom; 3rd when fell 12* . . . . F
Minella Storm (IRE) (7x) 50-1 T Vaughan *Ld to 3; lost plce rap; t.o & pu 12* P
Nousayri (IRE) 50-1 C Wadland *(xnb) Midfield til crashing fall 7; fell agn when loose* . . . . F
Paddies Boy (IRE) (7x) 25-1 J Trice-Rolph *Last when hmpd & ur 2* . . . . . . U
Robins Pride (IRE)(bl) 50-1 S McHugh *Cl up; 5th when mist 10; sn wknd; t.o & pu 14* . . . . P
11P Running Times (USA) (7x) 100-1 A Sansome *Prom til wknd rap 6; t.o 8; pu 12* P
Smile Pleeze (IRE) (4x) 20-1 T Stephenson *Last pr & tk no interest; t.o 8; 16th 10; pu 14* . . . . P
Waders (IRE) 25-1 James Tudor *Fell 2* . . . . F

OFFICIAL DISTANCES: 15*l*, 15*l* **TIME:** 6min 24.6s

35 Panacur/TBA PPORA Club Members Maiden Mares, 12st - 16J 16 ran

ITCHEN MILL (5a) 2-1F **T Dreaper** *4s-2s; hld up; mist 2; blun bad 8; 8th 11; clsd 14 to 2nd aft 3 out; ld aft nxt; 2l clr at last; hld on wl* 1
Knighton Star (5a) 100-30 **G Barfoot-Saunt** *Prsd ldrs gng wl; 4th 11; ld 14 til rdn & hdd app last; kpt on flat* 1¼ 2
Kayleigh (IRE) (5a) 10-1 **P York** *Hld up; mist 10; 6th 11; eff 13; sn cl up; just outpcd app 2 out til rallied & r.o wl flat* 1 3
Scarlet Glory (5a) 12-1 H Fry *2 handlers; oht; ld til mist & hdd 14; still cl 2nd 3 out; wknd app nxt* 15 4
Rio Pops (5a) 10-1 Miss A Goschen *Hld up; 7th 11; outpcd 14 til rallied aft 2 out; stayed on; promising* 4 5
Hilarity (5a) 12-1 M Miller *(xnb,bf) Fat; prom; 3rd 11; still cl 5th 3 out; sn wknd* 12 6
Royal Squeeze (IRE) (5a) 6-1 Miss P Gundry *(xnb) 2 handlers; keen & prom; 5th 11; jmpd slow 12; 6th & wkng 3 out* . . . . ½ 7
Shy Lizzie (5a) 16-1 P Mason *Bckwd; towards rr; hit 6; 9th 11; still just in tch 15; sn tired* 12 8
Any Other Business (5a) 16-1 R Stephens *(xnb) Bckwd; sn bhnd; 12th & strugg 11; t.o & pu 13* . . . . P
Eastern Apple (5a) 50-1 B King *Midfield til hit 5 & ur* . . . . U
Emma's Dream (12a) 7-1 N Williams *Lw; 20l last 2; kpt swishing tail in rr; last aft mist 10; t.o & pu 14* . . . . P
Love Potion (5a) 8-1 Miss R Davidson *Turned somersault 1; dead* . . . . F
Miss Chloe (IRE) (5a) 25-1 R Bliss *(xnb) Sn bhnd; 9th & btn when mist & ur 12* U
Mountain Lily (5a)(tt) 8-1 J Cook *Lw; prsd ldr til drpd out rap aft 12; t.o & pu last* . . . . P
Run River Run (5a)(tt) 50-1 S Graham *Swtng bad & lkd dreadful; jmpd v slow 4; sn wl t.o; pu 9* . . . . P
Sixes And Sevens (IRE) (5a) 20-1 N Pearce *Hld up & bhnd; 10th 11; pu qckly 12* . . . . P

OFFICIAL DISTANCES: 1*l*, 1½*l* **TIME:** 6min 34.9s

Fences 9 & 17 omitted - fallen horse

36 PPORA Club Members Restricted 67&8yo (Div 1), 12st 8 ran

KINGSTON-BANKER 2-1 **D Jacob** *(xnb) 4s-2s; hmpd 3; mist 4; hld up in rr in slow rce; clsd 10; 2nd 14; ld 3 out; ½l ahd & rdn last; stayed on wl* . . . 1
I Am Said I (IRE) 7-4F **A Farrant** *(xnb) Pulled hrd; hld up in tch; 3l 5th 14; went 2nd 2 out; rdn & ev ch aft til nt qckn aft last* 2 2
Leading Case 5-1 **S Morris** *Tchd 7s; lw; ld to 14; cl up til rdn & nt qckn frm 2 out* . . . . nk 3
Bolide Du Aunay (FR) 5-1 T Vaughan *Prom; ld 14; hdd 3 out; wknd qckly* . 15 4
Grey Fandango (IRE) 16-1 M Rimell *(xnb) Bckwd; prom; jmpd slow 7; ev ch til pckd bad 13 & imm lost tch; t.o 3 out; pu nxt* . . . . P
Jim's Gift (IRE) (5a) 7-1 T Lane *Prom til crashing fall 2* . . . . F
Moscow's Return (IRE) 40-1 J Trice-Rolph *Sn last; lost tch & jmpd slow 6; rallied brief 10; lost tch aft mist 12 & sn t.o; pu 13* . . . . P
Treble Trouble 14-1 P Millington *Lkd awful; tk keen hld; hld up & cl up; nt jw; ev ch til terrible mist 13 & lost all ch; t.o 3 out; pu last* . . . . P

OFFICIAL DISTANCES: 2½*l*, nk **TIME:** 6min 40.5s

Return The Call (very late to paddock & start) was withdawn not under orders

37 PPORA Club Members Restricted 67&8yo (Div 2), 12st - 16J 12 ran

HIGHWAY OAK 16-1 **N Mitchell** *Ld/disp to 12; 2nd til ld agn app 3 out; rdn & hld on wl on long run-in* . . . 1
Pot Shot 2-1F **R Burton** *Tchd 5/2; hld up; 6th 9; eff 14 to 5l 2nd app 2 out; rdn & tried to chall app last; no imp* . . . 2½ 2
Sutton Courtenay (IRE) 10-1 **J Jenkins** *Hld up in tch; went 3rd & mist 13; 5l 3rd nxt; wknd 3 out* . . . 25 3
Nickit (IRE) 5-1 S Morris *(xnb) Bckwd; mists; hld up; 9th 9; strugg frm 11* 3 4
Cloudy Bay Boy 9-2 R Cope *Prom; ld 13 til app 3 out; wknd bad; hvly eased flat* . . . 15 5
Alpenstock (FR) 16-1 Miss K Jones *Ur gng down & bolted; strugg in last pr; t.o 7; pu 9* . . . P
Anflora (5a) 5-1 N Williams *8s-5s; ld/disp to 11; stpd to nil nxt; pu 13* . . . P
Handy Hill 25-1 A Sansome *Chsd ldrs; 7th 9; went 4th 13; pu rap nxt* . . . P
Jimmy Cricket 33-1 N Oliver *Cl up when crashing fall 2* . . . F
Lord Of The Bride (IRE) 7-2 A Farrant *(xnb) Lw; jmpd slow 4; settled cl up; 4th 9; stpd to nil 12; pu 13* . . . P
Mister Bruce (IRE) 10-1 F Hutsby *Prom; cl 4th 13; wknd rap; pu 15* . . . P
Top Light 50-1 D I Turner *(xnb) Bad mover; hmpd 2; blun bad 3; a strugg in last pr; drvn 9; t.o & pu 12* . . . P

OFFICIAL DISTANCES: 3*l*, 20*l* **TIME:** 6min 27.5s
Fences 10 & 18 omitted - fallen rider

Dunston Harriers

Ampton (RH 7F,20J)

Sun, 25 Jan (GOOD to FIRM, GOOD in places)

38 Confined, 12st 10 ran

MININO (IRE) (3x) 6-1 **N Bloom** *(xnb) Bit bckwd; prom; ld 11-15; w ldr when lft 8l clr 17; rdn 2 out; hld on game flat* . . . 1
1P **Colonel Conca** 9-2 **A Braithwaite** *(xnb) Hld up; hdwy 10; 2nd/3rd frm 12; 12l 3rd & outpcd aft 17; rallied nxt; drvn & no imp flat* . . . 1½ 2
Rathnally Park (7x) 6-1 **C Gordon** *Tk keen hld; hld up; mist 9; went prom nxt; outpcd in 6l 2nd 3 out; rallied app last; kpt on one pce flat* . . . 2 3
Wilton Bridge (IRE) 4-1 Mrs S Hodge *(xnb) Hit 2; sn cl up; lost plce 11; 7th & strugg 14; rem when mist & nrly ur 2 out* . . . 25 4
Avondale Illusion (IRE) 20-1 R Stearn *Ld 1; reluct & sn bhnd; mist 11; cont t.o; pu 15* . . . P
Lone Star (IRE)(bl) 20-1 H Fowler *Midfield; 6th & just in tch 14; strugg frm nxt; t.o & pu 2 out* . . . P
Lord Valnic (IRE) 5-2F G Johnson Houghton *Bit bckwd; ld/disp to 10; 4th 14; rjnd ldr nxt til rn out 17* . . . R
Mai Point (5a) 6-1 N Moore *(xnb) Prom; 2nd 13; wkng when mists 15 & 16; t.o & pu 2 out* . . . P
Prologue (IRE) 12-1 N King *Prom brief; drpd to rr & blun 8; t.o & pu 15* . . . P
Westfield John (3x) 4-1 J Owen *Bckwd; bhnd; drvn & strugg 12; t.o & pu 2 out* P

OFFICIAL DISTANCES: 1*l*, 1½*l* **TIME:** 6min 24.0s **TOTE:** £5.40

39 Open Maiden (Div 1), 12st 11 ran

SPECIAL FRIEND (IRE) 2-1F **R Burton** *(xnb) Rcd keen; a gng str; hld up in rr til stdy prog 11; ld 3 out; clr app nxt; easily* . . . 1
Lindron 9-2 **P Bull** *2 handlers; hit 11; set modest pce to 16; sn dem 3rd; battled to tk 2nd agn cl home; no ch w wnr* . . . 10 2
6P **Arctic Snip** 5-1 **N Moore** *Prom til ld 16; hdd 3 out; chsd wnr vain aft til dem cl home* . . . 2½ 3
8P Shallee Term (IRE) 7-1 P Millington *Lkd awful; mists towards rr; 6th & rdn 13; strugg 15* . . . 10 4
27P Sharp Sarah (5a) 10-1 P Chinery *Bckwd; oft jb lft on outside; prom in 2nd/4th; jb lft & wknd qckly 17* . . . 3 5
Arctic Sun (IRE) 5-1 N Bloom *Nt a fluent; prom; blun bad 7; ev ch til wknd 16; no ch aft nxt* . . . 8 6
Charango Star 9-2 P York *Trckd ldrs til mist & ur 8* . . . U

	Hi Tech Man (IRE) 5-1 G Wigley *Ur gng down; bhnd; niggled along & just in tch 14; nt pushed aft; pu 17; easy debut*		P
	Pendils Charm (5a) 10-1 D Kemp *Bckwd; cl up early; rdn 9; strugg 11; t.o 14; pu 3 out*		P
	Pernickety King (7a) 14-1 P Cowley *Lkd awful; jmpd erratic in rr; t.o 6; pu 9*		P
26^{2}	What Next (IRE) 3-1 A Hickman *Handy til blun & ur 3*		U

OFFICIAL DISTANCES: 10*l*, 1*l* **TIME:** 6min 38.0s **TOTE:** £2.80

40 Open Maiden (Div 2), 12st — 10 ran

21^{U}	**RHYTHM KING** 9-4 **G Maundrell** *(xnb) Hld up early; 3rd/4th & gng wl frm 7 til 2nd 16; ld 3 out; sn clr; easily*		1
	Cosmic Sky 14-1 **R Stearn** *Ld 2; hdd 3 out; no ch w wnr aft*	20	2
26^{3}	**Golden Shred** (5a) 7-1 **A Braithwaite** *Hld up towards rr; 5th & outpcd 12; 15l 5th 14; plodded on*	5	3
2^{12}	Ginger Bug (5a) 12-1 P Chinery *Ld to 3; stdly lost plce; 7th & strugg 12; t.o 16*	runin	4
	Bright Torino (IRE) (5a) 25-1 J Bevan *A bhnd; hopelessly t.o 12; pu 14.*		P
20^{P}	Dolitanlad 14-1 P Millington *Lkd dreadful; jmpd erratic in rr; 17l 6th 14; t.o 17; pu 2 out*		P
	Gunner Be True 7-1 C Gordon *V bckwd; hld up; prog 10; cl 4th & rdn 12; blun 15; hung lft & stpd rap app nxt; pu 17*		P
6^{8}	Manhatton Storm (IRE) 7-1 A Merriam *Settled 2nd/4th; 3rd when nt fluent 16; still 3rd but stpng rap when fell 3 out*		F
6^{2}	Morph evensF P York *Hld up; fell 5*		F
	Sleeping Panther 14-1 P Cowley *Lkd ghastly; jmpd appalling; sn t.o; pu 14*		P

OFFICIAL DISTANCES: 15*l*, dist **TIME:** 6min 29.0s **TOTE:** £5.00

41 Intermediate, 12st — 9 ran

	HOT TODDY (IRE) 9-4 **R Burton** *(xnb) Bckwd; a gng wl; settled rr; 5th & eff 14; trckd ldrs aft til ld 2 out; sn in comm*		1
28^{2}	**Fine And Dandy (IRE)** 4-1 **J Owen** *Sn 2nd/3rd; chsd ldr frm 16; ev ch 3 out; one pce nxt*	4	2
4^{2}	**Aughmor River (IRE)**(bl) 8-1 **N Moore** *Bckwd; ld to 7; 2nd/3rd til ld agn 17; rdn & hdd 2 out; sn wknd*	10	3
	Glenmont (IRE) 10-1 Ms L Stock *Bhnd; last & outpcd 14; wl bhnd 17; some late prog & stayed on stdly*	2	4
	Colonel Carats(cp) 10-1 A Merriam *(xnb) A drvn along; chsd ldrs til outpcd 14; 5th & btn nxt; plugged on*	8	5
	Airoski evensF N Bloom *Hld up; blun bad 7; 5th when blun & ur 9*		U
19^{P}	Jack Hackett (IRE)(bl) 16-1 P Hall *2nd til ld 7; hdd 17; wknd qckly & sn v tired; t.o & pu last*		P
	Kirkharle (IRE) 14-1 Miss A Bowles *A rr & sn strugg; t.o 12; pu 15.*		P
	Viking Lily (IRE) (5a) 16-1 Mrs D Rowell *Sn bhnd; strugg 12; t.o & pu 16.*		P

OFFICIAL DISTANCES: 3*l*, 8*l* **TIME:** 6min 30.0s **TOTE:** £2.60

42 Ladies Open - 19J — 8 ran

	KINCORA (IRE) 20-1 **Ms L Stock** *(xnb) Jmpd bold; made all frm 3; rdn & kpt on game frm 2 out*		1
	Bush Hill Bandit (IRE) 3-1 **Miss A Stennett** *Ld to 3; settled trckng ldrs; 4th & gng wl 15; rdn & outpcd in 3rd 3 out; rallied to chse wnr nxt; no imp*	$2\frac{1}{2}$	2
	Andsuephi (IRE) 7-2 **Mrs S Hodge** *Sn cl up; mostly 3rd frm 7; ev ch 2 out; wknd app last*	3	3
5^{5}	Sea Tarth (5a)(cp) 16-1 Miss H Kinsey *(xnb) A bhnd; strugg 14; 5th & t.o 3 out; some late prog*	10	4
	Le Prince 10-1 Miss E Jones *Pulled hrd & sn prom; went 2nd 7; 2l down 3 out; fdd qckly nxt*	nk	5
	Dunrig (IRE) 3-1 Mrs J Gordon *Bckwd; nvr gng wl; blun bad 4 & rr aft; mist 6; u.p 10; t.o 13; pu 16*		P
	Jolly Minster 7-4F Mrs D Rowell *Lost shoe 1; settled midfield; niggled along in 5th & lkd outpcd 15; fell 17*		F
5^{6}	Village Copper 10-1 Miss H Grissell *(xnb) 3rd/4th til fell 8.*		F

OFFICIAL DISTANCES: 2*l*, 2*l* **TIME:** 6min 25.0s **TOTE:** £25.00

Fence 15 omitted - fallen rider

43 Mens Open — 8 ran

Form	Runner	Dist	Pos
1^{3}	**PENDLE HILL** 10-1 **J Owen** *Ld 3-5; 2nd/3rd til ld agn 15; forged clr 2 out; comf*		1
	Fair Exchange 5-2 **P Taiano** *Fat; went 2nd 7; ld 11-15; nt fluent 17; releg 3rd app 2 out; stayed on to 2nd flat; btr for rce*	5	2
	Carthago (IRE) 25-1 **M Harris** *Strong; prom; rdn 3 out; went 2l 2nd & flatt app nxt; rdn & no ex*	1	3
	Paddy For Paddy (IRE) 4-6F R Burton *Ld to 3; nvr gng wl aft & sn pushed along; 4th & rdn 17; 10l 4th & btn app 2 out*	8	4
24^{P}	Fatalistic (IRE)(tt) 12-1 H Fowler *(xnb) Jmpd erratic & sn last; nvr went a yd; t.o when climbed 12 & 13; pu 16.*		P
	King Of The Dawn 25-1 J Sole *Hld up towards rr; mist & ur 8*		U
3^{7}	Little Worsall (IRE) 6-1 F Marshall *Ss; rr til rfo 8*		U
	Woodward Street (AUS) 33-1 A Braithwaite *(xnb) Tk str hld; ld 5-11; wknd 13; rr when jmpd v slow 16; t.o & pu last*		P

OFFICIAL DISTANCES: 3*l*, 1/2*l* **TIME:** 6min 26.0s **TOTE:** £14.00

44 Restricted, 12st — 14 ran

Form	Runner	Dist	Pos
2^{9}	**TEACH ALTRA (IRE)** 7-1 **C Gordon** *10s-7s; hld up & bhnd; 7th & prog 11; went 3rd gng str 16; ld nxt; 12l clr 2 out; quite impressive*		1
	Holy Moses (IRE) 4-1 **G Wigley** *Bckwd; sn prom; made virt all frm 8 til hdd 17; 3l 2nd 3 out; sn wl outpcd by wnr; plugged on*	6	2
	Carlton Brae (5a) 6-1 **P Hall** *Prom; 5th 16; 9l 3rd & outpcd 3 out; plugged on stdly*	3	3
	Filou Du Bois (FR) 5-2 Ms A Embiricos *(xnb) Ld to 8; cl 4th 16; rdn & sn wknd*	15	4
29^{r}	Josh's Choice (IRE) 6-1 A Braithwaite *Cl up; 3rd 11; 6th & rdn 16; sn btn.*	1/2	5
6^{U}	Street Smart (IRE) 4-1 Miss B Donnelly *(xnb) Hld up in rr div; strugg 13; poor 8th 16*	10	6
	Glad All Over (5a) 8-1 D Hays *Bckwd; last most of way; no ch frm 13; poor 10th 16*	3	7
	Maharajah (IRE) 3-1 A Bealby *Tkn v stdly in last pr; poor last 16; nvr gvn any ch*	2	8
29^{3}	General Confusion (IRE) 8-1 R Stearn *Cl up early; drpd to midfield 9; 7th & wl outpcd 16*	2	9
27^{1}	Jacob's Choice (7a) 2-1F P York *Prom; w ldr 11-13; 2nd 16; wknd qckly nxt; pu 2 out*		P
22^{1}	Lambrini King (IRE) 6-1 Miss L Barrett-Nobbs *(xnb) Midfield; 6th 11; mist & ur 13*		U
	Red Square Prince (IRE) 5-1 D Dunsdon *Towards rr; strugg aft bad blun 10; t.o & pu 16*		P
	Sootsir 6-1 R Hawker *10s-6s; jmpd mod in rr & rdr little help til f.o 10.*		U
2^{5}	Teeton Fizz (5a) 6-1 N Bloom *Cl up til wknd 10; poor 9th 16; pu 3 out.*		P

OFFICIAL DISTANCES: 8*l*, 3*l* **TIME:** 6min 34.0s **TOTE:** £27.00

45 PPORA Club Members 6yo&up (Nov Rdrs), 12st — 9 ran

Form	Runner	Dist	Pos
23^{2}	**ROYAL ACTION** 9-4F **P Chinery** *Hld up; eff 13; went 2nd 15; ld & nt fluent 17; sn 12l clr; only 2l up aft 3 out; in comm agn nxt*		1
16^{5}	**Quick Response (IRE)** 3-1 **Miss B Donnelly** *(xnb) 2nd & gng too fast til ld 7; hdd 16; outpcd aft nxt; rallied to flatt app 2 out; eff short-lived*	8	2
16^{U}	**Brown Chieftain (IRE)** 7-1 **Miss C Haydon** *Bhnd; some prog in 4th 15; 3rd 17; 18l 3rd & no imp nxt*	20	3
	Garrison Friendly (IRE)(bl) 9-2 N Wilson (South) *Bhnd & nvr gng wl; rdn & strugg 12; 27l 5th 3 out; nt r.o; needlessly belted home*	2	4
33^{U}	Optimistic Thinker(cp) 14-1 G Wigley *3rd/4th bhnd tearaway pr; rdn & outpcd 16; 25l 4th 3 out.*	12	5
	J-Okay (IRE) 3-1 W Kinsey *Keen in last til rn out 3.*		R
32^{3}	Legal Storm (IRE) 5-1 Richard Green *Set breakneck pce w 1 rival to 7; releg 3rd & wkng when rfo 15*		U
	Monsukh (IRE) (5a) 14-1 Mrs L Spence *Sn detach last; t.o 10; furlongs bhnd when pu 3 out*		P
23^{3}	Pampered Gale (IRE) 8-1 Miss N Barnes *Towards rr when ur 3*		U

OFFICIAL DISTANCES: 8*l*, 20*l* **TIME:** 6min 33.0s **TOTE:** £2.50

Heythrop

Dunthrop (RH 9F,18J)

Sun, 25 Jan (GOOD to FIRM)

46 Hunt Members, 12st — 3 ran

RYANS STAR 4-9F **Mrs J Parris** *Hld up & mostly last; eff to ld 2 out; hdd brief app last; pushed out str flat* 1

Rockfield Lane (IRE) 5-2 **J Trice-Rolph** *Trckd ldr mostly; disp ld 2 out; unable to qckn app last; stayed on to tk 2nd nr fin* 2½ 2

Marlmont Lad (IRE) 6-1 **I Howe** *Ld; set crawl to 15; hdd 2 out; rallied to ld brief app last; one pce flat* . . . . ½ 3

OFFICIAL DISTANCES: 2½*l*, ½*l* **TIME:** 7min 39.2s

47 Confined, 12st — 6 ran

16^{3} **KUSTOM KIT GRIZZLY (IRE)**(cp) 10-11F **A Barlow** *(xnb) Opened 5/4; prsd ldr 3 til terrible blun & nrly ur nxt; drpd to 4th; eff agn 14; ld 2 out; in comm app last; rdn out* 1

Dinsey Finnegan (IRE)(vis) 5-2 **G Phillips** *(bf) Warm; pckd 1; ld to 12; ld 14-2 out; kpt on u.p flat; a hld* 3 2

34^{P} **Dons Delight (IRE)** 5-1 **G Kerr** *(xnb) Tchd 10s; bit bckwd; trckd ldrs; cl 3rd when blun 10; mist 14; cl 3rd 2 out; kpt on u.p flat* . . . . ½ 3

Maltby Son 20-1 Miss K Branson *Swtng; nov rdn; last pr; rdr nrly f.o 7; nvr on terms w ldrs; tried to cl 14; sn outpcd* 6 4

Esterelle (USA) (5a) 8-1 J Jenkins *(xnb) Fat; warm; last pr; wkng when jmpd slow 12 & 13; t.o when crawled over 14 & pu* . . . . P

10^{P} Northern Bluff 33-1 D I Turner *Bit bckwd; mostly prsd ldr; ld 12; hdd & mist 14; wknd rap & mist nxt; pu 3 out* . . . . P

OFFICIAL DISTANCES: 3*l*, ½*l* **TIME:** 6min 46.3s

48 Ladies Open, 3m5f70y - 21J — 12 ran

WHAT A MOVER (5a) 7-4F **Miss P Gundry** *Nt a fluent; settled midfield; wl in tch; chsd ldrs 12; lft 2nd 16; ld 2 out; 2l up when nt fluent last; drvn clr flat* 1

5^{3} **Garolo (FR)**(bl) 6-1 **Miss V Tremlett** *Bit bckwd; jmpd slow 1; sn wl bhnd; stdy prog frm 12; chsd ldrs 15; chall & w wnr 2 out; sn nt qckn; lft w ch agn last; outrdn flat; eased nr fin* 5 2

18^{2} **Killerine (FR)** 4-1 **Miss H Irving** *A.p; ld to 2; lft in ld 16; hdd & wknd 2 out* 6 3

Starpath (NZ) 12-1 Miss R Green *(xnb) Ss; sn wl bhnd; virt t.o 3; r.o frm 15; chsd clr ldng trio 3 out; no imp nxt; kpt on flat* 3½ 4

Lugs Brannigan (IRE) 33-1 Mrs G Harvey *Prom; ld 13-14; outpcd frm 16; fdd 2 out* 15 5

Six Clerks (IRE)(cp) 25-1 Miss A de Lisle Wells *Prsd ldr 2-11; lost tch w ldrs frm 18; nd aft; virt pu nr fin* 10 6

Borderline Breeze (IRE) 33-1 Miss H Watson *Sn wl bhnd; last frm 11; t.o frm 15* 20 7

3^{4} Silver Lake (IRE) 11-2 Miss S Beddoes *Ldng group til wknd rap 15; t.o* 4 8

Allotrope (IRE) (1ow) 33-1 Miss L Brooke *Sn wl bhnd; t.o last 6; ground to a halt & pu 8* . . . . P

3^{6} Grand Gousier (FR) 10-1 Miss J Williams *8th when rfo 2* . . . . U

10^{7} Polo Pony (IRE) 33-1 Miss Gemma Hutchinson *Prom when mist rfo 3* . . . . U

Watchyourback (NZ)(vis,tt) 8-1 Miss A Frieze *Ld 2-13; ld agn nxt; 2l up when blun & ur 16* . . . . U

OFFICIAL DISTANCES: 4*l*, 5*l* **TIME:** 7min 51.8s

49 Mens Open (Lord Ashton of Hyde's Cup), 4m - 23J — 7 ran

BRIGHT APPROACH (IRE) 1-5F **Julian Pritchard** *Patient rdn; in tch; lft disp 2nd 18; ld & nt fluent 20; drew 4l clr aft 2 out; rdn out str to keep dwindling advant flat* 1

Mr Smudge 8-1 **B King** *Prom; prsd ldr 11; lft in ld 18; hdd 20; lkd hld aft 2 out; rallied wl flat clsng nr fin* 1 2

Seabrook Lad 8-1 **T Lane** *Ww; chsd ldng pr 15; rmdr nxt; lft disp 2nd 18; ev ch app 2 out; sn btn* 10 3

34[P] Running Times (USA) 33-1 J Jenkins *Sn rr but in tch; pckd 17; outpcd 19; eff to 7l 4th 2 out; one pce aft; gd eff* 2 4

Absolutely Hopeful(bl) 33-1 P Callaghan *Jw; made most; 2l up & still gng str when blun 18 (ditch) & shot rdr over front* . . . . U

Darrell Boy (IRE) 25-1 S Blackwell *In tch; mist 10; wknd rap 15; pu nxt* . . P

Harry Hotspur (IRE)(vis) 20-1 M Barber *W ldr to 10; in tch til wknd app 18; sn t.o; pu aft 2 out* . . . . P

OFFICIAL DISTANCES: 1*l*, 8*l* **TIME:** 8min 36.8s

50 Intermediate, 12st — 14 ran

RODNEY TROTTER(cp) 14-1 **H Dowty** *In tch in midfield; prog to chse ldrs 11; rdn 2 out; chall last; drvn & r.o to ld last 50yds* 1

Camden Carrig (IRE) 3-1F **N Phillips** *(bf) Chsd ldr; ld 5-12; disp ld agn 14; mist 3 out; ld 2 out; jnd last; hrd rdn flat; hdd final 50yds*. 3/4 2

26[1] **Esendi** 7-1 **L Payter** *(xnb) Fractious lvng padd; tk keen hld; prom; trckd ldr 9; ld 12; made most aft til hdd 2 out; rallied & ev ch last; one pce u.p final 100yds* 3 3

Grizzly Golfwear (IRE) 6-1 M Barber *(xnb) Outpcd in mid-div; 8th & wl bhnd 1/2way; stayed on frm 14; chsd ldrs 2 out; 4l 4th last; no ex flat* 1 1/4 4

16[4] Tanager 4-1 J Docker *Swtng; out of tch in midfield; lost plce & wl bhnd 8; sn virt t.o in 10th 1/2way; some prog u.p 15; nvr on terms; mulish display*. . 25 5

Aztec Rule (IRE) 8-1 S Joynes *(xnb) Ld at fast pce to 5; lost plce frm 9; wknd 13; t.o 6th when pu last* . . . . P

Baccarat (IRE) 25-1 M Wall *(xnb) A wl bhnd in last trio; t.o & pu 12*. . . . . P

Carew Lad 12-1 D Jones *(xnb) Trckd ldrs; eff 12; in ldng quartet & clr of rest nxt; still ev ch when pu imm aft 2 out; broke down* . . . . P

11[P] Chaucers Miller 33-1 D I Turner *Warm; ldng group to 12; sn wknd; t.o & pu 2 out* P

Cloak And Dagger 33-1 D Harvey *Bckwd; a t.o; mist 1; mist 10; ambled round disp last aft & miles bhnd til pu last* . . . . P

Itsallupintheair 7-1 T Vaughan *(xnb) Warm; midfield; rdn & no prog 10; wknd aft nxt; pu 13* . . . . P

Rian Bo Padraig (IRE) 33-1 G Barfoot-Saunt *(xnb) 2 handlers; ld in start; a bhnd; t.o in last pr 1/2way; ambled round miles bhnd; pu last* . . . . P

Vercheny (5a) 8-1 L Jefford *(xnb) Jb & sn wl in rr; prog frm 8; rchd 5th at 12; no imp; pu 3 out* . . . . P

Who Let The Dogout 33-1 Miss F Wilson *Rr when blun & ur 1* . . . . U

OFFICIAL DISTANCES: 3/4*l*, 3*l* **TIME:** 6min 39.5s

51 Open Maiden 6yo&up (Div 1), 12st — 12 ran

ABBEYKNOCK BOY (IRE) 2-1F **Miss P Gundry** *Jmpd big early; chsd clr ldr; ld aft 8; wl clr aft 11; 15l up 14; back w rivals 2 out; 3l up last; hrd prsd flat; drvn & hld on wl*. 1

Johnsair (IRE) 12-1 **G Perkins** *(xnb) Midfield; 4th 1/2way; eff to chse wnr 3 out; clsd to 3l down last; rdn to chall & ev ch flat; outrdn nr fin* 1/2 2

12[P] **Bally Blue** 5-1 **L Jefford** *(xnb) Chsd ldrs; 3rd 9; outpcd 11; chsd wnr 15-3 out; clsd & in tch in 3rd 2 out; wknd last*. 15 3

Igam Ogam 12-1 W Hill *Midfield; 5th 1/2way; outpcd 11; sn wknd; t.o* . . . 250y 4

20[P] Gloves Off (IRE) 14-1 Miss H Irving *Jmpd slow 1 & 3; sn toiling in rr; wl bhnd in 7th 13; t.o*. 3 5

Blue Monk (IRE) 14-1 Miss E Bell *(xnb) 20s-14s; bit bckwd; ld & blazed into clr ld; hdd & stpd to nil aft 8; t.o last when pu 11* . . . . P

Kuwait Faith (IRE) 20-1 T Stephenson *(xnb) Rr when sltly hmpd & rfo 1* . . U

Misty Ramble (IRE) 4-1 G McPherson *Hmpd in melee & rfo 1* . . . . U

Northsprite(bl) 6-1 J Trice-Rolph *(xnb) 2 handlers; fell 1* . . . . F

Sales Dodger (IRE) 8-1 S Hughes *Mist & ur 1* . . . . U

35[P] Sixes And Sevens (IRE) (5a) 8-1 N Pearce *Prom in chsng group; chsd wnr aft 8; no imp 13; lost plce aft nxt; 4th & wkng when fell 15* . . . . F

Wannabe Gangster 8-1 S Gray *A last; t.o 1/2way; pu 15* . . . . P

OFFICIAL DISTANCES: 1/2*l*, 10*l* **TIME:** 6min 47.5s

52 Open Maiden 6yo&up (Div 2), 12st — 9 ran

6[6] **GREENKEYS (AUS)** 8-1 **T Stephenson** *Tk keen hld; trckd ldrs; disp frm 11 til narrow ld 2 out; hit last & jnd; hld on wl u.p nr fin* 1

6[3] **Jolly Jake** 3-1F **E Walker** *(xnb) 2 handlers; a.p; made most to 11; rmdrs 13; eff to chall last & ev ch flat; resolutely refused to go by nr fin*. 1 2

35^{8}	**Shy Lizzie** (5a) 7-1 **P Mason** *W ldrs; chall frm 14; mists 3 out & nxt; unable to qckn app last; kpt on*	4	3
35^{U}	Eastern Apple (5a) 25-1 B King *Sev v slow js; w ldrs; disp ld 11-2 out; one pce aft*	1½	4
20^{P}	On A Full Wager 9-2 J Docker *(xnb) Warm; trckd ldrs; went 3rd 13; rdn aft nxt; 5th & btn when mist 2 out; wknd rap*	30	5
	Moorepark Joy (IRE) 16-1 R Bandey *Warm; prog to disp ld 5 til mist 9 & lost plce; wknd 13; t.o*	1	6
	North Pass 6-1 Julian Pritchard *School in last pr; disp last & wl bhnd when fell 10*		F
	Plenty Inn Hand 7-2 Miss P Gundry *(xnb) A last pr; sn wl bhnd; pu 2 out; school.*		P
	Westington 7-1 Miss C Hart *(xnb) Nvr on terms w ldrs; wl bhnd ½way; t.o last when mist 13; fell last*		F

OFFICIAL DISTANCES: 1*l*, 4*l* **TIME:** 7min 00.0s

53 Open Maiden 56&7yo, 2m4f, 12st - 14J — 16 ran

	GILLIE'S NEPHEW 7-1 **James Tudor** *(xnb) W ldrs til stdd bhnd pce 4; lft 2nd 6; ev ch frm 10; ld 2 out; drvn & hld on wl flat*		1
	Gentlemans Relish 4-1 **T Lane** *Prom in chsng group; clsd 8; ld 10-2 out; rallied & ev ch last; nt qckn flat*	1	2
	Beauchamp Oracle 7-1 **S Hughes** *12s-7s; midfield; mist 3; prog to jn ldrs 9; ev ch frm 3 out; upsides ldng pr last; one pce flat.*	3	3
	The Lords Cross (IRE) 25-1 M Barber *(xnb) 2 handlers; swtng; midfield; eff 8; chsd clr ldrs 11; no imp 2 out*	20	4
	Which Pocket (IRE) 20-1 M Wall *Midfield; out of tch frm 9; r.o flat to snatch poor 5th on post.*	2	5
	Prince Of Beal 7-1 B King *Midfield; eff aft 8; no imp on ldrs aft 10; wknd 2 out*	s hd	6
	Millys Filly (5a) 14-1 Miss F Wilson *A wl in rr; t.o frm 7*	20	7
	Serves You Right (7a) 12-1 J Docker *School & a wl bhnd; t.o frm 6.*	1	8
	Bubble Brook 25-1 J Jenkins *Bit bckwd; jmpd slow; a wl bhnd; t.o 6; pu 10*		P
	Clare's Memory (5a) 7-1 Miss P Gundry *Prom in chsng group when fell 6*		F
	Jazz Night 2-1F Julian Pritchard *(xnb) Jmpd slow 1; ld til crashed thro wing 5*		R
	Jeune Premier (FR) 16-1 G Perkins *(xnb) W ldrs; lft disp ld 5; clr of rest when fell 7*		F
	Little Word (12a, 2ow) 25-1 T Vaughan *Jmpd v slow 1; a bhnd; t.o & pu 10*		P
	Nearly Dark (5a) 20-1 D Harvey *Ur bef start; set off in detach last (wisely) til pu 10 (still plenty lft in tank however).*		P
	Norbert (IRE) 12-1 G Barfoot-Saunt *(bf) Pulled hrd; jnd ldrs 4; lft disp ld nxt; lft clr 7; hdd & wknd rap 10; t.o when fell last*		F
8^{P}	Potter's Wheel (7a) 33-1 T Stephenson *A wl bhnd in rr group; t.o & pu 10.*		P

OFFICIAL DISTANCES: 1*l*, 2*l* **TIME:** 5min 04.7s

Lincolnshire United Hunts Club

Market Rasen (LH 7F,18J)

Sun, 25 Jan (GOOD to FIRM, FIRM in places)

54 LUHC Club Members, 12st — 5 ran

	RAMIREZ (IRE) 7-1 **N Kent** *Hld up; 10l 3rd 8; prog to jn ldr 14; lft in ld nxt; 5l clr 2 out; sn in comm; hvly eased last 100yds*		1
	Near And Phar (IRE) (5a) 14-1 **Miss S Buckley** *(xnb) Hld up; 15l last 13; gd hdwy & cl 4th nxt; outpcd when lft 3rd 15; rdn & r.o wl flat; snatched 2nd last 100yds; no ch w wnr.*	6	2
	Its-On-The-Cards (IRE) 11-4 **A Sansome** *Ld to 1; lft in ld 6; 15l clr 10; hdd app 14; lft cl 2nd nxt; rdn & btn 2 out; dem flat.*	2	3
	Fine Times (7x)(tt) 5-4F M Mackley *Lw; 3rd til lft 2nd 6; ld app 14; 2l up when mist & ur nxt*		U
	Stevie Dee 5-1 O Williams *Bckwd; pulled hrd; dashed into ld 1; 20l clr when blun & ur 6*		U

OFFICIAL DISTANCES: 5*l*, 1*l* **TIME:** 6min 41.0s

Racing was delayed by 30 minutes awaiting paramedic cover

55 Confined, 12st — 9 ran

	RIDGEWAY (IRE) (7x)(cp) 7-4F **Miss J Foster** *(xnb) Chsd ldrs til ld app 7; made rest; rdn clr aft 2 out; 6l clr at last; pushed out*		1
5[2]	**Winter Gale (IRE)** 7-2 **Miss L Eddery** *Hld up bhnd; prog to 5l 5th 14; 4l 4th 2 out; nt clr rn last bend; switched & r.o flat; no ch w wnr.*	3½	2
	Glacial Dancer (IRE) 20-1 **R Clark** *Oht; ww in tch; hit 10; prog 12; cl 3rd 15; one pce u.p app last*	1½	3
	Springlea Tower (3x) 7-1 R Hunnisett *Lw; ld to 1; stayed prom; ev ch 14; one pce frm 3 out.*	1	4
	Contingency 9-2 R Cope *6s-9/2; ld 1-7; chsd ldrs til hrd rdn & wknd 15; 5th & wl btn nxt*	15	5
	Amarettoforanna (IRE) (7x) 10-1 Miss Rachel Clark *Swtng; mid-div; mist 7; 7th & outpcd app 14; wl bhnd when pu 3 out*		P
	Gus Berry (IRE)(bl) 12-1 C Mulhall *Sltly bckwd; jmpd slow & nvr lkd happy; sn detach; t.o 6 til pu 11.*		P
	Macfin (IRE) 16-1 Miss L Allan *Nvr gng wl; 8l 7th & pushed along 11; lost tch nxt; t.o & pu 3 out*		P
	Panooras Lord (IRE) 50-1 N Docker *Trckd ldrs; 6l 6th & wkng app 14; wl bhnd when pu 15*		P

OFFICIAL DISTANCES: 3*l*, ½*l* **TIME:** 6min 22.0s

Merry Minstrel (12-1, bolted to start & completed 2 circs of course) was withdrawn not under orders - Rule 4 deduction of 5p in pound; the stewards interviewed the owner and rider and recorded that steps were to be taken to avoid a repeat

56 Dodson & Horrell PPORA Club Members, 12st — 6 ran

3[1]	**GUILSBOROUGH GORSE** (7x) 10-11F **M Walford** *Opened 5/4; a gng wl; chsd ldr til jmpd to ld 3 out; sn in comm; v easily*		1
	Red Rebel (7x) 7-4 **R Cope** *Ld; 2l clr 15; hdd & rdn nxt; btn app last.*	10	2
19[P]	**Mr Naborro (IRE)** (3ow)(cp) 14-1 **A Wintle** *Trckd ldrs; 4l 3rd & rdn 15; no ch w ldng pr aft.*	3	3
	Wibbley Wobbley (4x) 10-1 T Ellis *Chsd ldrs; blun 3; mist 5; 6l 5th app 14; sn outpcd*	10	4
	Supreme Silence (IRE) 20-1 N Kent *Hld up last; prog to trck ldrs 11; 4th & rdn 14; sn outpcd*	15	5
	Bidin' My Time (NZ) 12-1 L Hicks *Hld up in tch; mist 7; cl 3rd 9; hit 13; wknd qckly app nxt; pu 15.*		P

OFFICIAL DISTANCES: 12*l*, 3*l* **TIME:** 6min 29.0s

57 Restricted, 12st — 12 ran

	NOBLE AFFAIR (5a) 10-1 **M Mackley** *Lw; patient rdn; bhnd til stdy prog 11; went 4l 2nd 3 out; chall & ld last; rdn out*		1
	Imps Way (5a) 4-1F **M Morley** *Chsd ldrs; 5l 5th 11; prog to ld app 14; hdd last; unable to qckn flat.*	2	2
	Snowtre (IRE) (3ow) 14-1 **A Wintle** *(xnb) Hld up & bhnd; stdy prog 13; lft 5th 2 out; went mod 3rd app last; nvr nrr*	8	3
	Miss Zarnni (5a) 16-1 L Hicks *Mists; rr but in tch; 10l 8th 10; outpcd app 14; stayed on agn app last.*	nk	4
	Henry Henbit 5-1 S Morris *Tk keen hld; chsd ldr; 2l 2nd 14; rdn 3 out; 3rd & btn app last*	2	5
	Colonel Ludlow (IRE)(tt) 14-1 C Cundall *(xnb) Chsd ldrs; 5l 3rd 14; wknd app 3 out*	7	6
	Agent Provocateur (NZ) 14-1 R Clark *A bhnd; 10l 9th 11; sn lost tch; t.o & pu 3 out*		P
	Approaching Land (IRE) 11-2 M Watson *Lw; knocked over handler in padd; nt fluent; pulling & chsd ldrs to 4; lost plce stdly & bhnd 7; prog & 10l 6th 15; 6l 4th & running on when fell hvly 2 out*		F
	Gale Damage (IRE) 12-1 O Williams *(xnb) Mid-div til rdn & wknd qckly 12; last frm nxt; pu 14*		P
	Purple Jean (5a) 14-1 G Brewer *(xnb) Prom; chsd ldr 7-8; wknd 15; 6th & wl btn nxt; pu last*		P
	Sounds Promising 6-1 A Sansome *Lw; jmpd rt; ld til aft 13; wknd rap & pu nxt*		P
	Table For Four 10-1 P Andrew *(xnb) Wl bhnd when pu 7*		P

OFFICIAL DISTANCES: 1½*l*, 8*l* **TIME:** 6min 30.0s

58 Open Maiden (Div 1), 12st — 10 ran

		Dist	Pos
HENRY MURPHY 7-2 **M Walford** *Jw; pulled to ld 1; made rest; 6l clr 2 out; sn drew rt away; v easy*			1
Dreamie Battle (5a) 14-1 **Miss S Sharratt** *Chsd ldrs 2-3 & 7 til app 14; 8l 3rd & btn 3 out; kpt on u.p to 2nd agn last 100yds*		20	2
Cashari (IRE) 7-4F **S Morris** *Ww wl bhnd; prog to 12l 5th 9; mist 11; lft 8l 4th 13; chsd wnr & mist 15; sn rdn; 6l down & btn nxt; lost 2nd last 100yds*		nk	3
Cloudkicker (IRE) 14-1 A Pennock *Ld to 1; chsd ldrs til 15l 4th & wkng app 14; no ch when blun 3 out.*		fence	4
Glen Canyon (IRE) 14-1 M Bennison *Oht; chsd ldr 3 til mist 7; 4th & in tch when blun bad & ur 13; dead.*			U
Mrs Fidget (5a) 14-1 O Williams *Mid-div til rdn & wknd qckly 11; sn t.o; pu 14*			P
Northern Breeze (5a) 8-1 M Mackley *12s-8s; hld up last; prog 10; 6th & in tch when fell 12*			F
Prince Mouse 14-1 J Howard *(xnb) Mid-div til blun & ur 6.*			U
Sherfield Lass (5a) 7-1 G Brewer *Mid-div til blun bad & drpd to last 5; lft mod 5th & rdn 13; no prog; t.o & pu 3 out*			P
Southern Ha'i (5a) 7-1 T Ellis *(xnb) Tk keen hld; hld up last pr; prog to 10l 6th 10; wknd app 14; t.o & pu last*			P

OFFICIAL DISTANCES: 24*l*, $\frac{1}{2}$*l* **TIME:** 6min 34.0s

59 Open Maiden (Div 2), 12st - 17J — 5 ran

		Dist	Pos
GOLDEN RIVET 1-2F **M Walford** *Oht padd & start; hld up last; prog 6; ld 10; made rest; 6l clr 15; wl in comm frm nxt; nt extended.*			1
Troubleshooter 7-2 **M Mackley** *Ld at crawl to 2; lft 7l 3rd 8; lft 2nd 13; 6l down & rdn 3 out; sn wl btn.*		30	2
Another Half (12a) 6-1 P Kinsella *Ur gng down; hld up; 10l 4th 3; blun & ur 5*			U
Eastern Royal (7a) 12-1 Miss Rachel Clark *Dashed into ld 2; sn clr; hit 7; hdd 10; 2l 2nd when blun & ur 13*			U
Lord Jurado (IRE) 20-1 O Williams *Chsd ldrs; 3l 3rd when ur 8*			U

OFFICIAL DISTANCE: dist **TIME:** 6min 37.0s

Fence 15 omitted - fallen rider; Man Of Spirit (following loss of connections' horse in previous rce) was withdrawn not under orders

60 Open Maiden (Div 3), 12st — 7 ran

		Dist	Pos
	NEWGATE WELLS (IRE) 3-1 **N Kent** *2 handlers; ld to 3; jmpd slow nxt; disp ld 15; sn rdn; slt ld 2 out; hdd app last; hld inner & kpt on to ld agn nr fin*		1
	Tap Dance 5-2JF **P Kinsella** *(xnb) Ww in mid-div; prog 9; disp ld 15 til ld on outer last bend; hdd & no ex last 50yds.*	hd	2
7[2]	**Tooley Park** 5-2JF **A Sansome** *Ww; mid-div; mist 6; prog 11; rdn 13; 8l 4th nxt; btn 3 out; went poor 3rd app last*	20	3
	Miss Danbys (5a) 6-1 M Walford *(xnb) Chsd ldr; 15l 2nd 9; ld aft 13; mist nxt; hdd 15; sn wknd; t.o.*	25	4
	Auntie Alba (5a) 10-1 M Mackley *Bhnd; 25l 6th 10; t.o & pu 14*		P
	Dextrous 16-1 Miss Rachel Clark *(xnb) Pulling; chsd ldr til ld 3; 30l clr 6; blun 8 & 9; hit 12 & 13; hdd & stpd to nil & pu nxt.*		P
	Tommy Flanders 20-1 Miss S Phizacklea *(xnb) Sn bhnd; mists 4 & 5; rdn & no prog 11; t.o & pu 14.*		P

OFFICIAL DISTANCES: nk, 10*l* **TIME:** 6min 45.0s

Silverton

Black Forest Lodge (RH 8F,19J)

Sun, 25 Jan (GOOD)

61 Hunt Members, 12st — 4 ran

		Dist	Pos
MIDNIGHT COUP(vis) 4-5F **A Farrant** *Ww; 4l last $\frac{1}{2}$way; eff to ld aft 16; clr 2 out; comf*			1
Calleva Star (IRE) 7-2 **S Kidston** *Lw; ld til hdd aft 15; rdn 3 out; one pce .*		7	2
Listen To Us (IRE) 7-4 **Miss L Gardner** *(xnb) Bckwd; went 2nd 3; rn wide bend aft 8; jnd ldr 13; mist 14; ld aft 15 til hdd aft nxt; wkng when mist 3 out*		12	3
Stone Valley 8-1 C Heard *Jmpd novicey; 2nd to 3; releg last & rmdrs nxt; tried to ref & blun bad & ur 6*			U

OFFICIAL DISTANCES: 6*l*, 10*l* **TIME:** 6min 12.6s

62 Confined, 12st — 8 ran

SIR WILLIAM (8x) 7-2 **R Woollacott** *(xnb) 5s-7/2; hld up; mist 6; hdwy 8; went 2nd 10; qcknd to ld 13; 5l clr 16; rdn 2 out; kpt on wl* . . . 1

Agile King (6x) 7-1 **Miss C Tizzard** *Ld to 6 & 8-13; rdn & no imp 2 out; fin v lame* . . . 7 2

Bak On Board 5-2 **Miss L Gardner** *(xnb) 2 handlers; hld up; mist 4; last to 6; hdwy & 5l 4th ½way; outpcd 14; lft poor 3rd 3 out* . . . 15 3

Virtuoso 6-1 R McCarthy *(xnb) Hld up; lost plce & 7l last ½way; outpcd 14; 19l 5th 16; lft poor 4th nxt* . . . 6 4

15P Eskimo Gold (5a) 20-1 M Sweetland *(xnb) Lw; 2 handlers; prom til lost plce 8; 6l 6th ½way; wknd u.p 12; wl bhnd when pu 14* . . . P

O So Bossy 8-1 Miss J Congdon *Lost plce 6; last 8; 6½l 7th ½way; mist 11; bhnd when pu 14* . . . P

Porlock Hill (15x) 2-1F N Harris *(xnb) 2nd til ld 6-8; 3l 3rd ½way; 7l 3rd & outpcd when mist 15; 20l 3rd when fell 3 out* . . . F

Tiger Talk 5-1 A Farrant *Lw; hld up; mist & releg last 6; 5½l 5th ½way; rdn 12; lost tch 15; t.o & pu 3 out* . . . P

OFFICIAL DISTANCES: 5*l*, 20*l* **TIME:** 5min 55.4s

63 Gerrard Ladies Open — 8 ran

JOLITAN(bl) 7-1 **Miss A Goschen** *Threw rdr lvng padd; hld up; went 2nd aft 8; eff 16; ld aft 3 out; 8l clr when swerved lft & reluct to rce flat; rdr lost irons; just hld on* . . . 1

Phoenix Phlyer(vis) 1-2F **Miss C Stucley** *(xnb,pricker n/s) 4/5-1/2; ld; 15l clr 8 til mist 12; 10l up 16; hdd aft nxt; rdn 2 out; rallied flat; just failed* . s hd 2

10U **Garethson (IRE)** 14-1 **Mrs S Heath** *Prom; went 2nd brief 8; 18l 3rd ½way; 11l 3rd when blun 14; nd aft; poor 3rd agn 2 out; stayed on* . . . 8 3

Market Springer (IRE) 7-1 Miss B Williams *(xnb) Hld up; last to 10; 22l 5th ½way; hdwy u.p 12; 15l 3rd when mist 16; wknd 2 out* . . . 7 4

Fair Wind (IRE) 6-1 Mrs S Brown *Lost plce 5; 26l last ½way; wl bhnd 13* . 15 5

Mr Ben Gunn 14-1 Miss V Heal *Hld up; 23l 6th ½way; rdn 12; sn wl bhnd; 31l last 16; t.o.* . . . 10 6

Father Jim 14-1 Miss C Tizzard *2nd to 8; 20l 4th ½way; rdn 12; 20l 5th & wkng when hit 16; wl bhnd when crashed thro wing last & collapsed; down for sev mins* . . . R

Iceni Queen (5a) 33-1 Miss S Robinson *Chsd ldrs til lost plce 8; 24l 7th ½way; last & rdn aft 12; t.o & pu 14* . . . P

OFFICIAL DISTANCES: s hd, 6*l* **TIME:** 5min 55.5s

64 Land Rover Mens Open, 12st — 10 ran

JUST THE JOB TOO (IRE) 6-1 **R McCarthy** *2nd/3rd til ld 13; hit last; rdn & r.o wl flat* . . . 1

Charlie Strong (IRE) (7x) 7-1 **N Williams** *(xnb) 2 handlers; hld up; jmpd slow 6; hdwy & 2l 3rd ½way; went 2nd aft 16; sust chall frm 3 out; unable to qckn flat* . . . 1 2

County Derry (7x) 4-7F **N Harris** *Swtng; 4/5-4/7; hld up; 5l 6th ½way; mist 12; sn rdn along; 13l 6th 15; hdwy u.p nxt; went 5l 3rd aft 3 out; hit 2 out; stayed on wl flat; nt rch ldrs* . . . 1 3

Perkys Pride (IRE) (7x) 7-1 A Farrant *2nd til ld 4; hdd 13; ev ch 16; rdn & wknd 3 out* . . . 15 4

The Pickled Duke (IRE) 33-1 M Miller *2 handlers; prom; 3l 4th ½way; mist 11; rdn 12; mist 14; 12l 5th nxt; sn wknd* . . . 20 5

Doublet 6-1 R Woollacott *(orbs) 8s-6s; hld up; blun 10; 4½l 5th ½way; 9l 4th 15; sn wknd; t.o & pu 2 out* . . . P

Lilardo (5a) 40-1 L Heard *(xnb) Hld up; mist 6; 7l 8th ½way; wknd 14; t.o & pu 16* . . . P

Lyringo (5a) 40-1 P Sheldrake *Blun & ur 1* . . . U

Marquis Max 16-1 W Smith *25s-16s; 2 handlers; jmpd lft; ld to 4; 2nd to 7; lost plce & 6l 7th ½way; lost tch 12; pu 14* . . . P

Welsh Warrior 40-1 R Richards *A bhnd; nrly ur 3; detach last & rdn 7; mist 9; lost tch 12; t.o when mist & ur 15* . . . U

OFFICIAL DISTANCES: 1*l*, 1*l* **TIME:** 5min 57.1s

65 Restricted (Nov Rdrs), 12st — 14 ran

	EARL'S TOY (IRE) 6-1 **H Fry** *Hld up & bhnd; 17½l 8th ½way; hdwy 12; lft 8l 3rd 14; jnd ldr aft 16; rdn to ld nr fin*		1
14^{2}	**Frankly Fear** 7-1 **N Heath** *(xnb) 2 handlers; lw; a.p; 7l 4th ½way; went 4l 2nd 14; ld 16 til outrdn & hdd nr fin*	s hd	2
16^{6}	**Sissinghurst Star (IRE)** 14-1 **P Mann** *Hld up & bhnd; 21l 10th ½way; hdwy 15; 9l 5th nxt; lft 10l 3rd 2 out; nvr able to chall*	12	3
	Alpine Fugue (IRE)(tt) 14-1 Miss S Lewis *Hld up & bhnd; 20l 9th ½way; 26l 8th 16; nvr on terms*	25	4
	Carling Elect (5a) 12-1 Miss L Hawkings *(xnb) Hld up & bhnd; 22l 11th ½way; hdwy & 14l 5th 15; wknd app 3 out*	4	5
15^{3}	Chief Suspect (IRE) 8-1 D Jacob *2 handlers; hld up; 17l 7th ½way; hdwy 14; 5l 4th & rdn 16; wknd app 3 out*	4	6
16^{P}	Always Good (IRE) 14-1 P Needham *(xnb) Chsd ldrs til lost plce 8; 16l 6th ½way; 21l 8th & rdn 15; t.o*	10	7
	Nice Approach (IRE) 33-1 Miss V Murphy *A wl bhnd; t.o 9*	25	8
	Mrs Peggoty (5a) 3-1 J Morgan *5s-3s; chsd ldrs; 14l 5th ½way; wknd 14; 20l 7th nxt; t.o*	2	9
	The Last Shout (IRE) 14-1 Miss A Hughes *Bckwd; 1st ride; last 5; t.o 7; cont v slow*	2fncs	10
	Barton Saint (NZ) 16-1 B Parsons *Prom; 6l 3rd ½way; went 2nd 12 til releg 5l 3rd & ur 14*		U
14^{P}	Magnemite (IRE)(bl) 7-4F J White *5s-7/4; hit 3; 2nd til ld 12; hdd 16; 8l 3rd & wkng when blun & ur 2 out*		U
	Mister Party 7-1 T Eades *(xnb) 14s-7s; lw; ld; 12l clr 8; stpd to nil & hdd 12 (& should have pu); bhnd when crashing fall 13*		F
	Return The Call (IRE) 20-1 N McDiarmid *(xnb) Mists; a bhnd; 29l 12th ½way; t.o & pu 14*		P

OFFICIAL DISTANCES: s hd, 8*l* **TIME:** 6min 03.2s

66 Open Maiden (Div 1), 12st — 11 ran

	OLLY MAY (5a) 4-1 **R Woollacott** *12s-4s; hld up; hdwy 9; 3l 3rd ½way; went 2nd 11-13 & agn frm 16; rdn 3 out; stayed on to ld nr fin*		1
	Our Weddingpresent (USA) (7a) 4-1 **A Farrant** *(xnb) Hld up & bhnd; 9l 9th ½way; 10l 7th 13; gd hdwy & 3l 3rd 16; ld 3 out; 3l clr & lkd wnr last; wknd & hdd nr fin*	s hd	2
	Merlins Bay (IRE) 12-1 **W White** *2 handlers; hld up; 4½l 5th ½way; went 2nd 13; ld 15-3 out; rdn 2 out; 7l 3rd & wkng when mist last*	10	3
	Western Frontier (IRE) (7a) 7-4F D Alers-Hankey *(xnb) Hld up & bhnd; 7l 8th ½way; disp 10l 7th 13; lost tch aft 15; stayed on frm 2 out*	12	4
20^{U}	Keegan Bearnais (FR) 6-1 T Mann *(xnb) Swtng; ld 3-10; 4l 4th ½way; sn lost plce; 13l 9th 13; wl bhnd 15*	2	5
12^{U}	Princess Hatie (12a) 16-1 M Sweetland *(xnb) 2 handlers; prom; mist 5; went 2nd 10-11; 6l 4th 13; wknd 15*	7	6
	Arthur-K 20-1 O Nelmes *(xnb) Swtng; hld up; 6½l 7th ½way; 8½l 6th 13; in tch when fell 14*		F
	Bristol Bridge 16-1 R Stephens *(xnb) A bhnd; 10l last ½way; lost tch 13; t.o & pu 16*		P
	Darcy Jones(bl) 3-1 Mrs O Jackson *Tubed; ld to 3; 2nd til ld 10; hdd 15; 5l 4th nxt; wknd qckly; wl bhnd when pu 2 out*		P
	Meadows Prince (IRE) (7a) 20-1 L Heard *(xnb) Hld up; 7th when rn out & ur 5*		R
	Saxon Gale (5a) 25-1 R Bliss *(xnb) 2 handlers; swtng; unruly when mounted padd; sn prom; 3rd when rn wide & lost plce bend aft 8; 6l 6th ½way; 8l 5th 13; wknd 15; t.o & pu 3 out*		P

OFFICIAL DISTANCES: s hd, 5*l* **TIME:** 6min 19.8s

67 Open Maiden (Div 2), 12st - 18J — 10 ran

	BESSIE BUNTER (5a) 9-2 **M Miller** *Hld up; hdwy 8; 7l 6th ½way; went 2nd 12; ld aft by-passing 15 til blun 3 out; ld aft 2 out; sn clr*		1
	The Sycophant (IRE) 10-1 **Miss E Tory** *Hld up; lost plce 8; 11l 8th ½way; hdwy 14; 2l 4th 16; ld aft 3 out til hdd & wknd aft nxt*	10	2

Royal Czarina (5a) 14-1 **J Snowden** *Chsd ldrs; went 2nd 10-12 & aft by-passing 15; ev ch 2 out; sn wknd* 2 3
Another Bit 9-1 Miss A Goschen *Mist 8; 2nd to 10; 4l 3rd 1/2way; wknd qckly 12; t.o 16* 1 1/2fs 4
Ballyknock Rose (IRE) (5a) 9-2 Miss V Shaw *(xnb) 8s-9/2; hld up; 8th when hmpd bad & ur 7* . . . . U
Red Stranger (FR)(cp) 7-4F A Farrant *4s-7/4; nvr gng wl; last & rdn 5; t.o & pu 11* . . . . P
State Affairs (IRE) 14-1 R McCarthy *Prom; 10l 3rd when fell 7* . . . . F
Summer Snow(cp) 7-1 O Nelmes *Ld; 8l clr when mist 6; hdd & wknd qckly aft by-passing 15; wl bhnd when fell 3 out* . . . . F
Tragic Belle (5a) 7-1 N Williams *(xnb) Hld up; mist 3; last to 5; hdwy & 6l 5th 1/2way; mists 11 & 12; 1 1/2l 3rd 16; sn rdn & wknd qckly; pu 3 out* . . . . P
13P Worthy Man(tt) 10-1 Miss L Hawkings *(xnb) Hld up; 8l 7th 1/2way; in tch til mist & rdr lost iron 12; wl bhnd when fell 14* . . . . F

OFFICIAL DISTANCES: 8*l*, 2*l* **TIME:** 6min 09.5s

Fence 15 omitted - fallen rider; Toon Society (C Heard 3-1 reluctant to line up & eventually galloped off riderless) was withdrawn not under orders - Rule 4 deduction 25p in pound

68 Open Maiden (Div 3), 12st — 9 ran

8[4] **CIMMAROON (IRE)** (7a) 4-5F **A Farrant** *Ww; hdwy 7; 1 1/2l 3rd 1/2way; ld 13; 5l clr 16; easily* 1
Stalbridge Rose (5a) 5-1 **Miss A Goschen** *2nd til ld 11; hdd 13; releg 3rd 16; one pce aft; 2nd agn frm 2 out; no ch w wnr* 10 2
Dursey Island (IRE) 8-1 **M Miller** *Hld up; 5l 7th 1/2way; hdwy 13; went 6l 3rd 15 & 5l 2nd nxt; rdn app 2 out; sn wknd* 7 3
Purslet (5a) 11-1 Miss N Stallard *(xnb) Ld to 11; mists 12 & 13; 5l 3rd 14; wknd 15; t.o* . . . . runin 4
Mo's O Friendly 14-1 Miss S Robinson *Chsd ldrs; 3 1/2l 5th 1/2way; 7l 5th 14; wknd 15; mist 2 out; t.o* 2 5
Hoteliers' Dream (5a) 10-1 M Sweetland *(xnb) 2 handlers; reluct to go to post; hld up & pulled hrd; mist 2; hdwy 9; 2 1/2l 4th 1/2way; wknd 13; 13l 6th 15; mist last; t.o* 7 6
Game Endeavour (IRE) 7-2 D Edwards *Hld up; last to 7; 4 1/2l 6th 1/2way; 10l last 14; wl bhnd when pu 16* . . . . P
Kerry Zulu Warrior 14-1 R Stephens *(xnb) 7th when ur 3* . . . . U
King Marlon 16-1 R Bliss *Bckwd; lost plce 5; last 7; sn t.o; pu 11* . . . . . . P

OFFICIAL DISTANCES: 8*l*, 4*l* **TIME:** 6min 16.6s

West Percy

Alnwick (LH 9F,18J)

Sun, 25 Jan (GOOD to SOFT)

69 Hunt Members, 12st — 6 ran

DERE STREET 7-4F **Miss R Davidson** *Opened 2s; a handy; ld 2-3; cl 2nd/3rd til ld & dived at 11; 1l up last; rdn & r.o flat* 1
Be A Better Boy (3x, 4ow) 5-2 **J Walton** *Chsd ldrs; 5l 4th 4; 6l 5th app 10; prog to disp ld brief 14; 2l 2nd 2 out; drvn & ev ch last; r.o; just failed* . 1/2 2
Timberley (3x)(tt) 8-1 **T Oates** *(citation) Swtng; ld brief; settled in 3rd/4th til disp ld brief 14; wknd aft 15; 8l 3rd & rmdrs 3 out* 15 3
Coquet Gold (5a) 20-1 Miss C Walton *Fat; 1st ride; mists; 8l last 1; a last pr; 8l 5th 10; outpcd 13; 30l last 15; pu nxt* . . . . P
Lively Dessert (IRE) (7x) 9-4 C Gillon *(xnb) Lw; oht; chsd ldrs; disp 4l 3rd 4; disp ld 7; sn 4l up; rdn & drpd to 8 1/2l 5th passing boxes 10; nt keen & outpcd aft; mist 13; 40l last 15; pu 3 out* . . . . P
Ramon Allones (IRE) 14-1 R Green *Trckd ldr; ld aft 3; 2l up 5; hdd aft 7; wknd qckly; 20l last aft 9; t.o & tired when jmpd lft & fell 11* . . . . F

OFFICIAL DISTANCES: 1/2*l*, 20*l* **TIME:** 6min 37.6s

70 Restricted — 9 ran

CREVAMOY (IRE) (5a) 12-1 **A Richardson** *A handy; pulling in 5l 4th mostly til eff app last; r.o wl flat; ld nr line; wl rdn* 1

Alittlebitopower evensF **C Storey** *9/4-evens; made virt all; jw at times; 2l up 7; 4l up 15; 2l up & lkd wnr 2 out; jmpd slow last; hrd prsd & one pce flat; hdd nr line; lkd to fin clr 2nd; btr for rce* . . . . 3/4 2†

Wilfie Wild 8-1 **Mrs L Ward** *In tch in rr early; cl 5th 9; 5l 3rd app 14; prog to 3l 2nd 3 out; sn rdn; 1l 2nd & ev ch last; r.o flat; lkd to fin 3rd* . . . . s hd 2†

Highland Brig 6-1 R Morgan *Trckd ldr; 2l 2nd 5-7; hit 10; outpcd app 3 out; rallied to 4l 3rd app last; fin tired; btr for rce* 3 1/2 4

Bermuda Blue 16-1 L Bates *(xnb) In tch in rr; 7l 7th & mist 9; outpcd 11; nd frm 13* 10 5

2[4] Hessac (FR) 7-2 N Tinkler *Prom; disp 3l 3rd 4; 5l 4th 11; pushed along nxt; outpcd & rdn 15; nd* 5 6

Captain Oates 8-1 T Oates *In tch in rr; prog to 3l 3rd aft 11; ev ch til wknd qckly app 3 out* 15 7

Cross River(tt) 9-4 N Saville *(xnb) Sis; rr when mist & ur 3* . . . . U

Mr Sonshine 8-1 P Frank *Mid-div; 8l last 4; mist 6; outpcd 11; bhnd when jmpd slow 15 & pu* . . . . P

OFFICIAL DISTANCES: 3/4l, d ht **TIME:** 6min 33.8s

71 Ladies Open — 7 ran

LIGHT THE RIVER (IRE)(bl,tt) 2-1 **Miss C Metcalfe** *(xnb) Trckd ldrs; disp 3l 3rd app 6 til 3l 2nd 10; 1/2l 2nd 14; ld aft nxt; 2l up 3 out; stayed on* . 1

Harden Glen 5-1 **Miss J Riding** *(xnb) Trckd ldr til disp ld 5; ld 7; 1/2l up 14; hdd 3 out; ev ch app last; kpt on wl; dem 3rd brief flat; nt trble wnr* . . . 2 2

5[7] **Balisteros (FR)** 5-4F **Miss P Robson** *Chsd ldrs; 5l 4th 4; cl 2nd/3rd til 3l 3rd 14; 6l 4th 3 out; kpt on; went 2nd brief flat; nt pce to chall* . . . . hd 3

Ledgendry Line 9-4 Miss S Brotherton *In tch in rr; hit 2; 7l 6th app 7; disp 4l 4th 10 til outpcd aft 15; kpt on but nd* 2 4

Baby John (IRE) 14-1 Miss L Horner *Towards rr; 6l 5th app 7; outpcd & 10l 6th 13; sn btn; tk poor 5th aft 3 out* 20 5

Marteeny (5a) 5-1 Miss C Walton *Rr; 10l last 2; prog to disp 4l 4th 10; outpcd aft 12; mist 14; sn 20l 5th; releg last aft 3 out* 3 6

Wheresbob(vis) 20-1 Miss L Kendall *2 handlers; hdstrng; jmpd rt at times; tk keen hld; ld; 5l up 2; hdd aft 5; cl up til rn wide & app 10; wknd & 20l last 12; t.o & pu 15* . . . . P

OFFICIAL DISTANCES: 2 1/2l, nk **TIME:** 6min 29.1s

72 Mens Open, 12st — 15 ran

GEORDIES EXPRESS (7x) 6-1 **K Anderson** *(xnb) A.p; cl 2nd/3rd til ld 3 out; sn 8l clr; unchall* 1

Just Barney Boy 16-1 **T Oates** *Towards rr; 18l 6th 13; 15l down nxt; stayed on wl frm 3 out; nrst fin* 8 2

Parade Racer (7x) 3-1JF **D Jewett** *Chsd ldrs; 6l 4th app 6; 3 1/2l 3rd 9; outpcd 14; 9l 5th nxt; went 8l 2nd aft 3 out; kpt on one pce* 8 3

Extra Jack (FR) (7x)(bl) 4-1 C Shirley-Beavan *Tried to make all at gd pce; 3l up 11; hdd 3 out & sn brushed aside; fin tired* 15 4

Meander (IRE) 20-1 J Mactaggart *Nvr btr than mid-div; t.o 13* 2 5

Who Dares Wins 8-1 L Bates *Rr & mist 1; t.o 13* 5 6

Dr Deductible (7x)(cp) 12-1 R Brown *Chsd ldrs; 5l 4th 5; 8l 5th 11; sn one pce; t.o 3 out* 2 7

Broken English (5a) 20-1 C Dawson *A rr; t.o 14; pu 3 out* . . . . P

Gaultier Gale (IRE) 16-1 A Findlay *Prom brief; rr & outpcd aft 10; t.o & pu 15* P

Indien Du Boulay (FR) (7x) 6-1 W Ramsay *Rr; pushed along 9; sn strugg & wl bhnd; pu 3 out* . . . . P

Missy Moscow (IRE) (5a) 4-1 R Tate *Ld early; 3l 2nd 4; 2l 2nd 6; 10l 6th & lsng tch 10; wl bhnd when pu 3 out* . . . . P

Mr Busby 8-1 R Morgan *Oht; ss; a rr; 20l last 3; some prog aft 12; t.o & pu 3 out* P

Starbuck 9-1 L Morgan *Mid-div; 8l 6th & rmdrs 8; sn strugg; wl bhnd when pu 3 out* P

Star Of Raven (5a) 5-1 N Saville *Rr; prog to 4l 3rd 12; outpcd 14; wknd qckly; bhnd when pu 3 out* . . . . P

Yorkshire Edition (IRE) (7x) 3-1JF N Tinkler *Mid-div; outpcd aft 9; 20l 11th & rdn 12; t.o 13; pu 14* . . . . P

OFFICIAL DISTANCES: 12l, 10l **TIME:** 6min 25.7s

73 Confined, 12st — 8 ran

DREAM OF MY LIFE (USA) (3x) 8-1 **R Morgan** *(xnb) Ld/disp frm 7; ½l 2nd 15; ld agn aft nxt; 2l up 2 out; rdn clr; comf* 1
Superior Weapon (IRE)(tt) 3-1JF **D Jewett** *Rr; 4l last 6; 3½l 5th 9; stdy prog to disp ld 14; ld nxt; hdd aft 3 out; 2l 2nd & wkng nxt; fin v tired* 10 2
Raging Torrent 5-1 **L Morgan** *Cl 3rd til disp ld brief 14; outpcd & 3l 3rd app nxt; 5l 3rd 3 out; fin tired* 1 3
Boulta (IRE)(cp) 4-1 T Oates *Ld/disp; 3l up 6; hdd nxt; 3½l 5th app 15; wknd qckly; 20l 4th at last* 8 4
Across The Card 20-1 W Ramsay *(xnb) Prom; 1l 2nd 6; 5l 6th 8; pushed along frm nxt; 6l 6th 10; outpcd frm 12; bhnd when slithered & fell 3 out* . . . F
Count Keni 3-1JF J Mactaggart *Oht; cl up til 8l last 9; sn outpcd & strugg; 15l last 12; t.o & pu 3 out; poor eff* . . . . P
Houselope Beck 20-1 Miss A Wanless *(xnb) 1st ride; 10l last 2; ur nxt* . . . U
Thats The Crack (IRE) 4-1 K Anderson *Hld up; 3l 4th 9; prog to 1l 3rd 14; 5l 4th w hd in air aft 15; wknd & pu 3 out* . . . . P

OFFICIAL DISTANCES: 12*l*, 1½*l* **TIME:** 6min 37.3s

74 Open Maiden (Div 1) — 13 ran

HALLRULE (IRE) 5-4F **Miss P Robson** *3s-5/4; ww in mid-div; 15l 5th 6; 7l 5th 9; prog to 1½l 4th 13; ld aft 3 out; 2l up at last; rdn clr* 1
Miss Mattie Ross (5a) 10-1 **R Green** *Made most; 8l up 5; ½l ahd 14; hrd prsd 3 out; hdd app nxt; kpt on; 2l down at last; no ex* 4 2
Anniejo (12a) 9-1 C Gillon *Oht; pulling; mist 1 & saddle slpd; pu 2* . . . . P
Borleagh Pilot (IRE) 10-1 L Bates *(xnb) Trckd ldrs; disp 12l 3rd app 6; 6½l 3rd 9; went cl 2nd 13; ev ch til wknd qckly aft 15; pu nxt* . . . . P
Carrow Garden (IRE) 10-1 C Dawson *Fat; a rr; mist 1; 20l 12th & pushed along when mist 7; lost tch; pu aft 9* . . . . P
French Chocolate (5a) 25-1 L Morgan *Oht; a rr; hit 1; 20l last 5; hrd rdn aft nxt; reluct & lost tch 9; t.o & pu 11* . . . . P
6P House Colours 5-1 N Saville *(xnb) Mid-div; lsng tch 12; t.o & pu 3 out* . . . P
Lethem Air 2-1 D Jewett *Oht; mid-div; prog to 6l 2nd 9; ev ch til outpcd aft 15; pu qckly 3 out; dism* . . . . P
Looking Deadly (5a) 12-1 R Nichol *Oht; a rr; strugg 9; bhnd & pu 3 out* . . P
Perfect Bear 16-1 K Anderson *Mid-div; rmdrs 9; outpcd 10; t.o 12; pu 13* . P
Red Jupiter 16-1 A Richardson *Chsd ldrs til wknd 10; mist nxt & pu* . . . . P
Scowlin Brig 9-2 S Huggan *Opened 5s; trckd ldrs; 8l 2nd app 5; 3l 3rd 3 out; 2l down & ev ch when fell nxt* . . . . F
Superstar Express (IRE) 10-1 A Findlay *Trckd ldrs; disp 12l 3rd app 6; outpcd 13; 15l 6th aft 15; bhnd & pu nxt; dism* . . . . P

OFFICIAL DISTANCE: 4*l* **TIME:** 6min 38.2s

The stewards interviewed the rider of House Colours for apparently seeking payment from the owner; his explanation that the payment was for schooling fees including diesel was referred to Portman Square who were satisfied this was in order

75 Open Maiden (Div 2) — 13 ran

NATIVE ALIBI (IRE) 5-2 **C Shirley-Beavan** *(xnb) Chsd ldrs; 30l 4th 4; 40l 4th 6; prog 12 to trck ldr aft nxt; lft in ld nxt; 1l up 2 out; stayed on wl* . . . 1
Little John 8-1 **A Richardson** *Pulling; chsd ldrs; 25l 7th 9; stdy prog to 4l 6th aft 13; sltly hmpd & lft 6l 4th nxt; went 3l 3rd 2 out; lft 2nd at last; no ch w wnr* 5 2
Miss Royello (5a) 5-2 **D Jewett** *Midfield; 45l 5th 6; went 10l 2nd brief 12; lft 1½l 3rd 14; grad wknd frm nxt; 15l 4th 2 out; lft 3rd agn at last* 10 3
Bob's Gray 12-1 F Arthur *Ld; pulling; 25l clr 7; 3l ahd aft 13; hrd prsd when fell nxt* . . . . F
Bright Dawn (IRE) (12a) 6-1 Miss A Armitage *Hld up; nt a fluent & school in rr; t.o 9; pu 2 out* . . . . P
Deep Design (IRE) 6-1 C Dawson *Fat; swtng; nt a fluent; 20l 2nd 3; stdy prog & lft 5l 5th when hmpd sltly 14; wknd qckly; wl bhnd when pu 3 out* . . P
Ginger Biscuit (7a) 8-1 P Frank *Chsd ldrs; outpcd 11; wl bhnd when bd 14* B
Harvest The Oak 8-1 T Coles *A rr; t.o & pu 14* . . . . P
Red Tyrant 9-2 Miss C Metcalfe *6s-9/2; rr; lsng tch 11; pu 13* . . . . P
Souden Lyric 8-1 K Anderson *Chsd ldrs off pce; 35l 3rd 5; stdy prog to 13; 2l 5th & ev ch when bd 14* . . . . B

Super Dolphin (7a) 8-1 R Tate *Rr; t.o 9; some prog 12; wl bhnd when bd 14* — B

Switchback (IRE) 7-1 N Saville *Chsd ldrs; 46l 6th 6; mist 11; stdy prog aft nxt; lft cl 2nd 14; 3l 2nd & btn when fell last* — F

Thorsgill 6-4F N Tinkler *2s-6/4; bhnd; stdy prog 13; 6l 8th & gng wl when bd nxt* — B

OFFICIAL DISTANCES: 4*l*, 6*l* **TIME:** 6min 44.7s

North Cornwall

Wadebridge (LH 8F,18J)

Sat, 31 Jan (SOFT)

76 Hunt Members, 12st — 8 ran

KESTICK 4-6F **Miss T Cave** *Ww; last to 6; 20l 6th ½way; wl bhnd til hdwy aft 11; went 15l 3rd nxt & 2nd app 2 out; ld last; sn clr; canter* — 1

Hasten Bak 7-2 **Miss L Gardner** *(xnb,bh) Ld til aft 1; 7l 4th ½way; went 2nd aft 11; ld aft 14; rdn 3 out; hdd last; no ch w wnr* — 8 — 2

It'snotsimple (IRE) (5a) 7-1 **Mrs T Trickey** *Ld aft 1 til hdd aft 14; ev ch 3 out; wknd nxt* — 3 — 3

Buckley's Chance (IRE) 20-1 J Tickle *(xnb) Lost plce 5; sn wl bhnd; 25l last ½way; t.o & pu aft 13* — P

Cornish Hope 33-1 A Glassonbury *(xnb) Tde; hld up; 14l 5th ½way; bhnd til fell 11* — F

Got Alot On (USA) 12-1 M Shears *Pulled hrd; went 2nd aft 4 til stpd to nil aft 11; t.o & pu aft 13* — P

Mister Cone 20-1 I Hambley *(xnb) Prom; mists 3 & 7; 4l 3rd ½way; wknd qckly aft 11; t.o & pu 15* — P

Rush Job 33-1 W Biddick *(Ran und the name TYPICAL WOMEN) Wl bhnd til fell 8* — F

OFFICIAL DISTANCES: 2*l*, 2*l* **TIME:** 6min 39.5s

77 Mens Open, 12st — 5 ran

POLAR CHAMP (7x)(bl) 4-5F **A Farrant** *Lw; went 2nd 5; ld aft 12; sn wl clr; fnce up 2 out; unchall* — 1

33P **Nearly Gold** (4x) 8-1 **G Maundrell** *Hld up; 7l 4th ½way; last & lost tch aft 11; went dist 2nd 15; nvr nr wnr* — 30 — 2

Bruthuinne (IRE) (7x) 16-1 **D McKenna** *(xnb) 2 handlers; ld to 4; 4l 3rd ½way; lost plce 12; sn wl bhnd; chall for rem 2nd 3 out; sn wknd* — 12 — 3

108 Dawn's Cognac (IRE) 8-1 Julian Pritchard *Hld up; 8l last ½way; went 12l 3rd app 12; lft 30l 2nd aft 14; last nxt; blun 2 out; t.o & pu last* — P

Sol Music (7x) 2-1 L Jefford *Bckwd; 2nd til ld 4; hdd aft 12; 25l 2nd & wkng when pu aft 14* — P

OFFICIAL DISTANCES: dist, 6*l* **TIME:** 6min 36.0s

78 Ladies Open — 6 ran

CENTO (IRE) 11-1 **Miss C Stucley** *W ldrs; lost plce & 7l 4th ½way; went 3rd aft 12 & 3l 2nd 14; rdn when mist 2 out; ld last; stayed on wl* — 1

Parte Prima 7-1 **Miss L Hawkings** *2nd to 14; 7l 3rd 3 out; rallied nxt; stayed on flat* — 1½ — 2

33F **Ballysicyos (FR)** 4-5F **Mrs O Jackson** *(xnb) Ld; 4l clr 3 out; dived lft 2 out; hdd last; nt qckn* — ½ — 3

Beadnell Bay 4-1 Miss A Goschen *Sn prom; 5l 3rd ½way; lost plce 12; 15l 4th 14; no ch aft; wl bhnd when blun 2 out; btr for rce* — 20 — 4

Romany Move 50-1 Mrs S Godfrey *A bhnd; 8l 5th ½way; lost tch 11; t.o & pu 15* — P

Wag The Brush 8-1 Miss T Cave *A bhnd; jmpd slow 2; mist 4; 10l last ½way; blun 12; t.o & pu aft 14* — P

OFFICIAL DISTANCES: ½*l*, ½*l* **TIME:** 6min 30.2s

79 Restricted, 12st — 11 ran

SIMPLY SAM 5-1 **H Fry** *(xnb) 8s-5s; hld up; stdy hdwy & 5l 5th ½way; went 2nd 13; ld 15; sn 5l clr; stayed on wl* — 1

Just Sally (5a) 4-1 **A Farrant** *A.p; went 2nd 8; ld app 12-15; sn outpcd* — 10 — 2

Beachtime 8-1 **L Jefford** *(xnb) Hld up; 7½l 7th ½way; hdwy 12; 7l 3rd 14; no imp* 10 3
Drumhorc (IRE) 7-1 Miss L Gardner *(xnb) Hld up; lost plce 6; 11l 10th ½way; hdwy u.p 12; 10l 4th 14; wknd 15* 12 4
Panto Pixie (5a) 8-1 Miss T Cave *Hld up; last to 4; 9l 8th ½way; lost tch 12; 15l 5th 15; nvr trbld ldrs* 3 5
Lingering Fog (IRE) 20-1 Miss M McCarthy *2nd to 6; 2½l 3rd ½way; wknd qckly 12; t.o 14* 25 6
37^{P} Anflora (5a) 7-2F Julian Pritchard *Hld up; 7l 6th ½way; wkng when hmpd 12; bhnd when pu 13* . . . . . P
65^{5} Carling Elect (5a) 10-1 Miss L Hawkings *(xnb) Prom; went 2nd 6-8; 3l 4th ½way; wknd qckly 13; bhnd when pu nxt* . . . . . P
Change 11-1 T Dennis *(xnb) Hld up; 10l 9th ½way; eff 12; went 12l 4th 15; wkng when mist nxt; wl bhnd when pu last* . . . . . P
Elegant Light (5a) 20-1 Miss S Robinson *2 handlers; a bhnd; t.o 8; pu 12* . . . . . P
Winning Leader (IRE) 6-1 R Skinner *Ld til hdd & blun & ur 12* . . . . . U

OFFICIAL DISTANCES: 8*l*, 6*l* **TIME:** 6min 33.1s

80 Confined, 12st — 5 ran

BILL ME UP (IRE) 7-2 **C Heard** *Ww; 2½l 3rd ½way; went 2nd 13; ld aft nxt; clr 3 out; comf* 1
Bengal Bullet (3x) 4-6F **Julian Pritchard** *Ld; clr w wnr 14; sn hdd; 7l 2nd & rdn 3 out; sn wknd; fin tired* 12 2
Squaddie 20-1 **L Heard** *Hld up; last to 9; 5l 4th ½way; went 12l 3rd aft 14; no imp* 15 3
Artic Ground (IRE) 25-1 D Doyne-Ditmas *(xnb) Hld up; releg 6l last ½way; lost tch u.p aft 11; t.o 14* 5 4
African Dawn 5-2 L Jefford *(xnb) 4s-5/2; hit 8; 2nd to 13; 12l 3rd & rdn nxt; wl bhnd when pu 15* . . . . . P

OFFICIAL DISTANCES: 20*l*, 10*l* **TIME:** 6min 38.7s

81 Intermediate, 12st — 5 ran

BRACEYS GIRL (IRE) (5a) 4-1 **Julian Pritchard** *7s-4s; lw; ww; last to 12; jnd ldrs nxt; qcknd to ld aft 15; sn in comm; rdn out* 1
Burley Don Carlos 4-5F **Miss C Stucley** *2nd/3rd til ld 13; hdd & nt qckn aft 15; stayed on frm 2 out* 5 2
Happy Team (5a) 5-1 **L Jefford** *Ld to 6 & 10-13; ev ch 14; went 7l 2nd 2 out; dem nr fin* . . . . . ¾ 3
Baldhu Jay Arr 5-1 Miss L Gardner *Hld up; hdwy 7; ld 8-10; last 12; rdn 14; wknd 3 out* 25 4
Commander Cully (IRE) 20-1 M Sweetland *(xnb) 2nd/3rd til ld 6; rn of course app 8* . . . . . R

OFFICIAL DISTANCES: 6*l*, ½*l* **TIME:** 6min 45.6s

82 Open Maiden (Div 1), 12st — 8 ran

SEA SNIPE (5a) 2-1F **Miss T Cave** *Sn prom; went 4l 2nd 8; ld 15; 5l clr when hit 3 out; rdly* 1
Gunners Mistake 3-1 **C Heard** *Hld up; 5½l 4th ½way; went 10l 3rd aft 12; hdwy 15; tk 2nd aft 2 out; nvr able to chall* 12 2
Jemannette (5a) 7-1 **T Dennis** *Ld; 5l clr to 11; hdd & stumbled bad 15; wknd 2 out* 2½ 3
Baldhu Bendy (5a) 16-1 A Glassonbury *A bhnd; 11l 7th ½way; t.o & pu 14* P
Hayling Star (5a) 14-1 M Sweetland *20s-14s; tde; ss; a wl bhnd; 20l last ½way; rdn 11; t.o & pu 12* . . . . . P
Menantol 7-1 R Morgan *2nd to 8; 5l 3rd ½way; lost plce u.p aft 11; bhnd when pu 12* . . . . . P
Pauls Legacy 7-1 D McKenna *Hld up; 8l 6th ½way; hdwy & 6l 4th when fell 12* F
Whats Up Maid (5a) 12-1 M Munrowd *(xnb) Hld up; 7l 5th ½way; hdwy 11; wknd qckly aft 12; pu 14* . . . . . P

OFFICIAL DISTANCES: 12*l*, 2*l* **TIME:** 6min 47.4s

83 Open Maiden (Div 2), 12st — 8 ran

BISHOP'S BLADE 2-1F **Miss S Gaisford** *(xnb) 3s-2s; ld 2-8; ld 9; rdly* . . . 1
O'ech (5a) 7-1 **C Heard** *Mist 2; 2nd/3rd til lost plce 8; 11l 4th ½way; rallied u.p & 5l 3rd 14; went 2nd app 3 out; ev ch last; one pce* 3 2

Go Positive (5a) 11-4 **L Heard** *Hld up & pulled hrd; hdwy 7; ld 8-9; ev ch 15; wkng when blun 2 out* . . . 20 3
Knockaun Wood (IRE) 8-1 M Sweetland *Chsd ldrs; 10l 3rd ½way; 15l 4th & rdn 14; sn t.o* . . . 25 4
Buddy Bear (IRE) 9-1 M Shears *Hld up; 12l 5th ½way; mist & lost tch 12; t.o 14; pu 2 out* . . . P
Silver Kracker 10-1 M Woodward *Ld to 2; 2nd to 6; stpd to nil und much tail swishing sn aft; t.o & pu 9* . . . P
Tom Dove 10-1 M Munrowd *A bhnd; 15l last ½way; rdn 11; t.o & pu 13* . . . P
Young Harry 9-2 L Jefford *Hld up; bhnd til pu 9; lame* . . . P

OFFICIAL DISTANCES: 3l, 6l **TIME:** 6min 51.0s

Royal Artillery

Larkhill (RH 13F,18J)

Sat, 31 Jan (GOOD becoming GOOD to SOFT)

84 King's Troop RHA Members, 2m4f, 12st - 15J 10 ran

CAPRIOLE (U) (5a) 6-4F **J Grantham** *3s-6/4; less cobby than rest; lkd fit; chsd ldrs; til ld brief 3; hdd nxt; ld 11; hdd last; ld agn flat w rdr lkng at rnr-up; cheeky* . . . 1
Brummel (U) 8-1 **N Collier** *(b4) Fat; pulling; 5th 4; chsd ldr frm 6; ld app last; sn hdd; a hld flat* . . . ¾ 2
Benetton (U) 6-1 **Miss B Tunley** *Ld to 3; disp ld agn nxt til lft in ld 7; hdd 11; ev ch til no ex app last* . . . 4 3
Champagne (U) (5a, 1ow) 8-1 J Chick *(orbs) 9th 1; hdwy 10; 5th nxt; cl up til no ex frm 2 out* . . . 1 4
Honiton (U) (5a) 9-1 C Mason *(xnb,orbs) 4th 4; cl up til wknd frm 2 out* . . . 10 5
Cheltenham (U) (5a) 8-1 Miss J Illingworth *(orbs) Chsd ldrs til grad wknd frm 2 out* . . . ½ 6
Churchill (U) 10-1 Miss C Trim *(orbs) A bhnd; t.o frm 12* . . . 25 7
Centurian (U) 11-2 Miss E Bridge *A bhnd; t.o frm 9; jmpd lft nxt; plodded home* . . . runin 8
Cleopatra (U) (5a) 4-1 Miss K Lancaster *(orbs) Prom; 2nd 3; disp ld nxt til ur 7* U
Happisburgh (U) 8-1 N Cross *Sa; climbed 1; detach last when ref nxt* . . . r

OFFICIAL DISTANCES: ½l, 2l **TIME:** 6min 59.0s **TOTE:** £1.50

All the horses for this race were late to the paddock for which the Commanding Officer of the King's Troop was fined £55

85 Hunt Members, 12st 3 ran

CARRINGTON HOUSE 4-1 **J O'Rourke** *Settled last; jmpd rt 9; clsd to ld 15-nxt; rdn & outpcd when lft clr last; plodded on* . . . 1
9⁵ **Alltime Dancer (IRE)** 7-4 **C Lambert** *(bnh) Prsd wnr to 15; kpt on one pce frm nxt; lft 2nd at last* . . . 4 2
Flora Macdonald (5a, 2ow) evensF H Wallace *2nd Pointing ride (other was in 2000 - 3rd ride in all) Ld to 15 & agn nxt; 4l clr & in comm when hit last & rfo; event tkn back & cont for bad 3rd but Judge had lft box* . . . U

OFFICIAL DISTANCE: 3l **TIME:** 6min 47.4s **TOTE:** £4.20

86 Open Maiden 567&8yo (Div 1), 12st 8 ran

12F **SPANISH DOLPHIN (IRE)** (7a) 2-1F **Miss P Gundry** *(xnb) Opened 3s; lw; pulled hrd & nt a fluent; went 2nd 5; ld 8; drew clr aft 2 out; mist last* . . . 1
Trumper 11-2 **P York** *Tchd 7s; a 2nd/4th; 2nd when jmpd slow 15; lft 2nd agn nxt; rdn & ev ch 2 out; v one-pcd* . . . 2 2
Radbrook Hall (7a) 12-1 **P Callaghan** *2 handlers; hrd hld & cl up; hit 13; 5th & ev ch app 15; wknd qckly nxt* . . . 15 3
Coffee Morning (IRE) 20-1 H Dowty *Hrd hld; in tch to 12; 15l last when blun & nrly ur 15; plugged on; ev ch of 3rd when blun agn last* . . . 12 4
20U Bloowit 20-1 M Legge *(xnb) Jmpd mod in rr; last when mist 6; t.o nxt; pu 13* P
Captain Wildow (IRE) (7a) 9-4 J Snowden *4s-9/4; 2 handlers; trckd ldrs; went 2nd app 15; ev ch jmpng when lost hind action jmpng 3 out; collapsed w back inj a stride later; destroyed* . . . F

Noble Action (7a) 7-2 N Williams *Hld up in rr & nt fluent; mist 8; eff 13; 4l 6th app 15; sn wknd; pu 2 out* . . . . P

Tudor Lucky Boy 10-1 N Mitchell *Set crawl 1; hdd 8; 2nd til stpd to nil app 15; pu 3 out; dism* . . . . P

OFFICIAL DISTANCES: 2*l*, 20*l* **TIME:** 6min 39.2s **TOTE:** £2.60

87 Open Maiden 567&8yo (Div 2), 12st — 13 ran

VINNIE BOY (IRE) 7-1 **Miss P Gundry** *Hld up gng wl; clsd to jn ldr 13; prsd ldr 15 til ld last; rdn & stayed on wl*. 1

Court Adjourn 10-1 **S Morris** *Tchd 12s; ld 3-5; stdd to trck ldrs; ld agn 15 til drvn & hdd last; kpt on* 1¼ 2

35[3] **Kayleigh (IRE)** (5a) 11-4 **P York** *Hld up; last 9; rap prog 13; cl up aft; 1l 3rd app last; nt qckn* 5 3

13[2] Roseacre (IRE) 8-1 D Alers-Hankey *Tchd 10s; cl up to 13; 5l 7th & wkng 15; eased app last* 20 4

The Luddite 20-1 H Dowty *Prom; 3l 6th 15; sn fdd* 8 5

Frere Du Cure 25-1 R Bliss *(xnb) Bckwd; nvr btr than midfield; wknd 12; t.o last 15; pu 2 out* . . . . P

Lord Ken (IRE) 12-1 N Phillips *Tchd 14s; bckwd; ld to 3 & 5-9; 10l 8th & wkng 15; ref & ur 2 out*. . . . . r

21[4] Lord Of The North (IRE) 20-1 N Benstead *Hit 5; handy; ev ch 13; cl 3rd when pckd 3 out; sn wknd; 8l 4th when rfo last* . . . . U

Rosetta (5a) 25-1 J Jenkins *Chsd ldrs to 10; t.o & pu 3 out*. . . . . P

Saffron Hill (IRE) (7a) 8-1 F Hutsby *Hdwy to ld 9; hdd app 3 out; sn wknd; pu last* . . . . P

The Jam Saheb 25-1 J Snowden *Jmpd slow 6; rr aft; t.o & pu 13*. . . . . . . P

Upton Crusader 20-1 S Joynes *(xnb) A bhnd; lost tch 13; t.o & pu 2 out* . . P

13[F] Wild Chimes (IRE) (7a) 5-4F N Williams *3s-5/4; lw; pulling in last til blun & ur 4* . . . . U

OFFICIAL DISTANCES: 1*l*, 5*l* **TIME:** 6min 35.4s **TOTE:** £2.00

88 Ladies Open — 7 ran

10[4] **SIR D'ORTON (FR)** 5-2 **Miss C Tizzard** *Went 2nd 6; ld 14; slt advant & drvn frm 2 out; kpt on game; lkd to be hdd nr fin* 1

Tales Of Bounty (IRE) 4-5F **Miss R Green** *5/4-4/5; mists 2 & 3; settled last pr til eff 13; chall 15; prsd wnr hrd frm nxt; rdn & stayed on flat; lkd to ld nr fin* hd 2

10[5] **Alska (FR)** (5a) 25-1 **Miss W Southcombe** *Rcd wide; cl up; disp 2nd & ev ch 3 out; wknd tame nxt*. 15 3

Storm Castle (IRE) 4-1 Miss J Wickens *Hld up & handy; 3rd 9; cl up 13 til wknd 3 out* 10 4

18[P] Robbie's Adventure 25-1 Miss E James *Mostly last; lost tch 12; brief eff 14; wknd agn aft nxt*. 7 5

Prah Sands 25-1 Mrs L Young *(xnb) Ld to 14; wknd rap; t.o & pu last* . . . . P

33[P] Sadler's Realm 14-1 Miss J Buck *Ur some way aft 1*. . . . . U

OFFICIAL DISTANCES: ½*l*, 3*l* **TIME:** 6min 23.5s **TOTE:** £1.80

89 Mens Open — 17 ran

11[3] **ABERFOYLE PARK (IRE)** 3-1 **D Jacob** *Opened 4s; midfield til impd qckly to 4th 7; ld 12; hrd prsd frm 14 til lft clr 3 out; unchall; impressive* 1

11[1] **Always On The Line (IRE)** 7-2 **A Merriam** *Settled 2nd/4th; w ldr 9-12; wknd nxt; 12l 4th 15; lft rem 2nd aft 3 out*. 25 2

Woodlands Beau (IRE) 8-1 **T Dreaper** *Bhnd; 13th & rdn 5; plugged into 30l 6th 15; staying on at fin; no ch w ldrs*. 12 3

11[2] Red Brook Lad 5-4F N Mitchell *Opened 2s in plce; hld up towards rr; hit 6; eff 12; wknd nxt; 10l 4th 15; fin tired*. 4 4

11[F] Arlequin De Sou (FR) 16-1 R Stephens *2nd/3rd til ld 6-12; wknd rap 14; rem last when pu last* . . . . P

Be My Dream (IRE) 25-1 P Cowley *Midfield; wknd 12; t.o & pu 14*. . . . . . P

11[U] Chism (IRE) 100-1 W King *A wl bhnd; lost tch 7; t.o 10; rn out & ur 3 out* R

Colombian Green (IRE) 50-1 G Barfoot-Saunt *Midfield; wknd 12; t.o & pu 14* P

Hot Plunge 25-1 J Owen *Cl up to 11; wknd aft nxt; pu 14*. . . . . P

Macgyver (NZ) 33-1 J Diment *Pulled hrd; ld to 6; wknd rap; t.o & pu 10*. . P

Mouseski 10-1 N Williams *(xnb) Midfield; 8th 7; eff 11; chall 13 til stpd to nil aft 15 & climbed nxt; pu 2 out*. . . . . P

Perching (IRE) 50-1 M Sheridan *Sn hopeless t.o; 2 fncs bhnd when pu 11.* P

Right To Reply (IRE) 3-1 N Harris *(xnb) 20s-3s; midfield; 9th 7; hdwy 11; pulled to chall 14; ev ch when ur 3 out; rn v wl* . . . . U

Rustic Revelry 20-1 C Whittaker *(xnb) A wl bhnd; 15th 5; t.o & pu 13* . . . P

Susies Melody (IRE) 20-1 R Bandey *A strugg bad; 16th 5; t.o 10; pu 13*. . P

Touring-Turtle (IRE) 33-1 W Procter *(xnb) Sis; 14th 5; t.o & pu 13* . . . . . . P

17[3] Travelling Jack 20-1 J Young *Chsd ldr to 7; qckly lost plce & blun 9; pu 10* P

OFFICIAL DISTANCES: 20*l*, 15*l* **TIME:** 6min 19.0s **TOTE:** £6.00

90 Intermediate, 12st — 9 ran

36[1] **KINGSTON-BANKER** 5-4F **D Jacob** *6/4-5/4,opened 5/2 in plce; lw; hdwy to 2nd 5; ld 10 til aft 12; ld agn 14; drew clr app 3 out; stayed on stdly*. . 1

19[P] **Live Wire (IRE)** 10-1 **P York** *Went 2nd/3rd 5 til ld aft 12; hdd 14; jmpd delib aft; wl hld by wnr* 10 2

Owenabue Valley (IRE) (5x) 10-1 **T Underwood** *Hld up in rr; hdwy 9 to 4th aft 12; 3rd & flatt 14; 13l 3rd & btn u.p nxt*. 10 3

Brockbuster 6-1 E Walker *(xnb) Rn in snatches; 5th & outpcd aft 12; 20l 5th 15; kpt on agn frm 2 out; no ch w ldrs* 1½ 4

37[1] Highway Oak 13-8 N Mitchell *Opened 2s; hdwy frm rr to ld 5-10; 3rd & wkng aft 12; 18l 4th 15; tired & eased flat* 20 5

O'flaherty's (IRE) 50-1 W Kavanagh *Towards rr; strugg 11; cont hopeless t.o frm 13* 40 6

Ashburton Lord (IRE) 66-1 M Legge *Tk keen hld & ld to 5; sn strugg in rr; t.o 9; pu 14*. . . . . P

Bright Flash (IRE) 50-1 D Luff *Lw; prsd ldrs to 10; wknd rap; pu 15* . . . . . P

Gutsy Dalton (IRE) 16-1 J Young *Tubed; t.o 6; pu 14* . . . . P

OFFICIAL DISTANCES: 4*l*, 10*l* **TIME:** 6min 27.0s **TOTE:** £2.50

Albrighton

Weston Park (LH 7F,18J)

Sun, 1 Feb (GOOD to SOFT)

91 Hunt Members — 6 ran

ASHGAN (IRE) 10-11F **R Burton** *Settled last to 9; a gng wl; clsd app 14 to ld 3 out; rdn app last; kpt on wl*. 1

Sharlom (IRE) 9-4 **W Hill** *Mist 3; settled towards rr; clsd 11; ev ch 14 til rdn & nt qckn app last*. 1½ 2

Mr Kermit 4-1 **Miss S Sharratt** *Hld up; clsd 11; nt fluent 13; ld app 15; hdd nxt; drvn & wknd app last* 8 3

35[P] Run River Run (5a)(bl) 33-1 S Graham *Swtng profuse & lkd dreadful; ld & 8l clr; jmpd rt 9 & sn u.p; blun bad 11 & hdd; lsng plce rap when crashing fall 12* . . . . F

Skippers Canyon (5a) 33-1 J R Barlow *Grad lost gd plce; strugg aft 11; t.o 13; pu aft 2 out*. . . . . P

Wraparound You (IRE) 16-1 S Prior *Pckd 2; went 2nd 5; ld aft 11 til hdd & nt fluent 15; wknd rap; t.o & pu aft 2 out* . . . . P

OFFICIAL DISTANCES: 2*l*, 8*l* **TIME:** 6min 56.0s

92 Intermediate, 12st — 11 ran

MEL IN BLUE (FR) 5-2 **S Waley-Cohen** *(xnb) 6s-5/2; lw; mist 1; jmpd safely aft; went 2nd 4; ld 6; rdn & stayed on str frm 2 out; impressive* 1

Finder Keeps (USA) 9-1 **J Jenkins** *Bckwd; midfield; blun 12; clsng grad aft & went 2nd 15; sn rdn; no imp app last; kpt on game* 2½ 2

Arctic King 8-1 **A Wintle** *Ur in false start & bolted; prom; 4th 13; 12l 3rd 3 out; no ch aft*. 15 3

48[7] Borderline Breeze (IRE) 20-1 Miss H Watson *Imm strugg; t.o 6; pu 14*. . . . P

Browns Boy 25-1 M Jackson *Ur padd; mounted on course & ld round start; jmpd slow in rr; sn t.o; pu 11*. . . . . P

Gee A Two (IRE) 14-1 N Chapman *(xnb) Midfield til ur 12*. . . . . U

Genereux(cp) 14-1 S Blackwell *Bckwd; sn wl bhnd; t.o 12; pu 15*. . . . . . . P

Life Of A River (IRE) 6-1 T Greenall *Tk keen hld in 3rd/4th; eff 13; prsd ldrs 15; wknd aft nxt; rem last when pu last*. . . . . P

Mister Moss (IRE) (5x) 4-1 G Hanmer *Ur in false start & bolted; ld; 6l clr 4; hdd 6; prsd wnr to 13; wknd qckly & eased; pu 14* . . . . P

Petrouge(cp) 2-1F R Burton *4s-2s; bckwd; midfield; outpcd when blun 11; mist 12; t.o & pu 14* . . . . P

Springwood White 12-1 Miss H Kinsey *Sn wl bhnd; t.o 12; pu 15* . . . . P

OFFICIAL DISTANCES: 2½l, dist **TIME:** 6min 41.0s

93 Mens Open — 19 ran

BAY ISLAND (IRE) 5-1 **A Wadlow** *Lw; 2nd til ld 5; clr w rnr-up when mist 15; drew ahd 2 out; rdly* 1

Irilut (FR)(cp) 2-1F **S Waley-Cohen** *Mist 5; cl up; went 2nd 11; prsd wnr til rdn 3 out; wl hld nxt* 8 2

An Capall Dubh (IRE) 5-1 **A Crow** *Lw; tk keen hld; 3rd when mist 5; nt fluent 12; ev ch til 4th & rdn app 14; sn wknd* 15 3

Brown Esquire 20-1 C Barlow *Prom; 6th 11; wknd 14; t.o.* 30 4

Oneanthreequarters (IRE) 10-1 R Jagger *Lw; stdd start & a t.o* 20 5

Benick (IRE) 33-1 W Hill *Mist 1; a bhnd; t.o when jmpd slow 10; pu nxt.* . . P

Caught At Dawn (IRE) 6-1 T Weston *Hld up & bhnd; prog 8; 8th 11; wknd 13; t.o & pu 2 out; btr for rce* . . . . P

Hors Concours (NZ) 33-1 N Oliver *(xnb) Wl bhnd early; 7th & prog 11; sn wknd; blun 13; t.o & pu nxt* . . . . P

Jemaro (IRE) 4-1 R Burton *Bckwd; set str pce; hdd 5; 8l 5th & wkng 13; t.o & pu 3 out* . . . . P

Jolly Jack (IRE) 33-1 R Hodges *(xnb) Midfield early; wknd u.p 9; t.o 11; blun bad nxt & pu lame* . . . . P

Knock It Back (IRE) 10-1 J Handley *(xnb) 2 handlers; midfield; mist 7; 13th & strugg 11; t.o & pu 14* . . . . P

Nicholls Cross (IRE) 8-1 G Hanmer *(xnb) Lw; hld up in rr; hdwy 5; 5th 11; eff & disp 2nd brief 14; wknd tame u.p nxt; t.o & pu 2 out* . . . . P

Pagermar (IRE)(tt) 14-1 R Cooper *Wl bhnd; 14th & drvn 11; blun bad 12; t.o & pu 14* . . . . P

Pekan Polly (5a) 33-1 J R Barlow *Mist 2; sn t.o; pu 11* . . . . P

Phyllis (5a) 20-1 D Greenway *Wl bhnd early; 9th 11; rchd mod 5th 14; nvr nr ldrs; t.o & pu 3 out* . . . . P

Raconteur (IRE) 16-1 W Puddifer *Midfield til 10th & wkng 10; t.o & pu 14* P

34[P] Smile Pleeze (IRE) 16-1 A Wintle *Nt keen in rr; t.o 6; pu 10* . . . . P

34[7] Tubber Roads (IRE) 14-1 J Diment *Handy brief; drpd to rr 8; 11th 11; t.o & pu 14* . . . . P

Wild Edric 14-1 A Beedles *Midfield til 12th & strugg 11; t.o & pu 15* . . . . P

OFFICIAL DISTANCES: 8l, dist **TIME:** 6min 40.0s

94 Ladies Open — 15 ran

ASK THE NATIVES (IRE) evensF **Miss C Roddick** *Hld up; stdy hdwy 8; went 12l 2nd 12; clsd grad & jmpd ahd w huge leap 3 out; imm clr; eased flat* 1

Cascum Lad (IRE) 20-1 **Miss S Holmes** *Midfield; 7th 11; outpcd til stayed on stout aft 3 out; went 2nd app last; no ch w wnr; game eff* 12 2

Euro Bob (IRE) 12-1 **Mrs A Rucker** *20s-12s; pulled hrd & cl up in chsng group; 5th 13; outpcd 15; kpt on stdly app last desp rdr* 12 3

Pennyahei (5a) 3-1 Miss S Beddoes *Bit bckwd; ld til app 7; drpd back 7th 13; kpt on agn 2 out; nd; btr for rce* 1 4

Jackie Jarvis (IRE) (5a) 13-2 Mrs K Diggle *Lw; rcd keen; hdwy to ld app 7; sn clr; 15l ahd 11; 3l up 15; hdd nxt; sn wknd.* 1 5

5[8] Dellone 50-1 Miss T Clark *Handy in chsng group; 4th 13; went 6l 3rd nxt; outpcd when nt fluent 15; sn wknd; fin lame* 4 6

Justin Mac (IRE) 16-1 Miss K Wood *Towards rr; 10th 11; no ch frm 13* . . . 6 7

Zamhareer (USA) 12-1 Miss T Harrison *Well bhnd; t.o 9; u.p 11; rem 10th 13* 15 8

Slaney Native (IRE) 12-1 Miss M Mullineaux *Sn wl bhnd; t.o last 9* . . . . . . dist 9

Dunston Heath (IRE) 50-1 Miss A Blake *Ss; wl t.o til jmpd slow & rfo 10.* . . U

Guest Alliance (IRE) 50-1 Miss R Reynolds *Prom til 7th & niggled 9; sn wknd; t.o & pu aft 13; lame* . . . . P

Midy's Risk (FR) 14-1 Miss S Davies *Bhnd; 8th 11; clsd stdly 13-14; nvr nr ldrs; t.o & pu 2 out* . . . . P

Nashville Star (USA)(vis) 50-1 Miss H Lewis *(xnb) Bckwd; prom; chsd clr ldr app 7-12; 8th & fdng bad 14; t.o & pu 2 out* . . . . P

The Proud Pound 50-1 Miss H Kinsey *Ur 4* . . . . U
Wychnor King (IRE) 50-1 Mrs D Caine *Bckwd; a bhnd; t.o 9; ur 13* . . . . . . U

OFFICIAL DISTANCES: 10*l*, 12*l* **TIME:** 6min 41.0s

95 Restricted, 12st — 17 ran

37^F **JIMMY CRICKET** 6-1 **N Oliver** *14s-6s; cl up; 5th when blun bad 9; ld aft 13; forged clr frm 3 out; hrd drvn needlessly app last; r.o game* 1
37^3 **Sutton Courtenay (IRE)** 6-1 **J Diment** *Hit 5; prsd ldrs; went 2nd aft 13; ½l down 3 out; sn wknd; tired & poor 2nd when nrly ref last* 25 2
2^6 **Donrico (IRE)** 5-1 **A Beedles** *Wl bhnd; rem 8th aft 13; plugged on as others defaulted* 3 3
Jubileeman (IRE) 20-1 Miss H Phizacklea *Cl up; 6th 8; lost plce nxt; mod 6th aft 13; plugged on* 6 4
What Will Be (IRE) 10-1 W Hill *(xnb) Sn bhnd; t.o 10; forced on app last to complete* . . . . dist 5
Bobtail (IRE) (7a) 4-5F R Burton *2nd/3rd til ld 8-9; disp ld when blun & ur 12* U
Highlands II (FR)(tt) 10-1 T Greenall *Ld to 7; 3rd aft 13; wknd rap; pu nxt* P
Hill Of Kilfeacle (IRE) 14-1 C Barlow *(xnb) Sis & wl bhnd; mist 5; t.o 10; pu 15* P
Lily Brown (5a) 12-1 Mrs S Johnson *Bit bckwd; midfield; prog 10; 5th aft 13; went cl 3rd 15; wknd aft nxt; poor 3rd when ref & ur last* . . . . r
Lord Castle (IRE) 10-1 A Wintle *A bhnd; t.o 10; pu 15* . . . . P
My Native Knight (IRE) 5-1 A Wadlow *(xnb) Tkn stdly in midfield; 4th & prog aft 13; 1l 3rd & gng wl 3 out; stpd to nil & pu nxt; choked* . . . . P
Robert The Rascal 20-1 J R Barlow *Swtng bad; sis; rem in last pr; t.o 10; ur 12* U
Rooneyran 12-1 S Joynes *A wl bhnd; t.o 10; pu 14* . . . . P
Satanas (FR) 7-1 G Hanmer *(xnb) Cl up to 11; 7th & wkng rap aft 13; pu nxt* P
Spizzichino 14-1 K Pearson *A wl bhnd; t.o last 10; pu 13* . . . . P
2^{11} Templenoe Hare (IRE) 12-1 R Cooper *Prom; ld 10; w ldr when blun & ur 12* U
Top Weld 12-1 Miss S Beddoes *A wl bhnd; t.o 6; pu 11* . . . . P

OFFICIAL DISTANCES: dist, 2*l* **TIME:** not taken

96 Confined Maiden (Div 1), 12st — 12 ran

HOME TOR 7-2JF **Miss S Beddoes** *Made virt all; urged along frm 2 out; hld on game flat* 1
Welcome News (5a) 7-2JF **B Shaw** *Hld up in midfield; nt fluent 12; went 4th & gng wl 14; tk 2nd aft 3 out; chall last; kpt on; outrdn* . . . . s hd 2
Ironbridge 5-1 **S Ross** *(xnb) Tubed; 2 handlers; tde; pulled v hrd; chsd ldrs; mist 7; went 2nd & nt fluent 12 til 3rd & lkd wkng 2 out; rallied app last & flatt brief; sn wknd* 12 3
Heathyards Element 4-1 G Hanmer *Tk keen hld; chsd ldr til stdd app 7; 6l 6th 13; went 4th & rdn 15; sn no resp* 8 4
4^P Mosscroft Jack 16-1 D Greenway *(xnb) Settled 3rd/4th; jb rt 5; nt fluent 10; ev ch 14; wknd qckly* 20 5
Bless Yourself (IRE) 4-1 A McArdle *Nt fluent in rr; 13l 8th 13; some prog aft 3 out; still last nxt; wl btn when ur last* . . . . U
Gosh Josh (IRE) 8-1 W Hill *Sn bhnd; 9th 10; blun bad & ur 11* . . . . U
No Keep (IRE)(tt) 8-1 C Barlow *3rd/4th til 2nd 10-12; 6th & wkng when mist 14; t.o & pu 3 out* . . . . P
Raiseapearl (2ow) 14-1 I Clyde *Fell 2* . . . . F
Ridware Rose (5a) 10-1 Miss S Sharratt *Last trio; t.o when jmpd v slow 9; jmpd slow agn nxt; pu 13* . . . . P
Superior Footwork (1ow) 6-1 P Morris *Oht; pulled hrd; nt fluent in last trio; blun 11; 10l 7th & brief eff 14; sn lost tch; pu nxt* . . . . P
Troubleinallenwood (IRE) (7a) 12-1 D Cook *Bckwd & lkd dreadful; ref 1; cont til pu 4* . . . . r

OFFICIAL DISTANCES: nk, 2*l* **TIME:** 7min 13.0s

97 Confined Maiden (Div 2), 12st — 12 ran

MASTER CLUB ROYAL(bl) 11-10F **G Hanmer** *Lw; 2nd & clr of rest til ld 12; 12l ahd 13-15; hdd u.p & nt keen aft 3 out; lkd btn til rallied & lft in ld app last; stayed on one pce* 1
Benbow 9-1 **B Shaw** *Hld up & bhnd; prog to 20l 4th 11; 15l 3rd 15; clsd gng wl to ld 2 out; lkd in comm til hung bad lft & hdd app last; nt rec* 5 2

Form	Runner	Dist	Pos
7^{4}	**Cousin George** 7-2 **R Burton** *Pulled hrd towards rr; mod 6th 11; went 20l 4th 13; rdn & short-lived eff 2 out*	10	3
30^{R}	Shaking Chief (IRE) 5-2 A Wintle *6s-5/2; trckd ldrs; went 3rd 10; 15l down 13; tk 2nd nxt; nd & wknd 3 out*	4	4
	Hokey Wokey 20-1 W Hill *Midfield early; 9th & strugg 11; plodded on wl bhnd*	5	5
	Iadora (5a) 10-1 Miss T Clark *A bhnd; 7th 11; 35l last 15; plugged on* . . .	6	6
	Brombil Lady (5a) 33-1 Miss R Reynolds *(xnb) 2 handlers; bckwd; ld & clr early; hdd 12; wknd rap; pu 14*		P
	Cool Archie 8-1 S Ross *Sn strugg in last pr; tlng off when pu 12*		P
	Coppice Lane (5a) 33-1 A Wadlow *Detach last til rn out 5*.		R
	Mervsintrouble(cp) 33-1 C Barlow *Detach 3rd til bad mist 9; 4th nxt; slpd up on turn bef 11*		S
	Ridware Boy 25-1 J R Barlow *4th when mist 5; 25l 5th & wkng 11; t.o & pu aft 13*.		P
	The Sky Is Blue 25-1 M Caldwell *Nt fluent in rr; 9th 8; slt mist & rfo 11*. .		U

OFFICIAL DISTANCES: 4*l*, 5*l* **TIME:** 7min 05.0s

Cambridge University Draghounds

Cottenham (RH 9F,19J)

Sun, 1 Feb (GOOD)

98 Hunt Members — 7 ran

Form	Runner	Dist	Pos
23^{P}	**HIGHLAND ROSE (IRE)** (5a) 11-10F **Ms A Embiricos** *(xnb) Tchd 6/4; ld 3; made rest; drew clr frm 12; v easy*		1
	Borrow Mine (IRE) 7-2 **Miss L Marriott** *Chsd ldrs; outpcd 10; disp mod 3rd frm 13 til went 2nd 2 out; no ch w wnr*.	35	2
	Ballad (IRE) 8-1 **G Haines** *Bit bckwd; 1st ride; set off last; in tch to 9; poor 5th final circ til stayed on frm 2 out; tk 3rd at last*	5	3
	Fiolino (FR) 4-1 Miss R Page *(xnb) 1st ride; ld to 3; chsd ldrs aft; outpcd 11; disp mod 3rd frm 13; chall for 2nd when mist & nrly ur 2 out; fdd*	7	4
	Campbellhill (IRE) 10-1 A Williams *Facing wrong way start; pulled hrd & prsd wnr 4; outpcd frm 13 & jmpng lft; wknd & lost 2nd 2 out; fin v tired*. . .	25	5
	Ardnut 16-1 R Page *(xnb) Last when mist & rdr up in air 6; sn t.o; crawled over fncs final circ; sprinted into v rem 6th nr fin*	400y	6
	J W (U) (5a) 33-1 Miss J Mills-Hewitt *(xnb) 1st ride; in tch to 7; t.o 10; disp hopelessly t.o last final circ; lkd sure to fin 6th til hdd nr fin*	4	7

OFFICIAL DISTANCES: dist, 3*l* **TIME:** 6min 20.4s **TOTE:** £2.60 **DF:**£4.10

99 Intermediate, 12st — 10 ran

Form	Runner	Dist	Pos
19^{4}	**SHEILA MCKENZIE** (5a) 8-1 **T Lane** *Mist 1; prom; chsd ldr & mist 9; chall frm 13; rdn & lkd hld in 5l 2nd 2 out; stayed on wl flat; ld last 20yds*. .		1
23^{1}	**The Red Boy (IRE)** (5x) 2-5F **A Braithwaite** *Trckd ldr; ld 6; clr w wnr frm 13; 5l up & btr j 2 out; 6l up last; rdn flat; hung rt & dogged it furiously; hdd last 20yds*.	1	2
	Offshore (IRE) 12-1 **P Cowley** *Chsd ldrs; went 3rd 13; outpcd by ldng pr & no imp aft; plugged on*.	20	3
	Oxendale (10x) 14-1 P Bull *Keen early; in rr; clsd & in tch 10; outpcd 13; nd aft; plugged on*.	2½	4
	Jack Of Kilcash (IRE) (5x) 7-1 N Benstead *Ld to 6; stdly lost plce frm 10; t.o last 15; snatched rem 5th on line*.	25	5
	Persian Hero (IRE) 7-1 J Owen *Rr til clsd & in tch 10; outpcd 13; nd aft; rem 5th 2 out; dem to last on line*.	s hd	6
28^{P}	Ballylesson (IRE) 33-1 N Moore *Chsd ldrs til wknd aft 12; 7th & lsng tch rap when pu 14*.		P
	Castle Road (IRE) 33-1 H Fowler *(xnb) A last pr; t.o 7; miles bhnd when pu 15*		P
	Claywalls 33-1 Miss O Maylam *Rdr waving at sev fncs; t.o in last pr 7; miles bhnd when pu 15*.		P
6^{9}	Going Primitive 33-1 P Callaghan *(xnb) Prom; chsd ldr 8-10; imm wknd u.p; pu 12*.		P

OFFICIAL DISTANCES: 1*l*, 15*l* **TIME:** 6min 14.5s **TOTE:** £17.80 **DF:**£4.30

The stewards fined the rider of The Red Boy £125 for not riding his mount out to achieve the best possible placing

100 Mens Open — 12 ran

OMNI COSMO TOUCH (USA) 7-1 **N Saville** *Hld up in rr group; stdy prog frm 9; went 4th 14; eff to tk 2nd 2 out; narrow ld last; rdn clr flat* 1

Little Farmer 9-2 **P Hall** *2 handlers; ld; hit 2; jnd 16; just hdd last; kpt on wl flat; a hld; rn wl* 3 2

3[2] **Cape Stormer (IRE)** 10-1 **M Gorman** *16s-10s; prom; prsd ldr 13; upsides frm 16; releg to cl 3rd 2 out; still ev ch last; wknd final 100yds* 5 3

Freedom Fighter 20-1 A Martin *Prom; chsd ldr 9; mist 11; lost 2nd 13; sn outpcd; kpt on agn flat* 2 4

Splash And Dash (IRE) 10-11F A Hickman *Trckd ldrs; went 3rd 13; 4l 3rd 3 out; tried to cl app nxt; sn wknd* 8 5

Route One (IRE) 8-1 P Cowley *Bit bckwd; nt a fluent in rr; lost tch by 13; no ch aft; plugged on frm 2 out* 12 6

Belvento (IRE) 12-1 M Sheridan *Mostly chsd ldr to 9; rdn & lsng plce nxt; wl in rr & toiling frm 14* 5 7

Northern Fleet 33-1 J Sole *Chsd ldrs; u.p & strugg 10; wl in rr frm 13* . . . 1 1/2 8

Esprit De Cotte (FR) 16-1 P York *Chsd ldrs; 6th & in tch 13; sn outpcd; no ch aft; wknd frm 3 out* 8 9

3[P] La Colina (IRE) 20-1 James Tudor *(xnb) Settled in rr; fell 7* . . . . . F

Leatherback (IRE) 12-1 J Owen *Reared in padd; settled in last group; lsng tch when pu 13; easy rn* . . . . . P

Vain Minstrel (IRE) 8-1 E Linehan *Bit bckwd; chsd ldrs; lost plce 6; rr when hit 9; wknd 12; t.o aft til pu 3 out* . . . . . P

OFFICIAL DISTANCES: 3*l*, 3*l* **TIME:** 6min 05.8s **TOTE:** £7.80 **DF:**£35.20

101 Ladies Open — 6 ran

SUPREME CITIZEN (IRE) 8-11F **Miss J Williams** *Disp ld at slow pce 5-9 & agn 13 til ld aft 16; clr 2 out; eased flat* 1

25[4] **The Wiley Kalmuck (IRE)** 7-1 **Miss Z Turner** *Ld/disp at slow pce to 9 & agn 12 til aft 16; btn when hit 2 out; just kpt 2nd* 6 2

24[3] **Gatchou Mans (FR)** 6-1 **Ms A Embiricos** *(xnb) Cl up; ld 9-12; outpcd 14; 12l 3rd 3 out; kpt on flat & nrly snatched 2nd* . . . . . nk 3

Stylish Dave (NZ) 8-1 Mrs D Rowell *(xnb) Jmpd sticky & bhnd early; clsd & in tch 6; outpcd 13; jmpd v slow 15; 27l 4th 3 out; r.o wl agn flat* 10 4

Grand Ambition (USA) 8-1 Miss L Allan *Pu 2; tack problems* . . . . . P

Ical (IRE) (5a) 7-1 Miss C Rogers *1st ride; jmpd big & rfo 1* . . . . . U

OFFICIAL DISTANCES: 8*l*, nk **TIME:** 6min 23.7s **TOTE:** £2.20 **DF:**£2.30

102 Restricted, 12st — 10 ran

STEP AND RUN (IRE) 7-1 **Miss J Williams** *(xnb) Mist 5; prom; chsd ldr 10; mist nxt; lost plce 12; rnwd eff 16; chsd ldr 3 out; disp cl 2nd at last; urged along & kpt on wl flat; ld final strides* 1

Pa Pierre (IRE) 3-1 **D Dunsdon** *5s-3s; hld up; stdy prog 12; trckd ldr 15; eff 2 out; disp 2nd last; rdn to ld flat; hdd final strides* . . . . . hd 2

Banana Ridge (5a) evensF **C Mulhall** *Opened 5s (10s in plce, off boards later); settled rr; prog 10; ld & pckd 15; 3l up & lkd in comm 2 out; rdn app last; hdd & wknd flat* 3 3

Killiney Bay (IRE) 10-1 P York *(xnb) Chsd ldr to 10 & agn 12-14; wl in tch 3 out; wknd app nxt* 15 4

River Bailiff (IRE) 10-1 Mrs J Gordon *Made most to 15; wknd qckly aft 3 out* 12 5

7[1] Gray Knight (IRE) 9-2 James Tudor *Cl up; outpcd 16; wknd nxt; sn bhnd* . . 1 6

2[7] Give Him A Chance (IRE) 14-1 N Moore *In tch til wknd 10; sn t.o; pu 14* . P

2[8] Imperial Prince 10-1 Miss K Smith *Disp 8th & in tch when fell 9* . . . . . F

The Grey Baron 20-1 P Bull *W ldrs til wknd rap 16; pu nxt* . . . . . P

What's The Problem (IRE) 8-1 S Spice *(bf) Mist 1; sn bhnd; t.o & pu 11* . . P

OFFICIAL DISTANCES: hd, 3/4*l* **TIME:** 6min 12.5s **TOTE:** £12.30 **DF:**£5.40

103 Open Maiden 8yo&up, 12st — 14 ran

LONGVILLE LAD 2-1F **P Cowley** *(xnb) Swtng; jmpd lft; made virt all; drew clr 14; in comm 3 out; r.o wl flat; fin w plenty in hand* 1

No Reward (IRE) 10-1 **A Hickman** *(xnb) Last group early; prog to 4th 1/2way; lft 22l 3rd 13; nt pushed & no prog til r.o to tk 2nd aft 2 out; no ch w wnr* 30 2

Form	Runner	Dist	Pos
	Tea Time (IRE) 12-1 **T Lane** *Bit bckwd; mists; prom; chsd wnr 8; blun 11; no ch w wnr frm 15; v tired & mist 2 out; sn dem*	10	3
	Latterly (USA) 20-1 I Bostock *(xnb) Settled rr; t.o 5th 1/2way; plodded rnd*	25	4
	Bailey's Of Cashel (IRE) 9-2 D Dunsdon *Chsng ldrs when hmpd bad & nrly brought to standstill 7; nt rec; crawled over 9 & pu*		P
	Granny Dick (5a) 8-1 H Fowler *Fell 1*		F
	Itsthebrass (5a) 20-1 G Wigley *Oht; sn last; jmpd appalling to 3; t.o & pu 4*		P
	Niteattheworkhouse (IRE) 14-1 C Thomson *Midfield when ur 5*		U
	Private Percival 10-1 P Blagg *Chsng ldrs when fell 7*		F
	See Red Billdan (IRE) 10-1 P Callaghan *2 handlers; chsd wnr to 8; 3rd when tried to rn off course bend aft 12; drpd to rr; t.o & pu 15*		P
26^{4}	Sister Ali (IRE) (5a) 8-1 S Gordon-Watson *Chsng ldrs when bd 7*		B
6^{P}	Society Scandal (IRE)(tt) 6-1 P Millington *10s-6s; a rr; last pr & wl bhnd 1/2way; ploughed on miles bhnd til pu last*		P
	The Flying Dragon (5a)(tt) 7-1 S Spice *Wl in rr; disp poor last 1/2way; sn t.o; v rem 5th when ur 16*		U
	Tidal Race (IRE) 12-1 N Moore *Chsd ldrs; wkng in 6th 1/2way; t.o & pu 14.*		P

OFFICIAL DISTANCES: dist, 10*l* **TIME:** 6min 27.7s **TOTE:** £2.40 **DF:**£46.60

104 Open Maiden 56&7yo (Div 1), 2m4f, 12st - 13J — 10 ran

Form	Runner	Dist	Pos
	IT'S MISSY IMP (12a) 10-1 **A Martin** *2 handlers; sn cl up; 3rd 5; disp ld (w 3 others) when mist 3 out & drpd to 4th; rallied nxt; ld last; stayed on wl*		1
8^{3}	**Drumdowney Lad (IRE)** (7a) 10-11F **P York** *Hld up; 9l 5th 8; prog nxt; disp ld 3 out & nxt; ld aft 2 out; hdd last; rdn flat; fnd nil*	5	2
	To The Top 5-1 **James Tudor** *Jmpd slow 1; ld 2-8; prsd ldr aft; disp agn 3 out; cl 3rd 2 out; still cl up last; one pce*	1 1/2	3
7^{F}	Rash Moment (FR) (7a) 10-1 C Ward-Thomas *Prsd ldr; ld 8; jnd 3 out; still ev ch 2 out; wknd app last.*	7	4
	Pusey Sance 10-1 J Newbold *Prom; 6l 4th 8; outpcd by ldng 4 frm 10; wknd app 2 out; fin tired*	35	5
	Half A Story (5a) 10-1 A Williams *Swtng; set off last; detach in last pr 5; sn t.o*	12	6
	Almazard 5-1 C Gordon *(xnb) Rr; mist 4; strugg frm 6; t.o 9*	15	7
	King Of The Sea (IRE) 10-1 A Merriam *(xnb) Chsd ldrs; lost tch frm 9; sn bhnd; poor 7th when pu last*		P
	Naughty Noah 5-1 P Cowley *Keen; ld 1; stdd; no room & rn out nxt*		R
	Shot Of Jollop (IRE) (7a) 8-1 N Bloom *(xnb) Jmpd slow 1 & 3; in tch til wknd & jb lft 8; t.o & pu 3 out*		P

OFFICIAL DISTANCES: 3*l*, 5*l* **TIME:** 4min 48.0s **TOTE:** £16.80 **DF:**£17.80

Fences 3 & 12 omitted - damaged

105 Open Maiden 56&7yo (Div 2), 2m4f, 12st - 15J — 9 ran

Form	Runner	Dist	Pos
12^{4}	**SONNANT (FR)** (7a) 6-4F **P Cowley** *Made all; clr w rnr-up 3 out; pushed along & stayed on wl flat*		1
	Nailed On (7a) 8-1 **A Martin** *2 handlers; in tch; prog 10; chsd wnr aft 11; 5l down 2 out; trying to cl & mist last; no imp aft.*	8	2
	Lady Baronette (5a) 4-1 **I Howe** *2 handlers; warm; disp 2nd to 6; sn drvn; grad lost plce; poor 6th 12; kpt on u.p to 3rd agn flat*	25	3
21^{P}	Donnini (IRE) 12-1 P Millington *(xnb) Tchd 20s; mostly in rr; outpcd in midfield frm 12; disp poor 3rd when mist 2 out; no prog aft*	10	4
	Alfie Moon (IRE) 5-2 T Lane *Trckd ldrs; went 2nd 9; hit 11 & drpd to 3rd; wknd 2 out*	5	5
	Trouble Loves Me (IRE) 14-1 J Newbold *Bit bckwd; disp 2nd to 6; sn wknd; wl bhnd aft; t.o*	10	6
	Inching Brook 8-1 P Taiano *(xnb) 2 handlers; drpd to detach last pr 6; schooled round wl t.o*	15	7
	Northall Lad 7-1 L Morgan *Bit bckwd; bucked rdr off in padd; disp 2nd to 6; sn wknd; 7th 9; t.o & pu 3 out*		P
	Queen's Shilling (5a) 10-1 P Hall *Jmpd slow & detach 1-3; t.o 7; crawled over 10 & pu*		P

OFFICIAL DISTANCES: 6*l*, 20*l* **TIME:** 4min 50.0s **TOTE:** £3.00 **DF:**£23.10

Midlands Area Club

Thorpe Lodge (LH 7F,19J)

Sun, 1 Feb (GOOD, STICKY in places)

106 Midlands Area Club Members, 12st — 10 ran

Form	Horse / Details	Dist	Pos
	NAUTICAL LAD (3x) 3-1 **J Docker** *Hld up; 16l 6th ½way; shkn up & hdwy aft 12; went 2nd aft nxt; ld 15; all out*		1
	Marston Moses 10-1 **A Bealby** *Ld; clr w a rival to 13; hdd 15; rdn 3 out; ev ch last; r.o wl nr fin*	½	2
	Fisherman Jack (7x) 3-1 **M Mackley** *Sn wl bhnd; 23l last ½way; stayed on frm 16; lft 17l 4th 2 out; went 3rd flat; nvr nrr*	20	3
	Minella Hotel (IRE) (3x) 7-1 R Cope *(xnb) Lw; hld up; 17l 7th ½way; hdwy 12; 2l 3rd 14; wknd aft 3 out*	4	4
	Weavers Choice 10-1 A Sansome *2nd til aft 13; sn lost plce; wl bhnd 16*	8	5
54^U	Stevie Dee 20-1 O Williams *Chsd ldrs; 12l 3rd ½way; wknd 14; wl bhnd 16; t.o*	15	6
	Euro Alert (IRE) 11-4F S Morris *(bh) Prom; mist 2; 13l 4th ½way; lost plce 12; rallied 14; 3½l 4th 16; wkng when pu 2 out; btr for rce*		P
1^P	Noble Colours 25-1 N Pearce *Still bckwd; hld up; 20l 8th ½way; hdwy 14; 7l 5th & rdn 16; wkng when pu 3 out*		P
	Preferred (IRE) 33-1 R Armson *Bckwd; nd; 15l 5th ½way; wknd aft 13; bhnd when pu 15*		P
58^U	Prince Mouse (1ow) 25-1 J Howard *(xnb,bf) Bhnd til fell 7*		F

OFFICIAL DISTANCES: 2*l*, 10*l* **TIME:** 6min 48.8s

107 Mens Open — 13 ran

Form	Horse / Details	Dist	Pos
45^R	**J-OKAY (IRE)** 14-1 **T Stephenson** *Hld up; last to 6; stdy hdwy & 5l 7th ½way; 4l 6th 14; jnd ldrs 16; ld 2 out; forged clr flat*		1
	Mr Pendleberry 6-1 **N Tinkler** *A.p; 2l 3rd ½way; ld 14-2 out; no ex flat*	8	2
	Parahandy (IRE) 9-1 **H Dowty** *Jnd ldrs 6; 2½l 4th ½way; went 2nd 12 til drvn 14; 3½l 5th 16; stayed on one pce frm 3 out*	2½	3
	Bold Tactics (IRE) 9-2 M Keel *Hld up; hdwy 8; 3½l 5th ½way; lft 2nd & ev ch 16; 2l 3rd 2 out; wknd flat*	nk	4
	Westerton (IRE) 7-1 F Hutsby *Ld 6-14; 2nd til blun 16; wknd 3 out*	15	5
	Araminta (5a) 5-4F M Mackley *3s-5/4; a bhnd; 9l 10th ½way; rdn & lost tch 12; 12l last 16; strugg on; subsq fnd to have a fracture of her pelvis; has been retired*	5	6
	Joy For Life (IRE) (5a) 16-1 Julian Pritchard *Ld to 6; 2nd to 12; 2½l 4th 14; wknd 16*	8	7
	Bold Action (IRE)(bl) 33-1 D Smith *Drpd to rr 6; lost tch 8; 25l ½way; t.o & pu 13*		P
	Folliday (FR) 25-1 R Wakeham *Hld up; mist 7; hdwy & 4l 6th ½way; mist 13; 6l 8th nxt; wkng when fell 15*		F
	Maquilleux 14-1 E Walker *Chsd ldrs; 5th when fell 6*		F
	Rosey Boy (IRE) 25-1 N Tutty *Prom; jmpd slow 4; mist & lost plce 9; 8l 9th & rdn ½way; lost tch 12; pu 13*		P
	Royaltino (IRE) 6-1 M Harris *Hld up; 7l 8th ½way; eff & 5l 7th 14; 5l 6th 16; wkng when pu 3 out*		P
	Young Tomo (IRE) 20-1 L Hicks *Prom; 3rd when rn out 6*		R

OFFICIAL DISTANCES: 4*l*, 2*l* **TIME:** 6min 41.7s

The connections of J-Okay, whose passport was found to be incorrect, was fined £70

108 Ladies Open — 8 ran

Form	Horse / Details	Dist	Pos
	WHETHER THE STORM (IRE) 6-1 **Miss E Jones** *Lw; hld up; 3½l 5th ½way; went 3rd 12; lft 2nd 16; rdn to ld aft 3 out; sn clr; stayed on wl*		1
17^2	**Find Me Another (IRE)** 7-2 **Miss A Stennett** *Swtng; ld til hdd aft 3 out; sn btn*	8	2
33^1	**Upton Adventure** (5a) 4-5F **Miss E James** *Lw; nvr gng wl; 3l 4th ½way; shkn up 11; lost plce u.p & 9½l 5th 14; lft 10l 3rd 16; no imp.*	15	3
	Lucky Master (IRE) 33-1 Miss G Swan *50s-33s; hld up; hdwy 8; 2l 3rd ½way; wknd & 14l 6th 14; lft poor 4th 3 out*	12	4
	Gortroe Guy (IRE) 25-1 Miss K Robinson *(xnb) Tde; last 4; lost tch 8; 22l last ½way; t.o 14; pu 2 out*		P

Mullensgrove 6-1 Miss S Phizacklea *Lost plce 6; mist 9; 10l 6th ½way; hdwy u.p 13; went 9l 4th nxt; stpd to nil 16; pu 3 out* . . . . P
Nokimover 14-1 Miss Gemma Hutchinson *Pulled hrd; prsd ldr til rn out 16* R
Silk Vestments (5a) 50-1 Miss H Dunning *(xnb) Ss; last to 4; jnd ldrs 6; lost plce 8; 20l 7th ½way; t.o when rfo 15* . . . . U

OFFICIAL DISTANCES: 10*l*, 20*l* **TIME:** 6min 37.9s

109 PPORA Club Members Restricted, 12st — 11 ran

CATECHIST (IRE) 9-4F **Julian Pritchard** *4s-9/4; ld 1-3; 2nd/3rd til ld aft 9; drvn & r.o wl flat* 1
Coolefind (IRE) 7-2 **S Morris** *Hld up & pulled hrd; 8½l 8th ½way; hdwy when mist 13; 2l 4th nxt; went 2nd 3 out; ev ch last; nt qckn* 1½ 2
65^{3} **Sissinghurst Star (IRE)** 14-1 **P Mann** *(xnb) Prom; went 2nd 7; ld brief 9; 3l 3rd ½way; 2½l 5th 14; 8l 4th 3 out; went 3rd at last; stayed on* 8 3
Budle Bay 7-2 R Cope *6s-7/2; 2 handlers; hld up; hdwy & 5l 4th ½way; went 2l 3rd 11 & 2nd 15 til rdn 3 out; 5l 3rd & wkng nxt* 10 4
Carebec (IRE) (5a) 14-1 M Mackley *Hld up; mists 7 & 9; 12l 10th ½way; lost tch u.p 11; wl bhnd when pu 13* . . . . P
Claire's Nomad(cp) 14-1 Miss Rachel Clark *(xnb) W ldrs; lost plce & 7l 6th ½way; mist 13; 7l last nxt; wknd 16; 20l 5th 2 out; pu last* . . . . P
Kalahari Ferrari 16-1 T Stephenson *Hld up; last to 4; mist 8; 11l 9th ½way; bhnd til hdwy & 6l 7th 14; in tch when pu nxt; lame* . . . . P
37^{P} Mister Bruce (IRE) 6-1 F Hutsby *Ld to 1; jmpd slow 5; mist 6; 5½l 5th ½way; lost plce 12; bhnd when pu 13* . . . . P
Paddy Bettalot 7-1 M Harris *Hld up; 8l 7th ½way; hdwy & 3½l 6th 14; wknd 16; wl bhnd when pu 2 out* . . . . P
Ricky B 12-1 W Kinsey *(xnb) Mist & nrly ur 2; ld 3-9; 2nd to 15; wknd qckly app 3 out; t.o & pu last* . . . . P
Waterloo Leader (IRE) 14-1 D Smith *Nt jw; lost tch 5; t.o 9; pu 11* . . . . . . P

OFFICIAL DISTANCES: 2*l*, 8*l* **TIME:** 6min 48.2s

110 PPORA Club Members (Nov Rdrs), 12st — 10 ran

32^{5} **GUIGNOL DU COCHET (FR)** 3-1 **G Slade-Jones** *7s-3s; a.p; lft 4l 2nd 7; ld 14-15; ld 16; drew clr 2 out; comf* 1
River Ness (5a) 8-1 **Mrs V Thirlby** *Chsd ldrs; 3½l 4th ½way; mist & nrly ur 13; went 4l 3rd 15; chsd wnr 2 out; no imp* 8 2
17^{5} **Picket Piece**(bl) 12-1 **M Goldstein** *2nd til ld aft 6; hdd & mist 14; ld 15-16; sn drvn; 5l 3rd 2 out; no ex* 2 3
34^{9} Drum Battle (3x) 2-1F T Messenger *Chsd ldrs; 2l 3rd ½way; 6l 4th & rdn 15; wknd app 3 out* 20 4
Better Future (IRE) (3x) 5-1 J Taylor *A wl bhnd; hit 1; rdn 6; 25l 7th ½way; 33l 7th 14; t.o 16; fin w flourish* 1½ 5
32^{U} Perfect Finisher 25-1 Miss R Lobley *Rdr lost iron & lost tch 5; 26l 8th ½way; 32l 6th 14; t.o.* 8 6
Energy Man 50-1 M Bennison *(xnb) Missed break; a wl bhnd; 20l 6th ½way; 20l 5th 14; sn wknd; releg last 2 out; t.o.* 20 7
31^{U} Nelsun 14-1 A Corbett *(xnb) Ld; rdr nrly f.o & lost irons 4; hdd aft 6; regained irons but rfo 7* . . . . U
Superior Risk (IRE) 12-1 R Stearn *Hld up; 7l 5th & rdn along ½way; lost tch 12; stpd to nil & pu 13* . . . . P
Welburn Boy(bl,tt) 25-1 Miss L Allfrey *1st ride; missed break; sn wl bhnd; t.o 5; pu 15* . . . . P

OFFICIAL DISTANCES: 10*l*, 2*l* **TIME:** 6min 50.7s

111 Open Maiden (Div 1), 12st — 12 ran

COOLE GLEN (IRE) 5-2F **S Morris** *4s-5/2; hld up & pulled hrd; hdwy to ld aft 5; 4l clr 15; drew away und hands & heels flat* 1
Fast Lane Harry (IRE) 8-1 **R Wakeham** *(xnb) A.p; mist 2; 2½l 3rd ½way; went 2nd 11; one pce 3 out* 8 2
Arctic Summer (IRE) 14-1 **J Trice-Rolph** *Ld til hdd aft 5; 2nd to 11; 6l 3rd 14; mist 15; one pce aft* 5 3
Tommy Hotspur (IRE) 6-1 N Docker *Chsd ldrs; 10l 5th ½way; went 6l 3rd aft 15; one pce aft* 1 4

Rosie Stroud (IRE) (5a) 12-1 Julian Pritchard *Hld up; lost tch & 17l 9th 1/2way; 16l 8th 14; wl bhnd 16; t.o* . . . 25 5

Coral Bay 8-1 R Cope *Hld up; jmpd slow 4; 11 1/2l 7th 1/2way; hmpd & lost plce 13; 20l last nxt; pu 15* . . . P

Fancy A Buck (5a) 5-1 M Mackley *10s-5s; 2 handlers; hld up; jmpd slow 3; 13l 8th 1/2way; in tch when fell 13; fracured nk vertebrae; has been retired* F

Festival Time 4-1 L Hicks *Hld up; 11l 6th 1/2way; hdwy 13; 7l 4th when mist nxt; wknd 16; 20l 6th 3 out; mist 2 out; t.o & pu last* . . . P

Horatio (IRE) 20-1 W Kinsey *(xnb) Hld up; hdwy 5; 5th when rfo 7* . . . U

New Lodge Express (IRE) 3-1 T Stephenson *(xnb) 10s-3s; hld up; last to 8; 19l 10th 1/2way; hdwy to 10l 7th 14; rn out 16* . . . R

No Mour Fooling 16-1 Miss L Robson *Hld up & bhnd; last 8; 25l last 1/2way; pu 12* . . . P

Two By Four 14-1 N Pearce *Swtng; prom; 5l 4th 1/2way; mist & rmdrs 11; 9l 6th & rdn 14; wknd & 13l 5th 3 out; pu 2 out* . . . P

OFFICIAL DISTANCES: 7*l*, 7*l* **TIME:** 7min 02.4s

The stewards interviewed the rider of New Lodge Express who appeared to pull up three fences from home; they accepted his explanation that the horse had actually run out

112 Open Maiden (Div 2), 12st — 14 ran

51^{U} **MISTY RAMBLE (IRE)** 100-30 **G McPherson** *Lw 2; mist & nrly ur 8; 10l clr 1/2way; unchall* . . . 1

66^{5} **Keegan Bearnais (FR)** 12-1 **T Mann** *(xnb) A 2nd/3rd; chsd wnr 14; no imp* 15 2

37^{4} **Nickit (IRE)** 3-1F **S Morris** *(xnb) Hld up & bhnd; 29l 8th 1/2way; rdn 13; 21l 8th nxt; went 20l 4th 3 out & 3rd flat; nvr nrr* . . . 7 3

The Green Goblin (NZ) 10-1 Julian Pritchard *(xnb) Hld up; 26l 7th 1/2way; hdwy & 16l 5th 14; went 15l 3rd 16; disp 12l 2nd 3 out; wkng when mist nxt* . . . 3 4

Midnight Moon 20-1 J Burley *A wl bhnd; 33l 12th 1/2way; rdn 13; 23l 9th nxt; t.o* . . . runin 5

Berry Hill Boy (IRE) 14-1 M Keel *A wl bhnd; mist 6; 31l 10th 1/2way; rdn 12; t.o & pu 16* . . . P

Claude (IRE) 14-1 M Briggs *(xnb) Sn prom; 2nd when mist 7; 13l 3rd 1/2way; lost plce aft 12; 17l 6th 14; 22l 5th & wkng when mist 16; pu 3 out* . . . P

Coombs Spinney 12-1 J Docker *Bckwd; a wl bhnd; 32l 11th 1/2way; 24l 10th 14; t.o & pu 16* . . . P

Gollinger 100-30 B Woodhouse *Chsd ldrs; 17l 4th 1/2way; went 15l 2nd 12; wknd rap 14; wl bhnd when pu 16* . . . P

59^{U} Lord Jurado (IRE) 33-1 O Williams *(xnb) V reluct to rce; set off fnce bhnd; pu 4* P

Red Rookie 10-1 M Mackley *A bhnd; 30l 9th 1/2way; 28l 11th 14; t.o & pu 15* P

Retribution 20-1 M Harris *2 handlers; swtng; ld to 2; lost plce 5; 22l 5th 1/2way; 18l 7th 14; wl bhnd 16; t.o & pu last* . . . P

Rundetto (IRE) 20-1 S Moreton *A wl bhnd; mist 1; 36l last 1/2way; t.o & pu 11* P

Supreme Vintage (IRE) 12-1 J Botham *Wl bhnd til hdwy & 23l 6th 1/2way; went 14l 3rd 14; wknd qckly 16; pu 3 out* . . . P

OFFICIAL DISTANCES: 10*l*, 8*l* **TIME:** 6min 54.4s

113 Open Maiden (Div 3), 12st — 10 ran

CASHEW CACHE (IRE) 7-1 **M Wall** *A.p; went 2nd 9; ld 14; rdn 3 out; mist 2 out; hdd last; rallied to ld nr fin* . . . 1

Jenny's Charmer 4-1CF **F Hutsby** *Hld up; 8l 6th 1/2way; hdwy & 5l 3rd 13; went 5l 2nd aft 16; ld last til hdd & no ex nr fin* . . . 3/4 2

51^{F} **Northsprite**(cp) 4-1CF **J Trice-Rolph** *(xnb) 2 handlers; ld til hdd aft 2; 2nd to 9; 4l 3rd 1/2way; lost plce & 10l 5th 14; wl bhnd 16; tk poor 3rd at last* 25 3

It's Norman 7-1 M Mackley *Hld up & bhnd; 11l 7th 1/2way; 11l 6th 14; went 12l 4th 16; nvr nr to chall* . . . 8 4

Billymax (IRE) 4-1CF R Wakeham *(xnb) 12s-4s; 2 handlers; 2nd til ld aft 2; hdd 14; 5l 2nd when mist 16; wknd 3 out* . . . 1 5

Clodagh Valley (IRE) 8-1 W Kinsey *(xnb) A bhnd; 12l last 1/2way; lost tch 12; t.o & pu 2 out* . . . P

58^{4} Cloudkicker (IRE) 12-1 A Pennock *Chsd ldrs; 6l 5th 1/2way; wknd & 12l 7th 14; t.o & pu last* . . . P

Currow Kate (5a) 5-1 L Hicks *8s-5s; hld up; hdwy & 5l 4th 1/2way; 8l 4th & mist 14; sn wknd; wl bhnd when pu 3 out* . . . P

Polly Tino (5a) 16-1 N Pearce *(xnb) Pu bef 1* . . . . P

51U Sales Dodger (IRE) 16-1 Miss S Carter *Rdr lost control start; rn out 1* . . . . . R

OFFICIAL DISTANCES: 1*l*, dist **TIME:** 7min 03.3s

Tango Bojangles (Miss L Robson, 10-1) was withdrawn not under orders; a truly shambolic start with three horses clearly ahead of the Starter as he dropped the flag, and those who rightly anticipated it would be declared a false start lost all chance

Tiverton

Chipley Park (RH 7F,18J)

Sun, 1 Feb (GOOD with SOFT patches with standing water)

114 Hunt Members — 3 ran

JABIRU (IRE) (5x) 1-6F **D Edwards** *Tchd 1/5; lw; cl up/disp ld til ld aft 12; drew clr aft 15; jmpd lft aft; hvly eased flat* 1

Rosalee Royale (5a) 9-1 **L Heard** *Bit bckwd; slt ld/disp to 12; in tch til mist 14; sn one pce* 5 2

Now Young Man (IRE) (5x) 5-1 **M Heuff** *Bit bckwd; cl 3rd mostly; hdwy 13; 2nd brief & mist 15; wl hld in 3rd when slt mist 3 out* 3 3

OFFICIAL DISTANCES: 10*l*, 3*l* **TIME:** 6min 49.0s

115 Mixed Open, 12st - 17J — 11 ran

MISS O'GRADY (IRE) (5a, 7x) 7-4F **M Miller** *Tchd 9/4; handy; cl 4th ½way; smooth hdwy 15; rdn to ld 2 out; drvn clr by-passing last* 1

Cherokee Run (IRE) (7x) 11-2 **Miss C Tizzard** *Tchd 6s; slt ld til aft 14; cl 3rd & rdn 3 out; stayed on game to 2nd agn 2 out* 3 2

34U **Le Cure** 8-1 **R Woollacott** *(xnb,ringbit) In tch; 3l 3rd 9; went 2nd 13; slt ld 15-16; ev ch til wknd 2 out* 5 3

Hobbycyr (FR) 3-1 Miss P Gundry *Tchd 4s; trckd ldr til lost plce 12; 4th & rdn 15; kpt on one pce frm 3 out* 4 4

Cherokee Boy 33-1 M Atkinson *Cl 5th ½way; no prog frm 13* 10 5

Fou Doux (FR) 25-1 N Wilmington *(xnb) Midfield; 6th 11; 25l 7th 15; no prog* 15 6

Royal Barge (7x) 9-1 M Barber *Opened 14s; lw; 8th ½way; 30l 10th 15; nd* 1 7

Kingdom Of Shades (USA) 14-1 A Phillips *Bit bckwd; bhnd frm 6; t.o 11 til pu 16* . . . . P

64P Lilardo (5a) 50-1 L Heard *(xnb) Midfield; just in tch in 7th 9; sn lost ground; 8th 15; bhnd when pu 3 out* . . . . P

Minderoo 13-2 A Farrant *16s-13/2; lw; hld up off pce; 10th 9; some hdwy when mist 13; poor 9th 15; bhnd when pu 3 out* . . . . P

34P Robins Pride (IRE)(bl) 25-1 S McHugh *Hld up towards rr; 9th ½way; hdwy to 5th when slt mist 14; wknd nxt; bhnd when pu 2 out* . . . . P

OFFICIAL DISTANCES: 3*l*, 4*l* **TIME:** 6min 27.0s

Fence 18 omitted - damaged

116 Intermediate, 12st — 16 ran

12 **THE KINGS FLING** (5x) 11-10F **Miss P Gundry** *(xnb) Opened 7/4; a handy; cl 6th on inner 9; hdwy to 3l 3rd 15; crept clsr on inner to chall 2 out; ld last; stayed on wl flat* 1

191 **Mensch (IRE)**(cp) 11-4 **E Williams** *(xnb) In tch; cl 3rd 9; ld 12 til rdn & jnd 2 out; no ex u.p app last* 2½ 2

Leon Garcia (IRE) (5a) 20-1 **T Bishop** *Hld up; hdwy to 5th 9; went 3rd 12; 1l 2nd & gng wl 15; disp 16-17; no ex app last* 3 3

Briary Boy (IRE) 25-1 Miss A Goschen *(xnb) Bit bckwd; rr; t.o 9; 11th 13; r.o past btn horses clsng stages; nrst fin* . . . . runin 4

33P Soul King (IRE) 12-1 R Bliss *Tchd 20s; midfield; 8th 6; no prog; poor 8th 15; nt rch ldrs* 2 5

Krystal Tip (5a) 10-1 Miss L Gardner *(ringbit) Tde; towards rr in wl grouped field; 8th 12; 7th 15; wl btn when wandered lft run-in* . . . . ½ 6

Silver Pot Black 16-1 M Barber *Ld/disp to 11; lost ground & 4th aft nxt; 6th 15; no ch aft* 4 7

19^{P}	Makhpiya Patahn (IRE)(cp) 20-1 D I Turner *(xnb) Rmdrs in mid-div aft 2; rn in snatches; drvn to disp 9th; sn dogged it agn & drvn along; no ch frm 15*	3	8
	Alexander Nevsky 50-1 D Dennis *(xnb) Bit bckwd; bhnd til pu 14*		P
19^{3}	Buckland Boy (5x) 6-1 T Vaughan *Hdwy to 3rd 6; 3l 2nd 12; wknd & 12l 4th 15; wl btn 4th when tried to ref, got stuck on fnce & ur 2 out*		r
	Glen Mist (IRE) 20-1 R Woollacott *Last & rdn 4; bhnd til pu 8*		P
	Rubian Princess (5a) 25-1 D Jones *10th 5; bhnd til pu 12*		P
	Russian Connection (IRE) (5x) 33-1 A Ward-Thomas *Bckwd; rr; bhnd frm 9; fnce bhnd 12; t.o & pu 14*		P
	Skip 'n' Tune (IRE) (5a) 8-1 M Miller *(boh) Lw; midfield; cl 7th 11; 5th 15; nt rch ldrs; btn 5th when hmpd bad 2 out & pu*		P
	Sporting Chance 16-1 M Munrowd *Bit bckwd; trckd ldr; disp 5; lost plce 7; bhnd when pu 12*		P
	Thunder Thighs (5a) 20-1 N Wilmington *(xnb) 2 handlers; prom til lost ground qckly 5; pu nxt*		P

OFFICIAL DISTANCES: 2*l*, 6*l* **TIME:** 6min 26.0s

117 Dodson & Horrell PPORA Club Members, 12st - 17J — 9 ran

	UNLIMITED FREE (IRE) (4x) 10-1 **Miss D Harding** *(xnb) Jw; ld 4; made rest in slt ld; kpt on wl when prsd frm 2 out; veered sharply lft cl home*		1
	Polka 10-1 **D Edwards** *Lw; rcd keen; hld up towards rr; hdwy to 4th 7; cl 4th 14; eff aft 15; sn rdn; $1\frac{1}{2}$l 2nd when pckd 2 out; no ex flat*	$2\frac{1}{2}$	2
16^{1}	**Quickswood (IRE)** (7x) 9-4F **G Maundrell** *Tchd 5/2; hld up in tch; cl 3rd on outer frm 7; went 2nd 13; ev ch 3 out; no hdwy u.p frm 2 out*	2	3
	Maggies Brother (7x) 4-1 D Barlow *Tchd 5s; prom til lost ground 8; 6th 13; wl btn 6th 3 out*	25	4
	Blackwater Brave (IRE) 8-1 H Fry *In tch towards rr; hdwy to 5th 13; unable to cl frm nxt; btn 5th when pu last*		P
	Coole'sabbot (IRE) 10-1 M Walters *Ld to 4; chsd ldr til wknd 8; bhnd when pu 13*		P
63^{R}	Father Jim 20-1 Miss C Tizzard *Prom; slt mist 2; disp 5th $\frac{1}{2}$way; rmdrs 10; blun & ur 11*		U
32^{6}	Frank Byrne (4x) 4-1 Miss A Goschen *Lw; in tch til lost ground 7; last 8; poor 7th 15; bhnd when pu last*		P
	Jentar Equilibra (IRE) (5a) 11-4 R Woollacott *(xnb) Opened 4s; lw; hld up towards rr; impd 8; went 2nd 9; cl up & ev ch til wknd rap aft 15; bhnd when pu last*		P

OFFICIAL DISTANCES: $2\frac{1}{2}$*l*, $2\frac{1}{2}$*l* **TIME:** 6min 34.0s

Fence 14 omitted - damaged

118 Restricted, 12st — 13 ran

14^{3}	**LITTLE NATIVE (IRE)** 8-1 **Miss P Gundry** *(xnb) 2 handlers; lw; hld up towards rr; 7th 12; gd hdwy to 2nd 13; disp ld nxt; cl 2nd & rdn 3 out; lkd hld frm 2 out til rallied on inner & drvn to ld cl home*		1
40^{1}	**Rhythm King** 7-4F **G Maundrell** *(xnb) Tchd 2s; lw; midfield; prog to 4th 12; 3rd & gng wl 14; eff & slt ld 3 out; lkd wnr til hit last; hdd nr post*	$\frac{3}{4}$	2
	Mister Swallow 4-1 **M Miller** *7s-4s; tk keen hld; ld to 5 & agn frm 8; disp ld 14 til wknd & rdn 3 out; tired when blun 2 out; eased*	12	3
44^{U}	Sootsir 25-1 R Hawker *(xnb) Towards rr; 8th 12; no prog; bhnd frm 15*	25	4
	Askers Jack 10-1 N Mitchell *Handy on outer; 5th 9; lost plce 12; poor 7th 15*	$1\frac{1}{2}$	5
	Almost A Day(bl) 10-1 D Mansell *Sn bhnd; t.o 4 til pu 15*		P
37^{P}	Alpenstock (FR) 14-1 D I Turner *Chsd ldr til ld 5-7; cl 4th 10; 5th & rdn 12; lost ground stdly frm 13; pu 15*		P
14^{P}	Hawkers Hill 14-1 Miss A Goschen *Prom; cl 3rd 10; lost plce 13; 25l 5th 15; pu 3 out*		P
14^{4}	Horrified 7-1 D Edwards *Midfield; 6th 13; went 5th nxt; nt rch ldrs; poor 6th when pu 3 out*		P
63^{P}	Iceni Queen (5a) 33-1 Miss S Robinson *Towards rr when blun & ur 9*		U
	Kilvoydan (IRE)(cp) 10-1 D Phelan *Rr; 9th 12; t.o & pu 14*		P
65^{9}	Mrs Peggoty (5a)(bl) 10-1 L Jefford *(xnb) Rr; slt mist 4; t.o & pu 9*		P
	Pulham Downe 16-1 Miss E Tory *Bit bckwd; sn wl in tch; cl 3rd $\frac{1}{2}$way; wknd 15; wl hld in 4th 3 out; pu last*		P

OFFICIAL DISTANCES: 1*l*, 8*l* **TIME:** 6min 31.0s

119 Open Maiden (Div 1), 12st — 15 ran

	HUG THE BEND 8-1 **D Edwards** *(xnb) Hld up; midfield; went 5th 11; prog in 4th aft 15; chall on inner 2 out; disp ld last; nt much room & hmpd cl home; fin nk 2nd; awarded rce.*		1
	A Romp Too Far (IRE) 7-1 **R McCarthy** *Patient rdn; 6th 11; went 4th 14; prog to 2nd & rdn 3 out; disp ld aft nxt til slt ld & edged rt cl home; won by nk; dem to 2nd by stewards.*	*	2
	Cargo Flight 2-1F **A Farrant** *Tried to make all; 2½l ld & rdn app 3 out; wknd & hdd aft 2 out*	6	3
	Strong Finish 12-1 Miss E Tuck *A.p; cl 3rd 9-11; 10l 3rd 13; lost ground aft 15; kpt on one pce*	8	4
	Sound Sense 12-1 J Young *5th ½way; in tch to 12; 7th 13; no ch w ldrs frm 15*	10	5
	Cappa Hill (IRE) 6-1 Miss P Gundry *Tchd 8s; in tch; 4th ½way; lost plce 13; poor 6th frm 3 out*	5	6
	Go Boy 4-1 M Holmes *(xnb) Sn rr; t.o frm 11*	4	7
	Dans Blarney (IRE) 8-1 D Jones *Tchd 10s; prom; cl 2nd frm 9; blun 14; 3rd when rn wide app 3 out; hrd rdn & wknd rap 2 out*	5	8
	B B Boy 7-2 S McHugh *(xnb) Midfield early; 7th 5; bhnd when pu 8*		P
	Black Hope (IRE) (5a) 10-1 T Vaughan *Ld til jmpd rt & rn off course 3*		R
	Golden Embers 7-1 D Mansell *Rr; 9th when pu 14*		P
53[P]	Little Word (12a) 10-1 A Charles-Jones *Towards rr til pu 13*		P
66[R]	Meadows Prince (IRE) (7a) 10-1 L Heard *(xnb,ringbit) Unruly in padd; towards rr when fell 2*		F
35[U]	Miss Chloe (IRE) (5a) 20-1 R Bliss *Towards rr til pu 16*		P
	Vexford Lucy (5a) 12-1 L Jefford *(xnb) Fell 1*		F

OFFICIAL DISTANCES: Originally s hd, 4*l* **TIME:** 6min 58.0s

** A Romp Too Far was the winner of this race from Hug The Bend, but following a stewards enquiry into interference on the run-in the first two placings were reversed*

120 Open Maiden (Div 2), 12st — 10 ran

35[4]	**SCARLET GLORY** (5a) 6-4F **H Fry** *(xnb) Tchd 2s; lw; jw; trckd ldr til ld 8; made rest; drew clr 2 out; stayed on wl; comf.*		1
	Deltic Arrow 10-1 **T Vaughan** *(xnb) Went 3rd 6; 9l 3rd ½way; 15l 3rd 15; blun 3 out; stayed on to tk 2nd at last.*	10	2
	Gunnerbe Posh 3-1 **J Maxse** *Tde; midfield; prog to 3rd 9; went 2nd 11; chsd ldr; 3l 2nd 3 out; tired & jmpd slow u.p 2 out*	3	3
	Warren Hill 7-2 R Tory *Towards rr; 6th 13; tk poor 4th 2 out; veered lft run-in*	15	4
	Maybe A Double (5a) 3-1 N Wilmington *(xnb) Towards rr; jmpd lft 5; 5th 11; prog to 4th 13; btn 4th when jmpd slow 2 out; walked in.*	20	5
	Black A Brook (IRE) (5a) 6-1 M Shears *In tch; 6th ½way; bhnd & pu 13*		P
	Evans The Coal 12-1 J Price *Towards rr when blun bad 7; blun bad & ur some way aft 8.*		U
	Pandeli 6-1 D Phelan *T.o & pu 7*		P
67[P]	Red Stranger (FR)(bl) 5-1 A Farrant *Ld to 8; 3rd & wkng when mist 11; lost plce rap & pu 13*		P
	Smokey Robot (IRE) 6-1 D Dennis *(xnb) Hdwy to 3rd 8; wl in tch in 5th 13; hld in 6th 15; bhnd when pu 16*		P

OFFICIAL DISTANCES: 8*l*, 1½*l* **TIME:** 6min 57.0s

121 Open Maiden (Div 3), 12st — 11 ran

	MARTBY 5-2 **M Atkinson** *Ld/disp til app 3 out; cl 2nd 2 out; rallied to disp ld last; stayed on wl to ld flat.*		1
	Sliema (IRE) 16-1 **N Wilmington** *A.p; cl 2nd til disp ld 9-11; disp ld agn brief 15; 1l 2nd 3 out; ld nxt; jnd agn last; hdd & no ex flat*	nk	2
	Lady Widd (IRE) (5a, 2ow) evensF **S McHugh** *Handy; cl 3rd 10; cl 3rd & gng wl on outer 11; disp ld 15; 1l ld 3 out; hdd & no ex frm 2 out*	8	3
	Forest Fortress (IRE) (5a) 12-1 D I Turner *5th ½way; just in tch in 5th 13; no hdwy frm 14*	20	4
	Random Trix (5a) 6-1 Miss S Robinson *6th ½way; wl bhnd frm 14*	runin	5
	Just Aretha (5a) 10-1 Miss P Gundry *6th & out of tch 12; wl bhnd frm 14.*	½	6
	Beaford Princess (5a) 14-1 J Young *Jmpd violent lft & hmpd rivals 1; sn prom; cl 4th 9; lost ground nxt; last when jmpd slow 12; pu nxt.*		P
21[P]	Huic Holloa (IRE) 14-1 T Vaughan *5th 12; lost ground frm nxt; no ch frm 15; pu 3 out*		P

	Just Caramel (5a) 5-1 M Barber *Hmpd & fell 1*		F
	Strand Onthe Green (IRE) 4-1 N Mitchell *Hmpd & fell 1*		F
	Willoughby Flyer 10-1 M Walters *Rr; 8th 12; some hdwy to 4th 13; pu 15*		P

OFFICIAL DISTANCES: 1½l, 8l **TIME:** 7min 07.0s

Wetherby (LH 8F,16J*)

Sat, 7 Feb (SOFT)

122 Wilmot-Smith Mem HC, 3m1f £1667 — 15 ran

72P	**STAR OF RAVEN** 10-12 16-1 **N Saville** *Hld up in rr; gd hdwy 9; ld 11; stayed on game frm 2 out*		1
	Master Wood 12-01 11-4F **T Greenall** *Mid-div; 4th & prog to chse ldrs 8; chall 3 out; ev ch nxt; kpt on same pce; mist last*	3	2
107³	**Parahandy (IRE)** 11-03 16-1 **H Dowty** *Chsd ldrs; 6th 8; went 3rd & ev ch app 3 out; drvn & a hld aft; kpt on stdly flat*	1¾	3
72⁶	Who Dares Wins 11-05 20-1 L Bates *Chsd ldrs; 8th & mist 8; rdn & outpcd aft 13*	16	4
	Bold Classic (IRE) 11-03 33-1 P Kinsella *Mid-div; hdwy 9; chsd ldrs 13; wknd app 3 out*	13	5
71¹	Light The River (IRE) 11-05(bl,tt) 11-1 Miss C Metcalfe *Chsd ldrs; 7th 8; outpcd when hmpd 12; t.o 3 out*	22	6
	Lord Of The River (IRE) 11-07 3-1 H Fowler *2nd/3rd to 13; wknd rap 3 out; fin tired & t.o*	8	7
33P	Tiraldo (FR) 11-11(cp) 66-1 S Hughes *Chsd ldrs; lost plce 5; sn bhnd & rdn; t.o 10*	dist	8
	Boogy Woogy 11-03(bl) 20-1 Miss J Foster *Ld to 5; 2nd to 10; lost plce 12; t.o & pu 3 out*		P
	Courage Under Fire 12-01(bl) 8-1 O Nelmes *Chsd ldrs; 5th 8; cl 6th when fell 12*		F
	Mr Cooney (IRE) 11-03(bl) 8-1 S Clements *Blun 2; hit 6; a bhnd; rdn & lost tch 7; pu aft nxt*		P
	Mr Mahdlo 11-11 20-1 B Woodhouse *Chsd ldr; ld 5-12; sn lost plce; t.o & pu 3 out*		P
	Primitive Rites 11-03 50-1 S Charlton *Chsd ldrs; mist 5; 10th 8; lost tch & blun 10; t.o & pu 13*		P
	Raffles Rooster 11-05 11-2 C Mulhall *Hld up; 9th & stdy hdwy 8; sn chsng ldrs; lost tch tame 3 out; t.o 7th when pu last*		P
56⁵	Supreme Silence (IRE) 11-03 100-1 N Kent *Bhnd when hit 6; rr & rdn 8; t.o & pu 13*		P

TIME: 6min 47.9s **TOTE:** £26.90; places £4.80,£1.80,££4.70 **Ex:**£188.20 **CSF:**£57.91

** Fences 5 and 15 were omitted - state of the ground; the stewards enquired into the improved form of the winner; they accepted the trainer's explanation that the mare was unsuited by the holding ground and stiff track*

Cambridgeshire with Enfield Chace

Horseheath (RH 10F,18J)

Sat, 7 Feb (GOOD)

123 Hunt Members — 7 ran

44⁹	**GENERAL CONFUSION (IRE)** 5-2 **T Lane** *Hld up in tch; 2l 3rd & eff 12; drvn to chall 2 out; sn ld; urged vigorously & hld on game cl home; rdr drpd whip flat*		1
	The Glen Road (IRE) 7-4F **A Sansome** *Cl up; 2nd 7; rdn 8; prom til lft in ld 2 out; sn hdd; 1l down at last; rallied u.p; a just hld*	nk	2
	Nowornever (IRE) 5-1 **D Kemp** *Settled prom; ld app 12; drawing 5l clr when blun & nrly ur 3 out; climbed nxt & hdd; imm btn; jmpd slow last*	7	3
	Royal Arctic (IRE) 25-1 Miss K Smith *Last & rdn 4; nt keen; pckd bad 6; t.o 11*	runin	4

101U	Ical (IRE) (5a) 4-1 Miss C Rogers *Tk keen hld; ld 4; sn 10l clr; prsd 7; hdd aft 11; cl 4th when rfo 12*		U
104P	King Of The Sea (IRE) 16-1 A Merriam *(xnb) Lw; last pr & sn lost tch; t.o 11; pu 13*		P
	Mr Know What (IRE) 20-1 Miss C Bartlett *1st ride; ld to 4; 2nd 9; lost plce app 11; handy to 15; exhaust nxt; t.o & crawling when crashing fall 2 out*		F

OFFICIAL DISTANCES: hd, 5*l* **TIME:** 6min 40.0s **TOTE:** £3.80 **DF:**£2.80

The stewards interviewed the rider of The Glen Road whose horscame into contact with Mr Know What; he was fined £75 for having struck the latter's rider (who fell later in the race and could not attend the enquiry) with his whip or arm

124 Dodson & Horrell PPORA Club Members Conditions, 12st — 12 ran

	BARD OF DRUMCOO (IRE) (5x) 9-2 **D Kemp** *Ld 3-7; 2nd/4th til ld agn 3 out; 2l clr nxt; rdn & kpt on wl*		1
23U	**Endeavour (FR)** (5x) 4-1 **G Cooper** *Bit bckwd; settled handy; went prom 11; 2½l 3rd when nt fluent 15; jmpd slow nxt; btn 2 out; tk 2nd nr fin; a hld by wnr.*	5	2
555	**Contingency** 6-1 **R Cope** *Prom; ld 10; rdn 15; hdd nxt; kpt on one pce; lost 2nd nr fin*	nk	3
	Light The Sky 16-1 Miss K Norris *Jw; midfield; 6l 5th 15; plugged on same pce*	10	4
382	Colonel Conca 5-2F C Ward-Thomas *(xnb) Prsd ldrs; 3½l 4th 15; rdn & wknd 3 out*	½	5
	Bruan (IRE) 20-1 Miss J Bevin *Bhnd; lost tch 10; t.o 15*	30	6
	Eastern Point (5a) 10-1 P York *Towards rr til hmpd & ur 6*		U
	Good Thyne Murphy (IRE) 16-1 A Braithwaite *Rearing in padd & at start; nt fluent 3; midfield til fell 6*		F
41P	Jack Hackett (IRE)(bl) 20-1 P Hall *Scrubbed along & v reluct; imm lost tch; jmpd slow 2; t.o 6; pu 3 out*		P
45P	Monsukh (IRE) (5a)(bl) 20-1 N Moore *Sn prom; 3rd 10; wknd 12; t.o 14; pu 3 out*		P
	Teeton Priceless (5a) 8-1 A Sansome *Ld to 3 & 7-10; prom til wknd rap aft 14; t.o & pu 3 out*		P
38P	Westfield John (5x) 6-1 J Owen *Towards rr; drvn & no resp 10; strugg aft; 15l 7th 14; t.o & pu last.*		P

OFFICIAL DISTANCES: 4*l*, hd **TIME:** 6min 42.0s **TOTE:** £5.40 **DF:**£10.40

125 Mens Open, 12st — 8 ran

241	**GALLANT GLEN (IRE)** (7x) 4-5F **M Mackley** *Hld up & confid rdn; 15l 3rd 10; clsd & jmpd slow 11; ld app 15; drew clr 3 out; impressive in v fast time*		1
34P	**Involved (IRE)** 3-1 **R Burton** *Jmpd sluggish; mostly cl 2nd; ev ch 14; rdn when jmpd slow 3 out; no ch w wnr aft*	12	2
	Owen's Pet (IRE) 12-1 **S Morris** *Slt ld til app 15; lost tch qckly w ldng pr but kpt on agn flat*	12	3
346	Choral Dream (IRE) 7-1 R Cope *Jmpd slow in rr & nvr gng wl; best plce when 27l 4th 15; nt r.o*	30	4
	Athenian Law (7x) 20-1 P Millington *Lkd appalling; last pr; t.o 10; pu 12*		P
34F	Manavite (IRE) 14-1 T Lane *Blun & nrly ur 4; last nxt; 22l 4th 10; some prog 14; sn fdd; tired when climbed 3 out; pu nxt*		P
	Millenium Way (IRE) 9-1 J Owen *Fat; mid-div; mist 8; mod 5th 10; t.o & pu 14*		P
381	Minino (IRE) 8-1 C Ward-Thomas *Ref to line up; tk no part*		r

OFFICIAL DISTANCES: 10*l*, 8*l* **TIME:** 6min 25.0s **TOTE:** £2.00 **DF:**£3.90

126 Ladies Open — 8 ran

55P	**MACFIN (IRE)**(cp) 20-1 **Miss L Allan** *Ld/2nd til ld 14; made rest; lft 4l clr 3 out; blun nxt; drvn out flat.*		1
181	**Tom Cobbler (IRE)** (4x) 2-1 **Mrs P Hall** *Hld up & bhnd; eff in cl 5th 12; 1l 3rd when jmpd slow 15; impeded nxt & lost ground; 5½l 3rd 2 out; stayed on agn to 2nd flat; nt rch wnr.*	2	2
	Spring Gale (IRE) (7x) 6-1 **Miss Z Turner** *Tde; ld 3-5, 8-10 & 12-14; ev ch til releg 3rd aft 15; lft 2nd nxt; 3l down last; wknd & dem flat*	7	3
982	Borrow Mine (IRE) 20-1 Miss L Marriott *Towards rr; jmpd slow 8; outpcd 11; t.o 14; stayed on quite wl flat.*	8	4
	Mister Audi (IRE) 16-1 Miss A Bowles *Prsd ldrs; 4th 12; wknd rap; 20l 5th 14*	20	5

42^{F} Jolly Minster (7x) 7-4F Mrs D Rowell *Hld up midfield; eff in cl 4th 14; niggled nxt; went 2nd & lkd wnr when rfo 3 out. . . . .* U

Mr Miller (IRE) (7x) 9-4 Ms A Embiricos *Prom; nt fluent 6; 3rd & rdn 12; no resp; wl bhnd when pu 14 . . . .* P

Pele Mele (FR) 33-1 Miss S Firmin *A last; lost tch 12; t.o & pu 14. . . . . .* P

OFFICIAL DISTANCES: 2*l*, 1*l* **TIME:** 6min 32.0s **TOTE:** £62.90 **DF:**£48.10

The stewards enquired into the improved form of the winner; they accepted the trainer's explanation that the horse 'never came to himself' in 2003 and had run with much more enthusiam wearing cheekpieces for the first time for two seasons

127 Restricted, 12st — 18 ran

FANE COUNSEL (IRE) 5-2F **R Burton** *(xnb) Jw; made all in clr ld; 10l ahd 11; 20l up 14; a cruising; most impressive . . . .* 1

Present Moment (IRE) 20-1 **N Moore** *Lw; went 22l 4th 5; 5th 10; chsd wnr vain frm nxt; 12l down & v tired when climbed 3 out. . . . .* 25 2

44^{4} **Filou Du Bois (FR)** 7-1 **Ms A Embiricos** *(xnb) Prom in chsng group; 4th 10; 34l 4th 14; poor 3rd frm nxt . . . .* 10 3

44^{2} Holy Moses (IRE) 6-1 N Bloom *Midfield; 8th 10; 57l 6th 14; no ch . . . . .* 25 4

44^{7} Glad All Over (5a) 33-1 D Hays *Bhnd; jmpd v slow 5; 16th & t.o 10; plodded on . . . .* 30 5

Hoplite 12-1 R Cope *Midfield; rdn 8; 7th 10; 67l 7th 14; pu 15 . . . .* P

102^{F} Imperial Prince 33-1 Miss K Smith *Strugg in rr; rem 12th 10; pu 13. . . . .* P

Ishma (IRE) 16-1 D Page (Kent) *Rem last when ref 7 . . . .* r

Jerome Jerome 10-1 N King *A bhnd; rem 13th 10; pu 12. . . . .* P

44^{5} Josh's Choice (IRE) 20-1 A Braithwaite *Midfield & nvr nr ldrs; 9th 10; 70l 8th 14; mist nxt & event ur . . . .* U

Kepi Royal (FR) 4-1 J Docker *(xnb) 2nd/3rd bhnd clr ldr; wknd 12; 32l 4th 14; t.o & pu 3 out . . . .* P

Mountain Trooper (7a) 25-1 J Owen *Bckwd; school in rr; rem 14th 10; pu 13* P

Nonplussed (5a) 25-1 P Andrew *A lagging bad; t.o last 10; event pu flat. .* P

19^{P} Phar Afield (IRE) 7-1 D Brightling *Fat; wl off pce in midfield; 10th 10; t.o & pu 13. . . . .* P

44^{P} Red Square Prince (IRE) 14-1 D Dunsdon *Towards rr; 11th & strugg 10; t.o & pu 12. . . . .* P

Rip Kirby(bl) 20-1 G Cooper *Hld up & wl bhnd; rem 15th 10; pu 14. . . . .* P

36^{P} Treble Trouble 20-1 P Millington *Lkd dreadful; off pce in midfield; 6th 10; 50l 5th 14; pu 3 out . . . .* P

What A Charmer (IRE) 4-1 N Pearce *Jmpd slow 6; 2nd/3rd to 10; lost plce rap nxt; pu 12; lost both front shoes. . . . .* P

OFFICIAL DISTANCES: dist, 10*l* **TIME:** 6min 31.0s **TOTE:** £3.30 **DF:**£1.90 (1+any)

128 Open Maiden 56&7yo, 12st — 16 ran

39^{P} **HI TECH MAN (IRE)** 14-1 **T Lane** *Towards rr til hdwy to trck ldrs 8; went 2nd 15; ld last; drvn & stayed on wl . . . .* 1

Briery Fox (IRE) 3-1 **J Docker** *Settled 2nd/4th; clsd to ld aft 14; rdn & hdd last; nt qckn . . . .* 1½ 2

Willow Ryde (IRE) 7-1 **N Pearce** *Chsd ldrs; 5th 12; went 3rd & rdn aft 15; plugged on; btn app 2 out; should improve. . . . .* 10 3

39^{U} What Next (IRE) 5-1 A Hickman *Midfield; 8th 12; kpt on to 4th & flatt brief aft 15; sn wknd . . . .* 12 4

39^{6} Arctic Sun (IRE) 6-1 N Bloom *Hld up midfield; 4th & prog 11; ev ch 14; wknd tame aft nxt. . . . .* nk 5

Arctic Penguin(tt) 20-1 P York *(xnb) Pulled v hrd in rr; rushed up to 2nd 5; ld 6-7; chsd ldr til ld brief 14; 1l 3rd nxt; wknd rap; pu 3 out . . . .* P

Ascoolasice 16-1 M Keel *Hld up in last pr & nvr put in rce; pu 11 . . . . . .* P

Bacarese 7-1 S Morris *Lw; ld to 2; 8l 3rd when fell 8 . . . .* F

7^{5} Beacon White(tt) 12-1 P Hall *Made virt all til hdd & lost plce rap 14; pu nxt* P

Homeleigh Meadow 10-1 A Merriam *Got loose padd; bhnd; strugg when mist & ur 10. . . . .* U

Jumping Jeffrey 12-1 M Mackley *Last when fell 5. . . . .* F

Killard Point (IRE) (7a) 5-2F R Cope *2 handlers; oht; 6th when bd 8. . . . .* B

Legolas (7a) 16-1 P Millington *Lkd ghastly; saddled with wrong number-cloth (only changed as other rnrs lft padd); bhnd & jmpd erratic; 9th 11; plugged on & still fair 6th when nrly ur 3 out; pu last . . . .* P

Little Heck (IRE) 16-1 A Sansome *Very skinny; lkd terrible; jb in rr; t.o & pu 11* P

On The Day (IRE) 5-1 J Owen *Quite attractive; oht; mid-div; 8l 7th 11; strugg 13; t.o & pu 2 out* . . . . P
Vintage Rock 12-1 T Ellis *A bhnd; lft poor last 11; t.o & pu 13* . . . . P

OFFICIAL DISTANCES: hd, 2*l* **TIME:** 6min 41.0s **TOTE:** £26.00 **DF:**£31.00 (1+any)

129 Open Maiden 8yo&up (Div 1), 12st — 10 ran

26F **BATTLE HONOURS** 8-1 **P Hall** *Hld up midfield; eff to duel for ld app 11 til drew clr app 3 out; 8l ahd nxt; rdn & wknd flat; just hld on* 1
Here Comes Choosey (IRE) 6-1 **N Bloom** *Prsd ldrs; clsd to chall app 11; w wnr til rdn & outpcd aft 15; jmpd slow nxt; 4l down last; r.o game & ev ch 50yds out; no ex nr fin* . . . . nk 2
Over The Rhee (IRE) 8-1 **P Taiano** *Fat; towards rr til prog 11; 6l 3rd 14; sn outpcd; 20l down app 3 out* 25 3
Penlet Too 14-1 T Ellis *(xnb) Towards rr; rdn 11; 15l 5th & btn 14; t.o* . . . 30 4
103P Bailey's Of Cashel (IRE) 2-1F D Dunsdon *Ld to 2 & 7 til rdn & hdd app 11; lost plce tame; pu 14* . . . . P
40P Bright Torino (IRE) (5a) 10-1 J Bevan *Mists in rr; t.o 5; furlongs bhnd when pu 13* . . . . P
Faircatcher 6-1 J Owen *Tk keen hld; cl up til fell 4* . . . . F
Frosty Fella 3-1 B Pollock *(xnb) Novicey in rr; blun 4; just in tch to 11; 20l last 14; t.o & pu 3 out* . . . . P
Sandyland 10-1 A Sansome *Cl up to 12; 8l 4th & wkng 14; t.o & pu 3 out* P
103P Tidal Race (IRE) 10-1 N Moore *(xnb) Ld 2-7; wknd qckly 11; t.o & pu 13* . P

OFFICIAL DISTANCES: hd, 10*l* **TIME:** 6min 39.0s **TOTE:** £13.80 **DF:**£11.10

130 Open Maiden 8yo&up (Div 2), 12st — 9 ran

WINCY SPIDER 5-2 **J Diment** *(xnb) Hld up gng wl; 2nd brief 11; rstrnd til ld app 3 out; 8l clr at last; rdn out* 1
Brass Razoo 5-4F **S Morris** *Vied for 2nd bhnd clr ldr; eff 13; ev ch app 3 out; chsd wnr aft; plugged on game; a hld* 3 2
32P **Igloux Royal (FR)** 12-1 **M Briggs** *(xnb) Tk str hld; ld & sn clr; 6l ahd 12; hdd aft 15; blun nxt; imm btn; mists 2 out & last* 15 3
40P Gunner Be True(bl) 4-1 T Lane *Nt jw; towards rr; rdn 10; clsd 13; 3rd & ev ch 15; finding nil u.p when jmpd v slow nxt; reluct aft* 10 4
404 Ginger Bug (5a) 8-1 P Chinery *Nrly ur 5 & drpd to rr; strugg 9; 15l last aft 15; r.o flat & nrly snatched rem 4th* . . . . nk 5
Erin's Surprise (IRE) 10-1 E Linehan *Hld up; mist 8; went 2nd brief nxt; eff 12; wknd 14; pu 3 out; lame* . . . . P
103F Granny Dick (5a) 5-1 N Pearce *Hld up & bhnd; outpcd 9; eff & jmpd slow 13; 5l 6th app 15; wknd qckly; t.o & pu 2 out* . . . . P
103P Itsthebrass (5a) 12-1 P York *(xnb) Blun 3; nt jw in rr; strugg frm 9; t.o when virt ref 3 out & pu* . . . . P
Sneeze (5a) 12-1 R Stearn *Cl up in chsng group; eff 13; 3l 5th when fell 15* F

OFFICIAL DISTANCES: 1*l*, 10*l* **TIME:** 6min 46.0s **TOTE:** £8.10 **DF:**£2.00

Jedforest

Friars Haugh (LH 8F,18J)

Sat, 7 Feb (GOOD)

131 Hunt Members — 4 ran

MOZIELAW (5a) 5-2 **Miss M Neill** *Trckd ldrs in mostly 3rd; went 2nd 8; 2l 2nd app 14; btr j to ld 3 out; 1l up nxt; rdn & stayed on* 1
751 **Native Alibi (IRE)** 4-5F **C Shirley-Beavan** *(xnb) Hld up in last; 4l last app 8; eff to disp 1l 2nd 11; ld brief aft 15; ev ch til nt qckn app last* 2 2
Sporty Spice (IRE) (5a) 4-1 **Miss L Hislop** *Made virt all til hdd aft 15; sn btn; walked in* 20 3
Exact (FR) 5-2 Miss V Russell *(xnb) Trckd ldr til wknd 8; 10l last & jmpd slow nxt; sn lost tch; wl bhnd when pu 12; lame* . . . . P

OFFICIAL DISTANCES: 1½*l*, dist **TIME:** 7min 04.9s

132 Dodson & Horrell PPORA Club Members Restricted, 12st — 7 ran

Form	Runner	Dist	Pos
	SNOOTY ESKIMO (IRE) 10-1 **H Norton** *Cl 2nd til ld 9; jnd 15; hdd nxt; 3l down 2 out; rallied to chall last; ld flat; r.o.*		1
	Wild Edgar (IRE) 5-1 **A Richardson** *Hld at start & ld in; a.p; ld to 8; jnd ldr 15 til ld 3 out; lkd wnr til prsd agn at last; hdd & no ex flat*	¾	2
69[3]	**Timberley**(tt) 3-1 **T Oates** *(citation) Trckd ldrs; 3l 3rd aft 7; blun bad & rdr lost iron 8; gd rcvry but lost plce; 10l 4th 11; prog to disp 4l 4th 14-15; wknd & 20l 4th app 2 out; kpt on wl app last; tk 3rd nr line*	10	3
	Faster Sweep (IRE) 7-4F R Morgan *In tch in mid-div; 4l 4th app 8; 6l 3rd 10; prog to 1l 3rd when pckd 15; sn pushed along & one pce; 10l 3rd app 2 out; dem cl home*	hd	4
	Anotherhandyman 4-1 Miss S Gledson *A rr; 15l last 1; t.o 8; 2 fncs adrift when pu aft 14*		P
	Hervey Bay (5a) 4-1 W Goldie *(xnb) Mid-div when pu aft 2; saddle slpd*		P
	Laura Lugs (IRE) (7ow) 10-1 T Mounsey-Heysham *Fat; nt jw; a rr; rmdrs 4; 6l 5th & mist nxt; drvn along aft; lsng tch 7; 20l 5th 8; pu aft 9*		P

OFFICIAL DISTANCES: ½*l*, 10*l* **TIME:** 6min 54.5s

133 Ladies Open — 9 ran

Form	Runner	Dist	Pos
	MYTIMIE (IRE) 5-4F **Miss P Robson** *Nt a fluent; disp last but in tch early; 4l 6th app 3; disp 4l 4th 8; eff 11 to ld 15; 3l up when stumbled sltly bend bef 2 out; rdn & r.o when prsd flat*		1
	Pharmistice (IRE) 4-1 **Miss N Stirling** *(xnb) Ld/disp til cl 2nd 7; ld 10; 1l ahd 12; hdd & outpcd aft 15; stayed on wl frm 2 out; prsd ldr last; r.o flat; a hld*	½	2
69[1]	**Dere Street** 7-2 **Miss R Davidson** *Hld up & disp last early; went 6l 6th 10 & 5l 6th 13; stayed on wl to 3l 2nd 2 out; 3rd & ev ch last; r.o flat*	1	3
71[3]	Balisteros (FR) 4-1 Miss J Williams *Prom; 1l 2nd 12; 3l 3rd 15; rdn & went 2nd nxt; sn outpcd; kpt on wl frm 2 out.*	1	4
	Commanche Law (IRE) 2-1 Mrs A Hamilton *Prom til outpcd 9; lsng tch 11; stayed on wl agn frm 3 out; 8l 5th nxt; clsd flat; nt rch ldrs*	s hd	5
72[5]	Meander (IRE) 10-1 Miss L Hislop *Mid-div; 8l 6th aft 8; outpcd aft 14; kpt on frm 3 out; 10l 6th 2 out*	10	6
	Miss Portcello (5a) 3-1 Miss J Hollands *Trckd ldrs; 3l 3rd app 8; ½l 2nd 10; outpcd 14; wknd aft nxt; bhnd when pu 2 out*		P
	Piper's Rock (IRE) 6-1 Miss V Russell *(xnb,boh) Ld/disp; mist & nrly ur 2; ½l up 7; wknd 13; bhnd when pu aft 15*		P
	Westie (5a) 10-1 Miss L Kendall *A rr; 12l last 3; detach 7; 20l last 3 out; t.o & pu last*		P

OFFICIAL DISTANCES: ½*l*, 1*l* **TIME:** 6min 50.9s

134 Mens Open — 12 ran

Form	Runner	Dist	Pos
	FALCON'S FLAME (USA) 20-1 **R Green** *(xnb) Prom; ld aft 8; 1l up 12 til drew clr frm 3 out; 6l up nxt; stayed on; 2½l ahd at last.*		1
	Epsilo De La Ronce (FR) 7-2 **W Ramsay** *Fat; in tch; gd prog to 3l 2nd aft 2 out; kpt on wl flat; nrst fin*	1½	2
	Welsh March (IRE) 8-1 **N Tutty** *2 handlers; in tch; prog to trck ldrs 10; outpcd app 3 out; kpt on app last; tk 3rd flat*	6	3
	Golf Land (IRE)(tt) 3-1 A Richardson *Mid-div; 4l 5th 8; mist 10; went 1l 2nd 15; sn outpcd & lost plce; prog to 3l 2nd agn 2 out; one pce & dem flat*	½	4
	Spring Double (IRE) (5ow) 25-1 T Mounsey-Heysham *Fat; ld til hdd aft 8; 2l 2nd nxt; outpcd 14; 20l last 3 out; kpt on wl frm nxt; one pce flat*	3	5
	Laganside (IRE) (3ow) 14-1 J Muir *Trckd ldrs; disp 4l 3rd app 10; outpcd 2 out; kpt on*	1½	6
72[7]	Dr Deductible(cp) 7-1 R Brown *In tch in rr; outpcd & nd aft 13; kpt on*	8	7
72[P]	Starbuck(cp) 10-1 R Morgan *Prom til grad wknd frm 15; bhnd app last*	1	8
	Derryrose 5-1 M McAlister *Greased legs; fat; oht; a rr; 15l last app 3; sn lost tch; rdn along 8; t.o & pu 3 out*		P
	Erzadjan (IRE) 12-1 T Craggs *1st ride; rr; 20l last aft 1; ur 2*		U
	Katinka (5a) 6-4F C Storey *(xnb) 2s-6/4; handy til fell 6*		F
69[P]	Lively Dessert (IRE) 12-1 C Gillon *(xnb) In tch; outpcd 13; 8l 8th when fell 15*		F

OFFICIAL DISTANCES: 1*l*, 6*l* **TIME:** 6min 56.3s

135 Confined (Nov Rdrs), 12st — 6 ran

PASSING DANGER (FR) (3x) 5-4F **Miss R Davidson** *Hld up; mist 1 & releg 8l last aft; 5th 5; 15l 5th & mist 8; clsd to 8l 5th 12 & 6l 3rd app 3 out; ld last; sn clr; comf; wl rdn* 1

Johnnys Gone (IRE) 5-2 **C Shirley-Beavan** *Mostly 3rd; disp 10l 3rd app 9; prog to trck ldr aft 14; lft in ld nxt; hrd prsd & hdd brief aft 3 out; hrd prsd til hdd agn last; brushed aside flat* 5 2

71^{2} **Harden Glen** (5x) 2-1 **Miss J Riding** *(xnb) Chsd ldrs; 16l 4th 5; disp 10l 3rd app 9; disp 4l 3rd 15; prog to ld brief 3 out; no ex app last* 1 1/2 3

In Demand 4-1 Miss J Balmer *Lw; a rr; 20l last 4; 10l last app 12; 25l 4th 3 out; nd* 10 4

73^{U} Houselope Beck 10-1 Miss A Wanless *Trckd ldr; 2l 2nd & mist 8; outpcd frm 14; sn wl bhnd.* 3 5

Lord Edwards Army (IRE) 7-2 G Willoughby *Ld; 3l up 9; 2l ahd 14; mist & ur 15* U

OFFICIAL DISTANCES: 6*l*, 2*l* **TIME:** 6min 57.8s

136 Open Maiden Mares, 12st — 7 ran

SHARP FOUNTAIN (5a) 6-4 **C Storey** *Prom; 3l 3rd app 3; ld aft 8; went 6l clr aft 3 out; stayed on* 1

Tallaburn (5a) 3-1 **A Findlay** *In tch in rr; 8l last & mist 8; 8l 5th 12; stdy prog frm nxt; prsd ldr app 3 out; 2l 2nd & outpcd aft nxt; wknd app last.* 8 2

Steady Lass (IRE) (5a) 4-1 **R Nichol** *Set sedate pce to 2; grad lost plce; 8l last app 9; clumsy nxt & sn t.o; 40l 4th 2 out; inherited v rem 3rd nxt* 1 1/2fs 3

74^{P} Anniejo (12a) 3-1 C Gillon *(xnb) In tch in rr; 6l 5th 6; prog to 2l 3rd 8; 6l 3rd & mist 15; rdn & jmpd slow nxt; wknd qckly; 30l 3rd when pu 2 out* . . . . P

Northern Lyne (5a) 3-1 Miss J Hollands *(xnb) Oht; prom; ld aft 2-8; outpcd & 10l 4th 15; wknd qckly & pu nxt* . . . . P

Solway Saffy (5a) 5-1 R Morgan *2 handlers; unruly padd; mid-div; disp 5l 4th app 4; strugg in 8l 5th & rmdrs aft 9; lost tch; pu aft 12.* . . . . P

Stanwick Gypsy (5a) 5-4F A Richardson *In tch in rr; 6l 5th 3; mist nxt; 3l 3rd when hit 11; handy when fell 13* . . . . F

OFFICIAL DISTANCES: 9*l*, dist **TIME:** 7min 10.3s

137 Open Maiden, 12st — 11 ran

BILINGUAL (7a) 2-1F **C Storey** *Unruly padd; green; rr til prog aft 9; went 3l 3rd 14; ld app nxt; sn clr; 10l up til wandered aft 2 out; hrd prsd & mist last; r.o str flat.* 1

Three Spires 4-1 **A Richardson** *2 handlers; ld in start; ww in rr; 10l 5th 15; stayed on wl past btn horses frm nxt; chall & ev ch aft last; imm outpcd* 1 2

Rutherford 4-1 **R Morgan** *Ld/disp til 1l 2nd 8; disp ld agn brief nxt; 1/2l 2nd 12 til 4l 3rd & wkng 15; kpt on one pce* 3 3

Toorak (USA) 6-1 R Trotter *(bf) Ld/disp til 2nd 8; ld agn 9-14; 8l 4th & outpcd 15; one pce.* 4 4

Storm Ahead (IRE) 7-2 C Shirley-Beavan *Oht; chsd ldrs; 5l 3rd app 11; 3 1/2l 4th & hit 14; trckd ldr nxt; sn rdn & outpcd* 1 5

Birkwood (7a) 3-1 C Gillon *Mists in rr; lsng tch 6; t.o when fell 3 out* . . . . F

Commanche Spirit (IRE) 4-1 F Arthur *Fat; chsd ldrs til wknd aft 10; t.o & pu 15* P

Jackofalltrades (IRE) 4-1 T Oates *In tch in rr when rn into 7 & ur* . . . . U

69^{F} Ramon Allones (IRE) 5-1 R Green *(xnb) Mid-div when ur 3.* . . . . U

Spring Rock 7-2 K Anderson *Mists; trckd ldrs; 5l 3rd 10; outpcd & wknd frm 15; wl bhnd when pu 2 out* . . . . P

The Panjshir 8-1 G Willoughby *Prom; 3l 3rd app 3; wknd aft 11; t.o 15; pu nxt* P

OFFICIAL DISTANCES: 1*l*, 3*l* **TIME:** 7min 04.4s

United Services

Larkhill (RH 13F,18J)

Sat, 7 Feb (GOOD, GOOD to SOFT becoming DEAD in places)

138 United Services Members, 12st — 7 ran

9^{2}† **NORSKI LAD**(bl,tt) 9-4 **J Snowden** *Tchd 5/2; ww; 2 1/2l 4th 1/2way; 3l 4th 15; qcknd to ld aft 2 out; sn clr (equipped with tongue strap rather than silk tie used last time (didn't make a noise this time* 1

Teller Of Tales 16-1 **Miss V Flood** *Fired; hld up; 6l 5th 1/2way; 5l 5th 15; outpcd nxt; went 7l 3rd aft 2 out; tk 2nd & stayed on wl flat* 4 2

$9^{2\dagger}$	**Puzzleman** 6-1 **S Wheeler** *Opened 8s; ld to 13; 2nd/3rd til ld 3 out; hdd aft nxt; sn outpcd*	6	3
19^{5}	The Vintage Dancer (IRE) 16-1 G Kerr *2nd til ld 14; hdd 3 out; wknd 2 out; lkd to fin 15½l 5th*	4	4
9^{1}	Strong Tea (IRE) (5x) 6-4F D Alers-Hankey *Tde; prom; 1½l 3rd ½way; lost plce u.p 13; 6l last 15; one pce 3 out; hung lft flat; lkd to fin 14l 4th.*	1½	5
	Friars Island (IRE) 33-1 H Wallace *Bckwd; jmpd slow 5; last & lost tch nxt; t.o 8; pu 11; bbv*		P
	Mister Pepper (IRE) 6-1 T Underwood *Opened 8s; hld up; last 2-6; 7l 6th ½way; hdwy 12; ld 13-14; ev ch 15; wknd qckly app 2 out; pu last*		P

OFFICIAL DISTANCES: 3*l*, 3*l* **TIME:** 6min 19.2s **TOTE:** £3.40

139 Restricted, 12st — 15 ran

12^{1}	**FREE GIFT** 8-11F **D Jacob** *(xnb) Opened evens; lw; sn prom; 8l 3rd ½way; went 2nd 11; ld 14; in comm when blun & lft clr at last*		1
	Slip The Ring 20-1 **M Hooper** *Hld up & bhnd; 18l 13th ½way; gd hdwy aft 12; 6l 3rd 14; one pce 3 out; lft 2nd at last*	8	2
604^{2}	**Milnstorm (IRE)** 16-1 **Miss P Gundry** *(xnb) Hld up; hdwy 7; 10l 5th ½way; went 8l 3rd 11; wknd & 18l 6th 14; lft dist 3rd at last*	30	3
35^{6}	Hilarity (5a) 25-1 M Miller *(xnb,bf) Chsd ldrs; 11½l 8th ½way; 15l 5th 14; 22l 4th & wkng when mist 3 out; t.o*	10	4
90^{P}	Bright Flash (IRE) 50-1 D Luff *(orbs) Prom; went 2nd aft 8-11; wknd & 12l 4th 14; t.o*	5	5
14^{P}	Withycombe(vis) 66-1 J Snowden *Nd; 12l 9th ½way; lost tch aft 12; 21l 8th 14; t.o*	8	6
	Ballyalbert 20-1 Miss A de Lisle Wells *Ld aft 1; 7l clr ½way; hdd 14; 3l 2nd when fell last*		F
	Final Magic 20-1 G Maundrell *(kineton) Tde; ld til aft 1; 2nd til wknd aft 8; wl bhnd when pu 11*		P
65^{2}	Frankly Fear 12-1 N Heath *(xnb) W ldrs; 10½l 6th ½way; lost plce 13; 25l 5th 3 out; dist 4th when rfo last*		U
37^{P}	Lord Of The Bride (IRE)(bl) 8-1 A Farrant *(xnb) Hld up; mists 8 & 9; 13l 10th ½way; rdn & no resp 12; wl bhnd when pu 14*		P
30^{1}	Out The Black (IRE) 100-30 D Alers-Hankey *Opened 6s in plce; hld up; 9th when mist & ur 5*		U
	Ruling The Roast 20-1 J Jenkins *Bckwd; a bhnd; 14l 11th ½way; t.o & pu 13*		P
	Sweet Kari (IRE) 66-1 G Weatherley *Ss; a wl bhnd; 30l last ½way; t.o & pu 11*		P
37^{P}	Top Light 33-1 Miss K Cuthbertson *(xnb) Jnd ldrs & almost ur 5; 11l 7th ½way; mid-div when ur 11*		U
	Trigger Again 8-1 Miss E Tory *(xnb) 2 handlers; a bhnd; jmpd slow 3; 15l 12th ½way; 24l 9th 14; t.o & pu 3 out.*		P

OFFICIAL DISTANCES: 5*l*, dist **TIME:** 6min 17.6s **TOTE:** £1.60

140 Mixed Open (Coronation Gold Cup), 12st — 7 ran

88^{2}	**TALES OF BOUNTY (IRE)** 9-2 **N Williams** *Lw; a.p; 2l 3rd ½way; went 2nd aft 12; ld 13; lft 15l clr 3 out; wknd flat; just hld on*		1
64^{3}	**County Derry** 9-4 **N Harris** *Tchd 5/2; 2 handlers; hld up; jmpd slow & rmdrs 3; last to 9; went 10l 3rd & rdn 14; lft 2nd & hmpd 3 out; storming rn & made up 12l flat; just failed*	½	2
63^{5}	**Fair Wind (IRE)** 20-1 **Miss P Gundry** *2nd til ld aft 5; hdd 7; sn lost plce; last 9; lost tch 12; went 20l 3rd aft 3 out; stayed on.*	8	3
63^{6}	Mr Ben Gunn 50-1 Miss V Heal *Ld; mist 5; sn hdd; ld 7-11; 8l 3rd 13; wknd 15; mist nxt; t.o*	40	4
89^{1}	Aberfoyle Park (IRE) 10-11F D Jacob *Opened evens, tchd 11/10; hld up; 2½l 4th ½way; ld 11-13; 1l 2nd & rdn when fell hvly 3 out; rdr broke collar-bone*		F
33^{2}	Chasing The Bride 16-1 Miss A Goschen *(xnb) Hld up; 6th when blun & ur 5*		U
47^{P}	Northern Bluff(tt) 100-1 D I Turner *Prom; went 2nd 8-11; stpd to nil aft 12; pu 13*		P

OFFICIAL DISTANCES: s hd, 10*l* **TIME:** 6min 17.3s **TOTE:** £2.60

141 Intermediate, 12st — 6 ran

	KELTIC LORD 5-4F **A Charles-Jones** *Hld up; hdwy to ld 9-13; ld 2 out til hdd flat; rallied to ld agn nr fin.*		1
	Pendragon 6-1 **N Mitchell** *Made most to 9; 2nd til ld 13; hdd aft nxt; rdn 3 out; ld & edged lft flat; hdd nr fin.*	hd	2

Stennikov (IRE) 7-4 **E Walker** *(xnb) Tchd 2s; prom; jmpd to ld 3 & 6; 5l 5th ½way; 4l 4th when blun 15; wkng when lft 20l 3rd 2 out* 30 3

116P Alexander Nevsky 33-1 D Dennis *(xnb) Hld up; 6l last ½way; lost tch 13; t.o* 25 4

50P Chaucers Miller 14-1 D I Turner *Hld up; 3l 4th ½way; went 3rd 11; rdn to ld aft 14; hdd & fell 2 out* . . . . F

Themaster's Choice (IRE) 9-1 S Joynes *(orbs) Tchd 10s; 2nd/3rd to 11; sn lost plce; 9l 5th & rdn 13; bhnd when blun 3 out; pu nxt* . . . . P

OFFICIAL DISTANCES: ½*l*, 20*l* **TIME:** 6min 19.5s **TOTE:** £2.20

142 Open Maiden 56&7yo (Div 1), 12st — 10 ran

WHO'S EDDIE (IRE) 3-1JF **M Harris** *(xnb) Tchd 7/2; a.p; went 2nd 8; mist 10; lft in ld 14; rdn aft 2 out; all out* 1

86P **Noble Action** (7a) 7-2 **N Williams** *Hld up; last to 11; hdwy 13; lft 4l 2nd nxt; rdn aft 2 out; kpt on* 2 2

Kyalami (FR) 3-1JF **Miss P Gundry** *(xnb) 5s-3s; 2 handlers; hld up; 11l 8th ½way; hdwy when lft 7l 3rd 14; disp 4l 2nd 3 out; one pce* 1¾ 3

Fourspice Allspice (IRE) (5a) 10-1 Miss A Goschen *Ld to 3; 2nd to 8; 2½l 3rd ½way; lost plce & 14l 5th 14; wknd 3 out* 15 4

Senior Moment 7-1 J Snowden *14s-7s; hld up; 7l 6th ½way; drpd to rr & rdn 11; 17l 7th 14; mist 2 out; t.o.* 30 5

Darcey Mae (5a) 5-1 Miss L Bridges *2nd til ld 3; went 10l clr 11; 5l up when mist & ur 14* . . . . U

Georges Pleasure (5a) 9-1 L Heard *Chsd ldrs til hit 5; 8th when fell nxt* . . . F

Keith's Dream (12a) 14-1 J Jenkins *Hld up; 10l 7th ½way; hdwy 12; wknd & 18l last 14; jmpd slow 3 out; t.o & pu 2 out* . . . . P

30F See More Fun 20-1 A Charles-Jones *Prom; 3l 4th ½way; wknd qckly 12; wl bhnd when pu 13* . . . . P

53⁴ The Lords Cross (IRE) 20-1 M Barber *Tde; hld up; hdwy 6; mist 8; 3½l 5th ½way; wknd & 15l 6th 14; wl bhnd when pu 2 out* . . . . P

OFFICIAL DISTANCES: ½*l*, 1*l* **TIME:** 6min 21.7s **TOTE:** £2.30

143 Open Maiden 56&7yo (Div 2), 12st — 6 ran

12²† **PREACHER BOY** (7a) 4-6F **Miss P Gundry** *Hld up; hit 5; went 2nd 7; jmpd lft 10; ld aft 14; jmpd lft 2 out; 6l clr when jmpd lft & v slow last; rdly* . . . 1

30P **No Pressure (IRE)** 9-2 **A Charles-Jones** *Tchd 6s; prom; went 2nd 5-7; 5l 3rd ½way; lost plce & 5l 4th w rdr sat motionless 15; 10l last aft 2 out; shkn up & stayed on wl flat* 5 2

Toon Society (IRE) 5-2 **N Harris** *7/2-5/2; hld up; last to 11; went 10l 4th nxt; jnd ldrs app 15; 2½l 3rd & rdn 3 out; one pce* 3 3

30³ Killough Hill (IRE) 6-1 W Hill *(bh) Swtng; ld til hdd aft 14; 4l 2nd & rdn 2 out; wknd tame flat* 15 4

53P Bubble Brook 25-1 J Jenkins *Hld up; jmpd slow 2 & 3; mist 8; 12l 5th ½way; rdn 12; wl bhnd when pu 14* . . . . P

Lothian Emerald (5a) 25-1 J Snowden *2nd to 5; lost plce & 10l 4th ½way; last 11; wl bhnd when pu 13* . . . . P

OFFICIAL DISTANCES: 4*l*, 8*l* **TIME:** 6min 28.6s **TOTE:** £1.50

Mid Devon

Black Forest Lodge (RH 8F,19J)

Sun, 8 Feb (GOOD)

144 Confined, 12st — 3 ran

62P **O SO BOSSY** 6-1 **Miss J Congdon** *2nd to 5 & frm 9; jmpd to ld 11; hdd 14; jmpd to ld 16; sn in comm; drew clr flat* 1

Friar Waddon (5x) 10-11F **C Heard** *(xnb) Jmpd lft; ld to 11; 2nd til 14; outj & hdd 16; releg last u.p 3 out; one pce; subsq promoted to 2nd.* 9½ 2

61¹ Midnight Coup(vis) 5-4 A Farrant *(xnb) Hld up; went 2nd 5-9; rdn 15; chsd wnr 3 out; nt resolute; btn when hit last; fin 7l 2nd; subsq disq - nt carry penalty* 2d

OFFICIAL DISTANCES: Originally 6*l*, 4*l* **TIME:** 6min 14.3s

Midnight Coup finished second but was disqualified by the Jockey Club Disciplinary Committee for failing to carry a 7lb penalty as required by the conditions; the owner was fined £200 and third horse was promoted

145 Mens Open — 6 ran

Form	Horse / Rider / Comment	Dist	Pos
77[1]	**POLAR CHAMP**(bl) 2-5F **A Farrant** *A.p; qcknd to ld 10; 6l clr 13; hrd rdn app 3 out; kpt finding ex*		1
11[P]	**Kingston Venture** 9-1 **J Barnes** *(xnb) Ld to 5 & 7-10; 7l 2nd 15; eff & lkd dangerous app 3 out; rdn 2 out; no ex*	5	2
	Ashbury Star (NZ) 14-1 **D Alers-Hankey** *(xnb) Went 2nd 4; ld 5-7; 6l 4th ½way; went 12l 3rd 13; wknd 16; t.o*	runin	3
77[3]	Bruthuinne (IRE) 8-1 Richard Darke *(xnb) 12s-8s; 2 handlers; swtng; tde; ld in start; 2nd to 4 & frm 8 til mist 10; 4l 3rd ½way; wknd 13; t.o.*	2	4
	Native King (IRE) 8-1 M Walters *Last to 5; 9l last ½way; rdn 12; wl bhnd when mist 15; t.o & pu 3 out*		P
	Questionaire (5a) 12-1 R Stephens *Blun 5; lost tch & rdn 7; wl bhnd when pu 9; saddle slpd*		P

OFFICIAL DISTANCES: 5*l*, dist **TIME:** 6min 02.5s

146 Ladies Open — 6 ran

Form	Horse / Rider / Comment	Dist	Pos
33[4d]	**SAILORS FOLLY (IRE)** 5-4F **Miss P Gundry** *(xnb) Made all; qcknd 5l clr aft 16; unchall*		1
	Sunburnt 8-1 **Miss J Houldey** *A chsng wnr; chall 14; one pce 3 out; wkng when mist last*	10	2
63[2]	**Phoenix Phlyer**(vis) 9-4 **Miss C Stucley** *(xnb,pricker n/s) Chsd ldrs; 5l 3rd ½way; mist & rmdrs 11; eff 16; no imp 3 out*	¾	3
48[2]	Garolo (FR)(bl) 7-2 Miss V Tremlett *Nvr on terms; 10l 4th ½way; rdn 12; lost tch 15; sn wl bhnd*	15	4
	Let's Fly (FR) 14-1 Mrs M Hand *Last 5; lost tch 8; rdn 12; wl bhnd 14.*	10	5
	Abkins Du Bois (FR) 100-1 Miss K Gordon-Quayle *Last til pu aft 4*		P

OFFICIAL DISTANCES: 10*l*, ½*l* **TIME:** 6min 02.1s

147 Intermediate, 12st — 7 ran

Form	Horse / Rider / Comment	Dist	Pos
	MORRIS PIPER (5x) 4-1 **R Woollacott** *6s-4s; lw; ld in start; rcd keen; last to 3; hdwy aft 8; went 2nd 10; ld 12; clr app 3 out; quite impressive*		1
65[1]	**Earl's Toy (IRE)** 9-4 **H Fry** *Hld up & bhnd; last 3-12; went 8l 3rd 14 & 10l 2nd 3 out; no imp*	12	2
116[7]	**Silver Pot Black** 10-1 **M Barber** *14s-10s; ld to 2; 2nd/3rd til lost plce 9; 4½l 6th ½way; 9l 5th & rdn 13; went 15l 4th 16; plodded on u.p*	7	3
62[3]	Bak On Board 7-4F Miss L Gardner *2 handlers; swtng; chsd ldrs; 2l 3rd ½way; lft 2nd 12; mist 15; 4l down nxt; wknd 3 out*	¾	4
116[4]	Briary Boy (IRE) 9-1 N Wilmington *(xnb) Hld up; 4l 5th ½way; lft 3rd 12-14; rdn & wknd qckly aft nxt*	6	5
	Early Morning Call (IRE) 6-1 J Barnes *(xnb) Ld 2 til hdd & blun & ur 12*		U
	Mr Evans 10-1 D Jones *Bckwd; 2nd to 9; 3l 4th ½way; wknd qckly aft 11; wl bhnd when pu 13*		P

OFFICIAL DISTANCES: 10*l*, 8*l* **TIME:** 6min 14.1s

148 Restricted, 12st - 18J — 11 ran

Form	Horse / Rider / Comment	Dist	Pos
	CANTERBURY JACK (IRE) 6-4F **A Farrant** *A.p; mist 3; 2l 3rd ½way; went 2nd aft 11; lft in ld 15; 8l clr when jmpd slow nxt; mist 3 out; nt fluent last 2; rdn out*		1
65[4]	**Alpine Fugue (IRE)**(tt) 20-1 **Miss S Lewis** *Rcd wide; w ldrs; 7l 5th ½way; 9l 4th 13; lft 4l 2nd 15; one pce & dem 3 out; went 2nd agn last*	10	2
67[1]	**Bessie Bunter** (5a) 2-1 **D Edwards** *4s-2s; hld up; lost plce 8; 10l 7th ½way; 10l 5th 13; lft 7l 4th & rdn 15; chsd wnr 3 out; 6l 2nd & wkng when mist nxt*	1½	3
118[P]	Mrs Peggoty (5a)(bl) 10-1 L Jefford *2nd to 9; 4l 4th ½way; 7l 3rd 13; wknd qckly aft 15.*	25	4
83[1]	Bishop's Blade 5-1 Miss S Gaisford *(xnb) Ld; 3l clr when fell 15.*		F
79[P]	Elegant Light (5a) 25-1 M Munrowd *2 handlers; hld up; hdwy 8; 7½l 6th ½way; lost tch u.p 12; pu 13*		P
	Liberty Livelihood (5a) 10-1 Miss L Gardner *(xnb) Hld up; 8th when fell 6; dead*		F
65[F]	Mister Party 14-1 C Heard *(xnb) Hld up; mist 7; drpd back 14l last ½way; pu 11*		P
68[5]	Mo's O Friendly 33-1 Miss S Robinson *Mist 2; chsd ldrs til lost plce 8; 12l 9th ½way; lost tch 12; pu 13*		P

Porto (IRE) 5-1 R Woollacott *Hld up & pulled hrd; hdwy 8; went 2nd 9 til aft 11; rdn & stpd to nil aft 12; pu 13* . . . . P
Socute (5a) 10-1 J Barnes *(xnb) Last to 10; 11l 8th ½way; lost tch 12; t.o & pu aft 16* . . . . P

OFFICIAL DISTANCES: 10*l*, 2*l* **TIME:** 6min 10.3s

Fence 14 omitted - fallen horse

149 Open Maiden (Div 1), 12st — 13 ran

51² **JOHNSAIR (IRE)** 2-1JF **G Perkins** *(xnb) Made all; r.o wl* 1
Coralinga (5a)(cp) 16-1 **N Wilmington** *Virt a 2nd; drew clr w wnr aft 16; rdn & ev ch app last; nt qckn* 5 2
My Moondancer (FR) (7a) 2-1JF **Miss P Gundry** *(xnb) 2 handlers; hld up & bhnd; 20l 7th ½way; hdwy & 7l 5th 14; outpcd aft 16; went 15l 3rd 2 out; wkng when mist last* 15 3
66³ Merlins Bay (IRE) 5-1 W White *Prom; 4l 4th ½way; 4l 3rd 14; disp 2l 2nd aft 16; wknd tame 3 out* 12 4
Orinoco's Flight (IRE) 12-1 M Holmes *Hld up; hdwy 8; 2l 3rd ½way; 6l 4th 14; wknd 15* 1 5
66^P Bristol Bridge 20-1 S Blackwell *(xnb) Lw; bhnd; rn wide bend aft 8; pu 9* . P
Challis Choice (IRE) 16-1 R Woollacott *(xnb) Hld up; hdwy & 8l 5th ½way; wknd & 10l 6th 14; bhnd when pu aft 15* . . . . P
Five Minutes (5a)(vis) 4-1 C Heard *Prom; lost plce & 9l 6th ½way; sn rdn & nt r.o; wl bhnd when pu 14* . . . . P
68^P King Marlon 25-1 G Barfoot-Saunt *Mist 3; wl bhnd 6; t.o 9; pu 12* . . . . . . P
Merlin Cider (5a) 14-1 Mrs M Hand *Sn last & wl bhnd; t.o 6; pu aft 10.* . . P
North Croft 20-1 D Doyne-Ditmas *Hld up; lost plce 8; mist 10; 25l 8th ½way; t.o & pu 12* . . . . P
Rody (IRE) 16-1 M Walters *(xnb) Prom til rn out 4* . . . . R
Roy My Boy (7a) 20-1 J Cole *Sn wl bhnd; 11th when mist & rfo 6* . . . . . . U

OFFICIAL DISTANCES: 4*l*, 20*l* **TIME:** 6min 16.3s

150 Open Maiden (Div 2), 12st - 18J — 10 ran

67^U **BALLYKNOCK ROSE (IRE)** (5a) 6-1 **Miss V Shaw** *(xnb) 2nd/3rd til ld aft 8; r.o wl* 1
Gipsy Girl (5a) 5-1 **R Stephens** *Hld up; 7l 4th ½way; went 4l 3rd 12 & 2nd 14; rdn to chall app 2 out; ev ch when outj last; one pce* 2 2
Smokey Joe (IRE) 12-1 **C Heywood** *Lost tch 7; t.o 9; 40l last ½way; 35l 6th 16; went rem 3rd 2 out; nvr nrr* . . . . runin 3
121^P Beaford Princess (5a) 16-1 J Young *Chsd ldrs; 6l 3rd ½way; 8l 5th & rdn 13; sn wknd; 23l 5th 16; mist 2 out; t.o* 15 4
67⁴ Another Bit 7-1 G Barfoot-Saunt *16s-7s; ld til tried to duck out & ur 7* . . . U
Fluted Edge (5a) 16-1 Mrs M Hand *Sn wl bhnd; t.o & pu 6* . . . . P
Highway Ten (5a) 20-1 T Dennis *Hld up; lost tch aft 8; 20l 7th ½way; t.o 15; pu 3 out* . . . . P
61³ Listen To Us (IRE) 7-1 Miss L Gardner *(xnb) Hld up; 8l 5th ½way; 7l 4th 13; went 10l 3rd aft by-passing 15; sn wknd; t.o & pu aft 2 out; dism* . . . . P
66² Our Weddingpresent (USA) (7a) 4-5F A Farrant *(xnb) Nt jw; hld up; mist 2; 9l 6th ½way; rdn & no hdwy 12; pu aft mist 13.* . . . . P
67^F Worthy Man(tt) 12-1 L Jefford *(xnb) Pulled hrd; went 2nd aft 2; lft in ld 7; hdd aft nxt; chsd wnr til wknd 14; 20l 4th 16; t.o & pu 2 out.* . . . . P

OFFICIAL DISTANCES: 3*l*, dist **TIME:** 6min 16.4s

Fence 15 omitted - fallen rider

North Norfolk Harriers

Higham (LH 8F,19J)

Sun, 8 Feb (GOOD)

151 Open Maiden (Div 1, Part 1), 12st — 9 ran

39^U **CHARANGO STAR** 4-1 **P York** *Settled midfield; clsd to 3rd 14 & 2nd nxt; ld aft 3 out; sn clr; mist 2 out; rdly.* 1
Sovereign Gale (IRE) (5a) 10-1 **M Harris** *(xnb) Made nrly all til drvn & hdd aft 3 out; sn outpcd; eased flat* 12 2

40^{3}	**Golden Shred** (5a)(bl) 5-1 **S Morris** *(xnb) 2nd/3rd til ld brief 12; ev ch til jmpd v slow 16; most reluct in rem 3rd aft.*	30	3
	Marciano 6-1 Miss L Allan *(xnb) Midfield early; rr & strugg 12; t.o 16*	3	4
39^{5}	Sharp Sarah (5a) 10-1 P Chinery *Jmpd lft; hld up towards rr; 6th 12; sn lost tch; t.o 16.*	5	5
	All Eyez On Me (IRE) 7-1 M Wall *Prsd ldrs til 5th & drvn 15; sn lost tch; t.o 3 out; pu last*		P
	Barry Lydon (IRE) 14-1 T Lane *Mists towards rr; rdr lost iron 4; strugg when blun 13; t.o & pu nxt*		P
	Divine Mist (IRE) 5-1 J Owen *Jmpd & hung rt; reluct in last til blun & ur 11*		U
	Madmidge 2-1F D Kemp *Chsd ldrs & nt a fluent; went 4th 14; fair 3rd when rn thro wing & ur 3 out*		R

OFFICIAL DISTANCES: 10*l*, dist **TIME:** 6min 14.0s **TOTE:** £4.00 **DF:**£29.00

152 Open Maiden (Div 1, Part 2), 12st — 9 ran

	ASTHEFELLOWSAID (IRE) 5-4F **A Hickman** *(xnb) Hld up last to 11; cruising aft; chall & lft 2nd 16; ld aft nxt; mist 2 out; drvn & in comm flat; all out*		1
59^{2}	**Troubleshooter** 5-2 **M Mackley** *Ld; rdn & hdd aft 3 out; kpt on stdly; a hld*	6	2
40^{F}	**Manhatton Storm (IRE)** 5-1 **N Bloom** *Chsd ldrs; jmpd slow 8; 12l 5th 14; fdd tame; flatt by posn*	30	3
103^{B}	Sister Ali (IRE) (5a) 10-1 S Gordon-Watson *Mist 2; a bhnd; 15l 6th 14; sn t.o*	runin	4
26^{F}	Castlediva (5a) 4-1 B Pollock *Mist 5; prsd ldr & ev ch til fell 16 (lkd hld)*		F
	Conquistador (IRE) 6-1 G Johnson-Houghton *Midfield til fell 3*		F
40^{P}	Dolitanlad 6-1 P Millington *Lkd awful; midfield; wknd rap 12; sn t.o; pu 3 out*		P
	Lancastrian Island (5a) 7-1 R Armson *Bckwd; settled 3rd til mist 12; sn wknd & nt jw aft; v tired when lft rem 3rd 16; pu 2 out*		P
	Miss Biddy (5a) 2-1 Miss O Maylam *Rr frm 6; releg last 11; t.o & pu 16.*		P

OFFICIAL DISTANCES: 3*l*, dist **TIME:** 6min 12.0s **TOTE:** £3.20 **DF:**£3.70

153 Open Maiden (Div 2, Part 1), 12st - 18J — 7 ran

	GREYBROOK LAD (IRE) 2-1F **Stuart Robinson** *A gng easy; sn ld; drew rt away frm 16; qckly dism aft fin; impressive*		1
	Vivaldi Rose (IRE) (5a) 5-1 **N Walker** *(xnb) Sn prsng wnr; nt fluent & rdr novicey; still ev ch 16; qckly outpcd & tired; plugged on*	30	2
29^{5}	**Bebe Bleu (IRE)** (5a) 3-1 **C Ward-Thomas** *(xnb) Mists in last; nvr gng wl; t.o 8*	15	3
105^{4}	Donnini (IRE) 5-1 P Millington *(xnb) V unimpressive padd; 4th when crashing fall 7; destroyed aft nxt rce*		F
39^{P}	Pendils Charm (5a) 10-1 D Kemp *Ld 1; nt jw & reluct; lost tch 5; strugg bad when hmpd & ur 8*		U
	Rumour Has It (IRE) 4-1 P Hall *(xnb) 2 handlers; re-bridled start; jmpd erratic in last pr & sn lost tch; t.o 8; pu 12*		P
28^{3}	Tartar Sabre 3-1 Miss L Barrett-Nobbs *Fat; chsd ldrs; 3rd when rfo 8.*		U

OFFICIAL DISTANCES: dist, 20*l* **TIME:** 6min 13.0s **TOTE:** £2.00 **DF:**£6.50

Fence 15 omitted - fallen horse; Marsden (bckwd, ur & bolted) was withdrawn not under orders

154 Open Maiden (Div 2, Part 2), 12st - 17J — 8 ran

40^{F}	**MORPH** 4-6F **P York** *Settled rr til smooth prog to ld app 12; drew wl clr aft jmpd slow 16; v easily.*		1
104^{6}	**Half A Story** (5a) 10-1 **A Williams** *Lft 3rd 13; went 6l 2nd aft mist 16; nvr nr wnr aft*	25	2
	Play Alone (IRE) (5a) 5-1 **N Bloom** *Mist 1; ld/2nd til app 12; lft 2nd nxt; wkng when mist 16; 3rd & btn aft.*	8	3
	Waterliner (12a) 6-1 A Merriam *Mist 2; cl up til wknd 12; poor 4th 16; plugged on sltly frm 2 out*	1½	4
	Cerasus Knight (IRE) 8-1 J Morgan *Jmpd wild rt 1; t.o aft til pu aft 11*		P
	General Hopkins (IRE) 8-1 W Pewter *Mists in midfield; wknd 12; rem last 16; pu last*		P
	Joves Shadow 4-1 T Lane *Hld up; went cl 3rd 10; ev ch & lkd gng wl when bd 13*		B
	No Penalty 5-1 A Braithwaite *(xnb) 2 handlers; ld/disp; cl 2nd when fell 13*		F

OFFICIAL DISTANCES: 20*l*, 10*l* **TIME:** 6min 13.0s **TOTE:** £1.20 **DF:**£7.50

Fences 7 & 15 omitted - fallen horse from previous race

155 Dodson & Horrell PPORA Club Members (Nov Rdrs), 12st - 18J

15 ran

45[1]	**ROYAL ACTION** 2-1F **P Chinery** *Settled 3rd; ld 10; lft clr 12; r.o stout & unchall aft*		1
	Naughty Dandy (IRE) 16-1 **Mrs C Andrews** *(xnb) Chsd ldrs; 10l 5th 11; sn outpcd; 27l 3rd 16; stayed on to poor 2nd app last*	20	2
45[U]	**Pampered Gale (IRE)** 12-1 **Miss N Barnes** *Nvr put in rce; poor 8th 11; 40l 5th 16*	10	3
42[F]	Village Copper 3-1 R Stearn *(xnb) Chsd ldrs; went 4th 10; lft 10l 2nd 12; chsd wnr vain til fdd bad aft 2 out*	2	4
22[2]	Treasure Dome (IRE) 20-1 Miss A Bowles *Prsd ldrs til 18l 4th & wkng 12; 30l 4th 16; t.o*	25	5
	Tomcappagh (IRE) (1ow) 14-1 J Wall *Nvr put in rce; rem 9th 11; plodded rnd*	1	6
99[P]	Castle Road (IRE) 10-1 Miss L Marriott *(xnb) Ss; a t.o*	½	7
	Buckland Bobby 33-1 Miss L Fear *Lkd terrible; a t.o*	30	8
	Brave Albert (IRE) 12-1 Miss K Keefe *(xnb) Unruly & dism to leave padd; ur 1*		U
45[3]	Brown Chieftain (IRE) 10-1 Miss C Haydon *Made most to 10; w wnr when fell 12*		F
	Coole Chief 10-1 Sam Gray *1st ride; mostly 2nd to 8; 7th & wkng rap 11; t.o & v tired when pu 14*		P
	Henwyn 5-1 A Humphrey *(xnb) Midfield; 6th 11; hmpd & ur 12*		U
	Mr Moonbeam (IRE) 12-1 M Buchan *V ss; a wl t.o; pu 8*		P
57[P]	Table For Four (1ow) 7-1 P Andrew *Imm wl bhnd; t.o & blun 9; pu 10*		P
	Thurles Pickpocket (IRE) 10-1 B Elson *A wl bhnd; rem 10th 11; pu 16*		P

OFFICIAL DISTANCES: dist, 20*l* **TIME:** 6min 13.0s **TOTE:** £2.80 **DF:**£50.00

Fence 9 omitted - fallen rider; declared runners Act In Time, Crackrattle (IRE), Little Worsall (IRE) and Win The Toss were balloted from this race so it no longer had to be divided

156 Mens Open

10 ran

	HOMME DE FER 5-1 **N Bloom** *Settled 3rd/4th; 9l 3rd 12; clsd gng wl 16; ld 3 out; rdn out flat*		1
	Philtre (IRE) 11-4 **A Wintle** *Ld to 6 & agn 12 til rdn & hdd 3 out; ev ch nxt; nt qckn aft*	5	2
24[F]	**Shanavogh** 11-10F **R Hunnisett** *2nd til ld 6-12; cl 2nd 16; wknd qckly app nxt; tired frm 2 out*	20	3
54[U]	Fine Times 16-1 T Lane *Hld up & nvr btr than midfield; 5th & outpcd 12; 45l 5th 16*	30	4
38[P]	Mai Point (5a) 16-1 N Moore *Hit 4; rr & nvr gng wl aft; rem last 12*	runin	5
24[B]	Galeaway (IRE) 20-1 J Barnard *Rdr v unstdy; a rr; t.o 10; rdr finally decanted 14*		U
3[P]	Glemot (IRE) 25-1 N Pearce *Chsd ldrs; 7th & outpcd 12; ur 14*		U
43[U]	King Of The Dawn 33-1 J Sole *Jmpd slow 8; handy to 10; 6th & fdng 12; wl t.o 16; pu 2 out*		P
	Militaire (FR) 20-1 J Owen *Reluct in rr; lost tch 5; t.o & pu 12*		P
38[3]	Rathnally Park 9-2 M Mackley *Tk keen hld; hld up in rr til hdwy 10; 4th 12; 25l 4th & tiring rap 16; jb rt nxt; t.o & pu last*		P

OFFICIAL DISTANCES: 5*l*, 15*l* **TIME:** 6min 03.0s **TOTE:** £4.80 **DF:**£10.00

157 Ladies Open

10 ran

25[1]	**PLACID MAN (IRE)** 5-4F **Ms A Embiricos** *Jw; made virt all & twice qcknd when prsd; easily drew 8l clr 14; virt solo frm 16; impressive*		1
	Celtic Duke 3-1 **Miss Z Turner** *Settled cl up; 3rd 11; outpcd 13 & 20l 3rd 16; nt chse wnr aft but went 2nd flat; btr for rce*	35	2
	Paradisio (FR) 20-1 **Miss A Stennett** *Rn 2nd; jnd wnr 4 & agn 12 but imm outpcd; chsd wnr vain to last; fin lame*	1½	3
42[5]	Le Prince 12-1 Miss E Jones *Pulled hrd; cl up; 4th & rdn 11; outpcd nxt; 23l 4th 16*	6	4
	Mackoy (IRE) 20-1 Miss H Hall *Midfield to 8; 8th & wkng 11; 43l 6th 16; t.o*	10	5
101[P]	Grand Ambition (USA) 10-1 Miss L Allan *Towards rr early; disp 7l 4th 12; outpcd when nt fluent 13 & 15; 36l 5th nxt; t.o & pu 2 out*		P
	Heaven Is Above (IRE) 4-1 Mrs D Rowell *Midfield til rfo 8*		U
	Hoodwinker (IRE) 7-2 Miss J Williams *Bhnd; mist 7 & drvn; mod 7th 11; nt fluent 13; t.o nxt; pu rap app 16; broke leg; dead*		P

	Karzhang 20-1 Miss H Kinsey *Bhnd; 9th 11; 33l 5th 16; t.o & pu last*		P
5P	Step In Line (IRE) 20-1 Mrs S Hodge *(xnb) Midfield; 15l 6th & strugg 12; t.o 14; pu 3 out*		P

OFFICIAL DISTANCES: dist, 1½l **TIME:** 5min 59.0s **TOTE:** £2.00 **DF:**£25.00

158 Countryside Alliance Club Members Conditions 12 ran

	MARTHA'S BOY (IRE) 5-4F **D Dunsdon** *Tkn stdly in rr; mists 8 & when 6l 6th 12; went 2nd 3 out; ld on bit aft nxt; comf*		1
31¹	**Lord Kilpatrick (IRE)** 3-1 **T Edwards** *Lw; cl up; went 2nd 10; ld 12; hdd aft 2 out; drvn along flat; a hld*	2	2
98¹	**Highland Rose (IRE)** (5a) 5-1 **Ms A Embiricos** *(xnb) Settled chsng ldrs; 5l 5th 12; still 5th 16; rdn & no imp aft*	10	3
100P	Leatherback (IRE) 14-1 J Owen *Prsd ldrs; 4th 12; 6l 4th 16; wknd qckly*	25	4
	Adamatic (IRE) (12ow) 14-1 C Jarvis *Midfield early; rr 8; t.o aft 11; pu 14*		P
1F	Merry Minstrel (IRE) 12-1 L Hicks *Fell 2*		F
56³	Mr Naborro (IRE)(cp) 20-1 A Wintle *Blun 4; towards rr; rdn & reluct 11; 7th & btn nxt; t.o & pu 15*		P
45⁵	Optimistic Thinker(cp) 10-1 M Harris *Cl up to 8; lost tch 10; t.o & pu 13*		P
	Persian Bandit (IRE) 10-1 M Mackley *Jmpd v erratic; sn t.o; pu 12*		P
	Santi (FR) 5-1 P Cowley *Chsd ldr to 10; 2nd 12; fdd rap aft 15; t.o & pu 3 out*		P
	Tea Box (IRE) 4-1 D Kemp *Ld to 12; cl 2nd when nt fluent 16; dem & wknd 3 out; wl btn 3rd when pu qckly & dism last*		P
	Valman (IRE) 12-1 P Millington *Lkd awful; sn bhnd; t.o 10; pu 12*		P

OFFICIAL DISTANCES: 2l, 10l **TIME:** 6min 07.0s **TOTE:** £4.20 **DF:**£4.80

159 Restricted 14 ran

	CANTARINHO 11-10F **D Kemp** *Trckd ldrs; lft 2nd aft 11; ld 2 out; rdn & jnd last; outbattled rnr-up flat*		1
57³	**Snowtre (IRE)**(cp) 4-1 **A Wintle** *(xnb) Hld up; 5th & prog 12; chall in 2l 3rd 16; rdn to jn wnr last; fnd little final 100yds; ur just aft post*	nk	2
	Captive (IRE) 14-1 **J Owen** *Settled handy; went 3rd 12; ev ch til wknd rap 3 out*	35	3
65⁷	Always Good (IRE) 20-1 P Needham *(xnb) Rcd keen; ld 3-6; sn lost plce; 6th & wkng 12; t.o 14*	8	4
31P	Sydney Hobart 8-1 A Vaughan-Jones *Imm lost tch; t.o 4; ab fnce bhnd final circ*	30	5
99P	Ballylesson (IRE) 20-1 N Moore *Prom; ld 6 til fell 11*		F
	Broad Edge (IRE) 8-1 R Stearn *(xnb) Threw rdr lvng padd; imm lost tch; t.o 4; pu 11*		P
	Camden Loch (IRE) 16-1 N Bloom *Cl up to 8; rr & strugg 12; t.o when jmpd v slow 13; pu nxt*		P
57⁵	Henry Henbit 6-1 S Morris *Ld to 3; 2nd/3rd to 11; wknd 13; t.o & pu 3 out*		P
44P	Jacob's Choice (7a) 6-1 P York *Nvr gng wl; lost tch qckly 8; t.o & pu 12*		P
2³	Jims Belief (IRE) 5-1 G Cooper *(xnb) Hld up; hdwy 10; lft in ld nxt; hdd & blun 2 out; cl 3rd but btn when ur last; stirrup leather broke*		U
44U	Lambrini King (IRE) 8-1 Miss L Barrett-Nobbs *(xnb) Midfield; hmpd 11 & lost tch; t.o 14; pu 16*		P
38P	Lone Star (IRE)(bl) 14-1 H Fowler *Midfield; strugg 10; t.o & pu 14*		P
	Regal Bride (5a) 10-1 R Armson *T.o 4; pu 11*		P

OFFICIAL DISTANCES: hd, 10l **TIME:** 6min 10.0s **TOTE:** £2.60 **DF:**£11.00

Old Raby Hunt Club

Witton Castle (RH 7F,19J)

Sun, 8 Feb (GOOD)

160 ORHC Club Members Maiden 13 ran

	MAGIC PERFORMER 6-4F **N Tinkler** *Last to 5; 12l 4th 14; pushed along 3 out; stayed on best to ld 2 out; ½l up at last; rdly drew clr flat*		1
	Stormy Sunrise (IRE) 16-1 **Miss A Armitage** *Cl 2nd 8; in tch til outpcd 13; 6th 14; hdwy to disp ld 3 out-nxt; tired bad & clambered over last; all out*	8	2
	Bobby Buttons 5-2 **N Tutty** *Chsd along in 25l 3rd 7; lft handy 2nd 8; 8l 2nd 14 til pushed along aft 15; lft in ld nxt; hdd aft 3 out; v tired nxt; just outpcd for 2nd flat; all out*	1	3

Red September 7-2 P Kinsella *A midfield; went cl 3rd 14; pushed along & wknd 15* 6 4
Legenda (7a) 8-1 T Craggs *(xnb) Tk keen hld; sn clr; 20l ahd when fell 8; cannoned into rival when loose; collapsed & died returning to unsaddle* . . . . F
Lothian Rising 12-1 L Morgan *Hld up early; stdy hdwy to handy 4th 9; in tch when fell 13* . . . . F
No Info (IRE) (5a) 14-1 C Mulhall *A rr; pushed along & lsng tch 8; t.o & pu 13* P
Nomadic Blaze 3-1 P Atkinson *Chsd ldr til lft in ld 8; 15l clr & galloping str when knocked over by loose horse app 16* . . . . B
Northern Castle (IRE) 10-1 R Clark *(xnb) Prom in 4th to 8; sn wknd; rr by 10; t.o & pu 13* . . . . P
Oaklands Ted 16-1 T Glass *A towards rr; rem 5th when pu last.* . . . . P
Parsifal (7a) 8-1 R Abrahams *Sa; hld up in rr; slt hdwy when fell 9.* . . . . F
Perky's Wish (IRE) 20-1 S J Robinson *(xnb) Midfield to 5; sn pushed along; last by 7; t.o 11; pu 12.* . . . . P
The Melting Pot (IRE)(cp) 8-1 L Bates *Midfield to 5; jmpd slow 6; rr & lsng tch 12; t.o 13; pu 15.* . . . . P

OFFICIAL DISTANCES: 8*l*, 1*l* **TIME:** 6min 40.0s

161 Intermediate, 12st — 13 ran

JUST CLIQUOT (5a) evensF **G Hanmer** *4s-evens; hld up; last to 4; still rr 9; grad prog to cl 4th 15; ld 3 out; sn clr; canter* 1
Infamelia (5a)(vis) 14-1 **Miss T Clark** *Rr; hdwy 8 to disp ld 10; ld 15; hdd 3 out; sn hrd rdn & one pce* 6 2
57P **Agent Provocateur (NZ)** 25-1 **R Clark** *(xnb) A.p; 1l 2nd 9; ev ch 16; cl 3rd 3 out; wknd app nxt.* 3 3
Sledmere (IRE) 50-1 J Botham *Handy in 2nd to 5; wknd frm 7; t.o 14; stayed on past btn horses; fin str; nrst fin* 6 4
Loose Cannon (IRE) 12-1 N Saville *Mid-div to 11; hdwy to cl 2nd & lkd dangerous 15; wknd 3 out* 2 5
Rising Talisker (5a)(cp) 50-1 Miss Rachel Clark *Mid-div & handy to 12; 4l 5th 14; grad wknd frm 16* 1 6
Heather Lad 20-1 R Wakeham *Last early; rap hdwy frm 15 to 3rd 3 out; wknd nxt* 4 7
Princess Derry (5a) 7-1 C Cundall *A midfield; nvr any ch* 8 8
Needsmoretime (IRE) 20-1 S J Robinson *A rr div; lsng tch 12; t.o 14* 2 9
Catosphere (IRE) 16-1 C Mulhall *A rr; t.o & pu 14* . . . . P
Emperor's Son 4-1 Miss S Brotherton *(xnb) A handy; 2l 3rd 15; 1l 2nd & gng wl when carried out bend bef 3 out* C
Sharpaman(bl) 7-1 C Shirley-Beavan *Jmpd slow & reluct at times; ld; jnd 10 til hdd 15; clambered over nxt; t.o & pu 2 out* . . . . P
T'nightsthenight 40-1 D Jewett *Rr early; good hdwy 14; cruised to ld aft 16; missed marker bef nxt.* . . . . R

OFFICIAL DISTANCES: 6*l*, 6*l* **TIME:** 7min 09.0s

Step Lively (W Burnell, 6-1, lost tongue-strap at start) was withdrawn not under orders

162 Ladies Open — 10 ran

SILVER GROOM (IRE) 2-1 **Miss J Coward** *Sa; wl bhnd; last 10; hdwy 13 to 20l 4th 15; rap hdwy nxt to 4l 2nd 2 out; ld last; qcknd wl flat; luckily horses in front stpd; rdr's 1st wnr* 1
70[6] **Hessac (FR)** 14-1 **Miss W Gibson** *Chsd ldng pr in 15l 3rd til lft in ld 13; 5l clr 3 out; wknd app nxt; hdd last; outpcd flat* 1½ 2
Wandering Wild (5a) 8-1 **Mrs L Ward** *Mid-div & mist 4; 20l 6th 11; lft 2nd 13; 2l 2nd 15; ev ch 3 out; wknd app nxt* 10 3
Dun Distinctly (IRE) 12-1 Miss L Horner *Rr; hdwy to handy 5th 13 & 4l 3rd 15; wknd app 3 out; fin tired* 10 4
108U Silk Vestments (5a) 10-1 Miss H Dunning *A rr; bhnd by 6; poor 6th 11; t.o 13; plodded on* 35 5
Wishful Thinker 10-1 Miss L Hislop *Chsd ldrs in 4th to 8; wknd 11; rr & lsng tch 13; t.o 16* 15 6
Over The Beck (IRE) 3-1 Miss C Metcalfe *Mid-div to 7; wknd qckly aft 9; lsng tch when pu 10* . . . . P
Pharlindo (IRE) 6-1 Miss A Armitage *(xnb) Ld to 4; 2l 2nd til blun & ur 13* U

Shining Light (IRE) 20-1 Miss A Vernon *Mid-div to 6; pushed along & rr by 10; lsng tch when blun bad & lost irons 12; pu 13* P

Texas Ranger 5-4F Miss J Foster *Tk keen hld; ld frm 5; bad blun 11; nt fluent 12; jmpd big, landed steep & ur 13* U

OFFICIAL DISTANCES: 1¼*l*, 10*l* **TIME:** 6min 41.0s

163 Mens Open 14 ran

107[2] **MR PENDLEBERRY** evensF **N Tinkler** *Mid-div to 8; went 10l 4th 13; pushed along 15; chall 2 out; 1l 2nd at last; rallied und str press to ld on line.* 1

San Francisco 6-1 **G Brewer** *Tried to make all; 6l clr 14; jnd 2 out; 1l up at last; drvn & r.o game flat; hdd nr line* ½ 2

Blank Cheque 10-1 **D Coates** *Sa; sn bhnd; t.o last 8; stayed on past defectors for rem 3rd* 40 3

Badge Of Fame (IRE) 25-1 P Kinsella *A rr; last early; hdwy to 6th 7; grad wknd; t.o & pu 16* P

Chadswell (IRE) 10-1 W Puddifer *A towards rr; t.o 16; pu 2 out* P

Erni (FR)(vis) 25-1 K Pearson *Cl 3rd/4th to 11; pushed along & wknd frm 14; t.o & pu 16* P

Feeling Grand (IRE) 33-1 F Arthur *In tch in rr div to 8; pushed along & lsng tch when pu 13* P

Flat Top 5-1 M Manton *Prom when ur 2* U

55[3] Glacial Dancer (IRE) 8-1 R Clark *A.p; handy 3rd til pushed along & outpcd 3 out; 15l 3rd & btn when fell last.* F

Mademist Sam 4-1 N Tutty *Chsd ldr; 2l 2nd til outpcd 13; 6l 2nd & wkng qckly nxt; v tired when pu 16* P

72[P] Mr Busby 16-1 R Morgan *Prom early; midfield frm 6; lsng tch & wknd 14; t.o & pu 16* P

Steel Rigg (IRE)(bl) 5-1 J Botham *A rr; t.o & pu 16.* P

Torn Silk 14-1 C Mulhall *A mid-div; stayed on to poor 5th 3 out; pu nxt.* P

Touchez Du Bois (IRE) 25-1 S Huggan *Handy early; cl up to 6; wknd qckly & t.o by 8; pu 12.* P

OFFICIAL DISTANCES: ½*l*, dist **TIME:** 6min 42.0s

164 Restricted, 12st 11 ran

PLACE ABOVE (IRE) 4-1 **L Bates** *Cl 2nd til ld 6-7; in tch til drpd back 13; hdwy 15 to ld agn 3 out; jnd 2 out-last; hrd rdn flat; stayed on to ld nr fin* 1

Just Fluster 20-1 **R Wakeham** *Hld up early; prog 12 to 6th 14; went cl 2nd 3 out; disp ld 2 out-last; hrd rdn & r.o flat; just outpcd.* ½ 2

109[P] **Claire's Nomad**(cp) 16-1 **Miss Rachel Clark** *(xnb) Handy 3rd til 1l 2nd 15; disp ld 16-3 out; wknd & outpcd by ldng pr frm nxt* 8 3

Lingham Lady (5a) 8-1 S Swiers *Sn rr; still last & all to do 15; stayed on wl; nrst fin* 8 4

70[7] Captain Oates 4-1 T Oates *Gng wl in mid-div to 8; cl 4th 12 til ld 15; jnd nxt; ev ch til hdd & wknd 3 out.* 3 5

70[4] Highland Brig 7-4F R Morgan *A midfield & nd; 7th 13 & pushed along; one pce aft* 8 6

Woodyouever (IRE) 8-1 S Todd *Sa; a rr; last by 7; lsng tch 8; t.o 15* 6 7

Minster Echo (5a) 20-1 G Brewer *Ld to 6 & 8-14; pushed along nxt; sn wknd; rr 2 out; coasted home* 12 8

Lord Scroop (IRE) 5-1 M Morley *Ur 1* U

70[P] Mr Sonshine 8-1 P Frank *A handy & lkd gng wl; cl 2nd 13; ev ch til wknd v qckly & pu 16* P

Tinarana Lord (IRE) 2-1 G Hanmer *Last by 2; mist 3 & rdr lost irons; failed to negotiate bend bef 6.* R

OFFICIAL DISTANCES: ½*l*, 5*l* **TIME:** 6min 51.0s

165 Open Maiden (Div 1), 12st 16 ran

TEN BOB (IRE) 3-1 **N Saville** *Hacked round in rr to 8; hdwy 11 to cl 3rd 13; cruised to ld on bridle 15; sn clr; impressive; toyed w rivals* 1

Ravenscar 7-1 **S Walker** *Midfield; 8l 5th 7 & 4l 4th 14; stayed on to 2nd 2 out; hrd rdn flat & fin str; flatt by prox.* 1½ 2

Oaklands Luis (7a) 12-1 **T Glass** *Rr; hdwy 12 to 4l 4th 16; ev ch 3 out; stayed on u.p to tk 3rd flat* 15 3

Indian Rope Trick 8-1 Miss J Foster *Ld 3-14; cl 2nd 16; pushed along & wknd to 6l 3rd 2 out; dem flat* 2 4

Bankersdraft 20-1 M Morley *Prom; 1l 2nd 6-11; pushed along & wknd 14; poor 5th 16; plodded on* 30 5
Born Special (7a) 6-1 P Kinsella *Midfield; wkng when fell 14* F
Castle Lodge 5-1 C Barlow *Blun & broke iron 2; pu 3* P
Hattie (5a) 14-1 P Cornforth *(xnb) Prom in 3rd/4th to 10; pushed along & wknd 11; sn bhnd & lsng tch; t.o & pu 16* P
High Peak 2-1F T Greenall *Fell 1* F
74P Lethem Air 5-1 D Jewett *Hld up in rr til hdwy 7; clsng & gng wl when ur 10* U
Littleton Zeus (IRE) (7a) 10-1 N Tutty *Handy; cl 5th 10; 6l 5th 14; sn wknd; pu 16* P
Melitma 16-1 T Oates *Ur 2* U
My Rock 10-1 N Tinkler *Lkd v novicey; sa; sn bhnd; jmpd slow & novicey; t.o & pu 9* P
75P Red Tyrant 7-1 Miss C Metcalfe *Ur 1* U
Rocky Fountain 8-1 L Morgan *Prom to 3; cl 2nd til pu app 6; broke leg; dead* P
Songino (IRE) 16-1 P Robinson *Ld to 3; in tch til wknd 8; rr 9; t.o & rem when pu last* P

OFFICIAL DISTANCES: 2l, 15l **TIME:** 6min 50.0s

166 Open Maiden (Div 2), 12st — 15 ran

70U **CROSS RIVER** 4-1 **N Saville** *(xnb) Midfield to 5; went 4l 3rd 9; ld 12; 3l up 16; jnd app last; pushed out & qcknd wl when chall flat* 1
Sir Alf 14-1 **T Glass** *Rr to 12; gd hdwy 14 to handy 3rd 16; chall app last; hrd rdn & outpcd flat* 3 2
Coastal Safari 25-1 **A Richardson** *Ld; 6l up 3 til hdd aft 6; ld agn 9-11; cl 2nd til wknd 3 out* 15 3
Clonshire Paddy (IRE) 5-2 T Greenall *Handy 5th 7; in tch to 12; 4l 4th 15; pushed along & outpcd nxt* 5 4
74F Scowlin Brig 9-2 S Huggan *2l 2nd 5; handy 3rd 13; u.p & pushed along nxt; wknd 16; dist 5th 3 out* 8 5
112P Gollinger 8-1 B Woodhouse *A midfield; nd* 20 6
1125 Midnight Moon 25-1 J Burley *Midfield to 10; sn wknd; t.o 16* 35 7
Almacash (IRE) (5a) 14-1 C Mulhall *(xnb) Rr & bhnd by 6; pushed along & wknd 12; t.o & pu 13* P
Atlantic Drift (IRE)(bl) 7-1 A Pennock *Cl up; handy 3rd til ld 7-8; in tch til wknd 13; t.o 16; pu 3 out* P
Caimins Well (IRE) 2-1F G Hanmer *Midfield til fell 11* F
Callitwatulike 25-1 C Dawson *Handy in 4th to 8; grad wknd; t.o & pu 16* P
59U Eastern Royal (7a) 14-1 Miss Rachel Clark *(xnb) Sa; hld up in rr; pushed along & lsng tch 11; t.o & pu 16* P
Fair Signet 16-1 P Cornforth *Tk v keen hld; pulled hrd to trck ldr; saddle slpd & rn out 5* R
Inverdante (IRE) 8-1 A Pickering *A towards rr & nd; lost tch frm 13; t.o & pu 16* P
Sweet Chestnut 14-1 Miss L Kendall *Jmpd slow in rr; last by 2; sn t.o; pu 16* P

OFFICIAL DISTANCES: 3l, 15l **TIME:** 6min 51.0s

167 Open Maiden (Div 3), 12st — 14 ran

753 **MISS ROYELLO** (5a) 7-2 **D Jewett** *A handy; 6l 4th 10; hdwy to chall 3 out; ld nxt; rdly drew clr* 1
Iron Trooper (IRE) 14-1 **T Glass** *(xnb) Lw; rr til stdy hdwy frm 10; disp ld 3 out; one pce frm nxt; sure to improve* 5 2
Irish Paddy (IRE) (7a) 14-1 **R Clark** *Handy 5th 7; ld 12-13; in tch til outpcd & wknd 2 out* 3 3
Drovers Road 14-1 C Mulhall *Rr to 7; gd hdwy frm 12; ev ch 3 out; one pce frm nxt; will improve* 5 4
Mademist Sparky (5a) 16-1 N Tutty *Cl 2nd to 12; ld 13-16; ev ch 3 out; sn wknd* 4 5
Bally Leader (IRE) 12-1 C Dawson *Cl 3rd to 12; in tch til wknd 13; t.o by 16* 20 6
74P Looking Deadly (5a) 16-1 R Nichol *A rr; lsng tch 12; t.o by 14* 50 7
High Fields (7a) 7-2 T Greenall *Midfield; went 8l 6th 9 & cl 5th 15; 3l 2nd & lkd hld when tried to rn out, screwed over fnce & ur 2 out* U
Kindle A Flame 7-2 G Brewer *Ld to 5; jmpd slow 6; blun bad & fell 9* F
Political Cruise 10-1 S Huggan *Fell 1* F
Search Party (FR) (7a) 12-1 S Walker *Prom to 7; went 1l 2nd 12; 3l 3rd 14; trckng ldng pr when ur 15* U

Form	Horse / Details	Dist	Pos
	Sizer (IRE) 3-1F N Saville *Tk keen hld; ld til rn out 4; bolted across course in direction of Piercebridge; rdr aimed for a wall & baled out when horse shaped to jump it*		R
	Stickwiyadad 16-1 T Craggs *Handy in mid-div to 11; pushed along & wknd 13; t.o & pu 16*		P
	Three Way Split 12-1 Miss Rachel Clark *(xnb) Dwelt & imm bhnd; gd hdwy 6 to 3rd 8; cl up til hung bad aft 12; wknd & pu 16*		P

OFFICIAL DISTANCES: 4*l*, 4*l* **TIME:** 7min 10.0s

South Midlands Area Club

Tweseldown (RH 9F,19J)

Sun, 8 Feb (GOOD to FIRM, GOOD in places)

168 SMAC Club Members — 9 ran

Form	Horse / Details	Dist	Pos
100^{4}	**FREEDOM FIGHTER** 5-1 **A Martin** *Lkd rough; keen early; rstrnd bhnd ldrs; trckd ldr 9; rdn 3 out; mist nxt; stayed on to ld sn aft last; kpt on game u.p*		1
50^{5}	**Tanager**(bl) 7-1 **J Docker** *Nr fluent 2; pulled way to ld 7; made most aft; drew 3l clr aft 2 out; hrd rdn & hdd sn aft last; nt qckn*	2	2
	Dancing Fosenby 11-4 **M Holdforth** *(xnb) 5s-11/4; tended to j lft; a.p; ld; mist 1; hdd 3; rdn 2 out; kpt on same pce app last*	1	3
90^{3}	Owenabue Valley (IRE) 14-1 T Underwood *Hld up in rr; outpcd 12; prog 15; clsd frm 2 out; tried to chall flat; one pce*	nk	4
	Prate Box (IRE) 3-1 F Hutsby *Cl up; trckd ldng pr 12; rdn & mist 2 out; one pce app last*	2	5
47^{1}	Kustom Kit Grizzly (IRE)(vis) 5-2F A Barlow *(xnb) Rcd wide; hld up in tch; outpcd 12; nvr on terms aft; eff 2 out; no imp*	4	6
16^{P}	Grand Canyon (IRE) 33-1 N Docker *Bckwd; ld 3-7; rdn 11; sn wknd; t.o & pu 16*		P
116^{P}	Russian Connection (IRE) 33-1 A Ward-Thomas *A rr; last & lsng tch when mist 9; t.o & pu 12*		P
	Sweet Reward 20-1 R Smith *Hld up in tch; wl in contention 15; sn wknd; t.o & pu 2 out*		P

OFFICIAL DISTANCES: 1½*l*, 1*l* **TIME:** 6min 24.0s

169 Restricted, 12st — 15 ran

Form	Horse / Details	Dist	Pos
20^{1}	**LAMBRINI MIST** 6-1 **R Burton** *A ldng trio; ld 3-4; ld agn aft 3 out; clr nxt; stayed on str*		1
19^{2}	**Denvale (IRE)** 7-4F **R Cope** *Settled midfield; prog & mist 7; 4th ½way; no imp on ldrs 16; kpt on to 2nd aft 2 out; no ch w wnr.*	12	2
21^{1}	**Sharp Seal** 6-1 **F Buckett** *Set off in last trio; prog & 8th ½way; 5th & chsng ldrs 15; kpt on frm 2 out; nrst fin.*	½	3
8^{1}	Viscount Bankes 7-1 A Martin *(xnb) Rcd free; ld 4; made most til hdd aft 3 out; wknd grad frm nxt*	2½	4
	Poppy Maroon (5a) 3-1 M Miller *Trckd ldrs; blun 7; prog to trck ldr nxt; cl 3rd when mist 3 out; wknd nxt.*	10	5
118^{P}	Kilvoydan (IRE) 20-1 D Phelan *Ld to 3; sn lost plce & in midfield; 8th & last of those in tch 15; no prog aft; blun bad last*	5	6
118^{P}	Alpenstock (FR) 33-1 D I Turner *Midfield; mist 4; 7th ½way; same & just in tch chsng ldrs 15; wknd app 3 out*	20	7
50^{P}	Cloak And Dagger 33-1 D Harvey *Set off last trio; a bhnd; t.o last ½way; pu 3 out*		P
	Hello Roscrea (IRE) 14-1 Mrs S Brown *A last trio; t.o in last pr ½way; pu 3 out*		P
	Master Grass 20-1 P Mason *Midfield; 10th & lsng tch ½way; jmpd v slow 12; t.o & pu 14*		P
13^{1}	Spiers Peace (IRE) (7a) 14-1 Miss A Goschen *Set off wl in rr; nvr put in rce; t.o in 13th ½way; no real prog final circ; pu 2 out.*		P
	Stormy Pass 16-1 S Waley-Cohen *Mist 1; chsd ldrs; 5th ½way; same & wl in tch 15; sn wknd; pu 2 out.*		P
44^{P}	Teeton Fizz (5a) 16-1 A Sansome *Jb; mist 1; lsng plce when jmpd slow 3; 11th & bhnd ½way; poor 10th when pu 16 (was still gng str but also demolishing fncs)*		P

Teeton Glaive (5a) 10-1 Miss H Irving *(xnb) Midfield; 7th ½way; in tch in 8th when fell 13* . . . . F

The Wee General (IRE)(tt) 20-1 A Charles-Jones *(xnb) A rr; 12th & wl bhnd ½way; t.o & pu 14* . . . . P

OFFICIAL DISTANCES: 10*l*, ½*l* **TIME:** 6min 20.2s

170 Mens Open — 11 ran

17^{1} **TITUS BRAMBLE**(bl,tt) 1-2F **Julian Pritchard** *Opened 4/6; ld/disp at stdy pce; mist & rdr waving 13; hdd & mist 14; drvn to ld agn 3 out; drew 5l clr app last; flagging flat; officially jnd on line; lkd to just hld on* . . . . 1†

GOT NEWS FOR YOU 20-1 **A Charles-Jones** *(xnb) Tchd 25s; trckd ldrs gng wl; 3rd ½way; same & outpcd 15; 6l 3rd 3 out; went 2nd aft 2 out; 5l down at last; str rn flat & officially jnd ldr on line; lkd to fin hd 2nd* . . . . hd 1†

Et Light (FR) 7-1 **A Barlow** *Ww; 8th ½way; prog to press ldr 12; ld 14; jmpd lft 15; hdd 3 out; 2l 2nd nxt; fdd app last* 10 3

49^{2} Mr Smudge 8-1 A Martin *Mostly midfield; 7th ½way; outpcd by ldrs 14; no imp aft; plodded on* 15 4

17^{P} Life's Work 25-1 M Gorman *Midfield; mist 8 & drpd to rr; 10th ½way; lost tch 12; plodded on.* 8 5

34^{5} Poppet (5a) 8-1 H Fowler *(xnb) Midfield; 6th ½way; outpcd frm 14; ab 6th & no ch when fell 3 out* . . . . F

Private Pete 6-1 J Docker *Drpd to rr 6; 9th & rdn ½way; nvr gng wl aft; lost tch 12; t.o & pu last.* . . . . P

Rolling Maul (IRE) 33-1 J Horton *(xnb) Set off last & stayed there; lost tch 12; t.o & pu 3 out* . . . . P

3^{P} Shiny Bay (IRE) 33-1 A Sansome *Prom; disp ld 5-11; wknd nxt; 8th & wl bhnd when pu 15.* . . . . P

48^{8} Silver Lake (IRE) 10-1 C Gordon *20s-12s; prsd ldrs; jmpd slow 3; 5th ½way; sn wknd; 10th & wl bhnd when pu 15.* . . . . P

Some Go West (IRE) 20-1 R Cope *Trckd ldrs; 4th ½way; outpcd frm 14; wl bhnd in 6th when pu 2 out* . . . . P

OFFICIAL DISTANCES: d ht, 10*l* **TIME:** 6min 22.7s

171 Ladies Open — 6 ran

MISTER BENJAMIN (IRE) 1-4F **Miss C Roddick** *Hld up; trckd ldr 7; stdd to last & mist 11; clsd 3 out; swept into ld on outer app last; sn clr; easily.* 1

Filscot 12-1 **Miss E Harbour** *Trckd ldrs; went 2nd 11; clsd 3 out; ev ch aft 2 out; easily outpcd by wnr app last.* 7 2

The Granby (IRE) 4-1 **Miss H Irving** *Keen; ld 5; made most aft & 4-5l up til hdd app last; easily outpcd* 2 3

33^{5} The Bounder 7-1 Miss C Tizzard *Settled in last; outpcd 13; eff & just in tch 15; wknd 3 out* 25 4

33^{P} Priestthorn (IRE)(cp) 33-1 Miss W Southcombe *Ld to 3; cl 2nd when mist & ur 6* . . . . U

Shy Paddy (IRE) 33-1 Miss E Tory *Pulled hrd; ld 3-5; drpd to rr 9; went prom agn 11 & still pulling; wknd app 3 out; disp poor 4th when fell last.* . . . . F

OFFICIAL DISTANCES: 6*l*, 2*l* **TIME:** 6min 23.8s

172 Open Maiden (Div 1), 12st — 13 ran

30^{2} **AGUA ARDENTE** 9-4F **R Cope** *Trckd clr ldr 3; clsd 12; ld 15; clr nxt; rdn aft 2 out; 5l up last; clsd down but in comm flat* 1

Simply The One (IRE) 4-1 **H Fowler** *6s-4s; chsd ldrs; 5th ½way; prog to 3rd 12; went 7l 2nd 16; tried to cl app last; clsng flat; a hld* 2½ 2

Galaxy Girl (5a) 7-1 **J Mahot** *Towards rr & wl off pce; poor 9th ½way; stdy prog frm 13; tk rem 3rd 2 out; no ch w ldng pr; btr for rn.* 30 3

68^{2} Stalbridge Rose (5a) 10-1 Miss A Goschen *Chsd clr ldrs; 4th ½way; same & no prog final circ; disp rem 3rd 2 out; wknd* 20 4

April Treasure (5a) 5-1 Julian Pritchard *Rcd free; ld & sn clr; hdd 15; blun nxt & went out like a light; poor 5th when pu aft 2 out* . . . . P

Cats Cross (5a) 20-1 N Mitchell *(xnb) 2 handlers; sn t.o; jmpd v slow 5; pu 7* P

Faugere 8-1 M Miller *(xnb) 2 handlers; gt loose in padd & galloped into car park; midfield; jmpd slow 3; prog to chse clr ldng pr 8; lsng plce when jmpd slow 12; gave up; t.o & pu 16* . . . . P

Form	Runner	Dist	Pos
	Floorex Carpetman 33-1 A Foster *A bhnd; t.o in 10th ½way; cont miles bhnd til pu 16*		P
120P	Pandeli 33-1 D Phelan *Bckwd; jmpd v slow & sn t.o; pu 6*		P
52P	Plenty Inn Hand 10-1 A Charles-Jones *(xnb) Chsd clr ldrs; 6th ½way; sn strugg; t.o & pu 13*		P
51F	Sixes And Sevens (IRE) (5a) 33-1 G Kerr *Chsd clr ldrs; 7th ½way; sn wknd; t.o & pu 14*		P
	Sneedham's Green 33-1 P Mason *(xnb) Many mists; midfield; wknd & mist 9; t.o when crawled over 11 & pu*		P
	Will Shakespeare 8-1 N Williams *(xnb) A towards rr & wl off pce; 8th ½way; no ch when mist 12 & imm pu*		P

OFFICIAL DISTANCES: 2½*l*, dist **TIME:** 6min 25.9s

173 Open Maiden (Div 2), 12st — 10 ran

Form	Runner	Dist	Pos
112²	**KEEGAN BEARNAIS (FR)** 7-2 **T Mann** *(xnb) Made virt all; jnd 8; btr j & lft clr 2 out; stayed on wl*		1
30P	**Kalypso De Laugere (FR)** 9-2 **H Fowler** *Trckd wnr 5; chall & upsides frm 9; clr of rest frm 14; still level when blun 2 out; btn when mist last*	12	2
67³	**Royal Czarina** (5a) 5-1 **J Snowden** *Chsd wnr to 5; 3rd ½way; outpcd frm 14; disp 8l 3rd & no imp nxt; kpt on*	4	3
52⁵	On A Full Wager 10-1 J Docker *Warm; chsd ldrs; 4th & outpcd 13; disp 8l 3rd & no imp ldng pr 15; one pce*	2	4
	Alfie Be 5-2F R Cope *Jmpd slow sev fncs & rn green; rr; clsd & wl in tch 10; blun nxt; outpcd 12; jmpd slow & sn wknd; t.o & pu 2 out*		P
86P	Bloowit 33-1 M Legge *(xnb) Last & sn bhnd; t.o & pu aft 9*		P
	Chicago's Padre 10-1 A Charles-Jones *9th when pu 3; saddle slpd*		P
52⁴	Eastern Apple (5a) 7-1 A Martin *Jmpd slow 3; drvn in rr; disp poor 7th ½way; t.o & pu 13*		P
53⁷	Millys Filly (5a) 16-1 Miss F Wilson *Midfield; blun 7; strugg aft; disp poor 7th ½way; miles bhnd when pu 15*		P
	Octane Booster (IRE) 7-1 C Gordon *Trckd ldrs; cl 6th when mist & ur 11*		U

OFFICIAL DISTANCES: 10*l*, 6*l* **TIME:** 6min 34.0s

174 Open Maiden (Div 3), 12st — 8 ran

Form	Runner	Dist	Pos
	RUNNING HOT 3-1CF **A Charles-Jones** *(xnb) Keen; made all & sn clr; 15l up ½way; blun & nrly ur 12; mist nxt; 20l up & in comm frm 15; unchall*		1
52³	**Shy Lizzie** (5a) 3-1CF **P Mann** *Jmpd awkward 2; wl in rr; jmpd slow 7; 6th ½way; wl bhnd 13; stdy prog 15; stayed on to 2nd at last; hopeless task*	20	2
	Lutteur Bleu (FR) (7a) 5-1 **A Michael** *(xnb) Chsd clr ldrs; disp 3rd ½way; chsd wnr 14; no imp frm nxt; lost 2nd at last*	1½	3
	Tupelov (IRE) 3-1CF D Dennis *(xnb) W wnr 1; lost plce; last 4; prog to 3rd ½way; chsd wnr 12-14; no ch aft; virt pu flat*	15	4
68⁴	Purslet (5a) 16-1 Miss N Stallard *(xnb) Bit bckwd; mounted on course & tde; chsd wnr 3-12; wknd & no ch aft*	hd	5
53F	Norbert (IRE) 8-1 W Hill *(xnb) Mostly rr; 7th ½way; poor 6th frm 15*	20	6
	Chasing Buttercups (5a) 7-1 Miss A Goschen *Set off last pr; prog to 3rd 3; lost plce frm 9; t.o last frm 15*	2	7
	Little Mister 12-1 N Mitchell *Drpd to last 9; lsng tch when pu 11*		P

OFFICIAL DISTANCES: 20*l*, 1¾*l* **TIME:** 6min 32.8s

175 PPORA Club Members (Nov Rdrs), 12st — 15 ran

Form	Runner	Dist	Pos
	NOMADIC STAR 5-1 **Miss Z Lilly** *Rr group & wl bhnd; some prog to 10th ½way; hdwy to poor 4th 14; r.o frm 3 out; chsd clr ldr aft 2 out; urged along & r.o to ld flat; sn clr.*		1
	Masalarian (IRE) 9-2 **Miss L Bridges** *(xnb) 16s-9/2; 2 handlers; rr; prog 6; 7th ½way; hdwy to 3rd 12; chsd ldr 15; ld 3 out; sn clr; 10l up aft 2 out; tired & hdd flat*	2½	2
	Lively Lord (IRE)(cp,tt) 6-1 **G Wigley** *Ld at fast pce to 3 out; jmpd slow 2 out & lost 2nd; fin tired*	20	3
110U	Nelsun 20-1 A Corbett *(xnb) Chsd clr ldr 4-15; grad wknd*	2	4
32⁷	Tale Bridge (IRE) 20-1 J Russell *Rr group & sn wl bhnd; rdr up in air 3; 13th & t.o ½way; r.o frm 3 out; snatched 5th in blanket fin*	15	5
48⁴	Starpath (NZ) 6-1 N McDiarmid *(xnb) Chsd ldrs; went 3rd ½way; outpcd frm 12; sn lost plce; no ch aft; kpt on frm 2 out*	nk	6

49^{3} Seabrook Lad 4-1JF N Docker *Rr group & sn wl bhnd; rdn & prog to 8th ½way; no imp on ldrs frm 12; stayed on frm 2 out* . . . . hd 7

Down (FR) (7x) 4-1JF Miss J Waley-Cohen *(xnb) 1st ride; midfield & nvr on terms w ldrs; 11th & wl off pce ½way; no imp final circ til r.o wl app last* hd 8

31^{2} Topical Tip (IRE) (1ow) 5-1 Mrs E Chugg *Rr group & sn wl bhnd; 14th & t.o ½way; no ch aft; kpt on* 15 9

47^{P} Esterelle (USA) (5a) 33-1 G Tumelty *(xnb) Warm; chsd ldrs; 5th ½way; no prog frm 12; wknd app 2 out* 2 10

5^{9} Solo Gent 25-1 Miss K Jones *Tkn to post 15mins early; chsd ldr to 4; 4th ½way; sn lost plce & bhnd*. 6 11

Gabaka De Thaix (FR) 33-1 M Caldwell *2 handlers; midfield & nvr on terms w ldrs; 9th ½way; wknd frm 13; t.o* 3 12

Angus Airways (IRE) 33-1 M Legge *(xnb) Blun 2; rr group & sn wl bhnd; poor 12th ½way; t.o aft; pu 2 out* . . . . P

Croft Court 33-1 D Renney *Rr group & sn wl bhnd; t.o last ½way; pu 2 out* P

31^{4} Forest Jump (IRE) 7-1 R Lee *12s-7s; chsd clr ldrs; blun 10; 6th ½way; ab same when ur 12* . . . . U

OFFICIAL DISTANCES: 2*l*, 12*l* **TIME:** 6min 24.2s

Ludlow (RH 8F,19J)

Wed, 11 Feb (GOOD)

176 pointtopoint.co.uk HC, 3m £3423 10 ran

GAME GUNNER 12-00 8-1 **Miss C Stucley** *(boh) Made all frm 6; darted 15l clr 15; prsd agn nxt but a gng wl; kpt on str flat; rdly* 1

10^{2} **Mrs Be (IRE)** 11-09 8-11F **Miss P Gundry** *Sn drpd towards rr; 3rd & prog 10; rdn & outpcd 12; rallied to chse wnr 16; drvn along & 2l down last; a hld flat* 3 2

108^{P} **Mullensgrove** 11-07 16-1 **Miss S Phizacklea** *Made most to 6; jmpd slow 11 (water); mist 13; chsd wnr vain 14-16; drvn & no imp frm 2 out*. 6 3

11^{U} Carbonado 11-09(tt) 20-1 Miss A Goschen *Wl outpcd 6; slt prog 10; 8th & rdn 12; plodded on in poor 4th aft pckng 16* 7 4

Caher Society (IRE) 11-09 (2ow) 11-1 P Morris *Hld up last & rdr oft waving; wl outpcd 6; blun 8; poor last when mist 13; t.o 16* 12 5

48^{U} Grand Gousier (FR) 12-00 9-1 R Burton *Prom til drvn & wknd 11; mist 13; rem 6th 16; pu 3 out* . . . . P

50^{4} Grizzly Golfwear (IRE) 11-07 13-2 M Barber *(xnb) Drvn aft 1; chsd ldrs; hit 7; mist 9; 7th & wkng 12; t.o & pu 16* . . . . P

Persona Pride 12-00 33-1 Julian Pritchard *Drpd rr 3; t.o 7; pu 12* . . . . . . P

Spilaw (FR) 11-07 50-1 Miss C Dyson *(xnb) Hdwy to disp 2nd 6; outpcd by wnr 14; releg 4th & wkng when fell nxt* . . . . F

Valjean (IRE) 11-07 66-1 A Hanly *(xnb) Blun 1; hdwy to chse ldrs 3; mist 7; 5th 12; sn wknd; pu 16* . . . . P

TIME: 6min 08.4s **TOTE:** £9.50; places £2.10,£1.40,£2.40 **Ex:**£18.90 **CSF:**£14.89

Huntingdon (RH 9F,17J*)

Thu, 12 Feb (SOFT, GOOD to SOFT in places)

177 Visit Our New Huntingdon Racecourse Website Nov HC, 3m £1407 17 ran

GATSBY (IRE) 11-11 11-2 **H Fowler** *Trckd ldrs; hmpd 1 & 8; clsd grad 13; rdn to ld app 2 out; rcd v idly flat but clr final furlong*. 1

Mighty Willing 11-09 12-1 **G Brewer** *Chsd ldrs; lft 2nd 11; ld 3 out; rdn & hdd app nxt; kpt on same pce* 7 2

57^{2} **Imps Way** 11-02 33-1 **M Morley** *Mist 6; wl in rr to 12; plugged on stdly to go 3rd & flatt brief app 2 out; sn tired passing omitted last* 15 3

106^{3} Fisherman Jack 11-07 8-1 M Mackley *Sn towards rr; no ch frm 13; inherited rem 4th app 2 out* 30 4

43^{1} Pendle Hill 11-09 9-2F A Hickman *Mists & nvr btr than midfield; strugg aft 12; t.o 3 out* 19 5

128^{P} Ascoolasice 11-07 100-1 M Keel *Jmpd extreme sticky; drvn along in last; t.o aft blun 7; pu 11* . . . . P

Bassey (IRE) 11-07 25-1 Miss F Hatfield *Lw; 5th when fell 3*. . . . . F

Beachcomber 11-07 33-1 W Hill *Went 2nd bhnd clr ldr & fell 8* . . . . F
Bohemian Spirit (IRE) 11-07 20-1 S Charlton *Swtng profuse; lft 15l 2nd 8; blun bad & ur 11* . . . . U
Handy Boy 11-07 25-1 M Jackson *6th & cl up in chsng bunch when fell 8* F
93[2] Irilut (FR) 11-07(cp) 15-2 S Waley-Cohen *Handy in chsng group; 4th 11; rdn 14; 6th & fdng aft 3 out; tired when pu nxt* . . . . P
38[R] Lord Valnic (IRE) 12-00 12-1 G Johnson-Houghton *(xnb) Fell hvly 1* . . . . . F
89[P] Macgyver (NZ) 11-11 14-1 J Diment *Tk fierce hld; ld & clr; still 6l ahd 12; hdd 3 out; 4th & tiring bad when pu nxt* . . . . P
116[2] Mensch (IRE) 11-11(cp) 16-1 E Williams *(xnb) Nt fluent; sn bhnd; lost tch 12; mist 14 (water); pu nxt* . . . . P
Preston Brook 11-11 15-2 T Greenall *(xnb) Hmpd 1 & 8; hld up off pce; mist 12; eff 14 to 5th & flatt brief 3 out; tired & btn 4th when fell 2 out* . . . F
Saxon Victory (USA) 11-09(vis) 20-1 R Armson *Nvr gng keen; t.o & pu 13.* P
106[5] Weavers Choice 12-00 66-1 A Sansome *Jmpd v ponderously; chsd clr ldr to 7; bad hmpd 8; strugg in rr aft; t.o & pu 13.* . . . . P

TIME: 6min 38.9s **TOTE:** £6.20; places £2.80,£3.30,£12.10 **Ex:**£90.80 **CSF:**£62.14

** Fences 10 & 19 omitted - fallen rider*

Wincanton (RH 9F,21J)

Thu, 12 Feb (GOOD, GOOD to SOFT in places)

178 Stewart Tory Mem HC, 3m1f110y £1561 10 ran

PHILSON RUN (IRE) 12-00 25-1 **N Harris** *Jmpd soundly; hld up in rr; 7th aft 12; stdy prog 14; ld 17; rdly; quite impressive (originally won by 2½l)*. . 1
Rathbawn Prince (IRE) 12-04 11-2 **Miss S Samworth** *Bhnd; hit 1, 2 & 8; hdwy 14; 9l 4th 18; one pce & nd frm 3 out; fin 3rd; promoted* 11½ 2
Good Time Melody (IRE) 12-02 50-1 **T Malone** *Bhnd; 8th aft 12; eff in 8l 5th 17; one pce frm 3 out; hit nxt; fin 4th; promoted* 1¾ 3
Hurricane Lamp 12-07 7-2 R Burton *Chsd ldrs; fine j to ld 9; hdd aft 12; cl 3rd 17; wknd app 3 out; fin 5th; promoted* 5 4
34[2] Garruth (IRE) 12-02 5-1 N Williams *Ld to 9; ld aft 12-17; rdn & ev ch when mist 3 out; sn lost weight-cloth; jmpd rt nxt & agn last; a hld flat; fin 2½l 2nd; disq & plcd last*. 2d
119[2] A Romp Too Far (IRE) 11-07 66-1 R McCarthy *Bhnd; hit 7; t.o aft; pu 3 out* P
49[1] Bright Approach (IRE) 12-07 2-1F Miss P Gundry *Prsd ldrs; mist 4; blun 11; 15l 3rd & rdn when jmpd slow 13; wknd nxt; t.o & pu 3 out*. . . . . P
115[2] Cherokee Run (IRE) 11-13 14-1 Miss C Tizzard *Prsd ldr to 9; 6th & wkng rap 12; blun 15; t.o & pu 18*. . . . . P
114[1] Jabiru (IRE) 12-00 9-1 D Edwards *Jmpd lft; in tch; hit 8; rdn & outpcd 11; 6th nxt; hit 14; t.o & pu 3 out* . . . . P
Soloman (IRE) 12-04 40-1 M Miller *Chsd ldrs; blun 5; 10l 3rd aft 12; hit 14; wknd qckly; t.o & pu 18* . . . . P

TIME: 6min 45.5s **TOTE:** £25.90; places £3.70,£2.30,£11.00 **Ex:**£343.00 **CSF:**£152.51

Garruth finished 2nd but was disqualified for failing to draw the correct weight (had lost weight cloth before the last fence); the later finishers were promoted accordingly, but no further action was taken

Haydock (LH 9F,17J)

Sat, 14 Feb (SOFT, GOOD to SOFT in places)

179 Walrus HC, 2m6f £8970 9 ran

GUN'N ROSES II (FR) 12-00(bl) 9-2 **J Jenkins** *Jw; w ldr; hit 4; ld 10; clr 2 out; idled; stayed on wl aft last*. 1
Torduff Express (IRE) 12-00(bl) 3-1F **N Williams** *Made most to 10; ev ch when blun 12; sn outpcd; rallied 2 out; wknd aft last* 13 2
The Butterwick Kid 11-12(bl) 12-1 **Richard Tate** *Went prom 7; outpcd 10; kpt on frm 3 out*. 7 3
72[1] Geordies Express 12-05 10-1 K Anderson *Chsd ldrs; lost plce 10; mod 4th when blun 12; t.o 3 out; kpt on flat* 5 4

110[1] Guignol Du Cochet (FR) 11-05 25-1 S Hughes *Chsd ldrs; outpcd 12; wknd qckly* . . . 6 5
Macgeorge (IRE) 12-05 5-1 R Burton *Chsd ldrs; blun & lost plce 6; bhnd frm 10; t.o 3 out* . . . 1/2 6
122[2] Master Wood 12-02 7-2 T Greenall *Hld up & bhnd; rdn 12; no resp; t.o 3 out* dist 7
33[3] Bosuns Mate 11-09 16-1 Mrs B Keighley *Mists; wl bhnd when blun & ur 12* U
107[P] Royaltino (IRE) 11-05 33-1 M Keel *Bhnd; t.o 3 out; pu nxt* . . . P

TIME: 5min 51.6s **TOTE:** £4.80; places £1.70,£2.00,£2.20 **Ex:**£22.10 **CSF:**£18.17

Mid Surrey Farmers Draghounds

Charing (LH 8F,19J)

Sat, 14 Feb (GOOD to FIRM)

180 Hunt Members (with Coakham Bloodhounds) 4 ran

102[P] **THE GREY BARON**(tt) 3-1 **P Bull** *(xnb) 6s-3s; tk keen hld; disp 2nd/3rd til chsd ldr 7; chall 3 out; ld on inner app last; stayed on u.p flat* . . . 1
Kenny Davis (IRE) 4-7F **P Blagg** *Chsd ldr; mist & rdr waved 9; ld 13; 4l clr app 16; rdn & hdd app last; one pce* . . . 1 1/2 2
Tuck Tin 3-1 **Stuart Robinson** *(xnb) Ww in last; clsd 12; 2l 3rd 16; outpcd frm nxt* . . . 10 3
Three Of Clubs (IRE)(bl) 8-1 Miss C Haydon *Jmpd lft; ld & clr til hdd 13; sn bhnd; lost tch app 16* . . . 15 4

OFFICIAL DISTANCES: 2*l*, 6*l* **TIME:** 6min 31.0s **TOTE:** £4.80 **DF:**£2.70

181 Restricted, 12st 10 ran

102[4] **KILLINEY BAY (IRE)** 6-4F **P York** *(xnb) Chsd ldr 5; ld app 11; 5l clr app 16; mist 3 out; 2l up & rdn nxt; stayed on* . . . 1
Rainbow Ranch (IRE) 5-1 **C Gordon** *(xnb) Ww in mid-div; prog 10; chsd wnr 15; rdn 3 out; 2l down nxt; unable to qckn; eased when btn nr fin* . . . 3 1/2 2
169[6] **Kilvoydan (IRE)** 8-1 **D Phelan** *Swtng; last early; prog to mid-div 7; drvn 12; 12l 3rd app 16; no imp til stayed on wl flat; nt rch ldrs* . . . 3 1/2 3
155[2] Naughty Dandy (IRE)(tt) 7-2 Mrs C Andrews *(xnb) 5s-7/2; chsd ldrs; mist 13; strugg aft; 13l 4th app 16; no ch aft* . . . 12 4
29[4] Zafan (IRE) 12-1 H Fowler *Fat; swtng; blun & lost plce 6; wl bhnd when jmpd slow 11; nd frm nxt* . . . 20 5
169[P] The Wee General (IRE) 20-1 S Cobden *Mid-div; mist 4; outpcd 12; 6th & no ch frm 15* . . . 10 6
Tonrin 20-1 J Sole *Ld til jmpd slow & hdd 11; wknd 13; t.o when jmpd slow 2 out* . . . 5 7
Namron (IRE) 6-1 A Sansome *Tubed; ww; brief eff 11; rdn & wl outpcd 13; wl bhnd & pu 15* . . . P
Shanrod View (IRE) 8-1 D Brightling *Mid-div til blun & lost plce 8; bhnd when mist & ur 9* . . . U
Simony Sam (IRE) 20-1 J Sarchet *(xnb) Rr; jmpd slow 5; lost tch qckly 7; pu 8* P

OFFICIAL DISTANCES: 3*l*, 3*l* **TIME:** 6min 25.0s
TOTE: £2.60; places £1.60,£2.10,£6.30 **DF:**£6.70

182 South East Hunts Club Members Conditions, 12st 14 ran

156[U] **GALEAWAY (IRE)** 12-1 **J Barnard** *Mid-div; prog 11; ev ch 16; 3l 3rd & lkd hld last; str burst last 100yds to ld on line* . . . 1
89[P] **Perching (IRE)** 6-1 **M Sheridan** *Prom; ld 8; 1l up 16; jnd app last; btr j to ld agn last; hdd on post* . . . hd 2
29[1] **Great Jubilee (IRE)** 5-4F **Stuart Robinson** *Chsd ldrs; 3l 3rd 16; rdn to chall on inner app last; slt ld when outj & hdd last; unable to qckn flat* . . . s hd 3
16[2] Tell The Nipper (IRE) 4-1 M Gorman *Mid-div; prog 11; 8l 6th app 16; outpcd app nxt* . . . 10 4
99[4] Oxendale (7x) 10-1 P Bull *Oht; chsd ldrs til outpcd 14; 8th & no ch app 16* 20 5
Alice Reigns (5a) 4-1 C Gordon *(xnb) Swtng; lkd v fit; oht; stdd start; hld up wl bhnd; smooth prog 11; 6l 4th app 16; wknd nxt* . . . 1/2 6
116[8] Makhpiya Patahn (IRE)(vis) 20-1 D I Turner *(xnb) Nt jw; blun 1; bhnd & rmdrs when blun 6; hrd rdn & lost tch 13; t.o* . . . 8 7
Scotch Bob (IRE) 10-1 P Hall *A rr; nd* . . . 1/2 8

Form	Horse	Dist	Pos
99[P]	Claywalls 33-1 Miss O Maylam *Prom; mist 9; lost plce qckly & bhnd frm nxt; t.o frm 13*	12	9
19[P]	Acuteangle (IRE) (5a) 33-1 J Morgan *Swtng; ld app 3-8; wknd 12; t.o when jmpd slow 2 out; pu last*		P
41[4]	Glenmont (IRE) 14-1 Ms L Stock *Bhnd; stdy prog frm 11; 4l 5th when mist & ur 3 out*		U
	Graphic Designer (IRE) 12-1 G Wigley *A bhnd; blun & rdn 13; no prog; pu 16*		P
99[5]	Jack Of Kilcash (IRE) (4x) 6-1 N Benstead *Mid-div; wkng when blun 13; bhnd when pu nxt.*		P
	Satcotino (IRE) (5a) 14-1 P York *Ld til app 3; sn drvn along; chsd ldrs til 7th & outpcd aft 15; blun & ur nxt*		U

OFFICIAL DISTANCES: s hd, s hd **TIME:** 6min 23.0s
TOTE: £14.00; places £4.00,£4.00,£1.40 **DF:**£32.10 (1+any)

183 Mens Open, 12st - 17J — 6 ran

Form	Horse	Dist	Pos
	SHERIFF'S FRIEND (IRE) 4-7F **C Gordon** *(xnb,pricker n/s) Ww; prog to trck ldrs 13; ld app 16; 1 1/2l up by-passing 2 out; a hldng rnr-up*		1
	Struggles Glory (IRE) 9-4 **Stuart Robinson** *2 handlers; lw; ld til app 16; 1 1/2l down by-passing 2 out; rdn & one pce aft*	3	2
100[7]	**Belvento (IRE)** 12-1 **M Sheridan** *Chsd ldrs 6-14; 4l 3rd app 16; sn outpcd by ldng pr*	20	3
43[U]	Little Worsall (IRE) 12-1 F Marshall *Hld up; eff & 6l last 13; outpcd 15; 15l 4th & no ch nxt*	4	4
	Tricky Trevor (IRE) 5-1 P York *Chsd ldr to 6; 4th & outpcd u.p 14; no ch aft*	1	5
	Tough Terms (IRE) 12-1 P Bull *(xnb) 2 handlers; fell 2; dead*		F

OFFICIAL DISTANCES: 2*l*, 4*l* **TIME:** 6min 20.0s
TOTE: £1.90; places £1.50,£1.40 **DF:**£2.20 **trio:**£1.40

Fences 10 & 18 omitted - fallen horse

184 Ladies Open — 2 ran

Form	Horse	Dist	Pos
140[U]	**CHASING THE BRIDE** 4-6F **Miss A Goschen** *Opened 5/4; ld 8-11 & frm 13; 7l clr app 16; drew rt away; v easily*		1
	Dick McCarthy (IRE) 5-4 **Mrs S Ashby** *Swtng; ld to 8 & 11-13; outpcd app 16; sn no ch; eased flat*	20	2

OFFICIAL DISTANCE: dist **TIME:** 6min 18.0s **TOTE:** £1.20 **DF:**£1.10

Kincora was withdrawn not under orders - rider injured in previous race

185 Panacur/TBA PPORA Club Members Mares Maiden, 12st — 5 ran

Form	Horse	Dist	Pos
87[3]	**KAYLEIGH (IRE)** (5a) 4-7F **P York** *Trckd ldrs; went 3l 2nd & blun 12; rdn 14; hit 16; ld aft 2 out; in comm when jmpd slow last; drvn & r.o wl flat*		1
	Granny Smith (IRE) (5a) 5-2 **C Gordon** *(xnb) Ld 3; jnd 8; btr j to ld agn nxt; hdd app last; no ex; eased when btn nr fin*	3	2
152[P]	**Miss Biddy** (5a) 10-1 **Miss O Maylam** *Ld to 3; stdly lost plce; 7l last 9; hdwy to chse ldng pr 11; strugg when mist 16; sn no ch*	20	3
103[U]	The Flying Dragon (5a)(tt) 10-1 S Spice *Cl up til 4th & outpcd 14; no ch app 16*	8	4
121[4]	Forest Fortress (IRE) (5a) 5-1 D I Turner *(xnb) Jmpng & hanging rt; cl up; disp ld 8 til mist 9; blun & lost plce 12; 4th & hanging app 16; wl bhnd when pu last*		P

OFFICIAL DISTANCES: 3*l*, dist **TIME:** 6min 29.0s **TOTE:** £1.30; places £1.10,£1.60 **DF:**£1.40

186 Open Maiden, 12st — 9 ran

Form	Horse	Dist	Pos
	LITTLE MICKEY 4-6F **C Gordon** *(xnb) Tk keen hld; ld til outj & hdd 3 out; 1l down & lkd btn when lft wl clr nxt; inj leg*		1
	Carvilla (IRE) 5-2 **A Sansome** *Prsd ldr to 9; 10l 3rd & outpcd 14; no ch 16; lft poor 2nd 2 out*	runin	2
104[7]	**Almazard** 12-1 **P Hall** *(xnb) Bhnd; 15l last & pushed along 8; blun 10; t.o 12; lft 3rd 2 out; jmpd slow last*	runin	3
	Intercity 10-1 J Morgan *Detach in last; eff to 15l 5th 11; lost tch nxt; t.o 14 til pu & dism flat*		P
87[U]	Lord Of The North (IRE) 6-1 N Benstead *Chsd ldrs; went 2nd 9; blun 13; gd j to ld 3 out; 1l up & lkd wnr when fell nxt.*		F
	Master Chief (IRE) 8-1 P Bull *(xnb) 2 handlers; tk keen hld; chsd ldrs; 4th & wkng when hit 13; t.o & pu 15*		P

103^{U}	Niteattheworkhouse (IRE) 20-1 C Thomson *Chsd ldrs; 4th when fell 5*		F
	Sloe Coach 20-1 G Wigley *In tch til blun & ur 5*		U
	Worth A Shot (IRE) 16-1 D Phelan *Bhnd; lsng tch when pu 12*		P

OFFICIAL DISTANCES: dist, dist **TIME:** 6min 36.0s
TOTE: £1.90; places £1.10,£1.10,£3.20 **DF:**£2.40

Oxford University Hunt Club

Kingston Blount (LH 8F,18J)

Sat, 14 Feb (GOOD)

187 Confined, 12st — 13 ran

47^{2}	**DINSEY FINNEGAN (IRE)**(cp) 4-1CF **G Phillips** *(bf) Warm; ld aft 1-5; ld 9 til app 14; ld app 2 out; hrd prsd last; hld on game*		1
34^{F}	**Nousayri (IRE)** 20-1 **J Trice-Rolph** *(xnb) Settled in last trio; prog frm 15; rap hdwy 2 out; prsd wnr flat; just hld final 75yds*	1/2	2
	Bullfinch 4-1CF **P Cowley** *In tch; prog to trck ldng pr 12 til ld 14; hdd app 2 out; one pce*	2 1/2	3
	Sunczech (IRE) (5a) 10-1 Miss S Phizacklea *(xnb) Ld til aft 1; sn lost plce & wl in rr; some prog 14; stayed on wl app last; nrst fin*	2	4
168^{P}	Grand Canyon (IRE) (3x) 14-1 N Pearce *Jmpd slow 3; towards rr; pushed along 8; no real prog frm 14 til stayed on frm 2 out; unable to chall*	3	5
	Bell Rock 10-1 James Tudor *(xnb) Hld up midfield; prog 12; chsd ldng pr 14; chall & w wnr 2 out; wknd app last*	2	6
	Route Two (IRE) 40-1 F de Giles *Chsd ldrs; mist 7; drpd to rr 11; no prog frm 15*	10	7
	Bold Statement (3x)(tt) 5-1 G Tawell *(xnb) Prom til lost plce rap frm 12; last pr 14; wl bhnd & pu 2 out*		P
	Camitrov (FR) 14-1 G Kerr *(xnb) Warm; prom; mist 8; midfield frm 14; eff & wl in tch in chsng group & ch of plce when slpd up bend bef last*		S
7^{F}	Cash 'n Carrots (7a) 10-1 A Martin *(xnb) Midfield; drpd to rr & jmpd slow 11; stayed in tch; 8th & btn but still in tch when fell 3 out*		F
103^{4}	Latterly (USA) 25-1 I Bostock *(xnb) Midfield; mist & rfo 2*		U
138^{P}	Mister Pepper (IRE) 4-1CF T Underwood *Hld up in last pr; brief eff to midfield 10; sn lost plce agn; last pr 14; bhnd when pu last*		P
31^{5}	One Of The Natives (IRE)(vis) 40-1 Miss J Jenner *(xnb) Ld 5-9; wknd rap aft 13; t.o & pu 2 out*		P

OFFICIAL DISTANCES: nk, 5*l* **TIME:** 6min 20.4s

Fog caused the start of racing to be delayed for 30mins

188 Mens Open, 12st — 7 ran

34^{4}	**FATHER ANDY (IRE)** 6-4F **S Morris** *(xnb) Trckd ldr & sn clr of rest; outj at sev fncs; eff to ld 2 out; clr last; drvn out*		1
93^{P}	**Tubber Roads (IRE)** (7x)(bl) 6-1 **J Owen** *Ld; sn clr w wnr; hdd 2 out; wknd last*	5	2
34^{U}	**Paddies Boy (IRE)** (7x) 2-1 **J Trice-Rolph** *Chsd clr ldng pr; 16l 3rd 1/2way; eff to 9l 3rd 14; sn lost tch agn & btn*	15	3
	Cotteir Chief (IRE) 14-1 R Hughes *Hld up & bhnd; 19l 4th 1/2way; wknd & jmpd slow 11; sn t.o*	fence	4
56^{P}	Bidin' My Time (NZ) 8-1 L Hicks *25s-8s; hld up bhnd; 20l 5th when fell 8*		F
	Full Egalite 20-1 G Disney *Bckwd; last & jmpd slow 1; t.o last when ref 5*		r
	Is Wonderful (USA)(tt) 4-1 Julian Pritchard *(xnb) Hld up & bhnd; 25l last 1/2way; wknd & jmpd rt 12; sn wl t.o; pu 14*		P

OFFICIAL DISTANCES: 6*l*, 15*l* **TIME:** 6min 24.3s

189 Ladies Open - 17J — 8 ran

48^{3}	**KILLERINE (FR)** 7-4 **Miss H Irving** *Disp 2nd frm 4 til lft clr 2nd 9; eff to ld 15; hit 3 out; jmpd slow & hdd last; rallied u.p to ld agn nr fin*		1
25^{3}	**Pride Of Kashmir** 9-2 **Miss S Phizacklea** *Chsd ldrs; lft 3rd 9; 8l 3rd 1/2way; clsd on ldng pr 14; no imp & lkd btn 3 out; drvn up & best j to ld last; hrd drvn flat; hdd nr fin*	nk	2
108^{2}	**Find Me Another (IRE)** 5-4F **Miss A Stennett** *Ld to 15; stayed prsng ldr; chall & level last last; nt qckn u.p flat*	3	3
	Cedar Chief(bl) 20-1 Miss E Harbour *Bckwd; nvr on terms; 27l 5th 1/2way; nd aft*	35	5

Moonlite Magic (IRE)(cp) 14-1 Miss J Wickens *Bckwd; keen early; jmpd slow 3; last frm 5; 35l 7th ½way; nrly ur 13; cont miles bhnd.* 200y 6

Lottie The Lotus (5a) 14-1 Miss R Goodwin *Bit bckwd; chsd ldrs but nvr on terms; 15l 4th ½way; no imp aft; fin 18½l 4th; disq - nt draw correct weight* 4d

33P Craven Hill (IRE) 33-1 Miss A Wells *(xnb) Reluct to rce & lft 20l; sn in tch in rr; mist 6; 33l 6th & wkng ½way; miles bhnd when pu 14* . . . . P

110[6] Perfect Finisher 20-1 Miss R Lobley *Disp 2nd frm 3 til mist & ur 9* . . . . U

OFFICIAL DISTANCES: nk, 3*l* **TIME:** 6min 19.5s

Fence 17 omitted - fallen rider; Lottie The Lotus finished fourth but was disqualified for failing to draw the correct weight (rider weighed-in over three pounds light); the owner was fined £125

190 OUHC Club Members 9 ran

175[8] **DOWN (FR)** 9-4 **S Waley-Cohen** *Opened 3s; jw; settled in last trio; stdy prog 11; hdwy to 2nd 15; ld 2 out; forged clr app last; comf* 1

117[3] **Quickswood (IRE)** 7-4F **G Maundrell** *Trckd ldrs; prog to ld app 14; hdd 2 out; one pce aft; wkng & just kpt 2nd flat* 6 2

Gunner Sid 20-1 **A Wadlow** *Bit bckwd; a.p; sn ld; hdd 11; eff to 3rd 3 out; stayed on & nrly caught rnr-up* . . . . ½ 3

53[1] Gillie's Nephew 6-1 James Tudor *(xnb) Midfield; mist 11; eff 14; went 4th aft 3 out; no imp on ldrs* 12 4

90[2] Live Wire (IRE) 10-1 Miss C Benstead *Towards rr; 7th ½way; lost tch 13; mist 15; kpt on frm 3 out; nt rch ldrs.* 5 5

19P Wild Blade (IRE)(cp) 33-1 R Jenkins *(xnb) Rcd free; prsd ldr; ld 11 til app 14; wknd rap 3 out.* 20 6

47[3] Dons Delight (IRE) 6-1 G Kerr *(xnb) Prom; chsd ldr 13 til app nxt; still wl there when blun bad 15; wknd* . . . . s hd 7

108P Gortroe Guy (IRE) 20-1 Miss K Robinson *(xnb) Bit bckwd; tde; a rr; rdr propping at fncs; last 12; t.o aft nxt* 25 8

Gangster 14-1 Miss S Tarry *Rdr unstdy 1; chsd ldrs; 4th when rfo 8* . . . . U

OFFICIAL DISTANCES: 8*l*, ½*l* **TIME:** 6min 20.3s

191 Restricted, 12st 14 ran

MR SPLODGE 7-1 **James Tudor** *(xnb) Hld up towards rr; prog to 3rd ½way; trckd ldrs gng wl til ld 2 out; pushed out* 1

32[2] **Boyne Banks (IRE)** 3-1JF **G Disney** *Ld/disp frm 2; hdd brief 14; hdd 2 out; one pce und feeble rdng flat* 4 2

57[4] **Miss Zarnni** (5a) 10-1 **L Hicks** *Tchd 14s; hld up; mist 7; 8th when mist 11 & str rmdrs; rap prog to ld & blun 14; sn hdd; cl 3rd 2 out; one pce aft* . . 4 3

Double Thatch (IRE) 5-1 Julian Pritchard *Mostly jw; disp ld frm 2-14; still cl up 3 out; wknd nxt* 25 4

Romany Pearl 8-1 J Owen *2 handlers; chsd ldrs; 4th & rdn ½way; outpcd app 14; no ch aft* 25 5

169P Stormy Pass 16-1 S Waley-Cohen *Ld to 2; 5th ½way; wknd rap app 14; t.o* 20 6

94[3] Euro Bob (IRE) 4-1 Mrs A Rucker *Midfield; 6th & wl in tch ½way; jnd ldrs 14; cl 4th when mist & rfo nxt* . . . . U

Kingfisher Star 20-1 Miss J Lodge *(xnb) Rr; 11th when fell 8* . . . . F

Madmariea (IRE) (5a) 7-1 T Underwood *Hld up in rr; 7th & in tch ½way; outpcd in 8th when blun bad & ur 13* . . . . U

20S Milamoss 16-1 R Hughes *Prom; cl 5th when blun & ur 8* . . . . U

Miss Man (5a) 16-1 Miss A Cavanagh *Sn hopeless t.o; miles bhnd 6; pu 8* P

Regal Rumour 16-1 M Wall *Bckwd; a rr; in tch til wknd 9; t.o last & pu 11* P

Rommel 3-1JF J Trice-Rolph *12th when mist & ur 1* . . . . U

109[3] Sissinghurst Star (IRE) 16-1 P Mann *(xnb) Sn rr; last ½way; sn outpcd; t.o aft 13; staying on in poor 5th but no ch when fell 3 out* . . . . F

OFFICIAL DISTANCES: 4*l*, 3*l* **TIME:** 6min 21.5s

192 Confined Maiden, 12st 8 ran

MURPHY'S MAGIC (IRE) 7-2 **Julian Pritchard** *Trckd ldrs; eff to disp ld 14 & qcknd; ld 2 out; clr last; rdn out* 1

174[2] **Shy Lizzie** (5a) 4-1 **P Mason** *Ld at slow pce to 5; prom til drpd to 6th 14; sn outpcd (rdr asleep); prog to 3rd 3 out; clsd stdly; tk 2nd & clsd on wnr fin; too much to do* 3 2

	Caraiyni (IRE) 5-2F **S Morris** *(xnb) Prom; ld brief 5 & agn 12; jnd 14 & qcknd; hdd 2 out; one pce aft.*	1	3
	Brownies Tale (IRE) 8-1 J Docker *Cl up; eff to disp ld brief aft 13; outpcd aft 14; wknd.*	25	4
51^{5}	Gloves Off (IRE)(bl) 10-1 Miss H Irving *In tch til mist & wknd 14; fin v slow; t.o*	40	5
	Blakes Romany Girl (5a, 3ow) 8-1 J Trice-Rolph *12s-8s; bit bckwd; keen; school in last; mist 9; wknd & mist 12; t.o & pu 15*		P
	Hermano (IRE) 14-1 N Pearce *(bh) Ss; hld up & pulling; pulled to ld aft 5; sn clr & jb; wknd & hdd 12; pu nxt*		P
20^{P}	Two Oceans (IRE) 4-1 R Cope *Tchd 6s; prom; disp ld brief aft 13; wknd rap aft nxt; t.o & pu aft 2 out*		P

OFFICIAL DISTANCES: 4*l*, 3/4*l* **TIME:** 6min 38.5s

South Pool Harriers

Buckfastleigh (RH 7F,18J)

Sat, 14 Feb (DEAD)

193 Intermediate, 12st — 11 ran

116^{3}	**LEON GARCIA (IRE)** (5a) 5-2F **T Bishop** *Tchd 3s; hld up in rr & a gng str; still 8th 15; str rn to ld aft 2 out; sn burst clr; easy.*		1
	Father Mansfield (IRE) 10-1 **Miss C Prouse** *Settled towards rr; 9th & outpcd app 15; str rn app last to snatch 2nd; no ch w wnr*	15	2
50^{P}	**Vercheny** (5a) 6-1 **Miss P Gundry** *(xnb) Hld up in rr; 7th 15; dashed up to 2nd & flatt brief aft 2 out; sn no ch w wnr; dem nr post*	hd	3
	Th'moons A Balloon (IRE) 4-1 S Partridge *Prom; ld 6-8 & 13 til hdd aft 2 out; rdn & one-pcd app last*	1	4
	Carefree Love (IRE) 9-2 Richard Darke *Bckwd; cl 2nd/4th til rdn 3 out; one pce frm nxt*	1/2	5
81^{3}	Happy Team (5a) 7-1 L Jefford *(xnb) Prsd ldrs; 4th app 15; rdn 3 out; no imp aft*	4	6
147^{U}	Early Morning Call (IRE) 12-1 J Barnes *(xnb) Settled midfield; 4l 6th app 15; flatt nxt; wknd 2 out*	2	7
81^{4}	Baldhu Jay Arr 14-1 Miss L Gardner *Tchd 16s; swtng; cl up; 4th 11; wknd 14; no ch frm 15*	20	8
90^{P}	Gutsy Dalton (IRE)(bl) 33-1 J Young *Tubed; ld to 6 & 8 til hmpd bad by loose horse 13; last nxt; t.o 15*	15	9
	Native Drum (IRE) (5x) 12-1 Miss S Gaisford *Jmpd slow 3; hld up & mostly last to 11; gd hdwy 13; went 2nd brief 15; wknd qckly; t.o & pu last.*		P
	Silver Man(cp) 20-1 Mrs M Hand *Chsd ldrs til hit 7 & ur*		U

OFFICIAL DISTANCES: 15*l*, 1/2*l* **TIME:** 6min 10.4s

194 Confined Maiden (Div 1), 12st — 14 ran

	VIVID IMAGINATION (IRE) (7a) evensF **A Farrant** *5/2-evens; ld to 8; 2nd til ld agn 16; drew clr aft nxt; pushed along app last; unchall.*		1
	Albamart Wood(tt) 16-1 **J Young** *Chsd ldng pr; 6l down & outpcd app 15; 12l 3rd 2 out; plugged into poor 2nd last*	12	2
51^{3}	**Bally Blue** 5-1 **L Jefford** *(xnb) Dwelt; hairy & v erratic 1 & 2; in tch by 5; went 8l 4th app 15; wknd to poor 5th 2 out; plugged on*	10	3
	Terino 25-1 Richard Darke *Hld up in midfield; 10l 5th & outpcd app 15; 22l 4th 2 out.*	6	4
82^{2}	Gunners Mistake 5-1 C Heard *2 handlers; pulled hrd in 2nd/4th; lost plce qckly 13; poor 7th app 15.*	3	5
	Advice Taken (IRE) 20-1 N Mitchell *Rcd keen; sn 2nd; ld 8 til nt fluent & hdd 15; wkng & lsng 2nd when terrible mist last; virt pu aft.*	8	6
	Virgos Bambino (IRE) (5a) 20-1 A Charles-Jones *Jmpd slow 3; strugg 11; t.o 15*	15	7
	Abigails Star 33-1 A Jones *(xnb) Sn bhnd; t.o 7; pu 11*		P
76^{P}	Buckley's Chance (IRE) 33-1 J Tickle *(xnb) Nt fluent in rr; strugg 12; t.o & pu 2 out*		P
	Commanche Summer (5a) 5-1 A Glassonbury *10s-5s; mounted outside padd; midfield; 6th 11; wknd 13; t.o & pu 16.*		P
	Joli Christmas 7-1 R Woollacott *Bckwd; midfield; 12l 6th & chsng ldrs when hung violent lft & unrideable aft 14; pu nxt*		P

Master Of Fashion 25-1 L Heard *Nt fluent in midfield; wknd 13; t.o & pu 15* P

83P Silver Kracker 33-1 M Woodward *(xnb) Handy early; drpd to rr 7; drvn & t.o 12; pu 14* P

83P Tom Dove 25-1 M Munrowd *(xnb) A bhnd; 9th 11; t.o & pu 15* P

OFFICIAL DISTANCES: 10*l*, 8*l* **TIME:** 6min 12.1s

195 Confined Maiden (Div 2), 12st — 14 ran

COOMBE QUEST 25-1 **T Dennis** *(xnb) Handy; drew clr w rival frm 14; slt ld aft btr j 3 out; level til rdn & outpcd aft nxt; 3l down when lft virt solo at last* 1

Think Commercial (IRE) (7a) 4-1 **A Farrant** *(xnb) Nt jw & seemed to be hanging lft; rr early; 5th 11; blun 13 & 14; 7l 3rd app nxt; no imp aft & eased frm 2 out; lft poor 2nd at last* 15 2

149⁵ **Orinoco's Flight (IRE)** 20-1 **M Holmes** *Hld up in midfield; 3rd by 11; outpcd by ldng pr 15; 10l 4th nxt* 2½ 3

119³ Cargo Flight 9-4F L Jefford *7/2-9/4; tk keen hld; prom to 11; wknd to poor last when pu 15* P

Four In Hand (5a) 20-1 D Edwards *Suddenly stpd & pu 5* P

Four Of A Kind 5-1 Miss S Gaisford *2 handlers; oht; knocked owner over padd; chsd ldrs til wknd aft 11; t.o & pu 15* P

Josanjamic (5a) 3-1 L Heard *10s-3s; ld til duelled w wnr frm 15; jmpd slow 3 out; rdn 3l clr aft 2 out; in comm when jmpd v slow & ur last* U

Little Apple Bay (5a) 33-1 C Heard *Swtng profuse; wl in rr til pu 9* P

Miss Ziggerson (5a) 20-1 Miss S Young *2 handlers; mist 7; mid-div til hmpd bad 8; nt rec; pu 10* P

Newhouse Lira (5a) 25-1 Richard Darke *Bckwd; bhnd; lost tch 7; pu 10* P

Satanass (IRE) (7a) 20-1 N Mitchell *Jmpd appalling 1 & 2; wisely pu 3* P

Sup Of Tea (IRE)(bl) 25-1 J Young *(xnb) Swtng; pulled hrd in 3rd to 7; 6th & wkng 11; t.o & pu 14* P

Truicear 5-1 R McCarthy *12s-5s; 2nd to 7; chsng ldrs when fell 8* F

Vero Beach 12-1 A Charles-Jones *5th when mist & ur 4* U

OFFICIAL DISTANCES: 20*l*, 4*l* **TIME:** 6min 22.6s

196 Mens Open — 12 ran

89U **RIGHT TO REPLY (IRE)** 4-5F **N Harris** *(xnb) Lw; confid rdn in rr; 7th & hdwy 11; ld 15; a gng str aft; in comm frm 2 out; impressive* 1

Monty's Lass (IRE) (5a) 7-2 **A Charles-Jones** *6s-7/2; pounded away in last pr & lkd outpcd to 11; still mod 5th 3 out; stayed on v str aft to 2nd at last; no ch w wnr; btr for rce* 6 2

5P **Polar Flight** 10-1 **J Young** *(xnb) Made most 5-15; chsd wnr vain aft; 3l down & drvn aft 2 out; dem last* 4 3

5F Colquhoun 7-1 A Farrant *Lw; ld to 5; prom til ld agn 13-14; sn hdd & u.p in 3rd; 9l 3rd 3 out; fnd little aft; dem app last* ¾ 4

145⁴ Bruthuinne (IRE) 40-1 Richard Darke *(xnb) 2 handlers; swtng; settled midfield; outpcd 13; mod 6th 3 out* 30 5

77² Nearly Gold(bl) 20-1 N Mitchell *Chsd ldr 5-11; qckly drpd to rr; t.o last 2 out* 12 6

117P Blackwater Brave (IRE) 16-1 H Fry *Tchd 20s; midfield early; rdn & outpcd 12; t.o 15; pu last* P

115⁶ Fou Doux (FR) 66-1 N Wilmington *(xnb) Last trio; 11th & slt detach when fell 11* F

Lead Story (IRE) 16-1 R Woollacott *V bckwd; 2nd/3rd to 6; wknd 12; t.o & pu 15* P

115³ Le Cure 12-1 J Barnes *(xnb) Hld up; hdwy to ld 11-12; lost plce rap; poor 7th 2 out; pu last* P

Major Belle (FR) (12a) 25-1 M Miller *(xnb) Midfield; brief eff in 4th 14; 15l 4th 3 out; no ch aft; pu last* P

Procedure (USA) 40-1 D Edwards *Midfield early; t.o & pu 12; v reluct* P

OFFICIAL DISTANCES: 5*l*, 2*l* **TIME:** 6min 04.9s

197 Restricted (Div 1), 12st — 10 ran

118⁴ **SOOTSIR** 14-1 **R Hawker** *(xnb) Bhnd early; 6th 12; eff to press ldrs frm 15; 2½l 4th 2 out; drvn & r.o to chall last; sn ld flat; r.o game* 1

148⁴ **Mrs Peggoty** (5a)(bl) 14-1 **D Edwards** *Rn in snatches; ld to 2 & 10-11; 5th nxt; rdn 14; ld agn 2 out & rdn 2½l clr; idled bad & ½l ahd last; hdd & lkd dem 3rd final 50yds* ½ 2

79^4	**Drumhorc (IRE)** 16-1 **Miss L Gardner** *(xnb) Ld 2-4, 8-10* & *12 til aft 15; brief outpcd nxt; mist 2 out; 7l 4th & rallying app last; kpt on flat; just failed; lkd to fin 2nd*	nk	3
	Baldara (IRE) 7-4 A Farrant *Prom; jnd ldr 12; ld brief app 6; 2½l 2nd & rdn app last; kpt on same pce aft*	nk	4
121^1	Martby evensF M Atkinson *5/2-evens; ld 4-8; 5th 11; prsd ldrs aft til ld 3 out; sn hdd & 1½l 3rd; 5l 3rd aft 2 out & kpt on game; rdr a hopeless passenger*	1	5
	Budghill 16-1 L Heard *(xnb) Prom; 2nd 7; 7th & wkng 12; t.o 15; pu last.*		P
83^4	Knockaun Wood (IRE) 20-1 M Sweetland *Fat; prom; ld brief 11; 6th & wkng rap 14; pu 15*		P
	Persian Dawn (5a) 25-1 J Young *Jmpd poor in last; strugg aft mist 8; t.o 11; pu 15*		P
	Winners Enclosure (IRE) 14-1 A Michael *2 handlers; a towards rr; 8th & outpcd 12; rem when ur 16*		U
83^P	Young Harry 20-1 R Woollacott *Rr when mist 5 (by boxes) & imm rdn & ref to rce*		r

OFFICIAL DISTANCES: s hd, s hd **TIME:** 6min 19.8s

198 Restricted (Div 2), 12st — 9 ran

2^2	**ONEMINUTETOFIVE** 4-7F **A Farrant** *(xnb) Opened evens in plce; lw; 3rd early; 2nd 7 til ld on bit 16; 15l clr aft 2 out; v easy*		1
118^3	**Mister Swallow** 8-1 **M Miller** *Jmpd tentatively in ld; hdd 16; 3l down & rdn when jmpd v slow 2 out; sn no ch w wnr*	20	2
82^1	**Sea Snipe** (5a) 4-1 **Miss T Cave** *Hld up towards rr; hit 12; 5th 14; outpcd nxt; 25l 4th aft 2 out; stayed on game aft & clsd on 2nd flat*	1¼	3
85^1	Carrington House 33-1 J O'Rourke *Chsd ldrs; went 3rd 11; 4l down & rdn when blun 15; 8l 3rd & outpcd 2 out; fdng when jmpd v slow last*	15	4
	Baron Ridge 50-1 Richard Darke *(xnb) A bhnd; 8th & strugg 11; t.o 15*	20	5
	Fortysixallout (IRE) 6-1 Mrs O Jackson *(xnb) Lw; slpd up gng down; a bhnd; 20l 6th & strugg aft 14; t.o 16; pu last*		P
	Lazy Lemon (5a) 16-1 R Woollacott *(xnb) Bit bckwd; settled 4th; drvn & outpcd app 15; t.o when jmpd v slow 2 out; pu last.*		P
	Timber Top (IRE) 50-1 Mrs P Swarbrick *Mounted outside padd; tde; chsd ldr to 7; sn lost plce; t.o 13; pu 3 out*		P
	Xraysauce (5a) 50-1 A Glassonbury *Nt jw in last trio; t.o 11; pu 12*		P

OFFICIAL DISTANCES: 25l, 1l **TIME:** 6min 12.8s

199 Ladies Open — 10 ran

94^1	**ASK THE NATIVES (IRE)** 8-11F **Miss C Roddick** *Lw; hld up in rr & gng str; clsd on bit 11; cl 2nd app 15 til ld 2 out; sn 10l clr; effortlessly*		1
	Balinova (IRE) 5-2 **Miss P Gundry** *11/2-5/2; rcd keen; 2nd 4; stdd til dashed ahd aft 11; hdd 2 out; imm outpcd & 11l 3rd app last; rallied flat; fin str to snatch 2nd frm dozing rival on line*	10	2
76^1	**Kestick** 9-2 **Miss T Cave** *Tchd 5s; hld up & bhnd; hdwy 12; 3l 4th app 15; outpcd by wnr 2 out; went 2nd app last; cert of 2nd til rdr stpd rdng last 100yds & pipped on post.*	hd	3
	Breteche (FR) (5a) 12-1 Miss T Newman *(xnb) Tchd 14s; midfield; 5th 11; outpcd 13; poor 5th 3 out*	25	4
	Sandy Duff 33-1 Miss M McCarthy *Bckwd; rcd keen & prom; pushed into ld app 8; hdd aft 11; wknd 15; 14l 4th 3 out*	1½	5
	Polar King (IRE) 66-1 Miss W Southcombe *Cl up til lost plce & mist 10; poor 6th app 15; plugged on stdly*	6	6
	Jack The Bear (IRE) 16-1 Miss C Tuffin *Bhnd; lost tch 7; wl adrift 11; some late prog; staying on at fin*	1	7
117^U	Father Jim 66-1 Miss C Tizzard *Sn cl up; 4th 11; blun 13 & wknd; poor 7th app 15; t.o*	15	8
88^P	Prah Sands 66-1 Mrs L Young *(xnb) Ld til app 8; lost plce rap; t.o 15; virt pu flat*	25	9
	Guru Rinpoche 20-1 Miss S Gaisford *Hld up; imp qckly 12; 2nd when blun & ur 14*		U

OFFICIAL DISTANCES: 15l, s hd **TIME:** 6min 04.7s

200 Confined, 12st — 13 ran

RONANS CHOICE (IRE) 14-1 **Richard Darke** *25s-14s; swtng; oht; 2 handlers; ld; hdd brief 15; drew 6l clr aft 2 out; rdn & stayed on wl* 1

80[1] **Bill Me Up (IRE)** (3x) 4-6F **C Heard** *2 handlers; reluct to line up; svs & set off ab fnce bhnd; hdwy 8 to disp ld 12; ld brief 15; prsd wnr til rdn & tired aft 2 out* 10 2

Province 16-1 **R Woollacott** *Cl up; 5th 14; chall nxt; $2\frac{1}{2}$l 3rd 2 out; wknd app last* 5 3

144[2d] Midnight Coup (7x)(bl) 7-1 A Farrant *10s-7s; cl up in ab 4th; drvn along 15; 7l 4th & fnding nil 2 out; plugged on* 4 4

147[4] Bak On Board 16-1 Miss L Gardner *(xnb) 2 handlers; 2nd/3rd to 14; grad wknd; 5th & btn 2 out*. 10 5

89[P] Travelling Jack 16-1 J Young *Swtng profuse; 2 handlers; midfield; 6th 14 & rdn; wknd qckly* 15 6

80[4] Artic Ground (IRE) 50-1 D Doyne-Ditmas *Nvr btr than mid-div; jmpd slow 7; 7th 12; sn lost tch; t.o* 10 7

80[P] African Dawn(tt) 33-1 N Harris *Settled midfield; 8th 12; slt prog in 12l 6th 15; sn wknd; wl bhnd when pu last*. . . . . P

61[2] Calleva Star (IRE) 25-1 S Kidston *A bhnd; 11th & strugg 14; t.o & pu last*. P

Damiens Pride (IRE) (5x) 12-1 T Dennis *(xnb) A bhnd; 10th 14; t.o & pu 15* P

It's-The-Biz (IRE) 20-1 D Summersby *(xnb) Chsd ldrs; 7th 11; 8th & strugg 14; pu 15* . . . . P

Itworked 14-1 A Glassonbury *12th when fell 3*. . . . . F

Millyhenry 14-1 Miss C Tizzard *Reluct & sn strugg in rr; lost tch 9; t.o & drvn 12; pu 13* . . . . P

OFFICIAL DISTANCES: 7*l*, 6*l* **TIME:** 6min 14.9s

Vale of Clettwr

Erw Lon (LH 8F,18J)

Sat, 14 Feb (HOLDING)

201 Hunt Members - 17J — 2 ran

ZOLA (IRE) 5-4 **P Sheldrake** *Made all; 3l up when slowed into 7; lft solo nxt; ambled on; jmpd slow 14*. 1

River Lossie 1-2F L Sloyan *1st ride; hld up in 3l last; slt mist 5; mist 7 & rdr lost iron; ur nxt* . . . . U

OFFICIAL DISTANCE: Finished alone **TIME:** 7min 09.0s

Fence 16 omitted - fallen rider; the start of racing was delayed by $1\frac{1}{2}$ hours awaiting the arrival of paramedic cover

202 Confined Maiden (Div 1), 12st — 13 ran

DAISY'S CHOICE (5a) 5-1 **P Sheldrake** *Hld up in midfield; 4l 4th 10; went 3rd 12; stayed on past tiring horse to 2nd 2 out; 5l 2nd when lft in ld last* 1

119[8] **Dans Blarney (IRE)** 2-1 **D Jones** *A.p; 3l 3rd frm 9; tk 2nd 12; wknd frm 2 out; fin tired* 25 2

St Palais (12a) 4-1 **T Faulkner** *Midfield early; rr frm 7; last frm 12 til r.o frm 2 out; chall for 2nd flat; no ch w wnr*. 3 3

Musical Sleuth (7a) 8-1 J Price *(xnb) Cl 2nd til ld 2; mist & hdd 6; mist 9 & picked up off floor by rdr; drpd to 4th; wknd 14; no ch when mist 2 out.* 25 4

Batchworth Lock 14-1 Mrs C Owen *(xnb) Fell 1* . . . . F

Indian Trix (IRE) (5a) 12-1 A Hanly *With odd wart on belly; rr & jmpd slow 2; a bhnd; school til pu 14*. . . . . P

Lady Palamon (IRE) (5a) 5-1 H Evans *A last pr; mist 6; pu 12*. . . . . P

Miss Barton Ridge (5a) 6-1 M Lewis *Midfield to 7; lost tch aft mist 12; t.o 5th when pu last* . . . . P

Mr Mackenzie (IRE) 11-10F T Vaughan *(xnb) Ld 1; stdd in cl 2nd til ld agn 6; mists 14 & 16; qcknd clr 2 out; 5l clr & lkd wnr when hmpd by loose horse & fell last; broke nk; dead* . . . . F

Royal Century (IRE) 10-1 C Penycate *Rr til ur 9; crashed thro ropes when loose & inj; destroyed* . . . . U

Willie The Kid (7a) 10-1 S Blackwell *A bhnd; school in rr til pu 11*. . . . . . P

Woodland Warrior 8-1 M Barber *Fell 1* . . . . F

Worcester Way (IRE) 8-1 Miss I Tompsett *Trckd ldrs; 3rd & mist 3; fdd 10; last pr 12; pu 14* . . . . P

OFFICIAL DISTANCES: dist, 3*l* **TIME:** 6min 32.0s

203 Confined Maiden (Div 2), 12st — 8 ran

CANNON BRIDGE (IRE) 4-5F **D Jones** *Stdd in 2nd til lft in ld 4-8; cl 3rd til went 4l 2nd 14; ld app 2 out; r.o wl* . . . 1
Beasley (7a) 6-1 **M Barber** *Cl 3rd mostly frm 5 til ld 13; sn 5l clr; hdd app 2 out; no ex* . . . 6 2
Chunito 5-2 **Miss F Wilson** *Detach 4th frm 6; 6l 4th 8; went 3rd 3 out; nt trble ldrs* . . . 30 3
Wiston Wizo 16-1 P Sheldrake *Cl 3rd til ld 10-12; 7l 3rd 14; blun 3 out; fdd; t.o when crawled over last; trotted in* . . . 10 4
Gay Abandon (5a) 25-1 C Penycate *Jb in last; 10l adrift 2; stdly lost tch; t.o & pu 11* . . . P
53F Jeune Premier (FR) 10-1 D Davies *Ld & sn 8l clr; fell 4* . . . F
Penny Poor (IRE) (7a) 3-1 T Vaughan *Mid-div; 5th & lsng tch when mist 14; pu nxt* . . . P
Sergwyn 8-1 T Faulkner *School in last pr til pu 11* . . . P

OFFICIAL DISTANCES: 8*l*, dist **TIME:** 6min 42.0s

204 Confined Maiden (Div 3), 12st — 12 ran

TRIAL TRIP (5a) evensF **E Williams** *(xnb) Hld up; tk 15l 2nd 2; mist & dem nxt; ld 14; sn clr; in comm when blun & sprawled sideways 2 out; kpt on* 1
Hill Top Flyer (IRE) 8-1 **N Oliver** *(bh) Trckd ldrs in 3rd mostly; rem 12; some hdwy frm nxt; tired & lft poor 2nd 16; nvr nr wnr* . . . runin 2
120U Evans The Coal 10-1 James Price *2 handlers; rr & jmpd slow 1; 15l adrift 5; blun 8; t.o til pu 13* . . . P
General Craig 4-1 T Faulkner *Ld; 12l clr 1; 30l ahd 5; still 6l up 12; tired & jmpd slow nxt; sn hdd & qckly lost posn; v tired when blun 15 & pu* . . . P
Hallbrook (5a) 5-1 A Hanly *A midfield; nvr clsr than 5th; lost tch 11; pu 13* P
Kerrygoldsovereign (5a) 10-1 R Richards *Midfield to 7; 18l 3rd 9; 8l 2nd & clsng 10; ur nxt* . . . U
Morristhemilk 6-1 M Lewis *(xnb) Poor 2nd to 7; settled mid-div til wknd 11; pu 13* . . . P
35P Mountain Lily (5a) 5-2 J Cook *Pu & dism aft 2; lame* . . . P
Mr Morgan 5-1 D Jones *Sn last trio; t.o 11; pu nxt* . . . P
Royal Tradition (IRE) 5-1 J Merry *Rr; 7th when ur 6* . . . U
Sadler's Vic 4-1 J Price *(b4) Jmpd slow in rr; 15l last when rn out 5* . . . R
Take The Gamble (5a)(cp) 6-1 Miss I Tompsett *Rr when fell 3* . . . F

OFFICIAL DISTANCE: dist **TIME:** 6min 50.0s

205 Mens Open, 12st — 7 ran

BRIGHT BEACON 1-2F **E Williams** *Midfield; 12l 4th 9; eff to ld 12; lft wl clr 2 out* . . . 1
Home Again (IRE) 7-1 **M Lewis** *2nd & mist 2; chsd ldr til wknd 14; 4l 3rd & tired 3 out; t.o when blun & lft 2nd 2 out* . . . 30 2
Aye Surely (IRE) 12-1 H Evans *Last pr 1; ww in midfield til ld 6; 3l clr 9; hdd aft nxt; 4th & wkng when ur 14* . . . U
Harfdecent(tt) 6-1 M Williams *Rr; 5th frm 9; prog 10; 1l 2nd 14; 4l 2nd when ur 2 out* . . . U
Head Gardener (IRE)(bl) 12-1 S Blackwell *Jmpd slow 1; 4th & mist 6; 15l 6th 9; wknd nxt; sn t.o last; pu 14* . . . P
64U Lyringo (5a) 25-1 P Sheldrake *A last; 8l adrift 2; rdn 6; no resp; t.o til pu 10* P
34F Waders (IRE) 6-1 M Barber *Ld 1-5; 3rd to 11; tired when blun 14; pu nxt.* P

OFFICIAL DISTANCE: dist **TIME:** 6min 23.0s

206 Ladies Open — 8 ran

77P **DAWN'S COGNAC (IRE)** 6-1 **Miss F Wilson** *A.p; ld 5; made rest; nvr more than 2l clr; kpt on game* . . . 1
No Fiddling (IRE) 10-1 **Miss R Reynolds** *Ww in mid-div; 5l 5th & hdwy 10; went cl 3rd 2 out & 2nd app last; nt rch wnr* . . . 2 2
Red Neck(tt) 2-1 **Miss E Jones** *Prom; 2½l 4th 10; went 2nd 15; 2l down 2 out; tired & dem app last* . . . 1½ 3
1081 Whether The Storm (IRE) 4-7F Miss S Samworth *Drpd out last 1-5; ww in last pr; 20l off pce 10; rdn & clsd stdly frm 14; too much to do* . . . 5 4
Hurdante (IRE) 8-1 Miss I Tompsett *(b4) Ld 1-5; cl 2nd til wknd aft 14; 7l 4th 2 out; dem aft* . . . 8 5

Cage Aux Folles (IRE) 10-1 Mrs B Lewis *Midfield; prog to 1l 2nd 6; prom to 10; fdd 12; sn rr; pu 15* . . . . . P
Cowanstown Prince 10-1 Miss J Hughes *4th early; 10l 6th 5; 30l last 9; pu 12* P
63^{4} Market Springer (IRE) 6-1 Miss B Williams *A rr; 15l 6th 10; sn wl bhnd; pu aft 15* P

OFFICIAL DISTANCES: 1*l*, 1*l* **TIME:** 6min 23.0s

207 Restricted, 12st — 9 ran

GILZINE 7-2 **J L Llewellyn** *(xnb) Hld up in last pr; prog 8; cl 2nd & rdn 13; chall 16; ld nxt; r.o wl* 1
176^{P} **Valjean (IRE)**(tt) 4-1 **A Hanly** *Settled 3rd; went 2nd 8; ld aft 12; 1l up til hdd 2 out; tired & hld aft* 10 2
Commanche Fox (IRE) 8-1 **N Oliver** *(xnb) Prom; mist 6; ld 10-12; cl 3rd & ev ch nxt til fdd 15; 12l 3rd 3 out; sn btn; eased hvly flat; walked in* . . . . . runin 3
All For Jake (IRE) 6-4F D Jones *Mid-div when fell 2* . . . . . F
79^{P} Anflora (5a) 4-1 M Barber *Midfield; 5th & jmpd slow 3; impd to ld 8-9; 3rd nxt; mist 11 & drpd to rr; t.o 4th 13; v tired & crawled thro 14; pu nxt* . P
Hail Stone (IRE) 3-1 S Blackwell *Rr; t.o last 3; bd 6* . . . . . B
Onward Bound 7-1 M Lewis *2l 2nd 5; 3rd when fell nxt* . . . . . F
65^{10} The Last Shout (IRE) 8-1 T Vaughan *Ld; 12l clr 1; 6l up aft nxt; hdd aft 7; sn rr; pu 11* . . . . . P
50^{U} Who Let The Dogout 6-1 Miss F Wilson *Rr when fell 6* . . . . . F

OFFICIAL DISTANCES: 14*l*, dist **TIME:** 6min 33.0s

208 Confined, 12st — 10 ran

HUNTER GOLD (FR) 4-1 **M Lewis** *Prom; ld 5; hdd brief 11; 4l clr 14; 12l up when lft virt solo 2 out; tired & jmpd v slow last* 1
Never In Debt(cp) 6-1 **M Barber** *Ld to 5; 3rd til 4l 2nd 14; 12l 2nd & tiring when ref 2 out; cont t.o* . . . . . fence 2
115^{P} Lilardo (5a)(tt) 12-1 D Jones *2nd & mist 3; cl 2nd til ld brief 11; rdn & no resp nxt; fdd 13; pu 15* . . . . . P
Mecca Prince (IRE) evensF E Williams *Mid-div; 15l 5th 11; sn fdd; t.o & pu 13* P
Minstrel's Quay (IRE) 20-1 H Evans *4th til wknd 9; rr 11; pu 14* . . . . . P
Rainbow Star (FR) 16-1 A Hanly *Dwelt; set off more than fnce bhnd; 30l last 6; mist 11; pu 13* . . . . . P
Rathgibbon (IRE) 10-1 J Merry *A last trio; t.o aft 11; pu 13* . . . . . P
Ribble Assembly 7-2 T Vaughan *Settled 4th frm 5 til 3rd by defection 14; pu 3 out* . . . . . P
Scarlet Emperor (IRE) 8-1 D Rochester *A bhnd; mist 2; pu 4* . . . . . P
64^{U} Welsh Warrior 10-1 R Richards *Nt fluent & a bhnd; 7th when mist 2; 25l 8th 6; pu 11* . . . . . P

OFFICIAL DISTANCE: dist **TIME:** 6min 41.0s

Hereford (RH 9F,18J)

Sun, 15 Feb (GOOD to SOFT, SOFT in places)

209 Julian Graves HC, 3m1f110y £1820 — 16 ran

LANCASTRIAN JET (IRE) 12-00 5-2F **M Barber** *Ld to 2; chsd ldr til ld agn app 8; clr frm 2 out; stayed on wl* 1
34^{P} **Minella Storm (IRE)** 12-00 50-1 **P Sheldrake** *Hld up midfield; 8th 10; hdwy 13; chsd wnr aft 3 out; no imp frm 2 out* 16 2
92^{3} **Arctic King** 11-09 12-1 **R Stephens** *Hld up mid-div; hit 6; 6th 10; hdwy when hit 14; outpcd 16; no ch when lft 3rd 2 out* 7 3
117^{4} Maggies Brother 12-04 8-1 D Barlow *Mid-div; drpd back 13th 10; hdwy app 3 out; stayed on flat; nd* . . . . . 1$\frac{1}{4}$ 4
49^{U} Absolutely Hopeful 11-11(bl) 25-1 T Greenall *Prom; chsd wnr aft 10 til aft 3 out; drvn & sn wknd* 19 5
Bold King (FR) 12-00 13-2 P Morris *Hit 1 & 2; rdn 8; a wl bhnd & rdr oft waving; 14th 10* . . . . . s hd 6
34^{8} Benson (IRE) 12-02 16-1 T Malone *A bhnd; poor 12th 10* . . . . . 2$\frac{1}{2}$ 7
122^{8} Tiraldo (FR) 12-02(cp) 25-1 D Mansell *Prom; hit 5 & 10; 4th nxt; rdn aft 13; wknd aft 15; t.o* 21 8
50^{P} Baccarat (IRE) 11-07(tt) 40-1 M Wall *Mid-div; 9th when hit 10; bhnd frm 13; t.o & pu 3 out* . . . . . P

Colonel Blazer 12-00(cp) 50-1 T Messenger *Bhnd; t.o 6; pu & dism 8. . . .* P
Fanion De Nourry (FR) 11-12 50-1 N Oliver *Chsd ldrs til 5th 10; wknd 14; t.o & pu 2 out. . . . .* P
Justjim 12-07 40-1 Julian Pritchard *Ld 2; blun 6; hdd app 8; chsd wnr til aft 10; wknd 12; t.o & pu 2 out . . . .* P
Master Jock 12-04 7-2 G Hanmer *Bhnd; 10th 10; hdwy app 3 out; 8l 3rd & btn when mist & ur 2 out. . . . .* U
Sip Of Brandy (IRE) 11-12 14-1 Miss J Hughes *Mid-div; 7th 10; hit 12 & ur* U
Speed Board (IRE) 12-00(bl) 33-1 J Cook *Mists; a bhnd; rdn 8; last 10; t.o 11; pu 15 . . . .* P
Tom's River (IRE) 12-00 16-1 M Jackson *A bhnd; 11th 10; rdn 14; t.o & pu aft 3 out . . . .* P

TIME: 6min 37.0s **TOTE:** £3.40; places £1.80,£29.60,£2.50 **Ex:**£332.50 **CSF:**£151.16
Fence 17 omitted - injured horse

College Valley & North Northumberland

Alnwick (LH 9F,18J)

Sun, 15 Feb (GOOD, GOOD to SOFT in places)

210 Confined, 12st 10 ran

134^{5} **SPRING DOUBLE (IRE)** (8ow) 16-1 **T Mounsey-Heysham** *Ld/disp til hdd 9; ld agn 13; prsd 15; hdd brief agn 2 out; 2l up at last; rdn out . . . .* 1
Dun Victory (3x) 9-4F **T Oates** *Chsd ldrs; 8l 4th 5; prog to ld 9; hdd 13; cl 2nd til ld agn brief 2 out; no ex flat; btr for rce. . . . .* 2 2
135^{2} **Johnnys Gone (IRE)** 7-1 **C Shirley-Beavan** *Opened 8s; hld up in last; 15l last 7; prog 9 to 7l 6th 11; trckd ldrs 14; 4l 4th nxt; ev ch 3 out; nt qckn frm nxt* 2 3
73^{1} Dream Of My Life (USA) (6x) 3-1 R Morgan *(xnb,orbs) Chsd ldrs; 5l 5th 15; prog & ev ch aft nxt; sn no ex. . . . .* 3 4
Hailstorm (IRE) 14-1 J Alexander *Carried condition; mist 2; ld/disp frm 3; ld brief 8-9; cl up & ev ch til outpcd frm 3 out. . . . .* 1½ 5
131^{1} Mozielaw (5a) 8-1 Miss M Neill *Lw; in tch in rr; 12l 9th app 7; outpcd 11; kpt on one pce frm 15 . . . .* 10 6
73^{4} Boulta (IRE)(cp) 7-1 K Anderson *Chsd ldrs; 6l 3rd 4; 3l 4th app 10; 2l 3rd & ev ch 15; sn pushed along & outpcd; 10l 6th 3 out; one pce . . . .* 3 7
70^{1} Crevamoy (IRE) (5a, 3ow) 5-1 J Galbraith *Swtng; oht; rfo aft 1. . . . .* U
134^{8} Starbuck (3x)(cp) 10-1 L Morgan *Mid-div; disp 10l 6th 6; rdn along 9; wknd frm 11; wl bhnd when pu 2 out . . . .* P
Wensley Blue (IRE) (7a, 5x) 12-1 A Richardson *Mists; chsd ldrs; blun 2; disp 10l 6th 6; rdn & wknd aft 12; wl bhnd when pu 3 out; dism . . . .* P

OFFICIAL DISTANCES: 2*l*, 3*l* **TIME:** 6min 28.0s

211 Dodson & Horrell PPORA Club Members, 12st 14 ran

DUN ROSE (5a, 2ow) 5-2F **T Oates** *Late to padd; trckd ldrs; 2l 2nd 11; ld aft 14; drew 8l clr 2 out; hit last; rdn out. . . . .* 1
Emperor's Magic (IRE)(tt) 6-1 **Miss S Ward** *Bckwd; rr; wl bhnd 11; outpcd 13; stayed on wl frm nxt; went 20l 3rd 15; rdn in comical fashion & clsng when hit last; nrst fin . . . .* 3 2
Noble Hymn 3-1 **C Mulhall** *(xnb) Opened 7/2; rr; wl bhnd 11; stdy prog frm 14; 20l 4th 15; kpt on past btn horses; nrst fin . . . .* 6 3
Briery Hill 20-1 T Morrison *2 handlers; tde; prom; 4l 2nd 7; 6l 3rd app 12; 15l 3rd & outpcd nxt; no ch aft . . . .* 6 4
Stormalong (IRE)(tt) 10-1 C Storey *In tch; 12l 6th 9; outpcd 12; kpt on one pce* 5 5
Hoh Tel (IRE)(cp) 7-2 K Anderson *Mid-div; 5l 6th app 7; 10½l 5th 9; outpcd 12; kpt on; nd . . . .* 4 6
Ben From Ketton (6ow) 7-1 S J Robinson *In tch in rr; 11l 7th 10; sn outpcd* 5 7
161^{P} Sharpaman(bl) 10-1 C Shirley-Beavan *In tch in rr; pushed along 9; outpcd aft; wl bhnd 11 . . . .* 8 8
71^{5} Baby John (IRE) 14-1 Miss L Horner *Chsd ldrs; 4l 5th 4; wkng 9; nd aft . .* 8 9
Dean Deifir (IRE) 8-1 R Morgan *(xnb,bf,orbs) Oht; ld; 5l up 9; 1l ahd 12; hdd aft 14; wknd frm nxt; wl bhnd when pu last . . . .* P
Freddie Muck 8-1 B Mounsey-Heysham *Prom; 3½l 4th 4; 10l 4th 9; outpcd 13; wl bhnd when pu last . . . .* P
Jethro Tull (IRE) (7a) 8-1 G Brewer *(xnb) A rr; bhnd 13; t.o & pu 15. . . . .* P

	Naomh Padraig (IRE) 10-1 J Cookson *In tch; 15l 7th 9; outpcd aft; wl bhnd when pu last*		P
160^{P}	Oaklands Ted 14-1 T Glass *A rr; t.o & pu aft 15*		P

OFFICIAL DISTANCES: 4*l*, 8*l* **TIME:** 6min 26.1s

PLATE 10 211 College Valley & N. Northumberland PPORA Club Members: The Recall Man runs for cover as the field bears down *PHOTO: Alan Mitchell*

212 Restricted, 12st — 15 ran

	DUMADIC 4-1 **N Tutty** *Lw; handy; cl 7th aft 9; 2l 2nd 15; sn ld; 8l up at last; r.o wl*		1
74^{1}	**Hallrule (IRE)** 4-1 **Miss P Robson** *Chsd ldrs; 5l 8th 6; disp 10l 8th app 13; prog to 8l 4th 15; kpt on wl; nt trble wnr*	5	2
132^{3}	**Timberley** 8-1 **T Oates** *Trckd ldrs; disp 3l 4th app 5; went 3l 2nd 14; outpcd & 6l 3rd nxt; kpt on one pce*	8	3
$70^{2\dagger}$	Alittlebitopower 6-4F C Storey *Sn ld; 2l up frm 6; prsd & bad mist 15; hdd & lost momentum; 20l 4th aft 2 out; kpt on*	hd	4
	Roscoe Burn 10-1 M McAlister *Prom til outpcd 13; sn no ch; bhnd 3 out*	25	5
69^{2}	Be A Better Boy (4ow) 5-1 J Walton *Chsd ldrs; disp 3l 4th app 5; outpcd 14 & sn btn*	1	6
57^{P}	Purple Jean (5a) 12-1 G Brewer *Trckd ldrs; 6l 6th 12; wknd 14; sn bhnd*	2	7
	Alex In Action 25-1 B Hall *Swtng; in tch in rr to 8; t.o 15*	20	8
	St Bee(cp) 12-1 A Richardson *Bckwd; sn rr; 20l last 9; strugg 11; t.o frm nxt*	1	9
	Eighty Days (IRE) (7a, 3ow) 14-1 R Morgan *(xnb) In tch in rr to 10; t.o & pu 14*		P
132^{P}	Laura Lugs (IRE) (8ow) 20-1 T Mounsey-Heysham *Ld brief; sn rr; 25l last app 10; sn t.o; pu 15*		P
	Offspringer 8-1 L Morgan *Mounted on course; rr; some prog frm 10; 10l 8th app 13; sn wknd; bhnd & pu 3 out*		P
	Royalecko 8-1 Miss J Hollands *Prom; 2l 2nd 6; outpcd aft 12; t.o & pu 15*		P
	The Broken Man 16-1 Miss K Bryson *Sis; a rr; t.o aft 11; pu 15*		P
133^{P}	Westie (5a) 12-1 Miss L Kendall *Mid-div; 7l 7th app 11; outpcd 13; t.o & pu 3 out*		P

OFFICIAL DISTANCES: 8*l*, 7*l* **TIME:** 6min 27.8s

213 Ladies Open — 4 ran

135^{3}	**HARDEN GLEN** 4-1 **Miss J Riding** *(xnb) Made all; 2l up 4; 1l ahd 10; jnd 15; hrd prsd frm 2 out; $1^{1}/_{2}$l up last; hld on wl flat*		1
	Donnegale (IRE)(cp) 3-1 **Miss J Foster** *Trckd ldr; $^{1}/_{2}$l 2nd 8; prsd ldrs frm 15; ev ch 2 out; outpcd app last; rallied flat; a hld*	$^{3}/_{4}$	2

133[3] **Dere Street** 4-6F **Miss R Davidson** *Trckd ldng pr; 4l 3rd 4; jmpd slow 9; 5l 3rd 14; eff to 2l 3rd 3 out & rmdrs; 4l 3rd & no imp nxt* 3 3

Manhattan Rainbow (IRE) 10-1 Miss J Hollands *Mists; in tch in last; disp 3l 3rd 9; mist 11; rdn & wknd 13; sn lost tch; 20l 4th 15; pu nxt* . . . . . . P

OFFICIAL DISTANCES: 1*l*, 3*l* **TIME:** 6min 35.1s

214 Mens Open 8 ran

72[2] **JUST BARNEY BOY** 5-1 **A Waugh** *1st ride; handy; 2l 3rd 9; disp ld 12; hdd brief aft 13 & 15-3 out; ld & gng wl nxt; qcknd clr app last; wl rdn* 1

Red Gauntlet 6-4F **K Anderson** *Ld; hdd aft 4; ld agn 7; 2l up 10; jnd 12; ld brief aft 13 & 15 til hdd 2 out; rdn & one pce aft; btr for rce* 4 2

Kilcaskin Gold (IRE) 5-1 **A Findlay** *Oht; in tch in rr; 12l 6th app 7; 15l 6th & pushed along 9; clsd u.p frm 3 out; nt able to chall* 8 3

Dorans Magic (3ow) 3-1 N Bannister *Lw; chsd ldrs; 10l 5th app 7; pushed along 9; went 6l 3rd app 3 out; sn outpcd* 3 4

Charlieadams (IRE) (3ow) 16-1 J Muir *Prom; ld aft 4-6; cl 2nd til 10l 4th & wkng 12; pu 3 out* . . . . P

134[1] Falcon's Flame (USA) 6-1 R Green *Trckd ldrs; 3l 4th 9; disp 1l 2nd 14; sn wknd & lost tch; pu 3 out* . . . . P

107[P] Rosey Boy (IRE) 7-1 N Tutty *Trckd ldr; 1l 2nd 3; crumpled on landing & fell 4* F

Royal Plum(bl) 14-1 S J Robinson *Rr; sltly detach 3; 15l last app 7; 40l last & jmpd slow 10; t.o & totally exhaust when ref 3 out* . . . . r

OFFICIAL DISTANCES: 4*l*, 12*l* **TIME:** 6min 30.3s

215 Open Maiden (Div 1), 12st 17 ran

FLYING PAST 10-1 **R Morgan** *Rr to 7; stdy prog to 15l 3rd aft 15; ld aft nxt; 8l up 2 out; lft wl clr at last* 1

Pure Steel (IRE) 4-1 **C Storey** *Mid-div; 6l 6th 10; outpcd & wl bhnd 15; poor 4th when lft 2nd at last* 25 2

137[U] **Jackofalltrades (IRE)** 5-1 **T Oates** *Oht; trckd ldrs; 4l 4th 9; outpcd aft 13; 16l 4th 15; poor 5th when lft 20l 3rd at last* 2½ 3

137[P] Commanche Spirit (IRE) 10-1 Mrs V Jackson *Ld early; sn hdd; outpcd aft 13; wl bhnd 3 out; t.o when lft 4th at last* 25 4

74[P] Carrow Garden (IRE) 10-1 C Dawson *Bckwd; prom to 9; wknd & rmdrs aft; lsng tch & pu 10* . . . . P

Derrys Choice (5a) 10-1 N Tutty *Unruly padd; in tch til mist & ur 11* . . . . U

75[P] Harvest The Oak 10-1 T Coles *Chsd ldrs; outpcd 13; t.o & pu 15* . . . . P

Hi Up Brenkley 10-1 A Richardson *Green; v unruly padd; nt jw in rr; t.o 12; pu 3 out* P

I'm Willie's Girl (5a) 10-1 Miss J Riding *Chsd ldrs; jmpd big 3; 6l 5th when blun & ur 11* . . . . U

167[F] Kindle A Flame 7-4F G Brewer *Ld frm 4 til hdd aft 3 out; sn btn; 10l 2nd when fell last* . . . . F

Midnight Reiver (5a)(tt) 8-1 Miss J Hollands *(xnb) 10s-8s; fat; sis; 20l last 2; bhnd when ur 12* . . . . U

Posh Stick (5a, 9ow) 5-1 J Walton *A rr; t.o 12; pu 15.* . . . . P

137[U] Ramon Allones (IRE) 10-1 R Green *(xnb) Mid-div; outpcd 10; t.o 12; pu nxt* P

Reeker Pike (5a) 10-1 J Thompson *In tch til outpcd 12; sn rr; t.o & pu 3 out* P

Seasmith 4-1 C Shirley-Beavan *Nt a fluent; prom; 3l 4th 6; disp 3l 2nd 9; 2l 2nd & mist 15; sn outpcd; 15l 3rd & btn when fell last* . . . . F

Seemore Sunshine 10-1 L Morgan *(xnb) Green; ur padd; ld to post & at start; midfield; outpcd aft 10; strugg aft 12; t.o & pu 3 out* . . . . P

Simply Silver Lady (5a) 10-1 S Huggan *Prom; disp 3l 2nd 9; cl up when blun & ur 12; rdr rolled und hedge* . . . . U

OFFICIAL DISTANCES: dist, 2*l* **TIME:** 6min 42.6s

216 Open Maiden (Div 2), 12st - 17J 13 ran

75[2] **LITTLE JOHN** 5-2F **A Richardson** *Rr; 15l 7th 9; stdy prog to 5l 3rd 15; ww til ld app last; sprinted clr flat* 1

Try Me And See 8-1 **G Crow** *Swtng; 1st ride; a.p; ld 9 & frm 12 til hdd & no ex app last.* 5 2

166[P] **Sweet Chestnut** 14-1 **Miss L Kendall** *(xnb) Mid-div; rdn & rmdrs 12; some prog to 10l 4th 15; kpt on one pce frm nxt* 6 3

Comfortably Numb (FR) (7a) 3-1 N Tinkler *Cl up; 3l 3rd 10; 1l 2nd 15; outpcd aft nxt; kpt on* 8 4

Sijujama (IRE) 5-1 Miss N Patterson *(xnb) 14s-5s; prom; 1/2l 2nd 9; ev ch 15; 8l 3rd & no ex nxt* 5 5
167[2] Iron Trooper (IRE) 7-2 T Glass *(xnb) Rr; 20l last aft 1; some prog aft 9; nd* 1/2 6
Can't Catch Me (IRE) (5a) 6-1 C Storey *A rr; strugg & 25l 11th 9; t.o 12* . . 15 7
165[U] Red Tyrant 4-1 Miss C Metcalfe *10s-4s; a rr; t.o 12; nd* 4 8
Alice's Old Rose (5a) 12-1 Mrs K Hargreave *Swtng; rr; t.o when mist & ur 13* U
74[P] French Chocolate (5a, 2ow)(bl) 25-1 L Morgan *Unruly padd; ld to 3; sn wknd; 30l last 9; rdn along aft; t.o & pu nxt* . . . . . . P
132[P] Hervey Bay (5a) 7-1 W Goldie *(xnb) Prom; 1l 2nd 5; 8l 4th 9; wknd nxt; t.o & pu 15* . . . . . . P
James Drummond (7a) 10-1 R MacDonald *Oht; rr; 20l 6th 11; t.o when hit 13 & ur* . . . . . . U
Jinful Du Grand Val (FR) 3-1 J Alexander *Oht; prom; ld aft 4; mist & ur 7* . U

OFFICIAL DISTANCES: 4*l*, 6*l* **TIME:** 6min 44.5s

Fence 16 omitted - fallen rider

Easton Harriers

High Easter (LH 9F,19J)

Sun, 15 Feb (GOOD, GOOD to FIRM in places)

217 Hunt Members 5 ran

GLENALLA BRAES (IRE) 4-1 **Miss R Page** *Ld to 5; drpd to last 7; eff to chse ldr 11; clsd to ld 3 out; sn clr; rdr's 1st wnr - 2nd ride* 1
Marsden 4-1 **N Moore** *Keen; ld 5; 6l clr 1/2way; hdd 3 out; sn btn; wknd flat* 20 2
127[P] **Rip Kirby**(bl) 4-6F **G Cooper** *(xnb) Trckd ldr 6-11; rmdrs & no resp 13; no prog & btn aft* 5 3
Arkay 12-1 Miss L Franks *Fat; 1st ride; w ldr to 4; in tch to 9; gng v slow nxt; plodded round miles bhnd* 55sec 4
Spring Frolic 10-1 R Cundy *1st ride; last when blun & ur 1* . . . . . . U

OFFICIAL DISTANCES: 15*l*, 4*l* **TIME:** 6min 57.4s **TOTE:** £4.40

218 Open Maiden 56&7yo (Div 1), 12st 8 ran

21[3] **JUST JOVE** 4-6F **R Cope** *Opened evens; made all; rdn clr aft 3 out; dived at 2 out; in comm aft* 1
Flaxley Abbey (5a) 16-1 **N Moore** *Late to padd; prsd wnr til rdn & outpcd app 3 out; fdd* 15 2
151[P] **Barry Lydon (IRE)** 16-1 **T Lane** *In tch; prog to press ldrs 11; cl 3rd til wknd 3 out; mist 2 out* 7 3
39[4] Shallee Term (IRE) 7-1 P Millington *Prom; outpcd 13; eff & in tch when mist 15; sn btn; rdr all over the plce 2 out* 4 4
Daisy Duke (5a) 16-1 A Merriam *Bit bckwd; cl up; mists 8 & 9; in tch when hmpd bad 12, brought to standstill & pu* . . . . . . P
7[R] Groovejet (7a) 16-1 Miss K Smith *(xnb) Swtng; rcd wide; hld up; prog & in tch when fell 12* . . . . . . F
20[P] San Malo (IRE) 7-1 Miss B Donnelly *In rr; last & lsng tch 11; t.o & pu 14* . P
60[3] Tooley Park 8-1 N Pearce *In tch in rr; mist 11; wknd 14; t.o & pu 15* . . . . P

OFFICIAL DISTANCES: 15*l*, 10*l* **TIME:** 6min 45.2s **TOTE:** £2.40

219 Open Maiden 56&7yo (Div 2), 12st 10 ran

8[U] **MISTER RINGA** 7-4F **A Merriam** *Nt fluent early; hld up rr; mist 7; prog to 4th 13; lft 3rd 15; chall & blun 3 out; rallied to press ldr 2 out; ld last; drvn & hld on wl* 1
King Freddy (7a) 4-1 **R Cope** *Midfield; prog to 3rd 13; lft 2nd nxt; ld 16; rdn & prsd 2 out; just hdd last; kpt on flat; a hld* 1 2
104[P] **Shot Of Jollop (IRE)** (7a) 16-1 **N Bloom** *(xnb) Ld til jmpd slow 3; chsd ldrs; outpcd 13; 6th nxt; stayed on agn frm 2 out* 25 3
Highland Dancer (IRE) (7a) 40-1 T Ellis *Midfield; prog to chse ldr 11; lft in narrow ld brief 15; wknd & mist 2 out; fin tired* 15 4
105[7] Inching Brook 33-1 P Taiano *(xnb) Keen; hld up; prog to chse ldr 9-11; sn drpd to rr; last 14; no ch aft* 4 5
151[U] Divine Mist (IRE) 14-1 J Owen *Jmpd rt 4; 9th when fell 5* . . . . . . F

Germany Park (IRE) 2-1 M Smith *(xnb) Ld 3; 8l up 9; came back to field 14; 2l up & still gng wl enough when carried out by loose horse 15* C

128[F] Jumping Jeffrey 40-1 M Mackley *In tch in rr til wknd & pu 12* . . . . P

Magic Lodge (7a) 12-1 R Stearn *(xnb) 4th when blun & ur 5* . . . . U

30[P] On The Deck 14-1 P Millington *Prom til jmpd slow 9 & lost plce; wl in rr 13; ploughed thro 15 & rdr all over the plce; t.o last when pu last* . . . . P

OFFICIAL DISTANCES: 1*l*, 15*l* **TIME:** 6min 49.7s **TOTE:** £4.00

220 Open Maiden 8yo&up, 12st — 8 ran

86[2] **TRUMPER** evensF **P York** *6/4-evens; trckd ldr 6; upsides 10 til ld 15; drew 8l clr 2 out; rdn app last; kpt on* 1

44[6] **Street Smart (IRE)** 16-1 **Miss B Donnelly** *(xnb) Mist 2; prom; trckd ldng pr 11-16; outpcd aft 3 out; stayed on to 2nd 2 out; clsd on wnr last; kpt on* 2½ 2

Glen Amber (IRE) 10-1 **A Sansome** *Ss & hld up 10l bhnd rest; stdy prog frm 11; went 4th aft 14 & clsd nxt; chsd wnr 3 out-nxt; wknd* 12 3

A Fine Story 3-1 A Williams *(xnb) Wl in tch til outpcd in 11l 4th 13; ab 15l 5th & btn when eased & pu 3 out* . . . . P

Fair Storm (IRE) 20-1 H Fowler *Rr; mist 7; last & lsng tch 9; t.o & pu 14* . P

39[2] Lindron 4-1 P Bull *2 handlers; ld 3; jnd 10; mist 14; hdd nxt; wknd 3 out; poor 4th when pu last* . . . . P

103[P] Society Scandal (IRE)(tt) 20-1 P Millington *2 handlers; ld til mist 3; cl up til wknd & jb rt 12 & 13; t.o & pu 3 out* . . . . P

111[P] Two By Four 14-1 R Cope *Warm; chsd ldrs; mists 6 & 9; rdn & no resp 10; pu 11* P

OFFICIAL DISTANCES: 2*l*, 6*l* **TIME:** 6min 47.0s **TOTE:** £2.00

221 Mens Open — 6 ran

DELGANY ROYAL (IRE) 5-1 **B Pollock** *Jmpd bold; ld 4; drew clr frm 15; r.o wl; comf* 1

125[r] **Minino (IRE)**(bl) 8-1 **C Ward-Thomas** *(xnb) V reluct to line up & even more reluct to rce; lft 30l; grad clsd; at rr of field 6; prog to chse wnr 9; outpcd & nd frm 16* 20 2

98[3] **Ballad (IRE)** 40-1 **A Williams** *In tch; 8l 4th aft 13; outpcd frm 15; went poor 3rd aft 3 out; plodded on.* 5 3

42[P] Dunrig (IRE) 6-1 J Owen *Ld til hdd & mist 4; 5l 3rd aft 13; outpcd 15; wknd 3 out; fin slow.* 25 4

Polo Ridge (IRE) 16-1 H Fowler *Prom; prsd wnr 6-9; 11l 5th & wkng aft 13; wl bhnd frm 16* 4 5

43[2] Fair Exchange 1-2F P Taiano *In tch; nt fluent 6 & 7; last aft 8; drpd away tame frm 11; 16l last aft 13; t.o & pu 16* . . . . P

OFFICIAL DISTANCES: 20*l*, 5*l* **TIME:** 6min 38.4s **TOTE:** £6.80

The stewards enquired into the running and riding of Fair Exchange; the rider's explanation that the horse 'had not travelled from the 1st fence, and had jumped right on ground that was too quick for him' was accepted

222 Ladies Open — 5 ran

88[4] **STORM CASTLE (IRE)** 4-1 **Miss J Wickens** *Keen; mist 2; went 2nd 7; still pulling 11; ld 15; lft 4l clr 3 out; hrd prsd 2 out; pushed out flat* 1

42[2] **Bush Hill Bandit (IRE)** 4-5F **Miss A Stennett** *Opened 5/4; ld 5; narrowly hdd when stumbled bad 15 & drpd to 4th; rallied to press wnr 2 out; ev ch last; no ex flat.* 1¼ 2

Corston Joker 33-1 **Mrs L Spence** *Ld to 5; stayed wl in tch til outpcd in 3rd app 2 out; wknd & walking nr fin* 20 3

101[2] The Wiley Kalmuck (IRE) 5-1 Miss Z Turner *Jmpd slow 7 & drpd to last; rmdr 11; no prog & outpcd 16; nrly caught toiling 3rd nr fin* . . . . ½ 4

25[2] Fair Kiowa (IRE) 9-2 Mrs S Hodge *Trckd ldrs; eff & lft 2nd 15; w wnr & ev ch when fell 3 out.* . . . . F

OFFICIAL DISTANCES: 1*l*, 5*l* **TIME:** 6min 38.5s **TOTE:** £3.20

223 Intermediate, 12st — 10 ran

124[U] **EASTERN POINT** (5a, 5x) 10-1 **P York** *Ss; sn drvn up to chse ldng pr; mists 6 & 7; went 2nd 13; ld on inner 3 out; outj & hdd nxt; rousted along to ld agn last; all out* 1

50[2] **Camden Carrig (IRE)** 4-5F **N Phillips** *(bf) Nt a fluent; ld at decent pce; narrowly hdd 3 out; btr j to ld agn 2 out; hdd last; kpt on flat; just hld.* . . 1 2

Bedtime Boys 6-1 **J Docker** *10s-6s; bckwd; hld up in midfield; 5th 1/2way; went 4th 14; outpcd when lft 3rd 3 out; no imp ldng pr.* 15 3
Libido 14-1 P Andrew *Prsd ldr to 13; sn wknd; wl bhnd frm 15* 25 4
159F Ballylesson (IRE) 33-1 N Moore *Rcd in 7th; wknd aft 11; tlng off when pu 13* P
41² Fine And Dandy (IRE) (5x) 3-1 J Owen *Chsd ldng trio; went 3rd 13; ab 3l down & wl in tch when fell 3 out.* F
127P Jerome Jerome 20-1 T Lane *Mostly in last trio; lost tch frm 12; t.o 14; pu 2 out* P
Lord Montagu (IRE) 16-1 M Mackley *A towards rr; wknd & pu 11* P
No Dramas (IRE)(tt) 12-1 C Gordon *Hld up last pr; some prog to 6th 1/2way; sn lost plce; pu 14* P
Stick Or Bust 33-1 M Smith *Midfield; drvn & strugg 10; sn btn; t.o 14; pu 3 out* P

OFFICIAL DISTANCES: 1*l*, 15*l* **TIME:** 6min 39.2s

224 Dodson & Horrell PPORA Club Members Confined Moderate — 6 ran

LORD EURO (IRE) 4-5F **A Merriam** *Pulled to ld 2 & sn 20l clr; nt fluent & jmpd rt sev fncs; jnd 15; drew away agn frm 3 out* 1
159P **Camden Loch (IRE)** 5-2 **N Bloom** *6s-5/2; hld up; 18l 4th 1/2way & pushed along; 16l 3rd & no imp 15; stayed on to 2nd 2 out; no ch w wnr* 10 2
38P **Prologue (IRE)** (9ow) 6-1 **C Jarvis** *Bhnd; 31l last aft 13; brief eff 16; sn plodding; tk poor 3rd at last.* 25 3
98⁶ Ardnut(bl) 33-1 R Page *2 handlers; ld til hdd & rfo 2* U
Skirmishing 10-1 N Moore *(xnb) Chsd clr wnr frm 2-11; sn wknd; hopelessly t.o 15; pu 2 out* P
155⁵ Treasure Dome (IRE) 14-1 T Lane *Disp 2nd frm 3 til clr 2nd frm 11; clsd on wnr 14; upsides 15; mist 3 out & sn btn; lost 2nd 2 out; poor 4th & exhaust when ref last* r

OFFICIAL DISTANCES: 10*l*, 20*l* **TIME:** 6min 47.0s

Meynell & South Staffordshire

Weston Park (LH 7F,18J)

Sun, 15 Feb (GOOD to SOFT)

225 Hunt Members — 6 ran

57F **APPROACHING LAND (IRE)** 11-10F **M Manton** *Pulling; trckd ldrs; hit 3 & 4; went 2nd 9; ld aft 2 out; sn qcknd clr; blun last; nt pushed flat; easily* 1
107R **Young Tomo (IRE)**(bl) 7-4 **Miss C Goodall** *Chsd ldr 3 til ld 5; 4l clr app 14; hdd & imm outpcd app last; kpt on flat; flatt by prox* 1 1/2 2
Ridware Pride 10-1 **W Hill** *Bckwd; ww in tch; 6l 3rd 14; rdn 3 out; kpt on one pce aft; bbv* 3/4 3
Needwood Neptune 14-1 P Bennett *Bckwd; ld to 5; chsd ldrs til 4th & wkng app 14; no ch aft* 20 4
Ballyhannon (IRE) 14-1 Miss J Froggatt *Bhnd; jmpd slow 3; 10l 5th 13; sn lost tch; t.o* 50 5
97P Ridware Boy 10-1 Miss S Sharratt *Tk keen hld; ww; mist 5; 12l last when mist 11; sn lost tch; t.o & pu 15* P

OFFICIAL DISTANCES: 1 1/2*l*, 3/4*l* **TIME:** 7min 00.00s

226 Confined Maiden (Div 1), 12st — 12 ran

NO REMORSE 9-4 **G Hanmer** *Hld up; 15l last 10; hdwy & 10l 7th app 14; ld aft 3 out; 2l up when jmpd slow & jnd nxt; kpt alongside rival w rdr lkng across; outj last & 2l down til shkn up & qcknd to ld nr fin; v cheekily* 1
111³ **Arctic Summer (IRE)** 5-1 **J Trice-Rolph** *Mid-div in tch; mist 4; went 2nd 3 out; lft disp ld nxt; outj rival & 2l up aft last; allowed to ld til hdd nr fin* nk 2
97⁶ **Iadora** (5a) 7-1 **Miss T Clark** *Ld to 2; mist 4; lft in ld 11-nxt; chsd ldrs til wknd 3 out* 15 3
Ridware George 6-1 W Hill *Bckwd; prom; chsd ldr 13; 5l 2nd nxt; wknd 3 out; lft 4th at last* 10 4
97² Benbow 2-1F B Shaw *Ld 2 til fell 11* F
Carrigafoyle 12-1 Miss S Talbot *Prom; ld 12; 5l clr app 14; hdd 3 out; sn outpcd; disp mod 3rd when blun & ur last* U

113P Currow Kate (5a) 12-1 L Hicks *Ww; chsd ldrs 11; 6l 3rd & rdn 14; sn wknd; bhnd & pu 2 out* . . . . P
Kissed By Moonlite (5a) 20-1 R Armson *(xnb) In tch; mist 6; cl 6th when hmpd 11; sn rdn; lsng plce when fell nxt* . . . . F
Master Lord (IRE) 16-1 M Briggs *(xnb) Mid-div; blun & drpd to rr 8; t.o & pu 14* P
96⁵ Mosscroft Jack 20-1 D Greenway *(xnb) Ww; jmpd slow 3; mist 6; prog to trck ldrs 11; jmpd rt nxt; rdn & wknd app 14; t.o & pu 2 out* . . . . P
91P Skippers Canyon (5a) 20-1 R Carey *2 handlers; blun 1; prom; chsd ldrs 7 til blun 11; sn wknd; t.o & pu 14* . . . . P
Well Said Sam 20-1 J Handley *Bhnd; hdwy to 8l 6th 7; wkng when blun 13; t.o & pu 15* . . . . P

OFFICIAL DISTANCES: 1/2l, 15l **TIME:** 6min 56.0s

227 Confined Maiden (Div 2), 12st — 11 ran

96² **WELCOME NEWS** (5a) 5-4F **B Shaw** *Cl up; ld 8; jnd 14; 1/2l up last; a hldng reluct rival* 1
Uncle Ada (IRE)(bl) 5-2 **R Burton** *Chsd ldrs; jnd wnr gng wl 14; rdn & hung rt app last; nt r.o* 3/4 2
Karinga Lane 8-1 **W Hill** *(xnb) Tk keen hld; prom; blun & nrly ur 11; 4l 3rd 13; rdn & wknd qckly app 2 out* 20 3
Single Man (IRE) 20-1 J Burley *In tch; 4l 5th & rdn 14; blun & outpcd nxt; sn no ch* 20 4
96U Bless Yourself (IRE) 5-1 A McArdle *16s-5s; nt jw; rr til rn out thro wing & ur 4* R
96U Gosh Josh (IRE) 12-1 J Jarrett *Rr; 50l 10th when mist 10; t.o & pu 12* . . . P
Magnatism 10-1 L Hicks *(xnb) Ww in rr; prog 9; 5l 6th 12; wknd 15; 20l 5th 2 out; pu last* . . . . P
Mountsorrel (IRE) (7a) 12-1 R Cooper *Tk keen hld; jnd ldrs 10-13; wknd qckly 14; 6th & no ch 2 out; pu last* . . . . P
93P Pekan Polly (5a) 10-1 A Wadlow *Rr; in tch; 8l last 13; sn wknd; t.o & pu 2 out* P
96F Raiseapearl 14-1 I Clyde *(citation) Ld round start; stdd & lost 20l; a wl detach in last; mist 6; t.o & pu 11* . . . . P
96P Ridware Rose (5a) 20-1 Miss S Sharratt *2 handlers; ld 3-8; prom til fell 11* F

OFFICIAL DISTANCES: 1l, 20l **TIME:** 6min 53.0s

228 Confined, 12st — 14 ran

106² **MARSTON MOSES** 3-1 **A Bealby** *W ldr to 3; outpcd 9; 12l 5th 11; prog app 14; 8l 4th & clsng 15; ld app last; stayed on* 1
Westcoast 20-1 **W Hill** *Ww; prog to trck ldrs 11; went 2nd 15; ld nxt; 4l clr 2 out; hdd & no ex app last* 2 1/2 2
Dainty Man (IRE) 33-1 **Miss T Clark** *Wl bhnd; 25l 11th 11; stayed on past btn horses frm 15; went 3rd app last; nvr nrr* 8 3
Fornaught Alliance (IRE) (5x)(bl) 20-1 Miss A Turner *1st ride; swtng; sn wl bhnd; 27l 12th 11; stayed on past btn horses frm 15; 4th app last; nvr nrr* 3/4 4
92P Springwood White 20-1 Miss H Kinsey *Mid-div; 20l 7th 13th; kpt on frm 15; nvr able to chall* 8 5
93P Pagermar (IRE)(tt) 6-1 R Cooper *Mid-div; rmdrs 4; jnd ldr 10 til blun 12; 3rd & rdn 14; wknd nxt* 10 6
Ballingale Dawn (IRE) 10-1 R Rogers *A bhnd; t.o & pu 14* . . . . P
City Gent 6-1 Mrs E Heaton *(xnb) Dashed into ld app 4; rn wide & hdd aft 6; 15l 8th & wkng 11; wl bhnd when pu 13* . . . . P
Easby Blue 33-1 J Buxton *Nt jw; sn bhnd; t.o & pu 13* . . . . P
125² Involved (IRE) (6x)(bl) 4-5F R Burton *Nt fluent; pckd 1; w ldr to 3; blun 6; lft in ld app nxt; hrd rdn & blun 15; hdd nxt; 7l 3rd & btn 2 out; wl bhnd when pu last* . . . . P
93P Knock It Back (IRE) (1ow) 10-1 J Handley *(xnb) Oht; chsd ldrs; 3l 3rd 11; 5th & wkng when pu 14* . . . . P
Lord Of The West (IRE) (10x) 12-1 W Puddifer *Bhnd; jmpd slow 9; t.o last 11; pu 14* . . . . P
Roll With It (IRE) 33-1 B Shaw *Mid-div; 14l 6th 11; sn lost tch; t.o & pu 2 out* P
Whatafellow (IRE)(bl) 12-1 Mrs S Edwards *Arrived in padd aft others had mounted; a wl bhnd; blun 9 & 11; t.o & pu last* . . . . P

OFFICIAL DISTANCES: 2l, 5l **TIME:** 6min 48.0s

229 Mens Open — 17 ran

Form	Horse	Dist	Pos
	STEP ON EYRE (IRE) 7-1 **S Morris** *Lw; lft in ld aft 5; made most aft to 15; ld agn nxt; sn hdd; 2l down & lkd hld when lft clr at last*		1
110[3]	**Picket Piece**(bl) 6-1 **M Goldstein** *Swtng; chsd ldrs; lft 2nd 11; ld 15 til blun & hdd nxt; 3rd & btn 2 out; lft 2nd at last*	10	2
93[P]	**Wild Edric** 20-1 **A Beedles** *Ww; 7th & prog 11; 5l 4th app 14; btn 3 out; lft 3rd at last*	20	3
	Iro Origny (FR) 20-1 A Phillips *(xnb) Chsd ldrs; blun & lost plce 10; no ch frm 14*	5	4
106[P]	Noble Colours 33-1 P Ikin *Sn wl bhnd; t.o frm 5*	2	5
91[1]	Ashgan (IRE) 3-1 R Burton *Mid-div; chsd ldrs 11; outpcd nxt; 15l 6th & btn 14; pu 2 out*		P
	Ceasers Reign (IRE) 16-1 T Faulkner *Rr; some hdwy to 10th 11; nvr trbld ldrs; wl bhnd when pu 2 out*		P
163[P]	Chadswell (IRE) 14-1 W Puddifer *Ld 3; 10l clr when missed markers aft 5; cont til blun & ur 11*		R
49[P]	Darrell Boy (IRE)(vis) 33-1 S Blackwell *Bhnd; rdn & no resp 11; wl bhnd & pu 14*		P
	Devonshire (IRE) 7-1 P Bennett *Mists; chsd ldrs early; bhnd 7; t.o 11; 7th & staying on 3 out; no ch when ur nxt*		U
	Do It Again (IRE)(bl) 8-1 R Cooper *Prom; ld aft 10 til blun & ur 11*		U
	Inthaar 33-1 M Hooper *Ww; prog & in tch 11; wknd nxt; t.o & pu 15*		P
32[1]	Mickthecutaway (IRE) 6-4F D Skelton *Chsd ldrs; 4l 3rd app 14; ld app 2 out; 2l up & lkd wnr when fell last*		F
	Mister Falcon (FR) 8-1 S Hughes *Mid-div; prog to trck ldrs 11; 6l 4th & hrd rdn 13; sn wknd; wl bhnd & pu 15*		P
33[P]	Shamel(tt) 20-1 K Pearson *(xnb) A bhnd; 15l 10th 12; t.o & pu 15*		P
	The Archdeacon (IRE) 33-1 T Stephenson *A bhnd; t.o & pu last*		P
	Yer 'umble (IRE) 33-1 O Williams *Blun 1; rdn 4; wl bhnd til pu 13*		P

OFFICIAL DISTANCES: 8*l*, 25*l* **TIME:** 6min 51.0s

230 Ladies Open - 17J — 13 ran

Form	Horse	Dist	Pos
101[1]	**SUPREME CITIZEN (IRE)** 1-2F **Miss J Williams** *Chsd ldrs; mist 13; disp ld 14 til ld 2 out; sn clr; lkd in comm when lft clr at last*		1
94[5]	**Jackie Jarvis (IRE)** (5a) 7-1 **Mrs K Diggle** *(xnb) Ld in start; bhnd; prog 9; 7l 3rd 2 out; kpt on; lft 2nd at last; nt trble wnr*	4	2
	Class Of Ninetytwo (IRE) 12-1 **Miss S Sharratt** *Ld to 4; jmpd rt 5 & 6; lft in ld 14; hdd 2 out; sn btn; lft 3rd at last*	8	3
108[4]	Lucky Master (IRE) 20-1 Miss G Swan *Prom 6; chsd ldrs 7-13; wknd nxt; lft poor 4th at last*	20	4
94[8]	Zamhareer (USA) 10-1 Miss T Harrison *Sn wl bhnd*	3	5
94[P]	Midy's Risk (FR) 20-1 Miss S Davies *(xnb) Mid-div; 8th & outpcd app 14; no ch aft*	20	6
94[2]	Cascum Lad (IRE) 5-1 Miss S Holmes *(xnb) In tch in mid-div; 8l 4th 15; no prog til str burst aft 2 out; 2l down & clsng when rn out last*		R
	Dancetillyoudrop (IRE) 8-1 Miss T Tellwright *(xnb) Ld 4 til mist & lost irons 14; sn hdd; pu nxt*		P
94[U]	Dunston Heath (IRE) 33-1 Miss A Blake *Cl up; nrly ur 4; mist 7; blun & ur 9*		U
94[P]	Guest Alliance (IRE) 33-1 Miss R Reynolds *Bhnd; rdn & lost tch 11; t.o & pu 14*		P
.	Joyce Bel (FR) 12-1 Miss K Crank *Chsd ldrs til fell 5*		F
94[7]	Justin Mac (IRE) 16-1 Miss K Wood *Ur 1*		U
94[9]	Slaney Native (IRE) 25-1 Miss M Mullineaux *Bhnd; prog 12; disp 8l 4th & staying on when fell 15*		F

OFFICIAL DISTANCES: 3*l*, 6*l* **TIME:** 6min 48.0s

Fence 12 omitted - fallen rider

231 Dodson & Horrell PPORA Club Members Restricted, 12st — 12 ran

Form	Horse	Dist	Pos
	HIJACKED 10-1 **S Morris** *Prom in main group; went 20l 2nd & hrd rdn 15; stayed on; hld when lft clr at last*		1
	Kasilia (FR) 7-1 **Miss V Simpson** *Prom in main group; lft 20l 2nd 9-15; nvr nr ldrs; lft 2nd agn at last*	5	2
95[3]	**Donrico (IRE)** 8-1 **A Beedles** *Ww in main group; nvr nr ldrs; lft 3rd at last.*	6	3
	Henbury Dancer (5a) 10-1 E Linehan *Hld up in rr; prog aft 13; went poor 3rd 3 out; dem app last; nd*	5	4

Gaetano (IRE) 5-1 R Burton *Hld up in main group; 7th & wkng aft 13; pu nxt* P
95P Hill Of Kilfeacle (IRE) 20-1 C Barlow *(xnb) A bhnd til pu 14* P
95[4] Jubileeman (IRE) 14-1 Miss H Phizacklea *Last frm 6; t.o 11 til pu 14* P
Magicien (FR) 12-1 R Hodges *Prom in main group; blun 13; wknd nxt; last when ref last* r
112[1] Misty Ramble (IRE) 5-4F G McPherson *Prsd ldr til ld 4; sn wl clr; blun 5 & 11; 20l up 14; tiring but still 10l up & in comm when blun bad & ur last* U
109P Paddy Bettalot 9-2 T Stephenson *Hld up; mist 2; went prom in main group 6; chsd ldr 13-15; wknd; pu last* P
109P Ricky B 8-1 W Kinsey *Ld to 4; 15l 2nd when stumbled & ur 9* U
95[5] What Will Be (IRE) 14-1 M Wilesmith *A wl bhnd; t.o 11 til pu 14* P

OFFICIAL DISTANCES: 4*l*, 6*l* **TIME:** 6min 53.0s

South Dorset

Milborne St Andrew (LH 8F,19J)
Sun, 15 Feb (GOOD)

232 Restricted, 12st — 12 ran

139U **OUT THE BLACK (IRE)** 5-1 **D Alers-Hankey** *Hld up as ldrs went off much too fast; 4th 11; clsd 16 & lft clr 2nd; ld aft rivals blun 2 out; in comm app last; rdn & all out* 1
Lord Of The Mist (IRE) 7-2 **N Williams** *Settled 3rd/4th & 20l frm tearaway pr; clsd grad 10; ld app 16; 3l clr when blun bad 2 out; hdd & drvn aft 2 out; one pce* 8 2
Proby Lady (IRE) (5a) 14-1 **Miss D Harding** *Bad outpcd in rr; jmpd slow 7; 8th 10; plugged on to 25l 4th 3 out; rdr bounced into 3rd nr fin* 20 3
Carat 9-4F Miss P Gundry *(xnb) Lw; novicey in midfield & off pce; 20l 4th 15; lft 3rd nxt; no imp aft; exhaust flat & dem nr fin* ½ 4
116P Thunder Thighs (5a) 16-1 N Wilmington *(xnb) Oht; tde; mists & wl off pce in midfield; 40l 5th when blun 15; blun bad 2 out* ¾ 5
Calfstown Lord 16-1 Miss S Lane *Ss; a t.o* fence 6
118[5] Askers Jack 20-1 N Mitchell *Blun & ur 2* U
65U Barton Saint (NZ) 33-1 B Parsons *Ss; a t.o & rdr v unenterprising; pu 16* P
Branski 100-1 G Weatherley *Rcd keen; ld & sn clr w one rival; hdd 11; drpd out qckly; pu 14* P
35[1] Itchen Mill (5a) 100-30 T Dreaper *Keen in 2nd; 20l clr of rest 5; ld 10; 6l ahd nxt; jmpd rt & blun 15; sn hdd; wkng when crashing fall 16* F
65P Return The Call (IRE) 100-1 R Bliss *Midfield & wl off pce; 7th when hit 10; t.o 14; pu 3 out* P
Sixth Sense (IRE) 50-1 Miss A Bush *Lw; crashing fall 2* F

OFFICIAL DISTANCES: 10*l*, dist **TIME:** 6min 14.5s **TOTE:** £9.00

233 Hunt Members — 9 ran

KESTLE MILL (IRE) 5-1 **N Mitchell** *(xnb) Bckwd; trckd ldrs; went 2nd aft 10; ld 14; 6l clr & in comm 2 out; easy* 1
Nimbus Stratus(cp) 11-4JF **N Wilmington** *Hld up & bhnd; 8l 7th 11; outpcd in 10l 6th 15; rdn & stayed on frm 2 out; nvr nr wnr; nvr in rce* 12 2
Contra Charge 11-2 **T Dreaper** *7s-11/2; keen hld & sn cl up; eff u.p 14; disp 2nd nxt; nt r.o; 7l 3rd & btn when hmpd 2 out; sn dem; fin v tired; lame* 8 3
Druid's Brook 16-1 Miss K Reynolds *(xnb) Ld aft 3-7; 2nd 11; drpd to 8l last 13; plodded on game; jnd eased 4th on line* 12 4†
11[6] Spring Marathon (USA) 9-2 D Green *Tended to j rt; ld to 3 & frm 7 til jmpd rt & pckd 14; wknd qckly; rem 3 out; clr 4th flat til eased & jnd on line; broke down* d ht 4†
89R Chism (IRE) 12-1 W King *Chsd ldrs; 4th 11; 6l 4th 15; no imp when fell hvly 3 out; lame* F
My Brother Jack 8-1 Miss K Lovelace *Lw; midfield til ur 8* U
Swan Song (5a) 50-1 Miss T Barnes *(xnb) Nt jw & imm lost tch; rem last til hit 12 & ur* U
120[4] Warren Hill 11-4JF R Tory *4s-11/4; settled towards rr; 6th 11; clsd stdly to disp 2nd 15; 6l 2nd & btn when blun, nrly ur & fell 2 out; rdr inj* F

OFFICIAL DISTANCES: 12*l*, 10*l* **TIME:** 6min 28.0s **TOTE:** £9.00

234 Ladies Open — 6 ran

EASE THE PRESSURE (IRE) 7-4 **Miss R Green** *Bit bckwd; tk keen hld & hld up trckng ldrs; went 2nd 16; 4l down 2 out; rdn & no imp aft til lft in comm last* 1

117^P **Frank Byrne** 16-1 **Miss A Goschen** *Ld 3; nt fluent 6; hdd 10; 2nd 15; wknd nxt; 14l 3rd 2 out; lft 2nd at last* . . . . 6 — 2

33^P **Wink And Whisper** (5a) 20-1 **Miss L Bridges** *Bit bckwd; handy; went 2nd brief; wknd 16; 16l 4th 2 out.* . . . . 2 — 3

Jackson Hill 16-1 Miss T Cave *(xnb) Lw; jmpd v sticky; last to 7; clsd & blun 11; rdn 12; lost tch 15; t.o 3 out* . . . . runin — 4

64² Charlie Strong (IRE) 10-11F Miss P Gundry *(xnb) Lw; ld to 3; 2nd til ld agn 10; r.o str frm 2 out; 5l clr & in comm when clouted last & ur* . . . . U

171^U Priestthorn (IRE)(cp) 40-1 Miss W Southcombe *Sn bhnd; releg last 7; 15l adrift & strugg 10; ur 13* . . . . U

OFFICIAL DISTANCES: 8*l*, 3*l* **TIME:** 6min 14.5s **TOTE:** £2.00

235 Mens Open, 12st — 7 ran

115¹ **MISS O'GRADY (IRE)** (5a, 7x) 2-1JF **M Miller** *Lw; hld up gng wl; 3rd 10; tk 2nd aft 15; jmpd ahd 2 out & qcknd clr; pushed out flat* 1

11⁵ **Oscar Wilde** 3-1 **D Drake** *Lw; made most to 7; 2½l 3rd aft 15; sn outpcd; 11l 3rd 2 out; kpt on to 2nd cl home* . . . . 15 — 2

Badger Beer (4x) 8-1 **N Mitchell** *W ldr 3 til ld 7; hdd 2 out; imm outpcd; tired when lost 2nd flat.* . . . . 1 — 3

89³ Woodlands Beau (IRE) (7x)(bl) 6-1 T Dreaper *Occasional mists; chsd ldrs; 6l 4th 10; drvn & lost tch 13; nt pushed frm 2 out.* . . . . 12 — 4

Caspers Case 2-1JF N Williams *(xnb) Trckd ldrs in 3rd til fell 9* . . . . F

81^R Commander Cully (IRE) 66-1 M Sweetland *(xnb) Bhnd; lost tch 6; wl t.o when jb lft 11 & 12; pu 13* . . . . P

Lily Lane 66-1 N McDiarmid *(xnb) V fat; hdwy til blun bad 4; sn t.o last & jmpd sticky; pu 12* . . . . P

OFFICIAL DISTANCES: 20*l*, 1½*l* **TIME:** 6min 15.7s **TOTE:** £4.00

The rider of Caspers Case was reported to the Jockey Club Disciplinary Committee for being unable to produce his Medical Record Book

236 Countryside Alliance Club Members (Nov Rdrs), 12st — 5 ran

115⁵ **CHEROKEE BOY** 11-1 **M Atkinson** *Rdn 3 & imm outpcd; went 20l 4th 10; t.o 13; plugged on & lft in ld 2 out; rdr sat still flat & lucky nt to be caught by remounter* 1

90¹ **Kingston-Banker** 10-11F **H Wallace** *Lw; 2nd til ld 7-11; 2l down & ev ch when slt hmpd 2 out & rfo; rmtd 12l bhnd wnr & tried valiantly to cl gap; just failed* . . . . 2 — 2

89^P **Rustic Revelry** 13-2 **C Whittaker** *(xnb) Ld to 7; 15l 3rd & wkng rap 10; ref 2 out; cont* . . . . 1½fs — 3

89^P Mouseski 9-4 H Fry *Rcd keen; 3rd frm 5 til 2nd 8; ld 11; 2l ahd when fell 2 out* . . . . F

Pearl Dante (IRE) 33-1 T Hampton *(xnb) 3rd til rdr got both legs on one side 4 & lost tch; t.o 12; crawled on jmpng v slow til event pu 16.* . . . . P

OFFICIAL DISTANCES: 1¾*l*, dist **TIME:** 6min 25.2s **TOTE:** £5.00

237 Confined Maiden (Div 1), 12st — 9 ran

CAPTAIN RANDOM 8-1 **Mrs J Reed** *(xnb) Bckwd; settled 3rd; 2nd 11; outpcd 16 & lkd hld nxt; stayed on game app last; urged ahd flat* 1

67² **The Sycophant (IRE)** 6-4F **Miss A Goschen** *5/2-6/4; ld to 2; lft in ld 5-7; ld 10; 3l clr 13; drew 15l ahd 2 out; rdn & wknd app last; tired when hdd flat* 1½ — 2

King Of Swing (IRE) 10-1 **Mrs F Vigar** *(xnb) Ld aft 2 til mist 5; ld 7-10; 4th & wkng nxt; t.o when pckd 15; plodded on & went hopeless 3rd aft 2 out .* runin — 3

Ashwicke Gambler 16-1 T Dreaper *(xnb) Bckwd; pulled hrd & hvly rstrnd in detach last pr; hit 2; clsd 9 to 4l 3rd 13; wknd 15 & 23l 3rd nxt; sn wl t.o; lft 3rd brief 2 out* . . . . 12 — 4

Cool Shuil (IRE) (5a) 11-1 M Miller *Chsd ldrs; 3rd 11; 8l 4th & wkng 14; mist nxt; 40l 3rd when ref 2 out* . . . . r

Deep Pockets (IRE) (7a) 4-1 D Alers-Hankey *(xnb) 6s-4s; hld up & wl bhnd in 8th when fell 8* . . . . F

Fanny By Gaslight (5a) 20-1 Miss S Derrick *(xnb) Hit 2; rcd wide in midfield; drpd back to 12l last 11; t.o 14; pu 3 out* . . . . P
Queens House (5a) 20-1 T Hampton *4th 4; ur 9* . . . . U
121F Strand Onthe Green (IRE) 4-1 N Mitchell *2 handlers; pulled v hrd & hvly rstrnd in poor last; 20l adrift 5; hdwy in 8l 6th 11; wknd qckly 14; t.o & pu 3 out* P

OFFICIAL DISTANCES: 1½l, dist **TIME:** 6min 27.4s **TOTE:** £9.00

238 Confined Maiden (Div 2), 12st - 18J — 9 ran

68[3] **DURSEY ISLAND (IRE)** 7-2 **M Miller** *6s-7/2; lw; set off in rr; hdwy & lft 10l 2nd 10; still 12l down 15; clsng when lft virt solo 3 out* 1
Emerald Mist (IRE) (12a) 7-1 **Miss P Gundry** *(xnb) Stdd in poor last; t.o 7; went v rem 2nd aft 2 out; nvr put in rce* . . . . runin 2
12[5] **Let's Rock** 8-1 **M Green** *Wl bhnd; poor 4th 10; lft 3rd 13; t.o 14; lft 2nd 3 out; dem aft omitted 2 out*. 12 3
119P B B Boy 5-1 Miss A Goschen *(xnb) 8s-5s; ld 1; 27l 3rd 10; poor 4th when fell 13* . . . . F
Bilton's Nap (7a) 6-1 T Dreaper *Bit bckwd; ur 1*. . . . . U
James Victor (IRE) 5-2F N Mitchell *Tk keen hld & sn 2nd bhnd lunatic; lft in clr ld 10; 12l ahd 15; tiring rap nxt; still just in front when fell 3 out; bad winded* . . . . F
78P Romany Move 7-1 Mrs S Godfrey *Chsd ldrs til ur 10*. . . . . U
Rydon Brook (5a) 25-1 J Snowden *Jmpd sticky & sn rr; 5th 10; went 25l 3rd & fell 13* . . . . F
Young Lirrup 8-1 R Woollacott *(xnb) Bolted into clr ld frm 1 & set maniacal pce; spreadeagling field when terrible mist 7; broke leg tkng off & fell 10; dead*. . . . . F

OFFICIAL DISTANCES: dist, 15l **TIME:** 6min 27.2s **TOTE:** £3.00

Fence 18 omitted - fallen horse

Folkestone (RH 7F,18J)

Tue, 17 Feb (GOOD to SOFT, SOFT in places)

239 R E Sassoon Mem HC, 3m1f £1561 — 12 ran

117[1] **UNLIMITED FREE (IRE)** 12-00 10-1 **Miss D Harding** *(xnb) J v wl; hld up til hdwy 7; impeded 8; ld 11; bumped along to draw clr aft 2 out* 1
Galapiat Du Mesnil (FR) 12-07 13-8F **R Burton** *Ld 2; jmpd lft & hmpd rival 9; hdd 11; prsd wnr aft; jmpd lft & nrly knocked over another rival 14; drvn & ev ch 2 out; sn tired & btn; blun last*. 11 2
Cloudy Creek (IRE) 11-11 25-1 **S Morris** *(xnb) Chsd ldrs; hmpd 8; outpcd 14; 7th nxt; plugged into poor 3rd aft last* 18 3
116[1] The Kings Fling 12-00 5-1 Miss P Gundry *(xnb) Lw; handy; mist 7; mist 11 & drvn; mist nxt & sn strugg; 5th & btn 15* 5 4
44[1] Teach Altra (IRE) 11-09 6-1 C Gordon *Lw; settled towards rr; eff & rdn aft 11; 6th & drvn 15; sn outpcd; poor 3rd 3 out; wknd & tired & t.o*. 18 5
Dunmanus Bay (IRE) 12-04 25-1 H Fowler *Fat; last when jmpd slow 5; blun bad nxt & lost tch; t.o & pu 12*. . . . . P
Harding 11-07 20-1 Mrs J Gordon *Bit bckwd; tk keen hld; mist 1; cl up til ld & fell 8* . . . . F
10U Hi Rudolf 12-02 20-1 J Jenkins *Bckwd; hld up; eff 12; chsng ldrs when bad hmpd & nrly ur 14; nt rec; hit nxt; poor 4th 3 out; pu last* . . . . P
Lordston (IRE) 11-07 14-1 W Kavanagh *Tk keen hld; nt fluent; pckd 7; cl up til rdn & wknd rap aft 11; t.o when crawled over 13 & pu*. . . . . P
99[3] Offshore (IRE) 11-07 50-1 P Hall *Settled rr; impd qckly & cl up aft 11; disp 4th & rdn 13; wkng qckly when jmpd v slow 3 out; pu nxt* . . . . P
3F Real Value (IRE) 12-02 8-1 A Hickman *Ld to 2; prsd ldr; bad hmpd 9; dem 11 & sn lost plce; hit 14; wl bhnd when jmpd slow & to lft 3 out; pu nxt*. . . P
170P Silver Lake (IRE) 11-11 33-1 P Cowley *Sn bhnd; hmpd 8 & lost tch; no ch aft; pu 12*. . . . . P

TIME: 6min 47.6s **TOTE:** £11.50; places £2.50,£1.40,£6.40 **Ex:**£47.10 **CSF:**£25.52

Musselburgh (RH 8F,18J)

Wed, 18 Feb (GOOD, GOOD to FIRM in places)

240 Anderson Strathern HC, 3m £2170 — 6 ran

Form	Runner	Dist	Pos
	BLYTH BROOK 12-00 5-2 **R Morgan** *Tk keen hld in 3rd/4th; went 2nd 12; hit 15; ld 3 out; rdn nxt; 6l clr last; comf*		1
	Son Of Anshan 12-04(tt) 9-4 **G Tuer** *2nd til ld app 11; rdn & hdd 3 out; one pce nxt; rallied to 2nd agn flat; btr for rce*	6	2
134^{2}	**Epsilo De La Ronce (FR)** 12-00 2-1F **W Ramsay** *Trckd ldrs; pushed along 14; eff 3 out; one pce frm nxt; went 2nd brief last*	½	3
72^{P}	Gaultier Gale (IRE) 11-07 12-1 A Findlay *Mists in last; blun 9; rdn & wknd 14*	26	4
	Mini Cruise 11-11 28-1 D Jewett *Ld til app 11; hit nxt; sn rdn & wknd; t.o*	28	5
	Tom's Man 11-09(tt) 14-1 T Oates *Tk keen hld in 3rd/4th; rdn 14; sn wknd; wl bhnd when pu 2 out*		P

TIME: 6min 06.9s **TOTE:** £3.90; places £1.40,£1.40 **Ex:**£7.50 **CSF:**£8.61

Sandown (RH 11F,16J)

Thu, 19 Feb (GOOD, GOOD to SOFT in places)

241 Ubique HC, 2m4f110y £2331 — 18 ran

Form	Runner	Dist	Pos
89^{4}	**RED BROOK LAD** 11-13 11-2 **N Mitchell** *Mist 1 & wl bhnd; 16th 7; mist 8; prog 10; hit 12; trckd ldng pr 3 out; ld bef last; rdn & stormed clr flat.*		1
	Hermes Ili (FR) 11-12 6-5F **T Greenall** *Prom; ld 7-11; ld agn bef 3 out; hdd & outpcd app last*	11	2
179^{U}	**Bosuns Mate** 11-08(bl) 20-1 **Mrs B Keighley** *Rcd keen; prom; hmpd 3; prsd ldr 8-11; eff agn & w ldr 3 out; one pce & btn when nt fluent 2 out; hit last*	6	3
100^{3}	Cape Stormer (IRE) 11-11 15-2 M Gorman *Hld up in midfield; mists 7 & 8; outpcd aft 14; kpt on frm 2 out; nd*	hd	4
	Irbee 11-13(bl) 10-1 Miss C Tizzard *Trckd ldrs; 6th 13; 4th & btn app 3 out*	5	5
10^{6}	Rock Rose 11-10 40-1 Miss P Gundry *Hld up in midfield; mist 7; eff aft 13; no imp on ldrs nxt; wl btn when mist last; rallied & stayed on wl flat*	s hd	6
	The Hearty Joker (IRE) 11-08 25-1 R Bandey *W ldrs til stdly fdd frm 12; mist 14*	5	7
102^{5}	River Bailiff (IRE) 10-13 100-1 Mrs J Gordon *Chsd ldrs; rdn 12; 5th nxt; wknd app 3 out*	6	8
89^{P}	Hot Plunge 11-01 50-1 J Owen *Tk str hld; ld to 7; ld agn 11 til app 3 out; sn wknd*	nk	9
178^{3}	Good Time Melody (IRE) 11-05 12-1 T Malone *Hit 4; a strugg; wl in rr frm 6; no prog aft 13*	2½	10
	Chief Of Justice 10-13 100-1 J Young *Chsd ldrs; mists 3 & 6; wknd frm 11*	6	11
33^{r}	Blackberry Way 11-07 40-1 P Cowley *Towards rr & nt gng wl frm 6; still in tch 11; wknd nxt*	7	12
100^{6}	Route One (IRE) 12-01 16-1 S Morris *Nt jw; hld up & wl off pce; brief eff 8; sn strugg*	8	13
100^{9}	Esprit De Cotte (FR) 11-07 50-1 P York *Prsd ldrs; rdn 10; 4th 13; wkng when blun 3 out*	2½	14
53^{R}	Jazz Night 11-03 66-1 S Joynes *Ss; t.o 4; pu 8*		P
91^{F}	Run River Run 10-11 (3ow)(bl) 100-1 S Graham *Mist 1 & imm lost tch; hopeless t.o when fell 7*		F
107^{5}	Westerton (IRE) 12-01 33-1 F Hutsby *Chsd ldrs; rmdrs 5; rdn & wknd 11; t.o & pu 3 out*		P
24^{2}	Win The Toss 11-03 100-1 Richard Green *Rcd wide; a in rr; wknd 9; t.o when mists 12 & nxt; pu 3 out*		P

TIME: 5min 22.2s **TOTE:** £6.00; places £1.50,£1.50,£5.50 **Ex:**£18.00 **CSF:**£11.73

Fence 9 was omitted - damaged

Fakenham (LH 6F,16J)

Fri, 20 Feb (GOOD, GOOD to FIRM)

242 Belvoir Castle Country Fair 12/13th June HC, 2m5f110y £2590 6 ran

UPHAM LORD (IRE) 11-09 10-11F **G Brewer** *Lw; jw except for mist 10; made all; clr 6; 15l ahd 11; breather app 2 out; sn clr agn* 1

Chicago City (IRE) 11-09 7-2 **Ms A Embiricos** *3rd/4th; mist 6; sn outpcd; 25l 3rd when jmpd v slow 11; t.o 13; hopeless t.o when lft 2nd last* 96½ 2

157P **Grand Ambition (USA)** 11-07 20-1 **Miss L Allan** *Tk keen hld in detach last; went 4th 9; 26l 4th 11; t.o when blun bad 13* 45 3

156¹ Homme De Fer 11-11 3-1 N Bloom *Chsd wnr; outpcd 6; rdn to flatt & 5l 2nd 2 out; sn btn; 15l 2nd when fell hvly last; event rmtd* . . . . dist 4

25P Attack 11-07(tt) 50-1 Miss A Stennett *Bckwd; jmpd mod; 3rd 7; last by 9; t.o & pu 13* . . . . P

Catherine's Way (IRE) 11-11 33-1 H Fowler *Ur 1* . . . . U

TIME: 5min 44.6s **TOTE:** £1.90; places £1.30,£2.20 **Ex:**£6.40 **CSF:**£4.31

East Essex

Marks Tey (LH 10F,20J)

Sat, 21 Feb (GOOD, GOOD to SOFT in places)

243 Hunt Members 4 ran

130⁵ **GINGER BUG** (5a) 4-1 **P Chinery** *Ld 4; sn clr; 8l clr 16; unchall* 1

102P **Give Him A Chance (IRE)** 2-1 **N Moore** *Hld up; went 15l 2nd 11; eff & 8l down 16; no hdwy frm 3 out; tired when jmpd slow last* 15 2

124P **Monsukh (IRE)** (5a)(bl) 5-1 **Mrs L Spence** *Ld to 3; drpd to last 8; t.o 11; lft 3rd & stpd aft last; gt gng agn to bt a remounter* 2½fs 3

155P Coole Chief 4-5F Sam Gray *Pulling; ld 3-4; 3rd & outpcd 10; t.o frm 14; blun & ur last; rmtd* 7 4

OFFICIAL DISTANCES: 12*l*, dist **TIME:** 6min 58.00s **TOTE:** £2.40

244 Confined Maiden (Div 1), 12st 13 ran

151R **MADMIDGE** 3-1JF **D Kemp** *Hld up; last 6; 8th ½way; trckd ldrs frm 11; ld 2 out; rdn & kpt on app last* 1

Catch On (IRE) 20-1 **P Taiano** *(chifney) Ww; 9th ½way; prog 11; 2l 4th 16; chsd wnr aft nxt; ev ch 2 out; kpt on one pce; improve* 2½ 2

128P **On The Day (IRE)** 3-1JF **J Owen** *Chsd ldrs; 5th ½way; ld 16-nxt; 3rd & outpcd app 2 out* 8 3

Montenegro 10-1 N Bloom *Chsd ldrs; 6th ½way; ld app 15-nxt; wknd app 2 out; improve* 12 4

154B Joves Shadow 4-1 T Lane *In tch; cl 3rd app 16; jmpd to ld gng wl 17; hdd app nxt; 4th & btn app 2 out; tired when jmpd slow last; improve* 1 5

Monarch Ruler (7a, 7ow) 12-1 G Cooper *(xnb) Prom; 2nd ½way; wknd app 3 out; improve* 6 6

151⁵ Sharp Sarah (5a) 14-1 P Chinery *Ld til app 15; stdly wknd; no ch frm 17* . 8 7

Epop (IRE) 16-1 R Stearn *In tch; 3rd ½way; blun 11; wknd 15; bhnd & pu 2 out* . . . . P

First And Fourmost (IRE) 8-1 J Docker *Bhnd; prog & 7th ½way; rdn & lost tch 12; t.o & pu 17* . . . . P

154P General Hopkins (IRE) 12-1 W Pewter *Bhnd; 10th ½way; no ch frm 14; t.o & pu 3 out* . . . . P

130⁴ Gunner Be True(bl) 8-1 M Mackley *Blun & ur 3* . . . . U

Looking Magic (IRE) (5ow) 16-1 C Lawson *Chsd ldr 4-6; sn lost plce; 11th ½way; t.o & pu 16* . . . . P

She's A Terror (12a) 16-1 C Ward-Thomas *Rr; last ½way; sn lost tch; t.o & pu 14* . . . . P

OFFICIAL DISTANCES: 2*l*, 4*l* **TIME:** 6min 58.0s **TOTE:** £5.00

245 Confined Maiden (Div 2), 12st — 13 ran

Form	Runner	Dist	Pos
219^{U}	**MAGIC LODGE** (7a) 12-1 **R Stearn** *Ww; 8th 1/2way; prog 11; cl 3rd when blun 15; outpcd app nxt; 3rd & rdn app 2 out; kpt on flat to 2nd last 100yds; fin 20l 2nd; awarded rce*		1
128^{5}	**Arctic Sun (IRE)**(cp) 6-1 **N Bloom** *Tchd 12s; w ldrs; 3rd 1/2way; 6l 4th 15; outpcd by ldr nxt; kpt on u.p flat; fin 3rd; promoted*	1	2
151^{3}	**Golden Shred** (5a)(bl) 12-1 **N Moore** *(xnb) 2 handlers; prom; chsd ldr 10; ev ch 16; outpcd nxt; 10l down when blun 2 out; lost 2 plces flat; fin 4th; promoted*	2	3
154^{3}	Play Alone (IRE) (5a) 8-1 D Kemp *In tch; 5th 1/2way; 6th & outpcd app 16; no ch aft*	1 1/2	5
128^{3}	Willow Ryde (IRE) evensF R Cope *In tch; 4th 1/2way; 7l 5th 15; sn rdn; no prog*	1/2	6
154^{F}	No Penalty 6-1 C Ward-Thomas *2 handlers; ld 2; made rest; clr frm 4; 6l clr 17; blun 3 out; 10l up 2 out; r.o str flat; won by 20l; disq - nt draw wt; had lost weight cloth app 15*		1d
	Assington Bay (IRE) 20-1 A Merriam *(xnb) A bhnd; t.o & pu 12*		P
129^{P}	Bright Torino (IRE) (5a)(bl) 33-1 J Bevan *Prom; jmpd rt 2; wkng & 9th 1/2way; jmpd slow 11; t.o when ur nxt*		U
219^{F}	Divine Mist (IRE) 20-1 J Owen *Rr; mist 1; 10th 1/2way; hrd rdn 11; no ch frm 15; pu nxt*		P
130^{P}	Granny Dick (5a) 14-1 M Mackley *Bhnd; prog & 7th 1/2way; lost tch 13; t.o & pu 3 out*		P
218^{F}	Groovejet (7a) 25-1 Miss K Smith *(xnb) Ld round start; a bhnd; 11th 1/2way; t.o & pu 17*		P
	Swanbank 25-1 H Fowler *(xnb) In tch; 6th 1/2way; outpcd 13; wl bhnd when pu 16*		P
103^{3}	Tea Time (IRE) 8-1 T Lane *Mid-div; in tch til lost plce qckly 9; pu 11; bbv*		P

OFFICIAL DISTANCES: Originally 3*l*, 1*l* **TIME:** 6min 57.00s **TOTE:** £59.00

No Penalty won by 20l but was disqualified when the rider failed to draw the correct weight - had lost weight cloth on the last circuit; the placed horses were promoted accordingly

246 Ladies Open — 12 ran

Form	Runner	Dist	Pos
157^{2}	**CELTIC DUKE** 2-1F **Miss Z Turner** *Ld to 6; handy til 2nd 3 out; ld app last; rdn & stayed on wl*		1
108^{R}	**Nokimover** 10-1 **Miss Gemma Hutchinson** *Chsd ldr 4; ld 6-11 & agn 13; hdd app last; no ex*	4	2
189^{1}	**Killerine (FR)** 4-1 **Miss H Irving** *Chsd ldr 6; ld 11-13; 4th & one pce app 2 out*	10	3
126^{U}	Jolly Minster 5-1 Mrs D Rowell *Bhnd; 14l 7th 1/2way; prog 11; 10l 5th 15; went 3rd 3 out; no hdwy app nxt; fin lame*	2	4
158^{3}	Highland Rose (IRE) (5a) 12-1 Ms A Embiricos *Prom; 4l 4th 1/2way; jnd ldr 16-nxt; sn rdn; wknd app 2 out*	8	5
126^{4}	Borrow Mine (IRE) 33-1 Miss L Marriott *Mid-div; 13l 6th 1/2way; nvr rchd ldrs; bhnd when pu 3 out*		P
222^{F}	Fair Kiowa (IRE) 4-1 Mrs S Hodge *Nvr gng wl; bhnd frm 7; rdn & 16l 8th 1/2way; no prog; pu 15*		P
98^{4}	Fiolino (FR) 33-1 Miss R Page *(xnb) A bhnd; t.o 9 til pu 17*		P
25^{P}	Hay Dance 33-1 Miss L Barrett-Nobbs *(xnb) Chsd ldrs; 9l 5th 1/2way; sn strugg; t.o & pu 17*		P
	Irish Sea (USA) 6-1 Mrs C Adam *1st ride; rr; mist 6; 20l 10th 1/2way; no ch frm 12; ur 2 out*		U
189^{6}	Moonlite Magic (IRE)(cp) 33-1 Miss J Wickens *A bhnd; 18l 9th 1/2way; sn no ch; t.o & pu 3 out*		P
	Over The Country 33-1 Mrs S Ashby *A bhnd; 22l 11th 1/2way; t.o & pu 13.*		P

OFFICIAL DISTANCES: 2*l*, 3*l* **TIME:** 6min 44.0s **TOTE:** £3.00

247 Mens Open — 5 ran

Form	Runner	Dist	Pos
	BALLINURE BOY (IRE) 4-5F **A Hickman** *Ww in tch; 8l 4th 10; ld 2 out; pushed out*		1
	Tod's Brother 5-1 **A Merriam** *Trckd ldrs; mist 9; went 2nd 13; ev ch 2 out; unable to qckn aft*	2	2
221^{2}	**Minino (IRE)** 3-1 **C Ward-Thomas** *(xnb) Reluct to line up & ld in; ld 2; rdn 3 out; blun & hdd nxt; sn wknd*	6	3

Form	Runner	Dist	Pos
125^{P}	Millenium Way (IRE) 4-1 J Owen *Ld to 2; rdn & blun 16; last aft; sn lost tch*	25	4
	Red Lake (IRE) 25-1 P Millington *Pulling; hld up in last pr; lost tch 7; t.o & pu 11*		P

OFFICIAL DISTANCES: 2*l*, 3*l* **TIME:** 6min 53.0s **TOTE:** £1.90

248 Confined, 12st — 9 ran

Form	Runner	Dist	Pos
124^{2}	**ENDEAVOUR (FR)** (6x) 6-4F **G Cooper** *Chsd ldr 6; ld 10; made rest; stayed on str app last*		1
	Ardkilly Warrior (IRE) 25-1 **N Bloom** *Chsd ldrs; ev ch frm 16; rdn app 2 out; kpt on one pce*	7	2
123^{3}	**Nowornever (IRE)** 4-1 **D Kemp** *Ww in tch; trckd ldrs app 16; chsd wnr aft 3 out; rdn & no ex app last; dem nr fin*	nk	3
124^{P}	Westfield John (3x) 6-1 J Owen *Ld to 8; mist 10; hrd rdn 16; wknd app 3 out*	3	4
224^{3}	Prologue (IRE) (14ow) 16-1 C Jarvis *Ur padd; stdd start & lost 30l; sn t.o*	fence	5
224^{U}	Ardnut(bl) 33-1 Miss R Page *Mists; 10l 6th ½way; still in tch when fell 13*		F
124^{5}	Colonel Conca 5-2 C Ward-Thomas *(xnb) Mists; prom; ld 8-10; mist 11; 6l 4th app 15; wkng when blun 16; bhnd & pu last*		P
155^{U}	Henwyn 6-1 A Humphrey *In tch; 13l 7th ½way; lost tch qckly 11; t.o when jmpd slow 16; pu 3 out*		P
159^{P}	Lambrini King (IRE) 16-1 Miss L Barrett-Nobbs *A bhnd; t.o 14 til pu 17*		P

OFFICIAL DISTANCES: 2*l*, ½*l* **TIME:** 6min 53.0s **TOTE:** £2.50

249 Countryside Alliance Club Members (Nov Rdrs), 12st — 16 ran

Form	Runner	Dist	Pos
155^{3}	**PAMPERED GALE (IRE)** 12-1 **Miss N Barnes** *Mid-div; 17l 6th ½way; hdwy 11; 8l 3rd 17; ld app last; sn clr; r.o wl*		1
155^{1}	**Royal Action** 5-4F **P Chinery** *Chsd ldrs; went 2nd 9; ld 15; sn clr; tired & blun 2 out; sn hdd & no ex*	3	2
4^{U}	**Crackrattle (IRE)** (7ow) 10-1 **A Brown** *Wl bhnd; blun 9; 27l 13th ½way; stayed on frm 16; nvr nrr*	2	3
175^{9}	Topical Tip (IRE) 6-1 Mrs E Chugg *Sn wl bhnd; 22l 10th ½way; stayed on frm 17; nvr nrr*	1	4
222^{3}	Corston Joker 10-1 Mrs L Spence *Ss; bhnd; 19l 8th ½way; hdwy nxt; went 7l 2nd 17 til app 2 out; no ex*	6	5
41^{3}	Aughmor River (IRE) 10-1 R Stearn *Ld to 5; blun 10; 3rd ½way; w ldrs til wknd 16*	10	6
175^{5}	Tale Bridge (IRE) 16-1 J Russell *Wl bhnd; 32l 14th ½way; stayed on frm 17; nd*	4	7
155^{8}	Buckland Bobby 25-1 Miss L Fear *(citation) Bhnd; some hdwy & 20l 9th ½way; nd*	½	8
217^{3}	Rip Kirby 33-1 R Hanley *(xnb) A bhnd; 26l 12th ½way; nd*	1	9
124^{6}	Bruan (IRE)(cp) 16-1 Miss J Bevin *Chsd ldr til ld 5-15; wknd app 17*	nk	10
45^{4}	Garrison Friendly (IRE) 12-1 N Wilson (South) *Chsd ldrs to 5; stdly lost plce; 17l 6th ½way; nd*	6	11
126^{5}	Mister Audi (IRE) 14-1 Miss A Bowles *(xnb) A bhnd; 25l 11th ½way; nd*	2	12
110^{4}	Drum Battle(tt) 9-2 T Messenger *Chsd ldrs; 5l 4th ½way; wknd 12; no ch frm 15*	1	13
155^{7}	Castle Road (IRE) 20-1 Miss L Marriott *(xnb) T.o frm 5*	12	14
123^{U}	Ical (IRE) (5a) 14-1 Miss C Rogers *Galloped past start gng down; mid-div; lost iron brief 3; 7th when ur 5*		U
155^{6}	Tomcappagh (IRE) 25-1 J Wall *Chsd ldng group; 15l 5th ½way; wknd 15; bhnd & pu 3 out*		P

OFFICIAL DISTANCES: 3*l*, 1*l* **TIME:** 6min 53.0s **TOTE:** £104.00

250 Restricted — 15 ran

Form	Runner	Dist	Pos
159^{U}	**JIMS BELIEF (IRE)** 7-1 **G Cooper** *Ld 4; made rest; drifted lft u.p flat; hld on game*		1
	Secrete Contract 5-2 **D Dunsdon** *Hld up; 10l 10th ½way; prog 14; went 2nd aft 3 out; mist nxt; rdn & unable to qckn flat*	¾	2
29^{6}	**Run Monty (IRE)** 7-1 **T Lane** *(xnb) Ww in tch; 6l 7th ½way; cl 3rd app 17; rdn & no ex frm 2 out*	8	3
	Bunratty's Sole (IRE) 2-1F N Bloom *Ww in tch; 3l 5th ½way; rdn & no prog frm 3 out*	8	4
159^{5}	Sydney Hobart 12-1 A Vaughan-Jones *Chsd ldrs; 4th ½way; outpcd 16; kpt on*	3	5

Form	Horse	Dist	Pos
31^{6}	Ferryhill (IRE) 20-1 Miss L Bridges *(xnb) Chsd ldrs; 4l 6th ½way; cl 4th & rdn 3 out; wknd app nxt*	2	6
127^{3}	Filou Du Bois (FR) 10-1 Ms A Embiricos *(xnb) Ld to 4; cl up til wknd app 16*	8	7
127^{5}	Glad All Over (5a) 20-1 D Hays *A bhnd; 23l 12th ½way; nd*	30	8
	Federal Case (FR) 3-1 C Ward-Thomas *(xnb) Prom; chsd ldr 11-14; sn wknd; bhnd when pu 2 out*		P
104^{R}	Naughty Noah 20-1 P Hall *Chsd ldrs 4 til app 11; sn wknd; bhnd & pu 14*		P
127^{P}	Nonplussed (5a) 14-1 P Andrew *Sn detach last; t.o 6 til pu 12*		P
103^{2}	No Reward (IRE) 8-1 A Hickman *(xnb) A bhnd; 27l 13th ½way; t.o & pu 13*		P
29^{2}	Paddy's Dream (IRE) 8-1 N Moore *Ww in tch; 7l 8th ½way; prog 11; chsd wnr app 15-16; sn wknd; pu 2 out*		P
181^{U}	Shanrod View (IRE) 12-1 D Brightling *Bhnd; 11th ½way; lost tch 12; t.o & pu 3 out*		P
127^{P}	Treble Trouble 16-1 P Millington *Mid-div; lost tch 12; t.o & pu 16*		P

OFFICIAL DISTANCES: 2*l*, 1*l* **TIME:** 6min 56.0s **TOTE:** £4.90

Harkaway Club

Chaddesley Corbett (LH 8F,18J)
Sat, 21 Feb (GOOD to FIRM)

251 Harkaway Club Members, 12st - 17J — 11 ran

Form	Horse	Dist	Pos
	THE CAMPDONIAN (IRE) 20-1 **E Walker** *Chsd ldrs; 20l 5th ½way; went 15l 4th 14; lft 4l 2nd 2 out; ld app omitted last; stayed on wl*		1
	Dare 16-1 **D Barlow** *Chsd ldrs; 18l 4th ½way; eff 12; went 10l 3rd nxt & 2nd aft 14; lft in ld 2 out; sn hdd & no ex*	4	2
156^{2}	**Philtre (IRE)** (7x) 4-6F **A Wintle** *Ld til aft 2; 5l 3rd ½way; chsd ldr 11 til stpd to nil aft 15; lft poor 3rd 2 out*	20	3
93^{P}	Phyllis (5a) 25-1 D Greenway *Nvr on terms; mist 9; 22l 6th ½way; no hdwy when mist 12*	2	4
48^{P}	Allotrope (IRE)(bl,tt) 50-1 Miss L Brooke *Sn wl bhnd; 35l 8th ½way; t.o & pu 12*		P
	Carnage (IRE) 20-1 W Hill *Pulled hrd & saddle slpd; went 2nd 3; mist 4; dem 11; 8l 3rd when mist 12; wknd & 20l 5th 14; wl bhnd when pu 15*		P
	Chelsea King (IRE) (7x) 16-1 R Garton *Last to 9; 36l 9th ½way; wl bhnd til blun & ur 10*		U
93^{5}	Oneanthreequarters (IRE) 16-1 R Jagger *Hld up; 20l 6th when mist 6; rfo on bend sn aft*		U
106^{P}	Preferred (IRE) 25-1 R Armson *Hld up; 23l 7th ½way; rdn 11; mist 13; wl bhnd when pu 14*		P
	Whitegates Willie 12-1 C Barlow *Sn wl bhnd; t.o last 10; pu 12*		P
	William Lionheart 5-1 Julian Pritchard *Ld aft 2; hit 8; qcknd clr 15; 5l up when fell 2 out*		F

OFFICIAL DISTANCES: 3*l*, 12*l* **TIME:** 6min 07.8s

Fence 18 omitted - fallen rider

252 Harkaway Club Members Restricted, 12st — 17 ran

Form	Horse	Dist	Pos
103^{1}	**LONGVILLE LAD** 4-1 **P Cowley** *7s-4s; oht; swtng; made all; sn 7l clr to 11; jnd 14; qcknd 7l clr 3 out; impressive*		1
95^{P}	**My Native Knight (IRE)**(tt) 10-1 **A Wadlow** *(xnb) Hld up & bhnd; 19l 11th ½way; stdy hdwy & 11l 9th 14; stayed on frm 3 out; went 15l 3rd nxt & 2nd last; no ch w wnr*	12	2
159^{2}	**Snowtre (IRE)**(cp) 10-1 **A Wintle** *(xnb) Hld up; 12l 6th ½way; stdy hdwy & 10l 6th 12; stayed on frm 3 out; nvr able to chall*	½	3
	Rushing Again 7-1 Miss P Gundry *Prom; mist 5; 8l 3rd ½way; 7l 4th 12; eff & disp 2½l 3rd 14; sn outpcd; lft 12l 3rd aft 3 out; no ex*	1½	4
	Alvero (FR) 5-1 R Armson *8s-5s; mist 2; 2nd til aft 11; chsd wnr 13; brushed aside aft 15; lost 2nd at last*	hd	5
228^{P}	Ballingale Dawn (IRE) 33-1 R Rogers *Swtng; hld up; 16l 9th ½way; hdwy & 10½l 7th 12; nvr nr to chall*	1½	6
95^{U}	Bobtail (IRE) (7a) 7-2F R Burton *Hld up & bhnd; 20l 12th ½way; hdwy & 11l 8th 12; jnd ldrs 14; 12l 5th & wkng when mist 3 out*	5	7
	Campden Kitty (5a) 6-1 F Hutsby *Hld up; hdwy 6; 9½l 5th ½way; prsd ldrs til wknd & 9l 7th 14*	3	8

Winning Town 14-1 Miss S Talbot *A wl bhnd; 25l 16th 1/2way; t.o 12* 4 9

15^{4} Not Yet Decent (IRE) 7-1 A Puddy *Lost plce 4; 23l 15th 1/2way; t.o 12* . . . 5 10

118^{P} Almost A Day(bl,tt) 16-1 D Mansell *2 handlers; fell thro padd railings & galloped off loose; nd; 14l 7th 1/2way; mist 10; wl bhnd when pu 12* . . . P

159^{4} Always Good (IRE) 25-1 P Needham *(xnb) Nd; jmpd slow 4; mist 9; 15l 8th 1/2way; wl bhnd 12; t.o & pu 2 out* . . . P

231^{r} Magicien (FR) 33-1 R Hodges *A wl bhnd; 21l 13th & rdn 1/2way; t.o & pu 2 out* P

95^{P} Rooneyran(tt) 25-1 R Cooper *Tubed; swtng; hld up; 18l 10th 1/2way; lost tch 12; t.o & pu 14* . . . P

Rosegrove Rooster 12-1 T Stephenson *Cannoned into & went over bckwds padd; unruly start; a last; t.o 12; pu 3 out* . . . P

Tom Brown (IRE) 10-1 D Barlow *Hld up; hdwy 8; 9l 4th 1/2way; went 2nd aft 11-13; 8l 3rd when pu aft 3 out; lame* . . . P

127^{P} What A Charmer (IRE) 12-1 N Pearce *Hld up & wl bhnd; 21 1/2l 14th 1/2way; hdwy & 12 1/2l 9th 12; wknd 14; pu 3 out* . . . P

OFFICIAL DISTANCES: 12*l*, nk **TIME:** 6min 07.9s

253 Ladies Open — 5 ran

1^{U} **PACON (GER)** 20-1 **Miss H Kinsey** *(xnb) Hld up; jmpd slow 4; went 8l 2nd 7; ld 14; 12l clr 3 out; easily* . . . 1

Octagonal (IRE) 4-1 **Miss R Reynolds** *Chsd ldr to 7; 8l 3rd 1/2way; wknd 14; lft poor 2nd 2 out* . . . 15 2

Ghutah 12-1 Miss J Owen *(xnb) Swtng; jmpd rt; ld; sn 10l clr to 1/2way; mist 10; hdd 14; wknd aft nxt; 15l 2nd when fell 2 out* . . . F

146^{1} Sailors Folly (IRE) 2-7F Miss P Gundry *(xnb) Fell 2* . . . F

56^{4} Wibbley Wobbley 8-1 Miss L Ellis *1st ride; hld up & bhnd; 20l last 1/2way; hdwy 11; went 7l 3rd & rfo 13* . . . U

OFFICIAL DISTANCE: 15*l* **TIME:** 6min 14.7s

254 Mens Open, 12st — 10 ran

93^{P} **JEMARO (IRE)** (7x) 3-1 **R Burton** *Lw; ld to 4; 2nd til ld 10; clr aft 15; easily* 1

Rusty Fellow (7x) 8-1 **D Mansell** *Sn wl bhnd; 22l 6th 1/2way; stayed on frm 3 out; went 2nd flat; no ch w wnr* . . . 12 2

Teme Willow (IRE) (4x) evensF **Julian Pritchard** *Jmpd rt; 2nd til ld 4; hdd 10; lost plce & 6l 4th 14; rallied aft nxt & sn 8l 2nd; wkng when jmpd slow last; dem flat* . . . 2 1/2 3

209^{8} Tiraldo (FR) (7x) 20-1 G Slade-Jones *Hld up & bhnd; 20l 5th 1/2way; gd hdwy 12; went 6l 3rd nxt; disp 2l 2nd 14; wknd qckly aft nxt.* . . . 7 4

170^{P} Rolling Maul (IRE) 25-1 J Horton *Chsd ldrs; 5l 4th & rdn 1/2way; went 2nd 11 til wknd qckly aft 15* . . . 3/4 5

O J Selym (IRE) (7x) 12-1 G Opperman *(xnb) Hld up; hdwy & 4l 3rd 1/2way; wkng when blun 12; 18l 5th 14; t.o* . . . runin 6

188^{4} Cotteir Chief (IRE) 25-1 R Hughes *Prom; mist 4; reluct to rce u.p aft 6; sn wl bhnd; 30l 7th 1/2way; t.o & pu 11* . . . P

Meadows Boy (7x) 7-1 A Beedles *(xnb) Ref to rce; event set off 2 fncs bhnd; pu 3* . . . r

Native Man (IRE) (7x) 6-1 C Barlow *7th when fell 2* . . . F

Theatreland (USA) 7-1 E Walker *(xnb) Ss; a wl bhnd; 34l last 1/2way; t.o 11; pu 14* . . . P

OFFICIAL DISTANCES: 12*l*, 2*l* **TIME:** 6min 07.5s

255 Harkaway Club Members Conditions, 12st — 6 ran

2^{1} **FERTILE VALLEY (IRE)** 11-10F **Miss P Gundry** *Tde; hit 3; went 2nd 5; mist 6; ld aft 7; mist 13; in comm 3 out; hit last; rdn out.* . . . 1

Cider Man 4-1 **Julian Pritchard** *(xnb) Ld til hdd aft 7; 4l 3rd 1/2way; chsd wnr 14; hit nxt; rdn 3 out; one pce* . . . 3 1/2 2

Beet De Bob (IRE) 4-1 **P Cowley** *Hld up & bhnd; last to 8; 10l 5th 1/2way; lost tch 14; lft 15l 3rd 3 out; no imp; bbv* . . . 12 3

158^{P} Mr Naborro (IRE)(cp) 20-1 A Wintle *Hld up; drpd to rr 8; 15l last & rdn 1/2way; nt r.o; wl bhnd when pu 11* . . . P

92^{P} Petrouge(vis) 7-1 R Burton *Chsd ldr to 5; went 2nd app 8-14; stpd to nil nxt; pu 3 out* . . . P

91^{2} Sharlom (IRE) 6-1 W Hill *Hld up; 7l 4th 1/2way; no hdwy when mist & ur 13* U

OFFICIAL DISTANCES: 3*l*, 12*l* **TIME:** 6min 04.6s

256 Harkaway Club Members Maiden 56&7yo (Div 1), 12st — 14 ran

JACKSON (FR) 5-4F **R Burton** *Jnd ldrs 5; lft 2nd 7-12; went 2nd agn nxt; ld app 15; sn clr; hit last; easily* . . . 1

111R **New Lodge Express (IRE)** 5-1 **T Stephenson** *(xnb) A.p; 2l 3rd ½way; went 2nd 12-13; 6l 3rd nxt; went 7l 2nd app 3 out; no imp* . . . 7 2

96P **No Keep (IRE)** 8-1 **C Barlow** *Hld up & bhnd; hdwy & 4½l 5th ½way; wknd & 15l 7th 12; sn wl bhnd; went rem 3rd at last* . . . 30 3

143⁴ Killough Hill (IRE)(tt) 4-1 Miss P Gundry *Hld up; hdwy 8; 3l 4th ½way; outpcd 12; 10l 4th 14; wknd 15; lft 25l 3rd 2 out; dem last* . . . 2 4

119P Golden Embers 12-1 D Mansell *Ld to 1; last when jmpd slow 4; sn drvn along; t.o 6; pu 12* . . . P

Gunsmoke 10-1 N Oliver *(xnb) Pulled hrd; ld 3 til hdd app 15; rdn & wknd 3 out; 15l 3rd when fell nxt* . . . F

Neeley (7a) 8-1 M Keel *Hld up; 10l 9th ½way; lost tch 12; 26l 7th 14; t.o when rn out last; rdr lost irons* . . . R

Nothing Better (IRE) (12a, 2ow) 12-1 T Weston *Last to 4; hmpd 5; t.o when ur 6* . . . U

104⁵ Pusey Sance 16-1 J Newbold *Mist 4; in tch til fell 8* . . . F

191P Regal Rumour 16-1 M Wall *Hld up; 8l 8th ½way; wkng when blun 11; wl bhnd when pu 12* . . . P

Stantons Church 10-1 M Barber *(xnb) 2nd/3rd til mist 8; 7l 7th ½way; wknd & 13½l 6th 12; sn wl bhnd; t.o & pu 3 out* . . . P

The Noble Roman 20-1 T Ellis *12th when fell 5* . . . F

Vaigly North (5a) 20-1 M Hammond *Swtng; chsd ldrs; 6l 6th ½way; mists 10 & 11; wknd & 13l 5th nxt; t.o & pu 15* . . . P

Wookey Woods (IRE) 20-1 R Hughes *Ld 1 til hdd & mist 3; 2nd til rn out thro wing & ur 7* . . . R

OFFICIAL DISTANCES: 6*l*, dist **TIME:** 6min 15.1s

257 Harkaway Club Members Maiden 56&7yo (Div 2), 12st — 8 ran

87² **COURT ADJOURN** 8-11F **S Morris** *Hld up; hit 4; 3l 4th ½way; hdwy 12; ld 13-14; w ldr 3 out til ld & lft clr at last* . . . 1

Primitive Son 12-1 **P Morris** *Hld up; 8l 7th ½way; bhnd til hdwy 15; 9l 4th & one pce nxt; lft 2nd at last* . . . 10 2

Shemardi 14-1 **R Hodges** *20s-14s; prom; 2l 3rd ½way; rdn 15; 8l 3rd nxt; no ex* . . . 3 3

87⁵ The Luddite 8-1 H Dowty *Chsd ldr to 12; 4l 5th 14; wknd rap nxt; t.o* . . . 30 4

Youwoudhavethat (IRE) (5a) 12-1 M Hammond *Hld up; 6l 5th ½way; 5l 6th 14; wknd 15; t.o* . . . 4 5

119R Black Hope (IRE) (5a) 8-1 T Vaughan *14s-8s; pulled hrd & jmpd rt; ld; blun 2; mist 12; hdd 13; ld 14 til stpd to nil app nxt; pu 3 out* . . . P

Joe Lively (IRE) (7a, 4ow) 7-1 A Wintle *Bckwd; school in rr; 9l last ½way; lost tch 13; 15l last nxt; wl bhnd when pu 3 out* . . . P

Martin Ossie 4-1 Julian Pritchard *(boh) Lw; hld up; mist 4; 7l 6th ½way; hdwy & 3l 4th 14; qcknd to ld app 15; hdd & fell last; rdr broke collar-bone* . . . F

OFFICIAL DISTANCES: 8*l*, 3*l* **TIME:** 6min 17.9s

258 Harkaway Club Members Maiden 8yo&up (Div 1), 12st — 15 ran

DORSET FERN (IRE) (5a) 12-1 **Miss E James** *Hld up & bhnd; 8l 9th ½way; hdwy & 3l 5th 12; went 7l 3rd aft 15; stayed on frm 3 out; rdn to ld flat* . . . 1

Stockton Wolf 12-1 **R Hodges** *Hld up; 5l 6th ½way; hdwy 11; went 2nd nxt; ld 13-14; lft w ev ch flat; nt qckn* . . . ½ 2

113² **Jenny's Charmer** 7-2 **F Hutsby** *(xnb) Hld up & bhnd; 11l last ½way; hdwy & 4½l 7th 12; ld 14; 5l clr & lkd wnr when hit 3 out; stdd into last; hdd & no ex flat* . . . 2½ 3

52² Jolly Jake 8-1 E Walker *(xnb) Chsd ldrs; 7½l 8th ½way; eff & 3½l 6th 12; mist 13; 7l 5th 15; one pce 3 out* . . . 8 4

52F Westington 25-1 M Wall *(xnb) Hld up; 4l 5th ½way; hdwy & 2½l 4th 12; wknd & 9l 6th 15* . . . 7 5

Barton Dream (IRE) 16-1 T Vaughan *(xnb) Pulled hrd; prom; 2l 3rd ½way; went 2nd aft 11-12; wknd qckly 14; t.o & pu 2 out* . . . P

Crotty (IRE) 10-1 Miss P Gundry *Pulled hrd; hdwy to ld 4; hdd & wknd rap 11; t.o & pu 14* . . . P

203P Gay Abandon (5a) 20-1 M Keel *Lkd awful; fell 1; fell agn 3 when loose* . . . F

35^{2}	Knighton Star (5a) 4-5F S Morris *6/5-4/5; ch ride; prom; 4th when fell 8.*		F
51^{U}	Kuwait Faith (IRE) 10-1 T Stephenson *(xnb) Hld up; 7l 7th ½way; lost tch 12; t.o & pu 15*		P
	Little Dish (5a)(tt) 20-1 H Dowty *Bhnd til fell 8*		F
191^{U}	Milamoss 20-1 R Hughes *Hld up; mist 4; hdwy 6; 3l 4th ½way; mist & lost plce u.p 11; wl bhnd 14; t.o when fell 3 out*		F
113^{R}	Sales Dodger (IRE) 12-1 S Hughes *Ld to 4; 2nd til ld 11; hdd 13; 4l 3rd 15; wknd qckly app 3 out; wl bhnd when fell last*		F
119^{4}	Strong Finish 14-1 Miss E Tuck *2nd to 3; 4th when rn out & ur 5*		R
	Trust Ger 25-1 D Mansell *Sn wl bhnd; jmpd v slow 4; t.o & pu 5*		P

OFFICIAL DISTANCES: ½l, 3l **TIME:** 6min 17.9s

259 Harkaway Club Members Maiden 8yo&up (Div 2), 12st - 17J 11 ran

	TENDER TANGLE 3-1 **S Morris** *2nd til ld 5; went 5l clr 15; drew rt away; unchall.*		1
	Craiova Comet (IRE) 12-1 **T Weston** *2 handlers; hld up; hdwy 8; 4½l 4th ½way; went 5l 3rd 14 & 2nd nxt; wkng when blun 3 out*	25	2
151^{2}	**Sovereign Gale (IRE)** (5a) 5-2F **R Burton** *(xnb) Ld to 5; 2nd to 11; 7l 4th 14; sn wknd; poor 3rd frm 3 out.*	8	3
121^{F}	Just Caramel (5a)(tt) 4-1 M Barber *Mist 2; prom til lost plce 8; 7l 6th ½way; 9l 5th 12; wknd 14; t.o.*	7	4
	Come On Boy 25-1 M Jackson *(xnb) Hld up; 5½l 5th ½way; hdwy & 2nd 11 til wknd rap 15; t.o.*	10	5
187^{U}	Latterly (USA) 16-1 I Bostock *(xnb) Lost tch 6; 16l last ½way; wl bhnd 12; t.o*	15	6
	City Standard (IRE)(cp) 7-1 Miss P Gundry *(xnb,bf) A bhnd; reluct to rce & hung rt bend aft 6; 7½l 7th ½way; mist 10; lost tch u.p 12; t.o when rn wide bend bef 3 out*	25	7
177^{F}	Beachcomber 8-1 W Hill *2 handlers; sn prom; 4l 3rd ½way; lost plce & mist 11; 20l 7th nxt; t.o & pu 14*		P
165^{P}	Castle Lodge 7-2 C Barlow *6s-7/2; 2 handlers; hld up; tried to rn out & ur 5*		U
	Little Poppy (5a) 10-1 F Hutsby *Lost tch 6; mist 7; pu 8.*		P
172^{P}	Sneedham's Green 20-1 P Mason *(xnb) 2 handlers; oht; prom; mist 4; lost plce 8; 14l 8th ½way; t.o & pu 12*		P

OFFICIAL DISTANCES: 20l, 8l **TIME:** 6min 14.6s

April Treasure was withdrawn not under orders - rider injured in previous race

Hursley Hambledon

Badbury Rings (LH 10F,19J)

Sat, 21 Feb (GOOD to FIRM, FIRM in places)

260 Hunt Members, 12st 5 ran

	LADY DOT (IRE) (5a) 14-1 **D Dennis** *(xnb) Ld/disp til 5l up 4; hdd brief 7; disp ld agn nxt til ld 13; made rest; 2½l up & lkng vulnerable when lft clr 3 out; mist nxt; coasted home*		1
	Dos Desperados (IRE) 8-1 **D Phelan** *Tchd 10s; reluct to line up; chsd ldr 2-6; disp ld 10-12; 4l down 15; 3rd & wkng nxt; lft 2nd 3 out; no ch w wnr.*	12	2
	Alpha Centauri (IRE) 7-2 Miss C Cowe *(xnb) Disp ld to 2; stdd to 4th 3; ld 7; jnd nxt; hung v wide aft 10; wknd qckly; pu 14*		P
	Juicy Lucy (5a) 10-1 M Sheridan *A last; 4½l down 8; jmpd slow 10; grad lost tch frm 12; t.o & pu 16.*		P
89^{P}	Susies Melody (IRE) (7x) 2-5F R Bandey *Opened 4/6; 6½l 3rd 4; chsd ldng pr frm 10; 7l 3rd 15; chsd wnr frm nxt; 2½l down & clsng rap when somersaulted twice 3 out; broke back; dead*		F

OFFICIAL DISTANCE: 10l **TIME:** 6min 35.5s

261 Confined, 12st 8 ran

116^{P}	**SKIP 'N' TUNE (IRE)** (5a) 5-2 **M Miller** *5s-5/2; hld up in mostly 5/6th; prog to ld 15; sn 5l clr; pushed out flat; rdly.*		1
182^{7}	**Makhpiya Patahn (IRE)** 10-1 **D I Turner** *(xnb) Prom; disp/ld 2-3; 2½l 3rd 8; rmdrs 10; chsd ldr frm 15; nt trble wnr*	3	2
	Coolteen Hero (IRE) (7x) 2-1F **T Dreaper** *(xnb) 9/2-2s; ld/disp to 3; 2l 2nd 8; outpcd & last 15; stayed on agn frm 2 out; nd*	5	3

171^F Shy Paddy (IRE) 33-1 R Bliss *(bf) Handy; 3rd 2; ld 5; 2l up 8; hdd 13; grad wknd frm 16* . . . 8 4
168^4 Owenabue Valley (IRE) (3x) 9-4 T Underwood *Last to 3; 7l 6th 8; 5th & outpcd 15; bhnd frm 2 out* . . . 6 5
10^R Gigi Beach (IRE) 12-1 Mrs S Reynoldson *Last 4; lsng tch when tried to ref & ur tk-off side 7* . . . U
Millcroft Regatta (IRE) 14-1 N Wilmington *(xnb) Hld up; prog to 4l 4th 8; chsd ldr 10; jmpd lft nxt; ld 14; hdd nxt; wknd qckly 3 out; bhnd when pu last* P
236^P Pearl Dante (IRE) 33-1 T Hampton *(xnb) Ld brief 4; sn lost plce; jmpd slow 7; t.o 10; pu 13* . . . P

OFFICIAL DISTANCES: 4*l*, 5*l* **TIME:** 6min 08.9s

262 Ladies Open — 6 ran

199^4 **BRETECHE (FR)** (5a) 2-1JF **Miss T Newman** *(xnb) Tde; disp 4l 3rd 4; impd to 1l 2nd 10; jnd ldr 3 out; ld aft nxt; stayed on str flat* . . . 1
78^1 **Cento (IRE)** 9-4 **Miss C Stucley** *Disp 4l 3rd 4; cl 4th 10; 1 1/2l 3rd 14; chsd wnr game frm 2 out; no ex u.p flat* . . . 1 1/4 2
Macaroni Beach (5a) 14-1 **Miss S West** *(xnb) Jw; disp ld to 3 & agn 6; bold j & 1l up 14; jnd 3 out; hdd aft nxt; stayed on u.p til no ex flat* . . . hd 3
140^4 Mr Ben Gunn (14ow) 25-1 Miss V Heal *(xnb) Last 4; chsd rivals til grad wknd frm 13; t.o frm 16* . . . 35 4
234^2 Frank Byrne 2-1JF Miss A Goschen *Disp ld til ld aft 3; hdd & fell 7* . . . F
169^P Hello Roscrea (IRE) 12-1 Mrs S Brown *(bf) 5th 4; rap hdwy to disp ld 6-nxt; chsd ldrs til wknd frm 14; 4th & btn when fell 16* . . . F

OFFICIAL DISTANCES: 1 1/2*l*, hd **TIME:** 6min 08.6s

263 Land Rover Mens Open, 12st — 7 ran

235^3 **BADGER BEER** (4x) 15-8 **N Mitchell** *Tchd 2s; made all; 2l up 5; bold j 14; still 1 1/2l up but lkng vulnerable when lft virt solo 2 out; hung & jmpd lft last; coasted home* . . . 1
138^3 **Puzzleman** 12-1 **S Wheeler** *2 handlers; trckd ldrs; 4l 3rd 4; disp 2nd frm 12; 1 1/2l down when fell 2 out; rmtd* . . . 1 1/2fs 2
Djeddah (FR) (7x)(bl) 9-2 P York *(boh) Chsd ldr; 2l down 4 til wknd frm 14; bhnd when pu 16; collapsed & died* . . . P
141^1 Keltic Lord 7-4F A Charles-Jones *9/2-7/4; 5l 4th 4; chsd ldrs; hdwy 15; 4l 4th & ev ch when hmpd & ur 2 out* . . . U
Lord Esker (IRE) (7x) 12-1 T Underwood *A bhnd; last when ur 6* . . . U
Merry Shot (IRE) 20-1 R Bliss *Tchd 25s; fat; last 6; 7l adrift 8; slt hdwy 13; last agn nxt; bhnd frm 16; t.o when lft 2nd 2 out; exhaust & ref last* . . . r
Shock's Pride (IRE) 9-1 M Miller *Tchd 10s; ld round start; last 2; 5l 5th 8; last 13; gd hdwy nxt to chse ldr; disp 1 1/2l 2nd & ev ch when fell 2 out* . . . F

OFFICIAL DISTANCE: dist **TIME:** 6min 15.8s

264 Confined Maiden, 12st - 18J — 13 ran

104^2 **DRUMDOWNEY LAD (IRE)** (7a) 7-2 **P York** *Tchd 4s; 12th 2; hdwy to 5th 9; chsd ldng pr frm 16; 2nd when lft in ld 2 out; drew clr by-passing last* . 1
139^U **Top Light** 7-1 **J Sole** *(xnb,bh) 12s-7s; chsd ldrs frm 6; 3rd 8; chsd clr ldr frm 11; ld 16; blun bad & hdd 2 out; no ex* . . . 5 2
120^3 **Gunnerbe Posh** 3-1F **J Maxse** *(xnb) 6s-3s; tde; lft rem 3rd 3; chsd ldr frm nxt; ld 8; sn 25l clr; hdd 16; stayed on one pce frm 2 out* . . . 1 1/2 3
142^4 Fourspice Allspice (IRE) (5a) 7-2 M Miller *Trckd ldrs frm 6; 4th 8; chsd ldrs frm 16; no ex frm 2 out* . . . 2 4
233^U My Brother Jack 12-1 Miss K Lovelace *Rr 7; t.o 9; plodded home* . . . 40 5
Busmans Holiday (IRE) 25-1 S Coady *Set suicidal pce & sn clr w rival; 1 1/2l up when lft clr 4; stdd nxt; hdd 8; wknd frm 11; t.o frm 14* . . . 3/4 6
Able Bob (IRE) 14-1 R Bliss *(xnb) Nvr btr than mid-div; 7th 8; t.o when pu 14* P
Amy's Gift (5a)(bl,tt) 25-1 J Barnes *(kineton) Set suicidal pce & sn clr w a rival; jmpd violent rt 3; rn out nxt* . . . R
Deep Fried 14-1 A Charles-Jones *Chsd ldng pr frm 5; 6th 8; pu nxt; collapsed & died* . . . P
173^U Octane Booster (IRE) 6-1 M Holdforth *(xnb) Nvr btr than mid-div; 8th 8; jmpd slow 10; fnce adrift when pu 14* . . . P
Peter Parkgate (7a) 14-1 D Drake *Last 1; rr when blun & ur 6* . . . U

237[U] Queens House (5a) 12-1 N Mitchell *A bhnd; t.o 9; pu 11* . . . . P
Sula Queen (5a) 25-1 D I Turner *3rd when blun & ur 3* . . . . U

OFFICIAL DISTANCES: 6*l*, 1*l* **TIME:** 6min 15.3s

Fence 19 was omitted - fallen horse

265 Restricted, 12st — 8 ran

118[P] **PULHAM DOWNE** 4-1 **N Wilmington** *(xnb) Tchd 9/2; ld to 2 & agn 4; hit 8 & jnd; ld agn frm 11; made rest; jnd 16; stayed on str frm 2 out* 1

118[P] **Hawkers Hill** 6-1 **N Mitchell** *12s-6s; chsd ldng pr til disp ld 8-9; chsd wnr til disp ld agn 16-2 out; no ex u.p frm last.* 2 2

151[1] **Charango Star** 6-4F **P York** *Hld up in 6th; hdwy to 4th 11; eff & disp ld 16; sn rdn & no ex; disapp.* 6 3

Bettie Blue (5a) 12-1 N McDiarmid *2 handlers; 7th mostly til pu aft 10; school* P

65[6] Chief Suspect (IRE) 11-2 A Charles-Jones *Tchd 7s; 4th 4; grad lost plce frm 8; last & wkng when mist 12; pu nxt.* . . . . P

Horsemans Green 20-1 J Barnes *(xnb) A last & sn detach; t.o 5; pu 11* . . . P

Just Lark 4-1 R Bliss *(kineton) Ld 3; trckd ldrs in 3rd/4th mostly til wknd qckly 14; pu nxt* . . . . P

The Nelson Touch 14-1 D I Turner *Near eye never formed (hence name); 5th 4; impd to 3rd 8; disp ld nxt-10; 4th & wkng when mist 14; t.o & pu last* P

OFFICIAL DISTANCES: 2½*l*, 5*l* **TIME:** 6min 10.5s

Sinnington

Duncombe Park (RH 9F,18J)
Sat, 21 Feb (GOOD)

266 Hunt Members — 6 ran

161[C] **EMPEROR'S SON** 5-4JF **Miss S Brotherton** *(xnb) Settled 3rd; 20l down 10; tk 2nd 14; chall 2 out; ld app last; clr flat.* 1

Shankly 5-4JF **M Walford** *Tk str hld in clr ld; 15l ahd 10; prsd 2 out; 5l clr agn brief til jnd & rn wide app last; imm hdd & fnd nil* 6 2

Landford Lad (IRE) 25-1 **G Armitage** *2 handlers; oht; chsd clr ldr to 14; sn wl outpcd; 15l 3rd 2 out* 30 3

Blue Bud 10-1 W Burnell *Jmpd v slow & a reluct in last; 25l adrift 9; t.o & pu 15* . . . . P

Grandmere (5a) 20-1 G Brewer *Mod 4th til 5th 9; rem when pu 15* . . . . . P

167[3] Irish Paddy (IRE) (7a) 20-1 R Clark *Jmpd sticky in poor 5th til 4th 9; rem 4th when pu 15; dism* . . . . P

OFFICIAL DISTANCES: 6*l*, dist **TIME:** 6min 18.0s

267 Confined, 12st — 14 ran

163[1] **MR PENDLEBERRY** (5x)(bl) 6-4F **N Tinkler** *Mist 2; confid rdn in 2nd/4th; chsd ldr & clr of rest frm 15; clsd smoothly to ld last; qcknd clr* 1

122[4] **Who Dares Wins** 14-1 **L Bates** *Hld up; prog 14; 6th 3 out; went 6l 2nd aft nxt; stayed on; no ch w wnr* 2½ 2

134[3] **Welsh March (IRE)** 8-1 **N Tutty** *Trckd ldrs frm 7; went 3rd 3 out; rdn & no imp frm nxt* 6 3

Royal Crimson 10-1 R Alers-Hankey *Ld to 15; sn drpd back 5th & outpcd; plugged on agn aft last; nd* . . . . ½ 4

177[U] Bohemian Spirit (IRE) 4-1 S Charlton *Swtng; hld up midfield; hdwy 12 to ld 15; 8l clr 2 out; hdd last; lost plce rap uphill* 5 5

Chaos Theory 10-1 T Collier *Novicey rdr & nt fluent in last trio; strugg 12; passed btn horses* 5 6

Quango (3x)(cp) 7-1 Miss J Foster *Midfield; cl up to 12; last of 7 who were clr 3 out; no ch w ldrs* . . . . s hd 7

Glendamah (IRE) 25-1 M Morley *Bhnd; hdstrng & went prom 10; wknd 12; rem 8th 3 out* 3 8

55[P] Gus Berry (IRE) 12-1 C Mulhall *A towards rr; strugg 14* 3 9

163[P] Erni (FR)(bl) 16-1 R Abrahams *2nd/3rd to 10; wknd tame 12; rem 9th 3 out* 5 10

214[r] Royal Plum(bl) 33-1 S J Robinson *Cl up to 9; drpd to rr & drvn 11; t.o 3 out* 7 11

Fayalie (IRE) (5a) 33-1 P Robinson *2nd/3rd to 8; lost tch 11* 20 12

163^{P} Steel Rigg (IRE) 33-1 Miss Rachel Clark *Mists in final trio; strugg 11; t.o 3 out* 2 13

Notation (IRE) 33-1 R Clark *Blun 2; chsd ldrs; eff 11; 4th & outpcd by ldng pr 3 out; fell nxt* . . . . F

OFFICIAL DISTANCES: 1½*l*, 6*l* **TIME:** 6min 12.0s

268 Restricted — 11 ran

177^{3} **IMPS WAY** (5a) 6-4F **C Mulhall** *A gng wl; handy til disp 2nd frm 11; ld on bit app last; sn clr* 1

70^{2†} **Wilfie Wild** 6-1 **Mrs L Ward** *Hld up; 6th 11; went 3rd nxt; ld 2 out til app last; no ch w wnr; virt pu nr fin til rdr went into frantic late overdrive to keep plce* 15 2

Journey 25-1 **N Tutty** *Ld; 1 of 3 clr 3 out; hdd aft nxt; kpt on same pce* . . 3 3

70^{5} Bermuda Blue(bl) 20-1 L Bates *(xnb) Midfield; rdn & outpcd 14; 18l 5th 2 out* 1½ 4

122^{P} Primitive Rites 6-1 S Charlton *(xnb) Prom; 3rd 12; releg 5th & rdn nxt; wl btn aft* 4 5

Don'ttellthetaxman (IRE) 5-1 A Richardson *Handy; went cl 4th 11 til wknd 3 out; nt pushed aft nxt* 10 6

Dolphin Square (IRE) 8-1 T Oates *Hld up towards rr; lost tch 14; sn wl bhnd* 7 7

General Gem 33-1 R Morgan *Sn labouring in rr; t.o & pu 9* . . . . P

In The Van 20-1 J Morley *(xnb) Unruly & threw rdr twice; mounted outside padd & tde; lft 100yds; a t.o; pu 15* . . . . P

164^{8} Minster Echo (5a)(bl) 33-1 G Brewer *2 handlers; oht & v mulish padd; chsd ldrs; 5th when blun 11; reluct u.p aft; climbed 14; t.o & pu 15* . . . . . . P

Norman Way 33-1 P Cornforth *Wl in rr & nt lk keen; 9th 11; t.o when jmpd v slow 14; pu nxt* . . . . P

OFFICIAL DISTANCES: 15*l*, 3*l* **TIME:** 6min 07.0s

269 Land Rover Mens Open, 12st — 12 ran

122^{P} **MR MAHDLO** (7x) 33-1 **B Woodhouse** *Settled 3rd/4th; went 2nd 14; ld app last; rdn & stayed on wl flat* 1

163^{2} **San Francisco** (7x) 7-2 **G Brewer** *Trckd ldrs; mist 10; 6th nxt; outpcd 14; 6l 4th & rallying aft 2 out; drvn into 2nd at last; no imp uphill* 1½ 2

Sad Mad Bad (USA) (7x) 8-1 **G Tuer** *Hld up & bhnd; 9th 11; 6th & lot to do 14; still 15l 6th aft 2 out; fin str flat* 1 3

163^{P} Mademist Sam 33-1 N Tutty *Sn 3rd/4th; ev ch 2 out; rdn & nt qckn app last* 1½ 4

72^{4} Extra Jack (FR) (7x)(bl) 10-1 C Shirley-Beavan *2nd til ld 9 & agn frm 11; 3l clr 3 out; hdd app last; sn wknd* 5 5

Go Nomadic (7x) 2-1F P Atkinson *Midfield; 8th 11; outpcd & strugg nxt; listless eff* 5 6

132^{4} Faster Sweep (IRE) 14-1 R Morgan *Rcd keen & made nrly all to 11; 8l 4th & wkng 3 out* 7 7

214^{3} Kilcaskin Gold (IRE) (7x) 5-1 A Findlay *A bhnd; strugg in last pr 8; plodded rnd* 8 8

Decoded (7x)(cp) 33-1 L Bates *Mist 4; midfield; 7th & in tch when fell hvly 11* F

Just Coming 33-1 C Mulhall *A bhnd; strugg in last pr 8; t.o & pu 15* . . . . . P

161^{9} Needsmoretime (IRE) 33-1 S J Robinson *Jmpd slow 3; a towards rr; 11th & bumped along 11; wl t.o when crawled 3 out; pu nxt* . . . . P

On The Mend (IRE) (7x) 10-1 R Wakeham *Midfield; went 5th 11; 8th & wkng rap 14; t.o 2 out; pu last* . . . . P

OFFICIAL DISTANCES: 1*l*, ½*l* **TIME:** 6min 08.0s

270 Ladies Open — 10 ran

133^{4} **BALISTEROS (FR)** 5-1 **Miss P Robson** *A gng keen in ldng trio; ld 2-6 & 11-14; ld agn 3 out; stayed on v str flat; sn clr* 1

Ballad Minstrel (IRE) 14-1 **Miss J Foster** *Ld to 2 & made most 6-11; ld agn 14-3 out; 1l 2nd & rdn app last; sn wl outpcd* 12 2

162^{U} **Pharlindo (IRE)** 4-1 **Miss A Armitage** *(xnb) Rcd keen & prom; ld brief aft 8; ev ch til wknd 3 out; wl btn app last* 3 3

122^{6} Light The River (IRE)(bl) 2-1F Miss C Metcalfe *(xnb) Hld up til stdy prog 9; cl 4th 12; rdn & bad outpcd 3 out; some prog flat* 12 4

162^{3} Wandering Wild (5a) 14-1 Mrs L Ward *A 4/5th; outpcd 14; releg mod 5th aft 2 out* 5 5

Form	Horse / Rider / Comment	Dist	Pos
	Knockholt 6-1 Miss M Neill *Midfield; 7th when mist 12; sn lost tch*	1	6
	Just Jake 8-1 Mrs L Tinkler *V feebly rdn & detach in last pr; t.o 8.*	20	7
162[5]	Silk Vestments (5a) 33-1 Miss H Dunning *(xnb) A wl bhnd; t.o 8.*	3	8
	Sharp Embrace 33-1 Miss S Rodman *Stdly drpd to rr; lost tch 10; t.o 15*	5	9
	Supercharmer 10-1 Miss S Brotherton *(xnb) Bhnd; eff in 6th 12; wknd 14; t.o*	20	10

OFFICIAL DISTANCES: 15*l*, 5*l* **TIME:** 6min 06.0s

271 Open Maiden (Div 1) 16 ran

Form	Horse / Rider / Comment	Dist	Pos
137[2]	**THREE SPIRES** 3-1 **A Richardson** *2 handlers; trckd ldrs; 5th aft 3 out; ld aft nxt; jnd & lft clr last; stayed on*		1
160[3]	**Bobby Buttons** 5-2F **N Tutty** *Mostly 2nd; releg 3½l 4th aft 2 out; lft 2nd agn last; drvn & nt qckn*	5	2
165[3]	**Oaklands Luis** (7a) 5-1 **T Glass** *Settled midfield; 7th 11; 7l 6th app 2 out; eff to 2l 3rd app last; sn wknd*	3	3
161[6]	Rising Talisker (5a)(cp) 12-1 Miss Rachel Clark *Settled 2nd/4th to 2 out; nt r.o & sn btn*	3	4
165[5]	Bankersdraft 14-1 M Morley *Lft in ld 5; hdd & fdd rap aft 2 out.*	3	5
74[P]	House Colours 20-1 T Oates *(xnb) Prsd ldrs; chall 13; sn btn; 10l 7th app 2 out*	3	6
166[7]	Midnight Moon 25-1 J Burley *(xnb) Rr div; 10th 9; no ch frm 13*	3	7
167[4]	Drovers Road 12-1 C Mulhall *Sn 20l last & nvr able to cl*	10	8
167[6]	Bally Leader (IRE) 14-1 C Dawson *4/5th to 11; sn wknd; rr when ur 15 & rdr ended up running alongside*		U
75[P]	Bright Dawn (IRE) (12a) 14-1 G Brewer *Trckd ldrs; hung lft & rn wide app 9; 10l 9th 11; rallied in 3rd app 2 out; jnd wnr app last but hung bad lft & rn out*		R
	Ellie Bee (12a) 12-1 B Woodhouse *Hld up & wl bhnd; 12th 9; t.o & pu 15*		P
166[R]	Fair Signet 12-1 P Cornforth *(xnb) Tk str hld; ld til rn out 5*		R
	Hendrix 9-1 Miss J Foster *Mists in rr; 11th 9; t.o & pu 14.*		P
167[U]	Search Party (FR) (7a) 7-1 S Walker *Nt fluent in midfield; 8th 11; brief eff 13; 8th & fdng app 2 out; t.o & pu last.*		P
	Staple Sound 16-1 W Burnell *(xnb) Last pr & wl adrift; bad t.o when pu 2 out*		P
137[P]	The Panjshir 16-1 G Willoughby *Prom brief; 13th & lsng tch 8; t.o & pu 15*		P

OFFICIAL DISTANCES: 5*l*, 3*l* **TIME:** 6min 18.0s

272 Open Maiden (Div 2) 16 ran

Form	Horse / Rider / Comment	Dist	Pos
	LE MILLENAIRE (FR) (7a) 20-1 **C Shirley-Beavan** *(xnb) Ur & bolted into car park; ld mounted to start; rcd keen; ld to 14; releg 4th app 2 out; 6l 3rd when lft 2nd at last; rallied & str rn uphill to ld cl home*		1
	Sevensider (IRE) 7-2 **R Wakeham** *Hld up; prog gng wl in 3rd 11; went 2nd app 2 out; lft in ld & lkd wnr at last; rdn & overwhelmed nr fin.*	1½	2
165[2]	**Ravenscar** 11-4F **S Walker** *Settled 3rd/4th; ev ch 3 out; 8l 4th & outpcd when lft 3rd at last; nt qckn.*	8	3
167[5]	Mademist Sparky (5a) 10-1 N Tutty *Midfield; 7th 11; outpcd 14; plugged on*	15	4
	Flat Stanley (7a) 16-1 Miss J Foster *Towards rr mostly; strugg & no ch 14*	5	5
166[6]	Gollinger(bl) 16-1 B Woodhouse *Cl up til releg 7th aft 8; 6th & last in tch 14; fdd tame*	15	6
	Dear Lord (IRE) 3-1 G Brewer *Settled midfield; eff in 5th 11; trckd ldrs til wknd rap 2 out; t.o & pu last*		P
	Devil's Perk (IRE) 8-1 T Glass *Bhnd early; prog in 2nd aft 8; ld 14; 2l clr when hung bad lft, crashed thro wing & ur last*		R
	Hidden Pearl (IRE) 5-1 J Davis *Nt fluent in rr; lost tch 10; nrly fell 11; pu 12*		P
	Jobee Jack 33-1 T Craggs *(xnb) Midfield til blun & ur 7*		U
	Just A Lady (5a) 16-1 C Mulhall *V novicey & imm lost tch; t.o 6; pu 14*		P
165[P]	My Rock 25-1 C Dawson *Pulled hrd; 2nd to 8; 8th & wkng rap 11; pu 13.*		P
75[B]	Super Dolphin (7a) 14-1 Richard Tate *Handy; 5th aft 8; rdr stepped off 10*		U
167[P]	Three Way Split 20-1 Miss Rachel Clark *Jmpd mod in rr; lost tch 8; t.o & pu 15*		P
	Uncle Neil (IRE) 20-1 A Richardson *Novicey in rr; 9th 11; sn wl bhnd; pu last*		P
	Zebs Lad 16-1 R Walker *Imm t.o & jmpd v poor; pu 5.*		P

OFFICIAL DISTANCES: 2*l*,8*l* **TIME:** 6min 18.0s

West Somerset & Minehead Harriers

Holnicote (LH 7F,19J)

Sat, 21 Feb (GOOD, GOOD to FIRM in places)

273 Hunt Members, 12st — 4 ran

	COOL WAGER 8-11F **D Edwards** *Hld up in tch; hmpd by loose horse bend aft 6; hdwy to disp ld 12-13; cl 2nd nxt til ld agn 2 out; easily*		1
	Caundle Chase 2-1 **W White** *Lft in ld 3; jnd brief 12-13; hdd & blun 2 out; sn btn*	15	2
10P	Ariann Sound (IRE) 5-1 R McCarthy *Slt ld til blun & ur 3*		U
	Sparkle (U) 12-1 D Ravenscroft *1st ride; cl up; impd to disp ld when blun & ur 6*		U

OFFICIAL DISTANCE: 20*l* **TIME:** 7min 09.0s **TOTE:** £2.30 **DF:**£1.10

Fences 10 & 17 omitted - damaged

274 Confined Maiden (Div 1), 12st - 18J — 10 ran

	INAGH ROAD (IRE) 10-1 **A Michael** *Ld/disp til def advant frm 16; hld on wl*		1
149P	**Challis Choice (IRE)** 8-1 **J Snowden** *(xnb) Bckwd; midfield & gng wl; hdwy 14; went 2nd 3 out; kpt on; a hld; fair eff*	1	2
	Execute (IRE) 12-1 **J Young** *Settled 3rd; lost plce 14; 4th 16; no ch w ldrs frm nxt*	8	3
197P	Knockaun Wood (IRE) 10-1 M Sweetland *Tchd 12s; bckwd; 8th 1/2way; just in tch 16; one pce frm 3 out; fin lame*	8	5
	Merry Melody (5a) 3-1F Miss S Robinson *(ringbit) In tch; hit 12; 5th & no imp 16; wl btn when mist last*	5	6
1395	Bright Flash (IRE) 5-1 D Luff *Ld/disp to 16; sn rdn; no ex frm 3 out; fin 15l 4th; disq - nt weigh-in*		4d
	Augathella 8-1 C Heard *(xnb) Sn rr; t.o & pu 14*		P
	Elegant Maid (5a, 4ow)(tt) 25-1 H Thomas *6th 1/2way; midfield when ur 10; rdr inj*		U
	General Short 100-30 R Woollacott *Sn rr; bhnd til pu 14; school*		P
	Rosehill Doorbell (5a) 7-2 D Edwards *(xnb) 7th 1/2way; bhnd frm 16 til pu 2 out; lame*		P

OFFICIAL DISTANCES: 1*l*, 10*l* **TIME:** 6min 53.0s **TOTE:** £9.00 **DF:**£14.00

Fence 17 omitted - fallen rider; Bright Flash finished 4th but was disqualified when the rider failed to weigh-in; he was fined £40

275 Confined Maiden (Div 2), 12st — 14 ran

87P	**ROSETTA** (5a) 50-1 **Miss L Gardner** *(xnb) Settled midfield; hdwy 15; went 2nd app 3 out; chall app last; str rn to ld last 75yds*		1
	Far Too Crowded (IRE) (5a) 8-1 **N Williams** *Tchd 10s; lw; hld up towards rr; hdwy 12; jnd ldrs nxt; slt ld 16; 2l up when blun last; no ex & hdd cl home*	1 1/2	2
1433	**Toon Society (IRE)** 7-4F **N Harris** *Tchd 2s; in tch; cl 2nd frm 10; cl up & ev ch 16; wknd nxt; no ch frm 2 out*	8	3
	Abu Dancer (IRE) (5a) 50-1 C Heard *Ch ride; handy; 4th 1/2way; cl 3rd 16; wknd nxt; wl hld frm 2 out*	6	4
	Polly Come Back (12a) 5-1 R Woollacott *(xnb) Hld up in midfield; 9th 1/2way; mist 11; 4th & ev ch 16; no ex frm 3 out*	nk	5
149P	Five Minutes (5a) 9-2 Miss T Cave *Tchd 5s; slt ld to 14; lost ground aft nxt; sn btn*	25	6
	Bickleigh Cottage (5a) 25-1 D Edwards *Quite attractive; rr; 11th 1/2way; t.o & pu 16*		P
	Chita's Flora (12a) 16-1 J Snowden *Rr group; bhnd frm 14; t.o & pu 3 out*		P
	Phanthom Walker 20-1 T Dennis *Rr; 10th 1/2way; hit 13; t.o & pu 15*		P
	Rocastle Lad (IRE) 20-1 Miss L Hawkings *Bckwd; prog 6; went 2nd 8; rn out 10*		R
	Rowleyrascal 12-1 M Sweetland *Chsd ldr to 4; sn wknd; last 9; t.o & pu 16*		P
	Viva Bingo (IRE)(bl) 14-1 A Michael *Oht; svs; scrambled over 1 & 2; t.o & pu nxt*		P
	Which Moscow (IRE) 6-1 D McKenna *Mid-div; 8th 9; hdwy to 4th 12; lost plce nxt; bhnd & pu 3 out*		P
	Whizzie Lite (5a) 20-1 W White *7th 1/2way; gd hdwy 15; hrd to steer & rn out bend aft 16*		R

OFFICIAL DISTANCES: 1 1/2*l*, 8*l* **TIME:** 6min 57.0s **TOTE:** £28.00 **DF:**£18.50

276 Ladies Open — 5 ran

LONGSTONE BOY (IRE) 7-1 **Miss J Hughes** *Tchd 9s; jw; made virt all in slt ld; 2l up 3 out; jnd nxt; drew clr app last; comf.* 1

62^{1} **Sir William**(tt) 11-4 **Miss T Cave** *(xnb) Tchd 3s; trckd ldr; cl up frm 11; ev ch when jinked rt app 2 out; no ex app last* . . . . . . 6 — 2

236^{1} **Cherokee Boy** 16-1 **Miss C Atkinson** *Prom; ld brief 4; rn wide on bend & lost plce aft 6; t.o 15; tk poor 3rd flat.* . . . . . . runin — 3

Hope Value 25-1 Miss G Edwards *Last til went 4th 13; nvr nr ldrs; t.o when lft 3rd 2 out; dem flat* . . . . . . 3 — 4

10^{1} Rimpton Boy 8-15F Miss R Green *Tchd 4/7; nt a fluent; hld up; rap hdwy 3 out; chall on inner when nt much room & crashed thro wing 2 out; rdr suffered facial injuries.* . . . . . . R

OFFICIAL DISTANCES: 7l, dist **TIME:** 6min 42.0s **TOTE:** £4.90 **DF:**£11.20

277 Mens Open, 12st — 6 ran

145^{1} **POLAR CHAMP** (7x)(bl) evensF **A Farrant** *(bh) Tchd 11/10; made all; went 4l clr aft 16; kpt on wl u.p* 1

140^{1} **Tales Of Bounty (IRE)** (7x) 5-4 **N Williams** *Lw; a trckng wnr; rdn 15; r.o wl u.p frm 2 out; a hld* . . . . . . 2½ — 2

144^{2} **Friar Waddon** 16-1 **C Heard** *Trckd ldrs; 4th & in tch 9; outpcd 13; poor 3rd frm 3 out.* . . . . . . 12 — 3

Vic's Brush (IRE) 25-1 W White *Trckd ldrs; 4th 11; bhnd & no ch frm 15* . . . . . . runin — 4

Nearly Noble (IRE) 8-1 R Woollacott *(xnb) Tchd 10s; hld up; cl 5th ½way; short-lived eff 14; lost tch frm 16; btn 3rd when pu nxt; btr for rce.* . . . . . . P

September Harvest (USA) 50-1 R Shute *Bckwd; sn strugg in last; t.o til pu 16* . . . P

OFFICIAL DISTANCES: 2l, 15l **TIME:** 6min 39.0s **TOTE:** £2.50 **DF:**£1.40

278 Intermediate (Nov Rdrs), 12st - 17J — 6 ran

OPAL'LOU (FR) (5a) 13-2 **R Pyman** *(xnb) Lw; jw; sn prom; ld 4; made rest; went 20l clr 16; kpt on wl; should progress* 1

117^{2} **Polka** 4-5F **R McCarthy** *Tchd evens; lw; hld up; 5l 3rd ½way; went 2nd 15; hrd rdn 2 out; no real imp* . . . . . . 5 — 2

The Grey Shadow 20-1 **W White** *Bckwd; last ½way; went poor 3rd 15; one pce.* . . . . . . 15 — 3

193^{9} Gutsy Dalton (IRE)(bl) 8-1 Miss J Buck *Tubed; 4th but in tch 10; lost ground 13; bhnd frm 16* . . . . . . 12 — 4

Evolution Lad (IRE) 12-1 Miss V Price *(xnb) Lw; last but in tch when blun & ur 3; rdr airlifted* . . . . . . U

79^{U} Winning Leader (IRE) (2ow) 7-2 R Skinner *Tchd 4s; ld to 4; trckd ldr nxt; 5l 2nd when blun bad 14; 3rd & wkng when pckd nxt; t.o & pu last* . . . . . P

OFFICIAL DISTANCES: 8l, 20l **TIME:** 6min 39.0s **TOTE:** £8.30 **DF:**£1.20

Fences 10 & 17 omitted - fallen rider

279 Restricted, 12st — 10 ran

232^{2} **LORD OF THE MIST (IRE)** 13-8F **N Williams** *Tchd 7/4; lw; hdstrng gng to post; hld up wl off pce; 8th 14; gd hdwy 16; 4th nxt; swooped on outer to ld last; drvn out.* 1

197^{2} **Mrs Peggoty** (5a)(bl) 14-1 **D Edwards** *Handy; cl 3rd ½way; went 2nd 13; disp ld 3 out to last; kpt on wl* . . . . . . 1 — 2

Ellofamonkey (5a) 11-2 **R Woollacott** *(xnb removed in padd when fractious) 7s-11/2; 6th ½way; impd to 3rd 14; disp ld aft 16; ev ch til wknd aft last* 2 — 3

118^{2} Rhythm King 9-4 G Maundrell *(xnb) Lw; hld up wl off pce; 8th 9; hdwy 16; 3rd 3 out; chall bet horses & ev ch when rivals clsd gap & forced him back app last.* . . . . . . 1½ — 4

Miss Illustrious (5a) 100-1 T Dennis *Ch ride; bit bckwd; 4th ½way; cl 4th frm 14; 3rd aft 16; lost plce frm 3 out; one pce (creditable eff for 100-1 shot)* 1½ — 5

Knight Of Kilcash (IRE) 40-1 J Jones *(xnb) Bhnd til pu 14.* . . . . . . P

My Jess (5a) 20-1 M Sweetland *(xnb) Oht; prom; distracted by loose marker tape flapping in front of fnce & jinked 2; slt ld 3-13; lost plce qckly; bhnd when pu 3 out* . . . . . . P

148^{P} Porto (IRE) 8-1 R McCarthy *(xnb) 5th when rn out in tape melee 2; cont without rtrcng; 10l 5th 4; cl 5th 8; hdwy to ld 13-15; lost plce qckly; pu 3 out; rdr fined* . . . . . . R

	River Dante (IRE) 9-1 Mrs O Jackson *(xnb) Lw; distracted by loose marker tape flapping across course & rn out 2*		R
114[2]	Rosalee Royale (5a) 25-1 C Heard *Ld til caught up in flapping tape 2 & hdd; cl up til ld agn 11-12; lost plce rap aft 13; t.o & pu 3 out*		P

OFFICIAL DISTANCES: 1*l*, 2*l* **TIME:** 6min 49.0s **TOTE:** £5.20 **DF:**£8.60

The stewards interviewed the rider of Porto who pulled up 3 fences out; they fined him £75 for continuing in the race after running out at the second fence

Fontwell (L&RH 7F,19J)

Sun, 22 Feb (GOOD)

280 Norma Dodd Birthday Celebration Foxhunters Trial HC, 3m2f110y £4065 — 9 ran

140[2]	**COUNTY DERRY** 12-07(cp) 5-1 **N Harris** *Prsd ldr til ld aft 10; hit 12; hrd prsd frm 3 out; nk ahd when btr j last; drvn clr*		1
	Earthmover (IRE) 12-02 5-4F **Miss A Goschen** *Made most til hdd aft 10; outpcd by ldng pr 13; sn 10l adrift; rallied to 2nd 3 out; hrd rdn & ev ch when ploughed thro last; nt rec*	4	2
	Forest Gunner 11-07 11-4 **S Hughes** *Hld up; hdwy 6; prsd wnr aft 13; nt fluent nxt; ev ch til rdn & wknd btn app 3 out*	21	3
176[3]	Mullensgrove 11-07 50-1 Miss S Phizacklea *Bhnd; mists 2 & 9; rdn & lost tch aft 10; nd aft.*	3	4
222[2]	Bush Hill Bandit (IRE) 12-02 33-1 Ms A Embiricos *Midfield; 4th & eff 12; wknd nxt*	17	5
100[5]	Splash And Dash (IRE) 12-02 12-1 A Hickman *Jmpd sluggishly in last; rdn 6; hdwy 11; sn strugg; 5th & btn when nt fluent 14*	3/4	6
18[3]	Bitofamixup (IRE) 12-00 8-1 Mrs J Gordon *Sn towards rr; mist & rdn 10; no ch frm 14; t.o & pu 17*		P
	Maidstone Monument (IRE) 12-04 8-1 E Williams *2nd/3rd to 10; lost plce rap 12; wl bhnd when pu 15*		P
88[5]	Robbie's Adventure 11-09 50-1 C Gordon *A bhnd; lost tch 10; t.o & pu 16*		P

TIME: 6min 45.3s **TOTE:** £7.80; places £1.90,£1.20,£1.70 **Ex:**£25.50 **CSF:**£14.10

The trainer of Bitofamixup reported that the horse had been unsuited by the going

Berwickshire

Friars Haugh (LH 9F,18J)

Sun, 22 Feb (GOOD)

281 Hunt Members — 6 ran

72[P]	**INDIEN DU BOULAY (FR)** 5-1 **W Ramsay** *Bit bckwd; ld to 2; jnd ldr 9 til ld agn 13; 2l clr nxt; drvn frm 2 out; all out but a hldng rnr-up*		1
137[4]	**Toorak (USA)** 4-1 **R Trotter** *(xnb) Hdwy to 2nd 6; ld 7; jnd 9-13; prsd wnr aft; drvn & no imp frm 2 out*	6	2
73[F]	**Across The Card** (1ow) 5-1 **C Ramsay** *(xnb) Hit 3; tkn stdly in last pr; outpcd 9; t.o 13; snatched 3rd nr fin*	25	3
	Planet Ireland (IRE) 7-1 Mrs J Wight *Oht; bckwd; 3rd to 6; outpcd 9; lft poor 3rd 12; plodded on; dem nr fin*	2	4
166[3]	Coastal Safari 10-1 M Ellwood *Pulled hrd & rdr novicey; ld 2-7; drpd back 5th 8; t.o when nrly ur 15*	25	5
215[1]	Flying Past 4-5F Miss D Calder *Hld up last to 6; went 3rd 9; 10l down when blun & ur 12*		U

OFFICIAL DISTANCES: 8*l*, 20*l* **TIME:** 6min 55.0s

282 Confined, 12st — 10 ran

134[F]	**KATINKA** (5a) 6-4F **C Storey** *(xnb) Keen & sn prom; ld 7; 5l clr when blun 12; 2l up app 2 out; rdn when blun last; bounced along & all out aft.*		1
210[3]	**Johnnys Gone (IRE)** 7-2 **C Shirley-Beavan** *Sn towards rr; mist 9; outpcd 11; rallied in 6l 3rd app 15; still 10l down app 2 out; urged along & str rn flat; too much to do*	1	2

	French Cedar 6-1 **W Ramsay** *2nd mostly; 2l down & rdn app 2 out; tried to chall last; kpt on one pce*	s hd	3
135[4]	In Demand 6-1 Miss J Balmer *Sn last; lost tch 8; wl bhnd 14; stayed on wl frm 3 out to poor 4th*	25	4
	Valley Erne (IRE) 10-1 J Thompson *(bh) Chsd ldrs; 4th & still in tch 15; sn wknd*	20	5
211[8]	Sharpaman(bl) 12-1 Miss K Bryson *Nvr btr than midfield; outpcd 11; wl bhnd aft 14*	4	6
134[P]	Derryrose(cp) 12-1 M McAlister *Prom early but nvr lkd keen; releg 5th 7; outpcd when hit 11; wl bhnd 15*	5	7
	Mr McDuff (IRE) 9-2 Miss J Hollands *Ld to 7; 3rd 12; prsd ldrs til wknd qckly 15*	5	8
	Colonel North (IRE) 7-1 A Richardson *Mists; nvr btr than midfield; outpcd 12; last when blun 14; t.o & pu aft 3 out*		P
210[U]	Crevamoy (IRE) (5a, 3ow) 5-1 J Galbraith *Shaky in last til inept rdr f.o 7*		U

OFFICIAL DISTANCES: 1*l*, s hd **TIME:** 6min 50.0s

283 Restricted — 6 ran

132[2]	**WILD EDGAR (IRE)** 4-6F **A Richardson** *Oht; 2 handlers; mist 2; made virt all; hrd prsd when lft virt solo 3 out*		1
	Musical Socks (5a) 6-1 **K Anderson** *Cl up to 14; 6l 3rd & wkng app nxt; t.o when lft 2nd 3 out*	30	2
212[P]	**The Broken Man** 5-1 **Miss K Bryson** *Bckwd; cl up to 12; 15l last & wl btn app 15; t.o when lft 3rd nxt*	20	3
	Harry's Mare (IRE) (5a) 4-1 S Huggan *Swtng profuse; jmpd rt; 2nd mostly; hit 11; ld brief & jmpd rt 15; cl 2nd when blun bad & ur 3 out*		U
212[P]	Offspringer 2-1 D Jewett *Settled cl up; 4th when nrly fell 14; 10l 4th app nxt; chall event 2nd when ur 3 out*		U
	Treble Vision (IRE) 5-1 J Thompson *(bf) Cl up in rr; rdn 9 & nt gng wl; hit 11 & lost tch; pu 12*		P

OFFICIAL DISTANCES: dist, 25*l* **TIME:** 6min 57.0s

284 Ladies Open — 6 ran

133[1]	**MYTIMIE (IRE)** evensF **Miss P Robson** *Lw; ld; nt fluent 1 & 2; hdd aft 4; ld agn 8; made rest; nt fluent 12; drew clr on bit 3 out; v easily*		1
135[1]	**Passing Danger (FR)** 4-1 **Miss R Davidson** *Opened 5s; settled 3rd/4th; 5l 3rd app 15; 12l 3rd app 2 out; kpt on to 2nd flat; no ch w wnr*	8	2
133[2]	**Pharmistice (IRE)** 3-1 **Miss N Stirling** *(xnb) Lw; ld 4-8; prsd wnr til outpcd 3 out; dem flat*	2	3
133[5]	Commanche Law (IRE) 4-1 Mrs A Hamilton *Opened 5s; hit 2; cl up til blun & rdr waved 14; 10l 4th & btn app nxt*	15	4
	Little Santa (IRE) (5a) 33-1 Mrs K Hargreave *Detach last mostly; no ch 10; t.o & jmpd slow frm 3 out*	1½fs	5
133[P]	Miss Portcello (5a, 4ow) 6-1 Miss J Hollands *Jmpd slow 4; handy til wknd 10; last when jmpd slow nxt; pu 13*		P

OFFICIAL DISTANCES: 6*l*, 2*l* **TIME:** 6min 41.0s

285 Mens Open — 3 ran

214[P]	**FALCON'S FLAME (USA)** 5-4F **R Green** *(xnb) Made all; drew 8l clr & lkd in comm aft 3 out; wknd last; drvn & all out; won on jockeyship*		1
134[7]	**Dr Deductible**(cp) 7-4 **R Brown** *Pckd 2; 2nd frm 5; 2l down 14; hit nxt; outpcd 3 out; rallied last & tried hrd to carry feeble rdr to front*	1	2
134[6]	**Laganside (IRE)** (3ow) 2-1 **J Muir** *Oht; jmpd rt; lost tch 6; t.o 14; slt late prog; rdr no help*	10	3

OFFICIAL DISTANCES: 1*l*, 12*l* **TIME:** 6min 57.0s

286 Confined Maiden (Div 1) — 11 ran

216[P]	**HERVEY BAY** (5a) 7-2 **W Goldie** *(xnb) Prom in chsng group; 15l 3rd app 10; lft 2nd 11; ld brief 14; ld agn aft last; drvn out*		1
137[3]	**Rutherford** 3-1 **R Morgan** *Oht; rdr knocked off by loose horse gng down & bolted; settled midfield; lft 6l 3rd aft 11; ld app 15-nxt; ld agn 2 out; one pce u.p aft; hdd & no ex flat*	1½	2
216[5]	**Sijujama (IRE)** 4-1 **Miss N Patterson** *(xnb) 10s-4s; ldng pr & sn clr; ld app 10 & lft clr brief nxt; hdd 14; ld agn 3 out-nxt; sn gave up*	10	3

136[2] Tallaburn (5a)(tt) 6-1 A Findlay *Jmpd slow 2; hld up; 7th 8; lft 8l 4th aft melee 11; eff & cl up 15; rdn & wknd app 2 out* 2 4
69[P] Coquet Gold (5a) 10-1 Miss C Walton *Rr but in tch to 14; wknd nxt; t.o aft 3 out* . . . . . runin 5
136[3] Steady Lass (IRE) (5a) 8-1 R Nichol *A bhnd; lost tch 10; t.o & reluct frm 14* 20 6
216[U] Alice's Old Rose (5a) 8-1 T Oates *A wl bhnd; lost tch 12; t.o when blun bad 15; pu aft nxt* . . . . . P
Blackhill Princess (5a) 4-1 K Anderson *(xnb) Rdr lost iron brief 2; midfield; mist 9; handy when hmpd bad & ur 11* . . . . . U
Chase The Moon (5a) 2-1F Miss L Hislop *Settled 3rd/4th & 10l frm ldng pr; hmpd v bad 11 & pu*. . . . . P
Hot Bricks 3-1 J Walton *Fat; rdr knocked off by loose horse gng down; re-saddled start; v nervous & climbed fncs; imm t.o; nrly 2 fncs bhnd when pu aft 7; schooling* . . . . . P
71[P] Wheresbob(bl) 16-1 Miss L Kendall *Jmpd rt at times; pulled hrd & sn clr in ldng pr; hdd app 10; fell hvly nxt* . . . . . F

OFFICIAL DISTANCES: 1*l*, 6*l* **TIME:** 7min 04.0s

Turbo Mower (J Thompson, 6-1, bckwd, ur gng down & kicked rdr breaking his hip, loose horse cannoned into & ur Hot Bricks - who needed resaddling - and Rutherford - who galloped off) was withdrawn not under orders

287 Confined Maiden (Div 2) 9 ran

74[P] **SUPERSTAR EXPRESS (IRE)**(tt) 5-1 **A Findlay** *(xnb) Hld up in rr; last 9; 10l 4th & prog app 15; 5l 4th app 2 out; rdn & str rn to ld aft 2 out; clr when pckd last*. 1
137[5] **Storm Ahead (IRE)** 4-1 **C Shirley-Beavan** *Handy & gng wl; 3rd 9; ld app 15; hdd brief nxt; hdd agn aft 2 out; sn outpcd & outrdn* 3 2
136[F] **Stanwick Gypsy** (5a) 7-4F **C Storey** *Hld up; hdwy & jmpd slow 8; 2nd 9; ld brief 14; ev ch app 2 out; drvn & nt qckn aft* 3 3
Camair Commander (IRE)(tt) 9-1 T Oates *Opened 10s; lw; trckd ldrs; 6th 9; fnd nil frm 14; poor 5th nxt*. 25 4
74[P] Red Jupiter 8-1 A Richardson *Nt jw; 2nd/3rd to 7; 7th 9; lost tch 14; t.o nxt* 15 5
215[U] I'm Willie's Girl (5a) 4-1 Miss J Riding *Nt fluent & last mostly; strugg 12; t.o aft 14; drpd shoulder & ur app last*. . . . . U
215[U] Simply Silver Lady (5a) 6-1 S Huggan *Nt fluent; 2nd/3rd to 7; 5th 9; lost tch 14; t.o & pu 3 out* . . . . . P
131[3] Sporty Spice (IRE) (5a) 6-1 Miss L Hislop *Oht; ld to 14; drpd out rap; t.o & pu 2 out* . . . . . P
161[R] T'nightsthenight 2-1 D Jewett *Hld up & bhnd; 4th & prog 9; chall 15; ld nxt; sn hdd & stpd to nil; poor 4th when pu 2 out* . . . . . P

OFFICIAL DISTANCES: 4*l*, 2*l* **TIME:** 6min 58.0s

Bicester with Whaddon Chase

Mollington (RH 8F,18J)

Sun, 22 Feb (GOOD)

288 Hunt Members 4 ran

SHORTCUT SHORTY 14-1 **P Cowley** *W ldr/2nd til aft 15; outpcd aft nxt; 5l 3rd 2 out; str rn flat; stayed on to ld nr fin*. 1
170[3] **Et Light (FR)** 1-3F **A Barlow** *Jmpd lft; made most til hdd nr fin* 3/4 2
True Chimes(cp) 7-1 **J Owen** *A.p; 1 1/2l 3rd 1/2way; shkn up aft 13; went 2nd aft 15; rdn & ev ch when hit last; nt qckn* 1 3/4 3
Hawthorn 3-1 B Clarke *(xnb,bf) A last; blun 11; mist & lost tch 12; pu 13* P

OFFICIAL DISTANCES: 1/2*l*, 1 1/2*l* **TIME:** 6min 32.7s

289 Confined Ladies 14 ran

171[3] **THE GRANBY (IRE)** 2-1F **Miss H Irving** *A.p; 2l 3rd 1/2way; ld 11; hit 2 out; stayed on wl*. 1
46[1] **Ryans Star** 5-1 **Mrs J Parris** *2 handlers; ld to 4; 2nd til ld 8; hdd 11; lft clr w wnr 14; ev ch 3 out; one pce* 5 2
171[2] **Filscot** 7-2 **Miss E Harbour** *Hld up & bhnd; 13l 9th 1/2way; 17l 6th 12; stayed on wl frm 3 out; went 18l 3rd app nxt; fin str; impossible task* 2 1/2 3

175^{10}	Esterelle (USA) (5a) 40-1 Miss S Beddoes *(xnb,bh) Pulled hrd; ld 4-8; 3l 4th 12; sn outpcd; no ch frm 14*	20	4
92^{P}	Borderline Breeze (IRE) 33-1 Miss H Watson *Chsd ldrs; 5l 5th ½way; outpcd 10; 15l 5th 12; wl bhnd 14*	6	5
189^{U}	Perfect Finisher 40-1 Miss E Jones *Hld up; hdwy & 5½l 6th ½way; outpcd 13; lft 12l 3rd nxt; wknd aft 3 out*	7	6
124^{4}	Light The Sky 16-1 Miss K Norris *A bhnd; 14l 10th ½way; t.o 15*	5	7
48^{U}	Polo Pony (IRE) 25-1 Miss T Habgood *Chsd ldrs to 8; 10l 7th ½way; wl bhnd 12; t.o 15*	5	8
190^{U}	Gangster 25-1 Miss S Tarry *Lost tch 5; 30l 12th ½way; t.o 11*	1½fs	9
43^{3}	Carthago (IRE) 9-2 Miss E James *6s-9/2; hld up; hdwy 8; 5th when ur nxt*		U
	Ela Agapi Mou (USA)(bl) 25-1 Miss D Ball *A wl bhnd; 31l last ½way; t.o 11; pu 15*		P
190^{8}	Gortroe Guy (IRE) 33-1 Miss K Robinson *(xnb) Tde; nd; 12l 8th ½way; wl bhnd when rfo 13*		U
47^{4}	Maltby Son 16-1 Miss K Branson *Nd; 16l 11th ½way; mist & lost tch 10; t.o & pu 13*		P
	My Best Buddy 8-1 Miss A Stennett *Lw; sn prom; 3l 4th ½way; went 2l 3rd 12; fell 14*		F

OFFICIAL DISTANCES: 6*l*, 3*l* **TIME:** 6min 13.5s

290 Confined Maiden 56&7yo (Div 1), 2m4f, 12st - 15J — 10 ran

128^{P}	**ARCTIC PENGUIN** 5-2F **P York** *4s-5/2; ld; jmpd slow 4; sn 10l clr to 7; hdd 11; 2nd til rallied & ld last; rdn out*		1
104^{3}	**To The Top** 4-1 **James Tudor** *2nd til ld 11; lkd wnr 2 out; mist & hdd last; kpt on*	2	2
105^{2}	**Nailed On** (7a) 3-1 **A Martin** *A.p; 2l 3rd ½way; mists 11 & 12; 5l down 3 out; blun 2 out; stayed on flat*	2	3
53^{2}	Gentlemans Relish 7-2 T Lane *Hld up; mist 6; 9½l 6th ½way; hdwy & 6l 4th 9; rdn 3 out; btn when hit 2 out*	10	4
	Earl Of Buckingham 8-1 P Cowley *Hld up & bhnd; 11l 8th ½way; lost tch 12; 20l 5th nxt; stayed on*	12	5
30^{U}	One For Olly (IRE) 33-1 G Walters *Chsd ldrs; 8½l 5th ½way; 9l 5th 10; wknd 11*	6	6
	Jewel Song 20-1 J Owen *Jmpd novicey; a bhnd; 13l last ½way; t.o*	15	7
111^{P}	Coral Bay 10-1 R Cope *Chsd ldrs; 8l 4th ½way; wknd qckly u.p 9; wl bhnd when pu 12*		P
	Ginger Miss (IRE) (12a) 8-1 F Hutsby *Hld up; 10l 7th ½way; jmpd slow 10; wl bhnd when pu 12*		P
	Red Ringa 33-1 H Fowler *(xnb) A bhnd; 12l 9th ½way; blun & ur 12*		U

OFFICIAL DISTANCES: 2*l*, 1¾*l* **TIME:** 5min 16.7s

291 Confined Maiden 56&7yo (Div 2), 2m4f, 12st - 15J — 8 ran

128^{B}	**KILLARD POINT (IRE)** (7a, 1ow) evensF **R Cope** *A.p; 2l 3rd ½way; lft 2l 2nd 11; ld last; rdly drew clr flat*		1
127^{P}	**Mountain Trooper** (7a) 5-1 **J Owen** *A.p; 2½l 4th ½way; lft 2½l 3rd 11; mist 3 out; rdn & ev ch 2 out; no ex flat*	5	2
	Kupto (FR) 10-1 **P Cowley** *(xnb) Hld up; 4l 6th ½way; lost plce & 12l 5th 12; hdwy 3 out; rdn & wknd 2 out*	15	3
	Jonno 14-1 T Lane *(xnb,orbs) Hld up; 3½l 5th ½way; mist 10; 8l 4th 12; wkng when mist 2 out*	2	4
	Fromrussiawithlove (12a, 4ow) 20-1 M Keel *2 handlers; nt jw; lost tch 5; 20l last ½way; t.o 11; pu 3 out*		P
143^{2}	No Pressure (IRE) (1ow) 3-1 D Harvey *Ld to 5; 2nd til mist & ur 11*		U
58^{P}	Southern Ha'i (5a) 16-1 T Ellis *(xnb) Pulled hrd; 2nd til ld 5; hdd & fell last*		F
	Tom's Gold 33-1 J Trice-Rolph *School in rr; lost tch 5; 15l 7th ½way; wl bhnd when pu 12*		P

OFFICIAL DISTANCES: 4*l*, 15*l* **TIME:** 5min 27.9s

292 Mixed Open, 12st — 16 ran

43^{4}	**PADDY FOR PADDY (IRE)** 11-8F **R Burton** *W ldrs; 5l 4th ½way; went 5l 3rd aft 15; stayed on wl to ld nr fin*		1
168^{1}	**Freedom Fighter** 3-1 **A Martin** *(orbof) Swtng; hld up; hdwy 8; 7l 5th ½way; ld 12-13; 2nd til ld 2 out; hdd nr fin*	½	2

48^{U}	**Watchyourback (NZ)**(vis,tt) 14-1 **S Gray** *Ld 2-3 & 6-8; 2nd/3rd til ld 13; hdd 2 out; no ex flat*	6	3
99^{1}	Sheila McKenzie (5a) 8-1 T Lane *Hld up; blun 7; 9l 7th ½way; jnd ldrs 13; 6l 5th & rdn 15; wknd 3 out*	15	4
	Crown And Cushion 16-1 J Owen *Ld to 2; ld 4-5 & 8-12; 5l 3rd 15; wknd qckly 3 out; fin tired*	6	5
31^{7}	Magical Approach (IRE) 40-1 T Phillips *(xnb,bf) Mist & lost tch 8; 17l 10th ½way; 16l 7th & no hdwy 13; wl bhnd 15*	8	6
124^{3}	Contingency(cp) 16-1 R Cope *Ld 3-4 & 5-6; 2nd/3rd til mist 11; 3l 5th 13; wknd & 10l 6th 15*	2	7
188^{3}	Paddies Boy (IRE) 10-1 Jack Young *Sn wl bhnd; t.o last 5*	runin	8
32^{8}	Lyphard's Fable (USA) 40-1 D England *(xnb) A wl bhnd; disp 35l 12th ½way; t.o 11*	3	9
	Aldington Charlie 40-1 C Sands *Lost tch 5; 35l 12th ½way; t.o 11; pu 15.*		P
187^{P}	Bold Statement(tt) 16-1 G Tawell *(xnb) A wl bhnd; 25l 11th ½way; t.o & pu 3 out*		P
90^{4}	Brockbuster(bl) 25-1 E Walker *(xnb) Chsd ldrs til lost plce 8; 12l 8th ½way; lost tch 12; t.o & pu 15*		P
229^{R}	Chadswell (IRE) 20-1 D Greenway *Nd; 13l 9th ½way; wl bhnd 12; t.o & pu 15*		P
	Fearless Bertie 40-1 N Pearce *Chsd ldrs; 7½l 6th ½way; wknd 11; wl bhnd when pu 13*		P
228^{P}	Lord Of The West (IRE) 40-1 W Puddifer *Sn wl bhnd; t.o 8; ur 15*		U
	Mr Max (IRE) 33-1 M Wall *Prom; 5th when fell 9*		F

OFFICIAL DISTANCES: ½l, 6l **TIME:** 6min 15.6s

293 Panacur/TBA PPORA Club Members Mares Maiden, 12st — 10 ran

	LEACHBROOK LADY (12a) 10-1 **G Phillips** *(bf) Sn prom; 2½l 3rd ½way; 3l 4th 15; hung lft frm 3 out; 3rd & btn when lft clr at last*		1
153^{2}	**Vivaldi Rose (IRE)** (5a) 4-1 **N Walker** *(xnb) Hld up; hdwy to ld 7; hdd aft 15; ev ch 2 out; stpd to nil; lft 2nd at last; fin v tired*	15	2
	Fun For Girls (12a, 4ow) 20-1 M Keel *Hld up; 8th when blun bad 5; wl bhnd when ref & ur 8*		r
	Hunca Munca (IRE) (12a) 5-1 T Lane *(xnb) 12s-5s; hld up; 5½l 7th ½way; w ldrs when fell 11*		F
142^{P}	Keith's Dream (12a) 20-1 G Tumelty *Prom; 3l 4th ½way; disp 2½l 3rd 13; 6l 5th & wkng when fell 15*		F
105^{3}	Lady Baronette (5a) 5-1 I Howe *Hld up; 5l 6th ½way; 3l 5th 13; went 2nd aft nxt; ld aft 15; 3l clr when rdr leapt over horses hd at last*		U
	Polly Flinders (5a) 9-2 R Cope *Ld; jmpd v slow 3; hdd 7; jmpd slow 8; 2nd til mist 14; jmpd slow 3 out; 3l 2nd & rdn when fell hvly last; down for sev mins*		F
	Siobhans Quinner (IRE) (5a) 9-4F D Phelan *2nd til lost plce & mist 7; 4l 5th ½way; 5l 6th 13; pu & dism 14*		P
	Stable Girl (5a) 16-1 H Fowler *A bhnd; 15l 8th ½way; t.o & pu aft 12*		P
	Wanna Be Bay (5a) 6-1 P York *Hld up; drpd to rr 5; t.o 9; pu 11*		P

OFFICIAL DISTANCE: 15l **TIME:** 6min 38.8s

294 Restricted, 12st — 17 ran

	MUSSEL BUOY (IRE) 10-1 **R Cope** *(xnb) A.p; 3l 4th ½way; went 2nd 10; ld 14; r.o wl*		1
191^{6}	**Stormy Pass** 25-1 **T Ellis** *Hld up; hdwy 8; 7l 6th ½way; went 2l 3rd 13 & 2nd aft 15; one pce 2 out*	4	2
	Daisy Fay (5a) 20-1 **J Owen** *Hld up; 11l 10th ½way; hdwy 12; 6½l 7th nxt; went 5l 3rd aft 3 out; wknd app last*	4	3
104^{1}	It's Missy Imp (12a) 5-1 A Martin *Hld up; mist 9; 12l 11th ½way; 8l 9th 13; hdwy 15; 3½l 5th nxt; one pce*	3	4
169^{4}	Viscount Bankes 8-1 James Tudor *(xnb) 12s-8s; lkd rough; pulled hrd; ld 2; mist 9; hdd 14; 2½l 4th 3 out; sn wknd*	6	5
191^{U}	Rommel 3-1F J Trice-Rolph *Hld up; 10l 9th ½way; 10l 10th 13; mist 14; 12l 9th 3 out; nvr able to chall*	4	6
36^{P}	Moscow's Return (IRE) 40-1 M Keel *2nd/3rd til wknd aft ev ch 3 out; mist 2 out*	½	7
	Tom Putt 10-1 N King *Lost plce 7; 14l 13th ½way; lost tch 12; hit 2 out*	2½	8
169^{P}	Cloak And Dagger 40-1 D Harvey *A wl bhnd; t.o 12; pu flat; lame*		P
	Cumberland Youth 40-1 T Messenger *A bhnd; 20l 15th ½way; t.o & pu 15*		P
149^{1}	Johnsair (IRE) 5-1 G Perkins *(xnb) Jnd ldrs 5; 4th when ur 7*		U

109P	Mister Bruce (IRE) 14-1 F Hutsby *2 handlers; mist 2; 13l 12th ½way; bhnd til pu 11*		P
154¹	Morph 9-2 P York *Hld up; 9l 8th ½way; hdwy to jn ldrs 11; 6l 6th 13; wknd 15; wl bhnd when pu last*		P
	Sutton Lighter 40-1 S Gray *Tde; ld to 2; 2nd to 10; wkng rap when blun 11; wl bhnd when pu 12*		P
169F	Teeton Glaive (5a) 12-1 Miss H Irving *Hld up; 8l 7th ½way; hdwy 11; lost plce & 7½l 8th 13; 9l 8th 3 out; bhnd when fell last*		F
	Weallwayswillbeone (IRE) 7-1 J Sole *W ldrs; 6l 5th ½way; 6l 7th 3 out; sn wknd; wl bhnd when pu last*		P
	Wood Buzzard 40-1 D Phelan *(xnb) A bhnd; 15l 14th ½way; pu 12*		P

OFFICIAL DISTANCES: 3*l*, 5*l* **TIME:** 6min 18.5s

295 Open Maiden (Div 1), 12st - 17J — 10 ran

	RIGHTUN 33-1 **T Ellis** *(xnb) Pulled hrd; ld to 6 & 7-10; 2nd til ld agn aft 15; stayed on wl*		1
	Sword Fighter 5-1 **P York** *Hld up; 7l 5th ½way; went 4l 3rd 11 & 2nd app 2 out; one pce*	5	2
226²	**Arctic Summer (IRE)** 6-4F **J Trice-Rolph** *2s-6/4; hld up; hdwy & disp 6l 3rd ½way; lost plce 13; rallied 15; disp 3l 3rd nxt; rdn 2 out; wkng when blun last*	4	3
203F	Jeune Premier (FR) 6-1 G Perkins *Hld up & bhnd; 15l 7th ½way; hdwy 11; jnd ldrs 13; went 2nd aft 15; 4th & wkng when blun 2 out*	6	4
52F	North Pass 10-1 H Dowty *Blun 4; mist 7; 2nd/3rd til mist 11; 5l 4th 13; wknd 14; wl bhnd when mist 2 out*	20	5
130³	Igloux Royal (FR) 9-2 M Smith *Went 2nd 2; ld 6-7; hit 8; ld 10 til hdd & wknd qckly aft 15*	4	6
173P	Chicago's Padre 9-2 P Cowley *Hld up; 12l 6th ½way; hdwy 11; 7½l 7th 13; wknd 14; wl bhnd when pu 3 out*		P
129F	Faircatcher 16-1 E Linehan *Ss; a wl bhnd; t.o & pu 14*		P
	Master Jay Jay (IRE) 8-1 M Keel *Bhnd til pu aft 10*		P
	Mister Sooty 7-1 Miss E Harbour *6th when fell 4; dead*		F

OFFICIAL DISTANCES: 6*l*, 3*l* **TIME:** 6min 30.9s

Fence 12 omitted - fallen horse and rider

296 Open Maiden (Div 2), 12st - 15J — 8 ran

	GREET YOU WELL 9-4 **R Cope** *Ld til aft 4; ld 6; rdn 2 out; kpt on wl*		1
112³	**Nickit (IRE)** 7-4F **S Morris** *(xnb,pricker n/s) 9/4-7/4; nt jw; hld up; 3½l 5th ½way; 5l 4th & rdn 15; went 2nd aft 2 out; kpt on u.p*	2½	2
113³	**Northsprite**(cp) 8-1 **J Trice-Rolph** *(xnb) 2 handlers; hld up; hit 3; last to 9; went 3l 4th ½way; lost plce 13; 10l last 15; stayed on frm 2 out; nt rch ldrs*	2	3
129⁴	Penlet Too 8-1 T Ellis *(xnb) Ld aft 4-5; 2nd/3rd til outpcd aft 3 out; stayed on flat*	¾	4
173²	Kalypso De Laugere (FR) 3-1 H Fowler *Hld up; hdwy & 2l 3rd ½way; went 2nd 13 til mist & rmdrs nxt; 2l 2nd agn 3 out; rdn & ev ch 2 out; no ex flat*	nk	5
139P	Ruling The Roast 8-1 G Tumelty *Hld up; 4l 6th ½way; hdwy 11; 4l 5th 13; w ldrs til wknd 3 out; eased when btn*	15	6
	Northern Prince 16-1 Miss C Allen *Sn prom; ld 5-6; w ldr when fell 8*		F
	Patum Peperium (7a) 10-1 T Lane *Hld up; mist 7; 5l last ½way; blun bad & lost tch 11; wl bhnd when pu 14*		P

OFFICIAL DISTANCES: 3*l*, 1*l* **TIME:** 6min 23.0s

Fences 2, 10 & 18 omitted - low sun

Burton

Market Rasen (LH 7F,18J)

Sun, 22 Feb (GOOD to FIRM, FIRM in places)

297 Hunt Members, 12st — 4 ran

	ABABOU (FR) (7x) 2-7F **S Charlton** *Ld 8; drew wl clr app 14; canter*		1
	Mister Rose (IRE)(tt) 6-1 **O Williams** *Set stdy pce to 8; chsd wnr aft; jmpd slow 11; no ch frm 14; v tired frm 3 out*	1½fs	2

60^{4}	Miss Danbys (5a) 16-1 S Walker *(xnb) Hld up; lft 12l 3rd 9; fell 11*		F
54^{2}	Near And Phar (IRE) (5a) 5-1 Miss S Buckley *(xnb) 6l 3rd when fell 10.*		F

OFFICIAL DISTANCE: dist **TIME:** 6min 41.0s

The rider of Near And Phar was fined £50 for being unable to produce her Medical Record Book

298 Confined, 12st — 9 ran

	THE NOBLEMAN (USA) 20-1 **N Docker** *Ld to 6 & 8-12 & agn app 14; made rest; hrd prsd frm 2 out; stayed on wl u.p flat.*		1
57^{1}	**Noble Affair** (5a) 6-4F **M Mackley** *3s-6/4; ww in rr of main group; prog 10; went 3rd 14; rdn to chall app last; no ex flat*	2½	2
55^{4}	**Springlea Tower** (3x) 6-1 **R Hunnisett** *Prsd ldrs; ld 6-8 & 12 til app 14; rallied & ev ch 2 out; one pce*	2	3
177^{P}	Saxon Victory (USA) (3x)(vis) 8-1 R Armson *Chsd ldrs; 6l 3rd & rdn app 14; sn outpcd; t.o frm 2 out.*	fence	4
107^{F}	Folliday (FR) 20-1 R Wakeham *2 handlers; mid-div; mists 3 & 7; lft 4th 13; wknd 15; t.o*	8	5
	Bowfell (5a) 40-1 G Brewer *Stdd start & lost 30l; a wl bhnd til pu 14.*		P
106^{4}	Minella Hotel (IRE) (3x) 7-2 J Docker *(xnb) Rr; mist & rmdrs 5; 12l 7th & rdn 10; no prog wl bhnd when pu 15*		P
	Rio's Lord (IRE) (3x)(bl,tt) 7-2 R Collinson *Oht; chsd ldrs; mist 4; 5th & wl in tch when pu & dism 13.*		P
	Valentines Vision 40-1 O Williams *Stdd start & lost 40l; hvly rstrnd; t.o til fell 5*		F

OFFICIAL DISTANCES: 3*l*, 2*l* **TIME:** 6min 28.0s

299 Ladies Open — 8 ran

122^{P}	**SUPREME SILENCE (IRE)** 33-1 **Miss Rachel Clark** *Jw; ld app 7; made rest; 5l clr 12; just hdd 2 out; ld agn app last; r.o wl*		1
55^{1}	**Ridgeway (IRE)**(cp) 4-5F **Miss J Foster** *(xnb) Ld to 2 & 4-5; mist 7; chsd ldr 13; just ld 2 out; hdd app last; unable to qckn flat*	1½	2
	Ardmayle (IRE) 5-2 **Miss L Coney** *Ww bhnd; 10l 6th 10; prog 12; went 3rd app 14; outpcd 15; lft 12l 3rd nxt; kpt on.*	8	3
	Master Adam (IRE) 20-1 Miss K Edminson *Ld 2-4; lost plce nxt; 6th & no ch 15; lft 4th aft 2 out*	20	4
	Anneka Louise (5a) 14-1 Miss L Allan *Chsd ldrs; 15l 4th & wkng app 14; wl btn when blun bad 2 out; pu aft.*		P
110^{2}	River Ness (5a) 8-1 Mrs V Thirlby *Chsd ldrs; 3rd when ur 13.*		U
	Sheskinqueen (IRE) (5a) 33-1 Miss A Wells *Bhnd til dashed up to ld 5-6; chsd ldrs til mist 12; pu nxt*		P
162^{1}	Silver Groom (IRE) 11-4 Miss J Coward *Bhnd; 14l last 10; prog 13; 10l 3rd & staying on when ur 3 out.*		U

OFFICIAL DISTANCES: 1*l*, 7*l* **TIME:** 6min 22.0s

300 Land Rover Mens Open, 12st — 7 ran

	OH HIGHLY LIKELY (IRE) (7x) 4-1 **N Kent** *Lft in 5-12; ld agn 15; hdd last; stayed on wl to ld agn last 100yds*		1
	Rigadoon (IRE) (7x)(cp) 16-1 **J Haley** *(xnb) Trckd ldrs; ld 12 til mist & hdd 15; just ld agn last; hdd & no ex final 100yds*	¾	2
56^{2}	**Red Rebel** (7x) 4-9F **J Docker** *Ld to 4; lft 2nd nxt; nt fluent 12 & sn pushed along; 3l 4th & hrd rdn 14; 3rd & btn 2 out.*	12	3
	Trouvaille (IRE) 12-1 M Mackley *Ww in tch; prog & cl 3rd 14; wkng when mist 3 out*	20	4
155^{P}	Thurles Pickpocket (IRE) 14-1 B Elson *In tch to 8; 5th & no ch 10; t.o*	15	5
160^{2}	Stormy Sunrise (IRE) (14ow) 14-1 P Hodgson *Pulling; ld 2; jnd 4; rn out nxt*		R
	Strong Chairman (IRE) 6-1 K O'Brien *Bhnd when mist 7; pu app nxt w rdr lkng down; circled & cont; hopeless t.o when pu 11*		P

OFFICIAL DISTANCES: 1*l*, 10*l* **TIME:** 6min 34.0s

301 Restricted, 12st — 8 ran

164^{3}	**CLAIRE'S NOMAD**(cp) 5-1 **Miss Rachel Clark** *(xnb) Chsd ldrs; went 2nd 7; lft in ld 8; hdd 3 out; ld agn nxt; hld on game flat.*		1
231^{P}	**Jubileeman (IRE)** 14-1 **Miss H Phizacklea** *Chsd ldrs; lft 2nd 8; 4l 3rd 2 out; chsd wnr frm 2 out; ev ch last; kpt on*	nk	2

Schoolhouse Walk 11-4 **M Manton** *Blun 1; chsd ldrs; slt ld 3 out; just hdd when blun bad nxt; nt rec; dem app last* . . . 10 3

110^{7} Energy Man 25-1 M Bennison *A rr group; 14l 5th 12; 4th & wl btn when blun 3 out* . . . 10 4

175^{12} Gabaka De Thaix (FR) 14-1 M Caldwell *2 handlers; mists; rr group; 15l last when blun 12; no ch aft* . . . 12 5

Fiesty Frosty (IRE) (5a) 7-1 J Docker *Mid-div; 12l 4th & rdn 12; lost tch app 14; t.o & pu 2 out* . . . P

54^{3} Its-On-The-Cards (IRE) 9-2 A Sansome *Ld; 7l clr til pu & dism app 8; dead* P

60^{1} Newgate Wells (IRE) 5-2F N Kent *Opened 5s; ld in start & lost 20l; rr; in tch when mist 7; pu app 9; dead* . . . P

OFFICIAL DISTANCES: 1/2l, 5l **TIME:** 6min 32.0s

302 Open Maiden (Div 1), 12st — 7 ran

165^{F} **HIGH PEAK** 4-6F **T Greenall** *5/4-4/6; tk keen hld; trckd ldrs; ld 11-15; ld agn nxt; 1l up when lft wl clr 2 out* . . . 1

Mother's Ruin 11-2 **S Charlton** *(xnb) In tch; 5l 4th when blun 12; mist nxt; outpcd 14; lft poor 2nd 2 out* . . . fence 2

112^{P} **Lord Jurado (IRE)**(tt) 33-1 **O Williams** *Pulling; ld app 7-11; wknd qckly app 14; lft poor 3rd 3 out; nursed home* . . . 1 1/2fs 3

Earl Token 12-1 R Armson *Ww; prog to chse ldr 10; ld 15-nxt; 1l 2nd when fell 2 out* . . . F

Runningwiththemoon(cp) 9-2 M Briggs *Ld at stdy pce til app 7; lost plce qckly aft 10; blun bad 11; pu 12* . . . P

95^{P} Satanas (FR) 7-1 S Joynes *Rr; 10l 5th & rdn 13; sn lost tch; pu nxt* . . . P

Twinkle Toe Titch (IRE) (12a) 16-1 A Pennock *Last when jmpd slow 2; rn out 5* R

OFFICIAL DISTANCES: dist, dist **TIME:** 6min 42.0s

Prince Mouse (rdr inj in prev rce) was withdrawn not under orders

303 Open Maiden (Div 2), 12st — 8 ran

GLENSAN (IRE) 2-1 **G Brewer** *6s-2s; pulled to ld 2; made rest; lft 10l clr 14; unchall aft* . . . 1

111^{4} **Tommy Hotspur (IRE)**(bl) 7-4F **N Docker** *Ld to 2; chsd ldrs; hmpd by loose horse app 11; lft 10l 2nd 14; 5l down when mist 3 out; btn app last* . . 8 2

112^{P} Claude (IRE) 8-1 M Briggs *Rr; mist 6; lost tch 13; 20l 4th nxt; lft 3rd 3 out; v tired when pu 2 out* . . . P

95^{P} Lord Castle (IRE)(cp) 7-1 Miss H Lewis *Blun & ur 1* . . . U

Mr Buckle (IRE) (7a) 12-1 N Pettitt *Chsd ldr 3 til rn out & ur 5* . . . R

Quel Regal (FR) 10-1 Miss Rachel Clark *(xnb) Lft 2nd 5; blun 10; 1l 2nd when fell 14* . . . F

130^{F} Sneeze (5a) 9-2 R Stearn *Ww; 12l last & rdn 12; sn lost tch; pu 14* . . . P

Snizort (USA) 10-1 D Thomas *(xnb) Blun & ur 3* . . . U

OFFICIAL DISTANCE: 8l **TIME:** 6min 43.0s

304 Open Maiden (Div 3), 12st - 15J — 12 ran

166^{P} **EASTERN ROYAL** (7a) 16-1 **M Briggs** *Chsd ldrs; ld 9; 6l clr 14; hld on wl flat* 1

167^{U} **High Fields** (7a) evensF **T Greenall** *Ww; jmpd slow 4; mist 12; lft 3rd nxt; went 6l 2nd 15; sn hrd rdn; kpt on; nt quite rch wnr* . . . 1 2

Orchestra's Boy (IRE) 2-1 **K Green** *Lw; prsd ldrs; 6l 2nd 14; wknd 3 out* . . 15 3

Aunt Gladys (IRE) (5a) 7-1 G Brewer *Unruly when mounted; ww; blun 12; 12l 4th app 14; sn lost tch* . . . 12 4

Tuftex King 16-1 A Pennock *2 handlers; mid-div; prog 10; 12l 3rd when blun 13; sn lost tch; no ch frm 14; t.o* . . . fence 5

Firle Phantasy 12-1 J Haley *Chsd ldrs til wknd qckly 7; pu nxt* . . . P

92^{U} Gee A Two (IRE) 16-1 S Joynes *(xnb) Rr; lost tch 6; t.o & pu 9* . . . P

Ghali (USA) 20-1 T Parr *Sn detach in last; t.o when jmpd slow 5; pu 11* . . P

113^{4} It's Norman 10-1 M Mackley *Bhnd frm 11; t.o last when pu 14* . . . P

152^{P} Lancastrian Island (5a) 8-1 R Armson *Chsd ldng group til wknd 12; pu 14.* P

Pour Chi Pas (5a) 20-1 O Williams *Ref & ur 1* . . . r

The Doc 20-1 A Sansome *2 handlers; ld to 9; 3rd & wknd qckly 11; t.o 13; pu 14* . . . P

OFFICIAL DISTANCES: 1/2l, 5l **TIME:** 6min 41.0s

Fences 3, 10 & 17 were omitted - state of ground on landing side

East Cornwall

Great Trethew (RH 7F,19J)

Sun, 22 Feb (GOOD to FIRM)

305 Hunt Members, 12st — 4 ran

Form	Runner	Dist	Pos
	FOSSY BEAR (5a, 10x) 1-8F **Miss S Young** *Bit bckwd; made all at stdy pce; drew clr 2 out; unchall*		1
	Little Rosie (5a) 14-1 **Miss D Mitchell** *Chsd wnr; 3l 2nd til wknd 2 out*	10	2
	Heidi Moo (U) (5a) 10-1 **S Rogers** *Bckwd; cl 3rd & in tch til lost ground 16; t.o*	runin	3
	Grey Valley 8-1 R McCarthy *(rn as Cornish Mist) Lost tch 9; t.o & pu 12*		P

OFFICIAL DISTANCES: 10*l*, dist **TIME:** 6min 47.0s

306 Open Maiden 56&7yo (Div 1), 2m4f, 12st - 16J — 8 ran

Form	Runner	Dist	Pos
142F	**GEORGES PLEASURE** (5a) 5-1 **L Heard** *Bit bckwd; hld up in tch; 7l 3rd 12; tk ld app 3 out; sn in comm; comf*		1
	Abseal 7-1 **A Charles-Jones** *(xnb) Bckwd; 5th ½way; 20l 4th 12; stayed on to tk 2nd app last*	8	2
	Nditlir (12a) 4-1 **C Heard** *Opened 8s; tk keen hld; ld til app 3 out; no ex app nxt; releg 3rd when tired & blun last*	10	3
194P	Joli Christmas 3-1JF R Woollacott *Lw; handy; cl 3rd & gng wl 11; cl 2nd 13; difficult to steer, rn v wide bend bef 3 out & lost tch; nt rec*	15	4
	Hooray Henry (7a) 3-1JF Miss P Gundry *Jmpd novicey; 4th & just in tch ½way; wknd aft 13; bhnd when pu last*		P
	Rock Dancer 12-1 M Sweetland *Bit bckwd; rr; slt mist 4; bhnd frm 7 til pu 11; school*		P
	Sandy's Way (12a) 14-1 I Hambley *Bhnd frm 7 til pu 9; school*		P
1724	Stalbridge Rose (5a) 7-2 N McDiarmid *Lw; fell 1*		F

OFFICIAL DISTANCES: 5*l*, 5*l* **TIME:** 5min 20.0s

307 Open Maiden 56&7yo (Div 2), 2m4f, 12st - 16J — 8 ran

Form	Runner	Dist	Pos
	SPOT THE BUSINESS 6-4F **Miss P Gundry** *(xnb) Tchd 2s; lw; ur padd; pulled hrd & sn prom; 3l 2nd 7; ld 9; made rest; 2l up 3 out; kpt on wl und str press frm nxt; all out*		1
1945	**Gunners Mistake** 8-1 **C Heard** *Ld to 3; 4th ½way; 8l 3rd 11; outpcd nxt; 17l 3rd 3 out; jmpd lft nxt; fin str to tk 2nd cl home*	1½	2
195P	**Four In Hand** (5a) 4-1 **D Edwards** *10s-4s; hdwy 9; 3l 2nd & gng wl 11; sust eff frm 3 out; drvn to cl 2 out; blun bad last; tired & dem cl home*	2	3
	Pharshu (IRE) (5a) 7-1 J Snowden *Rr; some hdwy to 12l 4th 11; jmpd violent lft 12; t.o frm 3 out*	20	4
	Baldhu Mynah (7a) 33-1 Miss L Gardner *(bf) Bckwd; towards rr; bhnd frm 8 til pu 11; school.*		P
12U	Jd Trout (12a) 16-1 R Woollacott *Prog to 5th 6; in tch in 5th 9; wknd; btn 6th when pu 12; school*		P
133	Kings Command 2-1 A Michael *Opened 4s in plce; ld 3-8; 5l 2nd 9; sn wknd; bhnd when pu 11*		P
	Wendys Dynamo 25-1 M Munrowd *(xnb) Midfield; 6th ½way; lost tch frm 9; pu 11*		P

OFFICIAL DISTANCES: 2*l*, 1*l* **TIME:** 5min 21.0s

308 Open Maiden 56&7yo (Div 3), 2m4f, 12st - 16J — 7 ran

Form	Runner	Dist	Pos
	TOUCH OF FLAME (7a) 6-1 **M Miller** *(xnb) Prom; cl 3rd 9; ld 12; stayed on wl; promising*		1
1195	**Sound Sense** 14-1 **J Young** *Hld up in tch; hdwy to ld brief 11; hdd nxt; cl 3rd 3 out; ev ch when lft clr 2nd nxt; mist last.*	1½	2
	Ebony Jack (IRE) evensF **G Barfoot-Saunt** *Tchd 5/4; lw; sn prom; cl 3rd 8-11; lost tch 13; stayed on agn clsng stages; fin str*	1½	3
823	Jemannette (5a) 11-4 T Dennis *Disp ld til ld 3-10; wknd; btn 5th 3 out; no ch*	6	4
	Bucket Awl (IRE) (7a) 10-1 R Woollacott *Mist 1; in tch; cl 4th ½way; prog 12; chall frm 3 out; disp 2nd & ev ch when fell 2 out; winded bad; promising*		F
	Elegant Apple (5a) 12-1 A Glassonbury *Bckwd; sn rr; rdn 8; t.o & pu 11; school*		P
82P	Whats Up Maid (5a) 12-1 M Munrowd *(xnb) 6th & just in tch 9; wknd nxt; bhnd when pu 3 out*		P

OFFICIAL DISTANCES: 1*l*, 1*l* **TIME:** 5min 21.0s

309 Open Maiden 56&7yo (Div 4), 2m4f, 12st - 16J — 8 ran

61U **STONE VALLEY** 7-1 **A Charles-Jones** *Hdwy to 4th 7; went 2nd 13; 2l 2nd 3 out; ld app nxt; sn drew clr; easily* . . . 1
Simply Bruno 11-4F **R Woollacott** *(xnb) 4s-11/4; bit bckwd; hld up in rr; prog 13; 5th 3 out; stayed on str; lft 2nd at last; promising* . . . 8 2
Retorrick Rose (5a) 9-1 **A Glassonbury** *Bit bckwd; hit 1; mists; midfield; 6th 9; some hdwy aft 13; 4th & no ch aft 3 out; lft 3rd at last* . . . 5 3
76P Got Alot On (USA) 4-1 G Barfoot-Saunt *(xnb) Bit bckwd; ld/disp 3-11; lost plce 13; bhnd frm 3 out* . . . 6 4
Cadravel (7a) 6-1 D Edwards *Lw; ld & blun 2; cl up; cl 3rd 9; ld 12 til rdn & hdd aft 3 out; 8l 2nd when fell last* . . . F
Indian Renegade (IRE) (5a) 6-1 D McKenna *Lw; last 7; bhnd frm 10 til pu 2 out* P
Merlin Meg (12a) 9-1 W Biddick *Prom; 3rd 4; disp ld 9; cl 2nd when blun bad & ur 11* . . . U
197r Young Harry(bl) 6-1 T Dennis *Lw; prom when blun 4; jmpd lft nxt; 5th 9; hung lft & reluct when pu 12* . . . P

OFFICIAL DISTANCES: 2*l*, 1*l* **TIME:** 5min 29.0s

310 Land Rover Mens Open, 12st — 9 ran

198[1] **ONEMINUTETOFIVE** 1-2F **A Farrant** *(xnb,ringbit) 4/6-1/2; lw; trckd ldr til ld 12; qcknd 16; 20l clr 3 out; v easily; impressive* . . . 1
Shobrooke Mill 5-1 **A Charles-Jones** *Hld up in tch; cl 4th 11; 10l 3rd 14; went 2nd aft 3 out; nt pce of wnr; stayed on wl; gd seasonal debut* . . . runin 2
Bouchasson (FR) (7x) 7-1 H Froud *Towards rr; 7th 8; strugg 12; bhnd & pu 14* P
Destin D'Estruval (FR) 20-1 I Hambley *Tchd 25s; 5th ½way; in tch to 13; wknd; poor 4th when pu 16* . . . P
200F Itworked 25-1 A Glassonbury *Sn prom; cl 3rd 10; cl 2nd & gng wl 14; outpcd nxt; 3rd & no ch frm 3 out; 20l 3rd & tired when fell last; winded; fair eff* F
196P Lead Story (IRE) 16-1 R Woollacott *Slt ld to 12; wknd; btn 4th when pu 15* P
115P Minderoo 12-1 D McKenna *(xnb) Tchd 20s; lw; sn rr; nt a fluent; poor 7th when pu 13* . . . P
196P Procedure (USA) 20-1 M Miller *Ch ride; midfield; 6th 12; nd; bhnd when pu 14* . . . P
Young General 33-1 Richard Darke *Sn lost gd early plce; last frm 7; bhnd when pu 13* . . . P

OFFICIAL DISTANCE: 15*l* **TIME:** 6min 17.0s

311 Ladies Open — 9 ran

171[1] **MISTER BENJAMIN (IRE)** 2-9F **Miss C Roddick** *Opened 1/4; lw; hld up; prog 8; 6th 11; gd hdwy to ld 15; qcknd 10l clr 3 out; unchall* . . . 1
199U **Guru Rinpoche** 16-1 **Miss L Gardner** *(bf) In tch; cl 4th 11; 5th 3 out; r.o to tk 2nd app 2 out; no ch w wnr* . . . 20 2
Lirsleftover 12-1 **Miss S Young** *Prom frm 5; slt ld 8-15; sn outpcd by wnr; 5th aft 3 out; no ch aft; snatched 3rd cl home* . . . 2 3
Just Bert (IRE) 12-1 Miss T Cave *Tchd 14s; hdwy 11; cl 4th 14; disp 10l 2nd 3 out; no ch w wnr; lost 3rd nr post* . . . ½ 4
76[3] It'snotsimple (IRE) (5a) 16-1 Mrs T Trickey *(xnb) Ld to 3; prom; cl 2nd ½way; lost plce aft 13; btn 6th 3 out; one pce* . . . 3 5
Defendtherealm 20-1 Miss A Mills *1st ride; a rr; jmpd safely; bhnd frm ½way* 6 6
199[5] Sandy Duff 14-1 Miss M McCarthy *Prog to 5th 8; jnd ldrs 11; cl 3rd to 15; wknd frm 3 out; lks non-stayer* . . . ½ 7
199[6] Polar King (IRE) 33-1 Miss W Southcombe *Ld aft 3-7; sn lost plce; 8th 15; poor 6th 3 out; fell nxt; rdr concussed & airlifted* . . . F
Roseta (IRE) 25-1 Miss V Shaw *Prom; cl 4th 7; lost plce 11; bhnd when fell hvly 14; rdr suffered back injury* . . . F

OFFICIAL DISTANCES: 10*l*, ½*l* **TIME:** 6min 06.0s

312 Confined Maiden 8yo&up, 12st — 12 ran

194P **COMMANCHE SUMMER** (5a) 15-2 **A Glassonbury** *Mounted on course; hld up in midfield; hdwy to 5th & gng wl 14; went 5l 3rd 16; chall 2 out; hrd rdn & stayed on game to ld on line; fin lame* . . . 1
119[6] **Cappa Hill (IRE)** 20-1 **R Woollacott** *Lw; midfield; prog to 3rd 9; ld/disp frm 14; battled bet horses to slt ld 2 out-last; edged lft flat; hdd on post* . . . hd 2

83^{2}	**O'ech** (5a) 11-4 **C Heard** *Tchd 3s; bckwd; prom frm 7; cl 4th 11; disp ld frm 13; ev ch app 2 out; wknd app last*	4	3
	Jaunty Janner 50-1 T Dennis *Sn prom; 2nd 9-11; lost tch w ldrs 14; kpt on*	6	4
120^{P}	Black A Brook (IRE) (5a) 20-1 R McCarthy *Bit bckwd; a towards rr; bhnd frm 14; t.o*	runin	5
82^{P}	Baldhu Bendy (5a) 50-1 Miss L Gardner *Rr frm 7; bhnd frm 13 til pu 3 out*		P
83^{P}	Buddy Bear (IRE) 25-1 G Barfoot-Saunt *Bit bckwd; ld 1; prom to 11; lost ground frm 13; bhnd 15 til pu 2 out*		P
195^{P}	Cargo Flight 7-4F A Farrant *(xnb) 5/2-7/4; lw; hld up in rr; prog 11; went 3rd 14; sn wknd; btn 4th 3 out; t.o & pu last; disapp*		P
194^{P}	Master Of Fashion(bl) 20-1 L Heard *Made most to 13; sn wknd; 7th when pu 15*		P
	Paddy's Glory 14-1 L Rowe *Bckwd; nt fluent; just in tch ½way; lost ground & blun bad 14; t.o & pu 16.*		P
	Small-Lir (5a) 20-1 Miss S Young *(b4) Bhnd frm 7 til pu 11*		P
195^{U}	Vero Beach(vis) 4-1 A Charles-Jones *8s-4s; prom early; 7th ½way; sn strugg; t.o & pu 3 out*		P

OFFICIAL DISTANCES: hd, 3*l* **TIME:** 6min 30.0s

Just Aretha (Miss P Gundry, 12-1 - bolted & ur before start) was withdrawn not under orders; Rule 4 deduction 5p in pound

313 Intermediate, 12st — 3 ran

148^{1}	**CANTERBURY JACK (IRE)**(bl) 6-4F **A Farrant** *Hld up; cl last til went 2nd 15; rdn to chall aft 3 out; drvn to ld app last; sn clr*		1
	Teninarow (IRE) 7-4 **Richard Darke** *Tchd 2s; ch ride; lw; set stdy pce in 2l ld til hdd app last; no ex*	2½	2
118^{1}	**Little Native (IRE)** 7-4 **Miss P Gundry** *2 handlers; trckd ldr to 15; cl 3rd & ev ch 3 out; hung lft & nt qckn app 2 out; eased*	6	3

OFFICIAL DISTANCES: 2*l*, 5*l* **TIME:** 6min 28.0s

314 Restricted (Div 1), 12st — 10 ran

68^{1}	**CIMMAROON (IRE)** (7a) 6-4F **A Farrant** *(xnb) In tch; cl 3rd 12; ld 15; drvn frm 3 out; 2l up at last; hld on game.*		1
148^{F}	**Bishop's Blade** 7-4 **Miss S Gaisford** *(xnb) Cl 4th & gng wl 11; hdwy to 4l 2nd 16; sust chall frm 3 out; fin wl; nt quite get up*	s hd	2
79^{5}	**Panto Pixie** (5a) 12-1 **Miss T Cave** *Towards rr; 8th 10; still 8th & wl off pce 14; stayed on past btn horses; tk 3rd cl home*	runin	3
118^{P}	Horrified(bl) 20-1 D Edwards *Sn prom; ld 5-15; sn one pce & 15l 3rd 3 out; dem flat*	2	4
148^{P}	Elegant Light (5a) 20-1 M Munrowd *Midfield; 7th ½way; went poor 4th 15; 40l 4th & no ch 3 out*	1½	5
79^{6}	Lingering Fog (IRE) 20-1 Miss M McCarthy *Sn prom; slt ld 2-4; in tch til rdn & wknd 12; bhnd frm 15*	8	6
79^{3}	Beachtime 4-1 N Mitchell *(xnb) 8s-4s; sn rr; 9th ½way; no prog; wl bhnd 14; t.o*	1	7
139^{P}	Sweet Kari (IRE) 33-1 G Weatherley *6th 10; just in tch to 13; sn wknd & poor 5th 15; no ch*	1	8
87^{4}	Roseacre (IRE) 5-1 Miss P Gundry *Tchd 7s; sn last & a strugg; t.o 14*	15	9
76^{P}	Mister Cone 10-1 I Hambley *(xnb) Mist 4; prom til rdn 12; poor 4th 14; bhnd 16 til pu last*		P

OFFICIAL DISTANCES: nk, 4*l* **TIME:** 6min 19.0s

315 Restricted (Div 2), 12st — 5 ran

79^{2}	**JUST SALLY** (5a) 6-4 **A Farrant** *(xnb) Ld/disp frm 9; forged clr frm 14; 4l up 3 out; kpt on wl u.p; drvn out*		1
	Butler Didit (5a) 6-1 **Miss T Cave** *(bf) Ld/disp to 13; prom til chsd ldr frm 3 out; 4l 2nd nxt; stayed on*	2	2
150^{1}	**Ballyknock Rose (IRE)** (5a) evensF **Richard Darke** *Ch ride; lw; prom; disp ld 7-11; cl 2nd when slt mist 14; hit 16; 12l 3rd 3 out; no ch w ldrs; eased flat*	12	3
	Handstand 7-1 M Sweetland *Lw; chsd ldrs in 4th mostly; just in tch til rdn 14; no hdwy; 20l 4th 3 out*	5	4
150^{4}	Beaford Princess (5a) 16-1 J Young *Prom to 5; last & stdly lost tch frm 8; bhnd when jmpd slow 14; t.o*	2fncs	5

OFFICIAL DISTANCES: 2*l*, 5*l* **TIME:** 6min 26.0s

Sedgefield (LH 8F,14J)

Tue, 24 Feb (GOOD to SOFT, SOFT in places)

316 John Smith's Extra Smooth Nov HC, 2m5f £1514 14 ran

	TOR HEAD 11-09 8-1 **C Mulhall** *A cl up; went 2nd/3rd frm 9; outpcd by ldng pr 3 out; lft poor 2nd nxt; stayed on to 9l 2nd; v flatt by prox; subsq awarded rce*		1
	Scottish Roots 11-11 7-1 **T Greenall** *W ldr 1; stdd in midfield; 6th & drvn & outpcd 3 out; plugged into 3rd at last; no ch w wnr; fin 3rd; subsq promoted*	4	2
163F	**Glacial Dancer (IRE)** 11-07 20-1 **R Clark** *Hld up; prog 8; disp 3rd but drvn & outpcd 3 out; lft w ev ch of 2nd nxt; wknd flat; fin 4th; subsq promoted*	7	3
1671	Miss Royello 11-06 12-1 D Jewett *Chsd ldrs til outpcd 11; 5th & btn nxt; hmpd 2 out; fin 5th; subsq promoted*	6	4
	Jupiter's Fancy 11-04 33-1 M McAlister *Prom; 5th 9; 7th & wkng qckly 3 out; fin 6th; subsq promoted*	1½	5
135U	Lord Edwards Army (IRE) 11-07 12-1 G Willoughby *Pulled hrd; rdr unstdy in rr; lost tch 9; fin 7th; subsq promoted*	1¼	6
	Orleans (IRE) 11-09 (2ow)(bl) 33-1 S J Robinson *Pulled v hrd in midfield; bumped along & wknd 10; fin 8th; subsq promoted*	nk	7
	The Preacher Man (IRE) 12-00 25-1 M Thompson *Rcd keen; ld to 7; wknd & mist 9; t.o; fin 9th; subsq promoted*	21	8
733	Raging Torrent 11-09 16-1 R Morgan *(xnb) Towards rr; rmdrs aft 6; mist 7; lost tch 9; t.o; fin 10th; subsq promoted*	½	9
1001	Omni Cosmo Touch (USA) 11-07 2-1F N Saville *Sltly reluct to set off; hld up in rr til smooth prog 7; prom nxt; w ldr & clr of rest 3 out til slt advant when lft w long ld nxt; sauntered home; won by 9l; subsq disq - tested positive*		1d
	Avenel 11-02 40-1 M Seston *Bhnd; rdn 7; sn strugg; blun 10; t.o & pu 11; lame*		P
	Enitsag (FR) 11-02 8-1 D Mansell *Sn prom; ld 7; nt fluent 9; drew clr w wnr 3 out; just hdd when fell nxt*		F
782	Parte Prima 11-07 11-2 R Woollacott *(xnb) Hld up in midfield; blun 7; stumbled bad, virt fell & ur 10*		U
	Thixendale 11-02 100-1 Miss J Foster *Mists; cl 2nd to 8; wknd rap aft nxt; t.o & pu 11*		P

TIME: 5min 37.5s **TOTE:** £2.50; places £1.60,£2.80,£2.80 **Ex:**£59.50 **CSF:**£17.51

Fences 6 & 14 omitted - damaged; the winner Omni Cosmo Touch was subsequently disqualified by the Jockey Club Disciplinary Committee for testing positive to felbinac, a prohibited substance; the owner (Mrs S. Smith) was fined £600

Ludlow (RH 8F,17J)

Wed, 25 Feb (GOOD, GOOD to FIRM in places)

317 Onny HC, 2m4f £2744 12 ran

1463	**PHOENIX PHLYER** 11-03(cp) 14-1 **Miss C Stucley** *Rcd keen; pulled to ld aft 4; drew 8l clr 13; kpt on str; unchall*		1
1795	**Guignol Du Cochet (FR)** 11-03 9-2 **S Hughes** *Off pce in midfield; 28l 4th 13; stayed on frm 3 out; went 2nd flat; no ch w wnr*	9	2
2419	**Hot Plunge** 11-05 25-1 **J Owen** *Pulled hrd; ld til aft 4; chsd wnr; hit 5; 20l clr of rest & rdn aft 13; no imp; nt fluent last; dem flat*	2½	3
77P	Sol Music 12-03 evensF L Jefford *Nt jw in 3rd/4th; lost tch w ldng pr & mist 10; 25l 3rd when mist 13; plugged on*	3½	4
209P	Justjim 11-03 50-1 M Barber *Mid-div; 5th & rdn & wl outpcd 11; no prog.*	6	5
89P	Arlequin De Sou (FR) 11-03(bl) 11-1 C Heard *Nvr btr than midfield; strugg 10*	5	6
	Silent Keys (SWE) 12-00(tt) 11-1 D Dunsdon *Imm lost tch; hopelessly t.o frm 5*	dist	7
	Chaparro Amargoso (IRE) 11-03 25-1 S Ross *Bhnd; mist 7; t.o 9; cont miles bhnd*	24	8
	Alpha Romana (IRE) 12-00 7-1 P Cowley *Nt fluent; chsd ldrs; mist 6; outpcd 9; 7th & eased 11; t.o & pu last*		P
93P	Nicholls Cross (IRE) 11-07 22-1 G Hanmer *Nt fluent 4; hld up & bhnd; mod 6th 11; crashing fall 12*		F

Form	Runner	Dist	Pos
208[P]	Rainbow Star (FR) 11-03(bl) 100-1 A Hanly *V reluct to line up; ref to rce .*		r
115[P]	Robins Pride (IRE) 11-05(bl) 100-1 Miss C Tizzard *A bhnd; rdn & lost tch app 10; t.o & pu 13*		P

TIME: 5min 00.0s **TOTE:** £17.10; places £2.90,£2.20,£4.40 **Ex:**£53.30 **CSF:**£74.25

The owner of Chaparro Amargoso, whose passport was found to be incorrect, was fined £110

East Devon

Bishops Court (LH 7F,19J)

Sat, 28 Feb (GOOD to SOFT becoming DEAD)

318 Hunt Members — 5 ran

Form	Runner	Dist	Pos
194[1]	**VIVID IMAGINATION (IRE)** (7a) 2-5F **A Farrant** *(xnb) Tchd 4/9; lw; made most to 5; ld agn 10; hit 13; dashed clr 16; hrd hld; impressive*		1
	Norlandic (NZ) 9-4 **L Jefford** *Tchd 5/2; bit bckwd; ld 5-12; prsd wnr til hopelessly outpcd 16 but wl clr of rest*	20	2
198[P]	**Lazy Lemon** (5a) 14-1 **Miss C Llewellin** *(xnb) Detach 4th til clsd brief 10; went 12l 3rd aft 12; 20l adrift & no ch 15*	12	3
62[P]	Eskimo Gold (5a) 33-1 M Sweetland *Ld brief 1 & agn when pckd 3; cl up til wknd 10; t.o 15*	runin	4
194[P]	Silver Kracker 66-1 M Woodward *(xnb) Jmpd slow in last; t.o 7; swishing tail & over fnce bhnd 11; pu aft 14*		P

OFFICIAL DISTANCES: 20*l*, 15*l* **TIME:** 6min 13.0s

319 Mens Open, 12st — 10 ran

Form	Runner	Dist	Pos
310[1]	**ONEMINUTETOFIVE** 2-1 **A Farrant** *(xnb) Lw; prom in 2nd/4th; went 2nd app 14; lkd 2nd best when lft clr 16; hvly eased flat*		1
236[F]	**Mouseski** (7x) 8-1 **N Williams** *(xnb) 12s-8s; trckd ldrs; cl 4th 13; lft 2nd 16; 10l down & rdn nxt; tired frm 2 out*	20	2
273[1]	**Cool Wager** 16-1 **D Edwards** *Handy in chsng group til 5th & outpcd 13; 30l 3rd 3 out*	20	3
196[5]	Bruthuinne (IRE) (7x) 50-1 D McKenna *(xnb) 2nd/3rd to 12; wknd rap 14; 42l 4th 3 out; t.o*	12	4
199[8]	Father Jim(bl) 66-1 L Heard *Lw; prom to 10; wkng u.p when mist 12; reluct aft; t.o & pu 16*		P
175[U]	Forest Jump (IRE) 75-1 R Lee *Bhnd & off pce; mod 9th when rfo 9*		U
235[P]	Lily Lane 120-1 R Coleridge *(xnb) Still fat; detach last; t.o 7; climbed 15 & pu*		P
	On His Toes 33-1 W White *2 handlers; towards rr & off pce; strugg 13; ur 16*		U
196[1]	Right To Reply (IRE) (7x) 4-6F N Harris *(xnb) Tchd 4/5; lw; settled off pce til smooth prog 10; sn prom; ld app 14; 4l up & gng str when pckd & ur 16*		U
188[2]	Tubber Roads (IRE) (7x)(bl) 33-1 J Owen *Ld til app 14; sn lost plce u.p & nt keen; t.o last 3 out; pu last*		P

OFFICIAL DISTANCES: 20*l*, 20*l* **TIME:** 6min 04.4s

320 Confined, 12st — 11 ran

Form	Runner	Dist	Pos
200[1]	**RONANS CHOICE (IRE)** (3x)(bl) 6-1 **Richard Darke** *Made all; prsd brief 3 out; sn 5l clr; r.o wl; comf*		1
235[F]	**Caspers Case** 5-2F **N Williams** *(xnb,bh) Tchd 3s; lw; trckd ldrs; hit 9; 9l 4th 10; chsd wnr frm 16; ch nxt; sn outpcd*	4	2
88[1]	**Sir D'Orton (FR)** (5x) 4-1 **Miss C Tizzard** *Tchd 9/2; chsd wnr to 7; 8l 3rd 10; rdn to 3l 3rd 3 out; imm outpcd*	8	3
193[1]	Leon Garcia (IRE) (5a) 9-2 T Bishop *Jmpd awkward in rr; stdy hdwy 11; 12l 5th 15; flatt brief 3 out; rdn & hanging lft aft*	5	4
200[4]	Midnight Coup(bl) 20-1 A Farrant *Prom; chsd wnr 7-16; drvn & nt r.o; 8l 5th & btn nxt*	15	5
89[P]	Touring-Turtle (IRE) 50-1 W Procter *(xnb) A bhnd; poor 7th 13; t.o 16.*	20	6
200[2]	Bill Me Up (IRE) (3x) 11-4 C Heard *Tchd 7/2; 2 handlers; cl up til hit 4 & ur*		U
	Boy Band (IRE) 50-1 C Dailly *1st ride; strugg in last pr; t.o when pckd 10; pu 12*		P
200[P]	Calleva Star (IRE) 50-1 S Kidston *Chsd ldrs til 15l 5th & wkng 12; t.o & pu 3 out*		P

232F Sixth Sense (IRE) 50-1 R Bliss *A last trio; t.o 9; pu 12* . . . . P
80³ Squaddie 50-1 L Heard *Prom brief; lsng plce when jmpd slow 6; t.o & pu 14* P

OFFICIAL DISTANCES: 4*l*, 5*l* **TIME:** 6min 09.8s

321 Intermediate, 12st 14 ran

232¹ **OUT THE BLACK (IRE)** evensF **J Snowden** *Tchd 6/4; settled trckng ldrs; went 4l 3rd app 15; chall 3 out; ld nxt; sn clr; impressive agn* 1
By My Side (IRE) 14-1 **A Charles-Jones** *Ld til app 15; rdn to ld agn 3 out-nxt; imm outpcd but a clr of rest* 8 2
200⁵ **Bak On Board** 25-1 **Miss L Gardner** *Hld up in midfield; went 3rd 13; outpcd 15; 12l 4th & u.p 3 out* 12 3
116⁵ Soul King (IRE) 33-1 R Bliss *Cl 3rd/4th til 5th 13; outpcd app 15; nd aft* . 1 4
Sherbourne Guest (IRE) 20-1 J Kwiatkowski *Trckd ldrs but rdr nvr in harmony w horse; handy til 8th & outpcd 13; plugged on* 6 5
193² Father Mansfield (IRE) 8-1 Miss C Prouse *12s-8s; nervously rdn & wl off pce in last quartet; strugg 7; kpt on; gvn no ch* 6 6
79¹ Simply Sam 5-1 N Williams *(xnb) Opened 7s in plce; went 2nd 4 til ld app 15; hdd 3 out; wknd rap; climbed last* 2 7
193⁷ Early Morning Call (IRE) 20-1 J Barnes *(xnb) A bhnd in last quartet; strugg 7; t.o 14; pu 3 out* . . . . P
193⁶ Happy Team (5a) 16-1 L Jefford *Midfield when mist 6; drpd back last & pu aft 7* P
Heisamodel (IRE) 7-1 M Miller *(xnb) Trckd ldrs; nt fluent 9; 5th when fell 10* F
141² Pendragon 8-1 N Mitchell *Last trio & nvr gng wl; lost tch 7; t.o 13; pu 16* . P
116P Sporting Chance 14-1 M Munrowd *20s-14s; last when jmpd slow 3; detach in final quartet to 10; 9th & just in tch 13; sn btn; t.o & pu 2 out* . . . . . . P
141³ Stennikov (IRE) 9-1 E Walker *(xnb) 20s-9s; midfield; 6th 13; outpcd app 15; 15l 5th 3 out; saddle slpd & ur bend bef 2 out* . . . . U
193⁴ Th'moons A Balloon (IRE) 8-1 S Partridge *12s-8s; midfield; 8l 7th 13; sn wknd; t.o & pu 3 out* . . . . P

OFFICIAL DISTANCES: 6*l*, 8*l* **TIME:** 6min 08.6s

322 Ladies Open 13 ran

234¹ **EASE THE PRESSURE (IRE)** 9-4 **Miss R Green** *Lw; settled trckng ldrs; eff 14; ld app 3 out; a gng str aft; comf* 1
234³ **Wink And Whisper** (5a) 16-1 **Miss E Tory** *Bhnd; stdy prog 11; cl up 15; disp 3l 3rd app 3 out; kpt on stdly to 2nd nr fin; nt rch wnr* 2 2
78⁴ **Beadnell Bay** 5-1 **Miss A Goschen** *Tchd 7s; ld to 4; 2nd til ld agn 9; rdn & hdd app 3 out; hit nxt; kpt on; no ch w wnr; dem nr fin* . . . . nk 3
Knight Of Passion 20-1 Miss C Tizzard *Slt ld 4-9; prom til disp 3l 3rd & drvn app 3 out; kpt on same pce* 5 4
88U Sadler's Realm 20-1 Miss L Gardner *Prom; prsd ldr 13-15; wknd nxt; 5th & btn 3 out* 12 5
311⁶ Defendtherealm 25-1 Miss A Mills *Sn midfield; strugg 11; t.o & pu 13* . . . P
Glenahary Rose (IRE) 40-1 Miss A Tory *(xnb) 1st ride; jmpd awkward in detach last & rdr v novicey; t.o 6; pu 11* . . . . P
234⁴ Jackson Hill(tt) 16-1 Miss T Cave *Handy; 5th & rdn 13; went 3rd brief nxt; nt r.o & lost tch 15; t.o & pu 2 out* . . . . P
146⁵ Let's Fly (FR) 25-1 Miss S Gaisford *A wl bhnd; strugg 5; t.o & pu 14* . . . . P
196P Major Belle (FR) (12a) 12-1 Miss L Bridges *Cl up; 3rd 13; wknd tame nxt; t.o & pu 3 out* . . . . P
253F Sailors Folly (IRE) evensF Miss P Gundry *(xnb) Tchd 6/5; prom; 3rd & ev ch 15; wknd nxt; mod 6th 3 out; pu last* . . . . P
Select Star (IRE)(cp,tt) 50-1 Miss J Congdon *Bhnd; nt fluent & nvr rcd keen; mist 6 & drvn; t.o 8; pu 13* . . . . P
Sparkling Missile (5a) 40-1 Miss S Robinson *Bhnd; jmpd slow 3; t.o 10; pu 12* P

OFFICIAL DISTANCES: 1*l*, 2*l* **TIME:** 6min 09.5s

323 Restricted (Div 1), 12st 15 ran

198³ **SEA SNIPE** (5a) 7-2 **Miss T Cave** *Handy; went 3rd 9; ld 16; drew clr rdly aft nxt; mist 2 out; nt prsd aft* 1
95² **Sutton Courtenay (IRE)** 4-1 **J Jenkins** *Hld up in midfield; 6th & eff 12; 6l 3rd 16; drvn & no imp aft; chsd wnr frm 2 out* 5 2
State Medlar 12-1 **R Woollacott** *20s-12s; prom; prsd ldr 5-13; 7l 4th 16; kpt on same pce* 1 3

197[4]	Baldara (IRE) 3-1F A Farrant *Tchd 7/2; prsd ldrs; 5th 12; eff to ld 15; blun nxt & hdd; ev ch til blun agn nxt & outpcd; wknd 2 out; climbed last*	15	4
148[P]	Socute (5a) 10-1 J Barnes *(xnb) Chsd ldrs; 7th 12; lost tch 15; 23l 5th aft 3 out*	1½	5
314[6]	Lingering Fog (IRE) 16-1 Miss M McCarthy *Rr of midfield; 11th & strugg 12; plodded on*	15	6
278[P]	Winning Leader (IRE) 10-1 R Skinner *Prom w v ungainly rdr forcing him into mists; wknd 9; 9th 12; t.o 3 out.*	15	7
197[P]	Persian Dawn (5a) 33-1 J Young *Wl bhnd; lost tch 9; 13th & t.o 12; wl t.o frm 16*	runin	8
273[U]	Ariann Sound (IRE) 20-1 R McCarthy *Nvr btr than midfield; 8th 12; wl bhnd when pu 16; broke down bad*		P
232[U]	Askers Jack 10-1 N Mitchell *Stdd start; jb in last; t.o 7; pu 14*		P
195[1]	Coombe Quest 7-1 T Dennis *(xnb) Lw; ld; blun bad 11; 7l clr nxt; hdd when blun & nrly ur 15; wkng when pu nxt.*		P
197[5]	Martby 6-1 M Atkinson *Chsd ldrs to 9; 10th & outpcd 12; pu 2 out*		P
279[P]	My Jess (5a) 10-1 M Sweetland *Jb; lost tch 5; t.o 7; pu 8.*		P
252[4]	Rushing Again 7-2 Miss P Gundry *Prsd ldrs; 4th 12; pu qckly & dism 14.*		P
	Wicked Imp 25-1 M Munrowd *A wl bhnd; 12th & t.o 12; pu 14*		P

OFFICIAL DISTANCES: 4*l*, 1*l* **TIME:** 6min 17.9s

324 Restricted (Div 2), 12st — 12 ran

279[4]	**RHYTHM KING** 11-4 **G Maundrell** *(xnb) Tchd 3s; mist 1; hdwy to go cl up 5; disp 2nd frm 9 til ld 16; 3l clr nxt; kpt on wl*		1
36[2]	**I Am Said I (IRE)** 4-5F **A Farrant** *Opened 6/4 in plce; ld 4-9 & app 14-16; 3l 2nd & drvn nxt; no ex; hit last*	1½	2
139[6]	**Withycombe**(vis) 50-1 **J Snowden** *Lw; midfield; 6th 9; lost plce tame 12; 45l 5th 3 out; lft 4th nxt & 3rd at last; drpd dead aft fin.*	runin	3
85[U]	Flora Macdonald (5a) 12-1 H Wallace *Jmpd slow & qckly lost tch; t.o 9; furlongs adrift 16*	20	4
198[5]	Baron Ridge(cp) 40-1 Richard Darke *Midfield; 7th & lsng tch 9; t.o 12; furlongs adrift 16*	10	5
	Aslapoftheeuro (IRE) 10-1 A Charles-Jones *(xnb) 2nd/4th til lost plce 9; strugg 12; wl bhnd when pu 14*		P
197[3]	Drumhorc (IRE) 10-1 Miss L Gardner *(xnb) Bhnd & nvr gng wl; poor 8th 9; t.o 12; pu 14*		P
200[P]	It's-The-Biz (IRE) 16-1 D Summersby *(xnb) Stdd start; detach last; t.o 9; pu 12*		P
	Pinmoor Hill 16-1 Miss S Robinson *Towards rr; strugg 9; t.o when mist 11; pu 12*		P
279[R]	River Dante (IRE) 10-1 Mrs O Jackson *(xnb) Settled 4/5th til 3rd & outpcd 15; 15l 3rd & v tired 3 out; unwisely cont; poor 3rd when crashing fall last; winded*		F
232[5]	Thunder Thighs (5a)(cp) 12-1 N Wilmington *(xnb) Tde; made most til app 14; wknd rap; 35l 4th 3 out; lkd v tired when fell 2 out; rdr cautioned for foul language*		F
	Tycoon Ted 16-1 R Woollacott *7th when fell 8*		F

OFFICIAL DISTANCES: 1*l*, dist **TIME:** 6min 18.0s

The rider of Thunder Thighs was officially cautioned for improper conduct (foul language after his mount had fallen - cf Pulham Downe Race 265)

325 Open Maiden (Div 1), 12st - 18J — 14 ran

	HEADWRECKER (IRE) 12-1 **G Maundrell** *Settled handy; ld 13; prsd but outj challenger 3 out; btr j agn nxt; in comm aft*		1
87[U]	**Wild Chimes (IRE)** (7a) 4-5F **N Williams** *5/4-4/5; lw; hvly rstrnd in last & tk keen hld; virt t.o 8; rap prog in 4th aft 11; mist 15; 8l 3rd nxt; clsd to chall & mist 2 out; drvn & ch when mist last; a hld aft*	3	2
	Nearly A Mildred (5a) 8-1 **Miss A Goschen** *(xnb) Made most 2-12; prsd wnr to 16; 7l 3rd & wkng nxt.*	20	3
172[P]	Will Shakespeare 11-1 Miss T Newman *Prom; ld aft 11-13; 4th & in tch when mist 15; no ex; 15l 4th 3 out.*	5	4
238[U]	Romany Move 10-1 Mrs S Godfrey *Sn bhnd; strugg 10; 30l 5th 3 out.*	10	5
306[F]	Stalbridge Rose (5a) 10-1 N McDiarmid *Nvr btr than midfield; strugg 13; plodded on*	6	6
	Early Rivers (12a) 16-1 Miss T Cave *Mist 1; detach 13th til crashed thro wing & ur 3.*		R

	Lipstick Lass (5a) 50-1 L Tibbatts *(xnb) Mists in rr; t.o 8; pu 13*		P
174^{P}	Little Mister 14-1 N Mitchell *(xnb) 2 handlers; bhnd; rdn 5; t.o 8; pu 14*		P
	Midnight Emperor (IRE) 16-1 M Munrowd *Midfield til pu rap aft 13; broke knee; destroyed*		P
	Mr Baloo(bl) 14-1 A Charles-Jones *Chsd ldrs til wknd 13; pu 16*		P
195^{3}	Orinoco's Flight (IRE) 10-1 M Holmes *(xnb) Tk keen hld; went 2nd 3; ld 5-7; 2nd when rdr lurched forward & f.o 10*		U
275^{R}	Rocastle Lad (IRE) 6-1 Richard Darke *10s-6s; towards rr; some hdwy 11; eff short-lived; t.o & pu 3 out*		P
87^{P}	The Jam Saheb(bl) 33-1 J Snowden *Ld to 2; nt jw & sn lost plce; poor 12th when fell 12*		F

OFFICIAL DISTANCES: 2*l*, 15*l* **TIME:** 6min 24.7s

Last fence omitted - fallen horse

326 Open Maiden (Div 2, Part 1), 12st — 9 ran

	COMBAT DRINKER (IRE) 6-4JF **N Williams** *Tchd 2s; lw; novicey & hld up towards rr; 6th 9; smooth prog in 4th app 14; ld app 16; 8l clr nxt; in comm when terrible mist 2 out; nt fluent last.*		1
	Flo Keen (12a) 12-1 **J Snowden** *Prsd ldrs; blun 12; cl 5th app 14; wknd nxt; 25l 4th 3 out; lft lucky 2nd*	25	2
82^{P}	**Hayling Star** (5a) 50-1 **M Sweetland** *Bckwd; tde; mists & sn last & labouring; t.o 10; hopeless rem frm 14*	2fncs	3
	Gunville (7a) 5-1 Miss P Gundry *(bf) 8s-5s; mostly 2nd/3rd; chsd wnr frm 16; outpcd nxt; assured of mod 2nd when fell 2 out*		F
	Lady Of Jazz (5a) 16-1 A Charles-Jones *(xnb) Cl 2nd/4th; tk slt ld & fell 15*		F
	Miss Karingaroo (5a) 33-1 N McDiarmid *V unruly & threw rdr padd; stdd start; v reluct & novicey in last early; a detach in final trio but jmpng impd frm 4; t.o 11; pu 14*		P
	Primitive Delight (5a) 16-1 D Edwards *Jmpd poor in rr; drvn & strugg 8; t.o 10; pu 13*		P
67^{F}	State Affairs (IRE) 14-1 R McCarthy *Prsd ldrs til mist 8; lsng plce when blun 12; poor 6th app 14; t.o & crawling 16; pu 3 out*		P
195^{2}	Think Commercial (IRE) (7a) 6-4JF A Farrant *(xnb) Tchd 2s; nt a fluent; ld til hdd & lft in ld 15; sn hdd agn; stpd to nil; 20l 3rd 2 out; pu last*		P

OFFICIAL DISTANCES: dist, dist **TIME:** 6min 33.2s

327 Open Maiden (Div 2, Part 2), 12st - 18J — 9 ran

	WAYWARD SPREE (5a) 9-1 **J Snowden** *Made all; drew 5l clr aft 3 out; pushed out (a gng best)*		1
195^{P}	**Four Of A Kind** 9-4F **Richard Darke** *Oht; settled trckng ldrs; 6l 3rd 15; went 2nd & pckd 16; rdn 3 out; a hld*	10	2
	Off The Hook (IRE) 7-1 **I Hambley** *Settled midfield; went 3rd 12 & 2nd brief 15; 7l 3rd & btn aft 3 out*	5	3
119^{P}	Miss Chloe (IRE) (5a) 16-1 R Bliss *2nd/3rd til lost plce app 15; 12l 4th aft 3 out*	2	4
314^{9}	Roseacre (IRE) 4-1 M Miller *Mists; 2nd/3rd til lost plce 10; 6l 5th 12; just in tch til 15l last & pckd bad 3 out.*	7	5
	Druid Pandora (5a) 8-1 M Munrowd *School in last pr; lost tch & pckd 9; t.o 12; pu 14*		P
	Harjach 6-1 N Wilmington *(xnb) 2 handlers; hld up; 6th when ur 7*		U
150^{P}	Highway Ten (5a) 14-1 T Dennis *Jmpd slow & a labouring; t.o last when pu 11*		P
237^{P}	Strand Onthe Green (IRE) 5-2 N Mitchell *(xnb) 7/2-5/2; last when pu 3; lame*		P

OFFICIAL DISTANCES: 10*l*, 4*l* **TIME:** 6min 32.7s

Fence 14 omitted - fallen rider

328 Open Maiden (Div 3), 12st — 17 ran

	LORD ANNER (IRE) (7a) 7-1 **N Williams** *(xnb) Lw; hld up midfield; 6th 10; prog nxt; went 2nd aft 15; ld app 3 out; shot 12l clr nxt; unchall*		1
	Zakley 6-4F **A Farrant** *(xnb) 14s-6/4; cl up; ld 10; rdn & hdd app 3 out; imm outpcd; btn when blun nxt*	20	2
150^{3}	**Smokey Joe (IRE)** 14-1 **C Heywood** *Midfield; 8th 10; 13l 4th 16; plugged into poor 3rd frm nxt*	1½	3

Up To The Minute 6-1 Miss A Goschen *Ld 5-7; lost plce rap; 9th 10; 25l 5th 3 out* 12 4

Just For Now (IRE) (7a) 20-1 Miss P Gundry *A wl bhnd; 13th 10; 45l 6th 3 out* 30 5

Lady Blackthorn (5a) 20-1 N McDiarmid *Nt fluent; chsd ldrs; 12l 5th 11; sn wknd; 55l last 3 out* . . . . . runin 6

April's Past (5a) 33-1 M Atkinson *Bckwd; novicey & imm strugg; t.o 8; pu 12* P

Calinash (IRE) 25-1 I Hambley *(xnb) Tchd 33s; reshod & delayed race by 20mins; hld up; impd to 3rd 10; lft 2nd brief 15; 9l 3rd 16; wknd rap; pu 2 out* . . . . . P

172P Cats Cross (5a) 33-1 N Mitchell *(xnb) 2 handlers; pu aft 3* . . . . . P

274P General Short 20-1 D Edwards *(xnb) Midfield early; poor 10th 10; t.o & pu 13* P

13P Leader Du Turf (FR) (7a) 4-1 T Dreaper *(xnb) 8s-4s; ld 2-11; drpd out qckly; pu 15* . . . . . P

82F Pauls Legacy 16-1 D McKenna *A wl bhnd; 14th 10; sn t.o; pu 15* . . . . . P

275P Phanthom Walker 25-1 T Dennis *A wl bhnd; rem 12th 10; t.o & pu 13* . . . P

Polly Dust (5a) 20-1 M Sweetland *(xnb) Midfield; 7th 10; mist 11 & sn lost tch; t.o & pu 14* . . . . . P

195F Truicear 7-1 R McCarthy *Cl up; 4th 10; went 2nd 14; ½l down when ur 15* U

233F Warren Hill 5-1 R Tory *Stdd start & a rem last; t.o 8; pu aft 13* . . . . . P

307P Wendys Dynamo 25-1 M Munrowd *(xnb) A bhnd; 11th 10; lost tch & mist nxt; t.o & pu 14* . . . . . P

OFFICIAL DISTANCES: 25l, 1l **TIME:** 6min 20.3s

Deep Pockets and See More Fun were balloted out of this race after declarations had closed so that it no longer had to be divided

329 Open Maiden (Div 4), 12st — 17 ran

1205 **MAYBE A DOUBLE** (5a) 25-1 **R Bliss** *(xnb) 2 handlers; hld up; prog 9; 3rd nxt; prsd ldr 12 til ld app 3 out; lft wl clr nxt* 1

1947 **Virgos Bambino (IRE)** (5a) 50-1 **A Charles-Jones** *(kineton) Prom; ld 10 til app 3 out; rdn & sn wknd; 4th when lft 2nd nxt* 12 2

355 **Rio Pops** (5a) 10-1 **Miss A Goschen** *Prom early; 7th when mist 10; rallied 12; cl 3rd 16; sn wknd; lft poor 3rd aft melee 2 out* 6 3

2383 Let's Rock 33-1 M Green *A bhnd; 13th 10; t.o 12th 16; event lft 4th; fin 33l 4th; disq - nt weigh-in* 4d

2374 Ashwicke Gambler 14-1 T Dreaper *(xnb) 33s-14s; set off in last pr; pulled hrd & rap hdwy to ld 4-10; sn stpd to nil; t.o & pu 15.* . . . . . P

Caracciola (NZ) 33-1 W White *Ur padd; hld up & bhnd; 14th 10; stdy prog 12; eff to disp 2l 2nd 3 out; 6th & wkng qckly when fell in melee nxt; rdr inj* F

Heliotrope (IRE) (12a) 12-1 A Farrant *(xnb) Midfield; jmpd slow 8; 11th 10; pu 12; broke leg; destroyed* . . . . . P

195U Josanjamic (5a) 6-1 L Heard *A wl bhnd; 16th 10; t.o & pu 3 out* . . . . . P

1423 Kyalami (FR) 5-2 Miss P Gundry *Tchd 3s; prsd ldrs; 4th 10; jmpd to 3rd 14; disp 2nd 3 out; btn when lft 2nd & fell 2 out* . . . . . F

195P Little Apple Bay (5a) 33-1 Miss T Cave *2 handlers; midfield; 10th 10; sn lost tch; pu 14.* . . . . . P

Nobody's Heroine (5a) 33-1 N McDiarmid *(xnb) Prsd ldrs; 5th 10; wknd 14; 9th 16; carried out by loose horse 3 out* C

Officer Cadet (IRE) (7a) 5-4F N Williams *4s-5/4; hvly rstrnd & sev mists & some gd js; blun 5; last trio to 10; eff 14; 7th & rdn 16; no resp; pu 3 out* P

Panhandle (5a) 14-1 N Mitchell *Settled midfield; 9th 10; prog to handy 6th when mist & ur 15* . . . . . U

Pitchfork Pete (7a) 20-1 Miss C Tizzard *Hld up & bhnd; 12th 10; still 8th 16; str rn to 2nd aft nxt; ev ch when crashing fall 2 out; dead* . . . . . F

275P Rowleyrascal 50-1 M Sweetland *Sn wl bhnd; t.o last 10; pu 15* . . . . . P

Sure How Bad (IRE) 50-1 L Tibbatts *Ld to 4; chsd ldrs; 6th 10; wknd 14; poor 10th 16; hmpd & ur 2 out.* . . . . . U

664 Western Frontier (IRE) (7a) 7-1 J Snowden *(xnb) 20s-7s; midfield; 8th 10; 7th & btn when mist & ur 3 out* . . . . . U

OFFICIAL DISTANCES: 7l, 4l **TIME:** 6min 33.5s

Darcey Mae was balloted out of this race after declarations had closed to avoid it being divided; Let's Rock finished 4th but was disqualified when the rider failed to weigh-in; no fine was imposed

Musselburgh (RH 8F,18J)

Sun, 29 Feb (FIRM, GOOD to FIRM in places)

330 Kronenbourg 1664 Open HC, 3m £2240 — 11 ran

56[1] **GUILSBOROUGH GORSE** 11-07 13-8F **M Walford** *Hld up in tch; stdy prog 14; rdn to chall nxt; ld 3 out; nt fluent 2 out; pushed clr flat* 1

Penny Native (IRE) 12-00 10-1 **C Storey** *Prom; 2nd 9 til ld aft 14; rdn & hdd nxt; nt fluent last; drvn & kpt on to snatch 2nd*. 2 2

Primitive Way 12-00(cp) 25-1 **P Maitland-Carew** *W ldr; ld 6 til hdd aft 14; ld agn 15-nxt; rdn & one pce app last; assured of 2nd til eased & dem by trainer-partnered rival final stride* . . . . s hd 3

179[4] Geordies Express 12-07 9-4 K Anderson *Trckd ldrs; chall 12; 2nd/3rd nxt til drvn & outpcd aft 15; rallied last; stayed on wl cl home*. . . . . nk 4

281[1] Indien Du Boulay (FR) 11-07 11-2 W Ramsay *A.p; drvn & ev ch 15; one pce frm nxt* . . . . $3\frac{1}{2}$ 5

210[P] Starbuck 11-11 33-1 D Jewett *Chsd ldrs to 12; wknd tame nxt; t.o* . . . . . dist 6

240[5] Mini Cruise 11-07 66-1 W Goldie *Disp ld to 6; prom to 12; 7th & wkng nxt; blun 14; t.o*. . . . . $2\frac{1}{2}$ 7

212[9] St Bee 11-07(cp) 200-1 H Norton *Nt fluent in last pr; lost tch & mist 8; t.o 10* dist 8

Another Justice (IRE) 11-07 100-1 D Da Silva *Last pr & strugg; jmpd slow 4; lost tch 8; t.o & pu 11* . . . . P

214[P] Charlieadams (IRE) 12-02 (9ow) 25-1 J Muir *Tk keen hld in midfield early; outpcd 10; t.o & pu 2 out* . . . . P

240[4] Gaultier Gale (IRE) 11-07 33-1 A Findlay *Mists; rr when blun 5; nvr gng wl aft; 9th & outpcd 11; t.o & pu 3 out*. . . . . P

TIME: 5min 57.2s **TOTE:** £2.30; places £1.10,£2.30,£4.50 **Ex:**£19.80 **CSF:**£15.92

The stewards agreed to a change of rider on St Bee but fined the trainer £75 for failing to properly engage the rider originally declared; the rider of Primitive Way was suspended for seven days for failing to achieve the best possible placing

Staff College & R.M.A. Sandhurst Draghounds

Larkhill (RH 13F,18J)

Sun, 29 Feb (GOOD to FIRM)

331 Hunt Members, 12st — 3 ran

24[r] **HATCH GATE** (7x) 1-2F **P York** *Nt a fluent; ld 1 & frm 5; 4l clr 13; rdr lkng round flat; easy* 1

45[U] **Legal Storm (IRE)** 7-4 **Richard Green** *Ld 2-5; w wnr to 10; wl hld frm 15* . 7 2

Nariar (U) (12ow) 12-1 A Draycott *(xnb,orbs) Fat; sis, scuttled up to be in tch 3; wkng when fell hvly 5* . . . . F

OFFICIAL DISTANCE: 8*l* **TIME:** 6min 06.2s

The start of racing was put back by one hour to allow the frost to come out of the ground

332 Confined, 12st — 4 ran

223[1] **EASTERN POINT** (5a, 3x) 7-4 **P York** *Lw; mostly cl 2nd; drvn furiously frm 14; 2l down & finding v little aft 2 out; chall on inner last; forced ahd on line* 1

175[1] **Nomadic Star** (3x) 6-4F **Miss Z Lilly** *Nt fluent 3; 3rd/4th til 3rd frm 7; dashed ahd uphill to 13; bumped along aft; lkd wnr aft 2 out; rdr v novicey & pipped on post* . . . . hd 2

Highcroft Boy 3-1 **C Gordon** *Made most to 13; sn 3rd & outpcd; 4l down 3 out; rdn & no imp* 30 3

263[U] Lord Esker (IRE) 10-1 T Underwood *Last pr til clr last & nt gng wl 7; t.o & pu 14*. . . . . P

OFFICIAL DISTANCES: hd, dist **TIME:** 6min 04.6s

333 Mixed Open, 4m, 12st - 22J — 2 ran

NEW ROSS (IRE)(bl) 1-4F **Miss A Turner** *2nd ride; lw; made all; lft virt solo 16; hit 3 out but otherwise v safe* 1

140^{P} Northern Bluff 3-1 D I Turner *Lkd exhaust padd; chsd wnr; jb lft 14 & 15; still in tch when jmpd violent lft 16 & rn off course lsng 25l; jmpd lft & rfo 17; rmtd; dived at 19 & rfo agn* . . . . . U

OFFICIAL DISTANCE: Finished alone **TIME:** 8min 14.0s

334 Open Maiden (Div 1), 12st — 3 ran

264^{U} **SULA QUEEN** (5a) 11-8F **D I Turner** *Bckwd; tk keen hld; jmpd rt; blun 3 & rdr drpd reins; 2nd frm 6; bad outpcd 13 & lkd no ch til drvn & rallied app last; caught stpng ldr on line* 1

Lydia's Echo (5a) 11-4 **A Michael** *Pulled hrd; 2nd til ld 6; drew 15l clr 14; drvn along frm 2 out; stpd to nil aft last; hdd nr post* 1½ 2

53^{P} **Nearly Dark** (5a) 13-8 **D Harvey** *Ld to 6; sn last; lost tch 12; jmpd poor aft; 40l adrift 14* 30 3

OFFICIAL DISTANCES: 1½l, dist **TIME:** 6min 32.5s

335 Open Maiden (Div 2), 12st — 2 ran

238^{F} **B B BOY** 5-6F **A Michael** *Made all at v slow pce; rmdr aft 14; rdn 2 out; plodded on* 1

174^{7} **Chasing Buttercups** (5a) evens **Miss A Goschen** *Novicey in last; 8l bhnd rival 13; rdn & trying vain to cl when climbed 2 out; no imp aft* 7 2

OFFICIAL DISTANCE: 8l **TIME:** 6min 43.0s

336 Countryside Alliance Club Members (Military Rdrs), 12st — 2 ran

138^{2} **TELLER OF TALES** 2-5F **Miss V Flood** *Oft jw; ld at gd pce; hdd brief aft 12; drew 7l clr 13; hit nxt; stayed on str* 1

100^{8} Northern Fleet 2-1 J Sole *Rdn 2 & nvr gng wl; ld brief aft 12; lost tch u.p nxt; crawled over 2 out; exhaust when fell last; broke back; destroyed* . . . . . F

OFFICIAL DISTANCE: Finished alone **TIME:** 6min 03.5s

337 Restricted, 12st - 15J — 5 ran

102^{6} **GRAY KNIGHT (IRE)** 6-4F **James Tudor** *Made nrly all; drew 5l clr 3 out; pushed along & stayed on stout flat* 1

262^{F} **Hello Roscrea (IRE)** 100-30 **Miss A Goschen** *Nt a fluent; ld brief 1, 10 & aft 12; releg 3rd 14; drvn into 8l 2nd aft 2 out; no ch w wnr* 7 2

265^{P} **Chief Suspect (IRE)** 15-2 **R Bliss** *Hld up; 4th 14; rdn to 6l 2nd 2 out; dem app omitted last; wknd* 10 3

198^{4} Carrington House 9-4 J O'Rourke *Tk keen hld; hld up; mist 8; went 2nd 14; wknd tame 3 out; 15l last aft nxt; eased flat* 15 4

Lord Of Heaven (USA) 14-1 Miss K Cuthbertson *Drpd back last 7; in tch til wknd 13; rem when pu 3 out* . . . . . P

OFFICIAL DISTANCES: 8l, 8l **TIME:** 6min 04.6s

Fences 5,6 & 18 omitted - low sun

West of Yore

Hornby Castle (LH 8F,18J)

Sun, 29 Feb (GOOD to FIRM)

338 Confined, 12st — 8 ran

134^{U} **ERZADJAN (IRE)** 5-1 **L Bates** *Hld up & bhnd; last to 7; pushed along & hdwy frm 13; 15l 3rd 15; went 4l 3rd & bad mist 3 out; chall app last; sprinted clr flat* 1

Darak (IRE) (5x) 5-1 **N Tutty** *Ld to 6; cl 2nd 7 til disp ld 14; ld agn 15; 2l up 3 out; prsd last; hdd & outpcd flat* 3 2

270^{2} **Ballad Minstrel (IRE)** 4-5F **Miss J Foster** *Handy in 3l 4th to 6; ld 7-13; disp ld 14-15; 1l 2nd to 3 out; wknd aft* 8 3

Abinger 20-1 M Morley *Chsd along in midfield to 6; 5l 6th 8; bad mist 9 & drpd of pce; poor 4th 15; stayed on frm 2 out; nrly snatched 3rd* 1 4

	Purevalue (IRE) 4-1 Miss J Coward *Cl up; handy 6th 8; blun 9; rr by 15; t.o 3 out*	20	5
	Given Grace (IRE) (5a) 33-1 J Davis *A rr; lsng tch 9; t.o & pu 14*		P
271^{4}	Rising Talisker (5a)(cp) 33-1 R Clark *Prom early; 3l 3rd 5; mists 7 & 8; 6l 3rd 12; wknd rap frm 14; poor 3rd nxt; t.o & pu last*		P
267^{13}	Steel Rigg (IRE) 33-1 J Botham *Prom early; 6l 5th 5; cl 3rd 7; bad mists 10 & 13; sn wknd; last by 14; t.o & pu last*		P

OFFICIAL DISTANCES: 3*l*, 10*l* **TIME:** 6min 52.0s

339 Ladies Open — 9 ran

270^{1}	**BALISTEROS (FR)** 7-4F **Miss P Robson** *Ld to 2; cl 2nd til disp ld 7; ld 8-14; outpcd 3 out; 3l 3rd nxt; hrd rdn & rallied flat; ld on line; v game*		1
299^{U}	**Silver Groom (IRE)** 11-4 **Miss J Coward** *Rr & bhnd early; last 8; hdwy 11 to 6th 14; went 6l 4th 15 & 3l 4th 2 out; qcknd wl to ld app last; outpcd nr fin*	½	2
162^{4}	**Dun Distinctly (IRE)** 50-1 **Miss L Horner** *Rr early; gd hdwy frm 12 to 3l 3rd 15 & 1l 2nd 3 out; ev ch nxt; raliied flat; one pce nr fin*	½	3
282^{4}	In Demand 25-1 Miss J Balmer *A midfield to rr; stayed on; nrst fin*	6	4
72^{P}	Yorkshire Edition (IRE) 8-1 Miss W Gibson *Set str gallop & jmpd v bold; ld 3; jnd 6-7; sn hdd; ld agn 15-2 out; wknd*	10	5
	Deputy Leader (IRE) 50-1 Miss S Brotherton *Prom early; 15l 5th 9; wknd frm 13; lsng tch 14; sn bhnd; t.o & pu 15*		P
213^{2}	Donnegale (IRE)(cp) 6-1 Miss J Foster *Chsd ldng pr in 6l 3rd to 6; 12l 4th 9; pushed along & wknd frm 13; t.o 3 out; pu 2 out*		P
270^{7}	Just Jake 10-1 Mrs L Tinkler *Lkd unenthusiastic; a last; t.o 10; pu 15; reportedly retired*		P
	Lord Dorcet (IRE) 7-1 Miss C Metcalfe *Gng wl in midfield til prog to 5l 3rd 7-12; in tch til wknd app 3 out; 5th & hld when fell 2 out*		F

OFFICIAL DISTANCES: ½*l*, ½*l* **TIME:** 6min 43.0s

340 Mens Open — 7 ran

	VICTORIA'S BOY (IRE) 5-4F **G Brewer** *Ld to 10; 1l 2nd til ld agn aft 3 out; rdly drew clr; easy*		1
210^{1}	**Spring Double (IRE)** (2ow) 3-1 **T Mounsey-Heysham** *Chsd ldng pr in 3l 3rd to 12; outpcd 14 & 8l adrift 15; pushed along to 5l 3rd 3 out; stayed on u.p to tk 2nd flat; no ch w wnr*	8	2
269^{5}	**Extra Jack (FR)**(bl) 5-1 **C Shirley-Beavan** *Chsd ldr; 2l 2nd til ld 11-15; easily outpcd by wnr frm 3 out; dem flat*	6	3
163^{U}	Flat Top 7-1 M Manton *Jmpd slow in rr; clambered over 9; outpcd & lsng tch 11; hdwy 13 to poor 4th 2 out; lkd unenthusiastic & unhappy*	15	4
	Stoney River (IRE) 7-1 C Mulhall *A midfield; pushed along 10; lsng tch 14; poor 6th 3 out; lft 5th at last*	10	5
163^{P}	Badge Of Fame (IRE) 40-1 P Kinsella *Last 4; slt hdwy 8 to 8l 5th 9; pushed along 13; last agn & lsng tch 14; t.o & pu 3 out*		P
162^{P}	Shining Light (IRE) 50-1 S J Robinson *Chsd ldrs in 4th to 12; pushed along & wkng 13; poor 5th & exhaust when fell last*		F

OFFICIAL DISTANCES: 8*l*, 6*l* **TIME:** 6min 48.0s

The stewards interviewed the rider of Shining Light as to why he continued in the race when his horse was obviously exhausted; he was warned as to his future conduct

341 Restricted — 16 ran

302^{1}	**HIGH PEAK** evensF **T Greenall** *V confid rdn; hld up & bhnd to 9; grad prog 11; went cl 8th 13 & trckng ldng quartet 15; cruising bhnd ldrs 3 out; ld aft nxt; clr by last; r.o u.p*		1
164^{2}	**Just Fluster** 5-1 **R Wakeham** *W ldrs early; lost plce 6; 6l 8th 12; went 1l 3rd 3 out; ld app 2 out; brushed aside by wnr; r.o one pce*	3	2
268^{7}	**Dolphin Square (IRE)** 14-1 **T Oates** *A ldng trio; 1l 3rd 12; ld 14 til wknd & outpcd app 2 out*	2	3
	The Singing Nun (IRE) (5a) 5-1 P Kinsella *Cl up; 3l 5th 9; ld 12-14; in tch til wknd 3 out; lft 4th flat*	6	4
161^{3}	Agent Provocateur (NZ) 14-1 R Clark *Prom to 12; 2l 4th 13; disp ld 14-15; wknd 3 out; 6th app last; lft 5th flat*	2	5
166^{4}	Clonshire Paddy (IRE) 14-1 Miss J Coward *Rr early; prog to cl 2nd 7-12; in tch til wknd 15; r.o one pce*	3	6
161^{4}	Sledmere (IRE) 20-1 J Botham *Prom early; 1l 3rd 7 til ld brief 13; grad wknd frm 15*	5	7

215^{4} Commanche Spirit (IRE) 50-1 F Arthur *A rr; t.o 15; plodded on* . . . . runin 8

268^{4} Bermuda Blue 14-1 L Bates *(xnb) Midfield to 9; went cl 6th 11 & handy 4th 15; pushed along & outpcd 3 out; hld in 4th when pu flat; bad lame* . . . P

215^{P} Carrow Garden (IRE) 50-1 C Dawson *Prom early; grad wknd & rr by 11; pushed along & lsng tch 12; t.o & pu 14* . . . . P

Hanisia (5a) 33-1 P Atkinson *(xnb) A last; jmpd sticky; sn bhnd; t.o & pu 12* P

Horton-Cum-Peel (IRE) 33-1 W Kinsey *(xnb) Ld to 12; wknd frm 13; t.o & pu 2 out* P

164^{4} Lingham Lady (5a) 10-1 S Swiers *(xnb) Midfield to 7; lost plce & rr by 9; pushed along; grad lost tch & pu 15* . . . . P

164^{U} Lord Scroop (IRE) 14-1 M Morley *Trckd ldrs in 5th to 12; mist 14; sn wknd; rr & wl adrift when pu last.* . . . . P

Mid Summer Lark (IRE) 40-1 R Nichol *(xnb) Tkn gently in midfield to 12; grad wknd frm nxt; lsng tch when pu 15.* . . . . P

Son Of Sam 40-1 C Mulhall *Rr by 12; sn bhnd; t.o when pu 12* . . . . P

OFFICIAL DISTANCES: $2\frac{1}{2}$*l*, $1\frac{1}{2}$*l* **TIME:** 6min 59.0s

342 Open Maiden 56&7yo (Div 1), 2m4f, 12st - 13J 9 ran

212^{P} **EIGHTY DAYS (IRE)** (7a) 2-1F **R Morgan** *(xnb) A ldng pr; 1l 2nd 9; disp ld 11; ld aft 2 out; 1l up at last; drvn flat; just hld on.* 1

Sweeping Storm (IRE) 6-1 **C Dawson** *Mid-div to 8; went cl 3rd 11; 1l 2nd 2 out; chall flat; hrd rdn & just outpcd nr fin.* . . . . hd 2

Clever Fella (7a) 3-1 **N Tinkler** *Rr; 7th & pushed along 8; went 5th 11; stayed on wl to tk 3rd app last* 8 3

215^{3} Jackofalltrades (IRE) 5-1 T Oates *(xnb) A midfield; in tch 11; outpcd 2 out; r.o one pce.* 8 4

215^{P} Hi Up Brenkley 25-1 A Richardson *Prom early; cl 2nd 4; last by 8; lost tch 10; bhnd frm 2 out.* 10 5

272^{U} Jobee Jack 33-1 P Kinsella *Jmpd big 1; mid-div 5; hdwy 7 to 2l 3rd 9; wknd frm 11; t.o 2 out* 3 6

113^{5} Billymax (IRE) 6-1 R Wakeham *(xnb) Ld; lkd wkng when fell 3 out* . . . . . . F

Ivory Cross 10-1 C Rae *Rr early; grad hdwy to prom 4th 7; 5th & in tch when fell 3 out.* . . . . F

Tony 14-1 S Charlton *(xnb) Mid-div early; t.o by 10; pu 3 out* . . . . P

OFFICIAL DISTANCES: hd, 10*l* **TIME:** 5min 06.0s

343 Open Maiden 56&7yo (Div 2), 2m4f, 12st - 13J 6 ran

272^{U} **SUPER DOLPHIN** (7a) 5-1 **Richard Tate** *Hvly rstrnd in last to 10; hdwy 3 out; 4th 2 out & 3l 2nd last; fin fast; ld on line* 1

Shirostran 6-1 **P Kinsella** *14s-6s; made virt all; 2l up 3 out; qcknd 4l clr last; wknd flat; hdd on line* . . . . $\frac{1}{2}$ 2

166^{P} **Callitwatulike** 10-1 **C Dawson** *Prom; 3l 3rd to 10; in tch til outpcd frm 2 out* 10 3

216^{4} Comfortably Numb (FR) (7a) 4-6F N Tinkler *3l 3rd 8; rmdrs 9; went 1l 2nd & pushed along 10; outpcd & wknd 2 out* 4 4

Whitleygrange Girl (5a) 7-1 N Tutty *Rr & bad mist 6; last & lsng tch 8; stayed on to 5th 11; nvr nrr.* 3 5

160^{P} Perky's Wish (IRE) 33-1 S J Robinson *Ld to 2; chsd ldr in 2l 2nd to 8; sn wknd; t.o & pu 3 out* . . . . P

OFFICIAL DISTANCES: $\frac{1}{2}$*l*, 12*l* **TIME:** 5min 12.0s

344 Open Maiden 56&7yo (Div 3), 2m4f, 12st - 13J 10 ran

304^{2} **HIGH FIELDS** (7a)(bl) evensF **T Greenall** *Hld up & patient rdn; 6th 8; hdwy to 3rd 10; cruising bhnd ldng pr 2 out; ld app last; jnd & qcknd best flat* . 1

211^{P} **Jethro Tull (IRE)** (7a) 8-1 **G Brewer** *A.p; 4th to 9; went 3l 4th 2 out; disp ld last; outpcd flat* 4 2

136^{P} **Anniejo** (12a) 10-1 **R Morgan** *20s-10s; ld to 2; prom to 10; ld agn 11 til mist 3 out; rallied app last; just hld for 2nd flat.* . . . . $\frac{1}{2}$ 3

Red Rose Dixie (5a) 20-1 C Dawson *A.p; cl 4th 10; pushed along & outpcd frm 3 out; r.o same pce.* 8 4

160^{P} Northern Castle (IRE) 8-1 R Clark *(xnb) Mid-div to 7; went cl 2nd 10; disp 3 out-nxt; wknd app last.* 4 5

160^{F} Parsifal (7a) 5-1 R Abrahams *(xnb) Ld frm 3-10; wknd v qckly app 11; poor 6th 2 out; crawled home* 10 6

216^{6} Iron Trooper (IRE) 10-1 L Bates *(xnb) A rr; last & lsng tch 8; pu 9* . . . . . . P

112^{P} Supreme Vintage (IRE) 11-1 J Botham *In mid-div when ur 5* . . . . U

Swordface (IRE) 7-2 N Tinkler *Lkd v novicey & slow; jmpd slow 2 & rmdrs; last & pushed along 8; t.o & pu 10* … P
272P Zebs Lad 33-1 R Walker *A rr; sn bhnd; t.o & pu 11* … P

OFFICIAL DISTANCES: 4*l*, nk **TIME:** 5min 08.0s

Folkestone (RH 7F,15J)

Wed, 3 Mar (GOOD, GOOD to FIRM in places)

345 Tenterden HC, 2m5f £1469 — 12 ran

316U **PARTE PRIMA** 11-11 7-2 **R Woollacott** *Trckd ldrs; eff to ld 10; gng best aft 3 out; prsd when mists 2 out & last; rdn & hld on wl flat (btr rdr prevailed)* 1
332 1 **Eastern Point** 11-06 13-2 **J Sole** *3rd mostly til chsd wnr 11; chall & mist 2 out; rdn & ev ch last; kpt on; outrdn & a hld.* … 3/4 2
Pistol Knight 11-12 (1ow) 66-1 **Stuart Robinson** *Midfield; 8l 6th & eff aft 10; outpcd & mist 3 out; urged into 3rd nxt; no ch w ldrs* … 20 3
191 1 Mr Splodge 11-11 7-2 James Tudor *Hld up in midfield; trckd ldrs 8; 5th aft 10; mist 12; outpcd nxt; rdn to chse ldng pr vain app 2 out; sn dem & wknd; hit last* 5 4
331 2 Legal Storm (IRE) 11-11 16-1 Richard Green *Made most to 10; wknd qckly 3 out* … 9 5
241P Jazz Night 11-13 20-1 J Jenkins *Tk keen hld; prsd ldr to 10; lost plce in 4th nxt; rallied to chse ldng pr brief 3 out; wknd qckly* … 7 6
90 6 O'flaherty's (IRE) 11-11 40-1 W Kavanagh *A rr; rdn & strugg aft 8; sn wl t.o* dist 7
182P Acuteangle (IRE) 11-06 66-1 P Hall *Midfield til rdn & strugg aft 6; sn wl bhnd; poor 7th when nrly ref & ur 3 out* … U
Highfield's Clover 11-07 14-1 C Gordon *Hld up last pr; mist 2; prog 5; mist 8; 7th & lsng tch 9; t.o & pu 3 out* … P
Iconic 11-11 50-1 D Page (Kent) *Tk keen hld; prom to 6; wknd to last 9; sn t.o; pu 3 out* … P
103P See Red Billdan (IRE) 11-11 50-1 P Callaghan *Mists; in tch to 8; wknd nxt; sn t.o; pu 3 out* … P
183 5 Tricky Trevor (IRE) 12-01 9-4F P York *Last pr when jmpd lft & fell 2.* … F

TIME: 5min 26.8s **TOTE:** £4.50; places £1.10,£3.10,£15.00 **Ex:**£19.30 **CSF:**£24.49

Ludlow (RH 8F,22J)

Thu, 4 Mar (GOOD, GOOD to FIRM in places)

346 Chase Meredith Mem HC, 3m1f110y £2999 — 10 ran

280 4 **MULLENSGROVE** 11-03 12-1 **Miss S Phizacklea** *Midfield til 3rd & prog 9; 2nd 14; ld nxt; 3l clr & drvn app 18; stayed on stout aft; hit last (galvanic ride).* … 1
Dam The Breeze 11-09 7-1 **N Williams** *Lw; set str pce; hdd 15; blun bad nxt; chsd wnr aft; drvn & nt qckn frm 2 out* … 2 2
299 2 **Ridgeway (IRE)** 11-03(cp) 8-1 **Miss J Foster** *(xnb) Mist 1; hld up in detach last trio; went 6th 12; stayed on frm 18; tk 3rd & blun last; rdn & r.o flat; unable to chall* … 1/2 3
176 4 Carbonado 11-05(tt) 28-1 Miss A Goschen *(xnb) Midfield; 6l 4th 13; wl outpcd 16; mod 6th last; urged along & fin v str.* … 1 4
254 1 Jemaro (IRE) 11-11 12-1 A Wintle *Settled 3rd; 7l down & rdn app 18; one pce aft; dem last* … 2 5
178 4 Hurricane Lamp 11-10 9-4 R Burton *Hld up in detach final trio; nt fluent 2; 15l 7th 13; nvr able to cl* … 5 6
209 6 Bold King (FR) 11-10(cp) 20-1 P Morris *Nt jw; detach in final trio; last when mist 6; mist 11 & rdr waved; t.o 14; pu 19* … P
93 4 Brown Esquire 11-03 66-1 Miss T Clark *Midfield til mist 10; rdn & wknd 12; t.o 14; pu 17.* … P
49P Harry Hotspur (IRE) 11-03(vis) 50-1 M Barber *Midfield til wknd & mist 9; t.o 13; pu 15* … P
Primaticcio (IRE) 11-07(bl) 7-4F T Greenall *Lw; settled 4th til nt fluent 11; 6l 5th 13; rdn nxt; strugg aft; t.o & pu 18.* … P

TIME: 6min 30.1s **TOTE:** £21.00; places £3.20,£2.10,£2.10 **Ex:**£94.20 **CSF:**£89.48

The trainer of the favourite, Primaticcio, was unable to account for the poor running of his horse

Taunton (RH 8F,17J)

Thu, 4 Mar (GOOD, GOOD to FIRM in places)

347 Mitford Slade Challenge Trophy HC, 3m £2027 — 14 ran

Form	Horse	Dist	Pos
199^{3}	**KESTICK** 11-07 5-2F **Miss T Cave** *Bhnd til 5th & prog 10; chsd clr ldr 13; stayed on to ld aft 2 out; comf*		1
	Tell Tale (IRE) 11-09 40-1 **T Malone** *Last & wl bhnd; 12th 10; hdwy 12; stayed on stout flat; tk 2nd final stride; nvr nr wnr*	7	2
178^{P}	**Jabiru (IRE)** 12-01(bl) 9-1 **D Edwards** *Jmpd & hung bad lft; w ldr; ld 4; 15l clr app 8; 12l ahd 3 out; wknd & hdd aft nxt; blun last; hung lft; no ex & dem on line*	hd	3
235^{1}	Miss O'Grady (IRE) 12-00 11-4 M Miller *Hld up towards rr; nt fluent 5; 10th 10; stayed on frm 3 out; nvr nr ldrs.*	3½	4
311^{3}	Lirsleftover 11-09 40-1 Miss S Young *Prom; 3rd 10; 4th & wkng 13; hung lft flat*	19	5
321^{P}	Sporting Chance 11-07 100-1 M Munrowd *Ld to 4; chsd clr ldr; jmpd lft 12; dem nxt; sn wknd*	12	6
157^{U}	Heaven Is Above (IRE) 12-03 8-1 A Hickman *Hld up in tch; 7th & rdn 10; sn wknd; pu 11*		P
144^{1}	O So Bossy 11-07 20-1 Miss J Congdon *Bhnd; 11th 10; some hdwy when fell 12*		F
317^{1}	Phoenix Phlyer 12-01(cp) 4-1 Miss C Stucley *Hld up; hdwy 9; 4th nxt; wknd 13; bhnd when hmpd & ur 3 out.*		U
	Polar Prospect 12-08 14-1 Miss P Gundry *Mid-div; mist 5; 9th 10; bhnd frm nxt; pu 14*		P
241^{6}	Rock Rose 11-10 33-1 Miss E Tory *Hld up & bhnd; mist 3; hdwy 8; 6th 10; no ch frm 13; 5th & wkng when blun & ur last*		U
	Severn Magic 11-02 66-1 J Cook *Last when jmpd awkward & ur 2*		U
317^{7}	Silent Keys (SWE) 12-08(bl,tt) 40-1 D Dunsdon *Mists; prom; blun 7 & drvn; 8th & rdn 10; t.o & pu 13*		P
308^{2}	Sound Sense 11-07 66-1 J Young *Bhnd; mist 5; last 10; t.o when mist 12; pu 3 out*		P

TIME: 5min 52.0s **TOTE:** £5.30; places £1.60,£12.40,£2.70 **Ex:**£345.30 **CSF:**£107.30

Newbury (LH 11F,18J)

Fri, 5 Mar (GOOD)

348 Rivar HC, 3m £1995 — 14 ran

Form	Horse	Dist	Pos
319^{U}	**RIGHT TO REPLY (IRE)** 11-12 2-1F **N Harris** *(xnb) Lw; mists 1 & 2 & oft nt fluent; v confid rdn in rr; 15l adrift 8; passed horses frm 11 but still mod 9th 14; clsd rap nxt & stormed ahd flat; eased cl home*		1
178^{2}	**Rathbawn Prince (IRE)** 11-09 7-2 **Miss S Samworth** *Prog in 4th 8; tk 2nd aft 13; chall 2 out; rdn to ld nxt til hdd & totally outpcd flat*	3½	2
100^{2}	**Little Farmer** 11-10 10-1 **P Hall** *Ld to 11; ld agn app 13; rdn & hdd 2 out; sn outpcd*	7	3
	Smarty (IRE) 11-09(cp) 9-1 A Wintle *Chsd ldrs; jmpd slow 7; 5th 8; mist 12; 4th & detach frm ldng trio 14; one pce nxt*	11	4
184^{1}	Chasing The Bride 11-07 25-1 Miss A Goschen *(xnb) Chsd ldrs; 8th 8; 7th & rdn 14; nd aft*	1¼	5
	Cimarrone Cove (IRE) 11-09 8-1 T Greenall *Nt fluent; chsd ldrs; 6th 8; hit 11; 6th 14; one pce & btn nxt*	5	6
242^{2}	Chicago City (IRE) 11-07 16-1 Ms A Embiricos *7th 8; 5th & rdn when hit 14; sn btn*	6	7
235^{2}	Oscar Wilde 11-05 33-1 D Drake *(xnb) Bhnd; 10th 8; hit 9; poor 11th 14*	nk	8
182^{1}	Galeaway (IRE) 11-07 (2ow) 50-1 J Barnard *Bhnd; 12th 8; last when hit 11; plugged on & t.o aft 13*	12	9
260^{P}	Alpha Centauri (IRE) 11-05 100-1 J Sole *Sn prom; went 2nd 7; ld 11 til app 13; stumbled bad aft fnce; nt rec; pu nxt.*		P
	Hastate 11-05 100-1 D I Turner *Bckwd; bhnd; nt fluent 6; 13th 8; poor 10th 14; pu nxt.*		P
175^{2}	Masalarian (IRE) 11-05 50-1 Miss L Bridges *(xnb) Rr when blun & nrly ur 3; nt fluent; 11th 8; 8th & wl btn 14 (tho still in front of wnr!); pu 15*		P

	Sea Haitch Em 11-12 6-1 N Williams *Swtng; pulled hrd in cl 2nd til 3rd 8; same & ev ch 14; wknd qckly; pu 3 out*		P
239^{P}	Silver Lake (IRE) 11-05 100-1 J Morgan *Towards rr; 9th & rdn 8; t.o & pu 15*		P

TIME: 6min 01.9s **TOTE:** £3.60; places £1.50,£2.50,£2.40 **Ex:**£15.00 **CSF:**£8.64

The owner of Masalarian, whose passport was found to be incorrect, was fined £110

Kelso (LH 8F,17J)

Sat, 6 Mar (GOOD to SOFT, GOOD in places)

349 K.O.S.B. Nov HC, 3m1f £1410 — 9 ran

74^{2}	**MISS MATTIE ROSS** 11-02 25-1 **M McAlister** *In tch; hit & outpcd 14; rallied & ev ch last; edged lft; ld nr fin*		1
210^{7}	**Boulta (IRE)** 11-07(cp) 14-1 **T Oates** *Made most; rdn app last; kpt on; hdd cl home*	hd	2
316^{4}	**Miss Royello** 11-04 9-1 **D Jewett** *Hld up; hdwy aft 3 out; rdn & no ex last*	9	3
316^{6}	Lord Edwards Army (IRE) 11-05 25-1 G Willoughby *Mists; cl up til wknd frm last*	12	4
177^{F}	Preston Brook 11-09 7-2 T Greenall *Hld up in tch; hit 14; stdy hdwy & cl up when blun last; nt rec*	4	5
132^{1}	Snooty Eskimo (IRE) 11-05 12-1 H Norton *Cl up; blkd bend aft 3 out; wknd last*	7	6
	Havetwotaketwo (IRE) 11-05 33-1 A Richardson *Hld up; blun & ur 11*		U
216^{U}	Jinful Du Grand Val (FR) 11-06 (1ow) 20-1 J Alexander *In tch; blun bad & ur 4*		U
316^{1}	Tor Head 11-07 evensF C Mulhall *Hmpd & fell 1*		F

TIME: 6min 35.5s **TOTE:** £43.30; places £4.70,£2.90,£3.00 **Ex:**£139.50 **CSF:**£280.58

Fences 10 & 19 omitted

Blackmore & Sparkford Vale

Charlton Horethorne (LH 8F,18J)

Sat, 6 Mar (GOOD to FIRM, FIRM in places)

350 Hunt Members, 12st — 8 ran

322^{3}	**BEADNELL BAY** 4-5F **Miss A Goschen** *Lw; ld & pckd bad 2; rdr rec wl; 2l up 7; made rest; drew clr frm 3 out; impressive*		1
178^{P}	**Cherokee Run (IRE)** 5-2 **Miss C Tizzard** *Opened 3s; ld 1; chsd ldr frm 3; 4l 3rd 7; trckd wnr frm 13; grad lost tch frm 3 out*	12	2
262^{4}	**Mr Ben Gunn** 25-1 **Miss V Heal** *Chsd ldrs; $2\frac{1}{2}$l 3rd 4; chsd ldr frm nxt-12; jmpd slow 14; stayed on one pce frm 3 out*	1	3
320^{4}	Leon Garcia (IRE) (5a) 9-2 T Bishop *Hld up; last 3; $7\frac{1}{2}$l 5th 7; disp 3rd 13; rdn & eff 3 out; tired when mist nxt; sn btn*	5	4
232^{P}	Barton Saint (NZ) 25-1 B Parsons *Tchd evens; freeze-marked; $6\frac{1}{2}$l 5th 4; rdr called cab 8 & sn last; waved agn at 11; lost tch frm nxt; bhnd frm 3 out*	10	5
322^{P}	Jackson Hill 10-1 Miss T Cave *(xnb) 8l 6th 4; blun 6; last nxt; no imp frm 14; t.o frm 3 out*	15	6
319^{P}	Lily Lane 50-1 R Coleridge *(xnb) Hdwy to chse ldr when slpd on bend aft 3; prom til wknd 10; sn last; t.o 15*	$1\frac{1}{4}$fs	7
	Brue Hound Boy 50-1 L Tibbatts *(boh) Last pr when ur 1*		U

OFFICIAL DISTANCES: 20*l*, nk **TIME:** 6min 39.2s **TOTE:** £2.00 **DF:**£2.40

351 Ladies Open — 6 ran

	ATAVISTIC (IRE) 9-2 **Miss R Booth** *1st ride; 3l 2nd 3; trckd ldrs frm nxt; disp 5l 2nd 13; qckly clsd on ldr aft 15; disp ld nxt; ld aft; drew clr flat (1st win for rdr & trainer frm 1st rnr)*		1
262^{F}	**Frank Byrne** 7-4F **Miss A Goschen** *Ld; 3l clr 6; gd j 10; 5l up 13; rmdr & jnd 3 out; hdd nxt; no ex frm last*	4	2
311^{4}	**Just Bert (IRE)** 9-1 **Miss T Cave** *Chsd ldr til lost plce 4; hdwy agn to 5l 4th 7; 2nd brief 9; 5l 3rd 3 out; stayed on one pce frm nxt*	nk	3
	Jorodama King 7-1 Miss T Newman *3l 3rd 5; chsd ldr frm 7; disp 5l 2nd 13; wknd 15; sn btn*	30	4

276^{3} Cherokee Boy 7-1 Miss C Atkinson *Sn last; strugg & 22l adrift 8; jmpd lft 11; t.o frm 13* . . . . . runin 5

261^{3} Coolteen Hero (IRE) 5-2 Miss R Green *(xnb) Opened 3s; disp 4l 4th 5; chsd ldrs til grad outpcd frm 12; 5th & wkng when fell 14* . . . . . F

OFFICIAL DISTANCES: 3*l*, nk **TIME:** 6min 37.1s **TOTE:** £9.40 **DF:**£10.40

352 Mens Open, 12st — 5 ran

145^{3} **ASHBURY STAR (NZ)** (7x) 10-1 **R Woollacott** *(xnb) Hld up in 8l 3rd 3; chsd ldng pr til hdwy 13; 2nd nxt; 2l down 15; chall 2 out; outj & hdd last; rallied flat; ld nr post* 1

263^{1} **Badger Beer** (7x) 11-8F **N Mitchell** *Opened 6/4; ld; dived at 2; 2l up 6; still 2l clr 15; jnd 2 out; gd j last; hdd & no ex nr line; game eff* . . . . . ½ 2

235^{4} **Woodlands Beau (IRE)** (7x) 6-4 **T Dreaper** *Nt jw; chsd ldr; hit 3 & 4; 1½l down 7; mists 12 & 13; releg 3rd 14; blun nxt; wknd 3 out* 20 3

319^{U} Forest Jump (IRE) 25-1 R Lee *A last pr; 12l 4th 3; last 8; t.o 11; pu nxt; broke leg; dead* . . . . . P

236^{3} Rustic Revelry (7x) 8-1 C Whittaker *(xnb) A last pr; 14l last 3; impd to 4th 7; rmdr 10; t.o 12 til rfo 3 out* . . . . . U

OFFICIAL DISTANCES: ½*l*, 12*l* **TIME:** 6min 44.6s **TOTE:** £8.50 **DF:**£5.00

353 Open Maiden 56&7yo, 12st — 7 ran

264^{4} **FOURSPICE ALLSPICE (IRE)** (5a) 5-1 **Miss R Green** *12l 3rd 4; chsd ldr frm 8; 1½l down 11; prsd ldr 3 out til hdd last; lft clr flat* 1

Annie Fleetwood (5a) 7-2 **Miss T Cave** *(xnb) Tchd 4s; swtng; chsd ldrs to 3; sn lost plce; mist 8; 4th & wkng 14; inherited rem 2nd by defections last* . . 25 2

237^{2} **The Sycophant (IRE)** evensF **Miss A Goschen** *Tchd 5/4; 2 handlers; ld & sn clr; jmpd lft 3; 12l up 5; only 1½l up 11; jnd 3 out & sn hdd; exhaust 3rd when ur last; rmtd* . . . . . dist 3

Ask Again (7a) 16-1 Miss L Gardner *A last; wknd 9; t.o nxt; pu 12* . . . . . P

265^{P} Bettie Blue (5a) 20-1 N McDiarmid *2 handlers; chsd clr ldr; 10l down 4-8; wkng when bad mist 10; t.o & pu 12* . . . . . P

121^{3} Lady Widd (IRE) (5a) 5-1 A Michael *Hld up; hit 2; 22l 6th 4; smooth hdwy to 8l 3rd 12 & 2l down 15; disp ld 2 out; just ld & prob wnr when blun & ur last; rdr airlifted* . . . . . U

142^{P} See More Fun 20-1 R Woollacott *Swtng; 18l 4th 4; grad lost plce frm 12; wknd 14; t.o & pu 3 out* . . . . . P

OFFICIAL DISTANCES: 20*l*, dist **TIME:** 6min 50.2s **TOTE:** £6.20 **DF:**c/f

354 Restricted, 12st — 8 ran

324^{P} **DRUMHORC (IRE)** 9-2 **Miss L Gardner** *(xnb) 4½l 5th 4; mist 6; hdwy to 2nd 7; rmdr 11; ld 14-15; disp ld 3 out til drew clr flat* 1

265^{2} **Hawkers Hill** 9-4F **Miss A Goschen** *Lw; ld 1 & agn 7; 2l up 11; mist & hdd 13; ld agn 15; jnd nxt; hdd & no ex flat* 2½ 2

237^{1} **Captain Random** 5-2 **Mrs J Reed** *(xnb) 7/2-5/2; hld up; last 2; hdwy to 5th 12; chsd ldng pr frm 15; hit nxt; one pce & nt trble ldrs* 6 3

232^{P} Return The Call (IRE) 20-1 J Barnes *(xnb) 5l 6th 4; disp 2nd 7; lft 5l 3rd 12; sn wknd; stayed on one pce frm 3 out* 5 4

65^{8} Nice Approach (IRE) 25-1 Miss V Murphy *2nd ride; ld 2-7; sn lost plce; bhnd frm 15* 5 5

265^{P} Just Lark 7-1 R Bliss *7th 4; last 12; nd; rem 5th 15* . . . . . ½ 6

139^{U} Frankly Fear 5-1 N Heath *(xnb) Opened 6s; 3rd 4; disp 2nd nxt; grad lost plce frm 11; last when blun bad 14; bhnd frm nxt* 3 7

264^{P} Queens House (5a) 25-1 D Drake *3l 4th 4; trckd ldrs; 2½l 3rd 11; cl up when fell nxt* . . . . . F

OFFICIAL DISTANCES: 3*l*, 8*l* **TIME:** 6min 48.9s **TOTE:** £7.00 **DF:**£49.20

B B Boy was withdrawn not under orders - rider injured in previous race

355 Confined Maiden 8yo&up, 12st — 3 ran

322^{P} **SPARKLING MISSILE** (5a) 3-1 **Miss S Robinson** *Opened 4s; disp ld to 2; chsd ldr aft; 1½l down 8; rdr called cabs 13 & nxt; 5l adrift 14; clsd app 3 out; wandered rt aft 2 out; chall last; stayed on u.p flat; ld nr line* 1

237^{3}	**King Of Swing (IRE)** 4-5F **Mrs F Vigar** *Disp ld til ld 3; virt made rest; 1l up 10; jnd last; no ex when hdd flat*	$^{1}/_{2}$	2
350^{U}	Brue Hound Boy 3-1 L Tibbatts *(boh) 2nd outing; disp ld to 2; mist nxt; jmpd slow 4; 5l down when jmpd rt 8; grad lost tch frm 10; jmpd slow 12; t.o when ref nxt*		r

OFFICIAL DISTANCE: $^{3}/_{4}$*l* **TIME:** 6min 57.1s **TOTE:** £3.00 **DF:**£1.30

Curre & Llangibby

Howick (LH 9F,18J)

Sat, 6 Mar (GOOD)

356 Hunt Members, 12st — 5 ran

117^{P}	**COOLE'SABBOT (IRE)**(bl) 6-4 **G Maundrell** *Ld 2; 6l clr 14; unchall*		1
	Steel Gem (IRE) 5-1 **J Price** *Mists & rdr oft waving; went 2nd 5; no imp when mist 15*	8	2
191^{P}	**Miss Man** (5a) 14-1 **Miss A Cavanagh** *Bckwd; lft 2nd 3-5; 9l 3rd $^{1}/_{2}$way; wl bhnd 11; t.o & crawling fncs aft*	2fncs	3
	Danny Gale (IRE)(tt) 20-1 James Price *Jmpd delib; sn detach last; t.o 8; pu 10*		P
145^{P}	Questionaire (5a)(vis) evensF R Stephens *Ld to 2; 2nd when fell 3*		F

OFFICIAL DISTANCES: 5*l*, dist **TIME:** 6min 38.5s

357 Restricted (Div 1), 12st — 11 ran

14^{P}	**TWILIGHT DANCER (IRE)** (5a) 4-1 **Miss F Wilson** *Ld aft 1; made rest; r.o wl*		1
	Pete The Painter (IRE) 2-1F **James Tudor** *3s-2s; sn prom; 5l 5th $^{1}/_{2}$way; 7l 4th & shkn up 12; went 3l 2nd 14; pckd 3 out; sn rdn & no imp*	3	2
202^{P}	**Lady Palamon (IRE)** (5a) 10-1 **R Stephens** *2nd to 8; 3l 3rd $^{1}/_{2}$way; chsd wnr 11; mist 13; dem u.p nxt; wknd 3 out*	20	3
207^{F}	Onward Bound 9-1 M Lewis *Nt fluent; prom; 5$^{1}/_{2}$l 6th $^{1}/_{2}$way; lost plce 11; 13l 6th nxt; sn wknd; t.o 15*	30	4
203^{4}	Wiston Wizo 20-1 P Sheldrake *(xnb) Chsd ldrs; mist 2; went 2nd 8-11; 6l 3rd nxt; wkng when mist 14; sn t.o.*	$^{1}/_{2}$	5
	Black Dan 25-1 D Underwood *Sn wl bhnd; mist 8; 20l 9th $^{1}/_{2}$way; t.o & pu 11 (lost a shoe).*		P
	Hay Bluff Lady (IRE) (12a) 8-1 D Jones *Bckwd; jmpd novicey; lost tch 5; 25l 10th $^{1}/_{2}$way; t.o & pu 12*		P
	Its A Handfull 14-1 J Price *Ld til aft 1; lost plce 5; 15l 8th $^{1}/_{2}$way; mist 10; t.o & pu 13*		P
	Johnston's Ville (IRE) 20-1 J Merry *Nvr trbld ldrs; 12l 7th $^{1}/_{2}$way; no hdwy 11; wl bhnd when pu 13*		P
	Rebel Yell (IRE) (5a) 33-1 James Price *Sn wl bhnd; t.o last when mist 6; pu 11*		P
	Runaway Ralph 7-2 T Faulkner *2 handlers; swtng; hld up; jb lft & blun 3; hdwy 8; 4l 4th $^{1}/_{2}$way; jmpd slow 10; wknd & 10l 5th 12; mist 14; t.o & pu 2 out*		P

OFFICIAL DISTANCES: 3*l*, 25*l* **TIME:** 6min 25.0s

358 Restricted (Div 2), 12st — 11 ran

139^{F}	**BALLYALBERT** evensF **Miss A de Lisle Wells** *2s-evens; ur padd; jmpd lft; ld aft 1; sn clr; 15l up 11-14; drew clr agn frm 2 out; unchall*		1
	Jerroboam (FR) 14-1 **S Gray** *(xnb) Went 7l 2nd aft 5; shkn up aft 10; eff 14; rdn 3 out; no ex*	15	2
202^{1}	**Daisy's Choice** (5a) 14-1 **P Sheldrake** *Hld up; hdwy 8; 17l 4th $^{1}/_{2}$way; 25l 4th when mist 12; mist 14; went 30l 3rd nxt; t.o*	25	3
	Norse 5-1 R Hodges *A bhnd; 21l 7th $^{1}/_{2}$way; 29l 6th 12; t.o*	2$^{1}/_{2}$	4
207^{P}	The Last Shout (IRE) 33-1 Miss A Hughes *Lost plce 6; 27l 9th $^{1}/_{2}$way; t.o 12*	runin	5
207^{P}	Anflora (5a) 25-1 J L Llewellyn *Hld up & bhnd; 22l 8th $^{1}/_{2}$way; hdwy & 20l 3rd 11; wkng when mist 15; t.o & pu 2 out*		P
	Fernhill Blaze (IRE) 12-1 S Hughes *Chsd ldrs; went 14l 3rd 6; blun 9; 15l 3rd $^{1}/_{2}$way; wkng when mist 11; blun 12; t.o & pu 13*		P
258^{F}	Gay Abandon (5a) 50-1 C Penycate *A last; t.o 4; pu 11.*		P
207^{B}	Hail Stone (IRE)(cp) 10-1 S Blackwell *Ld til aft 1; lost plce 7; 20l 5th $^{1}/_{2}$way; t.o & pu 12*		P

Tigersun 12-1 D Jones *(xnb) Nvr on terms; disp 20l 5th ½way; 27l 5th 12; t.o & pu 13* P

Under Milk Wood 12-1 J Price *(xnb) 2nd to 5; mist & lost plce 7; 7th when pu 8; lame* P

OFFICIAL DISTANCES: 25*l*, dist **TIME:** 6min 27.6s

359 Confined, 12st — 11 ran

SOHAPARA (5a) 4-6F **D Jones** *(xnb) Lw; a.p; went 2nd 9; ld 10; lft 6l clr 2 out; hld on wl u.p flat* 1

Inis Cara (IRE) 20-1 **M Hooper** *Hld up; 14l 8th ½way; bhnd til hdwy & 9l 6th 12; went 6l 3rd nxt; lft 6l 2nd 2 out; stayed on wl flat; nt rch wnr* 1 2

207[1] **Gilzine** 3-1 **J L Llewellyn** *(xnb) Swtng; hld up; stdy hdwy & 4½l 5th ½way; went 2nd 12; 2l down when blun & slithered on landing 2 out; nt rec* 20 3

208[P] Mecca Prince (IRE) (3x) 20-1 James Tudor *2nd til ld 9; hdd 10; rdn & releg 3rd 12; wknd & 15l 4th 14; sn wl bhnd* 2 4

147[3] Silver Pot Black 20-1 R Stephens *Prom; 2½l 4th ½way; mist 11; 7l 5th nxt; wknd 13; sn wl bhnd* 4 5

Chief Predator (USA) (3x) 9-1 T Faulkner *Hld up; 16l 9th ½way; lost tch 10; wl bhnd 12* 7 6

116[P] Rubian Princess (5a) 20-1 James Price *Nd; mist & lost plce 7; 10l 7th ½way; lost tch 12; t.o* 20 7

116[P] Glen Mist (IRE)(bl) 16-1 L Stephens *Ld to 9; 2l 3rd ½way; 5l 4th 12; wknd 13; t.o & pu 3 out* P

205[U] Harfdecent (3x)(tt) 7-1 M Williams *Chsd ldrs; 5½l 6th ½way; lost plce & 10l 7th 12; wl bhnd when mist 14; sn pu* P

208[P] Scarlet Emperor (IRE) 33-1 D Rochester *Last til tried to ref & fell 3* F

190[6] Wild Blade (IRE)(cp) 20-1 R Jenkins *(xnb) A bhnd; blun 2; 20l last ½way; t.o & pu 3 out* P

OFFICIAL DISTANCES: 1*l*, 20*l* **TIME:** 6min 22.1s

360 Mens Open, 12st — 11 ran

SIR DANTE (IRE) 2-1 **A Martin** *2 handlers; mists; a.p; 2l 4th ½way; 2nd/3rd 11 til lft in ld 15; 5l clr 3 out; drvn & hld on wl flat* 1

190[2] **Quickswood (IRE)** (7x) 5-1 **G Maundrell** *10s-5s; hld up; 10l 7th ½way; hdwy & 7l 5th 12; went 8l 3rd aft nxt; lft 4l 2nd 15; r.o one pce* 1½ 2

93[P] **Smile Pleeze (IRE)** (4x) 20-1 **R Stephens** *Lost plce 6; 13l 8th ½way; 10l 6th 12; went 9l 3rd 3 out; no imp aft til str rn flat; nt rch ldrs* 1½ 3

Moon Tiger (4x) 8-1 D Jones *Chsd ldrs; 4l 5th ½way; 5l 4th 12; lft 10l 3rd 13; wknd 3 out* 20 4

209[5] Absolutely Hopeful (7x)(bl) 33-1 S Hughes *2 handlers; 2nd til ld 5; hdd & stpd to nil app 11; t.o 15* 20 5

254[P] Cotteir Chief (IRE) 25-1 James Price *Mist 6; sn last & reluct; jmpd slow 8; t.o when pulled himself up 10* P

229[4] Iro Origny (FR) 25-1 A Phillips *(xnb) Prom; went 2nd 9; ld app 11 til hdd & ur 13* U

Lord Of Love 12-1 T Faulkner *Last til mist & ur 3* U

177[P] Mensch (IRE) 7-4F E Williams *(xnb) Hld up; 6l 6th ½way; hdwy 11; went 2l 2nd nxt; ld 13; mist 14; pu & dism 15; lost shoe* P

208[P] Rathgibbon (IRE) 50-1 J Merry *A bhnd; 15l 9th ½way; pu 12* P

The Writer (IRE) 12-1 R Hodges *(xnb) Ld to 5; 2nd to 9; 1½l 3rd ½way; w ldrs when pu & dism 11* P

OFFICIAL DISTANCES: 1½*l*, 1½*l* **TIME:** 6min 27.4s

361 Ladies Open - 17J — 8 ran

ASHFIELD ORCHESTRA (IRE) (5a) 10-1 **Miss I Tompsett** *14s-10s; hld up; last to 5; hdwy & 2½l 4th ½way; went 3rd 10; ld 13; clr 2 out; easily* 1

206[P] **Cowanstown Prince** 8-1 **Miss J Hughes** *Hld up; lft 3rd 9; went 2nd app nxt; ld app 13; sn hdd; 3l 2nd when hit 3 out; no ex.* 15 2

Andre Laval (IRE) 9-1 **Miss H Watson** *(bf) Bit bckwd; jw; ld til aft 1; ld 3-4 & 5 til app 13; wknd 14* 20 3

Young Manny (4x) 12-1 Mrs B Lewis *Hld up; 4½l 5th ½way; rdn 10; lost tch & mist 12; lft poor 4th 2 out* 1 4

Flockmaster (IRE) 8-1 Miss G Morris *Ld aft 1 til hdd & mist 3; mist & drpd to rr 6; 5l 6th ½way; stumbled bend bef 10; sn wl bhnd; t.o 13* 1½fs 5

116^{r} Buckland Boy evensF Miss A Frieze *Ld & pckd 4; hdd 5; ld & blun & ur 6* . . . U

208^{P} Lilardo (5a) 16-1 Miss R Reynolds *(xnb) Prom; lft 2nd 6 til app 10; mist 11; 6l 4th nxt; sn wknd; wl bhnd when fell 2 out* . . . F

Nigel's Boy 5-2 Miss F Wilson *6s (in plce)-5/2; hld up; hdwy 7; ld & fell 9* F

OFFICIAL DISTANCES: 25*l*, 20*l* **TIME:** 6min 24.8s

Fence 15 omitted - fallen rider

362 Confined Maiden (Div 1), 12st — 16 ran

150^{2} **GIPSY GIRL** (5a) 5-4F **R Stephens** *A.p; mist 3; 2l 3rd 1/2way; ld 12; 10l clr 14; mist 15; drew rt away; unchall* . . . 1

204^{P} **Mountain Lily** (5a) 10-1 **J Cook** *Ld to 10; 6l 3rd 12; wknd & 18l 4th 14; lft poor 3rd nxt; chsd wnr vain 2 out* . . . runin 2

202^{2} **Dans Blarney (IRE)** 8-1 **D Jones** *Tde; 2nd til ld 10; hdd 12; wknd 14; 20l 2nd when blun 3 out; dem nxt* . . . 3 3

Cooleen Strong (IRE) 14-1 C Penycate *(xnb) A bhnd; 18l 9th 1/2way; disp 22l 6th & rdn 12; t.o 14* . . . 12 4

Capacoostic (5a) 20-1 P Sheldrake *Hld up; mist 5; hmpd 7; 9l 6th 1/2way; wknd & 20l 5th 12; wl bhnd when pu 13* . . . P

203^{3} Chunito 9-1 James Tudor *Chsd ldrs; hmpd 7; 10l 7th 1/2way; wknd 10; t.o & pu 12* . . . P

Cottage Boy (IRE) 14-1 James Price *Sn wl bhnd; mist 6; t.o & pu 11* . . . P

Croesy Pennant 33-1 Miss F Wilson *Hld up; hdwy 9; 7l 5th 1/2way; wknd & 22l 6th 12; wl bhnd when pu 13* . . . P

204^{P} Hallbrook (5a) 14-1 A Hanly *(bnh,bnf) A bhnd; 23l 10th 1/2way; pu 10* . . . P

Ian's Boy 12-1 J L Llewellyn *Sn wl bhnd; 14th & t.o 1/2way; pu 13* . . . P

149^{P} King Marlon 20-1 T Faulkner *(xnb) A bhnd; mist 1; rmdrs 3; hit 6; 28l 11th 1/2way; t.o & pu 11* . . . P

202^{4} Musical Sleuth (7a) 20-1 J Price *Hld up & pulled hrd; a wl bhnd; 32l 12th 1/2way; t.o when blun 12; pu 13* . . . P

Pams Oak 5-2 T Vaughan *2 handlers; prom; 3l 4th 1/2way; 7l 4th 12; went 15l 3rd nxt; wkng when pu 15* . . . P

67^{P} Tragic Belle (5a) 20-1 L Stephens *(xnb) A wl bhnd; blun 3; mist 6; 36l 13th 1/2way; t.o & pu 10* . . . P

202^{F} Woodland Warrior 12-1 S Hughes *2 handlers; chsd ldrs; mist 4; 5th when fell 7* . . . F

256^{R} Wookey Woods (IRE) 20-1 R Hughes *(xnb) 2 handlers; hld up & pulled hrd; 17l 8th 1/2way; bhnd til pu 10; struck into himself; dead* . . . P

OFFICIAL DISTANCES: dist, 1 1/2*l* **TIME:** 6min 27.3s

363 Confined Maiden (Div 2), 12st — 16 ran

CALL ME SONIC 6-4F **D Jones** *2nd to 4; disp 8l 3rd 1/2way; went 6l 2nd 12; lft 20l clr 3 out; kpt on* . . . 1

259^{4} **Just Caramel** (5a)(tt) 5-1 **R Stephens** *Prom; 8l 3rd 1/2way; 10l 3rd 12; wknd & 15l 4th 14; lft 20l 2nd 3 out* . . . 20 2

173^{P} **Millys Filly** (5a) 14-1 **Miss F Wilson** *Lost tch 8; 27l 11th 1/2way; t.o 13; lft dist 3rd 3 out* . . . 30 3

Start It Up 14-1 J Price *(xnb) A wl bhnd; blun 3; t.o 10* . . . 1 4

Belle's Last (5a) 20-1 James Tudor *(xnb) Compact; 2 handlers; a wl bhnd; mist 2; t.o last 1/2way; pu 15* . . . P

Cedar Grove 7-1 P Sheldrake *10s-7s; nt fluent; nvr nr ldrs; 22l 8th 1/2way; no hdwy 11; wl bhnd when pu 13* . . . P

204^{P} Evans The Coal 14-1 James Price *(xnb) 2 handlers; swtng; ld; blun 8; hdd & mist 11; 5th & stpng qckly when blun & almost ur 12; t.o & ditto nxt; pu 15* P

Glastrian 14-1 G Perkins *Lost tch 8; 30l 12th 1/2way; 28l 9th 11; t.o & pu 15* P

202^{P} Indian Trix (IRE) (5a) 20-1 A Hanly *A wl bhnd; 32l 13th & rdn 1/2way; t.o & pu 13* . . . P

258^{P} Kuwait Faith (IRE) 20-1 M Wilesmith *(xnb) W ldrs; jmpd slow 3; lost plce 6; 25l 9th 1/2way; t.o & pu aft 12* . . . P

Lynwood Legend 8-1 J L Llewellyn *(xnb,bf) Blun 3; lost tch 8; 26l 10th 1/2way; t.o & pu 11* . . . P

Maloney (IRE) 16-1 Miss C Evans *Ss; blun 3; t.o 5; pu 11* . . . P

258^{F} Milamoss 8-1 T Vaughan *Nvr nr ldrs; 20l 6th 1/2way; wl bhnd when pu 11* . P

Ruby Dante (IRE) (5a) 12-1 S Hughes *Swtng; a.p; went 2nd 5; ld app 11; 5l clr when blun 13; 1l up when fell hvly 3 out* . . . F

203P Sergwyn 14-1 T Faulkner *(bh) Hld up; 21l 7th ½way; 25l 6th 11; wl bhnd when pu 13* . . . P
Sumerian Lad 8-1 J Sole *Chsd ldrs; 14l 5th ½way; went 4th 12 & 10l 3rd nxt; 4l down & clsng when hmpd & ur 3 out* . . . U

OFFICIAL DISTANCES: 30*l*, 20*l* **TIME:** 6min 41.2s

Duke of Beaufort's

Didmarton (LH 10F,18J)

Sat, 6 Mar (FIRM, GOOD to FIRM in places)

364 Hunt Members — 5 ran

	MACHALINI 7-4 **A Morley** *(xnb) Jw; went 2nd 4; ld 7; 6l clr 12; staying on str when lft virt solo 3 out*		1
	Che Guevara 6-4F **A Wintle** *3s-6/4; 2 handlers; hld up in tch; 8l 3rd 12; plodded on; lft rem 2nd 3 out; hit nxt; dem app last*	30	2
	Mr Magget (IRE) 7-1 **R Hawker** *(xnb) Ld 2-7; lost tch 12; tlng off when blun 13*	runin	3
145P	Native King (IRE) 7-4 M Walters *Jmpd slow at times; ld to 2; 5l 2nd 11; lost plce 12; no ch frm 14; went rem 2nd app last; fin 25l 2nd; disq - nt draw wt*		2d
	Mazury (USA) (7a) 12-1 Miss E Tuck *(xnb) Pulled hrd; last to 11; went 2nd nxt; chsd wnr vain aft; 5l down 15; blun & ur 3 out*		U

OFFICIAL DISTANCES: Originally 35*l*, 5*l* **TIME:** 6min 04.0s

Native King finished second but was disqualified for failing to draw the correct weight (had carried no weights and was more than five pounds light); the stewards decided (wrongly) not to impose a fine as there had been no intention to break the rules

365 Intermediate, 12st — 11 ran

261¹	**SKIP 'N' TUNE (IRE)** (5a) 4-1 **M Miller** *Hld up; 7th 8; smooth prog in 3rd 12 & 2nd app 15; rdn to ld flat; drew clr*		1
14¹	**Kerstino Two** 5-4F **J Snowden** *2 handlers; hit 7; ld & keen til bad mist 11 & hdd; ld agn app 15; drvn aft 2 out; hdd & outpcd flat*	2	2
265¹	**Pulham Downe** 14-1 **Miss E Tory** *(xnb) Mostly 2nd/3rd til lft in ld 11; mist 14; sn hdd; wknd 2 out*	10	3
223²	Camden Carrig (IRE) 2-1 N Phillips *Rn in snatches; went 2nd 2-4; 6th 8; wide when nt fluent 10; chsd ldrs til 8l 4th & outpcd app 15*	2	4
	Rain Delay 5-1 R Rogers *Mostly 2nd to 8; lost plce 10; strugg in 8th 14; plugged on*	3	5
	Lava (5a) 5-1 M Wall *(xnb) Tk keen hld in midfield; wknd 14; 5th & btn app nxt*	10	6
50P	Itsallupintheair 12-1 T Vaughan *Trckd ldrs; 5th 12; wknd 14; pu 3 out*		P
261P	Millcroft Regatta (IRE) 20-1 N Wilmington *(xnb) Last by 5; nvr gng wl; poor 10th 14; pu 2 out*		P
	Mister Rf (IRE) 12-1 E Kenney-Herbert *Bckwd; prom; 4th 8; wknd 12; 7th 14; 35l last when ur last*		U
187²	Nousayri (IRE) 12-1 J Trice-Rolph *(xnb) Nt fluent 2; last trio; strugg 14; wl bhnd when pu 2 out*		P
193³	Vercheny (5a) 14-1 C Heard *(xnb) Mostly last trio; wknd 12; poor 9th 14; pu 15*		P

OFFICIAL DISTANCES: 3*l*, 10*l* **TIME:** 6min 01.0s

366 Mixed Open, 12st — 5 ran

277³	**FRIAR WADDON** 15-8 **C Heard** *(xnb) Settled last til qcknd to disp ld 12-14; stdly drew clr; 8l ahd 2 out; easily*		1
310²	**Shobrooke Mill** 5-6F **A Charles-Jones** *(xnb) Cl up til ld 11; w wnr 12-14; rdn & outpcd nxt*	8	2
254⁶	**O J Selym (IRE)** (7x) 40-1 **G Opperman** *Ld 2 til jmpd slow 3; ld 9-11; cl up til 13 3rd & wkng 14; rallied brief nxt; hit 3 out; sn fdd*	7	3
254⁵	Rolling Maul (IRE) 12-1 J Horton *Ld to 2 & 3-9; lost tch 13; 16l last 15*	20	4
254²	Rusty Fellow 4-1 D Mansell *Cl up in rr when fell 3*		F

OFFICIAL DISTANCES: 8*l*, 10*l* **TIME:** 6min 07.0s

367 Open Maiden 56&7yo (Div 1), 12st — 7 ran

Form	Horse	Dist	Pos
86[3]	**RADBROOK HALL** (7a) 7-4F **P Callaghan** *2nd/3rd til ld 11; blun 13 & hdd; ld agn app 15; nk ahd 2 out; rdn to gain upper hand flat*		1
173[P]	**Eastern Apple** (5a) 8-1 **B Pauling** *2nd/3rd; prsd wnr & ev ch frm 15 til hopelessly outrdn flat*	1	2
174[3]	**Lutteur Bleu (FR)** (7a) 5-2 **M Miller** *(xnb) Mid-div & hld up; 3rd 11; ev ch 14; wknd nxt; jmpd mod aft.*	25	3
	Brer Bear (7a) 8-1 M Walters *Settled in tch; hmpd 9; 6l last 11; lost tch 12; pu 14*		P
	Ham Lane (7a) 7-2 F Hutsby *(xnb) Stdd start; jmpd sketchy; last to 6; pulled to 3rd nxt; lft in ld 8; hdd & fell 9*		F
	Panto 12-1 Miss K Lovelace *Nt fluent early; chsd ldrs; hmpd 9; 5th 11; wknd nxt; wl bhnd when pu 14*		P
	Silk St Bridget (5a) 16-1 G Tumelty *Ld & hit 1; hung rt & wanted to rn out 8 & hdd; ld agn nxt; hdd 12; lft in ld 13; hit 14; sn passed & wknd; pu 3 out*		P

OFFICIAL DISTANCES: 1*l*, 30*l* **TIME:** 6min 23.0s

368 Open Maiden 56&7yo (Div 2), 12st - 17J — 11 ran

Form	Horse	Dist	Pos
329[U]	**WESTERN FRONTIER (IRE)** (7a) 5-2 **J Snowden** *(xnb) Hld up; 6th aft 9; clsd 13; chall & jmpd slow 2 out; 4th & rdn & lkd btn app omitted last; drvn & kpt on game to ld nr fin.*		1
87[P]	**Saffron Hill (IRE)** (7a) 6-1 **F Hutsby** *Cl up; ld aft 9; hdd brief 12; slt advant aft; drvn frm 2 out; hdd cl home.*	nk	2
121[P]	**Willoughby Flyer** 7-1 **M Walters** *Prom; mostly 3rd frm 9; mist 14; ev ch 2 out; wknd passing omitted last*	3	3
	Victim (IRE) 7-1 D England *Hld up; 4th 11; went 2nd 14; rdn & ev ch passing omitted last; sn wknd*	4	4
257[2]	Primitive Son 6-4F P Morris *Opened 2s; stdd start; a t.o; blun 13; pckd nxt*	30	5
237[F]	Deep Pockets (IRE) (7a) 7-1 M Miller *(xnb) Hld up; 7th & in tch when blun & ur 9*		U
290[6]	One For Olly (IRE) 14-1 G Walters *Prom til ur 8*		U
149[R]	Rody (IRE) 16-1 M Keen *(xnb,pricker o/s) Tk keen hld in ld til rn out 7*		R
112[P]	Rundetto (IRE) 25-1 S Moreton *(xnb) 2 handlers; chsd ldrs; blun 2, 4 & when 5th 10; sn wknd; pu 12*		P
	Spencive 16-1 G Tumelty *Lkd appalling; nrly ref 1, 2 & 3; a completely t.o; pu 5*		P
257[4]	The Luddite(bl) 14-1 H Dowty *2nd til lft in ld 7; hdd aft 9; ld brief 12; stpd to nil nxt; pu 15.*		P

OFFICIAL DISTANCES: nk, 5*l* **TIME:** 6min 10.0s

Fence 18 omitted - fallen rider

369 Restricted, 12st — 14 ran

Form	Horse	Dist	Pos
294[3]	**DAISY FAY** (5a) 20-1 **H Dowty** *Hld up towards rr til smooth prog to disp 2nd 13; ld app 15 & sn 3l clr; hit nxt; nt rdn & hung rt app last & hdd; rallied to ld & draw clr flat (wl-handled)*		1
252[8]	**Campden Kitty** (5a) 7-1 **F Hutsby** *Handy; ld aft 10; hdd aft 15; kpt on & lft in ld last; drvn & sn hdd; no ex*	2½	2
294[6]	**Rommel** 4-1 **J Trice-Rolph** *Hld up & bhnd; last 10; still wl adrift 13; 13l 4th 3 out; kpt on to 3rd flat; too much to do.*	1	3
294[7]	Moscow's Return (IRE) 14-1 M Keel *Handy; went 2nd app 11-13; 9l 3rd 3 out; rdn & clsd app last; put hd in air & nt go thro*	2½	4
169[P]	Master Grass 14-1 P Mason *Chsd ldrs; went 3rd 11; prsd ldrs til disp 7l 3rd 15; sn btn*	6	5
252[5]	Alvero (FR) 8-1 R Armson *Midfield; jmpd slow 5; hit 6 & 7; 5th app 11; outpcd 13; 15l 6th 15*	20	6
252[P]	Almost A Day(bl,tt) 25-1 D Mansell *Reluct to line up but dashed in & gt flyer; ld to 1 but sn stdd; midfield when blun 9; rr & drvn 11; nt keen; pu 12.*		P
	Black Optimist (IRE) 7-1 Mrs K Baimbridge *Bckwd; ld 2-8; lft in ld 9 til jb rt 10 & stpd to nil; t.o & pu 14*		P
250[6]	Ferryhill (IRE) 20-1 Miss L Bridges *(xnb) V sis; a t.o; pu 9.*		P
119[1]	Hug The Bend 10-1 D Edwards *(xnb) A towards rr; wl bhnd when pu 12*		P
262[3]	Macaroni Beach (5a) 10-1 Miss E Tory *Ld to 2; dived rt & nrly ur 3; lost plce 8; 7th app 11; pu 13*		P

198[2] Mister Swallow 3-1JF M Miller *Hld up; prog to 3rd 10; jmpd slow 12; nt r.o; wl btn when pu 14* . . . . P
231[U] Misty Ramble (IRE) 3-1JF G McPherson *Went 2nd & rdr nrly f.o 4; ld 8 til rfo 9* U
252[3] Snowtre (IRE)(cp) 6-1 A Wintle *(xnb) A towards rr; brief eff in 6th app 11; wknd nxt; pu 14*. . . . . P

OFFICIAL DISTANCES: 3½l, 2l **TIME:** 6min 07.0s

370 Open Maiden 8yo&up, 12st — 15 ran

130[2] **BRASS RAZOO** 9-4F **S Morris** *2nd/4th; chall & ½l 2nd 15; outpcd aft nxt; 6l down & btn when lft 3l clr 2 out; hrd prsd & jmpd delib last; drvn & fnd ex cl home*. 1
Beau Jake (IRE) 10-1 **R Armson** *Settled handy; 6th 8; went prom 11 & 2nd/3rd aft; outpcd 3 out; lft 2nd nxt; drvn to chall last; no ex final 100yds*. 1 2
258[3] **Jenny's Charmer** 11-4 **F Hutsby** *(xnb) Tk keen hld in midfield; 8th 8; eff in 6l 4th 13; pckd nxt; lost tch aft mist 15* 25 3
295[3] Arctic Summer (IRE) 7-2 J Trice-Rolph *Midfield; 9th & outpcd 8; 20l 6th 13; rem last when pu last* . . . . P
Billy Whitelies (IRE) 6-1 S Joynes *12s-6s; ld to 2; 2nd/3rd til ld agn 11; drew clr 3 out; 6l ahd & in comm when fell nxt* . . . . F
264[6] Busmans Holiday (IRE) 16-1 S Coady *Chsd ldrs; 7th 8; wknd 10; pu 12* . . P
Dun Aengus 10-1 H Tett *Last when blun 2; poor 12th when rn out & demolished wing 10* . . . . R
139[P] Final Magic 5-1 A Charles-Jones *(xnb) Pulled hrd & chsd ldrs; blun 6; 5th 8; went 2nd brief 10; wknd 13; rem 5th when fell 15* . . . . F
General Ben 12-1 M Miller *Wl bhnd; poor 13th 8; t.o & pu 13*. . . . . P
Green Ice 12-1 H Kinchin *(xnb) Rcd free; ld 3-4; 2nd til ld agn aft 9-11; wknd rap; 25l 3rd 13; pu nxt*. . . . . P
Masitat (5a) 14-1 P Mason *Novicey; towards rr; mod 10th 8; t.o & pu 13* . P
295[P] Master Jay Jay (IRE) 14-1 M Keel *Bhnd; blun 6; 11th & strugg 8; t.o & pu 13* P
Oneforthefrog (IRE) 25-1 G Tumelty *Ld 2-3; lost plce rap; 14th & t.o 8; pu 9* P
Phar And Away (5a) 33-1 Miss H Bevan *Ss & lost 25l; rushed up to ld 4; hdd aft 9; stpd to nil; t.o & pu 12*. . . . . P
Polar Bright (IRE) 33-1 D Edwards *(xnb) A rr; t.o when mist 9; pu 10* . . . . P

OFFICIAL DISTANCES: 1l, 20l **TIME:** 6min 11.0s

Thurlow

Horseheath (RH 10F,18J)

Sat, 6 Mar (GOOD, GOOD to FIRM in places)

371 Open Maiden 56&7yo, 12st — 10 ran

219[C] **GERMANY PARK (IRE)** 4-6F **M Smith** *(xnb) 2 handlers; made all; mostly 2l up til lft 12l clr 14; 20l ahd when hit 3 out; v easily*. 1
Round The Isles 5-1 **R Cope** *V green; reluct to enter padd til called sweetheart by trainer; sis; 8l 5th 6; pushed along & hdwy 11; 12l 4th & outpcd 15; kpt on stdly; 21l 3rd 3 out; went 2nd nxt; improve - lks nice prospect*. 20 2
Just Lute 25-1 **G Wigley** *2nd til 3rd 5; sn outpcd by ldng pr; kpt on to 20l 2nd 3 out; dem nxt*. 3 3
218[3] Barry Lydon (IRE) 8-1 T Lane *Jb; 4th & blun 3; drpd to rr & blun 6; last when blun bad 10; pu 11* . . . . P
218[P] Daisy Duke (5a) 16-1 A Braithwaite *Last pr; t.o & pu 14*. . . . . P
245[P] Divine Mist (IRE) 16-1 J Owen *Jmpd poor & to rt; rr; hdwy 12; 10l 3rd 13; lft 2nd nxt; wknd 15; releg last 3 out; reluct & climbed 3 out & nxt; t.o & pu last* . . . . P
219[5] Inching Brook 20-1 P Taiano *(xnb) Hld up towards rr; eased & pu aft 10* . . P
219[P] Jumping Jeffrey 25-1 M Mackley *(xnb) In tch; 6l 5th 9; wl in rr when rn out thro wing & fell 14* . . . . R
105[P] Northall Lad 6-1 P Cowley *Sn prom; 2l 2nd 5; chsd ldr aft; still 2l down when fell 14* . . . . F
40[P] Sleeping Panther 25-1 P Millington *Prom til lost plce & drpd to rr 9; t.o & pu 12* P

OFFICIAL DISTANCES: 20l, 3l **TIME:** 6min 41.0s **TOTE:** £1.60 **DF:£7.60**

372 Intermediate, 12st — 5 ran

Form	Runner	Dist	Pos
127[1]	**FANE COUNSEL (IRE)** 1-4F **R Burton** *Made all & a in comm; 2-3l ahd til qcknd downhill & 6l clr 15; pushed out*		1
159[1]	**Cantarinho** 4-1 **D Kemp** *Chsd wnr vain in 2-3l 2nd til outpcd & 6l 2nd 14; pckd nxt; rdn & kpt on frm 2 out; a hld*	4	2
161[8]	**Princess Derry** (5a) 12-1 **C Cundall** *Reared & ur padd; last pr til 3rd 3; 6l down 7; stdly lost tch; 15l 3rd 11; t.o 13*	fence	3
248[5]	Prologue (IRE) (12ow) 25-1 C Jarvis *Fell 1; rdr inj*		F
158[P]	Valman (IRE) 25-1 P Millington *3rd til last 3; 8l mists 5 & 6; blun bad & reins flew over horse's hd 10; hopelessly t.o 11; pu 3 out*		P

OFFICIAL DISTANCES: 2½l, dist **TIME:** 6min 18.0s **TOTE:** £1.30 **DF:**£1.10

373 Gerrard Ladies Open — 7 ran

Form	Runner	Dist	Pos
126[1]	**MACFIN (IRE)**(cp) 2-1 **Miss L Allan** *3s-2s; ld; jnd aft 3 out; hdd nxt; 1l 2nd at last; r.o game flat; ld cl home*.		1
126[3]	**Spring Gale (IRE)** evensF **Miss Z Turner** *Opened 5/4; tde; cl 2nd til 4l 3rd 6; prsd ldr 12 til jmpd to ld 2 out; 1l ahd last; outbattled & hdd cl home*. .	¾	2
246[P]	**Borrow Mine (IRE)** 33-1 **Miss L Marriott** *Mostly 3rd til 5l 4th & nt qckn aft 15; 3rd agn nxt; kpt on game flat; just hld*.	2	3
123[1]	General Confusion (IRE) 16-1 Miss B Czepulkowski *1st ride; prom; 2l 2nd 6; 5l 4th 12; jmpd to 3rd 15; nt qckn uphill & dem agn nxt; one pce aft*. .	10	4
249[12]	Mister Audi (IRE) 20-1 Miss A Bowles *Nrly a 5th; 6l 5th 7; nvr nrr*.	4	5
	Dook's Delight (IRE) 6-1 Miss L Horsfall *1st ride (what a name for a new jockey); a last pr; 8l 6th 7; outpcd 14; kpt on one pce frm nxt*	8	6
126[P]	Pele Mele (FR) 20-1 Miss S Firmin *Imm last & nt keen; t.o & blun 10; pu 11*		P

OFFICIAL DISTANCES: nk, 1l **TIME:** 6min 30.0s **TOTE:** £3.30 **DF:**£1.70

374 Mens Open, 12st — 6 ran

Form	Runner	Dist	Pos
	TEMPLEBREEDY (IRE) 4-5F **R Burton** *Made all in 2-3l ld; kpt on resolute frm 3 out*		1
124[P]	**Teeton Priceless** (5a) 5-1 **R Cope** *3l 2nd til 3rd 6; trckd ldrs aft; jmpd to 2l 2nd 14; prsd wnr 3 out-nxt; no ex last*.	2	2
156[P]	**Militaire (FR)** (7x) 7-1 **J Owen** *Trckd ldrs in 3rd/4th; hdwy 11; 2nd 13; 1l down when sprawled on landing & dem 14; ev ch 3 out; nt qckn nxt* . . .	4	3
89[P]	Be My Dream (IRE) (7x) 2-1 P Cowley *Cl 4th to 5; dashed to 6l 2nd 6 til outpcd 12; 8l 4th & one pce 14*.	6	4
	Exclusive Air (USA) (7a) 3-1 P Millington *Lkd utterly miserable padd; jmpd atrocious in rr; blun bad 2; last nxt; hopeless t.o & pu 11*		P
177[P]	Weavers Choice 6-1 N Pearce *Swtng; reared up start & lost 15l; sn in tch; 5th 3; 5l 4th 10; pushed along & nt r.o 12; wknd qckly; last 14; t.o & pu 3 out*		P

OFFICIAL DISTANCES: 2l, 2l **TIME:** 6min 37.0s **TOTE:** £1.70 **DF:**£9.60

375 Restricted, 12st — 14 ran

Form	Runner	Dist	Pos
	PRISTEEN SPY 12-1 **R Burton** *(xnb) Disp ld til ld 5-12; jnd ldr agn 14; ½l up when lft wl clr 15; easily*		1
169[P]	**Teeton Fizz** (5a) 12-1 **N Pearce** *Prom; 5l 4th 5; 10l 3rd & outpcd 14; lft poor 2nd 15; chsd wnr vain aft*	25	2
127[2]	**Present Moment (IRE)** 4-1 **N Moore** *(xnb) Sn outpcd & bhnd; t.o 5th 14; plodded into 4th nxt & rem 3rd 3 out*	30	3
224[2]	Camden Loch (IRE) 20-1 N Bloom *Trckd ldrs; 6l 6th 6; outpcd by ldng pr 10; t.o 4th 14; lft 3rd brief nxt*	6	4
245[P]	Granny Dick (5a) 25-1 T Messenger *Nt jw; sn wl in rr; hopelessly t.o 14* . .	5	5
172[1]	Agua Ardente 7-4F R Cope *Swtng; disp ld to 4; 1l 2nd & pckd 5; prsd ldr til ld agn 13; jnd nxt; ½l 2nd when blun & ur 15*.		U
159[P]	Broad Edge (IRE) 14-1 R Stearn *(xnb) Sn prom; 5th when blun 5; wkng when blun 11; pu 12*		P
249[U]	Ical (IRE) (5a) 12-1 T Lane *Mid-div til outpcd frm 10; dist 8th when pu 13*		P
223[P]	Jerome Jerome(cp) 16-1 P York *Mist 1; mid-div; wl in rr by 15; 7th & last when pu 3 out*		P
223[P]	Lord Montagu (IRE) 8-1 M Smith *Prom to 4; sn lost plce; wl bhnd when pu 11*		P
219[1]	Mister Ringa 3-1 A Braithwaite *Sa; a wl bhnd & nvr gng wl; last pr 2; blun 5; t.o & pu 14*		P
155[P]	Mr Moonbeam (IRE) 12-1 M Buchan *2 handlers; last 2; sn t.o; pu 14*. . . .		P

250^{3}	Run Monty (IRE) 8-1 M Mackley *(xnb) In tch in mid-div til lost plce 10; eased & pu nxt*		P
252^{P}	What A Charmer (IRE) 12-1 J Burley *Prom; 4l 3rd 5; outpcd 13; sn rr; disp rem 5th when pu 2 out*		P

OFFICIAL DISTANCES: 20*l*, 25*l* **TIME:** 6min 34.0s **TOTE:** £25.40 **DF:**£14.40

376 Confined, 12st — 7 ran

	ALGAN (FR) 7-1 **P York** *Pulling; hit 1; handy; went 2nd 7 til lft in ld 12; sn wl clr; v easily*		1
124^{1}	**Bard Of Drumcoo (IRE)** (6x) 4-7F **D Kemp** *2 handlers; trckd ldrs in 2nd/3rd til 2nd 12; lost tch qckly; btn when blun & dem brief 14*	20	2
158^{4}	**Leatherback (IRE)** 7-1 **J Owen** *(xnb) 6th; rdn along 9; hdwy 11; 2nd brief aft 14; qckly lost tch; reluct & clambered fncs frm 3 out*	30	3
39^{3}	Arctic Snip 20-1 N Moore *Towards rr til last 9; blun 13; sn t.o & climbing fncs*	15	4
224^{1}	Lord Euro (IRE) (3x) 5-2 A Merriam *(xnb) Ld til fell 11*		F
158^{P}	Persian Bandit (IRE) 12-1 M Mackley *Imm last; 5th brief 7; pu 12*		P
123^{2}	The Glen Road (IRE) 4-1 A Sansome *Trckd ldr til 4th & rdn 10; lost tch qckly; t.o & pu 14*		P

OFFICIAL DISTANCES: 25*l*, dist **TIME:** 6min 46.0s **TOTE:** £16.50 **DF:**£7.40

Market Rasen (RH 8F,19J)

Sun, 7 Mar (GOOD to SOFT, SOFT in places)

377 Sharpen The Mind: Betfair Nov HC, 3m1f £1340 — 9 ran

297^{1}	**ABABOU (FR)** 11-07 9-2 **S Charlton** *Hld up; last when blun 3; hdwy 7; hit 9 & 10; sn rdn; chsd ldr 12; lft 20l clr nxt; rdn app 2 out; jmpd slow last; idled v bad flat; all out*		1
299^{1}	**Supreme Silence (IRE)** 11-07 13-2 **Miss L Allan** *Prom; mist 1; nt fluent 4; outpcd aft 12; lft 20l 2nd nxt; stayed on frm 2 out & made 12l flat but nvr lkd like catching stpng wnr*	$3\frac{1}{2}$	2
292^{3}	**Watchyourback (NZ)** 11-07(vis,tt) 6-1 **S Gray** *Ld/disp til jmpd slow 11; wknd nxt; lft rem 3rd 13; virt pu flat*	dist	3
	Fountain Street (IRE) 11-11 12-1 O Nelmes *W ldr til ld 11; sn hdd & wknd rap; t.o & pu 3 out*		P
256^{1}	Jackson (FR) 11-09 7-2 T Malone *Hld up; hit 2; jmpd slow 4; hdwy in 4th 10; ld aft 11; mist nxt; slt ld when mist & ur 13*		U
55^{P}	Panooras Lord (IRE) 11-07 33-1 B King *Tk keen hld; hld up; pckd 6; 6th & strugg 10; fell hvly 12*		F
316^{2}	Scottish Roots 11-11 5-2F T Greenall *Mists; bhnd; rmdrs 7; nvr lkd keen; poor 8th 10; t.o & pu 13*		P
341^{7}	Sledmere (IRE) 11-07 66-1 M Seston *Chsd ldrs to 9; 7th & lsng tch u.p nxt; t.o & pu 13*		P
106^{6}	Stevie Dee 11-07 33-1 O Williams *Mist 5 & rdr lurched forward; rr aft; drvn 6; sn t.o; pu aft 10*		P

TIME: 6min 59.6s **TOTE:** £4.90; places £1.70,£2.00,£1.50 **Ex:**£22.70 **CSF:**£31.91

Cottesmore

Garthorpe (RH 8F,18J)

Sun, 7 Mar (GOOD)

378 Hunt Members, 12st — 8 ran

	OVER THE MASTER (IRE) 8-1 **T Coles** *Ld to 2; chsd ldrs; ld 14-15; lft disp ld nxt; sn ld; drew clr frm 2 out; rdn out; rdr's 1st wnr*		1
	Jumping Jack 8-1 **S Morris** *Chsd ldrs; went 2nd 11; mist 14; lft in ld 3 out; sn hdd; wknd nxt*	10	2
	Theridamas (IRE) 20-1 **R Collinson** *(xnb) Tk keen hld; ld 2nd; 8l clr 7; hdd 14; wknd frm nxt; lft 15l 3rd 2 out*	15	3
250^{P}	Treble Trouble (3x) 12-1 P Millington *Mid-div; eff to 2nd 9-11; wknd qckly app 13; t.o*	30	4
	Codys Castle(bl) 33-1 Miss L Collinson *Swtng; 2 handlers; ld in start; in tch to 7; 15l last 8; blun 9; t.o frm 12*	$2\frac{1}{2}$	5

Form	Runner	Dist	Pos
249[8]	Buckland Bobby (3x) 14-1 Miss L Fear *Last til pu 5*		P
	Holywell Girl (5a) 6-1 R Armson *Nvr gng wl; jmpd slow 3; rmdrs nxt; 12l 6th & rdn 8; no resp; t.o & pu 11*		P
298[2]	Noble Affair (5a, 5x) 2-5F M Mackley *Ww; mist 5; blun 10; hdwy nxt; ld 15; 3l clr & gng wl when fell nxt*		F

OFFICIAL DISTANCES: 14*l*, 18*l* **TIME:** 6min 31.0s

379 Intermediate, 12st — 11 ran

Form	Runner	Dist	Pos
106[1]	**NAUTICAL LAD** (5x) 9-4F **J Docker** *A gng wl; mid-div; chsd ldr frm 11; ld app 2 out; clr last; easily; impressive*		1
	Miss Hoity Toity (5a) 14-1 **A Sansome** *Ld; clr 4; 4l ld aft 15; hdd & hit 2 out; no ch w wnr aft*	10	2
92[2]	**Finder Keeps (USA)** 4-1 **J Jenkins** *Mid-div; mist 6; mist & rmdrs 9; hdwy 11; chsd ldrs 13; outpcd by ldng pr app 3 out*	8	3
289[F]	My Best Buddy 7-1 R Cope *Ww in tch; blun 3; jnd ldrs 11; 3rd & rdn app 3 out; btn nxt*	2	4
231[2]	Kasilia (FR) 14-1 Miss V Simpson *A bhnd; r.o frm 2 out; nvr nrr*	12	5
289[7]	Light The Sky 25-1 Miss K Norris *A mid-div; no ch frm 12*	hd	6
249[3]	Crackrattle (IRE) (6ow) 20-1 A Brown *Bhnd; stayed on frm 2 out; nd*	½	7
228[3]	Dainty Man (IRE) 20-1 Miss T Clark *Chsd ldrs to 10; 6th & outpcd app 13; sn no ch*	10	8
11[P]	Mustang Molly (5a) 16-1 A Martin *Chsd ldr til mist 11; wknd app 13; 7th & no ch 15*	3	9
228[1]	Marston Moses (5x) 4-1 A Bealby *Prom to 3; stdly lost plce; 16l 9th 8; last 11; t.o when blun 15*	15	10
	Saxon Gold 8-1 L Hicks *Chsd ldrs; mist 6; wknd 12; wl bhnd frm 14; pu 3 out*		P

OFFICIAL DISTANCES: 15*l*, 12*l* **TIME:** 6min 21.0s

380 Ladies Open — 10 ran

Form	Runner	Dist	Pos
146[4]	**GAROLO (FR)**(bl) 3-1 **Miss V Tremlett** *Prom; 2l 2nd aft 15; ld 2 out; idled & jnd 100yds out; fnd ex & ld final 50yds*		1
299[3]	**Ardmayle (IRE)** 11-10F **Miss L Coney** *Mist 1; trckd ldrs; mist 8; lft in ld 15; hit nxt; hdd & mist 2 out; rallied & ev ch flat til outpcd last 50yds*	½	2
254[F]	**Native Man (IRE)** 12-1 **Miss T Clark** *(xnb) Ld 2; clr 5; hdd 14; outpcd by ldng pr frm 3 out*	10	3
299[U]	River Ness (5a) 6-1 Mrs V Thirlby *Ld to 2; chsd ldrs; ld 14 til blun bad & releg 4th nxt; nt rec & one pce aft*	3	4
249[10]	Bruan (IRE)(cp) 25-1 Miss J Bevin *A mid-div; 20l 5th & mist 10; nvr on terms*	15	5
299[P]	Sheskinqueen (IRE) (5a) 40-1 Miss A Wells *Stdd start; wl bhnd; some prog & 25l 6th 10; nvr nr ldrs*	8	6
289[P]	Ela Agapi Mou (USA)(bl) 16-1 Miss D Ball *A bhnd; t.o 11; r.o flat; nd*	½	7
289[U]	Gortroe Guy (IRE) 25-1 Miss K Robinson *(xnb) A bhnd; mist 5; t.o*	15	8
33[U]	Sunshine Leader (IRE) (5a) 6-1 Miss S Samworth *Bhnd; mist 2; blun 8; 30l 7th when blun 11; t.o & pu 3 out*		P
	Veredarius (FR) 40-1 Mrs S Tyler *Last frm 5; t.o aft 7 til pu 11*		P

OFFICIAL DISTANCES: ¾*l*, 14*l* **TIME:** 6min 22.0s

381 Land Rover Mens Open (Div 1), 12st — 11 ran

Form	Runner	Dist	Pos
156[3]	**SHANAVOGH** (7x) 5-2 **R Hunnisett** *Chsd ldrs; went 2nd 11; ld app 13; sn clr; 10l up 15; in comm aft*		1
228[6]	**Pagermar (IRE)** 8-1 **R Burton** *Chsd ldrs; 4th & outpcd 13; went 2nd 2 out; no ch w wnr*	30	2
	Gillone 4-1 **J Docker** *Rdn in padd; swtng; tde; in tch; went 2nd app 13; 7l down & rdn 14; no ch w wnr aft; dem & blun 2 out; just kpt 3rd*	6	3
	Grecian Star (7x) 9-4F J Tarry *Ww in tch; 10l 6th & pushed along app 13; sn no ch; nrly snatched 3rd*	hd	4
249[13]	Drum Battle (7x)(cp) 8-1 R Cope *(xnb) Ld; mist 9; hdd app 13; sn outpcd by wnr; 3rd & no ch 3 out; t.o*	20	5
229[U]	Devonshire (IRE) 7-1 P Bennett *A bhnd; t.o 13*	20	6
300[P]	Strong Chairman (IRE) 8-1 K O'Brien *Bhnd; last frm 6; t.o 9*	30	7
228[P]	Easby Blue 33-1 J Buxton *(xnb) Last & jmpd slow 1; prog & in tch 8; 12l 7th & strugg 11; t.o.*	1	8
	Deel Quay (IRE) 20-1 N Docker *A bhnd; mist 6; 9th & no ch 12; pu 14*		P

Itsforu 20-1 J Jenkins *Chsd ldrs 4 til app 13; 8l 3rd & strugg when blun & ur 14* . . . . . U
158F Merry Minstrel (IRE) (7x) 20-1 L Hicks *2 handlers; ww; prog 9; 8l 7th when blun 10; lost tch 12; t.o & pu 3 out* . . . . . P

OFFICIAL DISTANCES: dist, 10l **TIME:** 6min 25.0s

382 Land Rover Mens Open (Div 2), 12st — 10 ran

PRINCE DUNDEE (FR) 10-1 **R Burton** *Opened 14s; ww in tch; cl 4th 11; trckd ldr frm 15; ld 3 out; rdn & qcknd clr app last; comf* 1
190[1] **Down (FR)** (7x) 5-4F **S Waley-Cohen** *Ww; last 4; prog 9; 4l 5th 13; chall 2 out; outpcd by wnr app last* 4 2
346P **Bold King (FR)** (7x)(cp) 5-1 **P Morris** *Jmpd lft; a.p; 3l 4th & rdn 3 out; kpt on one pce* 8 3
170P Private Pete (7x) 5-2 S Morris *Chsd ldrs; rmdrs 9; 7l 6th & rdn 14; wl outpcd frm nxt* 10 4
187[3] Bullfinch (7x) 8-1 P Cowley *Rr; in tch; 7th & rdn 11; 10l 7th app 3 out; no ch nxt; passed btn horses flat* . . . . . nk 5
170P Some Go West (IRE) 6-1 R Cope *Cl up; ld app 13; hdd 3 out; imm btn; t.o* 6 6
Bengal Boy 16-1 B Pollock *Ld; mist 6; hdd app 13; 2nd when blun 15; wknd app nxt* 5 7
4[3] Storm Forecast (IRE) 12-1 P Andrew *In tch til 8th & outpcd 12; no ch aft; t.o* 40 8
Lord Of The Chase (IRE) 33-1 T Messenger *Prom to 4; bhnd frm 8; t.o & pu 13* P
251P Preferred (IRE) 33-1 R Armson *Mid-div; in tch when fell 8* . . . . . F

OFFICIAL DISTANCES: 4l, 9l **TIME:** 6min 27.0s

383 Restricted (Div 1), 12st — 16 ran

CHRISTY BEAMISH (IRE) 2-1F **R Burton** *Keen; hld up; last 3; smooth prog to 3rd app 3 out; stalked ldr 2 out; qcknd to ld last; cruised clr; v impressive* 1
191[2] **Boyne Banks (IRE)** 5-1 **G Disney** *A.p; ld 2-7; cl up til ld 3 out; hdd last; brushed aside flat* 4 2
King's Hero (IRE) 20-1 **N Docker** *Prom; ld 7-3 out; wknd app nxt & sn no ch* 6 3
142[1] Who's Eddie (IRE) 6-1 F Hutsby *(xnb) Chsd ldrs; 5l 5th when hit 14; outpcd app 3 out* 12 4
250[4] Bunratty's Sole (IRE) 10-1 N Bloom *2 handlers; in tch; rdn 14; 7l 6th app 3 out; no ch frm nxt* 6 5
218[1] Just Jove 8-1 R Cope *Ld to 2; prom; mist 8; 6l 4th 3 out; sn wknd* . . . . . hd 6
I'm Dreaming (IRE) 8-1 A Martin *Chsd ldrs; cl 5th 11; outpcd frm nxt; no ch frm 15* 20 7
164R Tinarana Lord (IRE) 10-1 G Hanmer *2 handlers; mid-div; in tch; 8th 11; sn outpcd; t.o* 12 8
Athenry Lass (5a) 33-1 P Newton *A bhnd; pckd 5; t.o 8 til pu 3 out* . . . . . P
Crested Manor 12-1 A Sansome *Bhnd; mist 8; rdn & no resp nxt; pu 11* . . P
Devils Domino 33-1 M Mackley *Rr when jmpd big & ur 1* . . . . . U
223[4] Libido 25-1 P Andrew *A bhnd; t.o 12 til pu 2 out* . . . . . P
191[3] Miss Zarnni (5a) 12-1 L Hicks *Nt jw; last when blun 7; t.o frm nxt til pu 12* P
Moscow Tradition (IRE) 12-1 J Docker *Strong-topped; ww bhnd; prog & 8l 10th 11; outpcd app 13; t.o & pu 3 out* . . . . . P
Rathbarry Lad (IRE) 7-1 S Morris *Ww in rr; prog 9; 7l 9th when blun 11; nvr rchd ldrs; 8th & no ch when blun 2 out; pu last* . . . . . P
Romanybaan 33-1 E Linehan *2 handlers; a bhnd; blun 10; rdn & lost tch nxt; pu 12* . . . . . P

OFFICIAL DISTANCES: 5l, 7l **TIME:** 6min 23.0s

384 Restricted (Div 2), 12st — 7 ran

109[2] **COOLEFIND (IRE)** 4-6F **S Morris** *Ww in tch; blun 11; went 2nd gng wl app 3 out; ld 2 out; qcknd clr; v easily* 1
Balmoral Spring (IRE)(bl) 10-1 **R Armson** *Cl up; chsd ldr app 8; disp ld 9 til ld aft 15; hdd & hit 2 out; no ch w wnr* 10 2
155P **Table For Four** 20-1 **B Pollock** *(xnb) Chsd ldr; mist 4; ld 7 til aft 15; 4th & btn 3 out; went poor 3rd at last* 15 3
37[5] Cloudy Bay Boy 3-1 R Cope *Ww in tch; trckd ldrs 11; 1l 3rd & gng wl aft 15; rdn & wknd qckly 3 out; walked in* 15 4
301P Fiesty Frosty (IRE) (5a) 20-1 J Docker *Nt fluent; 8l last & rdn 9; blun nxt; lost tch 12; t.o & pu 3 out* . . . . . P

294[F]	Teeton Glaive (5a) 16-1 Miss H Irving *(xnb) Mists 1 & 2; chsd ldr 6; 10l 5th & outpcd 13; no ch aft; pu last*		P
	The Lord Roberts (IRE) 12-1 Miss T Clark *Ld to 7; lost plce nxt; 6l 6th 11; lsng tch when blun 13; pu nxt*		P

OFFICIAL DISTANCES: 12*l*, 15*l* **TIME:** 6min 34.0s

385 Open Maiden 567&8yo (Div 1), 12st — 16 ran

	FRANCO (IRE) 3-1F **P Cowley** *6s-3s; tk keen hld; chsd ldrs 6; ld 9; 10l clr app 13; 4l up & rdn 2 out; fnd ex & in comm last; comf*		1
293[U]	**Lady Baronette** (5a) 6-1 **I Howe** *In tch; 9l 3rd 11; chsd wnr app 13; only dang aft; 4l down 2 out; one pce*	7	2
128[F]	**Bacarese** 12-1 **S Morris** *Mist 1; chsd ldrs; 12l 7th 11; went 28l 3rd app 3 out; no hdwy aft; dism aft fin; lame*	35	3
	King's Reply 6-1 R Burton *Settled wl bhnd; 24l 10th 11; went poor 4th 2 out; nvr put in rce*	5	4
219[2]	King Freddy (7a) 7-2 R Cope *Mid-div; 11l 6th 11; outpcd nxt; 20l 4th 13; nvr nr ldrs; dem 2 out; t.o*	20	5
	Abitofahike (IRE) 20-1 A Martin *(xnb) Chsd ldrs; 11l 5th 11; lost tch app 13; t.o & pu 3 out*		P
	Catalan Girl (12a) 16-1 M Mackley *2 handlers; rr; 22l 9th 11; lsng tch when pu nxt*		P
	College Superman 14-1 L Hicks *Chsd ldrs; 10l 4th 11; sn wknd; wl bhnd when pu 13*		P
219[4]	Highland Dancer (IRE) (7a) 16-1 T Ellis *Mid-div; 15l 8th 11; no ch frm 13; pu 3 out*		P
295[6]	Igloux Royal (FR) 10-1 M Briggs *(xnb) Chsd ldr to 4; blun 3 & 7; lost plce app 8; t.o & pu 13*		P
12[F]	Jupiter Jay 10-1 A Sansome *Ld to 9; 3rd & wkng 13; blun nxt; wl bhnd when pu 3 out*		P
	Russian Friend(bl) 6-1 R Collinson *2nd when rn out thro wing & ur 5*		R
302[P]	Satanas (FR) 7-1 G Hanmer *(xnb) Hld up; rr when fell 5*		F
	Silver Styx (7a) 20-1 J Docker *Mists; sn bhnd; t.o 8 til pu 11*		P
96[P]	Superior Footwork 20-1 P Morris *Mists; sn bhnd; t.o 8 til pu 13*		P
60[P]	Tommy Flanders 25-1 N Docker *(xnb) Prom to 5; bhnd frm 8; t.o & pu 12.*		P

OFFICIAL DISTANCES: 8*l*, dist **TIME:** 6min 31.0s

386 Open Maiden 567&8yo (Div 2, Part 1), 12st — 10 ran

	INTERROGATOR 8-1 **J Docker** *Jw; chsd ldrs; went 2nd 10; ld 15; drew clr app last; comf*		1
219[3]	**Shot Of Jollop (IRE)** (7a) 3-1 **N Bloom** *Mists; chsd ldrs; 12l 3rd when mist 11; rdn app 3 out; rallied & cl 3rd when blun 2 out; hung bad lft & nt r.o app last; nt rec*	15	2
151[4]	**Marciano** 5-1 **R Cope** *(xnb) Slt ld to 3; in tch; 8l 4th app 3 out; 3rd & ch 2 out; sn outpcd*	2	3
192[P]	Hermano (IRE) 8-1 J King *Tk keen hld; stdd start; pulled to ld app 4; 10l clr 11; blun 13; hdd 15; wknd app nxt; pu 2 out*		P
58[P]	Mrs Fidget (5a) 10-1 E Linehan *A bhnd; t.o & pu 15*		P
58[F]	Northern Breeze (5a) 3-1 M Mackley *Ww; prog & 8l 4th app 13; mist 14; jnd ldr & pckd 3 out; wknd qckly aft; 4th & btn when ur last*		U
	Pennyago (IRE) 14-1 D Renney *Bhnd; last when pu 6*		P
	Sassy's Circle (12a) 5-1 B Pollock *Mists; a bhnd; 9th when blun 8; t.o & pu 3 out*		P
172[P]	Sixes And Sevens (IRE) (5a) 14-1 G Kerr *Mists; chsd ldr 4-10; wknd nxt; wl bhnd when pu 14*		P
	Teeton Diamond (5a) 6-4F P Cowley *Ww; 20l last app 8; prog 9; 3rd 12; rdn & wknd 15; pu 3 out*		P

OFFICIAL DISTANCES: 14*l*, 1½*l* **TIME:** 6min 42.0s

387 Open Maiden 567&8yo (Div 2, Part 2), 12st — 9 ran

97[3]	**COUSIN GEORGE** 4-1 **R Burton** *Ld round start; ld; jmpd big 1 & 2; jnd 6; lft in ld 9; made rest; 2l clr 2 out; in comm when drifted lft flat*		1
128[2]	**Briery Fox (IRE)** 4-5F **J Docker** *Tchd 6/4; trckd ldrs; went 2nd & mist 12; 2l down 2 out; one pce u.p*	1	2

302F **Earl Token** 5-1 **R Armson** *In tch; mist 7; 10l 4th & btn app 3 out; went mod 3rd app last* . . . 15 3

Hever Road (IRE) (7a) 7-1 S Morris *In tch; 5l 3rd aft 15; outpcd by ldng pr nxt; dem app last* . . . 10 4

304P Gee A Two (IRE) 7-1 G Hanmer *(xnb) Tk keen hld; chsd ldrs; lft 2nd 9 til wknd app 12; 6th & wl btn 14* . . . 30 5

Martha Jane (5a) 20-1 P Newton *A last pr; 12l last when mist 11; no ch frm 15* . . . 8 6

226P Currow Kate (5a) 20-1 N Docker *Ww in tch; 5th & outpcd 13; no ch aft* . . . 15 7

227P Magnatism 10-1 L Hicks *(xnb) Jnd ldrs 6 til fell 9* . . . F

247P Red Lake (IRE) 20-1 P Millington *(kineton) Nt jw; a last pr; lost tch 12; t.o & pu 15* . . . P

OFFICIAL DISTANCES: 1l, 9l **TIME:** 6min 43.0s

Derwent

Charm Park (LH 9F,19J)

Sun, 7 Mar (GOOD)

388 Hunt Members — 4 ran

2681 **IMPS WAY** (5a, 8x) 1-3F **M Morley** *Lw; jmpd v wl; made virt all; drew rt away frm 15* . . . 1

268P **In The Van** (5x)(cp) 10-1 **J Morley** *(xnb) Tde; nt a fluent; last til chsd wnr frm 9; 15l adrift & no ch 16* . . . 15 2

166P Atlantic Drift (IRE)(bl) 4-1 J Swiers *Cl up in bunch til rfo 8* . . . U

113P Cloudkicker (IRE) 10-1 A Pennock *Rdr lurching ev fnce; cl up til 12l last & labouring 10; jmpd lft aft & sn t.o; exhaust 16; ab 2 fncs bhnd when crashing fall last; winded bad; rdr insisted saddle kpt on so he could remount* . . . F

OFFICIAL DISTANCE: dist **TIME:** 6min 36.0s

The stewards enquired into the riding of Cloudkicker who fell at the last fence; the rider was fined £200 for failing to pull up an obviously exhausted horse

389 Confined, 12st - 17J — 15 ran

591 **GOLDEN RIVET** 7-2 **M Walford** *V cantankerous & hrd to saddle & bridle; settled rr early; prog to 3rd/4th 9 til 2nd 14; rdn passing 3 out; ld & jw last; hld on wl* . . . 1

Maitre De Musique (FR) (3x) 7-1 **Richard Tate** *Ld til aft 3; prom til ld agn 11-15; 7l 3rd & outpcd passing 3 out; rallied app last; stayed on flat; a just hld* 1 2

2121 **Dumadic** 5-2F **N Tutty** *(xnb) Settled midfield; 7th 10; sn cl up; ld aft 15; 2l clr 2 out; hrd rdn & hdd app last; wknd flat* . . . 4 3

2661 Emperor's Son 3-1 Miss S Brotherton *(xnb) Midfield; 5th 10; one pce 15; 10l 4th & rdn & btn 2 out* . . . 2 4

Nip On 14-1 G Brewer *Hld up & bhnd; 12th 10; prog in 6th aft 15; sn wknd* 1 5

2682 Wilfie Wild 7-1 Mrs L Ward *Hld up; 9th 10; eff 14; 5th & no ex passing 3 out* 1/2 6

2672 Who Dares Wins 5-1 L Bates *Cl up; 6th 10; wknd 13; 8th passing 3 out; plugged on* . . . 4 7

2678 Glendamah (IRE) 20-1 M Morley *Pulled hrd & prom; lft in ld 5-11; prom to 14; wknd qckly* . . . 1 1/2 8

2985 Folliday (FR)(cp) 33-1 R Wakeham *2 handlers; midfield; 8th 10; wknd to rr 14; blun nxt* . . . 30 9

Choice Cut (IRE) 33-1 Miss K Pickersgill *Rn free & prom; 3rd 10; wknd 12; rem aft 15* . . . 12 10

2676 Chaos Theory 14-1 T Collier *Rcd wide & pulled hrd; ld aft 3 til hit 5 & ur* . U

1617 Heather Lad 33-1 N Smith *Sn lost gd plce; 11th 10; strugg when fell 12* . F

269P Just Coming 50-1 B Woodhouse *A bhnd; 10th 10; t.o & pu 2 out* . . . P

267F Notation (IRE) 20-1 R Clark *Bhnd; blun bad 3; poor 13th 10; t.o & pu 14.* P

338P Steel Rigg (IRE) 33-1 Miss Rachel Clark *A bhnd; bad mist 4; last & strugg when ur 10* . . . U

OFFICIAL DISTANCES: 1l, 4l **TIME:** 6min 27.0s

Fences 8 & 17 omitted - damaged

390 Restricted (Nov Rdrs) — 7 ran

Form	Horse	Dist	Pos
341^{6}	**CLONSHIRE PADDY (IRE)** 7-4 **Miss J Coward** *Settled midfield; went 3rd app 13; still 3rd & plugging on 3 out; ld app last; sn clr*		1
	Mandate Man (IRE) 14-1 **D Thomas** *Made virt all; terrible mist & nrly ur 3 out; hdd app last; sn outpcd.*	10	2
266^{3}	**Landford Lad (IRE)** 8-1 **G Armitage** *Swtng; prsd ldr frm 4; $^{1}/_{2}$l down 3 out; wknd qckly nxt*	8	3
267^{12}	Fayalie (IRE) (5a) 33-1 P Robinson *Midfield & in tch til 10l 4th & outpcd app 13; plodded on.*	1	4
266^{P}	Blue Bud 14-1 T Collier *Nt jw in rr; last & labouring 10; ur 11.*		U
304^{1}	Eastern Royal (7a) 4-5F Miss Rachel Clark *(xnb) Cl up til mists 8 & 9 & rdr v unstdy; 8l 4th & outpcd app 13; no prog when rdr nrly f.o 16; last when pu last*		P
268^{P}	Minster Echo (5a) 16-1 J Haley *In tch to 10; last by 12; nt r.o; t.o & pu 16*		P

OFFICIAL DISTANCES: 8*l*, 8*l* **TIME:** 6min 44.0s

391 Mixed Open, 12st — 14 ran

Form	Horse	Dist	Pos
269^{1}	**MR MAHDLO** 4-1 **B Woodhouse** *Trckd ldrs; 7th 9 but 2nd by 11; ld 13; $2^{1}/_{2}$l clr 2 out; outstayed rivals.*		1
267^{1}	**Mr Pendleberry**(vis) 2-1F **N Tinkler** *Trckd ldrs; 6th 10; mist 12; sn drvn along & little resp; 3rd & no imp frm 15; went 2nd last; no ch w wnr.*	6	2
162^{U}	**Texas Ranger** 5-1 **Miss J Foster** *Tk keen hld; ld aft 3-13; chsng wnr vain when tired j 2 out; dem & tired j last.*	4	3
211^{2}	Emperor's Magic (IRE) 8-1 Miss S Ward *Rcd v wide & prom; 3rd 10; lost plce qckly & 30l 7th when mist 13; wl bhnd aft*	30	4
266^{2}	Shankly 4-1 M Walford *Hld up midfield; 8th 10; sn went 4th; wknd aft 12; 12l 5th aft mist 13; wknd; t.o; fin lame*	30	5
211^{9}	Baby John (IRE)(cp) 50-1 Miss L Horner *Bhnd; rem last & drvn & v reluct 10; pu aft 12*		P
	Don Rio (IRE) 50-1 M Morley *(xnb) Bhnd; poor 13th 10; t.o & pu aft 12.*		P
267^{10}	Erni (FR)(bl) 66-1 A Morris *Jmpd rt; ld til aft 3; chsd ldr to 10; gave up rap; t.o & pu 13*		P
	Hadeqa 50-1 P Robinson *A wl bhnd; 12th 10; t.o & pu 14*		P
	Londolozi Lad (IRE) (7a) 10-1 P Kinsella *(xnb) Hld up & wl in rr; 11th 10; t.o & pu 15*		P
	Mr McDuck (IRE) 5-1 L Bates *Hld up towards rr; 10th 10; sn lost tch; t.o & pu 15*		P
269^{P}	On The Mend (IRE) 33-1 R Wakeham *Prsd ldrs; 5th 10; 12l 4th & wkng 13; rem when pu 3 out*		P
269^{2}	San Francisco 6-1 G Brewer *Prom brief; 9th & labouring 10; t.o & pu 13.*		P
267^{3}	Welsh March (IRE) 16-1 N Tutty *Pulled hrd; prom; 4th 10; lost tch qckly 12; poor 6th nxt; pu 2 out.*		P

OFFICIAL DISTANCES: 7*l*, 4*l* **TIME:** 6min 30.0s

392 Confined Maiden 5&6yo (Div 1), 12st - 18J — 12 ran

Form	Horse	Dist	Pos
272^{2}	**SEVENSIDER (IRE)** 5-4F **R Wakeham** *Set v slow pce til app 4; prom til ld agn 13; 6l clr 3 out; wl in comm aft*		1
59^{U}	**Another Half** (12a) 10-1 **M Walford** *Novicey; hld up off pce til clsd 10; 7th nxt; went 3rd 14 & 2nd 16; mist nxt; tired when dem last*	40	2
	Vics Fane (IRE) 6-1 **B Woodhouse** *(xnb) Novicey; ld 7-9; cl 4th app 16; 3rd & btn when terrible mist 3 out.*	2	3
266^{P}	Irish Paddy (IRE) (7a) 10-1 R Clark *Prom; ld 9; nrly carried out by loose horse app 10; hdd 13; 2nd 16; fdng rap when bad mist 2 out*	3	5
344^{6}	Parsifal (7a) 14-1 R Abrahams *Tk keen hld & settled wl off pce; clsd 10; 3rd 12; mist & wknd tame 15*	3	6
60^{2}	Tap Dance 7-4 P Kinsella *(xnb) Trckd ldrs; 4th & rdn w little resp 14; 5l 5th app 16; plugged into poor 2nd last; nt lk keen; btn 20l; disq - nt weigh-in*		2d
	Brown's Beck 14-1 M Morley *Fat; spooky in padd; v novicey; crawled fncs & a t.o; pu 11*		P
271^{R}	Fair Signet 33-1 P Cornforth *(xnb) Pulled hrd; prsd ldrs til fell 10.*		F
	Knight Crossing (IRE) 14-1 N Tutty *Blun & ur 1*		U
	Milliners Guide (5a) 14-1 C Cundall *(xnb) Crashing fall 2.*		F

Raggy Jumper 14-1 L Bates *Bit bckwd; blun & ur 1* . . . . U
344P Zebs Lad 33-1 R Walker *Ld app 4-7; rr 11; t.o & pu 14* . . . . P

OFFICIAL DISTANCES: Originally 20*l*, 20*l* **TIME:** 6min 49.0s

Fence 11 omitted - fallen rider; Tap Dance finished second but was disqualified when the rider failed to weigh-in; he was fined £60

393 Confined Maiden 5&6yo (Div 2), 12st — 8 ran

BLACK COLLAR (12a) 7-1 **M Walford** *Tkn stdly in rr; 6l 4th aft 13; prog gng wl in 2nd 16; jmpd to ld 2 out; hrd prsd but still gng wl when lft virt solo app last.* 1
303U **Snizort (USA)** 25-1 **G Brewer** *Prom; w ldr 15; rdn 3 out; 6l 3rd & wkng nxt; lft poor 2nd app last* 30 2
272³ **Ravenscar** 3-1 **S Walker** *Prom but jmpd delib at times; slt ld 11-13; wknd tame aft 15; sn wl bhnd* 25 3
165F Born Special (7a) 10-1 P Kinsella *Trckd ldrs til fell 9* . . . . F
272R Devil's Perk (IRE) 8-11F T Glass *V free to post; rcd keen & made most on outer; jmpd v slow 5; hrd prsd by wnr 16 til hdd 2 out; trying to rally on inner when slpd up turn bef last* . . . . S
God Of War 16-1 P Robinson *Bckwd; novicey; rr but in tch to 9; sn wknd; t.o when crawled 11 & 12; pu nxt* . . . . P
Just A Man 14-1 B Woodhouse *(xnb) Novicey in rr; lost tch 11; wl bhnd when pu 13* . . . . P
303F Quel Regal (FR) 12-1 Miss Rachel Clark *(xnb) Keen & cl up but nt a fluent; mist 3; 5th & outpcd 11; t.o & pu 16* . . . . P

OFFICIAL DISTANCES: dist, 20*l* **TIME:** 6min 37.0s

394 Confined Maiden 7yo&up (Div 1) — 11 ran

74P **BORLEAGH PILOT (IRE)** 6-1 **P Collins** *Wl bhnd; mod 7th 10; still 15l 5th aft 15; 4th but clsng & gng best 2 out; ld last; kicked clr of floundering rivals; rdr's 1st wnr* 1
271⁵ **Bankersdraft** 5-1 **M Morley** *(xnb) Prom; 3rd 10; lft in ld 2 out; rdn & hdd last; desperately one-pcd* 2½ 2
272P **Hidden Pearl (IRE)** 7-1 **J Davis** *2nd mostly; blun 11; lft in ld 15-nxt; 2nd but tired 2 out; fdd app last* 5 3
272⁶ Gollinger(cp) 3-1 B Woodhouse *Ld at fast pce early; 4l clr when bad mist 13 & stpd in trcks; ld agn 16; 4l ahd when jmpd v slow 3 out; climbed nxt; sn hdd & gave up* 3 4
161P Catosphere (IRE) 10-1 L Bates *Well bhnd; poor 10th 10; t.o & pu 14* . . . . P
111² Fast Lane Harry (IRE) 7-4F R Wakeham *(xnb) Cl up; 4th 10; lft in ld 13 til crashing fall 15; broke nk; dead* . . . . F
Nomiret (IRE) 16-1 N Tutty *Pulled hrd in rr; mists 3 & 8; poor 8th 10; pu 11* P
271P Staple Sound 3-1 P Kinsella *Labouring bad in last trio; 9th 10; t.o when blun bad 12; pu 14* . . . . P
167P Stickwiyadad 12-1 T Craggs *Jmpd poor in rr; t.o last when pu 11* . . . . P
344U Supreme Vintage (IRE) 14-1 J Botham *Cl up; 5th 10; 3rd 14 til hmpd & ur nxt* U
304⁵ Tuftex King 14-1 A Pennock *Midfield; 6th & rdn 10; hung on til 7l 4th 16; wknd qckly; t.o & climbed 2 out; pu last* . . . . P

OFFICIAL DISTANCES: 3*l*, 6*l* **TIME:** 6min 54.0s

Dextrous (xnb, small sturdy, ur twice & bolted bef start) was withdrawn not under orders

395 Confined Maiden 7yo&up (Div 2) - 15J — 10 ran

MISTER BROMLEY 2-1F **Miss S Brotherton** *(xnb) Blun 2; hdwy in 3rd 6; ld & nt fluent 13; sn hdd; 3l 3rd 15; bad outpcd nxt; went 20l 2nd & lft 3l clr 2 out; wl in comm & nt pushed aft; unimpressive; v lucky* 1
300R **Stormy Sunrise (IRE)** 5-2 **Miss A Armitage** *Pulled hrd; tanked ahd & nt fluent 4; hdd app 13; 2nd til aft 3 out; lft 3l 2nd nxt; frantically rdn & a hld aft* 4 2
266P **Grandmere** (5a) 10-1 **G Brewer** *Sn wl bhnd; 7th 9; t.o 13; 25l 6th 15; plugged on.* 20 3
272P Just A Lady (5a) 20-1 B Woodhouse *(xnb) Novicey; towards rr; 5th 10; 14l 4th & tired 15; t.o 16.* 35 4
Dinan (IRE) 20-1 Mrs J Brown *(xnb) Ld to 4; 2nd to 12; 13l 4th & tired 15; t.o 16* 8 5
304P Firle Phantasy(bl) 20-1 J Haley *Prom til nrly ref 5 & rfo sn aft; crashed thro wire fnce when loose* . . . . U

Form	Entry	Dist	Pos
	Sams Way 3-1 P Kinsella *Settled 4th til 3rd 11; ld passing 14; 20l ahd when fell 2 out*		F
	Stately Biv 20-1 R Wakeham *Jmpd hesitant & sn rr til blun & ur 4*		U
160^{P}	The Melting Pot (IRE)(bl) 8-1 T Glass *Midfield; 6th 10; strugg when ur 12*		U
	Vals Whispa 8-1 D Thomas *Bckwd; bhnd; poor last 8; t.o when blun & ur 11*		U

OFFICIAL DISTANCES: 4*l*, 20*l* **TIME:** 6min 51.0s

Fences 1, 10 & 19 omitted - low sun; fence 14 omitted - damaged; Billymax (rdr inj in prev rce) was withdrawn not under orders

Granta Harriers

Higham (LH 8F,19J)

Sun, 7 Mar (GOOD to FIRM)

396 Hunt Members — 3 ran

Form	Entry	Dist	Pos
221^{3}	**BALLAD (IRE)** 4-5F **A Williams** *Made all & a in comm; pushed along 16; comf*		1
	Wise Advice (IRE) evens **Miss L Marriott** *(xnb) 2nd frm 2; prsd ldr; 4l down 11; chsd wnr vain aft; wknd 2 out*	6	2
249^{14}	**Castle Road (IRE)** 11-2 **H Fowler** *Last frm 2; detach frm 5; 15l adrift 16; minor hdwy 2 out; a hld*	3	3

OFFICIAL DISTANCES: 5*l*, 3*l* **TIME:** 6min 35.0s **TOTE:** £2.60

397 Mens Open — 6 ran

Form	Entry	Dist	Pos
221^{4}	**DUNRIG (IRE)** 9-2 **J Owen** *Ld to 3; 4l 5th 9; 2l 3rd 11; ld 14-15; 2nd nxt; nt qckn & 4l down app last; drvn & r.o flat to catch stpng ldr cl home*		1
99^{2}	**The Red Boy (IRE)** 2-5F **A Braithwaite** *Hld up bhnd ldrs; cl 2nd frm 11; ld 16; drvn & qcknd 4l clr last; rdn flat; flashed tail, hung rt & nt r.o; hdd cl home*	½	2
183^{4}	**Little Worsall (IRE)** 8-1 **F Marshall** *Cl up; prsd ldr 7; ld 10-13; 2½l 3rd nxt; nt qckn 2 out; r.o flat w minimal assist frm rdr; just failed*	hd	3
38^{P}	Avondale Illusion (IRE)(bl) 33-1 R Stearn *Ld 4-8; releg 4th 11; lsng tch when blun 13; t.o 16*	25	4
221^{5}	Polo Ridge (IRE) 16-1 H Fowler *Nt jw; a last pr; jmpd slow 10; rem 5th frm 16*	10	5
43^{P}	Woodward Street (AUS) 33-1 T Lane *Nt jw; a last pr & nvr gng wl; last 15; lost tch qckly; t.o & pu 16*		P

OFFICIAL DISTANCES: ½*l*, hd **TIME:** 6min 20.0s **TOTE:** £4.80 **DF:**£2.00

398 Restricted, 12st - 18J — 13 ran

Form	Entry	Dist	Pos
244^{1}	**MADMIDGE** 9-2 **D Kemp** *Trckd ldrs; 5th when hit 6; jnd ldrs 11; ld 13; a gng best aft; kpt on wl*		1
159^{3}	**Captive (IRE)** 5-1 **J Owen** *Sn prom; 2l 2nd when carried wide bend aft 11 & lost 8l; sn chsng ldr agn; 1l 2nd 15; rdn 2 out; a hld*	2	2
187^{6}	**Bell Rock** 4-1 **James Tudor** *(xnb) Prom; 2l 3rd 8; ld 10; hung rt & rn wide bend aft 11; chsd ldr aft; 4l 3rd 14; no ex frm 2 out*	15	3
	Hollyhock (5a) 10-1 P Taiano *(xnb) Towards rr when blun 6; nvr on terms; plodded into v rem 4th 16*	30	4
128^{1}	Hi Tech Man (IRE) 5-2F T Lane *Opened 3s; cl up; 3l 4th 11; hmpd & lost plce app 12; blun & no ch frm nxt; 25l 5th 14*	15	5
127^{U}	Josh's Choice (IRE)(bl) 16-1 A Braithwaite *Mid-div; sn strugg to go pce; hit 11; rem 6th when blun 16; plodded on*	1	6
248^{P}	Lambrini King (IRE) 25-1 Miss L Barrett-Nobbs *(xnb) Cl 4th 3; blun & lost plce 7; rr aft; t.o*	2	7
220^{P}	A Fine Story 8-1 A Williams *(xnb) Rr; 12th 3; a bhnd & nt able to gt into rce; t.o 12*	3	8
223^{P}	Ballylesson (IRE) 33-1 C Ward-Thomas *Jb; imm detach in rr; plodded rnd*	8	9
248^{P}	Henwyn 16-1 A Humphrey *(xnb) Blun 2; ld to 4; lost plce 6; bhnd 8; sn hopelessly t.o*	15	10
	Chasing Bailey's 8-1 M Smith *Prom; ld 5-7; sn lost plce; rr when blun bad 14 & 15; t.o & pu 16*		P
22^{3}	No Nay Never (IRE) 33-1 Miss A Bowles *Cl 3rd til ld 8; fell 9*		F
250^{P}	Paddy's Dream (IRE) 10-1 N Moore *(xnb) Handy; 2l 3rd 9; prsd ldr aft til lft in ld bend aft 11; hmpd by loose horse & ur 12*		U

OFFICIAL DISTANCES: 4*l*, 8*l* **TIME:** 6min 14.0s **TOTE:** £5.60 **DF:**£15.00

Fence 17 omitted - fallen rider

399 Gerrard Ladies Open - 17J — 6 ran

222[4]	**THE WILEY KALMUCK (IRE)** 5-1 **Miss Z Turner** *Lft in ld 2-12; trckd ldr aft til chall by-passing 2 out; ld last; qcknd clr; rdn out*		1
246[P]	**Hay Dance** 33-1 **Miss L Barrett-Nobbs** *(xnb) Mostly 3rd; on heels of ldrs til ld 13; jnd by-passing 2 out; sn hdd; nt qckn last*	2	2
156[5]	**Mai Point** (5a) 10-1 **Mrs S Hodge** *(xnb) Hld up in rr of tightly-grouped field; 1l 3rd 8; prsd ldr 11; cl 4th til outpcd 3 out; went dist 3rd app nxt; kpt on one pce*	15	3
242[U]	Catherine's Way (IRE) 20-1 Miss L Marriott *2nd 4; prsd ldr 11; cl 3rd 13 til outpcd & lost tch 3 out; releg last app 2 out*	6	4
249[5]	Corston Joker 14-1 Mrs L Spence *2nd 3; reluct on bend & lost plce app 4; 5l 4th 5; last 8; v reluct & ref to rce bend aft 11*		r
157[1]	Placid Man (IRE) 1-4F Ms A Embiricos *Ld til ur 2*		U

OFFICIAL DISTANCES: 3*l*, 8*l* **TIME:** 6min 14.0s **TOTE:** £2.60 **DF:**£84.00

Fences 10 & 17 omitted - fallen rider

400 Countryside Alliance Club Members — 7 ran

248[4]	**WESTFIELD JOHN**(bl) 6-1 **J Owen** *9s-6s; ld aft 1; 15l clr 3; unchall aft (galvanised by 1st time blinkers)*		1
249[2]	**Royal Action** 5-2 **P Chinery** *Chsd ldr 2; unable to go early pce & qckly detach; sent in vain pursuit 8; hit 2 out; nt able to chall*	10	2
248[F]	**Ardnut**(bl) 40-1 **Miss R Page** *Last 2; 5th 4; qckly detach; 30l 5th 8; plodded on; went 40l 3rd 3 out*	30	3
	Gin N Ice (IRE) 9-2 J Turcan *Mostly 3rd; sn wl bhnd; 20l 3rd 8; 4th 12 til 30l 3rd agn 16; dem agn 3 out; plodded on; just kpt 4th*	5	4
124[F]	Good Thyne Murphy (IRE) 20-1 T Lane *Mid-div; 25l 4th 8; went 3rd 12; 4th agn 16; dem rem last 3 out; plodded on; nrly snatched 4th*	½	5
248[1]	Endeavour (FR) 7-4F G Cooper *Ld & ur 1*		U
	Secret Streams (IRE) 7-2 A Braithwaite *Last 4; 35l 6th 8; blun 11; hopeless t.o & pu 12; dism*		P

OFFICIAL DISTANCES: 15*l*, dist **TIME:** 6min 10.0s **TOTE:** £6.60 **DF:**£5.00

401 Open Maiden 56&7yo, 12st — 8 ran

245[1d]	**NO PENALTY** 6-4F **A Braithwaite** *2 handlers; made all; a gng wl; 8l up 14; drew clr frm 3 out*		1
153[U]	**Tartar Sabre** 8-1 **Miss L Barrett-Nobbs** *Chsd ldr til blun & releg 4th 11; sn 3rd; 6l 2nd 16; one pce & sn no ch w wnr*	25	2
244[3]	**On The Day (IRE)** 7-4 **J Owen** *4l 3rd 3; 2nd & chsd ldr 9; outpcd 12; no ch when dem 3rd 16; lft poor last nxt*	15	3
245[P]	Groovejet (7a) 33-1 Miss K Smith *(xnb) Hld up in 7th; dashed up to jn ldrs 11; 3rd 12; qckly outpcd; 10l 4th when fell hvly 15; rdr inj*		F
154[2]	Half A Story (5a) 6-1 A Williams *In tch in 4th til til releg 5th 8; 15l 7th when fell 10*		F
	Lightning Fork (IRE) (5a) 16-1 T Lane *Settled 5th; 8l 5th 8; hdwy 11; 8l 3rd & clsng when fell 13; encouraging start*		F
	Straw Exchange (12a) 16-1 P Chinery *Imm last; t.o 8; hmpd by loose horse bend aft 11; miles bhnd when lkd reluct bend aft 15; pu 3 out*		P
	Victory March 16-1 H Fowler *Rr; 25l 7th 8; 15l 5th 13; nt pushed aft; t.o & barely galloping when pu 3 out*		P

OFFICIAL DISTANCES: 20*l*, 15*l* **TIME:** 6min 18.0s **TOTE:** £3.00 **DF:**£20.00

Ross Harriers

Garnons (LH 7F,18J)
Sun, 7 Mar (GOOD)

402 Hunts Members (with S. Herefordshire), 12st — 3 ran

110[5]	**BETTER FUTURE (IRE)** (7x) 3-1 **J Taylor** *Made all; oft drvn out of fncs; jmpd slow 12; rdn 15; blun 3 out; stayed on wl*		1
229[P]	**Darrell Boy (IRE)** (7x)(vis) 5-2 **D Mansell** *4s-5/2; nt keen; lft last 1; jnd sole rival 13; rdn 15; ev ch aft 3 out; nt r.o; eased when btn final 100yds*	8	2
	Gipsy Cricketer (7x) evensF T Symonds *(xnb) 1st ride; 2nd when rfo 1*		U

OFFICIAL DISTANCE: 9*l* **TIME:** 6min 34.2s

403 Confined, 12st — 16 ran

323^{P}	**RUSHING AGAIN** 5-1 **Miss P Gundry** *A.p; 3l 4th ½way; 2½l 3rd 14; went 2nd aft nxt; ld 2 out; rdn out*		1
92^{P}	**Genereux**(cp,tt) 20-1 **S Blackwell** *Ld to 3; 2nd til ld 13; hdd 2 out; nt qckn u.p*	2½	2
31^{P}	**Henry Bruce**(bl) 25-1 **A Brown** *Rn in snatches; mist 1; 7l 8th ½way; 10½l 8th 14; stayed on frm 3 out; went 3rd flat; nvr able to chall*	15	3
	Southern Cross 10-1 T Stephenson *Jnd ldrs 5; 4½l 6th ½way; 3½l 4th 14; outpcd aft nxt; went 12l 3rd 2 out; wknd & dem flat*	2½	4
	Felix Randal (IRE) 7-1 Miss R Reynolds *Ld 3-13; 1l 2nd when jmpd slow nxt; 5l 3rd 3 out; wknd qckly*	1½	5
205^{P}	Head Gardener (IRE)(bl) 20-1 D Mansell *Nvr on terms; 10l 11th ½way; lost tch & 16l 10th 14; plodded on*	1	6
	Go Go Gallant (IRE) 16-1 M Wilesmith *Ss; 9l 10th ½way; bhnd til hdwy 12; 9l 6th 14; wknd 15*	3	7
	Felloo (IRE) 8-1 E Walker *W ldrs; 4l 5th ½way; lost plce 13; 10l 7th nxt; wknd app 3 out*	1	8
	Tirley Gale (3x) 10-1 J Jones *(xnb) Mounted on course & tde (reluctantly); hld up; 7½l 9th ½way; eff 12; lost plce & 13l 9th 14; t.o*	7	9
258^{2}	Stockton Wolf 12-1 R Hodges *W ldrs; mist 1; 5l 7th ½way; lost plce 12; 18l 11th 14; t.o.*	8	10
277^{P}	September Harvest (USA) 20-1 R Shute *Ss; a wl bhnd; last ½way; t.o 14*	12	11
229^{P}	Inthaar 20-1 A Phillips *(xnb) A bhnd; 14l 13th ½way; 25l 12th 14; t.o*	8	12
	A Bit Of Fluff (5a) 20-1 Miss L Brooke *Lost plce 5; 15l 14th ½way; lost tch 11; t.o & pu 14*		P
1^{U}	High Mood (3x) 10-1 A Wintle *Prom; 2l 3rd ½way; 4½l 5th 14; wknd app 3 out; wl bhnd when pu lame aft last*		P
	Perry Of Troy (12a) 20-1 R Rogers *Mist 5; jmpd slow 7; 10½l 12th ½way; lost tch 11; pu 12*		P
50^{1}	Rodney Trotter(cp) 2-1F H Dowty *Hld up; 9th when pu 7; broke down*		P

OFFICIAL DISTANCES: 2*l*, 12*l* **TIME:** 6min 26.5s

The stewards enquired into the improved form of the winner; they noted the trainer's explanation that the horse kept changing legs between jumps the previous weekend and had leg problems so had been pulled up; two substantial bets were reported

404 Mens Open, 12st — 14 ran

122^{3}	**PARAHANDY (IRE)** 3-1 **H Dowty** *A.p; shkn up aft 6; went 6l 2nd aft 8; ld 2 out; all out*		1
251^{1}	**The Campdonian (IRE)** 6-1 **E Walker** *Hld up; 13l 7th ½way; hdwy 11; 11l 5th & rdn 14; went 6l 3rd 3 out; disp ld 2 out til mist last; outrdn & one pce flat*	¾	2
252^{6}	**Ballingale Dawn (IRE)** 20-1 **R Rogers** *25s-20s; hld up; 10l 4th ½way; went 3rd 11 til 9l 4th 14; outpcd app 3 out; stayed on wl flat*	6	3
	Warner For Players (IRE) (7x)(cp) 5-1 A Wintle *Sn prom; ld 3; lft 6l clr 8-12; qcknd 5l clr 14; jmpd slow 3 out; hdd 2 out; wknd flat*	3	4
	Act In Time (IRE) (7x) 5-2F T Edwards *Hld up; 15l 8th ½way; 15l 7th 14; nvr nr to chall*	12	5
292^{6}	Magical Approach (IRE) 25-1 T Phillips *(xnb) Nvr trbld ldrs; 12l 6th ½way; 14l 6th & rdn 14; wkng when mist 15.*	1½	6
229^{P}	The Archdeacon (IRE) 25-1 T Stephenson *Ld; mist 1; hdd 3; 2nd/3rd to 11; sn lost plce; wknd & 16l last 14*	7	7
	Ballydoole (IRE) 25-1 M Wilesmith *Sn wl bhnd; t.o when hmpd & fell hvly 7*		F
360^{U}	Lord Of Love (7x) 6-1 N Williams *8s-6s; jb; sn wl bhnd; ref 7*		r
	On The Run (IRE) (5a, 7x)(tt) 20-1 A Wadlow *(xnb) Blun bad 5 (snapped guard rail); lost tch; t.o 8; pu 12*		P
292^{8}	Paddies Boy (IRE) (7x) 12-1 J Trice-Rolph *A bhnd; t.o 8; pu 12*		P
229^{2}	Picket Piece(bl) 7-1 M Goldstein *Ref to rce aft shambles at start.*		r
170^{P}	Shiny Bay (IRE) 33-1 N Pearce *Hld up; hdwy & 11l 5th ½way; blun 12; went 7l 3rd 14; 2½l 4th & rdn when ur 2 out*		U
	Time Can Tell(bl) 25-1 S Graham *2nd/3rd til terrible blun 8; 16l 9th ½way; wl bhnd when pu 12*		P

OFFICIAL DISTANCES: 1*l*, 4*l* **TIME:** 6min 24.3s

The trainer of Picket Piece formally complained about the start (many horses were already beyond the Starter, who shouted 'false start' causing some to pull up, then changed his mind); the stewards were satisfied the start was satisfactory

405 Intermediate (Nov Rdrs) (Div 1), 12st — 10 ran

STAR CHANGES (5x) 7-1 **Miss N Lloyd** *1st ride; tde; ld to 4; lft in ld 5-6; 2nd til ld brief agn 10; 7l 3rd 14; went 6l 2nd aft 3 out; dem last; stayed on to ld nr fin* 1
Stride To Glory (IRE) (5x) 2-1 **M Hooper** *3s-2s; hld up; 8½l 6th ½way; went 9l 4th 14; eff app 3 out; went 3l 2nd at last; stayed on to ld flat; hdd nr fin* ¾ 2
Double Rich 4-1 **O Greenall** *(xnb) 1st ride; hld up & bhnd; hdwy 6; 5l 4th ½way; outpcd 14; 10l 5th 3 out; stayed on wl u.p flat; just failed.* . . . . . hd 3
Guard A Dream (IRE) 25-1 P Mason *A.p; mist 7; 1l 3rd ½way; ld 11; qcknd 4l clr 14; 5l clr when mist 2 out; hdd & no ex flat* 2 4
187^{7} Route Two (IRE) 12-1 F de Giles *Hdwy to ld aft 6; hdd 10; 2nd til wknd qckly aft 3 out* 20 5
227^{P} Raiseapearl 25-1 I Clyde *(kineton) Hld up; lost shoe 7; 11l 7th ½way; lost tch 12; wl bhnd 14; t.o* 25 6
Cariad Cymru 6-4F S Evans *Hld up & bhnd; 15l last ½way; 25l last 14; sn t.o* 3 7
259^{5} Come On Boy 20-1 G Davies *(xnb) Hld up; 8l 5th ½way; lost tch 12; 20l 6th 14; sn t.o* 30 8
Ard Na Carrig (IRE) 25-1 Miss A Parkes *1st ride; rdr nrly f.o sideways 3; ld 4 til collided w rival & rfo 5* . . . . U
Foxy Royale 16-1 Miss R Reynolds *2nd til hmpd & ur 5* . . . . U

OFFICIAL DISTANCES: nk, s hd **TIME:** 6min 33.8s

406 Intermediate (Nov Rdrs) (Div 2), 12st — 9 ran

107^{4} **BOLD TACTICS (IRE)** 4-7F **T Weston** *Ww; 4l 5th ½way; hdwy 12; went 2nd aft nxt; ld 14 til hung rt bend app 2 out; rallied to ld flat; stayed on* . . . 1
15^{2} **Love At Dawn** 4-1 **P Mason** *Hld up; rmdrs 8; 5½l 6th ½way; hdwy 12; 2l 3rd when mist 14; went 3l 2nd nxt; lft in ld app 2 out; hdd flat; kpt on.* . . . ½ 2
Arctic Grey (IRE) 6-1 **M Goldstein** *Prom; 2½l 3rd ½way; wknd & 8l 6th 14; lft dist 3rd flat* 40 3
252^{P} Magicien (FR) 10-1 S Gray *Went 2nd 5; ld 6-12; 6l 4th 14; sn wknd; t.o* . 7 4
289^{5} Borderline Breeze (IRE) 12-1 Miss H Watson *(bf) Ld to 6; blun 7; 2nd til ld 12; hdd 14; 5l 3rd when blun nxt; stpd to nil; wl bhnd when pu aft 3 out* . . P
Hedzamarley (IRE) 12-1 Miss S Davies *8th when fell 1* . . . . F
Huntersway (IRE) 6-1 D Greenway *10s-6s; prom; 3l 4th ½way; lost plce u.p 11; 7l 5th when rdr leapt off 14.* . . . . U
252^{10} Not Yet Decent (IRE) 10-1 A Puddy *Hld up; rdr almost f.o 6; 9l 7th ½way; rdr nrly lurched off agn 12; 15l last 14; went 25l 3rd 3 out; comedy partner finally f.o 50yds aft last.* . . . . U
Scholar Green 20-1 R Hughes *A wl bhnd; blun 5; t.o 8; pu 12.* . . . . P

OFFICIAL DISTANCES: nk, dist **TIME:** 6min 24.8s

407 Ladies Open — 12 ran

108^{3} **UPTON ADVENTURE** (5a, 7x) 4-6F **Miss E James** *Sn prom; 5l 4th ½way; went 2nd 11; ld 14; rdly* 1
189^{2} **Pride Of Kashmir** 5-1 **Miss S Phizacklea** *A.p; 4l 3rd ½way; went 2l 2nd aft 14; rdn 3 out; one pce* 2½ 2
230^{5} **Zamhareer (USA)** 16-1 **Miss T Harrison** *Sn wl bhnd; 25l last ½way; stayed on wl frm 3 out; went 3rd flat; nrst fin.* 20 3
289^{4} Esterelle (USA) (5a) 12-1 Miss S Beddoes *(xnb) Swtng; w ldrs; 6l 5th ½way; 3l 4th 14; went 5l 3rd u.p 3 out; wknd aft 2 out; dem flat.* 5 4
230^{3} Class Of Ninetytwo (IRE) (7x) 6-1 Miss S Sharratt *Jmpd slow 2; lost plce 5; rdn 7; 13l 8th ½way; lost tch 11; rallied & 9l 8th 14; wknd & 12l 6th 3 out* 6 5
252^{9} Winning Town 20-1 Miss S Talbot *Nvr on terms; 19l 9th ½way; wl bhnd 14* ¾ 6
Camden Fellow (IRE) 14-1 Miss C Hurley *(xnb) Hld up & nvr trbld ldrs; 10l 7th ½way; 8l 7th 14; wknd aft 15* 1 7
206^{P} Cage Aux Folles (IRE) 33-1 Mrs B Lewis *(xnb) Nt jw; hld up & bhnd; hdwy & 7l 6th ½way; 3½l 5th 14; wknd qckly 3 out; t.o* 12 8
253^{2} Octagonal (IRE) (7x)(bl) 10-1 Miss R Reynolds *Ld to 1; blun 7; 2nd til ld 9; mist 12; hdd 14; 6l 4th 3 out; wknd qckly; t.o & virt pu flat* 6 9
Fair Charmeur (IRE) (5a) 9-1 Miss I Tompsett *Hld up; 7th when blun & ur 8* U
230^{P} Guest Alliance (IRE) 33-1 Miss H Lewis *A bhnd; 20l 10th ½way; t.o 14; pu 3 out* P
Owl Vulgan (IRE) 10-1 Mrs K Baimbridge *Swtng; ld 1-9; 2nd/3rd to 12; 4l 6th 14; sn wknd; t.o & pu 2 out.* . . . . P

OFFICIAL DISTANCES: 2*l*, 16*l* **TIME:** 6min 21.3s

408 Panacur/TBA PPORA Club Members Mares Maiden (Div 1), 12st — 12 ran

	SHAFTS CHANCE (IRE) (5a) 4-1 **S Ross** *Hld up; stdy hdwy 8; 5l 6th ½way; qcknd to ld 15; sn 4l clr & in comm; rdly*		1
	Brendas Nightmare (5a) 20-1 **A Wadlow** *Hld up; hdwy 8; 2l 3rd ½way; 4l 5th 14; chsd wnr 3 out; one pce*	4	2
	Toffee Lady (5a) 20-1 **R Rogers** *(xnb) Hld up; mist 6; 6l 7th ½way; jnd ldrs 11; 3½l 4th 14; outpcd 15; stayed on flat*	2	3
	Cathy Come Home (IRE) (5a) 6-1 Miss P Gundry *(xnb) Swtng; hld up; hmpd 4; 11l 8th ½way; hdwy 12; 2½l 3rd 14; ev ch 15; one pce 3 out*	2½	4
97[P]	Brombil Lady (5a) 12-1 Miss R Reynolds *(xnb) Ld to 7; ld aft 8; blun 14; hdd & wknd 15; t.o*	30	5
	Will You Come On (IRE) (5a) 5-1 D Mansell *Prom; mist 5; blun bad & lost plce 7; jmpd slow 8; 12l 9th ½way; wl bhnd 14; t.o*	1½	6
	Babs Wheal (5a) 4-1 A Wintle *9th when fell 1*		F
	Beauty Star (IRE) (5a) 6-4F N Williams *2 handlers; hld up & bhnd; blun bad 6; hdwy & mist 9; 4l 5th ½way; went 2nd app 12 til stpd to nil app 3 out; poor 5th when pu 2 out*		P
	Caveat Graeci (IRE) (5a) 10-1 M Barber *Prom; mist 8; 2½l 4th ½way; wkng when mist 12; wl bhnd when pu aft nxt*		P
226[3]	Iadora (5a) 6-1 I Clyde *(bh) 2nd til ld 7; hdd aft nxt; wknd & 6l 7th 14; wl bhnd when pu 2 out*		P
	Knickers (5a) 20-1 J Trice-Rolph *Hld up; drpd to rr 5; 15l last ½way; 20l 8th 14; pu 15*		P
	Lady Archenfield (5a) 8-1 S Graham *(bf) Detach last & rmdrs aft 1; hdwy when fell 4*		F

OFFICIAL DISTANCES: 4*l*, 1½*l* **TIME:** 6min 39.4s

409 Panacur/TBA PPORA Club Members Mares Maiden (Div 2), 12st — 11 ran

192[2]	**SHY LIZZIE** (5a) 3-1CF **P Mason** *Hld up; 5½l 7th ½way; outpcd 14; went 13l 4th nxt; 20l off pce 3 out; stayed on wl aft; ld flat; sn clr*		1
111[5]	**Rosie Stroud (IRE)** (5a) 10-1 **G Barfoot-Saunt** *Sn prom; mist 6; 2l 3rd ½way; outpcd & lost plce 14; 15l 6th nxt; rallied 2 out; went 2nd nr fin*	7	2
172[P]	**April Treasure** (5a) 3-1CF **N Williams** *(xnb) Swtng; ld til aft 1; ld 4; qcknd 7l clr 14; wandered u.p aft 2 out; hung lft & hdd & no ex flat; eased prematurely & lost 2nd nr fin*	1	3
	Chatabit (5a) 7-1 A Beedles *Chsd ldrs; 5l 6th ½way; outpcd 14; 14l 5th nxt; w event wnr 3 out; no imp*	6	4
	Laurelgirl (IRE) (5a) 11-2 M Barber *Chsd ldr; 7l 2nd & outpcd 14; no imp 3 out; still 5l 2nd at last; wknd flat*	½	5
27[F]	Charlotte Russe (5a) 16-1 N Pearce *Hld up; mist 8; 7l 8th ½way; lost tch 11; pu 12*		P
	Frogsmarsh (5a) 20-1 Miss R Reynolds *Mist 2; sn last; lost tch 11; t.o when ref 14*		r
	Howgreenismyvalley (12a) 8-1 M Jackson *School in rr; 7½l 9th ½way; lost tch 12; 22l 7th 14; t.o & pu 2 out*		P
204[U]	Kerrygoldsovereign (5a) 20-1 R Stephens *(xnb,bf) Hld up; hdwy 8; 3l 4th ½way; went 6l 3rd 12; outpcd 14; releg 10l 4th when blun & ur last*		U
	McGinty All Stars (IRE) (5a) 3-1CF M Hooper *6s-3s; hld up; 9½l 10th ½way; bhnd til fell 11*		F
227[F]	Ridware Rose (5a) 10-1 Miss S Sharratt *Ld aft 1-4; 4l 5th ½way; wknd 12; 24l 8th 14; t.o & pu last*		P

OFFICIAL DISTANCES: 2*l*, 1*l* **TIME:** 6min 36.5s

410 Confined Maiden 56&7yo, 2m4f, 12st - 14J — 15 ran

257[3]	**SHEMARDI** 9-4F **R Hodges** *3s-9/4; a.p; ld 2-3; 3l 4th ½way; ld app 3 out; 6l clr nxt; drvn out; rfo aft fin*		1
256[U]	**Nothing Better (IRE)** (12a) 12-1 **T Weston** *Chsd ldrs; went 2l 3rd ½way & 4l 2nd aft 3 out; stayed on wl flat*	3	2
	Jump For Paddy (7a) 5-1 **A Wadlow** *Hld up; lost tch 8; 14l 10th ½way; some hdwy 11; 18l 6th 3 out; went 3rd flat; fin wl*	20	3
	Evanly Miss (5a) 12-1 M Jackson *Hld up; hdwy & 7l 6th ½way; 5l 6th & hmpd 11; sn outpcd; 15l 5th 3 out; went poor 3rd last; wknd & dem flat*	8	4

151^{P} All Eyez On Me (IRE) 10-1 M Hammond *Ld to 2; 2nd/4th til ld 12; hdd & wknd qckly app 3 out; t.o* . . . 12 5

256^{P} Stantons Church 8-1 M Barber *(xnb) Swtng; prom; ld 3-4 & 8-12; wknd qckly 3 out; t.o.* . . . 2 6

Crystal Brook (5a) 12-1 S Graham *A bhnd; 13l 9th ½way; t.o 11* . . . 15 7

Bally Cyrano 10-1 M Hooper *Last when blun & ur 2* . . . U

Force Ten 10-1 T Stephenson *Swtng bad; tk fierce hld; rap hdwy to ld 4; hdd aft 5; 4l 5th ½way; 6l 7th when pu 11* . . . P

Lord Saxbury (7a) 8-1 Miss S Beddoes *A wl bhnd; 28l last ½way; t.o & pu 11* P

256^{R} Neeley (7a) 10-1 M Keel *6th when blun 2; iron broke 4; wl bhnd when pu 7* P

53^{P} Potter's Wheel (7a) 12-1 D Mansell *Hld up & pulled hrd; 9l 7th ½way; hdwy & 4l 5th when rn out 11* . . . R

8^{P} Terimon's Dream 6-1 G Barfoot-Saunt *(xnb) Pulled hrd & saddle sn slpd; last aft 1; mist 3; jnd ldrs 4; ld aft 5-8; lost plce & 11l 8th ½way; pu 11* . . P

The Maverick 6-1 Miss P Gundry *Sn wl bhnd; pu 8* . . . P

87^{P} Upton Crusader 5-1 S Joynes *(xnb) Hld up; 16l 11th ½way; bhnd when pu aft 10* . . . P

OFFICIAL DISTANCES: 3*l*, 12*l* **TIME:** 5min 25.7s

Fence 9 omitted - fallen rider; the stewards interviewed the rider of Charlotte Russe who pulled up before the last circuit when apparently full of running; the rider, who felt the horse was not going at all well, was cautioned as to his future riding

South Devon

Black Forest Lodge (RH 8F,19J)

Sun, 7 Mar (GOOD to FIRM)

411 Hunt Members — 3 ran

319^{4} **BRUTHUINNE (IRE)** (5x) 6-4 **D McKenna** *(xnb,ringbit) Tchd 2s; made all at stdy pce; went 7l clr 16; pegged back frm 2 out; kpt on; drifted rt last; drvn out* . 1

Knock Star (IRE) (5x) 4-5F **S Partridge** *Disp last til trckd clr ldr frm 8; outpcd aft 15; r.o clsng stages; nt rch wnr* . . . 3 2

Digitalis (5a)(bl) 5-2 **Miss S Gaisford** *Disp last til last 8; lost tch 14; t.o* . . 20 3

OFFICIAL DISTANCES: 5*l*, 30*l* **TIME:** 6min 07.0s

412 Confined, 12st — 4 ran

147^{1} **MORRIS PIPER** (3x) 4-6F **R Woollacott** *Lw; hld up in tch; hdwy to slt ld 14; jnd brief aft 16; 4l clr when mist last; pushed out.* . . . 1

311^{7} **Sandy Duff** 4-1 **Miss M McCarthy** *Tchd 11/2; 2nd til hdwy to disp ld 16; rdn & cl 2nd 3 out; ev ch til outpcd frm 2 out; r.o wl flat* . . . 1½ 2

320^{5} **Midnight Coup** (7x)(bl) 7-2 **A Farrant** *(bnh) Tchd 4s; disp 3rd; impd 11; rmdrs nxt; no resp; lost tch & strugg frm 15* . . . 20 3

200^{P} Damiens Pride (IRE) (5x) 9-2 T Dennis *(xnb) Ld to 14; sn rdn & wknd; 26l 3rd 16; t.o* . . . 12 4

OFFICIAL DISTANCES: 1*l*, 20*l* **TIME:** 5min 59.0s

413 Open Maiden 56&7yo, 2m4f, 12st - 17J — 6 ran

150^{U} **ANOTHER BIT** 11-2 **Miss A Goschen** *10s-11/2; a gng wl; lft in ld 4; rdr lost whip at ½way; 3l clr 2 out; stumbled & nrly ur last; rec wl & edged lft flat; all out.* . . 1

275^{3} **Toon Society (IRE)** evensF **N Harris** *Tchd 11/8; lw; hld up in tch; 5l 3rd 12; outpcd & lost plce nxt; drvn to 4l 2nd aft 14; dem aft 2 out; hrd rdn to chall agn app last; nt much room flat* . . . ¾ 2

173^{3} **Royal Czarina** (5a) 7-2 **J Snowden** *Lw; ld 1; settled 4th; pckd 9; 5th frm 12; 13l 5th 13; no ch frm 15* . . . 12 3

Dubious Deal 20-1 L Tibbatts *(xnb) Bckwd; keen & hld up last early; mist 10; went 4th 12; rap hdwy to 2nd nxt; 4th & wkng when fell hvly 14; winded* F

295^{4} Jeune Premier (FR) 5-1 G Perkins *(kineton) Tchd 8s; jnd ldrs 6; went 2nd 9; cl up & gng wl frm 12; lost plce & rdn aft 14; hdwy agn to 3l 2nd aft 2 out; 3rd when fell last; winded* . . . F

150^{P} Our Weddingpresent (USA) (7a)(vis) 7-2 A Farrant *(xnb) Swtng; ld 2; 8l clr when fell hvly 4; died in lorry gng home.* . . . F

OFFICIAL DISTANCES: ½*l*, 15*l* **TIME:** 5min 31.0s

414 Mixed Open, 12st — 6 ran

145^{2}	**KINGSTON VENTURE** 7-4 **J Barnes** *(xnb) Ld 1; trckd ldr gng str; rdn 3 out; hit nxt; still 3l 2nd when drvn & jmpd btr last; sn clr*		1
64^{4}	**Perkys Pride (IRE)** 4-1 **A Farrant** *(xnb) Tchd 5s; ld frm 2; slt mist 14; went 5l clr 16; rdn 3 out; tiring & jmpd lft nxt; still slt ld when outj last; no ex flat; nt disg*	2	2
322^{P}	**Let's Fly (FR)** 20-1 **W Biddick** *Tchd 25s; 10l 3rd ½way; no hdwy; mist 14; 25l 3rd 16; t.o.*	runin	3
175^{11}	Solo Gent 33-1 Miss K Jones *3rd to 5; poor last frm 8; wl bhnd frm 14; schoolmastering*	1½fs	4
322^{P}	Select Star (IRE)(cp,tt) 20-1 D Edwards *Rr; rdn 9; 25l 5th 10; t.o & pu 14*		P
276^{2}	Sir William(tt) evensF R Woollacott *(xnb) Tchd 5/4; hld up; nvr nr ldrs; 20l 4th & rdn 11; poor 4th when pu 14*		P

OFFICIAL DISTANCES: 2*l*, dist **TIME:** 5min 52.0s

415 Restricted, 12st — 8 ran

314^{5}	**ELEGANT LIGHT** (5a) 10-1 **N Harris** *2 handlers; prom in chsng group til clr 2nd 10; clsng menacingly & wl clr of rest when lft wl clr 16; blun nxt; unchall; enterprisingly rdn*		1
314^{8}	**Sweet Kari (IRE)** 25-1 **G Weatherley** *Chsd ldr to 6; settled 3rd; 12l 3rd 12; lost tch 14; poor 3rd 3 out; tk 2nd nxt; no ch w wnr*	25	2
66^{1}	**Olly May** (5a) 3-1 **R Woollacott** *Lw; impd to 4th 10; 14l 4th & wkng 12; lft 25l 2nd 16; wknd & dem 2 out*	6	3
238^{1}	Dursey Island (IRE) 2-1F M Miller *Tchd 3s; hld up & a bhnd; went 5th 12; poor 5th 16; poor 4th & tired when jmpd slow 2 out & last; disapp.*	2	4
76^{F}	Cornish Hope 4-1 A Glassonbury *(xnb) Bckwd; went 3rd 5; prom in chsng group to 10; wkng in last when mist 11; bhnd & pu nxt*		P
265^{P}	Horsemans Green 20-1 J Barnes *(bf) Towards rr; detach frm 5; pu 8*		P
279^{2}	Mrs Peggoty (5a)(bl) 9-4 D Edwards *Hit 2; nt gng wl; 6th 10; rdn in 6th 13; last when pu 14*		P
279^{R}	Porto (IRE)(tt) 8-1 R McCarthy *(xnb) Ld at fair pce; 8l clr 11; pegged back frm 14; just hdd when blun & ur 16*		U

OFFICIAL DISTANCES: 30*l*, 5*l* **TIME:** 6min 02.0s

416 Panacur/TBA PPORA Club Members Mares Maiden, 12st — 8 ran

185^{P}	**FOREST FORTRESS (IRE)** (5a) 5-1 **D I Turner** *(xnb,pricker o/s) Prom; slt ld frm 5; slt mist 8; w ldrs til lost ground & rdn 11; rmdrs nxt; disp ld 16 til forged ahd 2 out; rdn 3l clr when dived at last; game*		1
309^{U}	**Merlin Meg** (12a) 9-2 **W Biddick** *6s-9/2; hld up in tch; went 3rd 12; hdwy to disp ld 16-3 out; cl 2nd & ev ch nxt; wknd app last*	1½	2
	Butleigh Rose (5a) 11-2 **J Snowden** *Lw; ld to 4; trckd ldr til ld agn 10; slt ld til disp 16-3 out; 2½l 3rd & wkng nxt.*	3	3
326^{3}	Hayling Star (5a) 20-1 M Sweetland *Last frm 5; sn strugg; t.o frm 12*	1½fs	4
264^{R}	Amy's Gift (5a) 14-1 J O'Rourke *(xnb) Bit bckwd; ref to rec; bhnd rest & fcng wrong way as rce started*		r
275^{6}	Five Minutes (5a) 7-2 Miss T Cave *Prom; 2½l 3rd 8; cl 3rd 10; went 2nd nxt; rmdr 12; cl 2nd til wknd 14; lost tch frm 16; 4th when pu & dism last; lame*		P
	Phar To Comfy (IRE) (5a) 7-4F T Vaughan *5/2-7/4; in tch in midfield; 5th ½way; no prog frm 14; btn 6th when pu 16; lame*		P
309^{3}	Retorrick Rose (5a) 9-2 R Woollacott *Hld up in tch; hdwy to 4th 10; 5th 12; lost tch w ldrs aft 15; bhnd & pu 2 out*		P

OFFICIAL DISTANCES: 2*l*, 3*l* **TIME:** 6min 12.0s

417 Confined Horses & Geldings Maiden, 12st — 5 ran

328^{P}	**PAULS LEGACY** 7-2 **D McKenna** *Trckd ldr frm 5; cl 2nd til lft solo 3 out; jmpd slow 2 out*		1
194^{6}	Advice Taken (IRE) 10-11F J Barnes *Tchd evens; lw; jw; ld; rcd keen & a gng wl; 1l up 15; fell 3 out; dead*		F
328^{P}	General Short 100-30 R Woollacott *(xnb) 5s-100/30; hld up in tch; impd to cl 3rd 9; 2½l 3rd & outpcd 16; eff & clsng when bd 3 out*		B
	Lamerton Quest 4-1 L Rowe *8s-4s; 4th & in tch 9; cl 4th 12; lsng ground when hit 15; btn when pu nxt*		P
149^{U}	Roy My Boy (7a) 20-1 J Cole *Last but in tch frm 6; wknd 12; mist 13; fell 14*		F

OFFICIAL DISTANCE: Finished alone **TIME:** 6min 28.0s

South East Hunts Club

Charing (LH 8F,19J)

Sun, 7 Mar (GOOD to FIRM becoming GOOD)

418 S E Hunts Club Members Maiden 56&7yo, 2m4f, 12st - 15J 7 ran

	TOUJOURS (IRE) evensF **C Gordon** *(xnb) 7/4-evens; hld up in tch; trck ldrs 9; ld 2 out; sn clr; easily*		1
	Royal Cruise (IRE) 3-1 **P York** *(xnb) Ld/disp til def advant 12; rdn & hdd 2 out; no ch wnr aft; wknd last; just kpt 2nd*	20	2
293P	**Siobhans Quinner (IRE)** (5a) 5-1 **D Phelan** *Ld/disp to 12; sn outpcd in 3rd; plugged on one pce app last*	1½	3
250P	Naughty Noah 10-1 G Gallagher *Cl up; mist 4; cl 4th aft 11; wknd & mist 12; fin v slow*	30	4
186³	Almazard 12-1 P Bull *W ldrs to 5; lost plce 8; sn bhnd; t.o last aft 11*	12	5
105P	Queen's Shilling (5a) 14-1 P Hall *In tch; blun & nrly ur 8; sn wknd; t.o last & pu 11*		P
186U	Sloe Coach 14-1 G Wigley *Rdr unstdy; rcd wide; in tch til rfo 8*		U

OFFICIAL DISTANCES: 12*l*, 2*l* **TIME:** 5min 10.2s **TOTE:** £2.00; places £1.70,£6.10 **DF:**£4.60

419 S E Hunts Club Members Restricted, 12st 10 ran

181²	**RAINBOW RANCH (IRE)** 5-4F **C Gordon** *(xnb) Stalked ldr; clr of rest frm 15; ld 2 out; sn rdn clr*		1
180¹	**The Grey Baron**(tt) 8-1 **P Bull** *(xnb) 12s-8s; pckd 2; chsd ldrs; 4th 13; chsd clr ldng pr 15; no imp til kpt on to 2nd flat*	15	2
290¹	**Arctic Penguin**(tt) 4-1 **P York** *Made most; nt a fluent; mist 12; clr w wnr frm 15; hdd 2 out; wknd last; dem flat*	2	3
	Lord Alpha (IRE) 14-1 A Ward-Thomas *Bckwd; set off last & sn detach; in tch in rr by 8; rdn 13; sn wknd; last aft 15; r.o frm 2 out*	12	4
181⁷	Tonrin 20-1 J Sole *Chsd ldrs; 5th & rdn 13; went 4th 15; no imp; wknd 2 out*	8	5
129¹	Battle Honours 7-1 P Hall *Midfield; rmdrs aft 6; chsd ldng pr 10 til wknd aft 15; wl bhnd & pu 2 out*		P
127r	Ishma (IRE) 20-1 D Page (Kent) *Sev slow js; prom early; toiling in rr frm 7; t.o last & pu 15*		P
	Kniveniven (IRE) 16-1 Mrs J Gordon *Keen early; chsd ldrs; wknd aft 12; t.o & pu 15*		P
191U	Madmariea (IRE) (5a) 4-1 T Underwood *Settled in rr; disp last when mist & rfo 8*		U
	Native Spin (IRE) 16-1 Miss C Cowe *(xnb) A rr; last pr & wkng 12; t.o & pu 15*		P

OFFICIAL DISTANCES: 8*l*, 2*l* **TIME:** 6min 32.9s
TOTE: £2.20; places £1.20,£1.90,£1.20 **DF:**£7.40

420 Land Rover Mens Open, 12st 6 ran

	SATCHMO (IRE) 4-1 **P Hall** *7s-4s; jw; trckd ldr; ld 8; gng wl when jnd & lft 20l clr 16; hvly eased flat (lkd prob wnr anyway)*		1
183²	**Struggles Glory (IRE)** (7x) 7-2 **Stuart Robinson** *Lw; ld to 8; nt fluent & lost plce nxt; chsd ldng pr 14; 9l 3rd aft nxt; sn outpcd; lft 20l 2nd 16; no ch w wnr*	10	2
241¹⁴	**Esprit De Cotte (FR)** 12-1 **P York** *Wl in tch; disp 3rd 13; sn outpcd & disp 19l 4th aft 15; one pce aft*	25	3
	Good Heart (IRE) 12-1 P Bull *Chsd ldrs; mist 10; disp 3rd 13; outpcd 14; disp 19l 4th aft 15; no ch aft; walked in*	8	4
188r	Full Egalite(bl) 12-1 G Gallagher *Bckwd; in tch; rdn 6; sn wknd; t.o & jmpd slow frm 11; crawled over last & rdr nrly f.o*	runin	5
183¹	Sheriff's Friend (IRE) (7x) 1-2F C Gordon *Hld up; trckd wnr 10; pushed up to chall & upsides when fell 16*		F

OFFICIAL DISTANCES: 10*l*, 5*l* **TIME:** 6min 21.6s **TOTE:** £4.80; places £2.00,£1.20 **DF:**£13.60

421 Ladies Open 9 ran

183³	**BELVENTO (IRE)** 4-1 **Miss E Jones** *Ld to 2; 3rd frm 4 til chsd clr ldr 9; clsd to ld 14-15; rdn to ld agn 2 out; 2l up at last; all out (won on jockeyship)*		1
42¹	**Kincora (IRE)** 5-2 **Ms L Stock** *(xnb) Ld 2 & sn clr; 12l up 9; hdd 14; eff to ld agn aft 15; hdd & mist 2 out; 2l down last; stayed on wl und flapping rdr flat; just failed*	nk	2

184^{2}	**Dick McCarthy (IRE)** 10-1 **Mrs S Ashby** *Wl in tch; chsd ldng pr 12; 7l 3rd 16; clsd stdly aft; 3l 3rd last; pushed along & stayed on wl flat; just failed*	s hd	3
222^{1}	Storm Castle (IRE) 6-4F Miss J Wickens *Hld up & nvr on terms; 14l 5th & no prog 13; rmdrs nxt; sn bhnd; disapp*	runin	4
182^{P}	Graphic Designer (IRE) 20-1 Miss H Gordon *1st ride; a last trio; pottered round wl t.o frm 13*	2fncs	5
32^{U}	Newby End (IRE) 20-1 Miss C Cowe *Jmpd slow 1; chsd ldr 4-9; 6th & wkng 13; pu aft 15*		P
241^{8}	River Bailiff (IRE) 10-1 Mrs J Gordon *Chsd ldrs; 8l 4th 13; 27l 4th & wkng 16; t.o 5th when pu last*		P
182^{8}	Scotch Bob (IRE) 20-1 Miss H Grissell *Pckd 1 & rdr nrly f.o; a last trio; wkng when pu 12*		P
180^{4}	Three Of Clubs (IRE) 20-1 Miss C Haydon *(xnb) Jmpd lft; a last trio; t.o 14; pu 16*		P

OFFICIAL DISTANCES: hd, hd **TIME:** 6min 27.8s
TOTE: £5.50; places £2.20,£1.70,£1.30 **DF:**£5.40

The rider of Graphic Designer was fined £50 for being unable to produce her Medical Record Book

422 S E Hunts Club Members Conditions, 12st — 14 ran

182^{4}	**TELL THE NIPPER (IRE)** 10-1 **M Gorman** *Midfield; 5th 13; sn outpcd; prog frm 15; went 2nd 2 out & ld app last; rdn clr; stayed on wl*		1
	Indian Wings (IRE) 3-1F **W Hill** *Disp 2-12; outpcd by ldr frm 14; lft 10l clr 16; hdd aft 2 out; jmpd slow last; fin tired*	6	2
187^{P}	**Mister Pepper (IRE)** 14-1 **T Underwood** *Hld up in tch; 7th 13; sn outpcd; stayed on frm 16; tk 3rd flat; nvr nrr*	3	3
168^{3}	Dancing Fosenby (4x) 7-2 M Holdforth *(xnb) Disp ld 2-12; outpcd in 16l 3rd aft 15; lft 20l 2nd nxt; one pce & no imp; dem app 2 out & agn flat*	1	4
182^{2}	Perching (IRE) 4-1 M Sheridan *2 handlers; trckd ldrs; 4th & wl in tch 13; outpcd aft 15; no imp aft; wknd last*	8	5
182^{U}	Satcotino (IRE) (5a) 16-1 P York *In tch in midfield; 6th 13; sn outpcd & btn*	8	6
190^{5}	Live Wire (IRE) 20-1 Miss C Benstead *Prom; jmpd slow 10 & lost plce; 8th & strugg 13; one pce aft*	hd	7
141^{4}	Alexander Nevsky 25-1 D Dennis *(xnb) A bhnd; t.o 9th aft 7; cont miles bhnd*	runin	8
	Caddy Man (IRE) (6ow) 25-1 A Coveney *A bhnd; hmpd 5; t.o 10th aft 7; mist 11; plodded on*	7	9
189^{5}	Cedar Chief (4x)(bl) 12-1 G Gallagher *Rchd padd as others were mounting; chsd ldrs; went 3rd 10; ld 12 & drew clr uphill; 12l up & gng str when fell 16*		F
182^{U}	Glenmont (IRE) 25-1 Ms L Stock *A rr; t.o last aft 7; pu 14*		P
180^{2}	Kenny Davis (IRE) 6-1 P Blagg *Tde; in tch in rr when hmpd & fell 5*		F
175^{3}	Lively Lord (IRE)(cp,tt) 6-1 G Wigley *Ld til blun & event ur 2*		U
	Spy Boy (IRE) 16-1 L Cornford *(bf) Set off last & imm detach; t.o 11th aft 7; pu aft 11*		P

OFFICIAL DISTANCES: 5l, 1/2l **TIME:** 6min 34.5s
TOTE: £6.10; places £3.40,£2.30,£3.90 **DF:**£28.80

423 S E Hunts Club Members Maiden (Div 1), 12st — 8 ran

97^{U}	**THE SKY IS BLUE** 3-1JF **P York** *Wl in tch; ld brief 11; ld aft 15; a gng best aft; drew clr app last; easily (trainer's 1st wnr)*		1
	Inis Eile (IRE) 3-1JF **A Charles-Jones** *Cl up; ld brief aft 7; chsd ldng pr 15; mist 16; sn outpcd; stayed on flat to tk 2nd nr fin*	10	2
186^{P}	**Master Chief (IRE)** 8-1 **P Bull** *2 handlers; tde; cl up; rmdrs 13; eff to press wnr aft 15; btn aft 2 out; wknd last; dem nr fin*	1/2	3
345^{P}	Iconic 8-1 D Page (Kent) *Pulled hrd; ld 4; made most aft to 15; went out like a light & t.o nxt; r.o agn 2 out*	10	4
	Fables Green 4-1 D Dennis *Mists 5 & 9; nvr gng wl in rr; went poor 4th brief app 16; sn no prog*	4	5
154^{P}	Cerasus Knight (IRE) 16-1 J Morgan *Ld to 4; wknd rap app 8; pu 10*		P
	Gale On The Lake (IRE) (5a) 4-1 P Hall *Prom; cl 4th when fell 8*		F
103^{F}	Private Percival 8-1 P Blagg *In tch til wknd 15; t.o & pu 2 out*		P

OFFICIAL DISTANCES: 5l, nk **TIME:** 6min 51.0s
TOTE: £3.50; places £2.40,£1.20,£1.80 **DF:**£3.00

424 S E Hunts Club Members Maiden (Div 2), 12st — 8 ran

Form	Runner	Dist	Pos
	DIAMOND STONE (IRE) 6-1 **P York** *Nt fluent in rr early; prog to 3rd 9; ld 15; mist 2 out & nrly jnd; drvn clr app last*		1
220^{3}	**Glen Amber (IRE)** 6-1 **C Gordon** *Hld up; mist 12; eff 16; sn rdn & no imp; went 2nd last; no ch w wnr*	8	2
174^{4}	**Tupelov (IRE)** 5-4F **D Dennis** *(xnb) Ld 3; set v stdy pce; hdd 15; rdn & v one pce frm nxt; kpt on agn flat*	1	3
	Nocash (IRE) 3-1 J Sole *Ld to 3; prom til chsd wnr & mist 16; ev ch aft 2 out; wknd & dem app last*	2	4
	Madam Attorney (5a) 16-1 G Wigley *Wl in tch; 4th & ev ch aft 15; blun 16 & wknd; t.o.*	30	5
	Midnight Lord (IRE) 16-1 Miss C Benstead *Keen; prom til rfo 7*		U
264^{P}	Octane Booster (IRE) 14-1 M Holdforth *(xnb) In tch; jmpd slow 11 & wknd; wl bhnd when pu 14*		P
186^{P}	Worth A Shot (IRE) 12-1 D Phelan *Trckd ldrs to 13; wknd & pu 15*		P

OFFICIAL DISTANCES: 6*l*, 1*l* **TIME:** 6min 53.4s
TOTE: £13.40; places £14.50,£1.10,£1.10 **DF:**£1.80 (1+any)

Tynedale

Corbridge (RH 9F,18J)

Sun, 7 Mar (GOOD, GOOD to SOFT in places)

425 Hunt Members, 12st — 7 ran

Form	Runner	Dist	Pos
	COOMAKISTA (5a) 20-1 **R Morgan** *Green; in tch; 5l off pce & gng wl 10; ld aft 13; ½l up 2 out; hdd brief app last; stayed on wl u.p flat*		1
340^{2}	**Spring Double (IRE)** (7x) 4-6F **T Mounsey-Heysham** *Ld; 2l up 4; hdd aft 13; trckd ldr; ld brief aft 2 out; no ex flat*	4	2
270^{6}	**Knockholt** 5-1 **Miss M Neill** *Mists; in tch in rr early; prog 10 to ld brief aft 15; ev ch til outpcd aft 2 out; 4l 3rd app last*	3	3
160^{F}	Lothian Rising 33-1 L Morgan *Chsd ldrs; outpcd 12; 10l 4th 15; kpt on; nd*	20	4
330^{8}	St Bee(cp) 25-1 A Richardson *Burly; chsd ldrs; pushed along 9; outpcd 12; sn nd; wl bhnd 15; 20l 5th 2 out; v one-pcd*	6	5
	Donallach Mor (IRE) (7x) 4-1 Mrs V Jackson *Cl 2nd early; drpd back 5l last app 8; some prog & mist 10; outpcd 12 & sn detach; 25l last 2 out*	8	6
163^{P}	Feeling Grand (IRE) 20-1 F Arthur *(xnb) Tubed; trckd ldrs; 4l 4th when fell 13*		F

OFFICIAL DISTANCES: 3*l*, 3*l*, 20*l* **TIME:** 6min 26.8s

426 Confined, 12st — 15 ran

Form	Runner	Dist	Pos
133^{6}	**MEANDER (IRE)**(cp) 14-1 **J Mactaggart** *Ld/disp; ½l up 4; 1½l 2nd 13; lft 2l clr 15; 2l up 2 out; 1l up last; rdn clr flat*		1
	Clifford Bay (IRE) 5-1 **Miss N Stirling** *(xnb) Oht; 2 handlers; unruly padd & gng to post; ld/disp; 4½l 4th 13; 8l 5th & outpcd 15; rallied 2 out; ev ch last; outpcd*	2½	2
214^{2}	**Red Gauntlet** (5x) 5-4F **K Anderson** *6/4-5/4; tde; a.p; ½l 2nd 4; 4l 3rd 13; ev ch til outpcd app last*	3	3
	Trivial (IRE) (5a) 12-1 L Morgan *Mid-div; outpcd 14; btn aft nxt; wl bhnd 3 out; stayed on stdly app nxt*	20	4
	Extra Stout (IRE) 14-1 C Storey *Mid-div; outpcd 13 & sn nd; wl bhnd 3 out*	10	5
330^{P}	Gaultier Gale (IRE) (6x) 20-1 A Findlay *Mid-div; 5l 7th 10; outpcd aft 13 & sn btn; t.o 3 out*	4	6
339^{F}	Lord Dorcet (IRE) 6-1 D Jewett *In tch; 4l 6th app 10; eff 12; outpcd aft 14; wknd 2 out; releg last & virt pu flat*	25	7
75^{F}	Bob's Gray 25-1 R Nichol *Ss; detach by 3; sn t.o; 50l last 6; slt late prog; pu last*		P
282^{3}	French Cedar (7x) 7-1 W Ramsay *Ld/disp til 1½l clr 13; 3l up when fell 15*		F
282^{2}	Johnnys Gone (IRE) 8-1 C Shirley-Beavan *Mid-div til fell 4*		F
285^{3}	Laganside (IRE) (5x) 25-1 J Muir *In tch in rr; strugg 11; wl bhnd 13; t.o & pu last*		P
284^{5}	Little Santa (IRE) (5a) 20-1 Mrs K Hargreave *A rr; wl bhnd 5-10; t.o & pu 2 out*		P
134^{F}	Lively Dessert (IRE)(cp) 25-1 C Gillon *Rr; 25l 12th 6; strugg & rmdrs 10; sn nd; t.o & pu last; dism*		P

133P Piper's Rock (IRE) 20-1 Miss V Russell *(xnb) Cl up; 6l 4th app 15; ev ch when ur 3 out* . . . U
162⁶ Wishful Thinker 33-1 Miss K Scott *1st ride; in tch in rr when ur 2* . . . U

OFFICIAL DISTANCES: 2*l*, 4*l*, 20*l* **TIME:** 6min 21.9s **TOTE:** £14.30

427 Intermediate, 12st — 7 ran

282U **CREVAMOY (IRE)** (5a) 6-4F **A Richardson** *Oht; 30l last 5; 20l 4th 10; went 5l 3rd 13; ld aft 3 out; hrd prsd app last; rdn clr flat* . . . 1
Trooper Collins (IRE) 5-2 **G Tuer** *Oht; 25l 4th 5; went 4l 3rd 14; prog to ld brief aft nxt; prsd ldr frm 3 out; ev ch app last; easily outpcd flat* . . . 5 2
211⁷ **Ben From Ketton** 10-1 **S J Robinson** *Chsd ldrs; 20½l 3rd 4; mist 11 & rmdrs; 8l 4th 15; kpt on one pce* . . . 12 3
Rainton 3-1 Miss N Stirling *(xnb) Oht; tde; unruly start; pulled hrd & sn wl clr; 20l ahd 4; 15l up 10; grad pegged back & 3l clr 14; hdd aft nxt; wknd qckly* 8 4
210⁶ Mozielaw (5a) 12-1 Miss M Neill *Chsd runaway ldr; 30l 2nd 7; 15l 2nd 10; 10l 5th & outpcd 15; wl bhnd 3 out* . . . 6 5
132P Anotherhandyman 12-1 Miss S Gledson *A rr; wl bhnd when mist & ur 4* . . . U
282⁶ Sharpaman(bl) 25-1 C Shirley-Beavan *A rr; pushed along 10; strugg 13; 10l last & wkng 14; t.o 16; pu last* . . . P

OFFICIAL DISTANCES: 5*l*, 14*l*, 7*l* **TIME:** 6min 24.0s **TOTE:** £3.00

428 Ladies Open, 3m5f - 21J — 10 ran

72³ **PARADE RACER** 11-2 **Miss J Riding** *Opened 6s; chsd ldrs; 3l 4th 9; went 3rd 16; 1l 2nd 18; chall last; hrd rdn & ld nr line* . . . 1
Lordberniebouffant (IRE) 4-5F **Miss P Robson** *Tchd evens; a.p; ½l 2nd 7; ld aft 12; 2l up 16; hrd prsd app last; hrd rdn flat; nt qckn & hdd nr line* . nk 2
284² **Passing Danger (FR)** 5-1 **Miss R Davidson** *In tch in rr; 8l 8th app 9; 15l 7th 17; stayed on wl app 2 out; 10l 3rd app last; too much to do* . . . 1 3
284⁴ Commanche Law (IRE) 9-1 Mrs A Hamilton *Chsd ldrs; 6l 6th 9; eff & 5l 5th 17; 8l 4th & outpcd 3 out; kpt on; lkd to snatch 4th* . . . 10 4†
270⁴ Light The River (IRE)(bl) 8-1 Miss C Metcalfe *(xnb) In tch; 6l off pce 13; prog to 4l 3rd 18; sn outpcd; lkd to fin 5th* . . . hd 4†
162² Hessac (FR) 14-1 Miss W Gibson *Ld to 12; 2l 2nd 16; 4l 4th & outpcd 18; kpt on* . . . 4 6
211P Dean Deifir (IRE)(cp) 20-1 Mrs V Jackson *(xnb) Trckd ldrs; 3½l 5th 9; 4l 5th 13; outpcd app 18; sn nd* . . . 3 7
135⁵ Houselope Beck 25-1 Miss A Wanless *(xnb) A rr; mist 1; 10l off pce 12; sn wknd; wl bhnd 3 out* . . . 3 8
270⁸ Silk Vestments (5a) 33-1 Miss H Dunning *A rr; 10l last 8; detach 10; rdn 12; t.o nxt* . . . 30 9
284³ Pharmistice (IRE) 5-1 Miss N Stirling *(xnb) Prom; 1½l 3rd 7 til outpcd & wknd 15; pu 2 out* . . . P

OFFICIAL DISTANCES: nk, 1*l*, 15*l* **TIME:** 7min 45.4s **TOTE:** £4.10

429 Land Rover Mens Open, 3m5f, 12st - 21J — 13 ran

269⁶ **GO NOMADIC** (7x) 7-2 **P Atkinson** *Ld/disp til ld 7; hdd 15; prog to ld agn 2 out; stayed on wl u.p* . . . 1
272P **Uncle Neil (IRE)** 33-1 **R Morgan** *Tchd 50s; nt a fluent; ld/disp early; lft in ld brief 17 & agn brief 3 out; outpcd app last; promising* . . . 5 2
240² **Son Of Anshan** (7x)(tt) 5-4F **G Tuer** *Handy; 6l 5th app 9; eff to chall 2 out; 2l 3rd & btn last* . . . 2½ 3
Just Whiskey (IRE) (7x) 6-1 C Shirley-Beavan *In tch in rr; prog 16 to 10l 5th 17; sn rdn; 4th & one pce 2 out* . . . 8 4
163³ Blank Cheque (4x) 12-1 D Coates *Mid-div & nvr plcd to chall; 20l off pce 11; stayed on stdly frm 3 out* . . . 3 5
269⁸ Kilcaskin Gold (IRE) 8-1 A Findlay *A rr; 30l last 7; some prog aft 12; sn nd; tired flat* . . . 12 6
211⁶ Hoh Tel (IRE)(cp) 20-1 C Gillon *Trckd ldrs; 2l 3rd 7; 2l 4th 10; wknd aft 15; t.o 3 out; tired & virt walking flat* . . . 1 7
214⁴ Dorans Magic (7x) 5-1 N Bannister *Opened 6s; handy; 6l 6th app 11; 2l 3rd 17; ld nxt; 2l clr & ev ch when fell hvly 3 out* . . . F
285¹ Falcon's Flame (USA) (4x) 25-1 R Green *Rr; stdy prog aft 13; outpcd 16; wl off pce when rn into by loose horse & ur app 19* . . . B
Idiot's Star 20-1 J Burley *A rr; wknd & pu aft 12; dism; lame* . . . P

214[1]	Just Barney Boy 3-1 A Waugh *Trckd ldrs; 2l 4th aft 9; prog 11; ld 15; 1l up when fell 17*		F
269[P]	Needsmoretime (IRE) 33-1 S J Robinson *Mid-div; rdn & 12l 8th 12; sn strugg; t.o & pu 16*		P
271[P]	The Panjshir 66-1 G Willoughby *Oht; chsd ldrs; strugg aft 11; sn t.o; pu 16*		P

OFFICIAL DISTANCES: 6*l*, 1½*l*, 10*l*, 4*l* **TIME:** 7min 52.0s **TOTE:** £19.50

430 Restricted (Div 1), 12st - 16J — 14 ran

212[2]	**HALLRULE (IRE)**(cp) evensF **Miss P Robson** *Trckd ldr; 2l 2nd 15; ld & lft 2l clr 2 out; rdn out*		1
164[6]	**Highland Brig** 7-1 **R Morgan** *Ld til hdd app 2 out; wknd app last*	10	2
	Distinct (IRE) 40-1 **Miss M Neill** *A.p; 5l 4th 15; outpcd 2 out; kpt on wl flat*	4	3
212[8]	Alex In Action 50-1 B Hall *Mid-div; outpcd aft 11; 25l off pce 14; nd; tired flat*	35	4
286[3]	Sijujama (IRE) 25-1 Miss N Patterson *(xnb) Mid-div; outpcd & nd frm 13.*	3	5
283[3]	The Broken Man 33-1 Miss K Bryson *Mid-div; t.o 11; climbed 14; rdn out flat to snatch 6th*	6	6
	Shylock (IRE) 25-1 A Richardson *Chsd ldrs; outpcd & nd aft 13; 20l 5th 3 out*	s hd	7
	Barwick Green (IRE) 33-1 Miss B Kendall *Oht; in tch til mist & fell 4*		F
164[5]	Captain Oates 8-1 T Oates *Prom; 2l 4th 6; 4l 3rd when pu & dism aft 10; destroyed.*		P
316[5]	Jupiter's Fancy (5a) 4-1 M Coglan *Rr; 20l last 5; gd prog 10; disp 2l 2nd aft 15; cl 2nd & ev ch when fell 2 out*		F
160[1]	Magic Performer 5-1 L Morgan *Trckd ldrs; rmdrs aft 9; 7l 5th 10; outpcd 13; t.o 15; pu 2 out; broke down; destroyed.*		P
271[7]	Midnight Moon 33-1 J Burley *Fell 3; broke nk; dead*		F
283[U]	Offspringer 10-1 D Jewett *Unruly start; a rr; rmdrs 8; lsng tch 11; pu nxt*		P
287[P]	Simply Silver Lady (5a) 33-1 S Huggan *A rr; mist 11; t.o aft; pu nxt*		P

OFFICIAL DISTANCES: 10*l*, 4*l*, dist **TIME:** 6min 24.3s **TOTE:** £1.80

Fence 12 omitted - fallen horse; fence 13 omitted - fallen rider

431 Restricted (Div 2), 12st — 12 ran

271[1]	**THREE SPIRES** 5-2F **A Richardson** *2 handlers; hld up; 12l 5th 7; gd prog to 1l 2nd 13; ld app 15; drew clr app last; comf*		1
131[2]	**Native Alibi (IRE)** 8-1 **C Shirley-Beavan** *Lw; rr; prog to ld aft 11-14; ev ch til one pce app last; tired flat.*	10	2
216[2]	**Try Me And See** 8-1 **G Crow** *Prom til ld aft 8-10; pckd 15 & outpcd in 3rd aft; hmpd 2 out; wknd nxt; tired flat; improve*	12	3
215[2]	Pure Steel (IRE) 14-1 C Storey *Chsd ldrs; 10l 4th 6-7; mist 13; t.o 6th & strugg aft*	runin	4
211[4]	Briery Hill 7-1 T Morrison *(xnb) In tch in rr; 13l 6th 7; mist 9; went 10l 4th 3 out; 8l 3rd & clsng stdly when fell 2 out*		F
	Distracting (5a) 10-1 L Morgan *Mists; in tch; 14l 7th 11; prog to 4l 3rd 13; sn pushed along & outpcd; 25l 4th & hmpd 2 out; pu last*		P
283[U]	Harry's Mare (IRE) (5a) 10-1 S Huggan *Nt a fluent; trckd ldrs; 4l 3rd 5; outpcd 13; 12l 5th nxt; sn wknd & jmpng slow; pu aft 3 out*		P
216[1]	Little John 7-1 J Galbraith *In tch til rfo aft 8*		U
	Silver Sovereign 20-1 C Dawson *Sn rr; pushed along 10; t.o & pu 11*		P
212[3]	Timberley(tt) 5-1 T Oates *Mid-div when fell 3*		F
283[P]	Treble Vision (IRE)(bl) 20-1 M McAlister *(bf) Nt jw; mist 1; 30l last 4; mists 6 & 7; pu 11*		P
286[F]	Wheresbob(vis) 20-1 R Nichol *Ld at gd pce til hdd aft 8; sn strugg; pu 15.*		P

OFFICIAL DISTANCES: 12*l*, 10*l*, dist **TIME:** 6min 27.2s **TOTE:** £7.40

432 Open Maiden 567&8yo (Div 1), 12st — 9 ran

	KING BARRY (FR) (7a) 4-5F **Miss P Robson** *Prom; 3l 4th 6; 1l 2nd 10 til ld aft 3 out; hdd brief aft nxt; ld last; rdn out; improve*		1
	River Alder (5a) 7-2 **C Storey** *Opened 4s; trckd ldr; ld aft 10; 1l up 13; hdd 3 out; ld agn brief aft 2 out; nt qckn last; sn eased when btn flat; improve*	5	2
344[4]	**Red Rose Dixie** (5a) 6-1 **C Dawson** *(bh) Cl up; 4l off pce 7; outpcd 15 & 10l 4th nxt; nd; kpt on wl app last*	25	3
	Air Leader (IRE) (7a) 12-1 L Morgan *Hmpd 1; chsd ldrs; disp 2l 3rd 10; outpcd 3 out; no ch when mist nxt; btr for rce*	2	4
	Justenough 6-1 K Anderson *(bf) Chsd ldrs; pulling; disp 2l 3rd 10; outpcd 14; grad wknd; t.o*	10	5

286P Alice's Old Rose (5a) 12-1 M McAlister *In tch; prog 13 & 3l 3rd nxt; mist 3 out; sn t.o* 4 6

341P Mid Summer Lark (IRE) 6-1 D Jewett *(xnb) Ld at sedate pce; ½l up 4 til hdd aft 10; outpcd 15; t.o & strugg aft; stayed on u.p frm 2 out* 5 7

216⁷ Can't Catch Me (IRE) (5a) 20-1 Miss J Riding *A rr; mists 1 & 4; jmpd slow 5; detach in 25l last when hit 6; climbed over nxt & rdr jmpd off* . . . . U

Suny Henry 12-1 J Tate *Mists; in tch in rr; wl bhnd 9; detach in 20l last 13; t.o & pu 2 out*. . . . . P

OFFICIAL DISTANCES: 6*l*, 15*l*, 1*l* **TIME:** 6min 50.4s **TOTE:** £1.60

Eastlands Rain (rdr inj in prev rce) was withdrawn not under orders

433 Open Maiden 567&8yo (Div 2), 12st — 12 ran

165U **LETHEM AIR**(tt) 7-1 **D Jewett** *Opened 8s; a handy; 4l 3rd when pckd 13; ½l 2nd app 15; chall & lft clr 2 out; eased flat; btr for rce* 1

160B **Nomadic Blaze** 4-5F **P Atkinson** *(xnb) Tchd 11/10; oht; tde; ld; 3l up 4; hdd & outpcd app 13; sn bhnd; stayed on agn past btn horses frm 2 out; no ch w wnr* 12 2

342² **Sweeping Storm (IRE)** 6-1 **C Dawson** *Handy; 10½l 4th 5; 8l 3rd 15 & outpcd; sn one pce* 8 3

287⁵ Red Jupiter 14-1 A Richardson *Lw; in tch in rr; pushed along 10; sn wl bhnd; kpt on*. 2½ 4

More Flair (5a, 5ow) 8-1 J Walton *Trckd ldrs; 10l 3rd 5; 4l off pce 10; outpcd 12 & sn wknd; trotted in* 15 5

Chief Seattle (IRE) 33-1 J Tate *In tch in rr; pushed along 10; mist 12; lost tch 13; pu aft* . . . . P

Imposa 16-1 J Stonehouse *Sn bhnd; rn down fnce to lft & climbed 2; rn out nxt* R

Misty Hills (7a) 11-1 C Gillon *Green; ur post; jmpd slow in rr til lost tch & pu aft 5*. . . . . P

215P Reeker Pike (5a) 25-1 Miss C Walton *Rn out aft 2* . . . . R

137P Spring Rock 20-1 T Scott *(xnb) A rr; 8l last 6; jmpd slow nxt & sn detach; pu aft 9*. . . . . P

287³ Stanwick Gypsy (5a) 7-1 C Storey *Cl up; ld app 13; prsd 15; jnd & fell 2 out* F

Tight Fisted Benny (IRE) 7-1 L Morgan *12s-7s; green; oht; trckd ldr; 3l 2nd 4; disp ld brief 12; outpcd 15; 15l 4th & wkng nxt; wl bhnd when pu last* . P

OFFICIAL DISTANCES: 15*l*, 6*l*, 2*l*, 20*l* **TIME:** 6min 33.6s **TOTE:** -

Detroit Storm (reared up & inj rdr) was withdrawn not under orders - Rule 4 deduction 15p in pound; House Colours (rdr inj in previous rce) was withdrawn not under orders

Hereford (RH 9F,19J)

Tue, 9 Mar (GOOD to FIRM, FIRM patches)

434 Arabian Racing Organisation HC, 3m1f110y £1561 — 5 ran

209² **MINELLA STORM (IRE)** 11-07 15-8JF **P Sheldrake** *Hld up trckng ldrs; went 2nd 15; ld aft nxt; gng clr when mist 2 out; comf*. 1

209U **Sip Of Brandy (IRE)** 11-11 5-1 **Miss J Hughes** *Ld aft 1 til jnd 11; hdd & mist 14; 3rd & rdn when nt fluent nxt; outpcd 3 out; mist 2 out; went 2nd agn flat; no ch w wnr* 10 2

205² **Home Again (IRE)** 11-07 6-1 **M Barber** *Ld 1; cl 2nd; disp ld 11 til ld 14-16; rdn & outpcd 2 out; dem flat* 3 3

168⁵ Prate Box (IRE) 11-11 15-8JF F Hutsby *Last pr; blun 16 & outpcd; hrd rdn & tried to rally aft 3 out; btn when blun nxt*. 7 4

Buckland Knight (IRE) 11-07 14-1 J Young *Last til mist & ur 3* . . . . U

TIME: 6min 29.9s **TOTE:** £2.40; places £2.20,£1.80 **Ex:**£9.60 **CSF:**£10.62

Bangor (LH 9F,16J)

Wed, 10 Mar (GOOD)

435 Hugh Peel Challenge Trophy HC, 3m110y £2299 — 9 ran

206⁴ **WHETHER THE STORM (IRE)** 11-11 16-1 **Miss S Samworth** *Hld up & bhnd; 14l 5th & prog 12; chall 2 out; disp ld when mist last; r.o to ld cl home* 1

Heidi III (FR) 12-00(cp) 7-2 **R Burton** *2nd/3rd til ld app 2 out; jnd last; r.o u.p; hdd cl home* . . . . s hd 2

242^{1} **Upham Lord (IRE)** 12-02 4-6F **G Brewer** *Hld up; hdwy 6; went 2nd 8; nt fluent 11; ld 12; rdn & hdd app 2 out; rallied & still ev ch when hung lft app last; fnd little; wknd flat; eased cl home* 12 3

209^{U} Master Jock 12-04 16-1 G Hanmer *Hld up & bhnd; 15l 6th 12; mod prog app 13; wknd app 2 out* 26 4

317^{5} Justjim 11-07 66-1 M Barber *Chsd ldrs; 4th & rdn when mist 10 (water); no ch aft; t.o 3 out* . . . . dist 5

176^{5} Caher Society (IRE) 11-08 (1ow) 100-1 P Morris *Cl 3rd when mist & rdr waved & f.o 6* . . . . U

Far Glen (IRE) 11-07 14-1 B Woodhouse *Ld at fast pce to 12; wkng rap when pckd 13; t.o & pu 3 out* . . . . P

95^{U} Robert The Rascal 11-07 100-1 Miss S Sharratt *Unruly bef start; ss; nt jw in 25l last; t.o & pu 13* . . . . P

229^{1} Step On Eyre (IRE) 11-11 11-1 S Morris *In tch; blun 6; jmpd slow 8 & rdn; sn lost plce & strugg; t.o & pu 2 out* . . . . P

TIME: 6min 20.8s **TOTE:** £16.70; places £2.40,£2.00,£1.10 **Ex:**£118.40 **CSF:**£70.95

Fences 5 & 14 omitted

Catterick (LH 8F,19J)

Wed, 10 Mar (GOOD to FIRM, GOOD in places)

436 John Wade Skip Hire Nov HC, 3m1f110y £1095 — 6 ran

GOLDEN CHIMES (USA) 11-11 7-2 **G Tuer** *Hld up; mist 1; clsd 13; ld 3 out; 10l clr nxt; v easily* 1

Corrie Mor (IRE) 11-11 14-1 **P Cowley** *V wound up start; made most til hdd & hit 12; nk 2nd 15; outpcd by wnr aft 3 out; kpt on u.p* 12 2

Taleban 11-07 7-1 **T Glass** *Hld up; mist 5; nt fluent 6; hdwy to 3rd 10; rdn & outpcd aft 16; tk poor 3rd flat* 8 3

Mydante (IRE) 11-02 15-8F S Hughes *Burly; blun 2; mist 3; prsd ldr til ld 12; hdd 3 out; imm outpcd by wnr; wknd aft 2 out; fin tired* 2½ 4

394^{3} Hidden Pearl (IRE) 11-07 50-1 J Davis *Sn 3rd; mist 8 & rdn; dem 10; lost tch 13; jmpd lft aft; t.o 15* . . . . dist 5

388^{1} Imps Way 11-02 5-2 M Morley *Hld up; 8l last 11; still in tch but lkd strugg when ur 13* . . . . U

TIME: 6min 36.3s **TOTE:** £3.70; places £1.80,£4.10 **Ex:**£17.80 **CSF:**£37.09

Towcester (RH 10F,18J)

Thu, 11 Mar (GOOD)

437 Grafton HC, 3m1f £2149 — 12 ran

209^{1} **LANCASTRIAN JET (IRE)** 11-09 5-6F **M Barber** *Ld to 2; 2nd til ld 8; mist 10; jnd 15; hdd 3 out; rdn to ld agn app nxt; 5l clr last; r.o game; all out* . . 1

289^{1} **The Granby (IRE)** 11-13 4-1 **Miss H Irving** *Went 3rd 7 & 2nd aft 11; ld 3 out; hdd & mist nxt; one pce und wild & unstylish urging flat* 1¾ 2

321^{4} **Soul King (IRE)** 11-05 100-1 **R Bliss** *Chsd ldrs; 3rd frm 12; rdn & outpcd 3 out; rallied flat; r.o wl cl home* . . . . hd 3

292^{2} Freedom Fighter 11-07 14-1 A Martin *Pulled hrd; sn stdd to midfield; 6th 9; went 3rd & mist 10; rdr waved 11; outpcd aft mist 12; 15l 5th 15; stayed on agn aft 2 out; hung rt flat* 2½ 4

209^{4} Maggies Brother 12-03 12-1 D Barlow *Chsd ldrs to 7; 7th 9; rallied in 7l 4th 15; rdn & sn outpcd; plugged on flat* 5 5

West Pal (IRE) 12-03 25-1 P York *(xnb) Hit 1; hmpd 3; jmpd slow 5; 5th & hdwy 9; mist 11; wknd & jmpd slow 13; t.o 3 out* . . . . dist 6

348^{6} Cimarrone Cove (IRE) 11-09(bl) 7-1 T Greenall *Fell 3; blinkers fell over horse's eyes effectively blinding him, but rn loose w field crashing into 3 separate sets of plastic rails* . . . . F

177^{4} Fisherman Jack 11-05 33-1 E Walker *In tch to 8; wkng when mist 10; wl bhnd when pu 12* . . . . P

292^{9} Lyphard's Fable (USA) 11-05 150-1 D England *Wl bhnd; jmpd slow 5; 10th when ur 6* . . . . U
239^{P} Offshore (IRE) 11-09 100-1 P Cowley *Last when hmpd 6; pu & dism sn aft* P
289^{8} Polo Pony (IRE) 11-05(cp) 100-1 Miss T Habgood *Mist 1; tore into ld 2; hdd 8; lsng plce when pckd 10; mist nxt; 6th when ur bend bef 12; rdr inj.* . U
225^{2} Young Tomo (IRE) 11-05(bl) 33-1 L Hicks *Bad hmpd 3; jmpd slow 5; bhnd; last & strugg when blun 8; hrd drvn & most reluct aft; sn t.o; pu 14* . . . P

TIME: 6min 47.4s **TOTE:** £1.80; places £1.10,£2.20,£26.10 **Ex:**£4.90 **CSF:**£4.06

The stewards interviewed the rider of Soul King concerning his use of the whip, but were satisfied he had complied with the Jockey Club Instructions

Wincanton (RH 9F,20J)

Thu, 11 Mar (GOOD to FIRM, GOOD in places)

438 Blue Square Dick Woodhouse HC, 3m1f110y £1470 6 ran

348^{5} **CHASING THE BRIDE** 11-09 5-2 **Miss A Goschen** *Ww; hdwy to 2nd 11; ld 15; 12l clr 18; ab fnce ahd frm 3 out* 1
88^{3} **Alska (FR)** 11-02 16-1 **Miss W Southcombe** *Last pr; virt t.o 4; slt prog 9-12; t.o agn 18; plugged into rem 2nd flat* 25 2
241^{12} **Blackberry Way** 11-09 20-1 **J Diment** *Virt t.o 4; clsd to 14l 4th 9; lost tch 15; rem 2nd brief last.* 3 3
Cherry Gold 12-02 2-1F N Williams *Ld; nt fluent 2 & 3; mist 12; hdd 15; lost tch rap w wnr app 18; jmpd rt nxt & sn t.o; lost 2 plces frm 2 out; eased flat* 9 4
352^{2} Badger Beer 11-11 7-2 N Mitchell *Trckd ldr; level when fell 8; dead* . . . . . F
10^{P} Caldamus 12-02 11-2 R Stephens *Chsd ldrs; hit 3; lft 2nd 8-11; rdn & wknd qckly aft 12; pu 13* . . . . P

TIME: 6min 28.3s **TOTE:** £5.30; places £2.20,£4.20 **Ex:**£47.00 **CSF:**£31.62

Fence 17 omitted fallen horse

Ayr (LH 9F,17J)

Fri, 12 Mar (GOOD to FIRM, GOOD in places)

439 Ayrshire Agricultural Association HC, 2m5f110y £1939 11 ran

267^{5} **BOHEMIAN SPIRIT (IRE)** 11-05 12-1 **S Charlton** *Midfield & gng wl; went 2nd 15; ld 3 out; 6l clr when lunged at last; kpt on stout.* 1
330^{2} **Penny Native (IRE)** 11-12 13-2 **L Morgan** *Cl 2nd/3rd til ld aft 16; hdd nxt; one pce.* 5 2
163^{P} **Mr Busby** 11-05 50-1 **M Seston** *Chsd ldrs; eff 15 & disp ld brief; 3rd & one pce frm nxt* . . . . ¾ 3
Monnaie Forte (IRE) 12-05 8-1 C Storey *Rcd keen; chsd ldr 5; ld brief 9 & agn 11 til aft 15; wkng when hit 3 out* 19 4
282^{5} Valley Erne (IRE) 11-12 25-1 A Richardson *Mists; sn bhnd; last & strugg 10; nvr on terms but fin fast* 5 5
330^{P} Charlieadams (IRE) 12-02 (4ow) 33-1 J Muir *Tk keen hld early & bhnd; dashed up on outside to chall app 10; 4th when bad mist nxt; sn wknd; rem when tried to rn out last* 10 6
240^{1} Blyth Brook 12-00 3-1 R Morgan *Ld to 9 & brief 10; wknd qckly 13; pu nxt* P
Hughie 11-01 66-1 C Gillon *Mists & imm lost tch; wl t.o when ur 8* . . . . . U
349^{4} Lord Edwards Army (IRE) 11-05 25-1 G Willoughby *Mists & rdr oft waving; chsd ldrs; in tch 15; sn btn; 15l 5th when fell hvly last* . . . . F
Strong Tartan (IRE) 12-05(cp) 2-1F K Anderson *Prom; went 2nd & blun bad 12; nt rec; 6th & strugg 14; pu 3 out (rdr reported horse had lost its action)* P
287^{P} T'nightsthenight 11-03 33-1 M McAlister *Mists in rr; 9th 9; brief hdwy aft; wknd 10; fell 11* . . . . F

TIME: 5min 37.3s **TOTE:** £16.80; places £2.30,£1.70,£10.20 **Ex:**£50.30 **CSF:**£73.30

Fence 17 omitted - fallen horse; the stewards enquired into possible interference entering the back straight; the rider of Penny Native who had switched his horse hampering Mr Busby was found guilty of careless riding and suspended for two days

Leicester (RH 10F)

Fri, 12 Mar (GOOD)

440 Sherwood Rangers Yeomanry Mdn HC, 2m7f110y - 18J £2203 8 ran

Form	Horse / details	Dist	Pos
345^{2}	**EASTERN POINT** 11-09 5-2 **P York** *Hld up gng wl; went prom 10; ld on bit 15; clr & rdr motionless flat; pushed out cl home*		1
	Black Smoke (IRE) 12-00 9-2 **D Jewett** *Trckd ldrs til rdn & outpcd 15; rallied to 2nd app last; kpt on; flattered by prox to wnr*	1¼	2
168^{2}	**Tanager** 11-10(bl) 16-1 **J Docker** *Hdwy to ld 7; mist 12; drvn & hdd 15; lost 2nd u.p aft 2 out; blun last*	21	3
187^{4}	Sunczech (IRE) 11-05 50-1 Miss S Phizacklea *(xnb) Bhnd when mist 6; strugg 12*	4	4
168^{6}	Kustom Kit Grizzly (IRE) 11-10(vis) 11-1 A Barlow *(xnb) Towards rr; nrly ur 7; nvr gng wl aft; rem frm 12*	20	5
187^{1}	Dinsey Finnegan (IRE) 11-10(cp) 10-1 G Phillips *Ld til aft 5; drpd to rr & rdn 8; t.o aft mist 12*	3	6
313^{1}	Canterbury Jack (IRE) 12-03(vis) 7-4F A Farrant *Jmpd poor; reluct & sn getting rmdrs; hdwy 7; drvn when jmpd v slow 11; rap lost tch; pu 3 out*		P
345^{5}	Legal Storm (IRE) 11-10 100-1 Richard Green *Chsd ldr til ld aft 5; hdd 7; 4th & drvn when fell hvly 15; dead*		F

TIME: 6min 00.9s **TOTE:** £3.10; places £1.40,£1.50,£2.90 **Ex:**£18.80 **CSF:**£13.27

441 Dick Saunders HC, 2m4f110y - 15J £2681 8 ran

Form	Horse / details	Dist	Pos
241^{4}	**CAPE STORMER (IRE)** 12-00 13-8F **M Gorman** *Hld up; hdwy to press ldrs 9; chall 12; ld & nt fluent 2 out; surged wl clr flat*		1
317^{2}	**Guignol Du Cochet (FR)** 11-07 11-2 **S Hughes** *Chsd ldr til ld app 3 out; rdn & hdd nxt; no ch w wnr flat*	20	2
317^{4}	**Sol Music** 12-07 9-4 **L Jefford** *Ld at gd pce; mist 11; hdd app 3 out; wknd nxt*	15	3
	Solvang (IRE) 11-07 50-1 M Wall *Midfield; rdn & outpcd by ldng trio app 12; no ch aft*	7	4
187^{S}	Camitrov (FR) 11-07 20-1 G Kerr *(xnb) Strugg frm 11; t.o.*	27	5
391^{P}	On The Mend (IRE) 12-00 14-1 D Thomas *Chsd ldrs; outpcd 9; hit 12; t.o when eased cl home*	½	6
94^{P}	Nashville Star (USA) 11-07(vis) 50-1 Miss H Lewis *(xnb) Cl up; hit 2 & 7; drpd out rap; wl t.o frm 11*	dist	7
	Thunderpoint (IRE) 12-00(bl) 9-1 Miss V Price *Strugg when nt fluent 3; hopelessly t.o frm 6*	14	8

TIME: 5min 14.1s **TOTE:** £2.10; places £1.10,£1.50,£2.20 **Ex:**£11.70 **CSF:**£10.18

442 Mallard Pawnbrokers HC, 2m7f110y - 18J £6864 6 ran

Form	Horse / details	Dist	Pos
221^{1}	**DELGANY ROYAL (IRE)** 11-12 4-1 **B Pollock** *Jw; made all; drvn along frm last; hld on game cl home*		1
122^{1}	**Star Of Raven** 11-04 5-2F **N Saville** *(xnb) Settled in last to 11; prog to chse wnr frm 3 out; drvn & stayed on wl flat; a just hld.*	nk	2
242^{4}	**Homme De Fer** 11-09 9-2 **N Bloom** *Rcd keen & prom til lost plce 10; 5th & outpcd app 15; rdn & stayed on agn frm last*	4	3
247^{1}	Ballinure Boy (IRE) 11-07 5-1 A Hickman *(xnb) Hld up; hdwy to trck ldrs frm 11; went 2nd app 15-nxt; hit 2 out; rdn & sn btn; eased flat*	18	4
289^{3}	Filscot 11-05 7-2 Miss S Phizacklea *Nt fluent 5; mist 12; chsd ldr til aft 14; drpd out qckly & sn wl bhnd*	19	5
	Traditional (IRE) 11-07 25-1 N Williams *(xnb) Cl up til squeezed for room aft 12; releg last & rdn & mist 13; t.o & pu 3 out*		P

TIME: 5min 59.5s **TOTE:** £6.50; places £1.70,£2.60 **Ex:**£21.70 **CSF:**£14.10

The stewards suspended the rider of Star Of Raven for one day for using his whip with excessive frequency and not giving the horse time to respond

443 Queens Royal Lancers Mdn HC, 2m4f110y - 15J £2229 15 ran

Form	Horse / details	Dist	Pos
276^{1}	**LONGSTONE BOY (IRE)** 11-12 11-4F **N Williams** *Cl up; ld 9; hit 11; rdn & slt advant frm 3 out til drvn ahd flat; all out*		1
189^{3}	**Find Me Another (IRE)** 12-00 100-30 **R Cope** *Prom; w wnr 3 out til rdn & ev ch last; kpt on same pce final 100yds*	1¼	2

138^{4}	**The Vintage Dancer (IRE)** 11-10 20-1 **G Kerr** *Bhnd; stayed on stdly frm 11; bumped into 3rd flat; no ch w ldrs*	11	3
345^{4}	Mr Splodge 11-10 9-1 James Tudor *(xnb) Prsd ldrs; rdn to chse ldng pr app 3 out; one pce & unable to chall*	2½	4
	Charlie's Angel 11-09 12-1 P York *Nt a fluent; outpcd 10; nd aft*	10	5
258^{4}	Jolly Jake 11-10 20-1 E Walker *(xnb) Drpd to rr 8; no ch aft*	2	6
270^{10}	Supercharmer 11-10 16-1 Miss A Armitage *(xnb) Mist 1; ld to 9; chsd ldr to 11; wknd nxt*	7	7
405^{8}	Come On Boy 11-12(bl) 66-1 D Mansell *Prom to 7; lost tch 10; t.o & pu 12*		P
166^{1}	Cross River 11-10 7-1 N Saville *(xnb) Pulled v hrd brief; mists & hld up in rr; outpcd 10; hit nxt 2; t.o & pu last*		P
345^{7}	O'flaherty's (IRE) 11-10(bl) 80-1 W Kavanagh *Tk keen hld early; hdwy to go prom 5; lost plce rap nxt; t.o when fell 8*		F
173^{4}	On A Full Wager 11-10 66-1 J Docker *Nt jw & detach in last pr; t.o 8; pu 3 out*		P
289^{6}	Perfect Finisher 11-10 50-1 T Ellis *Rcd keen & cl up; nt a fluent; ev ch til hit 11; sn wknd; wl bhnd when pu 2 out.*		P
255^{P}	Petrouge 12-03(vis) 12-1 R Burton *Bhnd; strugg when mist 9; rdn & nt keen aft; t.o & pu 3 out*		P
324^{F}	River Dante (IRE) 11-10 25-1 Mrs O Jackson *(xnb) Chsd ldrs til mist 6 (water); lost tch 10; 9th when fell 12*		F
410^{6}	Stantons Church 11-10 40-1 M Barber *Detach in last pr; t.o 8; pulled up 3 out*		P

TIME: 5min 15.3s **TOTE:** £5.30; places £2.30,£1.60,£11.90 **Ex:**£17.70 **CSF:**10.28

444 Francis Suzuki HC, 2m - 12J £2240 13 ran

241^{13}	**ROUTE ONE (IRE)** 12-03 4-1 **S Morris** *Hdwy 4; chsd clr ldr frm nxt; clsd 9; ld aft 3 out; drvn & kpt on wl flat*		1
345^{6}	**Jazz Night** 11-07 33-1 **J Jenkins** *(xnb) Chsd ldrs; eff 9; ch nxt; rdn to go 2nd last; no imp*	1½	2
345^{1}	**Parte Prima** 11-11 9-2 **R Woollacott** *(xnb) Hld up; 6th & prog 6; went 3rd last; kpt on but unable to chall*	7	3
317^{3}	Hot Plunge 11-07 6-1 J Owen *Tk keen hld & prom; 3rd 9; chall nxt; rdn & nt qckn aft 2 out*	½	4
230^{2}	Jackie Jarvis (IRE) 11-04 7-2JF Mrs K Diggle *(xnb) Reluct to go to post & set off; hdwy when mist 6; 5th 9; urged along & nt qckn frm nxt; hit 2 out*	3½	5
177^{P}	Macgyver (NZ) 11-12 7-2JF J Diment *Tk fierce hld & rcd 6l clr; hdd aft 3 out; wknd nxt*	5	6
395^{2}	Stormy Sunrise (IRE) 11-05 20-1 Miss A Armitage *A wl bhnd; no ch frm 8.*	6	7
378^{5}	Codys Castle 11-05(bl) 80-1 R Collinson *Stdd start & a wl bhnd; t.o aft mist 8*	dist	8
20^{r}	Be Bop Bentley 11-05 100-1 A Maskill *(xnb) Stdd start; a rem last*	15	9
304^{P}	It's Norman 11-05 100-1 R Armson *Jmpd lft; midfield to 4; strugg bad nxt; t.o & pu 3 out.*		P
	Jay Man (IRE) 11-05 20-1 N Saville *Chsd ldrs; pckd 6; 6th & outpcd when blun & ur 9*		U
229^{5}	Noble Colours 11-05 20-1 N Pearce *A bhnd; no ch 8; t.o & pu 3 out; dism*		P
229^{P}	Shamel 11-05(tt) 50-1 S Hughes *Strugg frm 8; hmpd nxt; t.o & pu last*		P

TIME: 4min 05.1s **TOTE:** £5.10; places £1.70,£8.20,£2.20 **Ex:**£166.10 **CSF:**£122.97

The owner of Jay Man, whose passport was found to be incorrect, was fined £110

Sandown (RH 11F,20J)

Fri, 12 Mar (GOOD)

445 Queen Elizabeth The Queen Mother Mem HC, 3m110y £5460 9 ran

277^{2}	**TALES OF BOUNTY (IRE)** 11-07(bl) 10-11F **J Snowden** *Prom; trckd ldr 12; ld 15; in comm frm 2 out; pushed out flat*		1
404^{5}	**Act In Time (IRE)** 11-07(bl) 9-1 **T Edwards** *Ld 4-15; chsd wnr aft; kpt on frm 2 out; a hld*	4	2
330^{5}	**Indien Du Boulay (FR)** 11-07 10-1 **W Ramsay** *Midfield; eff to chse ldng pr in 7l 3rd & rdn 19; bumped along & nt qckn nxt; stayed on agn aft last.*	2½	3
267^{4}	Royal Crimson 11-08 (1ow) 33-1 R Alers-Hankey *Prom; hit 11 & rdn & lost plce brief; chsd ldng pr 12-3 out; bumped along aft; wknd app 2 out*	23	4
122^{P}	Raffles Rooster 11-09 100-30 M Manton *Jmpd slow 4; trckd ldrs; outpcd & jmpd slow & mists frm 12; no ch frm 16*	3½	5
170^{4}	Mr Smudge 11-07 16-1 R Sturgis *In tch in rr; 7th & rdn aft 11; strugg frm 14*	4	6

Braes Of Mar 11-07 20-1 E Andrewes *Ld til jmpd slow 4; mostly 2nd to 12; wknd nxt; t.o* . . . 19 7
422F Cedar Chief 11-07(bl) 25-1 F Wheeler *Hit 2; hld up in last pr; eff 11; no prog when blun 15; cont t.o* . . . 12 8
398⁸ A Fine Story 11-11 50-1 J Trice-Rolph *A last; t.o 10; pu 17* . . . P

TIME: 6min 38.0s **TOTE:** £1.80; places £1.20,£3.10,£2.50 **Ex:**£9.70 **CSF:**£9.32
Fences 10 & 21 omitted

Brecon & Talybont
Llanfrynach (RH 8F,18J)
Sat, 13 Mar (GOOD)

446 Hunt Members, 12st — 4 ran

363¹ **CALL ME SONIC** 2-1 **D Jones** *Jmpd path app 4; 2nd til ld 5; hit 14; qcknd 4l clr nxt; rdn out* . . . 1
Glacial Boy (3x) 1-2F **E Williams** *Ld to 5; jmpd slow 8; mists 12 & 13; rdn aft 15; one pce* . . . 6 2
363P **Lynwood Legend** 12-1 **J L Llewellyn** *(xnb,bf) Hld up; jmpd path app 4; 9l 3rd ½way; lost tch 12; 25l last 14; t.o* . . . 1½fs 3
Prickly Green 12-1 G Barfoot-Saunt *Jmpd delib; a bhnd; 17l last ½way; t.o & pu 11* . . . P

OFFICIAL DISTANCES: 5*l*, dist **TIME:** 6min 50.3s

447 Confined, 12st — 18 ran

360P **MENSCH (IRE)** (3x) 7-4F **E Williams** *A.p; 2nd/3rd 8 til ld 14; hdd app last; rallied to ld flat; stayed on wl* . . . 1
Noaff (IRE) 2-1 **T Vaughan** *(xnb,bf) Lw; hld up; hdwy 5; 10l 6th ½way; jnd ldrs 11; 2l 3rd 14; went 4l 2nd nxt; rdn to ld app last; hdd & no ex flat* 2½ 2
403² **Genereux**(cp,tt) 8-1 **T Faulkner** *Chsd ldrs; 10½l 7th & rdn ½way; went 4l 4th 14l; 5l 3rd 3 out; one pce* . . . 8 3
359⁵ Silver Pot Black 20-1 G Barfoot-Saunt *2nd to 8; 7½l 5th ½way; lost plce & 12l 6th 14; sn wl bhnd* . . . runin 4
403⁵ Felix Randal (IRE) 7-1 Miss R Reynolds *2 handlers; swtng; hld up; lost plce & 20l 9th ½way; 16l 7th 14; sn wl bhnd* . . . 1 5
Aficionado (IRE) 33-1 H Oakes *Rdr in voluminous breeches; a wl bhnd; 33l last ½way; t.o 11* . . . runin 6
Against The Agent 6-1 A Wintle *Ld; 6l clr 8; hdd 14; wknd nxt; 20l 4th when pu 2 out* . . . P
Chesnut Wood 14-1 M Barber *Hld up & bhnd; 13th when fell 5* . . . F
Fassan (IRE) 20-1 W Oakes *Rdr slpd & landed up on his backside on way to saddle horse; a bhnd; mist 3; hmpd 5; 32l 14th ½way; t.o when mist 12; pu 14* . . . P
359P Glen Mist (IRE)(bl) 33-1 L Stephens *11th when mist & ur 1* . . . U
408F Lady Archenfield (5a) 33-1 S Graham *(bf) Jb; rmdrs aft 1; sn t.o; ref 5* . . . r
359⁴ Mecca Prince (IRE) 16-1 James Tudor *Prom; 6½l 4th ½way; 6l 5th 14; sn wknd; wl bhnd when pu 2 out* . . . P
229P Mister Falcon (FR)(bl) 14-1 S Hughes *Nd; mist 8; 16l 8th & rdn ½way; 25l 9th when pu aft 14* . . . P
147P Mr Evans 14-1 J Cook *Lost tch 8; 29l 12th ½way; t.o & pu aft 11* . . . P
317r Rainbow Star (FR) 50-1 A Hanly *Reluct to rce; a wl bhnd; 30l 13th & u.p ½way; t.o 11; pu 15* . . . P
360P Rathgibbon (IRE)(bl) 33-1 J Merry *Nvr nr ldrs; 23l 10th & u.p ½way; wl bhnd when pu 10* . . . P
Reefer Dancer(vis) 14-1 D Jones *20s-14s; 2nd/3rd to 10; sn lost plce; 17l 8th 14; t.o & pu 15* . . . P
359⁷ Rubian Princess (5a) 33-1 R Hodges *A bhnd; 24l 11th ½way; t.o & pu 12* . . . P

OFFICIAL DISTANCES: 2*l*, 4*l*, dist **TIME:** 6min 27.4s

448 Land Rover Mens Open, 12st — 12 ran

32P **TICTAC (FR)** 5-1 **P Sheldrake** *(xnb,bf) 8s-5s; 2nd/3rd til ld 15; rdn 2 out; stayed on wl* . . . 1
115⁷ **Royal Barge** (7x) 20-1 **M Barber** *Lw; ld til aft 1; 2nd/3rd til ld aft 14; hdd nxt; ev ch 2 out; edged lft & no ex flat* . . . 2 2

Drumlin (IRE) 20-1 **R Hodges** *W ldrs; 3l 5th ½way; mist 12; 8l 4th & rdn when mist 14; sn wknd; lft poor 3rd 2 out; t.o* . . . runin 3
359^{6} Chief Predator (USA) 25-1 T Faulkner *9th when mist & ur 3* . . . U
360^{P} Cotteir Chief (IRE)(bl) 50-1 R Hughes *Reluct to rce; climbed fncs & t.o til pu 3* P
Dat My Horse (IRE) (7x) evensF E Williams *10th when ur 1* . . . U
Dexter Gordon (IRE) 14-1 James Tudor *Chsd ldrs; mist 5; 5l 6th & drvn along ½way; lost tch & pu 12* . . . P
Doc Ryan's 25-1 T Vaughan *7th when fell 3* . . . F
Farnando (IRE) 8-1 G Barfoot-Saunt *(xnb) 20s-8s; ld aft 1 til hdd aft 14; wknd & 8l 3rd 3 out; pu 2 out* . . . P
359^{P} Harfdecent(tt) 14-1 M Williams *Ss; a wl bhnd; t.o 5; pu 11* . . . P
360^{4} Moon Tiger (4x) 4-1 D Jones *Blun 2; 7th when pu & dism aft 4* . . . P
Thatsforeel (7x) 4-1 A Wintle *11/2-4s; prom; 2½l 4th ½way; w ldrs til pu aft 12* . . . P

OFFICIAL DISTANCES: 1½*l*, dist **TIME:** 6min 26.7s

449 Ladies Open 10 ran

407^{1} **UPTON ADVENTURE** (5a, 7x) 1-2F **Miss E James** *Hld up; hdwy 7; went 7l 2nd nxt; dem 13; went 2nd agn 15; ld aft 2 out; stdly drew clr.* . . . 1
361^{1} **Ashfield Orchestra (IRE)** (5a) 9-2 **Miss I Tompsett** *Hld up; last to 4; 12l 6th ½way; hdwy 12; went 2nd & mist nxt; dem 15; 2l 3rd 3 out; nt qckn aft; went 2nd agn at last* . . . 6 2
208^{1} **Hunter Gold (FR)** 8-1 **Mrs B Lewis** *(xnb) 2 handlers; ld; clr 8-11; hdd aft 2 out; no ex; dem flat* . . . 2 3
361^{U} Buckland Boy 7-1 Miss F Wilson *Prom til lost plce 6; went 9l 3rd ½way; 10l 4th & outpcd 14; stayed on one pce 3 out* . . . 3½ 4
206^{3} Red Neck(tt) 9-2 Miss R Thomas *(xnb) 1st ride; hld up; disp 10l 4th ½way; hdwy 11; lost plce & 12l 5th 14; stayed on one pce 3 out* . . . 1 5
Three Saints (IRE) 14-1 Miss T Clark *A bhnd; 16½l 8th ½way; 21l 7th 14; t.o* runin 6
Do It Once (IRE) (7x) 20-1 Mrs A Rucker *Sn bhnd; 16l 7th ½way; 25l last 14; t.o & pu 15* . . . P
Flying Pennant (IRE) 25-1 Miss S Davies *4th when ur 3* . . . U
La Maestra (FR) (5a) 33-1 Miss H Lewis *2nd to 8; 10l 4th ½way; wknd 12; 20l 6th 14; t.o & pu 2 out* . . . P
206^{P} Market Springer (IRE) (7x) 16-1 Miss B Williams *(xnb) A bhnd; rdn 8; 22l last ½way; t.o & pu 12* . . . P

OFFICIAL DISTANCES: 6*l*, 2*l*, 6*l* **TIME:** 6min 26.4s

450 Restricted (Div 1), 12st 13 ran

203^{1} **CANNON BRIDGE (IRE)** 5-4F **D Jones** *Made all; 4l clr when hit 15; drew rt away 2 out; unchall* . . . 1
252^{2} **My Native Knight (IRE)**(tt) 2-1 **A Wadlow** *(xnb) Hld up; 4½l 6th ½way; went 4l 2nd aft 14; no imp 3 out* . . . 12 2
Roboastar (USA) 16-1 **T Vaughan** *Hld up; 9l 9th ½way; mist 12; hmpd 13; sn wl bhnd; stayed on wl 2 out; nvr nrr* . . . 15 3
405^{U} Foxy Royale 10-1 T Faulkner *Prom; went 2nd 9; lost plce 11; 5½l 6th 14; rallied app nxt; disp 3l 2nd 3 out; wknd qckly* . . . 4 4
406^{4} Magicien (FR) 14-1 R Hodges *2nd/3rd to 13; 7l 4th & u.p 15; sn btn.* . . . 2 5
Running On Red 14-1 S Gray *Hld up & bhnd; jmpd slow 2; 11l 10th ½way; 8l 7th & rdn 14; wknd 15* . . . 6 6
363^{P} Milamoss 25-1 R Hughes *Prom; 4l 5th ½way; went 2nd 11 til mist 14; wknd qckly & 13l 7th nxt.* . . . 5 7
202^{F} Batchworth Lock 20-1 M Lewis *Hld up; hdwy & 3½l 4th ½way; went 4l 3rd 13; wknd & 10l 5th 15; wl bhnd when pu last* . . . P
Blazing Pride 12-1 P Haynes *Lost tch 6; 20l 11th ½way; pckd 10; wl bhnd when pu 11* . . . P
Camden Caramel (IRE) (5a) 10-1 S Hughes *Swtng; chsd ldrs; lost plce & 8l 7th ½way; in tch til fell 13* . . . F
408^{P} Caveat Graeci (IRE) (5a) 10-1 G Barfoot-Saunt *Lost tch 6; 25l last ½way; t.o & pu 12* . . . P
Far From Perfect (IRE) (5a) 7-1 A Wintle *11th when mist & ur 5* . . . U
New World Comet 11-1 T Stephenson *(xnb) Hld up; 8½l 8th ½way; wknd & 15l 8th 14; t.o & pu 2 out; v easy rn.* . . . P

OFFICIAL DISTANCES: dist, dist **TIME:** 6min 40.6s

451 Restricted (Div 2), 12st — 8 ran

Form	Runner	Dist	Pos
	THEREALBAT (IRE) 5-1 **G Barfoot-Saunt** *(xnb) A gng wl; mist 2; 2l 3rd ½way; went 2nd 15; ld 3 out; sn clr; easily*		1
356^{2}	**Steel Gem (IRE)** 5-4F **J Price** *A.p; went 2nd 7; ld 8-9 & 11; hit 14; hdd 3 out; no ch w wnr*	12	2
	Risk Advisory (IRE)(cp) 5-1 **R Hodges** *(xnb) 2nd/3rd til ld 7; hdd 8; ld 9-11; rdn 15; 5l 3rd & wkng 3 out; blun 2 out*	25	3
357^{P}	Black Dan 14-1 D Underwood *Sn wl bhnd; rfo 6*		U
358^{P}	Gay Abandon (5a) 40-1 C Penycate *4th when ur 1*		U
358^{P}	Hail Stone (IRE)(cp) 7-4 James Price *Sn wl bhnd; jmpd v slow 5; t.o 7; pu 12*		P
406^{P}	Scholar Green 12-1 R Hughes *Ld; mist 4; mist & hdd 7; sn drvn along; lost plce & 4l 5th ½way; lost tch und str press 13; t.o & pu 3 out*		P
363^{P}	Sergwyn 12-1 T Faulkner *Hld up; 3l 4th ½way; mist 10; 8l 4th when mist & ur 14*		U

OFFICIAL DISTANCES: dist, dist **TIME:** 6min 46.8s

452 Restricted (Div 3), 12st — 15 ran

Form	Runner	Dist	Pos
	VICARS CHALET (IRE) 20-1 **A Wintle** *Hld up; 11l 9th ½way; hdwy & 5l 7th 14; 5l 4th 3 out; str rn to ld aft 2 out; rdn out*		1
410^{1}	**Shemardi** 3-1 **R Hodges** *2nd til ld 3; hdd 8; ld 11 til aft 14; ld 2 out; sn hdd & nt qckn*	2	2
	Plain Chant 2-1 **S Blackwell** *(xnb) Ld; blun 1; hdd 3; 2nd til ld 8; hdd 11; ld agn aft 14-2 out; wkng when mist last*	10	3
258^{1}	Dorset Fern (IRE) (5a) evensF Miss E James *5/2-evens; w ldrs; 7l 6th ½way; lost plce 10; 6l 8th 14; 7l 5th & rdn 3 out; wknd aft 2 out*	4	4
	Alleywell 25-1 A Wadlow *A.p; 3l 3rd ½way; disp 1½l 2nd 3 out; wkng qckly when mist nxt*	8	5
294^{P}	Sutton Lighter(tt) 14-1 S Gray *Tde; prom; 5l 5th ½way; 4l 5th when mist 14; sn wknd; 25l 6th 3 out; t.o*	runin	6
	Golden Pride (5a, 5ow) 25-1 T Haynes *A bhnd; 20l last ½way; t.o 14*	8	7
403^{P}	A Bit Of Fluff (5a) 16-1 Miss L Brooke *Hld up; lost plce & 13½l 11th ½way; 15l 10th 14; sn wl bhnd; t.o & pu 2 out*		P
	Clarky's Choice (IRE) 25-1 T Vaughan *W ldrs; 4l 4th ½way; 3l 3rd when fell 14*		F
	Fort Apache (IRE) 14-1 D Marsh *Fell 3*		F
362^{P}	Ian's Boy 33-1 J L Llewellyn *Sn wl bhnd; mist 6; t.o & pu 8*		P
252^{P}	Rosegrove Rooster 12-1 T Stephenson *Mounted on course & tde; hld up; jmpd slow 5; 8½l 8th ½way; hdwy 10; wknd & 11l 9th 14; t.o & pu last*		P
	Teg (5a) 20-1 D Davies *A bhnd; bad hmpd 2; hmpd 3; 13l 10th ½way; mist 12; t.o & pu 15*		P
	Tormoss Lady (5a) 33-1 J Price *9th when tried to stop & ur 2*		U
357^{5}	Wiston Wizo 25-1 P Sheldrake *(xnb) Hld up; 8l 7th ½way; hdwy 10; 4½l 6th 14; wkng when mist & ur 15*		U

OFFICIAL DISTANCES: 2*l*, 8*l* **TIME:** 6min 46.4s

453 Confined Maiden 56&7yo (Div 1), 12st — 12 ran

Form	Runner	Dist	Pos
362^{P}	**MUSICAL SLEUTH** (7a) 8-1 **J Price** *Hld up; mist 9; 6l 5th ½way; hdwy 11; went 2nd 14; ld app 15; blun 3 out; stayed on wl*		1
	Gumlayloy (7a) 6-1 **S Hughes** *(xnb) 8s-6s; hld up; mist 1; hdwy 8; 7l 6th ½way; jnd ldrs 11; went 4l 3rd aft 15 & 3l 2nd app last; kpt on*	1½	2
202^{3}	**St Palais** (12a) 6-4 **T Faulkner** *Chsd ldr 5-11; went 2nd aft 14 til wknd app last*	4	3
119^{F}	Meadows Prince (IRE) (7a)(cp) 16-1 D Mansell *(xnb) Prom; 5l 4th ½way; 8l 5th 14; 9l 4th & rdn 3 out; nt r.o*	10	4
362^{2}	Mountain Lily (5a) 5-4F J Cook *Ld to 3; lft in ld 4; hdd aft 14; drpd out tame*	6	5
363^{P}	Belle's Last (5a) 20-1 James Tudor *(xnb,bof) Hld up; 10l 8th ½way; lost tch 11; wl bhnd when pu 14*		P
362^{P}	Capacoostic (5a) 20-1 M Barber *W ldrs; 4l 3rd ½way; went 2nd 11-14; mist & stpd to nil 15; wl bhnd when pu 2 out*		P
68^{U}	Kerry Zulu Warrior 12-1 A Wadlow *(xnb) Pulled hrd; hdwy to ld 3; pu 4; saddle slpd*		P
363^{P}	Maloney (IRE) 12-1 Miss C Evans *Rdr lost iron 2; wl bhnd when rfo 5*		U
	Mo's Grey (5a) 8-1 Miss F Wilson *Ld to post; nt jw; bhnd til pu & dism 5*		P

204P Mr Morgan 14-1 D Jones *Lost plce 5; 12l last 1/2way; lost tch 12; t.o 15; pu 2 out* . . . . P
Sefton Clover (5a) 10-1 J Jones *Hld up; 9l 7th 1/2way; mist 10; 12l 6th when mist & ur 14* . . . . U

OFFICIAL DISTANCES: 1*l*, 3*l* **TIME:** 6min 49.7s

Penny Poor (rdr inj in previous rce) was withdrawn not under orders

454 Confined Maiden 56&7yo (Div 2), 12st — 10 ran

13W **ROSTOCK (IRE)** 7-1 **Miss F Wilson** *(xnb) 2 handlers; ld to post; tk keen hld; ld aft 1-5 & 8-9; 2nd til jnd ldr 2 out; a gng best aft; stayed on to ld flat* . 1
Rescindo (IRE) (7a) 11-10F **W Oakes** *Went 2nd 3; ld 5-8; ld 9; jnd 2 out; sn hrd rdn; hdd & nt qckn flat* 1/2 2
Whitebarn Vixen (IRE) (5a) 7-1 **C Penycate** *Threw herself down padd; nvr on terms; 25l 5th 1/2way; lft dist 3rd 3 out; t.o* 1 1/2fs 3
Crystal Soldier (5a) 12-1 D Jones *Ld til hdd aft 1; 17l 4th 1/2way; fell 10* . F
363P Indian Trix (IRE) (5a)(tt) 20-1 A Hanly *Lost plce 5; jmpd v slow 7; sn t.o; pu 11* P
Kiss This (5a) 14-1 R Hodges *Ref 1* . . . . r
409⁵ Laurelgirl (IRE) (5a) 9-4 M Barber *Prom; 9l 3rd 1/2way; eff 10; 4l 3rd 14; wknd qckly 15; 20l 3rd when pu 3 out* . . . . P
Malvic (IRE) (7a) 10-1 S Hughes *Bckwd; mist 2; 8th when slpd up bend bef 5* S
Red Salmon Dancer (7a) 5-1 D Mansell *Hld up; lost plce 6; t.o 8; mist 10; pu 12* . . . . P
362F Woodland Warrior 3-1 A Wintle *6s-3s; hld up & bhnd; 7th when fell 6* . . . F

OFFICIAL DISTANCES: 1/2*l*, dist **TIME:** 6min 43.3s

New Forest

Larkhill (RH 13F,18J)

Sat, 13 Mar (GOOD to FIRM, GOOD in places)

455 Confined, 12st — 4 ran

2612 **MAKHPIYA PATAHN (IRE)** 5-4F **D I Turner** *(xnb) Ld & jmpd v lft 1; hdd aft 4; ld agn 7; drew 10l clr app 13; in comm when dogged it furiously & tried to pull himself up flat; forced home; unchall* 1
332P **Lord Esker (IRE)** 8-1 **T Underwood** *Towards rr; lft 5l last 5; sn chsng ldrs; eff & lkd gng quite wl aft 12; sn wknd; plodded into 15l 2nd 14; nvr nr wnr aft* 40 2
3323 Highcroft Boy 7-4 C Gordon *7/2-7/4; cl 2nd til ld 4-6 outjmpng rivals; cl 2nd nxt til wknd rap uphill app 13; t.o & pu 3 out.* . . . . P
2332 Nimbus Stratus (3x)(cp) 4-1 Miss J Sims *1st ride; weighed out originally without penalty; v sa; a detach last; 10l bhnd 2; rdr pitched in saddle 4; jinked lft & rfo in wings 5* . . . . U

OFFICIAL DISTANCE: dist **TIME:** 6min 24.1s **TOTE:** £2.30

456 Open Maiden, 12st — 2 ran

VIEW HOLLO 3-1 **E Walker** *(xnb) Bit bckwd; ld/disp at crawl til ld brief 7; ld agn 15; sn clr; easily; sore & dism aft line; quite promising* 1
2642 **Top Light** 1-4F **J Sole** *(xnb) Constantly stdd to ld/disp at crawl; hdd brief 7; hdd agn 15; sn btn.* 15 2

OFFICIAL DISTANCE: 20*l* **TIME:** 6min 45.6s **TOTE:** -

This and all subsequent races were put back 35min because of local traffic congestion

457 Mixed Open, 12st — 3 ran

1403 **FAIR WIND (IRE)** 4-1 **Miss A Goschen** *Tchd 5s; cl 2nd mostly til jmpd to ld 7; jnd brief 11; jnd agn & drvn 3 out; ld aft 2 out; kpt on game* 1
140F **Aberfoyle Park (IRE)** 2-5F **D Jacob** *Opened 4/9; disp cl 2nd til 1l 3rd 5; jnd ldr 11; drpd back 4l 3rd 13; sn clsd agn; prsd ldr 3 out-nxt; btn app last; v disapp* 2 2
3361 **Teller Of Tales** 4-1 **Miss V Flood** *Ld to 6; 2nd nxt til disp ld 11; 2l 2nd 13; ev ch til dem last 3 out; drpd away tame nxt; pckd & rdr nrly f.o last* 20 3

OFFICIAL DISTANCES: 2*l*, 20*l* **TIME:** 6min 12.2s **TOTE:** £5.00

458 Intermediate, 12st — 3 ran

Form	Horse / Comment	Dist	Pos
139[1]	**FREE GIFT** 2-7F **D Jacob** *(xnb) Opened 4/6 in plce; made all; a gng easy; 10l clr 3 out; cruised clr; canter*		1
261[5]	**Owenabue Valley (IRE)** (5x) 3-1 **T Underwood** *5l 3rd 4; blun bad 6; went 2nd 9; disp 2nd 10 & 13-14; 10l 2nd & no imp 3 out*	30	2
	Cabille (FR) 12-1 **J Owen** *(xnb) Chsd clr ldr; 6l 2nd 11; dem last aft 14; 11l last & wkng qckly 3 out*	15	3

OFFICIAL DISTANCES: 30*l*, 15*l* **TIME:** 6min 18.8s **TOTE:** £1.10

Stennikov (connection's previous rnr had fin sore) was withdrawn after declarations closed

459 Restricted, 12st — 5 ran

Form	Horse / Comment	Dist	Pos
232[3]	**PROBY LADY (IRE)** (5a) 7-2 **Miss D Harding** *Tchd 4s; cl up; ld 6; 2nd nxt til ld agn 10; made rest; rdn & r.o wl flat*		1
337[2]	**Hello Roscrea (IRE)** 3-1 **Miss A Goschen** *5l 4th 4; cl up aft; 1l 2nd 14; prsd ldr frm nxt; rdn aft 2 out; kpt on; a hld*	1¾	2
294[4]	**It's Missy Imp** (12a, 1ow) 11-10F **A Martin** *Jmpd & hung bad lft; disp 2nd 5; 4l 3rd 8; cl 2nd & jb lft 12; prsd ldr aft & ev ch 15; no ex last*	1¼	3
337[P]	Lord Of Heaven (USA) 20-1 Miss K Cuthbertson *Imm last; 6l 5th 12; went 4th 13; no imp aft*	25	4
335[1]	B B Boy 11-1 J Owen *(xnb) Ld to 5 & 7-9; blun 13 & releg last; lost tch rap; pu 3 out*		P

OFFICIAL DISTANCES: 2*l*, 1*l* **TIME:** 6min 18.8s **TOTE:** £3.90

460 Dodson & Horrell PPORA Club Members, 12st — 3 ran

Form	Horse / Comment	Dist	Pos
196[P]	**BLACKWATER BRAVE (IRE)** 7-4JF **H Fry** *Tchd 2s; made all at stdy pce in narrow ld; kpt on wl flat; wl rdn*		1
263[r]	**Merry Shot (IRE)** 2-1 **J Snowden** *Fat; cl last til 1l 2nd 8; prsd ldr 3 out; switched to chall last; rdn & no ex flat*	¾	2
288[3]	**True Chimes**(cp) 7-4JF **J Owen** *(xnb) 2l 2nd 3; dem 1½l last 8; rdn 15; imm btn*	12	3

OFFICIAL DISTANCES: 1*l*, 15*l* **TIME:** 6min 39.0s **TOTE:** £1.80

Oakley

Brafield-on-the-Green (LH 8F,18J)
Sat, 13 Mar (GOOD to SOFT)

461 Hunt Members — 5 ran

Form	Horse / Comment	Dist	Pos
191[5]	**ROMANY PEARL**(cp) 11-8F **Miss R Goodwin** *Prom; disp ld 10-11; ld 14; ploughed on und ungainly rdr aft; wl clr frm 3 out*		1
	Uncle Den 10-1 **Miss J Dallow** *1st ride; lost tch 6; t.o 40l 4th 14; plodded on to tk 2nd flat*	30	2
292[P]	**Bold Statement** 2-1 **G Tawell** *(xnb) Lkd awful; made most to 11; outpcd & btn 13; blun 15; lft 2nd app 2 out; dem flat*	3	3
259[6]	Latterly (USA) 14-1 I Bostock *(xnb) Wknd rap 4; pu nxt*		P
	Lottery Lil (5a) 3-1 T Lane *(xnb) Prom; ld 11; hdd & mist 14; sn wknd; v tired 3 out; still poor 2nd when pu 2 out*		P

OFFICIAL DISTANCES: 30*l*, 3*l* **TIME:** 7min 17.0s

462 Open Maiden (Div 1) — 9 ran

Form	Horse / Comment	Dist	Pos
	BORN TO DREAM (IRE) (5a) 10-1 **R Cope** *(xnb) Tchd 14s; trckd ldrs & a gng wl; ld 11; drew rt away frm 15; impressive debut*		1
296[2]	**Nickit (IRE)** 10-11F **R Burton** *(xnb) Midfield & jmpd slow early; jnd ldrs 10; chsd wnr frm 12; easily outpcd frm 15*	25	2
	Native Thunder (IRE) 4-1 **Miss S Duckett** *(xnb) Made most to 11; 3rd aft nxt; eff to disp 2nd & mist 15; sn wknd*	8	3
192[5]	Gloves Off (IRE)(bl) 16-1 Miss H Irving *Sn lost plce & toiling in rr; 21l 7th 10; wknd & pu 12*		P
	Herpen (5a) 16-1 T Ellis *2 handlers; mist 1; a rr; mist 7; 25l 8th 10; t.o & pu 12*		P

	Lord Stroller 33-1 Miss E Bell *Prom to 6; sn wknd; t.o last when pu aft 10*		P
129[P]	Sandyland 25-1 A Sansome *Prsng ldr mostly to 9; wknd 11; wl bhnd when pu 15*		P
	Sandy Lark 33-1 J Diment *Last & strugg 4; rchd 17l 6th 10; sn wknd; pu 12*		P
	Shady Minx (12a) 5-1 F Hutsby *Hld up; prog 8; trckd ldrs 10; cl 4th when fell 12*		F

OFFICIAL DISTANCES: 25*l*, 8*l* **TIME:** 6min 51.0s

463 Open Maiden (Div 2) — 13 ran

227[2]	**UNCLE ADA (IRE)**(bl) 5-2F **R Burton** *Settled midfield; 5l 7th 10; prog to trck ldr aft 12; ld 15; rdn & 2l up last; dogging it flat; just hld on*		1
296[3]	**Northsprite**(cp) 6-1 **J Trice-Rolph** *(xnb) 2 handlers; chsd ldrs; cl 4th 10; eff to ld 12; hdd 15; 2l down last; urged along & kpt on reluct flat; just failed*	s hd	2
	Jurist 25-1 **M Keen** *(xnb) Ld/disp to 11; chsd ldng pr frm 13; outpcd 3 out; clsd stdly frm 2 out but nvr able to chall agn*	5	3
385[F]	Satanas (FR) 25-1 G Hanmer *(xnb) Hld up wl in rr; 10l 9th 10; some prog 12 but outpcd; 4th frm 14; no imp on ldrs; t.o; fin dist 4th; disq - nt draw weight*		4d
	Bethin (5a) 20-1 P Newton *2 handlers; chsd ldrs; cl 5th 1/2way; mist 11; sn wknd; t.o & pu 15*		P
244[U]	Gunner Be True(cp) 12-1 J Diment *In tch; 8l 8th 10; wknd 12; t.o & pu 3 out*		P
367[F]	Ham Lane (7a) 6-1 F Hutsby *Mist 2; hld up; prog to cl 6th 10 & gng wl; fell nxt*		F
244[5]	Joves Shadow 7-1 T Lane *Midfield til mist & event ur 4*		U
	Letsgeton (5a) 10-1 A Sansome *In tch in rr; 10l 10th 10; wknd aft nxt; wl bhnd when pu 13 (though nt as tired as some)*		P
291[U]	No Pressure (IRE) 5-1 D Harvey *Hld up wl in rr; 15l 11th 10; pu 12; dism*		P
296[4]	Penlet Too 6-1 T Ellis *(xnb) Ld/disp to 11; wknd aft nxt; poor 7th 13; pu 3 out*		P
	Whatamonkey(cp) 8-1 P Morris *Prom; 3rd & rdn 10; wknd 12; t.o & pu 3 out*		P
	Winleah 14-1 Miss S Phizacklea *Ss; a t.o; pu 12*		P

OFFICIAL DISTANCES: hd, 6*l* **TIME:** 7min 03.0s

Satanas finished 4th but was disqualified when the rider was unable to draw the correct weight (was four pounds light); the stewards accepted that there had been confusion between the rider and Clerk whist weighing-out; no fine was imposed

464 Ladies Open — 7 ran

246[3]	**KILLERINE (FR)**(bl) 9-2 **Miss H Irving** *Made most; 6l clr aft 10; stayed on relentlessly aft; rdn out flat; unchall*		1
230[R]	**Cascum Lad (IRE)** 9-4F **Miss S Holmes** *Hld up; went 3rd 8; chsd wnr & 8l down 12; no imp aft; dem last; flapped along & tk 2nd agn nr fin*	10	2
289[2]	**Ryans Star** 4-1 **Mrs J Parris** *Hld up in detach last & wl off pce; mist 10 & 20l last; prog 15; r.o to tk 2nd last; flapped along & dem nr fin*	nk	3
380[8]	Gortroe Guy (IRE) 33-1 Miss K Robinson *(xnb) Chsd wnr 6-12; wknd aft 15; t.o*	25	4
280[5]	Bush Hill Bandit (IRE) 4-1 Miss A Stennett *Sn in rr; lost tch 6; pu 8*		P
373[4]	General Confusion (IRE) 20-1 Miss B Czepulkowski *Chsd wnr to 6; stdly lost plce; last frm 12; t.o when rfo 15*		U
	Phar From Chance 9-2 Miss E Jones *(xnb) Lkd awful; in tch in rr; jmpd slow 3; wknd rap & pu aft 7*		P

OFFICIAL DISTANCES: 10*l*, nk **TIME:** 6min 49.0s

465 Mens Open — 8 ran

300[3]	**RED REBEL** 4-1 **R Cope** *Prom; ld 12; hdd brief aft 15; hrd rdn 2 out; kpt on wl u.p flat*		1
292[4]	**Sheila McKenzie** (5a) 10-1 **T Lane** *Hld up; prog 7; trckd wnr 13; ld brief aft 15; ev ch & rdn 2 out; btn when jmpd slow last*	6	2
404[r]	**Picket Piece**(bl) 14-1 **M Goldstein** *Mists; in tch; outpcd aft 10; drvn & rap prog to press wnr 12-nxt; sn lost tch w ldng pr; no ch frm 15; r.o agn flat*	12	3
229[F]	Mickthecutaway (IRE) 5-4F D Skelton *Last & jmpd ponderous; t.o frm 6*	200y	4
229[U]	Do It Again (IRE)(bl) 5-1 R Burton *Hld up; prog to trck ldrs 10; wknd rap 12; pu nxt*		P
	Iorana (FR) 33-1 T Mastoras *Hld up in rr; prog to trck ldrs 11; wkng when mist 13; imm pu*		P

319^{P} Tubber Roads (IRE)(bl) 25-1 J Diment *Ld aft 3-7; rdn & nt r.o aft 10; t.o & pu 12* . . . . P
100^{P} Vain Minstrel (IRE) 4-1 G Hanmer *Ld til aft 3; ld 7-12; wknd rap; t.o when crawled over 15 & pu* . . . . P

OFFICIAL DISTANCES: 6*l*, 10*l* **TIME:** 6min 54.0s

The stewards enquired into the running and riding of Mickthecutaway which was always last; the rider's explanation that the horse was 'unsuited by the soft and sticky ground having won on the firm at Barbury Castle' was accepted

466 Confined, 12st — 8 ran

125^{4} **CHORAL DREAM (IRE)** (5x) 10-11F **R Cope** *Nt a fluent; cl up; ld aft 11; drew clr frm 14; in comm but still drvn along 2 out; eased flat* 1
253^{U} **Wibbley Wobbley** (3x) 4-1 **T Ellis** *Hld up; jmpd slow 6; prog & prom 10; prsd wnr 12; outpcd frm 14; no ch nxt; fin v tired* 30 2
187^{5} **Grand Canyon (IRE)** (3x) 7-1 **T Lane** *Jmpd slow 3; prog frm rr to chse ldrs 10; outpcd nxt; went 3rd 13; trying to cl when mist 14; no imp aft & wknd 3 out* 12 3
375^{P} Jerome Jerome 33-1 A Sansome *Made most til aft 11; 4th & wl btn frm 13; stdly wknd* 6 4
249^{7} Tale Bridge (IRE)(cp) 14-1 J Russell *In tch; outpcd 11; sn toiling in rr; poor 6th 13; plodded on* 1/2 5
382^{P} Lord Of The Chase (IRE) 20-1 T Messenger *Hld up; prog 7; 5th & in tch when ur 12* . . . . U
289^{P} Maltby Son 12-1 Miss K Branson *In tch; drpd to last 7; lost tch 11; poor 5th aft nxt; plodded on to tk rem 3rd when rfo last* . . . . U
Rakaposhi Raid (5a) 8-1 P Newton *Prom til wknd 10; t.o & pu 15* . . . . P

OFFICIAL DISTANCES: 30*l*, 15*l* **TIME:** 6min 55.0s

467 Dodson & Horrell PPORA Club Members Restricted, 12st — 7 ran

37^{2} **POT SHOT** 4-5F **R Burton** *Lw; in tch; trckd ldr 7; ww til chall & upsides gng btr 3 out; rdn nxt; still disp ld last; hrd rdn to ld nr fin* 1
296^{1} **Greet You Well** 2-1 **R Cope** *Ld; 3-4l up frm 6; rdn & jnd 3 out; disp ld u.p aft til just hld nr fin* 3/4 2
Inspector Blake 12-1 **G Hanmer** *Hld up bhnd; prog to 4th 6; went 3rd & in tch 12; outpcd nxt; nd aft; t.o* 45 3
191^{F} Sissinghurst Star (IRE) 12-1 P Mann *Jmpd slow 3; chsd ldr to 7; dem 4th 12; blun nxt & wknd; t.o* 8 4
250^{P} Nonplussed (5a, 4ow) 40-1 P Newton *Jmpd slow; bhnd frm 7; miles bhnd when pu 13* . . . . P
295^{1} Rightun 10-1 T Ellis *(xnb) Keen; w ldrs when mist & rfo 2* . . . . U
109^{P} Waterloo Leader (IRE) 25-1 D Smith *A bhnd; t.o 7; miles bhnd when pu 15* P

OFFICIAL DISTANCES: 3/4*l*, 30*l* **TIME:** 6min 57.0s

Race was run in torrential downpour

Quantock Staghounds

Cothelstone (LH 7F,19J)

Sat, 13 Mar (GOOD)

468 Hunt Members, 12st — 5 ran

273^{2} **CAUNDLE CHASE** 2-5F **J Snowden** *Trckd ldng pr; 3 1/2l 3rd 5 til chsd ldr frm 13; ld 16; sn clr; easily* 1
317^{P} **Robins Pride (IRE)**(bl) 5-1 **Miss C Tizzard** *Ld; 1 1/2l up 5 til hdd 16; sn brushed aside* 15 2
Lingering Laughter (IRE) 33-1 Miss J Buck *Last 2; sn lost tch; jmpd slow 7; fnce adrift 11; clambered over 13 & imm pu* . . . . P
355^{1} Sparkling Missile (5a) 4-1 Miss S Robinson *Chsd ldr; 1 1/2l down 6; blun & rdr called cab 11; rdn & wknd qckly; bhnd when pu 16* . . . . P
275^{P} Viva Bingo (IRE)(bl) 14-1 N McDiarmid *Reared over bckwds padd & kicked rdr; mounted on course; jmpd slow 1; rap hdwy & erratic j nxt; disp 2nd when fell 3* . . . . F

OFFICIAL DISTANCE: 10*l* **TIME:** 6min 22.2s **TOTE:** £1.20

469 Open Maiden 56&7yo, 2m4f110y, 12st - 16J — 11 ran

329^{2}	**VIRGOS BAMBINO (IRE)** (5a) 5-2JF **A Charles-Jones** *(kineton) Ld & sn 8l clr; hdd 5; chsd ldr aft; 2l down 10; ld flat; kpt on wl*		1
	Miss Flinders (5a) 12-1 **R Bliss** *(xnb) Chsd ldr frm 3; ld 5 & sn clr; blun bad 8; 3l up nxt til hdd & no ex flat*	$1\frac{1}{2}$	2
306^{4}	**Joli Christmas** 5-2JF **R Woollacott** *(xnb) Chsd clr ldr frm 2; mist 3 & rdr rec wl; 6l 4th 5; lft 3rd 3 out; nt trble ldrs*	15	3
327^{U}	Harjach 7-2 N Wilmington *(xnb) 2 handlers; nvr btr than mid-div; 22l 8th 10; lft rem 4th by defections 3 out*	8	4
	Tarpon Tale (IRE) 12-1 R Stephens *(xnb,bf) A mid-div; 17l 6th 10; nd.*	hd	5
274^{P}	Augathella 12-1 D Edwards *(xnb) Mid-div 3; 7l 5th 5; hdwy to 10l 3rd 9; still 3rd when blun bad 11; pu nxt*		P
	Margery's Opera (5a) 8-1 E Kenney-Herbert *Mist 1; last trio 3; stdy hdwy to 11l 4th 9; lft 3rd 11; chsng ldng pr when fell 3 out*		F
	Midnight Eclipse (IRE) (7a) 6-1 M Miller *3rd 2; 5l 3rd 5; lost plce & bhnd frm 10; pu 13*		P
174^{6}	Norbert (IRE) 10-1 N McDiarmid *Last 2; 20l 7th 10; bhnd when ur 11*		U
325^{F}	The Jam Saheb(cp) 8-1 Mrs O Jackson *Prom; jmpd rt 1 & 2; lsng plce when mist 5; rr 9; t.o & pu 10*		P
	Theydon Star (NZ) (4ow)(bl) 10-1 R Skinner *2 handlers; a rr; last 7; blun & rdr called cab 10; t.o & pu 13.*		P

OFFICIAL DISTANCES: 2*l*, 12*l* **TIME:** 5min 15.8s **TOTE:** £4.80 **DF:**£c/f

470 Ladies Open — 6 ran

320^{3}	**SIR D'ORTON (FR)** 7-4JF **Miss C Tizzard** *Ld to 5; disp ld 8 til ld agn 10; made rest; 3l up 13; stayed on wl frm 2 out*		1
351^{2}	**Frank Byrne** 3-1 **Miss R Green** *Chsd ldr til jmpd into ld 6; jnd 8; hdd 10; releg 3rd 13; rnwd eff to 2nd app 3 out; no ex frm last*	$1\frac{1}{4}$	2
322^{5}	**Sadler's Realm** 14-1 **Miss C Stucley** *Last; 10l down 3; disp 3rd 9; chsd ldr frm 13 til wknd 3 out; one pce frm nxt*	10	3
	Ardross Gem (IRE) (5a) 12-1 Miss W Southcombe *4th when ur 1*		U
78^{3}	Ballysicyos (FR) 7-4JF Mrs O Jackson *(xnb) Disp ld when ur 1*		U
64^{P}	Doublet 8-1 Miss J Buck *(orbs) 6l 3rd 3; clsd on ldng pr 6; last 13; grad wknd frm 14; bhnd when pu 2 out*		P

OFFICIAL DISTANCES: $1\frac{1}{2}$*l*, 8*l* **TIME:** 6min 17.5s **TOTE:** £3.00 **DF:**£36.00

471 Mens Open, 12st — 7 ran

	KINGSBRIDGE (IRE) 14-1 **T Eades** *(xnb) Chsd ldr til ld 2; made rest; 10l up 5; only 1l up 12; jnd 2 out; fnd ex u.p flat; wl rdn*		1
	Gladiatorial (IRE) 4-1 **T Bishop** *(xnb) Hld up; 15l 6th 5; stdy hdwy to 4th 14; chsd ldr frm 16; chall 2 out; ev ch til rdn & no ex flat*	$1\frac{1}{2}$	2
62^{F}	**Porlock Hill** (7x) 2-1JF **N Harris** *(xnb) 9l 4th 3; chsd ldr frm 7; 1l down 12; mist 15; one pce frm 3 out*	15	3
319^{3}	Cool Wager 5-1 D Edwards *3rd 2; chsd ldrs frm 7; disp 5l 3rd 12; wkng when rmdrs nxt; bhnd frm 3 out*	2	4
233^{F}	Chism (IRE) 33-1 W King *Sn outpcd & last 2; t.o frm 9; pu 3 out*		P
196^{6}	Nearly Gold (4x) 14-1 A Charles-Jones *Ld to 2; chsd ldr til lost plce qckly 7; bhnd when pu 11*		P
277^{P}	Nearly Noble (IRE) 2-1JF R Woollacott *(xnb) Hld up; last 1; 14l 5th 5; disp 5l 3rd 12; wknd frm 15; bhnd when pu 2 out*		P

OFFICIAL DISTANCES: 2*l*, 15*l* **TIME:** 6min 19.5s **TOTE:** £7.70 **DF:**c/f

472 Confined, 12st — 8 ran

196^{3}	**POLAR FLIGHT** 7-4F **A Charles-Jones** *(xnb) Bhnd til hdwy to chse ldr 6-8; cl 3rd 13; ld & mist 3 out; sn in comm; comf*		1
317^{6}	**Arlequin De Sou (FR)** (7x) 4-1 **R Stephens** *12s-4s; trckd ldrs; $2\frac{1}{2}$l 3rd 6; chsd ldr frm 8; ld 13; hdd 3 out; no ex frm nxt.*	3	2
350^{4}	**Leon Garcia (IRE)** (5a) 9-2 **T Bishop** *Hld up last & nd; rem 5th 13; stayed on frm 3 out; nt trble ldng pr*	4	3
278^{2}	Polka 5-2 D Edwards *$3\frac{1}{2}$l 4th 6; mist 12; chsd ldng trio frm nxt; cl up til one pce frm 3 out.*	10	4
171^{4}	The Bounder 8-1 Miss C Tizzard *Ld; $1\frac{1}{2}$l up 6; hdd 13; grad wknd frm 15; walked in.*	12	5

321[5] Sherbourne Guest (IRE) 16-1 J Kwiatkowski *Chsd ldr to 5; jmpd slow 7; releg 6th nxt; t.o 14* 2 6
321[P] Happy Team (5a) 14-1 S Kidston *(xnb) 5th when fell 3* F
318[3] Lazy Lemon (5a) 33-1 Miss C Llewellin *(xnb) 6l 6th 6; wkng when mist 12; t.o & pu nxt* P

OFFICIAL DISTANCES: 4*l*, 5*l* **TIME:** 6min 16.9s **TOTE:** £3.40 **DF:**c/f

473 Restricted, 12st — 10 ran

279[3] **ELLOFAMONKEY** (5a) 5-2F **R Woollacott** *8l 4th 5; chsd ldng pr frm 9; disp ld brief 12; chsd ldr 15 til chall 3 out; sn clr; easily* 1
329[1] **Maybe A Double** (5a) 3-1 **N Wilmington** *(xnb) Prom; 5l 3rd 4; chsd ldrs frm 13; lft 2nd app 2 out; no ch w wnr* 12 2
337[3] **Chief Suspect (IRE)** 12-1 **R Bliss** *4th 4; sn lost plce & outpcd; 9th 8; stayed on one pce frm 16; nd* 3 3
Milldalus (IRE) 4-1 S Kidston *Chsd ldr til disp 5; ld 9; jnd 12; hdd nxt; grad wknd frm 16* nk 4
324[P] Aslapoftheeuro (IRE) 10-1 A Charles-Jones *(xnb) Disp 12l 5th 5; grad wknd frm 13; bhnd frm 15; pu 2 out* P
232[6] Calfstown Lord 20-1 Miss S Lane *Nov rdn; a last; t.o frm 9; pu 13* P
274[1] Inagh Road (IRE) 7-2 J White *(xnb) Tde; ld; 2l up 4; jnd nxt; hdd 9; wknd rap 11; pu 13* P
Kildysart Lady (IRE) (5a) 8-1 N Harris *Hld up; 9th 2; hdwy to 4th 7; disp ld 12; ld app nxt; tried to slip field 15; jnd 3 out; stpd to nil & pu nxt* P
My Nad Knows 14-1 D Edwards *14l 7th 5; nvr btr than mid-div; bhnd when collapsed app 13; dead* P
198[P] Timber Top (IRE) 33-1 Mrs P Swarbrick *Mounted on course; disp 12l 5th 5; grad wknd frm 14; bhnd when jmpd slow 16; t.o when ref nxt* r

OFFICIAL DISTANCES: 15*l*, 3*l* **TIME:** 6min 23.5s **TOTE:** £3.00 **DF:**£10.00

474 Open Maiden (Div 1), 12st — 9 ran

325[5] **ROMANY MOVE** 5-1 **Mrs S Godfrey** *Ld; jnd 3; 2l up 7; dived at 10; hdd 16; disp ld agn 2 out; lkd vulnerable when lft clr last* 1
327[4] **Miss Chloe (IRE)** (5a) 9-2 **R Bliss** *Chsd ldr to 3; 6th 6; $1\frac{1}{2}$l 3rd 12; chsd ldr frm 13; ld 16-nxt; sn hdd; lft 2nd last* 4 2
Collier 9-2 **T Atkinson** *(xnb) Chsd ldng pr 3; $2\frac{1}{2}$l 4th 12; outpcd 14; lft 3rd last; fin fast* 15 3
326[P] Miss Karingaroo (5a) 10-1 J White *Reluct to leave padd; dism & rmtd on course; disp $1\frac{1}{2}$l 3rd 5; chsd ldr frm 11; rdn 13; bhnd frm 16* 5 4
Sula Hill (5a) 12-1 Miss J Buck *Tde; disp ld 3-5; chsd ldr til wknd 10; last nxt; t.o frm 14* $1\frac{1}{4}$fs 5
312[P] Master Of Fashion(bl) 14-1 D Edwards *8th 3; impd to disp $1\frac{1}{2}$l 3rd 5; wknd qckly 9; bhnd when pu 10* P
326[P] Primitive Delight (5a) 4-1JF A Charles-Jones *3rd 2; sn lost plce; last 5; pu 8* P
354[F] Queens House (5a) 4-1JF D Drake *6th when fell 5* F
325[P] Rocastle Lad (IRE) 5-1 R Woollacott *(xnb) 2 handlers; vsa; hdwy to 5th 11; cl 3rd 14; disp ld 2 out; lkd prob wnr when fell hvly last; destroyed* F

OFFICIAL DISTANCES: 4*l*, 15*l* **TIME:** 6min 35.8s **TOTE:** £6.00 **DF:**£16.00

475 Open Maiden (Div 2), 12st — 6 ran

329[U] **PANHANDLE** (5a) 4-5F **R Stephens** *11/10-4/5; $2\frac{1}{2}$l 4th 5; chsd ldr frm 7; ld 11; 2l up 15; u.p when lft clr 2 out; eased flat* 1
121[5] **Random Trix** (5a) 5-1 **Miss S Robinson** *Chsd ldr 2; jmpd slow nxt; 1l down 5; chsd ldr when mist 12; 3rd & labouring 14; lft 2nd 2 out* 8 2
329[F] Caracciola (NZ) 4-1 R McCarthy *Ld 2; mist 5; ld to 10; wknd qckly & pu aft 12* P
Gone On (IRE) 4-1 A Charles-Jones *$1\frac{1}{2}$l 3rd 5; chsd ldng pr 11 & ldr frm 13; 2l down 15; gd j nxt & clsd on ldr; ev ch when fell 2 out; winded* F
Greenhopper(tt) 6-1 M Atkinson *(xnb) Set slow pce 1; sn releg 5th; lsng tch when fell 10* F
264[U] Peter Parkgate (7a) 12-1 D Drake *A last; jmpd novicey; t.o & pu 10* P

OFFICIAL DISTANCE: 7*l* **TIME:** 6min 47.2s **TOTE:** £3.00 **DF:**£4.50

South Wold

Brocklesby Park (LH 8F,18J)

Sat, 13 Mar (GOOD to SOFT, HOLDING patches)

476 Confined Maiden 56&7yo, 12st — 16 ran

293F	**HUNCA MUNCA (IRE)** (12a) 5-1 **N Pearce** *(xnb) Handy; went 3rd 8; disp 2nd 12 til ld app 3 out; kpt on game*		1
	Thanks Jim (IRE) (7a) 9-2 **M Walford** *Set off last; 7th & prog 8; went cl up 13; chsd wnr app 3 out; rdn & ev ch nxt; no imp aft*	$1^3/_4$	2
393³	**Ravenscar** 8-1 **S Walker** *Cl up in chsng group; 4th 11; outpcd 13; 15l 5th 15; stayed on agn frm 2 out*	15	3
271R	Bright Dawn (IRE) (12a) 5-2F G Brewer *Nt jw; hld up & bhnd; jmpd v slow 7; mod 5th 14; kpt on to 3rd & no ch 3 out; jmpd rt nxt*	10	4
152²	Troubleshooter 10-1 O Williams *Rcd keen in clr ld; 12l ahd 12; hdd & wknd rap aft 15; t.o*	30	5
342F	Billymax (IRE) 14-1 B Woodhouse *(xnb) 2 handlers; midfield; 8th 11; sn wknd; t.o 14; pu 3 out*		P
	Caipiroska (7a) 16-1 M Briggs *(xnb) Novicey; 3rd/4th til blun & ur 7*		U
	Combe Florey (12a, 2ow) 16-1 J Docker *Hld up towards rr; 10th 11; pu 14; school*		P
112P	Coombs Spinney 16-1 N Docker *(xnb) Chsd clr ldr to 12; lsng plce when blun & ur nxt*		U
244P	First And Fourmost (IRE)(bl) 14-1 N Bloom *Chsd ldrs til 7th & rdn 11; nt keen aft; t.o 14; pu 3 out*		P
	Hougham George (7a) 10-1 S Morris *Midfield & jmpd safely; 11th 11; pu 14; school*		P
128P	Little Heck (IRE) 20-1 N Kent *Strugg in last pr; t.o & pu 10*		P
	Quizzal (5a) 8-1 R Armson *Prom in chsng group; disp 2nd 12 til wknd rap 15; pu 3 out*		P
371P	Sleeping Panther 20-1 P Millington *V unimpressive padd; jmpd poor; strugg in last pr aft 5; t.o & pu 11*		P
	Stingo (5a) 10-1 E Linehan *Pu aft 5; saddle slpd*		P
	Whats The Fuss (IRE) (5a) 16-1 M Bennison *Chsd ldrs early; 9th 8; wknd & pu 11*		P

OFFICIAL DISTANCES: 2l, 5l **TIME:** 6min 42.0s

477 PPORA Club Members (Nov Rdrs), 12st — 10 ran

301¹	**CLAIRE'S NOMAD**(cp) 8-1 **Miss Rachel Clark** *(xnb) Settled 3rd; mist 11; ld aft 13; forged clr app last; stayed on wl*		1
55²	**Winter Gale (IRE)** 5-2JF **Miss L Eddery** *Hld up off pce til prog 8; went 2nd 14; ½l down & rdn 2 out; sn btn*	$3^1/_2$	2
298¹	**The Nobleman (USA)** 5-2JF **N Docker** *Ld; jmpd v slow 6; jmpd slow 7; hdd aft 13; lost tch app 3 out; nt lk keen aft*	40	3
338⁵	Purevalue (IRE)(bl) 5-1 Miss J Coward *Midfield; 8l 5th 11; wl bhnd frm 14*	½	4
301⁴	Energy Man 20-1 M Bennison *2nd til 4th & drvn 14; stayed prom to 3 out; gave up rap*	4	5
	Galeshan (IRE) (7x)(tt) 10-1 C Huxley *(xnb) 1st ride; nt jw & rdr novicey; midfield; outpcd 9; 7th & btn 11; t.o 14*	25	6
304P	Ghali (USA)(tt) 20-1 T Parr *Nt fluent & rdr v novicey; 20l last 5 & a last pr; rdn & no resp 9; t.o & pu 12*		P
225⁴	Needwood Neptune 40-1 P Bennett *Prom brief but strugg in rr 5; t.o last when ducked out at marker & ur app 12*		R
333¹	New Ross (IRE) (4x)(bl) 12-1 Miss A Turner *Chsd ldrs; 10l 6th & outpcd 11; mist & ur 13*		U
251⁴	Phyllis (5a) 10-1 D Greenway *Prom til pu aft 2 (tendon inj)*		P

OFFICIAL DISTANCES: 3l, 15l, ½l **TIME:** 6min 46.0s

478 Confined, 12st — 9 ran

298³	**SPRINGLEA TOWER** (3x, 1ow) 6-1 **R Hunnisett** *Chsd ldr to 6; rap drpd to rr & poor 8th 9; rnwd eff in 20l 4th 15; plugged on wl frm nxt & ld last; urged ahd flat; all out*		1
54¹	**Ramirez (IRE)** (3x) 8-1 **N Kent** *Hld up; hdwy 8 to 2nd 9; clr w 1 rival 14; ld app 3 out but tired & rdn nxt; hdd last; rallied nr fin*	¾	2

	The Graduate 9-4F **S Walker** *(xnb) Ld; rdn & hdd app 3 out; sn tired but plugged on & ev ch til no ex app last*	$1\frac{1}{2}$	3
389^{9}	Folliday (FR)(bl) 33-1 B Woodhouse *Jmpd v slow 3; went 2nd 6-9; drvn & nt keen when jmpd slow 11; releg 4th & blun bad 13; t.o aft 15*	40	4
248^{2}	Ardkilly Warrior (IRE) 10-1 N Bloom *Cl up to 7; 7th & wkng 9; wl bhnd when pu aft 11*		P
	Blue Royal (FR)(tt) 9-2 S Morris *Bit bckwd; nt fluent 2; nvr btr than midfield; 12l 5th & strugg 12; rem when pu aft 15*		P
298^{P}	Bowfell (5a)(bl) 20-1 G Brewer *Pulled hrd & prom; still 3rd aft 10; sn lost plce; pu 12*		P
156^{4}	Fine Times (5x)(tt) 9-1 R Armson *Last & nvr gng wl; lost tch 9; pu 11*		P
	Silver Buzzard (USA) (7a, 7x) 10-1 Miss Gemma Hutchinson *Tk keen hld in rr; prog 8; 5th 10; went 14l 3rd & jmpd slow 14; sn wknd; releg v tired 4th when fell 3 out*		F

OFFICIAL DISTANCES: $\frac{1}{2}$*l*, 1*l* **TIME:** 6min 46.0s

479 Ladies Open — 8 ran

230^{1}	**SUPREME CITIZEN (IRE)** (7x) 4-5F **Miss J Williams** *Prom & gng wl; ld 9-12 & app 3 out; drew clr frm nxt; rdly*		1
246^{2}	**Nokimover** (7x) 6-1 **Miss Gemma Hutchinson** *Tk keen hld towards rr til prog 9; went 2nd 11; ld 12 til app 3 out; tired & btn when mist nxt*	15	2
	Edmond (FR) 7-1 **Miss H Campbell** *2nd/3rd til ld brief app 8; prom to 13; 6l 4th aft mist nxt; mist 15 & lost tch; rem 5th app 3 out; fin str*	25	3
380^{2}	Ardmayle (IRE) 3-1 Miss L Coney *Hld up in tch; jnd ldrs 12; ev ch til 5l 3rd when pckd & ur 3 out*		U
338^{3}	Ballad Minstrel (IRE) 14-1 Miss J Foster *Settled trckng ldrs; cl 5th 12; wknd 14; lft rem & tired 3rd app 3 out; pu last*		P
299^{4}	Master Adam (IRE) 25-1 Miss K Edminson *Jmpd bold & made most to 7; lsng ground qckly when pu 10*		P
	What A Fuss (7x) 33-1 Miss J Coward *Handy; 4th app 8; wknd nxt; pu 11*		P
	Zabadi (IRE) (7x, 2ow) 25-1 Miss R Napier *Bckwd; a last; lost tch 11; pu 13*		P

OFFICIAL DISTANCES: 20*l*, 20*l* **TIME:** 6min 41.0s

480 Land Rover Mens Open, 12st — 3 ran

379^{1}	**NAUTICAL LAD** 2-7F **J Docker** *2 handlers; lw; keen in 2nd til ld 13; rdn frm 3 out; in comm aft but all out*		1
391^{P}	**San Francisco** (7x) 5-2 **G Brewer** *Ld to 13; prsd wnr aft; rdn & hld frm 3 out*	10	2
	Cateel Bay (5a) 16-1 P Millington *A last; keen early; lost tch & mist 11; mist 12; pu 13*		P

OFFICIAL DISTANCE: 8*l* **TIME:** 6min 46.0s

481 Restricted, 12st — 14 ran

165^{1}	**TEN BOB (IRE)** 5-4F **N Saville** *Pulled hrd in 3rd til 2nd & gng str 8; ld aft 13; hit 15; 5l clr bef nxt where jmpd bad lft; stayed on stout*		1
303^{1}	**Glensan (IRE)** 10-1 **G Brewer** *(xnb) Off pce in midfield; 5th 11; nvr able to cl; 25l 4th app 3 out*	15	2
383^{P}	**Moscow Tradition (IRE)** 25-1 **J Docker** *4th bhnd clr ldrs; 25l adrift 11; lft 3rd aft 15; clsd to 12l 3rd app 3 out; rdn & sn floundering; jmpd rt nxt*	10	3
111^{1}	Coole Glen (IRE) 5-1 S Morris *Set brisk pce; hdd 11; chsd wnr vain frm 13; stuck on wl; fin 8l 2nd; disq - nt weigh-in*		2d
338^{4}	Abinger 20-1 M Morley *Wl bhnd; poor 9th 11; bad mist nxt; t.o & pu 14*		P
390^{U}	Blue Bud 40-1 W Burnell *Jmpd v slow & sn last; t.o & pu aft 11*		P
109^{4}	Budle Bay 4-1 N Pearce *Lw; 2nd/3rd til disp ld 11-12; wknd rap aft 14; pu aft nxt*		P
	Cawkwell Princess (5a) 12-1 R Stearn *Midfield & wl off pce; 8th 11; t.o & pu 14*		P
	General Carats 33-1 M Walford *Set off last; prog 9; 6th when mist 11; no ch aft; t.o & pu 3 out*		P
	Gentleman Charles (IRE) 12-1 S Walker *Bhnd til pu 10*		P
	Ravensworth(tt) 33-1 N Docker *A wl bhnd; t.o & pu aft 11*		P
377^{P}	Stevie Dee 33-1 O Williams *Handy in chsng group; til u.p 9; sn strugg; t.o 14; lkd exhaust when saddle slpd & ur app 3 out*		U

343^{1}	Super Dolphin (7a) 10-1 Richard Tate *Off pce in midfield; 7th 11; blun 13 & rdr up horses nk; pu 14*		P
	The Bombers Moon 25-1 L Hicks *Bad mist 4; sn outpcd; t.o & pu aft 11*		P

OFFICIAL DISTANCES: Originally 4*l*, 5*l* **TIME:** 6min 54.0s

Coole Glen who finished 2nd was disqualified when the rider failed to weigh-in; he was fined £55; the placings were amended

482 Open Maiden 8yo&up, 12st — 10 ran

	LIGHTS ON 5-1 **M Manton** *Tkn stdly in rr of midfield; still 12l 5th 15; clsd to ld 3 out; 12l clr nxt; comf*		1
215^{F}	**Kindle A Flame** 2-1F **G Brewer** *Settled handy; went prom 11; ld aft 15-nxt; rdn & sn outpcd; fin tired*	15	2
129^{P}	**Frosty Fella** 10-1 **B Pollock** *Prom; ld 13 til mist 15; releg 3rd nxt & no ch w wnr; plugged on & clsng on 2nd nr fin*	nk	3
394^{2}	Bankersdraft 8-1 M Morley *(xnb) Prsd ldr to 8; prom til 3rd & u.p 15; sn v tired; plodded on*	12	4
	Ecclesiastes 16-1 J Howard *(xnb) Last pr; tlng off when nrly carried out by loose horse 11 & pu*		P
129^{2}	Here Comes Choosey (IRE) 7-2 R Morgan-Evans *2nd/4th til ld 12; jmpd v slow 13 & hdd; wknd 15; poor last & tired when pu 2 out*		P
390^{3}	Landford Lad (IRE) 8-1 G Armitage *Detach last til ur 6*		U
302^{3}	Lord Jurado (IRE)(tt) 33-1 O Williams *Rcd keen & sn ld; hdd 12 & stpd to nil; t.o & pu 14*		P
	Mount Alpha (IRE) 12-1 R Armson *7th 5; pu 8*		P
220^{P}	Two By Four 12-1 N Pearce *Towards rr; 10l last 7; strugg when mist 10; t.o & pu 12*		P

OFFICIAL DISTANCES: 10*l*, 1*l* **TIME:** 6min 58.0s

Western

Wadebridge (LH 8F,18J)

Sat, 13 Mar (GOOD to SOFT)

483 Confined, 12st — 3 ran

320^{U}	**BILL ME UP (IRE)** (3x) 4-9F **C Heard** *Made virt all; drew clr app 15; v easily*		1
	Karadin (FR) (7x) 11-4 **Mrs M Hand** *Settled 3rd; 10l 3rd $^{1}/_{2}$way; went 2nd app 15; no ch w wnr*	15	2
311^{5}	**It'snotsimple (IRE)** (5a) 3-1 **B Trickey** *(xnb) Tchd 4s; trckd ldr; slt ld brief app 12; lost ground frm 13; 3rd & btn 15*	15	3

OFFICIAL DISTANCES: 10*l*, 11*l* **TIME:** 6min 21.0s

484 Ladies Open — 7 ran

311^{2}	**GURU RINPOCHE** 3-1 **Miss L Gardner** *(bf) Made all; 2l up $^{1}/_{2}$way; drew clr frm 14; 10l ahd 3 out; pushed out; comf*		1
262^{1}	**Breteche (FR)** (5a) evensF **Miss T Newman** *(xnb) Tchd 6/4; lw; mounted on course; 2nd til 3rd 7; 13l 3rd & lot to do aft 14; went 2nd aft nxt; kpt on one pce*	10	2
322^{P}	**Defendtherealm** 7-1 **Miss A Mills** *Nov rdn; lw; in tch early; 7l 4th 9; outpcd 13; 23l 4th 14; lft poor 3rd 2 out; gd schoolmaster*	6	3
347^{5}	Lirsleftover 4-1 Miss S Young *5th 7; detach 6th 12; 35l 6th 14; nrst fin*	3	4
62^{P}	Tiger Talk(bl) 8-1 Miss L Bridges *(xnb) Last to 9; some hdwy 12; 17l 5th 13; no prog frm 14*	12	5
	Dark Challenger (IRE) 6-1 Miss S Gaisford *10s-6s; lost plce 7; last frm 11; t.o 14; pu 2 out*		P
62^{4}	Virtuoso 12-1 Mrs S Corcoran *Tchd 16s; lw; prom; chsd ldr frm 7; cl 2nd 12; 8l 2nd when blun 15; wknd; 4th & wkng when fell 2 out*		F

OFFICIAL DISTANCES: 8*l*, 3*l* **TIME:** 6min 18.0s

485 Open Maiden (Div 1), 12st — 11 ran

	FLASH POINT (IRE) (7a) 3-1 **Miss P Gundry** *Opened 4s; hld up in rr & bit novicey early; 6th 11; gd hdwy nxt; mist 14; jmpd to 2nd 15; disp ld nxt; rn wide bend app 2 out; r.o to ld last; drvn out*		1
	Prioritisation (IRE) (7a, 4ow) 5-2 **A Farrant** *(xnb) Hld up in tch; prog 7; 2l 2nd 9; ld 11; went 3l clr but nt fluent 15; jnd nxt; disp 2 out til app last; lkd hld til r.o agn cl home*	1$^{1}/_{2}$	2

307^{2} **Gunners Mistake** 2-1F **C Heard** *Tchd 5/2; handy; 4th 9; 3rd & rdn 14; 5l 3rd 15; one pce* 20 3

275^{4} Abu Dancer (IRE) (5a) 7-1 L Heard *2 handlers; ld 1; in tch in mid-div; 5th 12; wknd aft 13; btn 6th when pu 3 out* . . . . P

Allied Imperial (5a) 7-1 D McKenna *Tchd 8s; lw; prom; 3rd 9; cl 2nd 11; lost plce aft 13; btn 5th when pu 3 out* . . . . P

415^{P} Cornish Hope 25-1 A Glassonbury *(xnb) Ld 5-10; sn lost plce; rmdr 11; 7th when pu 12* . . . . P

305^{2} Little Rosie (5a) 10-1 Miss D Mitchell *Tchd 14s; last when ref 8* . . . . r

149^{P} North Croft 25-1 D Doyne-Ditmas *Nt jw; 7th & rdn when mist 8; sn strugg; 9th when pu 12* . . . . P

Port Valenska (IRE) 14-1 T Dennis *(b4) Midfield; rmdrs 7; 8th 9; no hdwy; 8th when pu 12* . . . . P

308^{P} Whats Up Maid (5a) 20-1 M Munrowd *(xnb) In tch; 6th 9; 4th frm 13; rdn nxt; no prog; poor 4th when pu last* . . . . P

198^{P} Xraysauce (5a, 16ow) 25-1 D Stephens (Devon) *Ld 2-5; sn lost plce; last aft 8; t.o & pu 12* . . . . P

OFFICIAL DISTANCES: 1*l*, 10*l* **TIME:** 6min 29.0s

486 Open Maiden (Div 2), 12st — 13 ran

AUNTIE KATHLEEN (12a, 5ow) 11-10 **A Farrant** *Sn handy on inner; cl 5th 9; jnd ldrs 11; slt ld frm nxt; went 4l clr but nt fluent 15; 3l clr 2 out; r.o flat; just hld on und str press* 1

That's My Boy (IRE) evensF **Miss P Gundry** *Hld up towards rr; 6th 11; hdwy to 3rd 13; crept clsr & went 2nd aft 3 out; stayed on str; nt quite rch wnr* 1/2 2

327^{3} **Off The Hook (IRE)** 6-1 **I Hambley** *2 handlers; swtng; 5th 1/2way; went cl 3rd 9 & 2nd 12; 2l 2nd & ev ch 3 out; wknd u.p frm nxt* 8 3

194^{P} Buckley's Chance (IRE) 8-1 J Tickle *(xnb) Slt ld frm 2-12; lost plce rap; 10l 4th aft 14; one pce; fin lame* 8 4

312^{4} Jaunty Janner 6-1 T Dennis *Prom; slt mist 3; 3rd 1/2way; lost plce 12; poor 5th frm 14* 8 5

121^{6} Just Aretha (5a) 16-1 Miss L Gardner *Tde; hdwy 8; 6th 13; bhnd frm nxt* 20 6

308^{P} Elegant Apple (5a, 18ow) 50-1 D Stephens (Devon) *Last frm 5; t.o & pu 12* . . . . P

274^{U} Elegant Maid (5a) 33-1 L Heard *Rr frm 7; mist 10; bhnd & pu 12* . . . . P

309^{P} Indian Renegade (IRE) (5a) 20-1 D McKenna *Ld 1; in tch; 5th 11; wknd; bhnd & pu 15* . . . . P

Little Lord Lewis (7a) 20-1 C Heard *2 handlers; mid-div; 7th & just in tch when hmpd & ur 12* . . . . U

Mr Rory 25-1 Miss P Moorhouse *(xnb) Prom frm 5; cl 2nd when slt mist 7; lost plce 12; rr & pu 14* . . . . P

Native Christy (IRE) 9-1 A Glassonbury *Midfield; 6th 9; wknd; rr & pu 14* . . . . P

328^{P} Wendys Dynamo 20-1 M Munrowd *(xnb) Rr frm 7; bhnd when pu 11* . . . . P

OFFICIAL DISTANCES: 1/2*l*, 2*l* **TIME:** 6min 34.0s

487 Mens Open, 12st — 4 ran

196^{4} **COLQUHOUN** 1-2F **A Farrant** *Lw; trckd ldr on inner til ld 11; drew 30l clr 14; canter; walked in* 1

Gotha (FR) 13-2 **M Sweetland** *Settled 3rd; disp 3 1/2l 3rd 11; went rem 2nd app 2 out; mist last* 40 2

411^{1} **Bruthuinne (IRE)** (7x) 3-1 **D McKenna** *(xnb,ringbit) Tde; slt ld to 11; rmdr; lost tch w ldr aft 13; btn 3rd frm 2 out; tired & wandered rt u.p flat* 8 3

351^{3} Just Bert (IRE) 4-1 W Biddick *Mostly 4th; lost tch 12; t.o frm 15; mist last* 1 1/2 4

OFFICIAL DISTANCES: dist, 2*l* **TIME:** 6min 24.0s

488 Restricted, 12st — 8 ran

314^{2} **BISHOP'S BLADE** 7-4 **Miss S Gaisford** *(xnb,bnh) Ld frm 2; jnd 11; disp ld & clr of rivals when hit 14; level last; sn hdd & lkd hld; rallied game to jn ldr agn on post* . . . . 1†

324^{2} **I AM SAID I (IRE)** 5-4F **A Farrant** *(xnb,ringbit) Lw; settled cl 3rd; mist 9; jnd ldr 11; rdn 14; hrd rdn & ld aft last; jnd agn final stride* . . . . d ht 1†

323^{6} **Lingering Fog (IRE)** 16-1 **Miss M McCarthy** *Tchd 20s; ld 1; cl up til rdn 11; lost ground aft 12; r.o stdly frm 3 out* 10 3

314^{3} Panto Pixie (5a) 3-1 Miss T Cave *5s-3s; 4th 7; 15l 4th 11; bhnd frm 14.* . . 30 4

Dear As Saffron (5a) 20-1 W Biddick *Last frm 7; bhnd when pu 12* . . . . P

314P	Mister Cone 12-1 I Hambley *(xnb) 4th & in tch 8; 5th when pu 12*		P
324P	Pinmoor Hill 14-1 M Munrowd *Bckwd; lost tch 7; bhnd when pu 12*		P
	The Only Option (IRE) (5a) 14-1 J Tickle *(xnb) In tch in 4th when ur 10*		U

OFFICIAL DISTANCES: d ht, 10*l* **TIME:** 6min 22.0s

489 Intermediate, 12st — 3 ran

315¹	**JUST SALLY** (5a) 2-5F **A Farrant** *Lw; nt a fluent; ld til jnd 12; lft wl clr 15; unchall*		1
	Touching Down (IRE) 9-2 **W Biddick** *Chsd ldr to 7; last & outpcd frm 9; 25l last 13; lft rem 2nd 15*	30	2
197P	Budghill 5-2 L Heard *Went 7l 2nd 7; hdwy to disp ld 12; rn wide bend aft 13; rdn nxt; upsides & ev ch when blun & ur 15*		U

OFFICIAL DISTANCE: dist **TIME:** 6min 49.0s

Warwick (LH 10F,18J)

Sun, 14 Mar (GOOD to SOFT)

490 Air Wedding HC, 3m2f £1603 — 14 ran

179⁶	**MACGEORGE (IRE)** 12-00 11-4 **M Barber** *Made all; drew 10l clr 16; nt fluent 2 out; stayed on wl; unchall*		1
280P	**Maidstone Monument (IRE)** 12-02 12-1 **R Stephens** *Prom; hit 9; chsd wnr 14 til wknd 3 out; 23l 3rd nxt; lft rem 2nd last*	20	2
239¹	**Unlimited Free (IRE)** 12-00 2-1F **Miss D Harding** *Jmpd rt; chsd ldrs; jmpd rt & knocked over rival 4; went 2nd 9-14; outpcd 16; lft rem 3rd at last; nrly caught runner-up*	hd	3
139²	Slip The Ring 11-07 20-1 M Hooper *Wl bhnd; t.o 8; blun 16*	22	4
360P	The Writer (IRE) 11-07 16-1 S Gray *Chsd ldrs; mist 11; 4th 13; wknd 16; wl t.o*	dist	5
347²	Tell Tale (IRE) 11-09 6-1 T Malone *Chsd ldrs; hmpd & lost plce 4; rem 8th 13; hopeless t.o*	22	6
434U	Buckland Knight (IRE) 11-07 25-1 J Young *Hld up; mist 1; hmpd 4; hdwy 11 to 5th 13; went 12l 2nd 3 out; no imp when mist nxt; 8l 2nd & tired but wl clr of rest when fell last*		F
	Chief Mouse 11-07 33-1 S Graham *Jb in rr; wl t.o when pu 10; fin lame*		P
292⁵	Crown And Cushion 11-11 33-1 P Cowley *Chsd wnr to 9; wkng when mist 11; t.o & pu aft 13*		P
	Nahthen Lad (IRE) 11-09(vis) 25-1 D Mansell *Handy; mist 2; hmpd & fell 4*		F
241F	Run River Run 11-02(bl) 100-1 R Hughes *Mists in rr; t.o when blun bad 9; pu 10*		P
	Scoundrel 11-07 50-1 A Price *Ss; a rr; bad mist 4; t.o 8; pu aft 13*		P
175⁷	Seabrook Lad 11-07(cp) 25-1 T Lane *Hld up; hdwy 6; mist 12; 6th & rdn nxt; sn wknd; t.o 17; pu 2 out*		P
176F	Spilaw (FR) 11-07 40-1 Miss C Dyson *Numerous mists; bhnd; 7th & eff app 13; sn wknd; t.o & pu 2 out*		P

TIME: 7min 05.7s **TOTE:** £4.00; places £2.50,£2.20,£2.00 **Ex:**£25.50 **CSF:**£28.36
Fences 5 & 15 omitted

Dart Vale & Haldon Harriers

Buckfastleigh (RH 7F,19J)

Sun, 14 Mar (GOOD to SOFT, SOFT in places)

491 Hunt Members, 12st — 3 ran

324⁵	**BARON RIDGE** 3-1 **Richard Darke** *(xnb) Ld/disp til 2nd frm 3 out; rallied game to ld inside last 50yds*		1
80²	**Bengal Bullet** 1-5F **Miss S Gaisford** *Lw; ld/disp til def advant 3 out; lkd wnr til no ex last 50yds*	½	2
329P	Little Apple Bay (5a) 8-1 C Heard *Swtng; 3rd when blun & ur 2*		U

OFFICIAL DISTANCE: ¾*l* **TIME:** 6min 43.0s

492 Open Maiden (Div 1), 12st - 17J — 15 ran

Form	Horse	Dist	Pos
325^{2}	**WILD CHIMES (IRE)** (7a) 4-5F **N Williams** *Tchd evens; lw; hld up in midfield; 6th 12; prog to 2nd 14; 5l 2nd when pckd 3 out; rdn & r.o wl to ld at last; stayed on wl.*		1
238^{U}	**Bilton's Nap** (7a) 8-1 **D Jacob** *16s-8s; hld up towards rr; hdwy to 4th 12; ld 14; went 5l clr 3 out; mist 2 out; hdd last; no ex flat*	3	2
329^{U}	**Sure How Bad (IRE)** 33-1 **L Tibbatts** *Ld/disp to 9; lost plce 12; 5th 15; r.o agn to 3rd 3 out; kpt on*	5	3
195^{P}	Miss Ziggerson (5a) 16-1 Miss S Young *Prom in ldng group; 4th 1/2way; lost ground frm 15*	12	4
326^{F}	Lady Of Jazz (5a) 15-2 A Charles-Jones *(xnb) Lw; prom; disp 4-14; lost ground stdly frm 16.*	10	5
172^{P}	Floorex Carpetman 25-1 A Foster *Prom early; lost plce 10; bhnd frm 15*	runin	6
	Burrow Corner 12-1 L Jefford *(xnb) Towards rr; mist 13; pu nxt; nt busy*		P
238^{2}	Emerald Mist (IRE) (12a) 10-1 Miss P Gundry *(xnb) Midfield; 7th when blun 11; bhnd frm 15 til pu last*		P
329^{C}	Nobody's Heroine (5a) 16-1 N McDiarmid *(xnb) In tch; 6th 1/2way; lost plce; pu 13*		P
325^{U}	Orinoco's Flight (IRE) 8-1 M Holmes *(xnb) Tchd 10s; hdwy 7; slt ld 12; w ldrs til wknd 15; 4th 2 out; pu last*		P
275^{5}	Polly Come Back (12a) 7-1 R Woollacott *(xnb) 10s-7s; mid-div; prog to 5th 12; just in tch til wknd 16; t.o & pu last*		P
	Red Risk 16-1 M Sweetland *(xnb) T.o 7 til pu 13*		P
238^{F}	Rydon Brook (5a) 25-1 J Snowden *Distracted by rival & crashed thro wing 1*		R
306^{P}	Sandy's Way (12a) 33-1 I Hambley *Mid-div; 8th 5; bhnd frm 10 til pu 14.*		P
265^{P}	The Nelson Touch 16-1 D I Turner *Rn out 1; rtrcd; t.o til pu 13*		R

OFFICIAL DISTANCES: 3l, 10l **TIME:** 6min 34.5s

Fences 8 & 15 omitted - damaged

493 Open Maiden (Div 2), 12st — 12 ran

Form	Horse	Dist	Pos
275^{2}	**FAR TOO CROWDED (IRE)** (5a) 2-1F **N Williams** *Tchd 5/2; lw; hld up midfield; gd prog 14; chall 15; ld nxt; 3l up when slt mist 2 out; rdn clr app last; tired flat; just hld on*		1
319^{U}	**On His Toes** 5-2 **R Woollacott** *Tchd 3s; 2 handlers; ur gng down; 7th 8; prog 12; went 4th 15; 2nd nxt; chsd wnr & lkd hld til r.o wl flat; just failed.*	1/2	2
370^{P}	**Polar Bright (IRE)** 20-1 **D Edwards** *(xnb) Sn prom; cl 2nd 8-14; slt mist 15; 4th & rdn nxt; one pce*	15	3
308^{3}	Ebony Jack (IRE) 5-2 G Barfoot-Saunt *Opened 9/2; lw; handy; hdwy to 4th 14; rdn nxt; stayed on one pce frm 3 out.*	6	4
306^{2}	Abseal 8-1 A Charles-Jones *Midfield; 5th 10; last frm 14; pu nxt*		P
232^{P}	Branski 33-1 G Weatherley *2 handlers; rap hdwy to ld 4; hdd 7; wknd rap & jmpd slow 9; bhnd & pu 12*		P
142^{U}	Darcey Mae (5a) 9-2 Miss L Bridges *Ld to 4 & agn 7-15; wknd & 3rd nxt; rdn & no resp; pu last*		P
87^{P}	Frere Du Cure 14-1 J Barnes *(xnb) 9th 8; 6th & just in tch 10; wknd; bhnd when pu 13.*		P
416^{4}	Hayling Star (5a) 50-1 M Sweetland *Sn trailing; t.o & pu 13*		P
308^{4}	Jemannette (5a) 10-1 T Dennis *Rr when pu 5*		P
	Starlight Striker 20-1 N McDiarmid *Lw; rr when hit 7; bhnd & pu 12.*		P
325^{4}	Will Shakespeare 10-1 Miss T Newman *(xnb) Tchd 11s; lw; 2 handlers; sn prom; cl 3rd 10-12; ur nxt.*		U

OFFICIAL DISTANCES: 1l, 10l **TIME:** 6min 33.0s

494 Open Maiden (Div 3), 12st — 14 ran

Form	Horse	Dist	Pos
	EUWILUWIL (IRE) 13-8F **A Farrant** *3s-13/8; hld up; hdwy 12; disp ld 14 til hdd aft 2 out; 2l 2nd app last; r.o str to ld 100yds out*		1
142^{2}	**Noble Action** (7a) 7-4 **N Williams** *Lw; hdwy to 3rd 10; smooth prog to ld aft 14; jnd 15 til rdn 2l clr aft 2 out; ld & lkd wnr last; v tired & hdd last 100yds*	3	2
329^{P}	**Josanjamic** (5a) 11-2 **L Heard** *Rr; 6th 14; went 4th nxt; poor 4th when jmpd slow 2 out; tk 3rd on post*	20	3
327^{5}	Roseacre (IRE)(bl) 16-1 Miss P Gundry *Prom; ld brief 8; cl 2nd 9; disp ld 14; lost plce qckly nxt; poor 3rd frm 3 out; dem on post*	s hd	4
353^{P}	Ask Again (7a) 25-1 Miss L Gardner *Sn rr; bhnd 1/2way; poor 6th when pu 15*		P
312^{5}	Black A Brook (IRE) (5a) 25-1 R McCarthy *Bhnd til pu 12.*		P

327[P]	Druid Pandora (5a) 20-1 Richard Darke *Prom to 5; lost ground 11; bhnd & pu 12*		P
	Forglori 50-1 L Tibbatts *Ld til jmpd lft 7; prom til ld agn 10-11; wknd; rr when jmpd lft 12; pu 14*		P
	Friendly Girl (IRE) (12a) 20-1 A Charles-Jones *In tch; lost ground 7; mist 8; pu nxt*		P
	Golden Sovereign 20-1 M Dennis *Towards rr til fell 11*		F
	Kingsmill Creek (5a) 20-1 T Dennis *Towards rr when rn out 8*		R
	Mrs Goldfarb (12a) 14-1 D Edwards *In tch; 4th 12; disp ld 13; slt ld when bad mist 14; pu nxt*		P
328[P]	Polly Dust (5a) 12-1 M Sweetland *20s-12s; sn prom; ld brief 8; 4th 10; lost plce 12; bhnd when pu 15*		P
	Winnie The Pooh 10-1 Miss S Gaisford *Hdwy to 2nd 10; ld 11-13; sn lost plce; btn when pu 14*		P

OFFICIAL DISTANCES: 4*l*, 15*l* **TIME:** 6min 34.0s

495 Intermediate, 12st — 13 ran

279[1]	**LORD OF THE MIST (IRE)** 9-4 **N Williams** *Lw; hld up in midfield; hdwy 8; 5th 13; gd prog & jmpd into ld 15; 8l ahd 2 out; drew wl clr app last; v easily*		1
321[6]	**Father Mansfield (IRE)** 14-1 **Miss C Prouse** *Midfield; 7th 10; went 5th 14; 19l 4th 2 out; stayed on wl; tk 2nd flat; no ch w wnr.*	15	2
313[2]	**Teninarow (IRE)** 6-4F **A Farrant** *Lw; in tch; cl 3rd 7-15; outpcd as ldrs qcknd 16; 13l 3rd 2 out; kpt on one pce; disapp*	3	3
90[5]	Highway Oak 16-1 M Miller *Lw; ld to 5, 7-10 & 12-14; 8l 2nd 2 out; tired & blun last; lost 2 plces flat*	3	4
321[3]	Bak On Board 20-1 Miss L Gardner *(xnb) Prom til ld 10-12; drpd back 4th 15; one pce*	12	5
147[2]	Earl's Toy (IRE) 12-1 H Fry *2 handlers; lw; midfield; 7th 13; one pce frm 15*	3	6
197[1]	Sootsir 14-1 R Hawker *(xnb) A rr; 10th 10; t.o 15*	15	7
320[P]	Boy Band (IRE) 66-1 C Dailly *Blun 4; disp ld 5-7; wknd; 6th 10; bhnd & pu 12*		P
193[5]	Carefree Love (IRE)(bl) 10-1 Richard Darke *Prom; cl 4th 7-13; wknd nxt; btn 6th when pu 3 out*		P
193[P]	Native Drum (IRE) 16-1 Miss S Gaisford *Bhnd til pu 11*		P
	Rudge Hill 50-1 D Jacob *Swtng; 7th 6; midfield when fell 9*		F
	Tabernacle 50-1 A Glassonbury *Bhnd frm 5; t.o when scrambled over 12; imm pu*		P
321[P]	Th'moons A Balloon (IRE) 8-1 S Partridge *Towards rr; 8th 1/2way; no prog; bhnd when pu 15*		P

OFFICIAL DISTANCES: 15*l*, 4*l* **TIME:** 6min 27.0s

496 Mixed Open, 12st - 17J — 7 ran

115[4]	**HOBBYCYR (FR)** 14-1 **Miss P Gundry** *Lw; 2 handlers; ld to 5; prom til lost plce 15; 4th nxt; 15l 3rd 2 out; str rn app last; swooped to ld last; sn clr; comf*		1
322[1]	**Ease The Pressure (IRE)** 11-8F **N Williams** *Lw; handy; went 2nd 10; disp ld 11-14; 1 1/2l 2nd 15; rdn to chse ldr 3 out; rdn to chall aft 2 out; ev ch til wknd last.*	8	2
	Red Native (IRE) 7-1 **A Farrant** *Lw; wl in tch; ld/disp 8-14; wknd; 12l 3rd & no ch 3 out*	15	3
276[R]	Rimpton Boy(bl) 2-1 Miss R Green *Tchd 9/4 in plce; lw; hld up; hdwy 11; ld app 15; 2 1/2l up 2 out; lkd wnr til wknd app last; exhaust flat; walked in*	10	4
199[7]	Jack The Bear (IRE) 20-1 Miss C Tuffin *Tchd 25s; sn rr; last when mist 14; no ch frm 15*	2	5
196[P]	Le Cure 16-1 J Barnes *(xnb) Ld 5-8; in tch til wknd 13; no ch frm 15*	5	6
278[1]	Opal'lou (FR) (5a) 5-1 R Pyman *(xnb) Tchd 6s; sn last; nvr on terms w ldrs; pu 15*		P

OFFICIAL DISTANCES: 10*l*, 10*l* **TIME:** 6min 29.0s

Fences 5 & 12 omitted - damaged

497 Confined, 12st — 6 ran

412[2]	**SANDY DUFF** 3-1 **Miss M McCarthy** *(xnb) Lw; jw; ld/disp til drew clr stdly frm 14; went 10l clr 2 out; r.o str.*		1
200[3]	**Province** evensF **R Woollacott** *Cl up/disp; mist 11; ev ch til lost ground aft 14; no ch w wnr frm 3 out; eased flat*	30	2

200[6]	**Travelling Jack** 4-1 **A Charles-Jones** *(ringbit) 6s-4s; in tch; 6½l 3rd 11; rdn nxt; jmpd slow 15; poor 3rd & scrambled over 2 out; fin tired*	25	3
200[7]	Artic Ground (IRE) 25-1 D Doyne-Ditmas *(xnb) Poor 4th frm 11; t.o*	2	4
	Fenny Royal 33-1 M Woodward *Mounted on course; tde; sn last & strugg; 2 fncs bhnd by 9; pu 12*		P
310[P]	Procedure (USA) 6-1 D Edwards *(xnb,ringbit) 12s-6s; prom to 7; jmpd slow 9; 4th & wkng when climbed 11; imm pu*		P

OFFICIAL DISTANCES: 10*l*, 10*l* **TIME:** 6min 33.0s

498 Restricted, 12st — 13 ran

318[1]	**VIVID IMAGINATION (IRE)** (7a) 8-11F **A Farrant** *(xnb) Opened evens; lw; sn prom; cl 2nd 8 til ld 14; 15l clr nxt; drew rt away; nt fluent 2 out; unchall; impressive*		1
	Jolie Roslin (5a) 25-1 **Mrs F Vigar** *Towards rr; 8th 9; poor 6th 14; jmpd into rem 2nd 2 out*	runin	2
	Knight Ofthe North 50-1 **Miss E Burrows** *Nov rdn; wl bhnd by 6; sn t.o; 2 fncs adrift 16; lft rem 3rd app last*	1½fs	3
369[P]	Black Optimist (IRE) 20-1 Mrs K Baimbridge *Saddle slpd & pu 5*		P
323[P]	Coombe Quest 25-1 T Dennis *(xnb,bf) Lw; sn rr; mist 9; 7th & btn when pu 14*		P
369[P]	Hug The Bend 12-1 D Edwards *Towards rr til pu 13*		P
	Indian Raider (IRE) 40-1 A Glassonbury *Mid-div; some hdwy to 5th 13; lft rem 2nd by defectors 16; releg 3rd 2 out; tired & pu last*		P
232[F]	Itchen Mill (5a) 16-1 T Dreaper *Lw; handy; 12l 6th ½way; 4th 14; tiring 3rd when pu 15*		P
328[1]	Lord Anner (IRE) (7a) 7-4 N Williams *(xnb) 4s-7/4; lw; nt a fluent; hld up; hdwy to 5l 3rd 8; went 2nd 14; 15l 2nd & nt gng wl when pu 15*		P
415[P]	Mrs Peggoty (5a)(bl) 16-1 Miss S Gaisford *Sn prom; disp ld brief 7; 9l 4th 9; wknd & pu 12*		P
143[1]	Preacher Boy (7a) 7-1 Miss P Gundry *Lw; 2 handlers; fell 3*		F
120[1]	Scarlet Glory (5a) 12-1 H Fry *(xnb) 20s-12s; 2 handlers; swtng; ld/disp to 14; wknd & lost ground app nxt; poor 3rd when pu 3 out*		P
	Silly Boy 25-1 A Foster *Prom til lost plce 7; bhnd 9 til pu 13*		P

OFFICIAL DISTANCES: dist, dist **TIME:** 6min 33.0s

Holderness

Dalton Park (RH 8F,20J)
Sun, 14 Mar (GOOD)

499 Hunt Members — 4 ran

341[3]	**DOLPHIN SQUARE (IRE)** 3-1 **N Saville** *Cl 2nd til ld 7; jmpd slow 9; rmdrs & pushed along 12; went 2nd agn 14; ld nxt; 3l clr 2 out; stayed on wl*		1
301[3]	**Schoolhouse Walk** 7-2 **M Manton** *Ld to 7 & agn 11-14; cl 2nd when bad mist 17; one pce aft*	5	2
	Nordic Crest (IRE)(tt) 4-6F **T Greenall** *Handy 3rd to 16; pushed along 17; 3l 3rd 2 out; r.o one pce*	2	3
	Procol's Boy 12-1 S Walker *In tch in last to 16; rmdrs & pushed along nxt; sn outpcd*	12	4

OFFICIAL DISTANCES: 3*l*, 2*l*, dist **TIME:** 7min 42.0s

500 Panacur/TBA PPORA Club Members Mares Maiden, 12st — 13 ran

297[F]	**NEAR AND PHAR (IRE)** (5a) 7-2 **Miss S Buckley** *Rr til stdy hdwy frm 10; 12l 5th 16; stormed into ld aft 3 out; sn clr; r.o str.*		1
304[4]	**Aunt Gladys (IRE)** (5a) 3-1F **G Brewer** *Mid-div; 8l 6th 7; went 4l 3rd 13; ld 15; jnd 3 out; sn hdd & easily outpcd by wnr*	8	2
338[P]	**Rising Talisker** (5a)(cp) 9-2 **Miss Rachel Clark** *Cl 2nd til lft in ld 13-15; handy til pushed along & wknd frm 3 out*	6	3
272[4]	Mademist Sparky (5a) 5-1 N Tutty *Handy in 3rd/4th to 11; went 1l 2nd 14-16; wknd nxt*	25	4
395[4]	Just A Lady (5a) 10-1 B Woodhouse *(xnb) Rr early; went 12l 7th 9 & 3l 4th 14; pushed along & outpcd by ldrs 16*	12	5
	Alizarin (IRE) (12a) 10-1 T Craggs *(xnb) Ld; 1l up til fell 13*		F
	Final Chorus (5a) 10-1 S Charlton *Prom in mid-div to 9; went 5l 5th 12; pushed along 13; sn wknd; t.o & pu 15*		P

341^{P}	Hanisia (5a) 10-1 P Atkinson *(xnb) Sn bhnd; t.o 10; pu 15*		P
165^{P}	Hattie (5a) 10-1 W Burnell *(xnb) Reluct & lft at start; 2 fncs adrift til pu 7*		P
	Lough Erin Shore (5a) 6-1 N Kent *Rr to 10; gd hdwy to handy 6th 14; stpd as if shot & pu 15*		P
392^{F}	Milliners Guide (5a) 8-1 D Thomas *(xnb) Mid-div when ur 13*		U
297^{F}	Miss Danbys (5a) 6-1 S Walker *(xnb,bf) A rr div; sn bhnd; lsng tch when pu 9*		P
316^{P}	Thixendale (5a)(cp) 10-1 Miss J Foster *Ld to 2; 3l 3rd til saddle slpd & pu 14*		P

OFFICIAL DISTANCES: 10*l*, 8*l*, 20*l* **TIME:** 7min 42.0s

501 Mens Open — 11 ran

341^{1}	**HIGH PEAK** 2-1JF **T Greenall** *A gng wl; cl 5th 10; 3l 3rd 14; outpcd 3 out; 3l 2nd when lft clr 2 out; idled flat; just hld on*		1
429^{5}	**Blank Cheque** 8-1 **D Coates** *Ld to 14; outpcd & 8l 4th 3 out; stayed on; fin v fast; just failed*	nk	2
391^{2}	**Mr Pendleberry**(bl) 2-1JF **N Tinkler** *Cl 2nd til ld 7 til jnd 15-16; sn hdd & pushed along; one pce; lft 4l 2nd 2 out; dem flat*	3	3
338^{1}	Erzadjan (IRE) 10-1 L Bates *Last to 5; slt hdwy 10; still all to do 14; r.o one pce; nt rch ldrs*	25	4
	Cadrillon (FR) 20-1 A McEntyre *1st ride; handy 6th to 12; wknd 13; lsng tch 14; bad mist & t.o 15*	5	5
391^{P}	Don Rio (IRE) 40-1 M Morley *A midfield; 12l 6th 13; pushed along & wknd 14; t.o & pu 16*		P
391^{P}	Hadeqa 33-1 S Charlton *Handy 4th til ur 6*		U
269^{4}	Mademist Sam 5-1 N Tutty *Cl 3rd/4th til disp ld 14; jw to ld 3 out; 3l clr & lkd wnr when fell 2 out*		F
389^{5}	Nip On 5-1 G Brewer *Mid-div to 15; 8l 4th when fell 2 out*		F
214^{F}	Rosey Boy (IRE) 40-1 P Kinsella *Cl 3rd to 11; grad wknd; t.o & pu 16*		P
	Sign Of The Tiger 40-1 R Clark *A rr; jb lft 9; bad mist 10 & imm pu*		P

OFFICIAL DISTANCES: nk, 2*l*, dist **TIME:** 7min 34.0s

502 Ladies Open — 5 ran

391^{3}	**TEXAS RANGER** 2-1 **Miss J Foster** *Cl 2nd til ld 5-7; qcknd 10l clr aft 10; 15l up 17; drew rt away*		1
339^{2}	**Silver Groom (IRE)** 5-4F **Miss J Coward** *Poor last by 7; t.o & rmdrs 10; rem 4th 14; r.o to dist 2nd app last; gvn far too much to do*	40	2
	Sally Scally (5a) 3-1 **Miss T Jackson** *A rr; dist 3rd by 11; rem 4th 17; lft 3rd app last*	30	3
395^{5}	Dinan (IRE) 20-1 Mrs J Brown *Ld to 3; last & lsng tch when pu 13*		P
270^{3}	Pharlindo (IRE) 6-1 Miss A Armitage *Prom to 6; ld 8-9; sn outpcd; chsd wnr vain; dist 3rd when pu last; dism*		P

OFFICIAL DISTANCES: dist, dist **TIME:** 7min 29.0s

503 Restricted — 9 ran

344^{1}	**HIGH FIELDS** (7a)(bl) 7-4F **T Greenall** *Sa; mid-div by 10; blun & rmdrs 11; went 4l 4th 15 & 1l 2nd 3 out; hrd rdn to chall last; drew clr flat*		1
212^{7}	**Purple Jean** (5a) 20-1 **G Brewer** *(xnb) A.p; 3l 2nd 10; disp ld 11-13; ld 2 out; jnd app last; hdd & outpcd flat*	3	2
389^{6}	**Wilfie Wild** 4-1 **Mrs L Ward** *A.p; 4l 3rd 10; rushed up to ld app 3 out; hdd nxt; wknd*	8	3
390^{4}	Fayalie (IRE) (5a) 33-1 P Robinson *Prom in 2nd/3rd to 7; wknd 9; poor 5th 15; plodded on*	25	4
57^{P}	Gale Damage (IRE) 20-1 O Williams *Slt ld to 15; pushed along & wknd nxt; rem 5th when pu last*		P
388^{2}	In The Van 20-1 J Morley *Tde; rr to 7; mid-div when bd bend aft 14*		B
341^{P}	Lord Scroop (IRE) 25-1 M Morley *Handy 4th when blun & ur 7*		U
	Redsands (IRE) 20-1 S Walker *Rstrnd in last; lsng tch when pu 15; nvr put in rce*		P
75^{F}	Switchback (IRE) 2-1 N Saville *Rr to 8; gd hdwy to 4l 4th 11; trckng ldrs when blkd & slpd up bend aft 14*		S

OFFICIAL DISTANCES: 3*l*, 10*l*, dist **TIME:** 7min 43.0s

504 Countryside Alliance Club Members Maiden (Div 1) — 8 ran

393^{2}	**SNIZORT (USA)** 5-1 **G Brewer** *A handy; cl 5th 12; went 1l 2nd 17; chall 2 out; qcknd to ld app last; rdly drew clr flat*		1
271^{2}	**Bobby Buttons** evensF **N Tutty** *Prom; 3l 3rd 4-11; went 1l 2nd 15; ld 16 til jnd & blun 2 out; hld when mist last; wknd flat*	8	2

272[5] **Flat Stanley** (7a) 8-1 **Miss J Foster** *Cl 2nd til ld 15-16; wknd nxt; 8l 3rd & one pce app last.* . . . 10 3
Karinga Leap 5-1 W Burnell *Cl 4th 3-7; mist 9; rr by 13; pushed up to cl 4th 15; lost tch 16; poor 4th 2 out.* . . . 20 4
394[4] Gollinger(cp) 5-1 B Woodhouse *Slt ld to 14; pushed along nxt; wknd frm 17; poor 4th 2 out* . . . 12 5
393[P] God Of War 20-1 S Charlton *Nt jw; a rr; bad mists 12 & 14; t.o & pu 16.* . . P
271[6] House Colours 6-1 N Saville *Mid-div to 6; jmpd slow 8 & rmdrs; rr when jmpd slow 12; pu nxt* . . . P
165[P] Songino (IRE) 20-1 P Robinson *A bhnd; last & mist 1; lost irons; lsng tch 11; t.o 14; pu 16.* . . . P

OFFICIAL DISTANCES: 6*l*, 10*l*, 25*l* **TIME:** 7min 40.0s

505 Countryside Alliance Club Members Maiden (Div 2) 8 ran

I'M NO FAIRY (7a) 7-2 **D Thomas** *Patient rdn; hld up in last to 17; gd hdwy to 5th 2 out; stayed on wl to chall last; just gt up in drvng fin* . . . 1
394[P] **Staple Sound**(cp) 7-1 **W Burnell** *Ld to 5; cl 2nd til outpcd & wknd 12; stayed on frm 17 to disp ld last; just hld in drvng fin* . . . nk 2
393[P] **Just A Man** 5-2F **B Woodhouse** *(xnb) Rr; went 3l 4th 14 & 2l 2nd 17; ld app 2 out til hdd & outpcd flat* . . . 4 3
392[P] Brown's Beck 5-1 M Morley *Mid-div to 10; went 1l 2nd 14; ev ch 2 out; wknd* ½ 4
Fairmile Star 5-1 R Wakeham *Cl 2nd til ld 5-17; 1l 2nd 2 out; rallied & ev ch when fell last.* . . . F
344[P] Swordface (IRE) 5-1 C Dawson *Prom in 3rd to 12; 3l 3rd when ur 15.* . . . U
342[P] Tony(tt) 10-1 S Charlton *(xnb) Unruly padd; mid-div when mist 9; rdn to 5l 4th 12; mist 13; wknd qckly aft nxt; pu 15; dism.* . . . P
343[5] Whitleygrange Girl (5a) 7-2 N Tutty *(xnb) Mulish & planted herself sev times padd; late to start; a midfield; in tch in 6th 14; pushed along 16; wknd 3 out; poor 5th when pu last.* . . . P

OFFICIAL DISTANCES: hd, 3*l*, ½*l* **TIME:** 8min 08.0s

Northern Point-to-Point Area Club

Musselburgh (RH 8F,18J)

Sun, 14 Mar (GOOD to FIRM, FIRM in places)

506 Northern P-t-P Area Club Members (Nov Rdrs), 12st 6 ran

426[6] **GAULTIER GALE (IRE)** 6-4F **A Findlay** *Trckd ldr; 4l 2nd 6; prog to disp ld 14 til ld aft 2 out; kpt on wl u.p* . . . 1
330[6] **Starbuck** 3-1 **W Goldie** *Ld; 2-3l up til jnd 14; hdd aft 2 out; no ex.* . . . 4 2
281[3] **Across The Card** 10-1 **Miss H Gray** *(xnb) Trckd ldrs; 4l 3rd 11; outpcd 14; disp 8l 3rd nxt; one pce; rdn out to snatch 3rd.* . . . 6 3
Try A Bluff (IRE) 5-2 M Nicholson *(xnb,bf) Lw; in tch in rr; 15l 4th 6; 8l 5th 10-11; short-lived to 6l 3rd app 14; 8l 3rd & wkng nxt; sn btn; dem cl home* hd 4
426[U] Wishful Thinker (1ow) 14-1 Miss K Scott *Burly; chsd ldrs; rn wide aft 2; 10l 5th 5; wknd 13; sn t.o; fnce bhnd 2 out* . . . runin 5
Dannicus (3ow) 4-1 A McElwee *Rdr v novicey; pulling; a rr; hit 1; jmpd big nxt; 15l last aft; 20l last app 7; lost iron aft 12; t.o 14; 2 fncs bhnd 3 out* runin 6

OFFICIAL DISTANCES: 3*l*, 10*l* **TIME:** 6min 06.1s

507 Intermediate, 12st 4 ran

212[5] **ROSCOE BURN** 2-1 **M McAlister** *Trckd ldr; 3l 2nd aft 6; disp ld aft 10; btr j to ld 12; 1l up & mist 15; 3l clr last; comf* . . . 1
Micky Mansions (IRE) evensF **A Richardson** *Opened 5/4; ld; pulling; 3l up 5; jnd aft 10; hdd 12; prsng ld when dived at 13 & nxt; hrd rdn 2 out; no ex app last; eased flat.* . . . 5 2
Hadaway Lad 3-1 **A Findlay** *Trckd ldrs; mist 3; 6l 3rd 6; outpcd aft 11; sn btn; 25l 3rd 14; t.o* . . . runin 3
281[5] Coastal Safari 5-1 M Ellwood *Ss; jb & to lft at times; pulling; sn detach last; 30l last 10; fnce bhnd 13; t.o when blun 15; pu aft* . . . P

OFFICIAL DISTANCES: 5*l*, dist **TIME:** 6min 01.4s

508 Ladies Open 4 ran

339[4] **IN DEMAND** 7-4 **Miss J Balmer** *3s-7/4; lw; jmpd lft at times; ww in rr; mist 5; 25l 3rd 14; rdn & prog aft nxt; gd hdwy app 2 out; prsd ldr last; sn ld; rdn clr; wl rdn* 1

Nisbet 3-1 **Miss J Riding** *(xnb) Bckwd; ld/disp til hit brief 10; ld 14; 3l up 2 out; tired & hdd flat; btr for rce* 4 2

339[5] **Yorkshire Edition (IRE)** 11-10F **Miss W Gibson** *Ld/disp at gd pce; 2l up aft 10; jnd nxt; 1/2l down 14; prsd ldr til mist 3 out; wknd nxt; sn btn* 10 3

Dukestown (IRE) 8-1 Miss E McWilliam *(bf) Pulling; ld early; hdd & rn wide aft 2; sn rr; 10l last by 4; stdly lost tch; fnce bhnd 14; sn t.o* . . . . runin 4

OFFICIAL DISTANCES: 4l, 10l **TIME:** 5min 56.1s

509 Mens Open 6 ran

426[P] **LAGANSIDE (IRE)** (1ow) 5-1 **J Muir** *Rn in snatches; 3l last 2; went 1l 2nd 5; disp 5l last 10; prog to 4th 14; chall app last; hrd rdn flat; ld cl home* . 1

282[P] **Colonel North (IRE)** 10-1 **A Richardson** *(bf) In tch in rr; 7l 6th 4; 3l 3rd 10; prsd ldrs 3 out; chall app last; hdd & no ex cl home* . . . . nk 2

210[4] **Dream Of My Life (USA)** 4-6F **R Morgan** *(xnb,orbs) Trckd ldr; hit 2; 1l 2nd 4; ld 15; 2l up nxt; hrd prsd & hdd app last; nt qckn flat* 3 3

Glacial Sygnet (IRE)(cp) 4-1 D Da Silva *Ld; 2l up 14; hdd nxt; cl up til no ex app last* 2 4

210[P] Wensley Blue (IRE) (7a) 3-1 K Anderson *4s-3s; chsd ldrs; disp 5l last 10; 7l last nxt; 8l 5th & outpcd 14; wknd & sn t.o* 20 5

282[7] Derryrose(cp) 5-1 M McAlister *Prom; niggled along on & off bridle; 4l 4th 6; pushed along 10; rmdrs 12; 10l last 14; lsng tch when blun 15; pu aft* . P

OFFICIAL DISTANCES: s hd, 3l **TIME:** 6min 03.5s

510 Open Maiden 56&7yo, 12st 7 ran

BAY OF DREAMS (7a) 4-1 **K Anderson** *(bf) Trckd ldrs; 5l 3rd app 3; 3l 2nd aft 10; ww til eff & lft solo 3 out* 1

137[F] Birkwood (7a) 8-1 A Richardson *In tch; 10l 5th when tried to duck out & ur 3* U

216[U] James Drummond (7a) 10-1 R MacDonald *A rr; 25l 4th 10-11; sn t.o; fnce bhnd when mist & ur 13* . . . . U

216[8] Red Tyrant(cp) 10-1 Miss C Metcalfe *Chsd ldrs; 8l 4th 3; 20l 4th 7; climbed nxt; poor 5th 10; lost action & pu app 11; lame* . . . . P

Slytherin Falls 14-1 S Clark *(xnb) Ld; pulling; 5l up 3; 10l clr app 7; mist 14; 2l up when mist & ur 3 out* . . . . U

75[B] Thorsgill evensF R Morgan *Jmpd lft at times; trckd ldr; 4l 2nd 3; 4l 3rd 10; sn outpcd; 15l 3rd app 13; climbed nxt; sn wknd; t.o & pu 15* . . . . P

Wild Imagination 9-2 C Storey *Green; a rr; 10l last 2; sn detach; 50l last 13; fnce bhnd when pu 14* . . . . P

OFFICIAL DISTANCE: Finished alone **TIME:** 6min 12.4s

511 Open Maiden Mares, 12st 8 ran

287[P] **SPORTY SPICE (IRE)** (5a) 6-4F **Miss L Hislop** *9/4-6/4; pulling; trckd ldr; 6l 2nd 10; 3l 2nd nxt; ww til ld 15; mist nxt; went 10l clr app last; easily* . 1

Queen Of Araghty (5a) 5-1 **W Goldie** *Ld in start; ld; 6l up 10; 3l ahd 12; hdd 15; sn btn* 12 2

286[5] **Coquet Gold** (5a) 5-1 **Miss C Walton** *In tch in midfield; 6l 3rd 11; outpcd app 15 & sn 15l down; kpt on one pce* 3 3

432[U] Can't Catch Me (IRE) (5a) 3-1 C Storey *Hdstrng; in tch; disp 5l last 11; short-lived eff in 6l 2nd 13; outpcd & sn nd; 20l 4th 3 out; no irons aft* . . . . runin 4

Beeches Dream (IRE) (12a) 7-1 Miss C Metcalfe *Jmpd slow in rr; sn t.o; fnce bhnd 7; jmpd slow 9; pu nxt* . . . . P

Fairy Bell (5a) 7-1 A Findlay *Chsd ldrs; 13l 6th 3; mist 9; disp 5l last 11; sn outpcd; 10l last & wkng 14; t.o & pu 2 out; dism; lame* . . . . P

Flying Respect (5a) 7-1 D Da Silva *Sis; in tch in rr when rn out thro wing 6* R

Gladys (5a) 5-1 S Huggan *(xnb) Prom early; 5l 3rd app 3; mist 5; rr 7; t.o 10; pu aft* . . . . P

OFFICIAL DISTANCES: 12l, 5l **TIME:** 6min 09.9s

Nodform Returns (rdr inj in previous rce) was withdrawn not under orders

North Herefordshire

Whitwick Manor (LH 8F,18J)

Sun, 14 Mar (GOOD to FIRM, FIRM in places)

512 Hunt Members, 12st — 2 ran

	MISS MOSS (5a) 4-5 **R Rogers** *Jmpd rt; trckd ldr; mist 3 out; slt ld 2 out; hld on wl*		1
206[2]	**No Fiddling (IRE)** 8-11F **Miss R Reynolds** *Ld til hdd 2 out; just outpcd*	nk	2

OFFICIAL DISTANCE: nk **TIME:** 6min 49.0s

513 Confined, 12st - 16J — 9 ran

93[P]	**CAUGHT AT DAWN (IRE)** 6-4F **T Weston** *A gng wl; chsd ldrs til ld 11; drew clr app 13; v easy*		1
404[7]	**The Archdeacon (IRE)** 14-1 **T Stephenson** *Chsd ldrs; went 2nd 12; outpcd by wnr app nxt; no ch aft*	fence	2
359[P]	**Wild Blade (IRE)**(cp) 16-1 **R Jenkins** *(xnb) Ww in tch; blun 10; 10l 4th app 13; no ch w wnr aft; went poor 3rd 2 out*	7	3
	Highbridge (IRE) (3x) 5-1 R Hughes *Ld 2-11; 8l 3rd app 13; sn no ch w wnr; dem 2 out*	5	4
	Ole Gunnar (IRE) 7-1 M Wilesmith *(xnb) Mid-div; 6l 6th 10; 5th & outpcd app 13; no ch aft*	1/2	5
50[P]	Aztec Rule (IRE) 7-1 S Joynes *(xnb) Ld to 2; chsd ldrs; blun & nrly ur 11; wknd nxt; t.o & pu 3 out*		P
229[P]	Ceasers Reign (IRE) (3x) 8-1 T Faulkner *2 handlers; tde; a bhnd; 11l 7th 10; sn lost tch; t.o & pu 13*		P
231[1]	Hijacked 4-1 D Mansell *Mid-div til pu 6*		P
	Hillcrest Manor (IRE)(cp) 12-1 Miss S Davies *A bhnd; 17l last 10; t.o frm 12 til pu 3 out*		P

OFFICIAL DISTANCES: dist, 9l **TIME:** 6min 32.0s

The start of this race was delayed by 15min; fence 7 was omitted from this and all subsequent races - state of the ground; revised fence numbers have been used in the comments-in-running

514 Mens Open, 12st - 16J — 4 ran

209[P]	**SPEED BOARD (IRE)** 6-4 **J Cook** *Chsd ldrs; disp ld brief 10; 8l 3rd & outpcd app 13; rallied nxt; ld app 2 out; in comm when lft clr 2 out*		1
437[U]	**Lyphard's Fable (USA)** 12-1 **D England** *W ldr til ld 10-12; 7l 2nd & rdn app 3 out; 3rd & btn aft nxt; lft 2nd 2 out*	25	2
176[P]	Persona Pride evensF J Trice-Rolph *Ld to 10; sn rdn & drpd to last; no ch app 13; t.o & pu 3 out*		P
444[P]	Shamel 3-1 S Hughes *Hld up last; hdwy to ld 12; sn clr; 6l up when blun 3 out; sn hdd; btn when fell nxt*		F

OFFICIAL DISTANCE: 20l **TIME:** 6min 47.0s

515 Ladies Open - 16J — 4 ran

303[U]	**LORD CASTLE (IRE)** 6-4F **Miss H Lewis** *Nt a fluent; chsd ldrs; lft 2nd 9; jnd ldr 11; ld 13; drew clr frm 3 out; easily*		1
251[P]	**Allotrope (IRE)**(bl,tt) 3-1 **Miss L Brooke** *(xnb) 2 handlers; ld to 5; lft in ld 9-13; wknd 3 out; dism aft fin; removed frm course by horse ambulance*	15	2
230[U]	Dunston Heath (IRE) 5-1 Miss A Blake *Rcd wide; chsd ldr 3; ld 5 til ur 9*		U
	Fuero Real (FR) 5-2 Miss H James *Bckwd; a last; 15l 3rd app 13; sn no ch; pu 2 out*		P

OFFICIAL DISTANCE: 18l **TIME:** 6min 53.0s

516 Restricted, 12st - 16J — 6 ran

294[8]	**TOM PUTT** 7-1 **B Pauling** *Chsd ldr til ld 14; made rest; clr when jmpd rt 2 out; comf*		1
231[P]	**Paddy Bettalot** 8-1 **T Stephenson** *Chsd ldrs; went 2nd app 13; outpcd by wnr app 3 out; no imp aft*	8	2
406[U]	**Huntersway (IRE)** 7-1 **R Hodges** *In tch; mist 10; rdn nxt; 8l 4th app 13; kpt on one pce frm 3 out*	2	3
	Ashor Ted 14-1 S Bush *(xnb) A last; jmpd slow 2; detach when ref 7*		r

Father Tom (IRE) 4-5F Julian Pritchard *Ww; prog to 3rd & in tch when slpd & fell 9* F
Slaney Lass (5a) 2-1 M Jackson *2 handlers; rcd free; ld; pckd 2; sn clr; hdd 13; wknd qckly; no ch when crawled over 3 out & pu.* P

OFFICIAL DISTANCES: 5*l*, 2*l* **TIME:** 6min 39.0s

517 Confined Maiden (Div 1), 12st - 16J 8 ran

53[3] **BEAUCHAMP ORACLE** evensF **S Hughes** *A gng wl; trckd ldrs 11; went 2nd 13; ld app 2 out; sn clr; v easily* 1
Classic Fable (IRE) (5a) 4-1 **A Hanly** *Ld; sn clr; 3l up 10; hdd app 2 out; no ch w wnr* 30 2
A Proper Charlie 8-1 T Stephenson *Mid-div; 8l 6th 10; outpcd 12; sn no ch; t.o & pu 3 out* P
Baron Kiss 7-1 H Dowty *Ww in last pr; lost tch 11; 4th & no ch aft 13; pu nxt* P
Corn General 20-1 J Trice-Rolph *A last; mist 2; lsng tch when pu 8.* P
358[4] Norse 4-1 R Hodges *Chsd ldrs; rdn & wknd 10; no ch 12; t.o & pu 3 out* P
Norton Wood (IRE) 20-1 Miss R Reynolds *Chsd ldr til app 11; 4th & wkng when pu 12* P
Snitton Salvo(bl) 16-1 M Jackson *In tch; chsd ldr app 11; ev ch til wknd aft 3 out; 3rd & btn when fell nxt; winded* F

OFFICIAL DISTANCE: dist **TIME:** 6min 43.0s

518 Confined Maiden (Div 2), 12st - 16J 5 ran

SNITTON WEST(vis) 8-1 **M Jackson** *Hld up; prog & cl up 10; chall 13; lft 5l clr nxt; sn hrd rdn & hanging; just hdd last; lft wl clr flat; v lucky* 1
Channel's Brook 3-1 **T Stephenson** *Ld til hdd 13; sn wknd; lft 3rd 3 out & poor 2nd 2 out* fence 2
410[U] Bally Cyrano 5-1 Miss R Reynolds *Tk keen hld; jnd ldr 3; rstrnd & bhnd 5; prog to jn ldr 10; mist nxt; sn wknd; bhnd & pu 12* P
172[3] Galaxy Girl (5a) evensF J Mahot *Ww; trckd ldng pr 11; ld 13; jnd but still gng wl when rn out & ur 3 out* R
Legend Of Light (IRE) (5a) 4-1 S Hughes *Chsd ldrs; disp ld 11-nxt; 3rd & outpcd aft 13; lft 5l 2nd nxt; ld when stumbled bad landing & ur 50 yds aft last* U

OFFICIAL DISTANCE: dist **TIME:** 6min 48.0s

The rider of Galaxy Girl objected to the winner for squeezing him out at the third last; the objection was overruled, but the deposit was returned

519 Confined Maiden (Div 3), 12st - 16J 5 ran

256[2] **NEW LODGE EXPRESS (IRE)** 4-6F **T Stephenson** *(xnb) Jmpd rt 1; ld/disp til app 3 out; rdn to ld app last; stayed on flat* 1
Kirkfield (IRE) (5a) 8-1 **A Hanly** *Chsd ldrs; jnd ldr 7 til ld app 3 out; hdd app last; unable to qckn* 1 2
403[10] **Stockton Wolf** 5-1 **R Hodges** *Trckd ldng pr; 5l 4th & rdn app 3 out; lft 3rd 2 out; no imp* 7 3
408[F] Babs Wheal (5a) 3-1 H Dowty *Ww in last; 8l 4th 10; prog to chall 3 out; wandered u.p app nxt; 3l 3rd & lkd btn when fell 2 out* F
259[P] Sneedham's Green 20-1 F de Giles *Cl up; blun 6; wknd qckly nxt; rdn when mist 9; sn t.o; pu 11.* P

OFFICIAL DISTANCES: 1*l*, 6*l* **TIME:** 6min 41.0s

The stewards enquired into the riding of Sneedham's Green and fined the rider £65 for using his whip when the horse was out of contention

Suffolk

Ampton (RH 7F,20J)

Sun, 14 Mar (GOOD, GOOD to FIRM in places)

520 Hunt Members 3 ran

223[F] **FINE AND DANDY (IRE)** 1-2F **J Owen** *Trckd ldr til lft in ld 7; made rest; 8l ahd of rival 9; eased clr 16; unchall* 1
155[4] **Village Copper**(bl) 5-4 **C Ward-Thomas** *Ld til hmpd bad by loose horse 7; 8l down & chsd rival vain frm 9; rdn & no imp 15.* 25 2
Neronian (IRE) 10-1 Mrs H Edwards *Fat; 2nd when saddle slpd & ur 1* U

OFFICIAL DISTANCE: dist **TIME:** 6min 50.0s **TOTE:** £1.30

521 Confined, 12st — 7 ran

Prev	Horse / Rider / Comment	Dist	Pos
376²	**BARD OF DRUMCOO (IRE)** (6x) 4-6F **D Kemp** *Made all; kpt on game frm 2 out; all out*		1
99⁶	**Persian Hero (IRE)** 3-1 **J Owen** *Hld up; 4th 8; hdwy to 3rd 10; 2l 2nd 12; prsd ldr frm 15; ev ch 2 out; kpt on game flat; just failed*	hd	2
	Nordic Spree (IRE)(cp) 12-1 **N Bloom** *Trckd ldr; 4l 3rd 5; outpcd & dem 8l 4th 15; kpt on to 3rd agn 2 out; no ch w ldrs.*	25	3
376ᴾ	The Glen Road (IRE) 8-1 A Sansome *Trckd ldr in 2nd til releg 3rd 10; chsd ldrs til wknd 17; dem 2 out*	6	4
	Gawngadinn (IRE) 10-1 R Morgan-Evans *Sn outpcd; 5l 4th 7; 5th 10; hit 13; rdn & one pce 16*	10	5
396³	Castle Road (IRE) 25-1 Miss L Marriott *Sa & imm last; t.o 2; pu 9*		P
22⁵	Musical Hit 25-1 J Bevan *A 6th; 10l 6th 9; hopeless t.o 15; pu & collapsed app 2 out; dead*		P

OFFICIAL DISTANCES: hd, 8l **TIME:** 6min 40.0s **TOTE:** £1.80

522 Ladies Open — 8 ran

Prev	Horse / Rider / Comment	Dist	Pos
399¹	**THE WILEY KALMUCK (IRE)** evensF **Miss Z Turner** *Trckd ldr in 2nd til ld 14; sn in comm; drew clr frm 3 out*		1
399ʳ	**Corston Joker** 20-1 **Mrs L Spence** *Ld til jnd 13; sn hdd; prsd ldr til wknd qckly 3 out*	25	2
242³	**Grand Ambition (USA)**(cp) 6-1 **Miss L Allan** *Sn 4th; chsd ldrs; pckd 10; cl up 12; nt qckn 14; 10l 3rd 16; no imp aft.*	15	3
373⁵	Mister Audi (IRE) 20-1 Miss A Bowles *(xnb) Sn strugg in 6th; 30l 7th 16; lft 5th 2 out; plodded into rem 4th app last*	fence	4
373³	Borrow Mine (IRE) 12-1 Miss L Marriott *Nvr gng wl in 5th mostly; 10l 5th 9; t.o 16*	8	5
378ᴾ	Buckland Bobby 33-1 Miss L Fear *Sa; t.o 7; pu 9.*		P
249¹	Pampered Gale (IRE) 5-2 Miss N Barnes *Sn wl in rr & nvr lkd happy; 20l 7th 3; slt hdwy frm 16; gng dist 5th when hung rt & rn out 3 out*		R
157ᴾ	Step In Line (IRE) 8-1 Mrs S Hodge *(xnb) Drpd out in 4th; 10l 4th 8; prsd ldrs frm 12-13; wknd qckly & lost tch frm nxt; 30l 4th when pu 2 out*		P

OFFICIAL DISTANCES: 20l, 15l **TIME:** 6min 33.0s **TOTE:** £2.20

523 Land Rover Mens Open, 12st — 5 ran

Prev	Horse / Rider / Comment	Dist	Pos
400²	**ROYAL ACTION** 15-8 **P Chinery** *Prom; ld 4; jnd 5; hdd aft 7; cl up til jnd ldr 15; slt ld aft nxt til pushed clr 3 out; kpt on wl.*		1
247⁴	**Millenium Way (IRE)** 5-2 **J Owen** *Hld up in cl 4th; went cl 2nd 9; prsd ldr til nt qckn aft 3 out*	4	2
396¹	**Ballad (IRE)** 10-1 **A Williams** *Cl 3rd mostly; ev ch 15; nt qckn aft nxt; 6l 3rd & one pce 3 out*	20	3
374ᴾ	Exclusive Air (USA) (7a) 33-1 P Millington *Lkd bored padd; cl last 2; hit 8 & 9; wkng when jmpd slow 14; t.o 15; pu 16*		P
247³	Minino (IRE) 13-8F C Ward-Thomas *(xnb) Ld to 3; disp ld 5 til ld agn 8; rn wide & hdd bend bef 16; pu qckly; inj hock*		P

OFFICIAL DISTANCES: 5l, 15l **TIME:** 6min 43.0s **TOTE:** £2.00

524 Restricted, 12st — 11 ran

Prev	Horse / Rider / Comment	Dist	Pos
375ᴾ	**MISTER RINGA** 4-1 **A Braithwaite** *Sn prom; cl 3rd 6; prsd ldr aft til ld 14; drew clr aft 17; easily*		1
243¹	**Ginger Bug** (5a) 25-1 **P Chinery** *Blun 2; 8l 7th 11; rr of main group aft; outpcd 15; kpt on stdly frm 17; picked off wkng rivals til dist 4th aft 3 out; went 2nd aft nxt; no ch w wnr*	20	2
250ᴾ	**Federal Case (FR)** 7-2 **A Merriam** *(xnb) Trckd ldrs in 5th; 5l 5th 10; outpcd 16; 15l 4th 17; kpt on to 3rd 2 out; no ex.*	2	3
375⁴	Camden Loch (IRE) 16-1 R Morgan-Evans *Ld 1; cl up; 4th 6; 2l 2nd 16; ch til outpcd 3 out; dem 4th nxt.*	1	4
243²	Give Him A Chance (IRE)(bl) 25-1 N Moore *Mid-div; 7l 6th 9; chsd ldrs aft; 4l 3rd 15; outpcd & no ch 17; wknd app 2 out*	4	5
248³	Nowornever (IRE) 2-1F D Kemp *Cl 2nd 4; prom til outpcd 14; 10l 4th 16; no imp aft*	½	6
243⁴	Coole Chief 25-1 Sam Gray *(xnb) Sn outpcd & strugg; 8th 7; last by 11; t.o & pu 14*		P
398¹⁰	Henwyn 25-1 M Smith *(xnb) Ld 2-13; wknd v rap; last 17; t.o & pu last*		P

398[5] Hi Tech Man (IRE) 11-4 N Bloom *Imm rr & nvr gng wl; 10l 10th 3; sn detach in trailing quartet; t.o & pu 14* . . . . . . P
375[P] Mr Moonbeam (IRE) (2ow) 12-1 M Buchan *2 handlers; imm rr; 9th 10; wl bhnd in last when slpd up bend bef 12* . . . . . . S
378[4] Treble Trouble 33-1 P Millington *Sa; sn detach in trailing quartet; 8th 10; t.o & pu 2 out.* . . . . . . P

OFFICIAL DISTANCES: 15*l*, 1½*l* **TIME:** 6min 43.0s **TOTE:** £9.00

The stewards enquired into the improved form of the winner; the connections' explanation that last time out 'the horse having been re-saddled at the start was left 30l and was never able to get into the race' was accepted

525 Open Maiden, 12st — 12 ran

EUROGAEDEL (IRE) (7a) 8-1 **R Stearn** *16s-8s; cl 2nd; prsd ldr til 6l 3rd & outpcd 16; rallied to chall 2 out; drvn & r.o game to ld flat; wl rdn* 1
376[4] **Arctic Snip** 5-2F **N Moore** *Ld; jnd 2 out; hdd flat; no ex* . . . . ¾ 2
398[F] **No Nay Never (IRE)** 5-1 **Miss A Bowles** *Chsd ldrs; 10l 5th 10; kpt on; 6l 4th 16; lft 3rd 2 out; no ch ldrs* 15 3
463[P] Gunner Be True(cp) 8-1 J Owen *(xnb) Hopeless outpcd in rr 6; plodded rnd; inherited dist 4th 2 out* 20 4
128[U] Homeleigh Meadow 25-1 W Pewter *(xnb) Last 3; slt hdwy 7; 8l 4th 10; sn bhnd; t.o* 15 5
245[P] Assington Bay (IRE) 16-1 A Braithwaite *(xnb) Prom early; 4l 4th 7; sn rr; virt t.o 14; crawled over 15 & imm pu.* . . . . P
186[2] Carvilla (IRE) 9-2 A Sansome *3rd 4; cl up bhnd ldng pr; prsd ldrs 14; went 2l 2nd & ev ch 16; wknd nxt; 3rd when stpd to nil & pu 2 out* . . . . P
152[3] Manhatton Storm (IRE) 4-1 A Merriam *9th when blun 4; seemed to lose confidence & nvr gng or jmpng wl aft; 8l 5th 14; 20l 5th & wkng when pu 2 out* . . . . P
217[2] Marsden 4-1 P Taiano *Sn bhnd; lsng tch in 9th 8; blun 10; t.o 11; pu 12.* . . . . P
Namche Bazaar (IRE) 14-1 M Smith *A rr; t.o & pu 12.* . . . . P
244[7] Sharp Sarah (5a) 20-1 P Chinery *Imm rr; nt jw & frequently diving out to lft; sn t.o; pu last.* . . . . P
293[2] Vivaldi Rose (IRE) (5a) 4-1 E Walker *Towards rr when ur 2.* . . . . U

OFFICIAL DISTANCES: 1*l*, 10*l* **TIME:** 6min 48.0s **TOTE:** £10.00

Tanatside

Eyton-on-Severn (LH 12F,17J)

Sun, 14 Mar (GOOD to SOFT becoming HOLDING)

526 Hunt Members — 3 ran

CUTINA (5a) evensJF **D Barlow** *Hld up; went 2nd 6; clsd 12; ld nxt; in comm frm 3 out.* 1
292[U] **Lord Of The West (IRE)** (7x) 7-2 **W Puddifer** *Ld & clr; 15l ahd 6; prsd 12; hdd nxt; plodded on v slow frm 3 out; rdr lurched forward nxt.* 15 2
228[P] **Whatafellow (IRE)** evensJF **B Shaw** *Hit 2; chsd ldr to 6; rdn & fnd nil 14; hanging rt frm nxt.* 3½ 3

OFFICIAL DISTANCES: 15*l*, 4*l* **TIME:** 6min 45.9s

Fence 6 was omitted from all races - state of the going

527 Intermediate, 12st — 5 ran

102[1] **STEP AND RUN (IRE)** 4-1 **Miss J Williams** *(xnb) 2nd 5 til jmpd slow 6 & 7; 6l 3rd 11 & sn outpcd; lft 15l 2nd 13; smooth rn to ld app 2 out; sn clr* . . 1
375[1] **Pristeen Spy** 10-11F **R Burton** *(xnb) Ld to 11; disp ld when lft 15l clr 13; drvn & hdd app 2 out; fnd nil* 7 2
324[1] Rhythm King 5-2 G Maundrell *(xnb) Hld up; eff 10; ld 11; disp ld when fell hvly 13; winded* . . . . F
228[5] Springwood White 20-1 Miss H Kinsey *Prom to 10; wknd rap & t.o aft 13; nrly 2 fncs bhnd when climbed 2 out & pu & dism* . . . . P
The Unamed Man 7-1 L Morgan *2 handlers; blun 1 & 4; a last; strugg 6; t.o 9; pu 10* . . . . P

OFFICIAL DISTANCE: 6*l* **TIME:** 6min 35.0s

528 Mens Open, 12st — 13 ran

404^{U}	**SHINY BAY (IRE)** 10-1 **N Pearce** *Hld up; 12l 7th ½way; hdwy & 9l 6th 11; jnd ldrs 13; ld 14; sn 3l clr; rdn out*		1
	Coole Venture (IRE) 5-4F **R Burton** *Hld up; stdy hdwy 7; 10l 5th ½way; went 6l 3rd 11 & 2nd aft nxt; ev ch 14; rdn when jmpd rt 3 out; nt qckn*	3	2
190^{3}	**Gunner Sid** 8-1 **A Wadlow** *Ld to 5; 2nd to 10; 7l 4th nxt; ev ch 14; bumped 3 out; one pce*	2½	3
229^{3}	Wild Edric(bl) 14-1 A Beedles *Hld up; 14l 8th ½way; bhnd til hdwy 13; 7l 4th & rdn 3 out; wknd aft 2 out*	12	4
251^{U}	Oneanthreequarters (IRE) 14-1 R Jagger *Chsd ldrs; 11l 6th ½way; 8l 5th 11; wknd 13*	8	5
228^{P}	Knock It Back (IRE) 20-1 J Handley *Rcd wide; 2nd to 4; 4l 3rd ½way; went 5l 2nd 10; wknd 14*	2½	6
251^{P}	Carnage (IRE) 12-1 W Hill *Prom; went 2nd 4; ld 5 til hdd & wknd qckly 14*	12	7
	Border Run 25-1 S Ross *Ss; a wl bhnd; 30l 11th ½way; t.o 11; pu 14*		P
188^{P}	Is Wonderful (USA) 20-1 M Munrowd *(xnb) Ss; a wl bhnd; t.o & pu 10*		P
	Jimmy Jumbo (IRE) (4x, 10ow) 7-1 N Cecil *(xnb) 1st ride (had shed 22lb on Atkins diet); lost plce 8; 17l 9th ½way; 25l 10th 11; sn t.o; pu aft 2 out*		P
	Kerres Noires (FR) (7x) 7-4 S Waley-Cohen *Lw; prom; 7l 4th ½way; wknd qckly & 12l 7th 11; t.o & pu 14*		P
254^{r}	Meadows Boy (7x) 7-1 D Barlow *20s-7s; 2 handlers; svs; a wl bhnd; 18l 10th ½way; 18l 9th 11; t.o & pu 3 out*		P
	Red Hare (NZ) (7x) 12-1 G Hanmer *Fat; wl bhnd & rdn along 7; 35l 12th ½way; t.o & pu 10*		P

OFFICIAL DISTANCES: 3*l*, 5*l* **TIME:** 6min 38.1s

529 Ladies Open — 13 ran

	STRETCHING (IRE) (4x) 6-1 **Miss J Williams** *10s-6s; 2nd/3rd; chsd ldr aft 10; ld app 13; 6l clr when mist nxt; 12l ahd last*		1
230^{U}	**Justin Mac (IRE)** (7x) 20-1 **Miss K Wood** *Chsd ldr 5-10; releg 4th nxt; 14l 3rd 14; kpt on stdly to 2nd agn flat; no ch w wnr*	10	2
191^{U}	**Euro Bob (IRE)** 4-1 **Mrs A Rucker** *Hld up; 8th 6; 6th 11; rchd 14l 4th 3 out; kpt on wl flat desp rdr*	4	3
380^{3}	Native Man (IRE) (7x) 14-1 Miss T Clark *(xnb) Hld up; 6th 6; prog 10 to 3rd nxt; chsd wnr vain 14 til mist last; fin tired*	hd	4
91^{3}	Mr Kermit 10-1 Miss S Sharratt *Wl bhnd; mod 10th 6; hdwy 11; nt rch ldrs; poor 5th 3 out; stayed on stdly flat*	2½	5
230^{F}	Slaney Native (IRE) 10-1 Miss M Mullineaux *Bhnd; jmpd v slow 5; poor 11th nxt; still wl bhnd 14; plugged on*	12	6
230^{P}	Dancetillyoudrop (IRE) (7x) 12-1 Miss T Tellwright *(xnb) Midfield; last of 9 in tch 6; no prog or ch frm 13*	1	7
94^{4}	Pennyahei (5a, 7x) evensF Miss S Beddoes *Midfield; 7th 6; brief eff in 5th 11; strugg frm 13; disapp*	2	8
5^{10}	China Lal (5a) 20-1 Mrs K Diggle *Cl up early; 5th 6; lost plce 10; poor 7th 14*	10	9
	Jelali (IRE) 20-1 Miss S Talbot *(xnb) Prom; 4th 6; wknd 10; wl bhnd 13*	2	10
230^{F}	Joyce Bel (FR) 20-1 Miss K Crank *Rdr v insecure; imm strugg; last 6; cont t.o; pu aft 11*		P
92^{P}	Life Of A River (IRE) 16-1 Miss H Kinsey *Ld til hdd & mist 13; wknd rap nxt; poor 6th 3 out; pu last*		P
94^{U}	Wychnor King (IRE) 25-1 Mrs D Caine *Wl bhnd; poor 12th 6; t.o & pu 11*		P

OFFICIAL DISTANCES: 12*l*, 3*l* **TIME:** 6min 38.5s

530 Restricted, 12st — 13 ran

	HEAVY WEATHER (IRE) 4-1 **W Hill** *Hld up; hdwy 6; 2l 3rd ½way; 3l 4th 11; blun 12; 3rd & rdn 3 out; ld nxt; sn clr*		1
231^{3}	**Donrico (IRE)** 6-1 **L Morgan** *8s-6s; chsd ldrs; jmpd slow 8; 6l 7th & drvn along ½way; eff & 4l 5th 11; 6l 4th 3 out; went 4l 2nd aft nxt; one pce*	6	2
97^{1}	**Master Club Royal**(bl) 9-4F **G Hanmer** *Prom; 2½l 4th ½way; 2½l 3rd 11; lost plce 14; 8l 5th & rdn 3 out; stayed on reluct u.p 2 out*	nk	3
231^{U}	Ricky B 20-1 W Kinsey *(xnb) Ld to 5; 2nd til ld 13; hdd 2 out; no ex*	2	4
95^{r}	Lily Brown (5a) 25-1 Mrs S Johnson *(xnb) Chsd ldrs til lost plce 8; 8½l 9th ½way; 13l 10th 11; rallied 14; 11l 6th 3 out; stayed on one pce*	2½	5
	Corky Browne 25-1 Miss J Perry *Hld up; hdwy 6; 5l 6th ½way; wknd & 10l 9th 11; t.o*	30	6

231^{P} Hill Of Kilfeacle (IRE) 20-1 D Greenway *Prom; 4$^{1}/_{2}$l 5th $^{1}/_{2}$way; 5l 6th 11; wknd 13; 22l 8th 3 out; t.o* . . . 2 7
96^{1} Home Tor 6-1 Miss S Beddoes *Mist 4; 2nd til ld 5; mist 6; hdd 13; 1l 2nd 3 out; wknd aft nxt; hung rt & virt stpd aft last; t.o* . . . 5 8
252^{P} Always Good (IRE) 25-1 P Needham *(xnb) Nt jw; sn wl bhnd; t.o last $^{1}/_{2}$way; pu 3 out* . . . P
301^{5} Gabaka De Thaix (FR) 25-1 M Caldwell *A bhnd; mists 1 & 3; 12l 12th $^{1}/_{2}$way; 20l 11th 11; t.o & pu 13* . . . P
231^{P} Gaetano (IRE) 6-1 R Burton *Hld up; 10l 11th $^{1}/_{2}$way; bhnd til hdwy & 6l 7th 11; wknd 14; 15l 7th 3 out; pu 2 out* . . . P
Italian Clover 20-1 B Shaw *(xnb) De-tubed; swtng; nd; 9l 10th & rdn $^{1}/_{2}$way; 21l 12th 11; t.o & pu 3 out* . . . P
294^{P} Weallwayswillbeone (IRE) 5-1 N Oliver *Hld up; mist 7; 8l 8th $^{1}/_{2}$way; 7l 8th 11; wknd 13; pu 14* . . . P

OFFICIAL DISTANCES: 6*l*, $^{1}/_{2}$*l* **TIME:** 6min 46.0s

The rider of Master Club Royal was fined £65 for using his whip with excessive force and causing his horse to be injured

531 Open Maiden (Div 1) 13 ran

ALONG THE LAWN (IRE) 3-1JF **A Crow** *Settled 3rd/4th til 2nd 11; ld app 13; jb rt 3 out & wildly rdn & hdd; ld agn aft 2 out; just hdd when lft virt solo last; lucky* . . . 1
408^{P} **Iadora** (5a) 10-1 **Miss T Clark** *3rd/4th to 5; 8th & wkng when mist 8; rem frm 14 but lft 2nd by default* . . . runin 2
227^{R} **Bless Yourself (IRE)** 7-1 **G Hanmer** *Trckd ldrs; went 3rd 12; drew clr w wnr frm nxt; rdn & ev ch when lft in ld 3 out; hdd aft nxt; stylishly drvn into nk advant when blun bad & ur last; event rmtd (unlucky)* . . . dist 3
227^{P} Gosh Josh (IRE) 20-1 A Wadlow *A bhnd; lost tch 10; t.o & pu 11* . . . P
97^{5} Hokey Wokey 14-1 D Sherlock *Lw; jmpd rt in rr & sn getting rmdrs; last 5; t.o & pu 12* . . . P
Hot Brandy (IRE) (7a) 3-1JF S Morris *Novicey in midfield; mist 4; 5th & eff 9; wknd aft 11; t.o & pu 3 out* . . . P
257^{P} Joe Lively (IRE) (7a) 20-1 A Wintle *Jmpd poor; t.o when nrly ref 13; pu nxt* P
259^{P} Little Poppy (5a) 20-1 F Hutsby *Midfield; u.p 5; no prog when fell 7* . . . F
226^{4} Ridware George 10-1 W Hill *Chsd ldr to 10; 4th & fdng rap app 13; t.o & pu 3 out* . . . P
368^{P} Rundetto (IRE) 14-1 S Moreton *(xnb) Nt jw in midfield & impeded by rdr; lost tch 11; blun bad 12; t.o & pu nxt* . . . P
Times Two 9-2 R Burton *(xnb) Rcd wide in ld; 6l clr 9; hdd app 13; wknd rap; 25l 3rd nxt; pu 3 out* . . . P
95^{P} Top Weld 10-1 Miss S Beddoes *A wl bhnd; last 8; rem 8th when fell 14* . . . F
Treasulier (IRE) 5-1 N Oliver *Settled midfield; impd to 4th 8; handy til wknd app 13; t.o & pu 3 out* . . . P

OFFICIAL DISTANCES: dist, dist **TIME:** 6min 53.3s

532 Open Maiden (Div 2) 12 ran

259^{P} **BEACHCOMBER** 5-1 **W Hill** *Ld 3-5; 12l 2nd when mist 9; dem & 6l 3rd 11; 2nd agn aft 14; ld aft 3 out; sn clr; comf* . . . 1
256^{F} **The Noble Roman** 12-1 **T Ellis** *Lashed out & kicked face of spectator learing over padd rails; hld up; hdwy 7; 13l 3rd $^{1}/_{2}$way; went 5l 2nd aft 10; ld 14 til aft 3 out; sn wknd* . . . 15 2
405^{6} **Raiseapearl** 8-1 **I Clyde** *Ld in start; hld up & bhnd; blun 5; 25l 8th $^{1}/_{2}$way; 20l 6th when mist 11; hdwy & 10l 5th 13; went 4l 3rd 3 out; wkng when mist nxt; blun last* . . . 3 3
Bank On Lady (5a) 10-1 Miss A de Lisle Wells *Mists & rdr most insecure; 12l 3rd when blun & ur 7* . . . U
259^{U} Castle Lodge 9-4JF G Hanmer *11/4-9/4; hld up & bhnd; 26l 9th $^{1}/_{2}$way; 7th when fell 10* . . . F
293^{r} Fun For Girls (12a) 12-1 M Keel *Lost plce aft 5; blun & lost tch 8; 23l 7th $^{1}/_{2}$way; 30l last 11; t.o & pu 12* . . . P
Ginmini (IRE) (5a) 12-1 N Oliver *Nvr on terms; 20l 5th $^{1}/_{2}$way; wl bhnd when pu 10* . . . P
Mayday Girl (5a) 6-1 J Handley *Tk str hld; went 2nd aft 3; ld 5; 12l clr 8-10; hdd & stpd to nil 14; poor 5th when pu 3 out* . . . P

409P Ridware Rose (5a) 10-1 Miss S Sharratt *Ld to 3; lost plce 6; 22l 6th ½way; 17l 5th 11; wl bhnd when pu aft 3 out* . . . . . . P
Spot The Native (IRE) 9-4JF P Hemmings *1st ride; nrly ur 1; rn out & ur 3* R
Strong Weld 12-1 D Sherlock *School in rr; 30l last ½way; 22l 7th 11; wl bhnd til fell 14* . . . . . . F
Whats Up Jake 8-1 A Wadlow *(xnb) Hld up; 17l 4th ½way; hdwy 12; rdn 14; 7l 4th & wkng when blun 3 out; jmpd v slow 2 out; pu last* . . . . . . P

OFFICIAL DISTANCES: 15l, 3½l **TIME:** 6min 54.5s

533 Confined Maiden 56&7yo, 2m4f, 12st - 13J — 10 ran

2273 **KARINGA LANE** 5-4F **W Hill** *(xnb) Settled 3rd; went 2nd & mist 9; mist nxt; ld on bit app 2 out; clr last* 1
227P **Mountsorrel (IRE)** (7a) 7-1 **B Shaw** *Trckd ldrs; clsd to ld 7; 4l clr 10; rdn & hdd app 2 out; fin tired* 12 2
Blue Jar 12-1 S Ross *(xnb) Detach in last pr; no ch frm 7; t.o & pu 3 out* . P
Fort Glendennon (7a) 13-2 R Burton *(xnb) Detach in last pr & gvn blatant school til pu 9* . . . . . . P
Grantie Boy (IRE) (7a) 6-1 J O'Brien *(xnb) Pulled hrd & prom brief; t.o & pu 8* P
Handsome Lad (IRE) 12-1 A Wadlow *Rcd free; ld app 2; jmpd v slow 3 & hdd brief; ld agn to 7; wknd 9; 20l 4th nxt; pu 3 out* . . . . . . P
387F Magnatism 6-1 L Hicks *Ld til app 2; 2nd til mist 6; wknd rap nxt; t.o & pu 9* P
97S Mervsintrouble(cp) 25-1 G Hanmer *Bhnd; some prog in 13l 5th 7; sn no imp; pu 9* . . . . . . P
410P Neeley (7a) 12-1 M Keel *Midfield; mist 4; outpcd when mist 5; no ch aft 7; t.o & pu 2 out* . . . . . . P
410R Potter's Wheel (7a) 7-1 L Morgan *Hld up; prog in 3l 4th 7; cl 3rd 10; wknd nxt & sn 8l adrift; crashing fall 2 out; winded* . . . . . . F

OFFICIAL DISTANCE: 10l **TIME:** 5min 34.8s

West Street Tickham

Detling (LH 9F,21J)

Sun, 14 Mar (GOOD becoming GOOD/SOFT)

534 Hunt Members — 5 ran

127P **PHAR AFIELD (IRE)** 7-4JF **J Sole** *Hld up in 4th; impd to trck ldr 13; ld 3 out; drew clr app nxt; easily* 1
Ocki 4-1 **D Page (Kent)** *Mostly 3rd; prsd ldr 10-12; ev ch til wknd 17; kpt on frm 3 out; disp 2nd when nrly ur last; rallied to tk 2nd cl home* 15 2
Lord Of The Flies (IRE) 7-4JF **D Brightling** *Ld; clr to 9; made rest til hdd 3 out; wknd rap app nxt* 1 3
Winward 10-1 J Merry *Chsd ldr to 9; wl in tch til 5l 4th & wkng 14; no ch frm 18* . . . . . . fence 4
Amandas Fancy (IRE) (5a, 4ow) 10-1 B Neaves *Imm lost tch; fnce bhnd by 9; kpt on stdly frm 18* 15 5

OFFICIAL DISTANCES: 8l, ½l **TIME:** 6min 49.0s **TOTE:** £2.60; places £1.60,£2.40 **DF:**£11.20

535 Mens Confined, 12st — 4 ran

345F **TRICKY TREVOR (IRE)** 2-1 **P York** *A prsd ldr; ld 2 out; slt advant last; r.o str flat* 1
1775 **Pendle Hill** (5x) 2-1 **A Hickman** *Hld up; cl 4th to 9; trckd ldng pr frm 13; gd hdwy to ld 3 out; hdd nxt; ev ch last; no ex flat* 2 2
239P **Real Value (IRE)** (7x) 7-4F **P Hall** *Narrow ldr til hdd 3 out; sn btn* 10 3
1825 Oxendale (6x) 8-1 P Bull *Cl 3rd to 9; 4th & ev ch 16; lost tch frm 18* 10 4

OFFICIAL DISTANCES: 1½l, 5l **TIME:** 6min 20.0s **TOTE:** £2.00; places £-,£- **DF:**£4.60

536 Ladies Confined — 7 ran

4213 **DICK MCCARTHY (IRE)** 4-5F **Mrs S Ashby** *Prsd ldr til ld aft 13; sn drew clr; 15l up 16; in comm frm 3 out* 1
2395 **Teach Altra (IRE)** 2-1 **Miss B Donnelly** *Towards rr; 16l 5th & pushed along 12; stayed on frm 18 to tk rem 2nd flat* 30 2
1014 **Stylish Dave (NZ)** 14-1 **Mrs D Rowell** *Chsd ldng pr frm 5; went 8l 2nd aft 14; no imp on wnr; 30l down app 3 out; dem flat* 2 3

182[P] Jack Of Kilcash (IRE) 14-1 Miss C Benstead *Ld to 13; sn wknd; 20l 3rd 16; wl bhnd frm 18* 25 4
Barron Bay (USA) 14-1 Miss N Moisey *A last; qckly lost tch; 20l bhnd field by 7; t.o frm 12* 2fncs 5
246[U] Irish Sea (USA) 14-1 Mrs C Adam *Midfield; 4th & in tch when ur 11* . . . . U
421[P] Newby End (IRE) 14-1 Miss C Cowe *Chsd ldrs; 14l 4th 12; wkng when climbed 14; wl bhnd when pu 16* . . . . . . P

OFFICIAL DISTANCES: 20*l*, 1*l* **TIME:** 6min 23.0s **TOTE:** £1.90; places £1.90,£1.40 **DF:**£3.20

537 Mixed Open, 4m, 12st - 28J 11 ran

280[P] **ROBBIE'S ADVENTURE** 20-1 **Mrs J Gordon** *A ldng trio; ld 6-10; prsd 2nd frm 19 til ld 24; made rest in narrow ld; hld on wl flat* 1
Dixon Varner (IRE) 10-1 **F Marshall** *A cl up; ld 11-23; prsd wnr rest of way; ev ch app last; kpt on game flat* 2 2
Brackenheath (IRE)(cp) 6-1 **P Hall** *Ld to 5; prsd ldr to 18; 5l 4th 21; wknd 23; kpt on frm 2 out to tk 3rd flat* 12 3
422[1] Tell The Nipper (IRE) 7-2 M Gorman *Hld up towards rr of main group; hdwy 14; 3l 3rd 21; lost tch w ldng pr frm 24; dem flat* 2 4
422[8] Alexander Nevsky 20-1 D Dennis *In tch in midfield to 18; 7th & wkng when fell 21* . . . . . . F
249[11] Garrison Friendly (IRE)(cp) 20-1 N Wilson (South) *A towards rr; lost tch 10; t.o 15 til pu 21.* . . . . . . P
332[2] Nomadic Star evensF Miss Z Lilly *Sa; 10l adrift of field when rmdrs aft 4; nvr able to gt in tch; some hdwy to 25l 5th 21; staying on to disp 15l 4th when ur 24* U
Nubro (IRE) 6-1 A Hickman *Sn lost tch; detach last frm 9; t.o & pu 16.* . . . P
Prime Course (IRE) (7x) 5-1 C Gordon *Cl up in midfield; niggled along 12; 4th when blun & ur 19* . . . . . . U
168[P] Russian Connection (IRE) 20-1 A Ward-Thomas *In tch to 12; 45l 6th 21; pu aft nxt.* . . . . . . P
249[P] Tomcappagh (IRE) (7x) 20-1 J Wall *Prom to 6; sn lost plce; rr when pu 11* P

OFFICIAL DISTANCES: 1*l*, 6*l* **TIME:** 8min 37.0s
TOTE: £20.40; places £6.00,£1.80,£2.10 **DF:**£4.90 (1+any)

538 Restricted, 12st 7 ran

152[1] **ASTHEFELLOWSAID (IRE)** 1-2F **A Hickman** *Hld up; detach last to 12; hdwy 14; trckd ldng pr 16; qcknd to ld 3 out; 6l up w rdr lkng round 2 out; easily* 1
185[1] **Kayleigh (IRE)** (5a) 7-4 **P York** *Hld up; a wl in tch; impd to jn ldr 14; ld app 3 out; sn hdd; kpt on one pce frm 2 out* 8 2
127[P] **Red Square Prince (IRE)** 14-1 **D Dunsdon** *Ld/disp to 9; cl up aft til outpcd app 3 out; some late hdwy* 3 3
Straight Baron 14-1 R Bandey *Cl up; ld/disp frm 13 til wknd qckly app 3 out; fin tired* 25 4
181[3] Kilvoydan (IRE) 3-1 D Phelan *Ur 1* . . . . . . U
181[P] Simony Sam (IRE) 14-1 J Sarchet *Ld 6-12; wknd & lost tch aft 15; pu 17.* P
419[5] Tonrin 14-1 J Sole *Cl 2nd 2 til ld 4; mist & ur 5* . . . . . . U

OFFICIAL DISTANCES: 10*l*, 1*l* **TIME:** 6min 44.0s
TOTE: £1.80; places £1.50,£2.00 **DF:**£2.60

539 Open Maiden, 12st 9 ran

BALAU (7a) 6-1 **P Bull** *Towards rr; hdwy 13; cl 4th 15; chsd ldr frm 17; stayed on to ld app 2 out; sn drew clr* 1
185[4] **The Flying Dragon** (5a)(tt) 5-1 **S Spice** *W ldrs to 6; in tch til lost plce 13; 15l 4th 18; stayed on frm 3 out; tk 2nd flat* 12 2
418[2] **Royal Cruise (IRE)** 5-4F **P York** *Hld up; hdwy 13; trckd ldng pr 15; lft in ld 17; 5l clr app 3 out; wknd rap uphill & hdd app nxt; lost 2nd cl home.* 2 3
423[F] Gale On The Lake (IRE) (5a) 5-2 P Hall *A in tch; impd to press ldr 12; lft in ld 16; fell nxt* . . . . . . F
423[4] Iconic 5-1 D Page (Kent) *Prom to 10; lsng plce when pu 13.* . . . . . . P
345[P] See Red Billdan (IRE) 10-1 J Merry *Ld/disp til rn out thro wing 16* . . . . . . R
Seymour Of Me 7-1 R Bandey *Sn lost tch; wl bhnd when pu 8* . . . . . . P
Spruce Goose (IRE) 8-1 N Wilson (South) *In tch to 12; sn wknd; t.o & pu 18* P
293[P] Wanna Be Bay (5a) 14-1 J Sole *A wl in tch; lft cl 3rd 17; wknd app 3 out; 4th & wl btn when fell nxt; winded* . . . . . . F

OFFICIAL DISTANCES: 5*l*, 2*l* **TIME:** 7min 19.0s
TOTE: £7.10; places £5.10,£-,£4.30 **DF:**£8.80 (2nd+any)

540 Confined Maiden, 12st — 9 ran

Form	Horse	Dist	Pos
220[2]	**STREET SMART (IRE)** evensF **Miss B Donnelly** *Wl in tch in 3rd/4th most of way; lft 2nd 16; hdwy app 3 out; jnd ldr nxt; ld last; drew clr flat*		1
153[P]	**Rumour Has It (IRE)** 12-1 **P Hall** *Midfield; 20l 4th 18; gd hdwy frm 3 out; tk 2nd cl home; fin wl.*	6	2
250[P]	**No Reward (IRE)** 3-1 **A Hickman** *Hld up; stdy hdwy 10; cl 4th 15; gd rn to ld app 3 out; jnd nxt; ev ch last; wknd flat.*	1	3
423[3]	Master Chief (IRE) 4-1 P Bull *Ld; clr 5-13; made rest til hdd & wknd qckly app 3 out*	20	4
130[P]	Itsthebrass (5a) 12-1 P York *A towards rr; lost tch frm 13; t.o*	fence	5
	Lightning Rebel 14-1 S Gordon-Watson *A towards rr; t.o frm 14*	fence	6
	Advanta Pride (IRE) 2-1 Mrs J Gordon *A in tch; chsd ldr frm 10; blun 12; 3l down when blun & broke hind leg 16; imm pu; dead*		P
129[P]	Bailey's Of Cashel (IRE) 4-1 D Dunsdon *Chsd ldr til wknd app 10; towards rr when pu 12*		P
172[P]	Pandeli 20-1 R Bandey *A towards rr; t.o when pu 18*		P

OFFICIAL DISTANCES: 6l, 1l **TIME:** 6min 50.0s
TOTE: £3.20; places £1.10,£2.00,£1.10 **DF:**£5.10

Stratford (LH 8F,16J)

Mon, 15 Mar (GOOD)

541 Steve Hammond Nov HC, 3m £3581 — 14 ran

Form	Horse	Dist	Pos
236[2]	**KINGSTON-BANKER** 11-10 5-4F **T Dreaper** *Lw; midfield; hit 5; went prom & gng wl app 10; hit 13; rdn to ld app 2 out; hung lft aft; hld on game; all out*		1
	Shraden Edition 12-00 20-1 **D Barlow** *Hdwy & prom 7-10; sn lost plce; 6th & outpcd app 12; rallied to cl 3rd app 2 out; hit last; stayed on game (splendid eff)*	¾	2
11[4]	**Don Royal** 12-03 20-1 **N Harris** *Prom; ld 5; hit 10; rdn & hdd 2 out; wknd last*	5	3
177[2]	Mighty Willing 11-12 3-1 G Brewer *Sis; stdy prog to chse ldrs 9; 3rd app 12; rdn 3 out; one pce app nxt.*	4	4
	Normania (NZ) 11-10 50-1 Miss S West *(xnb) Chsd ldrs; hit 7; 5th app 12; sn wknd; eased aft 2 out*	27	5
346[4]	Carbonado 12-00(tt) 10-1 Miss A Goschen *(xnb) Prom early; drpd to rr & jmpd slow 7; 11th app 12; t.o & pu 2 out*		P
239[3]	Cloudy Creek (IRE) 12-00 18-1 S Morris *(xnb) Bhnd; poor last app 12; t.o & pu 2 out*		P
314[4]	Horrified 11-10(bl) 66-1 D Edwards *Mists; midfield; strugg 10; 9th & t.o when blun 12 & pu.*		P
383[7]	I'm Dreaming (IRE) 11-12 50-1 A Martin *Prom til blun frm 8 & sn lost plce; 8th app 12; t.o & pu 2 out*		P
161[2]	Infamelia 11-05(vis) 33-1 Miss T Clark *(xnb) Mists in rr; 10th & t.o when blun 12; pu nxt.*		P
263[U]	Keltic Lord 12-03 9-1 A Charles-Jones *Ld to 5; chsd ldr to 9; 4th app 12; wknd & mist 13; poor 5th when fell 3 out*		F
164[1]	Place Above (IRE) 11-12 20-1 L Bates *Blun & ur 2*		U
48[6]	Six Clerks (IRE) 12-00(cp) 50-1 J Trice-Rolph *Fell 1*		F
247[2]	Tod's Brother 11-10 18-1 A Merriam *Numerous mists & rr mostly; 7th & no ch app 12; t.o & pu last*		P

TIME: 6min 27.9s **TOTE:** £2.50; places £1.50,£4.20,£4.40 **Ex:**£56.00 **CSF:**£33.86
Fences 3 & 11 omitted

Sedgefield (LH 8F,21J)

Tue, 16 Mar (GOOD, GOOD to SOFT patches run-in)

542 Westwood Timber HC, 3m3f £1512 — 10 ran

Form	Horse	Dist	Pos
269[3]	**SAD MAD BAD (USA)** 12-04 13-8JF **G Tuer** *Nt a fluent; hld up; 5th aft 13; outpcd nxt & sn 15l adrift; still 5th 3 out; clsd rap to ld app last; sn clr; easily*		1
429[1]	**Go Nomadic** 12-02(tt) 13-8JF **P Atkinson** *Ld til aft 13 & agn 17; hdd aft 2 out; wknd flat; fin tired*	10	2

389[7] **Who Dares Wins** 12-02 12-1 **L Bates** *Prom til hit 7; chsd ldrs til 12l 3rd & outpcd 15; hit nxt; rallied aft 3 out; one pce aft nxt* 1¼ 3
267[9] Gus Berry (IRE) 12-00 25-1 N Saville *2nd/3rd til ld aft 13; qcknd nxt; hdd 17; sn u.p; wknd app 2 out* 23 4
211[3] Noble Hymn 12-00 7-1 N Tutty *Trckd ldrs; 14l 5th & outpcd 15; went 6l 3rd u.p 3 out; sn fdd* 9 5
341[8] Commanche Spirit (IRE) 11-07 66-1 F Arthur *Detach in last pr; t.o 11; pu 14* P
349[U] Havetwotaketwo (IRE) 11-07 50-1 M Seston *2nd/3rd to 12; 4th & wkng when blun bad 14; t.o & pu 18.* . . . . P
429[6] Kilcaskin Gold (IRE) 11-11 12-1 A Findlay *Midfield; rn wide aft 5 & agn aft 13; strugg aft; t.o & pu 2 out* . . . . P
267[11] Royal Plum 11-07(bl) 33-1 S J Robinson *Midfield; rdn & strugg when hit 13; jmpd slow 16; t.o when blun nxt; ref 2 out* . . . . r
Sean's Minstrel (IRE) 11-07 33-1 M Lurcock *Sn detach last; mist 4 & went rt; t.o 11; blun & Lurcock lurched off 13* . . . . U

TIME: 7min 11.7s **TOTE:** £2.70; places £1.50,£1.10,£2.20 **Ex:**£3.60 **CSF:**£4.31

Cheltenham (LH 10F,22J)

Thu, 18 Mar (GOOD, GOOD to SOFT in places)

543 Christie's Foxhunter HC, 3m2f110y £23,200 24 ran

280[2] **EARTHMOVER (IRE)** 12-00 14-1 **Miss A Goschen** *Settled rr; stdy prog 12; mist nxt; jnd ldrs 16; ld aft 18; rdn 3 out; jnd last; battled clr flat (supremely game)* 1
Never Compromise (IRE) 12-00 9-2 **A Crowe** *Wl plcd; w ldrs frm 17; trckd wnr gng wl aft 3 out; rdn to chall & upsides last; unable to qckn flat* . . . 4 2
280[1] **County Derry** 12-00(cp) 16-1 **N Harris** *Chsd ldrs; lsng plce u.p when mist 13; hmpd 16; wl bhnd 18; stayed on str frm 2 out; tk 3rd flat* 12 3
319[1] Oneminutetofive 12-00 12-1 G Elliott *Cl up; mist 8; 3rd/4th 15 til trckd wnr gng str 19; rdn & wknd app 2 out; lost 3rd flat*. 6 4
Spot Thedifference (IRE) 12-00 8-1 J McNamara *Settled rr; eff 9; nvr on terms w ldrs; no prog & wl bhnd 18; poor 8th 19; plugged on frm 3 out* 14 5
241[5] Irbee 12-00(bl) 100-1 Miss C Tizzard *Prom; chsd ldr frm 6; nt fluent 7; chsd wnr aft 18-nxt; 2nd/4th & ev ch til wknd u.p 3 out; fin tired*. 10 6
178[P] Bright Approach (IRE) 12-00 14-1 Miss P Gundry *Mists & nvr gng particularly wl in midfield; strugg when hit 13; no ch aft; t.o.* 14 7
179[2] Torduff Express (IRE) 12-00(bl) 33-1 N Williams *Mist 2; midfield; eff 10; hit 13; jnd ldrs nxt; drvn & wknd aft 18; t.o* 10 8
346[1] Mullensgrove 12-00 100-1 Miss S Phizacklea *Rcd wide in midfield; blun 8 & drvn; sn lost plce & strugg; t.o 18.* 5 9
277[1] Polar Champ 12-00(vis) 25-1 T Malone *Ld to 2; ld 4 & set str pce; 10l clr brief 8; mist 13; hdd & wknd rap 18; t.o.* 2 10
89[2] Always On The Line (IRE) 12-00 50-1 A Merriam *Mists; towards rr when fell 9* F
Arctic Times (IRE) 12-00 14-1 W O'Sullivan *Midfield; prog 14; 10l 7th & rdn when fell 18* . . . . F
241[3] Bosuns Mate 12-00(bl) 100-1 Mrs B Keighley *A.p; ld 2-4; mist 6; 6th but lkd wkng when blun & ur 17* . . . . U
Castle Weir (IRE) 12-00 33-1 J Codd *Midfield; wkng when mists 12 & 13; t.o & pu 15* . . . . P
234[U] Charlie Strong (IRE) 12-00 66-1 A Charles-Jones *A bhnd; hmpd 9; strugg when hmpd 17; pu nxt* . . . . P
176[1] Game Gunner 12-00 50-1 Miss C Stucley *Mist 2; nr fluent 3; rcd wide & a wl in rr; rdn & toiling bad aft 12; t.o & pu 18*. . . . . P
330[4] Geordies Express 12-00 100-1 D Jewett *Mist & ur 1*. . . . . U
34[1] Lord Atterbury (IRE) 12-00 3-1F A Farrant *Trckd ldrs; nt fluent 8; blun 9; mist 10; 4th & u.p 13; sn wknd; nt fluent 15; t.o & pu 18* . . . . P
316[1d] Omni Cosmo Touch (USA) 12-00 50-1 N Saville *Reluct to rce; last when blun & ur 5*. . . . . U
Quetal (IRE) 12-00 50-1 J Young *A bhnd; t.o frm 9; pu 13* . . . . P
241[1] Red Brook Lad 12-00 14-1 N Mitchell *Mists; last when blun 2 & 3; wl bhnd til prog 13; hmpd 16; chsd ldrs vain nxt; 7th & no ch 19; t.o & pu 2 out*. . P
420[F] Sheriff's Friend (IRE) 12-00 20-1 C Gordon *Chsd ldrs til wknd 14; 9th & strugg nxt; wl bhnd when pu 18*. . . . . P

435[3] Upham Lord (IRE) 12-00 33-1 G Brewer *Hld up towards rr; prog to midfield when blun bad 15; no ch aft; t.o when fell 2 out* . . . . F
352[3] Woodlands Beau (IRE) 12-00(bl) 200-1 T Dreaper *Jb; a wl bhnd; hopeless t.o when fell 17* . . . . F

TIME: 6min 57.1s **TOTE:** £11.30; places £2.90,£2.30,£4.10 **Ex:**£48.70 **CSF:**£70.28

The stewards interviewed the trainer of Lord Atterbury who was unable to offer any explanation for the horse pulling up; they ordered it be routine tested

Fakenham (LH 6F,15J)

Fri, 19 Mar (GOOD to SOFT)

544 William Bulwer-Long Mem Nov HC, 2m5f110y £2444 10 ran

316[F] **ENITSAG (FR)** 10-13 5-2 **D Mansell** *Hld up on outer; last when mist 6; mist 7; nt fluent 9; hdwy 11; nt fluent 13; ld 2 out; sn clr; v easily* 1
Lindsay (FR) 12-00 9-4F **R Burton** *Hld up; hdwy 6; chsd ldr 9; ld app 3 out; hdd nxt; no ch w wnr; wknd & nrly dem flat* 8 2
379[5] **Kasilia (FR)** 11-02 33-1 **Miss V Simpson** *Hld up; hdwy 7; 2l 2nd app 3 out; outpcd in 8l 3rd nxt; catching runner-up flat* . . . . ½ 3
378[F] Noble Affair 10-11 10-1 M Mackley *Hld up; hdwy to ld passing omitted 10; hdd app 3 out; sn wknd; t.o* . . . . dist 4
444[P] Noble Colours 11-02(tt) 40-1 M Scales *Pulled hrd; chsd ldrs; lft 2nd 4; ld 7 til passing omitted 10; wknd rap aft blun 12; wl t.o* . . . . dist 5
447[P] Mister Falcon (FR) 11-02 33-1 S Hughes *Chsd ldrs til bd 4* . . . . B
379[9] Mustang Molly 11-01 (2ow) 33-1 A Martin *Hld up in tch; hmpd 4; rdn & wknd 11; t.o & pu last* . . . . P
Rooster 11-02 9-1 A Braithwaite *Ld til fell 4* . . . . F
Round The Bend 11-02 9-1 Miss L Allan *Keen in 2nd til lft in ld 4; hdd 7; wknd rap 9; sn pu* . . . . P
377[2] Supreme Silence (IRE) 11-02 11-2 Miss Rachel Clark *Ss; sn wl t.o; pu 2 out* P

TIME: 5min 55.5s **TOTE:** £3.00; places £1.90,£1.10,£5.10 **Ex:**£9.70 **CSF:**£8.54

Fence 10 omitted

Ascot (RH 10F,14J)

Sat, 20 Mar (GOOD to SOFT)

545 Silwood Park Nurseries Mahonia HC, 2m3f110y £2170 7 ran

SIKANDER A AZAM 11-11 11-4F **T Greenall** *Hld up in rr; stdy hdwy 11; trckd ldrs 3 out; went 2nd nxt; sn ld; pushed clr flat; rdly* 1
406[1] **Bold Tactics (IRE)** 11-07 7-2 **M Keel** *Trckd ldrs; ld 11; 4l clr aft 3 out; rdn & hdd aft nxt; sn no ch w wnr* 10 2
347[4] **Miss O'Grady (IRE)** 11-06 4-1 **T Dreaper** *Hld up in rr; hdwy 10; 3l 3rd 12; drvn & minimal resp frm nxt; no imp aft* 2 3
441[2] Guignol Du Cochet (FR) 11-09 5-1 D Mansell *Bhnd; last 10; rdn 3 out; some prog frm nxt; nvr rchd ldrs* 3 4
348[7] Chicago City (IRE) 12-00 9-2 D Dunsdon *Ld; slt mist 7 & rdr nrly f.o both sides; hld slt advant til hdd 11; wknd tame aft 3 out; mist last* 4 5
445[8] Cedar Chief 11-07(bl) 33-1 G Gallagher *Chsd ldrs; hit 3; 4th when blun 12; wknd qckly* 15 6
348[P] Alpha Centauri (IRE) 11-07 50-1 M Sheridan *Prom; nt fluent 8; blun 9; 5th & wkng when mist 11; t.o when fell 2 out* . . . . F

TIME: 5min 13.6s **TOTE:** £3.00; places £2.00,£2.20 **Ex:**£10.00 **CSF:**£11.73

Fences 3 & 13 omitted; the rider of Alpha Centauri was suspended for six days for failing to pull up and then falling on a clearly exhausted horse

Newcastle (LH 11F,18J)

Sat, 20 Mar (HEAVY)

546 Unison/NHS HC, 3m £1904 6 ran

179[3] **THE BUTTERWICK KID** 11-06(bl) 6-4F **Richard Tate** *Cl up; ld 10; drew clr app 2 out; unchall* 1
330[3] **Primitive Way** 11-09(cp) 7-1 **P Maitland-Carew** *Prom; pckd 11; outpcd 14; 12l 3rd 3 out; went 2nd at last; no ch w wnr* 12 2

391[1] **Mr Mahdlo** 11-03 5-2 **B Woodhouse** *Chsd ldrs; nt fluent 12; sn drvn; eff to jn wnr 15; outpcd aft nxt; wknd & dem flat* 3 3
349[2] Boulta (IRE) 11-05(cp) 10-1 M McAlister *Ld to 10; rdn when pckd 11; prsd wnr to 14; wknd qckly app nxt; t.o & fin v tired* . . . . dist 4
428[1] Parade Racer 11-13 5-1 O Nelmes *Ref to rce; tk no part*. . . . . r
541[U] Place Above (IRE) 11-03 20-1 M Seston *Ref to rce; tk no part*. . . . . r

TIME: 6min 53.1s **TOTE:** £1.70; places £1.50,£2.80 **Ex:**£17.60 **CSF:**£11.53

Fences 10 & 11 omitted

Duke of Buccleuch's

Friars Haugh (LH 7F,15J)

Sat, 20 Mar (SOFT)

547 Hunt Members 4 ran

285[2] **DR DEDUCTIBLE**(cp) 2-1 **R Brown** *Ld; 1l up 6; 2l ahd 8; lft virt solo 10; 20l up aft; 15l up 3 out-nxt; unchall* 1
427[1] **Crevamoy (IRE)** (5a) 2-1 **J Galbraith** *Oht; rdr v novicey; jmpd big 2; last 3 til 10l 3rd 7; lft 20l 2nd & sltly hmpd 10; still 15l 2nd 2 out; rdn & r.o flat; nvr plcd to chall* 6 2
506[5] **Wishful Thinker**(tt) 14-1 **Miss K Scott** *Cl 3rd early; dem 12l last 8; outpcd & no ch when lft 25l 3rd 10; kpt on frm 3 out*. 15 3
Natiain (7a) evensF A Richardson *Trckd ldr in cl 2nd til fell 10; rmtd fnce bhnd; 40l last when tired & mist 3 out; t.o & pu aft 2 out (mistakenly plcd 4th by Judge)*. . . . . P

OFFICIAL DISTANCES: 7*l*, 15*l* **TIME:** 7min 24.0s

Racing was put back 30 mins because of high winds; fences 2 (9 & 16) were omitted from all races - state of the ground

548 Restricted 10 ran

342[1] **EIGHTY DAYS (IRE)** (7a) 6-1 **Miss R Davidson** *(xnb) Sn mid-div; 7l 7th 8; prog 13 & 4l 2nd 3 out; lkd hld til stayed on wl to ld app last; rdn clr flat* 1
430[2] **Highland Brig** 2-1F **K Anderson** *Lw; trckd ldr til ld aft 5; sn 5l clr; 4l up 3 out; tired & hit nxt; lkd wnr til hdd app last; wknd flat*. 2 2
427[U] **Anotherhandyman** 6-1 **Miss S Gledson** *Sn lost tch; 30l 8th 7; nd but kpt on past btn horses frm 3 out; tk 3rd flat* . . . . runin 3
287[1] Superstar Express (IRE)(tt) 6-1 A Findlay *(xnb) Prom in 3rd/4th til outpcd 12; 10l 3rd 2 out; wknd nxt; dem flat; fin v tired* 8 4
431[U] Little John 5-1 A Richardson *Trckd ldrs; 4l 4th 7; outpcd aft 12; 12l 4th & wkng 3 out; tired & climbed last; walked in* 25 5
330[P] Another Justice (IRE) 14-1 R Westwood *Fat; a rr; 25l last app 2; t.o 6; 2 fncs bhnd 9; pu 3 out* . . . . P
Good Morning (5a) 10-1 R Dickson *A rr; t.o 6; fnce bhnd 8; climbed 11 & 12; jmpd slow nxt & pu*. . . . . P
286[1] Hervey Bay (5a) 6-1 W Goldie *(xnb) Ld til hdd aft 5; 2l 2nd 10; wknd qckly aft 12; pu nxt*. . . . . P
430[7] Shylock (IRE) 8-1 C Storey *Chsd ldrs; 6l 5th app 8; sn strugg; 15l 4th 11; pu aft nxt*. . . . . P
431[F] Timberley(tt) 4-1 T Oates *Chsd ldrs; nt jw & sn lsng tch; 25l 7th 7; t.o & pu aft 12*. . . . . P

OFFICIAL DISTANCES: 2*l*, 25*l* **TIME:** 7min 15.7s

549 Panacur/TBA PPORA Club Members Maiden Mares, 12st 8 ran

432[2] **RIVER ALDER** (5a) 4-6F **C Storey** *Trckd ldrs; 3l 3rd 2; prog to chall 3 out; ld nxt; sn clr; stayed on*. 1
433[F] **Stanwick Gypsy** (5a) 9-4 **C Shirley-Beavan** *Ld til jnd 3 out; hdd nxt; sn 3l down & btn; kpt on one pce*. 8 2
286[P] **Chase The Moon** (5a) 6-1 **Miss L Hislop** *Trckd ldr; 8l 2nd 7; outpcd 12; sn wknd; 20l 3rd & no ch 3 out* 25 3
215[P] Posh Stick (5a) 5-1 J Walton *A rr & nd; 15l last 1; 25l 4th 3 out*. 3½ 4
433[R] Reeker Pike (5a) 8-1 W Goldie *Trckd ldrs; 6l 4th 3; outpcd 10; sn lost tch; t.o 3 out* . . . . runin 5

Another Daffodil (5a) 7-1 Miss J Hollands *A rr; jmpd slow 1; 15l last 7; sn lost tch; pu 10* . . . P

286U Blackhill Princess (5a)(bl) 8-1 K Anderson *(bf) Bckwd; in tch; 6l 4th 8; outpcd aft; wknd & pu 12* . . . P

2864 Tallaburn (5a) 5-1 A Findlay *Towards rr; 12l 7th & outpcd 7; sn wknd; lost tch & pu 2 out* . . . P

OFFICIAL DISTANCES: 10*l*, dist **TIME:** 7min 24.8s

Detroit Sam withdrawn - ur going down & rider injured

550 Gerrard Ladies Open 6 ran

428P **PHARMISTICE (IRE)** 3-1 **Miss N Stirling** *(xnb) 2 handlers; ld/2nd to 6; 8l 3rd 12; prog to 2l 3rd nxt; chall 2 out; ld app last; stayed on* . . . 1

2133 **Dere Street** 6-4F **Miss R Davidson** *Handy in 2nd/3rd til ½l 2nd 3 out; kpt on wl; nt pce to chall* . . . 2½ 2

5081 **In Demand** 5-1 **Miss J Balmer** *Vied for ld til ld aft 5; 5l up when hit 9 & rdr lost iron; prsd 3 out; jnd nxt; hdd & no ex app last* . . . 2½ 3

284P Miss Portcello (5a) 5-2 Miss J Hollands *Chsd ldrs; 4½l 5th 7; 7l 4th 9; outpcd 12; 20l 4th & jmpd slow 3 out; fin wl* . . . 25 4

4288 Houselope Beck 16-1 Miss A Wanless *(xnb) In tch; 6l 5th app 2; 4l 4th to 7; outpcd 12 & sn nd; 25l 5th 3 out* . . . 5 5

5064 Try A Bluff (IRE) 10-1 Miss E McWilliam *(bf) A rr; 20l last aft 1; t.o 8; fnce bhnd nxt* . . . 30 6

OFFICIAL DISTANCES: 3*l*, 2*l* **TIME:** 7min 13.2s

551 Mens Open 5 ran

429F **JUST BARNEY BOY** evensF **A Waugh** *Ww in last; 15l last 9; prog to 12l 3rd aft 3 out; 6l 2nd app nxt; ld app last; rdn clr flat; wl rdn* . . . 1

2111 **Dun Rose** (5a, 2ow) 7-4 **T Oates** *Lw; oht; cl 2nd til jnd ldr aft 6; ld aft 12; qcknd 10l clr aft nxt; prsd 14 til hdd app last; hrd rdn & nt qckn flat* . . 1 2

4261 **Meander (IRE)**(cp) 5-2 **J Mactaggart** *Trckd ldrs; cl up til 3l 2nd 13; sn 10l down & outpcd; no imp & dem app 3 out* . . . 12 3

4396 Charlieadams (IRE) (4ow) 12-1 J Muir *Ld to 3; handy in 3rd/4th til 8l 4th & wkng 12; releg 12l last app 2 out; walked in* . . . runin 4

429B Falcon's Flame (USA) 6-1 R Green *(xnb) Prom ld aft 3; jnd aft 6; ld agn 9 til hdd & outpcd aft 12; 10l 4th app 2 out; wknd qckly; pu last* . . . P

OFFICIAL DISTANCES: 1*l*, 25*l* **TIME:** 7min 16.0s

552 Confined, 12st 5 ran

4262 **CLIFFORD BAY (IRE)** 4-6F **Miss N Stirling** *(xnb) 2 handlers; oht; ld 2; nvr more than 2l up til hdd aft 3 out; rallied nxt; ld agn last; rdn clr flat* . . . 1

2102 **Dun Victory** (3x) 6-4 **T Oates** *Rr; 6l last 2; 4l 3rd 4; prog to disp 1l 2nd 7; 12l 2nd 12; drvn to ld aft nxt; prsd 2 out; hdd last; no ex* . . . 2½ 2

426U **Piper's Rock (IRE)** 8-1 **Miss V Russell** *(xnb) Ld to 2; cl 2nd til 3rd 9; 8l 3rd & wkng 3 out; sn btn* . . . 25 3

5063 Across The Card 8-1 C Ramsay *(xnb) A rr; 5l 4th 2; last 7; detach 12; 20l 4th & no imp aft 3 out* . . . 1½ 4

Olympic Storm (IRE) 8-1 J Alexander *(xnb) Pulling; chsd ldrs in 3rd/4th; 7l 4th 10; 5l 3rd & hdwy when bad mist nxt; pu aft 12* . . . P

OFFICIAL DISTANCES: 1½*l*, dist **TIME:** 7min 22.9s

553 Confined Maiden (Div 1), 12st 8 ran

CAPYBARA (IRE) 5-4F **F Arthur** *Mid-div; 6l 5th 2; prog to ld aft 10-3 out; lft 2l clr agn nxt; kpt on wl; eased nr fin* . . . 1

510U **Birkwood** (7a) 6-4 **C Storey** *Arrived in padd rce early; mid-div; 10l off pce 6; prog to 4l 3rd 3 out; eff & lft 2l 2nd & ev ch nxt; a hld* . . . 1 2

Lord Lane 5-1 **Miss N Stirling** *Opened 6s; ld; hit 6 & hdd brief; hdd aft 10; drpd to 8l 4th 3 out; lft 10l 3rd nxt; stayed on str app last; nt quite rch ldrs* nk 3

4255 St Bee (3ow) 8-1 T Scott *Prom; 1l 2nd 5; 3l 3rd 10; 10l 5th & outpcd 3 out; plodded on* . . . 20 4

433P Chief Seattle (IRE) 5-1 J Tate *Mists in rr; jmpd v slow & nrly stpd 7; t.o & pu aft 11* . . . P

511P Gladys (5a) 10-1 S Huggan *(xnb) Prom; ld brief 6; sn hdd; wknd qckly & sn strugg; hit 11; pu nxt* . . . P

287U I'm Willie's Girl (5a) 4-1 Miss J Riding *Hdstrng; chsd ldrs; 4l 4th 3-5; went 1l 2nd 12; ld aft nxt; ½l up & ev ch when mist & ur 2 out* . . . . U
The Midnite Grocer 8-1 R Westwood *(xnb) Fat; jmpd v slow 1; sn detach; t.o & pu 3 out* . . . . P

OFFICIAL DISTANCES: 1*l*, ½*l* **TIME:** 7min 29.6s

554 Confined Maiden (Div 2), 12st — 6 ran

DECENT BOND (IRE) 7-1 **R Green** *Chsd clr ldrs; 42l 3rd 7; 21l 3rd & gd hdwy app 12; went cl 2nd 2 out; ld app last; rdn clr flat* 1
286² **Rutherford** 2-1JF **T Oates** *(xnb) Trckd clr ldrs in 4th mostly; went 8l 4th app 2 out; prsd ldr til hung & one pce app last* 6 2
Redhouse Chevalier (7a) 5-2 **C Storey** *Ld brief; sn chsng runaway ldr; 40l 2nd 7; 20l 2nd 3 out; drvn to ld brief 2 out; sn btn*. 12 3
431³ Try Me And See 2-1JF G Crow *Sn ld & clr; fnce ahd 9; mist 11; 20l clr app 3 out; sn hdd & wknd rap; fin tired* 3 4
433⁴ Red Jupiter 5-1 A Findlay *A rr; 15l 5th 3; 22l 5th nxt; wl bhnd & 50l 5th 7; t.o & pu 3 out*. . . . . P
432P Suny Henry 10-1 J Tate *(xnb) Unruly gng down; sis; a detach last; 52l last 7; t.o & pu 2 out* . . . . P

OFFICIAL DISTANCES: 4*l*, 7*l* **TIME:** 7min 25.8s

Fitzwilliam (Milton)

Cottenham (RH 9F,19J)

Sat, 20 Mar (GOOD)

555 Hunt Members, 12st — 4 ran

223P **STICK OR BUST**(cp) 3-1 **M Smith** *Ld/disp til ld 15; rdn & drew clr app 2 out; rdn out* 1
375P **Lord Montagu (IRE)**(cp) 3-1 **N Walker** *Ld/disp to 15; prsd wnr til aft 3 out; btn nxt* 12 2
386³ **Marciano** evensF **Miss L Allan** *Nvr gng wl; a 3rd/4th; mist & rmdr 9; rdn 13; mist 3 out; kpt on one pce aft* 1 3
Sea Victor 12-1 M Grange *A 3rd/4th; 7l 3rd 3 out; no imp aft; dem app last* 6 4

OFFICIAL DISTANCES: 15*l*, ¾*l* **TIME:** 6min 31.0s **TOTE:** £5.90 **DF:**£4.60

556 Confined, 12st — 5 ran

376¹ **ALGAN (FR)** (3x) 4-7F **P York** *Disp ld 7 til ld app 14; 2l up 2 out; pushed out flat; comf* 1
376F **Lord Euro (IRE)** (3x) 2-1 **A Merriam** *Mist 1; prom; ld 6-7; chsd wnr app 14; 2l down 2 out; no imp flat*. 5 2
381P **Merry Minstrel (IRE)** 20-1 **L Hicks** *2 handlers; tde; tk keen hld; chsd ldrs; blun 10; 4th & outpcd 13; sn no ch; went poor 3rd at last*. 25 3
376³ Leatherback (IRE) 10-1 J Owen *Prom; disp ld 7 til app 13; 3rd & strugg when blun bad 16; no ch aft; dem app last* 12 4
479P Zabadi (IRE) 33-1 Miss R Napier *Ld 2; clr nxt; hdd 6; sn bhnd; t.o frm 14 til ur 3 out* . . . . U

OFFICIAL DISTANCES: 4*l*, 25*l* **TIME:** 6min 24.0s **TOTE:** £1.70 **DF:**£1.80

557 Mens Open — 9 ran

374³ **MILITAIRE (FR)** 4-1 **J Owen** *7s-4s; tk keen hld; in tch; prsd ldr 14; ld app last; sn clr; eased nr fin*. 1
464P **Bush Hill Bandit (IRE)** 7-2 **H Fowler** *Ww; prog & in tch 11 4l 3rd 15; outpcd app 2 out; went 2nd flat; no ch w wnr*. 10 2
397² **The Red Boy (IRE)** 5-4F **A Braithwaite** *Ww; prog 11; 6l 5th 16; went 2nd brief last; nvr nr wnr* 2 3
478P Fine Times(tt) 8-1 M Mackley *Chsd ldrs; disp ld 9; clr w wnr aft 3 out; hdd app last; wknd* 12 4
Catchphrase 33-1 R Armson *(xnb) Ww in rr; 8l 6th 13; outpcd nxt; no ch 3 out; kpt on flat*. 3 5
Vital Issue (IRE) 14-1 P Johnson *Ld 2-5; bhnd frm 10; no ch 14* 25 6

Form	Runner	Dist	Pos
397^{5}	Polo Ridge (IRE) 33-1 A Sansome *In tch when mist 7; bhnd 10; no ch 14.*	12	7
381^{8}	Easby Blue 33-1 R Dobney *Cl up; ld 5-9; wkng when blun 11; sn bhnd; pu 15*		P
520^{2}	Village Copper(bl) 10-1 C Ward-Thomas *Cl up til wknd app 3 out; 6th & no ch when pu last*		P

OFFICIAL DISTANCES: 8*l*, 1*l* **TIME:** 6min 28.0s **TOTE:** £5.00 **DF:**£11.10

558 Ladies Open — 12 ran

Form	Runner	Dist	Pos
246^{5}	**HIGHLAND ROSE (IRE)** (5a) 8-1 **Ms A Embiricos** *(xnb) Chsd ldrs; 4th ½way; ld app 13; sn kicked clr; unchall aft; r.o str*		1
373^{2}	**Spring Gale (IRE)** 6-4JF **Miss Z Turner** *Tde; ww rr of main group; 6th ½way; chsd wnr aft 13; 10l down 16; wl btn nxt*	35	2
	Free 6-4JF **Miss Gemma Hutchinson** *Ld to 5 & 9 til app 13; 3rd & outpcd nxt; no ch aft; kpt on flat.*	6	3
157^{5}	Mackoy (IRE) 40-1 Miss H Hall *Rcd wide; prom; ld 5-9; outpcd app 13; 4th & no ch frm 15*	7	4
380^{5}	Bruan (IRE)(cp) 33-1 Miss J Bevin *Chsd ldrs; 8th ½way; sn lost tch; no ch 14*	12	5
466^{U}	Maltby Son 25-1 Miss K Branson *Wl bhnd til stayed on frm 3 out; nvr nrr.*	½	6
399^{2}	Hay Dance 12-1 Miss L Barrett-Nobbs *(xnb) Prom; 3rd ½way; outpcd app 13; sn no ch; lost 2 plces nr fin*	nk	7
522^{3}	Grand Ambition (USA)(cp) 10-1 Miss L Allan *In tch; 6th ½way; outpcd 12; no ch frm 14*	12	8
399^{4}	Catherine's Way (IRE) 20-1 Miss L Marriott *Wl bhnd frm 7; t.o.*	10	9
	Lateen (5a) 40-1 Miss L Collinson *(xnb) A bhnd; t.o frm 13*	30	10
	Ruth's Boy (IRE) 33-1 Miss N McGoldrick *1st ride; a bhnd; t.o when ur 16*		U
380^{6}	Sheskinqueen (IRE) (5a) 40-1 Miss A Wells *Ww rr of main group; 7th ½way; same & no ch when ur 15*		U

OFFICIAL DISTANCES: dist, 5*l* **TIME:** 6min 13.0s **TOTE:** £5.10 **DF:**£6.10

559 Restricted, 12st — 10 ran

Form	Runner	Dist	Pos
	ARCHBISHOP(cp) 3-1 **S Morris** *(xnb) Chsd ldrs; 4l 4th 13; ld 15; made rest; drew clr flat.*		1
294^{P}	**Morph** 5-2 **P York** *Prog to trck ldrs 7; ld 14-nxt; w wnr 2 out til hung lft & wknd flat.*	12	2
398^{7}	**Lambrini King (IRE)** 33-1 **Miss L Barrett-Nobbs** *(xnb) Mid-div; outpcd 13; lft poor 4th 2 out; went 3rd nr fin.*	40	3
371^{1}	Germany Park (IRE) 6-4F M Smith *(xnb) Tchd 2s; 2 handlers; ld; mist 9; hdd 14; rdn & wknd 16; lft poor 3rd 2 out; dem nr fin.*	½	4
383^{P}	Libido 33-1 P Andrew *Last frm 6; t.o frm 11*	25	5
	Albarden 12-1 N Pearce *Bhnd; prog & 8l 7th 11; sn rdn & lost tch; pu 14*		P
398^{4}	Hollyhock (5a) 10-1 P Taiano *(xnb) Mid-div; in tch til ur 9.*		U
398^{6}	Josh's Choice (IRE) 12-1 A Braithwaite *A bhnd; lost tch 12; pu aft 13*		P
245^{1}	Magic Lodge (7a) 8-1 R Stearn *Chsd ldrs; ev ch 3 out; cl 3rd when fell nxt*		F
181^{5}	Zafan (IRE)(cp) 25-1 M Mackley *Prom; rdn 10; bhnd frm 13; t.o & pu 3 out*		P

OFFICIAL DISTANCES: 10*l*, dist **TIME:** 6min 26.0s **TOTE:** £4.30 **DF:**£4.50

560 Open Maiden (Div 1) — 12 ran

Form	Runner	Dist	Pos
401^{2}	**TARTAR SABRE** 4-1 **Miss L Barrett-Nobbs** *Chsd ldrs; lft in ld 16; rn wide & jnd app last; forged ahd last 50yds*		1
218^{P}	**Tooley Park** 5-1 **N Pearce** *In tch; 3rd & ev ch 3 out; w wnr last; no ex last 50yds*	nk	2
226^{F}	**Kissed By Moonlite** (5a) 20-1 **R Armson** *(xnb) Ww; prog & in tch 13; wknd app 3 out; t.o.*	50	3
105^{5}	Alfie Moon (IRE)(tt) 3-1 S Morris *Trckd ldrs; hmpd & lost plce 11; bhnd 13 til pu 15*		P
367^{P}	Brer Bear (7a) 8-1 D Barlow *2 handlers; last frm 4; t.o 7 til pu 11.*		P
525^{P}	Carvilla (IRE) 5-1 C Gordon *Tk keen hld; prom; ld 10 til app 13; 2nd & ev ch 3 out; wknd rap nxt; pu last*		P
371^{P}	Divine Mist (IRE) 8-1 J Owen *Jmpd rt; ww in mid-div; prog to ld app 13; just ahd when fell 16*		F
	Ernford Smokinjoe 33-1 A Braithwaite *(bf) Ld 3 til rn wide & hdd app 10; jb lft nxt; bhnd & jmpd lft 12; pu 13*		P
401^{F}	Lightning Fork (IRE) (5a) 2-1F T Lane *Ww in mid-div; jnd ldrs gng wl 11; ev ch 16; 4th & btn nxt; blun 2 out & pu*		P

Form	Runner	Dist	Pos
244^{P}	Looking Magic (IRE) 20-1 M Mackley *Chsd ldrs; 5th & wkng aft 16; pu nxt*		P
462^{P}	Sandyland 25-1 A Sansome *Chsd ldrs to 10; sn bhnd; pu 16*		P
401^{P}	Straw Exchange (12a) 25-1 P Chinery *A bhnd; lost tch 11; t.o & pu 3 out*		P

OFFICIAL DISTANCES: nk, dist **TIME:** 6min 33.0s **TOTE:** £13.70 **DF:**£14.50

561 Open Maiden (Div 2) — 12 ran

Form	Runner	Dist	Pos
476^{5}	**TROUBLESHOOTER** 7-4F **M Mackley** *Made virt all; 5l clr 15; mist 2 out; rdn & kpt on flat*		1
	Dream On Then (5a) 3-1 **J Newbold** *14s-3s; 2 handlers; keen; cl up; mist 11; 3l 2nd 3 out; rdn & wandered app last; no imp flat*	6	2
152^{F}	**Conquistador (IRE)** 4-1 **N Moore** *Chsd ldrs; 3rd & blun 13; 5l 3rd 3 out; outpcd app nxt; kpt on agn flat*	4	3
	Memsahib Ki Behan (5a) 10-1 H Fowler *Chsd ldrs til outpcd 13; no ch 16; hung lft flat*	20	4
375^{5}	Granny Dick (5a) 14-1 T Messenger *Nvr trbld ldrs*	20	5
444^{8}	Codys Castle 16-1 R Collinson *Prom; ld brief 4; wknd 13; t.o & pu 3 out*		P
463^{U}	Joves Shadow 3-1 T Lane *In tch; blun 6; pckd 11; 5th & rdn 13; sn outpcd; no ch when pu 15*		P
463^{P}	Letsgeton (5a) 10-1 A Sansome *2 handlers; a bhnd; pu 10*		P
123^{F}	Mr Know What (IRE) 10-1 Miss C Bartlett *Sn wl bhnd; t.o & pu 11*		P
244^{P}	She's A Terror (12a) 12-1 C Ward-Thomas *(xnb) 2 handlers; chsd ldrs to 8; bhnd when pu 11*		P
385^{P}	Silver Styx (7a) 10-1 J Docker *Ww; 8th when fell 9*		F
154^{4}	Waterliner (12a) 4-1 A Merriam *A bhnd; t.o & pu 3 out*		P

OFFICIAL DISTANCES: 5*l*, 2*l* **TIME:** 6min 30.0s **TOTE:** £2.30 **DF:**£14.20

Hurworth

Hutton Rudby (LH 8F,20J)
Sat, 20 Mar (SOFT)

562 Hunt Members, 12st — 3 ran

Form	Runner	Dist	Pos
389^{2}	**MAITRE DE MUSIQUE (FR)** (10x) 1-2F **M Tate** *Ld; 2-3l up til blun 16; hdd nxt; sn 4l down & lkd hld; clsd to 1½l 2nd at last; tired & wandered flat; passed exhaust ldr 75yds out; sn clr*		1
391^{P}	**Welsh March (IRE)** 6-4 **N Tutty** *Jw mostly; trckd wnr til ld 17; 4l clr nxt; lkd in comm til wknd last; exhaust & hdd flat; walked over line*	5	2
391^{P}	**Baby John (IRE)** 10-1 **Miss L Horner** *A last; in tch til outpcd 15; 20l bhnd 3 out; kpt on wl frm nxt; clsd on exhaust 2nd flat*	2	3

OFFICIAL DISTANCES: 5*l*, 2*l* **TIME:** 7min 11.0s

563 Restricted — 12 ran

Form	Runner	Dist	Pos
268^{3}	**JOURNEY** 6-1 **N Tutty** *Jw; sn prom; disp ld 4 til ld app 3 out; made rest; r.o str frm 2 out*		1
316^{7}	**Orleans (IRE)**(bl) 10-1 **S J Robinson** *Pulled hrd; a ldng trio; chsd wnr in 3rd 3 out-last; kpt on; went 2nd flat*	3½	2
395^{1}	**Mister Bromley** 2-1 **Miss S Brotherton** *(xnb) Hld up in rr; hdwy to 3l 6th app 14; went 2nd 3 out; ev ch app last; no ex; dem flat*	1½	3
57^{6}	Colonel Ludlow (IRE)(tt) 14-1 G Brewer *Ld; jnd 4-17; releg 4th 3 out; 6l down nxt; fdd app last*	15	4
481^{P}	Abinger 20-1 M Morley *Prom; 2l 3rd app 14; wknd stdly frm nxt; 6th & wl btn 3 out; lft poor 5th at last*	12	5
211^{P}	Oaklands Ted 20-1 T Glass *A bhnd; 5l 7th app 14; plugged on same pce frm 16; no ch frm 3 out*	3	6
430^{F}	Jupiter's Fancy (5a) 3-1 M Coglan *Nvr gng wl; lost tch 4; wl bhnd aft; t.o frm 15*	1	7
341^{P}	Son Of Sam 5-1 L Bates *Sa & a wl bhnd; hopeless t.o frm 15*	20	8
341^{5}	Agent Provocateur (NZ) 14-1 R Clark *(xnb) In rr of main group; strugg frm 12; 10l 8th app 14; lost tch & pu 17*		P
503^{B}	In The Van(cp) 20-1 J Morley *Tde; prom brief 5; in rr by 7; 10½l 9th app 14; wl bhnd frm nxt; t.o & pu last*		P

341[2] Just Fluster 6-4F S Charlton *Midfield; 2½l 5th app 14; outpcd app 3 out; 10l 5th nxt til fell last.* . . . F
Sylcanny (5a) 10-1 S Gibbon *A rr; 16l 10th & strugg app 14; tlng off when pu 15* . . . P

OFFICIAL DISTANCES: 5*l*, 2*l* **TIME:** 7min 12.0s

564 Ladies Open — 8 ran

502[1] **TEXAS RANGER** 4-5F **Miss J Foster** *Made all; 10-15l clr to 12; 3l up 14 til qcknd clr app last; easily* . . . 1
389[4] **Emperor's Son** 11-4 **Miss S Brotherton** *(xnb) Hld up; hdwy to 16l 3rd 7; 10l 2nd 11; prog 14; chsd wnr til outpcd app last* . . . 10 2
428[6] **Hessac (FR)** 16-1 **Miss W Gibson** *Disp 3rd to 7; lost plce & rr by 10; 25l 5th app 14; no hdwy til r.o frm 3 out; tk poor 3rd at last* . . . 25 3
506[6] Dannicus 20-1 Miss C Metcalfe *Tk keen hld; disp 3rd to 6; 20l 4th app 14; lft 30l 3rd 16; 45l bhnd 3 out; plodded on; releg last app last* . . . 15 4
389[10] Choice Cut (IRE) 66-1 Miss K Pickersgill *A last pr; 30l last app 14; rem frm 3 out til pu & dism last; collapsed & died in box park* . . . P
Miorbhail 50-1 Miss T Gray *Chsd ldr in 10-15l 2nd 3-10; wknd rap 11-12; last when mist 13 & pu* . . . P
502[3] Sally Scally (5a) 7-2 Miss T Jackson *(xnb) Last & wl off pce; hdwy app 11; went 20l 3rd nxt; wknd 14; wl bhnd when pu 16* . . . P
270[5] Wandering Wild (5a)(cp) 16-1 Mrs L Ward *Jmpd big & sent rdr into orbit 1* U

OFFICIAL DISTANCES: 15*l*, 25*l* **TIME:** 7min 02.0s

565 Land Rover Mens Open, 12st — 7 ran

436[U] **IMPS WAY** (5a) 7-4 **L Bates** *A gng wl; trckd ldng pr; went 2nd 7; ld 14; 10l clr 16; 15l ahd 2 out; unchall.* . . . 1
501[F] **Mademist Sam** 4-7F **N Tutty** *In tch in rr; went 3rd 11; pushed along in 4l 3rd app 14; 2nd nxt; sn outpcd & chsd wnr vain aft; 15l down last; eased flat* 25 2
478[P] Bowfell (5a)(bl) 14-1 G Brewer *(xnb) Prom; ld 5-13; 2nd nxt; wknd rap aft 15; 40l 3rd when pu 3 out* . . . P
501[U] Hadeqa 20-1 S Charlton *Last pr but wl in tch to 13; disp 13l 5th app nxt; sn wl bhnd; lft rem 3rd & pu 3 out* . . . P
389[F] Heather Lad 25-1 N Smith *Ld to 4; cl up til wknd 7; last by 10; lsng tch 12; 20l last when pu 14* . . . P
391[P] Londolozi Lad (IRE) (7a, 7x) 12-1 P Kinsella *(xnb) In tch til wknd 13; disp 13l 5th app nxt; wkng when ur 15* . . . U
389[P] Notation (IRE) 33-1 R Clark *Handy in 3rd/4th; 9l 4th & wkng when pu 14.* P

OFFICIAL DISTANCE: dist **TIME:** 7min 10.0s

The rest of the meeting was abandoned due to continuing high winds

Lamerton

Kilworthy (LH 8F,18J)

Sat, 20 Mar (SOFT becoming tacky)

566 Hunt Members, 12st — 4 ran

315[2] **BUTLER DIDIT** (5a) 1-2F **L Jefford** *(bf) Tchd 4-7; ld frm 2; went 6l clr 14; blun bad 2 out; r.o; drvn out* . . . 1
412[4] **Damiens Pride (IRE)** 5-2 **T Dennis** *(xnb) Settled 3rd; in tch; disp 2nd frm 3 out; 2nd & ev ch aft nxt; one pce* . . . 5 2
Lydford Castle 9-2 **L Heard** *Lw; a.p; ld to 2; disp 2nd frm 3 out; last & no ex frm nxt* . . . 2½ 3
417[P] Lamerton Quest 20-1 L Rowe *Bckwd; lost tch 10; t.o & pu 12* . . . P

OFFICIAL DISTANCES: 2*l*, 1*l* **TIME:** 6min 52.0s

567 Confined Maiden (Div 1), 12st — 13 ran

328[2] **ZAKLEY** 2-1F **A Farrant** *(xnb) Lw; ld/disp; ½l 2nd 2 out; ld app last; drvn clr flat* . . . 1
329[F] **Kyalami (FR)** 4-1 **Mrs M Hand** *Ld/disp; slt advant aft 15; hdd aft 2 out; 1½l 2nd last; sn outpcd; r.o agn cl home* . . . 2 2
194[2] **Albamart Wood**(tt) 3-1 **J Young** *(xnb) Lw; chsd ldng pr frm 9; 20l 3rd 12; clsd sltly frm 3 out; no ch w ldrs* . . . 10 3

309^{2} Simply Bruno(hd) 9-2 R Woollacott *(xnb) Opened 5s; sn rr; some hdwy to 6th 11; no ch w ldrs frm 15* . . . 30 4
Abbey's Girl (IRE) (5a) 20-1 D McKenna *Midfield; bhnd frm 10 til pu 14.* . . P
328^{P} Calinash (IRE) 14-1 I Hambley *(xnb) Prom; 10l 3rd 7; lost ground frm 10; bhnd & pu 15* . . . P
486^{P} Indian Renegade (IRE) (5a) 20-1 D Edwards *Midfield; prog to 18l 5th 10; lost ground frm nxt; bhnd & pu 15* . . . P
King Tudor 25-1 M Woodward *Bhnd frm 10 til pu 13* . . . P
Lilabet (5a) 8-1 Miss C Prouse *Lw; towards rr; bhnd 10 til pu 13* . . . P
148^{P} Mo's O Friendly 33-1 M Munrowd *5th $\frac{1}{2}$way; lost ground stdly frm 11; t.o & pu 3 out* . . . P
306^{3} Nditlir (12a) 7-1 C Heard *Sn rr; bhnd til pu 13* . . . P
469^{5} Tarpon Tale (IRE) 14-1 Miss D Clark *(xnb) Some hdwy to 4th when ur 9* . . U
312^{P} Vero Beach(vis) 12-1 A Charles-Jones *Prom; jmpd into at 2; pu nxt.* . . . P

OFFICIAL DISTANCES: 2*l*, 8*l* **TIME:** 6min 51.0s

568 Confined Maiden (Div 2), 12st — 9 ran

RAREGEM 10-1 **Miss T Cave** *Handy; cl 5th $\frac{1}{2}$way; stdy prog frm 12; tk ld 3 out; drew clr flat; easily; quite impressive* . . . 1
347^{P} **Sound Sense** 6-1 **J Young** *In tch; disp 2nd 10; trckd ldr frm 12; cl up & ev ch 3 out; hld when blun last.* . . . 10 2
312^{3} **O'ech** (5a) 3-1 **C Heard** *5s-3s; ld to 3 out; 3rd & one pce frm nxt* . . . 4 3
Dancing Dasi (IRE) (12a) 14-1 Miss L Gardner *Tchd 16s; rr; jmpd slow 3; lost tch 13; t.o.* . . . 40 4
327^{2} Four Of A Kind 5-2F Richard Darke *Tchd 3s; lw; prom; cl 2nd 8; cl 4th 12; lost plce nxt; pu 15* . . . P
Longstone Lady (IRE) (5a) 10-1 D McKenna *2 handlers; midfield; 6th 10; lost tch 13; last when pu 15* . . . P
474^{P} Master Of Fashion(bl) 33-1 L Heard *Bckwd; sn prom; jmpd rt & lost ground 5; bhnd when pu 7.* . . . P
492^{4} Miss Ziggerson (5a) 3-1 Miss S Young *6s-3s; handy; cl 3rd 8; in tch when ur 9* U
486^{3} Off The Hook (IRE) 6-1 I Hambley *Handy; cl 4th 6; 3l 4th 10; chsd ldrs; cl 3rd when ur 3 out* . . . U

OFFICIAL DISTANCES: 5*l*, 2*l* **TIME:** 6min 56.0s

569 Mixed Open, 12st — 8 ran

470^{U} **BALLYSICYOS (FR)** 9-4JF **A Farrant** *(xnb) Tchd 3s; lw; went 2nd 3; ld 8; went clr aft 11; drew rt away frm 15; unchall; eased cl home; impressive* . . . 1
483^{1} **Bill Me Up (IRE)** 9-2 **C Heard** *Tchd 5s; lw; 2 handlers; ld to 8; chsd ldr vain aft; 8l 2nd 13; lost tch 15; one pce* . . . 30 2
305^{1} **Fossy Bear** (5a) 3-1 **Miss S Young** *Tchd 7/2; midfield; 15l 5th 9; no real imp; poor 4th 15; tk 3rd flat; fin wl* . . . 4 3
483^{2} Karadin (FR) 20-1 Mrs M Hand *Lw; went 4th 8; chsd ldrs; 16l 4th 11; went 3rd 14; no imp; dem flat.* . . . 4 4
196^{2} Monty's Lass (IRE) (5a) 9-4JF Miss C Prouse *Tchd 3s; lw; detach last aft 2 & nvr gng wl; 40l last 9; poor 7th 12; wl bhnd 15; nrst fin; rdr fined* . . . 6 5
76^{2} Hasten Bak 14-1 Miss L Gardner *(xnb) Bit bckwd; prom; 3$\frac{1}{2}$l 3rd $\frac{1}{2}$way; lost ground frm 11; wknd; poor 5th 2 out.* . . . 20 6
Belarus (IRE) 16-1 D Harvey *Prom early; 20l 6th 9; lost tch w ldrs 12; t.o.* 1 7
Longstone Lad 7-1 R Woollacott *24l 7th 9; jmpd slow 11; releg last 12; last when pu 14.* . . . P

OFFICIAL DISTANCES: 25*l*, 3*l* **TIME:** 6min 41.0s

The stewards enquired into the running and riding of Monty's Lass; the rider was fined £125 for failing to ride the horse to achieve the best possible placing; she appealed to the Jockey Club Disciplinary Committee who upheld the local decision

570 Confined, 12st — 6 ran

484^{4} **LIRSLEFTOVER** (3x) 5-1 **Miss S Young** *Hld up & bhnd; prog 13; went 2nd 3 out; ld last; rdn clr; drifted lft flat.* . . . 1
484^{P} **Dark Challenger (IRE)** (3x) 8-1 **Miss S Gaisford** *Hld up & bhnd; prog 13; went 4th 3 out; stiil 4th last; r.o wl flat.* . . . 3 2
414^{3} **Let's Fly (FR)** 8-1 **Mrs M Hand** *Handy; cl 3rd $\frac{1}{2}$way; 1$\frac{1}{2}$l 3rd 11; ev ch 3 out; one pce frm nxt* . . . $\frac{1}{2}$ 3

366[2] Shobrooke Mill (5x) 4-6F A Farrant *(xnb,boh) Tchd 8-11; went 2nd 3; prom til ld 13; went 4l clr 3 out; hdd & no ex app last; wknd flat* 4 4
310[P] Destin D'Estruval (FR) 8-1 A Charles-Jones *Slt ld to 13; cl up & ev ch 15; wknd nxt* 30 5
495[P] Th'moons A Balloon (IRE) 6-1 S Partridge *2 handlers; in tch; 3½l 4th 11; wknd frm 13; bhnd when pu 15* . . . . P

OFFICIAL DISTANCES: 8*l*, ½*l* **TIME:** 6min 56.0s

571 Restricted (Div 1), 12st — 9 ran

323[3] **STATE MEDLAR** 5-4 **R Woollacott** *5/2-5/4; lw; a.p; ld to 14; 1l 2nd 2 out; ld app last; pushed clr flat; stayed on* 1
488[P] **Pinmoor Hill** 7-1 **M Munrowd** *Sn prom; ½l 2nd 10; disp ld 15; slt ld frm nxt til hdd app last; tired flat.* 8 2
323[2] **Sutton Courtenay (IRE)** 11-10F **J Jenkins** *Lw; chsd ldrs; wl in tch 9; 6l 6th 11; prog to 3rd & flatt brief 3 out; sn btn* 6 3
337[4] Carrington House 8-1 J O'Rourke *Prom; cl 3rd 9; w ldrs frm 11; disp ld 15; ev ch til wknd rap nxt* 5 4
488[P] Dear As Saffron (5a) 16-1 W Biddick *Wl in tch; blun bad 8; cl 4th 10; lost ground stdly frm 14; bhnd frm 16.* 25 5
Big Mossy 16-1 J Cole *Towards rr in wl bunched field; 7th & just in tch 10; rmdr nxt; last when pu 12* . . . . P
Mad Jack(tt) 7-1 L Heard *(xnb) Midfield in wl bunched field; 4l 5th 10; lost ground nxt; bhnd when pu 14.* . . . . P
492[P] Red Risk 20-1 M Sweetland *(xnb) Rr; last but just in tch when fell 8* . . . . F
309[P] Young Harry(vis) 25-1 T Dennis *Lw; rr til ref to rce aft 5* . . . . r

OFFICIAL DISTANCES: 15*l*, 8*l* **TIME:** 7min 04.0s

572 Restricted (Div 2), 12st — 12 ran

309[1] **STONE VALLEY** 6-1 **A Charles-Jones** *Hld up just off pce; hdwy to 5th 10; gd prog aft 14; disp ld 3 out; ld nxt; 2l up at last; drew clr flat; comf* 1
Aller Coombe (5a) 2-1F **L Jefford** *4s-2s; hld up; 8th ½way; hdwy frm 14; went 3rd 3 out; eff & ev ch nxt; no ex frm last.* 8 2
488[3] **Lingering Fog (IRE)** 7-1 **Miss M McCarthy** *Sn prom; 1½l 3rd 10; eff & disp ld 3 out; ev ch til one pce frm 2 out; no ex flat* 6 3
79[P] Change 6-1 T Dennis *Rr frm 7; lost tch 12; sn t.o last; lft rem 4th when blun bad last; walked in* . . . . runin 4
Baldhu Jack 20-1 Miss P Moorhouse *Sn last; t.o frm 7 til pu 15* . . . . P
318[4] Eskimo Gold (5a) 16-1 Miss L Gardner *Prom to 8; 7th 10; sn wknd; bhnd frm 12 til pu last* . . . . P
Hachley (FR) 7-1 J Jenkins *Midfield; 6th 10; no prog; pu 15* . . . . P
Lirkimalong 3-1 Miss S Young *Tchd 4s; in tch; cl 3rd 8; 1l 2nd 10; wknd 13; pu 15* . . . . P
139[P] Lord Of The Bride (IRE)(bl) 4-1 A Farrant *Disp ld when blun & ur 1* . . . . . . U
498[P] Mrs Peggoty (5a)(vis) 7-1 D Edwards *Cl 4th when blun & ur 2* . . . . U
417[1] Pauls Legacy 12-1 D McKenna *(ringbit) In tch; cl 4th ½way; lost plce frm 12; pu 15* . . . . P
Village Queen (IRE) (5a) 12-1 D Harvey *(bnh) Ld frm 4; went 4l clr 14; hdd & wknd rap aft nxt; btn 4th 2 out; fell last; winded.* . . . . F

OFFICIAL DISTANCES: 12*l*, 8*l* **TIME:** 6min 54.0s

573 Intermediate, 12st — 10 ran

495[5] **BAK ON BOARD**(bl) 16-1 **Miss L Gardner** *(xnb,ringbit) Patient rdn; in tch in 7th ½way; gd hdwy 15; swept into ld aft nxt; drew clr app last; stayed on str* 1
321[2] **By My Side (IRE)** 100-30 **A Charles-Jones** *Lw; sn prom; trckd ldrs; disp ld 8-11; cl 4th 13; 7l 3rd aft 3 out; r.o & jmpd to 2nd at last; kpt on* 12 2
323[1] **Sea Snipe** (5a) 2-1 **Miss T Cave** *3s-2s; lw; sn prom; cl 4th 10; 1l 2nd 13; disp ld nxt; prsd ldr frm 15; lft in ld brief 3 out; sn outpcd; 10l 2nd app last; no ex flat.* 10 3
The Earth Moved (IRE) 20-1 Mrs S Godfrey *Lw; hdwy to 5th 9; in tch in 5th 13; lost tch 15; kpt on; btr for rce* 12 4
488[1†] Bishop's Blade 4-1 Miss S Gaisford *Tchd 5s; ld/disp til slt ld frm 11; ld & gng str when fell 3 out* . . . . F
314[1] Cimmaroon (IRE) (7a) 6-4F A Farrant *(xnb) Lw; ld/disp til mist 11; sn rdn; wkng when mist 14; rdn & no resp; pu nxt; v disapp* . . . . P

497P Fenny Royal 20-1 M Woodward *Tde; sn rr; detach & jmpd novicey; t.o & pu 11* P
495P Native Drum (IRE) 20-1 R Woollacott *Lw; in tch; cl 6th 10; just in tch 13; pu nxt* . . . . P
Ross Poldark 12-1 T Dennis *Planted in padd; reluct to go down; towards rr; 8th ½way; mist 12; pu nxt* . . . . P
329P Rowleyrascal 33-1 D Edwards *Tchd 50s; prom early; sn towards rr; 9th & rdn 10; bhnd & pu 12* . . . . P

OFFICIAL DISTANCES: 12*l*, 6*l* **TIME:** 6min 51.0s

Wilton

Badbury Rings (LH 10F,19J)
Sat, 20 Mar (GOOD)

574 Hunt Members, 12st — 3 ran

459² **HELLO ROSCREA (IRE)** 1-5F **Miss A Goschen** *Disp ld til ld 3; set sedate pce; 1½l up 11; grad drew clr frm 3 out; easy; rdr waving at fin* 1
Some Tourist (IRE) 5-1 **S Gordon-Watson** *Disp ld to 3; chsd wnr aft; jmpd rt 5; 1½l down 12; grad wknd frm 2 out; sn no ch; game eff.* 15 2
Charlie Hawes (IRE) 11-1 **Miss G Russell-Holmes** *(bf) A last; jmpd rt 5; disp 2nd brief 7; 20l bhnd & strugg 11; t.o frm 13; plodded home; rdr jubilant* 40 3

OFFICIAL DISTANCES: 20*l*, dist **TIME:** 6min 53.3s

575 Open Maiden 56&7yo, 12st — 8 ran

419⁴ **LORD ALPHA (IRE)** 2-1F **D Phelan** *4s-2s; prom; 2l 3rd 4; chsd ldrs til ld 10-14; cl up when lft in ld 2 out; sn clr; eased flat* 1
492R **The Nelson Touch** 12-1 **D I Turner** *(xnb) Hdwy to disp 4th 10; ld 15-nxt; lft 2nd 2 out; sn btn; flatt by prox.* 2½ 2
367P **Panto** 14-1 **Miss K Lovelace** *Ld; 2l up 5 til jnd 9; hdd nxt; grad wknd frm 15; lft rem 3rd 2 out* 30 3
142⁵ Senior Moment 5-1 J Snowden *Chsd ldrs; 4½l 4th 4; grad wknd frm 15; bhnd frm 3 out.* 2½ 4
My Little Lady (5a) 14-1 Miss A Bush *Last trio 2; 5l 6th 9; grad wknd frm 12; t.o 14 til pu 2 out* . . . . P
475P Peter Parkgate (7a) 10-1 N Mitchell *Releg last 4; mist 13; t.o nxt til pu 2 out* P
The Cooling Agent 3-1 M Miller *Tchd 7/2; last trio 2; disp 4l 4th 9; trckng ldrs when blun bad & ur 13* . . . . U
353³ The Sycophant (IRE) 9-4 Miss A Goschen *Trckd ldr; 1½l down 4; disp ld brief 9; ld 14-15 & agn 3 out; narrow ld when fell nxt* . . . . F

OFFICIAL DISTANCES: 2½*l*, 20*l* **TIME:** 6min 37.4s

576 Mens Open, 12st — 6 ran

321¹ **OUT THE BLACK (IRE)** 4-5F **D Alers-Hankey** *(b4) Tchd evens; hld up; 18l 4th 11; hdwy to chse ldr 14; disp ld 16; ld nxt; drew clr frm 2 out; impressive* 1
365¹ **Skip 'n' Tune (IRE)** (5a) 9-4 **M Miller** *4th 7; chsd ldrs frm 10; 12½l 3rd nxt; disp ld 16; hdd nxt; sn rdn & no ex; nt disg* 5 2
366¹ **Friar Waddon** (4x) 5-1 **N Harris** *(xnb) Tchd 6s; hld up; last 4; jmpd slow 8; eff to chse ldng pr 16; no imp frm 2 out* 8 3
455¹ Makhpiya Patahn (IRE) 33-1 D I Turner *(xnb) Ld & sn clr; 10l up 4; dogged it & drvn along aft 10; jmpd slow 14; hdd nxt; stayed on one pce frm 2 out .* 8 4
348⁸ Oscar Wilde 13-2 D Drake *12l 3rd 4; chsd ldr frm 6-8; releg last 12; bhnd frm 16* 4 5
460² Merry Shot (IRE) 50-1 J Snowden *Bit bckwd; chsd clr ldr; 20l down 5 til wknd qckly 14; sn t.o; pu 3 out* . . . . P

OFFICIAL DISTANCES: 4*l*, 8*l* **TIME:** 6min 18.6s

577 Countryside Alliance Club Members (Nov Rdrs), 12st — 5 ran

321⁷ **SIMPLY SAM** 7-4 **H Fry** *(xnb) 4l 4th 4; trckd ldng pr frm 6; disp ld 10 til ld 12; clr frm 15; easy* 1
351F **Coolteen Hero (IRE)** 6-4F **D Jacob** *(xnb) Opened 2s; 3l 2nd 4; releg 3rd 9; chsd wnr vain frm 15* 15 2
472⁶ **Sherbourne Guest (IRE)** 5-1 **J Kwiatkowski** *Jmpd lft early; ld til pckd & jnd 10; hdd 12; grad wknd frm 15; untidy j last.* 12 3

114^{3} Now Young Man (IRE) 14-1 M Heuff *2 handlers; $3\frac{1}{2}$l 3rd 4; outpcd 7 15l 4th 11; t.o when blun & ur 15* . . . . U

294^{P} Wood Buzzard(tt) 33-1 R Bandey *(xnb) A last; 20l adrift 11; t.o when clambered over 14; imm pu* . . . . P

OFFICIAL DISTANCES: 15*l*, 12*l* **TIME:** 6min 22.8s

578 Ladies Open — 3 ran

319^{2} **MOUSESKI** 6-4F **Miss R Green** *Ww; 2l 2nd 4; jmpd slow 8; clsd stdly frm 16; chall on inner final turn; ld last; sn clr; eased nr fin; wl rdn* 1

484^{2} **Breteche (FR)** (5a) 7-4 **Miss T Newman** *(xnb) Mounted on course; ld; 2l up 4; 7l clr & lkd in comm 13; pegged back stdly frm 15; jnd final bend; sn hdd & no ex* . . . . $3\frac{1}{2}$ 2

347^{U} Rock Rose (5a) 9-4 Miss C Tizzard *(xnb) Chsd ldr til 4l last 4; 5l adrift when pu rap aft 10; inj nr hind leg; removed by horse ambulance* . . . . P

OFFICIAL DISTANCE: 4*l* **TIME:** 6min 22.7s

579 Restricted, 12st — 6 ran

324^{F} **THUNDER THIGHS** (5a) 11-2 **N Wilmington** *(xnb) 2 handlers; mounted on course; ld til outj & hdd 8; chsd ldr; 2l down 12; chall 16; ld 2 out; pushed out* 1

354^{2} **Hawkers Hill** 9-4 **N Mitchell** *Chsd ldr til jmpd to ld 8; 2l up 11; jnd 16; hit 2 out & hdd; rdn & no ex frm last* 6 2

314^{7} **Beachtime** 8-1 **Miss C Tizzard** *(xnb) 2 handlers; 3l 3rd 4; trckd ldng pr; 4l 3rd 15; grad wknd frm 3 out* . . . . $2\frac{1}{2}$ 3

148^{3} Bessie Bunter (5a) 7-4F M Miller *Tchd 2s; rr when jmpd awkward & fell 1* . F

260^{1} Lady Dot (IRE) (5a) 20-1 D Dennis *(xnb) Jmpd rt 3; 5l 4th when mist nxt; disp 3rd brief 9; 10l adrift 14; t.o 3 out; pu last* . . . . P

Shillelah Law 9-2 R Bliss *(xnb) 7l last 4; followed loose horse & rn out & ur 5* R

OFFICIAL DISTANCES: 6*l*, 3*l* **TIME:** 6min 29.8s

580 Open Maiden, 12st — 8 ran

LORD BEAU (IRE) 6-4F **R Stephens** *Lw; 4l 3rd 4; disp ld 10; ld nxt; made rest; stayed on wl frm 2 out* 1

540^{P} **Pandeli** 10-1 **D Phelan** *10l 5th 4; chsd ldrs in 3rd mostly frm 11; kpt on frm 2 out; much improved* 3 2

474^{F} **Queens House** (5a) 5-1 **D Drake** *Chsd ldr frm 4; ld 8; jnd 10; hdd nxt; chsd ldr til tired & dem app last* . . . . $1\frac{3}{4}$ 3

Coastal Flight 7-2 Miss R Green *Tchd 4s; lft & lost 20l start; jmpd rt 6; 18l last 8; mist 10; stayed on one pce to 4th 15; nvr nr to chall; fin tired* 20 4

485^{P} Port Valenska (IRE) 6-1 N Harris *A bhnd; 15l 7th 8; last 11; jmpd slow 13; t.o frm 15* 30 5

264^{P} Able Bob (IRE) 20-1 R Bliss *(xnb) 9l 4th 4; chsd ldrs til wknd qckly 15; t.o frm 3 out* 10 6

494^{P} Forglori 12-1 L Tibbatts *Ld to 3; sn lost plce; $4\frac{1}{2}$l 6th 8; jmpd lft 13; wknd 15; exhaust 5th when scrambled over 2 out & pu* . . . . P

325^{P} Little Mister(bl) 7-1 N Mitchell *10s-7s; chsd ldr til ld 3; hdd 8; blun bad 9; imm pu* . . . . P

OFFICIAL DISTANCES: 3*l*, $1\frac{1}{2}$*l* **TIME:** 6min 43.9s

Fontwell (L&RH 7F,15J)

Sun, 21 Mar (GOOD, GOOD to SOFT in places)

581 Heathorns HC, 2m4f £1491 — 6 ran

399^{U} **PLACID MAN (IRE)** 11-13 6-4 **Ms A Embiricos** *V exhuberant & lkd too much of a handful for rdr; prom; pckd 2; ld 7; hit 10; hdd 3 out; 2l down & rdn when lft virt solo & hmpd last; drvn out flat; unconvincing* 1

441^{7} **Nashville Star (USA)** 11-05(vis) 66-1 **R McCarthy** *(xnb) Ld aft 3-7; wknd alarming aft 9; lft rem 3rd & hmpd 11; lft 2nd at last; drvn to keep gng flat; walked over line (desperate eff)* . . . . dist 2

422^{P} **Spy Boy (IRE)** 11-05 25-1 **T Hampton** *Ld til aft 3; rdn & fdng rap when blun 8; t.o 10; event walked in* . . . . dist 3

209^{7} Benson (IRE) 11-11 9-1 T Dreaper *Sn rr; u.p 8; 10l 4th nxt; 3rd when fell 11* F

156P King Of The Dawn 11-11 20-1 J Sole *Last til blun & ur 4* . . . . U
Silence Reigns 11-07 evensF J Jenkins *Hld up in rr til prog to 2nd aft 9; mists 11 & 12; ld 3 out; 2l ahd & lkd in comm when blun & ur last; rdr furious* U

TIME: 5min 20.0s **TOTE:** £2.50; places £1.40,£10.60 **Ex:**£58.50 **CSF:**£69.03

The stewards i) warned the rider of the winner for using the whip on a horse that was clearly winning; ii) interviewed the rider of Spy Boy for racing an apparently exhausted horse; following veterinary evidence they decided no offence had occurred

Grafton

Mollington (RH 8F,18J)

Sun, 21 Mar (GOOD, SOFT in places)

582 Hunt Members, 12st — 7 ran

374⁴ **BE MY DREAM (IRE)** (10x)(cp) 9-2 **P Cowley** *Made all; sn clr; drew 20l ahd aft 11; drvn to keep advant 13; in comm 3 out; enterprising ride* 1
Fours Are Wild (IRE) 8-1 **J Trevor-Roper** *Rdr unstdy; chsd clr ldrs; disp poor 4th 13; eff 3 out; kpt on to 2nd aft last.* 20 2
Court Alert 4-7F **S Morris** *Nt fluent; chsd wnr; outpcd frm 11; no imp aft; dem aft last* 1 3
437U Polo Pony (IRE)(cp) 10-1 T Ellis *Hld up til chsd clr ldng pr 7; eff 14; disp mod 2nd 2 out; one pce aft* 2 4
383P Crested Manor 8-1 J Tarry *Mists in chsng group; disp poor 4th frm 13; eff 3 out; ch of 2nd nxt; wknd last* 4 5
380⁷ Ela Agapi Mou (USA)(bl) 20-1 Miss D Ball *A last; t.o frm ½way* 20 6
443P Perfect Finisher 20-1 Miss R Lobley *In chsng group; 6th & wkng when rfo 12* U

OFFICIAL DISTANCES: 15*l*, 1½*l* **TIME:** 6min 24.0s

583 Confined, 12st — 8 ran

437⁴ **FREEDOM FIGHTER** 5-4F **A Martin** *Trckd ldng pr 5; went 2nd 10; ld 12; narrowly hdd 3 out; rdn to ld agn nxt; drvn clr flat.* 1
Kentford Busy B (5a) 10-1 **N Pearce** *Patient rdn in midfield; prog to cl 4th ½way; prsd wnr 15; narrow ld nxt; rdn & hdd 2 out; no ex last* 4 2
382⁵ **Bullfinch** 5-2 **P Cowley** *4s-5/2; set off last; prog to press ldr 4-10; dem to 4th 15; 3rd & outpcd by ldng pr nxt* 10 3
Rectory Garden (IRE) 20-1 Miss G Emtage *Off pce in midfield; 17l 6th ½way; kpt on frm 13; nvr rchd ldrs* 2 4
175P Croft Court 20-1 D Renney *Prsd ldr to 4; awkward nxt; sn lost plce; 7th ½way; sn lost tch; t.o 13; just kpt rem 5th* 30 5
466⁵ Tale Bridge (IRE)(cp) 33-1 J Russell *A last pr; 33l last ½way; cont t.o.* 1 6
Rough Tiger (IRE) (6x) 5-1 B Tuckey *1st ride; midfield; cl 5th ½way; sn lost tch; 6th & wkng when ur bend bef 13* . . . . U
460³ True Chimes(cp) 12-1 J Owen *(xnb) Made most to 12; lost 2nd 15; mist & wknd 3 out; wl btn 5th when pu last* . . . . P

OFFICIAL DISTANCES: 5*l*, 10*l* **TIME:** 6min 27.5s

The stewards fined the rider of Freedom Fighter £100 for improper riding having found him guilty of striking the rider of True Chimes during the race

584 Intermediate, 12st — 9 ran

379³ **FINDER KEEPS (USA)** 7-2 **J Owen** *Cl up; ld 12-13; drvn to ld narrowly 2 out; jnd on both sides flat; won on the nod* 1
321U **Stennikov (IRE)** 5-2 **E Walker** *4s-5/2; mostly trckd ldr til 3rd aft 12; went 2nd brief & mist 15; eff to chall 2 out; jnd wnr flat; just pipped in drvng fin.* s hd 2
Sing High (5a) 33-1 **A Martin** *(xnb) Hld up; prog ½way; ld 13; rdn & narrowly hdd 2 out; nt much room on inner app last; jnd wnr flat; just pipped nr fin* s hd 3
379² Miss Hoity Toity (5a) 9-4F A Sansome *Planted herself on way to start; ld to 12; sn dem 4th; still ch 3 out; wknd app nxt* 20 4
365P Nousayri (IRE) 9-2 J Trice-Rolph *(xnb) Keen; hld up; prog to trck ldrs 12; no imp 14; wknd aft 3 out* 6 5
36P Grey Fandango (IRE) 8-1 M Rimell *(xnb) Wl in tch til wknd 12; sn t.o; jmpd slow frm 14* 300y 6
383U Devils Domino 33-1 N Pearce *Hld up last; prog to jn ldng pr 8; wknd rap 10; pu 11* . . . . P

	Major Reno (IRE) 25-1 J Newbold *In tch til mist & wknd 8; t.o & pu 11 . .*		P
	Sams Sister (5a) 16-1 P Cowley *Jmpd lft; drpd to last 7; wknd nxt; t.o & pu 11*		P

OFFICIAL DISTANCES: s hd, s hd **TIME:** 6min 28.0s

The rider of the third objected to the rider of the winner for striking him with his whipduring the race; the stewards overruled the objection but returned his deposit; they reported the behaviour of both riders to the Stewards of the Jockey Club

585 Gerrard Ladies Open — 5 ran

464[1]	**KILLERINE (FR)**(bl) 1-4F **Miss H Irving** *Nt a fluent; ld 3; made rest at mod pce; prsd brief aft 3 out; in comm agn nxt; rdn out . . . .*		1
311[F]	**Polar King (IRE)** 7-1 **Miss W Southcombe** *16s-7s; mostly chsd ldng pr; eff to chse wnr app 3 out; flatt brief aft 3 out; sn btn . . . .*	3½	2
289[9]	**Gangster** 10-1 **Miss S Tarry** *Ld to 3; chsd wnr aft; dem to 3rd app 3 out; bumped along & one pce aft . . . .*	4	3
380[P]	Veredarius (FR) 33-1 Mrs S Tyler *A last pr; tlng off by-passing 12; sn miles bhnd . . . .*	250y	4
373[6]	Dook's Delight (IRE) 7-1 Miss L Horsfall *Last pr til blun 4 & shot rdr over front*		U

OFFICIAL DISTANCES: 4*l*, 4*l* **TIME:** 6min 34.0s

Fence 12 omitted - fallen rider

586 Mens Open — 8 ran

437[P]	**FISHERMAN JACK** 3-1 **S Morris** *Prom; drvn into fncs; ld 9; made rest; drvn 2l clr at last; wkng nr fin; just hld on . . . .*		1
381[4]	**Grecian Star** 7-4F **J Tarry** *Chsd ldrs; pushed along ½way; chsd wnr aft 14; tried to chall 2 out; outj last; stayed on flat; just failed . . . .*	½	2
445[6]	**Mr Smudge** 100-30 **A Martin** *Midfield; prog to jn ldrs 9; outpcd 12; jmpd slow 13 & drvn; eff 3 out; r.o frm 2 out; clsng fast on ldng pr nr fin . . . .*	¾	3
381[2]	Pagermar (IRE) 7-2 R Burton *(xnb) Jmpd slow 3; chsd ldrs; 4th & outpcd 13; eff 3 out; one pce & no imp frm nxt; wl btn when mist last. . . . .*	5	4
403[8]	Felloo (IRE) 20-1 E Walker *Rr; 7th ½way; outpcd 13; eff in chsng group 3 out; no prog app nxt . . . .*	8	5
404[P]	Paddies Boy (IRE)(cp) 14-1 Jack Young *Rdr nrly f.o 1; last & nt gng wl; stayed just in tch; btn when rdr nrly f.o agn 3 out. . . . .*	3	6
366[3]	O J Selym (IRE) 20-1 G Opperman *Prom; prsd wnr 9 til aft 14; sn lost plce; wknd. . . . .*	12	7
292[P]	Fearless Bertie 33-1 P Cowley *Made most to 9; wknd u.p nxt; t.o & pu 14.*		P

OFFICIAL DISTANCES: ½*l*, ¾*l* **TIME:** 6min 31.5s

587 Restricted, 12st - 17J — 15 ran

375[U]	**AGUA ARDENTE** 100-30 **N Pearce** *Made virt all; jnd & clr of rest frm 10; lft 20l clr 14; reeled in 3 out; rdn 2l clr agn last; idled flat; just hld on; all out*		1
375[2]	**Teeton Fizz** (5a) 25-1 **H Fowler** *Hld up in rr; 8th gng wl ½way; stdy prog aft; went 3rd 15; clsd to 2nd 2 out; 2l down last; kpt on wl flat; just failed .*	½	2
288[1]	**Shortcut Shorty** 14-1 **C Wadland** *Prom; blun 5; 5th ½way; lft 20l 2nd 14; clsd on wnr 3 out; dem 3rd nxt; wknd last . . . .*	10	3
95[U]	Templenoe Hare (IRE) 20-1 R Burton *Prom; chsd ldng pr 7 til by-passing 13; one pce & no imp on ldrs frm 15 . . . .*	4	4
467[P]	Waterloo Leader (IRE) 33-1 D Smith *Wl in rr; 11th & wl bhnd ½way; slt prog 14; r.o aft 3 out; nrst fin . . . .*	5	5
467[4]	Sissinghurst Star (IRE) 33-1 P Mann *(xnb) Midfield; 9th ½way; nvr on terms aft; plodded on frm 3 out. . . . .*	2½	6
369[3]	Rommel 4-1 J Trice-Rolph *6s-4s; hld up in rr; 10th & wl off pce ½way; no real prog aft 12; unenterprisingly rdn. . . . .*	12	7
173[1]	Keegan Bearnais (FR) 8-1 T Mann *(xnb) Prom til 6th & lsng plce ½way; no prog agn 12; wknd 3 out . . . .*	2	8
	Button Boy 20-1 P Cowley *Mist 1; chsd ldrs; 7th ½way; wknd 12; t.o in last pr frm 3 out. . . . .*	20	9
294[P]	Cumberland Youth 25-1 T Messenger *Midfield; jmpd slow 6 & drpd to last trio; sn bhnd; pu 11 . . . .*		P
	Fawsley Lake (5a) 33-1 A Sansome *2 handlers; a last trio; wl bhnd when pu 11*		P
31[8]	Mind The Gate 14-1 M Rimell *Reluct to line up; last & nt gng wl early; wknd ½way; t.o & pu aft 12. . . . .*		P

369U Misty Ramble (IRE) 5-2F L Payter *5s-5/2; hld up til prog to press wnr 6; clr of rest frm 10; cl 2nd & ev ch when fell 14* . . . F
369[4] Moscow's Return (IRE) 12-1 S Morris *Chsd ldrs; 4th ½way; wknd 13; t.o in last pr 3 out; pu nxt* . . . P
383P Romanybaan 33-1 J Newbold *(xnb) 2 handlers; midfield; blun 6 & 7; wknd; t.o & pu 10* . . . P

OFFICIAL DISTANCES: nk, 6/ **TIME:** 6min 26.5s

Fence 13 omitted - damaged

588 Confined Maiden (Div 1), 12st - 11J — 13 ran

462[3] **NATIVE THUNDER (IRE)** 5-1 **Miss S Duckett** *(xnb) Made all; clr frm ½way; in comm frm 13; unchall.* . . . 1
258F **Little Dish** (5a)(tt) 14-1 **J Owen** *Midfield; 7th ½way; eff 13; chsd wnr aft last; no ch* . . . 25 2
385P **Abitofahike (IRE)** 12-1 **A Martin** *Midfield; last of main group ½way; rap prog to chse wnr by-passing 14; wknd aft last; fin v tired* . . . 12 3
367[2] Eastern Apple (5a) 7-1 B Pauling *Chsd ldrs; 4th ½way; still w chsng group when blun bad 15; no ch aft* . . . 10 4
386P Teeton Diamond (5a) 7-1 N Pearce *Prom in chsng group til wknd aft 13; t.o* 6 5
Beechbrook Gale (IRE) 4-1 N Bell *(xnb) 7s-4s; mostly chsd wnr til aft 12; sn wknd; 7th & t.o when ref last* . . . r
370R Dun Aengus 33-1 L Payter *Mist 6; nt rec; wknd & pu 8* . . . P
Galevanter (IRE) 25-1 Miss J Hitchman *(xnb) Reluct to leave padd; ss; a last trio; t.o frm 7; plodded round til pu last.* . . . P
462P Herpen (5a) 33-1 T Ellis *2 handlers; a last trio; t.o 7; pu aft 12.* . . . P
371F Northall Lad 5-4F P Cowley *Chsd ldrs; 6th ½way; lost plce & strugg frm 11; no ch aft; poor 5th when mist & ur last* . . . U
296P Patum Peperium (7a) 14-1 S Morris *Chsd ldrs; 5th ½way; wknd 13; t.o & pu last* . . . P
Portway Sadie (5a) 16-1 H Dowty *Bckwd; chsd ldrs; wkng u.p & 8th ½way; crawled over 11 & pu* . . . P
291P Tom's Gold 33-1 J Trice-Rolph *Last trio; t.o frm 7; blun & nrly fell 12; imm pu* P

OFFICIAL DISTANCES: 25/, 12/ **TIME:** 6min 22.5s

Fences 1, 2, 9, 10, 17 & 18 omitted - low sun; fence 14 omitted - damaged; the original fence numbers are used in these comments-in-running, but the last fence referred to would be normally the third last

589 Confined Maiden (Div 2), 12st — 13 ran

LAH DI DAH LAD 7-1 **J Tarry** *Prom; ld 13; made most aft; clr frm 2 out; comf* 1
291[2] **Mountain Trooper** (7a) 7-2 **J Owen** *Hld up bhnd ldrs; 6th ½way; eff & mist 15; rnwd eff to chse wnr 2 out; hld when nt fluent last* . . . 3½ 2
Velvet Dove (12a) 8-1 **N Pearce** *Settled wl in rr; 10th ½way; prog 11; chsd ldrs 15; outpcd 3 out; stayed on stdly frm nxt.* . . . 3 3
291[3] Kupto (FR) 10-1 T Ellis *(xnb) Midfield; 7th & chsng ldrs ½way; outpcd aft 15; some prog frm 2 out; stayed on flat.* . . . 3 4
192[3] Caraiyni (IRE) 5-2F S Morris *(xnb) 4s-5/2; ld at stdy pce to 7; stayed prom; chall frm 13 til fdd frm 3 out* . . . 1 5
463P Penlet Too(bl) 7-1 E Walker *(xnb) Prom; ld 7-13; 4th 3 out; fdd* . . . 3 6
290[5] Earl Of Buckingham 7-2 P Cowley *W ldrs til aft 12; wknd 14; wl bhnd 3 out; kpt on flat* . . . 2 7
385P Jupiter Jay(cp) 25-1 A Sansome *Hld up in midfield; 9th & wl in tch ½way; wknd 14; t.o 3 out* . . . runin 8
386P Sixes And Sevens (IRE) (5a) 20-1 G Kerr *Hld up in rr; prog when blun 6; 5th ½way; wknd aft 12; t.o 3 out; crawled over last; walked in.* . . . 20 9
295P Faircatcher 25-1 L Payter *Wl in tch til wknd 11; wl bhnd when pu 14.* . . . P
Keno Du Moy (FR) 4-1 J Diment *(xnb) 10s-4s; green in padd; settled wl in rr; 12th & in tch ½way; sn wknd w rdr motionless; pu 14* . . . P
Leasebourne (12a) 12-1 T Messenger *Green in padd; last & drvn 3; nvr on terms; t.o last when pu 12.* . . . P
295[5] North Pass 20-1 H Dowty *In tch; 11th & rdn ½way; sn wknd u.p; t.o 13; pu 2 out* . . . P

OFFICIAL DISTANCES: 6/, 3/ **TIME:** 6min 34.0s

Grove & Rufford

Welbeck (RH 8F,19J)

Sun, 21 Mar (GOOD)

590 Hunt Members — 4 ran

523^{3}	**BALLAD (IRE)** 4-11F **Mrs L Howard** *Cl 2nd to 10; outpcd 11; 3l 3rd 15; ld app 2 out; rdly drew clr; easy*		1
	Crown Rule (IRE) 7-1 **A Williams** *Ld; 1l up to 12; cl 2nd 13-15; ld agn 16 til easily outpcd app 2 out; clr 2nd at last but rdr nrly caught napping*	8	2
	Roebucks Way 4-1 **J Howard** *3l 3rd to 10; ld 13-15; mist 16 & wknd; pushed along 3 out; stayed on & nrly caught dozing 2nd*	1	3
	San Antonio (U) (2ow) 10-1 S Clement *1st ride; a last; lsng tch 8; t.o 14; hunted rnd*	$2\frac{1}{2}$fs	4

OFFICIAL DISTANCES: 12*l*, $\frac{1}{2}$*l* **TIME:** 6min 42.0s

591 Dodson & Horrell PPORA Club Members Restricted — 12 ran

393^{1}	**BLACK COLLAR** (12a) 5-4F **M Walford** *Ww in mid-div to 10; went 5l 4th 11; chsd ldr in 6l 2nd 14; disp ld 2 out-last; easily drew clr flat; lks useful*		1
499^{2}	**Schoolhouse Walk** 7-1 **G Brewer** *Chsd ldr in 1l 2nd to 9; ld 10; scooted 10l clr 13-3 out; jnd nxt til rdn & outpcd flat*	5	2
482^{1}	**Lights On** 5-1 **M Manton** *Chsd ldng pr in 3l 3rd 9; outpcd 14; 10l 3rd 16; r.o one pce*	12	3
390^{2}	Mandate Man (IRE) 8-1 D Thomas *Prom 4th to 7; outpcd 9; bhnd 13; poor 8th 14; lft dist 5th 2 out & 4th at last*	runin	4
	Big Horn (IRE) 12-1 N Kent *(xnb) Last when bad mist 8; lsng tch 12; t.o & pu 13*		P
109^{P}	Carebec (IRE) (5a)(tt) 33-1 M Mackley *A towards rr; nvr in rce; t.o & pu 2 out*		P
390^{P}	Eastern Royal (7a) 8-1 Miss Rachel Clark *(xnb) Ld; 1l up to 9; cl up til outpcd & wknd 13; dist 5th when pu 15*		P
524^{P}	Hi Tech Man (IRE) 14-1 T Lane *Midfield early; 8l 6th 7 & 12l 5th 9; stayed on to poor 4th 3 out; still 4th when ref last*		r
467^{P}	Nonplussed (5a) 33-1 P Andrew *A rr; last by 12; pu 13*		P
499^{4}	Procol's Boy 25-1 S Walker *A rr; lsng tch 11; t.o & pu 13*		P
431^{P}	Silver Sovereign 25-1 C Dawson *Mid-div to 8; rr & lsng tch 12; t.o & pu 13*		P
524^{P}	Treble Trouble 33-1 Miss L Fear *Last to 5; hdwy 8 to 12l 7th 9-12; t.o 14; pu 2 out*		P

OFFICIAL DISTANCES: 2*l*, 12*l* **TIME:** 6min 20.0s

592 Mens Open, 12st — 13 ran

478^{2}	**RAMIREZ (IRE)** 6-1 **N Kent** *Hld up in mid-div; went 1l 2nd 13 til ld 2 out; jnd last; hrd rdn flat; just hld on*		1
	Mashwe (IRE) (5a) 4-1 **S Charlton** *Hld up; 8th 7; stdy prog to 3l 4th 15 & 1l 3rd 16; went cl 2nd 2 out; chall & lkd wnr last; just outpcd*	hd	2
465^{1}	**Red Rebel**(vis) 5-2F **R Cope** *Cl 2nd til ld 9-3 out; pushed along & wknd frm nxt*	10	3
372^{3}	Princess Derry (5a)(vis) 14-1 G Brewer *Hld up in rr to 11; went 2l 3rd 15 & 4th nxt; pushed along & wknd app 3 out; r.o one pce*	2	4
340^{5}	Stoney River (IRE) 9-1 S Walker *Midfield to 8; stayed on to 4th 3 out; dem flat*	3	5
298^{4}	Saxon Victory (USA) 12-1 R Armson *Ld; 1l up to 8; in tch til outpcd & wknd 15*	8	6
477^{3}	The Nobleman (USA) 11-2 N Docker *Handy 3rd to 6; 5th 7; outpcd by 13; r.o one pce*	2	7
437^{P}	Young Tomo (IRE)(bl) 14-1 L Hicks *Handy 4th to 9; pushed along 13; grad wknd*	5	8
382^{8}	Storm Forecast (IRE) 20-1 P Andrew *Prom; 5th til ld 5-6; disp ld 11-13; wknd rap; rr by 14; lost tch 16*	4	9
382^{7}	Bengal Boy 14-1 T Lane *A rr; 10th 8; last & lsng tch 14; t.o & pu 16*		P
381^{P}	Deel Quay (IRE) 12-1 N Docker *A rr; pushed along aft 8; t.o 9; pu 13*		P
477^{5}	Energy Man 25-1 M Bennison *Rr by 4; rdn to keep up 7; lsng tch 9; t.o 14; pu 3 out*		P
523^{P}	Exclusive Air (USA) (7a) 25-1 P Millington *Last & bhnd by 3; completely t.o 8; pu 10*		P

OFFICIAL DISTANCES: s hd, 12*l* **TIME:** 6min 21.0s

593 Ladies Open — 7 ran

Form	Runner	Dist	Pos
479^{2}	**NOKIMOVER**(cp) 6-4F **Miss Gemma Hutchinson** *Mid-div early; 5l 5th 7; ld frm 8; 6l clr 16; 20l clr 2 out; tired sltly aft last but r.o u.p*		1
373^{1}	**Macfin (IRE)**(cp) 11-4 **Miss L Allan** *A ldng pr; ld to 5; 2l 2nd 13; outpcd 17; bad mist 3 out; one pce & no ch w wnr aft*	10	2
479^{P}	**Master Adam (IRE)** 16-1 **Miss K Edminson** *A handy; 1l 2nd 11; outpcd 13; 6l 3rd 14; grad drpd back; t.o 3rd 2 out; clambered last; fin exhaust*	35	3
502^{P}	Pharlindo (IRE) 10-1 Miss A Armitage *Handy; ld 6-7; wknd 11; 6l 5th 12 & 20l 4th 15; poor 4th 3 out; hacked home*	6	4
	Farfields Prince 25-1 Miss S Sharratt *Prom when bad mist 7; 3l 4th 11; pushed along & wknd frm 13; t.o last 15*	1	5
	Bloomfield Storm (IRE) 11-4 Mrs J Dawson *Hld up & last; sn bhnd; t.o 6; pu 10*		P
390^{1}	Clonshire Paddy (IRE) 8-1 Miss J Coward *Sn adrift; t.o 7; pu 8*		P

OFFICIAL DISTANCES: 6*l*, 17*l* **TIME:** 6min 30.0s

594 Open Maiden 8yo&up (Div 1), 12st — 10 ran

Form	Runner	Dist	Pos
500^{2}	**AUNT GLADYS (IRE)** (5a) 11-4 **G Brewer** *A.p; 1l 2nd 13 til ld 3 out; 1l up nxt; jnd last; rallied & drew clr flat; game*		1
466^{P}	**Rakaposhi Raid** (5a) 10-1 **P Newton** *A.p; 2l 3rd 4; 3l 3rd 13; jnd ldr last; rdn & outpcd flat*	3	2
	Man At The Top 20-1 **M Bennison** *Mostly mid-div; 12l 6th 12; 10l 5th 14; lost tch 16; stayed on past btn horses to 3rd app last*	8	3
370^{2}	Beau Jake (IRE) evensF R Armson *Cl up; 4l 4th 8; ld 11-17; wknd rap app 2 out; all out; fin exhaust*	15	4
270^{9}	Sharp Embrace 12-1 Miss S Rodman *Ld to 2; handy in 6l 5th 6; t.o by 11; plodded on*	12	5
385^{P}	College Superman 33-1 L Hicks *Ld; 2l up to 10; in tch til pushed along 13; t.o 3 out; pu 2 out*		P
	Fairfields Boy 14-1 Miss Rachel Clark *Nt jw in rr; last 4; lost tch 7; t.o & pu 10*		P
	Grey Snipe 16-1 T Lane *Sn towards rr; bhnd by 4; lost tch 8; t.o & pu 10*		P
297^{2}	Mister Rose (IRE) 12-1 M Mackley *A.p; 3l 3rd 14; in tch til wknd aft 3 out; 8l 3rd & hld when ref 2 out*		r
258^{P}	Trust Ger 25-1 Miss H Phizacklea *A rr; 8th & lsng tch 11; t.o & pu 14*		P

OFFICIAL DISTANCES: 1*l*, 12*l* **TIME:** 6min 36.0s

595 Open Maiden 8yo&up (Div 2), 12st — 12 ran

Form	Runner	Dist	Pos
	ALTHREY DANDY (IRE) 4-1 **L Hicks** *Made all; 8l clr 9; gvn breather 10-13; 8l clr agn 15; drew rt away frm nxt; galloped on str; unextended*		1
531^{P}	**Ridware George** 5-1 **Miss S Sharratt** *Chsd ldr in 2l 2nd to 7; outpcd 16; dist 3rd 3 out; stayed on to 2nd aft nxt; prsd at last; just kpt 2nd in drvng fin*	30	2
387^{3}	**Earl Token** 5-2F **R Armson** *Hld up & bhnd; hdwy frm 10 to 15l 4th 14; went dist 4th 3 out; jnd 2nd app last; hrd rdn flat; dem nr line*	½	3
463^{P}	Bethin (5a) 6-1 P Newton *Midfield to 11; went 16l 5th 16 & 20l 2nd 3 out; wknd app last*	10	4
436^{5}	Hidden Pearl (IRE) 7-2 J Davis *In tch in 4th to 9; pushed along 10; poor 6th 15; lft rem 5th 2 out; coaxed home; all out*	20	5
152^{P}	Dolitanlad 20-1 P Millington *Prom in 4th til fell 15*		F
482^{P}	Ecclesiastes 12-1 J Howard *Bhnd 4; last by 8; lost tch 10; t.o & pu 14*		P
395^{U}	Firle Phantasy 16-1 M Lurcock *Cl 3rd when rn out 6*		R
500^{P}	Miss Danbys (5a) 12-1 S Walker *A rr; last 2; wkng when pu 12*		P
	Shalabibubbly 3-1 N Kent *Mid-div when bad mist 5; outpcd 11; poor 5th 15; t.o & pu 16*		P
227^{4}	Single Man (IRE) 10-1 J Burley *A rr div; outpcd & wknd frm 14; t.o & pu 2 out*		P
	Wonderful Remark (5a) 12-1 G Moloney *Cl up early; 5th when ur 7*		U

OFFICIAL DISTANCES: 15*l*, ½*l* **TIME:** 6min 30.0s

596 Open Maiden 56&7yo (Div 1), 2m5f, 12st - 17J — 9 ran

Form	Runner	Dist	Pos
167^{R}	**SIZER (IRE)** 5-2 **N Saville** *V sa; hld up & sn bhnd; gd hdwy frm 6; last but in tch 7; went 8l 5th 13; cruised up to disp ld 3 out; gd j & sn clr; cantered home; nvr off bridle; v impressive*		1
387^{2}	**Briery Fox (IRE)** 7-4F **J Docker** *Cl 3rd 8; ld 13; jnd 3 out; sn hdd & pushed along; r.o one pce; no ch w wnr*	5	2

	Civil Gent (IRE) (7a) 12-1 **G Brewer** *Ld to 7; cl 2nd til ld agn 11-13; ev ch 3 out; wknd nxt*	8	3
75P	Deep Design (IRE) 8-1 C Dawson *W ldrs to 9; pushed along & wknd 13; poor 5th 2 out; lft 4th at last*	35	4
4764	Bright Dawn (IRE) (12a) 5-2 M Walford *A midfield; in tch to 16; pushed along & outpcd 17; 30l 4th 2 out; pu last*		P
60P	Dextrous 16-1 R Clark *Hld up & sa; bhnd to 5; pulled to ld aft 7 til fell 10*		F
392U	Knight Crossing (IRE) 16-1 N Tutty *In tch in rr to 11; outpcd & lsng tch 13; t.o 14; pu 2 out*		P
	Minella Leader (IRE) 8-1 J Docker *Cl up; 1l 2nd 5; 3l 4th 8; tired aft 10; rr & wkng 11; t.o & pu 12*		P
476P	Stingo (5a) 12-1 M Mackley *A rr; v tired by 12; t.o & pu 14*		P

OFFICIAL DISTANCES: 4*l*, 4*l* **TIME:** 5min 56.0s

597 Open Maiden 56&7yo (Div 2), 2m5f, 12st - 17J — 8 ran

3442	**JETHRO TULL (IRE)** (7a) 1-2F **G Brewer** *Cl up; 4th 5; 2l 3rd 12; chall 13; ld 14; jnd 3 out-nxt; stayed on best; clr at last; r.o u.p; still green*		1
	Tom Tobacco 7-2 **R Cope** *Mid-div to 5; went 1l 2nd 7; disp ld 3 out-nxt; pushed along & wknd app last*	4	2
3433	**Callitwatulike** 5-1 **C Dawson** *Rr to 9; gd hdwy 12; 2l 3rd 13; rmdrs & pushed along nxt; outpcd frm 3 out*	8	3
304P	Lancastrian Island (5a) 14-1 R Armson *Prom; 1l 3rd 9; in tch 14; pushed along & wknd frm 15*	12	4
3876	Martha Jane (5a) 14-1 P Newton *Sa; sn bhnd; 10l 5th 7; mist 10; lost tch 12; stayed on wl frm 15; nrst fin*	2	5
385P	Catalan Girl (12a) 14-1 M Mackley *Hld up in cl last to 12; wknd 14; t.o & pu last; will improve*		P
	Cruising Along (5a) 12-1 L Hicks *Mid-div when ref 2.*		r
386P	Mrs Fidget (5a) 12-1 O Williams *Cl up; ld 3-10; wknd rap; t.o 14; pu 2 out*		P

OFFICIAL DISTANCES: 4*l*, 10*l* **TIME:** 6min 03.0s

Mendip Farmers

Ston Easton (RH 7F,18J)

Sun, 21 Mar (GOOD, GOOD to SOFT in places)

598 Hunt Members, 12st — 5 ran

	SPRINGFORD (IRE) (5x) 2-5F **D Alers-Hankey** *(xnb) 2 handlers; lw; jmpd rt; made all; clr 7-10; qcknd 13; drew clr agn 3 out; easily*		1
321P	**Early Morning Call (IRE)** 6-1 **J Barnes** *W wnr to 6; 2nd til app 14; 9l 3rd nxt; chsd wnr aft 3 out; no imp.*	15	2
4163	**Butleigh Rose** (5a) 6-1 **J Snowden** *Chsd ldrs; 8l 3rd 1/2way; went 5l 2nd app 14 til wknd aft 3 out; eased when btn flat*	20	3
459P	B B Boy 14-1 T Edwards *(xnb,bnh) A bhnd; 14l 4th 1/2way; rdn 11; mist 13; sn wl t.o; fin v tired*	2 1/2fs	4
	Sunleys Quest (5a) 20-1 L Tibbatts *(xnb) Shkn up aft 4; mist & lost tch 5; 15l last 1/2way; wl bhnd when pu 13.*		P

OFFICIAL DISTANCES: 15*l*, 25*l* **TIME:** 6min 31.4s

599 Open Maiden 56&7yo (Div 1), 2m4f, 12st - 15J — 12 ran

	SMART CAVALIER (7a) 2-1F **N Williams** *(xnb) Hld up; 5 1/2l 8th 1/2way; hdwy & mist 10; 7 1/2l 5th nxt; went 2l 3rd 3 out; sn qcknd 3l clr on inner; flagged flat; hld on wl*		1
	Trust Fund (IRE) 5-1 **D Jacob** *Swtng; prom; 1l 3rd 1/2way; 6l 3rd 11; 4th & outpcd aft 3 out; rallied 2 out; stayed on wl flat; nt rch wnr*	3/4	2
3682	**Saffron Hill (IRE)** (7a) 7-2 **F Hutsby** *Sn prom; went 2nd aft 3; ld 8-11; blun 12; ev ch 3 out; kpt on*	2	3
4133	Royal Czarina (5a) 33-1 J Snowden *Ld to 8; 2nd til ld 11; hdd aft 3 out; wknd last.*	5	4
2907	Jewel Song 33-1 J Barnes *Hld up & bhnd; mist 2; hdwy & 4 1/2l 6th 1/2way; lost plce & 10l 7th 11; 11l 6th 3 out; kpt on stdly*	2	5
	Kentford Bracken (5a) 33-1 D I Turner *(xnb) Hld up & bhnd; 9l 11th 1/2way; hdwy & 8l 6th 11; 9l 5th 3 out; no ex.*	4	6

Countryside Counts 40-1 Miss L Gardner *(xnb) Bckwd; nt jw; a bhnd; 15l last ½way; t.o & pu 12* . . . . P

326F Gunville (7a) 11-2 Miss P Gundry *Hld up; mist 1; hdwy 6; 4l 5th ½way; 7l 4th 11; pu 12* . . . . P

Hellofajob (IRE) (7a) 11-1 R Stearn *Hld up; hdwy & 3l 4th ½way; wknd qckly & 16l 9th 11; t.o & pu 2 out* . . . . P

119P Little Word (12a) 25-1 T Vaughan *Lw; 2nd & mist 2; lost plce 6; 6l 9th ½way; lost tch 11; 17l 7th 3 out; pu 2 out* . . . . P

325³ Nearly A Mildred (5a) 7-1 A Charles-Jones *(xnb) W ldrs; lost plce & 5l 7th ½way; bhnd when pu 11* . . . . P

Regardez-Moi (5a) 25-1 J White *(xnb) Hld up & pulled hrd; hdwy 7; lost plce & 8l 10th ½way; wkng when mist 9; wl bhnd when pu 11* . . . . P

OFFICIAL DISTANCES: 1*l*, 2*l* **TIME:** 5min 20.8s

600 Open Maiden 56&7yo (Div 2), 2m4f, 12st - 14J — 13 ran

BODDIDLEY (IRE) 11-10F **Miss C Roddick** *6/4-11/10; hld up; 7½l 6th ½way; hdwy 10; 3l 4th nxt; went 2nd aft omitted 3 out; stayed on to ld cl home* 1

Herswell Castle (7a) 10-1 **R Woollacott** *(xnb) Hld up; 9l 7th ½way; hdwy & 4l 5th 11; went 8l 3rd aft 3 out; kpt on* 8½ 2

3294d **Let's Rock** 20-1 **M Green** *Chsd ldrs; 6l 4th ½way; lost plce 10; 9l 6th nxt; wknd u.p 3 out* 15 3

121² Sliema (IRE) 6-1 N Wilmington *14s-6s; a.p; 5l 3rd ½way; ld aft 10; missed marker & went 6l clr aft 3 out; wknd flat; hdd cl home; fin ½l 2nd; disq* 2d

353² Annie Fleetwood (5a) 8-1 Miss T Cave *(xnb) 20s-8s; hld up; 7l 5th ½way; went 2nd & fell 10* . . . . F

257P Black Hope (IRE) (5a) 20-1 T Vaughan *(xnb) Swtng; ld; blun 7; hdd aft 10; 2nd til stpd to nil aft 12; t.o & pu 2 out* . . . . P

53F Clare's Memory (5a) 9-1 Miss P Gundry *(xnb) Hld up & bhnd; 12l 8th ½way; gd hdwy 10; went 2nd aft 12; dem & wknd qckly aft omitted 3 out; t.o & pu last* . . . . P

Just Champ 10-1 A Charles-Jones *(xnb) Prom; 3rd when rn out thro wing & ur 6* R

Questionit (12a) 14-1 Miss L Gardner *Sn wl bhnd; 30l last ½way; t.o 10; pu 2 out* . . . . P

531P Rundetto (IRE) 50-1 S Moreton *(xnb) 2nd til wknd & hmpd 10; 20l 7th nxt; t.o & pu 2 out* . . . . P

Run Four (7a) 7-1 J Barnes *Fell 1* . . . . F

Running Earth (IRE) (7a) 8-1 N Williams *Hld up; 10l 6th when carried out by loose horse 7* C

Senor Cid (7a) 8-1 Mrs J Reed *(xnb) Hld up; lost tch 7; 20l 9th ½way; 25l 8th 11; t.o when fell last* . . . . F

OFFICIAL DISTANCES: Originally ½*l*, 6*l* **TIME:** 5min 23.0s

Fence 13 omitted - damaged; Sliema finished second but was disqualified for missing a marker after the omitted third last

601 Restricted, 12st — 7 ran

197U **WINNERS ENCLOSURE (IRE)** 10-1 **M Miller** *Hld up; last to 11; hdwy & 3l 4th 14; went 2nd aft 3 out; rdn to ld last; buffeted by gale force winds & wandered flat; just hld on* 1

498F **Preacher Boy** (7a) 2-1F **Miss P Gundry** *Hld up; 5l 6th ½way; hdwy & 2nd 13; ld aft 15; hit 2 out; hdd last; rallied flat; just failed* . . . . hd 2

383⁴ **Who's Eddie (IRE)** 9-2 **M Harris** *(xnb) 2nd til ld 9; hdd aft 15; sn outpcd* . 10 3

323⁴ Baldara (IRE)(tt) 7-1 A Farrant *Hld up; hdwy & 2l 3rd ½way; chsd ldr 11-13; 2l 3rd nxt; went 2nd u.p & jmpd slow 3 out; wknd 2 out* 1 4

368¹ Western Frontier (IRE) (7a) 11-4 D Alers-Hankey *(xnb) 2 handlers; ld til hdd & jmpd slow 9; lost plce & mist 11; 5l 5th & rdn 14; no imp* 1 5

334¹ Sula Queen (5a) 40-1 D I Turner *Jmpd rt; prom; 2½l 4th ½way; stpd to nil 11; last & lsng tch rap when blun & ur 12* . . . . U

473r Timber Top (IRE) 25-1 Mrs P Swarbrick *Mounted on course & tde; hld up; 3½l 5th ½way; hdwy 11; lost plce aft 13; 8l last nxt; v reluct to rce aft 15; wl bhnd when ref 3 out* . . . . r

OFFICIAL DISTANCES: hd, 7*l* **TIME:** 6min 34.0s

Running Hot (A. Charles-Jones, 9-2 - ref to line up) was withdrawn not under orders; Rule 4 deduction 15p in pound

602 Mixed Open, 12st — 10 ran

Form	Horse / Rider / Comment	Dist	Pos
464P	**PHAR FROM CHANCE** 14-1 **Miss P Gundry** *(xnb) A.p; 3l 4th ½way; rdn to ld app 14; drew clr & hung lft flat; all out*		1
4963	**Red Native (IRE)** evensF **N Williams** *Sn prom; 2l 3rd ½way; went 2nd aft 11 til app 14; chsd wnr app 3 out; ev ch last; wknd flat; virt stpd to nil nr fin*	8	2
89P	**Colombian Green (IRE)** 20-1 **N Mitchell** *W ldrs; 5l 6th ½way; 10l 4th & outpcd 14; went 20l 3rd app 2 out; stayed on*	5	3
	Bankit 12-1 A Charles-Jones *Ld til hdd app 14; 5l 3rd & wkng when mist 3 out*	10	4
3502	Cherokee Run (IRE) 8-1 Miss C Tizzard *2nd to 11; sn lost plce; disp 13l 6th 14; plodded on*	1	5
4712	Gladiatorial (IRE) 9-2 T Bishop *(xnb) 8s-9/2; hld up; last til 7½l 9th ½way; 15l last 14; 20l 5th 3 out; wl bhnd when pu last*		P
3506	Jackson Hill 20-1 J Snowden *(xnb) Hld up; 5½l 7th ½way; wknd & 13l 6th 14; t.o & pu 2 out*		P
	Simons Castle (IRE) 25-1 A Farrant *Hld up; 6½l 8th ½way; eff u.p 13; disp 10l 4th nxt; sn wknd; wl bhnd when pu & dism 2 out*		P
3601	Sir Dante (IRE) 2-1 F Hutsby *(xnb) Hld up; 4l 5th ½way; rdn 11; sn lost plce; disp 13l 6th 14; wl bhnd when pu 2 out; v disapp*		P
645	The Pickled Duke (IRE) 33-1 M Miller *Nd; releg 8l last ½way; lost tch & jmpd slow 13; pu 14*		P

OFFICIAL DISTANCES: 6*l*, 5*l* **TIME:** 6min 27.1s

603 PPORA Club Members (Nov Rdrs), 12st — 12 ran

Form	Horse / Rider / Comment	Dist	Pos
4723	**LEON GARCIA (IRE)** (5a) 11-2 **T Bishop** *Hld up; 7l 6th ½way; hdwy 13; 2½l 4th nxt; jnd ldr app 2 out; ld last; stayed on wl*		1
1381	**Norski Lad**(bl,tt) 5-4F **H Fry** *Sn prom; 3l 5th ½way; 2l 3rd 14; went 2nd nxt; ld aft 3 out til hdd last; hung rt & no ex flat*	2½	2
3503	**Mr Ben Gunn** 12-1 **Miss V Heal** *Ld to 4 & 7 til aft 3 out; btn when hit nxt*	7	3
496P	Opal'lou (FR) (5a, 3ow) 5-1 R Pyman *(xnb) Hld up; hdwy 9; went 1l 3rd ½way & 2nd aft 13-15; wknd 3 out*	20	4
4965	Jack The Bear (IRE) 5-1 Miss C Tuffin *8s-5s; lost plce & mist 6; 17l 10th ½way; wl bhnd 12*	8	5
200P	Millyhenry 20-1 R Lee *Nvr on terms; 16l 9th ½way; wl bhnd 12*	nk	6
322P	Glenahary Rose (IRE) (2ow) 33-1 Miss A Tory *(xnb) Nd; 12l 7th ½way; lost tch 11; 23l 9th 14; t.o*	30	7
	Zingibar(vis) 25-1 Miss J Houldey *Spurs; dogged it furiously & sn last & u.p; t.o ½way*	8	8
292P	Aldington Charlie (8ow) 50-1 C Sands *Lost plce 5; sn wl bhnd; 25l 11th ½way; t.o & pu 13*		P
	Rainbow Frontier (IRE) 33-1 Miss J Janes *(xnb) Nd; 13l 8th ½way; mist & lost tch 11; wl bhnd when pu aft 12*		P
352U	Rustic Revelry(bl) 16-1 C Whittaker *(xnb) Swtng; stayed on; 2l 4th ½way; lost plce 12; 14l 6th 14; t.o & pu 2 out*		P
	Supreme Storm (IRE) 16-1 R Bandey *Ld 4-7; 2nd to 13; 7l 5th nxt; wkng when mist & ur 15*		U

OFFICIAL DISTANCES: 5*l*, 5*l* **TIME:** 6min 31.5s

The stewards enquired into possible interference between Norski Lad and Leon Garcia on the home turn; they decided that the former had caused interference but could not say if it had been accidental or not; the rider was cautioned but not fined

604 Open Maiden 8yo&up, 12st — 12 ran

Form	Horse / Rider / Comment	Dist	Pos
139P	**TRIGGER AGAIN** 5-1 **Miss E Tory** *(xnb) 2 handlers; hld up; hdwy 6; 3l 5th ½way; went 2nd 12; ld aft 2 out; sn clr; kpt on wl*		1
1393	**Milnstorm (IRE)** 3-1 **Miss P Gundry** *(xnb) 9/2-3s; ld to 8; 2nd to 12; 4l 3rd & rdn 14; outpcd 3 out; rallied 2 out; went 2nd nr fin*	4	2
258F	**Knighton Star** (5a) 5-4F **A Charles-Jones** *(xnb) 2nd til ld 8; hdd aft 2 out; no ex*	¾	3
416r	Amy's Gift (5a) 50-1 J O'Rourke *(xnb) Tde; hld up & pulled hrd; mist 5; 5th when fell 8*		F
172P	Faugere 8-1 M Miller *(bh) 2 handlers; almost bolted out of padd & tde; a bhnd; 12l 8th ½way; pu 13*		P
1394	Hilarity (5a) 7-1 N Mitchell *(xnb) Hld up; 6l 7th ½way; hdwy 12; wknd & 8l 4th 14; wl bhnd when pu 2 out; broke down*		P
415P	Horsemans Green(cp) 7-1 J Barnes *(xnb) A bhnd; rmdrs 4; 13l 9th ½way; 20l 7th when pu 14*		P

350[7] Lily Lane 25-1 N Heath *(xnb) 2 handlers; swtng; lost plce 7; 14l 10th ½way; wl bhnd 13; almost ur 14 & 15; t.o & pu 3 out; rdr lost irons* . . . . P
474[4] Miss Karingaroo (5a) 20-1 W White *Chsd ldrs; 2½l 4th ½way; disp 8l 4th 14; sn wknd; wl bhnd when ref & ur 2 out* . . . . r
495[F] Rudge Hill 14-1 J White *2 handlers; pulled hrd; prom to 8; 4l 6th ½way; stpd to nil u.p 11; pu 12* . . . . P
The Real Murphy (IRE) 12-1 S Rogers *Sn wl bhnd; 30l last ½way; t.o & pu 13* P
Turn It On (IRE) 16-1 M Harris *Hld up; hdwy 8; 2l 3rd ½way; wknd qckly 13; 17l 6th when pu nxt* . . . . P

OFFICIAL DISTANCES: 3*l*, ½*l* **TIME:** 6min 41.6s

Southdown & Eridge

Godstone (RH 6F,18J)

Sun, 21 Mar (GOOD to SOFT)

605 Hunt Members 7 ran

124[P] **JACK HACKETT (IRE)**(bl) 10-1 **P Hall** *Chsd ldr; mist 12 & rmdrs; mist 15; 4l down & rdn 3 out; hung lft flat but kpt on to catch ldr nr fin* 1
182[6] **Alice Reigns** (5a) 1-2F **C Gordon** *Jmpd lft; rcd keen; ld; clr 10 til hung lft app 2 out; rdn app last; wknd & hdd nr fin.* . . . . nk 2
538[4] **Straight Baron** 4-1 **P Bull** *Chsd ldng pr; mist 11; rdn app 2 out; staying on when nt clr rn last 50yds; possibly unlucky.* . . . . ½ 3
419[P] Kniveniven (IRE) 10-1 Mrs J Gordon *Chsd ldrs & a ab same; 10l 4th app 13; sn lost tch* 25 4
Mambo (U) (5a, 31ow) 14-1 D Campbell *Imm t.o; ur 6; rmtd; miles bhnd til pu 13* . . . . U
Royal Dew (IRE) 14-1 D Evatt *Jmpd slow 3; a bhnd; t.o 8 til pu 3 out.* . . . . P
Tidal Reef (IRE) 7-1 G Wigley *Bhnd; jmpd slow 4; t.o 8 til pu 13* . . . . P

OFFICIAL DISTANCES: nk, ½*l* **TIME:** 6min 58.0s **TOTE:** £15.40; places £6.20,£1.70 **DF:**£16.40

The stewards enquired into possible interference between the winner and second on the run-in, the rider of the winner was found guilty of careless riding and cautioned but not fined; the result was allowed to stand

606 Restricted, 12st 5 ran

418[1] **TOUJOURS (IRE)** evensF **C Gordon** *Tk keen hld; trckd ldrs; ld 9; made rest; drew clr 2 out; v easy* 1
36[3] **Leading Case** 2-1 **P Bull** *In tch; ld app 7-9; ev ch 3 out; btn nxt* 5 2
400[5] Good Thyne Murphy (IRE) 10-1 A Braithwaite *Ld til app 7; blun 9; 3rd & no ch 12; t.o when fell hvly 15; winded* . . . . F
419[P] Ishma (IRE) 10-1 D Page (Kent) *Chsd ldr til app 7; sn bhnd; ref 9; cont; pu nxt* r
538[U] Kilvoydan (IRE) 7-1 D Phelan *Bhnd; virt ref to rce aft 7; t.o aft til pu 13.* . P

OFFICIAL DISTANCE: 6*l* **TIME:** 6min 51.0s **TOTE:** £3.10; places £2.60,£1.70 **DF:**£1.10

607 Confined, 12st 7 ran

422[U] **LIVELY LORD (IRE)** (6x)(cp,tt) 5-2F **C Gordon** *Chsd ldr 4; ld 7; made rest; clr 13; rdn & stpng flat; just hld on* 1
541[P] **Cloudy Creek (IRE)** 4-1 **P Bull** *Chsd ldrs; mist 3; chsd wnr frm 13; mist 15; rdn 2 out; kpt on flat; just failed.* . . . . nk 2
250[1] **Jims Belief (IRE)** 3-1 **G Cooper** *Prom; ld 4-7; 7l 3rd 14; wl btn frm nxt* . . 25 3
537[P] Garrison Friendly (IRE) (3x)(bl) 14-1 N Wilson (South) *Ld to 4; 12l 4th 10; no ch frm 13; t.o* . . . . fence 4
422[P] Glenmont (IRE) 14-1 Ms L Stock *A last; detach 4; t.o & pu 14.* . . . . P
534[3] Lord Of The Flies (IRE) 14-1 D Brightling *A bhnd; 14l 6th 10; sn lost tch; t.o & pu 13* . . . . P
45[2] Quick Response (IRE) 7-2 Miss B Donnelly *(xnb) Mid-div; 13l 5th 10; 4th & no ch when pu 15.* . . . . P

OFFICIAL DISTANCES: nk, 20*l* **TIME:** 6min 48.0s **TOTE:** £3.60; places £4.00,£3.00 **DF:**£14.60

The rider of Garrison Friendly was fined £65 for using the whip with excessive force and not giving his horse time to respond

608 Ladies Open — 7 ran

Form	Runner	Dist	Pos
126[2]	**TOM COBBLER (IRE)** (4x) 9-4 **Mrs P Hall** *Patient rdn; 15l 5th 9; prog nxt; lft in ld 15; sn clr; easily*		1
239[F]	**Harding** 6-4F **Mrs J Gordon** *(xnb) Jmpd lft; ld to 3 & aft 14 til blun bad & hdd nxt; no ch w wnr aft*	20	2
	Glory Trail (IRE) 12-1 **Miss H Grissell** *Chsd ldrs; 12l 5th & outpcd 13; no ch aft; lft 3rd 15*	20	3
	Castle Arrow (IRE) 14-1 Miss N Moisey *Last frm 7; t.o & pu 13*		P
	Forest Run Forest(bl) 14-1 Miss A Sansom *A bhnd; t.o when jmpd slow 10; pu 11*		P
421[2]	Kincora (IRE) (7x) 3-1 Ms L Stock *Ld 3 til aft 14; 5l 3rd when mist & ur 15*		U
536[3]	Stylish Dave (NZ) 8-1 Mrs D Rowell *(xnb) Chsd ldrs; 12l 3rd 7; outpcd app 13; 4th & no ch when pu 2 out*		P

OFFICIAL DISTANCES: 20*l*, 20*l* **TIME:** 6min 48.0s **TOTE:** £2.40; places £1.30,£1.90 **DF:**£5.20

609 Mens Open, 12st — 4 ran

Form	Runner	Dist	Pos
420[2]	**STRUGGLES GLORY (IRE)** (7x) 5-2 **Stuart Robinson** *Spurs; chsd ldrs til ld app 13; 8l clr 3 out; stayed on wl*		1
348[3]	**Little Farmer** (7x) 1-2F **P Hall** *Ld til app 13; 4l down 14; btn 3 out*	8	2
420[5]	Full Egalite(bl) 8-1 G Gallagher *Trckd ldng pr; jmpd slow 4; ref & ur 9; rmtd & cont; ref & ur 10*		r
422[F]	Kenny Davis (IRE) 8-1 P Blagg *4th when hmpd by rival & ur 50 yds aft 4*		U

OFFICIAL DISTANCE: 8*l* **TIME:** 6min 56.0s **TOTE:** £2.10 **DF:**£1.30

The stewards interviewed the rider of Full Egalite whose horse refused and got stuck in the second open ditch, then after remounting refused at the next fence; they cautioned him for behaviour prejudicial to ther good reputation of the sport

610 Countryside Alliance Club Members (Vet & Nov Rdrs), 12st - 17J — 9 ran

Form	Runner	Dist	Pos
400[U]	**ENDEAVOUR (FR)** 5-4 **G Cooper** *Prom; ld 7; made rest; blun 9; 4l clr last; r.o wl u.p flat*		1
523[1]	**Royal Action** (7x) 4-5F **P Chinery** *In tch; 3rd when blun 9; chsd wnr frm 13; chall 3 out; mist nxt; no imp aft*	8	2
537[P]	**Russian Connection (IRE)** 20-1 **A Ward-Thomas** *Bhnd; 10l last aft 12; hdwy app nxt; 10l 3rd 15; no prog aft*	8	3
414[4]	Solo Gent 20-1 Miss K Jones *W ldrs; 5l 3rd 13; wknd bef nxt; 4th & no ch 15*	15	4
421[5]	Graphic Designer (IRE) 8-1 Miss H Gordon *W ldrs to 12; sn outpcd; no ch 15*	25	5
537[P]	Tomcappagh (IRE) 20-1 J Wall *Prom til wknd 12; 6th & no ch 14*	1	6
422[9]	Caddy Man (IRE) (3ow) 20-1 A Coveney *(xnb) Rcd wide; prom til fell 8; dead*		F
	Crewski (13ow) 20-1 A Gibbons *1st ride; last when nrly ur 3; imm t.o til pu 8*		P
538[P]	Simony Sam (IRE) 20-1 J Sarchet *In tch; 6th & wkng when pu 13*		P

OFFICIAL DISTANCES: 8*l*, 10*l* **TIME:** 6min 58.0s
TOTE: £3.00; places £1.40,£1.10,£1.90 **DF:**£1.60

Fence 14 omitted - fallen horse

611 Open Maiden, 12st — 15 ran

Form	Runner	Dist	Pos
185[2]	**GRANNY SMITH (IRE)** (5a) 2-1F **C Gordon** *(xnb) Chsd ldrs; ld 5; sn clr; 8l up 15; sn in comm; r.o str*		1
345[3]	**Pistol Knight** 7-2 **Stuart Robinson** *Wl bhnd; hdwy 10; 20l 3rd 13; went 2nd app last; nd*	fence	2
539[P]	**Spruce Goose (IRE)**(tt) 33-1 **N Wilson (South)** *Sn wl bhnd; kpt on frm 13; 30l 4th 15; went 3rd app last; nd*	4	3
423[P]	Private Percival 33-1 P Blagg *Chsd ldrs; 2nd & only danger to wnr frm 12; wknd 15; tired & lost 2 plces app last*	6	4
418[5]	Almazard 16-1 P Bull *Mid-div til blun & ur 4*		U
540[P]	Bailey's Of Cashel (IRE) 10-1 Mrs J Gordon *14s-10s; mid-div when blun bad 5; bhnd & pu 9*		P
	Baron Bernard 5-1 P Chinery *A wl bhnd; t.o 7 til pu 15*		P
423[2]	Inis Eile (IRE) 6-1 P Hall *Mid-div; nvr nr ldrs; 6th & no when crawled over 13 & pu*		P
371[3]	Just Lute 14-1 G Wigley *Prom; mist 3; stdly lost plce; mid-div when mist & ur 9*		U
540[6]	Lightning Rebel 33-1 S Gordon-Watson *(xnb) Prom; 3rd when fell 8*		F
418[4]	Naughty Noah 33-1 G Gallagher *(xnb) Bhnd; t.o 10 til pu 13*		P

539[P] Seymour Of Me 33-1 Ms L Stock *Ld 3-5; 3rd & wkng 12; 5th & no ch 13; pu 14* . . . P
418[U] Sloe Coach 33-1 Miss B Donnelly *Sn bhnd; t.o & pu 11* . . . P
27[P] Victory Salute (5a) 33-1 F Wheeler *Chsd ldrs to 9; wknd 11; t.o & pu 13.* . . P
424[P] Worth A Shot (IRE) 33-1 D Phelan *A wl bhnd; t.o & pu 13.* . . . P

OFFICIAL DISTANCES: dist, 5*l* **TIME:** 7min 04.0s
TOTE: £3.90; places £2.90,£3.70,£1.50 **DF:**£7.10 **tc:**£105.80

South Herefordshire
Garnons (LH 7F,18J)
Sun, 21 Mar (GOOD with HOLDING patches)

612 Confined, 12st — 12 ran

161[1] **JUST CLIQUOT** (5a) 5-4F **G Hanmer** *Lw; stdd start; stdy prog 6; 4l 4th & gng best aft 13; ld app 3 out & imm 8l clr; dived at last; eased flat* . . . 1
359[2] **Inis Cara (IRE)** 7-2 **M Hooper** *Nt jw; handy; clsd to ld aft 11; hdd & blun 15; 3rd when jmpd slow nxt; urged to snatch mod 2nd nr fin* . . . 8 2
Haste Ye Back (IRE)(vis) 16-1 **Miss V Price** *(xnb) 2nd/3rd til ld 7-9; 3l 3rd aft 13; ld agn 14-15; imm outpcd; rdr drpd hands & dem nr fin* . . . hd 3
107[7] Joy For Life (IRE) (5a) 8-1 Julian Pritchard *Prsd ldrs; 5l 5th aft 13; rdn & wknd app 3 out* . . . 8 4
512[2] No Fiddling (IRE) 9-1 Miss R Reynolds *Towards rr; poor 7th aft 13; clsd brief 14-15; rdn & nt r.o; sn btn* . . . 3 5
403[3] Henry Bruce(bl) 20-1 A Brown *V reluct in last; t.o 6; passed 2 rivals in clsng stages* . . . 20 6
403[4] Southern Cross 14-1 T Stephenson *11th when bad mist 2; t.o 9th aft 13; jmpd lft & mist last* . . . 2 7
356[1] Coole'sabbot (IRE)(bl) 12-1 M Walters *Sn 2nd; ld aft 6-7; ld 9 til aft 11; chsd ldr til wknd app 14; t.o 3 out* . . . 1 8
405[7] Cariad Cymru 9-1 M Jackson *Mid-div; 5th 11; 6l 6th aft 13; mist nxt & sn btn; t.o & pu last* . . . P
402[2] Darrell Boy (IRE)(vis) 25-1 D Mansell *Midfield early; nt keen frm 9; wl bhnd when pu aft 13* . . . P
403[12] Inthaar 33-1 A Phillips *(xnb) Ld til aft 6; wkng when mist 9; 10th & tailing off aft 13; pu 3 out* . . . P
Pear Tree Percy 25-1 R Rogers *Lw; cl up to 6; drvn & wkng 11; nt r.o; rem 8th aft 13; pu 3 out* . . . P

OFFICIAL DISTANCES: 10*l*, nk **TIME:** 6min 36.0s

The stewards interviewed the rider of Haste Ye Back who dropped her hands before the finish and forfeited second place; she had been unaware of the horse behind her and was severely cautioned as to her future riding

613 Ladies Open — 9 ran

449[1] **UPTON ADVENTURE** (5a) 2-5F **Miss E James** *Trckd ldrs; chsd clr ldr frm 9; niggled 15; clsd nxt; ld app 2 out; sn clr; pushed out; easily.* . . . 1
402[U] **Gipsy Cricketer** 10-1 **Miss C Stucley** *(xnb) V keen; ld at gd gallop aft 1; pckd 2; hdd app 2 out; sn btn; tired when mist last* . . . 12 2
230[4] **Lucky Master (IRE)** 25-1 **Miss G Swan** *Sn t.o; last til slt prog 11; 35l 6th aft 13; no imp aft; nvr put in rce* . . . 15 3
How To Run (IRE) 7-1 Miss F Wilson *Bckwd; 3rd/4th; mist 9; 28l 4th & strugg aft 13; plodded on; t.o 3 out* . . . 4 4
407[4] Esterelle (USA) (5a) 16-1 Miss S Beddoes *(xnb) Ld 1; chsd ldr to 9; wknd to 34l 5th aft 13; t.o aft 15* . . . 8 5
452[1] Vicars Chalet (IRE) 8-1 Miss H Lewis *Midfield; eff 10; 18l 3rd & outpcd aft 13; t.o 3rd 3 out; fin lame* . . . 12 6
176[P] Grand Gousier (FR)(bl,tt) 12-1 Miss J Williams *A bhnd; 40l 8th aft 13; t.o & pu 2 out* . . . P
Rosemead Tye (5a) 33-1 Miss N Stallard *Hdwy to 3rd 7; hit 8; wknd rap 11; t.o 13; pu 15* . . . P
110[P] Welburn Boy(bl,tt) 33-1 Miss L Allfrey *Rdr pitched forwards nrly ev fnce; wl bhnd til hdwy 8; 36l 7th & strugg agn aft 13; t.o & pu 2 out* . . . P

OFFICIAL DISTANCES: 15*l*, 25*l* **TIME:** 6min 30.0s

614 Restricted, 12st — 12 ran

Prev	Horse / details	Dist	Pos
406[2]	**LOVE AT DAWN** 2-1F **P Mason** *Hld up; impd to disp 3rd 9; ld aft 11; gng str frm 14; 5l ahd 3 out; rdn out; rdly*		1
404[3]	**Ballingale Dawn (IRE)** 7-2 **R Rogers** *Prom; 3l 3rd aft 13; chsd wnr til 5l down & btn 3 out; fin v tired*	15	2
516[2]	**Paddy Bettalot** 12-1 **T Stephenson** *Prom; ld aft 7 til aft 11; 2l 2nd aft 13; v one-pcd aft; 8l 3rd 3 out; fin tired*	6	3
383[8]	Tinarana Lord (IRE) 4-1 G Hanmer *Lw; hld up in rr; 9l 8th aft 13; wknd & no ch frm 15; 20l 4th 3 out*	20	4
231[4]	Henbury Dancer (5a) 25-1 E Linehan *Mounted on course & unruly; hld up last pr; jmpd slow 9; slt prog nxt; 8l 7th aft 13; terrible mist 14; cont t.o*	10	5
	Merry Major 10-1 M Keel *(xnb) Ld 5 til app 7; disp 5l 4th aft 13; nt r.o; t.o aft 15*	12	6
452[P]	A Bit Of Fluff (5a) 20-1 Miss L Brooke *Prom til ur 2*		U
530[P]	Always Good (IRE) 20-1 Julian Pritchard *Jmpd v poor; ld; climbed 2; hdd 5; ld agn & jmpd v slow 7 & hdd; drpd to rr aft 11; 12l 9th aft 13; pu 15*		P
	Exclusively (5a) 20-1 M Munrowd *Rr div; 9th 8; fell 11*		F
408[1]	Shafts Chance (IRE) (5a) 9-1 S Ross *Hld up towards rr; prog to disp 5l 4th aft 13; 4th but lkng outpcd when fell 15*		F
369[P]	Snowtre (IRE)(cp) 7-1 A Wintle *(xnb) Towards rr; clsd 11; 6l 6th aft 13; outpcd when bd 15*		B
358[5]	The Last Shout (IRE) 33-1 Miss A Hughes *Prom til jmpd v slow 2; climbed 7; t.o nxt; furlongs bhnd when pu & dism 12*		P

OFFICIAL DISTANCES: 14*l*, 6*l* **TIME:** 6min 41.0s

The rider of Henbury Dancer was fined £50 for being unable to produce his Medical Record Book

615 Mens Open, 12st — 8 ran

Prev	Horse / details	Dist	Pos
205[1]	**BRIGHT BEACON** (4x) 4-5F **E Williams** *Jw; tkn stdly; impd to 2nd 8; chsd clr ldr til ld 3 out; sn wl clr; canter frm last*		1
404[P]	**Time Can Tell**(bl) 12-1 **S Graham** *Rr div; eff in 10½l 3rd aft 11; 12l 4th & wkng aft 13; lft 3rd nxt & plugged on; t.o when lft 2nd at last; virt pu flat*	14sec	2
93[P]	Benick (IRE) 20-1 M Wilesmith *3rd brief; already strugg when mist 5; last 6; t.o when broke leg & slpd up app 7; dead*		S
	Berkeley Frontier (IRE) (7x) 12-1 D Jones *Chsd clr ldr to 7; 6th & wkng rap when pu 12*		P
292[P]	Chadswell (IRE) (7x) 14-1 D Greenway *3rd/4th; 10l 3rd when pckd bad & ur 14*		U
	Freestyler (IRE)(tt) 12-1 G Hanmer *Detach in last pr; some hdwy 9; 6th when ref 11*		r
403[6]	Head Gardener (IRE)(bl) 20-1 D Mansell *Last pr; t.o 7; 25l last aft 11; pu 14*		P
448[P]	Thatsforeel (7x) 9-4 A Wintle *Bckwd; ld & clr; 15l ahd 8; 6l up aft 13; hdd app 3 out; plodded on; poor 2nd & tired when fell last*		F

OFFICIAL DISTANCE: dist **TIME:** 6min 37.0s

616 Dodson & Horrell PPORA Club Members, 12st — 7 ran

Prev	Horse / details	Dist	Pos
513[P]	**HIJACKED** 13-2 **T Stephenson** *Trckd ldrs; went 2nd aft 11; disp 1l 2nd aft 13; ld gng best aft 15; 3l clr nxt; idled flat; drvn out*		1
447[3]	**Genereux**(cp,tt) 7-1 **R Hodges** *Drvn at sev stages; handy; 3l 4th aft 13; 6l 3rd 3 out; stayed on und str press to 2nd flat; no ch w wnr*	5	2
209[3]	**Arctic King** 7-4F **D Jones** *Nt fluent; 2nd til ld aft 11; drvn 15; sn hdd; 3l 2nd nxt; wknd app last; dem flat*	10	3
409[1]	Shy Lizzie (5a) 7-1 P Mason *Trckd ldrs; 3½l 5th aft 13; 12l 4th & outpcd 15; plugged on*	¾	4
	Joshua's Vision (IRE)(tt) 14-1 Miss L Brooke *Bckwd; 6th when hit 5; pu & dism 6*		P
	Prominent 2-1 G Hanmer *V reluct to line up; last away & nvr btr; rmdr 10 & no resp; 10l last when rdn & reluct aft 13; t.o 15; pu flat*		P
	Top Of The Charts 14-1 Julian Pritchard *Made most til aft 11; disp 1l 2nd aft 13; wknd rap 15; t.o & pu 3 out*		P

OFFICIAL DISTANCES: 3*l*, 6*l* **TIME:** 6min 43.0s

617 Open Maiden 56&7yo (Div 1, Part 1), 2m4f, 12st - 15J — 9 ran

111P **FESTIVAL TIME** 5-2F **G Hanmer** *Ld; 3l clr 8; prsd aft blun 11; hdd aft 12; 3l 3rd when lft 3l clr nxt; drvn flat; plugged on; lucky* . . . 1
362³ **Dans Blarney (IRE)** 4-1 **D Jones** *Pulled hrd; chsd wnr 8 til aft 12; lft 3l last 3 out; hrd rdn & no imp aft* . . . 2½ 2
143P Bubble Brook 6-1 N Oliver *Last by 6; strugg when pu 9* . . . P
Chance Fortune 4-1 A Wadlow *Fell 2* . . . F
291P Fromrussiawithlove (12a) 4-1 M Keel *2nd when fell 7* . . . F
Just Henry 4-1 Julian Pritchard *Fell 2* . . . F
Mr Tobias 7-1 J Cook *(xnb) Wl t.o when climbed 4; ref 5* . . . r
454P Red Salmon Dancer (7a) 7-1 D Mansell *Hld up; 5½l 4th aft 10; chall nxt; rdn to cl 2nd when fell 3 out* . . . F
408³ Toffee Lady (5a) 3-1 R Rogers *Trckd ldrs; 9l 3rd aft mist 8; chall 12; ld aft 12; slt advant when fell nxt* . . . F

OFFICIAL DISTANCE: 2*l* **TIME:** 5min 47.0s

618 Open Maiden 56&7yo (Div 1, Part 2), 2m4f, 12st - 15J — 9 ran

JUSTADREAM 8-1 **T Stephenson** *(xnb) Hld up towards rr til prog 9; 2l 3rd app 11; ld app 2 out; sn clr; hvly eased flat* . . . 1
364² **Che Guevara** 2-1JF **G Barfoot-Saunt** *Drpd out last to 8; prog to 2½l 4th app 11; bad mist nxt & nt rec; 12l 3rd 3 out; kpt on to 2nd flat; v flatt by prox* 3 2
You Can Call Me Al 4-1 **D Mansell** *Bad mist 3; ld to 5; 1½l 2nd app 11; sn fdd; disp 18l 4th 3 out; plodded home* . . . 12 3
Jack's The Boy (IRE) 5-1 G Hanmer *(xnb) 2nd til ld 5; 5l clr 11; mist 12; hdd app 2 out; fdd rap; v tired & jmpd rt last* . . . 2½ 4
Lucky Wyn 10-1 M Walters *Mists in rr; eff 8; 6l 6th app 11; sn fdd* . . . 1 5
149P Bristol Bridge 10-1 M Barber *(xnb) Lw; hld up towards rr; went prom 8; 5l 5th when mist 11; fdd bad; t.o & pu 3 out* . . . P
Calamint (7a) 10-1 J Merry *Pulled hrd; 2nd 5 til fell 7* . . . F
256³ No Keep (IRE) 2-1JF D Greenway *Prom; 2nd when fell 9* . . . F
128P Vintage Rock 10-1 D Sherlock *Towards rr; t.o when nrly ref 9; pu 12* . . . P

OFFICIAL DISTANCES: 4*l*, 10*l* **TIME:** 5min 47.0s

619 Open Maiden 56&7yo (Div 2), 2m4f, 12st - 15J — 13 ran

GAYNOR'S GAMBLE (IRE) 6-1 **G Hanmer** *Hld up; eff to disp 2½l 3rd aft 10; disp ld 12; ld aft 3 out; hrd rdn & wandering bad flat; all out (won on jockeyship)* . . . 1
452P **Rosegrove Rooster** 12-1 **T Stephenson** *Mounted on course; hld up towards rr; eff & disp 2½l 3rd aft 10; 4l 3rd app 3 out; chsd wnr u.p aft nxt; v one-pcd & no imp cl home* . . . ¾ 2
295P **Chicago's Padre** 10-1 **A Hanly** *Prom; 1½l 2nd aft 10; jnd ldng pr 12; rdn & ld brief 3 out; wknd qckly* . . . 12 3
453⁴ Meadows Prince (IRE) (7a)(cp) 7-1 D Mansell *Ld to 7; 3½l 5th aft 10; wknd bad 12; t.o 3 out; reluct* . . . 40 4
Borrisimo (IRE) 10-1 M Wall *Fat; jb & detach in last pr; jmpd v slow 6 & cont t.o; pu 9* . . . P
Countess Kiri (5a) 4-1 M Barber *Fell 2* . . . F
Kotori (IRE) (7a) 12-1 S Gray *Fell 3* . . . F
Mandagus (IRE) 5-1 D Barlow *Prom; ld 7-12; stpd to nil; pu 3 out* . . . P
409F McGinty All Stars (IRE) (5a) 6-1 M Hooper *Detach in last pr; nrly fell 7; 15l last aft 10; t.o & pu 3 out* . . . P
533P Neeley (7a) 10-1 M Keel *Nt jw towards rr; in tch til mist 9; blun 10 & qckly pu (inj hind leg)* . . . P
410² Nothing Better (IRE) (12a) 7-4F T Weston *Bd 2* . . . B
Sett Aside 8-1 Julian Pritchard *Awkward start; ur app 1* . . . U
The Brooklet 10-1 G Barfoot-Saunt *Carried out by loose horse app 1* . . . C

OFFICIAL DISTANCES: 1*l*, 15*l* **TIME:** 5min 46.0s

620 Open Maiden 8yo&up (Div 1), 12st — 9 ran

296F **NORTHERN PRINCE** 13-2 **Miss C Allen** *Lw; ld/disp til ld 7; mist 15; rdn & hdd last; kpt on as ldr gave up; v tired but ld agn final 50yds* . . . 1
409² **Rosie Stroud (IRE)** (5a) 2-1 **Julian Pritchard** *Hld up towards rr; eff 13 to disp 2l 2nd nxt; prsd wnr til pushed ahd last; hung violent rt & dogged it flat; hdd final 50yds* . . . 6 2

451[3]	**Risk Advisory (IRE)**(cp,tt) 11-2 **R Hodges** *Hit 1; mist 2; ld/disp til aft 6; 3rd & rdn 11; ev ch til wknd aft 15; fin v slow*	35	3
	Autcaesar Autnihil (IRE) 7-1 M Munrowd *Mists in last pr; strugg aft errors 8 & 9; pu 12*		P
408[2]	Brendas Nightmare (5a) 7-4F A Wadlow *Prsd ldrs; 3l 6th aft 13; wknd tame nxt; t.o & pu 3 out*		P
517[P]	Corn General 20-1 D Jones *Hld up; impd qckly to 2nd 9 til aft 13; pu rap nxt*		P
363[P]	Evans The Coal 20-1 R Carey *(xnb) Mounted on course; unruly; pulled hrd; prom til aft 13; stpd to nil nxt; t.o & pu 3 out*		P
	Its Mr Blobby 20-1 J Cook *Bckwd; last & lsng tch aft 6; pu 8*		P
	Tensing 5-1 G Barfoot-Saunt *(xnb) Midfield to 7; lost tch 10; t.o when mist 13; pu 3 out*		P

OFFICIAL DISTANCES: 6*l*, dist **TIME:** 7min 00.0s

621 Open Maiden 8yo&up (Div 2), 12st — 9 ran

259[2]	**CRAIOVA COMET (IRE)** 3-1 **T Weston** *Midfield; hdwy 7; pckd 9; 1/2l 2nd aft mist 13; ld nxt & dashed 10l clr 15; rdn flat & fin slow; all out but unchall*		1
	Lord Woodyard 6-1 **Julian Pritchard** *(xnb) Ld aft 1-2; prom; 3l 3rd aft 13; chsd wnr aft 15; mist nxt; drvn & a hld aft; fin tired*	8	2
357[P]	**Johnston's Ville (IRE)** 5-1 **J Merry** *Ld 1; towards rr aft 6; 5l 6th aft 13; wknd nxt; 18l 3rd 3 out; plugged on*	8	3
	Wind On The Common 7-2 T Stephenson *Hld up in rr; clsd 11; 6l 7th aft 13; sn wknd; 24l 4th 3 out; nt pushed flat & could have been poor 3rd*	nk	4
258[F]	Sales Dodger (IRE)(cp) 5-1 R Hughes *Nt fluent early; hld up; 4l 5th aft 13; lost tch nxt; 30l 5th 3 out*	2 1/2	5
443[P]	Come On Boy 7-1 G Davies *Made most frm 4; pckd 9; hdd 14; 10l 2nd when mist nxt; wknd rap; t.o & exhaust when pu imm bef 2 out*		P
	Cosmic Flight (IRE) 5-2F G Hanmer *Tk keen hld; prom; ld 7-8; pckd 9; 3 1/2l 4th aft 13; wknd qckly aft nxt; t.o & pu 2 out*		P
	Himalayan Heights 9-2 R Rogers *Ld 2 til hit 4; 2nd 8; lost tch 12; blun 13; t.o when jmpd v slow nxt; pu 15*		P
517[P]	Norton Wood (IRE) 10-1 T Faulkner *(xnb) Bhnd; mist 8; rdn & strugg 11; 16l 8th aft 13; t.o & pu 3 out*		P

OFFICIAL DISTANCES: 10*l*, 15*l* **TIME:** 6min 58.0s

Vale of Aylesbury with Garth & S. Berks

Tweseldown (RH 9F,19J)

Sun, 21 Mar (GOOD to FIRM, GOOD & SOFT in places)

622 Hunt Members, 12st — 4 ran

422[3]	**MISTER PEPPER (IRE)** 2-5F **T Underwood** *Hld up in rr; hdwy frm 16; ld app 2 out; pushed out flat*		1
100[F]	**La Colina (IRE)** (7x) 2-1 **James Tudor** *(xnb) Opened 11/4; lw; jw; ld til app 2 out; stayed on one pce*	2	2
	Steve Ford 16-1 **Miss E Harbour** *Trckd ldng pr; mist 13; nt fluent nxt; outpcd frm 16*	10	3
191[F]	Kingfisher Star 10-1 Miss J Lodge *(xnb) Cl 2nd til wknd frm 16; wl btn when ur 2 out*		U

OFFICIAL DISTANCES: 2*l*, 5*l* **TIME:** not taken

623 Confined, 12st — 4 ran

422[4]	**DANCING FOSENBY** 4-7F **M Holdforth** *(xnb) Evens-4/7; made virt all; hrd prsd frm 14; qcknd 2l clr & in comm 2 out; hrd hld*		1
422[6]	**Satcotino (IRE)** (5a) 2-1 **P York** *Oht; trckd ldrs in 3rd; rdn to 2nd 12; drvn along & prsd ldr 14 til no ex frm 2 out; stayed on one pce*	2 1/2	2
175[P]	**Angus Airways (IRE)** 16-1 **M Legge** *(xnb) Tchd 20s; mostly cl 2nd til wknd frm 12*	25	3
455[2]	Lord Esker (IRE) 4-1 T Underwood *A last; rn into bottom of sev fncs; wl bhnd frm 12; pu 3 out; bbv*		P

OFFICIAL DISTANCES: 3*l*, dist **TIME:** 6min 14.0s

624 Mens Open, 12st

440^{3} **TANAGER James Tudor** *Walked over.* 1

625 Ladies Open — 5 ran

157^{4} **LE PRINCE** 6-1 **Miss E Jones** *Hld up in rr; stalked ldr frm 12 til qcknd to ld 3 out; drvn out & r.o wl flat; wl rdn* 1

438^{P} **Caldamus** (7x) 9-4 **Miss A Goschen** *Tchd 5/2; v late in padd; trckd ldr; jmpd slow 13; outpcd 15 & sn rdn; rallied app last; no ex flat* 1½ 2

407^{2} **Pride Of Kashmir** evensF **Miss S Phizacklea** *Tchd 5/4; tkn wide; trckd ldr; rdn frm 16; ev ch app last; one pce* 2 3

361^{3} Andre Laval (IRE) 33-1 Miss H Watson *A last pr; outpcd 14; sn btn* 10 4

536^{4} Jack Of Kilcash (IRE) 5-1 Miss A Stennett *10s-5s; lw; ld & set sedate pce; qcknd 12; hdd 3 out; wknd rap* 5 5

OFFICIAL DISTANCES: 1*l*, ½*l* **TIME:** 6min 20.0s

626 Thames Valley Combined Hunts Club Members (Nov Rdrs), 12st — 6 ran

435^{4} **MASTER JOCK** (7x) 4-6F **W Kinsey** *Trckd ldr; pckd 8; cl 2nd frm 13; ld 3 out; rdn out* 1

355^{2} **King Of Swing (IRE)** 10-1 **Mrs F Vigar** *(xnb) 25s-10s; trckd ldr; ld 5; qcknd 14; hdd 3 out; stayed on one pce* 4 2

17^{6} **Toscanini (GER)** (7x) 5-1 **M Legge** *8s-5s; ww; prog frm 9; outpcd 14; stayed on one pce frm 3 out* ½ 3

Golden Jack (FR) 5-1 C Morris *Hld up last; outpcd 14; some mod late hdwy frm 3 out.* 6 4

Lyrical Seal (5a)(bl) 5-1 H Wallace *Ww; pushed along frm 11; bhnd frm 14* 6 5

536^{P} Newby End (IRE)(vis) 20-1 Miss C Cowe *Made most to 5; blun bad & nrly ur nxt; trckd ldr til outpcd 14; sn btn* 2 6

OFFICIAL DISTANCES: 5*l*, ½*l* **TIME:** 6min 29.0s

627 Open Maiden, 12st — 9 ran

THYNE MAN (IRE) evensF **W Hill** *Parrot-mouthed; opened 5/4; hld up early & nt fluent; stdy prog frm 11 & jmpd btr; rdn to ld last; drvn out* 1

424^{U} **Midnight Lord (IRE)** 14-1 **P York** *Disp ld 1-4; prom til lft in ld 14; hrd drvn frm 3 out; hdd last; no ex* 3 2

424^{P} **Octane Booster (IRE)** 10-1 **M Holdforth** *(xnb) Tchd 12s; disp ld 1-4; trckd ldrs til prog to chall 16; blun 2 out; nt rec* 4 3

459^{4} Lord Of Heaven (USA) 16-1 Miss K Cuthbertson *Ss & a rr; blun & rdr lost irons brief 13; stayed on one pce frm 16* 2 4

Barbed Broach (IRE) 16-1 M Sheridan *Trckd ldr; rap prog to ld 4; hdd 8; qckly lost ground frm 12; pu 14* P

Ministerial (IRE) 8-1 Miss A Goschen *14s-8s; ld; blun bad & ur 1* U

443^{P} On A Full Wager(bl) 8-1 B King *2 handlers; ww; prog to ld 8; hdd 12; lsng ground when blun & rdr lost iron 15; pu nxt* P

290^{2} To The Top 7-4 James Tudor *Disp ld 1-4; prom til qcknd to ld agn 12; 2l clr & gng best when carried out by loose horse 14.* C

463^{P} Winleah 20-1 Miss S Phizacklea *V sa; wl bhnd when pu 2* P

OFFICIAL DISTANCES: 5*l*, 2*l* **TIME:** 6min 32.0s

Hereford (RH 9F,13J)

Mon, 22 Mar (GOOD to SOFT)

628 Julian Graves HC, 2m3f £2009 — 15 ran

470^{3} **SADLER'S REALM** 11-07 6-1 **Miss L Gardner** *Chsd clr ldr 5 til clsd to ld passing 11; drew 8l clr nxt; unchall* 1

294^{5} **Viscount Bankes** 11-09 7-1 **A Martin** *(xnb) Chsd ldrs; eff app 9; jnd wnr brief passing 11; sn outpcd u.p but a wl clr of rest* 21 2

241^{7} **The Hearty Joker (IRE)** 12-00(bl) 5-1 **R Bandey** *Chsd ldrs to 6; 7th & strugg 8; t.o aft 11; snatched 3rd nr fin* 28 3

442^{P} Traditional (IRE) 11-09(cp) 14-1 N Williams *Nt fluent in midfield; 6th & lsng tch app 9; rdn along aft; went 28l 3rd app 3 out; sn t.o; dem nr fin* ½ 4

544^{B} Mister Falcon (FR) 11-09 12-1 D Mansell *Nt jw; 8th & u.p 6; strugg & nt keen 9; t.o app 3 out* 18 5

317^{8} Chaparro Amargoso (IRE) 11-07 25-1 S Ross *Mist 1; hmpd & ur 2* U

490[P]	Chief Mouse 11-07(cp) 40-1 S Graham *Reluct to start & barely able to gallop; sn hopeless t.o; event pu 11*		P
450[4]	Foxy Royale 11-07 25-1 T Faulkner *Fell hvly 2; lkd inj*		F
	Hill Trail 11-07(tt) 33-1 R Bliss *(xnb) Off pce in midfield; 10th when mist 5; pu nxt*		P
434[3]	Home Again (IRE) 11-09 9-2JF M Barber *Chsd ldr to 5; lsng plce when mist 8 (water); t.o 6th & exhaust when jb lft 3 out & pu*		P
444[6]	Macgyver (NZ) 12-00 9-2JF J Diment *Ld & clr; 5l ahd 8; hdd passing 11; 4th & fdng rap when pu 3 out*		P
450[5]	Magicien (FR) 11-07 50-1 R Hodges *Hmpd 2; sn t.o; pu 9*		P
65[U]	Magnemite (IRE) 11-07(bl) 11-1 J White *Off pce in midfield; 9th & strugg u.p 6; t.o & pu 8*		P
230[6]	Midy's Risk (FR) 11-07 20-1 Miss S Davies *Mist 1; nt jw & sn t.o; pu 11*		P
158[P]	Santi (FR) 11-11 28-1 P Cowley *Midfield; lost tch rap app 9; t.o & pu 3 out*		P

TIME: 5min 00.8s **TOTE:** £6.90; places £1.60,£5.30,£1.50 **Ex:**£68.40 **CSF:**£46.43

Fence 11 omitted - fallen horse

Exeter (RH 11F,18J)

Tue, 23 Mar (GOOD to SOFT, GOOD in places)

629 Robert Webb Travel Open HC, 3m1f110y £3640 — 11 ran

490[1]	**MACGEORGE (IRE)** 12-00 7-2 **M Barber** *Made all; 10l clr 12; mist 14; rdn app nxt; stayed on v game; unchall*		1
437[2]	**The Granby (IRE)** 11-05 12-1 **Miss H Irving** *3rd/4th til chsd wnr 8; rdn 12; dem nxt; 2nd agn & hmpd 2 out; no ch w wnr; fin tired*	27	2
348[1]	**Right To Reply (IRE)** 12-02 5-4F **N Harris** *Hld up in rr; smooth prog app 11; chsd wnr 13; 6l down & rdn when mist 15; sn wknd; tired & nt fluent nxt; jmpd rt & dem 2 out*	9	3
178[2d]	Garruth (IRE) 11-07 4-1 N Williams *Chsd wnr to 8; 4th & u.p 13; no resp & sn wl btn*	1	4
437[5]	Maggies Brother 11-13 50-1 D Barlow *A bhnd; t.o 10*	28	5
537[U]	Nomadic Star 11-05 100-1 Miss Z Lilly *A bhnd; nt fluent 4; t.o 10*	24	6
318[2]	Norlandic (NZ) 12-02 12-1 L Jefford *Prom; nt fluent 4; wkng when mist 10; t.o & pu 3 out*		P
292[1]	Paddy For Paddy (IRE) 12-02 12-1 R Burton *Hld up; hdwy aft 10; 5th & drvn nxt; wknd app 12; t.o & pu 15*		P
321[P]	Pendragon 11-09 66-1 N Mitchell *A bhnd; t.o 10; pu 3 out*		P
495[7]	Sootsir 11-05 100-1 J Barnes *Sn rdn & a wl bhnd; t.o last 10; pu 14*		P
437[3]	Soul King (IRE) 11-05 50-1 R Bliss *Hld up; blun 4; 20l 6th when hit 8; strugg aft; t.o & pu 3 out*		P

TIME: 6min 41.1s **TOTE:** £5.70; places £2.20,£2.30,£1.50 **Ex:**£39.60 **CSF:**£41.50

Fence 11 omitted; the owner of Sootsir, whose passport was found to be incorrect, was fined £110

Ludlow (RH 8F,17J)

Thu, 25 Mar (GOOD to SOFT)

630 Magnus-Allcroft Mem Trophy HC, 2m4f £3125 — 17 ran

543[9]	**MULLENSGROVE** 11-11 10-1 **Miss S Phizacklea** *Hld up; 5th & clsng 9; ld 12; drvn 15l clr 14; kpt on str aft; unchall (another galvanic ride)*		1
347[U]	**Phoenix Phlyer** 11-11(cp) 13-2 **Miss C Stucley** *Prom but nvr able to dominate; 4th 9; 2nd brief 10; 12l 4th 13; chsd wnr vain 3 out*	25	2
435[U]	**Caher Society (IRE)** 11-08 (1ow) 33-1 **P Morris** *Mists & rdr oft waving; prom; ld 9; blun 11; hdd 12; 15l 2nd 14; dem & mist 3 out*	13	3
444[1]	Route One (IRE) 12-04 13-2 S Morris *Nt jw; prom in group chsng 4 clr ldrs; 6th 9; strugg nxt*	¾	4
545[4]	Guignol Du Cochet (FR) 11-07 9-1 G Slade-Jones *Nvr went pce; poor 11th 9; plugged on*	2	5
436[4]	Mydante (IRE) 11-02 12-1 S Hughes *Midfield; 9th 9; 35l 6th 13; blun nxt*	14	6
347[P]	Polar Prospect 12-00 33-1 Miss P Gundry *Midfield; bad mist 6; nt rec; 13th 9; t.o 13*	dist	7

479P Ballad Minstrel (IRE) 11-07 33-1 Miss J Foster *Bhnd; 14th & strugg 9; t.o & pu 14* . . . . P
439¹ Bohemian Spirit (IRE) 11-11 6-1 S Charlton *Swtng; hld up; mod 12th 9; brief eff 12; 32l 5th nxt; rem 8th when pu 2 out* . . . . P
441⁵ Camitrov (FR) 11-07 50-1 G Kerr *Bhnd; t.o 16th & drvn 9; pu 12* . . . . P
437F Cimarrone Cove (IRE) 11-11(bl) 9-1 T Greenall *Midfield; 8th 9; rem 9th 13; blun nxt; pu 15* . . . . P
377P Fountain Street (IRE) 11-07 100-1 W Kinsey *Rdn & strugg 7; 15th & t.o 9; pu 12* . . . . P
441⁶ On The Mend (IRE) 12-00 66-1 R Wakeham *Nt fluent 7; chsd ldrs til 7th & u.p 9; wkng when blun nxt; t.o & pu 3 out* . . . . P
490P Scoundrel 11-07 100-1 A Price *Fat; imm rdn in last & strugg; wl t.o 9; ab 1½ fncs bhnd when event pu 12* . . . . P
348P Sea Haitch Em 11-13 11-2F N Williams *2nd til ld 8-9; ev ch til 3rd & rdn 13; wknd rap; poor 6th when pu 2 out* . . . . P
441⁴ Solvang (IRE) 11-07 66-1 M Wall *Midfield & nvr gng pce; 10th 9; same 13; t.o & blun 14; pu 2 out* . . . . P
374¹ Templebreedy (IRE) 12-00 7-1 R Burton *Set frenetic pce to 8; stpd rap aft 9; t.o & pu 12* . . . . P

TIME: 5min 12.0s **TOTE:** £15.40; places £4.10,£3.10,£7.60 **Ex:**£71.30 **CSF:**£71.45

Newbury (LH 11F,17J)

Fri, 26 Mar (GOOD, GOOD to SOFT in places)

631 Montpelier Re HC, 2m6f110y £1934 — 10 ran

581U **SILENCE REIGNS** 11-07(bl) 15-8F **N Williams** *Hld up in tch; went 2nd 10; ld gng wl 14; 5l clr 2 out; eased flat; v easily* 1
347³ **Jabiru (IRE)** 11-12(bl) 3-1 **D Edwards** *Jmpd lft; ld 3; 6l clr & rdn 13; hdd nxt; sn no ch w wnr; went lft 2 out; kpt on to retain 2nd flat* 16 2
438³ **Blackberry Way** 11-11(tt) 14-1 **J Diment** *Hld up in rr; hdwy 9; 3rd 13; sn rdn & outpcd; rallied frm 2 out to cl on runner-up flat; no ch w wnr* . . . . ½ 3
541⁵ Normania (NZ) 11-05 25-1 Miss S West *Chsd ldrs; 3rd 12; outpcd nxt; stayed on agn aft 2 out; kpt on flat; nd* 2½ 4
541³ Don Royal 11-12 7-2 N Harris *Prom; 2nd 9; releg 5th 11; wknd tame nxt.* 11 5
434² Sip Of Brandy (IRE) 11-09 14-1 Miss J Hughes *Rdr nrly f.o 2; waved 3; nt fluent aft; a bhnd; t.o 8* 30 6
187P One Of The Natives (IRE) 11-05(vis) 50-1 Miss J Jenner *Pulled hrd & rcd wide; ld to 3; 2nd til wknd 8; wl bhnd frm 10; t.o* 21 7
Shu Gaa (IRE) 11-13 10-1 S Morris *Bad hmpd & nrly fell 2; nt rec; wl bhnd in last pr; t.o 8* . . . . dist 8
288P Hawthorn 11-05 50-1 A Hanly *Fell 2* . . . . F
581U King Of The Dawn 11-09 33-1 J Sole *Bhnd; 6th but in tch when rfo 9* . . . U

TIME: 5min 46.0s **TOTE:** £2.40; places £1.30,£1.60,£2.80 **Ex:**£7.60 **CSF:**£7.61

Avon Vale

Larkhill (RH 13F,18J)

Sat, 27 Mar (GOOD to FIRM, GOOD in places)

632 Hunt Members — 4 ran

527F **RHYTHM KING** evensF **G Maundrell** *(xnb) 6/4-evens; lw; hld up in tch; jw; tk ld app 13; drew clr 15; easily* 1
138⁵ **Strong Tea (IRE)** 11-10 **A Charles-Jones** *Tde; prom; slt ld 6 til app 13; 3l 2nd nxt; sn outpcd; 10l 2nd 16; kpt on one pce* 5 2
610⁴ **Solo Gent** 25-1 **Miss K Jones** *2 handlers; rcd keen; nt a fluent; slt ld frm 2 til hmpd by loose horse aft 5; in tch til wknd 14; sn one pce* 15 3
261U Gigi Beach (IRE) 12-1 Mrs S Reynoldson *Slt ld 1; cl 2nd nxt til rfo 4* . . . . U

OFFICIAL DISTANCES: 6*l*, 20*l* **TIME:** 6min 13.0s **TOTE:** £1.60

633 Confined Maiden 56&7yo, 2m4f, 12st - 15J — 6 ran

Form	Horse / Rider / Comment	Dist	Pos
493^{P}	**DARCEY MAE** (5a) 2-1F **Miss L Bridges** *(xnb) Tchd 5/2; lw; cl up til ld 5; made rest; hmpd app nxt & nrly carried off course by loose horse app 7; 2l up 12; drew clr 3 out; v easily*		1
494^{P}	**Mrs Goldfarb** (12a) 5-2 **D Edwards** *Opened 3s; keen early; hld up in tch; hdwy to 3rd 7; trckd ldr frm 9; 2l 2nd & ev ch 12; wkng when mist 3 out; sn no ch*	30	2
368^{P}	**Spencive** 14-1 **J Jenkins** *Bckwd; trckd ldr to 4; lost plce 7; 24l 3rd 10; t.o frm 14; v tired & scrambling fncs frm 3 out*	30	3
469^{F}	Margery's Opera (5a) 6-1 E Kenney-Herbert *Cl 5th when blun & ur 2*		U
	Ring Off 12-1 J O'Rourke *Tchd 16s; tk keen hld; prom; 3rd & hit 3; stdd & just in tch to 7; 5th when pu 9; school*		P
575^{F}	The Sycophant (IRE) 5-2 R Bliss *Lw; nt fluent & jmpd lft; ld to 5; 8l 2nd 8; blun & ur 9*		U

OFFICIAL DISTANCES: dist, dist **TIME:** 5min 19.1s **TOTE:** £3.70

634 Mens Open, 12st — 5 ran

Form	Horse / Rider / Comment	Dist	Pos
458^{1}	**FREE GIFT** 5-4 **D Jacob** *(xnb) Tchd 6/4; lw; jw; made all frm 2 at gd pce; 5l ahd 3 out; coasted clr frm nxt; impressive*		1
495^{1}	**Lord Of The Mist (IRE)** evensF **N Williams** *Lw; 3½l 3rd when hit 3; jmpd to 2nd 7; chsd wnr & ev ch to 15; nt qckn frm nxt*	12	2
471^{3}	**Porlock Hill** (7x) 9-1 **N Harris** *(xnb) Slt ld 1; prom; cl 3rd 7 til rdn & lost plce app 13; 7l 3rd agn 14; jmpd slow nxt; tired & t.o frm 3 out*	30	3
487^{2}	Gotha (FR) 40-1 M Sweetland *In tch in 4th; went 3rd brief aft 12; sn btn; t.o frm 3 out*	7	4
445^{7}	Braes Of Mar 25-1 R McEwen *Imm outpcd; bhnd & strugg frm 4 til ref 8*		r

OFFICIAL DISTANCES: 12*l*, dist **TIME:** 6min 08.7s **TOTE:** £1.40

635 Ladies Open — 7 ran

Form	Horse / Rider / Comment	Dist	Pos
48^{1}	**WHAT A MOVER** (5a) evensF **Miss P Gundry** *2s (in a plce)-evens; lw; hld up in tch; 4th ½way; 12l 4th 14; gd hdwy to 3rd but still bit to do aft 3 out; clsd stdly to ld flat; r.o; wl rdn*		1
470^{1}	**Sir D'Orton (FR)** 9-2 **Miss C Tizzard** *Lw; trckd ldr; cl up til ld 14; went 3l clr 3 out; jmpd slow & hdd nxt; rallied & slt ld last; hdd & no ex flat*	2	2
496^{4}	**Rimpton Boy**(bl) 5-2 **Miss R Green** *(xnb) Tchd 3s; mist 1; hld up in tch; cl 5th ½way; impd to 3rd 15 & 2nd nxt; ld 2 out; just hdd last; dem agn & no ex flat*	1½	3
234^{U}	Priestthorn (IRE) 40-1 Miss W Southcombe *(bf) In tch; disp 8l 3rd 6; went cl 2nd aft 12; drpd out qckly uphill & 5th 14; kpt on one pce*	25	4
442^{5}	Filscot 20-1 Miss E Harbour *Tchd 25s; ld & set suicidal pce til app 14; lost plce & rmdrs 3 out; btn 4th nxt; fin tame*	4	5
459^{1}	Proby Lady (IRE) (5a) 7-1 Miss D Harding *10s-7s; jmpd rt; last & mist 3; lost tch 12; t.o*	8	6
	Timpani (IRE) 33-1 Miss T Cave *(xnb) Hld up in last pr; just in tch to 12; sn wknd; bhnd when pu 15*		P

OFFICIAL DISTANCES: 3*l*, 2*l* **TIME:** 6min 06.7s **TOTE:** £1.40

636 Restricted (Nov Rdrs), 12st — 8 ran

Form	Horse / Rider / Comment	Dist	Pos
383^{2}	**BOYNE BANKS (IRE)** 11-10F **G Disney** *Tchd 5/4; made virt all; slt ld til went 3l clr 15; kpt on wl; 3l up when lft clr at last*		1
616^{4}	**Shy Lizzie** (5a) 9-2 **P Mason** *Lw; cl up in midfield; 4th 9; ½l 2nd 11; cl 3rd & mist 13; rdn & wknd 15; 3rd agn 2 out; lft mod 2nd at last*	10	2
354^{4}	**Return The Call (IRE)** 14-1 **C Dailly** *(xnb) In tch; 6th 9; hdwy to 4th 14; disp 8l 3rd 15; mist 2 out; sn wknd; hmpd last*	8	3
473^{P}	Calfstown Lord 33-1 Miss S Lane *Sn last; pckd 4; detach 11; t.o 12; plodded on best of stragglers; nrst fin*	20	4
587^{8}	Keegan Bearnais (FR) 5-1 T Mann *(xnb) Tchd 6s; sn prom; cl 3rd 6; 4th 10; lost plce; poor 5th frm 14; lft poor 3rd & blun bad last*	nk	5
354^{7}	Frankly Fear 8-1 N Heath *(xnb) Prom to 5; 7th ½way; lost tch 11; t.o.*	5	6
443^{F}	O'flaherty's (IRE)(bl) 50-1 W Kavanagh *Tde; cl up; jmpd slow 4; cl 2nd & mist 8; wknd qckly 12; t.o when jmpd slow 16*	40	7
328^{P}	Warren Hill 5-1 R Tory *Hld up in tch; cl 5th 9; gd hdwy aft 12; went 2nd 13; chsd wnr vain aft; 3l down & hld when fell last*		F

OFFICIAL DISTANCES: 12*l*, 8*l* **TIME:** 6min 11.2s **TOTE:** £3.70

637 Panacur/TBA PPORA Club Members Mares Maiden, 12st — 6 ran

SAUCY ARETHUSA (5a) 11-10F **N Harris** *(xnb) Tchd 5/4; lw; hld up in tch; 3rd 9; hdwy 12; jmpd to ld 14; went 4l clr & mist 2 out; rec wl; in comm when blun agn last; r.o wl* 1

492^{P} **Emerald Mist (IRE)** (12a) 6-4 **Miss P Gundry** *Lw; hld up; slt mist 2; last & jmpd slow 5; impd 9; cl 3rd & nt jw 14; went 2nd aft 15; ev ch til nt qckn app last.* 3½ 2

Autumn Flame (IRE) (5a) 16-1 **Miss S Duckett** *2 handlers; ld/disp; rcd free; slt ld 4-14; one pce frm nxt.* 20 3

Inner State (5a) 10-1 D Edwards *Tchd 12s; 2 handlers; hld up towards rr; 4th 9; no ch frm 13; t.o & pu last* . . . . . P

370^{P} Masitat (5a) 6-1 P Mason *(xnb) Sn prom; 2nd & blun 6; cl 2nd 12; disp ld 13; 1l 2nd & when fell 15.* . . . . . F

Vitinsel (5a)(tt) 9-1 L Tibbatts *Towards rr; nt jw 4; detach 6; jmpd lft 11; bhnd frm 14 til fell hvly last* . . . . . F

OFFICIAL DISTANCES: 2½l, 20l **TIME:** 6min 31.5s **TOTE:** £1.60

Crawley & Horsham

Parham (RH 8F,18J)

Sat, 27 Mar (GOOD to SOFT)

638 Hunt Members — 5 ran

535^{1} **TRICKY TREVOR (IRE)** (5x) 1-3F **P York** *Cl up; ld 8; fiddled 11 & almost ur; hdd 13; rmdrs & ld agn app 15; made rest in narrow ld; rdn along frm 3 out; all out to hld on flat* 1

537^{4} **Tell The Nipper (IRE)** (5x) 5-2 **M Gorman** *Cl up; impd to jn ldr aft 11; btr j to ld 13; rdn & hdd app 15; prsd wnr rest of way; ev ch flat; kpt on one pce* 2 2

605^{P} **Royal Dew (IRE)** 10-1 **D Evatt** *Ld to 2; prsd ldr to 11; sn wknd; 20l 4th 13; lft 35l 3rd 15; t.o.* . . . . . fence 3

177^{P} Ascoolasice 10-1 J Morgan *Jmpd delib; cl up; pckd 8; lost tch aft 10; 25l 5th 13; lft rem 4th 15* 15 4

623^{2} Satcotino (IRE) (5a) 10-1 Miss C Pointing *1st ride; ld 2-7; lost plce app nxt; chsd ldng pr frm 12; 30l adrift when mist & ur 15* . . . . . U

OFFICIAL DISTANCES: 1l, dist, 25l **TIME:** 6min 39.0s
TOTE: £1.40; places £1.10,£1.20 **DF:**£1.30

639 Restricted, 12st — 7 ran

2^{10} **MAGNUS VERITAS (IRE)** 5-2 **Stuart Robinson** *Cl up in midfield; impd to trck ldr 12; ld 14; qckly drew clr aft nxt; in comm frm 3 out.* 1

220^{1} **Trumper** 2-1 **P York** *Settled towards rr; hdwy 8; cl 3rd when mist 12; rdn & lost tch w ldng pr aft nxt; 18l 3rd aft 15; stayed on frm 3 out to tk 2nd app last.* 20 2

611^{1} **Granny Smith (IRE)** (5a) 6-4F **Mrs J Gordon** *Ld to 14; 4l down nxt; sn lost tch w wnr; wkng frm 3 out; lost 2nd app last* 1 3

Ginger Sprout (IRE) (5a) 14-1 C Thomson *Last til ur 6.* . . . . . U

538^{3} Red Square Prince (IRE)(vis) 8-1 D Dunsdon *Prom to 9; 6l 5th & rmdrs app 11; lost tch frm 13; t.o & pu aft 15* . . . . . P

538^{U} Tonrin 14-1 J Sole *A towards rr; 12l 6th & lsng tch when rmdrs app 11; t.o & pu 14* . . . . . P

577^{P} Wood Buzzard(tt) 14-1 D Phelan *Cl up; prsd ldr 8-11; 6l 4th when mist 13; sn wknd; t.o & pu 2 out.* . . . . . P

OFFICIAL DISTANCES: 28l, 2l **TIME:** 6min 39.0s
TOTE: £3.90; places £2.00,£1.10 **DF:**£6.40

640 Confined, 12st — 7 ran

538^{1} **ASTHEFELLOWSAID (IRE)** 7-4F **A Hickman** *Hld up in last; gd hdwy aft 11 to press ldr frm nxt; ld 14; narrow advant til blun & hdd 3 out; rallied app last; r.o str to ld flat.* 1

443^{5} **Charlie's Angel** (5a, 3x) 7-2 **P York** *Hld up; impd to trck ldng pr frm 13; ld & lft 3l clr 2 out; hrd rdn app last; no ex & hdd flat* 1 2

607^{2} **Cloudy Creek (IRE)** 3-1 **S Morris** *Jmpd stickily at times; cl 3rd/4th most of way; rmdrs & hdwy 14; prsd wnr aft 15; lft in ld 3 out; jnd & blun 2 out; rallied app last; kpt on one pce flat.* 1½ 3

624[1] Tanager (5x)(bl) 4-1 J Docker *Cl 5th til gd hdwy aft 7; ld 8-13; chsd ldng trio frm 15; 6l 4th app 3 out; kpt on wl frm nxt; nrst fin* . . . 1 4
170[5] Life's Work 8-1 M Gorman *Cl 2nd/3rd to 11; lost tch w ldrs frm 14; kpt on one pce frm 3 out.* . . . 8 5
537[3] Brackenheath (IRE)(cp) 10-1 Miss H Grissell *Prsd ldr/disp to 7; cl 4th when ur 9* . . . U
610[6] Tomcappagh (IRE) 14-1 J Wall *Ld/disp to 7; lost plce aft 9; t.o 13 til blun & ur 15* . . . U

OFFICIAL DISTANCES: 1*l*, ½*l*, 1½*l* **TIME:** 6min 36.0s
TOTE: £2.90; places £2.70,£1.80 **DF:**£6.00

641 Ladies Open — 6 ran

608[1] **TOM COBBLER (IRE)** (7x) 13-8F **Mrs P Hall** *Rr early; sn in midfield; 5l 4th 10; hdwy 12; ld 14; def advant aft nxt; made rest; pushed clr flat; comf* 1
536[1] **Dick McCarthy (IRE)** 9-4 **Mrs S Ashby** *Ld to 14; chsd wnr rest of way; only 2l down last; no ex flat* . . . 5 2
470[2] **Frank Byrne** 7-4 **Miss A Goschen** *Detach last to 8; 11l 6th 10; no prog frm rr til hdwy to 20l 3rd 15; nvr nr ldng pr* . . . 15 3
626[6] Newby End (IRE)(vis) 12-1 Miss C Cowe *Prom to 5; sn towards rr; 10l 5th 10; lost tch frm 13; wl bhnd frm 15* . . . fence 4
608[P] Castle Arrow (IRE) 12-1 Miss N Moisey *Cl up; 4l 3rd 10; lost tch frm 13; no ch frm 15* . . . 1 5
126[P] Mr Miller (IRE) (7x) 7-1 Mrs J Gordon *Prsd ldr; slpd on bend bef 12; lost plce frm 14; 25l 4th & wkng aft nxt; t.o & pu 2 out* . . . P

OFFICIAL DISTANCES: 5*l*, 15*l*, dist **TIME:** 6min 37.0s
TOTE: £2.50; places £1.10,£1.80 **DF:**£2.60

642 Mens Open, 12st — 8 ran

280[6] **SPLASH AND DASH (IRE)** (7x) 4-5F **A Hickman** *Rr early; impd to cl 3rd aft 7; jnd ldr 14; btr j to ld 15; made rest; drew clr frm 3 out; easily* . . . 1
623[1] **Dancing Fosenby** 6-1 **M Holdforth** *Cl 2nd/3rd; prsd wnr 15; 5l down app 2 out; kpt on one pce.* . . . 6 2
440[1] **Eastern Point** (5a, 7x) 6-4 **P York** *Prom; ld 4; blun & jnd 14; mist & hdd 15; sn rdn; lost tch w ldng pr app 3 out; poor eff* . . . 15 3
583[5] Croft Court 16-1 D Renney *Midfield most of way; blun 9; rmdrs 13; 8l 4th aft 15; lost tch frm nxt.* . . . 5 4
471[P] Nearly Gold (4x) 16-1 N Mitchell *A ab same plce; 12l 6th aft 12; lost tch frm 15* . . . 8 5
535[4] Oxendale 16-1 P Bull *Ld to 3; prsd ldr to 11; 12l 5th & wkng aft 15; no ch frm 3 out* . . . 2 6
626[4] Golden Jack (FR) 16-1 C Morris *A rr; 18l 7th aft 12; lost tch frm 14* . . . 3 7
545[6] Cedar Chief 16-1 G Gallagher *Blun & ur 2.* . . . U

OFFICIAL DISTANCES: 6*l*, 12*l*, 6*l* **TIME:** 6min 41.0s
TOTE: £2.40; places £1.30,£1.30,£1.20 **DF:**£4.70

643 South East Hunts Club Members, 12st — 4 ran

182[3] **GREAT JUBILEE (IRE)** 9-4 **Stuart Robinson** *Made all; narrow advant most of way til drew clr aft 15; in comm frm 3 out.* . . . 1
556[1] **Algan (FR)** (7x) 4-6F **P York** *Trckd wnr frm 5; btr j to disp ld aft 12 & 13; pushed along frm nxt; 2l down 15; sn lost tch* . . . 15 2
609[r] Full Egalite 8-1 G Gallagher *Cl 2nd/3rd til jmpd slow 8; back on terms when ref 9.* . . . r
348[9] Galeaway (IRE) (4x) 5-1 J Barnard *A last; out of tch by 6; 20l adrift when mist & rfo 11* . . . U

OFFICIAL DISTANCE: 22*l* **TIME:** 6min 45.0s **TOTE:** £2.10 **DF:**£1.10

644 Open Maiden, 12st — 11 ran

627[U] **MINISTERIAL (IRE)** 9-2 **C Gordon** *A.p; cl 3rd/4th til ld 15; blun & hdd 3 out; 3l down nxt; rallied to jn ldr last; sn hdd; hrd rdn flat; r.o wl to ld cl home* 1
387[4] **Hever Road (IRE)** (7a) 5-2JF **S Morris** *Towards rr til stdy hdwy 12; trckd ldr 14 til lft in ld 3 out; made rest gng wl; jnd last; sn ld agn; pushed out flat; no ex & hdd cl home* . . . nk 2
295[2] **Sword Fighter** 5-2JF **P York** *Cl 3rd mostly til rdn to ld 14; sn hdd; chsd ldng pr frm 15; wknd aft 3 out* . . . 30 3

120P Smokey Robot (IRE) 14-1 D Dennis *Towards rr; hdwy to cl 5th 11; lost tch aft 13; stayed on frm 15 to tk rem 4th app 3 out* 15 4
370P Busmans Holiday (IRE) (1ow) 20-1 S Coady *Prsd ldr til wknd aft 13; wl bhnd when pu 3 out* . . . . . P
335² Chasing Buttercups (5a) 8-1 Miss A Goschen *Midfield; 7th 11; no prog; wl bhnd 14 til pu 2 out* . . . . . P
Merlots Mystery (IRE) 8-1 Stuart Robinson *A rr; last 11; t.o & pu 15* . . . . . P
611⁴ Private Percival 25-1 P Blagg *Ld to 13; sn wknd; t.o & pu 2 out* . . . . . P
53⁸ Serves You Right (7a) 5-1 J Docker *Midfield; 8th 11; slt hdwy to mod 6th 15; wknd sn aft; wl bhnd when pu 2 out* . . . . . P
Sleeping Music (FR) 8-1 A Hickman *A rr; 9th 11; lsng tch when pu 14* . . . P
539² The Flying Dragon (5a) 7-1 S Spice *Mists; a rr; 10th 11; slt hdwy frm 15; rem 5th when ur 2 out.* . . . . . U

OFFICIAL DISTANCES: s hd, dist, dist **TIME:** 6min 49.0s
TOTE: £4.50; places £2.30,£1.40,£1.40 **DF:**£14.30

645 Chiddingfold, Leconfield & Cowdray and Kent & Surrey Bloodhounds Hunts Members 3 ran

422⁷ **LIVE WIRE (IRE)** 3-1 **Miss C Benstead** *Made all at stdy pce; lft 6l clr 13; drew further away frm 3 out; easily.* 1
608² **Harding** (7x) 1-3F **C Gordon** *Jb lft; settled 2nd; 3l down when blun 13; rdn aft nxt; 8l down when rmdrs 3 out; no resp; eased aft 2 out* 25 2
Diamond Road (IRE) 6-1 M Sheridan *A last; lost tch frm 9; t.o & pu 15* . . P

OFFICIAL DISTANCE: dist **TIME:** 6min 48.0s **TOTE:** £4.20 **DF:**£1.10

Essex

High Easter (LH 9F,19J)
Sat, 27 Mar (GOOD)

646 Hunt Members, 12st 6 ran

249⁹ **RIP KIRBY** (13ow) 9-2 **R Cundy** *Settled 2nd bhnd tearaway ldr; prsd ldr frm 13; hit 15; just ld last; rdn & r.o flat.* 1
Top Boots (IRE) (7a) 5-2F **A Braithwaite** *2 handlers; green; jinked lft start & v novicey at fncs early; settled rr early; cl up 10; lft in ld nxt; hdd brief 3 out; mist & hdd 2 out; r.o; 1l 2nd & ev ch last; nt pushed* 2½ 2
560P **Looking Magic (IRE)** 5-1 **C Lawson** *Trckd ldrs; 35l 3rd 6; 2nd 8; cl 4th 15; ld brief 3 out & agn aft nxt; ev ch last; no ex* 3 3
Changing Fashion (IRE) 4-1 Miss N Barnes *Fat; hld up in 3rd/4th bhnd tearaway ldr; 3rd 12; kpt on to 2l 2nd 15; ev ch 2 out; wknd app last* . . 6 4
610P Crewski (5ow) 7-2 A Gibbons *Rdr v unstdy; last frm 5; 15l adrift 14; t.o & pu 2 out* . . . . . P
Trojan Love (IRE) (5a) 10-1 Miss R Page *(xnb) Bolted into clr ld 1; hit 3; 30l up 5 w rdr vain tkng pull at fncs; wknd qckly frm 9; still 2l up but exhaust when pu 11* . . . . . P

OFFICIAL DISTANCES: 2*l*, 3*l* **TIME:** 7min 09.0s **TOTE:** £4.20 **DF:**£7.00

647 Confined 8 ran

400¹ **WESTFIELD JOHN**(bl) 6-4JF **J Owen** *Sn prom; 3rd 4; prsd ldr 15; just ld & blun last; r.o game; all out* 1
521¹ **Bard Of Drumcoo (IRE)** 6-4JF **D Kemp** *Cl 2nd til ld 3-14; 5l 4th 15; 3rd 2 out; 2l 3rd & lkd hld at last; rallied game flat; tk 2nd cl home* 1 2
Tom De Savoie (IRE) 4-1 **N Bloom** *Mid-div; 4l 4th 14; prsd ldr nxt; ld 3 out til hdd app last; wknd & dem 3rd cl home* . . . . . ½ 3
521⁴ The Glen Road (IRE) 16-1 A Sansome *Settled in cl 4th to 10; 10l 5th 11; wknd qckly & sn t.o* . . . . . fence 4
400³ Ardnut(bl) 20-1 Miss R Page *Imm last; t.o 5; fin w breast-girth dangling round legs* 25 5
478P Ardkilly Warrior (IRE) 9-1 A Merriam *2nd 4; prsd ldr aft til ld 15-16; wknd rap nxt; 15l 4th & v tired when pu 2 out* . . . . . P

521^{5}	Gawngadinn (IRE) 20-1 R Morgan-Evans *(xnb) Nt jw; hit 2 & 4; 7th 5; 8l 6th 9; lost tch ldng group 11; t.o 14; pu 2 out*		P
520^{U}	Neronian (IRE) (7ow) 20-1 Mrs H Edwards *Fat; ld to 2; stdly drpd back thro field & 6th 5; 15l 7th 8; t.o & pu 10*		P

OFFICIAL DISTANCE: $1\frac{1}{2}$*l* **TIME:** 6min 37.0s **TOTE:** £3.00 **DF:**£3.40

The stewards interviewed the owner of Ardnut who arrived 10min late in the parade ring and not fitted with its declared blinkers causing further delay; he was fined £25

648 Restricted, 12st — 12 ran

383^{5}	**BUNRATTY'S SOLE (IRE)** 2-1F **N Bloom** *7/2-2s; sn prom; 2l 2nd 5; prsd ldr 14; ld 2 out; sn in comm; clr last; comf.*		1
383^{6}	**Just Jove** 5-1 **R Cope** *Made all in narrow ld til jnd 3 out; hdd nxt; 6l 2nd when blun bad last; fin v tired*	10	2
524^{3}	**Federal Case (FR)** 4-1 **A Braithwaite** *(xnb) Sn prom; cl 3rd 5; 7l 4th 13; sn outpcd; 8l 3rd 15; no hdwy aft.*	2	3
384^{3}	Table For Four(bl) 10-1 B Pollock *Mid-div & sn outpcd; 8th 7; rr 14; r.o past btn rivals frm 3 out; tk 4th cl home*	8	4
	Trinity Buoy (IRE)(cp) 7-2 M Mackley *In tch in mid-div; 6th 8; 8l 4th 14; chsd ldrs 15-nxt; sn wknd; dem flat*	5	5
524^{4}	Camden Loch (IRE) 8-1 R Morgan-Evans *In rr; 11th 5; nt pce to rch ldrs; kpt on one pce frm 15; nvr nrr.*	$\frac{1}{2}$	6
524^{2}	Ginger Bug (5a) 6-1 P Chinery *Tde; in rr; 10th 6; lost tch frm 12; t.o last when hmpd by rival 3 out; pu nxt*		P
524^{5}	Give Him A Chance (IRE)(bl) 12-1 N Moore *Cl up; 3l 4th 9; 6l 3rd 13; stdly wknd rem 5th & v tired when blun bad 2 out & imm pu*		P
606^{r}	Ishma (IRE)(bl) 25-1 D Page (Kent) *Chsd ldrs; 4l 5th when hit 8; wknd 13; t.o when ref 3 out*		r
466^{4}	Jerome Jerome(bl) 20-1 A Sansome *Rr of main group; 9th 7; same when rdn & no resp 11; t.o & pu 15.*		P
524^{S}	Mr Moonbeam (IRE) 14-1 M Buchan *Sis & imm last; t.o 12; pu 3 out.*		P
250^{P}	Shanrod View (IRE) 10-1 D Brightling *Mid-div; in tch in 8l 6th 9; stdly wknd; t.o last when pu last*		P

OFFICIAL DISTANCES: 20*l*, 2*l* **TIME:** 6min 38.0s **TOTE:** £3.10 **DF:**£13.60

649 Ladies Open — 7 ran

246^{1}	**CELTIC DUKE** 1-2F **Miss Z Turner** *Jw; made all; qcknd 16; 3l up 2 out; rdn & r.o flat.*		1
246^{P}	**Fair Kiowa (IRE)** 4-1 **Mrs S Hodge** *4th when blun 2; 3l 3rd 6; 2l 2nd 14; prsd ldr app 2 out; nt qckn app last; rdn & r.o agn flat; a hld*	2	2
250^{7}	**Filou Du Bois (FR)** 8-1 **Ms A Embiricos** *Hld up in tch in 5th; 5l 3rd 14; outpcd by ldng pr 16; 10l 3rd 3 out; no imp aft*	10	3
522^{4}	Mister Audi (IRE) 16-1 Miss A Bowles *Settled rr of main group; 5l 6th 9; rmdrs 11; 12l 4th 16; no imp aft*	8	4
464^{U}	General Confusion (IRE) 12-1 Miss B Czepulkowski *Cl up; 2l 3rd 5; 4l 5th 10 til saddle slpd & rfo app 13*		U
375^{P}	Ical (IRE) (5a) 25-1 Miss C Rogers *Lft 20l start; t.o til blun & rfo 5*		U
396^{2}	Wise Advice (IRE) 12-1 Miss L Marriott *Sn prom; 1l 2nd 4; prsd ldr aft til wknd v rap & drpd to last 16; t.o & pu last.*		P

OFFICIAL DISTANCES: 2*l*, 15*l* **TIME:** 6min 41.0s **TOTE:** £1.70 **DF:**£1.90

650 Mens Open, 12st — 9 ran

372^{2}	**CANTARINHO** 4-5F **D Kemp** *2 handlers; tde; sn prom; 3l 3rd 5; ld 6; made rest; 10l clr 14; blun & nrly ur 3 out; drew clr agn aft 2 out.*		1
466^{1}	**Choral Dream (IRE)** 5-2 **R Cope** *Hld up; last 4; 8l 7th 6; rdn 10; 8th & rmdrs 11; hdwy to 12l 2nd 16; r.o; 3l 2nd & ev ch app 2 out; wknd qckly; no ch app last.*	10	2
397^{1}	**Dunrig (IRE)** (7x) 4-1 **J Owen** *Sn chsng ldrs; $4\frac{1}{2}$l 5th 8; outpcd by ldng pr frm 14; 10l 3rd & one pce 2 out*	20	3
522^{P}	Step In Line (IRE) 33-1 N Bloom *(xnb) Mid-div; 10l 6th 8; outpcd & bhnd frm 14; went dist 4th 15; no imp aft*	4	4
607^{P}	Lord Of The Flies (IRE) 33-1 D Brightling *5th 4; 4l 4th 8; stdly outpcd frm 12; 15l 3rd 14; wkng when blun nxt; sn wl bhnd*	1	5
557^{7}	Polo Ridge (IRE)(bl) 40-1 A Sansome *Ld to 2 & frm 4-5; cl up til hopelessly outpcd frm 14; plodded on*	10	6
372^{P}	Valman (IRE) 33-1 P Millington *(xnb) Sn rr; last 5; t.o 10; pu 12*		P

374P Weavers Choice 25-1 P Cowley *Ld 3; trckd ldr in 2nd aft; 3l 2nd when fell 13* F
466² Wibbley Wobbley 20-1 T Ellis *2 handlers; sn in rr; 9l 8th 7; rmdrs & no resp 11; t.o & pu 15* . . . . P

OFFICIAL DISTANCES: 15*l*, dist **TIME:** 6min 36.0s **TOTE:** £1.80 **DF:**£2.00

651 Open Maiden (Div 1), 12st — 11 ran

534² **OCKI** 33-1 **D Page (Kent)** *Rr; 10l 7th 10; 8l 4th 3 out; stayed on stdly uphill to 2½l 4th 2 out; ld app last; drvn flat; all out.* 1
525P **Manhatton Storm (IRE)** 33-1 **A Merriam** *Mid-div; 7l 5th 10; chsd ldrs in 4th 14; 3l 3rd brief 3 out; stayed on to 3rd agn last; kpt on grimly to grab 2nd* 3 2
385P **Highland Dancer (IRE)** (7a) 33-1 **T Ellis** *Cl up; 5l 3rd 10; 4l 2nd 13; prsd ldr aft; ld 3 out til hdd app last; v tired & dem flat* . . . . ½ 3
401³ On The Day (IRE) 4-1 J Owen *Hld up off early pce; 9l 6th 10; smooth hdwy to 4l 3rd 14; prsd ldr nxt; ld brief 16; cl 2nd 3 out; 2l 3rd & drvn aft 2 out; dem last; no ex* 1 4
385⁵ King Freddy (7a) 5-2F R Cope *Trckd ldrs; 6l 4th 10; went 3rd 13; nt qckn 3 out; wknd & dem 5th 2 out* 8 5
525² Arctic Snip 3-1 N Moore *Prom; prsd ldr 5; disp ld 6-7; cl up til outpcd 13; 8l 6th 15; sn btn* 2 6
482³ Frosty Fella(bl) 5-1 B Pollock *(xnb) Ld to 4; disp 2l 3rd when bd 9* . . . . . . B
611U Just Lute 8-1 M Smith *Lft & set off fnce bhnd; jmpd slow 2; event pu 8* . . P
539R See Red Billdan (IRE) 7-1 J Merry *(xnb) 2 handlers; cl up; 3l 3rd 7; prsd ldr & lft in 9; wkng when tried to rn out 16; rr when pu 2 out.* . . . . P
386² Shot Of Jollop (IRE) (7a)(bl) 8-1 N Bloom *(xnb) Prom; ld 5; jnd 6-7; fell 9.* F
220P Society Scandal (IRE) 33-1 P Millington *Rr; blun 4; wl bhnd when jmpd rt 13; t.o & pu last* . . . . P

OFFICIAL DISTANCES: 2*l*, 1*l* **TIME:** 6min 48.0s **TOTE:** £15.00 **DF:**£37.00

652 Open Maiden (Div 2), 12st — 12 ran

185³ **MISS BIDDY** (5a) 6-1 **Miss O Maylam** *Keen; ld to 2; declined suicidal pce & 20l 2nd 6; clsd stdly frm 10; ld 15; kpt on frm 2 out racing w loose horses; rdr's 1st wnr* 1
561P **Mr Know What (IRE)** 12-1 **Miss C Bartlett** *Hld up mid-div; 8th 8; 14l 6th 14; stdy hdwy to 10l 2nd 3 out; stayed on frm nxt; nrst fin; gvn far too much to do* . . 3 2
371² **Round The Isles** 3-1F **R Cope** *Prom; 4th bhnd clr early ldr; 14l 4th 11; stdy hdwy to 8l 3rd 14; nt qckn 16; 8l 3rd & no ch 2 out; nt pushed* 8 3
525P Marsden 16-1 N Moore *Prom in pack bhnd runaway ldr; 22l 3rd 7; 10l 4th 14; sn btn; one pce frm 3 out* 25 4
525³ No Nay Never (IRE) 7-1 Miss A Bowles *Mid-div; 7th 8; no prog & 16l 7th 14; plodded on* 8 5
104⁴ Rash Moment (FR) (7a) 4-1 A Merriam *Handy in main group; 5th 8; 15l 5th 10; 12l 5th 14; chsd ldrs frm nxt; 10l 4th & no imp 2 out; wknd qckly & lost 2 plces last* 4 6
27³ Another Leader (IRE) 4-1 G Cooper *(xnb) Tk ferocious hld; pulled to ld 3; 10l clr 5; 20l clr nxt; grad wknd & jmpng rt frm 11; 5l up 14; hdd nxt; 2nd & wkng rap when fell 15.* . . . . F
476P First And Fourmost (IRE) 10-1 R Morgan-Evans *Mid-div when fell 3* . . . . . F
Green Leader (IRE) (5a) 10-1 M Mackley *A rr of pack; 9th 8; no prog when pu 12* P
461P Latterly (USA) 33-1 I Bostock *Mid-div; 6th 8; stdly lost plce; dist last by 14; t.o & pu 2 out* . . . . P
476P Little Heck (IRE) 33-1 A Sansome *Mid-div when fell 3.* . . . . F
387P Red Lake (IRE) 25-1 P Millington *Last by 5; plodded round til event pu 2 out* P

OFFICIAL DISTANCES: 3*l*, 10*l* **TIME:** 6min 52.0s **TOTE:** £6.00 **DF:**£7.80

Lanarkshire & Renfrewshire and Eglinton

Overton (LH 8F,19J)

Sat, 27 Mar (GOOD/GOOD to SOFT in places)

653 Hunts Members — 6 ran

212P **WESTIE** (5a) 9-4 **L Morgan** *Ld brief early; ld agn 5; 4l up 12; clr 14; mist 3 out; 20l up & rdn nxt; hit last* 1
Tursal (IRE) (7x) 7-4F **Miss J Campbell** *1st ride; rdr nodded most fncs & lkd likely to f.o; sn ld; mist 2; hdd 5; 1l 2nd 6; slt mist & nrly ur 14; sn outpcd; t.o when slt mist & nrly ur 2 out* 25 2

	Poppers 12-1 **W Goldie** *(bf) Chsd ldrs; hit 4; 8l 4th 8; hit 10; lft 12l 3rd nxt; hit 12; 25l 3rd 15; t.o & rdn aft.*	25	3
	Jamie Browne (IRE) 3-1 J Thompson *(bf) Trckd ldrs; mist 2; 6l 3rd 6; 5l 3rd 10; fell nxt*		F
	Scooby Doo (U) 10-1 D Jewett *Fat; a rr; 10l last 2; sn detach; 15l last 8-12; t.o 15; eased aft; pu aft 3 out*		P
553^{P}	The Midnite Grocer 14-1 R Westwood *(xnb) Fat; mid-div; mist 2; mist & ur 3*		U

OFFICIAL DISTANCES: dist, dist **TIME:** 6min 30.7s

654 Confined, 12st — 8 ran

425^{2}	**SPRING DOUBLE (IRE)** (3x) 7-4F **B Mounsey-Heysham** *Ld/disp til 8l 3rd 15; 2½l 3rd & gng wl aft nxt; ld 3 out; 2l up nxt; comf; rdr gave victory wave to family*		1
426^{4}	**Trivial (IRE)** (5a) 7-2 **L Morgan** *(xnb) Trckd ldrs; 3l 2nd 14; 2l 2nd 16; rdn to press ldrs aft; u.p nxt; no ex app last.*	5	2
426^{5}	**Extra Stout (IRE)**(tt) 5-1 **C Storey** *Ld/disp til 3l up 14; 6l clr aft nxt; hdd & hit 3 out; kpt on one pce*	3	3
163^{P}	Touchez Du Bois (IRE) 20-1 T Morrison *Chsd ldrs; 7l 5th 8; went 4l 3rd 10; rdn & rmdrs nxt; outpcd 15 & sn no ch*	25	4
425^{F}	Feeling Grand (IRE) 16-1 F Arthur *(xnb) Tubed; in tch; 5l 5th 10; outpcd 15; 15l 4th 3 out; wknd aft nxt*	4	5
542^{P}	Havetwotaketwo (IRE) 10-1 M Smith *(xnb) Prom til swerved, stumbled, lost footing & ur app 4*		U
552^{P}	Olympic Storm (IRE) 10-1 J Alexander *(xnb) Unruly start; ur & rn loose; caught & unruly agn; wrs; ref to rce.*		r
547^{3}	Wishful Thinker(tt) 16-1 Miss K Scott *Hmpd & sis; sn lost tch; 25l last 2; wl bhnd 15; some prog when ur 3 out*		U

OFFICIAL DISTANCES: 4*l*, 3*l* **TIME:** 6min 23.8s

655 Ladies Open — 7 ran

428^{3}	**PASSING DANGER (FR)** 2-1JF **Miss R Davidson** *(bof) In tch; 8l 5th 3; went 1½l 2nd 8; trckd ldr til ld 3 out; gd j nxt; stayed on wl; comf.*		1
391^{4}	**Emperor's Magic (IRE)**(cp) 5-1 **Miss S Ward** *Mid-div; 6l 5th 9; prog to 4l 3rd 14; ld brief app 3 out; 1l 2nd nxt; eff & nt pce to chall aft*	3	2
339^{1}	**Balisteros (FR)** 2-1JF **Miss P Robson** *Ld; 4l up 11; hdd app 3 out & imm outpcd; kpt on but nd aft; 6l 3rd app 2 out*	4	3
427^{4}	Rainton 5-1 Miss N Stirling *(xnb) 2 handlers; hdstrng; in tch; 9l 6th 3; 5l 4th 9; bumped into 12; prog to 2l 3rd 16; short-lived eff app nxt; sn rdn; 10l 4th & no ex app 2 out.*	8	4
425^{6}	Donallach Mor (IRE)(bl) 12-1 Mrs V Jackson *Fat; trckd ldrs; lft 2l 2nd 7; bumped into rival 12; grad wknd aft; lost tch 16; 30l 5th 2 out*	15	5
550^{3}	In Demand 5-1 Miss J Balmer *(orbs) A rr; outpcd; 8l last aft 1; 15l last & jmpd slow 8; 25l last 10; t.o 15; 50l last 2 out*	25	6
282^{8}	Mr McDuff (IRE) 20-1 Miss J Hollands *(orbs) Trckd ldr; 1½l 2nd 2; slithered to ground 7*		F

OFFICIAL DISTANCES: 2*l*, 6*l* **TIME:** 6min 17.1s

656 Land Rover Mens Open — 6 ran

506^{1}	**GAULTIER GALE (IRE)** 5-1 **A Findlay** *Oht; mid-div; 4l 4th 9; 5l 5th nxt; prog to 2l 3rd 16; chall aft nxt; ld 2 out; all out*		1
506^{2}	**Starbuck** 5-1 **L Morgan** *Ld/disp; 1l 2nd aft 16; eff nxt to disp ld; ½l 2nd agn 2 out; outpcd app last; nt qckn flat*	2½	2
509^{4}	**Glacial Sygnet (IRE)**(cp) 4-1 **J Thompson** *Ld/disp; 1l up 14; jnd 3 out; hdd aft & 5l 3rd nxt; kpt on one pce*	8	3
429^{4}	Just Whiskey (IRE) 2-1 C Shirley-Beavan *In tch; 10l 5th 7; disp 2l 3rd 10; mist 12 & pushed along; ev ch til outpcd aft 3 out; 8l 4th & one pce nxt*	1	4
546^{r}	Parade Racer 5-4F D Jewett *Virt ref to start; sis & lost 30l; stdy prog; 20l last 8; 5l last 15; 5l 5th & rdn app 3 out; sn wknd*	1	5
439^{5}	Valley Erne (IRE) 8-1 C Storey *(bh) Trckd ldrs; disp 2l 3rd 10; mist 15; 12l last & outpcd nxt; one pce*	3	6

OFFICIAL DISTANCES: 2*l*, 3*l* **TIME:** 6min 19.9s

657 Restricted, 12st — 12 ran

Form	Runner	Dist	Pos
349^{3}	**MISS ROYELLO** (5a) 5-1 **D Jewett** *In tch in rr; 7l 6th app 10; prog to 1l 2nd 16; ld aft 3 out; prsd frm nxt; jnd last; hdd flat; rallied to ld agn cl home*		1
554^{1}	**Decent Bond (IRE)** 6-1 **R Green** *Chsd ldrs; 15l 6th 11; smooth prog to 5l 4th 16-3 out; 4l 3rd app nxt; 1l down 2 out; chall last; ld brief flat; hdd & nt qckn cl home*	nk	2
433^{1}	**Lethem Air** 5-1 **K Anderson** *Mid-div; prog to trck ldrs & lft in ld app 14; hdd aft 3 out; sn outpcd; kpt on*	6	3
548^{3}	Anotherhandyman(cp) 20-1 Miss S Gledson *A rr; nd; lost tch 11; 40l 5th 3 out; t.o*	runin	4
212^{4}	Alittlebitopower 3-1 C Storey *(xnb) A.p; 2l 4th 6; ld nxt; 2l up 10; clr in ldng pr when loose horse jmpd rail & knocked him over app 14*		B
281^{U}	Flying Past 5-2F R Morgan *Lw; mid-div; disp 6l 4th 9; prog to press ldrs in 2l 3rd 3 out; sn rdn & no ex; wknd qckly; btn 4th when pu last*		P
548^{P}	Good Morning (5a) 14-1 R Dickson *A rr; lost tch 11; sn t.o; ur 16*		U
	Gudasmum (5a) 10-1 Miss R Davidson *Cl up; 4l 2nd 2; disp ld 8; mist & ur 10; rn loose across course jmpd rail & bd rival*		U
	Jimmy Blues 10-1 W Goldie *Bckwd; swtng; a rr; 10l last 1; lost tch 11; t.o & pu aft 15*		P
212^{P}	Laura Lugs (IRE) 20-1 L Morgan *Fat; ld early; 4l up 2; hdd 7; outpcd 11; sn t.o; 100l 6th 3 out; pu nxt.*		P
212^{P}	Royalecko 12-1 Miss J Hollands *Prom; 6l 3rd 3; 5l 3rd 8; prog to disp ld brief 12; trckng ldr when v bad hmpd & ur app 14*		U
548^{4}	Superstar Express (IRE) 5-1 A Findlay *(xnb) In tch in rr; 8l 7th when fell 10*		F

OFFICIAL DISTANCES: nk, 10*l* **TIME:** 6min 21.2s

658 Open Maiden (Div 1) — 12 ran

Form	Runner	Dist	Pos
	THE CINCINNATI KID 12-1 **R Green** *(xnb) In tch; prog 8 to ld 13; 6l up 16; 3l up 2 out; stayed on wl.*		1
554^{2}	**Rutherford** 4-1 **R Morgan** *Trckd ldrs; 6l 3rd app 4-7; $3\frac{1}{2}$l 3rd 10; went 6l 2nd aft 3 out; sn no ex; kpt on wl app last*	3	2
553^{P}	**Chief Seattle (IRE)** 14-1 **J Tate** *Mid-div; 5l 5th 2; 4l 4th app 8; disp 4l 4th 10; eff & 7l 3rd 16-3 out; kpt on*	1	3
211^{5}	Stormalong (IRE)(tt) 5-4F C Storey *(xnb) In tch; disp 4l 4th 10; blun 15 & outpcd; 10l 4th app 3 out; jmpd slow nxt; kpt on flat; improve*	1	4
	Freeway 8-1 Mrs V Jackson *(orbs) A rr; jmpd slow 9; outpcd 11; sn lost tch; 25l 5th 2 out; one pce*	25	5
542^{P}	Commanche Spirit (IRE) 16-1 A Findlay *In tch; pushed along 9; sn btn; t.o 16*	25	6
	Alizarine Blue(bl) 12-1 Miss L Kendall *Lw; ld; 2l up 4; 3l ahd 9; hdd 13 & sn wknd; t.o & pu 16*		P
	Ellemford (5a) 16-1 W Goldie *A rr; detach in 25l last 8; t.o & pu 12*		P
	Em'sgem (5a) 8-1 T Morrison *A rr; 18l 11th 8; outpcd aft & sn nd; t.o & pu 3 out*		P
	Mystical Spot (5a) 6-1 K Anderson *Mid-div; 6l 6th app 11; lost action & pu nxt*		P
549^{5}	Reeker Pike (5a) 8-1 J Thompson *Rr; 12l last 1; 8l 4th 6; outpcd aft 10 & sn ch; t.o & pu 16*		P
429^{P}	The Panjshir 16-1 L Morgan *Trckd ldrs; 2l 2nd 3-4; 3l 2nd 9; 6l 2nd & ev ch when fell 16*		F

OFFICIAL DISTANCES: 3*l*, 1*l* **TIME:** 6min 28.6s

659 Open Maiden (Div 2) — 9 ran

Form	Runner	Dist	Pos
	RAINHA (5a) 2-1F **Miss P Robson** *Lw; ld til hdd aft 3; trckd runaway pr aft; 8l 3rd 6; 20l 3rd 8; prog to 15l 3rd 14 & 6l 2nd when lft 6l clr 16; canter*		1
349^{U}	**Jinful Du Grand Val (FR)** 6-1 **J Alexander** *(xnb) Chsd ldrs; 10l 5th app 4; 25l 4th 15; tk 8l 2nd 3 out; no ch w wnr*	25	2
432^{5}	**Justenough** 6-1 **S Huggan** *(bf) Chsd ldrs; 12l 6th 4; wkng in 20l 4th 16-3 out; one pce.*	20	3
510^{U}	Slytherin Falls 6-1 S Clark *(xnb,bf) Pulling; trckd ldr til ld 3; ldng pr sn wl clr; hdd 15 & wknd; lft 6l 2nd nxt; jmpd slow 3 out; fin tired.*	1	4
549^{3}	Chase The Moon (5a) 6-1 Miss L Hislop *Lw; a rr; detach 4; t.o 8; pu 9*		P
	Hapthor (12a) 3-1 M McAlister *(xnb) Lw; swtng; trckd runaway ldr & sn clr of rest; 3l 2nd 8; 1l 2nd 14; ld nxt; 6l up when fell 16.*		F
	Nodform Returns (5a) 10-1 A Findlay *Lw; rr; 25l last 9; t.o & pu 15*		P

431^{4}	Pure Steel (IRE) 8-1 C Storey *Tubed; lw; in tch; 4l 4th app 3; mist 9; outpcd in 25l 7th nxt; sn btn; 30l 6th when climbed 3 out; tired & pu nxt*		P
	What A Night (7a) 3-1 K Anderson *In tch in rr; pckd & slid along & nrly fell 10; 20l 6th aft; lost tch & pu 13*		P

OFFICIAL DISTANCES: dist, dist **TIME:** 6min 20.7s

Teme Valley

Brampton Bryan (RH 8F,18J)

Sat, 27 Mar (DEAD)

660 Confined, 12st — 13 ran

513^{1}	**CAUGHT AT DAWN (IRE)** (3x) 5-1 **T Weston** *A.p; went 2nd aft 8; ld 10; mist 2 out; rdn out*		1
289^{U}	**Carthago (IRE)** 14-1 **M Harris** *A.p; ld 8-10; ev ch 3 out; rdn aft nxt; one pce*	3½	2
251^{2}	**Dare**(tt) 5-1 **D Barlow** *8s-5s; hld up; 8l 7th ½way; 7l 6th 12; stdy hdwy 15; jnd ldrs 3 out; went 2nd & switched rt aft 2 out; mist last; wknd flat*	6	3
228^{2}	Westcoast 12-1 W Hill *Hld up; 10l 8th ½way; 8½l 7th 12; mist 13; 12l 7th 15; no hdwy 3 out*	15	4
514^{P}	Persona Pride (3x) 25-1 Julian Pritchard *Ld til aft 2; 2nd to 8; 3l 4th ½way; 4l 5th 12; wknd app 3 out*	5	5
615^{P}	Head Gardener (IRE)(bl) 50-1 D Mansell *Chsd ldrs; blun 9; 7l 6th ½way; 10l 8th & rdn 12; lost tch 13; 22l 9th 15; t.o*	25	6
406^{P}	Borderline Breeze (IRE) 50-1 Miss H Watson *(xnb,bf) A bhnd; 17l last ½way; 20l 8th 15; t.o.*	2	7
628^{U}	Chaparro Amargoso (IRE) 25-1 S Ross *A bhnd; 16l 10th & rdn ½way; 25l last 15; t.o*	12	8
616^{3}	Arctic King 14-1 A Wintle *(bnh) Prom; lft in ld app 8; sn hdd; blun 9; 2l 3rd ½way; 3½l 4th 12; mist 14; 10l 6th when fell 15*		F
372^{1}	Fane Counsel (IRE) 1-3F R Burton *(xnb) 1/2-1/3; lw; 2nd til ld aft 2; cocked jaw & rn out bend bef 8.*		R
	Slave's Adventure (5a) 40-1 R Hodges *Swtng; ur 50 yds aft 1*		U
	Storm Valley (IRE) 40-1 M Jackson *A bhnd; 15l 9th ½way; pu 13*		P
528^{4}	Wild Edric(bl) 25-1 A Beedles *Chsd ldrs; 4l 5th ½way; 2½l 3rd 12; 6l 4th & wkng when fell 3 out.*		F

OFFICIAL DISTANCES: 2½l, 6l **TIME:** 6min 58.7s

Racing was delayed by 45 mins awaiting paramedic cover; the stewards interviewed the rider of Fane Counsel; they accepted his explanation that the horse had cocked his jaw and run out on the bend by the river

661 Countryside Alliance Club Members (Nov Rdrs), 12st — 13 ran

612^{3}	**HASTE YE BACK (IRE)** 2-1F **Miss V Price** *(xnb) Went 2nd aft 4; ld 5-8 & 10-15; 2l 3rd nxt; ld agn last; hld on wl flat*		1
465^{3}	**Picket Piece**(bl) 7-2 **M Goldstein** *Ld to 3 & 4-5; 2½l 3rd ½way; went 2nd 12; ld 15-last; rallied cl home*	nk	2
516^{3}	**Huntersway (IRE)** 20-1 **R Hughes** *Swtng; hld up & bhnd; 14l 10th ½way; gd hdwy 12; went 4l 3rd 14 & 1l 2nd when mist 3 out; ev ch aft 2 out; no ex*	4	3
528^{5}	Oneanthreequarters (IRE) 10-1 R Jagger *Nvr on terms; 13l 9th ½way; 10l 7th 12; lost tch 14; sn wl bhnd; snatched 4th nr fin.*	30	4
477^{6}	Galeshan (IRE)(tt) 33-1 C Huxley *W ldrs; 6l 5th ½way; disp 3l 4th 12; 6l 4th & rdn 14; wknd app 3 out; eased & lost 4th nr fin*	1	5
403^{9}	Tirley Gale 10-1 J Jones *A wl bhnd; blun 1; 25l 12th ½way; 28l 9th 12; t.o 14*	25	6
465^{P}	Iorana (FR) 10-1 T Mastoras *Hld up & bhnd; 17l 11th ½way; hdwy 11; 5l 6th nxt; wknd 14; t.o*	3	7
	Cadougold (FR) 8-1 T Weston *Chsd ldrs; 5l 4th ½way; pu 11; saddle slpd.*		P
529^{7}	Dancetillyoudrop (IRE) 12-1 Miss T Tellwright *(xnb) Sn prom; ld 8-10; mist 11; 2l 3rd nxt; sn lost plce; 12l 5th when ur 15.*		U
	Jovian Pond 25-1 R Sealey *Nd; 10l 7th ½way; lost tch & pu 11*		P
158^{P}	Optimistic Thinker (17ow) 25-1 A Shaw *1st ride; 2nd til ld 3; hdd 4; lost plce 8; 9l 6th ½way; wknd 11; sn wl bhnd; t.o when fell 14.*		F

Shekels (IRE) 8-1 T Gretton *Prom til mist 4; lost plce 7; 12l 8th ½way; lost tch 11; t.o & pu 13* . . . P

405^{2} Stride To Glory (IRE) 7-2 M Hooper *Lw; ss; a wl bhnd; 30l last ½way; t.o & pu 12* . . . P

OFFICIAL DISTANCES: hd, 3*l* **TIME:** 7min 03.8s

The rider of Shekels was fined £50 for being unable to produce his Medical Record Book

662 Mens Open, 12st — 12 ran

528^{2} **COOLE VENTURE (IRE)** 4-6F **R Burton** *Hld up; went 5l 4th ½way & 2nd at 15; lft in ld 3 out; 5l clr aft nxt; all out* . . . 1

L'idefix (IRE) 20-1 **P Callaghan** *Swtng; 2nd/3rd til ld 14; hdd aft nxt; chsd wnr 3 out; mist last; stayed on* . . . 3 2

Well Ted (IRE) (7x) 3-1 **Julian Pritchard** *(bnf) Hld up & bhnd; hit 5; 12l 8th ½way; hdwy 13; qcknd to ld aft 15 til blun bad 3 out; nt rec; wknd last* 12 3

251^{3} Philtre (IRE) (7x) 5-1 A Wintle *Ld to 14; wknd & 15l 4th 3 out* . . . 8 4

513^{2} The Archdeacon (IRE) 20-1 T Stephenson *Hld up; 10l 7th ½way; no hdwy 12; 11l 6th 15; sn wl bhnd* . . . 4 5

528^{6} Knock It Back (IRE) 20-1 J Handley *Prom; went 3l 2nd 8-11; wknd qckly 15; mist 3 out* . . . 10 6

Bansha House 16-1 S Joynes *Chsd ldrs; mist 6; 6l 5th ½way; 8l 5th & rdn when mist 12; wkng when mist nxt; bhnd when pu 14* . . . P

382^{3} Bold King (FR) (7x)(cp) 8-1 P Morris *8th when pu & dism aft 6* . . . P

586^{5} Felloo (IRE) 14-1 E Walker *Lost tch 7; 25l 9th ½way; t.o & pu 12* . . . P

513^{4} Highbridge (IRE) 12-1 R Hughes *Prom to 8; 7l 6th ½way; 8½l 6th & rdn 12; sn wknd; t.o & pu 3 out* . . . P

Lifebuoy (IRE) 20-1 T Mastoras *A bhnd; 10th ½way; t.o & pu 12* . . . P

Robsand (IRE) 33-1 M Wilesmith *A bhnd; blun 9; last ½way; t.o & pu 12* . . . P

OFFICIAL DISTANCES: 2½*l*, 10*l* **TIME:** 7min 05.8s

663 Intermediate, 12st — 14 ran

SAPEGA (IRE) 4-1 **Miss J Williams** *Swtng; sn prom; 5l 6th ½way; mist 10; went 5l 3rd aft 12; ld app 14; rdly* . . . 1

443^{P} **Petrouge** 12-1 **G Hanmer** *Hld up & bhnd; 11th ½way; 13l 9th 12; hdwy u.p & 5½l 6th 3 out; stayed on; went 2nd nr fin; no ch w wnr* . . . 1½ 2

365^{5} **Rain Delay** 7-1 **R Rogers** *2 handlers; hld up; lost plce 8; 8l 9th ½way; 10l 8th 12; hdwy 15; 3½l 5th nxt; went 2nd at last; dem cl home* . . . ½ 3

420^{4} Good Heart (IRE) 33-1 N Oliver *Hld up; 6l 7th ½way; 9½l 7th 12; hdwy 15; went 3l 4th nxt; one pce 2 out* . . . 3 4

616^{2} Genereux(cp,tt) 6-1 R Hodges *Sn cajoled along in 2nd/3rd til ld aft 4; hdd 9; chsd wnr 14-last; wknd flat* . . . 2½ 5

255^{U} Sharlom (IRE) 6-1 W Hill *2 handlers; hld up; 7l 8th ½way; hdwy 12; 5l 4th 15; went 2l 3rd nxt; wknd 2 out* . . . 4 6

358^{1} Ballyalbert 7-2 Miss A de Lisle Wells *Bd 1* . . . B

405^{4} Guard A Dream (IRE) 20-1 E Walker *Nt jw; a bhnd; last & rdn ½way; 13½l 10th 12; lost tch 14; t.o & pu 3 out* . . . P

513^{P} Hillcrest Manor (IRE)(cp) 33-1 A Brown *Prom; jmpd slow 6; 2l 3rd ½way; dem aft 12; wknd 15; wl bhnd when pu 2 out* . . . P

255^{P} Mr Naborro (IRE)(cp) 20-1 A Wintle *Hld up; hdwy 7; 3l 4th ½way; lost plce & 8l 5th 12; 12l 9th 15; wknd aft 3 out; wl bhnd when pu last* . . . P

513^{5} Ole Gunnar (IRE)(cp) 16-1 M Wilesmith *(xnb) Ld in start; prom; went 2nd 8; ld 9; mist 13; hdd app nxt; 6l 7th & rdn when mist 3 out; bhnd when ref & ur 2 out* . . . r

467^{1} Pot Shot 6-4F R Burton *Swtng; fell 1* . . . F

Rusty Buck 16-1 M Keel *Ld til aft 4; 2nd to 8; 3½l 5th ½way; wknd qckly u.p 11; wl bhnd when pu 12* . . . P

527^{P} The Unamed Man 12-1 G Barfoot-Saunt *Hld up; mist 2; drpd to rr aft 7; 10th ½way; lost tch 12; wl bhnd when pu 3 out* . . . P

OFFICIAL DISTANCES: 1½*l*, ½*l* **TIME:** 7min 12.4s

664 Ladies Open — 6 ran

527^{1} **STEP AND RUN (IRE)** 1-2F **Miss J Williams** *(xnb) Hld up; went 2nd aft 7; blun 13; ld app 15; drew 8l clr 2 out; comf* . . . 1

529^{8} **Pennyahei** (5a) 7-2 **Miss S Beddoes** *Chsd ldrs; 6l 3rd ½way; 4th & shkn up aft 12; rdn 15; went 5l 3rd nxt; stayed on one pce; went 2nd nr fin* . . . 5 2

Form	Runner	Dist	Pos
529[P]	**Life Of A River (IRE)** 12-1 **Miss H Kinsey** *Ld til app 15; 4l 2nd nxt; sn outpcd; dem nr fin*	s hd	3
	Gay Baratineur (FR) 7-2 Mrs K Baimbridge *Hld up; 9l 5th ½way; hdwy & 5l 3rd 12; went 2nd 15; wknd & 6l 4th nxt; mist 2 out; t.o & virt pu flat.*	runin	4
593[5]	Farfields Prince 16-1 Miss S Sharratt *Blun 3; 2nd til aft 7; 7l 4th ½way; wknd 12; t.o & pu 3 out*		P
515[P]	Fuero Real (FR) 33-1 Miss H James *A last; lost tch 11; t.o & pu 14*		P

OFFICIAL DISTANCES: 5*l*, s hd **TIME:** 7min 07.7s

665 Restricted, 12st — 14 ran

Form	Runner	Dist	Pos
377[U]	**JACKSON (FR)** 4-6F **R Burton** *Hld up; 9th ½way; hdwy 11; went 4l 3rd nxt & 2nd aft 15; ld 3 out; qcknd clr 2 out; impressive*		1
526[1]	**Cutina** (5a) 5-1 **D Barlow** *Hld up; 8th ½way; hdwy 11; 6l 5th nxt; jnd ldrs 3 out; nt qckn aft; tk 2nd nr fin*	12	2
519[1]	**New Lodge Express (IRE)** 3-1 **T Stephenson** *(xnb) 6s-3s; jnd ldrs 6; 4th ½way; lost plce 11; 9l 8th nxt; rallied 15; went 2l 3rd nxt; one pce*	nk	3
530[P]	Weallwayswillbeone (IRE) 10-1 N Oliver *Sn prom; 3rd ½way; ld aft 11-14; disp 2l 3rd 3 out; chsd wnr vain 2 out; dem nr fin; dism*	s hd	4
614[B]	Snowtre (IRE)(cp) 8-1 A Wintle *(xnb) Hld up & bhnd; 11th ½way; hdwy & 7l 6th 12; went 5l 4th 15; wknd app 2 out*	7	5
452[2]	Shemardi 5-1 R Hodges *A.p; went 2nd 3; ld 5-8 & 10-11; ld 14-3 out; rdn 2 out; sn wknd*	5	6
614[P]	Always Good (IRE)(tt) 20-1 P Needham *Nt jw; ld 2-5 & 8-10; disp 4l 3rd 12; mist 13; wknd & 11l 7th 15; t.o.*	20	7
252[P]	Rooneyran 16-1 S Joynes *(xnb) Tubed; a bhnd; 12th ½way; 10l 9th 12; lost tch 15; t.o.*	2	8
450[6]	Running On Red 20-1 S Gray *Hld up; 10th ½way; 12l 10th 12; wl bhnd 15; t.o when mist 2 out.*	12	9
	Finne Gaoithe (IRE) (5a) 12-1 M Munrowd *Hld up; hdwy & 6th ½way; 8l 7th 12; wkng when mist nxt; bhnd when pu 14*		P
530[8]	Home Tor 14-1 Miss S Beddoes *Prom; 5th ½way; lost plce qckly 11; 13l 11th nxt; wl bhnd when pu 14.*		P
	Lift The Latch (IRE) 14-1 M Wall *Tubed; ld to 2; mist & rmdrs 8; 7th ½way; wknd qckly 11; t.o & pu 13*		P
	Sabena Canyon 8-1 G Hanmer *Hld up & pulled hrd; last ½way; 13½l 12th 12; bhnd til fell 13.*		F
	Watergate Boy (IRE) 14-1 W Hill *Ur 1.*		U

OFFICIAL DISTANCES: 10*l*, hd **TIME:** 7min 10.6s

666 Open Maiden (Div 1, Part 1), 12st — 10 ran

Form	Runner	Dist	Pos
368[5]	**PRIMITIVE SON** 3-1 **Miss E James** *Hld up; 18l 7th ½way; mist 11; 11l 8th nxt; stdy hdwy 14; went 12l 3rd 3 out; ld aft 2 out; rdn clr flat*		1
453[P]	**Kerry Zulu Warrior** 12-1 **H Tett** *(xnb) Pulled hrd; ld; 12l clr 8-11; qcknd 12l clr 14; mist 2 out; sn hdd; wknd flat.*	15	2
518[2]	**Channel's Brook** 5-1 **H Dowty** *2nd til aft 11; 6l 4th nxt; outpcd 14; wknd & 17l 4th 3 out; lft poor 3rd nxt*	20	3
	Thyny Glen (IRE) 5-1 Miss J Houldey *Mist & drpd to rr 3; jmpd slow 7; 22l 9th & rdn ½way; 10l 7th when blun 12; last when mist 15; t.o*	25	4
450[P]	Blazing Pride 12-1 P Haynes *Chsd ldrs; 15l 4th ½way; 8l 5th 12; outpcd when fell 13*		F
620[P]	Corn General 7-1 Julian Pritchard *(xnb) Hld up; 16l 5th ½way; 9l 6th 12; wknd 14; t.o & pu 3 out*		P
93[P]	Hors Concours (NZ) 6-1 N Oliver *(xnb) 8s-6s; hld up & bhnd; 23l last ½way; hdwy 14; went 10l 2nd aft nxt; 12l 3rd & wkng when fell 2 out*		F
	Scallyweld 4-1 M Jackson *6s-4s; swtng; hld up & bhnd; 20l 8th ½way; 12l 9th 12; lost tch 15; 20l 5th when fell 2 out.*		F
617[F]	Toffee Lady (5a) 5-2F R Rogers *Prom; mist 2; 14l 3rd ½way; 5l 3rd 12; outpcd 14; 10l 5th when mist & ur 15*		U
257[5]	Youwoudhavethat (IRE) (5a) 8-1 M Hammond *Swtng; 17l 6th ½way; hdwy 11; went 4l 2nd nxt; mist 13; wknd qckly aft 15; t.o & pu 2 out.*		P

OFFICIAL DISTANCES: 15*l*, 25*l* **TIME:** 7min 27.0s

667 Open Maiden (Div 1, Part 2), 12st — 10 ran

	Horse	Dist	Pos
97^{4}	**SHAKING CHIEF (IRE)** 4-1 **A Wintle** *Hld up; hdwy 8; went 5l 3rd ½way & 2nd 11; ld aft 15; qcknd 10l clr 2 out; jmpd rt last; comf*		1
	Red Square Knight (IRE) 5-2 **R Burton** *(xnb) Hld up; 8l 5th ½way; went 8l 3rd 13 & 3l 2nd app 3 out; sn outpcd.*	12	2
	Penny Blue (12a) 6-1 **G Barfoot-Saunt** *(xnb) Hld up; blun 1; last to 13; 9l last & still nt asked a question 15; went 6l 3rd nxt; sn outpcd; wkng when mist last*	2½	3
621^{P}	Come On Boy 8-1 G Davies *Prom; went 2nd aft 7; ld 9; rdn 5l clr 11; jmpd slow 14; hdd aft 15; wknd qckly u.p 3 out.*	30	4
	Catch The Bus (IRE) 8-1 Miss S Sharratt *Pulled hrd; lft 2nd 5; ld 8-9; 8l 3rd 12; wknd app 3 out; bhnd when pu nxt*		P
	Missilebrook Lass (5a) 5-1 B Shaw *Hld up; 12l 8th ½way; 16l 7th & rdn w tail-swishing 12; mist 13; wl bhnd when pu 14*		P
	Our Friend Vinc (IRE) 8-1 S Joynes *Hld up; mist 9; 10l 6th ½way; 13l 6th & rdn 12; mist 13; short-lived eff 15; t.o & pu 2 out*		P
6^{5}	Ski Pass 6-4F T Stephenson *5/2-6/4; ld to 3; 2nd when fell 5*		F
	The Hare (IRE) 8-1 N Oliver *Chsd ldrs; 7l 4th ½way; mist 11; 10l 5th 12; wknd qckly aft 15; wl bhnd when pu 3 out.*		P
	Tigre Bois 8-1 R Carey *(xnb) Pulled hrd; blun 1; ld 3-8; 11l 7th & wkng ½way; wl bhnd when fell 11*		F

OFFICIAL DISTANCES: 12*l*, 3*l* **TIME:** 7min 28.0s

The stewards interviewed the rider of Tigre Bois who fell at the 11th fence; his explanation that the horse was going well enough to attempt the fence was not accepted and he was severely cautioned about his future riding of tired horses

668 Open Maiden (Div 2), 12st — 18 ran

	Horse	Dist	Pos
	BROWN SEAL (5a) 2-1F **N Oliver** *Sn prom; 5l 4th ½way; went 2nd 13; ld 3 out; drew clr flat; dism aft fin.*		1
	Bill Haze(bl) 9-2 **Julian Pritchard** *(bf) Ld 2 til mist 5; 2nd til ld 10; hdd 3 out; ev ch 2 out; nt r.o.*	10	2
	News Flash (IRE) 10-1 **Miss L Brooke** *Oht; swtng; sn prom; went 2nd aft 4; lft in ld 5; mist 7; hdd 10; 3l 3rd 12; outpcd aft 15; lft 20l 3rd 2 out; stayed on*	2	3
621^{5}	Sales Dodger (IRE)(cp) 7-1 R Hughes *Hld up & bhnd; 18½l 13th ½way; 11l 9th & rdn 14; stayed on frm 3 out; lft 4th nxt; nvr nrr*	8	4
	Lou Biarnes (FR) 20-1 B Shaw *Jmpd lft; 2nd/3rd to 8; 7l 6th ½way; 5l 5th 12; wknd aft 15*	15	5
	Four Opinions 6-1 H Dowty *Hld up; hdwy 8; 9l 8th ½way; 8l 6th 12; wknd 14; t.o*	8	6
621^{P}	Norton Wood (IRE)(tt) 20-1 R Hodges *(xnb) Hld up; 15l 9th ½way; 13l 11th & rdn 12; hdwy & 8½l 7th 14; wknd aft nxt; t.o*	6	7
	Romabit Tom 10-1 R Rogers *14s-10s; 2 handlers; a bhnd; 17l 11th ½way; lost tch 15; t.o*	3	8
410^{5}	All Eyez On Me (IRE) 14-1 M Hammond *20s-14s; hld up; gd hdwy 8; 4l 3rd ½way; went 2nd aft 11-13; stpd to nil aft 15; t.o & pu 2 out*		P
92^{P}	Browns Boy(cp) 12-1 M Jackson *Lost tch aft 7; 22l 14th ½way; t.o & pu 12*		P
533^{P}	Grantie Boy (IRE) (7a) 20-1 J O'Brien *(xnb) W ldrs; 6l 5th ½way; wknd & 9l 7th 12; blun 13; wl bhnd when pu 15.*		P
409^{U}	Kerrygoldsovereign (5a) 10-1 H Tett *(xnb,bf) Nt jw; wl bhnd til blun & ur 9*		U
	Nealie Mac (IRE) 20-1 Miss S Sharratt *(xnb) 2 handlers; lost tch aft 7; t.o & pu 10*		P
	Seymour Roses (5a) 20-1 J Handley *(xnb) Mounted on course & reluct to go down; ur & event ld to post; v reluct to rce; ref 1*		r
532^{F}	Strong Weld 20-1 D Sherlock *(xnb) A bhnd; hmpd 5; 16l 10th ½way; 15l 12th 12; lost tch 14; t.o & pu last*		P
	Tiger Ted 20-1 S Gray *Bckwd; blun & rdr lost iron 1; sn prom; 5th when fell 5*		F
258^{5}	Westington 10-1 M Wall *(xnb) Ld to 1; mist 9; 8l 7th ½way; 10l 8th & rdn 12; lost tch 14; t.o & pu 2 out*		P
	Withybrook Lass (5a) 5-1 R Burton *Hld up & bhnd; mist 3; 18l 12th ½way; hdwy & 8l 6th 14; went 10l 3rd app 3 out; wkng when pu nxt*		P

OFFICIAL DISTANCES: 10*l*, 2½*l* **TIME:** 7min 18.8s

Tivyside

Cilwendeg (RH 7F,19J)

Sat, 27 Mar (GOOD to SOFT becoming STICKY)

669 Hunt Members, 12st — 8 ran

Form	Horse	Dist	Pos
205P	**WADERS (IRE)**(bl) evensF **M Barber** *(xnb) Lw; made all; hit 9; jmpd slow 10 & agn when gng clr 16; 12l ahd nxt; unchall but nvr lkd v keen*		1
	Minster Belle (5a) 5-4 **P Sheldrake** *Settled 4th & off pce; 10l down & clsng 13; went 3rd aft 16 & chsd wnr nxt; wl hld when jmpd lft last*	25	2
	War Bride (5a) 10-1 **Miss I Tompsett** *Bhnd in final trio; 15l 5th 13; no ch frm 16 but urged along to snatch 3rd*	3	3
3574	Onward Bound(bl) 5-1 M Lewis *Prsd wnr; hit 9; hung lft bend bef 14; drvn & dem 2 out; nt r.o; lost 3rd cl home*	¾	4
	Betabug (IRE) 10-1 Miss G Morris *Bckwd; rem last when nrly ref 2; hopelessly t.o when rn out & ur 4*		R
	Calhoun (FR) 5-1 J Price *Bckwd; cl 3rd to 14; outpcd & dem 16; tired when pu 2 out*		P
	Coolarne Leader (IRE) 4-1 Miss R Davies *6th & out of control when rn out 3*		R
	Diamond Dot (5a) 10-1 S Hughes *Scruffy; mists in rr quartet; strugg 11; 20l last aft 13; virt ref & stuck on nxt; imm pu*		P

OFFICIAL DISTANCES: dist, 4*l* **TIME:** 6min 42.0s

670 Confined, 12st — 7 ran

Form	Horse	Dist	Pos
4495	**RED NECK**(tt) 1-2F **T Vaughan** *(xnb) Settled 6th to 9; prog on inner to chall 14; ld 16; drew clr 2 out; easily*		1
449P	**La Maestra (FR)** (5a) 12-1 **M Barber** *3rd til 2nd 9; ld 14-16; wknd qckly 2 out; eased flat*	15	2
4078	Cage Aux Folles (IRE) 20-1 Mrs B Lewis *Pulled to ld aft 1; 8l clr when jmpd slow 4; hdd & blun 14 & str rmdrs; 4l 4th 16; poor 3rd & tired when fell hvly & bad winded 2 out*		F
3612	Cowanstown Prince 3-1 Miss J Hughes *Bckwd; swtng; 3rd/4th til releg 5th & mist 11; cl up til blun 14; 12l 4th & tiring 16; jmpd v slow 3 out; rem 4th when ref nxt*		r
447P	Fassan (IRE)(cp) 20-1 W Oakes *Jmpd poor in detach last; u.p 6; t.o 9; pu 2 out*		P
2065	Hurdante (IRE) 6-1 D Jones *V fat; ld til app 2; 2nd to 9; hung bad lft app 14; rallied & 2l 3rd 16; pu qckly aft nxt; dism*		P
	Umbopa (USA)(bl) 7-1 M Lewis *Cl up early; drpd to rr 9; lost tch 11 & reluct; sn t.o; pu aft 13*		P

OFFICIAL DISTANCE: dist **TIME:** 6min 47.0s

671 Intermediate, 12st — 7 ran

Form	Horse	Dist	Pos
407U	**FAIR CHARMEUR (IRE)** (5a) 6-1 **Miss I Tompsett** *Set str pce & jmpd v bold in clr ld; 12l ahd 13; hdd nxt & imm outpcd; still 8l down last; drvn & str rn final 200yds; ld nr fin; v game*		1
628P	**Home Again (IRE)** 7-2 **P Sheldrake** *Lw; mist 11; 2nd bhnd tearaway til clsd qckly to ld 14; sn clr; 10l ahd when mist 3 out; 8l up & rdn last; flagged flat; hdd nr line*	1	2
447P	**Mecca Prince (IRE)** 12-1 **James Tudor** *Went 10l 3rd 5; disp 17l 3rd & rdn aft 13; no imp u.p frm 16; jmpd slow last*	10	3
	Candlestone Castle 6-4F T Faulkner *Mist 5; jmpd lft at times; last til 25l 6th aft 13; clsd sltly 3 out & chall for 2nd when blun bad nxt; lost any ch but had nvr lkd happy; trotted in*	15	4
4494	Buckland Boy 3-1 T Vaughan *Jmpd slow 5; mist 10; rr til prog to disp 17l 3rd aft 13; rn v wide nxt bend & nrly pulled himself up; cont t.o til almost ref 16 & imm pu*		P
	Cool General (IRE) 20-1 M Lewis *Settled 4th; mist 8; wkng when blun 13; t.o & pu nxt*		P
	Know Thyne (IRE) 7-2 J Cook *10l 3rd 4; dem nxt; midfield til lost tch 13; t.o & pu 3 out*		P

OFFICIAL DISTANCES: nk, 8*l* **TIME:** 6min 39.0s

672 Mens Open, 12st — 7 ran

434^{1} **MINELLA STORM (IRE)** (7x) 1-3F **P Sheldrake** *Went 2nd 5; ld 7; 8l ahd 16; kpt on stdly; unchall* 1

448^{F} **Doc Ryan's** 12-1 **T Vaughan** *Bckwd; handy; went 5l 2nd 13; chsd wnr vain aft; 10l down & wl hld app 2 out* . . . . 12 — 2

448^{U} **Chief Predator (USA)** 8-1 **T Faulkner** *A 3rd/4th; 12l 3rd & drvn 15; no resp & wl hld aft.* . . . . 3 — 3

448^{P} Harfdecent(tt) 8-1 M Williams *Sn last trio; 15l 5th aft 13; 27l 4th 16; sn t.o* 30 — 4

447^{6} Aficionado (IRE) 33-1 H Oakes *Rdr wears what lks to be father's enormous breeches (ex-rider now of epic proportions); jmpd slow in last; 10l adrift 7; 26l bhnd when rn wide app 14; cont wl t.o; pu last.* . . . . P

404^{r} Lord Of Love 16-1 L Stephens *Jmpd slow in last trio; u.p 6; nrly ref 9 & 10 & when t.o 11; succeeded nxt & ur* . . . . r

447^{P} Rathgibbon (IRE)(bl) 33-1 M Lewis *Fat; ld til jmpd lft & rmdr 7; jmpd slow 11; 2nd til aft 13; 4th & reluct when blun 15; 5th & tlng off when nrly ref 16 & pu* . . . . P

OFFICIAL DISTANCES: dist, 4*l* **TIME:** 6min 42.0s

673 Ladies Open — 5 ran

206^{1} **DAWN'S COGNAC (IRE)** (7x) 4-5F **Miss F Wilson** *Lw; ld 1; hvly rstrnd; lft 2nd 2; handy til rdn to chall 16; nk down when brief lft solo 3 out; virt pu flat* 1

615^{P} **Berkeley Frontier (IRE)** (7x)(tt) 25-1 **Mrs E Jones** *1st ride for 9 yrs; last & unable to raise gallop; 35l bhnd aft 7; fnce adrift 14; by-passed 3 out.* . . 10sec — 2

449^{3} Hunter Gold (FR) evens Mrs B Lewis *(xnb) Ld aft 1; nt fluent 11; 4l clr aft 13; hrd prsd but still gng wl when fell 3 out.* . . . . F

Never Sayaarr (IRE) (5a) 25-1 Miss G Morris *Lw; sn out of control; went 2nd & wide aft 1; blun & ur 2* . . . . U

Rusnetto (IRE) (7x)(vis) 20-1 Miss R Davies *15l last when hit 4 & ur.* . . . . U

OFFICIAL DISTANCE: dist **TIME:** 6min 46.0s

Fence 17 was omitted by the runner-up - fallen horse and rider

674 Restricted, 12st — 9 ran

454^{1} **ROSTOCK (IRE)** evensF **Miss F Wilson** *2 handlers; ld to start where tk off brief; made all & consistently outj rival frm 10; 8l clr 16; rdn aft last; kpt on stdly & a in comm* 1

357^{2} **Pete The Painter (IRE)** 3-1 **James Tudor** *Bckwd; mists; 3rd til 2nd frm 10; consistently outj aft; 5l down & drvn 3 out; tried to rally last but kpt hanging lft flat; a hld* . . . . $3\frac{1}{2}$ — 2

204^{1} **Trial Trip** (5a) 6-1 **J Cook** *(xnb) Midfield; 3rd brief 11; wknd bad 15; t.o 3 out; lft 3rd flat* . . . . 40 — 3

Carl's Boy 7-1 J L Llewellyn *(xnb) Hld up towards rr; 4th & prog 11; 3rd 13; 6l 3rd 3 out; wknd qckly nxt; eased to walk flat & dem* . . . . 10 — 4

207^{F} All For Jake (IRE) 8-1 D Jones *Tk keen hld & prom brief; blun 4; rn wide app 8; cont last & u.p; t.o 13; pu 15* . . . . P

452^{F} Clarky's Choice (IRE) 12-1 T Vaughan *Mists in midfield; rmdrs 7; u.p 11; no resp; t.o & pu 14* . . . . P

358^{3} Daisy's Choice (5a) 10-1 P Sheldrake *Mist 8; 2nd til terrible mist 10 & rdr nrly f.o bckwds; 8th nxt; t.o & pu 14* . . . . P

357^{P} Runaway Ralph 10-1 T Faulkner *2 handlers; tk keen hld; hld up; tended to j & hang lft; brief eff in 5th aft 13; nt r.o; wl btn when jmpd lft 15 & pu.* . . . . P

358^{P} Tigersun 20-1 J Price *(xnb) Jmpd sticky in rr w rdr lurching; prog 12 to 4th aft nxt; wknd qckly; t.o when climbed 3 out & pu.* . . . . P

OFFICIAL DISTANCES: 3*l*, dist **TIME:** 6min 42.0s

675 Confined Maiden (Div 1), 12st — 8 ran

453^{5} **MOUNTAIN LILY** (5a) 3-1 **J Cook** *Nt a fluent; hld up; clsd 11; 5l 3rd aft 13; mist nxt; went 2nd aft 3 out; drvn to jnd ldr & lft virt solo last* 1

Gilly Weet (5a) 5-2 **M Lewis** *Prsd wnr but nt a fluent; mist 3 out & dem; tired when jmpd lft nxt; lft poor 2nd last; eased flat* . . . . 25 — 2

600^{P} **Black Hope (IRE)** (5a)(tt) 10-1 **James Tudor** *Ld & jmpd rt; hung lft app 14; went 7l clr 3 out; prsd nxt; rdn & tired when jnd & jmpd rt & fell last; rmtd* runin — 3

Bold Flirtation 8-1 D Jones *Bckwd; svs & lost 30l; 7th when rn out 5* . . . . R

Champagne King (7a) evensF T Vaughan *Tk keen hld & hld up; disp 15l 3rd aft 7; 6l 4th aft 13; lkd strugg when fell hvly 15* . . . . F

451[U]	Gay Abandon (5a) 66-1 C Penycate *Lkd horrific in padd; t.o 2; rn thro wing 9*		R
	Mister Julius 4-1 M Barber *Unruly padd; v novicey in midfield; disp 15l 3rd aft 7; strugg when pckd 12 & rdn brief; pu aft nxt*		P
204[F]	Take The Gamble (5a) 8-1 Miss I Tompsett *(xnb) Outpcd 7; blun 8 & lost tch; t.o & mist 9; barely crawled over nxt 3; pu 13*		P

OFFICIAL DISTANCES: dist, dist **TIME:** 6min 56.0s

676 Confined Maiden (Div 2), 12st — 9 ran

357[3]	**LADY PALAMON (IRE)** (5a) 10-1 **S Hughes** *Settled midfield; 3rd frm 11; 3l 3rd 16; lft 2nd nxt; disp ld frm 2 out til forged clr though tired frm last; all out*		1
203[2]	**Beasley** (7a) 4-1 **M Barber** *Ld til mist 2; cont cl 2nd/3rd; rdn 13; 1l 2nd 16; lft in ld nxt; jnd nxt & duelled for ld u.p til hdd aft last; v tired & plugged home*	2½	2
120[2]	**Deltic Arrow** 4-1 **T Vaughan** *(xnb) Prom til 7l 4th & wkng 14; u.p aft mist nxt; 18l 4th 16; lft dist 3rd 3 out*	40	3
	Poacher's Pride (5a) 33-1 D Jones *Cl up in midfield; still ev ch when pu aft 13*		P
454[2]	Rescindo (IRE) (7a) 4-6F W Oakes *Nt a fluent; made nrly all; mist 15; 1l ahd 16; fell nxt (would prob have won)*		F
	Spicey Case (12a) 16-1 J Cook *School in rr; nrly ur 3 & 4; in tch to 8; t.o 10; pu 11*		P
	Stand On 12-1 James Tudor *Novicey & school in rr; 8l last aft 7; jmpd slow 8; lost tch app 14; t.o & pu aft 16*		P
	Swingingbridge (5a) 7-1 L Stephens *Swtng bad; blun & ur 3*		U
	Tiger Rag (5a) 20-1 P Sheldrake *(xnb) Mists in rr; t.o when blun 10; jmpd v slow nxt & pu*		P

OFFICIAL DISTANCES: 2*l*, dist **TIME:** 6min 54.0s

677 Confined Maiden (Div 3), 12st — 8 ran

450[P]	**BATCHWORTH LOCK** 7-1 **M Lewis** *(xnb) Ld to 4; mostly 2nd til outpcd aft 15; rdn & rallied to jn ldr 2 out; drew clr flat & outstayed rival*		1
	Westar Lad (IRE) 2-1 **T Vaughan** *(xnb) Tk str hld w rdr upright; pulled to ld 4; set slow pce; went 8l clr aft 15; hrd prsd 3 out; jnd nxt; hdd last; fin tired*	20	2
452[U]	**Wiston Wizo** 3-1 **P Sheldrake** *(xnb) Pulled hrd & prom; 2nd when hung violent lft app 8 & lost plce; rallied in 1l 3rd 13; 2nd when bad mist & veered wildly lft 15; terrible mist 3 out finally sealed fate; cont rem*	15	3
619[F]	Countess Kiri (5a) 6-4F M Barber *Mists in 2nd/4th; 3l 3rd aft 13; pckd bad nxt; wkng 16; 11l 3rd app 2 out where releg last & fell hvly*		F
	Final Mick 6-1 D Jones *(xnb) Pulled v hrd; anchored towards rr; 15l 5th aft 13; t.o & pu 16*		P
	Ladygal (IRE) (12a) 6-1 D Davies *Towards rr; wkng when rdr nrly f.o front 12 & agn 13; sn t.o; pu 16*		P
	Ridge Manor (IRE) (7a) 7-1 James Price *Jmpd slow 4; last by 5; t.o & reluct frm 7; ab 2 fncs bhnd when event pu 16*		P
	Sky Sorcerer (7a) 7-1 T Faulkner *7th when rn out 6*		R

OFFICIAL DISTANCES: dist, dist **TIME:** 7min 04.0s

Kelso (LH 8F,19J)

Sun, 28 Mar (GOOD, GOOD to SOFT in places)

678 Kelso Golf Club HC, 3m1f £2310 — 10 ran

349[1]	**MISS MATTIE ROSS** 11-06 8-1 **M McAlister** *Chsd ldrs; lft 2nd 6; stayed on to ld aft last; drvn out*		1
543[U]	**Geordies Express** 11-09 9-4 **W Kavanagh** *Chsd ldrs; lft in ld 6; qcknd 14; hdd aft last; no ex*	2½	2
542[2]	**Go Nomadic** 11-11(tt) 6-4F **P Atkinson** *Hdwy 9; sn chsng ldrs; wl outpcd aft 2 out*	16	3
509[1]	Laganside (IRE) 12-01 (12ow) 20-1 J Muir *Outpcd & pushed along when hmpd aft 13; sn bhnd*	20	4
122[5]	Bold Classic (IRE) 11-03 9-1 P Kinsella *Chsd ldrs; outpcd when hmpd by loose horse aft 13; sn bhnd*	4	5
552[3]	Piper's Rock (IRE) 11-03 20-1 Miss V Russell *Ld to 4; hit nxt; lost plce aft 13; sn bhnd; t.o 2 out*	dist	6

Ballymenagh (IRE) 11-07 20-1 D Jewett *Chsd ldrs; blun & ur 2* . . . . U
444U Jay Man (IRE) 11-05 33-1 K Mercer *Chsd ldrs; blun & ur 3* . . . . U
213P Manhattan Rainbow (IRE) 11-03 20-1 Miss J Hollands *Hit 4; t.o 10; pu 13* P
5544 Try Me And See 11-03 33-1 G Crow *Ld 4; blun & ur 6* . . . . U

TIME: 6min 24.2s **TOTE:** £8.20; places £1.70,£1.60,£1.10 **Ex:**£25.00 **CSF:**£24.62

Market Rasen (RH 8F,19J)

Sun, 28 Mar (GOOD to SOFT)

679 Beaumontcote HC, 3m1f £1529 — 18 ran

4371 **LANCASTRIAN JET (IRE)** 12-02 13-8F **M Barber** *Cl 2nd til ld app 10; shkn up app 3 out; stayed on str & wl clr frm nxt* 1
3404 **Flat Top** 12-02 25-1 **M Manton** *In tch; hit 6; mist 8; hdwy nxt; rdn & outpcd 15; 14l 3rd 3 out; plugging on when mist nxt; went poor 2nd aft last* . . 27 2
5651 **Imps Way** 11-06 9-2 **T Greenall** *Jmpd rt at times; hmpd 2 & bhnd; stdy prog when hit 12; chsd wnr 16; rdn nxt; wknd 2 out; v tired when dem sn aft last* dist 3
4376 West Pal (IRE) 12-00 50-1 M Smith *T.o 4; plodded round in own time* . . . dist 4
3771 Ababou (FR) 12-00 8-1 S Charlton *Midfield; brief eff 10; rdn 12; wknd 15; t.o & pu last* . . . . P
2496 Aughmor River (IRE) 11-09 33-1 N Moore *Chsd ldrs til hmpd 3; lost all interest; t.o 4; pu aft 10* . . . . P
Badworth Gale (IRE) 11-07 100-1 J Burley *Prom; rdn & lost plce rap 7; t.o & pu aft 10* . . . . P
3163 Glacial Dancer (IRE) 11-07 33-1 Miss Rachel Clark *Blun & ur 1* . . . . U
Imperial Line (IRE) 11-09(tt) 33-1 Miss T Jackson *Midfield; rdn 8; sn strugg; t.o & pu 12* . . . . P
Just Strong (IRE) 12-02 18-1 R Armson *Fell 3* . . . . F
5652 Mademist Sam 12-00 22-1 N Tutty *Chsd ldrs; mist 5 & rdr lost iron; rdn & wknd 10; t.o & pu 12* . . . . P
1253 Owen's Pet (IRE) 12-00 12-1 Miss E Jones *Tk keen hld; ld til app 10; rdn 14; hit nxt; sn wknd; 5th & tired 3 out; pu 2 out* . . . . P
Primitive Satin 12-02(bl) 25-1 L Bates *Fell 2* . . . . F
4455 Raffles Rooster 11-11 8-1 Miss S Brotherton *Hld up; hdwy to chse ldrs 8; rdn 15; no resp; rem 4th when ur 2 out* . . . . U
5003 Rising Talisker 11-04(bl) 66-1 Miss C Metcalfe *Chsd ldrs; blun 8; sn lost plce; t.o & pu 11* . . . . P
544P Supreme Silence (IRE) 11-07 25-1 N Kent *Chsd ldrs; mist 11; sn rdn & wknd; t.o & pu 3 out* . . . . P
The Sea Club (IRE) 11-07 50-1 M Seston *Jmpd rt & flung rdr into orbit 1* . U
226P Well Said Sam 11-07 66-1 J Handley *Bhnd; hit 10; t.o & pu 15* . . . . P

TIME: 6min 37.4s **TOTE:** £2.40; places £1.60,£6.80,£2.00 **Ex:**£119.20 **CSF:**£51.83

Belvoir

Garthorpe (RH 8F,18J)

Sun, 28 Mar (GOOD)

680 Hunt Members — 10 ran

592P **BENGAL BOY** 8-1 **N Pearce** *14s-8s; 2 handlers; a.p; ld to 3; ld agn 11; kicked clr 13; 10l up aft 15; 8l up at last; wkng flat; all out* 1
Eco Warrior (IRE) 6-1 **N Bell** *(xnb) 10s-6s; settled trckng ldrs; outpcd in 20l 5th app 13; eff aft 15; rdn to 2nd app last; clsd flat; nt rch wnr.* 3 2
302P **Runningwiththemoon** 16-1 **M Briggs** *Swtng; nt lw; prom; 2nd 4; chsd wnr frm 11; no imp frm 15; 8l down 3 out; dem app last; kpt on flat* 2½ 3
3861 Interrogator 10-11F J Docker *Nt a fluent; midfield; 14l 4th & no imp app 13; stdly lost tch aft; poor 4th 3 out; walked in* 25 4
3005 Thurles Pickpocket (IRE)(vis) 10-1 B Elson *Ld 3; hit 8 & rdr unstdy; hdd 11; outpcd when jmpd slow 15; stdly wknd* 5 5
4634d Satanas (FR) 16-1 M Chapman *(xnb,bf) Bit bckwd; a last pr; t.o aft 12; plodded rnd* 50 6
592P Deel Quay (IRE) 8-1 N Docker *Nvr went a yard & jmpd hesitant in last pr; t.o aft jmpd slow 11; pu 13* . . . . P

481P	General Carats 12-1 M Walford *Set off last; prog to jn ldrs 4; 6th & wkng 10; poor 7th when pu 15*		P
444P	It's Norman 20-1 M Mackley *Swtng; towards rr; 7th 10; jb lft & wknd 12; t.o & pu nxt*		P
481P	The Bombers Moon 9-1 L Hicks *Midfield; jmpd slow 6; 8th & drvn 10; sn wknd; pu 13*		P

OFFICIAL DISTANCES: 4*l*, 2½*l* **TIME:** 6min 31.7s

The stewards enquired into the running and riding of Interrogator; they accepted the owner's explanation that the horse had failed to act on the course

681 Intermediate, 12st — 3 ran

252¹	**LONGVILLE LAD** 1-3F **P Cowley** *2 handlers; oht; warm; made all; oft jmpd exuberantly; mist 10; drew clr frm 14; 25l up last; hvly eased to walk nr fin*		1
378¹	**Over The Master (IRE)** (5x) 6-1 **T Coles** *Chsd wnr; pckd 1 & 9; lost 2nd 13 & sn outpcd; went rem 2nd agn 3 out; blun & nrly ur 2 out (same fnce); plugged on*	15	2
379P	**Saxon Gold** 4-1 **L Hicks** *Bit bckwd; ur padd; outpcd in last; clsd 8; eff to chse wnr 13; rdn nxt; mist 15 & btn; last agn & blun 3 out; fin tired*	4	3

OFFICIAL DISTANCES: 20*l*, 3*l* **TIME:** 6min 28.5s

682 Ladies Open — 6 ran

380⁴	**RIVER NESS** (5a) 8-1 **Mrs V Thirlby** *Made all; set mod pce but nvr less than 3l up; drew clr frm 15; mist 2 out & rdr nrly f.o; r.o wl*		1
479³	**Edmond (FR)** 4-1 **Miss H Campbell** *Chsd wnr 2 til jmpd slow 3; went 2nd agn 13 til aft 15; sn outpcd in 3rd; no imp til r.o str flat to snatch 2nd agn*	8	2
443⁷	**Supercharmer** 14-1 **Miss A Armitage** *(xnb) Chsd wnr aft 3; outpcd frm 15; no imp aft; lost 2nd nr fin*	¾	3
478F	Silver Buzzard (USA) (7a) 8-1 Miss S Phizacklea *Trckd ldrs; 4th & outpcd 15; stdly wknd*	25	4
380¹	Garolo (FR)(bl) 2-1JF Miss V Tremlett *3s-2s; nt fluent & nvr gng wl; last & detach frm 8; t.o 15*	20	5
	Fami (FR) 2-1JF Miss Gemma Hutchinson *Chsd wnr to 2; pckd 9; wknd & mist 14; disp t.o 5th when pu 3 out*		P

OFFICIAL DISTANCES: 7*l*, nk **TIME:** 6min 20.2s

683 Mens Open, 12st — 9 ran

543U	**OMNI COSMO TOUCH (USA)** (7x) 5-4JF **A Sansome** *Set off w rest & no reluctance; hld up bhnd ldrs; ld aft 12; drew clr frm 15; impressive*		1
381¹	**Shanavogh** (7x) 5-4JF **R Hunnisett** *2s-5/4; prom; ld to 2; eff to disp ld app 13; sn brushed aside by wnr; vain pursuit frm 15*	25	2
389⁸	**Glendamah (IRE)** (7x) 33-1 **M Morley** *(xnb) In tch; 6th 10; outpcd 12; went poor 3rd aft 15; kpt on; no ch when mist 3 out*	15	3
298P	Minella Hotel (IRE)(cp) 7-1 J Docker *10s-7s; ld 2; made most aft til hdd & imm outpcd by ldng pr app 13; lost 3rd aft 15; tired aft; walked in*	40	4
477R	Needwood Neptune 100-1 P Bennett *Last frm 3; jmpd slow 5; t.o 7; still app 2 out as wnr crossed line*	30	5
565P	Bowfell (5a)(bl) 50-1 G Brewer *In tch til outpcd 12; sn wl bhnd; t.o 5th when crawled over 3 out; pu nxt*		P
	Gavroche Collonges (FR) 7-1 S Morris *(xnb) 33s-7s; oht; keen; prsd ldr 3; ld brief 8; went out like a light app 12; pu 15*		P
382F	Preferred (IRE) 25-1 N Docker *Bit bckwd; mists; in tch; 7th & drvn 10; no resp; tlng off when pu 14*		P
381⁷	Strong Chairman (IRE) 22-1 K O'Brien *Mist & ur 1*		U

OFFICIAL DISTANCES: 25*l*, 20*l* **TIME:** 6min 19.1s

The rider of Omni Cosmo Touch, who had been held up in traffic on the A1, was fined £40 for not weighing-out within the allowed time

684 Restricted — 9 ran

385¹	**FRANCO (IRE)** 9-4 **J Diment** *3s-9/4; sn prom; ld 5; made rest; clr frm 14; drew rt away frm 2 out; impressive*		1
504¹	**Snizort (USA)** 8-1 **G Brewer** *(xnb) Hld up; prog to 4th 10; no hdwy & outpcd 13; went 3rd 3 out; plodded on to tk rem 2nd flat*	40	2
501P	**Don Rio (IRE)** 25-1 **M Morley** *(xnb) Prom; chsd wnr 10; mist 14; sn easily outpcd; no ch aft; lost 2nd flat; fin v tired*	4	3

384P Fiesty Frosty (IRE) (5a) 16-1 J Docker *Chsd ldrs; 5th 10; mist nxt & rdn; outpcd 13; rem 5th aft 15; r.o flat* 1/2 4

3983 Bell Rock 20-1 James Tudor *(xnb) Hld up; 6th 10; went 4th & outpcd 13; 3rd brief but no imp aft 15; wknd 2 out; mist last* 20 5

5595 Libido 25-1 P Andrew *Mist 3; prom to 5; last by 10; wl t.o frm 13* 2 6

559P Albarden(bl) 25-1 N Pearce *Drvn in rr & no resp 6; wknd 11; t.o & pu 13* . . . . . P

4672 Greet You Well 4-1 R Cope *Mists; ld to 5; chsd wnr to 10; stdly wknd; mist 15 & sn pu; dism* . . . . . P

5961 Sizer (IRE) 11-10F N Saville *Lkd fit; late in padd; keen; hld up 15l bhnd rest; pu 4; saddle slpd* . . . . . P

OFFICIAL DISTANCES: dist, 2*l* **TIME:** 6min 24.4s

685 Open Maiden (Div 1), 12st — 9 ran

3833 **KING'S HERO (IRE)** 8-11F **S Morris** *2 handlers; made all; sn clr; gvn breather 10; drew rt away agn frm 13; 30l up aft 15; hvly eased flat* 1

2456 **Willow Ryde (IRE)** 5-1 **R Cope** *Chsd wnr to 8; rdn in 3rd 10; wl outpcd 13; no hdwy aft; lft v rem 2nd 2 out; tired* . . . . . runin 2

3922 Another Half (12a) 4-1 M Walford *Mist 3; prom in chsng group; went 2nd 8; clsd & 4l down 11; easily outpcd frm 13; tired frm 15; v rem 2nd when pu 2 out* . . . . . P

597P Catalan Girl (12a) 12-1 M Mackley *2 handlers; in tch in rr; nt fluent 8; wknd 10; t.o & pu 12* . . . . . P

Golden Dawn 20-1 Miss S Phizacklea *Keen early; midfield; 6th 10; wl outpcd aft 12; disp v rem 5th when pu 3 out* . . . . . P

500U Milliners Guide (5a) 12-1 G Brewer *Rr; prog & 5th 10; wl outpcd 13; poor 5th aft 15 til pu 2 out* . . . . . P

Past Forte (5a) 12-1 N Pearce *(xnb) School in last pr; mist 2; wknd & pu 11* P

Playaway (IRE) 25-1 R Collinson *Keen early; midfield; 4th 10; sn wknd; t.o & pu 14* . . . . . P

595P Shalabibubbly 14-1 S Walker *Midfield; nt fluent 6 & 7; 8th 10; wknd 13; disp v rem 5th when pu 3 out* . . . . . P

OFFICIAL DISTANCE: dist **TIME:** 6min 34.6s

686 Open Maiden (Div 2), 12st — 11 ran

476U **CAIPIROSKA** (7a) 7-2 **J Docker** *(xnb) 12s-7/2; trckd ldrs & a gng wl; 3rd 1/2way; gd j to ld 3 out; sn clr; veered lft nr fin; comf.* 1

293F **Polly Flinders** (5a) 7-1 **R Cope** *Ld; mist 2; hdd & outj 3 out; no ch w wnr aft* 10 2

476P **Hougham George** (7a) 10-1 **S Morris** *Settled midfield; outpcd but nt pushed aft 12; poor 5th aft 15; mist 3 out; lft poor 3rd 2 out; rdn & flashed tail flat* 30 3

3877 Currow Kate (5a) 20-1 L Hicks *Last pr when stumbled & nrly fell 1; gd rec; rchd 6th 10; outpcd aft 12; wl bhnd aft* 4 4

595U Wonderful Remark (5a) 25-1 G Moloney *Mists; a in rr; last & wl bhnd 10; plodded on* 15 5

589P Faircatcher 20-1 R Collinson *In tch; hmpd 7 & lost plce; wknd & mist 11; sn t.o; cont miles bhnd* 250y 6

560P Brer Bear (7a) 16-1 A Sansome *2 handlers; a rr; mists 8 & 11; wknd nxt; t.o & pu 15* P

2442 Catch On (IRE) 2-1F P Taiano *Keen early; prom; lft 2nd 7; dem app 3 out; sn outpcd; 3rd & hld when fell 2 out* . . . . . F

3875 Gee A Two (IRE) 12-1 J Diment *(xnb) Chsd ldrs; 3rd 1/2way; wknd 12; pu 14* P

4822 Kindle A Flame 3-1 G Brewer *(xnb) Cl up; hmpd 7; 5th 10; jnd ldrs aft 12; outpcd by ldng trio 15; 4th & wl btn when hmpd & rfo 2 out* . . . . . U

112P Red Rookie 25-1 M Mackley *Trckd ldr til fell 7* . . . . . F

OFFICIAL DISTANCES: 14*l*, dist **TIME:** 6min 35.0s

Cattistock

Littlewindsor (RH 7F,19J)

Sun, 28 Mar (GOOD with SOFT patches)

687 Hunt Members, 12st — 6 ran

4954 **HIGHWAY OAK** (7x) 11-8F **N Mitchell** *Made all; jnd 5-7; 2l up 12; gd j 16 & gained 2l; in comm frm nxt; drew clr frm 2 out.* 1

4601 **Blackwater Brave (IRE)** (7x) 5-2 **H Fry** *Settled in 4/5th til lft 3rd 9; disp 2nd 11; chsd wnr frm 14; no imp frm 3 out* 6 2

Alex Thuscombe(vis) 50-1 **Mrs R Barclay** *1st ride; 3rd to 3; sn lost plce; 7½l 5th 7; lft 4th 9; grad wknd frm 13; lft poor 3rd at last; game try* 20 3

351^{5} Cherokee Boy (7x) 9-1 Miss C Atkinson *A last; sn detach; 18l adrift 7; jmpd slow 13; t.o 15* 8 4

498^{2} Jolie Roslin (5a) 9-1 Mrs F Vigar *Trckd ldrs; 2l 3rd 5 til blun & ur 9* . . . . . U

323^{P} Martby 9-2 M Atkinson *Prom; disp ld 5-7; chsd ldr til rdn & wknd frm 16; still poor 3rd but exhaust when pu last* . . . . . P

OFFICIAL DISTANCES: 8*l*, 20*l* **TIME:** 6min 35.6s

688 Open Maiden 56&7yo, 2m4f, 12st - 16J — 7 ran

494^{2} **NOBLE ACTION** (7a) 1-2F **N Williams** *Hld up; 8½l 6th 4; stalked ldrs frm 11; chall app 2 out w rdr lkng round; sn clr; easy* 1

492^{P} **Orinoco's Flight (IRE)** 12-1 **M Holmes** *(xnb) Ld 4; 2½l up nxt; jnd 8-11; hdd 3 out; sn btn* 12 2

Apatura Joe 8-1 **N Mitchell** *(xnb) Prom; disp ld to 2; chsd ldr frm 11; wknd app 2 out; nt disg* 4 3

Foston Second (IRE) (5a) 14-1 M Sweetland *A last; 10l adrift 4; t.o 11* . . . 15 4

495^{P} Boy Band (IRE) 25-1 C Dailly *Chsd ldrs; 4l 3rd 4; disp 2nd 7; jnd ldr 8-11; grad wknd frm nxt; tired & jmpd slow 3 out; pu nxt* . . . . . P

575^{2} The Nelson Touch 9-2 D I Turner *(xnb) Swtng; ld 3; jmpd slow nxt & releg 5th; hdwy to 3rd 11; wknd qckly 13; 4th & tired when pu 2 out; dism* . . . . . P

Velvet Victory (IRE) (12a) 8-1 M Miller *Disp ld to 2; 6l 4th 4; mist 6 & climbed fncs aft; pu 10* . . . . . P

OFFICIAL DISTANCES: 15*l*, 3*l* **TIME:** 5min 43.0s

689 Restricted, 12st — 8 ran

498^{P} **SCARLET GLORY** (5a) 7-4F **H Fry** *(xnb) 2 handlers; swtng; 6l 4th 5; hdwy to 3l 3rd 10; chsd ldr frm 12; 8l down 14; clsd nxt; ld 16; sn clr; tired but stayed on wl frm 2 out* 1

Howya Matey (IRE) 9-4 **A Farrant** *Trckd ldrs; 2½l 3rd 5; chsd ldr frm 7; 1½l 2nd 10; outpcd 13 & 18l 3rd nxt; stayed on one pce frm 16; passed toiling rival app 2 out; nt trble wnr* 8 2

474^{1} **Romany Move** 11-1 **Mrs S Godfrey** *Disp 9l 5th 5; chsd ldng trio frm 10; 28l 4th 14; stayed on one pce frm 16; nd* 3 3

579^{3} Beachtime 11-2 N Mitchell *(xnb) Ld; jnd 5-7; 3l up 12; qcknd 8l clr 14; hdd 16; blun bad nxt; exhaust & virt ref last; walked in* 30 4

415^{4} Dursey Island (IRE) 9-1 M Miller *Disp 9l 5th 5; wknd 10; bhnd when pu 12* P

15^{P} Gami (FR) 12-1 J Snowden *Chsd ldr til disp ld 5-7; stumbled on downhill rn to nxt; wknd 11; jmpd slow 12; pu 13* . . . . . P

320^{P} Sixth Sense (IRE) 12-1 C Dailly *Last 2; sn outpcd; t.o 7; pu 11* . . . . . P

Winsley Spirit (5a) 20-1 G Weatherley *(xnb) A last pr; rdn 6; lsng tch when jmpd lft nxt; sn t.o; pu 11* . . . . . P

OFFICIAL DISTANCES: 10*l*, 4*l* **TIME:** 6min 38.7s

690 Ladies Open — 8 ran

603^{2} **NORSKI LAD**(bl,tt) 5-2 **Miss R Green** *Disp 6l 3rd 5; trckd ldrs frm 13; clsd app 3 out; ld nxt; sn clr; easy* 1

262^{2} **Cento (IRE)** 7-2 **Miss C Stucley** *Disp 6l 3rd 5; trckd ldng pr til ld 14; hdd aft 3 out; sn brushed aside* 12 2

351^{1} **Atavistic (IRE)** 6-4F **Miss R Booth** *Hld up; 14l 6th 7; hdwy to 2½l 5th 13; chsd ldr nxt; outpcd app 3 out; stayed on one pce frm nxt* 15 3

484^{F} Virtuoso 33-1 Mrs S Corcoran *Chsd ldrs; 4l 2nd 5; ld aft 7; jnd 10-13; sn hdd; bhnd frm 16* 3 4

470^{U} Ardross Gem (IRE) (5a)(vis) 20-1 Miss W Southcombe *(bf) Chsd ldr frm 3; disp 6l 3rd 5; jmpd lft 12 & 14; grad wknd; bhnd frm 16* 5 5

484^{3} Defendtherealm 16-1 Miss A Mills *Prom; disp ld 2; ld 3-6; jnd ldr agn 10 til ld brief 14; wknd qckly frm nxt; fin tired* 15 6

$233^{4\dagger}$ Druid's Brook 40-1 Miss K Reynolds *(xnb,b4) Swtng; a last; 40l adrift 7; t.o & pu aft 13* . . . . . P

603^{5} Jack The Bear (IRE) 10-1 Miss C Tuffin *Ld to 3; sn lost plce; outpcd & 25l 7th 7; t.o 12; pu & dism flat* . . . . . P

OFFICIAL DISTANCES: 15*l*, 12*l* **TIME:** 6min 30.3s

691 Mens Open, 12st — 3 ran

569^{1} **BALLYSICYOS (FR)** (7x) 1-4F **A Farrant** *(xnb) Chsd ldr; 2½l down 5 til ld aft 7; made rest; 3l up 12; grad drew clr frm 14; in comm 16; doddle* 1

263^{F} **Shock's Pride (IRE)** 4-1 **M Miller** *Last til chsd ldr vain frm 8; 5l 2nd 14; lost tch frm nxt; t.o & tired 3 out* . . . . runin 2

603^{6} Millyhenry (7x) 12-1 R Lee *Ld to 7; releg last nxt; mist 10; outpcd 14; 30l adrift when blun & ur 3 out* . . . . U

OFFICIAL DISTANCE: 30*l* **TIME:** 6min 37.5s

692 Intermediate, 12st — 6 ran

498^{1} **VIVID IMAGINATION (IRE)** (7a) 2-5F **A Farrant** *(xnb) Lw; made all; 1½l up 5; 5l clr 14; drew rt away frm 16; impressive* 1

468^{1} **Caundle Chase** 10-1 **W White** *Trckd ldr; 2l 2nd 7; sn 3rd & outpcd; t.o 15; went v rem 2nd past flagging rival aft 3 out* 1½fs 2

147^{5} Briary Boy (IRE) 14-1 N Wilmington *(xnb) 2 handlers; 7l 5th 5; releg last 7; t.o & pu 12* . . . . P

495^{6} Earl's Toy (IRE) 8-1 H Fry *Last 6; 4th & outpcd 10; bhnd when pu 15* . . . . P

321^{F} Heisamodel (IRE) 6-1 M Miller *Last til 6½l 4th 5; chsd ldng pr frm 8 & wnr vain frm 13; tiring when clambered over 3 out; pu nxt* . . . . P

Vansell (5a) 20-1 N Mitchell *2 handlers; chsd ldrs; mist 5; 5l 3rd 7; wkng & jmpd slow 10; clambered over 13 & pu* . . . . P

OFFICIAL DISTANCE: dist **TIME:** 6min 30.4s

693 Open Maiden, 12st — 11 ran

ROSE OF THE HILL (IRE) (7a) 6-5F **A Farrant** *(xnb) Chsd ldrs; 1½l 4th 7; ld app nxt; hdd 9; disp ld agn 12 til ld 15; sn clr; rn green frm 2 out; lks useful recruit* 1

474^{3} **Collier** 12-1 **T Atkinson** *(xnb) 4th 3; 5l 5th 7; chsd ldng trio 12; outpcd 14; stayed on frm nxt; lft 2nd 2 out; nvr nr wnr* 12 2

328^{P} April's Past (5a) 16-1 M Atkinson *(xnb) Ld/disp 3 til ld 5; jnd 7; hdd app nxt; grad wknd frm 12; clambered over 14 & imm pu.* . . . . P

237^{r} Cool Shuil (IRE) (5a) 20-1 M Miller *Jmpd lft; 7th 5; jmpd violent lft nxt & imm pu* . . . . P

119^{7} Go Boy 20-1 M Holmes *(xnb) Last 1; a bhnd; t.o 12; pu 15* . . . . P

580^{P} Little Mister(cp) 25-1 D Drake *Chsd ldr 3; 7½l 6th 7; wknd qckly 12; bhnd when pu 14* . . . . P

493^{3} Polar Bright (IRE) 4-1 N Mitchell *(xnb) Disp ld 3-5; ½l 3rd 7; ld agn 9; jnd 12-14; sn hdd & wknd; exhaust 4th when blun & ur 3 out* . . . . U

494^{P} Polly Dust (5a) 16-1 M Sweetland *8th 6; jmpd slow 9; t.o 12; pu 3 out* . . . . P

475^{2} Random Trix (5a) 10-1 Miss S Robinson *9th 5; a bhnd; t.o & pu 13* . . . . P

492^{3} Sure How Bad (IRE) 4-1 N Williams *Ld to 2; disp ld brief 7 & agn 12-14; sn wknd; 3rd & tired when pu 2 out* . . . . P

233^{U} Swan Song (5a) 25-1 Miss E Tory *10th 2; a bhnd; t.o & pu 13* . . . . P

OFFICIAL DISTANCE: 15*l* **TIME:** 6min 46.7s

Curre & Llangibby

Howick (LH 9F,18J)

Sun, 28 Mar (GOOD to SOFT)

694 Hunt Members, 12st — 4 ran

356^{F} **QUESTIONAIRE** (5a) 7-4F **R Stephens** *Trckd ldrs gng wl; ld app 13; sn clr; v easily* 1

148^{2} **Alpine Fugue (IRE)**(tt) 2-1 **Miss S Lewis** *Cl up til 3rd & outpcd app 13; chsd wnr app 15; no imp* 25 2

453^{1} **Musical Sleuth** (7a) 4-1 **J Price** *Jmpd rt; ld til app 13; sn wknd; t.o frm 3 out* 1½fs 3

Mikes Acre (5a) 8-1 Miss B Williams *(bf) In tch; mist 3; wknd qckly app 10; wl bhnd when pu 11* . . . . P

OFFICIAL DISTANCES: 25*l*, dist **TIME:** 6min 35.0s

695 Restricted, 12st — 10 ran

362[1] **GIPSY GIRL** (5a) 4-6F **R Stephens** *A gng wl; trckd ldrs; went 2nd aft 12; ld 14; in comm when lft wl clr nxt; v easily* 1
451[P] **Hail Stone (IRE)** 25-1 **L Stephens** *Ld to 3; chsd ldr; rmdr 8; 3rd & rdn 13; sn outpcd; lft poor 2nd 15* 30 2
Niloufer (5a) 6-1 **R Bliss** *Hld up; prog 8; rdn 12; went mod 4th 14; lft 3rd nxt; nd* 15 3
446[1] Call Me Sonic 4-1 D Jones *Chsd ldrs; rdn & outpcd 12; 5th & no ch 14; lft poor 4th nxt* 6 4
498[3] Knight Ofthe North 25-1 Miss E Burrows *Bhnd; lost tch 10; no ch frm 13* . 15 5
Deep Dale 25-1 T Vaughan *Chsd ldrs; 6th 10; wknd app nxt; bhnd when pu 13* P
358[P] Fernhill Blaze (IRE) 20-1 T Faulkner *A rr; mist 5; rdn & no resp 9; pu 11* . P
Phase Three (IRE) 7-1 T Edwards *(xnb) Ld 4-14; 3l 2nd & lkd btn when blun bad & ur nxt* . . . . U
452[3] Plain Chant(cp) 6-1 J L Llewellyn *Ww; prog to 4th 11; rdn & outpcd app 13; 5th & no ch when pu 3 out* . . . . P
357[P] Rebel Yell (IRE) (5a) 40-1 J Cook *Bhnd frm 5; rmdrs nxt; t.o & pu 10*. . . . P

OFFICIAL DISTANCES: 30*l*, 15*l* **TIME:** 6min 29.0s

696 Land Rover Mens Open, 12st — 3 ran

359[1] **SOHAPARA** (5a) 1-4F **D Jones** *(xnb) Set stdy pce to 5; ld agn 10; sn wl clr; canter* 1
Andy's Lad (IRE) 6-1 **T Vaughan** *(xnb) Pulled hrd; ld 5-10; imm btn; t.o frm 15* 40 2
360[U] Iro Origny (FR) 5-1 A Phillips *(xnb) Trckd ldrs; cl 3rd when pulled himself up app 10* . . . . P

OFFICIAL DISTANCE: dist **TIME:** 6min 44.0s

697 Ladies Open — 4 ran

322[4] **KNIGHT OF PASSION** 2-5F **Miss C Tizzard** *Made all; clr 10; 10l up 14; unchall* 1
448[P] **Dexter Gordon (IRE)**(bl,tt) 3-1 **Mrs C Owen** *Chsd ldrs; went 2nd 14; no imp frm 3 out*. 12 2
361[4] **Young Manny** 10-1 **Mrs B Lewis** *Chsd wnr to 11; sn outpcd; no ch frm 14* 3 3
613[P] Welburn Boy(bl,tt) 20-1 Miss L Allfrey *Last til prog to 2nd 11-13; sn lost tch; last & no ch frm 14* 10 4

OFFICIAL DISTANCES: 12*l*, 3*l* **TIME:** 6min 31.0s

698 Intermediate (Nov Rdrs), 12st — 6 ran

COLDABRI (IRE) (5a) 2-1JF **S Evans** *In tch; 6l 3rd 10; went 2nd 12; ld 3 out; rdn app last; stayed on wl* 1
447[4] **Silver Pot Black** 3-1 **Miss H Lewis** *Chsd ldrs til ld 11; hdd app 15; one-pcd u.p frm 3 out*. 6 2
447[F] **Chesnut Wood** (5x) 2-1JF **Miss A Hughes** *Ww; 10l 4th 9; hdwy & 5l 3rd 13; wknd 3 out* 40 3
447[U] Glen Mist (IRE)(bl) 20-1 Miss R Athay *Bhnd; eff & in tch 11; sn lost tch; t.o* 30 4
410[7] Crystal Brook (5a) 10-1 S Graham *(xnb) 20s-10s; 2 handlers; ld; rmdrs 7; hdd 11; sn wknd; wl bhnd when pu 15* . . . . P
Miss Foley (5a) 5-1 Miss A Gibbons *In tch til ur 8* . . . . U

OFFICIAL DISTANCES: 4*l*, dist **TIME:** 6min 34.0s

699 Confined Maiden (Div 1), 12st - 17J — 15 ran

413[F] **JEUNE PREMIER (FR)** 10-1 **G Perkins** *(citation) 2 handlers; chsd ldrs; ld 10; 5l clr 14; stayed on wl frm 2 out* 1
368[3] **Willoughby Flyer** 4-5F **M Walters** *Cl up; lft 6l 2nd 12; rdn app 15; one pce u.p frm 3 out*. 5 2
454[F] **Crystal Soldier** (5a) 25-1 **D Jones** *Chsd ldrs; cl 5th 11; outpcd frm nxt; 4th & no ch 15; lft 3rd nxt*. 40 3
356[3] Miss Man (5a) 8-1 Miss A Cavanagh *A rr; 6th & no ch 13; lft poor 4th 3 out; t.o* 12 4
362[P] Cottage Boy (IRE) 33-1 T Edwards *Pulled hrd; ld 2; clr nxt; hdd aft 9; sn wknd; bhnd & pu 11* . . . . P
362[P] Croesy Pennant 25-1 Miss F Wilson *Sn wl bhnd; t.o til pu 2 out*. . . . . P
620[P] Evans The Coal(tt) 25-1 James Price *Tongue-tie refitted start; pulled hrd; hld up in rr; prog to trck ldrs 10; cl 2nd when fell 12* . . . . F

Form	Horse	Dist	Pos
409r	Frogsmarsh (5a)(cp) 25-1 Miss R Reynolds *(xnb) A bhnd; lost tch & no ch 11; t.o & pu 3 out*		P
362P	Hallbrook (5a) 20-1 A Hanly *Chsd ldrs to 10; wknd nxt; bhnd & pu 13*		P
452P	Ian's Boy(tt) 12-1 L Stephens *Bhnd frm 6; t.o & pu 10*		P
	Itsdigitalis (5a) 6-1 J L Llewellyn *Mid-div to 5; sn lost plce; bhnd & pu 11.*		P
3632	Just Caramel (5a)(tt) 5-1 R Stephens *Ww in mid-div; 5th app 13; stayed on frm nxt; 5l 3rd when fell 3 out*		F
362P	King Marlon 10-1 T Vaughan *(xnb) Ld 1; sn hdd; last when fell 6; dead.*		F
454S	Malvic (IRE) (7a) 12-1 T Faulkner *Fell 1*		U
3634	Start It Up 10-1 J Price *(xnb) Cl up; chsd ldrs 5; 4th & outpcd 12; no ch when bd 3 out*		B

OFFICIAL DISTANCES: 4*l*, dist **TIME:** 6min 33.0s

Fence 15 omitted - fallen horse

700 Confined Maiden (Div 2), 12st — 14 ran

Form	Horse	Dist	Pos
258P	**BARTON DREAM (IRE)** 5-1 **T Vaughan** *(xnb) 2 handlers; chsd ldrs; went 2nd 11; chall 14; ld 3 out; clr last; r.o wl.*		1
363F	**Ruby Dante (IRE)** (5a) 9-4F **D Jones** *Prom; lft in ld 7; jnd 14; hdd 3 out; one pce u.p*	4	2
599P	**Little Word** (12a) 8-1 **R Stephens** *Prom; lft 2nd 4-11; 2l 3rd 13; outpcd app 15*	20	3
454P	Indian Trix (IRE) (5a)(tt) 20-1 A Hanly *Chsd ldrs; 7l 4th & rdn app 13; sn outpcd; no ch frm 15*	4	4
	Pharailde (5a) 16-1 J Price *2 handlers; mid-div; in tch; 6th & outpcd app 13; r.o flat; fin wl; btr for rce*	2	5
4533	St Palais (12a) 5-1 T Faulkner *Chsd ldrs; 5th & rdn app 13; no ch frm nxt.*	3	6
363U	Sumerian Lad 3-1 G Perkins *Ww in tch; lost plce & bhnd 10; 20l 8th app 13; some hdwy 15; 5th & no ch when blun bad 3 out*	3	7
453U	Maloney (IRE) 14-1 Miss C Evans *In tch; cl 5th 10; outpcd 12; no ch when nrly ur 3 out*	12	8
618P	Bristol Bridge(bl) 20-1 T Edwards *Prom; lft in ld 4 til blun, stumbled & ur 7*		U
6194	Meadows Prince (IRE) (7a)(bl) 10-1 R Bliss *In tch to 10; strugg when mist 12; t.o & pu 15*		P
368R	Rody (IRE) 25-1 M Walters *Ld til rn out 4*		R
	Saronica's Boy 20-1 James Price *Nt jw; sn detach in last pr; t.o 6 til pu 9.*		P
	The Leazes (7a) 20-1 L Stephens *Rr in tch; jmpd slow 6 & 9; 8l last 10; 7th & no ch when pu 13*		P
452U	Tormoss Lady (5a, 2ow) 20-1 C Penycate *Jmpd slow & reluct; sn detach in last pr; t.o when fell 6.*		F

OFFICIAL DISTANCES: 5*l*, 15*l* **TIME:** 6min 39.0s

East Cornwall

Great Trethew (RH 7F,19J)

Sun, 28 Mar (GOOD)

701 Open Maiden 56&7yo (Div 1), 2m4f, 12st - 16J — 13 ran

Form	Horse	Dist	Pos
1943	**BALLY BLUE** 9-4JF **L Jefford** *Trckd ldrs; hdwy to 2nd 3 out; chall nxt; r.o und str drvng to ld cl home*		1
568U	**Miss Ziggerson** (5a) 4-1 **Miss S Young** *Trckd ldr; hdwy to ld 9; 4l up 11; jnd 2 out; hdd cl home*	nk	2
4943	**Josanjamic** (5a) 9-4JF **L Heard** *Made most to 10; 2nd 11; 3rd & outpcd 3 out*	10	3
	Alfies Rocket 12-1 J Young *Hld up towards rr; hdwy to 5th 11 & 4th 2 out; no ex*	nk	4
5684	Dancing Dasi (IRE) (12a) 8-1 Miss L Gardner *Mid-div til hdwy to 5th 11 & 4th 14; no ex; wknd 2 out.*	6	5
568P	Longstone Lady (IRE) (5a) 12-1 D McKenna *Prom early; outpcd 8; 5th & lsng tch 11; kpt on*	8	6
150P	Fluted Edge (5a) 25-1 W Biddick *A towards rr; lost tch aft 10; kpt on*	8	7
	Brits Mate (5a, 8ow) 25-1 D Stephens (Devon) *Bit bckwd; sn rr; lost tch frm 6; t.o & pu 10*		P
	Just Fable (5a) 12-1 R Woollacott *Outpcd aft 7; rr when pu 11*		P
584P	Major Reno (IRE) 20-1 T Dennis *Trckd ldrs in 4th mostly til lost tch aft 11; rr when pu 3 out*		P

	Northern Thatch (12a) 12-1 I Hambley *Lost tch frm 10; rr when pu 12*		P
	Some Tool 50-1 R Ross *Mid-div; lost tch aft 9; rr when pu 11*		P
	Westwood Lir (5a)(tt) 20-1 A Glassonbury *Mist 5; lost tch aft 6; t.o & pu 10*		P

OFFICIAL DISTANCES: hd, 2*l* **TIME:** 5min 25.0s

The owner of Westwood Lir was fined £50 for having billet hook attachments on the reins and not stitched or buckled fastenings as required; the stewards allowed the reins to be changed so that the horse could run delaying the race by around seven minutes

702 Open Maiden 56&7yo (Div 2), 2m4f, 12st - 16J — 12 ran

	IMPATIENT LADY (5a) 12-1 **A Glassonbury** *Hld up; hdwy to 4th 11 & 3rd 3 out; ld aft nxt; sn clr*		1
	My Whisper (IRE) (12a) 7-2 **L Jefford** *Trckd ldrs in 3rd mostly; hdwy to chall 2 out; no ex app last*	5	2
491U	**Little Apple Bay** (5a) 14-1 **Miss S Gaisford** *Swtng; made most to 10; outpcd in 4/5th til r.o to 3rd frm 2 out; nt trble ldrs*	6	3
600P	Questionit (12a) 7-1 Miss L Gardner *Mid-div; hdwy to 4th 9; r.o one pce*	1	4
486U	Little Lord Lewis (7a) 4-1 C Heard *Hdwy to ld 11-3 out; wknd qckly*	6	5
493P	Abseal 5-2F Richard Darke *Trckd ldrs; hdwy to 2nd 12; outpcd & wknd frm 3 out*	2	6
	Beehawk (7a) 10-1 J Young *Hmpd 2 & sn rr; plugged on*	5	7
307P	Baldhu Mynah (7a) 16-1 M Woodward *Lost tch aft 10; t.o & pu 3 out*		P
13W	Dart View Lass (5a) 12-1 L Heard *Rr by 3; t.o & pu 11*		P
306P	Hooray Henry (7a) 5-1 T Dennis *Mid-div when ur 2*		U
	Silver Tray (IRE) (12a) 16-1 R Ross *Blun 4; lost tch 10; t.o & pu 3 out*		P
469P	Theydon Star (NZ)(bl) 16-1 R Skinner *Swtng; lost tch frm 11; t.o & pu 15*		P

OFFICIAL DISTANCES: 5*l*, 2*l* **TIME:** 5min 32.0s

703 Mixed Open, 12st — 7 ran

497²	**PROVINCE** 10-1 **L Jefford** *Hld up; hdwy to 3rd 15 & 20l 2nd 3 out; rap prog to ld last; r.o game*		1
487¹	**Colquhoun** 7-4 **Mrs O Jackson** *Made most; 20l clr 3 out; wkng but still 8l clr when blun, slowed & swerved lft nxt; no ex frm last*	2	2
569⁶	**Hasten Bak** 6-1 **Miss L Gardner** *Chsd ldrs in 3rd mostly; 20l 3rd 3 out; some late hdwy*	8	3
487³	Bruthuinne (IRE) (7x) 20-1 D McKenna *Prom; 2nd mostly til wknd aft 13; t.o last when pu 15*		P
320P	Calleva Star (IRE) 25-1 S Kidston *Lost tch frm 14; t.o & pu 3 out*		P
	Dale Creek (IRE) 10-1 R Woollacott *Nvr gng wl & sn pushed along; bhnd when pu 6*		P
569³	Fossy Bear (5a, 4x) 5-4F Miss S Young *Nvr plcd to chall; outpcd & 25l down when pu 3 out*		P

OFFICIAL DISTANCES: 2*l*, 4*l* **TIME:** 6min 25.0s

The stewards enquired into the running of the favourite, Fossy Bear; the rider's explanation that the mare was 'well in season, neighing at the start', had not jumped well on the ground nor responded to the whip almost pulling herself up, was noted

704 Confined Maiden 8yo&up, 12st — 10 ran

	LADY MISPRINT (5a) 5-1 **D McKenna** *12s-5s; hdwy to trck ldrs 5; ld 13; drew clr frm nxt; 6l up 16; r.o wl when chall 2 out*		1
568³	**O'ech** (5a) 7-4F **C Heard** *A.p; ld early; outpcd aft 13; r.o wl frm 3 out; 2l 2nd & ev ch 2 out; no ex cl home*	5	2
494P	**Winnie The Pooh** 3-1 **Miss S Gaisford** *Outpcd aft 13; 6th 15; r.o agn frm 3 out*	12	3
312P	Small-Lir (5a) 12-1 Miss S Young *Sn rr & nd; kpt on past pullers-up*	20	4
312P	Buddy Bear (IRE) 10-1 L Jefford *Prom in 2nd mostly til wknd frm 3 out; 25l 4th when pu nxt*		P
494P	Druid Pandora (5a) 10-1 R Woollacott *Prom; hdwy to ld 11; wknd frm 12; 5th 15; rr when pu 3 out; lkd sore*		P
	Je Suis (IRE) (5a) 16-1 I Hambley *Bit bckwd; in tch when mist & virt stpd 10; rr when pu nxt*		P
486⁶	Just Aretha (5a) 10-1 Miss L Gardner *Lost tch aft 13; rr when pu 3 out*		P
485r	Little Rosie (5a) 14-1 Miss D Mitchell *Lost tch frm 13; rr when pu 3 out*		P
567P	Vero Beach(vis) 9-1 Richard Darke *Prom early; lost tch aft 13; 30l 5th when pu 2 out*		P

OFFICIAL DISTANCES: 3*l*, 5*l* **TIME:** 6min 39.0s

705 Intermediate, 12st — 7 ran

495[3] **TENINAROW (IRE)** 6-4F **Richard Darke** *Trckd ldr; hdwy to ld aft 14; r.o str when chall aft 2 out* . . . 1
495[2] **Father Mansfield (IRE)** 3-1 **Miss C Prouse** *Hld up; hdwy to 3rd 12 & 2nd 2 out; chall at last; no ex flat* . . . 1 2
495[P] **Carefree Love (IRE)**(bl) 10-1 **Miss S Gaisford** *Ld 5-12; 4th 15; lost tch frm 16; went 3rd agn app last* . . . 25 3
354[1] Drumhorc (IRE)(cp) 4-1 Miss L Gardner *A rr; detach last 10; kpt on* . . . 2 4
573[P] Ross Poldark 8-1 T Dennis *Cl up/disp ld til wknd aft 13; 20l down when pu 15* P
193[U] Silver Man(cp) 10-1 Mrs M Hand *Trckd ldrs til lost tch 14; rr when pu 3 out* P
365[P] Vercheny (5a) 6-1 L Jefford *Hdwy to 3rd 15 & 2nd aft 3 out; 15l 3rd & wkng rap when pu last; distressed* . . . P

OFFICIAL DISTANCES: 1*l*, 5*l* **TIME:** 6min 34.0s

706 Restricted, 12st — 12 ran

488[U] **THE ONLY OPTION (IRE)** (5a) 16-1 **J Tickle** *Hld up; last 7; smooth hdwy to 2nd 13; ld 2 out; drew clr; comf* . . . 1
469[1] **Virgos Bambino (IRE)** (5a) 5-1 **R Woollacott** *Lw; sn ld; made most til hdd 2 out; no ex* . . . 10 2
541[P] **Horrified**(bl) 8-1 **D Edwards** *Trckd ldrs in 4/5th; hdwy to 3rd 16; no ex frm 3 out* . . . 2 3
572[P] Lirkimalong 4-1 Miss S Young *In tch to 11; outpcd; some late hdwy; nrst fin* 1/2 4
306[1] Georges Pleasure (5a) 8-1 L Heard *Trckd ldrs; 3rd 15; no ex frm 3 out* . . . 4 5
Indiana John (FR) 14-1 T Dennis *Mist & lost tch frm 13; kpt on* . . . 5 6
491[1] Baron Ridge(cp) 8-1 Richard Darke *Cl up to 10; lost tch aft 13; 35l adrift when pu last* . . . P
566[1] Butler Didit (5a) 2-1F L Jefford *Cl up & blun 7; outpcd & strugg towards rr when pu 3 out* . . . P
Chapners Cross 16-1 J March *Cl up & gng wl 13; sn lost tch; rr when pu 3 out* P
443[F] River Dante (IRE) 8-1 Mrs O Jackson *In tch to 14; rr when pu 3 out* . . . P
Star Of Kilcash (IRE) 9-1 C Heard *In tch to 10; rr & mist 13; t.o & pu 3 out* P
495[P] Tabernacle 10-1 A Glassonbury *A towards rr; 40l down when pu last* . . . P

OFFICIAL DISTANCES: 3*l*, 1*l* **TIME:** 6min 36.0s

707 Confined, 12st — 8 ran

570[3] **LET'S FLY (FR)** 11-1 **Mrs M Hand** *Ld to 7; disp ld on inner agn frm 10; ld 2 out; 1l up at last; r.o game up final hill* . . . 1
497[1] **Sandy Duff** (3x) evensF **Miss M McCarthy** *Mist 5 & rdr lost iron brief; rcd free on wide outside; ld frm 7; jnd frm 10 til out-stayed frm 2 out* . . . 2 1/2 2
483[3] **It'snotsimple (IRE)** (5a) 20-1 **B Trickey** *Hld up towards rr; hdwy to 4th 13 & 3rd 15; nvr able to chall* . . . 15 3
200[P] African Dawn(tt) 10-1 L Jefford *Chsng group til wknd aft 13; rr when pu 15* P
193[8] Baldhu Jay Arr 20-1 Miss L Gardner *Chsd ldrs in 3rd to 4; wknd; t.o & pu 3 out* P
489[U] Budghill 5-1 L Heard *Chsd ldrs in 4th mostly til wknd & pu 16* . . . P
570[2] Dark Challenger (IRE) (3x) 7-1 Miss S Gaisford *Sn rr; 30l down when pu 10* P
570[1] Lirsleftover (6x) 7-2 Miss S Young *Sn rr; 50l adrift when pu 14* . . . P

OFFICIAL DISTANCES: 2*l*, 6*l* **TIME:** 6min 34.0s

Flint & Denbigh

Eaton Hall (RH 8F,18J)

Sun, 28 Mar (GOOD)

708 Hunts Members (with Sir W.W. Wynn's) — 9 ran

405[1] **STAR CHANGES** 9-2 **Miss N Lloyd** *Ld to post; hld up; jmpd slow 6; 6l 5th 1/2way; mist 14; lft 6l 4th nxt; 3rd & rdn 2 out; ld last; r.o wl* . . . 1
Major Adams 9-2 **Miss T Clark** *Swtng; a.p; 2 1/2l 3rd 1/2way; lft 2nd 15; ld aft 3 out til wandered & hdd last; kpt on* . . . 3/4 2
449[6] **Three Saints (IRE)** 5-1 **G Hanmer** *(bnf) Went 2nd 3; ld 6 til hdd aft 3 out; one pce* . . . 6 3
405[3] Double Rich 4-1F O Greenall *(xnb) Hld up; 7l 6th 1/2way; lft 7l 5th 15; rdn 3 out; nvr able to chall* . . . 1 4

	Merry Christmas (5a, 4ow) 6-1 R Owen *Chsd ldrs; 5l 4th ½way; lft 3l 3rd 15; wknd qckly 3 out*	25	5
530^{7}	Hill Of Kilfeacle (IRE) 33-1 D Greenway *(xnb) Hld up; 8l 7th ½way; mist 13; in tch til rdn & wknd aft 15*	¾	6
477^{U}	New Ross (IRE) (7x)(bl) 14-1 Miss A Turner *V reluct to rce; a t.o*	20	7
	Orton House 100-1 S Kelly *Bckwd; lost tch 7; 20l 8th ½way; t.o & pu 13.*		P
530^{4}	Ricky B 6-1 W Kinsey *(xnb) Jmpd lft; ld til hdd & mist 6; mists 8 & 11; 2nd til blun & ur 15*		U

OFFICIAL DISTANCES: 1*l*, 7*l* **TIME:** 6min 19.5s

709 Open Horses & Geldings Maiden (Div 1), 12st — 13 ran

	MEENTAGH LOCH 8-1 **J Jarrett** *12s-8s; hld up; 9l 5th ½way; hdwy 13; went 3rd 15 & 2nd app 2 out; rdn to ld flat; r.o*		1
532^{R}	**Spot The Native (IRE)** 6-1 **P Hemmings** *A.p; went 2nd aft 4; lft in ld app 6; hdd flat; r.o*	nk	2
504^{3}	**Flat Stanley** (7a) 6-1 **Miss J Foster** *(xnb) Swtng; 2nd/3rd to 13; rallied aft 15; one pce 3 out*	1½	3
385^{4}	King's Reply 6-1 R Burton *Hld up; hdwy 7; 8l 4th ½way; went 3rd 13 & 2nd nxt; dem app 2 out; no ex*	5	4
517^{F}	Snitton Salvo(bl) 20-1 M Jackson *Hld up; 13l 9th ½way; hdwy & 6½l 6th 12; jnd ldrs 14; 4th & rdn 3 out; sn btn*	1	5
532^{3}	Raiseapearl 20-1 I Clyde *(kineton) Hld up & bhnd; 13½l 10th ½way; mist 10; hdwy & 5½l 6th 15; wkng when mist 2 out*	5	6
532^{F}	Castle Lodge 7-2 K Pearson *10s-7/2; 2 handlers; hld up & bhnd; 15l 11th ½way; 11l 10th 12; some hdwy 15; wknd 3 out.*	7	7
226^{P}	Mosscroft Jack(tt) 20-1 D Greenway *(xnb) Hld up; 11l 7th ½way; 11½l last 12; wl bhnd 14*	5	8
531^{3}	Bless Yourself (IRE) 5-2F G Hanmer *Hld up; jmpd slow 5; 12l 8th ½way; mist & rmdrs 13; short-lived eff 15; 7th & no ch when blun 2 out; pu last*		P
97^{P}	Cool Archie(bl) 14-1 S Ross *Ld til nrly rn wrong side of running rail app 6; 2nd til wknd 14; t.o & pu last.*		P
410^{P}	Lord Saxbury (7a) 20-1 M Keel *Chsd ldrs; 10l 6th ½way; mist 11; 6l 5th nxt; lost plce & mist 14; wl bhnd when pu 3 out.*		P
225^{3}	Ridware Pride 20-1 Miss S Sharratt *Swtng; chsd ldrs; mist 4; 10l 4th when fell 6*		F
532^{2}	The Noble Roman 10-1 T Ellis *Lft 100yds; t.o til pu 9*		P

OFFICIAL DISTANCES: nk, 6*l* **TIME:** 6min 22.8s

710 Open Horses & Geldings Maiden (Div 2), 12st - 17J — 15 ran

	BORDER FUSION (7a, 2ow) 5-1 **G Hanmer** *2 handlers; jmpd novicey & sn wl bhnd; 13th ½way; 17l 11th 12; hdwy aft 15; went 8l 4th 2 out; str rn to ld on bit flat; sn clr*		1
96^{4}	**Heathyards Element** 4-1JF **R Burton** *(bf,boh) Hld up; 8th ½way; hdwy 11; went 4l 3rd 13; stayed on one pce 3 out; went 2nd nr fin*	2½	2
343^{4}	**Comfortably Numb (FR)** (7a) 4-1JF **N Tinkler** *(xnb) Hld up; hdwy & 6th ½way; went 2nd 10; ld 14; mist 3 out; hung lft & hdd 2 out; ev ch when wandered app last; nt qckn*	1	3
531^{P}	Times Two 5-1 A Wadlow *(xnb) Ld 1; hit 3; hdd 14; 2nd til ld agn 2 out; hdd & no ex flat.*	nk	4
618^{F}	No Keep (IRE) 5-1 D Greenway *Hld up; 10th ½way; hdwy & 7l 6th 12; went 5l 4th 14; wknd u.p 3 out.*	15	5
435^{P}	Robert The Rascal 10-1 Miss S Sharratt *Did nt enter padd; hld up; mists 4 & 6; 11th ½way; 10l 8th 12; no hdwy 14; wknd 3 out.*	4	6
226^{U}	Carrigafoyle 10-1 Miss S Talbot *Ld to 1; 2nd/3rd to 13; wknd 15; t.o*	20	7
533^{P}	Blue Jar 25-1 S Ross *(xnb) A wl bhnd; 14th ½way; t.o & pu 12.*		P
113^{P}	Clodagh Valley (IRE) 11-1 W Kinsey *(xnb) Swtng; jnd ldrs 7; 4th ½way; disp 7l 6th 12; rdn 14; sn wknd; wl bhnd when pu 2 out*		P
	Cromaboo Count 20-1 D Cook *Hld up; hdwy & 5th ½way; mist 11; wknd & 11l 9th nxt; mist 13; wl bhnd when pu 14*		P
	Fortykix 25-1 K Pearson *A wl bhnd; rmdrs 2; t.o 9; pu 12*		P
531^{P}	Gosh Josh (IRE)(tt) 25-1 R Carey *Chsd ldrs til lost plce & rdn along 8; 12th ½way; wl bhnd when pu 11.*		P

271P Hendrix 6-1 Miss J Foster *Prom; blun 5 (broke fnce); lost plce 7; 9th ½way; blun & rdr lost irons 10; t.o & pu 12* . . . P
531F Top Weld 25-1 J Jarrett *(xnb) 2 handlers; blun 4; mist 6; 2nd/3rd to 10; wkng when mist 11; 15l 10th nxt; t.o & pu 3 out* . . . P
529P Wychnor King (IRE) 20-1 Mrs D Caine *Hld up; 7th ½way; hdwy 11; 6l 5th 12; one pce 15; 9l 5th when hmpd & ur 2 out* . . . U

OFFICIAL DISTANCES: 1½*l*, ½*l* **TIME:** 6min 18.4s

Fence 12 omitted - damaged

711 Land Rover Mens Open, 12st — 5 ran

SOUNDTRACK (IRE) 7-4F **G Hanmer** *2 handlers; made all; qcknd 12; 10l clr 15; drew rt away; unchall* . . . 1
527P **Springwood White** 25-1 **T Park** *1st ride; swtng; went 2nd 4 til aft 11; 6l 3rd nxt; sn outpcd; chsd wnr 3 out; no imp* . . . 25 2
4044 **Warner For Players (IRE)** (7x)(cp) 7-2 **A Wadlow** *Chsd wnr to 4; went 2nd aft 11; rdn 14 & sn gave up; dem 3 out* . . . 20 3
5262 Lord Of The West (IRE) 10-1 W Puddifer *Jb; releg last 6; sn wl bhnd; t.o 15* 15 4
465P Do It Again (IRE) (7x)(bl) 2-1 R Burton *Nt jw; hld up; last to 6; 7l 4th ½way; lost tch 11; sn shkn up & no resp; wl bhnd when pu 14* . . . P

OFFICIAL DISTANCES: 30*l*, 25*l* **TIME:** 6min 15.1s

712 Ladies Open — 9 ran

4445 **JACKIE JARVIS (IRE)** (5a) 7-2 **Mrs K Diggle** *(xnb) Hld up; 7l 6th ½way; hdwy 11; 2l 3rd nxt; ld 14; clr 2 out; wandered app last; rdly* . . . 1
5294 **Native Man (IRE)** 5-1 **Miss T Clark** *(xnb) Hld up & bhnd; last to 5; 12l 6th ½way; stdy hdwy 12; went 5l 4th 15; chsd wnr 2 out; no imp* . . . 7 2
Wandering Light (IRE) 10-1 **Miss S West** *Swtng; chsd ldrs; 6l 4th ½way; stayed on one pce 3 out; went 3rd flat; btr for rce* . . . 6 3
339P Donnegale (IRE)(bl) 4-1 Miss J Foster *Ld to 5; 2nd/3rd to 12; rallied & 3l 2nd 15; dem u.p 2 out; no ex* . . . 1½ 4
228P City Gent 11-2 Mrs E Heaton *Sn prom; went 2nd 7; ld 8 til aft 11; 2nd when nrly ur 13; lost plce & nrly ur agn nxt; wknd 15* . . . 6 5
4075 Class Of Ninetytwo (IRE) 14-1 Miss S Sharratt *2nd til ld 5; hdd 8; ld aft 11-14; 3rd & rdn nxt; wknd 3 out* . . . 3 6
229P Yer 'umble (IRE) 50-1 Miss M Hugo *Bckwd; nt jw; sn bhnd; 24l 8th ½way; t.o 13* runin 7
4642 Cascum Lad (IRE) 3-1F Miss S Holmes *Prom til lost plce & jmpd slow 5; last 8; t.o & pu aft 11; bbv* . . . P
424 Sea Tarth (5a)(cp) 7-1 Miss H Kinsey *(xnb) A bhnd; 20l 7th ½way; t.o & pu 2 out* . . . P

OFFICIAL DISTANCES: 8*l*, 7*l* **TIME:** 6min 08.8s

The stewards enquired into the running and riding of the favourite, Cascum Lad who was pulled up; the rider's explanation that the horse had bled from the nose was accepted

713 Confined, 12st — 11 ran

5272 **PRISTEEN SPY** 4-6F **R Burton** *(xnb) 6/4 (in a plce)-4/6; ld 3; mists 4 & 11; clr aft 3 out; easily* . . . 1
5283 **Gunner Sid** 7-2 **A Wadlow** *Swtng; ld to 3; chsd wnr vain aft; rdn when mist 3 out; stayed on one pce* . . . 8 2
5295 **Mr Kermit** (3x) 16-1 **Miss S Sharratt** *Chsd ldrs; 8l 4th ½way; went 5l 3rd 12; rdn 13; wknd u.p 3 out* . . . 10 3
Nicky The Kip (IRE)(tt) 20-1 W Puddifer *(xnb) Prom; 6l 3rd ½way; 7l 4th 12; outpcd w rdr motionless 15; sn wl bhnd* . . . 8 4
2284 Fornaught Alliance (IRE) (5x)(bl) 10-1 Miss A Turner *Swtng; a wl bhnd; 32l last ½way; t.o 11* . . . 20 5
4077 Camden Fellow (IRE) 6-1 Miss C Hurley *(xnb) 8s-6s; a bhnd; 23l 6th ½way; nrly ur & rdr lost irons 13; sn t.o.* . . . 1 6
Applefort (IRE) 50-1 Miss K Wood *(xnb) 2 handlers; 6th when ur 4* . . . U
528P Border Run 25-1 S Ross *Mists; hld up; hdwy 6; 7l 4th when blun & rdr lost iron 9; steered round 10; saddle slpd* . . . P
557P Easby Blue 50-1 J Buxton *(xnb) W ldrs to 8; 11l 5th ½way; lost tch 11; t.o last (but u.p) 15; pu 2 out* . . . P

	Excuse Me Sir (IRE) 14-1 Miss T Clark *(xnb) Bckwd; a bhnd; 30l 7th ½way; t.o last 11; pu 13*		P
	Jona Holley(cp) 25-1 E Bourne *(xnb) 1st ride; rcd wide & rdr unstdy; 8th when rfo 4*		U

OFFICIAL DISTANCES: 10*l*, 12*l* **TIME:** 6min 14.5s

714 Panacur/TBA PPORA Club Members Mares Maiden, 12st — 13 ran

259^{3}	**SOVEREIGN GALE (IRE)** (5a) 3-1 **A Wadlow** *(xnb) Jmpd lft; ld 3; mist 10; drew clr 2 out; r.o wl*		1
500^{P}	**Thixendale** (5a)(cp) 10-1 **Miss J Foster** *Ld to 3; 2nd/4th aft; one pce 3 out; tk 2nd at last*	10	2
532^{P}	**Ridware Rose** (5a) 10-1 **Miss S Sharratt** *2nd/3rd to 11; 4½l 6th & rdn nxt; rallied to 2nd 13; one pce u.p 3 out; dem at last*	3	3
531^{2}	Iadora (5a) 6-1 Miss T Clark *(bh) Chsd ldrs; 7l 5th ½way; 3l 4th when mist 12; hit 15; no ex u.p 3 out*	1	4
227^{P}	Pekan Polly (5a) 12-1 E Linehan *Hld up; 12l 8th ½way; 10l 7th 12; eff & 9l 5th 15; wknd 3 out*	10	5
410^{4}	Evanly Miss (5a) 8-1 M Jackson *Swtng; hld up & bhnd; blun 4; 17l last ½way; some hdwy & 13l 8th 12; wknd u.p 3 out; t.o.*	20	6
	Bromley Supreme (IRE) (12a) 14-1 K Pearson *Hld up; hdwy & 6l 4th ½way; 4l 5th 12; wknd & 12l 6th 15; wl bhnd when pu 2 out*		P
	Final Belle (12a) 4-1 R Burton *(boh) A bhnd; 15l 9th ½way; t.o & pu 13*		P
617^{F}	Fromrussiawithlove (12a, 3ow) 14-1 M Keel *2 handlers; prom; 5th & mist 8; pu 9*		P
532^{P}	Ginmini (IRE) (5a, 7ow) 12-1 R Ward-Dutton *Hld up; 8l 6th ½way; hdwy 11; went 2nd & mist nxt; nrly ur 14; wknd qckly 15; t.o & pu 2 out*		P
	Grey Tarquin (5a, 2ow) 9-4F G Hanmer *Nt jw & oft to lft; a bhnd; 16l 10th ½way; t.o & pu 13*		P
532^{P}	Mayday Girl (5a) 10-1 B Shaw *Hld up; hdwy 6; 5l 4th when mist & ur 9*		U
226^{P}	Skippers Canyon (5a) 20-1 R Carey *2 handlers; nd; 9l 7th ½way; wknd aft 11; wl bhnd when pu 14*		P

OFFICIAL DISTANCES: 8*l*, 4*l* **TIME:** 6min 30.2s

715 Restricted, 12st - 17J — 14 ran

530^{3}	**MASTER CLUB ROYAL**(bl) 3-1JF **G Hanmer** *2nd til ld 3; hdd 5; ld & nrly followed loose horse out 7; made rest; jnd 9 til qcknd 12; all out*		1
518^{1}	**Snitton West**(vis) 25-1 **M Jackson** *Hld up & pulled hrd; hdwy & mist 8; 2l 3rd ½way; 6l 5th 12; went 3rd 14 & 2nd u.p app 2 out; ev ch last; edged lft & nt go thro flat*	1	2
541^{P}	**Infamelia** (5a)(vis) 8-1 **Miss T Clark** *(xnb) Chsd ldrs; 7l 6th ½way; went 3l 2nd 12; rdn & ev ch 3 out; wknd 2 out*	12	3
407^{6}	Winning Town 14-1 Miss S Talbot *Prom; went 2nd 7; disp ld 9-11; 5l 4th 12; outpcd 15; plodded on*	6	4
530^{2}	Donrico (IRE) 9-2 R Burton *Hld up; 15l 9th ½way; rdn 11; 15½l 10th nxt; 15l 7th 15; nvr on terms*	7	5
614^{5}	Henbury Dancer (5a) 16-1 E Linehan *Hld up & bhnd; mist 6; 17l 11th ½way; mist 10; 15l 9th 12; wknd 15*	6	6
95^{P}	Spizzichino 20-1 K Pearson *(xnb) Hld up; 6l 5th ½way; 7l 6th 12; wknd 14; t.o*	8	7
530^{P}	Gabaka De Thaix (FR) 40-1 M Caldwell *A bhnd; blun 4; 18l 12th ½way; 20l 11th 12; t.o 15*	12	8
531^{1}	Along The Lawn (IRE)(bl) 3-1JF A Crow *Sn prom; ld & blun & ur 6*		U
	Edward Bear 25-1 Miss K Wood *(xnb) A wl bhnd; 30l last ½way; t.o 11; pu 3 out*		P
95^{P}	Highlands II (FR)(tt) 20-1 A Wadlow *(xnb) Hld up; disp 8l 7th ½way; eff u.p & 7l 5th 15; wknd aft 3 out; pu last*		P
	Holding The Fort (IRE) 9-2 D Barlow *Ld; mist 1; hdd 3; ld 5-7; 3l 4th ½way; disp 3l 2nd 12; 6l 4th & rdn 15; sn wknd; bhnd when pu 2 out*		P
341^{P}	Horton-Cum-Peel (IRE) 33-1 W Kinsey *(xnb) A bhnd; disp 15l 9th ½way; lost tch aft 11; t.o 14; pu last*		P
	Silver Sirocco (IRE) 20-1 S Kelly *Prom til lost plce 7; 8l 7th ½way; wknd & 14l 8th 12; wl bhnd when pu 14*		P

OFFICIAL DISTANCES: ½*l*, 8*l* **TIME:** 6min 13.3s

Fence 13 omitted - fallen rider

Hampshire

Hackwood Park (LH 7F,18J)

Sun, 28 Mar (GOOD)

716 Hunt Members, 12st — 6 ran

606P **KILVOYDAN (IRE)** 7-2 **D Phelan** *Tchd 4s; mostly 2nd; rmdrs 10 & 11; went on 13; jmpd rt & rdr drpd whip 3 out; qcknd clr app last; pushed out* 1
2643 **Gunnerbe Posh** 2-1F **J Maxse** *(xnb) Opened 5/2; mounted early & tde; hvly rstrnd start; hld up last; stdy hdwy frm 9; nt fluent 13; went 2nd & ev ch frm 3 out; nt qckn app last* 3 2
6103 **Russian Connection (IRE)** 3-1 **A Ward-Thomas** *Rstrnd in 3rd; nt fluent 8; lost ground frm 12 & sn rdn; btn frm 15; stayed on agn one pce frm 2 out.* . . 3 3
4235 Fables Green 16-1 Mrs C Evans *Trckd ldrs; bad mist 6; nt fluent & strugg frm 13; sn btn* 12 4
545F Alpha Centauri (IRE) 4-1 M Sheridan *6s-4s; trckd ldrs; prom frm 5; bad mist 12; sn pushed along; 3rd & wkng when bad mist 3 out; stpd qckly; pu nxt* P
627P Barbed Broach (IRE) 25-1 Miss C Cowe *(xnb,ringbit) Ld til hdd 13; sn wknd; t.o & pu last* . . . . P

OFFICIAL DISTANCES: 3*l*, 3*l* **TIME:** 6min 43.4s

The rider of Alpha Centauri was fined £50 for being unable to produce his Medical Record Book

717 Confined, 12st — 7 ran

19R **BALLY WIRRAL (IRE)** 7-4F **G Maundrell** *A gng wl; ww in 2nd; rdr lkng round frm 14; ld 3 out; 4l clr nxt; pushed out flat* 1
455P **Highcroft Boy**(bl) 12-1 **C Gordon** *Ld; nt fluent 9; hrd drvn frm 13; mist & hdd 3 out; sn brushed aside*. . . . 30 2
6221 **Mister Pepper (IRE)** 2-1 **T Underwood** *Hld up; prog to 3rd 6; mists 12 & 13; wknd & sn btn* 4 3
6233 Angus Airways (IRE) 33-1 M Legge *(xnb) Trckd ldrs; pushed along frm 5; hit 13; sn t.o* 20 4
537F Alexander Nevsky 33-1 D Dennis *(xnb) Nt jw; bhnd & hrd drvn 9; pu 11* . . P
381U Itsforu 7-1 J Jenkins *Disp 2nd when blun & ur 1* . . . . U
4573 Teller Of Tales (3x) 3-1 Miss V Flood *Hld up in rr; 5th when pu 11; broke down; dead* . . . . P

OFFICIAL DISTANCES: 30*l*, 4*l* **TIME:** 6min 34.7s

718 Mixed Open, 12st — 2 ran

3602 **QUICKSWOOD (IRE)** (7x) 6-4 **G Maundrell** *Ww; niggled along frm 7; shkn up 15 & clsd rdly to jn rival 2 out; qcknd 3l clr app last; pushed out* 1
3501 **Beadnell Bay** 1-2F **Miss A Goschen** *V edgy padd; 2 handlers; ld; jmpd slow 14; mist & rmdr 3 out; went 4l clr but jnd & untidy nxt; hdd app last where untidy agn; hung lft flat*. . . . 4 2

OFFICIAL DISTANCE: 4*l* **TIME:** 6min 39.5s

719 Countryside Alliance Club Members (Nov Rdrs), 12st — 4 ran

1894d **LOTTIE THE LOTUS** (5a) 4-7F **Miss R Goodwin** *Hld up in last; nt fluent 2; mist 8 & rdr nrly f.o; pushed up to cl 2nd 15; qcknd to ld 2 out; rdn out* 1
6414 **Newby End (IRE)**(vis) 3-1 **Miss C Cowe** *Trckd ldr in 2nd; outpcd & pushed along 15; kpt on frm 2 out*. . . . 6 2
3545 **Nice Approach (IRE)** 5-2 **Miss V Murphy** *Jw; ld; a pushed along; hdd 2 out; wknd* 4 3
610P Simony Sam (IRE) 5-1 J Sarchet *(xnb) 10s-5s; cl 3rd when blun & ur 3* . . U

OFFICIAL DISTANCES: 6*l*, 4*l* **TIME:** 6min 48.7s

720 Restricted, 12st — 5 ran

4611 **ROMANY PEARL**(cp) 3-1 **J Owen** *Trckd ldrs; rdn along frm 12; prog to ld 15; hrd drvn app last; eased cl home; wl rdn* 1
419P **Native Spin (IRE)** 16-1 **D Dennis** *(xnb) Jb rt; ld; jnd 10-13; hdd aft 15; one pce*. . . . 12 2
3251 **Headwrecker (IRE)** evensF **G Maundrell** *(xnb) Trckd ldrs; nt qckn frm 14; sn btn; disapp* 10 3

	Darkarrow (IRE) 12-1 T Underwood *Tk str hld; hld up last; nt fluent; bhnd frm 10; pu 14*		P
579[2]	Hawkers Hill 3-1 Miss A Goschen *Mostly cl 2nd til disp ld 10-13; cl 3rd & ev ch when fell 3 out (prob 2nd best)*		F

OFFICIAL DISTANCES: 12*l*, 10*l* **TIME:** 6min 46.4s

721 Open Maiden, 12st — 9 ran

325[6]	**STALBRIDGE ROSE** (5a) 9-1 **Miss A Goschen** *A.p; 2nd frm 7; rdn to ld bend aft 3 out; jnd aft nxt; fnd ex to ld agn cl home; all out; game*		1
424[4]	**Nocash (IRE)** 2-1F **P York** *Hld up; stdy hdwy frm 9; hrd rdn to jn ldr aft 2 out; hdd & no ex nr line*	hd	2
463[3]	**Jurist** 7-1 **M Keen** *(xnb) Jw; ld til hdd bend aft 3 out; stayed on one pce*	3	3
627[3]	Octane Booster (IRE) 8-1 M Holdforth *(xnb) Trckd ldr; wknd 13; mist 15; sn t.o*	40	4
567[U]	Tarpon Tale (IRE) 8-1 Miss D Clark *(xnb,bf) Lacklustre in padd; hld up; bhnd frm 13; t.o 3 out*	40	5
370[F]	Final Magic 16-1 G Maundrell *(xnb) Tk str hld; mid-div; strugg frm 14; t.o when ur 2 out*		U
456[2]	Top Light 6-1 J Sole *(xnb) Trckd ldrs; wknd frm 14; pu last*		P
105[6]	Trouble Loves Me (IRE) 25-1 C Wadland *Mid-div; lost ground frm 9; t.o & pu 15*		P
424[3]	Tupelov (IRE) 8-1 D Dennis *(xnb,ringbit) Sn bhnd; jmpd v slow 8; pu 11*		P

OFFICIAL DISTANCES: hd, 3*l* **TIME:** 6min 41.2s

Ledbury

Maisemore Park (LH 7F,18J)

Sun, 28 Mar (GOOD with SOFT patches)

722 Hunt Members, 12st — 6 ran

199[2]	**BALINOVA (IRE)** 1-3F **Miss P Gundry** *(xnb) Keen & jw; sn 2nd; ld app 10; qcknd 6l clr 3 out; nt fluent nxt & rdn; in comm when hit last*		1
360[3]	**Smile Pleeze (IRE)** 7-1 **T Stephenson** *Lw; 3rd mostly; 3l 3rd 15; rdn & 8l down nxt; rallied to mod 2nd flat; no ch w wnr*	6	2
612[4]	**Joy For Life (IRE)** (5a) 14-1 **Julian Pritchard** *Ld til app 10; 1l 2nd 15; outpcd nxt; dem flat*	2	3
513[3]	Wild Blade (IRE)(cp) 33-1 R Jenkins *(xnb) Cl up; 3l 4th 11; jmpd slow 12; 3rd when jmpd slow 14; wknd rap nxt; poor 4th 3 out*	25	4
366[F]	Rusty Fellow 9-1 Mrs M Finch *Jmpd slow 1 & 6; last pr aft; 20l last 12; t.o 3 out*	10	5
	Executive Days (12a, 5ow) 16-1 S Joynes *School in last; shkn up 4; 10l down 7; 25l bhnd when pu 12*		P

OFFICIAL DISTANCES: 5*l*, 2*l* **TIME:** 7min 03.0s

Phar Lord (M Wilesmith, xnb, tall heavy-topped; 33-1, bckwd) was withdrawn at the start not under orders

723 Open Maiden 56&7yo (Div 1, Part 1), 12st - 17J — 9 ran

87[r]	**LORD KEN (IRE)**(vis) 6-1 **H Dowty** *Nt a fluent; made nrly all; jmpd slow 7; jmpd rt 13; hdd brief aft 15; 5l clr & nt rdn aft 2 out; shkn up when jnd & pckd last; lft clr*		1
	Blackanblue (7a) 12-1 **T Stephenson** *Hmpd bad 2; hld up; hmpd agn 7; 7l 4th 11; eff in 4l 3rd aft 15; outpcd app 2 out; drvn to chall & ev ch when blun & nrly ur last.*	2	2
	Foreign Field (FR) (7a) 10-1 **G Barfoot-Saunt** *Settled mid-div; went 2nd 11; 9l 3rd passing 14; clsd qckly to ld aft nxt; hdd aft 3 out; fdd bad*	30	3
516[r]	Ashor Ted 14-1 S Bush *(xnb) Prom but often jmpd v slow; releg last 9; 10l down 11; wknd 14; t.o & jmpd wild lft 3 out; pu nxt*		P
	Definite Flash (IRE) (5a) 14-1 J Mahot *Mist 1; blun & ur 3*		U
619[F]	Kotori (IRE) (7a) 20-1 M Munrowd *Last pr; hmpd 3; mist 4; jmpd v slow 5 & pu*		P
619[B]	Nothing Better (IRE) (12a) 9-2 T Weston *Midfield when fell 2*		F
619[U]	Sett Aside 12-1 Julian Pritchard *Jmpd v nervously & sn last; t.o 5; spooked at 7 & ref & ur.*		r
486[2]	That's My Boy (IRE) 4-5F Miss P Gundry *Prsd wnr; 6l down passing 14; drew level & fell nxt*		F

OFFICIAL DISTANCES: 1½*l*, 20*l* **TIME:** 7min 12.0s

Fence 14 omitted - damaged

724 Open Maiden 56&7yo (Div 1, Part 2), 12st — 9 ran

Form	Horse / details	Dist	Pos
385^{2}	**LADY BARONETTE** (5a) 7-4F **A Martin** *3rd til 2nd 6; jnd ldr & jmpd hesitant 3 out; sn virt solo; hit last hrd*		1
290^{U}	**Red Ringa** 12-1 **S Waley-Cohen** *(xnb) Settled 4th; hit 11; $2\frac{1}{2}$l down & rdn 15; lft 2nd nxt but stpd to nil; rem when rn v wide & unsteerable app 2 out; just lasted home; most unimpressive*	runin	2
532^{U}	**Bank On Lady** (5a) 8-1 **D Mansell** *Mists in rr; releg 22l last 12; t.o 14; fin event*	25	3
	Cashew Kid (IRE) 12-1 N Oliver *Nt jw; hld up; nrly ur 3; pckd 7; 13l 5th 12; strugg when mists 14 & 15; pu & dism nxt*		P
453^{2}	Gumlayloy (7a) 3-1 S Hughes *Oht; 2 handlers; tk keen hld & sn ld; jnd when barely rose & fell hvly 3 out*		F
617^{F}	Just Henry 12-1 S Joynes *(xnb) Pulled hrd & nt jw; last to 9; rmdr aft 10; no resp; 17l 6th 12; pu 14*		P
	Matrix (AUS) 3-1 Julian Pritchard *5s-3s; originally saddled w no number-cloth; tkn stdly in rr; 19l 7th 12; 8l 5th & prog 15; crashed into faller & ur 3 out*		U
367^{P}	Silk St Bridget (5a) 8-1 G Tumelty *(xnb) Ref to rce*		r
493^{U}	Will Shakespeare 6-1 A Charles-Jones *(xnb) Ld 1; settled 2nd/3rd; nt fluent 6 & 7; $1\frac{1}{2}$l 3rd & gng wl 15; ev ch when hmpd & ur nxt*		U

OFFICIAL DISTANCES: dist, 17*l* **TIME:** 7min 06.0s

725 Open Maiden 56&7yo (Div 2), 12st — 14 ran

Form	Horse / details	Dist	Pos
493^{4}	**EBONY JACK (IRE)** 2-1F **G Barfoot-Saunt** *Lw; settled handy; went 4th 14; chall aft 3 out; rdn to ld nxt; imm drew clr*		1
575^{U}	**The Cooling Agent** 5-2 **Miss P Gundry** *Novicey in rr; rdn 4; jmpd slow 7; hmpd 14; poor 9th nxt; stayed on frm 2 out to rem 2nd flat*	20	2
408^{P}	**Knickers** (5a) 20-1 **J Trice-Rolph** *Midfield; pckd 8; drpd to rr when hmpd bad 14; 20l 8th nxt; stayed on app 2 out to 2nd brief last; tired & dem nr fin*	1	3
368^{P}	The Luddite(tt) 10-1 H Dowty *(xnb) Mostly 2nd til rdn & ev ch aft 3 out; stpd to nil nxt; fin exhaust*	20	4
	Hobo 10-1 S Joynes *Hld up & bhnd; 7th & prog gng wl 14; 3l 4th aft 3 out; stpd to nil bef nxt; fin exhaust*	6	5
410^{P}	Force Ten 8-1 T Stephenson *Swtng; ld; drvn & hdd 2 out; wknd alarmingly; fin exhaust*	3	6
150^{P}	Worthy Man(tt) 12-1 J Jones *Hdwy to 2nd/3rd 5-12; wknd rap aft 14; t.o aft 3 out; walked in*	runin	7
518^{P}	Bally Cyrano 14-1 D Mansell *Lw; mists in last trio; t.o 8; impd brief to rr of bunch 11; pu 13*		P
353^{P}	Bettie Blue (5a) 14-1 A Harris *Nt fluent & lost ground most fncs; hld up & bhnd early; 5th & prog 8; mist 13; sn rallied; slowed agn & failed to rise 14 giving 61yo rdr v hvy fall*		F
619^{P}	Borrisimo (IRE) 14-1 M Wall *Prom; 7th 12; wknd qckly 14; nrly ref 3 out & pu*		P
589^{P}	Leasebourne (12a) 20-1 R Rogers *Cl up; hit 5; wknd 12; hmpd 14; pu nxt*		P
619^{P}	McGinty All Stars (IRE) (5a) 8-1 R Hughes *Pulling; went 2nd when hit 4 & ur*		U
	Ski Country (5a) 12-1 B Pauling *Jmpd v slow 1; sticky in rr til hdwy 5; 3rd/4th 10 til 2nd brief 14; drvn & wknd nxt; pu 3 out*		P
619^{C}	The Brooklet 7-1 Julian Pritchard *Jmpd poor in rr; t.o 8; pu 12; easy rn*		P

OFFICIAL DISTANCES: 20*l*, 1*l* **TIME:** 7min 17.0s

726 Restricted, 12st — 20 ran

Form	Horse / details	Dist	Pos
517^{1}	**BEAUCHAMP ORACLE** 8-1 **R Hughes** *Hld up midfield; mist 8; 9th 12; qcknd thro field to ld 15; 10l clr aft nxt; stayed on str*		1
498^{P}	**Black Optimist (IRE)** 25-1 **Mrs K Baimbridge** *Gd prog to 3rd/4th frm 7 til chsd wnr frm 15; outpcd aft nxt but kpt on stdly*	5	2
529^{3}	**Euro Bob (IRE)** 8-1 **Mrs A Rucker** *Midfield; hmpd 11; 6th & eff 12; went 4th 15; stayed on game at one pce frm nxt*	3	3
587^{6}	Sissinghurst Star (IRE) 25-1 P Mann *(xnb) Midfield; 8th 12; passed btn horses aft 3 out; nd*	5	4
369^{2}	Campden Kitty (5a) 4-1 F Hutsby *2 handlers; oht; ld to 2; prom; hmpd 11; 2nd 12; ld 14-15; drvn 3 out; sn wknd; tired when hit last*	2	5
367^{1}	Radbrook Hall (7a) 5-1 P Callaghan *Lw; handy; 2nd 7 til lft in ld 11-14; lost plce rap; wl btn aft 3 out*	5	6
	Native Isle (IRE) 16-1 J Mahot *Chsd ldrs; 5th 12; hit 3 out; sn wknd u.p.*	8	7

	Echo Blu (IRE) 4-1 W Hill *Midfield; mist 7; 7th & rdn 12; plugged on one pce; no ch frm 3 out*	6	8
498P	Silly Boy 25-1 A Foster *Rr & rdr v cumbersome; 12th 12; plodded rnd*	12	9
4462	Glacial Boy 8-1 H Dowty *Chsd ldrs to 10; 11th & wkng 12; t.o*	20	10
614U	A Bit Of Fluff (5a) 33-1 Miss L Brooke *Nt lw; a wl bhnd; 14th 12; bad mist 14; t.o & pu nxt*		P
	Certain Surprise (5a) 9-1 Miss E James *Midfield; 10th 12; sn wknd; t.o & pu 3 out*		P
	Derrys Prerogative 33-1 Miss N Rudge *A wl bhnd; t.o last 12; pu 15*		P
614F	Exclusively (5a) 33-1 M Munrowd *Jmpd atrocious in rr; last when pu 8*		P
450U	Far From Perfect (IRE) (5a) 12-1 A Charles-Jones *Hmpd 1; midfield til hmpd & ur 11*		U
516F	Father Tom (IRE) 9-4F Julian Pritchard *Ld 2 til fell 11*		F
541P	I'm Dreaming (IRE) 14-1 A Martin *2nd/4th to 12; rdn & sn lost plce; t.o & pu last*		P
450P	New World Comet 14-1 T Stephenson *Hld up & wl bhnd; 16th & t.o 12; pu 14*		P
	Raymond James 16-1 D Mansell *A wl bhnd; 15th & t.o 12; pu 14*		P
660U	Slave's Adventure (5a) 20-1 R Hodges *A strugg in rr; 13th 12; t.o & pu 15*		P

OFFICIAL DISTANCES: 5*l*, 6*l* **TIME:** 6min 58.0s

727 Mixed Open, 12st — 16 ran

4721	**POLAR FLIGHT** 9-2 **A Charles-Jones** *Midfield; 5th 11; clsd to ld 13; prsd & lkd vulnerable when lft clr app last; rdn out*		1
4042	**The Campdonian (IRE)** 10-1 **E Walker** *Settled rr; prog to midfield 11; gd hdwy aft 14 to 1l 2nd aft 3 out; rdn & ev ch nxt; no ex; lft 2nd app last*	5	2
4961	**Hobbycyr (FR)** 2-1JF **Miss P Gundry** *Off pce in midfield; 9th 14; rdn in 20l 7th aft 3 out; nvr able to chall*	8	3
292F	Mr Max (IRE) 33-1 M Wall *Wl bhnd; 11th 14; 25l 9th aft 3 out; slt late prog*	7	4
1701†	Titus Bramble(bl,tt) 2-1JF T Stephenson *Lw; cl up; 4th 14; 8l 4th & drvn aft 3 out; fnd nil & sn btn*	1	5
5142	Lyphard's Fable (USA) 33-1 D England *Chsd ldrs to 11; sn hopeless outpcd; t.o 15*	runin	6
	Clear Blue Water (IRE) 25-1 G Barfoot-Saunt *Ld to 10; drpd out rap; pu 13*		P
4406	Dinsey Finnegan (IRE)(cp) 16-1 G Phillips *2nd/3rd til ld 10-11; urged & nt r.o; 6th & btn 14; t.o & pu last*		P
5151	Lord Castle (IRE) 25-1 J Trice-Rolph *Promptly lost tch in last trio; t.o & pu 13*		P
3641	Machalini 6-1 A Morley *(xnb) Midfield; impd qckly to ld 11-13; releg 5l 3rd & nt rdn aft 3 out; rallied nxt; prsng wnr when rdr lost iron & f.o app last*		U
	Macy (IRE) 16-1 J Mahot *Ur lvng padd; cl up til drvn & lost plce 8; nt keen aft; t.o & pu 13*		P
404P	On The Run (IRE) (5a)(tt) 33-1 Miss A de Lisle Wells *A wl bhnd; t.o 14; pu 3 out*		P
5834	Rectory Garden (IRE) 14-1 Miss G Emtage *Wl bhnd til 8th & gd prog 14; 15l 5th & clsng aft 3 out; 4th but no further hdwy when fell nxt*		F
4031	Rushing Again 12-1 Mrs K Baimbridge *Nt a fluent; sn 2nd/3rd; 3rd when mist 15; wknd rap; 23l 8th aft 3 out; pu nxt*		P
	Stormy Session 20-1 J Benfield *A nr last; strugg when mist 9 & pu*		P
6152	Time Can Tell(bl) 33-1 R Hodges *Cl up; 5th 14; 9l 5th & u.p aft 3 out; poor 7th & tired when fell nxt*		F

OFFICIAL DISTANCES: 4*l*, 10*l* **TIME:** 6min 54.0s

The stewards interviewed the rider of Machalini, who had unseated; his explanation that he had lost his left stirrup was accepted

728 Intermediate, 12st — 12 ran

3831	**CHRISTY BEAMISH (IRE)** 6-4F **Miss P Gundry** *Confid rdn in rr; 8th & prog 11; smooth rn to 2nd 3 out; ld nxt; sn pushed clr; easily; impressive agn*		1
251F	**William Lionheart** 3-1 **G Barfoot-Saunt** *Set fast pce 2-11; ld agn 14; 5l clr aft 3 out; hdd nxt; one pce & no ch w wnr*	12	2
5842	**Stennikov (IRE)** 12-1 **E Walker** *(xnb) Hdwy to 3rd/4th 8; 3rd & u.p 14; 9l 3rd aft 3 out; nd aft*	4	3
	Glacial Pearl (IRE) 50-1 P Mason *Midfield; went 12l 3rd 11; 4th when mist 15; wknd aft nxt*	15	4
5121	Miss Moss (5a) 7-1 R Rogers *Jmpd rt 6; cl up to 8; 7th 11; wknd 14; rem aft 3 out*	15	5
603P	Aldington Charlie (6ow) 50-1 C Sands *A last; t.o 7; pu 3 out*		P

365[4] Camden Carrig (IRE) 8-1 G Phillips *Lw; 2nd/3rd til rfo 3* . . . . U
530[1] Heavy Weather (IRE) 5-1 Miss J Williams *Lw; impd qckly to jn ldr 4 til blun bad 7; mist 9; 5th 11; rdn & strugg 14; t.o & pu 2 out* . . . . P
616[1] Hijacked 8-1 T Stephenson *A wl bhnd; strugg 10; pu 13* . . . . P
Imago II (FR) 20-1 M Harris *Hld up; impd to midfield 8; 6th 11; no ex 14; 18l 5th app 2 out; pu last* . . . . P
107[F] Maquilleux 14-1 H Dowty *Bckwd; volatile padd; set fast pce to 2; 2nd/3rd til ld agn 11-14; wkng qckly when mist 3 out; t.o & pu last* . . . . P
141[P] Themaster's Choice (IRE) 20-1 S Joynes *Drpd to rr 9; u.p nxt; poor 9th 11; mist 12; t.o & jmpd rt 3 out; pu nxt* . . . . P

OFFICIAL DISTANCES: 10*l*, 4*l* **TIME:** 6min 52.0s

729 Open Maiden 8yo&up (Div 1, Part 1), 12st — 9 ran

518[U] **LEGEND OF LIGHT (IRE)** (5a) 6-4F **D Mansell** *2nd to 3; hld up; 13l 4th aft 9; went 2nd 13; ld 15; duelled for ld aft nxt til drvn ahd app last; all out* . 1
Red Spark 6-1 **E Walker** *(xnb) Hld up; mist 8; 18l last aft 9; clsd 11; jnd wnr aft 3 out til rdn & hdd app last; no ex flat* 3/4 2
370[P] **Arctic Summer (IRE)** 3-1 **J Trice-Rolph** *Hld up & bhnd; 17l 5th aft 9; clsd to disp 4½l 4th 11; handy til fdd tame aft 3 out* 20 3
492[6] Floorex Carpetman 12-1 A Foster *Rdr v untidy; chsd clr ldr 3; blun 8; lft in ld 10; sn hdd; ev ch to 13; releg last 15; wknd app 2 out* . . . . ½ 4
Scotsbrook Lass (5a) 11-1 R Hughes *Rcd wide; nt jw; jmpd slow 2; 23l 3rd 4; mist 9 & terrible blun 10; sn ld til jnd & slow 15; jmpd slow agn nxt; drpd out qckly* 5 5
Monster Moss 14-1 D England *Jmpd v erratic; sn wl t.o; pu 5* . . . . P
370[P] Phar And Away (5a) 14-1 Miss H Bevan *(xnb) Jmpd rt & out of control; sn 10l clr; blun 9; hung rt & rn out 10* . . . . R
Sylvias Dream (5a) 10-1 P Morris *Fell 2* . . . . F
This One Is A Boy (IRE) 5-2 M Wilesmith *(xnb) Hld up & wl detach in last pr til hmpd & ur 2* . . . . U

OFFICIAL DISTANCES: ½*l*, 10*l* **TIME:** 7min 09.0s

The stewards enquired into the running out of Phar And Away who continued to race bypassing the fences; the rider's explanation that she had not been strong enough to pull the horse up was accepted

730 Open Maiden 8yo&up (Div 1, Part 2), 12st — 8 ran

370[P] **ONEFORTHEFROG (IRE)** 12-1 **G Tumelty** *Midfield; went 3rd 11 & 2nd aft 13; ld 3 out; jnd last; surprisingly fnd ex to forge clr flat* 1
370[F] **Billy Whitelies (IRE)** 4-6F **S Joynes** *Mists; ld to 2; 2nd til ld agn 8 til blun 11 & 12; ld 15-nxt; drvn 2 out; jnd wnr last; wknd* 3 2
The Grandson (IRE) 12-1 **D Mansell** *Chsd ldrs til mist 10 & rmdrs; 7l 7th nxt; lost tch rap in 26l 4th aft 3 out* 25 3
Mainlier 6-1 F Hutsby *Rmdrs 2; bhnd til clsd to press ldrs 11-14; nt r.o; 25l 3rd aft 3 out* 12 4
517[P] Baron Kiss 10-1 H Dowty *Hmpd start; towards rr but wl in tch to 13; gave up qckly nxt; rem last when ref 3 out* . . . . r
363[P] Kuwait Faith (IRE)(bl,tt) 12-1 T Stephenson *Mists; prom to 11; releg 7th & nt keen aft 13; rem aft blun 15; pu 3 out* . . . . P
588[P] Portway Sadie (5a) 12-1 M Wall *Reluct to start but ld by 2; hdd 8; hit 10; ld 11 til hdd & blun 15; btn when bad mist nxt; pu aft 3 out* . . . . P
620[2] Rosie Stroud (IRE) (5a) 3-1 G Barfoot-Saunt *Stdd in detach last; hit 8 & nt a fluent; 20l adrift 11; nvr asked to cl; pu 3 out* . . . . P

OFFICIAL DISTANCES: 2½*l*, 25*l* **TIME:** 7min 08.0s

731 Open Maiden 8yo&up (Div 2), 12st — 15 ran

ALLEZ TOUJOURS (IRE) 6-1 **N Oliver** *(xnb) 14s-6s; settled 3rd/4th til 2nd app 10; gng wl when lft 15l clr 15; unchall aft; eased flat* 1
463[2] **Northsprite**(cp) 4-1 **J Trice-Rolph** *(xnb) Chsd ldrs; 17l 4th 13; went 10l 2nd but nt pushed aft 3 out; plugged on & nvr nr wnr* 10 2
621[4] **Wind On The Common** 4-1 **T Stephenson** *Prom to 8; 14l 3rd 13; nt rdn in 16l 4th aft 3 out; tried to cl nxt; fdd v tame* 12 3
Ron Miel (IRE) 12-1 D Mansell *Bckwd; wl bhnd til some prog & bad mist 12; 24l 6th 13; strugg 3 out* 12 4

Form	Horse / comment	Dist	Pos
	Marty's Lamp (5a) 20-1 F de Giles *Stdd 15l bhnd rest in final pr; wl bhnd til 25l 7th 13; prog & lft 15l 2nd 15; dem aft nxt; fdd bad*	8	5
	B So Bold 16-1 M Munrowd *Midfield; drvn 8; no resp & sn lost tch; pu 11*		P
	Contrary King 14-1 T Weston *2 handlers; oht; threw rdr when mounted; chsd ldrs to 10; 8th & fdng 13; nt pushed; pu 14*		P
258P	Crotty (IRE) 6-1 Miss P Gundry *(xnb) 2 handlers; stdd 15l bhnd rest in final pr; hdwy to midfield 8; wknd rap; t.o & pu 14*		P
6043	Knighton Star (5a) 2-1F A Charles-Jones *(xnb) Lw; midfield; pckd bad 5; 15l 8th app 10; pu 11*		P
370P	Master Jay Jay (IRE) 20-1 S Joynes *Jb & detach in final trio; t.o & pu 7*		P
4507	Milamoss 14-1 R Hughes *Bckwd; bhnd til some prog in 12l 7th & rdn in app 10; 19l 5th 13; lft 3rd 15; lost tch u.p nxt; t.o last when pu 2 out*		P
517P	Norse 14-1 R Hodges *Mists in rr; blun 7; u.p nxt; rem 12th app 10; pu 14*		P
	Riches To Rags (IRE)(bl) 8-1 P Mason *Nt jw in rr; t.o & pu 9*		P
613P	Rosemead Tye (5a) 20-1 Miss N Stallard *2 handlers; dashed to ld 5; 3l clr of well strung out field 14; lkd vulnerable when fell 15*		F
620P	Tensing 12-1 G Barfoot-Saunt *(xnb) Ld to 5 but kpt hanging rt; mist 7; 2nd to 9; 9th & wkng rap 13; pu nxt*		P

OFFICIAL DISTANCES: 12*l*, 12*l* **TIME:** 7min 03.0s

Aintree (LH 7F,18J)

Thu, 1 Apr (GOOD)

732 Martell Cognac Fox Hunters HC, 2m5f110y £19,430 25 ran

Form	Horse / comment	Dist	Pos
2803	**FOREST GUNNER** 12-00 13-2 **Mrs C Ford** *Pckd 2; jw rest; hdwy 5; ld 8; 12l clr app 2 out; stayed on str; rdn out (fine ride)*		1
5451	**Sikander A Azam** 12-00 11-2JF **T Greenall** *In tch; lost plce 10 (Bechers); 7th 13; hdwy 15; drvn & stayed on to 2nd app last; no ch w wnr*	8	2
1791	**Gun'n Roses II (FR)** 12-00(bl) 11-2JF **J Jenkins** *Mists; chsd ldrs; 5th 11; pckd 13; went 2nd aft 15; nvr nr wnr aft; wknd app last*	7	3
4201	Satchmo (IRE) 12-00 16-1 P Hall *Hit 2; chsd ldrs; 3rd 11; 2nd when blun & nrly fell 15; nt rec*	8	4
5438	Torduff Express (IRE) 12-00(bl) 12-1 Miss P Gundry *Ld 2-4; w ldrs; hit 6, 11th when hit 11 (Foinavon); sn outpcd; 17l 3rd & rdn app 2 out; plugged on*	3	5
3462	Dam The Breeze 12-00 25-1 E Williams *Prom; disp 10l 2nd 3 out; sn wknd; mist nxt*	6	6
5461	The Butterwick Kid 12-00(bl) 20-1 R Tate *Sn wl bhnd; rem 14th 11; mod prog frm 15; nvr nr ldrs*	12	7
4411	Cape Stormer (IRE) 12-00 7-1 M Gorman *Midfield; strugg when hmpd 10 (Bechers); 10th nxt; btn when mist 12 (Canal Turn)*	3½	8
4903	Unlimited Free (IRE) 12-00 33-1 Miss D Harding *Mid-div; bhnd when hmpd 10 (Bechers); t.o when jmpd slow 12 (Canal Turn)*	1½	9
6261	Master Jock 12-00 100-1 G Hanmer *A towards rr; lft 9th & no ch 12 (Canal Turn)*	½	10
4902	Maidstone Monument (IRE) 12-00 66-1 R Stephens *Bhnd & nt jw; bad mist 6; lost tch & nt fluent nxt; hmpd 10 (Bechers); t.o frm 12 (Canal Turn)*	1½	11
	Itsmyturnnow (IRE) 12-00 100-1 C Gordon *Ld to 2; ld 4-6; 2nd when blun 10 (Bechers); 4th when mist 15; wknd rap; t.o*	15	12
4482	Royal Barge 12-00 100-1 M Barber *Jmpd rt in rr; t.o 7 (rcd incredibly wide to Bechers)*	2	13
2403	Epsilo De La Ronce (FR) 12-00 66-1 W Ramsay *A bhnd; t.o 7*	2	14
679P	Imperial Line (IRE) 12-00(tt) 100-1 Miss T Jackson *Prom on outside; 3rd when blun 10 (Bechers); nt rec; 6th nxt; wknd rap; t.o*	dist	15
	Atomic Breeze (IRE) 12-00 200-1 J Codd *Chsd ldrs; hmpd 10 (Bechers); 10th & outpcd when fell 12 (Canal Turn)*		F
280P	Bitofamixup (IRE) 12-00(tt) 50-1 Mrs J Gordon *Mists & wl bhnd; t.o 7; pu 13*		P
439P	Blyth Brook 12-00 100-1 R Morgan *W ldrs; blun 3 (Chair); ld 6-8; 4th when fell 10 (Bechers)*		F
448P	Farnando (IRE) 12-00 100-1 G Barfoot-Saunt *Midfield on inside when fell 10 (Bechers)*		F
1881	Father Andy (IRE) 12-00(tt) 66-1 S Morris *In tch; prsng ldrs when fell 10 (Bechers)*		F
	General Claremont (IRE) 12-00 16-1 Miss A Goschen *Last pr early; sn midfield; bd 10 (Bechers)*		B

543^{6}	Irbee 12-00(bl) 20-1 Miss C Tizzard *Chsd ldrs; outpcd in 8th 11; blun & ur 12 (Canal Turn)*		U
546^{3}	Mr Mahdlo 12-00 100-1 B Woodhouse *Jmpd v sticky & to lft in last pr; nt keen & a strugg; nrly ref 7; t.o & pu 8*		P
630^{1}	Mullensgrove 12-00 16-1 Miss S Phizacklea *Last away; nt fluent 1; nvr lkd happy; wl bhnd til fell 8*		F
631^{1}	Silence Reigns 12-00(bl) 8-1 N Williams *Blun 3; mid-div when mist & bd 10 (Bechers)*		B

TIME: 5min 33.5s **TOTE:** £8.10; places £3.30,£2.20,£2.20 **Ex:**£33.00 **CSF:**£37.82

All the riders in this race were fined £100 each for failing to obey the instructions of the Starter

Taunton (RH 8F,17J)

Thu, 1 Apr (GOOD, GOOD to SOFT in places)

733 Captain Ronnie Wallace HC, 3m £2404 — 9 ran

347^{1}	**KESTICK** 11-12 6-4F **Miss T Cave** *Hld up in rr; hdwy 10; hit 11; trckd ldr 14; chall nxt; slt ld 2 out; hmpd by loose horse & hit last; easily*		1
598^{1}	**Springford (IRE)** 11-11 7-1 **D Alers-Hankey** *Hit 3; bhnd; hdwy to chse ldrs 7; ld 14; hmpd by loose horse; blun & hdd 2 out; one pce when hit last.*	4	2
443^{1}	**Longstone Boy (IRE)** 11-12 8-1 **D Edwards** *Ld to 3; hit 9; lft in slt ld 12; hdd 14; wknd frm 3 out*	13	3
545^{3}	Miss O'Grady (IRE) 11-11 15-2 M Miller *Chsd ldrs to 14; wknd app nxt*	2½	4
543^{U}	Bosuns Mate 11-12(cp) 13-2 Mrs B Keighley *Chsd ldrs til jmpd slow 4 & 5; bhnd; hit 8; hdwy 11; wknd 12*	17	5
543^{F}	Always On The Line (IRE) 11-07 11-2 A Merriam *Ld 3; hit 9; slt ld but drvn along when blun & ur 12*		U
566^{3}	Lydford Castle 11-09(bl) 50-1 T Dennis *Sn bhnd; t.o 7; pu 11*		P
630^{P}	Sea Haitch Em 11-12 16-1 P Sheldrake *Chsd ldrs to 11; no ch when blun 14; t.o & pu 3 out; dism; subsq destroyed*		P
328^{U}	Truicear 11-07 33-1 R McCarthy *Chsd ldrs; hit 10; blun 12 & bhnd; t.o & pu 3 out*		P

TIME: 5min 59.4s **TOTE:** £1.70; places £1.10,£2.20,£2.40 **Ex:**£13.70 **CSF:**£12.79

Hereford (RH 9F,12J)

Sat, 3 Apr (GOOD)

734 Sun Valley Feed Milling HC, 2m £2205 — 11 ran

444^{2}	**JAZZ NIGHT** 11-09 13-2 **J Jenkins** *Chsd ldrs; ld sn aft 9; blun 2 out; str chall sn aft; hung lft u.p*		1
628^{2}	**Viscount Bankes** 11-09 7-1 **A Martin** *Chsd ldrs; nt much room & lost plce aft 6; rallied to chse wnr 3 out; upsides frm nxt til carried lft & nt rec flat.*	¾	2
630^{3}	**Caher Society (IRE)** 12-00 9-1 **P Morris** *Jmpd slow 1; blun 4; bhnd; hdwy app 3 out; stayed on frm 2 out; nt pce to rch ldrs*	3	3
545^{2}	Bold Tactics (IRE) 11-07 13-8F M Keel *Chsd ldrs til rdn & outpcd 5; stayed on frm 9; sn no imp*	8	4
	Saint-Declan (IRE) 11-07 16-1 A Wadlow *Ld to 9; wknd nxt.*	7	5
444^{3}	Parte Prima 12-02 11-2 R Woollacott *Chsd ldrs til wknd app 9*	2	6
384^{4}	Cloudy Bay Boy 11-11 9-1 R Cope *Chsd ldrs; mist 6; chall 7; ld 9; nt fluent & hdd sn aft; 5th & wkng when fell 2 out*		F
667^{4}	Come On Boy 11-07 33-1 M Jackson *A bhnd; t.o & pu 3 out.*		P
698^{P}	Crystal Brook 11-02 66-1 S Graham *Hit 4 & bhnd; t.o & pu 3 out*		P
264^{1}	Drumdowney Lad (IRE) 11-08 20-1 P York *Hit 2; bhnd; chsd ldrs 4; wknd 6; t.o & pu last*		P
465^{2}	Sheila McKenzie 11-02 11-1 T Lane *Hit 2; bhnd when mist & ur 3.*		U

TIME: 4min 03.6s **TOTE:** £7.00; places £1.70,£3.00,£2.90 **Ex:**£42.50 **CSF:**£53.21

The stewards enquired into possible intereference between the first two on the run-in; they cautioned the rider of the winner for careless riding, but since it had not improved his horses's placing they allowed the result to stand

Glamorgan

Ystradowen (LH 7F,18J)

Sat, 3 Apr (GOOD)

735 Confined Maiden 56&7yo, 12st — 8 ran

700^{5}	**PHARAILDE** (5a) 7-4F **J Price** *Still bckwd; ld to 13; lost plce to 9l 3rd app 15; rallied to ld & mist 2 out; sn clr & rdn out in inimitable fashion*		1
699^{3}	**Crystal Soldier** (5a) 3-1 **D Jones** *Prsd ldr; mist 6; ld 13; rdn & hdd app 2 out; fin wkly*	8	2
453^{P}	**Capacoostic** (5a) 14-1 **P Sheldrake** *Hld up; went 3rd aft 11; 2l 2nd app 15; rdn nxt; sn wknd.*	7	3
700^{4}	Indian Trix (IRE) (5a) 4-1 A Hanly *3rd/4th til rdn & lost plce 10; hmpd 13; t.o aft 15; slt late prog.*	10	4
618^{F}	Calamint (7a) 14-1 J Merry *(xnb) Pulled v hrd & mists in detach last; blun bad 5; 22l bhnd 10; t.o & pu 15*		P
363^{P}	Cedar Grove(cp) 4-1 T Faulkner *Jmpd slow in rr; nvr lkd keen; 10l 6th 10; nt r.o; t.o & pu 15*		P
699^{P}	Cottage Boy (IRE) 12-1 M Barber *Mist 5; cl 3rd til fell hvly 13; dead*		F
700^{8}	Maloney (IRE) 6-1 Miss C Evans *Sn 6/7th; rdr v insecure til f.o 9*		U

OFFICIAL DISTANCES: 8*l*, 10*l* **TIME:** 6min 56.0s

736 Confined Maiden 8yo&up, 12st - 17J — 10 ran

	ALJOASH (IRE) (5a) 2-1 **T Vaughan** *(xnb) Lw; pulled hrd; ld to 3; prog in 8l 3rd 11; went 2nd 15; ld passing omitted nxt; sn clr*		1
	Blakeney Hill (5a) 16-1 **J Price** *Lw; ld til passing omitted 3 out; rdn & desperately one-pcd aft*	12	2
677^{3}	**Wiston Wizo**(bl) 8-1 **P Sheldrake** *Hld up towards rr til prog 12; 2nd brief 14; 12l 3rd nxt; reluct aft & sn wl bhnd; nrly ref last*	25	3
699^{F}	Just Caramel (5a)(tt) 6-4F M Barber *Bhnd & nvr gng wl; mist 9; 5th 14; nt r.o; 30l 5th & u.p 3 out; rn atrociously*	8	4
731^{P}	Milamoss 10-1 R Hughes *Mists in rr; 8th 11; t.o 15.*	6	5
674^{P}	Clarky's Choice (IRE) 13-2 James Tudor *2nd to 6; cl up til 3rd 14; wknd rap; 28l 4th passing 3 out; pu last*		P
699^{P}	Croesy Pennant 14-1 Miss F Wilson *Tk keen hld; hdwy to 2nd 6-8; wkng rap when mist 11; last when slpd up bef 13; dead*		S
699^{F}	Evans The Coal 10-1 James Price *(xnb & other restraining tack) Mounted on course & tde; tk str hld; midfield til dashed up to 2nd 8-11; wkng bad when terrible mist 13; sn t.o; pu 15*		P
699^{P}	Itsdigitalis (5a) 11-2 L Stephens *Prom; blun & nrly ur 2; rmdrs aft 3; drvn & drpd to rr 10; t.o when pu & dism 12*		P
	Miss Charlotte (5a) 14-1 R Bliss *Detach last aft blun 3; t.o when mist 9; pu 12*		P

OFFICIAL DISTANCES: 15L, DIST **TIME:** 6min 46.0s

Fence 16 omitted - damaged

737 Ladies Open — 5 ran

	DE CHELLY (5a) 4-1 **Mrs C Owen** *2nd/3rd til hit 13; ld 14; kpt finding ex when prsd frm 3 out; stayed on game*		1
613^{1}	**Upton Adventure** (5a) 1-4F **Miss E James** *Hld up; went 2nd 12; pushed along frm 3 out; 1l down & drvn last; a hld.*	$1\frac{1}{2}$	2
697^{3}	**Young Manny** 12-1 **Mrs B Lewis** *Ld to 5; last & outpcd nxt; nrly ur 8; 20l adrift 12; t.o & mist 15; went 3rd flat*	$1\frac{1}{4}$fs	3
364^{U}	Mazury (USA) (7a) 16-1 Miss E Tuck *(xnb) Tk keen hld; hung lft & lost tch in 15l 4th aft 11; no ch aft; went dist 3rd 3 out til mist last*	10	4
361^{F}	Nigel's Boy 5-1 Miss F Wilson *Impd qckly to ld 5; nt fluent 9; hdd 14; wknd rap nxt; rem 4th when jmpd v slow 3 out; pu nxt*		P

OFFICIAL DISTANCES: 1*l*, dist **TIME:** 6min 37.0s

738 Mens Open, 12st — 3 ran

628^{5}	**MISTER FALCON (FR)** (7x) 4-6F **R Hughes** *Ld 5-7 & frm 10; drew clr 3 out; v easily*		1
670^{P}	**Fassan (IRE)** 6-4 **James Tudor** *Ld til jmpd slow 5 & rmdr; slt ld 7-10; rdn to chse wnr frm 14; nt keen aft; 12l down 2 out.*	15	2

672^{P} **Aficionado (IRE)** 3-1 **H Oakes** *Cl up in crawl; jmpd slow 4 & v slow 6; strugg in last when mist 15; 12l down 3 out; 20l adrift nxt; rdn & clsng on rnr-up flat* 1½ 3

OFFICIAL DISTANCES: 8*l*, 1*l* **TIME:** 7min 09.0s

739 Intermediate (Nov Rdrs), 12st — 3 ran

698^{2} **SILVER POT BLACK** 1-3F **Miss H Lewis** *Ld to 3 & frm 5; drew clr 15; v easily* 1

698^{3} **Chesnut Wood** (5x) 7-4 **Miss A Hughes** *Lkd poor; nt fluent; ld & jmpd slow 4; 2nd/3rd aft; ev ch aft 14; 12l 2nd & strugg 3 out* 8 2

698^{4} **Glen Mist (IRE)**(bl) 5-1 **Miss R Athay** *Rn in snatches; made most 3 til wide app 5; 12l last 9; rallied to 5l 2nd 12; releg last 14 & sn wl bhnd* 15 3

OFFICIAL DISTANCES: 12*l*, 25*l* **TIME:** 7min 15.0s

740 Restricted, 12st — 8 ran

TINDER-BOX 6-4F **Miss T Cave** *(xnb) Gng wl in rr til clsd to 3rd 11; ld 13; 12l clr 3 out; hit nxt; easily* 1

695^{2} **Hail Stone (IRE)** 13-2 **L Stephens** *Ld to 8 & agn 11-13; drvn & outpcd aft nxt; 12l 2nd 3 out* 12 2

Like The Buzz (IRE) (5a) 6-1 **James Tudor** *Nt fluent & hld up in rr; 6th 11; outpcd & mist nxt; went 35l 3rd 15* 8 3

451^{2} Steel Gem (IRE) 6-1 J Price *Cl up til drvn & drpd to rr 10; wl t.o 14* 1½fs 4

674^{P} Daisy's Choice (5a) 16-1 P Sheldrake *Sn cl up; ld 8 til blun 9; 5th & wkng 11; no ch when mist 13; pu nxt* . . . . P

530^{P} Italian Clover 8-1 Miss S Carter *Tubed; prom brief; lost tch 7; t.o 9; pu 12.* P

674^{P} Tigersun 14-1 D Jones *(xnb) Mists in 2nd/3rd til ld brief 10; drvn & wkng rap when mist 12; pu nxt* . . . . P

Troedrhiwdalar (5a) 5-2 M Barber *Hit 4; hld up; eff & jmpd slow 11; went 6l 3rd 13; wknd qckly nxt; just dem rem 4th when fell 15* . . . . F

OFFICIAL DISTANCES: 15*l*, 10*l* **TIME:** 6min 51.0s

Gay Abandon could not take his intended place in this race as no jockey present was prepared to ride her

Puckeridge

Horseheath (RH 10F,18J)

Sat, 3 Apr (GOOD, GOOD to FIRM in places)

741 Hunt Members, 12st — 3 ran

524^{1} **MISTER RINGA** 1-5F **A Braithwaite** *Made all; blun 3; jmpd lft 13; 3l clr 15; in comm nxt; easily* 1

561^{5} **Granny Dick** (5a) 14-1 **T Messenger** *Hld up; mist 7; chsd wnr frm 10; rdn 3 out; wl btn nxt* 15 2

651^{P} Just Lute 5-1 M Smith *Trckd wnr to 10; mist 5; rdn app 11; 8l 3rd 12; pu aft nxt; lame* . . . . P

OFFICIAL DISTANCE: 10*l* **TIME:** 6min 44.0s **TOTE:** £1.10 **DF:**£1.10 (1+any)

742 Intermediate, 12st — 7 ran

398^{1} **MADMIDGE** 3-1 **D Kemp** *Ww; trckd ldng pr 11; ld 2 out; stayed on wl* . . . 1

521^{2} **Persian Hero (IRE)** 9-4 **J Owen** *In tch; rdn 13; 6l 4th 15; stayed on u.p to chse wnr last; no imp flat* 6 2

607^{3} **Jims Belief (IRE)** 10-1 **G Cooper** *(xnb) Disp ld to 3; chsd ldr 10; upsides when outj 15; sn ld; blun 3 out; hdd nxt; wknd & lost 2nd at last* 2½ 3

556^{2} Lord Euro (IRE) 4-1 A Merriam *Ld 3; mist 9; hdd app 3 out; wknd nxt.* . . . 12 4

559^{1} Archbishop(cp) 2-1F S Morris *Ww; rmdrs & hdwy 10; 6l 6th 11; outpcd app 14; sn no ch* 25 5

559^{3} Lambrini King (IRE) 33-1 Miss L Barrett-Nobbs *(xnb) In tch; 5l 5th 11; rdn 12; outpcd & no ch frm 14* 15 6

650^{P} Valman (IRE)(vis) 33-1 P Millington *(xnb) Disp ld to 3; cl up when mists 8 & 9; sn drpd out; t.o & pu 11* . . . . P

OFFICIAL DISTANCES: 5*l*, 3*l* **TIME:** 6min 24.0s **TOTE:** £2.80 **DF:**£7.80

743 Ladies Open — 9 ran

Form	Horse / Rider / Comment	Dist	Pos
593^{2}	**MACFIN (IRE)** (4x)(cp) 4-1 **Miss L Allan** *Ld to 11; prsd ldr til ld agn app 3 out; hrd prsd when gd j last; hld on game u.p flat*		1
239^{4}	**The Kings Fling** 5-4F **Miss P Gundry** *Mists; ww in tch; went cl 3rd 14; chall 3 out; hit nxt & last; unable to qckn u.p flat*	1	2
	Linlathen (7x) 3-1 **Miss Gemma Hutchinson** *Pckd 1; mid-div; hdwy to 2nd 10; ld nxt; mist 12; hdd 3 out; one pce aft*	8	3
522^{1}	The Wiley Kalmuck (IRE) (7x) 7-2 Miss Z Turner *Chsd ldrs; 7l 5th 15; no hdwy aft*	$2\frac{1}{4}$	5
649^{4}	Mister Audi (IRE)(bl) 33-1 Miss A Bowles *In tch; mist 2; 6th & outpcd 15; no ch aft*	25	6
522^{5}	Borrow Mine (IRE) 25-1 Miss L Marriott *In tch til 7th & outpcd app 15; no ch aft*	1	7
536^{2}	Teach Altra (IRE) 12-1 Miss B Donnelly *Chsd ldrs; mist 10; 6l 4th 15; rallied nxt; no ex frm 2 out; fin 11l 4th; disq - nt weigh-in.*		4d
522^{2}	Corston Joker (7x) 25-1 Mrs L Spence *Reluct to line up; tk no part*		r
585^{4}	Veredarius (FR) 33-1 Mrs S Tyler *Sn detach last; t.o 7 til pu 15*		P

OFFICIAL DISTANCES: 1*l*, 3*l* **TIME:** 6min 27.0s **TOTE:** £4.60 **DF:**£9.70

Teach Altra who finished fourth was disqualified when the rider failed to weigh-in; she admitted her error and was reprimanded and cautioned as to her future conduct, but in view of her inexperience was not fined

744 Mens Open, 12st — 7 ran

Form	Horse / Rider / Comment	Dist	Pos
647^{2}	**BARD OF DRUMCOO (IRE)** 5-2 **D Kemp** *7/2-5/2; disp ld til app 11; ld agn 13; mist 14; stayed on wl frm 2 out*		1
557^{2}	**Bush Hill Bandit (IRE)** (7x) 6-1 **H Fowler** *Ww; prog & 4l 4th 13; chsd wnr 3 out; no imp u.p frm nxt*	3	2
586^{2}	**Grecian Star** (7x) 7-4F **J Tarry** *In tch; bustled along at times; 8l 4th 15; went 3rd 2 out; kpt on; nt pce to chall ldng pr*	7	3
610^{2}	Royal Action (4x) 5-1 P Chinery *In tch; cl 3rd frm 10; 5l 3rd 3 out; wknd & dem nxt*	7	4
537^{2}	Dixon Varner (IRE) 10-1 F Marshall *Disp ld til ld app 11; hdd 13; 5l 4th 15; outpcd app 3 out*	8	5
590^{1}	Ballad (IRE) 25-1 A Williams *Ww; rr but in tch til app 15; bhnd when pu last*		P
523^{2}	Millenium Way (IRE) 10-1 J Owen *Cl up; rdn app 11; wknd 14; bhnd & pu last*		P

OFFICIAL DISTANCES: 3*l*, 3*l* **TIME:** 6min 26.0s **TOTE:** £2.60 **DF:**£20.20

745 Restricted, 12st — 14 ran

Form	Horse / Rider / Comment	Dist	Pos
649^{3}	**FILOU DU BOIS (FR)** 4-1 **Ms A Embiricos** *(xnb) In tch; cl 4th 11; lft in ld nxt; drew clr 3 out; stayed on wl*		1
560^{1}	**Tartar Sabre** 5-1 **Miss L Barrett-Nobbs** *14s-5s; chsd ldrs; lft 2nd 12; mist 13; upsides wnr & ev ch 15; outpcd frm nxt.*	15	2
	Magnus Maximus 20-1 **R Collinson** *2 handlers; ww in rr; prog app 11; lft 4th 15; sn rdn & no hdwy nxt; went 3rd 2 out; no imp on ldrs*	6	3
159^{P}	Lone Star (IRE)(bl) 33-1 H Fowler *In tch; cl 6th 11; lft 3rd 15; wknd u.p app nxt*	5	4
524^{6}	Nowornever (IRE) 7-2F D Kemp *Ww in mid-div; 12l 6th app 14; sn lost tch; no ch aft*	3	5
540^{1}	Street Smart (IRE) 4-1 Miss B Donnelly *(xnb) Mid-div; 8th & outpcd 12; no ch aft*	2	6
481^{P}	Cawkwell Princess (5a) 20-1 S Morris *Bhnd; no ch frm 11; t.o*	25	7
648^{P}	Ginger Bug (5a) 20-1 P Chinery *A bhnd; t.o frm 11*	3	8
375^{P}	Broad Edge (IRE)(cp) 20-1 R Stearn *(xnb) Chsd ldr 5-7; 8th & wkng 13; pu 15*		P
522^{P}	Buckland Bobby 33-1 P Millington *Chsd ldng group; mist 10; lft 12l 5th 15; fell nxt*		F
559^{4}	Germany Park (IRE) 5-1 M Smith *(xnb) 2 handlers; ld/disp til fell 12.*		F
649^{U}	Ical (IRE) (5a) 14-1 Miss A Stennett *Disp ld til wknd qckly 12; sn bhnd; pu 14*		P
648^{P}	Mr Moonbeam (IRE) (1ow) 25-1 M Buchan *A wl bhnd; t.o & pu 14.*		P
646^{1}	Rip Kirby 20-1 R Hanley *Chsd ldrs; 4l 3rd when fell 15*		F

OFFICIAL DISTANCES: 10*l*, 5*l* **TIME:** 6min 29.0s **TOTE:** £13.10 **DF:**£20.30

The rider of Magnus Maximus was fined £65 for misuse of the whip causing his horse to be marked

746 Open Maiden, 12st — 16 ran

561[3] **CONQUISTADOR (IRE)** 4-1 **N Moore** *In tch gng wl; ld 13; sn clr; 25l clr 3 out; blun nxt; tiring & jmpd slow last; unchall* . . . 1
555[3] **Marciano**(cp) 8-1 **J Docker** *Chsd ldrs; jnd ldrs app 11; 10l 4th & rdn 14; went 20l 2nd 15; kpt on u.p frm 2 out; nt rch wnr* . . . 4 2
588[U] **Northall Lad** 5-1 **P Cowley** *Hld up wl in rr; mist 5; went 15l 5th 14 & poor 3rd 3 out; tired frm nxt; just kpt 3rd; nvr nr ldrs* . . . 40 3
611[2] Pistol Knight 5-1 Stuart Robinson *Mid-div; 8l 7th & pushed along 10; no ch 14; plodded on flat; nrly snatched 3rd* . . . nk 4
245[5] Play Alone (IRE) (5a) 10-1 D Kemp *Chsd ldrs; ld 10-13; 3rd & outpcd 14; no ch aft* . . . 15 5
611[P] Baron Bernard 16-1 P Chinery *Ld to 3; cl up til wknd qckly 9; wl bhnd frm 14; pu 2 out* . . . P
Call Me Again 14-1 N Pearce *Ww in rr; prog to 6th & wl in tch 10; fell 12* F
560[F] Divine Mist (IRE) 3-1F J Owen *Mid-div til blun & ur 4* . . . U
128[P] Legolas (7a) 20-1 P Millington *Mid-div; in tch til blun & ur 6* . . . U
Marbank Lad (IRE) 20-1 M Mackley *A bhnd; poor 9th 10; t.o & pu 12* . . . P
589[6] Penlet Too(bl) 6-1 T Ellis *(xnb) Pulled hrd; ld 3-10; chsd ldr 13-15; v tired nxt; wl bhnd & pu last* . . . P
Plain Polly (IRE) (5a) 20-1 A Williams *Ur start* . . . U
River Deed (7a) 12-1 M Smith *Cl up til 5th & wkng aft 13; pu 15* . . . P
303[P] Sneeze (5a) 14-1 A Braithwaite *A bhnd; t.o & pu 11* . . . P
217[U] Spring Frolic 14-1 R Stearn *Bhnd when jmpd slow & ur 7* . . . U
245[P] Swanbank 8-1 H Fowler *Mid-div; in tch to 8; wl bhnd frm 10; pu 11* . . . P

OFFICIAL DISTANCES: 3*l*, dist **TIME:** 6min 34.0s **TOTE:** £3.00 **DF:**£30.30

Wincanton (RH 9F,21J)

Sun, 4 Apr (GOOD, GOOD to SOFT in places)

747 Red Mills Nov HC, 3m1f110y £2054 — 7 ran

541[1] **KINGSTON-BANKER** 11-13 15-8JF **T Dreaper** *Ld aft 3; jmpd slow 9; hit 12 & 14; drvn & stayed on wl frm 3 out* . . . 1
490[6] **Tell Tale (IRE)** 11-09 10-1 **T Malone** *Bhnd; hdwy 15; disp 2nd when lft chsng wnr 18; rdn & kpt on frm 3 out; no imp* . . . 4 2
435[1] **Whether The Storm (IRE)** 12-03 15-8JF **Miss S Samworth** *Bhnd; hdwy frm 15; kpt on frm 3 out; nt rch ldrs* . . . 10 3
602[3] Colombian Green (IRE) 11-11 14-1 N Mitchell *Bhnd when hit 5; hdwy 10; blun nxt when chsng ldrs; no ch frm 17* . . . 8 4
438[2] Alska (FR) 11-02 25-1 Miss W Southcombe *Ld 2 til aft 3; bhnd 8; lost tch 13; some hdwy agn frm 3 out; nd* . . . 2 5
81[2] Burley Don Carlos 11-07 7-1 Miss C Stucley *Blun 3; w ldr frm nxt til jmpd slow 9; chsng ldrs when ur 11* . . . U
602[2] Red Native (IRE) 11-11(bl) 13-2 N Williams *Hit 2; in tch; chsd ldr 12; blun 16; disp 8l 2nd & drvn when fell 18* . . . F

TIME: 6min 53.6s **TOTE:** £2.30; places £1.80,£4.10 **Ex:**£28.50 **CSF:**£21.11

Cheshire Forest

Tabley (RH 7F,20J)

Sun, 4 Apr (GOOD becoming SOFT)

748 Hunt Members — 7 ran

ANALYSTIC (IRE) 10-11F **G Hanmer** *(xnb) Jmpd lft & nt a fluent; ld to 2; went 2nd 8; lft in ld 16; shkn up aft 2 out; comf* . . . 1
711[2] **Springwood White** 10-1 **T Park** *2nd to 8; 7l 3rd ½way; lft 7l 2nd 16; rdn app 2 out; hung lft app last; one pce* . . . 7 2
251[U] **Chelsea King (IRE)** 5-1 **Miss G Garton** *Chsd ldrs; 8l 4th ½way; went 10l 3rd 17; no imp* . . . 15 3
715[P] Horton-Cum-Peel (IRE) 40-1 W Kinsey *(xnb) Hld up; releg last 8; lost tch u.p 13; went poor 4th last; stayed on* . . . ½ 4
715[8] Gabaka De Thaix (FR) 33-1 M Caldwell *Hld up; 11l 5th ½way; lft 10l 3rd 16; wknd 3 out* . . . 15 5

712[5] City Gent 3-1 J R Barlow *Ld 2 til blun & ur 16* . . . U
Strong King (IRE) 16-1 A Wadlow *25s-16s; last to 8; 14l 6th ½way; lost tch u.p 13; t.o & pu 16* . . . P

OFFICIAL DISTANCES: 8*l*, 15*l* **TIME:** 6min 59.5s

749 Confined, 12st — 9 ran

422[2] **INDIAN WINGS (IRE)** 6-4F **R Burton** *3s-6/4; hld up; 12l 6th ½way; hdwy 13; 8l 4th 15; went 7l 2nd & rdn aft 3 out; ld app last; all out* . . . 1
92[P] **Mister Moss (IRE)** (3x) 3-1 **G Hanmer** *Ld; sn up to 8l clr to 12; qcknd 16; 8l up 3 out; hdd & no ex app last* . . . 2½ 2
709[6] **Raiseapearl** 33-1 **I Clyde** *(kineton) Hld up; hdwy 8; 10l 4th ½way; went 3rd 12; hit 13 & 15; mist 17; one pce 3 out* . . . 10 3
501[2] Blank Cheque 5-2 D Coates *Releg last & rmdrs 7; sn wl bhnd; t.o 15; fin wl* 10 4
662[6] Knock It Back (IRE) 10-1 J Handley *Hvly greased legs; 2nd til wknd qckly aft 3 out* . . . 12 5
630[P] Fountain Street (IRE) 12-1 W Kinsey *(xnb) 3rd/4th to 8; 11l 5th ½way; lost tch u.p 13; 30l 5th 15; sn t.o; pu last* . . . P
708[7] New Ross (IRE) (8x)(bl) 16-1 Miss A Turner *A bhnd; 16l 7th ½way; t.o last 15; pu 2 out* . . . P
93[P] Raconteur (IRE) 16-1 W Puddifer *Chsd ldrs; 8l 3rd ½way; 4th when rfo 12* U
428[9] Silk Vestments (5a) 33-1 Miss H Dunning *8th when rdr leapt off 1* . . . U

OFFICIAL DISTANCES: 2½*l*, 10*l* **TIME:** 6min 54.7s

750 Land Rover Mens Open, 12st — 5 ran

616[P] **PROMINENT** 10-1 **G Hanmer** *(xnb) Made all; qcknd 15; 8l clr 2 out; drvn out* 1
340[1] **Victoria's Boy (IRE)** (7x) 10-11F **D Coates** *5/4-10/11; a chsng wnr; nt qckn 15; stayed on one pce 2 out* . . . 5 2
663[4] **Good Heart (IRE)** 5-1 **N Oliver** *Hld up; last 10-12 & 14-17; rdn aft 3 out; went 3rd at last; nvr nr to chall* . . . 8 3
630[P] Templebreedy (IRE) 9-4 R Burton *Ww; last to 10; 6l 4th ½way; last 12 til went 6l 3rd aft 14; rdn & fnd nil 2 out; dem last* . . . 1 4
251[P] Whitegates Willie 10-1 D Greenway *Hld up & pulled hrd; 5l 3rd ½way; 10l 4th & outpcd 15; wknd u.p 17; t.o* . . . runin 5

OFFICIAL DISTANCES: 4*l*, 7*l* **TIME:** 7min 02.5s

751 Ladies Open — 7 ran

PALISANDER (IRE) 6-1 **Miss C Hurley** *14s-6s; tde; ld to 2 out; ld last; r.o wl* 1
253[1] **Pacon (GER)** 100-30 **Miss H Kinsey** *(xnb) Hld up; 5l 4th ½way; went 3rd 17 & 3l 2nd aft nxt; ld 2 out til hdd & jmpd lft last; no ex flat* . . . 2 2
529[2] **Justin Mac (IRE)** 8-1 **Miss K Wood** *2nd til aft 3 out; rdn 2 out; no ex* . . . 12 3
529[P] Joyce Bel (FR) 12-1 Miss K Crank *(xnb) Nt a fluent; prom til lost plce 10; 8l last ½way; lost tch 17* . . . 20 4
712[1] Jackie Jarvis (IRE) (5a, 7x) 4-5F Mrs K Diggle *(xnb) Ref to rce* . . . r
157[P] Karzhang 13-2 Miss S Sharratt *Hld up; hdwy 6; blun 8; 4l 3rd ½way; 6l 4th & rdn 3 out; wknd qckly; blun 2 out; pu last* . . . P
594[5] Sharp Embrace 25-1 Miss S Rodman *Rmdrs 3; lost tch u.p 8; last til ur 11* U

OFFICIAL DISTANCES: 2½*l*, 12*l* **TIME:** 6min 59.0s

752 Restricted, 12st — 10 ran

533[1] **KARINGA LANE** 3-1 **R Burton** *(xnb,bf) 8s(in plce)-3s; hld up; 10l 6th ½way; jnd ldrs 13; ld 15; drew clr 2 out; stayed on wl* . . . 1
Lima Bravo (5a) 9-2 **P Morris** *Nt fluent; hld up; last to 13; hdwy 15; went 2nd aft 3 out; wknd app last* . . . 7 2
715[7] **Spizzichino** 14-1 **K Pearson** *(xnb) Ld aft 4 til jb lft 7; 2nd til ld 11; jb lft & hdd 14; one pce 3 out* . . . 10 3
Barty Boy (IRE) 20-1 B Shaw *Hld up; 11l 7th ½way; hdwy 13; lft in ld 14-15; 2nd til aft 3 out; sn rdn & btn; rdr failed to weigh-in but horse nt disq.* . . 1 4
708[6] Hill Of Kilfeacle (IRE)(tt) 16-1 D Greenway *2 handlers; prom til lost plce 9; 12l 8th ½way; rallied & 3l 6th 15; wknd 3 out* . . . 12 5
452[5] Alleywell 9-1 A Wintle *14s-9s; prom; 5l 3rd ½way; disp 2l 4th 15; wknd aft 17; wl bhnd when pu 2 out* . . . P
715[P] Edward Bear 20-1 Miss K Wood *(xnb) Ld til aft 4; 2nd/3rd to 10; 9l 5th ½way; wknd 12; wl bhnd when pu aft 15* . . . P

715P Highlands II (FR)(vis) 14-1 A Wadlow *Prom; lft in ld 7-11; hit 12; 2l 4th 15; wkng when fell 17* . . . F
2261 No Remorse 4-5F G Hanmer *Hld up; 15l 9th ½way; hdwy 15; 5th & wkng when mist 2 out; pu last* . . . P
91P Wraparound You (IRE) 12-1 N Oliver *(xnb) Hld up; hdwy & 8l 4th ½way; went 2nd 13; wknd 15; bhnd when pu 3 out* . . . P

OFFICIAL DISTANCES: 8*l*, 8*l* **TIME:** 7min 06.8s

The rider of Barty Boy was reprimanded by the stewards for failing to weigh-in; the horse was not disqualified and no fine was imposed

753 Open Maiden — 8 ran

709F **RIDWARE PRIDE** 11-2 **Miss S Sharratt** *2nd til aft 14; 3l 4th & rdn 3 out; went 2nd app last; stayed on to ld flat* . . . 1
679P **Well Said Sam** 14-1 **J Handley** *Hld up; hdwy 9; went 6l 4th ½way & 2nd aft 14; ld 3 out til hdd & no ex flat* . . . 2½ 2
7104 **Times Two** 6-4F **A Wadlow** *(xnb) Jmpd lft; ld to 3 out; ev ch 2 out; sn wknd* 8 3
7106 Robert The Rascal 11-2 I Clyde *Hld up; 10l 7th ½way; hdwy 13; lost plce & 12l 6th 15; lft poor 4th 2 out* . . . 15 4
714P Ginmini (IRE) (5a) 12-1 R Ward-Dutton *Hld up; hdwy 7; 7l 5th ½way; wknd 13; 13l last 15; rdr lost irons nxt; pu 17* . . . P
Leicaree (IRE) 9-4 G Hanmer *(xnb) Prom til lost plce 7; 8l 6th ½way; rallied & 4l 3rd 15; rdn 3 out; sn wknd; pu 2 out* . . . P
595P Single Man (IRE) 14-1 J Burley *2 handlers; prom; disp 3l 2nd ½way; wknd u.p & 10l 5th 15; mist 16; t.o & pu 2 out* . . . P
729F Sylvias Dream (5a) 6-1 P Morris *Ss; 20l last ½way; wl bhnd til pu 12* . . . P

OFFICIAL DISTANCES: 3½*l*, 10*l* **TIME:** 7min 31.5s

754 Open Maiden 56&7yo, 12st — 9 ran

BEST ACCOLADE (7a) 3-1 **R Burton** *Hld up; hmpd 1; 8l 4th ½way; went 3rd 14 & 8l 2nd aft 3 out; clsd rap to ld 2 out; sn clr; rdn out* . . . 1
226F **Benbow** 9-4F **B Shaw** *7/2-9/4; a.p; went 2nd 10; ld 16; qcknd 8l clr 3 out; hdd 2 out; no ex* . . . 7 2
4103 **Jump For Paddy** (7a) 5-2 **A Wadlow** *Hld up; bhnd when jb lft 7; 11l last ½way; hdwy & 4l 5th 15; went 12l 3rd aft 3 out; no imp when blun last* 6 3
531P Treasulier (IRE) 5-1 N Oliver *Prom; went 2nd 5-10; 5l 3rd ½way; 3l 4th 15; wknd qckly 3 out; t.o* . . . runin 4
Button Lady (12a) 14-1 D Gaiter *6th when tried to stop & ur 1* . . . U
533P Fort Glendennon (7a, 5ow) 10-1 A Wintle *Hld up; drpd to rr 6; 10l 6th ½way; lost tch 14; pu 16* . . . P
533P Handsome Lad (IRE) 12-1 G Hanmer *Rap hdwy to ld aft 4; hdd 16; mist 17; 8l 2nd & wkng nxt; poor 4th when pu last* . . . P
714U Mayday Girl (5a) 12-1 J Handley *Wrs but ld til aft 4; 2nd/4th til fell 9; broke off-hind leg; dead* . . . F
Missuslarge (5a) 20-1 E Linehan *(xnb) Jmpd v slow 2; rdn 8; 9l 5th ½way; 9l 6th when jmpd v slow 15; pu 16* . . . P

OFFICIAL DISTANCES: 7*l*, 7*l* **TIME:** 7min 54.5s

No rider was keen to make the running and it took the field 28 seconds to reach the first fence

Cotswold

Andoversford (RH 9F,19J)

Sun, 4 Apr (GOOD with SOFT patches)

755 Hunt Members, 12st — 8 ran

4452 **ACT IN TIME (IRE)** 5-4F **T Edwards** *2s-5/4; w ldrs; stdy prog to ldng group 13; ld 3 out; clr nxt; stayed on wl when chall flat* . . . 1
4041 **Parahandy (IRE)** (5x) 2-1 **H Dowty** *Chsd ldrs; outpcd brief ½way; stayed on to tk 2nd 2 out; r.o wl und str drvng flat* . . . 1 2
587F **Misty Ramble (IRE)** 7-1 **G McPherson** *Bad mist 2; cl 5th ½way; eff frm 3 out to 4th app last; stayed on wl to tk 3rd in shadow of post* . . . 25 3
Pretoria Dancer(bl) 6-1 M Goldstein *Ld & set str pce til caught 12; dist 3rd 2 out; dem cl home* . . . nk 4

	Alpha Leather 20-1 J Grassick *Strugg as ldrs qcknd frm ½way; outpcd frm 14; wl bhnd when pu 2 out*		P
406[3]	Arctic Grey (IRE) 20-1 Mrs C Mackness *1st ride; sn completely t.o; hunted rnd t.o til pu 9.*		P
636[1]	Boyne Banks (IRE) 6-1 G Disney *Cl 2nd til ld 10-12; ev ch til wknd rap frm 3 out; 20l last when pu last*		P
	Not For Parrot (IRE) 20-1 H Tett *Mid-div when ur 6*		U

OFFICIAL DISTANCES: 1½*l*, 15*l* **TIME:** 6min 39.0s

756 Confined, 12st — 10 ran

660[1]	**CAUGHT AT DAWN (IRE)** (6x) 7-4F **T Weston** *Jw; prom til ld 12; drew away frm 15; clr 2 out; easily.*		1
727[P]	**Rushing Again** (3x) 6-1 **Mrs K Baimbridge** *Mostly 5th 1st circ; prog to 2nd 13; ev ch til outpcd frm 2 out*	4	2
727[2]	**The Campdonian (IRE)** (3x) 3-1 **E Walker** *Sev posns 1st circ; rmdrs 11; 4th 16 & 3rd nxt; stayed on one pce.*	20	3
584[1]	Finder Keeps (USA) 4-1 J Barnes *Disp 3rd; ev ch til wknd frm 3 out; pu last*		P
660[6]	Head Gardener (IRE)(vis) 16-1 D Mansell *Rr of ldng group til lost tch & pu 12*		P
662[2]	L'idefix (IRE) 4-1 H Dowty *Cl 5/6th to ½way; pushed along to stay in tch 12; wknd grad; last when pu 2 out*		P
46[3]	Marlmont Lad (IRE) 10-1 J Trice-Rolph *Strugg til pu 13*		P
729[R]	Phar And Away (5a) 10-1 G Tumelty *Hdstrng; ld 4; stride shortened 9; hdd 11; lsng tch when fell 12*		F
584[3]	Sing High (5a) 4-1 A Martin *Ld to 4; cl 2nd to 11; wknd 13; wl bhnd when pu 3 out*		P
	Stay Lucky (NZ)(cp) 7-1 N Phillips *Detach by 7; last when pu 15*		P

OFFICIAL DISTANCES: 6*l*, 12*l* **TIME:** 6min 33.0s

757 Ladies Open — 9 ran

625[2]	**CALDAMUS** 11-8 **Miss A Goschen** *Cl up; prog to jn ldrs 12; 2l clr frm 16; rdn frm 2 out; r.o wl*		1
382[1]	**Prince Dundee (FR)** evensF **Mrs B Keighley** *Mist 6; 5th & mist 11; 3l 3rd 13; eff to cl 2nd 3 out; ev ch nxt; level last; outpcd flat*	1½	2
	Arctic Burner (IRE) 20-1 **Mrs J Chapman** *Trckd ldrs; prog to 4th frm ½way; stayed on to 3rd app last*	30	3
727[P]	Macy (IRE)(cp) 20-1 Miss E James *Disp ld til 2l clr 6; jnd 13; wknd frm nxt; no ex frm 3 out.*	15	4
628[P]	Midy's Risk (FR) 20-1 Miss S Davies *Chsd ldrs; 5th 15; no ex*	10	5
632[3]	Solo Gent 20-1 Miss K Jones *5th mostly to ½way; grad drpd away*	8	6
490[F]	Nahthen Lad (IRE)(vis) 16-1 Miss A de Lisle Wells *Prom in ldng group til wknd 9; t.o & pu 2 out*		P
407[P]	Owl Vulgan (IRE) 16-1 Mrs K Baimbridge *Mist 2; disp ld frm nxt til drpd back to 3rd 12; wkng when fell 13.*		F
373[P]	Pele Mele (FR) 20-1 Miss S Firmin *A bhnd; t.o ½way til pu last*		P

OFFICIAL DISTANCES: 1½*l*, 30*l* **TIME:** 6min 39.0s

758 Land Rover Mens Open, 12st — 9 ran

583[1]	**FREEDOM FIGHTER** 5-1 **A Martin** *Mid-div to ½way; stdy prog frm 15 to 4l 3rd 2 out; swept thro on inner final bend; clr last; idled flat*		1
661[2]	**Picket Piece**(bl) 20-1 **M Goldstein** *Jmpd lft; ld frm 2 til jnd 13; drpd back to 4th 14; still 4th 2 out; r.o str u.p app last*	2	2
254[3]	**Teme Willow (IRE)** (4x) 5-1 **G Barfoot-Saunt** *Jmpd rt sev fncs; cl 2nd to 9; 4th 13-15; rnwd eff to ld 3 out; 2l clr when bad mist 2 out; sn hdd & unable to qckn*	10	3
602[1]	Phar From Chance (7x) 9-2 D Jones *Mostly 4th 1st circ; disp ld 12; ld 14; jnd agn 15; hdd aft nxt; disp ld agn aft 2 out; wknd app last*	2	4
727[6]	Lyphard's Fable (USA) 20-1 D England *Cl up in mid-div to 12; stayed on one pce frm 3 out.*	1	5
612[6]	Henry Bruce(bl) 20-1 A Brown *Bhnd by 6; t.o by ½way; r.o past btn horses frm 3 out*	2	6
586[6]	Paddies Boy (IRE) (7x) 20-1 Jack Young *8th ½way; mod late prog; nrst fin*	4	7
727[P]	Dinsey Finnegan (IRE)(cp) 20-1 G Phillips *3rd 7 & 4th 9; detach 5th 14; wknd*	2	8
576[1]	Out The Black (IRE) 4-7F D Alers-Hankey *Saddle slpd 4; cl 5th til eff to go 2nd brief 15; 3l 3rd & ev ch when mist & ur 3 out*		U

OFFICIAL DISTANCES: 2*l*, 8*l* **TIME:** 6min 43.0s

759 Intermediate, 12st — 10 ran

614[1]	**LOVE AT DAWN** 7-4F **P Mason** *Cl 3rd to ½way; prog to ld frm 14; bad mist nxt; in comm frm 2 out*		1
728[U]	**Camden Carrig (IRE)** 9-2 **N Phillips** *Ld; 2l up til jnd 13; hdd nxt; cl 2nd & ev ch til brushed aside frm 2 out*	6	2
726[P]	**I'm Dreaming (IRE)** 14-1 **A Martin** *Mostly 6th 1st circ; prog to 4th 3 out; tk 3rd nxt*	15	3
629[6]	Nomadic Star 10-1 Miss Z Lilly *Chsd ldrs; 8l 3rd 13; no ex frm 3 out*	4	4
516[1]	Tom Putt 8-1 B Pauling *Strugg to go pce 1st circ; rmdrs ½way; nvr plcd to chall*	10	5
602[4]	Bankit 5-2 J Barnes *2nd/3rd til wknd 11; lsng tch when pu 15*		P
406[F]	Hedzamarley (IRE) 20-1 D Jones *Cl 3rd to 12; drpd back qckly frm 13; bhnd when pu 15*		P
447[P]	Reefer Dancer(bl) 20-1 D Mansell *Lost 10l start; in vain pursuit aft; t.o & pu 16*		P
	Silent Action (USA) 14-1 D Smith *Cl 7th ½way; drpd back qckly & pu aft 13*		P
	Spring Cabbage (IRE) 16-1 G Barfoot-Saunt *Bhnd 1st circ; disp dist 3rd 13; wkng 6th when clambered over 2 out & imm pu*		P

OFFICIAL DISTANCES: 8*l*, 20*l* **TIME:** 6min 35.0s

760 Open Maiden, 12st — 16 ran

409[3]	**APRIL TREASURE** (5a) 2-1F **G Barfoot-Saunt** *3s-2s; jw til ld 11; grad drew clr frm 14; in comm frm nxt*		1
700[R]	**Rody (IRE)**(bl) 14-1 **D Mansell** *Disp ld to 9; cl 2nd 13; completely outpcd frm nxt*	30	2
731[4]	**Ron Miel (IRE)** 10-1 **M Hooper** *Imm outpcd; still wl bhnd ½way; stdy prog to tk 3rd 2 out*	15	3
588[3]	Abitofahike (IRE) 14-1 A Martin *Ld/disp to ½way; wknd frm 13; wl bhnd when pu 2 out*		P
517[P]	A Proper Charlie 14-1 T Stephenson *Hdwy & prom 10-12; wknd frm 15 til pu last*		P
644[P]	Busmans Holiday (IRE) 20-1 S Coady *Completely t.o by 14 til pu 3 out*		P
	Cash On Demand 20-1 Miss H Bevan *Ref to start*		r
731[P]	Contrary King 8-1 T Weston *Prom to 11; grad wknd; pu 15*		P
588[P]	Dun Aengus 12-1 M Wall *Short-lived eff to ldrs app 14; wknd & pu last*		P
621[P]	Himalayan Heights(cp) 6-1 R Rogers *Sn bhnd & nd; t.o & pu 2 out*		P
	Isefoul De Bellevue (FR) 10-1 J Horton *7th ½way; disp 4/6th when pu last*		P
627[4]	Lord Of Heaven (USA) 4-1 Miss K Cuthbertson *Rr by 2; t.o ½way; pu 2 out*		P
	Mr Kent 14-1 J Trice-Rolph *Lsng tch w ldrs when pu 13*		P
	Pipers Boy 20-1 D Morris *Ref 1*		r
580[5]	Port Valenska (IRE)(cp) 10-1 M Harris *Prom til wknd qckly 9; 30l detach by 13; t.o & pu 2 out*		P
627[P]	Winleah 12-1 T Lane *A bhnd til pu 12*		P

OFFICIAL DISTANCES: dist, 12*l* **TIME:** 6min 51.0s

Cumberland Farmers

Dalston (RH 8F,18J)

Sun, 4 Apr (GOOD)

761 Hunt Members, 12st — 4 ran

654[4]	**TOUCHEZ DU BOIS (IRE)**(cp) 5-2 **T Morrison** *Ld/disp; mist 9; hdd 11; ld agn nxt; drew 10l clr aft 2 out; unchall*		1
	Valley Garden 4-6F **R Nichol** *Ld/disp; ½l 2nd 7; ld brief 11; hrd rdn 15; no resp & sn btn; 15l down & jmpd slow last*	20	2
216[P]	French Chocolate (5a) 8-1 K Anderson *Nt a fluent; chsd ldrs; blun 1; 10l last & rmdrs aft nxt; 3l 3rd 5; blun bad & nrly fell 10; 8l last & outpcd 14; 20l last when pu 3 out*		P
286[6]	Steady Lass (IRE) (5a) 4-1 D Jewett *Ld/disp at suicidal pce til paddled 3 & ur*		U

OFFICIAL DISTANCE: 20*l* **TIME:** 6min 31.7s

762 Intermediate, 12st — 9 ran

427[P]	**SHARPAMAN**(bl) 6-1 **C Shirley-Beavan** *Ld til hdd 6; ld agn 9; 1l up nxt; 1l up & mist 15; 3l up 2 out; stayed on*		1
349[6]	**Snooty Eskimo (IRE)** 2-1F **H Norton** *Cl up; 2l 4th 4; 4l 5th 12; 3l 3rd & ev ch 3 out; 10l 4th & outpcd nxt; kpt on wl app last; fin 3rd; promoted*	7½	2

427^{3}	**Ben From Ketton** 5-1 **S J Robinson** *Prom; disp 4l 4th app 9; outpcd frm 3 out; fin 4th; promoted*	6	3
	How Burn 3-1 Mrs V Jackson *Prom early; sn in tch in rr; outpcd 12; 8l last app 15; kpt on app last*	8	5
507^{3}	Hadaway Lad 5-1 A Findlay *Prom; ld brief 4; 3l 3rd 8; 2l 2nd 3 out; outpcd nxt; 5l down app last; rdn out flat; fin $2\frac{1}{2}$l 2nd; disq - nt weigh-in*		2d
678^{U}	Ballymenagh (IRE) 6-1 S Huggan *In tch; 6l 8th 5; outpcd 13; wkng in 10l last 3 out; t.o & pu last*		P
268^{P}	General Gem 10-1 R Morgan *Prom; ld 6; hdd 9; wknd 10; 10l last 12; pu 13*		P
	Tartan Rising (7a, 3ow) 4-1 C Dawson *Lw; sis; a rr; nt a fluent; 20l last app 2; sn detach; t.o 9; mist 11 & nrly fell; pu aft*		P
658^{1}	The Cincinnati Kid 7-1 M Thompson *(xnb) Oht; mid-div; 5l 6th aft 7; outpcd 15; wknd qckly aft nxt; t.o & pu last*		P

OFFICIAL DISTANCES: Originally $2\frac{1}{2}$l, 6l, 5l **TIME:** 6min 17.4s

Hadaway Lad finished second but was disqualified when the rider failed to weigh-in; he was fined £55

763 Ladies Open — 8 ran

655^{3}	**BALISTEROS (FR)** 11-10F **Miss J Williams** *Prom; 3l 4th 5; cl 2nd mostly til ld app 2 out; sn clr; 10l up & mist last; comf.*		1
682^{3}	**Supercharmer** 3-1 **Miss J Riding** *Ld; mist 2; 1l up 3 out; hdd app nxt; sn brushed aside*	10	2
550^{2}	**Dere Street** 5-2 **Miss R Davidson** *Trckd ldrs; 2l 2nd 5; disp 1l 2nd 11; outpcd & 12l 4th aft 3 out; mod 3rd nxt; kpt on wl flat; nt trble ldrs*	4	3
425^{3}	Knockholt 10-1 Miss A Pattinson *Mid-div; 6l 6th 11-12; outpcd app 3 out & sn no ch; kpt on one pce*	3	4
550^{4}	Miss Portcello (5a) 7-1 Mrs A Hamilton *In tch in rr; 5l 5th app 4; outpcd 15; wl bhnd 2 out*	4	5
655^{F}	Mr McDuff (IRE) 20-1 Miss J Hollands *(orbs) Cl up; 4l 4th 9; 2l 4th 11; 4l 3rd & jmpd rt 15; outpcd app 3 out; wknd qckly app nxt*	25	6
339^{P}	Deputy Leader (IRE) 10- Miss L Kendall *Bit bckwd; rr; 15l last 3; detach 7; mist 10; rmdrs aft nxt; sn t.o; fin v tired*	25	7
564^{4}	Dannicus 14-1 Miss C Metcalfe *Trckd ldr; disp 2l 2nd 5; lost plce 11; sn rdn & btn; t.o & pu 2 out; bbv.*		P

OFFICIAL DISTANCES: 10l, 5l, 2l **TIME:** 6min 11.1s

764 Mens Open, 12st — 17 ran

426^{3}	**RED GAUNTLET** 7-2 **K Anderson** *Made virt all; mist & hdd brief 14; hit 15; 1l up 3 out; prsd nxt; rdn & stayed on wl flat; wl rdn.*		1
551^{2}	**Dun Rose** (5a) 5-2F **R Morgan** *Lw; oht; prom; 3l 3rd 8; 1l 2nd 15; prsd ldr & ev ch 2 out; outpcd app last; rdn & no ex flat.*	3	2
431^{1}	**Three Spires** 3-1 **A Richardson** *Handy in 5/6th til 3l 3rd 3 out; outpcd aft 2 out; kpt on wl flat.*	1	3
509^{3}	Dream Of My Life (USA) 10-1 D Jewett *(xnb,orbs) Prom; hit 4; disp 5l 5th app 9; 4l 4th 2 out; kpt on one pce*	$\frac{1}{2}$	4
547^{2}	Crevamoy (IRE) (5a) 8-1 J Galbraith *Mid-div til outpcd 13; nd frm 15; kpt on; nvr really put in rce.*	6	5
	Batoutoftheblue 20-1 S Huggan *Mid-div til outpcd 12; sn nd; kpt on.*	$\frac{1}{2}$	6
656^{1}	Gaultier Gale (IRE) 12-1 A Findlay *Mid-div til outpcd 13; sn nd; kpt on*	6	7
678^{4}	Laganside (IRE) (7x) 20-1 J Muir *Prom til outpcd 11; wknd aft 15; sn wl bhnd*	6	8
547^{1}	Dr Deductible (7x)(cp) 7-1 R Brown *Prom; disp 5l 5th 9; outpcd 13; sn wl bhnd*	10	9
	Finest Of Men (4x) 4-1 J Walton *Rr; nvr btr than mid-div; t.o 15; btr for rce*	4	10
509^{5}	Wensley Blue (IRE) (7a) 20-1 W Goldie *Rr & mist 2; 15l last nxt; 15l 10th 11; sn t.o; kpt on wl flat*	$\frac{1}{2}$	11
	Boyup Brook (4x) 20-1 T Morrison *A rr; last 7; t.o 9; fnce bhnd 13; pu nxt*		P
654^{5}	Feeling Grand (IRE) 33-1 F Arthur *(xnb) Prom; 1l 2nd 5; outpcd 12; sn wknd; t.o & pu 2 out*		P
656^{4}	Just Whiskey (IRE) (7x) 10-1 C Shirley-Beavan *A rr; lost tch 10; t.o & pu 2 out*		P
282^{1}	Katinka (5a) 7-1 C Storey *(xnb) Handy; 4l 4th 8; prog to 2l 2nd 12; ld brief 14; sn wknd; wl bhnd when pu last.*		P
542^{r}	Royal Plum (7x)(bl) 25-1 S J Robinson *A rr; lost tch 10; 25l 14th nxt; t.o & pu 14*		P
542^{U}	Sean's Minstrel (IRE) 25-1 T Scott *A rr; wl bhnd 7; t.o 9; pu 14*		P

OFFICIAL DISTANCES: 5l, 2l, 2l **TIME:** 6min 13.2s

765 Restricted (Div 1), 12st — 11 ran

431F **BRIERY HILL** 7-1 **T Morrison** *(xnb) Opened 8s; 2 handlers; handy; disp 1l 2nd 3; outpcd 2 out; lft in slt ld last; hrd rdn & hdd brief flat; ld agn & hld on wl cl home* . . . 1

429² **Uncle Neil (IRE)** evensF **R Morgan** *Prom; disp 1l 2nd 3; 3l 2nd & rmdr aft 7; outpcd & rmdrs in 8l 4th 2 out; lft v cl 2nd & ev ch last; hrd rdn & ld flat; hdd u.p cl home* . . . s hd 2

Lucky Brush (IRE) 6-1 **J Alexander** *(bf) Mid-div; 5l 8th 3; stdy prog to 6l 3rd app 3 out; lft v cl 3rd & ev ch last; no ex flat* . . . 2 3

216³ Sweet Chestnut 8-1 Miss L Kendall *(xnb) Mid-div; 4l 4th 7; outpcd aft 14; one pce aft* . . . 25 4

657U Gudasmum (5a) 10-1 Miss R Davidson *(xnb) Ld; 1l up 3; 5l up 3 out; clr & in comm when rn thro lft hand wing last* . . . R

431P Harry's Mare (IRE) (5a) 10-1 Mrs J Hedley *(xnb) 1st ride; a rr; detach 2; t.o & pu aft 15* . . . P

Jupiter Jo 6-1 J Walton *Trckd ldrs; cl 3rd til 2l 2nd 14; ev ch til outpcd 3 out; wknd qckly & pu nxt* . . . P

Milbrig (5a) 10-1 Miss L Hislop *Rr; prog when fell 4* . . . F

Mrs Sherman (5a) 10-1 S Huggan *(xnb) Handy; 2 1/2l 4th 8; 4l 3rd aft nxt; bad mist & nrly ur 12; drpd to 15l 7th; t.o & pu 2 out* . . . P

136P Solway Saffy (5a) 14-1 C Storey *A rr; hit 9; strugg aft; 20l 9th & rdn 11; pu aft* P

563P Sylcanny (5a) 10-1 S Gibbon *2 handlers; oht; in tch; 3l 5th 8; 12l 8th & strugg 11; lost tch & pu 3 out* . . . P

OFFICIAL DISTANCES: s hd, 3/4l, dist **TIME:** 6min 18.2s

766 Restricted (Div 2), 12st — 14 ran

657U **ROYALECKO** 5-1 **Miss J Hollands** *Oht; trckd ldrs; 3l 3rd aft 7; ld 11; made rest; 3l up 15; went 10l clr aft nxt; idled & only 4l ahd app 2 out; stayed on wl when prsd aft* . . . 1

657F **Superstar Express (IRE)** 5-1 **A Findlay** *(xnb) Hld up in mid-div; 8l 5th & gng wl 11; gd prog to 7l 3rd 15 & 2l 2nd aft 2 out; no ex app last* . . . 8 2

564³ **Hessac (FR)** 4-1CF **Miss W Gibson** *Rr; bhnd 8; hit 10; stdy prog frm 12; kpt on wl to 3rd app last; nt trble ldng pr* . . . 8 3

653¹ Westie (5a) 4-1CF D Jewett *Lw; ld/disp; 1/2l 2nd 11; 3l 2nd 15; 10l 2nd & outpcd aft nxt; grad wknd* . . . 1 1/2 4

431P Distracting (5a) 4-1CF R Morgan *Mid-div; 4l 4th aft 7; 10l 4th 11; outpcd aft nxt; bhnd 3 out* . . . 2 5

430³ Distinct (IRE) 8-1 Miss J Crosier *A rr; wl bhnd 3 out* . . . nk 6

548⁵ Little John 9-2 J Galbraith *Chsd ldrs til mist & lost tch 13; btn 15 & sn t.o* 20 7

271U Bally Leader (IRE) 14-1 C Dawson *Mid-div; 6l 5th 9; outpcd 12 & 15l 6th nxt; sn wknd & lost tch; t.o & pu last* . . . P

510¹ Bay Of Dreams (7a) 5-1 K Anderson *(bf) Prom til hit 4; pu & dism aft; removed by horse ambulance* . . . P

432⁷ Mid Summer Lark (IRE) 12-1 Miss L Kendall *A rr; mist & nrly ur 1; hit 2; mist nxt & rdr lost iron; 20l last 4; lost tch & pu 8* . . . P

654r Olympic Storm (IRE) 5-1 J Alexander *(xnb) Ur start; reluct & virt ref to rce; trotted up embankment bef 1* . . . r

215F Seasmith 7-1 C Shirley-Beavan *Ld/disp til 5l 3rd 11-12; hit nxt; wknd qckly & pu 3 out* . . . P

548P Shylock (IRE) 12-1 S Huggan *Mid-div; outpcd aft 9; t.o & pu 15* . . . P

553⁴ St Bee 14-1 H Norton *Bit bckwd; a rr; t.o 9; pu 3 out* . . . P

OFFICIAL DISTANCES: 5l, 8l, 1l **TIME:** 6min 18.6s

767 Open Maiden 56&7yo (Div 1), 2m4f, 12st - 15J — 12 ran

433³ **SWEEPING STORM (IRE)** 5-1 **C Dawson** *A handy; 8l 3rd 5; prog to 1l 2nd 3 out; chall last; rdn clr flat; quite comf; rdr gave victory salute* . . . 1

433P **Tight Fisted Benny (IRE)** 3-1 **R Morgan** *Ld rnd start; ld; 3l up 4; 1l ahd 3 out; hrd prsd & hdd last; nt qckn flat* . . . 5 2

433⁵ **More Flair** (5a) 6-1 **J Walton** *Opened 7s; sn trckng ldrs; 12l 5th 10; 15l 3rd & outpcd 2 out; kpt on wl; nt rch ldrs* . . . 1 1/2 3

549² Stanwick Gypsy (5a) 4-1 Miss M Neill *Prom til 6l 3rd 3 out; 10l 4th & outpcd nxt; kpt on; no ex flat* . . . 5 4

338P Given Grace (IRE) (5a) 12-1 J Davis *In tch til outpcd aft 8; t.o 10* . . . 1 1/2fs 5

	Dom Pilippe (FR) 14-1 R Nichol *A rr; jmpd slow & lost ground most fncs til bhnd & pu 7; did some dressage practice in centre of track*		P
	Eastlands Rain (5a) 12-1 T Morrison *Green; a rr; jmpd slow 1; wl bhnd 8; t.o 11; pu aft nxt; subsq destroyed*		P
659^{F}	Hapthor (12a) 5-2F M Bennison *(xnb) Oht; prom til ur 3*		U
342^{4}	Jackofalltrades (IRE) 7-1 D Jewett *Oht; in tch; $8^{1}/_{2}$l 4th 5; ur 9*		U
658^{P}	Mystical Spot (5a) 9-2 K Anderson *In tch; 8l 4th 10; outpcd app 12; lost tch & pu 3 out*		P
	Ofcoursehekhan (IRE) 10-1 Miss N Stirling *(xnb) Rr early; pulled to trck ldr in 3l 2nd 4; nrly rn off course & virt pu app 9; 25l 7th aft nxt; lost tch & pu 13; improve*		P
	Teasdale House (IRE) (7a) 7-1 A Findlay *Lkd poor in coat; ld down; ur start; in tch; mist 2; fell 8*		F

OFFICIAL DISTANCES: 4*l*, $1^{1}/_{2}$*l*, 6*l* **TIME:** 5min 20.4s

768 Open Maiden 56&7yo (Div 2), 2m4f, 12st - 15J — 15 ran

549^{4}	**POSH STICK** (5a) 3-1F **J Walton** *9/2-3s; mid-div; prog to 3l 3rd 8-10; ld 3 out; drew clr app last; pushed out; easily*		1
659^{2}	**Jinful Du Grand Val (FR)** 9-2 **J Alexander** *(xnb) 2 handlers; ld to 3; handy 4th til outpcd 2 out; kpt on wl to poor 2nd flat*	15	2
553^{2}	**Birkwood** (7a) 9-2 **Miss M Neill** *Ld 6; bad mist nxt & nrly ur; hdd app 9; went 1l 2nd app 2 out; sn 3rd & outpcd; kpt on flat*	1	3
	General Jake (IRE) 10-1 J Innes *(xnb) Mid-div; bad mist & nrly ur 8; 5l 5th 10; sn outpcd; kpt on wl frm 3 out; btr for rce*	nk	4
554^{3}	Redhouse Chevalier (7a) 7-2 C Storey *(xnb) Prom; 4l 4th app 6; 1l 2nd 8; ld app 9; hdd 3 out; sn wknd*	3	5
554^{P}	Suny Henry 20-1 J Tate *(xnb) Chsd ldrs; 3l 2nd 2; 12l off pce & wkng 12; sn bhnd*	15	6
596^{4}	Deep Design (IRE) 10-1 C Dawson *Mid-div; 12l off pce & outpcd 12; sn bhnd*	2	7
	Muscadin 8-1 S Huggan *Mid-div; outpcd aft 12; t.o 2 out*	2	8
215^{P}	Ramon Allones (IRE) 14-1 Miss R Davidson *(xnb) A rr; wknd qckly 12; sn t.o*	3	9
432^{6}	Alice's Old Rose (5a) 16-1 T Scott *A rr; outpcd 10; bhnd 12; t.o & pu nxt*		P
549^{P}	Blackhill Princess (5a)(bl) 14-1 K Anderson *(xnb,bf) Mid-div; outpcd aft 8; t.o & pu 3 out*		P
	Good Thyne Charlie (IRE) (7a) 10-1 A Findlay *Rr; detach 5; lost tch & pu 6; dism*		P
	Inglemotte Miss (5a) 8-1 D Jewett *10s-8s; handy til outpcd 9; sn wknd; pu 3 out*		P
342^{F}	Ivory Cross 5-1 C Rae *In tch in rr til lost plce & pu aft 8*		P
343^{P}	Perky's Wish (IRE) 10-1 S J Robinson *(xnb) Ld 4 til hdd 6; sn wknd; lost tch & pu aft 12*		P

OFFICIAL DISTANCES: 15*l*, $^{1}/_{2}$*l*, $^{1}/_{2}$*l* **TIME:** 5min 19.5s

Middleton

Whitwell-on-the-Hill (RH 9F,18J)

Sun, 4 Apr (SOFT)

769 Hunt Members — 6 ran

377^{P}	**SCOTTISH ROOTS** 7-1 **O Greenall** *Hld up in rr; last to 11; went 8l 3rd 14; gd hdwy 15 to 3l 3rd 3 out; ld app nxt; rdly drew clr app last; rdr's 1st wnr*		1
503^{1}	**High Fields** (7a)(bl) 7-4F **T Greenall** *Rr; blun 2; pushed along 9; went 4l 3rd 11 & 3l 2nd 15; disp ld 3 out-nxt; wknd & outpcd app last*	6	2
689^{2}	**Howya Matey (IRE)** 4-1 **B Woodhouse** *Tk keen hld; ld to 15; jnd & pushed along 16; wknd & v tired by nxt*	20	3
679^{2}	Flat Top 7-2 Miss J Coward *Cl up; 2l 3rd 5; hdwy to disp ld 10 til rn out 12; rtrcd; cont 2 fncs adrift*	2fncs	4
478^{4}	Folliday (FR)(bl) 66-1 R Wakeham *Cl 2nd to 5; disp ld 6-7; in tch til blun & fell 10; collapsed in box park; dead*		F
	Multi Franchise 10-1 S Charlton *Handy in 5l 4th to 11; wknd 12; sn last & pushed along; t.o & pu 16*		P

OFFICIAL DISTANCES: 8*l*, 12*l* **TIME:** 6min 48.0s

770 Confined — 12 ran

436[1] **GOLDEN CHIMES (USA)** 7-2 **G Tuer** *Hld up in mid-div; hdwy 7 to 2nd 9; ld 14; sn qcknd clr; stayed on wl* 1

440[P] **Canterbury Jack (IRE)**(vis) 3-1 **A Farrant** *Mid-div til hdwy 9; 8l 2nd 11; disp ld 13-15; easily outpcd by wnr; kpt on* 5 2

389[U] **Chaos Theory** 25-1 **D Thomas** *A mid-div; went 15l 5th 15; stayed on past btn horses; fin str; nrst fin* 4 3

340[P] Badge Of Fame (IRE) 33-1 P Kinsella *(xnb) Cl 2nd/3rd to 6; handy til wknd frm 11; t.o & pu 15* ...... P

71[4] Ledgendry Line 8-1 Miss S Brotherton *Midfield; wknd & lsng tch 14; t.o & pu 15* ...... P

391[P] Mr McDuck (IRE) 10-1 L Bates *Mid-div; went 12l 5th 10; pushed along & outpcd 14; poor 4th when clambered over 2 out & imm pu* ...... P

501[P] Rosey Boy (IRE) 33-1 N Tutty *Prom in 3l 3rd to 6; wknd rap aft 7; rr & lsng tch 9; t.o 13; pu 15* ...... P

445[4] Royal Crimson 33-1 R Alers-Hankey *Cl up to 6; went 20l 2nd 8; pushed along 10; 8l 4th 11; wknd frm 13; rem when pu 3 out* ...... P

501[P] Sign Of The Tiger 33-1 R Clark *A rr; lost tch aft 9; t.o & pu 11* ...... P

481[1] Ten Bob (IRE) 2-1F N Saville *Hld up in rr; last to 3; blun 7; hdwy 9; disp ld 13-15; pushed along & rmdrs aft; wknd qckly & pu 3 out; disapp.* ...... P

478[3] The Graduate 4-1 S Walker *(xnb) Bit bckwd; sn clr; 20l up frm 5; jnd 14; wknd qckly; pu 15* ...... P

479[P] What A Fuss 33-1 Miss J Coward *A rr; lost tch aft 5; pushed along 7; t.o 14; pu 3 out* ...... P

OFFICIAL DISTANCES: 6*l*, 6*l* **TIME:** 6min 46.0s

771 Restricted, 12st — 10 ran

499[1] **DOLPHIN SQUARE (IRE)** 7-1 **N Saville** *Mid-div early; hdwy 12 to 5l 4th 14; ld 2 out; clr last; stayed on str* 1

Hellodock (IRE) 20-1 **B Woodhouse** *Jw; hld up & last til hdwy 14; 6l 5th 15; gd hdwy to disp ld 3 out-nxt; 3rd & outpcd app last; rallied & stayed on str to snatch 2nd* 5 2

494[1] **Euwiluwil (IRE)** 6-4F **A Farrant** *(boh) Handy til disp ld 8; ld nxt-3 out; sn outpcd; 2nd app last; hrd rdn & dem flat* 1/2 3

591[3] Lights On 8-1 M Manton *Ld to 8; cl up to 13; 6l 4th 15; outpcd app 3 out & poor 4th nxt* 15 4

481[P] Blue Bud(vis) 50-1 W Burnell *Mid-div to 11; rr by 14; plodded on one pce* 10 5

684[3] Don Rio (IRE) 20-1 M Morley *Prom early; cl 2nd to 9; pushed along & wknd 11; lsng ground when fell 12* ...... F

481[P] Gentleman Charles (IRE) 25-1 S Walker *Prom early; rr by 12; pushed along & lsng tch 14; t.o & pu 3 out* ...... P

481[2] Glensan (IRE) 8-1 G Brewer *(xnb) Prom when rn out 3* ...... R

392[1] Sevensider (IRE) 7-4 T Greenall *Mid-div to 8; went 8l 6th 15; pushed along & outpcd app 3 out; t.o & exhaust when pu last* ...... P

564[U] Wandering Wild (5a)(cp) 33-1 Mrs L Ward *(xnb) Handy 4th til 2nd 4-7; disp ld 13-14; outpcd & wkng when fell 15* ...... F

OFFICIAL DISTANCES: 4*l*, 1/2*l* **TIME:** 6min 50.0s

772 Mixed Open (Grimthorpe Gold Cup), 4m1f, 12st - 24J — 17 ran

542[1] **SAD MAD BAD (USA)** 6-4F **G Tuer** *Midfield to 8; rr by 10; prog 14 to 8l 8th 19; cruised up to disp ld 3 out; ld app nxt; qcknd app last; stayed on str* 1

429[F] **Dorans Magic** 5-1 **Miss A Armitage** *Cl 2nd til disp ld 9-10; clr 2nd 16; disp ld 3 out; sn outpcd; 3rd app last; stayed on to 2nd flat; nt trble wnr* 5 2

593[P] **Clonshire Paddy (IRE)** 14-1 **T Greenall** *Nt jw in rr; hdwy 16 to 7th 20; stayed on to disp 2nd 3 out-last; wknd flat* 3 3

501[3] Mr Pendleberry(vis) 8-1 N Tinkler *Rr to 16; hdwy to 8th 20; stayed on one pce to 4th app last; nvr nrr* 4 4

541[4] Mighty Willing 8-1 G Brewer *Rr to 8; hdwy to 5l 4th 12 & cl 3rd 19; ld 21 til jnd & wknd app 2 out* 1/2 5

630[P] Cimarrone Cove (IRE) 7-1 O Greenall *In tch; handy 5th 9; went cl 3rd 16; in tch til pushed along & wknd frm 20* 2 6

501[4] Erzadjan (IRE) 12-1 L Bates *A mid-div; outpcd 19; stayed on one pce; nvr able to chall* 1 7

542[3] Who Dares Wins 5-1 P Kinsella *Cl 4th to 8; 12l 8th 11; in tch til outpcd 21; r.o one pce* 8 8

592^{4}	Princess Derry (5a) 33-1 B Woodhouse *Midfield to 14; in tch to 18; pushed along & outpcd 20; r.o one pce*	4	9
562^{3}	Baby John (IRE) 100-1 Miss L Horner *A last; t.o when pu 20*		P
477^{1}	Claire's Nomad(cp) 7-1 Miss Rachel Clark *Prom; ld frm 7-17; wknd 19; qckly lost tch aft; pu 21*		P
712^{4}	Donnegale (IRE)(bl) 20-1 Miss J Foster *Prom to 9; 4l 4th 11; in tch w ldrs; grad wknd frm 17; t.o & pu 21*		P
$488^{1\dagger}$	I Am Said I (IRE) 12-1 A Farrant *Mid-div to 14; hdwy to cl 4th 16; wknd frm 21; wl bhnd & v tired when pu last*		P
591^{4}	Mandate Man (IRE) 100-1 D Thomas *Cl up; 2l 3rd 6; in tch til wknd 13; rr 14; grad lost tch; pu 19*		P
565^{P}	Notation (IRE) 100-1 S Charlton *Ld to 6; cl 3rd/4th to 12; sn wknd; t.o & pu 18*		P
	Rubon Prince (IRE) 100-1 R Clark *A rr div; t.o & pu 15*		P
562^{2}	Welsh March (IRE) 33-1 N Tutty *Mid-div to 12; rr by 18; lost tch; rem when pu 21*		P

OFFICIAL DISTANCES: 6*l*, 4*l* **TIME:** 9min 31.0s

773 Dodson & Horrell PPORA Club Members Maiden 56&7yo (Div 1), 2m4f88y, 12st - 15J 10 ran

393^{S}	**DEVIL'S PERK (IRE)** 5-4F **T Glass** *Cl up to 5; 4l 3rd 8; ld 9; qcknd clr 2 out; blun last; gd rec; stayed on wl*		1
271^{P}	**Search Party (FR)** (7a) 20-1 **S Walker** *Hld up rr; last by 7; hdwy to 4th 11; stayed on past btn horses to 2nd 2 out; no ch w wnr*	8	2
596^{3}	**Civil Gent (IRE)** (7a) 8-1 **G Brewer** *Ld to 8; mist 9; chsd ldr in 2l 2nd to 3 out; sn wknd*	12	3
500^{5}	Just A Lady (5a) 20-1 B Woodhouse *Last & lsng tch 9; t.o 10; plodded on.*	15	4
500^{F}	Alizarin (IRE) (12a) 8-1 T Craggs *Cl up; 5th 5; went 2l 3rd 7; in tch til wknd 9; t.o & pu 12*		P
	Black Leopard (IRE) (7a) 2-1 A Farrant *Rr to 9; hdwy 11; cruised up to cl 2nd 3 out; wknd qckly & pu 2 out*		P
	Moraira (IRE) (7a) 6-1 N Tinkler *Mid-div & mist 6; pushed along 7; went 8l 6th 9; cl 3rd & blun 12; sn wknd; pu 2 out*		P
	Primitive Choice (5a) 8-1 L Bates *Sa; jmpd green; sn bhnd; rem when clambered over 6 & pu*		P
394^{U}	Supreme Vintage (IRE) 10-1 R Wakeham *Cl 4th to 6; 5l 5th 9; pushed along & hld in 5th when ur 12*		U
272^{P}	Three Way Split 20-1 Miss Rachel Clark *Tk keen hld; pulled to cl 3rd 2 & 1l 2nd 8; pushed along & wknd 10; t.o & pu 12*		P

OFFICIAL DISTANCES: 10*l*, 12*l* **TIME:** 5min 49.0s

774 Dodson & Horrell PPORA Club Members Maiden 56&7yo (Div 2), 2m4f88y, 12st - 15J 10 ran

504^{4}	**KARINGA LEAP** 7-1 **P Cornforth** *Handy in mid-div to 4; went 5l 5th 8-11; ld app 3 out; clr nxt; r.o wl*		1
	Magic Route (IRE) 12-1 **Miss T Jackson** *(xnb) Cl 3rd to 5 & 3l 3rd 11; disp ld 12-2 out; one pce aft*	5	2
343^{2}	**Shirostran** evensF **P Kinsella** *Handy 2nd/3rd to 8; ld 10 til jnd 3 out; wknd; 4th app last; rallied & tk 3rd flat*	8	3
563^{6}	Oaklands Ted 12-1 T Glass *A handy; 1l 2nd 11; 3l 3rd 2 out-last; wknd bad & dem 4th flat*	8	4
	Biddy (12a) 14-1 N Smith *A last; t.o 12; poor 5th 2 out*	15	5
476^{P}	Billymax (IRE) 6-1 R Wakeham *Ld; jnd 9-10; 5l 4th 11; sn wknd; t.o & pu 2 out*		P
165^{P}	Littleton Zeus (IRE) (7a) 10-1 N Tutty *Mid-div when blun & ur 9*		U
393^{P}	Quel Regal (FR) 8-1 Miss Rachel Clark *Mid-div til mist 6; sn rr; bd 8*		B
392^{U}	Raggy Jumper 10-1 L Bates *A bhnd; last 5; lost tch; t.o 12; pu 2 out*		P
	Springbok Noodles (7a, 2ow) 12-1 P Frank *Reluct to start; sa; ref 1*		r

OFFICIAL DISTANCES: 6*l*, 8*l* **TIME:** 6min 05.0s

775 Confined Maiden (Div 1), 12st 9 ran

271^{3}	**OAKLANDS LUIS** (7a, 3ow) 8-1 **T Glass** *Cl up; ld frm 3; jnd 2 out & lkd hld til btr j last; rdn & hld on wl.*		1
	Forty Shakes (IRE) (7a) 10-1 **L Bates** *Mid-div to 8; cl 3rd 11; sn 1l 2nd; ld 2 out; 3l up when blun last & came to standstill; event rallied & just failed*	1	2

Edstone (IRE) 25-1 R Clark *Mid-div to 3; last by 5; t.o & pu 13* . . . . P

505[3] Just A Man 8-1 B Woodhouse *Handy in mid-div to 7; went 2l 3rd 11 & 8l 4th 3 out; wknd & tired rap; pu 2 out* . . . . P

485[2] Prioritisation (IRE) (7a) 4-6F A Farrant *Cl 2nd til lost plce 9; went cl 2nd agn 11-13; pushed along 14; 15l 4th 3 out; t.o & pu 2 out* . . . . P

Queenies Girl (5a) 20-1 P Frank *A rr; stayed on to poor 3rd & clambered exhaust over 2 out; imm pu* . . . . P

476[3] Ravenscar 5-1 S Walker *Handy til disp ld 8-9; went 1l 2nd 11; in tch til outpcd 15; 10l 3rd 3 out; poor 3rd & exhausted when pu 2 out* . . . . P

Sea Princess (5a) 20-1 N Tutty *Mid-div to 6; mist 7 & rr by 10; bad mist 11; t.o & pu 13* . . . . P

505[2] Staple Sound 10-1 W Burnell *Ld to 2; in tch til wknd 6; last by 10; t.o 14; pu 2 out* . . . . P

OFFICIAL DISTANCE: 1*l* **TIME:** 7min 11.0s

776 Confined Maiden (Div 2), 12st — 11 ran

395[F] **SAMS WAY** 5-4F **P Kinsella** *Handy 4th to 8; went 1l 2nd 10 til disp ld 14; qcknd 5l clr 15; jnd 3 out; drew 3l clr at last; stayed on wl* 1

679[P] **Rising Talisker** (5a)(cp) 7-1 **R Clark** *Mid-div to 8; went 5l 5th 11; hdwy to 2l 3rd 3 out-nxt; outpcd by wnr app last* 5 2

Duchess Account (5a) 10-1 **R Wakeham** *Rn green in rr early; gd hdwy 11 to cl 2nd 15; disp ld gng wl 3 out; wknd & tired app last; coaxed home; sure to improve & should win* 10 3

482[4] Bankersdraft 7-1 M Morley *Cl up; went 1l 2nd 9; in tch to 14; 4l 4th 15; grad lost tch & poor 4th by last* 8 4

Cloigeann Rua (IRE) (5a) 20-1 S Charlton *(xnb) Oht; swtng bad; sn clr; 20l up to 8; wknd 9; sn t.o; pu 11* . . . . P

French Venture 7-2 B Woodhouse *(xnb) Rr when ur 5* . . . . U

344[P] Iron Trooper (IRE) 10-1 T Glass *A rr; last & lsng tch 12; t.o by 15; pu 3 out* P

342[6] Jobee Jack 33-1 T Craggs *(xnb) Rr early; hdwy to 6l 5th 7 & 2l 3rd 10; outpcd & wknd 13; sn pu* . . . . P

685[P] Milliners Guide (5a) 14-1 G Brewer *(xnb) A rr; lost tch 11; poor 5th when pu 2 out* P

Nought To Ninety 14-1 L Bates *A last; t.o by 8; pu 11* . . . . P

714[2] Thixendale (5a)(cp) 7-1 Miss J Foster *Cl up; ld 9-13; sn wknd aft 14; t.o & pu 3 out* . . . . P

OFFICIAL DISTANCES: 5*l*, 8*l* **TIME:** 7min 04.0s

Old Surrey, Burstow & West Kent

Penshurst (LH 7F,18J)

Sun, 4 Apr (HOLDING, GOOD in places)

777 Hunt Members — 5 ran

631[U] **KING OF THE DAWN** 5-1 **J Sole** *Made all; narrow advant most of way til drew clr aft 2 out* 1

420[3] **Esprit De Cotte (FR)** 4-5F **P York** *A prsng wnr; pushed along 14; hrd rdn frm 3 out; 3l down 2 out; wknd app last; eased flat* 12 2

348[P] **Silver Lake (IRE)** 8-1 **Miss K Pegram** *Detach last most of way; lost tch 9; lft rem 3rd aft 12; sn t.o* . . . . fence 3

611[F] Lightning Rebel 10-1 S Gordon-Watson *In tch in 4th til wknd 8; lft v dist 4th aft 12; t.o & pu 15* . . . . P

419[2] The Grey Baron(tt) 7-4 P Bull *Chsd ldrs in 4-6l 3rd til wknd aft 11; 12l adrift when pu aft 12* . . . . P

OFFICIAL DISTANCES: 12*l*, dist **TIME:** 7min 18.0s **TOTE:** £5.30; places £1.60,£1.90 **DF:**£4.80

The stewards interviewed the rider of The Grey Baron who was pulled up; they accepted his explanation that the horse 'was never going properly'

778 PPORA Club Members Conditions, 12st — 8 ran

541[P] **TOD'S BROTHER** 5-1 **A Merriam** *Midfield; blun 8; 11l 5th aft 10; hdwy to 6l 4th 12; sn rdn along but no further prog; mist 15; chsd ldng pr frm 3 out; lft 12l 2nd nxt; kpt on to jn ldr last; ld & drew clr flat* 1

610[1] **Endeavour (FR)** (7x) 6-4F **G Cooper** *A.p; trckd ldr frm 7 til ld 15; hdd brief nxt; disp ld when lft 12l clr 2 out; nt r.o; jnd & jmpd slow last; sn hdd & no ex* 4 2

345U Acuteangle (IRE) (5a) 16-1 P Hall *Chsd ldr to 7; sn wknd; 23l 8th aft 10; pu nxt* . . . . . P
717⁴ Angus Airways (IRE) 16-1 M Legge *A rr; 17l 6th aft 10; t.o 13 til pu 15* . . . . . P
607P Glenmont (IRE) 16-1 Ms L Stock *Prom to 4; sn lost plce; 19l 7th aft 10; t.o 12 til pu 15* . . . . . P
607¹ Lively Lord (IRE) (7x)(cp,tt) 3-1 C Gordon *Ld til hdd 15; 6l 3rd 3 out; wknd rap; 4th & no ch when pu nxt* . . . . . P
537P Nubro (IRE) 12-1 A Hickman *Midfield; 9l 4th aft 10; 5th & wkng when pu aft 11* . . . . . P
632¹ Rhythm King 5-2 G Maundrell *Midfield; cl 3rd frm 8 til impd to ld 3 out; sn jnd; w ldr when rn thro wing 2 out; unlucky* . . . . . R

OFFICIAL DISTANCE: 4l **TIME:** 7min 16.0s **TOTE:** £6.60; places £2.70,£1.90 **DF:**£7.40

779 Restricted, 12st — 8 ran

421P **RIVER BAILIFF (IRE)**(cp) 8-1 **P York** *Hld up; last to 7; 12l 5th aft 10; impd to trck ldrs 12; ld aft 15; 5l clr 2 out; jnd last; hrd rdn & sn ld agn flat; all out* — 1
716¹ **Kilvoydan (IRE)** 9-2 **D Phelan** *Trckd ldr til disp ld frm 8; ld 12-15; 6l 3rd 3 out; rallied to 5l 2nd nxt; hrd rdn to jn wnr last; no ex flat* . . . . . 1 — 2
539¹ Balau (7a) 11-4F P Bull *Midfield; 10l 3rd aft 10; hdwy to press ldr 13; blun 15; dived at 3 out; 6l 3rd & wkng when fell 2 out; winded bad & down 10mins* . . . . . F
419P Battle Honours 10-1 F Wheeler *Prom to 6; sn lost plce; 19l 8th aft 10; wl bhnd when pu 12* . . . . . P
605⁴ Kniveniven (IRE) 14-1 Mrs J Gordon *Midfield; 11l 4th aft 10; sn wknd; pu 12* — P
559F Magic Lodge (7a) 4-1 R Stearn *In tch; 13l 6th aft 10; wknd 13; no ch when pu 15* . . . . . P
720² Native Spin (IRE) 5-1 D Dennis *Ld; jnd 8 til hdd aft 11; jb rt 13; sn wknd; wl bhnd when pu 15* . . . . . P
534¹ Phar Afield (IRE) 7-2 J Sole *A towards rr; 16l 7th aft 10; lsng tch when pu 13* — P

OFFICIAL DISTANCE: ¾l **TIME:** 7min 22.0s
TOTE: £23.60; places £4.90,£8.40 **DF:**£5.60 (1+any)

The stewards enquired into the improved form of the winner; they accepted the connections' explanation that the horse had been dropped in class and different tactics had been employed to enable him to get the trip

780 Mens Open — 6 ran

642U **CEDAR CHIEF**(bl) 7-1 **J Merry** *Made all; 10l clr aft 10; nvr seriously chall; stayed on wl frm 3 out* 1
535³ **Real Value (IRE)** 9-4 **P Hall** *A 2nd/3rd; 14l 3rd aft 10; pushed along & chsd wnr frm 13; slt hdwy to 6l 2nd app 3 out; kpt on one pce & nvr able to chall* — 8 — 2
609¹ **Struggles Glory (IRE)** 4-5F **D Robinson** *Hld up; 22l 4th aft 10; impd to 12l 2nd 12; no further prog; lost 2nd aft 13; wknd aft 15; no ch frm 3 out* . — 30 — 3
626³ Toscanini (GER) 12-1 M Legge *Last most of way; 24l 5th aft 10; nvr gt nr ldrs* — 6 — 4
Lord George(cp) 12-1 G Gallagher *In tch til wknd 8; 34l 6th aft 10; pu 11* — P
Majadou (FR) 5-1 P Bull *Chsd wnr frm 5; 10l down aft 10; sn wknd; 5th & no ch when pu 13* . . . . . P

OFFICIAL DISTANCES: 8l, dist **TIME:** 7min 18.0s **TOTE:** £8.60; places £2.10,£1.60 **DF:**£12.40

The stewards fined the rider of Lord George £65 for using the whip with excessive force and frequency

781 Ladies Open — 10 ran

543P **SHERIFF'S FRIEND (IRE)** 4-7F **Mrs J Gordon** *Last to 4; sn cl up; prsd ldr 10 til ld app 2 out; rdn clr flat* 1
649² **Fair Kiowa (IRE)** 9-2 **Mrs S Hodge** *A.p; cl 3rd frm 14; went 2nd & chall app last; kpt on one pce flat* . . . . . 5 — 2
421⁴ **Storm Castle (IRE)** 6-1 **Miss J Wickens** *A in tch; hdwy to ld 14; hdd app 2 out; no ex app last* . . . . . 2 — 3
641² Dick McCarthy (IRE) 4-1 Mrs S Ashby *Cl up til ld 7-13; back into cl 4th nxt; prsd ldrs til fdd app 2 out* . . . . . 4 — 4
Commasarris 16-1 Miss F Hatfield *Mist & lost irons 4; pu nxt* . . . . . P
608P Forest Run Forest(bl) 20-1 Miss A Sansom *W ldrs to 10; lost tch qckly aft nxt; pu 13* . . . . . P
610⁵ Graphic Designer (IRE) 20-1 Miss H Gordon *In tch til wknd 9; wl bhnd when pu 11* . . . . . P

536^{U} Irish Sea (USA) 8-1 Mrs P Hall *Prom til pu aft 11* . . . . P
719^{2} Newby End (IRE)(vis) 16-1 Miss C Cowe *Wl in tch til wknd 11; t.o & pu 14* P
4^{P} Red Channel (IRE) 20-1 Miss B Donnelly *Ld to 6; sn wknd; wl bhnd when pu 11* P

OFFICIAL DISTANCES: 2*l*, 3*l* **TIME:** 7min 17.0s
TOTE: £2.80; places £1.60,£4.50,£1.40 **DF:**£11.10

782 Open Maiden, 12st - 16J 15 ran

627^{2} **MIDNIGHT LORD (IRE)** 5-2CF **J Pemberton** *A in tch; hdwy 9; ld 11; made rest in narrow ld; jmpd slow & rmdrs 3 out; drew clr app last* 1
345^{P} **Highfield's Clover** (7a) 5-2CF **C Gordon** *In tch in 4/5th most of way; stayed on frm 2 out to chse wnr app last; kpt on one pce flat* 6 2
539^{F} **Gale On The Lake (IRE)** (5a) 9-2 **P Hall** *A.p; chsd ldng pr frm 5; hdwy to press wnr app 2 out; wknd app last* 4 3
Sugar Toi (5a) 14-1 D Brightling *Midfield; hdwy 10; jnd wnr brief aft 3 out; wknd app nxt* 8 4
611^{U} Almazard 25-1 Mrs J Gordon *Midfield til fell 7* . . . . F
534^{5} Amandas Fancy (IRE) (5a) 25-1 Miss K Keefe *Rr when somersaulted & crashing fall 1; dead* . . . . F
423^{P} Cerasus Knight (IRE) 25-1 J Morgan *A towards rr; lost tch aft 8; wl bhnd when pu 10* . . . . P
639^{U} Ginger Sprout (IRE) (5a) 8-1 C Thomson *Ld; 6-10l clr frm 2-9; hdd & mist 11; wknd rap; pu 13* . . . . P
539^{P} Iconic 7-1 D Page (Kent) *A towards rr; lost tch aft 8; wl bhnd when pu 12* . P
611^{P} Naughty Noah 14-1 G Gallagher *A.p; chsd ldr frm 7; mist 9; prsd wnr frm 11 til wknd qckly app 3 out; exhaust when fell last* . . . . F
580^{2} Pandeli 10-1 D Phelan *Chsd ldr to 7; wknd 11; no ch when pu 13* . . . . . . P
539^{3} Royal Cruise (IRE) 5-2CF P York *Swtng; hld up in midfield; some hdwy in 6th 12; no further prog; wknd 3 out; pu nxt* . . . . P
Sawbridge(tt) 25-1 G Wigley *A rr; blun 7; wl bhnd when pu 10* . . . . P
Selfcertified (7a) 20-1 P Bull *Tkn stdly; in tch towards rr til fdd 11; pu 13.* P
611^{P} Seymour Of Me 10-1 J Merry *Tkn v stdly; detach last to 7; rr when ur 11* . U

OFFICIAL DISTANCES: 2*l*, 2*l* **TIME:** 7min 30.0s
TOTE: £12.30; places £3.80,£2.40,£2.80 **DF:**£17.70

Fences 8 & 15 omitted - fallen horse

Pytchley

Guilsborough (LH 8F,19J)
Sun, 4 Apr (GOOD)

783 Hunt Members 7 ran

384^{1} **COOLEFIND (IRE)** 4-7F **S Morris** *Hld up in rr; blun 7; clsng when mists 10 & 12; cl 3rd nxt; drvn aft 15; ld app 2 out; drew clr flat* 1
379^{4} **My Best Buddy** 3-1 **R Cope** *Cl 2nd til ld & nt fluent 13 & 15; rdn & hdd app 2 out; one pce & sn dem 3rd; went 2nd agn last; no ch w wnr* 8 2
374^{2} **Teeton Priceless** (5a) 5-1 **P Cowley** *Slt ld to 13; 2nd/3rd & ev ch til rdn & nt qckn 2 out; jmpd slow & dem last* 1 3
583^{6} Tale Bridge (IRE)(cp) 40-1 J Russell *Reluct & sn last; t.o 9* 150y 4
Hostetler 40-1 T Messenger *Nt fluent 3; towards rr; hit 5; outpcd 8; 15l 5th 11; pu 12* . . . . P
556^{3} Merry Minstrel (IRE) 20-1 N Pearce *Cl 3rd/4th to 13; wkng when jmpd slow 15; t.o when crashed over 2 out & pu* . . . . P
589^{9} Sixes And Sevens (IRE) (5a) 40-1 G Kerr *Chsd ldrs; pckd bad 6; wknd 9; 20l 6th 11; fell hvly nxt* . . . . F

OFFICIAL DISTANCES: 6*l*, ¾*l* **TIME:** 6min 39.0s **TOTE:** £1.50 **DF:**£3.70

784 Confined, 12st 13 ran

528^{1} **SHINY BAY (IRE)** (5x) 7-2 **N Pearce** *Nt fluent early; hld up; prog when mist 11; 3l 3rd app 13; ld 15; sn drvn; outj rival 2 out to forge clr; stayed on wl; all out.* 1
481^{2d} **Coole Glen (IRE)** (3x) 3-1F **S Morris** *Ld 3-15; prsd wnr til rdn & outj 2 out; sn btn; tired when jmpd slow last* 8 2
583^{3} **Bullfinch**(vis) 8-1 **P Cowley** *Tchd 10s; cl up til mists 6 & 11; 12l 4th & outpcd app 13; 15l 5th app 3 out; plodded on but no ch w ldrs* 8 3

	Emperor Roscoe 5-1 R Armson *Opened 6s; lw; hld up in rr; 15l 6th & prog app 13; went 3rd 15; flatt brief app 3 out; sn wknd; promising re-appearance*	3	4
249[4]	Topical Tip (IRE) 16-1 Mrs E Chugg *A wl bhnd; t.o 13; stayed on frm 2 out; no ch w ldrs*	10	5
478[1]	Springlea Tower (6x) 7-2 R Hunnisett *Sn drpd to rr; hit 9; t.o 13; some late prog*	3	6
	Colombe D'Or 40-1 T Ellis *Bckwd; midfield; outpcd aft 12; poor 6th when pu 15*		P
379[7]	Crackrattle (IRE) 14-1 A Brown *Chsd ldrs; 5th 8; lkd strugg when hmpd & ur 12*		U
490[P]	Crown And Cushion 14-1 J Owen *Ld to 3; cl 2nd/3rd til outpcd app 15; 4th app 3 out; tired when pu nxt*		P
466[U]	Lord Of The Chase (IRE) 40-1 T Messenger *Towards rr; 9th 8; strugg when jmpd slow 10; t.o & pu 16*		P
582[4]	Polo Pony (IRE)(cp) 20-1 J Diment *2nd/3rd; 2nd & rdn when fell 12*		F
587[P]	Romanybaan 40-1 P Ikin *(xnb) Oht; 2 handlers; towards rr til pckd bad & rfo 10*		U
555[4]	Sea Victor 40-1 M Grange *Fat; a nr last; t.o 12; pu 14*		P

OFFICIAL DISTANCES: 8*l*, 5*l* **TIME:** 6min 44.0s **TOTE:** £8.40 **DF:**£11.80

785 Ladies Open — 14 ran

443[2]	**FIND ME ANOTHER (IRE)** 7-2 **Miss A Stennett** *Cl 2nd/4th; jmpd slow 13; ld app 3 out; 5l clr nxt; kpt on stout*		1
558[3]	**Free**(cp) 6-1 **Miss Gemma Hutchinson** *3rd/4th til 2nd 15; ld nxt; hdd when ploughed thro 3 out; drvn & a hld aft*	7	2
585[1]	**Killerine (FR)**(bl) 5-4F **Miss H Irving** *Nt a fluent in 2nd/4th; rdn & nt lkng keen when mist 11; fnd nil aft jmpd slow 13; 16l 3rd app 3 out*	20	3
558[6]	Maltby Son 14-1 Miss K Branson *Off pce in midfield; poor 8th 11; went 4th app 3 out; no ch when jmpd v slow nxt*	10	4
582[6]	Ela Agapi Mou (USA)(bl) 40-1 Miss D Ball *Reluct in last pr; t.o 7; fin str to snatch 5th*	15	5
558[5]	Bruan (IRE)(bl) 40-1 Miss J Bevin *Rcd wide; ld at fast pce; hdd 16; wknd rap; poor 5th & v tired bef nxt; fin exhaust*	2	6
585[3]	Gangster 33-1 Miss S Tarry *Off pce in midfield; rem 10th 11; plodded on*	5	7
407[P]	Guest Alliance (IRE) 40-1 Miss R Reynolds *Outpcd in midfield; mod 6th 11; t.o 15*	25	8
464[4]	Gortroe Guy (IRE) 33-1 Miss K Robinson *A bhnd; rem 11th when mist 11; cont t.o*	6	9
255[3]	Beet De Bob (IRE) 9-2 Miss S Phizacklea *12th when blun & ur 1*		U
585[U]	Dook's Delight (IRE) 25-1 Miss L Horsfall *A last & sn t.o; pu 2 out*		P
581[2]	Nashville Star (USA)(vis) 40-1 Miss H Lewis *Prom in group chsng clr ldrs; 5th & outpcd 11; t.o 15; pu 2 out*		P
582[U]	Perfect Finisher 40-1 Miss R Lobley *Off pce in midfield; 9th & tlng off 11; rfo 14*		U
558[U]	Sheskinqueen (IRE) (5a) 33-1 Miss A Wells *Well bhnd til prog in mod 7th 11; rchd 5th 14; nvr nr ldrs & sn wknd; t.o & pu 16*		P

OFFICIAL DISTANCES: 6*l*, 15*l* **TIME:** 6min 32.0s **TOTE:** £2.50 **DF:**£23.30

786 Mens Open — 8 ran

480[1]	**NAUTICAL LAD** 1-3F **J Docker** *Lw; trckd ldrs; gng wl in 3rd mostly; ld 3 out; strode clr nxt; impressive*		1
382[6]	**Some Go West (IRE)** 14-1 **R Cope** *Settled cl up; ev ch 16; rdn & one-pcd 3rd nxt; lft poor 2nd at last; hvly eased flat*	40	2
648[P]	**Jerome Jerome**(bl) 40-1 **A Sansome** *Prsd ldr to 8; rdn & drpng out rap when mist 12; t.o 15*	20	3
	Catchatan (IRE)(tt) 12-1 J Dillon *Mists; last pr to 9; eff nxt; handy brief bef 13; wkng bad when blun 15; t.o nxt*	20	4
	Gallion's Reach (IRE)(tt) 12-1 T Ellis *Cl up; jnd ldr brief 9; ev ch to 13; wknd v rap nxt; t.o 5th 15; pu last*		P
156[U]	Glemot (IRE) 40-1 N Pearce *Jw; ld to 16; wknd rap to poor 4th; pu nxt*		P
683[5]	Needwood Neptune 40-1 P Bennett *Nt fluent 3; last pr & nvr keen; 15l last 9; sn t.o; crawled 15; pu nxt*		P
681[3]	Saxon Gold 6-1 L Hicks *Hld up in rr til prog 10; cl up when blun 13; ld 16-nxt; drvn & outpcd app 2 out; clr 2nd but exhaust when pu last*		P

OFFICIAL DISTANCES: dist, 8*l* **TIME:** 6min 43.0s **TOTE:** £1.50 **DF:**£14.60

787 Dodson & Horrell PPORA Club Members Restricted, 12st — 8 ran

169^{2}	**DENVALE (IRE)** 6-4F **R Cope** *Prom; ld 7; jmpd safe but nt a fluent; drew clr 2 out; comf*		1
587^{2}	**Teeton Fizz** (5a) 3-1 **N Pearce** *Tchd 4s; hld up towards rr til prog to 3rd 9; drvn 13; 8l 4th & outpcd app 16; rallied to 2nd & jmpd delib 2 out; no ch w wnr aft*	5	2
294^{2}	**Stormy Pass** 6-1 **T Ellis** *(xnb) Prom; lft in ld 5-7; prsd wnr aft; 2l down app 3 out; kpt on same pce*	$2^{1}/_{2}$	3
589^{1}	Lah Di Dah Lad 5-1 J Tarry *Cl up; bad mist 10; jmpd into 3rd 13; 6l down straight; rdn & ev ch of 2nd 2nd; sn wknd; eased flat*	5	4
159^{P}	Henry Henbit 12-1 S Morris *(xnb) Hld up last to 10; brief eff in 5th 14; t.o 16; clambered 2 out*	runin	5
591^{P}	Nonplussed (5a)(bl) 40-1 P Andrew *Jmpd slow; ld til crawled 5; last by 11; wl t.o 14*	250y	6
	Dante's Banker (IRE) 14-1 R Armson *(xnb) Hit 2; hld up 7th til eff 9 & cl up brief; rmdrs 12 & sn lost tch; t.o & pu 3 out*		P
481^{3}	Moscow Tradition (IRE) 8-1 J Docker *2 handlers; prsd ldrs gng wl; hit 6 & 9; ev ch til wknd rap app 14; t.o & pu 3 out*		P

OFFICIAL DISTANCES: 6*l*, $3^{1}/_{2}$*l* **TIME:** 6min 48.0s **TOTE:** £2.00 **DF:**£6.90

788 Confined Maiden (Div 1), 12st — 12 ran

462^{2}	**NICKIT (IRE)**(cp) 13-8F **S Morris** *Opened 5/2 (3s in plces); ld/disp til lft clr 3 out; drvn & prsd agn when outj rival nxt; all out & unimpressive*		1
589^{3}	**Velvet Dove** (12a) 11-4 **N Pearce** *Tchd 7/2; chsd ldrs; went 3rd 12; lft 2l 2nd & hmpd bad 3 out; rallied & ch when jmpd v slow nxt; kpt on game but rather slow last; unlucky*	2	2
172^{P}	**Plenty Inn Hand** 25-1 **A Hanly** *Tde; ld/disp to 13; slowed rap frm 16 & poor 4th app nxt; t.o*	runin	3
685^{P}	Past Forte (5a) 25-1 T Ellis *Bckwd; prsd ldrs; 5th 13; blun bad 15; nt rec; rem 6th app 3 out*	15	4
594^{P}	College Superman 25-1 L Hicks *Midfield; 8l 6th 13; wknd qckly u.p 15; rem 5th app 3 out; pu nxt*		P
	Cowslip Lace (5a) 20-1 J Owen *Fat; 2 handlers; veered bad start & lost 30l; v green in last pr; clsd 6; t.o & pu 13*		P
595^{F}	Dolitanlad 40-1 P Millington *Bhnd; 8th & strugg 13; t.o 15; jmpd v slow 2 out; pu last*		P
370^{3}	Jenny's Charmer 4-1 F Hutsby *(xnb) Mist 2; cl up; jnd ldr 15 til fell hvly 3 out*		F
596^{P}	Minella Leader (IRE) 20-1 J Docker *(xnb) Midfield; 10l 7th & outpcd when blun 13; pu nxt*		P
	Pudding And Pie (5a) 25-1 R Armson *Bckwd; novicey; cl up til hit 10; 5th & drvn nxt; pu 12*		P
386^{P}	Sassy's Circle (12a) 25-1 James Tudor *(xnb) Easy rn in rr; pu 12*		P
588^{5}	Teeton Diamond (5a) 12-1 P Cowley *Carried condition; 2 handlers; bhnd; mist 3; strugg 11; t.o & pu 15*		P

OFFICIAL DISTANCES: 3*l*, 25*l* **TIME:** 6min 49.0s **TOTE:** £2.80 **DF:**£5.50

789 Confined Maiden (Div 2), 12st — 11 ran

476^{P}	**QUIZZAL** (5a) 4-1 **R Armson** *Rcd keen; cl up; ld 11; mist 15; rdn & kpt on stdly frm 2 out*		1
	Sir Lancelot 14-1 **A Sansome** *Hld up midfield; 5th 12; 6l 4th 16; sn outpcd; rallied frm mod 3rd 2 out to 2nd at last; too much to do*	5	2
627^{C}	**To The Top** 9-4F **James Tudor** *Nt fluent; ld to 3; prom; ld 9-11; cl 2nd til nt fluent 3 out; drvn & wknd nxt; blun last*	6	3
595^{4}	Bethin (5a) 8-1 P Newton *Bhnd; 9th 12; plugged on as others gave up; nvr on terms*	$^{1}/_{2}$	4
584^{P}	Devils Domino 20-1 N Pearce *Midfield; 6th when mist 12; qckly eased; pu nxt*		P
587^{P}	Fawsley Lake (5a) 20-1 J Owen *2 handlers; novicey in last pr; lost tch aft 12; t.o & pu 14*		P
588^{P}	Herpen (5a) 33-1 T Ellis *Mounted outside padd & tde; reluct to go down then virt bolted to start; oft jmpd v slow; lft in ld 4; hdd & blun 9; 3rd 12; wknd rap nxt; mist 15; t.o & pu 3 out*		P
378^{2}	Jumping Jack 3-1 R Cope *Ld 3 til hdd & carried off course aft 4 & lost ab 150 yds; rjnd & caught tail of field 8; went 3rd 13 & ev ch til 6l 4th app 3 out; wknd qckly; pu nxt*		P

	Murphymeboy (IRE) 5-1 S Morris *Mist 4; hld up; prog 8; 4th 12; ev ch til 5l 3rd app 3 out; sn tired & btn; poor 5th when pu last*		P
652^P	Red Lake (IRE) 33-1 P Millington *Mists; nvr btr than midfield; no ch aft blun 14; t.o & pu 2 out*		P
584^P	Sams Sister (5a) 16-1 P Cowley *Tk str hld; ld 4; bit pulled thro mouth & rn off course just aft nxt*		R

OFFICIAL DISTANCES: 6*l*, 8*l* **TIME:** 7min 03.0s **TOTE:** £4.30 **DF:**£3.30 (1st+any)

Red Rookie (lame at start) was withdrawn not under orders

Spooners & West Dartmoor

Cherrybrook (LH 7F,18J)

Sun, 4 Apr (GOOD to SOFT)

790 Hunt Members, 12st — 2 ran

313³	**LITTLE NATIVE (IRE)** 4-9F **Miss P Gundry** *(xnb) Set v slow pce; jmpd rt; jnd by rival aft 3 out; edged rt & slt ld 2 out; 1½l up at last; drvn out*		1
415¹	**Elegant Light** (5a) 13-8 **N Harris** *Trckd rival in 3l last; impd 15; chall aft 3 out; carried wide nxt; ev ch til no ex u.p flat*	½	2

OFFICIAL DISTANCE: ¾*l* **TIME:** 6min 40.0s

791 Restricted, 12st - 17J — 12 ran

568¹	**RAREGEM** 4-6F **Miss T Cave** *Opened evens; hld up towards rr; impd 12; went 3rd 14; disp ld 15 til gd j to ld 16; sn pushed clr; easily*		1
	Mystic Warrior (USA) 10-1 **L Jefford** *In tch; 6th when slt mist 10; 5th & gng wl 11; impd to 3rd 16; 5l 3rd 17; went 2nd by-passing last; fin wl; nt trble wnr*	2	2
572⁴	**Change** 20-1 **T Dennis** *Sn prom; cl 4th ½way; hdwy to ld 13; jnd 15; outj & hdd 17; wknd & releg 3rd by-passing last*	5	3
323⁷	Winning Leader (IRE) 12-1 Mrs O Jackson *In tch; cl 4th 7; disp/slt ld 9-12; cl up & ev ch til wknd 15*	12	4
572^F	Village Queen (IRE) (5a) 8-1 D Harvey *(bnh) Opened 10s; sn prom; cl 5th 10; lost plce 12; bhnd frm 15*	6	5
706^P	Tabernacle 33-1 A Glassonbury *Chsd ldrs; 6th & in tch 11; just in tch in 6th 14-15; wknd*	2	6
324^F	Tycoon Ted 6-1 R Woollacott *10s-6s; rcd on inner; ld/disp to 6; disp ld agn 9-12; cl up til wknd 16*	6	7
	Farley Water 25-1 D Edwards *Sn rr; bhnd when mist 9; poor 10th 10; t.o & pu 12*		P
	Milla's Man (IRE) 7-1 M Dennis *Midfield; 8th 10; bhnd frm 11 til pu 15*		P
571^F	Red Risk 33-1 M Sweetland *(xnb) Sn bhnd; t.o frm 10 til pu 15*		P
415²	Sweet Kari (IRE) 12-1 G Weatherley *Ld/disp til slt advant 7-9; cl 3rd 10; lost ground 13; 7th & wkng 15; t.o & pu nxt*		P
	Wynford Eagle (7a) 16-1 Miss P Gundry *(xnb) Tkn stdly in rr til pu aft 12; school*		P

OFFICIAL DISTANCES: 2½*l*, 8*l* **TIME:** 6min 17.0s

Fence 18 omitted - damaged

792 Mixed Open, 12st — 8 ran

707²	**SANDY DUFF** 3-1 **Miss M McCarthy** *Opened 4s; lw; tk keen hld; trckd ldr clsly til ld aft 14; went clr nxt; jnd agn aft 3 out; pushed clr aft 2 out; stayed on wl*		1
491²	**Bengal Bullet** 6-5F **A Charles-Jones** *Tchd 13/8; ld til hdd aft 14; 4l 2nd 15; rallied to disp ld aft 3 out; outj 2 out; sn no ex*	5	2
569^P	**Longstone Lad** 15-2 **R Woollacott** *Sn prom on inner; cl 3rd 4; disp 5l 3rd & rmdr 11; rdn & lost ground aft 12; 25l 3rd 3 out; no imp*	30	3
472⁵	The Bounder 8-1 Miss C Tizzard *In tch; 4th mostly; disp 5l 3rd 11; lost ground aft 12; poor 4th frm 13*	6	4
687²	Blackwater Brave (IRE) 10-1 G Fry *1st ride; a last & sn off pce; jmpd rnd safe; t.o 12*	10	5
	Dom Shadeed 20-1 M Sweetland *Lft at start; tk no part*		r
472^F	Happy Team (5a) 20-1 L Jefford *(xnb) Trckd ldrs; 15l 5th 7; lsng ground in 5th when pu 9*		P
414^P	Select Star (IRE)(vis,tt) 25-1 Miss J Congdon *Sn rr; poor 5th frm 9; t.o & pu 3 out*		P

OFFICIAL DISTANCES: 10*l*, dist **TIME:** 6min 12.0s

Wag The Brush (Miss T Cave, 5-1 - broke a blood vessel at start) was withdrawn not under starters orders

793 Confined, 12st — 9 ran

411^{2}	**KNOCK STAR (IRE)** 16-1 **S Partridge** *Prom; went 3rd 6; slt ld frm 8; 2l up 16; jnd & btr j 2 out; ½l ahd last; stayed on game flat; all out*		1
569^{4}	**Karadin (FR)** (7x) 11-2 **Mrs M Hand** *Tchd 6s; sn prom; disp ld 5-7; trckd ldr in cl 2nd frm 8; cl 3rd 2 out; str chall flat; a just hld*	s hd	2
573^{1}	**Bak On Board**(bl) 5-2F **Miss L Gardner** *(xnb,ringbit) 2 handlers; hld up in rr; impd 11; went 3rd 14; cl 3rd on outer 3 out; chall & nt jw 2 out; cl 3rd at last; rallied & ev ch flat; no ex last 50yds.*	nk	3
347^{F}	O So Bossy (3x) 5-1 Miss J Congdon *Hld up towards rr; 7th ½way; gd hdwy to 3rd brief 14; 4th & one pce frm 15*	8	4
573^{2}	By My Side (IRE)(tt) 11-4 A Charles-Jones *Tchd 3s; in tch; disp 3rd 11; rdn & wknd 14; bhnd frm 3 out; disapp*	2½	5
487^{4}	Just Bert (IRE) 20-1 Miss T Cave *Ld to 4; disp ld 5-6; disp cl 3rd & rmdrs 11; lost ground 13; bhnd frm 15*	8	6
	Belitlir (5a) 7-1 Miss S Young *Last but in tch to 7; wknd; bhnd when pu 9.*		P
570^{5}	Destin D'Estruval (FR) 25-1 I Hambley *Midfield; 6th 6; wknd 9; last when pu 12*		P
	S B S By Jove 15-2 S Kidston *(bf) Prom in chsng group; disp 3rd 8 til lost plce aft 15; bhnd & pu 2 out; btr for rce*		P

OFFICIAL DISTANCES: s hd, nk **TIME:** 6min 18.0s

794 Intermediate (Nov Rdrs), 12st — 8 ran

577^{1}	**SIMPLY SAM** 4-5F **H Fry** *Tchd evens; confid rdn; hld up in tch; went 3rd 9; ld 10; drew clr effortlessly aft 15; 15l clr & wl in comm frm nxt; hvly eased flat*		1
705^{3}	**Carefree Love (IRE)**(bl) 6-1 **W White** *Handy; rcd just bhnd ldrs; 5th 11; went 18l 3rd 3 out & 2nd app nxt; kpt on wl; flatt by prox.*	5	2
79^{P}	**Carling Elect** (5a) 10-1 **Miss L Hawkings** *(xnb) Disp ld to 9; cl 4th to 11; went 2nd 15; 15l 2nd 3 out; tired & dem 2 out*	20	3
572^{3}	Lingering Fog (IRE) 5-1 Miss M McCarthy *Disp ld; slt mist 8; cl 3rd 10; rdn nxt & chsd ldr 12-14; sn wknd; 23l 4th 3 out; t.o*	15	4
571^{P}	Big Mossy 25-1 J Cole *Sn rr; last frm 4 til pu 12*		P
411^{3}	Digitalis (5a)(bl) 16-1 W Biddick *Tk keen hld; disp ld to 9; cl 2nd to 11; wknd stdly frm 13; bhnd & pu 3 out*		P
573^{P}	Native Drum (IRE) 20-1 J Tickle *Sn rr; just in tch to 9; 6th 10; bhnd & pu 14*		P
571^{1}	State Medlar 11-4 Miss C Heywood *Ur 1*		U

OFFICIAL DISTANCES: 5*l*, dist **TIME:** 6min 22.0s

795 Confined Maiden 8yo&up, 12st — 11 ran

494^{P}	**BLACK A BROOK (IRE)** (5a)(cp) 14-1 **L Jefford** *Handy; cl 2nd 9; ld 10; jnd at times frm 11 til hdd 2 out; rallied wl und str drvng; ld agn flat; r.o; won on jockeyship*		1
493^{2}	**On His Toes** 10-11F **W White** *Tchd evens; 2 handlers; oht; rcd keen; slt ld 8 til mist 10; cl 2nd/disp ld frm 11 til eff & slt ld 2 out-last; sn hdd; no ex last 75yds.*	1½	2
312^{2}	**Cappa Hill (IRE)** 2-1 **Miss P Gundry** *Ld 1; cl 3rd 11; wknd 13; 15l 3rd 15; poor 4th frm nxt til tk rem 3rd cl home*	1¼fs	3
567^{P}	Mo's O Friendly(tt) 25-1 M Munrowd *Towards rr; 8th 9; prog 11; disp 3½l 3rd 13; wknd nxt; 22l 3rd 3 out; rem 3rd & tired 2 out; dem cl home*	¾	4
567^{P}	Abbey's Girl (IRE) (5a) 10-1 A Glassonbury *Handy; cl 4th 9; rdn 11; in tch to 14; wknd; bhnd when pu 3 out.*		P
194^{P}	Abigails Star 20-1 A Jones *Bckwd; veteran rdn; ur 1*		U
	Dammitu (5a) 10-1 L Heard *25s-10s; hdwy to 3rd 6; sn lost plce; 7th 9; poor 8th 11; t.o & pu aft 12*		P
	Finbar (IRE) 6-1 Miss L Gardner *Ld to 8; lost plce 11; bhnd in 7th 13; t.o & pu 15*		P
704^{P}	Je Suis (IRE) (5a) 20-1 I Hambley *Sn rr; bhnd & nt jw 9; pu nxt.*		P
567^{P}	King Tudor 33-1 M Woodward *Prom to 5; sn lost plce; last frm 6; t.o & pu 12*		P
566^{P}	Lamerton Quest 20-1 L Rowe *Mid-div; 6th 9; some hdwy when mist 11; 4th brief app nxt; sn lost plce; poor 6th when pu 3 out*		P

OFFICIAL DISTANCES: 1½*l*, dist **TIME:** 6min 26.0s

796 Confined Maiden 56&7yo, 12st — 7 ran

485^{3}	**GUNNERS MISTAKE** 2-1 **C Heard** *Opened 5/2; lw; ld 1-8 & frm 10; drew clr frm 15; comf; appreciated stamina test*		1
568^{2}	**Sound Sense** 11-10F **J Young** *(bf) Tchd 5/4; trckd ldr to 9; cl 3rd 11; cl 2nd & ev ch 13-14; rdn & one pce frm 15; no ch w wnr frm 2 out*	10	2

485[P]	**Whats Up Maid** (5a) 33-1 **M Munrowd** *(xnb) Prom on inner; 1½l 2nd 11; cl up til wknd 14; lft poor 3rd 3 out; exhausted & trotted in*	20	3
	Mighty Mack (IRE) (7a) 11-1 M Sweetland *(xnb) Mists; last & jmpd slow 3; t.o 11*	runin	4
	Ercon (IRE) 14-1 J Tickle *(xnb) Bckwd; sn rr; last frm 10; bhnd when pu 12*		P
	Madame Cholet (5a)(tt) 14-1 M Woodward *Fractious when mounted padd; tde; prom; 4th when jmpd rt 7; ld 8-10; 5th & wkng when blun & ur 12*		U
702[4]	Questionit (12a) 9-2 Miss L Gardner *In tch in 5th 9; cl 4th 11; hdwy to 3rd 15; 10l 3rd when blun & ur 3 out*		U

OFFICIAL DISTANCES: 15*l*, dist **TIME:** 6min 33.0s

Kelso (LH 8F,18J)
Mon, 5 Apr (GOOD)

797 Roxburghe Hotel Buccleuch Cup Mdn HC, 3m1f £2096 — 9 ran

508[2]	**NISBET** 11-07 11-1 **Miss J Riding** *Bhnd early; went prom 7; ld 8; hmpd by loose horse app 14; mist 3 out & hdd; sn ld agn; rdn & stayed on wl*		1
657[1]	**Miss Royello** 11-07 (1ow) 9-2 **D Jewett** *Trckd ldrs; outpcd app 3 out; 10l 3rd nxt; rallied to chse wnr frm last; drvn & no imp aft*	7	2
431[2]	**Native Alibi (IRE)** 11-07 5-1 **Miss J Hollands** *Rcd keen; prom; ld 3 out; sn hdd; ev ch nxt; wknd app last*	9	3
546[4]	Boulta (IRE) 11-11(cp) 7-2JF M McAlister *Ld to 8; mostly 2nd til 3rd & rdn 16; strugg app nxt; plodded on*	1½	4
548[2]	Highland Brig 11-09 7-1 R Morgan *Rr when mist 3; last when mist 14; no ch aft*	6	5
657[2]	Decent Bond (IRE) 12-00 10-1 M Thompson *Mists 1 & when last at 4; blun & ur nxt*		U
552[2]	Dun Victory 12-00 7-2JF K Anderson *5th when mist 7; rmdrs 9; last when blun 12; sn lost tch; t.o & pu 14*		P
654[U]	Havetwotaketwo (IRE) 11-07 50-1 M Seston *Pulled hrd; hit 5; cl 5th when fell 6*		F
678[U]	Try Me And See 11-07 25-1 G Crow *Hit 2 & ur*		U

TIME: 6min 29.4s **TOTE:** £8.40; places £2.20,£1.50,£1.90 **Ex:**£77.10 **CSF:**£60.83

Fence 11 omitted - fallen rider

798 J Rutherford (Earlston) HC, 3m1f - 19J £2373 — 15 ran

678[1]	**MISS MATTIE ROSS** 11-11 6-1 **M McAlister** *Hld up midfield; mists 3 & 8; chall 15; jnd ldr aft nxt; ld last; rdn & r.o game flat*		1
439[F]	**Lord Edwards Army (IRE)** 11-07 50-1 **R Morgan** *Ld app 5-8, 10-11 & frm 12; hdd last; stayed on wl u.p*	2	2
284[1]	**Mytimie (IRE)** 11-12 5-2F **Miss P Robson** *Midfield; chsd ldrs frm 11; rdn 16; disp 4th when blun 3 out; nd aft; 3rd frm last but was nvr lkng v keen*	6	3
445[3]	Indien Du Boulay (FR) 11-05 12-1 W Ramsay *Midfield; bumped along violent in 6th 16; one-pcd aft; rdr v unstylish*	1½	4
546[2]	Primitive Way 11-09(cp) 16-1 P Maitland-Carew *Chsd ldrs til lost plce to 9th & switched outside app 12; rallied brief & in tch 14; strugg frm nxt*	16	5
429[3]	Son Of Anshan 12-02(tt) 5-1 G Tuer *Towards rr; slt prog 3 out; nvr in contention*	2	6
678[2]	Geordies Express 11-09 9-2 W Kavanagh *Cl up; ld 8 til blun & hdd 9; ld agn 11; pckd 12 & hdd; prom til wknd 3 out; wl btn when mist last*	8	7
679[F]	Just Strong (IRE) 11-13 33-1 O Nelmes *Strugg in last pr; t.o 11*	11	8
656[5]	Parade Racer 11-13 33-1 D Jewett *Rmdrs early; midfield; hdwy to chse ldrs 7; disp 2nd 15; wknd app 2 out*	1¾	9
551[4]	Charlieadams (IRE) 12-02 (11ow) 100-1 J Muir *Ld til hdd app 5; wknd rap 8; t.o 14*	7	10
	I'm The Man 11-05 12-1 J Cookson *Cl up early; lost plce 9; t.o aft mist 14*	24	11
439[2]	Penny Native (IRE) 11-12 16-1 C Storey *Midfield; eff 11; chsng ldrs when mist 13; sn wknd; wl t.o*	dist	12
269[F]	Decoded 11-07(cp) 100-1 L Bates *Wl in rr til fell 13*		F
439[3]	Mr Busby 11-05 40-1 M Seston *Midfield; blun 15; no ch aft; t.o & pu last*		P
550[1]	Pharmistice (IRE) 11-05 20-1 Miss N Stirling *Last pr & sn wl bhnd; t.o 11; pu 14*		P

TIME: 6Min 28.2s **TOTE:** £5.90; places £2.30,£10.30,£1.40 **Ex:**£683.10 **CSF:**£270.32

Exeter (RH 11F,14J)

Tue, 6 Apr (GOOD, GOOD to SOFT in places)

799 Countryside Alliance Open HC, 2m3f110y £3679 16 ran

578[1]	**MOUSESKI** 11-09 12-1 **N Williams** *Chsd ldrs; 6th aft 6; ld aft 10; 10l clr nxt; drvn 3 out; jmpd slow last; hung on game though v tired*		1
569[2]	**Bill Me Up (IRE)** 11-05 20-1 **L Heard** *Hld up; 5th & prog aft 6; went 2nd 3 out; 7l down nxt; clsng flat; post came just too sn*	nk	2
628[1]	**Sadler's Realm** 11-09 15-2 **Miss L Gardner** *Prom; 4th aft 6; chsd wnr 11-nxt; wknd 2 out; eased nr fin*	23	3
441[3]	Sol Music 12-05 12-1 L Jefford *Chsd ldr frm 4; mist 9; ld brief 10; wknd app 11*	3½	4
630[2]	Phoenix Phlyer 11-09(cp) 16-1 Miss C Stucley *Mist 2; nvr gng wl; 14th aft 6*	6	5
444[4]	Hot Plunge 11-07 33-1 J Owen *Hld up; 8th aft 6; hrd rdn & strugg app 11*	s hd	6
543[P]	Red Brook Lad 12-02 7-2 N Mitchell *Hld up & bhnd; 11th aft 6; stdy hdwy to 5th & threatened brief app 11; sn rdn & floundering*	2½	7
628[3]	The Hearty Joker (IRE) 11-09(vis) 40-1 R Bandey *Ld; 8l clr 5; hdd 10; wknd rap*	13	8
602[P]	Gladiatorial (IRE) 11-05 50-1 T Bishop *Blun bad 1 & rdr drpd reins; lost plce 4; 9th aft mist 6; sn strugg; t.o & pu 11*		P
541[F]	Keltic Lord 11-12 25-1 A Charles-Jones *A bhnd; 10th aft 6; t.o & pu 11*		P
412[1]	Morris Piper 11-07 14-1 R Woollacott *Reluct to set off & lost 20l; 12th aft 6; hdwy app 8; wkng when pu 11*		P
365[3]	Pulham Downe 11-05 50-1 Miss E Tory *Sn labouring; t.o aft 6; pu 10*		P
629[3]	Right To Reply (IRE) 12-02 11-8F N Harris *Mist 1; wl bhnd til 15th & rdn aft 6; pu nxt*		P
630[P]	Solvang (IRE) 11-05 100-1 M Wall *Chsd ldrs; 7th aft 6; mist 7; sn wknd; t.o & pu 11*		P
347[6]	Sporting Chance 11-05 100-1 M Munrowd *Prom; 3rd aft 6; wknd 8; rr when jmpd lft 10; t.o & pu 2 out*		P
628[4]	Traditional (IRE) 11-07(cp) 100-1 R Stephens *Chsd ldrs; sn rdn; 13th & nt keen aft 6; t.o & pu 11*		P

TIME: 5min 03.2s **TOTE:** £15.40; places £4.60,£5.40,£2.00 **Ex:**£283.00 **CSF:**£220.47

The stewards ordered that Right To Reply, whose rider reported was never travelling, be routine tested

Fontwell (L&RH 7F,19J)

Wed, 7 Apr (GOOD, GOOD to SOFT in places)

800 Build Centre HC, 3m2f110y £1526 9 ran

241[10]	**GOOD TIME MELODY (IRE)** 11-07 7-1 **T Dreaper** *5th & rdn aft 7; eff 13 & sn clr w rnr-up; hrd rdn to ld 15; hdd brief 3 out; plugged on*		1
320[1]	**Ronans Choice (IRE)** 11-07(bl) 9-2 **Richard Darke** *Ld; rdn & hdd 15; ld brief 3 out; wobbling u.p frm nxt; tried to rally app last; no imp*	2	2
679[P]	**Owen's Pet (IRE)** 11-11 25-1 **S Morris** *2nd/3rd; 3rd & lost tch w ldng pr 14; sn t.o & lkd disinterested*	dist	3
428[2]	Lordberniebouffant (IRE) 12-00 9-4F Miss P Robson *Chsd ldrs; nt fluent 7 & rmdrs; nt fluent 9; wknd 13; 4th & t.o frm nxt; v lacklustre*	1¼	4
537[1]	Robbie's Adventure 11-10 16-1 Mrs J Gordon *Sn strugg in last pr; t.o aft 10*	17	5
347[P]	Silent Keys (SWE) 12-02 33-1 C Gordon *Drvn in last & strugg 6; nvr lkd keen; t.o aft mist 9*	22	6
158[1]	Martha's Boy (IRE) 12-00 9-2 D Dunsdon *Bhnd; poor 6th when mist 10; last when pu & dism aft 13 (split a shoe)*		P
642[1]	Splash And Dash (IRE) 12-00 4-1 A Hickman *Hld up; fell 3*		F
581[3]	Spy Boy (IRE) 11-07(vis) 66-1 J Morgan *Chsd ldr to 8; lsng plce when mist 13; stpd to nil; t.o & pu nxt*		P

TIME: 7min 04.6s **TOTE:** £7.10; places £1.70,£2.40,£2.70 **Ex:**£51.50 **CSF:**£37.97

Ludlow (RH 8F,19J)

Thu, 8 Apr (GOOD)

801 Abberley Hall Old Boys Association HC, 3m £2905 10 ran

630[5] **GUIGNOL DU COCHET (FR)** 11-11 10-1 **D Mansell** *Hld up last; 12l adrift 6; 6th & prog 11; smooth rn frm nxt & squeezed thro to ld aft 15; well in comm aft; patted home.* . . . 1
755[1] **Act In Time (IRE)** 11-07 3-1 **T Edwards** *Chsd ldrs; 5th 11; went 2nd 16; rdr v feeble & no ch w wnr aft* . . . 4 2
635[5] **Filscot** 12-00 16-1 **J Diment** *Midfield; rmdrs aft 5; 8th 11; eff 12; 5th & hrd drvn aft 15; 2nd brief app nxt; wknd 3 out* . . . 4 3
Simber Hill (IRE) 11-09 2-1F R Stephens *Rr aft bad mist 3; sn drvn along; 7th & u.p 11; rchd 5l 6th 15 but nvr lkd keen; outpcd nxt; mist 2 out* . . . hd 4
732[F] Mullensgrove 12-02 100-30 P Cowley *Chsd ldrs; jmpd lft 9; eff 11; went 2nd nxt; rdn & ev ch when hmpd bend aft 15; lost plce & hit nxt; drpd out rap; blun 2 out* . . . 25 5
435[5] Justjim 11-07(cp) 50-1 M Goldstein *Jmpd lft; ld til aft 15; lost plce rap; hit 2 out* . . . 1¾ 6
631[6] Sip Of Brandy (IRE) 11-12 33-1 Miss J Hughes *Rdr nrly f.o 5 & lost iron; drpd to rr & waved nxt; mist 8; t.o 11 & more waving aft; stayed on frm 3 out* 5 7
532[1] Beachcomber 11-11 16-1 H Fowler *2 handlers; 2nd/3rd & rcd keen; mist 7; 3rd 11; rn out 12* . . . R
581[F] Benson (IRE) 11-12 20-1 T Dreaper *(xnb) Last pr; t.o & strugg when pu aft 11* P
668[3] News Flash (IRE) 11-07 100-1 Miss L Brooke *Bckwd; oht; chsd ldr 3-11; prom when carried out nxt* . . . C

TIME: 6min 18.3s **TOTE:** £12.00; places £1.90,£1.70,£3.80 **Ex:**£37.80 **CSF:**£39.23

Ashford Valley

Charing (LH 8F,19J)

Sat, 10 Apr (GOOD)

802 Restricted, 12st 8 ran

779[2] **KILVOYDAN (IRE)** 2-1 **D Phelan** *3rd til ld aft 7; made rest; hung rt & rmdrs aft 11; narrow advant til drew clr frm 2 out; comf* . . . 1
639[2] **Trumper** evensF **P York** *In tch; impd to press wnr 12; rdn 16; 1l down when blun 2 out; kpt on one pce app last.* . . . 5 2
540[4] **Master Chief (IRE)** 6-1 **P Bull** *In tch; chsd ldng pr frm 12; 10l adrift 15; wknd aft 3 out; t.o* . . . fence 3
779[P] Battle Honours 16-1 F Wheeler *Detach last to 7; hdwy to 10l 4th 12; fdd frm 15; wl bhnd when pu 2 out* . . . P
782[P] Ginger Sprout (IRE) (5a) 14-1 C Thomson *Prsd ldr to 7; sn wknd; t.o & pu 11* P
639[P] Tonrin 8-1 P Hall *Ld to 7; chsd wnr til rdn & lost plce qckly aft 11; t.o 15 til pu last* . . . P
Two Of Diamonds 16-1 J Sole *Midfield til rdn & wknd 9; last when pu aft 12* P
534[4] Winward 16-1 J Merry *Midfield til lost plce 6; last frm 8; t.o & pu 11* . . . P

OFFICIAL DISTANCES: 4*l*, dist **TIME:** 6min 23.0s
TOTE: £5.50; places £1.80,£1.10,£1.10 **DF:**£2.50

803 Open Maiden 56&7yo, 2m4f, 12st - 15J 5 ran

186[F] **LORD OF THE NORTH (IRE)** 4-6F **C Gordon** *Rce keen; hld up; 2nd frm 6 til ld aft 3 out; sn clr; v easily* . . . 1
611[P] **Worth A Shot (IRE)** 10-1 **D Phelan** *Chsd ldr to 5; 15l 3rd & lsng tch 7; wl bhnd 11 til r.o frm 2 out; tk 2nd flat.* . . . 15 2
782[F] **Naughty Noah** 8-1 **G Gallagher** *Ld; clr frm 3-10; blun & hdd 3 out; wknd rap aft nxt; mist & lost 2nd at last* . . . 5 3
782[F] Almazard 8-1 Mrs J Gordon *Jb lft; drpd to rr 7; lost tch 9; no ch frm 11* . . 30 4
Lady Mordaunt (IRE) (5a) 7-4 P York *Hld up; went 20l 3rd 8; stdy hdwy 10; 6l down when fell 16* . . . F

OFFICIAL DISTANCES: 18*l*, 4*l*, dist **TIME:** 5min 23.0s
TOTE: £2.00; places £1.10,£4.20 **DF:**£15.50

804 Mens Open, 12st — 3 ran

780[3] **STRUGGLES GLORY (IRE)** (7x) 4-5F **D Robinson** *Made all; 2-4l up til jnd 15; lft wl clr nxt* 1

716[3] **Russian Connection (IRE)** 6-1 **A Ward-Thomas** *A last; lost tch frm 12; wl bhnd frm 15; lft rem 2nd nxt* . . . . fence 2

421[1] Belvento (IRE) (7x) 11-10 M Sheridan *Trckd wnr; impd to disp ld 15; outj when blun & ur nxt* . . . . U

OFFICIAL DISTANCE: dist **TIME:** 6min 33.0s **TOTE:** £1.50 **DF:**£1.70

805 Ladies Open — 5 ran

780[1] **CEDAR CHIEF** (7x)(bl) 4-5F **Ms L Stock** *Ld/disp til mist & lost plce 8; prsd ldr 12 til ld 14; sn clr; stdd app 16; drew clr agn frm 3 out; easily* 1

608[3] **Glory Trail (IRE)** 9-4 **Miss H Grissell** *Last to 15; hdwy to chse wnr when blun & lost plce 3 out; rallied app last; tk 2nd flat* 20 2

781[P] **Commasarris** 9-2 **Mrs J Gordon** *A.p; prsd ldr 11-13; lft 8l 2nd 3 out; wkng when jmpd slow last; dem flat* 1 3

641[5] Castle Arrow (IRE) 10-1 Miss N Moisey *Cl 2nd/3rd to 10; lost plce 13; hdwy app 16; chsd ldng pr frm 3 out; wknd app last* 2 4

421[P] Scotch Bob (IRE) 8-1 Mrs P Hall *Cl 2nd/3rd til ld 10-14; chsng wnr when blun 16; wknd aft nxt* 4 5

OFFICIAL DISTANCES: dist, ½l, ½l **TIME:** 6min 32.0s
TOTE: £2.30; places £1.70,£2.00 **DF:**£2.40

806 S.E. Hunts Club Members, 12st — 5 ran

640[2] **CHARLIE'S ANGEL** (5a, 4x) 5-4F **P York** *Hld up; mist 4; cl 2nd/3rd frm 7 til disp ld aft 14; lft 10l clr 3 out; pushed out app last; easily* 1

419[1] **Rainbow Ranch (IRE)** 7-4 **C Gordon** *Ld 3-14; lost tch w ldng pr aft nxt; lft 2nd 3 out; rdn & slt hdwy app last; no ch w wnr* 6 2

643[U] **Galeaway (IRE)** (4x) 13-2 **J Barnard** *Cl 2nd/3rd til lost tch frm 12; 15l adrift when blun 15; wl bhnd frm nxt* 20 3

609[U] Kenny Davis (IRE) 10-1 P Blagg *Ld to 2; settled in rr til hdwy 11; disp ld aft 14; rdn to ld brief 16; jnd when blun bad & ur nxt* . . . . U

650[5] Lord Of The Flies (IRE) 10-1 D Brightling *A.p; prsd ldr frm 5 til fell 8* . . . . F

OFFICIAL DISTANCES: 5l, dist **TIME:** 6min 34.0s **TOTE:** £2.30; places £1.30,£1.10 **DF:**£3.10

807 Hunt Members, 12st — 5 ran

781[4] **DICK MCCARTHY (IRE)** (4x) 4-9F **Mrs S Ashby** *Hld up early; 2nd frm 7 til ld aft 14; 6l up app 16; drew rt away frm 3 out* 1

642[6] **Oxendale** 7-2 **Mrs C Andrews** *3rd most of way; lost tch w ldng pr frm 10; stayed on frm 3 out to tk rem 2nd app last* 30 2

Nicodemus 9-2 **G Wigley** *Ld 4; sn def advant; hdd aft 14; chsng wnr when blun 16; wknd qckly frm nxt; lost 2nd app last; fin tired* 25 3

648[r] Ishma (IRE)(bl) 10-1 D Page (Kent) *Ld to 3; sn lost plce; last frm 7; blun 8; jmpd stickily 9 & 10; t.o & pu 13* . . . . P

648[P] Shanrod View (IRE) 10-1 J Sole *A last pr; 25l 4th 11; wl bhnd when climbed 14; pu nxt* . . . . P

OFFICIAL DISTANCES: dist, dist **TIME:** 6min 35.0s **TOTE:** £1.60; places £1.20,£1.70 **DF:**£2.30

Bedale

Hornby Castle (LH 8F,18J)

Sat, 10 Apr (GOOD, GOOD to FIRM in places)

808 Confined Conditions, 12st — 6 ran

389[3] **DUMADIC** 6-4F **N Tutty** *Last when slpd bend bef 9; still last 13; hdwy to 2l 2nd 3 out; hrd rdn to ld app last; rdly drew clr flat* 1

427[2] **Trooper Collins (IRE)**(tt) 7-4 **G Tuer** *Cl up; ld 9; 1l up 3 out til jnd app last; outpcd flat* 2 2

592[5] **Stoney River (IRE)** 7-1 **S Walker** *Mid-div to 11; went 2nd 13 & cl 3rd 3 out; one pce frm 2 out* 6 3

564[2] Emperor's Son 7-2 Miss S Brotherton *A rr; pushed along 14; 8l 5th 15; went 4th app 2 out; r.o one pce* 4 4

565P Heather Lad 14-1 N Smith *Cl 2nd til pushed along 11 & blun; last & lsng tch 14; t.o & pu last* . . . . P
429P Needsmoretime (IRE)(cp) 50-1 S J Robinson *4l clr by 2; ld til jnd 9; pushed along & wknd frm 13; t.o & pu last* . . . . P

OFFICIAL DISTANCES: 1½*l*, 6*l* **TIME:** 6min 50.0s

809 Hunt Members 3 ran

770P **ROYAL CRIMSON** 1-2F **R Alers-Hankey** *Made all; 4l ld to 12; pushed along 13; 1l ld 3 out; just ld & gng best when lft solo 2 out* 1
Scenic Storm (IRE) 9-4 P Kinsella *Chsd ldr in 4l 2nd to 13; hdwy to disp ld 15; pushed along & hld in 2l 2nd when ur 2 out* . . . . U
Sweet Solitaire (U) (5a) 6-1 Miss J Crosier *Sn bhnd; jmpd slow 2 & 5; t.o by 6; fnce adrift when pu 11* . . . . P

OFFICIAL DISTANCE: Finished alone **TIME:** 6min 56.0s

810 Restricted, 12st 10 ran

503² **PURPLE JEAN** (5a) 6-4F **G Brewer** *Ld to 12; 3l 3rd 3 out; rallied to ld app last; stayed on wl u.p* 1
592P **Energy Man** 25-1 **M Bennison** *Cl 2nd til ld 13; jnd app last; one pce flat* . 1 2
563² **Orleans (IRE)**(bl) 5-1 **S J Robinson** *Prom in 3rd to 11; went 2l 2nd 15; disp ld 3 out til wknd app last* . . . . ½ 3
Lord Nick 7-1 N Tutty *Mid-div to 8; rr & pushed along 12; stayed on to 4th 2 out; r.o one pce* 12 4
766⁶ Distinct (IRE) 16-1 Miss J Crosier *Mid-div early; rr by 13; pushed along 15; stayed on str; nrst fin* 2 5
503U Lord Scroop (IRE) 16-1 M Morley *A last; lsng tch 6; jmpd slow & reluct 7; sev rmdrs aft; t.o & pu 8* . . . . P
503P Redsands (IRE) 12-1 S Walker *A midfield to rr; nd; pu 3 out* . . . . P
563⁸ Son Of Sam 12-1 L Bates *Handy in 4th early; outpcd 11; 2l 5th 13; blun 15; hld in 4th when fell 3 out* . . . . F
Vintage Choice (IRE) 25-1 P Cornforth *Last & lsng tch 11; t.o & rem when pu 14* . . . . P
503³ Wilfie Wild 3-1 Mrs L Ward *Rr early; hdwy to 10l 4th 11; hld in 15l 5th when pu last* . . . . P

OFFICIAL DISTANCES: 1*l*, nk **TIME:** 6min 41.0s

811 Ladies Open 6 ran

564¹ **TEXAS RANGER** 1-3F **Miss J Foster** *Ld frm 8; 2l ld 13; jnd 3 out; stayed on str; clr by last* 1
565P **Hadeqa** 50-1 **Miss S Brotherton** *Last to 7; hdwy to 8l 3rd 12 & 1l 2nd 15; disp ld 3 out; pushed along & wknd frm 2 out* 5 2
The Minister (IRE) 4-1 **Miss T Jackson** *Chsd ldr; 2l 2nd til mist 9; cl 2nd 13; wknd frm 15; 8l 3rd 3 out; r.o one pce* 12 3
630P On The Mend (IRE) 20-1 Miss F Hartley *Mid-div til outpcd 11; 15l 4th 13; dist 4th by 2 out* 20 4
564P Miorbhail 33-1 Miss T Gray *Ld to 2; handy 3rd til mist 9; wknd & poor 5th 13; rem 5th when ur last* . . . . U
477⁴ Purevalue (IRE)(bl) 6-1 Miss J Coward *Nt jw; blun 2 & rdr lost irons; last by 5; mists 9 & 10; sn lost tch; rem 6th when pu 14* . . . . P

OFFICIAL DISTANCES: 6*l*, 15*l* **TIME:** 6min 52.0s

The stewards enquired into the improvement in form of the runner-up; they noted the owner's explanation that it could not handle the soft ground at the Hurworth and had benefited from a change of rider

812 Land Rover Mens Open, 12st 7 ran

501¹ **HIGH PEAK** 7-4 **R Wakeham** *V confid rdn; hld up til ld 13; sn clr; 3l up 2 out; prsd at last; pushed clr flat; impressive* 1
679P **Mademist Sam**(bl) 4-1 **N Tutty** *A.p; 4l 3rd 14; 3l 2nd 3 out; mist nxt; hrd rdn to chall last; easily outpcd* 2½ 2
Backsheesh (IRE)(tt) evensF **G Tuer** *Ld to 14; ev ch 3 out; outpcd app nxt* . 1 3
683³ Glendamah (IRE) 20-1 M Morley *Prom 3rd to 12; outpcd 14; 8l 4th 3 out; stayed on str; fin fast; nrst fin* 1 4
Kuwait Millennium 12-1 W Burnell *Last to 10; hdwy 12 to 5th 14; 8l 5th 3 out; r.o one pce* 12 5

798^{9}	Parade Racer 8-1 P Kinsella *Mid-div to 7; bad mist 9; last 10; t.o 15*	6	6
764^{P}	Royal Plum(cp) 50-1 S J Robinson *Midfield to 9; pushed along & rmdrs 11; lsng tch 13; last & hrd rdn 15; t.o & pu last.*		P

OFFICIAL DISTANCES: 2*l*, $\frac{1}{2}$*l* **TIME:** 6min 41.0s

813 Open Maiden (Div 1) — 10 ran

	THE MURPHY MEISTER (IRE) 4-1 **G Tuer** *Mid-div to 8; ld frm 10; qcknd clr 14; 5l up 2 out; 10l clr at last; v easy.*		1
160^{P}	**No Info (IRE)** (5a) 10-1 **N Tutty** *Mid-div to 9; went 4l 4th 13 & 2nd 2 out; r.o one pce; no ch w wnr*	10	2
394^{P}	**Catosphere (IRE)** 12-1 **L Bates** *Rr early; hdwy 14 to 5l 4th & bad mist 3 out; rallied to 3rd app last*	8	3
594^{3}	Man At The Top 2-1F M Bennison *Cl up early; outpcd & rr by 9; hdwy 10 to 1l 2nd 13; ev ch 3 out; wknd.*	5	4
	Snow Nymph (5a) 4-1 W Burnell *Rr to 8; hdwy 10 to 6th 12; in tch 15; outpcd app 3 out*	5	5
	Tullineaskey Kitty (IRE) (5a) 10-1 C Dawson *Handy 3rd to 11; 2l 2nd 13; wknd 14; rr & lsng tch 15; hacked home*	35	6
	Ellfiedick (5a) 20-1 Miss T Jackson *Last & lsng tch 2; sn t.o; pu 11*		P
776^{P}	Iron Trooper (IRE)(bl) 6-1 T Glass *Handy; 3l 3rd when ur 5*		U
	Selectric (IRE) 16-1 S Gibbon *Pulled v hrd; ld to 9; wknd & lsng tch 13; t.o & pu 3 out*		P
591^{P}	Silver Sovereign 16-1 P Kinsella *Prom; 2l 3rd 8; cl up til wknd qckly 14; t.o & pu nxt.*		P

OFFICIAL DISTANCES: 15*l*, 10*l* **TIME:** 7min 00.0s

814 Open Maiden (Div 2) — 10 ran

342^{3}	**CLEVER FELLA** (7a) 11-8 **N Tinkler** *7/2-11/8; mid-div to 8; pushed along 12; went 8l 4th 13; sev hrd rmdrs; hdwy to 2nd 15; ld 3 out; clr by last; hrd rdn & stayed on*		1
504^{2}	**Bobby Buttons** 5-4F **N Tutty** *Chsd clr ldr; 10l 2nd 14; went 4l 3rd 3 out; ev ch nxt; outpcd app last.*	4	2
500^{P}	**Hattie** (5a) 20-1 **P Cornforth** *Pulled hrd; 2l ld to 7; went 10l clr aft 8; mist 9; jnd aft 15; mist 3 out; wknd*	10	3
500^{P}	Hanisia (5a) 20-1 P Atkinson *A rr; lft poor 4th 2 out; struggled home*	15	4
	Amaretto Express (IRE) (7a) 20-1 P Kinsella *A rr; last by 8; lsng tch when pu 11*		P
	Crake Way (7a) 9-1 G Brewer *Rr to 13; slt hdwy to 15l 5th 15; easily outpcd; t.o & pu 2 out; will improve*		P
	Highland Wonder 20-1 Mrs L Ward *Planted & lft at start; tk no part*		r
	Madaar (USA) (7a) 9-1 P Collins *Unruly start & lft; tk no part*		r
394^{P}	Nomiret (IRE) 20-1 Miss L Horner *Tde; chsd ldr in 2l 2nd to 7; mists 9 & 11; wknd qckly & pu 12*		P
432^{3}	Red Rose Dixie (5a) 9-1 C Dawson *Mid-div to 10; went 12l 3rd 13; grad wknd frm 14; dist 4th 3 out; pu nxt*		P

OFFICIAL DISTANCES: 5*l*, 10*l* **TIME:** 6min 48.0s

Nought To Ninety (rdr inj in previous rce) was withdrawn not under starters orders

Cotswold Vale Farmers

Andoversford (RH 9F,19J)

Sat, 10 Apr (GOOD with SOFT patches)

815 Hunt Members — 4 ran

661^{6}	**TIRLEY GALE** 11-10 **J Jones** *Hld up; eff to disp ld 14; jnd 2 out; r.o str app last.*		1
757^{3}	**Arctic Burner (IRE)** 5-2 **Mrs J Chapman** *Ld to 3; disp 2nd to 13; 3l 2nd til eff to disp ld brief 2 out; no ex*	$1\frac{1}{2}$	2
757^{4}	**Macy (IRE)**(cp) evensF **J Mahot** *Disp 2nd til lost tch w ldrs frm 13*	30	3
519^{P}	Sneedham's Green 7-1 P Mason *14s-7s; tubed; jw; clr ldr til bad mist 7; jnd 10; wknd qckly; pu 12*		P

OFFICIAL DISTANCES: 1*l*, dist **TIME:** 6min 49.0s

816 Confined, 12st — 5 ran

755² **PARAHANDY (IRE)** (5x) 4-9F **H Dowty** *Cl 2nd til disp ld 13; drew clr frm 3 out; easily* . . . 1
Mostyn (7x) 9-4 **G Barfoot-Saunt** *Hld up; 4th ½way; str rn frm 2 out to tk 2nd flat* . . . 25 2
664⁴ **Gay Baratineur (FR)** (6x)(cp) 2-1 **Mrs K Baimbridge** *Ww in 4th; prog to 3l 3rd 15 & 2nd 2 out; wknd & dem flat* . . . 4 3
755ᵁ Not For Parrot (IRE) 10-1 P Callaghan *Stdd in cl 3rd til disp ld frm 14; wknd qckly frm 2 out* . . . 12 4
756ᶠ Phar And Away (5a) 10-1 G Tumelty *Hdstrng; ld & jw til jnd 10; bad mist 11; imm pu* . . . P

OFFICIAL DISTANCES: dist, 1*l* **TIME:** 6min 41.0s

817 Dodson & Horrell PPORA Club Members (Nov Rdrs), 12st — 2 ran

661⁵ **GALESHAN (IRE)** (4x) 1-3F **C Huxley** *Ld; lft wl clr 4 & lft solo nxt* . . . 1
Hubbly Bubbly 7-4 S Howe *Bad mist 2; slowed dramatic & ref & ur 4; rmtd & cont; ref 5* . . . r

OFFICIAL DISTANCE: Finished alone **TIME:** 7min 48.0s

818 Mixed Open, 12st — 2 ran

229ᴾ **ASHGAN (IRE)** 1-4F **G Barfoot-Saunt** *Cl 2nd til ld 14; 2l clr 3 out; pushed out frm nxt* . . . 1
662ᴾ **Felloo (IRE)** 7-4 **E Walker** *Ld; jnd 13; 2l 2nd 14; eff agn 2 out; a hld* . . . 3 2

OFFICIAL DISTANCE: 3*l* **TIME:** 7min 02.0s

819 Restricted, 12st — 4 ran

587⁵ **WATERLOO LEADER (IRE)** 4-6F **D Smith** *4th 1st circ; prog to disp ld 13-14; 2l 2nd til ld 2 out; sn clr* . . . 1
Ballyblack (IRE) 2-1 **E Walker** *Trckd ldrs; 2l 3rd 9; eff to disp ld 14 til outpcd frm 2 out* . . . 12 2
Floodgate 3-1 **Miss V Flood** *Ur padd; disp ld til mist 7; 6l 3rd 2 out; short-lived eff frm nxt; wknd* . . . 2½ 3
740ᴾ Italian Clover 2-1 Miss S Carter *Cl 2nd to ½way; ld brief 13; wknd to 4th nxt; virt pu flat* . . . 50 4

OFFICIAL DISTANCES: 6*l*, 2*l* **TIME:** 6min 51.0s

820 Open Maiden, 12st — 4 ran

668⁴ **SALES DODGER (IRE)**(cp) 2-1 **R Hughes** *Hld up; prog to 4l 3rd 16; lkd hld 2 out; stayed on wl frm last; ld final strides* . . . 1
443⁶ **Jolly Jake** 6-4 **E Walker** *2s-6/4; chsd ldrs; 3l 2nd frm 8 til ld 3 out; 3l clr nxt til hdd final strides* . . . hd 2
721³ **Jurist** evensF **M Keen** *5/4-evens; ld 2; 2l up til hdd 3 out; wknd* . . . 30 3
667ᶠ Tigre Bois 12-1 R Carey *Ld brief to 2; cl 2nd til rmdrs 9; wknd & pu 10* . . . P

OFFICIAL DISTANCES: hd, dist **TIME:** 6min 43.0s

Eggesford

Lifton (RH 7F,19J)

Sat, 10 Apr (GOOD, GOOD to SOFT in places)

821 Hunt Members, 12st — 4 ran

705² **FATHER MANSFIELD (IRE)** 4-7F **Miss C Prouse** *Tchd 4/6; jw; ld to 4 & agn frm 10; in comm frm 16; pushed out* . . . 1
320ᴾ **Squaddie** 2-1 **C Heard** *Tchd 9/4; tk keen hld; hld up in tch; 5l 3rd when hit 8; went 2nd 13; rdn 16; kpt on same pce* . . . 2½ 2
Fern Leader (IRE) (2ow) 9-1 **R Skinner** *Trckd ldr til ld 4-10; releg 3rd 13; kpt in tch; 3½l 3rd 3 out; kpt on one pce* . . . 10 3
323⁸ Persian Dawn (5a) 12-1 Miss J Congdon *Tchd 14s; last but in tch; hdwy to 4½l 3rd aft 3 out; wknd rap nxt* . . . 35 4

OFFICIAL DISTANCES: 2*l*, 20*l* **TIME:** 6min 24.0s

822 Ladies Open 11 ran

793^{2} **KARADIN (FR)** 4-1 **Mrs M Hand** *7s-4s; lw; jw; ld/disp til cl 2nd frm 13; trckd ldr til chall aft 2 out; ld last; r.o str u.p flat* 1

578^{2} **Breteche (FR)** (5a) 13-2 **Miss T Newman** *(xnb) Tchd 7s; lw; tde; jw; ld/disp; slt ld 13; went $1\frac{1}{2}$l clr & lkd wnr aft 3 out; jnd & rdn aft nxt; ev ch last; no ex flat* . . . . $1\frac{1}{2}$ 2

635^{1} **What A Mover** (5a) 4-7F **Miss P Gundry** *Lw; ww in tch; nt a fluent; $4\frac{1}{2}$l 4th 10; went $7\frac{1}{2}$l 3rd 3 out; no imp on ldrs* 6 3

690^{4} Virtuoso 25-1 Mrs S Corcoran *In tch; chsng ldrs; cl 5th 9; went 5l 4th 13; 10l 4th 3 out; kpt on; nt trble ldrs* 6 4

484^{5} Tiger Talk(bl) 14-1 Mrs O Jackson *(xnb) Sn prom; cl 3rd $\frac{1}{2}$way; cl 2nd 13; rmdrs nxt; lost plce aft 15; 13l 5th 3 out; one pce* 1 5

635^{6} Proby Lady (IRE) (5a) 10-1 Miss D Harding *Sn rr; a bhnd; t.o* . . . . runin 6

690^{6} Defendtherealm 20-1 Miss A Mills *9th 5; lost tch stdly aft 9; t.o & pu last*. P

470^{P} Doublet 16-1 Miss C Heywood *In tch in midfield; cl 7th 9; lost tch frm 14; bhnd when pu last* . . . . P

484^{1} Guru Rinpoche 5-1 Miss L Gardner *(bf) Lw; disp 3rd when blun & ur 6* . . . U

635^{4} Priestthorn (IRE) 25-1 Miss W Southcombe *Towards rr; bhnd frm 9 til pu 16* P

705^{P} Vercheny (5a) 12-1 Miss T Cave *(xnb) In tch in midfield; cl 5th 10; 10l 6th 13; tail-swishing nxt; wknd & pu 15* . . . . P

OFFICIAL DISTANCES: 1*l*, 3*l* **TIME:** 6min 01.0s

823 Confined, 12st - 17J 10 ran

566^{2} **DAMIENS PRIDE (IRE)** (5x) 10-1 **T Dennis** *(xnb) Ld aft 1; made rest; 2-3l ld frm $\frac{1}{2}$way; 2l up when jmpd lft 2 out & last; r.o game flat; all out*. 1

489^{1} **Just Sally** (5a) 6-4F **A Farrant** *(xnb) Tchd 7/4; lw; hld up; prog to 4th 12; rdn aft 14; 5l 4th 15; still 4th & chsng ldrs 2 out; disp 3rd last; r.o u.p flat.* $\frac{3}{4}$ 2

705^{4} **Drumhorc (IRE)** 7-1 **Miss L Gardner** *(xnb) Ld 1; chsd ldr; pckd 13; 2l 2nd & eff & rdn 3 out; ev ch 2 out; nt qckn flat*. 1 3

Inter Rock (FR) (3x) 20-1 M Sweetland *Hld up towards rr of tightly grouped field; 7l 7th 12; 6th 3 out; hdwy frm 2 out; kpt on* . . . . hd 4

707^{P} African Dawn(cp,tt) 16-1 Miss L Hawkings *Lw; wl in tch; 4l 3rd 10; disp 2nd & gng wl 14; ev ch til rdn & wknd app 2 out* 4 5

794^{P} Digitalis (5a) 16-1 Richard Darke *In tch; 4l 5th 12; cl up til wknd aft 16* . runin 6

793^{P} Destin D'Estruval (FR) 16-1 L Heard *In tch in mid-div; 5l 6th 12; rdn 14; wknd aft nxt; bhnd & pu aft 3 out*. . . . . P

790^{2} Elegant Light (5a) 4-1 Miss P Gundry *2 handlers; 5th when slt mist 7; lost plce 10; last frm 11; t.o & pu 3 out*. . . . . P

792^{P} Select Star (IRE)(vis,tt) 33-1 Miss J Congdon *Rr when fell 2; rdr broke collar-bone* . . . . F

572^{1} Stone Valley 2-1 Miss T Cave *Facing wrong way in appalling start; rr & rdn when fell 2* . . . . F

OFFICIAL DISTANCES: $1\frac{1}{2}$*l*, 1*l* **TIME:** 6min 13.0s

Fences 9 & 16 omitted - fallen rider

824 Restricted, 12st 12 ran

601^{4} **BALDARA (IRE)**(tt) 2-1F **A Farrant** *Opened 5/2; hld up in tch; cl 5th 12; hdwy & poised in 3rd frm 15; eff & ld aft 3 out; sn clr; comf* 1

Ivans Dream 6-1 **L Jefford** *Prom; disp ld 5-8; trckd ldr til disp ld agn 12-14; cl 2nd til ld 3 out; hdd & outpcd app 2 out* 6 2

488^{P} **Mister Cone**(tt) 12-1 **I Hambley** *(xnb) Disp 5th $\frac{1}{2}$way; cl 4th 12; chsd ldrs; 4th & ev ch 3 out; stayed on u.p frm 2 out* . . . . $\frac{3}{4}$ 3

198^{P} Fortysixallout (IRE) 6-1 Mrs O Jackson *(xnb) Prom; disp ld 5 til ld 8; mist 10; disp ld 12-14; lost plce nxt; one pce frm 3 out*. 8 4

706^{P} Star Of Kilcash (IRE) 10-1 C Heard *Swtng; prog to 3rd 9; disp ld 14; slt ld to 16; wknd rap app 2 out*. 5 5

791^{3} Change 4-1 T Dennis *Trckd ldrs; 6th 14; in tch til wknd aft 15* 3 6

604^{P} The Real Murphy (IRE) 20-1 S Rogers *Rcd on outer & in tch; 7th 12; wknd nxt; t.o 16*. 25 7

Dark Comedy (5a) 20-1 W Biddick *Mid-div in wl-bunched field; 7th 14; wknd; t.o when mist 3 out*. . . . . runin 8

Derrilady (5a) 20-1 L Rowe *Sn rr; bhnd til pu 11* . . . . P

Feels Like Rain 12-1 L Heard *Sn rr; last pr & bhnd til pu 16; school* . . . . . P

791P Milla's Man (IRE) 7-2 M Dennis *Midfield; 9th in wl-grouped field 12; towards rr when blun & ur nxt* . . . U
323P My Jess (5a) 12-1 M Sweetland *(xnb) Ld to 4; prom; cl 6th 12; wknd 15; bhnd when pu 2 out* . . . P

OFFICIAL DISTANCES: 7*l*, ½*l* **TIME:** 6min 17.0s

825 Mens Open, 12st — 3 ran

733² **SPRINGFORD (IRE)** (7x) 5-2 **D Alers-Hankey** *(xnb) Trckd ldr til ld 13; slt ld & jmpd btr than rival 15-17; jnd 2 out; battled on wl u.p; lkd to win by nk* 1†
543⁴ **ONEMINUTETOFIVE** (4x) 1-3F **A Farrant** *(xnb,ringbit) Lw; hld up in tch; nt a fluent; hdwy & cl 2nd when outj 15-3 out; drvn to chall 2 out; upsides last; hdd flat; no ex cl home; lkd btn a nk* . . . nk 1†
629P **Norlandic (NZ)** (7x) 5-1 **L Jefford** *Ld & nt a fluent; hdd 13; sn wknd; 10l 3rd & strugg 3 out; eased* . . . 30 3

OFFICIAL DISTANCES: d ht, 15*l* **TIME:** 6min 09.0s

826 Open Maiden 56&7yo, 12st — 5 ran

494P **ASK AGAIN** (7a) 5-1 **Miss L Gardner** *2 handlers; swtng; tk keen hld; 2nd to 5; 10l 3rd ½way; hdwy u.p aft 3 out; disp 2nd when lft disp ld last; drvn to ld last 50yds* . . . 1
575P **My Little Lady** (5a) 4-1 **Miss A Bush** *Went 2nd 5; 4l 2nd when mist 9; chsd ldr & little imp til clsd to disp 2nd 2 out; ev ch when lft disp ld at last; outrdn & no ex cl home* . . . ½ 2
567P **Nditlir** (12a) 5-2 **C Heard** *Tried to make all; 4l up & hit 9; 5l clr 16-3 out; pegged back & str prsd when fell last; rmtd* . . . runin 3
702P Dart View Lass (5a)(cp) 12-1 L Heard *(xnb) 20l 4th & rmdrs aft 5; 15l 4th when blun 8; nt keen & releg last when pu nxt* . . . P
368U Deep Pockets (IRE) (7a) 6-4F D Alers-Hankey *(xnb) Tchd 2s; sn trailing in last; went poor 4th aft 8; no hdwy; t.o & pu 16* . . . P

OFFICIAL DISTANCES: nk, dist **TIME:** 6min 32.0s

827 Confined Maiden, 12st - 18J — 10 ran

702² **MY WHISPER (IRE)** (12a) 9-4F **L Jefford** *Prom; went 2nd 8; chsd ldr; hdwy to chall aft 3 out; ld aft nxt; pushed clr flat* . . . 1
701³ **Josanjamic** (5a)(vis) 5-2 **L Heard** *Tried to make all; went 6l clr 15; blun bad 16; slt ld & hrd prsd aft 3 out; hdd & no ex aft 2 out* . . . 2 2
194⁴ **Terino** 7-2 **Richard Darke** *In tch; cl 4th 9; 4½l 4th 12; went 8l 3rd 15; stayed on frm 3 out; nt trble ldrs; may improve* . . . 3½ 3
Countryside March (5a) 20-1 Miss L Gardner *In tch; cl 5th & gng wl 9; wknd 15; btn 4th frm 3 out* . . . 30 4
312P Cargo Flight 9-2 A Farrant *(xnb) Tchd 5s; hld up; hdwy 9; wl in tch in 6th when fell 13* . . . F
573P Fenny Royal 20-1 M Woodward *2 handlers; midfield; 7th 8; wknd 10; poor 8th when pu 12* . . . P
Harnage (IRE) 10-1 Miss C Prouse *2nd to 8; 6l 6th 12; lost tch 14; t.o & pu 16* P
567P Lilabet (5a) 6-1 Mrs M Hand *Sn rr; lost tch 6; t.o & pu 13* . . . P
312P Paddy's Glory 20-1 L Rowe *(xnb,bf) Towards rr; hdwy to 3½l 3rd 12; in tch in 4th 15; wknd nxt; pu 2 out* . . . P
Pebble Dasher (5a) 10-1 C Heard *(xnb) Rr & nt fluent; last pr til fell 10* . . . F

OFFICIAL DISTANCES: 2*l*, 3*l* **TIME:** 6min 19.0s

Fence 17 omitted - fallen rider

Essex & Suffolk

Higham (LH 8F,19J)

Sat, 10 Apr (GOOD to FIRM, GOOD in places)

828 Hunt Members — 4 ran

778² **ENDEAVOUR (FR)** 2-7F **G Cooper** *Made all; narrow advant til rdn out flat; unimpressive* . . . 1
Johnny Ross (IRE) 9-1 **D Kemp** *Prsd ldr to 7; 2l down 8-12; prsd ldr agn & ev ch to last; outpcd* . . . 3 2

Spikey Passage 14-1 **Miss S Keay** *1st ride; last to 4; 2l 3rd 6; outpcd 14; 25l 3rd when blun & rdr lost irons 2 out* 35 3
559U Hollyhock (5a) 3-1 P Taiano *(xnb) Cl 3rd to 5; 4th nxt til 3rd agn 8; 6l 3rd when pu & dism 12* . . . . P

OFFICIAL DISTANCES: 3*l*, dist **TIME:** 6min 34.0s **TOTE:** £1.20 **DF:**-

829 Restricted, 12st — 5 ran

648[6] **CAMDEN LOCH (IRE)** 2-1 **D Kemp** *Prsd ldr til ld 9; made rest; drew clr 3 out; easily* 1
648[5] **Trinity Buoy (IRE)**(cp) evensF **M Mackley** *(xnb) Trckd ldng pr; 2l 3rd 11; 2nd 14; sn outpcd; btn 2 out* 12 2
647[5] **Ardnut**(bl) 12-1 **Miss R Page** *Last til 4th 2-3; last agn 4; 15l adrift 11; 20l 4th 15; kpt on frm 2 out to catch a faltering rival cl home* 10 3
559P Zafan (IRE) 7-1 A Braithwaite *Ld to 8; cl 2nd aft til dem 14; wknd v rap; t.o 2 out; dem agn cl home* 3/4 4
648P Give Him A Chance (IRE)(bl) 5-1 N Moore *4th when blun & releg last 2; sn 4th agn; 10l 4th & blun 10; last by 15; rap t.o; crawled over 16 & imm pu* . P

OFFICIAL DISTANCES: 15*l*, 10*l* **TIME:** 6min 20.0s **TOTE:** £3.00 **DF:**£1.40

830 Mens Open, 12st — 3 ran

442[3] **HOMME DE FER** 2-1 **G Greenock** *1st ride & rdr constantly lkng rnd; rcd wide; 2nd til ld 4; narrow advant til jnd 3 out-nxt; qcknd to ld app last; kpt on wl; rdr watching rnr-up flat* 1
442[4] **Ballinure Boy (IRE)**(bl) 4-6F **A Hickman** *(xnb) Hld up in cl 3rd; went 1l 2nd 13; prsd ldr 16; disp ld 3 out-nxt; nt qckn app last* 1 2
650[3] **Dunrig (IRE)**(bl) 7-2 **J Owen** *Ld to 3; cl 2nd aft til dem 3rd & rdn 13; 20l down 2 out; rap lost tch; nt keen* 35 3

OFFICIAL DISTANCES: 1*l*, dist **TIME:** 6min 09.0s **TOTE:** £2.20 **DF:**-

831 Ladies Open — 4 ran

558[2] **SPRING GALE (IRE)** 1-2F **Miss Z Turner** *Mounted on course; reluct at start; 30l adrift when mist & nrly ur 1; 8l 3rd by 11; ld 15; 2nd nxt; ld agn app 2 out; qcknd clr last* 1
399[3] **Mai Point** (5a) 5-2 **Mrs S Hodge** *(xnb) Trckd ldr; 5l 3rd 4; ½l 2nd 8; disp ld 9 til ld brief 14; jmpd to ld agn 16; hdd & outpcd 2 out; no ex last; collapsed & died* 5 2
558[9] **Catherine's Way (IRE)**(cp) 10-1 **Miss A Stennett** *Ld to 8; disp ld frm 9-13; hopeless outpcd nxt; 25l 3rd 16; plodded on* 35 3
649P Wise Advice (IRE) 4-1 Miss L Marriott *Cl 2nd to 7; 3rd aft til dem last 11; 15l 4th 12; t.o 14* 10 4

OFFICIAL DISTANCES: 4*l*, dist **TIME:** 6min 17.0s **TOTE:** £1.40 **DF:**-

832 Confined — 7 ran

556[4] **LEATHERBACK (IRE)** 6-1 **J Owen** *10s-6s; cl up; 6l 4th 10; 3rd 13; ld 16; a gng best aft; drvn out* 1
744P **Ballad (IRE)** 5-2 **A Williams** *9/2-5/2; cl up; 2l 3rd 8; prsd ldr aft til ld frm 14-15; ev ch til nt qckn 2 out; sn btn* 5 2
650[6] **Polo Ridge (IRE)**(bl) 16-1 **H Fowler** *Ld to 10; outpcd & drpd to 4th 12; no ch 3 out; went 3rd 2 out* 8 3
643[2] Algan (FR) (5x) 5-4F J Ryan *Prom; prsd ldr frm 2; ld 11-13; nt qckn nxt; cl up aft til dem 4th 2 out; one pce; inept rdn* 6 4
246P Fiolino (FR) 20-1 Miss R Page *(xnb) Rr; 15l last 5; sn t.o; pu 2 out* . . . . . P
646P Trojan Love (IRE) (5a) 25-1 A Braithwaite *(xnb) Tk str hld; 3l 4th 4; dem 11; rap lost tch & pu 12* . . . . P
557[6] Vital Issue (IRE) 6-1 P Johnson *(xnb) Reluct to go down; last pr when cocked jaw & rn out 2* . . . . R

OFFICIAL DISTANCES: 4*l*, 6*l* **TIME:** 6min 21.0s **TOTE:** £7.20 **DF:**£82.00

833 Open Maiden, 12st — 14 ran

MR HAWKEYE (USA) (7a) 12-1 **N Moore** *(xnb) Ld in start; cl up til ld 6; made rest; spreadeagled field; 20l clr 16; eased flat; v impressive* 1
651[4] **On The Day (IRE)** 5-2F **J Owen** *Prsd ldr til completely outpcd frm 5; 2nd aft; no imp frm 12; 20l down 16; hung rt & drvn out flat* 35 2

651[2] **Manhatton Storm (IRE)** 4-1 **A Merriam** *Mid-div; 9th & mist 5; hdwy frm 9; 10l 3rd 11; sn outpcd bhnd clr ldr; 10l 3rd 16; stayed on frm 2 out; nrly caught hanging 2nd* . . . ½ 3
746[5] Play Alone (IRE) (5a) 8-1 D Kemp *Narrow ld to 5; chsd runaway ldr aft; 15l 3rd 12; one pce aft; dem 4th flat* . . . 3 4
652[5] No Nay Never (IRE) 8-1 Miss A Bowles *Cl up in mid-div til outpcd 11; lft 30l last by 2 out* . . . 6 5
560[P] Carvilla (IRE) 16-1 A Braithwaite *(xnb) Mid-div to 10; stdly lost tch frm 11; t.o & pu 3 out* . . . P
401[F] Half A Story (5a) 10-1 A Williams *Sn bhnd; virt t.o in 12th when rdn 9; plodded on til event pu 16* . . . P
777[P] Lightning Rebel 33-1 S Gordon-Watson *(xnb) Prom to 9; wknd rap; rr & detach aft 11; t.o & pu 16* . . . P
646[3] Looking Magic (IRE) 33-1 M Mackley *Imm rr; 13th 8; t.o by 11; pu 16* . . . P
561[4] Memsahib Ki Behan (5a) 10-1 H Fowler *Prom to 8; stdly lost plce; rr & detach aft 11; t.o & pu 16* . . . P
540[3] No Reward (IRE) 3-1 A Hickman *(xnb) Hld up in rr; 9l 8th 11; no hdwy when fell 14* . . . F
561[P] She's A Terror (12a) 16-1 M Smith *(xnb) Cl up bhnd ldrs; 4l 4th 11; sn lost plce; rr 13; t.o & pu 16* . . . P
746[U] Spring Frolic(bl) 16-1 R Stearn *Prom early; 3l 4th 8; outpcd frm 12; stdly lost tch; wl in rr when pu 3 out* . . . P
560[P] Straw Exchange (12a, 3ow) 20-1 P Chinery *Last 3; t.o 12; plodded rnd til event pu 3 out* . . . P

OFFICIAL DISTANCES: dist, ½*l* **TIME:** 6min 12.0s **TOTE:** £14.00 **DF:**£16.00 (1st+3rd/4th)

Ludlow

Bitterley (LH 8F,18J)
Sat, 10 Apr (GOOD)

834 Hunt Members — 6 ran

661[P] **CADOUGOLD (FR)**(tt) 6-4F **M Keel** *Hld up; went 3rd 6 & 2nd 14; ld app 2 out; sn rdn clr* . . . 1
513[P] **Ceasers Reign (IRE)** 7-2 **T Stephenson** *2 handlers; nt fluent 7; prom til outpcd 14; 12l 4th nxt; plugged into 2nd app last; no ch w wnr* . . . 15 2
586[7] **O J Selym (IRE)** (7x) 6-1 **G Opperman** *Mist 10; hld up last to 11; outpcd 14; 12l 5th nxt; plugged on desp rdr* . . . 4 3
517[2] Classic Fable (IRE) (5a) 10-1 A Hanly *2 handlers; 2nd bhnd clr ldr; clsd 7; ld 8; hdd aft 3 out; tired & mist nxt; fin slow* . . . 3 4
665[F] Sabena Canyon 5-1 M Wall *Hld up; eff to chall for cl 3rd & blun 14; nt rec; 10l 3rd nxt; no ch when blun agn 3 out; eased & t.o* . . . 30 5
613[P] Grand Gousier (FR) 4-1 E Andrewes *Bckwd; ld; 12l clr 4; prsd 7; hdd 8; wkng when hit 11; sn t.o last; pu 2 out* . . . P

OFFICIAL DISTANCES: 10*l*, 2*l* **TIME:** 6min 30.0s

835 Confined, 12st — 11 ran

95[1] **JIMMY CRICKET** 5-4F **N Oliver** *2s-5/4; lw; hdwy in 3rd 5; went 15l 2nd 9; niggled nxt; clsd 13; ld 3 out; in comm nxt; kpt on stout; game* . . . 1
663[2] **Petrouge**(cp) 3-1 **A Wintle** *Settled towards rr; clsd to 4th 9 & 3rd 13; 2nd aft 3 out; drvn & plugged on with little zest aft* . . . 6 2
Asthefellasays (IRE) 5-1 **Julian Pritchard** *Midfield; 6th 10; eff 13 to 6l 3rd nxt; outpcd 15; plugged into poor 3rd & jmpd slow last* . . . 20 3
660[7] Borderline Breeze (IRE) 20-1 Miss H Watson *(xnb) Last early; impd to 3rd/4th 10 til 8l 4th 14; wknd nxt; plodded home* . . . 5 4
660[F] Wild Edric(bl) 6-1 A Beedles *Prom early; drpd back 8th 10; wl bhnd frm 14* 2 5
663[5] Genereux(cp,tt) 5-1 R Hodges *Sn drvn in rr; blun 8; detach 9th 10; rem frm 13; nvr keen* . . . 15 6
447[P] Against The Agent 12-1 S Gray *Bit bckwd; ld & sn clr; 12l ahd when mist & went rt 11; prsd frm 13; pckd & hdd 3 out; wknd rap; eased flat* . . . 3 7
663[P] Hillcrest Manor (IRE)(cp) 20-1 Miss S Davies *Nt fluent; chsd clr ldr 4-9; strugg when mists 12 & 13; t.o last 15* . . . runin 8
515[2] Allotrope (IRE)(bl,tt) 20-1 Miss L Brooke *Last by 5; t.o & pu 12* . . . P

Beyond The Stars 5-1 Miss K Phillips *Fat; unruly when mounted; prom early; lost plce to 7th 11; still just in tch when pu nxt* . . . . P

346^{P} Harry Hotspur (IRE)(bl) 20-1 M Dearden *(xnb) 2 handlers; ss & lost 25l; crashed thro wing & ur 2* . . . . R

OFFICIAL DISTANCES: 4*l*, 8*l* **TIME:** 6min 29.0s

836 Land Rover Mens Open, 12st — 7 ran

377^{3} **WATCHYOURBACK (NZ)**(vis,tt) 6-1 **S Gray** *10s-6s; 3rd/4th & way off pce; 42l 3rd 13; clsd grad frm 15; made 15l frm nxt to ld last; sn clr und ecstatic rdr* 1

346^{5} **Jemaro (IRE)** (7x) 6-4 **A Wintle** *Lw; swtng; jw; ld & wl clr w 1 rival; lft 15l ahd 3 out; tired & rdn aft; hdd last; imm btn* 8 2

612^{7} **Southern Cross** 20-1 **T Stephenson** *A wl bhnd; drvn 9; 63l last 13* 30 3

727^{F} Time Can Tell(bl) 25-1 S Graham *Chsd clr ldng pr to 7; u.p nxt; 56l 4th 13* 20 4

662^{P} Robsand (IRE) 50-1 M Wilesmith *Bckwd; lumbered along in last; t.o 4; pu 12* P

727^{5} Titus Bramble (4x)(bl,tt) 4-5F Julian Pritchard *Prsd ldr but constantly outj; nk down & drvn 15; ev ch when fell nxt* . . . . F

201^{1} Zola (IRE) 12-1 M Jackson *Went 30l 3rd 7-10; rdn & reluct aft nxt; t.o 12; pu last* . . . . P

OFFICIAL DISTANCES: 5*l*, 20*l* **TIME:** 6min 28.0s

837 Open Maiden 56&7yo, 12st — 10 ran

53^{5} **WHICH POCKET (IRE)** 2-1F **M Wall** *4s-2s; lw; rcd keen & cl up; went 2nd 8; ld app 13; went 4l clr 2 out; rdn & stayed on wl* 1

Fergal's Find (IRE) (7a)(tt) 6-1 **M Goldstein** *(xnb) Hld up in tch; 3l 3rd aft 15; chsd wnr vain aft 2 out; one-pcd* 12 2

709^{P} **The Noble Roman** 3-1 **T Ellis** *Opened 4s; tk keen hld; cl up; went 2l 2nd aft 15; drvn nxt; no ex; dem last* 5 3

Geal Farraige (IRE) (12a) 4-1 N Oliver *(xnb) Midfield; cl 4th when mist 13; releg $3\frac{1}{2}$l 4th aft blun 15; nt pushed frm nxt; mist last* 2 4

723^{U} Definite Flash (IRE) (5a) 16-1 P Morris *Mists in rr; strugg 11; t.o when mist 12* 25 5

Analan (12a) 5-1 T Weston *Midfield; mists 6, 7 & 8; cl up til 4l 5th aft 15; sn wknd; will improve w experience* 2 6

725^{P} Bally Cyrano 14-1 Miss R Reynolds *Chsd ldr to 8; fdng rap when mist 11; pu 12* . . . . P

725^{6} Force Ten 5-1 T Stephenson *Swtng; ld til app 13 where mist when last; wkng rap; t.o & pu 15* . . . . P

Street Parade (12a) 6-1 R Hodges *Bckwd & lkd horrible; t.o when nrly ref 4; scrambled over nxt; pu 7* . . . . P

725^{P} The Brooklet 6-1 A Wintle *Lw; jmpd rt & numerous mists in rr; last & strugg 11; pu & dism 12* . . . . P

OFFICIAL DISTANCES: 7*l*, 2*l* **TIME:** 6min 36.0s

838 Ladies Open — 6 ran

737^{2} **UPTON ADVENTURE** (5a) 1-3F **Miss E James** *Jw; made all; drew 6l clr 14; in comm frm nxt* 1

650^{P} **Wibbley Wobbley** 12-1 **Miss H Watson** *Hld up; went 3rd 10; 8l down & drvn 14; tk poor 2nd 3 out; no ch w wnr* 20 2

490^{5} **The Writer (IRE)** 5-2 **Miss C Stucley** *(xnb) 10s-5/2; went 2nd 4; jmpd slow 5; niggled 10; ev ch til hit 13; sn outpcd; dem 3 out* 12 3

449^{U} Flying Pennant (IRE) 16-1 Miss S Davies *Nt fluent 7; cl up til wknd qckly 10; t.o 12; pu 15* . . . . P

616^{P} Joshua's Vision (IRE) 8-1 Miss L Brooke *A last; strugg 7; t.o 9; pu 12* . . . . P

751^{P} Karzhang(tt) 8-1 Miss S Talbot *Pulled hrd; cl up; hit 6; 8l 4th 12; lost tch nxt; t.o & pu 15* . . . . P

OFFICIAL DISTANCES: 16*l*, 8*l* **TIME:** 6min 25.0s

839 Restricted, 12st — 9 ran

726^{F} **FATHER TOM (IRE)** 11-8F **Julian Pritchard** *Opened 7/4; nt a fluent; detach in last pr; clsd 10; 7th & mist 12; hdwy on bit to pass most of field frm 3 out; ld last; imm strode clr; fine ride* 1

Belle Moss (5a) 5-1 **N Oliver** *Cl up; 6th when jmpd slow 7; trckng ldrs when hit 14; sn rdn; disp 2nd 2 out; ev ch app last; no match for wnr flat* . . . 8 2

618^{1} **Justadream** 3-1 **T Stephenson** *(xnb) Ld til app 3; prsd ldrs aft; 4th & rdn 2 out; one-pcd* 1 3

661³	Huntersway (IRE) 11-2 R Hodges *Swtng; 2nd/4th til ld 13-14; ld agn 3 out; sn hrd rdn; hdd & nt qckn last*	½	4
726P	Certain Surprise (5a) 12-1 Miss E James *Chsng ldrs when blun 8; 4th 12; rdn to chall on outside app 3 out; disp 2nd nxt; wknd tame*	15	5
715²	Snitton West(bl) 4-1 M Jackson *6s-4s; ld app 3-13; ld agn nxt; hrd rdn & hdd 3 out; imm gave up.*	½	6
614³	Paddy Bettalot 12-1 A Hanly *Hld up; 3rd & prog 10; 2nd brief 13; hit nxt; rdn & wknd app 3 out.*	1	7
726P	A Bit Of Fluff (5a) 20-1 Miss L Brooke *Bhnd; lost tch 6; clsd brief on sufferance 10; jmpd rt nxt & sn t.o; jmpd rt & v slow 15 & pu*		P
726U	Far From Perfect (IRE) (5a) 14-1 A Wintle *Blun bad 4; nt striding out aft; last when jmpd slow 5; pu 6*		P

OFFICIAL DISTANCES: 5*l*, 1*l* **TIME:** 6min 38.0s

840 Open Maiden 8yo&up, 12st — 14 ran

729U	**THIS ONE IS A BOY (IRE)** 5-2CF **M Wilesmith** *(xnb) Opened 3s; settled wl off pce early; prog in 4th 10; lft in ld 14; just hdd 3 out-nxt; r.o u.p flat; all out*		1
	Clever Dickie 5-2CF **M Jackson** *4s-5/2; hld up way off pce; t.o 4; still last but clsng 10; 20l 2nd app 13; sn chsng wnr; outj 15; drvn & slt ld 3 out til mist nxt; nt qckn.*	4	2
668⁵	**Lou Biarnes (FR)** 12-1 **B Shaw** *Prom in chsng group; went 2nd & mist 12 & releg 4th; mist nxt; 8l 3rd & rdn app 15; sn floundering*	25	3
661P	Jovian Pond(tt) 7-1 R Sealey *Prom in chsng group; 3rd 12; 6th & wkng qckly app nxt; rem 4th 3 out*	25	4
668⁷	Norton Wood (IRE)(tt) 10-1 R Hodges *(xnb) Nt jw; nvr btr than midfield; 8th & u.p app 13; 15l last app 15; sn t.o & v tired*	10	5
760P	A Proper Charlie 14-1 T Stephenson *Hld up in rr til rn out 5*		R
730r	Baron Kiss 20-1 S Gray *Towards rr; strugg 10; t.o & pu 13*		P
731P	B So Bold 12-1 A Hanly *Mist 3; midfield til fell 5*		F
666³	Channel's Brook 6-1 N Oliver *14s-6s; bhnd; lost tch 11; mist nxt; t.o when pu & dism 14.*		P
734P	Come On Boy 20-1 G Davies *Cl up; 2nd brief 10; 7th & wkng rap app 13; mist nxt; t.o & jb rt 15; pu nxt*		P
621²	Lord Woodyard 5-2CF Julian Pritchard *(xnb) Lw; hld up in rr; 10th aft mist 10; eff app 13; 13l 4th & strugg app 15; pu nxt*		P
668P	Nealie Mac (IRE) 20-1 M Wall *2 handlers; hit 9; chsd ldr til lost plce & mist 10; last aft nxt; pu 12*		P
112P	Retribution 20-1 Miss R Reynolds *Ld; 8l clr 10; 20l ahd when pu rap & dism 14*		P
753P	Sylvias Dream (5a) 20-1 P Morris *Hrd hld in last pr; t.o 4; rn out 5*		R

OFFICIAL DISTANCES: 2½*l*, 20*l* **TIME:** 6min 37.0s

Contrary King (2 handlers, T Weston, 6-1 - ur & bolted at start - agn almost unrideable in prelims) was withdrawn not under orders; Rule 4 deduction 10p in pound

Monmouthshire

Llanvapley (LH 7F,18J)

Sat, 10 Apr (GOOD to SOFT - stretch of plough)

841 Confined, 12st — 8 ran

671P	**BUCKLAND BOY**(vis) 4-1 **W Oakes** *Hld up in rr; last frm 4; prog 11 to 5l 2nd 14; sn ld & clr; 6l up 3 out; tying up nxt; rallied flat*		1
672³	**Chief Predator (USA)** (3x) 7-2 **T Faulkner** *4l 3rd 4; grad drpd to rr; last pr 11; r.o frm 3 out; 3rd nxt; went 2nd at last; nt rch wnr*	4	2
739³	**Glen Mist (IRE)**(bl) 16-1 **L Stephens** *Ld 3-13; mist 5; 2nd & u.p 15; 6l down 3 out; no ex & dem nxt*	4	3
672²	Doc Ryan's 11-10F T Vaughan *6/4-11/10; 5th early; last 9; hdwy u.p to 4th 13; no further prog*	8	4
738²	Fassan (IRE)(cp) 10-1 James Price *Settled 4th; fdd 11; last frm 14*	6	5
612P	Darrell Boy (IRE)(vis) 8-1 D Jones *Ld 1; midfield & rmdrs 2; 2l 2nd & pulling 4; 5l 2nd when rdn & rmdrs 11; sn t.o; pu 14*		P
670²	La Maestra (FR) (5a) 11-2 M Barber *Midfield; went 3rd 12; u.p 14; no resp; wknd & pu 2 out*		P
699⁴	Miss Man (5a) 20-1 Miss A Cavanagh *2 handlers; swtng sltly; a bhnd; rn out 7*		R

OFFICIAL DISTANCES: 3*l*, 3*l*, 3*l* **TIME:** 6min 45.0s

842 Mens Open, 12st — 5 ran

735^{1}	**PHARAILDE** (5a) 6-1 **J Price** *Tk 3rd app 5; disp 3rd 9; ld aft 11; slt mist nxt; 2l up 16; brushed thro 3 out; sn clr; comf*		1
660^{5}	**Persona Pride** 7-2 **D Jones** *Ld/disp to 11; 8l 4th 14; went 2nd u.p 2 out*	6	2
669^{1}	**Waders (IRE)**(bl) evensF **M Barber** *Opened 5/4; ld/disp to 11; 3rd & rdn nxt; 2nd 14; u.p 16; dem app 2 out*	8	3
	Khatani (IRE) (7x) 5-2 L Stephens *(xnb) Mostly 3rd; 6l away & rdn 16; no ex; walked in*	8	4
356^{P}	Danny Gale (IRE) 25-1 M Williams *Last & jmpd slow 1; 8l adrift 2; jmpd delib & sn t.o; 2 fncs bhnd when pu 10*		P

OFFICIAL DISTANCES: 4*l*, 6*l*, 6*l* **TIME:** 6min 41.0s

843 Ladies Open — 9 ran

	DETROIT DAVY (IRE) 6-1 **Miss F Wilson** *Hld up in 6th; prog to 5l 3rd 14; 2nd 16; ½l down at last; ld und str drvng nr post*		1
449^{2}	**Ashfield Orchestra (IRE)** (5a) 5-4F **Miss I Tompsett** *Swtng sltly; hld up in 4th; disp 3rd 4; tk 2nd 9; ld & slt mist 13; 5l up 3 out; prsd at last; hdd cl home*	nk	2
361^{5}	**Flockmaster (IRE)** 16-1 **Mrs C Owen** *Settled midfield; 4th frm 11; 3rd 3 out; r.o; just kpt 3rd*	3	3
	Millennium Gold 4-1 Miss A Frieze *Last early; last pr 3-9; went 4th frm 11; clsng flat & nrly snatched 3rd*	s hd	4
449^{P}	Do It Once (IRE) (7x)(tt) 10-1 Mrs A Rucker *(xnb) Ld 1; disp 3-4; 2l 2nd 14; outpcd aft; 5th frm nxt*	3	5
697^{4}	Welburn Boy(bl,tt) 25-1 Miss L Allfrey *Last to 13; stayed on past wkng horses frm 15*	4	6
756^{P}	Head Gardener (IRE)(bl) 25-1 Miss J Hughes *Chsd ldrs; 2l 2nd frm 4; ld brief 11; sn wknd; no ch frm 14*	8	7
739^{1}	Silver Pot Black 5-1 Miss H Lewis *Nd; 6th to 8; drpd to last 14*	12	8
737^{3}	Young Manny (4x) 16-1 Mrs B Lewis *Ld 2-10; 4th when ur 11*		U

OFFICIAL DISTANCES: nk, 3*l*, s hd **TIME:** 6min 40.0s

844 Restricted, 12st — 19 ran

700^{1}	**BARTON DREAM (IRE)** 5-2F **T Vaughan** *(xnb) 2 handlers; a ldng trio; ld 3 out; kpt on u.p frm last*		1
695^{U}	**Phase Three (IRE)** 3-1 **T Edwards** *(xnb) Ld 3 til hdd app 3 out; kpt on; a hld*	1	2
450^{F}	**Camden Caramel (IRE)** (5a) 12-1 **T Faulkner** *9th early; hdwy 8; settled 5th til wknd 14; went 3rd flat; all out*	12	3
674^{3}	Trial Trip (5a) 10-1 J Cook *Ld early; settled cl 2nd; lost plce 3 out; dem agn flat*	1	4
694^{2}	Alpine Fugue (IRE)(tt) 12-1 Miss S Lewis *A last trio; t.o last 10; pu 2 out*		P
674^{4}	Carl's Boy 6-1 J L Llewellyn *(xnb) Bhnd to 5; went 6th frm 8; fdd 14; pu nxt*		P
450^{P}	Caveat Graeci (IRE) (5a) 15-1 M Barber *Prom early; 3rd 4; rdn in mid-div 8; no resp; pu 13*		P
666^{P}	Corn General 25-1 D Jones *(xnb) Settled 6th; hdwy 8; 4th & blun 9; wknd qckly; pu 13*		P
	Daisy Leigh (5a) 16-1 N Williams *Prom; 4th frm 7; lost tch 14; pu nxt*		P
726^{10}	Glacial Boy(vis) 6-1 W Oakes *Last quartet 4; impd to 7th 10; no imp aft; pu 3 out*		P
	Jim Dore (IRE)(tt) 12-1 C Penycate *Unruly padd; sa; midfield when fell 2*		F
695^{5}	Knight Ofthe North 20-1 Miss E Burrows *Mid-div; ab 10th mostly; mist 10; detach 12; pu 15*		P
694^{P}	Mikes Acre (5a)(tt) 10-1 Miss B Williams *(xnb) Midfield; 11th when ur 7*		U
731^{P}	Riches To Rags (IRE) 20-1 M Hooper *(bf) A last; sn detach; t.o & pu 5*		P
674^{P}	Runaway Ralph 10-1 P Sheldrake *Midfield when bd 2*		B
700^{P}	Saronica's Boy 16-1 James Price *Mid-div; 12th 4; nvr btr; pu 11*		P
	Satco Prince (IRE) 12-1 L Stephens *Last pr; lost tch 5; pu 11*		P
451^{P}	Scholar Green 25-1 D Mansell *Spurs; 8th; a midfield; mist 12; pu nxt.*		P
740^{4}	Steel Gem (IRE) 10-1 J Price *Became tangled in ropes on way to post (too many horses in padd); chsd ldrs; 7th til wknd to last trio & mist 12; pu 2 out; drpd dead aft.*		P

OFFICIAL DISTANCES: 1*l*, 4*l*, 3*l* **TIME:** 6min 37.0s

Gay Abandon would have been declared for this race but no jockey could be found who was prepared to take the ride

845 Confined Maiden 56&7yo, 12st — 13 ran

	Horse / Rider / Comment	Dist	Pos
	RAG WEEK (IRE) 6-1 **J Cook** *Ld 1-2; sn 10l 2nd; cl 2nd 8 til lft in ld 13; drew 3l clr 3 out; blun & down on knees 2 out; tired but kpt on u.p*		1
450³	**Roboastar (USA)** 6-1 **T Vaughan** *Hld up in rr; prog 10; cl 5th 12; went 2nd 14; 3l 2nd 3 out; tired & no imp u.p nxt*	3	2
700³	**Little Word** (12a) 7-1 **Miss F Wilson** *Nt fluent; 3rd early; sn rr; t.o 14; plodded on; scrambled over last*	runin	3
700ᵁ	Bristol Bridge(bl) 16-1 T Faulkner *2 handlers; midfield to 8; sn fdd; rr til pu 15*		P
	Celtic Knight 12-1 James Price *(xnb) Fat; a last; t.o 7; pu 10*		P
	Celtic Prince (IRE) 8-1 N Williams *Rr early; settled 7th 6; detach in 5th & u.p 14; no resp; pu 15*		P
	Finlays Folly 20-1 C Penycate *A last trio; mist 2; pu 11*		P
666²	Kerry Zulu Warrior 6-1 H Tett *(xnb) Ld 2; 10l up 4; hdd 8; 4th when ur 9*		U
446³	Lynwood Legend 14-1 J L Llewellyn *(xnb,bf) Hld up in 8th; hdwy 8; cl 3rd 10; wknd 15; sn lost tch; pu 3 out*		P
735ᵁ	Maloney (IRE) 16-1 Miss C Evans *A last trio; pu 13*		P
617ᶠ	Red Salmon Dancer (7a) 7-2 D Mansell *Midfield; mostly 6th; in tch to 12; 4th 14; wknd & 20l 4th 16; pu nxt*		P
700²	Ruby Dante (IRE) (5a) 7-4F D Jones *A.p; ld 9 til ur 13*		U
700⁶	St Palais (12a) 12-1 P Sheldrake *Midfield; 5th mostly; cl 6th 12; no ex aft; lost tch & pu 14*		P

OFFICIAL DISTANCES: 3*l*, dist **TIME:** 6min 48.0s

846 Hunt Members, 12st — 2 ran

	Horse / Rider / Comment	Dist	Pos
613⁶	**VICARS CHALET (IRE)** 1-3F **Miss H Lewis** *Just ld rival frm 2 & jmpd btr; jmpd low 12 & 14; drew clr frm 14; 15l up 3 out; easy*		1
	Modesty Forbids (5a) 2-1 **M Hooper** *Just ld 1; virt level w rival til outpcd frm 14; 3l down nxt; 15l down 3 out; jmpd slow last*	runin	2

OFFICIAL DISTANCE: dist **TIME:** 6min 55.0s

North Staffordshire

Sandon (LH 8F,19J)

Sat, 10 Apr (DEAD)

847 Hunt Members, 12st — 4 ran

	Horse / Rider / Comment	Dist	Pos
715⁶	**HENBURY DANCER** (5a) 4-6F **E Linehan** *Mounted on course; tk keen hld; ld to 6; ld agn 13; fnce clr by 16; unchall*		1
713ᵁ	**Jona Holley**(cp) 5-1 **Miss A Blake** *(xnb) Last & sn outpcd; 38l bhnd 13; plodded on past wkng rivals to rem 2nd 2 out*	2fncs	2
710ᴾ	Cromaboo Count 9-2 D Cook *(xnb) Cl up; went 2nd 13; wknd qckly; jmpd v slow 14; releg last app 2 out & pu*		P
713ᴾ	Easby Blue(tt) 5-1 R Dobney *Pulling; cl up; disp ld 6; gd j to ld nxt; wknd qckly & hdd 13; poor 3rd nxt; 2nd agn 3 out; poor 3rd when staggered over 2 out & pu*		P

OFFICIAL DISTANCE: dist **TIME:** 7min 06.0s **TOTE:** £1.70

848 Open Maiden, 12st — 10 ran

	Horse / Rider / Comment	Dist	Pos
749³	**RAISEAPEARL** 3-1JF **I Clyde** *Cl up; ld 7 til jmpd slow & hdd 16; rallied app last; ld flat; r.o wl; rdr's 1st wnr*		1
686⁵	**Wonderful Remark** (5a) 16-1 **G Moloney** *(xnb) Hld up in mid-div; hdwy 14; went 2nd 16; ld 2 out til hdd flat; no ex*	2	2
595²	**Ridware George** 3-1JF **Miss S Sharratt** *Ld to 6; cl 2nd/3rd aft; ev ch app last; one pce flat*	3	3
532ᴾ	Whats Up Jake 8-1 A Wadlow *(xnb) Hld up in rr; hdwy to 5th 3 out; nt pce to chall*	5	4
	Tisallover (IRE) 12-1 M Hammond *(xnb) Prom; ld app 3 out; wknd & hdd nxt*	10	5
594ᴾ	Grey Snipe 14-1 L Hicks *A last trio; jmpd slow 7; rdn along aft; last & lsng tch 11; clambered over nxt & pu*		P
714ᴾ	Grey Tarquin (5a) 7-2 G Hanmer *Trckd ldrs in 4/5th til wknd 3 out; lost tch & pu nxt*		P
	Owens Invader 4-1 R Burton *Rr to 6; cl 4th 10 til wknd 13; sn bhnd; lost tch & pu 2 out*		P

714[5] Pekan Polly (5a) 8-1 S Ross *Rr most of way; lost tch 13; bhnd when pu 3 out* P
714[P] Skippers Canyon (5a) 20-1 R Carey *Tubed; a last pr; lost tch 13; t.o & pu 15* P

OFFICIAL DISTANCES: 2½*l*, 4*l* **TIME:** 7min 24.0s **TOTE:** £4.00

849 Ladies Open — 4 ran

712[3] **WANDERING LIGHT (IRE)** 7-2 **Miss T Clark** *Hld up in tch; hdwy to 2nd 15; ld app 2 out; stayed on wl flat* . . . 1
712[P] **Cascum Lad (IRE)** 2-1JF **Miss S Holmes** *Chsd ldr in 2nd til ld 13; 6l clr nxt; hdd app 2 out; rnwd eff last; no ex flat* . . . 1¼ 2
708[1] **Star Changes** 2-1JF **Miss N Lloyd** *Tde; last pr but in tch; off pce frm 13; chsd ldrs frm 16; nvr nr to chall.* . . . 10 3
664[3] Life Of A River (IRE) 3-1 Miss H Kinsey *Jmpd bold; tk keen hld; ld; wl clr 2-10; hdd 13; wknd 16; last nxt; v tired & clambered over last* . . . 35 4

OFFICIAL DISTANCES: 1½*l*, 10*l* **TIME:** 6min 58.0s **TOTE:** £4.00

850 Open Maiden 56&7yo, 2m5f, 12st - 15J — 9 ran

FLY FOR PADDY 7-2 **A Wadlow** *Oht; hld up in rr; hdwy 10; went 2nd app 2 out; chall & ld last; sn clr* . . . 1
668[P] **All Eyez On Me (IRE)**(bl) 6-1 **M Hammond** *A ldng pr; ld 11 til hdd last; qckly btn* . . . 6 2
668[P] **Grantie Boy (IRE)** (7a) 6-1 **J O'Brien** *(xnb) In tch; trckd ldrs 10 til wknd 3 out; sn bhnd; fin 4th; promoted* . . . 40 3
386[P] Hermano (IRE) 7-1 J King *(xnb) Tk keen hld; ld; wl clr 3-8; hdd 11; cl up til wknd app 2 out; fin 36l 3rd; disq - nt weigh-in.* . . . 3d
619[3] Chicago's Padre 7-1 Miss V Price *Prom til wknd qckly 10; wl bhnd when pu 12* P
686[4] Currow Kate (5a) 8-1 L Hicks *Lw; hld up in last pr; hdwy 10; 1½l 3rd & poised to chall when veered rt & crashed thro wing 3 out* . . . R
618[4] Jack's The Boy (IRE) 7-2 G Hanmer *(xnb) Cl up til wknd 11; bhnd & tired when fell 3 out* . . . F
709[P] Lord Saxbury (7a) 12-1 S Ross *A rr; lost tch app 10 & pu* . . . P
Nocando (IRE) (5a) 2-1F R Burton *(xnb) Nt fluent in last pr; 15l last when pu aft 9* P

OFFICIAL DISTANCES: Originally: 8*l*, 30*l* **TIME:** 5min 36.0s **TOTE:** £4.00

Hermano finished third but was disqualified when the rider failed to weigh-in; he was fined £55; the stewards enquired into the running of the favourite, Nocando, they accepted the rider's explanation that the mare had not felt right and had over-reached

851 Mens Open, 12st — 2 ran

662[1] **COOLE VENTURE (IRE)** 4-7F **R Burton** *Trckd rival in 2l last; eff & level 16; sn ld; drew clr app 2 out; 8l up last; pushed out flat; eased nr fin* . . . 1
711[1] **Soundtrack (IRE)** 11-8 **G Hanmer** *Jw; ld; qcknd 9; great j & went 4l clr 14; hdd 16; sn rdn; no ch w rival frm 2 out* . . . 6 2

OFFICIAL DISTANCE: 7*l* **TIME:** 6min 55.0s **TOTE:** £1.20

852 Confined, 12st — 3 ran

665[1] **JACKSON (FR)** 2-7F **R Burton** *A gng wl; hld up in cl 3rd; mist 13; sn rec; ld 15; 4l clr 2 out; eased cl home; unextended.* . . . 1
586[4] **Pagermar (IRE)** 7-2 **A Wadlow** *(xnb) Ld to 4; disp ld aft til ld 14; hdd 15; chsd wnr aft; easily hld* . . . 2½ 2
713[5] **Fornaught Alliance (IRE)** (5x)(bl) 9-1 **Miss A Turner** *Cl up; disp ld 5-13; one pce & lost tch app 2 out* . . . 12 3

OFFICIAL DISTANCES: 2½*l*, 12*l* **TIME:** 7min 15.0s **TOTE:** £1.20

853 Restricted, 12st — 8 ran

595[1] **ALTHREY DANDY (IRE)** 6-4F **L Hicks** *(xnb) Tde; tk keen hld; made all; kpt on str frm 2 out* . . . 1
383[P] **Miss Zarnni** (5a) 4-1 **Miss S Sharratt** *Rr mostly; 8l 7th 3 out; rap hdwy to press wnr nxt; ev ch last; no ex flat* . . . 2½ 2
715[5] **Donrico (IRE)** 6-1 **A Wadlow** *Rr to 11; hdwy to cl 3rd 13; ev ch til wknd app 2 out* . . . 20 3
614[4] Tinarana Lord (IRE) 7-1 G Hanmer *Prom; disp 2nd 3-11; lost plce 13; in tch til wknd app 2 out* . . . 1½ 4
614[F] Shafts Chance (IRE) (5a) 6-1 Miss K Wood *Last early; disp 2nd 5-11; wl in tch aft til wknd app 2 out* . . . 4 5

665[7]	Always Good (IRE)(tt) 12-1 P Needham *Prom til lost plce 12; last but in tch 14; one pce frm 3 out*	5	6
530[P]	Gaetano (IRE) 7-1 R Burton *In tch; went 2nd 12; chsd ldr til wknd qckly app 2 out; pu last*		P
715[3]	Infamelia (5a)(vis) 9-1 Miss T Clark *(xnb) A rr group; 6th & in tch 3 out; fdd & pu nxt*		P

OFFICIAL DISTANCES: 3*l*, 20*l* **TIME:** 6min 56.0s **TOTE:** £2.00

Percy

Alnwick (LH 9F,18J)

Sat, 10 Apr (GOOD)

854 Hunt Members, 12st — 5 ran

797[U]	**DECENT BOND (IRE)** evensF **R Green** *Trckd ldrs; prog 3 out; ld & lft clr nxt; easily*		1
429[7]	**Hoh Tel (IRE)** (4x)(cp) 3-1 **Miss R Davidson** *Handy til outpcd aft 15; one pce when lft 2nd 2 out*	8	2
	Kings Minstral (IRE) (7x)(tt) 9-2 **J Walton** *Trckd ldr til wknd aft 15; sn bhnd; lft poor 3rd 3 out*	2½	3
426[P]	Little Santa (IRE) (5a, 4x) 6-1 Mrs K Hargreave *Tried to make all; hdd & 1l down when mist & ur 2 out*		U
	Wexford (IRE) 25-1 Miss S Lamb *In tch til outpcd 12; sn wknd; t.o & pu 3 out*		P

OFFICIAL DISTANCES: 8*l*, 3*l* **TIME:** 6min 33.4s

855 Restricted — 6 ran

659[1]	**RAINHA** (5a) 4-5F **Miss P Robson** *Ld to 5; cl up til 1l down last; rdn flat; lkd to ld nr line*		1†
	PEPPERNICK 5-2 **C Storey** *Handy til prog to disp ld 13; 2l up 15; 1l up last; rdn & lkd to be hdd nr line*	nk	1†
762[P]	**The Cincinnati Kid** 7-1 **R Green** *(xnb) Oht; in tch in rr; prog to 3l 4th 14; 4l 3rd & ev ch 3 out; one pce aft nxt*	10	3
430[6]	The Broken Man 20-1 Miss K Bryson *Trckd ldr til ld 6; hdd 13; outpcd app 3 out; nd*	20	4
765[P]	Mrs Sherman (5a) 12-1 S Huggan *(xnb) Trckd ldrs; disp 3l 3rd app 15; wknd qckly app nxt; one pce aft*	4	5
	C L B Jemilla (5a) 20-1 Miss G Craggs *Fat; in tch in rr; outpcd 12 & sn lost tch*	runin	6

OFFICIAL DISTANCES: d ht, 10*l*, dist **TIME:** 6min 32.1s

856 Open Maiden 56&7yo, 2m4f, 12st - 15J — 10 ran

659[P]	**NODFORM RETURNS** (5a) 8-1 **A Findlay** *Oht; in tch; prog 10 to disp ld 3 out; ld nxt; stayed on wl*		1
344[3]	**Anniejo** (12a) 5-2JF **R Morgan** *(xnb) Ss; in tch in rr; prog to ld 9; ev ch til hdd 2 out; sn btn*	6	2
	Izzuthefox (IRE) 7-2 **C Storey** *In tch in rr; prog 10 to disp ld 3 out; hdd nxt & no ex*	4	3
768[9]	Ramon Allones (IRE) 10-1 Miss R Davidson *Ld til hdd 6; 5l 5th 12; wknd nxt; sn nd*	15	4
659[P]	What A Night (7a) 5-2JF K Anderson *In tch in rr; mist 12 & outpcd aft; kpt on; nd*	10	5
432[4]	Air Leader (IRE) (7a) 4-1 D Jewett *Cl up til slpd & ur bend bef 7*		U
	Copybook (7a, 5ow) 5-1 J Walton *Bckwd; in tch til saddle slpd & pu 3*		P
768[P]	Inglemotte Miss (5a) 6-1 Miss J Riding *Cl up til carried out by loose horse app 7*		C
554[P]	Red Jupiter 10-1 A Richardson *(bf) Swtng; prom til ld 6; hdd 9; 8l 4th when mist & ur 2 out*		U
	River Bandit 5-1 B Hall *Lw; oht; cl up when fell 10*		F

OFFICIAL DISTANCES: 4*l*, 2*l*, 15*l* **TIME:** 5min 42.2s

857 Mixed Open, 4m, 12st - 24J — 9 ran

655[1]	**PASSING DANGER (FR)** 7-4F **Miss R Davidson** *Hld up in rr; 6l 5th 12; 3l 5th 18; prog 21 & 3l down & lkd hld app last; rallied & ld; rdn out flat*		1
654[1]	**Spring Double (IRE)** (1ow) 3-1 **B Mounsey-Heysham** *4s-3s; ld til hdd 9; ld agn app 13; hdd 16; ld agn 21; hdd 3 out; no ex; kpt on u.p*	3	2

655^{2} **Emperor's Magic (IRE)**(cp) 4-1 **Miss S Ward** *Swtng; hld up in rr; 15l 6th 18; gd prog nxt to ld 3 out; 3l up & lkd wnr app last when stpd to nil & hdd; one pce flat* 5 3

766^{P} St Bee(bl) 25-1 A Richardson *Trckd ldr til ld 16; hdd nxt; ld agn 18; hdd 21 & outpcd aft; kpt on* 1 4

427^{5} Mozielaw (5a) 12-1 Miss M Neill *Lw; in tch in rr; 15l 7th 16; nd aft; sn one pce* 25 5

552^{4} Across The Card 14-1 W Ramsay *(xnb) In tch in rr; 10l last 6; 6l 6th 8; grad wknd; lost tch & pu 19* P

657^{4} Anotherhandyman(cp) 10-1 Miss S Gledson *Bckwd; in tch in rr; lsng tch in 15l last 13; wl bhnd 17; t.o & pu 3 out* P

654^{3} Extra Stout (IRE)(tt) 8-1 C Storey *Trckd ldrs; 3l 4th 11; $4\frac{1}{2}$l 6th 15; wknd aft 21; bhnd when pu last* P

653^{2} Tursal (IRE) 10-1 R Morgan *Handy til prog to ld 9; hdd app 13; 2l 3rd 15; ld 17; hdd nxt; wknd qckly aft 20; pu nxt* P

OFFICIAL DISTANCES: 2*l*, 4*l*, 1*l* **TIME:** 9min 13.7s

858 Confined, 12st — 4 ran

426^{P} **LIVELY DESSERT (IRE)** 8-1 **K Anderson** *Lw; oht; in tch in rr; went 3l 2nd app 10; 4l 3rd 12; prog to 1l 2nd 15; ld & lft clr 2 out* 1

762^{1} **Sharpaman**(bl) 9-4 **C Shirley-Beavan** *Ld early; 4l 2nd 5; 5l 3rd 15; outpcd nxt; nd when lft 2nd 2 out* 15 2

764^{4} **Dream Of My Life (USA)** (6x) 6-4F **R Morgan** *(xnb,orbs) Trckd ldrs til 8l last & outpcd 10; 10l last 15; kpt on; nt pce to chall* 8 3

764^{P} Katinka (5a, 5x) 2-1 C Storey *(xnb) Trckd ldr til ld aft 2; made rest til hdd & blun 2 out; imm pu* P

OFFICIAL DISTANCES: 20*l*, 7*l* **TIME:** 6min 35.3s

859 Confined Maiden, 12st — 10 ran

767^{4} **STANWICK GYPSY** (5a) 9-2 **Miss M Neill** *Chsd ldrs; 5l 3rd 9; 4l 2nd 15; prog to disp ld brief nxt; 2l down when lft clr 2 out* 1

342^{5} **Hi Up Brenkley** 10-1 **A Richardson** *(xnb) Fat; in tch in rr; prog to 5l 3rd 15; one pce nxt; nd when lft poor 2nd 2 out* 25 2

430^{5} **Sijujama (IRE)** 7-1 **Miss N Patterson** *(xnb) Trckd ldr til ld 9; hdd nxt; ld agn 13; hdd & outpcd app 15; lft poor 3rd 3 out; v one-pcd* 8 3

553^{U} I'm Willie's Girl (5a) 7-2 Miss J Riding *In tch in rr; 8l 5th when mist & ur 10* U

Kanturk Star (IRE) 7-1 Mrs V Jackson *In tch in rr; strugg 11; t.o & pu 3 out* P

553^{3} Lord Lane 9-2 Miss N Stirling *Swtng; chsd ldrs; 6l 4th 13; stdy prog to ld app 15; jnd brief nxt; 2l up when fell 2 out* F

Luckenburn 6-1 S Huggan *A rr; 15l last 9; mist 12; t.o aft; pu aft 13* P

765^{F} Milbrig (5a) 12-1 Miss L Hislop *(bnh) Ld til hdd 9; ld agn nxt; hdd 13; wknd aft; bhnd when pu 3 out* P

761^{U} Steady Lass (IRE) (5a) 14-1 R Nichol *Trckd ldr til rmdrs in 4l 4th 9; grad wknd; lost tch 14; t.o & pu 3 out* P

658^{4} Stormalong (IRE) 2-1F C Storey *(xnb) Pu & dism aft 1; lame* P

OFFICIAL DISTANCES: dist, 6*l* **TIME:** 6min 31.7s

Portman

Badbury Rings (LH 10F,19J)
Sat, 10 Apr (GOOD to FIRM)

860 Confined, 12st — 4 ran

348^{P} **MASALARIAN (IRE)** 5-1 **Miss L Bridges** *(xnb,bf) Chsd ldr; hit 6; 2l 3rd 8; disp ld 15-2 out; ld app last; stayed on u.p flat* 1

576^{2} **Skip 'n' Tune (IRE)** (5a, 3x) 1-2F **M Miller** *Tchd 4/7; disp 2nd mostly; gd j 7; $1\frac{1}{2}$l down 14; jnd ldr nxt; ld aft 2 out; slpd bend bef last & hdd; no ex u.p flat* nk 2

602^{P} **Jackson Hill** 10-1 **Miss A Goschen** *(xnb) Tchd 11s; a last; 4l down 4; mist 10; brief eff to cl 13; stayed on one pce frm 16; nd* 12 3

689^{1} Scarlet Glory (5a) 7-4 H Fry *(xnb) 4s-7/4; 2 handlers; swtng; ld; jmpd rt to 4; $1\frac{1}{2}$l up 8; rn wide aft 10; jnd 15; fell nxt; rdr broke collar-bone* F

OFFICIAL DISTANCES: $\frac{1}{2}$*l*, 12*l* **TIME:** 6min 17.6s

861 Hunt Members, 12st — 4 ran

733^{4}	**MISS O'GRADY (IRE)** (5a, 7x) 1-2F **M Miller** *3½l 3rd 4; chsd ldr frm 6; disp ld brief 10; ld 13; grad drew clr frm 16; easy*		1
577^{2}	**Coolteen Hero (IRE)** (7x) 3-1 **D Jacob** *(xnb) Tchd 7/2; ld; 3l up 5; jnd brief 10; hdd 13; grad wknd frm 16*	12	2
579^{1}	**Thunder Thighs** (5a) 2-1 **N Wilmington** *(xnb) Tchd 3s; 2 handlers; mounted on course; tde; chsd ldrs to 5; releg last nxt; lft 3rd 10; outpcd 12; 15l down 14; one pce frm nxt*	8	3
603^{7}	Glenahary Rose (IRE) 12-1 Miss A Tory *(xnb) Last to 5; 3l 3rd 7; still disp 3rd when ur 10*		U

OFFICIAL DISTANCES: 15*l*, 7*l* **TIME:** 6min 06.7s

862 Countryside Alliance Club Members (Nov Rdrs), 12st — 4 ran

634^{1}	**FREE GIFT** 2-5F **D Jacob** *(xnb) Jw; made all; 1½l up 4; bold j 7; hung rt aft 10; 7l up 14; clr when slt mist 3 out; eased flat*		1
687^{4}	**Cherokee Boy** 6-1 **Miss C Atkinson** *Chsd ldr; 4l down 8 til outpcd frm 15; sn btn; flatt by prox*	5	2
792^{5}	**Blackwater Brave (IRE)** 5-2 **G Fry** *2nd ride; a last; 7l adrift 8; brief eff to cl 16; stayed on one pce frm nxt*	6	3
636^{4}	Calfstown Lord 8-1 Miss S Lane *6½l 3rd 4; clsd on ldng pr 6; blun & ur 8*		U

OFFICIAL DISTANCES: 6*l*, 8*l* **TIME:** 6min 16.4s

863 Mixed Open, 12st — 4 ran

576^{3}	**FRIAR WADDON** (4x) 6-4 **M Miller** *(xnb) Hld up in last; hdwy 5; mist nxt; last agn 10; hdwy to chse ldr 12; 3l down 15; chall last; stayed on game u.p to ld flat*		1
718^{2}	**Beadnell Bay** 4-5F **Miss A Goschen** *Tchd evens; 2 handlers; mounted on course; tde; ld 2; gd j 4; 4l up 14; prsd at last; veered lft flat; sn hdd & no ex*	nk	2
543^{F}	**Woodlands Beau (IRE)** (7x) 4-1 **N Mitchell** *Ld to 2; chsd ldr til releg last 11; 12½l adrift 14; stayed on one pce frm 16; nt trble ldng pr*	5	3
576^{P}	Merry Shot (IRE) 8-1 J Snowden *Mostly 3rd to 5; 2nd brief 10; 10l 3rd 14; wknd qckly 16; tired when mist 2 out; pu last*		P

OFFICIAL DISTANCES: nk, 5*l* **TIME:** 6min 11.0s

864 Restricted, 12st — 8 ran

574^{1}	**HELLO ROSCREA (IRE)** 5-2 **Miss A Goschen** *Hld up; 8½l 6th 4; chsd ldng pr frm 13 & ldr frm 15; smooth hdwy to ld aft 3 out; slt mist nxt; sn clr; easy*		1
701^{1}	**Bally Blue** 3-1 **Miss R Green** *Tchd 7/2; hld up last to 10; chsd ldrs frm 16; stayed on frm 2 out; passed flagging rival flat; nt trble wnr*	12	2
633^{1}	**Darcey Mae** (5a) 5-2 **Miss L Bridges** *(xnb) Opened 3s; oht; reluct to leave padd; ld 2; 1½l up 8; 10l clr 14; blun bad 3 out; wknd & hdd app nxt; dem flat*	2½	3
369^{P}	Macaroni Beach (5a) 9-4F Miss E Tory *(xnb) Disp ld to 2; 4l 3rd 8; disp 2nd 11-14; grad wknd frm 16*	15	4
689^{4}	Beachtime 10-1 N Mitchell *(xnb) Tchd 12s; disp ld to 2; chsd ldr; jmpd slow 10; wknd 13; t.o & pu 3 out*		P
689^{P}	Gami (FR)(vis) 12-1 J Snowden *6l 4th 4; grad wknd frm 13; last nxt; bhnd when pu 16*		P
720^{F}	Hawkers Hill 7-2 D Jacob *Opened 4s; trckd ldrs in 4/5th mostly; still chsng ldng trio when blun & ur 13*		U
	Pool Of Lyphe (5a) 12-1 D I Turner *A last pr; 11l 7th 4; mist 7; releg last 10; sn lost plce; t.o when jmpd rt 12; pu nxt*		P

OFFICIAL DISTANCES: 10*l*, 2*l* **TIME:** 6min 06.6s

865 Open Maiden, 12st — 9 ran

599^{2}	**TRUST FUND (IRE)** 4-5F **D Jacob** *2 handlers; swtng; mounted on course; ld; hdd brief 6; 1½l up 8; jnd 10; hdd nxt; ld agn 15; sn clr; impressive*		1
688^{P}	**The Nelson Touch** 10-1 **D I Turner** *(xnb) Chsd ldrs; 1½l 2nd 8; disp ld 10; ld nxt; 1½l up 14; hdd nxt; sn hrd rdn & brushed aside*	15	2
633^{U}	**The Sycophant (IRE)** 7-2 **Miss A Goschen** *Hld up last to 5; releg last agn 9; gd hdwy to chse ldng pr 11; grad outpcd frm 15; bhnd frm 3 out*	20	3
580^{6}	Able Bob (IRE) 12-1 J Snowden *(xnb) Nd; disp 12l 6th 8; grad wknd & releg 8th 11; t.o frm 14; plodded home*	50	4

580^{4} Coastal Flight 12-1 Miss R Green *(bh) 7th 3; releg last 5; 12l 6th 8; still in tch when bd 13* . . . . . B

575^{3} Panto 4-1 Miss K Lovelace *8s-4s; trckd ldng pr til ld brief 6; $3\frac{1}{2}$l 4th 8; wknd qckly 13; pu 15; dism.* . . . . . P

760^{P} Port Valenska (IRE)(cp,tt) 12-1 N Wilmington *Tubed; prom; chsd ldr; $2\frac{1}{2}$l 3rd 8; grad wknd frm 13; t.o 15; clambered over 2 out; pu last* . . . . . P

580^{3} Queens House (5a) 8-1 D Drake *Mid-div; 8l 5th 8; still chsng ldrs when fell 13* F

693^{P} Swan Song (5a) 12-1 Miss E Tory *8th 3; last 8; mist nxt; t.o 11; pu 13* . . P

OFFICIAL DISTANCES: 15*l*, 20*l* **TIME:** 6min 12.8s

The stewards enquired into the riding of The Nelson Touch; having interviewed the rider they imposed a fine of £65 on him for excessive use of the whip from three out to the last on a horse that was showing no response

Vale of Aylesbury with Garth & South Berks

Kimble (LH 9F,19J)

Sat, 10 Apr (GOOD, GOOD to SOFT in places)

866 Hunt Members, 12st — 3 ran

MR SNOWMAN 1-3F **James Tudor** *Trckd ldr; nt fluent 12; ld nxt; clr 15; tired 2 out; pushed out flat* 1

622^{U} **Kingfisher Star** 13-2 **Miss J Lodge** *(xnb) Ld to 13; outpcd by wnr frm 15; 12l down app 2 out; kpt on agn last* 3 2

622^{3} **Steve Ford** 4-1 **Miss E Harbour** *A last; nt fluent 4 & lost tch; 25l down 14; r.o aft 3 out; clsng stdly flat* 2 3

OFFICIAL DISTANCES: 3*l*, 2*l* **TIME:** 6min 56.5s

867 Intermediate, 12st — 6 ran

663^{3} **RAIN DELAY** 7-2 **R Rogers** *2 handlers; trckd ldr 4; ld 8; jnd 3 out & nxt; rdn & drew clr last.* 1

728^{P} **Imago II (FR)** 6-1 **M Harris** *8s-6s; hld up in 5th; mist 7; prog to trck wnr 14; chall & outj 3 out; upsides 2 out; wknd last* 8 2

720^{1} **Romany Pearl**(cp) 3-1 **Miss R Goodwin** *Chsd ldr to 4; sn lost plce; outpcd frm 12; flapped along & no ch frm 3 out; tk poor 3rd app last* 30 3

443^{4} Mr Splodge 6-4F James Tudor *(xnb) Tk keen hld; hld up; 5th when mist & rfo 4* U

785^{U} Perfect Finisher 20-1 Miss R Lobley *Ld to 8; chsd wnr to 14; sn outpcd; poor 4th when rdr toppled off last* . . . . . U

Phar Lord (IRE) 8-1 T Messenger *(xnb) Chsd ldrs; mist 2; blun 5; blun & ur 10* U

OFFICIAL DISTANCES: 8*l*, 20*l* **TIME:** 6min 44.5s

868 Land Rover Mens Open — 8 ran

640^{4} **TANAGER**(bl) 5-2 **B King** *Cl up; trckd ldr 9; ld 12; forged clr frm 3 out; comf* 1

602^{P} **Sir Dante (IRE)** 7-4F **F Hutsby** *(xnb) Trckd ldr; ld 4-12; blun 14; ev ch & outj 3 out; btn aft; wknd & mist last.* 20 2

603^{U} **Supreme Storm (IRE)** 10-1 **R Bandey** *A rr; 19l 7th $\frac{1}{2}$way; wl outpcd frm 13; tk poor 3rd last* 20 3

461^{3} Bold Statement(tt) 20-1 G Tawell *(xnb) Swtng; nvr on terms; disp 15l 5th $\frac{1}{2}$way; sn lost tch; went poor 3rd 2 out; dem agn last; broke leg; dead.* . 8 4

583^{U} Rough Tiger (IRE) (1ow) 7-2 B Tuckey *Chsd ldrs; mist 6; disp 15l 5th $\frac{1}{2}$way; sn wknd; t.o.* . . . . . fence 5

466^{3} Grand Canyon (IRE) 8-1 C Wadland *Oht; sn lost plce; jmpd slow 5; last & mist 7; wknd 12; t.o & pu 16* . . . . . P

622^{2} La Colina (IRE) 7-1 James Tudor *(xnb) Late in padd; ld to 4; chsd ldr to 9; wknd 14; poor 5th when pu 2 out.* . . . . . P

490^{P} Seabrook Lad(cp) 7-1 N Docker *Sn chsd ldrs; 7l 4th $\frac{1}{2}$way; rmdrs 12; outpcd nxt; went 20l 3rd & fell hvly 15* . . . . . F

OFFICIAL DISTANCES: 15*l*, 12*l* **TIME:** 6min 40.0s

869 Ladies Open — 9 ran

629^{2} **THE GRANBY (IRE)** evensF **Miss H Irving** *Ld til aft 3; mostly trckd ldr; ld 15; 3l up 3 out; prsd agn nxt; rdn flat; a hldng on* 1

781^{3} **Storm Castle (IRE)** 5-1 **Miss J Wickens** *Tk keen hld; ld aft 3; made most til hdd 15; 3l down & nt fluent 3 out; rallied nxt; ev ch last; r.o; a just hld.* $\frac{3}{4}$ 2

Form	Runner	Dist	Pos
464[3]	**Ryans Star** 4-1 **Mrs J Parris** *Trckd ldrs; 3rd ½way; dem 4th 13; outpcd 3 out; no ch nxt; tk 3rd agn flat*	25	3
78[P]	Wag The Brush 5-1 Miss E Jones *Nt fluent 1; hld up; prog & 4th ½way; chsd ldng pr 13; 5l 3rd when mist 3 out; wknd app nxt.*	1	4
613[3]	Lucky Master (IRE) 12-1 Miss G Swan *In tch in midfield; 7th ½way; outpcd 13; disp 5th & no ch frm 15; rdr nrly f.o last*	15	5
	Aircon (IRE) 20-1 Miss R Hutsby *Prsd ldrs; lost plce 7; 5th ½way; outpcd aft 12; nd aft; wknd 2 out*	15	6
785[9]	Gortroe Guy (IRE) 33-1 Miss K Robinson *A rr; 8th & in tch ½way; sn outpcd & bhnd; t.o in last pr 15.*	8	7
541[F]	Six Clerks (IRE)(cp) 25-1 Miss A de Lisle Wells *In tch; 6th ½way; sn outpcd; mists 14 & 15; t.o in last pr aft; virt pu nr fin*	15	8
440[4]	Sunczech (IRE) (5a) 10-1 Miss H Phizacklea *(xnb) Lost plce rap 3; last nxt; lost tch 6; t.o & pu 13*		P

OFFICIAL DISTANCES: ½l, 10l **TIME:** 6min 33.5s

870 Restricted, 12st — 3 ran

Form	Runner	Dist	Pos
257[1]	**COURT ADJOURN** 4-5F **Miss H Irving** *Cl up; eff to disp ld 15; just ld 3 out; hit 2 out; jnd last; rdn clr.*		1
587[P]	**Moscow's Return (IRE)** 5-1 **J Trice-Rolph** *Ld at slow pce; hdd & outpcd 15; 8l down 3 out; r.o agn nxt; jnd wnr last; hung lft & fnd nil flat*	5	2
192[1]	**Murphy's Magic (IRE)** 6-4 **James Tudor** *Cl up; disp ld 15; narrowly hdd 3 out; lost 2nd & wknd last.*	5	3

OFFICIAL DISTANCES: 4l, 5l **TIME:** 7min 09.0s

871 Open Maiden — 8 ran

Form	Runner	Dist	Pos
82[P]	**MENANTOL** 25-1 **Miss A de Lisle Wells** *Prom; w ldr aft 9-13; eff to ld aft 15; drew clr frm 2 out; nt fluent last; kpt on*		1
731[2]	**Northsprite**(cp) 7-2 **J Trice-Rolph** *(xnb) Hld up in cl tch; jnd ldr & mist 13; eff to jn wnr aft 15; rdn & fnd nil 2 out*	8	2
462[P]	**Sandy Lark** 33-1 **G Tawell** *Lkd rough; in tch; outpcd 12; mod 5th 16; kpt on to 3rd 2 out; no imp on ldng pr last*	8	3
	Rockford (IRE) 5-1 C Wadland *Hld up in tch; eff & cl 4th 16; wknd nxt.*	25	4
	Cabin Boy 8-1 T Allanson *(xnb) 1st ride; keen; cl up; mist 10 & rdr unstdy; mist 12 & rfo some way aft*		U
291[4]	Jonno 5-1 N Docker *(xnb) Ld at slow pce aft 9; sn drpd out; last frm 11; t.o & pu 13*		P
627[P]	On A Full Wager(bl) 4-1 B King *2 handlers; prom; ld aft 9; mist 14; hdd aft nxt; wknd 3 out; pu aft 2 out; lame.*		P
599[3]	Saffron Hill (IRE) (7a) 5-2F F Hutsby *Hld up in tch; blun & ur 7.*		U

OFFICIAL DISTANCES: 6l, 5l **TIME:** 6min 54.5s

Vale of Lune

Whittington (LH 8F,18J)

Sat, 10 Apr (GOOD to SOFT)

872 Hunts Members (with Holcombe) - 17J — 5 ran

Form	Runner	Dist	Pos
713[6]	**CAMDEN FELLOW (IRE)** 7-2 **Miss C Hurley** *Chsd ldr to 6 & agn 9; ld 10; clr when jmpd slow 2 out; unchall aft*		1
	Aly Daley (IRE) 2-1 **Mrs C Gardner** *Ld to 6; lost plce 10; sn rdn along; wl bhnd when jmpd slow 15; mist nxt; lft poor 2nd 2 out.*	20	2
	Lion (U) 9-1 L Metcalfe *V bckwd; bhnd when jmpd slow 1; ref nxt; cont; wl t.o til pu 11*		P
	Marzibits (5a) 10-1 K Pearson *In tch til rn out 3*		R
709[2]	Spot The Native (IRE) 4-5F P Hemmings *Chsd ldrs; ld 6; clr 8-9; hdd 10; wkng & wl hld in 2nd when blun & ur 2 out*		U

OFFICIAL DISTANCE: 20l **TIME:** 7min 14.9s **TOTE:** £4.80

Fence 11 omitted - damaged

873 Confined, 12st — 7 ran

749^{4} **BLANK CHEQUE** (7x) 2-1 **D Coates** *Ld to 6; lost plce nxt; 5th 3 out; rallied aft 2 out; str rn aft last; ld flat; r.o.* . . . 1
713^{P} **Border Run** 16-1 **K Pearson** *Hld up; hdwy aft 10; chall aft 3 out; ld aft nxt; 4l clr when mist last; sn rdn; hdd & no ex flat* . . . 3½ 2
684^{P} **Sizer (IRE)** evensF **N Saville** *Hld up; hdwy 8; ld 11; hdd aft 2 out; sn wknd* 10 3
615^{U} Chadswell (IRE) (7x) 6-1 W Puddifer *In tch; tk clsr ord 6; str chall 3 out; wknd app last.* . . . 1½ 4
529^{9} China Lal (5a) 6-1 Mrs K Diggle *Cl up til rdn & wknd 15* . . . 6 5
Barneys Gold (IRE) 10-1 Miss G Garton *In tch; tk clsr ord 6; mist 10; hit 11; strugg & bhnd aft* . . . 5 6
761^{1} Touchez Du Bois (IRE)(cp) 7-1 T Morrison *Prom; ld 6-11; wkng when fell 3 out* F

OFFICIAL DISTANCES: 3½l, 10l **TIME:** 7min 03.8s **TOTE:** £1.70

874 Ladies Open — 4 ran

508^{3} **YORKSHIRE EDITION (IRE)** 5-2 **Miss W Gibson** *A.p; ld app 10; prsd frm 3 out; r.o flat* . . . 1
751^{r} **Jackie Jarvis (IRE)** (5a) 4-6F **Mrs K Diggle** *Chsd ldrs frm 3; went 2nd 14; str chall frm 3 out; ev ch flat; nt qckn nr fin* . . . 2½ 2
710^{U} **Wychnor King (IRE)** 10-1 **Mrs D Caine** *Jmpd slow 2; mist & drpd to rr 3; wkng when jmpd slow 15; tk poor 3rd 2 out* . . . 25 3
763^{7} Deputy Leader (IRE) 7-2 Miss L Kendall *Ld; hdd app 10; lost plce 14; wknd app 2 out* . . . 3 4

OFFICIAL DISTANCES: 2½l, 25l **TIME:** 7min 02.0s **TOTE:** £3.00

875 Land Rover Mens Open, 12st — 4 ran

772^{2} **DORANS MAGIC** (7x) evensF **N Saville** *Made all; drew clr app 3 out; v easily* 1
750^{2} **Victoria's Boy (IRE)** (7x) 5-4 **D Coates** *Prom; lost plce 13; wknd app 3 out; tk poor 2nd flat* . . . 25 2
317^{F} **Nicholls Cross (IRE)** (7x) 5-1 **M McAlister** *Tk keen hld; trckd ldrs; mist 3; went cl 2nd 13; pushed along when mist 3 out; no ch w wnr aft; lost 2nd flat* 1½ 3
711^{4} Lord Of The West (IRE) (4x) 8-1 D Greenway *Bhnd; mist 4; sulked & rdn along aft; mist 11; t.o 13; pu 3 out* . . . P

OFFICIAL DISTANCES: 25l, 1½l **TIME:** 6min 54.4s **TOTE:** £3.20

876 Intermediate, 12st — 3 ran

771^{1} **DOLPHIN SQUARE (IRE)** 11-10 **Miss H Bethell** *Chsd ldr 3-7; jmpd slow 10; stumbled bend bef 11; shkn up app 14; went 2nd aft 15; blun nxt; chall 2 out; upsides last; ld flat; eased cl home; cheekily* . . . 1
715^{1} **Master Club Royal**(bl) 4-5F **M McAlister** *Ld; dived at 9; qcknd app 11; rdn when prsd app last; hdd flat; hld cl home* . . . 1¼ 2
766^{5} **Distracting** (5a) 5-1 **K Pearson** *Chsd ldr to 3 & agn 7; rmdrs app 14; lost 2nd app 3 out; wknd app nxt* . . . runin 3

OFFICIAL DISTANCES: 1¼l, dist **TIME:** 7min 03.5s **TOTE:** £1.80

877 Open Maiden — 6 ran

710^{P} **CLODAGH VALLEY (IRE)** 9-2 **W Kinsey** *A handy; mist 6; ld aft 15; clr app 2 out; v easily* . . . 1
Mon Performer 6-1 **J Davis** *Swtng; prom; ld 6; hdd aft 15; 2nd when blun bad nxt; wknd qckly* . . . 25 2
754^{U} Button Lady (12a) 5-2F D Gaiter *In tch; tk clsr ord 4; cl up when fell 10* . . F
709^{P} Cool Archie(bl) 11-4 K Pearson *Tk keen hld; handy; drvn app 14; wknd aft 15; lft 3rd nxt; t.o & pu 2 out* . . . P
658^{P} Em'sgem (5a) 5-1 T Morrison *Tk keen hld; ld to 6; lost plce qckly; rr aft 8; niggled along app 10; mist nxt; t.o app 14; fell 15* . . . F
Longdale 3-1 N Saville *Hld up; cl up app 11; went 2nd 14 til rdn aft nxt; 3rd & u.p when fell 3 out* . . . F

OFFICIAL DISTANCE: 25l **TIME:** 7min 14.3s **TOTE:** £7.90

The rider of Button Lady was fined £50 for being unable to produce his Licence and Medical Record Book

West Somerset Vale

Cothelstone (LH 7F,19J)

Sat, 10 Apr (GOOD)

878 Hunt Members — 3 ran

Form	Horse	Dist	Pos
604^{r}	**MISS KARINGAROO** (5a) 5-1 **W White** *Swtng; mounted on course; disp ld 8-10; rmdrs 11; went 2nd aft nxt; mist 13 & outj aft; rdn to ld & edged lft flat; r.o*		1
	Butterwick King (IRE) 4-9F **D Alers-Hankey** *Bit bckwd; ld to 2 & 5-6; disp ld 8 til ld 12; 3l clr & lkd wnr 3 out; sn rdn; edged rt app last; hdd & no ex flat*	2	2
274^{6}	**Merry Melody** (5a) 2-1 **Miss S Robinson** *Ld 2-5 & 6-12; wknd & 8l last 14; t.o*	runin	3

OFFICIAL DISTANCES: 3*l*, dist **TIME:** 6min 34.4s **TOTE:** £2.60 **DF:**£12.60

879 Restricted, 12st — 11 ran

Form	Horse	Dist	Pos
473^{P}	**KILDYSART LADY (IRE)** (5a) 6-1 **B Woodhouse** *Swtng; hld up; 6l 8th ½way; last aft 12; hdwy & 5l 4th 16; went 2nd aft nxt; ld aft 2 out; sn rdn clr.*		1
323^{P}	**Askers Jack** 16-1 **R Stephens** *Jmpd lft; a.p; 3l 5th ½way; 1½l 3rd 13; ld & mist 14; hdd 15; 3l 2nd when mist 3 out; kpt on*	3½	2
706^{P}	**River Dante (IRE)** 10-1 **S Kidston** *(xnb) Pulled hrd; sn prom; ld 7 til aft 12 & 15 til aft 2 out; no ex flat*	¾	3
473^{2}	Maybe A Double (5a) 7-2 R Bliss *(xnb) Swtng; 2 handlers; hld up; last 2 til hdwy 12; 2l 4th nxt; 1½l 3rd 16; wknd aft 3 out*	10	4
	Bally Lir Lady (5a) 6-1 D Edwards *Hld up; 7l 9th ½way; hdwy 12; 4l 6th nxt; lost plce u.p & 10l 7th 16; no ch when mist 2 out*	4	5
278^{3}	The Grey Shadow 6-1 W White *8s-6s; chsd ldrs til lost plce & mist 9; 8l 10th ½way; last 13; nd aft*	3	6
275^{1}	Rosetta (5a) 3-1 J Jenkins *(xnb,bnh) Swtng; hld up; 4l 6th ½way; lost plce aft 12; eff & disp 9l 5th 16; sn wknd.*	2	7
199^{9}	Prah Sands(bl) 8-1 J Young *(xnb) Hld up; mist 10; 5l 7th ½way; wknd & 13l 9th 16; eased when btn; t.o.*	20	8
598^{4}	B B Boy 20-1 A Charles-Jones *(xnb) Ld to 2 & 4-7; 2½l 4th ½way; wknd aft 12; bhnd when pu 14*		P
720^{3}	Headwrecker (IRE) 5-2F G Maundrell *(xnb) Prom; went 2nd 7; ld aft 12-14; wknd & 9l 5th 16; mist 3 out; pu 2 out.*		P
689^{3}	Romany Move 6-1 Mrs S Godfrey *Ld 2-4; 2nd/3rd to 14; wknd & 12l 8th 16; wl bhnd when pu 2 out*		P

OFFICIAL DISTANCES: 2½*l*, 1*l* **TIME:** 6min 16.4s **TOTE:** £40.00 **DF:**£14.70 (1st+any)

880 Mixed Open, 12st — 7 ran

Form	Horse	Dist	Pos
414^{P}	**SIR WILLIAM** (4x) 7-2 **R Woollacott** *(xnb) Nt fluent; hld up; 6l 5th ½way; went 2nd & mist 13; ld 15; jmpd rt 2 out & last; r.o wl*		1
799^{P}	**Gladiatorial (IRE)** 6-1 **T Bishop** *Prom; went 3l 2nd 9-12; sn lost plce; rallied & 3l 4th 14; went 2nd aft 16; switched lft flat; one pce*	2½	2
	Delaware (FR) (7x)(bl) 5-1 **S Kidston** *Hld up; 8l last ½way; hdwy aft 12; 2l 3rd 14; stumbled bend bef 16; no ex 3 out*	12	3
472^{2}	Arlequin De Sou (FR) (7x)(bl) 5-2F R Stephens *Swtng; prom; 4l 3rd ½way; went 2nd brief 12; hmpd 13; 4l 5th when mist nxt; wknd 15; poor 4th frm 2 out*	8	4
	Shanavoher (IRE) 12-1 D Edwards *Hld up; 6½l 6th ½way; hmpd bad 13; 11l last nxt; nt rec*	1½	5
471^{1}	Kingsbridge (IRE) 3-1 T Eades *(xnb) Ld aft 1; sn 8l clr til aft 5; hdd 15; wknd 3 out; blun nxt*	5	6
602^{5}	Cherokee Run (IRE) (7x) 6-1 Miss C Tizzard *Ld til aft 1; 2nd to 9; mist 10; 5l 4th ½way; lost plce 12; 9l 6th & hrd rdn 14; wknd 15*	10	7

OFFICIAL DISTANCES: 2*l*, 10*l* **TIME:** 6min 13.3s **TOTE:** £6.30 **DF:**£1.60 (1st+any)

881 Intermediate (Nov Rdrs), 12st — 6 ran

Form	Horse	Dist	Pos
472^{4}	**POLKA** 2-1CF **Miss J Buck** *A.p; 4l 4th ½way; went 2nd 13; ld 2 out; rdn out*		1
692^{2}	**Caundle Chase** 2-1CF **W White** *2nd/3rd til ld 12; hdd 2 out; sn rdn & one pce*	2½	2
601^{1}	**Winners Enclosure (IRE)** 2-1CF **N McDiarmid** *Swtng; stdd start & rcd wide; pulled hrd; jnd ldrs 6; ld 7; mist 9; hdd 12; disp 2l 2nd 16; wknd app 2 out*	8	3

577[3] Sherbourne Guest (IRE) 8-1 J Kwiatkowski *Ld to 7; 2nd to 10; 3l 3rd ½way; 6l 4th 13; wknd 16* 20 4
598[2] Early Morning Call (IRE) 7-1 S Wheeler *2nd/4th to 6; 10l last ½way; wl bhnd 15; t.o* 15 5
Pavillion Pride (12a) 10-1 Mrs T Rowe *Ss; detach last til rn out 10* . . . . . . R

OFFICIAL DISTANCES: 3*l*, 7*l* **TIME:** 6min 26.4s **TOTE:** £2.10 **DF:**£8.40

882 Dodson & Horrell PPORA Club Members, 12st — 6 ran

778[R] **RHYTHM KING** 4-5F **G Maundrell** *A.p; went 2nd 6; ld 10; qcknd 5l clr 13; hung bad lft & virt unrideable frm 3 out; hld on wl flat* 1
319[P] **Father Jim** 12-1 **Miss C Tizzard** *Swtng; ld to 10; lost plce 14; rallied u.p & 7l 3rd 16; went 4l 2nd aft 2 out; r.o; flatt by prox* . . . . . . ¾ 2
635[P] **Timpani (IRE)**(vis) 11-2 **R Woollacott** *(xnb) Hld up; hdwy 8; 3l 4th ½way; went 2nd aft 13; wknd aft 2 out*. 10 3
694[1] Questionaire (5a) 5-2 R Stephens *2nd til mist 6; lost plce 8 & sn drvn along; hit 10; went 2l 3rd ½way; blun 14; mist 15; 8l 4th nxt; wknd 3 out*. . . 8 4
632[U] Gigi Beach (IRE) 12-1 A Charles-Jones *Drpd to rr 6; 9l last ½way; lost tch 13; t.o* 20 5
603[P] Rainbow Frontier (IRE)(tt) 12-1 Miss J Janes *(xnb) Bhnd til hdwy 6; 4l 5th ½way; wkng when mist 12; t.o 15; pu 3 out* . . . . . . P

OFFICIAL DISTANCES: 1*l*, 10*l* **TIME:** 6min 20.2s **TOTE:** £1.60 **DF:**£8.20

883 Open Maiden (Div 1), 12st — 12 ran

SO PEACEFUL (5a) 7-1 **R Stephens** *Ld to 8; 2nd til ld 15; sn 10l clr; drew rt away 3 out; unchall* 1
626[2] **King Of Swing (IRE)** 6-1 **Mrs F Vigar** *(xnb) 2nd til ld 8; clr w wnr 14; hdd 15; btn when mist 3 out* 30 2
701[4] **Alfies Rocket** 6-1 **J Young** *10s-6s; hld up; 9l 10th ½way; lost tch & 15l 7th 13; t.o 15; went dist 3rd last*. 20 3
474[2] Miss Chloe (IRE) (5a) 7-1 R Bliss *Hld up; hdwy & 4½l 6th ½way; 6l 5th 13; rdn & wknd 15; went dist 3rd 2 out; dem last; t.o*. 4 4
598[3] Butleigh Rose (5a) 8-1 R Woollacott *12s-8s; swtng; chsd ldrs; 3l 4th ½way; 4l 3rd 13; sn outpcd; wknd 15; 25l 3rd 3 out; t.o; fin tired* 5 5
721[U] Final Magic 16-1 G Maundrell *(xnb) Chsd ldrs to 8; 7l 8th ½way; lost tch aft 12; wl bhnd when pu 14* . . . . . . P
307[3] Four In Hand (5a) 2-1F D Edwards *Nt jw; hld up & bhnd; 10l 11th ½way; hdwy & 11l 6th when blun & ur 13*. . . . . . U
571[P] Mad Jack(tt) 7-1 W White *(xnb) Swtng; svs; hld up; hdwy 8; 4l 5th ½way; 5l 4th 13; went 10l 3rd 15; sn wknd; wl bhnd when blun & ur 3 out*. . . . . U
599[P] Nearly A Mildred (5a) 7-1 J Barnes *(xnb) Hld up; 8l 9th ½way; lost tch aft 12; t.o 15; pu 2 out*. . . . . . P
702[P] Silver Tray (IRE) (12a) 12-1 R Ross *Jmpd rt; prom; blun 6; 2l 3rd ½way; wkng when mist 12; wl bhnd when pu 13* . . . . . . P
474[5] Sula Hill (5a) 20-1 Miss J Buck *(xnb) Swtng; 2 handlers; tde; ss; a bhnd; t.o 9; pu aft 12* . . . . . . P
The Gilly Smith 4-1 A Charles-Jones *(kineton) Hld up & bhnd; hdwy 9; 5l 7th ½way; wkng when blun 12; sn pu w rdr patting him down nk* . . . . . . P

OFFICIAL DISTANCES: 25*l*, 20*l* **TIME:** 6min 22.1s **TOTE:** £5.80 **DF:**£18.90 (1st+any)

884 Open Maiden (Div 2), 12st — 8 ran

353[U] **LADY WIDD (IRE)** (5a) 11-8F **D Edwards** *Hld up; hdwy 8; 2l 3rd ½way; ld 14; 3l clr when hit 2 out; drvn out* 1
600[2] **Herswell Castle** (7a) 3-1 **R Woollacott** *(xnb) Hld up; 6l 7th ½way; went 7l 4th aft 14 & 2nd 3 out; stayed on one pce* 2 2
633[U] **Margery's Opera** (5a) 8-1 **E Kenney-Herbert** *Ld aft 1; jmpd slow 10; mist 13; hdd nxt; 2nd to 3 out; kpt on one pce*. . . . . . ¾ 3
475[F] Gone On (IRE) 9-4 A Charles-Jones *Prom; went 2nd aft 10-14; mist 15; wknd 3 out; blun nxt*. 20 4
580[P] Forglori 20-1 R Bliss *Hld up; 5l 6th ½way; 7l 5th 13; wknd 15; t.o*. 15 5
Jag (5a) 12-1 J Barnes *School in rr; 10l last ½way; wl bhnd 13; t.o*. 1 6
693[P] Random Trix (5a) 12-1 Miss S Robinson *Ld til aft 1; 2nd to 10; lost plce & 3½l 5th ½way; wknd & 11l 7th 13; t.o*. 10 7
325[P] Mr Baloo(bl) 8-1 Miss C Tizzard *Jnd ldrs 6; hit 9; 2½l 4th ½way; jmpd v slow 13; 7l 5th when blun 16; nt r.o; wl bhnd when ref 2 out* . . . . . . r

OFFICIAL DISTANCES: 1½*l*, 1*l* **TIME:** 6min 30.4s **TOTE:** £3.10 **DF:**£10.50

Woodland Pytchley

Dingley (RH 8F,18J)

Sat, 10 Apr (GOOD to SOFT, SOFT in places)

885 Hunts Members (with Fernie) — 12 ran

	FRILEUX ROYAL (FR) 5-1 **G Morrison** *Made all; ldng pr clr frm 9; drew 8l ahd 3 out; sn in total comm*		1
785^{6}	**Bruan (IRE)**(cp) 14-1 **Miss J Bevin** *Chsd ldrs to 7; 12l 3rd & outpcd 11; no ch aft; went mod 2nd app last*	25	2
	Mystic Isle (IRE) 14-1 **R Cope** *Chsd ldrs; 15l 5th & rdn 10; no ch frm 13; went poor 3rd app last*	7	3
745^{F}	Buckland Bobby 33-1 P Millington *Mid-div; 20l 6th 10; nvr nr ldrs; lft poor 4th app last*	½	4
787^{6}	Nonplussed (5a)(vis) 33-1 P Andrew *Bhnd & jmpd slow 9; t.o 11; blun 3 out; kpt on past btn horses frm nxt*	fence	5
784^{U}	Romanybaan 33-1 P Ikin *(xnb) 2 handlers; sn bhnd; 30l 7th 10; t.o.*	12	6
786^{P}	Glemot (IRE) 33-1 J Dillon *Mid-div; prog to 8l 4th 10; wknd 12; 5th & no ch frm nxt*	3	7
	Mr Baldwin (IRE) 33-1 J Turcan *Jmpd slow 3; a bhnd; t.o frm 7*	10	8
743^{P}	Veredarius (FR) 33-1 Mrs S Tyler *Sn bhnd; t.o frm 7*	8	9
	Mullover 12-1 T Lane *(xnb) 25s-12s; pulling; chsd ldrs to 6; 20l 7th 10; wl bhnd when pu 12*		P
593^{1}	Nokimover(cp) 2-5F Miss Gemma Hutchinson *Chsd ldrs; went 2nd 7; 3l down when mist 15; btn nxt; 4th & wl btn when pu & dism app last*		P
	Simply A Star (IRE) 33-1 Miss N Chapman *A bhnd; 32l 8th 10; no ch when ur 14*		U

OFFICIAL DISTANCES: dist, 8*l* **TIME:** 6min 32.0s **TOTE:** £3.70 **DF:**£75.00

The stewards fined the owner of Bruan £60 for declaring the horse to race in blinkers but running it in cheekpieces

886 Confined, 12st — 8 ran

587^{1}	**AGUA ARDENTE** 5-2F **R Cope** *Swtng; chsd ldrs; mist 3; ld 13; blun nxt; clr frm 3 out; kpt on u.p app last; all out*		1
647^{3}	**Tom De Savoie (IRE)** 5-1 **N Bloom** *Mid-div; 8l 4th & pushed along 11; hdwy nxt; chsd wnr frm 3 out; 4l down app last; btn when jmpd v slow last*	8	2
584^{4}	**Miss Hoity Toity** (5a) 3-1 **A Sansome** *Chsd ldr til ld 12-13; 6l 3rd & rdn app 2 out; one pce*	1	3
544^{4}	Noble Affair (5a) 4-1 N Pearce *Ww in mid-div; prog 10; 7l 4th 2 out; one pce u.p aft*	1	4
650^{F}	Weavers Choice (5x) 10-1 P Cowley *Ld; clr & mist 6; hdd 12; sn drpd out; t.o frm 3 out.*	30	5
557^{5}	Catchphrase(vis) 33-1 R Armson *(xnb) Bhnd; 7th & lost tch 8; t.o & pu 14; dism*		P
587^{P}	Cumberland Youth 33-1 P Ikin *A last; t.o 6 til pu 13.*		P
	Shoemaker (IRE) 3-1 S Morris *Ww in tch; 12l 6th 10; mist nxt; lost tch 13; sn no ch; pu last*		P

OFFICIAL DISTANCES: 15*l*, 2*l* **TIME:** 6min 30.0s **TOTE:** £3.10 **DF:**£9.00

887 Confined Maiden — 13 ran

789^{2}	**SIR LANCELOT** 3-1 **A Sansome** *Ww; cl 6th 13; 6l 3rd aft 2 out; chall last; sn ld; r.o wl*		1
	Bathtime Boys 6-4F **R Cope** *In tch; chsd ldr 3 out; rdn to ld app last; hdd & no ex flat.*	2½	2
	Midnight Cowboy 5-1 **N Kent** *Swtng; ww; prog to trck ldrs 13; ld 3 out; 3l clr nxt; hdd app last; no ex flat*	1½	3
58^{3}	Cashari (IRE) 3-1 S Morris *Ww in tch; 7l 4th & rdn 2 out; wknd app last.*	15	4
476^{U}	Coombs Spinney 20-1 J Docker *(xnb) Keen; trckd ldrs; cl 7th 13; wknd 3 out*	8	5
	Shambob 20-1 J Burley *(xnb,pricker o/s) Mid-div; in tch; 5l 8th 15; outpcd frm nxt*	8	6
600^{P}	Rundetto (IRE) 33-1 S Moreton *(xnb) 2 handlers; keen; rcd wide; w ldr to 13; wknd 15; sn no ch*	1	7
788^{P}	Dolitanlad 20-1 P Millington *Jmpd violent rt 1; chsd ldrs til wknd qckly 15; no ch nxt*	8	8

Form	Horse	Dist	Pos
560[3]	Kissed By Moonlite (5a) 16-1 R Armson *(xnb) Ww; prog & in tch 10; wknd 14; bhnd & pu 3 out*		P
	Mr Match 33-1 D Hockridge *Ld at stdy pce; blun 7; hdd 15; sn wknd; bhnd & pu last*		P
	North Peak (7a) 14-1 S Pile *Chsd ldrs til wknd 9; bhnd & pu 12*		P
746[U]	Plain Polly (IRE) (5a) 33-1 P Cowley *Sn detach in last; jmpd slow 7; t.o 9 til pu 12*		P
783[F]	Sixes And Sevens (IRE) (5a) 33-1 G Kerr *Chsd ldrs til wknd 12; t.o & pu 2 out*		P

OFFICIAL DISTANCES: 2*l*, 1*l* **TIME:** 6min 44.0s **TOTE:** £3.20 **DF:**£7.00

888 Land Rover Mens Open, 12st — 6 ran

Form	Horse	Dist	Pos
683[2]	**SHANAVOGH** (7x) 7-4 **R Hunnisett** *Ld 3-5; w ldr; 3l 2nd when lft wl clr 14; in comm aft*		1
680[5]	**Thurles Pickpocket (IRE)** 33-1 **B Elson** *Chsd ldrs; 12l 3rd 11; sn outpcd by ldng pr; lft poor 2nd 14; no imp*	35	2
	Browjoshy (IRE)(cp) 12-1 **J Newbold** *Tchd 20s; last & drvn 6; rallied & in tch 9; outpcd 12; lft poor 3rd 14*	3	3
683[P]	Gavroche Collonges (FR) 12-1 S Morris *Ld to 3; bhnd frm 12; lft poor 4th 14; t.o*	40	4
786[4]	Catchatan (IRE) (7x)(cp) 20-1 J Dillon *Cl up til 10l 5th & rdn 10; hmpd 12; pu nxt*		P
684[1]	Franco (IRE) 1-2F J Diment *Cl up; ld 5; 3l clr & gng str when rn out 14*		R

OFFICIAL DISTANCES: dist, 3*l* **TIME:** 6min 35.0s **TOTE:** £2.30 **DF:**c/f

889 Dodson & Horrell PPORA Club Members Restricted, 12st — 8 ran

Form	Horse	Dist	Pos
291[1]	**KILLARD POINT (IRE)** (7a) 3-1 **R Cope** *In tch; went 2nd 13; ld aft 3 out; blun & hdd nxt; rallied to ld app last; hld on wl*		1
587[P]	**Mind The Gate**(bl) 7-1 **M Rimell** *Ld in start; jw; ld til aft 3 out; lft in ld nxt; hdd app last; kpt on one pce flat*	2	2
785[7]	**Gangster** 20-1 **Miss S Tarry** *Prsd ldr to 12; 4th & outpcd 14; went mod 3rd last; kpt on*	15	3
383[P]	Rathbarry Lad (IRE) 7-1 S Morris *Chsd ldrs; jmpd big 2; mist 11; 6th & outpcd 14; no ch aft; went mod 4th flat*	8	4
476[1]	Hunca Munca (IRE) (12a) evensF N Pearce *(xnb) 2 handlers; ww; smooth prog to 3rd 14; pushed along nxt; 5l 3rd 2 out; wknd app last; tired & lost 2 plces flat*	1	5
384[2]	Balmoral Spring (IRE)(vis) 6-1 R Armson *In tch; chsd ldrs 8 til rdn & btn 15*	12	6
684[4]	Fiesty Frosty (IRE) (5a) 20-1 J Docker *Rr; mists 6 & 7; lost tch 12; pu nxt*		P
591[P]	Treble Trouble 33-1 Miss L Fear *Pulling; bhnd; prog to jn ldrs 10-12; bhnd frm 14; t.o when fell last*		F

OFFICIAL DISTANCES: 2*l*, 10*l* **TIME:** 6min 37.0s **TOTE:** £3.30 **DF:**c/f

890 Open Maiden 56&7yo, 2m4f, 12st - 16J — 16 ran

Form	Horse	Dist	Pos
584[6]	**GREY FANDANGO (IRE)** 6-1 **M Rimell** *Made all; 7l clr 3 out; rdn app last; kpt on game flat; just hld on*		1
589[7]	**Earl Of Buckingham** 6-1 **P Cowley** *In tch; 6th & rdn 3 out; rallied to chse wnr aft 2 out; 2l down last; r.o flat; just failed*	nk	2
290[4]	**Gentlemans Relish** 6-1 **T Lane** *Trckd ldrs; 7l 4th & drvn 3 out; 3rd & one pce app last*	5	3
597[2]	Tom Tobacco 5-2F R Cope *Chsd ldrs in 2nd/3rd; 3rd & rdn 2 out; one pce*	1/2	4
651[F]	Shot Of Jollop (IRE) (7a)(bl) 3-1 S Morris *Mid-div; mist 4; prog & in tch 9; rdn 13; 7th & wl btn nxt*	20	5
701[P]	Major Reno (IRE) 33-1 J Newbold *(xnb) Ww mid-div; outpcd frm 11; no ch frm 3 out; t.o*	20	6
106[F]	Prince Mouse 33-1 N Kent *(xnb) A bhnd; lost tch 9; t.o*	7	7
500[P]	Lough Erin Shore (5a) 20-1 J Burley *(xnb) Ww in rr; prog & in tch 9; outpcd frm 12; no ch aft*	3	8
	All Alight (IRE) (7a) 14-1 N Bloom *A bhnd; t.o 8; last when pu aft 10*		P
685[P]	Golden Dawn 33-1 R Armson *Chsd ldrs til wknd qckly 10; bhnd & pu 12*		P
	Izzyizzenty (7a) 33-1 O Williams *A bhnd; lost tch 10; pu 12*		P
597[P]	Mrs Fidget (5a) 33-1 N Pettitt *W ldrs til wknd 8; wl bhnd when pu 3 out.*		P
789[P]	Red Lake (IRE) 25-1 A Sansome *Ww; prog & in tch 8; blun nxt; sn outpcd; wl bhnd & pu 12*		P
680[6]	Satanas (FR) 25-1 M Chapman *(xnb) Last when mist 6; sn t.o; pu 8*		P

	Sir Harry Henbit 33-1 J Diment *Chsd ldrs; disp 2nd 7 til wknd qckly app 2 out; no ch when pu last*		P
476[P]	Sleeping Panther(vis) 33-1 P Millington *Nt jw; chsd ldrs to 8; wkng when blun nxt; wl bhnd & pu aft 10*		P

OFFICIAL DISTANCES: hd, 1l **TIME:** 5min 32.0s **TOTE:** £10.80 **DF:**£100.00

Towcester (RH 10F,18J)

Sun, 11 Apr (SOFT)

891 Mortgage Solutions Open HC, 3m1f £2282 10 ran

457[1]	**FAIR WIND (IRE)** 11-09 8-1 **Miss A Goschen** *Jw; lft 2nd at 7; ld 10; drew rt away frm 3 out; unchall.*		1
632[2]	**Strong Tea (IRE)** 11-12 16-1 **A Charles-Jones** *Mounted v late; last frm 7; pckd 11; t.o 13; still last 3 out; mist nxt; drvn into 2nd flat.*	25	2
209[P]	**Fanion De Nourry (FR)** 11-05 40-1 **Miss S Sharratt** *Bhnd early; 3rd & mist 10; sn wl bhnd; rallied u.p 3 out; rem 2nd nxt; dem flat*	2	3
629[P]	Soul King (IRE) 11-05 20-1 R Bliss *Pckd 4; 2nd til lft in ld 7; reluct u.p aft 9; hdd nxt; mists aft; tired 2nd when mist 3 out*	8	4
727[4]	Mr Max (IRE) 11-05 40-1 M Wall *Chsd ldrs; rmdrs 10; rem 4th aft nxt; plodded on*	5	5
490[F]	Buckland Knight (IRE) 11-05 10-1 J Young *Fell 1.*		F
583[2]	Kentford Busy B 11-00 14-1 N Pearce *Climbed over 2 & 3; poor last when hmpd & ur 4*		U
679[1]	Lancastrian Jet (IRE) 12-01 8-13F M Barber *Rcd keen in ld til crossed by loose horse, bumped & ur 7*		U
465[4]	Mickthecutaway (IRE) 11-05 9-1 D Skelton *Bolted towards 1; blun & ur 1.*		U
543[P]	Quetal (IRE) 12-02 9-1 N Harris *5th when fell 4*		F

TIME: 6min 58.4s **TOTE:** £7.20; places £1.80,£2.00,£8.90 **Ex:**£68.40 **CSF:**£120.55

Fakenham (LH 6F)

Mon, 12 Apr (GOOD becoming SOFT)

892 Hood, Vores & Allwood Nov HC, 2m5f110y - 16J £3421 13 ran

630[P]	**BOHEMIAN SPIRIT (IRE)** 12-01 10-1 **Miss S Brotherton** *In tch; prog 10; nrly carried out & ld 11; drew clr app last; rdn out*		1
544[3]	**Kasilia (FR)** 11-05 12-1 **Miss V Simpson** *In tch; lost plce frm 7; hdwy 3 out; stayed on to tk 2nd cl home; nt trble wnr.*	8	2
443[3]	**The Vintage Dancer (IRE)** 11-05 12-1 **G Kerr** *Chsd ldrs; went 2nd 12; outpcd by wnr app last; dem cl home.*	hd	3
544[1]	Enitsag (FR) 11-11 13-8F D Mansell *Chsd ldrs; mist 2; rdn app 3 out; one pce aft*	$2^1/_2$	4
557[3]	The Red Boy (IRE) 11-05 8-1 A Braithwaite *Towards rr; stdy hdwy 12; kpt on frm 2 out; nvr able to chall*	nk	5
544[F]	Rooster 11-05 12-1 M Mackley *Prom til wknd 13*	5	6
	Bering Gifts (IRE) 11-09 13-2 H Fowler *Mist 2; a bhnd; t.o*	dist	7
679[P]	Badworth Gale (IRE) 11-05 50-1 J Burley *Midfield; blun 5; lost plce 9; t.o & pu 12*		P
742[1]	Madmidge 11-05 7-1 D Kemp *A bhnd; t.o & pu 3 out*		P
738[1]	Mister Falcon (FR) 11-05 20-1 R Hughes *Prom; rdn to ld brief aft 10 & nrly tk wrong course; wknd app 12; t.o & pu 2 out*		P
544[5]	Noble Colours 11-05(tt) 50-1 M Scales *Bhnd; blun 3; t.o when blun 3 out; pu 2 out*		P
631[4]	Normania (NZ) 11-05 12-1 Miss S West *Midfield; mist & lost plce 7; sn bhnd; t.o & pu 9*		P
647[1]	Westfield John 11-07(bl) 11-2 J Owen *Ld; hdd & hmpd aft 10; wkng when blun 12; t.o & pu 2 out*		P

TIME: 5min 30.5s **TOTE:** £10.40; places 2.50,£8.40,£5.90 **CSF:**£138.81

The stewards enquired into interference with a circuit remaining by Mister Falcon on Westfield John, also affecting the winner; they found the rider of the former guilty of careless riding and of riding a finish too soon; he was suspended for 15 days

893 Queen's Cup, An Eastern Counties HC, 3m110y - 18J £3328 7 ran

650[1] **CANTARINHO** 11-01 5-2 **D Kemp** *Prom; ld 6; hit 13; drew clr app last; easily* 1
122[F] **Courage Under Fire** 11-09(bl) 7-4F **O Nelmes** *Rn in snatches; in tch; mist 2; jmpd slow 7; kpt on u.p to tk 2nd cl home; no ch w wnr* 14 2
557[1] **Militaire (FR)** 11-07 11-2 **J Owen** *Trckd ldrs; chsd wnr app 4 out; btn app last; lost 2nd cl home* . . . . ½ 3
649[1] Celtic Duke 11-07 4-1 Miss Z Turner *Ld to 6; prom til rdn & wknd aft 3 out* 8 4
744[2] Bush Hill Bandit (IRE) 11-09 8-1 H Fowler *Prom to 8; rdn app 15; no imp aft* 3 5
648[1] Bunratty's Sole (IRE) 11-05(cp) 14-1 N Bloom *In tch; blun 10; mist 12; mist & wknd 14* 17 6
239[P] Dunmanus Bay (IRE) 11-11(vis) 33-1 M Mackley *Hit 7; a bhnd; t.o & pu 11* P

TIME: 6min 55.5s **TOTE:** £4.40; places £2.10,£1.60 **Ex:**£8.30 **CSF:**£8.36

Sedgefield (LH 8F,21J)

Mon, 12 Apr (GOOD, GOOD to SOFT patches run-in)

894 Cantor Index Open HC, 3m3f £1463 6 ran

798[6] **SON OF ANSHAN** 11-09(tt) 5-4F **G Tuer** *Cl up frm 5; ld 13; clr 16; rdn aft 2 out; stayed on* 1
678[3] **Go Nomadic** 11-07 2-1 **P Atkinson** *Hld up in tch; went 2nd 18; rdn aft 2 out; stayed on; no imp on wnr last 100yds* 3 2
772[8] **Who Dares Wins** 11-05 11-2 **D Da Silva** *Made most til hdd 13; chsd wnr til wknd frm 18* 19 3
769[4] Flat Top 11-07 9-1 M Manton *Bhnd; rdn aft 14; no hdwy* 19 4
798[F] Decoded 11-05(cp) 25-1 M Seston *Chsng ldng pr when blun & ur 8* . . . . . U
656[6] Valley Erne (IRE) 11-12 20-1 C Storey *Ld/disp ld to 4; blun 6; lost tch frm 9; t.o & pu 15* . . . . P

TIME: 6min 57.7s **TOTE:** £2.50; places £2.00,£1.70 **Ex:**£4.00 **CSF:**£4.27

East Kent

Aldington (LH 9F,19J)

Mon, 12 Apr (GOOD, GOOD to FIRM in places)

895 Open Maiden, 12st 8 ran

782[P] **PANDELI** 5-1 **D Phelan** *Hdwy 8; cl 2nd/3rd frm 11 til ld app 3 out; jnd & outj last; hrd rdn to ld agn flat* 1
803[4] **Almazard**(bl) 12-1 **C Gordon** *2nd/3rd til ld 11-12; ld agn 14; rmdrs & hdd app 3 out; rallied u.p to jn wnr last; no ex flat* 1 2
782[U] **Seymour Of Me** 16-1 **J Merry** *Hld up; stdy hdwy 13; prsd ldrs 16; ld brief aft 3 out; disp ld 2 out; ev ch last; wknd flat* 2 3
Arctic Drift(tt) 7-2 D Dunsdon *Ld; sn clr; blun 3; mists 6 & 10; hdd app nxt; wknd qckly; pu 13* . . . . P
Blakes Road (IRE) 10-1 G Gallagher *In tch; lft 2nd 9; ld 13; sn hdd; 4th & wkng when pu 16* . . . . P
540[2] Rumour Has It (IRE) 2-1F P Hall *Jmpd sticky; sn in rr; detach last 9; wl bhnd when pu 13* . . . . P
644[P] Sleeping Music (FR) 8-1 Miss B Donnelly *A towards rr; lost tch frm 12; 5th & no ch when pu 15* . . . . P
611[3] Spruce Goose (IRE)(tt) 5-1 N Wilson (South) *A.p; chsd ldr frm 6 til rn out 9* R

OFFICIAL DISTANCES: 1*l*, 2*l* **TIME:** 6min 51.0s
TOTE: £5.40; places £1.30,£6.10,£1.60 **DF:**£30.80

896 S.E. Hunts Club Members Conditions, 12st 4 ran

606[1] **TOUJOURS (IRE)** 1-4F **C Gordon** *Jw; settled in last pr; impd 11; ld 13; ww in ld til qcknd away flat; v easily* 1
778[P] **Glenmont (IRE)**(cp) 8-1 **Ms L Stock** *Chsd ldr most of way; 3l down 3 out; kpt on one pce; no ch w wnr* 5 2
608[P] **Stylish Dave (NZ)** 7-1 **Mrs D Rowell** *Jmpd rt; last frm 5; lost tch aft 10; went mod 3rd 16; nvr nr ldrs* 15 3
806[F] Lord Of The Flies (IRE) 8-1 D Page (Kent) *Ld til hdd app 13; blun nxt; sn wknd; last frm 16* 2 4

OFFICIAL DISTANCES: 3*l*, 8*l* **TIME:** 6min 46.0s **TOTE:** £1.70 **DF:**£5.80

897 Confined (Vet & Nov Rdrs), 12st — 7 ran

778P **LIVELY LORD (IRE)** (9x)(cp,tt) 7-4F **G Wigley** *Ld 4; made rest at gd pce in 2-3l ld; drew clr frm 2 out; comf* 1
625⁵ **Jack Of Kilcash (IRE)** (3x) 4-1 **N Benstead** *Ld to 3; prsd wnr rest of way; 3l down when rmdrs 3 out; kpt on one pce app last.* 5 2
779P **Kniveniven (IRE)** 14-1 **Miss B Donnelly** *Sn lost tch; 30l 4th 8; t.o 13; tk v dist 3rd flat* 1½fs 3
640U Tomcappagh (IRE) 14-1 J Wall *Chsd ldng pr frm 4; 20l adrift 8; t.o 15; dem flat* 4 4
182⁹ Claywalls 12-1 Miss O Maylam *Midfield when pu & dism aft 3.* . . . . . . P
537U Prime Course (IRE) (5x) 5-2 Miss H Gordon *Midfield when blun 3; pu nxt; saddle slpd* . . . . . . P
804² Russian Connection (IRE) 6-1 A Ward-Thomas *Jmpd sticky; sn lost tch; 45l 5th 8; climbed 10; pu nxt* . . . . . . P

OFFICIAL DISTANCES: 6*l*, dist **TIME:** 6min 34.0s **TOTE:** £2.80; places £1.50,£2.70 **DF:**£7.30

The stewards enquired into the pulling-up of (i) Claywalls - accepting the rider's explanation that the horse had lost its action, and (ii) Prime Course - accepting the rider's explanation that her saddle had slipped

898 Mens Open, 12st — 3 ran

780² **REAL VALUE (IRE)** (7x) 6-4 **P Hall** *Jmpd delib at times; last most of way; 6l adrift of ldng pr & pushed along frm 15; no prog til hdwy 3 out; jnd ldr & outj last; r.o game flat; ld cl home.* 1
535² **Pendle Hill** 4-7F **P Bull** *Mostly 2nd & gng wl til jnd ldr 15; ld aft nxt; 4l up 2 out; rdn app last; no ex flat; hdd cl home.* . . . . . . ½ 2
607⁴ **Garrison Friendly (IRE)**(bl) 6-1 **N Wilson (South)** *Ld; mist 10; 2-4l ahd til jnd 15; prsd ldr 16-2 out; wknd qckly u.p last* 15 3

OFFICIAL DISTANCES: nk, 13*l* **TIME:** 6min 34.0s **TOTE:** £2.90 **DF:**£1.10

899 Ladies Open - 18J — 4 ran

781¹ **SHERIFF'S FRIEND (IRE)** (7x) 1-4F **Mrs J Gordon** *Hld up; 2nd frm 9; ld 2 out; jnd last; qcknd flat; easily* 1
777³ **Silver Lake (IRE)**(cp) 8-1 **Miss K Pegram** *Ld/disp at stdy pce to 9; lost tch 11; 15l 3rd aft 13; gd hdwy frm 15 to press ldrs app 2 out; jnd wnr last; outpcd flat.* 3 2
781P **Irish Sea (USA)** (7x) 5-1 **Mrs P Hall** *Last til hdwy to ld & mist 10; clr 12-15; hdd app 2 out; sn btn; wkng when mist last* 15 3
781P Red Channel (IRE) 8-1 Miss B Donnelly *Prsd ldr til rn thro wing 8.* . . . . . . R

OFFICIAL DISTANCES: 3*l*, 12*l* **TIME:** 6min 44.0 **TOTE:** £1.30 **DF:**£2.10

Fence 17 omitted - damaged

900 Restricted, 12st — 4 ran

575¹ **LORD ALPHA (IRE)** 2-1 **D Phelan** *2nd til ld aft 16; made rest; 3l up 2 out; r.o str when chall app last* 1
605³ **Straight Baron** 8-1 **P Bull** *3rd til hdwy to chse wnr app 2 out; ev ch app last; no ex flat.* 4 2
Sliabh Foy (IRE) 4-1 **P Hall** *Ld; 5-8l up to 7; slt advant 11 til hdd aft 16; ev ch when blun 3 out; kpt on one pce frm nxt* 4 3
644¹ Ministerial (IRE) evensF C Gordon *A last; sev slt mists; 10l 4th aft 15; no prog; pckd 3 out; eased app last.* 25 4

OFFICIAL DISTANCES: 3*l*, 5*l* **TIME:** 6min 44.0s **TOTE:** £2.00 **DF:**£7.50

Essex Farmers & Union

Marks Tey (LH 10F,20J)
Mon, 12 Apr (GOOD)

901 Open Maiden — 9 ran

244⁶ **MONARCH RULER** (7a) 5-2 **G Cooper** *Trckd ldr in 2nd; chall 15 til ld 17; drew clr app last.* 1
445P **A Fine Story** 3-1 **A Williams** *A.p; trckd ldr; 4l 3rd 7; 2l 2nd 3 out; ev ch til one pce app last.* 3 2

746P **Baron Bernard** 8-1 **P Chinery** *Hld up in rr; 7th 10; stdly lost tch; t.o 15; plodded on; ploughed thro last* . . . fence 3
Catley Cross (5a) 8-1 A Merriam *(xnb) In tch; 8l 6th 7; hit 10; wknd; t.o & pu 12* . . . P
Lolloping Lad 8-1 M Smith *Rr & nt jw; rdn along & no resp; drpd to last 10; t.o & pu 11* . . . P
Mai Cure (12a) 8-1 N Moore *(xnb) In tch; 7l 5th 7; lost tch 11; t.o & pu 14* P
Peats Ridge (IRE) 9-4F R Stearn *Hld up; 5l 4th 7; 8l 4th 12; wknd 13; t.o & pu 3 out* . . . P
Phatic (IRE) 5-1 A Sansome *Pulled to ld 1; set fast pce; wknd 15; 15l 3rd when lost action & pu 2 out; horse collapsed twice aft; event removed by horse ambulance - nxt rce delayed 20 mins* . . . P
6462 Top Boots (IRE) (7a) 3-1 Miss N Barnes *Last 1; t.o when jmpd slow & to lft 3; 30l last 6; 25l 5th 15; 4th & exhaust when ref & ur last* . . . r

OFFICIAL DISTANCES: 2*l*, dist **TIME:** 6min 51.0s **TOTE:** £4.00

902 Restricted, 12st 10 ran

745F **RIP KIRBY** 7-1 **G Cooper** *Hld up in rr; stdy hdwy 13; 4l 3rd 16; ld 2 out; stayed on wl last* . . . 1
7458 **Ginger Bug** (5a) 5-1 **P Chinery** *Hld up in rr; chsd ldrs frm 12; 8l 4th 16; stayed on to 3rd 2 out; went 3l 2nd app last; a hld* . . . 2 2
6483 **Federal Case (FR)** 5-2F **A Merriam** *Prsd ldr frm 1 til ld 10-15; cl 2nd til ld frm 3 out-nxt; wknd & dem 3rd app last* . . . 8 3
5551 Stick Or Bust(cp) 5-1 R Stearn *3l 3rd 4; chsd ldr aft; 6l 5th 16; no imp 3 out* 5 4
5552 Lord Montagu (IRE)(cp) 8-1 A Williams *Prom; 4l 4th 7; ld brief 10; prsd ldr nxt; 1l 2nd 15; wknd qckly; dem 4th app 2 out* . . . 6 5
745F Germany Park (IRE) 4-1 M Smith *Hld up; 6l 5th 7; 12l 6th 10; no hdwy frm 15; trailed home; v disapp* . . . 30 6
6464 Changing Fashion (IRE) 14-1 Miss N Barnes *2 handlers; last 1; t.o 5; pu 11* P
745P Ical (IRE) (5a) 10-1 N Moore *Prom; ld frm 7-9; wknd 11; 4th & lsng tch when ur 13* U
7426 Lambrini King (IRE) 5-1 Miss L Barrett-Nobbs *(xnb) Ld to 6; cl 3rd 10; lsng tch when blun bad & v nrly ur 14; t.o aft; pu 2 out* . . . P
375P Run Monty (IRE) 3-1 A Sansome *(xnb) 5th 10; sn lost tch; t.o & pu 12* . . . P

OFFICIAL DISTANCES: 1*l*, 10*l* **TIME:** 6min 54.0s **TOTE:** £3.50

903 Mens Open 3 ran

523P **MININO (IRE)** 2-5F **A Merriam** *Disp ld to 4; trckd ldr til lft in ld 10; drew 8l clr aft 15; 20l clr 2 out; v easily* . . . 1
5213 **Nordic Spree (IRE)**(bl) 5-2 **A Sansome** *Disp ld to 4; narrow ld 5; 3rd aft til lft 2nd 10; cl up til totally outpcd 15; 20l down & rdn 2 out; no resp* . . . 25 2
8322 Ballad (IRE) 6-4 A Williams *Trckd ldng pr to 5; ld 6; jnd when iron snapped & rfo 10* . . . U

OFFICIAL DISTANCE: dist **TIME:** 6min 50.0s **TOTE:** £1.50

904 Ladies Open 3 ran

743r **CORSTON JOKER** 6-4 **Mrs L Spence** *Ld; jnd 13-15; 4l 2nd 17; 3l 2nd & hld when lft in ld 2 out; nt keen flat; rdr's 1st wnr* . . . 1
7436 **Mister Audi (IRE)**(bl) 3-1 **Miss A Bowles** *Trckd ldrs in last; 3l 3rd 7; 10l adrift 17; chsd rivals vain til lft 6l 2nd 2 out; kpt on one pce* . . . 3 2
7812 Fair Kiowa (IRE) 1-3F Mrs S Hodge *Trckd ldr in 2nd; prsd ldr frm 8; disp ld 13 til ld 16; 3l up & in comm when blun & ur 2 out* . . . U

OFFICIAL DISTANCE: 2½*l* **TIME:** 6min 54.0s **TOTE:** £3.00

905 Confined, 12st 4 ran

384 **WILTON BRIDGE (IRE)** 7-2 **Mrs S Hodge** *Sis; hld up in 4th; 6l 4th 10; hdwy to press ldr 15; jmpd to ld 17; qckly drew clr; unchall* . . . 1
7424 **Lord Euro (IRE)** (3x) 4-5F **A Merriam** *Ld & jmpd rt; 3l up 10; jnd 15; disp ld when tried to demolish 17 & lost 20l; 3rd aft til r.o to dist 2nd aft 3 out; no ch w wnr* fence 2
Thyne Express (IRE) 10-1 **M Smith** *Sis; 1l 2nd 4; 5l 3rd 10; 2nd agn 11; ld brief 14; 3rd when lft 2nd 17; dem agn aft 3 out; sn lost tch; exhaust & climbed over last* 25 3
Sir Williamwallace (IRE) (3x) 6-4 N Moore *2l 3rd 4; 3l 2nd 10; 4l 4th 12; wknd 14; rap lost tch nxt; virt t.o 3 out* . . . ½ 4

OFFICIAL DISTANCES: dist, 15*l* **TIME:** 6min 54.0s **TOTE:** £5.00

906 PPORA Club Members (Nov Rdrs), 12st — 4 ran

Form	Horse / Rider / Comments	Dist	Pos
744^{4}	**ROYAL ACTION** 1-2F **P Chinery** *Settled last; 6l 2nd 6; clsd 10; ld 11; made rest; drew clr frm 3 out; unchall*		1
557^{P}	**Village Copper** 2-1 **R Stearn** *Ld to 10; chsd ldr aft; wknd 3 out; 15l down & btn 2 out*	30	2
745^{P}	Mr Moonbeam (IRE)(cp) 6-1 M Buchan *2nd til dem 3rd 5; 15l 3rd 9; 20l 4th when rfo 20yds aft 13*		U
556^{U}	Zabadi (IRE) 7-1 Miss R Napier *Sis; rdr unstdy early; 4th 5; 16l 4th 9; went 3rd 10; v rem 3rd when pu 17*		P

OFFICIAL DISTANCE: 25*l* **TIME:** 6min 50.0s **TOTE:** £1.50

Four Burrow

Trebudannon (LH 8F,20J)

Mon, 12 Apr (GOOD/GOOD to FIRM)

907 Hunt Members, 12st — 7 ran

Form	Horse / Rider / Comments	Dist	Pos
707^{1}	**LET'S FLY (FR)** 4-5F **Mrs M Hand** *Trckd ldr; hdwy to ld 13; drew clr frm 3 out*		1
498^{P}	**Indian Raider (IRE)** 7-2 **A Glassonbury** *Hdwy to 2nd 16; outpcd aft 3 out*	10	2
707^{P}	**Baldhu Jay Arr**(bl) 3-1 **Miss L Gardner** *7s-3s; ld to 12; wknd & lost tch aft 16*	20	3
701^{7}	Fluted Edge (5a) 20-1 W Biddick *A rr; t.o aft 14; plodded on*	50	4
486^{P}	Elegant Apple (5a, 14ow) 33-1 D Stephens (Devon) *Towards rr when ref 3*		r
794^{P}	Native Drum (IRE) 10-1 Miss S Gaisford *Sa; a rr; t.o & pu 13*		P
492^{P}	Sandy's Way (12a) 25-1 I Hambley *Disp 3rd to 11; 25l down & lsng tch when pu 14*		P

OFFICIAL DISTANCES: 8*l*, dist **TIME:** 5min 53.0s **TOTE:** £2.00

908 Confined, 12st — 5 ran

Form	Horse / Rider / Comments	Dist	Pos
707^{3}	**IT'SNOTSIMPLE (IRE)** (5a, 5x) 9-2 **Mrs T Trickey** *Trckd ldr; ld & blun 14; ld agn 15; 4l up 3 out; just hld on*		1
705^{1}	**Teninarow (IRE)** 8-11F **Richard Darke** *Blun 2; mists 4 & 11; ld brief aft 14; chsd ldr; mist 16; hdwy to chall aft last; just failed*	s hd	2
	Moorland Rose (5a) 5-1 **Miss D Mitchell** *Rr; kpt on to tk 3rd aft last*	25	3
498^{P}	Coombe Quest 7-1 T Dennis *Rcd free in ld to 13; 10l 3rd 3 out; wknd*	2	4
794^{2}	Carefree Love (IRE)(bl) 9-4 Miss S Gaisford *In tch to 13; wknd aft nxt*	6	5

OFFICIAL DISTANCES: ½*l*, 3*l* **TIME:** 5min 53.0s **TOTE:** £3.00

909 Open Maiden 56&7yo (Div 1), 2m4f, 12st — 8 ran

Form	Horse / Rider / Comments	Dist	Pos
701^{6}	**LONGSTONE LADY (IRE)** (5a) 9-4F **D McKenna** *Trckd ldrs; hdwy to ld 13; r.o u.p frm 2 out*		1
702^{U}	**Hooray Henry** (7a) 11-4 **T Dennis** *Hdwy to 2nd 12; chall 2 out; outpcd*	1½	2
701^{P}	**Northern Thatch** (12a)(tt) 12-1 **I Hambley** *Rr; hdwy to 3rd 2 out; nt pce to chall*	8	3
701^{P}	Some Tool 10-1 R Ross *Disp ld to 10; sn wknd*	8	4
307^{P}	Jd Trout (12a, 4ow) 10-1 A Charles-Jones *Mostly 3rd til wknd aft 13*	2	5
701^{P}	Brits Mate (5a) 10-1 J Tickle *In tch to 8; t.o when rn out & ur 11*		R
	French Guest (7a) 6-1 Mrs M Hand *Sn towards rr; 12l 5th when fell 13*		F
	That's Cash (IRE) 5-1 A Glassonbury *Jw; ld/disp to 10; wkng when pu 13*		P

OFFICIAL DISTANCES: ½*l*, 2*l* **TIME:** 4min 56.0s **TOTE:** £2.50

The stewards enquired into the pulling-up of That's Cash; they accepted the rider's explanation that the horse had lost its action after a mistake at the 10th fence and he thought it had broken down but it was sound when eased

910 Open Maiden 56&7yo (Div 2), 2m4f, 12st — 7 ran

Form	Horse / Rider / Comments	Dist	Pos
	RYDERS HILL (12a) 5-1 **Richard Darke** *Mists in rr; hdwy to 3rd 12; ld app last; r.o wl*		1
796^{3}	**Whats Up Maid** (5a) 9-2 **M Munrowd** *Hdwy to ld 10 til hdd & outpcd last.*	3	2
702^{3}	**Little Apple Bay** (5a) evensF **Miss S Gaisford** *Ld/disp to 11; still cl up 3 out; r.o one pce*	4	3
	Sex Kitten (5a) 7-1 R McCarthy *Cl 3rd mostly til lost tch aft 10; kpt on*	6	4

796P	Ercon (IRE) 12-1 J Tickle *Towards rr when blun 10; sn lost tch; kpt on*	15	5
492P	Burrow Corner(tt) 5-1 L Jefford *Mostly 3rd til wknd aft 10; t.o & pu 2 out*		P
567P	Indian Renegade (IRE) (5a) 10-1 D McKenna *Lost tch aft 6; t.o & pu 11*		P

OFFICIAL DISTANCES: ½*l*, 2*l* **TIME:** 5min 00.0s **TOTE:** £5.00

911 Mixed Open, 12st — 5 ran

733¹	**KESTICK** (7x) 2-5F **Miss T Cave** *Hld up in rr; tk clsr ord 11; went 3rd 3 out; ld app nxt; pushed out*		1
703³	**Hasten Bak** 3-1 **Miss L Gardner** *Ld 11; mist 14; hdd app 2 out; outpcd*	6	2
707P	**Dark Challenger (IRE)** 6-1 **Miss S Gaisford** *Cl up til outpcd aft 3 out.*	8	3
703P	Calleva Star (IRE) 25-1 S Kidston *Made most to 10; 2nd to 14; wknd*	20	4
793⁶	Just Bert (IRE) 12-1 W Biddick *Mostly 2nd/3rd; disp 2l 2nd but lkng btn when rn out 2 out*		R

OFFICIAL DISTANCES: 3*l*, 4*l* **TIME:** 5min 55.0s **TOTE:** £1.50

912 Restricted, 12st — 11 ran

704¹	**LADY MISPRINT** (5a) 2-1F **D McKenna** *Chsd runaway ldr til ld 10; sn clr; eased; v impressive*		1
706²	**Virgos Bambino (IRE)** (5a) 9-2 **A Charles-Jones** *Chsng runaway ldrs in 3rd; 30l down 11; hdwy to 2nd app 2 out; r.o wl u.p*	30	2
706⁶	**Indiana John (FR)** 12-1 **T Dennis** *Mid-div til hdwy to 4th 16 & 3rd 2 out; outpcd in duel for 2nd flat*	½	3
706P	Chapners Cross 16-1 Miss S Young *Chsd ldrs in mostly 5th; kpt on*	6	4
824U	Milla's Man (IRE) 12-1 M Dennis *Towards rr; some late hdwy; nrst fin*	5	5
706P	Butler Didit (5a) 9-1 I Hambley *Chsd ldrs in mostly 4th; no hdwy frm 12.*	5	6
323P	Wicked Imp 20-1 M Munrowd *A outpcd in rr; no hdwy*	6	7
415U	Porto (IRE)(tt) 8-1 Richard Darke *Rcd free in ld to 9; wkng in 2nd to 3 out; lost tch aft 2 out*	1	8
572P	Baldhu Jack 16-1 Miss P Moorhouse *Sn t.o; plodded on*	2	9
473⁴	Milldalus (IRE) 8-1 S Kidston *Towards rr when pu 2 out.*		P
488⁴	Panto Pixie (5a) 7-1 Miss T Cave *In rr; no prog; pu 15*		P

OFFICIAL DISTANCES: dist, ½*l* **TIME:** 5min 47.0s **TOTE:** £2.00

Aller Coombe (orignal rdr inj in padd; bolted with substitute) was withdrawn not under orders; Rule 4 deduction 20p in pound

913 Open Maiden, 12st — 10 ran

	CHARMINSKY 7-1 **Miss S Young** *Trckd ldrs; hdwy to 4th 16; 3rd 17 & 2nd 2 out; ld last; r.o wl*		1
704³	**Winnie The Pooh** evensF **Miss S Gaisford** *Made most; lkd in comm til chall & hdd last; r.o one pce*	2	2
733P	**Truicear**(tt) 5-1 **R McCarthy** *Trckd ldrs in mostly 3rd desp some slow js; hdwy to 2nd 15; outpcd aft 3 out*	8	3
704P	Buddy Bear (IRE)(cp) 9-1 L Heard *Cl up to 14; lost tch; rr when pu 17*		P
824⁸	Dark Comedy (5a) 14-1 W Biddick *Rr when rn straight on bend aft 6*		R
	Golden Tanu 20-1 D McKenna *Hdwy to 2nd 10; 6l down in 3rd 16; 15l down when pu 3 out*		P
494R	Kingsmill Creek (5a) 7-1 T Dennis *Prom to 10; sn wknd; tlng off when pu 17*		P
795P	Lamerton Quest 25-1 L Rowe *Lost tch frm 14; rr when pu 3 out.*		P
486P	Native Christy (IRE) 7-1 A Glassonbury *Sn pushed along; rr & tlng off when pu 15*		P
194P	Tom Dove 12-1 M Munrowd *Sn strugg in rr; tlng off when pu 15*		P

OFFICIAL DISTANCES: 1*l*, 4*l* **TIME:** 6min 01.0s **TOTE:** £7.00

Morpeth

Tranwell (LH 9F,18J)

Mon, 12 Apr (GOOD to SOFT, SOFT in places)

914 Hunt Members, 12st — 5 ran

655⁵	**DONALLACH MOR (IRE)**(bl) 7-4 **Mrs V Jackson** *Swtng; handy til ld/disp aft 4; went clr 15; prsd app last; rdn out flat*		1
658²	**Rutherford** 4-1 **Miss J Balmer** *Oht; ld til hdd 4; lost plce & 15l last by 9; stdy prog to chall app last; one pce flat*	2	2

762^{2} **Snooty Eskimo (IRE)** 11-8F **H Norton** *Trckd ldr til ld/disp aft 4; ev ch 14 til rmdrs & sn wknd aft; tired & virt pu flat.* 30 3
549^{P} Another Daffodil (5a) 14-1 Miss S Hunt *1st ride; in tch in rr; crumpled on landing & fell 3* . . . . . . F
426^{P} Bob's Gray (4ow) 14-1 G Scantlebury *Mists; disp ld app 5; fell nxt* . . . . . . F

OFFICIAL DISTANCES: 2*l*, dist **TIME:** 6min 30.1s

915 Confined, 12st — 9 ran

552^{1} **CLIFFORD BAY (IRE)** (3x) 5-4F **Miss N Stirling** *(xnb) 2 handlers; oht; ld/disp til lft 6l clr 12; 5l up last; comf* 1
316^{9} **Raging Torrent** 8-1 **A Findlay** *Oht; chsd ldrs; 8l 3rd 11; rdn & prog & ev ch 14; outpcd nxt; kpt on; no ch w wnr* 6 2
426^{F} **Johnnys Gone (IRE)** 5-1 **C Shirley-Beavan** *Opened 11/2; hld up; 12l 5th & pushed along 12; prog to 1l 2nd 14; short-lived eff; sn outpcd* 1/2 3
857^{2} Spring Double (IRE) 6-1 B Mounsey-Heysham *In tch in rr; 10l off pce 9; prog & ev ch 14; sn outpcd; tired flat* 1/2 4
762^{P} Ballymenagh (IRE) 25-1 S Huggan *Hld up in rr; mist & 15l 8th 9; nd aft 14; t.o & pu 3 out* . . . . . . P
Calko 20-1 W Goldie *(xnb) Chsd ldr; 8l 3rd 5; wknd 11; t.o & pu 15* . . . . . . P
Driminamore (IRE) 66-1 C Ramsay *Oht; a rr; t.o 7; pu aft 11.* . . . . . . P
767^{U} Hapthor (12a) 6-1 C Dawson *(xnb) Oht; unruly padd; hdstrng; ld/disp til fell 12* F
283^{1} Wild Edgar (IRE) 6-1 A Richardson *2 handlers; oht; mid-div; 9l 4th 11; wkng in 15l 5th 14; lost tch & pu nxt* . . . . . . P

OFFICIAL DISTANCES: 6*l*, 1/2*l*, 1/2*l* **TIME:** 6min 21.9s

916 Ladies Open — 6 ran

428^{4†} **COMMANCHE LAW (IRE)** 5-1 **Mrs A Hamilton** *Prom; trckd ldr aft 9; disp 2l 2nd app 14; stdy prog to chall last; rdn & r.o flat to ld last 50yds* 1
548^{1} **Eighty Days (IRE)** (7a) 9-4 **Miss R Davidson** *(xnb) Lw; oht; trckd ldr til ld aft 9; 2l up app 14; 2l up last; rdn & hdd last 50yds.* 3 2
763^{1} **Balisteros (FR)** evensF **Miss P Robson** *Cl up; 3l 4th 9; disp 2l 2nd 14; 7l 3rd nxt; pushed along & some prog til one pce app last* 6 3
655^{6} In Demand 14-1 Miss J Balmer *In tch in rr; 6l last 9; 12l 5th 15; kpt on one pce aft* 12 4
550^{5} Houselope Beck 33-1 Miss A Wanless *(xnb) Ld til hdd 9; cl up til outpcd in 10l 4th 15; wknd aft* 6 5
854^{P} Wexford (IRE) 50-1 Miss S Lamb *In tch in rr; prog to 5l 5th 9; outpcd aft 14 & 15l last nxt; wknd aft* 25 6

OFFICIAL DISTANCES: 3*l*, 6*l*, 15*l* **TIME:** 6min 26.4s

917 Mens Open — 10 ran

340^{3} **EXTRA JACK (FR)**(bl) 8-1 **C Shirley-Beavan** *Made virt all; went 10l clr 9; 20l up 12; qcknd wl clr aft 14; unchall.* 1
426^{F} **French Cedar** 6-1 **W Ramsay** *Oht; chsd ldr; 18l 3rd 9; 20l 2nd 12; no ch w wnr* 15 2
656^{2} **Starbuck** 14-1 **W Goldie** *Chsd ldrs; 17l 2nd 9; 22l 3rd 13; no ch w wnr* . . 6 3
764^{9} Dr Deductible(cp) 20-1 R Brown *A rr; pushed along in 15l last 5; wl bhnd 15; kpt on.* 3 4
656^{3} Glacial Sygnet (IRE)(bl) 16-1 J Thompson *Handy til blun 7 & lost sev posns; outpcd aft 9; 40l 4th 15; kpt on one pce.* 1 5
764^{10} Finest Of Men 3-1 J Walton *Opened 7/2; a rr; 15l last & hmpd 5; wl bhnd 14; nd* 25 6
764^{6} Batoutoftheblue 14-1 S Huggan *Chsd ldrs til fell 5* . . . . . . F
764^{7} Gaultier Gale (IRE) 12-1 A Findlay *Mid-div; hrd rdn aft 9; wl bhnd 14; t.o & pu last* . . . . . . P
551^{1} Just Barney Boy 5-4F A Waugh *2s-5/4; mid-div; prog when blun & ur 11.* . U
340^{F} Shining Light (IRE) 33-1 S J Robinson *Prom early; sn rr; t.o aft 11; numerous rmdrs aft 13; exhaust & ref 15.* . . . . . . r

OFFICIAL DISTANCES: 15*l*, 5*l*, 2*l* **TIME:** 6min 21.2s

918 Restricted — 8 ran

432^{1} **KING BARRY (FR)** (7a) evensF **Miss P Robson** *7/4-evens; lw; oht; pulling in mid-div; 12l 5th 6; went 1l 2nd app 14; prog to ld aft 2 out; rdn clr flat* 1
425^{1} **Coomakista** (5a) 4-1 **R Morgan** *Lw; in tch; 10l 4th app 6; prog 9 to 2l 3rd app 14; ev ch til no ex app last* 5 2

765R **Gudasmum** (5a) 6-1 **Miss R Davidson** *Lw; ld/disp til 3l up 5; 3l ahd app 12; hdd aft 2 out; no ex* 4 3
657U Good Morning (5a) 33-1 R Dickson *Ld/disp til 8l 3rd 6; 5l 5th 9; in tch when ur 12* . . . . . U
Incroyable Mais Vrai (FR)(cp,tt) 5-1 K Anderson *(xnb) Hld up in rr; prog to 5l 4th 14; ev ch when ur 3 out* . . . . . U
766P Shylock (IRE)(bl) 20-1 J Thompson *Trckd ldr; 3l 2nd aft 5; wknd aft 11; t.o & tired when pu 3 out* . . . . . P
7662 Superstar Express (IRE) 16-1 A Findlay *(xnb) In tch in rr when pu aft 10* . . P
548P Timberley 16-1 R Green *In tch in rr; pushed along in 12l last 9; outpcd 13; sn strugg; 20l 5th 15; t.o & tired when pu 2 out* . . . . . P

OFFICIAL DISTANCES: 5*l*, 3*l* **TIME:** 6min 25.5s

919 Dodson & Horrell PPORA Club Members Maiden, 12st — 6 ran

7673 **MORE FLAIR** (5a, 2ow)(tt) 4-5F **J Walton** *(xnb) Trckd ldrs; 4l 3rd 6; went 1l 2nd 10; disp ld 13; lft clr app nxt; unchall* 1
5113 **Coquet Gold** (5a) 7-1 **Miss C Walton** *In tch in rr; 6l last 9; lft 25l 2nd 14; no ch w wnr; tired & virt pu flat* 40 2
659P Chase The Moon (5a) 5-1 Miss L Hislop *In tch in rr; 5l 4th app 6; outpcd & 15l last 12; lft poor 3rd 14; ur nxt* . . . . . U
766P Mid Summer Lark (IRE)(bl) 4-1 Miss L Kendall *Ld; 3l up app 3; jnd 13; disp ld when ducked out app nxt* . . . . . R
549P Tallaburn (5a) 7-2 A Findlay *(xnb) In tch in rr; prog to 4l 3rd 12; bad mist nxt; lft poor 3rd 15; ref & ur 3 out* . . . . . r
762P Tartan Rising (7a) 7-1 C Dawson *Trckd ldr; 1l 2nd 9; pushed along 11; wknd nxt; t.o & pu 15* . . . . . P

OFFICIAL DISTANCE: dist **TIME:** 6min 31.5s

The stewards enquired into the running out of Mid Summer Lark when in contention; they accepted the rider's explanation that the horse wearing blinkers seemed to catch sight of the horse on his outside and ducked inside the turning flag

920 Open Maiden 56&7yo, 2m4f, 12st - 15J — 10 ran

TWO HOOTS (5a) 8-1 **C Dawson** *Green; mid-div; 12l 5th 6; prog to 3l 2nd app 12; prsd ldr frm 2 out; disp ld last; ld flat* 1
7683 **Birkwood** (7a) 5-2F **Miss M Neill** *Trckd ldr til ld 6; qcknd pce; 5l up 8; hrd prsd frm 2 out; jnd last; hdd & nt qckn flat* 1 2
767P **Ofcoursehekhan (IRE)** 6-1 **Miss N Stirling** *(xnb) Handy til ld 4; hdd 6; ev ch til outpcd 3 out; r.o flat* . . . . . ½ 3
8592 Hi Up Brenkley 7-1 A Richardson *(xnb) Chsd ldrs; 6l 4th 11; outpcd aft nxt; grad wknd* 25 4
5973 Callitwatulike 4-1 T Glass *Mid-div; 8l 5th 11; outpcd aft nxt; grad wknd* . . 6 5
215U Midnight Reiver (5a)(tt) 12-1 Miss J Hollands *(xnb) In tch in rr; 25l 6th 10; nd* 25 6
856P Copybook (7a, 4ow) 9-2 J Walton *Nt a fluent; a rr; nd; t.o 10* 1 7
Stately Progress (IRE) 6-1 R Dickson *A rr; nd; t.o 10* 15 8
768P Perky's Wish (IRE) 33-1 S J Robinson *Ld early; trckd ldr til fell 10* . . . . . F
The Milecastle (IRE) (7a) 7-1 R Morgan *Green; 2 handlers; nt a fluent; a rr; nd; t.o 10; pu 2 out* . . . . . P

OFFICIAL DISTANCES: 1*l*, ½*l*, dist **TIME:** 5min 33.5s

North Cotswold

Paxford (LH 8F,18J)

Mon, 12 Apr (GOOD)

921 Hunt Members — 7 ran

7283 **STENNIKOV (IRE)** evensJF **E Walker** *(xnb) Settled 3rd til 2nd 9; ld 13; 10l clr app 15; hrd prsd 2 out; rdn & slt advant when lft clr last* 1
663B **Ballyalbert** evensJF **Miss A de Lisle Wells** *Oht; re-saddled start; rdr nrly off 1; tended to j lft; rcd keen in ld til hdd & mists 13 & 14; sn outpcd; rallied & cl up 3 out til jmpd lft nxt; imm btn; lft 2nd at last* 20 2
728P **Aldington Charlie** (16ow) 33-1 **C Sands** *Imm lost tch in 6th; t.o 7* 1½fs 3
Mr Fearless (16ow) 33-1 G Lockwood *(xnb) Bckwd; imm lost tch; t.o 4; fnce bhnd 7* 25 4

Cracking Day (U) (5a) 7-1 G Disney *20l 4th 6; 35l 5th & mist 10; pu 12* . P
661^{P} Shekels (IRE) 7-1 T Gretton *Chsd ldr to 9; wknd rap aft 11; 4th & t.o when pu 14* P
Sparkling Cascade (IRE) (5a) 16-1 Miss A Lindner *1st ride; hld up 4/5th; lost tch 7; went 25l 3rd 12; 30l down app 15; str rn to chall 2 out; ev ch but lkd hld when rfo last* . . . . U

OFFICIAL DISTANCES: 10*l*, 25*l* **TIME:** 6min 27.0s

922 Intermediate, 12st 9 ran

728^{2} **WILLIAM LIONHEART** 1-2F **Julian Pritchard** *Oht; made all at str gallop; still gng wl when lft virt solo 3 out; hvly eased last* 1
759^{5} **Tom Putt**(cp) 7-1 **B Pauling** *Chsd ldrs but nt a fluent; rdn 7; 9l 4th app 12; wl bhnd aft 14; lft rem 2nd 3 out*. 20 2
759^{P} **Silent Action (USA)**(tt) 10-1 **D Smith** *Towards rr; 20l 5th app 12; t.o 15* . . 25 3
728^{P} Themaster's Choice (IRE) 14-1 S Joynes *A bhnd; t.o when jmpd slow 12; btn nrly 2 fncs*. 20 4
Border Farmer (IRE) 9-1 N Wain *Tk off bef start; ss; inept rdr f.o 1*. . . . . . U
663^{P} Mr Naborro (IRE)(bl) 12-1 A Wintle *3rd early; 2nd 6; 3l down app 12; pu & dism 15* . . . . P
544^{P} Mustang Molly (5a) 12-1 A Martin *(xnb) Lw; 2nd to 6; sn lost tch w ldng pr; releg 5th 9 & strugg aft; t.o app 15; disp 4th & nrly 2 fncs bhnd when pu last* P
663^{r} Ole Gunnar (IRE) 9-1 M Wilesmith *(xnb) Jmpd slow in detach last; t.o 4; pu 11* P
451^{1} Therealbat (IRE) 7-1 G Barfoot-Saunt *Midfield; went 3rd 9; chsd wnr aft 14; ab 5l down when blun bad & ur 3 out* . . . . U

OFFICIAL DISTANCES: dist, dist **TIME:** 6min 20.0s

923 Ladies Open 3 ran

722^{1} **BALINOVA (IRE)** 1-6F **Miss P Gundry** *Lw; sauntered rnd in ld; hit 13; 6l clr 3 out; hrd hld*. 1
664^{P} **Fuero Real (FR)** 9-1 **Miss H James** *3rd til lft 3l 2nd on sufferance app 15; outclassed by wnr aft* 12 2
726^{P} Derrys Prerogative 7-2 Miss N Rudge *Pckd 5 & 13; chsd wnr til pu w difficulty 15; dism brief* . . . . P

OFFICIAL DISTANCE: 10*l* **TIME:** 6min 47.0s

924 Mens Open, 12st 5 ran

662^{3} **WELL TED (IRE)** (7x) 4-7F **Julian Pritchard** *Stdd last; blun 2; mist 5; hit 10; went 4th 13; hit 15; smooth rn nxt to ld & mist last; sn rdn clr*. 1
662^{4} **Philtre (IRE)** (7x) 5-2 **A Wintle** *Ld; rdn 2 out; hdd last; nt qckn* 2 2
727^{P} **Stormy Session** 7-1 **J Benfield** *Prsd ldr 5 til app 15; wknd app 2 out* 15 3
Captain's Log 12-1 M Wall *Pulled hrd in 4th til 3rd brief 9; wknd 12; last nxt; t.o 14; pu 15*. . . . . P
582^{2} Fours Are Wild (IRE) 7-2 A Martin *Rcd keen; chsd ldr to 5 & app 15; drvn & ab to lose 2nd when fell 2 out* . . . . F

OFFICIAL DISTANCES: $1\frac{1}{2}$*l*, 8*l* **TIME:** 6min 23.0s

925 Restricted, 12st 9 ran

232^{4} **CARAT** 9-2 **Miss P Gundry** *Settled midfield; went 2nd aft 14; ld nxt; just hdd 3 out; ld agn 2 out; jmpd delib last & jnd; rdn & fnd ex*. 1
787^{3} **Stormy Pass** 4-1 **T Ellis** *Midfield; went 2nd aft 11 til 3rd aft 14; lft 2nd nxt; slt ld 3 out til drvn & hdd 2 out; ev ch last; v one-pcd*. . . . . $1\frac{3}{4}$ 2
665^{3} **New Lodge Express (IRE)** 6-1 **T Stephenson** *(xnb) Hld up; hmpd 10; eff in 5l 5th aft 14; 5l 3rd & rdn 3 out; no imp* 4 3
601^{3} Who's Eddie (IRE) 11-2 M Harris *(xnb) Lft last aft 2; stdy prog app 15; 7l 3rd nxt; sn wknd* 12 4
726^{5} Campden Kitty (5a) 5-1 F Hutsby *2 handlers; rr aft mist 4; eff in cl 4th aft 14; fdd tame app 3 out*. 6 5
760^{1} April Treasure (5a) 5-2F Julian Pritchard *(xnb) Ld; 5l clr 11; just hdd when fell 15* F
756^{P} Marlmont Lad (IRE) 25-1 D Harvey *Chsd ldr to 11; drpd rap to rr & jmpd slow 12; t.o 14; pu 15*. . . . . P
755^{3} Misty Ramble (IRE) 6-1 G McPherson *(xnb) Mostly 3rd til fell 11* . . . . F
665^{4} Weallwayswillbeone (IRE) 6-1 N Oliver *(xnb) Planted & set off as rest jmpd 1; pu aft 2* . . . . P

OFFICIAL DISTANCES: $1\frac{1}{2}$*l*, $2\frac{1}{2}$*l* **TIME:** 6min 24.0s

926 Open Maiden 56&7yo, 12st — 11 ran

637[2] **EMERALD MIST (IRE)** (12a) 6-4F **Miss P Gundry** *(xnb) Settled handy; ld app 12-14 & aft 3 out; 2l clr nxt; hrd drvn last; hld on game; all out* 1
618[2] **Che Guevara** 3-1 **A Wintle** *Settled towards rr; trckd ldrs frm 11; went 2nd app 2 out; r.o to cl u.p flat; just hld* . . . . . . ½ 2
725[4] **The Luddite**(tt) 10-1 **Julian Pritchard** *(xnb) Prom; ld 10 til app 12 & 14 til aft 3 out; rdn & wknd rap* 30 3
589[P] North Pass(bl) 12-1 H Dowty *Ld; und constant press frm 6; hdd 10; cl up til app 15; drpd out rap* 15 4
Aiming High (5a) 9-1 G Barfoot-Saunt *Last when mist 5; school in rr; disp last when fell 8* . . . . . . F
725[P] Borrisimo (IRE) 12-1 M Wall *Swtng profuse; jmpd v slow 2; mist 9; prom to 10; lost tch rap aft nxt; t.o & pu 13* . . . . . . P
725[P] Leasebourne (12a) 12-1 T Ellis *Pulled hrd & prom; 4th aft 11; ev ch app 15; wknd qckly; pu 3 out* . . . . . . P
Nessarc (IRE) (7a) 10-1 N Oliver *(xnb) Midfield; went 2nd & fell 7* . . . . . . F
Scuttlebrook (IRE) (12a) 6-1 F Hutsby *Hld up; lost tch aft 11; 12l last app 15; pu 2 out; easy rn* . . . . . . P
666[U] Toffee Lady (5a) 5-1 R Rogers *Chsd ldr til mist & ur 7* . . . . . . U
588[P] Tom's Gold 14-1 J Trice-Rolph *Hit 2; last trio; lost tch aft 11; t.o when blun 13; pu nxt* . . . . . . P

OFFICIAL DISTANCES: ½l, 20l **TIME:** 6min 40.0s

927 Open Maiden 8yo&up, 12st — 12 ran

667[F] **SKI PASS** 7-4F **T Stephenson** *Tk keen hld; 2nd 4 til ld 9; hdd 15; ev ch when lft in ld nxt; drew 5l clr app 2 out; kpt on* 1
729[3] **Arctic Summer (IRE)** 5-2 **J Trice-Rolph** *7/2-5/2; pulling in ld to 3; sn stdd; 7th 10; outpcd aft; still 17l 4th app 2 out; fin wl but rdr gave him no ch.* . . . 6 2
700[7] **Sumerian Lad** 12-1 **J Sole** *Cl up; 2nd/3rd frm 9; 2l 3rd app 15; 5l 2nd & wkng when mist 2 out* 3 3
710[7] Carrigafoyle 10-1 Miss S Talbot *Prom in ab 4th; 2½l 4th & drvn app 15; fdd tame aft nxt* 5 4
Bolebec Ice Falcon 12-1 S Joynes *(xnb) Hld up in rr til gd prog 13; went 2nd nxt; ld 15; slt advant when fell 3 out* . . . . . . F
760[P] Himalayan Heights(tt) 10-1 F Hutsby *Swtng; prsd ldrs til 6½l 4th app 15; wknd qckly (as always); pu 3 out* . . . . . . P
385[P] Igloux Royal (FR) 10-1 A Martin *(xnb) Blun & nrly ur 2; blun 8; cl up til 4th & terrible mist 10 & nrly ur agn; lost plce & mist nxt; last app 15; pu 3 out* P
652[P] Latterly (USA) 16-1 I Bostock *(xnb) Last trio; last & strugg 10; t.o 14; pu 3 out* P
Margery Copse (5a) 14-1 M Wall *Midfield to 8; rr 10; blun 12; cont t.o; pu 15* P
730[P] Portway Sadie (5a) 12-1 H Dowty *Reluct & set off over fnce bhnd; a t.o; pu 9* P
731[P] Tensing 8-1 G Barfoot-Saunt *(xnb) Swtng; ld 3 til hdd, blun & ur 9* . . . . . . U
604[P] Turn It On (IRE) 5-1 M Harris *Sn prom; disp 2nd app 14; pu rap bhnd the rhubarb sheds aft 14; collected in horse ambulance* . . . . . . P

OFFICIAL DISTANCES: 5l, 3l **TIME:** 6min 39.0s

North Shropshire

Eyton-on-Severn (LH 12F,17J*)

Mon, 12 Apr (GOOD becoming GOOD to SOFT)

928 Hunt Members, 12st — 3 ran

713[1] **PRISTEEN SPY** 1-4F **R Burton** *(xnb) 2 handlers; jw; made all & sn 8l clr; canter* 1
753[2] **Well Said Sam** 4-1 **J Handley** *Disp 2nd 6-8; 10l last ½way; lost tch 11; lft 15l 2nd aft nxt; wknd 3 out* 30 2
665[P] Home Tor 4-1 J Jarrett *Chsd wnr; mist 8; 8l 2nd & rdn when swerved rt into hedge & ur aft mist 12; galloped off; rmtd sev mins later; event coaxed home w much tail swishing & declared official 3rd desp Judge having lft box; subsq disq* . . . U

OFFICIAL DISTANCES: Originally dist, dist **TIME:** 6min 27.6s **TOTE:** £1.50

**Fence 6 was omitted from all races - state of ground; Home Tor was originally placed officially third, but was disqualified by the Jockey Club Disciplinary Committee as the Judge had left his box when the horse crossed the line*

929 Open Maiden 56&7yo, 2m4f, 12st - 13J — 11 ran

Form	Horse	Dist	Pos
533^{2}	**MOUNTSORREL (IRE)** (7a) 5-2JF **B Shaw** *6s-5/2; hld up; hdwy 4; 2 1/2l 5th 1/2way; went 2nd 8; ld 9; in comm 3 out; 4l clr when pckd nxt; rdly*		1
	Reflected Glory (IRE) (7a) 7-2 **R Burton** *2 handlers; hld up; 5l 6th 1/2way; hit 9; stayed on frm 10; lft 3rd at last; snatched 2nd nr fin; btr for rce*	12	2
533^{P}	**Mervsintrouble**(cp) 16-1 **D Greenway** *Swtng; 2nd til ld 7; hdd 9; no ex 3 out; lft 12l 2nd when hmpd & rdr lost irons last; dem nr fin*	hd	3
	Silver Orchid (7a) 4-1 J O'Brien *(xnb) Ld to 7; wknd & 8l 4th 10; btr for rce*	15	4
619^{P}	Mandagus (IRE) 10-1 D Barlow *2 handlers; swtng; stdd start; hld up last to 5; 14l last 1/2way; wl bhnd 8*	1	5
	Beauchamp Brook 6-1 A Phillips *A.p; 1l 3rd 1/2way; chsd wnr 9; no imp 3 out; 8l 2nd & wkng when fell last*		F
	Chicago's Madam (5a) 8-1 A Hanly *(xnb) Jmpd v slow 1 & sn pushed along; lost plce 4; 13l 9th 1/2way; wl bhnd when pu 8*		P
714^{P}	Fromrussiawithlove (12a, 3ow) 10-1 M Keel *(xnb) Tde; hld up; mist 5; 8l 7th 1/2way; lost tch u.p aft 8; poor 8th when fell 10*		F
723^{F}	Nothing Better (IRE) (12a) 5-2JF T Weston *Nt jw; lost plce 4; 11l 8th 1/2way; wl bhnd 8 til hmpd & ur 10*		U
385^{P}	Superior Footwork 20-1 P Morris *Prom; 4th when ur 4*		U
666^{P}	Youwoudhavethat (IRE) (5a) 12-1 M Hammond *Swtng; prom; 2l 4th 1/2way; wknd & 10l 5th 10; blun 3 out & nxt; t.o & pu last*		P

OFFICIAL DISTANCES: 15*l*, hd **TIME:** 5min 18.0s **TOTE:** £5.00

The owner of Chicago's Madam, whose passport was found to be not in order, was fined £100

930 Land Rover Mens Open, 12st — 4 ran

Form	Horse	Dist	Pos
612^{1}	**JUST CLIQUOT** (5a) 1-3F **G Hanmer** *Swtng; ss; ww; last to 12; ld on bit 14; sn 5l clr; canter*		1
661^{4}	**Oneanthreequarters (IRE)** 5-1 **R Jagger** *Ld; jmpd slow 6 & 8; hdd aft 12; 5l 3rd & rdn 14; went 2nd app last; no ch w wnr*	5	2
660^{8}	**Chaparro Amargoso (IRE)** 12-1 **S Ross** *Hld up; 4l 3rd 1/2way; lft 3l 2nd brief 11; outpcd aft 12; one pce u.p 3 out; mist nxt*	6	3
711^{P}	Do It Again (IRE) (7x)(bl) 5-2 A Beedles *2nd til jmpd v slow 11; ld aft 12-14; gave up tame aft 2 out*	1/2	4

OFFICIAL DISTANCES: 6*l*, 8*l* **TIME:** 6min 44.3s **TOTE:** £1.50

931 Ladies Open — 6 ran

Form	Horse	Dist	Pos
751^{2}	**PACON (GER)** 4-1 **Miss H Kinsey** *(xnb) Ww; 7l last 1/2way; hdwy 11; hit 12; went 2nd nxt; ld 14; 4l clr 2 out; comf*		1
751^{3}	**Justin Mac (IRE)** 8-1 **Miss K Wood** *2nd til ld 7; hdd 13; one pce 3 out; lft 2nd last*	8	2
529^{1}	**Stretching (IRE)** 4-7F **Miss J Williams** *Prom; 2l 3rd 1/2way; went 2nd 12; ld 13-14; wknd u.p 2 out*	5	3
661^{U}	Dancetillyoudrop (IRE) 8-1 Miss T Tellwright *Nt a fluent; chsd ldrs; 5l 4th 1/2way; outpcd 12; wl bhnd 14*	25	4
664^{P}	Farfields Prince 16-1 Miss S Sharratt *Hld up; 6l 5th 1/2way; last 11; sn lost tch; t.o & pu 3 out*		P
664^{2}	Pennyahei (5a) 5-2 Miss T Clark *Swtng; ld to 7; 2nd to 12; rdn 14; 5l 3rd nxt; chsd wnr 2 out; no imp when fell last*		F

OFFICIAL DISTANCES: 12*l*, 6*l* **TIME:** 6min 19.3s **TOTE:** £4.00

932 Confined, 12st — 7 ran

Form	Horse	Dist	Pos
660^{3}	**DARE**(tt) 5-1 **D Barlow** *Hld up; last 5-10; 10l 6th nxt; hdwy aft 12; went 2nd 14; ld 3 out; drvn out*		1
749^{1}	**Indian Wings (IRE)** (3x) 8-11F **R Burton** *Hld up; hdwy 6; 2l 3rd 1/2way; went 2nd 11; ld 12-3 out; ev ch 2 out; nt qckn*	2	2
663^{6}	**Sharlom (IRE)** 6-1 **G Hanmer** *Hld up; 8l 6th 1/2way; last 10; hdwy 13; lft 8l 3rd aft 3 out; no imp*	7	3
713^{2}	Gunner Sid 9-2 A Wadlow *Ld to 12; 6l 4th when pu aft 3 out; lame*		P
662^{P}	Lifebuoy (IRE) 20-1 T Mastoras *Hld up; last to 4; hdwy 9; 2 1/2l 4th 1/2way; 2l 3rd 11; wknd qckly 14; pu 3 out*		P

708[2] Major Adams 7-2 Miss T Clark *2nd/3rd to 6; 4½l 5th ½way; eff 12; ev ch 14; 2l 3rd when fell nxt* . . . . F
749[U] Raconteur (IRE) 14-1 W Puddifer *Went 2nd aft 2 til wknd qckly 11; t.o & pu 3 out* . . . . P

OFFICIAL DISTANCES: 2½l, 7l **TIME:** 6min 26.5s **TOTE:** £3.50

933 Dodson & Horrell PPORA Club Members Restricted, 12st — 8 ran

627[1] **THYNE MAN (IRE)** 7-4 **G Hanmer** *Ww; 5l 7th ½way; gd hdwy 11; ld 14; sn qcknd clr; impressive* 1
587[4] **Templenoe Hare (IRE)** 10-1 **A Wadlow** *Hld up; 4l 6th ½way; hdwy aft 10; disp 2l 3rd nxt; 5l 4th 14; chsd wnr u.p 3 out; no imp* 25 2
752[5] **Hill Of Kilfeacle (IRE)**(tt) 25-1 **D Greenway** *W ldrs; 3l 5th ½way; ld aft 10-14; sn outpcd* 3 3
665[2] Cutina (5a) 4-5F R Burton *6/4-4/5; hld up; hdwy 6; went 2nd nxt; ld 10; sn hdd; 4l 3rd & rdn 14; sn btn* . . . . ¾ 4
748[5] Gabaka De Thaix (FR) 20-1 W Kinsey *2nd to 7; 2l 4th ½way; 4l 5th 11; wknd 13; t.o* 15 5
752[P] Edward Bear 25-1 Miss K Wood *(xnb) Spurs; prom; 1l 3rd ½way; wknd qckly aft 10; t.o 14; pu 2 out.* . . . . P
715[P] Holding The Fort (IRE) 4-1 D Barlow *2 handlers; swtng; ld to 10; lost plce & 7l 6th nxt; wl bhnd when pu 13* . . . . P
467[3] Inspector Blake 5-1 P Morris *Ss; nt fluent; last to 11; blun & lost tch 12; t.o & pu 3 out* . . . . P

OFFICIAL DISTANCES: 30l, 3l **TIME:** 6min 30.5s **TOTE:** £3.00

934 Open Maiden, 12st — 10 ran

463[P] **WHATAMONKEY**(cp) 4-1 **P Morris** *A.p; went 2nd 7-10; 4l 3rd nxt; sn outpcd; went 12l 2nd 13; stayed on frm 3 out; ld app last; sn clr.* 1
530[6] **Corky Browne** 7-1 **Miss J Perry** *Hld up; 8l 6th ½way; outpcd & 12l 6th 11; went 15l 3rd 3 out & 2nd flat; stayed on* 6 2
754[2] **Benbow** 2-1 **B Shaw** *Jw; a.p; 1l 3rd ½way; ld 10; qcknd clr app 12; 15l up 14; still 8l clr 2 out; stpd to nil, hung rt & hdd app last.* 5 3
848[3] Ridware George 7-1 Miss S Sharratt *2nd til ld 6; hdd 10; 6l 4th nxt; sn outpcd; 20l 3rd 14; wknd 3 out* 20 4
452[7] Golden Pride (5a) 16-1 T Haynes *A last & sn wl bhnd; t.o ½way* 1½fs 5
666[F] Blazing Pride 16-1 P Haynes *8th when mist & ur 4.* . . . . U
408[5] Brombil Lady (5a) 12-1 Miss R Reynolds *(xnb) Ld to 6; wknd & 18l 7th ½way; wl bhnd when carried out by loose horse 10* C
709[7] Castle Lodge 6-1 K Pearson *2 handlers; hld up; 5l 5th ½way; 7l 5th 11; rdn & wknd aft nxt; t.o & pu 3 out.* . . . . P
709[4] King's Reply evensF R Burton *3s-evens; hld up; hdwy & 4l 4th ½way; went 2nd aft 10; ld brief nxt; wknd qckly aft 13; wl bhnd when pu 2 out.* . . . . P
447[r] Lady Archenfield (5a)(bl) 20-1 S Graham *(bnf) Spurs; 8th when tried to stop & fell 1; rmtd; ref 2* . . . . F

OFFICIAL DISTANCES: 7l, 5l **TIME:** 6min 35.1s **TOTE:** £4.00

Old Berkshire

Lockinge (LH 9F,18J)
Mon, 12 Apr (GOOD)

935 Hunt Members, 12st — 5 ran

726[9] **SILLY BOY** 5-1 **A Foster** *Ld 2; made rest; 1½l up 5; mist 11; 7l up 14; 5l up & lkd in comm frm 3 out; hld on u.p flat; rdr's 1st wnr* 1
Pillager 7-4JF **Miss E Freeman** *Sa; last; 9l adrift 5 til hdwy to rem 3rd 13; chsd wnr frm 3 out; 5l down nxt; eff & clsd flat; nt rch wnr* 1¼ 2
Romanys Chance (5a) 7-1 **Miss E Pring** *2nd ride; ld 1; sn hdd; dived & jmpd rt 2; lft 2nd 4; 2l down 10; chsd ldr til wknd qckly frm 3 out; t.o frm nxt* 40 3
613[5] Esterelle (USA) (5a) 7-4JF G Tumelty *(xnb,orbnh) Swtng profuse; chsd ldr frm 2 til saddle slpd & pu 4.* . . . . P
729[4] Floorex Carpetman 7-1 Miss L Harfield *4½l 3rd 5; grad outpcd frm 9; wknd qckly frm 12; t.o & pu aft 14* . . . . P

OFFICIAL DISTANCES: 1l, 25l **TIME:** 6min 31.6s **TOTE:** £3.50 **DF:**£10.20

936 Intermediate, 12st — 4 ran

Form	Runner	Dist	Pos
759^{2}	**CAMDEN CARRIG (IRE)** evensF **N Phillips** *(bf) Swtng; mulish start & ld in by trainer; gt flyer; 3l up 5; jnd nxt-11; made rest; drew clr frm 16; easy*		1
799^{P}	**Pulham Downe** 2-1 **N Wilmington** *Chsd ldr; 3l down 5; disp ld nxt-10; trckd ldr & clsd brief 15; sn brushed aside*	40	2
817^{r}	Hubbly Bubbly 7-1 S Howe *Fcng wrong way start; last & sn lost tch; clambered over 4; t.o when ref nxt*		r
458^{2}	Owenabue Valley (IRE) (5x) 3-1 T Underwood *3rd & sn outpcd; 12l adrift 5; jmpd lft nxt; labouring frm 8; t.o & pu 14*		P

OFFICIAL DISTANCE: dist **TIME:** 6min 20.2s **TOTE:** £1.90 **DF:**£4.40

937 Countryside Alliance Club Members (Nov Rdrs), 12st — 4 ran

Form	Runner	Dist	Pos
758^{8}	**DINSEY FINNEGAN (IRE)**(vis) 4-6F **G Phillips** *(bf) Ld 2; hdd brief 5; hdd 10; disp ld 11; drew clr frm 2 out; pushed out flat*		1
642^{7}	**Golden Jack (FR)** 5-2 **C Morris** *Mist 1; last aft; hld up in tch til rem 4th 14; stayed on str frm 2 out; nt rch wnr*	4	2
616^{P}	**Top Of The Charts** 6-1 **G Tumelty** *Ld to 2; chsd ldr frm 8 til ld brief 10; jnd nxt; hdd 14; wknd qckly frm 2 out*	$2\frac{1}{2}$	3
631^{7}	One Of The Natives (IRE)(vis) 5-1 Miss J Jenner *(xnb) Sa; disp 2nd 4; ld brief 5; grad outpcd frm 13; t.o frm 2 out*	25	4

OFFICIAL DISTANCES: 3*l*, $2\frac{1}{2}$*l* **TIME:** 6min 21.5s **TOTE:** £1.30 **DF:**£2.00

938 Mixed Open, 12st — 8 ran

Form	Runner	Dist	Pos
642^{2}	**DANCING FOSENBY** 9-2 **M Holdforth** *(xnb) Chsd ldr til ld 4; hdd 6; trckd ldng pr til sust rn frm last; ld nr line; wl rdn*		1
734^{U}	**Sheila McKenzie** (5a) 7-2 **J Diment** *7th 5; gd prog to 3rd 6; chsd ldr frm 13; ld 2 out; hdd & no ex flat*	1	2
576^{5}	**Oscar Wilde** 5-1 **D Drake** *Last 1; impd qckly to chse ldr frm 4; ld 6; gd j 16; hdd nxt; stayed on til no ex flat*	2	3
625^{3}	Pride Of Kashmir 6-1 Miss A Stennett *6th 6; nd; chsd ldrs til no ex frm 2 out*	6	4
582^{1}	Be My Dream (IRE) (7x)(cp) 3-1F P Cowley *Ld; jmpd wildly rt 2 & 3; hdd 4; sn lost plce; rdn 10; bhnd frm 15*	15	5
869^{P}	Sunczech (IRE) (5a) 14-1 C Wadland *(xnb) 7th 6; a bhnd; t.o frm 15*	8	6
440^{5}	Kustom Kit Grizzly (IRE)(bl) 5-1 A Barlow *(xnb) A.p; trckd ldrs; $2\frac{1}{2}$l 4th 10; mist nxt; 5th & wkng when fell last*		F
	Scallybuck (IRE) 16-1 T Underwood *(kineton) Last 3; a bhnd; pu 13*		P

OFFICIAL DISTANCES: 1*l*, 2*l* **TIME:** 6min 13.9s **TOTE:** £4.40 **DF:**£59.00

939 Restricted, 12st — 3 ran

Form	Runner	Dist	Pos
384^{P}	**TEETON GLAIVE** (5a) 3-1 **Miss H Irving** *(xnb) Ld 1; chsd ldr til disp ld brief 10-nxt; 2l down 14; 4l down & lkd hld when lft solo 2 out*		1
498^{P}	Itchen Mill (5a) 11-10F T Dreaper *(bh) Hld up; 10l adrift 5; clsd on ldng pr 7; in tch when blun & ur 11*		U
723^{1}	Lord Ken (IRE)(vis) 7-4 N Phillips *(bf) Lw; mist 1; ld 2 & set crawl; 3l up 5; jnd 10-nxt; made rest; 4l up & lkd in comm when distracted by loose horse & ref & ur 2 out*		r

OFFICIAL DISTANCE: Finished alone **TIME:** 6min 36.2s **TOTE:** £3.00 **DF:**c/f

940 Open Maiden, 12st — 8 ran

Form	Runner	Dist	Pos
686^{P}	**BRER BEAR** (7a) 16-1 **J Diment** *Last 5; hdwy to 4th 7; $1\frac{1}{2}$l 3rd 10; disp ld nxt-13; ld agn 16; sn clr; easy*		1
721^{2}	**Nocash (IRE)** 6-4F **C Wadland** *Ch ride; hld up; hdwy to 3rd 7; disp ld 9; ld nxt; hdd 11; ld agn 13 til hdd 3 out; sn btn*	15	2
589^{5}	**Caraiyni (IRE)** 11-4 **J Jenkins** *(xnb) Mid-div 4; 3l 4th 10; trckd ldng pr frm 14; no imp frm 3 out*	6	3
637^{3}	Autumn Flame (IRE) (5a) 9-1 Miss S Duckett *2 handlers; chsd ldr til ld 3; $\frac{1}{2}$l 2nd 10; disp ld nxt-12; grad wknd; t.o frm 16*	25	4
	Crystal Vein 16-1 N McDiarmid *(xnb) 2 handlers; last 1; rap hdwy to disp ld 4; cl 2nd when blun & ur 5*		U
789^{R}	Sams Sister (5a) 9-2 P Cowley *Chsd ldrs til lost plce & last 7; grad outpcd frm 12; t.o & pu 16*		P

760^{P} Winleah 16-1 F de Giles *Ld 3 & agn nxt; lft clr 5; jnd nxt; hdd & sn lost plce; t.o & pu aft 14* . . . . P
Winnick (IRE) (3ow) 6-1 N Deacon *Chsd ldr 5; 2l down 3; disp ld 6; fell nxt* F

OFFICIAL DISTANCES: 20*l*, 8*l* **TIME:** 6min 20.8s **TOTE:** £6.60 **DF:**£178.00

South Notts

Thorpe Lodge (LH 7F,19J)
Mon, 12 Apr (GOOD)

941 Hunt Members, 12st

299^{P} **ANNEKA LOUISE** (5a) **N Kent** *(bf) Walked over* 1

942 Confined, 12st — 10 ran

223^{3} **BEDTIME BOYS** 4-1 **J Docker** *Ww; lft 3rd 9; chsd ldr 12; lft 4l clr 16; a in comm aft; pushed out flat* 1
681^{2} **Over The Master (IRE)** 8-1 **T Coles** *Prom; lft 2nd 9-12 & agn 16; 4l down nxt; one pce u.p aft.* 6 2
683^{P} **Preferred (IRE)** 40-1 **R Armson** *Ww; mid-div; lft 10l 3rd 16; sn rdn & no prog; wl btn when blun 2 out* 15 3
941^{1} Anneka Louise (5a) 7-1 N Kent *(bf) Nvr btr than mid-div; 15l 5th 12; no ch frm 14* fence 4
680^{1} Bengal Boy 3-1 N Pearce *(xnb) 5s-3s; 2 handlers; chsd ldr til blun & ur 9.* U
784^{U} Crackrattle (IRE) (2ow)(tt) 14-1 A Brown *Rn out & ur 2* . . . . R
686^{6} Faircatcher 40-1 R Collinson *In tch to 8; t.o & pu 13* . . . . P
685^{1} King's Hero (IRE) evensF S Morris *Ld; sn clr; 8l up & gng str when fell 16* . F
592^{7} The Nobleman (USA) (3x) 8-1 N Docker *A bhnd; rmdrs & no resp 6; t.o & pu 13* P
742^{P} Valman (IRE)(vis) 40-1 P Millington *(xnb) Nt jw; chsd ldrs; blun 7; sn drpd out; t.o 9 til pu 13* . . . . P

OFFICIAL DISTANCES: 6*l*, 10*l* **TIME:** 6min 31.0s

943 Mixed Open, 12st — 6 ran

381^{3} **GILLONE** 4-1 **J Docker** *Late & rdn in padd; swtng; lw; keen; trckd ldrs in 3rd; hdwy to ld 16; rdn nxt; $^{1}/_{2}$l up when jmpd rt & lft clr last* 1
Noel's Pride 5-2 **N Bell** *Lft in ld 1; hdd 16; 8l 3rd & btn nxt; lft 2nd at last* 15 2
592^{1} **Ramirez (IRE)** 6-4F **N Kent** *Nt fluent & nvr lkd happy; rmdr 4; eff & 5l 4th 12; rdn & btn 16; lft 3rd at last* 8 3
381^{5} Drum Battle(cp) 8-1 T Messenger *(xnb) A last pr; 8l last & rdn 12; sn lost tch; t.o & pu 15* . . . . P
592^{3} Red Rebel 7-4 R Cope *Ld til crashing fall 1* . . . . F
682^{4} Silver Buzzard (USA) (7a)(cp) 16-1 Miss Gemma Hutchinson *Chsd ldr 1; disp ld 11-16; still ev ch when fell last; winded* . . . . F

OFFICIAL DISTANCES: 25*l*, 5*l* **TIME:** 6min 31.0s

Fence 8 omitted - fallen rider

944 Restricted, 12st — 6 ran

787^{P} **DANTE'S BANKER (IRE)** 6-1 **R Armson** *Ww in rr; lft 4th 14; went 2nd app 2 out; ev ch last; no ex last 50yds; lkd btn by $^{1}/_{2}$l.* 1
787^{P} **Moscow Tradition (IRE)** 4-1 **J Docker** *Mid-div; jmpd rt 13; lft 3rd nxt; ld 16; jnd last; forged ahd u.p last 100yds; lkd to win by $^{1}/_{2}$l* . . . . * 2
503^{P} **Gale Damage (IRE)** 5-1 **O Williams** *2 handlers; mist 2; mid-div; lft 2nd 14; rdn & wknd nxt; lkd to fin 35$^{1}/_{2}$l 4th* . . . . * 3
481^{P} Ravensworth 4-1 R Collinson *(xnb) Tubed; prsd ldr til ld 6; lft in ld 14; hdd 13; 3rd & btn 2 out; lkd to fin 10$^{1}/_{2}$l 3rd (nt originally plcd by Judge, but aft appeal by rdr was plcd 4th!)* . . . . * 4
885^{4} Buckland Bobby 16-1 P Millington *Ld to 6; chsd ldrs to 13; last & lsng tch when blun & ur 14* . . . . U
500^{1} Near And Phar (IRE) (5a) 4-5F Miss S Buckley *(xnb) Pulling; chsd ldrs 4; went 2nd 9; ld & rn out 14; cont missing fncs til jmpd last (at first awarded rce by Judge, but later he changed his mind)* . . . . R

OFFICIAL DISTANCES: 2*l*, nk, 4*l* **TIME:** 6min 37.0s

** Distances are given in comments; the stewards interviewed the rider of Near And Phar who jumped the last and finished the race despite having run out at the 14th; her explanation that the horse was hanging badly was not accepted and she was fined £75*

945 Open Maiden 56&7yo, 12st — 7 ran

Form	Horse / details	Dist	Pos
385R	**RUSSIAN FRIEND**(bl) 3-1 **R Collinson** *Jmpd bold; rcd wide; ld 3; sn clr; 20l up 8; unchall*		1
596²	**Briery Fox (IRE)** 4-5F **J Docker** *Disp ld to 3; chsd clr ldr aft; rdn & clsd frm 3 out; nvr able to chall*	8	2
	Spinosa (5a) 9-1 **N Kent** *Mid-div; 25l 5th 12; poor 3rd frm 15; nd*	40	3
	For A Pagan Song 9-2 S Morris *Prom in chsng group; 25l 6th & mist 11; no hdwy aft; t.o & pu last*		P
597⁴	Lancastrian Island (5a) 12-1 R Armson *Tk keen hld; disp ld to 3; prom in chsng group aft til rdn 13; last & no ch when tried to ref & ur 2 out*		U
	Stylino (USA) 6-1 N Docker *2 handlers; pulling; prom in chsng group; 24l 3rd 12-15; t.o & pu 3 out*		P
685²	Willow Ryde (IRE) 9-2 N Pearce *Prom to 3; last & rdn 9; t.o & pu 14*		P

OFFICIAL DISTANCES: 8*l*, dist **TIME:** 6min 39.0s

946 Open Maiden, 12st — 10 ran

Form	Horse / details	Dist	Pos
680³	**RUNNINGWITHTHEMOON** 2-1 **M Briggs** *Chsd ldng pr; clsd 11; went 2nd 13; chall 3 out; ld flat; r.o wl*		1
304³	**Orchestra's Boy (IRE)** evensF **K Green** *2 handlers; keen; chsd ldr til ld 13; ½l ld 3 out til hdd & no ex flat*	2	2
651P	**Society Scandal (IRE)**(tt) 20-1 **P Millington** *Nt fluent; bhnd; hdwy 12; went 12l 3rd 15; no hdwy frm nxt*	20	3
409P	Charlotte Russe (5a) 25-1 N Pearce *A bhnd; mist 3; blun 10; t.o & pu 13*		P
788P	College Superman 25-1 L Hicks *(bf) Mid-div; mist 9; rmdrs & hdwy 12; blun nxt; sn no ch; pu 16*		P
680P	It's Norman 8-1 S Morris *(ringbit) Coughing in padd; ww; prog & cl 6th 13; sn outpcd; 4th & no ch when pu 3 out*		P
594r	Mister Rose (IRE)(bl) 7-1 O Williams *(xnb) Ld; jmpd slow 1; clr 3 til rdn & hdd 13; sn no ch; t.o & pu 16*		P
788P	Pudding And Pie (5a) 10-1 R Armson *Mid-div; 13l 4th 7; clsd 12; wknd 14; 5th & no ch when pu 16*		P
685P	Shalabibubbly 8-1 N Kent *5th when fell 5*		F
304P	The Doc 20-1 R Collinson *Hld up in rr til bd 5*		B

OFFICIAL DISTANCES: 2*l*, 8*l* **TIME:** 6min 38.0s

South Pembrokeshire

Lydstep (LH 8F,19J)

Mon, 12 Apr (GOOD to FIRM)

947 Hunt Members, 12st — 7 ran

Form	Horse / details	Dist	Pos
676²	**BEASLEY** (7a) 7-4F **M Barber** *Hld up in 4th; went 1l 2nd 13; ld nxt; lft 5l ahd app 16; clr when mist 2 out; comf*		1
208P	**Ribble Assembly** 16-1 **J Cook** *Last pr; 4l adrift & jmpd slow 6; 3rd 15; stayed on past tiring horse to 2nd 2 out; nd to wnr*	15	2
674P	**All For Jake (IRE)** 5-1 **D Jones** *Prom; ld 4-6 & agn 10; lft 5l 2nd app 16; tired 3 out; mist nxt; dem flat*	¾	3
	Bold Knight 12-1 H Evans *(xnb) Last early; ld aft 6; hdd 9; sn rr; ur 12*		U
	Camden Bus (IRE) 7-2 L Stephens *(xnb,bf) 3rd when mist 3; prog 11; ld 12; hdd nxt; 1l 2nd 15; ev ch when slpd up bend bef 16; dead*		S
208²	Never In Debt(cp) 5-2 Miss J Hughes *(bf) Ld 3; cl 3rd til jmpd to ld 10; hdd brief 11; ld agn 13; hdd; wknd qckly; rem 4th when ref last*		r
670P	Umbopa (USA)(bl) 20-1 M Lewis *Midfield; rr frm 8 til pu 3 out*		P

OFFICIAL DISTANCES: 15*l*, ½*l* **TIME:** 6min 15.0s

948 Open Maiden, 12st — 15 ran

Form	Horse / details	Dist	Pos
699P	**IAN'S BOY** 20-1 **H Evans** *Rr; 10th 9; poor 6th 14; r.o str frm 16; jmpd to ld 2 out; in comm when mist last*		1
736³	**Wiston Wizo**(bl) 14-1 **P Sheldrake** *(xnb) Rr early; settled 5th 8; 10l 4th 14; rdn 16; r.o to 2nd flat; nt trble wnr*	4	2
	Clarice Starling (5a) 8-1 **W Oakes** *(xnb,bf) Last early; cont rr; r.o wl frm 3 out to 3rd at last*	6	3

Billy Coleman (IRE) 11-4F James Tudor *Midfield; went 5th 9 & 5l 3rd 12; ld 16; hdd nxt; no ex* . . . 1 4
Market Value (IRE) 8-1 J Price *Rr; 10th 9; hdwy frm 11 & 5th 14; wknd frm 16; sn btn* . . . 12 5
370P General Ben(bl) 16-1 J Cook *Ld 2; sn midfield; grad wknd; rr 9; pu 14* . . . P
675² Gilly Weet (5a) 6-1 M Lewis *Ld 3-5; 4l 2nd to 9; fdd; pu 13* . . . P
677P Ladygal (IRE) (12a) 25-1 D Davies *8th when mist 9 & drpd to rr; pu 11* . . . P
Millenium Run (IRE) 5-1 E Williams *Settled 5th; mist 4; wknd & pu 9* . . . P
675P Mister Julius 12-1 M Barber *A rr; pu 11* . . . P
673U Never Sayaarr (IRE) (5a) 12-1 T Faulkner *Midfield; 7th 10; fdd 14; rr aft; pu 16* P
204U Royal Tradition (IRE) 25-1 James Price *5th when fell 2* . . . F
Tenacious Melody 25-1 Miss I Tompsett *Prom; ld 5-14; mist 12; outpcd frm 15; pu nxt* . . . P
Too Phar To Touch (5a) 12-1 T Vaughan *4th to 8; grad wknd & rr 14; pu 2 out* P
669³ War Bride (5a) 7-1 D Jones *(orbs) Settled 6th; prog 7 & 6l 3rd 8; went 2nd 12; fdd & pu 2 out; broke down* . . . P

OFFICIAL DISTANCES: 3*l*, 8*l* **TIME:** 6min 22.0s

The stewards enquired into the improved form of the winner; they accepted the explanation that the horse had recently changed stables

949 Ladies Open — 5 ran

737¹ **DE CHELLY** (5a) 4-6F **Mrs C Owen** *Ld 1; mostly 3rd to 11; ld brief 16; battled on game; chall last; ld cl home* . . . 1
843² **Ashfield Orchestra (IRE)** (5a) 7-2 **Miss I Tompsett** *Hld up in rr; went 2nd 11; jmpd to ld 3 out; mist nxt; jnd last; hdd flat; just hld* . . . ½ 2
673² **Berkeley Frontier (IRE)** 14-1 **Miss E Jones** *Trckd ldr to 4; cl 4th to 12; went poor 3rd 2 out; nt trble ldrs* . . . 15 3
673F Hunter Gold (FR) 5-2 Mrs B Lewis *(xnb) Ld 3-15; 3rd & no ex frm 16; dem 2 out* . . . 10 4
669R Coolarne Leader (IRE) 8-1 Miss R Davies *1l 2nd 6; mist 8; rr aft; detach 10; rn wide bend aft 11; fnce bhnd when mist 12; pu aft nxt* . . . P

OFFICIAL DISTANCES: ½*l*, 15*l* **TIME:** 6min 04.0s

950 Open Maiden 56&7yo, 2m4f, 12st - 16J — 9 ran

362P **PAMS OAK** 5-2 **Miss F Wilson** *2 handlers; prom; trckd ldrs in 3rd; ld 13; forged clr frm 2 out* . . . 1
617² **Dans Blarney (IRE)** 2-1F **D Jones** *Ld 1-7 & agn 9-12; hdd 13; outpcd clsng stages; eased flat* . . . 30 2
142P **The Lords Cross (IRE)** 5-1 **H Evans** *Tde; last to 8; rem 5th 11; some hdwy & 3rd 2 out; no ch w ldrs* . . . 2 3
675R Bold Flirtation 10-1 J Price *(xnb) Mid-div; 6th mostly; detach frm 11; lft 4th by defections 13; pu 2 out* . . . P
735P Calamint (7a) 10-1 James Price *Nt jw in 4th; fell 12* . . . F
677F Countess Kiri (5a) 6-1 M Barber *Last trio; detach frm 8; last when pu 2 out* P
Orient Express (IRE) 3-1 James Tudor *Trckd ldrs til ld 8; sn 2l 2nd; went cl 3rd & fell hvly 13; dead* . . . F
677R Sky Sorcerer (7a) 5-1 T Faulkner *(xnb) Last pr til pu 12* . . . P
Supreme Robber (IRE) 3-1 T Vaughan *(xnb) Tubed; chsd ldrs; 14l 5th when rn wide bend aft 8; lost posn & pu 11* . . . P

OFFICIAL DISTANCES: 25*l*, 2½*l* **TIME:** 5min 07.0s

951 Mens Open, 12st — 3 ran

670¹ **RED NECK**(tt) 1-2F **T Vaughan** *(xnb) Hld up in last; drvn 14; 2l 2nd nxt; ld 16; r.o; easy* . . . 1
669P **Calhoun (FR)** 6-1 **J Price** *Pulled to ld 3; mist 9; hdd 14; 1l 2nd nxt; tired 16; sn btn* . . . runin 2
365P **Itsallupintheair** 11-4 **D Jones** *(xnb) Lw; ld 1-3; cl 2nd til ld 15; sn hdd & outpcd* . . . 10 3

OFFICIAL DISTANCES: 30*l*, 8*l* **TIME:** 6min 07.0s

952 Intermediate, 12st — 5 ran

671² **HOME AGAIN (IRE)** 2-1 **M Lewis** *Made all; 2l up frm 14; mist last; kpt on game* 1
674¹ **Rostock (IRE)** evensF **Miss F Wilson** *(xnb) 2 handlers; mostly 2nd/3rd; jmpd to 2nd 14; ev ch; mist 16; nvr able to rch wnr* . . . 3 2

660[F] **Arctic King** 9-2 **D Jones** *(bnh) Swtng; 2nd/3rd; mist 9; 4l 3rd nxt; jmpd slow 14 & lost plce; wknd & sn btn* . . . 10 3

671[3] Mecca Prince (IRE) 6-1 James Tudor *Rr; lost tch frm 5; rdn 8; no resp; t.o frm 15* . . . 8 4

677[P] Final Mick(tt) 14-1 J Price *(xnb) Mists in last; detach frm 10; rn off course bend bef 12* . . . R

OFFICIAL DISTANCES: 3*l*, 8*l* **TIME:** 6min 10.0s

953 Restricted, 12st — 7 ran

674[2] **PETE THE PAINTER (IRE)**(bl) 9-4F **James Tudor** *Settled 2nd; ld 10; made rest; drew wl clr frm 15; easy* . . . 1

677[1] **Batchworth Lock** 3-1 **T Vaughan** *(xnb) Chsd ldrs; 20l 4th 8; rmdrs 10; lft dist 3rd 14 & v rem 2nd at last; nvr any ch* . . . runin 2

740[P] **Daisy's Choice** (5a) 6-1 **P Sheldrake** *Bhnd; 25l 5th 8; went 10l 3rd 10; wknd & sn t.o; slt hdwy 15; 25l 2nd 3 out; fell last; rmtd; walked in* . . . 2fncs 3

451[U] Black Dan 16-1 D Underwood *A last pr; last 1-6; 25l 6th when pu 10* . . . P

699[1] Jeune Premier (FR) 5-2 G Perkins *(kineton) Pulled to ld 3; 15l clr 6; only 1/2l up 9; hdd nxt; 6l 2nd when crashing fall 14* . . . F

669[4] Onward Bound 6-1 M Lewis *Chsd ldrs in 4th; 16l 3rd 8; sn fdd; jmpd v slow 13; pu 16* . . . P

614[P] The Last Shout (IRE)(bl) 12-1 D Jones *Trckd ldrs; 3rd & rmdrs 3; drpd to last 8; t.o & pu 10* . . . P

OFFICIAL DISTANCES: 30*l*, dist **TIME:** 6min 14.0s

Gay Abandon was an intended runner in this race, but once again no rider could be found to partner it

Staintondale Goathland

Charm Park (LH 9F,19J)

Mon, 12 Apr (GOOD)

954 Hunt Members, 12st — 7 ran

390[P] **MINSTER ECHO** (5a) 7-4F **G Brewer** *Made all; 8l clr aft 9; 2l up 15; jnd 3 out; stayed on & clr by last* . . . 1

500[P] **Final Chorus** (5a) 7-1 **R Wakeham** *Mid-div to 13; chsd ldr in 4l 2nd 15; chall 3 out; ev ch nxt; wknd app last* . . . 5 2

302[R] **Twinkle Toe Titch (IRE)** (12a) 4-1 **A Pennock** *Last by 3; jmpd slow 5 & 6; bhnd 12; hdwy 14 to 2l 3rd 16; wknd 3 out* . . . 12 3

Oswald 4-1 M Morley *Chsd ldr in 2nd to 13; sn pushed along & wknd* . . . 4 4

Emperor's Castle (7a) 4-1 Miss A Armitage *Mid-div when ur 2* . . . U

Palmand (5a) 10-1 N Tinkler *Mid-div when mist 10; 10l 3rd 12; wknd 14; poor 5th when pu 2 out* . . . P

Sizzling River 20-1 W Burnell *Rr by 8; bhnd when fell 11* . . . F

OFFICIAL DISTANCES: 2*l*, 8*l*, 2*l* **TIME:** 6min 51.0s

955 Restricted — 12 ran

443[P] **CROSS RIVER** 6-4F **N Saville** *Mid-div to 5; ld frm 6; 4l clr 15; r.o str flat; eased nr line; impressive* . . . 1

771[P] **Sevensider (IRE)** 7-4 **R Wakeham** *Mid-div to 8; went 15l 7th 9; hdwy to 3rd 15 & cl 2nd 2 out; easily outpcd by wnr app last* . . . 4 2

772[P] **Mandate Man (IRE)**(cp) 14-1 **D Thomas** *Ld to 7; handy 3rd til outpcd 15; 4th 2 out; stayed on wl to tk 3rd flat* . . . 10 3

771[F] Don Rio (IRE) 10-1 M Morley *A.p; 3rd & bad mist 8; went 4l 2nd 15-3 out; wknd nxt; just kpt 4th* . . . 4 4

563[5] Abinger 14-1 W Burnell *Mist 1; mid-div to 10; rr by 12; hdwy frm 15; stayed on str; nrst fin* . . . 1/2 5

684[2] Snizort (USA) 7-2 G Brewer *Last by 6; rr to 14; hdwy to 5th 2 out; nvr in w a ch* 1 6

591[P] Procol's Boy 20-1 S Walker *Rr to 10; hdwy 11 to 6th 13; wknd aft* . . . 4 7

563[P] In The Van(cp) 33-1 J Morley *Prom in 4th to 13; wknd frm 15* . . . 15 8

591[P] Big Horn (IRE)(tt) 33-1 N Tinkler *Rr & lsng tch when pu app 13; broke leg; dead* . . . P

394[1] Borleagh Pilot (IRE) 14-1 P Collins *A rr; mist 11; lsng tch frm 14; t.o & pu 2 out* . . . P

Form	Runner	Dist	Pos
766^{3}	Hessac (FR) 10-1 Miss W Gibson *Prom early; in tch to 12; outpcd & wknd 14; t.o & pu 2 out*		P
481^{P}	Super Dolphin (7a) 14-1 Richard Tate *A rr; mist 2; last by 4; t.o & pu 16*		P

OFFICIAL DISTANCES: 2*l*, 10*l*, s hd **TIME:** 6min 37.0s

956 Mixed Open, 12st — 6 ran

Form	Runner	Dist	Pos
772^{4}	**MR PENDLEBERRY**(cp) 2-1 **N Tinkler** *Ld frm 3; 1l ahd 3 out; 2l up at last; hrd rdn flat; lkd to be hdd on line*		1
499^{3}	**Nordic Crest (IRE)**(tt) 7-4F **M Walford** *Last & in tch 12; jmpd slow 13; 6l 4th 15; went 2nd app last; fin v fast; lkd to ld on line*	hd	2
679^{F}	**Primitive Satin** 4-1 **L Bates** *Trckd ldrs in 1l 2nd to 2 out; wknd app last*	3	3
772^{3}	Clonshire Paddy (IRE)(bl) 3-1 Miss J Coward *Cl 4th to 9; last & lsng tch 10; t.o 15; stayed on; nrst fin*	25	4
769^{P}	Multi Franchise 10-1 G Brewer *Cl 5th to 9; went 4l 3rd 15; pushed along & wknd 16; dem 5th nr fin*	2	5
	Wynyard Dancer (5a)(cp) 10-1 Miss T Jackson *Ld til blun & ur 2*		U

OFFICIAL DISTANCES: hd, 2*l*, 15*l* **TIME:** 6min 34.0s

957 Confined, 12st — 6 ran

Form	Runner	Dist	Pos
477^{2}	**WINTER GALE (IRE)** 2-1 **Miss L Eddery** *Made all; stayed on str when chall flat*		1
501^{F}	**Nip On** 3-1 **G Brewer** *Cl 3rd to 11; went 1l 2nd 13 & gng easy app 2 out; chall last; just outpcd flat*	$^{1}/_{2}$	2
562^{1}	**Maitre De Musique (FR)** 6-4F **M Tate** *Cl 2nd to 16; 1l 2nd 3 out; outpcd & wknd app last*	2	3
874^{1}	Yorkshire Edition (IRE) 4-1 Miss W Gibson *Hld up & last to 13; hdwy to 4l 4th 15; outpcd & wknd 3 out*	4	4
771^{5}	Blue Bud 16-1 W Burnell *In tch til outpcd & wknd 13; t.o by 16*	35	5
	Perchancer (IRE) 5-1 Miss A Armitage *Pulled hrd; saddle slpd & pu 2*		P

OFFICIAL DISTANCES: nk, 2*l*, 2*l* **TIME:** 6min 46.0s

958 Open Maiden (Div 1) — 10 ran

Form	Runner	Dist	Pos
773^{3}	**CIVIL GENT (IRE)** (7a) 3-1 **G Brewer** *A.p; 5l 3rd 11; went cl 2nd 14; ld 16; stayed on str flat*		1
482^{U}	**Landford Lad (IRE)** 8-1 **G Armitage** *Ld to 12; outpcd 14 & 5l 4th 16; stayed on frm 2 out; 4l 3rd at last; fin fast; just failed*	$1^{1}/_{2}$	2
775^{P}	**Ravenscar** 5-2F **S Walker** *Prom to 9; went 1l 2nd 10; ld 13-16; ev ch 2 out; wknd app last*	1	3
	Silogue (IRE) 8-1 N Tutty *Pulled hrd; prom; 3l 3rd 3 out; wknd nxt*	8	4
776^{P}	Thixendale (5a)(cp) 5-1 Miss J Foster *Prom 1st circ; handy 5th 13; outpcd & wknd 15; poor 5th 2 out*	40	5
774^{P}	Billymax (IRE) 16-1 R Wakeham *Last & mist 5; rr & rmdrs 13; lsng tch aft nxt; t.o & pu 3 out*		P
	Exmoor Express (7a) 16-1 A Pennock *V green; jmpd slow 2 & 3; last by 11; t.o when pu 13*		P
775^{P}	Just A Man 6-1 B Woodhouse *Prom in mid-div to 11; wknd frm 14; t.o & pu 3 out*		P
	Market Poseur (IRE) 14-1 N Tinkler *Mid-div til lost tch 14; t.o & pu 3 out*		P
773^{P}	Primitive Choice (5a) 14-1 L Bates *Rr & mist 2; lost tch 9; bhnd when fell 12*		F

OFFICIAL DISTANCES: $^{3}/_{4}$*l*, 1*l*, 6*l* **TIME:** 6min 47.0s

959 Open Maiden (Div 2) — 9 ran

Form	Runner	Dist	Pos
773^{2}	**SEARCH PARTY (FR)** (7a) 7-2 **S Walker** *Rr til pushed along 15; went 4l 4th 2 out; chall last; stayed on wl to ld flat*		1
392^{5}	**Irish Paddy (IRE)** (7a) 10-1 **R Clark** *Mid-div to 10; went 1l 2nd 13; ld 14 til jnd last; outpcd flat*	3	2
504^{P}	**Songino (IRE)** 16-1 **P Robinson** *A handy; went 1l 2nd 14; ev ch 2 out; wknd app last*	4	3
776^{4}	Bankersdraft 12-1 M Morley *Cl 2nd to 11; ld 12-14; 1l 2nd 2 out; wknd app last*	6	4
392^{6}	Parsifal (7a) 8-1 R Abrahams *Pulled hrd; a rr; detach & jmpd slow 7; stayed on one pce; nrst fin*	3	5
775^{P}	Edstone (IRE) 10-1 Miss Rachel Clark *Prom early; rr & lsng tch 14; t.o & pu 3 out*		P
	Light-O-Day 16-1 P Kinsella *Ld & sn clr; hdd aft 10; wknd qckly aft 12; pu nxt*		P

	Perfect Picture (7a) 16-1 O Dukes *Blun & ur 1*		U
476²	Thanks Jim (IRE) (7a) 4-7F M Walford *Hld up in mid-div; went 3rd 15; 6l 5th & u.p when fell 3 out; broke nk; dead*		F

OFFICIAL DISTANCES: 1*l*, 2*l*, 4*l* **TIME:** 6min 45.0s

960 Open Maiden Conditions, 12st — 14 ran

776P	**NOUGHT TO NINETY** 33-1 **L Bates** *Rr 1st circ; rr of ldrs 15; still 15l 6th 2 out; went 6l 4th app last; flew up run-in; ld nr line*		1
776U	**French Venture** 2-1 **B Woodhouse** *Nt jw; last to 12; hdwy to 5th 16; ld on bridle aft 2 out; 3l up at last; wknd & hdd nr line*	1	2
679U	**The Sea Club (IRE)** 12-1 **Miss L Robson** *Mid-div to 13; went 7th app 2 out; fin v fast; nrst fin*	3	3
773P	Moraira (IRE) (7a) 10-1 N Tinkler *Rr early; hdwy 9 to 4th 10; cl 3rd 16; outpcd 3 out; stayed on agn frm 2 out; fin wl*	1	4
774⁵	Biddy (12a) 10-1 N Smith *Last & lsng tch 7; jmpd slow 12; struggled on*	8	5
773⁴	Just A Lady (5a) 5-1 Miss J Foster *Ld to 5; cl 2nd 6-9; in tch til wknd 15*	4	6
	Gipsy Wood (5a) 33-1 G Brewer *A midfield to rr; t.o & pu 2 out*		P
814r	Highland Wonder 33-1 T Craggs *Cl up; ld 6 til wknd 15; t.o & pu last*		P
	Honeyfantastic (12a) 16-1 P Kinsella *Prom; 2nd 1st circ; handy 3rd 14; grad wknd; lsng tch when pu 2 out*		P
	Lilly Beach (5a) 8-1 N Tutty *Mid-div 1st circ; cl 3rd but wkng when fell 2 out*		F
	Pampered Lad (7a) 33-1 A Pennock *Rr & lsng tch 9; last & adrift when ur 11*		U
774P	Raggy Jumper 33-1 Miss T Jackson *Mid-div to 8; went 6th 14; hld in 6th when bd 2 out*		B
773U	Supreme Vintage (IRE) 12-1 R Wakeham *Rr 1st circ; hdwy 13 to 4l 4th & lkd dangerous 15; wknd 3 out; t.o & pu last*		P
503S	Switchback (IRE) evensF N Saville *Handy; 1l 2nd 13; ld 16-2 out; broke down & imm pu*		P

OFFICIAL DISTANCES: ½*l*, ½*l*, ½*l* **TIME:** 6min 49.0s

Taunton Vale

Kingston St Mary (RH 8F,19J)
Mon, 12 Apr (GOOD to FIRM)

961 Hunt Members — 3 ran

747U	**BURLEY DON CARLOS** 1-4F **Miss C Stucley** *Hld up; hdwy to disp ld 12; ld nxt; went 6l clr 16; easily*		1
	Blin (CZE) 9-2 **D Alers-Hankey** *Chsd ldr to 11; cl 3rd nxt til went 2nd 15; no imp*	8	2
	Jenko (FR) 5-1 **Miss R Green** *(xnb) Ld; slt mist 10; hdd 13; wknd 15; poor 3rd frm 3 out*	20	3

OFFICIAL DISTANCES: 7*l*, 11*l* **TIME:** 6min 23.0s **TOTE:** £1.30

962 Open Maiden 56&7yo, 12st — 13 ran

326P	**THINK COMMERCIAL (IRE)** (7a) 3-1 **A Farrant** *(xnb) Hld up; prog 13; ld 16; r.o*		1
688²	**Orinoco's Flight (IRE)** 5-1 **M Holmes** *(xnb) Sn prom; disp 2nd 9; 5l 2nd when mist 12; lft in ld 14; mist nxt; prom til cl 3rd 2 out; went 2nd aft last.*	2	2
688⁴	**Foston Second (IRE)** (5a) 16-1 **M Sweetland** *Swtng; midfield; 9l 6th 14; gd hdwy aft 16; chall & mist 2 out; ev ch when blun last*	½	3
618⁵	Lucky Wyn 11-1 M Walters *(bf) Bit bckwd; midfield; 4th 11; 5th when mist 15; 11l 4th 3 out; no prog.*	25	4
693P	April's Past (5a) 16-1 M Atkinson *(xnb) Reared up & ur bef start; went 2nd 8; 5l 3rd 14; wknd; pu 16.*		P
	Charliebob (12a) 16-1 J Barnes *(xnb) Bhnd til pu 9*		P
	Double Bubble (IRE) 16-1 J March *Swtng; last when fell 1*		F
	Judy's Lad (7a) 16-1 N Mitchell *(xnb) Nt jw 1 & 2; rn out 3*		R
633P	Ring Off 20-1 J O'Rourke *Prom when bad mist 5; 15l 2nd 7; sn wknd; bhnd; pu 9*		P
494⁴	Roseacre (IRE)(bl) 3-1 D Alers-Hankey *(xnb) Tch 9/2; nvr gng wl in midfield; bhnd frm 8; mists 9 & 10; pu nxt*		P
195P	Sup Of Tea (IRE) 16-1 J Young *Lw; 2 handlers; prom early; sn towards rr; 30l last 16; t.o 5th when pu nxt.*		P

721^{5} Tarpon Tale (IRE)(cp) 16-1 Miss D Clark *(xnb) Ld/disp til went 8l clr 5; 2l up when blun & ur 14* . . . . U

275^{P} Which Moscow (IRE) 5-2F D Edwards *6s-5/2; midfield; 7th ½way; 12l 7th when rdn 13; bhnd & pu 15.* . . . . P

OFFICIAL DISTANCES: ½*l*, nk **TIME:** 6min 26.0s **TOTE:** £3.00

963 Confined, 12st — 8 ran

634^{2} **LORD OF THE MIST (IRE)** 4-5F **N Williams** *(xnb) 6/4-4/5; lw; hld up in tch; prog 13; went 2nd 14; jmpd to ld 16; stdd & jnd brief 3 out; sn qcknd clr; impressive* 1

473^{1} **Ellofamonkey** (5a) 4-1 **R Woollacott** *Opened 5s; lw; hld up; prog to cl 5th 14; gd hdwy nxt; cl 3rd & ev ch aft 16; went 3l 2nd 2 out; nt pce of wnr.* . . . 12 2

573^{P} **Cimmaroon (IRE)** (7a) 7-2 **A Farrant** *(xnb) Lw; hld up in tch; cl 4th 11; ld 13; blun bad 15; disp ld 3 out; sn wknd u.p* 6 3

603^{1} Leon Garcia (IRE) (5a, 3x) 11-2 T Bishop *Keen; hld up in rr; last to 13; went 5th but lot to do aft 16; nrst fin* . . . . s hd 4

691^{2} Shock's Pride (IRE) 8-1 M Miller *Sn prom; ld/disp to 9; slt mist 10; wl in tch til wknd 14; one pce frm 3 out.* 1 5

634^{4} Gotha (FR) (3x) 14-1 M Sweetland *Tchd 16s; handy; cl 5th ½way; hdwy aft 16; one pce frm nxt* 4 6

Primero (IRE)(tt) 16-1 G Weatherley *(xnb) Jw; sn prom; slt ld 10-12; wknd 15; bhnd frm 3 out.* 8 7

Link Copper 16-1 Mrs O Jackson *Ld/disp to 9; rdn 11; wknd & 7th 13; bhnd frm 16* 1 8

OFFICIAL DISTANCES: 8*l*, ½*l* **TIME:** 6min 18.0s **TOTE:** £2.30

964 Mens Open, 12st — 5 ran

691^{1} **BALLYSICYOS (FR)** (7x) 2-5F **A Farrant** *Made all; went clr 3 out; jmpd sltly lft clsng stages; comf* 1

Hylters Chance (IRE) (4x) 3-1 **R Stephens** *Disp 2nd; 1½l 2nd & ev ch 16; rdn nxt; no imp; btr for rce* 8 2

352^{1} **Ashbury Star (NZ)** 11-2 **R Woollacott** *(xnb) Lw; disp 2nd; cl up 14; 3l 3rd 16; rdn & no resp frm 3 out.* 7 3

471^{4} Cool Wager 6-1 D Alers-Hankey *4th but in tch; slt mist 10; wknd & rdn 14; btn 4th when pu 16* . . . . P

792^{r} Dom Shadeed(bl) 16-1 M Sweetland *Ld in; ref to rce; tk no part.* . . . . r

OFFICIAL DISTANCES: 10*l*, 10*l* **TIME:** 6min 11.0s **TOTE:** £1.70

965 Ladies Open — 5 ran

613^{2} **GIPSY CRICKETER** 3-1 **Miss C Stucley** *(xnb) 5s-3s; ld to start early; made all; drew clr 16; unchall* 1

822^{2} **Breteche (FR)** (5a) 2-1 **Miss T Newman** *(xnb) Lw; tde; a chsng wnr; ev ch when impd to 4l 2nd 15; sn outpcd; no ex u.p frm 3 out* 6 2

690^{5} **Ardross Gem (IRE)** (5a)(vis) 9-1 **Miss W Southcombe** *Settled rr; 30l last 13; went 4th 15; stayed on stdly to 3rd app 3 out; nrst fin* 1½ 3

322^{2} Wink And Whisper (5a) 6-4F Miss E Tory *Hld up; went 3rd & hit 12; poor 3rd frm 14; t.o; dism aft post* 20 4

468^{2} Robins Pride (IRE)(bl) 14-1 Miss J Buck *Swtng; settled 3rd; 12l 3rd 10; wknd 13; bhnd frm 15 til pu & dism 3 out.* . . . . P

OFFICIAL DISTANCES: 3*l*, ½*l* **TIME:** 6min 07.0s **TOTE:** £5.00

966 Restricted, 12st — 11 ran

688^{1} **NOBLE ACTION** (7a) evensF **N Williams** *6/4-evens; lw; hld up midfield; prog when hit 12; 5l 3rd 13; hdwy to disp ld 16; ld & hit 3 out; ½l up at last; r.o u.p flat* 1

369^{P} **Mister Swallow** 5-1 **M Miller** *Opened 6s; lw; ld 2; ½l up when slt mist 7; hdd 11; disp ld 14 til aft 16; rallied & ev ch app last; no ex cl home.* . . . . . . ¾ 2

567^{1} **Zakley** 3-1 **A Farrant** *(xnb) Sn prom; w ldrs til ld 11-14; cl up til outpcd aft 16; no ch frm 2 out; eased* 20 3

791^{P} Sweet Kari (IRE) 16-1 G Weatherley *Ld 1; cl up to 9; 7l 4th 13; wknd nxt; no ch frm 16* 25 4

572^{P} Eskimo Gold (5a) 16-1 M Sweetland *In tch; cl 4th 9; lost plce 13; bhnd frm 16* 12 5

354^{3} Captain Random 6-1 Mrs J Reed *(xnb) Tchd 8s; hld up; 7th ½way; hdwy 13; stayed on to 5th 16; 4th & rng on when blun & ur 3 out* . . . . U

706^{3}	Horrified(bl) 10-1 D Edwards *6th 8; wknd & rdn 11; last when pu 13*		P
687^{P}	Martby 16-1 M Atkinson *(xnb) Rr; outpcd in 9th 8; bhnd frm 9 til pu 12.*		P
572^{U}	Mrs Peggoty (5a)(bl) 10-1 Miss C Tizzard *Prom til lost plce 8; last when pu 14*		P
604^{1}	Trigger Again 4-1 Miss E Tory *Tchd 9/2; last til pu 11*		P
601^{5}	Western Frontier (IRE) (7a) 9-1 D Alers-Hankey *(xnb) 2 handlers; lw; midfield; 10l 5th 9; rdn 11; went 10l 4th 16; no further hdwy; pu 3 out.*		P

OFFICIAL DISTANCES: $^1/_2$l, 20l **TIME:** 6min 12.0s **TOTE:** £3.50

967 Open Maiden 8yo&up, 12st — 16 ran

	AVEC PLAISIR (IRE) 12-1 **Miss A Clifford** *Blun 3; hdwy 6; ld 8; slt ld til jnd aft 16; 2l up 2 out; mist last; r.o flat.*		1
	Bradford Bridge (5a) 16-1 **R Woollacott** *In tch; 5th 11; went 3rd 13; gd hdwy to disp ld aft 16; 2l 2nd & u.p 2 out; ev ch last; no ex flat.*	1	2
264^{5}	**My Brother Jack** 12-1 **Miss K Lovelace** *Midfield; hdwy to 4th 11; went 2nd 13-15; 3$^1/_2$l 3rd 16; 7l 3rd 2 out; one pce.*	5	3
	Golden Spirit (5a) 8-1 Miss R Green *Lw; hld up & bhnd; last $^1/_2$way; hdwy 13; went 5th but lot to do 16; r.o stdly without trblng ldrs; promising*	6	4
794^{P}	Big Mossy 16-1 J Cole *9th $^1/_2$way; poor 6th & rdn 16; no ch w ldrs.*	2	5
567^{3}	Albamart Wood(tt) 6-4F J Young *(xnb) Ld aft 5; fell 6; rdr dislocated shoulder*		F
329^{P}	Ashwicke Gambler 20-1 J Barnes *(xnb) Rr til blun bad & ur 11*		U
	Famous Deal (IRE) 16-1 M Heuff *Good sort; mid-div; 8th $^1/_2$way; rr when pu 12*		P
493^{P}	Hayling Star (5a) 16-1 Miss C Tizzard *Tde; 9th 5; bhnd frm 9 til pu 13.*		P
604^{P}	Horsemans Green(cp) 16-1 J O'Rourke *(xnb) Prom til rn out 3*		R
637^{P}	Inner State (5a) 16-1 D Edwards *Prom; slt ld 4-5; wl in tch til fell 12.*		F
325^{P}	Lipstick Lass (5a) 16-1 C Dailly *(xnb) 2 handlers; a rr; t.o & pu 2 out*		P
492^{P}	Nobody's Heroine (5a) 8-1 D Alers-Hankey *(xnb) Handy; 6th $^1/_2$way; in tch in 4th when mist 15; went 3rd aft 16; in tch when rn out bend bef nxt; dumped rdr in ditch & disappeared over hedge into road*		R
693^{U}	Polar Bright (IRE) 3-1 N Mitchell *(xnb) Tchd 4s; sn prom; lft in ld 6-7; prom til lost plce 13; rr when hit 15; t.o & pu 3 out*		P
693^{P}	Polly Dust (5a) 16-1 M Sweetland *Hdwy to 2nd aft 8; cl 3rd 13; lost plce 14; t.o & pu 2 out*		P
	The Gambling Lady (5a) 8-1 Miss S Robinson *(ringbit) Ur 2; rdr tkn to hospital w suspected broken ankle*		U

OFFICIAL DISTANCES: $^1/_2$l, 6l **TIME:** 6min 27.0s **TOTE:** £11.40

Vine & Craven

Hackwood Park (LH 7F,18J)

Mon, 12 Apr (GOOD to FIRM, GOOD in places)

968 Hunt Members, 12st — 3 ran

717^{P}	**ALEXANDER NEVSKY** 2-5F **D Dennis** *(xnb,ringbit) Oht; made all; mist 7; jmpd rt frm $^1/_2$way; mists 11; 8l clr when slt mist & lft solo 15; pushed out flat*		1
	Ballinvella 3-1 J Casemore *Chsd wnr in 2nd; outpcd frm 13; 8l down & hld when fell 15*		F
	Diplodocus 4-1 H Tett *Fat; a last; outpcd 5; t.o 8; pu 14.*		P

OFFICIAL DISTANCE: Finished alone **TIME:** 6min 52.0s

969 Countryside Alliance Club Members (Nov Rdrs), 12st — 6 ran

719^{1}	**LOTTIE THE LOTUS** (5a) 4-6F **Miss R Goodwin** *Trckd ldrs; prog to 2nd 12; went on 14; blun nxt; 4l clr last; rdn out*		1
781^{P}	**Newby End (IRE)**(vis) 7-1 **Miss C Cowe** *Spurs; ld til aft 2; cl up & ev ch til outpcd bend bef 2 out; stayed on one pce*	10	2
471^{P}	**Chism (IRE)** 8-1 **W King** *Trckd ldrs; outpcd frm 14; stayed on one pce frm 2 out; tk mod 3rd last*	2$^1/_2$	3
719^{3}	Nice Approach (IRE) 7-1 Miss V Murphy *Opened 8s,tchd 10s(in a plce); oht; ld aft 2; rdn along frm 10; hdd 14; blun & wknd nxt*	4	4
626^{5}	Lyrical Seal (5a)(bl) 3-1 H Wallace *4s-3s; trckd ldrs; outpcd frm 7; bhnd frm 13*	15	5
780^{4}	Toscanini (GER) (7x) 3-1 M Legge *A last; nvr gng wl; pu 12.*		P

OFFICIAL DISTANCES: 10l, 2l **TIME:** 6min 33.0s

970 Mixed Open, 12st

642^{3} **EASTERN POINT** (5a) **P York** *(ringbit) Walked over* 1

971 Open Maiden, 12st — 6 ran

599^{4} **ROYAL CZARINA** (5a) 6-4 **J Snowden** *Tchd 2s in plce; swtng; mostly cl 2nd til jmpd to ld & qcknd clr 14; nrly jnd 2 out; sn ld agn; dived & jmpd rt last; all out* . . . 1

716^{2} **Gunnerbe Posh** evensF **J Maxse** *(xnb) Tchd 11/10 in a plce; tde; tk v str hld & hvly rstrnd in rr; prog frm 14; nrly jnd wnr 2 out; nt qckn app last; hrd drvn & stayed on agn flat* . . . . hd 2

716^{P} **Barbed Broach (IRE)** 12-1 **Miss C Cowe** *(xnb,ringbit) Ld to 14; imm outpcd & mist nxt; sn btn; lkd to fin 4th by hd*. 15 3

716^{4} Fables Green 7-1 Mrs C Evans *Dull in coat; trckd ldrs; rmdr 13 & sn strugg; stayed on frm 2 out; lkd to fin dist 3rd* . . . . hd 4

760^{P} Isefoul De Bellevue (FR) 12-1 J Horton *Lw; trckd ldrs; nt qckn frm 14; btn frm 2 out* . . . . hd 5

644^{4} Smokey Robot (IRE) 6-1 D Dennis *(xnb) Swtng; edgy; nt jw; trckd ldrs; rdn to cl 2nd 12; hrd drvn & wknd rap frm 14; pu last*. . . . . P

OFFICIAL DISTANCES: hd, 15*l* **TIME:** 6min 35.0s

972 Confined, 12st — 5 ran

717^{1} **BALLY WIRRAL (IRE)** (3x) 2-5F **G Maundrell** *Lw; jw & a gng wl; mostly cl 2nd til jmpd to ld 12; shkn up 2 out; pushed out* 1

728^{4} **Glacial Pearl (IRE)** 5-1 **P Mason** *Swtng bad start; last early; went 3rd 6; chsd wnr in 2nd frm 14; drvn & one pce frm 3 out; no ch w wnr* 5 2

576^{4} **Makhpiya Patahn (IRE)** (3x) 5-2 **D I Turner** *(xnb) A hrd drvn; made most to 12; btn frm 2 out; virt pu flat; walked in* 35 3

778^{P} Angus Airways (IRE) 14-1 M Legge *(xnb) Mostly 4th; rdn frm 9; outpcd 12; bad mist 14; pu nxt* . . . . P

138^{P} Friars Island (IRE) 16-1 H Wallace *Fat; sn bhnd; t.o 7; pu imm aft 9*. . . . . P

OFFICIAL DISTANCES: 10*l*, dist **TIME:** 6min 28.0s

973 Restricted, 12st — 4 ran

721^{1} **STALBRIDGE ROSE** (5a) 4-7F **Miss A Goschen** *Reluct to line up & ld in; rn in snatches; hld up; rap prog to ld 4-7; rdn 15; nt fluent 2 out; disp ld last; r.o to ld last 50yds; hung lft cl home; all out*. 1

159^{P} **Jacob's Choice** (7a) 3-1 **P York** *V lean; made most to 4 & 11 til mist 13; ld agn 3 out; jnd last; no ex when hdd 50yds out* 1½ 2

779^{P} **Native Spin (IRE)** 5-2 **D Dennis** *(xnb) Opened 3s; rushed up to ld 7; hdd 11; mist 13; drvn to ld agn 14-3 out; wknd rap* 12 3

473^{P} Aslapoftheeuro (IRE) 12-1 R Bliss *Swtng; last frm 7 & sn rdn; no ch frm 3 out* 3 4

OFFICIAL DISTANCES: 1*l*, 12*l* **TIME:** 6min 36.0s

Chepstow (LH 11F,18J)

Tue, 13 Apr (GOOD)

974 Dunraven Bowl HC, 3m £3367 — 10 ran

438^{4} **CHERRY GOLD** 12-04(cp) 3-1 **E Williams** *Made virt all; clr 15; unchall* . . 1

696^{1} **Sohapara** 11-09 5-1 **D Jones** *Hld up; hdwy aft 7; chsd wnr app 8; hit 14; wknd nxt*. 16 2

447^{2} **Noaff (IRE)** 11-07(tt) 7-1 **T Vaughan** *Hld up; hdwy 10; mod 3rd frm 12* . . 6 3

671^{1} Fair Charmeur (IRE) 11-02 25-1 Miss I Tompsett *Prom; mist 4; outpcd 11; wl btn when mist 15*. . . . . s hd 4

672^{1} Minella Storm (IRE) 11-12 5-2F P Sheldrake *Hld up; rdn 10; sn bhnd; t.o*. dist 5

668^{2} Bill Haze 11-06(bl) 40-1 J Jenkins *Pulled hrd; sn prom; mist 4; wknd 11; t.o & pu 14* . . . . P

673^{1} Dawn's Cognac (IRE) 11-12 14-1 Miss F Wilson *Hld up & bhnd; some hdwy app 14; mod 4th when fell last*. . . . . F

740^{2} Hail Stone (IRE) 11-02(cp) 50-1 T Faulkner *Prom; nt fluent 2; drpd to rr 8; t.o when fell 11* . . . . F

612^{2} Inis Cara (IRE) 11-11 7-1 N Williams *Hld up; hdwy 9; wknd 11; t.o & pu 15* P

669^{2} Minster Belle 10-13 16-1 M Barber *Hld up; rdn 10; sn bhnd; t.o & pu 2 out* P

TIME: 6min 06.0s **TOTE:** £4.40; places £1.90,£1.30,£2.00 **Ex:**£22.90 **CSF:**£18.57

Exeter (RH 11F,16J)

Tue, 13 Apr (GOOD to FIRM, FIRM in places)

975 gg.com Future Stars Nov HC, 2m7f110y £2782 — 9 ran

747[1] **KINGSTON-BANKER** 11-13 4-6F **T Dreaper** *Ld aft 2; hdd 6; ld agn 12; kpt up to work frm 3 out; stayed on wl* 1
747[2] **Tell Tale (IRE)** 11-07 11-2 **T Malone** *Hld up; some hdwy app 12; stayed on to 2nd flat* 2 2
733[U] **Always On The Line (IRE)** 11-05 6-1 **A Merriam** *A.p; ld 6; hdd 12; hit 4 out; kpt on but no ch w wnr; lost 2nd flat* . . . . ¾ 3
570[4] Shobrooke Mill 11-12 16-1 A Farrant *In tch; rdn 8; wknd 12; t.o* . . . . dist 4
436[2] Corrie Mor (IRE) 11-09 14-1 P Cowley *Ld til aft 2; rdn 11; sn wknd; t.o & pu last* . . . . P
Johns Legacy 11-09 5-1 N Mitchell *Hld up in rr; hdwy on outside to trck ldrs 8; 3rd but hld when fell 3 out* . . . . F
724[1] Lady Baronette 11-02 20-1 A Martin *In rr; lost tch 6; t.o when ref & ur last* r
239[P] Lordston (IRE) 11-12 40-1 Miss E Jones *Chsd ldrs to 7; stdly wknd; t.o & pu 13* . . . . P
793[P] S B S By Jove 11-12 25-1 A Charles-Jones *Chsd ldrs to 9; wknd 12; t.o & pu last* . . . . P

TIME: 5min 46.1s **TOTE:** £1.80; places £1.10,£1.80,£2.70 **Ex:**£5.30 **CSF:**£6.22
Fence 9 omitted

Croome & West Warwickshire

Upton-on-Severn (RH 10F,18J)

Tue, 13 Apr (GOOD to FIRM)

976 Hunt Members — 6 ran

JALCANTO 4-6F **D Mansell** *Bckwd; 2 handlers; hld up off pce; clsd sltly 8; 12l 5th 10; went 4th & rdn 14; same & lkd btn 3 out; galvanised to ld nxt; sn hdd; 1l down aft last; kpt on v game to ld on line* 1
Ashwell Boy (IRE) 33-1 **B Gallagher** *1st ride; settled 3rd; ld 3 out; hdd nxt; sn ld agn; lkd wnr last; one pce & hdd on line; splendid debut for rdr but horse unfortunately drpd dead in unsaddling enclosure* . . . . s hd 2
Coddington Girl (5a) 7-2 **M Wilesmith** *Ld & jw; hdd 3 out; wknd qckly app nxt* 30 3
254[P] Theatreland (USA) 33-1 H Phipps *(xnb) 1st ride for 15yrs; imm lost tch; t.o 6; fnce bhnd 12; mist 3 out* . . . . runin 4
621[1] Craiova Comet (IRE) 9-2 T Weston *2 handlers; 20l last 1; clsd & hit 9; 3rd brief 13; lost tch rap 15; t.o & pu 2 out* . . . . P
Prempted 25-1 M Harris *(xnb) Rcd keen; hit 7; prsd ldr to 3 out; wknd nxt; 4th when pu last* . . . . P

OFFICIAL DISTANCES: s hd, dist **TIME:** 6min 32.0s

977 Restricted, 12st — 12 ran

726[2] **BLACK OPTIMIST (IRE)** 3-1 **Mrs K Baimbridge** *Nt fluent 3; went 2nd 5 til ld 14; prsd ldr aft; rdn & lkd hld last; rallied game & ld final 50yds* 1
369[6] **Alvero (FR)** (5x) 7-1 **M Harris** *Ld; nt fluent 6; hdd 14; releg 5th nxt; rallied app 2 out; kpt on wl to 2nd flat* . . . . ¾ 2
614[2] **Ballingale Dawn (IRE)** 100-30 **R Rogers** *2nd/4th frm 5 til ld 15; drvn & lkd wnr last; wknd to lose 2 plces flat* 1 3
729[1] Legend Of Light (IRE) (5a) 6-1 D Mansell *2 handlers; chsd ldrs; went cl up 13 til 7l 3rd app 3 out; drvn & one-pcd nxt* 4 4
666[1] Primitive Son 12-1 Miss E James *Cl up; 7th 13; eff in 4l 3rd app 3 out; rdn & nt qckn nxt* 3 5
730[1] Oneforthefrog (IRE) 9-1 G Tumelty *Midfield; cl 6th 13; wknd 15; plodded on* 10 6
725[1] Ebony Jack (IRE) 11-4F G Barfoot-Saunt *5s-11/4; prsd ldrs; 5th 13; rdn & wknd 15* 2 7
695[3] Niloufer (5a) 10-1 R Bliss *Last trio; lost tch 12* 12 8
668[F] Tiger Ted 20-1 S Gray *Hld up last trio; hit marker & nrly ur aft 9; eff & 8l 8th 13; wknd aft 15; t.o* 20 9
279[P] Knight Of Kilcash (IRE) 20-1 J Jones *(xnb) A last trio; t.o 10; pu 14* . . . . P

665P Lift The Latch (IRE) 25-1 M Wall *Tubed; towards rr; strugg u.p 12; t.o & pu 2 out* P
726P Raymond James 8-1 Julian Pritchard *Prom early; drpd to rr app 7; hrd drvn & no resp nxt; t.o & pu 13* . . . P

OFFICIAL DISTANCES: ½l, 1l **TIME:** 6min 29.0s

978 Panacur/TBA PPORA Club Members Maiden Mares, 12st 14 ran

519F **BABS WHEAL** (5a, 3ow) 6-1 **A Wintle** *Hld up wl in rr; last 8; 28l 8th 12; still 20l 5th 15; sust rn aft; 4th app 2 out but kpt on for drvng; ld aft last* . . 1
River Treasure (IRE) (5a) 8-1 **A Wadlow** *Hit 4; hld up midfield; impd to 2nd/3rd 10 til ld app 2 out; drvn & hdd aft last; nt qckn* . . . 1 2
724³ **Bank On Lady** (5a) 14-1 **D Mansell** *Mist 6; nt fluent in rr; eff 10; 20l 5th 12; hdwy aft 3 out; nt rch ldrs but kpt on* . . . 4 3
Greensleeves (5a) 6-1 Miss P Gundry *Prom; 2nd 12 til ld 15; blun bad nxt & hdd; wknd 2 out; lks sure to win* . . . 7 4
518R Galaxy Girl (5a) 5-2F J Mahot *Hld up midfield; prog in 3rd/4th frm 11; 4l 4th 15; disp 3rd & one pce when mist 2 out; broke down & virt pu flat* . . . 10 5
453U Sefton Clover (5a) 20-1 M Hooper *Jmpd slow 3; prom to 6; 10th 12; no ch aft* 10 6
561P Letsgeton (5a) 20-1 A Sansome *2 handlers; midfield; mist 7 & rdn; 24l 6th 12; no ch aft* . . . 2 7
725³ Knickers (5a) 14-1 J Trice-Rolph *Hld up in rr; bad mist 5; 25l 7th 12; no ch aft; mist 3 out* . . . 6 8
Coddington Susie (5a) 5-1 Julian Pritchard *A last pr; t.o 10; pu 3 out* . . . P
Dinnys Double (5a) 16-1 N Oliver *(xnb) 2nd/3rd to 8; still prom when put brakes on app 10 & sent rdr into orbit* . . . r
326² Flo Keen (12a) 4-1 J Snowden *Cl up to 6; wknd 9; 11th & t.o 12; pu 14* . P
588² Little Dish (5a)(tt) 20-1 J Owen *Midfield to 8; sn btn; wl t.o when fell 15* . F
927P Portway Sadie (5a) 25-1 M Wall *Ld in & gt flier; hdd & mist 15; lft in ld nxt; sn re-passed & stpd to nil; pu last* . . . P
Portway Sorrel (5a) 25-1 M Keel *Bckwd; ur padd & dragged rdr brief; bhnd; jmpd slow 10; poor 9th 12; t.o & pu 2 out* . . . P

OFFICIAL DISTANCES: 1½l, 2l **TIME:** 6min 37.0s

979 Mixed Open (Nov Rdrs), 12st 13 ran

756¹ **CAUGHT AT DAWN (IRE)** 8-13F **T Weston** *Midfield til smooth prog to 2nd 11; ld 13; went 3l clr app 2 out; sn in comm; hrd hld; impressive* . . . 1
755⁴ **Pretoria Dancer** (4x)(bl) 16-1 **M Goldstein** *3rd til ld 5; mist 12; hdd nxt; releg 8l 3rd & outpcd 3 out; rallied to 2nd agn at last; no ch w wnr* . . . 12 2
759¹ **Love At Dawn** 5-2 **P Mason** *Rr & mist 3; sn midfield; 5th & prog 11; 3rd 12 til prsd wnr 14; rdn & wknd aft 3 out; gng v slow & dem nxt; blun last* . . . 5 3
629⁵ Maggies Brother (7x) 12-1 Mrs M Finch *Chsd ldrs; outpcd 12; 11l 4th 14; kpt gng stdly; nvr clsd* . . . 7 4
758⁶ Henry Bruce 33-1 A Brown *Ld to 4; cl up; 4th when jmpd slow 11; downed tools & lost plce; 35l 6th 15; stayed on agn frm 2 out* . . . 3 5
403⁷ Go Go Gallant (IRE) 33-1 J Jones *Ss & lost 15l; prog to midfield 8; outpcd 11; 23l 5th 14; plugged on* . . . 15 6
661P Stride To Glory (IRE) 20-1 M Hooper *A wl bhnd; lost tch 7; nvr able to cl.* . 4 7
603⁸ Zingibar(vis) 33-1 Miss J Houldey *Last trio & nvr in tch; t.o 13* . . . 15 8
835R Harry Hotspur (IRE) (7x)(bl) 33-1 S Gray *(xnb) Ld 4-5; cl 2nd til rdn 9; nt keen aft; t.o & pu 12* . . . P
759P Hedzamarley (IRE) 40-1 Miss S Davies *Midfield; lost tch 7; mist 12; poor 7th 15; rem 7th when mist & ur last* . . . U
528P Jimmy Jumbo (IRE) (4x, 4ow) 9-1 N Cecil *(xnb) Prom early; 8th & wkng 11; rem 8th 15; 9th when fell last* . . . F
Knight's Crest (IRE) 20-1 Miss R Hutsby *(xnb) Hdwy to 3rd 5-11; wkng when blun 13; t.o & pu 3 out* . . . P
758⁷ Paddies Boy (IRE) (7x)(cp) 40-1 Jack Young *Ss & lost 20l; t.o til passed 1 & pu 9* . . . P

OFFICIAL DISTANCES: 8l, 4l **TIME:** 6min 25.0s

980 Confined, 12st 9 ran

663¹ **SAPEGA (IRE)** 7-2 **Miss J Williams** *Swtng; midfield; eff & hmpd 10; ld 11-12; 3rd til rallied & rdn aft 2 out; ld last; kpt on game* . . . 1
Stag Party (IRE) 25-1 **H Fowler** *Cl up til drpd to rr 6; nt fluent 8; rallied 12; ld app 14 & sn 4l clr; rdn & jnd last; nt qckn* . . . 1 2

756^{2}	**Rushing Again** (3x) 7-2 **Miss P Gundry** *2nd/3rd til ld 13; sn hdd; rdn & eff in 1l 2nd 2 out; nt qckn*	3	3
722^{5}	Rusty Fellow 12-1 D Mansell *Bhnd; rdn 7; 10l last 12; 20l last 15; hrd drvn & stayed on too late frm 2 out*	4	4
722^{2}	Smile Pleeze (IRE) (5x) 9-1 T Stephenson *Jmpd slow 1; rr but in tch; rdn 7; lost tch app 14; stayed on frm 2 out*	4	5
727^{U}	Machalini evensF A Morley *(xnb) Swtng; chsd ldrs til outpcd app 14; mod 5th when pckd 3 out; kpt on but rdr no use to him*	2	6
615^{F}	Thatsforeel (7x) 10-1 A Wintle *Swtng; prsd ldrs; ld brief aft 8; 5th 12; last of 4 gng clr app 14; plugged on v one-pcd frm 3 out*	2	7
513^{P}	Aztec Rule (IRE)(bl) 33-1 Julian Pritchard *(xnb) Ld; 10l clr 3; hit 5 & ld reduced; jmpd rt 10; hdd nxt; ld agn 12 til hdd & blun 13; imm gave up; t.o 3 out*	runin	8
	Tortugas (FR) 25-1 N Oliver *Last trio but in tch til blun bad 11 & pu*		P

OFFICIAL DISTANCES: 1½*l*, 2*l* **TIME:** 6min 19.0s

981 Open Maiden 8yo&up, 12st — 10 ran

731^{3}	**WIND ON THE COMMON** 5-2 **T Stephenson** *Ld to 2; trckd ldrs; nt fluent 7; 6l 3rd 11 til eff aft 3 out; ld app last; drvn out*		1
	Chateau Burf 6-1 **H Dowty** *Swtng; bucking broncho act lvng padd; midfield outpcd 11; 6l 4th & rdn 3 out; sn wl bhnd ldng pr but rallied nxt & snatched 2nd*	5	2
620^{P}	**Autcaesar Autnihil (IRE)** 12-1 **M Munrowd** *Nt fluent 1; bhnd til hdwy to 4th aft 8; ld 10-12 & agn 15; 2l clr when mist 2 out; rdn & hdd app last; sn btn*	hd	3
668^{8}	Romabit Tom 12-1 R Rogers *2 handlers; bckwd; bhnd & hld up; wknd 11; no ch 15*	20	4
621^{P}	Cosmic Flight (IRE) 8-1 J Jones *(xnb) Swtng; tk keen hld & rcd wide; went 3rd 6 til lost plce 9; 6l 5th app 3 out; fdd qckly; pu nxt*		P
668^{6}	Four Opinions 5-1 S Gray *Hld up towards rr; mist 10; 5th & prog 11; fell 12; rdr airlifted*		F
788^{3}	Plenty Inn Hand 7-1 A Hanly *Ld 2-7; prom til 4th & rdn 11; reluct aft; t.o 15; pu 3 out*		P
760^{3}	Ron Miel (IRE) 11-2 M Hooper *Bhnd; 6l last aft 8; sn lost tch; t.o & pu 14*		P
731^{F}	Rosemead Tye (5a) 9-4F H Fowler *Tk keen hld in midfield til hdwy to ld 7-10; ld 12 til jmpd slow 15; ev ch when hit nxt; wknd rap; pu last*		P
	The Footsy 10-1 Julian Pritchard *(xnb) Prom to 8; drpd to rr & mist 10; t.o & pu 13*		P

OFFICIAL DISTANCES: 8*l*, s hd **TIME:** 6min 38.0s

982 Open Maiden 56&7yo (Div 1), 2m5f, 12st — 12 ran

30^{P}	**COTTON ON** 7-4F **M Wilesmith** *(xnb) 9/4-7/4; 30l last when mist 1; hdwy to midfield 5; went 32l 3rd 11 & 20l 2nd 3 out; relentless prog aft; passed stpng ldr nr fin*		1
256^{4}	**Killough Hill (IRE)**(bl) 3-1 **Miss P Gundry** *Ld & clr; went 25l ahd 11; 20l clr but rdn 3 out; wknd app last; hrd drvn & nt r.o flat; just caught; fin v lame*	2	2
	Fencethegap (IRE) 10-1 **M Hooper** *Wl bhnd; poor 8th 8; t.o 11; lft 3rd by default*	15	3
469^{U}	Norbert (IRE) 14-1 A Hanly *(xnb) Went 2nd 5 but nvr within 8l of ldr; releg 30l 3rd app 3 out; fin tired*	12	4
	Stanley Island 20-1 Miss J Buck *Awkward padd; swtng; last pr; nrly ur 3; t.o 8; kpt gng v slow*	runin	5
723^{P}	Ashor Ted 20-1 S Bush *(xnb) Midfield & usual attempts to ref; 5th & outpcd 8; nrly stpd 10; t.o & pu 3 out*		P
	Design X Press 16-1 Miss R Reynolds *(xnb) 2 handlers; 2nd til jmpd erratic 3; lost plce qckly aft 5; mist nxt; pu 7*		P
723^{3}	Foreign Field (FR) (7a) 6-1 G Barfoot-Saunt *Midfield; 7th & outpcd 8; t.o & pu 3 out*		P
256^{P}	Golden Embers 10-1 D Barlow *Prom to 6; 20l 4th & wkng 8; t.o & pu 3 out*		P
	Pollerton Run (IRE) 11-1 G Davies *Midfield til ducked out 4*		R
619^{2}	Rosegrove Rooster 4-1 T Stephenson *Cl up til 18l 3rd & outpcd 8; tlng off when jmpd v slow 12; clambered over nxt; pu 2 out*		P
408^{6}	Will You Come On (IRE) (5a) 14-1 D Mansell *A wl bhnd; t.o 9; pu 12*		P

OFFICIAL DISTANCES: 3*l*, 8*l* **TIME:** 5min 22.0s

983 Open Maiden 56&7yo (Div 2), 2m5f, 12st — 12 ran

723^{r}	**SETT ASIDE** 10-1 **Julian Pritchard** *Hld up & wl in rr; 20l 7th 10; pckd 8; still 7th 3 out; stayed on & lft 2nd nxt; drvn ahd last; forged clr; v lucky*		1
443^{P}	**Stantons Church** 10-1 **Miss R Reynolds** *Swtng; 4/5th til went 5l 3rd 11; outpcd in 13l 3rd 3 out; hrd drvn when lft in ld nxt; hdd last; fnd nil*	2½	2
714^{6}	**Evanly Miss** (5a) 12-1 **M Jackson** *Midfield; 12l 6th 7; hit 8; 4th & strugg 3 out; wkng aft*	20	3
	Sulalah Sunrise (12a) 10-1 H Dowty *(xnb) V bckwd; school & wl off pce in last trio; strugg 7; t.o 10*	25	4
837^{P}	Force Ten 10-1 T Stephenson *2 handlers; swtng; handy; mist 6; 5th nxt; went 3rd 9-10; fdd rap; t.o 3 out*	3	5
408^{4}	Cathy Come Home (IRE) (5a) 5-1 Miss C Tizzard *Bhnd; 8th 7; t.o last 11; pu 2 out*		P
724^{F}	Gumlayloy (7a) 7-4F R Hughes *(xnb) Swtng; rcd keen; ld 5; pckd 10; hdd nxt; chsd ldr aft; ab 3l down & u.p when both blun & ur 2 out*		U
723^{P}	Kotori (IRE) (7a) 16-1 A Hanly *(xnb) Mist 3; towards rr; 7th & outpcd 7; t.o & pu 12*		P
403^{P}	Perry Of Troy (12a) 14-1 R Rogers *V sticky & reluct in last; t.o 4; trying to ref app 6; pu 10*		P
724^{r}	Silk St Bridget (5a) 10-1 G Tumelty *Pulled hrd; ld 3-5; 2nd til ld agn 3 out; 5l clr nxt; drvn when blun & ur 2 out*		U
754^{4}	Treasulier (IRE) 7-2 N Oliver *Lft in ld 1-3; prom til 10l 4th & outpcd 11; lft rem 4th & pu 2 out.*		P
725^{7}	Worthy Man(tt) 14-1 D Mansell *Ld & fell 1*		F

OFFICIAL DISTANCES: 2*l*, 10*l* **TIME:** 5min 20.0s

High Peak

Flagg Moor (LH 9F,18J)
Tue, 13 Apr (GOOD)

984 Hunt Members (stone walls), 3m4f, 12st - 13J — 6 ran

	TELLITASITIS 4-1 **Miss N Brady** *(xnb) Ld 8-10; ld 2 out; tk direct route to last; sn clr*		1
	Quinn (U) 7-1 **N Fogg** *Lft in ld 4-8; ld 11-2 out; tk long route to last; r.o*	8	2
	Lily (U) (5a) 5-1 **Miss D McKenna** *2nd til nrly followed ldr wrong way 4; ld 10-11; tk long route to last; stayed on*	5	3
	Fable (U) (5a) 12-1 Miss P Winn *Chsd ldrs; 6l 4th 10; ev ch last; wknd final furlong*	3	4
753^{P}	Single Man (IRE) 4-6F Miss S Rodman *Evens-4/6; 2 handlers; ld til tk wrong course 4; rtrcd & cont miles bhnd; gt lost agn aft 11 & waited for fattie rival; cont*	4min	5
	Alidiamond (U) (5a, 26ow) 33-1 L Hopkins *Fat; imm t.o; ref 2; cont; ref 5; cont; miles bhnd when ref last; cont; ref & ur demolishing top 2ft of stone wall; rmtd*	5min	6

OFFICIAL DISTANCES: 10*l*, 8*l* **TIME:** 7min 12.7s **TOTE:** £3.60

985 Open Maiden, 12st — 8 ran

714^{4}	**IADORA** (5a) 4-1 **Miss T Clark** *2nd/3rd til ld app 6; drew 7l clr 3 out; stayed on wl*		1
714^{3}	**Ridware Rose** (5a) 5-1 **Miss S Sharratt** *Ld til app 6; lost plce 8; 7l 5th ½way; went 8l 4th aft 14; btn when mist 3 out; hit 2 out; went poor 2nd app last*	20	2
303^{R}	**Mr Buckle (IRE)** (7a) 6-1 **R Armson** *8s-6s; hld up; hit 1; disp 3l 3rd ½way; 6l 3rd & no ex 15; rdn to chse wnr 2 out; dem app last*	1	3
775^{P}	Staple Sound(cp) 12-1 W Burnell *(xnb) Hld up; 10l last ½way; mist 11; wl bhnd 14*	7	4
651^{B}	Frosty Fella(vis) 6-4F M Mackley *(xnb) Went 2nd 2; ev ch til wknd qckly 3 out; t.o & virt pu flat*	25	5
709^{8}	Mosscroft Jack 14-1 D Greenway *(xnb) Hld up; hdwy 8; 3l 3rd ½way; 8l 4th 13; wknd u.p aft 14; wl bhnd when pu 3 out*		P
753^{4}	Robert The Rascal 8-1 J R Barlow *Swtng; ur 2*		U
710^{P}	Top Weld 20-1 K Pearson *(xnb) 2 handlers; fell 2*		F

OFFICIAL DISTANCES: 20*l*, 1*l* **TIME:** 7min 36.5s **TOTE:** £6.40

986 Confined — 5 ran

	MINELLA SILVER (IRE) 4-7F **R Burton** *Made all; went 3l clr 3 out; sn rdn & lkd vulnerable; jmpd lft 2 out; jnd last; fnd ex final 50yds*		1
786P	**Saxon Gold** 4-1 **Miss S Sharratt** *8s-4s; hld up; mists 8 & 9; last to 10; 5l 4th 15; went 3l 2nd aft mist 3 out; jnd wnr last; ev ch til no ex final 50yds*	1	2
7083	**Three Saints (IRE)** 11-2 **G Hanmer** *Went 2nd 3-11; chsd wnr 12 til wknd aft 3 out*	20	3
5928	Young Tomo (IRE)(cp) 5-1 L Hicks *(boh) 8s-5s; 2nd to 3; jmpd slow 4; 1½l 3rd ½way; chsd wnr 11-12; rdn 14; 2l 3rd nxt; sn wknd*	8	4
749U	Silk Vestments (5a) 33-1 J Burley *Hld up; mists 5 & 7; 2½l 4th ½way; mist & rmdrs 10; lost tch 14*	7	5

OFFICIAL DISTANCES: 1½l, 20l **TIME:** 7min 28.1s **TOTE:** £1.60

987 Ladies Open — 8 ran

6821	**RIVER NESS** (5a) 5-2F **Mrs V Thirlby** *Lw; a.p; disp ld 7; went 2nd ½way; ld 11; 5l clr 3 out; comf*		1
7126	**Class Of Ninetytwo (IRE)** 12-1 **Miss S Sharratt** *2nd til ld 5; hdd aft 9; 2½l 3rd 14; went 5l 2nd app 3 out; one pce*	10	2
7431	**Macfin (IRE)**(cp) 7-2 **Miss L Allan** *Ld to 5; 2nd/disp ld til ld aft 9; hdd 11; drvn along 15; releg 6l 3rd app 3 out; sn wknd*	15	3
679P	Supreme Silence (IRE) 7-2 Miss Rachel Clark *Swtng; detach last til aft 14; 15l 6th nxt; nvr nr to chall*	½	4
712P	Sea Tarth (5a)(cp) 12-1 Miss H Kinsey *(xnb) Hld up; 4l 5th ½way; outpcd & 10l 4th 14; wknd 3 out*	2½	5
4073	Zamhareer (USA) 7-1 Miss T Harrison *Hld up; hdwy & 3l 4th ½way; mist 11; sn lost plce; 13l 5th & rdn 14; wknd app 3 out; t.o.*	15	6
682P	Fami (FR) 4-1 Miss Gemma Hutchinson *Ld & ur 1*		U
7127	Yer 'umble (IRE) 33-1 Miss M Hugo *Chsd ldrs to 5; 11l 6th ½way; lost tch 14; 20l last when ur nxt*		U

OFFICIAL DISTANCES: 12l, 25l **TIME:** 7min 22.5s **TOTE:** £3.40

988 Mens Open, 12st — 3 ran

435P	**STEP ON EYRE (IRE)** (7x) 6-4 **R Burton** *Ld til aft 5; cl 2nd til ld 13; rdn 3l clr 2 out; all out*		1
7482	**Springwood White** 9-2 **T Park** *Rcd wide; w ldr til ld aft 5; hdd 13; ev ch 3 out; kpt on game flat*	1½	2
7501	**Prominent** 4-5F **G Hanmer** *(xnb) Ld in start; ww; sat 10l off rivals til hdwy 14; 2l last nxt; rdn & fnd nil aft 3 out; mist 2 out; eased when btn flat*	12	3

OFFICIAL DISTANCES: 1¾l, 20l **TIME:** 7min 28.1s **TOTE:** £1.70

989 Countryside Alliance Club Members (Nov Rdrs), 12st — 9 ran

8493	**STAR CHANGES** 7-4F **Miss N Lloyd** *Lw; mist & rdr lost iron 5; 2nd til ld 3 out; rdn out*		1
6424	**Croft Court** 10-1 **D Renney** *Hld up; hdwy 6; 3½l 3rd ½way; went 1l 2nd & rdn aft 3 out; ev ch last; nt qckn*	2½	2
7484	**Horton-Cum-Peel (IRE)** 12-1 **W Kinsey** *(xnb) Hld up; 9l 7th ½way; 7l 6th 12; stayed on frm 3 out; went 8l 3rd nxt; nvr nr to chall*	10	3
6846	Libido 8-1 P Andrew *Hld up; 8l 6th ½way; hdwy & 3½l 4th 12; no ex 3 out*	1½	4
7483	Chelsea King (IRE) 6-1 Miss G Garton *8s-6s; lw; ld 2; 8l clr 7-9; hdd 3 out; sn wknd*	15	5
786P	Needwood Neptune 10-1 P Bennett *Ld to 2; lost plce 6; 10l 8th & rdn ½way; lost tch aft 15*	8	6
7084	Double Rich 3-1 O Greenall *(xnb) Prom; 6l 4th ½way; lost plce 11; 10l 7th nxt; short-lived eff 15; wl bhnd when pu & dism aft 2 out*		P
753P	Ginmini (IRE) (5a) 25-1 R Ward-Dutton *Svs; jmpd rt; wl bhnd to 5; 10½l last ½way; lost tch 14; t.o & pu 3 out*		P
683U	Strong Chairman (IRE) 8-1 K O'Brien *Hld up; hdwy & 6½l 5th ½way; 6l 5th 14; no imp when ur 3 out*		U

OFFICIAL DISTANCES: 4l, 10l **TIME:** 7min 32.6s **TOTE:** £2.10

990 Dodson & Horrell PPORA Club Members Restricted, 12st 5 ran

463[1] **UNCLE ADA (IRE)**(bl) 5-2 **R Burton** *Hld up; last to 2 & 7-12; went 2nd 15; ld app 3 out; lkng v vulnerable when swerved lft causing challenger to fall app last; lft clr; fin w inj hind leg* 1
680[2] **Eco Warrior (IRE)** 2-1JF **N Bell** *(xnb) Nt fluent; 2nd to 9; last 12-14; 3l last agn 3 out; no ex; lft 2nd aft 2 out.* 8 2
594[1] **Aunt Gladys (IRE)** (5a) 2-1JF **G Brewer** *Swtng; hld up; last 2-7; went 2nd 9; ld 10-11 & 14 til app 3 out; sn wknd* 15 3
753[1] Ridware Pride 6-1 Miss S Sharratt *Swtng; ld to 9 & 11-14; last nxt; went 2l 2nd aft 3 out; rdn & clsng qckly on inner when ldr swerved lft app last; no ch of avoiding him & crashed to ground* . . . . . . S
648[4] Table For Four(vis) 14-1 M Mackley *(xnb) 4th when ur 4* . . . . . . U

OFFICIAL DISTANCES: 10*l*, 20*l* **TIME:** 7min 43.0s **TOTE:** £2.70

Cheltenham (LH 10F,22J)

Thu, 15 Apr (GOOD, GOOD to FIRM in places)

991 Jacuzzi UK HC, 3m2f110y £4936 6 ran

543[7] **BRIGHT APPROACH (IRE)** 11-12 7-1 **T Malone** *Last & nt fluent 2; 5th 8; 10l down 12; tk 3rd 16 & 2nd 18; stdy prog app 2 out; sn ld flat & edged clr; rdn out; game* 1
629[1] **Macgeorge (IRE)** 12-02 4-1 **M Barber** *Lw; ld to 2 & frm 8; drew clr 17; 10l ahd 19; drvn & prsd 2 out; sn hdd flat; kpt on game but one pce* 2 2
543[1] **Earthmover (IRE)** 12-04 5-4F **Miss A Goschen** *Lw; hld up; nt a fluent; outpcd by ldng pr 8; clsd 11; went 2nd 16; hit 17 & nxt & dem; rdn to chall 2 out; wknd app last* 10 3
543[3] County Derry 12-07(cp) 3-1 N Harris *Oht; 2 handlers; hld up; mist 5 & rdn; last & hit 8; 16l down 12; drvn & nvr gng wl aft; t.o aft 3 out.* 29 4
442[1] Delgany Royal (IRE) 12-07 20-1 R Burton *Lw; ld 2-8; chsd ldr to 16; wknd qckly; t.o & pu 2 out.* . . . . . . P
732[11] Maidstone Monument (IRE) 12-04 50-1 N Williams *Chsd ldrs; outpcd 8; 10l 4th when hit 12; dem & drvn nxt; t.o & pu 17* . . . . . . P

TIME: 6min 38.9s **TOTE:** £7.90; places £2.70,£2.20 **Ex:**£41.30 **CSF:**£32.33

Ayr (LH 9F,21J)

Fri, 16 Apr (GOOD to SOFT, GOOD in places)

992 Royal Scots Dragoon Guards ILPH HC, 3m3f110y £3432 6 ran

798[2] **LORD EDWARDS ARMY (IRE)** 11-09 11-2 **R Morgan** *Rcd keen; cl up; ld 13 til mist 17; rdn app nxt; rallied to ld app last; kpt on stout.* 1
772[1] **Sad Mad Bad (USA)** 12-02 4-6F **G Tuer** *Pckd 2; nvr fluent in last; outpcd 14; went 10l 5th but u.p app 17; 20l down 3 out; rallied app nxt; kpt on str flat; too much to do.* 1½ 2
678[5] **Bold Classic (IRE)** 11-07 16-1 **P Kinsella** *Prom; ld 17; sn rdn 3l clr 3 out; hdd app last; wknd flat* 1¾ 3
439[P] Strong Tartan (IRE) 12-03(cp,tt) 7-1 K Mercer *Cl up; outpcd 15; 4th & no imp when blun 18; 18l 4th nxt; kpt on frm 2 out* 2 4
179[7] Master Wood 12-03 14-1 L Bates *Ld 3-13; chsd ldrs til 15l 3rd & outpcd 3 out; plugged on agn aft nxt* 1½ 5
798[5] Primitive Way 11-12(cp) 14-1 P Maitland-Carew *Ld to 3; mists 7 & 12; drvn & lost plce app nxt; last & btn 17* 7 6

TIME: 7min 20.0s **TOTE:** £5.80; places £3.30,£1.10 **Ex:**£14.10 **CSF:**£9.30

Taunton (RH 8F,15J)

Fri, 16 Apr (GOOD to FIRM, FIRM in places)

993 Royal Devon Yeomanry HC, 3m £2383 8 ran

747[5] **ALSKA (FR)** 11-02 25-1 **Miss W Southcombe** *Sn wl bhnd; t.o & rmdrs 6; gd hdwy app 3 out; tk mod 3rd nxt; fin like a rocket & made 8l frm last; ld on line* . . 1
Dantie Boy (IRE) 12-02 7-2 **Miss S Young** *3rd til lft 2nd bend bef 11; clsd to press ldr app 3 out; sn ld flat; rdn & pipped on post* . . . . . . s hd 2

631[2] **Jabiru (IRE)** 12-00(bl) 2-1F **D Edwards** *Ld to 3; chsd ldr til lft 12l clr app 11; jmpd lft frm nxt; rdn & 2l ahd app 3 out-last; sn hdd & hung bad lft; fin tired* 8 3
799[P] Sporting Chance 11-07 40-1 M Munrowd *Hld up; hdwy in 3rd & mist 10; outpcd 13; mist 3 out; jmpd lft nxt* . . . 20 4
801[4] Simber Hill (IRE) 12-00(bl) 4-1 B Woodhouse *Hld up; 7th 9; hdwy u.p to 3rd brief 13; nt r.o & sn wl bhnd* . . . $1^{3}/_{4}$ 5
799[P] Keltic Lord 12-00 10-1 A Charles-Jones *Hit 1 & 2; midfield; pckd 8; rdn 10; sn btn; pu 12* . . . P
800[2] Ronans Choice (IRE) 12-00(bl) 7-2 Richard Darke *Rcd keen; ld 3; hit 9; slpd up bend bef 11* . . . S
799[P] Traditional (IRE) 11-11(cp) 50-1 N Williams *Chsd ldrs til rdn & strugg aft 10; mist 12; nt keen; t.o & pu passing omitted 14* . . . P

TIME: 6min 06.6s **TOTE:** £21.40; places £3.20,£1.80,£1.40 **Ex:**£80.20 **CSF:**£112.69
Fences 7 & 14 omitted - slippery ground

Bangor (LH 9F,16J)

Sat, 17 Apr (SOFT, GOOD to SOFT in places)

994 Jane McAlpine Mem HC, 3m110y £2404 — 14 ran

801[5] **MULLENSGROVE** 12-02 12-1 **Miss S Phizacklea** *A.p; ld app 4 out; cl bef 2 out; stayed on wl* . . . 1
683[1] **Omni Cosmo Touch (USA)** 11-11 7-1 **N Saville** *Reluct to rce; bhnd; hdwy 11; chsd clr wnr 2 out; no imp* . . . 14 2
732[7] **The Butterwick Kid** 12-00(bl) 7-1 **Richard Tate** *Ld 2-8; ld agn 10 (water); hdd app 13; wknd 2 out* . . . 9 3
435[2] Heidi Ili (FR) 11-11(cp) 9-4F G Hanmer *Cl up; rdn 11; wknd app 3 out* . . $1^{1}/_{2}$ 4
543[F] Upham Lord (IRE) 11-13 9-1 G Brewer *Prom; ld 8; hdd 10 (water); wknd aft 3 out* . . . nk 5
631[3] Blackberry Way 11-06(tt) 22-1 J Jenkins *Midfield; bhnd frm 11; t.o & pu 3 out* P
891[F] Buckland Knight (IRE) 11-07 20-1 D Edwards *Bhnd; some hdwy app 13; no imp when fell nxt* . . . F
838[P] Joshua's Vision (IRE) 11-07(tt) 50-1 Miss L Brooke *A bhnd; t.o & pu aft 8.* P
727[P] Lord Castle (IRE) 11-07 66-1 R McCarthy *Ld to 2; tch til wknd aft 8; t.o & pu 12* . . . P
798[P] Mr Busby 11-07 66-1 M Seston *A bhnd; t.o & pu 12; sore (lost a shoe)* . . P
630[P] Scoundrel 11-07 100-1 S Ross *A bhnd; t.o & pu aft 8* . . . P
784[1] Shiny Bay (IRE) 11-07 20-1 N Pearce *Mists; in tch; rdn 12; sn wknd; bhnd when pu 13* . . . P
541[2] Shraden Edition 11-11 9-1 D Barlow *Hld up midfield; hit 5; wknd aft 9; t.o & pu 12* . . . P
445[1] Tales Of Bounty (IRE) 12-04(bl) 4-1 N Williams *Chsd ldrs 3; wknd qckly aft 3 out; pu nxt* . . . P

TIME: 6min 41.3s **TOTE:** £16.60; places £3.00,£3.30,£3.30 **Ex:**£71.90 **CSF:**£91.01
Two fences were omitted

Aldenham Harriers

Cottenham (RH 9F,19J)

Sat, 17 Apr (GOOD, GOOD to FIRM in places)

995 Hunt Members — 2 ran

525[4] **GUNNER BE TRUE** evens **A Corbett** *Set v slow pce; jnd 11; hdd 13; rallied 2 out; pushed ahd last; plugged on* . . . 1
833[P] **Carvilla (IRE)** 4-7F **A Sansome** *(xnb) 5/4-4/7; jmpd slow 5; jnd wnr 11; ld 13; went 6l clr 3 out; rmdr & swished tail nxt; hdd last & curled up completely* 5 2

OFFICIAL DISTANCE: 4*l* **TIME:** 6min 43.0s **TOTE:** £1.50 **DF:**-

996 Panacur/TBA PPORA Club Members Mares Maiden, 12st — 10 ran

833[4] **PLAY ALONE (IRE)** (5a) 7-2 **N Bloom** *A ldng pr; ld to 3 & 10 til hdd 2 out; rdn & rallied last; ld flat; all out* . . . 1
386[U] **Northern Breeze** (5a) 6-1 **M Mackley** *Swtng bad; settled rr; 20l last 8; prog 10; $3^{1}/_{2}$l 4th 16; clsd to ld 2 out-last; drvn & hdd flat* . . . nk 2

782[3] **Gale On The Lake (IRE)** (5a) 7-4F **P Hall** *2s-7/4; chsd ldrs; hit 7; went 2nd brief 14; 2l 3rd & nt fluent 16; 4l down 2 out; fdd tame* 25 3
833[P] Memsahib Ki Behan (5a) 10-1 H Fowler *Ld 3-10; w wnr agn brief 16; rdn & wkng in 6l 4th 2 out* 6 4
887[P] Kissed By Moonlite (5a) 20-1 R Armson *(xnb) Hld up towards rr; outpcd 14; plodded on* 8 5
539[F] Wanna Be Bay (5a) 10-1 P York *Hld up & nvr btr than midfield; strugg in last & rdn 13; t.o 16* 15 6
652[P] Green Leader (IRE) (5a) 10-1 S Morris *Drpd to rr & strugg 8; rdn 13; rem last when mist 3 out; pu nxt* . . . . P
Pink Mosaic (5a) 2-1 J Diment *Nt a fluent; midfield; wknd 14; strugg when pu 3 out* . . . . P
Scalby Croft (5a) 12-1 Miss N Barnes *Prom; 4th 10; wknd rap; t.o & pu 15* P
832[P] Trojan Love (IRE) (5a) 25-1 A Braithwaite *Pulled hrd & prom to 8; stpd to nil 10; t.o & pu 11* . . . . P

OFFICIAL DISTANCES: ½*l*, 10*l* **TIME:** 6min 16.0s **TOTE:** £3.30 **DF:**£20.40

997 Land Rover Mens Open, 12st 10 ran

804[U] **BELVENTO (IRE)** (7x) 4-1 **M Sheridan** *Lw; hld up; 9th 10; prog in 4th & rdn 14; went 2nd aft 3 out; ld app last; sn rdn clr* 1
331[1] **Hatch Gate** (7x) 3-1 **P York** *Hld up; mist 3; prog in 2nd 10; ld & mist 11; 7l clr 3 out; drvn & hdd app last; nt qckn* 7 2
Gratomi (IRE) 10-1 **N Kent** *Fat; jw; ld to 11; chsd ldr til app 2 out; kpt battling on* 1 3
758[1] Freedom Fighter 6-4F A Martin *Prom; 13l 3rd 8; rdn 10; nvr really gng wl aft; outpcd 15; 20l 4th 3 out* 1½ 4
903[U] Ballad (IRE) 16-1 A Williams *Midfield; hit 9 & 10; 6th & outpcd nxt; no ch frm 15* 5 5
832[3] Polo Ridge (IRE)(bl) 16-1 H Fowler *2nd/3rd til 4th 10; rdn & wknd 15; jmpd slow nxt; plodded on* 3 6
783[P] Merry Minstrel (IRE) (7x) 33-1 L Hicks *Midfield & off pce; 5th 13; no ch frm 15* 6 7
480[P] Cateel Bay (5a) 33-1 P Millington *(citation) Lkd poor; a last; 25l adrift 4; t.o nxt; bad mist 7; pu 11* . . . . P
557[4] Fine Times(tt) 14-1 M Mackley *Midfield; 10l 5th & rdn 10; nvr gng wl aft; strugg 13; pu 15* . . . . P
832[R] Vital Issue (IRE) (7x) 16-1 P Johnson *(xnb) Chsd ldrs; 15l 4th when mist 8; drpd to rr 10; last & blun 13; pu 2 out* . . . . P

OFFICIAL DISTANCES: 5*l*, 1*l* **TIME:** 6min 03.0s **TOTE:** £6.70 **DF:**£8.80

998 Ladies Open 8 ran

558[1] **HIGHLAND ROSE (IRE)** (5a) 8-11F **Ms A Embiricos** *(xnb) 2nd til 3rd 4-10; chsd ldr til level 15-nxt; drew 8l clr 2 out; r.o str; impressive* 1
906[2] **Village Copper** 6-1 **Miss H Grissell** *(xnb) 2 handlers; midfield; disp 4th 10; 13l 3rd 3 out; went 2nd aft nxt; no ch w wnr* 12 2
750[4] **Templebreedy (IRE)** 5-2 **Miss S Beddoes** *Ld at fast pce; jnd 15-16; 1l 2nd when pckd nxt; rdn & wknd 2 out* 7 3
743[5] The Wiley Kalmuck (IRE) 7-2 Miss Z Turner *Midfield; disp 6l 4th 10; rdn 12 & no resp; 12l 5th 14; nd aft* 2½ 4
607[P] Quick Response (IRE) 20-1 Miss B Donnelly *Rcd keen; chsd ldr 4-10; hit nxt; 7l 3rd 14; wknd stdly aft* 2 5
743[7] Borrow Mine (IRE) 16-1 Miss L Marriott *A 6th; 20l adrift 10; wl t.o 14* . . . 35 6
831[3] Catherine's Way (IRE)(cp) 25-1 Miss F Hatfield *Carries condition; 2 handlers; a 7th; 25l adrift 10; wl t.o 14* 2 7
832[P] Fiolino (FR)(bl) 33-1 Miss R Page *(xnb) A last & rdr nt an asset; 15l adrift 2; wl t.o 13* 12 8

OFFICIAL DISTANCES: 15*l*, 10*l* **TIME:** 5min 59.0s **TOTE:** £1.50 **DF:**£13.80

999 Restricted, 12st 10 ran

130[1] **WINCY SPIDER** 5-2 **J Diment** *Ld to 6; 2nd til ld agn 14; 6l clr 2 out; nt fluent last; rdn & stayed on wl* 1
190[4] **Gillie's Nephew** 8-1 **James Tudor** *(xnb) Hld up; 5th 10; eff 14 to 4l 2nd & blun 16; drvn & no imp frm 2 out* 2 2
680[4] **Interrogator** 10-1 **J Docker** *Chsd ldrs in 4/5th; eff to disp 5l 3rd 14; rdn & wknd 16; 18l 3rd 2 out* 35 3

561[1] Troubleshooter 8-1 M Mackley *Hld up towards rr; 7th 10; wknd 14; 26l 4th 2 out* . . . . . $2^1/_2$ 4
745[4] Lone Star (IRE)(bl) 20-1 H Fowler *Towards rr; 6th 10; mist 12; wknd aft 13; rem 6th 16* 15 5
829[3] Ardnut(bl) 33-1 Miss R Page *Nr jw & rdr no help; sn last pr; t.o & mist 7; kpt plugging on* 10 6
745[5] Nowornever (IRE) 10-1 D Kemp *Prom; 3rd & rdn 10; wknd bad 13; t.o 16* 2 7
405[U] Ard Na Carrig (IRE) 20-1 Miss A Parkes *Sn strugg in last pr; t.o 9; rfo 13* . U
779[P] Magic Lodge (7a) 10-1 R Stearn *Nt jw; prom til 10l 8th & wkng 10; blun bad 13 & rdr lost irons; pu nxt* . . . . . P
734[2] Viscount Bankes 5-4F A Martin *(xnb) Pulled hrd; went 2nd 3; ld 6 til hdd & mist 14; 6l 3rd & wkng 16; midfield when pu 2 out* . . . . . P

OFFICIAL DISTANCES: $1^1/_2$l, 20l **TIME:** 6min 04.0s **TOTE:** £3.10 **DF:**£23.20

1000 Open Maiden, 12st — 6 ran

MILL LORD (IRE) 12-1 **M Mackley** *Jmpd stdy; imm 6l clr; at least 15l ahd frm 9; a in comm* 1
560[2] **Tooley Park** 4-5F **S Morris** *Jmpd sticky in 2nd; chsd wnr vain & nvr within 12l frm 3; lumbered on & nvr lkd like clsng* 12 2
760[P] **Abitofahike (IRE)** 6-1 **A Martin** *(xnb) Rcd keen & mists; 18l 4th 10; poor 4th when mist 16; 27l 3rd 2 out* 10 3
946[3] Society Scandal (IRE)(tt) 14-1 P Millington *V scraggy; went mod 3rd 9; mist 11; releg 4th 13; 33l adrift & violent drvn 2 out* 12 4
746[U] Divine Mist (IRE) 7-4 J Owen *Nr jw in rr; 19l 5th 10; went poor 3rd 13-3 out; fdd bad; t.o & pu aft climbing nxt* . . . . . P
685[P] Playaway (IRE) 14-1 R Armson *2 handlers; rn last; mist 5; 23l adrift 10; t.o 16; pu 3 out* . . . . . P

OFFICIAL DISTANCES: 10l, 10l **TIME:** 6min 11.0s **TOTE:** £12.50 **DF:**£23.60

Dartmoor

Flete Park (RH 8F,20J)

Sat, 17 Apr (GOOD, GOOD to FIRM in places)

1001 Hunts Members (with Modbury Harriers), 12st — 4 ran

702[1] **IMPATIENT LADY** (5a) 4-5F **A Glassonbury** *Tchd evens; lw; hld up in tch; went 2nd aft 13; cl up when pckd 3 out; chall aft 2 out; ld last; sn clr; rdly; lost a front shoe; should win agn* 1
794[4] **Lingering Fog (IRE)** 2-1 **Miss M McCarthy** *Opened 5/2; jw; tried to make all; 2-3l up frm 15 til str prsd 2 out; hdd last; no ex* . . . . . $2^1/_2$ 2
Hickory (IRE) 5-1 Richard Darke *Cl up trckng ldrs; wl in tch when blun & ur 13* U
Steponthebandit (5a) 7-1 D McKenna *(boh) 2 handlers; settled last but in tch; some hdwy 12; 3l 3rd 14; wknd nxt; bhnd frm 17; pu 2 out; easy rn* . . . P

OFFICIAL DISTANCE: $2^1/_2$l **TIME:** 6min 48.0s

1002 Restricted, 12st — 9 ran

791[2] **MYSTIC WARRIOR (USA)** 11-4 **Miss T Cave** *Lw; hld up in tch; hdwy to disp ld 8; ld 17; slt ld til pushed clr app 2 out; stayed on wl* 1
706[P] **Baron Ridge** 10-1 **Richard Darke** *(xnb) Ld/disp to 6; prom; cl 3rd 12; rdn & outpcd 15; rallied to 2nd app 2 out; one pce* 6 2
791[4] **Winning Leader (IRE)** 8-1 **Mrs O Jackson** *Ld/disp frm 6-17; cl 3rd when rn wide bend aft 3 out; nt rec* 20 3
795[1] Black A Brook (IRE) (5a)(cp) 9-4F L Jefford *Tchd 3s; last til pu 3* . . . . . P
707[P] Budghill 16-1 C Heard *Lw; towards rr; last $^1/_2$way; 6th & hdwy 14; just in tch in 6th when blun & ur 16* . . . . . U
Cut Down The Sound (IRE) 10-1 Miss S Gaisford *Midfield; lost plce 9; last frm 12; t.o & pu 3 out* . . . . . P
494[F] Golden Sovereign 50-1 M Dennis *2 handlers; towards rr; 6th 10; prog 14; just in tch in 5th when blun & ur 16* . . . . . U

796[1] Gunners Mistake 5-2 L Heard *Lw; 2 handlers; tde; disp ld to 8; cl 4th 10; lost plce nxt; poor 7th 14; t.o & pu 3 out; disapp* . . . . P
791[6] Tabernacle 16-1 A Glassonbury *Wl in tch; cl 3rd & gng wl 11 til went 2nd & nt fluent 3 out; ev ch til pu app 2 out; dism.* . . . . P

OFFICIAL DISTANCES: 8*l*, 20*l* **TIME:** 6min 44.0s

The stewards enquired into the pulling-up of the favourite, Black A Brook; the rider's explanation that the mare was continually changing her legs and he thought she had lost her action was noted (the on-course vet confirmed the mare was sound)

1003 Mens Open, 4m, 12st - 25J — 6 ran

703[1] **PROVINCE** (4x) evensF **L Jefford** *Tchd 11/10; jw; slt ld 2-12; ld agn aft 15; forged clr frm 3 out; stayed on str.* 1
911[3] **Dark Challenger (IRE)** 4-1 **A Charles-Jones** *Tchd 5s; hld up; disp 7l 3rd 12; 16l 3rd 17; prog 20; went 7l 3rd 3 out; rdn to 2nd app last; stayed on; nt trble wnr; lks indolent & a hrd ride* . . . . $3^1/_2$ 2
770[2] **Canterbury Jack (IRE)**(bl) 2-1 **G Weatherley** *In tch; hdwy 15; went 2nd 16; chsd ldr; 5l 2nd & rdn 22; 3l 2nd & ev ch when hit 3 out; no further hdwy; dem 3rd app last; nt lk keen* 5 3
642[5] Nearly Gold (4x)(cp) 12-1 N McDiarmid *Tchd 14s; settled rr but just in tch to 11; hit 14; disp 18l 4th 15; t.o & strugg frm 20.* . . . . runin 4
235[P] Commander Cully (IRE) 25-1 M Sweetland *(xnb) In tch; ld 12; mist 14; wknd rap aft 15; t.o when jmpd lft 22; btn ab 3 fncs* 2fncs 5
733[P] Lydford Castle 16-1 L Heard *Ld 1; trckd ldr & rmdr 5; rdn to keep in tch 11; wknd nxt; bhnd frm 17 til pu 19.* . . . . P

OFFICIAL DISTANCES: 4*l*, 7*l* **TIME:** 8min 10.0s

1004 Gerrard Ladies Open — 5 ran

792[1] **SANDY DUFF** evensF **Miss M McCarthy** *Lw; jw; ld frm 2; 2-3l up til drew clr 17; easily* 1
822[P] **Defendtherealm** 12-1 **Miss A Mills** *Tde; ld in start; disp 2nd; rn wide bend aft 3; chsd wnr gng wl 12; 4l 2nd & slt mist 17; one pce frm 3 out* 8 2
641[3] **Frank Byrne** 9-2 **Miss A Goschen** *Ww in tch in 4th; shkn up 11; no real prog; 20l 4th 3 out; tk poor 3rd nr line* 20 3
322[P] Sailors Folly (IRE) 7-4 Miss P Gundry *(xnb) Lw; 2 handlers; ld 1; settled disp 2nd til wknd 12; 7l 3rd 15-16; rallied brief 3 out; dem 4th cl home* . . . 2 4
792[P] Happy Team (5a) 20-1 Mrs O Jackson *A last; just in tch til wknd & rdn frm 11; rmdrs 15; no imp; t.o* 3 5

OFFICIAL DISTANCES: 12*l*, 15*l* **TIME:** 6min 32.0s

1005 Confined, 12st — 6 ran

412[3] **MIDNIGHT COUP** (7x)(bl) 7-1 **G Weatherley** *Lw; hld up in tch; went 2nd aft 14; trckd ldr til ld & rn wide bend aft 3 out; stayed on wl u.p.* 1
Barton Rose 16-1 **I Chanin** *1st ride; tde; sn bhnd; prog 13; went 18l 4th 3 out; kpt on to 2nd at last.* 4 2
705[P] **Silver Man**(cp) 10-1 **D McKenna** *Ld/disp; slt ld & qcknd 15; hdd aft 3 out; 4l 2nd & hit nxt; fin tame* 5 3
277[4] Vic's Brush (IRE) 2-1 W White *2 handlers; oht; tk keen hld; wl in tch; cl 3rd & ev ch 13 til 7l 3rd & outpcd aft 3 out; btn when mist nxt; releg 4th app last* 4 4
790[1] Little Native (IRE) 4-5F Miss P Gundry *(xnb) Lw; nt a fluent; prom; disp ld frm 6 til wknd 15; bhnd 3 out; disapp.* 8 5
821[3] Fern Leader (IRE) 25-1 Miss L Woodward *1st ride; ss; disp 5th when ur 3 .* U

OFFICIAL DISTANCES: 6*l*, 7*l* **TIME:** 6min 42.0s

1006 Confined Maiden, 12st - 19J — 9 ran

702[6] **ABSEAL** 8-1 **A Charles-Jones** *In tch; impd to disp 2nd 10; ld 15; $1^1/_2$l up 3 out; prsd & hrd rdn 2 out; stayed on game flat* 1
824[P] **Feels Like Rain** 12-1 **L Heard** *Hld up in tch; 3rd & gng wl 11; hdwy to 2nd 3 out; chall nxt; ev ch til no ex flat; fair eff.* . . . . $2^1/_2$ 2
913[2] **Winnie The Pooh** 5-4F **Miss S Gaisford** *Ld to 15; cl 2nd & ev ch til wknd app 2 out* 6 3
571[5] Dear As Saffron (5a) 14-1 W Biddick *Midfield; 4th $^1/_2$way; in tch when pckd 16; clsd to $2^1/_2$l 3rd 3 out; rn v wide bend aft 3 out; nt rec* 15 4
962[U] Tarpon Tale (IRE)(cp) 9-1 D McKenna *(xnb,b4) Rr frm 6; last but just in tch $^1/_2$way; lost tch 3 out.* 3 5

910[3] Little Apple Bay (5a) 9-2 Miss T Cave *2 handlers; swtng; prom; 2l 2nd 6 til fell 9* F
796[U] Madame Cholet (5a)(tt) 6-1 M Woodward *Oht; tde; prom; cl 5th 11; 3rd & slt mist 13; sn rdn & wknd; bhnd when pu 16* . . . . P
195[P] Newhouse Lira (5a)(tt) 16-1 Richard Darke *(xnb) Svs; sn t.o; pu 9* . . . . . . P
568[U] Off The Hook (IRE) 3-1 I Hambley *2 handlers; swtng; cl 5th 6; wl in tch when bd 9* B

OFFICIAL DISTANCES: 3*l*, 6*l* **TIME:** 6min 45.0s

Fence 17 omitted - fallen riders

Seavington

Littlewindsor (RH 7F,19J)

Sat, 17 Apr (GOOD to FIRM)

1007 Open Maiden 56&7yo, 2m4f, 12st - 16J 5 ran

367[3] **LUTTEUR BLEU (FR)** (7a) 5-6F **M Miller** *(xnb) Ld; sn 8l clr; 5l up 9; hdd brief 11; drew clr frm 2 out.* 1
600[F] **Senor Cid** (7a) 9-1 **Mrs J Reed** *(xnb) 2 handlers; mounted on course; tde & ld to start; chsd clr ldr til clsd app 5; rdr called cab 10; blun nxt & dem 3rd; jmpd to 2nd agn 3 out; no imp on wnr.* 5 2
962[R] **Judy's Lad** (7a) 11-1 **J Barnes** *(xnb) Chsd ldrs; 3rd 4; 2¹/2l down 6; ld brief 11; 2nd til outj & dem 3 out; wknd frm nxt* 15 3
Heartleys Quest (IRE) (12a) 5-1 N Wilmington *(xnb) Last 2; 5 1/2l down 7; 4th 8; grad lost tch frm 11; t.o 4th when ref & ur 3 out* . . . . r
796[4] Mighty Mack (IRE) (7a) 4-1 J Snowden *(xnb) Jmpd novicey; 3rd til lost plce 4; releg last 8; grad wknd; t.o & pu 3 out* . . . . P

OFFICIAL DISTANCES: 5*l*, 15*l* **TIME:** 5min 26.6s

1008 Hunt Members, 12st 2 ran

573[4] **THE EARTH MOVED (IRE)** 13-8 **Mrs S Godfrey** *Jogged rnd trckng family rival til disp ld 10-14 & agn nxt; qcknd & rcd properly frm 2 out; ld & outj rival at last; just hld on* 1
966[U] **Captain Random** 1-2F **Mrs J Reed** *(xnb) Jogged rnd ldng family rival at crawl; jmpd lft 7; jnd 10; slt ld 14; event started racing 2 out; hrd prsd til hdd last; r.o; just failed* . . . . s hd 2

OFFICIAL DISTANCE: s hd **TIME:** 7min 15.7s

1009 Open Maiden, 12st 4 ran

469[4] **HARJACH** 6-1 **N Wilmington** *(xnb) 2 handlers; ld 2; made rest; 4l up 5; fnd ex when prsd 15; tired when jmpd lft 2 out & last; all out; rdr celebrated passing post.* 1
693[2] **Collier** 2-1 **T Atkinson** *Ld 1; sn hdd; chsd ldr; 3l 2nd 7; dem last 12; 8l last 15; stayed on to chse wnr frm 3 out; nt able to chall.* 6 2
775[P] **Prioritisation (IRE)** (7a) 4-7F **A Farrant** *(xnb) 5l 3rd 3; rmdrs 12; 2nd & mist nxt; clsd 15; sn rdn; last & rmdrs 3 out; one pce; another disapp eff* . . . 2 1/2 3
967[U] Ashwicke Gambler 7-1 T Dreaper *(xnb) Ld rnd start; sa; a last; 15l adrift & hanging lft 3; jmpd lft 7; bhnd when pu 12* . . . . P

OFFICIAL DISTANCES: 6*l*, 2 1/2*l* **TIME:** 6min 28.9s

1010 Mens Open, 12st 2 ran

747[F] **RED NATIVE (IRE)** 1-6F **A Farrant** *Jw; made all; 12l up 3; drew rt away frm 7; 30l up 14; canter.* 1
703[P] **Dale Creek (IRE)** (7x) 5-1 **R Woollacott** *Bckwd; qckly outpcd; 15l adrift 5; drpd back 30l last 11; no imp* 1 1/4fs 2

OFFICIAL DISTANCE: dist **TIME:** 6min 30.3s

1011 Ladies Open 3 ran

690[2] **CENTO (IRE)** 4-6F **Miss C Stucley** *Hld up in last; 5 1/2l adrift 5; clsd 8; 2l 2nd 12; lft last 16; eff to ld 2 out; 2 1/2l up & lkd prob wnr when lft solo last* 1
882[2] **Father Jim** 3-1 **Miss C Tizzard** *Jw; ld; jnd brief 3; 4l up 5; hdd aft 14; ld agn 16-3 out; 2 1/2l down & lkd hld when pckd bad & rfo front last; event rmtd* 4min 2
965[3] Ardross Gem (IRE) (5a)(vis) 7-2 Miss W Southcombe *(bf) Chsd ldr mostly; disp ld brief 3; 2 1/2l down 7; ld aft 14; hdd & fell hvly 16; rdr airlifted* . . . . . F

OFFICIAL DISTANCE: dist **TIME:** 6min 25.4s

1012 Dodson & Horrell PPORA Club Members (Nov Rdrs), 12st — 5 ran

862^{3} **BLACKWATER BRAVE (IRE)** 3-1 **G Fry** *Ld to 2; disp 4l 4th 5; gd hdwy to 1½l 2nd 12; lost plce 14; chsd ldr frm 3 out; blun bad nxt; rallied v wl to ld last; rdn out; rdr's 1st wnr* . . . 1

603^{3} **Mr Ben Gunn** 2-1 **Miss V Heal** *(xnb) Chsd ldrs; 3l 3rd 5; ld 9; 1½l up 12; hdd last; r.o u.p flat; a just hld* . . . ½ 2

691^{U} **Millyhenry** 25-1 **R Lee** *Ld 2-8; 1l down 14; sn outpcd; stayed on one pce frm 3 out; snatched 3rd flat* . . . 15 3

Keitho (IRE) 5-4F D Green *(xnb) 5/2-5/4; disp 4l 4th 5; gd j 8; lost plce but still in tch 13; chsd ldr frm nxt til wknd 2 out; dem flat* . . . 1½ 4

455^{U} Nimbus Stratus(bl) 20-1 Miss J Sims *Last 2; rap hdwy to chse ldr nxt; ld 8-9; rn wide app 11; 3l 3rd 12; releg last 14; wknd qckly; t.o 3 out* . . . runin 5

OFFICIAL DISTANCES: ½l, 12l **TIME:** 6min 34.0s

This race was delayed for 45mins by the deployment of the air ambulance

1013 Restricted, 12st — 3 ran

693^{1} **ROSE OF THE HILL (IRE)** (7a) 2-9F **A Farrant** *(xnb) Chsd ldr; 1½l down 5; ld brief 7; disp ld 11-12; hit nxt; eff to ld agn 16; drvn & gd j last; pushed out flat* . . . 1

879^{P} **Romany Move** 5-1 **Mrs S Godfrey** *Last; 4½l down 5; hit nxt; lkd outpcd 8; hdwy to disp ld 11; ld nxt; hdd 16; ev ch 2 out; one pce* . . . 2½ 2

687^{U} **Jolie Roslin** (5a) 6-1 **Mrs F Vigar** *Ld; hdd brief 7; hdd 11; sn releg last; stdly lost tch frm 13; t.o 16* . . . 25 3

OFFICIAL DISTANCES: 3l, 25l **TIME:** 6min 34.3s

Worcestershire

Chaddesley Corbett (RH 8F,18J)

Sat, 17 Apr (GOOD, GOOD to SOFT in places)

1014 Hunt Members, 12st — 7 ran

660^{2} **CARTHAGO (IRE)** 8-15F **M Harris** *Ld 2; shkn up 3 out; r.o wl* . . . 1

726^{3} **Euro Bob (IRE)** 11-4 **Mrs A Rucker** *4s-11/4; went 4l 2nd 6; no imp und feeble handling frm 3 out* . . . 2½ 2

853^{6} **Always Good (IRE)**(tt) 33-1 **P Needham** *Ld to 2; 2nd til mist 6; disp 5l 3rd ½way; outpcd 12; wl bhnd 15* . . . runin 3

625^{4} Andre Laval (IRE) 16-1 Miss H Watson *(bf) Swtng; prom; jmpd slow 5; 7l 5th ½way; 15l 4th & drvn 12; t.o 15* . . . 25 4

614^{6} Merry Major 14-1 M Keel *(xnb) Hld up; hdwy 7; 5l 3rd & shkn up ½way; wknd u.p aft 11; t.o & pu 13* . . . P

661^{F} Optimistic Thinker (14ow) 40-1 A Shaw *A bhnd; 25l 6th ½way; t.o 11; furlongs bhnd when fell 2 out* . . . F

Waky Lady (IRE) (5a) 25-1 M Hammond *(xnb) Bckwd; jmpd delib in last pr; lost tch 7; t.o & pu 11* . . . P

OFFICIAL DISTANCES: 2½l, 30l **TIME:** 6min 14.1s

1015 Confined, 12st — 9 ran

41^{1} **HOT TODDY (IRE)** 7-4F **R Burton** *(xnb) 9/4-7/4; hld up; 5th ½way; hdwy 12; 2l 3rd nxt; ld aft 15; comf* . . . 1

756^{3} **The Campdonian (IRE)** (3x) 9-2 **E Walker** *Ld 4-6; 2nd/3rd to 13; chsd wnr 3 out; outj & one pce aft* . . . 3½ 2

662^{5} **The Archdeacon (IRE)** 25-1 **T Stephenson** *2nd/4th til lost plce 11; rallied nxt; jnd ldr 13; ev ch when blun 3 out; sn wknd* . . . 15 3

728^{P} Hijacked 13-2 Julian Pritchard *Ch ride; ld to 4 & 6-10; lost plce & 9l 7th 12; no ch aft; tk poor 4th last* . . . 1 4

834^{3} O J Selym (IRE) 40-1 G Opperman *2 handlers; hld up; 7th ½way; hdwy 11; 8l 6th & rdn 12; lost plce 14; lft poor 4th 3 out; dem last* . . . 4 5

752^{1} Karinga Lane 3-1 W Hill *(xnb,bf) 4s-3s; hld up; last 3-13; disp 8l 7th nxt; wknd 15* . . . 6 6

Blue Orleans 33-1 A Phillips *(xnb) Hld up; 8th ½way; wknd u.p 12; t.o & pu 3 out* . . . P

734^{4}	Bold Tactics (IRE) 3-1 M Keel *Hld up; 6th $^{1}/_{2}$way; shkn up 11; 6l 5th & rdn 14; blun & ur 15*		U
	Rubissimo (IRE)(bl) 25-1 M Harris *Went 2nd 5; ld 10 til hdd & stpd to nil aft 15; pu 3 out*		P

OFFICIAL DISTANCES: 4*l*, 15*l* **TIME:** 6min 23.3s

1016 Mens Open (Lady Dudley Cup), 3m2f - 20J — 11 ran

979^{1}	**CAUGHT AT DAWN (IRE)** 3-1 **T Weston** *Hld up; 6th $^{1}/_{2}$way; shkn up aft 12; hdwy & lft 3rd 14; ld 16; r.o wl*		1
758^{U}	**Out The Black (IRE)** 9-4JF **D Alers-Hankey** *Hld up; 5th $^{1}/_{2}$way; mist 11; blun & lost plce 12; hdwy 14; 6l 5th 16; went 3l 2nd nxt; switched inside 3 out; mist 2 out; btn when blun last*	5	2
836^{1}	**Watchyourback (NZ)**(vis,tt) 20-1 **R Hodges** *Chsd ldrs; 4th $^{1}/_{2}$way; lft 2nd 14-16; jmpd slow 17; sn wknd*	20	3
661^{1}	Haste Ye Back (IRE)(vis) 6-1 N Oliver *(xnb) Prom; went 2nd 5; ld 9-11; 5l 4th & rdn 16; wknd 17*	hd	4
758^{2}	Picket Piece(bl) 20-1 M Goldstein *2nd til ld 2; jmpd slow 5; hdd 9; ld 11; drvn 14; hdd 16; wknd aft nxt.*	7	5
615^{1}	Bright Beacon 5-1 E Williams *Hld up; 9th when carried out thro wing & ur 7*		C
734^{3}	Caher Society (IRE) 25-1 P Morris *Hld up; mist & rdr waved 5; last til aft 13; short-lived eff & 8l 7th 16; wl bhnd when pu 3 out.*		P
851^{1}	Coole Venture (IRE) 9-4JF R Burton *Hld up; hdwy 6; lost plce 9; 7th $^{1}/_{2}$way; went 2nd aft 12 til jmpd v slow 14; sn lost plce; 7l 6th 16; wl bhnd when pu 3 out*		P
597^{5}	Martha Jane (5a) 66-1 P Newton *(xnb,bh) Lw; 10th when fell 3*		F
836^{3}	Southern Cross 50-1 T Stephenson *Hld up; hdwy 8; 3rd $^{1}/_{2}$way; lost plce 13; 11l 8th 16; t.o when fell 2 out.*		F
743^{2}	The Kings Fling 16-1 Julian Pritchard *(xnb) Ld to 2; lost plce 6; 8th $^{1}/_{2}$way; lost tch aft 13; 20l last 16; t.o & pu 3 out.*		P

OFFICIAL DISTANCES: 5*l*, 25*l* **TIME:** 6min 52.5s

1017 Ladies Open, 3m2f - 20J — 7 ran

838^{1}	**UPTON ADVENTURE** (5a) 5-4 **Miss E James** *2nd til ld 6; hdd 8; ld 11; 5l clr 14; drew rt away 17; unchall*		1
869^{5}	**Lucky Master (IRE)** 33-1 **Miss G Swan** *Sn wl bhnd; 30l 5th 14; went dist 3rd 3 out; stayed on to 2nd nr fin.*	runin	2
664^{1}	**Step And Run (IRE)** 8-11F **Miss J Williams** *Evens-8/11; nt jw; hld up; rmdrs 8; 10l 3rd $^{1}/_{2}$way; went 15l 2nd app 17; no imp & nursed home aft; shkn up & dem nr fin*	hd	3
843^{6}	Welburn Boy(bl,tt) 25-1 Miss L Allfrey *Nd; 20l 5th $^{1}/_{2}$way; went poor 4th 12; lft 3rd 17; releg t.o last nxt*	20	4
891^{3}	Fanion De Nourry (FR) 11-1 Miss S Sharratt *Ld to 6; ld 8; mist 10; hdd 11; hit 13; wknd 16; 15l 3rd when ref & ur 17.*		r
923^{2}	Fuero Real (FR) 50-1 Miss H James *(bf) Sn wl bhnd; t.o 7; pu 10*		P
727^{P}	On The Run (IRE) (5a)(tt) 33-1 Mis A De Lisle Wells *Sn prom; lost plce 8; 15l 4th $^{1}/_{2}$way; wknd u.p 12; t.o & pu 14*		P

OFFICIAL DISTANCES: dist, nk **TIME:** 6min 53.4s

1018 Restricted, 12st — 8 ran

628^{P}	**MAGICIEN (FR)** 25-1 **Miss R Reynolds** *Hld up; hdwy & 4th $^{1}/_{2}$way; went 2nd 10; ld aft 11-2 out; rallied u.p to ld nr fin*		1
839^{7}	**Paddy Bettalot** 8-1 **T Stephenson** *A.p; went 2nd aft 6; ld 8-10; disp ld 14 & 15; ld 2 out til hdd nr fin*	hd	2
667^{1}	**Shaking Chief (IRE)** 3-1 **A Wintle** *Hld up; 6th $^{1}/_{2}$way; mist 10; hdwy & 1l 3rd 12; rdn 3 out; ev ch last; nt qckn*	s hd	3
665^{6}	Shemardi 9-4 R Hodges *3s-9/4; hld up; hdwy 8; 3rd $^{1}/_{2}$way; 2$^{1}/_{2}$l 5th 12; rdn 15; ev ch when blun last; nt rec*	7	4
715^{4}	Winning Town 20-1 Miss S Talbot *Jmpd v slow 2; rmdrs 3; hdwy to ld 4; hdd 8; ld 10 til aft nxt; wknd & 8l 5th 14*	12	5
387^{1}	Cousin George 2-1F R Burton *Ld to 3; 5th $^{1}/_{2}$way; drpd to rr aft 10; wl bhnd when pu 12*		P
384^{P}	The Lord Roberts (IRE) 7-1 Miss T Clark *(xnb) 2nd; ld 3-4; 2nd til rn v wide bend aft 6; 7th $^{1}/_{2}$way; 3l 6th 12; wknd 14; wl bhnd when pu 3 out* . . .		P
665^{U}	Watergate Boy (IRE) 20-1 D Mansell *(xnb) Hld up; last to 10; 5l 7th 12; wknd 14; wl bhnd when pu 3 out*		P

OFFICIAL DISTANCES: hd, hd **TIME:** 6min 25.7s

1019 Countryside Alliance Club Members Mares, 12st — 6 ran

714[1] **SOVEREIGN GALE (IRE)** (5a) 6-1 **M Harris** *(xnb) Ld to 11; 2nd til ld 3 out; drew 4l clr nxt; drvn out* . . . 1

925[5] **Campden Kitty** (5a) 9-2 **F Hutsby** *2 handlers; hld up; 5th ½way; went 3rd 11-14; releg last & rdn nxt; stayed on one pce 3 out; went 2nd flat* . . . 7 2

853[P] **Infamelia** (5a)(vis) 16-1 **Miss T Clark** *(xnb) Prom; went 2nd 7; ld 11; 4l clr 14; hdd 3 out; wknd & lost 2nd flat* . . . 2 3

668[1] Brown Seal (5a) 9-4JF N Oliver *Mist 3; 2nd/3rd to 7; 6l 5th 12; 4th & rdn aft 15; no imp* . . . 6 4

Proper Primitive (5a) 5-1 Miss E James *(bf) Sn prom; went 2nd 4-7; 5l 4th 12; went 5l 3rd 14; rdn & wkng when mist 2 out* . . . 3 5

728[5] Miss Moss (5a) 9-4JF R Rogers *Nt jw; rmdrs 3; lost tch u.p 11; wl bhnd when pu aft 13* . . . P

OFFICIAL DISTANCES: 8*l*, 2*l* **TIME:** 6min 19.7s

1020 Open Maiden, 12st — 16 ran

667[P] **CATCH THE BUS (IRE)** 5-1 **Miss S Sharratt** *10s-5s; 2 handlers; tk keen hld; 2nd/3rd to 8; 6l 4th ½way; went 7l 3rd 13; ld app 2 out; sn clr; rdn out* 1

982[P] **Rosegrove Rooster** 8-1 **T Stephenson** *W ldrs; 5l 3rd ½way; went 2nd aft 11; rdn when lft in ld 3 out; hdd app nxt; sn btn* . . . 10 2

981[P] **Ron Miel (IRE)** 16-1 **Miss R Reynolds** *Hld up; mist 3; hdwy 7; 8l 5th ½way; 6l 5th 12; went 8l 3rd 15; no ex 3 out* . . . 6 3

760[P] Contrary King 14-1 T Weston *Unruly padd & start; hld up; 11l 8th ½way; lost tch & 15l 9th 12; wl bhnd when pu 15* . . . P

Franco Lady (IRE) (5a) 10-1 Miss E James *(xnb) Hld up; hdwy & 9l 6th ½way; 8l 6th 12; wknd & 15l 5th 14; pu 15* . . . P

929[F] Fromrussiawithlove (12a, 3ow) 20-1 M Keel *(xnb) 2 handlers; hld up; mist 9; 12l 9th ½way; lost tch 11; t.o & pu 13* . . . P

754[P] Handsome Lad (IRE) 10-1 R Burton *Ss; a wl bhnd; 20l 12th ½way; 22l 10th 12; t.o & pu 14* . . . P

Holly Park (5a) 16-1 P Newton *(xnb) Bckwd; 13th when rn out 3* . . . R

840[P] Lord Woodyard(bl) 8-1 A Wintle *(xnb) Mist 3; 2nd til ld 5; hdd 9; 4l 3rd & drvn 12; nt r.o; wl bhnd when pu 14* . . . P

667[3] Penny Blue (12a, 4ow) 5-2F N Oliver *(xnb) 13th when blun & ur 1* . . . U

729[2] Red Spark 7-1 E Walker *(xnb) 12th when followed loose horse & rn out aft 3* R

760[2] Rody (IRE)(bl) 12-1 D Mansell *(xnb) Ld; mist 1; hdd 5; 2nd til ld 9; u.p when rn out 3 out* . . . R

519[3] Stockton Wolf 6-1 R Hodges *A bhnd; 18l 11th ½way; mist 11; 25l 11th nxt; t.o & pu 14* . . . P

929[U] Superior Footwork 20-1 P Morris *Ss; sn wl bhnd; jmpd v slow 3; 25l last ½way; t.o & pu aft 11* . . . P

The Well Lad (IRE) (7a, 1ow) 14-1 M Hammond *Hld up; mist 4; 13l 10th ½way; 12l 8th 12; pu 13* . . . P

256[P] Vaigly North (5a) 14-1 M Harris *Hld up; 10l 7th ½way; wknd 13; wl bhnd when pu 15* . . . P

OFFICIAL DISTANCES: 10*l*, 8*l* **TIME:** 6min 28.8s

Ystrad Taf Fechan

Ystradowen (LH 7F,18J)

Sat, 17 Apr (GOOD)

1021 Hunt Members, 12st — 7 ran

362[4] **COOLEEN STRONG (IRE)** 2-1 **L Stephens** *Ld to 4; stdd in 2nd til ld agn 14; drvn clr frm nxt; sn in comm* . . . 1

Foggy Hill (IRE) 6-1 **M Whitehouse** *1st ride; in tch 5; r.o frm 14 to 8l 2nd nxt; one pce & no ch w wnr aft* . . . 30 2

Orphan Spa (IRE) 20-1 **J Cook** *Hld up in 2nd til just ld 12; hdd aft 13; no ex uphill; lost tch clsng stages* . . . 25 3

Saffron Moss 11-2 R Bliss *Nt fluent & sev slow js; mostly last; lost tch 14; blun 2 out; completed in own time* . . . 6 4

695[P] Deep Dale(tt) 7-4F Miss F Wilson *Tde; mid-div til cl 3rd 6; tk 5l 2nd 14; wknd aft; pu aft 15* . . . P

736^{P} Evans The Coal 14-1 James Price *Jmpd rt; midfield; ld 5-11; wknd qckly & last 13; fnce bhnd when pu 15* . . . . P
982^{R} Pollerton Run (IRE) 12-1 G Davies *A rr; t.o when scrambled over 10; pu 11* P

OFFICIAL DISTANCES: 30*l*, 30*l* **TIME:** 6min 37.0s

1022 Restricted, 12st — 7 ran

740^{3} **LIKE THE BUZZ (IRE)** (5a) 10-1 **J Cook** *Settled 4th frm 3; mist 9; prog 14; 1l 2nd frm 3 out; $^{1}/_{2}$l down 2 out; ld flat* 1
736^{1} **Aljoash (IRE)** (5a) 4-5F **T Vaughan** *(xnb) Ww; mostly 5th til r.o 14; disp ld nxt; $^{1}/_{2}$l up 16 til hdd & hld flat* 2 2
354^{6} **Just Lark** 10-1 **R Bliss** *Rn in snatches; rr; went 2nd brief 13; 5th nxt & 3rd frm 3 out; nt trble ldrs* 12 3
819^{4} Italian Clover(bl) 33-1 Miss S Carter *Tubed; 2 handlers; swtng; ld 3; jnd 6; sn hdd; prom to 9; drvn & mist 11; rn wide downhill app 12; rr aft; nd* . . . runin 5
357^{P} Its A Handfull(tt) 33-1 J Price *A last pr; last frm 5; 8l adrift 7; lost tch 9; rallied frm 2 out to v dist 4th flat; disq - nt weigh-in* 4d
695^{4} Call Me Sonic 2-1 D Jones *A.p; ld 1-3 & 7-14; wknd 15; pu 2 out (reported to have twisted a shoe)* . . . . P
676^{1} Lady Palamon (IRE) (5a) 13-2 M Barber *(boh) A.p; 2nd 10 til disp ld 15; outpcd & jmpd slow 2 out; pu imm* . . . . P

OFFICIAL DISTANCES: 2*l*, 12*l* **TIME:** 6min 45.0s

Its A Handfull finished fourth but was disqualified when the rider failed to weigh-in; he was fined £40

1023 Confined, 12st — 6 ran

882^{4} **QUESTIONAIRE** (5a) evensF **M Barber** *A.p; ldng trio til ld 11; forged clr 14; fnce ahd 3 out; unchall.* 1
672^{P} **Rathgibbon (IRE)** 33-1 **J Merry** *Sn bhnd; detach 4; r.o downhill & sn w field; went rem 2nd but tired 3 out; nvr nr wnr; mist last* . . . . fence 2
Jakes Progress (IRE) 5-1 **Miss F Wilson** *Wl bhnd early; hdwy downhill to 5 & agn to 12; 7l 3rd 13; tired 15; blun last; eased flat; walked in* 30 3
612^{8} Coole'sabbot (IRE)(bl) 4-1 M Walters *Ld; hdd brief 5; hdd aft 10; 2nd to 12; 5th & fdng 13; pu 3 out; lame; has been retired* . . . . P
841^{3} Glen Mist (IRE)(bl) 6-1 L Stephens *Chsd ldrs in 3rd mostly; ld brief 5; rdn & rmdrs 11; went 2nd 13; sn fdd; pu 15* . . . . P
Pride Of Pennker (IRE) (5a) 33-1 M Flynn *In tch in 4th mostly til wkng & mist 12th; t.o & pu nxt.* . . . . P

OFFICIAL DISTANCES: dist, dist **TIME:** 6min 56.0s

1024 Mens Open, 12st — 6 ran

892^{P} **MISTER FALCON (FR)** (7x) 8-1 **R Hughes** *Trckd ldrs; 3rd to 7; cl 5th til rdn 14; ld nxt; qcknd clr frm 2 out.* 1
842^{4} **Khatani (IRE)**(tt) 5-2 **L Stephens** *Settled 4th; disp 3rd 10 & went 6l 2nd 12; chsd wnr vain aft; tired when mist last* 4 2
842^{2} **Persona Pride** 5-2 **D Jones** *Jw; ld; 6l up 12; 2l ahd 14; hdd 15 & outpcd aft; no ex* 6 3
841^{5} Fassan (IRE)(cp) 50-1 James Price *Trckd ldr in 2nd to 11; lost tch frm 13; t.o nxt.* 12 4
403^{11} September Harvest (USA) 50-1 R Shute *A last & sn strugg; t.o 9; jmpd slow 12; 50l adrift 3 out* 15 5
Shafi (IRE) 7-4F M Barber *Tk str hld & rstrnd in cl 4th; mist 4; disp 3rd brief 10; fell 13.* . . . . F

OFFICIAL DISTANCES: 4*l*, 7*l* **TIME:** 6min 51.0s

1025 Ladies Open — 5 ran

739^{2} **CHESNUT WOOD** 3-1 **Miss F Wilson** *Greased hind legs; trckd ldrs in 4th mostly; 2$^{1}/_{2}$l 4th 10; disp 2nd 14; ld nxt; sn 6l clr; mist 3 out & untidy last; unchall.* 1
843^{8} **Silver Pot Black** 4-1 **Miss H Lewis** *Mostly 2nd; disp 2nd 14; 3rd & no ex nxt; went 2nd agn app 2 out; a hld* 6 2
843^{7} **Head Gardener (IRE)**(bl) 14-1 **Miss J Hughes** *A last; lost tch 9; drvn & no resp 11; completed in own time* . . . . fence 3

952[1] Home Again (IRE) 10-11F Miss A Francis *1st ride; ld; nrly ur 1 & rdr rnd horses nk; mist 3; rn wide app 8; hdd aft 14; 2nd til tired 2 out; 18l 3rd & btn when ur last* . . . U
843[U] Young Manny 14-1 Mrs B Lewis *Cl 3rd til wknd qckly 12; pu & dism 13* . . . P

OFFICIAL DISTANCES: 6*l*, dist **TIME:** 6min 55.0s

1026 Open Maiden 56&7yo, 12st — 3 ran

CHANCY GUY 7-4 **L Stephens** *Ld 1; rn sltly wide bend bef 5; mist 6 & hdd aft nxt; cl 2nd til rdn 10; 3l 3rd 14; drvn to ld agn aft 15; 6l ahd nxt; drew clr; rdly* . . . 1
Coal Queen (12a) 9-2 **T Vaughan** *Last & jmpd slow 2; in tch 3; chsd ldr 11; 4l 2nd when lft in ld brief 15; sn outpcd & btn* . . . 25 2
735[2] Crystal Soldier (5a) 4-5F D Jones *Greased hind legs; 2nd til ld 8; 4l clr when fell 15* . . . F

OFFICIAL DISTANCE: 30*l* **TIME:** 7min 14.0s

1027 Open Maiden 8yo&up, 12st — 13 ran

621[3] **JOHNSTON'S VILLE (IRE)** 10-1 **J Merry** *Ww; settled 6th frm 7; hdwy to 4th 14 & 3rd 15; ld nxt; 1l up when lft clr at last* . . . 1
699[B] **Start It Up** 12-1 **J Price** *(xnb) 2nd til ld 8-15; 2nd til lost plce 2 out; no ch aft* 12 2
844[P] Caveat Graeci (IRE) (5a)(bl) 50-1 P Callaghan *Midfield & rmdrs 3; 4th 5; sn drpd to rr; t.o when jmpd slow 10 & pu* . . . P
840[P] Come On Boy 33-1 G Davies *A bhnd; 7th 9; t.o 13; pu 15* . . . P
844[P] Corn General(tt) 20-1 M Barber *(xnb,orbof) 5th to 5; in tch in midfield til fdd 9; rr when pu 12* . . . P
Drom Island (5a) 10-1 Miss F Wilson *Mid-div; 6th 6; hdwy to 3rd 12; wknd uphill; pu 14* . . . P
Imustgeton (5a)(tt) 14-1 D Davies *Reared up padd & mounted outside; rr; 9th 3; impd to cl 3rd 9 til outpcd uphill frm 13; wknd qckly; pu 15* . . . P
948[5] Market Value (IRE)(bl) 10-1 L Stephens *Last trio; mist 8; hdwy to 5th 12 & 3rd 14; sn btn; t.o 4th & tired when pu 2 out* . . . P
948[P] Millenium Run (IRE) 7-2 J Cook *Mostly 7th; hdwy to 4th 15 & 3rd nxt; tk 2nd app 2 out; 1l down & ev ch when fell hvly last; down for sev mins* . . . F
736[P] Miss Charlotte (5a) 3-1 R Bliss *A bhnd; ur 10* . . . U
Newmarket Magic (IRE) evensF D Jones *Trckd ldrs; mist 6; ld 14; hdd u.p 15; wknd rap; pu 3 out* . . . P
844[P] Saronica's Boy 33-1 James Price *T.o last by 3; jmpd v slow & mist 5; fnce bhnd when pu 8* . . . P
677[2] Westar Lad (IRE) 3-1 T Vaughan *(xnb) Pulling; ld; 10l clr 2; stdd & 1l up 5; hdd 8 & releg 4th; rr when crashing fall 12; down for sev mins* . . . F

OFFICIAL DISTANCE: 15*l* **TIME:** 7min 00.0s

Carlisle (RH 9F,18J)

Sun, 18 Apr (GOOD to SOFT)

1028 Cumberland Mdn HC, 3m £1624 — 6 ran

440[2] **BLACK SMOKE (IRE)** 11-11 15-8F **D Jewett** *Cl up; hit 4; outpcd aft 14; rallied to ld 2 out; kpt on wl* . . . 1
919[R] **Mid Summer Lark (IRE)** 11-00(vis) 16-1 **M Seston** *Made most til hdd 2 out; one pce last* . . . 6 2
797[2] **Miss Royello** 11-09 9-4 **Miss P Robson** *Chsd ldrs; outpcd 8; rallied 12; wknd frm 4 out* . . . 26 3
762[5] How Burn 11-04 14-1 Mrs V Jackson *Bhnd frm 5; t.o & pu aft 9* . . . P
657[3] Lethem Air 11-00 4-1 P Kinsella *Sn prom; mist 12; sn btn; t.o & pu 3 out* P
507[1] Roscoe Burn 11-04 8-1 M McAlister *Disp ld to 5; hit 7; cl up til outpcd 11; t.o & pu 4 out* . . . P

TIME: 6min 30.2s **TOTE:** £2.40; places £1.70,£4.30 **Ex:**£66.10 **CSF:**£24.69

Stratford (LH 8F,18J)

Sun, 18 Apr (GOOD to FIRM, GOOD in places)

1029 John & Nigel Thorne Mem HC, 3m £2926 10 ran

438[1] **CHASING THE BRIDE** 12-02 5-2 **Miss A Goschen** *Hld up; hdwy 10; went 2nd app 14; ld & lft clr 3 out* . . . 1
801[C] **News Flash (IRE)** 11-07 50-1 **Miss L Brooke** *Ld 2 til app 9; chsd ldr til app 14; hit 14; wkng when mist 15; lft 2nd 3 out* . . . 29 2
891[U] **Mickthecutaway (IRE)** 11-07 11-1 **D Skelton** *Ld to 2; lost plce 4; bhnd when mist 15* . . . 15 3
706[4] Lirkimalong 11-09 25-1 Miss S Young *Sn wl bhnd* . . . 12 4
843[4] Millennium Gold 11-07 20-1 Miss A Frieze *Prom; hit 8; rdn 11; mist 12; sn wknd* . . . 17 5
444[9] Be Bop Bentley 11-07 125-1 A Maskill *Prom; nt fluent 2; sn lost plce; t.o when ref & ur 13* . . . r
545[5] Chicago City (IRE) 11-09 15-2 Ms A Embiricos *Fell 1* . . . F
866[3] Steve Ford 11-07 40-1 Miss E Harbour *Sn wl bhnd; fell 8* . . . F
869[1] The Granby (IRE) 11-07 10-11F Miss H Irving *Prom; went 2nd 4; ld app 9; rdn & hdd when blun & ur 3 out* . . . U
679[4] West Pal (IRE) 12-01 50-1 A Humphrey *Fell 1* . . . F

TIME: 6min 16.8s **TOTE:** £3.60; places £1.60,£12.10,£1.80 **Ex:**£106.00 **CSF:**£111.77

Bicester with Whaddon Chase

Mollington (RH 8F,18J)

Sun, 18 Apr (GOOD, GOOD to SOFT in places becoming SOFT)

1030 Hunt Members 3 ran

583[P] **TRUE CHIMES**(bl) 9-4 **J Owen** *(xnb) Made most at little more than a walk to 13; releg 3rd 14 til aft 3 out; sn prsd ldr; 1l down last; drvn to ld flat* . . 1
587[3] **Shortcut Shorty** 4-7F **C Wadland** *Mostly trckd ldr; ld 13; started rcng properly frm 15; 1l up last; hdd & nt qckn flat* . . . 3/4 2
Tellaporky 5-1 **H Owen** *(xnb) 1st P-t-P ride (27yrs aft hanging up boots und Rules); hld up; went 2nd 14 til aft 3 out; outpcd 2 out* . . . 6 3

OFFICIAL DISTANCES: 1/2*l*, 5*l* **TIME:** 8min 18.0s

This race was a farce, the first 1 1/2 miles too more than five minutes

1031 Confined, 12st 7 ran

783[3] **TEETON PRICELESS** (5a) 2-1 **P Cowley** *Ld; jnd 15; rdn & hdd 2 out; rallied to ld agn last; stayed on wl* . . . 1
717[3] **Mister Pepper (IRE)** 7-1 **T Underwood** *Hld up in detach last pr; prog to chse clr ldng pr 13; no imp til eff 2 out; r.o & ev ch last; nt qckn flat* . . . 2 2
783[2] **My Best Buddy** 4-5F **N Pearce** *Cl up; mists 10 & 11; eff to disp ld 15; drvn to ld 2 out; hdd & mist last; wknd* . . . 3 1/2 3
783[4] Tale Bridge (IRE)(vis) 33-1 J Russell *Detach 5th; eff to chse ldng pr brief aft 12; sn outpcd in 4th; nd aft* . . . 20 4
630[P] Camitrov (FR) 14-1 G Kerr *(xnb) Chsd ldr to 2 & agn 8-11; wknd 13; sn wl t.o* runin 5
869[7] Gortroe Guy (IRE) 33-1 Miss K Robinson *(xnb) Chsd wnr 2-8; 4th when blun 10; wknd 12; t.o 6th when fell 15* . . . F
784[P] Sea Victor 33-1 M Grange *A detach in last pr; wknd rap 12; t.o nxt; rfo 15* U

OFFICIAL DISTANCES: 1 1/2*l*, 3*l* **TIME:** 6min 38.0s

1032 Mens Open 7 ran

650[2] **CHORAL DREAM (IRE)** 4-6F **N Pearce** *Cl up; eff to ld 13; jnd 3 out; drvn nxt; finally fnd ex to ld last 50yds* . . . 1
867[3] **Romany Pearl**(cp) 6-1 **J Owen** *Towards rr; nt fluent 7; 7l 5th & pushed along 10; kpt on u.p frm 14; clsd 3 out; ev ch last; no ex final 50yds (gd eff & wl rdn)* . . . 1 1/2 2

784^{3}	**Bullfinch** 4-1 **P Cowley** *Made most to 13; jnd wnr agn 3 out; ev ch last; nt qckn final 50yds*	nk	3
979^{P}	Paddies Boy (IRE)(cp) 16-1 Jack Young *Rcd wide; w ldrs; ld brief 12; awkward nxt; cl 4th aft 3 out; kpt on game und feeble rdng flat.*	¾	4
922^{U}	Border Farmer (IRE) 33-1 N Wain *Rdr wobbled 4 & drpd to last; t.o & miles bhnd when pu 9*		P
18^{U}	Celtic Season 6-1 C Wadland *(xnb) Chsd ldrs; wknd aft 13; jmpd slow aft; t.o & pu last*		P
818^{2}	Felloo (IRE) 20-1 E Walker *Settled off pce; 15l 6th & no prog when slithered on landing 13; nt rec; pu nxt*		P

OFFICIAL DISTANCES: 1½l, ½l **TIME:** 6min 44.0s

1033 Ladies Open - 14J — 4 ran

869^{3}	**RYANS STAR** 5-4 **Mrs J Parris** *Hld up; mostly chsng ldr frm 8; eff 2 out; narrow ld & mist last; tired flat but hld on*		1
891^{U}	**Kentford Busy B** (5a) 4-5F **Miss S Phizacklea** *Cl up; ld 8; 3l clr 3 out; narrowly hdd & blun last; tired but kpt on flat; just hld.*	nk	2
785^{5}	**Ela Agapi Mou (USA)**(bl) 20-1 **Miss D Ball** *Ld 4-5; outpcd & wl bhnd 13; 25l last by-passing 15; no ch aft; stayed on wl flat & clsng on tiring ldng pr.*	12	3
	Handley Park 12-1 Miss L Ellis *Ld to 4; ld 5-8; cl 3rd when slithered on landing 12; nt rec; last & wkng when fell 13*		F

OFFICIAL DISTANCES: ½l, 10l **TIME:** 6min 40.0s

Fences 3 & 11 and 7 & 15 (ditch) were omitted from this and all subsequent races - state of going

1034 Restricted, 12st - 13J — 6 ran

582^{5}	**CRESTED MANOR** 6-1 **A Sansome** *Wl in tch; chsd ldr 14; rdn to ld aft 2 out; kpt on wl*		1
787^{2}	**Teeton Fizz** (5a) 4-5F **N Pearce** *Disp 2nd bhnd clr ldr; pushed along 10; drvn 12; ld by-passing 13; hdd & btn aft 2 out; fin tired.*	8	2
787^{4}	**Lah Di Dah Lad** 6-4 **J Tarry** *3s-6/4; in tch; went cl 4th 14; sn chsd ldng pr; no imp 2 out; btn when mist last*	5	3
587^{9}	Button Boy 8-1 P Cowley *Disp 2nd bhnd clr ldr; drvn 12; sn wknd; t.o 14.*	35	4
467^{U}	Rightun 4-1 T Ellis *(xnb) 2 handlers; noseband came loose padd & horse v unsettled; keen; ld & sn 6l clr; mist 12; hdd by-passing 13; wknd rap*	6	5
720^{P}	Darkarrow (IRE) 14-1 J Owen *(xnb) Hld up in last; wknd 12; t.o & pu 14*		P

OFFICIAL DISTANCES: 6l, 4l **TIME:** 6min 38.5s

Fence 13 also omitted - damaged

1035 Open Maiden, 12st - 12J — 10 ran

172^{2}	**SIMPLY THE ONE (IRE)** 1-2F **H Fowler** *Prom; ld 10; blun 12; shkn up 2 out; in comm app last*		1
	Sovereign Dove (12a) 8-1 **F Hutsby** *2 handlers; settled in rr; prog & 3rd ½way; chsd wnr app 2 out; kpt on stdly; a hld*	4	2
788^{P}	**Teeton Diamond** (5a) 8-1 **N Pearce** *Prom; ld 9-10; chsd wnr til app 2 out; wknd app last*	12	3
788^{P}	Cowslip Lace (5a) 16-1 J Owen *Jmpd slow 4; last pr; wkng when hit 12 & pu*		P
789^{P}	Fawsley Lake (5a) 16-1 P Cowley *Mist 2; midfield; 6th & in tch ½way; wknd 13; t.o & pu 3 out*		P
	Gerry Watson 14-1 J King *Sn ld; hdd 9; reluct & imm gave up aft nxt; pu by-passing 11*		P
	Les The Lizard 14-1 T Allanson *2 handlers; midfield; 6th when mist & ur 6*		U
871^{4}	Rockford (IRE) 4-1 C Wadland *Chsd ldrs; mist 2; jmpd lft 4; 4th ½way; wknd 13; poor 4th when slpd up bef 3 out*		S
725^{P}	Ski Country (5a) 7-1 A Martin *Chsd ldrs; mist 10; 5th & pushed along ½way; lost tch 12; t.o 5th when slpd up bef 3 out*		S
594^{P}	Trust Ger 33-1 Miss H Phizacklea *2 handlers; a rr; bhnd frm 8; t.o when mist & ur 12*		U

OFFICIAL DISTANCES: 3l, 6l **TIME:** 6min 50.0s

Fences 5 & 13 were also omitted - damaged

Braes of Derwent

Corbridge (RH 9F,18J)

Sun, 18 Apr (GOOD, GOOD to FIRM in places)

1036 Hunt Members — 4 ran

Form	Horse	Dist	Pos
857^{3}	**EMPEROR'S MAGIC (IRE)**(cp,tt) 2-5F **Miss S Ward** *Settled detach last; still 12l down 13; clsd qckly 15 to ld app 2 out; sn clr*		1
762^{2d}	**Hadaway Lad** 3-1 **Miss C Metcalfe** *Ld til app 6; cl 2nd til ld agn 3 out; hdd app nxt; imm outpcd*	12	2
763^{P}	**Dannicus** (4ow) 12-1 **A McElwee** *Ld at slow pce app 6; nt fluent 7; hdd 3 out; tired rap*	15	3
	Seaburn 20-1 W Barron *(xnb) Bckwd; rn loose rnd boxes bef rce; fat; 2 handlers; pulling in 2nd til insecure rfo front 6*		U

OFFICIAL DISTANCES: 15*l*, 20*l* **TIME:** 6min 24.0s **TOTE:** £1.50

1037 Intermediate, 12st — 7 ran

Form	Horse	Dist	Pos
764^{3}	**THREE SPIRES** 5-4F **A Richardson** *Lw; cl up & gng wl; went 2nd 14; rdn to ld last; kpt on stout*		1
808^{2}	**Trooper Collins (IRE)**(tt) 3-1 **G Tuer** *Lw; settled in tch; went $1\frac{1}{4}$l 3rd 15; rdn & fnd little app 2 out; snatched 2nd.*	$1\frac{1}{2}$	2
766^{1}	**Royalecko** 7-1 **Miss J Hollands** *Jw; ld app 4; hrd prsd frm 15; drvn & hdd last; nt qckn*	hd	3
655^{4}	Rainton 10-1 Miss N Stirling *(xnb) 2 handlers; oht; mounted on course; tde; pulled hrd; went 2nd brief 6; cl up til 4l 4th 15; wknd app 2 out*	7	4
765^{1}	Briery Hill 7-1 T Morrison *(xnb) 2 handlers; tde & mounted on way; jmpd slow 3; ld til app 4; nrly a 2nd to 14; sn fdd; last when mist 3 out.*	15	5
855^{3}	The Cincinnati Kid 10-1 R Green *(xnb) Rr but in tch til wknd aft 14; wl bhnd when eased flat*	7	6
563^{7}	Jupiter's Fancy (5a) 12-1 M Coglan *Swtng; rdr unstdy & sn last; 10l down 9; hit 12 & ur*		U

OFFICIAL DISTANCES: 1*l*, nk **TIME:** 6min 17.0s **TOTE:** £1.40

1038 Mens Open — 7 ran

Form	Horse	Dist	Pos
764^{5}	**CREVAMOY (IRE)** (5a) 12-1 **J Galbraith** *Hld up last; 12l down 9; went 5th 14; str rn frm 3 out; sn ld flat; sprinted clr; impressive (1st win for 48yo rdr)*		1
915^{P}	**Wild Edgar (IRE)** 25-1 **A Richardson** *Swtng profuse; ld rnd start; rcd free; ld to 6; 2nd til ld agn app 13; hdd nxt; drvn & ld brief last; imm outpcd flat*	$1\frac{1}{2}$	2
894^{1}	**Son Of Anshan**(tt) 5-4F **G Tuer** *Lw; 2nd/3rd til ld 14; rdn & hdd when hit last; imm btn*	7	3
917^{U}	Just Barney Boy 2-1 A Waugh *2 handlers; prom; ld 6 til app 13; 2l 3rd app 2 out; sn wknd*	4	4
858^{1}	Lively Dessert (IRE) 6-1 K Anderson *Opened 7s; lw; midfield; rmdrs 12; no resp; wknd aft 15*	10	5
764^{11}	Wensley Blue (IRE) (7a) 33-1 W Goldie *Last trio; strugg app 13*	15	6
917^{P}	Gaultier Gale (IRE) 12-1 A Findlay *Towards rr; outpcd 13 & last nxt; poor 6th when crashing fall 3 out*		F

OFFICIAL DISTANCES: $3\frac{1}{2}$*l*, 3*l* **TIME:** 6min 08.0s **TOTE:** £8.30

1039 Ladies Open — 5 ran

Form	Horse	Dist	Pos
798^{P}	**PHARMISTICE (IRE)** (7x) 6-4 **Miss N Stirling** *(xnb) Hld up in tch; ld 12; jmpd best aft; outbattled rival frm 2 out; stayed on wl*		1
916^{3}	**Balisteros (FR)** (7x) evensF **Miss P Robson** *Cl up; jmpd slow 5; ld 7-12; rdn app nxt; outj aft; ev ch when mist 3 out; drvn along but nt keen frm nxt; a hld.*	4	2
763^{4}	**Knockholt** 7-1 **Miss A Pattinson** *Handy; 2nd brief 11; 6l 3rd 13; nd frm 15*	8	3
916^{5}	Houselope Beck 20-1 Miss A Wanless *(xnb) Mostly 2nd til lost plce 11; 15l last & strugg 15; ur 3 out*		U
678^{6}	Piper's Rock (IRE) 20-1 Miss V Russell *(xnb) Rn free & made most til mist 6 & hdd; last by 9; pu 10*		P

OFFICIAL DISTANCES: 3*l*, 6*l* **TIME:** 6min 10.0s **TOTE:** £4.60

1040 Restricted — 6 ran

563[3]	**MISTER BROMLEY** 5-2 **Miss S Brotherton** *3s-5/2; cl up; ld 7; drew 10l clr 3 out; stayed on str; v easily*		1
766[7]	**Little John** 7-1 **J Galbraith** *Cl up; ld app 6 til jmpd slow 7; outpcd frm 13; 16l 4th 3 out; some rnwd prog to 2nd flat*	12	2
855[4]	**The Broken Man** 16-1 **Miss K Bryson** *Jmpd slow 5; ld til app 6; rdn frm 9; outpcd in 9l 3rd 15; chsd wnr vain 2 out til mist last*	4	3
856[1]	Nodform Returns (5a) 7-2 K Anderson *Hld up in tch; lft 2nd 14; 7l down & outpcd nxt; wknd & lost 2 plces frm 3 out*	4	4
855[6]	C L B Jemilla (5a) 33-1 Miss G Craggs *Stdd & lost 10l start; a last & wl bhnd frm 13*	nk	5
854[1]	Decent Bond (IRE) 5-4F R Green *Hld up; eff 11; went 2nd 13; 1l down when rfo nxt.*		U

OFFICIAL DISTANCES: 10*l*, 4*l* **TIME:** 6min 26.0s **TOTE:** £3.60

1041 Open Maiden — 7 ran

768[4]	**GENERAL JAKE (IRE)** 4-1 **J Innes** *Ld 5; drew 3l clr 15; stayed on wl*		1
765[2]	**Uncle Neil (IRE)** 4-6F **R Morgan** *Opened evens; ld to 5; chsd wnr aft but rcd awkward frm 9 & nvr lkd v keen; 3l 2nd when mist 15; hrd rdn & fnd nil frm nxt*	5	2
857[4]	**St Bee** 4-1 **A Richardson** *A 3rd; hit 10; ev ch til 6l down & outpcd 14; rdn & desperately one-pcd aft*	6	3
856[U]	Red Jupiter 16-1 T Scott *Midfield; wknd 12; 20l 4th 15*	12	4
859[P]	Kanturk Star (IRE) 16-1 Miss L Kendall *Tubed; 15l last when pckd 4; clsd 8 to 5th nxt; wknd 14; 22l last 15; plugged on*	2	5
658[P]	Ellemford (5a) 40-1 W Goldie *Bhnd; mist 1; hit 4; lost tch 9; t.o & pu 12.*		P
433[P]	Spring Rock 33-1 C Shirley-Beavan *(xnb) Towards rr & some errors; wknd u.p 12; t.o 3 out; pu last*		P

OFFICIAL DISTANCES: 7*l*, 4*l* **TIME:** 6min 19.0s **TOTE:** £5.10

1042 Panacur/TBA PPORA Club Members Mares Maiden, 12st — 6 ran

814[3]	**HATTIE** (5a) 3-1 **P Cornforth** *(xnb) Ld & pulled hrd; hvly rstrnd til allowed to stride 15l clr 4; 30l ahd when hit 10, skidded & nrly came to halt; 12l up 15; drew clr agn aft nxt.*		1
919[2]	**Coquet Gold** (5a) 9-2 **Miss C Walton** *Chsd wnr frm 4 but nvr within 12l; brief eff 15; rdn & wknd 2 out.*	20	2
856[2]	Anniejo (12a) 9-4F R Morgan *(xnb) Ref to rce*		r
920[6]	Midnight Reiver (5a)(tt) 10-1 Miss J Hollands *(xnb) Cl up in chsng group; blun 8; nt fluent 9; stpd to nil 10; t.o 11; pu 13*		P
658[P]	Reeker Pike (5a) 25-1 J Thompson *Nt fluent; cl up in chsng group til 15l last 4; went 3rd nxt but hit 3 out; wl btn when blun bad & ur nxt*		U
813[6]	Tullineaskey Kitty (IRE) (5a) 7-2 C Dawson *Opened 4s; jmpd lft in chsng quartet; 13l 3rd 14; last frm nxt; t.o & pu last*		P

OFFICIAL DISTANCE: 20*l* **TIME:** 6min 35.0s **TOTE:** £5.20

Cheshire

Alpraham (RH 7F,16J*)
Sun, 18 Apr (SOFT)

1043 Hunt Members — 2 ran

848[1]	**RAISEAPEARL** 7-4 **I Clyde** *Trckd ldr; ld 5-9; ld 12; 10l clr 3 out; v easily.*		1
876[2]	**Master Club Royal** 2-5F **G Hanmer** *Ld at stdy pce; jmpd slow & hdd 5; ld 10; rmdrs 11; mist & hdd nxt; sn btn; hrd rdn & no resp frm 3 out*	20	2

OFFICIAL DISTANCE: 20*l* **TIME:** 8min 15.8s

** Fences 5 & 13 (fences 1 & 9 in 2m4f) were omitted from all races - state of going*

1044 Open Maiden, 12st — 7 ran

934[4]	**RIDWARE GEORGE**(bl) 6-4F **Miss S Sharratt** *Opened 2s; made virt all; hdd brief last; stayed on u.p*		1
985[F]	**Top Weld** 20-1 **J Jarrett** *(xnb) 2 handlers; in tch; last 10; mist 12; hdwy & chall 2 out; ld brief last; unable to qckn flat.*	nk	2

Mullarts Lad (IRE) (7a) 20-1 **S Ross** *Ww in tch; blun 12; 5l 6th 3 out; chall & ev ch nxt; unable to qckn flat* . . . 1 3
751U Sharp Embrace 8-1 J Burley *Prsd ldr; jmpd slow 7; blun 8; cl 4th when blun bad 3 out; sn rdn; 5th nxt; kpt on u.p frm last* . . . 1½ 4
748P Strong King (IRE)(cp) 7-1 W Kinsey *Trckd ldrs; ld brief 9; ev ch 3 out; wknd app last* . . . 1 5
848⁴ Whats Up Jake 5-2 A Wadlow *(xnb) Hld up in last; prog to 4th app 11; cl 3rd 3 out; wknd app last* . . . 2 6
985U Robert The Rascal 8-1 J R Barlow *Ww in tch; 4l 5th when blun bad & rdr lost iron 3 out; nt rec; pu nxt* . . . P

OFFICIAL DISTANCES: nk, 1½l **TIME:** 8min 15.0s

1045 Confined, 12st — 7 ran

748¹ **ANALYSTIC (IRE)** (3ow) 9-4 **G Hanmer** *(xnb) Made all; mists 7 & 12; drew clr app 3 out; in comm aft* . . . 1
873⁶ **Barneys Gold (IRE)** 20-1 **Miss G Garton** *(xnb) Mist 2; chsd ldr 3-5; 7l 5th 11; sn outpcd; stayed on frm 3 out; went 2nd at last; no ch w wnr* . . . 20 2
852² **Pagermar (IRE)** evensF **R Burton** *Opened 6/4; ww; prog to 2nd 9-10; 4th & rdn nxt; 8l 3rd when jmpd slow 13; no ch aft* . . . 12 3
750⁵ Whitegates Willie 12-1 D Greenway *Pckd 1; hld up; 10l 6th 9; lost tch app 12; t.o* 15 4
847² Jona Holley(cp) 33-1 Miss A Blake *(xnb) Bhnd; jmpd slow 5; last & t.o frm nxt; pu & dism 10* . . . P
986³ Three Saints (IRE) 6-1 D Barlow *Chsd ldr 5-9; mist nxt; outpcd by wnr 13; tired when blun bad 2 out; 4th & no ch when pu last* . . . P
711³ Warner For Players (IRE) (5x) 6-1 A Wadlow *Ww in tch; cl 4th 10; outpcd 12; 5th & no ch when pu & dism last* . . . P

OFFICIAL DISTANCES: 20l, 12l **TIME:** 7min 58.3s

1046 Ladies Open — 3 ran

849¹ **WANDERING LIGHT (IRE)** 4-5F **Miss T Clark** *Trckd ldr 4; ld 8; 2l clr 3 out; drew wl clr app last; eased flat* . . . 1
849² **Cascum Lad (IRE)** 2-1 **Miss S Holmes** *Mist & drpd to last 4; 5l 3rd when mist 12; still in tch & rdr motionless app 2 out; outpcd by wnr app last; rdn & went 2nd nr fin* . . . 6 2
987² **Class Of Ninetytwo (IRE)** 2-1 **Miss S Sharratt** *Ld to 8; chsd wnr aft; drvn along 13; outpcd by wnr app last; lost 2nd nr fin* . . . nk 3

OFFICIAL DISTANCES: 6l, nk **TIME:** 8min 00.0s

1047 Mens Open, 12st — 3 ran

873² **BORDER RUN** 5-2 **S Ross** *Hld up in 3rd; a gng wl; went 2nd on bridle 3 out; jnd wnr app nxt; ld last; rdn clr* . . . 1
988¹ **Step On Eyre (IRE)** (7x) 1-3F **R Burton** *Chsd ldr; ld 8-9 & agn 13; rdn app 2 out; hdd last; sn btn* . . . 8 2
873⁴ **Chadswell (IRE)** (7x) 11-2 **W Puddifer** *Ld; jmpd slow 7; hdd nxt; ld agn 9 til hdd & mist 13; btn 3 out; no ch when crawled over last* . . . 20 3

OFFICIAL DISTANCES: 8l, 25l **TIME:** 8min 01.0s

1048 Restricted, 12st — 7 ran

933⁴ **CUTINA** (5a) 5-2JF **D Barlow** *Chsd ldrs; 4l 3rd 13; ev ch 2 out; ld last; drifted lft flat; hld on wl* . . . 1
877¹ **Clodagh Valley (IRE)** 10-1 **W Kinsey** *Ww in tch; prog to 3l 3rd 11; went 2nd 13; ld 2 out; hdd last; switched rt flat; r.o; just failed* . . . ½ 2
985¹ **Iadora** (5a) 5-2JF **Miss T Clark** *Tk keen hld; trckd ldrs til ld 5; hdd 13; ld agn aft 3 out; hdd & blun nxt; sn wknd* . . . 20 3
847¹ Henbury Dancer (5a) 6-1 G Hanmer *Tde; hld up; smooth prog to ld 13; hdd aft 3 out; imm btn; no ch when pu 2 out* . . . P
990S Ridware Pride 7-2 Miss S Sharratt *2 handlers; ld to 5; cl up til rdn 13; 6l 5th when blun nxt; no ch aft; pu 2 out* . . . P
933² Templenoe Hare (IRE) 7-2 R Burton *Hld up; blun bad 2; trckd ldrs 9; rdn & outpcd app 12; 6th & no ch 3 out; pu nxt* . . . P
423¹ The Sky Is Blue 6-1 M Caldwell *In tch; last frm 5; blun 11; sn lost tch; wl bhnd when pu nxt* . . . P

OFFICIAL DISTANCES: ½l, 20l **TIME:** 8min 03.0s

1049 Open Maiden 56&7yo, 2m4f, 12st - 12J — 10 ran

985P **MOSSCROFT JACK**(tt) 8-1 **Miss T Clark** *(xnb) Ww in tch; prog 6; cl 3rd 9; ld 2 out; stayed on u.p flat* 1

Carnalway (IRE) 4-1 **D Barlow** *Chsd ldrs; mist 4; ld nxt; hdd 2 out; hung lft & no ex u.p flat; fin tired* 1½ 2

Neminos (IRE) (7a)(tt) 9-2 **A Wadlow** *Ld; clr to 4; hdd nxt; cl up; lft 6l 3rd 3 out; wknd nxt; fin tired* 20 3

710P Blue Jar 12-1 S Ross *Mid-div; wl in tch til outpcd 8; sn no ch; went mod 4th nr fin* 4 4

929[5] Mandagus (IRE) 5-2F G Hanmer *5s-5/2; 2 handlers; hld up; prog 7; 5th & outpcd 9; lft mod 4th nxt; no ch aft* . . . . . ½ 5

Bradogue (IRE) 14-1 W Kinsey *Prom til wknd qckly app 8; wl bhnd when pu 9* P

877F Button Lady (12a) 7-1 D Gaiter *Rcd wide; in tch til hanging & wknd qckly app 8; sn wl bhnd; t.o & pu 3 out* . . . . . P

929[3] Mervsintrouble(cp) 3-1 D Greenway *Rcd wide; chsd ldrs; 3rd & ev ch when rn out thro wing & ur 3 out* . . . . . R

754P Missuslarge (5a) 10-1 R Burton *(xnb) Cl up til 5th & wknd 9; no ch nxt; t.o & pu 2 out* . . . . . P

Muqadars Delight (7a) 10-1 B Shaw *Nt a fluent; rr but in tch; mist 3; wknd 8; t.o & pu 2 out* . . . . . P

OFFICIAL DISTANCES: 2*l*, 25*l* **TIME:** 6min 00.0s

East Sussex & Romney Marsh

Catsfield (RH 8F,18J)

Sun, 18 Apr (GOOD to SOFT)

1050 Hunt Members, 12st — 5 ran

744[5] **DIXON VARNER (IRE)** (3ow) 7-4 **F Marshall** *Jw; made all; rdr kpt lkng rnd; narrow advant til rmdrs aft 14; stayed on wl frm 3 out* 1

640U **Brackenheath (IRE)**(cp) 6-4F **Miss H Grissell** *Prsd wnr; mist 9; niggled along 14; 5l down & hrd rdn 3 out; slt prog & ch when mist last; kpt on one pce flat* 3 2

Daydreamer (USA) 9-4 **A Hickman** *Hld up; trckd ldng pr frm 9; 6l 3rd 3 out; wkng u.p when jmpd slow 2 out; eased app last* 15 3

778P Acuteangle (IRE) (5a) 10-1 J Wall *Cl 3rd to 8; 10l 4th aft 11; lsng tch when blun & almost fell 12; imm pu* . . . . . P

Jojo (IRE) (11ow) 10-1 G Barker *1st ride; last frm 6; lost tch 9; t.o 12; 2 fncs bhnd when ref 2 out* . . . . . r

OFFICIAL DISTANCES: 3*l*, 20*l* **TIME:** 7min 08.0s **TOTE:** £2.30; places £2.50,£1.50 **DF:**£3.70

1051 Restricted, 12st — 5 ran

639[3] **GRANNY SMITH (IRE)** (5a) 6-4F **C Gordon** *Narrow advant to 11; disp ld 12 til hdd aft 15; hrd rdn frm 3 out; prsd ldr app nxt; kpt on game to ld agn flat* 1

803[1] **Lord Of The North (IRE)** 2-1 **P York** *Hld up in detach last to 9; impd to 5l 3rd aft 12; smooth hdwy to jn ldr 3 out; sn ld; slt advant 2 out; pushed along & jnd last; wknd flat* 2 2

897[3] Kniveniven (IRE) 10-1 Mrs J Gordon *Cl 2nd to 10; 4l 3rd aft 11; lost tch frm nxt; wl bhnd when pu aft 15* . . . . . P

900[2] Straight Baron 5-1 P Hall *Cl 3rd to 9; 6l 4th aft 11; wknd & lost tch 13; wl bhnd when pu 15* . . . . . P

777P The Grey Baron(tt) 5-1 P Bull *Cl 4th til hdwy 9; w wnr 12 til ld aft 15; dived at 3 out; sn hdd & wknd; pu & dism 2 out* . . . . . P

OFFICIAL DISTANCE: 2*l* **TIME:** 7min 02.0s **TOTE:** £2.30; places £1.20,£1.70 **DF:**£1.40

1052 Land Rover Mens Open, 12st — 5 ran

609[2] **LITTLE FARMER** (7x) 2-1 **P Hall** *Jw; made all; 4l up app 3 out; stayed on str & drew clr frm nxt* 1

800F **Splash And Dash (IRE)** (7x) 4-5F **A Hickman** *Hld up; last to 8; hdwy 12; niggled along & went 3l 2nd aft 14; hrd rdn & rmdrs 3 out; little resp; 6l down & btn when jmpd lft 2 out; eased app last* 12 2

732[12] **Itsmyturnnow (IRE)** (7x) 4-1 **C Gordon** *Cl 2nd/3rd; rdn 14; 10l 3rd & wkng aft 15; jb lft frm 3 out* 30 3

805[4] Castle Arrow (IRE) 10-1 J Sole *Cl up to 7; pushed along & lost tch 9; wl bhnd when pu aft 11* . . . . . P
397[3] Little Worsall (IRE) (7x) 10-1 F Marshall *Sev slt mists; prsd wnr most of way to 11; 4th & lsng tch when blun 14; pu nxt* . . . . . P

OFFICIAL DISTANCES: 15*l*, 25*l* **TIME:** 7min 00.0s **TOTE:** £2.70; places £2.90,£1.10 **DF:**£3.90

1053 Ladies Open — 6 ran

807[1] **DICK MCCARTHY (IRE)** 9-2 **Mrs S Ashby** *Hld up in last pr til hdwy 7; 7l 4th aft 11; prog to chse ldr 15; hrd rdn & hdwy 3 out; 1l down 2 out; ld & btr j last; hld on wl flat* 1
805[1] **Cedar Chief** (4x)(bl) 9-4 **Mrs J Gordon** *Ld to 3; disp ld frm 4 til ld agn 13; 4l up aft 15; hrd prsd frm 2 out; just hdd when mist last; no ex flat* 2 2
641[1] **Tom Cobbler (IRE)** (7x) evensF **Mrs P Hall** *Hld up early; chsd ldng pr frm 8; 5l 3rd aft 11; pushed along & lost plce 14; 8l 3rd aft nxt; kpt on one pce frm 3 out* 8 3
807[2] Oxendale 12-1 Mrs C Andrews *Prom to 6; lost tch frm 9; 17l 5th aft 11; wl bhnd frm 15* 25 4
608[U] Kincora (IRE) (7x) 8-1 Ms L Stock *A.p; disp ld 4-12; ev ch til wknd qckly 15; mod 4th when pu 3 out* . . . . . P
897[P] Prime Course (IRE) (7x) 12-1 Miss H Gordon *Prom when mist 2; last frm 6; 25l 6th aft 11; no ch when mist & ur 14* . . . . . U

OFFICIAL DISTANCES: 2*l*, 10*l* **TIME:** 6min 54.0s **TOTE:** £3.40; places £1.90,£1.80 **DF:**£8.80

1054 Confined, 12st — 9 ran

778[1] **TOD'S BROTHER** (3x) 3-1 **A Merriam** *A cl up; ld 11-12; mist & rmdrs 14; prsd ldr frm 15; mist 3 out; gd rn to ld app nxt; kpt on str app last* 1
638[1] **Tricky Trevor (IRE)** (8x) 7-4F **P York** *Cl up in midfield; impd to trck ldr 11; ld 13 til hdd app 15; sn rdn along & drpd back 3rd; hdwy u.p into 3l 2nd app 2 out; kpt on one pce app last* 3 2
806[U] **Kenny Davis (IRE)** 8-1 **P Blagg** *Hld up towards rr; hdwy to cl 4th aft 15; ev ch app 2 out; no ex app last* 3 3
645[1] Live Wire (IRE) 10-1 Miss C Benstead *Cl up in midfield til lost plce aft 14; 13l 6th aft 15; stayed on frm 3 out; nrst fin* 4 4
638[2] Tell The Nipper (IRE) (3x) 6-1 M Gorman *Cl up in midfield til 10l 5th & no prog aft 15; kpt on same pce frm 3 out* 5 5
779[1] River Bailiff (IRE)(cp) 10-1 P Hall *A in tch; hdwy 9; trckd ldng pr 11 til ld 15; hdd app 2 out; wknd qckly app last* 4 6
806[3] Galeaway (IRE) (3x) 16-1 J Barnard *Ld/disp to 10; lost plce qckly frm 12; t.o when pu 3 out* . . . . . P
800[P] Spy Boy (IRE)(vis) 16-1 G Wigley *Sn prom; w ldr 4-7; wknd qckly aft 8; t.o & pu 11* . . . . . P
605[P] Tidal Reef (IRE) (3x) 16-1 D Slattery *Detach last; wl in tch to 7; sn fdd; t.o & pu 11* . . . . . P

OFFICIAL DISTANCES: 3*l*, 3*l* **TIME:** 7min 00.0s
TOTE: £3.80; places £1.50,£1.90,£2.20 **DF:**£4.10

1055 Open Maiden, 12st - 16J — 11 ran

418[3] **SIOBHANS QUINNER (IRE)** (5a) 6-1 **D Phelan** *Cl up in midfield; hdwy to jn ldrs 13; ld aft 15; lft wl clr 3 out* 1
782[P] **Royal Cruise (IRE)**(cp) 7-1 **P Hall** *Cl up in midfield; 13l 3rd aft 15; no prog; lft poor 2nd 3 out; no ch w wnr* 25 2
274[3] Execute (IRE) 10-1 L Cornford *Ld/disp til wknd qckly 13; wl bhnd when pu aft 15* . . . . . P
746[4] Pistol Knight 6-1 Stuart Robinson *Prom when pckd & ur 1* . . . . . U
644[P] Private Percival 16-1 P Blagg *Hld up; hdwy to press ldrs 11; wknd 13; no ch when pu 15* . . . . . P
782[P] Sawbridge(tt) 20-1 Miss A Sansom *Rr til blun & ur 6* . . . . . U
782[P] Selfcertified (7a) 20-1 P Bull *A wl in tch; hdwy 11; w ldrs 13 til 15l 4th & wkng aft 15; pu 3 out* . . . . . P
895[R] Spruce Goose (IRE)(tt) 8-1 N Wilson (South) *Ur 1* . . . . . U
644[3] Sword Fighter 3-1F P York *Prsd ldr/disp; reluct, str rmdrs & lost plce brief aft 11; disp ld 13 til v reluct & further rmdrs aft 15; 10l 2nd when almost ref & ur 3 out* . . . . . U

802P Two Of Diamonds 12-1 J Sole *Cl up til wknd qckly 10; rr when pu 12. . . .* P
1284 What Next (IRE) 5-1 A Hickman *Jb lft at times; a last; detach but in tch to 12; no prog; wl bhnd when pu 15. . . . .* P

OFFICIAL DISTANCE: dist **TIME:** 7min 19.0s **TOTE:** £6.10; places £2.60,£5.30 **DF:**£39.90

Fences 9 & 17 omitted - fallen rider; the stewards fined the rider of Sword Fighter £65 for misuse of the whip - not giving the horse time to respond

Quorn

Garthorpe (RH 8F,18J)

Sun, 18 Apr (GOOD, GOOD to FIRM in places becoming SOFT)

1056 Hunt Members, 12st — 6 ran

8896 **BALMORAL SPRING (IRE)**(vis) 2-1 **R Armson** *A.p; 2l 3rd ½way; ld app 12; qcknd clr 15; 12l up 2 out; idled bad flat; hld on wl . . . .* 1
7846 **Springlea Tower** (3ow) 6-4F **R Hunnisett** *Ld til aft 1; ld 8-10; urged along 13; 7l 3rd & outpcd 15; stayed on 2 out; went 2nd flat; nt rch wnr. . . . . . .* 4 2
7845 **Topical Tip (IRE)** 6-1 **Mrs E Chugg** *Ld aft 1-6 & aft 7-8; ld 10 til app 12; 6l 2nd & outpcd 15; stayed on 2 out; dem flat. . . . .* nk 3
Brilliant Star (NZ) (7x) 7-1 P Millington *Nt jw; drpd to rr 6; went 3l 4th ½way; wkng when mist 13; wl bhnd when pu 15 . . . .* P
789P Devils Domino 33-1 M Mackley *Hung lft in last pr; mist 3; 5th ½way; lost tch 12; pu 13 . . . .* P
945P Stylino (USA) 16-1 Miss R Botterill *(orbs) Rcd wide; went 2nd 4; ld 6 til aft 7; drpd to rr 9; lost tch 11; t.o & pu 15 . . . .* P

OFFICIAL DISTANCES: 3½*l*, nk **TIME:** 6min 29.06s

1057 Mens Open — 4 ran

7861 **NAUTICAL LAD** 10-11F **J Docker** *Ww; last til app 12; went 2nd 14; ld 15-2 out; ld app last; clr when idled & hung lft flat; rdn out. . . . .* 1
888R **Franco (IRE)** evens **J Diment** *2nd til ld 6; hdd 15; rdn to ld 2 out; hdd & no ex app last. . . . .* 4 2
7862 **Some Go West (IRE)** 14-1 **R Cope** *20s-14s; prom; 1l 3rd ½way; went 2nd aft 11-14; sn outpcd; t.o . . . .* runin 3
8882 Thurles Pickpocket (IRE) 33-1 B Elson *Ld to 6; 2nd til aft 11; sn last; wl bhnd 15; t.o . . . .* 7 4

OFFICIAL DISTANCES: 4½*l*, dist **TIME:** 6min 20.04s

The stewards cautioned the rider of Franco concerning his use of the whip on a horse which was out of contention

1058 Gerrard Ladies Open — 4 ran

7852 **FREE**(cp) 5-2 **Miss Gemma Hutchinson** *Jw; 2nd til ld 3; hdd 11; ld 13; drew clr 2 out; 7l up last; comf . . . .* 1
593P **Bloomfield Storm (IRE)** 13-2 **Miss S Buckley** *Hld up; lost tch 8; 15l last ½way; hdwy 14; outpcd aft nxt; stayed on 2 out; went 2nd nr fin . . . . .* 5 2
9874 **Supreme Silence (IRE)** 5-1 **Miss L Allan** *Ld to 3; 2nd til ld 11; hdd 13; outpcd aft 15; 10l 3rd nxt; stayed on 2 out; went 2nd flat; dem nr fin. . . . . . .* nk 3
7851 Find Me Another (IRE) 4-5F Miss A Stennett *Nt a fluent; prom; mist 9; 4l 3rd & shkn up ½way; went 2nd aft 15; ev ch when outj 3 out; wknd app last; lost 2 plces & eased when btn flat . . . .* 10 4

OFFICIAL DISTANCES: 4*l*, nk **TIME:** 6min 20.07s

The stewards spoke to the owners of Bloomfield Storm concerning the horse's improvement in form; they accepted their explanation that the horse had been disappointing when pulled up at Welbeck and that this was more like its real form

1059 Intermediate, 12st — 5 ran

7871 **DENVALE (IRE)** 11-8F **R Cope** *Nt a fluent; 2nd to 13; ev ch 3 out; sn outpcd; stayed on to ld last; all out. . . . .* 1
692P **Heisamodel (IRE)** 6-1 **M Miller** *Hld up; went 3rd 5-11; blun nxt; 3l 4th 14; mist 3 out; stayed on flat; nt rch wnr. . . . .* ½ 2†
770P **The Graduate** 7-2 **S Walker** *(xnb) Tk keen hld; ld 3-3 out; rallied flat; stayed on* d ht 2†

784[4] Emperor Roscoe 3-1 R Armson *Hld up; last to 7; hit 9; 5l 4th ½way; went 2nd 13; ld 3 out; 4l clr nxt; faltered & hdd last; no ex* . . . 2½ 4
819[1] Waterloo Leader (IRE) 5-1 D Smith *8s-5s; nt jw; ld to 3; last & strugg 7; wl bhnd ½way; t.o 13; pu 3 out* . . . P

OFFICIAL DISTANCES: 1*l*, dd ht **TIME:** 6min 43.7s

Following heavy rain the official going was changed to good to soft before the next race

1060 Restricted, 12st - 16J — 6 ran

686[1] **CAIPIROSKA** (7a) 5-4 **J Docker** *(xnb) A.p; 3l 4th ½way; ld 15; drew clr 2 out; rdly* . . . 1
788[1] **Nickit (IRE)**(cp) evensF **R Cope** *Nt jw & nvr gng keen; ld to 13; ev ch u.p app omitted 3 out; no ex 2 out* . . . 6 2
Have A Chat 5-1 **S Morris** *Hld up; lost plce 7; last & rmdrs ½way; jmpd slow 11; eff u.p 15; went 7l 3rd aft omitted 3 out; sn wknd* . . . 20 3
745[3] Magnus Maximus 7-1 T Lane *(xnb) 2 handlers; 2nd til ld 13; hdd 15; wknd by-passing 3 out* . . . 5 4
745[7] Cawkwell Princess (5a) 16-1 M Mackley *Hld up last pr; went 7l 4th 15; sn wknd* 7 5
771[P] Gentleman Charles (IRE) 8-1 S Walker *Hld up last pr to 7; went 2l 3rd ½way; wknd qckly 15* . . . 6 6

OFFICIAL DISTANCES: 6*l*, 15*l* **TIME:** 6min 51.08s

Fences 8 & 16 omitted - state of ground: Coole Chief (8-1) and Quizzal (3-1) were withdrawn after declarations closed - state of ground; no penalties were imposed

1061 Open Maiden, 12st - 16J — 12 ran

686[3] **HOUGHAM GEORGE** (7a) 12-1 **T Lane** *Hld up; 6th ½way; jnd ldrs aft 12; 3l 4th 14; rdn 15; stayed on & lft in ld app last; veered lft & stumbled nr fin; just hld on* . . . 1
789[P] **Jumping Jack** 7-4JF **R Cope** *5/2-7/4; a.p; ld aft 12-14; rdn & lkd btn app 2 out; lft w ev ch last; nt qckn* . . . nk 2
887[3] **Midnight Cowboy** 5-1 **N Kent** *Hld up; 7th ½way; hdwy 11; went 2nd 13; lft in ld 2 out til hmpd by loose horse app last; no ex flat* . . . 2 3
887[8] Dolitanlad 20-1 P Millington *A bhnd; 20l last ½way; t.o 14* . . . runin 4
588[r] Beechbrook Gale (IRE) 10-1 J Diment *20s-10s; w ldr til mist 11; stpd to nil; wl bhnd when pu 13* . . . P
887[5] Coombs Spinney 8-1 N Docker *20s-8s; w ldrs to 7; lost plce & 8th ½way; lost tch 12; 5th when blun & ur 15* . . . U
942[P] Faircatcher(tt) 20-1 R Collinson *Hld up; mist 3; 10th ½way; lost tch & pu 11* P
644[2] Hever Road (IRE) (7a) 7-4JF S Morris *5/2-7/4; hld up; hdwy aft 7; 5th ½way; ld 14; 1½l up & lkd wnr when blun & ur 2 out* . . . U
746[P] Marbank Lad (IRE)(cp) 20-1 M Mackley *Ld; mist 9; hdd aft 12; sn wknd; wl bhnd when pu 15* . . . P
746[2] Marciano(cp) 4-1 J Docker *Nvr gng wl; 9th & u.p ½way; lost tch 12; rem 5th when pu 2 out* . . . P
887[P] Plain Polly (IRE) (5a) 20-1 M Briggs *Sn wl bhnd; hit doll & ur aft 3* . . . U
890[P] Satanas (FR) 20-1 L Hicks *(xnb) Chsd ldrs; 4th ½way; mist 10; wknd & 8l 6th 13; pu 14* . . . P

OFFICIAL DISTANCES: nk, ¾*l* **TIME:** 7min 04.9s

Fences 8 & 16 were omitted - state of the going: Orchestra's Boy (4-1) was withdrawn after declarations closed - state of the going; no penalty was imposed

Tedworth

Barbury Racecourse (LH 8F,18J)

Sun, 18 Apr (GOOD to FIRM becoming DEAD)

1062 Hunt Members

972[P] **FRIARS ISLAND (IRE) H Wallace** *Walked over; rdr's 1st wnr* . . . 1

1063 Restricted, 12st — 7 ran

87[1] **VINNIE BOY (IRE)** 4-6F **Miss P Gundry** *Hld up; hdwy to trck ldrs 8; 3l 2nd 10; hit 13 & nxt; ld 15; jnd app last; stayed on flat* . . . 1
939[r] **Lord Ken (IRE)**(vis) 5-1 **N Phillips** *Sn prom; ld frm 3-4; jmpd slow & dem 3rd 5; ld agn 8-15; prsd ldr aft til no ex flat* . . . 1 2

636[2] **Shy Lizzie** (5a) 6-1 **P Mason** *Settled 4/5th; outpcd 9; 10l 4th 10; sn lost tch w ldng pr; rem 3rd 3 out; plodded on* . . . 15 3
969[4] Nice Approach (IRE) 25-1 Miss V Murphy *Ld to 2; 2nd aft til ld agn 6-7; rap outpcd & last 11; blun 13 & 3 out; t.o* . . . runin 4
864[U] Hawkers Hill 10-1 N Mitchell *Prom; 4l 2nd 8; ld 10-11; dem 3rd & labouring 12; wknd rap; pu 14* . . . P
628[P] Hill Trail(tt) 16-1 R Bliss *A last pr; lost tch & tlng off when pu 9* . . . P
665[5] Snowtre (IRE)(cp) 8-1 A Wintle *Imm rr & nvr gng wl; jmpd awkward 1 & 2; 5th 11; 30l 4th blun 3 out; t.o & pu last* . . . P

OFFICIAL DISTANCES: 1½l, 20l **TIME:** 6min 25.0s **TOTE:** £1.60

1064 Ladies Open — 3 ran

869[2] **STORM CASTLE (IRE)** 5-2 **Miss J Wickens** *Made all; crawled to 5; prsd frm 2 out; kpt on game last* . . . 1
176[2] **Mrs Be (IRE)** (5a) 1-3F **Miss P Gundry** *Hld up in 2-3l last; eff app 3 out; went 2l 2nd app nxt; ev ch & rdn app last; drvn & no ex flat* . . . ¾ 2
838[P] **Flying Pennant (IRE)** 12-1 **Miss S Davies** *Jw; ld brief app 1; prsd ldr til dem last aft 3 out; sn outpcd & btn* . . . 15 3

OFFICIAL DISTANCES: ½l, 15l **TIME:** 6min 44.0s **TOTE:** £3.90

1065 Mens Open, 12st — 2 ran

880[2] **GLADIATORIAL (IRE)** 3-1 **T Bishop** *Disp ld to 5; made rest; 6l up 13; 15l clr 3 out; unchall* . . . 1
543[10] **Polar Champ**(bl) 1-4F **A Farrant** *Mists; disp ld to 5; last aft; rmdrs app & aft 10; pushed along & no resp; sn lost tch w rival; t.o 3 out* . . . 30 2

OFFICIAL DISTANCE: 30l **TIME:** 6min 33.0s

1066 Countryside Alliance Club Members Conditions, 12st — 7 ran

496[6] **LE CURE** 2-1F **J Barnes** *Opened 5/2; trckd ldng pr; 5l 3rd & blun 5; 4th nxt; chsd ldrs 10; went 3l 2nd 14; ld 3 out; sn clr; comf* . . . 1
465[P] **Tubber Roads (IRE)**(bl) 5-1 **A Charles-Jones** *Prsd ldr til ld frm 5-7; prsd ldr nxt til disp ld 11; ld 13-3 out; brushed aside aft 3 out; one pce* . . . 15 2
Perryman (IRE) 3-1 **Miss P Gundry** *Ld to 4; prsd ldr nxt til ld frm 8; jnd 11-12; cl up til 3rd & outpcd 3 out; lost tch qckly; sn btn* . . . 10 3
881[4] Sherbourne Guest (IRE) 10-1 J Kwiatkowski *Sn detach bhnd ldrs; 10l 6th 7; kpt on one pce 2 out; nrst fin* . . . 3 4
755[P] Arctic Grey (IRE) 12-1 M Goldstein *Trckd ldng pr; 5l 3rd 8; fell 9* . . . F
Hillview Hut (IRE) 16-1 R Bandey *Imm last; blun 3; t.o & pu 10* . . . P
Urban Hunter (IRE) 5-1 D Alers-Hankey *Sn off pce & nvr gng wl; 8l 5th 11; rmdrs aft 12; stdly lost tch; t.o & pu 2 out* . . . P

OFFICIAL DISTANCES: 20l, 12l **TIME:** 6min 32.0s **TOTE:** £10.00

1067 Open Maiden, 12st — 11 ran

ALHERI 3-1 **F de Giles** *Sis; pulled to ld 2; made rest; 6l ahd 12; 25l clr when lft solo at last* . . . 1
Born Winner 16-1 R Bandey *Rr; 20l 8th 8; t.o 12; pu 15* . . . P
760[r] Cash On Demand 16-1 N Mitchell *Reluct to jn others start; sa & imm virt t.o; v slow & reluct at all fncs; miles bhnd when tried to ref & jmpd violent rt 9; imm pu* P
736[P] Clarky's Choice (IRE) 8-1 D Davies *Mid-div when fell 2* . . . F
940[U] Crystal Vein 10-1 N McDiarmid *Mid-div; lsng tch w pack when blun 9 & 11; lft rem 5th by 15; t.o & pu 3 out* . . . P
599[P] Gunville (7a) 7-4F Miss P Gundry *Hld up off pce; trckd clr ldr frm 8; 8l 3rd 11; stayed on to chse ldr frm 15; 2nd nxt; 25l down when fell hvly last* . F
John Builder 10-1 R Rogers *Tde & kpt on move start; chsd ldrs to 10; wknd v qckly; t.o & pu 15* . . . P
760[P] Lord Of Heaven (USA) 7-2 Miss K Cuthbertson *Hld up off pce; 10l 4th & chsd ldrs 11; went 3rd aft 3 out; last of survivors but exhaust when pu last; rdr keen to cont aft rival fell at last but was waved rnd fnce* . . . P
575[4] Senior Moment 7-2 J Snowden *Mid-div; trckd ldr frm 8; 15l 3rd 14; dem 4th nxt; qckly lost tch; exhaust when pu 2 out* . . . P
633[3] Spencive 6-1 P Mason *Ld 1; 2nd & chsd ldr nxt; blun 5 & 6; wknd qckly 8; t.o & pu 13* . . . P
202[P] Willie The Kid (7a) 8-1 H Dowty *Mid-div when fell 3* . . . F

OFFICIAL DISTANCE: Finished alone **TIME:** 6min 43.0s **TOTE:** £5.50

Perth (RH 8F,18J)

Fri, 23 Apr (GOOD to SOFT, GOOD in places)

1068 Standard Life Bank Champion Stayers HC, 3m2f110y £4186

10 ran

241[2] **HERMES III (FR)** 11-07 7-4F **T Greenall** *Hld up; nt fluent 6; prog gng str 15; lft 3rd nxt; tk 2nd 3 out; ld on bit last; lft wl clr; hvly eased* 1
797[1] **Nisbet** 11-08 12-1 **Miss J Riding** *(xnb) Ld 4; clr passing 9; hdd passing 17; lost 2nd nxt; wknd 2 out; lft rem 2nd & nt fluent last* . . . . dist 2
894[2] **Go Nomadic** 11-13(tt) 6-1 **P Atkinson** *Made most to 4; hit 7; 4th 13; bad outpcd aft mist 15; t.o passing 17; lft 3rd at last* 26 3
798[3] Mytimie (IRE) 11-10 6-1 Miss P Robson *Pushed along in rr; nvr keen; 15l 8th 13; t.o aft 16; drvn rt out in desperate duel for 4th*. 1½ 4
894[U] Decoded 11-05 50-1 L Bates *Bhnd & nt fluent; eff in 6th & rdn 14; strugg aft; t.o aft 16* . . . . nk 5
875[1] Dorans Magic 11-03 6-1 N Saville *Sn stdd to trck ldrs; 4th when mist 8; went 2nd 13; ld passing 17; still nt rdn but just hdd when fell last (was gng wl, but nt as wl as wnr)* . . . . F
764[8] Laganside (IRE) 12-04 (15ow) 100-1 J Muir *Prom v brief; jmpd slow & drpd to rr 5; last & strugg 9; mist 10; t.o 14; pu 2 out*. . . . . P
798[1] Miss Mattie Ross 11-10 5-1 M McAlister *Swtng bad; prom; 2nd 6-13; cl 3rd when fell 16* . . . . F
812[6] Parade Racer 12-01 33-1 D Jewett *Midfield; 6th & outpcd 13; wknd rap; pu 15*. . . . . P
The Met Man (IRE) 11-03 25-1 M Seston *(xnb) Bolted to 1; virt fell & ur 1* U

TIME: 7min 10.3s **TOTE:** £2.50; places £1.50,£3.00,£2.20 **Ex:**£27.20 **CSF:**£22.31

Fences 9 & 17 omitted

Berkeley

Woodford (LH 10F,19J)

Sat, 24 Apr (GOOD)

1069 Restricted, 12st

13 ran

498[P] **LORD ANNER (IRE)** (7a, 1ow) 3-1 **A Farrant** *Lw; jmpd lft; hld up; hdwy 7; 2l 4th ½way; hit 14; ld 16; sn 4l clr; rdn out* 1
459[3] **It's Missy Imp** (12a) 9-1 **A Martin** *Lft 2nd 4; ld 6 til hdd & mist 12; lost plce & 5l 6th 15; rallied 3 out; went 2nd app nxt; stayed on* 3 2
977[P] **Raymond James** 25-1 **D Mansell** *2nd til lft in ld 4; hdd 6; shkn up 8; 3l 5th ½way; lost plce u.p & 13l 8th 15; stayed on frm 2 out* 10 3
853[5] Shafts Chance (IRE) (5a) 33-1 Miss K Wood *(xnb) Wl bhnd til stayed on frm 3 out; nvr gvn a ch* 1 4
879[4] Maybe A Double (5a) 25-1 N Wilmington *(xnb) Hld up; 5l 7th ½way; 8l 7th 15; went 2nd aft nxt; mist 3 out; sn wknd* 6 5
601[2] Preacher Boy (7a) 5-2 Miss P Gundry *Hld up; 10th when mist 3; hdwy & 3½l 6th ½way; jmpd slow 11; mists 12 & 14; ev ch 15; wknd 3 out* 2 6
819[2] Ballyblack (IRE) 33-1 E Walker *(xnb) Hld up; 5½l 8th ½way; lost tch u.p 15; wl bhnd when pu 3 out* . . . . P
600[1] Boddidley (IRE) 2-1F Miss C Roddick *Hld up; 6l 9th ½way; hdwy & 3l 5th 15; ev ch when bd nxt* . . . . B
844[P] Daisy Leigh (5a) 33-1 G Barfoot-Saunt *Prom; 1½l 3rd ½way; went 2nd & ev ch 15; bd nxt*. . . . . B
923[P] Derrys Prerogative 33-1 Miss N Rudge *A bhnd; 10th ½way; lost tch 12; t.o & pu 2 out* . . . . P
684[P] Greet You Well 6-1 R Cope *Prom; went 2nd 7; ld 12 til hdd & fell 16* . . . . F
Make Up Your Mind (IRE) 25-1 B Gallagher *(bf) Bhnd til pu aft 10*. . . . . . P
327[1] Wayward Spree (5a) 20-1 Mrs O Jackson *Swtng; tk str hld; ld til blun & ur 4* U

OFFICIAL DISTANCES: 2½l, 10l **TIME:** 6min 35.8s

The stewards enquired into the running of Make Up Your Mind who was pulled up after the 10th fence; they noted the rider's explanation that he thought the horse had lost its action and appeared lame, but found it was sound after pulling-up

1070 Hunt Members, 12st — 5 ran

Form	Runner	Dist	Pos
922[1]	**WILLIAM LIONHEART** 2-7F **G Barfoot-Saunt** *Lw; made all; qcknd 11; 6l clr when hit 13; drew rt away 15; unchall.*		1
666[4]	**Thyny Glen (IRE)** 14-1 **Miss J Houldey** *Jmpd rt; last to 4; 4½l 4th ½way; went 3rd 11; lost tch 14; lft dist 2nd 3 out*	runin	2
979[8]	**Zingibar**(vis) 9-1 **C Dailly** *Spurs; 12s-9s; rn in snatches & rdn all the way; jmpd slow 4; hdwy u.p 9; 4l 3rd ½way; lost tch 13; t.o 16; fin wl*	3	3
844[P]	Knight Ofthe North 14-1 Miss E Burrows *Rcd wide; 2nd/3rd til hmpd & rdr lost iron 8; 7l last ½way; lost tch 13; t.o 16*	15	4
967[1]	Avec Plaisir (IRE) 3-1 Miss A Clifford *Prom; went 2nd aft 6; no ch 14; 30l down when fell 3 out.*		F

OFFICIAL DISTANCES: dist, 3*l* **TIME:** 6min 35.2s

1071 Intermediate, 12st — 8 ran

Form	Runner	Dist	Pos
1031[3]	**MY BEST BUDDY** 3-1 **R Cope** *A.p; 2l 3rd ½way; went 2nd 13; ld 16; qcknd 5l clr 2 out; rdn out*		1
861[3]	**Thunder Thighs** (5a) 16-1 **N Wilmington** *(xnb) 2 handlers; mounted on course; tde; 2nd to 13; 4th & rdn 16; 5l 3rd nxt; went 2nd agn flat; stayed on.*	6	2
921[1]	**Stennikov (IRE)** 5-2 **E Walker** *(xnb) Hld up; mist 3; hit 9; hdwy & 2½l 4th ½way; 3rd & ev ch when hmpd bad 16; nt rec; hung lft frm 3 out; stayed on one pce.*	2	3
972[2]	Glacial Pearl (IRE) 8-1 P Mason *Swtng; hld up; 5l 6th ½way; mist 13; rdn aft nxt; went 2nd aft 16; ev ch 3 out; wknd & lost 2 plces flat.*	3	4
1015[4]	Hijacked 5-1 G Hanmer *Hld up; mist 8; 7l last ½way; 8l 7th & rdn 13; wknd 16*	20	5
629[P]	Sootsir 20-1 R Hawker *(xnb) Last 6-9; 6½l 7th & rdn ½way; last agn 11; lost tch u.p 14; sn wl bhnd*	½	6
977[1]	Black Optimist (IRE) 5-4F Mrs K Baimbridge *3s-5/4; jmpd rt; ld til hdd & hung bad rt 16; imm pu & dism*		P
882[3]	Timpani (IRE)(vis) 12-1 R Woollacott *(xnb) 2 handlers; w ldrs; 3l 5th ½way; rdn 14; wknd app 16; wl bhnd when pu 2 out*		P

OFFICIAL DISTANCES: 6*l*, 2*l* **TIME:** 6min 33.0s

1072 Ladies Open — 5 ran

Form	Runner	Dist	Pos
758[4]	**PHAR FROM CHANCE** 9-4 **Miss P Gundry** *(xnb) Ld to 2; 2nd to 13; went 7l 2nd nxt; ld 16; 3l clr 2 out; all out*		1
836[F]	**Titus Bramble**(bl,tt) 5-2 **Mrs K Baimbridge** *Ld 2; qcknd 11; 8l clr 14; mist nxt; hdd 16; rallied u.p aft 2 out; just failed.*	s hd	2
965[2]	**Breteche (FR)** (5a) 9-1 **Miss T Newman** *(xnb) Mounted on course; tde; hld up; went 3rd 6 & 6l 2nd 13-14; wknd u.p 3 out*	20	3
931[2]	Justin Mac (IRE) 20-1 Miss K Wood *Nrly ur 1; 3rd to 6; 5l 4th ½way; 10l down 13; hdwy u.p 15; wknd 3 out.*	6	4
690[1]	Norski Lad(bl,tt) 11-10F Miss R Green *Jmpd rt; hld up last; reluct & hanging 11; lost tch 12; pu 14*		P

OFFICIAL DISTANCES: s hd, 20*l* **TIME:** 6min 26.7s

1073 Mens Open, 12st — 11 ran

Form	Runner	Dist	Pos
936[1]	**CAMDEN CARRIG (IRE)** 8-1 **N Phillips** *Swtng; ld 1; drew rt away frm 2 out; quite impressive*		1
1015[2]	**The Campdonian (IRE)** 10-1 **E Walker** *Prom til lost plce & 10l 7th ½way; rdn 13; lft 10l 4th nxt; stayed on one pce 3 out; went 2nd nr fin*	20	2
924[1]	**Well Ted (IRE)** (7x) 3-1 **G Hanmer** *Hld up; hdwy & 6l 4th ½way; lft 4l 2nd 14; wkng when hit 2 out; dem nr fin.*	½	3
868[2]	Sir Dante (IRE) (4x) 7-1 F Hutsby *(xnb) A.p; went 2nd 3-6; 2½l 3rd ½way; 7l down 15; wknd u.p 2 out.*	4	4
994[P]	Lord Castle (IRE) 33-1 R McCarthy *Nd; 12l 8th ½way; 11l 7th 13; 5th & no hdwy 15; sn wl bhnd.*	15	5
980[4]	Rusty Fellow (7x) 12-1 D Mansell *Ld to 1; mist 3; lost plce & mist 7; 13l 9th & drvn ½way; mist 11; lost tch 12; t.o.*	6	6

924F	Fours Are Wild (IRE) 33-1 J Jones *Sn prom; went 2nd 6 til mist 9; 7l 5th 1/2way; wkng when mist 13; pu aft nxt*		P
9372	Golden Jack (FR) 25-1 C Morris *A bhnd; lost tch 8; 20l last 1/2way; t.o 14; pu last*		P
8164	Not For Parrot (IRE) 33-1 P Callaghan *(xnb) Hld up & bhnd; 15l 10th 1/2way; 14l 9th 13; lost tch w rdr motionless 15; 25l 7th when pu nxt*		P
9764	Theatreland (USA) 33-1 G Barfoot-Saunt *(xnb) Hld up; hdwy 6; 8l 6th 1/2way; 12l 8th & rdn 13; lost tch & jb rt 16; mist 3 out; wl bhnd when pu nxt*		P
6921	Vivid Imagination (IRE) (7a) 4-9F A Farrant *(xnb) Hld up; hdwy 9; went 2l 2nd nxt; mist & ur 14*		U

OFFICIAL DISTANCES: 20*l*, 1/2*l* **TIME:** 6min 26.3s

1074 Open Maiden (Div 1), 12st — 14 ran

	LORD OF THE ROAD (7a) 7-1 **S Morris** *(xnb) 10s-7s; 2 handlers; hld up; 11l 6th 1/2way; hdwy 14; went 2nd 16; ld 3 out; forged clr nxt; kpt on wl*		1
6992	**Willoughby Flyer** 5-4F **M Walters** *Ld to 3; 2nd til outpcd 16; 8l 3rd 2 out; stayed on; 2nd agn nr fin*	10	2
8485	**Tisallover (IRE)** 5-1 **M Hammond** *(xnb) Pulled hrd; ld 3-3 out; wknd aft nxt; lost 2nd nr fin*	1/2	3
926U	Toffee Lady (5a) 7-1 R Rogers *(xnb) Hld up; 14l 8th 1/2way; hdwy & 6l 5th aft 15; 12l 4th & wkng when mist 3 out; hit nxt*	8	4
6003	Let's Rock 6-1 M Green *Prom til lost plce 6; 13l 7th 1/2way; mist 12; sn wl bhnd; t.o 15*	20	5
1067P	Crystal Vein 20-1 N McDiarmid *(xnb) Pulled hrd; mists 1 & 5; jnd ldrs 6; wknd qckly 10; 16l 9th 1/2way; wl bhnd when mist 12; pu 13*		P
8846	Jag (5a) 8-1 J Barnes *Jmpd rt; a bhnd; mist 6; t.o & pu aft 10*		P
	Laggan More (7a) 6-1 F Hutsby *Hld up; hdwy & 9l 4th 1/2way; went 6l 3rd 14; rdn nxt; wknd app 3 out; poor 5th when pu nxt*		P
	Make It Plain (12a, 6ow) 10-1 G Hanmer *Ref & ur 1*		r
7315	Marty's Lamp (5a) 10-1 F de Giles *Prom; 5l 3rd 1/2way; wknd qckly 14; blun 16; t.o & pu 3 out*		P
	Our Girl Fleur (12a)(tt) 12-1 N Wilmington *(xnb) Hld up & bhnd; 17l 10th 1/2way; hdwy 13; 9l 6th aft 15; wknd nxt; pu aft mist 3 out*		P
865P	Panto 20-1 Miss K Lovelace *W ldrs; disp 9l 4th 1/2way; 10l 5th 13; wknd & 15l 7th 15; wl bhnd when pu 3 out*		P
9825	Stanley Island 25-1 Miss J Buck *5th when fell 1*		F
	The Squab 16-1 Mrs O Jackson *11th when fell 2*		F

OFFICIAL DISTANCES: 10*l*, 1*l* **TIME:** 6min 40.9s

1075 Open Maiden (Div 2), 12st — 12 ran

7232	**BLACKANBLUE** (7a) 11-10F **G Hanmer** *Hld up & bhnd; stdy hdwy & 8l 7th 1/2way; 5l 6th 13; went 2nd 16; qcknd to ld last; cleverly*		1
1020R	**Rody (IRE)**(bl) 2-1 **D Mansell** *(xnb) Ld til hdd last; nt qckn*	1/2	2
	Throwaparty (7a) 14-1 **N Wilmington** *(xnb) Hld up; 10l 9th 1/2way; hdwy & 5l 6th aft 15; went 8l 3rd aft 3 out; nvr able to chall*	7	3
9814	Romabit Tom 25-1 R Rogers *2 handlers; chsd ldrs; 6l 5th 1/2way; 3 1/2l 4th 13; wknd aft 15*	10	4
883U	Mad Jack(tt) 7-1 W White *(xnb) Hld up; 7l 6th 1/2way; hdwy & disp 3 1/2l 4th 13; 6l 3rd & rdn 3 out; wkng qckly when mist nxt*	8	5
9715	Isefoul De Bellevue (FR) 12-1 J Horton *Hld up; 9l 8th 1/2way; no hdwy 13; wl bhnd 16*	2	6
8502	All Eyez On Me (IRE)(bl) 7-1 M Hammond *Prom; 5l 3rd when fell 4*		F
840F	B So Bold 20-1 N McDiarmid *Hld up; mists 9 & 10; 17l 10th & rdn 1/2way; wl bhnd when pu 13*		P
7015	Dancing Dasi (IRE) (12a) 8-1 Miss L Gardner *Hld up; hdwy & 5l 4th 1/2way; lost plce & 7l 7th 13; last 15; 20l 4th & staying on when fell last*		F
881R	Pavillion Pride (12a) 25-1 Mrs T Rowe *Sn wl bhnd; 25l last 1/2way; t.o & pu 13*		P
1020R	Red Spark 9-2 E Walker *(xnb) Chsd ldrs; 4l 3rd 1/2way; mist 15; rdn & wknd 3 out; pu aft nxt*		P
	The Croppy(tt) 20-1 G Barfoot-Saunt *(xnb) 2nd to 16; sn pu; lame*		P

OFFICIAL DISTANCES: 1/2*l*, 8*l* **TIME:** 6min 40.8s

Fife

Balcormo Mains (RH 8F,18J)
Sat, 24 Apr (GOOD, SOFT in places)

1076 Hunt Members — 3 ran

Form	Runner	Dist	Pos
550^{6}	**TRY A BLUFF (IRE)** 4-1 **Miss E McWilliam** *(bf) 5s-4s; sn detach in last; 30l last 7; clsr 10-13; 12l last agn 15; gd prog to 6l down & pushed along nxt; 3l 2nd 2 out; ld last; eased cl home; comf*		1
	Solsgirth 11-10F **M Alexander** *(bf) Swtng; chsd ldr; $2\frac{1}{2}$l 2nd 9; hit 11; $\frac{1}{2}$l 2nd 13; ld app nxt; hdd 15; ld agn 3 out; hdd last; imm outpcd*	4	2
659^{4}	**Slytherin Falls** 5-4 **S Clark** *(xnb,bf) Nt a fluent; ld; 6l up & jmpd rt 8; hdd brief 14; 1l up nxt; hdd 3 out; & drpd to last; btn 3rd when fell last; rmtd aft 5min*	5min	3

OFFICIAL DISTANCES: 4*l*, dist **TIME:** 6min 56.5s

1077 Restricted, 12st — 8 ran

Form	Runner	Dist	Pos
1040^{U}	**DECENT BOND (IRE)** 3-1CF **R Green** *In tch; 6l 7th 6; prog frm 12; 4l 4th app 14; 3l 3rd 3 out; prsd ldr nxt; sn ld & rdn clr*		1
919^{1}	**More Flair** (5a) 6-1 **J Walton** *In tch in rr; 5l last 3; stdy prog to 4l 3rd 13; pushed into ld 15; hrd prsd 2 out; sn hdd; no ex.*	3	2
1040^{3}	**The Broken Man** 10-1 **Miss K Bryson** *Trckd ldrs; disp 3l 3rd aft 4; 2l 2nd app 13; outpcd & 8l 4th 3 out; kpt on; nt trble ldrs.*	4	3
765^{3}	Lucky Brush (IRE) 3-1CF J Alexander *(bf) Chsd ldrs; 8l last 7; sltly detach & lsng tch 9; 20l off pce 14; kpt on wl past btn horses frm 3 out.*	6	4
797^{5}	Highland Brig 7-1 R Morgan *Oht; swtng; ld til hdd 7; nrly fell & pckd bad 10; hmpd aft; 5l 4th 13; outpcd 3 out; one pce*	$1\frac{1}{2}$	5
810^{5}	Distinct (IRE) 12-1 Miss J Crosier *Chsd ldrs; 5l 5th app 5; lsng tch 12; nd aft*	2	6
918^{3}	Gudasmum (5a) 3-1CF Miss R Davidson *Trckd ldrs; disp 3l 3rd aft 4; fell hvly 10*		F
766^{4}	Westie (5a) 8-1 D Jewett *A.p; ld 7; 3l up 13; hdd 15; cl up when fell 2 out*		F

OFFICIAL DISTANCES: 2*l*, 4*l* **TIME:** 6min 50.3s

1078 Ladies Open — 5 ran

Form	Runner	Dist	Pos
1039^{1}	**PHARMISTICE (IRE)** 6-4 **Miss N Stirling** *(xnb) Made virt all; 1l up & hit 8; $1\frac{1}{2}$l ahd 13; prsd brief 2 out; stayed on wl*		1
857^{1}	**Passing Danger (FR)** evensF **Miss R Davidson** *In tch; disp 4l last aft 5; $1\frac{1}{2}$l last 11; went 1l 2nd app 13; hit nxt; sn outpcd; eff & rallied brief 2 out; nt pce to chall*	3	2
763^{5}	**Miss Portcello** (5a) 5-1 **Mrs A Hamilton** *Nt a fluent; in tch on last frm 6; hit 8 & pushed along; rmdr aft; 4l 3rd 13; 8l 3rd & rdn along aft 15; wknd app last.*	12	3
508^{4}	Dukestown (IRE) 12-1 Miss E McWilliam *(bf) Oht; swtng; sis; hdstrng & sn prom; 1l 2nd 6; 3l last app 13; 8l last & outpcd 14; grad lost tch.*	runin	4
1028^{P}	How Burn 10-1 Mrs V Jackson *Prom; 3l 3rd 8; fell nxt*		F

OFFICIAL DISTANCES: 3*l*, 15*l* **TIME:** 6min 49.1s

1079 Land Rover Mens Open, 12st — 6 ran

Form	Runner	Dist	Pos
917^{3}	**STARBUCK** 7-4F **L Morgan** *Trckd ldrs; disp 3l 2nd 5; 3l 3rd app 12; prog nxt to ld 3 out; sn clr; lft virt solo nxt*		1
764^{P}	**Just Whiskey (IRE)** (7x) 7-2 **C Shirley-Beavan** *In tch; hmpd app 4 & 8l last nxt; prog to 5l 4th app 7; 1l 2nd 13; 5l 3rd & outpcd 15; wkng when lft 2nd agn 2 out*	25	2
798^{10}	**Charlieadams (IRE)** (7x) 7-1 **J Muir** *In tch in rr; 10l last 6; 20l last 11; some prog frm 3 out; nd*	2	3
857^{P}	Tursal (IRE) 5-1 R Morgan *Trckd ldr; disp 3l 2nd 5; outpcd 12; 15l 4th & pushed along nxt; mist 15; poor 5th when jmpd slow nxt; wknd*	25	4
915^{P}	Calko 12-1 W Goldie *Chsd ldrs; 3l 3rd 3; 10l 5th aft 9; 15l 5th & wkng 11; fnce bhnd 14; t.o & pu aft 2 out.*		P
917^{2}	French Cedar (7x) 5-2 W Ramsay *Swtng; ld; 3l up 5; jmpd awkward 9; 1l up & hit 13; rmdrs 15; hdd nxt; 8l 2nd & btn when rn out 2 out*		R

OFFICIAL DISTANCES: 20*l*, 1*l* **TIME:** 6min 45.3s

1080 Confined 7 ran

1037[3] **ROYALECKO** 2-1F **Miss J Hollands** *Lw; oht; jw; made virt all; 4l up app 13; stayed on wl.* 1
915[3] **Johnnys Gone (IRE)** 11-4 **C Shirley-Beavan** *In tch; disp 8l 6th 8; pushed along app 10; 3l 3rd nxt; 6l 2nd 14; rdn 3 out; kpt on wl; nt trble wnr* . 3 2
657[P] **Flying Past**(tt) 9-2 **R Morgan** *(xnb) Opened 5s; lw; sis; 12l last 3; disp 8l 6th 8; 10l 4th & outpcd 13; sn btn; 20l 3rd 2 out* 25 3
857[P] Extra Stout (IRE)(tt) 7-1 C Storey *Opened 8s; trckd ldrs; rmdrs aft 4; disp 4l 3rd nxt; 2l 3rd app 11; outpcd 15; 20l 4th 3 out* 6 4
914[1] Donallach Mor (IRE) (3x)(bl) 9-1 Mrs V Jackson *Opened 10s; in tch; disp 4l 3rd app 5; outpcd aft 12; 20l 5th aft 15; t.o & pu 2 out* .... P
857[5] Mozielaw (5a) 6-1 Miss M Neill *Prom early; pckd 2; sn lost plce; 12l last 8; lost tch & pu 11* .... P
654[U] Wishful Thinker(tt) 14-1 Miss K Scott *Hdstrng; trckd ldr; 1½l 2nd 5; pckd 9; sn wknd; lost tch frm 12; t.o & ur 2 out* .... U

OFFICIAL DISTANCES: 3*l*, 15*l* **TIME:** 6min 47.1s

1081 Open Maiden 56&7yo 7 ran

768[2] **JINFUL DU GRAND VAL (FR)** 6-4F **J Alexander** *(xnb) 9/4-6/4; 2 handlers; oht; made all; mist 4; 2l up 14; 5l clr 2 out; stayed on; comf.* 1
768[5] **Redhouse Chevalier** (7a) 4-1 **C Storey** *Opened 9/2; prom; 3l 2nd 7; eff 15 & 5l 2nd nxt; rdn & no imp aft* 5 2
920[7] **Copybook** (7a) 10-1 **J Walton** *In tch in rr; hld up; jmpd lft 3; 8l last app 5; 5l 6th 9; 6l 4th 13; grad lost tch aft; 20l 3rd 2 out; kpt on* 12 3
658[3] Chief Seattle (IRE) 5-1 J Tate *Trckd ldrs; 3½l 3rd 7; rmdrs aft 12; 6l 3rd nxt; outpcd 14; wknd 3 out; 20l 4th 2 out; 25l 4th when mist last & ur some way aft* .... U
856[C] Inglemotte Miss (5a) 8-1 L Morgan *Trckd ldr; 4l 3rd 5; cl up when fell 10* . F
856[4] Ramon Allones (IRE) 8-1 Miss R Davidson *Tde & ld to start; in tch til outpcd 10; 20l 5th when pu 13* .... P
Temple Glen (7a) 7-1 Miss J Hollands *In tch in rr; 8l last app 5; 6l last 8; lost tch 10; pu aft 12* .... P

OFFICIAL DISTANCES: 5*l*, 14*l* **TIME:** 6min 53.3s

1082 Open Maiden 8yo&up 5 ran

859[F] **LORD LANE** 5-4F **Miss N Stirling** *Trckd ldrs; 4l 3rd 5; went 2l 2nd nxt; lft in ld 9; jnd 12; hdd brief nxt; 8l clr 3 out; 15l up & in comm last; easy* 1
859[U] **I'm Willie's Girl** (5a) 2-1 **C Storey** *3s-2s; in tch in rr; 5l 4th 5; cl up til disp ld 12; ld brief nxt; 1l 2nd & pushed along 14; mist nxt; sn btn; pckd 2 out; eased flat* 25 2
658[5] **Freeway** 5-1 **Mrs V Jackson** *Burly; in tch; 8l last app 5; sltly detach 8; 15l 4th 11; 20l 3rd & btn 15* 8 3
919[U] Chase The Moon (5a) 7-1 Miss L Hislop *Trckd ldr; 3l 2nd app 5; 8l 4th 9; outpcd & 20l last 13; jmpd v slow 3 out & mist nxt; tired & virt pu flat* . 25 4
653[U] The Midnite Grocer 8-1 W Goldie *(xnb) Oht; ld; 4l up 4; jmpd big nxt; 2l up when fell 9* .... F

OFFICIAL DISTANCES: dist, 10*l* **TIME:** 7min 00.6s

Old Surrey, Burstow & West Kent

Penshurst (LH 7F,18J)

Sat, 24 Apr (GOOD to SOFT)

1083 Confined, 12st 7 ran

1053[4] **OXENDALE** (3x)(bl) 14-1 **P Bull** *Cl 3rd til prsd ldr frm 12; lft in ld aft 15; 5l up 3 out; hrd rdn & nrly jnd when btr j last; all out* 1
802[1] **Kilvoydan (IRE)** 5-2 **D Phelan** *Prsd ldr/disp til ld 10; made rest til reluct, rmdrs & hdd aft 15; chsd wnr frm 3 out; hdwy to chall when jmpd slow & lost 3l last; r.o flat; too much to do* 1½ 2
1054[4] **Live Wire (IRE)** (3x) 7-1 **Miss C Benstead** *Cl 4th til lost tch brief aft 9; hdwy to press ldng pr 13; mist 14; drpd back 7l 4th nxt; hrd rdn & some hdwy 3 out; kpt on one pce app last* 4 3

805[3] Commasarris 10-1 Mrs J Gordon *A towards rr; blun 8; 12l 5th aft 11; lsng tch when pu 13* . . . . P
896[2] Glenmont (IRE)(cp) 14-1 Ms L Stock *Last frm 4; lsng tch when ur 10* . . . . U
805[2] Glory Trail (IRE) 11-2 P Hall *In last pr most of way; mist 9; 17l 6th & rdn along aft 11; t.o 14 til pu last* . . . . P
1051[1] Granny Smith (IRE) (5a) 13-8F C Gordon *Ld/disp to 9; prsd ldr to 12; 4l 4th & pushed along app 14; wknd 3 out; pu nxt* . . . . P

OFFICIAL DISTANCES: 1½l, 2l **TIME:** 7min 05.0s
TOTE: £19.50; places £7.00,£1.40 **DF:**£16.00

1084 Restricted, 12st — 6 ran

900[3] **SLIABH FOY (IRE)** 5-2 **P Hall** *Made all; 2-4l up to 15; 8l clr 2 out; stayed on wl* 1
782[1] **Midnight Lord (IRE)** 7-4F **J Pemberton** *Last to 2; impd to trck ldr gng wl frm 4; hrd rdn 15; little resp; lost tch aft nxt* 10 2
902[P] Changing Fashion (IRE) 12-1 Miss N Barnes *Last frm 3; sn lost tch; t.o 6; nrly fnce bhnd when pu 9* . . . . P
779[P] Phar Afield (IRE) 8-1 J Sole *Cl 4/5th til lost tch aft 11; wl bhnd when pu 13* P
639[P] Red Square Prince (IRE) 8-1 C Gordon *Chsd ldr to 3; cl 3rd/4th rest of way; rdn along frm 7; prsd ldng pr 11; rmdrs 13; lost tch app 15; no ch when pu 2 out* P
1055[1] Siobhans Quinner (IRE) (5a) 9-4 D Phelan *Cl 3rd/4th most of way; pckd 12; rmdrs 13; 8l 4th when fell nxt* . . . . F

OFFICIAL DISTANCE: 5l **TIME:** 7min 06.0s **TOTE:** £3.70; places £2.30,£1.30 **DF:**£15.50

1085 S.E. Hunts Club Members (Vet & Nov Rdrs) — 9 ran

897[1] **LIVELY LORD (IRE)**(cp,tt) 5-2 **G Wigley** *Made all; 2-4l up til narrow advant aft 14; drew clr agn app 3 out; 4l up when faltered & nrly jnd app last; rallied flat; hld on game* 1
640[3] **Cloudy Creek (IRE)**(bl) 6-4F **P Bull** *A trckng wnr; clsng when mist 14; 1l down & rdn aft nxt; 4l adrift 2 out; kpt on to chall app last; ev ch flat; just outbattled* . . . . hd 2
832[4] **Algan (FR)** 10-1 **J Ryan** *Chsd ldng pr frm 4; 9l 3rd aft 11; rmdrs & clsd brief 12; lost tch frm 14; stayed on one pce frm 3 out* 10 3
902[1] Rip Kirby 11-2 G Cooper *A 3rd/4th; 17l 4th aft 11; lost tch frm 13* 20 4
1053[U] Prime Course (IRE) 16-1 Miss H Gordon *Ducked away frm app ambulance & could nt avoid jmpng 6th fnce whilst gng down; a towards rr; 30l 7th aft 11; slt prog frm 3 out* 4 5
902[2] Ginger Bug (5a) 8-1 P Chinery *A midfield; 27l 5th aft 11; same plce til wknd aft 3 out* 8 6
1051[P] The Grey Baron(tt) 16-1 Miss F Field *A last; 44l 9th aft 11; hrd rdn flat & impd a plce cl home* 15 7
897[P] Russian Connection (IRE) 16-1 A Ward-Thomas *Sn out of tch; 32l 8th aft 11; t.o frm 14* 1 8
Celtic Bounty (IRE) 16-1 D Slattery *Mid-div; 29l 6th & wkng aft 11; rr when pu 13* . . . . P

OFFICIAL DISTANCES: nk, 5l **TIME:** 7min 09.0s
TOTE: £4.30; places £1.80,£1.10,£4.40 **DF:**£2.40

The stewards interviewed the rider of Prime Course who spooked at a vehicle going to the start and jumped the open ditch; they accepted that the incident was unavoidable but cautioned her to be more careful in future

1086 Ladies Open — 5 ran

831[1] **SPRING GALE (IRE)** 7-4 **Miss Z Turner** *Mounted on course & tde; hld up in 3rd/4th; hdwy to 6l 2nd & rmdrs 12; lft in ld aft 14; 4l up nxt; made rest; kpt on str app last* 1
1053[2] **Cedar Chief**(bl) 6-4F **Mrs J Gordon** *Chsd ldr til ld 7; 10l clr aft 10; 4l up when jmpd slow 14; brief reluct & hdd bend bef nxt; chsd wnr rest of way; kpt on one pce frm 3 out* 5 2
1053[P] **Kincora (IRE)** 6-1 **Ms L Stock** *Set gd pce; ld to 6; chsd ldr til 10l 3rd 12; lost tch aft nxt; no ch frm 15* 12 3
904[U] Fair Kiowa (IRE) 7-2 Mrs S Hodge *Chsd ldrs; cl up to 9; 4th & lsng tch when pu 13* . . . . P
246[P] Moonlite Magic (IRE)(cp) 10-1 Miss J Wickens *A last; lost tch qckly; t.o 5 til pu 9* P

OFFICIAL DISTANCES: 2l, 8l **TIME:** 6min 59.0s **TOTE:** £2.10; places £1.40,£1.30 **DF:**£1.40

1087 Land Rover Mens Open — 4 ran

899[1] **SHERIFF'S FRIEND (IRE)** 1-4F **C Gordon** *Rcd keen; hld up in 3rd til prsd ldr brief 12; stdd aft nxt; 5l 3rd 3 out; qcknd 2 out; sn ld; 4l up app last; rdn out flat* 1

777[1] **King Of The Dawn** 8-1 **J Sole** *Ld; 2-5l up to 14; narrow advant aft til hdd app 2 out; sn outpcd & back in 3rd; r.o to 2nd flat* 5 2

906[1] **Royal Action** 6-1 **P Chinery** *Chsd wnr; pushed along frm 13; ld app 2 out; sn hdd; wknd app last* 2 3

832[1] Leatherback (IRE) 8-1 J Owen *A last; rmdrs & hrd rdn 15; no resp; lost tch aft nxt* 10 4

OFFICIAL DISTANCES: 3*l*, 5*l* **TIME:** 7min 09.0s **TOTE:** £1.70 **DF:**£2.70

1088 Open Maiden, 12st — 8 ran

901[3] **BARON BERNARD** 2-1F **P Chinery** *Disp ld at stdy pce; qcknd aft 11; ld 14; made rest; drew clr aft 3 out* 1

27[4] **Abbey Days (IRE)** 5-2 **J Owen** *Hld up towards rr; outpcd 13; 20l 5th aft 15; gd hdwy frm 3 out to chse wnr in 10l 2nd app last; no further prog* 12 2

895[P] **Blakes Road (IRE)** 9-2 **G Gallagher** *Settled in rr; smooth hdwy to trck ldng pr 12; mist 15; rdn to press wnr when blun 3 out; wknd app nxt* 8 3

424[5] Madam Attorney (5a) 6-1 S Gordon-Watson *Prsd ldr/disp to 15; ev ch 3 out; wknd qckly app nxt* 6 4

996[P] Scalby Croft (5a) 16-1 Miss N Barnes *Tde; disp ld to 7; cl up til lost tch frm 13; no ch frm 3 out* 10 5

782[P] Cerasus Knight (IRE)(cp) 16-1 J Morgan *Last pr most of way; cl up to 11; sn lost tch as pce qcknd; t.o frm 15* 20 6

1055[U] Sawbridge(tt) 4-1 C Gordon *Cl up til wknd 13; wl bhnd when pu 2 out* . . . P

Sir Henrik (IRE) 10-1 B Garner *Cl up in midfield; mist 10; sn wknd; last & lsng tch when pu aft nxt* . . . . . P

OFFICIAL DISTANCES: 6*l*, 5*l* **TIME:** 7min 35.0s
TOTE: £2.60; places £1.10,£1.10,£2.20 **DF:**£1.40

Pentyrch

Bonvilston (RH 7F,18J)
Sat, 24 Apr (GOOD)

1089 Hunt Members, 12st — 6 ran

450[1] **CANNON BRIDGE (IRE)** (3x) 4-6F **D Jones** *Disp ld til ld 4; jmpd lft 6; hdd 14; nt fluent 15; jnd ldr & pckd bad 3 out; 2l clr nxt; hit last; rdn out (lkd v lame aft but sound later)* 1

1024[2] **Khatani (IRE)**(tt) 10-1 **L Stephens** *Handy; rdn 9; went 2nd 10; ld 14 til jnd & drvn 3 out; outpcd app last* 8 2

675[1] **Mountain Lily** (5a) 33-1 **J Cook** *Rr but cl up til nt fluent 11 & 12 & rdn; outpcd & mist 13; t.o 15* . . . . . runin 3

Cefn Coch 66-1 W Oakes *Bckwd; ss & lost 20l; rushed up to others 3 til jmpd slow 5 & hung lft; lost tch; t.o when jmpd v slow 7; pu 8* . . . . . P

843[1] Detroit Davy (IRE) (5x) 9-2 Miss F Wilson *Hld up; went 2nd & mist & ur 7.* U

1022[1] Like The Buzz (IRE) (5a, 3x) 3-1 E Williams *Nt a fluent; w ldr til blun 4; hmpd 6; mist 8; rem 3rd 10; rdn & wknd 15; rem 3rd 2 out; pu last* . . . . . P

OFFICIAL DISTANCES: 6*l*, dist **TIME:** 6min 15.0s

1090 Confined, 12st — 12 ran

952[2] **ROSTOCK (IRE)** 2-1 **N Williams** *(xnb) 3s-2s; 2 handlers; rcd keen; disp w 2 rivals til ld 5; hdd & hit 12; sn ld agn; 4l clr 2 out; drvn & kpt on; all out* 1

974[3] **Noaff (IRE)**(tt) 6-4F **T Vaughan** *(xnb) Lw; hld up; 6th 12; eff 14; 4½l 4th & drvn; chsd wnr frm nxt; no imp* 2 2

974[P] **Inis Cara (IRE)** 7-1 **M Hooper** *Midfield; 7th 12; prog in 3rd 15; rdn to 2nd nxt; dem 2 out; sn btn* 8 3

841[2] Chief Predator (USA) (3x) 25-1 T Faulkner *Disp ld to 5; 3rd 12; chsd ldrs til 6l 5th & drvn 3 out; one-pcd* . . . . . nk 4

836[P] Zola (IRE) 16-1 P Sheldrake *Handy early; jmpd slow 8; 8th & outpcd 12; sn rdn; some prog 2 out; nd* 1 5

Form	Runner	Dist	Pos
949^{4}	Hunter Gold (FR) (3x) 10-1 Mrs B Lewis *(xnb) Hld up; impd to 2nd 9; ld 12; chsd wnr to 3 out; sn wknd; tired when mist last*	6	6
843^{3}	Flockmaster (IRE) 25-1 Mrs C Owen *Bhnd; 7th & outpcd 12; plugged into 8l 6th 3 out; sn btn; nt fluent 2 out & last*	10	7
613^{4}	How To Run (IRE) (3x) 12-1 Miss H Lewis *Chsd ldrs; 5th 12; wknd 14; nd aft*	$1\frac{1}{2}$	8
	Gold Kriek 6-1 D Jones *Bhnd til pu 12*		P
	Harppy (FR) 50-1 M Barber *(xnb) Swtng; chsd ldrs; 4th 12; wknd nxt; t.o & pu last*		P
1023^{P}	Pride Of Pennker (IRE) (5a) 40-1 M Flynn *(xnb) Lw; disp ld to 5; wknd 8; t.o 12; event pu last*		P
1021^{4}	Saffron Moss 25-1 R Carey *Imm lost tch; mist 5; jmpd slow 6 & rdn; t.o 12; cont v slow til event ur last*		U

OFFICIAL DISTANCES: 2*l*, 8*l* **TIME:** 6min 14.0s

1091 Panacur/TBA PPORA Club Members Mares Maiden, 12st — 11 ran

Form	Runner	Dist	Pos
845^{U}	**RUBY DANTE (IRE)** (5a) 6-4F **D Jones** *Nt jw; trckd ldrs; went 2nd & hit 10; ld 12; 7l clr when mist 15; mist nxt; a in comm; eased flat*		1
950^{P}	**Countess Kiri** (5a) 25-1 **P Sheldrake** *Bhnd; hdwy 11; 6th 13; no prog til went 15l 2nd app 2 out; flatt by prox*	8	2
846^{2}	**Modesty Forbids** (5a) 6-1 **Miss F Wilson** *Bhnd; last 12; still poor 8th 15; plugged past btn horses; nvr nr ldrs*	20	3
948^{P}	Ladygal (IRE) (12a) 20-1 D Davies *Jmpd poor in rr; mists 11 & 12; 7th nxt; some prog in 4l 4th 15; rchd mod 3rd 3 out til mist last; dem cl home*	$\frac{1}{2}$	4
736^{2}	Blakeney Hill (5a) 5-1 J Price *Ld to 12; sn outpcd by wnr; lost 2nd app 2 out; fin v wkly*	15	5
	Ballet Red (5a) 5-2 L Stephens *Swtng; prom early; drpd back last 7; rallied 12; 8th nxt; 7th & wkng 15; pu 3 out*		P
837^{4}	Geal Farraige (IRE) (12a) 12-1 N Oliver *(xnb) Settled rr; hdwy 9; 6l 5th 12; 10l 3rd & drvn 15; wknd tame; pu 2 out*		P
454^{P}	Laurelgirl (IRE) (5a) 12-1 M Barber *Swtng bad; chsd ldr to 10; 4th & u.p 12; pu nxt; dism*		P
883^{4}	Miss Chloe (IRE) (5a) 10-1 J Jenkins *Jmpd mod in last trio; u.p 6; strugg 13 & nt lk keen; t.o & pu 2 out*		P
676^{U}	Swingingbridge (5a) 7-1 N Williams *Hld up in rr til hdwy 9; 4th 13; drvn & wknd aft nxt; poor 6th 3 out; pu 2 out*		P
362^{P}	Tragic Belle (5a) 25-1 James Price *(xnb) Settled 3rd; rmdrs 12; still 3rd when fell 14 & broke leg; dead*		F

OFFICIAL DISTANCES: 10*l*, 20*l* **TIME:** 6min 23.0s

1092 Intermediate, 12st — 11 ran

Form	Runner	Dist	Pos
695^{1}	**GIPSY GIRL** (5a) evensF **M Barber** *A gng wl; trckd ldrs; went 2nd 9; ld 11; drew clr app 2 out; easily*		1
844^{1}	**Barton Dream (IRE)** 5-1 **T Vaughan** *(xnb) 2 handlers; chsd ldrs; 3rd 11; went 2nd 13; drvn & outpcd aft 3 out*	8	2
109^{1}	**Catechist (IRE)** 4-1 **Julian Pritchard** *Ld to 4 & 6-11; releg 5th 14; 5l 4th 3 out; rallied to 3rd at last; no ch w wnr*	5	3
870^{1}	Court Adjourn 5-1 J Newbold *Nt jw; rr til hdwy 9; 5l 5th 12; 2nd brief 14; 2l 3rd & drvn nxt; 12l 3rd & tired 2 out; blun last & eased*	12	4
922^{4}	Themaster's Choice (IRE) 40-1 M Goldstein *Prom til hmpd 7 & lost plce; 8l 6th 12; strugg 14*	15	5
841^{1}	Buckland Boy (5x)(vis) 10-1 W Oakes *Sn last pr; last when jmpd v slow 11; t.o when scrambled over 13 & pu*		P
671^{4}	Candlestone Castle 10-1 N Williams *Midfield; 4th & eff 12; nt fluent nxt; 7l 5th & drvn when nt fluent 3 out; tired aft; pu last*		P
1023^{P}	Glen Mist (IRE)(bl) 25-1 L Stephens *(xnb) Ld 4-6; 2nd when jmpd v slow & to lft nxt; caused some mayhem; pu 8*		P
1029^{5}	Millennium Gold 16-1 Miss A Frieze *Midfield til hmpd 7; nt rec; rr & hit 8; 8th 12; t.o & pu 15*		P
846^{1}	Vicars Chalet (IRE) 8-1 E Williams *Towards rr; rdn 11; 7th nxt; t.o & pu 14*		P
948^{2}	Wiston Wizo(bl) 40-1 P Sheldrake *(xnb) Swtng; a last pr; strugg 13; jmpd v slow frm nxt; t.o & pu 2 out*		P

OFFICIAL DISTANCES: 8*l*, 3*l* **TIME:** 6min 11.0s

1093 Mixed Open (Welsh P-t-P Grand National), 4m, 12st - 24J — 10 ran

382^{2} **DOWN (FR)** 4-5F **S Waley-Cohen** *Confid rdn in midfield; tk 4th 19; niggled nxt; clsd to ld 3 out; drew rt away frm nxt; hvly eased flat* 1

514^{1} **Speed Board (IRE)** 16-1 **J Cook** *Went 3rd 6-12; chsd ldrs; 5th & eff 19; 13l 6th & rdn nxt; still 28l 4th 2 out; plugged into 2nd at last; flatt by prox.* 10 2

951^{1} **Red Neck**(tt) 4-1 **T Vaughan** *(xnb) Hld up; eff in 10l 5th 20; tk 3rd 3 out; drvn & sn wknd; fin exhaust; walked in* 25 3

738^{3} Aficionado (IRE) 100-1 H Oakes *Jmpd slow in last pr; lost tch rap 14; t.o when ref 20 & ended up in open ditch* . . . . r

989^{2} Croft Court 33-1 D Renney *Cl up; 6th 12; rdn & wknd 16; t.o 18; pu 3 out* P

Daisys Rainbow (7a) 66-1 D Jones *Bckwd & nt lw; jmpd stickily in detach last; t.o 7 (v green); hung violent lft aft 12 & unrideable; sn pu* . . . . P

974^{F} Dawn's Cognac (IRE) 6-1 N Williams *Ld/2nd til ld 17; drvn & hdd 3 out; 3l 2nd & 15l clr of rest nxt; fdd rap uphill; pu last* . . . . P

842^{1} Pharailde (5a) 10-1 J Price *Tk keen hld; cl up; mostly 3rd 12 til hit 18; wkng when mists nxt 2; t.o & tired when pu 2 out* . . . . P

1016^{5} Picket Piece(bl) 16-1 M Goldstein *Midfield; 5th & eff 18; cl 2nd & ev ch when fell 21* F

842^{3} Waders (IRE)(tt) 14-1 M Barber *Ld/cl 2nd to 20; drvn & sn wknd; 16l 4th 3 out; v tired when pu last* . . . . P

OFFICIAL DISTANCES: 10*l*, dist **TIME:** 8min 32.0s

1094 Restricted (Div 1), 12st — 10 ran

974^{P} **BILL HAZE**(cp) 6-1 **D Jones** *Midfield til 3rd & prog 7; went 2nd 8; hung violent lft & nrly pulled himself up aft 12; ld 14; sn 8l clr; swishing tail when jmpd v slow 2 out; still 5l clr but hanging & drvn when hit last* . . . 1

845^{1} **Rag Week (IRE)** 6-4JF **E Williams** *Jmpd poor; 2nd to 7; 3rd til lft 8l 2nd aft 14; drvn & tried to rally to gt within 4l 2 out; sn brushed aside* 8 2

974^{F} **Hail Stone (IRE)** 8-1 **L Stephens** *3rd/4th; u.p 11 & dem nxt; nt r.o; 30l 4th 15; tk rem 3rd last* 25 3

473^{3} Chief Suspect (IRE) 12-1 J Jenkins *Swtng; towards rr; 6th 11; rdn & reluct aft; 32l 6th 15* 12 4

953^{P} Black Dan 50-1 D Underwood *Imm strugg in last; t.o 11; btn 2 fncs (rdr's 1st completion)* 2fncs 5

953^{2} Batchworth Lock 10-1 M Lewis *(xnb) Rr & nvr gng wl; sn drvn; t.o & pu aft 12* P

953^{3} Daisy's Choice (5a) 12-1 P Sheldrake *Bhnd; jmpd slow 4 & rdn; drvn & nvr gng wl aft; pu 11* . . . . P

952^{R} Final Mick 33-1 J Price *(xnb) Ref to rce* . . . . r

950^{1} Pams Oak 6-4JF Miss F Wilson *Ld at fast pce early; mist 11; just hdd when terrible mist 14; swerved lft & nrly rn off course; 28l 4th 15; still 4th but t.o when jmpd v slow last; pu flat* . . . . P

844^{P} Satco Prince (IRE) 25-1 N Williams *(xnb) Rmdrs 4; midfield; 15l 4th aft 12; lft 16l 3rd aft 14; still rem 3rd but v tired when pu 2 out* . . . . P

OFFICIAL DISTANCES: 8*l*, 30*l* **TIME:** 6min 20.0s

A woman (obviously with a death wish) waddled across the course near the fourth fence in the path of the oncoming runners

1095 Restricted (Div 2), 12st — 8 ran

844^{3} **CAMDEN CARAMEL (IRE)** (5a) 5-2F **T Faulkner** *Settled midfield; clsd & lft 2nd 12; rdn 14; ld 3 out; drew wl clr nxt; virt pu flat* 1

1022^{P} **Lady Palamon (IRE)** (5a) 4-1 **M Barber** *2nd/3rd til lft in ld 12; 4l clr 14; hdd & rdn 3 out; imm outpcd; jmpd slow last* 10 2

948^{P} **Tenacious Melody** 14-1 **Miss I Tompsett** *(xnb) Stdd & lost 12l start; pulled hrd & mists; blun bad 13 & lost tch; t.o 3 out; crashed thro last* 20 3

Clear Away (IRE) 3-1 T Vaughan *Midfield; jmpd slow 10; 5th & wkng 14; last when pu nxt* P

949^{P} Coolarne Leader (IRE) 14-1 D Jones *2nd/3rd til hit 11; sn lost plce; 4th & strugg 14; t.o & pu 3 out* . . . . P

1021^{P} Evans The Coal 25-1 R Carey *(xnb) Mounted outside padd; mists in last pr; rmdrs 3; rdr stepped off 6* . . . . U

974^{P} Minster Belle (5a) 4-1 P Sheldrake *Hld up; lft 3rd 12; 12l 3rd 14; wknd rap; wl bhnd when pu 2 out* . . . . P

694^{3} Musical Sleuth (7a) 5-1 J Price *Keen early; hit 11; ld til fell hvly 12* . . . . . F

OFFICIAL DISTANCES: 15*l*, 25*l* **TIME:** 6min 21.0s

Beehive Lad (James Price, 5-1, unruly padd & hit rdr in fce drawing blood) was withdrawn not under orders; Rule 4 deduction 10p in pound

1096 Open Maiden 56&7yo, 12st — 14 ran

845[2]	**ROBOASTAR (USA)**(bl) 7-2 **T Vaughan** *Settled 3rd; lft 2nd aft 7 & lft in ld 11; 30l clr by 14; unchall; rdr stood up in irons & in ecstasies of delight passing post.*		1
950[3]	**The Lords Cross (IRE)** 20-1 **M Barber** *Mounted outside padd & tde; midfield; 15l 5th 10; went 12l 2nd 13; sn wl adrift; mist 3 out*	20	2
675[3]	Black Hope (IRE) (5a)(tt) 12-1 N Williams *(xnb) Stdd start; squeezed for room & rn out 1; cont to bolt brief*		R
950[P]	Bold Flirtation 50-1 J Price *(xnb) Sis; veered & caused mayhem 1; jmpd v stickily; hopelessly t.o when nrly stuck on top of 7 & imm pu*		P
845[P]	Celtic Prince (IRE) 12-1 Julian Pritchard *(xnb) Carried out 1*		C
950[2]	Dans Blarney (IRE) 7-1 D Jones *(xnb) 2 handlers; midfield; 13l 4th 10; lft 3rd 13 but 40l adrift when mist nxt; ref 15; cont; crawled over 2 out & pu*		r
676[3]	Deltic Arrow 12-1 D Davies *(xnb) Pckd bad 5; ld/disp til lft in ld aft 7; blun bad & ur 11*		U
	Essence Of Time (7a) 33-1 Miss I Tompsett *Sis; sn t.o; blun bad & ur 7*		U
845[P]	Finlays Folly 33-1 C Penycate *Mounted early & ur padd; sis; a rr; wl t.o 8; pu 11*		P
845[P]	Maloney (IRE) 33-1 Miss C Evans *Midfield; 23l 7th 10; t.o when crawled 12 & 13; pu nxt*		P
363[3]	Millys Filly (5a) 25-1 Miss F Wilson *Ref & ur 1*		r
676[F]	Rescindo (IRE) (7a) 4-6F W Oakes *Ld/disp til slpd up aft 7*		S
676[P]	Stand On 10-1 E Williams *Mists in rr; 21l 6th 10; blun 11 & pu*		P
700[P]	The Leazes (7a) 14-1 L Stephens *2 handlers; tkn to horse boxes to be mounted; 3rd/4th; 10l 3rd 10; hit 12; releg 4th & wkng when blun 13 & pu*		P

OFFICIAL DISTANCE: 25*l* **TIME:** 6min 25.0s

South & West Wilts

Larkhill (RH 13F,18J)

Sat, 24 Apr (GOOD to FIRM)

1097 Hunt Members, 12st — 4 ran

1022[3]	**JUST LARK** 5-1 **R Bliss** *Trckd ldrs in 3rd mostly; 3½l 3rd 4; chsd ldr frm 13; disp ld nxt; ld 3 out; drew clr frm nxt; rdr celebrating at post*		1
864[3]	**Darcey Mae** (5a) 4-5F **Miss L Bridges** *(xnb) Tchd 11/10; swtng; ld; 3l up 4; still 1½l up 13; jnd nxt; hdd 3 out; one pce frm nxt*	8	2
863[P]	**Merry Shot (IRE)** 9-4 **J Snowden** *Fat; chsd ldr; 1½l 2nd 6; mist 13; wknd frm 15; one pce frm nxt*	10	3
969[5]	Lyrical Seal (5a)(bl) 6-1 Miss A Goschen *A last; 6l bhnd 4; mist 12; nvr able to chall; has been retired.*	2½	4

OFFICIAL DISTANCES: 10*l*, 10*l* **TIME:** 6min 10.9s **TOTE:** £4.00

1098 Open Maiden, 12st — 10 ran

791[P]	**WYNFORD EAGLE** (7a) 10-1 **A Merriam** *Disp 3rd 3; lft disp ld 8; hdd 12; lft in ld agn 13; made rest; stayed on u.p flat.*		1
1067[P]	**Lord Of Heaven (USA)** 12-1 **Miss K Cuthbertson** *Tchd 14s; 9th 2; slt hdwy 10; rap prog 12; lft 2nd 13; chsd wnr til no ex frm last; fin lame on off-fore*	6	2
962[P]	**Roseacre (IRE)**(bl) 4-1 **Miss A Goschen** *(xnb) Disp 3rd 3; lft 2nd 5; trckd ldrs frm 8; wknd qckly 14; plodding on in last when inherited rem 3rd 16*	40	3
865[4]	Able Bob (IRE) 20-1 R Bliss *(xnb) 8th 3; sn last; mist 6; t.o frm 10 til pu 3 out*		P
927[F]	Bolebec Ice Falcon 5-1 S Joynes *(xnb) Last 1; 18l 8th 4; stdy hdwy to 5th 9; wknd qckly frm 14; bhnd when pu 2 out*		P
	Calling Home (IRE) 8-1 W Kavanagh *Swtng; 10½l 5th 4; chsd ldng pr frm 8 til wknd qckly frm 15; bhnd when pu last*		P
413[F]	Dubious Deal 14-1 J Snowden *(xnb) Ld & pulled v hrd; sn clr; 20l up when mist & rn lft 6; still clr when ref & ur nxt.*		r
865[F]	Queens House (5a) 6-1 D Drake *Tchd 13/2; 17l 7th 4; a bhnd; mist 10; bhnd when pu & dism aft 13; ld back but reported sound aft*		P
871[U]	Saffron Hill (IRE) (7a) 4-5F R Bandey *(xnb) 5/2-4/5; pckd bad 1; chsd ldr; jmpd bold 3; saddle slpd & rn out app 5*		R
598[P]	Sunleys Quest (5a) 16-1 Miss L Bridges *(xnb) 12l 6th 4; lft 4th 5; lft disp ld 8; ld aft 12; pu aft nxt; saddle slpd*		P

OFFICIAL DISTANCES: 6*l*, dist **TIME:** 6min 18.5s **TOTE:** £6.30

1099 Ladies Open — 5 ran

Form	Runner	Dist	Pos
822^{4}	**VIRTUOSO** 12-1 **Mrs S Corcoran** *Chsd ldr; hvly rstrnd; 1½l down 5; dem 3rd 13; ld 3 out; hrd prsd dem nxt til pushed out flat; cosily; rdr's 1st wnr. .*		1
860^{1}	**Masalarian (IRE)** 9-2 **Miss L Bridges** *(xnb) Re-saddled padd; disp 3rd 2; 4½l last 6; trckd ldng trio 13 til 2nd frm 2 out; ev ch last; no ex. . . . .*	2½	2
757^{1}	**Caldamus** 2-1 **Miss A Goschen** *Ld; 1½l up 4; mist 8; hdd 3 out; still ch aft nxt; sn btn; fin lame . . . .*	8	3
635^{2}	Sir D'Orton (FR) 4-5F Miss C Tizzard *6/4-4/5; disp 3rd 2; 3l 4th 6; chsd ldr frm 13; mist & lost plce 15; still ch aft 2 out; rdn & fnd nil . . . .*	3	4
816^{2}	Mostyn 11-2 Miss C Stucley *Hld up til disp 1½l 2nd 5; chsd ldrs til wknd 13; drpd out qckly; bhnd when pu 15 . . . .*		P

OFFICIAL DISTANCES: 2½*l*, 5*l* **TIME:** 6min 05.6s **TOTE:** £5.50

1100 Mens Open, 12st — 6 ran

Form	Runner	Dist	Pos
$825^{1\dagger}$	**SPRINGFORD (IRE)** (7x) 4-7F **D Alers-Hankey** *(xnb) Chsd ldng pr; 5l 3rd 5; hdwy to ld aft 12; made rest; sn clr; eased flat. . . . .*		1
863^{3}	**Woodlands Beau (IRE)** (7x) 5-1 **T Dreaper** *Ld 1 & agn 4; hit 5; jnd & hit nxt; hdd 11; stayed on to chse wnr vain frm 14; mist nxt; one pce frm 2 out*	8	2
938^{3}	**Oscar Wilde** 4-1 **D Drake** *Hld up in last; impd to 4th 7; stayed on one pce frm 15; nvr trbld ldng pr . . . .*	6	3
972^{3}	Makhpiya Patahn (IRE) 12-1 D I Turner *(xnb) Chsd ldr til ld 2-4; drvn up to disp ld agn 6; hdd 12; chsd wnr til grad wknd frm 14; bhnd frm 2 out. .*	25	4
585^{2}	Polar King (IRE) 12-1 R Bandey *9l 5th 4; mist 8 & sn last; bhnd frm 13; t.o & pu aft 2 out. . . . .*		P
963^{7}	Primero (IRE) (7x)(tt) 7-1 G Weatherley *(xnb) 12s-7s; mostly 4th; 8l adrift 5-7; bhnd frm 13; t.o & pu aft 2 out . . . .*		P

OFFICIAL DISTANCES: 8*l*, 5*l* **TIME:** 5min 58.7s **TOTE:** £1.50

1101 PPORA Club Members (Nov Rdrs), 12st — 12 ran

Form	Runner	Dist	Pos
1012^{2}	**MR BEN GUNN** (7x) 3-1 **Miss V Heal** *(xnb) 6s-3s; hld up; disp 15l 7th 5; rdr called cab 8; hdwy to 12l 6th 13; staying on str when lft in ld 2 out; rdn out; rdr's 1st wnr . . . .*		1
963^{4}	**Leon Garcia (IRE)** (5a) 5-4F **T Bishop** *Tchd 11/8; trckd ldrs; 12½l 5th 5; chsd ldr frm 15; no ex frm last . . . .*	5	2
861^{2}	**Coolteen Hero (IRE)** (7x) 5-1 **D Jacob** *(xnb) Tchd 6s; chsd ldrs; 5th 9; 5½l 3rd 13; stayed on one pce frm 3 out. . . . .*	1½	3
603^{4}	Opal'lou (FR) (5a) 6-1 R Pyman *(xnb) 8s-6s; swtng; sa; sn in tch; disp 15l 7th 5; rap hdwy frm 7; 4th 9; ld 12; hdd nxt; sn wknd; one pce frm 3 out. .*	5	4
1012^{3}	Millyhenry (7x) 20-1 R Lee *Mist 3 & mostly towards rr; 8th 13; nrst fin; nd*	½	5
862^{2}	Cherokee Boy 10-1 Miss C Atkinson *Tchd 12s; 11th 5; some hdwy to mid-div 9; 7th 13; kpt on; nd; carried wide by loose horse flat . . . .*	½	6
969^{3}	Chism (IRE) 20-1 W King *Disp 15l 7th 5; a bhnd; nvr trbld ldrs. . . . .*	10	7
922^{3}	Silent Action (USA) 20-1 D Smith *Prom; 2½l 3rd 5; grad lost plce frm 13; t.o frm 2 out. . . . .*	25	8
687^{3}	Alex Thuscombe(vis) 20-1 Mrs R Barclay *(bf) Prom; ld 3; 2l up 8; hdd 12; ld agn nxt; still 3l up when blun & ur 2 out; unlucky. . . . .*		U
862^{U}	Calfstown Lord 20-1 Miss S Lane *A bhnd; last frm 2; t.o 6; blun & ur 12 .*		U
1066^{P}	Hillview Hut (IRE)(bl) 20-1 W Kavanagh *Prom; ld 2; 1l 2nd 5; chsd ldr til mist 9; wknd frm 12; t.o & pu 15 . . . .*		P
989^{4}	Libido 20-1 P Andrew *Ld to 2; sn lost plce; bhnd frm 9; clambered over 12; t.o & pu 15 . . . .*		P

OFFICIAL DISTANCES: 3*l*, 1½*l* **TIME:** 6min 07.8s **TOTE:** £2.80

1102 Restricted, 12st — 10 ran

Form	Runner	Dist	Pos
802^{2}	**TRUMPER** 100-30 **Miss A Goschen** *2 handlers; swtng; ld 4; jnd 6; hdd nxt; chsd ldng pr frm 15; sust rn on inner frm 2 out; ld flat; wl rdn . . . .*		1
637^{1}	**Saucy Arethusa** (5a) 5-2 **N Harris** *(xnb) Hld up; hdwy to chse ldrs 10; 3l down & clsng 3 out; disp ld when hmpd last; no ex flat . . . .*	1¼	2
879^{3}	**River Dante (IRE)** 14-1 **S Kidston** *(xnb) Trckd ldrs; disp ld 6; ld nxt; hdd 13; ld agn 15; jnd & mist last; sn btn. . . . .*	2	3
579^{R}	Shillelah Law 10-1 A Charles-Jones *(xnb) Swtng; hld up; a bhnd; some late hdwy; nd . . . .*	25	4
794^{3}	Carling Elect (5a) 25-1 Miss L Hawkings *(xnb) Prom; disp ld to 3; 2l 3rd 7; ld 13; hdd 15; sn wknd; bhnd frm 2 out . . . .*	¾	5

864^{2} Bally Blue 2-1F L Jefford *(xnb) 3s-2s; 5th 7; nd; one pce frm 15; disapp* . . . 7 6
973^{4} Aslapoftheeuro (IRE) 25-1 R Bliss *Swtng profuse; a towards rr; 9th 6; t.o & pu 2 out* . . . P
791^{P} Farley Water 25-1 D Edwards *Last frm 6; mist 8; t.o 12 til pu 15* . . . P
819^{3} Floodgate 20-1 J Diment *(bnh) Tde; 6th 4; hdwy to disp ld 6; hdd nxt; still cl up when pu 12* . . . P
871^{1} Menantol 7-1 Miss A de Lisle Wells *Prom; disp ld to 3; grad lost plce; wknd frm 14; bhnd frm nxt; pu 2 out* . . . P

OFFICIAL DISTANCES: 1½*l*, 1½*l* **TIME:** 6min 07.1s **TOTE:** £2.20

Thames Valley Combined Hunts Club

Kingston Blount (LH 8F,18J)

Sat, 24 Apr (GOOD to FIRM)

1103 Thames V. Combined Hunts Club Members, 12st — 4 ran

867^{U} **MR SPLODGE** 2-1 **James Tudor** *(xnb) 3rd til went 2l 2nd aft 5; jmpd to ld 6; made rest; hit 11; jnd 15-nxt; 2 up & gng best when lft wl clr 2 out; eased to walk flat* . . . 1
938^{P} **Scallybuck (IRE)** 12-1 **T Underwood** *A last; 8l adrift 5; blun 9; t.o when jmpd lft 13; hopelessly t.o frm 14; lft 2nd & jmpd lft 2 out* . . . runin 2
.806^{1} Charlie's Angel (5a) 1-2F P York *(xnb) 2nd til drpd to 3rd 6; trckd ldrs aft til went 2l 2nd 13; prsd ldr nxt; hit 15; 2l 2nd & hld when fell hvly 2 out* . . . F
938^{6} Sunczech (IRE) (5a) 10-1 Miss S Phizacklea *(xnb) Ld to 6; cl 2nd nxt; pushed along frm 11-13; no resp & lost tch qckly w ldng pr; 25l 3rd when pu & dism 14* . . . P

OFFICIAL DISTANCE: dist **TIME:** 6min 20.0s

1104 Thames V. Combined Hunts Club Members (Nov Rdrs), 12st — 7 ran

838^{2} **WIBBLEY WOBBLEY** 3-1 **Miss L Ellis** *Opened 7/2; hit 2; mid-div til hdwy 11; 3l 2nd aft 13; prsd ldr frm 15; nipped thro on inner to ld last; r.o wl; wl rdn; rdr's 1st wnr* . . . 1
868^{P} **La Colina (IRE)** 7-2 **N Docker** *Opened 4s; ld; jnd 15; hdd app last; no ex cl home* . . . 1½ 2
1032^{P} **Border Farmer (IRE)** 16-1 **N Wain** *Swtng; tde; 2nd 4; lost plce 6; 8l 5th 11; r.o agn 14; 15l 4th 2 out; went 3rd app last; no imp on ldng pr* . . . 15 3
969^{1} Lottie The Lotus (5a) 2-1F Miss R Goodwin *(xnb) Cl up til lost plce 4; 6th nxt; 10l last 13; rdn & r.o frm 14; kpt on to 4th cl home; nvr plcd to chall* . . . 1 4
1029^{F} Steve Ford 10-1 Miss E Harbour *Rr; last 3; 9l 6th 12; no ch frm nxt; stayed on to poor 3rd 2 out; wknd & dem app last & agn flat* . . . 3 5
892^{P} Noble Colours (1ow) 14-1 P Ikin *In tch; 5l 5th 6; hdwy nxt; 2l 2nd 10; outpcd ldng pr 13; 10l 3rd 15; wknd qckly nxt* . . . 12 6
868^{5} Rough Tiger (IRE) (4ow) 4-1 B Tuckey *Prsd ldr to 3; 3rd frm 5; drpd to 5th 11 & last by 14; blun & rdr shot up in air 15; bumbled on; rdr a liability* . . . 8 7

OFFICIAL DISTANCES: 2*l*, 10*l* **TIME:** 6min 18.0s

1105 Mens Open, 12st — 6 ran

777^{2} **ESPRIT DE COTTE (FR)** 8-1 **P York** *Confid rdn; cl 2nd til ld aft 13; pushed along 15; stayed on wl frm 2 out* . . . 1
866^{1} **Mr Snowman** 7-4F **James Tudor** *Cl up; 3rd frm 2; trckd ldrs til went 2l 2nd app 14; ev ch frm nxt til wknd tame 2 out* . . . 7 2
1032^{4} **Paddies Boy (IRE)** (7x)(cp) 4-1 **Jack Young** *Rr frm 1; plodded rnd & a wl bhnd; went dist 5th 12; lft rem 3rd by 3 out* . . . runin 3
867^{U} Perfect Finisher 33-1 T Ellis *Settled 4th; 6l down 9; 15l 4th when blun 13; dem last nxt; t.o* . . . 30 4
Ball In The Net 2-1 M Holdforth *Ld to 12; 2l 2nd nxt; dem 3rd 14; rap lost tch w ldng pr; dist 4th when pu 2 out* . . . P
938^{F} Kustom Kit Grizzly (IRE)(bl) 6-1 T Lane *(xnb) 5th 2; jmpd slow 6; rdn 8; last 11; nt keen aft; t.o 13; pu 3 out* . . . P

OFFICIAL DISTANCES: 6*l*, dist **TIME:** 6min 08.0s

1106 Ladies Open — 2 ran

Form	Runner	Dist	Pos
785^{3}	**KILLERINE (FR)** (7x) evens **Miss H Irving** *Ld to 14; cl 2nd aft; pushed along 3 out; r.o to ld last; rdn & r.o best cl home; fin sore & nr fore bandaged aft rce*		1
743^{3}	**Linlathen** (7x) 8-11F **Miss Gemma Hutchinson** *(xnb) Cl 2nd; hit 8; rdn to ld 14; 2l up 3 out; rdn app nxt; jnd last; no ex cl home.*	1	2

OFFICIAL DISTANCE: nk **TIME:** 6min 15.0s

1107 Restricted, 12st — 7 ran

Form	Runner	Dist	Pos
853^{2}	**MISS ZARNNI** (5a) 2-1 **Miss S Sharratt** *Hld up; last 5; 10l adrift 9; rap hdwy to press ldr 11; drpd back to 4th 13; chsd ldrs nxt; 3l 3rd 14; ld 2 out; kpt on wl*		1
684^{5}	**Bell Rock** 6-1 **James Tudor** *(xnb) Hld up rr; hdwy frm 12; chsd ldrs 14; 5l 4th 15; rdn & r.o to 3l 2nd app last; a hld.*	2½	2
587^{7}	**Rommel** 7-4F **J Trice-Rolph** *Prom; trckd ldrs in cl 3rd frm 5; 3l 3rd & still ev ch 3 out; wknd qckly aft nxt.*	15	3
990^{U}	Table For Four(vis) 20-1 M Mackley *Ld 2; narrow advant aft til hdd app 2 out; imm btn; v one-pcd & dem 4th app last.*	6	4
1030^{2}	Shortcut Shorty 5-1 C Wadland *Cl up; 4th 5; jmpd slow & drpd to rr 10; nvr gng wl aft; went dist 5th aft 2 out.*	15	5
1051^{P}	Kniveniven (IRE) 33-1 Miss B Donnelly *Prom; 2nd frm 5; trckd ldr aft til outpcd aft 13; dem 4th & blun 14; wknd qckly.*	8	6
866^{2}	Kingfisher Star 10-1 Miss J Lodge *(xnb) Ldng when sprawled on landing & ur 1*		U

OFFICIAL DISTANCES: 2½l, 6l **TIME:** 6min 27.0s

1108 Open Maiden, 12st — 8 ran

Form	Runner	Dist	Pos
940^{3}	**CARAIYNI (IRE)**(tt) 6-1 **J Jarrett** *Mid-div; 4½l 5th 9; trckd ldrs in 4l 3rd 13; ld 2 out; stayed on wl u.p frm app last*		1
58^{2}	**Dreamie Battle** (5a) 6-1 **Miss S Sharratt** *Hld up; 5th 5; 1½l 3rd nxt; ld frm 11-3 out; dem 3rd aft nxt; rnwd chall on inner app last; ev ch but no ex flat*	hd	2
871^{3}	**Sandy Lark** 5-1 **G Tawell** *Prom; 3rd 4; 4l 4th 8; nt qckn & lost tch ldng trio aft 13; no ch nxt; kpt on one pce frm 3 out; lft 3rd at last*	8	3
1035^{P}	Fawsley Lake (5a) 12-1 P Cowley *Rr; last frm 5; sn t.o; lft 4th by defections*	35	4
971^{3}	Barbed Broach (IRE) 33-1 Miss C Cowe *(xnb) 2 handlers; tde; 2nd til ld frm 7-10; 3l 2nd when fell 12*		F
588^{4}	Eastern Apple (5a) 5-1 B King *In tch in 3rd 5; drpd to 6th 9; rmdrs 10; hit 11; lost tch qckly; t.o & pu 14*		P
1061^{P}	Marbank Lad (IRE)(cp) 12-1 M Mackley *2 handlers; a rr; 10l 5th 13; labouring aft; t.o & pu 3 out*		P
789^{3}	To The Top 7-4F James Tudor *Ld til blun bad & drpd to 3rd 6; 3½l 3rd when lft 2nd 12; prsd ldr frm 14; ev ch til wknd v qckly aft 2 out; 8l 3rd & v tired when ref last*		r

OFFICIAL DISTANCES: hd, 12l **TIME:** 6min 23.0s

United Pack

Brampton Bryan (RH 8F,19J)
Sat, 24 Apr (GOOD/GOOD to FIRM)

1109 Hunts Members — 4 ran

Form	Runner	Dist	Pos
835^{5}	**WILD EDRIC**(bl) 3-1 **A Beedles** *5s-3s; made all; qcknd clr app 3 out; hrd prsd when lft clr 2 out; kpt on (loose horse prob helped); unimpressive*		1
977^{4}	**Legend Of Light (IRE)** (5a) 4-6F **S Hughes** *Evens-4/6; hld up in 3rd; rdn frm 14; nt stride out & sn no ch; lft 2nd 2 out*	8	2
731^{P}	**Norse** 25-1 **R Hodges** *Bhnd frm 13; t.o 3 out; fin lame & dism imm aft post*	10	3
1018^{1}	Magicien (FR) 11-4 Miss C Taylor *1st ride; rdr insecure; a.p; lkd outpcd aft 16; hdwy agn to chall & rfo 2 out*		U

OFFICIAL DISTANCES: 8l, 10l **TIME:** 7min 17.0s

1110 Mens Open, 12st — 5 ran

Form	Runner	Dist	Pos
994^{P}	**SHINY BAY (IRE)** 9-4 **N Pearce** *Hld up; jmpd slow 5; mist 7; prog to 2nd 10; 3½l 3rd 12; went 2nd 14 & ld 3 out; sn clr; kpt on str*		1
1024^{3}	**Persona Pride** 6-1 **R Hodges** *Ld; 6l clr 5; mist 7; hdd 3 out; kpt on one pce*	10	2

612^{P} Inthaar(bl) 33-1 A Phillips *8l 3rd 4; went 2nd 5; 2nd when blun & ur 9* . . U

979^{F} Jimmy Jumbo (IRE) 10-1 N Cecil *2nd early; grad lost tch frm 11; rem 3rd when fell last* . . . . . F

629^{P} Paddy For Paddy (IRE) 4-5F R Burton *Hld up; went 3l 2nd 12; rdn along frm 13; no hdwy frm nxt; btn 3rd when pu 2 out* . . . . . P

OFFICIAL DISTANCE: 8 **TIME:** 7min 10.0s

1111 Ladies Open — 5 ran

839^{5} **CERTAIN SURPRISE** (5a) 7-1 **Miss E James** *16l 3rd 6; grad hdwy frm 8; 8l 3rd 12; went 2nd 2 out; 3l 2nd & staying on wl when lft clr last* 1

849^{4} **Life Of A River (IRE)** 9-2 **Miss H Kinsey** *Ld; 10l clr 5; 4l clr 12; mist 16; hdd 3 out; lost 2nd nxt; no ch when lft 2nd agn at last* 7 2

835^{P} Allotrope (IRE)(cp,tt) 25-1 Miss H Kinsey *Mist 5 & drpd back last; 21l last 7; t.o & pu 13* . . . . . P

999^{U} Ard Na Carrig (IRE) 20-1 Miss A Parkes *20l 4th 7; grad drpd further bhnd; t.o & pu 11* . . . . . P

479^{1} Supreme Citizen (IRE) 2-7F Miss J Williams *Mostly 2nd; ld 3 out; ab 3l clr when tried to rn out last, hit wing & ur; horse scrambled over* . . . . U

OFFICIAL DISTANCE: 7*l* **TIME:** 7min 01.0s

1112 Dodson & Horrell PPORA Club Members, 12st — 4 ran

972^{1} **BALLY WIRRAL (IRE)** 8-11F **G Maundrell** *Jw; prom; 4l 2nd 8; jmpd to ld 16; sn lft wl clr (nearest pursuer pu); v easily; dism aft fin* 1

886^{5} **Weavers Choice**(bl) 8-1 **N Pearce** *Ld; 4l clr & mist 8; mist & hdd 12; sn wknd & drpd back 3rd; no ch when lft 2nd aft 16* 20 2

1015^{P} Blue Orleans 14-1 A Phillips *Rmdrs aft 2; last 5; jmpd slow 8; grad lost tch; t.o & pu 12* . . . . . P

Sams Day (IRE)(bl) 13-8 R Burton *Hld up; 3rd 5; 6l 3rd & mist 11; went 2nd 12; ld app 13-nxt; 2nd when pu app 15; lame* . . . . . P

OFFICIAL DISTANCE: 20*l* **TIME:** 7min 04.0s

1113 Confined, 12st — 7 ran

835^{2} **PETROUGE**(cp) 6-4F **R Burton** *A.p; ld/disp til ld 12; went clr aft 2 out; kpt on str* 1

1018^{4} **Shemardi** 6-1 **R Hodges** *Prom; disp ld 10; ev ch when bad mist 13; 3rd & grad outpcd frm nxt; went 2nd agn flat; no ch w wnr* 6 2

834^{1} **Cadougold (FR)**(tt) 2-1 **M Keel** *Jw; hld up; 4th 4; went 2nd 14; eff frm 3 out; no hdwy u.p frm 2 out; dem flat* 3 3

834^{2} Ceasers Reign (IRE) 10-1 T Stephenson *4th early; ld 4 til jnd 9; jmpd slow 12 & lost plce; r.o agn frm 14; no ch frm 2 out* 15 4

922^{P} Mr Naborro (IRE)(cp,tt) 10-1 A Wintle *5th early; jmpd slow 8; went 4th & ev ch 13; v one-pcd frm 3 out* 4 5

839^{P} A Bit Of Fluff (5a) 20-1 Miss L Brooke *Last frm 4; lost tch frm 7; clsd to 8l last 11; lost tch agn 12; t.o & pu 3 out* . . . . . P

528^{P} Meadows Boy 14-1 A Beedles *Ld in start; ref to rce; tk no part* . . . . r

OFFICIAL DISTANCES: 6*l*, 2*l* **TIME:** 7min 02.0s

1114 Restricted, 12st — 6 ran

839^{4} **HUNTERSWAY (IRE)** 4-5F **R Hodges** *Jw; prom til jmpd to ld brief 12; ld agn 16; str prsd frm 2 out; kpt on und str drvng* 1

1014^{3} **Always Good (IRE)**(tt) 10-1 **P Needham** *Ld & sn clr; hdd brief 12; hdd aft 15; kpt on frm 2 out to bustle up wnr* . . . . . $1\frac{1}{2}$ 2

853^{P} Gaetano (IRE) 4-1 R Burton *Hld up; jw; cl 3rd when stumbled on landing & ur 9* U

977^{P} Lift The Latch (IRE)(cp) 9-2 M Wall *Fell 1* . . . . . F

665^{9} Running On Red 14-1 S Gray *8l 3rd when fell 8* . . . . . F

1018^{P} Watergate Boy (IRE) 6-1 W Hill *Bad hmpd & ur 1* . . . . . U

OFFICIAL DISTANCE: $1\frac{1}{4}$*l* **TIME:** 7min 18.0s

1115 Open Maiden (Div 1), 12st — 6 ran

736^{5} **MILAMOSS** 6-1 **R Hughes** *Hld up; grad prog to jn ldrs 13; 2l 2nd when lft in ld 16; 2l clr at last; kpt on one pce u.p* 1

934^{U} **Blazing Pride** 6-1 **P Haynes** *Last 6; stdy prog to 4th 13; lft 3rd nxt; went 2nd 2 out; sust chall but rdr of little assistance* 3 2

845U	**Kerry Zulu Warrior** 2-1 **H Tett** *Tore off into clr ld; 50l up 4; grad brought und control; hit 5; hit 10 hrd; jmpd slow 12 & hdd; lft 2nd & ev ch 14; wknd rap frm 2 out.*	20	3
981F	Four Opinions 6-4F S Gray *Opened 2s; prom in main group; went 3rd 10 & 2nd 13; jmpd to ld 14; 2l clr when fell nxt*		F
983P	Kotori (IRE) (7a) 10-1 A Hanly *2nd til wknd qckly frm 12; lsng tch when pu aft 13.*		P
	Peggys Gold (5a) 6-1 S Graham *Last when rn out thro wing 9.*		R

OFFICIAL DISTANCES: 3½l, 15l **TIME:** 7min 24.0s

1116 Open Maiden (Div 2), 12st - 16J — 5 ran

531P	**JOE LIVELY (IRE)** (7a) 6-1 **A Wintle** *Jmpd slow at times; ld; 10l clr 3; hdd 5; ld agn 7-10; 7l 4th app 2 out; lft 2nd at last & easily passed floundering rival*		1
847P	**Cromaboo Count** 10-1 **D Cook** *Hld up; hdwy to jn ldrs 11; mist 12; disp ld 13 til app 2 out; lft in ld last; dogged it furiously & hdd ½way up run-in.*	4	2
	Teeton Toast 3-1 **N Pearce** *Novicey; nvr btr than 3rd; outpcd frm 16; no ch frm nxt; lft 3rd agn at last*	15	3
840⁵	Norton Wood (IRE)(tt) 5-1 R Hodges *2nd til jmpd to ld 5; hit 7 hrd & lost 2 plces; 6l 3rd 3 out; v one-pcd & hung v bad lft flat*	8	4
668P	Withybrook Lass (5a) 4-5F R Burton *Jw; ld 10 til jnd 12; qcknd clr frm 2 out desp much tail-swishing & hanging towards boxes by-passing 2 out; in comm when crumpled on landing last; unlucky*		F

OFFICIAL DISTANCES: 4l, 12l **TIME:** 7min 41.0s

Fences 1,9 & 15 omitted - low sun; Scotsbrook Lass (lame at start, but rdn back to boxes!) was withdrawn not under orders

Ludlow (RH 8F,22J)

Sun, 25 Apr (GOOD to FIRM)

1117 Ludlow Gold Cup HC, 3m1f110y £2576 — 8 ran

931F	**PENNYAHEI** 11-02 14-1 **Miss S Beddoes** *Hld up; pushed along & outpcd app 18; over 12l off pce 19; mist nxt; str rn frm last to ld cl home*		1
994¹	**Mullensgrove** 11-12 10-11F **Miss S Phizacklea** *Hld up; mist 1; hdwy 9; ld 17; lft clr 2 out; hdd cl home.*	½	2
924²	**Philtre (IRE)** 11-09 (2ow) 8-1 **A Wintle** *Ld; blun 4; hdd nxt; wknd app 18*	18	3
835⁶	Genereux 11-03(cp,tt) 40-1 R Hodges *Sn bhnd & nvr gng wl; t.o*	dist	4
994P	Joshua's Vision (IRE) 11-03(tt) 40-1 Miss L Brooke *A bhnd; t.o & pu 17*		P
801⁷	Sip Of Brandy (IRE) 11-07 16-1 Miss J Hughes *Trckd ldrs; lost plce 13; strugg aft; poor 5th when fell 19*		F
1064¹	Storm Castle (IRE) 11-03 4-1 Miss J Wickens *Prom; ld 5; hdd 17; rdn & 1l down when blun & ur 2 out*		U
448¹	Tictac (FR) 11-03 11-2 P Sheldrake *Trckd ldrs; cl 3rd & pushed along when pu aft 18.*		P

TIME: 6min 35.5s **TOTE:** £18.10; places £2.10,£1.10,£2.30 **Ex:**£32.30 **CSF:**£29.46

Atherstone

Clifton-on-Dunsmore (LH 8F,19J)

Sun, 25 Apr (GOOD)

1118 Hunt Members — 5 ran

886P	**CATCHPHRASE**(vis) 14-1 **L Hicks** *(xnb) Jw; made most; hdd brief 8 & 16; forged clr frm 3 out; wandered app last; kpt on.*		1
942³	**Preferred (IRE)** 7-2 **R Armson** *6s-7/2; lkd rough; warm; hld up; jnd wnr 12; outj aft til gd j to ld brief 16; wknd frm 3 out.*	12	2
	Shallow River (IRE) 3-1 **Miss H Phizacklea** *Rcd wide; prom; rdr waving 6; wknd 12; mist & bhnd aft*	35	3
944²	Moscow Tradition (IRE) 4-5F N Docker *Tk keen hld; hld up; pulled way to disp ld & j rt 5; disp ld agn when mist & ur 8*		U
989U	Strong Chairman (IRE) 16-1 K O'Brien *Prom til blun & rfo 9.*		U

OFFICIAL DISTANCES: 8l, dist **TIME:** 6min 16.0s

1119 Panacur/TBA PPORA Club Members Mares Maiden, 12st — 15 ran

Form	Horse	Dist	Pos
848[2]	**WONDERFUL REMARK** (5a) 4-1 **G Moloney** *(xnb) Swtng; wl in tch; 5th 12; eff 15; outpcd 3 out; lft 2nd 2 out; 20l down & no ch when lft clr at last*		1
946[P]	**Pudding And Pie** (5a) 12-1 **R Armson** *Midfield; 7th 12; cl up 15; outpcd nxt; lft 2nd by defections*	20	2
789[4]	**Bethin** (5a) 12-1 **P Newton** *2 handlers; settled rr; mist 11; 9th & in tch nxt; cl up 15; wknd nxt; lft 3rd by defections; fin tired*	10	3
940[P]	Sams Sister (5a) 6-1 P Cowley *14s-6s; prsd ldrs; jmpd rt 7; 2nd 12; wknd 16; fin tired*	1 1/2	4
	Charlestown Lass (5a) 5-2F T Vaughan *(xnb) 8s-5/2; wl in tch; 4th 12; eff to ld 15; in comm when lft clr 2 out; 20l ahd when crashed thro wing last*		R
929[P]	Chicago's Madam (5a) 20-1 A Hanly *(xnb) 2 handlers; jb; bhnd frm 6; t.o last when pu 10*		P
	Classic Maid (12a) 10-1 B Gallagher *A bhnd; t.o last when pu 11*		P
741[2]	Granny Dick (5a) 10-1 T Messenger *Mists; sn rr & nvr gng keen; t.o 13; pu 3 out*		P
789[P]	Herpen (5a) 33-1 T Lane *2 handlers; tde; in tch to 9; wkng rap when blun 12; last & pu nxt*		P
978[F]	Little Dish (5a)(tt) 10-1 H Dowty *(xnb) Jmpd rt; made most to 15; chsd ldr aft; 4l down & hld but clr of rest when fell 2 out*		F
788[4]	Past Forte (5a) 10-1 T Ellis *(xnb) Hld up in rr; prog & 8th 12; same & just in tch when fell 14*		F
985[2]	Ridware Rose (5a) 7-1 Miss S Sharratt *2 handlers; nt jw; a rr; blun 11; t.o when blun & rdr event f.o 12*		U
788[P]	Sassy's Circle (12a)(vis) 8-1 N Pearce *Prsd ldr; ld brief 8; 3rd 12; stpd as if shot aft 15; pu 3 out*		P
887[P]	Sixes And Sevens (IRE) (5a) 33-1 G Kerr *Mists; prom to 8; sn wknd; t.o 12; pu 3 out*		P
945[3]	Spinosa (5a) 12-1 N Kent *Swtng; jmpd rt 3; in tch; 6th 12; 5th & wkng when blun & ur 16*		U

OFFICIAL DISTANCES: 8*l*, 1/2*l* **TIME:** 6min 19.5s

1120 Confined, 12st — 14 ran

Form	Horse	Dist	Pos
942[R]	**CRACKRATTLE (IRE)** (4ow)(tt) 33-1 **A Brown** *Chsd ldng pr; 8l 3rd 12; lkd btn in 4th 16; rallied 3 out; stayed on to ld aft last; hrd rdn & kpt on*		1
986[4]	**Young Tomo (IRE)**(cp) 14-1 **L Hicks** *33s-14s; chsd clr ldrs; 10l 4th 12 & u.p; chsd ldr 3 out; kpt on to ld last; sn hdd; no ex nr fin*	1	2
943[1]	**Gillone** (5x) 5-4F **J Docker** *Late to padd (as usual) but nt swtng; ww in midfield; prog & 10l 5th gng wl 12; eff to ld 16 & lkd cert wnr; hrd rdn 2 out; hdd last; no ex; fin lame*	2	3
886[3]	Miss Hoity Toity (5a) 4-1 A Sansome *Prsd ldr; ld 4; jmpd rt 7; hdd nxt; stayed w ldrs; ev ch 16; one pce frm nxt*	8	4
	Danzante (IRE) 33-1 S Moreton *2 handlers; warm; midfield; 18l 6th 12; stayed chsng ldrs; no prog & btn frm 16*	10	5
	Majestic Approach (IRE) 20-1 Miss H Campbell *(xnb) Towards rr; blun 9; 25l 11th 12; nd aft but kpt plugging away frm 14*	20	6
885[2]	Bruan (IRE)(bl) 16-1 Miss J Bevin *(xnb) Pulled hrd; ld to 4; ld agn 8; hdd & wknd 16*	2	7
886[P]	Shoemaker (IRE) 9-2 S Morris *Warm; midfield; rn in snatches; 24l 10th & strugg bad 12; nd aft; plodded on*	2	8
885[U]	Simply A Star (IRE) 25-1 Miss N Chapman *Ss & lft 10l; a bhnd; 13th & wl bhnd 12; t.o*	10	9
784[P]	Lord Of The Chase (IRE) 33-1 T Messenger *Nvr on terms; 23l 9th 12; toiling in rr aft*	2	10
885[P]	Mullover 33-1 T Lane *(xnb) 2 handlers; hld up; mist 2; 20l 8th & gng wl enough 12; 7th frm nxt; nt pushed & no prog; hvly eased frm 3 out*	2	11
1031[5]	Camitrov (FR)(bl) 33-1 G Kerr *(xnb) Chsd clr ldrs; 18l 7th & wkng 12; sn t.o*	25	12
989[6]	Needwood Neptune 25-1 P Bennett *Last & tlng off 5; cont miles bhnd*	20	13
939[1]	Teeton Glaive (5a) 8-1 Miss H Irving *(xnb) Nvr gng wl & a wl in rr; 12th & tlng off 12; poor 11th when rfo 15*		U

OFFICIAL DISTANCES: 3/4*l*, 2*l* **TIME:** 6min 11.0s

Topical Tip (Miss E Chugg, 2ow, kicked & inj in padd) was withdrawn not under orders; the stewards cautioned the riders of the winner (not giving horse time to respond) and runner-up (causing horse to be marked) concerning their use of the whip

1121 Land Rover Mens Open, 12st — 6 ran

888[1] **SHANAVOGH** (7x) 5-2 **R Hunnisett** *Jw; prsd ldr aft 4; ld 6; hrd prsd 3 out; urged along & kpt on game flat* 1
681[1] **Longville Lad** 11-10F **P Cowley** *2 handlers; warm; ld to 6; prsd wnr aft; gd j 16; chall aft; hrd rdn 2 out; kpt on wl u.p; just hld* .... nk 2
478[P] **Blue Royal (FR)** 7-1 **S Morris** *Chsd ldr & mist 4; 3rd & outpcd nxt; went 5l 3rd 12; same & eff 16; no ex frm 2 out; rn wl* 10 3
980[5] Smile Pleeze (IRE) (4x) 12-1 N Pearce *Mostly 4th; str rmdrs 10; stayed in tch; 9l 4th 12; 8l 4th 16; sn outpcd; kpt on flat* 2 4
944[1] Dante's Banker (IRE) 20-1 R Armson *A last pr; 11l 5th & drvn 12; sn wknd; t.o when mist & rdr nrly f.o 15* 30 5
943[F] Red Rebel (7x) 5-1 R Cope *Lost plce 3; pushed along & nvr gng wl aft; 15l last & u.p 12; sn t.o; pu 3 out* .... P

OFFICIAL DISTANCES: nk, 5l **TIME:** 6min 05.0s

1122 Ladies Open — 5 ran

869[6] **AIRCON (IRE)** 8-1 **Miss R Hutsby** *(xnb) 16s-8s; swtng; a.p; disp ld to 10; 4l 3rd 16; eff 2 out; ld last; stayed on wl* 1
987[U] **Fami (FR)** 2-1 **Miss Gemma Hutchinson** *Tchd 5/2; trckd ldrs; slpd thro on inner to ld 12; 2l up 16; rdn 2 out; hdd last; fnd little* 1½ 2
479[U] **Ardmayle (IRE)** 11-8F **Miss L Coney** *Disp ld def advant 10; hdd 12; chsd ldr aft; 2l down 16; rdn 2 out; kpt on same pce* .... nk 3
682[2] Edmond (FR) 11-4 Miss H Campbell *2 handlers; trckd ldrs til hopelessly outpcd frm 10; 20l 4th 12; sn wl t.o.* .... runin 4
684[P] Albarden 20-1 Miss H Irving *Hld up; jmpd slow 3; lost tch 8; reluct & t.o 12; pu 15* .... P

OFFICIAL DISTANCES: 1½l, nk **TIME:** 6min 08.0s

1123 Restricted, 12st — 7 ran

734[F] **CLOUDY BAY BOY** 11-2 **R Cope** *(xnb) Tchd 7s; made all; jmpd rt 7; rdn & hrd prsd when lft 3l clr 2 out; prsd agn last; kpt on wl* 1
789[1] **Quizzal** (5a) 9-4 **R Armson** *Hld up in tch; trckd wnr aft 12; rdn 3 out; chall when stumbled on landing 2 out; kpt on & ev ch agn last; no ex* 2 2
870[2] **Moscow's Return (IRE)** 6-1 **M Keel** *Trckd wnr til mist 12; sn rdn & reluct; mists aft; in tch 16; sn btn* 20 3
Astley Gold (IRE) 6-4F J Docker *(xnb) Hld up; 5th & wl in tch when bd 11.* B
787[5] Henry Henbit 13-2 S Morris *(xnb) Nt a fluent; in tch; last of 4 at 12; wknd rap nxt; t.o & pu 16* .... P
836[P] Robsand (IRE) 33-1 N Pearce *Fat; last & rdn 4; sn toiling; t.o & pu 10* .... P
885[6] Romanybaan 20-1 P Ikin *(xnb) 2 handlers; trckd ldng pr til fell 11* .... F

OFFICIAL DISTANCES: 2l, 20l **TIME:** 6min 12.0s

1124 Open Maiden (Div 1), 12st - 18J — 14 ran

945[2] **BRIERY FOX (IRE)** 9-4F **J Docker** *Trckd ldrs; ld 10; drew clr aft 16; in comm frm 2 out.* 1
651[3] **Highland Dancer (IRE)** (7a) 12-1 **T Ellis** *2 handlers; warm; pulled hrd; cl up; eff 14; chsd wnr 3 out; no imp; kpt on* 15 2
985[3] **Mr Buckle (IRE)** (7a) 10-1 **Miss S Sharratt** *Mist 1; jmpd slow 3; in rr; prog 12; outpcd 16; one pce aft* 10 3
Miaheyyun(tt) 3-1 T Vaughan *(xnb) 7s-3s; 2 handlers; swtng; pulled hrd; hld up in tch; eff 14; rdn 16; sn btn* 1 4
850[R] Currow Kate (5a) 14-1 L Hicks *(bnh) Tchd 20s; prom; chsd wnr 11-3 out; sn outpcd & btn* .... ½ 5
752[4] Barty Boy (IRE) 8-1 B Shaw *Warm; in tch; last of main group 12; wknd 14; t.o when virt pu flat.* 30 6
927[2] Arctic Summer (IRE) 10-1 J Trice-Rolph *Prom til lost plce rap aft 11; tlng off when wrestled to a halt 13.* .... P
595[3] Earl Token 8-1 R Armson *Hld up; prog & cl 3rd when mist 12; iron broke; nt rec; pu nxt.* .... P
1016[F] Martha Jane (5a) 20-1 Miss N Hickling *(xnb) Last pr when rfo 7.* .... U
789[P] Murphymeboy (IRE) 5-1 S Morris *Mist 2; last when jmpd slow 3; nvr gng aft; bhnd til pu 9; disapp* .... P
890[7] Prince Mouse 33-1 N Kent *(xnb) Midfield; eff 13; 5th & outpcd when fell 16* F

746P River Deed (7a) 20-1 P Cowley *Pulled hrd; rcd wide; made most to 7; wknd 9; t.o & pu 13* . . . . . P
192P Two Oceans (IRE)(vis) 12-1 R Cope *Prom; ld 7-10; wknd rap aft 14; t.o & pu aft 16; disapp* . . . . . P
Usedtobeasweetboy (7a) 20-1 J Newbold *Nt jw in rr; pckd 5; blun 8; t.o & pu 11* . . . . . P

OFFICIAL DISTANCES: 15*l*, 10*l* **TIME:** 6min 15.0s

Fence 15 omitted - fallen rider

1125 Open Maiden (Div 2), 12st 15 ran

7345 **SAINT-DECLAN (IRE)** 5-1 **S Morris** *(xnb) Tchd 7s; made all at gd pce; blun 12; drew clr nxt; 15l up 16; tired frm 2 out; clambered over last; unchall* 1
8712 **Northsprite**(cp) 6-1 **J Trice-Rolph** *(xnb) Hld up in rr; prog to trck ldrs 12; 3rd & outpcd nxt; eff & blun 3 out; chsd wnr 2 out; clsng flat but nvr any ch.* . 5 2
8902 **Earl Of Buckingham** 2-1F **P Cowley** *Hld up in midfield; prog to chse wnr 12; outpcd nxt; no imp 16; lost 2nd 2 out; kpt on* 3 3
8904 Tom Tobacco 9-2 R Cope *Prom; chsd wnr 11-12; wknd 16; fin v tired.* . . . 30 4
5944 Beau Jake (IRE) 4-1 R Armson *Tchd 6s; hld up in rr; mist 6; outpcd frm 13; nd aft; fin tired.* 5 5
746F Call Me Again 10-1 N Pearce *Hld up; a wl in rr; jmpd rt 11; 11th & lsng tch nxt; pu 13.* . . . . . P
1035P Gerry Watson 50-1 J King *2 handlers; just in tch to 7; wknd alarm; t.o & pu 9* P
1020R Holly Park (5a) 14-1 P Newton *2 handlers; fat; t.o in last pr frm 5; pu 10.* P
8404 Jovian Pond(tt) 40-1 R Sealey *Midfield; 8th 12; outpcd nxt; eff into v mod 5th when ur 15* . . . . . U
927P Latterly (USA) 40-1 C Wadland *A wl in rr; in tch til wknd 12; t.o 14; miles bhnd when pu 2 out* . . . . . P
8877 Rundetto (IRE) 40-1 S Moreton *(xnb) 2 handlers; chsd wnr to 11; sn wknd; wl t.o when pu 3 out.* . . . . . P
1061P Satanas (FR) 33-1 L Hicks *(xnb) Midfield; outpcd 13; sn bhnd; t.o & pu 3 out; dism.* . . . . . P
946F Shalabibubbly 33-1 N Kent *Chsd ldrs; outpcd 13; 8th & wkng when ur 14.* U
561F Silver Styx (7a) 12-1 J Docker *Tk keen hld; a rr; 10th 12; sn wknd; t.o & pu 15* P
1035U Trust Ger 40-1 Miss H Phizacklea *T.o frm 5; pu 9.* . . . . . P

OFFICIAL DISTANCES: 6*l*, dist **TIME:** 6min 09.0s

Axe Vale

Stafford Cross (RH 8F,18J)

Sun, 25 Apr (GOOD, GOOD to FIRM in places)

1126 Hunt Members, 12st 3 ran

9622 **ORINOCO'S FLIGHT (IRE)** 4-6F **M Holmes** *(xnb) Tchd evens; pulled hrd; ld frm 3; jmpd rt; went 20l clr 11; rdn 2 out; 6l clr at last; tired flat; rdn out* 1
692P **Vansell** (5a) 6-4 **Mrs O Jackson** *2 handlers; swtng; slt ld to 3; chsd ldr; 20l adrift 11; clsd grad frm 3 out; still 6l adrift at last; nrst fin* 4 2
686 Hoteliers' Dream (5a) 7-1 M Sweetland *Tchd 8s; unruly lvng padd; tk keen hld & rstrnd in 3rd; nt fluent; fnce bhnd 10; t.o when fell 11.* . . . . . F

OFFICIAL DISTANCE: 5*l* **TIME:** 6min 06.0s **TOTE:** £1.50 **DF:**£1.20

1127 Confined, 12st 5 ran

9631 **LORD OF THE MIST (IRE)** (3x) 30-100F **N Williams** *Tchd 4/11; lw; hld up in tch; hdwy & gng wl 9; disp ld 13 til ld aft 3 out; rdn clr app last; pushed out* 1
799P **Morris Piper** (6x) 7-2 **R Woollacott** *Swtng; hld up in tch; cl 3rd on inner & gng wl 11; disp ld 13-16; 1l 2nd & ev ch 2 out; no ex & jmpd rt last; eased last 100yds* 12 2
3505 **Barton Saint (NZ)** 12-1 **Miss S West** *Tchd 16s; prom to 4; 4th 1/2way; wknd 12; 25l 4th 3 out; tk mod 3rd nr post.* 10 3
Agent 25-1 M Munrowd *Swtng; ld & went 20l clr 7; 10l ld when mist 10; hdd aft 12; kpt on one pce frm 3 out; releg 4th cl home* 2½ 4
Magical Fun (IRE) 20-1 Miss T Hayes *(xnb) Rr; in tch til wknd 13; t.o.* . . . 30 5

OFFICIAL DISTANCES: 15*l*, 15*l* **TIME:** 6min 04.0s **TOTE:** £1.40 **DF:**£1.60

1128 Mixed Open, 12st — 7 ran

414[1]	**KINGSTON VENTURE** 7-2 **J Barnes** *(xnb) Tchd 4s; handy; went 2nd 9; trckd ldr; eff 2 out; ld app last; sn clr*		1
964[1]	**Ballysicyos (FR)** (7x) 1-2F **A Farrant** *(xnb,boh) Lw; ld/disp til ld 7; went 4l clr 12; hit 15; hrd rdn when prsd 2 out; no ex app last; eased last 50yds*	8	2
799[3]	**Sadler's Realm** (7x) 10-1 **Miss L Gardner** *Lw; ld/disp to 7; wknd & 17l 3rd 11; wl bhnd frm 15; walked in*	runin	3
880[3]	Delaware (FR) (7x)(bl) 12-1 S Kidston *40s-12s; blun & ur 1*		U
880[5]	Shanavoher (IRE) 14-1 R McCarthy *In tch in 5th when fell 9*		F
975[4]	Shobrooke Mill 16-1 N Williams *(xnb) Prom; 3rd when fell 10*		F
602[P]	The Pickled Duke (IRE) 66-1 N Wilmington *Bhnd til pu 9*		P

OFFICIAL DISTANCES: 10*l*, dist **TIME:** 5min 47.0s **TOTE:** £3.00 **DF:**£2.30

1129 Intermediate, 12st — 12 ran

821[1]	**FATHER MANSFIELD (IRE)** 9-1 **Miss C Prouse** *Rr; 9th ½way; 12l 6th 3 out; went 4th & running on aft 2 out; str rn on inner flat; ld last stride*		1
966[1]	**Noble Action** (7a) 11-10F **N Williams** *Tchd 11/8; lw; hld up; stdy hdwy 12; cl 3rd 14; ld 16; 1½l up 2 out; drvn 3l clr last; hrd rdn; lkd wnr til wknd & hdd on line*	hd	2
963[3]	**Cimmaroon (IRE)** (7a) 8-1 **A Farrant** *(xnb) Hld up in tch; 6th ½way; went 5th & rdn 14; hdwy u.p 16; went 1½l 2nd & ev ch 2 out; no ex flat*	2½	3
936[2]	Pulham Downe 16-1 Miss E Tory *(xnb) Ld 4-15; wl in tch til no ex frm 2 out*	6	4
963[2]	Ellofamonkey (5a) 7-1 R Woollacott *Lw; hld up in midfield; prog to 3rd 10; went 2nd 14; wknd aft 3 out; one pce*	8	5
740[1]	Tinder-Box 7-2 Miss T Cave *Tchd 4s; midfield; hdwy 8; went 4th 14; wknd 16*	2	6
793[5]	By My Side (IRE) 14-1 A Charles-Jones *(xnb) Swtng; ld to 3; wknd & rcd in midfield frm 7; bhnd frm 12; poor 7th when pu 2 out*		P
1003[5]	Commander Cully (IRE) 50-1 M Sweetland *(xnb) Sn rr; bhnd frm 6 til pu 11*		P
823[6]	Digitalis (5a) 66-1 M Munrowd *In tch; cl 5th 10; wknd 14; bhnd when pu 15*		P
881[5]	Early Morning Call (IRE) 25-1 J Barnes *(xnb) Towards rr; 10th 8; bhnd when pu 11*		P
907[P]	Native Drum (IRE) (5x) 40-1 Miss S Gaisford *(xnb) Lost plce 4; 10th 6; bhnd frm 8; t.o & pu 15*		P
570[P]	Th'moons A Balloon (IRE)(tt) 25-1 S Partridge *Prom; ½l 2nd 8; disp ld 9-10; wknd 11; 6th & strugg 14; bhnd & pu 2 out*		P

OFFICIAL DISTANCES: s hd, 4*l* **TIME:** 5min 56.0s **TOTE:** £6.40 **DF:**£10.10

1130 Countryside Alliance Club Members (Nov Rdrs), 12st — 7 ran

907[1]	**LET'S FLY (FR)** 2-1F **W Biddick** *11/4-2s; ld/disp til lft clr 2 out; pushed out flat*		1
1065[1]	**Gladiatorial (IRE)** 9-4 **T Bishop** *(xnb) Tchd 5/2; handy; 5l 4th 12; hdwy to cl 3rd 14; disp ld & pckd 3 out; rdn & no ex when lft 2nd 2 out*	6	2
908[1]	**It'snotsimple (IRE)** (5a) 5-1 **B Trickey** *Towards rr but in tch; 5th & tail-swishing 13; no real prog; lft poor 3rd 2 out; r.o u.p flat*	8	3
883[2]	King Of Swing (IRE) 14-1 Mrs F Vigar *(xnb) Tchd 20s; prom; disp ld 8-11; lost plce 13; bhnd frm 16*	40	4
823[5]	African Dawn(cp,tt) 8-1 Miss L Hawkings *Lw; 5th & mist 7; in tch in 3rd when stumbled & ur bend bef 9; rdr broke ankle*		U
690[3]	Atavistic (IRE) 4-1 Miss R Booth *Lw; hld up in tch; 3rd 9; gd hdwy to 2nd & gng wl 12; chall aft 3 out; level & ev ch when fell hvly nxt; rdr inj & delayed nxt rce nrly an hour.*		F
577[U]	Now Young Man (IRE) 16-1 Miss P Moore *Tack problems & pu 3*		P

OFFICIAL DISTANCES: 6*l*, 6*l* **TIME:** 6min 05.0s **TOTE:** £2.30 **DF:**£3.20

1131 Restricted (Div 1), 12st — 10 ran

771[3]	**EUWILUWIL (IRE)** 11-4 **A Farrant** *(xnb,boh) Tchd 3s; lw; jw; prog 6; cl 3rd & gng wl 11; jmpd to ld 12; r.o wl u.p when chall app last; drvn out*		1
879[2]	**Askers Jack** 5-1 **J Snowden** *Tchd 9s; slt ld 1; trckd ldr 2-12; cl 3rd til rallied to chall 2 out; ev ch last; r.o*	2	2
912[4]	**Chapners Cross** 20-1 **Miss S Young** *Chsd ldrs; 4th when slt mist 10; lost plce 12; 13l 4th 16; kpt on*	5	3
324[4]	Flora Macdonald (5a) 12-1 Miss P Gundry *In tch; 5th ½way; chsd ldrs til wknd 3 out*	8	4

864^{4} Macaroni Beach (5a) 16-1 N Wilmington *(xnb) 2 handlers; mounted on course; ld 2-12; lost plce 15; bhnd frm 2 out* 30 5
Emali 16-1 W White *(xnb) Towards rr; 7th 11; bhnd 15 til pu 2 out* . . . . P
706^{5} Georges Pleasure (5a) 12-1 L Heard *Rr; last when pu 12* . . . . P
827^{P} Lilabet (5a) 50-1 Miss C Prouse *Detach last frm 4 til crashed thro wing 8* . R
599^{1} Smart Cavalier (7a) 4-6F N Williams *(xnb) Tchd evens; lw; nt a fluent; hld up in midfield; prog to 4th & gng wl 11; went 2nd & prsd ldr frm 13; ev ch til wknd rap app 2 out; eased & pu last* . . . . P
967^{U} The Gambling Lady (5a) 25-1 R Woollacott *Rr; bhnd when pu 12* . . . . P

OFFICIAL DISTANCES: 2l, 10l **TIME:** 5min 57.0s **TOTE:** £4.10 **DF:**£6.10

1132 Restricted (Div 2), 12st — 10 ran

HOLD ON HARRY 4-1 **L Heard** *(ringbit) Wl in tch; cl 3rd 9; 3l 3rd & gng wl 12; went 2nd 14; pckd 3 out; ld app 2 out; sn clr* 1
879^{8} **Prah Sands**(bl) 12-1 **D Edwards** *(xnb) Chsd ldr til disp 10; ld 12; nt fluent nxt; went 3l clr 3 out; sn rdn; wknd & hdd app 2 out; wl btn when clambered over last; fin lame* 30 2
879^{5} Bally Lir Lady (5a) 3-1 R McCarthy *7s-3s; chsd ldrs; mist 8; cl 4th when fell 11* . . . . F
827^{F} Cargo Flight 11-2 A Farrant *7s-11/2; lw; ld til jnd 10; cl up til wknd & rdn 16; poor 3rd when pu 2 out* . . . . P
824^{P} Derrilady (5a) 33-1 L Rowe *Bhnd when pu 6* . . . . P
369^{P} Ferryhill (IRE) 16-1 Miss L Britton *1st ride; hmpd 3; bhnd when ur 6* . . . . U
827^{P} Harnage (IRE) 20-1 Miss C Prouse *6th ½way; rr when bd 11* . . . . B
824^{2} Ivans Dream 6-4F L Jefford *Midfield; 5th ½way; no prog; poor 4th when pu 15* P
693^{P} Little Mister(cp) 10-1 D Drake *Prom when hmpd & ur 3* . . . . U
791^{P} Red Risk 40-1 M Sweetland *(ringbit) Prom when fell 3* . . . . F

OFFICIAL DISTANCE: 20l **TIME:** 5min 59.0s **TOTE:** £3.00 **DF:**£27.50

1133 Open Maiden 56&7yo (Div 1), 12st — 14 ran

600^{2d} **SLIEMA (IRE)** 5-1 **N Wilmington** *Disp ld til ld aft 3; made rest in 3-4l ld; 4l clr at last; easily* 1
Here's To Lucy (5a) 33-1 **R Woollacott** *Midfield; 7th 11; prog & went 7l 4th 16; still 4th last; stayed on wl flat; snatched 2nd cl home* 10 2
909^{2} **Hooray Henry** (7a) 5-1 **T Dennis** *(xnb) Chsd ldr frm 4; 3l 2nd 12-16; no imp; lost 2nd nr post* . . . . nk 3
633^{2} Mrs Goldfarb (12a) 16-1 D Edwards *Went 4th 11; prog 15; 3½l 3rd 16; ev ch 2 out; wknd app last* 5 4
644^{P} Chasing Buttercups (5a) 33-1 Miss A Goschen *Prom; 3rd 9; 6th & just in tch 12; grad wknd* 20 5
599^{P} Countryside Counts 33-1 Miss L Gardner *(xnb) 2 handlers; sn rr; 8th 11; t.o frm ½way* 3 6
1007^{P} Mighty Mack (IRE) (7a) 14-1 M Sweetland *(xnb) Sn rr; rmdrs 4; trailed rnd last; t.o frm ½way* 10 7
688^{3} Apatura Joe 5-1 A Farrant *(xnb) Lw; disp 2-3; carried out bend bef 4* C
688^{P} Boy Band (IRE) 33-1 J Tickle *In tch; 4th ½way; lost plce & 7th 15; t.o & pu last* . . . . P
826^{P} Dart View Lass (5a)(cp) 33-1 A Charles-Jones *Carried out bend bef 4* C
962^{F} Double Bubble (IRE) 33-1 Miss J Buck *Swtng; tde; out of control & rn out bend bef 4* . . . . R
600^{C} Running Earth (IRE) (7a) 2-1F N Williams *Midfield; nt a fluent; prog 9; cl 5th 11; rdn but no real hdwy 15; 5th when pu 2 out* . . . . P
909^{4} Some Tool 20-1 R Ross *Lw; prom; carried out bend bef 4* C
725^{2} The Cooling Agent 7-2 M Miller *Tchd 5s; rr; 9th ½way; no prog; poor 7th 16; t.o & pu 2 out* . . . . P

OFFICIAL DISTANCES: 15l, ½l **TIME:** 6min 05.0s **TOTE:** £4.20 **DF:**c/f

1134 Open Maiden 56&7yo (Div 2), 12st — 11 ran

796^{U} **QUESTIONIT** (12a) 9-1 **Miss L Gardner** *Hld up in midfield; 6th 11; gd hdwy 15; went 2nd aft 16; sust chall til ld & edged lft run-in* 1
913^{3} **Truicear**(tt) 7-1 **R McCarthy** *Handy; cl 4th 11; went 2nd 13; slt ld 16; hrd prsd frm 2 out; ev ch last; hdd & no ex flat* 3 2
791^{5} **Village Queen (IRE)** (5a) 9-2 **D Harvey** *(bnh) Ld & slt mist 1; ld/disp til slt ld 11-15; ev ch til wknd u.p 2 out* 5 3

308[F]	Bucket Awl (IRE) (7a) 9-4 R Woollacott *(xnb) Hld up in tch; cl 3rd 9; 2½l 3rd 16; eff & ev ch 2 out-last; wknd flat*	s hd	4
827[2]	Josanjamic (5a)(vis) 6-4F L Heard *Opened 9/4; ld/disp to 11; sn rdn; lost plce 14; kpt on same pce frm 3 out*	2	5
962[P]	Charliebob (12a) 20-1 J Barnes *Rr; mist 7; bhnd frm 11 til pu 15*		P
	Joyful Jade (FR) (5a) 16-1 A Farrant *Prom when blun & ur 3*		U
328[6]	Lady Blackthorn (5a) 14-1 Miss P Gundry *Ss; sn bhnd; 7th 12; t.o & pu 2 out*		P
575[P]	Peter Parkgate (7a) 33-1 D Drake *Prom when blun & ur 3*		U
962[P]	Sup Of Tea (IRE) 25-1 A Charles-Jones *2 handlers; chsd ldrs; 5th 8; in tch til wknd 14; bhnd frm 15 til pu 2 out*		P
688[P]	Velvet Victory (IRE) (12a) 16-1 M Miller *6th 5; midfield when fell 8*		F

OFFICIAL DISTANCES: *2l, ½l* **TIME:** 6min 11.0s **TOTE:** £11.90 **DF:**£15.00

Clifton-on-Teme

Upper Sapey (RH 8F,18J)

Sun, 25 Apr (GOOD to FIRM)

1135 Hunt Members — 3 ran

838[3]	**THE WRITER (IRE)** 6-4JF **R Hodges** *(xnb) 2s-6/4; swtng; 2nd til ld 13; drvn out*		1
937[3]	**Top Of The Charts** 6-4JF **M Harris** *2s-6/4; ld to 13; rdn aft 15; ev ch 2 out; one pce*	2	2
663[P]	**Guard A Dream (IRE)** 5-2 **E Walker** *2 handlers; a last; hit 10 & 11; rdn 12; mist 15; v one-pcd 3 out*	4	3

OFFICIAL DISTANCES: 1½l, 5l **TIME:** 6min 15.8s

1136 Restricted, 12st — 5 ran

1019[2]	**CAMPDEN KITTY** (5a) 7-2 **F Hutsby** *Ld to 9; 2nd til ld & lft clr 13; drew rt away 15; unchall*		1
1063[P]	**Snowtre (IRE)**(cp) 9-1 **A Wintle** *(xnb) Hld up; 8l 4th ½way; went 3rd 12 & 8l 2nd aft nxt; jb lft 15; nt rec*	30	2
925[F]	**April Treasure** (5a) 6-4F **Julian Pritchard** *(xnb) 2s-6/4; 2nd/3rd til ld 9; 5l clr 11; mist 12; hdd & bad mist 13; nt rec & 15l 3rd nxt; sn wl bhnd; t.o & virt pu flat*	25	3
820[1]	Sales Dodger (IRE)(cp) 5-1 S Hughes *(b4) Nt jw; a last; pushed along 5; mist & lost tch 7; t.o 14; ref 2 out*		r
925[P]	Weallwayswillbeone (IRE) 7-4 P York *5s-7/4; mist 6; hrd rdn aft 10; 2nd/3rd to 12; wknd & 17l 4th 14; t.o & pu 2 out*		P

OFFICIAL DISTANCES: 20l, 20l **TIME:** 6min 11.6s

1137 Ladies Open — 3 ran

843[5]	**DO IT ONCE (IRE)**(tt) 8-13F **Mrs A Rucker** *(xnb) Ld 1 til mist 2; ld 4-7; 2nd til ld 12; qcknd last; rdly*		1
1017[4]	**Welburn Boy**(bl,tt) 3-1 **Miss L Allfrey** *Hld up; 3l last ½way; hit 10; nt fluent 12; went 2nd aft 2 out; rdn & nt qckn flat*	3	2
1064[3]	**Flying Pennant (IRE)** 3-1 **Miss S Davies** *Ld to 1 & 2-4; ld 7-12; 2nd til aft 2 out; wknd flat*	7	3

OFFICIAL DISTANCES: 2l, 6l **TIME:** 6min 20.8s

1138 Mens Open, 12st — 4 ran

758[3]	**TEME WILLOW (IRE)** (7x) 6-4JF **Julian Pritchard** *Jmpd rt; ld 1; drew clr 2 out; comf*		1
979[2]	**Pretoria Dancer** (4x)(bl) 6-4JF **M Goldstein** *Went 2nd aft 2; rdn 15; blun 3 out; one pce*	8	2
732[F]	**Farnando (IRE)** 5-2 **G Barfoot-Saunt** *5s-5/2; hld up; last to 4; hdwy 8; 2½l 3rd ½way; mist 11; lost tch 13; 20l 3rd & rdn aft 15; t.o*	25	3
759[P]	Reefer Dancer(bl) 14-1 D Mansell *Ld to 1; last & rdn 4; reluct u.p when mist 11; lost tch 12; t.o & pu 2 out*		P

OFFICIAL DISTANCES: 8l, 25l **TIME:** 6min 07.3s

The stewards fined the rider of Reefer Dancer £65 for using the whip with excessive force and frequency and at times hitting the horse in the wrong place

1139 Open Maiden 56&7yo, 12st — 6 ran

1020U	**PENNY BLUE** (12a) 7-4F **G Barfoot-Saunt** *(xnb) Hld up; jmpd slow 4; 6l 4th 1/2way; mist 11; jmpd lft frm 12; hdwy 13; ld & saddle slpd rnd & rdr lost iron 3 out; hdd app nxt; rdn to ld flat; r.o wl*		1
926F	**Nessarc (IRE)** (7a) 11-2 **P York** *A.p; 4l 3rd 1/2way; went 2nd & hung lft aft 10; ld 12 til app 3 out; ld app 2 out til hdd & no ex flat*	3	2
	Dunmanus Supreme (IRE) 4-1 **T Faulkner** *2nd/3rd to 5; drpd to rr 8; 9l last 1/2way; rallied 12; went 2nd nxt; ev ch last; wknd flat*	7	3
666F	Hors Concours (NZ) 9-4 N Oliver *(xnb) Hld up; last to 8; 7l 5th 1/2way; 6l last 14; wknd 15; t.o*	30	4
820P	Tigre Bois 10-1 R Carey *(xnb) Pulled hrd; went 2nd 4; ld 5 til aft 10; wknd rap 12; last when pu nxt*		P
1014P	Waky Lady (IRE) (5a) 12-1 M Hammond *(xnb) Jmpd slow 1 & 2; ld to 5; 2nd til ld aft 10; hdd 12; wkng when fell nxt*		F

OFFICIAL DISTANCES: 2*l*, 6*l* **TIME:** 6min 28.8s

1140 Confined, 12st — 8 ran

8391	**FATHER TOM (IRE)** 8-13F **Julian Pritchard** *Ww; 10l last 1/2way; 11l 6th 12; went 12l 3rd 15 & 7l 2nd aft nxt; qcknd to ld last; sn clr*		1
922U	**Therealbat (IRE)** 7-2 **G Barfoot-Saunt** *(xnb) Hld up; mist 3; hdwy & disp 4l 3rd 1/2way; qcknd to ld aft 10; 7l clr aft 3 out; hdd & no ex last*	7	2
756P	**L'idefix (IRE)** 9-2 **M Goldstein** *Ld to 8 & 9 til aft 10; rdn 15; 2nd til outpcd aft 3 out*	12	3
8171	Galeshan (IRE) (10x)(tt) 6-1 C Huxley *Went 2nd 3; ld 8-9; 2nd/3rd to 13; wknd 15*	15	4
8364	Time Can Tell(bl) 20-1 Miss R Reynolds *Hld up; mists 7 & 8; 6l 5th 1/2way; 10l 5th 12; lost tch 14*	7	5
980P	Tortugas (FR) 20-1 P York *Swtng; hld up; 5l 5th 1/2way; rdn 12; went 5l 3rd nxt; wknd qckly 15*	2	6
924P	Captain's Log 16-1 M Wall *Hld up; lft 3rd 5-10; wkng when mist 11; t.o 13*	runin	7
979U	Hedzamarley (IRE) 16-1 Miss S Davies *2nd/3rd til ur 5*		U

OFFICIAL DISTANCES: 5*l*, 12*l* **TIME:** 6min 03.7s

PLATE 11 1140 Clifton-on-Teme Confined: L'Idefix leads Galeshan, Hedzamarley, Time Can Tell, Captain's Log, The Real Bat, Father Tom and Tortugas *PHOTO: Kathleen Mullen*

1141 Open Maiden 8yo&up, 12st — 6 ran

Form	Horse & comment	Dist	Pos
820[2]	**JOLLY JAKE** 6-4F **E Walker** *(xnb) Hld up; hdwy 8; 4l 3rd 1/2way; lft in ld 14; sn drvn clr; 10l up 3 out; kpt on wl.*		1
840[R]	**A Proper Charlie** 4-1 **T Stephenson** *6s-4s; hld up last to 5; 7l 5th 1/2way; went 5l 4th 12 & 7l 2nd aft 15; rdn 2 out; no imp.*	5	2
730[P]	**Rosie Stroud (IRE)** (5a) 2-1 **Julian Pritchard** *Ld to 1; chsd ldr to 9; went 2nd aft 11; lft w ev ch 14; 5l 2nd nxt; sn rdn & wknd qckly.*	25	3
699[P]	Frogsmarsh (5a)(cp) 12-1 Miss R Reynolds *(xnb) Swtng; ld 1 til wknd qckly 11; t.o & pu 14; removed by horse ambulance.*		P
981[P]	Rosemead Tye (5a) 7-2 Miss N Stallard *Prom; went 2nd 9; ld 11 til ur 14.*		U
844[P]	Scholar Green 10-1 D Mansell *Last 5; lost tch 7; t.o when mist 11; pu 12.*		P

OFFICIAL DISTANCES: 5*l*, 20*l* **TIME:** 6min 13.2s

Sir W.W. Wynn's

Eaton Hall (RH 8F,18J)

Sun, 25 Apr (GOOD to FIRM)

1142 Open Maiden (Div 1) — 7 ran

Form	Horse & comment	Dist	Pos
1044[P]	**ROBERT THE RASCAL** 9-1 **J R Barlow** *Trckd ldrs in cl 3rd; ld 14; made rest; kpt on wl flat.*		1
709[5]	**Snitton Salvo**(bl) 7-1 **M Jackson** *Hld up in 4/5th; 3 1/2l 4th app 12; went 2nd 15; prsd wnr aft; 1l down last; just outpcd flat.*	1/2	2
710[2]	**Heathyards Element** 5-4F **G Hanmer** *Hld up in 4/5th; lost plce 11 & 14l last app nxt; hdwy 3 out; prsd ldrs til outpcd app last; wknd flat; fin lame.*	10	3
872[U]	Spot The Native (IRE) 4-1 P Hemmings *Ld/disp to 12; lost plce 15; last but ev ch 2 out; sn outpcd; late burst to snatch 3rd*	nk	4
	Tidal Beach (7a, 1ow) 14-1 W Hill *Last pr 1st circ; 8l 5th app 12; cl 4th & ev ch 2 out; kpt on same pce.*	1	5
1049[P]	Bradogue (IRE)(tt) 14-1 W Kinsey *Jw; disp ld; slt advant 12-13; hdd & blun nxt; rdr lost iron, swerved & hit rival, saddle slpd & rdr baled out nxt.*		U
934[P]	Castle Lodge 4-1 K Pearson *10s-4s; wrs & lost 20l; in tch in last pr 5; no imp when hit by rival & knocked over 14*		B

OFFICIAL DISTANCES: 1/2*l*, 8*l* **TIME:** 6min 26.0s **TOTE:** £6.00

1143 Open Maiden (Div 2) — 5 ran

Form	Horse & comment	Dist	Pos
1044[3]	**MULLARTS LAD (IRE)** (7a) 2-1F **S Ross** *4s-2s; hld up in last pr; hdwy to 2nd 15; trckd wnr til chall last; ld & sprinted clr flat.*		1
710[P]	**Hendrix** 4-1 **N Saville** *Lft in ld app 5; made rest til jnd last; sn hdd; no ch w wnr flat; eased.*	12	2
1044[2]	**Top Weld** 4-1 **J Jarrett** *(xnb) Cl 2nd 5-10; 2nd agn 12 til wknd & releg last 15; stdly lost tch; lft 3rd 2 out.*	20	3
	Commander Conn 100-30 G Hanmer *Ld to 4; eased, pu & dism app nxt; lame*		P
850[3]	Grantie Boy (IRE) (7a) 6-1 J O'Brien *(xnb) Oht; trckd ldrs; rmdr app 10; 2nd nxt til outj & dem 12; ev ch 3 out; wknd qckly & pu app nxt; dism; lame*		P

OFFICIAL DISTANCES: 12*l*, 20*l* **TIME:** 6min 20.0s **TOTE:** £2.50

1144 Confined, 12st — 3 ran

Form	Horse & comment	Dist	Pos
932[1]	**DARE** (3x) 1-2F **D Barlow** *Disp poor last to 14; trckd ldrs nxt til ld 3 out; went clr app last; comf.*		1
852[3]	**Fornaught Alliance (IRE)** (5x)(cp) 6-1 **Miss A Turner** *Ld 1; sn hdd & outpcd; disp dist last til ld brief 15; 1l down nxt; outpcd aft 2 out; no ch w wnr when jmpd slow last.*	15	2
875[3]	**Nicholls Cross (IRE)** (7x) 5-2 **G Hanmer** *(xnb) Pulled v hrd; fly-jmpng to 1; rdr tried to hld him but tore into 15l ld 2; 40l up 6 til began to tire & ld reduced frm 11; hdd app 15; sn t.o last; gvn oxygen aft.*	25	3

OFFICIAL DISTANCES: 15*l*, 30*l* **TIME:** 6min 18.0s **TOTE:** £1.50

1145 Mens Open, 12st — 4 ran

Form	Horse & comment	Dist	Pos
836[2]	**JEMARO (IRE)** (7x) 1-3F **R Burton** *Disp ld at gd pce; went 3l up 15; drew rt away nxt; 25l ahd 2 out; easily.*		1
979[P]	**Harry Hotspur (IRE)** (7x)(bl) 20-1 **M Jackson** *(xnb) Nt keen in 3rd; lost tch 4; dem to 12l last 8; t.o 11; rdn & no resp nxt; mist & nrly stpd aft 15; fnce last when lft 2nd tkng 2 out.*	2fncs	2

875P Lord Of The West (IRE) (4x) 4-1 G Hanmer *Disp ld w wnr; wknd app 3 out; 40l down & exhaust when ref & collapsed on to last fnce; sn rec.* . . . . r
1113r Meadows Boy (7x) 10-1 A Beedles *(xnb) Reluct to rce & lost 30l; rchd 15l 3rd 8; nvr nr ldrs; 30l 3rd 15; v tired when lft 2nd & pu last* . . . . P

OFFICIAL DISTANCE: dist **TIME:** 6min 11.0s **TOTE:** £2.00

The stewards enquired into the refusal of Lord Of The West; they decided no further action was required

1146 Ladies Open 3 ran

874² **JACKIE JARVIS (IRE)** (5a) 5-4 **Mrs K Diggle** *(xnb) A gng wl; hld up in last; qcknd to ld aft 11; gd j & went 5l clr nxt; 10l up 14; sn in comm* 1
1039² **Balisteros (FR)** 10-11F **Miss J Williams** *Trckd ldr til ld 5; hdd aft 11 & rdn along; outpcd 12-14; chsd game aft; no imp frm 3 out* 10 2
873⁵ **China Lal** (5a) 8-1 **Mrs S Johnson** *Ld to 4; mist nxt; releg last 11; 20l bhnd 12; t.o aft* 40 3

OFFICIAL DISTANCES: 12*l*, dist **TIME:** 6min 00.0s **TOTE:** £5.00

1147 PPORA Club Members (Nov Rdrs), 12st 5 ran

749P **NEW ROSS (IRE)** (4x)(bl) 9-4 **Miss A Turner** *Jw; ld to 8; ld agn 12; made rest; 3l clr at last; kpt on wl when prsd cl home* 1
874³ **Wychnor King (IRE)** 3-1 **Mrs D Caine** *Trckd ldrs in 3rd; ld brief 10-11; chsd wnr frm 15; 3l down last; str rn & chall flat; no ex cl home* 1 2
989⁵ **Chelsea King (IRE)** 7-4F **Miss G Garton** *Prom; ld brief 9; cl up til outpcd 14; kpt on same pce frm 3 out.* 8 3
933⁵ Gabaka De Thaix (FR) 10-1 M Caldwell *A 4th; 6l down when mists 12 & 13; kpt on one pce frm 14; nvr able to chall* 3 4
1045P Jona Holley 25-1 E Bourne *Last & imm lost tch; 15l detach & rdn along frm 5 til pu aft 3 out* . . . . P

OFFICIAL DISTANCES: 1*l*, 6*l* **TIME:** 6min 20.0s **TOTE:** £2.60

1148 Restricted, 12st 5 ran

1018P **THE LORD ROBERTS (IRE)** 7-2 **Miss T Clark** *(xnb) Swtng; made all; 4-5l up frm 8; r.o str frm 3 out; drew clr app last.* 1
Royrace 7-2 **G Hanmer** *Trckd ldrs in 3rd/4th; ev ch 3 out; outpcd app nxt; kpt on flat to snatch 2nd.* 15 2
839⁶ **Snitton West**(vis) 2-1F **M Jackson** *Hld up; 6-8l detach last to 9; hdwy 13; went 2nd 15; chsd wnr aft; btn off app last; lost 2nd nr line* . . . . ½ 3
530⁵ Lily Brown (5a) 6-1 Mrs S Johnson *A 3rd/4th; in tch & ev ch til fdd tame app 2 out* 12 4
933³ Hill Of Kilfeacle (IRE)(tt) 7-2 D Greenway *Chsd ldr in 2nd til wknd 13; last nxt; stdly lost tch aft* 2½ 5

OFFICIAL DISTANCES: 15*l*, nk **TIME:** 6min 11.0s **TOTE:** £2.20

1149 Intermediate, 12st

838P **KARZHANG R Burton** *Walked over* 1

West Norfolk

Fakenham (LH 6F,18J)

Sun, 25 Apr (GOOD)

1150 Hunt Members 5 ran

886² **TOM DE SAVOIE (IRE)** 4-7F **N Bloom** *Trckd ldrs; went 2nd 13; nt lk keen when rdn frm 15 til ld 2 out; grad forged clr.* 1
745P **Broad Edge (IRE)**(bl) 20-1 **R Stearn** *(xnb) Jw; mostly 2nd til rdn 13; outpcd 2 out; drvn into 2nd app last; no ch w wnr* 6 2
829¹ **Camden Loch (IRE)** 7-4 **D Kemp** *Ld; rdn & hdd 2 out; wknd & dem last; eased flat; dism* 15 3
906P Zabadi (IRE) 20-1 Miss R Napier *Lw; cl up til wknd qckly app 15; sn rem; all out to keep 4th* 25 4
Doctor Dunklin (USA)(bl) 20-1 Miss D Bulwer-Long *1st ride; rdr untidy 2 but safe aft; a last & sn detach; 25l adrift 11; tried hrd to catch 4th flat.* . . . ½ 5

OFFICIAL DISTANCES: 8*l*, 6*l* **TIME:** 6min 36.0s **TOTE:** £2.00 **DF:**£10.00

1151 Confined — 8 ran

893^{6}	**BUNRATTY'S SOLE (IRE)**(cp) 5-2 **N Bloom** *2nd/3rd til ld 5; went clr 3 out; kpt on frm nxt; rdly*		1
744^{P}	**Millenium Way (IRE)**(bl) 7-1 **J Owen** *Ld to 5; chsd wnr; mist 10; urged final circ; outj 3 out; drvn & tried to rally app last; wl hld & outbattled*	2	2
742^{2}	**Persian Hero (IRE)** 3-1 **J Diment** *Swtng; a 2nd/4th; drvn & lst tch aft 14; 20l 3rd 3 out*	10	3
745^{1}	Filou Du Bois (FR) 10-1 Ms A Embiricos *(xnb) Bhnd & rmdrs 6; in tch but nvr lkd v keen; 12l 6th 12; sn btn*	15	4
905^{2}	Lord Euro (IRE) 12-1 A Merriam *(xnb) Hld up in rr; prog in 3rd 9; ev ch til releg 5th 14; sn lost tch; t.o & pu last*		P
741^{1}	Mister Ringa 9-4F A Braithwaite *Chsd ldrs; mists 10 & 11; went 3rd 14; rdn & outpcd when bad mist nxt; nt rec; t.o & pu last*		P
1031^{U}	Sea Victor 33-1 M Grange *Bhnd; lost tch 10; t.o & pu 13; saddle problem.*		P
905^{4}	Sir Williamwallace (IRE) 20-1 R Stearn *Jmpd slow 4 & rmdrs; nvr lkd happy; midfield til strugg 11; t.o & pu 13*		P

OFFICIAL DISTANCES: 2*l*, 5*l* **TIME:** 6min 20.0s **TOTE:** £4.00 **DF:**£8.00

1152 Restricted, 12st — 12 ran

999^{7}	**NOWORNEVER (IRE)** 12-1 **D Kemp** *Ld to 3 & 6-8; rdn frm 12; 15l 3rd & outpcd 15; lft 8l 2nd nxt; lkd hld til drvn & clsd app last; ld flat; all out (1st win in 4yrs for present connections*		1
746^{1}	**Conquistador (IRE)** 4-1 **N Moore** *Chsd ldrs; clsd to 2nd aft 12; 10l down when lft 8l clr 3 out; rdn & wknd app last; hdd & no ex flat*	½	2
990^{2}	**Eco Warrior (IRE)** 5-1 **N Bell** *(xnb) Hld up & bhnd; 12l 6th 10; poor 8th aft 12; lft 18l 5th aft 3 out; stayed on wl frm nxt til no imp last; gvn too much to do*	2	3
902^{4}	Stick Or Bust(cp) 20-1 M Smith *Prom til lost plce 8; 6th & outpcd aft 12; tried to rally 14; lft 12l 3rd aft nxt; sn no imp*	12	4
652^{1}	Miss Biddy (5a) 7-2 Miss O Maylam *9/2-7/2; jmpd v stickily & imm lost tch; 30l adrift 6; t.o 9*	runin	5
885^{5}	Nonplussed (5a)(vis) 20-1 P Andrew *Jmpd v slow & imm lost tch; 25l adrift 6; t.o 9*	15	6
892^{P}	Badworth Gale (IRE) 10-1 J Burley *(xnb) Bhnd; mist 4; 8th & strugg 11; t.o 14; pu 2 out*		P
944^{3}	Gale Damage (IRE) 33-1 O Williams *Nvr btr than midfield; 7th & strugg aft 12; 26l 7th aft 3 out; t.o & pu last*		P
996^{1}	Play Alone (IRE) (5a) 8-1 N Bloom *Midfield; 5th & outpcd aft 12; sn rdn; lft 16l 4th aft 3 out; no prog; pu last*		P
945^{1}	Russian Friend(bl) 11-4F R Collinson *(xnb) Hld up; impd qckly to jn ldrs 6; ld 8 & jw aft; 10l clr 10; lkd in comm when fell 3 out*		F
745^{2}	Tartar Sabre 5-1 Miss L Barrett-Nobbs *Midfield; niggled 6; fell 9*		F
999^{4}	Troubleshooter(cp) 10-1 M Mackley *Ld 3-6; 2nd/3rd til releg 4th & drvn aft 12; sn strugg; lft 24l 6th aft 3 out; t.o & pu last.*		P

OFFICIAL DISTANCES: ½*l*, 1*l* **TIME:** 6min 30.0s **TOTE:** £25.00 **DF:**£50.00

1153 Mens Open, 12st — 10 ran

744^{1}	**BARD OF DRUMCOO (IRE)** 3-1 **D Kemp** *Jw; ld to 2 & frm 4; a gng best frm 12; 4l clr 3 out; kpt on stout*		1
830^{1}	**Homme De Fer** (7x) 5-4F **G Greenock** *Settled 3rd/4th & jmpd safe; 7l 4th aft 12; one pce & no imp frm 15; kpt on game to be lft 2nd flat*	12	2
893^{3}	**Militaire (FR)** (7x) 4-1 **J Owen** *2nd/3rd; niggled aft 12; 4l 2nd & u.p 3 out; no resp; lft 3rd flat*	hd	3
	Avalon Buck (IRE) (7x) 33-1 P Johnson *Imm strugg in last trio; virt t.o 9; plodded rnd*	runin	4
892^{5}	The Red Boy (IRE)(cp) 6-1 A Braithwaite *Jmpd rt & slow; prom; ld 2-4; 5l 4th & u.p 3 out; went 2nd aft nxt; no ch w wnr when ref to rce aft last; stpd to a walk*	3	5
397^{4}	Avondale Illusion (IRE) 33-1 R Stearn *Rr & most reluct frm 4; t.o 6; pu 10*		P
1056^{P}	Brilliant Star (NZ) (7x) 33-1 P Millington *Fat; lkd awful; 2 handlers; nt jw & imm lost tch in last trio; pu 5*		P
997^{P}	Fine Times (7x) 33-1 M Mackley *Mist 3; rr & nvr gng wl; rem 7th 9; pu 12; lifeless*		P

885[7] Glemot (IRE) (7x) 50-1 J Burley *Off pce in midfield; rdn 6; 33l 5th 9; wl t.o 13; pu last* . . . . P
943[2] Noel's Pride (7x) 10-1 N Bell *(xnb) Stdd start; hdwy in 15l 5th but out of control when rn out 7* . . . . R

OFFICIAL DISTANCES: 10*l*, hd **TIME:** 6min 22.0s **TOTE:** £2.50 **DF:**£2.50

1154 Ladies Open — 6 ran

893[4] **CELTIC DUKE** 6-4 **Miss Z Turner** *2nd to 10; 3½l 3rd aft 12; 2nd agn nxt; urged ahd aft 2 out; sn in comm.* 1
785[P] **Sheskinqueen (IRE)** (5a) 20-1 **Miss A Wells** *Hld up; hdwy to 3rd 8 & 2nd 10; ld app 15 til rdn & hdd aft 2 out; no ch w wnr* 5 2
998[1] **Highland Rose (IRE)** (5a) 4-7F **Ms A Embiricos** *(xnb) V free to post; numerous mists or slow js; in tch; blun 10; 5l 4th aft 12; outpcd in 9l 3rd 15; rdn & tried to rally 2 out; sn fnd little.* 7 3
904[2] Mister Audi (IRE)(bl) 20-1 Miss A Bowles *3rd/4th & in tch til wknd 11; 17l 5th aft nxt; sn t.o.* . . . . runin 4
998[7] Catherine's Way (IRE)(cp) 25-1 Miss A Stennett *Ld; hdd app 15; wknd rap to 4th; t.o & pu last* . . . . P
650[4] Step In Line (IRE) 20-1 Mrs S Hodge *(xnb) A last; blun 9; 20l down aft 12; t.o & pu 2 out.* . . . . P

OFFICIAL DISTANCES: 4*l*, 5*l* **TIME:** 6min 23.0s **TOTE:** £2.00 **DF:**£32.00

1155 Open Maiden 56&7yo, 12st — 10 ran

244[4] **MONTENEGRO** 5-2 **N Bloom** *Tk keen hld; went 2nd 5; a ldng pr aft; ld 7-9; outpcd 15-nxt; rallied to chall & jmpd slow 2 out; came agn last; lkd hld til gt up nr fin; game* 1
833[2] **On The Day (IRE)** 2-1F **J Owen** *7/2-2s; ld to 7 & frm 9; drvn aft 2 out; nk ahd last; over 1l ahd flat til caught u.p nr fin* . . . . hd 2
652[2] **Mr Know What (IRE)** 7-2 **Miss C Bartlett** *Jw; drpd to rr 6; poor last 11; lft 15l last 14; stayed on to make 2 plces frm 2 out; set impossible task* 25 3
901[P] Peats Ridge (IRE) 6-1 R Stearn *Bckwd; chsd ldr to 5; rdn frm 9; 6l 4th & outpcd aft 12; 17l 4th 15; plodded on; walked in* 15 4
652[6] Rash Moment (FR) (7a) 20-1 A Merriam *Tde; hld up midfield; impd rap to jn ldrs 12 til 7l 3rd & wkng bad u.p 15; t.o app 2 out.* 3 5
652[F] First And Fourmost (IRE) 14-1 R Morgan-Evans *2 handlers; chsd ldrs to 7; 6th & nt keen 11; wl bhnd when pu 13.* . . . . P
Geordie Macgregor (7a) 8-1 P Millington *Bckwd; lkd horrible; blun rnd in last pr; bad mist 6; t.o & pu 13; school* . . . . P
560[P] Lightning Fork (IRE) (5a) 5-1 M Mackley *2 handlers; midfield; 6th when mist & ur 9.* . . . . U
901[P] Lolloping Lad 12-1 M Smith *Sn 3rd/4th; drvn & ev ch aft 12; wkng rap when blun nxt & pu.* . . . . P
39[P] Pernickety King (7a) 20-1 A Williams *Nt fluent in last trio; t.o & pu 13; school* P

OFFICIAL DISTANCES: hd, 10*l* **TIME:** 6min 37.0s **TOTE:** £3.30 **DF:**£2.50

1156 Open Maiden 8yo&up — 5 ran

1000[4] **SOCIETY SCANDAL (IRE)**(tt) 10-1 **Miss L Fear** *V scraggy; imm detach last; 25l down 4; slt prog frm 12; lft 3rd 15 & 2nd bhnd stablemate nxt; sn ld; rdr more composed than rival & forged clr app last; rdr's 1st wnr.* 1
Macrobert's Reply (IRE) 10-1 **P Millington** *(xnb) Lkd dreadful; chsd ldng pr til 13l 3rd & strugg aft 12; lft poor 2nd 15; lft in ld nxt; hdd & wildly rdn app 2 out; wknd app last* 20 2
901[2] A Fine Story 11-8F A Williams *Lw; ld & mostly ab 8l clr; jmpd v awkward 13; lft uncatchable when pursuer fell 15; ploughing on in virt isolation when fell nxt* . . . . F
813[4] Man At The Top(bl) 6-4 M Bennison *Chsd ldr but lkd reluct & niggled along; blun 6 & u.p; mist 11; 6l down & hrd rdn nxt; 10l adrift when desperate blun & ur 15* . . . . U
652[4] Marsden 10-1 R Hanley *Swtng; went 2nd aft 2 til rfo 3* . . . . U

OFFICIAL DISTANCE: 20*l* **TIME:** 6min 57.0s **TOTE:** £10.00 **DF:**£37.50

York & Ainsty (North and South)

Easingwold (LH 8F,18J)

Sun, 25 Apr (GOOD)

1157 Hunts Members — 9 ran

772[P]	**CLAIRE'S NOMAD**(cp) 5-4F **Miss Rachel Clark** *(xnb) Mid-div early; 8l 4th 8-13; mist 14; 8l 4th 3 out; all to do app last; fin str und v hrd drvng to ld on line*		1
591[P]	**Eastern Royal** (7a) 12-1 **M Briggs** *(xnb) Cl up; 4l 3rd 6; hdwy 9; ld frm 11; 3l up 3 out; clr last; hrd rdn flat; wknd & hdd on line*	hd	2
502[P]	**Dinan (IRE)** 50-1 **Mrs J Brown** *(xnb) Cl 2nd to 11; 2l 3rd 14-3 out; 1l 2nd app last; ev ch but wknd flat*	2	3
1042[1]	Hattie (5a) 6-1 P Cornforth *Nt fluent early; ld; sn 3l clr; jnd 11; sn hdd; cl 2nd & ev ch til wknd 2 out*	1/2	4
679[U]	Glacial Dancer (IRE) 5-2 R Clark *Nvr btr than mid-div; 10l 5th 8; pushed along & lsng tch 12; 10l 5th 3 out; r.o same pce*	8	5
955[6]	Snizort (USA) 6-1 G Brewer *A midfield to rr; 9l 5th 8; pushed along & drpng off pce 13; rr & no ch 14*	15	6
814[4]	Hanisia (5a) 50-1 P Atkinson *(xnb) A towards rr; mist 6; lsng tch aft 8; t.o 13; rem when pu 2 out*		P
505[1]	I'm No Fairy (7a) 8-1 D Thomas *A last; hrd rdn & pushed along 7; lsng tch 9; t.o when virt ref 12; clambered over & ur*		U
	Noggler (7a) 25-1 S Charlton *Oht; swtng bad; rr when blun & ur 4*		U

OFFICIAL DISTANCES: hd, 4*l* **TIME:** 6min 03.0s

1158 Open Maiden 56&7yo (Div 1), 12st — 14 ran

709[3]	**FLAT STANLEY** (7a) 5-1 **Miss J Foster** *Handy in 4th to 8; went 2l 2nd 12; chall last; ld & qcknd clr flat & r.o wl*		1
959[2]	**Irish Paddy (IRE)** (7a) 6-1 **R Clark** *Hld up in mid-div; 6l 5th 8; hdwy 10; ld 12; 1l up app last; hdd & easily outpcd flat*	6	2
774[2]	**Magic Route (IRE)** 6-1 **Miss T Jackson** *A.p; trckd ldr in 2l 2nd to 8; handy 3rd 9-14; disp ld 15-2 out; outpcd & wknd app last*	3	3
814[2]	Bobby Buttons 3-1F N Tutty *Cl 3rd to 8; pushed along 11; outpcd & 10l 4th 14; wknd qckly; poor 4th 2 out*	15	4
776[P]	Milliners Guide (5a) 33-1 G Brewer *(xnb) Tk keen hld; hld up to 4; pulled to handy 5th 7; in tch til outpcd & wknd frm 14*	8	5
813[3]	Catosphere (IRE) 10-1 L Bates *Rr & bhnd to 7; lsng tch 8; poor 6th by 15; r.o one pce*	3	6
919[P]	Tartan Rising (7a) 33-1 C Dawson *Tk keen hld; ld to 11; mist 12; sn wknd; t.o by 15*	2 1/2fs	7
773[P]	Alizarin (IRE) (12a) 33-1 T Craggs *(xnb) A towards rr; pushed along & lsng tch when ur 14*		U
504[P]	God Of War 33-1 P Robinson *Mid-div when blun & ur 2*		U
960[P]	Honeyfantastic (12a) 33-1 P Kinsella *Rr by 9; pushed along 12; lsng tch 13; t.o & pu 3 out*		P
813[U]	Iron Trooper (IRE)(bl) 14-1 T Glass *Mid-div til fell 7*		F
813[2]	No Info (IRE) (5a) 8-1 B Woodhouse *(xnb) Handy in mid-div to 7; blun 11; sn pushed along; lsng tch 12; t.o & pu 14*		P
960[B]	Raggy Jumper 33-1 N Smith *Last by 3; bad mist 4; lsng tch 7; t.o when pu 12*		P
960[P]	Supreme Vintage (IRE) 33-1 R Wakeham *Prom in mid-div; 8l 7th 11; gng wl when ur 12*		U

OFFICIAL DISTANCES: 6*l*, 3*l* **TIME:** 6min 02.0s

1159 Open Maiden 56&7yo (Div 2), 12st — 14 ran

776[3]	**DUCHESS ACCOUNT** (5a) 2-1F **R Wakeham** *Nt jw early; mid-div when mist 3; 8th 10; hdwy 12 to 4th 14 & 1l 2nd 3 out-last; hrd drvn & stayed on game; ld & drew clr nr fin*		1
774[3]	**Shirostran** 7-2 **P Kinsella** *Handy in mid-div to 10; drpd to rr by 12; hdwy frm 13 to 5th 15; ld 3 out; 1l ahd last; hung rt & hdd flat; one pce*	1	2
920[5]	**Callitwatulike** 20-1 **T Glass** *Mid-div early; 12l 8th 9; hdwy frm 11 to 4th 15; outpcd by ldng pr 3 out; went 3rd app 2 out; r.o one pce*	8	3
959[5]	Parsifal (7a) 14-1 R Abrahams *Mid-div 1st circ; hdwy to 8l 3rd 14-3 out; sn wknd & dem aft nxt*	6	4

814[r] Madaar (USA) (7a) 6-1 N Smith *Sa; ld 2-12; cl 2nd to 15; wknd aft.* 7 5
768[P] Ivory Cross 14-1 C Rae *Cl 3rd to 8; handy to 11; wknd 13; wl bhnd 15* . . 1 6
954[U] Emperor's Castle (7a) 12-1 G Brewer *Ur gng down & galloped loose; sa; rr to 4; rap hdwy frm 7 til 1l 3rd 9; in tch til wknd frm 15* 5 7
768[7] Deep Design (IRE)(bl) 12-1 C Dawson *Cl 2nd to 7; handy & in tch; ld 13-14; wknd nxt* 6 8
Brandnewplan (IRE) (7a) 8-1 B Woodhouse *Rr; 15l 7th 11; gng wl bhnd ldrs 12; in tch til wknd 15; will improve* . . . . ½ 9
776[P] Jobee Jack 20-1 T Craggs *Sa; rr by 6; t.o by 14; fell on flat aft 3 out; down for 45 mins & delayed nxt rce; event gt up but inj* . . . . F
958[F] Primitive Choice (5a) 14-1 L Bates *Sn bhnd; last by 11; t.o by 13; pu 3 out* P
774[B] Quel Regal (FR) 12-1 Miss Rachel Clark *Rr by 6; pushed along 11; lsng tch 14; t.o & pu 2 out; dism* . . . . P
775[P] Sea Princess (5a) 14-1 N Tutty *Fell 1* . . . . F
392[P] Zebs Lad 33-1 R Walker *Cl 4th to 8; wknd 9; rr by 11; last & lsng tch 13; t.o & pu 14* . . . . P

OFFICIAL DISTANCES: 1*l*, 10*l* **TIME:** 6min 14.0s

1160 Ladies Open — 8 ran

811[2] **HADEQA** 5-1 **Miss S Brotherton** *Trckd ldr in 2l 2nd til disp ld 13-14; ld aft 3 out; qckknd rt away app nxt; r.o str; fin wl* 1
564[P] **Sally Scally** (5a) 8-1 **Miss T Jackson** *Last & in tch to 14; hdwy to 8l 3rd 3 out; went 2nd nxt; one pce & no ch w wnr* 6 2
957[P] **Perchancer (IRE)** 16-1 **Miss A Armitage** *Tk keen hld; hld up & bhnd til hdwy 9; 3rd 14; outpcd 3 out; lft 3rd agn last; r.o str flat & nrly snatched 2nd* nk 3
811[4] On The Mend (IRE) 33-1 Miss F Hartley *A.p; 3l 3rd 10; cl 4th 14; pushed along & wknd 15; lft 4th agn last; r.o one pce* 5 4
957[4] Yorkshire Edition (IRE) 8-1 Miss W Gibson *Rr but in tch to 14; pushed along & outpcd 15; wknd frm 3 out* 2 5
811[U] Miorbhail 33-1 Miss T Gray *Handy in mid-div til outpcd & wknd 15* 8 6
957[5] Blue Bud(bl) 50-1 Miss C Metcalfe *Lkd reluct; jmpd slow & sn bhnd; lsng tch 5; t.o 7; rem when pu 10* . . . . P
811[1] Texas Ranger 2-5F Miss J Foster *Tried to make all; ld; jnd 13-14 & agn 3 out; easily outpcd; mist 2 out & wknd; hld in 4th when fell last* . . . . F

OFFICIAL DISTANCES: 5*l*, nk **TIME:** 5min 54.0s

1161 Mens Open — 10 ran

956[2] **NORDIC CREST (IRE)**(tt) 2-1F **M Walford** *V confid rdn; hld up last to 12; stdy hdwy to cl 3rd 3 out; easily ld app last; drew clr flat* 1
917[1] **Extra Jack (FR)**(bl) 5-1 **C Shirley-Beavan** *Sn clr; set str gallop; 8l up 8-14; 2l clr 3 out; jnd aft nxt; sn hdd & easily outpcd; rallied & stayed on game flat* 1½ 2
679[P] **Ababou (FR)** 4-1 **S Charlton** *Chsd ldr in 4l 2nd to 7; & 3l 2nd 15; ev ch 3 out; wknd nxt* 3 3
770[P] Mr McDuck (IRE) 8-1 L Bates *Midfield; prom in 4th til outpcd & wknd 3 out* 8 4
565[U] Londolozi Lad (IRE) (7a) 66-1 P Kinsella *A towards rr; pushed along 14; 12l 5th 3 out; r.o one pce* 2 5
955[5] Abinger 66-1 M Morley *Mid-div til trckd ldrs 10; last & pushed along 12; t.o by 15; rem when pu 2 out; lame; removed in horse ambulance* . . . . P
338[2] Darak (IRE) 5-1 N Tutty *Chsd ldrs; 12l 3rd to 9; went 5l 3rd 14; in tch til wknd qckly 15; t.o & pu 2 out* . . . . P
957[2] Nip On(cp) 5-1 G Brewer *Rr by 3; pushed along 5; lsng tch when blun & fell 13* F
772[P] Notation (IRE) 66-1 R Clark *Rr to 8; pushed along & resp 12; went 5l 4th 3 out; wknd app nxt; bhnd when pu last* . . . . P
772[P] Rubon Prince (IRE)(cp) 66-1 T Glass *Mid-div 1st circ; rr & hrd rmdrs 11; sn t.o; pu 14* . . . . P

OFFICIAL DISTANCES: 1½*l*, 2*l* **TIME:** 5min 55.0s

1162 Restricted — 13 ran

960[1] **NOUGHT TO NINETY** 5-1 **L Bates** *Last & bhnd to 8; lost tch 9; t.o 11; hdwy 13 to 10l 5th 2 out; 3l down last; flew up run-in; ld & drew clr nr fin* . . 1
958[1] **Civil Gent (IRE)** (7a) 7-1 **G Brewer** *Mid-div to 7; hdwy 8; went 1l 2nd 9 til ld 11; 3l clr 14-last; hrd drvn flat; hdd nr line* 2 2
955[2] **Sevensider (IRE)** 2-1F **R Wakeham** *Mid-div; hdwy 10 to 3l 2nd 15; 2nd & ev ch 2 out; one pce aft; dem flat* 1 3

955P Hessac (FR) 10-1 J Davis *Prom in 4th to 9; went 2l 3rd 11; outpcd 12; stayed on to 4th 2 out; one pce aft* . . . ½ 4

Office Hours 33-1 S Charlton *Hld up in rr; hdwy frm 8 to 5th 13; cruised up to 2l 3rd 3 out; sn wknd* . . . 4 5

955⁴ Don Rio (IRE)(tt) 10-1 M Morley *Chsd ldr in 8l 2nd to 12; pushed along & wknd 14; stayed on one pce frm 2 out* . . . ½ 6

776¹ Sams Way 5-2 P Kinsella *A midfield; 6th 9 & 8th 12; pushed along & rmdrs 13; lsng tch 15; nd aft* . . . 8 7

563⁴ Colonel Ludlow (IRE) 50-1 C Cundall *Handy in 3rd to 8; in tch 13-15; sn wknd; bhnd by 3 out* . . . 3 8

563P Agent Provocateur (NZ) 20-1 R Clark *Rr by 6; a bhnd; lsng tch 14; t.o & pu 3 out* . . . P

955⁸ In The Van(cp) 33-1 J Morley *Mounted on course; tde; mid-div when fell 7* F

810P Redsands (IRE) 50-1 S Walker *Ld & sn clr; 6l up 9; hdd aft 12; sn wknd; t.o & pu 15* . . . P

810P Vintage Choice (IRE) 50-1 P Cornforth *Handy & in tch early; 5th 6; rr 11; last & lsng tch 13; t.o & pu 2 out* . . . P

505P Whitleygrange Girl (5a) 66-1 N Tutty *Rr when mist 3; bhnd by 10; lsng tch 13; t.o & pu 14* . . . P

OFFICIAL DISTANCES: 1*l*, 2*l* **TIME:** 6min 04.0s

1163 Confined, 12st — 9 ran

563¹ **JOURNEY** 7-2 **N Tutty** *Made all; 8l clr 11; drew rt away 15; 30l clr 3 out; coasted run-in & nrly caught napping* . . . 1

812⁴ **Glendamah (IRE)** 3-1JF **M Morley** *Chsd ldrs in 3rd to 13; went 12l 2nd 14; outpcd & 30l 2nd 3 out; hrd rdn frm nxt; fin str & nrly caught wnr napping* nk 2

732¹⁵ **Imperial Line (IRE)** 10-1 **Miss T Jackson** *Rr & bhnd 12; hdwy to dist 4th 3 out; stayed on to 3rd app last; no ch w ldrs* . . . 10 3

809¹ Royal Crimson 8-1 R Alers-Hankey *Chsd ldr in 8l 2nd to 11; outpcd & wknd 13; 15l 3rd 15; r.o one pce* . . . 1 4

377F Panooras Lord (IRE) 33-1 Miss Rachel Clark *Prom in 4th to 11; pushed along & wknd 14; dist 5th by 3 out* . . . 15 5

770³ Chaos Theory 3-1JF D Thomas *Midfield when blun bad & ur 3* . . . U

771R Glensan (IRE) 5-1 G Brewer *Prom in 3rd to 8; went 2nd & chsng ldr when slpd up bend bef 9* . . . S

772⁹ Princess Derry (5a) 12-1 C Cundall *A rr; last by 4; lsng tch 13; t.o 15; pu 2 out* P

772P Welsh March (IRE) 8-1 P Kinsella *Last by 3; bhnd when bd bend bef 9* . . . B

OFFICIAL DISTANCES: nk, 8*l* **TIME:** 5min 57.0s

1164 Open Maiden (Div 1) — 10 ran

809U **SCENIC STORM (IRE)** 6-1 **P Kinsella** *Cl 4th til 3l 3rd 11-14; rushed up to disp ld 2 out; ld last; hrd rdn & drew clr flat* . . . 1

504⁵ **Gollinger**(cp) 6-1 **B Woodhouse** *Ld; 2l up til jnd 2 out; hdd & easily outpcd app last; rallied & stayed on wl flat; just failed* . . . 1 2

766P **Seasmith** 4-1 **C Shirley-Beavan** *Trckd ldr in 2l 2nd til disp ld 10-12; in tch & ev ch til wknd frm 3 out* . . . 4 3

960P Gipsy Wood (5a) 14-1 T Glass *(nosenet) Rr to 6; 7th 10; hdwy aft 11 to 8l 4th 3 out; r.o one pce* . . . 3 4

504P House Colours 6-1 S Charlton *A mid-div; 8l 5th 13; pushed along 14; nvr able to chall* . . . 8 5

960⁵ Biddy (12a) 4-1 N Smith *Prom early; cl 2nd & mist 4; rr by 6; nd aft* . . . 25 6

959P Edstone (IRE) 20-1 N Tinkler *Prom in 2l 2nd 5-9; wknd 12 & rr 13; sn t.o; pu 2 out* . . . P

Fair Grand 20-1 P Cornforth *Sn bhnd; last by 3; pushed along 10; t.o by 14; pu 3 out* . . . P

960F Lilly Beach (5a) 5-2F N Tutty *Handy in 3rd/4th to 10; went 2l 3rd 13; wknd rap aft 14; t.o & pu 2 out* . . . P

813P Selectric (IRE) 20-1 S Gibbon *A rr; lsng tch 11; t.o 14; pu 3 out* . . . P

OFFICIAL DISTANCES: 1*l*, 3*l* **TIME:** 6min 07.0s

1165 Open Maiden (Div 2) — 11 ran

444⁷ **STORMY SUNRISE (IRE)** 3-1 **Miss A Armitage** *A.p; 2l 2nd 15 & 1l 2nd 2 out; gng wl on bridle app last; scooted clr flat* . . . 1

Black Rainbow (IRE) (5a) 10-1 **Miss T Jackson** *Mid-div to 5; 8l 5th 7; hdwy to 2l 2nd 9; cl 2nd 15; disp ld last; easily outpcd flat* . . . 6 2

595[5] **Hidden Pearl (IRE)**(bl) 10-1 **J Davis** *Sn ld; 6l clr to 8; 2l up til jnd app last; sn hdd & outpcd* . . . 2 3
960[3] The Sea Club (IRE) 5-2F Miss L Robson *Hld up last til hdwy 8; 12l 5th 11; outpcd 14; 12l 5th 2 out; r.o one pce* . . . 4 4
959[4] Bankersdraft 6-1 M Morley *Mid-div early; hdwy 9 to cl 3rd 14; in tch til wknd app 3 out* . . . 6 5
813[5] Snow Nymph (5a) 6-1 W Burnell *A midfield; nvr able to chall* . . . 8 6
877[2] Mon Performer 7-1 N Tinkler *Mid-div to 14; rdn 3 out to 6l 4th 2 out; hrd drvn to disp ld & gng wl when pckd bad & nrly fell last; brilliant rcvry but lost all ch* 1 7
1158[U] God Of War 20-1 P Robinson *Rr by 3; lsng tch 10; t.o 14; 2 fncs adrift by last; plodded on* . . . 2½fs 8
954[2] Final Chorus (5a) 16-1 R Wakeham *Rr & mist 3; pushed along & lsng tch 12; t.o 14; pu 3 out* . . . P
394[P] Stickwiyadad 20-1 T Craggs *Sn bhnd; t.o by 8; pu 9* . . . P
Trigger Castle (5a) 20-1 S Walker *Rr 5; jmpd slow 6; pushed along & lsng tch 8; t.o & pu 13* . . . P

OFFICIAL DISTANCES: 6*l*, 2*l* **TIME:** 6min 06.0s

Newton Abbot (LH, 11F)

Tue, 27 Apr (GOOD, GOOD to FIRM in places)

1166 One and Only Handicap HC, 2m5f110y - 14J £10,205 13 ran

801[1] **GUIGNOL DU COCHET (FR)** 10-04 3-1JF **T Greenall** *Ld 1; sn stdd in midfield; 15l 4th when jmpd slow 6; 5th 9; eff in 3rd app 3 out; ld app last; sn clr; rdly* . . . 1
993[3] **Jabiru (IRE)** 10-08 (5ow)(bl) 4-1 **D Edwards** *3rd when blun 5; went 2nd 9-10; sn rdn; 2nd agn 13; nt fluent nxt; hrd drvn & ev ch 2 out; btn when jmpd lft last* . . . 6 2
799[4] **Sol Music** 11-02 7-1 **L Jefford** *Ld aft 1; set fast pce; hdd 5; ld 7; jmpd rt 8; hdd 10; ld agn app 13; 3l clr when hit 2 out; hdd app last; wknd flat* . . . 4 3
799[5] Phoenix Phlyer 10-11(cp) 14-1 Miss C Stucley *Ld 3-7 & app 10; hdd & mist 13; wknd 2 out* . . . 4 4
732[B] Silence Reigns 12-04(bl) 3-1JF N Williams *Hld up in tch; hdwy in 4th when mist 11; 8l 5th 3 out; wknd nxt; eased flat* . . . 12 5
892[4] Enitsag (FR) 11-00 15-2 D Mansell *Mists in rr; 8th 9; strugg aft blun 10; t.o* 28 6
994[P] Blackberry Way 10-07(tt) 25-1 J Diment *Sn poor last; jmpd rt 3; t.o 5; pu 13* P
823[1] Damiens Pride (IRE) 10-00 25-1 C Heard *Chsd ldrs; lost plce 6; 6th 9; bhnd frm 11; pu 2 out* . . . P
636[7] O'flaherty's (IRE) 10-00(bl) 66-1 W Kavanagh *Bhnd; mist 6; pu 8; bbv* . . . P
734[6] Parte Prima 10-02 14-1 R Woollacott *Mist 1; sn bhnd; blun 8; poor 10th nxt; t.o & pu 13* . . . P
799[7] Red Brook Lad 11-09 6-1 N Mitchell *Bhnd; mist 8; 9th nxt; nvr gng wl aft; t.o & pu 2 out* . . . P
993[4] Sporting Chance 10-00 50-1 Miss T Cave *Pckd 1; mid-div; blun 2 & rdr rt up nk & lost iron; outpcd 7; 7th 9; rallied in 13l 6th 3 out; 5th & staying on when blun & ur last* . . . U
993[P] Traditional (IRE) 10-00 66-1 Miss R Green *Jmpd v slow 3; sn wl bhnd & nt keen; t.o & pu 13* . . . P

TIME: 5min 18.2s **TOTE:** £4.70; places £1.50,£2.10,£2.00 **Ex:**£32.60 **CSF:**£17.84

Fences 4 & 11 omitted

1167 Totnes & Bridgetown Races Co Nov HC, 3m2f110y - 17J £2801 12 ran

792[2] **BENGAL BULLET** 11-07 10-1 **Miss T Cave** *Jmpd rt; ld 3; mist 3 out (water); 3l clr last; stayed on game* . . . 1
975[F] **Johns Legacy** 11-07 12-1 **Miss S Robinson** *Hld up; hdwy 9; chsd wnr app 2 out; 3l 2nd when mist & pckd bad last; no imp* . . . 3 2
1064[2] **Mrs Be (IRE)** 11-09 9-4 **Miss P Gundry** *Hld up in tch; lost plce 7; sn bhnd; 9th 12; some hdwy app 14; too much to do; stayed on flat* . . . 10 3
975[1] Kingston-Banker 12-02 5-4F T Dreaper *Chsd ldr; nt fluent 14; rdn 16; dem 3rd & drvn & wkng 2 out* . . . hd 4
793[1] Knock Star (IRE) 11-07 16-1 S Partridge *Hld up; hdwy 6; brief eff in 5th 14; wknd 16* . . . 6 5

860[2] Skip 'n' Tune (IRE) 11-06 10-1 M Miller *Hld up & bhnd; 5th & hdwy 16; wknd app 3 out* . . . 7 6
961[1] Burley Don Carlos 11-07(cp) 10-1 Miss C Stucley *Prom; mist 9; 3rd 14; lost plce qckly aft mist 16; t.o* . . . dist 7
793[3] Bak On Board 11-07(bl) 20-1 Miss L Gardner *A towards rr; 7th 11; t.o 13; pu 2 out* . . . P
908[5] Carefree Love (IRE) 11-09(bl) 20-1 Miss S Gaisford *Nvr went a yard; last & rdn 4; t.o & pu 7* . . . P
864[1] Hello Roscrea (IRE) 11-11 12-1 Miss A Goschen *Ld to 3; nt fluent 6; wknd 7; t.o & pu 3 out* . . . P
907[2] Indian Raider (IRE) 11-07(cp) 50-1 A Glassonbury *Hld up in tch; rdn 5; lost plce u.p 12; hit 13; t.o & pu 15* . . . P
1006[B] Off The Hook (IRE) 12-00 33-1 A Charles-Jones *A wl bhnd; 10th 11; t.o & pu aft 3 out* . . . P

TIME: 6min 41.0s **TOTE:** £14.40; places £3.30,£3.70,£1.10 **Ex:**£144.80 **CSF:**£132.01
Fences 1, 8 & 15 omitted

Cheltenham (LH 10F)

Wed, 28 Apr (GOOD to SOFT)

1168 Peter Davies Media 10th Anniversary HC, 2m5f - 17J £3570

19 ran

892[1] **BOHEMIAN SPIRIT (IRE)** 12-00 11-1 **S Charlton** *Prom; went 2nd 10; jnd 3 out; gng best when lft clr nxt; blun last; kpt on str.* . . . 1
732[8] **Cape Stormer (IRE)** 12-00 3-1F **M Gorman** *Chsd ldrs; outpcd 11; rallying & lft 12l 4th when hit 14; lft 12l 3rd & hit 2 out; rdn & stayed on to tk 2nd final 75yds; no ch w wnr.* . . . 8 2
543[P] **Charlie Strong (IRE)** 12-00 14-1 **Miss P Gundry** *2 handlers; mists & detach in final quartet; prog to poor 6th app 11; str rn aft 3 out; went 3rd cl home; too much to do* . . . 1¾ 3
732[U] Irbee 12-02(bl) 14-1 Miss C Tizzard *Trckd ldrs; eff when mist & hmpd 14; nt qcknd when lft 5l 2nd 2 out; hung rt & lost 2 plces flat.* . . . ½ 4
799[2] Bill Me Up (IRE) 11-07 5-1 L Heard *2 handlers; midfield & nt fluent; drvn 9; outpcd nxt; passed btn horses frm 14; nvr nr ldrs* . . . 15 5
Iron N Gold 11-11 33-1 Mrs R Powell *Hld up last; no prog til passed wkng rivals frm 11; rdr nvr gave him any ch* . . . 3½ 6
1029[U] The Granby (IRE) 11-07 9-1 Miss H Irving *Mist 2 & rn in snatches; mist 5; 9th & rdn 9; no ch frm 11; lost a front shoe* . . . ½ 7
747[3] Whether The Storm (IRE) 12-04 8-1 Miss E Jones *Cl up; 5th when mist 11; jmpd slow 13; sn lost plce & strugg.* . . . 1 8
1029[2] News Flash (IRE) 11-07 66-1 Miss L Brooke *Prom til lost plce 8; 10th nxt; rallied to chse clr ldrs aft 14; sn wknd.* . . . 9 9
755[P] Boyne Banks (IRE) 11-07 66-1 G Disney *Keen; ld 2-3; chsd ldr to 9; lost plce rap; t.o 3 out* . . . 21 10
868[3] Supreme Storm (IRE) 11-07 66-1 R Bandey *Detach in final quartet; no ch 11; t.o 3 out* . . . 12 11
880[4] Arlequin De Sou (FR) 11-07(bl) 33-1 B Woodhouse *Midfield; drvn 10; sn lost tch; t.o 3 out* . . . ½ 12
975[P] S B S By Jove 12-00 100-1 A Charles-Jones *Cl up til lost plce 8; wl bhnd 11; t.o 3 out* . . . 10 13
997[7] Merry Minstrel (IRE) 11-07 100-1 L Hicks *2 handlers; mists & towards rr; lost tch 10; t.o 3 out* . . . dist 14
937[1] Dinsey Finnegan (IRE) 11-07(vis) 66-1 G Phillips *Sn cl up; mist 10; rdn & sn wknd; rem 11th when fell 3 out* . . . F
801[3] Filscot 12-00 33-1 J Diment *Detach in final quartet; nvr gng wl; t.o last when ref 13* . . . r
965[1] Gipsy Cricketer 11-07 20-1 Miss C Stucley *Tde & ld to start; mid-div; lost tch 10; t.o & pu 3 out* . . . P
528[P] Kerres Noires (FR) 12-00 20-1 S Waley-Cohen *(xnb) Lw; oht; tk str hld; prsd ldrs; eff app 11; cl 3rd & gng wl when fell 14* . . . F
994[5] Upham Lord (IRE) 11-13 11-1 G Brewer *Lw; ld to 2 & frm 3; jnd 3 out; rdn & just hdd when fell nxt (lkd 2nd best)* . . . F

TIME: 5min 28.8s **TOTE:** £11.60; places £3.80,£2.60,£6.00 **Ex:**£54.70 **CSF:**£40.01

1169 Faucets The Leading Independant Brassware Distributor Champion HC, 3m2f110y - 22J £4800 — 7 ran

732^{5}	**TORDUFF EXPRESS (IRE)** 11-11(bl) 9-2 **N Williams** *Settled 3rd; went 2nd 11; ld 17; drawing clr when nt fluent 19; distance ahd app 2 out; rdn & waved tail in triumph nr fin; fin tired*		1
1117^{2}	**Mullensgrove** 12-01 13-2 **Miss S Phizacklea** *Reluct in prelims; nt a fluent & nvr lkd v keen; drvn final 2m; poor 10th 5; t.o 17; 4th 3 out; late prog to snatch 2nd*	22	2
991^{2}	**Macgeorge (IRE)** 12-01 11-8F **M Barber** *Nt jw; chsd ldr to 11; rdn 13; 20l 3rd 19; rem 2nd agn app 2 out til dem nr fin*	½	3
893^{1}	Cantarinho 11-13 7-2 D Kemp *Ld; mist 9; hdd 17; outpcd when blun 19; v tired when lost 2nd app 2 out; t.o & fin exhaust*	dist	4
994^{P}	Tales Of Bounty (IRE) 11-13(bl) 10-1 J Snowden *Chsd ldng trio; mist 9; rdn & lost tch 15; t.o 17*	8	5
	Native Daisy (IRE) 11-02 66-1 E O'Grady *A 6th; mist 12; lost tch 15; t.o 17; fin lame*	10	6
997^{2}	Hatch Gate 11-11 33-1 P York *V reluct to start & lost 30l; bustled up to be just in tch 3-5; strugg when mist 8; t.o 10; pu 16*		P

TIME: 7min 12.1s **TOTE:** £5.80; places £2.40,£2.90 **Ex:**£47.70 **CSF:**£29.87

The stewards suspended the rider of Macgeorge for four days for misuse of the whip causing the horse to be injured

1170 Winning Post at Cheltenham HC, 4m1f - 27J £4982 — 11 ran

991^{4}	**COUNTY DERRY** 12-07(cp) 2-1F **N Harris** *Hld up towards rr; nt fluent 12; prog in 4th 18; ld 23; rdn & hrd prsd 2 out; drvn & stayed on flat*		1
732^{B}	**General Claremont (IRE)** 11-11 3-1 **Miss A Goschen** *Blun 2; hld up; eff in 4th gng wl 19; went 2nd app 2 out; sn ev ch; sn rdn & no resp*	2½	2
727^{3}	**Hobbycyr (FR)** 12-00 7-1 **Miss P Gundry** *Settled 3rd/4th; went 2nd 16-23; nt fluent nxt 2; drvn & one pce aft*	5	3
993^{1}	Alska (FR) 11-02 12-1 R Bandey *Bhnd; prog to handy 6th 22; drvn 24 & sn wl outpcd; some rnwd prog flat*	11	4
800^{5}	Robbie's Adventure 11-07 25-1 Mrs J Gordon *Oft jmpd rt; sn 2nd; ld 11; hdd 23; wknd rap; t.o*	dist	5
744^{3}	Grecian Star 11-07 10-1 J Docker *Midfield; 5th & handy 22; wknd 24; tired when mist 3 out; t.o*	11	6
1032^{3}	Bullfinch 11-11 25-1 P Cowley *Ld to 11; 2nd 15; rdn & wknd 17; tlng off when blun bad 21 & pu*		P
786^{P}	Gallion's Reach (IRE) 11-07(tt) 66-1 T Ellis *Mists in rr; blun 11; lost tch 18; t.o & pu 24*		P
1071^{5}	Hijacked 11-11 25-1 G Hanmer *Sn 20l last; a labouring; t.o 19; pu 23*		P
1029^{3}	Mickthecutaway (IRE) 11-07 12-1 D Skelton *Tk keen hld in midfield; 6th when pu & dism 6*		P
899^{2}	Silver Lake (IRE) 11-09(cp) 40-1 C Gordon *Cl up; 4th 15; wknd nxt; t.o & pu 20*		P

TIME: 9min 14.6s **TOTE:** £2.90; places £1.70,£1.70,£2.30 **Ex:**£7.10 **CSF:**£7.15

1171 Land Rover Gentlemans Open P-t-P Championship Final HC, 3m2f110y - 22J £7150 — 9 ran

629^{4}	**GARRUTH (IRE)** 12-01(bl) 7-2F **N Williams** *Midfield; jmpd slow 8; 10l 5th when jmpd slow 17 & drvn; sn outpcd; rallied 19; ld app 3 out; rdn clr app nxt; unchall*		1
875^{2}	**Victoria's Boy (IRE)** 11-09 15-2 **G Brewer** *Rcd wide; handy; went 3rd 9 & 2nd 15 til nt fluent nxt; lft cl 2nd 19; rdn & sn outpcd; mist 2 out; fin tired*	19	2
997^{4}	**Freedom Fighter** 11-13 20-1 **A Martin** *Detach in last pr; rdn & no resp 15; sn t.o; snatched rem 3rd nr fin*	24	3
1052^{1}	Little Farmer 11-07 4-1 P Hall *Hdwy to 2nd 6; ld 11-18; lft in ld nxt; sn hdd; blun 3 out & wknd; tired 3rd & mist nxt; lost rem 3rd nr fin*	1	4
93^{1}	Bay Island (IRE) 11-11 4-1 A Wadlow *Chsd ldr to 6; 4th 10; blun 12; nt rec; strugg when pu 15*		P
1057^{1}	Nautical Lad 11-07 13-2 J Docker *Nt fluent & nvr went a yd; detach in last pr; drvn & strugg 9; t.o & pu 18*		P

851^{2}	Soundtrack (IRE) 12-01 8-1 G Hanmer *Set ridiculously fast pce in conditions; hdd 11; bad mist 13; wknd 18; t.o & pu last*		P
988^{2}	Springwood White 11-07 33-1 T Park *2nd/3rd to 6; sn wknd; jmpd slow 8; bad t.o 10; pu 13.*		P
868^{1}	Tanager 11-07(bl) 16-1 B King *Swtng; handy; 3rd/4th 9 til eff & ld 18; 5l clr & gng wl when hit nxt & ur.*		U

TIME: 7min 25.0s **TOTE:** £4.60; places £1.90,£2.00,£3.80 **Ex:**£25.90 **CSF:**£28.86

1172 Colin Nash Mem HC, 3m1f110y - 21J £3526 — 15 ran

1016^{1}	**CAUGHT AT DAWN (IRE)** 11-10 5-1 **T Weston** *Settled trckng ldrs; 7l 6th 16; chall 18; disp ld frm nxt til slt advant last; rdn & hld on brave aft*		1
923^{1}	**Balinova (IRE)** 12-03 7-2 **Miss P Gundry** *Pulled hrd; hld up; prog to trck ldrs 13; nt fluent 17; chall nxt; slt ld 3 out-last; battled on game flat; a just hld*	$\frac{3}{4}$	2
979^{4}	**Maggies Brother** 12-00 13-2 **D Barlow** *Sn cl up; went 2nd 10-16; rdn & sn btn; stayed on agn to snatch poor 3rd nr fin*	22	3
980^{3}	Rushing Again 12-00 33-1 A Wintle *Prom; 4th 16; blun nxt; wknd app 3 out; jmpd rt 2 out & last; dem cl home*	nk	4
732^{10}	Master Jock 12-00 17-2 G Hanmer *Hld up towards rr; stdy prog 16; handy when mist 18; sn wknd*	14	5
1067^{1}	Alheri 11-10 66-1 F de Giles *(xnb) Mist 1; last pr early; prog 12; went 2nd 16-18; wknd rap app nxt*	2	6
891^{2}	Strong Tea (IRE) 12-03 28-1 A Charles-Jones *Chsd ldrs to 14; 10l 7th & outpcd 16; no ch aft.*	$2\frac{1}{2}$	7
974^{1}	Cherry Gold 12-00(cp) 100-30F E Williams *Jmpd scrappy at times; ld; hdd & blun 3 out; drvn & imm btn; virt pu nr fin; t.o*	29	8
755^{P}	Alpha Leather 12-00 66-1 T Malone *Bhnd; jmpd slow 6; labouring 11; tlng of when blun 14; pu 16*		P
541^{P}	Carbonado 12-00(tt) 16-1 Miss A Goschen *Set off last & nvr gng wl; blun 2; t.o 12; pu 18*		P
759^{3}	I'm Dreaming (IRE) 11-12 33-1 A Martin *Chsd ldr 4-10; hrd rdn & wkng when mist 14; t.o & pu 17.*		P
177^{P}	Irilut (FR) 11-10(cp) 16-1 S Waley-Cohen *(xnb) Hld up; eff 9; wknd 13; wl bhnd when pu 16.*		P
815^{3}	Macy (IRE) 12-03(cp) 40-1 Julian Pritchard *Trckd ldrs; nt fluent 10; wknd 15; t.o & pu 18*		P
938^{2}	Sheila McKenzie 11-05 33-1 T Lane *Mists 1 & 2; 9th when bad mist 14; nt rec; last when pu 3 out*		P
1066^{2}	Tubber Roads (IRE) 12-03(bl) 25-1 J Diment *Nvr went a yd; drpd to rr u.p 4; cont reluct; t.o 9; pu 14*		P

TIME: 7min 09.4s **TOTE:** £6.10; places £2.30,£2.20,£1.90 **Ex:**£21.40 **CSF:**£21.47

The rider of Balinova was cautioned concerning her use of the whip

1173 Amateur Jockeys Association Investing In Racing HC, 2m110y - 14J £3136 — 10 ran

799^{1}	**MOUSESKI** 11-13 11-8F **N Williams** *Lw; handy & gng wl; ld 3 out; cantered clr app nxt.*		1
799^{6}	**Hot Plunge** 11-07 10-1 **J Owen** *Mist 3; rcd keen & prom; ld 10; hdd 3 out; no ch w wnr aft*	26	2
757^{2}	**Prince Dundee (FR)** 11-12 4-1 **R Burton** *(xnb) Towards rr; clsd in 5l 5th 9; mist 11; lft 3rd nxt; no ch w ldrs aft*	$2\frac{1}{2}$	3
999^{P}	Viscount Bankes 11-07(cp) 10-1 A Martin *Midfield & rdn aft 4; prog to cl 3rd 9; blun nxt & sn wknd; t.o*	dist	4
914^{3}	Snooty Eskimo (IRE) 11-05 22-1 H Norton *Mist 2; lost plce qckly 5; t.o 8.*	dist	5
734^{1}	Jazz Night 11-13 6-1 J Jenkins *Prom to 6; 6th & wkng nxt; jmpd slow 9; sn t.o; hacked on*	dist	6
834^{4}	Classic Fable (IRE) 11-00(tt) 66-1 A Hanly *Made most to 7; wknd rap nxt; wl t.o when pu 2 out.*		P
1024^{F}	Shafi (IRE) 11-09 14-1 D Mansell *Bhnd; lost tch 5; t.o when fell 9*		F
241^{P}	Win The Toss 11-09 25-1 P York *Prom; ld 7-10; 3l 3rd & rdn when blun & ur 3 out*		U
983^{F}	Worthy Man 11-05(tt) 100-1 R Hodges *Jb in rr; t.o 6 & und wild press; pu 11*		P

TIME: 4min 26.4s **TOTE:** £2.30; places £1.40,£3.00,£1.60 **Ex:**£15.20 **CSF:**£14.79

Kelso (LH 8F,19J)

Wed, 28 Apr (GOOD, GOOD to FIRM in places)

1174 Charlie Brown Utd Border HC, 3m1f £2299 — 4 ran

797^{4} **BOULTA (IRE)** 11-05(cp) 5-1 **M Seston** *Made all; rdn & hit last; hld on game; all out* — 1

1068^{F} **Miss Mattie Ross** 11-10 evensF **M McAlister** *Chsd ldrs; hit 14; blun bad 16; went 2nd 2 out; eff & ev ch last; drvn & r.o but no imp cl home* . . . . . . ¾ — 2

657^{B} **Alittlebitopower** 11-12 6-1 **C Storey** *(xnb) Rcd keen; jmpd rt; lft 2nd 1; nt fluent 10; hit 11; releg 3rd & wknd rap 2 out; t.o* . . . . dist — 3

798^{4} Indien Du Boulay (FR) 11-05 3-1 W Ramsay *2nd when fell 1* . . . . F

TIME: 6min 17.9s **TOTE:** £7.30; **Ex:**£15.50 **CSF:**£10.53

The stewards cautioned the rider of Boulta, who had caused interference to Miss Mattie Ross after the last fence, for careless riding; and suspended the rider of the latter for five days for using his whip with excessive force and frequency

Hereford (RH 9F,19J)

Thu, 29 Apr (GOOD to SOFT)

1175 Arabian Racing Organisation HC, 3m1f110y £1561 — 5 ran

891^{U} **LANCASTRIAN JET (IRE)** 12-02 2-5F **M Barber** *Jmpd lft; made all; jmpd slow 7; drew clr 3 out; v easily* 1

1003^{1} **Province** 12-00 10-1 **L Jefford** *Chsd ldrs 9 til mist 13; one pce aft; mod 4th when mist 2 out; lft 2nd at last* . . . . 15 — 2

891^{F} **Quetal (IRE)** 12-04 9-1 **N Harris** *Settled cl up; lft 2nd aft 13; rdn & lost 2nd 3 out; btn when mist last; sn eased* . . . . 21 — 3

822^{1} Karadin (FR) 11-07 11-2 Mrs M Hand *Mostly last pr; rdn 14; no resp; poor last when pu 3 out; reported to have struck into itself & lost a shoe*. . . . P

975^{r} Lady Baronette 11-04 50-1 A Martin *2nd to 9; 4th aft mist 12; went 2nd & nt fluent 3 out; wl hld when mist nxt; jmpd lft last; veered lft & ur* . . . . . . U

TIME: 6min 40.3s **TOTE:** £1.40; places £1.10,£2.60 **Ex:**£2.90 **CSF:**£4.87

Bangor (LH 9F,17J)

Fri, 30 Apr (GOOD, GOOD to FIRM in places)

1176 James Griffith Mem Nov HC, 3m110y £1514 — 11 ran

930^{1} **JUST CLIQUOT** 11-06 5-2F **G Hanmer** *Lw; jmpd slow 4; hld up wl off pce; 20l last 6; eff in 12l 6th aft 12; went 2nd 2 out; rdn & stayed on game to ld nr fin* 1

1016^{P} **Coole Venture (IRE)** 12-00(bl) 100-30 **R Burton** *Lw; sn prom; lft in ld 11; 4l clr aft nxt; rdn app 2 out; outbattled flat & caught cl home* . . . . ½ — 2

892^{3} **The Vintage Dancer (IRE)** 11-07 8-1 **G Kerr** *Ld til bad mist 11 (water); prsd ldr to 2 out; urged along & one-pcd when hit last* . . . . 6 — 3

1043^{1} Raiseapearl 11-07 16-1 I Clyde *Chsd ldrs; jmpd slow 7; went 10l 3rd aft 3 out; rdn & btn when blun nxt* . . . . 4 — 4

1092^{3} Catechist (IRE) 12-00 10-1 Julian Pritchard *(xnb) Wl bhnd; virt t.o 9; some hdwy u.p aft 3 out; no ex app nxt* . . . . hd — 5

1142^{1} Robert The Rascal 11-08 (1ow) 33-1 J R Barlow *Swtng & lkd awful; quirky in prelims; midfield; eff in 9l 4th aft 12; rdn & btn app 3 out* . . . . hd — 6

801^{R} Beachcomber 11-07 16-1 W Hill *2 handlers; oht; tk str hld; 2nd/3rd til 8l 3rd aft 12; sn wknd; no ch 3 out* . . . . 3 — 7

1044^{5} Strong King (IRE) 11-07(cp) 66-1 S Ross *Cl up to 7; wknd & mist 10; 7th & btn aft 12* . . . . 27 — 8

1024^{1} Mister Falcon (FR) 11-07 10-1 S Hughes *Trckd ldrs til pushed along & wknd 10; 8th & btn aft 12; last when jmpd slow 3 out; t.o*. . . . . 12 — 9

1029^{r} Be Bop Bentley 11-07 66-1 A Maskill *(xnb) Prom til jmpd lft, blun & ur 5*. U

852^{1} Jackson (FR) 12-00(tt) 11-2 G Barfoot-Saunt *Lw; hld up in midfield til hmpd & ur 5* . . . . U

TIME: 6min 22.1s **TOTE:** £3.40; places £1.60,£1.10,£3.50 **Ex:**£6.90 **CSF:**£10.71

Fence 14 omitted - fallen rider

Sedgefield (LH 8F,16J)

Fri, 30 Apr (GOOD, GOOD to FIRM places, GOOD to SOFT patches run-in)

1177 Saltwell Signs HC, 2m5f £1547 11 ran

102[3] **BANANA RIDGE** 11-04 9-4F **C Mulhall** *Hld up in tch; jnd ldrs gng wl 10; ld 2 out; drvn out frm last* 1

Buddy Girie 11-07 9-2 **P Cornforth** *Hld up in rr; hdwy to midfield ½way; outpcd app 12; rallied aft 3 out; went 2nd app last; no imp on wnr* 3½ 2

810[3] **Orleans (IRE)** 11-07(bl) 25-1 **S J Robinson** *Hld up; hdwy ½way; chsng ldrs & ch 13; kpt on same pce* 3½ 3

858[P] Katinka 11-09 16-1 C Storey *In tch; wknd aft 3 out; no ch when hmpd aft nxt* 19 4

1165[1] Stormy Sunrise (IRE) 11-07 14-1 Miss A Armitage *Cl up; ld ½way; hdd 10; wknd aft 13* 12 5

1158[U] Alizarin (IRE) 10-12 50-1 P Kinsella *Bhnd when mist 10; t.o & pu 3 out* . . P

955[1] Cross River 11-07 5-1 N Saville *Ld til hdd ½way; wknd aft 13; wl bhnd when pu 2 out* . . . . P

1161[4] Mr McDuck (IRE) 11-13 13-2 L Bates *Mist 1; sn towards rr; staying on u.p but no ch when hmpd bad & bd app last* . . . . B

240[P] Tom's Man 11-11(tt) 25-1 O Nelmes *In tch til wknd aft 11; wl bhnd when pu 2 out* . . . . P

1038[2] Wild Edgar (IRE) 11-07 11-2 A Richardson *Cl up; blun 7; ld 10; hdd 2 out; wkng when stumbled & fell app last* . . . . F

956[U] Wynyard Dancer 11-08(cp) 14-1 Miss T Jackson *Mist 1; midfield when blun & ur 11* U

TIME: 5min 23.2s **TOTE:** £2.90; places £2.10,£2.50,£5.10 **Ex:**£19.40 **CSF:**£13.23

The stewards enquired into an incident approaching the last when Wild Edgar fell and hampered Katinka who then interfered with Mr McDuck causing him to fall; they decided that the interference was accidental and that no action need be taken

Hexham (RH 9F,19J)

Sat, 1 May (GOOD)

1178 George F White Heart of All England Mdn HC, 3m1f £2483 12 ran

1028[2] **MID SUMMER LARK (IRE)** 11-07(vis) 7-1 **M Seston** *Made all; hit 3 out; rdn nxt; 1l up when lft 4l clr last; hung rt flat; kpt on wl* 1

915[2] **Raging Torrent** 11-07 16-1 **L Morgan** *Chsd ldrs; eff app 2 out; 4l 3rd & hld when lft 2nd at last; kpt on* 5 2

769[1] **Scottish Roots** 12-00 3-1F **T Greenall** *Hld up in tch; eff 2 out; 5l down & hld when lft 3rd at last; one pce* 2½ 3

876[1] Dolphin Square (IRE) 11-07 6-1 N Saville *Mists in rr; hdwy aft 4 out; mist & outpcd 2 out; no imp frm last* 7 4

679[3] Imps Way 11-04 100-30 C Mulhall *Hld up midfield; stdy hdwy ½way; chsng ldrs when blun bad 3 out; nt rec* 10 5

548[P] Hervey Bay 11-02 33-1 W Goldie *Chsd ldrs to ½way; sn lost tch; t.o* . . . . dist 6

1152[3] Eco Warrior (IRE) 11-07 12-1 N Bell *Mists; in tch til hit & lost plce 9; blun & ur 12* . . . . U

854[2] Hoh Tel (IRE) 10-11(cp) 7-1 O Nelmes *Nt jw in rr; hdwy & prom ½way; still in tch when fell 15* . . . . F

1037[U] Jupiter's Fancy 11-06 25-1 M McAlister *Hld up; hdwy & prom 13; rdn 2 out; 1l down & staying on when fell last* . . . . F

808[P] Needsmoretime (IRE) 11-07 50-1 S J Robinson *Mists; sn bhnd; t.o when ref 15* r

659[P] Pure Steel (IRE) 12-00(cp) 14-1 C Storey *Chsd ldrs; hit & wknd 14; sn btn; t.o & pu last* . . . . P

918[P] Superstar Express (IRE) 11-07(tt) 20-1 A Findlay *Midfield; blun bad 14; sn strugg; pu last* . . . . P

TIME: 6min 34.8s **TOTE:** £8.80; places £3.20,£5.60,£1.30 **Ex:**£66.60 **CSF:**£103.97

1179 Red Squirrel HC, 3m1f £1246 9 ran

894[3] **WHO DARES WINS** 11-09 8-1 **L Bates** *Hld up; hmpd bad 3; hdwy app 14; lft cl 3rd 3 out; ld aft nxt; r.o str.* 1

992[2] **Sad Mad Bad (USA)** 12-02 5-4F **G Tuer** *Hld up; outpcd 8; rallied 16; chsd wnr flat; no imp* 5 2

956^{3}	**Primitive Satin** 11-07(bl) 14-1 **N Saville** *Cl up; 4l down when lft in ld 3 out; hdd aft nxt; one pce*	4	3
1153^{R}	Noel's Pride 11-07 11-2 N Bell *Tk keen hld; hdwy to disp ld 7; hmpd bad by loose horse & lost plce bend bef 9; rallied 14; lft cl 2nd 3 out; outpcd nxt*	$2\frac{1}{2}$	4
992^{1}	Lord Edwards Army (IRE) 12-00 9-2 G Willoughby *Mists in rr; outpcd 8; rallied app 3 out; nvr rchd ldrs*	$3\frac{1}{2}$	5
772^{6}	Cimarrone Cove (IRE) 12-00(bl) 7-1 T Greenall *Ld; 4l up & still gng wl when blun & ur 3 out*		U
1038^{5}	Lively Dessert (IRE) 12-00 22-1 K Anderson *Chsd ldrs to 16; sn wknd; pu nxt*		P
994^{P}	Mr Busby 11-07 40-1 M Seston *Chsd ldrs to 16; sn btn; t.o & pu last*		P
654^{2}	Trivial (IRE) 11-02 20-1 L Morgan *Prom when blun & ur 3*		U

TIME: 6min 36.5s **TOTE:** £11.30; places £2.20,£1.60,£2.90 **Ex:**£21.10 **CSF:**£19.82

Devon & Somerset Staghounds

Holnicote (RH 7F,19J)

Sat, 1 May (GOOD to FIRM)

1180 Hunt Members — 7 ran

863^{1}	**FRIAR WADDON** 5-2 **M Miller** *(xnb) Lw; hld up; last 4-7; 4l 5th ½way; rdn & outpcd 15; went 6l 3rd aft nxt; lft 5l 2nd 3 out; stayed on to ld nr fin*		1
881^{1}	**Polka** 7-2 **D Edwards** *9/2-7/2; a.p; 2nd 5; lft in ld brief 10; ld 14; hdd but lft 5l clr 3 out; hdd agn nr fin*	nk	2
1002^{3}	**Winning Leader (IRE)** 5-1 **S Kidston** *20s-5s; 2nd/3rd to 7; 3l 4th ½way; ld 11-13; ev ch when mist 16; sn wknd*	15	3
1004^{5}	Happy Team (5a) 20-1 R Ross *2nd/3rd to 5 & frm 7 til mist 14; 9l 5th & hrd rdn 16; sn wknd*	4	4
1005^{U}	Fern Leader (IRE) 33-1 R Skinner *Ld til blun & nrly ur 10; sn lost plce; lost tch 14; blun 3 out; t.o*	20	5
273^{U}	Sparkle (U) 40-1 Miss J Buck *Hld up; last to 4; 5l 6th ½way; last agn 11; lost tch & mist 14; t.o.*	10	6
880^{1}	Sir William(tt) 11-8F R Woollacott *(xnb) Opened 6/4; hld up; last 7-11; qcknd to jn ldrs 14; ld & fell 3 out*		F

OFFICIAL DISTANCES: hd, 20*l* **TIME:** 6min 51.2s **TOTE:** £7.00 **DF:**£2.60

1181 Intermediate, 12st — 6 ran

772^{P}	**I AM SAID I (IRE)** 4-5F **A Farrant** *(xnb) 11/10-4/5; ld 1; mists 9 & 16; rdn 4l clr nxt; kpt on wl*		1
891^{4}	**Soul King (IRE)** 5-1 **R Bliss** *Ld to 1; mists 2 & 14; prsd wnr til mist 15; rdn 3 out; no imp*	6	2
1071^{6}	**Sootsir** 33-1 **R Hawker** *(xnb) 2nd/3rd to 4; sn lost plce; last & strugg 7; lost tch u.p 13; went poor 4th last; promoted to 3rd*	18	3
879^{1}	Kildysart Lady (IRE) (5a) 9-2 B Woodhouse *Opened 5s; swtng; hld up; mist 7; 9l 4th ½way; hdwy & 4l 3rd 12; disp 3l 2nd aft 15; stpd to nil app 3 out*	5	5
881^{2}	Caundle Chase 9-2 W White *Prom; mist 9; 6l 3rd ½way; 5l 4th 14; rdn 16; went 8l 3rd app nxt; no ex; fin 16l 3rd; disq - nt weigh-in*		3d
1005^{2}	Barton Rose 11-1 I Chanin *16s-11s; tde; hld up; last to 7; 15l 5th ½way; bhnd til fell 13*		F

OFFICIAL DISTANCES: Originally 7*l*, 10*l* **TIME:** 6min 34.4s **TOTE:** £2.20 **DF:**£3.20

Caundle Chase finished third but was disqualified when the rider failed to weigh-in; he was fined £55

1182 Panacur/TBA PPORA Club Members Mares Maiden, 12st — 9 ran

469^{2}	**MISS FLINDERS** (5a) 7-4F **R Bliss** *(xnb) Bit bckwd; hld up & pulled hrd; went 2nd 7; lft in ld 8; 6l clr 12; unchall*		1
878^{3}	**Merry Melody** (5a) 10-1 **Miss S Robinson** *A.p; 4l 3rd ½way; went 6l 2nd 13; no imp 3 out; mist last*	8	2
967^{F}	**Inner State** (5a) 6-1 **D Edwards** *12s-6s; ld 3 til aft 6; 2nd to 13; mist 14; 8l 3rd 16; wkng when blun 3 out*	12	3
883^{P}	Silver Tray (IRE) (12a) 16-1 R Ross *Hld up; mists 1 & 6; hdwy & 6l 4th ½way; 7l 5th 14; went 9l 4th & rdn aft 16; sn wknd.*	$2\frac{1}{2}$	4
1006^{P}	Madame Cholet (5a)(tt) 14-1 M Woodward *Tde; hld up; last 2-6; 8l 6th ½way; mist 10; last agn nxt; 9l 6th & rdn 14; sn wknd*	15	5

962[P] April's Past (5a) 5-1 M Miller *(xnb) 10s-5s; lw; 2 handlers; hld up; 9l 7th ½way; hdwy 12; 6l 4th 14; wknd qckly 16; wl bhnd when pu 3 out . . .* P
967[P] Hayling Star (5a) 25-1 Miss C Tizzard *Mounted on course & tde; ld; mist 2; hdd 3; lost plce 7; 7l 5th ½way; rdn 12; last when mist 14; wl bhnd when ur 16 . . .* U
826[2] My Little Lady (5a) 2-1 Miss A Bush *Hld up; last 8-11; hdwy & jmpd lft 12; lost plce & 10l 7th when ur 14. . .* U
119[F] Vexford Lucy (5a) 18-1 J Barnes *(xnb) Hld up & pulled hrd; mist 1; went 2nd 5; ld & rn wide bend aft 6; jmpd slow 7; blun & ur 8. . .* U

OFFICIAL DISTANCES: 10*l*, 10*l* **TIME:** 6min 54.3s **TOTE:** £4.70 **DF:**£5.50

1183 Confined — 4 ran

1065[2] **POLAR CHAMP**(bl) 4-7F **A Farrant** *Made all; stumbled 5; qcknd 14; drew wl clr 16; unchall. . .* 1
1011[2] **Father Jim** 4-1 **Miss C Tizzard** *Pckd 4; 2nd til app 14; chsd wnr app 16; no imp . . .* 15 2
964[P] **Cool Wager** 9-2 **D Alers-Hankey** *Hld up; 7l 3rd ½way; mist 13; 11l last & rdn nxt; went 15l 3rd 16; no imp; mist last. . .* 6 3
1128[U] Delaware (FR)(bl) 11-2 S Kidston *Hld up; mist 3; last til went 6l 2nd & rdn app 14; nt r.o; stpd to nil & releg last 16. . .* 25 4

OFFICIAL DISTANCES: 15*l*, 6*l* **TIME:** 6min 33.7s **TOTE:** £1.50 **DF:**£2.90

1184 Restricted, 12st — 9 ran

883[1] **SO PEACEFUL** (5a) 6-4F **C Heard** *5/2-6/4; prom; 5l 4th ½way; blun & lost plce 13; 9l 5th nxt; rallied aft 16; went 7l 2nd app nxt; ld aft 2 out; sn clr; drvn out . . .* 1
1063[P] **Hill Trail** 33-1 **J Barnes** *(xnb) Pulled hrd; went 2nd 3; ld aft 6 til app 15; lost plce & 15l 4th 3 out; rallied & went 3l 2nd at last; no ex flat. . .* 4 2
579[F] **Bessie Bunter** (5a) 4-1 **M Miller** *11/2-4s; hld up; 5½l 6th ½way; 7l 4th 14; went 9l 3rd 16; one pce 3 out . . .* 8 3
1102[3] River Dante (IRE) 8-1 S Kidston *Tchd 10s; 2nd til ld 5; hdd aft 6; rn wide bend aft 13; qcknd to ld app 15; 7l clr aft nxt; hung lft & mist 3 out; hdd aft 2 out; no ex . . .* 2½ 4
884[1] Lady Widd (IRE) (5a) 5-1 D Edwards *Hld up; 5¼l 5th ½way; went 3rd 13 til 11l 4th & rdn 16; sn wknd . . .* 8 5
926[1] Emerald Mist (IRE) (12a) 4-1 Miss P Gundry *Tchd 5s; nt fluent; hld up; last to 15; 15l 6th nxt; nvr on terms. . .* 4 6
1094[4] Chief Suspect (IRE) 33-1 R Bliss *Hld up; 8l 8th & pushed along ½way; 11l 6th & rdn 14; wl bhnd when pu 3 out . . .* P
878[1] Miss Karingaroo (5a) 25-1 W White *Swtng; mounted v late; hld up; 7l 7th ½way; rmdrs 11; 12l 7th 14; wl bhnd when pu 2 out . . .* P
966[P] Mrs Peggoty (5a)(tt) 16-1 Miss C Tizzard *Ld to 5; 4l 3rd ½way; w ldrs til blun & ur 12. . .* U

OFFICIAL DISTANCES: 5*l*, 8*l* **TIME:** 6min 42.1s **TOTE:** £1.80 **DF:**£18.50

1185 Mixed Open, 12st — 5 ran

1128[2] **BALLYSICYOS (FR)** 1-2F **A Farrant** *(xnb,boh) Tchd 4/7; ld 5; drew clr 16; unchall . . .* 1
938[1] **Dancing Fosenby** 4-1 **M Holdforth** *(xnb) Ld to 5; 2nd to 9; chsd wnr 11; no imp 16 . . .* 12 2
497[3] **Travelling Jack**(bl) 25-1 **D Edwards** *2 handlers; hld up; hdwy 5; blun 6; went 2nd 9 til app 11; sn hrd rdn & nt r.o; t.o 15 . . .* runin 3
880[7] Cherokee Run (IRE) 14-1 Miss C Tizzard *2nd/3rd to 5; lost plce 7; 10l 4th ½way; wl bhnd 11; t.o 15. . .* 2½ 4
964[2] Hylters Chance (IRE) 9-2 C Heard *Nvr gng wl; jmpd slow 2; last 3 til pu 10* P

OFFICIAL DISTANCES: 15*l*, dist **TIME:** 6min 27.3s **TOTE:** £2.00 **DF:**£1.70

1186 Open Maiden 567&8yo, 12st — 9 ran

795[2] **ON HIS TOES** 7-4JF **W White** *Lw; 2 handlers; hld up; went 2nd 8; ld 11; drew clr 3 out; comf. . .* 1
967[F] **Albamart Wood**(tt) 3-1 **D Edwards** *(xnb) 6s-3s; hld up; jb lft 6; 4l 5th ½way; lft 3rd 13; went 2nd 15; rdn aft 3 out; one pce . . .* 12 2
Safawi (12a) 12-1 **Miss A Bush** *2nd to 8; 3l 4th ½way; lost plce 12; 8l 5th 14; lft 8l 3rd 16; no ex. . .* 15 3

Aftermeyourfirst 7-4JF A Farrant *(xnb) 3s-7/4; nt fluent; hld up; disp 4l 5th ½way; mist & rmdrs 11; 3l 4th & rdn 14; wknd 16; wl bhnd when pu 3 out* P
826P Deep Pockets (IRE) (7a) 10-1 D Alers-Hankey *(xnb) Ld til app 2; lost plce 6; 8l 7th ½way; wl bhnd when pu 14* . . . . . . P
7214 Octane Booster (IRE) 20-1 M Holdforth *(xnb) Ld app 2-11; 2nd when blun bad & ur 13* . . . . . . U
328P Phanthom Walker 20-1 Miss C Tizzard *Hld up; mist 7; last nxt; wl bhnd when pu 10* . . . . . . P
1131P The Gambling Lady (5a) 20-1 R Woollacott *A.p; 2l 3rd ½way; lft 2nd 13-15; 2l 3rd when fell nxt* . . . . . . F
Tilly Time (5a) 16-1 L Heard *Bit bckwd; hld up & bhnd; last to 8; 7l 6th ½way; hmpd 13; 9l 6th nxt; wknd 16; pu 3 out* . . . . . . P

OFFICIAL DISTANCES: 20*l*, 25*l* **TIME:** 6min 49.3s **TOTE:** £1.80 **DF:**£1.10

Llangeinor

Laleston (LH 6F,18J)

Sat, 1 May (GOOD to FIRM)

1187 Hunt Members — 3 ran

9531 **PETE THE PAINTER (IRE)** (3x)(bl) 1-2F **James Tudor** *Ld 3; made most; rmdrs 13; 4l clr 15; lft virt solo app nxt; eased 3 out; cantered home* 1
953P **The Last Shout (IRE)**(cp) 16-1 **Miss A Davies** *1st ride; ld to 3; 2nd 7; sn last; 16l last when lft 2nd 15; hmpd by loose horse app last* . . . . . . fence 2
10251 Chesnut Wood (3x) 6-4 Miss F Wilson *Mostly 2nd; 4l 2nd 15; slpd up bend aft 15* . . . . . . S

OFFICIAL DISTANCE: dist **TIME:** 6min 39.0s

1188 Confined, 12st — 6 ran

10231 **QUESTIONAIRE** (5a, 3x) 4-6F **M Barber** *Hld up in 3rd; disp ld 12; just ld nxt; drew clr 3 out; sn in comm* 1
10232 **Rathgibbon (IRE)** 33-1 **James Tudor** *Ld 2; jnd 4; hdd 6; ld agn 8; jnd brief 10 & agn 12; hdd nxt; a hld aft* 6 2
1089P **Like The Buzz (IRE)** (5a) 7-4 **J Cook** *Cl 3rd mostly; outpcd frm 15; 10l 3rd & no imp nxt* 15 3
10244 Fassan (IRE)(cp) 20-1 James Price *Cl 5th; rdn 11; mist 13; 10l 4th 14; fdd; t.o 3 out* 15 4
1093P Daisys Rainbow (7a) 20-1 D Jones *A last; mist 3; rn v wide & pu app 6* . . P
1092P Glen Mist (IRE)(bl) 10-1 L Stephens *Ld 1; 2nd til jnd ldr agn 4; ld 6; mist & hdd nxt; disp ld brief 10; sn wknd; 4th & rmdrs 13; pu 15; bbv* . . . . . . P

OFFICIAL DISTANCES: 8*l*, dist **TIME:** 6min 25.0s

1189 Ladies Open — 5 ran

10723 **BRETECHE (FR)** (5a, 7x) 9-4 **Miss T Newman** *(xnb) Jw; disp ld 2; ld 3; enormous j 15; qcknd bend aft 2 out & sn clr; rdly* 1
9491 **De Chelly** (5a) 4-5F **Mrs C Owen** *Ld 1-4; cl 2nd aft; 4l away 3 out; rdn to chall nxt; slpd sltly bend bef last; no ex* 6 2
1089U **Detroit Davy (IRE)** 3-1 **Miss F Wilson** *Settled 4th; 6l 3rd 11; in tch til outpcd frm 3 out* 4 3
9493 Berkeley Frontier (IRE) (7x) 25-1 Mrs E Jones *Chsd ldrs in 3rd; slpd sltly bend aft 3; last frm 9; slt mist nxt; r.o to 2nd 13; sn last; lost tch 15* . . . . . . runin 4
1095P Coolarne Leader (IRE)(tt) 20-1 Miss R Davies *Last frm 4; ur 9* . . . . . . U

OFFICIAL DISTANCES: 5*l*, 4*l* **TIME:** 6min 25.0s

1190 Mens Open, 12st — 5 ran

10892 **KHATANI (IRE)** (7x)(tt) 2-1 **L Stephens** *4s-2s; swtng; ww; mostly 3rd; tk 3l 2nd 14; jmpd to ld 2 out; hld inner on tight bend bef last; kpt on* 1
9742 **Sohapara** (5a) 2-5F **D Jones** *Ld 5; hdd brief 10; hdd 2 out; no ex* 1½ 2
10213 **Orphan Spa (IRE)** 66-1 **J Cook** *Ld 1-4 & agn 10; cl 2nd til mist 13; wknd; lft rem 3rd 14* . . . . . . fence 3
1092P Candlestone Castle 12-1 R Evans *1st ride; last; 10l adrift 1; mist & nrly ur 3; t.o aft; 2 fncs bhnd 9; mist 10; 3 fncs adrift 14; ur nxt* . . . . . . U
1093P Pharailde (5a) 12-1 J Price *Chsd ldrs; 4l 3rd when fell 14* . . . . . . F

OFFICIAL DISTANCES: ½*l*, dist **TIME:** 6min 18.0s

1191 Restricted — 8 ran

Form	Horse / rider / comments	Dist	Pos
947[3]	**ALL FOR JAKE (IRE)** 12-1 **D Jones** *Prom; ld brief 7; 6l 4th 10; ld aft 3 out; 4l clr nxt; drew clr; rdly*		1
1021[P]	**Deep Dale** 25-1 **Miss F Wilson** *Ww; prog 9; ld 11-12; 2l 2nd nxt; sn lost plce aft; went 2nd agn 2 out; nt trble wnr*	6	2
1018[5]	**Winning Town** 12-1 **Miss S Talbot** *Midfield; fdd 8; 15l 6th 10; lsng tch 12; rallied 15; went 3rd 2 out; r.o*	3/4	3
450[2]	My Native Knight (IRE)(tt) evensF A Wadlow *(xnb) Fcng wrong way & wrs; clsd grad; in tch frm 7; ld 15-3 out; wknd*	4	4
935[1]	Silly Boy 6-1 A Foster *A bhnd; slpd & nrly ur bend aft 3; t.o 8; plodded on*	runin	5
	Cresswell Gold (5a) 3-1 P Sheldrake *3rd til mist & dem 3; ld brief 10 & 13-14; sn wknd; pu 3 out*		P
1022[4d]	Its A Handfull(tt) 25-1 J Price *Handy; went 3rd 5; sn rr; t.o frm 10; pu 15.*		P
844[4]	Trial Trip (5a) 4-1 J Cook *Ld 1; hdd brief 7; hdd aft 10; 3rd & rdn 12; wkng when fell 15*		F

OFFICIAL DISTANCES: 6*l*, 1*l* **TIME:** 6min 29.0s

The owner of Winning Town, whose passport was found to be not in order, was fined £100

1192 Open Maiden 56&7yo — 7 ran

Form	Horse / rider / comments	Dist	Pos
740[F]	**TROEDRHIWDALAR** (5a) 5-2 **D Jones** *Settled 3rd frm 5; ld 10; 3l up 15; gng clr when lft virt solo app 2 out*		1
735[3]	**Capacoostic** (5a) 5-2 **P Sheldrake** *3rd & mist 1; ld brief 4 & agn 8-10; 2nd & blun 13 & 14; sn 3rd & wkng; lft poor 2nd app 2 out*	fence	2
1089[P]	Cefn Coch 10-1 W Oakes *Ld 2 til rn wide aft 3; 3rd & mist nxt; last 8; jmpd slow til pu 10.*		P
203[P]	Penny Poor (IRE) (7a) evensF T Vaughan *Hld up in rr; prog & slt mist 9; 5l 3rd 11; mist 12; went 3l 2nd 15; wkng & btn when slpd & fell hvly app 2 out*		S
	Plynlimon 25-1 James Price *Rr; cl 3rd when fell 7*		F
676[P]	Spicey Case (12a) 12-1 J Cook *Ld 1; settled 4th; lost plce 7; 14l 5th 11; pu nxt.*		P
1139[F]	Waky Lady (IRE) (5a) 10-1 M Wall *(xnb) 3rd & jmpd delib 4; ld 5-7; fdd to 4th & rmdrs 11; no resp; fnce bhnd when jmpd v slow 14; fell nxt*		F

OFFICIAL DISTANCE: dist **TIME:** 6min 31.0s

1193 Open Maiden 8yo&up — 13 ran

Form	Horse / rider / comments	Dist	Pos
1027[P]	**DROM ISLAND** (5a) 9-2 **Miss F Wilson** *Hld up in rr; 5th & prog 13; tk 2nd 15; ld 2 out; kpt on*		1
1067[F]	**Clarky's Choice (IRE)** 12-1 **L Stephens** *Settled 3rd frm 7; jmpd slow 11; mist 13; went 2nd aft 3 out; nt trble wnr*	8	2
841[R]	**Miss Man** (5a) 20-1 **J Price** *Trckd ldr til disp ld 13; ld nxt til wknd & hdd 2 out; no ex*	12	3
927[4]	Carrigafoyle 10-1 Miss S Talbot *A last trio; 4th 16; mist nxt; no ch w ldrs aft; chall for 4th flat*	3	4†
1027[F]	Millenium Run (IRE) 9-2 J Cook *8th til mist 10; last aft; r.o frm 15; chall for 4th flat; nrst fin*	d ht	4†
935[P]	Floorex Carpetman 16-1 A Foster *Chsd ldrs in 3rd til rdn 11; sn rr & btn*	15	6
	Beehive Lad 6-1 James Price *Mounted on course; ld 4; jnd 13; hdd nxt; cl 2nd when fell 15*		F
736[4]	Just Caramel (5a)(tt) 2-1F M Barber *Mists in 5th; went 4th 11; rdn 13; fdd 15; 5th when mist 2 out; pu nxt*		P
948[P]	Never Sayaarr (IRE) (5a) 8-1 T Faulkner *Midfield when ur 3*		U
	Right To Reason (IRE) (5a) 20-1 W Oakes *Ur when mounted outside padd; sa; detach 1; in tch when blun 5; pu aft*		P
948[F]	Royal Tradition (IRE) 12-1 D Jones *Mist 1; managed to clamber over 2 & pu*		P
815[P]	Sneedham's Green 16-1 P Mason *Mid-div; 7th when ur 9*		U
1027[F]	Westar Lad (IRE) 6-1 T Vaughan *(xnb) Tk str hld in ld to 3; hdd nxt; rstrnd frm 5; 6th when pu 14*		P

OFFICIAL DISTANCES: 10*l*, 20*l* **TIME:** 6min 31.0s

The owner of Royal Tradition, whose passpost was found to be not in order, was fined £100

Modbury Harriers

Flete Park (RH 8F,20J)

Sat, 1 May (GOOD)

1194 Confined, 12st — 4 ran

1167[P]	**BAK ON BOARD**(bl) 11-10F **Miss L Gardner** *(xnb,ringbit) Hld up in tch; went 1½l 2nd 16; ld 17; hdd aft 3 out; rallied to ld agn nxt; rdn clr.*		1
1005[1]	**Midnight Coup** (10x)(bl) 2-1 **G Weatherley** *Lw; rcd keen; ld/disp; def advant frm 13 til hdd 17; ld agn aft 3 out; rdn & hdd 2 out; sn one pce*	3	2
1005[3]	**Silver Man**(cp) 11-2 **Mrs M Hand** *8s-11/2; in tch; cl 3rd 12; 4l 3rd 17; wknd nxt; one pce.*	12	3
912[6]	Butler Didit (5a) 3-1 L Jefford *8s-3s; ld/disp to 13; wknd 16; bhnd frm 3 out*	7	4

OFFICIAL DISTANCES: 4*l*, 15*l* **TIME:** 6min 40.0s

1195 Intermediate, 12st — 4 ran

823[P]	**ELEGANT LIGHT** (5a) 4-1 **Miss S Gaisford** *Made all; sn clr; fnd ex when prsd app 2 out; rdn out*		1
791[1]	**Raregem** 2-9F **Miss T Cave** *Opened 1/4; lw; hld up & bhnd; went 12l 2nd 15; chsd ldr & clsd to 2l 2nd aft 3 out; rdn & fnd little app nxt*	3	2
1129[P]	**Commander Cully (IRE)** 25-1 **M Sweetland** *(xnb) Nt a fluent; chsd ldr 6 til jmpd lft & rdn 14; sn wknd; t.o & nt jw frm 17.*	2fncs	3
822[P]	Vercheny (5a) 9-1 L Jefford *(xnb) 3rd when jmpd slow 7; mist 10; poor 4th when pu 15.*		P

OFFICIAL DISTANCES: 5*l*, dist **TIME:** 6min 38.0s

The stewards enquired into the running and riding of odds-on favourite Raregem which was dropped out early; the rider's explanation that the horse had made mistakes early on and had no more to give when joining the leader three out was noted

1196 Restricted, 12st — 11 ran

1001[1]	**IMPATIENT LADY** (5a) 7-2 **A Glassonbury** *Lw; ld in start; hld up in tch; cl 7th ½way; hdwy to 4th 14; jnd ldr 17; slt ld frm nxt; qcknd u.p aft 2 out; pushed clr flat*		1
1001[2]	**Lingering Fog (IRE)** 8-1 **Miss M McCarthy** *Lw; ld til jnd 17; ev ch til rdn & no ex app last.*	3	2
912[3]	**Indiana John (FR)** 8-1 **T Dennis** *Tk keen hld; prom; cl 2nd 12; slt ld 14; cl up til rdn 3 out; kpt on one pce*	15	3
912[9]	Baldhu Jack 25-1 Miss P Moorhouse *2 handlers; rcd keen; hld up in rr; last ½way; some hdwy to 20l 6th 3 out; stayed on*	½	4
1006[1]	Abseal 6-1 A Charles-Jones *Lw; midfield; hdwy to cl 4th 12; cl 3rd 16; ev ch til outpcd aft 3 out*	nk	5
1002[2]	Baron Ridge 10-1 Richard Darke *(xnb) In tch; cl 4th 10; rdn & lost plce 14; 12l 5th 3 out; kpt on same pce*	1½	6
966[4]	Sweet Kari (IRE) 33-1 G Weatherley *Prom; 6th 11; wl in tch til rdn 16; wknd*	20	7
1069[B]	Boddidley (IRE) evensF Miss C Roddick *Opened 6/4; lw; hld up towards rr; 8th 12; smooth hdwy to 4th & gng wl when fell 15; rdr broke collar-bone. . .*		F
	Cath's Lass (5a) 100-1 W Biddick *Last when pu & dism 4.*		P
1002[P]	Gunners Mistake 10-1 Miss T Cave *Chsd ldr to 7; prom til wknd 14; 5th 16; last when pu 3 out*		P
1013[3]	Jolie Roslin (5a) 20-1 Mrs F Vigar *Midfield; 6th ½way; 12l 7th 16; just in tch in 7th when ur 17*		U

OFFICIAL DISTANCES: 5*l*, 15*l* **TIME:** 6min 39.0s

1197 Ladies Open, 4m - 25J — 6 ran

1011[F]	**ARDROSS GEM (IRE)** (5a) 10-1 **Miss R Green** *Hld up in tch; hdwy to 2nd 20; trckd ldr til wl-timed chall to ld aft last; pushed out*		1
822[U]	**Guru Rinpoche** 5-2CF **Miss L Gardner** *Ld & tried to make all; str prsd aft 2 out; jnd last; sn hdd; kpt on game.*	¾	2
1004[2]	**Defendtherealm** 3-1 **Miss A Mills** *In tch; went 2nd 9-16; cl up til wknd 20; 14l 3rd 3 out; one pce*	12	3

908^{3} Moorland Rose (5a, 5ow) 16-1 Miss S Young *Sn last & strugg; wl bhnd frm 15* 2fncs 4
1003^{3} Canterbury Jack (IRE)(bl) 5-2CF Mrs O Jackson *A handy; 4l 3rd $^{1}/_{2}$way; went 2nd 16; rdn nxt; in tch when broke hind leg on flat bef 19; destroyed . .* P
1003^{2} Dark Challenger (IRE) 5-2CF Miss S Gaisford *In tch til wkng & jmpd slow 14; poor 5th when pu 19 . . . .* P

OFFICIAL DISTANCES: $^{1}/_{2}$*l*, 18*l* **TIME:** 8min 05.0s

1198 Mens Open, 12st — 2 ran

912^{1} **LADY MISPRINT** (5a) 1-5F **D McKenna** *Made all & toyed w rival; gvn breather 12-13; drew rt away 16; hvly eased app last . . . .* 1
1006^{4} **Dear As Saffron** (5a) 4-1 **W Biddick** *Chsd rival; allowed to cl 12-13; sn outpcd; rdn & clsd on eased rival aft 2 out; flatt by prox; nvr any ch . . .* 6 2

OFFICIAL DISTANCE: 7*l* **TIME:** 6min 36.0s

1199 Pegasus Club Members — 3 ran

1004^{1} **SANDY DUFF** 2-7F **Miss M McCarthy** *Opened 1/3; lw; trckd ldr; ld 11; drew clr 16; canter. . . . .* 1
582^{3} **Court Alert** 7-2 **S Brodie** *Lw; ld to 11; sn wknd; lft last 14; no ch frm 16; fin tired. . . . .* runin 2
925^{F} Misty Ramble (IRE)(bl) 13-2 G McPherson *(xnb,bf) Nt a fluent; poor last when rn out 14. . . . .* R

OFFICIAL DISTANCE: dist **TIME:** 6min 33.0s

1200 Open Maiden, 12st — 7 ran

871^{U} **CABIN BOY** 7-2 **T Allanson** *(xnb) 4s-7/2; nov rdn; sn prom; trckd ldr frm 3 til ld aft 10; slt ld til rn wide bend aft 3 out; ld agn app last; rdn out; rdr's 1st wnr . . . .* 1
795^{P} **Je Suis (IRE)** (5a) 8-1 **I Hambley** *(xnb) 11s-8s; 4th & rmdrs 6; 3l 3rd 12; rmdrs agn 13; 6l 3rd when blun bad 16; stayed on to 3rd app 2 out; tk 2nd flat. . . . .* $2^{1}/_{2}$ 2
795^{P} **Abbey's Girl (IRE)** (5a) 9-2 **A Glassonbury** *Lw; in tch; cl 3rd $^{1}/_{2}$way; chsd ldr 12; lft in ld aft 3 out; 4l clr 2 out; wknd rap; fnd nil & blun last. . . . . .* $^{3}/_{4}$ 3
967^{P} Famous Deal (IRE) 10-1 M Heuff *(xnb) Ld 2 til aft 10; wknd rap; last when pu 12 . . . .* P
1006^{P} Newhouse Lira (5a)(tt) 6-1 Richard Darke *(xnb) Ld 1; cl up when slt mist 4; 6th 8; sn detach; t.o & pu 12 . . . .* P
Over The Weld (5a) 7-1 M Sweetland *(xnb) Sn bhnd & jmpd lft; t.o 8; jmpd novicey til pu 12 . . . .* P
1001^{P} Steponthebandit (5a) 2-1F D McKenna *Lw; in tch in midfield; cl 5th 10; rdn 13; hdwy to 3rd 17; ev ch when rn v wide bend aft 3 out; nt rec; pu nxt* P

OFFICIAL DISTANCES: 4*l*, s hd **TIME:** 7min 03.0s

Pendle Forest & Craven

Heslaker (LH 6F,19J)

Sat, 1 May (GOOD)

1201 Hunt Members — 2 ran

873^{1} **BLANK CHEQUE** 4-6F **D Coates** *Ld 1; chsd rival & niggled at times; ld 3 out; sn wl clr . . . .* 1
1158^{1} **Flat Stanley** (7a) evens **Miss J Foster** *Ld aft 1; blun 13; hdd 3 out; imm outpcd in last. . . . .* runin 2

OFFICIAL DISTANCE: 25*l* **TIME:** 7min 27.0s

1202 Confined, 12st — 6 ran

1045^{4} **WHITEGATES WILLIE** 7-1 **D Greenway** *Tk keen hld; last pr til went 6l 4th aft 13; lkd outpcd 3 out; rallied to 2nd nxt; sn ld; drvn & r.o wl. . . . .* 1
957^{3} **Maitre De Musique (FR)** (3x) 7-4F **M Tate** *Ld 3-9 & 11-13; prsd ldr til ld app 2 out; hdd sn aft; kpt on game desp feeble partner . . . .* 4 2
772^{7} **Erzadjan (IRE)** (3x) 4-1 **L Bates** *Last pr; 12l 5th aft 13; eff nxt; flatt brief 3 out; 3rd & wl btn 2 out; stayed on agn last. . . . .* $1^{1}/_{2}$ 3
1043^{2} Master Club Royal(bl) 2-1 G Hanmer *Trckd ldrs; eff & ev ch 3 out; hrd rdn & nt r.o; 4th & btn nxt . . . .* 25 4

1161P	Rubon Prince (IRE)(bl) 12-1 R Clark *Cl up; ld 9-11 & aft 13; hdd app 2 out; drpd out rap.*	$\frac{1}{2}$	5
1163[4]	Royal Crimson(cp) 8-1 R Alers-Hankey *Ld to 3; 2nd 7; t.o frm 11*	25	6

OFFICIAL DISTANCES: 5*l*, $1\frac{1}{2}$*l* **TIME:** 7min 26.0s

1203 Ladies Open — 7 ran

751[1]	**PALISANDER (IRE)** evensF **Miss C Hurley** *(xnb) Swtng; tde; made all at v fast pce; 20l clr when hit 7; virt solo aft; impressive*		1
1046[3]	**Class Of Ninetytwo (IRE)** 5-1 **Miss S Sharratt** *Chsd wnr but a outpcd; tried to cl 3 out; nvr any imp.*	12	2
987[6]	**Zamhareer (USA)** 8-1 **Miss T Harrison** *Bad outpcd in 4/5th; 36l 5th 7; lft 45l 3rd 11; plugged rnd*	40	3
1045P	Three Saints (IRE) 5-1 Miss N Lloyd *(xnb) 30l adrift 3; 50l down 7; cont wl t.o; btn 28 secs by 3rd*	100	4
1047[3]	Chadswell (IRE) 5-2 Miss H Kinsey *Jmpd slow 4; bad outpcd in 4/5th; 34l 4th 7; blun bad & ur 13*		U
772P	Donnegale (IRE)(bl) 4-1 Miss J Foster *Ur 1*		U
986[5]	Silk Vestments (5a) 8-1 Miss H Dunning *Chsd ldng pr; 32l adrift 7; ur 11*		U

OFFICIAL DISTANCES: 15*l*, dist **TIME:** 7min 14.0s

1204 Mens Open — 6 ran

163P	**TORN SILK** 10-1 **N Kent** *Lw; hld up; 4th 13; eff 3 out; went 6l 2nd nxt; stayed on stdly aft; ld nr fin*		1
808[1]	**Dumadic** 7-2 **N Tutty** *Lw; mist 1; pulled v hrd in 2nd/3rd; shot into ld 3 out & sn 6l clr; lkd in comm though rdn app last; hung rt & mist; hung rt flat; drvn & hdd nr line*	$\frac{3}{4}$	2
810[1]	**Purple Jean** (5a) 9-2 **G Brewer** *(xnb) Ld; mist 13; hdd 3 out; imm outpcd; rdn & rallied app last; kpt on flat*	$1\frac{1}{2}$	3
1047[1]	Border Run 4-1 S Ross *Mist 1; hld up last; 12l adrift when nt fluent 13; clsd app nxt & in tch brief; wknd u.p 15*	$3\frac{1}{2}$	4
1068F	Dorans Magic 4-6F N Saville *Lw; 2nd til mist & ur 2*		U
990[1]	Uncle Ada (IRE)(bl) 6-1 R Burton *Lw; 2nd/3rd; ev ch 15; blun nxt; imm btn; poor 5th when pu 2 out*		P

OFFICIAL DISTANCES: $\frac{3}{4}$*l*, $1\frac{1}{2}$*l* **TIME:** 7min 22.0s

1205 Dodson & Horrell PPORA Club Members Restricted — 7 ran

754[1]	**BEST ACCOLADE** (7a) 4-6F **R Burton** *Mist 1; last to 11; rdn 15; still 12l 5th & strugg app nxt; kpt on aft 2 out but nt gng wl enough til determined late eff; ld final stride*		1
1060[6]	**Gentleman Charles (IRE)** 12-1 **S Walker** *Settled 6th; jmpd slow 9; eff in 4th aft 13 & 2nd 16; ld & lkd wnr aft 2 out; drvn & hdd final stride*	s hd	2
680P	**General Carats**(bl) 14-1 **M Walford** *Ld by ab 15l; still clr 15; rdn & hdd aft 2 out; fnd nil*	10	3
933P	Edward Bear 16-1 Miss K Wood *(xnb) Spurs; handy early; drpd back last 12; sn 15l adrift; t.o 16*	50	4
990[3]	Aunt Gladys (IRE) (5a) 9-2 G Brewer *Midfield; 6th & rdn aft blun 13; sn btn; t.o & pu 16*		P
	Barrys Lord (IRE) 3-1 G Hanmer *Mist 1 & rdr lost iron; pulled hrd early; 30l 3rd 7; eff 14; 4th when hmpd bad 16; nt rec; pu aft 3 out*		P
989[3]	Horton-Cum-Peel (IRE) 8-1 W Kinsey *(xnb) Ab 15l 2nd til releg 3rd & lkd wkng when blun bad & ur 16*		U

OFFICIAL DISTANCES: s hd, 10*l* **TIME:** 7min 30.0s

1206 Open Maiden — 5 ran

686U	**KINDLE A FLAME**(tt) 6-4F **G Brewer** *A ldng pr; ld 3-6, 12-16 & sn aft 2 out; rdn & in comm app last*		1
	Luck In Run'in 7-2 **G Hanmer** *Hld up 3rd/4th; went 2nd 15; ld 16 til sn aft 2 out; drvn & desperately one-pcd*	8	2
1164[6]	**Biddy** (12a) 3-1 **Miss J Foster** *(xnb) Set v slow pce to 3; ld agn 6; mist 10; hdd 12; lost tch qckly app 3 out; eased app last*	20	3
1165P	Trigger Castle (5a) 8-1 S Walker *Settled 3rd/4th; brief eff 13; stpd to nil aft 3 out & sn t.o; mist last*	15	4
	Springwood Hill 7-2 P Kinsella *(xnb) A last; climbed 2; jmpd slow 4; 15l adrift aft 13; pu nxt*		P

OFFICIAL DISTANCES: 8*l*, 20*l* **TIME:** 7min 46.0s

Surrey Union

Peper Harow (LH 8F,18J)

Sat, 1 May (GOOD with HEAVY patches)

1207 Hunt Members, 12st — 4 ran

1086^{2}	**CEDAR CHIEF** (7x)(bl) 1-3F **F Wheeler** *Made all; sn clr; jmpd slow 4; mist 9; jmpd slow 10; 20l clr 13; unchall.*		1
781^{P}	**Graphic Designer (IRE)** 5-2 **Mrs J Gordon** *Ww; went 2nd 10; 6l down nxt; outpcd app 13; last & no ch 15*	fence	2
1085^{P}	Celtic Bounty (IRE) 8-1 D Slattery *Chsd ldr; jmpd slow 8; mist & dem to 3rd 10; lost tch app 13; t.o & pu 15*		P
1055^{P}	Two Of Diamonds 8-1 Miss R Williams *A last; 12l last 10; sn lost tch; t.o & pu 15*		P

OFFICIAL DISTANCE: dist **TIME:** 7min 02.0s **TOTE:** £1.60 **DF:**£1.70

1208 Restricted, 12st — 6 ran

265^{3}	**CHARANGO STAR** 7-4F **P York** *Trckd ldng pr to 4; went 2nd 13; ld 3 out; 3l clr nxt; stayed on wl*		1
1051^{2}	**Lord Of The North (IRE)** 2-1 **N Benstead** *Hld up in tch; chsd ldr 7-13 & agn app 2 out; unable to qckn flat*	2½	2
971^{1}	**Royal Czarina** (5a) 3-1 **J Snowden** *Ld; hdd 3 out; 4l 3rd & btn when fell last; rmtd*	fence	3
1034^{P}	Darkarrow (IRE) 12-1 T Underwood *(xnb) A last; lost tch 7; mist 10; 20l last 11; no ch when rn out 13*		R
1107^{6}	Kniveniven (IRE) 12-1 Mrs J Gordon *(xnb) Chsd ldrs; mist & rmdrs 10; blun 14; sn lost tch; no ch when blun 3 out; virt stpd aft; pu 2 out*		P
1048^{P}	The Sky Is Blue 8-1 M Caldwell *In tch; 10l 4th & outpcd 15; lft poor 3rd & fell hvly last; winded.*		F

OFFICIAL DISTANCES: 3*l*, dist **TIME:** 7min 00.0s
TOTE: £3.90; places £3.40,£1.60 **DF:**£2.30 **trio**:£4.40

1209 Mens Open, 12st — 6 ran

750^{3}	**GOOD HEART (IRE)** 6-1 **N Oliver** *In tch; prog to cl 3rd 15; ld app 2 out; faltered & jnd last; r.o u.p flat*		1
1054^{6}	**River Bailiff (IRE)**(cp) 10-1 **P York** *Ww; stdy prog in 6l 4th 13; chall 3 out; ev ch last; unable to qckn*	1	2
1085^{1}	**Lively Lord (IRE)**(cp,tt) 11-8F **C Gordon** *Ld; blun 3 out; sn hdd; ev ch nxt; btn last; eased flat.*	5	3
830^{3}	Dunrig (IRE) (7x) 2-1 J Owen *Chsd ldrs; 6l 4th 10; hrd rdn 13 & reluct; no ch frm 15*	25	4
1003^{4}	Nearly Gold (4x)(cp) 5-1 J Snowden *In tch; 8l last 11; sn outpcd; no ch frm 15*	15	5
1052^{P}	Little Worsall (IRE) (7x) 12-1 F Marshall *Chsd ldr 3-15; 4l 3rd aft nxt; sn wknd; eased frm 2 out.*	3	6

OFFICIAL DISTANCES: 1*l*, 5*l* **TIME:** 6min 55.0s **TOTE:** £10.90; places £3.60,£2.70 **DF:**£5.20

1210 Gerrard Ladies Open — 3 ran

998^{4}	**THE WILEY KALMUCK (IRE)** (7x) evensJF **Miss Z Turner** *Ld/disp til ld app 3 out; chall app nxt; in comm last; r.o wl*		1
1004^{3}	**Frank Byrne** evensJF **Miss A Goschen** *Trckd rivals til went 2nd 3 out; chall app nxt; outpcd by wnr app last*	2	2
805^{5}	**Scotch Bob (IRE)** 6-1 **Mrs P Hall** *Ld/disp til hdd app 3 out; sn outpcd*	30	3

OFFICIAL DISTANCES: 2*l*, dist **TIME:** 7min 18.0s **TOTE:** £2.30 **DF:**£1.10

1211 Open Maiden, 12st — 8 ran

1055^{2}	**ROYAL CRUISE (IRE)** 3-1 **P York** *(xnb) Pulling; hld up in rr; prog 8; went 2nd 13; ld aft 3 out; 4l clr nxt; rdn out*		1
971^{2}	**Gunnerbe Posh** 7-4F **J Maxse** *Tde & ld to start; pulled hrd; chsd ldrs; mist 7; ld 10; sn clr; blun 3 out; sn hdd & no ex; fin lame*	7	2
1055^{P}	**Private Percival** 12-1 **P Blagg** *Hld up; prog 12; 8l 3rd 14; 4th & no hdwy frm 3 out; went 3rd agn flat.*	15	3
1000^{P}	Divine Mist (IRE) 10-1 J Owen *Ww in tch; 6l 3rd when mist 13; sn rdn; wknd 3 out; btn when jb rt 2 out; nrly stpd last; dem flat.*	1	4

989[P] Ginmini (IRE) (5a) 16-1 N Oliver *Rr; jmpd slow & rmdr 3; 5th & outpcd 14; kpt on frm 3 out; nrly snatched 3rd* 1/2 5
802[3] Master Chief (IRE) 4-1 P Bull *Pulled hrd; chsd ldrs til lost plce 9; 6th & outpcd 11; no ch frm 13* 5 6
1108[F] Barbed Broach (IRE) 16-1 Miss C Cowe *Ld to 10; cl up til wknd app 13; sn no ch* 3 7
418[P] Queen's Shilling (5a) 16-1 F Wheeler *Chsd ldr; blun 4; wknd qckly 9; last when pu 11* . . . . P

OFFICIAL DISTANCES: 5*l*, 12*l* **TIME:** 7min 15.0s
TOTE: £2.70; places £1.10,£1.10,£4.70 **DF:**£2.10

The stewards fined the rider of Divine Mist £65 for improper use of the whip (not giving the horse time to respond); the owner of Ginmini was wrongly fined £50 for changing the rider, who was not fit following an earlier fall, after close of declarations

1212 Confined, 12st — 6 ran

1031[2] **MISTER PEPPER (IRE)** 7-2 **T Underwood** *Ww in last; gd hdwy 11; ld 14; in comm app 2 out; rdr celebrating flat; comf* 1
1083[2] **Kilvoydan (IRE)** 2-1F **D Phelan** *Swtng; ld to 2, 7-9 & agn app 11; hdd 14; 2l 2nd 3 out; unable to qckn* 2 2
1054[3] **Kenny Davis (IRE)** 3-1 **P Blagg** *Tde; hmpd & drpd to last 2; prog to 3rd 8; 4th & outpcd 14; no imp on ldng pr frm 3 out* 10 3
968[1] Alexander Nevsky 12-1 D Dennis *(xnb) In tch; mist 10; 5th & outpcd 12; no ch aft; went poor 4th 2 out* 15 4
897[2] Jack Of Kilcash (IRE) (3x) 7-2 N Benstead *Ld & blun 2; hdd 7; ld agn 9 til app 11; 3rd & wkng app 3 out; last frm 2 out* 2 5
1085[8] Russian Connection (IRE) 12-1 A Ward-Thomas *3rd when fell hvly 2* . . . . . F

OFFICIAL DISTANCES: 1*l*, 6*l* **TIME:** 7min 08.0s
TOTE: £2.80; places £1.90,£7.70 **DF:**£2.60 **trio**:£4.40

Fernie

Dingley (RH 8F,18J)

Sun, 2 May (DEAD)

1213 PPORA Club Members (Nov Rdrs) — 13 ran

862[1] **FREE GIFT** 1-2F **D Jacob** *(xnb) Settled wl off pce til 5th & smooth prog 9; ld 11; qcknd 8l clr 2 out; sn drvn & tired but lkd in comm when lft clr at last* 1
1031[1] **Teeton Priceless** (5a) 7-1 **T Messenger** *Chsd ldr to 10; 13l 3rd & wl outpcd 15; lft 2nd at last.* 6 2
889[3] **Gangster** 25-1 **Miss S Tarry** *Chsd ldrs but nd; 20l 7th 10; 40l 4th 15; lft rem 3rd at last* 30 3
1101[P] Libido 10-1 P Andrew *Wl outpcd & nt a fluent; 25l 8th 10; plugged past btn horses for rem 4th* 3 4
1031[4] Tale Bridge (IRE)(vis) 40-1 J Russell *Plodded rnd reluct in rr; 9th & t.o 10.* 1 1/2 5
713[4] Nicky The Kip (IRE)(tt) 20-1 W Puddifer *Nt fluent & imm strugg; t.o 7* . . . runin 6
1057[4] Thurles Pickpocket (IRE) 40-1 B Elson *Midfield; 5th 10; lost tch 12; sn t.o* 10 7
1120[13] Needwood Neptune 40-1 P Bennett *Imm strugg; t.o last 7* 25 8
1088[1] Baron Bernard 14-1 P Chinery *Cl 5th 10; 17l 4th & wkng 12; t.o & pu last* P
885[1] Frileux Royal (FR) 5-1 G Morrison *Swtng; set str gallop & spreadeagled field; hdd 11; cl up til outpcd 2 out; rallied & 4l down but lkng hld when ref last* r
477[P] Ghali (USA)(tt) 40-1 T Parr *Ld rnd padd by rdr; a labouring in rr; t.o 10th when jmpd slow 10; ur 14* . . . . U
979[P] Knight's Crest (IRE) 33-1 Miss R Hutsby *(xnb) Swtng; 2 handlers; prom brief; rr & strugg 4; t.o 11th 10; pu last* . . . . P
1104[6] Noble Colours(tt) 40-1 P Ikin *Midfield; last of 6 w any ch 10; sn rem; t.o & pu 2 out* . . . . P

OFFICIAL DISTANCES: 2 1/2*l*, dist **TIME:** 6min 35.0s
TOTE: £1.50; places £1.10,£1.50,£3.50 **DF:**£5.00

1214 Confined, 12st — 9 ran

942[F] **KING'S HERO (IRE)** 5-4F **S Morris** *Made all at fast pce; lft 5l clr 3 out & galloped on in great style til eased flat.* 1
886[1] **Agua Ardente** (3x) 7-4 **R Cope** *Chsd wnr; hit 7; ev ch til rdn & blun 3 out; no ch aft* 20 2

885[3]	**Mystic Isle (IRE)** 12-1 **N Pearce** *A 3rd; outpcd 13; 15l down 15; eased flat & nrly caught napping*	4	3
1034[1]	Crested Manor (5x) 4-1 A Sansome *Blun 3; midfield; 20l 5th & outpcd 12; 30l 5th 15; stayed on wl & nrly caught dozing 3rd*	nk	4
886[4]	Noble Affair (5a)(tt) 14-1 M Mackley *Midfield; eff in 10l 4th 12; 25l 4th when jmpd v slow 15; cont wl bhnd*	12	5
1120[5]	Danzante (IRE) 40-1 S Moreton *Bhnd; jmpd slow 7; 30l 7th & drvn 12; rem aft; no zest*	8	6
1120[9]	Simply A Star (IRE) 25-1 Miss N Chapman *Stdd start & detach in last pr; nt fluent 6; t.o 10; cont fncs bhnd*	fence	7
592[P]	Exclusive Air (USA) (7a) 40-1 P Millington *(citation) Lkd dreadful; midfield & nd; 26l 6th & tired 12; pu nxt*		P
1118[3]	Shallow River (IRE) 25-1 Miss H Phizacklea *Midfield early; lost tch rap 10; t.o & pu 13*		P

OFFICIAL DISTANCES: 20*l*, 5*l* **TIME:** 6min 31.0s
TOTE: £2.40; places £1.10,£1.40,£3.20 **DF:**£1.80

1215 Confined Maiden — 12 ran

1108[3]	**SANDY LARK** 8-1 **J Owen** *12s-8s; settled 3rd/4th; chall 14 & lft in ld brief; ev ch aft til drvn ahd app last where tried to rn out & lost action brief; stayed on cl home; all out*		1
887[2]	**Bathtime Boys** evensF **R Cope** *Cl 2nd til ld 12; bad mist 14 & hdd brief; rdn & repassed aft 2 out; lft w ev ch last; no ex flat*	5	2
1035[3]	**Teeton Diamond** (5a) 20-1 **N Pearce** *Hld up & bhnd; clsd 10 & sn prsng ldrs; 3l 4th 15; rdn & fdd tame aft nxt*	7	3
1124[6]	Barty Boy (IRE) 10-1 R Wakeham *Hld up towards rr til prog in 4th 14; 2l 3rd nxt; wknd tame aft 3 out*	1/2	4
	Broadspeed (5a) 10-1 S Morris *Hld up towards rr; wl in tch to 12; wknd rap; pu 14*		P
1061[4]	Dolitanlad 25-1 Miss L Fear *Hat-rack; virt a t.o last; 15l adrift 1; jmpd slow 9; ur 14*		U
1061[P]	Faircatcher 33-1 R Collinson *Chsd ldrs; mist 10; 6th when blun 13; nt rec; t.o & pu last*		P
885[8]	Mr Baldwin (IRE) 12-1 J Turcan *Bit bckwd; ld to 12; cl 3rd 14; tired nxt; rem 5th 2 out; pu last*		P
219[P]	On The Deck(vis) 33-1 P Millington *Lkd dire; nt fluent; cl up til stpd to nil & tried to pu aft 10; t.o & pu 12*		P
1061[U]	Plain Polly (IRE) (5a) 33-1 A Sansome *Lkd v dull; rcd wide & handy to 11; sn wknd; t.o 15; pu last*		P
887[6]	Shambob 10-1 J Burley *(xnb) Chsd ldrs til rdn & wknd 10; t.o & pu 14*		P
1056[P]	Stylino (USA) 16-1 N Docker *Drpd to rr & jmpd v slow 6; reluct u.p aft 8; sn lost tch; t.o & pu 12*		P

OFFICIAL DISTANCES: 4*l*, 1/2*l* **TIME:** 6min 45.0s
TOTE: £22.00; places £4.00,£1.10,£1.20 **DF:**£7.50

1216 Mixed Open, 4m100y, 12st - 24J — 11 ran

956[4]	**CLONSHIRE PADDY (IRE)**(bl) 7-2 **T Greenall** *Settled towards rr; hdwy 12; 7l 3rd 18; clsd to 3rd 20; drvn ahd aft 2 out; sn in comm*		1
1122[3]	**Ardmayle (IRE)** 7-2 **Miss L Coney** *Chsd ldrs; lost plce 10; 10l 5th 18; still mod 4th 2 out; kpt on stout; lkd to fin 3rd; gvn too much to do*	4	2
1032[1]	**Choral Dream (IRE)** 4-1 **R Hunnisett** *Lw; hld up midfield; hdwy 12; ld 18; sn 4l clr; urged & hdd aft 2 out; kpt on same pce; lkd to fin 2nd*	1/2	3
888[3]	Browjoshy (IRE)(cp) 20-1 J Newbold *Bhnd; hdwy 12; 8l 5th 18; 12l 5th & btn 21; plugged on*	20	4
1163[P]	Princess Derry (5a)(bl) 7-1 C Cundall *Chsd ldrs til lost plce 16; wl bhnd 18*	12	5
786[3]	Jerome Jerome 40-1 A Sansome *3rd til 2nd 15-17; lost tch rap nxt; sn wl bhnd*	7	6
1045[1]	Analystic (IRE) 3-1F G Hanmer *(xnb) Lw; sn ld; hdd 18; mist 20; still 2l 3rd & rdn 3 out; wkng when broke down bad aft nxt; dead*		P
938[5]	Be My Dream (IRE)(cp) 6-1 P Cowley *Ld 1; chsd ldr to 15; lost plce rap & nt r.o; t.o & pu 21*		P
835[4]	Borderline Breeze (IRE)(cp) 25-1 Miss H Watson *(xnb) Towards rr; strugg 16; t.o 19; pu last*		P
1121[5]	Dante's Banker (IRE) 10-1 R Armson *A detach in last pr; strugg 12; t.o & pu 17*		P
1152[6]	Nonplussed (5a)(vis) 40-1 P Andrew *Jmpd stickily & detach in last pr; t.o 8; pu 11*		P

OFFICIAL DISTANCES: 2*l*, nk **TIME:** 8min 40.0s
TOTE: £6.50; places £1.70,£1.80,£1.40 **DF:**£14.00

1217 Restricted 11 ran

1163[S] **GLENSAN (IRE)** 7-1 **G Brewer** *(xnb) Jw & cl up; went 2nd 13; ld nxt; prsd 2 out but kpt finding ex; r.o game flat* . . . 1

887[1] **Sir Lancelot** 4-1 **A Sansome** *Opened 9/2; trckd ldrs; 5th 10; 5l 5th 13; rdn to 2nd 2 out; 1l down app last; sn outpcd flat* . . . 4 2

853[4] **Tinarana Lord (IRE)** 8-1 **G Hanmer** *Lw; 2 handlers; bhnd; mist 7; 20l 8th 10; hdwy u.p 13; flatt brief 2 out; sn wknd & poor 3rd* . . . 15 3

1034[2] Teeton Fizz (5a) 9-2 N Pearce *Cl up; 3rd & u.p 10; still 3rd & drvn 3 out; fdd qckly nxt* . . . 2 4

1034[4] Button Boy 40-1 P Cowley *Ld; mist 11; hdd 13; wknd nxt; t.o when jb rt 2 out; pu last* . . . P

524[P] Coole Chief 16-1 K Green *(xnb) Hld up wl bhnd; 25l 9th 10; t.o 13; pu last* P

886[P] Cumberland Youth(cp) 40-1 P Ikin *Chsd ldr to 8; 18l 7th & fdng 10; t.o when ref 14* . . . r

1069[F] Greet You Well 3-1F R Cope *2nd/3rd til ld 13-14; 2nd & rdn 3 out; wknd qckly nxt; pu last* . . . P

It'sallinthestars (IRE) (7a) 16-1 N Bloom *20s-16s; school in rr; 10th & t.o 10; pu 12* . . . P

1118[U] Moscow Tradition (IRE) 7-1 J Docker *2 handlers; swtng; midfield; mist 7; 12l 6th 10; wknd rap nxt; pu 13; bbv* . . . P

944[R] Near And Phar (IRE) (5a) 9-2 Miss S Buckley *Stdd 30l bhnd rest & a wl t.o; finally pu last* . . . P

OFFICIAL DISTANCES: 3l, 10l **TIME:** 6min 42.0s
TOTE: £51.00; places £6.00,£1.20,£10.00 **DF:**£14.00

The stewards enquired into the running and riding of Near And Phar which was never put in the race before pulling up; the explanation that the horse did not like the ground was not accepted and the trainer and rider were each fined £125

1218 Open Maiden 9 ran

1061[3] **MIDNIGHT COWBOY** 6-4F **N Kent** *Rough & swtng; settled towards rr; clsd 10; 4l 4th 14; went 2nd 3 out; sust chall aft; nk down & rdn last; kpt on to ld cl home; all out* . . . 1

945[P] **Willow Ryde (IRE)**(cp) 4-1 **N Pearce** *Set v slow pce; rdn & hrd prsd frm 3 out; hdd cl home* . . . nk 2

1061[U] **Coombs Spinney** 14-1 **T Coles** *(xnb) Prsd ldr to 10; 4th 12; 9l 5th & wkng 14; 25l 3rd 2 out* . . . 25 3

652[3] Round The Isles 9-4 R Cope *Lw; chsd ldrs; rdn frm 6; 6th & strugg 12; nvr lkd keen aft; mist 15; t.o* . . . 25 4

890[P] All Alight (IRE) (7a) 8-1 N Bloom *Cl up; 6l 5th 12; went 2nd brief 14; 10l 3rd 3 out; sn wknd & nt pushed; t.o* . . . 6 5

1155[P] Geordie Macgregor (7a) 12-1 P Millington *Lame off fore padd & had a scabby staring coat; mists in rr; lost tch 11; 16l 7th nxt; t.o & pu 14* . . . P

890[P] Izzyizzenty (7a) 14-1 O Williams *(xnb,pricker o/s) Bckwd; cl 3rd/4th; 3l 3rd 14; stpd to nil 3 out; pu nxt* . . . P

887[P] Mr Match (3ow) 25-1 D Hockridge *Bckwd; a detach last; t.o 12; climbed 15; pu 2 out* . . . P

Slingsby Lady (12a) 14-1 A Sansome *Another w scabby staring coat; jmpd alarm in rr; jmpd v slow 10 & lost tch rap; pu nxt* . . . P

OFFICIAL DISTANCES: hd, 20l **TIME:** 6min 56.8s
TOTE: £2.20; places £1.10,£1.40,£3.00 **DF:**£9.00

Lauderdale

Mosshouses (LH 8F,19J)

Sun, 2 May (GOOD)

1219 Hunt Members 2 ran

1079[1] **STARBUCK** 1-3F **L Morgan** *Ld/disp w rival til 1l up 15; rmdrs & qcknd clr aft 3 out* . . . 1

1068[P] **Laganside (IRE)** (2ow) 2-1 **J Muir** *Oht; ld/disp w rival til 1l down 15; pushed along & outpcd aft 3 out* . . . 4 2

OFFICIAL DISTANCE: 4l **TIME:** 6min 23.9s

1220 Northern Area P-t-P Association Club Members, 12st — 11 ran

Prev	Horse / Rider / Comment	Dist	Pos
1077[1]	**DECENT BOND (IRE)** 4-1 **R Green** *Oht; rr; 15l 7th 15; gd prog aft; str rn to ld last; rdn clr; wl rdn*		1
800[4]	**Lordberniebouffant (IRE)** 7-4F **Miss P Robson** *A.p; hrd rdn & prsd ldr & ev ch last; outpcd flat*	1	2
798[12]	**Penny Native (IRE)** 5-1 **L Morgan** *Handy til ld aft 15; hrd prsd & hrd rdn app last; hdd & no ex flat*	½	3
1028[P]	Roscoe Burn 20-1 M McAlister *Chsd ldrs; 12l 4th 6; prog to disp 1l 2nd 14; outpcd aft 2 out; kpt on; nd*	10	4
858[3]	Dream Of My Life (USA) 8-1 R Morgan *(xnb,orbs) In tch; 12l 5th 9; kpt on one pce aft 3 out*	2	5
915[P]	Ballymenagh (IRE) 33-1 S Huggan *Chsd ldrs til pu bad lame aft 9; dead*		P
764[P]	Boyup Brook 40-1 T Morrison *A rr; lsng tch 12; t.o & pu aft 16; lame*		P
915[P]	Driminamore (IRE) 33-1 Miss H Gray *Oht; a rr; t.o 8; pu aft nxt*		P
1081[1]	Jinful Du Grand Val (FR) 8-1 J Alexander *(xnb) 10s-8s; 2 handlers; oht; ld aft 2; 5l up 6; hdd aft 13; outpcd 16; wknd & pu 2 out*		P
1080[2]	Johnnys Gone (IRE) 6-1 C Shirley-Beavan *Lw; chsd ldrs; 12l 5th app 9; prog to disp 1l 2nd 14; 2l down when slpd on bend & ur aft 16*		U
761[2]	Valley Garden 50-1 R Nichol *Sn detach; t.o 7; pu aft 3 out*		P

OFFICIAL DISTANCES: 1*l*, ½*l* **TIME:** 6min 12.6s

PLATE 12 1220 Lauderdale Northern Area P-t-P Association Club Members: The grey Dream Of My Life is prominent as the flag falls *PHOTO: Alan Mitchell*

1221 Ladies Open - 18J — 5 ran

Prev	Horse / Rider / Comment	Dist	Pos
1078[1]	**PHARMISTICE (IRE)** 4-6F **Miss N Stirling** *(xnb) Trckd ldr til ld aft 13; qcknd clr aft 3 out; comf*		1
763[3]	**Dere Street** 9-2 **Miss R Davidson** *Lw; chsd ldng pr; 5l 3rd 12; prog to 1l 2nd 16; short-lived eff aft nxt; no ch w wnr aft*	6	2
916[4]	**In Demand** 10-1 **Miss J Balmer** *In tch in rr; 10l 4th 12; prog to 6l 4th 14; outpcd aft; pushed along to 10l 3rd app 3 out; one pce*	3	3
1036[1]	Emperor's Magic (IRE)(cp,tt) 5-2 Miss S Ward *Blun & ur 1*		U
	Wester Lad 33-1 Miss J Riding *Lw; ld; 1l up 11; hdd aft 13; still ev ch til wknd aft 16; wl bhnd when pu last*		P

OFFICIAL DISTANCES: 8*l*, 4*l* **TIME:** 6min 13.6s

Fence 9 omitted - fallen rider

1222 Restricted, 12st — 12 ran

Form	Horse, price, rider and comment	Dist	Pos
918^{2}	**COOMAKISTA** (5a) evensF **R Morgan** *6/4-evens; trckd ldr til 2l 3rd 8; prog to ld 12; made rest; clr last; comf*		1
1077^{4}	**Lucky Brush (IRE)** 8-1 **J Alexander** *(bf) Chsd ldrs; outpcd 14; 8l 7th 16; kpt on wl aft; went 2nd app last; no ch w wnr*	3	2
918^{P}	**Timberley**(tt) 20-1 **R Green** *In tch; 12l 7th 12; prog & ev ch 16; outpcd aft nxt; kpt on; nt trble ldrs.*	5	3
768^{1}	Posh Stick (5a) 4-1 J Walton *In tch in rr; prog to 5l 4th 11; 2l 2nd 15; eff & ev ch app 3 out; outpcd aft; one pce app last.*	10	4
876^{3}	Distracting (5a) 12-1 L Morgan *In tch; hdwy to disp 3l 3rd 15; eff & ev ch 3 out; outpcd nxt; kpt on one pce*	1	5
1040^{2}	Little John 8-1 J Galbraith *In tch in rr; prog to 6l 7th 14; sn outpcd & nd aft 16*	6	6
272^{1}	Le Millenaire (FR) (7a) 7-2 C Shirley-Beavan *(xnb) Lw; oht; trckd ldr til ld aft 7; hdd 12 & rdn along aft; still ev ch app 3 out; sn wknd.*	$^{1}/_{2}$	7
918^{P}	Shylock (IRE) 33-1 S Huggan *Ld; 2l up 6; hdd aft nxt; disp 3l 3rd 15; wknd app 3 out*	8	8
918^{U}	Good Morning (5a, 3ow) 25-1 R Dickson *Oht; a rr; bhnd 9; t.o 16*	10	9
1040^{5}	C L B Jemilla (5a) 50-1 Miss G Craggs *A rr; lsng tch 13; t.o 16*	3	10
857^{P}	Anotherhandyman(cp) 33-1 Miss S Gledson *A rr; t.o 11.*	12	11
765^{P}	Harry's Mare (IRE) (5a) 25-1 Mrs J Hedley *(xnb) Rr; sn lost tch; jmpd slow 5; jmpd v slow nxt; pu aft*		P

OFFICIAL DISTANCES: 4*l*, 5*l* **TIME:** 6min 14.9s

1223 Mens Open — 5 ran

Form	Horse, price, rider and comment	Dist	Pos
1179^{U}	**TRIVIAL (IRE)** (5a) 2-1JF **L Morgan** *A handy; prog to 1l 2nd app 8; 2l 2nd app 16; ww gng wl til qcknd clr app 2 out; 10l clr last; rdly*		1
1080^{4}	**Extra Stout (IRE)**(tt) 3-1 **C Storey** *Ld/disp til 1l 2nd 6; releg to 4l last 12; still ev ch 3 out; sn outpcd; kpt on wl aft to tk 2nd flat; nt trble wnr*	8	2
854^{3}	**Kings Minstral (IRE)**(tt) 6-1 **R Morgan** *Ld/disp til 1l up 6; $1^{1}/_{2}$l clr 15; hdd & easily brushed aside by wnr app 2 out; lost 2nd flat*	4	3
858^{2}	Sharpaman(bl) 2-1JF C Shirley-Beavan *In tch; 4l last 6; sn rdn along; 2l 3rd 12; hrd rdn nxt; outpcd aft 16; kpt on u.p*	3	4
1079^{3}	Charlieadams (IRE) 8-1 J Muir *Prom when ducked out thro wing 2; tried to j wall & became caught in wire.*		R

OFFICIAL DISTANCES: 10*l*, 5*l* **TIME:** 6min 18.7s

1224 Open Maiden (Div 1), 12st — 10 ran

Form	Horse, price, rider and comment	Dist	Pos
920^{3}	**OFCOURSEHEKHAN (IRE)** 2-1F **Miss N Stirling** *(xnb) Green; oht; trckd ldr til ld aft 8; made rest; 2l clr 16; in comm nxt; wl clr when nrly rn off course flat; improve*		1
1041^{3}	**St Bee**(bl) 5-1 **A Richardson** *Trckd ldrs; 4l 3rd 6; 8l 4th aft 16; kpt on one pce; no ch w wnr*	10	2
919^{r}	**Tallaburn** (5a) 16-1 **A Findlay** *(xnb) In tch in rr; stdy prog to chse ldr 16; one pce frm nxt*	10	3
856^{3}	Izzuthefox (IRE) 6-1 C Storey *Chsd ldrs; 5l 3rd 12; prog to trck ldr 16; eff aft; wknd aft nxt; one pce*	6	4
856^{U}	Air Leader (IRE) (7a) 3-1 L Morgan *4s-3s; ld; 2l up 6; hdd aft 8; 3l 2nd 12; wknd aft nxt; pu aft 14*		P
1042^{r}	Anniejo (12a) 5-1 R Morgan *(xnb) In tch in rr til saddle slpd & pu aft 8.*		P
	Hardy Mouse (IRE) (5a) 12-1 R Green *(xnb) Nt fluent in rr; detach 7; t.o & pu 10*		P
1041^{5}	Kanturk Star (IRE)(bl) 12-1 Mrs V Jackson *Oht; chsd ldrs; 8l 4th 5; strugg aft 12; wl bhnd 14; pu sn aft*		P
920^{8}	Stately Progress (IRE) 20-1 S Huggan *Oht; a rr; 13l 6th 16; t.o & pu nxt.*		P
287^{2}	Storm Ahead (IRE) 5-1 C Shirley-Beavan *Mid-div; stdy prog & 5l 3rd 15; ev ch nxt; sn outpcd; btn 4th when fell last*		F

OFFICIAL DISTANCES: dist, 15*l* **TIME:** 6min 23.5s

1225 Open Maiden (Div 2), 12st — 8 ran

Form	Horse, price, rider and comment	Dist	Pos
914^{2}	**RUTHERFORD**(cp) 4-6F **R Morgan** *Jw; trckd ldr til ld app 7; made rest; 6l up 15; kpt on wl.*		1
	Rich Song (IRE) 6-1 **A Findlay** *In tch in rr; 8l 6th 11; gng wl aft & hdwy & ev ch 2 out; kpt on u.p; promising*	4	2

	Moorfoot Blaze 6-1 **Miss J Hollands** *(xnb) Prom; 1l 2nd 14; eff aft nxt; outpcd & 10l 2nd 16; kpt on wl aft; promising*	8	3
1041^{P}	Ellemford (5a) 20-1 W Goldie *Ld til hdd app 7; 2l 2nd 12; outpcd & 12l 4th 15; sn nd*	25	4
768^{P}	Alice's Old Rose (5a) 10-1 M McAlister *In tch; 6l 5th 8; still in tch when blun & ur 13*		U
767^{U}	Jackofalltrades (IRE) 11-2 C Storey *Oht; mid-div; 4l 4th 13; outpcd aft 15; wl bhnd & pu last*		P
	The Babbler (5a) 7-2 Mrs V Jackson *Sn detach; t.o & pu aft 14*		P
916^{6}	Wexford (IRE) 14-1 Miss S Lamb *Rr; prog to 6l 6th 9; outpcd aft; lsng tch 13; t.o & pu 3 out*		P

OFFICIAL DISTANCES: 6*l*, 8*l* **TIME:** 6min 30.2s

Radnor & West Herefordshire

Cold Harbour (RH 8F,18J)

Sun, 2 May (GOOD to SOFT)

1226 Hunt Members, 12st — 10 ran

1110^{2}	**PERSONA PRIDE** 4-5F **Julian Pritchard** *2nd til ld 5-8; ld agn 10; drew wl clr 3 out; unchall*		1
752^{P}	**Alleywell** 7-2 **A Wadlow** *A.p; went 2nd aft 7; ld 9; hdd nxt; ev ch 15; wknd u.p 3 out; fin tired*	30	2
	Scarlet Boy (7a) 15-1 **S Gray** *Bit bckwd; hld up; mist 6; 22l 7th $^1/_2$way; bhnd til hdwy 11; went 20l 4th 13 & 30l 3rd 15; kpt on stdly*	15	3
	Trevveethan (IRE) 25-1 T Rogers *1st ride; ss; pulled hrd; jnd ldrs 3; lost plce 8; disp 10l 4th $^1/_2$way; lost tch 12; t.o 15; plodded on*	nk	4
1022^{5}	Italian Clover(cp) 10-1 Miss S Carter *Swtng; a bhnd; mists 7 & 9; 23l 8th $^1/_2$way; 30l 6th 12; t.o 14*	20	5
1027^{P}	Come On Boy 20-1 G Davies *W ldrs; 2l 3rd $^1/_2$way; 10l 3rd & wkng 12; dem 15; t.o*	5	6
1115^{2}	Blazing Pride 6-1 P Haynes *A wl bhnd; 30l 9th $^1/_2$way; t.o 12*	$1^1/_4$fs	7
1113^{P}	A Bit Of Fluff (5a) 25-1 Miss L Brooke *2 handlers; jmpd delib; drpd to rr & rmdrs 3; t.o & pu aft 11*		P
835^{7}	Against The Agent 10-1 A Hanly *Ld to 5; lost plce & 10l 4th $^1/_2$way; stpd to nil aft 10; t.o last 12; pu 13*		P
667^{P}	Missilebrook Lass (5a) 8-1 B Shaw *16s-8s; nvr gng wl; rmdrs 5; mist 8; 20l 6th $^1/_2$way; wl bhnd when blun & ur 11*		U

OFFICIAL DISTANCES: dist, 8*l*, $^1/_2$*l* **TIME:** 6min 32.9s

1227 Confined, 12st — 9 ran

1140^{1}	**FATHER TOM (IRE)** (3x) 4-7F **Julian Pritchard** *Ww; last to 11; hdwy & 9l 5th 14; jnd ldrs app 3 out; qcknd to ld last; rdly*		1
867^{1}	**Rain Delay** 7-2 **R Rogers** *2 handlers; a.p; 2l 3rd $^1/_2$way; qcknd to ld aft 11; hdd last; one pce*	$2^1/_2$	2
1114^{1}	**Huntersway (IRE)** 11-1 **R Hughes** *Swtng; hld up; 6l 6th $^1/_2$way; hdwy & 5l 4th 12; went 2nd app 3 out; ev ch last; unable to qckn*	1	3
952^{3}	Arctic King 14-1 A Wintle *Swtng; ld to 2; 2nd to 11 & frm 13 to app 3 out; sn outpcd*	7	4
1109^{U}	Magicien (FR) 9-1 R Hodges *W ldrs; 3l 5th $^1/_2$way; $6^1/_2$l 5th 12; lost plce & 10l 6th 14; no ch aft*	2	5
1135^{3}	Guard A Dream (IRE) 20-1 E Walker *Hld up; disp 3l 5th $^1/_2$way; lost plce & 8l 6th 12; rdn 13; wl bhnd 15; t.o*	runin	6
728^{P}	Heavy Weather (IRE) 4-1 W Hill *Ld 2 til aft 11; 6l 3rd 14; rdn 3 out; mist nxt; 6l 4th when fell last; rdr broke collar-bone*		F
696^{P}	Iro Origny (FR) 33-1 A Phillips *(xnb) Hld up; mist 5; shkn up 7; 9l 7th & rdn $^1/_2$way; mist 10; last when fell 12*		F
1090^{P}	Pride Of Pennker (IRE) (5a) 33-1 M Flynn *(xnb) Prom; $2^1/_2$l 4th $^1/_2$way; wknd qckly 12; wl bhnd when fell 15*		F

OFFICIAL DISTANCES: 3*l*, $^1/_2$*l*, 5*l* **TIME:** 6min 33.4s

1228 Mens Open, 4m, 12st - 24J — 9 ran

Form	Horse / Rider / Comment	Dist	Pos
1117[4]	**GENEREUX**(cp,tt) 12-1 **R Hodges** *Ld 2-3; sn lost plce & off bridle; 9l 7th ½way; lost tch 14; went 15l 4th 19 & 8l 3rd 2 out; str rn to ld flat; sn clr; wl rdn*		1
977[7]	**Ebony Jack (IRE)** 12-1 **Julian Pritchard** *Sn prom; blun 8; went 2nd nxt; ld 18; hit 2 out; lkd wnr til overwhelmed flat*	3	2
1047[2]	**Step On Eyre (IRE)** (7x) 13-8F **R Burton** *Hld up; went 4l 3rd 12 til aft 16; lft 10l 3rd 18; went 2l 2nd & rdn 3 out; ev ch when blun last; eased when btn flat*	7	3
979[5]	Henry Bruce 12-1 Adam Brown *16s-12s; lost plce 5; last 9; rdn 10; lost tch 14; 23l 6th 20; stayed on 3 out; went 4th last; nt rch ldrs.*	hd	4
1109[1]	Wild Edric(bl) 16-1 A Beedles *Hld up; mist 4; hdwy & 6½l 5th ½way; went 4l 3rd aft 16; lft 3l 2nd 18-3 out; sn wknd*	7	5
758[5]	Lyphard's Fable (USA) 33-1 D England *Hld up; hdwy 9; 6l 4th ½way; wkng when lft 15l 4th 18; mist 19; t.o 21*	25	6
1048[1]	Cutina (5a) 7-4 D Barlow *5/2-7/4; hld up; last to 9; 12l 8th ½way; lost tch 14; mists 15 & 16; 20l 5th & no hdwy 20; t.o & pu 2 out*		P
663[P]	The Unamed Man 20-1 G Barfoot-Saunt *Ld 3-4 & 6 til aft 8; lost plce 11; 7l 6th ½way; lost tch 14; wl bhnd when pu 18*		P
660[4]	Westcoast 7-1 T Stephenson *(bf) Ld to 2 & 4-6; ld aft 8 til hdd & fell 18*		F

OFFICIAL DISTANCES: 3*l*, 6*l*, ½*l* **TIME:** 8min 47.2s

1229 Ladies Open — 8 ran

Form	Horse / Rider / Comment	Dist	Pos
980[1]	**SAPEGA (IRE)** 4-9F **Miss J Williams** *Swtng; hld up; 4½l 4th ½way; went 2nd 11; ld 13; qcknd clr flat*		1
932[F]	**Major Adams** 5-1 **Miss T Clark** *Hld up; 6l 5th ½way; hdwy 11; went 2nd 14; ev ch app 3 out; unable to qckn*	5	2
1019[5]	**Proper Primitive** (5a) 14-1 **Miss E James** *(bf) Went 2nd app 4; ld aft 10-13; 6l 3rd 15; wknd 3 out.*	12	3
1025[3]	Head Gardener (IRE)(bl) 33-1 Miss J Hughes *Prom til jmpd slow & lost plce 7; mist 9; 13l last & rdn ½way; lost tch 12; t.o 15.*	25	4
1137[1]	Do It Once (IRE)(tt) 10-1 Mrs A Rucker *(xnb) Ld to 1; 4l 3rd ½way; 3l 4th when mist 12; sn lost plce; wl bhnd 15; eased & lost 4th nr fin*	1	5
974[4]	Fair Charmeur (IRE) (5a) 4-1 Miss I Tompsett *Ld 1 til aft 10; lost plce & 6l 5th 12; wl bhnd when mist 14; pu 15.*		P
1117[P]	Joshua's Vision (IRE) 25-1 Miss L Brooke *Tubed; sn wl bhnd; t.o 4; pu 6*		P
987[5]	Sea Tarth (5a)(cp) 14-1 Miss H Kinsey *(xnb) Jmpd delib; a bhnd; 12l 6th ½way; rdn & lost tch 12; t.o & pu 3 out*		P

OFFICIAL DISTANCES: 5*l*, 15*l*, dist **TIME:** 6min 33.5s

1230 Restricted, 12st — 10 ran

Form	Horse / Rider / Comment	Dist	Pos
1014[2]	**EURO BOB (IRE)** 2-1F **Mrs A Rucker** *Swtng; a.p; 5l 3rd ½way; went 2nd app 11-13; 3l 4th nxt; lft 2nd 15; ld last; stayed on*		1
1113[2]	**Shemardi** 3-1 **R Hodges** *A.p; disp 5l 3rd ½way; ld 14; 3l clr & rdn 3 out; hdd & no ex last*	2	2
726[7]	**Native Isle (IRE)** 20-1 **J Mahot** *2nd til lost plce & blun 11; u.p when mist 12; sn wl bhnd; t.o aft 15*	runin	3
752[P]	Wraparound You (IRE) 33-1 G Disney *(xnb) Ld; 10l clr 6-9; hdd 14; 4th & wkng when hmpd nxt; fin tired & walked in*	20	4
369[P]	Almost A Day(bl) 12-1 D Mansell *(xnb) 2 handlers; a bhnd; rdn 8; 20l last ½way; t.o & pu 13*		P
978[1]	Babs Wheal (5a) 7-2 A Charles-Jones *Hld up; 10l 5th ½way; clsng when fell 10*		F
1027[1]	Johnston's Ville (IRE) 20-1 J Merry *A bhnd; 17l 9th ½way; pu 14*		P
1069[3]	Raymond James(cp) 10-1 D Barlow *Nvr gng wl; rmdrs 4; 13l 8th ½way; lost tch aft 10; wl bhnd when pu 12*		P
927[1]	Ski Pass 4-1 T Stephenson *Hld up; mist 7; 12l 7th ½way; hdwy 11; went 3rd aft nxt & 2nd 14; ev ch when fell 15.*		F
1114[U]	Watergate Boy (IRE) 25-1 R Carey *(xnb) Hld up; hdwy 6; 10½l 6th ½way; wknd 12; pu 13*		P

OFFICIAL DISTANCES: 2*l*, dist, dist **TIME:** 6min 34.4s

1231 Open Mares Maiden, 12st — 8 ran

1116F	**WITHYBROOK LASS** (5a) evensF **R Burton** *Sn prom; went 2nd aft 7; lft in ld 8; qcknd last; rdly*		1
1020P	**Franco Lady (IRE)** (5a) 7-2 **Miss E James** *2nd/3rd til aft 7; 7l 4th ½way; went 2nd 13; ev ch when hit 2 out; sn rdn & nt qckn*	2	2
929P	**Youwoudhavethat (IRE)** (5a) 12-1 **M Wall** *W ldrs; jmpd slow 2; lft 2nd 8-10; 4l 3rd 14; mist 15; wkng when mist 2 out*	25	3
840R	Sylvias Dream (5a) 12-1 P Morris *Hld up & bhnd; 20l last ½way; hdwy 11; 7l 5th nxt; went 7l 4th aft 14; wknd 3 out*	6	4
734P	Crystal Brook (5a) 8-1 S Graham *(xnb) 2 handlers; hld up; hdwy 8; 5l 3rd ½way; went 2nd 10 til aft 12; 5l 4th 14; wknd rap u.p 15; sn t.o*	runin	5
1096R	Black Hope (IRE) (5a)(tt) 10-1 L Stephens *(xnb) Jmpd rt; ld; sn 12l clr; reduced advant when blun bad & ur 8*		U
620P	Brendas Nightmare (5a) 7-2 A Wadlow *Hld up; 10l 5th ½way; 10l last & rdn 12; no resp; pu aft 13*		P
1049P	Missuslarge (5a) 6-1 Julian Pritchard *(xnb) Nt jw; 2nd/3rd to 3; 6th when jmpd slow & ur 4*		U

OFFICIAL DISTANCES: 2*l*, dist, 8*l* **TIME:** 6min 47.3s

1232 Open Maiden (Div 1), 12st — 13 ran

934P	**KING'S REPLY** 5-1 **R Burton** *2nd/3rd til ld 11; hdd 12; w ldr til ld & mist 2 out; 2l clr last; wknd nr fin; just hld on*		1
9294	**Silver Orchid** (7a) 4-1 **J O'Brien** *(xnb) 2nd/3rd til ld 9; hdd 11; ld 12 til app 2 out; 2l 2nd when mist last; rallied flat; just failed*	hd	2
8402	**Clever Dickie** 9-4F **M Jackson** *Hld up & bhnd; mist 7; 11l 9th ½way; hdwy & 8l 5th 12; lft 5l 3rd 15; rdn 3 out; wkng when blun last*	12	3
10446	Whats Up Jake 8-1 A Wadlow *Hld up; hdwy & 5l 7th ½way; went 3l 3rd aft 11-14; wknd u.p 15*	7	4
9345	Golden Pride (5a) 20-1 T Haynes *A bhnd; 16l 11th ½way; t.o 12*	25	5
10754	Romabit Tom 10-1 R Rogers *W ldrs; 4l 6th ½way; 6l 4th & rdn 12; went 3rd 14; wknd aft 15; t.o*	1	6
	But Me No Buts 16-1 J Mahot *2 handlers; swtng; nt jw; a wl bhnd; rmdrs 3; 25l last ½way; blun 10; t.o & pu 11*		P
	Can You Talk 16-1 R Hodges *Rn out 1*		R
1115F	Four Opinions 5-1 S Gray *Nt jw; hld up; rmdrs 7; 10l 8th ½way; no hdwy when blun & ur 12*		U
	Tejaque (5a) 10-1 D Mansell *Bckwd; a bhnd; 14l 10th ½way; t.o & pu 12*		P
927U	Tensing 10-1 G Barfoot-Saunt *(xnb) Ld; mist 3; hdd 9; wknd & 10l 7th 12; wl bhnd when pu 15*		P
981P	The Footsy 14-1 Julian Pritchard *Chsd ldrs; 3½l 5th ½way; fell 10*		F
1067F	Willie The Kid (7a) 10-1 H Dowty *Hld up; mist 3; hdwy 7; 3l 4th ½way; lost plce & 10l 6th 12; rallied & 5l 3rd when mist & ur 15*		U

OFFICIAL DISTANCES: nk, 8*l*, 6*l* **TIME:** 6min 46.4s

1233 Open Maiden (Div 2), 12st — 8 ran

8403	**LOU BIARNES (FR)** 5-1 **B Shaw** *Hld up; 22l 4th ½way; went 8l 2nd 11; ld 14; stayed on wl 3 out*		1
7543	**Jump For Paddy** (7a) 4-5F **A Wadlow** *Hld up; 23l 5th ½way; hdwy & 6l 5th 12; went 2l 3rd aft 15; chsd wnr u.p 3 out; chall & outj last; wknd flat*	5	2
850P	**Chicago's Padre** 8-1 **A Hanly** *(xnb) Hld up & pulled hrd; 20l 3rd ½way; hdwy 11; went 1l 2nd aft 14 til rdn & wknd 3 out; fin tired*	25	3
982P	Golden Embers 8-1 D Barlow *2nd/3rd to 3; lost plce 5; 28l last ½way; rdn & lost tch 11; wl bhnd when pu 14*		P
600R	Just Champ(bl) 3-1 D Mansell *(xnb) Hld up & pulled hrd; mist 2; went 2nd nxt; ld 4; 6l clr 8-12; hdd 14; wknd aft nxt; dist 4th when fell hvly last; winded*		F
11153	Kerry Zulu Warrior 7-2 H Tett *(xnb) Pulled hrd; ld; 10l clr when blun 2; hdd 4; mists 6 & 10; 2nd til stpd to nil 11; pu 12*		P
1115R	Peggys Gold (5a) 7-1 S Graham *(xnb,bf) Last til fell 7*		F
666F	Scallyweld 7-1 M Jackson *Hld up; 24l 6th ½way; blun 10; hdwy & 5l 4th 12; mist 13; wknd 14; t.o & pu 2 out*		P

OFFICIAL DISTANCES: 4*l*, dist **TIME:** 6min 50.2s

Banwen Miners

Pentreclwydau (LH 7F,18J)

Mon, 3 May (GOOD with FIRM patches)

1234 Hunt Members

1022^{2}	**ALJOASH (IRE)** (5a) **T Vaughan** *(xnb,bh) Walked over*		1

1235 Confined, 12st — 6 ran

1090^{7}	**FLOCKMASTER (IRE)** 6-1 **Mrs C Owen** *Prom; ld 8; 1l up til lft 8l clr app 3 out; in comm aft*		1
1090^{5}	**Zola (IRE)** 9-4 **P Sheldrake** *Rr; 12l last 11; rdn & clsd 14; lft 8l last app 3 out; r.o u.p; nt rch ldr; all out*	3	2
1090^{P}	Harppy (FR) 16-1 M Barber *(xnb,bh) Cl 3rd; lft 1l 2nd 10; jnd ldr 15; slpd & ur bend bef nxt*		U
1090^{6}	Hunter Gold (FR) (3x) 2-1F Mrs B Lewis *Ld 1-6; rstrnd in cl 2nd til fell 10*		F
	Ile Distinct (IRE) 3-1 Miss B Williams *(xnb) 6s-3s; 4th early; sn strugg & lsng tch 4; pu nxt*		P
841^{P}	La Maestra (FR) (5a) 10-1 Miss H Lewis *Swtng; in tch in last til shot rdr out of saddle 7*		U

OFFICIAL DISTANCE: $2\frac{1}{2}$*l* **TIME:** 6min 14.0s

1236 Mixed Open (West Wales Grand National), 4m, 12st - 25J

1025^{2}	**SILVER POT BLACK Miss H Lewis** *Walked over*		1

1237 Restricted, 12st — 9 ran

1094^{3}	**HAIL STONE (IRE)** 14-1 **L Stephens** *Prom; settled 2nd til ld 15; 4l up 2 out; kpt on wl*		1
1091^{1}	**Ruby Dante (IRE)** (5a) 3-1JF **D Jones** *Trckd ldrs; 4th & mist 7; 2l 4th 11; went 3rd 13; 2nd & ev ch aft 3 out; sn no imp*	5	2
1234^{1}	**Aljoash (IRE)** (5a) 3-1JF **T Vaughan** *In tch in rr; 4th 15; went 3rd & ev ch aft 3 out; outpcd*	2	3
947^{1}	Beasley (7a) 4-1 M Barber *6s-4s; rr; went 3rd 7-11; drpd to last but in tch 13; outpcd frm 3 out*	3	4
1191^{P}	Cresswell Gold (5a) 7-1 P Sheldrake *Lft in ld 4; mist 13; u.p & hdd 15; wknd 3 out*	4	5
1094^{P}	Pams Oak 8-1 Miss F Wilson *(xnb,bh) 2nd outing; rstrnd in rr early; settled 6th; no ex frm 3 out*	1	6
1094^{5}	Black Dan(cp) 33-1 D Underwood *A last; t.o 9; pu 12*		P
844^{P}	Carl's Boy 12-1 T Faulkner *A bhnd; detach frm 9; pu 3 out*		P
1094^{2}	Rag Week (IRE) 4-1 J Cook *Ld til fell 4*		F

OFFICIAL DISTANCES: 4*l*, $2\frac{1}{2}$*l* **TIME:** 6min 16.0s

1238 Intermediate, 12st — 4 ran

882^{1}	**RHYTHM KING** 6-4 **G Maundrell** *(xnb) Jw; ld 9 & qcknd clr; 8l up 11; pegged back 12 til qcknd away agn aft 3 out*		1
1092^{2}	**Barton Dream (IRE)** 4-5F **T Vaughan** *(xnb) Opened evens; ld 4; hdd 9; lft flat-footed by ldr frm 10; clsd 12 but nvr able to gt back on terms; outpcd frm 3 out*	7	2
1095^{1}	**Camden Caramel (IRE)** (5a) 6-1 **T Faulkner** *Nt fluent; sn outpcd in 3rd; 16l 3rd 11; t.o 15; r.o stdly aft; nt rch ldrs*	5	3
1094^{P}	Daisy's Choice (5a) 14-1 P Sheldrake *A last; 20l adrift 11; sn t.o*	runin	4

OFFICIAL DISTANCES: 7*l*, 4*l* **TIME:** 6min 27.0s

1239 Open Maiden (Div 1), 12st — 9 ran

1095^{3}	**TENACIOUS MELODY** 4-1 **Miss I Tompsett** *(xnb) 6s-4s; prom; ld 5; 3l ahd 12; sn qcknd clr; 15l up & in comm 15*		1
1091^{5}	**Blakeney Hill** (5a) 9-2 **J Price** *Ld 1-4; settled 3rd til 14l last 12; clsd to 3rd agn nxt; 15l 2nd 15; nvr nr wnr*	30	2
1027^{P}	**Imustgeton** (5a)(tt) 12-1 **D Davies** *Mounted on course; mostly 4th; 12l 4th 12; dem nxt; no ch aft but stayed on to rem 3rd agn 2 out*	30	3
452^{F}	Fort Apache (IRE) 16-1 R Carey *Midfield; went 2nd 5 til jmpd slow 13; rem 3rd 15; lost a plce frm 2 out*	2	4
1096^{P}	Bold Flirtation 25-1 L Stephens *(xnb) A rr; t.o 3; pu 5*		P
948^{3}	Clarice Starling (5a) 11-10F D Jones *(xnb) Opened 2s; nt jw; 6th mostly; went 6l 3rd & mist 11; jmpd slow nxt & last pr aft; pu 3 out*		P

	Honary Secretary 25-1 P Sheldrake *Fat; jmpd v slow 1; ref 3*		r
735[4]	Indian Trix (IRE) (5a) 7-1 M Barber *2nd early; 5th 4-8; drvn in rr 9; pu 11*		P
950[P]	Supreme Robber (IRE) 7-1 T Vaughan *Tubed; 2 handlers; a bhnd; last when mist 6; pu 8*		P

OFFICIAL DISTANCES: 30*l*, 30*l*, 1*l* **TIME:** 6min 18.0s

1240 Open Maiden (Div 2), 12st — 10 ran

1091[P]	**BALLET RED** (5a) 8-1 **L Stephens** *12s-8s; a.p; ld 4-6; drpd back; chsd ldr 12; 5l 2nd 3 out; r.o str u.p frm nxt; ld final strides*		1
1193[4†]	**Millenium Run (IRE)** 5-4F **James Tudor** *7/4-5/4; prom; ld brief 3; settled 5th; ld agn 15; 5l up & rdn nxt; jnd last; hdd cl home*	¾	2
1092[P]	**Wiston Wizo**(bl) 6-1 **P Sheldrake** *2nd; ld 8 & agn 12-14; 3rd & wkng 15; outpcd aft*	5	3
1026[2]	Coal Queen (12a) 3-1 T Vaughan *6s-3s; 4th; ld 6-8; drpd to 7th 9; pu 13*		P
1096[P]	Finlays Folly 25-1 Miss I Tompsett *(bh) Midfield; lost tch 12; t.o & pu 3 out*		P
845[P]	Lynwood Legend 20-1 J L Llewellyn *(xnb,bf) Rr early; went 4th 9; rdn 12; sn wknd; rr when pu 3 out*		P
1049[3]	Neminos (IRE) (7a)(tt) 5-1 T Faulkner *Ld til rn out 2*		R
676[P]	Poacher's Pride (5a) 14-1 D Jones *(xnb) 4th; ld 9-11; wknd qckly & sn rr; pu 15*		P
844[P]	Riches To Rags (IRE) 16-1 S Graham *A last; hmpd 3; detach 8; mist 11 & pu aft*		P
	Top Commander (IRE) 10-1 M Barber *Mid-div & mist 3; went 3rd 9; 5th & wkng 12; pu 15*		P

OFFICIAL DISTANCES: ¾*l*, 3*l* **TIME:** 6min 25.0s

PLATE 13 1240 Banwen Miners Open Maiden (Div 2): L to R: Ballet Red, Poacher's Pride, Top Commander, Coal Queen, Millenium Run, Wiston Wizo and Lynwood Legend PHOTO: Liz Howard

Cambridgeshire with Enfield Chace

Northaw (LH 8F,18J)

Mon, 3 May (SOFT with HEAVY patches)

1241 Hunt Members, 12st — 4 ran

902[U]	**ICAL (IRE)** (5a) 4-1 **A Merriam** *Ld app 5; made rest; drew clr app 2 out*		1
123[P]	**King Of The Sea (IRE)** 4-1 **Miss E Bell** *Hld up; went 2nd 8; jnd wnr 14; wknd 2 out*	15	2

649^{U}	General Confusion (IRE) (3x) 2-5F Miss B Czepulkowski *Mist & ur 1*		U
401^{F}	Groovejet (7a) 4-1 A Braithwaite *Ld til app 5; mist 7; 3rd frm 8; wkng when jmpd v slow 3 out; pu nxt*		P

OFFICIAL DISTANCE: 15*l* **TIME:** 7min 53.0s **TOTE:** £4.70 **DF:**£5.90

There was $4\frac{1}{2}$ hours of continuous heavy rain before and during this meeting and the stewards are to be commended for their actions which allowed it to be successfully completed despite the extreme conditions

1242 Confined, 12st — 5 ran

997^{6}	**POLO RIDGE (IRE)** (5x)(bl) 8-1 **H Fowler** *Ld rnd start; made all; mist 8; went 8l clr 12; unchall aft.*		1
	Oranbay (IRE) (2ow) 6-1 **G Freeney** *In tch; chsd ldr 11; no imp app 2 out; just won battle for 2nd flat; fin tired*	12	2
1087^{4}	**Leatherback (IRE)** (3x) 7-4 **J Owen** *In tch; 8l 3rd app 13; rdn aft 3 out; no imp on wnr; tired when jmpd rt last; just lost battle for 2nd flat*	nk	3
742^{3}	Jims Belief (IRE) 5-4F G Cooper *(xnb) Tk str hld; chsd ldr to 11; wknd app 13; 4th & no ch when pu 14*		P
936^{P}	Owenabue Valley (IRE) 11-2 T Underwood *A last & detach; no ch frm 12; t.o & pu 2 out*		P

OFFICIAL DISTANCES: 15*l*, $\frac{1}{2}$*l* **TIME:** 7min 54.0s **TOTE:** £13.60 **DF:**£3.80

1243 Mens Open, 12st - 16J — 3 ran

997^{5}	**BALLAD (IRE)** 7-4 **A Williams** *Ld/disp til ld 2 out; sn clr.*		1
1030^{1}	**True Chimes**(bl) 9-2 **A Sansome** *(xnb) Ld/disp; mists 14 & 15; hdd 2 out; sn btn; tired when blun last*	15	2
1209^{4}	**Dunrig (IRE)** (7x)(bl) 4-6F **J Owen** *Hld up in 3rd; jmpd slow 7; 3l 3rd when jmpd slow 3 out; sn hrd rdn; no prog.*	2	3

OFFICIAL DISTANCES: 20*l*, 3*l* **TIME:** 8min 01.0s **TOTE:** £3.30 **DF:**£7.10

Fences 5 & 12 were omitted from this and all subsequent races - state of the going; for clarification in these and all subsequent race comments-in-running revised fence numbers have been used

1244 Ladies Open - 11J — 4 ran

1086^{1}	**SPRING GALE (IRE)** (7x) 4-9F **Miss Z Turner** *Tde; ld rnd start; lft disp 2nd 3; rdn to chall app last; ld flat; r.o u.p.*		1
998^{6}	**Borrow Mine (IRE)** 8-1 **Miss L Marriott** *Lft disp 2nd 3; hdwy to ld app 3 out; 4l clr app 2 out; rdn & hdd flat; one pce*	2	2
998^{2}	**Village Copper** 5-2 **Miss H Grissell** *(xnb) Lft in ld 3; hdd app 3 out; wknd app 2 out; t.o*	40	3
1241^{U}	General Confusion (IRE) 8-1 Miss B Czepulkowski *2nd outing; tk keen hld; ld app 2 til pu 3*		P

OFFICIAL DISTANCES: 2*l*, dist **TIME:** 7min 45.0s **TOTE:** £1.80 **DF:**£12.80

Fences 2, 8, 9, 15 & 16 were also omitted from this race and all subsequent races - state of the ground

1245 Restricted, 12st - 11J — 8 ran

944^{U}	**BUCKLAND BOBBY** 14-1 **A Sansome** *Ww in mid-div; lft 2nd 3 out; 4l down app nxt; ld app last; sn clr.*		1
995^{1}	**Gunner Be True** 10-1 **A Corbett** *Ww wl in rr; gd hdwy 8; lft 2nd 3 out; sn ld; hdd app last; no ex.*	10	2
1156^{1}	**Society Scandal (IRE)** 14-1 **P Millington** *Ww in mid-div; went 3rd app 8; lft cl 3rd 3 out; wknd 2 out.*	5	3
999^{6}	Ardnut(bl) 14-1 Miss R Page *Wl bhnd; last frm 4; t.o & pu 3 out*		P
902^{3}	Federal Case (FR) 7-4F A Braithwaite *(xnb) Chsd ldr to 3; mist 6; wknd app 8; t.o & pu 2 out*		P
999^{5}	Lone Star (IRE)(bl) 7-1 H Fowler *Ld; sn wl clr; jnd & blun 3 out but lft clr agn; sn hdd & stpd to nil; pu nxt*		P
1152^{4}	Stick Or Bust(bl) 3-1 M Smith *Chsd clr ldr frm 3; mist 6; 10l down 8; prog to jn ldr when blun & ur 3 out*		U
1030^{3}	Tellaporky(cp) 5-1 J Owen *(xnb) Mid-div; went 3rd 4; jmpd slow 7; wknd app nxt; t.o & pu 2 out*		P

OFFICIAL DISTANCES: 10*l*, 5*l* **TIME:** 7min 53.0s **TOTE:** £16.70 **DF:**£7.70 (1st+any)

1246 Open Maiden, 12st - 10J — 10 ran

1156F **A FINE STORY** 9-2 **A Williams** *Ww in mid-div; went 3rd 5; clsd app 2 out; ld app last; drew clr u.p flat* . . . 1
652F **Another Leader (IRE)** 16-1 **G Cooper** *Ld; sn wl clr; furlong clr 4; still 30l up 3 out; wknd app nxt; 2l ahd 2 out; sn hdd; 3rd & btn last; went 2nd agn nr fin; fin lame* . . . 10 2
1155U **Lightning Fork (IRE)** (5a) 10-1 **M Mackley** *2 handlers; ww wl bhnd; prog to 5th 6; went 2nd 3 out; clsd app nxt; 2l down 2 out; rdn app last; tired & hung rt flat; lost 2nd nr fin* . . . ½ 3
1155² On The Day (IRE) 5-4F J Owen *Chsd clr ldr til app 3 out; sn rdn & no prog* 20 4
1119P Granny Dick (5a) 10-1 A Braithwaite *Reluct to start & lost 30l; hdwy to 4th 6; 3rd 3 out; sn rdn & no prog; 5th & no ch when pu 2 out* . . . P
996P Green Leader (IRE) (5a) 16-1 T Lane *Bhnd til stumbled & ur 6* . . . U
371P Inching Brook 20-1 P Taiano *(xnb) A wl bhnd; t.o & pu 7* . . . P
1155³ Mr Know What (IRE) 6-1 Miss C Bartlett *Mid-div; nvr nr ldrs; lost plce & bhnd 6; t.o & pu aft 3 out* . . . P
525P Namche Bazaar (IRE) 25-1 M Smith *Chsd ldrs in 3rd til wknd qckly aft 4; pu nxt* . . . P
1155P Pernickety King (7a) 25-1 P Millington *A bhnd; nvr nr ldrs; t.o & pu 3 out* . P

OFFICIAL DISTANCES: 3l, nk **TIME:** 7min 44.0s **TOTE:** £4.80 **DF:**£28.80

Fence 1 was also omitted from this race; the rider of Lightning Fork was fined £65 for using the whip excessively in the soft conditions with no response; the rider of A Fine Story, which was slightly marked, was warned about his future use of the whip

Cotley

Cotley Farm (LH 9F,18J)

Mon, 3 May (GOOD)

1247 Hunt Members — 3 ran

697¹ **KNIGHT OF PASSION** 1-4F **Miss C Tizzard** *Made all; 1½l up 6; gd j 13; 6l clr 3 out; lft solo nxt* . . . 1
1010² Dale Creek (IRE) 7-2 M Miller *Chsd ldr; 2l 2nd 5; in tch til grad wknd 14; 6l down when ref 2 out; bbv* . . . r
884⁵ Forglori 12-1 L Tibbatts *A last; sn detach; 10l adrift 6; jmpd violent lft 9; t.o when scrambled over nxt; imm pu* . . . P

OFFICIAL DISTANCE: Finished alone **TIME:** 6min 51.8s **TOTE:** £1.50

1248 Open Maiden 56&7yo, 12st — 5 ran

353P **SEE MORE FUN** 7-2 **N Williams** *7s-7/2; 5½l 3rd 5; chsd ldr nxt; ld 15; hdd nxt; ld agn 2 out; hld on u.p flat* . . . 1
865² **The Nelson Touch** 5-4F **D I Turner** *Last 2; hdwy to 4th 5; disp 3l 3rd 9; rdn app 15; eff & chsd wnr frm 2 out; jmpd lft last; no ex flat* . . . nk 2
1074P **Panto** 12-1 **Miss K Lovelace** *Ld & set mod pce; sn clr; 5l up 5; 1½l up 14; hdd nxt; ld agn brief 3 out; sn hdd & wknd* . . . 15 3
1133C Dart View Lass (5a)(cp) 12-1 N Wilmington *(xnb) Chsd ldr til lost plce & releg last 3; jmpd rt 8; grad lost tch frm nxt; t.o & pu 10* . . . P
Rings Of Power (IRE) 6-4 N Mitchell *Hld up til chsd ldr fm 4; disp 3l 3rd 9; gng wl & clsng on ldr when fell 3 out; poss unlucky* . . . F

OFFICIAL DISTANCES: ½l, 10l **TIME:** 6min 57.6s **TOTE:** £5.00

1249 Mixed Open, 12st — 4 ran

732⁹ **UNLIMITED FREE (IRE)** (7x) 6-4JF **Miss D Harding** *(xnb) Jw; made all; 2l up 6; prsd frm 15; kpt finding ex; drew clr frm last* . . . 1
1010¹ **Red Native (IRE)** (4x) 6-4JF **N Williams** *Chsd ldr til releg last 3; chsd ldr agn frm 9; 3l 2nd 15; rdn & ev ch app 2 out; sn btn* . . . 5 2
1128F **Shanavoher (IRE)** 12-1 **R McCarthy** *Last til hdwy to 2nd 3; 3l 3rd 9; last 10; lost tch 13; t.o frm 15; stayed on one pce to pass toiling rival flat* . . . runin 3
794¹ Simply Sam 11-4 H Fry *(xnb) Mostly 3rd; 3l down 6; releg last 7; 2l 3rd 10; grad outpcd frm 14; t.o frm 3 out; dem flat* . . . 2½ 4

OFFICIAL DISTANCES: 5l, dist **TIME:** 6min 38.2s **TOTE:** £2.50

1250 Countryside Alliance Club Members 10yo&up, 12st — 8 ran

1127^{1}	**LORD OF THE MIST (IRE)** 2-5F **N Williams** *Disp 2½l 3rd 5; chsd ldr 8; mist nxt; gd j 10; ld 15; sn in comm*		1
1100^{2}	**Woodlands Beau (IRE)** (7x) 11-2 **N Mitchell** *Ld til hdd 2; ld agn 8; hdd 15; chsd wnr til no ex frm 2 out*	6	2
1101^{5}	**Millyhenry** (7x) 20-1 **Miss C Tizzard** *Re-plated bef rce; disp 2½l 3rd 5; 2l 2nd 9; grad lost tch w ldng pr frm 14; mist 3 out; stayed on one pce*	20	3
963^{5}	Shock's Pride (IRE) 14-1 M Miller *Chsd ldrs in mostly 3rd to 6; 5½l 5th 9; grad lost tch frm 13; bhnd frm 15*	20	4
1012^{1}	Blackwater Brave (IRE) (7x) 6-1 G Fry *Hld up; 12l 7th 5; nvr trbld ldrs; t.o frm 14*	2½	5
1101^{6}	Cherokee Boy 12-1 Miss C Atkinson *20s-12s; 7l 6th 5; nd & a bhnd; t.o frm 14*	5	6
320^{6}	Touring-Turtle (IRE) (7x) 25-1 W Procter *Chsd ldr til ld 2; blun bad 6; hdd 8; grad wknd frm 12; t.o frm 16*	10	7
1130^{P}	Now Young Man (IRE) (7x) 33-1 Miss P Moore *A rr; 15l last 5; t.o frm 10; plodded home*	1¼fs	8

OFFICIAL DISTANCES: 5*l*, 20*l* **TIME:** 6min 34.5s **TOTE:** £1.40

1251 Restricted, 12st — 6 ran

1008^{2}	**CAPTAIN RANDOM** 2-1 **Mrs J Reed** *(xnb) Chsd ldrs; 6l 3rd 5; chsd ldr frm 11; 2½l down 14; ld nxt; in comm when lft virt solo last*		1
912^{7}	**Wicked Imp** 12-1 **Miss S Robinson** *Chsd ldr; blun 6; ½l down 9; disp ld brief app nxt; wknd qckly 12; t.o frm 14; mist 3 out; lft rem 2nd last*	30	2
689^{P}	**Dursey Island (IRE)** 9-2 **M Miller** *Mostly 4th; 12l adrift 5; outpcd frm 12; t.o frm 14; plodded home*	15	3
1009^{1}	Harjach 6-4F N Wilmington *(xnb) 5/2-6/4; 2 handlers; ld; 2½l up 5; jnd brief app 10; sn clr agn; hdd 15; chsng wnr & hld when pu last; broke down; collected by horse box*		P
1098^{P}	Queens House (5a) 20-1 D Drake *Chsd ldr 1; lost plce qckly; jmpd slow nxt; 20l 5th 6; t.o frm 9; pu aft 11*		P
689^{P}	Winsley Spirit (5a) 6-1 N Mitchell *(xnb) A last & outpcd qckly; t.o frm 9; pu nxt*		P

OFFICIAL DISTANCES: 25*l*, 20*l* **TIME:** 6min 46.0s **TOTE:** £1.60

1252 Open Maiden 8yo&up, 12st — 9 ran

1009^{2}	**COLLIER** 2-1F **T Atkinson** *Trckd ldr frm 4; 1l down 6; ld 9; 6l clr nxt; sn drew away; stayed on wl frm 3 out*		1
967^{2}	**Bradford Bridge** (5a) 11-4 **D Alers-Hankey** *Ld; 1l up 6; hdd 9; 8½l 3rd 11; mist 12; chsd wnr vain frm nxt; brief eff app 3 out; btn when mist last*	8	2
967^{3}	**My Brother Jack** 10-1 **Miss K Lovelace** *Mostly mid-div; hdwy to 3rd 7; chsd ldng pr frm 14; one pce frm nxt*	20	3
1009^{P}	Ashwicke Gambler 10-1 T Dreaper *(xnb) 20s-10s; sa; last til stdy hdwy to 6th 10; staying on when pu 14; saddle slpd*		P
1132^{F}	Bally Lir Lady (5a) 5-1 R McCarthy *Towards rr; hdwy to disp 4l 3rd 9; chsd ldr & mist nxt; wknd 13; t.o & pu 2 out*		P
865^{B}	Coastal Flight 8-1 Miss R Green *(bh) Hld up; hdwy & disp 3l 4th 6; chsd ldng pr 9; wknd 12; bhnd when pu 14*		P
1132^{U}	Little Mister(cp) 33-1 D Drake *Chsd ldr til grad lost plce frm 5; jmpd slow nxt; rmdr 8; t.o & pu 12*		P
967^{R}	Nobody's Heroine (5a) 12-1 N Wilmington *(xnb) Chsd ldrs; disp 3l 4th 6; wkng when mist 9; t.o last when pu 11*		P
693^{P}	Sure How Bad (IRE) 10-1 L Tibbatts *Prom; 1½l 3rd 6; grad lost plce frm 9; wknd 11; bhnd when pu 14*		P

OFFICIAL DISTANCES: 15*l*, 20*l* **TIME:** 6min 47.5s **TOTE:** £2.00

North Ledbury

Maisemore Park (LH 7F,18J)

Mon, 3 May (GOOD to SOFT)

1253 Hunt Members, 12st — 8 ran

835^{P}	**BEYOND THE STARS** (5x) 3-1 **Miss K Phillips** *Tde; hld up; last 8; 7l 6th ½way; went 8l 4th 13 & 9l 3rd aft 3 out; str rn to ld aft nxt; clr when blun last; rdly*		1
1137^{2}	**Welburn Boy**(bl,tt) 7-2 **Miss L Allfrey** *2nd til aft 8; 3½l 4th ½way; went 4l 3rd aft 12; qcknd to ld app 3 out; sn 7l clr; hdd & no ex app last*	7	2

662P	**Bansha House**(tt) 5-1 **S Joynes** *Nt fluent; hld up; went 2nd aft 8; mist 12; ld 14 til app 3 out; disp 2l 2nd & rdn 2 out; sn wknd*	12	3
410P	Terimon's Dream 12-1 D Mansell *(xnb) Tde; ld; sn 7l clr to 8; blun 13; hdd 14; wknd 3 out*	15	4
927P	Himalayan Heights(tt) 20-1 R Rogers *(xnb) Prom til lost plce 9; 7½l last & rdn ½way; lost tch 14; t.o.*	runin	5
1069P	Derrys Prerogative 14-1 Miss N Rudge *Prom til lost plce & 6l 5th ½way; 10l 6th & rdn 12; wl bhnd when pu 14.*		P
1069P	Make Up Your Mind (IRE) 16-1 B Gallagher *Swtng; ss; mist 1; hmpd bend aft 6; hdwy 9; 2½l 3rd ½way; wknd qckly aft 12; wl bhnd when tried to ref & ur 14*		U
1016F	Southern Cross 2-1F T Stephenson *3s-2s; fcng wrong way start & lft 40l; t.o til pu aft 7*		P

OFFICIAL DISTANCES: 5*l*, 10*l* **TIME:** 7min 11.7s

1254 Confined, 12st — 8 ran

726¹	**BEAUCHAMP ORACLE** 4-7F **S Hughes** *Hld up; last to 4; 5l 7th ½way; 5l last 14; went 2l 4th nxt; ld aft 3 out; 5l clr 2 out; rdn out*		1
1073²	**The Campdonian (IRE)** (3x) 3-1 **Miss P Gundry** *Ld to 6; 2nd to 14; 1l 3rd 3 out; chsd wnr 2 out; kpt on wl*	3	2
1135¹	**The Writer (IRE)** 10-1 **R Hodges** *(xnb) W ldrs; 4l 6th ½way; 3l 4th 14; rdn when mist nxt; went 6l 3rd 2 out; one pce*	5	3
1071³	Stennikov (IRE) 7-2 E Walker *(xnb) Prom; 2l 3rd ½way; 4l 5th & rdn 14; wknd 2 out; eased when btn flat*	12	4
662P	Highbridge (IRE) (3x) 20-1 R Hughes *(xnb) Went 2nd 5; ld 6 til aft 3 out; wknd 2 out*	3	5
921³	Aldington Charlie (3ow) 20-1 C Sands *2nd to 3; last nxt; lost tch & mist 11; t.o & pu aft 13*		P
1172P	Macy (IRE) (3x)(cp) 20-1 A Wintle *Prom; 3l 4th ½way; went 1l 2nd & drvn 14; wknd qckly u.p 3 out; t.o & pu last*		P
1015³	The Archdeacon (IRE) 14-1 T Stephenson *Hld up; disp 3l 4th ½way; 5l 7th & rdn when fell 13.*		F

OFFICIAL DISTANCES: 4*l*, 5*l* **TIME:** 7min 04.9s

1255 Ladies Open — 4 ran

1017¹	**UPTON ADVENTURE** (5a) 1-6F **Miss E James** *Lw; oft jw; ld til aft 1; ld 7; qcknd 7l clr 14; unchall aft; lft virt solo 2 out*		1
1141U	**Rosemead Tye** (5a) 16-1 **Miss A de Lisle Wells** *Ld aft 1-2; 8l 3rd ½way; went 2nd aft 10 til aft nxt; wknd 14; lft rem 2nd 2 out.*	1¼fs	2
757F	Owl Vulgan (IRE) 10-1 Mrs K Baimbridge *Ld 2-7; 2nd & rmdrs ½way; releg last 11; lost tch & pu aft nxt*		P
	Scarrots 10-1 Miss E Tuck *Bckwd; ss; last til went 2nd aft 11; outpcd 14; no imp 3 out; stpd to nil & pu in wings 2 out*		P

OFFICIAL DISTANCE: dist **TIME:** 7min 08.4s

1256 Restricted, 12st — 7 ran

1063²	**LORD KEN (IRE)**(vis) 5-2F **N Phillips** *(bf) Nt jw; went 2nd 3; ld 5 til downed tools & hdd 7; mist 12; 2nd/3rd til mist & lost plce 14; 10l 6th & rdn nxt; rallied u.p 2 out; stayed on to ld nr fin*		1
839³	**Justadream** 3-1 **T Stephenson** *Hld up; hdwy 8; 4½l 5th ½way; mist 10; disp 3l 4th 12; went 4l 2nd 15; ld app last; hdd nr fin*	nk	2
925⁴	**Who's Eddie (IRE)** 3-1 **M Rimell** *(xnb) Lw; a.p; went 2nd 7 til 2l 3rd ½way; qcknd to ld aft 14; sn 4l clr; hdd u.p app last; one pce*	1¼	3
921U	Sparkling Cascade (IRE) (5a) 7-2 Mrs K Baimbridge *Hld up; 5l 6th ½way; hdwy 14; 6l 4th nxt; went 4l 3rd 3 out; rdn 2 out; kpt on*	nk	4
977⁵	Primitive Son 5-1 Miss E James *Hld up; last to 7; hdwy & 4l 4th ½way; went 5l 3rd 15; 6l 4th & wkng when mist nxt; pu 2 out*		P
	Rocky Balboa 14-1 G Barfoot-Saunt *Nt fluent; 2nd to 3; last 7; mist & lost tch 13; t.o & pu 2 out*		P
759P	Spring Cabbage (IRE) 8-1 Julian Pritchard *Ld; blun 4; hdd 5; ld 7 til hdd & stpd to nil aft 14; wl bhnd when pu 3 out*		P

OFFICIAL DISTANCES: ½*l*, 1*l* **TIME:** 7min 14.6s

1257 Mens Open, 12st — 3 ran

1066[1] **LE CURE** 7-2 **J Barnes** *(xnb) Last til jmpd to ld 8; hdd aft nxt; ld 11; 4l clr 15; a in comm aft; hld on wl flat* . . . 1
1138[1] **Teme Willow (IRE)** (7x) 4-11F **Julian Pritchard** *Jmpd rt; ld to 8 & 10-11; lkd labouring 14; swished tail u.p aft 3 out; drvn & stayed on 2 out; unable to qckn flat* . . . ¾ 2
1168[F] **Dinsey Finnegan (IRE)**(cp) 11-2 **N Phillips** *(bf) Jmpd rt; nvr gng particularly keen; 2nd to 8; 9l 3rd ½way; rdn & no resp 12; sn wl bhnd.* . . . 20 3

OFFICIAL DISTANCES: ¾*l*, 20*l* **TIME:** 7min 08.5s

1258 Open Maiden 8yo&up, 12st — 8 ran

981[3] **AUTCAESAR AUTNIHIL (IRE)** 9-2 **M Munrowd** *Hld up; last 2-4; hdwy 6; lft in ld 7-10; ld 12; qcknd 14; 7l clr nxt; stayed on wl 2 out.* . . . 1
730[2] **Billy Whitelies (IRE)** 5-4F **S Joynes** *Ld til blun 7; 2nd til ld app 11; hdd nxt; lost 2nd 15; 10l 3rd & no imp 3 out; went 2nd nr fin* . . . 10 2
981[2] **Chateau Burf** 2-1 **H Dowty** *2 handlers; swtng; went 2nd aft 1-6; lost plce 8; hdwy & disp 2l 3rd ½way; went 7l 2nd 15; rdn & fnd nil 2 out; dem nr fin* ½ 3
Master Cruise 12-1 Julian Pritchard *Hld up; 3½l 5th ½way; 8l 5th 14; went 14l 4th aft nxt; no imp* . . . 7 4
Chief Wallah 12-1 Miss A de Lisle Wells *(bh) Swtng; 2nd/3rd 4-9; 2½l 4th ½way; wknd 11; pu aft nxt* . . . P
1020[P] Contrary King(vis) 14-1 T Weston *Tde; v unruly start; prom; mist 8; 2l 3rd ½way; 7l 4th & rdn 14; wkng when mist nxt; 17l 5th when pu 3 out.* . . . P
730[3] The Grandson (IRE) 12-1 D Mansell *(bf) 2nd til aft 1; jmpd slow & rmdrs 2; 5l 6th ½way; rdn 10; lost tch & pu aft 12; dism* . . . P
940[F] Winnick (IRE) 7-1 G Barfoot-Saunt *(xnb) Hld up; last 4; lost tch 12; t.o & pu 3 out; bbv* . . . P

OFFICIAL DISTANCES: 10*l*, ½*l* **TIME:** 7min 16.5s

1259 Open Maiden 56&7yo, 12st — 9 ran

837[P] **THE BROOKLET** 10-1 **Julian Pritchard** *Ld aft 3-7; 2nd til ld 15; qcknd 6l clr aft nxt; blun 2 out; r.o wl.* . . . 1
926[2] **Che Guevara**(tt) 5-4F **A Wintle** *Hld up; last to 4; stdy hdwy 8; went 5l 3rd ½way & 2nd aft 15; outpcd aft nxt; rdn 2 out; no imp.* . . . 12 2
983[P] **Treasulier (IRE)** 8-1 **R Hodges** *Pulled hrd; w ldrs; 5½l 4th ½way; lost plce 12; wl bhnd 15; went poor 3rd app last.* . . . 15 3
982[3] Fencethegap (IRE) 7-1 M Hooper *Sn prom; went 2nd 6; ld 7-15; wknd aft 3 out* 10 4
982[P] Ashor Ted(cp) 14-1 S Bush *(xnb) Hld up; mists 6 & 8; 7½l 7th & rdn ½way; blun 11; lost tch 13; wl bhnd when pu 15* . . . P
983[P] Cathy Come Home (IRE) (5a) 7-1 G Barfoot-Saunt *Hld up & sev posns; 7l 6th ½way; 8l 5th when tried to ref & blun bad & ur 12.* . . . U
724[P] Just Henry(tt) 16-1 S Joynes *(xnb) Ld til aft 3; 2nd/3rd to 9; 6½l 5th ½way; wknd qckly 10; last when pu 11* . . . P
883[P] Nearly A Mildred (5a) 13-2 Miss A Goschen *(xnb) 8s-13/2; drpd back last 4; 9l 6th 12; went 8l 4th nxt; wknd 15; t.o & pu 2 out* . . . P
392[2d] Tap Dance 5-2 Adam Brown *Hld up; rmdrs 9; 10l 8th ½way; mist 10; last when pu aft 12; lame* . . . P

OFFICIAL DISTANCES: 12*l*, 14*l* **TIME:** 7min 14.5s

South Shropshire

Eyton-on-Severn (LH 12F,17J)

Mon, 3 May (GOOD with GOOD to SOFT patches)

1260 Hunt Members, 12st — 3 ran

932[2] **INDIAN WINGS (IRE)** (5x) 1-4F **R Burton** *Ww; 4l last til clsd up 10; 2nd 11; ld 2 out; pushed out; unimpressive* . . . 1
930[2] **Oneanthreequarters (IRE)** 5-2 **R Jagger** *Ld; jnd 6; hdd 8; ld agn 9-2 out; kpt on one pce* . . . 3 2
668[P] **Strong Weld** 12-1 **D Sherlock** *(xnb) Pulling; 2nd til jmpd to disp ld 6; ld brief 8; dem last 11; outpcd app 3 out; imm btn* . . . 10 3

OFFICIAL DISTANCES: 4*l*, 15*l* **TIME:** 6min 39.0s **TOTE:** £1.20

1261 Open Maiden, 12st — 13 ran

934^{2}	**CORKY BROWNE** 9-2 **Miss J Perry** *Cl up; ld frm 7-9; prsd ldr aft; ldng pr wl clr 3 out; 2l 2nd nxt; ld last; drvn out*		1
934^{3}	**Benbow** 9-4F **B Shaw** *Hld up in mid-div; trckd ldrs frm 7; cl 4th 12; ld 14 til hdd last; no ex; easily outbattled.*	4	2
	Money Magic (5a) 8-1 **J R Barlow** *Sn prom; ld frm 3-6; prom bhnd ldrs til outpcd frm 12; no ch aft; dist 4th 3 out; lft rem 3rd nxt*	30	3
1142^{2}	Snitton Salvo(bl) 10-1 M Jackson *A rr of main group; 10l 6th 12; plodded on; tk dist 4th at last*	15	4
1119^{U}	Ridware Rose (5a) 10-1 Miss S Sharratt *Ld 1; chsd ldrs aft; 2l 2nd 11; outpcd by ldng pr frm 13; wknd rap; lft dist 4th by 2 out; jmpd slow & dem at last*	5	5
709^{P}	Bless Yourself (IRE)(bl) 4-1 R Burton *Sn prom bhnd ldrs; cl 6th 7; ld frm 10-13; wknd qckly to 3rd nxt; 25l 3rd & v tired when pu 2 out*		P
	Castle Frome (IRE) (7a) 20-1 Miss R Reynolds *Prom til blun 3; rap lost plce; t.o when ref 6*		r
	Effessbee 8-1 Mrs E Gilruth *(xnb) Sn prom; ld frm 5-6; lost plce rap & t.o 10; blun & ur 12*		U
	Gunnaballright 12-1 N Pearce *Jmpd stickily in rr; lsng tch 6; virt t.o when bd 8*		B
753^{P}	Leicaree (IRE) 6-1 G Hanmer *Sn strugg & last 5; t.o & pu 8.*		P
981^{P}	Plenty Inn Hand 12-1 A Hanly *Tde; sn prom; chsd ldrs til outpcd & drpd to rr 10; t.o & pu 13*		P
1148^{2}	Royrace 10-1 W Kinsey *Prsd ldrs to 6; still cl up when fell 7*		F
984^{5}	Single Man (IRE) 20-1 J Burley *Cl up in mid-div; 4l 5th 7; 7th & wkng when fell hvly 12*		F

OFFICIAL DISTANCES: 5*l*, 20*l* **TIME:** 6min 27.0s **TOTE:** £3.00

1262 Mens Open, 12st — 4 ran

1015^{1}	**HOT TODDY (IRE)** 4-9F **R Burton** *Ww; 4l 3rd 9; went 2nd 10; hit 3 out; rdn & disp ld 2 out; slt advant last; rdn out; unimpressive.*		1
932^{P}	**Raconteur (IRE)** 5-1 **D Greenway** *12s-5s; pulling; hld up in 5l 3rd 3; 3l 3rd 11; prsd ldrs 14; rdn & ev ch 2 out; nt qckn last*	2	2
1121^{4}	**Smile Pleeze (IRE)** (4x) 4-1 **N Pearce** *Prsd ldr til ld brief 6; disp ld 8; ld agn 9; jnd 2 out; hdd app last; no ex flat.*	1½	3
1145^{2}	Harry Hotspur (IRE) (7x)(bl) 12-1 M Dearden *(xnb) Ld at crawl to 5; ld agn 7; jnd 8; dem last 10; wknd v qckly; t.o 13*	1½fs	4

OFFICIAL DISTANCES: 2*l*, 10*l* **TIME:** 6min 44.0s **TOTE:** £1.50

1263 Ladies Open — 11 ran

931^{3}	**STRETCHING (IRE)** (7x) 5-1 **Miss J Williams** *7s-5s; trckd ldng pr in 3rd; 10l 3rd 8; stdy hdwy frm 12; narrow advant aft 3 out; 2l up nxt; stdd last; stayed on.*		1
1146^{1}	**Jackie Jarvis (IRE)** (5a, 7x) 5-2 **Mrs K Diggle** *2 handlers; mounted on course; ld in start; sn chsng ldrs; 10l 5th 6; hdwy 12; went 4th 14; disp 2nd 3 out; ½l 2nd when blun 2 out; rdn & kpt on app last; no ex cl home.*	2	2
931^{4}	**Dancetillyoudrop (IRE)** (7x) 14-1 **Miss T Tellwright** *(xnb) Ld 2; prsd ldr aft til outpcd frm 13; no ch 3 out; kpt on one pce; tk 3rd app last.*	10	3
1046^{1}	Wandering Light (IRE) (7x) 3-1 Miss T Clark *Opened 7/2; nvr able to go pce; 8l 4th 6; 8l 5th 10; kpt on one pce frm 3 out; went 4th at last*	2	4
748^{U}	City Gent 6-1 Miss S Sharratt *Ld 1 & frm 3 til app 3 out; imm outpcd by ldng pr; wknd qckly to 5th last; fin tired*	5	5
253^{F}	Ghutah 14-1 Miss J Owen *(xnb) Rr; 22l last 4; went dist 10th 6; plodded rnd*	35	6
1046^{2}	Cascum Lad (IRE) 6-1 Miss S Holmes *Mid-div; outpcd frm 9; 20l 7th 11; t.o & pu 14*		P
1137^{3}	Flying Pennant (IRE) 33-1 Miss S Davies *Chsd ldrs in mid-div til hopelessly outpcd 9; t.o by 10; hmpd & ur 12*		U
931^{1}	Pacon (GER) (7x) 2-1F Miss H Kinsey *(xnb) Opened 5/2; rr; 15l 7th 10; brief eff nxt; no hdwy; t.o & pu 2 out*		P
	Shady Affair (IRE) 10-1 Miss C Hurley *(xnb) 20l 10th 4; last nxt; trudged rnd in rr til event pu last*		P
1118^{U}	Strong Chairman (IRE) 14-1 Mrs V Thirlby *Chsd ldrs to 6; sn completely outpcd; t.o when fell 12*		F

OFFICIAL DISTANCES: 3*l*, dist **TIME:** 6min 21.0s **TOTE:** £6.00

1264 Confined, 12st — 2 ran

928^{1} **PRISTEEN SPY** (3x) 1-5F **R Burton** *(xnb) Made all; a 5-6l clr of rival; unchall* — 1
989^{P} **Double Rich**(tt) 5-2 **O Greenall** *(xnb) A 5-6l last; rdn 2 out; no imp* . . . . . — 6 — 2

OFFICIAL DISTANCE: 6*l* **TIME:** 6min 29.0s **TOTE:** £1.20

1265 Restricted, 12st — 18 ran

994^{P} **SHRADEN EDITION** evensF **D Barlow** *2s-evens; a handy & gng wl; trckd clr ldr in 3rd/4th to 8; smooth hdwy 9 to ld 3 out; stayed on wl* . . . . — 1
834^{5} **Sabena Canyon** 20-1 **M Wall** *Oht; trckd ldrs; hdwy 10; 5l 4th 14; prsd ldr aft; 1l 2nd & ev ch 3 out; no ex last* . . . . — 2 — 2
John Foley (IRE) 3-1 **P Morris** *Ld frm 2; 6l up 8; ld cut to 2l 10; hdd 14; chsd ldng pr vain aft; no ch 2 out; btr for rn* . . . . — 10 — 3
929^{1} Mountsorrel (IRE) (7a) 7-1 B Shaw *2 handlers; mid-div; 8l 6th 11; no imp 3 out* . . . . — 8 — 4
1148^{4} Lily Brown (5a) 14-1 Mrs S Johnson *(xnb) Trckd ldrs in 5/6th; 5l 5th 11; wknd 3 out* . . . . — 6 — 5
1044^{1} Ridware George(vis) 6-1 Miss S Sharratt *Chsd ldrs in 2nd/3rd to 11; lost tch v qckly & no ch by 14; plodded on.* . . . . — 3 — 6
1048^{2} Clodagh Valley (IRE) 6-1 W Kinsey *Mid-div; 11th 7; outpcd & bhnd 10; 25l 7th 3 out.* . . . . — 2 — 7
928^{U} Home Tor 4-1 J Jarrett *Trckd ldrs; 6l 5th 9; 2l 2nd 13; ld brief nxt; imm wknd v rap & sn wl in rr; virt t.o last* . . . . — 20 — 8
1148^{5} Hill Of Kilfeacle (IRE)(tt) 12-1 D Greenway *2 handlers; sn strugg to go pce; 9th 7; t.o frm 12* . . . . — 3 — 9
1114^{U} Gaetano (IRE) 20-1 J O'Brien *Chsd ldrs in 2nd/3rd to 12; wknd v rap; hopelessly t.o 3 out; staggered on; barely cantering last* . . . . — fence — 10
252^{7} Bobtail (IRE) (7a) 6-1 R Burton *(xnb) Mid-div; outpcd ldrs 7; nvr gng aft; wknd 14; dist 8th when pu 2 out* . . . . — P
889^{P} Fiesty Frosty (IRE) (5a) 20-1 N Pearce *Nt fluent & a rr; 30l 17th 7; last when pu 14* . . . . — P
1147^{4} Gabaka De Thaix (FR) 20-1 M Caldwell *Jmpd poor; last 6; t.o 7; miles bhnd when pu 12* . . . . — P
1048^{P} Henbury Dancer (5a) 10-1 G Hanmer *20l 6th 5; a wl in rr; t.o & pu 3 out* . — P
Rich Return (IRE) 14-1 C Faulkner *Barely raised a gallop & imm t.o; jmpd appalling; ref 6* . . . . — r
1069^{4} Shafts Chance (IRE) (5a) 6-1 Miss K Wood *(xnb) Sn bhnd; t.o 12; rn out thro wing & ur 14; hdd into distance* . . . . — R
1148^{3} Snitton West 16-1 M Jackson *Sn outpcd in mid-div; rr 12; t.o & pu last* . . — P
1048^{P} Templenoe Hare (IRE) 12-1 A Wadlow *Nvr gng wl in rr; rem 16th when fell 10* — F

OFFICIAL DISTANCES: 3*l*, 8*l* **TIME:** 6min 22.0s **TOTE:** £3.00

1266 Open Maiden 56&7yo, 2m4f, 12st - 13J — 14 ran

929^{2} **REFLECTED GLORY (IRE)** (7a) 9-4 **R Burton** *2 handlers; hld up in 4/5th; clsd up 7; ld 10; jmpd rt 3 out; jmpd violent rt & nrly rn off course 2 out; sn in comm agn; rdn out* . . . . — 1
1049^{R} **Mervsintrouble**(cp) 6-1 **D Greenway** *Prom in 5/6th; chsd ldr frm 7; no ch w wnr 3 out; kpt on one pce; tk 2nd flat; nrst fin* . . . . — 10 — 2
1049^{2} **Carnalway (IRE)** 5-1 **D Barlow** *Opened 6s; hld up; chsd ldrs 8; 4l 2nd 10; ev ch til wknd 2 out; dem 3rd flat.* . . . . — 1 — 3
1049^{P} Button Lady (12a) 16-1 D Gaiter *Sn outpcd in mid-div; no ch frm 7; plodded on miles bhnd; lft v rem 4th by defections last* . . . . — fence — 4
929^{F} Beauchamp Brook 5-1 A Phillips *Opened 6s; ld 3; prsd ldr aft til wknd 10; no ch aft; 35l 4th when barely rose, crashed over & ur last.* . . . . — U
1142^{U} Bradogue (IRE)(tt) 8-1 D Sherlock *Rr; v slow & rdn 2; labouring aft; t.o & pu 8* — P
983^{3} Evanly Miss (5a)(bl) 12-1 M Jackson *Ld to 2 & frm aft 3-9; sn lost plce; wknd v rap; t.o & pu 2 out* . . . . — P
1115^{P} Kotori (IRE) (7a) 10-1 S Gray *(xnb) A wl in rr; t.o 6; pu 9* . . . . — P
890^{6} Major Reno (IRE) 16-1 J Newbold *(xnb) 20s-16s; mid-div; ab 8l 7/8th when fell 7* . . . . — F
Mistress Return (12a) 2-1F G Hanmer *Mounted on course; 11th & mist 1; nvr gng & a wl in rr aft; pushed along & no resp 5; t.o & pu 2 out* . . . . — P
1049^{P} Muqadars Delight (7a) 10-1 B Shaw *Mid-div; chsd ldr to 5; wknd; virt t.o when fell 10* . . . . — F
982^{4} Norbert (IRE) 12-1 A Hanly *20s-12s; chsd ldrs; 4l 3rd when fell 7* . . . . . . — F

	Rouge Lady (5a) 20-1 K Pearson *A rr; t.o 8; rn out 10*		R
	Smarties Surprise (IRE) 20-1 W Kinsey *Imm last; t.o & pu 9*		P

OFFICIAL DISTANCES: 10*l*, 1*l* **TIME:** 5min 18.0s **TOTE:** £1.50

Stevenstone

Vauterhill (RH 7F,19J)

Mon, 3 May (GOOD/GOOD to FIRM)

1267 Hunt Members, 12st — 4 ran

	RICE POINT 3-1 **L Heard** *Hld up; hdwy to ld 3 out; comf*		1
793^{4}	**O So Bossy** 4-6F **Miss S Young** *Set stdy pce; hdd 3 out; r.o one pce*	2½	2
824^{6}	**Change** 7-2 **T Dennis** *Chsd ldrs in mostly 2nd; mists; lost tch aft 16*	25	3
1133^{C}	Some Tool 14-1 R Ross *Lost tch aft 13; 25l down in 4th when pu 16*		P

OFFICIAL DISTANCES: 2*l*, 20*l* **TIME:** 6min 28.0s

1268 Restricted, 12st - 18J — 11 ran

1002^{U}	**BUDGHILL** 8-1 **C Heard** *Hld up; hdwy aft 13; 3rd 3 out; chall last; r.o str.*		1
1167^{P}	**Indian Raider (IRE)** 6-1 **A Glassonbury** *Trckd ldrs mostly in 2nd & 3rd; ld app last; hdd cl home*	½	2
824^{P}	**My Jess** (5a) 16-1 **M Sweetland** *Hld up; hdwy aft 14; 4th 3 out; rap late hdwy to tk 3rd on line*	5	3
966^{P}	Horrified(bl) 10-1 D Edwards *A.p; lft in ld 9; hdd app last; no ex & wknd flat; dem on line*	s hd	4
572^{2}	Aller Coombe (5a) 4-1 L Jefford *Trckd ldrs; cl 4th 14; outpcd aft 16*	8	5
	Take The Brush (IRE) (5a) 14-1 Miss T Hayes *Hld up & mostly rr; kpt on final stages*	8	6
1131^{3}	Chapners Cross 9-2 Miss S Young *Ld 6 til fell 8*		F
1132^{P}	Derrilady (5a) 66-1 L Rowe *Disp ld when fell 4*		F
821^{4}	Persian Dawn (5a) 20-1 S Kidston *In tch til wknd app 3 out; tlng off when pu last*		P
912^{8}	Porto (IRE)(tt) 14-1 Richard Darke *In tch til wknd 16; 30l down when pu 3 out*		P
966^{3}	Zakley 11-10F A Farrant *Cl up to 14; wknd app 16; 25l down when pu 3 out; lame.*		P

OFFICIAL DISTANCES: ½*l*, 5*l* **TIME:** 6min 29.0s

Fence 15 omitted - fallen horse

1269 Mixed Open, 12st — 4 ran

1073^{U}	**VIVID IMAGINATION (IRE)** (7a) 2-5F **A Farrant** *A cl up; ld 14; 5l up 3 out; qcknd when chall app last*		1
911^{2}	**Hasten Bak** 8-1 **Miss L Gardner** *Hld up; hdwy to 2nd 15; rdn to chall aft 2 out; no ex last*	8	2
634^{3}	**Porlock Hill** (7x) 7-1 **D Edwards** *Disp ld to 14; sn rdn & wknd*	15	3
1127^{2}	Morris Piper 7-2 R Woollacott *Jmpd slow at times; rr; rdn by 13; lost tch & wknd app 16; 25l down when pu 3 out*		P

OFFICIAL DISTANCES: 8*l*, 15*l* **TIME:** 6min 15.0s

1270 Confined, 12st — 3 ran

1129^{1}	**FATHER MANSFIELD (IRE)** 4-9F **Miss C Prouse** *Cl up; pulled ahd 14; hdd 3 out; ld agn nxt; r.o wl*		1
821^{2}	**Squaddie** 7-4 **A Farrant** *Trckd ldrs; ld 3 out; jmpd slow & hdd 2 out; r.o one pce*	2	2
911^{4}	**Calleva Star (IRE)** 12-1 **S Kidston** *Disp ld til wknd app 14*	25	3

OFFICIAL DISTANCES: 1½*l*, 20*l* **TIME:** 6min 29.0s

1271 Intermediate, 12st — 5 ran

1002^{1}	**MYSTIC WARRIOR (USA)** 3-1 **Miss T Cave** *A cl up; disp ld frm 15; ld last; rdn out*		1
794^{U}	**State Medlar** 4-1 **R Woollacott** *Jw; made most; outpcd app last; r.o game .*	½	2
823^{3}	**Drumhorc (IRE)** 3-1 **Miss L Gardner** *Mist 3; chsd ldrs mostly in 3rd; outpcd frm 16*	15	3
823^{F}	Stone Valley 13-8F A Charles-Jones *Hld up; hdwy to 3rd 15; no ex*	s hd	4
1002^{P}	Black A Brook (IRE) (5a)(cp) 7-1 L Jefford *In tch til wknd aft 13; 25l down when pu 16*		P

OFFICIAL DISTANCES: hd, 8*l* **TIME:** 6min 18.0s

1272 Open Maiden, 12st — 12 ran

Form	Horse	Dist	Pos
796^{2}	**SOUND SENSE** 2-1F **A Charles-Jones** *Trckd ldrs; ld 3 out; r.o wl*		1
967^{P}	**Polar Bright (IRE)** 14-1 **D Edwards** *A.p; ld 15; hdd 3 out; kpt on*	4	2
827^{3}	**Terino** 3-1 **Richard Darke** *Mid-div; hdwy to 4th 15 & 3rd at last; stayed on*	½	3
826^{3}	Nditlir (12a) 9-2 C Heard *Made most; outpcd aft 16; r.o game aft 2 out*	1	4
795^{P}	Finbar (IRE) 10-1 Miss L Gardner *Trckd ldrs; outpcd aft 14; r.o final stages*	8	5
795^{4}	Mo's O Friendly 16-1 A Glassonbury *A mid-div; outpcd aft 16*	3	6
913^{P}	Golden Tanu 16-1 D McKenna *Rr when pu 10*		P
486^{5}	Jaunty Janner 10-1 T Dennis *Cl up; some slow js; 20l down & fdng when pu 16*		P
913^{P}	Lamerton Quest 50-1 L Rowe *Hld up; a towards rr; tlng off when pu 15*		P
	National Debt 5-1 R Woollacott *Hld up; hdwy to disp ld 14; cl up when wknd qckly & pu 16*		P
1186^{P}	Phanthom Walker(bl) 12-1 L Jefford *A rr; t.o when pu 16*		P
	Roberts Return 20-1 M Woodward *Rn out 1*		R

OFFICIAL DISTANCES: 4*l*, ½*l* **TIME:** 6min 27.0s

Warwickshire

Ashorne (RH 8F,18J)

Mon, 3 May (GOOD to SOFT, HOLDING patches)

1273 Open Maiden (Div 1), 12st — 7 ran

Form	Horse	Dist	Pos
589^{4}	**KUPTO (FR)** 7-4F **P Cowley** *3s-7/4; ld to 3; prsd ldr til outpcd 3 out; rallied last; finally wore down rival u.p nr fin*		1
837^{2}	**Fergal's Find (IRE)** (7a)(tt) 9-4 **M Goldstein** *Oft nt fluent; ld 3; drew 5l clr & lkd wnr 3 out; hrd prsd frm last; hdd cl home*	nk	2
1125^{P}	**Holly Park** (5a) 33-1 **Miss N Hickling** *Sn last pr; 30l 5th 8; mist 11; t.o & show-jmpng frm 14*	1min	3
	Froghole Flyer (7a) 5-1 S Morris *(xnb) Unruly padd & lkd a character; hld up & at least 10l frm ldng pr; oft jmpd novicey; strugg when mist 13; jmpd slow nxt; 25l 3rd 3 out; pu nxt*		P
	Lagan Lady (5a) 16-1 J King *Mists in last pr; 32l last 8; t.o & mist 12; pu nxt*		P
1035^{S}	Rockford (IRE)(bl) 5-1 C Wadland *10s-5s; midfield; hmpd 5; jmpd slow 7; 13l 4th & strugg aft 10; hit 11 & ur*		U
1035^{S}	Ski Country (5a) 14-1 B Pauling *Mist 4; 4th when fell 5*		F

OFFICIAL DISTANCES: ½*l*, dist **TIME:** 7min 09.0s

1274 Confined, 12st — 6 ran

Form	Horse	Dist	Pos
783^{1}	**COOLEFIND (IRE)** 11-10F **S Morris** *Lw; hld up; last to 7; went cl 3rd aft 10 & 2nd app 15; ev ch when pckd bad 2 out; ld last; drvn clr.*		1
1014^{1}	**Carthago (IRE)** 6-5 **M Harris** *Ld 1 & agn 8; hrd prsd frm 3 out; hdd & nt fluent last; eased when btn cl home*	5	2
922^{2}	**Tom Putt** 7-1 **B Pauling** *Mostly cl 2nd to 14; 6l 3rd & wkng nxt; fin tired*	15	3
943^{P}	Drum Battle (5x)(vis) 16-1 T Messenger *(xnb) Lw; ld aft 1-8; reluct u.p 11 & lost tch; t.o 13*	runin	4
1120^{12}	Camitrov (FR) 33-1 G Kerr *(xnb) Last frm 7; hit 9; lost tch & mist 10; sn t.o; mist 12; toddled on fncs bhnd*	runin	5
	Regency Rake 14-1 Miss R Davidson *Bckwd; cl up; 2l 4th 14; wknd rap app nxt; t.o & pu last*		P

OFFICIAL DISTANCES: 2½*l*, 20*l* **TIME:** 6min 47.0s

1275 Open Maiden (Div 2), 12st — 10 ran

Form	Horse	Dist	Pos
1125^{2}	**NORTHSPRITE**(cp) 5-2 **J Trice-Rolph** *(xnb) 7/2-5/2; sn cl up; ld 9; 4l clr 3 out; prsd nxt but a gng the btr*		1
1035^{2}	**Sovereign Dove** (12a) 2-1JF **F Hutsby** *2 handlers; hld up; went 4th 12; disp 3rd 14; chsd wnr app nxt; tried to chall & rdn 2 out; sn btn; nt punished*	20	2
746^{P}	**Penlet Too**(bl) 20-1 **T Ellis** *(xnb) Tk keen hld & prom; disp 2½l 3rd 14; fdd rap app nxt; t.o*	30	3
1108^{P}	Eastern Apple (5a) 20-1 B Pauling *3rd 4; lost plce & mist 8; t.o & pu 14*		P
978^{4}	Greensleeves (5a) 2-1JF Miss P Gundry *Hit 3 & nt fluent in last; 10l bhnd rest 6; pu 10*		P
	Gregory Peckory (IRE) 7-1 M Goldstein *(xnb) Pulled hrd in 2nd/3rd; 1l 2nd 14; 12l 3rd & wkng qckly when fell nxt*		F

927P Igloux Royal (FR) 20-1 M Briggs *(xnb) Mist 2; ld to 9; lost plce rap; t.o & pu 3 out* . . . P
Orton Playboy 16-1 L Hicks *Ur gng down; rr & jmpd lft 3; nt fluent; mist 10; t.o & pu 13* . . . P
890P Sir Harry Henbit 20-1 J Diment *Nvr btr than midfield; lost tch 13; t.o when hmpd 15 & pu* . . . P
Wellfield Lad 16-1 R Smith *Mist 4; towards rr; last 12; t.o & pu 3 out* . . . P

OFFICIAL DISTANCES: 18*l*, dist **TIME:** 6min 59.0s

1276 Hunt Members 7 ran

434⁴ **PRATE BOX (IRE)** 5-4F **F Hutsby** *Hld up; went 2nd aft 10 til releg 3l 3rd 3 out; rallied nxt; ld last; rdn clr* . . . 1
925² **Stormy Pass** 9-4 **T Ellis** *Hld up; mist 9 & nrly ur; 6th aft 10; chall 13 & went 2nd 3 out; rdn & ev ch nxt; nt qckn app last; plugged into 2nd* . . . 6 2
Stonesby (IRE) 12-1 **Miss S Duckett** *Bckwd; last early; hdwy to ld 5; 1½l clr 3 out; rdn & hdd last; wknd* . . . ½ 3
584⁵ Nousayri (IRE) 6-1 C Wadland *(xnb) Hld up; last 8; eff 10; wknd app 14 & sn mod 4th; hit 3 out* . . . 10 4
1031F Gortroe Guy (IRE) 8-1 J Trice-Rolph *(xnb) Ld to 3 & brief app 5; jmpd slow 7; mist 11; 5th & wkng 13; pu 15* . . . P
887P North Peak (7a) 16-1 S Pile *Oht; mist 2; ld 3 til app 5; last & strugg when mist 10 but hung on to tails of ldrs to 12; pu nxt* . . . P
Notable Exception 14-1 Miss K Henry *Bckwd; cl up til wknd qckly 11; t.o nxt; pu 13* P

OFFICIAL DISTANCES: 5*l*, nk **TIME:** 7min 09.0s

1277 Mixed Open, 12st 3 ran

1073⁴ **SIR DANTE (IRE)** (4x) 5-4F **F Hutsby** *(xnb) Lw; made all; drew clr 14; unchall* 1
1032P **Celtic Season**(tt) 3-1 **S Morris** *Chsd wnr 7-8 & frm 9; 6l down 13 but 12l adrift 15; jmpd v slow nxt & nt pushed aft; mist 2 out* . . . 25 2
1121P Red Rebel (7x) 11-8 R Cope *Mounted on course & tde; mostly 2nd to 9; sn drvn along & reluct; wl bhnd when pu 13* . . . P

OFFICIAL DISTANCE: 25*l* **TIME:** 7min 00.0s

1278 South Midlands Area Club Members (Nov Rdrs), 12st 5 ran

1033³ **ELA AGAPI MOU (USA)**(bl) 7-2 **Miss D Ball** *Ld brief & jmpd v slow 5; chsd ldr to 12; lft 4l 2nd 15; clsd 2 out; ld last & sn clr* . . . 1
1122¹ **Aircon (IRE)** (5x) 1-2F **Miss R Hutsby** *(xnb) 2 handlers; made most to 2; 15l 4th 8; went 2nd 12; lft in ld 14; jmpd slow nxt; hdd & rdr flopped over last; imm btn* . . . 6 2
1107U **Kingfisher Star** 6-1 **Miss J Lodge** *(xnb) Lw; ld aft 2 til app 5; 13l 3rd 8; 4th & nt fluent 11; lft 20l 3rd 14; fin tired* . . . 40 3
Final Escapade 12-1 Miss K Garner *Sn last; lost tch & mist 12; t.o 14* . . . 5 4
757P Pele Mele (FR) 12-1 Miss S Firmin *Ld 5; 5l clr 13; mist & ur nxt* . . . U

OFFICIAL DISTANCES: 3½*l*, dist **TIME:** 7min 08.0s

1279 Restricted, 12st 3 ran

1119¹ **WONDERFUL REMARK** (5a) 2-1 **G Moloney** *2nd til ld 11; rdn clr aft 2 out* 1
977² **Alvero (FR)** 2-5F **M Harris** *(xnb) Set crawl & numerous slow js; jb lft 9 & agn when hdd 11; pckd 15; prsd wnr til rdn & fnd nil 2 out* . . . 6 2
1123F **Romanybaan** 10-1 **P Ikin** *(xnb) Str hld in last; lost tch aft mist when 7l down 15; mist 2 out* . . . 12 3

OFFICIAL DISTANCES: 6*l*, 12*l* **TIME:** 7min 25.0s

West Street Tickham

Aldington (LH 9F,19J)

Mon, 3 May (GOOD becoming GOOD to SOFT)

1280 Hunt Members 4 ran

1083U **GLENMONT (IRE)**(cp) 4-6F **Ms L Stock** *Hld up; cl 3rd frm 7 til ld 15; sn clr; 10l ahd 3 out; easily* . . . 1
896⁴ **Lord Of The Flies (IRE)** 5-1 **D Page (Kent)** *Ld; clr to 5; hdd 15; sn wknd; 13l 3rd 3 out; kpt on to tk 2nd app last* . . . 20 2

1084P **Phar Afield (IRE)** 11-4 **S Spice** *2nd most of way; chsd wnr frm 15; no imp; wknd & lost 2nd app last* . . . 5 3
802P Winward 8-1 J Merry *Prom to 6; last frm nxt; lost tch aft 9; t.o frm 15* . . . fence 4

OFFICIAL DISTANCES: 20*l*, 6*l* **TIME:** 6min 54.0s **TOTE:** £1.40 **DF:**£2.50

1281 Confined 4 ran

1050² **BRACKENHEATH (IRE)**(bl) evensF **P Hall** *Ld; 2-4l up til hdd aft 14; chsd ldr til hrd rdn & ld agn 2 out; drew clr u.p flat* . . . 1
778P **Nubro (IRE)**(bl) 7-2 **P Bull** *Trckd wnr; blun 10; ld aft 14; mist 15; hdd app 2 out; ev ch last; wknd flat* . . . 5 2
1050³ **Daydreamer (USA)** 2-1 **A Hickman** *Hld up; detach 3rd frm 6; hdwy to press ldng pr app 16; wknd aft 3 out; fin tired* . . . 30 3
969² Newby End (IRE)(vis) 8-1 Miss C Cowe *Jmpd stickily; last frm 6; lost tch aft 10; t.o & pu 13* . . . P

OFFICIAL DISTANCES: 3*l*, dist **TIME:** 6min 49.0s **TOTE:** £2.00 **DF:**£4.50

1282 Restricted, 12st 4 ran

1051P **STRAIGHT BARON** 7-2 **P Bull** *Ld to 10; prsd ldr til 6l 3rd & wkng aft 15; wl btn when lft effectively solo 2 out; fin tired* . . . 1
900⁴ **Ministerial (IRE)** 6-4F **P York** *Sev slt mists; trckd ldr til ld 11; drew clr aft 16; 10l up when fell 2 out; rmtd* . . . fence 2
973³ Native Spin (IRE) 7-2 D Dennis *Cl 3rd/4th til trckd wnr frm 15; lost tch app 3 out; lft in ld & ref 2 out* . . . r
895¹ Pandeli 2-1 D Phelan *Cl up in last pr; pushed along & rmdrs aft 10; lost tch frm 14; t.o & pu 16* . . . P

OFFICIAL DISTANCE: dist **TIME:** 7min 02.0s **TOTE:** £2.00 **DF:**£3.50

1283 Ladies Open 5 ran

1086³ **KINCORA (IRE)** (7x) 9-2 **Ms L Stock** *Ld to 1 & frm 5; made rest; 3-5l up til hrd prsd app 3 out; drew clr agn app last; stayed on str* . . . 1
1053¹ **Dick McCarthy (IRE)** (4x) 5-4JF **Mrs S Ashby** *Hld up; 18l 5th aft 10; gd hdwy 12; chsd wnr 14; impd to hld ev ch 3 out; no ex u.p app last* . . . 4 2
1053³ **Tom Cobbler (IRE)** (7x) 5-4JF **Mrs P Hall** *Hld up; 17l 4th aft 10; gd hdwy 12; chsd ldng pr frm 14; 8l 3rd 16; kpt on one pce frm 3 out* . . . 6 3
1085⁵ Prime Course (IRE) (7x) 10-1 Miss H Gordon *Ld 2-5; chsd wnr til lost plce aft 13; 14l 4th 16; wknd frm nxt* . . . 30 4
899R Red Channel (IRE) 10-1 Miss B Donnelly *Chsd ldng pr; 15l 3rd aft 10; sn wknd; t.o 13 til pu 16* . . . P

OFFICIAL DISTANCES: 4*l*, 6*l* **TIME:** 6min 48.0s **TOTE:** £4.70; places £1.10,£1.40 **DF:**£5.40

1284 Mens Open, 12st 3 ran

1054² **TRICKY TREVOR (IRE)** evensJF **P York** *Settled last; qcknd to ld aft 10; made rest; 2-3l up frm 12 til drew clr app last; comf* . . . 1
1083¹ **Oxendale**(bl) 5-1 **P Bull** *Spurs; disp ld til ld aft 6; jnd & mist 10; cl 3rd frm nxt til chsd wnr 14; ev ch 2 out; rdn & no ex app last* . . . 5 2
898¹ **Real Value (IRE)** (7x) evensJF **P Hall** *Disp ld til prsd ldr frm 6; pushed along 12; last aft 14; lost tch frm nxt* . . . 10 3

OFFICIAL DISTANCES: 4*l*, 8*l* **TIME:** 7min 00.0s **TOTE:** £2.00 **DF:**£5.60

1285 Open Maiden, 12st 7 ran

833F **NO REWARD (IRE)** 4-1 **A Hickman** *Hld up; detach in last pr til stdy hdwy 15; prsd ldr 3 out; ld aft nxt; drew clr app last; comf* . . . 1
1055U **Sword Fighter**(vis) 7-2 **P York** *Mostly 2nd til ld 13; hrd rdn & hdd aft 2 out; kpt on one pce u.p app last* . . . 6 2
803² **Worth A Shot (IRE)** 5-2F **D Phelan** *3rd til prsd ldr 11-16; ev ch when blun 3 out; wknd qckly* . . . 25 3
1088³ Blakes Road (IRE) 3-1 G Gallagher *Midfield til fell 6* . . . F
645P Diamond Road (IRE) 14-1 M Sheridan *Jmpd slow; last frm 4; lost tch frm 8; t.o & pu 11* . . . P
996³ Gale On The Lake (IRE) (5a) 9-2 P Hall *Midfield til bd 6* . . . B
802P Ginger Sprout (IRE) (5a) 14-1 C Thomson *Ld; clr 3-7; hdd aft 12; sn wknd; dist 4th when pu 16* . . . P

OFFICIAL DISTANCES: 7*l*, 20*l* **TIME:** 7min 11.0s **TOTE:** £5.50; places £2.40,£1.30 **DF:**£5.70

Zetland

Witton Castle (RH 7F,19J)
Mon, 3 May (GOOD)

1286 Hunt Members — 6 ran

762[3] **BEN FROM KETTON** 4-6F **S J Robinson** *Chsd ldr in 4l 2nd to 12; hdwy to ld 14; sn clr; stayed on wl* 1

593[3] **Master Adam (IRE)** 6-4 **Miss K Edminson** *Ld to 13; jnd 14; outpcd nxt; dist 2nd & tired by 3 out* 35 2

1164[P] **Selectric (IRE)** 25-1 **S Gibbon** *T.o & rem by 13; bad mist 14; poor 4th last; stayed on to snatch 3rd cl home* 40 3

Harry Jay 25-1 C Dawson *(xnb) A towards rr; rem 3rd 15; v tired & clambered last; dem flat* 3 4

767[5] Given Grace (IRE) (5a) 33-1 J Davis *Sn outpcd; 15l 3rd 10-16; v tired & last by 3 out; pu nxt* . . . . P

Red Seven (U) (7a) 12-1 Miss S Williamson *(xnb) A last; jmpd slow 10; t.o & pu 13* . . . . P

OFFICIAL DISTANCES: dist, dist **TIME:** 6min 25.0s

1287 Intermediate, 12st — 5 ran

808[4] **EMPEROR'S SON** 7-2 **Miss S Brotherton** *Chsd ldr in 5l 2nd to 3 out; rdn to ld app last & nt fluent; hrd rdn flat; just gt up in drvng fin* 1

1059[2†] **The Graduate** 5-2 **S Walker** *Sn clr; 5l ld to 3 out; jnd & jmpd rt 2 out; gd j last; ld flat; hrd rdn & hdd on line* . . . . hd 2

73[P] **Count Keni**(tt) 5-1 **Miss P Robson** *Last & mist 5; poor 3rd by 15; plodded on* 50 3

1036[2] Hadaway Lad 10-1 A Findlay *Ur 1* . . . . U

769[2] High Fields (7a)(bl) 5-4F T Greenall *15l 3rd to 7; mist 8; rmdrs & hrd rdn; lsng tch when pu 14* . . . . P

OFFICIAL DISTANCES: hd, dist **TIME:** 6min 14.0s

1288 Restricted — 13 ran

767[1] **SWEEPING STORM (IRE)** 7-2 **C Dawson** *Handy in mid-div til pushed along 14; disp ld 16; ld app 2 out; 1l up at last; forged clr flat* 1

773[1] **Devil's Perk (IRE)** 5-4F **T Glass** *Prom; hdwy to disp ld 10; ld 11; jnd 16; disp ld til hdd app 2 out; ev ch last; outpcd flat; dism aft line; lame* 4 2

774[1] **Karinga Leap** 10-1 **P Cornforth** *Handy to 8; cl up & mist 13; 1l 2nd 15; outpcd app 3 out; r.o one pce* 5 3

771[F] Wandering Wild (5a) 12-1 Mrs L Ward *Mid-div to 11; mist 13 & 8th 15; stayed on to 15l 4th 2 out* 6 4

959[1] Search Party (FR) (7a) 12-1 S Walker *Rr early; rdn 12; handy 5th 14; pushed along & outpcd 15; 12l 4th 3 out; wknd nxt* 8 5

1162[6] Don Rio (IRE) 10-1 M Morley *Rn in snatches; prom to 4 but rr by 9; hdwy 14 to 6th 15; r.o one pce aft* 3 6

1159[1] Duchess Account (5a) 8-1 R Wakeham *A midfield to rr; nvr able to chall* 1/2 7

810[F] Son Of Sam 25-1 L Bates *Last & adrift by 7; t.o 14; fin wl; nrst fin; school* 6 8

955[3] Mandate Man (IRE)(cp) 20-1 D Thomas *Ld to 3; in tch til wknd 13; rr by 15* 4 9

810[4] Lord Nick 14-1 N Tutty *Trckd ldrs to 8; went 2l 3rd 12; in tch til outpcd & wknd 14; pu 16; lame* . . . . P

954[1] Minster Echo (5a) 33-1 G Brewer *Ld frm 4-10; in tch til wknd frm 15; t.o & pu 2 out* . . . . P

164[P] Mr Sonshine 25-1 P Frank *A rr; pushed along & lsng tch when fell 13* . . . . F

1164[1] Scenic Storm (IRE) 4-1 P Kinsella *A rr; lsng tch 8; t.o & pu 16; lame* . . . . P

OFFICIAL DISTANCES: 5l, 5l **TIME:** 6min 18.0s

1289 Mens Open — 10 ran

ROYAL SNOOPY (IRE)(bl) 3-1 **R Abrahams** *Made all; 6l clr 2 out; r.o str* . . 1

1163[2] **Glendamah (IRE)** 5-1 **M Morley** *Hld up in rr til hdwy 9; 5l 4th 12-16; outpcd 3 out; stayed on one pce; tk 2nd flat* 10 2

1163[U] **Chaos Theory** 3-1 **D Thomas** *Last early; rr til hdwy 11; 8l 3rd 14; chsd ldr in 8l 2nd 3 out; hld in 2nd when bad blun last; dem flat* 6 3

956[1] Mr Pendleberry(cp) evensF N Tinkler *Chsd ldrs in 5th 13; pushed along 14; poor 5th 3 out; stayed on u.p to 4th app last* 15 4

1163[B] Welsh March (IRE)(cp) 20-1 N Tutty *Prom in 3rd to 8; went 1l 2nd to 10; 6l 2nd & outpcd 14; grad wknd; v tired by 2 out* . . . 4 5
917[F] Batoutoftheblue 12-1 S Huggan *Last & pushed along 9; t.o by 13; plugged on* 10 6
1036[3] Dannicus 100-1 A McElwee *Last when rn out 6* . . . R
My Shenandoah (IRE) 16-1 P Kinsella *Mid-div when pu qckly 8; broke down* P
1161[P] Notation (IRE) 100-1 R Clark *Handy in 4th til mist 4; sn wknd; rr when pu 10* P
917[r] Shining Light (IRE) 100-1 S J Robinson *Trckd ldr in cl 2nd to 8; rr & pushed along 13; rem last when pu last* . . . P

OFFICIAL DISTANCES: 10*l*, 10*l* **TIME:** 6min 13.0s

1290 Ladies Open 9 ran

763[2] **SUPERCHARMER** 5-1 **Miss J Riding** *Pulled to ld 3; 5l clr to 10; 2l up til jnd last; hung lft but stayed on game flat* . . . 1
1160[1] **Hadeqa** 5-4F **Miss S Brotherton** *Hld up in 15l 3rd to 8; hdwy to 3l 3rd 14; ev ch last; outpcd flat* . . . 2 2
630[P] **Ballad Minstrel (IRE)** 8-1 **Miss J Foster** *A.p; 3l 3rd 12; pushed along & ev ch last; nt clr rn flat; r.o one pce* . . . 1 3
1160[5] Yorkshire Edition (IRE) 6-1 Miss W Gibson *Rr by 9; t.o 14; stayed on frm 3 out; nrst fin* . . . 15 4
874[4] Deputy Leader (IRE) 50-1 Miss L Kendall *Hld up in rr; gd hdwy to 8l 5th 16; pushed along & outpcd 3 out* . . . 4 5
956[5] Multi Franchise 50-1 Miss F Hartley *Mid-div to 11; pushed along 14; lsng tch 3 out* . . . 3 6
593[4] Pharlindo (IRE) 14-1 Miss A Armitage *In tch til outpcd & wknd 14; t.o by 3 out; clambered over last & hacked in* . . . 30 7
732[F] Atomic Breeze (IRE) 14-1 Miss A Vernon *Last by 13; lsng tch; t.o & pu 2 out* P
957[1] Winter Gale (IRE) 4-1 Miss L Eddery *Ld to 2; chsd ldr in 2l 2nd to 16; upsides when ur 3 out* . . . U

OFFICIAL DISTANCES: 2*l*, 1½*l* **TIME:** 6min 15.0s

The stewards enquired into the possible interference to the third by the winner after the last fence; they decided that the interference was accidental and had not affected the result so the placings remained unaltered

1291 Open Maiden (Div 1), 12st 11 ran

958[3] **RAVENSCAR** 4-1 **S Walker** *Hld up; gd hdwy to 1l 2nd 13; ld 16; 2l up 2 out; stayed on u.p flat; impressive* . . . 1
433[2] **Nomadic Blaze** 5-4F **P Atkinson** *Trckd ldr in 2l 2nd to 13; ld 14 til jnd & outpcd frm 3 out* . . . 4 2
859[P] **Milbrig** (5a) 33-1 **Miss L Hislop** *Ld to 13; easily outpcd by ldng pr; 20l 3rd by 3 out; one-pcd* . . . 20 3
Arewetoolate 16-1 P Kinsella *Mid-div to 10; pushed along & wknd frm 13; t.o & pu 3 out* . . . P
505[F] Fairmile Star 10-1 R Wakeham *Sa; a rr; t.o & pu 14* . . . P
775[2] Forty Shakes (IRE) (7a) 5-2 T Glass *Rr to 8; hdwy 11 to 15l 7th 13; sn wknd; t.o & pu 16* . . . P
1159[5] Madaar (USA) (7a)(tt) 12-1 N Smith *Prom til blun 2; last & lsng tch 9; lft poor 4th 3 out; rem when ref last* . . . r
920[F] Perky's Wish (IRE) 50-1 S J Robinson *Prom to 10; rr & lsng tch 13; t.o & pu 14* P
775[P] Queenies Girl (5a) 14-1 P Frank *Mid-div when ur 6* . . . U
1042[U] Reeker Pike (5a) 50-1 J Thompson *A mid-div; pushed along & lsng tch 14; t.o & pu 3 out* . . . P
1159[F] Sea Princess (5a) 50-1 N Tutty *Mid-div to 8; went 3l 4th & mist 13; drpd back to 8l 4th 14; hrd rdn 15; sn wknd; t.o & pu 3 out* . . . P

OFFICIAL DISTANCES: 4*l*, dist **TIME:** 6min 24.0s

1292 Open Maiden (Div 2), 12st 12 ran

1159[4] **PARSIFAL** (7a) 5-1 **R Abrahams** *Tk keen hld; mid-div to 8; gd hdwy to handy 5th 13; ld & mist 3 out; jnd nxt; drew clr app last; r.o wl* . . . 1
1158[4] **Bobby Buttons**(cp) 2-1F **N Tutty** *A handy; went 1l 2nd 14-3 out; chall nxt; outpcd app last* . . . 5 2
1157[3] **Dinan (IRE)** 9-2 **Mrs J Brown** *Handy; ld 4-16; outpcd & wknd app 3 out* . . 15 3
1158[F] Iron Trooper (IRE) 12-1 T Glass *A rr; went poor 5th 14; lft rem 4th app 2 out* 25 4

1158^{6}	Catosphere (IRE) 12-1 L Bates *Ld to 3; cl 2nd to 7; handy in 3rd til wknd 15; t.o & pu 3 out*		P
1164^{P}	Fair Grand 12-1 P Cornforth *Mid-div when mist 7; rr by 14; rem when pu 3 out*		P
	Fiddler Crab 8-1 M Ellwood *Sn t.o; jmpd slow 3; fnce adrift when pu 11*		P
	Gardor (FR) 9-2 Miss J Foster *Ur 1*		U
958^{P}	Just A Man 14-1 C Mulhall *Mid-div to 9; pushed along 11; rr & lsng tch 13; t.o & pu 16*		P
959^{P}	Light-O-Day 14-1 P Kinsella *A to rr; poor 4th when fell 3 out*		F
	She's No Lady (12a) 20-1 C Dawson *Handy in 3rd to 7; sn cl up; 2l 3rd when saddle slpd & rn wide bend bef 14 & pu*		P
1159^{P}	Zebs Lad 25-1 R Walker *Handy in 5th to 5; mist 6; rr & lsng tch 9; t.o & pu 16*		P

OFFICIAL DISTANCES: 5*l*, dist **TIME:** 6min 30.0s

Exeter (RH 11F,16J)

Tue, 4 May (GOOD)

1293 Westcountry Ladies Club and Holne Chase Hotel Open HC, 2m7f110y £3406 — 9 ran

1130^{2}	**GLADIATORIAL (IRE)** 11-07 25-1 **T Bishop** *Hld up & bhnd til hdwy 12; ld 14; 5l clr 2 out; rdn app last; stayed on wl*		1
891^{1}	**Fair Wind (IRE)** 12-02 3-1 **Miss A Goschen** *2nd/3rd to 13; outpcd nxt; 5th 3 out; rallied bef last; stayed on wl to snatch 2nd; nt rch wnr*	$1\frac{1}{2}$	2
993^{2}	**Dantie Boy (IRE)** 11-07 7-1 **D Edwards** *Hld up towards rr; hdwy 11; 4th & gng wl bef 14; rdn app 2 out; no resp; 2nd & btn when blun last; dem nr fin*	hd	3
1166^{P}	Blackberry Way 11-02(tt) 25-1 W Kavanagh *Cl up; went 2nd aft 13; rdn & nt qckn 3 out; lost 2 plces aft*	$1\frac{1}{4}$	4
991^{1}	Bright Approach (IRE) 12-05 evensF T Malone *Niggled aft 2 & aft 8; bhnd; 12l 8th 12; rdn & laboured hdwy bef 14; nvr trbld ldrs*	6	5
993^{S}	Ronans Choice (IRE) 11-07(bl) 9-2 Richard Darke *Ld to 14; rdn & wknd nxt*	13	6
1117^{U}	Storm Castle (IRE) 11-07 14-1 Miss J Wickens *Tk keen hld; prom; nt fluent 7; wknd qckly aft 13*	15	7
1175^{2}	Province 12-00 12-1 L Jefford *2nd/3rd to 11; wknd qckly; poor 8th aft 13*	6	8
1129^{P}	Th'moons A Balloon (IRE) 11-07(tt) 50-1 S Partridge *A last; lost tch aft 8; t.o 10*	dist	9

TIME: 6min 12.1s **TOTE:** £24.60; places £6.60,£1.20,£2.30 **Ex:**£206.60 **CSF:**£112.47

Fence 9 omitted

Chepstow (LH 11F,18J)

Wed, 5 May (GOOD to SOFT, SOFT in places)

1294 Countryside Alliance Nov HC, 3m £1456 — 7 ran

1073^{1}	**CAMDEN CARRIG (IRE)** 11-07 5-2 **N Phillips** *Made all; sn clr; unchall.*		1
1176^{U}	**Jackson (FR)** 12-00(tt) 7-2 **R Burton** *Hld up in rr; hdwy 8; lft chsng wnr 12 but no ch*	28	2
571^{2}	**Pinmoor Hill** 12-00 20-1 **N Harris** *Chsd ldrs frm 3; wknd 10; t.o & tk poor 3rd frm 3 out*	dist	3
629^{P}	Pendragon 11-11 16-1 N Mitchell *In tch early; blun & wl bhnd 8; hopeless t.o 13; stayed on for poor 4th frm 2 out*	11	4
881^{3}	Winners Enclosure (IRE) 11-11 11-1 M Miller *Bhnd; nt fluent 5; some hdwy 9; lft t.o 3rd 13-15; prematurely eased*	11	5
1016^{C}	Bright Beacon 11-11 15-8F E Williams *Chsd ldrs 3; went 2nd 4; hit 6; 20l 2nd when fell & broke leg 12; dead.*		F
1281^{P}	Newby End (IRE) 11-07(vis) 12-1 D Dennis *Chsd ldrs to 4; wknd 10; t.o & pu 15*		P

TIME: 6min 20.0s **TOTE:** £3.40; places £1.50,£2.40 **Ex:**£20.80 **CSF:**£11.61

The rider of Winners Enclosure was banned for four days for failing to ride the horse out for fourth position

Fakenham (LH 6F,17J)

Wed, 5 May (GOOD, GOOD to SOFT)

1295 Eldred Wilson Mem HC, 3m110y £2520 — 5 ran

1154[1] **CELTIC DUKE** 11-13 11-2 **Miss Z Turner** *Jw; lft 2nd 4; ld 6; hdd brief app 11-12; drew 6l clr 3 out & a in comm aft* 1

1151[2] **Millenium Way (IRE)** 11-03(bl) 10-1 **J Owen** *Nvr jmpd w any zest; lft in ld 4-6; jmpd slow 7 & rdn; ld app 11-12; drvn frm 3 out but a outj & outbattled; tried to rally bef last where 2l down; sn brushed aside & eased* 4 2

815[1] **Tirley Gale** 11-05 25-1 **J Jones** *(xnb) Mounted on course & reluct to go down til ld by huntsman's horse; mostly 3rd; cl up til wknd tame app 2 out* . . 9 3

1153[1] Bard Of Drumcoo (IRE) 11-01 3-1 D Kemp *Sn last; mist 5; blun bad 13 & cont 8l adrift; rdn 3 out; nvr able to cl although catching 3rd nr fin* 2 4

1168[F] Upham Lord (IRE) 11-13 4-5F G Brewer *Lw; ld til blun & ur 4* . . . . . . U

TIME: 6min 38.9s **TOTE:** £4.90; places £2.50,£3.30 **Ex:**£16.30 **CSF:**£43.99

Fence 10 omitted - fallen rdr

Kelso (LH 8F,19J)

Wed, 5 May (GOOD)

1296 Z Hinchliffe & Sons HC, 3m1f £2257 — 5 ran

1068[2] **NISBET** 11-11 9-4F **Miss J Riding** *Jw; made all; hit 15; hld on wl final furlong* 1

1068[3] **Go Nomadic** 11-13(tt) 7-2 **P Atkinson** *Prom; outpcd ½way; rallied 15; prsd wnr app last; rdn & kpt on same pce flat* 2½ 2

1219[1] **Starbuck** 11-07 7-1 **W Goldie** *Blun 1; in tch; hdwy to chse wnr ½way; outpcd app last* 4 3

1174[F] Indien Du Boulay (FR) 11-07 7-2 W Ramsay *Chsd ldrs; eff app 2 out; outpcd when blun last; sn btn* 1½ 4

992[5] Master Wood 12-07 4-1 T Greenall *In tch; hit 11; wknd frm 15; t.o & pu aft 2 out* P

TIME: 6min 20.3s **TOTE:** £3.10; places £1.50,£1.60 **Ex:**£7.10 **CSF:**£9.95

The rider of Go Nomadic was found guilty of using his whip with excessive force; he was suspended for four days

Wetherby (LH 9F,18J)

Thu, 6 May (GOOD to SOFT, GOOD in places)

1297 The Yorkshire Area P-t-P Association HC, 3m1f £1526 — 7 ran

1204[U] **DORANS MAGIC** 11-07 5-2 **N Saville** *Trckd ldrs; 4th & niggled 10; went 2nd gng wl 14; nt fluent nxt; ld 2 out; 3l clr last; stayed on wl* 1

772[5] **Mighty Willing** 11-09 7-1 **G Brewer** *Hld up; went prom 7; 2nd 11; pckd bad 13; 6l 3rd when jmpd lft 3 out & hung rt aft; kpt on to tk 2nd flat; no ch w wnr* . . . 6 2

994[3] **The Butterwick Kid** 12-00(bl) 7-4F **J Tate** *Ld; shkn up app 15; hdd 2 out; one pce & sn btn; dem und str press flat* 2 3

1177[2] Buddy Girie 11-07 7-1 P Cornforth *Bhnd & rdn 5; eff 9; outpcd & strugg 14* 3½ 4

1178[5] Imps Way 11-06 9-1 C Mulhall *Jmpd slow 2; towards rr but in tch; lost plce app 15; poor 5th when pu last* . . . . . . P

812[2] Mademist Sam 12-00(bl) 25-1 N Tutty *Mist 8; 2nd/3rd to 12; lost tch 14; last when pu nxt* . . . . . . P

1179[3] Primitive Satin 11-09(bl) 14-1 L Bates *Fiddled 1; chsd ldrs; lost plce 9; t.o & pu 14* P

TIME: 6min 31.3s **TOTE:** £3.30; places £2.30,£4.60 **Ex:**£16.20 **CSF:**£18.54

Wincanton (RH 9F,21J)

Fri, 7 May (GOOD)

1298 R K Harrison West Country Championship HC, 3m1f110y £3367 — 5 ran

1100[1] **SPRINGFORD (IRE)** 11-09 2-1 **D Alers-Hankey** *(xnb) Lw; ld 4; oft jw & a btr than pursuer; hit 11; gng str final circ; nt fluent 17; in comm nxt; hit 2 out* 1

1171[1] **Garruth (IRE)** 12-02(bl) 10-11F **N Williams** *Jmpd rt (& oft bad so frm 15); ld to 4; chsd wnr aft but nvr gng wl; many urgings & rmdrs final circ; ch til jmpd v slow 18; no ex* 17 2

1170[4] **Alska (FR)** 11-04 10-1 **R Bandey** *Sn last; 12l down 5 & 20l adrift 8; went 4th 13 & 18l 3rd 15; t.o 18* . . . . . dist 3
1072[1] Phar From Chance 12-02 9-1 Miss P Gundry *(xnb) Lw; sn 3rd; rdn & nt gng wl 12; releg 4th & mist 13 (water); last & mist nxt; 24l adrift 17; t.o 18* . . 24 4
965[4] Wink And Whisper 11-04 14-1 Miss E Tory *Jmpd slow 6; 12l 4th 12; went 3rd nxt; still 12l down when pckd sltly & rfo 15* . . . . . U

TIME: 6min 42.4s **TOTE:** £3.40; places £1.40,£1.50 **Ex:**£5.00 **CSF:**£4.52

The rider of Garruth was found gulity of using his whip with excessive frequency and when the horse was showing no response; he was suspended for two days

Warwick (LH 10,17J)

Sat, 8 May (GOOD)

1299 Childrens Society HC, 2m4f110y £1582 — 8 ran

581[1] **PLACID MAN (IRE)** 12-02 100-30 **N Moore** *Chsd ldr to 4; hit 6; went 2nd agn 8; ld 11; drvn out flat* 1
732[2] **Sikander A Azam** 12-07 5-6F **T Greenall** *Hld up; hdwy 10; chsd wnr 13; hrd app last; one pce* 3 2
1168[4] **Irbee** 12-00(bl) 10-1 **L Heard** *Hld up; hdwy app 11; wknd 2 out* 15 3
818[1] Ashgan (IRE) 12-07 20-1 G Barfoot-Saunt *Hld up & bhnd; rdn & hdwy aft 3 out; no further prog frm 2 out* 3 4
732[14] Epsilo De La Ronce (FR) 12-00 20-1 W Ramsay *Jmpd slow 3; hit 4; sn bhnd; t.o frm 14* . . . . . dist 5
1168[F] Kerres Noires (FR) 11-12 8-1 S Waley-Cohen *Tk keen hld; ld; clr when hit 6; hdd 11; wknd 3 out; t.o; fin distressed* 5 6
785[P] Nashville Star (USA) 11-12(vis) 200-1 R McCarthy *Chsd ldr 4-8; rdn aft 10; wknd 11; t.o* 4 7
784[P] Colombe D'Or 11-07 150-1 T Ellis *A bhnd; mist 2; t.o & pu 11* . . . . . P

TIME: 5min 12.2s **TOTE:** £3.60; places £1.70,£1.02,£2.70 **Ex:**£12.20 **CSF:**£6.11

Bilsdale

Easingwold (LH 8F,18J)

Sat, 8 May (GOOD)

1300 Open Maiden 56&7yo, 12st — 9 ran

958[4] **SILOGUE (IRE)** 7-2 **N Tutty** *Hld up in mid-div; went 3l 3rd 8 & 1l 2nd 10-12; ld 14; jnd & lft dist clr 15; canter.* 1
958[5] **Thixendale** (5a)(cp) 14-1 **Miss J Foster** *Cl up; 4l 4th til outpcd 9; hdwy to 8l 4th 14; lft 3rd nxt & 30l 2nd by 2 out; no ch w wnr* 40 2
1165[8] **God Of War** 6-1 **S Charlton** *Mid-div early; 5l 5th 8 til mist 11; outpcd aft 13; dist 3rd by 2 out; r.o one pce* 3 3
774[U] Littleton Zeus (IRE) (7a) 14-1 P Collins *A towards rr; last to 12; lsng tch 13; rem 4th by 2 out* 6 4
1291[P] Perky's Wish (IRE) 33-1 S J Robinson *(xnb) Cl 3rd to 5; went 1l 2nd 7; pushed along & wknd frm 11; rem 5th 3 out* 20 5
Been Supreme (IRE) (5a) 14-1 L Bates *Sn bhnd; clambered over 1; jmpd 2 & pu* . . . . . P
1158[2] Irish Paddy (IRE) (7a) evensF R Clark *Mid-div early; 8l 6th 8; hdwy 9 to 4l 3rd 10; cl 2nd 13; disp ld & gng like wnr when fell 15* . . . . . F
960[U] Pampered Lad (7a) 14-1 A Pennock *Rr by 3; bhnd & lsng tch 10; t.o & pu 14* P
773[P] Three Way Split 33-1 Miss Rachel Clark *(xnb) Ld; 2l up to 12; jnd 13; sn wknd; lft 25l 2nd 15; poor 3rd when blun 3 out & imm pu; lame* . . . . . P

OFFICIAL DISTANCES: dist, 3*l* **TIME:** 6min 15.0s

1301 Confined, 12st — 6 ran

1160[6] **MIORBHAIL** 25-1 **Miss T Gray** *Ld to 2; 3l 3rd to 11; ld 15; 2l clr 3 out; hrd rdn & hld on wl flat.* 1
1161[P] **Darak (IRE)** (5x) 6-4JF **N Tutty** *Ld frm 3; 2l up 12; jnd 15; 2l 2nd & pushed along 3 out; chsd wnr vain aft* 3 2
1157[5] **Glacial Dancer (IRE)** 4-1 **R Clark** *Mid-div; 12l 4th 6; hdwy 9 to 4l 3rd 10; pushed along & outpcd 13; poor 3rd 3 out; r.o one pce* 35 3

1290[3] Ballad Minstrel (IRE) 6-4JF Miss J Foster *Nvr gng wl; 15l 5th 6; slt hdwy 11 to 8l 4th 13; pushed along & outpcd app 14; rem 4th 3 out; broke down. .* 20 4
1202[5] Rubon Prince (IRE)(bl) 16-1 T Glass *Cl 3rd til 1l 2nd 4-8; wkng & hvy rmdrs 11; rap lost tch 13; t.o 15. . . . .* 3 5
812[P] Royal Plum 50-1 S J Robinson *Lkd reluct; sn pushed along; detach last & lsng tch when jmpd slow & ur 4 . . . .* U

OFFICIAL DISTANCES: 3*l*, dist **TIME:** 6min 08.0s

1302 Mens Open 3 ran

1161[1] **NORDIC CREST (IRE)**(tt) 1-4F **M Walford** *Patient rdn; hld up; handy in last to 14; easily ld app 3 out; sn clr w rdr lkng rnd; canter . . . .* 1
1203[U] **Donnegale (IRE)**(bl) 4-1 **N Smith** *Slt ld to 14; pushed along & outpcd 15; 2l 3rd 3 out; hrd rdn & tk 2nd app nxt; stayed on und hrd drvng; flatt by prox* 3 2
1153[P] **Fine Times**(tt) 8-1 **O Williams** *Trckd ldr in 1l 2nd til disp ld 3 out; sn outpcd & wknd qckly; 20l last 2 out; tired j last; fin exhaust . . . .* 20 3

OFFICIAL DISTANCES: 3*l*, 20*l* **TIME:** 6min 12.0s

1303 Ladies Open 3 ran

1160[4] **ON THE MEND (IRE)** 3-1 **Miss F Hartley** *Made all; 2l up 3 out; prsd app nxt; hrd rdn & r.o game flat (rdr drpd whip at open ditch). . . . .* 1
346[3] **Ridgeway (IRE)** 1-5F **Miss J Foster** *A trckng ldr; 2l 2nd to 3 out; pushed along app nxt; no resp; did nt want to pass ldr . . . .* 3 2
1159[P] **Quel Regal (FR)**(cp) 14-1 **Miss Rachel Clark** *Chsd ldng pr in 3l 3rd to 12; pushed along & outpcd 13; 12l 3rd 2 out; r.o one pce . . . .* 25 3

OFFICIAL DISTANCES: 3*l*, 20*l* **TIME:** 6min 12.0s

1304 Dodson & Horrell PPORA Club Members Restricted 9 ran

1162[2] **CIVIL GENT (IRE)** (7a) 7-4F **G Brewer** *(xnb) Tk keen hld; hld up in mid-div; 8l 6th 8; hdwy 11 to 3l 3rd 13; ld 14; clr 3 out; jnd app nxt; rdly drew clr flat* 1
1292[1] **Parsifal** (7a) 5-1 **R Abrahams** *Rr; hdwy 10 to 4l 5th 14 & 5l 2nd 3 out; rdn to chall 2 out; wknd app last; easily outpcd flat . . . .* 6 2
1201[2] **Flat Stanley** (7a) 9-4 **Miss J Foster** *Mid-div early; 5l 4th 8 til mist 12; rdn to 2l 2nd 14; 3rd & ev ch 3 out; outpcd nxt; hrd rdn & stayed on flat . . . . . .* 1 3
1152[P] Troubleshooter 25-1 O Williams *Chsd ldr in 2l 2nd to 12; handy til pushed along & outpcd 14; 12l 4th 2 out; v tired & clambered over last; strugg home. . . . .* 25 4
1288[4] Wandering Wild (5a) 20-1 Mrs L Ward *(xnb) Mid-div; 8l 6th 7 & 4l 5th 11; pushed along & wknd 14; poor 5th 3 out . . . .* 12 5
1162[P] Redsands (IRE) 33-1 S Charlton *Ld; 2l up to 13; sn hdd & wknd qckly; poor 6th 3 out. . . . .* 8 6
1162[4] Hessac (FR) 7-1 J Davis *Handy in 6l 5th when slpd up bend bef 9. . . . . .* S
1162[F] In The Van(cp) 50-1 M Morley *(xnb) Mounted on course; ur & galloped loose in box park; tde; 3l 3rd to 11; 4th & pushed along 13; grad lost tch; t.o & pu 2 out . . . .* P
1162[5] Office Hours 9-2 S Walker *Sa; a last; pushed along & lsng tch 11; hvy rmdrs 12; no resp; t.o & pu 14 . . . .* P

OFFICIAL DISTANCES: 6*l*, 1*l* **TIME:** 6min 09.0s

1305 Open Maiden, 12st 10 ran

1165[4] **THE SEA CLUB (IRE)** 4-1 **Miss L Robson** *Ld; 4l up 8; hdd nxt & sn outpcd; chsd ldr in 5l 2nd 14; easily ld app 3 out; 4l up 2 out; galloped on str; drew clr flat; rdr's 1st wnr. . . . .* 1
1156[U] **Man At The Top** 5-1 **M Bennison** *Rr early; 12l 7th 9; hdwy 12 to 3rd 14 & 4l 2nd 3 out; chsd wnr vain aft; one pce . . . .* 8 2
1292[U] **Gardor (FR)** 3-1 **N Smith** *Jmpd big 1; cl up in mid-div to 7; went 3l 2nd 9; ld 10; sn 4l clr; jnd 15; sn hdd; wknd v qckly frm 3 out; bbv. . . . .* 25 3
960[P] Highland Wonder 12-1 Mrs L Ward *Prom early; drpd back 4; 6th & lsng tch 14; lft poor 5th 3 out; tk 4th app last . . . .* 20 4
Oaklands Billy 50-1 T Glass *Mid-div to 9; pushed along to 8l 3rd 12; easily outpcd & poor 4th 3 out; dem app last . . . .* 25 5
954[3] Twinkle Toe Titch (IRE) (12a) 6-1 A Pennock *A rr; last to 10; outpcd 13; bhnd when mist 15; t.o aft . . . .* 10 6

1292[P] Fair Grand(bl) 33-1 P Cornforth *In tch to 10; 10l 5th & pushed along 11; sn wknd; t.o & pu 14* . . . . P
1143[2] Hendrix evensF N Saville *Tde; hld up in rr til hdwy 6; went 6th 8 & 8l 4th 13; v tired 3rd & hld when fell 3 out* . . . . F
954[F] Sizzling River 50-1 W Burnell *A last; qckly lost tch 7; t.o & pu 11* . . . . . . P
1206[4] Trigger Castle (5a) 20-1 S Walker *Mid-div when slpd up bend bef 9* . . . . . S

OFFICIAL DISTANCES: 20*l*, dist **TIME:** 6min 20.0s

Cumberland

Aspatria (LH 8F,17J*)

Sat, 8 May (GOOD, SOFT in back straight)

1306 Hunt Members — 3 ran

1222[5] **DISTRACTING** (5a) 1-2F **R Morgan** *Lw; ld/disp; pckd 10; 1l up 16; sn 8l clr; 10l up at last; easily* 1
Pilot's Harbour 2-1 **C Storey** *Bckwd; ld/disp to 15; 1l 2nd nxt; outj & outpcd aft; sn btn* 12 2
Polly Peacock (5a) 7-1 C Dawson *(xnb) Trckd ldng pr; 3l last 3; 2l down 13 & pushed along aft; sn wl bhnd; 25l last aft 15; tired when broke down & crashing fall 16* . . . . F

OFFICIAL DISTANCE: 20*l* **TIME:** 6min 38.1s

** Fences 6 & 14 omitted from all races - state of going; original fence numbers have been retained for comments-in-running*

1307 Confined, 12st — 9 ran

1037[5] **BRIERY HILL** 10-1 **T Morrison** *Mounted outside padd; tde; a.p; 1l up 5; hdd 7; ld agn 13; 3l up 16; hdd 3 out; ½l down nxt; rallied & ld app last; gd j & stayed on game* 1
1223[1] **Trivial (IRE)** (5a) 2-1 **L Morgan** *A handy; disp 4l 4th app 7 & 3l 3rd nxt; 5l 4th aft 13; went 2l 2nd 15; ld 3 out; hrd prsd nxt; ev ch til hdd app last; nt qckn flat* 2 2
1037[1] **Three Spires** 11-10F **A Richardson** *2 handlers; oht; swtng; hld up in rr; prog to 5l 5th 7 & 4l 3rd 11; went 2l 2nd aft 13; 4l 3rd app 16; ev ch til mist 3 out; no ch aft; 6l 3rd & no imp app last* 6 3
1221[2] Dere Street (3x) 6-1 Miss R Davidson *In tch in rr; 8l 8th 7; 10l 7th nxt; ev ch til rdn & 5l 5th 16; sn btn; wknd 2 out* 12 4
1223[2] Extra Stout (IRE)(tt) 16-1 C Storey *Prom til ld 7; 2l up nxt; hdd 13; ev ch til wknd aft nxt* 20 5
1179[P] Lively Dessert (IRE) (3x) 16-1 R Morgan *Mid-div; disp 4l 4th app 7; lost plce & rmdr aft 12; sn strugg* 10 6
1287[U] Hadaway Lad 16-1 A Findlay *Oht; a rr; 10l last 3; outpcd & rmdrs in 10l 8th 12; lost tch aft* 8 7
1287[3] Count Keni (5x)(tt) 33-1 C Dawson *Oht; swtng; tde; trckd ldr til lost plce aft 11; rmdrs aft nxt; wknd qckly; pu aft 13* . . . . P
1220[P] Valley Garden 33-1 R Nichol *Carried condition; prom til outpcd 7; drpd to rr nxt; sn strugg & bhnd; lost tch & pu aft 13* . . . . P

OFFICIAL DISTANCES: 2*l*, 12*l* **TIME:** 6min 21.6s

1308 Ladies Open — 9 ran

915[1] **CLIFFORD BAY (IRE)** 4-6F **Miss N Stirling** *(xnb) 5/4-4/6; 2 handlers; trckd ldr; ½l 2nd app 7; ld brief 10; 2l 2nd nxt; 5l 2nd 16; prog app 2 out & sn prsng ldr; btr j to ld last; comf* 1
1080[1] **Royalecko** 3-1 **Miss J Hollands** *A.p; ld 11; 5l clr 16; hrd prsd frm 2 out; mist & hdd last; wknd flat* 3 2
1078[2] **Passing Danger (FR)** 5-2 **Miss R Davidson** *(xnb) Sev posns til gd hdwy app 2 out; went 6l 3rd app last; stayed on u.p; nt rch ldr* . . . . ½ 3
1039[3] Knockholt 12-1 Miss A Pattinson *Mists; chsd ldrs; 3l 4th app 7; hit 13; rdn along when mist 15; sn outpcd; kpt on* 3 4

1039^{P}	Piper's Rock (IRE) (3ow) 25-1 Miss V Russell *(xnb) Jmpd lft at times; prom; ld brief 7; 3l 3rd 13; outpcd aft 15; kpt on but nd*	3	5
1221^{3}	In Demand 12-1 Miss J Balmer *Nt jw; a rr; 25l 8th 8; strugg & nd frm 11.*	20	6
1290^{5}	Deputy Leader (IRE) 33-1 Miss L Kendall *(bf) In tch; disp 8l 5th 9; prog to 5l 4th 13 & 4l 4th 15; sn rdn along & wknd*	3	7
1078^{4}	Dukestown (IRE) 66-1 Miss E McWilliam *(bf) Reluct to start & sis; a rr; detach & 25l last 3; t.o 11; pu 3 out.*		P
1039^{U}	Houselope Beck 50-1 Miss A Wanless *(xnb) In tch; 7l 5th app 7; disp 8l 5th when rn out 9*		R

OFFICIAL DISTANCES: 4*l*, 2*l* **TIME:** 6min 24.0s

1309 Mens Open 4 ran

798^{7}	**GEORDIES EXPRESS** 11-8 **T Scott** *(xnb) Made all; 3l up 3; 6l up aft 5; 2l up & rmdr 15; hrd prsd 2 out; 2l up app last; stayed on wl*		1
1220^{1}	**Decent Bond (IRE)** 5-4F **R Green** *Trckd ldr; 5l 2nd 11; bad mist & nrly ur 13; 8l last aft til prog to 2l 2nd 16; prsd ldr & ev ch 2 out; no ex app last* . .	5	2
917^{6}	**Finest Of Men** 4-1 **J Walton** *Trckd ldrs on inner; $5\frac{1}{2}$l 3rd 11; disp 3l 2nd aft 13; brief eff to 1l 2nd 15; 8l last & outpcd nxt; sn nd; hrd rdn to tk poor 3rd flat*	20	3
134^{4}	Golf Land (IRE)(tt) 16-1 A Richardson *In tch in last; 8l last 11; disp 3l 2nd aft 13; rdn along aft nxt; 10l 3rd aft 16; sn btn; 25l 3rd app last; hrd rdn flat; dem nr line*	1	4

OFFICIAL DISTANCES: 5*l*, 25*l* **TIME:** 6min 28.9s

1310 Restricted 7 ran

1077^{2}	**MORE FLAIR** (5a) 6-4F **J Walton** *9/4-6/4; a handy; 3l 2nd 5; clr in ldng pr aft 13; ld brief app 15; ld agn app 3 out; sn 8l up; 10l up & in comm last* .		1
1041^{1}	**General Jake (IRE)** 3-1 **J Innes** *Ld; 3l up 5; clr in ldng pr frm 13; hdd brief 15; hdd agn app 3 out; easily brushed aside*	12	2
1222^{10}	**C L B Jemilla** (5a) 25-1 **Miss G Craggs** *Chsd ldrs; 7l 6th 7; some prog aft 11; outpcd aft 13 & sn lost tch; went poor 3rd 16; kpt on frm nxt*	15	3
1222^{9}	Good Morning (5a) 33-1 R Dickson *Trckd ldrs; 3l 3rd 3; lost plce & 6l last app 6; pckd 9; 10l last & outpcd 11; 15l 6th & strugg aft 13; lost tch aft* . .	3	4
	Ben Buckley 8-1 R Sinton *(xnb) 1st ride; 2 handlers; tde; prom; rcd wide til outpcd aft 13; 15l last app 15; sn lost tch; t.o 5th 2 out*	20	5
597^{1}	Jethro Tull (IRE) (7a) 3-1 R Morgan *(xnb) Dism & saddle adjusted padd; unruly; in tch; prog to disp 3l 2nd 7; $2\frac{1}{2}$l 4th 11; 6l 3rd & pushed along aft 13; wknd qckly; lost tch & pu aft 16*		P
136^{1}	Sharp Fountain (5a) 3-1 C Storey *10s-3s; oht; chsd ldrs; disp 3l 2nd 7; $2\frac{1}{2}$l 3rd & hit nxt; 10l 4th & wkng aft 13; poor 4th & climbed 15; lost tch & pu nxt*		P

OFFICIAL DISTANCES: 25*l*, 12*l* **TIME:** 6min 28.2s

1311 Open Maiden 8 ran

1224^{P}	**ANNIEJO** (12a) 5-2 **R Morgan** *(xnb) In tch; 4l 4th app 7; prog to 2l 3rd app 15; sltly outpcd aft; hdwy frm nxt; ld 2 out; rdn clr*		1
1224^{2}	**St Bee**(bl) 2-1F **A Richardson** *Trckd ldr; 2l 2nd 3; ld 6; hdd 10; 1l 2nd 15; ld agn & lkd wnr app nxt; hdd 2 out; tried to rally aft; no imp app last.* . . .	2	2
1041^{4}	**Red Jupiter** 4-1 **T Scott** *Trckd ldr; 3l 3rd 3; went 1l 2nd 11; ld aft 12; hdd aft 15; ev ch til outpcd 2 out; kpt on one pce*	4	3
1081^{P}	Temple Glen (7a) 6-1 Miss J Hollands *10s-6s; mists; mid-div; $6\frac{1}{2}$l 5th 3; hit 5; some prog to 6l 4th app 15; 12l 4th & outpcd nxt; kpt on*	6	4
920^{P}	The Milecastle (IRE) (7a) 14-1 L Morgan *In tch; 8l 6th 7; some prog 13 til outpcd in 15l 5th 15; sn wknd; walked in*	25	5
286^{P}	Hot Bricks 9-2 J Walton *A rr; 15l last 3; lost tch 5; 25l last 7; t.o 11; 2 fncs bhnd when nrly fell last*	2fncs	6
658^{F}	The Panjshir 8-1 G Willoughby *Mid-div; 6l 4th 3; lsng tch aft 6; t.o & pu 12*		P
1221^{P}	Wester Lad 12-1 Miss J Riding *Ld til hdd 6; disp 6l 3rd 8; ld 10; hdd aft 12; 10l 6th & outpcd aft 13; wknd aft 15; t.o & pu 2 out*		P

OFFICIAL DISTANCES: 3*l*, 5*l* **TIME:** 6min 39.5s

Essex Farmers & Union

Marks Tey (LH 9F,18J*)

Sat, 8 May (GOOD to SOFT, SOFT in places)

1312 Hunt Members — 3 ran

1085[4] **RIP KIRBY** 3-1 **M Cobbald** *Chsd ldr til blkd by loose horse & ref 3; jmpd it at 2nd attempt; cont solo; tail swishing frm 10* . . . 1

828[1] Endeavour (FR) 2-5F G Cooper *Ld rnd start; ld; jmpd rt & cannoned into rival 1; blkd by loose horse & ur 3* . . . U

833[P] Spring Frolic(bl) 14-1 R Cundy *(xnb) Bumped & ur 1* . . . U

OFFICIAL DISTANCE: Finished alone **TIME:** 9min 05.0s

** Fences 9 and 19 were omitted from all races - state of the ground (original fence numbers have been retained in comments-in-running); Marsden (6-1, bolted bef start) was withdrawn not under orders - Rule 4 deduction 10p in pound*

1313 Confined, 12st — 7 ran

892[P] **MADMIDGE** 6-4F **D Kemp** *Ww; prog to 4th 8; 8l 3rd 14; clsd 3 out; ld app last; rdn clr; eased flat* . . . 1

1150[1] **Tom De Savoie (IRE)** 3-1 **N Bloom** *Chsd ldng pr; went 2nd 11; clsd & ev ch 2 out; wknd app last* . . . 10 2

1085[3] **Algan (FR)** (6x) 6-1 **J Ryan** *Chsd ldr til ld 6; mist 10; 7l clr 14; hdd aft 2 out; no ex; blun last* . . . 4 3

903[2] Nordic Spree (IRE)(bl) 12-1 R Morgan-Evans *Ld to 6; 4th & wkng 13; no ch frm 15* . . . 30 4

1153[P] Avondale Illusion (IRE) 16-1 R Stearn *In tch; 12l 5th when jmpd slow & rdn 9; lost tch 13; no ch aft* . . . 3 5

998[8] Fiolino (FR) 33-1 R Page *(xnb) Ld in start; sn detach in last; t.o frm 7* . . . 2fncs 6

1151[3] Persian Hero (IRE) 3-1 J Owen *Ref to rce; tk no part* . . . r

OFFICIAL DISTANCES: 10*l*, 5*l* **TIME:** 7min 00.0s

1314 Ladies Open — 6 ran

1017[2] **LUCKY MASTER (IRE)** 16-1 **Miss G Swan** *33s-16s; lft 3rd 4; prsd ldr 10; ev ch frm 2 out; ld last 100yds; stayed on wl* . . . 1

221[P] **Fair Exchange** 3-1 **Miss J Wickens** *Chsd ldr til lft in ld 4; slt ld frm 14; gd j last; hdd & no ex last 100yds* . . . ½ 2

1210[1] **The Wiley Kalmuck (IRE)** evensF **Miss Z Turner** *Trckd ldrs; 3l 3rd 16; rdn & no prog nxt; eased when btn flat* . . . 15 3

1086[P] Fair Kiowa (IRE) 5-2 Mrs S Hodge *Hld up in tch; trckd ldrs frm 7; 4l 3rd when mist 15; 4th & btn frm nxt* . . . 6 4

1244[2] Borrow Mine (IRE) 10-1 Miss L Marriott *Last frm 7; lost tch 10; t.o 16 til pu last* . . . P

1244[P] General Confusion (IRE) 25-1 Miss B Czepulkowski *Set off last; tk keen hld; ld aft 1 til rn out 4* . . . R

OFFICIAL DISTANCES: ½*l*, 12*l* **TIME:** 7min 01.0s

1315 Mens Open — 3 ran

1052[2] **SPLASH AND DASH (IRE)** 11-10 **A Hickman** *Nt fluent; ww in 3rd; rmdrs 9 & 11; went 2nd 14; 10l down & btn when lft in ld 3 out; hrd rdn app last; just prevailed* . . . 1

1243[1] **Ballad (IRE)** 10-1 **A Williams** *Chsd ldr to 14; 3rd & btn nxt; lft cl 2nd 3 out; kpt on u.p; just hld* . . . nk 2

991[P] Delgany Royal (IRE) 4-5F M Mackley *Set stdy pce; qcknd 11; clr 14; 10l clr & in comm when fell 3 out* . . . F

OFFICIAL DISTANCE: nk **TIME:** 7min 29.0s

1316 Restricted, 12st — 6 ran

1107[4] **TABLE FOR FOUR**(vis) 9-4F **M Mackley** *Chsd ldrs; went 2nd 7; clsd 15; ld 3 out; sn clr & in comm* . . . 1

1245[P] **Ardnut**(bl) 16-1 **Miss R Page** *Chsd ldr to 7; 4th & outpcd 9; no ch 13; kpt on frm 3 out; went mod 2nd flat; nt trble wnr* . . . 15 2

1245[U] **Stick Or Bust**(bl) 5-2 **M Smith** *Ld; sn clr; 8l clr 10; hdd 3 out; sn no ch w wnr; lost 2nd flat* . . . 2 3

1245^{2}	Gunner Be True 7-2 A Corbett *Wl bhnd; eff & 15l 5th $\frac{1}{2}$way; sn lost tch; no ch frm 12; nd.*	20	4
1314^{R}	General Confusion (IRE) 3-1 J Owen *2nd outing; keen; ww in tch; went 3rd 9; jmpd rt 13; 5l 3rd & rdn 3 out; wknd app nxt; 4th & no ch when pu last*		P
906^{U}	Mr Moonbeam (IRE)(cp) 14-1 M Buchan *Chsd ldrs to 4; mist 6; last & lsng tch when ur 12*		U

OFFICIAL DISTANCES: 15*l*, $2\frac{1}{2}$*l* **TIME:** 7min 13.0s

The stewards gave permission for General Confusion, who had run in the Ladies Open, to start in this race with the proviso that it had stronger handling

1317 Confined Maiden, 12st — 7 ran

1246^{4}	**ON THE DAY (IRE)** 5-2 **J Owen** *Ld to 2; w ldr til ld agn 11; made rest; drew clr 2 out*		1
833^{3}	**Manhatton Storm (IRE)** 5-4F **A Merriam** *2s-5/4; oht; trckd ldrs; mist 9; blun nxt; cl 3rd 14; outpcd by ldng pr nxt; kpt on to disp mod 2nd app last; just won battle for 2nd*	12	2
1155^{4}	**Peats Ridge (IRE)** 9-2 **R Stearn** *Trckd ldrs; 3l 4th 14; outpcd nxt; kpt on to disp mod 2nd app last; dem 3rd nr line*	hd	3
1155^{P}	Lolloping Lad 12-1 M Smith *Trckd ldrs; jmpd rt 3; chsd wnr app 14; 3l 2nd 3 out; wknd aft nxt; dem 4th app last*	8	4
1088^{5}	Scalby Croft (5a) 14-1 Miss N Barnes *Hld up in last pr; wl in tch til outpcd 14; 5th & no ch nxt*	$\frac{1}{2}$	5
1156^{U}	Marsden 8-1 A Braithwaite *Tde; ld 2-11; wknd 13; wl bhnd when pu 15*		P
746^{P}	Swanbank 12-1 H Fowler *(xnb) Hld up; in tch til wknd 13; wl bhnd when pu 15*		P

OFFICIAL DISTANCES: 15*l*, hd **TIME:** 7min 25.0s

Gelligaer Farmers

Bonvilston (RH 7F,18J)

Sat, 8 May (GOOD to SOFT - sticky)

1318 Hunt Members, 12st — 7 ran

1235^{1}	**FLOCKMASTER (IRE)** 5-2F **Mrs C Owen** *Made all; 3-4l clr frm 7 til qcknd clr 12; 12l up nxt; grad drew away; in comm when mist last*		1
1237^{1}	**Hail Stone (IRE)** 9-2 **J L Llewellyn** *Prom; 2nd 1-3; chsd ldr agn 8; 3l 2nd 12; outpcd frm nxt; no ch aft*	30	2
1236^{1}	**Silver Pot Black** 5-1 **Miss H Lewis** *Chsd ldrs; 4th & u.p 9; 6l last 12; u.p 14; no ex in gluey ground 3 out; eased flat*	20	3
620^{P}	Its Mr Blobby 6-1 T Vaughan *(xnb) A bhnd; last frm 5; lost tch frm 10; pu 11*		P
1235^{U}	La Maestra (FR) (5a) 10-1 S Hughes *Prom; 4l 2nd 7; 3rd 8 til disp 2nd u.p 12; wknd; 30l 4th & tired 2 out; pu last*		P
1237^{6}	Pams Oak 5-1 W Oakes *2 handlers; 3rd early; rdn 3 & last nxt; hung violent lft & tried to pull himself up aft 5; crashed thro wing 6*		R
	Shadar (IRE) (7a) 20-1 G Marsh *(bf) Prom; settled 2nd 3; mist 5 & rdr lost iron; pu nxt*		P

OFFICIAL DISTANCES: 30*l*, 20*l* **TIME:** 6min 16.0s

1319 Intermediate, 12st — 3 ran

	SILVER CASTLE 4-7F **L Stephens** *Ld; 1-2l up til slt mist 15; rdn clr 3 out; 5l ahd when slt mist nxt; rn wide bend bef last; v comf*		1
1094^{1}	**Bill Haze**(cp) 6-4 **D Jones** *(bf) Trckd ldr in cl 2nd; squeezed up on bend aft 12; slt mist 15 & sn outpcd; no imp aft.*	10	2
1092^{5}	**Themaster's Choice (IRE)** 8-1 **M Goldstein** *(orbs) A last & nd; mist & drvn frm 11; detach & rmdrs nxt; 8-10l adrift til wknd frm 3 out*	15	3

OFFICIAL DISTANCES: 8*l*, 15*l* **TIME:** 6min 13.0s

1320 Confined, 12st — 11 ran

1026^{1}	**CHANCY GUY** 6-1 **L Stephens** *Mid-div to 6; settled 4th; u.p in 3rd 15; stayed on game u.p to ld & mist last; rdly*		1
1090^{P}	**Gold Kriek** 4-1 **D Jones** *A.p; ld 2; ld agn 5 til hdd app last; hld flat*	4	2
1090^{3}	**Inis Cara (IRE)** 4-1 **M Hooper** *Midfield; 7th to 8; hdwy to 5th 12; btn 4th 3 out; kpt on; went mod 3rd nr line*	12	3
1090^{8}	How To Run (IRE) 12-1 Miss H Lewis *(bf) 4th early; prog to 2nd & mist 10; lost tch frm 15*	6	4

1188[4] Fassan (IRE)(cp) 33-1 James Price *3rd 1-5; 5th to 11; u.p & fdd aft; last frm 15* . . . . . runin 5
1093[r] Aficionado (IRE) (1ow) 33-1 H Oakes *A last; lost tch frm 7; t.o 11; pu 15*. P
Columna (5a) 50-1 J Price *Mist 1; a last pr; detach frm 7; pu 10*. . . . . . . P
Cream Supreme (IRE) (3x) 6-4F E Williams *Stole sev lengths at start; ld; hdd brief 2 & aft 5; cl 2nd til dem 4th 13; rallied 14 to 2nd; wknd 2 out; 20l 4th last; eased to walk flat, pu & dism nr line* . . . . . P
948[1] Ian's Boy (3x) 12-1 H Evans *Towards rr when ur 1* . . . . . U
1023[3] Jakes Progress (IRE) 14-1 Miss F Wilson *Swtng; a bhnd & last trio; pu 13* . P
1190[3] Orphan Spa (IRE) 50-1 P Sheldrake *4th early & 2nd 6; sn rr & rdn; last pr 11; lost tch & pu 3 out* . . . . . P

OFFICIAL DISTANCES: 3*l*, 15*l* **TIME:** 6min 17.0s

1321 Mixed Open, 12st 6 ran

1090[1] **ROSTOCK (IRE)** evensF **L Stephens** *(xnb) 2 handlers; made all; mist 14; qcknd clr 3 out; sn in comm; slt mist last; trotted in* 1
1235[2] **Zola (IRE)** 25-1 **P Sheldrake** *3rd; rmdrs 5 & went 2nd nxt; in tch to 14; outpcd 3 out; no ex u.p; tired & jmpd v slow last*. 25 2
1099[P] **Mostyn** 14-1 **Mrs T Rowe** *Jmpd slow 1; detach aft; t.o last til snatched 3rd final strides* 15 3
1189[4] Berkeley Frontier (IRE)(tt) 16-1 Mrs E Jones *Ld & jmpd slow & mist 1; 2nd 2-5; 4th when rn wide app 6 & agn 13; mist 12; lost tch aft; 3rd til hvly eased run-in; walked in & dem nr line* 3/4 4
1093[3] Red Neck(tt) 3-1 T Vaughan *(xnb) Nvr gng wl in rr; 6l 3rd 7; mist 9; u.p & wkng 10; pu 11* . . . . . P
1093[2] Speed Board (IRE) 4-1 E Williams *A bhnd; pu & dism 6; lame* . . . . . P

OFFICIAL DISTANCES: 30*l*, 20*l* **TIME:** 6min 18.0s

The stewards enquired into the pulling-up of i) Red Neck, whose rider reported was 'never travelling' and ii) Speed Board, whose rider reported was lame; both explanations were accepted

1322 Restricted, 12st 10 ran

1237[F] **RAG WEEK (IRE)** 5-2 **E Williams** *Mounted outside padd; made virt all; hdd brief 12; 4l up 15; drvn clr 2 out* 1
1094[P] **Batchworth Lock** 14-1 **M Lewis** *(xnb) Cl 2nd 1 til ld 12; hdd 14; 4l 2nd nxt; no ex u.p & tired; scrambled over last* 20 2
1096[1] **Roboastar (USA)**(bl) 7-2 **T Vaughan** *A.p; settled 4th to 10; clsd to 2nd 13-14; 5l 3rd 15; tired frm nxt & sn btn* 15 3
1191[P] Its A Handfull(tt) 25-1 J Harris *1st ride; mist 1; a last pr; detach frm 2; mist 7; t.o 10; plodded on* 2fncs 4
1021[1] Cooleen Strong (IRE) 6-4F L Stephens *(xnb) Nvr gng wl; in last trio to 8; drvn in 6th 12; wknd & pu 3 out*. . . . . P
1074[P] Crystal Vein 25-1 N McDiarmid *(xnb) 6th to 7; lost tch frm nxt; pu 10* . . . P
1188[P] Daisys Rainbow (7a) 25-1 D Jones *A last pr; jmpd lft 6; lost tch; rn violent lft bend aft 12 (exactly as he did here bef); tried to pull himself up; hvy rmdrs; fnce bhnd & pu nxt*. . . . . P
1095[2] Lady Palamon (IRE) (5a) 12-1 S Hughes *(boh) Chsd ldrs; mostly 4th; 12l 4th 15; wknd further; pu last*. . . . . P
1230[3] Native Isle (IRE) 12-1 J Mahot *6th til lost tch 13; t.o & pu 15*. . . . . P
1094[P] Satco Prince (IRE) 25-1 T Faulkner *(xnb,bf) 7th to 11; stayed on past wkng horses to 5th 12; 14l 5th 15; tired & pu 2 out*. . . . . P

OFFICIAL DISTANCES: 15*l*, 12*l* **TIME:** 6min 19.0s

1323 Confined Maiden (Div 1), 12st 6 ran

1027[P] **NEWMARKET MAGIC (IRE)** 6-4F **D Jones** *Trckd clr ldr; clsd frm 7; 2l 2nd 9; u.p 12; 6l 2nd when lft virt solo 2 out; blun thro last; lucky*. 1
1193[F] **Beehive Lad** 5-2 **James Price** *Tde; rr early; settled ab 6l 3rd frm 7; 11l 3rd & wkng 14; v tired & no ch when blun bad & nrly fell 2 out; clambered over last; staggered home*. . . . . runin 2
1231[U] Black Hope (IRE) (5a)(tt) 5-2 L Stephens *(xnb) Ld & sn 12l clr; blun 5 & 5l up nxt; 2l ahd & jmpd slow 9; kpt on frm 14; 6l clr when fell 2 out*. . . . . F
1239[P] Clarice Starling (5a) 5-1 T Vaughan *(xnb,bf) Nt fluent in rr; last frm 6; went 14l 4th & rdn 12; no resp; pu 13*. . . . . P

363P Glastrian 10-1 G Perkins *Ld to start by rdr; a last pr; last & u.p 12; tried to ref 13; scrambled over & pu* . . . P
699U Malvic (IRE) (7a) 10-1 R Carey *Dwelt; last when mist 3; rdr lost irons & pu* P

OFFICIAL DISTANCE: dist **TIME:** 6min 38.0s

This race was delayed for 25 mins with the horses at the start while the medical team attended to a stricken racegoer

1324 Confined Maiden (Div 2), 12st — 13 ran

1095P **CLEAR AWAY (IRE)** 5-4F **T Vaughan** *5s-5/4; a.p; settled 2nd frm 7; jnd ldr 11; ld 13; 6l up 15; drew clr frm 3 out; unchall*. . . 1
Dunmanus Sound (IRE) 3-1 **L Stephens** *In tch in 5th; clsd frm 13; 6l 2nd 15; tired thro gluey ground frm 3 out; sn t.o* . . . runin 2
Peaceful Bow (IRE) 6-1 **D Jones** *Swtng; mostly 2nd til lft in ld 8; jnd 11; hdd 13; lost tch frm 3 out; fin tired* . . . 30 3
453P Belle's Last (5a) 25-1 James Price *(xnb) A bhnd; last trio frm 3; mist 11; btn frm 12; t.o & pu last*. . . P
1096C Celtic Prince (IRE) 7-1 James Tudor *(xnb) A last trio; lost tch 12; wl btn when pu 15* P
1096U Essence Of Time (7a) 33-1 G Perkins *A bhnd; last pr frm 7; pu 11* . . . P
1095U Evans The Coal 33-1 R Carey *Mounted outside padd; reared up & ur; reluct to go down; 6th; clsd to 3l 3rd 9-13; dem but in tch til tired rap 15; wl btn 3rd when pu 2 out* . . . P
1193P Just Caramel (5a)(tt) 14-1 S Hughes *Chsd ldrs; mostly 4th to 9; fdd & lost tch 12; last 13; no ch when pu 15*. . . P
1240² Millenium Run (IRE)(cp) 3-1 E Williams *Nt fluent; 6th when mists 3 & 5; u.p 11; sn lost tch; pu last* . . . P
1240P Riches To Rags (IRE)(bl) 25-1 S Graham *Midfield when blun & ur 1* . . . U
451U Sergwyn 25-1 T Faulkner *Last frm 3; becoming detach when rn out 12* . . . R
1318P Shadar (IRE) (7a, 3ow) 25-1 M Whitehouse *(xnb) 2nd outing; prom; jnd ldr 3; 4l clr 5; ur 8* . . . U
1027² Start It Up 14-1 J Price *Ld 1-4; stdd in 3rd; fdd 12; detach 5th frm nxt; t.o & pu last* . . . P

OFFICIAL DISTANCES: dist, dist **TIME:** 6min 24.0s

Minehead Harriers & West Somerset

Holnicote (LH 7F,19J)

Sat, 8 May (GOOD to FIRM)

1325 Restricted, 12st — 6 ran

1184² **HILL TRAIL** 6-4F **J Barnes** *(xnb) Made all & a 8-15l clr; unchall frm 14* . . . 1
1127³ **Barton Saint (NZ)** 4-1 **Miss S West** *Nt v fluent; mostly 3rd but nvr nr wnr; 2nd brief 14; 20l 3rd app 3 out; rdn into 2nd at last*. . . 12 2
1184U **Mrs Peggoty** (5a) 11-2 **Miss C Tizzard** *Nrly a 2nd but nvr able to get nr wnr; 15l down app 3 out; dem last* . . . 2 3
1131P Georges Pleasure (5a) 8-1 C Heard *In tch in chsng group til rdn & lost tch rap aft 16; pu 3 out*. . . P
Loxley-Lad 20-1 W White *(xnb) Bckwd; midfield & handy in chsng group til 21l 4th & wkng app 3 out; pu & dism last* . . . P
1013² Romany Move 7-2 Mrs S Godfrey *Lw; last til ur aft 6*. . . U

OFFICIAL DISTANCES: 15l, 1½l **TIME:** 6min 34.0s **TOTE:** £2.50 **DF:**£9.80

1326 Open Maiden (Div 1), 12st — 9 ran

413² **TOON SOCIETY (IRE)** 4-5F **N Harris** *Confid rdn; hld up & handy; went 2nd 12; ld 14; hdd 2 out; ld last; rdn clr*. . . 1
884r **Mr Baloo**(bl) 20-1 **A Charles-Jones** *Lft in ld 4; set slow pce; hdd 14; allowed to ld agn 2 out-last; drvn & sn no ch w wnr* . . . 3 2
827⁴ Countryside March (5a) 6-1 Miss L Gardner *2 handlers; 2nd/3rd; hit 11; 5l 4th 12; prob strugg when fell 14* . . . F
1133R Double Bubble (IRE) 25-1 Miss J Buck *(xnb) Tde & unruly; tk no part* . . . r
1182U Hayling Star (5a) 50-1 M Sweetland *Tde; hld up in midfield til blun bad & ur 4* U
Merv's Magic 33-1 M Woodward *(xnb) Pu 2* . . . P
1098³ Roseacre (IRE) 6-1 D Alers-Hankey *Lw; ld til jnkd rt, ref & ur 4* . . . r
1098P Sunleys Quest (5a) 7-2 R Woollacott *(xnb) Hld up; went 2nd 9-12; 3l 3rd aft 16; 8l down & wkng when fell 2 out* . . . F

1186P Tilly Time (5a) 14-1 C Heard *Tk keen hld in detach last; 8l down aft 16; pu 3 out; blatant school* . . . . P

OFFICIAL DISTANCE: 2½l **TIME:** 6min 49.0s **TOTE:** £1.30 **DF:**£9.80

1327 Open Maiden (Div 2), 12st — 12 ran

8844 **GONE ON (IRE)** 5-2 **A Charles-Jones** *5s-5/2; trckd ldrs; 6l 4th 12; went 2nd 15; ld 2 out; pushed out* 1

1133P **The Cooling Agent** 4-1 **Miss P Gundry** *Last early; 12l 5th & niggled 12; eff in 3½l 3rd aft 16; bad outpcd nxt; drvn & stayed on agn to 2nd flat & catching wnr cl home*. 1½ 2

12522 **Bradford Bridge** (5a) 6-4F **R Woollacott** *Lw; 2nd/3rd til ld 11; 2l clr aft 16; rdn & hdd 2 out; one pce aft; dem flat* 1 3

1126F Hoteliers' Dream (5a) 33-1 M Sweetland *Set mod pce; blun 4; hdd 11; 6l 4th aft 16; stayed on agn frm last* . . . . ¾ 4

11823 Inner State (5a) 8-1 D Edwards *Nrly ref 3 & drpd to rr; rdn & reluct 5; u.p nxt; 25l last 12; t.o 16* . . . . runin 5

469P Augathella 25-1 C Heard *(xnb) Chsd ldrs to 9; lsng plce when pu 11* . . . . P

11335 Chasing Buttercups (5a) 10-1 Miss A Goschen *Midfield; 20l 5th & outpcd 12; some prog & 8l 5th aft 16; wknd & ref 2 out* . . . . r

Lansdowne Park (12a) 20-1 Miss A Bush *Pulled hrd in midfield; 5th 10; blun nxt & rfo long way aft 11* . . . . U

1252P Little Mister(bl) 50-1 D Drake *Sn 2nd; dem 12; rdn aft nxt; mist 14 & lost tch; t.o & pu 16* . . . . P

865P Port Valenska (IRE)(cp) 50-1 N Wilmington *Tubed; Millington-esque padd; handy brief; rdn & lost tch aft 6; jmpd slow 7; t.o & pu 10*. . . . . P

Rifton Bramble (5a) 20-1 G Weatherley *Rn off course app 1*. . . . . R

Six Of Tother 16-1 R Ross *Bhnd; mist 6 & lost tch; jmpd slow 7; t.o & pu 9* P

OFFICIAL DISTANCES: 2l, 1l **TIME:** 6min 49.0s **TOTE:** £7.20 **DF:**£5.30

PLATE 14 1327 Minehead Harriers & W. Somerset Open Maiden (Div 2): L to R, Inner State, Port Valenska, The Cooling Agent and Six of Tother *PHOTO: Baths Photographic*

1328 Mixed Open, 12st — 5 ran

822P **DOUBLET** 7-1 **R Woollacott** *Settled 3rd/4th on inner til ld & blun bad 3 out; 3rd nxt; rallied to ld agn last; drvn & r.o; gd ride*. 1

12693 **Porlock Hill** 1-2F **A Farrant** *(xnb) Late rdr change; lw; ld to 7; v cl 2nd til rdn 14; ld agn nxt; hdd 3 out & drvn & lft in ld; jnd last; kpt on; outbattled nr fin* hd 2

1185^{3}	**Travelling Jack**(bl) 6-1 **D Edwards** *Mist 4; 2nd til narrow ld 7-15 where nt fluent; rdn & lkd outpcd 3 out; rallied & ev ch last; no ex final 50yds*	1	3
1209^{5}	Nearly Gold 10-1 Miss V Murphy *Last 3; lost tch 5; t.o 7; snatched rem 4th*	40	4
	Ringside View (IRE) 7-2 A Charles-Jones *(xnb) Hit 1; cl 3rd/4th til 7l 4th & rdn 12; lost tch 15; virt pu flat & dem nr fin*	2	5

OFFICIAL DISTANCES: hd, 1*l* **TIME:** 6min 33.0s **TOTE:** £9.50 **DF:**£1.70

1329 Countryside Alliance Club Members (Nov Rdrs), 12st — 8 ran

1101^{4}	**OPAL'LOU (FR)** (5a) 11-10F **R Pyman** *(xnb) Lw; jw; went prom 4; ld app 10; 6l clr app 14; hdd 16; ld agn nxt & easily drew clr*		1
1127^{5}	**Magical Fun (IRE)** 25-1 **Miss T Hayes** *(xnb) Lw; cl up; went 2nd 12; ld & wl clr w wnr nxt; hdd 3 out; sn btn; fin rather tired; game try*	15	2
1101^{7}	**Chism (IRE)** 28-1 **W King** *Prom to 12; 5th & outpcd app 14; 27l 4th aft 16; plugged into mod 3rd at last*	3	3
692^{P}	Earl's Toy (IRE) 3-1 H Fry *12l last 4; hdwy in 5th but niggled 11; went mod 3rd 15 but 20l down aft nxt; drvn & nvr lkd clsng; dem last*	$1\frac{1}{2}$	4
882^{5}	Gigi Beach (IRE) 20-1 Mrs S Reynoldson *Ld til app 10; 3rd app 14; sn wknd; 34l 5th aft 16*	15	5
1073^{P}	Golden Jack (FR) 9-2 C Morris *Lft padd bckwds at rate of knots; ss & a last pr; sn in tch; wknd app 14; 37l 6th aft 16*	1	6
1250^{8}	Now Young Man (IRE) 25-1 Miss P Moore *2 handlers; handy til drpd to rr 9; 10l last 12; wl bhnd 14; 40l last aft 16*	10	7
603^{P}	Rustic Revelry(bl) 8-1 C Whittaker *(xnb) 14s-8s; last when rfo 3.*		U

OFFICIAL DISTANCES: 25*l*, 6*l* **TIME:** 6min 34.0s **TOTE:** £2.10 **DF:**£10.20

1330 Intermediate, 12st — 5 ran

1129^{5}	**ELLOFAMONKEY** (5a) evensF **A Farrant** *Jw; went 2nd aft 5; ld app 14 & sn in comm; hvly eased flat; quite impressive*		1
921^{2}	**Ballyalbert** 2-1 **Miss A de Lisle Wells** *Jmpd lft (oft bad so); ld & clr to 8; hdd app 14; 10l last aft 16; no hope aft*	10	2
878^{2}	Butterwick King (IRE) 10-1 R Woollacott *12s-10s; nvr really gng wl; 22l 4th aft 9; t.o & pu 11*		P
1012^{5}	Nimbus Stratus(bl) 50-1 N Wilmington *2 handlers; mist 1 & rdn rest of way & a reluct; jmpd lft; 26l last aft 9; t.o & pu 14*		P
1129^{6}	Tinder-Box 7-2 Miss T Cave *Jmpd lft & nvr gng wl; blun 8; 16l 3rd aft nxt; blun 12; 18l 3rd app 14; t.o & scraped over 16; pu nxt*		P

OFFICIAL DISTANCE: 10*l* **TIME:** 6min 32.0s **TOTE:** £2.20 **DF:**£8.40

1331 Confined, 12st — 4 ran

703^{2}	**COLQUHOUN** (7x) 1-4F **A Farrant** *(xnb) Went 2nd 7; ld 15; rdn & hdd aft nxt; scrubbed along aft & forged clr 2 out; $2\frac{1}{2}$l ahd last; idled agn flat; all out; unimpressive (reported lost a shoe)*		1
1168^{13}	**S B S By Jove** 9-2 **A Charles-Jones** *2nd til ld 7; mist 15 & hdd; ld brief aft nxt; rdn & outpcd 2 out; stayed on flat.*	$1\frac{1}{2}$	2
1100^{P}	**Primero (IRE)** 14-1 **G Weatherley** *(xnb) Set slow pce to 7; mist 8; cl up til wknd rap 14; sn t.o*	runin	3
1272^{R}	Roberts Return 25-1 M Woodward *Oht; strangled to canter along in last; jmpd appalling & 24 secs bhnd by 5; rn off to boxes aft 6*		R

OFFICIAL DISTANCES: $1\frac{1}{2}$*l*, dist **TIME:** 6min 41.0s **TOTE:** £1.10 **DF:**£1.10

Vale of Aylesbury with Garth & South Berks

Kingston Blount (LH 8F,18J)

Sat, 8 May (SOFT)

1332 Confined, 12st — 6 ran

1170^{P}	**BULLFINCH** 4-1 **T Lane** *Trckd ldng pr; went 2nd 13-15; eff agn 2 out; drvn to ld last; kpt on u.p*		1
756^{P}	**Finder Keeps (USA)** 7-2 **J Jenkins** *Hld up in tch; nt fluent 7; trckd ldrs 13; went 2nd 15; ld 3 out; narrowly hdd last; no ex*	$1\frac{1}{2}$	2
1172^{P}	**Irilut (FR)**(bl) 5-4F **S Waley-Cohen** *(xnb) In tch; outpcd app 14 & niggled along; tried to rally 3 out; disp 5l 4th when blun 2 out; no imp aft*	8	3

1104^{3} Border Farmer (IRE) 33-1 N Wain *Jmpd rt; ld to 9; ld brief 11; last frm 13; no ch when rfo some way aft 2 out* . . . . U

Golden Savannah 33-1 Miss L Sleep *(xnb) A last; wknd 12; t.o & pu nxt* . . P

337^{1} Gray Knight (IRE) 5-1 James Tudor *Prsd ldr; ld 9; made most to 3 out; wknd & jmpd slow 2 out; pu last* . . . . P

OFFICIAL DISTANCES: $1\frac{1}{2}$*l*, 5*l* **TIME:** 6min 43.4s

1333 Restricted, 12st — 8 ran

571^{3} **SUTTON COURTENAY (IRE)** 8-1 **J Jenkins** *Tchd 12s; rr; pushed along $^{1}/_{2}$way; mist 11 & rmdrs; strugg aft 13; eff u.p to 4th nxt; drvn & clsd 2 out; ld last; just hld on; all out* 1

1282^{2} **Ministerial (IRE)** 3-1 **P York** *Trckd ldr to 3 & agn 9; ld nxt; 4l up & gng wl 14; mist nxt; blun 3 out; hrd prsd nxt; hdd last; rallied u.p nr fin; just failed* hd 2

870^{3} **Murphy's Magic (IRE)** 6-1 **Julian Pritchard** *Tchd 10s; midfield; mist 7; trckd ldr 10 til blun 13; 5th 14; rdn & prog agn to press ldr 2 out; ev ch last; no ex flat* 4 3

779^{F} Balau (7a) 9-1 P Bull *(xnb) Hld up; prog to 3rd 10; trckd ldr aft 13-15; cl up & ev ch app 2 out; sn wknd* 20 4

1107^{5} Shortcut Shorty 12-1 C Wadland *Midfield; drpd to last 10; lost tch 13; wl bhnd & no ch frm nxt* 5 5

1191^{5} Silly Boy 40-1 A Foster *Pushed up to press ldr 3-9; prom til went 2nd agn 15; wknd rap aft 3 out* 7 6

50^{3} Esendi 2-1F J Diment *Ld to 10; sn lost plce; wknd rap 13; pu sn aft* . . . . P

1034^{3} Lah Di Dah Lad 5-1 J Tarry *Last pr; nt fluent 9; 6th & outpcd aft 13; eff u.p nxt; no imp on ldrs 3 out; wknd & pu last* . . . . P

OFFICIAL DISTANCES: nk, 5*l* **TIME:** 6min 44.2s

1334 Ladies Open — 4 ran

1106^{2} **LINLATHEN** 7-4 **Miss Gemma Hutchinson** *(xnb) Made virt all; qcknd 14; 3l clr when hit 3 out; hrd prsd aft; gd j last; hld on nr fin* 1

938^{4} **Pride Of Kashmir** 11-4 **Miss A Stennett** *Hld up in tch; cl 3rd frm 13; chsd wnr aft 3 out; outj last; stayed on wl flat; just hld* . . . . nk 2

1033^{1} **Ryans Star** 11-8F **Mrs J Parris** *Trckd wnr; jmpd awkward 13; stumbled 3 out & lost 2nd; still ch at last; wknd flat* 8 3

1104^{4} Lottie The Lotus (5a) 12-1 Miss R Goodwin *A 3rd/4th; in tch to 14; sn outpcd; one pce aft* 8 4

OFFICIAL DISTANCES: nk, 4*l* **TIME:** 6min 46.2s

1335 Land Rover Mens Open, 12st — 3 ran

1207^{1} **CEDAR CHIEF** (7x)(bl) 1-4F **C Gordon** *Trckd ldr; ld 6; made rest; easily drew clr frm 15* 1

1168^{11} **Supreme Storm (IRE)** (7x) 4-1 **R Bandey** *Cl up; trckd wnr 7; outpcd 15; nd aft* 10 2

1228^{6} **Lyphard's Fable (USA)** 12-1 **D England** *Ld; hdd & jmpd slow 6; last & rdn 12; lft bhnd frm 15* 12 3

OFFICIAL DISTANCES: 8*l*, 12*l* **TIME:** 6min 46.5s

1336 Intermediate, 12st — 4 ran

1059^{P} **WATERLOO LEADER (IRE)** 12-1 **D Smith** *Cl up; hmpd 6; chall frm app 14; ld 2 out; sn clr; rdn out* 1

1120^{4} **Miss Hoity Toity** (5a) 2-1 **A Sansome** *Reluct to line up; cl up; eff to ld 15; hdd & stumbled bad 2 out; drpd to 3rd & no ch aft; went mod 2nd flat* 15 2

1103^{F} **Charlie's Angel** (5a, 5x) 8-11F **P York** *(xnb) Reluct to line up; trckd ldr; lft in ld 6; mist & hdd 15; rdn to chall agn nxt; ev ch 2 out; sn wknd; lost 2nd flat & eased* 8 3

717^{U} Itsforu 11-2 J Jenkins *8s-11/2; ld; 1l up when fell 6* . . . . F

OFFICIAL DISTANCES: 12*l*, 5*l* **TIME:** 6min 47.6s

1337 Open Maiden, 12st — 9 ran

1261^{B} **GUNNABALLRIGHT** 7-4F **N Pearce** *6s-7/4; hld up; a gng wl; prog & 3rd 12; ld 14; clr nxt; rdn aft 3 out; in comm aft nxt* 1

1273^{U} **Rockford (IRE)** 3-1 **C Wadland** *Chsd ldr to 6; jmpd slow 7; 2nd agn aft 8 til app 14; chsd wnr 15; no imp frm 3 out* 12 2

1075^{6} **Isefoul De Bellevue (FR)** 7-1 **J Horton** *Chsd ldrs; 4th & wl in tch aft 13; 3rd & outpcd aft 15; no ch aft* 7 3

1211[7] Barbed Broach (IRE) 12-1 Miss C Cowe *(xnb,boh) Ld to 14; last & wkng 3 out; v tired* 20 4
978[r] Dinnys Double (5a) 6-1 P York *Rn out 1 & sent rdr flying into hedge* . . . . R
Hunter Gatherer 8-1 B King *2 handlers; prom; chsd ldr & jmpd slow 6; lost plce bend aft 8; rmdrs & prom agn 10; wknd 12; pu aft nxt* . . . . P
1035[U] Les The Lizard 8-1 A Sansome *Last when ref & ur 2* . . . . r
1273[F] Ski Country (5a) 8-1 B Pauling *Hld up; 6th 10; same & wl in tch when rfo 12* U
971[P] Smokey Robot (IRE) 10-1 D Dennis *(xnb) Swtng; nt jw; a rr; lost tch 11; miles bhnd when pu 14* . . . . P

OFFICIAL DISTANCES: 12*l*, 5*l* **TIME:** 6min 55.5s

1338 Hunt Members — 2 ran

892[7] **BERING GIFTS (IRE)** 2-1 **R Cope** *Made all; 20l clr aft 5; jmpd slow & came back to rival frm 8; kicked 6l clr agn 15; drvn 3 out; slowed into last & swishing tail; kpt on wl agn flat* 1
1212[1] **Mister Pepper (IRE)** 4-11F **T Underwood** *Hld up; clsd on rival 9; mist 15 & outpcd; rdn 3 out; clsd & 1l down at last; no ex flat* 2½ 2

OFFICIAL DISTANCE: 2½*l* **TIME:** 6min 48.0s

Wheatland

Chaddesley Corbett (LH 8F,18J)
Sat, 8 May (GOOD to SOFT)

1339 Open Maiden 56&7yo, 12st — 13 ran

962[4] **LUCKY WYN** 10-1 **M Walters** *A.p; 6l 3rd ½way; lft in ld 10; in comm when lft clr at last* 1
Copper Grove (IRE) 20-1 **D Barlow** *2 handlers; hld up; 13l 7th ½way; hdwy 11; 4l 6th nxt; rdn & one pce 3 out; lft 2nd at last* 4 2
Jolejoker 5-2 **R Burton** *(xnb) Mounted outside padd; hld up & bhnd; 19l 9th ½way; hdwy & 7l 8th 12; jnd ldrs 14; rdn 3 out; one pce* 7 3
Teeton Prince (7a) 16-1 R Cope *Hld up; hdwy 5; 9l 4th ½way; 1½l 3rd 12; ev ch when pckd 3 out; sn wknd* 8 4
1124[U] Martha Jane (5a) 12-1 Miss N Hickling *(xnb) 2 handlers; a bhnd; lost tch 6; t.o last when mist 10; blun on* 1½fs 5
887[4] Cashari (IRE) 3-1 S Morris *Swtng; hld up; 10l 5th ½way; jnd ldrs 11; 2½l 4th nxt; went 2nd 13; ev ch 2 out; 2l down & hld when fell last* . . . . F
890[P] Golden Dawn 25-1 Miss S Phizacklea *Sn bhnd; 19½l 10th ½way; 11l 9th when ur 12* . . . . U
652[F] Little Heck (IRE)(tt) 20-1 P Mason *A bhnd; 20l 11th ½way; 9th when slpd up bend aft 11* . . . . S
1266[2] Mervsintrouble(cp) 7-1 D Greenway *Mist 3; w ldrs til lost plce 6; 16l 8th & rdn ½way; rallied aft 10; went 2nd 11-13; wknd & 10l 7th 15; pu 3 out; lame* P
1246[P] Pernickety King (7a) 25-1 P Millington *Hld up & bhnd; 22l 12th ½way; hdwy & 5l 7th 12; 7l 6th & wkng when mist 15; t.o & pu last* . . . . P
Petrie 25-1 R Hodges *(xnb) Mist 4; 2nd/3rd til wknd qckly & bad mist 11; 10th when pu 12* . . . . P
1075[2] Rody (IRE)(bl) 2-1F D Mansell *(xnb) Ld; 5l clr 8 til rn out 10* . . . . R
1116[3] Teeton Toast 8-1 N Pearce *Hld up; 12l 6th ½way; hdwy 11; 3½l 5th nxt; wknd 14; 15l 8th when pu 15* . . . . P

OFFICIAL DISTANCES: 4*l*, 6*l* **TIME:** 6min 27.6s

The stewards interviewed the owner and rider of Rody who ran out; since this had happened before they reported the horse to the Portman Square

1340 Open Maiden 8yo&up (Div 1), 12st — 8 ran

1255[2] **ROSEMEAD TYE** (5a) 8-1 **Mrs K Baimbridge** *Ld to 3; 2nd to 12 & frm 14; ld 15; sn clr; hit last; unchall* 1
1173[P] **Classic Fable (IRE)** (5a)(tt) 4-1 **A Hanly** *Pulled hrd; a.p; 7l 3rd ½way; went 4l 12-14 & 7l 2nd when blun 3 out; sn btn* 12 2
1261[F] **Royrace** 5-4F **G Hanmer** *5/2-5/4; hld up; disp 12l 4th ½way; rdn 12; 6l 5th 13; wknd u.p 15; went poor 3rd aft nxt* 10 3
1119[4] Sams Sister (5a) 7-1 P Cowley *Hld up; 13½l 7th ½way; hdwy 12; 7l 6th nxt; rdn & wknd 15* 2½ 4

1075P Red Spark 9-2 E Walker *(xnb) Hld up; last to 10; hdwy 12; 5l 4th nxt; rdn & wknd 15; virt pu flat* . . . 12 5

Liscombe (5a) 8-1 Miss H Watson *(xnb) Bit bckwd; tk str hld; ld 3; 8l clr 6-8; qcknd 8l clr 11; jmpd slow 12; hdd & wknd rap 15; t.o when mist 2 out* 5 6

848P Pekan Polly (5a) 12-1 S Ross *Nd; 13l 6th 1/2way; rdn & wknd 12; 15l 7th nxt; wl bhnd when pu aft 15* . . . P

668P Westington 7-1 Miss C Hart *(xnb) Mist 3; jmpd slow 4; 12l 4th 1/2way; drpd to rr 10; t.o 12; pu 14* . . . P

OFFICIAL DISTANCES: 15*l*, 12*l* **TIME:** 6min 38.7s

1341 Open Maiden 8yo&up (Div 2), 12st — 11 ran

11689 **NEWS FLASH (IRE)** 11-10F **Miss L Brooke** *2 handlers; swtng; made all; qcknd 13; 6l clr 15; hit nxt; unchall* . . . 1

10003 **Abitofahike (IRE)** 9-1 **A Martin** *(xnb,orbs) A chsng wnr; mists 8 & 3 out; no imp aft* . . . 10 2

1119F **Little Dish** (5a) 7-1 **H Dowty** *(xnb) A.p; 6l 3rd 1/2way; mist 10; one pce 3 out* 1 1/4 3

1215U Dolitanlad 20-1 P Millington *2 handlers; a bhnd; 18l 10th 1/2way; 13l 8th 12; t.o aft 15* . . . runin 4

1258P Contrary King 14-1 T Weston *Mounted outside padd; tde; unruly start; hld up; 15l 7th 1/2way; 12l 7th 12; lost tch nxt; wl bhnd when pu aft 14* . . . P

189P Craven Hill (IRE) 14-1 Miss S Phizacklea *Ss; a bhnd; 20l last 1/2way; t.o & pu 3 out* P

1232U Four Opinions 8-1 D Mansell *Hld up; 12l 5th 1/2way; hdwy 11; 6l 4th nxt; wknd u.p 3 out; 15l 4th when fell nxt* . . . F

12115 Ginmini (IRE) (5a, 4ow) 20-1 M Caldwell *Hld up & bhnd; 16l 8th 1/2way; hdwy 11; 9l 5th nxt; wknd 13; t.o & pu 3 out* . . . P

631F Hawthorn 10-1 A Hanly *(xnb,bf) Chsd ldrs; mists 4 & 5; 8l 4th 1/2way; fell 11* F

1193U Sneedham's Green 20-1 P Mason *Tubed; 2 handlers; nd; mist & rmdrs 7; 14l 6th & hrd drvn 1/2way; stpd to nil u.p aft 10; t.o & pu aft 11* . . . P

7533 Times Two 4-1 A Wadlow *(xnb) Hld up & bhnd; 17l 9th 1/2way; some hdwy & 11l 6th 12; wknd 14; 20l 5th when pu nxt* . . . P

OFFICIAL DISTANCES: 6*l*, 1 1/4*l* **TIME:** 6min 24.3s

1342 Mens Open, 12st — 6 ran

9861 **MINELLA SILVER (IRE)** 7-2 **A Wintle** *2nd til ld 13; hdd 15; ld app 3 out; drvn out* 1

12542 **The Campdonian (IRE)** 7-1 **E Walker** *Last 3-6; 10l 5th 1/2way; bhnd til hdwy u.p 12; 6l 3rd nxt; stayed on wl 3 out; went 2nd flat; nt rch wnr* . . . 2 1/2 2

660R **Fane Counsel (IRE)** 2-5F **R Burton** *(xnb) Jmpd rt; ld to 13; ld 15 til app 3 out; ev ch nxt; switched lft last; wknd flat* . . . 7 3

12635 City Gent 16-1 G Hanmer *Prom; 5l 3rd 1/2way; lost plce 12; went 10l 4th 14; no imp 3 out* . . . 7 4

1214P Exclusive Air (USA) (7a) 50-1 P Millington *(citation) Nt jw; a last pr; rdn & lost tch 8; t.o & pu 12* . . . P

1170P Gallion's Reach (IRE) (7x)(bl,tt) 33-1 T Ellis *(xnb,bf) Chsd ldrs; 8l 4th 1/2way; hit 9; 4l 3rd & drvn 12; wknd & 12l 5th 14; wl bhnd when pu 3 out* . . . P

OFFICIAL DISTANCES: 2 1/2*l*, 4*l* **TIME:** 6min 18.3s

1343 Ladies Open — 8 ran

11361 **CAMPDEN KITTY** (5a) 6-4F **Miss J Williams** *2s-6/4; made all; qcknd 7l clr 3 out; comf* . . . 1

12295 **Do It Once (IRE)** (7x)(tt) 8-1 **Mrs A Rucker** *(xnb) Hld up; hdwy 5; 5l 3rd 1/2way; lost plce 11; 7l 6th nxt; lost tch 14; stayed on wl 2 out; went 2nd nr fin* . . . 5 2

1203U **Chadswell (IRE)** (7x) 11-1 **Miss T Clark** *A 2nd/3rd; chsd wnr 8; rdn 3 out; one pce; dem nr fin* . . . nk 3

12532 Welburn Boy(bl,tt) 12-1 Miss L Allfrey *Chsd ldrs; 6 1/2l 4th 1/2way; 4l 3rd 12; 6l 4th 14; one pce* . . . 2 4

1263P Pacon (GER) (7x)(tt) 3-1 Miss H Kinsey *(xnb) Hld up; 10l 7th 1/2way; hdwy when mist 12; went 4l 3rd nxt; rdn 3 out; sn btn* . . . s hd 5

12294 Head Gardener (IRE)(bl) 25-1 Miss J Hughes *2nd/3rd to 6; 7l 5th 1/2way; no hdwy 12; lost tch 14; t.o* . . . 25 6

10332 Kentford Busy B (5a) 100-30 Miss S Phizacklea *W ldrs; jmpd v slow 4; disp 7l 5th 1/2way; shkn up 11; lost tch 12; t.o 15* . . . runin 7

11071 Miss Zarnni (5a) 5-1 Miss S Sharratt *A last; wl bhnd 7; t.o 11; pu 13* . . . P

OFFICIAL DISTANCES: 3*l*, nk **TIME:** 6min 19.9s

1344 PPORA Club Members 8yo&up, 12st — 8 ran

	BROOK BEE 10-1 **D Sherlock** *Ld 2 til app 8; 2nd til ld aft 3 out; 1½l up last; hld on wl nr fin*		1
364^2d	**Native King (IRE)**(bl) 5-1 **M Walters** *Ld 1-2; 2nd til ld app 8; reluct & hdd aft 3 out; rallied nr fin*	½	2
815^2	**Arctic Burner (IRE)** 10-1 **Mrs J Chapman** *Ld to 1; lost plce 5; went 4l 3rd ½way; drpd back 9l 5th 12; went 7l 3rd aft 15; no imp*	10	3
1262^2	Raconteur (IRE) 3-1 D Greenway *(bh) Hld up; last to 6; 8l 7th ½way; 12l 6th & rdn when mist 12; wknd u.p 15*	12	4
722^4	Wild Blade (IRE)(cp) 16-1 R Jenkins *Hld up; hdwy & 5l 5th ½way; 8l 4th 12; wknd aft 15; t.o & virt pu flat*	25	5
1276^P	Gortroe Guy (IRE)(bl) 20-1 M Keel *Jmpd slow 4; last 6; sn rdn & no resp; lost tch 10; t.o 12; pu 14*		P
1015^P	Rubissimo (IRE)(bl) 3-1 M Harris *10s-3s; hld up; hdwy 5; 4½l 4th ½way; 2l 3rd 12; wknd qckly aft 15; poor 4th when jmpd slow 2 out; pu last*		P
1228^F	Westcoast 5-4F R Burton *(bf) W ldrs til lost plce & 7l 6th ½way; 15l 7th 12; wl bhnd when pu 14*		P

OFFICIAL DISTANCES: ½l, 8l **TIME:** 6min 24.6s

1345 Restricted, 12st — 10 ran

981^1	**WIND ON THE COMMON** 8-1 **T Stephenson** *2nd to 3; went 7l 2nd 7-11; 22l 4th nxt; went 12l 3rd 15; ld app 3 out; rdn out*		1
1265^7	**Clodagh Valley (IRE)** 10-1 **W Kinsey** *Prom til lost plce 6; 12½l 5th ½way; went 18l 3rd 11 & 15l 2nd 14; chsd wnr 3 out; one pce*	2½	2
839^2	**Belle Moss** (5a) 9-4 **N Oliver** *5s-9/4; hld up; last 6 til 27l 7th 12; stayed on 3 out; went 3rd last; nt rch ldrs*	10	3
1230^P	Almost A Day(bl) 14-1 D Mansell *(xnb) 2 handlers; rdn 8; 15l 6th ½way; 24l 5th 12; bhnd til hdwy u.p 15; went 10l 3rd app 2 out; sn wknd*	12	4
1265^10	Gaetano (IRE)(bl) 33-1 J O'Brien *Ld 4; sn clr; 15l up 11-15; hdd & wknd rap app 3 out*	8	5
850^1	Fly For Paddy 10-1 A Wadlow *2 handlers; hld up; 7th when bd 5*		B
1265^P	Gabaka De Thaix (FR) 33-1 M Caldwell *Swtng; a bhnd; 15½l 7th ½way; 30l last 12; t.o 14; pu 3 out*		P
1143^1	Mullarts Lad (IRE) (7a) 100-30 S Ross *5th when fell 5*		F
1048^P	Ridware Pride 12-1 Miss S Sharratt *Swtng; ld to 4; 2nd to 7; 12l 4th ½way; lost plce 11; 25l 6th nxt; wl bhnd when blun & ur 3 out*		U
39^1	Special Friend (IRE) 6-4F R Burton *(xnb) 9/4-6/4; hld up; last 5; hdwy 7; went 11l 3rd ½way & 15l 2nd 11; wknd qckly 14; t.o & pu 3 out*		P

OFFICIAL DISTANCES: 2l, 6l **TIME:** 6min 28.4s

1346 Hunt Members, 12st — 2 ran

840^P	**NEALIE MAC (IRE) M Wall** *2 handlers; oft outj rival; ld to 14; ld 15; clr 2 out; hung lft; kpt on wl*		1
1015^6	**Karinga Lane A Wadlow** *(xnb) Ld 14-15; hrd rdn aft 3 out; sn btn*	10	2

OFFICIAL DISTANCE: 8l **TIME:** 6min 44.6s

The one bookmaker offering prices on this race was betting solely on the forecast

Market Rasen (RH 8F,14J)

Sun, 9 May (SOFT)

1347 Geostar HC, 2m6f110y £1603 — 10 ran

1160^3	**PERCHANCER (IRE)** 11-07 12-1 **Miss A Armitage** *Stdd start; hld up & bhnd; tk keen hld; hdwy 10; lft in ld last; stayed on wl*		1
1177^B	**Mr McDuck (IRE)** 11-13 12-1 **L Bates** *Chsd ldrs; went 2nd 9; blun 3 out; lft w ev ch last; no ex*	8	2
1169^2	**Mullensgrove** 12-05 2-1F **Miss S Phizacklea** *Sn pushed along; hdwy to chse ldrs 7; wl outpcd 11*	4	3
1290^U	Winter Gale (IRE) 11-07 10-1 Miss L Eddery *Stdd start; hld up & bhnd; hdwy 5; outpcd frm 14*	1¼	4

992[3] Bold Classic (IRE) 12-00 4-1 T Greenall *Bhnd; some hdwy 9; sn lost plce; virt pu flat* . . . . . dist 5
1068[5] Decoded 12-00(cp) 33-1 N Tutty *Chsd ldrs; blun 7; lost plce nxt; t.o 14; pu nxt* P
997[3] Gratomi (IRE) 11-07 14-1 N Kent *Chsd ldrs; wknd 9; bhnd when pu 3 out* P
Pats Cross (IRE) 11-07 33-1 Miss Rachel Clark *Ld to 4; blun 6; pu aft nxt.* P
776[2] Rising Talisker 11-04(cp) 33-1 Miss C Metcalfe *Bhnd frm 7; t.o when ref 9* r
1289[1] Royal Snoopy (IRE) 11-07(bl) 3-1 R Abrahams *Chsd ldrs; ld 4; clr 10; 18l ahd when blun & ur last* . . . . . U

TIME: 6min 07.6s **TOTE:** £13.20; places £3.90,£3.00,£1.60 **Ex:**£91.70 **CSF:**£138.23

Tetcott

Lifton (RH 7F,19J)

Sun, 9 May (GOOD, FIRMER & SOFTER in places)

1348 Confined, 12st — 4 ran

1168[5] **BILL ME UP (IRE)** (6x) 2-5F **L Heard** *Lw; 2 handlers; jw & made all; drew rt away frm 3 out; hvly eased; v easy* 1
1128[F] **Shobrooke Mill** (5x)(cp) 9-4 **A Farrant** *(xnb) Settled 3rd; hit 10; went 2nd 12; hit 14 & 5l down & u.p nxt; no ch w wnr aft.* 20 2
1197[4] **Moorland Rose** (5a) 20-1 **Miss S Young** *20l adrift & rdn aft 2; nt jw; fnce bhnd 6; t.o* 30sec 3
907[3] Baldhu Jay Arr 16-1 Miss L Gardner *Chsd wnr to 12; nt fluent 14 & 20l 3rd nxt; sn t.o; blun 2 out; pu last* . . . . . P

OFFICIAL DISTANCES: 12*l*, dist **TIME:** 6min 04.3s

1349 Mens Open — 2 ran

1166[P] **DAMIENS PRIDE (IRE)** 11-10 **D Dennis** *(xnb,boh) Made all & a gng btr than rival; 4l clr when jmpd lft 2 out & rdn; jmpd lft last; hld on wl* 1
1194[2] **Midnight Coup**(bl) 8-11F **A Farrant** *Chsd rival & outj; niggled frm 5; rdn 12; outpcd u.p 3 out; some imp frm nxt but a dogging it* 1 1/4 2

OFFICIAL DISTANCE: 1*l* **TIME:** 6min 17.0s

1350 Ladies Open — 6 ran

1130[3] **IT'SNOTSIMPLE (IRE)** (5a) 7-1 **Mrs T Trickey** *(xnb) Ld 2-8 & frm 10; drew clr app 2 out; rdly* 1
1189[1] **Breteche (FR)** (5a) 5-2 **Miss T Newman** *(xnb) Tde; ld to 2 & 8-9; prsd wnr aft; 1l down & rdn aft 3 out; sn outpcd* 6 2
1197[3] **Defendtherealm** 16-1 **Miss A Mills** *In tch; last brief 10; eff 13; 4 1/2l 4th aft 3 out; one pce & no imp aft* 3/4 3
1166[P] Traditional (IRE) 20-1 Miss R Green *(xnb) Lw; cl 3rd & rdn 15; blun nxt; 4l 3rd aft 3 out; sn btn* 3 4
1166[4] Phoenix Phlyer(cp) 7-4F Miss C Stucley *Hld up; 10l last 5 & nvr lkd happy; 6l bhnd rest aft jmpd slow 11; eff 12-13 but rdn & no resp nxt; 8l 5th & btn aft 3 out; jmpd slow nxt* 4 5
1197[2] Guru Rinpoche 5-2 Miss L Gardner *Swtng; cl up til lost plce 12; last & jmpd slow nxt; fnd nil u.p 15; sn rem* 25 6

OFFICIAL DISTANCES: 2*l*, 1*l* **TIME:** 5min 58.2s

1351 Intermediate (Nov Rdrs), 12st — 6 ran

1196[2] **LINGERING FOG (IRE)** 9-4 **Miss M McCarthy** *Ld to 4; slt ld 7 til rdn ahd aft 12 (hit 8); 6l clr 15; prsd brief 2 out; stayed on stout* 1
912[5] **Milla's Man (IRE)** 11-2 **M Dennis** *Ld 4-7; w wnr to 11; rdn & kpt trying to gt back on terms aft; u.p to flatt brief 2 out; sn btn* 7 2
1101[8] **Silent Action (USA)**(tt) 8-1 **D Smith** *Nd in midfield; 20l 3rd 11; nvr any imp* 30 3
1196[4] Baldhu Jack 14-1 Miss P Moorhouse *Swtng; lost tch & rdr waved 5; 20l last 7; pu 9* . . . . . P
1268[F] Derrilady (5a) 50-1 L Rowe *Tk keen hld early; 3rd 6; mist 7; fdd to 40l 4th 11; wl t.o when pu aft 14* . . . . . P
860[F] Scarlet Glory (5a) 4-5F H Fry *(xnb) Lw; 2 handlers; nt jw in last pr; lost tch 5; mist 8 & rdn; strugg when jmpd v sticky 10 & pu* . . . . . P

OFFICIAL DISTANCES: 4*l*, 15*l* **TIME:** 6min 08.0s

1352 Restricted, 12st — 3 ran

1102^{P}	**MENANTOL** 11-8 **Miss A de Lisle Wells** *Slt ld frm 4; hit 3 out; sn 4l clr; in comm aft*		1
1102^{5}	**Carling Elect** (5a) evensF **Miss J Buck** *(xnb) Ld til jnd 4; last 9; 2nd agn 13; ev ch til mist 3 out & rdn; strugg aft; eased flat*	8	2
824^{7}	**The Real Murphy (IRE)** 4-1 **S Rogers** *Mist 5; w rivals til 2l last & tired 15; sn rem*	20	3

OFFICIAL DISTANCES: 6*l*, 18*l* **TIME:** 6min 15.3s

1353 Open Maiden, 12st — 10 ran

1248^{F}	**RINGS OF POWER (IRE)** evensF **N Mitchell** *Hit 1; pulled hrd; last to 9; mist 10; smooth eff 12 to jn ldr 15; level aft mist 3 out; sn rdn clr; comf*		1
1132^{B}	**Harnage (IRE)** 10-1 **Miss C Prouse** *Towards rr; hdwy in 3rd brief 11; 7th aft 14; 25l 5th aft 3 out; fin str to 2nd flat; no ch w wnr; gvn v inept ride*	4	2
1006^{5}	**Tarpon Tale (IRE)**(cp) 10-1 **G Weatherley** *(xnb,b4) Ld; 6l clr brief 11; nt fluent 13; jnd 15; hdd aft 3 out; hrd drvn & btn nxt; jmpd slow last; dem flat*	8	3
910^{P}	Indian Renegade (IRE) (5a) 25-1 Miss L Gardner *Prom; went 2nd 12 til 3l 3rd 15; 10l down aft 3 out; v one-pcd*	3	4
1252^{P}	Coastal Flight 3-1 Miss R Green *Towards rr; 7th & rdn 12; strugg & no ch frm 15; mist 3 out*	12	5
913^{R}	Dark Comedy (5a) 33-1 W Biddick *Mist 10; prsd ldr to 12; wknd qckly 15 & sn wl bhnd*	7	6
909^{F}	French Guest (7a) 10-1 Richard Darke *Midfield; mist 9; in tch til 9l 4th & outpcd 15; 22l 4th aft mist 3 out; 5th when pu 2 out*		P
795^{P}	King Tudor 33-1 M Woodward *Prom to 9; last & rdn 12; t.o & pu 16*		P
1272^{6}	Mo's O Friendly 7-1 M Munrowd *(xnb) Tk keen hld in last trio til fell 6*		F
486^{P}	Mr Rory 20-1 Miss P Moorhouse *Lw; oht; pulled hrd in midfield til rn out 4*		R

OFFICIAL DISTANCES: 3*l*, 4*l* **TIME:** 6min 20.0s

Towcester (RH 10F)

Mon, 10 May (HEAVY)

1354 Gibbs & Dandy HC, 2m110y - 11J £1855 — 9 ran

1087^{2}	**KING OF THE DAWN** 11-05 15-2 **J Sole** *Cl up; disp ld frm 6 til urged clr frm last*		1
1173^{U}	**Win The Toss** 11-09 10-1 **P York** *Handy; jnd wnr & nt fluent 6; still level at last; drvn & wknd; fin tired*	5	2
1166^{3}	**Sol Music** 11-12 4-6F **L Jefford** *Ld; hit 4; mist & hdd 6; cl up til rdn & wknd 2 out; fin tired*	10	3
1173^{4}	Viscount Bankes 11-07(cp) 9-2 A Martin *(xnb) Swtng bad; tk keen hld & prom; hit 5; rdn & wknd rap 2 out; fin v tired*	4	4
1154^{P}	Catherine's Way (IRE) 11-05(cp) 33-1 Miss A Stennett *Prom til wknd aft 7; t.o & pu last*		P
847^{P}	Easby Blue 11-05(tt) 40-1 J Buxton *(xnb) Imm lost tch; 7th when hit 7 & ur*		U
757^{5}	Midy's Risk (FR) 11-05 28-1 Miss S Davies *Tde; brief speed; strugg 4; jmpd v slow 6; sn t.o; pu 2 out*		P
628^{P}	Santi (FR) 11-09 25-1 P Cowley *Hld up in tch; wknd 7; t.o & pu 2 out*		P
1207^{P}	Two Of Diamonds 11-07 100-1 M Harris *Imm lost tch; t.o 6; pu 3 out*		P

TIME: 4min 36.6s **TOTE:** £10.20; places £1.70,£3.10,£1.10 **Ex:**£45.20 **CSF:**£64.07

Fence 8 omitted - state of ground

1355 Martin Moore 50th Birthday HC, 3m1f - 16J £2149 — 4 ran

1105^{2}	**MR SNOWMAN** 11-07 7-4F **James Tudor** *Lft in ld 4; set crawl; jmpd slow 9; hdd aft 3 out; ld agn nxt; rdn & stayed on game*		1
1263^{4}	**Wandering Light (IRE)** 11-11 11-4 **Miss T Clark** *Lft 2nd 4; nt a fluent; jmpd slow 10; prsd wnr til ld aft 3 out; hdd nxt; tried to rally flat; edged lft; no ex*	2	2
1090^{4}	**Chief Predator (USA)** 11-07 8-1 **T Faulkner** *A last; lost tch 11; 9l 3rd 3 out; stayed on aft last; nt rch ldrs*	2½	3
1185^{2}	Dancing Fosenby 11-11 2-1 M Holdforth *(xnb) Ld & sn clr; jmpd slow 1 & 2; climbed 3; 34l ahd when ref & ur 4*		r

TIME: 7min 34.4s **TOTE:** £2.10; **Ex:**£5.40 **CSF:**£6.74

Fences 4 & 14 omitted - state of ground

1356 Severn Valley Catering Nov HC, 2m6f - 15J £1904 — 5 ran

1213[2] **TEETON PRICELESS** 10-10 7-2 **N Pearce** *Hld up & cl up; went 2nd 12; rdn & ev ch but lkd hld when lft clr 2 out; kpt on one pce.* . . . 1
1294[P] **Newby End (IRE)** 11-03 (2ow)(vis) 5-1 **D Dennis** *Chsd ldr til jmpd slow 3; prom til rdn & wknd 3 out; lft 11l 2nd but exhaust 2 out; climbed last* . 14 2
759[P] **Bankit** 11-05 9-1 **J Jenkins** *Ld at v slow pce; mist 5; hdd 12; wknd bad 3 out; climbed nxt; fin v tired & btn 55l* . . . dist 3
1256[P] Rocky Balboa 11-05 40-1 D Mansell *Clambered over sev fncs; last til clsd 6; rdn 9; lost tch & slow 13; climbed 3 out & nxt; t.o & pu last* . . . P
1171[U] Tanager 11-01(bl) 5-6F B King *Cl up; ld 13; 1l ahd & lkd to be gng btr when pckd & ur 2 out* . . . U

TIME: 6min 25.5s **TOTE:** £3.70; places £1.20,£2.40 **Ex:**£14.30 **CSF:**£18.19

Fences 2 & 12 omitted - state of ground

1357 Wayside HC, 3m1f - 16J £2177 — 4 ran

1171[3] **FREEDOM FIGHTER** 11-09 6-4JF **A Martin** *Tk keen hld & rcd wide; w ldr to 5; ld 9; hdd & hit 11; ld app 2 out; sn clr; stayed on stout.* . . . 1
1170[6] **Grecian Star** 11-11 6-4JF **J Docker** *Pckd 3 & 6; cl up til ld 11; hdd 3 out; chsd wnr vain app nxt; v tired* . . . 17 2
1170[P] **Hijacked** 11-11 6-1 **G Hanmer** *Settled cl last til eff 10; ld brief 3 out; tired bad up hill aft* . . . 8 3
1017[r] Fanion De Nourry (FR) 11-07 8-1 Miss S Sharratt *Disp ld til ld 5; hdd & mist 9; strugg when mist 11; plodded on; nt fluent 2 out* . . . 1¾ 4

TIME: 7min 33.3s **TOTE:** £1.90; **Ex:**£1.50 **CSF:**£4.03

Fences 4 & 14 omitted - state of ground; it took a minute for the runners to reach the first fence

Hereford (RH 9F,19J)

Tue, 11 May (GOOD)

1358 Betfred Early Prices from 9am HC, 3m1f110y £1470 — 7 ran

1190[2] **SOHAPARA** 11-06 5-4F **D Jones** *In tch; chsd ldrs 10; went 2nd 12; ld nxt; drew clr frm 3 out; easily.* . . . 1
1175[3] **Quetal (IRE)** 12-00 5-1 **D Edwards** *Chsd ldr til hit 11; prom til outpcd frm 16; stayed on to 2nd agn cl home; nt trble wnr.* . . . 10 2
1166[P] **Parte Prima** 12-02 9-1 **R Woollacott** *In tch 6; chsd wnr 15; outpcd frm 3 out; sn no ch; dem cl home* . . . ½ 3
1341[1] News Flash (IRE) 11-07 13-2 Miss L Brooke *Ld to 13; wknd 16; nd aft* . . 2½ 4
1228[1] Genereux 11-07(cp,tt) 12-1 R Hodges *Nvr gng wl & sn rdn in rr; t.o & pu aft 14* P
1226[1] Persona Pride 12-00 7-1 Julian Pritchard *Chsd ldrs til drpd to rr 10; sn no ch; t.o & pu 3 out* . . . P
934[1] Whatamonkey 11-07(cp) 16-1 P Morris *Rr but in tch; hit 9; wknd 13; t.o & pu 16* . . . P

TIME: 6min 21.9s **TOTE:** £1.80; places £1.30,£3.90 **Ex:**£9.40 **CSF**£7.51

Huntingdon (RH 9F)

Tue, 11 May (GOOD to SOFT, GOOD in places)

1359 27th May Live Evening Entertainment Nov HC, 2m4f110y - 16J £1407 — 14 ran

1169[4] **CANTARINHO** 12-00 5-2F **D Kemp** *2 handlers; lw; ld & a gng wl; ldng pr wl clr app 2 out; hmpd by loose horse flat; kpt on game.* . . . 1
1058[4] **Find Me Another (IRE)** 11-07 7-1 **Miss A Stennett** *Prom; lft 2nd 13; clr w wnr & ev ch when hmpd app last; nt fluent; hld hd on one side flat; rallied cl home.* . . . 1 2
1173[5] **Snooty Eskimo (IRE)** 11-07 33-1 **H Norton** *Prom; 10l 4th 5-12; rdn & wknd app 2 out* . . . 16 3
892[6] Rooster 11-07 14-1 M Mackley *Carries too much condition; midfield & wl off pce; niggled 8; prog to mod 4th app 2 out; sn no imp* . . . 2 4

1173^{2} Hot Plunge 11-09 7-1 J Owen *Reluct & lost 20l start; last til some hdwy frm 8; disp 5th aft 3 out; no prog aft* $2^{3}/_{4}$ 5
784^{2} Coole Glen (IRE) 11-11 14-1 S Morris *Rcd keen; chsd ldr til blun 13 & drpd back 4th; fdd app 2 out; eased flat* 19 6
1244^{3} Village Copper 11-07 40-1 Miss H Grissell *Nt fluent & a wl bhnd; no ch frm 12* 7 7
1172^{P} I'm Dreaming (IRE) 11-09 33-1 A Martin *Midfield; rdn 9; strugg 11; t.o* 14 8
995^{2} Carvilla (IRE) 11-09 66-1 C Gordon *Off pce in midfield; lost tch bad frm 12* 16 9
1166^{6} Enitsag (FR) 12-01 15-2 D Mansell *Hld up midfield; 5th & in tch when fell 7* F
572^{P} Hachley (FR) 12-00 25-1 J Diment *Off pce in midfield; eff 10; wknd 3 out; rem when pu nxt* P
544^{2} Lindsay (FR) 11-11 7-2 B Shaw *Lw; ur 1* U
1060^{4} Magnus Maximus 11-07 50-1 T Lane *(xnb) 2 handlers; jmpd poor & nvr gng wl; rdn 5; last 8; t.o & pu 12* P
1275^{3} Penlet Too 11-07 100-1 T Ellis *(xnb) Chsd ldrs to 11; sn wknd; t.o & pu last* P

TIME: 5min 09.3s **TOTE:** £2.90; places £1.30,£2.00,£11.20 **Ex:**£21.50 **CSF:**£19.09

1360 Gerrard Ladies Championship HC, 3m - 19J £3412 9 ran

916^{1} **COMMANCHE LAW (IRE)** 10-10 9-1 **Mrs A Hamilton** *Trckd ldrs; mist 11; rdn 15; outpcd nxt; rallied app last; str rn to ld flat; sn clr* 1
1011^{1} **Cento (IRE)** 10-10 14-1 **Miss C Stucley** *Prom; went 2nd 14; ld app 2 out; 2l clr & rdn last; hdd & outpcd final 100yds* 2 2
1099^{4} **Sir D'Orton (FR)** 11-02 5-1 **Miss C Tizzard** *Prom; mist 8; 2nd 12; lost plce aft mist 15; lft mod 3rd last* 13 3
625^{1} Le Prince 11-03 10-1 Miss E Jones *Chsd ldrs; rdn & wknd 3 out; lft tired 4th & jmpd slow last* 6 4
1249^{1} Unlimited Free (IRE) 11-00 2-1F Miss D Harding *(xnb) Nt a fluent & nvr gng wl; poor last & bumped along 6; slt hdwy 11; strugg agn 13* 22 5
1146^{2} Balisteros (FR) 11-00 11-1 Miss J Williams *Nt a fluent in rr; niggled 6; hdwy to 4th & u.p 12; hit 14; wknd nxt; 6th when hit rail & slpd up app 2 out* S
1295^{1} Celtic Duke 11-02 9-2 Miss Z Turner *Last pr & nvr gng wl; nt fluent 10 & lost tch; scrambled over 12; t.o & pu 14* P
1058^{1} Free 11-00(cp) 10-1 Miss Gemma Hutchinson *Prom; hit 8; rdn & wknd aft 12; wl bhnd when pu 15* P
1290^{1} Supercharmer 10-10 20-1 Miss J Riding *Set str pce & jmpd bold; hit 3 out; hdd app nxt; disp 2l 2nd & btn when fell last* F

TIME: 6min 12.4s **TOTE:** £15.70; places £2.70,£4.40,£1.70 **Ex:**£151.10 **CSF:**£118.01

The stewards interviewed the rider of Celtic Duke, who was unable to offer any explanation why she had had to pull up; they ordered the horse to be routine tested

1361 Huntingdon Racecourse Confined Series HC, 3m - 19J £2961 8 ran

1274^{1} **COOLEFIND (IRE)** 11-11 7-2 **S Morris** *Lw; hld up towards rr; prog gng wl in 3rd aft 12; tk 2nd 3 out; ld app nxt; level but gng btr when lft clr sn aft last* 1
1214^{1} **King's Hero (IRE)** 12-00 2-1F **T Greenall** *Made most; just hdd when hung lft app 2 out; drvn & level when stumbled last; sn hung bad lft; nt rec* 13 2
1284^{1} **Tricky Trevor (IRE)** 12-01 11-1 **P York** *Chsd ldrs; nt fluent 9; mist 12; outpcd nxt; lft poor 3rd aft 3 out* 17 3
1287^{2} The Graduate 11-11 20-1 S Walker *(xnb) Hld up towards rr; eff 11; mist nxt; lft 3rd 3 out; sn wknd* 5 4
1059^{4} Emperor Roscoe 11-11 40-1 R Armson *Detach last & nvr gng wl; strugg 12; t.o when jmpd lft 16; pu 2 out* P
1295^{2} Millenium Way (IRE) 11-09(bl) 9-1 J Owen *Lw; nt jw; chsd ldr to 5; hit 8 & u.p; last 11; t.o & pu 13* P
1110^{1} Shiny Bay (IRE) 11-11 11-1 N Pearce *(xnb) Hld up towards rr; jmpd slow 7; prog to 3rd brief & nt fluent 12; sn rdn; 5th & wkng when hit 15; pu nxt* P
1168^{7} The Granby (IRE) 11-11 4-1 Miss H Irving *Lw; w ldr; hit 10; releg to cl 3rd & rdn but ev ch when fell 3 out* F

TIME: 6min 09.4s **TOTE:** £5.50; places £1.40,£1.30,£2.40 **Ex:**£15.50 **CSF:**£10.42

1362 31st October Countryside Day HC, 3m6f110y - 25J £2317 8 ran

1110^{P} **PADDY FOR PADDY (IRE)** 12-04 10-1 **R Burton** *Settled cl up; went 2nd 22; rdn app 2 out; chall last & sn ld; stayed on game to draw clr* 1
1179^{U} **Cimarrone Cove (IRE)** 12-00(bl) 15-8 **T Greenall** *Jw; ld 4; rdn aft 2 out; hit last; sn hdd; fin wkly* $3^{1}/_{2}$ 2

1038^{3} **Son Of Anshan** 12-04(tt) 7-4F **G Tuer** *Tk keen hld; hld up towards rr til prog 13; 2nd 20-22; rdn & wknd aft 3 out; plugged home* 9 3
1175^{U} Lady Baronette 11-04 20-1 A Martin *Midfield; rdn & outpcd aft 18; rem 4th aft 3 out* . . . . dist 4
1073^{6} Rusty Fellow 11-11 12-1 D Mansell *Rather reluct to set off; rr & sn rdn; nt a fluent; strugg when hit 17; t.o 22* 24 5
1154^{4} Mister Audi (IRE) 11-07(bl) 25-1 Miss A Stennett *Cl up; went 2nd 10-20; drpd out rap; hopelessly t.o aft 3 out; btn 127l* . . . . dist 6
1216^{6} Jerome Jerome 12-00(bl) 66-1 A Sansome *Ld to 4; chsd ldr to 10; t.o 15; pu 17* . . . . P
1250^{3} Millyhenry 11-09 7-1 Miss C Tizzard *Some mists & nvr keen; rr & drvn at sev stages; strugg 16; t.o & pu 20* . . . . P

TIME: 8min 13.9s **TOTE:** £10.30; places £2.60,£1.50,£1.10 **Ex:**£43.10 **CSF:**£28.46

Exeter (RH 11F,14J*)

Wed, 12 May (GOOD, GOOD to SOFT in places)

1363 Westcountry Business Network Nov HC, 2m3f110y £2736 8 ran

1167^{1} **BENGAL BULLET** 11-13 1-3F **Miss T Cave** *(xnb) Lw; cl 2nd til ld 6; drew clr frm 10; v easily* 1
1131^{5} **Macaroni Beach** 11-00 16-1 **R Bliss** *(xnb) Settled 3rd; outpcd 8 & 16l bhnd 10; disp poor 2nd nxt & chsd wnr vain frm 3 out; all out* 17 2
1029^{4} **Lirkimalong** 11-08 (1ow) 14-1 **Miss S Young** *Swtng; oht; hld up in rr; 6th aft 7; 15l 5th 9; hdwy app 12; rdn & tried hrd to tk poor 2nd flat; just hld* . $\frac{1}{2}$ 3
1130^{4} King Of Swing (IRE) 11-05 12-1 Mrs F Vigar *(xnb) Midfield; outpcd aft 6; 10l 4th 9; jmpd slow 10; lft poor 4th nr line* 13 4
1182^{P} April's Past 11-04 25-1 O Nelmes *(xnb) Sn t.o & v reluct & drvn; hung lft aft 4; pu 7* . . . . P
1129^{P} Digitalis 11-00(bl) 50-1 M Munrowd *Reluct to go down; bhnd; reluct u.p aft 6; t.o & pu 8* . . . . P
1293^{9} Th'moons A Balloon (IRE) 11-05(tt) 16-1 S Partridge *2 handlers; slt ld to 6; rdn & outpcd aft 10; lost 2nd & wknd aft 3 out; mod 4th when hung lft flat; swerved lft to padd gate & ur nr fin; trotted loose back down course* . . . U
1173^{P} Worthy Man 11-09(tt) 50-1 D Mansell *Chsd ldrs til wknd & nt fluent 7; u.p nxt; 18l 6th 9; t.o & pu 11* . . . . P

TIME: 4min 46.8s **TOTE:** £1.30; places £1.10,£2.20,£2.00 **Ex:**£9.10 **CSF:**£5.96

** Fence 7 omitted - state of ground; the rider of Th'Moons A Balloon was found guilty of using the whip with excessive frequency and when his horse was not responding; he was suspended for three days*

Weston & Banwell Harriers

Cothelstone (LH 7F,19J)

Wed, 12 May (GOOD to FIRM)

1364 Hunt Members 4 ran

892^{P} **NORMANIA (NZ)** 2-1 **Miss S West** *(xnb) Jw; ld/disp til clr advant 5; went 15l clr 13; 8l up but wl in comm 16; drew away agn 2 out; comf* 1
879^{7} **Rosetta** (5a) 5-4F **J Jenkins** *(xnb) Hld up in last; went 3rd but nt fluent 7; 8l 3rd $\frac{1}{2}$way; tk 2nd 12; clsd to 8l 2nd 16; sn rdn & no imp* 10 2
365^{U} Mister Rf (IRE) 5-2 R Isgar *Disp ld to 5; slt mist nxt; trckd ldr til wknd 12; sn strugg; t.o 15; pu nxt* . . . . P
1075^{P} Pavillion Pride (12a) 25-1 Mrs T Rowe *3rd to 6; last & just in tch when rfo 8* U

OFFICIAL DISTANCE: 10*l* **TIME:** 6min 20.2s

1365 Countryside Alliance Club Members 7yo&up (Nov Rdrs), 12st - 18J 12 ran

980^{6} **MACHALINI** 5-4F **A Morley** *(xnb) Made all; jw; 10l clr 8; kpt on str; unchall* 1
1212^{2} **Kilvoydan (IRE)** 6-1 **A Ward-Thomas** *Rr; 8th 12; poor 7th 16; 30l 6th nxt; went 5th 2 out; r.o stdly past btn horses to 2nd cl home* 25 2
1181^{3d} **Caundle Chase** 5-1 **W White** *Handy; went 2nd 10; chsd ldr & no imp; one pce frm 3 out; releg 3rd cl home* . . . . $\frac{3}{4}$ 3

1250[5]	Blackwater Brave (IRE) 7-1 H Fry *Hld up bhnd ldrs; went 3rd 15; 25l 3rd 3 out; one pce*	5	4
976[1]	Jalcanto 3-1 M Hooper *(xnb) Mid-div; 7th 8; some hdwy 15; went 4th but lot to do 2 out; no further prog*	6	5
1250[7]	Touring-Turtle (IRE) 50-1 W Procter *(xnb) Bhnd frm 8; t.o*	8	6
1180[5]	Fern Leader (IRE) 40-1 Miss L Woodward *Sn last; 8l detach by 2; t.o when ur 8*		U
1329[5]	Gigi Beach (IRE) 50-1 Mrs S Reynoldson *Prom to 4; lost plce aft 6; 9th 8; t.o & pu 13*		P
1149[1]	Karzhang(tt) 16-1 R Stearn *(xnb) Ur lvng padd; rdr had to search for whip in long grass; reluct to go down; a rr; t.o & pu 3 out*		P
1063[4]	Nice Approach (IRE) 25-1 Miss V Murphy *Oht; chsd ldr to 6; 5th & wkng 10; 6th when blun & ur 14*		U
1274[P]	Regency Rake 12-1 Miss R Davidson *(xnb) Chsd ldrs; 7th ½way; 16l 5th 13; no real hdwy; btn 6th when fell 3 out*		F
1329[U]	Rustic Revelry(bl) 50-1 C Whittaker *(xnb) 2nd frm 6-10; 11l 3rd 13; wknd 15; poor 6th when pu 2 out*		P

OFFICIAL DISTANCES: 10*l*, ½*l* **TIME:** 6min 03.7s

Fence 13 omitted - damaged

1366 Restricted, 12st — 12 ran

516[P]	**SLANEY LASS** (5a) 7-4JF **R Burton** *(xnb) Made all; ab 6l up til drew clr frm 3 out; hvly eased flat*		1
1325[2]	**Barton Saint (NZ)** 12-1 **Miss S West** *Lw; bhnd; 7th 12; still 6th but some prog 16 til 10l 3rd app 2 out; stayed on to mod 2nd flat*	10	2
1184[4]	**River Dante (IRE)** 8-1 **S Kidston** *Chsd ldrs; 6th 12; wl outpcd 14; rallied in 3rd 16; chsd wnr vain 3 out til dem flat*	3	3
1325[3]	Mrs Peggoty (5a)(tt) 20-1 Miss C Tizzard *2nd/4th til releg 5th & drvn & outpcd 14; 11l 3rd & jmpd slow 3 out; sn gave up*	15	4
1131[P]	Emali 16-1 W White *Lw; settled 3rd/4th; outpcd 13 & 15l 4th nxt; 5th & drvn 16; fdd & t.o when pu 2 out*		P
1063[P]	Hawkers Hill 4-1 Miss A Goschen *14s-4s; 2 handlers; midfield; prog 10; 3rd 12; went 5l 2nd nxt & chsd wnr til wknd app 16, t.o & pu 2 out*		P
1141[1]	Jolly Jake 8-1 E Walker *(xnb) Swtng; chsd ldrs; 5th 12; fell 13*		F
1327[P]	Little Mister(bl) 50-1 D Drake *V reluct & sn drvn along in rr; slow 7; t.o 8; pu 10*		P
572[U]	Lord Of The Bride (IRE)(bl) 7-1 A Farrant *Bhnd; jmpd v slow 2; last & slow 3; gd hdwy 6; 5th 8; blun 10; 8th & u.p 12; cont v reluct; t.o & pu 16*		P
966[2]	Mister Swallow 7-4JF M Miller *Tde; rn in snatches; hdwy in 4th 6; jmpd slow 7; drpd back to poor 9th & dogging it 12; v reluct past boxes; t.o when ref & ur 13*		r
599[P]	Regardez-Moi (5a) 40-1 J Jenkins *Prom to 5; wl t.o when drvn & v reluct 12; pu 13*		P
1325[U]	Romany Move 10-1 Mrs S Godfrey *Lw; last pr & nvr went pce; t.o 8; pu 16*		P

OFFICIAL DISTANCES: 8*l*, 3*l* **TIME:** 6min 10.0s

1367 Mens Open, 12st - 17J — 9 ran

1180[F]	**SIR WILLIAM** (4x) 6-4 **R Woollacott** *(xnb) Settled 3rd; mist 7; 2½l down 12; went cl 2nd 16; sn ld & 3l clr; in comm 2 out; nt rdn flat*		1
1185[P]	**Hylters Chance (IRE)** (4x) 6-1 **C Heard** *Ld to 4; chsd ldr; chall agn 14 & ld brief 16; rdn & kpt on game frm nxt; no ch w wnr*	5	2
880[6]	**Kingsbridge (IRE)** 6-1 **A Farrant** *(xnb) Lw; ld 4; jnd 14; rdn & hdd 16; gave up qckly & 6l 3rd nxt; nt r.o*	7	3
1101[3]	Coolteen Hero (IRE) (7x) 20-1 D Jacob *(xnb) Sn lost tch in poor last; some prog in 22l 5th 12; sn wknd agn; rem & v tired frm 16*	25	4
1100[4]	Makhpiya Patahn (IRE) 20-1 D I Turner *(xnb) Rdn all way; hmpd 3; bhnd; pckd & on nose 9; mist 10; last 12; t.o nxt*	6	5
1093[P]	Dawn's Cognac (IRE) 5-1 N Williams *Lw; 3rd when fell 3*		F
1183[4]	Delaware (FR) (7x)(bl) 25-1 S Kidston *Towards rr; bad mist 10 & nvr lkd keen; 23l 6th & strugg 12; t.o nxt; pu 14*		P
1145[1]	Jemaro (IRE) (7x) 5-4F R Burton *Lw; swtng; tde; w ldr til rn out & ur 1; demolished wing*		R
1249[3]	Shanavoher (IRE) 50-1 D Edwards *Midfield but nvr on terms w ldrs; 10l 4th 12; staggered nr post & drpd dead*		P

OFFICIAL DISTANCES: 5*l*, 6*l* **TIME:** 6min 08.0s

Fences 8 & 15 omitted - damaged; the stewards enquired into the running-out of the favourite, Jemaro, and fined the rider of Hylters Chance £140 for dangerous riding; this decision was later overturned by the Jockey Club Disciplinary Committee

1368 Ladies Open — 6 ran

1350[4] **TRADITIONAL (IRE)** 10-1 **Miss R Green** *(xnb) Lw; jmpd slow 3; chsd ldrs; went 15l 2nd app 13; clsd stdly frm 3 out; ld last; pushed clr* 1
1168[P] **Gipsy Cricketer** 13-8F **Miss C Stucley** *Tde; ld & clr; 15l ahd when mist 14; nt fluent aft; 10l ahd but rdn app 2 out; tired & jnd app last; sn hdd & btn* 5 2
1210[2] **Frank Byrne** 8-1 **Miss A Goschen** *Chsd ldrs; niggled 5; went 2nd brief app 6; 13l 3rd 10; 2nd brief & rdn 12; nt keen aft; jmpd slow 14; 27l 3rd 16*. 20 3
1099[1] Virtuoso 3-1 Mrs S Corcoran *Chsd ldr 4-10; sn last & strugg; t.o 16; jmpd slow nxt* . . . . runin 4
1250[4] Shock's Pride (IRE) 22-1 Miss C Tizzard *Last pr; 15l last & rdn aft 5; nvr keen; t.o 8; pu 12*. . . . . . . P
1016[P] The Kings Fling 7-4 Miss P Gundry *(xnb) Lw; chsd ldr til hit 4; rdn & outpcd 7; poor 5th when pu 12* . . . . P

OFFICIAL DISTANCES: 2½l, 20l **TIME:** 6min 08.0s

1369 Confined, 12st — 9 ran

1331[1] **COLQUHOUN** 7-4JF **A Farrant** *(xnb) Lw; a gng wl; oft nt fluent; settled 4th; went 2nd 12; ld app 16 & imm 5l clr; v easy* 1
1181[5] **Kildysart Lady (IRE)** (5a) 8-1 **B Woodhouse** *Swtng; hld up; 5th & prog 11; stdy rn to 2nd 16; no ch w wnr frm nxt; tired flat & lkd to fin 3rd* 12 2
993[P] **Keltic Lord** 4-1 **A Charles-Jones** *2nd/3rd til releg 5l 4th app 16; kpt on agn aft 2 out; lkd to fin 2nd; no ch w wnr*. . . . . . . s hd 3
863[2] Beadnell Bay 7-4JF Miss A Goschen *2 handlers; tk off in false start; ld; rdn & hdd app 16; wknd qckly; hit 2 out; eased flat*. 15 4
1101[1] Mr Ben Gunn 5-1 Miss V Heal *(xnb) Bhnd; lost tch 10; 30l 8th 12; t.o nxt* 5 5
961[2] Blin (CZE) 25-1 D Alers-Hankey *Jmpd slow 2; lost tch 4; mist 7; t.o 9* . . . 20 6
1195[3] Commander Cully (IRE) 40-1 M Sweetland *(xnb) 3rd/4th to 7; 8l 6th 12; wknd qckly nxt; t.o* 12 7
1129[P] Early Morning Call (IRE) 25-1 J Barnes *Hdwy to 2nd/3rd 5-11; wknd 15; t.o & pu last* . . . . P
963[8] Link Copper 25-1 Mrs O Jackson *Midfield; rdn 9; strugg aft; 20l 7th 12; t.o nxt; pu 3 out* . . . . P

OFFICIAL DISTANCES: 6l, hd **TIME:** 6min 09.0s

1370 Open Maiden (Div 1), 12st - 18J — 9 ran

1339[R] **RODY (IRE)**(bl) 2-1F **D Mansell** *(xnb,pelham) Ld & clr but stdd at stages & set v slow pce; drew 12l clr 16; unchall aft (rdr did flying dism)*. 1
1231[3] **Youwoudhavethat (IRE)** (5a) 4-1 **N Williams** *Settled 3rd; went 2nd 13; blun nxt; jmpd poor & lkd hanging lft aft; 12l down & mist 16; nvr able to cl; jmpd crooked 2 out*. 20 2
1200[3] **Abbey's Girl (IRE)** (5a) 6-1 **A Glassonbury** *Chsd ldrs; 5th 12; outpcd nxt; t.o 16; just won duel for fnce 3rd* . . . . runin 3
1182[5] Madame Cholet (5a) 6-1 M Woodward *Tde; towards rr; dashed into 2nd brief aft 12; releg 4th & jmpd slow nxt; sn lost tch; t.o 16*. . . . . . . nk 4
1326[F] Countryside March (5a) 2-1 Miss L Gardner *6s-2s; 2 handlers; pulled hrd & handy; 5th when fell 3* . . . . F
967[R] Horsemans Green(cp) 33-1 B Woodhouse *Bckwd; bhnd but in tch; cl 6th 12; outpcd 14; 18l 3rd 16; fell 3 out* . . . . F
827[F] Pebble Dasher (5a) 8-1 R Woollacott *(xnb) Rr but in tch; 6l last aft 12; pu 13; lame*. . . . . . . P
1134[U] Peter Parkgate (7a) 10-1 N Mitchell *Jb & to rt; imm lost tch; t.o 6; pu 13; dreadful* . . . . P
Spinning Silver 10-1 D Edwards *Chsd wnr to 12; wknd 15; 22l 4th nxt; fell 3 out* . . . . F

OFFICIAL DISTANCES: 15l, dist **TIME:** 6min 24.0s

Fence 10 omitted - fallen rider

1371 Open Maiden (Div 2), 12st — 9 ran

KEEP THE DAY JOB (12a) 14-1 **N Wilmington** *(xnb) Settled rr but cl up; lft 2nd 16; level aft 3 out til slt ld nxt; drvn & lkd to be pipped on post* . . . 1
910[4] **Sex Kitten** (5a) 4-1 **R McCarthy** *Hdwy to 2nd 7; ev ch til lft in ld 16; jnd aft 3 out; cl 2nd last; kpt on u.p & lkd to snatch ld on line* . . . . hd 2
1134[F] **Velvet Victory (IRE)** (12a) 14-1 **M Miller** *Settled 3rd/4th; mist 14; cl up to 15; wknd nxt & 12l adrift aft 3 out*. 12 3

1251[P]	Queens House (5a) 11-1 Miss R Green *Towards rr but wl in tch to 15; strugg bad nxt; mist 3 out*	15	4
1324[P]	Celtic Prince (IRE) 5-2JF N Williams *(xnb) 8s-5/2; hld up; imp to 3rd 9; blun 10; still prsng ldrs when nrly fell 16; nt rec; eased aft nxt*	30	5
1007[3]	Judy's Lad (7a) 8-1 J Barnes *(xnb) Jmpd rt in ld; v slow pce; blun 13 & 14; still just ldng when rn out 16*		R
1182[2]	Merry Melody (5a) 5-2JF Miss S Robinson *2nd til pu & dism 6*		P
	Quantock's Return (5a) 16-1 Miss J Buck *V bckwd; a t.o; barely gt over 1 & 2; clambered over 3; ref 4*		r
1200[P]	Steponthebandit (5a) 7-2 D McKenna *Rr but cl up to 12; lost tch qckly nxt; t.o & pu 3 out*		P

OFFICIAL DISTANCES: *½l, 6l* **TIME:** 6min 40.0s

Ludlow (RH 8F,17J)

Thu, 13 May (GOOD)

1372 Shukers Land Rover of Ludlow HC, 2m4f £2786 — 15 ran

1173[1]	**MOUSESKI** 12-04 4-5F **N Williams** *Lw; midfield; clsd to 2nd/3rd frm 10; a cruising aft; ld 14; v easily*		1
1168[r]	**Filscot** 12-00(cp) 16-1 **J Diment** *2nd/4th til ld 13; drvn & hdd nxt; no ch w wnr aft; just kpt 2nd*	6	2
630[4]	**Route One (IRE)** 12-04 7-2 **S Morris** *Midfield; eff 10; 6th & outpcd 13; sn drvn; rallied & stayed on cl home*	nk	3
1209[1]	Good Heart (IRE) 11-07 25-1 N Oliver *Lw; midfield; 7th 13; kpt on frm 2 out; unable to chall*	½	4
1276[4]	Nousayri (IRE) 11-07 50-1 T Ellis *(xnb) Tk keen hld; handy; jmpd slow 10; 5th 13; kpt on flat; nd*	½	5
1166[1]	Guignol Du Cochet (FR) 12-00 11-2 G Slade-Jones *Towards rr; 8th & u.p 13; hdwy nxt; kpt on flat; nt able to chall*	2½	6
1140[5]	Time Can Tell 11-07 100-1 R Hodges *In tch til lost plce & rdn 8; sn strugg in rr; t.o*	23	7
1058[3]	Supreme Silence (IRE) 11-07 40-1 N Kent *Nvr gng wl; bhnd; drvn frm 5; no ch 13*	9	8
931[P]	Farfields Prince 11-07 100-1 M Wall *Cl up; 5th 11; hit nxt; drvn & sn wknd; pu 3 out*		P
1067[P]	John Builder 11-07 100-1 R Rogers *(xnb) Last trio; t.o when crawled over 10; pu 12*		P
1111[2]	Life Of A River (IRE) 12-00 25-1 T Greenall *Trckd ldrs; 4th & drvn app 14; sn wknd; poor 7th when blun & ur 2 out*		U
630[7]	Polar Prospect 12-00 50-1 Miss P Gundry *W ldr early; 2nd til mist 11; sn wknd; t.o & pu 14*		P
1229[3]	Proper Primitive 11-02 50-1 Miss E James *Mist 2; jmpd lft; chsd ldrs til lost plce 9; t.o & pu 14*		P
1173[F]	Shafi (IRE) 11-11 40-1 D Mansell *Jmpd stickily in last pr; t.o 10; pu 12*		P
1057[3]	Some Go West (IRE) 11-11(vis) 33-1 R Cope *Made most to 13; stpd to nil; wl bhnd when pu nxt*		P

TIME: 5min 11.7s **TOTE:** £2.00; places £1.20,£2.80,£1.30 **Ex:**£15.10 **CSF:**£15.57

Perth (RH 8F,15J)

Thu, 13 May (GOOD)

1373 Ineralmond Brewery Ossian's Ale Nov HC, 2m4f110y £3380 9 ran

1296[1]	**NISBET** 11-11 9-4 **Miss J Hollands** *Cl up; ld 7; made rest; stayed on str; easy*		1
1174[3]	**Alittlebitopower** 11-10 16-1 **C Storey** *Jmpd rt; mists; prom; eff to ch wnr aft 12; drvn & no imp frm nxt*	16	2
1178[F]	**Jupiter's Fancy** 11-00 8-1 **P Callaghan** *Bhnd; niggled 7; 6th & rdn 10; hdwy 3 out; fin str & nrly snatched poor 2nd*	nk	3
1177[1]	Banana Ridge 11-07 6-5F C Mulhall *Hld up in tch; hdwy to chse ldrs 9; rdn & wknd frm 3 out; jmpd lft nxt; rdr reported mare has had a breathing problem*	11	4
1178[6]	Hervey Bay 10-12 66-1 W Goldie *Prom to 8; 5th & rdn 10; strugg aft; t.o.*	dist	5
1220[P]	Jinful Du Grand Val (FR) 11-12 (9ow) 20-1 J Alexander *Mists; ld to 7; wknd rap; t.o & pu 10*		P

1177[4]	Katinka 11-02 25-1 K Mercer *Blun 1; 7th when fell 7*		F
1028[P]	Lethem Air 11-07 25-1 D Jewett *A bhnd; t.o & pu 9*		P
1179[P]	Mr Busby 11-05 33-1 M Seston *Chsd ldrs til wknd aft 12; blun 2 out; t.o & pu last; lame*		P

TIME: 5min 18.1s **TOTE:** £3.20; places £1.10,£3.60,£2.00 **Ex:**£42.20 **CSF:**£27.19

Aintree (LH 7F,19J)

Fri, 14 May (GOOD)

1374 Great People Nov HC, 3m1f £5152 — 6 ran

1168[1]	**BOHEMIAN SPIRIT (IRE)** 11-07 7-4F **S Charlton** *Chsd ldr to 12 & frm 16; chall 3 out; ld gng wl nxt; sn clr; easily*		1
442[2]	**Star Of Raven** 11-02 11-2 **N Saville** *Hld up; hdwy 11; chsd ldr 12-16; lft 2nd & hmpd 2 out; sn wknd*	17	2
1178[2]	**Raging Torrent** 11-07 16-1 **L Morgan** *In tch; rdn 10; drvn app 12; hit nxt; sn outpcd; poor 4th 16*	12	3
1174[1]	Boulta (IRE) 11-09(cp) 10-1 M Seston *Chsd ldrs in 3rd til niggled 11; hit 12 & wknd; t.o & pu 3 out*		P
1294[1]	Camden Carrig (IRE) 11-07 2-1 N Phillips *Swtng; ld at gd pce; pckd 1; nt fluent 3 out & rmdrs; just hdd when fell nxt*		F
1265[1]	Shraden Edition 11-11 9-1 D Barlow *Last pr; mist 4; 8l last 11; strugg 12; pu 3 out*		P

TIME: 6min 30.4s **TOTE:** £2.50; places £1.70,£2.20 **Ex:**£6.80 **CSF:**£11.27

Bangor (LH 9F,18J)

Sat, 15 May (GOOD)

1375 North Western Area P-t-P Championship HC, 3m110y £4231 — 11 ran

853[1]	**ALTHREY DANDY (IRE)** 11-07 10-1 **L Hicks** *A.p; ld 13; rdn app last; stayed on wl*		1
933[1]	**Thyne Man (IRE)** 11-11 100-30 **P Cowley** *In tch; mist 14; rdn aft 3 out; hdwy to chse wnr app nxt; one pce flat*	4	2
1171[P]	**Soundtrack (IRE)** 11-11 9-1 **G Hanmer** *Ld; hdd 13; still ev ch app 3 out; wknd nxt*	19	3
1176[2]	Coole Venture (IRE) 11-11 11-8F N Williams *Chsd clr ldrs; rdn & hdwy aft 3 out; wknd app nxt*	2½	4
1176[4]	Raiseapearl 11-07 12-1 I Clyde *Chsd clr ldrs til wknd app 14*	24	5
1260[2]	Oneanthreequarters (IRE) 11-07 20-1 R Jagger *Sn bhnd; t.o*	dist	6
1228[P]	Cutina 11-02 20-1 J Jarrett *Midfield; mist 6; rmdrs aft nxt; bhnd 11; t.o*	2	7
1048[3]	Iadora 11-02 40-1 Miss T Clark *A bhnd; t.o*	¾	8
1261[2]	Benbow 11-07 14-1 B Shaw *Midfield; blun & ur 11*		U
928[2]	Well Said Sam 11-07 40-1 J Handley *Midfield; mist 6; fell 10*		F
1202[1]	Whitegates Willie 11-07 20-1 D Greenway *A bhnd; rdn aft 8; t.o & pu 12*		P

TIME: 6min 26.6s **TOTE:** £13.00; places £3.40,£1.20,£3.30 **Ex:**£66.30 **CSF:**£41.76

Uttoxeter (LH 8F)

Sat, 15 May (GOOD to SOFT)

1376 Mount Argus Open HC, 4m2f - 21J £3393 — 9 ran

991[3]	**EARTHMOVER (IRE)** 12-02 3-1 **Miss A Goschen** *Trckd ldrs; ld 12; clr 18; rdn app last; stayed on game*		1
1170[1]	**County Derry** 12-03(cp) 2-1F **N Harris** *Hld up in tch; chsd wnr 15; blun 18; sn rdn; stayed on one pce frm last*	6	2
1297[1]	**Dorans Magic** 11-08 8-1 **N Saville** *Hld up; hdwy 7; rdn 3 out; nt fluent last; wknd flat*	3½	3
1172[3]	Maggies Brother 11-09 11-1 D Barlow *Hld up; hdwy 15; stayed on one pce frm 2 out*	hd	4
1179[2]	Sad Mad Bad (USA) 11-12 4-1 G Tuer *Hld up; mist 5; eff app 18; nvr trbld ldrs*	4	5
1216[1]	Clonshire Paddy (IRE) 11-12(bl) 25-1 T Greenall *Hld up; a rr; t.o & pu 3 out*		P

1170[3] Hobbycyr (FR) 11-12 12-1 Miss P Gundry *Prom; lost plce 10; bhnd when pu 3 out* P
1092[P] Millennium Gold 11-05(vis) 100-1 Miss A Frieze *Ld aft 1; mist 3; clr 5; hdd 12; wkng when mist 14; hit nxt; sn pu* . . . . P
1294[4] Pendragon 11-05(bl) 100-1 D Jacob *Ld til aft 1; chsd ldr; mist 3; drvn along 14; hit 16; bhnd when jmpd slow nxt; t.o & pu 18* . . . . P

TIME: 9min 06.9s **TOTE:** £3.60; places £1.40,£1.60,£2.90 **Ex:**£6.50 **CSF:**£9.30

Fences 7, 15 & 23 omitted; the stewards interviewed two riders regarding their use of the whip: (i) Dorans Magic's rider was cautioned for using excessive force, and (ii) Maggies Brother's was suspended for one day for using it with excessive frequency

1377 Friends of St Giles Hospice Mdn HC, 2m5f - 16J £2200 7 ran

1178[3] **SCOTTISH ROOTS** 12-03 7-4F **T Greenall** *Prom; drpd to rr 7; hdwy & hit 4 out; sn rdn; lkd hld when jmpd rt 2 out; sn lft in ld; jmpd rt last; all out* 1
1254[1] **Beauchamp Oracle** 11-10 4-1 **S Hughes** *Hld up; hdwy 8; chsd ldr 10; rdn 3 out; 2nd & lkd hld when lft in ld & hmpd 2 out; sn hdd; hmpd last; r.o* . nk 2
1123[B] Astley Gold (IRE) 11-10 14-1 J Docker *Hld up; blun 1; hdwy 7; wknd aft 10; t.o & pu 3 out* . . . . P
1261[P] Bless Yourself (IRE) 12-00(bl) 33-1 O Nelmes *Hld up; mist 2; fell 6* . . . . . F
1092[1] Gipsy Girl 11-07 5-2 M Barber *Chsd ldr; ld 8; clr when fell 2 out*. . . . . . . F
1275[P] Igloux Royal (FR) 11-10 80-1 M Briggs *Ld; mist 3; hdd 8; wknd 13; t.o when fell 2 out*. . . . . F
567[2] Kyalami (FR) 12-03 7-1 Miss P Gundry *Prom; hit 11; sn rdn; lft 3rd when hmpd & fell 2 out*. . . . . F

TIME: 5min 35.3s **TOTE:** £2.80; places £1.40,£2.20 **Ex:**£6.80 **CSF:**£8.39

Dulverton West

Bratton Down (LH 8F,19J)
Sat, 15 May (GOOD to FIRM)

1378 Hunts Members 7 ran

1267[1] **RICE POINT** 9-4 **T Dennis** *Tchd 5/2; lw; jmpd bold; hld up; went 2nd 6; hit 9; rn wide bend aft 13; ld on bit last; sauntered clr flat; v easily*. 1
1180[4] **Happy Team** (5a) 20-1 **R Ross** *Tchd 25s; went 2nd 2; ld 6; mist 9; hrd rdn aft 2 out; hdd last; no ch w wnr* 12 2
1268[3] **My Jess** (5a) 12-1 **M Sweetland** *(xnb) Mounted on course; tde; ld to 6; 4l 3rd ½way; wkng when mist 3 out*. 2½ 3
1184[3] Bessie Bunter (5a) 5-1 G Maundrell *Lw; hld up; jmpd slow 1; 6th when blun bad & ur 3*. . . . . U
1328[1] Doublet 4-5F R Woollacott *5/4-4/5; jmpd rt; hld up; last when jmpd slow 7 & 8; lost tch & 15l 4th 14; wl bhnd when pu 16* . . . . P
Lady Pamroy (5a) 100-1 A Charles-Jones *(xnb) Hld up; releg last & fell 9* . F
1251[P] Winsley Spirit (5a) 50-1 Miss T Cave *(bh) Tchd 66s; 2nd/3rd to 5; 6l 4th ½way; mist 10; rmdrs 11; lost tch 13; last when pu aft nxt* . . . . P

OFFICIAL DISTANCES: 10*l*, 4*l* **TIME:** 6min 17.0s

1379 Mixed Open, 12st 7 ran

822[3] **WHAT A MOVER** (5a) 3-1 **Miss P Gundry** *Nt fluent; hld up; 6l 5th ½way; hdwy & 5l 3rd 13; went 2nd aft 3 out; rdn to ld flat; r.o wl (rdr had drpd whip aft 13)* 1
1183[1] **Polar Champ**(bl) 5-4F **A Farrant** *2s-5/4; swtng; ld; qcknd 5l clr 14; jmpd slow 16; sn drvn along; hdd u.p flat; one pce* 5 2
727[1] **Polar Flight** 3-1 **A Charles-Jones** *(xnb,bf) Swtng; hit 4; 2nd til mist 3 out; 6l 3rd when mist nxt; wknd flat* 15 3
1180[1] Friar Waddon 7-1 C Heard *(xnb) Tchd 9s; hld up; 5l 4th ½way; jmpd slow 12; outpcd 14; wknd 3 out* 1 4
1100[P] Polar King (IRE) 100-1 R Bandey *(bf) Nd; 12l 6th & rdn ½way; lost tch 13; wl bhnd 15* 5 5
196[F] Fou Doux (FR) 120-1 N Wilmington *(xnb) Hld up; hdwy 8; 4l 3rd ½way; hit 11 & 13; 10l 6th nxt; wknd 3 out; virt pu flat*. 40 6
703[P] Fossy Bear (5a) 10-1 Miss S Young *(b4,pelham) Last 3; lost tch 8; wl bhnd 14; t.o & pu 3 out* . . . . P

OFFICIAL DISTANCES: 4*l*, 15*l* **TIME:** 6min 01.7s

1380 Open Maiden (Div 1), 12st — 14 ran

	LORD OSCAR (IRE) (7a) 11-10F **A Farrant** *(xnb) Opened 6/4; ld 2-3; hit 4; disp 4l 3rd ½way; mist 11; ld 14; qcknd 8l clr 3 out; pckd nxt; impressive*		1
1327^U	**Lansdowne Park** (12a) 33-1 **Miss A Bush** *Hld up; 12th & rmdrs 3; gd hdwy 8; 5l 5th ½way; eff 15; went 12l 2nd 2 out; kpt on; no ch w wnr*	8	2
962³	**Foston Second (IRE)** (5a) 12-1 **M Sweetland** *Swtng; ld aft 1-2 & 3 til aft 5; 2nd/3rd til ld 13; hdd nxt; 8l 2nd when mist 3 out; wknd u.p & hung bad rt flat*	10	3
1252³	My Brother Jack 14-1 Miss K Lovelace *2nd/4th til ld 7; hdd 10; lost plce & 7l 6th 14; poor 4th frm 2 out*	5	4
1134³	Village Queen (IRE) (5a) 8-1 D Harvey *(bnh) Hld up; lost plce 6; 12l 9th ½way; lost tch 14; wl bhnd 16.*	10	5
1248²	The Nelson Touch 5-1 D I Turner *(xnb) Swtng; 2nd/3rd til ld aft 5; hdd 7; ld 10-13; 7l 4th 16; wknd nxt.*	½	6
1134^P	Sup Of Tea (IRE) 25-1 A Charles-Jones *(pelham) Swtng; hld up; 8l 6th ½way; mist 13; hdwy & 5l 4th nxt; wknd 3 out.*	4	7
1067^F	Gunville (7a) 12-1 Miss P Gundry *(bf) Ss; last to 5; 14l 12th ½way; wl bhnd 14; t.o*	15	8
1133⁶	Countryside Counts 33-1 Miss L Gardner *(xnb) Nt jw; a bhnd; mists 2 & 4; last 9; t.o 16*	1	9
1327^P	Augathella 66-1 C Heard *(xnb) Hld up; hdwy 6; disp 8l 6th ½way; wknd 13; 15l 8th nxt; pu 15*		P
1326^P	Merv's Magic 50-1 M Woodward *Ld til fell 1*		F
1272^P	National Debt 5-1 R Woollacott *Opened 6s; hld up; 13½l 11th ½way; mist 11; hdwy & 9l 7th nxt; pu aft 15; lame*		P
	Silver Image 50-1 M Dennis *2 handlers; hld up; last 5-9; 13l 10th ½way; hmpd & rdr lost iron 10; saddle slpd & ur bend bef 11*		U
	Sonnet Supreme (IRE) (12a) 25-1 D Alers-Hankey *Hld up; 10l 8th ½way; in tch til fell 10*		F

OFFICIAL DISTANCES: 6*l*, 10*l* **TIME:** 6min 12.7s

1381 Open Maiden (Div 2), 12st — 9 ran

704²	**O'ECH** (5a) 5-2F **A Farrant** *A.p; ld aft 5; qcknd 14; clr 3 out; rdn out.*		1
702⁷	**Beehawk** (7a) 20-1 **A Charles-Jones** *Lw; hld up & tk keen hld; hdwy 8; disp 3l 3rd ½way; chsd wnr 11; lft 4l 2nd 14; no imp 3 out.*	6	2
1353²	**Harnage (IRE)** 5-1 **Miss C Prouse** *Ld aft 1-3 & 4 til aft 5; lost plce & mist 9; 9l 7th ½way; last 11-14; went 20l 4th aft 3 out & 3rd at last; stayed on*	6	3
1006²	Feels Like Rain 3-1 L Heard *Swtng; ld til aft 1; lost plce 7; 5l 5th ½way; lft 7l 3rd 14; no imp 3 out; wknd & dem last.*	15	4
1326^r	Roseacre (IRE)(bl) 16-1 Miss P Gundry *(xnb) Jmpd rt; a last pr; 10½l last ½way; lost tch u.p 14; t.o 16*	30	5
1326^r	Double Bubble (IRE) 33-1 A Glassonbury *Mounted on course; tde; swtng; nt jw; ld 3-4; mists 7 & 10; 2nd til mist 11; blun 13; lft 8l 4th nxt; wknd u.p 16; t.o*	2½	6
1252^P	Ashwicke Gambler 16-1 T Dreaper *(xnb) Tchd 20s; hld up; 10l 8th ½way; last pr to 11; 10l 6th 14; wknd 16; t.o*	6	7
883^U	Four In Hand (5a) 7-2 D Edwards *(xnb) Sn prom; 3l 3rd ½way; went 3l 2nd when blun & ur 14*		U
	Swift Wood (7a) 8-1 M Miller *(xnb) Tchd 10s; bit bckwd; hld up; 7l 6th ½way; 5th when blun & ur 13*		U

OFFICIAL DISTANCES: 8*l*, 5*l* **TIME:** 6min 13.8s

1382 Intermediate, 12st — 8 ran

1063¹	**VINNIE BOY (IRE)** 9-4 **Miss P Gundry** *Nt fluent; hld up; 5½l last ½way; hdwy & 2½l 5th 14; went 2l 3rd 2 out; rdn to ld aft last; hung rt flat; all out.*		1
1132¹	**Hold On Harry** 8-1 **L Heard** *Hld up; 4l 5th ½way; hdwy 12; 1½l 3rd 14; releg 4th 2 out; rallied flat; went 2nd 50yds out; r.o*	1	2
1126²	**Vansell** (5a) 40-1 **Mrs O Jackson** *2 handlers; swtng; hld up; hdwy & 2nd 6; lft in ld nxt; mist 12; hdd 2 out; lft in ld last; sn hdd & one pce*	1½	3
1251¹	Captain Random 12-1 Mrs J Reed *(xnb) Lw; prom; 3l 4th ½way; lost plce 13; 5l 6th nxt; 11l 5th & outpcd 3 out; lft mod 4th at last*	15	4
1066⁴	Sherbourne Guest (IRE) 33-1 J Kwiatkowski *Nt jw; ld to 3; went 2nd 8 til aft 15; nrly ur nxt; 12l 6th 3 out; sn wknd*	5	5

1329[4] Earl's Toy (IRE) 25-1 H Fry *Drpd to rr 4; 4½l 6th ½way; last 14; lost tch 3 out; t.o & pu last* . . . . P

1129[2] Noble Action (7a) 4-6F A Farrant *Opened 4/5; hld up; hdwy & 2½l 3rd ½way; 2l 4th 14; went 2nd 16; ld 2 out til saddle slpd & rn out app last; unlucky* R

1071[2] Thunder Thighs (5a) 10-1 N Wilmington *(xnb) 2 handlers; mounted on course; tde; 2nd til ld 3; cocked jaw & rn out 7* . . . . R

OFFICIAL DISTANCES: 1*l*, ½*l* **TIME:** 6min 12.7s

1383 Dodson & Horrell PPORA Club Members (Nov Rdrs), 12st — 8 ran

1181[F] **BARTON ROSE** 10-1 **I Chanin** *Opened 12s; tde; hld up; 8l 6th ½way; hdwy & 3½l 4th 14; qcknd to ld on inner 3 out; just hld on* 1

1101[U] **Alex Thuscombe**(vis) 20-1 **Mrs R Barclay** *(bf) Rcd wide; prom; 2nd when carried wide bend aft 5; 5l 4th ½way; lost plce & 5½l 6th 14; went 5l 3rd aft 3 out; stayed on wl desp weak rdr flat; just failed* . . . . hd 2

1329[3] **Chism (IRE)** 16-1 **W King** *A.p; 4l 3rd ½way; went 2nd 12-15; chsd wnr 3 out; rdn & ev ch flat; nt qckn* . . . . ½ 3

1270[1] Father Mansfield (IRE) 1-2F Miss C Prouse *(bnh) Tchd evens; 2 handlers; hld up & rcd wide; last to 6; 10l 7th ½way; 7l last 14; outpcd 3 out; still 9l 5th last; stayed on wl flat; too much to do* 1 4

1329[6] Golden Jack (FR) 20-1 C Morris *Ld to 4; 6l 5th ½way; ld on inside aft 13-3 out; 7l 4th last; one pce* 6 5

861[U] Glenahary Rose (IRE) 25-1 Miss A Tory *(xnb) 2nd/3rd til ld 4; rn wide & hdd bend aft nxt; chsd ldr til ld app 12; rn wide & hdd bend aft nxt; ev ch app 3 out; wkng when mist nxt* 20 6

1365[U] Fern Leader (IRE) 33-1 R Skinner *2nd/3rd til ld aft 5; mist 11; hdd app nxt; 4½l 5th 14; wknd 15; mist 3 out; t.o & pu flat* . . . . P

1249[4] Simply Sam 3-1 H Fry *(xnb) Nvr gng wl; last 6; rdn 8; lost tch & pu aft 13* P

OFFICIAL DISTANCES: hd, ½*l* **TIME:** 6min 19.6s

1384 Confined, 12st — 7 ran

1269[1] **VIVID IMAGINATION (IRE)** (7a, 5x) 1-3F **A Farrant** *(xnb) Tchd 2/5; lw; hld up & sev posns; 4l last ½way; went 2nd aft 13; ld aft 16; qcknd 5l clr & mist 3 out; 15l up last; hvly eased flat* 1

1183[3] **Cool Wager** (5x) 8-1 **D Alers-Hankey** *Tchd 10s; ld to 6; lft in ld 7 til aft nxt; 2½l 3rd ½way; went 2nd 12 til aft 13; releg last nxt; went 12l 2nd & pckd 2 out; kpt on; no ch w wnr* 4 2

961[3] **Jenko (FR)** 50-1 **A Charles-Jones** *(xnb) Hld up & pulled hrd; went 2nd aft 7; ld aft 8 til aft 16; releg 3rd 2 out; sn wknd* 15 3

Khayal (USA) 8-1 L Jefford *Hld up; 3l 4th ½way; disp 2l 2nd 14; blun nxt; 6l 3rd & rdn 3 out; sn wknd* 5 4

569[7] Belarus (IRE) (5x) 10-1 D Harvey *Tchd 11s; 2nd til ld 6; rn out & ur app 7* R

1268[P] Persian Dawn (5a) 66-1 Miss S Young *Hld up; mist 3; went 2nd app 9-12; lost plce & pu 13* . . . . P

306[P] Rock Dancer 33-1 M Sweetland *(xnb) Tchd 50s; mist 1; sn last; pu & dism 4* P

OFFICIAL DISTANCES: 6*l*, 12*l* **TIME:** 6min 15.3s

1385 Restricted (Div 1), 12st - 18J — 8 ran

1131[4] **FLORA MACDONALD** (5a) 7-1 **A Farrant** *Ch ride; sn prom; 1l 3rd ½way; 4th when mist 14; sn rdn; 6l 3rd 3 out; went 3l 2nd at last; drvn to ld flat; all out; wl rdn* 1

1180[3] **Winning Leader (IRE)** 5-1 **Mrs O Jackson** *Blun 2; ld 4-7; 2nd til ld 12; 3l clr at last; hdd flat; no ex* 2½ 2

791[7] **Tycoon Ted** 9-1 **R Woollacott** *Ld til app 4; disp 1l 3rd ½way; went 2nd aft 13; ev ch 2 out; no ex u.p flat; fin lame* 4 3

1271[P] Black A Brook (IRE) (5a)(cp) 20-1 L Jefford *Drpd to rr 3; 3½l last ½way; eff u.p 12; went 8l 4th 16; wkng when mist 3 out* 40 4

1196[5] Abseal 5-1 A Charles-Jones *10s-5s; jnd ldrs 6; ld 7-12; disp 2l 2nd 14; wknd 16; pu 3 out* . . . . P

864[P] Beachtime 16-1 N Mitchell *(xnb) Hld up; 2½l 5th ½way; jmpd slow 10; blun 15; sn rdn & wknd; jmpd v slow & pu 3 out* . . . . P

1268[4] Horrified(bl) 12-1 D Edwards *2nd til swerved rt & ur aft 5* . . . . U

308[1] Touch Of Flame (7a) evensF M Miller *(xnb) Opened 5/4; 6th when fell 1* . . F

OFFICIAL DISTANCES: 3*l*, 3*l* **TIME:** 6min 19.5s

Fence 13 omitted - fallen rider

1386 Restricted (Div 2), 12st - 18J — 7 ran

1366P **ROMANY MOVE** 14-1 **Mrs J Reed** *Lw; hld up; 11l 5th ½way; jmpd rt 12 & 13; hdwy & 6l 4th 15; outpcd aft nxt; lft 6l 3rd 2 out; went 4l 2nd at last; ld flat; stayed on wl* 1

1007[1] **Lutteur Bleu (FR)** (7a) 5-1 **M Miller** *(xnb) Tchd 7s; 2nd/3rd til ld 13; hdd by-passing nxt; lft in ld 2 out; hdd u.p flat; one pce* 2 2

1196U **Jolie Roslin** (5a) 25-1 **H Fry** *Tchd 33s; hld up; 9l 4th ½way; 7l last 15; hdwy to jn ldrs 3 out; lft 3l 2nd nxt; wknd flat* 7 3

966[5] Eskimo Gold (5a) 33-1 M Sweetland *Tchd 40s; jmpd rt; pulled hrd; ld; sn 8l clr to 5; hdd 13; wknd aft 16.* 15 4

1131[2] Askers Jack 6-4F N Mitchell *Tchd 7/4; jmpd lft & oft v low; 2nd/3rd til ld by-passing 14; blun & ur 2 out.* . . . . . U

1378U Bessie Bunter (5a) 5-1 G Maundrell *Tchd 7s; 2nd outing; nt jw; a last; lost tch 8; t.o & pu 10* . . . . . P

1272[1] Sound Sense 2-1 A Charles-Jones *Tchd 9/4; prom; 4th when fell 6; broke nk; dead* . . . . . F

OFFICIAL DISTANCES: 2*l*, 8*l* **TIME:** 6min 10.6s

Fence 14 omitted - fallen horse and rider

Golden Valley

Bredwardine (RH 8F,18J)

Sat, 15 May (GOOD)

1387 Hunt Members — 8 ran

1254[5] **HIGHBRIDGE (IRE)** 7-2 **P Crozier** *(xnb) Made all & 15l clr at times to 9; pckd 14 & rdr nrly f.o front; 1½l clr app 2 out; prsd when lft clr at last; wknd; all out.* 1

1114F **Running On Red** 20-1 **R Hughes** *Midfield; 7½l 3rd & rdn 13; eff 3 out; 3½l 3rd & drvn app nxt; sn outpcd; lft 2nd at last; rallied flat; catching wnr nr fin* 2 2

1232[5] **Golden Pride** (5a) 25-1 **T Haynes** *Chsd clr ldr to 11; last by 13; 28l adrift app 2 out; rallied game & plugged on wl frm last.* 1 3

1231[5] Crystal Brook (5a) 25-1 S Graham *Mists in last; hmpd app 6; eff 11 & 2nd brief 13; 10l 4th & fdng app 2 out; plodded on* 20 4

1226[7] Blazing Pride 12-1 P Haynes *Swtng; 2 handlers; cl up in chsng group til 13l 5th & wknd 13; 25l 5th app 2 out* 10 5

1227[4] Arctic King 4-7F A Wintle *Cocked jaw start & ref to rce* . . . . . r

Bronllys Skyvor (U) 12-1 H Evans-Bevan *Hld up; went 2nd 11; tried valiantly frm 3 out; 2l down but lkd hld when hit last & rfo.* . . . . . U

978[6] Sefton Clover (5a) 10-1 M Hooper *Hld up; blun & ur 4* . . . . . U

OFFICIAL DISTANCES: 1*l*, 1*l* **TIME:** 7min 03.0s

1388 Restricted (Div 1), 12st — 14 ran

752[2] **LIMA BRAVO** (5a) 7-1 **P Morris** *Ss; rr til stdy prog 10; pckd 12; 4th & rdn nxt; ld aft 3 out; qcknd 6l clr; jmpd lft & mist last; drvn out.* 1

1230[2] **Shemardi** 3-1JF **R Hodges** *Sn 2nd/3rd; ld & mist 12; rather wide app nxt & hdd; ld agn 15 til aft 3 out; rdn & no imp frm nxt.* 2½ 2

1230P **Raymond James** 16-1 **D Mansell** *Swtng; midfield; eff 10; 5th & u.p 13; outpcd when lft 7l 3rd 2 out; hrd rdn & fnd nil.* 5 3

1345[3] Belle Moss (5a)(cp) 3-1JF N Oliver *Chsd ldrs; 4th 9; wknd 13 & releg 7th; unable to cl aft; 15l 5th app 2 out* 6 4

1226[2] Alleywell 14-1 A Wadlow *Chsd ldrs; eff 11; 3rd 13; wknd 15; 15l 6th app 2 out* 12 5

1191[2] Deep Dale 8-1 Miss F Wilson *Hdwy to 3rd/4th 7-11; 9th & fdng rap 13; t.o & pu 15* . . . . . P

1226[5] Italian Clover(cp) 33-1 Miss S Carter *Tubed; rr & rdn 9; t.o 13; pu 15* . . . . P

1232[1] King's Reply 5-1 R Burton *Prom to 5; stdly lost plce; rr & strugg aft 9; pu 11* P

844U Mikes Acre (5a)(tt) 33-1 James Price *(xnb) Swtng; last trio; blun 3; rdn 9; t.o & pu 12* . . . . . P

1115[1] Milamoss 20-1 R Hughes *Nvr gng wl; detach last by 4; nvr able to cl; t.o & pu 3 out* . . . . . P

1089[3] Mountain Lily (5a) 16-1 J Cook *Ld to 2; prom to 9; 9th & fdng bad 13; t.o & pu 15* . . . . . P

1346[1]	Nealie Mac (IRE) 10-1 M Wall *Midfield; 6th & getting outpcd 13; wl bhnd when pu 3 out*		P
1340[1]	Rosemead Tye (5a) 7-1 Mrs K Baimbridge *Rcd keen; ld 2-12; 8th & fdng rap 13; blun nxt & pu*		P
1230[F]	Ski Pass 5-1 T Stephenson *Hld up; hdwy 11; ld on inner 13; hdd 15; disp 2nd & rdn when fell 2 out*		F

OFFICIAL DISTANCES: 3*l*, 2*l* **TIME:** 6min 44.0s

1389 Restricted (Div 2), 12st — 15 ran

1035[1]	**SIMPLY THE ONE (IRE)** 7-4F **H Fowler** *Hld up; 6th & smooth prog 11; went 2nd 15; ld aft 3 out; strode clr app last; rdly*		1
1239[1]	**Tenacious Melody** 9-2 **Miss I Tompsett** *(xnb) Tk str hld; ld & sn clr; 12l ahd 14; wknd & hdd aft 3 out; kpt on same pce aft*	10	2
925[3]	**New Lodge Express (IRE)** 4-1 **T Stephenson** *(xnb) Swtng; chsd clr ldr; clsd & eff 15; 6l 3rd app 2 out; one pce & nd aft*	3	3
1256[P]	Primitive Son 10-1 Miss E James *Midfield; hdwy 10; 5th 13; wknd 15; poor 5th app 2 out*	2	4
1116[1]	Joe Lively (IRE) (7a) 33-1 A Wintle *A towards rr; slt prog 12; wknd 14; rem aft 3 out*	30	5
1258[1]	Autcaesar Autnihil (IRE) 5-1 M Munrowd *Chsd ldrs; went 2nd 11-12; wknd qckly nxt; pu 3 out*		P
1230[F]	Babs Wheal (5a) 9-2 Julian Pritchard *Hld up last trio & wl off pce; t.o & pu 14*		P
1237[P]	Black Dan(bl) 33-1 D Underwood *Jmpd erratic & labouring in last trio; t.o 9; pu 12*		P
1193[1]	Drom Island (5a) 10-1 Miss F Wilson *Sn bhnd; t.o & pu 14*		P
1014[P]	Merry Major 10-1 M Keel *(xnb) Jmpd slow 7; chsd ldrs til 7th & wkng 9; no ch 12; t.o & pu 3 out*		P
1095[P]	Minster Belle (5a) 33-1 P Sheldrake *Sn bhnd; t.o & pu 12*		P
1322[P]	Native Isle (IRE) 20-1 J Mahot *Cl up in chsng group; 4th 13; wknd 15; 20l 4th app 2 out; 5th when pu last*		P
1136[r]	Sales Dodger (IRE)(cp) 16-1 R Hughes *A wl bhnd; no ch 12; t.o & pu 3 out*		P
1265[F]	Templenoe Hare (IRE) 12-1 R Burton *Bhnd; some prog in 7th 12; wknd 14; t.o & pu 2 out*		P
1230[P]	Watergate Boy (IRE) 33-1 R Carey *(xnb) Prom; 3rd 9; wknd nxt; t.o & pu 13*		P

OFFICIAL DISTANCES: 10*l*, 2*l* **TIME:** 6min 43.0s

1390 Mens Open, 12st - 16J — 16 ran

1257[2]	**TEME WILLOW (IRE)** (7x) 7-2 **Julian Pritchard** *Jmpd rt in 2nd; ld app omitted 14; rdn & a hldng rivals frm 2 out*		1
1117[3]	**Philtre (IRE)** (7x) 8-1 **A Wintle** *Ld 3 til rdn & hdd passing omitted 14; 2½l 2nd app 2 out; drvn along & no imp aft*	2½	2
1277[1]	**Sir Dante (IRE)** (7x) 5-1 **F Hutsby** *Nrly a 3rd; sust eff frm 15; 3½l down app 2 out; nvr able to cl*	2½	3
980[2]	Stag Party (IRE) 3-1F H Fowler *Wl bhnd & niggled 5; poor 11th 12; 30l 7th app 2 out; stayed on wl aft; too much to do*	6	4
1073[5]	Lord Castle (IRE) 25-1 R McCarthy *Hdwy to 5th 10; nd frm 15; 15l 4th app 2 out*	2	5
979[3]	Love At Dawn 4-1 P Mason *Midfield but nvr on terms; 8th 11; no prog & 26l 6th app 2 out*	12	6
1335[3]	Lyphard's Fable (USA) 25-1 D England *A bhnd; 10th 11; t.o 15*	25	7
835[3]	Asthefellasays (IRE) 14-1 R Burton *Midfield but nd; 7th 11; strugg when pu 15*		P
1261[r]	Castle Frome (IRE) (7a) 33-1 M Jackson *Poor last aft jmpd v slow 1; t.o 7; pu 10*		P
	Celtic Song (IRE) (7x) 33-1 E Walker *(xnb) Ld brief aft 2; 5th when mist 6; lost plce rap; pu 10*		P
1110[F]	Jimmy Jumbo (IRE) (4x, 8ow)(tt) 33-1 N Cecil *(xnb) Ld to start; midfield early; lsng tch when rfo 10*		U
974[5]	Minella Storm (IRE) (7x) 7-2 P Sheldrake *Settled ab 4th til rdn & wknd app omitted 14; 20l 5th when blun & ur 2 out*		U
1187[1]	Pete The Painter (IRE)(bl) 7-1 James Tudor *Midfield til crashed thro wing & fell 7*		R
1190[F]	Pharailde (5a) 8-1 J Price *Chsd ldrs; 6th 11; wknd app omitted 14; t.o & pu 3 out; broke down*		P

979[7] Stride To Glory (IRE)(vis) 12-1 M Hooper *Sn bhnd; t.o last 12; pu 15* . . . . P
1073[P] Theatreland (USA) 33-1 G Barfoot-Saunt *(xnb) Cl up to 9; 9th & wkng 11; t.o & pu 15* . . . . P

OFFICIAL DISTANCES: 1½l, 4l **TIME:** 6min 38.0s

Fences 13 & 14 omitted - damaged

PLATE 15 1390 Golden Valley Mens Open: Teme Willow leads after two miles from Philtre, Sir Dante, Minella Storm, Pharailde and Lord Castle (with a commendably shoulder-high whip) and the rest of the field *PHOTO: Kathleen Mullen*

1391 Ladies Open - 17J 13 ran

1255[1]	**UPTON ADVENTURE** (5a, 7x) 4-7F **Miss E James** *Lw; prsd ldr; chall 14; ld app 2 out; rdly drew clr; rdn out; impressive*		1
1263[1]	**Stretching (IRE)** (7x) 6-1 **Miss J Williams** *Settled 3rd; went 2nd app 2 out; sn u.p & outpcd; nt fluent last*	10	2
1314[1]	**Lucky Master (IRE)** 8-1 **Miss G Swan** *Midfield; 7th 12; some prog in 10l 5th app 2 out; nvr able to chall*	10	3
1189[2]	De Chelly (5a, 7x) 6-1 Mrs C Owen *Settled 3rd/4th; ev ch til jmpd slow 13 & 14; 9l 4th & outpcd app 2 out*	12	4
1263[6]	Ghutah (7x) 33-1 Miss J Owen *(xnb) Swtng; wl bhnd til some prog 11; 9th nxt; lost tch 15*	2	5
976[3]	Coddington Girl (5a) 20-1 Miss S Sharratt *Ld; drvn & hdd app 2 out; drpd out qckly*	3	6
1320[4]	How To Run (IRE) 14-1 Miss H Lewis *Midfield; 8th 12; wknd 14*	½	7
1343[4]	Welburn Boy(bl,tt) 16-1 Miss L Allfrey *Last & sn wl detach; t.o 10-3 out; stayed on clsng stages; v negative ride*	12	8
1278[2]	Aircon (IRE) 9-1 Miss R Hutsby *(xnb) Chsd ldrs; rdr waving at times; 10l 6th 13; slt mist & rfo nxt*		U
1343[1]	Campden Kitty (5a) 13-2 Miss A de Lisle Wells *Chsd ldrs; 4th 13; wknd nxt; poor 8th when pu last*		P
1278[4]	Final Escapade 33-1 Miss K Garner *Towards rr til pu 4*		P
1017[P]	Fuero Real (FR) 33-1 Miss H James *A bhnd; t.o 11; pu 15*		P
1235[P]	Ile Distinct (IRE)(tt) 25-1 Miss B Williams *Bhnd til fell 9*		F

OFFICIAL DISTANCES: 8l, 5l **TIME:** 6min 40.0s

Fence 16 omitted - fallen rider

1392 Welsh Border Counties Area Club Members (Confined Hunts Championship), 12st — 12 ran

Form	Horse	Dist	Pos
1227[1]	**FATHER TOM (IRE)** (6x) 4-7F **Julian Pritchard** *Nt fluent; hld up last to 7; 12l 7th 13; smooth prog 15; ld aft 2 out; sn clr; easily*		1
1227[3]	**Huntersway (IRE)** 7-1 **R Hughes** *Swtng; hld up & wl bhnd; hdwy 11 to 4½l 4th 13; went 2nd 15; ld app 2 out; hdd aft 2 out; no ch w wnr*	8	2
1227[5]	**Magicien (FR)** 12-1 **Miss R Reynolds** *Midfield; 10l 5th 13; 6l 5th app 2 out; one pce & nd aft*	6	3
1358[P]	Persona Pride (3x) 8-1 Miss E James *Ld & jw; hdd app 2 out; sn wknd*	nk	4
1358[P]	Genereux (5x)(cp) 12-1 R Hodges *Drvn all way & nvr keen; prom to 8; nt r.o; poor 8th & u.p 13*	30	5
979[6]	Go Go Gallant (IRE) 25-1 J Jones *Midfield; wknd 11; poor 9th 13; t.o.*	10	6
1228[5]	Wild Edric(bl) 12-1 A Beedles *Cl 2nd/3rd to 13; wkng when jmpd v slow nxt; reluct aft; t.o*	nk	7
1113[3]	Cadougold (FR) (3x)(tt) 14-1 M Keel *Lw; midfield; 11l 6th 13; wknd app 2 out; poor 6th when bd by unseater at last*		B
1320[3]	Inis Cara (IRE) 12-1 J Harris *Numerous slovenly js; releg last aft mist 7; t.o & u.p 10; pu 15*		P
1110[U]	Inthaar(bl) 25-1 A Phillips *(xnb) Jb in rr; t.o 10; blun bad 12; pu 14*		P
1113[1]	Petrouge (3x)(cp) 5-1 R Burton *Lw; prom; 4th when blun & ur 12*		U
1344[5]	Wild Blade (IRE)(cp,tt) 20-1 R Jenkins *(xnb) Towards rr to 10; gd prog to 2nd 12-15; 2½l 3rd app nxt; nt r.o; poor 5th when jmpd rt & ur last*		U

OFFICIAL DISTANCES: 5l, 3l **TIME:** 6min 41.0s

1393 Open Maiden 56&7yo (Div 1), 12st — 11 ran

Form	Horse	Dist	Pos
1240[R]	**NEMINOS (IRE)** (7a) 7-1 **A Wadlow** *Jmpd sluggish stdly lost gd early plce; 6th 13; rallied 15; ld app 2 out & sn clr; a in comm; rn green clsng stages*		1
1096[S]	**Rescindo (IRE)** (7a)(vis) 6-4F **W Oakes** *Prom; ld app 10; drew clr aft 12; 12l ahd aft 15; wknd rap app 2 out; sn hdd & threw in the towel*	10	2
	Courseman (IRE) 20-1 **D Painter** *Rr & hmpd 2; 15l last 4; hdwy 10 to 3rd 13 & 12l 2nd aft 15; releg 10l 3rd app 2 out; wknd*	25	3
1259[4]	Fencethegap (IRE) 7-1 M Hooper *Swtng; towards rr when mist 4; 20l last 8; 12l 6th 13; wknd; wl bhnd 15*	6	4
1323[P]	Glastrian 20-1 G Perkins *Hdwy to 4th 6; 3rd app 10 til mist 13; hit nxt & sn wknd; poor last when pu last*		P
983[U]	Gumlayloy (7a) 3-1 D Mansell *(xnb) Oht; tk keen hld; ld & nt fluent; hit 7; hdd app 10; chsd ldr to 14; wknd tame; wl bhnd when pu 2 out*		P
1233[P]	Kerry Zulu Warrior 8-1 H Tett *(xnb) Pulled v hrd (as always); hdwy to 3rd 6; lost plce aft 9; 8th 12; pu 13*		P
1266[P]	Kotori (IRE) (7a) 20-1 S Gray *(xnb) Mist 4; chsd ldr 4-9; 25l last & fdng rap 13; pu 3 out*		P
	One Minute Man (IRE) 10-1 R Hughes *Strugg in rr; wl bhnd when pu 8*		P
	Scally's George 6-1 Julian Pritchard *Pulled hrd & novicey in rr; hmpd 2; wl bhnd when pu 11; reins broke*		P
983[2]	Stantons Church 5-1 Miss R Reynolds *(xnb) Prom til blun & ur 2*		U

OFFICIAL DISTANCES: 6l, 20l **TIME:** 6min 51.0s

Fences 9 & 16 omitted - fallen rider

1394 Open Maiden 56&7yo (Div 2), 12st — 11 ran

Form	Horse	Dist	Pos
1253[4]	**TERIMON'S DREAM** 12-1 **D Mansell** *Tde & went v fast to start; tk keen hld; ld; rn wide app 6; hdd 12; ld agn on inner nxt; mist 14; hrd drvn to go clr frm 2 out; wandering clsng stages (good ride)*		1
1074[2]	**Willoughby Flyer** 5-4F **M Walters** *Swtng; prom; jmpd slow 5; ld 12-13; ev ch til rdn & outpcd 2 out; rallied last; no ex cl home; outrdn*	1	2
1091[4]	**Ladygal (IRE)** (12a) 8-1 **D Davies** *3rd aft 9; 6l 4th & outpcd 13; t.o app 2 out; lft rem 3rd at last*	15	3
1266[P]	Evanly Miss (5a)(vis) 12-1 M Jackson *Sn bhnd; lost tch 12; 12l 6th nxt; t.o app 2 out*	8	4
837[P]	Bally Cyrano 25-1 J Jones *(xnb) Wl bhnd; jmpd v slow 6; t.o & pu 7*		P
1091[P]	Geal Farraige (IRE) (12a) 9-2 N Oliver *Chsd ldrs; went 2nd & ev ch 12-3 out; rdn in 6l 3rd & wkng app nxt; tired & no imp when fell last*		F
1275[P]	Greensleeves (5a) 9-2 Miss J Pearson *1st ride; hit 2; nt fluent in rr; 8th aft 9; saddle slpd & fell on flat bef 11*		F

1239P	Indian Trix (IRE) (5a) 20-1 M Munrowd *Mists & sn bhnd; poor last aft 9; t.o & pu 11*		P
1139²	Nessarc (IRE) (7a) 4-1 R Hodges *(xnb) Mists; chsd ldrs; 5l 5th 12 but 11l down & drvn nxt; wknd rap; t.o when mist 15; pu 2 out*		P
1192F	Plynlimon 14-1 James Price *A bhnd; 27l 7th 13; t.o & mist 14; pu nxt*		P
	Sea Grit (7a) 12-1 P Morris *(xnb) Ss & lost 20l; novicey in poor last til pu 6*		P

OFFICIAL DISTANCES: 1½*l*, dist **TIME:** 6min 50.0s

1395 Open Maiden 8yo&up, 12st - 16J — 17 ran

1239²	**BLAKENEY HILL** (5a) 6-1 **J Price** *Made all; blun 15; 1l up app 2 out; drvn clr*		1
1232³	**Clever Dickie** 7-4F **R Burton** *Hld up & bhnd; 7th 11; prog in 16l 4th but niggled 14; went 2nd & ev ch app 2 out; drvn & sn outpcd; fin wkly*	6	2
1125U	**Jovian Pond** 25-1 **R Sealey** *Swtng; cl up; 3rd 11; went 2nd 14; ev ch nxt til 4l 3rd & wkng app 2 out; plodded on*	3	3
1320P	Columna (5a) 25-1 James Price *Mist 7; midfield til drpd to rr 11; 23l 7th 13; t.o when lft 4th nr fin*	30	4
1258⁴	Master Cruise 4-1 Julian Pritchard *Prom til 6th & outpcd 11; 22l 6th 13; no prog; walked in & lost 4th nr fin*	2	5
1232⁶	Romabit Tom 12-1 R Rogers *2 handlers; a bhnd; t.o 11; jmpd v slow 14; jb rt 2 out*	runin	6
1226⁶	Come On Boy 25-1 G Davies *Cl up til tried to ref, jb rt & ur 4*		U
1324P	Evans The Coal 16-1 R Carey *Tk keen hld; hung lft & rn v wide on bends; prom; 2nd when nrly rn off course app 10; sn prom agn; 8l 3rd & wkng 13; pu 15*		P
1231²	Franco Lady (IRE) (5a) 7-2 Miss E James *Cl up when fell 2*		F
	Golden Host(bl) 25-1 H Dowty *Chsd ldrs til 8th & drvn 8; t.o & pu 11*		P
730P	Kuwait Faith (IRE)(bl) 25-1 G Barfoot-Saunt *(xnb) Nt fluent; prom; blun 5; mist 7; 4th & outpcd 11; t.o & pu 14*		P
927P	Margery Copse (5a) 20-1 M Wall *(xnb) Midfield when bd 4; lkd to be fatally inj*		B
1116⁴	Norton Wood (IRE) 20-1 R Hodges *Midfield til bd 4*		B
1233F	Peggys Gold (5a) 25-1 S Graham *Jmpd stickily in last pr; t.o 11; pu 15*		P
1055U	Spruce Goose (IRE)(tt) 10-1 M Walters *(xnb) Swtng; rdr insecure; chsd ldrs; blun 12; 20l 5th & outpcd 13; pu 15*		P
927³	Sumerian Lad 7-1 J Sole *Midfield when rn thro wing & ur 2*		R
	Your Turn Rosie (5a) 20-1 A Brown *Bckwd; a last trio; hmpd bad 2; nrly fell 5; t.o 13; pu 3 out*		P

OFFICIAL DISTANCES: 4*l*, 6*l* **TIME:** 6min 55.0s

Fences 11 & 18 Omitted - fallen rider

Melton Hunt Club

Garthorpe (RH 8F,18J)

Sat, 15 May (GOOD to FIRM)

1396 Melton Hunt Club Members Conditions — 18 ran

885P	**NOKIMOVER**(cp) 6-1 **Miss Gemma Hutchinson** *Lw; ldng group; ld 11; kicked 10l clr app 13; rdn & lkd vulnerable 3 out; 2l up 2 out; stayed on; drew clr flat*		1
1071¹	**My Best Buddy** 5-1 **R Cope** *Ldng group; mist 7; chsd wnr 13; rdn aft 15; clsd & mist 3 out; 2l down when mist 2 out; hld when mist last.*	8	2
868F	**Seabrook Lad**(cp) 14-1 **N Pearce** *Ldng group; outpcd 13; 3rd & nt on terms w ldng pr 15; kpt on same pce*	8	3
1216²	Ardmayle (IRE) 3-1F Miss L Coney *7th & last of clr ldng group; outpcd frm 13; poor 5th & nd aft 15; stayed on to snatch 4th*	6	4
1347P	Gratomi (IRE) 8-1 N Kent *Swtng; w ldrs; outpcd 13; poor 4th aft 15; same til wknd & dem on post*	s hd	5
1120⁶	Majestic Approach (IRE) 20-1 Miss H Campbell *(xnb) Off pce in midfield; nvr on terms; wl bhnd frm 15; stayed on frm 2 out.*	6	6
889⁴	Rathbarry Lad (IRE) 10-1 S Morris *20s-10s; warm; off pce in midfield; nvr on terms; wl bhnd frm 15; mod late prog*	2	7
1056²	Springlea Tower (2ow) 10-1 R Hunnisett *Nvr gng pce in midfield; no ch frm 15; one pce.*	15	8
1202⁶	Royal Crimson 25-1 R Alers-Hankey *Wl off pce in rr; no ch frm 13; plodded on*	5	9
1217P	Coole Chief 25-1 K Green *(xnb) A off pce in midfield; no prog 11; t.o frm 15*	20	10

1213^{4}	Libido (2ow) 25-1 P Andrew *(xnb) Sn wl bhnd; t.o in last quintet 1/2way; plodded rnd*	20	11
997^{P}	Vital Issue (IRE) 50-1 P Johnson *(xnb) Mounted on course; ss; imm t.o in last group; wobbled rnd safely*	1/2	12
1213^{r}	Frileux Royal (FR) 7-1 G Morrison *Ld to 2; ld 5-11; wknd & jmpd slow 14; 7th when ref nxt*		r
1241^{2}	King Of The Sea (IRE) 50-1 Miss E Bell *(xnb) Imm miles bhnd & jmpng wildly; t.o til pu 13*		P
1245^{P}	Lone Star (IRE)(bl) 33-1 A Sansome *Nvr on terms in midfield; 10th & strugg when fell 11*		F
1000^{1}	Mill Lord (IRE) 8-1 M Mackley *Ld 2-4; prom til wknd rap 13; pu 15*		P
1218^{P}	Mr Match (2ow) 50-1 D Hockridge *Sn wl bhnd; t.o in last quintet 1/2way; pu 12*		P
1279^{3}	Romanybaan 40-1 P Ikin *(xnb) 2 handlers; swtng; imm t.o w rdr waving; pu 11*		P

OFFICIAL DISTANCES: 10*l*, 8*l* **TIME:** 6min 06.0s

1397 Intermediate, 12st — 8 ran

1361^{P}	**EMPEROR ROSCOE** 3-1JF **N Docker** *Cl up; chse ldr 10; ld 15; sn kicked 6l clr; jmpd slow 3 out & prsd; hrd rdn frm 2 out; hld on wl flat*		1
946^{2}	**Orchestra's Boy (IRE)** 4-1 **K Green** *6s-4s; prom; trckd ldr 4-10; chsd wnr aft 15; rn wide bend aft 3 out; drvn to chall agn & ev ch last; no ex flat*	2	2
1151^{4}	**Filou Du Bois (FR)** 7-2 **Ms A Embiricos** *(xnb) Sn shuffled to rr but in tch; eff to 4th 15; ch 3 out; nt qckn app nxt; stayed on wl flat*	3	3
1274^{3}	Tom Putt 7-1 B Pauling *Rn in snatches; ld to 2; sn lost plces; 10l adrift of rest & strugg 10; kpt on frm 15; stayed on wl flat*	4	4
1056^{1}	Balmoral Spring (IRE)(vis) 3-1JF R Armson *Hld up last pr; prog to trck ldrs 8; 3rd aft 15; clsd to chall & ev ch app 2 out; wknd last*	3/4	5
1216^{P}	Dante's Banker (IRE)(cp) 8-1 M Mackley *Mist 3 & rmdrs; in tch; blun 11 & wknd; pu 13*		P
1205^{3}	General Carats(bl) 25-1 M Walford *Hld up; pulled to ld 3; hdd & jmpd slow 15; wknd rap; pu 3 out*		P
1216^{5}	Princess Derry (5a)(bl) 7-1 C Cundall *In tch; mist 11; sn pushed along; mist 14 & wknd; t.o & pu last*		P

OFFICIAL DISTANCES: 1 1/2*l*, 2*l* **TIME:** 6min 16.5s

1398 Panacur/TBA PPORA Club Members Mares Final, 12st — 5 ran

1019^{1}	**SOVEREIGN GALE (IRE)** (5a) 11-8F **M Harris** *(xnb) Jw; made all; drew 8l clr aft 15; prsd brief 3 out; sn clr agn; rdn & tired last; kpt on flat*		1
1102^{2}	**Saucy Arethusa** (5a) 15-8 **N Harris** *(xnb) Warm; hld up in 4th; outpcd & mist 10; eff 13; chsd wnr 15; 3l 2nd & mist 3 out; mist nxt; kpt on agn flat; nvr able to chall; fin lame*	4	2
1157^{4}	**Hattie** (5a) 9-1 **P Cornforth** *(xnb) Prsd wnr 2-4 & frm 7; cl 2nd 13; hit 14 hrd; lost 2nd nxt; one pce aft*	10	3
1119^{3}	Bethin (5a) 33-1 P Newton *Chsd wnr to 2 & agn 4 til mist 7; wknd rap 12; crawled over 14 & pu*		P
1217^{P}	Near And Phar (IRE) (5a) 5-2 K Green *(xnb) Hld up in last; blun bad & ur 8*		U

OFFICIAL DISTANCES: 4*l*, 8*l* **TIME:** 6min 16.8s

1399 Ladies Open — 7 ran

1347^{3}	**MULLENSGROVE** 10-11F **Miss S Phizacklea** *Tchd evens; lw(!); prom; ld 5-7; bumped along frm 9; ld 10; jnd nxt; duelled w rival & pr sn wl clr; drvn & 1l up when lft wl clr 3 out; eased flat (prob would have won anyway)*		1
1058^{2}	**Bloomfield Storm (IRE)** 7-1 **Miss S Buckley** *In tch; 9l 5th & pushed along 10; sn wl outpcd; no ch aft; stayed on frm 2 out to tk 2nd final 100yds*	25	2
987^{3}	**Macfin (IRE)**(cp) 5-1 **Miss L Allan** *Lft in ld 3-5; ld agn 7-10; sn brushed aside by ldng pr; lost poor 3rd 15; kpt on to rem 2nd 2 out; dem flat*	1	3
1060^{5}	Cawkwell Princess (5a) 33-1 Miss A Stennett *Chsd ldrs; 7l 4th 10; sn wl outpcd; went poor 3rd 15; lft dist 2nd 3 out; dem nxt*	2	4
1104^{5}	Steve Ford 50-1 Miss E Harbour *A last; in tch to 11; sn wknd; t.o*	30	5
1122^{2}	Fami (FR) 5-2 Miss Gemma Hutchinson *4s-5/2; lw; cl up gng wl; eff to disp ld 11; sust duel w wnr aft & pr sn miles clr of rest; 1l down when blun & ur 3 out*		U
1290^{7}	Pharlindo (IRE) 20-1 Miss A Armitage *(xnb) Ld til blun & ur 3*		U

OFFICIAL DISTANCES: dist, 3/4*l* **TIME:** 6min 10.2s

1400 Melton Hunt Club Members Novices — 9 ran

1057[2] **FRANCO (IRE)** 4-7F **J Diment** *Mostly jw; ld/disp til 1l up 10; drew 10l clr aft 15; rdn app 2 out; nvr in serious danger but drvn out flat* 1

1168[10] **Boyne Banks (IRE)** 7-1 **G Disney** *Rcd free; ld/disp aft 2-10; 4l down 13; rdn & outpcd 15; 7l 2nd & prsd 3 out; kpt on wl frm nxt* 4 2

1092[4] **Court Adjourn** 5-1 **S Morris** *8s-5s; swtng; hld up off pce; went 3rd 8; 18l 3rd 10; eff & pushed along 13; clsd to disp 2nd app 3 out; one pce aft.* 2 1/2 3

1135[2] Top Of The Charts 25-1 M Harris *Lkd rough; w ldng pr to 3; sn outpcd; lost plce 8; disp 24l 5th 10; dist 4th 15; t.o* . . . . fence 4

1060[2] Nickit (IRE)(cp) 8-1 J Docker *(xnb) Nt jw & nvr went a yd; 40l 8th 1/2way; wl t.o aft* 25 5

997[P] Cateel Bay (5a) 50-1 A Sansome *Off pce in midfield; disp 24l 5th 10; 6th & wkng when fell hvly 12* . . . . F

1246[P] Granny Dick (5a)(bl) 50-1 T Messenger *Last & drvn 3; 42l last 10; blun nxt; t.o & pu 15* . . . . P

1218[1] Midnight Cowboy 16-1 N Kent *Nt on terms in midfield; 24l 4th 10; no prog; v dist 5th 15; pu 2 out* . . . . P

1245[3] Society Scandal (IRE) 50-1 P Millington *Sn wl in rr; 39l 7th 1/2way; sn t.o; missed out 15 (w rdr drvng along).* . . . . P

OFFICIAL DISTANCES: 5*l*, 1 3/4*l* **TIME:** 6min 05.0s

The time of this race equalled the course record

1401 Mens Open — 4 ran

1121[3] **BLUE ROYAL (FR)** 7-2 **S Morris** *Jw; ld 5; made rest; 4l up aft 15; drvn 2 out; prsd aft last; kpt on wl; fin sore* 1

1171[P] **Nautical Lad** 10-11F **J Docker** *Lw; ww in last; nt fluent 6 & 7; prog to chse wnr 13; nt fluent 15 & sn pushed along; eff 2 out; tried to chall flat; a hld* . 1 1/4 2

924[3] **Stormy Session** 50-1 **J Benfield** *Warm; ld to 5; chsd wnr to 11; sn wl outpcd; went poor 3rd agn app 3 out; t.o* 45 3

1121[1] Shanavogh 2-1 R Hunnisett *Cl up; chsd wnr 11 til nt much room bend aft nxt; sn wl outpcd; drpd to poor last when collapsed jmpng 3 out; dead.* . . . . . F

OFFICIAL DISTANCES: 1 1/2*l*, 20*l* **TIME:** 6min 07.5s

1402 Open Maiden 56&7yo (Div 1), 2m4f, 12st - 15J — 13 ran

1125[4] **TOM TOBACCO** 7-4F **R Cope** *3s-7/4; jmpd slow 3; ld/disp til 2l clr 3 out; lft 5l clr 2 out; drvn & jmpd slow last; sn prsd; strugg home.* 1

1218[3] **Coombs Spinney** 6-1 **T Coles** *Prom; cl 3rd 1/2way; 4th & outpcd frm 12; rallied 2 out; stayed on to press wnr flat; a just hld.* 2 2

1125[P] **Silver Styx** (7a) 10-1 **R Armson** *Cl up; jnd wnr 9-3 out; 2l down when blun 2 out; kpt on wl but dem agn flat.* 1/2 3

1266[F] Major Reno (IRE) 16-1 J Newbold *(xnb) Wl in tch; cl 5th gng wl 8; eff to chse ldng pr 12; sn no imp; fdd & mist 2 out* 10 4

1339[U] Golden Dawn 20-1 Miss S Phizacklea *Disp ld to 8; outpcd frm 12; 5th & wl btn 3 out.* 7 5

1215[P] Shambob 8-1 J Burley *(xnb) Warm; midfield; 8th 8; outpcd frm 10; nd aft* 10 6

1233[3] Chicago's Padre 8-1 A Hanly *(xnb) Midfield; 6th 8; lost tch app 10; t.o 8th when blun bad 3 out & pu* . . . . P

1119[P] Herpen (5a) 20-1 T Ellis *A rr; 11th & lsng tch 8; t.o & pu 11* . . . . P

1275[P] Orton Playboy 20-1 P Newton *A wl in rr; 10th & strugg 8; t.o frm 12; pu 2 out* P

1339[P] Pernickety King (7a) 20-1 P Millington *Sev slow js in midfield; 7th & in tch 8; outpcd 10; drvn & no prog 12; poor last when pu last* . . . . P

1218[P] Slingsby Lady (12a, 4ow) 14-1 A Sansome *Ur gng to post; a rr; t.o last & pu 8* P

1119[U] Spinosa (5a) 4-1 N Kent *Swtng; midfield; 9th & lsng tch 8; t.o & pu 12* . . P

1124[P] Usedtobeasweetboy (7a) 12-1 C Wadland *Reluct to rce & lft 25l; caught up in rr by 6; 12th & strugg 8; sn t.o; 9th when blun & ur 3 out* . . . . U

OFFICIAL DISTANCES: 1 1/2*l*, 3/4*l* **TIME:** 5min 13.5s

1403 Open Maiden 56&7yo (Div 2), 2m4f, 12st - 15J — 12 ran

1000[2] **TOOLEY PARK** 4-1 **J Diment** *6s-4s; rn in snatches; in tch; prog to chse clr ldr 9; clsd 12; chall & 1l down when lft in unassailable ld 3 out; dogged it furiously & hrd drvn frm 2 out; all out* 1

1125[P] **Call Me Again** 5-1 **N Pearce** *Prom; chsd ldr 7-9; sn outpcd by ldng pr; t.o when lft 2nd 3 out; prsd flat & just kpt 2nd* 30 2

945P **For A Pagan Song** 6-1 **S Morris** *Tk keen hld; cl up; lost plce 7; outpcd frm 9; poor 6th aft 12; stayed on frm 3 out; disp rem 2nd when blun 2 out; nt pushed but kpt on flat.* ½ 3
1124⁵ Currow Kate (5a) 8-1 N Docker *Trckd ldrs; outpcd aft 9; disp poor 4th aft 12; no prog* 2½ 4
1215P Mr Baldwin (IRE) 8-1 J Turcan *Chsd ldrs; 5th & outpcd 9; 1 of 4 disp poor 4th aft 12; wknd 3 out; t.o* 25 5
685P Another Half (12a) 5-2F M Walford *(xnb) Ld; drew 10l clr 9; prsd aft 12; 1l up when fell hvly 3 out (prob would have won)* F
Dynamic Sea 16-1 P Millington *Lkd awful; last trio of main group (w stable companions) & sn detach; rdr waving frantic 7; t.o & pu 11* P
James Pine (IRE) (7a) 14-1 A Sansome *Lkd awful; last trio & sn detach; wl bhnd & pu 7* P
1273P Lagan Lady (5a) 16-1 J King *Drpd to rr 5; sn bhnd; t.o when jmpd slow 12; pu 3 out* P
1339S Little Heck (IRE) (6ow)(tt) 14-1 C Weaver *Jb & a in rr; t.o & pu 11* P
1266F Norbert (IRE) 8-1 A Hanly *Wrs; reluct to rce; set off 200yds bhnd; jmpd wildly; no hdwy; pu 11* P
996² Northern Breeze (5a) 3-1 M Mackley *Warm; midfield; outpcd 9; disp poor 4th aft 12; t.o & pu 3 out; disapp* P

OFFICIAL DISTANCES: dist, nk **TIME:** 5min 12.7s

Following a complaint by the trainer of Norbert the stewards enquired into the start of this race, having interviewed the Starter it was confirmed the horse was given every opportunity to start with the rest of the field

Southdown & Eridge

Godstone (RH 6F,18J)

Sat, 15 May (GOOD)

1404 Open Maiden (Div 1), 12st - 15J — 9 ran

1211³ **PRIVATE PERCIVAL** 16-1 **P Blagg** *Hld up; a in tch; hdwy 12; prsd ldr aft 13 til lft 6l clr 15; rdn along frm by-passed 3 out* 1
1337⁴ **Barbed Broach (IRE)** 16-1 **Miss C Cowe** *Ld/disp to 10; 4th & lsng tch aft 13; lft 12l 3rd 15; r.o; chsd wnr by-passing 3 out; no imp* 6 2
803F **Lady Mordaunt (IRE)** (5a) 7-4F **P York** *Sn prom; w ldr 9-13; 6l 3rd & wkng when lft 2nd 15; dem by-passing 3 out* 8 3
1098P Calling Home (IRE) 3-1 W Kavanagh *Cl up when mist & ur 5* U
1211⁴ Divine Mist (IRE) 6-1 J Owen *Prsd ldr/disp til ld & jmpd slow 13; narrow advant when fell 15* F
1091P Miss Chloe (IRE) (5a) 6-1 R Bliss *A towards rr; in tch to 10; rdn along & no resp 12; wl bhnd when pu 14* P
1317⁵ Scalby Croft (5a) 16-1 Miss N Barnes *Tde; a rr; lost tch 8; wl bhnd when pu aft 12* P
1088P Sir Henrik (IRE) 8-1 B Garner *Cl up in midfield til rn out 12* R
1285³ Worth A Shot (IRE) 5-1 D Phelan *Mists; prsd ldrs; rdn along aft 12; sn lost plce; rr when pu 14* P

OFFICIAL DISTANCES: 5l, 8l **TIME:** 6min 42.0s
TOTE: £17.40; places £3.10,£5.80,£1.60 **DF:**£4.50 (1st+any)

Fences 10 & 16 omitted - fallen rider; fence 18 omitted - damaged

1405 Open Maiden (Div 2), 12st — 8 ran

1246P **MR KNOW WHAT (IRE)** 4-1 **Miss C Bartlett** *A.p; lft cl 3rd aft 12; trckd ldr 13 til ld 3 out; made rest; drew clr flat; comf* 1
1067P **Born Winner** 12-1 **P York** *A.p; lft disp ld aft 12; ld 13 til hdd 3 out; ev ch when mist nxt; no ex app last* 3 2
1088P **Sawbridge**(tt) 10-1 **C Gordon** *Midfield; lft cl 4th aft 12; prsd ldng pr 13; hrd rdn & ev ch 2 out; wknd app last* 4 3
Cowanstown King (IRE) 5-1 J Morgan *Prom to 3; sn lost plce; t.o 9 til pu 12* P
1285B Gale On The Lake (IRE) (5a) 7-4F A Merriam *Sn in rr; rdn along aft 4; no resp; wl bhnd when pu aft 9* P
1317P Marsden 6-1 A Braithwaite *Ld to 4; chsd ldr til lft disp aft 12; sn wknd; rem 4th when pu 15* P

Form	Horse / Comment	Dist	Pos
651[P]	See Red Billdan (IRE) 8-1 J Pemberton *Cl up; ld aft 4; sn clr; 25l ahd 9; mist 10; hung bad lft & rn out to horse boxes aft 12*		R
1280[4]	Winward 16-1 J Merry *Prom to 3; sn towards rr; wl bhnd 12 til pu 14*		P

OFFICIAL DISTANCES: 3*l*, 3*l* **TIME:** 6min 45.0s **TOTE:** £4.20; places £2.30,£3.20 **DF:**£37.00

The stewards enquired into the running and riding of i) Gale On The Lake, they accepted that the horse was never going and had come into season; and ii) Cowanstown King, they accepted that the horse had made a bad mistake and lost its action

1406 Intermediate, 12st — 7 ran

Form	Horse / Comment	Dist	Pos
1313[r]	**PERSIAN HERO (IRE)** 7-2 **J Owen** *Last away; cl 3rd frm 5; hrd rdn 15; chall & jmpd lft 2 out; ld last; r.o str flat*		1
759[4]	**Nomadic Star** 7-2 **Miss Z Lilly** *Prsd ldr/disp frm 3; ev ch when bumped & nrly ur 2 out; rallied flat to tk 2nd cl home.*	3	2
1084[1]	**Sliabh Foy (IRE)** 6-4F **P Hall** *Ld/disp til hdd last; wknd flat*	nk	3
1152[1]	Nowornever (IRE) 9-2 D Kemp *A ab same plce; 7l 4th 13; lost tch aft nxt.*	20	4
1280[1]	Glenmont (IRE)(cp) 6-1 Ms L Stock *Prsd ldrs; mist 10; pushed along 12; 8l 5th 13; fdd frm nxt.*	2	5
1212[4]	Alexander Nevsky 14-1 D Dennis *A last pr; rmdrs 12; 20l 6th 13; t.o & pu 15*		P
1242[P]	Owenabue Valley (IRE) (5x) 6-1 T Underwood *A last; 22l 7th 13; pu aft nxt*		P

OFFICIAL DISTANCES: 3*l*, nk **TIME:** 6min 30.0s **TOTE:** £3.30; places £1.10,£3.10 **DF:**£14.80

The stewards enquired into possible interference between Persian Hero and Nomadic Star at the second last; they concluded that any interference had been accidental and the result had not been affected

1407 Ladies Open — 7 ran

Form	Horse / Comment	Dist	Pos
1244[1]	**SPRING GALE (IRE)** (7x) 10-11F **Miss Z Turner** *Tde; cl up in midfield; trckd ldng pr 12; hdwy to ld 15; made rest; 5l up aft 3 out; easily*		1
1335[1]	**Cedar Chief** (7x)(bl) 6-4 **Mrs J Gordon** *Cl up in midfield til impd to ld aft 12; jnd & outj 15; sn rdn & outpcd; hit 3 out; kpt on one pce over last 2.*	3	2
1083[P]	**Glory Trail (IRE)** 14-1 **Miss H Grissell** *Cl last to 12; hdwy to chse ldng pr aft 14; 10l adrift 15; kpt on one pce frm 3 out*	20	3
1283[4]	Prime Course (IRE) (7x) 12-1 Miss H Gordon *Ld to 2; prsd ldr/disp frm 3; rmdrs aft 12; drpd back 5th nxt; no ch frm 15*	1	4
757[6]	Solo Gent (7x) 14-1 Miss K Jones *Ld/disp frm 3 til chsd ldr aft 12; fdd frm 14*	2	5
1283[P]	Red Channel (IRE) 14-1 Miss B Donnelly *Prom to 11; sn wknd; t.o frm 15.*	fence	6
1332[P]	Golden Savannah 14-1 Miss L Sleep *A last pr; lost tch aft 12; no ch when pu aft 14*		P

OFFICIAL DISTANCES: 3*l*, 10*l* **TIME:** 6min 31.0s **TOTE:** £3.00; places £2.20,£2.00 **DF:**£1.50

1408 Mens Open, 12st — 5 ran

Form	Horse / Comment	Dist	Pos
1295[4]	**BARD OF DRUMCOO (IRE)** (4x) evensF **D Kemp** *Made all in narrow ld; blun 12; kpt on str frm 3 out*		1
1209[2]	**River Bailiff (IRE)**(cp) 5-1 **P York** *Hld up; detach last frm 3 til hdwy 9; cl 4th aft 12; prsd wnr frm nxt; rdn aft 15; jnd wnr brief 3 out; kpt on one pce*	2	2
1172[P]	**Sheila McKenzie** (5a) 8-1 **T Lane** *Prsd wnr/disp 2nd to 12; cl 3rd when mist 15; lost tch app nxt*	10	3
1242[2]	Oranbay (IRE) (2ow) 10-1 G Freeney *A last pr; lost tch frm 12; wl bhnd 15; r.o frm 3 out; nrst fin.*	5	4
1153[3]	Militaire (FR) (7x) 2-1 J Owen *Cl 2nd/3rd til lost plce aft 13; mod 4th when pu 3 out*		P

OFFICIAL DISTANCES: 3*l*,5*l* **TIME:** 6min 35.0s **TOTE:** £2.80; places £1.10,£3.40 **DF:**£2.60

1409 Dodson & Horrell PPORA Club Members Restricted, 12st — 6 ran

Form	Horse / Comment	Dist	Pos
999[P]	**MAGIC LODGE** (7a) 12-1 **R Stearn** *In last pr; hdwy 9; cl 3rd frm 12 til qcknd to ld app 3 out; made rest in narrow ld; kpt on str flat.*		1
1317[1]	**On The Day (IRE)** 6-4 **J Owen** *Made most til hdd aft 15; hrd rdn & ev ch last; no ex flat.*	1½	2
1208[2]	**Lord Of The North (IRE)** 10-11F **C Gordon** *Hld up; hdwy 10; prsd ldr 13; ev ch 3 out; kpt on one pce*	2	3
1101[P]	Hillview Hut (IRE)(bl) 12-1 T Lane *Cl up; rmdrs 6; lost tch aft 12; wl bhnd when pu 14.*		P
1278[3]	Kingfisher Star 10-1 Miss J Lodge *Prom til lost plce qckly aft 8; t.o 12 til pu 15*		P
1208[P]	Kniveniven (IRE) 12-1 P York *Cl up; prsd ldr/disp frm 9 til blun & ur 12*		U

OFFICIAL DISTANCES: 2*l*, 3*l* **TIME:** 6min 31.0s **TOTE:** £10.60; places £7.40,£1.60 **DF:**£29.10

1410 Confined, 12st — 6 ran

1212^{3} **KENNY DAVIS (IRE)** 5-1 **P Blagg** *Tde; cl 3rd/4th til rap hdwy to ld 14; made rest in narrow ld; hld on wl flat* 1

1281^{1} **Brackenheath (IRE)** (3x)(bl) 2-1F **P Hall** *Ld to 12; chsd ldng pr frm 14; hrd rdn to nrly jn ldr 2 out; ev ch flat; nvr quite on terms* .... ½ 2

1054^{5} **Tell The Nipper (IRE)** (3x) 7-1 **M Gorman** *A cl 3rd/4th; lost plce brief 14; hdwy app 3 out; chall last; no ex cl home* .... ½ 3

1338^{2} Mister Pepper (IRE) (3x) 3-1 T Underwood *Detach last til gd hdwy 11; ld 13-14; prsd wnr rest of way til no ex u.p app 2 out* 2 4

806^{2} Rainbow Ranch (IRE) 5-2 C Gordon *Trckd ldr til lost plce aft 12; 5th & wkng 14; no ch when pu 3 out* .... P

897^{4} Tomcappagh (IRE) 12-1 J Wall *In tch til rdn & lost plce qckly aft 12; t.o & pu 14* .... P

OFFICIAL DISTANCES: ½*l*, ½*l* **TIME:** 6min 34.0s **TOTE:** £6.20; places £3.80,£1.70 **DF:**£4.60

1411 Hunt Members — 4 ran

1209^{3} **LIVELY LORD (IRE)**(cp,tt) 4-11F **Mrs J Gordon** *Ld 2; made rest; 2-3l up most of way; pushed out flat; comf* 1

1054^{P} **Spy Boy (IRE)**(vis) 8-1 **J Morgan** *Last til went 3rd 11; prsd wnr frm 13; rdn 3 out; 3l down when mist last; kpt on one pce flat* 4 2

1282^{1} **Straight Baron** 5-2 **P Bull** *Ld to 2; prsd wnr to 12; lost tch w ldng pr frm 14* 30 3

1054^{P} Tidal Reef (IRE) 8-1 G Wigley *3rd til last frm 11; lost tch app 13; t.o frm 15* fence 4

OFFICIAL DISTANCES: 4*l*, dist **TIME:** 6min 40.0s **TOTE:** £1.20 **DF:**£1.50

South Durham

Mordon (LH 8F,20J)

Sat, 15 May (GOOD, GOOD to FIRM patches)

1412 Hunt Members, 12st — 3 ran

166^{2} **SIR ALF** 6-4 **T Glass** *(xnb) Patient rdn; hld up in 10l 3rd 5 & 4l 3rd 13; hdwy to 1l 2nd 16; ld aft 3 out; 2l clr app nxt; r.o wl u.p.* 1

1347^{2} **Mr McDuck (IRE)** (7x) 1-2F **L Bates** *Ld to 15; 1l ld 16; jnd 17; sn pushed along; 2l 2nd 3 out; r.o one pce* 4 2

1292^{P} **Catosphere (IRE)** 14-1 **N Tutty** *Trckd ldr in 1l 2nd to 8; mist 10; 2l 2nd 13; gd j to ½l 2nd 15; outpcd 17; wknd frm 3 out; poor 3rd at last* 25 3

OFFICIAL DISTANCES: 4*l*, 25*l* **TIME:** 6min 18.0s

1413 Confined — 3 ran

1301^{2} **DARAK (IRE)** 15-8 **N Tutty** *Made all; 4l ahd 2; 1l up frm 8 til drew 3l clr 3 out; jnd app last; hrd rdn flat; just hld on* 1

1286^{1} **Ben From Ketton** 5-1 **S J Robinson** *Chsd ldr; 4l down til clsd to 1l 2nd 8-17; outpcd app 3 out; rdn to chall agn last; drvn & outrdn flat* .... ½ 2

1179^{1} Who Dares Wins 4-6F L Bates *A last; 5l 3rd to 6; 10l 3rd 10; pushed along 13; sn lost tch; 15l 3rd & wkng 17; hit 2 out; fnce adrift when pu last (rdr thought horse lame; lkd sound aft)* .... P

OFFICIAL DISTANCE: nk **TIME:** 5min 55.0s

1414 Mens Open — 8 ran

1204^{2} **DUMADIC** 5-4F **N Tutty** *(xnb) Rr to 4; 11l 7th 8; 6th & hdwy 14; went 3l 4th 16; rdn to chall last; hrd rdn & drew clr flat* 1

1204^{1} **Torn Silk** 3-1 **C Mulhall** *Last to 5; still bhnd 16; rap hdwy frm nxt to ld 3 out; jnd app nxt; hdd & outpcd flat* 2 2

1304^{1} **Civil Gent (IRE)** (7a) 4-1 **G Brewer** *(xnb) Trckd ldrs; 3l 4th to 8; disp 3rd 12; outpcd 14 & 6l 3rd 15; went 1l 2nd 3 out; disp ld brief nxt; pushed along & ev ch last; one pce flat* .... nk 3

1299^{5} Epsilo De La Ronce (FR) 14-1 W Ramsay *Midfield & nd; pushed along 10; rr & outpcd 14; stayed on to 5th 16 & mod 4th app last* 15 4

1301^{3} Glacial Dancer (IRE) 40-1 R Clark *Rr to 4; hdwy 8 to 3l 4th 10 & 2l 3rd 16; wknd app 2 out* 3 5

1201[1]	Blank Cheque 6-1 D Coates *Chsd ldr; 1l 2nd to 10; pushed along 12; releg last & lsng tch 13; t.o 16; stayed on to 6th app last*	6	6
1302[3]	Fine Times(tt) 20-1 O Williams *Ld to 17; grad wknd; wl bhnd app last.*	12	7
1289[P]	Shining Light (IRE) 50-1 S J Robinson *Handy in 3rd to 5; jmpd slow 6; pushed up to 1l 2nd 12; mist 14; sn wknd; rr by 17; t.o 2 out*	3	8

OFFICIAL DISTANCES: 3*l*, nk **TIME:** 6min 02.0s

1415 Ladies Open — 4 ran

1290[2]	**HADEQA** evensF **Miss S Brotherton** *Hld up; 3l 3rd to 12; went 2l 3rd 14; easily ld 15; 2l up til qcknd rt away 2 out; v easy*		1
1302[2]	**Donnegale (IRE)**(bl) 5-1 **Miss J Foster** *Ld to 7; 1l 2nd til disp ld 13-14; sn outpcd; rallied to 1½l 2nd 2 out; sn brushed aside; 15l 2nd & no ch last*	20	2
1289[R]	**Dannicus**(cp) 20-1 **Miss C Metcalfe** *Trckd ldr in 1l 2nd til ld 8; jnd 13; hdd aft nxt & releg last; in tch til wknd frm 17*	15	3
1221[U]	Emperor's Magic (IRE)(cp,tt) 6-4 Miss S Ward *Sn last; 12l last when blun & ur 7*		U

OFFICIAL DISTANCES: 20*l*, 20*l* **TIME:** 6min 02.0s

1416 Restricted, 12st — 7 ran

1300[1]	**SILOGUE (IRE)** 4-5F **N Tutty** *Rr; blun 8; last when mist 12; blun 15 & bhnd 16; pushed along & lkd no ch nxt; went 4l 2nd 2 out; 1l down last; hrd rdn flat; ld on line (brilliant ride)*		1
955[7]	**Procol's Boy** 12-1 **S Walker** *Mid-div early; last by 8; hdwy to 1l 2nd 13; 2l 2nd when lft in ld app 17; 8l clr 3 out; 4l clr nxt; just ld last; hdd & outpcd nr line; unlucky*	½	2
1288[6]	**Don Rio (IRE)** 7-1 **M Morley** *(xnb) Chsd ldng pr in 8l 3rd to 7; went 4l 2nd 10; outpcd 13 & 4th 16; lft 3rd app 17; chsd ldrs vain aft*	25	3
1304[4]	Troubleshooter 6-1 M Mackley *Rr early; 8l 4th 6; in tch til 12l 6th & outpcd 16; lft poor 4th app nxt.*	6	4
1288[P]	Minster Echo (5a) 20-1 G Brewer *Cl up til ld 3-8; handy 3rd 10; 5l 3rd 14; sn wknd; t.o 17*	8	5
1304[P]	Office Hours 9-2 S Charlton *Mid-div; went 5th 9; releg last by 12; hdwy to 5l 3rd 16; cl up & ev ch when bd bend bef 17.*		B
1288[8]	Son Of Sam 6-1 L Bates *Jmpd appalling; ld to 2; 1l 2nd til mist 5; jmpd slow 6; mist 8; ld agn 9; 2l up & gng wl when slpd up bend bef 17*		S

OFFICIAL DISTANCES: ½*l*, dist **TIME:** 6min 01.0s

1417 Open Maiden, 12st — 11 ran

1165[5]	**BANKERSDRAFT** 10-1 **M Morley** *Prom til 1l 2nd 6; ld 11; 1l clr 17; jnd 2 out; hdd last; hrd rdn & rallied flat; ld nr line*		1
1291[U]	**Queenies Girl** (5a) 16-1 **P Kinsella** *Rr to 8; stdy hdwy to 3l 3rd 16; ld app 2 out; prsd at last; hrd rdn flat; hdd nr line.*	1	2
1292[3]	**Dinan (IRE)** 5-1 **Mrs J Brown** *A rr; sn bhnd; t.o 14; stayed on past btn horses to rem 3rd app last.*	40	3
814[P]	Crake Way (7a) 3-1F C Mulhall *Sn bhnd; last by 2; t.o 4; rdr lkng down app 5; pu 8 & dism*		P
1164[P]	Edstone (IRE) 20-1 G Brewer *Midfield to 9; went 5l 4th 10 & cl 2nd 11; 2l 2nd & gng wl when pu app 17; broke down*		P
1291[P]	Fairmile Star 10-1 R Wakeham *Jmpd terribly; rn down fncs & jmpd rt; bhnd by 4; t.o 13; rem when pu 3 out.*		P
1292[4]	Iron Trooper (IRE) 6-1 T Glass *(xnb) Mid-div to 8; went 3l 3rd 10; 1l 2nd 16; mist 17; 3l 3rd 2 out; rallied to 1l 3rd & ev ch when fell last*		F
946[P]	Mister Rose (IRE) 12-1 O Williams *Cl 2nd til ld 4-9; pushed along 13; wknd qckly; t.o & pu 17*		P
1157[U]	Noggler (7a) 7-2 S Charlton *Sn bhnd; t.o by 4; jmpd slow 6; rem & 1½ fncs adrift when pu 13.*		P
1291[P]	Sea Princess (5a) 10-1 N Tutty *Midfield to 8; hdwy 12 to 5l 4th 13; pushed along & outpcd 15; 12l 5th when blun 16; lost tch qckly; poor 5th when pu last*		P
1300[2]	Thixendale (5a)(cp) 6-1 Miss J Foster *Ld to 3; cl up til wknd 8; rr & lsng tch 11; bad mist 12; t.o & pu 14.*		P

OFFICIAL DISTANCES: ½*l*, dist **TIME:** 6min 04.0s

Border

Hexham (LH 8F,19J)

Sun, 16 May (GOOD to FIRM, GOOD in places)

1418 Confined, 12st — 8 ran

1310[1] **MORE FLAIR** (5a) evensF **J Walton** *Trckd ldrs; disp 6l 3rd app 4; 3l 3rd 7; disp 3l 3rd agn nxt; went 1l 2nd app 15; ld aft 3 out; rdn & stayed on wl flat* — 1

1415[U] **Emperor's Magic (IRE)** (7x) 9-2 **Miss S Ward** *Hld up in tch; disp 12l 6th app 9; stdy prog aft to 10l 6th 12 & 6l 3rd app 2 out; went 2nd flat; prsd wnr cl home; just hld* — ¾ — 2

1223[3] **Kings Minstral (IRE)**(tt) 6-1 **R Green** *Mid-div; 6l 5th aft 8; 5l 4th 14; went 1l 2nd aft 16; 2l 3rd 3 out; ev ch til no ex app last* — 8 — 3

1307[5] Extra Stout (IRE)(tt) 8-1 C Storey *Ld; 1l up 7; 2l ahd 12; 1l clr 3 out; sn hdd; kpt on til no ex app last.* — 2 — 4

1223[4] Sharpaman(bl) 14-1 C Shirley-Beavan *Handy; disp 6l 3rd app 4; 4l 4th 7; disp 8l 3rd agn nxt; outpcd in 8l 5th app 3 out; wknd app last; tired & virt pu flat* — 20 — 5

1220[5] Dream Of My Life (USA) (6x) 8-1 R Morgan *(xnb,orbs) Trckd ldr; 1l 2nd 7; 2l 2nd 12; outpcd 15; sn btn; hit 3 out; sn t.o.* — 4 — 6

The Timberman 14-1 L Morgan *Mid-div; 8l 5th 6; disp 12l 6th app 9; lsng tch in 18l 7th when pu 11* — P

1076[1] Try A Bluff (IRE) (3x) 14-1 Miss E McWilliam *(bf) A rr; 15l last 3; detach 7; t.o 9; pu 13* — P

OFFICIAL DISTANCES: ¾l, 8l **TIME:** 6min 46.3s

1419 Restricted — 8 ran

1306[1] **DISTRACTING** (5a) 7-1 **R Morgan** *In tch; disp 8l 3rd app 9; disp ld brief 16 & agn aft 3 out; 3l up nxt; hrd rdn flat; hld on wl.* — 1

1224[1] **Ofcoursehekhan (IRE)** 7-2F **Miss N Stirling** *(xnb) Green; trckd ldr; 6l 2nd 4; prog to ld aft 8; hdd aft 14; 3l 3rd 3 out; 2l 2nd aft nxt; chall app last; no ex cl home.* — 2½ — 2

813[1] **The Murphy Meister (IRE)** 6-1 **G Tuer** *(xnb) Chsd ldrs; disp 8l 3rd app 9; prog to ld aft 14; 1l up 3 out; sn hdd; rdn along & wknd app nxt; tired flat; fin exhaust.* — 25 — 3

1310[4] Good Morning (5a) 16-1 R Dickson *A rr; disp 10l last app 4; sltly detach 9; 25l last 15; t.o aft nxt; kpt on to tk poor 4th flat* — 4 — 4

1222[3] Timberley(tt) 8-1 R Green *Hld up; 10l 6th app 10; prog to 3l 5th 12; 5l 4th app 15; outpcd & 15l 4th aft nxt; wknd.* — 3 — 5

765[P] Jupiter Jo 4-1 J Walton *6s-4s; in tch in rr; disp 10l last app 4; prog to chse ldrs when fell 7* — F

1068[U] The Met Man (IRE) 8-1 A Richardson *(xnb) Ld; jmpd & hung rt; 6l up when mist 5; 10l up nxt; hdd aft 8; wkng when mist 12; pu nxt* — P

1077[F] Westie (5a) 8-1 L Morgan *Trckd ldrs; mist 3; 7l 3rd 4; disp 8l 3rd app 9; rmdrs nxt; drpd to rr & strugg aft; pu aft 12* — P

OFFICIAL DISTANCES: 2½l, 15l **TIME:** 6min 49.6s

Gudasmum (5-2F, Miss R Davidson, xnb, bbv, rdr unable to produce Medical Record Book, fined £50) was withdrawn from the paddock - Rule 4 deduction 25p in pound; the stewards cautioned the rider of Distracting for using his whip above shoulder height

1420 Ladies Open — 5 ran

1160[F] **TEXAS RANGER** 5-4 **Miss J Foster** *Made all at decent pce; 10l clr 12; 4l ahd 14; only ½l up aft 16; prsd agn app last; rdn & hld on wl flat* — 1

1221[1] **Pharmistice (IRE)** evensF **Miss N Stirling** *(xnb) A trckng wnr; 12l 2nd 7; prog to 4l 2nd app 14; ½l down aft aft 16; chall agn app last; a hld* — 1 — 2

1308[6] **In Demand** 12-1 **Miss J Balmer** *Chsd ldrs; 12l 3rd 4; mist 6 & no ch aft; 25l last 8; 30l 4th 12; went poor 3rd aft 3 out* — 30 — 3

1163[3] Imperial Line (IRE)(tt) 12-1 Miss F Hartley *(xnb) Rr; 8l last 2; 13l 4th 4; 15l 3rd aft 8; 25l 3rd app 15; dem poor 4th aft 3 out* — 5 — 4

1289[6] Batoutoftheblue 11-1 Miss C Metcalfe *Mid-div when blun & ur 1.* — U

OFFICIAL DISTANCES: 1l, 25l **TIME:** 6min 39.7s

1421 Mens Open 7 ran

764[1]	**RED GAUNTLET** 2-1F **K Anderson** *Made virt all; 2l up 4; jnd brief aft 11; 2l ahd 15; 4l clr 3 out; hrd prsd flat; rdn & just hld on cl home*		1
1038[4]	**Just Barney Boy** 5-1 **A Waugh** *Swtng; trckd ldr; 2l 2nd 4; 1l 2nd app 7; disp ld brief aft 11; 2l 2nd 15; 4l down 3 out; prog to chall last; hrd rdn cl home; just failed*	nk	2
1309[2]	**Decent Bond (IRE)** 5-2 **R Green** *Hld up in rr; 10l 6th app 4; 25l 6th 14; went 20l 4th 16; gd prog app 3 out; 12l 3rd app last; stayed on; too much to do*	6	3
1220[4]	Roscoe Burn 20-1 M McAlister *Trckd ldrs; disp 5l 3rd 7; went 3l 2nd aft nxt; 3l 3rd app 12; 5l 3rd app 15; outpcd & 8l 3rd 3 out; one pce & dem 4th at last*	6	4
1178[F]	Hoh Tel (IRE)(vis) 6-1 R Morgan *Trckd ldrs; disp 5l 3rd 7; lost plce; pushed along in 8l 5th app 10; rmdrs aft; disp 12l 4th app 13; disp 20l 4th 15; grad lost tch*	20	5
1309[3]	Finest Of Men 5-1 J Walton *Mid-div; 8l 5th app 4; 5l 4th 8; disp 12l 4th & outpcd app 13; sn nd; t.o last aft 16*	10	6
1301[U]	Royal Plum(bl) 66-1 S J Robinson *Blun 1; sn last; 12l last 3; strugg & rmdrs when ref & ur 6*		r

OFFICIAL DISTANCES: nk, 8*l* **TIME:** 6min 46.9s

1422 Open Maiden 8 ran

	BENBEOCH (7a) 6-1 **K Anderson** *Hld up; 10l 7th 8; stdy prog to 3l 4th 12; disp 4l 3rd 3 out; r.o to chall app last; ld flat; wl rdn; nice intro*		1
1178[P]	**Pure Steel (IRE)**(cp) 5-1 **C Storey** *Ld & tried to make all; hit 8; 1l up app 15; 2l clr nxt; hrd prsd last; hdd & nt qckn flat*	4	2
1311[2]	**St Bee**(bl) 9-4F **A Richardson** *Trckd ldr; mist 4; 1l 2nd 8; hit nxt; ½l 2nd 3 out; no ex app last*	2	3
	Sixties Melody 5-1 M McAlister *(xnb) Trckd ldrs; 8l 3rd 6; 3l 3rd nxt; 2l 3rd 15; disp 4l 3rd 3 out; sn 4th & outpcd*	12	4
1082[4]	Chase The Moon (5a) 16-1 Miss L Hislop *Mid-div; strugg 12; lost tch & 20l last 15; tired & clambered over 3 out; t.o last aft 2 out*	40	5
1224[P]	Hardy Mouse (IRE) (5a) 14-1 R Green *In tch in rr; 15l last 3; strugg aft 10; lost tch & pu aft 12*		P
	Mr Kaar 3-1 L Morgan *6s-3s; late in padd; oht; in tch in rr; 12l 5th 9; rdn along in 7l 7th 12; strugg when pu nxt*		P
1224[3]	Tallaburn (5a) 6-1 A Findlay *(xnb) Chsd ldrs; 8l 3rd 2; 4l 4th app 7; 15l last app 9; 5l 5th 15; outpcd in 15l 5th app nxt; sn wknd; t.o & pu last*		P

OFFICIAL DISTANCES: 4*l*, 2*l* **TIME:** 6min 52.8s

1423 Hunt Members, 12st 8 ran

1220[2]	**LORDBERNIEBOUFFANT (IRE)**(cp) 4-6F **Miss P Robson** *Made virt all; 1l up 9; 3l ahd 16-3 out; rmdrs aft nxt; sn clr*		1
1222[4]	**Posh Stick** (5a) 4-1 **J Walton** *Hld up in tch; 10l 7th 2; disp 8l 3rd 7; 6l 4th 9; 7l 4th 12; went 3l 3rd app 15; 3l 2nd & ev ch 3 out; no ex u.p app last.*	10	2
1222[P]	**Harry's Mare (IRE)** (5a) 25-1 **Mrs J Hedley** *(xnb) A rr; hit 1; 12l last nxt; detach 7; 15l last 9; t.o 13; kpt on past btn horses; tk poor 3rd flat*	40	3
1311[3]	Red Jupiter 16-1 T Scott *Chsd ldrs; disp 8l 3rd 7; 5l 3rd nxt; 6l 5th & pushed along 12; outpcd 15; lost number cloth amongst other things frm 16-3 out; t.o aft; releg poor 4th flat*	1	4
1308[R]	Houselope Beck 25-1 Miss A Wanless *(xnb) Chsd ldrs; 2l 3rd app 4; 3l 6th 8; 9l 6th app nxt; rn out 10.*		R
377[P]	Sledmere (IRE) 16-1 J Botham *(xnb) Trckd ldr; 1l 2nd 9; wknd qckly 15; 20l 5th & pu nxt*		P
1178[P]	Superstar Express (IRE)(tt) 5-1 A Findlay *Hld up in rr; 12l 5th 8; 7l 5th nxt; gd prog to 1l 2nd 14-15; ev ch til 8l 3rd & outpcd app 3 out; 15l 3rd & btn when blun, nrly fell & ur last*		U
1311[P]	Wester Lad 33-1 R Sinton *Hld up in rr; 15l 7th 8; 10l 7th when hit nxt; strugg aft; detach 11; lost tch & pu 13.*		P

OFFICIAL DISTANCES: 10*l*, dist **TIME:** 6min 45.8s

North West Point-to-Point Club

Tabley (RH 7F,20J)

Sun, 16 May (GOOD)

1424 Open Maiden (Div 1), 12st — 10 ran

Form	Runner	Dist	Pos
1075^{F}	**ALL EYEZ ON ME (IRE)**(bl) 3-1 **R Burton** *A ldng trio; disp ld 6 til ld 9; jnd 2 out; rdn ahd flat; r.o wl*		1
1124^{P}	**Earl Token** 9-4F **R Armson** *Hld up in rr; hdwy 11; handy 5th nxt; prsd ldrs frm 15; w wnr 2 out-last; no ex flat*	¾	2
1206^{2}	**Luck In Run'in** 7-2 **G Hanmer** *A handy; 2nd 11; mostly 3rd aft til 2nd agn 17; dem 2 out; ev ch last; no ex flat*	1¼	3
1124^{F}	Prince Mouse 20-1 N Kent *(xnb) Mid-div; went 4th & ev ch 17; nt pce to chall frm nxt*	7	4
1341^{P}	Ginmini (IRE) (5a) 20-1 M Caldwell *A last trio; outpcd 16; plugged on same pce frm 3 out.*	4	5
1261^{5}	Ridware Rose (5a) 6-1 Miss S Sharratt *Ld/disp to 8; prom til lost plce app 15; in tch til wknd app 2 out*	20	6
1266^{4}	Button Lady (12a) 20-1 D Gaiter *A rr; jb lft frm 7; lost tch 9; 15l adrift 12; t.o & pu aft 14*		P
1273^{3}	Holly Park (5a) 20-1 Miss N Hickling *Mid-div; moved thro qckly to disp ld 5-8; drpd back nxt; lost tch app 13; sn t.o; pu aft nxt*		P
1292^{F}	Light-O-Day 20-1 P Kinsella *Mid-div; 3l 4th 6-8; rr frm 14; outpcd 16; lost tch nxt; pu 2 out*		P
1231^{4}	Sylvias Dream (5a, 3ow) 20-1 P Morris *A rr trio; strugg 16; sn lost tch; pu 3 out*		P

OFFICIAL DISTANCES: ¾*l*, 1¼*l* **TIME:** 6min 51.0s

1425 Open Maiden (Div 2), 12st — 11 ran

Form	Runner	Dist	Pos
	JUPITER GEORGE 11-4F **R Burton** *W ldrs frm 6; disp ld 14-16; ld nxt; 6l up app 2 out; drew clr flat; eased cl home*		1
1261^{4}	**Snitton Salvo**(bl) 8-1 **M Jackson** *Rr til hdwy to 2½l 4th 14; cl 3rd nxt til outpcd app 2 out; 6½l 3rd at last; tk 2nd flat; nt trble wnr*	8	2
1020^{3}	**Ron Miel (IRE)** 10-1 **Miss R Reynolds** *Ld/disp 6-14; prsd wnr nxt til outpcd app 2 out; dem flat.*	nk	3
1020^{P}	The Well Lad (IRE) (7a) 25-1 M Wall *Sn prom; cl 4th 15 til wknd 2 out*	20	4
1291^{P}	Arewetoolate 16-1 P Kinsella *A towards rr; 5l 6th 14; lost tch 16; pu nxt*		P
1215^{4}	Barty Boy (IRE) 7-1 B Shaw *Rr til went 2nd 9-11; lost plce nxt; 8th & wkng 13; bhnd 14 til pu 2 out*		P
1125^{5}	Beau Jake (IRE) 6-1 R Armson *Cl up; disp ld 10-12; 5th & trckng ldrs when fell 16*		F
1142^{B}	Castle Lodge 4-1 K Pearson *10s-4s; a rr; 7l 9th 13; lost tch app 16; 20l bhnd nxt; pu 3 out*		P
710^{P}	Gosh Josh (IRE) 25-1 J R Barlow *Pulled hrd; disp ld 1; stdd to 5th by 4; last when mist & rmdrs 7; sn detach; 15l adrift when jmpd v slow 8; pu nxt.*		P
1339^{5}	Martha Jane (5a) 25-1 P Newton *Ld/disp 2-6; prom til wknd qckly app 12; sn lost tch; 15l bhnd 14; t.o & pu nxt*		P
1232^{4}	Whats Up Jake 12-1 A Wadlow *(xnb) Rr most of way; 6l 7th 14; lost tch 16; mod 5th nxt; pu last*		P

OFFICIAL DISTANCES: 8*l*, nk **TIME:** 6min 42.0s

1426 North West Point-to-Point Club Members, 12st — 9 ran

Form	Runner	Dist	Pos
1191^{4}	**MY NATIVE KNIGHT (IRE)** 7-1 **A Wadlow** *(xnb,tt) 10s-7s; hld up in rr; outpcd 15 til hdwy 2 out; str rn to 1½l 3rd at last; qcknd to ld flat*		1
1264^{1}	**Pristeen Spy** (6x) 4-7F **R Burton** *(xnb) Evens-4/7; jw; ld til hdd flat; no ex cl home.*	1	2
1229^{2}	**Major Adams** 7-2 **Miss T Clark** *A w ldrs; 2nd & chsd ldr frm 16; 1l down at last; no ex flat*	1½	3
1344^{4}	Raconteur (IRE) 12-1 D Greenway *Trckd ldrs; went 3rd 15; outpcd by ldng pr app 3 out; rallied to cl 4th at last; no ex flat*	¾	4
1263^{P}	Shady Affair (IRE) 33-1 K Pearson *Prom 4 til wknd 17; nd aft*	15	5
1346^{2}	Karinga Lane 11-1 P Callaghan *Handy to 6; rr but in tch aft til wknd app 2 out*	7	6
1345^{P}	Gabaka De Thaix (FR) 33-1 M Caldwell *Rr but in tch when blun & ur 7*		U

1205[U] Horton-Cum-Peel (IRE) 33-1 W Kinsey *Prom; 2nd 2-8; cl up aft til wknd 16; last nxt; sn lost tch; pu 2 out* . . . . P

932[P] Lifebuoy (IRE) 33-1 T Mastoras *A last pr; lsng tch when mist 15; imm pu & dism; removed by horse ambulance* . . . . P

OFFICIAL DISTANCES: 1*l*, 1½*l* **TIME:** 6min 38.0s

1427 Mens Open, 12st — 7 ran

1372[8] **SUPREME SILENCE (IRE)** 6-1 **N Kent** *Rr til hdwy to 3rd 14; disp ld frm 15; ld 3 out; drew 6l clr app last; r.o wl* 1

General Wolfe (7x) 5-2 **P Callaghan** *A ldng trio; mist 3; cl 2nd 5 til ld 12; jnd 15; hdd aft 17; 2l 2nd 2 out; outpcd app last; kpt on* 7 2

749[5] **Knock It Back (IRE)** 20-1 **J Handley** *Oht; prom; cl 2nd 12 til releg 4th 15; lft 7l 3rd 3 out; outpcd by ldng pr app nxt* 10 3

Ash Branch (IRE) (7x) 14-1 D Barlow *Cl up in 4/5th; went 3rd gng wl 15 til wknd qckly 3 out; pu nxt; btr for rce* . . . . P

1262[4] Harry Hotspur (IRE) (7x)(bl) 100-1 M Dearden *(xnb) Imm last; 20l detach by 4; stdly lost tch; 2 fncs bhnd when pu 14* . . . . P

749[2] Mister Moss (IRE) 3-1 R Burton *Set str pce; some chancy js; pckd bad 9; hdd 12; wknd qckly & last by nxt; pu 14* . . . . P

988[3] Prominent 2-1F G Hanmer *(xnb) 5s-2s; hld up last of main group; mist 11; mist & rmdr 14; rdn along aft; lost tch 17; bhnd when pu last* . . . . P

OFFICIAL DISTANCES: 6*l*, 8*l* **TIME:** 6min 31.0s

1428 Ladies Open — 9 ran

1263[3] **DANCETILLYOUDROP (IRE)** (7x) 8-1 **Miss T Tellwright** *(xnb) Pulling; ld/disp 2-13; disp 2l 3rd 15; outpcd & 8l 3rd app 2 out; clsd to 1l 2nd last; stayed on str to ld last 25yds* 1

1203[2] **Class Of Ninetytwo (IRE)** (7x) 13-2 **Miss S Sharratt** *Trckd ldrs in 5/6th; hdwy to cl 3rd 14; 1l 2nd nxt; ld 3 out til hdd & no ex nr line* 1 2

1138[2] **Pretoria Dancer** (4x)(bl) 2-1F **Miss A de Lisle Wells** *Ld 1; disp ld 7 til ld 14; 1l up nxt; jnd 17; sn hdd; cl 3rd & ev ch last; one pce flat* 3 3

1203[U] Silk Vestments (5a) 50-1 Miss H Dunning *Mid-div to 8; rr aft; bhnd 16; stayed on wl frm 2 out to 4th flat; nrst fin* 3 4

1203[3] Zamhareer (USA)(vis) 14-1 Miss T Harrison *Sn last & rdn to stay in tch; mist 8; hdwy frm 15; went 4th 2 out; nt rch ldrs; dem flat* 4 5

1343[3] Chadswell (IRE) (7x) 7-2 Miss T Clark *8s-7/2; cl up frm 6; disp 2l 3rd 15; mist nxt; outpcd by ldng trio nxt; stdly wknd* 12 6

1214[P] Shallow River (IRE) 20-1 Miss H Phizacklea *Cl up til lost plce 6; rr aft; bhnd frm 16* 15 7

816[3] Gay Baratineur (FR)(cp) 13-1 Mrs K Baimbridge *Prom; disp ld 6-11; wknd & lost tch 16; pu aft 3 out* . . . . P

751[4] Joyce Bel (FR) 20-1 Miss H Kinsey *Tde; a rr; disp 9½l 8th 15; bhnd 16 til pu last* . . . . P

OFFICIAL DISTANCES: 1½*l*, 4*l* **TIME:** 6min 36.0s

1429 PPORA Club Members 6yo&up (Nov Rdrs), 12st — 10 ran

1204[4] **BORDER RUN** 2-1F **S Ross** *4s-2s; confid rdn in rr; stdy hdwy frm 7; cl 3rd on tight rein 16; went 2nd app 2 out; ld app last; rdn clr flat* 1

1171[P] **Springwood White** 6-1 **T Park** *Jw; trckd ldrs in cl 4th til ld 9; made rest til hdd app last; one pce flat* 10 2

1120[1] **Crackrattle (IRE)** (4ow) 5-1 **A Brown** *Midfield to 7; drpd to rr & last 10; 6th & outpcd 16; hdwy u.p app 2 out; went 3rd app last; nvr nrr* 5 3

1202[4] Master Club Royal(bl) 7-1 D Greenway *A ldng trio; ld 8; cl 2nd aft til releg 3rd aft 3 out; one pce frm 2 out* 8 4

1264[2] Double Rich 9-1 O Greenall *(xnb) A rr; no ch frm 16* 3 5

1208[F] The Sky Is Blue 20-1 M Caldwell *A last pr; 20l last 16; t.o 3 out; plodded on* 25 6

1140[4] Galeshan (IRE) (7x)(tt) 12-1 C Huxley *(xnb) Ld to 4; cl up aft; 6l 4th 3 out; clsng when fell nxt* . . . . F

1265[8] Home Tor 20-1 J Jarrett *Cl up; 5th & ev ch 16; wknd nxt; pu 3 out* . . . . P

1147[1] New Ross (IRE)(bl) 10-1 Miss A Turner *A rr; 9th when hit 14 & pu* . . . . P

1093[F] Picket Piece(bl) 4-1 D England *Prom; ld 5-7; cl up til wknd 15; sn lost tch; pu 3 out* . . . . P

OFFICIAL DISTANCES: 10*l*, 4*l* **TIME:** 6min 40.0s

1430 Intermediate, 12st — 11 ran

932[3] **SHARLOM (IRE)** 12-1 **G Hanmer** *Hld up in rr; gd hdwy frm 3 out; ld nxt; drew clr app last; r.o wl.* . . . 1

1019[P] **Miss Moss** (5a) 6-1 **R Rogers** *10s-6s; a handy; chsd ldrs frm 15; ld brief app 2 out; sn hdd; outpcd app last* . . . 5 2

1019[3] **Infamelia** (5a)(vis) 25-1 **Miss T Clark** *(xnb) Rr most of way; outpcd in last pr app 3 out; gd hdwy to 3rd & ev ch nxt; no ex app last* . . . 3½ 3

1345[U] Ridware Pride 16-1 Miss S Sharratt *Cl up til lost plce 11; last but still in tch 16; wknd frm nxt* . . . 30 4

1176[5] Catechist (IRE) 11-8F Julian Pritchard *(xnb) Hld up in midfield; hdwy 7; 2nd 9 til ld 14; 3l up when pu qckly & dism app 2 out; broke leg; dead* . . . P

1018[P] Cousin George 6-1 R Burton *(xnb) Midfield; jnd ldrs brief 14-15; in tch til wknd & pu 2 out* . . . P

749[P] Fountain Street (IRE) 20-1 W Kinsey *Mounted on course; tde; prom; lft in ld 7; hdd 14; chsd ldr aft; lft in ld v brief app 2 out; sn hdd & wknd; pu last* . . . P

1227[F] Heavy Weather (IRE) 10-1 M Harris *Fcng wrong way & rdr nt ready when Starter let them go; missed break; set off slow & pu 1* . . . P

1345[F] Mullarts Lad (IRE) (7a) 8-1 S Ross *A last trio; rdn & tried to cl app 16; sn wknd; pu 3 out.* . . . P

1140[2] Therealbat (IRE) 4-1 G Barfoot-Saunt *(xnb) 6s-4s; gt flier in ragged start; pulling; ld til blun & ur 7* . . . U

1228[P] The Unamed Man 20-1 J Jarrett *Mists in rr; rmdr 11; hrd rdn to 4th app 15; cl up aft til wknd 2 out; pu last* . . . P

OFFICIAL DISTANCES: 5*l*, 3*l* **TIME:** 6min 44.0s

South Cornwall

Trebudannon (LH 8F,20J)

Sun, 16 May (GOOD to FIRM)

1431 Intermediate, 12st — 7 ran

1059[2†] **HEISAMODEL (IRE)** 6-4F **M Miller** *5/2-6/4; hld up; clsd to 3rd 9; nt fluent 10; ld 16; drew clr app 2 out; rdn out.* . . . 1

1271[2] **State Medlar** 2-1 **R Woollacott** *Chsd ldr 6-15; prom to 17; chsd wnr vain frm nxt* . . . 6 2

1363[3] **Lirkimalong** 12-1 **Miss S Young** *2 handlers; ld 2-6; cl up til outpcd 17; nd aft but went 3rd app last* . . . 12 3

1194[3] Silver Man(cp) 33-1 Mrs M Hand *Jw; ld 6-16; rdn & wknd app 2 out* . . . 7 4

1268[1] Budghill 5-1 C Heard *Cl up; 5th 14; nt fluent nxt & rdn; lost tch 17.* . . . 12 5

1129[P] By My Side (IRE) 10-1 T Bishop *(xnb) Jmpd slow 1; mist 4; last til pu 5* . . . P

1167[P] Carefree Love (IRE) 12-1 W White *Swtng; rr but cl up til 6l last & drvn 14; nt keen aft; t.o & pu 2 out.* . . . P

OFFICIAL DISTANCES: 2*l*, 3*l* **TIME:** 6min 05.0s

1432 Open Maiden 56&7yo, 12st - 18J — 8 ran

1134[U] **JOYFUL JADE (FR)** (5a) 10-1 **A Charles-Jones** *3rd/4th; lft in ld 9 til rdr mistook fin & pu aft 13; cont last; 2nd agn 15; 4l down & rdn 3 out; ld app nxt; sn clr (saving rdr's blushes - his 100th P-t-P wnr).* . . . 1

1272[4] **Nditlir** (12a) 7-2 **L Heard** *Made virt all to 6; lft in ld app omitted 14 (rdr lkd rnd & stdd his mount); 12l clr nxt; drvn & wkng when hit 3 out; sn hdd; crawled last & fin exhaust* . . . 25 2

702[P] Baldhu Mynah (7a) 20-1 M Woodward *Ld brief app 4; hit 7; prom til wknd rap app 10; t.o & pu 12* . . . P

Good Gracious 12-1 T Dennis *Towards rr; blun 5; mist 8; 5th & strugg when bad mist 10; pu mxt* . . . P

Havabash 12-1 Miss L Gardner *Green; jmpd mod; sn detach last; 15l adrift aft 9; t.o & pu 14* . . . P

702[5] Little Lord Lewis (7a) 5-1 C Heard *Chsd ldrs; lft 2nd brief aft omitted 14; 18l 3rd nxt & wkng rap; sn t.o; pu 2 out* . . . P

	Student Night (IRE) (7a) 8-11F A Farrant *(xnb) Tk keen hld & erratic; ld 6 til rn out & ur 9*		R
909[P]	That's Cash (IRE) 10-1 A Glassonbury *Bckwd; ref to rce*		r

OFFICIAL DISTANCE: 10*l* **TIME:** 6min 21.0s

Fences 14 (damaged) & 16 (fallen rider) omitted; field initially taken to wrong start; the stewards interviewed the riders of the winner (who mistook the finish) & Nditlir; they recommended that the former fully acquaint himself with the course in future

1433 Confined, 12st — 6 ran

1195[1]	**ELEGANT LIGHT** (5a) 7-2 **Miss S Gaisford** *Jmpd bold; made all; went 5l clr 17; rdn last; hld on bravely*		1
908[2]	**Teninarow (IRE)** 6-4JF **Richard Darke** *Jw; chsd ldr to 11; niggled 13; 2nd agn 15; 5l down 17; rdn to cl app last; sust chall flat; a just hld*	nk	2
1271[1]	**Mystic Warrior (USA)** 6-4JF **Miss T Cave** *Trckd ldrs; disp 3rd 13; hit 16; outpcd aft; nt fluent nxt; rdn & no imp frm 2 out*	2½	3
1267[3]	Change 6-1 T Dennis *Mostly ab 5l 5th to 16; lost tch frm 3 out*	15	4
1348[3]	Moorland Rose (5a) 33-1 Miss S Young *Imm drvn; nvr keen; lost tch 3; t.o 8; pu 17*		P
1129[P]	Native Drum (IRE) 33-1 R Woollacott *(xnb) Prom; went 2nd 11-15; sn drvn; wknd rap app 3 out; pu nxt*		P

OFFICIAL DISTANCES: ½*l*, ½*l* **TIME:** 6min 02.0s

Squaddie (rdr inj in prev rce) was withdrawn not under orders

1434 Mixed Open, 12st — 3 ran

1269[2]	**HASTEN BAK** 7-4 **Miss L Gardner** *(xnb) Lw; cl 2nd til ld 12; nt fluent 17 & rmdrs; mist 3 out; drew clr nxt; eased flat*		1
1130[1]	**Let's Fly (FR)** 8-13F **Mrs M Hand** *Ld to 12; rdn app 15; 5l down 3 out; no ch aft*	10	2
1349[2]	**Midnight Coup** (7x)(bl) 4-1 **C Heard** *A last & jmpd unwillingly; rdn 5; jmpd slow 11 & lost tch; drvn & tried to rally 15; no ch aft; mist nxt; 25l down 3 out.*	15	3

OFFICIAL DISTANCES: 10*l*, 12*l* **TIME:** 6min 00.0s

1435 Restricted, 12st — 7 ran

912[2]	**VIRGOS BAMBINO (IRE)** (5a) 5-4F **A Charles-Jones** *Rdr knocked off gng to start & horse rn loose, crossed brook & galloped into far field; returned und a woman who was - unwisely - nt wearing a crash helmet; swtng; tk keen hld; made all; hrd prsd frm 3 out; rdn & kpt on game; all out*		1
1196[3]	**Indiana John (FR)** 7-1 **T Dennis** *Mist 1; handy; went 2nd 12; drvn & sust chall frm 3 out; a just hld*	1½	2
1268[2]	**Indian Raider (IRE)** 3-1 **A Glassonbury** *Handy; lft 2nd 8; mist 11; dem 12; cl up til 2½l 3rd 3 out; sn wknd*	10	3
1251[2]	Wicked Imp 16-1 M Munrowd *Cl up; 6l last & rdn 14; brief eff nxt; wknd qckly 3 out; jmpd rt last*	7	4
1196[P]	Cath's Lass (5a) 33-1 M Woodward *Fat; swtng; oht; 2 handlers; wonky walker; blind nr eye; a last; mist 4; 25l ahd 6; t.o & pu 8.*		P
913[1]	Charminsky 4-1 Miss S Young *(xnb) Towards rr; mist 11; cl 4th 14; lost tch nxt; wl bhnd when mist 16; pu 17*		P
1196[P]	Gunners Mistake(cp) 12-1 C Heard *Prsd wnr til rn out 8*		R

OFFICIAL DISTANCES: 1½*l*, 3*l* **TIME:** 6min 06.0s

1436 Open Maiden 8yo&up, 12st — 5 ran

1006[3]	**WINNIE THE POOH** 4-6F **Miss M McCarthy** *Made virt all; urged clr frm 3 out; easily*		1
1353[F]	**Mo's O Friendly** 6-1 **M Munrowd** *(xnb) Hld up last to 7; went 3rd & mist 11; tk 2nd 16; 3l down when hit 3 out; sn wknd; all out to keep 2nd*	15	2
704[4]	**Small-Lir** (5a) 10-1 **Miss S Young** *Hdwy to ld aft 7-9; chsd wnr to 16; 10l 3rd when hit 3 out; rallied app last & fin quite str*	2	3
567[P]	Calinash (IRE)(tt) 9-4 A Charles-Jones *(xnb) Rdr enjoying cigarette in padd bef mounting; settled 3rd/4th til 6l 4th & outpcd 15; still just in tch when pu 17*		P
1353[R]	Mr Rory 33-1 Miss P Moorhouse *Tde; pulling; went 2nd 2-6 but last aft hitting nxt; t.o when ur 12; veered rt & slpd up; rdr returned limping bad.*		U

OFFICIAL DISTANCES: 8*l*, ½*l* **TIME:** 6min 15.0s

The rider of Mo's O Friendly was fined £65 for excessive use of the whip and not giving the horse time to respond

Newton Abbot (LH 7F,16J)

Mon, 17 May (GOOD)

1437 Newton Abbot Racecourse Nov HC, 2m5f110y £2795 — 14 ran

1166^{U}	**SPORTING CHANCE** 11-07 25-1 **M Munrowd** *Lw; jw; 2nd til ld 5; 5l clr 13; r.o str & nvr lkd like being caught aft*		1
1348^{1}	**Bill Me Up (IRE)** 11-07 5-2 **L Heard** *Lw; settled 3rd/4th; went 5l 2nd 3 out; drvn & no imp aft*	14	2
1359^{F}	**Enitsag (FR)** 11-12 6-1 **D Mansell** *Bhnd early; 7th & prog 9; hit 11 & drvn; mist 12; went mod 4th & mist 13; chsd ldng pr app 2 out but nvr able to cl*	2½	3
1369^{2}	Kildysart Lady (IRE) 11-02 25-1 B Woodhouse *Bhnd; 12l 10th 9; passed btn horses frm 13; nvr nr ldrs*	13	4
1167^{5}	Knock Star (IRE) 11-07 20-1 S Partridge *Bhnd; bad mist & nrly ur 9 & releg 12l 11th; t.o 13; mist 2 out; needlessly whipped home by rdr.*	½	5
1268^{F}	Chapners Cross 11-07 50-1 J Barnes *Lw; chsd ldrs; went 8l 4th aft 10; sn lost plce; mist 12; t.o & pu 2 out*		P
1293^{1}	Gladiatorial (IRE) 11-11 7-1 T Bishop *(xnb) Towards rr; 9th 9; outpcd when bad mist 11; t.o & pu 2 out*		P
707^{P}	Lirsleftover 11-09 40-1 Miss S Young *Swtng; bhnd; last 5; t.o 7; pu & dism last*		P
1250^{1}	Lord Of The Mist (IRE) 11-11 7-4F N Williams *Lw; bumped rival & fell 1*		F
1351^{2}	Milla's Man (IRE) 11-09 25-1 T Dennis *Midfield; jmpd slow 4; 6th 9; wknd 11; jmpd v slow 12; t.o when jb rt 2 out; pu last*		P
1176^{9}	Mister Falcon (FR) 11-07 25-1 R Hughes *Midfield; 8th 9; u.p app nxt; nvr gng wl; t.o 13; pu 2 out*		P
1294^{3}	Pinmoor Hill 11-09 50-1 Miss S Gaisford *Towards rr; 12th & strugg when fell 8*		F
1129^{4}	Pulham Downe 11-07 50-1 Miss E Tory *(xnb) 2nd/4th til hit 9; sn lost plce; t.o 13; pu 2 out*		P
1354^{4}	Viscount Bankes 11-09(cp) 20-1 A Martin *(xnb) 2 handlers; swtng; ld to 5; chsd wnr to 3 out; drvn & wknd qckly; pu last*		P

TIME: 5min 28.2s **TOTE:** £30.20; places £6.80,£1.10,£2.80 **Ex:**£122.50 **CSF:**£86.89

Folkestone (RH 7F)

Wed, 19 May (GOOD to FIRM)

1438 Tiger Inn Nov HC, 3m2f - 19J £1722 — 11 ran

1355^{r}	**DANCING FOSENBY** 11-10 6-1 **M Holdforth** *(xnb) Ld to 2; stayed prom; chsd ldr aft 3 out; rdn to ld last; stayed on wl*		1
1365^{2}	**Kilvoydan (IRE)** 11-10 12-1 **D Phelan** *Trckd ldrs; pushed along aft 12; mists 14, 16 & 3 out; outpcd aft; stayed on wl frm 2 out; tk 2nd nr fin*	2	2
1407^{4}	**Prime Course (IRE)** 11-12 40-1 **C Gordon** *Hld up; jmpd slow 6; rdn & prog frm 13; eff to ld sn aft 3 out; jmpd lft 2 out; hdd last; rdr drpd hands & horse virt pulled himself up & dem nr line*	1¼	3
1283^{1}	Kincora (IRE) 11-10 7-1 Ms L Stock *(xnb) Ld 4; nt fluent frm 13; hdd sn aft 3 out; bumped along & wknd 2 out*	11	4
1054^{1}	Tod's Brother 11-10 13-2 A Merriam *In tch; blun 9 & 10; in rr & nt jmpng wl aft; no ch frm 16*	18	5
1284^{2}	Oxendale 11-10(bl) 18-1 Mrs J Gordon *Ld 2-4; chsd ldr to 15; rdn when mist nxt; wknd qckly*	1	6
1338^{1}	Bering Gifts (IRE) 11-10 3-1F James Tudor *Rcd in midfield; in tch 14; rdn & outpcd frm nxt; no ch when blun 2 out*	3	7
1151^{1}	Bunratty's Sole (IRE) 12-00(cp) 4-1 N Bloom *Hld up; terrible mist 4 & lost tch; nvr jmpd fluent aft; eff 12; btn 14; wknd 2 out; hung lft flat; t.o*	17	8
1406^{P}	Alexander Nevsky 11-10 33-1 D Dennis *(xnb) A rr; mist 9; t.o frm 12; pu 14*		P
1242^{3}	Leatherback (IRE) 11-12 15-2 J Owen *Chsd ldrs; nt fluent 10; rdn & strugg & nt keen aft 12; sn wknd; t.o & pu 14*		P
651^{1}	Ocki 11-10 22-1 D Page (Kent) *(xnb) Oht; swtng; nt fluent & rdr waving; a last; t.o frm 5; pu 16*		P

TIME: 6min 31.3s **TOTE:** £8.80; places £3.00,£3.20,£13.70 **Ex:**£121.30 **CSF:**£73.09

The rider of Prime Course was suspended for 10 days for dropping his hands and failing to ride his horse out to achieve the best possible placing

1439 Grants Cherry Brandy S E Nov HC, 2m5f - 15J £2697 8 ran

Form	Horse / Details	Dist	Pos
1213[1]	**FREE GIFT** 11-10 4-7F **D Jacob** *(xnb) Lw; jmpd v bold; ld aft 2; lobbed along aft; easily; impressive*		1
1172[6]	**Alheri** 11-10(tt) 6-1 **F de Giles** *(xnb) Nt jw (oft dragged hind legs thro fncs); chsd ldng pr; rdn aft 3 out; kpt on to tk 2nd flat; no ch w wnr*	9	2
1208[3]	**Royal Czarina** 11-05 12-1 **J Snowden** *Swtng; ld til aft 2; chsd wnr vain aft; no imp 2 out; hung lft & lost 2nd flat*	1½	3
1285[1]	No Reward (IRE) 11-12 6-1 A Hickman *(xnb) Hld up in last pr; prog to chse clr ldng trio aft 9 & clsd on them 11; rdn 3 out; in tch app 2 out; wknd; hung lft flat*	12	4
1061[P]	Marciano 11-10(cp) 25-1 D Kemp *(xnb) Mist 4; chsd clr ldng trio to 9; sn strugg; wl bhnd frm 11*	11	5
1359[9]	Carvilla (IRE) 11-12 40-1 C Gordon *Pulled hrd; in tch; rdn to chse clr ldng trio brief 9; sn btn; wl bhnd when pu last*		P
1055[U]	Pistol Knight 11-10 14-1 Mrs J Gordon *A rr; nt fluent 3; rdn 7; wknd 9; t.o & pu 3 out*		P
1429[6]	The Sky Is Blue 11-10 14-1 J Diment *A rr; nt fluent 3; strugg frm 9; wl bhnd when pu last*		P

TIME: 5min 16.6s **TOTE:** £1.60; places £1.20,£1.60,£2.30 **Ex:**£4.90 **CSF:**£4.85

Royal Cruise (P York, could nt be identified frm its passport) was withdrawn not under orders; the stewards were not satisfied with the trainer's explanation and reported the matter to Portman Square

1440 Stuart Adamson Mem Open HC, 3m1f - 18J £1926 7 ran

Form	Horse / Details	Dist	Pos
1167[4]	**KINGSTON-BANKER** 12-03 11-8F **T Dreaper** *(xnb) In tch; chsd ldng pr 12; mist nxt & rdn; clsd aft 3 out; ld & nt fluent 2 out; drvn clr*		1
997[1]	**Belvento (IRE)** 12-06 9-1 **Miss E Jones** *Cl up; prsd ldr 11; upsides frm 13 til ld 3 out; rdn & hdd 2 out; fin tired*	5	2
893[5]	**Bush Hill Bandit (IRE)** 12-03 16-1 **H Fowler** *Drpd to 4th last; strugg & lost tch 11; wl bhnd 13; kpt on aft 3 out; tk poor 3rd flat*	3½	3
1293[7]	Storm Castle (IRE) 11-13 22-1 Miss J Wickens *Tk keen hld; trckd ldr to 11; outpcd frm 13; no ch & eased aft 3 out; kpt on agn frm 2 out*	½	4
1171[4]	Little Farmer 11-13 7-4 P Hall *Lw; tde; ld; jnd 13; hdd & rdn 3 out; wknd nxt; sn tired; lost 2 plces nr fin*	½	5
830[2]	Ballinure Boy (IRE) 12-01 9-1 A Hickman *(xnb) In tch til lost action & pu aft 11*		P
1283[2]	Dick McCarthy (IRE) 11-10 10-1 Mrs S Ashby *Trckd ldng pr til blun & ur 9*		U

TIME: 6min 19.9s **TOTE:** £2.30; places £1.60,£3.40 **Ex:**£10.00 **CSF:**£15.11

1441 Shepherd Neame Utd Hunts Open Champion HC, 3m7f - 22J £3497 9 ran

Form	Horse / Details	Dist	Pos
1170[2]	**GENERAL CLAREMONT (IRE)** 11-11 10-11F **Miss A Goschen** *Mist 1; prom frm 5; trckd ldr 11; clr of rest frm 17; eff to ld aft 2 out; clr last; pushed out*		1
975[2]	**Tell Tale (IRE)** 11-11 7-2 **T Malone** *Hld up; detached in last til prog 16; hit 19; 25l 5th 3 out; went v mod 3rd app 2 out; rdn & stayed on to tk 2nd flat; hopeless task*	3½	2
	Monks Error (IRE) 12-00 16-1 **J Diment** *Prom; ld 10; drew 5l clr 17; rdn 3 out; hdd sn aft 2 out; wknd & mist last; fin tired*	4	3
1298[3]	Alska (FR) 11-05 16-1 R Bandey *In tch; outpcd frm 16; went 22l 4th aft 3 out; stayed on wl frm nxt; nd*	1¼	4
1170[5]	Robbie's Adventure 11-07 25-1 Mrs J Gordon *Ld to 10; chsd ldng pr frm nxt; bumped along & outpcd 17; wknd aft 3 out*	25	5
1283[3]	Tom Cobbler (IRE) 11-07 10-1 Mrs P Hall *Jmpd delib; hld up; eff to disp 3rd when mist 17; sn btn*	¾	6
1250[2]	Woodlands Beau (IRE) 11-11 6-1 N Mitchell *Mists; in tch; rcd wide frm 7; outpcd 17; sn wl bhnd; t.o 3 out; eased flat*	23	7
1243[3]	Dunrig (IRE) 11-12(bl) 20-1 J Owen *Swtng; mostly chsd ldr til mist & drvn 8; nvr lkd keen aft; u.p 10; last 16; t.o & pu 18*		P
1029[F]	West Pal (IRE) 11-10(bl) 33-1 M Smith *In tch; wkng when mist 16; t.o & pu 18*		P

TIME: 7min 52.9s **TOTE:** £2.20; places £1.20,£1.30,£2.90 **Ex:**£3.80 **CSF:**£4.78

1442 Hobbs Parker Mdn HC, 2m5f - 15J £1755 — 11 ran

1332P	**GRAY KNIGHT (IRE)** 11-10 5-2F **James Tudor** *Prom; chsd ldr 4-6; nt fluent 7; went 2nd agn 9; ld nxt; clr 3 out; drvn & prsd nxt; kpt on to go clr last*		1
1396P	**Mill Lord (IRE)** 11-10 6-1 **M Mackley** *Tk keen hld; ld 2; mist 5; hdd 10; outpcd 3 out; rallied & ch 2 out; sn btn; fin tired*	12	2
1097¹	**Just Lark** 11-10 4-1 **R Bliss** *Prom; chsd ldr 6-9; cl up when mist 10; mist & outpcd 12; 10l 3rd 3 out; no ch aft*	8	3
579P	Lady Dot (IRE) 11-05 20-1 D Dennis *(xnb) Swtng; in tch; chsd clr ldng trio aft 9; no imp u.p when mist 2 out*	4	4
1285F	Blakes Road (IRE) 11-10 10-1 Ms L Stock *(xnb) Outpcd & bhnd; mist 3; virt t.o 11; mod late prog*	9	5
1212⁵	Jack Of Kilcash (IRE) 11-10 11-2 N Benstead *Lw; hld up; prog to chse ldrs 8; outpcd nxt; sn strugg*	3/4	6
1354P	Two Of Diamonds 11-10 40-1 J Sole *Wrs; v reluct to rce & lft 200yds; ambled rnd & jb; tkng 2 out as wnr fin*	dist	7
1050P	Acuteangle (IRE) 11-05 50-1 J Morgan *Outpcd & a wl bhnd; jmpd slow 6; t.o & pu 3 out*		P
1083P	Commasarris 11-10 8-1 Mrs J Gordon *Fat; chsd ldrs; wknd 8; t.o & pu 3 out*		P
1211⁶	Master Chief (IRE) 11-10 14-1 P Hall *(xnb) Ld; jmpd lft & hdd 2; strugg frm 7; t.o 7th when pu 2 out*		P
1404R	Sir Henrik (IRE) 12-00 14-1 P Cowley *Jmpd lft; sn bhnd; eff & in tch 7; wkng when jb lft 9; t.o & pu nxt*		P

TIME: 5min 23.5s **TOTE:** £3.70; places £1.70,£1.80,£1.90 **Ex:**£18.00 **CSF:**£18.48

1443 Kelly's Boy Celebration Open HC, 2m5f - 15J £1901 — 10 ran

1099²	**MASALARIAN (IRE)** 11-10 12-1 **Miss L Bridges** *(xnb) Hld up; prog to jn ldrs 9; ld 3 out; drew clr frm 2 out; stayed on wl*		1
1359⁵	**Hot Plunge** 11-12 9-1 **J Owen** *Made most; set str pce early; hdd 3 out; no ch w wnr frm nxt*	10	2
732⁴	**Satchmo (IRE)** 11-12 2-1 **G Wragg** *(xnb) Sev posns & nt fluent; outpcd aft mist 9; no ch aft; r.o frm 2 out; fin full of running*	5	3
1168²	Cape Stormer (IRE) 12-03 11-10F M Gorman *Nvr gng pce in rr; pckd 6; rdn 9; sn outpcd; stayed on aft 3 out; just pipped for 3rd*	s hd	4
1359⁴	Rooster 11-10 20-1 M Mackley *Burly as ever; prom; chsd ldr 6-12; wknd aft 3 out*	17	5
1354²	Win The Toss 12-00 14-1 P York *Nt a fluent; hld up; blun 7; prog to jn ldrs 9; mist 11; sn wknd*	7	6
1100³	Oscar Wilde 11-10 11-1 D Drake *Lw; chsd ldrs; rdn & strugg frm 9; sn wknd*	1 1/4	7
1372⁴	Good Heart (IRE) 12-03 12-1 J Diment *Lw; mists; chsd ldrs to 7; strugg frm 9; t.o & pu 3 out*		P
1125P	Latterly (USA) 12-03(cp) 50-1 A Sansome *Chsd ldr to 6; last & lsng tch 8; jmpd v slow nxt; t.o & pu 10*		P
1411²	Spy Boy (IRE) 11-10(vis) 50-1 J Morgan *Outpcd & bhnd; mist 4; prog & in tch 8; sn wknd; t.o & pu 12*		P

TIME: 5min 13.4s **TOTE:** £12.90; places £2.10,£2.80,£1.10 **Ex:**£199.00 **CSF:**£121.62

Kelso (LH 8F,19J)

Wed, 19 May (GOOD to FIRM)

1444 Glengoyne Single Highland Malt HC, 3m1f £2373 — 6 ran

1309¹	**GEORDIES EXPRESS** 12-00 11-10F **W Kavanagh** *Jmpd lft 4 & nt a fluent; ld/cl 2nd til ld & hit 3 out; rdn last; drew clr final 100yds*		1
992⁶	**Primitive Way** 12-00(vis) 13-2 **P Maitland-Carew** *Ld/cl 2nd; rdn app 2 out; ev ch til outpcd aft last*	5	2
1307²	**Trivial (IRE)** 11-09 4-1 **Miss P Robson** *Prsd ldrs; 2l 3rd when blun 15; rallied & nt fluent 2 out; sn rdn; fnd little flat*	3/4	3
1347P	Decoded 11-09 25-1 L Bates *Nt fluent; sn wl bhnd; hmpd 9; cont t.o; pu aft 13*		P
1306²	Pilot's Harbour 11-07 10-1 C Dawson *Chsd ldrs; hit 14; rdn & getting outpcd in 6l 3rd when ur & then fell 16*		U
1297P	Primitive Satin 11-07(bl) 7-1 N Saville *Prom when pu rap 9*		P

TIME: 6min 19.6s **TOTE:** £2.00; places £1.30,£2.40 **Ex:**£7.70 **CSF:**£7.74

Taunton Vale Harriers

Kingston St Mary (RH 8F,19J)

Wed, 19 May (FIRM)

1445 Hunt Members — 3 ran

Form	Horse / Details	Dist	Pos
1129^{3}	**CIMMAROON (IRE)** (7a) 1-8F **A Farrant** *(xnb) Mist 3; went 4l 2nd aft nxt; ld 13; sn wl clr; lft virt solo 16*		1
1326^{U}	**Hayling Star** (5a) 12-1 **Miss P Gundry** *Mounted on course; tde; 2nd til aft 4; sn wl bhnd; t.o 8; lft rem 2nd 16; plodded on slow*	2fncs	2
1369^{7}	Commander Cully (IRE) 14-1 J Tickle *(xnb,pricker n/s) Jmpd & hung lft; ld; sn 4l clr til mist 11; hdd & mist 13; sn tired; 25l 2nd when pu 16*		P

OFFICIAL DISTANCE: dist **TIME:** 6min 35.5s

1446 Confined, 12st — 6 ran

Form	Horse / Details	Dist	Pos
1181^{1}	**I AM SAID I (IRE)** 1-4F **A Farrant** *(xnb) Lw; mist 3; went 2nd aft 5; ld app 14; drew wl clr 16; doddle*		1
1365^{6}	**Touring-Turtle (IRE)** 33-1 **W Procter** *(xnb) A.p; ld 7 til app 14; 5l 2nd 16; sn brushed aside*	15	2
1250^{6}	**Cherokee Boy** (3x) 8-1 **Miss C Atkinson** *Spread plate padd; sn outpcd; lost tch 5; went 20l 4th 11 & 35l 3rd aft 16; kpt on game*	8	3
1369^{P}	Link Copper 14-1 Mrs O Jackson *Ld til mist 2; ld 3-4; 2nd/3rd til mist 7; 16l 4th & rdn ½way; wl bhnd when pu aft 12*		P
1331^{3}	Primero (IRE) 10-1 G Weatherley *(xnb) 16s-10s; ld 2 til mist 3 & 4-7; 4l 3rd ½way; wknd 14; wl bhnd when jmpd v slow 16; t.o & pu 3 out*		P
1331^{R}	Roberts Return 66-1 M Woodward *(xnb) Kpt napping to box park padd; imm wl t.o und iron grip & lkng to rn out; jmpd mod; fncs bhnd when pu 11*		P

OFFICIAL DISTANCES: 15*l*, 8*l* **TIME:** 6min 28.3s

1447 Mens Open, 12st — 4 ran

Form	Horse / Details	Dist	Pos
1185^{1}	**BALLYSICYOS (FR)** (7x) 4-9F **A Farrant** *(xnb,boh) Jmpd lft at times; ld to 2; 2nd til ld aft 5; qcknd 10l clr 14; drew rt away 16; unchall*		1
1367^{1}	**Sir William** (7x)(tt) 13-8 **R Woollacott** *(xnb) Last to 8; went 6l 2nd app nxt; unable to cl 14; eased when btn aft 16; nursed home*	runin	2
1359^{8}	**I'm Dreaming (IRE)** 33-1 **A Martin** *3rd to 8; 13l last ½way; rdn & lost tch 13; t.o 15*	25	3
1073^{P}	Fours Are Wild (IRE) 25-1 J Trevor-Roper *Nt fluent & rdr oft tangled w reins; ld 2 til aft 5; 12l 3rd ½way; mist 11; lost tch 13; 25l 3rd when rfo 15*		U

OFFICIAL DISTANCES: dist, 25*l* **TIME:** 6min 12.0s

1448 Ladies Open — 5 ran

Form	Horse / Details	Dist	Pos
	EPICURE (FR) 3-1 **Mrs O Jackson** *2nd/3rd til ld aft 8; mist 15; lft 5l clr nxt; rdn 2 out; kpt on wl*		1
1185^{4}	**Cherokee Run (IRE)** 6-1 **Miss C Tizzard** *Ld til hdd aft 8; chsd wnr til aft 15; lft 5l 2nd nxt; rdn app 2 out; one pce*	3	2
1368^{1}	**Traditional (IRE)** 11-10F **Miss R Green** *(xnb) Hld up; last 8 til eff & jmpd slow 14; went 2nd aft 15 til blun 16; rdn 2 out; rn wide bend bef last; one pce; dism aft fin (lost a shoe)*	½	3
1368^{4}	Virtuoso 5-1 Mrs S Corcoran *Hld up; last to 8; last when mists 15 & 16; wknd app 3 out*	30	4
1350^{3}	Defendtherealm 8-1 Miss A Mills *2nd/3rd til rn out 7*		R

OFFICIAL DISTANCES: 2½*l*, nk **TIME:** 6min 19.8s

1449 Restricted, 12st — 4 ran

Form	Horse / Details	Dist	Pos
1136^{2}	**SNOWTRE (IRE)** 6-4F **R Burton** *(xnb) Hld up last pr; mist 7; went 2nd app 14; ld on inner 2 out; rdn out*		1
756^{P}	**Sing High** (5a) 7-4 **A Martin** *(xnb) Pulled hrd; ld aft 3-6; 2nd til lft in ld 12; hdd 2 out; one pce*	2½	2
1352^{2}	**Carling Elect** (5a) 5-2 **Miss J Buck** *Tk keen hld; ld til aft 3; ld 6 til blun 12; 4l 3rd 15; wknd app 2 out*	20	3
1345^{4}	Almost A Day(bl) 4-1 D Mansell *(xnb) 2 handlers; hld up last pr; mist 8; went 2nd aft 12 til lost plce u.p & mist 14; wkng when mist 16; t.o & pu 3 out*		P

OFFICIAL DISTANCES: 2½*l*, 15*l* **TIME:** 6min 28.8s

1450 Open Maiden, 12st — 7 ran

1341^{2} **ABITOFAHIKE (IRE)** 7-2 **A Martin** *(xnb) Ld 2; mist 7; lkng vulnerable when lft wl clr app 3 out* 1
1371^{4} **Queens House** (5a) 20-1 **Miss R Green** *Went 2nd aft 4 til blun 15; 8l 3rd nxt; sn wknd; lft poor 2nd app 3 out* . . . . . . runin 2
1327^{P} **Port Valenska (IRE)**(tt) 50-1 **M Harris** *2nd/3rd to 9; 8l 4th $^{1}/_{2}$way; lost tch rap aft 12; t.o 15.* . . . . . . runin 3
1327^{R} Rifton Bramble (5a) 20-1 M Sweetland *Drpd to rr 5; releg last nxt; t.o 13* . runin 4
1186^{P} Aftermeyourfirst(vis) 11-10F A Farrant *(xnb) 6/4-11/10; nt fluent; hld up; last to 6; 9l 5th $^{1}/_{2}$way; 6l 4th when mist 14; imm pu* . . . . . . P
1327^{3} Bradford Bridge (5a) 9-4 R Woollacott *Hld up; 6l 3rd $^{1}/_{2}$way; shkn up 11; lft 2nd 15; ev ch when slpd up bend bef 3 out* . . . . . . S
1370^{F} Spinning Silver 10-1 M Woodward *Ld til blun & ur 1* . . . . . . U

OFFICIAL DISTANCES: dist, dist **TIME:** 6min 41.9s

Stratford (LH 8F)

Fri, 21 May (GOOD, GOOD to FIRM in places)

1451 Dodson & Horrell PPORA P-t-P Series Final HC, 3m - 18J £3376 — 4 ran

1372^{6} **GUIGNOL DU COCHET (FR)** 12-00 2-1 **G Slade-Jones** *Lw; ld to 4; 2nd til lft in ld 13; $2^{1}/_{2}$l clr 3 out; rdn & in comm nxt; rdr busy doing victory salutes & eased prematurely; just hld on* 1
1347^{4} **Winter Gale (IRE)** 11-07 15-2 **Miss L Eddery** *Ld 4 til mist 13; wl hld by wnr frm 3 out til urged & allowed to cl wl aft aft last; flatt by prox.* . . . . . . $^{3}/_{4}$ 2
1375^{2} **Thyne Man (IRE)** 11-11 4-6F **G Hanmer** *Last & nt fluent; stumbled 10; drvn 17; hit nxt; still last 2 out; kpt on u.p nr fin.* . . . . . . $^{3}/_{4}$ 3
1097^{3} Merry Shot (IRE) 11-07 33-1 J Snowden *Cl 3rd/4th; slpd app 13; rdn & wknd rap 2 out.* 13 4

TIME: 6min 12.0s **TOTE:** £3.10; **Ex:**£7.40 **CSF:**£13.28

1452 Weatherbys Chase John Corbet Champion Nov HC, 3m4f - 21J £13,682 — 12 ran

1359^{1} **CANTARINHO** 11-07 6-1 **D Kemp** *Chsd ldrs 5; fiddled 11; ld 14; ldng pr wl clr 3 out; outpcd rnr-up app nxt; rdn & kpt on game* 1
1358^{4} **News Flash (IRE)** 11-07 66-1 **Miss L Brooke** *Swtng; oht; ur in false start; ld & rcd keen; hit 8; mist 12; hdd 14; prsd wnr game til ev ch 3 out; outpcd app nxt; a hld aft but kpt trying game* 3 2
1167^{3} **Mrs Be (IRE)** 11-09 12-1 **Miss P Gundry** *Towards rr; drvn frm 12; wl outpcd nxt; 7th 17; 25l 6th 3 out; str rn aft; went 3rd 2 out; fin best but set herself hopeless task* 7 3
631^{5} Don Royal 12-00 50-1 N Harris *Hld up towards rr; 5th & prog 11; chsd ldng trio 15; went 10l 3rd app 3 out; drvn & wknd app nxt* 19 4
1374^{1} Bohemian Spirit (IRE) 11-07 7-4F S Charlton *Swtng; settled midfield; went 4th gng wl 11 but 5th & wkng when blun 16; sn wl bhnd.* 11 5
Mucky Man (IRE) 11-07(tt) 16-1 M O'Connor *Mists; nd in midfield; blun 8 & rdr bet ears; 4th when ditto 10; no ch 16* 4 6
1356^{U} Tanager 11-07(bl) 16-1 J Docker *Mists in rr; nvr gng wl; drvn 14; last when hit nxt; sn t.o* 21 7
1373^{4} Banana Ridge 11-06 20-1 C Mulhall *(xnb) Hld up towards rr; 9th 11; nrly fell nxt & imm pu.* . . . . . . P
1363^{1} Bengal Bullet 11-09 5-2 Miss T Cave *(xnb) Lw; 2nd/3rd til blun & ur 8* . . . U
1375^{4} Coole Venture (IRE) 12-00(bl) 16-1 R Burton *Handy; lft cl 3rd 8 til rdn 15; wknd tame 17; 20l 4th & tired 3 out; pu nxt* . . . . . . P
1356^{2} Newby End (IRE) 11-07(vis) 66-1 D Dennis *Jmpd slow in rr; 25l last 7; sn t.o; pu 10* . . . . . . P
1374^{2} Star Of Raven 11-02 10-1 N Saville *Hld up & bhnd; last 11; strugg 16; t.o & pu 2 out* . . . . . . P

TIME: 7min 06.4s **TOTE:** £7.00; places £3.10,£9.00,£2.00 **Ex:**£1827.40 **CSF:**£333.54

The stewards found the rider of Mucky Man guilty of using his whip with excessive force and suspended him for one day

Stratford (LH 8F)

Sat, 22 May (GOOD to FIRM, GOOD in places)

1453 46th Intrum Justitia Cup Champion HC, 3m4f - 21J £21,664 — 11 ran

1169^{1} **TORDUFF EXPRESS (IRE)** 12-00(bl) 11-1 **N Williams** *Trckd ldrs; went prom 13; slt ld 16; drvn & slender advant when lft clr last; eased cl home . . .* — 1

1298^{1} **Springford (IRE)** 12-00 16-1 **D Alers-Hankey** *(xnb) Settled rr til gd prog aft 13; ld 15-nxt; cl up til wknd & mist 2 out; 8l 4th when lft 2nd at last; kpt on stdly.* — 3 — 2

1293^{5} **Bright Approach (IRE)** 12-00 5-1 **T Malone** *Trckd ldrs; rdn 13; drvn & wknd 16; lft poor 3rd at last . . .* — 12 — 3

543^{P} Lord Atterbury (IRE) 12-00 5-4F A Farrant *Blun bad 1; settled rr; nt fluent 6; hdwy 13; rdn nxt; wknd app 3 out; mist nxt . . .* — 14 — 4

1390^{2} Philtre (IRE) 12-00 100-1 A Wintle *Ld 5-13; rdn & wknd 15; wl bhnd 3 out* — 2½ — 5

1166^{2} Jabiru (IRE) 12-00 40-1 D Edwards *Lw; handy til blun & nrly ur 8; rr when hmpd 10 & rdn; nt fluent nxt; stayed in tch til wknd 15. . . .* — 2 — 6

1399^{1} Mullensgrove 12-00 33-1 Miss S Phizacklea *Rcd wide; midfield; a urged frm 6; mist 11; rdn & fdd aft 14; sn rem. . . .* — nk — 7

1376^{1} Earthmover (IRE) 12-00 9-2 Miss A Goschen *Lw; bhnd; hdwy 16; lft 4th & rdn 3 out; pckd 2 out; 3l 3rd & staying on brave but lkd hld when bd last . .* — B

1179^{5} Lord Edwards Army (IRE) 12-00 50-1 R Morgan *Set slow pce 2-5; blun 9 & lost iron brief; dem when blun & ur nxt . . .* — U

1299^{1} Placid Man (IRE) 12-00 14-1 N Moore *Lw; a.p; ld til hdd & hit 2; trckd ldrs; 3l 4th & still gng wl enough when mist & ur 2 out. . . .* — U

799^{P} Right To Reply (IRE) 12-00 18-1 N Harris *(xnb) Tk keen hld; hld up in rr & nt a fluent; eff 14 & cl up nxt; hit 18; w wnr 3 out til fell last; drpd dead aft* — F

TIME: 7min 02.1s **TOTE:** £13.60; places £2.60,£2.80,£1.80 **Ex:**£115.80 **CSF:**£150.54

1454 Oi Oi Ladies HC, 3m - 18J £3649 — 10 ran

1369^{1} **COLQUHOUN** 10-07 9-1 **Mrs O Jackson** *Sn trckng ldng pr; mists 8 & 12; clsd u.p 15; 2nd nxt; blun 2 out; 4l down when lft clr last; drvn out . . . . . .* — 1

1437^{F} **Lord Of The Mist (IRE)** 11-00 9-2 **Miss P Gundry** *Nt fluent; sn midfield; rdn 9; went 2nd & blun 11; clsd 15 but nt gng easily; dem app 2 out; lft poor 2nd at last . .* — 14 — 2

1429^{2} **Springwood White** 10-07 66-1 **Miss T Clark** *Chsd ldr to 10; wknd stdly; t.o 15* — 24 — 3

1360^{2} Cento (IRE) 10-07 12-1 Miss C Stucley *(xnb) Towards rr; mist 7; wknd 11; t.o when jmpd slow 13. . . .* — 8 — 4

1372^{7} Time Can Tell 10-07 80-1 Miss R Reynolds *Blun along in rr; t.o frm 6 . . .* — 16 — 5

921^{P} Shekels (IRE) 10-07 66-1 Miss H Lewis *(xnb) Midfield & off pce; wknd 11; hopelessly t.o frm 13 . . .* — dist — 6

1372^{1} Mouseski 11-00 2-1F Miss R Green *Lw; last when fell 1 . . .* — F

1379^{2} Polar Champ 10-07(vis) 9-2 Miss L Bridges *Ld; tk keen hld & jmpd rt; clr 7 til prsd & only 5l up 15; rdn app 2 out; 4l up when nt fluent & ur last. . . .* — U

1166^{5} Silence Reigns 10-10(bl,tt) 9-2 Miss C Roddick *Ur 3. . . .* — U

1342^{2} The Campdonian (IRE) 10-07 25-1 Miss J Williams *Mist & ur 1 . . . .* — U

TIME: 5min 56.7s **TOTE:** £9.60; places £2.70,£1.60,£9.60 **Ex:**£36.50 **CSF:**£48.02

The trainer of Master Jock and the owner of Ridgeway were both fined £120 for declaring their horses for this race but not running them without giving the required notification

Badsworth & Bramham Moor

Heslaker (LH 6F,19J)

Sat, 22 May (GOOD to FIRM)

1455 Hunt Members, 12st

SALER SAL (5a) **I Bennett** *Walked over . . .* — 1

1456 Restricted — 7 ran

708^{U} **RICKY B** 7-2 **R Burton** *7s-7/2; made all; 2l clr to 16; 2l up when nt fluent last; r.o wl . . .* — 1

1157^{6} **Snizort (USA)**(bl) 7-1 **G Brewer** *Hld up last to 2; midfield til hdwy 12; 4l 3rd 13; 2l 2nd & still on bridle 2 out; ev ch last; r.o one pce . . .* — 2 — 2

1205[2] **Gentleman Charles (IRE)** 7-2 **S Walker** *Mid-div to 6; went 5l 4th 7 & 4l 3rd 14; pushed along & outpcd frm 3 out* 5 3
1416[3] Don Rio (IRE) 10-1 M Morley *(xnb) Handy early; lost posn & 6th 7; rdn to cl 5th 14; pushed along & outpcd 3 out; 6l 4th 2 out; r.o one pce* 6 4
1265[9] Hill Of Kilfeacle (IRE) 20-1 D Greenway *Chsd ldng pr in 4l 3rd to 12; pushed along & wknd 14; qckly lost tch; t.o & pu 2 out* . . . . P
1416[2] Procol's Boy 5-1 C Mulhall *Nvr travelling; a rr; last by 3; lsng tch 12; t.o & pu 14* . . . . P
1305[1] The Sea Club (IRE) 3-1F Miss L Robson *Trckd ldr in 2l 2nd to 13; bad mist 14; sn towards rr; wknd qckly by 16; t.o 2 out; pu last* . . . . P

OFFICIAL DISTANCES: 2*l*, 8*l* **TIME:** 7min 26.0s

1457 Mens Open — 6 ran

1414[2] **TORN SILK** 6-4F **C Mulhall** *Hld up; 8l 4th 5; chsng ldng trio aft 10 & 12l 4th 11; gd hdwy to handy 3rd 14; went 1l 2nd 2 out; ld app last; sn clr; r.o str flat* 1
1396[9] **Royal Crimson**(vis) 25-1 **R Alers-Hankey** *Cl 2nd til ld 7-10; cl 2nd to 12; ld agn 13-14; ev ch 2 out; outpcd app last; r.o one pce; gd rn* 1½ 2
1413[1] **Darak (IRE)** 5-1 **N Tutty** *Ld to 6; cl 2nd til ld agn 11-13 & frm 15; jnd 2 out; sn hdd; outpcd & 2l 3rd at last; r.o one pce* . . . . nk 3
1202[3] Erzadjan (IRE) 9-1 L Bates *Last by 6; pushed along & lsng tch 7; still last 15; slt hdwy 16; stayed on; tk 4th app last; nrst fin* 8 4
1289[2] Glendamah (IRE) 5-1 M Morley *Chsd ldng pr; 5l 3rd to 8; handy 3rd 11; ev ch 16; wknd app 2 out; 4th app last; dem agn flat* 3 5
1375[P] Whitegates Willie 5-2 R Burton *Last to 5; 15l 5th & lsng tch 12; last agn 13; t.o & pu 14* . . . . P

OFFICIAL DISTANCES: 1*l*, nk **TIME:** 7min 13.0s

1458 Open Maiden, 12st — 5 ran

1305[2] **MAN AT THE TOP** 2-1 **M Bennison** *Trckd ldr in 1l 2nd to 13; outpcd 14 & 4th 15; pushed up to ld 2 out; ½l clr last; drew clr flat.* 1
1417[2] **Queenies Girl** (5a) 7-4F **P Kinsella** *Mid-div when mist 4; last by 5; hdwy 12 to 4l 3rd 13; blun 14; rdn to cl 2nd 2 out; ev ch last; outpcd flat; hanging & did nt lk resolute* 2 2
1417[P] **Noggler** (7a) 6-1 **Miss S Brotherton** *Bckwd; last to 13; gd hdwy 14 to disp ld 15-16; 3l 3rd 2 out; wknd app last; sure to improve* 10 3
1417[P] Thixendale (5a)(cp) 5-1 Miss J Foster *Set v slow pce; ld to 6; handy 3rd to 10; last 11; went 3l 3rd 14; one pce frm 2 out* 2½ 4
1425[P] Castle Lodge 5-1 R Burton *Cl 3rd til ld 7-3 out; outpcd app nxt; wknd v qckly & pu last* . . . . P

OFFICIAL DISTANCES: 2½*l*, 12*l* **TIME:** 7min 51.0s

1459 Ladies Open — 8 ran

1415[1] **HADEQA** 7-2 **Miss S Brotherton** *Chsd clr ldr early; 4l 2nd 10; hdwy 13; brilliant j 14; sn clr; 3l up 2 out; r.o str.* 1
1420[1] **Texas Ranger** 4-6F **Miss J Foster** *Ld til mist 13; outj by wnr 14; 3l 2nd 2 out; a chsng wnr vain aft; dism aft line; lame* 3 2
1415[2] **Donnegale (IRE)**(bl) 20-1 **Miss A Armitage** *A towards rr; lft poor 4th 16; tk rem 3rd flat.* 50 3
1428[6] Chadswell (IRE) 20-1 Miss C Hurley *Chsd ldr in ½l 2nd to 7; 5l 3rd 9; wknd 12; poor 3rd 3 out; rem 3rd when blun last; dem 4th flat* 2 4
808[3] Stoney River (IRE) 10-1 Miss F Hartley *A last; lsng tch 7; t.o 13; rem 5th 16* 35 5
1301[1] Miorbhail 12-1 Miss T Gray *Blun & ur 1* . . . . U
1428[4] Silk Vestments (5a) 20-1 Miss H Dunning *A mid-div; outpcd by ldng pr 13; 15l 3rd & clr of rest when rn out 16* . . . . R
1177[U] Wynyard Dancer (5a) 12-1 Mrs L Ward *A rr; pushed along 7; lsng tch 9; poor 6th 13; rem when pu 14.* . . . . P

OFFICIAL DISTANCES: 3*l*, dist **TIME:** 7min 09.0s

1460 Intermediate, 12st — 4 ran

1413[2] **BEN FROM KETTON** 9-4 **S J Robinson** *Last til went 1l 2nd 7; ld frm 10; 2l up to 2 out; r.o game.* 1
1204[3] **Purple Jean** (5a) 4-6F **G Brewer** *Ld to 5; chsd ldr in 2l 2nd; pushed along 3 out; hanging bad lft app last; a hld* 2½ 2

1397P	**Princess Derry** (5a) 8-1 **C Cundall** *Last to 10; jmpd slow 11; mist 13 & outpcd by ldng pr; rdn to 3l 3rd 15-2 out; wknd app last*	15	3
1301[5]	Rubon Prince (IRE) 10-1 Miss J Foster *Handy in 1l 2nd to 5; ld 6-9; wknd & rmdrs 12; last by 13; poor 4th 14*	5	4

OFFICIAL DISTANCES: 4*l*, 20*l* **TIME:** 7min 25.0s

Dulverton Farmers

Mounsey Hill Gate (RH 7F,20J)
Sun, 23 May (FIRM)

1461 Hunt Members, 12st — 2 ran

1431[2]	**STATE MEDLAR** 1-2F **R Woollacott** *Made all; jnd brief by rival 6; hung lft to boxes aft 13; kicked 10l clr 15; 25l up when lft solo app 2 out*		1
1437P	Chapners Cross 5-4 J Barnes *(xnb,orbs) Trckd rival in 2l last til disp ld brief 6; 2-3l down agn aft til jmpd slow 15 & v slow 16; imm lost tch; t.o 3 out; pu nxt*		P

OFFICIAL DISTANCE: Finished alone **TIME:** 6min 55.0s

1462 Ladies Open — 4 ran

1368[3]	**FRANK BYRNE** 5-2 **Miss A Goschen** *Ld til hdd aft 7; 2nd aft; prsd ldr 15; ld nxt; drew clr app 2 out; easily*		1
	Kandy Four (NZ) 6-5F **Miss C Roddick** *Rstrnd in 3rd til went 2nd 4; pulled to ld on downhill rn app 7; jnd 15; cl 2nd nxt til wknd v qckly app 2 out; imm btn*	25	2
1183[2]	Father Jim 9-4 Miss C Tizzard *Trckd ldr in 2nd til drpd to 3rd 4; stdly lost tch & 20l down 11; virt t.o when ref 14*		r
1366P	Regardez-Moi (5a)(cp) 33-1 Miss J Buck *A last; slt mist & rdr shot up horse's nk 2; 10l last 4; 20l 4th when rfo bend aft 11*		U

OFFICIAL DISTANCE: dist **TIME:** 6min 33.0s

1463 Mens Open, 12st — 5 ran

1249[2]	**RED NATIVE (IRE)** (4x) 4-5F **A Farrant** *Made all; mostly 2-3l up; rmdrs 15; jnd & jmpd slow & to lft last; drvn out*		1
	Haydn James (USA) (7x) 6-1 **L Heard** *(xnb) Jw; cl up; disp 2nd 7; went clr 2l 2nd 10; trckd ldr aft; still 2l down & gng wl 17; chall last; rdn & no ex flat*	1¼	2
1367[2]	**Hylters Chance (IRE)** (4x) 11-4 **C Heard** *Hld up; disp 2nd 7; 5l 3rd 11; pushed along & no resp 17; no ch aft; dism imm aft line*	15	3
1434[3]	Midnight Coup (7x)(vis) 20-1 G Weatherley *Trckd ldr til drpd to last 8; pushed along & no resp 12; 15l last 13; t.o 15*	12	4
1348[2]	Shobrooke Mill(cp) 16-1 D Edwards *(xnb) Cl up when stumbled & ur imm aft 5*		U

OFFICIAL DISTANCES: 1*l*, 25*l* **TIME:** 6min 32.0s

1464 Intermediate, 12st — 2 ran

1364P	**MISTER RF (IRE)** 1-2F **R Isgar** *Swtng; made all at v stdy pce; 10l clr of rival 10; 6l ahd 17; 3l up 2 out; kpt on (rdr's 1st wnr frm 2nd ride)*		1
1445P	**Commander Cully (IRE)** 5-4 **M Sweetland** *(xnb) Pulling; a chsng rival & jmpd v lft; cl up til jmpd slow 9; 10l down 10; 6l down 17; clsd to 3l last 2 out; no ex*	4	2

OFFICIAL DISTANCE: 3*l* **TIME:** 7min 12.0s

Cimmaroon (A Farrant) was withdrawn not under orders; the trainer was unable to give a satisfactory reason and the stewards fined him £155

1465 Restricted, 12st — 3 ran

1366[2]	**BARTON SAINT (NZ)** 1-2F **Miss S West** *Cl 2nd til ld 7; jnd 8-13; 3l up 14; lft clr 3 out; rdn out*		1
1366[4]	**Mrs Peggoty** (5a)(bl,tt) 7-4 **Miss C Tizzard** *Narrow ld to 6; disp ld 8-13; dived over 16; dem 3rd nxt; outpcd & no ch when lft 2nd agn 3 out*	10	2
	Another Bula (IRE) 9-1 Miss J Buck *Cl 3rd til 3l 2nd 17; ev ch & gng wl when rfo 3 out*		U

OFFICIAL DISTANCE: 10*l* **TIME:** 6min 44.0s

1466 Open Maiden (Div 1), 12st — 3 ran

Form	Details	Dist	Pos
1381[3]	**HARNAGE (IRE)** 4-5F **Miss C Prouse** *11/10-4/5; made all; 4l up 9; drew clr 14; 25l clr 2 out; v easily*		1
1445[2]	**Hayling Star** (5a) 25-1 **M Sweetland** *Mounted on course; tde; jmpd poor; a last; 8l 3rd 9; lft dist 2nd 14; plodded on*	25	2
1186[3]	Safawi (12a) 6-5 Miss A Bush *Jmpd v big in 2nd & lkd ill-suited to ground; 8l 2nd when pu & dism 14*		P

OFFICIAL DISTANCE: 20*l* **TIME:** 7min 05.0s

This race was delayed by 25min due to lack of ambulance cover (attending to collapsed spectator); Over The Weld (Miss L Gardner, 5-1; reported to have spread a plate at start) was withdrawn not under orders - Rule 4 deduction 15p in pound

1467 Open Maiden (Div 2), 12st — 2 ran

Form	Details	Dist	Pos
1380[3]	**FOSTON SECOND (IRE)** (5a) 1-3F **M Sweetland** *Distracted by elastic gate & lft 20l; jmpd slow 1; blun 2; clsd on rival & 4l last 4; disp ld 5; ld brief 6; cl last when lft virt solo aft 7; 2 fncs clr frm nxt*		1
1450[U]	**Spinning Silver** 6-4 **M Woodward** *Jmpd poor in ld at crawl; jnd 5; cl 2nd nxt; ld agn 7; missed marker bend bef nxt; rtrcd & cont 2 fncs bhnd; btn 42 secs*	41sec	2

OFFICIAL DISTANCE: dist **TIME:** 7min 35.0s

Harborough Race Club

Dingley (RH 8F,18J)

Sun, 23 May (GOOD)

1468 Harborough Race Club Members — 5 ran

Form	Details	Dist	Pos
1356[1]	**TEETON PRICELESS** (5a) 4-6F **N Pearce** *Lw; jw; cl 2nd til jmpd to ld 3 out; 5l clr nxt; drvn & in comm when nt fluent last*		1
1336[2]	**Miss Hoity Toity** (5a) 7-4 **A Sansome** *Ld til outj & hdd 3 out; rdn & a 2nd best aft; fnd little*	12	2
1213[5]	**Tale Bridge (IRE)**(vis) 33-1 **J Russell** *Rdn & nt keen frm 5; rr but in tch to 11; 20l last app 13; went 22l 3rd 3 out & kpt on; nvr nr ldrs*	10	3
1245[1]	Buckland Bobby 12-1 P Millington *(citation) Lkd awful; trckd ldrs; mists 8 & 11; outpcd nxt; 35l 4th when jmpd slow 15*	20	4
1168[14]	Merry Minstrel (IRE) 16-1 L Hicks *Jmpd slow 5; last pr; rdn 11; strugg nxt; 34l 4th 3 out; pu last*		P

OFFICIAL DISTANCES: 15*l*, 10*l* **TIME:** 6min 23.0s

1469 Restricted, 12st — 16 ran

Form	Details	Dist	Pos
933[P]	**HOLDING THE FORT (IRE)** 20-1 **D Barlow** *Ld; rdn & hdd app 2 out; ld agn app last; hung on game*		1
1304[3]	**Flat Stanley** (7a) 14-1 **Miss J Foster** *(xnb) A.p; tkn wide; chsd wnr 6-13; rallied aft 2 out; 1l 3rd at last; kpt on to 2nd flat; a just hld*	nk	2
1377[P]	**Astley Gold (IRE)** 7-1 **J Docker** *Tk keen hld; handy 6th 11; went 2nd & hmpd app nxt; ld app 2 out; sn drvn & dem; ev ch last; nt qckn & dem agn flat*	2	3
1217[2]	Sir Lancelot 5-1 A Sansome *Hld up in rr; 12th 11; some prog to 6th app 2 out; kpt on stdly; unable to chall*	4	4
1217[P]	Button Boy 40-1 P Cowley *Prom; 4th 11; eff 2 out; 3rd & flatt brief app last; sn wknd*	1	5
1333[5]	Shortcut Shorty 25-1 C Wadland *Chsd ldrs; 5th 11; same but outpcd aft 3 out; plugged on*	hd	6
1400[5]	Nickit (IRE)(cp) 12-1 S Morris *Nt jw; cl up til lost plce & blun 7; mist 10; 7th nxt; strugg frm 13*	8	7
1077[6]	Distinct (IRE) 33-1 Miss J Crosier *Nt fluent 2; wl bhnd; 13th 11; nd frm nxt*	5	8
1228[2]	Ebony Jack (IRE) 4-1 Julian Pritchard *Cl up early; 8th & wkng 11; no ch aft*	15	9
1279[2]	Alvero (FR) 5-1 B Gallagher *Chsd ldrs; 9th 11; outpcd nxt; t.o & pu last*		P
1316[2]	Ardnut(bl) 33-1 Miss R Page *A wl bhnd; t.o last when mist 12; pu last*		P
810[P]	Lord Scroop (IRE) 40-1 M Morley *Tde; a wl bhnd; 15th 11; t.o & pu 14*		P
752[P]	No Remorse 5-1 G Hanmer *Nt fluent 2; hld up in rr; 14th 11; t.o & pu 14*		P
1416[B]	Office Hours 14-1 S Walker *Set off last; brief eff in 10th 11; wknd 13; t.o & pu last*		P

Form	Runner	Distance	Place
1265^{2}	Sabena Canyon 11-4F R Burton *Rr & nt fluent 5; 12l 11th & rdn & nt gng wl 11; strugg 14; rem when pu last.*		P
1215^{1}	Sandy Lark 14-1 J Owen *3rd/4th to 11; lost plce rap aft nxt; t.o & pu last.*		P

OFFICIAL DISTANCES: 1*l*, 1/2*l* **TIME:** 6min 28.0s

1470 Ladies Open — 8 ran

Form	Runner	Distance	Place
1314^{3}	**THE WILEY KALMUCK (IRE)** 5-1 **Miss Z Turner** *Settled 3rd; clsd 13; went 2nd 3 out; ld aft nxt; sn rdn clr*		1
1342^{P}	**Gallion's Reach (IRE)** 40-1 **Miss H Watson** *Ld 3; sn clr; 15l ahd 10; 6l up 13; drvn & hdd aft 2 out; a hld aft but in comm of rest*	4	2
1361^{F}	**The Granby (IRE)** 4-7F **Miss H Irving** *Ld to 3; chsd clr ldr; niggled 10 & nvr lkd keen aft; clsd 13; mist nxt; disp 1l 2nd 3 out; gave up aft nxt; hvly eased flat & just kpt 3rd.*	30	3
1391^{3}	Lucky Master (IRE) 5-1 Miss G Swan *28l 6th & outpcd 7; nvr able to cl; plodded on towards rr; nrly caught eased 3rd*	1/2	4
785^{P}	Dook's Delight (IRE) 20-1 Miss L Horsfall *A last; 37l adrift 7; t.o 9; pu last*		P
785^{8}	Guest Alliance (IRE) 40-1 Miss S Sharratt *Fat; wl bhnd; 31l 7th 7; pu & dism 10*		P
1343^{5}	Pacon (GER) 6-1 Miss H Kinsey *(xnb) 27l 5th 7; nvr able to cl; 4th & t.o 15; pu last*		P
1177^{5}	Stormy Sunrise (IRE) 12-1 Miss A Armitage *23l 4th 7; nvr nr ldrs; 29l 4th 13; t.o 15; pu last*		P

OFFICIAL DISTANCES: 4*l*, 1/2*l* **TIME:** 6min 27.0s

1471 Mens Open — 8 ran

Form	Runner	Distance	Place
1073^{3}	**WELL TED (IRE)** 5-2 **Julian Pritchard** *Stdd in 20l last; hdwy 8; went 2nd 10; gng wl til rdn to ld aft 2 out; qcknd 4l clr; jmpd slow last; kpt on wl*		1
1367^{R}	**Jemaro (IRE)** 6-4F **R Burton** *Jmpd bold in ld; sn clr; 15l ahd 5-9; 4l up frm 13 til rdn & hdd aft 2 out; kpt on game; a hld.*	3	2
1332^{1}	**Bullfinch** 8-1 **T Lane** *Chsd clr ldr 6-10; sn outpcd; 16l 3rd & btn 13*	20	3
1357^{1}	Freedom Fighter 3-1 A Martin *Midfield & off pce; 5th & rdn 10; nd aft; 18l 4th 14; plugged on.*	15	4
1216^{P}	Be My Dream (IRE) 10-1 P Cowley *Chsd clr ldr to 6; 4th & wkng 10; 28l 5th & no ch 13.*	4	5
1342^{P}	Exclusive Air (USA) (7a) 40-1 P Millington *Lkd utterly depressed; rr div; strugg 8; t.o & pu 12*		P
1213^{8}	Needwood Neptune 40-1 P Bennett *T.o 4; cont furlongs bhnd til pu 15*		P
	Silent Voice (IRE) 20-1 D Barlow *Fat; hld up & nvr nr ldrs; went 4th 7-8; 6th & lsng tch when pu 11*		P

OFFICIAL DISTANCES: 2*l*, 15*l* **TIME:** 6min 17.0s

1472 Intermediate, 12st — 6 ran

Form	Runner	Distance	Place
1199^{2}	**COURT ALERT** (5x)(bl) 8-1 **S Morris** *Chsd ldr til ld & hit 12; sn hdd; cl up when lft in ld 15; 8l clr 2 out; drvn & v idle app last.*		1
1361^{P}	**Millenium Way (IRE)** (5x)(bl) 4-1 **J Owen** *Blun 5; niggled & nvr keen aft; cl up; 3 1/2l 3rd & drvn 13; outpcd 15; went 8l 2nd & jmpd v slow 2 out; allowed to cl by wnr app last; a hld flat*	2 1/2	2
925^{1}	**Carat** 2-1 **Miss P Gundry** *Lw; hld up in tch; cl 4th 13; lft 2nd 15; ch nxt; wknd tame 2 out; eased flat.*	20	3
1332^{U}	Border Farmer (IRE) 25-1 N Wain *Tde; last frm 4; detach by 9; t.o 12; stayed on frm 2 out*	1 1/2	4
1140^{U}	Hedzamarley (IRE) 40-1 M Keel *Cl up til 4l 5th 13; wknd qckly; 18l 4th 3 out; lsng 4th when fell nxt*		F
1366^{1}	Slaney Lass (5a) 11-10F R Burton *(xnb) Ld; jmpd & hung lft; jmpd violent lft & nrly rn off course 5; hdd brief 12; mist 14; slt advant when blun & ur nxt*		U

OFFICIAL DISTANCES: 3*l*, 20*l* **TIME:** 6min 27.0s

1473 Open Maiden — 10 ran

Form	Runner	Distance	Place
1339^{4}	**TEETON PRINCE** (7a) 9-4 **R Cope** *(xnb) Bit bckwd; settled midfield; nt fluent 6; went 3rd 9 & 2nd 12; ld 15; rdn & kpt on wl frm nxt*		1
1404^{F}	**Divine Mist (IRE)** 8-1 **J Owen** *Trckd ldrs; went cl up 8; 3l 3rd & drvn 2 out; nt r.o; v one-pcd.*	3 1/2	2
1061^{2}	**Jumping Jack** 5-4F **S Morris** *Tde; tk keen hld; ld to 14; 1/2l 2nd 3 out; drvn & wknd aft nxt*	2 1/2	3

1215^{P} Broadspeed (5a) 8-1 J Docker *Hld up towards rr; hdwy 9; slt ld 14 til blun nxt; 5l 5th 2 out; v one-pcd* . . . . . nk 4
1340^{3} Royrace(cp) 6-1 G Hanmer *Hld up towards rr; eff to disp 2l 3rd 13; outpcd 15; rdn & a hld aft* 3 5
1215^{P} Faircatcher 40-1 R Collinson *Rcd wide; 2nd/3rd til wknd 12; t.o 15* . . . . . runin 6
1337^{r} Les The Lizard 20-1 A Sansome *Nt fluent; midfield til wknd 10; sn drvn; tlng off when pu 12* . . . . . P
1424^{P} Light-O-Day 33-1 L Payter *Tde; last pr; in tch to 11; sn fdd; t.o 15; pu 2 out* P
1402^{P} Slingsby Lady (12a) 33-1 P Millington *Lkd in abject despair; sn last pr & nt gng wl; nt fluent; rdn & jmpd slow 10; t.o & pu 12* . . . . . P
1125^{P} Trust Ger 33-1 Miss H Phizacklea *Pckd 1; jmpd v slow 2; midfield til blun & ur 7* . . . . . U

OFFICIAL DISTANCES: $2\frac{1}{2}$l, 3l **TIME:** 6min 39.0s

Haydon

Hexham (LH 8F,19J)

Sun, 23 May (GOOD)

1474 Open Maiden 56&7yo, 2m4f, 12st - 14J — 10 ran

1076^{3} **SLYTHERIN FALLS** 10-1 **S Clark** *(xnb,bf) Made virt all; went 4l up aft 3; 6l up & mist 2 out; rdn & kpt on wl flat* 1
1412^{3} **Catosphere (IRE)**(cp) 12-1 **L Bates** *Chsd ldrs in mid-div; outpcd in 15l 3rd 3 out; some prog aft; kpt on wl app last; nt rch ldr* 3 2
1311^{4} **Temple Glen** (7a) 4-1 **Miss J Hollands** *Oht; mid-div; 5l 6th app 2; prog 4 to 1l 2nd 10; 1l 2nd 3 out; mist & hung rt aft; outpcd app nxt; kpt on wl agn app last; stayed on stout flat; nt rch ldrs* 1 3
1081^{P} Ramon Allones (IRE) 20-1 Miss R Davidson *(xnb) Tde; rr; 10l last 3; detach nxt; kpt on wl aft 3 out; nd* 6 4
1081^{3} Copybook (7a) 6-4F J Walton *2s-6/4; lw; hld up in rr; 8l 9th 3; mist 6; outpcd 10 & 25l 4th 3 out; nd; mist last; kpt on flat* 8 5
1292^{P} Fiddler Crab 33-1 M Ellwood *A rr; pckd 3; lsng tch 7; blun nxt & strugg aft; t.o aft 9; pu 10* . . . . . P
1291^{P} Forty Shakes (IRE) (7a, 5ow) 4-1 T Glass *Chsd ldrs; 4l 4th 6; outpcd 11 & wknd aft; t.o & pu 2 out* . . . . . P
1422^{P} Mr Kaar 10-1 L Morgan *Trckd ldrs; 3l 3rd 3; wknd aft 9; t.o & pu 2 out* . . P
1300^{P} Pampered Lad (7a, 1ow) 33-1 A Pennock *A rr; nt lk keen 6; lsng tch aft nxt; t.o & pu aft 9* . . . . . P
1292^{P} She's No Lady (12a, 5ow) 10-1 C Dawson *Pulling; trckd ldr; 4l 2nd aft 3; wandered & hung & nt lk keen aft 10; tried to rn out when pu qckly app 11* P

OFFICIAL DISTANCES: 3l, $1\frac{1}{2}$l **TIME:** 5min 32.0s

1475 Open Maiden — 7 ran

1422^{3} **ST BEE**(bl) 5-2 **A Richardson** *Trckd ldr; rmdr aft 3; 1l 2nd nxt; mist 9; mist 13 & rmdr aft; hrd rdn & ev ch 2 out; 4l down & lkd hld last; stayed on stout flat to catch ldr on line* 1
1422^{2} **Pure Steel (IRE)**(cp) 6-4F **C Storey** *2s-6/4; jw at times; made virt all; 1l up app 7; went 4l up aft 3 out; 4l up & lkd wnr last; kpt on flat; caught on line* s hd 2
1422^{P} **Tallaburn** (5a) 12-1 **A Findlay** *(xnb) Chsd ldrs; disp 4l 4th aft 3; 4l 3rd 7; outpcd in 15l 3rd 9; some prog agn 12 to 5l 4th 15; outpcd aft; sn btn.* 20 3
1417^{F} Iron Trooper (IRE) 4-1 T Glass *(xnb) In tch in rr; disp 6l 3rd 12; outpcd in 15l 5th 15; sn nd; t.o aft 3 out* 25 4
1311^{6} Hot Bricks 25-1 J Walton *A rr; 12l last & jmpd slow 1; detach in 25l last aft 8; swished tail & fnce bhnd 11* 2fncs 5
1159^{3} Callitwatulike 6-1 C Dawson *In tch; went 4l 4th app 7; disp 6l 3rd 12; 4l 3rd app 15; outpcd & 8l 3rd when blun & ur nxt* . . . . . U
1225^{4} Ellemford (5a) 25-1 W Goldie *Oht; nt a fluent; chsd ldrs; disp 4l 4th app 3; outpcd in 10l 6th 8; lsng tch when blun 11; pu 14* . . . . . P

OFFICIAL DISTANCES: s hd, 20l **TIME:** 7min 05.0s

1476 Restricted, 12st — 10 ran

1419^{5} **TIMBERLEY**(tt) 14-1 **R Green** *Trckd ldr; 5l 4th aft 8; went 1l 2nd agn 15; prog to ld 3 out; prsd brief aft; stayed on wl* 1

1077^{F} **Gudasmum** (5a) 2-1F **Miss R Davidson** *Mid-div; 6l 6th app 6; prog to 2l 3rd 15; prsd ldr in $1\frac{1}{2}$l 2nd aft 3 out; rdn & nt qckn flat* . . . . $2\frac{1}{2}$ 2

1419^{F} **Jupiter Jo** 4-1 **J Walton** *In tch; disp 5l 5th 12; outpcd in 12l 9th 12; some prog aft 3 out; kpt on wl to tk 3rd flat* 15 3

1416^{S} Son Of Sam 5-1 L Bates *Ld; 1l up 4; 2l up 15; hdd 3 out & 4l 3rd aft; wkng in 10l 3rd app last; one pce & dem flat* 1 4

1373^{5} Hervey Bay (5a)(tt) 20-1 W Goldie *Mid-div; 5l 5th & hit 7; outpcd in 12l 9th 12; sn bhnd & nd; t.o 3 out* 25 5

1177^{3} Orleans (IRE)(bl) 4-1 S J Robinson *Pulling; trckd ldrs; 3l 3rd app 7; outpcd 15 & sn bhnd; nd; t.o 3 out; rdn out flat* . . . . $2\frac{1}{2}$ 6

1310^{5} Ben Buckley 10-1 R Sinton *(xnb) Tde; in tch til wknd 9; sn btn; 20l last 11; sn lost tch; t.o 16* . . . . nk 7

1310^{3} C L B Jemilla (5a) 33-1 Miss G Craggs *Greased hind legs; prom; 1l 2nd 4; 4l 3rd aft 8; outpcd 10; strugg aft nxt; lsng tch 14; t.o 16* 2 8

1311^{1} Anniejo (12a) 6-1 R Morgan *(xnb) In tch in rr; 10l last & hit 8; pushed along 12; lsng tch aft; pu 15* . . . . P

1412^{1} Sir Alf 5-1 T Glass *(xnb) In tch in rr; 8l 8th 9; stdy prog to 5l 5th 12 & 8l 4th when bad mist 16; lost all ch; pu aft* . . . . P

OFFICIAL DISTANCES: 3*l*, 15*l* **TIME:** 6min 55.0s

1477 Mens Open, 12st — 6 ran

1296^{3} **STARBUCK** 1-2F **L Morgan** *Made virt all at stdy pce; $\frac{1}{2}$l up 16; 1l up nxt; rmdr nxt & hrd prsd aft; jnd last; hrd rdn to ld cl home* 1

1421^{5} **Hoh Tel (IRE)** 4-1 **R Morgan** *Trckd ldr; $\frac{1}{2}$l 2nd 9; mist 12; $\frac{1}{2}$l 2nd 16; rmdrs & hrd rdn to press ldr aft 2 out; disp ld last; hrd drvn flat; no ex cl home* $1\frac{1}{2}$ 2

1420^{U} **Batoutoftheblue** 16-1 **S Huggan** *Trckd ldrs; mists 1 & 3; 2l 3rd 9; disp 3l 3rd nxt; strugg in 5l last & rmdrs 12; outpcd nxt & detach app 15; 25l last aft nxt; kpt on past btn horses frm 2 out; tk poor 3rd flat* 20 3

1414^{4} Epsilo De La Ronce (FR) (7x) 7-2 W Ramsay *Trckd ldrs; 5l 3rd 6; disp 3l 3rd 10; 1l 3rd app 15; rdn & rmdrs in 5l 3rd app 3 out; wknd nxt; releg to poor 4th flat* . . . . $1\frac{1}{2}$ 4

1373^{P} Mr Busby 10-1 A Richardson *Hld up in rr; 8l last 6; 5l 5th 9; disp 3l 3rd nxt; prog aft 16; 8l 4th 3 out; outpcd aft; releg flat* 6 5

1421^{r} Royal Plum (5x)(cp) 25-1 S J Robinson *Dism start; nt jw; chsd ldrs; disp 3l 3rd app 4; jmpd slow 7 & 8 & pushed along; lsng tch nxt; jmpd ponderous agn 10 & pu aft* . . . . P

OFFICIAL DISTANCES: $1\frac{1}{2}$*l*, 10*l* **TIME:** 7min 03.0s

The stewards fined the rider of Hoh Tel £100 (second offence) and the rider of Starbuck £65 for using the whip with excessive force causing their horses to be marked

1478 Ladies Open — 4 ran

1308^{3} **PASSING DANGER (FR)** (4x)(cp) 9-4 **Miss R Davidson** *Trckd ldrs; 3l 3rd app 2; 3l 3rd app 7; stumbled gng downhill & 6l 3rd app 9; went 1l 2nd 11-12; 2l 3rd app 15-3 out; prog to ld nxt; sprinted clr flat* 1

1308^{5} **Piper's Rock (IRE)** 25-1 **Miss V Russell** *(xnb) Ld; 1l up 3; hdd 7 & 1l 2nd nxt; 3l 3rd 11; ld agn aft 14; hdd & 1l 2nd aft 16; ld agn nxt; hdd 2 out; ev ch & 1l 2nd last; nt qckn flat* 6 2

1420^{2} **Pharmistice (IRE)** (7x) 2-5F **Miss N Stirling** *(xnb) Trckd ldr; 1l 2nd 3; $\frac{1}{2}$l ld 7; 1l up nxt; hdd agn aft 14; ld & 1l up aft 16; hdd agn nxt; 2l 3rd aft-last; no ex flat* . . . . $\frac{1}{2}$ 3

1420^{3} In Demand 25-1 Miss J Balmer *A rr; nd; 4l last 2; 6l last 7; 10l last app 9; rdn along aft 11; outpcd 14 & 25l last aft; some prog aft but nd* 20 4

OFFICIAL DISTANCES: 6*l*, $\frac{3}{4}$*l* **TIME:** 7min 00.0s

1479 Confined, 12st — 6 ran

1423^{1} **LORDBERNIEBOUFFANT (IRE)**(cp) 1-2F **Miss P Robson** *Jw; made virt all; 1l up 9; 2l up when hit 3 out & hdd aft; sn ld agn; stayed on wl to hld on cl home* 1

1418^{2} **Emperor's Magic (IRE)** (7x) 3-1 **Miss S Ward** *4s-3s; cl up; 3l 3rd 9; prog nxt to $\frac{1}{2}$l 2nd 12; 2l 2nd app 3 out where btr j to ld; sn hdd; stayed on stout flat; nt rch ldr* . . . . nk 2

1307^{6} **Lively Dessert (IRE)** (3x) 10-1 **K Anderson** *In tch in rr; 6l last app 3; disp 5l last aft 6; prog to 1l 2nd 8-14; rmdr nxt; 3l 3rd 16; outpcd aft; sn nd.* . 30 3

1418[4] Extra Stout (IRE)(tt) 10-1 C Storey *Cl up; disp 5l last aft 6 & rmdrs; 5l 5th app 9; 8l 4th & outpcd 12; 20l last 15; 25l last 3 out; one pce* . . . . $2^1/_2$ 4
1307[7] Hadaway Lad 16-1 A Findlay *Trckd ldr; ½l 3rd app 4; 1l 2nd app 7; 4l 4th 9; outpcd aft & pushed along; lsng tch & pu aft 13* . . . . P
1418[P] The Timberman 14-1 L Morgan *Trckd ldr; ½l 2nd 4; outpcd 7; pushed along aft; lsng tch aft 9; t.o & pu 11* . . . . P

OFFICIAL DISTANCES: nk, 30*l* **TIME:** 6min 54.0s

1480 Hunts Members (with North Tyne), 12st — 4 ran

1419[4] **GOOD MORNING** (5a, 2ow) 5-2 **R Dickson** *Jmpd rt; ld (possibly the first time ever!); made virt all; 6l up 7; 5l up 11; jnd aft 15; 1l up aft nxt; 3l up app last; rdn clr flat; easy* 1
1040[4] **Nodform Returns** (5a) 1-3F **A Findlay** *Trckd ldr; 4l 2nd 4-6; 2l 2nd 9; disp ld aft 15; 1l 2nd agn aft nxt; prsd ldr brief 2 out; nt qckn app last* 8 2
Lottie (U) (5a, 1ow) 14-1 **R Walton** *A rr; nt a fluent; 20l last 4; disp 30l last 8-12; fnce bhnd 13; 40l 3rd 15; some prog & 30l 3rd app 3 out; nd* . . runin 3
Warkswoodman 16-1 Mrs H Dickson *Fat; oht; chsd ldrs; 15l 3rd 3-5; sn bhnd; disp 30l last 8-12; fnce bhnd nxt; 50l last 15; hunted rnd & plodded on; completed in own time* . . . . runin 4

OFFICIAL DISTANCES: 8*l*, dist **TIME:** 7min 26.0s

Tredegar Farmers
Rhydygwern (LH 7F,18J)
Sun, 23 May (FIRM)

1481 Hunt Members, 12st — 4 ran

1321[P] **RED NECK** (7x) 4-6F **T Vaughan** *(xnb,bf) Settled 3rd; went 2nd aft 13; jmpd to ld 3 out; rdn out* 1
1355[3] **Chief Predator (USA)** 5-2 **T Faulkner** *4s-5/2; ld to 8; 2nd til drpd back last aft 11; lost tch 13; went 10l 3rd aft 15; rallied u.p 2 out; went 4l 2nd app last; nt rch wnr* . . . . $2^1/_2$ 2
1389[P] **Drom Island** (5a) 14-1 **Mrs L Rowsell** *Hld up last til went 2nd aft 11; ld 12-3 out; no ex 2 out* 5 3
Northern Motto 5-1 N Williams *(xnb) Rmdrs 6; 2nd til ld 8; mist 11; hdd 12; wknd u.p 14; jmpd slow nxt; t.o & pu last; lame* . . . . P

OFFICIAL DISTANCES: 2*l*, 4*l* **TIME:** 6min 45.8s

1482 Restricted, 12st — 9 ran

1237[3] **ALJOASH (IRE)** (5a) 2-1 **T Vaughan** *(xnb,bh) A.p; 7l 4th ½way; 10l 3rd 12; went 7l 2nd nxt; rdn to ld app last; drew clr & hung lft flat (saddle slpd)* 1
1388[P] **Deep Dale** 6-1 **Miss F Wilson** *Jmpd lft; tk str hld; ld 3; 7l clr 10-14; hdd & no ex app last* 4 2
1322[P] **Satco Prince (IRE)** 33-1 **T Faulkner** *(xnb,bf) Chsd ldrs; 9l 5th ½way; 15l 4th & outpcd 12; went 15l 3rd 3 out; stayed on; nvr able to chall* 4 3
1424[1] All Eyez On Me (IRE)(bl) 6-1 M Wall *Ld til hdd & bumped 3; 2nd to 10; 8l 3rd when slpd up bend aft 11* . . . . S
1238[4] Daisy's Choice (5a) 25-1 Miss I Tompsett *Hld up; 10l 7th ½way; lost tch & mist 12; 25l 5th when rfo 14* . . . . U
1208[R] Darkarrow (IRE) 33-1 T Underwood *(xnb) A bhnd; last to 8; 11l 8th ½way; 25l 6th 12; t.o & pu 15* . . . . P
1322[4] Its A Handfull(tt) 33-1 J Harris *Bhnd; 12l last & rdn ½way; mist 10; 6th when bad hmpd & ur bend aft 11* . . . . U
1366[F] Jolly Jake 6-1 E Walker *(xnb) Swtng; hld up; disp 9l 5th ½way; hmpd bend aft 11; lost tch & pu 12* . . . . P
1237[2] Ruby Dante (IRE) (5a) 7-4F D Jones *Nt fluent; w ldrs; 6l 3rd ½way; went 7l 2nd 10-13; 8l 3rd when blun nxt; wknd 15; wl bhnd when pu aft 3 out.* P

OFFICIAL DISTANCES: 4*l*, 4*l* **TIME:** 6min 14.3s

1483 Ladies Open — 3 ran

1190[1]	**KHATANI (IRE)** (7x)(tt) 1-3F **Mrs L Rowsell** *Swtng; ww; 4l last 1/2way; went 5l 2nd 12; ld app 2 out; rdn out*		1
1344[3]	**Arctic Burner (IRE)** 12-1 **Mrs J Chapman** *Ld at v slow pce; qcknd 5l clr 12; jmpd slow nxt; hdd app 2 out; no ex*	4	2
1391[U]	**Aircon (IRE)** 5-2 **Miss R Hutsby** *(xnb) 2 handlers; blun 4; 2nd to 12; 6l last 14; sn outpcd; t.o.*	runin	3

OFFICIAL DISTANCES: 3*l*, dist **TIME:** 6min 49.3s

1484 Mens Open, 12st — 8 ran

1320[1]	**CHANCY GUY** 4-6F **L Stephens** *Hld up; shkn up aft 3; 3l 5th 1/2way; went 2nd 11; hrd rdn aft 3 out; ld aft nxt; nursed home; fin lame*		1
1390[U]	**Jimmy Jumbo (IRE)** (4x)(tt) 6-1 **G Barfoot-Saunt** *(xnb) A.p; ld 9 til aft 2 out; ev ch last; r.o.*	3/4	2
952[4]	**Mecca Prince (IRE)**(cp) 6-1 **James Tudor** *Ld to 5 & 8-9; 2nd to 11; rdn 12; 5l 4th nxt; one pce 15*	6	3
1321[2]	Zola (IRE) 4-1 M Barber *6s-4s; 2nd til ld 5; hdd 7; 2l 3rd 1/2way; lost plce 12; 6l 5th & rdn nxt; no hdwy 15; fin lame*	1	4
1103[2]	Scallybuck (IRE) 20-1 J Sole *(hackamore) Hld up; 4l 6th 1/2way; hdwy 10; disp 2l 2nd 12; 4l 3rd 15; wknd app 2 out; fin lame*	3/4	5
1227[6]	Guard A Dream (IRE) 20-1 E Walker *Hld up; lost plce 9; last 1/2way; wl bhnd 12; t.o & pu 3 out*		P
1320[P]	Orphan Spa (IRE) 50-1 J Cook *Prom; ld 7-8; 2 1/2l 4th 1/2way; wknd aft 11; 18l 6th 13; t.o & pu last*		P
844[B]	Runaway Ralph 25-1 T Faulkner *2 handlers; swtng; jmpd lft; bhnd til pu & dism aft 9*		P

OFFICIAL DISTANCES: 1*l*, 7*l* **TIME:** 6min 14.0s

1485 PPORA Club Members (Nov Rdrs), 12st — 12 ran

	WEND'S DAY (IRE) (7x)(tt) 9-4 **M Hooper** *4s-9/4; workmanlike; w ldrs til ld aft 9; qcknd 6l clr 12; nvr seriously chall aft*		1
1387[r]	**Arctic King** 9-1 **R Hughes** *Hld up; hdwy 7; 4l 5th 1/2way; 7l 3rd 12; went 5l 2nd 14; hrd rdn 2 out; no imp*	6	2
1318[1]	**Flockmaster (IRE)** 2-1F **Mrs C Owen** *A.p; ld 3-8; 2nd to 14; 8l 3rd & rdn 3 out; one pce*	5	3
1024[5]	September Harvest (USA) 33-1 R Shute *Lost tch 6; 18l 10th 1/2way; 20l 7th 12; t.o 15; stayed on wl frm 2 out; nrst fin*	6	4
1429[P]	New Ross (IRE) (4x)(bl) 12-1 Miss A Turner *Nd; 8th 1/2way; lost tch & 15l 6th 12; lft 20l 4th 15; dem flat*	4	5
1362[5]	Rusty Fellow 7-1 Mrs M Finch *Sn wl bhnd; t.o last 9; nvr nrr*	12	6
1276[P]	Notable Exception 33-1 Miss K Henry *Hld up; hdwy & 5l 6th 1/2way; lost plce & 14l 5th 12; wl bhnd 15*	4	7
1389[P]	Black Dan(bl) 66-1 D Underwood *Jnd ldrs 5; lost plce & mist 9; 10l 9th & rdn 1/2way; wl bhnd when mist 11; t.o 12*	2fncs	8
1214[6]	Danzante (IRE)(bl) 14-1 S Moreton *2 handlers; ld to 3; 2nd/3rd til ld 8; hdd aft nxt; 7l 4th when slpd & ur bend aft 11*		U
1320[5]	Fassan (IRE)(cp,tt) 33-1 James Price *2nd/3rd to 7; sn lost plce; 7th 1/2way; 25l 8th 12; t.o 14; pu 2 out*		P
1318[2]	Hail Stone (IRE) 6-1 M Whitehouse *Prom; 3l 4th 1/2way; 10l 4th & outpcd 12; 20l bhnd when rfo 15*		U
359[F]	Scarlet Emperor (IRE) 33-1 D Rochester *Nt jw; a bhnd; lost tch 6; 30l 11th 1/2way; t.o & pu aft 11*		P

OFFICIAL DISTANCES: 4*l*, 6*l* **TIME:** 6min 10.0s

1486 Open Maiden (Div 1), 12st — 5 ran

1259[3]	**TREASULIER (IRE)** 10-11F **P York** *Made all; r.o wl*		1
1096[P]	**Maloney (IRE)** 5-2 **L Stephens** *Nt fluent; chsd wnr to 9; 4l 3rd 1/2way; went 2nd und str press 13; no ex 2 out.*	5	2
1394[P]	**Indian Trix (IRE)** (5a) 9-2 **M Barber** *Hld up; blun 7; 7l 4th 1/2way; 10l last 14; sn wl bhnd; lft rem 3rd at last*	30	3

1395U	Come On Boy 6-1 G Davies *Prom; went 2nd 9 til jmpd slow 13; wknd & 8l 3rd 16; wl bhnd when ur last; rmtd*	2min	4
1395P	Golden Host 16-1 R Cummings *Declared to rn in blinkers but didn't wear them (owner should have been fined); a last; mist & lost tch 8; nt r.o u.p; t.o & pu aft 11*		P

OFFICIAL DISTANCES: 4*l*, dist **TIME:** 6min 32.2s

1487 Open Maiden (Div 2), 12st — 6 ran

1395R	**SUMERIAN LAD** 16-1 **J Sole** *Swtng; went 2nd aft 4; lft in ld aft 12; clr app 2 out; easily*		1
1324²	**Dunmanus Sound (IRE)** 5-2 **Mrs L Rowsell** *Hld up; hmpd 9; 5l 4th ½way; lft 2l 2nd aft 12; rdn & wknd app 2 out; fin lame*	runin	2
1324P	**Start It Up** 20-1 **J Price** *(xnb) Ld to 1; lost plce 7; 7l 5th ½way; lft 12l 3rd aft 12; wl bhnd 15*	7	3
1393U	Stantons Church 10-1 Miss R Reynolds *(xnb) Jmpd rt; hld up & bhnd; 12l last ½way; lost tch 12; went poor 3rd aft 3 out; dem flat.*	1½	4
1074³	Tisallover (IRE) 1-2F N Williams *(xnb) 5/4-1/2; ld 1 til pu aft 12; lame...*		P
1240³	Wiston Wizo(bl) 10-1 M Barber *(xnb) Mists 8 & 9; 2nd/3rd til blun & ur 10*		U

OFFICIAL DISTANCES: 20*l*, 8*l* **TIME:** 6min 30.0s

Fence 17 omitted - fallen rider

1488 Open Maiden (Div 3), 12st — 12 ran

1393P	**KERRY ZULU WARRIOR** 20-1 **T Faulkner** *(xnb) Tde; 2nd til ld app 3; sn spreadeagled field; 10l up 5; 30l clr 10-12; tired 2 out; unchall.*		1
1192²	**Capacoostic** (5a) 10-1 **M Barber** *Hld up; disp 44l 5th ½way; 30l 4th 12; went 3rd 15 & 15l 2nd aft nxt; no imp u.p 2 out*	10	2
1340⁵	**Red Spark** 16-1 **E Walker** *(xnb) Swtng; hld up & bhnd; 49l 9th ½way; 38l 6th 12; stayed on u.p frm 3 out; went 25l 3rd app nxt; nrst fin*	6	3
1324P	Just Caramel (5a)(tt) 20-1 J Cook *Hld up; 44l 5th ½way; hdwy 10; went 25l 2nd 12; dem aft 3 out; sn wknd*	8	4
1239⁴	Fort Apache (IRE) 5-1 Miss I Tompsett *Chsd clr ldrs; 41l 4th ½way; 33l 5th 12; wknd 14; t.o*	runin	5
676P	Tiger Rag (5a) 40-1 M Lewis *(xnb) Tde; chsd clr ldrs; 25l 3rd 6; 40l bhnd ½way; wknd u.p 10; t.o 12*	runin	6
1371⁵	Celtic Prince (IRE) 2-1F N Williams *(xnb) 6s(in plce)-2s; nvr gng wl; u.p when blun 5; 47l 8th ½way; t.o & pu aft 11*		P
1193²	Clarky's Choice (IRE) 3-1 L Stephens *Rmdrs 5; 45l 7th ½way; no hdwy when pu 12; dead.*		P
1340²	Classic Fable (IRE) (5a)(tt) 8-1 A Hanly *Ss; a wl bhnd; mist 6; 58l last ½way; t.o & pu 12*		P
760P	Dun Aengus(bl) 33-1 M Wall *Chsd ldrs til lost plce & mist 7; stpd to nil u.p & 51l 10th ½way; t.o last & dogging it furiously aft 11; pu 15*		P
1318P	Its Mr Blobby(cp) 12-1 T Vaughan *(xnb) 2 handlers; ld til 3; chsd wnr to 12; 16l 3rd & wkng when mist 14; wl bhnd when pu 3 out*		P
1323P	Malvic (IRE) (7a) 25-1 D Jones *Ss; 11th when pu & dism 2.*		P

OFFICIAL DISTANCES: 10*l*, 6*l* **TIME:** 6min 18.4s

Sedgefield (LH 6F,15J*)

Tue, 25 May (GOOD to FIRM, FIRM in places)

1489 Northern Echo Open HC, 3m3f £1484 — 9 ran

1460¹	**BEN FROM KETTON** 11-07 12-1 **S J Robinson** *Rcd wide; chsd ldrs; went 2nd 15; ld 18; rdn & a outbattling rival frm 2 out*		1
1362³	**Son Of Anshan** 12-04(tt) 8-13F **G Tuer** *Nt fluent 5; last 7; prog in 4th 15; str rmdrs nxt 2; went 2nd 19; urged along frm 2 out; nvr wanted to overtake*	5	2
1427¹	**Supreme Silence (IRE)** 11-07 10-1 **N Kent** *Bhnd; rdn 13; rem 6th 18; stayed on frm 2 out; no ch w ldrs*	16	3
1202²	Maitre De Musique (FR) 11-07 7-1 M Tate *Ld to 12; 3rd & nt rdn 15; lost tch w ldng pr 17*	5	4
1418³	Kings Minstral (IRE) 11-07(tt) 14-1 A Richardson *Bhnd; last aft 13; hdwy in 4th 19; 10l 3rd 3 out til hit nxt & wknd*	2	5
	Cregg Rose (IRE) 11-02 100-1 O Williams *Tk keen hld early; nt fluent 2; chsd ldrs til nt fluent 8; last & rdn 10; t.o & pu 13*		P

1414⁵ Glacial Dancer (IRE) 11-07 20-1 R Clark *Chsd ldrs; 4th 13; sn btn; t.o & pu 2 out* . . . . . . P
1421⁴ Roscoe Burn 11-11 33-1 M McAlister *In tch; hdwy to chse ldrs 9; 5th 13; wknd 15; t.o & pu 2 out* . . . . . . P
1120² Young Tomo (IRE) 11-07(cp) 10-1 L Hicks *Cl up; ld 12-18; wknd rap aft nxt; t.o & pu long run-in* . . . . . . P

TIME: 6min 57.8s **TOTE:** £10.00; places £2.20,£1.10,£1.60 **Ex:**£22.40 **CSF:**£20.93

** Fences 3 & 5 were omitted on all three circuits - false ground/ground under repair; original fence numbers used in the comments-in-running; the trainer of Maitre De Musique, whose passport was found to be incorrect, was fined £110*

Cartmel (LH 6F,18J)

Wed, 26 May (GOOD, GOOD to FIRM in places)

1490 Holker Hall Garden Festival 2004 HC, 3m2f £1512 — 8 ran

1444³ **TRIVIAL (IRE)** 11-02 14-1 **L Morgan** *Trckd ldrs; ld 14; 5l clr 2f out; drvn & kpt on wl when hrd prsd last 200 yds* 1
1160² **Sally Scally** 11-02 20-1 **Miss F Hartley** *Bhnd; hdwy 15; 4th nxt; chall 1f out; no ex nr fin* . . . . . . ½ 2
1171² **Victoria's Boy (IRE)** 11-13 3-1JF **G Brewer** *Ld to 14; nt fluent nxt (water); 3l 2nd when hmpd by loose horse aft last; rallied & ev ch 1f out; kpt on same pce* 1½ 3
894ᴾ Valley Erne (IRE) 11-07 33-1 A Richardson *Handy; eff & ev ch in 3rd 15; 2nd nxt; rdn & blun 2 out; sn outpcd* 5 4
1296⁴ Indien Du Boulay (FR) 11-09 10-1 R Morgan *W ldr; level brief 12; rdn & outpcd when hit 14; nd aft* . . . . . . ½ 5
1444¹ Geordies Express 12-00 3-1JF N Saville *Chsd ldrs; 6th app 13; mist & ur nxt* U
1176¹ Just Cliquot 11-10 7-2 G Hanmer *Hld up towards rr but wl in tch til blun & ur 11* . . . . . . U
1303² Ridgeway (IRE) 11-11(cp) 7-1 Miss J Foster *Chsd ldrs; 2nd app 13; hmpd bad by loose horse & ur nxt* . . . . . . U

TIME: 6min 34.4s **TOTE:** £11.90; places £2.90,£3.90,£1.30 **Ex:**£204.20 **CSF:**£196.48

14 Regiment Royal Artillery

Larkhill (LH 13F,18J)

Wed, 26 May (FIRM)

1491 Restricted, 12st — 4 ran

1366ᴾ **HAWKERS HILL** 3-1 **Miss A Goschen** *2 handlers; swtng; ld to 15; ld aft 2 out; rdn out (without resort to whip)* 1
1366³ **River Dante (IRE)** 6-4F **S Kidston** *Hld up last to 9; went 2nd 12; ld 15 til hrd rdn aft 2 out; nt qckn* 5 2
962¹ **Think Commercial (IRE)** (7a) 7-4 **G Weatherley** *(xnb,pricker n/s) Opened 2s; hld up; mist 5; last 9 til hdwy 13; ev ch when mist 15; drpd out tame app 2 out* 20 3
1184ᴾ Chief Suspect (IRE) 14-1 R Bliss *Tchd 16s; chsd wnr to 12; lost tch u.p aft 13; wl bhnd when pu 15* . . . . . . P

OFFICIAL DISTANCES: 4*l*, 25*l* **TIME:** 6min 09.0s **TOTE:** £2.00

Current Point-to Pointers Belle Moss, Northern Bluff, Darkarrow (IRE), 3rd, and Spy Boy (IRE), and former Point-to Pointers J'Accuse (IRE) and Monty's Theme (IRE), 2nd, featured in a 10-runner charity flat race over 9f prior to this race

1492 Confined, 12st — 4 ran

1383⁵ **GOLDEN JACK (FR)** 5-2 **D Dunsdon** *5s-5/2; ld; 7l clr 6; stdd aft 12; rdn to ld 3 out; kpt on wl* 1
1369⁵ **Mr Ben Gunn** (10x) 2-1 **Miss V Heal** *(xnb) Tchd 9/4; 2nd/3rd til ld 15; hdd 3 out; nt rdn til aft last; unable to qckn* 2 2
1410⁴ **Mister Pepper (IRE)** (3x) 5-4F **T Underwood** *9/4-5/4; hld up last to 8; ld aft 12-15; ev ch 3 out; wknd aft 2 out* 8 3
1399⁵ Steve Ford 20-1 Miss E Harbour *2nd/3rd to 8; 5l last 15; sn wknd* 15 4

OFFICIAL DISTANCES: 3*l*, 6*l* **TIME:** 6min 12.4s **TOTE:** £2.10

1493 Ladies Open — 5 ran

	MOUNTHENRY STAR (IRE) 6-4F **Miss C Tizzard** *Tchd 7/4; oft jmpd v low; ld 2; hit 5 & 7; qcknd 10l clr 1/2way; at least 20l up frm 14; unchall*		1
1363[2]	**Macaroni Beach** (5a) 4-1 **Miss S West** *(xnb) 7s-4s; ld to 2; a in vain pursuit of wnr aft; outpcd 1/2way; no ch frm 14; tired 2 out but a hldng 3rd*	20	2
1407[5]	**Solo Gent** 40-1 **Miss K Jones** *2 handlers; only half a tail; w ldrs til outpcd 7; 15l 3rd 1/2way; wl bhnd 12; rdn 14; unable to cl on rnr-up til stayed on flat*	1	3
1483[2]	Arctic Burner (IRE) 9-2 Mrs J Chapman *Sn outpcd & out of tch; 30l last 1/2way; nvr able to cl*	15	4
1321[3]	Mostyn 7-4 Miss A Goschen *4s-7/4; v reluct to rce; jmpd poor & wl t.o til ref 9*		r

OFFICIAL DISTANCES: 25*l*, 1*l* **TIME:** 5min 59.6s **TOTE:** £3.00

1494 Mens Open, 12st — 2 ran

1328[2]	**PORLOCK HILL** (7x) 4-5JF **N Harris** *(xnb) Ld sole rival to 8 & 9-11; disp ld 13 til jmpd ahd 3 out; went 5l clr aft 2 out; stdd into last & mist; drvn clr final 50yds*		1
1367[3]	**Kingsbridge (IRE)** 4-5JF **A Farrant** *(xnb) Jw; trckd rival til ld 8-9; ld agn 11 til rdn & hdd 3 out; lft w ch at last; nt qckn*	2	2

OFFICIAL DISTANCE: 1 1/2*l* **TIME:** 6min 06.4s **TOTE:** -

1495 Open Maiden, 12st — 9 ran

1405[2]	**BORN WINNER** 7-1 **W Kavanagh** *Hld up & bhnd; disp 10l 6th 1/2way; hdwy & 10l 4th 14; went 6l 2nd nxt; rdn to ld final 50yds*		1
1425[3]	**Ron Miel (IRE)** 7-2 **Miss R Reynolds** *Hld up; hdwy 6; 6l 3rd 1/2way; went 7l 2nd 11-12; ld 13; sn 7l clr; jmpd slow last; hdd & no ex final 50yds.*	3/4	2
1395[3]	**Jovian Pond**(tt) 7-1 **R Sealey** *Hld up & bhnd; 10l 6th 1/2way; gd hdwy 13; went 7l 2nd app 14-15; one pce 3 out*	6	3
1450[2]	Queens House (5a) 7-1 Miss R Green *Hld up; hdwy & disp 6l 3rd 1/2way; went 15l 2nd 12; wknd & 13l 5th 14; lft dist 4th last*	40	4
1450[3]	Port Valenska (IRE)(tt) 33-1 M Harris *Ld; jmpd v slow 1; hdd app nxt; lost plce rap 7; 22l last 1/2way; t.o 11; forced on*	runin	5
1337[R]	Dinnys Double (5a) 7-1 P York *(martin) Ss; jmpd lft; pulled hrd; ld app 2; qcknd 15l clr aft 12; hdd & mist 13; hung bad lft & stpd to nil; t.o & pu 15*		P
978[P]	Portway Sadie (5a) 25-1 M Wall *Tchd 33s; ld in; ss; 2nd til mist 10; 8l 3rd 14; 12l 4th & wkng 3 out; blun 2 out; wl bhnd when pu last*		P
	Star Of William (IRE) (7a) 2-1F T Vaughan *(xnb,bh) 4s-2s; hld up (w rdr oft stood bolt upright in irons); mist 2; 8l 5th 1/2way; mist 10; 20l 5th aft 12; wl bhnd when pu 14*		P
1326[F]	Sunleys Quest (5a) 7-2 J Snowden *(xnb) Swtng; hld up; 7th when ur 6*		U

OFFICIAL DISTANCES: 3/4*l*, 8*l* **TIME:** 6min 13.2s **TOTE:** £4.80

1496 Intermediate, 12st — 4 ran

1449[1]	**SNOWTRE (IRE)**(cp) 4-5F **R Burton** *(xnb) Hld up; last pr til went 2nd aft 8; dem & hit 3 out; rdn to ld aft 2 out; kpt on wl*		1
1390[P]	**Stride To Glory (IRE)** (5x)(bl) 5-1 **M Hooper** *Hld up; last pr til 2nd aft 5; dem aft 8; 3rd & rdn aft 14; went 2nd 3 out; one pce*	8	2
1404[U]	**Calling Home (IRE)** 7-1 **W Kavanagh** *10s-7s; tk keen hld in 2nd; jmpd past ldr 1 & 3; ld 5 til hdd u.p aft 2 out; sn wknd*	12	3
1367[5]	Makhpiya Patahn (IRE) (5x) 5-2 D I Turner *(xnb) Tchd 3s; ld; jmpd v slow 1 & 3; hdd u.p 5; last nxt; lost tch 14; t.o & pu last*		P

OFFICIAL DISTANCES: 5*l*, 12*l* **TIME:** 6min 07.8s **TOTE:** £2.00

Huntingdon (RH 9F,19J)

Thu, 27 May (GOOD to FIRM)

1497 huntingdon-racecourse.co.uk HC, 3m £1526 — 16 ran

1359[2]	**FIND ME ANOTHER (IRE)** 11-07 11-4F **Miss A Stennett** *Trckd ldrs; mist 12; 5th nxt; eff 3 out; sn jnd ldr; narrow ld 2 out; drvn & stayed on wl to go clr flat*		1
1360[F]	**Supercharmer** 11-09 16-1 **Miss A Armitage** *Set str pce; hdd 2 out; rdn & ev ch last; kpt on game but nt qckn*	2 1/2	2

1376[4]	**Maggies Brother** 12-04 10-1 **D Barlow** *Bhnd; 8th & prog 13; stayed on 3 out to 4th nxt; plugged on at end; nvr able to chall*	6	3
1347[U]	Royal Snoopy (IRE) 11-07(bl) 4-1 R Abrahams *Settled 3rd/4th; mist 16; rdn when lft 3rd app 2 out; no ch aft*	1½	4
1372[3]	Route One (IRE) 12-04 11-1 S Morris *Mist 3; midfield; 7th 13; rdn & impeded app 2 out; kpt on same pce*	1½	5
1443[4]	Cape Stormer (IRE) 12-00 3-1 M Gorman *Lw; midfield; rdn 9; 9th 13; rchd 6th 2 out; nvr nr to chall*	nk	6
1179[4]	Noel's Pride 11-07 14-1 N Bell *(xnb) Towards rr; no ch frm 13; unadventurously rdn as always*	16	7
1105[P]	Ball In The Net 11-07 66-1 M Holdforth *(xnb) Hld up towards rr; slt prog 14; nvr nr ldrs; sn btn*	7	8
1396[5]	Gratomi (IRE) 11-07 50-1 N Kent *Chsd ldr to 10; 4th when nt fluent 13; wknd 15*	2½	9
1168[6]	Iron N Gold 12-00 25-1 Mrs R Powell *Rr & nt fluent 2; t.o 7; nvr put in rce*	5	10
1344[P]	Rubissimo (IRE) 11-09 100-1 M Harris *Bhnd; bad mist 7; strugg 13*	4	11
1295[3]	Tirley Gale 11-07 50-1 J Jones *(xnb) Tk keen hld early; cl up to 7; sn lost plce; no ch 13*	1½	12
1333[P]	Esendi 12-00 25-1 J Diment *(xnb) Chsd ldrs; rdn 11; 6th 13; sn wknd; t.o & pu 3 out*		P
1372[2]	Filscot 11-09(cp) 16-1 J Owen *Settled 2nd/4th; chsd ldr 10; rdn 14; ev ch til dem aft 3 out; 3rd but wkng when slpd up turn bef nxt*		S
1354[P]	Santi (FR) 11-11(tt) 100-1 P Cowley *Midfield; nt fluent 8 & 9; sn bhnd; t.o & pu 12*		P
1441[P]	West Pal (IRE) 12-00(bl) 66-1 M Smith *(xnb) Reluct to start & lost 15l; a last; mist 4; t.o when crawled 7 & pu; bbv*		P

TIME: 6min 01.8s **TOTE:** £5.70; places £1.90,£3.60,£2.50 **Ex:**£90.30 **CSF:**£45.83

Newton Abbot (LH 7F,20J)

Thu, 27 May (GOOD, GOOD to FIRM in places)

1498 Levitation Champion HC, 3m2f110y £2877 — 5 ran

1453[6]	**JABIRU (IRE)** 12-00(bl) 11-8JF **D Edwards** *Made all; drew 25l clr 16; rdn app last; hvly eased flat*		1
1437[2]	**Bill Me Up (IRE)** 11-07 11-8JF **L Heard** *Chsd wnr to 3 & frm 6; drvn & no ch frm 15; fnce bhnd 2 out*	dist	2
1437[P]	**Lirsleftover** 11-09 20-1 **Miss S Young** *Chsd wnr 3-6; lost plce nxt; t.o 11; lft hopeless 3rd app 15*	19	3
1382[2]	Hold On Harry 11-07 7-1 C Heard *Hld up; went 3rd 7; 17l down 10; u.p 13; strugg bad when pu 15*		P
1384[4]	Khayal (USA) 12-00 11-1 L Jefford *Nvr went a yd; rdn 5; t.o & pu 9*		P

TIME: 6min 48.2s **TOTE:** £2.60; places £1.10,£1.70 **Ex:**£4.40 **CSF:**£3.74

The owner of Jabiru, whose passport was found to be incorrect, was fined £110

Hexham (RH 9F,15J)

Sat, 29 May (GOOD to FIRM)

1499 Fying Ace HC, 2m4f110y £1249 — 14 ran

1377[1]	**SCOTTISH ROOTS** 12-07 7-2 **T Greenall** *Hld up; 10th 9; hdwy app 3 out; 2nd & drvn nxt; ld app last; surged clr flat; confid handled*		1
1475[2]	**Pure Steel (IRE)** 12-00(cp) 11-1 **C Storey** *Ld 1 & agn 5; hdd app last; wknd flat*	10	2
1476[5]	**Hervey Bay** 11-02(tt) 33-1 **W Goldie** *Prom; 3rd 9; eff app 3 out; 4l 3rd nxt; one pce when hit last*	1¾	3
1288[1]	Sweeping Storm (IRE) 11-07 13-2 C Dawson *Cl up; 4th & rdn 9; outpcd app 3 out; no imp aft*	1	4
1374[3]	Raging Torrent 11-07 5-1 L Morgan *(xnb) Chsd ldrs; 7th 9; wknd 11*	15	5
1412[2]	Mr McDuck (IRE) 12-02 9-1 L Bates *Hit 1; bhnd & nvr gng wl; jmpd slow 6; last & rdn 9*	½	6
1373[3]	Jupiter's Fancy 11-06 6-1 M McAlister *Mist 2; 11th 9; a bhnd*	11	7
1359[3]	Snooty Eskimo (IRE) 11-07 16-1 H Norton *Midfield; hmpd 3; 8th 9; no ch aft; t.o*	25	8

1459U	Miorbhail 11-07 20-1 Miss T Gray *Tk keen hld; ld aft 1-5; 5th 9; sn wknd; t.o*	3½	9
1452P	Banana Ridge 11-13(tt) 3-1F C Mulhall *Hld up; hit 8 & rmdr; 6th nxt; hdwy & prom 11; chsd wnr aft 12-2 out; wknd alarm; pu last*		P
1299P	Colombe D'Or 11-07 66-1 N Saville *Cl up; chsd ldr 6-11; wknd nxt; blun 3 out; pu 2 out*		P
14186	Dream Of My Life (USA) 11-09(tt) 14-1 R Morgan *Bhnd; 9th & drvn 9; pckd bad nxt; pu 11*		P
14224	Sixties Melody 12-00 20-1 Miss P Robson *Hld up; hmpd 3; hit 5 & pu*		P
1456P	The Sea Club (IRE) 11-09 25-1 M Seston *Handy til blun bad & ur 3*		U

TIME: 5min 13.5s **TOTE:** £3.40; places £1.70,£3.10,£7.80 **Ex:**£46.10 **CSF:**£46.39

Blankney

Garthorpe (RH 8F,18J)

Sat, 29 May (GOOD to FIRM, GOOD in places)

1500 Confined, 12st — 10 ran

13971	**EMPEROR ROSCOE** 5-1 **R Armson** *Shkn up aft 2; last pr to 4; hdwy 7; 4l 3rd 1/2way; ld 11; drew clr 2 out; rdn out.*		1
14143	**Civil Gent (IRE)** (7a) 7-2 **G Brewer** *(xnb) Hld up & bhnd; hdwy & 6l 5th 1/2way; 5l 4th 13; went 5l 3rd & rdn aft 15 & 8l 2nd at last; one pce*	8	2
13962	**My Best Buddy** 6-4F **R Cope** *2s-6/4; nt fluent; hld up; hdwy 7; 5l 4th 1/2way; went 2nd 12; rdn & ev ch 3 out; wknd aft nxt*	2	3
13964	Ardmayle (IRE) 5-1 Miss L Coney *Prom; lft 2nd app 9-12; 4l 3rd & rdn nxt; wknd & 11l 4th 3 out*	10	4
13968	Springlea Tower (6x, 1ow) 12-1 R Hunnisett *Ld to 3; lost plce 7; 10l 7th & drvn urgently 1/2way; wl bhnd 13.*	25	5
14287	Shallow River (IRE) 33-1 Miss H Phizacklea *Prom til lost plce 6; 9l 6th 1/2way; wl bhnd 13; t.o when mist 15*	10	6
942P	The Nobleman (USA) (3x) 14-1 N Docker *(bf) Ld 3-6 & 7-11; nt r.o u.p; 20l 5th 13; t.o 15*	15	7
1153P	Brilliant Star (NZ) 33-1 P Millington *Sn bhnd; last 7; 15l 9th 1/2way; lost tch 11; t.o & pu 13*		P
14147	Fine Times (5x)(tt) 33-1 M Mackley *Sn bhnd; 12l 8th 1/2way; lost tch 11; t.o & pu 13*		P
1397P	General Carats(bl) 33-1 N Pearce *Went 2nd aft 4; ld 6-7; v reluct to rce & hung bad lft bend bef 9; last 1/2way; rallied u.p 11; wknd & 25l 6th 13; pu 14*		P

OFFICIAL DISTANCES: 5*l*, 1½*l* **TIME:** 6min 09.8s

1501 Ladies Open — 5 ran

14512	**WINTER GALE (IRE)** 2-1 **Miss L Eddery** *Ld aft 1; ldng pr wl clr 11; rdn 2 out; kpt on game*		1
1399U	**Fami (FR)** evensF **Miss Gemma Hutchinson** *(bf,bnh) Ld til 2nd aft 1; drew clr w wnr 11; drvn to gain inner 13; ev ch u.p 2 out; one pce*	3	2
14595	**Stoney River (IRE)** 9-1 **Miss F Hartley** *Swtng; nd; 11l 4th 1/2way; lost tch 11; fnce bhnd 13; went dist 3rd 15; nvr able to cl*	30	3
13344	Lottie The Lotus (5a) 9-1 Miss R Goodwin *Swtng; last & outpcd 3; lost tch 8; wl bhnd 11; tk rem 4th flat*	5	4
13994	Cawkwell Princess (5a) 16-1 Miss A Stennett *Chsd ldrs; 7l 3rd 1/2way; outpcd & lost tch 11; fnce bhnd 13; dem 15 & releg last flat*	4	5

OFFICIAL DISTANCES: 2*l*, dist **TIME:** 6min 12.5s

1502 Mens Open, 12st — 7 ran

1391P	**CAMPDEN KITTY** (5a) 4-1 **F Hutsby** *Sn declined early pce; hdwy & went 2nd aft 7; ld 11; 5l clr 15; unchall*		1
14893	**Supreme Silence (IRE)** 3-1 **N Kent** *4s-3s; jnd ldrs aft 7; 3l 4th 1/2way; mist 12; went 5l 3rd app nxt & 10l 2nd aft 15; drvn & no imp; mist last*	12	2
1428P	**Gay Baratineur (FR)** 13-8F **Julian Pritchard** *(pricker n/s) 4s-13/8; ld to 2 & 5-11; 2nd til rdn & wknd aft 15; t.o.*	30	3
1471P	Needwood Neptune 100-1 P Bennett *Jmpd lft; blun 2; sn wl t.o.*	2½fs	4
1400F	Cateel Bay (5a) 50-1 P Millington *(citation) Sn wl bhnd; 30l 6th 1/2way; t.o 11; pu 13*		P

1497[9] Gratomi (IRE) 14-1 M Mackley *Chsd ldrs; mists 7 & 8; 4l 5th ½way; mist 10; wknd u.p & 14l 5th 13; wl bhnd when pu 15* . . . . P
998[3] Templebreedy (IRE) 3-1 R Burton *Ld 2-5; 2l 3rd ½way; wknd & 10l 4th 13; t.o & pu 3 out* . . . . P

OFFICIAL DISTANCES: 12*l*, dist **TIME:** 6min 13.6s

1503 Restricted — 12 ran

1402[1] **TOM TOBACCO** 12-1 **R Cope** *Hld up; hdwy 8; 4th ½way; went 2nd aft 12; ld 3 out; all out* 1
1397[5] **Balmoral Spring (IRE)**(vis) 9-2 **R Armson** *Hdwy 5; went 2nd 9; ld 12; 5l clr 15; hdd 3 out; nt qckn* 2½ 2
1396[7] **Rathbarry Lad (IRE)** 9-2 **S Morris** *7s-9/2; drpd to rr & rmdrs aft 4; hdwy 8; 7th ½way; eff u.p 13; went 10l 4th 15 & 7l 3rd nxt; stayed on wl flat; nt rch wnr* hd 3
1439[P] The Sky Is Blue 33-1 M Caldwell *Hld up & bhnd; 10th ½way; hdwy & 8l 6th 13; outpcd 15* 20 4
1396[10] Coole Chief 33-1 K Green *(xnb) Hdwy to ld 4; hdd 12; 6l 4th when hit 14; wknd 15* 3 5
1396[11] Libido 33-1 P Andrew *Lost plce 5; last 8; wl bhnd & u.p 12; t.o 15* 25 6
1400[P] Society Scandal (IRE)(tt) 33-1 P Millington *A bhnd; drvn frantically 7; 11th ½way; lost tch 12; t.o.* 6 7
1469[5] Button Boy 4-1 P Cowley *Chsd ldrs; mist 2; 5th ½way; 12l 9th & wkng when mist 13; pu 14* . . . . P
1425[1] Jupiter George 7-4F R Burton *Hld up; 6th ½way; hdwy 12; 4l 3rd 14; wknd qckly & 12l 4th 3 out; pu 2 out* . . . . P
1359[P] Magnus Maximus 20-1 T Lane *(xnb) 2 handlers; hld up; 9th ½way; 13l 10th 13; wl bhnd when pu 3 out* . . . . P
1405[1] Mr Know What (IRE) 7-1 Miss C Bartlett *Ld 2-4; lost plce 8; 8th ½way; 10l 8th 13; lost tch 15; t.o & pu last* . . . . P
1416[4] Troubleshooter 16-1 M Mackley *Ld to 2; 2nd to 9; rdn 11; wknd & 9l 7th 13; wl bhnd when pu 3 out* . . . . P

OFFICIAL DISTANCES: 2*l*, nk **TIME:** 6min 16.7s

The riders of Jupiter George, Society Scandal and The Sky Is Blue returned to scale to re-weigh-out at 12st5lb having originally done so at 12st

1504 Open Maiden 56&7yo, 2m4f, 12st - 15J — 12 ran

1402[4] **MAJOR RENO (IRE)** 9-1 **J Newbold** *(xnb) 2nd til ld aft 9; rdn 2 out; kpt on wl* 1
1474[2] **Catosphere (IRE)**(cp) 3-1F **N Tutty** *Sn prom; disp 5l 3rd ½way; 4l 4th 10; went 2nd aft 12; one pce 2 out* 1½ 2
850[3d] **Hermano (IRE)** 16-1 **J King** *25s-16s; ld til hdd aft 9; 2nd & ev ch til wknd aft 12; fin tired.* 30 3
1402[P] Pernickety King (7a) 33-1 P Millington *A bhnd; mist 3; 22l 11th ½way; t.o 12* 2½ 4
1458[3] Noggler (7a) 4-1 Miss S Brotherton *Hld up; 9l 8th ½way; lost tch & 16l 7th 10; t.o 12* 3 5
1266[U] Beauchamp Brook 7-1 R Burton *(xnb) A bhnd; t.o & pu 8; dism* . . . . P
1403[P] James Pine (IRE) (7a) 33-1 A Sansome *Ur & rn loose padd; prom; 5l 3rd ½way; 5th & wkng when fell 9* . . . . F
1124[P] Murphymeboy (IRE) 5-1 S Morris *Hld up; 7l 5th ½way; hdwy 9; 2l 3rd when mist nxt; wknd & 10l 4th 12; bhnd when pu 3 out* . . . . P
1403[P] Northern Breeze (5a) 6-1 M Mackley *Jmpd slow 3; mist 4; lost tch 6; 20l 10th ½way; wl bhnd when pu 11* . . . . P
1402[P] Orton Playboy 14-1 L Hicks *Swtng; hld up; mist 5; 8½l 7th ½way; 8l 5th 10; 17l 6th & wkng when hmpd & ur 3 out* . . . . U
1124[P] River Deed (7a) 20-1 M Smith *Swtng; hld up & pulled hrd; 10l 9th ½way; in tch when pu aft 9; dead* . . . . P
1402[U] Usedtobeasweetboy (7a) 25-1 C Wadland *(xnb) Hld up; 8l 6th ½way; 9l 6th 10; hdwy 12; 10l 4th when fell nxt.* . . . . F

OFFICIAL DISTANCES: 1½*l*, dist **TIME:** 5min 16.2s

1505 Open Maiden 8yo&up, 12st — 12 ran

1397[2] **ORCHESTRA'S BOY (IRE)** 4-7F **K Green** *Evens-4/7; ld 5-8; 2nd til ld agn 13; made rest; rdly.* 1
1425[P] **Arewetoolate** 14-1 **J Owen** *Hld up; 12l 7th ½way; mist 10; hdwy 13; went 2nd aft 15-3 out; stayed on one pce flat* 4 2

1425F **Beau Jake (IRE)** 11-2 **R Armson** *Ww; mist 5; 9l 6th ½way; 7l 4th aft 15; went 3l 2nd & gng wl nxt; fnd nil & dem flat* 1 3
1473[6] Faircatcher 40-1 R Collinson *Hld up; 8l 5th ½way; hdwy 11; 2½l 3rd 13; rdn & wknd aft 15* 20 4
1341[4] Dolitanlad 25-1 P Millington *A bhnd; 14l 8th ½way; t.o 14* . . . . . . runin 5
1061P Beechbrook Gale (IRE) 12-1 S Morris *(xnb) Ld to 5 & 8-13; mist 14; 2nd til wknd qckly u.p aft nxt; wl bhnd when pu last* . . . . . . P
1377F Bless Yourself (IRE)(bl) 13-2 R Burton *Jmpd v slow in last til pu aft 4* . . . . P
1488P Dun Aengus 25-1 M Wall *Mist 2; lost plce & rdn along 6; 17l last & u.p ½way; t.o & pu 13* . . . . . . P
1424[5] Ginmini (IRE) (5a, 9ow) 16-1 R Ward-Dutton *Ur 1 (galloped 3 circuits whilst loose)* . . . . . . U
833P Looking Magic (IRE) 25-1 M Mackley *Chsd ldrs; 7l 4th ½way; 4l 5th when fell 13; dead* . . . . . . F
1119F Past Forte (5a)(tt) 14-1 T Ellis *(xnb) Prom; 5l 3rd ½way; 3l 4th & rdn 13; wknd u.p 3 out; bhnd when pu last* . . . . . . P
1473U Trust Ger 33-1 P Cowley *Rmdrs 2; jmpd slow 4; lost tch u.p 7; pu 8* . . . . P

OFFICIAL DISTANCES: 5*l*, ½*l* **TIME:** 6min 28.5s

Exmoor

Bratton Down (LH 8F,19J)
Sat, 29 May (FIRM)

1506 Countryside Alliance Club Members, 12st — 4 ran

117P **JENTAR EQUILIBRA (IRE)** (5a) 4-5F **R Woollacott** *(xnb) Tchd 11/10; lw; tk keen hld; jmpd hesitantly on slippery ground; ld til slpd & blun bad 8; trckd riaval nxt; disp ld 3 out; eff & ld app last; sn rdn clr* 1
1329[2] **Magical Fun (IRE)** 4-1 **Miss T Hayes** *Lw; lft last aft 5; ld aft 8 & outj rival; jnd 3 out; hdd app last; sn btn* 12 2
1378[2] Happy Team (5a) 11-4 R Ross *(xnb) Cl 2nd til slpd up bend aft 5* . . . . . . S
1378[3] My Jess (5a) 12-1 M Sweetland *(xnb) Mounted on course; cl 3rd til fell 5* . F

OFFICIAL DISTANCE: 12*l* **TIME:** 6min 22.0s

1507 Restricted, 12st — 3 ran

1465[2] **MRS PEGGOTY** (5a)(bl) 9-4 **Miss C Tizzard** *Tchd 5/2; last & nt fluent on slippery ground; lft 2nd aft 7 & lft virt solo 8; kpt fnce clr; hit 15; still 30l clr 2 out; stdly pegged back but unchall.* 1
1386U **Askers Jack** 2-5F **J Snowden** *Trckd ldr; mist 4; lft in ld 7; slpd, ref & ur into ditch 8; rmtd & chsd wnr vain; hit 13; made up considerable ground; nt able to chall.* 20 2
1002U Golden Sovereign 8-1 M Dennis *Ld; rn v wide bend & hdd aft 5; hdwy agn on outer to slt ld when rn out 7.* . . . . . . R

OFFICIAL DISTANCE: 25*l* **TIME:** 6min 55.3s

1508 Intermediate, 12st — 4 ran

1386[1] **ROMANY MOVE** 11-2 **Mrs S Godfrey** *Lw; disp ld aft 3-12; lost ground nxt; outpcd & grad wkng in 3rd aft 14; 23l 3rd 2 out; no ch when lft in ld at last* 1
1071P **Timpani (IRE)**(cp) 12-1 **R Woollacott** *(xnb) Ld/disp aft 3-12; chsd ldr frm nxt; 4l 2nd 16; some prog u.p 2 out; 2l 2nd when fell last; rmtd; walked & trotted in.* 45 2
1445[1] **Cimmaroon (IRE)** (7a) 8-11F **A Farrant** *(xnb) Hit 1; hld up in tch; ld 12; went 3-4l clr; rdn aft 2 out; 2l up when fell last; rmtd; walked & cantered in* . 15 3
1325[1] Hill Trail 5-2 R Bliss *(xnb) Lw; rcd free; ld til fell 3.* . . . . . . F

OFFICIAL DISTANCES: dist, 20*l* **TIME:** 6min 36.8s

1509 Ladies Open — 2 ran

1350[6] **GURU RINPOCHE** 4-5F **Miss L Gardner** *(b4) Last & jmpd slower than rival; slpd into 15; eff to ld on inner app last; edged rt u.p; rdn out.* 1
1364[1] **Normania (NZ)** 10-11 **Miss S West** *(xnb) Jmpd btr than rival; ld; slpd & blun bad 8; 2-3l up til 2 out; hdd app last; carried wide run-in; switched & nt qckn last 200yds* 3 2

OFFICIAL DISTANCE: 4*l* **TIME:** 6min 21.4s

1510 Mens Open, 12st — 5 ran

1379^{4} **FRIAR WADDON** (7x) 3-1 **C Heard** *(xnb) Ld 2; slt ld & hugged inner; hdd aft 14; cl up til ld agn on inner 3 out; 2l up 2 out; stayed on wl; a in comm flat* — 1

1447^{1} **Ballysicyos (FR)** (7x) 4-9F **A Farrant** *(xnb,boh) Hld up in tch; went 2nd 10; qcknd to ld 14; drvn 16; hrd rdn & hdd 3 out; one pce frm nxt; btn & eased cl home* — 6 — 2

1498^{P} Khayal (USA)(bl) 10-1 L Jefford *Ld 1; settled trckng ldr; cl up til reluct & rmdrs 11; sn wknd; mist 15; t.o & pu nxt* — P

1380^{F} Merv's Magic 33-1 M Sweetland *(xnb) Dwelt; clambered over 1 & 2; t.o when rn out 3; rtrcd & ref 3* — R

Stepasideboy 25-1 G Weatherley *(bf) Last but in tch aft 3; went 3rd 13; hdwy to disp 2nd 16; wknd nxt; btn 3rd when fell 2 out; nt disg* — F

OFFICIAL DISTANCE: 6l **TIME:** 6min 06.5s

1511 Open Maiden, 12st — 5 ran

1186^{2} **ALBAMART WOOD**(tt) 4-6F **D Edwards** *(xnb) Tchd 10/11; lw; jw; lft in ld 5; made rest; hrd hld & rcd stdly on inner; drew clr w rnr-up aft 14; 3l clr 2 out; comf* — 1

1380^{7} **Sup Of Tea (IRE)** 3-1 **A Charles-Jones** *(pelham) Tchd 100/30; trckd ldr frm 5; slow pce & disp 11-16; ev ch 3 out; outpcd nxt; rdn & kpt on flat* — 5 — 2

1450^{4} **Rifton Bramble** (5a) 33-1 **M Sweetland** *Ld & climbed 1; sn hdd; rn wide bend aft 2; $3\frac{1}{2}$l 4th 11; wknd & bhnd frm 16; just kpt rem 3rd* — 30 — 3

1432^{P} Good Gracious 8-1 Miss L Gardner *Chsd ldrs; $1\frac{1}{2}$l 3rd 11; wkng & slt mist 15; bhnd frm 16; battled for rem 3rd flat; a hld* — $\frac{3}{4}$ — 4

1381^{6} Double Bubble (IRE) 7-2 A Glassonbury *(xnb) Tchd 4s; pulled hrd; ld 2; mist 3; jmpd violent lft 4; hung bad & blun 5; imm pu & dism* — P

OFFICIAL DISTANCES: 6l, 25l **TIME:** 7min 02.0s

Uttoxeter (LH 8F,16J)

Sun, 30 May (GOOD to FIRM)

1512 Country Mutual Insurance Brokers HC, 2m6f110y £2780 — 9 ran

1441^{3} **MONKS ERROR (IRE)** 11-11 15-2 **N Williams** *W ldr til ld 6-10; ld agn 13; made rest; all out* — 1

1169^{3} **Macgeorge (IRE)** 12-02 2-1F **M Barber** *Ld to 6; hit 9; sn rdn; outpcd & hit 10; rallied 2 out; no ex flat* — 1 — 2

1443^{1} **Masalarian (IRE)** 12-00 9-4 **Miss L Bridges** *Hld up in tch; hdwy 5; ld 10-13; wknd 2 out* — 19 — 3

1454^{5} Time Can Tell 11-07 66-1 R Hodges *Hld up; mist 8; rdn & strugg 10; sn lost tch; t.o* — dist — 4

1357^{4} Fanion De Nourry (FR) 11-07 66-1 Miss S Sharratt *A bhnd; rdn 8; sn lost tch; t.o & pu 3 out* — P

994^{4} Heidi Ili (FR) 12-00(bl) 9-2 T Greenall *Prom; lost plce 5; t.o frm 9; pu 3 out* — P

1172^{5} Master Jock 12-04 8-1 G Hanmer *Rmdrs aft 4; rdn aft 8; sn lost tch; t.o & pu 12* — P

1176^{6} Robert The Rascal 11-07 20-1 J R Barlow *A bhnd; t.o 9; pu 3 out* — P

1255^{P} Scarrots 11-07 66-1 Miss E Tuck *A bhnd; reluct aft 8; sn pu* — P

TIME: 5min 48.6s **TOTE:** £8.90; places £2.10,£1.50,£1.20 **Ex:**£28.50 **CSF:**£23.35

Berks & Bucks Draghounds

Kingston Blount (LH 8F,18J)

Sun, 30 May (GOOD to FIRM)

1513 Hunt Members

1276^{3} **STONESBY (IRE) M Keen** *Walked over (rdr's 1st wnr)* — 1

1514 Confined, 12st — 5 ran

1103^{1} **MR SPLODGE** (3x) 11-10F **James Tudor** *(xnb) Hld up; went 3rd 4 & 2nd 9; ld 10; qcknd 15; 7l clr nxt; comf* — 1

1257^{3} **Dinsey Finnegan (IRE)** (6x)(vis) 5-1 **G Phillips** *(bf) 2nd til ld 6; hdd 10; drvn 14; chsd wnr to 2 out; rallied & 2nd agn flat* — 6 — 2

1492[3]	**Mister Pepper (IRE)** (3x) 4-1 **T Underwood** *Hld up & bhnd; 12l last ½way; hdwy 11; went 4th aft nxt & 6l 3rd 15; chsd wnr 2 out; dem & eased flat*	2½	3
1336[F]	Itsforu(bl) 6-1 J Owen *10s-6s; ld to 6; 4l 3rd ½way; mist 13; wknd u.p 15; t.o*	30	4
1277[2]	Celtic Season(tt) 10-1 S Morris *3rd to 4; 7l 4th ½way; sn pushed along; hit 12; sn last; lost tch 15; t.o*	7	5

OFFICIAL DISTANCES: 5*l*, 2*l* **TIME:** 6min 15.5s

1515 Mens Open — 8 ran

1452[7]	**TANAGER**(bl) 9-4 **B King** *2 handlers; a gng wl; 1½l 3rd ½way; ld 12; drew 4l clr 15 & rt away frm 2 out; easily*		1
1438[P]	**Leatherback (IRE)** 16-1 **J Owen** *Chsd ldrs; 3l 4th ½way; lft 5l 3rd aft 12; sn outpcd; wl bhnd 15; drvn into poor 2nd flat*	30	2
1355[1]	**Mr Snowman** 4-1 **James Tudor** *Ld 3 til aft 5; mist 7; drvn & ev ch 14; wknd bad 2 out; dem flat; fin tired*	8	3
1442[P]	Acuteangle (IRE) (5a) 40-1 J Sole *(xnb) Swtng; lost tch u.p 8; 13l 5th ½way; wl bhnd when pu 11*		P
1471[3]	Bullfinch 7-1 P Cowley *Hld up & pulled hrd; hdwy 6; 4th when fell 8*		F
1169[P]	Hatch Gate(tt) 5-1 P York *(xnb) V reluct to rce; a wl bhnd; drvn & no resp 4; t.o & pu 12*		P
528[P]	Is Wonderful (USA)(tt) 2-1F Julian Pritchard *33s-2s; hld up; hdwy to ld aft 5; hdd & pu imm aft 12; lame*		P
1172[P]	Tubber Roads (IRE) 20-1 A Charles-Jones *Ld to 3; hmpd & lost plce 6; 7th when pu nxt*		P

OFFICIAL DISTANCES: dist, 6*l* **TIME:** 6min 13.7s

1516 Ladies Open — 11 ran

1360[P]	**FREE**(cp) 5-2 **Miss Gemma Hutchinson** *Swtng; ld to 6; 2nd til ld 9; forged clr 15; galloped on str*		1
1438[4]	**Kincora (IRE)** 8-1 **Ms L Stock** *(xnb) A.p; 2l 3rd ½way; went 2nd 10; ev ch 14; mist 3 out; no ex*	15	2
1407[1]	**Spring Gale (IRE)** 11-8F **Miss Z Turner** *Mounted on course & tde (reluctantly); hmpd 3 & nvr gng wl aft; 14l 8th & rdn ½way; eff & 7l 5th 14; 11l 6th & no hdwy 3 out; tk poor 3rd at last*	12	3
1513[1]	Stonesby (IRE) 7-1 Miss S Duckett *2nd outing; hld up; mist 4; 10l 6th ½way; hdwy & 5l 4th 13; went 8l 3rd aft 3 out; wknd & dem last*	3	4
1497[S]	Filscot(cp) 7-1 Miss E Harbour *Hld up & bhnd; 13l 7th ½way; hdwy 11; 9l 6th 13; 10l 5th 3 out; sn wknd*	½	5
1468[2]	Miss Hoity Toity (5a) 9-1 Miss H Irving *Pulled hrd; ld 6-9; outpcd 14; 8l 3rd 3 out; sn wknd*	½	6
1406[5]	Glenmont (IRE)(cp) 40-1 Miss L Allan *Chsd ldrs; jmpd slow 6; 6l 5th & drvn along ½way; lost plce & 10l 7th 13; wl bhnd 15; t.o.*	25	7
1485[7]	Notable Exception 40-1 Miss K Henry *(xnb) A wl bhnd; t.o 9*	runin	8
1391[P]	Final Escapade 40-1 Miss K Garner *Sn wl bhnd; t.o 9*	6	9
1442[6]	Jack Of Kilcash (IRE) 25-1 Miss A Stennett *2nd/3rd to 8; 3l 4th ½way; wknd qckly aft 13; t.o & pu 2 out*		P
885[9]	Veredarius (FR) 40-1 Mrs S Tyler *A bhnd; t.o 7; pu 11*		P

OFFICIAL DISTANCES: 20*l*, 10*l* **TIME:** 6min 08.0s

1517 Restricted, 12st — 9 ran

1482[P]	**DARKARROW (IRE)** 8-1 **J Sole** *(xnb) Went 2nd 4; lft in ld 7; hdd brief aft 8; hdd aft 2 out; rallied u.p flat; caught ldr napping & ld nr fin*		1
1333[P]	**Lah Di Dah Lad** 5-1 **J Tarry** *A.p; ld brief aft 8; trckd ldr; mist 15; ld agn 2 out; 3l clr & in comm last; idled flat; shkn up & hdd nr fin*	½	2
1409[P]	**Kingfisher Star** 10-1 **Miss J Lodge** *Rn in snatches; 7l 5th ½way; eff u.p & 3l 4th 11; wknd & 15l 4th 14; lft poor 3rd nxt*	30	3
1469[P]	Ardnut(bl) 33-1 Miss R Page *A bhnd; t.o 9; pu 15*		P
424[1]	Diamond Stone (IRE) 5-1 P York *Hld up; shkn up 6; 9l 6th & rdn ½way; hdwy 11; wknd u.p 13; t.o & pu 15*		P
1442[4]	Lady Dot (IRE) (5a) 25-1 Miss C Cowe *(xnb) Nt jw; sn wl bhnd; t.o 8; pu 11*		P
1409[3]	Lord Of The North (IRE) 5-2JF L Hicks *Hld up; 5th when hit 7; pu 8; broke off-hind fetlock; dead.*		P

Notsotiny 12-1 J Newbold *Ld til mist 7; 1l 3rd ½way; wknd qckly u.p 10; 20l 6th when pu 12* . . . P
1469P Sandy Lark 5-2JF J Owen *Chsd ldrs; shkn up 3; 3l 4th ½way; 2l 3rd & rdn 11; wkng when fell 15; broke shoulder; dead* . . . F

OFFICIAL DISTANCES: ½l, 25l **TIME:** 6min 20.3s

1518 Open Maiden, 12st — 10 ran

820³ **JURIST** 4-1 **M Keen** *(xnb) Swtng; stdd start; last to 5; 3½l 5th ½way; hdwy to ld 14; 5l clr when hit 3 out & nxt; kpt on wl* . . . 1
1337² **Rockford (IRE)** 4-1 **C Wadland** *Prom; 2l 3rd ½way; lost plce 14; went 6l 2nd aft 3 out; stayed on one pce.* . . . 4 2
1439P **Carvilla (IRE)**(bl) 25-1 **C Gordon** *Ld 2; hit 11; hdd 14; gave up rap* . . . 11½ 3
1337³ Isefoul De Bellevue (FR) 14-1 J Horton *Ld to 2; 2nd/3rd to 14; wkng when blun 3 out* . . . 10 5
1442⁵ Blakes Road (IRE) 7-1 G Gallagher *Hld up; blun 5; 5l 6th ½way; rdn 11; went 2nd aft 13 til aft 3 out; wknd u.p 2 out.* . . . 3d
1473² Divine Mist (IRE) 7-2F J Owen *9/2-7/2; jb & to rt; hld up; jmpd v slow 7; 12l 8th & rdn ½way; lost tch & pu 10* . . . P
1405P Gale On The Lake (IRE) (5a) 14-1 P Hall *Nd; 9l 7th & rdn ½way; lost tch u.p 13; t.o & pu 15* . . . P
1337P Hunter Gatherer 8-1 B King *Jmpd slow & drpd to rr 6; lost tch u.p 8; t.o & pu 12* . . . P
1404³ Lady Mordaunt (IRE) (5a) 4-1 P York *6s-4s; hld up; 3l 4th ½way; w ldrs til fell 13* . . . F
1442⁷ Two Of Diamonds 40-1 M Harris *Swtng; v unruly start; reversed ½way to 1; tk no part* . . . r

OFFICIAL DISTANCES: Originally 4l, 12l **TIME:** 6min 26.7s

Craven Hill (Miss S Phizacklea, 33-1, ur lvng padd) was withdrawn not under orders; Blakes Road finished third but was disqualified when the rider failed to weigh-in; he was fined £55

Carmarthenshire

Lydstep (LH 8F,19J)

Sun, 30 May (GOOD to FIRM, GOOD in places - watered)

1519 Hunt Members — 2 ran

1321⁴ **BERKELEY FRONTIER (IRE)**(tt) 1-5F **Mrs E Jones** *Made all; 20l ahd of rival 1; jnd brief 3; 5l up 6; sn clr; dived over 14; unchall* . . . 1
Chief Gale (IRE) 7-2 **Mrs M Stephens** *Sa & 20l last 1; jnd rival brief 3; 5l down 6; 10l down 14; wknd 16; t.o* . . . runin 2

OFFICIAL DISTANCE: dist **TIME:** 6min 38.0s

1520 Mens Open, 12st — 2 ran

1481¹ **RED NECK**(tt) 1-5F **T Vaughan** *Pulling; disp ld at crawl 2-4, 7-8 & 10-11; hvly rstrnd & switched to inner aft 11 forcing rival wide; lft virt solo.* . . . 1
1235U **Harppy (FR)** 7-2 **D Jones** *Ld in; pulling; ld 1; jnd by rival 2; disp at crawl til ld 5; jmpd slow 6; jnd 7-8 & 10 til forced wide, hung to exit & ref to cont desp vigorous rein-waving by handler bend bef 12; event cont 2 fncs bhnd; btn 35 secs.* . . . 2½fs 2

OFFICIAL DISTANCE: dist **TIME:** 7min 35.0s

1521 PPORA Club Members (Nov Rdrs), 12st — 3 ran

1188³ **LIKE THE BUZZ (IRE)** (5a) 4-5F **James Price** *Hld up in last til 1l 2nd frm 4; rdn to disp ld 3 out; r.o btr to ld flat* . . . 1
1188² **Rathgibbon (IRE)** evens **Mrs C Owen** *2nd til lft in ld aft 3; 1l up aft; jmpd slow 16; jnd 3 out; hdd & no ex flat.* . . . 1 2
1485⁸ Black Dan(bl) 20-1 D Underwood *Ld til slpd up bend aft 3* . . . S

OFFICIAL DISTANCE: 1l **TIME:** 6min 40.0s

1522 Ladies Open — 3 ran

KOVACH (IRE) 10-1 **Miss J Hughes** *Trckd ldr; disp ld 7; ld 9; made rest; qcknd 12; a gng btr aft; wl clr & in comm 3 out; wl rdn* 1

1483[1] **Khatani (IRE)** (4x) 4-9F **Mrs L Rowsell** *Hld up in last; 4l 3rd 7; went 2nd 9; chsd ldr in 6l 2nd 14; totally outpcd & no ch frm 3 out* 20 2

1367[F] Dawn's Cognac (IRE) (7x) 2-1 Miss F Wilson *2 handlers; ld; jnd 7; hdd 9; dem 3rd 9; outpcd 12; 15l adrift 13; mist nxt; fnce last & pu 16* . . . . P

OFFICIAL DISTANCE: 15*l* **TIME:** 6min 05.0s

1523 Restricted, 12st — 4 ran

1323[1] **NEWMARKET MAGIC (IRE)** evens **D Jones** *Swtng; ld to 2; lft in ld agn aft 3; made rest in narrow ld; drvn frm 3 out; kpt on flat* 1

1482[U] **Its A Handfull**(tt) 12-1 **J Harris** *3rd til lft 2nd aft 3; jmpd slow 6; 2l 2nd 8; prsd ldr frm 11; 1 1/2l down & ev ch 3 out; no ex last* 3 2

1521[S] **Black Dan** 25-1 **D Underwood** *2nd outing; hld up in rr; 25l last 6; fnce bhnd 12; plodded on.* 2fncs 3

1318[R] Pams Oak 4-5F Miss F Wilson *Tk str hld; pulled to ld 3; rn off course bend bef nxt; event cont fnce bhnd; pu 5* . . . . P

OFFICIAL DISTANCES: 3*l*, dist **TIME:** 6min 31.0s

1524 Open Maiden Mares, 12st — 5 ran

1091[2] **COUNTESS KIRI** (5a) 4-5F **R Burton** *Nt fluent; settled in 5l 4th 3; hdwy to 3l 3rd 11 & 2nd 14; prsd ldr nxt til ld 16; eased clr frm 3 out; comf* 1

1323[P] **Clarice Starling** (5a) 7-1 **D Jones** *(xnb) Jmpd poor in rr; 20l last & jmpd slow 7; plodded on frm 15 to 20l 3rd 3 out; tk 2nd at last; nrst fin* 10 2

Blackchurch Lass (IRE) (5a) 6-4 **J Cook** *2s-6/4; 4l 3rd til went 2nd 8; ld 15; hdd nxt; imm outpcd; dem 3rd at last; dism aft post; lame*. 3 3

1488[6] Tiger Rag (5a) 20-1 M Lewis *Mounted outside padd; tde; tk str hld; ld to 14; wknd v rap; labouring in last 3 out; t.o* . . . . runin 4

948[P] Too Phar To Touch (5a) 6-1 T Vaughan *Trckd ldr in 3l 2nd; dem 3rd 8 & 4th 11; lost tch v qckly 13; t.o 15; pu 2 out* . . . . P

OFFICIAL DISTANCES: 5*l*, 2*l* **TIME:** 6min 28.0s

1525 Open Maiden Horses & Geldings, 12st — 7 ran

1324[3] **PEACEFUL BOW (IRE)**(tt) 3-1 **D Jones** *Trckd ldr in 2nd til 2l 3rd 8; cl up til ld 14; sn 5l clr; rdn app 2 out; stayed on* 1

1324[P] **Millenium Run (IRE)** 9-2 **J Cook** *Settled 6th; last 9; stayed on to 8l 3rd 16; rdn & r.o to 3l 2nd 2 out; no ex last* 2 1/2 2

1495[P] **Star Of William (IRE)** (7a) 6-1 **T Vaughan** *(xnb) Ld to 14; outpcd by wnr & no ch 16; dem 3rd 2 out*. 12 3

1189[U] Coolarne Leader (IRE)(tt) 25-1 H Evans *Jmpd poor in rr; 20l last 3; plodded on to jn rr of pack 14; lft 15l 4th 2 out*. 6 4

1487[3] Start It Up 8-1 J Price *(xnb) Cl 4th; went 1l 2nd 6; chsd ldr til wknd v qckly 15; drpd to rr nxt; pu 3 out* . . . . P

1425[4] The Well Lad (IRE) (7a) evensF R Burton *Cl 5th til went 5l 4th 9; gng wl enough when blun & ur 12*. . . . . U

1487[U] Wiston Wizo(bl) 10-1 P Sheldrake *(xnb) Prom; prsd ldr 4; mist & drpd to 4l 4th 6; 5th & in tch 11; rdn & no resp 15; 10l 4th when stpd to nil & pu 2 out* P

OFFICIAL DISTANCES: 3*l*, 15*l* **TIME:** 6min 21.0s

Cartmel (LH 6F,18J)

Mon, 31 May (GOOD)

1526 Sticky Toffee Pudding Mdn HC, 3m2f £1456 — 12 ran

1177[P] **CROSS RIVER** 11-07(tt) 9-1 **N Saville** *(xnb) 12s-9s; nt fluent 2; hld up midfield; 10l 4th 12; stdy prog frm nxt; went 10l 2nd 15; stayed on stdly; sn ld flat; rdn clr* 1

1297[2] **Mighty Willing** 11-09 5-2F **G Brewer** *Came frm stable yard already saddled; cl 2nd til ld 6; drew 8l 13; pckd bad 15 (water); wandering & wobbling aft; sn hdd flat; r.o one pce; just hld 2nd (girth broke starting final circuit)* . 6 2

1469[2] **Flat Stanley** 11-00 14-1 **Miss J Foster** *(xnb) Towards rr; 8th 9; 25l 8th 13; r.o str frm last; nrly caught 2nd; gvn far too much to do* . . . nk 3
1477[1] Starbuck 11-09(cp) 6-1 L Morgan *Prom; 3rd 12; went 2nd nxt til rdn & dem 15; sn wknd* . . . 13 4
1420[4] Imperial Line (IRE) 11-07(tt) 66-1 Miss Rachel Clark *(xnb) Nvr btr than midfield; 9th 9; outpcd 12; plugged on* . . . 9 5
1490[2] Sally Scally 11-02 6-1 Miss F Hartley *Stdd rr; 6th & prog 9; hit nxt; outpcd 12; 4th & no ch 15* . . . 16 6
1475[1] St Bee 11-07(bl) 25-1 A Richardson *Nt jw; sn midfield; 7th 9; outpcd 12; rem frm 15* . . . 15 7
1477[2] Hoh Tel (IRE) 11-09 12-1 R Morgan *Bhnd; rmdrs 6; nvr lkd keen; 12l last nxt; t.o 12; pu 14* . . . P
1424[3] Luck In Run'in 11-09 50-1 M Barber *Ld to 3; mist 7; 3rd 9; 5th & wkng 12; strugg when blun & ur nxt* . . . U
1321[1] Rostock (IRE) 11-11 3-1 N Williams *(xnb) 2 handlers; tkn down gingerly; tk off for 1f at start; ld in & knocked handler over; rcd keen; ld 3-6; prsd wnr to 13; wknd rap; poor 5th 15; pu nxt (rdr reported horse had lost its action)* P
1460[4] Rubon Prince (IRE) 11-11 (4ow) 100-1 T Glass *Nt fluent in last pr; strugg 7; t.o 12; pu 15* . . . P
1418[5] Sharpaman 11-11(bl) 50-1 M McAlister *9th when ref 7; lame* . . . r

TIME: 6min 36.1s **TOTE:** £15.40; places £4.80,£1.70,£3.10 **Ex:**£91.10 **CSF:**£31.93

The stewards accepted the trainer's explanation that the improved form of the winner was due to the horse settling better and being suited by the step up in distance; they ordered it to be routine tested

Albrighton Woodland

Chaddesley Corbett (LH 8F,18J)

Mon, 31 May (FIRM)

1527 Hunt Members, 12st 4 ran

1389[4] **PRIMITIVE SON** evensF **Miss E James** *5/4-evens; swtng; ld 4-7 & 8-9; ld 11; qcknd 7l clr aft 15; mist last; rdn out* . . . 1
1191[3] **Winning Town** (4x) 5-2 **Miss S Talbot** *Last 3 til hdwy 8; ld 9-11; ev ch 14; outpcd aft nxt; no imp* . . . 7 2
1114[2] **Always Good (IRE)**(tt) 11-4 **P Needham** *(xnb) Ld til aft 2; mist 3; ld 7-8; 4l 3rd ½way; lost plce u.p 11; wknd 15; t.o* . . . 1¼fs 3
1424[P] Holly Park (5a) 33-1 Miss N Hickling *2 handlers; ld aft 2-4; last 8; wkng when mist 10; t.o & pu 12* . . . P

OFFICIAL DISTANCES: 7*l*, dist **TIME:** 6min 11.3s

1528 Confined, 12st 9 ran

1496[1] **SNOWTRE (IRE)**(cp) 5-1 **R Burton** *Hld up; hdwy 8; 2½l 4th ½way; 2l 3rd 12; lft 2nd 15; ld aft 2 out; rdn clr flat* . . . 1
1454[U] **The Campdonian (IRE)** (3x) 6-4F **E Walker** *A.p; ld 8-11 & 13 til aft 2 out; no ex flat* . . . 5 2
1430[1] **Sharlom (IRE)** 9-4 **G Hanmer** *2 handlers; hld up; last to 5; mist 8; 6l 7th ½way; hdwy 11; 3l 4th nxt; 2nd & ev ch when mist 15; rdn 3 out; no ex* . . . 3½ 3
1512[P] Fanion De Nourry (FR)(cp) 16-1 Miss S Sharratt *Ld 4-8; 2nd/3rd to 11; 4½l 5th nxt; 4th & rdn 3 out; wknd 2 out* . . . 3 4
1390[P] Theatreland (USA) 25-1 G Barfoot-Saunt *(xnb) Hld up; disp 6l 7th ½way; mist 10; 14l 8th 12; wl bhnd 15* . . . 15 5
1400[4] Top Of The Charts 11-1 M Harris *Swtng; ld to 1; 2nd/3rd to 10; rdn 11; 12l 6th nxt; wl bhnd 15* . . . 1 6
1485[6] Rusty Fellow 10-1 Mrs M Finch *Ld 1 til hdd & jmpd v slow 4; last nxt; lost tch 7; wl bhnd 12; t.o* . . . 20 7

1392U	Wild Blade (IRE)(cp,tt) 20-1 R Jenkins *(xnb) Hld up; hdwy & 3l 5th ½way; went 2nd 10; ld 11-13; wknd qckly 15; t.o*	6	8
1014F	Optimistic Thinker 25-1 Miss S Talbot *Swtng; chsd ldrs; mist 7; 4l 6th ½way; lost plce 11; 13l 7th nxt; wl bhnd when pu 15*		P

OFFICIAL DISTANCES: 5*l*, 4*l* **TIME:** 5min 55.7s

1529 Mixed Open, 12st — 7 ran

1471²	**JEMARO (IRE)** 3-1 **R Burton** *Swtng; made all at str gallop; lft 3l clr 3 out; drvn & hld on wl flat*		1
1453⁵	**Philtre (IRE)** 5-2F **A Wintle** *A.p; 4l 3rd ½way; rdn 13; lft 3l 2nd 3 out; unable to qckn*	1½	2
1390¹	**Teme Willow (IRE)** 3-1 **Julian Pritchard** *Ss; jmpd rt; sn wl bhnd; 22l 5th ½way; went 25l 4th aft 15; lft rem 3rd nxt*	runin	3
1429F	Galeshan (IRE)(tt) 25-1 C Huxley *Sn outpcd & wl bhnd; 28l 6th ½way; t.o 15*	8	4
1484²	Jimmy Jumbo (IRE)(tt) 16-1 G Barfoot-Saunt *(xnb) W ldrs to 7; 10l 4th ½way; wknd 14; t.o*	10	5
1502P	Cateel Bay (5a) 50-1 P Millington *(citation) Sn wl bhnd; last aft 4; t.o 11; pu 15*		P
1365¹	Machalini 3-1 A Morley *Chsd wnr; mist 10; 2l 2nd when mist & shot rdr over hd 3 out*		U

OFFICIAL DISTANCES: 1½*l*, dist **TIME:** 5min 46.8s

1530 Intermediate, 12st — 8 ran

1429⁵	**DOUBLE RICH** 16-1 **O Greenall** *Prom; went 2nd 6-10; 7l 4th & outpcd 12; rallied u.p 3 out; went 5l 3rd nxt; ld flat; r.o wl*		1
1430U	**Therealbat (IRE)**(bl) 7-2 **G Barfoot-Saunt** *(xnb) Hld up; 4l 5th ½way; went 2nd 10; ld 11; qcknd 5l clr 14; pegged back frm 2 out; hdd & no ex flat*	2½	2
1392U	**Petrouge** (5x)(cp) 6-4F **R Burton** *A.p; 4l 3rd when jmpd slow 12; 7l down & rdn 15; wknd & hung rt 2 out*	15	3
1254P	Aldington Charlie (8ow) 25-1 C Sands *Sn wl bhnd; t.o 5; pu 10*		P
867²	Imago II (FR) 7-1 B Gallagher *Hld up; 4th when slpd up bend aft 6*		S
1430²	Miss Moss (5a) 5-2 R Rogers *Jmpd rt; lost plce 5; 8l 6th ½way; lost tch 11; t.o 14; pu 3 out*		P
1456¹	Ricky B 10-1 W Kinsey *Swtng; ld to 11; 2nd til jnd ldr, rn out thro wing & ur last*		R
1148¹	The Lord Roberts (IRE)(tt) 8-1 E Walker *(xnb) Swtng; 2nd/3rd to 6; mist 9; 3l 4th ½way; lost plce & 10l 5th 12; wknd 15; wl bhnd when pu 2 out*		P

OFFICIAL DISTANCES: 2½*l*, 12*l* **TIME:** 5min 58.3s

1531 Restricted, 12st - 16J — 8 ran

1469P	**SABENA CANYON** 5-2F **R Burton** *Swtng; a.p; mist 9; 3l 4th ½way; went 2nd 12; ld aft 15; sn 5l clr; mist 2 out; kpt on wl*		1
1482P	**Jolly Jake** 5-1 **E Walker** *(xnb) 8s-5s; hld up; last 8-11; hdwy & 5l 4th nxt; went 5l 2nd aft 3 out; no imp*	3½	2
1482S	**All Eyez On Me (IRE)**(bl) 12-1 **M Wall** *2nd til ld 9; hdd aft 15; wknd app 2 out*	12	3
1388³	Raymond James 11-2 D Mansell *Chsd ldrs; 4l 5th ½way; rdn 12; 9l 5th 14; no imp 3 out*	¾	4
452⁴	Dorset Fern (IRE) (5a) 3-1 Miss E James *4s-5/2; hld up; hdwy 7; 2l 3rd ½way; went 2nd 11-12; ev ch 15; sn wknd*	8	5
	Hydemilla (5a) 10-1 R Rogers *(xnb) Jw; ld to 9; 2nd to 11; wknd & 10l 6th 14*	1½	6
1114F	Lift The Latch (IRE)(bl) 20-1 M Harris *Prom to 7; 5l 6th ½way; last 11; lost tch 14; wl bhnd when pu 3 out*		P
1265P	Snitton West(vis) 10-1 R Hodges *Last til fell 2*		F

OFFICIAL DISTANCES: 4*l*, 15*l* **TIME:** 6min 02.2s

Fences 10 & 18 omitted - fallen rider; Rosemead Tye (8-1, lame at start) was withdrawn not under orders; Rule 4 deduction 10p in pound

1532 Open Maiden 12 ran

1395F **FRANCO LADY (IRE)** (5a) 2-1F **Miss E James** *3s-2s; hld up; lost plce 7; 7th 1/2way; rmdrs 10; went 2nd app 12; ld 15; all out; fin lame* 1
1258P **Winnick (IRE)** 4-1 **G Barfoot-Saunt** *(xnb) Hld up; hdwy 7; 5th 1/2way; 4l 5th 12; went 2l 3rd 14 & 2nd 3 out; ev ch last; nt qckn* 3/4 2
1488³ **Red Spark** 4-1 **E Walker** *(xnb) Hld up & bhnd; 10th 1/2way; stdy hdwy 11; 2l 3rd nxt; ld 13-15; rdn 3 out; no ex* 7 3
1473P Slingsby Lady (12a, 2ow)(vis) 12-1 P Millington *Hld up; mist 8; 6th 1/2way; lost plce & 8l 9th 12; rallied & 5l 6th 14; 4th & no hdwy 3 out* 10 4
1393P Kotori (IRE) (7a) 14-1 S Gray *(nosenet) Swtng; hld up & pulled hrd; 8th 1/2way; hdwy to ld app 12-13; 3l 4th nxt; wknd 15* 12 5
1232F The Footsy 7-1 D Mansell *(xnb) 2nd til mist 9; 5l 7th 12; wknd & 9l 9th 14* 6 6
1020P Superior Footwork (1ow) 14-1 P Morris *Sn prom; 4th 1/2way; went 2nd 10 til lost plce & mist 12; wknd & 7l 8th 14* 7 7
1403P Dynamic Sea(tt) 12-1 J Owen *Hld up; 9th 1/2way; mist 10; 6l 8th 12; hdwy & 4l 5th 14; wknd 15; bhnd when pu 2 out* . . . . P
1486P Golden Host(bl) 20-1 R Cummings *Prom; mist 3; jmpd v slow 4; 3rd when slpd up bend aft 6.* . . . . S
1403P Little Heck (IRE)(tt) 10-1 P York *Ch ride; prom; 3rd 1/2way; ld 10 til app 12; wknd & 6l 7th 14; bhnd when pu 3 out.* . . . . P
1261P Plenty Inn Hand (1ow) 7-1 A Hanly *Ld to 10; wknd qckly u.p 11; sn wl bhnd; t.o 14; pu 3 out* . . . . P
1074F Stanley Island 12-1 Miss J Buck *A last pr; rdn 11; 15l 10th nxt; wl bhnd 14; t.o & pu last* . . . . P

OFFICIAL DISTANCES: 1*l*, 7*l* **TIME:** 6min 19.6s

Countryside Alliance Club (Wales)

Bonvilston (RH 7F,18J)

Mon, 31 May (GOOD - watered)

1533 Open Maiden 56&7yo, 12st 8 ran

1096P **STAND ON** 6-1 **James Tudor** *Hld up in 4th; cl 3rd frm 13; r.o to 2nd 2 out; ld last; kpt on game* 1
1324U **Shadar (IRE)** (7a) 12-1 **D Jones** *(xnb,bnf) 2nd 1 til ld 5; hdd last; no ex u.p* 2 2
1487⁴ **Stantons Church** 2-1 **Miss R Reynolds** *(xnb) 3rd 1-8; 4th & in tch til outpcd aft 3 out* 5 3
1486² Maloney (IRE) 6-1 Miss C Evans *Midfield til 2nd brief 8; 3rd til fdd 14; sn btn* 7 4
950F Calamint (7a) 20-1 James Price *Dwelt sltly; nt fluent; rr & mist 6; lost tch 15; no ch aft* 3 5
1096U Deltic Arrow evensF L Stephens *(xnb) Swtng; ld 1-4; mostly 2nd aft; mists 9 & 12 (rdr lost irons); wknd 16; pu aft* . . . . P
1387U Sefton Clover (5a) 8-1 M Hooper *A bhnd; jmpd slow 6; lost tch 8; ur 11* . . U
1192P Spicey Case (12a) 10-1 J Cook *Jmpd delib in 6th early; wknd 13; pu 3 out* P

OFFICIAL DISTANCES: 1½*l*, 8*l* **TIME:** 6min 13.0s

1534 Open Maiden 8yo&up, 12st - 17J 7 ran

WELLHESEEMEDSOLOW (IRE) 2-1F **L Stephens** *Hld up in last; bhnd but in tch til 4th 2 out; r.o str u.p to ld last; kpt on wl* 1
1525² **Millenium Run (IRE)** 3-1 **J Cook** *Ld 1; 2nd 2 til dem 3rd aft 5; mist & rmdrs 11; went 2nd aft 15; no ex clsng stages* 6 2
1488⁴ **Just Caramel** (5a)(tt) 4-1 **James Tudor** *Prom; 8l 2nd 7 til jnd ldr 15; sn ld til hdd & outpcd frm 2 out.* 1 3
1395P Evans The Coal 20-1 R Carey *Ld 2; 8l clr 5-14; tired & hdd aft nxt; sn rr* . 6 4
1486⁴ Come On Boy 6-1 G Davies *Chsd ldrs; 4th 4 til fell 10* . . . . F

1488[5] Fort Apache (IRE) 3-1 D Jones *3rd early; settled 5th; in tch to 13; wknd & sn rr; pu 2 out* . . . . . . P
1395[P] Spruce Goose (IRE)(tt) 4-1 Miss E Tuck *(xnb) A rr; last 6; detach 7; pu 8.* . . P

OFFICIAL DISTANCES: 1*l*, 5*l* **TIME:** 6min 13.0s

Fence 16 omitted - fallen rider; the stewards enquired into an erroneous announcement of the withdrawal of the favourite at the start; they decided the broadcast was premature and an unfortunate incident which care should be taken to avoid in future

1535 Mens Open, 12st

1358[1] **SOHAPARA** (5a, 7x) **D Jones** *Walked over*. 1

1536 Ladies Open — 5 ran

1343[2] **DO IT ONCE (IRE)**(tt) 4-1 **Mrs A Rucker** *(xnb) 3rd frm 5; tk 3l 2nd 10; 6l away 16; r.o wl to ld last; drew clr flat*. 1
1376[P] **Millennium Gold**(vis) 4-1 **Miss A Frieze** *(xnb) Napped & planted himself lvng padd; ld; mist & rmdrs 10; hdd aft 13; ld agn 15; 6l clr nxt; mist & hdd last; one pce*. 6 2
1189[3] **Detroit Davy (IRE)** 6-1 **Miss F Wilson** *2nd frm 5-9; 6l 3rd nxt; ld 13 & 14; slpd nxt bend & hdd & 16l 3rd 16; no ex aft* 20 3
1391[F] Ile Distinct (IRE)(tt) 33-1 Mrs C Owen *2nd to 4; sn last; t.o 7; plodded on; 2 fncs adrift frm 15*. 2fncs 4
1319[1] Silver Castle 1-2F Mrs L Rowsell *Mid-div when slpd up bef 2* . . . . . . S

OFFICIAL DISTANCES: 8*l*, dist **TIME:** 6min 06.0s

1537 Countryside Alliance Club Members, 12st — 3 ran

1481[2] **CHIEF PREDATOR (USA)** 4-1 **T Faulkner** *Last; 2½l 3rd & mist 5; rdn frm 15; 8l 3rd 17 & lft 2nd app last; r.o to ld flat; rdr celebrated w salute to crowd*. 1
841[4] **Doc Ryan's** 4-1 **T Vaughan** *2l 2nd to 15; drvn to stay in tch & 4l away 2 out; lft in ld gng to last; hdd flat & outpcd; rdr celebrated w usual salute!!* . . ½ 2
1535[1] **Sohapara** (5a, 17x) 1-2F **D Jones** *(xnb) Jw; made all; 2l up frm 5; drew 4l clr 2 out; lkd wnr when slpd up bend bef last; rmtd; plcd 3rd (although Judge had lft his post)* 4mins 3

OFFICIAL DISTANCES: nk, dist **TIME:** 6min 07.0s

1538 Restricted, 12st — 6 ran

1388[5] **ALLEYWELL**(tt) 4-1 **D Jones** *8s-4s; ld early; cl 2nd 5 til 3l 3rd 10; ld agn 15; made rest & drvn clr; 4l up 2 out; wandered u.p flat* 1
1395[1] **Blakeney Hill** (5a) 3-1 **J Price** *Ld 4-14; hdd & nt rch wnr u.p clsng stages.* 3 2
1481[3] Drom Island (5a) 6-1 Miss F Wilson *Open sore on top of off-hind; hld up in rr; prog 7; 3rd & mist 8; tk 1l 2nd 10; wknd v qckly 2 out; pu last* . . . . . . P
1393[4] Fencethegap (IRE) 20-1 M Hooper *Ur 1; horse rn thro car park & into road; event recaptured* . . . . . . U
1233[1] Lou Biarnes (FR) 2-1F L Stephens *2nd 1-4; mist in 3rd 6; 7l 4th 10; t.o 14; pu nxt*. . . . . . P
207[F] Who Let The Dogout 20-1 W Oakes *A rr; jmpd slow in last 7; trailed hind legs thro 12; fell nxt; cracked shoulder bone; retired* . . . . . . F

OFFICIAL DISTANCE: 2½*l* **TIME:** 6min 15.0s

Satco Prince (xnb,bf, T Faulkner, 4-1, lame at start) was withdrawn not under orders; Rule 4 deduction 15p in pound

1539 Intermediate, 12st - 17J — 5 ran

1322[1] **RAG WEEK (IRE)** 5-4F **J Cook** *Ld 2; jnd 11; sn hdd; ld agn aft 13; 5l ahd 14; qcknd 25l clr frm 3 out; eased flat* 1
1485[U] **Hail Stone (IRE)** 5-2 **L Stephens** *2nd 1-4; 3rd til lft 2nd agn 8; disp ld 12; ld & drvn 13; hdd nxt; outpcd aft*. 30 2
1392[4] **Persona Pride** 5-2 **D Jones** *Ld 1; settled 4th; lft 3rd 8; 5l 3rd 10; drvn 11; no ex* 20 3

1066F Arctic Grey (IRE) 8-1 D England *Chsd ldrs; 3rd 1-4; cl 2nd til ur 8* . . . . . . U
1181³ Sootsir 16-1 R Hawker *(xnb) Detach & jmpd v slow 1; 30l adrift 5; 2 fncs bhnd when pu 9* . . . . P

OFFICIAL DISTANCES: 20*l*, 15*l* **TIME:** 6min 02.0s

Fence 15 omitted - fallen rider

South Tetcott

Lifton (RH 7F,19J)

Mon, 31 May (GOOD - watered)

1540 Confined, 12st — 6 ran

1270² **SQUADDIE** 5-2 **A Farrant** *Hld up in tch; 4th 11; hdwy 14; went 2nd 15; rdn to chall aft 3 out; ld app nxt; drvn out flat* 1
1463U **Shobrooke Mill** (5x)(cp) 3-1 **D Edwards** *(xnb) 5s-3s; wl in tch; 2nd 10; ld aft 14; went 2½l clr 3 out; sn rdn & hdd; ev ch last; kpt on one pce* . . . . . ½ 2
1435¹ **Virgos Bambino (IRE)** (5a) 5-4F **A Charles-Jones** *Tchd 11-8; jmpd to ld 3; ld/disp to 13; wknd nxt; drpd away tame 15; no ch frm 3 out.* 20 3
1362P Millyhenry 12-1 Miss C Tizzard *In tch; cl 4th 10; wknd 13; 20l 4th 16; one pce* 1 4
1270³ Calleva Star (IRE) 40-1 S Kidston *Prom to 2; 4th 8; wknd 12; bhnd frm 15* 12 5
497P Procedure (USA) 6-1 C Heard *(xnb,ringbit) Tchd 33s in plce; tk keen hld; ld to 3; ld/disp frm nxt; hit 11; hdd aft 14; lsng plce when jmpd slow 15; pu nxt* P

OFFICIAL DISTANCES: ½*l*, 20*l* **TIME:** 6min 05.0s

1541 Mens Open, 12st — 2 ran

1454U **POLAR CHAMP** (7x)(bl) 1-5F **A Farrant** *Nt fluent early; nk & nk w rival at fast pce to 6; went 4l clr 10; lft solo frm 12.* 1
Finewood (IRE) 3-1 R Woollacott *(xnb) Jmpd btr than rival & disp ld at brisk pce to 6; mist & lost 3l 9; drpd away qckly aft 10; pu & dism 12* . . . . . P

OFFICIAL DISTANCE: Finished alone **TIME:** 6min 03.0s

1542 Ladies Open — 4 ran

1199¹ **SANDY DUFF** 4-6F **Miss M McCarthy** *Opened 5-6; lw; wl-greased off-hind; hld up in tch; went 2nd & gng wl 14; eff 3 out; sn ld; drew clr 2 out; comf* 1
1434² **Let's Fly (FR)** 7-2 **Mrs M Hand** *Jw; made most in slt ld til hdd brief 6-7; disp ld nxt til def advant frm 11; ½l ld 3 out; sn hdd; kpt on one pce* 8 2
1434¹ **Hasten Bak** 2-1 **Miss L Gardner** *(xnb,ringbit) Lw; dwelt; rcd keen & sn cl up; mist 5; settled cl 3rd & hrd hld; prog to disp 2nd 15; rdn nxt; outpcd frm 3 out* 6 3
1367P Delaware (FR) 25-1 Mrs O Jackson *Hdwy to ld on outer 6-7; disp ld 8-11; rdn nxt; cl 4th 15; sn outpcd; no ch frm 3 out* 8 4

OFFICIAL DISTANCES: 15*l*, 10*l* **TIME:** 6min 00.0s

1543 Restricted, 12st — 10 ran

1366P **EMALI** 16-1 **W White** *Hld up gng wl; cl 6th ½way; gd hdwy 13; ld aft 14; drew 6l clr 3 out; v easily* 1
1435³ **Indian Raider (IRE)** 5-1 **A Glassonbury** *Tchd 6s; hdwy to 4th & gng wl 9; went 3l 2nd 11; disp ld 13; chsd ldr frm 14; hrd rdn 2 out; no imp* 15 2
1385P Abseal 12-1 A Charles-Jones *Tchd 14s; lw; prom til fell 6* . . . . F
1002P Cut Down The Sound (IRE) 6-1 Miss L Gardner *Tchd 13/2; nvr gng wl; last frm 4; t.o & pu 13* . . . . P
Gayble 16-1 W Biddick *Tk keen hld; ld til jnd 13; lost plce qckly 14; poor 4th 3 out; t.o when pu 2 out* . . . . P
1132P Ivans Dream 3-1 L Jefford *Lw; sn prom; cl 3rd 9; 1½l 3rd 14; outpcd & 6l 2nd 16-17; hrd rdn & no imp; 20l 3rd when pu & dism app last* . . . . P
1432¹ Joyful Jade (FR) (5a) 11-8F A Farrant *Opened 5/2; lw; just in tch; 5th ½way; hdwy to cl 4th 13; sn wknd; no ch frm 16; t.o & pu 2 out* . . . . P
1272P Lamerton Quest 66-1 L Rowe *Prom; chsd ldr frm 6 til rdn 10; 5th & rmdrs 12; sn wknd; t.o & pu 14* . . . . P

1384P Persian Dawn (5a) 50-1 S Kidston *Mists 2 & 3; last when pu 4* . . . . P
1436[1] Winnie The Pooh 7-1 Miss M McCarthy *Cl 4th when bd 6* . . . . B

OFFICIAL DISTANCE: 12*l* **TIME:** 6min 10.0s

1544 Intermediate, 12st — 7 ran

1461[1] **STATE MEDLAR** 2-1F **R Woollacott** *Tchd 9/4; ld/disp til ld 7; jnd 12; 2l 2nd 14; r.o wl to chall 16; ld 2 out; drifted lft flat; all out* 1
1352[1] **Menantol** 100-30 **Miss A de Lisle Wells** *Tchd 5s; lw; sn prom; cl 3rd ½way; went 2l 2nd 14; ev ch til no ex frm 2 out.* 3 2
1435[2] **Indiana John (FR)** 11-2 **L Heard** *Lw; hld up towards rr in tightly bunched field; hdwy to 4th 15; 11l 4th 3 out; no ch w ldrs frm nxt; tk 3rd flat* 8 3
1431[4] Silver Man(cp) 15-2 Mrs M Hand *Opened 12s; disp ld to 7; cl 3rd on inner 11; lost plce 14; 14l 5th 3 out; no ch frm nxt* . . . . s hd 4
824[1] Baldara (IRE)(tt) 3-1 A Farrant *Ur & gt loose padd & rn off rnd boxes; hld up; went 4th 11; sltly hmpd 13; cl 3rd & rdn 15; 7l 3rd & one pce 3 out; no ch w ldrs frm 2 out; eased flat* 1½ 5
1198[2] Dear As Saffron (5a) 4-1 W Biddick *14s-4s; hld up in tch; gd hdwy 12; disp ld & gng wl when fell 13; collapsed walking back & gvn oxygen; removed by horse ambulance* . . . . F
1369P Early Morning Call (IRE) 12-1 J Barnes *(xnb) Tchd 14s; cl 4th 10; 6th & wl in tch 12; hmpd bad & ur some way aft 13* . . . . U

OFFICIAL DISTANCES: 4*l*, 6*l* **TIME:** 6min 09.0s

1545 Open Maiden, 12st — 8 ran

1272[3] **TERINO** 5-4F **A Farrant** *Opened 6/4 in plce; lw; sn prom; settled cl 3rd/4th; 4th ½way; gd hdwy 14; jmpd to ld 16; drew clr 2 out; easily* 1
Waddon Hill 6-1 **Richard Darke** *8s-6s; blun 2; last when mist 6; 6th & niggled along ½way; hdwy & hit 14; 12l 3rd 3 out; r.o to 15l 2nd & blun last* . . 20 2
1232R **Can You Talk** 7-1 **L Rowe** *10s-7s; prom; mist 3; 1l 2nd 10; cl 3rd ½way; cl up when blun 15; lost plce; 30l 4th 3 out; fin wl* 2 3
1370[3] Abbey's Girl (IRE) (5a) 6-1 A Glassonbury *10s-6s; ld/disp til slt ld frm 4; ½l up 12; hdd 16; wknd nxt; tired & jmpd lft 2 out; fin tame* 8 4
907r Elegant Apple (5a) 25-1 J Tickle *6l 5th when rmdrs 11; 6th when pu 13.* . P
1134[5] Josanjamic (5a) 9-4 L Heard *Tchd 5-2; prom; disp cl 3rd ½way; cl 2nd when ur 13* . . . . U
1432P Little Lord Lewis (7a) 8-1 C Heard *Mist 1; towards rr when blun & ur 4* . . . U
76F Rush Job 10-1 W Biddick *Prom when fell 5; rmtd; cont t.o til rn past 13; cont without rtrcng & jmpd all fncs* . . . . R

OFFICIAL DISTANCES: dist, 1*l* **TIME:** 6min 33.0s

1546 Hunts Members (with Tetcott), 12st

328[3] **SMOKEY JOE (IRE) Miss M McCarthy** *Walked over.* 1

Pembrokeshire

Trecoed (RH 7F,18J)

Sat, 5 Jun (GOOD to FIRM)

1547 Hunt Members, 12st — 5 ran

732[13] **ROYAL BARGE**(tt) 1-3F **M Barber** *Jmpd sltly rt; ld 1 & frm 7; 8l clr 13; 30l ahd 15; unchall; hvly eased flat* 1
1394[3] **Ladygal (IRE)** (12a) 6-1 **D Davies** *Mists & rdr waving; last to 6; 3rd when hit 11; lft 2nd aft nxt; 8l 2nd 13; t.o 15* 30 2
1525P **Wiston Wizo**(bl) 8-1 **Miss I Tompsett** *(xnb) Clsd to ld 6-7; drvn & lost tch 11; 40l 3rd 15; rdr nvr stpd trying* 25 3
1524[4] Tiger Rag (5a) 10-1 M Lewis *(xnb) Tde; keen early; ld aft 1-6; last when jmpd slow 7; t.o 10; fnce bhnd 3 out* 35 4
Barafundle Bay 12-1 P Sheldrake *(xnb) Bckwd; cl up til 2nd 8-12; v reluct to rce bend bef nxt & sn t.o; pu 3 out (gurgled 3 times).* . . . . P

OFFICIAL DISTANCES: dist, 30*l* **TIME:** 6min 22.0s

1548 Restricted, 12st — 5 ran

1534[1] **WELLHESEEMEDSOLOW (IRE)** evensF **L Stephens** *4th frm 2; hit 7; clsd to 2nd 13; hit nxt; ld 15 & sn clr; 12l ahd 2 out; eased flat.* 1
1487[1] **Sumerian Lad** 5-1 **J Sole** *Hit 4; chsd ldr to 12; wkng when blun & nrly ur nxt; 15l 3rd 14; mist 3 out; hrd rdn frm nxt; went 2nd past dozing rival final strides* 20 2
1538[P] **Drom Island** (5a) 10-1 **Miss F Wilson** *Settled 3rd; ld 12-15; imm outpcd; 20l clr of rnr-up 2 out but eased flat & dem.* 1/2 3
1531[6] Hydemilla (5a) 20-1 M Wall *(xnb) Ld; 8l clr 5; niggled & hdd 12; sn last; t.o 3 out; fell last; rmtd* .... runin 4
1524[1] Countess Kiri (5a) 7-4 R Burton *Jmpd slow; last frm 2; 15l down 9; t.o when jmpd slow nxt; pu 13* .... P

OFFICIAL DISTANCES: 25*l*, nk **TIME:** 6min 18.0s

1549 Mens Open, 12st — 5 ran

1514[3] **MISTER PEPPER (IRE)** 5-1 **T Underwood** *8s-5s; hld up in detach last; clsd aft 11; ev ch frm 14; ld app 2 out; sn clr; rdly* 1
1522[2] **Khatani (IRE)** (7x)(tt) evensF **L Stephens** *Settled 3rd til 2nd 12; rdn to ld app 2 out; sn hdd & outpcd* 6 2
1520[1] **Red Neck** (4x)(tt) 5-4 **T Vaughan** *(xnb) Trckd ldrs; jmpd slow 8; rdn 12; 6l 4th aft jmpd slow 14; nvr gng wl enough aft; tk 3rd aft 2 out* 2 3
1520[2] Harppy (FR)(bl) 25-1 D Jones *(xnb) Bit bckwd; ld 4 til rdn & hdd app 2 out; gave up qckly* 4 4
1521[2] Rathgibbon (IRE) 14-1 James Price *Ld to 4; chsd ldr til drvn 12; last & strugg nxt; plodded on* 20 5

OFFICIAL DISTANCES: 7*l*, 2*l* **TIME:** 6min 12.0s

1550 Open Maiden 56&7yo, 12st — 5 ran

1393[2] **RESCINDO (IRE)** (7a)(vis) 5-4F **W Oakes** *Hld up last to 12; 2nd nxt; rdn to ld 2 out; fnd little in front* 1
1524[2] **Clarice Starling** (5a) 5-1 **D Jones** *(boh) Tk keen hld; settled cl up; sltly outpcd 15 & 6l 3rd nxt; rallied app last; drvn & kpt on flat* 1½ 2
1488[2] **Capacoostic** (5a) 2-1 **R Burton** *Ld 3 til hdd & blun 2 out; tired rap; mod 3rd when mist last* 12 3
1533[4] Maloney (IRE) 16-1 Miss C Evans *Reared & fell padd; ld to 3; cl up til last & rdn aft 12; strugg when hit 14; went poor 4th 2 out* 25 4
1533[P] Spicey Case (12a) 7-1 J Cook *Chsd ldr 5-13; lost tch nxt; eased in last frm 2 out; t.o* 12 5

OFFICIAL DISTANCES: 2*l*, 7*l* **TIME:** 6min 20.0s

1551 Ladies Open — 8 ran

1537[2] **DOC RYAN'S** 16-1 **Mrs C Owen** *Settled towards rr; 4th & eff 13; cl 2nd 15 til ld aft 2 out; sn rdn clr* 1
1536[S] **Silver Castle** 2-1 **Mrs L Rowsell** *Swtng; cl up; went 2nd 7; hit 10; ld 14; mist 2 out & hdd; drvn & wknd app last* 10 2
1298[4] **Phar From Chance** 2-1 **Miss P Gundry** *(xnb) Ld 1; sn towards rr; niggled aft 11; went 3rd 13; rdn & outpcd 15; plugged on* 6 3
1497[2] Supercharmer 7-4F Miss A Armitage *Ld aft 1-14; rdn nxt; 3½l 3rd 3 out; strugg aft* 15 4
1146[3] China Lal (5a) 20-1 Mrs K Diggle *Midfield; 3rd brief aft 11; wknd 14; sn wl btn* 2½ 5
1493[3] Solo Gent 25-1 Miss K Jones *Bckwd; swtng; 2nd/3rd to 7; last aft 11; sn t.o* .... runin 6
1519[1] Berkeley Frontier (IRE)(tt) 25-1 Mrs E Jones *Midfield; drpd to rr 10; lost tch qckly app 13; pu 14* .... P
1519[2] Chief Gale (IRE) 66-1 Mrs M Stephens *Lost 15l start; unable to raise gallop & hopeless t.o til pu 7* .... P

OFFICIAL DISTANCES: 8*l*, 4*l* **TIME:** 6min 02.0s

1552 Intermediate, 12st — 5 ran

1521[1] **LIKE THE BUZZ (IRE)** (5a) 9-2 **J Cook** *Settled handy; eff to ld 15; 5l clr 2 out; ploughed thro last; kpt on wl* 1
1539[2] **Hail Stone (IRE)** 12-1 **L Stephens** *Rdn most of way; ld 6-7; 2nd aft 12; releg 4th 15; rallied to 2nd nxt; drvn & a hld* 2 2

1517[1]	**Darkarrow (IRE)** 8-1 **T Underwood** *(xnb) Last when jmpd slow 2; nrly fell 8; 4l last aft 12; ld 14-15; wkng when mist 3 out; sn strugg u.p*	12	3
1482[1]	Aljoash (IRE) (5a) 9-4 T Vaughan *(bf) Made virt all to 14; lost plce qckly to poor last 3 out*	25	4
1531[1]	Sabena Canyon 5-4F R Burton *Hld up & cl up; 3rd when ducked out 13*		R

OFFICIAL DISTANCES: 2*l*, 12*l* **TIME:** 6min 14.0s

1553 Open Maiden 8yo&up, 12st — 6 ran

1239[3]	**IMUSTGETON** (5a) 8-1 **D Davies** *(xnb) Swtng; went 3rd 6; lft 2nd 13; mists aft; ld app 2 out; sn clr; collapsed aft rce*		1
1534[2]	**Millenium Run (IRE)** 11-8F **J Cook** *Mists; last frm 8; 15l adrift & v idle aft 12; some late prog & went poor 2nd at last*	15	2
1488[P]	**Classic Fable (IRE)** (5a) 11-2 **A Hanly** *Made most til aft 12; lft in ld 13; hdd u.p app 2 out; sn wknd; pckd last & lost 2nd*	4	3
1534[4]	Evans The Coal 4-1 R Burton *Stdd 12l bhnd; last to 8; pushed up to ld 9-11 & aft 12 til terrible blun & ur 13*		U
1488[P]	Its Mr Blobby(cp) 5-2 T Vaughan *(xnb,orbs) Prom til rdn & lost plce 6; 5th & just in tch when pu 12*		P
1495[P]	Portway Sadie (5a) 20-1 M Wall *Cl up; 2½l 3rd 14; stpd to nil & staggered over nxt & pu*		P

OFFICIAL DISTANCES: 10*l*, 3*l* **TIME:** 6min 25.0s

Tiverton Staghounds

Bratton Down (LH 8F,19J)
Sun, 6 Jun (FIRM)

1554 Hunt Members — 7 ran

1466[1]	**HARNAGE (IRE)** 4-1 **Miss C Prouse** *6s-4s; ld to 3; 2nd to 7; 12l 3rd 12; rallied 15 to ld aft nxt; drew rt away app 2 out; rdn out*		1
1510[F]	**Stepasideboy** 4-1 **G Weatherley** *6s-4s; hld up; went 2nd 7; rdn 15; chall & ld brief nxt; chsd wnr vain frm 3 out*	15	2
1506[2]	**Magical Fun (IRE)** 12-1 **Miss T Hayes** *(xnb) Midfield; 13l 4th 12; 3rd 15; 9l 4th 3 out; sn wknd; snatched 3rd*	5	3
1506[1]	Jentar Equilibra (IRE) (5a) 4-5F J Barnes *(xnb) 6/4-4/5; jmpd rt at times; ld & hit 3; 8l clr 9-12; jb rt 16 & hdd; wknd rap; lost 3rd nr fin; lame*	s hd	4
1465[U]	Another Bula (IRE) 16-1 Miss J Buck *Tde; bhnd; rdr nrly f.o 3; 15l 6th 8; 25l 5th 12; t.o 13*	20	5
	Daktari (U) (3ow) 66-1 R Williams *(xnb) T.o aft 3; sn furlongs bhnd*	2fncs	6
1268[5]	Aller Coombe (5a) 8-1 L Jefford *Fat; sn bhnd; 6th & strugg 10; t.o & pu aft 13*		P

OFFICIAL DISTANCES: 25*l*, 8*l* **TIME:** 6min 01.1s

1555 Intermediate, 12st — 8 ran

1508[3]	**CIMMAROON (IRE)** (7a) 11-10F **A Farrant** *(xnb) Swtng; hld up midfield; jmpd slow 6; went 3rd/4th 8 til jmpd ahd 16; drvn clr aft last*		1
1498[P]	**Hold On Harry** 3-1 **L Heard** *Tchd 5s; tk keen hld & prom in chsng group; went 2nd 9; clsd 12 to ld aft 14 til jb rt 16; chsd wnr aft; hrd rdn & ev ch last; outpcd final furlong*	6	2
1382[5]	**Sherbourne Guest (IRE)** 25-1 **J Kwiatkowski** *Ld til jmpd slow 2; sn rr; 15l last 12; t.o 3 out; plugged into 3rd*	40	3
1507[1]	Mrs Peggoty (5a)(bl,tt) 16-1 Miss C Tizzard *Lft in ld 2-4; drpd back 6th 10; nrly ur 11; strugg when hit 13; t.o when blun last*	12	4
1545[R]	Rush Job 25-1 W Biddick *Stdd start; novicey in last pr 10; lost tch 13; t.o when jmpd v slow 3 out*	15	5
1365[3]	Caundle Chase 6-1 W White *Midfield; outpcd 13; 5th 16; some prog in 17l 3rd when fell 2 out*		F

Form	Entry	Dist	Pos
1363[U]	Th'moons A Balloon (IRE)(bl,tt) 6-1 S Partridge *8s-6s; tk str hld; rushed up to ld 4; missed marker aft 7; cont without rtrcng; 10l clr 8-10; hdd aft 14; wknd qckly app 3 out; fin 5l ahd of the last finisher; rdr fined*		R
1508[2]	Timpani (IRE)(cp) 9-2 R Woollacott *(xnb) Tchd 5s; midfield; hdwy to disp 3rd frm 8; 3l 3rd 14; wknd qckly 16; rem when pu 2 out*		P

OFFICIAL DISTANCES: 6*l*, dist **TIME:** 6min 03.7s

Th'moons A Balloon finished the course but had missed a marker before the seventh fence; the rider was fined £75 for continuing in the race without retracing

1556 Mixed Open, 12st — 9 ran

Form	Entry	Dist	Pos
1542[2]	**LET'S FLY (FR)** 5-1 **W Biddick** *Opened 6s; a ldng trio; ld 4-6, 10-16 & agn nxt; lft 2l clr 2 out; in comm til idled inside final furlong & drvn along; fnd ex nr fin*		1
1454[1]	**Colquhoun** 4-6F **A Farrant** *(xnb) Opened 4/5; nt fluent; bhnd to 9; quick move in 2nd 12; ld 16-nxt; w wnr when blun 2 out & lost 2l; rallied u.p inside final furlong & lkd dangerous; no imp cl home*	1¼	2
1485[1]	**Wend's Day (IRE)**(tt) 7-2 **M Hooper** *Tchd 4s; sn bhnd; 6th & in tch 12; hit bale aft nxt & lost tch; blun 15; rem 3 out; kpt on past strugglers*	20	3
1437[5]	Knock Star (IRE) 25-1 S Partridge *Midfield; drpd to rr 12; outpcd 14; 37l 4th 3 out*	4	4
1508[1]	Romany Move 20-1 Mrs S Godfrey *Settled 3rd/4th; outpcd aft 13; rem frm 16*	hd	5
1441[7]	Woodlands Beau (IRE) 16-1 D Drake *Ld to 4; jmpd slow 8; 5th 12; outpcd & mist 14; rem frm 16*	2½	6
1351[1]	Lingering Fog (IRE) 10-1 Miss M McCarthy *Prom; ld 6-10; prom til 5l 3rd & outpcd 16; wknd bad app 2 out; fin v lame*	6	7
1464[1]	Mister Rf (IRE) 50-1 R Isgar *Swtng; last pr & rdr most ungainly; nrly f.o 11; t.o 15*	10	8
1492[2]	Mr Ben Gunn 20-1 Miss V Heal *(xnb) Rn out & ur 3*		R

OFFICIAL DISTANCES: ½*l*, 6*l* **TIME:** 6min 07.4s

1557 Confined — 5 ran

Form	Entry	Dist	Pos
1446[1]	**I AM SAID I (IRE)** (7x) 1-4F **A Farrant** *(xnb) Tchd 1/3; handy; jmpd slow 6; nt fluent 7; tried to rn out 8 & last brief; ld 15 & sn 8l clr; 15l ahd 2 out; hrd drvn & slowing bad inside final furlong; all out; lame*		1
1540[4]	**Millyhenry** 10-1 **Miss C Tizzard** *Ld to 4; sn niggled along; cl up til wnr qcknd clr aft 15; 15l down when hit 2 out; rdn & plugged on & catching wnr quite qckly final 100yds*	2	2
1510[P]	**Khayal (USA)** 7-1 **Miss R Green** *Cl up; ld 11-12 & 14-15; no ch w wnr frm nxt; 18l 3rd 2 out; plodded on*	15	3
1506[S]	Happy Team (5a) 5-1 R Ross *Tchd 6s; made nrly all 4-14; outpcd nxt; 4th & fdng when mist & ur 3 out*		U
1543[P]	Persian Dawn (5a) 50-1 S Kidston *Bckwd; nrly a last; u.p 11; 11th aft 13; pu 16*		P

OFFICIAL DISTANCES: 4*l*, 20*l* **TIME:** 6min 06.4s

1558 Restricted, 12st — 8 ran

Form	Entry	Dist	Pos
1268[P]	**PORTO (IRE)**(tt) 9-2 **N Harris** *(xnb) 10s-9/2; tk keen hld; ld; 7l clr 9; hrd prsd 12 til hdd 16; lkd wl btn 2 out; urged & rallied final furlong; passed stpng ldr 50yds out*		1
1491[2]	**River Dante (IRE)**(vis) 5-2 **S Kidston** *Opened 3s; handy; chsd ldr most frm 9; chall 12; ld 16; drew 20l clr 3 out; drvn & dogged it furiously final furlong; hdd final 50yds*	4	2
1365[U]	**Nice Approach (IRE)** 12-1 **Miss V Murphy** *Lost tch 5; t.o 8; plugged into rem 3rd 16*	30	3
1543[P]	Gayble 4-1 W Biddick *Opened 5s; tk keen hld; mist 7; mostly 2nd to 11; 8l 3rd nxt; lost tch aft bad mist 13; wl t.o 4th 16; fin lame*	65	4
1543[P]	Lamerton Quest(bl,tt) 66-1 L Rowe *Awkward padd; midfield; lost tch 9; 20l 6th & drvn 12; v reluct frm 14 but forced on; hopelessly t.o 16*	15	5
1507[2]	Askers Jack 6-4F J Snowden *2s(in plce)-6/4; mists; impd to 3rd 7 til blun 8; 13l 4th & rdn when mist 12; saddle slpd rt round bend aft nxt; ur 14*		U

1098[r] Dubious Deal 66-1 R Woollacott *(kineton) Pulled hrd; prom til slpd up turn aft 5; horse bad inj hind legs* . . . . . . S
1435[4] Wicked Imp 8-1 M Munrowd *Jmpd slow 1; 6th & strugg 9; rem 4th when pu 13* P

OFFICIAL DISTANCES: 5*l*, dist **TIME:** 6min 08.9s

Golden Sovereign (D Edwards, 25-1, at start; vet's advice) and Winnie The Pooh (5-2, A Farrant, rdr dehydrated) were both withdrawn not under orders; Rule 4 deduction 30p in pound on bets struck before withdrawal

1559 Open Maiden, 12st — 11 ran

1467[2] **SPINNING SILVER** 14-1 **M Woodward** *(xnb) Stdd start & lost 20l; rcd keen & ld app 4; 2l up 2 out; rdn & drew clr flat* 1
1532[6] **The Footsy** 10-1 **G Barfoot-Saunt** *(xnb) Tchd 11s; ld 2 til app 4; cont 2nd/3rd; blun bad 8; mist 10; 2l 2nd & rdn 2 out; wknd last; dem flat; fin slow in 3rd; subsq promoted* 14½ 2
1495[4] **Queens House** (5a) 6-1 **Miss R Green** *Hld up til eff in 4th 12; 3l 3rd 14; wknd 16; 9l 4th 2 out; fdd; subsq promoted* 4 3
1511[4] Good Gracious 8-1 Miss L Gardner *Jmpd poor in midfield; impd to 2nd brief 10; 5th 12; lost tch & jmpd slow 16; 30l 6th 2 out* 15 5
1466[2] Hayling Star (5a)(bl,tt) 14-1 M Sweetland *Ld to 2; made several terrible js & sn rr; 10l last 12; blun nxt 2; 40l last 3 out* 10 6
1450[P] Aftermeyourfirst 11-2 G Weatherley *(xnb) Tchd 6s; ch ride; hld up & nt jw; went 3rd/4th 9 til lost plce 14; nrly fell 15 & strugg aft; jmpd slow nxt; 10l 5th 2 out; fdd bad & t.o* 5 7
1380[P] National Debt 3-1 R Woollacott *Opened 4s; nt fluent; midfield; jmpd slow 6; 6th 12; saddle slpd 16; eff & cl up 14 til outpcd 3 out; plugged into 12l 2nd flat; disq - nt draw correct weight (lost weights on run-in)* 2d
143[P] Lothian Emerald (5a)(tt) 16-1 J Snowden *Nrly ref 1 & releg to last pr; blun & ur 5* . . . . . . U
1380[U] Silver Image 10-1 M Dennis *Bckwd; 2 handlers; sn labouring in rr; t.o when nrly ref 8 & pu aft* . . . . . . P
1327[P] Six Of Tother 12-1 J Barnes *Tchd 14s; rr & oft jb; mist 11 & lost tch; pu 12* P
1511[2] Sup Of Tea (IRE) 2-1F A Charles-Jones *3rd when blun bad & ur 7* . . . . . . U

OFFICIAL DISTANCES: Originally 15*l*, 6*l* **TIME:** 6min 26.5s

National Debt finished second but was disqualified when the rider was unable to draw the correct weight (had lost weight-cloth on run-in); no fine was imposed

Torrington Farmers

Umberleigh (LH 6F,18J)

Sat, 12 Jun (GOOD to FIRM - mechanically lifted - with stretch of arable)

1560 Confined — 2 ran

1557[3] **KHAYAL (USA)** 3-1 **Miss R Green** *Jmpd rt; made all; 4l clr 12; jnd app 2 out til jmpd much btr last; r.o wl* 1
1540[1] **Squaddie** 1-4F **A Farrant** *Opened 2/5; settled 3l off rival; mist 13; hrd rdn to chall aft 3 out; ev ch when outj last; nt qckn* 2½ 2

OFFICIAL DISTANCE: 2*l* **TIME:** 6min 37.1s

1561 Restricted, 12st — 8 ran

1554[1] **HARNAGE (IRE)** evensF **Miss C Prouse** *Tchd 5/4; ld til stdd downhill aft 12; 4l 3rd 14; qcknd to ld aft 3 out; sn clr; quite impressive* 1
1558[U] **Askers Jack** 7-2 **J Snowden** *Tchd 4s; chsd wnr 4-7; went 2nd aft 10; ev ch 3 out; sn brushed aside* 12 2
1554[5] **Another Bula (IRE)** 50-1 **Miss J Buck** *Tde; hld up; 2nd/3rd 7-12; lost plce & 9l 5th 14; no ch aft* 15 3
1531[2] Jolly Jake 3-1 E Walker *(xnb) 5s-3s; 2 handlers; prom; 2½l 4th ½way; 5l 4th when jmpd slow 14; sn rdn & outpcd; went 15l 3rd app 2 out; no imp.* . . hd 4
1548[3] Drom Island (5a) 11-1 Miss F Wilson *Tchd 5/4; hld up; last to 4; stdy hdwy & disp 2½l 4th ½way; ld aft 12 til hdd aft 3 out; stpd to nil; t.o & virt pu flat* 15 5
1558[3] Nice Approach (IRE) 33-1 Miss V Murphy *2 handlers; last pr to 10; 9l 6th ½way; wl bhnd 13; t.o* 1½ 6

1433^{4} Change 28-1 T Dennis *(xnb) Jmpd v slow & drpd to rr 4; blun 6; 11l 7th ½way; bhnd til pu aft 12.* . . . P

1543^{P} Cut Down The Sound (IRE) 12-1 A Charles-Jones *Tchd 14s; 2nd/3rd til lost plce 7; sn rdn & no resp; mist 8; 13l last ½way; bhnd when pu 11.* . . . P

OFFICIAL DISTANCES: 15*l*, 10*l* **TIME:** 6min 14.3s

1562 Mens Open, 12st - 16J — 5 ran

1276^{1} **PRATE BOX (IRE)** 4-1 **F Hutsby** *Ld to 2; lft 2nd 4; mist & rmdrs 11; outpcd & dem aft 12; went 3l 2nd 14; ld app 2 out; 5l clr last; rdn out* . . . 1

1554^{2} **Stepasideboy** 11-1 **G Weatherley** *(bh) Jmpd sticky; hld up; hdwy 8; 5l 3rd ½way; went 2nd aft 12; lft in ld nxt; jmpd slow 14 & 15; hdd app 2 out; kpt on wl flat.* . . . 1¾ 2

1510^{2} Ballysicyos (FR) (7x) 4-9F A Farrant *(xnb,bh) Tchd 1/2; 2nd til lft in ld 4; mist 9; shkn up aft 12; blun & hdd nxt; releg last 14; wknd aft omitted 3 out; pu nxt.* . . . P

1529^{5} Jimmy Jumbo (IRE) (4x) 7-1 N Cecil *(xnb) Tde; ld 2 til rn out thro wing & ur 4* R

1556^{8} Mister Rf (IRE) 50-1 R Isgar *Swtng; a bhnd; 30l last ½way; t.o & pu 13* . . P

OFFICIAL DISTANCE: 2*l* **TIME:** 6min 09.6s

Fences 10 & 16 omitted - damaged

1563 Ladies Open — 8 ran

1549^{2} **KHATANI (IRE)**(tt) 8-1 **Mrs L Rowsell** *Hld up; hdwy 8; 2½l 3rd ½way; went 2nd aft 12-14; lft in ld 3 out; 5l clr at last; rdn out* . . . 1

1502^{1} **Campden Kitty** (5a) 13-8F **Miss J Williams** *7/2-13/8,tchd 6/4; ld til app 5; went 2nd 7 til aft 12; 3½l 4th 14; 2nd agn & ev ch app 2 out; one pce* 2½ 2

1448^{1} **Epicure (FR)** 7-2 **Mrs O Jackson** *(xnb) 9/2-7/2; stdd start; last to 8; 7l 5th ½way; hdwy 12; went 2nd 14; lft w ev ch 3 out; wknd nxt; mist last*. . . 8 3

1542^{4} Delaware (FR) 25-1 Miss P Gundry *50s-25s; 2nd to 7; 5l 4th & pushed along ½way; 6l 5th & drvn along 14; nt r.o* . . . 35 4

1509^{1} Guru Rinpoche 14-1 Miss L Gardner *(bf) Swtng; jmpd slow 2 & 3; 5th when ur 4* . . . U

1494^{2} Kingsbridge (IRE) 25-1 Miss L Bridges *(xnb) Pulled hrd; ld app 5 til ducked out, hit wing & ur 3 out*. . . . R

1463^{1} Red Native (IRE)(bl) 2-1 Miss R Green *7/2-2s; hld up; 7th when hmpd & ur 4* U

1492^{4} Steve Ford 150-1 Miss E Harbour *Mist 1; mist & releg last 8; lost tch & pu 12; lame*. . . . P

OFFICIAL DISTANCES: 3*l*, 10*l* **TIME:** 6min 09.6s

1564 Intermediate, 12st — 3 ran

1491^{1} **HAWKERS HILL** evensJF **Miss A Goschen** *Swtng; 2nd to 3 & frm 7; ld aft 10-15; ld 3 out; 6l clr nxt; stdd to tk last; drvn out* . . . 1

1544^{2} **Menantol** evensJF **Miss A de Lisle Wells** *5/4-evens; went 2nd 3; ld 5-6; last nxt til jmpd to ld 10; sn hdd; releg last 13; went 2nd & outpcd aft 3 out; rallied u.p aft nxt; stayed on flat*. . . . ½ 2

1555^{3} **Sherbourne Guest (IRE)** 8-1 **J Kwiatkowski** *Tchd 9s; ld to 5; ld 6; pckd 8; hdd 10; 2l last ½way; mist 11; chsd wnr 13; ld 15-3 out; sn btn; mist last* . 12 3

OFFICIAL DISTANCES: nk, 3*l* **TIME:** 6min 23.2s

1565 Open Maiden (Div 1), 12st — 8 ran

1545^{U} **JOSANJAMIC** (5a) evensF **L Heard** *6/4-evens; hld up; hdwy & 5l 3rd ½way; went 2nd 11; ld 14; drew rt away frm 3 out; easily*. . . . 1

1518^{3} **Carvilla (IRE)** 9-1 **C Gordon** *Tchd 10s; ld 1; jmpd slow 9; hdd 14; mist 15; sn caved in* . . . 30 2

1559^{6} **Hayling Star** (5a) 33-1 **A Charles-Jones** *Mounted on course; tde; jmpd delib; 2nd to 5; lft 5l 2nd 10-11; 12l 3rd 14; sn wl bhnd* . . . 2½ 3

1545^{4} Abbey's Girl (IRE) (5a) 14-1 A Glassonbury *Tchd 16s; jmpd delib; a bhnd; rdn & no resp 7; pu 9*. . . . P

1558^{5} Lamerton Quest(bl,tt) 50-1 J Cole *Prom; went 2nd 5; mists 8 & 9; leather broke & dem 10; pu 11*. . . . P

1370^{P} Pebble Dasher (5a) 12-1 R Woollacott *(xnb) Pulled up lame aft 1* . . . P

1532^{3} Red Spark 6-1 E Walker *(xnb) A bhnd; 12l last ½way; t.o & pu 2 out* . . . P

1525^{3} Star Of William (IRE) (7a) 2-1 T Vaughan *(xnb) Tchd 5/2; ld til hdd & fell 1* F

OFFICIAL DISTANCES: dist, 4*l* **TIME:** 6min 21.0s

1566 Open Maiden (Div 2), 12st — 8 ran

637^{F} **VITINSEL** (5a)(tt) 10-1 **J Snowden** *Lft in ld 1; hdd 9; 2nd til blun 13; 2l 3rd nxt; ld app 2 out; sn clr.* 1

1550^{4} **Maloney (IRE)** 3-1 **Miss C Evans** *Tchd 4s; chsd wnr 2-9; 2l 3rd ½way; 5l 4th & outpcd 14; rdn 3 out; went 7l 3rd nxt & 10l 2nd last; no imp* 20 2

1323^{2} **Beehive Lad** 2-1 **J Sole** *(bf) 8s-2s; hld up; hdwy 7; ld 9 til aft 3 out; sn wknd* 3 3

1534^{3} Just Caramel (5a)(tt) 7-4F James Tudor *Opened 2s; ld til jmpd slow 1; 2½l 4th ½way; went 2nd 14; ld aft 3 out; sn hdd; wknd u.p nxt* . . . . . . ½ 4

1507^{R} Golden Sovereign 7-1 A Charles-Jones *(xnb,bh) 14s-7s; hld up; 7l last ½way; lost tch 12; t.o & pu 3 out* . . . . . . P

1370^{F} Horsemans Green(cp) 16-1 D Edwards *(xnb) Swtng; hld up; mist 10; 5l 6th ½way; disp 7l 4th & rdn when blun 3 out; sn wknd; wl bhnd when pu last* P

1559^{3} Queens House (5a) 5-1 Miss R Green *Tchd 6s; jnd ldrs 5; 3½l 5th ½way; mist 12; disp 5l 4th 14; wknd 15; t.o & pu last.* . . . . . . P

318^{P} Silver Kracker 20-1 M Woodward *Drpd to rr 5; sn reluct & lost tch; t.o & pu 8* P

OFFICIAL DISTANCES: 15*l*, 2*l* **TIME:** 6min 37.0s

Runners

An alphabetical list of all the horses that raced in Hunter Chases and Point-to-Points in 2004 together with a list of Handicap Ratings for all horses with measurable form

How to Read the Form

The description of each horse commences with details of age (from January 1st 2005), colour and sex. All male animals have been assumed to be geldings in the absence of definite knowledge to the contrary. Complete details of pedigree are given for all except unregistered horses (when any part of the pedigree is omitted it is non-thoroughbred or not registered). The latter, indicated by the abbreviation (U) after their name, may run only in Members races and such details of age and breeding as have appeared on racecards are given for them.

b	brought down	**R**	ran out
c	carried out	**s**	slipped up
d	disqualified (after finishing position)	**u**	unseated rider
f	fell	**v**	void
p	pulled up	**w**	withdrawn under orders
r	refused, took no part		

Form figures in italics refer to races, other than Hunter Chases, under NH Rules from 1st February 2004 to the end of the Point-to-Point season.

A synopsis of the horses previous racing history under all Rules, together with that of the dam and near relatives where notable, follows a brief physical description. When relative's names are given without qualification (*ie* flat winner, Hurdles winner, etc.) they have at some time appeared in *Hunter Chasers & Point-to-Pointers* (back editions of the Annual are available from Weatherbys Chase.

Past form details are given thus

FLAT r4 w1 (12f) p1 (2nd) = ran four times on flat, won once (at 12 furlongs) and placed once (second).

NH '80/2 r6 w1 (2m Ch) p2 = ran six times under National Hunt rules from 1980 to 1982, won once (a two mile Chase) and placed twice.

P-t-P/HUNT CH '82 r12 w2 (Maiden and Restricted) p6 = ran 12 times in Point-to-Point or hunter chases in 1982, won a Maiden and a Restricted Open and placed six times.

All Sales prices are in guineas unless otherwise stated.

Many' details will, of course, remain unchanged from year to year and pressure of space necessitates some abbreviation and omission. Generally the most comprehensive histories will be given in the horse's first season of Point-to-Pointing.

All races are run over three miles unless specifically stated otherwise. The following abbreviations have been used for races under NH Rules:

Amat	Amateur Riders	**HCap**	Handicap	**Nov**	Novices
Ch	Chase	**Hdle**	Hurdle	**Opp**	Opportunity
Condit	Conditions	**Mdn**	Maiden	**Sell**	Seller

The owner's name and the qualifying Hunt(s) complete the description followed by the trainer's name or qualifying livery yard, where applicable, and finally the numbers and types of races in which the horse appeared. Owners and trainers are not officially recorded and we cannot guarantee the accuracy of this information. The following race type abbreviations or combinations are used:

C	Club Members	**L**	Ladies Open	**N**	Novices
Cf	Confined	**m**	Mares	**NCM**	Natural Country Members
CL	Ladies Members	**M**	Members	**nr**	Novice Riders
CO	Gentlemen Member	**Ma**	Maiden	**O**	Mens Opens
H	Hunter Chase	**MO**	Mixed Open	**R**	Restricted
I	Intermediate	**Mod**	Moderate	**Vet**	Veteran Horses

These abbreviations are prefixed by the race distance for races not run over three miles. The corresponding races with detailed comments-in-running can be found in the Results section.

HANDICAP MARKS, where merited, appear after the horse's names. These are expressed as weights in stones and pounds, and are derived directly from Geoffrey Sale's original Handicap first published in 1959, but based on work going back several years previously. They are intended to represent the merit of the horse at the beginning of 2005, but should give a valuable guide to racing throughout the season. Some ratings include the symbols which means ungenerous or unreliable — cannot be relied on to do its best or run up to its rating, and — totally ungenuine — unrateable and to be avoided.

As the season progresses some horses will be seen to have improved, some to have deteriorated, and new horses will appear and the Handicap is updated accordingly. The new and revised ratings are issued in Weekly and Fortnightly Supplements which may be obtained from Weatherbys Chase, (*qv* advertisement inside rear cover).

MODIFYING THE RATINGS

The higher the handicap mark given, the better is the previous form. If all the handicap marks are listed for all the runners in a level weight race, the highest-rated will have the best chance on previous form, though due consideration must be given to any qualifying remarks given in the Annual regarding going preferences, riders, etc.

Where a horse has incurred a penalty his chance is theoretically diminished in comparison with the others by the amount of the penalty, whilst an allowance increases the animal's chance. In practice, the good horses are usually capable of giving more weight to their opponents in Point-to-Points than would be expected — class tells.

Point-to-Points

It is therefore suggested that Handicap Marks (ratings) should be reduced for Point-to-Point penalties, on the following scale:

penalty	deduction
1lb — 4lb	0
5lb — 9lb	1
10lb — 14lb	2

Hunter Chases

Deductions in Hunter Chases should be greater, since the task is more testing and the following scale should be applied:

penalty	deduction	penalty	deduction
1lb	1lb	**5lb**	3lb
2lb	2lb	**6lb**	4lb
3lb	2lb	**7lb**	4lb
4lb	3lb		

and for higher penalties 4lb should be deducted from the rating for each whole 7lb extra carried and to scale for any balance. Overweights should be treated in the same way.

Dealing with Allowances. The ratings are calculated including the seven pounds allowance for five-year-olds and the five pounds allowance for mares. No adjustment is therefore required in Point-to-Points, but a discrepancy arises when these horses run in Hunter Chases. To correct any anomaly, we recommend that for Hunter Chases only:

3lb should be deducted from the ratings of mares aged six years and over
4lb should be deducted from the ratings of five-year-old geldings
7lb should be deducted from the ratings of five-year-old mares

before any further adjustments are made.

All horses carrying more weight than the lowest-weighted are considered to be carrying a penalty of the difference and their ratings modified using the above table. An example of this is given below.

Having worked out the top-rated horses in this fashion, the comments on each horse in the Annual must be checked to discover any other factors that might affect the result. Despite the small profit which might accrue from blindly backing the top-rated, the discriminating punter using his own discretion to decide between the top few horses will be much more successful.

BANGOR — Friday 30th April 2004

11176 JAMES GRIFFITH MEMORIAL NOVICES HUNTER CHASE

	Original Handicap Rating	Actual Weight Carried	Weight Carried in excess of Bottom Weight	Adjustment Necessary (from table)	Revised Handicap Rating	Fate
JUST CLIQUOT (mare)	10-5*	11-06	0	0	10-5	1
COOLE VENTURE (IRE)	10-8	12-00	+8lb	-5	10-3	2
THE VINTAGE DANCER (IRE)	10-1	11-07	+1lb	-1	10-0	3
RAISEAPEARL	10-2	11-07	+1lb	-1	10-1	4
CATECHIST (IRE)	10-0	12-00	+8lb	-5	9-9	5
ROBERT THE RASCAL	9-5	11-08	+2lb	-2	9-3	6
BEACHCOMBER	9-2	11-07	+1lb	-1	9-1	7
STRONG KING (IRE)	8-13	11-07	+1lb	-1	8-12	8
MISTER FALCON (FR)	9-8	11-07	+1lb	-1	9-7	9
BE BOP BENTLEY	7-6	11-07	+1lb	-1	7-5	U
JACKSON (FR)	10-1	12-00	+8lb	-5	9-9	U

* reduced from 10-8 because of mares allowance (see above)

Just Cliquot (top-rated at a modified 10-5) won by ½l from Coole Venture (second top-rated at a modified 10-3) with The Vintage Dancer (4th top-rated at 10-0) 6l away in third, just a head in front of Raiseapearl (third top-rated at a modified 10-1).

The winner was returned at 5-2 (Tote £3.40), the Computer Straight Forecast paid £10.71, and the Tote Exacta £6.90.

ABABOU (FR) ..10-4.. 9 ch.g. Synefos (USA) — Racine Carree (FR) (Dom Racine FR) 11p3. Tall rangy. FRENCH NH '99/00 r12 p0; pulled up 2. P-t-P/HUNT CH '02/3 r8 w5 (inc Open) p1 (2nd); 6th and pulled up. Completed a Pointing six-timer when retaining his Members title with the expected minimum of fuss, and overcame some uncharacteristically sloppy fencing when successful in a Market Rasen Hunter Chase. Disappointed in a more competitive event there next time and had his speed blunted by the strong gallop set by the runner-up in his bid to extend his winning sequence when returned to Points. Can front run or come from behind, but has looked ill at ease on a sound surface, and averages only four outings per annum since leaving his homeland. All his wins have been gained at either Brocklesby Park or Market Rasen. *Mrs L. Latchford — Burton.* 297 (M), 377 (3m1fH), 679 (3m1fH), 1161 (O).

ABBEY DAYS (IRE) ..8-9.. 8 ch.g. Be My Native (USA) — Abbey Emerald (Baptism) 42. Lengthy. Dam won 2m3f Hdle in Ireland. NH FLAT '02 r2 p0. NH '03 (for Mrs H. Dalton) r2 p0; fell 1. Possesses a little ability, but worryingly manages only two outings per annum, and had been off the course for three months prior to his second in a bad race at Penshurst. There may be a Maiden for him if he can be produced fit. *J.M. Turner — Suffolk.* 27 (OMa), 1088 (OMa).

ABBEYKNOCK BOY (IRE) .10-1.. 7 b/br.g. Alphabatim (USA) — Haha Dash (IRE) (Lord Ha Ha) 1. Workmanlike. NH FLAT '01 r2 p0. NH '01/3 (for I. Williams, and M.F. Harris) r13 p3 (3rds). Put his experience under Rules when third at between five and ten lengths in two Chases to good use when winning a Maiden at Dunthrop in January, where the superior jockeyship of Polly Gundry proved vital, but failed to reappear. Should have a chance in Restricteds if problem-free. Visored once in '02. *Clock House Racing Group (A. Gould) — Bicester with Whaddon (Bradley Clarke).* 51 (OMa).

ABBEY'S GIRL (IRE) ..—.. 8 b.m. Elbio — Abbey Trinity (IRE) (Tender King) pp334p. Small neat. IRISH NH '00 and '03 r6 p0. IRISH P-t-P '03 r5 p0 (pulled up 4). HUNT CH '03 (for Mr K.M. Bourke) r1 p0 (fell). NH '03 (for J.D. Frost) r2 p0; last and pulled up. Tailed off last in her only Irish Pointing completion last year, and had previously survived only the first fence when ambitiously shipped to Haydock. Not surprisingly exposed as a blatant non-stayer in the new yard, and having floundered badly from the second last when a close third at Flete did so again when a market springer at Lifton, and appeared to take an instant dislike to Umberleigh. Only once better than last in 11 outings over fences, but has even performed without distinction in a Selling Hurdle. Has been tried in cheekpieces. *J.D. Frost — Dartmoor (Nicky Frost).* 567 (CfMa), 795 (CfMa), 1200 (OMa), 1370 (OMa), 1545 (OMa), 1565 (OMa).

ABERFOYLE PARK (IRE) .11-0.. 11 b.g. Riverhead (USA) — Go For Doe (Whistling Deer) 31f2. Big lengthy. P-t-P '99/01 (for Mr A.J. Sendell) r8 w3 (inc Open and Mixed Open) p3 (2nd twice); pulled up 2. NH '02/3 (for R.H. Alner) r4 p1 (last of 3); fell 1, pulled up 1. Blighted by all manner of physical flaws — very prone to bleed — and unable to operate in an anti-clockwise direction, but a very smart Pointer on his day, and returned from a short and unproductive spell under Rules to clock much the quickest time of the day when recording his third success at Larkhill. Tipped up at the final ditch there next time, and beaten at odds-on subsequently, and tragically met his end in a freak accident at home. A.J. Sendell & L. Sutopo — H.J. Irish — Quantock (Sally Alner). 11 (O), 89 (O), 140 (MO), 457 (MO).

ABIGAILS STAR .—.. 13 b.g. Arctic Lord — Bronze Age (Celtic Cone) pu. Compact well-made half-brother to Hurdles winner, Bronzesmith. NH FLAT '96/8 r3 p1 (2nd). NH '98/00 (for P.G. Murphy, and G.A. Ham) r11 p2 (inc 3rd in Ch); fell/unseated 3, and pulled up 3. A veteran maiden who has finished the course in less than half of his attempts over jumps, and went missing for four years after an appearance in a Selling Hurdle. Unrewarding for an elderly novice in Points. *A.J. Jones — Modbury H.* 194 (CfMa), 795 (CfMa).

ABINGER ..9-7§.. 13 ch.g. Absalom — Western Singer (Chief Singer) 4p55p. Sturdy. Dam is a half-sister to Ronaldsway (*qv* '99 Annual). FLAT '94/5 r4 p0. NH '95/9 r14 p5 (4 3rds); pulled up 3. P-t-P '02/3 r10 w1 (Members) p4 (2 2nds, of 3 once; 3rd of 4 once); 4th, 7th, slipped up 1, pulled up 1, and fell 1. Gifted his only success to date when left clear on the run-in in his Members last year, but usually fails to stay and cannot be relied upon to jump clear, and appeared to suffer a career-threatening injury at Easingwold. Blinkered once in '98. *D.N. Wilkinson — York & Ainsty N. (Sylvia Robinson).* 338 (Cf), 481 (R), 563 (R), 955 (R), 1161 (O).

ABITOFAHIKE (IRE) ..9-9.. 9 b.g. Valville (FR) — Born Early (IRE) (Western Promise VII) p3p321. Small light. Making a late start, but had shown a little ability before (appropriately enough) a bit of a hike to Kingston St Mary paid off when he stumbled across an appalling Maiden on firm in which he may have been lucky as a potential danger slipped up. Wears a cross-noseband and can be keen, and connections have probably done well to get a race out of him. *Mrs R. Gasson — Farmers Bloodhounds.* 385 (OMa), 588 (CfMa), 760 (OMa), 1000 (OMa), 1341 (OMa), 1450 (OMa).

A BIT OF FLUFF ..—.. 13 b.m. Green Adventure (USA) — Cantabile (Bustino) ppupppp. Small light sister to Adventure Princess. Dam, half-sister to Denberdar (*qv* '95 Annual), won 3 2m Hdles (hat-trick, including a Sell) and a 2m Ch and 2 Ladies and placed total of 8 for Sue Brooke. NH FLAT '98 r1 p0. NH '98 r3 p0. P-t-P/HUNT CH '97, '00 and '02/3 r15 w1 (Maiden) p3 (2 3rds); pulled up 8, fell/unseated 2 and refused 1. Won a bad Maiden in holding at Garnons in '02, but a regular non-finisher since and in common with most of her stable companions ran and jumped as though something was drastically amiss this year. Afflicted by sore shins in the past, but looks gutless now, and not worth bothering with again. Has been tried in cheekpieces. *Lady Susan Brooke — Radnor & W. Herefords.* 403 (Cf), 452 (R), 614 (R), 726 (R), 839 (R), 1113 (Cf), 1226 (M).

ABKINS DU BOIS (FR) ..—.. 17 b.g. Carmont (FR) — Quirida Du Bois (FR) (Diaghilev) p. FRENCH FLAT '91 r9 w1 (11f) p4. FRENCH NH (blinkered latterly) '91/00 r56 w7 (2m1f-3m1f Chses) p20. NH '00/1 r7 p1 (2nd); pulled up 3, and fell 1. P-t-P '03 r1 p0 (pulled up). Well served by lashings of mud when successful on a regular basis in the French provinces to '98, but appeared just once last year, and jumped only four fences before disappearing into the box-park on his solitary foray at Black Forest Lodge this term. Ancient and most unlikely to revive again. *Miss K.G. Quayle — Windsor & Chiltern.* 146 (L).

ABLE BOB (IRE) ..7-0.. 9 b.g. Alphabatim (USA) — Blaithin (Le Bavard FR) p64p. Compact. IRISH P-t-P '02 r2 p0; last, and fell. P-t-P '03 r4 p0 (pulled up 4). Sent off favourite in his first three Points, and held every chance when falling two out on his final Irish appearance, but often stops in a matter of strides or takes no interest at all, and has still to beat a rival. Almost certainly defective in some shape or form and should be shunned. Wears a cross-noseband. *C.A. Green — S. & W. Wilts.* 264 (CfMa), 580 (OMa), 865 (OMa), 1098 (OMa).

ABSEAL ..9-5.. 8 ch.g. Absalom — Sparta Seal (Privy Seal) 2p615pf. Compact. P-t-P '03 r2 p0 (last, and ran out 1). A beaten favourite in what turned out to be an above average short Maiden at Great Trethew on his third start, but a relatively unfancied 8-1 chance when leading throughout the final mile at Flete next time. Again let supporters down when a market springer at Bratton Down, and gives the impression that a lack of stamina will prove to be a stumbling block in competitive events. *The Miles Apart Partnership (J. Miles) — Spooners & W. Dartmoor (Verity Nicholls).* 306 (2m4fOMa), 493 (OMa), 702 (2m4fOMa), 1006 (CfMa), 1196 (R), 1385 (R), 1543 (R).

ABSOLUTELY HOPEFUL ..9-6.. 12 ch.g. Nearly A Hand — Owena Deep (Deep Run) u55. Workmanlike rangy half-brother to Hurdles winner, Karolena Bay. Dam won NH flat and 2m2f Hdle. 8300 4yo. NH FLAT '98 r2 p1 (3rd). NH '98 & '00/02 (for C.P. Morlock) r26 w1 (2m6f Hdle) p4 (inc 2nd of 3 in Ch); pulled up 7, and fell 2. Won a Folkestone Hurdle in soft by a heavily eased seven lengths in February '02, but beaten in all his 30 other attempts, and gave the impression of having something wrong with him in Points. Error-prone, and will probably prove to be the antithesis of his name if he reappears at 12. Wears blinkers, and used to be tongue-tied. *S. Jones — S. Pembs.* 49 (4mO), 209 (3m1f110yH), 360 (O).

ABU DANCER (IRE) .9-0.. 9 b.m. Vestris Abu — Oonagh's Teddy (Quayside) 4p. Small half-sister to Hurdles winner, Time Warrior (IRE). NH FLAT '01 r1 p0. NH '01/2 r4 p0; pulled up 1, unseated 1. P-t-P '03 r2 p0 (unseated 1, and pulled up 1). Sold cheaply out of Henrietta Knight's yard after just a handful of attempts, and despite showing up well for a long way on her reappearance at Holnicote has already had a soft palate operation, and has no other tangible form to her credit. *H.R. & Mrs B. Thomas — Exmoor (Hugh Thomas).* 275 (CfMa), 485 (OMa).

ACROSS THE CARD .9-5.. 17 b.g. Lir — Cornish Susie (Fair Season) f334p. Neat brother to Ewhonosebest. FLAT r4 p0. NH '91/4 r21 p8 (inc 2 Sells). P-t-P/HUNT CH '95/00 and '02 r42 w12 (inc 3m1f Hunt Ch, and 2 4m Mixed Opens) p14 (8 2nds; and inc 4 Hunt Chses 2m5f-3m2f); unseated 3, and pulled up 1. An out-and-out stayer, and unbeaten in five previous attempts in the Berwickshire Members, but in virtual retirement since '00, and able only to amble along at one pace nowadays. Was utterly ungenuine under Rules, and often wore headgear, but normally very sure-footed and has long been the ideal mount for an inexperienced rider. Wears a cross-noseband, and has previously run tongue-tied. *Major General C.A. Ramsay — Berwicks.* 73 (Cf), 281 (M), 506 (Cnr), 552 (Cf), 857 (4mMO).

ACT IN TIME (IRE) ..10-3.. 13 b.g. Actinium (FR) — Anvil Chorus (Levanter) 521272. Lengthy half-brother to Lady Dot (IRE) (*qv*). NH FLAT '97 r1 p0. NH '97/03 r37 w6 (2m5f-3m4f Chses) p9; pulled up 5, unseated 1. NH '04 r2 p1 (2nd in 3m2f Ch: *ld to 6, rdn app 2 out, one pce*); and 7th in 3m7f Ch: *prom til rdn & wknd 4 out, t.o.* In fair form in '04, and gained a first success for 28 months when taking a competitive Members at Andoversford. Also did well when runner-up in two Hunter Chases, but the rider was too weak to be of any assistance in the closing stages. A very thorough stayer, and the highlight of his career was when he captured the Durham National worth £11,164 at Sedgefield. A very reliable jumper, and appreciates some give in the ground. Occasionally wears headgear, including cheekpieces once. Does not take a lot out of himself, and could probably hold his form at 13. *T.R. George — Cotswold.* 404 (O), 445 (3m110yH), 755 (M), 801 (3mH).

ACUTEANGLE (IRE) ..—§.. 9 br.m. Cataldi — Sharp Mama VII (unknown) ppupppp. Small neat half-sister to Plessey Rose Lee (IRE), Ballysillan (IRE) and Just Reuben (IRE). NH '01 r1 p0 (11th in 2m110y Hdle). P-t-P '01/3 r7 w1 (Club Mares) p0; last, and pulled up 5 — inc in void Maiden once). Sprang a 33-1 surprise in a slow Mares only event at Godstone in '02, but tailed off in three previous attempts, and pulled up in all but one of her 10 subsequent starts. Has been troubled by a back problem, and looks unwilling to put one foot in front of another nowadays. *J.P.C. Wall — E. Sussex & Romney Marsh (Sarah Wall).* 19 (CMod), 182 (CCon), 345 (2m5fH), 778 (CCon), 1050 (M), 1442 (2m5fH), 1515 (O).

ADAMATIC (IRE) ..—.. 14 b.g. Henbit (USA) — Arpal Magic (Master Owen) p. Big rangy brother to NH flat and jumping winner, Bit O Magic (IRE), and half-brother to Arpal Breeze and One Last Chance, to Chasing winner, Arpal Forever, and to Hurdles winner, Pat's Gesture. Dam half-sister to Polar Nomad (*qv* '94 Annual). NH FLAT '95 r4 w1 p2. NH '96/01 r42 w8 (2 Hdles, 2m110y-2m2f, and 6 Chases, 2m-2m1f; also disqualified once) p14 (8 2nds); pulled up 4, fell/unseated 5. P-t-P/HUNT CH '02 r10 p0 (5th, 6th, last pair 5, and pulled up 3). A fair Chaser at around the minimum trip under Rules, but his last success dates back to June '00, and has proved too cagey for infinitely more talented riders than his current partner in the past. Effective on a sound surface, but no more than a safe conveyance nowadays. Visored once in '00. *C. Jarvis — Suffolk (Caroline Fryer).* 158 (CCon).

ADVANTA PRIDE (IRE) ..—.. 9 ch.g. Pips Pride — Mia Gigi (Hard Fought) p. Tall rangy half-brother to NH flat winner, Mister Gigi, and 2 flat winners. 2200 5yo. NH FLAT '01 (for J.R. Best) r2 p0. Resumed after a three-year absence only to break a leg at Detling. H.J. Jarvis — Ashford V. (Louise Best). 540 (CfMa).

ADVICE TAKEN (IRE) ..9-3.. 8 ch.g. Rashar (USA) — Cyrenaics (IRE) (Cyrano De Bergerac) 6f. Unfurnished. IRISH NH FLAT '01/2 r5 p0. NH '02/3 (for R.H. Alner) r2 p0 (pulled up 2). Bought Doncaster, May for 1400. The only one of six finishers behind Vivid Imagination at Buckfastleigh who did not go on to win a race, and would doubtless have done so, but unfortunately fell with fatal consequences at Black Forest Lodge next time. A real hard luck story. J.B. Shears — Mid Devon (Mark Shears). 194 (CfMa), 417 (CfMah).

AFICIONADO (IRE) ..8-0§.. 11 b.g. Marju (IRE) — Haneena (Habitat) 6p3rp. Small compact half-brother to Simply Perfect, and to 4 flat winners (one in France), including Antester and Doulab's Image. Dam, a smart sprinter, won at 6f in France, and later ran in USA. IR16000y. FLAT '96/9 r25 w1 (8f Sell) p7. NH '97/03 (for R.J. Hodges, and R. Williams) r25 p2 (3rds, inc Ch). The history books tell of him winning a Newmarket Seller with 21 runners by a head in November '96, but has always been temperamental, and a 54-time loser otherwise. Blinkered on four occasions in the past, and regularly beaten by huge margins if completing over jumps. Predictably would not try a yard in Points, but at least his slow safe jumping was of benefit to a beginner. The diminutive Howard Oakes will probably ride winners if his no longer diminutive father buys him something competitive. *W.D. Oakes — Llangeinor.* 447 (Cf), 672 (O), 738 (O), 1093 (4mMO), 1320 (Cf).

A FINE STORY ..9-11.. 9 b/br.g. Le Moss — Kelly's Story (Netherkelly) p8p2f1. Stocky lengthy half-brother to Half A Story. Dam is half-sister to 6 Pointers, including Moonlight Story (*qv* '02), won Maiden and placed 4 over 5 seasons. Grandam, Fixby Story, won 2 Points and 3rd 3. P-t-P '02 (for Mr H. Hill & Mr T. Williams) r4 p3 (2nds); and pulled up 1. Runner-up on four previous occasions, and fell when unassailable once, so was not winning out of turn in a Northaw quagmire. Conditions meant that nearly half the obstacles had to be omitted, but stamina seems to be his forte, and similar terrain may be imperative. *B. Munro-Wilson — Cambridge Univ (Henry Hill).* 220 (OMa), 398 (R), 445 (3m110yH), 901 (OMa), 1156 (OMa), 1246 (OMa).

AFRICAN DAWN ..9-5.. 7 b.g. Spectrum (IRE) — Lamu Lady (IRE) (Lomond USA) ppp5u. Compact attractive half-brother to flat winners Much Ado and Thekryaati. Dam won 7f race. FLAT '01/3 r7 w1 (12f) p4 (inc 3 2nds; inc Sell). NH '02 r3 p0; pulled up 2. FLAT '04 (for L.G. Cottrell) r4 p0. Bought Ascot, Aug for 1904. An all-weather winner for John Gosden in November '01, and four placings on the flat include head and short head defeats (including a Seller), but has finished only twice, with a total of one behind him in eight attempts over jumps, and seems to struggle to get the trip in Points. Wears a tongue-tie, and tried in a visor, and most recently in cheekpieces. Broke his rider's ankle when stumbling and unseating on a bend at Stafford Cross. *The Tribe Partnership (J. Rees) — Mid Devon (Leslie Jefford).* 80 (Cf), 200 (Cf), 707 (Cf), 823 (Cf), 1130 (Cnr).

AFTERMEYOURFIRST .7-0.. 8 b.g. Alflora (IRE) — Highland Waters (High Line) pp7. Tall angular brother to Westhall Belle, and half-brother to Hurdles winner, Madge McSplash. Started favourite or joint-favourite in his first two Points, but has given consistently shoddy displays of jumping, and suffered the supreme indignity of finishing behind Hayling Star at Bratton Down. Looks a camel, and will have to do immeasurably better to achieve anything. *D. Pipe — E. Devon.* 1186 (OMa), 1450 (OMa), 1559 (OMa).

AGAINST THE AGENT ..—.. 15 ch.g. Buckley — Calametta (Oats) p7p. Big rangy brother to NH flat and jumping winner, Skillwise, and half-brother to Irish NH flat winner, Beechcourt. P-t-P/HUNT CH '95, '97/00 and '02 r15 w4 (inc 2m Hunt Ch, and Confined) p4 (2nds, inc Hunt Ch); pulled up 1, ran out 1, and fell 1. A useful front-running performer in his prime, and recorded a hat-trick of wins at Whitwick to '99, but has never been easy to train, and four outings in a season is his record. Can still go a brisk gallop for a veteran, but blew up in the final mile when looking on the burly side on his first two starts this year, and appeared to suffer yet another setback in his Members. *J.P. Price — Radnor & W. Herefords (Clive Davies).* 447 (Cf), 835 (Cf), 1226 (M).

AGENT ..9-0.. 12 ch.g. Anshan — Maria Cappuccini (Siberian Express USA) 4. Small light close-coupled. Dam won 2 5f races. FLAT r19 w1 (7f) p7. NH '98 r5 p0 (inc Sells; broke blood vessel and withdrawn on intended debut). P-t-P '00 and '02 r9 p1 (3rd of 4); 4th, pulled up 6, and unseated. A headstrong individual who has been taken to post early, but predictably unable to get the trip in Points, and has stood his racing incredibly badly. If the current trend is anything to go by he is not due to return until '06. *R.O. Oliver — S. Devon.* 1127 (Cf).

AGENT PROVOCATEUR (NZ) ..9-0.. 9 b.g. Racing Is Fun (USA) — Silver Crest (NZ) (Silver Dream) p35pp. Workmanlike lengthy half-brother to winner in New Zealand. NH FLAT '00/01 r2 p1 (3rd). NH '02 r4 p1 (poor 3rd). P-t-P '03 r6 w1 (2m4f Maiden) p0; 5th, pulled up 3, and unseated. Left clear at the last when springing a 33-1 shock over 2m4f at Hornby Castle last year, but has often appeared less than co-operative, and gives the strong impression that the full trip is beyond his stamina limitations. *S.B. Clark — York & Ainsty S. (Liz Clark).* 57 (R), 161 (I), 341 (R), 563 (R), 1162 (R).

AGILE KING ..10-4.. 14 b.g. Rakaposhi King — My Aisling (John De Coombe) 2. Small unfurnished half-brother to Bridge House and The Ugly Gunner, to Hurdles winner, Lady Remainder, and to flat winner, Petal's Jarred. Dam won 2 flat, 7-10f, including a Seller, but was disqualified from both for causing interference. P-t-P/HUNT CH '96/03 r42 w5 (up to Confined) p13 (7 3rds, last twice); fell/unseated 4, and pulled up 3. Enjoyed something of an Indian summer when successful on three occasions last year (his first wins since recording a double in '98), but finished so lame that he had to be removed from the course by ambulance on his reappearance at Black Forest Lodge, and a comeback at 14 seems highly unlikely. Often lacks fluency over big fences, but basically safe, and has the virtue of being able to operate on all types of going. *A.J. Tizzard — Eggesford.* 62 (Cf).

AGUA ARDENTE ..10-7.. 8 ch.g. Afzal — Armagnac Messenger (Pony Express) 21u112. Lengthy half-brother to Vital, Armagnac Express and Jess Express, and to Hurdles winner, Colnside Bonnie. Dam won 2 Ladies and placed 4 (ended up on floor in 4 of her last 5 attempts). Grandam, Armagnac Queen, won Members (very lucky) and placed 5. P-t-P '02/3 r6 p5 (2nds, of 3 once); and fell when clear 2 out once. Amazingly frustrating in both previous campaigns, but has always been blessed with above average ability, and finally got his act together at Tweseldown when providing his handler with her first success of the season. Defeated only once subsequently, and despite still finding little in the closing stages of most of his races looks sure to win again. Sometimes too bold for his own good, but may be worth trying in a sub-3m Hunter Chase. A right-handed track is essential. *R.G. Russell — Pytchley (Caroline Bailey).* 30 (CMah), 172 (OMa), 375 (R), 587 (R), 886 (Cf), 1214 (Cf).

AIMING HIGH ..—.. 7 b.m. North Col — Thetford Chase (Relkino) f. Small neat homebred sister to Tensing (*qv*). Looked green before falling at halfway on her debut at Paxford. *Mrs A. Jackson & J.P. Thorne — N. Ledbury (Sarah Jackson).* 926 (OMa).

AIRCON (IRE) ..10-3§.. 10 ch.g. Moscow Society (USA) — Corrielek (Menelek) 612u3. Strong compact brother to Irish NH flat and jumping winner, Moscow Express (IRE), and half-brother to Baptist John (IRE) and Butler John (IRE), and to Hurdles winner, Molly Fitz Lad and two Irish Pointing winners.(IRE). IRISH NH '00 r1 p0. NH '00/3 (for R. Dickin) r29 w1 (2m5f Ch) p9; fell/unseated 3, pulled up 4. Has been a most expensive failure, but gained his second success in five years (the first was in a three-runner two-finisher Chase in soft in which the possible scorer fell two out and the other completer broke a blood vessel) when taking a five-runner Ladies at Clifton-on-Dunsmore. Has always been inconsistent and a sketchy jumper, and duly beaten at 1-2 next time. Visored under Rules. His partner Rebecca Hutsby made a successful debut in '95 and then retired for nine years and she does not always seem very confident of her own ability. *G. Hutsby — Warwicks (Rebecca Hutsby).* 869 (L), 1122 (L), 1278 (Cnr), 1391 (L), 1483 (L).

AIR LEADER (IRE) .7-8.. 6 b.g. Air Display (USA) — Paro's Leader (IRE) (Supreme Leader) 4up. Bought Tattersalls Ireland, Aug for 4000. Beaten 32 lengths on his debut, but a non-finisher when 4-1 or less twice subsequently. Will possibly do better at six. *S. Waugh — Morpeth.* 432 (OMa), 856 (2m4fOMa), 1224 (OMa).

AIROSKI ..10-5.. 9 b.g. Petoski — Thames Air (Crash Course) u. Good-topped workmanlike half-brother to Lord Max, and to NH flat and Hurdles winner, Alta. Dam, half-sister to Carswell's Choice (*qv* '96 Annual), won 2 Opens and 3m5f Hunt Ch. NH FLAT '01/2 r2 p0 (btn 37*l* plus). NH '02 r2 p0; pulled up 2. P-t-P '03 r6 w2 (Maiden and Restricted) p3 (2nds); and fell. Most progressive in his debut season between the flags, and displayed plenty of stamina when successful twice, but a beaten favourite in all three subsequent attempts, and remains prone to take the fences by the roots. Presumably laid low after the latest faux pas, but in a successful yard, and a revival in fortunes could not be discounted. *J. Beasley — Albrighton (Caroline Robinson).* 41 (I).

ALBAMART WOOD .9-9.. 9 gr.g. Gran Alba (USA) — Marty's Round (Martinmas) 23f21. Rangy half-brother to Lufah Wood and Marty's Lamp. NH '02/3 (for R.J. Hodges) r5 p1 (last of 3); last pair 2, fell 1 and brought down 1. Can boast a third that earned him £1,704 behind Edredon Bleu in a Chase, but unsurprisingly was soon tailed off on that occasion and beat only one horse in five attempts under Rules. A safe enough jumper who appreciated a drop to Maidens, and eventually scored on firm at Bratton Down (very bad race in which only five ran), but only moderate and will need to do better for Restricteds. Wears a tongue-tie. *The Dozen Dreamers Club (Mrs P. Stocker) — Eggesford (Laura Young).* 194 (CfMa), 567 (CfMa), 967 (OMa), 1186 (OMa), 1511 (OMa).

ALBARDEN .—§.. 8 ch.g. Mujtahid (USA) — Aljood (Kris) ppp. Rangy plain half-brother to 4 flat winners, including Society Snoop and Desert Invader. Dam, lightly raced, was 4th in Prix Marcel Boussac. FLAT '99/00 r7 p0. NH '00 r1 p0 (pulled up). P-t-P '02/3 (for Mr R.T. Dennis) r9 w1 (Maiden) p2; 4th, 5th, 6th, 7th and pulled up 2. Came with a late rattle to secure the spoils on firmish at Easingwold on his final appearance in '02, but became increasingly reluctant in the previous yard, and has not bucked the trend since changing hands. Has been tried in headgear. *J.T.B. Hunt — Pytchley (Carol Elderton).* 559 (R), 684 (R), 1122 (L).

ALDINGTON CHARLIE ..—.. 16 gr.g. Baron Blakeney — Aldington Princess (Cavo Doro) ppp3pp. Compact home-bred brother to Aldington Baron and Aldington Annie, and half-brother to Aldington Spot. P-t-P '94/6, '98/9 and '03 r18 w2 (Maiden and PPORA) p4 (2 3rds, last once); pulled up 7, unseated 1. A dual scorer going right-handed to '99, but had to wait until he was 15 before he raced more than four times in a season, and has become painfully slow. The lanky owner-rider tucks himself up quite neatly, but then sits in a state of inertia, and needs to become much more dynamic if he is ever to get competitive. *C. Sands — N. Cotswold (Harry Wheeler).* 292 (MO), 603 (Cnr), 728 (I), 921 (M), 1254 (Cf), 1530 (I).

ALEXANDER NEVSKY ..9-3.. 9 b.g. Be My Native (USA) — Tsarella (Mummy's Pet) p48fp14pp. Strong half-brother to Hurdles winner, Mulligan Express. Dam, half-sister to The Tsarevich (smart Chaser), won 2 Hdles (2-2m5f) and 6 Chses (2-3m). NH FLAT '00/1 r3 w1 p1 (3rd). NH '02 r2 p0 (8th, and pulled up). P-t-P '03 (for Mr R.J. Brown) r2 p0 (pulled up 1, and fell 1). Bred to be smart, and looked a bright prospect when making a successful racecourse debut, but until '04 never managed more than two outings in a year, and is clearly still physically troubled. In command when left solo in his Members, but error prone and otherwise well beaten. Wears a cross-noseband. *R.J. Brown & A. West — D.S. Dennis — Vine & Craven (Dan Dennis; -).* 116 (I), 141 (I), 422 (CCon), 537 (4mMO), 717 (Cf), 968 (M), 1212 (Cf), 1406 (I), 1438 (3m2fH).

ALEX IN ACTION .8-9.. 12 b.g. Fearless Action (USA) — Berata (New Member) 84. Compact light half-brother to River Bandit. Dam, half-sister to Dubata (*qv* '97 Annual), failed to finish in 6 of 9 Points. NH '99 r2 p0; pulled up 1. P-t-P '02/3 r5 w1 (Maiden) p0; and pulled up 2, unseated 2. Survived a bad mistake when successful on his Pointing debut at Musselburgh in '02, but was reappearing from a three-year hiatus then, and has been seen only on a handful of occasions since. At least jumped round in both starts this year but was beaten out of sight, and it is impossible to envisage a follow up. Reported to be a bad traveller, and tends to sweat excessively. *C. Hall — Braes (Carolyn Hall).* 212 (R), 430 (R).

ALEX THUSCOMBE ..9-12.. 17 ch.g. Takachiho — Portate (Articulate) 3u2. Small compact brother to Ben Tirran and Wayward Edward, and half-brother to Eborneezer's Dream. NH FLAT r1 p0. NH '93/4 r7 p0. P-t-P/HUNT CH '95/02 r39 w4 (up to Confined) p12 (7 2nds, inc Hunt Ch); failed to finish 9 (on floor 6, and carried out 1). Has not won since '97, and looked to have slid into an irreversible decline when last seen, but a year off has done him no harm at all, and gave the new rider a great introduction. Unlucky not to record back-to-back 20-1 wins on his last two starts, as he was in control when unseating two out at Larkhill, and despite taking the scenic route at Bratton Down failed only by a head to overhaul Barton Rose. Regained a visor in '04, and has previously worn blinkers. Wears bandages and stands only light campaigns on his favoured sound surface. *P. & Mrs F. Shaw — Cattistock (Fiona Shaw).* 687 (M), 1101 (Cnr), 1383 (Cnr).

ALFIE BE ..—.. 7 b.g. Alflora (IRE) — Might Be (Gunner B) p. Big. Favourite for his early February debut, but let down by his jumping and eventually pulled up two out. Can possibly do better with experience. *Mrs C.R. Saunders — Pytchley (Caroline Bailey).* 173 (OMa).

ALFIE MOON (IRE) ..8-9.. 7 gr.g. Arctic Lord — Aunty Babs (Sexton Blake) 5p. Half-brother to winning Hurdlers, Kyle David (IRE) and Jan's Dream (IRE). Virtually tailed off on a Cottenham debut, and failed to shine on a return visit when sent off second favourite. *M. McCaffrey — Aldenham H. (Simon Andrews).* 105 (2m4fOMa), 560 (OMa).

ALFIES ROCKET ..9-0.. 8 ch.g. Hatim (USA) — Run Pet Run (Deep Run) 43. Good-topped. Dam won 2m4f Hunt Ch and 3 2m4f-3m Chses, and is half-sister to Tierna's Respect (*qv* '04 Annual). Grandam, Tierna's Pet, failed to finish in three Points. NH FLAT '02 (for D.M. Grissell) r1 p0. Sold Ascot, Apr '02 for 1238. Had five horses including one subsequent scorer behind him when completing, but his 50 lengths third suggests that he will only be moderate at best. *Mrs K. Squire — Torrington F. (Laura Young).* 701 (2m4fOMa), 883 (OMa).

ALGAN (FR) ..10-1.. 17 b/br.g. Le Pontet (FR) — Djaipour II (FR) (Gaur) 112433. Compact good-sized half-brother to 8 winners in France including the dam of Imago II (*qv*). Dam won 4 flat in France. FRENCH FLAT w1. FRENCH NH '93/7 and '99/00 r20 w12 (5 Hdles and 7 Chses). NH '94/7 r5 w1 (3m Ch) p0. An incredible old horse who earned over a quarter of a million pounds in win money alone when owned by the Marquesa de Moratella and trained by Francois Doumen, and was the lucky victor in the '94 King George VI Gold Cup at Kempton, in which he was a beaten second until Barton Bank unseated at the final fence. A regular star at Auteuil, where he revelled in the ever-present muddy ground, but had not scored since October '99 until his heroic double for Phil York at Horseheath and Cottenham, where he came romping home in exuberant fashion to belie his years. Despite valiant attempts was unable to overcome the riding of his trainer on his last three outings. Used to wear blinkers, but has no need of them. How he and the late Djeddah ended up in the present yard is an amazing mystery — will Edredon Bleu and Best Mate finish their days Pointing for Frank Matthews?! *Miss R. Heikkola — Cambridge Univ (James JJ Ryan).* 376 (Cf), 556 (Cf), 643 (C), 832 (Cf), 1085 (Cv&nr), 1313 (Cf).

ALHERI ..9-12.. 14 gr.g. Puget (USA) — Miss Haddon (Free Boy) 1622. Strong compact. FLAT '94 r1 p0. NH '98/02 r18 p7 (4 Hdles, inc 3 Sells); pulled up 4. NH '04 r1 p1 (10l 2nd to Gallion's Reach in 3m1f110y Sell Ch: *a.p, went 2nd 9, btn when hit 2 out*). An old-stager who was often able to produce placed efforts in the lowest grade under Rules, and deservedly got off the mark at 13 when the only one of 11 contestants to manage a clear round at Barbury. Not the best of jumpers, but continued in good heart subsequently, and it may be worth bringing him out again at 14. Wears a tongue-tie now. *J.A.T. de Giles — V.W.H.* 1067 (OMa), 1172 (3m1f110yH), 1439 (2m5fH).

PLATE 16 182 Mid Surrey Farmers Draghounds S.E. Hunts Club Members Conditions: Alice Reigns (Chris Gordon), 6th PHOTO: Brian Armstrong

ALICE REIGNS .9-8§.. 8 b.m. Sir Harry Lewis (USA) — Richards Kate (Fidel) 62. Owner-bred half-sister to Kates Fancy, and to NH flat winner, Jane Lechat. Dam, sister to Sperrin View (*qv* '98 Annual), won

2 2m Hdles in Ireland (first past the post in another, but had taken the wrong course early). NH FLAT '02 r1 w1. NH '02 (from Mrs A.J. Perrett's) r1 p0 (4th in 2m1f110y Hdle). Won first time out at Folkestone, but like her half-sister Jane Lechat who also scored on her debut, has proved to be most disappointing, and there are plenty of doubts about her enthusiasm for a battle. Takes a keen hold, but can jump left, and looked to give away her Members to doggy old Jack Hackett when 1-2. Has ability, but must not be trusted. *S.P. Tindall — Southdown & Eridge (Jenny Gordon).* 182 (CCon), 605 (M).

ALICE'S OLD ROSE ..7-2.. 8 b.m. Broadsword (USA) — Rosie Marchioness (Neltino) up6pu*4*. Stocky sister to Nell Gwynne. Dam is half-sister to Glenrowan Lad and Kelly's Honor. Grandam, Maid Of Honor II, won 2 Points and 3rd twice. P-t-P '03 r2 p0 (unseated, and pulled up). NH '04 (for Mrs H.O. Graham) r1 p0 (4th in 2m1f110y Sell Hdle: *hdwy 4, one pce 3 out*). Has shown some speed, but to date her progress has been halted by earth-shattering mistakes, and beaten 46 lengths on her only Pointing completion. Subsequently beaten 21 lengths in a Cartmel Seller, and might just be able to improve enough to carve out a modest career under Rules. *C.J. Pickering — W. Percy (Kirstie Hargreave).* 216 (OMa), 286 (CfMa), 432 (OMa), 768 (2m4fOMa), 1225 (OMa).

ALIDIAMOND (U) ..—.. 10 gr.m. unknown 6. Massive shire-cross. Lucky not to break all his legs in his stone-wall Members, in which he eventually completed the course ten minutes after the winner following a series of refusals. *L.A.E. Hopkins — High Peak.* 984 (3m4fNCM).

PLATE 17 212 College Valley & N. Northumberland Restricted: L to R, Alittlebitopower (C. Storey), 4th, leads Roscoe Burn (M. McAlister), 5th, and Timberley (T. Oates), 3rd PHOTO: Alan Mitchell

ALITTLEBITOPOWER ..10-4.. 8 ch.g. Alflora (IRE) — What A Moppet (IRE) (Torus) 24b32. Dam, half-sister to Ali's Alibi (*qv* '00 Annual). P-t-P '02/3 r4 w1 (Maiden) p2; and 4th. Yet to miss the frame when completing, but has failed to add to his '03 Mosshouses success, and tends to race too keenly for his own good. Probably unlucky when bowled over by a loose horse at Overton, and compensation in a Restricted, at least, awaits. A bold jumper, but occasionally gets it wrong, and hopefully his habit of going away to the right does not portend trouble. Wears a cross-noseband. *Mrs A.D. Wauchope — College V. & N. Northumberland (Clive Storey).* 70 (R), 212 (R), 657 (R), 1174 (3m1fH), 1373 (2m4f110yH).

ALIZARINE BLUE ..—.. 12 b.g. Tina's Pet — Rhiannon (Welsh Pageant) p. Lengthy brother to successful Hurdler, Alcian Blue, and half-brother to King of Shadows, Malachite Green and Cash 'N Carrots, to flat winner, Prince Of The Lake, and to a winner in Italy. NH FLAT '98 r1 p0. P-t-P '00/3 r11 p1 (3rd); unseated 1, and pulled up 6. Frequently bombs off at high speed, but always runs out of gas after a maximum of two miles and for the third time in five seasons was restricted to a solitary appearance. Acquired blinkers in '04. *R.S. Kendall — Cumberland (Lynsey Kendall).* 658 (OMa).

ALIZARIN (IRE) ..—.. 6 b.m. Tagula (IRE) — Persian Empress (IRE) (Persian Bold) fpup. IR19000y. Half-sister to 3 flat winners (one in Italy), including Scotty's Future and Rhodamine. FLAT '01/3 r11 p1 (3rd). NH '03 (for A.C. Wilson) r1 p0 (pulled up). Third on her flat debut, but tried a Seller without success subsequently, and was blinkered once. Has never finished over jumps, and there must be grave doubts about her getting the trip in Points. *P. Cartmell — Hurworth.* 500 (CMam), 773 (2m4fCMa), 1158 (OMa), 1177 (2m5fH).

ALJOASH (IRE) ..9-13.. 9 b.m. Unblest — Party Guest (What A Guest) 121314. Small neat. Dam won 2m Hdle in Ireland. P-t-P '02/3 r5 p1 (last of 2); last of 4, and pulled up 3. Clocked fair times when successful at Ystradowen and Rhydygwern, and has not missed the frame in eight completions, but always starts at a false price, and only gets the trip when conditions aren't testing. Needs to improve again, and lacks physical scope, but her ability to handle a sound surface should ensure further success. Wears bandages and a cross-noseband,. *R. Scrine — Banwen Miners (John Moore).* 736 (CfMa), 1022 (R), 1234 (M), 1237 (R), 1482 (R), 1552 (I).

ALL ALIGHT (IRE) ..7-12.. 6 b.g. Fourstars Allstar (USA) — Villamont (USA) (Roanoke USA) p5. Strong compact. 56 lengths last on his second outing at Dingley, but did enough to suggest he might improve in time. *W.J. Turcan — Dunston H. (Nigel Bloom).* 890 (2m4fOMa), 1218 (OMa).

ALLER COOMBE .9-4§.. 11 b.m. Teamster — Ragsi (Amerian USA) 25p. Small weedy half-sister to Ragamuff, Huffin And Puffin and Artic Princess. Dam was placed in a Ladies and 3 Restricteds (rarely tried Maidens, or could probably have won). P-t-P '99/00 and '03 r10 w1 (Maiden) p3 (2 3rds; and 2nd of 3); last of 4, pulled up 4, and fell. Highly unpredictable and clearly not easy to train, but retains ability, and not disgraced when sent off favourite on her first start for Leslie Jefford. Promptly went missing for six weeks, and ran miserably on sound surfaces when returned. Her age and temperament suggests a Restricted success is not on the cards. *S.O. Sampson — Tiverton Stag (Leslie Jefford).* 572 (R), 1268 (R), 1554 (M).

ALL EYEZ ON ME (IRE) ..9-4.. 8 b.g. Torus — Ella Rosa (Le Bavard FR) p5p2f1s3. Compact. Dam won 2m Hdle at Bellewstown. IR11000 4yo. IRISH NH '02 r3 p0. NH '02/3 (for Dr P. Pritchard) r9 p0; inc last 2, fell/unseated 3, and pulled up 3. Very bad under Rules in the previous yard and only once better than last in nine attempts including a Seller (was a hairy ride over fences), and generally stopped to nothing in his Points, but managed to last home in a very slowly-run Maiden at Tabley under a fine ride on the only occasion Richard Burton partnered him. Used to wear cheekpieces, and has now switched to blinkers. Connections have done well to get a race out of him. *Mr & Mrs B. Edwards — N. Ledbury (Michael Hammond).* 151 (OMa), 410 (2m4fCfMa), 668 (OMa), 850 (2m5fOMa), 1075 (OMa), 1424 (OMa), 1482 (R), 1531 (R).

ALLEYWELL ..9-4.. 10 b.g. Petoski — Housemistress (New Member) 5p251. Tall half-brother to Rons Venture, Peter Pointer and House Colours (*qv*), and to Hurdles winner, Chain Line. Dam won 2 Hunt Chses and 14 Points (13 Ladies, 3m-3m3f) and placed 11 (inc a Hdle). IRISH P-t-P '00 r3 w1 (5yo&up Maiden) p0; pulled up and carried out. IRISH NH FLAT '00 r1 p0. IRISH NH '00/2 (for J.A. Berry) r11 p0. Persistently poor in Ireland and always struggling to get the trip in Points, and was 30 lengths second in his Members, but seemed to benefit from a first time tongue-tie when backed from eights to fours and wandering home in front of the only other finisher in a Bonvilston Restricted. Is surely going to find matters difficult in the future. *The Ideal Racing Club (J.W. Delahay) — Radnor & W. Herefords (Richard Mathias).* 452 (R), 752 (R), 1226 (M), 1388 (R), 1538 (R).

ALLEZ TOUJOURS (IRE) ..9-12.. 10 b.g. Castle Keep — Adapan (Pitpan) 1. Unfurnished half-brother to 2 Irish Pointing winners. IRISH NH '99/00 r4 p1 (3rd). NH '02/3 (for M. Sheppard) r9 p2 (3rds); pulled up 4. Has never run much and ended his career under Rules when blinkered in a Selling Hurdle, but found the ideal opportunity on his 14th outing in a Maiden for eight-year-olds plus at Maisemore, and was well supported before scoring easily in a good time. Definitely good enough for other Pointing successes if the chances arise. *S. Gegg — Ledbury (Nicky Sheppard).* 731 (OMa).

ALL FOR JAKE (IRE) ..9-11.. 10 ch.g. Sirsan (IRE) — Kelly's Gift (Santa's Sleigh) fp31. Tall rangy brother to Irish Pointing winner, Ardlea. IRISH P-t-P '00/2 r12 w1 (7yo geldings Maiden) p4; pulled up 5, ran out 1. IRISH NH FLAT '02 r1 p0. IRISH NH '02 (for Miss M.P. O'Toole) r1 p0. Has joined a stable who has persistently done well with sow's ears, and managed a ready success at Laleston, but very rarely aspires to his current rating, and has given the impression that all is not always well with him. Seems best on a firmish surface. *T.F. Mathias — S. Pembs (Richard Mathias).* 207 (R), 674 (R), 947 (M), 1191 (R).

PLATE 18 1191 Llangeinor Restricted: All For Jake and David Jones take the last
PHOTO: John Mullen

ALLIED IMPERIAL ..9-0.. 9 b.m. Morpeth — Super Sarena (IRE) (Taufan USA) p6. FLAT '99 r1 p0 (tailed off). NH '99/01 r13 p2 (Sell Hdles). P-t-P '03 (for Mrs S. Dix (Aqua Fresh Partners) r1 p0 (4th of 5). NH '04 r1 p0 (last of 6 in 2m110y Maiden Ch: *a bhnd, mist 7, t.o*). Usually gets round, but in her own time, and has not shown anywhere near enough stamina to warrant another attempt in Points. Has become very lightly raced in recent years, and a win under any code would be a shock. Has been tried in a visor. *J.D. Frost — Modbury H. (Jimmy Frost).* 485 (OMa).

ALLOTROPE (IRE) .7-7§.. 10 b.g. Nashwan (USA) — Graphite (USA) (Mr Prospector USA) pp2pp. Small half-brother to 4 flat winners (2 abroad), including Rose Quartz (in Ireland). Dam won 9f race. IRISH FLAT '98 r4 w1 (14f) p1 (2nd). FLAT '99/01 r14 p0. NH '99/02 r14 w1 (2m6f110y Hdle) p3. P-t-P/HUNT CH '03 r9 p0 (last of 4, pulled up 6, and fell 2). Cost a small fortune off the flat, but has won once only in 28 starts over jumps, and rarely shows any interest at all nowadays. Broke Emma James's collarbone in a fall last year, and appeared to have done himself a mischief when removed by ambulance following his only '04 completion, but was fit to resume a month later. Has been tried in blinkers and cheekpieces, and acquired a tongue-strap on his last four starts. *Lady Susan Brooke — Radnor & W. Herefords.* 48 (3m5f70yL), 251 (C), 515 (L), 835 (Cf), 1111 (L).

ALLTIME DANCER (IRE) .9-1§.. 13 b.g. Waajib — Dance On Lady (Grundy) 520. Close-coupled. Dam won at 14f and a 2m1f Hdle in Ireland. FLAT r12 w2 (8-10f) p1 (2nd in Sell). NH '95/7 and '01 r23 w6 (2m1f-2m4f Hdles) p3 (2 3rds). NH '02 r1 p0 (9th in Grand Military Gold Cup). P-t-P/HUNT CH '01/3 r13 w1 (3-finisher Members) p4 (2 2nds, dead-heat once; and 2 3rds, last once); 5th of 6, and pulled up 2. NH '04 r1 p0 (10th in Grand Military Gold Cup: *a wl bhnd, t.o 9*). A very safe conveyance, and most adept at course completion, but has always possessed a moody streak, and has consented to win only once from 20 attempts for present connections. His decline is certain to be permanent. Blinkered on four occasions in '97, including his last hurdling success, but not since. *Major & Mrs C.F. Lambert — R.A. (Moddi Lambert).* 9 (C), 85 (M).

ALMACASH (IRE) ..—.. 8 b.m. Clearly Bust — Buskin's Pride (IRE) (Altountash) p. Not seen since pulling up after two miles on an early February debut. *J. Mackley — S. Durham (Sarah Dent).* 166 (OMa).

ALMAZARD ..8-8§.. 8 b.g. Mazaad — Almanot (Remainder Man) 735uf42. Lengthy. NH FLAT '02/3 r2 p0. NH '03 (for L. Wells) r2 p0; pulled up 1. Bought Ascot, Jun for 2285. Good riders have been unable to prevent some consistently poor jumping (kept diving violently left once in '04), and was twice hopelessly tailed off when making the frame, but blinkers (which he wore once over hurdles) brought about some improvement when he was one length second of three at Aldington. Clearly not without a modicum of ability, but unreliable and very untrustworthy. *P. Hughes — E. Sussex & Romney Marsh (Alison Hickman).* 104 (2m4fOMa), 186 (OMa), 418 (2m4fCMa), 611 (OMa), 782 (OMa), 803 (2m4fOMa), 895 (OMa).

ALMOST A DAY .—§§.. 11 b.g. Nearly A Hand — Maranzi (Jimmy Reppin) pppp4p. Compact well-made brother to Joss Bay. Dam won 2m4f Hdle and 6 Chses, 2m-2m4f (4 at Worcester). IRISH NH FLAT '99 r2 p0. IRISH NH '99 r1 p0 (unseated). NH '99 r2 p0; 7th, and pulled up. P-t-P '02/3 r19 w1 (Maiden) p4 (2nds of 3 once); 4th, last 4, pulled up 7, and fell 2. Ended a frustrating run of seconds when successful (at the 24th attempt) on his final appearance last year, but never went a yard willingly in '04, and his 9-10 rating has been withdrawn. Most unlikely to reform and even Dave Mansell must be hoping connections do not persevere for another season. Wears a tongue-tie and blinkers, and despite having two handlers still managed to escape through the paddock fencing and gallop off at Chaddesley. *K. Bayliss — Ledbury (Roy Shail).* 118 (R), 252 (CR), 369 (R), 1230 (R), 1345 (R), 1449 (R).

ALONG THE LAWN (IRE) ..9-4.. 7 b.g. Commanche Run — Northcha Lady (IRE) (Brush Aside USA) 1u. Small. IRISH P-t-P '03 r5 p4 (inc 3 3rds); and pulled up. Left the lucky winner of two-finisher Maiden at Eyton after a rival had unseated at the last when a neck in front, and evidently did not impress connections with his attitude, as he was blinkered next time. Unfortunately he unseated after a mile and broke his pelvis when trying to jump a gate whilst running loose, and had to be destroyed. N. Morgan - N. Salop (Sheila Crow). 531 (OMa), 715 (R).

ALPENSTOCK (FR) .9-5.. 9 b.g. Mister Mat (FR) — Altaraza (FR) (Jolie Mars FR) pp7. Workmanlike. Dam was a leading Anglo-Arab at 4/5 in France. FRENCH FLAT '99 r1 p0. NH '99/01 r6 p1 (3rd) in Hdles. P-t-P '02/3 (for Mr D. Wellon) r4 w1 (Club Maiden) p2 (3rds); and pulled up 1. Made a winning debut in Points, and reached the frame in his first two Restricted completions, but finished lame in the latter, and after three quick runs for new connections his season was over by the first week in February. Dumped the trainer on the way to post on his reappearance, and she did not renew her acquaintance on the track again, and his own well being can never be guaranteed. *R. Grant — Avon V. (Kayley Jones).* 37 (CR), 118 (R), 169 (R).

ALPHA CENTAURI (IRE) ..—.. 11 ch.g. Alphabatim (USA) — Barna Glen (Furry Glen) ppfp. Tall lengthy workmanlike. Dam won NH Flat, 2 Hurdles (2m-2m3f) and 2m4f Ch in Ireland. IRISH NH FLAT '00 r2 w1 p0. NH '01/2 (for Miss V. Williams) r5 p0; pulled up 4. Looked promising when he won a Naas bumper in soft, but has clearly endured major problems since, and only once able to complete the course in nine attempts over jumps (pulled up seven, including in both Members Points). Liable to make bad errors, and hopefully retired. *Mrs J. Butler MFH — Hursley Hambledon (Peter Butler).* 260 (M), 348 (3mH), 545 (2m3f110yH), 716 (M).

ALPHA LEATHER .—.. 14 gr.g. Zambrano — Harvey's Choice (Whistlefield) pp. Tall rangy. Dam sister to Ham Hill Prince (*qv* '95 Annual). NH FLAT '95 r2 p0. NH '95/9 and '01/2 r42 p4. HUNT CH '03 r3 p0 (last of 7, unseated 1 and pulled up 1). A long-standing maiden who has been over ambitiously placed in recent years, and has found regulation fences too demanding on most occasions. Looks finished now. Visored once in '97. *D. & Mrs C.J. Lloyd — Cotswold (Mark Grassick).* 755 (M), 1172 (3m1f110yH).

ALPHA ROMANA (IRE) ..10-9.. 11 b.g. Alphabatim (USA) — Stella Romana (Roman Warrior) p. Strong-topped compact half-brother to Baronburn and Zojila. IRISH NH '98/9 r9 p1 (3rd). P-t-P/HUNT CH '01/3 r14 w4 (2m110y-2m5f110y Hunt Chses) p3 (2 2nds in Hunt Chses, and 3rd of 4); 5th, 7th, pulled up 4, and fell. A dual sub-3m Hunter Chase winner in the two previous seasons, and does best on sound surfaces, but not built to appreciate such terrain and evidently suffered a setback in '04. Does not have many miles on the clock, and his legs have probably always been a problem, but unlikely to have deteriorated enough to rule out another success provided connections can nurse him back to health. *Mrs S. Busby & K.H. Hutsby — Farmers Bloodhounds (Sue Busby).* 317 (2m4fH).

ALPINE FUGUE (IRE) .9-5§.. 11 b.g. Classic Music (USA) — Val Gardena (Ahonoora) 422p. Small neat close-coupled. IRISH NH FLAT '98 r3 p0. NH '99/00 r18 p8 (5 2nds); pulled up 1, unseated 1. P-t-P '02/3 r16 w1 (Horses & Geldings Maiden) p6 (5 2nds, beaten neck once); 4th, pulled up 4, fell/unseated 2, slipped up 1 and refused 1. Required 25 attempts to open his account, but has been runner-up seven times since, and consistently gives the impression that he is taking the mickey out of the owner-rider. Might be worth trying with stronger handling. Visored latterly under Rules, and acquired a tongue-tie in '04. *Miss S.D. Lewis — Curre & Llangibby (Bethan Williams).* 65 (Rnr), 148 (R), 694 (M), 844 (R).

PLATE 19 1298 R K Harrison West Country Championship HC, Wincanton: Alska and Richard Bandey, 3rd, take the 15th *PHOTO: Tim Holt*

ALSKA (FR) ..10-1.. 12 br.m. Leading Counsel (USA) — Kolkwitzia (FR) (The Wonder FR) 535251434. Tall. FRENCH FLAT '95/8 r18 w2 (6f) p13. FRENCH NH '96/8 r21 w3 (2m Hdles) p7 (inc 2 Chses). NH '00/3 r4 p1 (2nd) and 7th twice and pulled up in R.A. Gold Cup. P-t-P/HUNT CH '99/03 r31 p9 (6 3rds, inc 5 Hunt Chses; and 3 2nds inc 2 Hunt Chses, last once); unseated 5, and pulled up 3. NH '04 r1 p0 (5th in 3m110y R.A. Gold Cup: *lost tch 9, t.o 12*). Above average in her homeland, and has always retained plenty of ability, but has consented to win only one of her 44 starts for the current yard. Did so in extraordinary circumstances, as she tailed herself off after a mile only to finish jet propelled and make up all of eight lengths from the last fence. Stays extremely well, but indolent, and the usual rider is normally most unenterprising on her, however has never fallen, and should continue to pay her way. Acts on any going. Visored twice in '00. *P.L. Southcombe — Cattistock.* 10 (L), 88 (L), 438 (3m1f110yH), 747 (3m1f110yH), 993 (3mH), 1170 (4m1fH), 1298 (3m1f110yH), 1441 (3m7fH).

ALTHREY DANDY (IRE) ..10-9.. 10 ch.g. Good Thyne (USA) — Hawthorn Dandy (Deep Run) 111. Tall angular plain half-brother to Fine And Dandy, and to jumping winner, Something Dandy (IRE). Dam, half-sister to Dunamase Dandy (*qv* '98 Annual). NH FLAT '01 r1 p1 (3rd). P-t-P '03 r1 p0 (ran out). Showed promise in his only bumper, but clearly went wrong in the process, and was subsequently rescued from the clutches of the Grim Reaper by present connections. Ran away with Carly Goodall on his only appearance last year, but Lennie Hicks has had no such problems, and the combination followed two unextended Pointing successes with a thoroughly meritorious win at Bangor. Races with tremendous enthusiasm, and the only pity is that his racecourse appearances have been strictly rationed. Kept to ground close to good, and should have little difficulty in winning again. Wears a cross-noseband, and has been taken to post early. *Mrs J.E. Goodall — Meynell & S. Staffs (Carly Goodall).* 595 (OMa), 853 (R), 1375 (3m110yH).

ALVERO (FR) .9-12.. 7 b.g. Genereux Genie — Mazal (Midyan USA) 5622p. Small close-coupled. FRENCH NH '01/2 r12 p1 (3rd); pulled up 3. P-t-P '03 r4 w1 (Maiden) p2 (3rds, of 4 once and last once); and 6th of 7. Placed over fences in his homeland, and his debut English campaign culminated in success at Chaddesley, but largely disappointing in '04 and particularly so when turned over at 2-5 in a three-runner Restricted at Ashorne. Lacked fluency all year, and may not have been right, but will need watching when he reappears. *O.P.J. Meli — Croome & W. Warwicks (Rob Summers).* 252 (CR), 369 (R), 977 (R), 1279 (R), 1469 (R).

ALWAYS GOOD (IRE) ..8-0§.. 9 ch.g. Riot Helmet — Another Struggle (Cheval) p74ppp76323. Light-framed half-brother to Struggles Glory (*qv*), and to Irish Pointing winner, All A Struggle. IRISH P-t-P '00/3 r17 w1 (6yo and upward Maiden) p4; pulled up 5. IRISH NH FLAT '02 r1 p0. IRISH NH '03 (for J. O'Callaghan) r2 p0. Almost always bad, despite his kinship to a star. Does not fall, but a consistently cumbersome jumper, and surprisingly looked at his worst on the only occasion Julian Pritchard partnered him. Occasionally tongue-tied. Ended the season with a flurry of placings, but they were nothing of note, as he had only one horse behind him and was twice adrift by a fence or more. Lacks enthusiasm. *P. Needham — Worcs (Helen Needham).* 16 (C), 65 (Rnr), 159 (R), 252 (CR), 530 (R), 614 (R), 665 (R), 853 (R), 1014 (M), 1114 (R), 1527 (M).

ALWAYS ON THE LINE (IRE) ..10-5.. 11 gr.g. Arapahos (FR) — Fiona's Waltz (General Ironside) 12fu3. Compact well-made half-brother to Thinkers Effort (IRE). IRISH P-t-P '00/2 r17 w1 (7yo&up Maiden) p5; pulled up 2, slipped up 2 and fell 2. IRISH HUNT CH '01 r2 p0. P-t-P '03 r10 w5 (inc Open, and inc hat-trick) p4 (2 2nds, of 3 once; and 2 3rds, last once); and 4th of 5. Left his Irish form well behind when trained in East Anglia last year where he won half the races he contested, and completed a four-timer when beating Red Brook Lad and Aberfoyle Park in the fastest 12st time of the day on his reappearance. Had the form well and truly reversed by the latter next time, and subsequently let down by his jumping technique when sent Hunter Chasing, but should continue to do well when returned to Points. Acts on any going. Stays 3m2f. *Mrs M. Merriam — Cattistock (Richard Barber).* 11 (O), 89 (O), 543 (3m2f110yH), 733 (3mH), 975 (2m7f110yH).

ALY DALEY (IRE) .9-0.. 17 ch.g. Roselier (FR) — Roses In June (Timobriol) 2. Small flashy brother to Lady Steel (IRE). Dam is an unraced half-sister to Grand National winner, Rag Trade. IRISH P-t-P '93/4 r7 w1 (6yo&up Maiden) p4; fell 2. NH '94/9 r32 w5 (2m5f-3m Chses) p8 (short-headed once). P-t-P/HUNT CH '00 and '02/3 r15 w4 (inc 2 Confineds) p2; last pair 5; unseated 3. Scoring for the first time since '00 when recording a Members race double last year, but had only to outplod hunters, and was made to look decidedly slow by the winner on his only appearance in '04. Formerly a very game front-runner under Rules, and whilst his speed has deserted him his zest certainly hasn't. *D.T. Greenwood — V. of Lune H., & Holcombe.* 872 (M).

AMANDAS FANCY (IRE) ..—.. 13 ch.m. Dry Dock — Myle Avenue (Push On) 5f. Small angular half-sister to French Myle (IRE) and O J Selym (IRE), and to Irish Pointing winner, The Yellow Bog. Dam is sister to Baying Hound (*qv* '91 Annual). IRISH P-t-P 98/00 r15 p2 (3rds, last once); pulled up 7, fell 1. IRISH NH FLAT r2 p0. P-t-P '02/3 r10 p2 (last of 2, and remote 3rd); last pair 4, pulled up 3, and unseated 1. A long-standing maiden who had never finished within 25 lengths of the winner when completing in England, and was killed outright by a crashing first-fence fall at Penshurst. B. Neaves — W. Street Tickham. 534 (M), 782 (OMa).

AMARETTO EXPRESS (IRE) ..—.. 6 b.g. Blues Traveller (IRE) — Cappuchino (IRE) (Roi Danzig USA) p. Brother to flat winner, Blue Bolivar. Dam won 7f race on all-weather. 9500y. FLAT '01/3 r12 p0. Temperamental and bad including a Seller on the flat, and started at 66-1 or more when trounced on his final four appearances (blinkered once and wore cheekpieces once). Unlikely to fare any better Pointing. *Mrs R.E. Barr — Cleveland (Ronald Barr).* 814 (OMa).

AMARETTOFORANNA (IRE) ..—.. 12 b.g. Satco (FR) — Candy Slam (Candy Cane) p. Lengthy brother to Pointing and jumping winner, Satcoslam, and half-brother to Grand value, Well Delayed and Finesse The King (IRE). IRISH NH FLAT '99 r3 p1 (3rd). IRISH NH '99 r5 p2 (inc 2nd in Ch). NH '99/03 (for F. Murphy) r18 w3 (3 2m1f-2m6f Chses) p3. Best at up to 2m6f if able to front-run in the previous yard (made all for her final two wins), but unreliable (refused once), and sometimes jumps left. Approaching the veteran stage, and disappeared after pulling up in January. *O.R. Dukes — York & Ainsty S.* 55 (Cf).

AMY'S GIFT ..—§.. 9 b.m. Lahib (USA) — Miss Amy Lou (IRE) (Gallic League) Rrf. Small. Dam won 5f race at 2. P-t-P/HUNT CH '03 (for Anderson Racing Club) r3 p0 (pulled up 2, and unseated 1). Looked on the dangerous side in her debut season, but on the deranged side in this, and failed to get beyond the eighth fence in a mercifully truncated campaign. Bolted until running out after half a mile on her reappearance, but steadfastly declined to jump off at all next time, and hopefully connections have called it a day before Portman Square are forced to intervene. Has been tried in blinkers and a tongue-tie, and wears a kineton. *Miss D. Miller — S. Dorset (Ken Nelmes).* 264 (CfMa), 416 (CMam), 604 (OMa).

ANALAN ..8-0.. 6 b.m. Lancastrian — Ancella (Tycoon II) 6. Unfurnished owner-bred half-sister to Anflora (*qv*). Made a series of early mistakes before finishing a remote last at Bitterley, but kept up for 2m4f, and given her breeding chances are that she will improve with experience. *Mrs C. Banks — Worcs.* 837 (OMa).

ANALYSTIC (IRE) ..10-6.. 15 br.g. Kambalda — Burlington Miss (Burlington II) 11p. Compact light-framed half-brother to Another Stubbs, Rugged Baron and Cool It A Bit, to jumping winners, Golden Raider and Ennereilly River (in Ireland), and to Irish Pointing winner, Caffery's Park. Dam won an Irish Point. P-t-P '99/00 and '02/3 r24 w5 (inc Restricted and Club) p9 (6 2nds; last of 3, and 3rd of 4 twice); fell/unseated 5, and pulled up 3. A useful if somewhat error-prone Pointer who had been successful in the last three runnings of his Members, and was fast advancing on a double figure tally on right-handed tracks until breaking down irreparably in the Fernie 4-miler. *Mrs J. Hankey — Cheshire Forest (Gary Hanmer).* 748 (M), 1045 (Cf), 1216 (4m100yMO).

AN CAPALL DUBH (IRE) ..10-5.. 9 br.g. Air Display (USA) — Lady Of Wales (Welsh Pageant) 3. Tall rangy half-brother to Meganaire, and to a winner in Belium. Dam won at 6f race. IRISH P-t-P '00/3 r11 w2 (in Winner of One) p5; pulled up 5. IRISH NH '01/3 (for G. Ducey) r8 w1 (3m Hunt Ch) p0. The winner of three races on easy surfaces in Ireland including a Hunter Chase confined to horses who had not won more than one Point, and his first run for the new stable suggested he would enjoy a similar level of success for the new yard, but vanished after his February 1st outing. Tongue-tied on occasions in his homeland. *D. Pugh — N. Salop (Sheila Crow).* 93 (O).

ANDRE LAVAL (IRE) ..9-8.. 16 ch.g. Over The River (FR) — French Academy (Le Bavard FR) 344. Compact half-brother to Bill Joyce (IRE) and Jimmy Dan (IRE), and to NH flat and jumping winner, Peace Lord (IRE). Dam, is sister to Ozier Hill (*qv* '02 Annual). IRISH P-t-P '95 r6 w4 (inc Open) p0; pulled up 2. NH '96/00 r28 w3 (2m5f110y-3m1f110y Chses) p10 (5 2nds); pulled up 1, unseated 1, also withdrawn not under orders once — broke a blood vessel. P-t-P '02/3 r11 w1 (Confined) p5 (4 2nds); 5th, and last pair 4. Won seven races consecutively to November '96, and picked up the winning thread when providing Hannah Watson with her first success in '02, but has suffered with leg problems, and is easy to beat nowadays. Jumps for fun and retains plenty of enthusiasm, but went down on the road and injured both front knees after the season, and despite being the apple of his rider's eye may have to be retired to the hunting field. Thrice blinkered in '00. *The Watson Family (J. Watson) — Worcs (Valerie Watson).* 361 (L), 625 (L), 1014 (M).

ANDSUEPHI (IRE) .10-2.. 13 b.g. Montelimar (USA) — Butler's Daughter (Rhett Butler) 3. Good-topped lengthy half-brother to Howaryadoon. NH FLAT '97 r2 w2. NH '97/01 r20 w6 (2 2m-2m110y Hdles, and 4 2m5f-3m Chses) p3. P-t-P/HUNT CH '03 r2 w1 (Ladies); and pulled up. Useful at best and has traditionally taken plenty of beating first time out, but his well-being has always been a major concern, and a racecourse appearance is a rarity nowadays. Laid low by a bout of hepatitis pre-season, and despite running well at Ampton in January was not up to turning out again. Has been tried tongue-tied. *Mrs I. Hodge, A.H.B. & Mrs S.A. Hodge — E. Anglian Bloodhounds (Sam Hodge).* 42 (L).

ANDY'S LAD (IRE) .9-7.. 13 br.g. Versailles Road (USA) — Ah Ye Know (Wolverlife) 2. Small compact attractive half-brother to Adore Me (IRE). IRISH NH FLAT '97 r4 w1 p2. IRISH NH '97/8 r10 p1 (2nd). NH '98/02 r18 w3 (2m3f Hdle, and 2 2m3f Chses) p4. P-t-P '03 r1 p1 (2nd). Lost his form latterly under Rules, and his last success dates back to January '00, but still retains some ability and has been runner-up in both Points at Howick. That said he was beaten out of sight in a three-runner affair in the latest, and throughout his career has never withstood long campaigns, and has never been effective beyond 2m4f. Successful on the only occasion he wore blinkers. *A. Jenkins & A. Murphy — Curre & Llangibby (Bethan Williams).* 696 (O).

ANFLORA ..—.. 8 b.m. Alflora (IRE) — Ancella (Tycoon II) pppp. Neat half-sister to Analan. Dam, half-sister to 4 Pointers including Andy (*qv* '94 Annual), won 10 Points (inc 7 Opens) and placed 7 to '94. Grandam, Indy-Ann won 4 Points and placed 5. P-t-P '03 r3 w1 (Maiden, 3 finished) p0; 4th, and 6th. Brought along steadily in a debut season that culminated in an easy success in a three-finisher Maiden at Rhydygwern, but stopped to nil on her reappearance, and has looked wrong since. Clearly thought to be above average, and is usually amongst the market leaders, but her 9-4 rating has been withdrawn until she shows signs of shaking off whatever is ailing her. *Maenllwyd Racing Club (N. Brookes) — Tredegar F. (Tim Jones).* 37 (CR), 79 (R), 207 (R), 358 (R).

ANGUS AIRWAYS (IRE) ..9-0§.. 12 b.g. Convinced — Clairalice (Abednego) p34pp. Small compact. Dam is sister to Meadow Green (*qv* '93 Annual). IRISH P-t-P '98 and '00 r9 w1 (5yo&up Maiden) p1 (3rd); pulled up 1, and fell 1. NH '98/9 r6 p1 (3rd in Hdle); pulled up 2. P-t-P '01/3 r17 w1 (Restricted) p3 (3rds; of 4 once and last once); 5th, 7th, last pair 3, pulled up 7 and unseated 1. Responded to the vigorous urgings of Phillip York when successful at Umberleigh in '02, but long exposed as ungenuine, and only once better than last in 11 subsequent appearances. Very prone to catastrophic blunders. Wears a cross-noseband, and has been tried visored. *P.E. Legge — I. of W.* 175 (Cnr), 623 (Cf), 717 (Cf), 778 (CCon), 972 (Cf).

ANNEKA LOUISE ..9-8.. 11 ch.m. Jendali (USA) — Scotgavotte (FR) (Dunbeath USA) p14. Lengthy owner-bred half-sister to Lady Gavotte. NH FLAT '98 r1 p0. NH '98 r4 p0 (inc Sell). P-t-P/HUNT CH '00 and '02/3 r23 w2 (Restricted and Members) p3 (3 2nds, of 3 once; and inc 3rd of 4 twice and last of 3); pulled up 4, and fell/unseated 2. Consistently seeing a rear-end view of Upham Lord in '03, but ordinarily struggles to get the trip in any case, and her local will once again afford her the best chance of success next year. Usually needs an outing to get fit. Suited by a sound surface. *R.J. Jackson — S. Notts.* 299 (L), 941 (M), 942 (Cf).

ANNIE FLEETWOOD ..8-12.. 7 ch.m. Anshan — Gold Luck (USA) (Slew O' Gold USA) 2f. Good-topped half-sister to flat winners Zalda and Top Hand. NH FLAT '03 r1 p0. NH '03 (for C.P. Morlock) r4 p1

(3rd). Ten lengths third in a Hurdle, but was very lucky to inherit 25 lengths second when last to go clear in a youngsters Maiden at Charlton Horethorne. Fell at halfway next time, and still has plenty to prove. *J.P.M. & J.W. Cook — Dulverton F. (Sue Maude).* 353 (OMa), 600 (2m4fOMa).

ANNIEJO ..9-5§.. 6 br.m. Presenting — Lorna's Choice (Oats) pp32rp1p. Small owner-bred half-sister to Tom's Man (*qv*). Dam ran for George White. NH FLAT '03 (for W. McKeown) r3 p0. A highly-strung little mare and refused to set off when favourite once, but not too bad on the occasions she can be persuaded to complete, and Ran Morgan managed to get the best out of her when she took a slowly-run Maiden at Aspatria. There should be a Restricted for her if she will co-operate. *The Rennington Racing Club (Mrs G.F. White) — W. Percy (George White).* 74 (OMa), 136 (OMam), 344 (2m4fOMa), 856 (2m4fOMa), 1042 (CMam), 1224 (OMa), 1311 (OMa), 1476 (R).

ANOTHER BIT ..9-4.. 8 ch.g. Henbit (USA) — Perrinpit Annapolis VII (unknown) 4u1. Compact well-made. NH FLAT '02/3 r3 p0; unseated 1. NH FLAT '03 (for J.C. Tuck) r3 p0; unseated 1. Bad under Rules, but survived an eventful round (Rilly Goschen lost her whip at halfway, and was almost unseated by a stumble at the last after which she crowded the runner-up) when beating two other finishers (both of whom went on to score) in a 2m4f Maiden at Black Forest Lodge in early March. Not seen again, but is possibly a shade under-rated. *R.J. Weaver — Berkeley (John Tuck).* 67 (OMa), 150 (OMa), 413 (2m4fOMa).

ANOTHER BULA (IRE) ..9-4.. 14 b.g. Cardinal Flower — Celtic Lace (Celtic Cone) u53. Plain angular goose-rumped brother to Dewdrop Lady (IRE) and Hil's Bluff (IRE). NH FLAT '96 r1 p0. NH '97/8 r5 p0 (Hdles, last 2, pulled up 2, and fell 1). P-t-P '00 and '02/3 r15 w1 (Members) p3 (2 2nds; and last of 3); 5th, last pair 2 and pulled up 8. Had failed to beat a rival in six starts immediately prior to winning his Members in '02, but restricted to just three appearances in each of the last two campaigns, and threw away probably his last chance of a follow up when Jo Buck fell off three out when holding every chance on his return in a three-runner Restricted. *D.J. Richards & Miss N. Dickenson — Tiverton Stag (Dean Richards).* 1465 (R), 1554 (M), 1561 (R).

ANOTHER DAFFODIL ..—.. 7 b.m. Puissance — Traumatic Laura (Pragmatic) pf. Failed to get beyond halfway with two lady riders, and decked one of them (on her first ride) at the third. *Miss S.J. & R.E. Blain — Morpeth (Simon Waugh).* 549 (CMam), 914 (M).

ANOTHER HALF ..9-6.. 6 b.m. Weld — Golden Valley (Hotfoot) u2pf. Compact sister to Golden Rivet (*qv*). Novicey, and very poor jumping has caused problems so far, but it looked as if she might have won had she not fallen heavily when leading three out at Garthorpe (favourite). Promoted from 40 lengths third to second on her only completion, but three miles seems too far at present, and although she should eventually get the trip shorter distances seem more suitable for the present. Will have strong claims to a Maiden success in '05. *Mrs G.B. Walford & Mrs R.W. Bromfield — Middleton (Gill Walford).* 59 (OMa), 392 (CfMa), 685 (OMa), 1403 (2m4fOMa).

ANOTHERHANDYMAN ..9-0§.. 11 ch.g. Jupiter Island — Handbelle (Nearly A Hand) pu34p0. Sturdy compact. Dam is sister to Bow Handy Man. NH FLAT '99 r2 p0 (tailed off). NH '99 and '02 r5 p0 (pulled up 2). P-t-P '00/1 and '03 r8 w1 (2m4f Maiden) p3 (2 2nds); last pair 2 and pulled up 2. Came from a seemingly impossible position to score over 2m4f in mud at Tranwell in '00, but has failed to co-operate fully since, and the application of cheekpieces failed to buck the trend on his last three starts. Might be worth another chance with stronger handling, but does not stand much racing. *J.L. Gledson — Border.* 132 (CR), 427 (I), 548 (R), 657 (R), 857 (4mMO), 1222 (R).

ANOTHER JUSTICE (IRE) ..—.. 9 ch.g. Dolphin Street (FR) — Unheard Melody (Lomond USA) pp. Small sturdy. P-t-P/HUNT CH '01/3 r10 w1 (Maiden) p0; pulled up 6, unseated 1 and ran out 1. Recorded the slowest time of the day when successful at Cilwendeg on his '02 reappearance, but had already been operated on for his wind, and has been pulled up in seven of 10 subsequent outings. The current yard appear unable to get him fit at home, and running him in Hunter Chases is utterly ridiculous. *R.V. Westwood — Fife.* 330 (3mH), 548 (R).

ANOTHER LEADER (IRE) ..9-5.. 8 b.g. Lord Americo — Moyglen (Furry Glen) 3f2. Dam won three Irish Points. Can take a ferocious hold and build up huge early leads, but error-prone and gallops himself into the ground, and was finally collared after two out when ten lengths second at Northaw. Would be fast enough to score if he settled better, but now has lameness to overcome. *G.I. Cooper — Essex F. & U. (Cherie Cunningham).* 27 (OMa), 652 (OMa), 1246 (OMa).

ANY OTHER BUSINESS .. -.. 9 ch.m. Gildoran — Wooden Minstrel (Black Minstrel) p. Lengthy half-sister to Hillview Star (IRE) (dam of Hillview Hut (IRE), *qv*). Dam won 2 Points (one in Ireland; and the Berkeley Members in '94) and placed in 7 various races, subsequently placed in 4 more Points '97/8. P-t-P '02/3 (for Mr R. Jones) r3 p0 (pulled up 2, and ran out). Difficult to steer and has been eliminated on two occasions when third prize was going begging, and appears nigh on impossible to train. *M.R. Churches — Mendip F. (Sue Popham).* 35 (CMam).

APATURA JOE ..9-0.. 7 b.g. Riverwise (USA) — Apatura Iris (Space King) 3c. Sparely-made brother to Apatura River, and half-brother to Apatura Hati, Apatura King, Apatura Cherry and Apatura Queen.

Dam won a Maiden and placed 4. Grandam, Veroni, won at 5f, and won Adjacent and placed total of 6. 16 lengths third of four on his debut, but soon carried out next time. A conceivable winner in lowly company. *Mrs R.O. Hutchings — S. Dorset (Elsie Mitchell).* 688 (2m4fOMa), 1133 (OMa).

APPLEFORT (IRE) ..—.. 15 b.g. Over The River (FR) — Sweet Apple (Menelek) u. Big good-looking brother to Irish Pointing and Chasing winner, Riverfort (IRE). Dam won 2m2f Hdle in Ireland (on a disqualification). IRISH P-t-P '94/5 r2 w1 (5yo Maiden) p0; fell 2 out (probable winner). IRISH NH FLAT '95 r2 p1 (2nd). IRISH NH '95 and '97/9 (blinkered final) r23 w1 (2m5f Ch) p5. P-t-P/HUNT CH '00 and '02 r6 p0 (last, and pulled up 5). A dual winner in Ireland to '97, but useless in a handful of appearances for present connections, and his '04 campaign was even more fleeting than usual. Wears a cross-noseband. *Mrs A.P. Glassford — Cheshire.* 713 (Cf).

APPROACHING LAND (IRE) ..9-13.. 10 ch.g. Dry Dock — Crash Approach (Crash Course) f13695. Half-brother to Crashballoo (IRE), and to Irish NH flat and Hurdles winner, Adamant Approach (IRE). NH '02 r1 p0 (pulled up in Hdle). P-t-P '02/3 (for Mr D. Easterby) r6 w2 (2m4f Maiden and Members) p1 (2nd); unseated 3. NH '04 (for M.W. Easterby) r4 p1 (3rd in 2m7f Hdle: *hld up, hdwy 7, ev ch 3 out, one pce*); 6th in 3m1f Hdle: *hld up, hdwy 9, wknd 4 out, t.o*, 9th in 2m Hdle: *chsd ldrs til wknd 5*, and 5th in 2m1f Hdle: *chsd ldrs til wknd app 2 out, t.o*. Beaten once only in four Pointing completions, but has always been a tricky ride, and his jumping in particular has proved a real let down. Can additionally be bolshie in the preliminaries and takes a strong hold, and after following up in his Members in the slowest time of the day again this year was transferred to hurdling where his form deteriorated after a promising debut. *Lord Manton — Meynell & S. Staffs (David Easterby).* 57 (R), 225 (M).

APRIL'S PAST ..— §.. 7 br.m. Past Glories — April's Crook (Crozier) ppppp. Good-bodied short-backed half-sister to Greenhopper (*qv*). From a stable which have produced many game winners over the years, but this one looks a complete yak, and was thoroughly reluctant and immediately tailed herself off in an Exeter Hunter Chase. *The Atkinson family (Mrs N. Atkinson) — Cattistock (Robert Atkinson).* 328 (OMa), 693 (OMa), 962 (OMa), 1182 (CMam), 1363 (2m3f110yH).

APRIL TREASURE ..9-5.. 10 b.m. Stani (USA) — Eleri (Rolfe USA) p31f3. Very small neat half-sister to Thebarringtonboys and Saucy Kirina, and to Hurdles winner, Winter Rose. FLAT '98 r6 p0. NH '99/03 (for Mrs P. Ford) r32 p2 (2nds); pulled up 9, fell 2. Bought Ascot, Oct for 1619. A multiple loser who gained one of her placings in the previous yard in a Selling Hurdle, and even Dick Baimbridge has struggled with her, but finally got off the mark at the 41st attempt in a three-finisher Maiden at Andoversford. Only a titch and does not help her cause by running too freely, but the essence of it is that she is moderate in the extreme, and certainly not worth supporting at cramped odds (beaten favourite in her last two attempts). Sometimes let down by her jumping. *T.S. Warner — Berkeley (Dick Baimbridge).* 172 (OMa), 409 (CMam), 760 (OMa), 925 (R), 1136 (R).

A PROPER CHARLIE ..8-11.. 9 b.g. Cashwyn — Kate's Girl (Lighter) ppR2. Tiny. Dam won two 2m4f-2m5f Chases, and also won 6 Points (4 Opens) and placed total of 5 for R.J. Lewis and is sister to Boys Rocks (*qv* '98 Annual). FLAT '99 r4 p0; last 3. NH '99 and '01 (for J.L. Spearing, and R.J. Price) r5 p0; last 2, and unseated 1. Trounced in his first 12 races including in blinkers twice, and beaten over 50 lengths in three Selling Hurdles, but finally gained a prize when five lengths second of three in a truly bad elders Maiden at Upper Sapey. Must have trouble coping with the weights, and a win looks a forlorn prospect. *R.J. Lewis — N. Ledbury (Tim Stephenson).* 517 (CfMa), 760 (OMa), 840 (OMa), 1141 (OMa).

ARAMINTA ..10-11.. 11 ch.m. Carlingford Castle — Abinovian (Ra Nova) 6. Sparely-made owner-bred half-sister to Noble Affair (*qv*). NH FLAT '98 r2 p0. NH '98 and '01/2 r10 p1 (3rd in 3m Hdle); unseated and brought down in 2 Chses. P-t-P/HUNT CH '99 and '03 r8 w5 (2m4f Maiden and 4 Opens) p1 (2nd); 7th, and last. A disappointment under Rules, but displayed tremendous versatility when unbeaten in Points in '03, and was gambled on to pick up where she had left off at Thorpe. Never looked likely to become involved, but it later transpired that she had fractured her pelvis, and has been retired to the paddocks. *Mrs A.J. Higgins — Cottesmore (Laura Pomfret).* 107 (O).

ARCHBISHOP ..9-12.. 8 ch.g. Minster Son — Elitist (Keren) 15. Tall well-made half-brother to Broken English (*qv*). NH FLAT '01 r2 p0. NH '02 r5 p1 (2nd). P-t-P '03 r4 w1 (Maiden) p0; last pair 2, and fell. A dual winner in cheekpieces for Stuart Morris, but has never looked particularly trustworthy, and their third appearance together resulted in a wide margin defeat when favourite at Horseheath. Might revive when fresh, but appears to have to go right-handed, and his well-being has to be taken on trust. *R. Hartop — Pytchley (Toby Saunders).* 559 (R), 742 (I).

ARCTIC BURNER (IRE) ..9-10§.. 11 b.g. Glacial Storm (USA) — Lucky Appeal (Star Appeal) 32324. Compact half-brother to 4 winners, including Shambo (useful flat), Run Free (also successful Hurdler), and one in Norway. Dam is half-sister to La Chance (*qv* 2000 Annual). NH FLAT '99 r1 p0. IRISH NH FLAT '99 r1 p0. NH '99/01 r21 w2 (2m110y Ch, and 2m3f Hdle) p2 (2nds); unseated 1, and refused to race 1. P-t-P '02/3 r9 p3 (3rds, remote last twice); 5th of 6, pulled up 4, and unseated 1. NH '03 (from J.C. Tuck's) r1 p0; last. A frustrating beast who has more ability than he cares to reveal, and lists self-preservation high on his list of attributes, but the owner-rider has never been able to get to the bottom of him. Ran better than in previous campaigns this year, but his losing sequence has been extended to 19. Has been tried in all types of headgear, but all aids were made redundant in '04. *Mrs J. Chapman — Cotswold V.F. (James Tuck).* 757 (L), 815 (M), 1344 (C), 1483 (L), 1493 (L).

ARCTIC DRIFT .—.. 10 b.g. Arctic Lord — Miss Blizard (Vitiges FR) p. Dam, half-sister to Black Arrow (*qv* '95 Annual), was 3rd in a Maiden and failed to finish in 3 other Points. P-t-P '03 r2 p0 (pulled up 2). Has shown good speed for two miles in all three appearances, but is then seemingly stopped in his tracks by a wind infirmity, and the application of a tongue-tie has been unable to alleviate the problem. *C.J. & Mrs J. Sandeman-Allen — E. Sussex & Romney Marsh (Paul Hacking).* 895 (OMa).

ARCTIC GREY (IRE) ..9-2.. 15 gr.g. Roselier (FR) — Our Hollow (Wolver Hollow) 3pfu. Tall good-topped half-brother to Claras Pride (IRE) (*qv*). IRISH NH FLAT '95/7 (blinkered) r14 p4. IRISH NH '97 r1 p0 (fell). IRISH P-t-P '98 r2 w1 (Maiden) p1 (2nd). P-t-P/HUNT CH '99 and '02/3 r14 w1 (Restricted) p5 (4 2nds, last once); ran out 1, pulled up 2, and fell 1. An expensive purchase who went wrong after dead-heating at Paxford in '99, and has failed to add to his score in just 13 subsequent appearances. Employed as a schoolmaster in '04, but only once got beyond the ninth, and looks finished now. *Mrs P. Duncan — Cotswold (Jelly Nolan).* 406 (Inr), 755 (M), 1066 (CCon), 1539 (I).

ARCTIC KING ..10-2§.. 12 b.g. Arctic Lord — Dunsilly Bell (London Bells CAN) 333f34r2. Well-made half-brother to Dragon King and Second Thoughts. NH FLAT '98 r2 p0. NH '00/1 r15 p3; pulled up 4, and fell/unseated 2. P-t-P/HUNT CH '03 r5 w3 (Maiden, Restricted — 3 ran and Members — 3 finished) p1 (2nd); and fell. Sweetened sufficiently to win three modest races last year, but previously a regular non-finisher under Rules, and looked decidedly mulish on occasions in '04. Tends to get worked up pre-race, and is nowhere near as fluent as 10 out of 13 Pointing completions suggests. Can still go a good gallop and best when allowed to dominate, but has no acceleration, and will struggle to raise his standards at 12. *A.M. Lloyd — Golden V.* 92 (I), 209 (3m1f110yH), 616 (C), 660 (Cf), 952 (I), 1227 (Cf), 1387 (M), 1485 (Cnr).

ARCTIC PENGUIN ..9-12.. 8 gr.g. Absalom — Sedge Warbler (Scallywag) p13. Strong-topped. Dam, half-sister to Arctic Teal (*qv* '95). Grandam, won Point and 2 Hunt Chses and 2nd (inc Hdle), (ran after producing Arctic Teal, and rated 11-0). Great-grandam, Arctic Actress, was short-headed in Open, but subsequently won 6 Chses, 2-3m. NH FLAT '01 r2 p0. NH '02 r3 p0. P-t-P '03 r5 p0 (last, pulled up 2, refused 1, and ran out 1). Stoutly bred on the distaff side, but by a sprinter, and had not shown sufficient stamina until landing a touch over 2m4f under Phillip York at Mollington. Rallied to regain the initiative having raced 10 lengths clear at one stage, but appears too impetuous to get the trip in full, although the application of a tongue-strap in '04 certainly proved beneficial. *Miss R. Murrell, S. Barfoot & Miss G. Cooper — Farmers Bloodhounds (Rebecca Murrell).* 128 (OMa), 290 (2m4fCfMa), 419 (CR).

ARCTIC SNIP ..9-4.. 10 b/br.g. Arctic Lord — Royal Snip (Royal Highway) p3426. Compact good-topped sister to Ailsae, and half-sister to Jukino. P-t-P '02/3 r4 p2; and pulled up 2. Knocking at the door in East Anglian Maidens, and collared only after the last when beaten just under a length at Ampton, but remains a weak finisher and will require a certain amount of luck to open his account in his fourth campaign. *J.K. Buckle — Essex & Suffolk.* 6 (OMa), 39 (OMa), 376 (Cf), 525 (OMa), 651 (OMa).

ARCTIC SUMMER (IRE) ..9-1.. 10 b.g. Insan (USA) — Annaleighs Nancy (IRE) (Duky) 323p32p. Compact. NH '01 r2 p0. P-t-P '02 (for Mr C. Jarvis) r4 p1 (last of 2); and pulled up 3. Undoubtedly has the ability to register a small success, and got to within a neck of doing so at Weston Park, but becoming most frustrating and is beginning to look very suspect. Has been ridden from the front and dropped out, but usually fades alarmingly and on the only occasion he galloped to the line the jockey (who seems to have lost the plot tactically) had set him too monumental a task. *Mrs M.S. Wilson — Meynell & S. Staffs (Jon Trice-Rolph).* 111 (OMa), 226 (CfMa), 295 (OMa), 370 (OMa), 729 (OMa), 927 (OMa), 1124 (OMa).

ARCTIC SUN (IRE) ..9-4§.. 8 b.g. Arctic Lord — Sherwood Express (IRE) (Cardinal Flower) 652. Good-topped half-brother to Irish Hurdles winner, Touchwoodexpress. IRISH P-t-P '02 r7 p2 (2nds); pulled up 2 of 5. IRISH NH FLAT '02 r1 p0. IRISH NH '03 (for T.J. O'Mara) r8 p0. Beaten one length or less in two Irish placings, but proving a big disappointment, and followed two poor lasts with a 21 lengths third in cheekpieces at Marks Tey (promoted to second). Tried blinkered and tongue-tied in previous campaigns, and does not seem to want to end his run of defeats which now stands at 19. *D.H. Gibbon — Dunston H. (Nigel Bloom).* 39 (OMa), 128 (OMa), 245 (CfMa).

ARCTIC TIMES (IRE) ..10-9.. 9 ch.g. Montelimar (USA) — Miss Penguin (General Assembly USA) 121f1b3. Sturdy compact brother to Irish NH Flat and jumping winner, Arctic Copper, and half-brother to Irish jumping winner, Wild Country. Dam, half-sister to Striking Chimes (*qv* '97 Annual). NH FLAT '01 r2 p0. NH '01/2 r4 p0. IRISH P-t-P '03 r3 w3 (Confined, Winners Of 1 and Open).

IRISH HUNT CH '03 r4 w2 p1 (2nd); and 5th. HUNT CH '03 r1 p1 (2nd). IRISH P-t-P '04 r4 w3 (beat No Messin' and Dan's Your Man 5*l* and 3*l* in Duhallow Open: *a.p, ld 3 out, clr last, r.o wl*; Spot Thedifference and Rockholm Boy 4*l* and 3*l* in North Tipperary Open: *hld up, hdwy 5, ld 10, stayed on wl*; and Dun Locha Castle and Dalian Dawn 10*l* and 6*l* in Doneraile Open: *hld up, hdwy 6, ld 11, clr aft 2 out, stayed on wl*) p1 (2nd to Glenduff Bridge in Muskerry Open: *hld up, went 2nd app 12, rdn & ev ch last, unable to qckn*). IRISH HUNT CH '04 r2 p1 (18*l* 3rd to Bemo One and Donishallprincess in Wexford Hunt Ch: *prom, 3rd when mist 3 out, sn wknd*); and brought down 1. Rated amongst the leading Pointers in Ireland since leaving Henrietta Knight in '02, and has scored on four occasions at Dromahane, but despite chasing home Lord Atterbury at Aintree last year has yet to break his duck over regulation fences. Fighting a losing battle when coming to grief five out in the Cheltenham Foxhunters, and appeared not to appreciate the sound surface when disappointing on his final start, but looks certain to bounce back to form in early '05. *T.J. Hemmings — Duhallow (Eugene O'Sullivan, in Ireland).* 543 (3m2f110yH).

ARDKILLY WARRIOR (IRE) .. -.. 12 b.g. Commanche Run — Dream Of Gold (Golden Love) 2pp. Smallish compact hobdayed. Dam won Mares Maiden and NH flat in Ireland. IRISH NH '98 r2 p0. IRISH P-t-P '98/99 r11 w2 (Confined, and Winners of One) p2 (3rds); pulled up 5, unseated 1, and refused 1. P-t-P '00 (for Mrs G. Fryer) r3 p0 (pulled up 3). A dual winner in Ireland in '00, but has literally ground to halt in all but one of eight subsequent attempts, and remains highly suspect. Worth 9-13 on his second to Endeavour at Marks Tey, but his breathing problems make it impossible to perform consistently. *Mrs A. Wales — W. Norfolk.* 248 (Cf), 478 (Cf), 647 (Cf).

ARDMAYLE (IRE) ..10-1.. 11 b.g. Be My Native (USA) — Serena Bay (Furry Glen) 32u3244. Workmanlike hobdayed. Dam is half-sister to Shallow River (*qv*). IRISH P-t-P '99/00 r6 p3; pulled up, and fell when disputing 2nd at last. P-t-P/HUNT CH '01/3 (for Mrs R. Arthur) r18 w4 (inc Restricted and Intermediate) p4 (3 2nds); pulled up 2, unseated 1. Won twice and runner-up twice for present connections after changing hands midway through last season, but has proved expensive to follow in the main, and often let down by sketchy jumping. Tends to hit a flat spot, but can finish strongly on his day, and has gone close in the last two runnings of the Fernie 4-miler, both times leaving the impression he could have won. Best suited by ground close to good. Has been tried in a tongue-tie. *Mrs S.A. Coney — Blankney (Jill Dawson).* 299 (L), 380 (L), 479 (L), 1122 (L), 1216 (4m100yMO), 1396 (C), 1500 (Cf).

ARD NA CARRIG (IRE) ..—.. 12 ch.g. Mister Lord (USA) — Coxtown Lass (IRE) (Selko) uup. Tall lengthy. IRISH NH '98/9 r3 p0 (inc 14th of 15 and pulled up in Chses). NH '00/2 r3 p1 (dist 3rd in 2m4f Ch); 4th, and pulled up. P-t-P/HUNT CH '00/3 (for Mr S. Gegg) r18 w2 (Club Maiden and Members) p2 (2nds); 4th, last pair 5, pulled up 5, and fell/unseated 3. Ending a losing run of 12 when the incredibly lucky winner of his Members last year, but often stops in a few strides, and has been tried in a tongue-strap. Went no more than two miles in '04, ejecting an unsafe beginner on the first two occasions, and looks a waste of time now. *Mrs M. Mitchell — Worcs (Nicky Sheppard).* 405 (Inr), 999 (R), 1111 (L).

ARDNUT .9-2.. 13 b.g. Phardante (FR) — Lady Tut (Fine Blade USA) 6uf3536p2pp. Small unfurnished. Dam won 3 flat, 7-12f (inc 2 Sells) and 3 Hdles, 2m-2m6f. NH FLAT '98 r2 p0. NH '99 r1 p0 (pulled up). P-t-P '99/00 and '02/3 (for Miss D.M. Foley) r16 w1 (Maiden) p1 (2nd of 3); pulled up 5, fell/unseated 4, and refused 1. Lightly raced in three previous Pointing yards, but has never looked anything but modest, and has always tended to make mistakes. Turned out 11 times in '04, and regained blinkers on the last 10 occasions, but usually remote from an early stage, and does not look likely to add to his '00 Mosshouses success. *R.A. & Mrs C.R. Page — Cambridge Univ (Ruth Page).* 98 (M), 224 (CMod), 248 (Cf), 400 (C), 647 (Cf), 829 (R), 999 (R), 1245 (R), 1316 (R), 1469 (R), 1517 (R).

ARDROSS GEM (IRE) ..10-3.. 11 b.m. Ardross — Forty Watts (Sparkler) u53f1. Sturdy compact half-sister to Near And Phar (IRE), and to Hurdles winner, Marksman Sparks. NH FLAT '99/00 r2 p0. NH '01 r3 p0. P-t-P '02/3 r12 w2 (Ladies) p2 (2nd of 3 and 3rd of 4); 4th, last pair 3, fell 1 and pulled up 3. Moody and lacks consistency as a result, but can finish strongly on occasions, and appeared to relish the extended trip when successful for a substitute rider on her final appearance at Flete Park. Has won in softish but drier ground suits best, and could maintain her sequence of having won in each of the three previous seasons next year. Regular partner Wendy Southcombe certainly had an eventful season, with a Hunter Chase success, and two air ambulance trips following spills at Great Trethew and Littlewindsor. Has been tried in cheekpieces, and visored thrice in '04. *Miss W. Southcombe & Mrs S.C. Cook — Cattistock (Peter Southcombe).* 470 (L), 690 (L), 965 (L), 1011 (L), 1197 (4mL).

AREWETOOLATE ..8-7.. 13 br.g. Gods Solution — Attavante (Derrylin) pp2. Owner-bred. Did not do at all badly for a 12-year old newcomer when four lengths second in an elders Maiden at Garthorpe, but unfortunately the answer to his name is yes, we probably are. *D. Lee — Bilsdale (Denis Grattan).* 1291 (OMa), 1425 (OMa), 1505 (OMa).

ARIANN SOUND (IRE) ..—.. 10 ch.g. Montelimar (USA) — Ariannrun (Deep Run) pup. Tall good-topped half-brother to Makin' Doo (IRE), to Hurdles winners, Keepatem (IRE), Shore Party (IRE) (also won Chasing) and Valerios King (IRE), and to NH flat winner, Poachin Again (IRE). IRISH P-t-P '01/3 r10 w1 (Maiden) p3; pulled up 1. IRISH NH '00/1 (for G.J. O'Keeffe) r3 p0; pulled up 1. Won an Irish Maiden in deep mud in '01, but ended a brief English campaign when breaking down badly, and it would be a big surprise if he was able to race again. *C. Stevens — Minehead H.* 10 (L), 273 (M), 323 (R).

ARKAY ..6-0.. 15 ch.g. Good Times (ITY) — Evening Crystal (Evening All) 4. Small compact. P-t-P '95/00 and '02 r17 p4 (remote last of 2; 3rd of 4; and last of 3 twice); failed to finish 8 (fell/unseated 5). As slow as befits an old age pensioner, but normally gets from A-B without mishap, and escorted a first-timer on a leisurely tour of High Easter when 245 lengths last in his Members, a feat he was repeating for the seventh time. *R.C. Kerry — Easton H.* 217 (M).

ARLEQUIN DE SOU (FR) ..9-9.. 11 b.g. Sir Brink (FR) — Colombine (USA) (Empery USA) fp6240. Good-topped. FRENCH NH '98 r4 w3 (2m2f-2m5f Chses) p0. NH '99/03 (for P.J. Hobbs; claimed for £19,192) r25 w5 (3 2m4f-2m6f Hdles and 2 2m5f-2m6f Chses) p9; fell 2. An accomplished front-runner in the mud at best, but none of his eight wins have been at further than 2m6f, and always struggling to get the trip in Points. Very much on the downgrade in his seventh season, and future opportunities look sparse. Often wears blinkers. *Mrs S.L. Hobbs & Mrs K. Vann — W. Somerset (Polly Curling).* 11 (O), 89 (O), 317 (2m4fH), 472 (Cf), 880 (MO), 1168 (2m5fH).

A ROMP TOO FAR (IRE) ..9-3.. 9 b.g. Eurobus — Saxa Princess (IRE) (Lancastrian) 2p. Strong. 3400 3yo. NH FLAT '01 r1 p0. NH '01/3 (for C.J. Mann, and K.C. Bailey) r5 p0; pulled up 3. Bought Doncaster, May for 2400. Won a Chipley Park Maiden at the start of February, but edged right close home and hampered the runner-up, and placings were reversed by the stewards. Outclassed in all his other races including a Seller and wore cheekpieces twice under Rules, and was tailed off after a mile on his Hunter Chase debut. Manages few outings, and needs a prompt return to the lowest grade if able to reappear. *G.M. Julian — Lamerton (Mark Ranger).* 119 (OMa), 178 (3m1f110yH).

ARTHUR-K .—§.. 8 ch.g. Greensmith — Classy Miss (Homeboy) f. Compact half-brother to Hawkers Hill. FLAT '00 r4 p1 (3rd). NH '02 r3 p0; last, and pulled up 2. P-t-P '03 r2 p0 (slipped up, and pulled up). Yet to beat a rival over jumps, or even complete in Points, and although he was still in touch when falling after 2m3f at Black Forest Lodge he promptly disappeared. Wears a cross-noseband. *M. Chaffey — S. Dorset.* 66 (OMa).

ARTIC GROUND (IRE) ..8-8§.. 13 b.g. Lord Americo — Frozen Ground (Arctic Slave) 474. Good-bodied half-brother to Usario, Arctic Quest (dam of The Cooling Agent *qv*), Frozen Drop and Over The Maine (IRE). Dam won 2 Hdles, 2-3m. NH FLAT '97/8 r4 p2 (2nds). NH '98/00 r14 w1 (2m3f Hcap Hdle) p2 (3rds); pulled up 4. P-t-P '02/3 r8 p1 (2nd of 3); last pair 5, and pulled up 2. His win dates back to '98, but has never shown much in the way of determination and only once better than last in nine appearances for present connections. Wears a cross-noseband, and has been tried in a near-side pricker and blinkers. *Mrs W. Doyne-Ditmas — E. Cornwall (Derek Doyne-Ditmas).* 80 (Cf), 200 (Cf), 497 (Cf).

ASCOOLASICE .7-0.. 7 b.g. Thethingaboutitis (USA) — Frozen Pipe (Majestic Maharaj) pp4. Rangy. Dam, half-sister to Cool Relation, won 4 Points and placed 4 for the Brewers (*qv* '98 Annual). A currently sticky jumper who has been badly placed, and was over a fence behind when last in his Members, but could possibly do better if sharpened up and allowed to concentrate on Maidens. *A. Brewer — Crawley & Horsham (Louise Brewer).* 128 (OMa), 177 (3mH), 638 (M).

AS DE LA GARENNE (FR) .8-12.. 6 b.g. Sleeping Car (FR) — Maria Theresa (FR) (Iron Duke FR) 4d. Half-brother to Mister Bean (FR). Backed from sevens to threes in a January Maiden and showed some ability before fading in the closing stages (completed for last, but disqualified when the jockey failed to weigh-in), but his stable were generally under a cloud in '04, and was not seen again. Probably worth another look. *R. Waley-Cohen — Warwicks.* 13 (OMa).

ASH BRANCH (IRE) ..—.. 11 ch.g. Shardari — Etnas Princess (The Parson) p*p*. Tall rangy half-brother to Bearys Cross (IRE), and to 4 winners (one in Macau) including No Tag (Irish jumping). Dam won 3 Irish flat, 10-12f. IR11,000 4yo. NH FLAT '00 r1 p0. NH '01/2 r5 w1 (2m4f Ch) p0; pulled up 1. NH '04 r1 p0 (pulled up in 3m Hdle: *a bhnd, mist 6, t.o 8, pu 10*). The winner of a six-runner Hurdle on firmish at Bangor, but beaten 20 lengths plus in seven other races. Off the course for 21 months before his outing at Tabley, and gives the impression that he could have been a decent performer had he managed regular outings. *Sir John & Lady Barlow — Cheshire (John Barlow).* 1427 (O).

ASHBURTON LORD (IRE) ..—.. 14 br.g. Lord Americo — Fiona's Wish (Wishing Star) p. Small neat brother to Prestige Lord (IRE), and half-brother to Chasing winner, River Bug (IRE), and to Irish Pointing winner, Northern Fiona. IRISH P-t-P '96/8 r7 p2 (inc last of 3); pulled up 1, slipped up 1, and brought down 1. P-t-P '00 and '02/3 r15 w1 (Maiden) p3 (2nd of 3, remote 3rd of 4 and last of 3); last 4, and pulled up 7. Remains highly charged and tends to make the running, but rarely keeps going for more than two miles, and looks to have reached the end of the line. *P.E. Legge — I. of W.* 90 (I).

ASHBURY STAR (NZ) ..10-0.. 10 ch.g. Sumayr — Piaf's Star (NZ) (Famous Star) 313. Big strong. Dam won in Australia. NZ FLAT '99/00 r20 w4 (7-11f). NH '00/3 (for Mrs N. Smith) r18 w1 (2m Hdle) p7 (inc 5 2nds); pulled up 2. Bought Ascot, Jun for 3428. Competent in his flat racing days down under, but has frequently looked jaded since, and blinkered once and wore cheekpieces once under Rules. Not endowed with great stamina, and was gaining a first success for three years when he rallied to re-pass another weak finisher in a Charlton Horethorne Open in which only three got round. 15 lengths last next time, and connections did well to extract another success. *P. Gooder — Taunton V. (Mel Dixon).* 145 (O), 352 (O), 964 (O).

ASHFIELD ORCHESTRA (IRE) ..10-1.. 9 b.m. Orchestra — Colour Clown (Random Shot) 1222. Half-sister to Dillons Bridge (IRE) and Cathy Come Home (IRE), and to Irish Pointing winners, Coloured Thyme and Le Sept. IRISH P-t-P '02 r3 w1 (5&6yo Maiden) p0; fell 2. IRISH HUNT CH '02 r1 p0. P-t-P '03 r2 p0 (4th, and unseated). Rather fortunate to open her account in a two-finisher Maiden in Ireland, but the time before would have finished in front of Just Cassandra (successful in three Irish Hunter Chases in '04) but for falling two out, and easily landed a touch on her reappearance in a weak Ladies at Howick. Twice beaten less than a length subsequently, and met Upton Adventure the other time, and should find further opportunities in Wales where the fences suit her sometimes erratic jumping. *J.L. Brown — Llandeilo F.* 361 (L), 449 (L), 843 (L), 949 (L).

ASHGAN (IRE) .10-5.. 12 br.g. Yashgan — Nicky's Dilemma (Kambalda) 1p14. Lengthy workmanlike half-brother to Leicaree (IRE), and to Irish Hurdles winners, Rusheen Bay (IRE) and Joe Bosky (IRE) (latter also Irish Pointing winner). Dam won NH flat and 2m4f Hdle in Ireland. P-t-P '98 r4 w2 (Maiden and Restricted) p1 (2nd); and refused. NH '98/02 (for I. Williams, one win and Mrs H. Dalton) r29 w8 (5 2m4f-2m6f110y Hdles, and 3 2m4f110y Chses) p5; pulled up 6. Won two Points as a five-year-old, but quirky and took a while to become confident over regulation fences, and was undoubtedly happier over hurdles. Off the track for 12 months with both shoulder and leg problems before scoring twice at Worcester in the summer of '02 (typically pulled up in between), but successful for the first time since an operation on his wind when readily justifying favouritism in his Members. Beat a solitary opponent at Andoversford, but firmly put in his place next time, and having left the yard again his winning days appear numbered. Has been tried successfully in blinkers, and once when not so in a visor. *A.J. & Mrs L. Brazier — Albrighton (Andrew Dalton).* 91 (M), 229 (O), 818 (MO), 1299 (2m4f110yH).

ASHGREEN ..10-4.. 8 b.g. Afzal — Space Kate (Space King) 3. Workmanlike Green-bred half-brother to Tigerwolf. Dam, sister to Space Fair, and half-sister to Kerry Hill (*qv* '98 Annual), won 3m2f Hdle on her final start in her fourth season, but finished lame. Grandam, Katie Fare, won 3 Hunt Chses and placed 10 (including Points and Hcap Ch). NH '01/2 r5 p0; pulled up 2, and fell 1. P-t-P/HUNT CH '03 r6 w3 (hat-trick Maiden and Intermediate and Restricted Nov Rdrs) p1 (2nd); 7th, and pulled up. Left his previous form under Rules behind when recording a hat-trick last year, and helped propel Sam Thomas onto a bigger stage, but subsequently disappointed when upped in class. Likes to bowl along at the head of affairs, and ran well for a long way behind Lord Atterbury at Barbury on his reappearance, but presumably met with a setback and was not seen again. Should easily prove capable of winning again provided he has come to no lasting harm. *C.J. Green & S. Turner — S. Herefords (Stan Turner).* 34 (O).

ASHOR TED ..— §§.. 8 ch.g. Romany Rye — Leatan (Leander) rppp. Robust lengthy half-brother to Senor Cid. Dam (*qv* '96 Annual) won Maiden, but last once and failed to finish 7 in her other Points. Keeps wanting to refuse (including with cheekpieces on final start), and even if the rider keeps trying until he is 100 (he can't be far off) he is going to struggle to get this villain to complete. *The Conker Club (S.H. Jarrett) — Beaufort (Joanna Bush).* 516 (R), 723 (OMa), 982 (2m5fOMa), 1259 (OMa).

ASHWELL BOY (IRE) ..10-1.. 14 b.g. Strong Gale — Billys Pet (Le Moss) 2. Lengthy brother to Hurdles winner, Macaw-Bay (IRE). Dam, half-sister to Woodlawn (*qv* '92 Annual). NH FLAT '95, r4 w1 p1 (2nd). NH '96/02 r45 w10 (3 2m Hdles, and 7 2m-2m5f110y Chses) p16. P-t-P/HUNT CH '03 r3 p0 (pulled up 3). A prolific winner under Rules, but lost his form and wore headgear on his final six attempts, and looked a pale shadow of his former self when pulled up on three occasions last year. Made a surprise return in his Members when a first ride for Brendan Gallagher, and was denied a first victory beyond 2m5f by only the minimum margin, but literally ran his heart out and keeled over in the unsaddling enclosure. *P. Surtees — Croome & W. Warwicks (Rob Summers).* 976 (M).

ASHWICKE GAMBLER ..7-12.. 9 b.g. Tout Ensemble — Miss Dollymouse (Nader) 4pupp7. Strong compact. P-t-P '02 r2 p0 (ran out, and pulled up). NH '03 r3 p0; pulled up 2. Can go one hell of a lick, but his ability has yet to be harnessed, and not better than last in three completions over obstacles. Twice well supported at long odds, but needs to learn to settle better if he is ever to challenge for honours. Wears a cross-noseband. *S.H. Jarrett — S. Dorset (Mary Tory).* 237 (CfMa), 329 (OMa), 967 (OMa), 1009 (OMa), 1252 (OMa), 1381 (OMa).

ASK AGAIN ..9-3.. 6 ch.g. Rakaposhi King — Boreen's Glory (Boreen FR) pp1. Half-brother to Saffron Glory, Border Glory and Little Dragon. 2500y. Made the most of an extremely simple opportunity in a very slowly-run youngsters Maiden at Lifton, (five started and only two went clear), in which Lucy Gardner outrode her rival after the narrow leader had fallen at the last. Very much a baby, so may have the scope to raise his rating. *Miss L. Gardner — Silverton.* 353 (OMa), 494 (OMa), 826 (OMa).

ASKERS JACK ..9-12.. 9 b.g. Karinga Bay — Martins Lottee (Martinmas) 5up22u2u2. Tiny. Dam is half-sister to Sea Barn (*qv* '94 Annual). P-t-P '02/3 r13 w1 (Maiden) p2; 4th, 6th, carried out, pulled up 4, and fell/unseated 3. Survived some indifferent jumping to score in the fastest of three Maidens at Cothelstone last year, but has been most expensive to follow since, and is not big enough to shrug aside his customary errors. Let slip winning opportunities at consecutive Bratton Down fixtures, and let favourite backers down for the third time in succession there subsequently, but tries hard and deserves to be rewarded again. Usually goes away to the left in an attempt to put himself right at the obstacles. *G.B. Foot — Seavington.* 118 (R), 232 (R), 323 (R), 879 (R), 1131 (R), 1386 (R), 1507 (R), 1558 (R), 1561 (R).

ASK THE NATIVES (IRE) ..11-3.. 11 br.g. Be My Native (USA) — Ask The Lady (Over The River FR) 11. Tall strong. IRISH NH FLAT '98 r1 p1 (2nd). NH FLAT '99 r1 w1. NH '99/03 (for P.F. Nicholls) r13 w3 (2 2m1f-2m3f Hdles and 2m6f Ch) p3; fell 2, brought down 1, and fell 1. A quality performer at best and was regarded as an Arkle prospect after winning his first three races in England, but then suffered a run of ten defeats in which errors were creeping in latterly, and made only one appearance in '03. Could hardly have been more impressive in his Pointing double, particularly when slamming Balinova and Kestick at Buckfastleigh, but is a martyr to physical problems (leg and blood vessels) and although his engine seems every bit as powerful as ever his future prospects obviously are very much dependent upon his health. Sadly, signs are not looking good. *P. Nicholls — Blackmore & Sparkford V. (Chloe Roddick).* 94 (L), 199 (L).

ASLAPOFTHEEURO (IRE) ..8-12.. 7 b.g. Eurobus — Slapoftheballot (Ragapan) pp4p. Small sturdy close-coupled. Dam, half-sister to Paul (*qv* '03 Annual). IRISH P-t-P '02/3 r7 w1 (5yo Maiden) p3; pulled up 2. NH '03 (for M.C. Pipe) r5 p0; last 3, and pulled up 1. Bought Doncaster, May for 15,500. Won his Irish Maiden in very soft ground, but made to look ridiculously expensive when beaten more than 50 lengths over hurdles in autumn '03 (visored on final start). Could not buck the trend in the latest yard, and was 15 lengths last on his only completion. Tends to sweat profusely. *The Fuzzy Logic Racing Partnership (Sue Freeman) — S. & W. Wilts (Sarah Waugh).* 324 (R), 473 (R), 973 (R), 1102 (R).

ASSINGTON BAY (IRE) ..—.. 7 b.g. Glacial Storm (USA) — Miss Nidee (Pollerton) pp. Brother to Irish Hurdles winner, Stormy Miss, and half-brother to Challis Choice (IRE), and to Irish Pointing winner, Boardroom Coup. 14,000 4yo. Tailed off and pulled up after 2m and 2m4f so far. *A. Kendrick — Essex F. & U. (Ruth Hayter).* 245 (CfMa), 525 (OMa).

ASTHEFELLASAYS (IRE) ..9-13.. 13 b/br.g. Good Thyne (USA) — Tiffany Downs (Green Shoon) 3p. Workmanlike brother to Alva (IRE). IRISH P-t-P '96/7 r6 w1 (5yo Maiden) p3; pulled up 1. P-t-P '98/9 and '02/3 r12 w3 (Members, Intermediate and Club restricted) p6 (4 2nds, of 3 twice); unseated 1, and pulled up 2. Broke down in '99 and despite not failing to reach the frame in seven subsequent completions has proved difficult to win with. Suited by conditions that put more of a strain on his legs, but has to be produced as late as possible, and looks to be on the downgrade. *Mrs P.G.D. & Miss A.J. Sykes — S. Salop (Pamela Sykes).* 835 (Cf), 1390 (O).

ASTHEFELLOWSAID (IRE) .10-6.. 8 ch.g. Glacial Storm (USA) — Celias Fancy (IRE) (Mandalus) 111. Neat attractive. IRISH P-t-P '02 r1 p1 (dead-heat 2nd). P-t-P '03 r1 p0 (pulled up). Reported to have pulled muscles when sent off favourite on his only appearance last year, but remained unbeaten in '04, and looks to have further improvement in him. Clearly held in high regard he was roughed off as soon as the ground firmed up, but appears to have the necessary jumping acumen to make his mark in Hunter Chases. Usually ridden from behind and produced for a turn of foot. *M.R. Smith — E. Sussex & Romney Marsh (Sara Hickman).* 152 (OMa), 538 (R), 640 (Cf).

ASTLEY GOLD (IRE) ..10-1.. 11 ch.g. Big Sink Hope (USA) — Ascot Princess (Prince Hansel) bp3. Tall rangy half-brother to 2 Irish Pointing winners, including Jim Jam Joey (IRE) (also successful English Hurdler). Dam won Mares Maiden in Ireland. NH FLAT '99 r1 p1 (2nd). NH '99/02 r10 p1 (2nd). P-t-P '03 r4 w1 (Maiden 3 — finished) p2 (2nds); and pulled up 1. An expensive failure in previous yards, but romped a bad Maiden at Dunthrop last year, and has been beaten a maximum of three lengths in two subsequent Restricted placings. Did not reappear until the end of April in '04, and a full season should afford him the opportunity to score again, but usually takes a keen hold, and struggles to get the trip. Wears a cross-noseband. *G. Whisker — Farmers Bloodhounds.* 1123 (R), 1377 (2m5fH), 1469 (R).

ATAVISTIC (IRE) ..10-2.. 13 b.g. Architect (USA) — Saceili (Saher) 13f. Neat. Dam won 2 12f races and 3 2m Hurdles in Ireland. NH FLAT '96 r4 w1 p1 (2nd). NH '96/03 (for C.L. Popham, first win; and P.J. Hobbs) r32 w9 (3 2m3f-3m Hdles and 6 3m-3m4f Chses) p10; pulled up 7, and fell 2. A very thorough stayer in the mud and had plenty to recommend him in his early career under Rules, but pulled up on his only start in '03 and was gaining a first success for over three years when providing Rosie Booth with a thrilling debut at Charlton Horethorne. Gamely showed himself to be no back number at 12, but unfortunately it all went pear-shaped at Stafford Cross, where he fell heavily two out and injured his partner (another participant broke her ankle; the damage caused to the former delayed the next race nearly an hour). Visored once in the past. *Miss R. Booth — Minehead H. (Aaron Bateman).* 351 (L), 690 (L), 1130 (Cnr).

ATHENIAN LAW .—.. 8 br.g. Darshaan — Titania's Way (Fairy King USA) p. Very small. Half-brother to flat winner, Andromeda's Way. Dam won 2 flat, 7-8f races. 74000y. NH FLAT '01 r1 w1. NH '01 and '03 (for P.J. Hobbs) r4 w1 (2m1f110y Hdle) p2 (inc neck 2nd); pulled up 1. Bought Doncaster, Aug for 2300. Ran twice and won twice in '01, but was not impressive at 2-5 in the Hurdle. Clearly very frail now, and was produced in a disgraceful state for his only Point. His former trainer would doubtless have had some pungent words to say if he could have seen him. *P.J. Millington — Quorn.* 125 (O).

ATHENRY LASS .—§.. 14 ch.m. Vouchsafe — Athenmore Lass (Athenien II) p. Quite attractive owner-bred half-sister to Scottishhighlander. Dam, half-sister to 3 Pointers, including the dam of Dunsbrook Lad, won 3 Points and placed 13 (including 2nd twice in 4m Heythrop Open). Grandam, Dunsmore Lass, won 4 Points. P-t-P '98/9 and '02/3 r11 w1 (Maiden) p5 (4 3rds, of 4 once, and last thrice); last pair 2, pulled up 3. Rated 9-10 after landing a seven-minute Maiden at Sandon in '02, but a tail-swisher and has refused to go a yard in her two most recent attempts, and would appear to be heading to the paddocks. Has always been incredibly lightly raced, and four outings in a year is her record. *Mrs R. Prince — Meynell & S. Staffs (Roy Prince).* 383 (R).

ATLANTIC DRIFT (IRE) ..9-2.. 11 b.g. Commanche Run — Cantafleur (Cantab) pu. Tall half-brother to Quetal (IRE) (*qv*). NH FLAT '99/00 r2 p1 (3rd) NH '00/2 r11 p1 (3rd). P-t-P '03 (for The Chase Club) r3 p2 (2nds, of 3 once); and fell 1. Placed on four occasions, and had three subsequent winners behind him when runner-up on his Pointing debut, but a beaten favourite on his next two starts, and failed to complete in both starts for new connections this year. Has the ability to win but seems ungenuine, and does not stand much racing. Wears blinkers. *J.F. Swiers — Derwent (Andrew Pennock).* 166 (OMa), 388 (M).

ATOMIC BREEZE (IRE) ..—.. 11 b/br.g. Strong Gale — Atomic Lady (Over The River FR) fpp. Tall heavy-topped half-brother to Irish NH flat and Chasing winner, Laochra. Dam won 4 2m-2m4f Irish Hurdles. NH '00/3 r27 w1 (3m2f Ch) p5; pulled up 11. NH '04 r1 p0 (pulled up in 3m3f Ch: *prom til lost pl 7, t.o when pu aft 11*). Possesses a little more ability than he usually shows, but inconsistent and lacks fluency, and finds it almost impossible to win (gained his sole success in a six-runner Chase on firmish at Carlisle). A faller twice including the Aintree Foxhunters, and pulled up in the better part of 50 per cent of his other attempts. *D.M. Forster — Zetland.* 732 (2m5f110yH), 1290 (L).

ATTACK ..—.. 9 gr.g. Sabrehill (USA) — Butsova (Formidable USA) pp. Strong-topped brother to Hurdles winner, Sabre Butt, and half-brother to 3 flat winners, including Heathyards Swing. Dam won 6f race (one in France). IRISH FLAT '02 r6 p2 (3rds). IRISH NH FLAT '02 r1 p0. IRISH NH '02 r2 w1 (2m Hdle) p0. FLAT '02/3 r7 p0. NH '02/3 (for P.J. Hobbs) r2 p2 (3rds in Chses). A Hurdling winner on firmish at Limerick, but tailed off last of three when gaining both Chasing prizes, and surely has physical problems. Blinkered once in '03, wears a tongue-tie, and looked fat in '04. *Mrs P. King — Suffolk (Julie Read).* 25 (L), 242 (2m5f110yH).

AUGATHELLA ..—.. 8 b.g. Out Of Hand — Choral Work (Song) pppp. Compact owner-bred brother to Koolilabah Lane. NH FLAT '02 (for W.S. Kittow) r2 p0. Useless in all his races to date, including when 66-1 in the latest. *Mrs S. Kittow — Tiverton.* 274 (CfMa), 469 (2m4fOMa), 1327 (OMa), 1380 (OMa).

AUGHMOR RIVER (IRE) .9-10.. 10 b.g. Over The River (FR) — Morego (Way Up North) 236p. Compact attractive brother to Family Business (IRE). IRISH P-t-P '99 and '01/2 r12 p6; pulled up 1, unseated 1. IRISH HUNT CH '00 r2 p0; pulled up 1. P-t-P '03 r6 w2 (Maiden — 3 finished and Restricted) p2 (2nds of 3); unseated, and pulled up. Twice runner-up on the opening day of the season, and has won two minor races, but appears to need everything his own way and does seem very willing to battle. Clearly goes well fresh, and may revive to some degree, but has ended both English campaigns on a downward note and may have suffered a setback on his Hunter Chase debut. Blinkered once in '04. *B. Belchem — E. Essex (Robert Gardiner).* 4 (Cnr), 41 (I), 249 (Cnr), 679 (3m1fH).

AUNT GLADYS (IRE) ..9-7.. 10 b.m. Glacial Storm (USA) — Salmons Pride (IRE) (Supreme Leader) 4213p. Small compact. Won a very poor elders Maiden in a slow time at Welbeck, but it was a gallant effort for a matron who had bred a foal by Zilzal in '03. Subsequent attempts suggest it will not be easy for her to unearth another opportunity. *J. Payne — Blankney (Mary Sowersby).* 304 (OMa), 500 (CMam), 594 (OMa), 990 (CR), 1205 (CR).

AUNTIE ALBA .—.. 7 b.m. Gran Alba (USA) — Auntie Lorna (Uncle Pokey) p. Compact good-topped attractive owner-bred. NH '03 (for N.J. Pomfret) r2 p0; pulled up 2. Pulled up in all her three races including a January Maiden, and does not give the impression of being a racehorse. *R.P. Brett — Belvoir (Laura Pomfret).* 60 (OMa).

AUNTIE KATHLEEN .9-9.. 6 gr.m. Terimon — Lady High Sheriff (IRE) (Lancastrian) 1. Unfurnished. Dam won Hurdle and Chase, both 2m4f. Bought Doncaster, Aug for 7800. Given a strong ride by the champion (putting up five pounds overweight) when winning a mid-March Maiden at Wadebridge, but none of the five behind even managed to complete the course subsequently, and went into hiding herself. Very difficult to evaluate, but her decent pedigree at least gives cause for optimism. *P.J. Finn — Middleton (David Pipe).* 486 (OMa).

AUTCAESAR AUTNIHIL (IRE) ..9-9.. 10 b.g. Supreme Leader — Monagey (Pimpernels Tune) p31p. Lengthy well-made. Dam won 2 Irish Hudles, 2m2f-2m4f. NH '02/3 (for N.T. Chance, and A.G. Juckes) r9 p0; pulled up 2, and fell 2. Totally outclassed under Rules (visored once; 29 lengths last, distant fourth, pulled twice and fell twice in Chases), but more effective in Points, and kept going stoutly to win a long elders Maiden at Maisemore. Seemed very unfit in early season (much huffing and puffing after his races), but not without a chance if he can find a weak Restricted. *Mr & Mrs D.C. Jeynes — Ledbury (Jo Jeynes).* 620 (OMa), 981 (OMa), 1258 (OMa), 1389 (R).

AUTUMN FLAME (IRE) ..8-10.. 14 ch.m. Henbit (USA) — Tartan Thistle (Ovac ITY) 34. Workmanlike sister to Restless Native (IRE). NH FLAT '96 r2 p0. NH '96/8 r8 p2 (3rds in Sells). P-t-P '99 and '02 r11 p1 (3rd); 4th, 5th, last pair 4, fell/unseated 2, pulled up 1 and carried out 1. Sent off favourite on two occasions in '99, but a non-stayer who stands her racing badly, and has beaten only one rival since. Has two paddock handlers. *Mr & Mrs R. Blanchard — Berks & Bucks (Albertine Blanchard).* 637 (CMam), 940 (OMa).

AVALON BUCK (IRE) ..9-6.. 12 b.g. Buckskin (FR) — Lilly's Way (Golden Love) 4. Strong rangy brother to Irish Pointing winner, Indian View. Dam won 2m6f Hurdles and 2 Chases (2m3f-3m) and 6 Points in Ireland. IRISH P-t-P '98/9 r7 w2 (5-6yo Maiden and Winners of One) p1 (2nd); pulled up 2. NH FLAT '99 r1 w1. NH '00/3 (for Miss V. Williams) r18 w4 (3 2m1f-2m4f Hdles and 3 3m Chses) p4; pulled up 4. Won seven races in the mud to December '01, but there were elements of luck in the final two successes, and ended his career in the previous yard in blinkers or cheekpieces. Tailed off from halfway when last in a Fakenham Open, and gave the strong impression that he would not be worth trying again. *P.S. Johnson — Cambridge Univ (Tim Bryce).* 1153 (O).

AVEC PLAISIR (IRE) ..9-3.. 10 ch.g. Grand Plaisir (IRE) — Ballinellard Lady (Fine Blade USA) 1f. Rangy. IR4000 3yo. NH FLAT '00 r1 p0. NH '01/3 (for T.R. George) r6 p1 (2nd); pulled up 4. A real mixed bag in his races. Put up a game display when second in a 22-runner Hurdle, but was pulled up in all four Chases, and blinkered in the latest (given reminders soon after the start). Overcame whatever ails him in an elders Maiden at Kingston St Mary (slow time), but then fell three out when labouring badly in his Members. Has managed only eight outings in five years. *P.R.H. Clifford — Berkeley.* 967 (OMa), 1070 (M).

AVENEL ..—.. 13 b.m. Decent Fellow — Mermaid (Furry Glen) p. Small neat home-bred half-sister to Decent Jane. Dam is half-sister to Nautical Belle (*qv* '96 Annual). IRISH NH '98 r1 p0. IRISH P-t-P '98/9 r5 p0 (pulled up 4, and fell 1). P-t-P '01/3 (for Mr J.T.H. Ainslie) r7 w1 (Mares Maiden) p3 (3rds, of 4 twice); last, pulled up 1 and fell 1. Rated 9-11 after belatedly opening her account on firmish at Musselburgh last year, but raced only once apiece in the two previous seasons, and immediately went wrong again in '04. *Mrs M. Wilson — Lanarks & Renfrews (Dick Allan).* 316 (2m5fH).

AVONDALE ILLUSION (IRE) ..8-13§§.. 13 b.g. Satco (FR) — Tattered Illusion (Our Mirage) p4p5. Good-topped half-brother to Irish Pointing winner, Real Deal. Dam won Mares Maiden and 4 Chases (2m3f-3m1f). IRISH P-t-P '97/8 and '02 r8 w2 (5yo Maiden, and Open) p0; pulled up 1, and fell 1. IRISH NH FLAT '97 and '99/00 r10 p6. IRISH NH '99/02 r16 w1 (2m4f Hdle) p4 (inc 2nd in Chse). P-t-P '03 r5 p1 (last of 3); 4th twice, 6th, and pulled up. Won three races over a four year period in Ireland to '02, but was never a by-word for reliability over there, and has been beaten a minimum of 28 lengths since joining present connections. Does not want to try any more and is not worth bothering with again. Has been tried in headgear. *Mrs S.J. Stearn — Suffolk.* 38 (Cf), 397 (O), 1153 (O), 1313 (Cf).

AYE SURELY (IRE) ..—.. 11 b.g. Legal Circles (USA) — Uno Navarro (Raga Navarro ITY) u. Workmanlike unfurnished half-brother to Not My Line (IRE). IRISH P-t-P '99 r2 p1 (sh hd 2nd).

IRISH NH '99/03 r26 w2 (2m Hdle and 2m4f Ch) p2; fell/unseated 5. NH '03 (for Mrs A.M. Thorpe) r4 p1 (2nd); pulled up 1. Bought Doncaster, Mar for 1500. Won twice in Ireland, three years apart (soft and heavy ground), and often blinkered there. Despite scoring over shortish trips he stays 3m3f, and would not be without a chance in a Point if fit, but that seems to be a problem for him now. *N. Evans — Carms.* 205 (O).

AZTEC RULE (IRE) .9-9§.. 12 b.g. Strong Gale — Monksville (Monksfield) pp8. Lengthy half-brother to Irish Hurdles winner, Nan Chero. Dam won 2m veteran jockeys flat race, 2 Hurdles (2m2f-2m4f) and 3 Chases (2m4f-3m) in Ireland, and is half-sister to Verrazano Bridge (*qv* '02 Annual). NH FLAT '99 r2 p0. NH '00/2 r8 p3. P-t-P '03 (for The Bean Club) r7 w2 (Maiden and Restricted) p1 (last of 3); unseated 1, refused 1, ran out 1 and pulled up 1. Cajoled into winning twice last year, and can still tank along when he chooses, but liable to give up without warning, and still inclined to root the odd fence. Looks too set in his ways to stage a revival in '05. Wears a cross-noseband, and has been tried in a tongue-strap, cheekpieces, and acquired blinkers on his latest appearance. *Mrs S. Bird — Ledbury (Nicky Sheppard).* 50 (I), 513 (Cf), 980 (Cf).

BABS WHEAL ..9-4.. 9 b.m. Petoski — Releta (Relkino) ff1fp*0*. Small light half-sister to Reluckino and Haydens Field (won 5 Hdles since Pointing), and to Hurdles winner, Reltic. Dam won 4 Points consecutively and placed in 2 Hunt Chses (rated 10-10), and is half-sister to Dereta's Dudley (*qv* '88 Season Annual). NH FLAT '01 r2 p0. NH '04 (for D.J. Wintle) r1 p0 (11th in 2m4f Hdle: *a bhnd, rmdrs aft 2, t.o* 6). Far from robust and tends to be the victim of some horrible errors, but came from a long way back to beat seven other finishers in a Mares Maiden at Upton-on-Severn in mid-April. The time was slow and none of those behind have managed to break their duck, and it was clearly a dreadfully weak contest. Has a good trainer and jockeys, but not one to have any faith in in future. *Mrs H. Hogben — Cotswold V.F. (Alison Dare).* 408 (CMam), 519 (CfMa), 978 (CMam), 1230 (R), 1389 (R).

BABY JOHN (IRE) ..9-6.. 12 b.g. Celio Rufo — Kings Princess (King's Ride) 59p3p. Close-coupled brother to Irish Pointing and Hurdles winner, Orafeno. IRISH P-t-P '98/9 r2 p1 (2nd); and fell when looking winner 2 out. NH FLAT '99 r1 p0. NH '99/02 r18 w1 (2m3f Ch) p7 (inc 5 Hdles). P-t-P '03 r3 p0 (last thrice). Looked promising in Ireland, and subsequently managed to land a Chase in '00, but only once better than last in Points, and looked decidedly reluctant when tried in cheekpieces once. Has yet to give the impression that three miles is suitable. *Mrs S. Horner-Harker — Hurworth.* 71 (L), 211 (C), 391 (MO), 562 (M), 772 (4m1fO).

BACARESE ..8-9.. 8 b.g. Good Thyne (USA) — The Little Bag (True Song) f3. Workmanlike lengthy owner-bred brother to Little Veralyn, and half-brother to Gill's Gale, Leading Case and Hever Road (IRE). Dam won 8 Points (inc an Open, and hat-trick) and placed 6, and grandam, Ruakura, won 6 Points (3 in Ireland) and placed 12. P-t-P '03 (for Prof D.B.A. Silk & Mr R. Perkis) r2 p0 (last, and pulled up 1). Ideally bred and has shown a modicum of talent, but makes too many mistakes, and finished lame at Garthorpe. *Prof D.B.A. Silk, W. Bellamy & W. Meadows — Kent & Surrey Bloodhounds (Emma Leppard).* 128 (OMa), 385 (OMa).

BACCARAT (IRE) ..—.. 11 b.g. Bob Back (USA) — Sarahlee (Sayyaf) pp. Tall strong brother to Irish flat winner, Tres Chick. Dam won 3 Irish flat, 12-17f. NH FLAT '98/9 r4 w1 p2. NH '99/01 and '03 (for J.G & T.J. Fitzgerald) r9 p4 (3rds in Chses); pulled up 3, and fell 1. Bought Ascot, Nov for 2476. Made a winning debut at Doncaster in a 18-runner bumper in November '98, but a bitter disappointment since, including when beaten between seven and 15 lengths in four Chasing thirds. An uncertain jumper. Stands his racing badly, and also has breathing problems (generally tongue-tied now). *Lady Susan Brooke — Teme V.* 50 (I), 209 (3m1f110yH).

BACKSHEESH (IRE) ..10-8.. 10 b.g. Bob Back (USA) — Kottna (USA) (Lyphard USA) 3. Tall hobdayed brother to Irish/English Hurdles winner, A Few Bob Back (IRE), and to Irish flat winner. Dam won 7f race in Ireland. IRISH NH FLAT '99/00 r4 w1 p0. IRISH NH '99/01 r11 p1 (2nd). NH '01 r2 p1 (3rd in Ch). P-t-P/HUNT CH '02/3 r4 w3 (Confined, 3m1f Hunt Ch, and Mixed Open) p0; and pulled up. Defeated for the first time in three attempts at Hornby Castle in '04, but suffers one setback after another, and has had his appearances strictly rationed since leaving Ireland. A sound jumper worth 11-0 at best, and is ideally suited by some give in the ground, but his problems appear insurmountable at present. Runs tongue-tied. *G. Tuer — Hurworth.* 812 (O).

BADGE OF FAME (IRE) ..—.. 11 gr.g. Caerleon (USA) — Infamy (Shirley Heights) ppp. Compact half-brother to 6 winners (one in Italy) to Hurdling winners, Rostropovich (IRE) (won £29,000 prize at Sandown), Kamikaze (latter also won flat and Chasing) Innuendo (won £119,713), Moon Queen and Barafamy (all flat). FLAT '97 r4 w1 (12f) p0. NH '98/01 (for K.C. Bailey, and J.L. Eyre) r11 w4 (2m3f-2m5f Hdles) p2 (3rds); pulled up 3. Despite being bred in the purple he was no great shakes on the flat, but made up for it in his hurdling career, gaining four victories on good or easy surfaces.

Has been useless over fences, pulling up in six of seven attempts and finishing 27 lengths fourth in the exception. Wore a tongue-tie on his final start in the previous yard, and is doubtless physically impaired now. *A. Clare — P. Cartmell — Hurworth.* 163 (O), 340 (O), 770 (Cf).

BADGER BEER ..10-4.. 13 b.g. Town And Country — Panda Pops (Cornuto) 312f. Compact half-brother to Nearly A Pop, Panda Shandy, Hops And Pops (subsequent useful jumping winner and dam of Rio Pops *qv*), Best Bitter, Inforapop and Mister Ringa. Dam won 2 Points and placed 5 for Sue Woodhouse. Grandam, Queen's Bounty, half-sister to Royal Heath, Armagnac Queen and April Gypsey (themselves the dams of several successful Pointers), won 2 Points and placed 7 (including 2 3rds for her). Great-grandam, April Queen, won Liverpool Foxhunters, 2 other Chases and 6 Points. P-t-P/HUNT CH '97/03 r50 w9 (inc 2 Hunt Chses, 2m3f110y-2m5f, 2 Opens and 2 Ladies) p14 (6 2nds, inc 3 Hunt Chses, and inc 2 3rds in Hunt Chses); pulled up 6, fell 2 and brought down 1. A bold-jumping front-runner with a fondness for firm ground, and took his winning tally into double figures when recording his fourth success at Badbury Rings. Tragically killed in a fall during the race run in memory of the owner-breeder's late husband two starts later. Mrs R.H. Woodhouse — Portman (John Dufosee). 235 (O), 263 (O), 352 (O), 438 (3m1f110yH).

BADWORTH GALE (IRE) ..—.. 11 br.g. Strong Gale — Badsworth Madam (Over The River FR) ppp. Tall rangy half-brother to Smokey Joe (IRE). IRISH P-t-P '00 r6 w1 (5&6yo Maiden) p0; pulled up 1, fell 2. NH '00 and '02 (for K.C. Bailey) r5 p0; pulled up 2. Badly bought by the previous yard, and has been a total flop since leaving his native land. Pulled up in five of eight races over fences and beaten more than 19 lengths if completing, and misses alternate years. Obviously defective. *J.E. Dillon — Fernie.* 679 (3m1fH), 892 (2m5f110yH), 1152 (R).

BAILEY'S OF CASHEL (IRE) ..—.. 10 ch.g. Husyan (USA) — Ballyharron (Deep Run) pppp. Lengthy half-brother to Irish Pointing winner, Shania's Run. IRISH P-t-P '01 r1 p1 (2nd). IRISH NH FLAT '00 r2 p0. IRISH NH '02 (for L. Wells) r1 p0 (pulled up). Bought Ascot, June 2000. Capable of showing a little early speed, but stops to nothing, and got no further than the 14th in '04. A waste of time on recent evidence. *Mrs N. Ford — The 500 Club (M.K. Titchner — Crawley & Horsham (Louise Brewer).* 103 (OMa), 129 (OMa), 540 (CfMa), 611 (OMa).

BAK ON BOARD ..10-0.. 9 b.g. Sula Bula — Kirstins Pride (Silly Prices) 3453513p1. Small owner-bred half-brother to Hasten Bak (*qv*). NH FLAT '01 r3 p0. NH '01/2 r6 p1 (3rd). P-t-P/HUNT CH '03 r8 w2 (Maiden and Restricted) p4 (2 3rds, of 4 once); 5th of 6, and fell. Not 100% following an early season double at Black Forest Lodge last year, and has not made significant progress since. Lacks acceleration, but stays well and responded to the application of first-time blinkers when springing a 16-1 surprise in soft at Kilworthy. Subsequently beaten no more than half a length next door but outbattled the runner-up when obliging at Flete Park. Should be able to find further opportunities when firing on all cylinders, but may not be able to raise his rating much higher. Has two paddock handlers. Wears a cross-noseband. *Miss L. Gardner — Silverton.* 62 (Cf), 147 (I), 200 (Cf), 321 (I), 495 (I), 573 (I), 793 (Cf), 1167 (3m2f110yH), 1194 (Cf).

BALAU ..9-7.. 6 br.g. Primitive Rising (USA) — Say Daphne (Say Primula) 1f4. Dam, sister to Say Sadie (*qv* '01), was second and fourth twice in Points. Bought Ascot, July 4619. Beat two other finishers in a Maiden at Detling which took one minute longer than the Confined, but a crashing fall when favourite at Penshurst left him winded on the ground for ten minutes. Not disgraced when tried again a month later, and should not be far away in Restricteds at six. Despite his tender years, he seems to possess stamina aplenty. *C. Cheesman — E. Sussex & Romney Marsh (Alison Hickman).* 539 (OMa), 779 (R), 1333 (R).

BALDARA (IRE) .9-8.. 8 b.g. Jurado (USA) — Inca Rose (IRE) (Strong Gale) 44415. Small half-brother to Irish Hurdling winner, Killaloe. IRISH P-t-P '03 r4 w1 (5&6yo Maiden) p1 (2nd); fell 1. IRISH NH FLAT '02 r1 p0. IRISH NH '02 (for J.P. Mangan) r2 p0. A proficient jumper who can handle soft ground, and was the comfortable winner of a truly dreadful Restricted at Lifton (the next four behind him managed seven other outings in '04 — all pulled ups!). Normally tongue-tied and a weak finisher, and may not find it easy to score again. *Miss L.E. Claydon — Dulverton F. (Ashley Farrant).* 197 (R), 323 (R), 601 (R), 824 (R), 1544 (I).

BALDHU BENDY ..—.. 9 b.m. Almoojid — St Christabelle (Golden Passenger) pp. Small sturdy owner-bred sister to Baldhu Luckystrike, and half-sister to Baldhu Prospector and Baldhu Mynah. Dam, half-sister to the dam of Baldhu Chance (*qv* '03 Annual), won her Members for Terry Long. P-t-P '02 r2 p0 (refused, and pulled up). Almost refused in both attempts in '02, and once again showed no aptitude when rank outsider in two starts this year. *T. Long — Four Burrow (Stephen Long).* 82 (OMa), 312 (CfMa).

BALDHU JACK ..9-8.. 12 b.h. Baldhu Cavalier — Little Stella (I'm Alright Jack) p94p. Small home-bred brother to Baldhu Jay Arr, and half-brother to Tinstreamer Johnny and Baldhu Bonnie. Dam won a

Maiden and 2nd for Terry Long. Sire is an unbroken brother to Baldhu Belle, and half-brother to Sancreed. P-t-P '98 and '00/3 r20 w2 (Maiden and Members) p2 (3rds, last once); pulled up 6, and fell/unseated 2. Showed he retains some ability when a staying-on fourth at Flete Park, but generally ridden with a lack of urgency in '04, and having previously suffered the odd setback his latest appearance, when pulled up before halfway, does not bode well for future excursions away from the covering sheds. Usually has two paddock handlers. *T. Long — Four Burrow (Stephen Long).* 572 (R), 912 (R), 1196 (R), 1351 (Inr).

BALDHU JAY ARR ..9-9.. 11 b.g. Baldhu Cavalier — Little Stella (I'm Alright Jack) 48p3p. Narrow light home-bred brother to Baldhu Jack (*qv*). P-t-P '00/2 (for Mr T. Long & Mr M.J. Stocker) r11 w2 (Maiden and Restricted) p4 (3 3rds; and last of 2); fell/unseated 4, and pulled up. Only once out of the frame when completing, but missed the entire '03 campaign, and appears nothing like as good as he was. Well supported when fitted with blinkers for the first time in his Members, but after leading for almost two miles was eventually beaten 30 lengths, and it is difficult to see him recapturing his best at 11. Has shown a tendency to hang and jump right. *M.J. Stocker — Four Burrow (Stephen Long).* 81 (I), 193 (I), 707 (Cf), 907 (M), 1348 (Cf).

BALDHU MYNAH ..—.. 6 b.g. Lir — St Christabelle (Golden Passenger) ppp. Small strong compact homebred half-brother to Baldhu Bendy (*qv*). Tailed off and pulled up thrice, twice in 2m4f contests and once in a Maiden in which there was considerable debate about the distance until the runners were finally despatched from the 3m start (!). *T. Long — Four Burrow (Stephen Long).* 307 (2m4fOMa), 702 (2m4fOMa), 1432 (OMa).

PLATE 20 199 South Pool Harriers Ladies Open: Balinova (Miss P. Gundry), 2nd, leads Ask The Natives (Miss C. Roddick), 1st, and the hidden Sandy Duff (Miss M. McCarthy), 5th
PHOTO: Tim Holt

BALINOVA (IRE) ..11-1.. 8 b.g. Lord Americo — Shuil Comeragh (Laurence O) 2112. Small neat half-brother to Daring Walk, Shuil Saor, Shuil Poipin (IRE), and to Irish Pointing winner, Shuil Le Laoi. Dam won 2m Hdle and 3 Chses (2m6f-3m) in Ireland. IRISH P-t-P '02/3 r9 w3 (Maiden, Winners of One and Ladies Open) p0; 4th, pulled up 3, unseated 1 and ran out 1. Failed to finish in his first five Irish Points, but has been in excellent heart since, and beaten in only two of his seven most recent ventures between the flags. Lost nothing in defeat when chasing home Ask The Natives at Buckfastleigh (re-passed the idling rider of Kestick close home), and then made the most of two easy tasks before a superb display at Cheltenham, where he lost out to Caught At Dawn only after a prolonged battle from three out (the telling factor was that his rider could not claim the seven pound allowance). Splendidly keen and enthusiastic, stays 3m2f, and there will be no justice if he does not capture a Hunter Chase in '05. *C.J. Bennett — Ledbury (Ben Tulloch).* 199 (L), 722 (M), 923 (L), 1172 (3m1f110yH).

PLATE 21 270 Sinnington Ladies Open: Superhero, Balisteros (Pauline Robson), 1st, in his last season of competition, maintains his unbeaten Duncombe Park record PHOTO: Roy Parker

BALISTEROS (FR) ..10-2.. 16 b.g. Bad Conduct (USA) — Oldburry (FR) (Fin Bon) 7341131322s*p*. Workmanlike. Dam won 2 races in France, including Grande Steeplechase de Lyon. NH FLAT r2 p0. NH '93/4 and '03 r8 p0 (fell/unseated 2 in Chses). P-t-P/HUNT CH '95/6, '98 and '00/3 r72 w30 (inc 4 Hunt Chses 2m5f-3m2f, and 23 Ladies, 3m-3m5f) p31 (18 2nds, inc 5 Hunt Chses; and inc 4 3rds in Hunt Chses); fell/unseated 3, pulled up 2. NH '04 r1 p0 (pulled up in 3m1f Hcap Ch: *hld up, hmpd 1, lost plce 11, bhnd when blun & pu 4 out*). A veteran of 92 races over jumps, and won no fewer than 33 times. The winning most performer in '00, and also prolific in '02, but moody and unpredictable between and since, and never approached Hunter Chasing with the same verve as he did Points. Retired with full honours after failing to complete for only the sixth time in 74 appearances for Billie Thomson in a race named after himself at Kelso. Thrived on racing, and was a credit to all concerned, and the scene north of the border will be much the poorer without his presence. *Mrs B.K. Thomson — Berwicks.* 5 (L), 71 (L), 133 (L), 270 (L), 339 (L), 655 (L), 763 (L), 916 (L), 1039 (L), 1146 (L), 1360 (3mH).

BALLAD (IRE) .9-11§.. 13 b.g. Salluceva — Song Of Love (Raise You Ten) 33131p2u512. Compact attractive half-brother to Hurdles winner, Torboy (IRE). P-t-P/HUNT CH '99/00 and '02/3 (for Mrs E.R. Featherstone) r22 w4 (Maiden, Restricted, Club Confined and 2-runner Members) p4 (2 2nds, fence last once; and last of 3 twice); pulled up 7, unseated 3 and refused 1. Has a fair record in minor Points, and appeared on better terms with himself than usual in the new yard, but flattered by an Open success, gained in a three-runner event in mud at Northaw. A safe ride for a novice and stands a good chance of maintaining his winning run in Members races in '05. Tongue-tied in the previous yard. *H. Hill & J.M. Ratcliffe — Granta H., & Cambridge Univ (Henry Hill).* 98 (M), 221 (O), 396 (M), 523 (O), 590 (M), 744 (O), 832 (Cf), 903 (O), 997 (O), 1243 (O), 1315 (O).

BALLAD MINSTREL (IRE) ..9-13.. 13 gr.g. Ballad Rock — Sashi Woo (Rusticaro FR) 23pp34. Tall strong brother to winner in Hong Kong, and half-brother to Sushi Bar (IRE), and to 4 flat winners (one in Hong Kong). NH FLAT '96/7 r4 w1 p1 (2nd). NH '97/01 and '03 (for J.G. & T.J. Fitzgerald) w4 (2m Hdle and 3 2m-2m4f Chses) p8; pulled up 2, fell/brought down 2. Enjoyed five wins under Rules to February '01 (often blinkered in that sphere, but not in Points), and showed he retained some ability in '04, but was inconsistent (beaten at 4-5 once), and the ground was doubtless never soft enough for him. Broke down at Easingwold. *Yorkshire P-t-P Club (Miss J.E. Foster) — Middleton (Jo Foster).* 270 (L), 338 (Cf), 479 (L), 630 (2m4fH), 1290 (L), 1301 (Cf).

BALLET RED ..9-2.. 8 b.m. Sea Raven (IRE) — Cailin Rua (IRE) (Montelimar USA) p1. Small light. NH FLAT '01 r2 p0. NH '01/2 (for R.D. Wylie) r5 p1 (2nd); pulled up 1. Finished a distant second over hurdles, and was having only her ninth outing in five years when she got up to pip a donkey in a three-finisher Maiden at Pentreclwydau. Will have a lot more to do if she returns for Restricteds. *A. Simpson — S. Pembs (Beverley Thomas).* 1091 (CMam), 1240 (OMa).

BALLINGALE DAWN (IRE) .10-0.. 9 b/br.g. Caesar Imperator (FR) — Gerise (Nishapour FR) p6323. Tall strong half-brother to Grandman (IRE), and to flat winner, Purchased By Phone. Dam won at 12f in Ireland, and won 2m fillies Hdle there. IRISH P-t-P '02 r3 w1 (6yo Maiden) p1 (2nd); pulled up 2. IRISH NH '02/3 (for R. Tyner) r6 p0; pulled up 2. Won his Irish Point in soft, but did not seem to appreciate holding patches when a very tired second at Garnons, and gave better displays in two thirds (once in an Open at Garnons, where he was staying on in the closing stages, and one at Upton-on-Severn, where he looked the winner when in front at the last but faded to lose two positions). A competent jumper, and surely has a good chance of collecting his Restricted. *C.F. Basterfield — Albrighton Woodland (Roy Tatlow).* 228 (Cf), 252 (CR), 404 (O), 614 (R), 977 (R).

BALL IN THE NET..9-9.. 12 b.g. Arctic Lord — Courtlands Girl (Crimson Beau) p8. Unfurnished brother to Queens House, and half-brother to Russian Friend and Prince Pluto. Dam won 3 Hdles at around 2m. IRISH P-t-P '99 r2 p0 (fell 2). IRISH NH FLAT '99 r1 p0. NH '01 r1 p0 (10th of 12). P-t-P/HUNT CH '00/3 r11 w5 (inc Open, and inc hat-trick '00) p1 (3rd); pulled up 2, ran out 1. Rather headstrong and goes a good gallop, and recorded a hat-trick in '00 and a double two years later, but a bleeder and stands only light campaigns. A good jumper in Points, but nowhere near as accurate over regulation fences, and will need his sights lowering if he is to bounce back to form at 12. Suited by top-of-the-ground. *D.A. Rees — Hursley Hambledon (Penny Lownds).* 1105 (O), 1497 (3mH).

BALLINURE BOY (IRE) ..10-7.. 12 b.g. Meneval (USA) — Sweet Cahore (General Ironside) 142p. Workmanlike. IRISH P-t-P '98/9 r8 p4 (beaten a head once); fell 3. P-t-P/HUNT CH '00/3 (for Mrs N.E. Turtle) r15 w9 (inc 2m5f Hunt Ch and 4 Opens, and inc hat-trick '02) p1 (3rd); pulled up 1, fell 1. A useful Pointer who goes well fresh and is usually ridden for a turn of foot, but less productive than usual in '04 despite pushing his winning tally into double figures. Tried blinkered on his penultimate start where everything looked to be in his favour, but was outgunned by a first-timer on a 12-year-old, and ended the campaign on a low note at Folkestone. Vulnerable on easy ground but should still find some easy pickings in the South-East next year. Wears a cross-noseband. *Mrs E. Smith — E. Sussex & Romney Marsh (Sara Hickman).* 247 (O), 442 (2m7f110yH), 830 (O), 1440 (3m1fH).

BALLINVELLA ..—.. 13 ch.g. Ballinvella Boy — The Lady Tara (Leabeg) f. Small stocky hunter. Fell at the 15th when struggling to keep tabs on a thoroughbred in a one-finisher Members. *J. Casemore — Vine & Craven.* 968 (M).

BALLYALBERT..9-13.. 10 ch.g. Gran Alba (USA) — Ballytina (Rugantino) f1b22. Compact half-brother to True Chimes (*qv*). NH FLAT '00 r2 p0. P-t-P '02/3 (for Mrs A. De Lisle Wells) r5 w1 (Maiden) p2 (2nds, beaten fence once); ran out and pulled up. Not out of the first two in six Pointing completions, and is not short of ability, but can be very headstrong and always jumps left-handed. Scored unchallenged at Howick, but failed to beat a serious rival otherwise, and still gives the impression that stronger handling would be beneficial. Best suited by genuinely good ground, but stands only light campaigns. *Mrs K.M. Price — N. Cotswold (Harry Wheeler).* 139 (R), 358 (R), 663 (I), 921 (M), 1330 (I).

BALLYBLACK (IRE) .8-11.. 11 b/br.g. Brush Aside (USA) — Buck Away (Buckskin FR) 2p. Workmanlike. P-t-P '00/1 and '03 r8 w1 (Maiden) p1 (3rd); 4th, and pulled up 5. Scored at Andoversford in '00 and runner-up in a weak Restricted there this year, but physical problems have meant he has failed to progress at all, and does not stand his racing well. Wears a cross-noseband. *Mrs M.J. Arnold — N. Cotswold (Emma Baker).* 819 (R), 1069 (R).

BALLY BLUE ..9-9.. 7 br.g. Roselier (FR) — Layston Pinzal (Afzal) p33126. Small. Dam, sister to Pin Up Boy (*qv* '99 Annual), was 2nd in Point from only 3 attempts. P-t-P '03 r4 p0 (pulled up 4). Clocked a time seven seconds faster than the unbeaten Impatient Lady when opening his account over 2m4f at Great Trethew, but has still to prove his effectiveness over the full trip. Bitterly disappointing on his final start, and it may be worth taking the weight off his back in Ladies races. Wears a cross-noseband. *R. & L. Newton — E. Devon (Monique Pike).* 12 (OMa), 51 (OMa), 194 (CfMa), 701 (2m4fOMa), 864 (R), 1102 (R).

BALLY CYRANO ..—.. 8 b.g. Cyrano De Bergerac — Iolite (Forzando) upppp. Strong compact brother to flat winner, Nose The Trade (subsequently successful in USA). Dam won 3 flat (5-6f) all on all-weather. 8800y. FLAT '99/00 r8 p1 (3rd). IRISH NH '02 (for R. Marrs) r1 p0 (pulled up). Bought Doncaster, Oct 2100. Third on his flat debut, but truly dire since, and often wore headgear and was tongue-tied once prior to '04. Bred to be a sprinter, and sending him Pointing was bally potty. *D. Drinkwater & A. Bowness — N. Ledbury (David Drinkwater).* 410 (2m4fCfMa), 518 (CfMa), 725 (OMa), 837 (OMa), 1394 (OMa).

BALLYDOOLE (IRE) .—.. 12 b.g. Invited (USA) — Kyle-More Beauty (Bishop Of Orange) f. Good-bodied. IRISH P-t-P '99/00 r9 w1 (5&6yo Maiden) p1 (distant 3rd of 3); 7th of 8, last 2, and pulled up 4. P-t-P '02 r4 p0 (pulled up 4). Had luck very much on his side when dead-heating in Ireland, but otherwise only once better than last, and may have been hurt in a heavy fall after a mile at Garnons on his return, by which time he was already tailed off. *A.L. Shaw — N. Cotswold.* 404 (O).

BALLYHANNON (IRE) ..7-0.. 16 b.g. Strong Gale — Chestnut Fire (Deep Run) 5. Compact well-made half-brother to NH flat and jumping winner, Abbot Of Furness, to jumping winner, Plastic Spaceage, to Hurdles winner, Flaming Hope (IRE), to Irish Pointing and Hurdles winner, Lisaleen River, and to NH flat winner, Lisaleen Lady. Dam won NH flat and 2m2f mares Mdn Hdle in Ireland. IRISH NH FLAT r4 p1 (2nd). IRISH NH '94 r1 p0. IRISH P-t-P '94 r2 w1 (5yo Maiden) p0; disqualified from 2nd — no Hunters Certificate! P-t-P/HUNT CH '96, '98/01 and '03 r38 w1 (Club) p7 (6 3rds, of 4 once, and last once); failed to finish 20 (on floor 7). Managed to outbattle two exhausted shirkers in a race taking well over eight minutes at Flagg in '00, but a regular non-finisher before and since, and presumably retired following a fourth unsuccessful assault on his Members. *E.W. Froggatt — Meynell & S. Staffs.* 225 (M).

BALLYKNOCK ROSE (IRE) .9-12.. 10 ch.m. Cardinal Flower — Annamkerrig (Stetchworth USA) u13. Tall unfurnished. IRISH P-t-P '99/02 r11 p3 (3rds); pulled up 6 and fell. NH '02/3 (for T.R. George, and B. Grassick) r3 p0 (pulled up 3). Bought Malvern, July for 800. Modest in Ireland and beaten between 15 and 21 lengths in her Pointing thirds, and was pulled up on nine occasions over there. Yet another success story with a cheap purchase for new connections, and her victory in a Black Forest Lodge Maiden was made to look very good indeed by the subsequent exploits of runner-up Gypsy Girl. Rather disappointing on firmer ground next time, and last seen in February, but will have strong claims to a Restricted if fit. *M. Weir — Dartmoor.* 67 (OMa), 150 (OMa), 315 (R).

BALLY LEADER (IRE) ..7-13.. 9 b.g. Supreme Leader — Ballybree (Buckskin FR) 6up. Small stocky. Dam, is half-sister to Orchestrated Chaos (*qv* '97 Annual). P-t-P '03 r1 p0 (fell). Still travelling purposefully when exiting six out on his only appearance last year, but has weakened after two miles in all three subsequent attempts, and beaten 37 lengths in his only completion. *Mrs P.M. Robinson — S. Durham.* 167 (OMa), 271 (OMa), 766 (R).

BALLYLESSON (IRE) .8-11.. 10 b.g. Erdelistan (FR) — Three Dieu (Three Dons) ppfp9. Compact well-made half-brother to Hand Over, Top Pryal and Bear's Picnic. P-t-P '00 and '02 (for Mr H. Page, Mr M. Dale, Mr T. Finch, Mr J. Vestey & Mrs P.M. Shirley-Beavan) r6 w1 (Maiden) p1 (2nd); pulled up and fell/unseated 3. NH '02/3 (from S.H. Shirley-Beavan's) r5 p1 (3rd in 2m2f Hdle); fell 1st only Ch. Landed a touch for previous connections at Musselburgh in '02 and ran well on his subsequent hurdling debut, but most disappointing since, and remains a most unconvincing jumper. Normally stops to nothing, in the manner of a horse with a major physical disability. Acts on a sound surface. *P. Curtis — E. Essex (Paula Twinn).* 28 (I), 99 (I), 159 (R), 223 (I), 398 (R).

BALLY LIR LADY..8-12.. 11 b.m. Lir — Ballyorney Girl (New Member) 5fp. Compact sister to jumping winner, Bally Lira. NH FLAT '99/00 r4 p0. NH '00/1 and '03 (for P.R. Rodford, and S.C. Burrough) r12 p2 (3rds); pulled up 1, fell 1. Still a Maiden after 19 attempts often in lowly company (including three Selling Hurdles in which she was beaten 24 lengths plus), and still does not look to be particularly close to that elusive first victory. *P.R. Rodford — Devon & Somerset.* 879 (R), 1132 (R), 1252 (OMa).

BALLYMENAGH (IRE) ..—.. 13 br.g. Buckskin (FR) — Breeze Dancer (Torus) uppp. Workmanlike half-brother to Fighting For Good (IRE). Dam, half-sister to Mossiman (*qv* '98 Annual). IRISH P-t-P '97/8 r4 w1 (dead-heat for 6yo&up Maiden) p1 (3rd); pulled up 1, and fell 1. IRISH NH FLAT '98/9 r6 w1 (2m1f) p1 (2nd). IRISH NH '98/9 r6 p0. NH '00/01 r5 p0; pulled up 1. P-t-P/HUNT CH '02/3 r8 p3 (2 3rds, inc Hunt Ch); 4th, slipped up 1 and unseated 1. Gained his Irish success in deep mud, but made to look incredibly slow without that commodity since, and broke down irreparably at Mosshouses. Mrs M. Armstrong — Tynedale (Kevin Robson). 678 (3m1fH), 762 (I), 915 (Cf), 1220 (C).

BALLYSICYOS (FR) ..10-7.. 10 b.g. Nikos — Bally Duke (FR) (Iron Duke FR) f3u1112112p. Tall lengthy brother to Hurdles winner, Mawlyska (FR). Dam won 12 French flat, 8-15f (ran 90 times in 8 consecutive seasons including 26 outings at 4!). FRENCH NH '98 r7 p1 (3rd); fell 3, pulled up 1. NH '99/03 (for M.C. Pipe) r25 w5 (3 2m-3m2f Hdles and 2 2m4f-2m1f Chses) p4; pulled up 1, fell/unseated 2. Five Pointing wins took his career total into double figures, and was a very helpful contributor to Ashley Farrant's championship bid, but by no means invincible, as punters found to their cost who saw him turned over at 4-5 or less on four occasions (4-9 in the two latest). Can sustain a great gallop and often returns very fast times when scoring, despite there being a maximum of five runners in four of his Open successes. Looked like beating Upton Adventure until he fell two out with Ollie Jackson at Barbury, but after disappointing badly for her twice subsequently (reported to have continually hung right once) their partnership was terminated. Seems indifferent to underfoot conditions, but occasionally jumps left. Had a long hard season from the middle of January until the final day, and looked fed up by the end of it, but very capable of running up another sequence when fresh. Blinkered once in France. *Mrs P.A. Deal — Taunton V.H. (David Pipe).* 33 (L), 78 (L), 470 (L), 569 (MO), 691 (O), 964 (O), 1128 (MO), 1185 (MO), 1447 (O), 1510 (O), 1562 (O).

PLATE 22 1185 Devon & Somerset Staghounds Mixed Open: Ballysicyos and Ashley Farrant are clear at the third last *PHOTO: Tim Holt*

BALLY WIRRAL (IRE) ..10-6.. 13 b.g. Carlingford Castle — Jillie James (The Parson) R111. Workmanlike. IRISH P-t-P '98 r3 w1 (5&6yo Maiden) p0; fell after a mile twice. P-t-P '99/03 r11 w5 (Restricted, 2 Members, Intermediate and Club) p3 (2nds, beaten a head once); unseated 2. Admirably consistent and has won half the Points he has contested, but has been rather unambitiously placed, and '04 has been the only season when he has raced on more than three occasions. Capable of jumping extra well, and should readily take his winning tally into double figures, even at 13. Appears to be able to handle all but extremes of going. *G.C. Maundrell — R.A. (Paul Thompson).* 19 (CMod), 717 (Cf), 972 (Cf), 1112 (C).

BALMORAL SPRING (IRE) ..9-10§.. 12 b.g. Royal Fountain — The Best I Can (Derring Rose) 26152. Narrow angular half-brother to Hurdles winner, Purple Ace (IRE), and Irish Pointing and Hurdles winner, No Messin' (IRE). NH FLAT '98/9 r4 p1 (3rd). NH '99 and '01/2 r5 p0. P-t-P '00 and '03 r10 w2 (Maiden and Members) p4 (2 2nds; and inc last of 3); 5th of 6, pulled up 2, and fell 1. Able enough on a going day, and has won three minor races since a visor was applied, but has attempted to pull himself up on the run-in in both Members successes, and remains largely untrustworthy. Suited by top-of-the-ground, and could win a Restricted if he chose in '05. *Mrs A.P. Balderstone — Quorn.* 384 (R), 889 (CR), 1056 (M), 1397 (I), 1503 (R).

BANANA RIDGE ..9-13.. 7 ch.m. Primitive Rising (USA) — Madison Girl (Last Fandango) 314pp. Good-topped half-sister to flat winners, Madly Sharp and Mirror Four Sport. Dam won 2 flat, 12-14f, and won 2m Hdle. P-t-P '03 r3 w1 (2m4f Maiden) p0; pulled up 1, and fell 1. NH FLAT '03 (for T.D. Walford) r1 p0 (4th). Backed off the boards in all four Pointing attempts, but able to reward the support only once, and a wind infirmity has severely hampered her development. Returned from almost 13 weeks off the course to oblige at Sedgefield, but twice a beaten favourite subsequently, and the fitting of a tongue-strap on her final start made no difference to the outcome. Can only be watched when she reappears. *P. Maddison — Middleton.* 102 (R), 1177 (2m5fH), 1373 (2m4f110yH), 1452 (3m4fH), 1499 (2m4f110yH).

BANKERSDRAFT .8-12.. 10 ch.g. Mazaad — Overdraft (Bustino) 55244451. Compact half-brother to Irish flat and Hurdles winner, Musical Banker. NH FLAT '00 r1 p0. NH '00/01 and '03 (for D. McCain, and R.C. Guest) r10 p1 (3m Ch); pulled up 4, fell 1. Bought Doncaster, May for 1000. Consistently moderate and very easy to beat, and barely has sufficient stamina, but after seven honourable Pointing completions he could not be begrudged the victory which finally came his way at Mordon. Wore cheekpieces latterly under Rules, and was tongue-tied twice (has had a soft palate operation), but not equipped with either in the new yard. It would be rather surprising if he could plug home in front again, unless a really feeble Restricted comes his way. *Mrs S. Robinson & D.N. Wilkinson — York & Ainsty N. (Sylvia Robinson).* 165 (OMa), 271 (OMa), 394 (CfMa), 482 (OMa), 776 (CfMa), 959 (OMa), 1165 (OMa), 1417 (OMa).

BANKIT ..9-8.. 12 ch.g. Gildoran — Game Trust (National Trust) 4p3. Small compact home-bred half-brother to Itsforu (*qv*). P-t-P '98/9 and '02/3 r11 w2 (Maiden and Restricted) p2; last 1, fell/unseated 3, pulled up 1 and ran out 1. Returned from a two-year period on the sidelines to score emphatically on his final appearance of the '02 season at Ston Easton, but a weak finisher and only once better than last in just four subsequent appearances. Goes a good gallop, and likes to make the running, but has never stood his racing well, and looks too old to revive successfully at 12. Always inclined to make mistakes. *Mrs S. Nash — O. Berks (Matt Hazell).* 602 (MO), 759 (I), 1356 (2m6fH).

BANK ON LADY .8-9.. 7 ch.m. Dromod Hill — Sail On Lady (New Member) u33. Small sturdy homebred half-sister to Jimmy Jumbo (IRE) (*qv*). NH FLAT '03 (from R.J. Smith's) r3 p0. A very sticky jumper whose tenuous link with his owner ended after a mile at Eyton, but after finishing an exceptionally remote last of three for Dave Mansell she was beaten only five lengths in a dreadful Mares Maiden at Upton-on-Severn. Strong handling might force her into the winners enclosure eventually. *Miss A. De Lisle Wells — N. Cotswold (Ali De Lisle Wells).* 532 (OMa), 724 (OMa), 978 (CMam).

BANSHA HOUSE ..9-8.. 13 ch.g. Ardross — Proverbial Rose (Proverb) p3. Lengthy half-brother to Hurdles winner, Flinders Chase. Dam won 4 Irish Points. NH FLAT '98 r2 p1 (3rd). NH '00 r4 w1 (2m4f110y Mdn Hdle) p1 (3rd); pulled up 1, and brought down 1. P-t-P/HUNT CH '02/3 r5 p1 (2nd); pulled up 3, and slipped up. Justified favouritism in the last of four appearances over hurdles, but has always proved extremely difficult to train and never as effective over fences. Guaranteed to make jumping errors in Points, and looks finished now. Wears a tongue-strap. *Mrs D. Brown — N. Ledbury (Caroline Chadney).* 662 (O), 1253 (M).

BARAFUNDLE BAY .—§§.. 16 ch.g. Afzal — Vinca (French Vine) p. Tall. Grandam, Grass Of Parnassus, won 2 Military Points and 2nd for Lt Col Bulkeley to '67. Great-grandam, Pampas Cat, was a Pointer. P-t-P '97/8 and '02/3 r15 p4 (3 3rds, remote 2 fences last once, and after refusing once); pulled up 9, refused 1 and fell 1. Unraced until he was eight and has made very few appearances, but afflicted by a breathing problem from an early stage in his career, and has proved a complete waste of time since '98. Wears a cross-noseband, and has been tried in a tongue-tie and blinkers. *Mrs C. Morgan — Pembs.* 1547 (M).

BARBED BROACH (IRE) ..8-4.. 12 b.g. Waajib — Miss Galwegian (Sandford Lad) pp3f742. Tall rangy half-brother to Youknowhatimean, to 3 flat winners, including A Bridge Too Far and Jubal Early, and to a successful Hurdler. Dam, half-sister to Rustino (*qv* '99 Annual). IRISH P-t-P '98 r2 p1 (2nd); and fell. IRISH FLAT '99/00 r5 p1 (3rd at Laytown). IRISH NH FLAT '99 r2 p0. IRISH NH '99/00 r9 p0 (Chses). P-t-P/HUNT CH '02/3 (for Mr N.W. Padfield) r10 p5 (3 2nds, beaten neck once, and 3rd of 4); last pair 2, and pulled up 3. A frustrating individual who has avoided winning any of the 35 races he has contested, and changes hands on a frequent basis. An inveterate front-runner but does not possess enough stamina for Points and usually grinds to an ignominious halt in the closing stages. Wears a cross-noseband, and has been tried in blinkers. *Mrs J. Butler MFH — Hursley Hambledon (Peter Butler).* 627 (OMa), 716 (M), 971 (OMa), 1108 (OMa), 1211 (OMa), 1337 (OMa), 1404 (OMa).

BARD OF DRUMCOO (IRE) ..10-4.. 10 ch.g. Orange Reef — Sporting Houdini (Monseigneur USA) 12121141. Lengthy. IRISH P-t-P '00/2 r8 w1 (7yoplus Maiden) p4; pulled up 3. IRISH NH FLAT '01 r1 p0. IRISH NH '01 r2 p0. P-t-P/HUNT CH '03 r7 w2 (Restricted and Confined) p1 (3rd); last pair 3, and fell. Has done well for present connections, and helped David Kemp to his best ever season in '04. A good jumper in Points, where he likes to make the running, but has had his limitation exposed in Hunter Chases. Difficult to pass once he gets the bit between his teeth, and his battling qualities should ensure further success, but can operate at his optimum only on good or sound surfaces. *Mr & Mrs J.R.M. Ridge — Suffolk (David Kemp).* 124 (CCon), 376 (Cf), 521 (Cf), 647 (Cf), 744 (O), 1153 (O), 1295 (3m110yH), 1408 (O).

BARGIN BOY .—.. 16 ch.g. Undulate (USA) — Chaddy (St Chad) p. Tall half-brother to a Hurdling winner. Dam won in Norway. NH FLAT '93 r1 p0. NH '93/4, 97 and '99 (for J.S. Moore, and P.C. Ritchens) r8 w1 (2m2f Ch) p1 (3rd); pulled up 2. Won a Chase on firmish at Exeter in October '97 (25-1), but making just the tenth appearance of his life when tailed off and pulled up after two miles in a hot Open at Larkhill. Blinkered once under Rules. Quickly scuttled back into hiding after his first airing for five years. *Mrs K. Blackman — R.A.* 11 (O).

BARNEYS GOLD (IRE) ..9-11.. 16 ch.g. Orchestra — Fair Corina (Menelek) 62. Tall half-brother to Waverley Mill, to English Hurdles and Irish Chasing winner, Programmed To Win, and to an Irish NH flat winner. NH FLAT '95 r2 p0. P-t-P/HUNT CH '96/8,'00 and '02/3 r31 w5 (up to Confined) p10 (7

3rds, of 4 thrice inc Hunt Ch, and last of 3 once); ran out 3, fell/unseated 4, and pulled up 2. A real handful as a novice, but sorted out in the hunting field, and rated 10-6 in his prime. Provided Gemma Garton with her first success, and retains some ability when the mud is flying on a long track, but has been very lightly raced since '00 and a sixth career win at 16 appears unlikely. Wears a cross-noseband. *Mrs A.B. Garton — Cheshire (Tim Garton).* 873 (Cf), 1045 (Cf).

BARON BERNARD ..8-13.. 8 b.g. Baron Blakeney — Rosie VII (unknown) pp31p. Workmanlike. NH FLAT '01 r2 p0. NH '01/2 (for C.A. Dwyer) r3 p0. Outclassed in bumpers and Hurdles and was not doing much better in his early Points (a fence behind when last of three once), but crawled round Penshurst in the slowest time of the day by almost half a minute when capturing a Maiden which was so bad that he actually deserved his place as market favourite. Will need to improve if he is not to struggle in Restricteds. *A.G. Chinery — E. Essex (Paul Chinery).* 611 (OMa), 746 (OMa), 901 (OMa), 1088 (OMa), 1213 (Cnr).

BARON KISS ..—.. 10 gr.g. Baron Blakeney — Blow A Kiss (Auction Ring USA) prp. Small compact owner-bred half-brother to Derring Kiss. Dam won Maiden and placed 3 (inc match on flat), but failed to finish in 9 of 12 Points and rarely got the trip. P-t-P '02/3 r8 p2 (3rds, remote last once); last, pulled up 3, and fell/unseated 2. An error-prone non-stayer who has beaten only one rival in 11 attempts. *Mrs C.J. Bibbey — Radnor & W. Herefords (Clive Davies).* 517 (CfMa), 730 (OMa), 840 (OMa).

BARON RIDGE .9-6.. 9 gr.g. Baron Blakeney — Coinridge (Charlie's Pal) 551p26. Compact good-bodied half-brother to Copper Two and Port Lane. Dam, half-sister to The Butler (*qv* '99 Annual), won 2 Points and placed 4 for the Darkes (also 3rd twice in Hdles). Great-grandam, Nickel Coin won Grand National. P-t-P '02/3 r10 w1 (Maiden) p0; last, pulled up 7, and ran out. The winner of two poor races on contrasting surfaces, and inflicted a shock defeat on a below par Bengal Bullet in the latest, but has beaten only five rivals in his 16-race career. Probably ungenuine and is best left alone. Wears a cross-noseband, and has been tried in cheekpieces. *R.C. & Mrs M. Darke — Dart V.H. & S. Pool H., & Dart V. & Haldon H. (Melissa Darke).* 198 (R), 324 (R), 491 (M), 706 (R), 1002 (R), 1196 (R).

BARRON BAY (USA) ..8-0.. 13 br.g. Track Barron (USA) — In Bay (ARG) (Halpern Bay USA) 5. Workmanlike half-brother to a winner in USA. Dam won 10 races in Argentina, including 7 Group races. NH FLAT '96 r1 p0. NH '01 r1 p0 (pulled up). P-t-P/HUNT CH '98/01 and '03 r12 w1 (Maiden) p2 (3rds); 6th, and pulled up 6. Won a poor Maiden in the slowest time of the day at Peper Harow in '98, but useless in just nine appearances since (pulled up in six), and quickly tailed off when fences last on his only appearance this year. *B. Tetley — Surrey U. (Pam Tetley).* 536 (CfL).

BARRY LYDON (IRE) ..9-1.. 7 ch.g. Hubbly Bubbly (USA) — Banner Katie (Carlingford Castle) p3p. Sturdy. IRISH P-t-P '03 r5 p0 (pulled up 3, and fell 2). Only finished in front of a Millington muppet when 22 lengths third in a youngsters Maiden, and his jumping is generally little better than deplorable. Already given the order of the boot by his stable. *R. Andrews — Cambs with Enfield Chace (Simon Andrews).* 151 (OMa), 218 (OMa), 371 (OMa).

BARRYS LORD (IRE) .9-8.. 7 b/br.g. Lord Americo — Quayfield (Monksfield) p. Tall workmanlike. Dam won 3 Irish Points. IRISH P-t-P '02/3 r5 w1 (5yo Maiden) p0; pulled up 2, fell 1. IRISH NH FLAT '03 r1 p0. IRISH NH '03 (for P. Nolan) r1 p0 (fell). Scored in soft in Ireland, but had to wait until May before making an appearance for the new yard, and did not look an easy ride before he pulled up. Does not look a bad type, but could do with jumping and settling. *Mrs B.L. Shaw — Cheshire (Gary Hanmer).* 1205 (CR).

BARTON DREAM (IRE) ..10-2.. 9 b.g. Le Bavard (FR) — Tax Dream (IRE) (Electric) p1122. Rangy. NH FLAT '01 r2 p0. NH '01/2 (for J. Allen) r7 p0; fell 2, pulled up 1. Bought Ascot, Oct for 1619. Improved by a switch to Points and completed a double in minor company, but then had to give best to the well above-average Gypsy Girl, and the rider then found himself outwitted by wily old Godfrey Maundrell when at 4-5 at Pentreclwydau. His stable has done well with him, and should not be pressed to recoup losses in an Intermediate. *Mrs E. Kulbicki — Curre & Llangibby.* 258 (CMa), 700 (CfMa), 844 (R), 1092 (I), 1238 (I).

BARTON ROSE ..9-9§.. 14 b.g. Derring Rose — Barton Sauce (Saucy Kit) 2f1. Workmanlike good-bodied half-brother to Saucy's Wolf and Flying Fair. Dam won 2 Points. P-t-P/HUNT CH '99/01 and '03 (for Mrs S.J. Evans) r23 w2 (Maiden and Restricted) p5 (2 2nds, of 3 once); pulled up 2, fell/unseated 5. Very quirky and has largely under-achieved, but retains ability, and appeared to race with more enthusiasm than normal in the new yard. Hit the deck when a market springer at Holnicote, but given a fine ride by the newcomer Ian Chanin when successful at Bratton Down, where he grabbed the inside when kicking for home at the third-last. Probably only third best on merit that day, and the rider may have to find a mount more fleet of foot in order to score again. Can get worked up in the preliminaries and is usually taken to post early. Blinkered once in '03. *I. Chanin & A.J.S. Knox — Silverton (Robert Chanin).* 1005 (Cf), 1181 (I), 1383 (Cnr).

BARTON SAINT (NZ) ..9-11.. 10 ch.g. St Hilarion (USA) — Aquatramp (NZ) (Pevero) up53221. Small neat freeze-marked half-brother to 3 winners in New Zealand, and another in Macau. Dam won a race in New Zealand. NEW ZEALAND FLAT '98 p1 (3rd). NH '00/01 r4 p0; pulled up 1. P-t-P '02 (for Mrs E. Harrington) r5 w1 (Maiden) p1 (2nd of 3); 4th twice, and pulled up. NH '02 r9 p3; pulled up 3. Beaten two lengths or less when runner-up in Chases at Southwell after winning a youngsters Maiden at Charlton Horethorne in '02, and reaped the benefit of a much needed wind operation when finally able to follow up in a bad two-finisher Restricted on his latest Pointing appearance. Jumps well, but thoroughly exposed and will find it hard to upgrade successfully. Acts on a sound surface. Has been tried tongue-tied. *Mr & Mrs B.G. Parsons — Blackmore & Sparkford V. (Patrick Rodford).* 65 (Rnr), 232 (R), 350 (M), 1127 (Cf), 1325 (R), 1366 (R), 1465 (R).

BARTY BOY (IRE) ..9-2.. 13 b.g. Buckskin (FR) — Black Tulip (Pals Passage) 464p. Compact half-brother to Man On The Line, Tale Of Endurance (IRE) and Mr Leroi (IRE), and to Hurdles winner, Black Frost (IRE). Dam, half-sister to Black Monkey (*qv* '92 Annual), won NH flat & 2 Hurdles (2m-2m4f) in Ireland. NH '97/8 r2 p0 (tailed off in Hdle and fell in Ch). P-t-P '03 r3 p0 (7th, slipped up 1, and pulled up 1). In contention for up to 2m4f in all attempts this year, but does not appear to stay any further, and it is hard to enthuse about his winning prospects at 13. *Miss S. Hogbin — Meynell & S. Staffs.* 752 (R), 1124 (OMa), 1215 (CfMa), 1425 (OMa).

BARWICK GREEN (IRE) ..—.. 10 ch.g. Orchestra — Clarrie (Ballyciptic) f. Angular workmanlike brother to No Pain No Gain (IRE) and Top Note (IRE), and to Hurdles winner, All Talk No Action (IRE), and half-brother to 3 Irish NH flat winners. Dam won 2m Hdle in Ireland. NH FLAT '00 r1 p0. NH '00/01 r4 p0. P-t-P '02 r5 p0 (fell/unseated 5). Displayed a modicum of ability over hurdles, but a total disaster in Points, and hopefully his latest, and earliest crash landing will be his last. *Mrs M.A. Kendall — Cumberland F. (Heather Sayer).* 430 (R).

BASSEY (IRE) .—.. 12 b.g. Be My Native (USA) — Evergreen Lady (Smartset) f. Tall workmanlike half-brother to Irish Pointing winner, Commanche Country. NH FLAT '97 r2 w1 p0. NH '98/01 (for N.J. Henderson) r8 w1 (3m Hdle) p3 (inc 2 2nds). Bought Ascot, June 1238. Blinkered once in a career under Rules in which he signed off with a win in soft, but his comeback after three years was ephemeral, and clearly did himself a mischief when falling at the third at Huntingdon. *M. Hemphill — Granta H. (Fiona Hatfield).* 177 (3mH).

BATCHWORTH LOCK .9-5.. 7 b.g. Beveled (USA) — Treasurebound (Beldale Flutter USA) fp12p2. Workmanlike brother to I'll Be Bound, and half-brother to sprint winners, Batchworth Belle and Batchworth Bound. FLAT '00/3 (for E.A. Wheeler) r11 p0. Bought Ascot, Nov for 1666. Never better than seventh at odds ranging from between 25-1 to 100-1 over four seasons on the flat, but rather surprisingly proved more adept at Pointing, and won a Maiden run in much the slowest time of the day at Cilwendeg (only three finished including Wiston Wizo). Inconsistent and possibly struggles to get the trip in truly-run contests, but remarkably both his remote seconds were behind horses who went on to much greater glory in Chasing victories (these Welsh Restricteds ooze class nowadays!). May find another opportunity. *Mrs H.E. & P.H. Williams — S. Pembs (Paul Williams).* 202 (CfMa), 450 (R), 677 (CfMa), 953 (R), 1094 (R), 1322 (R).

BATHTIME BOYS ..9-10.. 7 gr.g. Relief Pitcher — Path's Sister (Warpath) 22. Well-made half-brother to Bedtime Boys (*qv*). Tarried behind Tarry maidens when runner-up twice at Dingley, and his first effort behind a nine-year-old looked better than his even money defeat at the hands of a 12-year-old. Certainly not helped by a bad mistake at the 14th on the latter occasion, and should plug home first eventually. *G.T.H. Bailey — Pytchley (Caroline Bailey).* 887 (CfMa), 1215 (CfMa).

BATOUTOFTHEBLUE ..9-10§.. 12 br.g. Batshoof — Action Belle (Auction Ring USA) 6f6u3. Good-topped half-brother to One For The Chief, and to flat winners, Holster and Shareoftheaction. FLAT '95/02 r45 w6 (1m6f-2m1f) p9. NH '99/2 r11 w1 (2m6f Hdle) p7 (3 2nds, beaten head once); pulled up 1, brought down 1. P-t-P/HUNT CH '03 r5 p2 (2nds); 6th, 8th, and unseated. An above average stayer on the level, but took a long time to transfer his ability to hurdling, and has still won only one of his 21 attempts over obstacles. Retains only a fraction of that ability now and still looks a most unnatural jumper of fences. Never fit in Points, and deserves pensioning off before he comes to any harm. *Mrs M. Armstrong — Tynedale (Kevin Robson).* 764 (O), 917 (O), 1289 (O), 1420 (L), 1477 (O).

BATTLE HONOURS ..9-6.. 9 ch.g. Past Glories — Hasty Salvo (Hasty Word) f1ppp. Compact good-looking brother to Victory Salute and Queen's Shilling. Dam, sister to Oaklands Word (*qv* '03 Annual), won 5 Points (inc 3 Opens) and placed 6 for Felix Wheeler; was also 3rd in Hdle and Chse. P-t-P '02/3 r4 p0 (4th of 5, and pulled up 3). Beat only one rival in his first five starts, and fell heavily on his reappearance, but held on to a dwindling advantage when successful in an elders Maiden at Horseheath. Pulled up in all three subsequent attempts, and has not looked at all keen on occasions. Possibly unsuited by an easy surface. *Major G.F. Wheeler — E. Sussex & Romney Marsh (Di Grissell).* 26 (OMa), 129 (OMa), 419 (CR), 779 (R), 802 (R).

BAY ISLAND (IRE) ..10-9.. 9 b.g. Treasure Hunter — Wild Deer (Royal Buck) 1p. Compact good-looking half-brother to Carton and Wild Bavard (IRE), to Chasing winner, Matta Mia Flier, and to Irish Hurdles winner, Dearborn Tec (IRE). Dam won an Irish Point. IRISH P-t-P '01 r2 w1 (5yo Maiden) p0 (pulled up). NH '02/3 (for Mrs H. Dalton) r9 w3 (3m-3m2f Ch) p2; pulled up 3. A great galloper who completed a hat-trick in Oct/Nov '02 (weak Chases), and was impressive when scoring in the fastest time of the day at Weston Park (even bettered Ask The Natives, who was carrying a stone less in the Ladies). Unfortunately he seems hard to train these days, and did not reappear for three months, when he made no impact in the Land Rover Final. Can be an erratic jumper, and sometimes dives right. Has been operated on for a wind infirmity. His top form would make him extremely difficult to beat in Points. *B.J. Perkins — N. Ledbury.* 93 (O), 1171 (3m2f110yH).

BAY MOUSE ..8-4.. 7 b.g. Karinga Bay — Mouse's Sister (Shaab) 4. Sparely-made. Dam is sister to Sharnish, earned £3000 for finishing 3rd in Marlborough Cup, but was last of 2, and failed to finish in 6 of 7 other Points for Rupert Nuttall (*qv* '92 Annual). P-t-P '03 r2 p0 (5th, and pulled up). Ran pleasingly on his debut last year, but subsequently let favourite backers down when well supported at Mounsey Hill Gate, and failed to reappear following a quiet re-introduction at Barbury. Well bred but lacks physical scope, and is clearly not that hardy either. *R.E. Nuttall — Blackmore & Sparkford V.* 30 (CMah).

PLATE 23 510 Northern P-t-P Area Club 56&7yo Open Maiden: Bay Of Dreams and Kevin Anderson, 1st, who were solo from the third last, win the penultimate race at Musselburgh, all six rivals having fallen by the wayside PHOTO: Alan Mitchell

BAY OF DREAMS ..9-5.. 6 ch.g. Salse (USA) — Cantico (Green Dancer USA) 1p. Brother to Hurdles winner, Sausalito Bay, and half-brother to 2 flat winners (plus others abroad). FLAT '01/2 r4 p1 (3rd). NH '02/3 (for R.M. Stronge) r5 p0. Poor on the flat (visored on final start) and over hurdles, but was left solo from three out in a youngsters Maiden on firm at Musselburgh. Impossible to evaluate, and jumped only four fences at Dalston before he went wrong and had to be collected in the horse ambulance. *J.P.G. Hamilton — Buccleuch (Alison Hamilton).* 510 (OMa), 766 (R).

B B BOY .6-8.. 9 br.g. Arctic Lord — Belle Muguet (Bargello) pf1p4p. Workmanlike. 33,0004yo. NH FLAT '02 r2 p0. NH '02/3 (for K.C. Bailey) r4 p0; pulled up 1, fell 1. Bought Doncaster, May for 7000. Sometimes leads for a short while, but essentially an awful performer who does not get the trip, and was nearly three fences last in his Members. Miraculously unearthed a match at the grizzly Staff College meeting (going firm to frosty) and crept round in front to outplod his rival. Would rank amongst the least deserving winners of the year. *D.R. Churches — Mendip F. (Sue Popham).* 119 (OMa), 238 (CfMa), 335 (OMa), 459 (R), 598 (M), 879 (R).

BE A BETTER BOY ..9-8.. 9 b.g. Primitive Rising (USA) — Carat Stick (Gold Rod) 26. Small close-coupled owner-bred brother to Pillaging Pict (Chasing winner since Pointing), and half-brother to

Price Of Gold, Coquet Gold and Posh Stick. Dam, half-sister to Ram The Thor (*qv* '90 Annual), won NH flat and 4 Hdles (2m1f-3m1f) for the Waltons. NH '02 r1 p0 (pulled up in Hdle). P-t-P '02/3 r9 w1 (Maiden) p5 (4 2nds, beaten neck once and 3/4*l* once; and last of 3); 8th, and pulled up 2. A secure jumper and won convincingly on firmish at Corbridge, but on the negative side has been beaten into second place in three tight finishes, and had disappeared by mid-February in '04. Will hopefully get another chance to prove himself but connections might be wishing they had gone to the well earlier with him. *J.B. & F.A. Walton — Border (Jimmy Walton).* 69 (M), 212 (R).

BEACHCOMBER ..9-11.. 10 b.g. Kuwait Beach (USA) — Miss Rupert (Solar Topic) fp1R7. Tall rangy. P-t-P '02 r1 p0 (last). Headstrong and nigh on impossible to train, but galloped to the line when successful in a three-finisher Maiden in holding ground at Eyton, and with sensible placing might be capable of following up. Tall enough to step over the fences but does not jump fluently enough for Hunter Chases. Has two paddock handlers. *F. Peate — Wheatland (John Groucott).* 177 (3mH), 259 (CMa), 532 (OMa), 801 (3mH), 1176 (3m110yH).

BEACHTIME ..9-0§.. 9 b.g. Lugana Beach — Time Warp (Town And Country) 3734pp. Compact owner-bred half-brother to Tony's Time, and to Hurdles winner, Time For A Flutter. Dam, sister to Norse Country (*qv* '95 Annual), 3rd on flat, pulled up and fell in Points 5 years later. NH FLAT '01 r2 p1 (2nd). NH '01 r2 p0 (7th and pulled up). P-t-P '03 r6 w1 (2-finisher Maiden) p1 (2nd); 7th of 8, pulled up 2, and unseated. Led throughout the final mile when landing a two-finisher Maiden in the slowest time of the day at Charlton Horethorne last year, but a major disappointment since, and is almost certainly ungenuine. Makes frequent blunders or deliberate jumps, and is best left well alone. Wears a cross-noseband. *Mr & Mrs N. Faulks — Dulverton F. (Sarah Faulks).* 79 (R), 314 (R), 579 (R), 689 (R), 864 (R), 1385 (R).

BEACON WHITE ..8-12.. 8 b.g. Homo Sapien — Sally Ho (Gildoran) 5p. Compact well-made. IRISH P-t-P '01/3 r10 p1 (2nd); last pair 2, pulled up 6, and fell. Can show early dash, but possesses no stamina even at 2m4f, and gave the clear impression of having problems when he pulled up at Horseheath in early February. Wears a tongue-tie, which suggests his wind is all to pot. *J. Pennells — E. Sussex & Romney Marsh (Zoe Anthony).* 7 (2m4fOMa), 128 (OMa).

BEADNELL BAY ..10-3.. 8 b.g. Past Glories — Sherry Season (Vital Season) 431224. Workmanlike. Dam (*qv* '96 Annual), failed to finish in 4 of 6 Points for the Dufosees (looked a non-stayer). Grandam, Pepe Lew, half-sister to 7 Pointers and 2 successful Hurdlers, was 2nd in a Ladies, but failed to finish in all 9 other Points. P-t-P '02/3 r7 w4 (Maiden, Restricted, Members and Intermediate, hat-trick '03) p0; pulled up 2 and unseated 1. Unbeaten in four completions prior to the start of the latest campaign, but has failed to maintain his progress, and was particularly disappointing when twice turned over at odds-on. Goes a strong gallop in front, but wastes a lot of nervous energy beforehand, and has developed into a relatively weak finisher with a tendency to hang left. Remains prone to novicey mistakes, and though he has form in soft all his winning has been done on a sound surface. Sure to win again when conditions are right, and could still prove to be useful if everything comes together. Has two paddock handlers, and has been mounted on course and taken down early in a bid to relax him. *Mr & Mrs S.W. Dufosee — Blackmore & Sparkford V. (John Dufosee).* 78 (L), 322 (L), 350 (M), 718 (MO), 863 (MO), 1369 (Cf).

BEAFORD PRINCESS ..8-0.. 9 b.m. Prince Of Peace — Bay Augusta (Langton Heath) p45. Sturdy attractive spotty sister to Peace Of Amber. P-t-P '02/3 r9 p1 (last of 3); 4th, 5th, last pair 3, pulled up 2, and fell. An exposed non-stayer with little jumping acumen, and beaten a minimum of 24 when completing. Running her again would be a complete waste of time. *L.W. Wickett — Torrington F. (Laura Young).* 121 (OMa), 150 (OMa), 315 (R).

BEASLEY .9-4.. 6 b.g. First Trump — Le Shuttle (Presidium) 2214. Small compact half-brother to flat winner, Mystery Pips. 7000y, 1000f, 13000 2yo. FLAT '01/2 r6 p0; ran out 1. NH '02/3 (for M. Pitman, and D. McCain) r10 p1 (last of 3); fell 1. Sold Doncaster, Jan for 900. Bought Ascot, Oct for 1238. Very doggy in previous yards and often needed early pressure (ran off the course and unseated on his racecourse debut, regularly contested Sellers, was 11 lengths last of three when gaining his only placing, and tried in headgear and with cheekpieces), but more cheerful in Points, and benefited from the association with Marc Barber when winning a three-finisher Members. Possibly needs decent ground to get the trip, and may have cause to regret missing out on a Maiden. *C. & Mrs C. Owen — S. Pembs (Charlotte Owen).* 203 (CfMa), 676 (CfMa), 947 (M), 1237 (R).

BEAT THE RETREAT ..9-6.. 10 b.g. Terimon — Carpet Slippers (Daring March) 4p. Compact. Dam won 3 flat, 10-12f (one on all-weather) and 2m Hdle. NH FLAT '99 r1 p0. NH '00 and '02/3 (for Mrs D. Haine, and A. King) r12 p7 (inc 2 Chses); pulled up 3, unseated 1. Managed plenty of placings, but was a moderate and inconsistent maiden, and suffered a fatal injury at the third when favourite at Higham. Mrs B. Abraham — Quorn (Laura Pomfret). 6 (OMa), 27 (OMa).

BEAUCHAMP BROOK ..—.. 8 b.g. Meadowbrook — Pandessa (Blue Cashmere) fup. Lengthy owner-bred sister to Brookessa. Dam, half-sister to Spy Dessa (*qv* '98 Annual), won 6 Hdles (2m-2m5f, the first a Sell). P-t-P '02/3 r2 p1 (2nd of 3); pulled up 1. Has ability but does not appear to get the trip, and has been prone to diabolical blunders when he tires. Encountered a sound surface for the first time on his final start, but appeared to take an instant dislike to it, and may well have suffered another setback. *Mrs N. Cull — N. Ledbury (Alan Phillips).* 929 (2m4fOMa), 1266 (2m4fOMa), 1504 (2m4fOMa).

BEAUCHAMP ORACLE ..10-5.. 8 gr.g. Mystiko (USA) — Beauchamp Cactus (Niniski USA) 31112. Lengthy half-brother to Hurdles winner, Beauchamp Noble (subsequently successful on flat in Italy). Dam won 2m2f race. 5300 5yo. NH FLAT '02 (for A.J. Chamberlain) r1 p0. Bought Ascot, Jun for 2857. A typically astute cheap purchase by Steve Flook, and followed an easy win in a two-finisher Whitwick Maiden with a double at Maisemore. Impressive when giving the promising Rhys Hughes his first winner in a 20-runner Restricted in which he showed some decisive acceleration, and then recorded the fastest time of the day (beating Upton Adventure in the Ladies) in a Confined. Tried a shorter trip in an incident-packed Maiden Hunter Chase at Uttoxeter, and eventually beaten a neck by Scottish Roots (who had hampered him at the last) after Gypsy Girl had fallen two out when in command. Game and speedy, and compensation surely awaits over the bigger obstacles. Could enjoy a profitable year in '05, and would surely have strong claims in Novices Chases. *E.C. & Mrs M.M. Everall — Ludlow (Steve Flook).* 53 (2m4fOMa), 517 (CfMa), 726 (R), 1254 (Cf), 1377 (2m5fH).

BEAU JAKE (IRE) ..8-6.. 10 b.g. Jolly Jake (NZ) — Cool Mary (Beau Charmeur FR) 245f3. Small half-brother to Mary Hand (IRE) and Irish Pointing & Chasing winner, Croc An Bir. IR4000 4yo. NH FLAT '01 r3 p0. NH '01/3 (for N.M. Babbage) r11 p2 (3rds); fell 1. Bought Doncaster, May 4000. Often makes the frame and sometimes gives the impression that he could win, but yet to do so after 19 opportunities, and deteriorated after finishing one length second on his seasonal reappearance. Later an exhausted 26 lengths fourth when even money favourite, and ultimately found nothing when five lengths third with a 12-year-old in his first season occupying the runner-up spot. Perhaps something will fall into his lap one day. *A.P. Garland — Atherstone.* 370 (OMa), 594 (OMa), 1125 (OMa), 1425 (OMa), 1505 (OMa).

BEAUTY STAR (IRE) ..—.. 8 b.m. Shalford (IRE) — Dream Academy (Town And Country) p. Small neat half-sister to flat winner, Academy (IRE) and Irish NH Flat and jumping winner, Sigma Dotcomm. Dam won 2m Hdle. NH FLAT '02 r2 p0. NH '02 (for N.M. Babbage) r1 p0. Sent off favourite for a bad Mares Maiden at Garnons, but made a bad blunder early and stopped as if shot when meeting the rising ground before three out. Missed '03, and evidently hard to train. *A. Lowrie — Glamorgan (Robert Williams).* 408 (CMam).

BEBE BLEU (IRE) .9-0.. 9 b.m. Terimon — Fu's Lady (Netherkelly) 53. Small neat half-sister to NH flat winner, Fu's Baby. Dam won 11 Chses (2m-2m4f) for Angie Malde; approximately £45,000 from Martin Pipe's. NH FLAT '01 r2 p1 (2nd). NH '02 r1 p0 (fell). P-t-P '03 (for Mrs A. Malde) r2 p0 (fell 2). NH '03 r2 p0 (pulled up and unseated in Hdles). Out of a splendid mare, and has shown speed on occasions, but is consistently thwarted by the obstacles and her previous connections are not renowned for entertaining swans unknowingly. *The Cherry Tree Partnership (Mrs T.H. Hayward) — N. Norfolk H. (Tina Hayward).* 29 (R), 153 (OMa).

BE BOP BENTLEY..7-6§.. 10 br.g. Arms And The Man — Playful Touch (Lepanto GER) r9ru. Compact. Dam, half-sister to Moonbribe (*qv* '90 Annual), pulled up 4, and fell 1 in Points. P-t-P '00 and '03 r4 p0 (pulled up 4). Can take a strong hold, and soon tailed off under an iron grip when last on his solitary completion, but is not averse to slamming the brakes on when fatigue sets in. Has no rights lining up in Hunter Chases. Wears a cross-noseband. *P.R. & Mrs R. Maskill — Bicester with Whaddon (P. Maskill).* 20 (OMa), 444 (2mH), 1029 (3mH), 1176 (3m110yH).

BEDTIME BOYS ..10-3.. 8 gr.g. Gran Alba (USA) — Path's Sister (Warpath) 31. Small attractive half-brother to Bathtime Boys, and to NH flat and Hurdles winner, Soeur De Sentier. Dam, sister to Copgrove (*qv* '93 Annual), won 10 flat, 15-18f. P-t-P '02/3 r6 w2 (Maiden and Restricted) p0; 4th, pulled up 1 and fell 2. Regained competent guidance in '04 and proved much too strong for the remainder after King's Hero had exited when going like a winner at Thorpe, but appears very difficult to keep sound, and averages fewer than three outings a year. Has the look of a Ladies horse, and still has enough time on his side to make the grade in that sphere. Suited by some cut in the ground. *Miss M. Samworth — Cottesmore.* 223 (I), 942 (Cf).

BEECHBROOK GALE (IRE) .—§§.. 9 b.g. Toulon — Swan Upping (Lord Gayle USA) rpp. Tall rangy angular half-brother to Irish Pointing winner, We Pay More, and to 3 flat winners (2 abroad). Dam won 3 flat, 7-9f. IRISH P-t-P '00/1 r5 p2 (3rds); pulled up 1. NH '01/3 r8 p1 (3rd); last 2, pulled up 2, fell 2. Third on three occasions in the past, but was beaten 35 lengths in a four-finisher Chase, and has been last twice and failed to finish on seven occasions in 11 outings for the current yard. Can show early speed, but pulls himself up immediately the going gets tough, and John Upson must now be terminally exasperated by him. *J.R. Upson — Grafton (Denis Grattan).* 588 (CfMa), 1061 (OMa), 1505 (OMa).

BEECHES DREAM (IRE) ..—.. 6 b/br.m. Executive Perk — Conna Bride Lady (IRE) (Phardante FR) p. Bought Tattersalls Ireland, Nov for 432. Ill-prepared for her Musselburgh debut, and jumped ponderously and was a fence behind after a mile before pulling up. *B. Bailey & T. Bushby — Braes (Russell Ross).* 511 (OMam).

BEEHAWK ..9-11.. 6 b.g. Gunner B — Cupids Bower (Owen Dudley) 72. Owner-bred brother to Irbee (*qv*), and half-brother to Chasing winner, Kingsmoor. Bred for the job, and his six lengths second at Bratton Down was given a very pleasing fillip by the third horse Harnage, who was unbeaten in his next three outings. Looks sure to win a race or two at six. *Mr & Mrs R.D. Cox — Eggesford (Laura Young).* 702 (2m4fOMa), 1381 (OMa).

BEEHIVE LAD .8-10.. 11 b.g. Then Again — Steel Typhoon (General Ironside) f23. Lengthy goose-rumped half-brother to Tactix (Hurdles winner since Pointing), General Typhoon and Baron Blitzkrieg, to Chasing winner, Errol Glamohr, and to Hurdles winner, Personal Assurance. NH FLAT '00 r2 p0. NH '01/3 (for R. Ford) r9 p3 (inc 3rd in Ch); fell 1. Bought Doncaster, Aug for 800. Looks rather a nasty individual and had to be withdrawn from his intended Pointing debut after hitting the rider in the face in the paddock and drawing blood, and tends to be an over-heated front-runner. His best display under Rules, when four lengths second to Noel's Pride in May '01 would make him a Maiden certainty, but it was never that simple, because he was also beaten 42 lengths plus twice in Selling Hurdles. Galloped himself into the ground in Points, including when a gamble from eights to 2-1 on the final day of the season (typically faded, and came home 23 lengths third). Tends to be mounted on the course and taken to post early now. *K. Richards & P. Williams — Llangeinor (Kevin Richards).* 1193 (OMa), 1323 (CfMa), 1566 (OMa).

BEEN SUPREME (IRE) ..—.. 8 b.m. Supreme Leader — Merton Mistress (Decent Fellow) p. Shocked by the look of the first fence at Easingwold, and after clambering over it negotiated one more and was wisely pulled up. *Miss C.C. Raw — S. Durham.* 1300 (OMa).

BEET DE BOB (IRE) ..10-3.. 7 b/br.g. Bob Back (USA) — Beet Statement (IRE) (Strong Statement USA) 3u. Close-coupled. Dam won 2 2m5f-2m6f Chses in Ireland and also won 7 Points there and is half-sister to Doonloughan (*qv* '99 Annual). IRISH P-t-P '03 r5 w2 (4&5yo Maiden, and Winner of One) p2 (3rds); unseated 1. His promising form as a five-year-old in Ireland resulted in a high price tag when he went to the sales, but has so far given new connections no joy, as he broke a blood vessel when he was last of three at Chaddesley Corbett, and got no further than the first at Guilsborough. Attractively bred and has shown he can handle an easy surface, and potentially quite useful if he can be got back on track. *Mrs S.E. Busby & G.P. Wright — Farmers Bloodhounds (Sue Busby).* 255 (CCon), 785 (L).

BELARUS (IRE) ..9-13§.. 13 b.g. Waajib — Kavali (Blakeney) 7R. Workmanlike compact half-brother to Mr Busker (IRE) and Noel's Pride, to Chasing winner, Careysville (IRE), and to Irish jumping winner, Market Mover. NH '97/8 r8 p0 (pulled up only Ch). P-t-P/HUNT CH '99/03 r34 w8 (up to Open) p13 (9 2nds, beaten neck once, and inc Hunt Ch); pulled up 2, refused 1 and unseated 1. An expert in self preservation and rarely fails to finish, but has always had more ability than he has been prepared to reveal, and illustrated his unreliable nature when ducking out and dumping Dominic Harvey at Bratton Down. Eight wins to date include three at Mounsey Hill Gate, but was denied a run there in '04, and will be hard pressed to recover his best form at 13. Often blinkered in the past. Acts on any going. *Mrs S. Ashburner — Devon & Somerset (Tessa White).* 569 (MO), 1384 (Cf).

BELITLIR .—.. 13 b.m. Lir — Kimberley Ann (St Columbus) p. Small neat home-bred sister to The Kimbler, Lady Lir, Saint Joseph, Lirkimalong, Small-Lir and Bedazlir. Dam, half-sister to Harringworth and 6 other Pointers, was placed in 3 very good Points (last after remounting once). Grandam, Dark Pointer, was 4th in big field for Oakley Maiden on only start. Great-grandam, Dark Rate, won 3 Points. NH '01/2 r10 p1 (2nd in 3m1f110y Ch). P-t-P/HUNT CH '97/01 and '03 r37 w2 (Maiden and Restricted) p14 (8 2nds, beaten ¾*l* once; and 5 3rds, last once); pulled up 14, unseated 1. A genuine little mare and worth 10-3 in her prime, but has not scored since '00, and appeared to meet with a setback on her reappearance. Has never fallen and stays all day, but seems likely to head to the paddocks where she should be an asset to the home-bred Young academy. *B.R.J. Young, Mrs K. Rogers & Miss S Young — E. Cornwall (Sue Young).* 793 (Cf).

BELLE MOSS ..9-8.. 10 b.m. Le Moss — Snow Princess (Julio Mariner) 234. Small neat. Dam, half-sister to Raba Riba (*qv* '98 Annual), did the only clear round in Teme Valley Members, but a prize cow when failing to finish in her 7 other Points (refused 3). P-t-P '02/3 r3 w1 (Maiden) p1 (last of 2); refused 1. Came from a seemingly impossible position to score on her debut at Brampton Bryan in '02, but has failed to co-operate fully since, and the application of cheekpieces on her final start had little effect. Had two subsequent winners behind when runner-up on her return at Bitterley, but failed to get going until it was too late when gambled on next time, and must be treated with caution. *Ms C. Walker & M. Dudley — Radnor & W. Herefords (Caroline Walker).* 839 (R), 1345 (R), 1388 (R).

BELLE'S LAST ..—.. 7 br.m. Tragic Role (USA) — Pokey's Belle (Uncle Pokey) ppp. Compact sister to Tragic Belle (*qv*). Never in sight of the leaders before pulling up in the final half-mile in Maidens. *M. Roberts — Ystrad Taf Fechan (David Gibbs).* 363 (CfMa), 453 (CfMa), 1324 (CfMa).

BELL ROCK .9-9.. 7 ch.g. Charmer — Sule Skerry (Scottish Rifle) 6352. Compact half-brother to 6 flat winners (one in Trinidad) including Sea Island (12 wins, inc 10 over jumps). Dam won 2 12f races. NH '01 r2 p0. FLAT '02 r1 p0 (tailed off). P-t-P '03 (for Mr P.J. Millington) r7 w1 (2m4f Maiden) p1 (2nd); 4th twice, fell 2, and pulled up 1. Coerced into numerous jumping errors by the previous coachman and benefited from the exit of Agua Ardente when successful at Garthorpe, but has been unable to stay the full trip to date. Still only a youngster and may yet follow up, but has only ever encountered sound surfaces, and was seen to cock his jaw and head for the exit at Higham once. Wears a cross-noseband. *A. Hill & I.R. Mann — V. of Aylesbury with Garth & S. Berks (Lawney Hill).* 187 (Cf), 398 (R), 684 (R), 1107 (R).

BELVENTO (IRE) ..10-10.. 13 b.g. Strong Gale — Salufair (Salluceva) 731u12. Tall strong half-brother to NH flat winner, Mister Sandrovitch (IRE), and to Chasing winner, Russell House (IRE). Dam is half-sister to Random Traveller (*qv* '93 Annual). NH FLAT '96 r1 p0. NH '97/9 and '03 r11 p0 (inc last twice, pulled up and fell in Chses — moderate jumper). P-t-P/HUNT CH '00/3 r17 w8 (inc 3m2f Hunt Ch and Open) p3 (2nds, inc 2 Hunt Chses); pulled up 3, and fell/unseated 3. A useful Pointer, and has won nine of 12 completions in that sphere, but much less effective over regulation fences where his record is one win from 13 attempts. Took his winning tally into double figures when successful at Cottenham and shows little sign of deteriorating with age. Has been treated for a kissing spine that probably accounts for his sometimes inaccurate fencing. Has won in soft but much more at home on a sound surface. *Mrs J. Plackett — Crawley & Horsham (Rachel Deakin).* 100 (O), 183 (O), 421 (L), 804 (O), 997 (O), 1440 (3m1fH).

BE MY DREAM (IRE) .10-0§.. 10 b.g. Be My Native (USA) — Dream Toi (Carlburg) p415p5. Well-made good-looking brother to Be The Dream (IRE), and half-brother to Minella Express (IRE), to Irish Pointing winners, Local Whisper (also won Chasing there) and Local Dream (also won NH flat and jumping there). Dam won 3 Points, a Hunter Chase, and 3 2m6f-3m1f Chases in Ireland. NH '01/2 r11 w3 (3m-3m1f Hdles and 3m Chase) p6. HUNT CH '03 r5 p2; 5th, 7th and last. An expensive purchase following three wins for Jonjo O'Neill to October '02, but prone to disappoint under Rules, and was a beaten favourite on five occasions. Forced to plunder his Members in order to pick up the winning habit, but otherwise only once better than last in '04, and will run up the white flag as soon as the going gets tough. Has been tried in cheekpieces and a visor. *C.W. Booth — Grafton (Richard Webb).* 89 (O), 374 (O), 582 (M), 938 (MO), 1216 (4m100yMO), 1471 (O).

BENBEOCH ..9-8.. 6 ch.g. Hatim (USA) — Phantom Singer (Relkino) 1. Owner-bred brother to Inglemotte Miss (*qv*). Given a model introduction by Kevin Anderson in a Hexham Maiden, and produced in the closing stages to beat some frustrating old characters without much fuss. Should build on this, and possibly a fair stayer in the making. *Mrs E.J. Deans — Dumfries (David Parker).* 1422 (OMa).

BENBOW ..9-12§§.. 8 ch.g. Gunner B — Juno Away (Strong Gale) 2f232u. Rangy dipped half-brother to NH flat winner, Shady Anne. Dam won 2m1f Hdle for Derek Pugh. NH FLAT '02 r1 p0. NH '02/3 (for F.T. Jordan) r4 p1 (last of 3); pulled up 1. Could easily have won any of the four Maidens in which he was placed, and was at least eight lengths clear three out in two of them, but a complete dog who stops and tends to hang violently in the closing stages, and loves to throw races away. Beaten at 9-4 or less on four occasions, and wise punters will lay not play in future. *D. Pugh — N. Salop (Gordy Edwards).* 97 (CfMa), 226 (CfMa), 754 (OMa), 934 (OMa), 1261 (OMa), 1375 (3m110yH).

BEN BUCKLEY ..9-0.. 13 b.g. Buckley — Koritsaki (Strong Gale) 57. Sturdy half-brother to Sylviss Dream. Dam was unbeaten in 2 Points, and subsequently won 2 2m4f Hdles; also placed total of 4, inc 2 Chses. P-t-P '99/00 and '02/3 (for Mr J.C. Hogg) r8 w1 (Maiden) p1 (3rd); pulled up 3, ran out 1 and fell 1. Won an average Maiden at Alnwick in '02, but has never been able to race on a regular basis, and despite not looking ideal schoolmaster material was used to teach the novice Ross Sinton in '04. Jumped round safely having been taken to post early twice, but ultimately tailed off on both occasions. *R. Bewley — Border (Kathryn Bewley).* 1310 (R), 1476 (R).

BENETTON (U) ..4-12.. 11 bl.g. unknown 3. Ran well for her lady Captain, but her colours were soon lowered when the chequered flag loomed. *The King's Troop RHA — R.A. (Neil Cross).* 84 (2m4fC).

BEN FROM KETTON ..10-5.. 10 b.g. Cruise Missile — Saucy Girl (Saucy Kit) 7331211. Tall plain. P-t-P/HUNT CH '00/3 r22 w2 (Maiden and 2-finisher Restricted) p6 (3 2nds, remote once); fell/unseated 3, refused 1, ran out 1, and pulled up 2. Required 10 attempts to lose his maiden status and two fewer to land a Restricted, but came within half a length of winning four races this May. A sound surface is paramount, and though flattered by a Hunter Chase success where the runner-up steadfastly refused to overtake looks destined to provide Simon Robinson with further success. His rise up the ratings has been aided by a greater understanding with the gyrating owner-rider, and improved fencing as a result. *S.J. Robinson — Zetland.* 211 (C), 427 (I), 762 (I), 1286 (M), 1413 (Cf), 1460 (I), 1489 (3m3fH).

PLATE 24 1413 South Durham Confined: With the favourite beaten, outsider of three, Ben From Ketton (Simon Robinson, left), 2nd, challenges Darak (Nigel Tutty), 1st, at the last

PHOTO: Roy Parker

BENGAL BOY ..9-11.. 9 b.g. Gildoran — Bengal Lady (Celtic Cone) 7p1u. Strong workmanlike brother to Fresh Brew, and half-brother to Royal Fireworks and Mistress Dasher (dam of Gillie's Nephew *qv*, also by Gildoran). Dam, half-sister to Teaplanter (*qv* '98 Annual) was placed in 5 Points. NH FLAT '00/1 r3 p0. NH '01/3 (for P. Beaumont) r31 w1 (2m2f Chse) p5; pulled up 6, unseated 3. Bought Doncaster, Oct 3200. Won a three-finisher Chase in soft in which only two went clear in the previous yard, and also pipped on the post when short-headed in a Hurdle, but was a poor jumper of regulation fences, wore blinkers twice and tried tongue-tied, and descended to Selling level once. Always finds it difficult to score, but gained a second success at the 37th attempt under an enterprising ride from Nick Pearce in his Members, in which he outwitted the runner-up by kicking clear with a mile to go and keeping his fading mount going on the flat. Remains prone to blunders, and not up to Open standard. *Mrs J. Knight — Belvoir.* 382 (O), 592 (O), 680 (M), 942 (Cf).

BENGAL BULLET ..10-13.. 8 b.g. Infantry — Indian Cruise (Cruise Missile) 22211u. Workmanlike rangy half-brother to Phar Away Cruise. Dam, won (2m5f) Chase and last of 2; and was placed in 2 Points after producing Phar Away Cruise ('may barely stay 3m'). Grandam, Indian Diva, won 3 Hunt Chses (2m4f-3m2f) and 5 Points and placed 8 (inc 2 Hunt Chses and Hcap). P-t-P '03 r6 w4 (4-timer inc Maiden, Restricted, Intermediate and Confined) p0; unseated, and pulled up. A cheap purchase who quickly went up through the ranks last year, but an odds-on failure in soft twice in '04, and appears able to maintain his relentless gallop only on better ground. Clicked immediately with Tabitha Cave (has only ever won for a girl) but has shown a tendency to jump one way or the other, and the combination was severed on the first circuit when well fancied for the John Corbet. By a stallion whose progeny tend to suffer with their legs, and his sometimes diagonal jumping style suggests he too may be afflicted, so it's fingers crossed that he remains sound as he is very talented on his day. *C. Blank — Dart V.H. & S. Pool H.* 80 (Cf), 491 (M), 792 (MO), 1167 (3m2f110yH), 1363 (2m3f110yH), 1452 (3m4fH).

BENICK (IRE) ..—.. 12 b.g. Yashgan — Sounds Symphonic (Orchestra) ps. Rangy well-made. IRISH P-t-P '99 r3 w1 (6yo Maiden) p1 (2nd); and fell. NH '99/02 (for R.J. Smith, and N.A. Twiston-Davies) r17 w2 (3m-3m4f Hdle) p2; pulled up 6, fell 2. Completed a Hurdling double in soft in November '00, but went to pieces completely in the previous yard, and was sometimes blinkered. Already tailed off when he broke a leg on the flat after a mile at Garnons. Mrs C.L. Goodinson — N. Hereford. 93 (O), 615 (O).

BENSON (IRE) .9-12.. 10 b/br.g. Hawkstone (IRE) — Erin St Helen (IRE) (Seclude USA) 87fp*80*. Big good-looking pin-fired. P-t-P '00 (for Mr H. Daly) r1 p1 (3rd of 4). NH '00/3 (for H.D. Daly) r11 w2 (2m3f-2m4f110y Chses) p1 (3rd); pulled up 2. NH '04 r2 p0 (8th in 2m3f110y Ch: *a bhnd, mist 7, t.o*; and last in 2m5f Hdle: *in tch til wknd u.p 10, t.o*). Lacked fluency when winning twice over fences for Henry Daly, but has shown form only on a sound surface, and cut no ice in the new yard. Acquired a visor when reverting to hurdling on his most recent appearance, and has yet to prove his effectiveness over three miles. *Miss D. Wilkins — R.A. (Seamus Mullins).* 34 (O), 209 (3m1f110yH), 581 (2m4fH), 801 (3mH).

BERING GIFTS (IRE) ..9-13§.. 10 b.g. Bering — Bobbysoxer (Valiyar) 717. Compact half-brother to Balsox. Dam, won 3 flat races consecutively, 10-12f. FLAT '97/9 r19 w3 (8-9f) p5. NH '99/02 r22 w5 (2m-2m1f Hdles) p3 (beaten head once). HUNT CH '03 r3 p2; and 5th of 6. Ridden with kid gloves and produced as late as possible when successful in five Hurdles for Charlie Mann to June '02, but would frequently down tools, and was scoring for the first time over fences and beyond the minimum trip when overturning the jolly in a match at Kingston Blount. That result was surprising for a number of reasons, as he made all and found extra when tackled and the ground was significantly softer than he prefers. Typically let favourite backers down next time and has to be kept at arms length as far as punting is concerned. *A. Hill — V. of Aylesbury with Garth & S. Berks (Lawney Hill).* 892 (2m5f110yH), 1338 (M), 1438 (3m2fH).

BERKELEY FRONTIER (IRE) ..9-7.. 12 ch.g. Imperial Frontier (USA) — Harristown Rose (Miami Springs) p23441p. Tall rangy half-brother to Irish jumping and English Chasing winner, Harristown Lady. Dam won 12f race and 2 Hdles (2m-2m4f) in Ireland. IR7400 3yo. IRISH NH FLAT r1 p1 (2nd). NH '98/03 (for N.A. Gaselee, and N.A. Twiston-Davies) r30 w3 (2m-3m Hdles) p5; pulled up 5, fell/unseated 3. A formerly competent Hurdler at best, and made all for three wins, including two at Towcester at odds of 16-1 and 20-1. Inconsistent, visored thrice, lacked confidence over fences, and was also pulled up five times and fell or unseated on three occasions. Barely able to breathe in Points (wears a tongue-tie), and tended to look a sorry spectacle, but made a very safe conveyance for Emma Jones (returning to the racing saddle after nine years), and faced only by Maggie Stephens on an old donkey in his Members even he could hardly fail to win. *Mrs E.K. Jones — Carms.* 615 (O), 673 (L), 949 (L), 1189 (L), 1321 (MO), 1519 (M), 1551 (L).

BERMUDA BLUE ..9-12.. 9 gr.g. Arzanni — Calora (USA) (Private Account USA) 54p. Tall half-brother to Pardon Me Son. Dam won flat and 2 Hurdles in France. NH '02 r1 p1 (3rd in 3m110y Mdn Hdle). P-t-P '02/3 r8 w2 (Maiden and Members) p2 (3rd of 4); 5th twice, pulled up and unseated. Sold cheaply after winning two Points for David Johnson in '02, but had already revealed the darker side of his nature in the West Country, and broke down badly when in the process of running a fair race at Hornby Castle. Visored twice when Pipe-trained and blinkered on one occasion in '04. Wears a cross-noseband. *J. Ashby — Bilsdale (Pat Tate).* 70 (R), 268 (R), 341 (R).

BERRY HILL BOY (IRE) ..—.. 7 b.g. Commanche Run — Picton Lass (Rymer) p. Attractive. Dam, half-sister to Lothian Jem (*qv* '99 Annual), won NH flat race in Ireland. P-t-P '03 r2 p0 (unseated, and pulled up). Showed a modicum of talent on his debut, but went no more than a mile next time and his '04 campaign was over on February 1. Error prone to date, and presumably faulty. *Miss J.M. Green — Ludlow (Penny Grainger).* 112 (OMa).

BESSIE BUNTER ..9-7.. 9 b.m. Rakaposhi King — Black H'Penny (Town And Country) 13f3up. Good-topped. Dam won 2m6f Hdle. NH FLAT '02 r2 p0. NH '02/3 (for J.A.B. Old) r7 p0. Beaten 21 lengths plus under Rules, but subsequently had a wind operation, and was able to land a weak January Maiden at Black Forest Lodge on her Pointing debut. Only moderate and has lost confidence in her jumping, and failed to get beyond halfway when making two appearances in an afternoon at Bratton Down. *Mrs J.M. Cumings & Mrs C. Dunsford — Devon & Somerset (Keith Cumings).* 67 (OMa), 148 (R), 579 (R), 1184 (R), 1378 (M), 1386 (R).

BEST ACCOLADE ..9-11.. 6 b.g. Oscar (IRE) — Made Of Talent (Supreme Leader) 11. Lightly-made lengthy. Dam, half-sister to Cedor Hicks (*qv* '01 Annual), won Maiden and 2nd twice for Edward Crow. Remarkably for a five-year-old has contested two races taking 7min30s plus, and after easily catching the reluctant dog Benbow at Tabley it took him a green age to get going at Heslaker, and despite apparently struggling in fifth four out the champion managed to force him ahead in the final stride (to the relief of his odds-on supporters). Has the right attitude, and will hopefully be able to get going in time in contests over less than 3m4f in future. *D. Rogers — N. Salop (Sheila Crow).* 754 (OMa), 1205 (CR).

BETABUG (IRE) ..—.. 7 ch.g. Alphabatim (USA) — Chatter Bug (Le Bavard FR) R. Strong half-brother to Irish Hurdling winner, Us And Mary. Fat in his Members, and after almost refusing at the second was hopelessly tailed off when running out and dumping Gwen Morris at the fourth. His partner is totally incompetent on difficult maidens, and was soon out of control before leaving the saddle at the second on her other ride at Cilwendeg. *Miss C. Morgan — Tivyside.* 669 (M).

BETHIN .8-7§.. 11 b.m. Henbit (USA) — Mandarling (Mandalus) p443p. Lengthy half-sister to Mankind and Captain Random. Dam, half-sister to Mandenka (*qv* '97 Annual), won 13f NH flat; and was a poor 3rd of 4 from her only completion in 5 Points in '92. NH FLAT '99 r4 p0. P-t-P '02/3 r11 p1 (2nd); 4th, last, pulled up 6, and fell/unseated 2. Has shown some ability, but regularly makes mistakes and only once beaten less than 30 lengths in '04. A weak finisher, and almost certainly another ungenuine product of her sire. *R. Harvey — Atherstone.* 463 (OMa), 595 (OMa), 789 (CfMa), 1119 (CMam), 1398 (Cm).

BETTER FUTURE (IRE) ..9-12§.. 16 br.g. Good Thyne (USA) — Little Else (Abednego) 51. Smallish compact. IRISH P-t-P '94/5 r10 w2 p3; pulled up 3. NH '97 and '01 r5 p0 (tailed off in Chses — pulled up 1, & 5th in Hdle). P-t-P '96 and '98/03 r27 w14 (inc 9 Opens, Mixed Open and 4m Open, hat-tricks '98 and '02) p6 (3 3rds, last once); and pulled up 5. A useful Pointer when in the right frame of mind, and aspired to 10-8 in '99, but famed for his mulish behaviour and needed mud and a long track to be most effective. Brought out of retirement to provide John Taylor with his first win when scoring for the seventh time at Garnons, but the rider of the favourite leapt off at the first, and the runner-up proved even more irresolute than himself. Has been tried in cheekpieces. *C.J. Hitchings — Ross H.* 110 (Cnr), 402 (M).

BETTIE BLUE ..—.. 8 b.m. Sula Bula — Bickfield Approach (Dubassoff USA) ppf. Sturdy compact owner-bred sister to Miss Biddy (*qv*). A shaky jumper in her first season, and batty 61-year-old Tony Harris should never have been allowed to partner her at Maisemore, where she failed to rise at the 14th and gave him a very heavy fall, which caused considerable delay to proceedings whilst the paramedics were in attendance. *A.G. Harris — Mendip F.* 265 (R), 353 (OMa), 725 (OMa).

BEYOND THE STARS ..10-0.. 14 b.g. Jupiter Island — MCA Lucky Star (Lucky Wednesday) p1. Compact good-bodied brother to Yonder Star, and half-brother to Mr Bumble. Dam won at 5f, but proved a madam after. FLAT r1 p0 (last). NH '94/6 (blinkered 1) and '97 r11 p2; inc last 6, and pulled up 2. P-t-P/HUNT CH '97/03 r13 w2 (Members and Restricted) p3 (2nds, of 3 once); last pair 2, pulled up 4, and fell 2. Plagued by leg trouble throughout his career and only able to run very infrequently, but retains plenty of ability, and has come from last to first and survived a last fence blunder in both successes at Maisemore Park. Unruly in the paddock on his '04 reappearance, and taken to post early next time. *Mrs E. Phillips & S. Joynes — N. Ledbury (Scott Joynes).* 835 (Cf), 1253 (M).

BICKLEIGH COTTAGE .—.. 8 b.m. Mahrajan — Salmon Spirit (Big Deal) p. Lengthy half-sister to Bert House. Dam is half-sister to 4 Pointers. Grandam, Spiritway, won 4 Points and placed 7. Started at 25-1 when tailed off and pulled up at Holnicote. *Exe Valley Racing (M. Rowe) — Tiverton (Mary Sanderson).* 275 (CfMa).

BIDDY ..8-1.. 6 b.m. Rock Hopper — Wanda (Taufan USA) 5563. Small neat half-sister to Hurdles winner, Jago. Dam won 4 flat (5-6f). FLAT '01/2 (for M.W. Easterby) r4 p0; last 2. 50-1 plus in her four flat races and tailed off in three of them, but the rider was suspended under the non-triers rule second time out (even if she had been allowed to try the result would have undoubtedly been the same). Does her best in Points, but it simply is not good enough, and in front of only two rivals to date, one of them partnered by her trainer. Lack of stamina is a major draw back. *Yorkshire P-t-P Club (Miss J.E. Foster) — Pendle Forest & Craven (Jo Foster).* 774 (2m4fCMa), 960 (OMa), 1164 (OMa), 1206 (OMa).

BIDIN' MY TIME (NZ) ..—.. 9 b.g. Centro (NZ) — Moet Heights (NZ) (Engagement USA) pf. Half-brother to winner in Australia, and to a winner in New Zealand. Dam won 2 races in New Zealand. NH FLAT '00 (for N.J. Henderson) r2 w1 p0. Sold Doncaster, May '01 for 25,000. Got off to a flying start with a bumper win, but 30 lengths eighth when 5-4 favourite next time, and promptly absented himself for four years. Unable to complete in early season Points, and fell after being backed from 25-1 to 8-1, after which it was hidin' time again. *J.S. Harlow — Atherstone.* 56 (C), 188 (O).

BIG BRENDAN (IRE) ..9-8.. 8 b.g. Insan (USA) — Small Slam (Buckskin FR) 2. Tall rangy. IRISH P-t-P '03 r4 p1 (2nd); pulled up 1. Bought Doncaster, May for 5500. Suffered a leg problem after finishing second on the opening day of the season, but as the third and fourth (Cimmaroon) were soon to score it is obvious that there is a Maiden at least for him when he can be produced sound. *B. & Mrs A. Watts — Weston & Banwell H. (Rose Vickery).* 8 (2m4fOMa).

BIG HORN (IRE) ..—.. 11 b.g. Little Bighorn — Fast Girl (IRE) (Tumble Gold) pp. Gigantic rangy. NH '01 r2 p0; 5th and pulled up in Hdles. P-t-P '00 and '02/3 r5 w1 (Maiden) p0; pulled up 4. Scored in the slowest time of the day at Witton Castle in '02, but has been virtually impossible to train, and snapped a leg when tried in a tongue-strap for the first time at Charm Park. *P. Sadler — Rockwood H. (Stephen Wiles).* 591 (CR), 955 (R).

BIG MOSSY ..8-8.. 10 b.g. Le Moss — Birniebrig (New Brig) pp5. Brother to jumping winner, Taramoss, and half-brother to Billieburn and Highland Brig (*qv*). Dam, half-sister to Earls Brig and Bronzeknowe, won a Maiden and 2nd 3 (inc 2 Chses; all her starts over fences). Grandam, Naughty

Tara, won Maiden and Hunter Chase and 2nd thrice (after unseating once) — fell in 8 of her 14 races. Bought Ascot, Oct 3333. A late starter who was last on his only completion, but not wholly disgraced on that occasion, and should concentrate exclusively on elders Maidens in future. *G. Mugleston — Devon & Somerset.* 571 (R), 794 (Inr), 967 (OMa).

BILINGUAL ..9-12.. 6 b.g. Prince Daniel (USA) — Gymcrak Cyrano (IRE) (Cyrano De Bergerac) 1. Dam won 2 flat (7-15f, including a Sell), and 2m6f Hdle. Bought Doncaster, Aug 9500. Novicey at Friars Haugh in early February, but maintained a stout gallop despite wandering in the closing stages to beat subsequent triple winner Three Spires by a length. Already stays well, and will be an interesting prospect in his second campaign. *I. Stark — Buccleuch.* 137 (OMa).

BILL HAZE ..9-11§.. 9 ch.g. Romany Rye — Brilliant Haze VII (unknown) 2p12. Plain light-framed home-bred brother to Gypsy Haze, and half-brother to Kristal Haze and Pearly Haze. P-t-P '02/3 r10 p4 (2 2nds; and inc last of 3 once); 5th, fell/unseated 2, refused 1, ran out 1 and pulled up 1. Possesses above average ability, but can be incredibly wayward and typically missed out on a Maiden success, and tried to pull himself up on several occasions when beating subsequent summer jumping winner Rag Week at Bonvilston. Hangs like a gate, and makes mistakes, and could not be trusted to follow up. Wears bandages in front, wore cheekpieces when successful and has been tried in blinkers. *Mr P. Dando — Pentyrch.* 668 (OMa), 974 (3mH), 1094 (R), 1319 (I).

BILL ME UP (IRE) ..10-4.. 9 b.g. Shardari — Little Credit (Little Buskins) 12u1225122. Small light-framed half-brother to Vatacan Bank, Minister For Fun (IRE) and Holy Sting (IRE), to Irish jumping winner, Ned Of The Hill, and to Irish Pointing winner, Mum's Eyes. Dam, won Irish Maiden. IRISH NH '01 r4 p0. IRISH HUNT CH '02 r1 p0 (unseated). IRISH P-t-P '02 r3 w1 (5&6yo Maiden) p0; brought down, and pulled up. P-t-P '03 r11 w3 (Restricted, Members and Intermediate) p6 (5 2nds, remote once and of 3 once); 5th, and 6th. Most consistent and is ideally suited by a flat galloping track and top-of-the-ground, but can handle softer conditions against minor opposition. Has shown signs of waywardness, and would have scored at Buckfastleigh had he not given the field a huge head-start, but is a very reliable jumper and should have no difficulty in finding further opportunities. Has two paddock handlers. *J.C. & K.C. Heard — Eggesford (John Heard).* 80 (Cf), 200 (Cf), 320 (Cf), 483 (Cf), 569 (MO), 799 (2m3f110yH), 1168 (2m5fH), 1348 (Cf), 1437 (2m5f110yH), 1498 (3m2f110yH).

BILLY COLEMAN (IRE) ..8-12.. 7 b.g. Hollow Hand — Little Treat (Miner's Lamp) 4. Half-brother to Evan's Collier Boy (IRE). Favourite for his debut at Lydstep in April, but could finish only 11 lengths fourth, with Wiston Wizo two places ahead of him. Not a great start, but may improve with time. *D. Brace — Llangeinor.* 948 (OMa).

BILLYMAX (IRE) ..—.. 8 ch.g. Eurobus — Yougotit (Orange Reef) 5fppp. Compact well-made. Dam won NH flat. IRISH NH FLAT '03 r1 p0. IRISH NH '03 (for R. O'Leary) r2 p0; pulled up 2. 35 lengths last (a totally uninspired gamble from 12s to fours) on his only completion from seven attempts over jumps. Does not even stay 2m4f, and there are also doubts about his enthusiasm. Not worth trying again. *D. Ward — Middleton (Chris Pimlott).* 113 (OMa), 342 (2m4fOMa), 476 (CfMa), 774 (2m4fCMa), 958 (OMa).

BILLY WHITELIES (IRE) ..9-5.. 10 gr.g. Ala Hounak — Mirella Parsons (Mirror Boy) f22. Tall strong. NH '00 r1 p0 (pulled up). P-t-P '03 r1 p0 (pulled up). Obviously difficult to train, but would have made a successful reappearance at Didmarton had he not been foiled by the final fence. Might have recovered losses had he jumped better in much softer ground next time, but beaten on merit on a return trip to Maisemore, and is becoming expensive to follow. Should find a race, but probably needs an easy three miles, and has to brush up his jumping. *Mrs P.M. Joynes & T. Goodman — N. Ledbury (Scott Joynes).* 370 (OMa), 730 (OMa), 1258 (OMa).

BILTON'S NAP ..9-9.. 6 b.g. Relief Pitcher — Sheer Water (Vital Season) u2. Heavy-topped compact Alner-bred half-brother to Okeford (IRE) and Twitchings (IRE). Dam won 8 Points (concluded with 4-timer in Ladies) and 2nd for Robert Alner (was rated 10-8). Exited at the first on his debut, but then chased home a fair maiden at Buckfastleigh (those behind him were rubbish). Given his connections there are causes for optimism that he can go one better soon. *Mrs B. Willcocks — Portman (Sally Alner).* 238 (CfMa), 492 (OMa).

BIRKWOOD ..9-5.. 6 b.g. Presidium — Wire Lass (New Brig) fu232. Brother to Thornton Bridge. Dam won Maiden and Restricted and 3rd twice ('a hot ride...a non-finisher in 22 of 31 attempts over fences'). Bought Doncaster, Aug 6500. Very green in early season and missed out on a great opportunity when he ducked out and unseated at the third in a Maiden in which only one horse completed, but his one length seconds put him on the verge of a victory. Taking longer than expected to break his duck, and connections evidently feel 2m4f is more suitable at present, but should reach the goal before too much longer. *I.D. Stark — Buccleuch.* 137 (OMa), 510 (OMa), 553 (CfMa), 768 (2m4fOMa), 920 (2m4fOMa).

BISHOP'S BLADE ..10-9.. 8 b.g. Sure Blade (USA) — Myrtilla (Beldale Flutter USA) 1f21f. Small sparely-made half-brother to Top Light (*qv*). FLAT '00/01 (for J.S. King) r6 p0. NH '03 (for M. Hill) r2 p0. Very modest flat and Hurdling, but gallops round with plenty of gusto in Points, and apart from two wins which included a gallant dead-heat with I Am Said I and a short head by Cimmaroon he also fell four out and three out when in front and apparently going strongly in both. A return to Hurdling in July and August has not suited him, but could make a cracking Ladies horse for the dynamic Sarah Gaisford. *E. Retter — Dartmoor.* 83 (OMa), 148 (R), 314 (R), 488 (R), 573 (I).

BITOFAMIXUP (IRE) ..10-6.. 14 br.g. Strong Gale — Geeaway (Gala Performance) 3p*f*pp. Tall brother to Laura Lugs (IRE) and Galeaway (IRE), and half-brother to Azurlordshipleases, and to NH flat winners, Skinaway and Stand Easy (IRE) (latter also won Chasing). NH '96 and '98/02 r19 w2 (3m-3m3f Chses) p5 (3 2nds); pulled up 3, unseated 1. P-t-P/HUNT CH '96/7, '01 and '03 r20 w11 (inc 5 Hunt Chses, 3m-3m4f, 3 Ladies and Open, inc 4-timer '03) p6 (4 2nds, remote once and inc Hunt Ch); 4th, pulled up 1 and unseated 1. NH '04 r2 p0 (fell in 3m Ch: *fell 1*; and pulled up in 3m110y Ch: *lost plce 3, t.o & pu 4 out*). A brilliant six-year-old, and remarkably rejuvenated when the ground dried out in the second half of '03, but has been hampered by wind problems for some time now, and will be hard pressed to reverse his decline in fortunes again. Usually a fine jumper, but has twice been unnerved by the fences at Aintree, and can lose interest if unable to dominate. Runs tongue-tied, and has been tried in blinkers. *M.J. Roberts — E. Sussex & Romney Marsh.* 18 (L), 280 (3m2f110yH), 732 (2m5f110yH).

BLACK A BROOK (IRE) ..8-9§.. 9 br.m. Good Thyne (USA) — Gladtogetit (Green Shoon) p5p1pp4. Compact owner-bred sister to Swincombe (IRE), and half-sister to Little Brown Bear (IRE) and Free Gift. Dam, sister to Green Sheen (IRE) (*qv* '00 Annual), won mares Maiden and NH flat in Ireland, and won 3 Chses (2m6f-3m) in England. P-t-P '02/3 (for Mr T.J. Whitley) r8 p1 (3rd of 4); 5th twice, 7th, pulled up 2, carried out 1 and fell 1. Beaten a minimum of 25 lengths in her first five completions, but related to two decent Chasers, and had clearly been reserving plenty for herself. Finally goaded into revealing all of her ability when acquiring Leslie Jefford and first-time cheekpieces at Cherrybrook, but their effects appear to have worn off already. *S. & Mrs J. Wood — Lamerton (Jane Wood).* 120 (OMa), 312 (CfMa), 494 (OMa), 795 (CfMa), 1002 (R), 1271 (I), 1385 (R).

BLACKANBLUE ..9-13.. 6 b.g. Alflora (IRE) — Emmabella (True Song) 21. Heavy-topped. Dam was 2nd in Maiden for Alan Hollingsworth, but ran only 7 times in 5 years. Hampered twice (badly once) and then blundered and almost unseated at the last when holding every chance at Maisemore (had a most unlucky passage throughout), but atoned with rather a cheeky success under Gary Hanmer in a modest contest at Woodford. Looks substantially better than mother, and gives the impression that he might make a successful Open horse when the time arises. *A. Hollingsworth — Worcs.* 723 (OMa), 1075 (OMa).

BLACKBERRY WAY..10-5§.. 11 ch.m. Almoojid — Prickly Path (Royal Match) r033pp4. Sturdy close-coupled owner-bred. Dam is half-sister to Eagle Tavern (*qv* '93 Annual). NH '00/1 r2 p0; pulled up 1. P-t-P/HUNT CH '99 and '02/3 r11 w3 (inc 2m4f110y Hunt Ch) p3 (2 3rds in Hunt Chses); 4th, last pair 2, pulled up 1 and unseated 1. Ambitiously placed since winning at Huntingdon in '02, but often drops herself out of contention from an early stage, and cannot handle soft ground. Returned to form when beaten less than three lengths at Exeter and if her mood is right a continued run in Ladies races could yield dividends in '05. Wears bandages, and acquired a tongue-tie on her last four starts. *C. & Mrs S. Watson — Wilton (Louise Cullen).* 33 (L), 241 (2m4f110yH), 438 (3m1f110yH), 631 (2m6f110yH), 994 (3m110yH), 1166 (2m5f110yH), 1293 (2m7f110yH).

BLACKCHURCH LASS (IRE) .8-2.. 7 b.m. Taum Go Leor (IRE) — Melons Lady (IRE) (The Noble Player USA) 3. Small well-made. NH FLAT '02 r1 p0 (tailed off). NH '02 r2 p1 (3rd); and pulled up. P-t-P '03 (for Mrs S. Stentiford) r3 p1 (last of 2); pulled up 1, and fell 1. Changed hands after an inauspicious debut, and ran passably when four lengths last of two next time, but did not reappear until the end of May this year, and immediately went lame. *K. Glastonbury — Pentyrch (Cath Williams).* 1524 (OMam).

BLACK COLLAR ..10-8.. 6 br.m. Bob's Return (IRE) — Rosemoss (Le Moss) 11*6*. Good-bodied half-sister to Daring Dilon. Dam, half-sister to The Hon Rose (*qv* '98 Annual) placed 2nd NH Flat and a Hdle, all her starts. NH FLAT '04 (for T.D. Walford) r1 p0 (6th over 2m1f100y at Market Rasen: *hld up, hdwy over 4f out, one pce final 3f, saddle slpd*). Placed to splendid advantage in a 5&6-year-old Maiden at Charm Park (was still going well when the only danger slipped up before the last) and PPORA Restricted at Welbeck, in which none of the three behind scored subsequently. The manner of her successes was decisive particularly as she was being looked after, and connections soon cashed in to take a highly pleasing profit. Based on concrete achievement her rating is much too high, but there looks to be plenty of potential for her to justify it. *N.L. Watson — Middleton.* 393 (CfMa), 591 (CR).

BLACK DAN ..—.. 13 b.g. Bay Spirit — Sian Melody VII (unknown) pup5pp8s3. Lengthy good-bodied owner-bred half-brother to Sing Cherry Ripe and Tiger Rag. P-t-P '98/00 and '02/3 r26 w1 (Maiden) p2 (last of 3 twice, remote once); pulled up 10, and fell/unseated 2. Sprang a surprise at Pentreclwydau in '00, but not better than a fence last in the present yard, and the application of cheekpieces (once) and blinkers failed to re-ignite his spark in '04. Error-prone and has a habit of dislodging his front shoes. *Mr & Mrs C.J. Underwood — Pembs (David Underwood).* 357 (R), 451 (R), 953 (R), 1094 (R), 1237 (R), 1389 (R), 1485 (Cnr), 1521 (Cnr), 1523 (R).

BLACKHILL PRINCESS ..7-10.. 8 b.m. Sharkskin Suit (USA) — Royal Vick (Royal Palace) upp. Small homebred. P-t-P '03 r4 p0 (5th of 6, pulled up 2, and unseated 1). Yet to go more than two miles on more than one occasion, and acquired blinkers on her last two appearances. Wears a cross-noseband, and bandages in front. *R. Vickers — Cumberland F.* 286 (CfMa), 549 (CMam), 768 (2m4fOMa).

BLACK HOPE (IRE) ..8-10.. 7 br.m. Presenting — All Black (Green Shoon) Rpp3Ruf. Lengthy unfurnished. IRISH NH FLAT '03 r1 p0. IRISH NH '02/3 (for J. Larkin) r2 p0. Has a deplorable completion record and failed to achieve a clear round in Devon, Worcestershire, Somerset, Pembrokeshire, Herefordshire and Glamorgan (did remount after crashing at the last once), but looked like making all until she fell two out when six lengths clear at Bonvilston on final start. Makes plentiful blunders and often jumps and hangs right, and tends to stop to nil in the manner of one with a severe breathing problem (wears a tongue-tie now). It is not inconceivable that she might emerge from the vale of tears eventually. Perhaps a wind operation would help. *Mr & Mrs K. Kelso — Pembs (Beverley Thomas).* 119 (OMa), 257 (CMa), 600 (2m4fOMa), 675 (CfMa), 1096 (OMa), 1231 (OMam), 1323 (CfMa).

BLACK LEOPARD (IRE) ..9-10.. 6 b/br.g. Presenting — Glen Laura (Kambalda) p*0p*. NH '04 (for P.D. Niven) r2 p0 (12th in 2m1f Hdle: *sn bhnd, t.o*; and pulled up in 2m4f110y Hdle: *stdd start, a bhnd, t.o & pu 3 out*). Bought Tattersalls Ireland, Aug for 4946. One of six losers for P.J. Finn and David Pipe at the Middleton (how the locals tittered), five of them partnered by Ashley Farrant, but this newcomer could have been second had he not pulled up two out when tiring quickly. Not seen again, but could be worth watching when he reappears. *P.J. Finn — Middleton.* 773 (2m4fCMa).

BLACK OPTIMIST (IRE) ..10-2§.. 11 br.g. Roselier (FR) — Borys Glen (Furry Glen) pp21p. Strong. IRISH P-t-P '00 r4 w1 (5&6yo Maiden) p0; pulled up 2, and ran out. NH '02 (for M. Bradstock) r2 p1 (2nd in 3m2f110y Ch); and refused. Appears bi-annually and regularly looks faulty and temperamental, but retains plenty of ability, and rallied gamely to catch the flagging leader close home at Upton-on-Severn. Tends to hang and jump right-handed, and may have suffered another setback when a well supported favourite at Woodford. *C.P. Maiden & Miss E. Croft — Berkeley (Susan Maiden).* 369 (R), 498 (R), 726 (R), 977 (R), 1071 (I).

BLACK RAINBOW (IRE) ..9-5.. 7 br.m. Definite Article — Inonder (Belfort FR) 2. Sturdy half-sister to 3 flat winners. 4000y. NH FLAT '02 r4 p2 (3rds). FLAT '03 r1 p0. NH '02/3 (for T.J. Etherington) r3 p0. Bought Doncaster, May for 4800. Has now achieved three placings, but a persistently weak finisher, and was typically fading on the run in after holding every chance at the last when six lengths second at Easingwold. Probably capable of a modest win if she can keep going a bit better. *Mrs P.A. Cowey — Cleveland (Howard Thompson).* 1165 (OMa).

BLACK SMOKE (IRE) ..10-9.. 8 gr.g. Ala Hounak — Korean Citizen (IRE) (Mister Lord USA) *88221b4*. Big stocky. Dam, half-sister to Call Me Citizen (*qv* '00 Annual), won Mares Maiden in Ireland but pulled up in 5 of 6 other attempts. P-t-P '03 r2 p0 (last, and pulled up 1). NH '04 r5 p1 (4*l* 2nd of 3 to Next To Nothing in 3m Ch: *nt fluent, 2nd to 10, rallied 2 out, ld flat, sn hdd & no ex*); 8th in 2m4f Hdle: *hld up, hdwy 5, wknd aft 3 out*; last of 8 in 2m4f Hdle: *hdwy 3, wknd u.p aft 7, t.o*; brought down in 3m1f Ch: *in tch til bd 12*; and last of 4 in 3m2f Ch: *chsd ldrs til wknd aft 12, t.o*. Given an easy time in his debut season, but followed two fair seconds with an emphatic win in a weak Hunter Chase in softish at Carlisle. The form received a boost when the runner-up went on to land the Heart at Hexham, and whilst his efforts under Rules have been modest to date the chances are that he has further improvement in him. *R & H Burridge and Bard Entertainments — Sinnington (Richard Guest).* 440 (2m7f110yH), 1028 (3mH).

BLACKWATER BRAVE (IRE) ..9-11.. 12 b.g. Commanche Run — Ardmore Lady (Quayside) pp1253154. Smallish lengthy. Dam, half-sister to Might As Well (*qv* '92 Annual). NH FLAT '98 r3 p1 (2nd). NH '98/02 r14 w3 (2m5f-3m1f Chases) p4. P-t-P '03 r6 w1 (3-runner Members) p3 (2 2nds); 4th, and 5th. Fired after striking into himself as a five-year-old, but has been successful six times going right-handed, and has become the ideal schoolmaster, but lacks a change of gear and is effective only in modest company. Lost the rider when blinkered once in '01, but otherwise as safe as houses, and provided 16-year-old George Fry with his first success at his third attempt at Littlewindsor. Suited by good or sound surfaces. *R.A. & Dr C.E. Fry — Cattistock (Caroline Fry).* 117 (C), 196 (O), 460 (C), 687 (M), 792 (MO), 862 (Cnr), 1012 (Cnr), 1250 (C), 1365 (Cnr).

BLAKENEY HILL ..9-0.. 10 ch.m. Baron Blakeney — Hillgate Lady (Rustingo) 25212. Well-made quite attractive. Dam won 4 Points and placed 4 for M.J. Ward (all wins in '92, but often highly reluctant before and after). NH FLAT '01 r2 p0. NH '02 r2 p0 (pulled up 2). P-t-P '03 r3 p1 (2 fences last of 3); and pulled up 2. Useless under Rules, and not better than last in her first five attempts over obstacles, but improved under Joe Price in '04 and outstayed bad opposition in a 17-runner elders Maiden at Bredwardine. Tends to race very keenly and generally a weak finisher herself otherwise, and will need to find further improvement for Restricteds. *Miss M.J. Ward — Curre & Llangibby.* 736 (CfMa), 1091 (CMam), 1239 (OMa), 1395 (OMa), 1538 (R).

BLAKES ROAD (IRE) ..8-13.. 8 b/br.g. Be My Native (USA) — Joyau (IRE) (Roselier FR) p3f53d. Small compact. NH FLAT '03 (for Miss V. Williams) r2 p0. Managed a couple of modest thirds (disqualified from the latest when the rider failed to weigh-in), but runs out of steam in the closing stages, and would need a bad Maiden to score. Could do with jumping better. *H.R. Neaves — W. Street Tickham (Lisa Stock).* 895 (OMa), 1088 (OMa), 1285 (OMa), 1442 (2m5fH), 1518 (OMa).

BLAKES ROMANY GIRL ..—.. 9 ch.m. Sula Bula — Ruby Celebration (New Member) p. Tall plain half-sister to Celebrate Summer. Dam, sister or half-sister to 8 winning Pointers (inc Romany Blues, (*qv* '99 Annual), failed to finish in 7 of 8 races including in 4 of 5 Points. P-t-P '02 r3 p0 (pulled up 3). Twice nibbled at in the ring and clearly thought to have some ability, but pulled up in all four attempts, and is proving impossible to train. *D.J. Jeffrey & R.B. Felmingham — V. of Aylesbury with Garth & S. Berks (Lynne Redman).* 192 (CfMa).

BLANK CHEQUE ..10-1.. 15 b.g. Idiot's Delight — Quickapenny (Espresso) 3524116. Small half-brother to Sneakapenny, Catchapenny and Shining Penny. Dam, from a great jumping family, won 7 Hdles (2-3m) and 2 3m1f Chses. NH '95 r4 p1 (3rd). P-t-P/HUNT CH '96/03 r41 w9 (inc 3 Opens) p17 (10 2nds, last once); failed to finish 6 (refused 1, ran out 1, and fell/unseated 3). A grand servant to connections, and took his score into double figures in '04, but can be very quirky and prepared to reveal his trademark barn-storming finish only when he feels like it. Failed by a neck to overhaul a rival half his age at Dalton Park, but passed four others from the third-last when successful for the fourth time at Whittington, and followed up when capturing his Members for the first time. Suited by a thorough test of stamina, and some cut in the ground. *J.J. Coates — Pendle Forest & Craven (Wendy Wild).* 163 (O), 429 (3m5fO), 501 (O), 749 (Cf), 873 (Cf), 1201 (M), 1414 (O).

BLAZING PRIDE .7-11.. 9 b.g. Blaze O'Gold (USA) — Percy's Pride (Rustingo) pfu275. Tall sparely-made brother to Golden Pride. Dam placed in Point for Mrs Haynes in '89. Grandam Our Fluff was 2nd in Members and pulled up 3. A slow coach, and was not helped by the novice rider when three lengths second of three in a Maiden (the only occasion he has finished ahead of another horse — was up to two fences last in two Members contests). It could at least be worth experimenting with a more experienced pilot in the saddle. *Mrs S.A. Haynes — Golden V., & Radnor & West Herefordshire (Sarah-Jayne Davies).* 450 (R), 666 (OMa), 934 (OMa), 1115 (OMa), 1226 (M), 1387 (M).

BLESS YOURSELF (IRE) ..8-12§§.. 9 b.g. Shardari — Wee Madge (Apollo Eight) uR3ppfp. Workmanlike. Dam won NH Flat and 4 Chses (2m2f-3m1f) in Ireland. NH FLAT '01 r1 p0. NH '02/3 r3 p0; pulled up 1. Would doubtless have won at Eyton-on-Severn had he not blundered badly and unseated at the last when a neck in front (eventually remounted in a race in which only two went clear), but a very shoddy jumper who has clearly shown how much he detests racing since, including when blinkered for the three most recent attempts. Only clambered over four fences before the champion pulled up him on final start, and could now be a lost cause. *Mrs J. Graves — Cheshire (Donald McCain Jnr).* 96 (CfMa), 227 (CfMa), 531 (OMa), 709 (Mah), 1261 (OMa), 1377 (2m5fH), 1505 (OMa).

BLIN (CZE) ..9-4.. 10 b.g. Lincoln (CZE) — Brenda (CZE) (Coulstry) 26. Small close-coupled. CZECH FLAT r3 p0. CZECH NH '00/2 r25 w2 (2m5f-2m7f Chses — inc at Pardubice) p4. NH '01 r1 p0. P-t-P '03 r3 p0 (last, unseated, and pulled up). A dual winner in his homeland but the form does not amount to a hill of beans, and has finished in front of only three rivals in six English starts. Took a crashing fall at the giant Taxis at Pardubice in '02, and his jumping at lowly Cothelstone lacked any confidence whatsoever. *D.G. Alers-Hankey — Taunton V. (Mel Dixon).* 961 (M), 1369 (Cf).

BLOOMFIELD STORM (IRE) ..10-3.. 12 b.g. Glacial Storm (USA) — Mylie's Response (Moyrath Response) p22. Compact well-made half-brother to Friary Lad (IRE), and to NH flat winner, Knock Lad. Dam won a 5yo Maiden and 2m Chase in Ireland. IRISH P-t-P '98/9 r6 w2 (inc Winners of One) p2 (3rds). NH '99/02 r10 w2 (2m-2m4f110y Chses) p2 (3rds); pulled up 1. P-t-P '03 r3 w1 (Ladies) p2 (inc 3rd of 4). Won his first two English Chases and had his next two starts in valuable Grade 2 events, but became disappointing under Rules, and was scoring for the first time since '00 when successful on his reappearance last year. Broke a blood vessel once in '03 and pulled up at halfway on his return this year, but runner-up twice at Garthorpe subsequently without ever looking likely to become seriously involved. Reported to need time between his races, and has not been seen more than thrice in a year since '00. Has won in soft but is suited by top-of-the-ground. *A.R. Lyons — Brocklesby (Jill Dawson; Sheila Mallet).* 593 (L), 1058 (L), 1399 (L).

BLOOWIT .—.. 7 b.g. Another Hoarwithy — Bellaloo (Privy Seal) upp. Small light half-brother to Hydemilla (*qv*). P-t-P '03 r1 p0 (unseated). Got over only one fence successfully in his first two races, and has subsequently jumped moderately until pulling up by the 13th. A real dud and already looks to have blown it. Wears a cross-noseband. *M. Legge — I. of W. (Phillip Legge).* 20 (OMa), 86 (OMa), 173 (OMa).

BLUE BUD ..9-0§.. 11 b.g. Lord Bud — Hodsock Venture (Major Portion) pup55p. Unfurnished half-brother to Park Mill, and to 3 flat winners, including Lady Locket and Chummy's Pet. NH FLAT '99 r3 p0. NH '99/01 r15 p3 (2 2nds); pulled up 1. P-t-P '02/3 r8 w1 (Maiden) p2 (2nds); 4th, last 2, pulled up and brought down. Awarded a Charm Park Maiden when the winning rider failed to weigh-in, but previously had a history of disappointments, and has failed to beat a rival since. Jumps reluctantly and pigs it furiously now, and looks a complete waste of time. Regained blinkers on his final appearance, and tried in a visor two starts earlier. *Mrs J. Cranage — Sinnington (John Cranage).* 266 (M), 390 (Rnr), 481 (R), 771 (R), 957 (Cf), 1160 (L).

BLUE JAR ..7-8.. 7 b.g. Royal Abjar (USA) — Artist's Glory (Rarity) pp4. Rangy light-framed half-brother to flat winners Zuno Noelyn, Zalara and winner in Italy. NH FLAT '02 r2 p0. NH '02/3 (for M. Mullineaux) r6 p0; pulled up 4, brought down, and last. Awful over Hurdles and in his first two Points (last, pulled up six times and brought down), and then finished 25 lengths fourth of five in a 2m4f Maiden. Had no chance from halfway, and still needs to improve a very great deal to make a racehorse. *R. Edwards — Cheshire.* 533 (2m4fCfMa), 710 (Mah), 1049 (2m4fOMa).

BLUE MONK (IRE) ..—.. 10 ch.g. Bluebird (USA) — High Habit (Slip Anchor) p. Big strong half-brother to a winner in Norway. FLAT r3 p0. P-t-P '01 and '03 (for Ms E. Bell) r2 p0 (pulled up and unseated). Has never been in the habit of racing on a regular basis, and having covered a circuit of Dunthrop at high speed promptly stopped to nil and went back into hiding. *M.S. Burman — Cambs with Enfield Chace.* 51 (OMa).

BLUE ORLEANS .— §.. 7 b.g. Dancing Spree (USA) — Blues Player (Jaazeiro USA) pp. Compact half-brother to 4 flat winners (3 abroad). Dam won 2m race. 5000y. FLAT '00/1 r10 p1 (3rd). NH '01 and '03 (for A.G. Newcombe when successful, and R. Brotherton) r3 w1 (2m1f Hdle) p0; pulled up 2. Showed battling qualities for a change when winning a Hurdle at 16-1, but has jumped poorly and pulled up in all four attempts over jumps since. Was ungenuine on the flat (blinkered in a Seller on his final attempt), and is not keen on Pointing (soon getting reminders in a four-horse race in the latest). *P. Tainton — N. Ledbury (Alan Phillips).* 1015 (Cf), 1112 (C).

BLUE ROYAL (FR) ..10-9.. 10 b.g. Dauphin Du Bourg (FR) — Before The Flag (IRE) (Lomond USA) p31. Rangy. FRENCH FLAT '98 r2 p0. FRENCH NH '98 r1 p1 (2nd). NH '99/00 and '02 (for N.J. Henderson) r8 w3 (2m-2m1f Hdles) p2; pulled up 1. A cracker in his youth, and like Ask The Natives was another for whom connections harboured pretentions as an Arkle winner, but following a hat-trick over Hurdles in '99 and good third to Istabraq in the '00 Champion it all went hideously wrong for him, and had made only one appearance under Rules (when pulled up) since. Seems riddled with problems still, and after breaking his pelvis in '02 he reappeared with a tongue-tie to give a rusty display in his first Point, but after a better effort when third connections were rewarded when he defeated the smart Nautical Lad in a four-runner Open at Garthorpe. Sadly he looked unsound after, which was desperate luck after all the years of nursing. *L. Wilson — Pytchley (Bill Warner).* 478 (Cf), 1121 (O), 1401 (O).

BLYTH BROOK ..10-8.. 13 b.g. Meadowbrook — The Bean-Goose (King Sitric) 1pf. Compact owner-bred brother to Beanley Brook, and half-brother to Victor Charlie, Good Fun and General Gem. NH '97/8 r3 p0. P-t-P/HUNT CH '99/03 r25 w5 (inc 2 Hunt Chses, 2m4f-2m4f110y) p10 (5 3rds, inc Hunt Ch; 5 2nds, beaten head once, inc 2 Hunt Chses); pulled up 3, brought down 1 and fell 1. Found to be suffering from a virus when pulled up in his Hunter Chase hat-trick bid last year, but bounced right back to form at Musselburgh (the first time he has won first-time out in six seasons). Sometimes let down by his jumping and his fall at Bechers, when running well, was no great surprise, but has never stood his racing particularly well and seems to leap from one setback to another. Suited by an easy three miles. Acts in soft and on firmish. *Mrs S.A. Sutton — Haydon (Tim Reed).* 240 (3mH), 439 (2m5f110yH), 732 (2m5f110yH).

BOBBY BUTTONS ..9-1.. 8 b.g. Primitive Rising (USA) — Lady Buttons (New Brig) 322242. Workmanlike owner-bred half-brother to Tudor Lord, Basil Grey, Lady Pokey (dam of Button Lady *qv*), Buster Buttons, Bonnie Buttons and Wayward Buttons. Dam won 6 Points (inc 4m2f Grimthorpe) and 3 Hunt Chses (3m-3m3f, inc John Corbet) and placed 12 for the Jones family. P-t-P '02/3 r6 p2; pulled up 4. In the frame in all eight completions, and only once beaten more than nine lengths, but a desperately weak finisher and a beaten favourite in his last five appearances. Races up with the pace, but it might be worth trying hold him up even though connections resorted to cheekpieces on his final start, and presumably think him ungenuine. *S.G. Jones — Cleveland (Jill Jones).* 160 (CMa), 271 (OMa), 504 (CMa), 814 (OMa), 1158 (OMa), 1292 (OMa).

BOB'S GRAY .—.. 11 gr.g. Scallywag — Summer Path (Warpath) fpf. Big strong hobdayed. Dam won 3 flat, 9-16f (the first a Sell), 2 Hdles (2m4f-3m) and 2m Ch, and ended her career in Points (beat 2 others from 5 attempts). NH FLAT '99 r2 p0. NH '00 r4 p0 (8th of 9, and pulled up 3). P-t-P/HUNT CH '01 and '03 r2 p0 (fell and pulled up). Useless and tongue-tied over hurdles, and has fallen in three of five subsequent attempts over fences. Has the usual Scallywag traits, and took off in front before crash landing after 2m2f on his reappearance. *G. Scantlebury — Morpeth.* 75 (OMa), 426 (Cf), 914 (M).

BOBTAIL (IRE) ..9-6.. 6 b.g. Topanoora — Death Or Glory (Hasdrubal) u7p. Compact half-brother to Glory Trail (IRE), and to Irish Pointing winner, Maria Hornell. IRISH P-t-P '03 r4 w1 (4yo Maiden) p0; pulled up 1. IRISH NH FLAT '03 (for T.J. Nagle) r1 p0. Unseated after two miles when disputing the lead on his first appearance for the new yard, but was disappointing in big fields twice subsequently (favourite once, and then absent for over two months). It is possible that he is better than he was able to show in '04. *R.J. French — N. Salop (Sheila Crow).* 95 (R), 252 (CR), 1265 (R).

BODDIDLEY (IRE) ..10-0.. 7 b.g. Be My Native (USA) — Boardwalker (IRE) (Waajib) 1bf. Compact well-made. Looked a promising recruit when getting up close home to catch a subsequently disqualified rival in a 2m4f Maiden at Ston Easton, but then departed twice with about half a mile to run when favourite and apparently going well in both (broke Chloe Roddick's collar-bone in the latest). Remains interesting, and could be worth noting if he turns up under Rules. *P. Nicholls — Blackmore & Sparkford V. (Chloe Roddick).* 600 (2m4fOMa), 1069 (R), 1196 (R).

BOHEMIAN SPIRIT (IRE) ..10-11.. 7 b.g. Eagle Eyed (USA) — Tuesday Morning (Sadler's Wells USA) u51p1115. Light-framed half-brother to flat winners, Purple Dawn and Ruby Estate. FLAT '00/1 r6 p0. P-t-P '03 r7 w2 (Maiden and Club Restricted) p3 (2 2nds); and fell/unseated 2. Vastly improved over fences since switching to sub-three mile Hunter Chases, and accrued more than 28 times his purchase price in winning prize money '04. Needs a flat track and top-of-the-ground in order to get the full trip, and patently did not get home at Stratford, but can handle a softer surface when stamina is not at a premium. Few inexpensive buys end up winning at Cheltenham and Aintree in the same year, and connections can be proud of their achievements. Tends to sweat up, and belts the odd fence, but still only a youngster and further success over regulation fences seems a formality. *P. Armitage — York & Ainsty N. (Michael Brown).* 177 (3mH), 267 (Cf), 439 (2m5f110yH), 630 (2m4fH), 892 (2m5f110yH), 1168 (2m5fH), 1374 (3m1fH), 1452 (3m4fH).

BOLD ACTION (IRE) ..—§.. 14 b.g. Denel (FR) — Loughan-Na-Curry (No Argument) p. Compact well-made brother to Kniveniven (IRE), and half-brother to Hurdles winner, Odstone Pear. NH FLAT '95/6 r4 p4. NH '97/02 r32 w5 (2m4f110y Hdle and 4 3m1f-3m2f Chases) p7 (5 2nds); pulled up 7, fell 1 and refused 1. P-t-P/HUNT CH '03 r5 p1 (3rd); and pulled up 4. A thorough stayer who was suited by a stiff uphill finish under Rules, and would not usually consent to hit the front until the closing stages, but a non-finisher in 11 of his last 14 starts and looks totally disenchanted nowadays. Usually wears headgear. *D.P. Smith — Heythrop (Sarah Kellard-Smith).* 107 (O).

BOLD CLASSIC (IRE) ..10-0.. 12 b.g. Persian Bold — Bay Street (Grundy) 55235. Tall half-brother to numerous winners, including Bex and Daarik (both flat). Dam won 2 flat, 7-9f, inc valuable race at Epsom. GERMAN FLAT '95 r2 p0. FLAT '96 and '01 r9 w1 (14f) p2 (2nds). NH '96/01 r20 w4 (3 2m4f110y-3m110y Hdles, and 3m2f Ch) p3 (2 3rds); pulled up 3. HUNT CH '02 r3 p1 (2nd); 4th, and 8th. NH '04 r1 p1 (3l 2nd to Hallrule in 3m1f Sell Ch: *hld up, hdwy 9, eff 3 out, stayed on to ch wnr flat*). As safe as they come, and has never fallen, but successful in only one of his last 23 starts, and the rot has well and truly set in. Might still be able to be competitive if switched to minor Points. Visored once in '96. *C. Grant — S. Durham.* 122 (3m1fH), 678 (3m1fH), 992 (3m3f110yH), 1347 (2m6f110yH).

BOLD FLIRTATION ..—§§.. 8 ch.g. Bold Fox — Final Flirtation (Clear Run) Rppp. Lengthy good-bodied half-brother to Final Mick (*qv*). An utter disgrace, and like stablemate Final Mick is completely mental. The trainer could at least ensure his horses do not endanger the other competitors. *D.H. Llewellyn — S. Pembs.* 675 (CfMa), 950 (2m4fOMa), 1096 (OMa), 1239 (OMa).

BOLD KING (FR) ..9-12§.. 10 gr.g. Turgeon (USA) — Vanila Fudge (USA) (Bold Bidder) 6p3p. Strong compact half-brother to 7 winners in France. FRENCH FLAT p2. FRENCH NH '98 r3 w1 (1m7f Hdle). NH '98/03 (for Mrs L.C. Jewell, N.A. Callaghan, and I. Williams) r40 w8 (5 2m-3m Hdles and 3 2m-3m2f Chses) p12; pulled up 1. Bought Doncaster, Nov for 5500. Won a Ff10,101 prize in a French Hurdle, and was at his peak in England when scoring four times in a five race spell in '00, but descended to a Claiming Hurdle for the penultimate of his nine wins. Not always keen and carries his head awkwardly and occasionally visored in previous yards, and was a disappointment when taking little interest in '04 (acquired cheekpieces after his seasonal debut). Looked to go wrong at Brampton

Bryan, and his best days are surely behind him. *Mrs N.J. Roberts — Albrighton (Paul Morris).* 209 (3m1f110yH), 346 (3m1f110yH), 382 (O), 662 (O).

BOLD KNIGHT ..—.. 12 b.g. Bold Fox — Harwall Queen (Tobique) u. Sturdy rangy. Dam, half-sister to Royal Oats (*qv* 2000 Annual), won a Restricted and a Members and placed 3 for Tudor Harries (to '97), and grandam, Knights Queen, won 11 Points (inc 2 dead-heats) and placed 10 (inc 3rd in Hunt Ch) for him. P-t-P '99/00 (for Mr E.T. Harries) r9 p2; pulled up 5 and fell 2. Placed on his only two completions, but they were way back in '00, and has been thwarted by the fences since. Appears to live life in semi-retirement nowadays. *Miss P.L. Philipps — S. Pembs (Owen Thomas).* 947 (M).

BOLD STATEMENT ..9-9.. 13 ch.g. Kris — Bold Fantasy (Bold Lad IRE) pp34. Compact half-brother to several flat winners, including Imaginary and Fetish. Dam won 2 7f races in Ireland. NH FLAT '96 r4 w1 p1 (2nd). NH '97/99 r20 w5 (3 Hdles, 2m-2m1f110y, and 2 3m Chses) p7 (4 2nds); fell/unseated 4. P-t-P/HUNT CH '02/3 (for Mr S.M. Flook, Mrs S.E. Vaughan, Mrs N. Carter & Mr T. Jones) r12 w1 (Confined; also disqualified from Club Members Nov Rdrs — tested positive) p2 (Hunt Chses, inc last of 3 once); 5th, last pair 3, pulled up 3 and unseated. Recording his first wins since '98 when successful twice for the previous yard last year, but failed to beat a rival under the owner-rider before breaking a leg in the closing stages at Kimble. *G.G. Tawell — Oakley.* 187 (Cf), 292 (MO), 461 (M), 868 (O).

BOLD TACTICS (IRE) ..10-2.. 9 br.g. Jurado (USA) — Bold Lyndsey (Be My Native USA) 4124u. Brother to Native Rain (IRE). Dam won 2 Irish Hdles, 2m-2m2f. P-t-P/HUNT CH '02/3 (for Mr K. Hutsby) r8 w2 (2m4f Maiden and Restricted) p4 (Hunt Chses, 3 2nds, beaten short head once); 5th, and fell. Won both his completed starts in softish in '02, but basically disappointing since, and was odds-on when gaining a narrow success under Tom Weston this year. Otherwise runner-up on four occasions, and having cocked his jaw and headed for the box-park at Garnons there is a suggestion that he is not entirely genuine. Appears suited by top-of-the-ground now and certainly worth a try in headgear, but remains prone to making mistakes. *N. Shutts — Warwicks (Penny Grainger).* 107 (O), 406 (Inr), 545 (2m3f110yH), 734 (2mH), 1015 (Cf).

BOLEBEC ICE FALCON ..—.. 9 gr.g. Arzanni — Bolebec Ayesha VII (unknown) fp. Tall rangy. P-t-P '03 (for Mr & Mrs S.C. Marler) r3 p0 (pulled up 2, and fell). Holding a narrow advantage when tipping up three out at Paxford, but disappointing in what looked to be an easier assignment next time, and presumably has a fault. Wears a cross-noseband, and tongue-tied once in the previous yard. *Mrs L.J.C. Tylor — Cury.* 927 (OMa), 1098 (OMa).

BOLIDE DU AUNAY (FR) .9-5.. 7 ch.g. Dadarissime (FR) — Upsilone (FR) (Chamberlin FR) 4. Strong. FRENCH NH '02/3 r 5 p1 (3rd). P-t-P '03 r1 w1 (2m4f Maiden). Had two subsequent winners behind when opening his Pointing account at the first time of asking last year, and not disgraced in a strong Restricted at Barbury on his return, but clearly hard to keep right, and has still to prove himself over the full trip. *The Emmanuel Family (Mr M. Emmanuel) — V. of Aylesbury with Garth & S. Berks (Lawney Hill).* 36 (CR).

BOOGY WOOGY ..9-10§.. 9 ch.g. Rock Hopper — Primulette (Mummy's Pet) p. Compact brother to flat winner, Rockette, and half-brother to flat and Hurdles winner, Primost, and to 7 other flat winners, including Proletariat, Martha Daly and B A Highflyer. FLAT '98/00 r23 w3 (7-12f) p7 (6 3rds). NH '99/02 r17 w2 (2m-2m1f110y Hdles) p7 (5 3rds; and inc 3 Chses). HUNT CH '03 r2 p1 (3rd of 4); and 4th. Relatively successful in a busy career for Tim Easterby to '02, but has never made a secret of his lack of resolve, and has not scored since October '00. An expensive flop for present connections, and his '04 campaign was his most truncated to date. Wears blinkers. *A. Bowling — Holcombe (Robert Bowling).* 122 (3m1fH).

BORDER BURN ..9-4.. 11 ch.g. Safawan — Burning Ryme (Rymer) 4. Deep-girthed lengthy half-brother to Effessbee. Dam is half-sister to 5 Pointers, including Burning Scally (*qv* '00 Annual). NH '01/3 r4 p0; 4th, 10th, last and pulled up in Chses. P-t-P/HUNT CH '00 and '02/3 r12 w2 (Maiden — 3 finished and Restricted) p2 (2nds, of 3 once); and 5th twice. A dual winner and runner-up twice in his first five Points, but indolent and error prone over big fences, and seems little more than a hunter nowadays. Has been tried tongue-tied. *Mr & Mrs J.M. Valdes-Scott — Waveney H. (Michael Valdes-Scott).* 22 (M).

BORDER FARMER (IRE) ..9-7.. 12 b.g. Riverhead (USA) — Double Figures (FR) (Double Form) up3u4. Lengthy half-brother to Can You Just (IRE), and to Irish flat winner, Mugnano. NH FLAT '98/9 r2 p0. NH '99 and '00/1 r7 p1 (3rd in Hdle); unseated 1. P-t-P/HUNT CH '00/1 and '03 (for Mr J. Richardson) r16 w2 (Maiden and Restricted) p4 (3 2nds, inc 2 Hunt Chses; and inc 3rd on 4 once); unseated 4, pulled up 3. NH '03 (for Mrs S. Richardson) r1 p0 (tailed off last). Successful once for both of his previous handlers, and has yet to miss the frame in eight Pointing completions, but can be hard to sit on and the new owner-rider quickly displayed his prowess for munching turf. A one-paced stayer at best and looks sure to deteriorate further. Took off on the way to post on his reappearance and has been taken down early since. *N.J. Wain — Farmers Bloodhounds (Robert Elwell).* 922 (I), 1032 (O), 1104 (Cnr), 1332 (Cf), 1472 (I).

BORDER FUSION ..9-12.. 6 b.g. Weld — Monteviot (Scallywag) 1. Compact attractive half-brother to Grey Tarquin (*qv*). Looked to be out for a jolly on his debut at Eaton Hall, and some novicey early jumping left him well behind, but he passed 12 rivals from halfway and eventually spurted through to lead on the bit after the last. It was an eye-catching performance, but let's not get carried away yet, as only one of the six behind (the sixth) was able to score subsequently. Will at least be of above average interest when he reappears. *G. Crawford — Cheshire (Gary Hanmer).* 710 (Mah).

BORDERLINE BREEZE (IRE) ..9-7.. 12 b.g. Mandalus — Barrow Breeze (Laurence O) 7p5p74p. Lengthy half-brother to jumping winners, Gimme (IRE) and Denham Hill (IRE), and to Irish Pointing winner, Bush Telegraph. Dam won Maiden and 2m Chase in Ireland. IRISH P-t-P '99/02 r18 w2 p6 (3rds). IRISH HUNT CH '01 r4 p0. IRISH NH FLAT '01 r2 p0. IRISH NH '01/2 r4 p0. P-t-P '03 (for Mrs V. Watson — The Watson Family) r6 p3 (2 2nds); 5th, 6th, and unseated 1. A dual winner in mud in Ireland in '00, but very one-paced and has accrued 33 defeats since. Often blinkered and tongue-tied prior to '03, and swallowed his tongue when in the process of running well at Garnons. Jumps safely but sometimes takes little interest, and the application of cheekpieces made no difference on his latest appearance. *Mrs V. Watson — Worcs (Valerie Watson).* 48 (3m5f70yL), 92 (I), 289 (CfL), 406 (Inr), 660 (Cf), 835 (Cf), 1216 (4m100yMO).

BORDER RUN ..10-1.. 8 b.g. Missed Flight — Edraianthus (Windjammer USA) pp2141. Compact half-brother to 2 flat winners (one in France and USA), and to successful Hurdles winner, Edwarda. 9500f, 1900y. FLAT '99/01 and '03 r13 p2 (3rds). NH '00/3 (for M. Mullineaux) r20 w1 (2m Hdle) p2 (3rds); pulled up 6, fell 1. Inconsistent and unpredictable and won only one of his first 36 races (a three-year-old Selling Hurdle in soft), and had been unplaced 19 times consecutively (including seven Chases in which he was beaten 36 lengths plus and failed to finish in four) before an unlucky defeat in a Confined at Whittington where he was four lengths clear when making a mistake at the last and then completely ran out of puff. Travelled supremely well in his two subsequent victories which included a three-runner Open taking eight minutes at Alpraham, and has forged a good relationship with Stuart Ross. Previously wore blinkers or cheekpieces. Should continue to enjoy success if his new enthusiasm can be sustained. *W. Padden — Cheshire (Richard Edwards).* 528 (O), 713 (Cf), 873 (Cf), 1047 (O), 1204 (O), 1429 (Cnr).

BORLEAGH PILOT (IRE) ..9-3.. 14 ch.g. Torus — Pilots Row (Tanavar) p1p. Compact brother to Irish Hurdles winner, Foyleclipper, and half-brother to 2 Irish winners (one NH flat and Hurdles, the other Chasing). IRISH NH FLAT '97 r1 p0. IRISH NH '97/8 and '00 r9 p1 (3rd); fell only Ch. NH '98 and '00/2 r6 p0; pulled up 2, fell 1. P-t-P '01 and '03 r7 p4 (3 3rds, last once); 4th of 5, and pulled up 2. Came from well off the pace to open his account at the 25th attempt in the slowest race of the day at Charm Park, but has been lightly raced since '98, and a follow up at 14 seems unlikely. The owner-rider, Paul Collins, is Mary Reveley's farrier. Blinkered once in '00. *P. Collins — Cleveland (Nick Smith).* 74 (OMa), 394 (CfMa), 955 (R).

BORN SPECIAL ..—.. 6 b.g. Bluebird (USA) — Dixie Eyes Blazing (USA) (Gone West USA) ff. Workmanlike. 12000y. FLAT '01/3 (for P.C. Haslam) r7 p0. Phillip Kinsella will be wishing he had never been born at all, having sustained two crashing falls on him (at least he was able to return to the saddle within a month of him being feared that he had broken an arm and a leg at Witton Castle). *P. Williamson — Bilsdale (Paul Williamson).* 165 (OMa), 393 (CfMa).

BORN TO DREAM (IRE) ..10-9.. 7 b.m. Supreme Leader — Ethel's Dream (Relkino) 1. Homebred. Dam, half-sister to Mr Splodge (*qv*). One of two youngsters launched to victory on their debut by James Richardson in '04 (the other was Lord Of The Road), and both were impressive. Achieved a remarkably fast time for a Maiden at Brafield-on-the-Green, when only Killerine in the Ladies got round the new course faster, and she looks a splendid prospect who could achieve plenty under Rules. *A Close Run Thing Racing Club (J. Richards) — V.W.H. (James Richardson).* 462 (OMa).

BORN WINNER ..8-13.. 10 b.g. Rainbow Quest (USA) — Tinaca (USA) (Manila USA) p21. Compact brother to flat winner, Lucky Rainbow (USA), and half-brother to flat winners, Quest Star (USA) (won $114,979 in USA) and Distant Cousin. FLAT '98 r2 p0. NH '00/2 r5 p0; pulled up 1. Beaten 29 lengths or more at 25-1 plus (including a Selling Hurdle) in previous brief campaigns, but showed his first form ever when plugging round Godstone for second of three, and then forced ahead on the run-in in a dreadful Maiden at Larkhill. The first winner for yonks plus ages for Lindsay Bower, who disappeared from her role as a professional trainer after she was warned off. Unlike the horse, his winning partner Wayne Kavanagh looks destined for better things. *Miss L. Bower — Hursley Hambledon.* 1067 (OMa), 1405 (OMa), 1495 (OMa).

BORRISIMO (IRE) .— §.. 8 ch.g. Phardante (FR) — Novelist (Quayside) ppp. Big strong brother to Novel Idea, and half-brother to The Writer. Tailed off and pulled up thrice, and is more intent in trying to refuse than he is to race properly. *N.D. Edden — V.W.H. (Sally Caton).* 619 (2m4fOMa), 725 (OMa), 926 (OMa).

BORROW MINE (IRE) ..9-7.. 13 b.g. Borovoe — Jasmine Girl (Jasmine Star) 24p35762p. Sturdy compact half-brother to Shalik (IRE). P-t-P '97/03 (for Mr N.A. Fyfe) r36 w2 (Maiden and PPORA Restricted) p10 (9 3rds, of 4 twice, and last once); pulled up 4, and fell 2. Won two of his first four Points, but has failed to score in 43 subsequent attempts, and despite his completion record remains a sketchy jumper. Ran remarkably well when a close third to Macfin at Horseheath, but otherwise had a distant view of him and the Turner horses, and usually races with minimal zest. Has been tried in headgear. *The Chequers Club (D. Marriott) — Cambridge Univ (Lisa Marriott).* 98 (M), 126 (L), 246 (L), 373 (L), 522 (L), 743 (L), 998 (L), 1244 (L), 1314 (L).

BOSUNS MATE ..10-0.. 12 ch.g. Yachtsman (USA) — Langton Lass (Nearly A Hand) 33u3u5. Well-made attractive half-brother to Ovahandy Man (jumping winner since Pointing) and Royal Scandal. Dam, is half-sister to Davimport (*qv* '97 Annual). NH FLAT '98 r3 w2 p0. NH '98/01 r26 w5 (2 3m110y Hdles and 3 3m110y-3m1f110y Chses) p7 (4 2nds). P-t-P/HUNT CH '03 r6 w1 (2m4f110y Hunt Ch) p3 (2 2nds, and 3rd of 4 in Hunt Chses); 7th of 8, and pulled up. A smart novice and regularly employed forcing tactics to great effect, but moody and unreliable, and has won only one of his last 15 races. Still retains plenty of ability, but lacks the toe to cope with the leading Ladies horses, and has tended to become error prone over big fences. Visored twice in '01, regained blinkers in '04, and acquired cheekpieces on his latest appearance. *M.H. Keighley — N. Cotswold.* 10 (L), 33 (L), 179 (2m6fH), 241 (2m4f110yH), 543 (3m2f110yH), 733 (3mH).

BOUCHASSON (FR) ..—.. 12 b.g. Big John (FR) — Kizil Ayak (FR) (Stratege USA) p. Workmanlike half-brother to a French Hurdling winner. Dam won 5 French flat at up to 11f. FRENCH FLAT '98 r2 p1 (2nd). FRENCH NH '97/8 r7 w1 (2m1f Hdle) p0. NH '99/02 (for P.J. Hobbs) r27 w3 (3 2m4f Chses) p9; pulled up 1, unseated 2. Untrustworthy and occasionally jumped markedly right when frequently equipped with headgear in the previous yard, but could produce decent form in mud at around 2m4f on his day, and was quite a little Euro-trotter with outings at such places at Cagnes-Sur-Mer (where he won) and Punchestown. Missed '03, and his one outing of '04 suggests he is seriously troubled now. *P.E. Froud — Blackmore & Sparkford V.* 310 (O).

BOULTA (IRE) ..10-3.. 11 ch.g. Commanche Run — Boulta View (Beau Chapeau) 472441p. Strong half-brother to Irish Pointing winner, Myalup. IRISH P-t-P '98 r1 p0 (4th). NH '03 r1 p0 (pulled up). P-t-P/HUNT CH '99 and '01/3 r18 w2 (Maiden and deadheat Restricted) p4 (2nds, beaten head once, inc 2 Hunt Chses); pulled up 7. Created an extremely favourable impression when making a winning debut for present connections at Alnwick in '99, but chronic leg and wind problems have severely hindered his progress, and was scoring for the first time since when successful on his reappearance last year. Twice beaten in photo finishes at Kelso after making most of the running before bravely lasting home there on his penultimate start, but lacks consistency and is a thoroughly unreliable betting proposition as a result. Acts on any going. Has been tried tongue-tied. *Mrs C. Moore — Percy.* 73 (Cf), 210 (Cf), 349 (3m1fH), 546 (3mH), 797 (3m1fH), 1174 (3m1fH), 1374 (3m1fH).

BOWFELL ..—.. 7 b.m. Alflora (IRE) — April City (Lidhame) pppp*08*. Compact well-made. Dam won 9f race and 2m Hdle, both Sellers. FLAT '00/2 r14 w1 (5f) p0. NH '02 r4 p0; fell/unseated 3. NH '04 (for M.E. Sowersby) r2 p0 (last of 13 in 2m5f110y Sell Hdle: *ld til hdd & mist 3 out, wknd qckly, t.o*; and 8th in 2m1f110y Sell Hdle: *a bhnd, t.o*). Won a five furlong Selling Nursery as a two-year-old, but useless in every other outing, and had fallen or unseated by the third in three of her Hurdles in '02. An equal waste of time in Points, in which she is not only outclassed but also totally lacking in stamina. *J. Payne — Blankney (Mary Sowersby).* 298 (Cf), 478 (Cf), 565 (O), 683 (O).

BOY BAND (IRE) .—.. 7 b.g. Desert Style (IRE) — Arab Scimetar (IRE) (Sure Blade USA) pppp. Compact unfurnished half-brother to flat winners, Take Manhattan and Mitcham, and to other winners, including abroad. IR30,000y. FLAT '00/1 r6 p0. NH '01/2 (for J.W. Mullins) r5 p0; pulled up 2, and unseated 1. Useless including in Sellers, and has only once been better than last in nine races over jumps. Sometimes leads early in Points, but does not stay, and although safe enough he is unrewarding for beginners. Not even a blur in the oasis of hope. *Mrs H.J. Merriman — Blackmore & Sparkford V.* 320 (Cf), 495 (I), 688 (2m4fOMa), 1133 (OMa).

BOYNE BANKS (IRE) ..10-9.. 10 ch.g. Boyne Valley — Pallatess (Pall Mall) 2221p02. Tall rangy half-brother to Spanish Pal (IRE), to Irish NH flat and Hurdles winner, Providence Lodge, and to Irish jumping winner, Canon Class (subsequently won English Chase). IR7200 3yo. IRISH P-t-P '00/1 r4 w1 (6yo Maiden) p0; pulled up 3. NH '01/3 (for N.A. Twiston-Davies) r6 p0; pulled up 3. A steady galloper who produced his best form in '04, and gained his first success in three years in a Novice Riders Restricted at Larkhill. Also headed near the line by Mickthecutaway in another race for inexperienced jockeys at Barbury, and gained a fourth second prize of the year in the Melton Novices (horses not jockeys). One-paced and finds it difficult to keep his head in front, but deserves to score again. Blinkered on his final start for the previous yard, and beat only three horses in six outings for them (pulled up thrice including his only Hurdle). *Mrs S. Stafford — Cotswold.* 32 (Cnr), 191 (R), 383 (R), 636 (Rnr), 755 (M), 1168 (2m5fH), 1400 (CN).

BOYUP BROOK ..—.. 16 ch.g. Meadowbrook — Terrona Lady (unknown) pp. Lengthy owner-bred half-brother to Polly's Lady. P-t-P '95, '97/00 and '02/3 r34 w4 (inc Open) p7 (5 2nds); failed to finish 11 (fell/unseated 3). A moody tail-swisher who recorded the last of his four victories in a two-runner Open at Ayr last year, but otherwise only once better than last in '03, and his downturn in fortunes was completed when he pulled up lame Mosshouses. *J.J. Paterson — Jedforest.* 764 (O), 1220 (C).

BRACEYS GIRL (IRE) ..10-2.. 8 b/br.m. Be My Native (USA) — Minigirls Niece (IRE) (Strong Gale) 1. Compact well-made half-sister to NH flat winner, Blue Derby (IRE). NH FLAT '01 r2 p1 (3rd). NH '02 r6 p1 (3rd). P-t-P '03 r6 w2 (Maiden and Restricted) p1 (2nd of 3); pulled up 2, and fell 1. Of little account under Rules, but beaten only once in four Pointing completions, and landed a touch in the latest. Originally purchased as a broodmare, and was promptly withdrawn from active service to be serviced by Luso. Acts in soft ground. Tongue-tied on her final appearance over hurdles. *D. Brace — Llangeinor.* 81 (I).

BRACKENHEATH (IRE) ..10-1§.. 14 b.g. Le Moss — Stable Lass (Golden Love) 3u212. Lengthy good-topped brother to Brackenfield, and to successful Hurdler, Shean Alainn (IRE), and half-brother to Bracken Run (IRE). Dam is half-sister to Shean Deas (*qv* '95 Annual). NH '96/01 r23 w2 (2m7f-3m Nov Hdles) p8 (inc 7 2nds; disqualified after winning once); pulled up 1, fell 3; blinkered latterly. P-t-P/HUNT CH '96 and '01/3 r16 w4 (inc 3m2f Hunt Ch and Open) p6 (2 3rds, of 4 once and inc Hunt Ch); last pair 3, pulled up 1, refused 1 and fell 1. Sold for a tidy sum after winning his only start of '96, and developed into a useful hurdler, but never really able to adapt to the bigger obstacles, and tends to sulk if things don't go his way. Emphasised his unreliability when a beaten favourite in his Members, but outbattled the runner-up when re-equipped with blinkers at Aldington, and could yet find another opportunity if he were to co-operate fully. Acts in soft and on firmish. Has been tried unsuccessfully in cheekpieces. *Mrs J. Grist — E. Sussex & Romney Marsh (Di Grissell).* 537 (4mMO), 640 (Cf), 1050 (M), 1281 (Cf), 1410 (Cf).

BRADFORD BRIDGE ..8-12.. 12 ch.m. Cruise Missile — Opt Out (Spartan General) 223s. Lengthy half-sister to General Option, Lost Fortune, Comers Gate, Decisive Spice and Heatherton Park. Dam won 2m3f Nov Hdle for Mr James. P-t-P '99 r3 p1 (2nd); 5th of 6, and fell. NH '03 (for W.S. Kittow) r1 p0 (pulled up). Thrice runner-up on sound surfaces, but has never had a subsequent winner in her wake, and let a golden opportunity slip by when coming down on the flat approaching three out when the only danger to the winner at Kingston St Mary. *Dhobiwallah Racing (N. James) — Quantock (Sarah Robinson).* 967 (OMa), 1252 (OMa), 1327 (OMa), 1450 (OMa).

BRADOGUE (IRE) ..—.. 8 b.g. Nucleon (USA) — Waweewawoo (IRE) (Rusticaro FR) pup. Sturdy. NH '02 (for F. Lloyd) r1 p0 (pulled up). Always wears a tongue-tie and never finishes, and from the way he performs he is presumably choking badly. *E.G. Dilworth — Sir W.W. Wynn's (Reg Crank).* 1049 (2m4fOMa), 1142 (OMa), 1266 (2m4fOMa).

BRAES OF MAR ..—.. 15 b.g. Bustino — Barbella (Barolo) 7r. Big strong good-looking owner-bred half-brother to jumping winner, Lunabelle. NH '94/9 and '01 r18 w4 (3 2m1f-2m5f Hdles, and 2m3f Ch; inc hat-trick) p5 (4 3rds, inc R.A. Gold Cup); last pair 3, pulled up, and fell 2 on final 6 attempts. P-t-P/HUNT CH '98/9 and '01/3 r9 w3 (inc 2 3m110y Hunt Chses) p3 (2nds); pulled up 1. Recorded his first success for three years when galloping on steadily to win his slowly-run Members in '02, but has a long history of unreliability, and made his feelings perfectly known when slamming on the brakes before halfway at Larkhill. Too old to tootle down The Mall, and will surely retire from all public engagements. *H.M. The Queen — V.W.H. (Bobby McEwen).* 445 (3m110yH), 634 (O).

BRANDNEWPLAN (IRE) ..7-6.. 6 b.g. Warcraft (USA) — Two-Penny Rice (Reformed Character) 9. Half-brother to My Man Tim (IRE), and to jumping winner, Copper Coin (IRE). Dam is half-sister to Two John's (*qv* '97 Annual). 6183 4yo. Last in a youngsters Maiden at Easingwold, but was still going well after two miles, and his shrewd trainer may be able to get considerably more out of him in future. *P.J. Finn — Saltersgate F. (Roger Marley).* 1159 (OMa).

BRANSKI ..—.. 14 b.g. Newski (USA) — Lady Cognac (NZ) (Smuggler) pp. Small neat. NH FLAT '95 r2 p0. P-t-P '00 (for Mrs S. Baxter) r1 p0 (pulled up). Goes missing for long periods, and stops to nothing after going like the clappers for a maximum of two miles in Points. *Miss F. Sotheran — Tiverton Stag.* 232 (R), 493 (OMa).

BRASS RAZOO ..9-10.. 11 ro/gr.g. Ra Nova — Bunched (Busted) 21. Small. Dam half-sister to Blakeneys Gift (*qv* '96 Annual). P-t-P '03 r1 p1 (2nd). Deserved his Didmarton success on firmish following two plucky seconds, but neither of the placed horses have gone on to frank the form, and his prolonged absences are disconcerting. *Ms J. Johnston & Ms S. Miles — Grafton (Joan Johnston).* 130 (OMa), 370 (OMa).

BRAVE ALBERT (IRE) .9-2§.. 9 b.g. Shalford (IRE) — Velia (Welsh Saint) u. Small light half-brother to 3 winners (one in Germany), including Unassisted (Irish Hurdles). IRISH FLAT CHARITY SWEEP '00 r1 p0. IRISH NH FLAT '00 and '02 r8 p0. IRISH NH '00 and '02 r7 p0. P-t-P '03 (for Mr R. Mathias) r3 w1 (3-runner, 2-finisher Members) p1 (3rd of 4); and 4th of 5. Often tongue-tied and blinkered when useless in 16 Irish attempts, but had enough ability to win a bad two-finisher Members in much the slowest time of the day on his first start since being bought off the White Elephant stall at Doncaster. The '04 Annual predicted that he was not the sort a novice would handle, and those words were borne out when he acted the goat in the paddock prior to decanting Kelly Keefe at the first at Higham. *Miss K. Keefe — E. Kent.* 155 (Cnr).

BRENDAS NIGHTMARE ..8-12.. 11 b.m. Tina's Pet — Clover Honey Bee (Winden) 2pp. Strong topped half-sister to Mister Bobs, My First Man and Broadleaf Clover. Dam is half-sister to Clobracken Lad (*qv* '00 Annual). P-t-P '03 r2 p0 (pulled up 1 and fell 1). Runner-up in a weak Maiden confined to mares where none of the finishers have even been placed since. Favourite on a return visit to Garnons but weakened tamely with a mile to run, and did not look at all keen when second-best in the ring subsequently. From a capable yard but looks unlikely winning material. *Mrs J.B. Badlan — Teme V. (Jo Priest).* 408 (CMam), 620 (OMa), 1231 (OMam).

BRER BEAR .9-13.. 6 b.g. Perpendicular — Nessfield (Tumble Wind) ppp1. Small compact half-brother to The Rising Scot. Dam won 3 2m4f-3m Hdles, and 2 2m4f-3m1f Chses. Bought Doncaster, Aug for 2500. Had a different rider each time and pulled up for the first three, but remarkably improved when James Diment took over at Lockinge, and scored by an easy 15 lengths (the silence from the Stewards was deafening). Bred from a likeable mare, and it seems very possible that he can progress further now that the brakes are off. *C. & Mrs E. Insley — O. Berks (Emma Insley).* 367 (OMa), 560 (OMa), 686 (OMa), 940 (OMa).

BRETECHE (FR) ..10-3.. 10 b.m. Fijar Tango (FR) — Foinery (Reference Point) 412222312. Small. Dam won at 13f in France. FRENCH FLAT '98 r5 p1 (2nd). FLAT '99 r1 p0 (Sell). NH '98/01 r35 w3 (2 2m1f110y Sell Hdles, and 2m110y Ch) p7 (3 2nds); pulled up 4, fell/unseated 2. P-t-P/HUNT CH '02/3 r15 w5 (Ladies) p8 (6 2nds; and 3rd of 4, and last of 3); 4th, and pulled up 1. A model of consistency and has not missed the frame in Points, and took her winning tally into double figures when travelled to Wales on her penultimate appearance. Easily put in her place by the best Ladies horses, but can handle fast ground so can easily avoid them, and should find further opportunities. Capable of superb jumping, and provided the novice Elise Newman, who promptly gave up, with her first wins last year. Has been mounted on course and is usually taken to post early. Frequently tried in headgear in the past, and has also run tongue-tied. Wears a cross-noseband. *Mrs R.J. Newman — Seavington (Chloe Newman).* 199 (L), 262 (L), 484 (L), 578 (L), 822 (L), 965 (L), 1072 (L), 1189 (L), 1350 (L).

BRIARY BOY (IRE) ..9-9.. 13 ch.g. Mister Lord (USA) — Aprolon Princess (IRE) (Duky) 45p. Workmanlike. Dam is an unraced half-sister to Many A Slip (*qv* '94 Annual). IRISH P-t-P '97 r3 p0 (5th of 6, and pulled up 2). IRISH NH '97/8 r3 p0. NH '02 r2 p0; fell and pulled up in Chses. P-t-P/HUNT CH '99/01 and '03 r18 w3 (Maiden, Restricted and Members) p6 (5 3rds, of 4 thrice, and last twice); pulled up 4, unseated 1 and ran out 1. Successful bi-annually for all three of his handlers, but easy to beat in competitive events, and beaten upwards of 25 lengths since his latest win. Tends to run in snatches at times and will have to target his Members to achieve a fourth success. Has two paddock handlers. Wears a cross-noseband. *C. Kendall & Miss M. Taylor — Wilton (Michelle Taylor).* 116 (I), 147 (I), 692 (I).

BRIERY FOX (IRE) ..9-7.. 7 ch.g. Phardante (FR) — Briery Gale (Strong Gale) 22221. Neat owner-bred. Dam, half-sister to dam of Briery Ella (*qv* '04 Annual). P-t-P '03 r2 p1 (2nd); and pulled up. Ended a most frustrating run of seconds (favourite in three and beaten a maximum of eight lengths) when successful at Clifton-on-Dunsmore, but has not progressed in the manner expected, and needs to find further improvement for Restricteds. Superior jumping should help in his quest, but has raced only on good ground, and seems unlikely to appreciate any cut. *Mrs H. Plumbly — Cottesmore (Holly Campbell).* 128 (OMa), 387 (OMa), 596 (2m5fOMa), 945 (OMa), 1124 (OMa).

BRIERY HILL ..10-5§.. 10 b.g. Buckley — Rippling Melody (Ardross) 4f151. Tall workmanlike. Grandam, Jimsleeves, won 2 bad Points and placed 2. P-t-P '02/3 r10 w1 (2m4f Maiden) p0; 5th, last 4, ran out, unseated and pulled up 2. Wayward, and came fitted with a defective steering column, but possesses plenty of ability, and left his '03 running (when he failed to beat a rival) well behind this year. Displayed plenty of spirit in both successes, and clocked the fastest time of the day at Aspatria, and now that his stamina does not have to be taken on trust can win again. Has been unruly in the preliminaries and is mounted on course and taken down early, and has two paddock handlers. Wears a cross-noseband, and has sported an off-side pricker and over-reach boots. *D.S. & Mrs M.J. Byers — Cumberland (Hector Barnfather).* 211 (C), 431 (R), 765 (R), 1037 (I), 1307 (Cf).

BRIGHT APPROACH (IRE) ..11-4.. 12 gr.g. Roselier (FR) — Dysart Lady (King's Ride) 1p7153. Small half-brother to Irish NH flat and jumping winner, It Takes Time (IRE). Dam won 2 Points (one at Castletown Geoghegan, scene of Bright Approach's victory), a NH flat, 2 2m Hdles and 3 Chses (2m3f-3m) in Ireland. IRISH P-t-P '98 r11 w1 (4&5yo Maiden) p3; pulled up 4, and unseated 1. P-t-P/HUNT CH '99/03 r29 w9 (inc 5 Hunt Chses, 2m7f110y-4m1f, and 2 Opens) p11 (5 3rds; inc 4 2nds in Hunt Chses); pulled 2, unseated 2. A top class stayer, and has landed back-to-back wins in the Cheltenham and Heythrop four-milers, but exposed as one dimensional now, and cannot act effectively unless the ground rides fast. Let down by his jumping when tailed off at the Festival, but a different kettle of fish next time, and turned the form with Earthmover upside down. Once again thwarted by precipitation at Exeter (could have been laid to lose a fortune on the exchanges after jumping just two fences had one been watching) but disappointed when conditions were in his favour in the Intrum Justitia Cup, and the balance of power in the staying division may be about to change. *J.H. Burbidge — Taunton V. (Grant Cann).* 49 (4m0), 178 (3m1f110yH), 543 (3m2f110yH), 991 (3m2f110yH), 1293 (2m7f110yH), 1453 (3m4fH).

BRIGHT BEACON ..10-8.. 11 br.g. Lighter — Pennulli (Sir Nulli) 11cf. Compact brother to Don'tcallmegeorge, and half-brother to Eighty Eight, Folly Furlong, Get On Lottie and Stand On. Dam is an unraced daughter of Pensham (won 44 Points and Hunt Ch and placed 26 for Pat Tollit). P-t-P/HUNT CH '99/03 r11 w5 (inc Open) p2 (3rds, last once); last 1, pulled up 3. Unbeaten in his six previous Pointing completions before he had the misfortune to be carried out in the Lady Dudley Cup, but tragically broke a leg when on a retrieving mission at Chepstow next time. Mrs P. Tollit — Pentyrch (Cath Williams). 205 (O), 615 (O), 1016 (3m2fO), 1294 (3mH).

BRIGHT DAWN (IRE) .9-5§.. 6 bl.m. Norwich — Bright Day (IRE) (Phardante FR) pR4p. Workmanlike. Bought Doncaster, Aug for 7500. Looked promising at Duncombe Park in her second Point, where she was hanging left on the turns but still had every chance of beating Three Spires until she went badly left and failed to negotiate the final bend, but very disappointing at 5-2 twice since (favourite once). Better jumping will help, and perhaps she may dispense with the early squiggle in her second campaign. *Rydeale P-t-P Club (P. Drury) — Middleton (Annabelle Armitage).* 75 (OMa), 271 (OMa), 476 (CfMa), 596 (2m5fOMa).

BRIGHT FLASH (IRE) ..9-3.. 12 b.g. Executive Perk — Bright Note (Buckskin FR) p54d. Tall workmanlike half-brother to Irish NH Flat and Hurdles winner, Mrs Battle (IRE). Dam, half-sister to Pepys, won 4 Irish Hdles, 2m-2m4f. IRISH P-t-P '99 r1 p1 (20/ 3rd). IRISH NH '98 r1 p0. IRISH NH FLAT '98/9 r3 p0. P-t-P '00 and '02/3 (for Mr & Mrs K. Smith) r8 p3 (2 3rds, of 4 once, and last once); last pair 4 and pulled up. A secure jumper, and often adopts a front-running role, but gone in the wind (has run tubed) and stops to nil after a maximum of 2m6f. Stands his racing badly, and wore over-reach boots on his latest appearance. *D.W. Kenny — W. Somerset V.* 90 (I), 139 (R), 274 (CfMa).

BRIGHT TORINO (IRE) ..—.. 10 b.m. Febrino — Bright Toro (Proverb) ppu. Workmanlike half-sister to Glynn Brae (IRE). P-t-P '00 and '02/3 r8 p0 (last 2, ran out, fell and pulled up 4). Unenterprisingly ridden and usually hopelessly tailed off from an early stage, and fared no better when blinkers were applied at Marks Tey. On most occasions the owner-rider would travel just as quickly if he got off and ran alongside. *J. Bevan — Waveney H. (John Ibbott).* 40 (OMa), 129 (OMa), 245 (CfMa).

BRILLIANT STAR (NZ) .—.. 13 b.g. Star Way — Karman Gal (Persian Bold) ppp. Good-bodied brother to 2 winners abroad (one in South Africa), and half-brother to 3 winners in Australia/New Zealand. Dam won 6 flat races in USA. NZ FLAT '96 w2 (7f). NH '98/02 (for S.A. Brookshaw) r29 w6 (2 2m Hdles and 4 2m-2m4f Chses) p5; pulled up 3, fell/brought down 3. Bought Doncaster, Aug for 900. It is easy to be positive about his past — two wins in his native New Zealand, six more in this country (four at Ludlow and two at Hereford; was unbeaten in three completed starts for A.P. McCoy), and also made the perfect excuse for enjoying the craic at Galway (six visits). Broke a blood vessel in one of his placings. Sadly he has now been plunged into the Millington mire, with the inevitable 'looked awful' and a string of pulled ups. *P.J. Millington — Quorn.* 1056 (M), 1153 (O), 1500 (Cf).

BRISTOL BRIDGE ..— §.. 8 b.g. Shannon Cottage (USA) — Plassey Bridge (Pitpan) pppup. Unfurnished owner-bred. Dam won 4 Points (2 in Ireland). Showed no ability or enthusiasm in Maidens, including when blinkered in the two latest. *Mrs L.P. Vaughan — Ross H. (Jane Evans).* 66 (OMa), 149 (OMa), 618 (2m4fOMa), 700 (CfMa), 845 (CfMa).

BRITS MATE .—.. 7 ch.m. Good Times (ITY) — Pinston Cove (Shaab) pR. Half-sister to Cool Cove and Play It Cool. Dam was placed in 4 Maidens. Tailed off when exiting after just under two miles in 2m4f Maidens. *D. Stephens — Four Burrow.* 701 (2m4fOMa), 909 (2m4fOMa).

BROAD EDGE (IRE) ..9-5§.. 9 ch.g. Broadsword (USA) — Portodamus (Porto Bello) ppp2. Compact rather unfurnished half-brother to Caldamus (*qv*). P-t-P '02/3 (for Mr D.G. Atkinson) r11 w1 (Maiden) p3 (2nds, last once); 4th, 9th 2, last pair 2, and pulled up 2. Made all and finished alone in a five-runner Maiden taking nearly eight minutes at Witton Castle on his '03 reappearance, but the effort appears to have left an indelible mark, and displayed minimal zest in the new yard. Wears a cross-noseband, and acquired cheekpieces and blinkers on his last two starts. Has been tried tongue-tied. *T.P. Whales — W. Norfolk.* 159 (R), 375 (R), 745 (R), 1150 (M).

BROADSPEED ..9-2.. 9 b.m. Broadsword (USA) — Bosom Friend (Bustomi) p4. Strong-topped attractive. Has good riders and her six and a half lengths fourth at Dingley was not a bad effort, but probably only moderate, and would need a poor race to score. *Mrs R.G. Saunders & D. Hockridge — Pytchley (Mrs P. Saunders).* 1215 (CfMa), 1473 (OMa).

BROCKBUSTER ..9-12.. 10 b.g. Syrtos — Ruby's Vision (Balinger) 4p. Small brother to Elliewelliewoo and Raregem, and half-brother to jumping winner, Act Of Faith. Dam is half-sister to Another Sword (*qv* '94 Annual). NH FLAT '01 r4 p2 (2nds). NH '01/2 r5 p0; pulled up 2. P-t-P '00 and '03 r7 w2 (Maiden and Restricted) p2 (3rds, of 4 once, and last once); 4th, 5th, and fell. Returned to Points in '03 and recorded a double on stiff tracks, but appears to require a severe test of stamina, and has found things happening too quickly for him since. Went in snatches on his return and no better when blinkers were applied next time, and will need watching when he reappears. Wears a cross-noseband. *Mrs M.J. Arnold — N. Cotswold (Emma Baker).* 90 (I), 292 (MO).

BROKEN ENGLISH .—.. 12 ch.m. Say Primula — Elitist (Keren) p. Plain rangy half-sister to Beyond Mombasa, Kralingen and Archbishop. P-t-P '99/00 and '02 r8 w1 (Restricted) p2 (last of 3 once); last and pulled up 4. Missed out on Maiden success and stands her racing incredibly badly, and able to resurface only once after a two-year hiatus. Used up her luck at Corbridge in '00. *Mrs G. Sunter — Cleveland (George Sunter).* 72 (O).

BROMBIL LADY ..8-0.. 9 gr.m. Tigerwood — Last Double (Neltino) p5c. Small light. Dam, half-sister to Shrill Whistle (*qv* '94 Annual), pulled up in 3 Points for the Tudors. NH FLAT '00 r1 p0 (tailed off). NH '01 r1 p0 (8th in 2m1f Hdle). P-t-P '01/3 r6 p2 (3rds; last once); last, fell/unseated 2, ran out 1. Impetuous and usually manages to pull her way to the front, but does not stay much more than two miles, and remains an error prone jumper. Wears a cross-noseband. *T.E. Wardall — Atherstone.* 97 (CfMa), 408 (CMam), 934 (OMa).

BROMLEY SUPREME (IRE) ..—.. 6 b.m. Supreme Leader — Susie's Well (IRE) (Buckskin FR) p. Lengthy. Kept up for two miles before fading and pulling up two out on a not displeasing debut. *Miss J. Froggatt — Meynell & S. Staffs.* 714 (CMam).

BRONLLYS SKYVOR (U) ..9-6.. 10 b.g. Blaze O'Gold (USA) — Bronllys Skyblue (unknown) u. Rangy. Made a brave stab at capturing his Members, and was only two lengths behind the winner when he hit the last and the beginner-rider toppled off. *H. Evans-Bevan — Golden V. (Nicky Sheppard).* 1387 (M).

BROOK BEE ..10-2§.. 13 br.g. Meadowbrook — Brown Bee III (Marcus Superbus) 1. Rangy brother to River Bee, and Procol's Boy, and to successful jumper, Regal Bee, and half-brother to Zam Bee and Moss Bee. Dam won 2m Hdle and placed 2, and won an Open. NH FLAT '97 r1 p0. NH '97/00 and '02 r23 w4 (3m1f-3m2f Chses) p6. P-t-P/HUNT CH '01/3 r16 p3 (2 3rds, of 4 once, and last once); last pair 6, unseated 5, pulled up 1 and carried out 1. Wildly inconsistent under Rules, and ineptly handled in his first season Pointing, but showed he retains ability when well-backed and making the frame twice last year, and outbattled the runner-up in a weak race at Chaddesley on his sole appearance in '04. Likes to dominate but the success was his first since '99, and would have been more prolific had he been more co-operative. Has been tried in blinkers. *The Muddy Patch Partnership (D. Sherlock) — Sir W.W. Wynn's (Steve Wynne).* 1344 (C).

BROOKFIELD BASS ..9-4.. 9 b.g. El Conquistador — Princess Singer (Prince Sabo) 2. Dam is half-sister to Abinger. P-t-P '02/3 r3 p0 (last, pulled up 1 and unseated 1). Ended Stuart Morris's season prematurely in '02 and laid low by sore shins himself last year, but far from disgraced when runner-up at Higham and clearly has the ability to win a small race if he can stand training. Wears a cross-noseband. *Mr & Mrs A.G.C. Howland Jackson — Suffolk (Ruth Hayter).* 27 (OMa).

BROWJOSHY (IRE) ..9-11§.. 12 b.g. Zaffaran (USA) — Keeping Company (King's Company) 34. Strong-topped half-brother to Firm Gale (IRE), and to a winner in Austria. Dam won 2 Irish flat, 11-12f. NH FLAT '97 r1 p0. NH '97/02 (for Mrs J. & M. Pitman, and K.C. Bailey) r32 w4 (2m5f Hdle and 3 2m5f-3m2f Chses) p8 (inc 7 3rds); pulled up 5, fell 2. Stays forever and does best in mud, and gained big prizes in two of his four wins (the £27,391 Warwickshire Gold Cup, and £15,570 race), as well as finishing third twice in cross-country Chases, one of them the La Touche. Always lazy and becoming increasingly temperamental, and although he plugged into the frame twice at Dingley he never had any hope of scoring. Often wore headgear in the previous yard, and acquired cheekpieces in Points. *The Laing Family (Miss V. Laing) — Woodland Pytchley (Vicky Laing).* 888 (O), 1216 (4m100yMO).

BROWN CHIEFTAIN (IRE) .9-8.. 12 b.g. Meneval (USA) — Brown Trout (IRE) (Beau Charmeur FR) u3f. Good-bodied. IRISH P-t-P '99/00 r12 p1 (2nd); pulled up 5, fell/unseated 2. IRISH NH '00 r5 p0. P-t-P/HUNT CH '02/3 (for Mr A.W.G. Geering & Mr A.E. Cowlishaw) r13 w4 (Maiden, Restricted, Members and Intermediate nov rdrs) p3 (3rds, of 4 once); last pair 2, and pulled up 4. A dual winner on sound surfaces in each of his two previous English campaigns, but thoroughly exposed now and presumably laid low by his Higham spill. Has won for four different riders, but all of them are well above average, and the present novice will be hard pressed to increase the total even if the combinations confidence is unaffected. *Mr & Mrs M.F. & Miss C. Haydon — Southdown & Eridge (Cynthia Haydon).* 16 (C), 45 (Cnr), 155 (Cnr).

BROWN ESQUIRE ..9-11.. 14 b.g. Broadleaf — Ana Brown (Souvran) 4p. Tall plain. Dam, half-sister to Chestnut Prince (*qv* '90 Annual), pulled up and unseated in Points for Gemma Dewhurst (was previously distant last of two in a Maiden). NH '98 r3 p0 (tailed off in Hdles — pulled up 2). NEWMARKET TOWN PLATE '01 10th. P-t-P/HUNT CH '98/03 r22 w2 (Maiden and Ladies) p7 (6 2nds, inc Hunt Ch); ran out 1, unseated 2, and pulled up 6. A thorough stayer and suited by lashings of mud, but was scoring for the first time in three years when snatching victory in the shadows of the post at Eyton in '02, and has performed well below the level of that form since. Averages only four outings per annum. *Miss G. Dewhurst — Cheshire (Olivia Dewhurst).* 93 (O), 346 (3m1f110yH).

BROWNIES TALE (IRE) ..8-3.. 9 b.g. Montelimar (USA) — Just A Brownie (IRE) (Orchestra) 4. Rangy. Faded when 29 lengths fourth in a mid-February Maiden, and approaches nine with just the one outing behind him. *Miss S. Williams, S. Boon, A. Conroy, P. Fullagar & R. Hildreth — V. of Aylesbury with Garth & S. Berks (Karen Lawther).* 192 (CfMa).

BROWN'S BECK ..7-11.. 7 b.g. Bollin William — Golden Chorus (Golden Mallard) p4. Strong-topped owner-bred half-brother to Final Chorus (*qv*). Fat and spooky and climbed the fences on his debut, but at least seemed more clued up when six lengths last in an incredibly slowly-run Maiden taking 8min08s at Dalton Park. Perhaps the Unplaced Maiden on his own ground at Charm Park should be the target for '05. *D.A.D. Brydon — Staintondale.* 392 (CfMa), 505 (CMa).

BROWNS BOY ..—§.. 7 b.g. Lancastrian — Merlins Girl (Feelings FR) pp. Close-coupled. Dam, half-sister to Spean Brig (*qv* '92 Annual), won Maiden and placed 5 (had 2 ways of running). P-t-P '03 (for Mr M. Brown) r2 p0 (unseated and pulled up). The subject of an unsuccessful gamble at Dingley last year, but threw a tantrum on his reappearance for the new yard, and acquired cheekpieces for his next start eight weeks later. A thoroughly nasty piece of work to date. *R.D. Griffiths — Ludlow (Geoff Evans).* 92 (I), 668 (OMa).

BROWN SEAL ..9-12.. 13 b.m. Arctic Lord — Brown Veil (Don't Look) 14. Compact half-sister to Brown Robber, Brown Bala, Brown Wren and Brown Blake. Dam won 2m4f Hdle and 4 Chses, 3m1f-3m4f. NH FLAT '98 r2 p0. NH '98/02 r9 p2 (3rds); pulled up 3, unseated 1. P-t-P '03 r3 p2 (short head 2nd of 3, and 3rd of 4); and pulled up. Deserved her moment of triumph when successful in a long 18-runner Maiden at Brampton Bryan, but has a history of leg trouble, and was dismounted after the line. Made it to the racecourse once more, but let favourite backers down, and is believed to have been retired to the paddocks. *Mrs P. Corbett — Radnor & W. Herefords (Caroline Walker).* 668 (OMa), 1019 (Cm).

BRUAN (IRE) ..8-8§.. 9 b.g. Be My Native (USA) — Celtic Cygnet (Celtic Cone) 6055627. Small sturdy close-coupled half-brother to Celtic Duke (*qv*). NH '00/01 r4 p0 (pulled up only Ch). P-t-P '02/3 (for Mr J.M. Turner) r14 w3 (Maiden, Restricted and Intermediate) p4 (3 2nds, of 3 once, and last twice; and last of 3); 6th, pulled up 4, and fell/unseated 2. An outright rogue who needed plenty of persuading to win three races in the previous ownership, but lit up by the application of blinkers in '04, and ran away with the novice lady rider on two occasions. Beaten a minimum of 25 lengths, and appeared less receptive to cheekpieces, and can be safely ignored in future. Suited by a sound surface. *Miss J. Bevin — Fernie.* 124 (CCon), 249 (Cnr), 380 (L), 558 (L), 785 (L), 885 (M), 1120 (Cf).

BRUE HOUND BOY ..—§.. 13 br.g. Brewery Boy (AUS) — The Deer Hound (Cash And Carry) ur. Tall half-brother to After The Fox (jumping winner since Pointing) and Frank Naylar, and to Hurdles winners, Daves Delight and Dear Deal. Dam lamed herself in the last of 4 unsuccessful Pointing efforts. P-t-P '98/9 and '02/3 r15 p2 (3rds, last once); pulled up 7, fell 2, brought down 1 and refused 2. Sent off at a shorter price than Bengal Bullet on his only appearance last year, but has never finished within 19 lengths of the winner, and has pulled up and refused twice in his last four starts. A non-staying waste of time, and has been tried in blinkers. *P.E. Froud — Blackmore & Sparkford V.* 350 (M), 355 (CfMa).

BRUMMEL (U) ..5-0.. 12 bl.g. unknown — unknown 2. P-t-P '99/02 r4 p0 (4th, 5th, pulled up and unseated). The '04 renewal of the King's Troop race was clearly a weaker affair than usual, as he had been beaten a minimum of 33 lengths in two previous completions. Waddled into the lead going to the last, but the favourite was toying with him, and was value for more than the winning margin. *The King's Troop RHA — R.A. (Neil Cross).* 84 (2m4fC).

BRUTHUINNE (IRE) ..9-7.. 10 ch.g. Vaquillo (USA) — Portane Miss (Salluceva) 345413p. Tall strong half-brother to useful jumping winner, Aghawadda Gold (IRE), and to Chasing winner, Churchtown Port (IRE). NH '99/03 (for Miss H.C. Knight, and B.G. Powell) r18 w2 (3m1f-3m2f Chses) p6; pulled up 4, fell/unseated 2. Completed a double in Chases in October '02 (three finished once, and three ran once; scored by a short head once), but was last, pulled up twice and fell in four subsequent attempts under Rules. Often front-runs and made all to beat two rivals in his Members, but essentially only a very poor Pointer, and there were just four horses behind him all year. Sometimes taken to post early. Firmish ground seems his preferred surface. *J.H. Berwick — S. Devon.* 77 (O), 145 (O), 196 (O), 319 (O), 411 (M), 487 (O), 703 (MO).

B SO BOLD ..—.. 11 b.g. Never So Bold — Gunner Girl (Gunner B) pfp. Tall half-brother to flat winner. Dam won 3 flat, 7-10f. NH FLAT '98/9 r2 p0. NH '02 (for late J. Neville) r1 p0 (pulled up). Very rarely seen prior to '04, when he maintained his bad record and additionally looked an unpleasant ride. *A.J. Williams — Curre & Llangibby (Sue Williams).* 731 (OMa), 840 (OMa), 1075 (OMa).

BUADHACH (IRE) ..—§.. 9 b.g. Petoski — Viking Rocket (Viking USA) p. Lengthy. Dam won 4 Hdles (2m-2m4f) and 2 3m1f Chses, and is half-sister to Bex Boy (IRE) (*qv* '01 Annual). NH FLAT '00/1 r4 p1 (2nd). NH '01/2 r7 w1 (2m4f Hdle) p1 (2nd); pulled up 2 . HUNT CH '03 r2 p0 (last and fell). His '01 Hurdling triumph at Ayr was a Seller in all but name, but his fortunes have taken a turn for the worse since, and restricted to three appearances for present connections, and pulled up lame in the latest. Has a wind problem to boot (tongue-tied in his penultimate bumper) and not surprisingly looks most reluctant. *M.A. Hill — Albrighton.* 31 (Cnr).

BUBBLE BROOK ..—.. 7 b.g. Alderbrook — Leinster Girl (Don) ppp. Unfurnished. NH FLAT '03 r1 p0. A slovenly jumper who has not shown any aptitude for racing yet. *A.J. Moffatt — O. Berks (Charles Cox).* 53 (2m4fOMa), 143 (OMa), 617 (2m4fOMa).

BUCKET AWL (IRE) ..9-0.. 6 ch.g. Lir — Upham Close (Oats) f4. Strong. Dam (*qv* '98 Annual) won 5 Points including 4m Ladies and placed 6. Was running well on his debut until a crashing fall two when holding every chance left him badly winded, and given two months to recover, but faded quickly on the run-in when eight lengths fourth at Stafford Cross. Gives the impression that he can win soon, possibly at 2m4f. Hate that name. *Mr & Mrs A. Walter — Taunton V.H. (Alan Walter).* 308 (2m4fOMa), 1134 (OMa).

BUCKLAND BOBBY ..9-4.. 7 b.g. Rakaposhi King — Lichen Moss (Le Moss) 88ppf4u14. Tiny brother to Buckland Boy (*qv*). P-t-P '03 (for Mr N.B. Jones) r11 w1 (3-finisher Maiden) p0; 4th of 5, pulled up 5, fell/unseated 3, and ran out 1. Little more than a Welsh mountain pony and subjected to no fewer than 11 outings in the Principality as a five-year-old, and must have sunk to his knees when he found out where he was to be based in '04. Performed dismally for a novice girl in the first half of the season and it was no fluke that the owner was not on board when notching his second three-finisher success at Northaw. Has no scope for improvement, but certainly does not lack heart. *P.J. Millington — Fernie.* 155 (Cnr), 249 (Cnr), 378 (M), 522 (L), 745 (R), 885 (M), 944 (R), 1245 (R), 1468 (C).

BUCKLAND BOY ..9-12§§.. 8 b.g. Rakaposhi King — Lichen Moss (Le Moss) 3ru4p1p. Small brother to Buckland Bobby. Dam is half-sister to China Gem (*qv* '03 Annual). P-t-P/HUNT CH '02/3 r8 w2 (Maiden and Restricted) p3 (2nds, of 3 once); pulled up, fell and ran out. Showed a determined attitude when recording a good ground double in '02, and responded in kind when equipped with a first-time visor at Llanvapley, but his '03 campaign was severely interrupted by back trouble which clearly still has not been alleviated. Stopped at Chipley Park and basically pulled himself up twice subsequently, and must be left alone until he shows signs of coming right. *N.B. Jones — Llangeinor (Paul Haskins).* 19 (CMod), 116 (I), 361 (L), 449 (L), 671 (I), 841 (Cf), 1092 (I).

BUCKLAND KNIGHT (IRE) ..—.. 9 b/br.g. Commanche Run — Myra Gaye (Buckskin FR) ufff. Half-brother to jumping winner, Keiran (IRE). NH FLAT '00/1 r2 p0. NH '01/3 (for D.M. Grissell) r9 w1 (2m2f Hdle) p0; pulled up 3, unseated 2. Most frustrating, and very rarely puts his best foot forward. Scored at 100-1 in heavy at Folkestone, and would have finished about eight lengths second to Macgeorge at Warwick had he not fallen when tired at the final fence, but has beaten only one horse in his ten most recent attempts and his always clumsy jumping had him in dire trouble in '04. Tends to hang, and was thrice blinkered in the previous yard. Jockeys will hardly be queuing up to ride him in future. *Mrs L.J. Young & Mrs S. White — Eggesford (Laura Young).* 434 (3m1f110yH), 490 (3m2fH), 891 (3m1fH), 994 (3m110yH).

BUCKLAND LAD (IRE) ..10-2.. 14 ch.g. Phardante (FR) — Belcraig (Foggy Bell) 4. Tall lengthy. Dam, won Hdle and 2 Chses, all over 2m in Scotland over 7 seasons. NH FLAT '95 r1 p0. NH '95/02 r28 w9 (2m1f110y Hdle and 8 2m-3m2f Chases) p10. P-t-P/HUNT CH '03 r3 w1 (dead-heat 2m5f Hunt Ch) p1 (3rd of 4); and 9th. Went awry under Rules, and had not scored since '99 until sharing the spoils at Folkestone last year, but struggles to get the trip in Points, and his '04 campaign was over after the opening day. Formerly tough and genuine, and owes connections nothing, and it would come as no surprise to see him retired with honours. Successful on fast ground over hurdles, but the bulk of his winning form has been in soft ground. *Mrs D.M. Grissell — E. Sussex & Romney Marsh.* 5 (L).

BUCKLEY'S CHANCE (IRE) ..9-2.. 11 b.g. Buckskin (FR) — Leadon Lady (Monksfield) pp4. Small. Dam, half-sister to L C Monro (*qv* '92 Annual). NH FLAT '99 r2 p0. NH '99/00 r5 p1 (3rd). P-t-P '02 (for Mr S. Heard) r4 p0 (5th of 6, unseated 2, and pulled up 1). Takes a keen hold, and has shown ability for two different beginner riders, but has never stood his racing well, and finished lame at Wadebridge. Wears a cross-noseband. Tongue-tied once in '00. *C.L. Dalley — N. Cornwall (Sarah Tickle).* 76 (M), 194 (CfMa), 486 (OMa).

BUDDY BEAR (IRE) .— §.. 9 br.g. Architect (USA) — Furry Dream (Furry Glen) pppp. Brother to Octane Booster (IRE), and half-brother to Irish Pointing winner, Sea Grass. IRISH P-t-P '02/3 r6 p0 (6th of 7, pulled up 4 and fell). Bought Ascot, July 1523. Pulled up in eight of ten Points, and does not seem to want to try. Acquired cheekpieces on his latest outing. *Mrs C. Hussey — N. Cornwall.* 83 (OMa), 312 (CfMa), 704 (CfMa), 913 (OMa).

BUDDY GIRIE ..10-1.. 12 b.g. Lord Bud — Hatsu-Girie (Ascertain USA) 24. Workmanlike half-brother to Hattie and Sola Topee. Dam, half-sister to Pepper Elder (*qv* '93 Annual), won 3 Chses, 2m4f-3m3f. NH '00 r1 p0 (fell). P-t-P/HUNT CH '00/3 r17 w4 (Members, Club Restricted, Confined conditions and Intermediate) p6 (5 2nds, inc 2 Hunt Chses); pulled up 1, fell 1, and ran out 2. Missed out on a Maiden success, but the winner of four weak Points on sound surfaces, and has been runner-up on three occasions in Hunter Chases. Better judged on his efforts over regulation fences, but his '04 campaign did not get under way until the end of April and lasted approximately seven days. *J. Cornforth — York & Ainsty N. (Philip Cornforth).* 1177 (2m5fH), 1297 (3m1fH).

BUDGHILL .9-0.. 12 b.g. Gold Dust — Celerity Lady (Lighter) pupu15. Robust half-brother to Bedtime Pixie. P-t-P '00/2 r14 w1 (Maiden) p4 (3 3rds, of 4 twice, and last once); pulled up 1, fell/unseated 3. Landed a gamble on his '01 reappearance at Black Forest Lodge, but then lost his way entirely, and was a relatively short price for an animal that had failed to get round in '04 when obliging in a weak Restricted at Vauterhill. Lacks fluency and looks unlikely to bridge the gap to the next level at 12. *Mrs K. Heard — Eggesford.* 197 (R), 489 (I), 707 (Cf), 1002 (R), 1268 (R), 1431 (I).

BUDLE BAY..9-6.. 9 b.g. Gran Alba (USA) — Sunylyn (Sunyboy) 4p. Tall rangy half-brother to Salcantay (dam of Wicked Surprise, *qv* '03 Annual), Uncle Norman and Sun Lark, and to NH flat winner, Smithlyn. Dam, sister to Elmboy, and half-sister to Aj's Boy, won 2 2m4f Hunt Chses and 5 Points and placed 7. P-t-P '03 r5 w1 (Maiden) p1 (2nd); last and pulled up 2. All out to win a Maiden at Guilsborough on his final start last year, but has stopped to nothing in the closing stages of both Restricteds, and gives the impression that he is too weak for his frame. *M. Scotney, D. Nightingale & C. Harrison — Pytchley (Caroline Bailey).* 109 (CR), 481 (R).

BULLFINCH ..10-1.. 12 ch.g. Anshan — Lambay (Lorenzaccio) 35333p13f. Small well-made half-brother to 7 flat winners, including My Lamb, Sultana Bayonet, Bayonne, Bay Bay and Toda (also a successful Hurdler). Dam won 7f race. FLAT '95/7 r10 w1 (7f) p2. NH '97/02 (for R.T. Phillips) r36 w6 (2-3m Hdle) p5 (inc 3rd in Ch); pulled up 4, unseated 1. A poor jumper of bigger fences and concentrated on Hurdling on his final 23 attempts in the previous yard, but safe enough to give some fun in Points, and gained an eighth career success (which includes his only Selling Hurdle) in a Confined at Kingston Blount. Can cope with soft ground or firm, but a bit of a thinker, and did not benefit from a visor once in '04. Will not find winning any easier at 12. *D.S. Frankland & M. Barratt — Grafton (Derek Frankland).* 187 (Cf), 382 (O), 583 (Cf), 784 (Cf), 1032 (O), 1170 (4m1fH), 1332 (Cf), 1471 (O), 1515 (O).

BUNRATTY'S SOLE (IRE) ..10-5.. 7 br.g. Phardante (FR) — Bucks Gift (IRE) (Buckley) 451618. Tall half-brother to Hurdles winner, Millcroft Seaspray (IRE). Dam, is half-sister to Granville Grill (*qv*). P-t-P '03 r2 w1 (Maiden) p1 (3rd). Highly regarded and easily disposed of poor opposition at Marks Tey last year, but laid low in the early part of this season, and was well supported when scoring at High Easter. Made mistakes in both Hunter Chase attempts, but a ready winner in between, and if his confidence can be restored will win plenty more races. Already seems best suited by top-of-the-ground. Wore cheekpieces on his last three starts. *R.P. Fryer — Dunston H. (Nigel Bloom).* 250 (R), 383 (R), 648 (R), 893 (3m110yH), 1151 (Cf), 1438 (3m2fH).

PLATE 25 961 Taunton Vale Members: Burley Don Carlos and Charlotte Stucley land the odds
PHOTO: Brian Armstrong

BURLEY DON CARLOS .10-2.. 9 b.g. Neltino — Burley Bianca (Kinglet) 2u17. Smallish compact. P-t-P '03 r3 w2 (Maiden and Restricted) p1 (2nd). An ex-eventer who immediately took to Pointing last year, and completed a double at Bratton Down, but suffered an interrupted campaign in '04, and faced a very simple task in his only success. Made mistakes in both Hunter Chase attempts, and acquired cheekpieces in the latter, but still looks to have the speed to score again when his sights are lowered. *Mrs C. Llewellyn — Taunton V. (David Pipe).* 81 (I), 747 (3m1f110yH), 961 (M), 1167 (3m2f110yH).

BURROW CORNER ..—.. 8 ch.g. Afzal — Elver Season (Vital Season) pp. Big strong half-brother to Sparkling Elver and Elverlena. Dam, half-sister to 6 Pointers, including Three Potato Four (*qv* '03 Annual), won 3 Hunter Chases, 2m4f-3m1f (hat-trick) and 11 Points (inc 6-timer, and 7 Opens) and placed 7. Grandam, Capelena, was 3rd in Sell Hdle, and won 6 Points (inc dead-heat) and 2 Hunter Chases (3m2f-4m) and placed 13 for late John Cork. Has plenty of size about him and an ideal pedigree, plus the assistance of Leslie Jefford, but on the debit side we are not seeing much of him, and it was discouraging that he already needed a tongue-strap for his second outing. *The Country Club (S. Redwood) — Tiverton Stag (Frederick Hollis).* 492 (OMa), 910 (2m4fOMa).

BUSH HILL BANDIT (IRE) ..10-5.. 10 b/br.g. Executive Perk — Baby Isle (Menelek) 225p2253. Sturdy half-brother to Deep Isle, to Irish Pointing winners, Baby Jamie and Chance Coffey (also won hurdling — won Coral Golden Cup at Festival), and to NH flat and jumping winner, Claverhouse (IRE). Dam won 2m2f NH flat and 2m Hdle in Ireland. NH FLAT '00 r2 p0. NH '00/1 r4 p0. P-t-P/HUNT CH '03 r7 w3 (hat-trick inc 3m110y Hunt Ch) p3 (2 2nds; and inc 3rd in Hunt Ch; also disqualified from 3rd once for not drawing correct weight). Lightly raced and beaten out of sight under Rules, but much improved in '03, and concluded his hat-trick with a typically game display in a Fakenham Hunter Chase. Did not appear to fire on all cylinders this season, and was pulled up before halfway when particularly listless once, but still runner-up in four Open events, and it will be a surprise if he cannot go one better again soon. Suited by top-of-the-ground conditions. *Mrs A.M. Hays — Thurlow.* 42 (L), 222 (L), 280 (3m2f110yH), 464 (L), 557 (O), 744 (O), 893 (3m110yH), 1440 (3m1fH).

BUSMANS HOLIDAY (IRE) ..—.. 9 b.g. Eurobus — Coolyhennan (Don) 6ppp. Good-bodied. IRISH P-t-P '01 r3 p0 (tailed off 3). IRISH NH '01/3 (for P. O'Keeffe) r6 p0; last 2, pulled up 3, and fell. Sometimes leads early, but quickly throws in the towel, and has a deplorable record. Tried blinkered and tongue-tied in Ireland. Permanent vacation looks the answer. *Miss Z.L. Urquhart — Tedworth (Nick Lampard).* 264 (CfMa), 370 (OMa), 644 (OMa), 760 (OMa).

BUTLEIGH ROSE ..8-10.. 10 ch.m. Nicholas Bill — Mistress McKenzie (Deep Run) 335. Small light. Dam is half-sister to Duchess Of Tubber (*qv* '01 Annual). NH '00 r4 p0; pulled up 2, fell 1. P-t-P/

HUNT CH '02/3 r10 p4 (3 3rds); 4th, 6th, pulled up and fell/unseated 3. An improved jumper and deserves a small success, but runs on her nerves and does not get the trip in full, and only once beaten less than ten lengths. Has been tried in an off-side pricker. *N. Searle & R. Napper — Mendip F. (Nikki Stephens).* 416 (CMam), 598 (M), 883 (OMa).

BUTLER DIDIT .9-2.. 11 ch.m. Pablond — Hungerdown Lady (New Member) 21p64. Sturdy compact half-sister to Donald Hawkins. Dam and grandam (Garton Lady) both won a Maiden (latter was also placed 3). P-t-P '00 and '02/3 r12 w1 (Maiden) p7 (4 3rds, of 4 twice, and last twice; inc 2nd of 3 once); 4th, last 2, and pulled up 1. Survived a bad blunder at the second-last when scoring outright for the first time at Kilworthy, but disappointing subsequently, and is a consistently weak finisher. A misplaced gamble on her latest appearance, and punters would be advised to leave well along despite the continued presence of Leslie Jefford in the saddle. Wears bandages in front. *Mrs K.R. Redwood — Lamerton (Kirsty Mathews).* 315 (R), 566 (M), 706 (R), 912 (R), 1194 (Cf).

BUT ME NO BUTS ..—.. 7 ch.g. Lancastrian — Decanna (Decoy Boy) p. Tall rangy. Dam won Maiden and p4 ('has enormous trouble getting the trip'). Looked very green and jumped moderately before pulling up after two miles at Cold Harbour. *Mrs J. Lawther — Ledbury.* 1232 (OMa).

BUTTERWICK KING (IRE) ..9-7.. 13 br.g. Roi Danzig (USA) — Girl On A Swing (High Top) 2p. Tall strong hobdayed half-brother to 5 flat winners (2 abroad), including Carbonate (also a successful jumper) and Fragonard. NH FLAT '96 r1 p0. NH '97 r3 p1 (3rd). P-t-P '99/00 and '02 r11 w2 (Maiden and Restricted) p3 (2 2nds, remote once); 4th twice, and pulled up 4. Quickened nicely to land an 18-runner Maiden at Bratton Down in '99, but has never stood his racing well, and appeared to suffer yet another setback at Holnicote. Previously run out of it on the flat having looked to be in control of his Members, and might have held on had he not blown up, but obviously impossible to get fully fit nowadays. *Mrs S. Lindley, Mrs D. Lewes, Mrs D. Little & Mrs M. White — W. Somerset V. (Anna Bucknall).* 878 (M), 1330 (I).

BUTTON BOY ..9-9.. 13 ch.g. Fearless Action (USA) — Maytide (Vimadee) 94p5p. Good-topped half-brother to Shipmate, Swordfish, Flashtide and Cabin Boy, and to Hurdles winner, Seachange. Dam won 2m6f Ch. P-t-P/HUNT CH '98 and '00/1 r6 w1 (Maiden) p4 (2 2nds, beaten head once, and inc Hunt Ch; and 2 3rds, inc Hunt Ch). Beat a subsequent Hunter Chase winner when comfortably landing a Maiden at Mollington in '98, but clearly impossible to train, and his '04 campaign has been his busiest to date. Ran with credit when fifth at Dingley, but no longer as accurate at the fences as he was, and has become a weak finisher. Races only on right-handed tracks. *P.W.E. Henn — Grafton (Sarah Higgs).* 587 (R), 1034 (R), 1217 (R), 1469 (R), 1503 (R).

BUTTON LADY ..—.. 6 br.m. Weld — Lady Pokey (Uncle Pokey) ufp4p. Dam, half-sister to Bobby Buttons (*qv*), won Maiden, but last and failed to finish 6 in her other Points. Ill-prepared for the job, and has been all over the place in Maidens (hanging once, and jumped badly left once; also unseated at the first when trying to stop on her debut). Last and over a fence behind on her only completion, and is not a suitable ride for a novice. *Mrs L. Williamson — Cheshire.* 754 (OMa), 877 (OMa), 1049 (2m4fOMa), 1266 (2m4fOMa), 1424 (OMa).

BY MY SIDE (IRE) ..9-6.. 11 b/br.g. Brush Aside (USA) — Stay As You Are (Buckskin FR) 225pp. Compact good-topped brother to Irish Pointing winner, Georges Brush, and half-brother to More People (IRE), to jumping winner, Stormtracker (IRE), and to Chasing winner, Gale Force (IRE). Dam is half-sister to General Highway (*qv* '97 Annual). IRISH P-t-P '99/00 r8 w1 (6&7yo Maiden) p2 (3rds); pulled up 2, fell 1. NH '00/01 r7 p1 (3rd); pulled up 2. P-t-P '02 r4 w1 (Restricted) p3 (2 3rds, of 4 once). Made all to land his Restricted in very holding ground at Great Trethew, and runner-up in his next three starts, but went missing in '03, and after his form nose-dived was pulled up after only a mile at Trebudannon. Might revive in mud when fresh, and worth 10-1 at best, but has been tried tongue-tied and is clearly a risky proposition at present. Blinkered in his last three Hurdles. *M.J. Lethbridge — Dart V.H. & S. Pool H.* 321 (I), 573 (I), 793 (Cf), 1129 (I), 1431 (I).

CABILLE (FR) ..9-4.. 13 ch.g. Lesotho (USA) — Ironique (FR) (Riverman USA) 3. Close-coupled hobdayed half-brother to 2 winners over jumps in France (one also successful on flat). IRISH P-t-P '97 r3 p1 (45l 3rd). NH FLAT '97 r1 p0. NH '98 r8 p2 (last of 3 once). P-t-P '99/00 (for Mr M.J. Tuckey) r7 w2 (Maiden and Restricted) p1 (2nd); 4th, pulled up 1 and fell 2. NH '03 r6 p0; pulled up 5 and unseated. Error prone and of no account under Rules, but managed to win two minor Points in '99, and could have won more had his wind been clean. Tailed off last in his first Point for four years and looks finished now. Has been tried in headgear. Wears a cross-noseband. *H.H.G. Owen — Bicester with Whaddon (Emma Owen).* 458 (I).**CABIN BOY ..8-5..** 10 ch.g. Royal Vulcan — Maytide (Vimadee) u1. Tall rangy half-brother to Button Boy (*qv*). P-t-P '02 r1 p0 (pulled up). Clocked a pedestrian time when winning a three-finisher Maiden at Flete Park, but it was his first completion, and there is a chance that improvement could be forthcoming if he stands his racing better. Provided Tom Allanson, who fell off him at his initial attempt, with his first winner. Wears a cross-noseband. *Sir Michael Connell — Grafton (Anne Connell).* 871 (OMa), 1200 (OMa).

CADDY MAN (IRE) ..—.. 16 ch.g. The Parson — Golfers Dream (Carnoustie) 9f. Strong half-brother to Gunner Stream, and to Irish NH flat winner, Ate Moscoe (IRE). Dam won at 5f. IRISH P-t-P '95/8 r12 p6; pulled up 3, and fell/unseated 2 (at last with every chance once). IRISH NH '96/8 r7 w2 (2-3m Chses, inc Hunt) p0. P-t-P/HUNT CH '00/3 (for Mr A. Coveney & Mrs H. Silk) r14 w1 (Club nov rdrs) p5 (2 3rds, of 4 once; and last of 2 thrice); pulled up 3. Recorded his first success for four years when successful in a match in '02, but had not beaten a rival in his five previous completions prior to meeting an untimely end at Godstone. *A. Coveney — O. Surrey, Burstow & W. Kent.* 422 (CCon), 610 (Cv&nr).

CADOUGOLD (FR) .9-7.. 14 b.g. Cadoudal (FR) — Fontaine Aux Faons (FR) (Nadjar FR) p13b. Small neat half-brother to jumping winner, Hugo De Perro (FR). FRENCH NH '94 r5 p1 (2nd). NH '94/8 and '00/02 r41 w9 (5 2m110y-2m4f Hdles and 4 2m-2m4110y Chses) p13. P-t-P '03 r7 w1 (Confined) p1 (2nd); 4th, 5th, pulled up 2, and unseated 1. A class performer in the previous yard, and made three appearances at the Cheltenham Festival (unplaced in the '95 Sun Alliance Hurdle, 10th in the '98 Champion Hurdle, and third in the '02 Kim Muir) but moody and error prone, and present connections have done well to sweeten him. Made the most of a relatively straightforward task in his Members, but very much into the veteran stage now, and his best days are distant memories. Acts on any going. Wears a tongue-strap. Visored once in '02. *N. Shutts — Ludlow (Katie Maund-Powell).* 661 (Cnr), 834 (M), 1113 (Cf), 1392 (C).

CADRAVEL ..8-9.. 6 b.g. Cadeaux Genereux — Space Travel (Dancing Dissident USA) f. Sturdy half-brother to flat winners, Tippitt Boy (also successful in Germany) and Reverie (later scored in Macau). FLAT '02/3 (for J. Gallagher) r6 p0. Useless on the flat (tailed off thrice; blinkered in a Seller on his final attempt), but did a little better at Great Trethew in February, where he was still second in a 2m4f Maiden when he fell at the final fence. Apart from the winner it looked a very bad race, and his failure to reappear suggests he may have hurt himself. *R. Rawle — Exmoor (Debbie Cole).* 309 (2m4fOMa).

CADRILLON (FR) ..9-7.. 15 br.g. Le Pontet (FR) — Jenvraie (FR) (Night And Day) 5. Small brother or half-brother to 3 French winners over obstacles. NH FLAT r2 p0. NH '94/5 and '99/01 r36 p4 (3m1f-4m Chses); pulled up 7, fell 1. P-t-P/HUNT CH '96/8 and '02/3 (for Miss J.E. Foster (Yorkshire P-t-P Club) r37 w9 (inc 3m1f Hunt Ch, Open and 4 Ladies) p12 (7 2nds, of 3 once; and inc 2 Hunt Chses); pulled up 5, unseated 1. An unpredictable out-and-out stayer who has often worn blinkers, but a relatively safe conveyance, and guided Alistair McEntyre round Dalton Park on his first race ride. Not seen again and having once gone 37 outings without success seems unlikely to push his winning tally into double figures at 15. *A. McEntyre — Pendle Forest & Craven.* 501 (O).

CAGE AUX FOLLES (IRE) ..9-1.. 10 b.g. Kenmare (FR) — Ivory Thread (USA) (Sir Ivor USA) p8f. Lengthy attractive. Dam won 14f race in Ireland. IR45,000y. FLAT '97/8 r11 w2 (11-12f) p2. NH '99/03 (for N. Williams, and R. Lee) r33 w5 (2m-2m1f Hdles) p8; pulled up 3. Bought Ascot, Jun for 1142. Competent when winning seven races on ground varying from firm to soft to April '01, but rarely attempted distances in excess of 2m1f, and a lack of stamina and some moderate jumping were his downfall in Points. Took a long time to stagger to his feet after a crashing fall two out at Cilwendeg in March, and not seen again. Tongue-tied and tried with headgear in the past. *H.J. Barton — Pembs.* 206 (L), 407 (L), 670 (Cf).

CAHER SOCIETY (IRE) ..10-2.. 13 ch.g. Moscow Society (USA) — Dame's Delight (Ballymoss) 5u33p. Big strong half-brother to flat winner, Starter's Image. IRISH P-t-P '97/8 r9 w2 (inc Winners of Two) p1 (3rd); pulled up 2, unseated 1, and ran out 1. IRISH NH '97 r1 p0 (last in Hdle). NH '99/00 r11 p3 (3rds); pulled up 3, fell 1. P-t-P/HUNT CH '02 r7 w1 (2m4f Hunt Ch) p1 (2nd in Hunt Ch); 4th, 6th, last 2, and pulled up. Gained his first success for four years when landing a 2m4f Hunter Chase at Ludlow in 02, and retains ability, but his frequent errors have Paul Morris hailing more cabs than the porters outside the Waldorf Astoria. Running in only his second English Point when pulled up in the Lady Dudley Cup, but will almost certainly have to concentrate on them if he is to score again. Suited by some cut in the ground. *R.D.J. Swinburne — Albrighton (Paul Morris).* 176 (3mH), 435 (3m110yH), 630 (2m4fH), 734 (2mH), 1016 (3m2fO).

CAIMINS WELL (IRE) ..—.. 8 b.g. Spanish Place (USA) — Pragownia (Pragmatic) f. IRISH P-t-P '03 r1 p0 (fell). A faller in both his races, including when favourite at Witton Castle in early February. Seems to have hurt himself. *D. Manning — Cheshire (Gary Hanmer).* 166 (OMa).

CAIPIROSKA ..10-1.. 6 b.g. Petoski — Caipirinha (IRE) (Strong Gale) u11. Compact. Dam won 3m Hurdle for Karen Roydon. Unseated after a mile on his debut, but then completed a double at Garthorpe, in the slowest time of the day once and in the second slowest once. It was a competent start and there may be more to come, but there will need to be judging from the ludicrous price he subsequently made at the sales (beat only Nickit in the Restricted!). Connections will be desperate for him to continue to do well, as they have four siblings tucked away at home. *Karen Roydon Racing (T.R. Roydon) — Cottesmore (Holly Campbell).* 476 (CfMa), 686 (OMa), 1060 (R).

CALAMINT ..7-6.. 6 gr.g. Kaldoun (FR) — Coigach (Niniski USA) fpf5. Close-coupled half-brother to Hurdles winner, Aston Mara, and to flat winner Motto. Dam won 3 flat, 8-15f, inc £16-21,000 prizes for H. Cecil. FLAT '01/3 r8 p1 (2nd). NH '02/3 (for K.C. Bailey) r4 p0; pulled up 2. Hopelessly tailed off over Hurdles including a Seller (only once better than last), and pulled very hard and jumped badly in Points, but did manage to scrape round Bonvilston when 17 lengths last. Tongue-tied on four occasions and visored once on the flat. A nail-biting ride for his jockeys. *J. Stephens — Carms (Maggie Stephens).* 618 (2m4fOMa), 735 (CfMa), 950 (2m4fOMa), 1533 (OMa).

PLATE 26 757 Cotswold Ladies Open: The grey Caldamus and Rilliy Goschen, 1st, battle it out with Prince Dundee and Belinda Keighley, 2nd PHOTO: David Jones

CALDAMUS ..10-3.. 13 gr.g. Scallywag — Portodamus (Porto Bello) pp213. Tall strong half-brother to Tanglefoot Tipple, Lady Porto and Broad Edge. Dam is half-sister to Midnight Bob (*qv* '00 Annual). NH FLAT '97/8 r3 p0. NH '99 r7 w1 (2m6f Hdle) p1 (3rd); inc 3 Chses. P-t-P/HUNT CH '01/3 r10 w2 (3m1f110y Hunt Ch and Ladies) p5 (2nds; beaten head once, of 3 in Hunt Ch once); pulled up 1. Races at or close to the head of affairs, and has a fine record in Points, but struggles to get the trip and can operate only on right-handed tracks. Won a weakly contested Ladies at Andoversford, but has never stood much racing, and finished lame when risked on a sound surface next time. *late J.W. Elliot & Friends (Miss R.D. Elliott) — S. & W. Wilts (Sarah Waugh).* 10 (L), 438 (3m1f110yH), 625 (L), 757 (L), 1099 (L).

CALFSTOWN LORD ..9-0.. 13 b.g. Arctic Lord — Calfstown Maid (Master Buck) 6p4uu. Lengthy half-brother to Heather Boy and Capstown Bay. Dam was unplaced in 14 races, including English/Irish Points. NH FLAT '98 r1 p0. NH '99/02 r21 p5 (Chses). P-t-P '03 r5 w1 (3-finisher Maiden) p1 (2nd of 3); 7th, unseated 1 and pulled up 1. Knocked at the door long enough under Rules, and finally gained his reward at the 26th attempt when scraping home under Richard Young at Littlewindsor last year, but beaten a minimum of 38 lengths since, and gets precious little assistance from the owner-rider. Visored once in '02, and subsequently tried in blinkers. Has also run tongue-tied. *Miss S.E. Lane — Portman (Alison Lane).* 232 (R), 473 (R), 636 (Rnr), 862 (Cnr), 1101 (Cnr).

CALHOUN (FR) ..9-2.. 10 b.g. Sheyrann — Blanche Dame (FR) (Saint Cyrien FR) p2. Tall lengthy. NH FLAT '99 r2 p2. NH '99/01 (for P.J. Hobbs) r15 w2 (2 2m Hdles) p2 (inc 3rd in Ch); fell 1, pulled up 1. A dual Hurdling winner at Wincanton to March '00, but although he finished in all his five Chases he was beaten 17 lengths plus and was a very poor jumper. Back in action after a three year break in '04, but did not seem to get the trip in Points, and was a fence behind the winner and tired in a three-runner Open. *R.E.B. Humfrey — Tivyside.* 669 (M), 951 (O).

CALINASH (IRE) .—.. 11 b.g. Insan (USA) — Hi Cal (Callernish) ppp. Tall rangy half-brother to Irish Pointing winners, Lommas River, Malenski and Fast Flow. IR6000 4yo. IRISH P-t-P '01 r1 p1 (2nd of 3). NH '02/3 (for Mrs L. Williamson) r6 p1 (2nd in 2m1f110y Ch); pulled up 2. Beaten 20 lengths plus when scraping into a couple of placings, but stopped quickly and looked all wrong when pulling up in his English Points. Tongue-tied in the latest. *P. Ansell — N. Cornwall (Ian Hambley).* 328 (OMa), 567 (CfMa), 1436 (OMa).

CALKO ..—.. 8 ch.g. Timeless Times (USA) — Jeethgaya (USA) (Critique USA) pp. Sturdy half-brother to winner in Scandinavia. 1200y. FLAT '99/02 r32 w4 (6-8f) p6. NH '02 (for R. Wilman) r2 p0. Bought Doncaster, Aug for 800. A twicer who tended to hang and frequently wore headgear on the level, but was in dashing form on the Southwell all-weather in the first three months of '00, when he gained all his four victories including two Sellers and including a hat-trick (blinkered each time). Predictably useless as a Pointer, and it would be amazing if he was tried again. *Miss J. Fisher — Lauderdale.* 915 (Cf), 1079 (O).

CALLEVA STAR (IRE) ..8-12.. 14 b.g. Over The River (FR) — Ask The Madam (Strong Gale) 2ppp435. Workmanlike half-brother to My Native Knight (IRE). Dam won mares Maiden in Ireland. NH '95/9 r22 w2 (3m2f Chses) p9. P-t-P/HUNT CH '00/3 (for Mr M. Abrahams) r31 w4 (inc Open) p8 (5 2nds, inc Hunt Ch; and 3rd in Hunt Ch once); unseated 4, brought down 1, and pulled up 5. Thrice successful at Hornby Castle for previous connections, and remains a safe jumper, but beat only one rival in '04 and all too quick to accept defeat. His rapid decline looks permanent and only of use as a schoolmaster now. *E.H. Cann — Silverton (Linda Blackford).* 61 (M), 200 (Cf), 320 (Cf), 703 (MO), 911 (MO), 1270 (Cf), 1540 (Cf).

CALLING HOME (IRE) .8-13.. 9 b.g. Executive Perk — Take Me Home (Amoristic USA) pu3. Tall half-brother to One Of The Natives (IRE) (*qv*). IRISH P-t-P '00 and '02/3 r9 p2; pulled up 2, fell 1. IRISH NH FLAT '01 (for L.J. Archdeacon) r2 p0. Beaten a head by a subsequent English Chasing winner on his Irish Pointing debut, but hugely disappointing since. Finished 20 lengths last of three in a Larkhill Intermediate, and would probably have had a chance in the preceding Maiden which was run in five seconds slower time, but as connections took that prize anyway they probably don't care. It is just possible that he might be rewarded at the lowest level. *Miss L. Bower — Hursley Hambledon.* 1098 (OMa), 1404 (OMa), 1496 (I).

CALLITWATULIKE ..8-7.. 8 b.g. Thethingaboutitis (USA) — Call Me Daisy (Callernish) p3353u. Workmanlike. Dam, sister to Savory, and half-sister to Queenofthedaises (*qv*). P-t-P '03 r3 p0 (pulled up 2 and refused 1). Would not have improved upon previous placings (beaten nine lengths minimum) had he not lost the rider on his final start, and does not look a good thing to get off the mark in his third season. *J.L. & Mrs H.D. Marks — S. Durham (Heather Marks).* 166 (OMa), 343 (2m4fOMa), 597 (2m5fOMa), 920 (2m4fOMa), 1159 (OMa), 1475 (OMa).

CALL ME AGAIN ..8-3.. 7 b.g. Past Glories — Emily's Niece (Balinger) fp2. Half-brother to Gunville (*qv*). Left a remote second three out and just managed to retain it to the finish in a 2m4f Maiden at Garthorpe, but will need to improve quite a bit more if he is to win. *K. Rolls & D. Tompkins — Grafton (Sam Loggin).* 746 (OMa), 1125 (OMa), 1403 (2m4fOMa).

CALL ME SONIC ..9-9.. 9 b.g. Henbit (USA) — Call-Me-Dinky (Mart Lane) 114p. Good-topped owner-bred. Dam, half-sister to Call Me Bertie (*qv* '01 Annual), won 4 Points and 2nd twice for Charlie Fuller. Grandam, Call-Me-Sally, was 3rd on flat (also disqualified from 2nd once); and pulled up 3 and unseated in Points for him. NH FLAT '01 r1 p0. NH '01/3 r6 p1 (3rd); pulled up 1. HUNT CH '03 r1 p0 (pulled up). Landed a weak 16-runner Maiden by a wide margin on his return at Howick, but only after two serious dangers had made their exits three out. Promptly doubled his score in his Members, but both successes were gained in the slowest times of the day, and will need to find more for Restricteds. Four outings in a year represents a busy schedule for him, and was reported to have twisted a shoe when pulled up latest. *A.C. & Mrs S. Fuller — Brecon & Talybont (Sue Fuller).* 363 (CfMa), 446 (M), 695 (R), 1022 (R).

CAMAIR COMMANDER (IRE) ..8-13.. 7 b.g. Beau Sher — Miss Josephine (IRE) (Kemal FR) 4. Strong compact. IR6200 3yo. NH FLAT '02 r1 p0. NH '03 (for W. McKeown) r6 p0; pulled up 1. Beaten 30 lengths plus in all of his eight races, and has often looked to have a poor attitude. Blinkered in a Selling Hurdle on his final start of '03, and wore a tongue-tie in the Maiden. *Mrs E. Melrose — W. Percy (George White).* 287 (CfMa).

CAMDEN BUS (IRE) ..9-7.. 9 ch.g. Eurobus — Miss Camden (IRE) (Camden Town) s. IRISH P-t-P '02 r4 p1 (3rd); fell 2. His 11 lengths third to Lord Atterbury in Ireland made him look interesting, but unfortunately slipped up with fatal consequences on the bend going to four out at Lydstep. Miss B.J. Thomas — S. Pembs. 947 (M).

CAMDEN CARAMEL (IRE) ..9-9.. 9 b.m. Camden Town — Sidhe Gaoth (Le Moss) f313. P-t-P '02/3 r9 w1 (Maiden) p2 (2nds, remote once); last 3, and pulled up 3. Favourite when landing two three-finisher events, but an edgy type, prone to jumping lapses, and lacks consistency. The sort to spring a surprise, but has been thumped in more competitive events, and will require sensible placing to score again. *M.G. Jones — Gelligaer F.* 450 (R), 844 (R), 1095 (R), 1238 (I).

CAMDEN CARRIG (IRE) ..10-9.. 10 b/br.g. Camden Town — Tinnecarrig Grove (Boreen FR) 224u2111f. Small well-made hobdayed and fired. Dam won mares Maiden in Ireland (raced for 5 seasons). IRISH P-t-P '00 and '02/3 r10 w2 (7yo&up Maiden and Winners of One) p6 (5 2nds); pulled up 1. A very consistent Irish Pointer who was first or second in eight of ten attempts, and new connections certainly got their monies worth with their new charge, particularly since it has been discovered that the best way to ride him is to let him bowl along at the head of affairs. Completed his hat-trick when taking a Chepstow Novices Hunter Chase which was reduced to a very bad affair after Bright Beacon had broken his leg, but was in the process of giving another commendable display when he fell two out having just been headed at Aintree. His partner Nick Phillips has blossomed since looking very weedy in early season, and the pair look sure to enjoy plenty more good times together. *J.G. Phillips — V.W.H. (Simon Bloss).* 50 (I), 223 (I), 365 (I), 728 (I), 759 (I), 936 (I), 1073 (O), 1294 (3mH), 1374 (3m1fH).

CAMDEN FELLOW (IRE) ..9-5.. 12 b.g. Camden Town — Decent Brandy (Decent Fellow) 761. Small light. NH FLAT '98 r2 p0. NH '98/00 (for P. Eccles, and R. Ford) r32 w6 (3 2m-3m4f Hdles and 3 2m-3m Chses) p5; pulled up 2, unseated 1. A very thorough stayer who progressed from gaining his first win in a Selling Hurdle to registering five successes in better company (four of them in contests with five or six runners), but a patch up job now, and it was a good feat of training to get him to the Vale of Lune Members in an almost racehorse like shape (the Ford name seems to have been associated with this trophy since time immemorial). Tongue-tied, and tried in headgear twice in the past. *Miss C. Hurley — Holcombe (Carrie Ford).* 407 (L), 713 (Cf), 872 (M).

CAMDEN LOCH (IRE) ..9-9.. 10 b/br.g. Camden Town — Poor Elsie (Crash Course) p244613. Tall good-topped brother to Irish NH flat and Hurdles winner, Camden Tanner (IRE), and half-brother to Mister RF, and to jumping winner, Blowing Rock (IRE). P-t-P '00/3 r10 w1 (Maiden) p3 (2 3rds, of 4 once); pulled up 5 and fell. Very lightly raced to '03, and only opened his account at the eighth attempt in his fourth season, but has failed to improve much despite managing a full campaign. An improved jumper, but gets the trip only when conditions are not testing, and gave the impression that he might have suffered a setback on his latest outing. *D.A. Wales — W. Norfolk.* 159 (R), 224 (CMod), 375 (R), 524 (R), 648 (R), 829 (R), 1150 (M).

CAMITROV (FR) .7-5.. 15 b.g. Sharken (FR) — Emitrovna (FR) (Buisson D'Or) s5p505. Compact attractive half-brother to 6 winners in France (including 3 Chasers). Dam won 2 flat and 3 Chses in France. FRENCH FLAT '93/4 r4 w1 (11f). FRENCH NH '94 r5 p4 (3 2nds); and unseated 1 in Chses. NH '94/9 r14 w3 (2m-2m4f Chses, inc £13,000 prize at Punchestown) p5 (inc 3rd in Arkle Ch, earned £8438). NH '00 r1 w1 (Grand Military Gold Cup). P-t-P/HUNT CH '00 and '02 r10 p3 (2 2nds, inc Hunt Ch); 4th, 7th, last 2, pulled up 2 and unseated 1. A very classy performer in his youth but has a list of physical faults as long as your arm and has deteriorated alarmingly after returning from another year on the sidelines. Seems to have lost all confidence after slipping up at Kingston Blount, and acquired blinkers on his penultimate start. Wears a cross-noseband. *G.R. Kerr — Pytchley (David Line).* 187 (Cf), 441 (2m4f110yH), 630 (2m4fH), 1031 (Cf), 1120 (Cf), 1274 (Cf).

CAMPBELLHILL (IRE) ..8-0§.. 13 ch.g. Torus — Gueranne (Green God) 5. Lengthy attractive half-brother to NH flat winner, Freelander (IRE). P-t-P '00/3 (for Mr H. Hill) r24 w1 (Maiden) p2 (2nds); refused 3, fell/unseated 7, and pulled up 8. Needed a race taking 8min21s in order to open his account, but a serial non-finisher, and usually grinds to a halt in a matter of strides. Has been tried in cheekpieces. *J. Purllant — Cambridge Univ.* 98 (M).

CAMPDEN KITTY ..10-6.. 11 b.m. Henbit (USA) — Catherine Tudor (Tudor Wood) 8255211p12. Compact half-sister to Allezscally, Tudor Mistress and Wellington Street. Dam, half-sister to Miss Berkeley (*qv* '93 Annual), won 9 Points (inc an Open and 5 Members) and placed 8. NH FLAT '99 r1 p0 (12th of 20). NH '01 r4 p0. P-t-P '99/00 and '03 r8 w1 (Maiden) p4 (3 2nds, beaten head twice, and ½*l* once; and last of 3); fell 2, and brought down. Runner-up in five Restricteds before she finally won one, but struck a rich vein of form once the ground dried out in '04, and is at her best when able to dominate over an easy three miles. Ultimately no match for Khatani at Umberleigh but seems better suited by the lighter weights in the Ladies division, and should have little difficulty winning again if her present mood extends to '05. Intelligently handled by the trainer and Jane Williams when successful. Has two paddock handlers. *Mrs S. Collett — N. Cotswold (Fred Hutsby).* 252 (CR), 369 (R), 726 (R), 925 (R), 1019 (Cm), 1136 (R), 1343 (L), 1391 (L), 1502 (O), 1563 (L).

CANDLESTONE CASTLE ..—.. 9 gr.g. Carlingford Castle — Nearly Time (Nearly A Hand) 4pu. Small compact. Dam is sister to King Of Diamonds (*qv* '92 Annual). Grandam, Half A Minute, won 8 Points and placed 10. Great-grandam, Another Minute, won 12 Points. P-t-P '02/3 r3 w2 (2m4f Maiden and Restricted) p0; and pulled up 1. Clocked the fastest time of the day when successful at Howick on his only appearance last year, but clearly in a malaise since, and entrusted to a beginner when soon tailed off on his latest start. Makes mistakes and his tentative 10-7 rating is withdrawn until he shows signs of renewed vigour. *R.H.P. Williams — Glamorgan.* 671 (I), 1092 (I), 1190 (O).

CANNON BRIDGE (IRE) ..10-1.. 7 ch.g. Definite Article — Hit For Six (Tap On Wood) 111. Lengthy half-brother to 2 winners of 28 races in Italy. Dam won 5f race in Ireland. NH FLAT '02 r1 p0. FLAT '02 r3 p0. NH '02 (for D. Shaw) r1 p1 (2nd). Sold Doncaster, Aug '02 for 4500, and resold Ascot, Oct '02 for 3238. Beaten 20 lengths plus in five races in '02, but emerged as quite a useful novice in Points, and seems ideally suited by forcing tactics. Won his Members only after a whole string of errors, and looked very lame after, but later seemed to come sound. Speedy enough for better contests, providing his jumping and legs are up to it. *K. Pritchard — Pentyrch (Nikki Hughes).* 203 (CfMa), 450 (R), 1089 (M).

PLATE 27 1452 Weatherbys Chase John Corbet Champion Nov HC, Stratford: Cantarinho and David Kemp, 1st, are clear two out *PHOTO: Tim Holt*

CANTARINHO .10-12.. 7 b.g. Alderbrook — Hot Hostess (Silly Season) 1211411. Tall lengthy half-brother to Arms Dealer. Dam, half-sister to Layston Pinzal (*qv* '97 Annual), was 2nd in 2 Points for Genie Collie, and great-grandam, RUCD, won 9 Hunt Chses and 3 Points for the late Robin Collie. P-t-P/HUNT CH '03 r3 w1 (Maiden) p1 (short head 2nd in Hunt Ch); and fell. A most progressive youngster whose early exuberance has been channelled in the right direction, and rounded off a fine second season with victory in the John Corbet at Stratford. Had the misfortune to run into an on-song Fane Counsel at Horseheath, but his only other defeat in '04 was attributed to the ever deteriorating ground at Cheltenham's evening fixture, and has the potential to develop into a smart staying handicapper should connections take that route. Has no real jumping deficiencies and races with great enthusiasm, but his trump card is his tenacity and has proved very hard to pass when it comes to a fight. Helped form part of an outstanding season for David Kemp. Has two handlers and has been taken to post early. *Mrs M. Harrison & D. Kemp — Suffolk (David Kemp).* 159 (R), 372 (I), 650 (O), 893 (3m110yH), 1169 (3m2f110yH), 1359 (2m4f110yH), 1452 (3m4fH).

CAN'T CATCH ME (IRE) ..7-0.. 7 b.m. Religiously (USA) — Rambling Polly (Pollerton) 7u4. Dam, half-sister to Ocheekobee (*qv* '93 Annual). P-t-P '03 r1 p0 (pulled up). Beaten a minimum of 49 lengths when completing, and whilst better jumping would help it can't be much fun trying to steer this unenviable ride to the finish. *The Should Be Fun Group (C. Storey) — College V. & N. Northumberland (Clive Storey).* 216 (OMa), 432 (OMa), 511 (OMam).

CANTERBURY JACK (IRE) ..10-0§.. 8 b.g. Supreme Leader — Crest Of The Hill (Prince Regent FR) 11p23p. Close-coupled half-brother to Irish Pointing winner, John Kelly. IRISH P-t-P '02 r4 w1 (5&6yo Maiden) p2; and pulled up. IRISH NH FLAT '01 r1 p0. NH '02 (for M.C. Pipe) r3 p3. Beat Newmarket Magic by a head in his Irish Maiden win, but was beaten favourite in all three Hurdles for the present owner, including at 4-9 once. Managed to collect a couple of modest Points in February (three ran once), but his doggy tendencies soon resurfaced, and did not seem to have any serious intention of scoring again. Wore headgear. Broke a hind leg at Flete Park and destroyed. P.J. Finn — Middleton (David Pipe). 148 (R), 313 (I), 440 (2m7f110yH), 770 (Cf), 1003 (4mO), 1197 (4mL).

CAN YOU TALK ..7-8.. 10 ch.g. Le Moss — Lady Lawyer (Mandamus) R3. Compact well-made half-brother to Rymer's Brief. Dam won 2m1f110y Hurdle and 2 2m-2m4f Chases, and was last of 3 from 4 Points. Ran out at the first on his belated debut, changed hands, and finished 22 lengths third of four at Lifton. Looks sub-standard at present, and has joined the stable of Lamerton Quest and Derrilady who failed to finish in 11 of their 12 combined outings in '04. *L. Rowe & A. Cole — Worcs (Martin Oliver).* 1232 (OMa), 1545 (OMa).

CAPACOOSTIC .9-4.. 8 ch.m. Savahra Sound — Cocked Hat Girl (Ballacashtal CAN) pp3223. Small compact scruffy half-sister to flat winner, Rex Is Okay. FLAT '99/02 r40 p5. NH '02/3 (for A.G. Juckes) r3 p0; pulled up 1. Bought Ascot, Jul for 761. Short-headed once at 50-1 and three-quarters of a length second of 24 amongst her flat placings, when she wore blinkers, but her prizes were gained at up to 8f, and is struggling to get the trip even in the bottom grade in Points. Tends to race prominently, but a very weak finisher, and has now accumulated 49 losses in six years. It looks as if she has bad feet, which cannot help. *Miss H.E. Roberts — Llangeinor.* 362 (CfMa), 453 (CfMa), 735 (CfMa), 1192 (OMa), 1488 (OMa), 1550 (OMa).

PLATE 28 441 Dick Saunders HC, Leicester: Cape Stormer (Marcus Gorman, right), 1st, and Guignol Du Cochet (Stephen Hughes), 2nd PHOTO: Brian Armstrong

CAPE STORMER (IRE) .10-4.. 10 b.g. Be My Native (USA) — My Sunny South (Strong Gale) 23418246. Compact half-brother to NH Flat and English Hurdling winner, Sunny Native, and to Hurdles winner, Corporation Pop (IRE). IR62,000 4yo. NH FLAT '01 r1 p0. NH '01/3 (for Miss H.C. Knight, and P.F. Nicholls) r13 w4 (2m4f Hdle and 3 2m4f-2m6f Chses) p5 (2nds). Although his five wins including a Leicester Hunter Chase have been at up to 2m6f he probably stays further, but often looks quirky, and seems to down tools in the middle stages before deciding to run on again when it is all too late. Sometimes lacks fluency, but plenty safe enough, and Aintree was not a problem jumping wise (although it taxed his enthusiasm). Tends to be sent off at unrewardingly short prices, and punters should seek out better value elsewhere. Could be edging towards a squiggle. *M.S. Gorman — Crawley & Horsham (Carolyn Gorman).* 3 (O), 100 (O), 241 (2m4f110yH), 441 (2m4f110yH), 732 (2m5f110yH), 1168 (2m5fH), 1443 (2m5fH), 1497 (3mH).

CAPPA HILL (IRE) ..9-0.. 9 ch.g. Dromod Hill — Swatter (IRE) (Over The River FR) 623. Compact well-made. 4400 3yo. IRISH P-t-P '01/2 r6 p2; pulled up 1, fell 1. NH '03 (for Mrs A.M. Thorpe) r3 p0 (pulled up 3). Sold Doncaster, May '02 2500. Very slow over Hurdles and beaten between 15 lengths and over a fence in three of his Pointing placings (last once), but failed by only a head to hang on in an elders Maiden at Great Trethew. Could win a poor race on that form, but nothing like so convincing next time, and averages only three outings per annum. *Mrs S. Smith & Mrs Z. Townsend — Spooners & W. Dartmoor (Sue Smith).* 119 (OMa), 312 (CfMa), 795 (CfMa).

CAPRIOLE (U) ..5-10.. 10 b.m. unknown 1. P-t-P '01/2 r2 w1 (2m4f Confined) p1 (3rd). Landed back-to-back runnings of the King's Troop race at Larkhill (the '03 event was abandoned due to the Firemen's strike), and was once again backed down to favouritism. Value for more than the winning margin, and presuming his pilot not required for a Green Goddess a follow-up looks to be on the cards in '05. *The King's Troop RHA — R.A. (Neil Cross).* 84 (2m4fC).

CAPTAIN OATES ..—.. 12 b.g. Arctic Lord — Captain's Cottage (Relkino) 75p. Unfurnished owner-bred. Dam is sister to Captain Teach, and half-sister to 5 other Pointers, including Cottage Joker (*qv* 2000 Annual). NH FLAT '97 r1 p0. NH '01 r1 p0 (8th in 3m Ch). P-t-P/HUNT CH '00/2 r10 w1 (Maiden) p2 (3rd of 4 once); last, pulled up 4, and on floor 2. Rated 9-13 after scoring at Brocklesby Park on his '02 reappearance, but never stood his racing particularly well, and broke down irreparably at Corbridge. W.A. Bethell — Holderness. 70 (R), 164 (R), 430 (R).

CAPTAIN RANDOM ..9-7.. 10 b.g. Le Moss — Mandarling (Mandalus) 13u214. Workmanlike half-brother to Bethin (*qv*). NH FLAT '01 r1 p0. P-t-P '02/3 r8 p2 (2nd of 3 and 3rd of 4); last pair 3, pulled up 2 and unseated. Roughed off after sustaining a minor injury on his only appearance last year, but has done well to make the frame in all but one of ten completions, and completed a ready double in minor events on good ground. Very one-paced and turned over at odds-on in a match run at a crawl for his Members, and will find it difficult to upgrade successfully. Wears a cross-noseband. *Mrs J.C. Reed & Mrs D. Bell — Seavington (Jane Reed).* 237 (CfMa), 354 (R), 966 (R), 1008 (M), 1251 (R), 1382 (I).

CAPTAIN'S LOG .8-7.. 10 b.g. Slip Anchor — Cradle Of Love (USA) (Roberto USA) p7. Small light half-brother to Velvet Jones, to flat winners, Ivory Dawn and School Days, and to a winner in Italy. Dam won 9f race. FLAT '98/02 (for M.L.W. Bell) r54 w11 (8-12f) p9 (inc 4 2nds). Admirable when a multiple winner over five years on the flat, but must have been alarmed to see obstacles in his way for the first time at the ripe old age of nine, and was hopelessly tailed off last in his completion. Still wants to try, but his chances of staying three miles are surely zero. *A.D. Peachey — N. Cotswold.* 924 (O), 1140 (Cf).

CAPTAIN WILDOW (IRE) ..—.. 6 b.g. Weldnaas (USA) — Veruna (IRE) (Strong Gale) f. Tall rangy. Dam won NH flat and 2m Hurdle in Ireland. 9347 3yo. Was shaping nicely until he had a horrible fall three out at Larkhill, and had to be destroyed. Had marked a welcome return to the course for the colours of Reg Wilkins, but tragic that it ended thus. Shortwood Family (R.C. Wilkins) — Mendip F. (Caroline Keevil). 86 (OMa).

CAPTIVE (IRE) ..9-12.. 9 br.g. Be My Native (USA) — La Capitana (Mon Capitaine) 32. Tall half-brother to Pin's Pride and Frisbee Dyke. Dam won 2m2f Hdle in Ireland. NH FLAT '02 r2 p0. NH '01/2 r8 p1 (3rd); pulled up 1. P-t-P '03 r4 w1 (3-finisher Maiden) p1 (½*l* last of 3); 5th of 6, and fell 1. A winner and placed twice from four attempts at Higham (fell three out with every chance in the exception) and clearly suited by the nature of the track, but looked suspect when tongue-tied under Rules, and continues to stand his racing badly. Can probably be safely ignored if returning from a new yard. Acts on a sound surface. *J.M. Turner — Suffolk.* 159 (R), 398 (R).

CAPYBARA (IRE) ..9-6.. 7 b.g. Commanche Run — The Pledger (Strong Gale) 1. Dam, half-sister to Greggs Boy (*qv* '93 Annual). P-t-P '03 r4 p2; and unseated 2. Improving with experience, and readily captured a long Maiden in soft when made favourite at Friars Haugh, but promptly went to ground. Although the third and fourth went on to score the form amounts to little, but he has claims in a Restricted at least if he is fit to resume in '05. *Mrs R. Arthur — Tynedale.* 553 (CfMa).

CARACCIOLA (NZ) ..—.. 9 ch.g. Fiesta Star (AUS) — Striking Princess (NZ) (Straight Strike USA) fp. Strong lengthy. 4000 5yo. Dam is half-sister to Grand National winner, Lord Gyllene. NH '01/3 (for G.M. McCourt, and J.L. Spearing) r8 p1 (2nd); pulled up 4. Finished ten lengths second in a Hurdle after the leaders had gone off at a suicidal pace, but beaten 28 lengths plus in seven other attempts, including a Seller (pulled up four). Stopped as if shot in both Points, and there is probably something wrong with him. *Mrs E. Scott — Minehead H.* 329 (OMa), 475 (OMa).

CARAIYNI (IRE) ..9-9.. 8 b.g. Be My Chief (USA) — Caraiyma (IRE) (Shahrastani USA) 3531. Small. Dam won 9f race in Ireland. IRISH P-t-P '02 r3 p2 (2nds). IRISH FLAT '01 r4 p0. IRISH NH FLAT '01 r1 p0. IRISH NH '01 (for D.T. Hughes) r1 p0. Fairly modest, but had achieved four placings in his first six Points, so it was no surprise when he clung on by a head in a Kingston Blount Maiden (tongue-tied for the first time). Not difficult to beat normally, but his safe jumping may give him a chance in Restricteds. Tried blinkered in Ireland. *P. Newton — Berks & Bucks (Roger Wernham).* 192 (CfMa), 589 (CfMa), 940 (OMa), 1108 (OMa).

CARAT ..10-0.. 7 b.g. Alflora (IRE) — Diamond Wind (USA) (Wind And Wuthering USA) 413. Tall workmanlike. Dam, won Maiden and Members for Count Konrad Goess-Saurau and previously won the £10,000 Marlborough Cup. P-t-P '03 r2 w1 (Maiden) p1 (2nd). Very much takes the eye in the paddock, and has readily reached Intermediate standard, but faded tamely eitherside of his Paxford success, and concerns are growing over what may be a problem with his wind. Young enough to atone and has still not reached his physical peak, but may need watching when he returns. *Count K. Goess-Saurau — V.W.H. (Countess Susie Goess-Saurau).* 232 (R), 925 (R), 1472 (I).

CARBONADO ..10-2.. 11 b.g. Anshan — Virevoite (Shareef Dancer USA) u44pp. Big workmanlike. NH FLAT '98 r3 p0. NH '98/9 r2 p0. P-t-P/HUNT CH '00 and '02/3 r19 w3 (Maiden, Restricted and Intermediate) p5 (2nds, inc 3 Hunt Chses); pulled up 3. Made a noise when landing his Maiden and broke down two starts later, and despite retaining much of his ability has consented to win only once from 18 subsequent starts. Capable of jumping well but also prone to shocking blunders, and has taken to dropping himself right out. Appears to have lost interest, but might revive if dropped back into Points. Usually needs at least one outing to put him right. Wears a cross-noseband, and a tongue-strap. *Mrs M.J. Tuck — Berkeley (Bill Tuck).* 11 (O), 176 (3mH), 346 (3m1f110yH), 541 (3mH), 1172 (3m1f110yH).

CAREBEC (IRE) .—.. 11 b.m. Good Thyne (USA) — Johns County (Crash Course) pp. Half-sister to 6 Pointing winners, including St Julien (IRE), Bold Caste (IRE) and Hilly Billy. Dam won an Irish NH flat. IRISH P-t-P '00 r6 w1 (5yo mares Maiden) p2 (3rds). P-t-P '02 r2 p0 (unseated 1 and pulled up 1). Won in deep mud in Ireland, but almost impossible to train since, and running her again would appear to be a waste of time. Produced a foal by Shambo in '02. *Mrs & Mrs N. Townsend & Mrs S. Platt — Cottesmore (Laura Pomfret).* 109 (CR), 591 (CR).

CAREFREE LOVE (IRE) ..9-4§.. 11 ch.g. Carefree Dancer (USA) — Eau D'Amour (Tall Noble USA) 5p325pp. Tall half-brother to Kingofnobles (IRE). P-t-P '00/3 r15 w2 (Maiden and Restricted) p3 (2 2nds, last once; and head & neck 3rd); pulled up 4, and fell 1. Lucky to have been adjudged the winner of two races at Buckfastleigh last year, but pulled up in half the races he has contested since and anything but keen on ground that was too fast in the last two. Never remotely consistent, but another swing in fortunes looks unlikely. Has been tried in blinkers. *Mrs A.P. Wakeham — Dartmoor (Gordon Chambers).* 193 (I), 495 (I), 705 (I), 794 (Inr), 908 (Cf), 1167 (3m2f110yH), 1431 (I).

CAREW LAD ..9-12.. 9 b.g. Arzanni — Miss Skindles (Taufan USA) p. Lengthy half-brother to Carrigafoyle (*qv*). P-t-P '02/3 r4 w1 (Maiden) p1 (2nd of 3); refused and fell. NH FLAT '02 r1 p0. NH '03 (for Mrs D.A. Hamer) r1 p0. A headstrong front-runner and scored totally unchallenged from one other finisher at Pentreclwydau last year, but has not looked the safest conveyance and shows a tendency to jump markedly to the right. Still holding every chance when breaking down after the second-last on his reappearance at Dunthrop. Wears a cross-noseband. *Mrs M. Hinchliffe — S. Pembs.* 50 (I).

CARGO FLIGHT ..9-1.. 10 br.g. Seymour Hicks (FR) — Lilac Wood (Precipice Wood) 3ppfp. Well-made half-brother to Lilac Lady. Dam, half-sister to Chasing winner, Clever Folly, won Maiden and p4. NH FLAT '00 r1 p0. NH '02 r2 p0. P-t-P '03 r4 p1 (2nd); unseated 1, refused 1 and pulled up 1. Speedy and has been in front jumping the second-last in both placings, but too headstrong to get the trip in full, and despite a novice being replaced by the likes of Ashley Farrant and Leslie Jefford has proved a costly failure since. Wears a cross-noseband. *T.W. Boon, R. White, & M.A. Bicknell — Lamerton (Tony Boon).* 119 (OMa), 195 (CfMa), 312 (CfMa), 827 (CfMa), 1132 (R).

CARIAD CYMRU ..—.. 11 b/br.g. Welsh Captain — Daddy's Darling (Mummy's Pet) 7p. Workmanlike owner-bred brother to Cymru Darling. Dam won 5 flat, 10-12f (the first 2 Sells). FLAT '96 and '98 r3 p0. NH '98/00 r8 p2. P-t-P '02/3 r6 w2 (Maiden and Restricted) p3 (2 3rds; and ¾*l* 2nd); and pulled up 1. Plumbed the lowest levels possible on the flat and over hurdles, but won two of his first three Points, and adjudged to have finished a close second on his final start last year. Very sparingly raced since '99, and clearly out of sorts in both trips to Garnons in '04, though has disappointed in the past and may be the sort to lose interest. Rated 10-4 on his best form, but best watched until he shows signs of a revival. Blinkered once in '00. *Mrs R. Evans — Croome & W. Warwicks (Charlotte Evans).* 405 (Inr), 612 (Cf).

CARLING ELECT ..9-2.. 9 ch.m. Carlingford Castle — Electress (Baron Blakeney) 5p3523. Small lengthy. Dam, sister to Going Around (*qv* '01 Annual), won Maiden and Restricted and p6 (was useless for Jeff Payne in her final season). NH '01/2 r6 p0; pulled up 1. P-t-P/HUNT CH '03 (for Mr J.S. Payne) r6 w1 (Maiden) p2 (2nds); fell/unseated 2, and pulled up 1. Scored all out from one other finisher when successful on firm at Ystradowen last year, but a persistently weak finisher, and only once beaten less than 22 lengths in the new yard (when evens favourite and second of three at Lifton). Wears a cross-noseband, and has been tried tongue-tied. Now dead. Mrs J. Walter — Taunton V.H. (Alan Walter). 65 (Rnr), 79 (R), 794 (Inr), 1102 (R), 1352 (R), 1449 (R).

CARL'S BOY ..9-0§.. 9 ch.g. Itsu (USA) — Adelbaran (FR) (No Pass No Sale) 4pp. Lengthy owner-bred brother to Baran Itsu. Dam won 8f Claimer in France (awarded race). FLAT '99/00 r4 p0 (beaten 24*l* plus). NH '99/02 r12 p5 (3 3rds); pulled up 1, and fell 1. P-t-P/HUNT CH '02/3 r8 w1 (Maiden) p4 (3rds; inc last of 3 and 3rd of 4); 5th, last and pulled up 1. Placed nine times previously, and made the most of a simple opportunity when landing a bad Maiden on firmish at Laleston on his 24th appearance, but only once tried beyond the minimum trip under Rules, and has otherwise failed to stay in Points. Has looked ungenuine in the past, and stands only light campaigns now. *F.H. Williams — Gelligaer F.* 674 (R), 844 (R), 1237 (R).

CARLTON BRAE ..9-10.. 10 b.m. Primitive Rising (USA) — Carlton Valley (Barolo) 3. Small compact half-sister to Thunderbird and Daisy Duke. Dam, half-sister to Chatterley, Prince Carlton, Carlton Bridge, Seventh Valley and Royal Battle, won Maiden and placed 5. Grandam, Non Such Valley, fell in 3 Points. P-t-P '00 and '03 r9 w1 (Maiden) p3 (2 2nds, remote once, and last once; and 3rd of 4); 4th twice, 5th, pulled up 1 and fell 1. Stays well and made a triumphant return from a three-year absence in a soft ground Maiden at Horseheath in '03, but has subsequently struggled to make much of an impression on sound surfaces, and may well have suffered another setback. Reported to be in foal to Shahrastani. *T.F.G. Marks & N. Dean — Fitzwilliam (Di Grissell).* 44 (R).

CARNAGE (IRE) ..9-0.. 8 b.g. Catrail (USA) — Caranina (USA) (Caro) p7. Close-coupled half-brother to Total Joy (IRE), to 6 flat winners, including Combative and Star Of Persia (and including 3 abroad), and to Irish Hurdles winner, Misniuil (IRE). Dam won 2 7f races in Ireland. IR5000y. FLAT '99/03 r17 w1 (14f) p4 (2 3rds Sells). NH '03 (for P. Bowen) r2 p0. Bought Ascot, Feb for 1904. Won on the Southwell all-weather in December '01 and gained two of his four placings in Sellers, but learned the habit of running too freely, and does not settle well enough to get the trip in Points (38 lengths last on his completion). Not eligible for Maidens or Restricteds, so future prospects look decidedly limited. *D.A. Smith — S. Salop (Willie Bryan).* 251 (C), 528 (O).

CARNALWAY (IRE) ..9-0.. 8 ch.g. Fourstars Allstar (USA) — Cora Domhain (Deep Run) 23. Half-brother to Super Trouper (IRE). IRISH NH '02 (for F. Flood) r9 p0; fell 1. Beaten 19 lengths plus and blinkered on his final three appearances in Ireland, but resumed after missing '03 to manage two reasonable placings in 2m4f Maidens. Tired in the closing stages of both, and it is far from certain that he will be able to get the trip when forced to tackle the full distance in '05. *C.J.B. Barlow — Cheshire.* 1049 (2m4fOMa), 1266 (2m4fOMa).

CARRIGAFOYLE .9-0.. 10 b.g. Young Senor (USA) — Miss Skindles (Taufan USA) u744. Workmanlike lengthy half-brother to Miss Panoo and Carew Lad (*qv*). Dam, half-sister to Il Bambino (*qv* '00 Annual), won 7f race. NH FLAT '00/1 r3 p0. NH '02/3 (for O. Brennan) r10 p2; pulled up 2. Bought Doncaster, Aug for 4600. Gave his best display over Hurdles when a strong finishing one and three-quarter lengths second, but lost his way badly, and pulled up and last in Sellers. Goes an adequate gallop in Points and has been able to contest some feeble ones, but does not have enough stamina to be in a prominent position where it matters. *K.V. & D.H. Wilkinson — Albrighton Woodland (Miss C.L. Wilkinson).* 226 (CfMa), 710 (Mah), 927 (OMa), 1193 (OMa).

CARRINGTON HOUSE ..9-4.. 12 b.g. Teenoso (USA) — Erica Superba (Langton Heath) 1444. Big rangy half-brother to Chasing winner, Lord Seamus, to NH Flat and Hurdling winner, Bay Kenny, and to Hurdles winners, Stac-Pollaidh and Quinag. Dam won 3m Chase, and is half-sister to smart Chaser The Tsarevich. NH FLAT '98 r1 p0 (unseated). NH '98/02 (for K.C. Bailey) r20 p2 (inc 3rd in Ch); pulled up 3, and fell/unseated 2. Ungenuine and tended to jump badly under Rules (blinkered once), and proved to be an extremely weak finisher in Points. There were only three horses behind him all season, but gifted the three-starter Royal Artillery Members when Harry Wallace (who seemed to like this sort of thing; see Kingston-Banker) fell off Flora MacDonald at the last when in clear command. The loss of his Maiden tag was most undeserved. *Mrs J.M. Bailey — R.A.* 85 (M), 198 (R), 337 (R), 571 (R).

CARROW GARDEN (IRE) ..—.. 8 b/br.g. Norwich — Garden Pit (Pitpan) ppp. Half-brother to Irish Pointing winners, Black Pit and Elkra. 2380 4yo. Pulled up in the ruck with more than half a mile or much more to travel in early season contests (looked fat on his debut). *C. Dawson — S. Durham.* 74 (OMa), 215 (OMa), 341 (R).

CARTHAGO (IRE) ..10-6.. 8 b.g. Roselier (FR) — Hi Cousin (Condorcet FR) 3u212. Small neat strong half-brother to Irish NH flat and jumping winner, Colin's Rock (17 wins), and to Irish NH flat winner Eoin's Orchestra. IR29,000 3yo. NH FLAT '01 r1 p0. FRENCH NH '01 (for F. Doumen) r15 w1 (2m2f Hdle) p4. Led virtually throughout when beating modest opposition in his Members, as one would have hoped from a horse who in his last season in France (where he was blinkered twice) had beaten the smart multiple English scorer Stormez by a neck in an 18-starter Hurdle worth £10,000 in very soft. Also performed very creditably in his placings, and unlucky to come up against Caught At Dawn and Coolefind when runner-up in Confineds. If future outings are chosen with care he should be able to score more regularly. *Mrs S. Cartridge & Miss T. McCurrich — Worcs (Theresa McCurrich).* 43 (O), 289 (CfL), 660 (Cf), 1014 (M), 1274 (Cf).

CARVILLA (IRE) .8-8§.. 10 b.g. Cardinal Flower — Villawood (Quayside) 2ppp29p32. Good-bodied brother to Mr McCarney (IRE). Dam won Point and 2m Hurdle in Ireland. IRISH P-t-P '01/2 r7 p2 (3rds); pulled up 4 and fell. IRISH NH FLAT '01 r1 p0. IRISH NH '02/3 (for Mrs J. Harrington) r8 p2

(3rds). Placed eight times including in blinkers on his penultimate appearance, but stops in a matter of strides after giving prominent displays (a replica of ex-stablemate Barbed Broach). It looked as if his day had come in the Aldenham Members where Andrew Sansome was faced with one spindley opponent, and sent off at 4-7, but in true Padfield Hunt race fashion he started swishing his tail after being six lengths clear three out and curled up like a limp lettuce after being headed at the last. His 30 lengths second at Umberleigh has surely taxed connections beyond their limit. *N.W. Padfield — Aldenham H.* 186 (OMa), 525 (OMa), 560 (OMa), 833 (OMa), 995 (M), 1359 (2m4f110yH), 1439 (2m5fH), 1518 (OMa), 1565 (OMa).

CASCUM LAD (IRE) ..10-1.. 14 b.g. Erin's Hope — Erins Shalom (Pas De Seul) 2R2p22p. Small. IRISH P-t-P '96/8 r15 w1 (7yo&up Maiden) p1 (3rd); pulled up 8, fell 1, and ran out 1. P-t-P '99 and '01/3 (for Mrs P.G.D. Sykes) r17 w3 (Intermediate, Club Restricted and Confined) p5 (3 3rds, last once); ran out 1, and pulled up 3. Developed a taste for ducking out in Ireland, and has done so twice under the present owner, but retains plenty of ability and might have scored given stronger handling in '04. Not an easy ride tactically, and only Richard Burton has mastered him since leaving his homeland, but left favourite backers with burnt fingers thrice this year, and burst a blood vessel on at least one occasion. Suited by an easy surface. *Miss S. Holmes — S. Salop (Pamela Sykes).* 94 (L), 230 (L), 464 (L), 712 (L), 849 (L), 1046 (L), 1263 (L).

CASHARI (IRE) ..9-7.. 7 b.g. Shardari — Somewhat Better (Rheingold) 34f. Half-brother to Chasing winner, Prince Sorinieres (FR). Ran fairly well in all three Maidens, including when falling at the last when two lengths down and beaten in the latest. Needs to toughen up a bit, but if he can get the trip somewhat better he should be able to score. *Mrs J. Wilson — Pytchley (Bill Warner).* 58 (OMa), 887 (CfMa), 1339 (OMa).

CASHEW CACHE (IRE) ..9-7.. 9 b.g. Phardante (FR) — Monks Lass (IRE) (Monksfield) 1. Lengthy unfurnished half-brother to Hurdles winner, Hardly (IRE), and to Irish NH flat and jumping winner, Carmelite (IRE). Dam, sister to Monk's Mistake (*qv* '97 Annual). P-t-P '02 (for Mr N. Shutts) r6 p1 (last of 2); last, pulled up 2, and fell/unseated 2. Failed to beat a rival and attained a squiggle in '02, and spent the next season on the sidelines with leg trouble, but did nothing wrong on his return when taking over seven minutes to succeed at Thorpe Lodge. Ominously failed to reappear and may not get the chance to prove his reformation is complete. *M.V. Darby — N. Ledbury.* 113 (OMa).

CASHEW KID (IRE) ..—.. 8 b.g. Persian Mews — No Honey (Dual) p. Small neat half-brother to No Bees and Two John's (IRE), to smart but ill-starred NH flat and Hurdles winners, Carobee (only beaten once in 6 starts) and Alekhine (won 5 Hurdles consecutively before falling fatally), and to winning Hurdlers, Zephyrus (IRE) and Winter Squall (also won NH flat). 15,000 4yo. NH FLAT '01/2 r3 p0. NH '02/3 (for Miss K. Marks, and S.E.H. Sherwood) r2 p0 (pulled up 2). Pulled up once a year over jumps (100-1 in the Hurdles), and after a highly unimpressive display of jumping he was dismounted with an apparent problem at Maisemore. *E.H. Lodder — Worcs (Mark Rodda).* 724 (OMa).

CASH 'N CARROTS ..9-7.. 6 b.g. Missed Flight — Rhiannon (Welsh Pageant) ff. Narrow close-coupled half-brother to Alizarine Blue (*qv*). 500 3yo. NH FLAT '02/3 r3 p0. NH '03 r1 p0 (last). Started his jumping career with a 64 lengths last in a Seller, but his Pointing debut was a lot more encouraging, as he fell at the last when two lengths second and closing in a 2m4f Maiden on the first day of the season (the runner-up and fourth scored later, whilst the winner went on to capture a Hunter Chase). Unfortunately broke down at Charing when crashing again. *R.C. Harper — Bicester with Whaddon.* 7 (2m4fOMa), 187 (Cf).

CASH ON DEMAND .—§§.. 13 ch.g. Gunner B — Morstons Maid (Morston FR) rp. Workmanlike half-brother to Hurdling winner, Buzzards Maid. NH FLAT '98 r2 p0. NH '98 r2 p0; refused to race and pulled up 1. P-t-P '03 r1 p0 (pulled up). Clearly annoyed at having his retirement interrupted and made his intentions perfectly clear when refusing to jump off for the second time in his career at Andoversford. Eventually persuaded to start next time, but would not consent to race properly, and presumably connections have taken the hint. *D.C. Stewart — Tredegar F.* 760 (OMa), 1067 (OMa).

CASPERS CASE ..10-5.. 12 gr.g. Neltino — Casket (Pannier) f2. Big strong brother to Olive Basket, and half-brother to Le Sac and Sacket. Dam won 5 Ladies (including dead-heat) and placed 3. P-t-P '03 r3 w3 (hat-trick, inc Maiden, Restricted and Intermediate) p0. Kept off the track by various means until he was ten, and thought too slow to catch a cold, but went through '03 unbeaten, and clocked some impressive times. Let down by his jumping on his return, and surprisingly unable to cope with Ronans Choice at Bishops Court, but unfortunately sidelined after, and may never be able to realise his full potential. Wears a cross-noseband, and bandages behind. *Sir Richard Cooper & R.J. Barber — Cattistock (Richard Barber).* 235 (O), 320 (Cf).

CASTLE ARROW (IRE) .9-2§.. 12 b.g. Mansooj — Soulful (So Blessed) p54p. Workmanlike half-brother to Irish Pointing winner, Private Yashkan, to an Irish flat winner, and to an Irish Hurdles winner. Dam won at 8f. IRISH P-t-P '97 r1 w1 (4yo Maiden). NH '97/'01 r10 p1 (3rd in Hdle); pulled up 3 and fell

2. P-t-P/HUNT CH '99/03 r19 w3 (up to Confined) p3 (2nds, inc 2 Hunt Chses); fell/unseated 2, and pulled up 5. Thrice successful for two previous champion riders at Kingston Blount to '00, but a confirmed villain, and will down tools if unable to dominate. Went wrong on his only appearance last year, and only once better than last in '04. Often blinkered in the past. *Miss R. Williams — Surrey U.* 608 (L), 641 (L), 805 (L), 1052 (O).

CASTLEDIVA ..9-10.. 8 ch.m. Carlingford Castle — Bivadell (Bivouac) ff*0p6*. Lengthy owner-bred sister to Bivacastle. Dam, half-sister to Dilly's Last (*qv* '99 Annual), was placed in 5 Points for Stewart Blyth. P-t-P '03 r2 p2 (head 2nd once). NH '04 (from B.N. Pollock's) r3 p0 (last of 11 in 2m7f Hdle: *prom til wknd 7, t.o*; pulled up in 2m Sell Hdle: *ld 2-6, sn wknd, bhnd when pu 2 out*; and 6th in 2m2f110y Sell Hdle: *nvr gng wl, rdn 4, v slow j 6, t.o*). Appeared to be wronged by the Judge when placed second on her debut, but disappointed next time, and spent the early part of '04 on the floor at Higham. In the process of giving Asthefellowsaid a race on the latter occasion, and may be able to atone, but her subsequent efforts under Rules suggest her resolve has been dented. *Mr & Mrs S.A. Blyth — S. Notts (Nicola Pollock).* 26 (OMa), 152 (OMa).

CASTLE FROME (IRE) ..— §.. 6 b.g. Spectrum (IRE) — Vendimia (Dominion) rp. Small neat half-brother to winner in Italy. IR20,000y. FLAT '03 (for Miss K.B. Boutflower) r7 p0. Beaten at long odds in his flat races (the last a Seller), and already tailed off when getting no further than halfway in Points. Not in love with the game and a waste of time. *M.J. Jackson — N. Ledbury (Geoff Evans).* 1261 (OMa), 1390 (O).

CASTLE LODGE ..8-8§.. 9 ch.g. Handsome Sailor — Chester Belle (Ballacashtal CAN) puf7pbpp. Workmanlike homebred. P-t-P '03 r1 p0 (pulled up). Must work like a good horse as he has been backed off the boards on several occasions, but beaten 20 lengths in his only completion, and has already developed some dirty tricks. Messrs Hanmer and Burton each had one bite at the cherry, but unlike his supporters were not keen to renew their association. Has two paddock handlers. *Mrs N. Jenkins & Mrs E.G. Tomlinson — Tanatside (Peter Morris).* 165 (OMa), 259 (CMa), 532 (OMa), 709 (Mah), 934 (OMa), 1142 (OMa), 1425 (OMa), 1458 (OMa).

CASTLE ROAD (IRE) ..8-2§.. 10 b.g. Good Thyne (USA) — Merry Miss (Deep Run) p703p. Compact half-brother to Mister Lew (IRE), to Chasing winner, Harrow Way (IRE), and to Irish NH flat winner, Tom Joad. IRISH P-t-P '99/00 r7 w2 (5yo Maiden and Winners of One) p2 (2nds); pulled up 2, and unseated 1. NH '01 r2 p0 (pulled up 2). P-t-P '02/3 r11 w1 (Members) p3 (2 2nds, of 3 once; and remote last of 3); 5th, 7th, last, fell 1 and pulled up 3. Signed off in Ireland with a double but consistently let down by poor jumping since, and is no longer prepared to try. Immediately remote in all attempts this year (twice after dwelling) and managed to beat only one rival. Wears a cross-noseband. *M. Ward & J. Glenister — Granta H. (Martin Ward).* 99 (I), 155 (Cnr), 249 (Cnr), 396 (M), 521 (Cf).

CASTLE WEIR (IRE) ..—.. 8 b.g. Lord Americo — Alchymya (Cosmo) 234p2. Sturdy half-brother to Loc A Lua (IRE), and to Irish Pointing winner, Bewleys Hotel. Dam won mares Maiden in Ireland. IRISH P-t-P '02/4 r3 w1 (5yo Maiden) p0; pulled up 1 and fell 1. IRISH HUNT CH '02 r2 w1 p0. IRISH HUNT CH '04 r4 p3 (3*l* 2nd to General Montcalm at Thurles: *a.p, ld 3 til hdd u.p app last, one pce*; 4½*l* 3rd to Never Compromise at Leopardstown: *a.p, 3rd when mist 5 out, hrd rdn 2 out, kpt on*; and 25*l* 2nd to General Montcalm at Gowran Park: *bhnd til hdwy aft 4 out, 3rd & rdn 3 out, went 2nd nr fin, no ch w wnr*); and 11½*l* 4th to Glenduff Bridge at Fairyhouse: *a.p, ld app 9 til hdd aft 4 out, no ex 2 out*. One of the better Irish Pointers, and beat subsequent English Chasing winner, Ankles Back in his Maiden there, but sometimes let down by his jumping, as he was when a 33-1 shot for the Cheltenham Foxhunters (tailed off and pulled up at the 15th). *Castle Racing Club — Premier (Willie Mullins, in Ireland).* 543 (3m2f110yH).

CATALAN GIRL ..—.. 6 ch.m. Lancastrian — Miss Vagabond (Scallywag) ppp. Half-sister to Castle Wanderer. Dam, half-sister to 3 Pointers including Rubian Princess (*qv*), was fence last of 3 in Maiden for Ian Crane. Had had enough by the time she pulled up in Maidens. Has two paddock handlers. *Mr I.P. Crane — Cottesmore (Laura Pomfret).* 385 (OMa), 597 (2m5fOMa), 685 (OMa).

CATCHATAN (IRE) ..8-11.. 10 b.g. Cataldi — Snowtan (IRE) (Tanfirion) 4p. Workmanlike. P-t-P '00 (for Mr M.T. & Mr K. Elliot) r2 w1 (3-finisher Maiden) p0; and pulled up. NH '00/3 (for P.R. Webber) r11 w1 (2m Ch) p1 (2nd); pulled up 4. Won impressively at Guilsborough as a five-year-old, but took exactly two years to open his account under Rules, and immediately lost his way again. Rendered hopeless by a wind problem, and acquired cheekpieces on his latest appearance. Wears a tongue-strap. *J.E. Dillon — Fernie.* 786 (O), 888 (O).

CATCH ON (IRE) ..9-12.. 7 b.g. Safety Catch (USA) — Delaross (IRE) (Delamain USA) 2f. Finished a promising second in an unusually competitive Maiden won by Madmidge at Marks Tey, and three of the next four home went on to score. Disappointing himself when favourite at Garthorpe, and fell two out when a modest third, but there are certainly races to be won with him when he returns to his best. *Mrs M.G. Sheppard — Cambs with Enfield Chace.* 244 (CfMa), 686 (OMa).

CATCHPHRASE ..9-8§.. 15 ch.g. Baron Blakeney — Aldington Miss (Legal Eagle) 5p1. Stocky brother to Catchword, and half-brother to Hurdles winner, Aldington Chapple. P-t-P/HUNT CH '97/00 and '02 r31 w3 (2m5f Maiden, Club Novices and Members) p4 (3rds, of 4 once); pulled up 12, and fell/unseated 4. Benefited from the exit of the odds-on jolly before halfway when recording his first success since '97 in his Members, but does little more than go through the motions in more competitive events, and can be safely ignored if returning at 15. Deserted by his regular partner (who chose to ride the much better fancied runner-up) at Cliton-on-Dunsmore, but seemed to go with more purpose for Lennie Hicks in any case. Wears a cross-noseband and a visor, and has been tried in blinkers. *Mrs K.D. Day — Atherstone.* 557 (O), 886 (Cf), 1118 (M).

CATCH THE BUS (IRE) ..9-6.. 8 b.g. Eurobus — Careful Biddy (IRE) (Buckskin FR) p1. Dam, half-sister to 4 Pointers, including Four North (IRE) (*qv* '01 Annual). IRISH P-t-P '03 r6 p0; pulled up 4, last 1. Trounced in Ireland and on his English debut, but did not let his supporters down when backed from tens to fives in a three-finisher Chaddesley Maiden, in which most of his 15 opponents were completely pathetic. A keen sort who has had two paddock handlers but may be up to Restricteds if maintaining progress. *M. Hingley — Ledbury (Heather Newell).* 667 (OMa), 1020 (OMa).

CATECHIST (IRE) ..10-4.. 10 b.g. Cataldi — Emily Bishop (IRE) (The Parson) 135p. Workmanlike half-brother to Irish Pointing winners, Grigori Rusputin and Emily Rose (IRE). P-t-P '00/1 and '03 r5 w1 (Maiden) p1 (3rd); ran out and pulled up 2. Had to endure a catalogue of problems, but was no mean performer (the only horse to lower Coolefind's colours in '04) and looked likely to register a third success until breaking a leg at Tabley. Rounded off a truly disastrous season for his trainer who deserves better luck in '05. *Mrs V. Ramm — Cotswold (Jelly Nolan).* 109 (CR), 1092 (I), 1176 (3m110yH), 1430 (I).

CATEEL BAY ..—.. 7 ch.m. Most Welcome — Calachuchi (Martinmas) ppfpp. Small scrawny half-sister to Hurdles winner, Calatagan (IRE),to flat winner Quezon City, and to a winner in Holland. Dam won 9 flat, 7-12f (Claimers and a Sell). FLAT '00/3 r10 w1 (8f) p0. NH '02/3 (for H. Alexander) r10 p0; pulled up 1, unseated 1. Bought Doncaster, Aug for 1400. Won a Maiden Claimer in August '01, and there would have been few direr contests that year, as the 14 runners had amassed 131 outings with no wins between them! Useless in Hurdles (nine of them Sellers), and went no more than 2m4f before pulling up in Opens (three ran once) and took a heavy fall in the Melton Novices. A pointless exercise. *P.J. Millington — Fernie.* 480 (O), 997 (O), 1400 (CN), 1502 (O), 1529 (MO).

CATHERINE'S WAY (IRE) ..8-7.. 13 b.g. Mandalus — Sharp Approach (Crash Course) u4937pp. Tall rangy. Dam, half-sister to Magical Approach (*qv*), won mares Maiden and 3m Hdle in Ireland. NH '97/00 r14 w3 (2m110y Hdle and 2 2m1f-2m6f110y Chases) p1 (2nd); pulled up 9, and fell/unseated 2. P-t-P/HUNT CH '02/3 r8 p1 (2nd); 5th thrice, 6th and pulled up 3. Won three times going right-handed during a four-race spell spread over 15 months to February '00, but breaks blood vessel on a regular basis, and rarely prepared to put his best foot forward now. Galvanised into a brisk gallop by Amy Stennett and the application of cheekpieces on a couple of occasions in '04, but carries plenty of condition, and has never proved his ability to stay three miles. *M. Ward & Mrs B. Martin — Granta H. (Martin Ward).* 242 (2m5f110yH), 399 (L), 558 (L), 831 (L), 998 (L), 1154 (L), 1354 (2m110yH).

CATH'S LASS ..6-3§.. 10 br.m. Lir — Veronica Ann (Henbit USA) pp. Small neat homebred sister to King Tudor (*qv*). P-t-P '03 r5 w1 (2-finisher Maiden) p0; and pulled up 4. Yet to go more than two miles without mishap, and makes some alarming blunders, but restarted after declining the 12th in a Maiden at Lifton last year and came home three fences ahead of another rejoiner. Blind in one eye, and in no state to be on a racecourse in '04, and should be humiliated no more. *Ms C. Bown — Lamerton.* 1196 (R), 1435 (R).

CATHY COME HOME (IRE) ..8-0.. 8 br.m. Bob's Return (IRE) — Colour Clown (Random Shot) 4pu. Small light half-sister to Ashfield Orchestra (IRE) (*qv*). P-t-P '03 r3 p0 (pulled up 2 and fell 1). Beaten under nine lengths when fourth in a weak Mares Maiden at Garnons, but went no further than a mile on two occasions in her debut season, and was in the process of stopping when unseating at the 12th on her latest appearance. Lacks scope and despite the presence of leading riders is not progressing on the right lines. *Mr & Mrs P.O. Perry — Ledbury (Maurice Perry).* 408 (CMam), 983 (2m5fOMa), 1259 (OMa).

CATLEY CROSS ..—.. 7 b.m. Shambo — Shamana (Broadsword USA) p. Half-sister to Greet You Well (*qv*). Tailed off and pulled up after two miles at Marks Tey. *Miss V.E. Hayter — Suffolk.* 901 (OMa).

CATOSPHERE (IRE) ..9-0.. 8 b.g. Catrail (USA) — Royaleffort (Dunphy) pp36p322. Tall plain. Dam, half-sister to Robchris (*qv* '95 Annual). IRISH NH FLAT '01 r2 p0; pulled up 1. P-t-P '03 r1 p0 (pulled up). Pulled up in four of his first five races, and improved by the application of cheekpieces when runner-up in 2m4f Maidens on his last two starts, but beaten a minimum of 18 lengths over the full trip and no longer has the option of the shorter version. Tongue-tied once in '01. *Mrs I. Sullivan &*

Mrs G.N. Lupton — S. Durham (Sarah Dent). 161 (I), 394 (CfMa), 813 (OMa), 1158 (OMa), 1292 (OMa), 1412 (M), 1474 (2m4fOMa), 1504 (2m4fOMa).

CATS CROSS .—.. 10 ch.m. Riverwise (USA) — Cut Above The Rest (Indiaro) pp. Very small light sister to Dart View Lass and Sex Kitten, and to Hurdles winner, Kittenkat. Dam was placed in 4 Points for Richard Mitchell. NH FLAT '01 r3 p0. NH '01/2 r4 p0; pulled up 2. Utterly devoid of ability, like several of her stablemates (*eg* Faugere, Peter Parkgate and Queens House). Connections are perfectly capable of doing a good job with the right material, but are never going to achieve much with this lot. *Mrs M.A. Cooke — S. Dorset (Elsie Mitchell).* 172 (OMa), 328 (OMa).

CAUGHT AT DAWN (IRE) ..10-12.. 11 b.g. Supreme Leader — Pharisee (IRE) (Phardante FR) p111111. Small neat half-brother to Phatic (IRE). NH FLAT '99 r1 p0. IRISH NH '01 r2 p0 (tailed off in 2m1f-2m4f Chses; pulled up 1). P-t-P '00 and '02/3 r12 w5 (Club Maiden, Restricted, 2 Members, and Intermediate) p2; 5th, 6th, pulled up 1 and fell/unseated 2. Originally bought as a humble schoolmaster for Tom Weston, but improved out of all recognition in his fourth campaign, and was successful in the finish of the night at Cheltenham on his latest appearance. Recorded much the fastest times of the day when galloping the opposition into the ground at Whitwick, Brampton Bryan and Andoversford, and became the first Lady Dudley Cup winner with a Worcestershire certificate since the wayward Darlingate in 1984. A more accurate jumper than he was, and usually in command throughout the final mile of proceedings, but fought bravely to fend off Balinova at Prestbury Park where the rider looked just as polished as Polly Gundry on the runner-up. Proven on all but extremes of going, and should continue to do well. *M.H. Weston — Worcs.* 93 (O), 513 (Cf), 660 (Cf), 756 (Cf), 979 (MOnr), 1016 (3m2fO), 1172 (3m1f110yH).

CAUNDLE CHASE ..10-0.. 10 gr.g. El Conquistador — Caundle Break (Rugantino) 21223d3f. Strong-topped owner-bred brother to Caundle Encore, and half-brother to Caundle Steps and Caundle's Hand. Dam is an unraced sister to Plot Lane. Grandam, Trudi Fair, won 6 Points and placed 25 for Peter Doggrell. P-t-P '02/3 r12 w2 (Restricted and Members) p7 (4 2nds, of 3 once; and inc last of 3 twice); last 2, and fell 1. Has a fair record in minor Points, but predictably struggling to win an Intermediate, and has to target his locals to rely on success nowadays. More robust than many by his sire, but lacks a change of gear, and remains liable to make mistakes. *P & Mrs S. Doggrell — W. Somerset (Gordon Chambers).* 273 (M), 468 (M), 692 (I), 881 (Inr), 1181 (I), 1365 (Cnr), 1555 (I).

CAVEAT GRAECI (IRE) ..— §.. 10 b.m. Ilium — Carrigconeen (Beau Charmeur FR) pppp. Half-sister to Dr Billy (IRE). IRISH P-t-P '00 r5 p0 (pulled up 4, and fell 1). A late starter who refuses to try, and her first season in Wales will doubtless be her last. Blinkered when pulling up for the eighth time. *N. Criddle — Tredegar F. (Lisa Day).* 408 (CMam), 450 (R), 844 (R), 1027 (OMa).

CAWKWELL PRINCESS .9-8.. 11 b.m. Cotation — Cawkwell Flower (Master Sing) p7545. Small neat. P-t-P '03 r4 w1 (Maiden) p0; 4th, and pulled up 2. Unraced until she was nine, and scored on her first completion on firm at Brocklesby Park, but the opposition was particularly weak and has been soundly beaten since. A sound jumper, but nowhere near quick enough to take advantage of the lighter weights in Ladies races, and may prove impossible to place successfully again. *M. Barthorpe & Mrs C. Wallis — S. Wold (Pat Barthorpe).* 481 (R), 745 (R), 1060 (R), 1399 (L), 1501 (L).

CEASERS REIGN (IRE) ..9-7.. 13 ch.g. Rhoman Rule (USA) — Dora Gayle (Lord Gayle USA) pp24. Lengthy. IRISH NH FLAT '97 r2 p0. IRISH P-t-P '97 and '99/00 r18 w2 (6yo&up Maiden and Winners of 2) p7; pulled up 2, and fell/unseated 2. IRISH NH '97/8 and '00 r10 p0. P-t-P/HUNT CH '02/3 (for Mr T.D.B. Underwood) r17 w2 (Intermediate and Club nov rdrs) p4 (2 2nds, last once; inc last of 3 once); last 4, pulled up 5, and fell/unseated 2. Exposed as moderate in Ireland, and gained his initial English success virtue of a walkover, but gets the trip only when conditions are not testing, and has scored just once in 18 subsequent attempts. Acquired a second paddock handler in the new yard, and has been taken to post early. *F. Lloyd & Mrs H. Taylor — Ludlow (Frank Lloyd).* 229 (O), 513 (Cf), 834 (M), 1113 (Cf).

CEDAR CHIEF ..10-3.. 8 b.g. Saddlers' Hall (IRE) — Dame Ashfield (Grundy) 5f86u1122112. Small neat half-brother to Hurdles winners, Valiant Dash and Rosina Mae (latter also won flat). Dam won 2 12f races in '83 and was sold soon after for 100,000. FLAT '99/00 r5 p0. NH '00/2 r20 w1 (2m6f110y Hdle) p3. P-t-P/HUNT CH '03 r5 w1 (3-finisher Confined, also won Members but disqualified for missing marker) p1 (3rd of 4); last, and fell 1. Required 16 attempts in order to get off the mark, but much more prolific since, and likes to dominate in small fields. Error prone, and particularly so in Hunter Chases, but sure to find further simple opportunities in his area. His ability to turn out on seven consecutive weekends from the beginning of April helped him establish enough points to land the Weatherbys Chase PPORA Young Horse Award. Has won on firmish but better suited by plenty of cut. Wears blinkers. *K. Tork — Surrey U.* 189 (L), 422 (CCon), 445 (3m110yH), 545 (2m3f110yH), 642 (O), 780 (O), 805 (L), 1053 (L), 1086 (L), 1207 (M), 1335 (O), 1407 (L).

CEDAR GROVE ..— §.. 8 b.g. Shirley Heights — Trojan Desert (Troy) pp. Small close-coupled half-brother to 3 flat winners (2 abroad), including Alberkinnie. Dam won 7f race and later successful in

USA. FLAT '00 and '02/3 r26 p4 (inc 2 Sells). NH '02 (for J.A. Harris) r2 p0. Bought Doncaster, Oct for 2000. Beaten between one length and 11 lengths in four flat placings (including two Sellers), but unreliable and has flashed his tail, and was tongue-tied once. Jumped sluggishly and decidedly unwilling in Maidens (regained cheekpieces in the latest), and there is no good reason for persevering with him. *Miss L. Llewellyn & V. Hughes — Llangeinor (Vivian Hughes).* 363 (CfMa), 735 (CfMa).

CEFN COCH ..—§.. 8 b.g. Deltic (USA) — Tommy's Last (Tom Noddy) pp. Small compact owner-bred. Dam, sister to Noddy's Daughter (*qv* '91 Annual). P-t-P '03 r2 p0 (ran out 1 and pulled up 1). An appalling creature with no manners and hangs at will, jumps with no conviction, and has yet to get beyond the tenth fence in four attempts. Not all his fault as he looks unfit and unschooled and reflects badly on connections. *A.D. Taylor — Pentyrch.* 1089 (M), 1192 (OMa).

CELTIC BOUNTY (IRE) ..—.. 9 b.g. Treasure Hunter — Welsh Glen (Furry Glen) pp. Very tall half-brother to Irish NH flat and Hurdling winner, Minister's Cross. IR10,000 3yo. NH FLAT '00/1 r2 p0. NH '02/3 (for R.J. Hodges) r3 p0; pulled up 2. Sold Ascot, Jun for 2857. Bought Ascot, Nov for 2285. Beaten 30 lengths plus twice on the flat, and 77 lengths last and pulled up on four occasions (including a four-horse Members in the latest) over jumps. Will never make a racehorse. *A.C. Simpson — Surrey U.* 1085 (Cv&nr), 1207 (M).

CELTIC DUKE ..10-8.. 13 b.g. Strong Gale — Celtic Cygnet (Celtic Cone) 211411p. Sturdy compact half-brother to Twice A Night and Bruan (IRE), to Hurdles winner, Stars Delight (IRE), and to NH flat winner, Sotattie. Dam, sister to smart winner, Celtic Isle, won NH flat and 2 Hdles (2m-2m4f). Grandam, Jo, completed a hat-trick in Points. NH '96/01 r18 w3 (3m-3m4f Chses) p9. P-t-P/HUNT CH '02/3 r19 w8 (3m110y Hunt Ch and 7 Ladies) p6 (2nds, beaten neck twice, inc Hunt Ch); 4th twice, fell 1 and pulled up 2. Rejuvenated in the present yard, and took his winning tally for Joe Turner into double figures when successful at Marks Tey in February. Achieved another notable success when retaining the Essandem Trophy at Fakenham's early May evening meeting, the 16th time that the yard has won the race. A thorough stayer, and prefers to dominate, but will not entertain going right-handed nowadays and was particularly reluctant at Huntingdon on his latest appearance. Gurgled in heavy ground once in '02, and resented a tongue-tie when pulled up next time, but usually placed and ridden to perfection, and is unbeaten in four trips to High Easter. *J.M. Turner — Suffolk.* 157 (L), 246 (L), 649 (L), 893 (3m110yH), 1154 (L), 1295 (3m110yH), 1360 (3mH).

CELTIC KNIGHT ..—.. 7 b.g. Gildoran — Bonny Beau (Kinglet) p. Dam, half-sister to Ruby Lady (*qv* '04 Annual), Last, fell and unseated in Points for Lyndon Williams 'deeply unpleasant'. Pulled up at halfway in a Maiden (fat, and tailed off after a mile). His stable have produced some decent homebreds over the years, and it could be a big mistake to write him off too quickly. *L.J. Williams — Curre & Llangibby.* 845 (CfMa).

CELTIC PRINCE (IRE) ..—.. 7 gr.g. Old Vic — No Slow (King's Ride) pcp5p. Tall well-made half-brother to jumping winner, Stratco (IRE). Sold Doncaster, May '02 for 15,000. Has not shown the faintest glimmer of ability on the racecourse so far, but was backed from 8-1 to 5-2 joint-favourite before finishing 57 lengths last (badly let down by his jumping) and then sent off 2-1 favourite (sixes available early) but was already under pressure when blundering at the fifth. Connections will be scratching their heads at present, but perhaps he is not as bad as he has looked so far. More fluent jumping would certainly help. *D. Walters — Tredegar F. (Tim Jones).* 845 (CfMa), 1096 (OMa), 1324 (CfMa), 1371 (OMa), 1488 (OMa).

CELTIC SEASON ..8-11.. 13 b.g. Vital Season — Welsh Flower (Welsh Saint) up25. Good-topped hobdayed brother to Agassi's Ace, and half-brother to Comedie Fleur, to Chasing winner, Snowdon Lily, and to flat and Hurdles winner, Flower Of Tintern. NH FLAT '97 r1 p0. NH '97/01 r28 w4 (2m4f-3m Chses) p6 (4 2nds); pulled up 5, and fell/unseated 4. P-t-P/HUNT CH '02/3 r9 w1 (dead-heat Open) p4 (3 2nds, inc Hunt Ch; and 3rd of 4); 5th, last pair 2, and pulled up 1. Formerly quite useful on his day, and successful four times racing in a clockwise direction, but has been dogged by wind trouble, and has failed to beat a rival in his last three completions. Ran to 10-10 when dead-heating with Minella Silver on his Pointing debut, but falls in a heap when pressure is applied now, and looks finished. Tried in headgear latterly under Rules, and often tongue-tied. *R. West — Bicester with Whaddon (Chris Loggin).* 18 (L), 1032 (O), 1277 (MO), 1514 (Cf).

CELTIC SONG (IRE) ..—.. 9 b.g. Cataldi — Iron Mariner (IRE) (Mandalus) p. Light-framed. Dam won 2 2m Hurdles in Ireland. 5000 4yo. NH FLAT '00 r3 p1 (3rd). NH '01/3 (for P.F. Nicholls) r3 w1 (2m6f Hdle) p0; fell 1. Pulled up at halfway at Bredwardine in May. Fell and broke a knee on his Hurdling debut and was absent for 18 months afterwards, but although he subsequently landed a four-runner Hurdle on firm he has been virtually untrainable, managing just one outing apiece in each of the last four years. *Mrs R.E. Walker — Clifton-on-Teme.* 1390 (O).

CENTO (IRE) .10-3§.. 12 b.g. Shernazar — Callianire (Sir Gaylord) 122124. Small compact brother to Irish flat and jumping winner, Chirkpar (won Irish Champion Hdle). Dam won 8f race in France. IRISH FLAT '95/7 r9 p4 (short-headed once). IRISH NH '96/7 r6 p4 (short-headed once) NH '98/01 r28 w3 (2m3f-2m3f110y Hdles) p9. P-t-P '03 r5 p3 (2 2nds, beaten short head once); 5th, and pulled up. Reached the winners enclosure for the first time since '00 (placed eight times in the interim) when springing an 11-1 surprise on his reappearance at Wadebridge, but remains a frustrating hold-up merchant, and gained his subsequent success in fortuitous circumstances. Probably in front too soon when cut down after the last at Huntingdon, but retains his ability well, and certainly worth another try in blinkers (used to wear them almost exclusively to '01). Suited by an easy surface. *Mr & Mrs N. Faulks — Dulverton F. (Sarah Faulks).* 78 (L), 262 (L), 690 (L), 1011 (L), 1360 (3mH), 1454 (3mH).

CENTURIAN (U) ..1-0.. 11 b.g. unknown 8. Has the speed of a 100-year-old and rider, Major Erica, was very soon demoted rear Gunner. *The King's Troop RHA — R.A. (Neil Cross).* 84 (2m4fC).

CERASUS KNIGHT (IRE) ..—.. 10 b.g. Arctic Lord — Cherry Field (Precipice Wood) ppp6. Tall. Dam won NH flat and 7 Chses (2m-2m4f) when Irish-trained (last win at Carlisle). NH FLAT '00 r4 p0. NH '00/01 r5 p0; last 2, pulled up 2 and unseated. P-t-P '02 r1 p0 (pulled up). Devoid of ability and has failed to beat a rival in ten starts over obstacles. Acquired cheekpieces on his most recent attempt. *Miss V.H. Smith — E. Kent.* 154 (OMa), 423 (CMa), 782 (OMa), 1088 (OMa).

CERTAIN SURPRISE ..9-13.. 11 b.m. Grey Desire — Richesse (FR) (Faraway Son USA) p51. Unfurnished sister to NH flat and Hurdles winner, Rich Desire, and half-sister to Johnny Grand, and to 3 flat winners (one in Belgium) including Rabirius (also successful Hurdler). FLAT '97/8 r7 p0. NH '97/01 r21 p5 (4 3rds). P-t-P '03 r3 w1 (Maiden) p1 (2nd); and last. Tried blinkered and descended to Sellers when unsuccessful in 28 events under Rules, but has found her level in Points, and was catching Supreme Citizen when that rival left her clear at the last in her first attempt in Ladies races at Brampton Bryan. Clearly not easy to train, but Emma James does well with her inexpensive purchases, and might just be able to score again. *Miss E.E.L. James & Mrs H. Albert — N. Ledbury (Emma James).* 726 (R), 839 (R), 1111 (L).

CHADSWELL (IRE) ..9-7§.. 12 b.g. Lord Americo — Marita Ann (Crozier) pRpu43u364. Small well-made. NH FLAT '99 r1 p0. NH '00/3 (for R. Ford) r25 w6 (3 2m4f-3m2f Hdles and 2 2m3f-2m4f Chses) p5; pulled up 3, fell 1. Formerly competent over extreme distances in the mud, and gained the last of his six victories on the technical disqualification of Master Club Royal (*qv*). Kept busy in Points and switched to Ladies Opens latterly (presumably in an attempt to get some weight off his back), but gave only one acceptable display all season (when five and a quarter lengths third), and his interest has waned badly. Tongue-tied once and wore cheekpieces once under Rules. Will probably decline further should he reappear at 12. *W. Puddifer Jnr — Sir W.W. Wynn's (Peter Morris).* 163 (O), 229 (O), 292 (MO), 615 (O), 873 (Cf), 1047 (O), 1203 (L), 1343 (L), 1428 (L), 1459 (L).

CHALLIS CHOICE (IRE) ..8-9.. 8 b.g. Executive Perk — Miss Nidee (Pollerton) p2. Good-bodied half-brother to Assington Bay (IRE) (*qv*). Bought Ascot, June 2476. Beaten one length in a dreadful Holnicote Maiden in February. The race threw up no subsequent winners, and at least two of the contestants went lame. Did not reappear himself, which looks rather ominous. *P. Gooder — Taunton V. (Mel Dixon).* 149 (OMa), 274 (CfMa).

CHAMPAGNE (U) .4-11.. 9 b.m. unknown 4. Fizzled out approaching the last. *The King's Troop RHA — R.A. (Neil Cross).* 84 (2m4fC).

CHAMPAGNE KING ..—.. 6 b.g. Prince Sabo — Champagne Season (USA) (Vaguely Noble) f. Lengthy brother to flat winners, Mis Chicaf and Champagne Prince, and half-brother to flat winners, Bubbly and Festive. FLAT '01/2 (for P.W. Harris) r5 p0. Sent off even money favourite for an eight-runner Maiden at Cilwendeg, but this was an indication of the rank awfulness of the opposition, as he had never shown any form on the flat. Took a keen hold, and looked to be struggling when taking a crashing fall at the 15th. Probably does not have the stamina for the job. *P. Richards — Banwen Miners (John Moore).* 675 (CfMa).

CHANCE FORTUNE ..—.. 8 b.g. Cap Diamant (USA) — Acrolight (Blakelight) f. Lengthy. Fell at the second in one of the five grief-stricken Maidens at the South Herefords (of the 49 who set off, only 19 made it to the finish in one piece). *Mrs M. Roberts — Wheatland.* 617 (2m4fOMa).

CHANCY GUY ..10-6.. 8 b.g. Tragic Role (USA) — Malacanang (Riboboy USA) 111. Dam won 2m Hdle. IRISH P-t-P '03 r1 p0 (pulled up). Made his Welsh debut in mid-April when taking a three-runner two-finisher youngsters Maiden, but then beat the subsequent Chasing winner Gold Kriek in a Confined, and nursed home in an Open on firm at Rhydygwern, which was a modest affair. Unfortunately finished lame, so his pleasing progress could be more difficult to maintain even if he can reappear in '05. *P. Roberts — Ystrad Taf Fechan (Robert Rowsell).* 1026 (OMa), 1320 (Cf), 1484 (O).

CHANGE ..9-7.. 11 b.g. North Briton — Karminski (Pitskelly) p43634p. Small neat half-brother to a winner in Norway. Dam won 3 flat, 13-17f. FLAT r2 p0. NH '98 r3 p0. P-t-P '00 and '02/3 r13 w1 (Members) p3 (2nds, of 3 once); pulled up 4, unseated 1. Outpaced the odds-on favourite when opening his account in his Members in '02, but ordinarily does not get the trip well, and only once better than last when making the frame this year. Wears a cross-noseband. *The Three To One Club (Mrs J.M. Wickett) - Stevenstone (Caroline Furse).* 79 (R), 572 (R), 791 (R), 824 (R), 1267 (M), 1433 (Cf), 1561 (R).

CHANGING FASHION (IRE) ..7-6.. 11 ch.g. Jamesmead — Sharp Fashion VII (unknown) 4pp. Tall strong-topped half-brother to Pointing winner, Bay Road. NH '99/00 r4 p0 (last in only Ch). P-t-P '01/2 r9 w1 (2-finisher Maiden) p0; last 2, and pulled up 6. Won the last Point of the year in foot-and-mouth afflicted '01, but not better than last in just ten subsequent attempts, and was carrying too much condition to take a hand in the finish of his Members this year. Indolent and quickly tailed off in more competitive events, and seems no more than a hunter now. Has been tried in blinkers. *The Marriage Family (Mrs J.K. Marriage) — Essex (Simon Marriage).* 646 (M), 902 (R), 1084 (R).

CHANNEL'S BROOK ..8-5.. 10 b.g. Tina's Pet — Bit Of Space (Space King) 23p. Workmanlike. Dam pulled up in 4 Hurdles, and subsequently ran badly in 5 Points at 12. Grandam, Collies Pet, won 2 Points and placed 6 (demoted after win once). P-t-P '02/3 r6 p1 (2nd of 3); last pair 3, unseated 1 and pulled up 1. In the frame in four Maidens, and can figure prominently for up to 2m4f, but stays no further, and appeared to suffer a setback when the subject of market support on his latest appearance. Managed only one outing in '03, and is obviously difficult to keep sound. *J.P. Price — Radnor & W. Herefords (Clive Davies).* 518 (CfMa), 666 (OMa), 840 (OMa).

CHAOS THEORY..10-2.. 10 b.g. Jupiter Island — Indian Orchid (Warpath) 6u3u3. Narrow unfurnished owner-bred. Dam, half-sister Desert Orchid. NH FLAT '99 r2 p0 (unseated 1). FLAT '02 r2 p0. NH '99/03 (for Mrs M. Reveley) r22 w3 (2 2m Hdles and 2m4f Chses) p2 (3rds); fell 4, pulled up 1. A triple winner at up to 2m4f under Rules to December '01, but unplaced on his final ten appearances, and showed a poor attitude and was blinkered thrice. Bad blunders make him a difficult ride in Points (hopeless for a novice), but would have been second in an Open at Witton Castle had he not crashed through the last. Retains ability and looks to stay three miles well, but it would be unwise to place any faith in him. For a graphic demonstration of the chaos theory, visit St Mary's Redcliffe Church in Bristol. *R. Burridge & Lady Henrietta Burridge — Sinnington (John Cranage).* 267 (Cf), 389 (Cf), 770 (Cf), 1163 (Cf), 1289 (O).

CHAPARRO AMARGOSO (IRE) ..8-7.. 12 b.g. Ela-Mana-Mou — Champanera (Top Ville) 8u83. Rangy half-brother to French flat winner. NH FLAT '97 r1 w1. FLAT '01 r1 p0. NH '00/2 (for B. Ellison) r20 w2 (2m Chses) p8 (inc 2 Hdles); pulled up 1, fell 1. Described as 'the best horse I've trained' by Brian Ellison after his successful bumper debut, but it turned out to be very wishful thinking, and his need for fast ground and inability to stay beyond two miles limited his prospects. A sketchy jumper of fences, and was often tongue-tied, and visored twice. Has stringhalt. Able to beat only one horse in the new yard, when 11 lengths third in an Open at Eyton-On-Severn which took far longer than both the Maidens run over the same trip. With an 8-7 rating, he could be the best horse Frank Matthews has ever trained. In an important location move, Frank has changed dwellings (now he's nearer the pub). *J.E. Wood — Wheatland (Frank Matthews).* 317 (2m4fH), 628 (2m3fH), 660 (Cf), 930 (O).

CHAPNERS CROSS ..9-7.. 9 b.g. Primitive Rising (USA) — Holly (Skyliner) p43fpp. Lengthy. Dam is half-sister to Saywhen (*qv* '01 Annual). P-t-P '02/3 r9 w1 (2m4f Maiden) p0; 7th, and failed to finish 7 (pulled up 4, ran out 1, unseated 1 and brought down 1). Won a 2m4f Maiden on firm at Great Trethew in '02, but otherwise a regular non-finisher, and could not manage to complete in a match for his Members on his latest appearance. Laid low by a virus in '03, and still does not appear to be that healthy. *Mrs E.M.F. & S. Roberts — Dulverton F. (Andrew Congdon).* 706 (R), 912 (R), 1131 (R), 1268 (R), 1437 (2m5f110yH), 1461 (M).

CHARANGO STAR .10-0.. 7 b.g. Petoski — Pejawi (Strong Gale) u131. Small plain half-brother to Safawi. Dam, half-sister to Moss-beau (*qv* '00), won 4 Points (one in Ireland) and placed 12 (inc and Irish Hurdle). Had a commendable first season, and his comfortable defeat of Sovereign Gale at Higham received a triple boost subsequently. A disappointing favourite next time, and absent for over two months before reappearing to take a weak Peper Harow Restricted in which only two went clear. Should find further opportunities, but insubstantial like several of the York runners, and has the look of a Ladies performer. *R.H. York — Staff College.* 39 (OMa), 151 (OMa), 265 (R), 1208 (R).

CHARLESTOWN LASS ..9-9.. 8 b.m. Bob Back (USA) — Prepare (IRE) (Millfontaine) R5. Compact half-sister to flat winner, Make Rady. Dam won 7f race. NH FLAT '01 r3 p1 (2nd). NH '02 (for late J. Neville) r3 p0. NH '04 (for C. Roberts) r1 p0 (5th in 2m5f110y Hdle: *hld up, blun 1, hdwy 6, wknd app last*). Clear entering the last furlong of a bumper, but was just caught and beaten a head. Less successful over Hurdles in '02, and visored on her final attempt, but a huge Welsh gamble in a Mares Maiden at Clifton-on-Dunsmore, where she was backed to take thousands out of the ring and the money was being counted when she came to the final fence with a 20 length advantage, but had already begun to waiver and crashed into the wing (to the joy of old cynics who cringe at the hooting and hollering of Tim Vaughan in victory mode!). Certainly deserves compensation which should not be hard to find in similar company, but the bookies are hardly likely to be chalking up 8-1 again. *Mrs M. Mulligan — Banwen Miners (John Moore).* 1119 (CMam).

CHARLIEADAMS (IRE) ..9-6.. 15 b.g. Carlingford Castle — Lucy Platter (FR) (Record Token) pp6403R. Rangy brother to Castle Stephen (IRE), and half-brother to Abbotsham, and to winning Hurdler, Betabatim (IRE). IRISH NH FLAT '95/6 r4 p0. IRISH NH '96 and '99 r4 p1 (2nd in Hunt Ch; 4th in only similar). IRISH P-t-P '98/9 r8 w2 (7yo&up Nov Rdrs Maiden, and Winners of Two) p2; pulled up 2, and fell 1. NH '02 r5 w3 (2m4f110y-2m5f Chses) p2 (2nds). P-t-P/HUNT CH '00/3 r31 w2 (2m4f110y Hunt Chses) p8 (4 3rds, of 4 once, and inc 2 Hunt Chses; and inc 2 2nds in Hunt Ch); fell/unseated 8, pulled up 4, and ran out 3. Acquired Tony Dobbin for five-race spell from Len Lungo's yard in '02 after failing to score in his previous 11 starts, and won three and was runner-up in the other two, but nowhere near as good for the owner who does a minimum of 12st2lb. Retains some speed and by virtue the rider is sometimes out of control, but basically a back number now, and beaten a minimum of 27 lengths in '04. *J.F.W. Muir — Lauderdale.* 214 (O), 330 (3mH), 439 (2m5f110yH), 551 (O), 798 (3m1fH), 1079 (O), 1223 (O).

CHARLIEBOB ..—.. 6 gr.m. Nomadic Way (USA) — Furry Bear (Rymer) pp. Owner-bred half-sister to Sootsir (*qv*). Pulled up after 1m4f and 2m4f in April Maidens. *Mrs S. Hawker — Beaufort (Richard Hawker).* 962 (OMa), 1134 (OMa).

CHARLIE HAWES (IRE) .6-7.. 16 b.g. Euphemism — Eyecap (King's Ride) 3. Rangy. IRISH P-t-P '96/7 r11 w1 (7yo&up Maiden) p2; fell/unseated 4 NH '97/9 r15 p0 (inc Sell; inc 5 Chses, inc pulled up 2, and fell). HUNT CH '00 and '03 r5 p0 (last 3, unseated 1 and pulled up 1). Hopeless since crossing the Irish Sea, but at least being able to travel at such slow speeds has meant he can concentrate on jumping which used to be very inaccurate. No more than a hunter now, and carried the triumphant owner (minus gumshield) to a remote last of three in his Members. Has been tried in headgear. *Miss G.A. Russell — Wilton.* 574 (M).

CHARLIE'S ANGEL ..9-13.. 7 gr.m. Rakaposhi King — Dunnohalm (Kalaglow) 521f3. Small sparely-made. Dam won NH FLAT. P-t-P '03 r5 w3 (Maiden, Restricted and Confined) p0; pulled up 1 and fell 1. NH FLAT '03 r2 p0. NH '03 r1 p0; tailed off last. Nothing to look at and was bought cheaply but has done well, and only Asthefellowsaid was able to lower her colours in her first five completed Points. Disappointed on her last two starts when looking for a third course win at Kingston Blount, and her attitude which was once admirable now appears compromised. Tends to make errors, and her stature suggests that the lesser weights in Ladies races would suit, but the likelihood is that she will be produced successfully again. Wears a cross-noseband. *C. Cheesman — Staff College (Phillip York).* 443 (2m4f110yH), 640 (Cf), 806 (C), 1103 (C), 1336 (I).

CHARLIE STRONG (IRE) ..10-9.. 12 b.g. Strong Gale — The Village Vixen (Buckskin FR) 2up3. Tall rangy. NH '99 r1 p0. P-t-P/HUNT CH '98/9 and '01/3 r16 w8 (inc 2 Hunt Chses, 2m5f-2m7f110y, Open and Ladies) p3 (3rds, inc Hunt Ch); pulled up 2, fell/unseated 2. A smart performer at his best, but needs regular nursing and like the rest of his trainers' string was under a cloud in '03. Involved in an exciting finish on his return, but made an uncharacteristic last-fence blunder when set for victory next time, and did not get into his stride until the race was over on his latest appearance. Thoroughly deserves to win again, but can ill afford clumsy mistakes, and has not scored going left-handed since '99. Best suited by some cut in the ground. Has two paddock handlers. Wears a cross-noseband. *R.G. Kelvin-Hughes — Spooners & W. Dartmoor.* 64 (O), 234 (L), 543 (3m2f110yH), 1168 (2m5fH).

CHARLOTTE RUSSE ..—.. 8 b.m. Rudimentary (USA) — Do Run Run (Commanche Run) fpp. Small sister to flat winner, Deeceebee. Dam won 8f race. 4700f, 2200y. FLAT '99/00 (for R.A. Fahey) r4 p0; last 3. Not better than tenth on the flat (visored once), and was tailed off last on her final three attempts. Jumped poorly for good jockeys in Points, and is clearly useless. *Miss C.C. Mills — Pytchley (Colin Potts).* 27 (OMa), 409 (CMam), 946 (OMa).

CHARMINSKY ..9-0.. 12 b.g. Karlinsky (USA) — Charmezzo (Remezzo) 1p. Good-topped lengthy owner-bred brother to Ashdown Boy and Sir William, and half-brother to Westcountry Lad and Late To Start. Dam is sister to Romany Anne (*qv* '00 Annual). P-t-P '02/3 r5 p1 (3rd of 4); pulled up 4. Unraced until he was nine, and pulled up in his first four attempts, but hinted at ability next time, and duly landed a three-finisher Maiden on firmish at Trebudannon. Clocked the slowest time of the day by far and a return visit resulted in another non-completion, whilst his nearest victim won the concluding Maiden. Wears a cross-noseband. *L. Bond — Stevenstone (Pen Bond).* 913 (OMa), 1435 (R).

CHASE THE MOON ..7-0.. 11 b.m. Super Sunrise — Bustle About (Bustino) p3pu45. Lengthy workmanlike owner-bred sister to Wakey Wakey. P-t-P '02/3 r8 p3 (2nds, of 3 twice); 5th of 6, unseated 1 and pulled up 3. Runner-up in three Maidens taking over seven minutes each, but not progressing, and beaten a minimum of 33 lengths in '04. Probably wrong and should be given a wide berth. *Miss D.M.M. Calder — Borders Bloodhounds.* 286 (CfMa), 549 (CMam), 659 (OMa), 919 (CMa), 1082 (OMa), 1422 (OMa).

CHASING BAILEY'S ..—.. 11 b.g. Neltino — Rosie Oh (Laurence O) p. Tall workmanlike half-brother to Oh So Vital, Oh No Rosie and Bentina. Dam won Maiden. NH '99/01 (for C. Grant) r8 p0; fell 2. Pulled up after bad blunders at the 14th and 15th on his first appearance for three years in a Restricted. Seems to be a martyr to physical problems and his legs and wind (tongue-tied once over Hurdles) both look dodgy. *Mrs S. Knowles — Suffolk (Helen Harris).* 398 (R).

CHASING BUTTERCUPS ..7-2§.. 7 b.m. Lyphento (USA) — Blue Breeze (USA) (Blue Times USA) 72p5r. Close-coupled owner-bred sister to Chasing Daisy, and half-sister to Golf Ball, Country Blue and Chasing Katie, and to a winner in Sweden. Dam won 5 flat, 12-15f, inc 3 Sells. Had a bad first season, and was beaten seven lengths in a match for a frosty Larkhill Maiden which was run at a crawl (her rival was subsequently three fences last and pulled up twice!). Not showing any desire to exert herself at present. *Mrs S. Hooper — Portman (John Dufosee).* 174 (OMa), 335 (OMa), 644 (OMa), 1133 (OMa), 1327 (OMa).

PLATE 29 438 Blue Square Dick Woodhouse HC, Wincanton: Chasing The Bride and Rilly Goschen), 1st, soar over the last open ditch PHOTO: Tim Holt

CHASING THE BRIDE ..10-12.. 12 b.g. Gildoran — Bride (Remainder Man) 2u1511. Compact owner-bred brother to Chasing A Bid, and half-brother to Chasing Charlie. Dam won at 12f, and won 2m Hdle at 50-1. P-t-P/HUNT CH '98/02 (for Mrs S. Hooper) r27 w8 (inc 2 Hunt Chses, 3m110y-3m1f110y, 4m Mixed Open, Mixed Open and Ladies) p10 (8 2nds, inc 4 Hunt Chses); fell/unseated 3, pulled up 2. Very much below par when last seen, and surprisingly had not scored since '00, but leased to a partnership run by Rilly Goschen on his return, and bounced back to something like his best with some shrewd placing. Skated up at Wincanton, and had taken the favourite's measure when left clear at Stratford next time, and whilst his early success were gained on easy surfaces he has matured into a lover of top-of-the-ground. A very genuine performer and it was good to see him overcome adversity. Wears a cross-noseband and has run tongue-tied, and previously had oxygen on standby after the finish. *The Florian Racing Partnership (Miss A. Goschen) — Blackmore & Sparkford V. (Rilly Goschen).* 33 (L), 140 (MO), 184 (L), 348 (3mH), 438 (3m1f110yH), 1029 (3mH).

CHATABIT .9-6.. 10 br.m. Henbit (USA) — Speakalone (Articulate) 4. Small half-sister to Gillone (*qv*). P-t-P '02/3 (for Mr A. Beedles & Mr W. Tuffin) r5 p1 (last of 3); 4th, last pair 2, and fell 1. Finished on the heels of a subsequent dual winning Chaser on her debut, but has been unable to reproduce that form in a handful of appearances since, and looks decidedly suspect now. Upside the eventual winner jumping the third-last on her return, but could not find an extra gear, and as in previous campaigns went missing subsequently. *M. Grange — Fitzwilliam (Michael Grange).* 409 (CMam).

CHATEAU BURF .9-4.. 9 ch.g. Cruise Missile — Headstrong Miss (Le Bavard FR) 23. Strong homebred half-brother to Burfords For Scrap. Dam won Irish NH flat. NH FLAT '02 (for D.G. Bridgwater) r2 p0. Tailed off in two bumpers in '02, but reappeared to finish five lengths second in an elders Maiden (gave a bucking bronco display leaving the paddock). Snatched second from Autcaesar Autnihil but disappointingly found nothing when they met again three weeks later, and was ten and a half lengths third behind him. Sweats up and has needed two paddock handlers, and seems a difficult ride, but there would probably be a weak Maiden for him if he co-operated. *M. Burford — Cotswold (Giles Smyly).* 981 (OMa), 1258 (OMa).

CHAUCERS MILLER ..9-13.. 9 ch.g. Baron Blakeney — Reine De Rosehill (Shack USA) ppf. Strong attractive half-brother to Brain Of Rosehill. Dam failed to finish in 4 of 7 Points for Hillary McCall. NH '01 r2 p0; pulled up 1. P-t-P '01/3 (for Mr H.M.F. McCall) r10 w3 (Maiden, Restricted and Members) p0 (10th, last pair 2, and pulled up 4). Well placed to win three bad races on firm ground in the previous ownership, but had looked moderate in more competitive events until falling two out when upsides the eventual winner on his latest appearance at Larkhill. His resulting absence does not bode well, and will need watching if he returns. *E.W. Smith — Beaufort (Richard Bryan).* 11 (O), 50 (I), 141 (I).

CHE GUEVARA ..9-7.. 7 b.g. Machiavellian (USA) — Girl From Ipanema (Salse USA) 2222. Tall rangy half-brother to flat winner, Ipanema Beach. Dam won 2 flat, 7-8f. 34000y. FLAT '01 r10 p1 (3rd). IRISH P-t-P '03 r3 p0 (5th of 6, and pulled up 2). IRISH NH '02 (for Lord Tyrone) r1 p0. Has had a busy career for a youngster, but placed only once in his first 14 attempts, when three-quarters of a length third of 16 on the flat. Not a fighter like his namesake, but has managed to plug into the runner-up spot in all four Points (favourite or second favourite each time). Often blinkered in the past, and regained a tongue-tie in his latest Maiden. His jumping is generally sound, and should plod home eventually (ought to try some trips to nearby Wales). *Miss J.E. Baker & J.R. Tuck — Beaufort (Jamie Tuck).* 364 (M), 618 (2m4fOMa), 926 (OMa), 1259 (OMa).

CHELSEA KING (IRE) ..9-5§.. 14 b.g. Riot Helmet — Chelsea Chick (London Bells CAN) u353. IRISH P-t-P 95, 97/8 and '00 r11 w1 (Maiden) p5 (3 2nds); pulled up 3, unseated 1. IRISH NH FLAT '95 r2 p0. IRISH HUNT CH '97/8 r3 p1 (3m1f Ch). IRISH NH '97/8 and '00/2 r19 w2 (2m6f-3m1f Chses) p2 (2 3rds). P-t-P '03 (for Mr E.H. Crow) r4 w1 (Club) p2 (last of 2; and last of 3); and 5th. Scoring for the first time since '00 when coaxed to victory by Richard Burton at Chaddesley Corbett last year, but ungenuine, and was a bad value favourite on his latest start. Does have the virtue of being ultra-safe, and has never fallen though Richard Garton managed to fall off him on his debut. Frequently blinkered in the past. *Mrs T. Garton — Cheshire Forest (Tim Garton).* 251 (C), 748 (M), 989 (Cnr), 1147 (Cnr).

CHELTENHAM (U) ..4-6.. 9 b.m. unknown 6. Cheltenham in January could not be further removed from the Festival in March. *The King's Troop RHA — R.A. (Neil Cross).* 84 (2m4fC).

CHEROKEE BOY ..9-1.. 13 gr.g. Mirror Boy — Cherry Side (General Ironside) 513542663. Tall attractive. Dam won 4 Points and placed 6 (inc 2 Hdles). NH '98/02 r28 w7 (3m1f110y-3m5f Chses) p8 (inc 6 2nds); pulled up 4 and refused 1. P-t-P '98 and '03 r10 w3 (Maiden, Restricted and Intermediate) p4 (3 3rds, of 4 once, and last twice); last pair 3. Recording his first success since '01 when left the amazingly fortunate winner at Milborne St Andrew, but plods very badly nowadays, and is easy to beat. Ultra-safe and has never fallen. Blinkered once in '98, and tried in cheekpieces last year. *The Atkinson Family (M. Atkinson) — Cattistock (Nicky Atkinson).* 115 (MO), 236 (Cnr), 276 (L), 351 (L), 687 (M), 862 (Cnr), 1101 (Cnr), 1250 (C), 1446 (Cf).

CHEROKEE RUN (IRE) ..10-2.. 11 b.g. Commanche Run — Hampton Grange (Boreen FR) 2p25742. Sturdy half-brother to Hurdles winner, Our Carol (IRE). Dam is half-sister to Carton (*qv* '99 Annual). P-t-P/HUNT CH '99/03 r31 w7 (inc 3m1f110y Hunt Ch and Mixed Open) p7 (4 2nds, last twice and of 3 once; 3 3rds, of 4 once); pulled up 7, and fell 2. Consistent in his grade and a sound jumper, and is happy to make the running, but easy to outpace nowadays and tends to sulk if things don't go his way. Suited by a sound surface and a right-handed circuit. Has run tongue-tied. *A.J. Tizzard & R.J. Bullock — Blackmore & Sparkford V. (Alan Tizzard).* 115 (MO), 178 (3m1f110yH), 350 (M), 602 (MO), 880 (MO), 1185 (MO), 1448 (L).

CHERRY GOLD ..10-11.. 11 b.g. Rakaposhi King — Merry Cherry (Deep Run) 4*u*18*f*. Workmanlike brother to Cherry Pie, and half-brother to Twelth Man and Cherrynut, to jumping winner, Cherry Dee, and to NH flat and Hurdles winner, Head For The Hills. P-t-P/HUNT CH '99/00 and '02/3 r17 w10 (inc 2 3m Hunt Chses and Open, hat-trick '03) p6 (2nds, last once); and 4th. NH '03 r4 w1 (3m Hdle) p2 (3rds). NH '04 r2 p0 (unseated in 3m Ch: *ld 2 til hdd & blun & ur 2 out*; and fell in 3m2f Ch: *ld to 9, 3rd when fell 13*). A smart Pointer who has been able to transfer his considerable ability to Hunter Chases, but nowhere near as infallible in them, and is frequently let down by his lack of fluency. Invariably makes all when successful, but has proved difficult to steer in the past, and never represents much in the way of value (nine times a beaten favourite). Has won in soft but seems ideally suited by a sound surface, and likely to find more opportunities under Rules where he can switch back to hurdling if needs be. *R.A. Mason — Glamorgan (Evan Williams).* 438 (3m1f110yH), 974 (3mH), 1172 (3m1f110yH).

CHESNUT WOOD ..9-11.. 11 ch.g. Tigerwood — Sally Haven (Haven) f321s. Small light-framed brother to Tiger Sally. Dam, half-sister to Lucky Rose (*qv* '94 Annual), won 2 Points and placed 7. Grandam, Trixy, pulled up in a Maiden. P-t-P/HUNT CH '00/3 r21 w3 (Maiden, Restricted and Confined) p7 (5 2nds, of 3 once; and inc 3rd of 4 once); fell/unseated 4, pulled up 2. Tough but clumsy, and predictably appreciated the extra weight off his back when making a successful debut in Ladies races at Ystradowen, where he was scoring for the third time. Thoroughly exposed, but stays well and has scored on firm and in softish, and well worth campaigning solely in 11st races in the Principality. *Miss H.E. Roberts — Llangeinor.* 447 (Cf), 698 (Inr), 739 (Inr), 1025 (L), 1187 (M).

CHICAGO CITY (IRE) ..10-2.. 12 br.g. Strong Gale — Orchardstown (Pollerton) 275f. Tall strong half-brother to Black Dante (IRE) (Hurdling winner since Pointing), and to Irish Pointing and Hurdles winner, Queenofclubs (IRE). Dam won 3 Irish Points. NH '97/01 (for J.T. Gifford) r22 w4 (2m-2m4f Chses) p5 (inc 4 in Hdles); pulled up 3, and fell 1. A decent Chaser at best until he went into a long hibernation, but his jumping was very much awry on his return, and inherited second only at the final fence when beaten about 100 lengths by Upham Lord at Fakenham. Unproven at beyond 2m4f, which is perhaps why he did not try Points. Reported to have had a breathing problem in the past. *Mr & Mrs S.N. Embiricos — Chid, Lec & Cowdray (Nick Gifford).* 242 (2m5f110yH), 348 (3mH), 545 (2m3f110yH), 1029 (3mH).

CHICAGO'S MADAM ..—.. 7 b.m. Tuam — Woven Gold (No Lute FR) pp. Small half-sister to My Sister Lucy. Got no further than the tenth in Maidens, and her jumping left a very great deal to be desired. *A. Gould — Bicester with Whaddon (Bradley Clarke).* 929 (2m4fOMa), 1119 (CMam).

CHICAGO'S PADRE ..8-0.. 7 b.g. Tuam — Garden Gate (IRE) (Don't Forget Me) pp3p3p. Small light. Can show early speed, but often wastes energy by pulling hard, and does not get the trip in consequence. His two thirds were acquired by default, as only one horse finished behind him. *A.J. Gould — Bicester with Whaddon (Bradley Clarke).* 173 (OMa), 295 (OMa), 619 (2m4fOMa), 850 (2m5fOMa), 1233 (OMa), 1402 (2m4fOMa).

CHIEF GALE (IRE) .—§.. 13 b.g. Strong Gale — Distant Lady (Buckskin FR) 2p. Tall workmanlike half-brother to Native Spin (IRE). Dam, half-sister to Summer Meadows (*qv* '93 Annual), won mares Maiden in Ireland, and 2 Chses (2m4f-3m) in England - all wins at 8, after having had both foals. IRISH NH '99 r1 p1 (3rd in Ch). NH FLAT '96 r4 p2. NH '96/99 r19 w1 (2m110y Nov Ch) p8 (3 2nds); pulled up 2. P-t-P '02/3 r6 p1 (last of 3); pulled up 3, and fell 2. Tried in headgear before gaining his solitary success in a bad four-runner Chase at Newton Abbot in '98, but beaten 19 times since, and has failed to beat a rival in the current yard. Becoming increasingly awkward at the start, and would not consent to break into a gallop at Trecoed. *Mrs M.B. Stephens — Carms.* 1519 (M), 1551 (L).

CHIEF MOUSE ..—.. 12 b.g. Be My Chief (USA) — Top Mouse (High Top) pp. Compact well-made half-brother to Last Of The Mice, to jumping winner, Die Fledermaus (IRE), to Irish NH flat and Pointing winner, Shere, and to 5 flat winners (2 abroad), including Pertemps FC. FRENCH FLAT '00 r2 p0. FRENCH NH '00 r5 p1. FLAT '95/7 and '99 r8 w1 (8f) p0. NH '96/02 (for Miss H.C. Knight, F.T. Jordan, I. Williams, and B.D. Leavy) r46 w9 (6 2m-2m4f Hdles and 3 2-3m Chses) p11; pulled up 4, and unseated 1. Sold Doncaster, Oct '02 for 800. An old monkey, but clever enough to win ten races (one on the all-weather) to July '00, including a hat-trick in '97. Also short-headed once, and was third in his only Selling Hurdle. One of the first English horses to score in cheekpieces, and has also been tongue-tied (was making a noise way back in '97) and blinkered. The sorriest of spectacles with his gormless partner in Hunter Chases, and should never have been taken to the racecourse. *J.E. Price — Suffolk.* 490 (3m2fH), 628 (2m3fH).

CHIEF OF JUSTICE ..9-10.. 8 b.g. Be My Chief (USA) — Clare Court (Glint Of Gold) 0. Strong half-brother to flat winner in Italy. Dam won 3 flat, 8-14f (and placed in 6 of her 7 other races, inc 2nd in £20,000 event final). FLAT '99/02 r17 w2 (11-12f) p4. P-t-P/HUNT CH '03 (for Mr J.C. Fretwell) r2 p0 (4th, and pulled up). Gained both flat successes on the all-weather, but presumably thought unlikely to get the trip in Points, and has made mistakes when well beaten in both sub-3m Hunter Chase efforts. *Mrs L.J. Young — Eggesford.* 241 (2m4f110yH).

CHIEF PREDATOR (USA) ..9-10§.. 11 ch.g. Chief's Crown (USA) — Tsavorite (USA) (Halo USA) 6u324321. Small half-brother to 3 winners in USA. FLAT r16 p5. NH '98/00 r30 w2 (2m-3m2f Hdles, the first a Sell) p4. P-t-P/HUNT CH '01/3 r15 w1 (Confined) p10 (5 2nds, of 3 once; 5 3rds, of 4 once); unseated 1. Moody and does not always respond to pressure, but stays well and is usually doing his best work in the closing stages. Collared the runner-up (whose rider thought he had won and duly celebrated with much arm-waving) in the shadows of the post at Bonvilston, but the long odds-on favourite was in command when slipping up turning for home, and usually prefers to settle for a placing. Predictably good at looking after number one, and has never fallen. Acts on any going. Has been tried in all types of headgear, but never successfully. *Mrs I.E.M. Hussey — Tredegar F. (Deborah Faulkner).* 359 (Cf), 448 (O), 672 (O), 841 (Cf), 1090 (Cf), 1355 (3m1fH), 1481 (M), 1537 (C).

CHIEF SEATTLE (IRE) ..9-4.. 7 b.g. Glacial Storm (USA) — Jubilaire (Gala Performance) pp3u. Half-brother to Anita's Son and Irish Hurdling and English Chasing winner, Mr Conductor. His four lengths third at Overton was reasonable, but gave a poor display next time (would have finished about 25 lengths last of four had the jockey not been unseated at the final fence). Not a proficient jumper so far, and stronger handling is worth a try. *R.H. Goldie — Cumberland F.* 433 (OMa), 553 (CfMa), 658 (OMa), 1081 (OMa).

CHIEF SUSPECT (IRE) ..8-11§.. 13 b.g. Yashgan — Clerihan Miss (Tarqogan) 36p334pp. Compact. Dam is half-sister to Paddy's Pond (*qv* '95 Annual). NH '00 r2 p0; last and fell. P-t-P/HUNT CH '02/3 r14 w1 (Maiden) p4 (3 2nds; and remote last of 3 once); 7th, last pair 2, fell/unseated 3, pulled up 2 and slipped up 1. Landed a weak Maiden in the slowest time of the day on firmish at Badbury Rings last year, but has never looked a natural over fences, and looks totally disinterested now. *Staverton Owners Group (M. Blake) — Avon V. (Michael Blake).* 15 (R), 65 (Rnr), 265 (R), 337 (R), 473 (R), 1094 (R), 1184 (R), 1491 (R).

CHIEF WALLAH .—§.. 9 b.g. Be My Chief (USA) — Arusha (IRE) (Dance Of Life USA) p. Good-topped half-brother to NH flat winner, Armageddon. Dam won 8f race at 2 and is half-sister 2000 Guineas winner, Don't Forget Me. FLAT '99/01 r10 p1 (2nd). NH '01 r2 p0. P-t-P '03 r1 p0 (pulled up). Frequently missed the break when racing out of stalls, and was an under-achiever on the flat, but has shown no aptitude for jumping and would be most unlikely to stay three miles in any case. Blinkered twice in '01. *R. Hancox — N. Ledbury.* 1258 (OMa).

CHINA LAL .9-7.. 13 b.m. Rakaposhi King — Doris Blake (Roscoe Blake) 09535. Very small owner-bred sister to Blacon Point, and half-sister to Mosscroft Jack. Dam, sister to Old Brig (*qv* '00 Annual), was 3rd in a Hunt Ch (in '95) and a Point (also disqualified from 2nd in a Point). NH '97 r1 p0. P-t-P/ HUNT CH '97/00 and '02/3 r28 w3 (Maiden, Restricted and Intermediate) p8 (4 2nds); brought down 1, unseated 3, and pulled up 6. Only modest but a sound jumper for one so small, and was recording her first successes since '99 when completing a double in April '03. Outclassed and tends not to get the trip too well in Ladies races, and will be difficult to place successfully again. Has been tried in a near-side pricker. *J.S. Swindells — Cheshire.* 5 (L), 529 (L), 873 (Cf), 1146 (L), 1551 (L).

CHISM (IRE) ..9-8§.. 14 br.g. Euphemism — Melody Gayle VII (unknown) uRfp3733. Sturdy half-brother to jumping winner, The Full Monty (IRE). P-t-P/HUNT CH '96/03 r45 w7 (inc 2m5f Hunt Ch, and Mixed Open) p13 (7 2nds, inc 6 Hunt Chses; inc 3rd of 4 twice); pulled up 7, ran out 1. A very frustrating individual who has not consented to score since landing a 2m5f Hunter Chase at Wincanton in '99, and retains more ability than he normally cares to reveal. Came perilously close to ending his losing sequence on his latest outing, but typically came off worst in a three-way finish, and continues to deteriorate with age. A sound jumper, but even his exemplary technique was not enough for the formidable fences at Milborne St Andrew where he suffered the first tumble of his long career. Has been tried in headgear, and with a tongue-tie. *Mrs S. King — S. Dorset (Richard King).* 11 (O), 89 (O), 233 (M), 471 (O), 969 (Cnr), 1101 (Cnr), 1329 (Cnr), 1383 (Cnr).

CHITA'S FLORA ..—.. 6 gr.m. Alflora (IRE) — Chita's Cone (Celtic Cone) p. Dam won 5 Points and placed 6 for I. Ham (*qv* '97 Annual). Tailed off and pulled up three out at Holnicote in February. Has an ideal pedigree, so perhaps she can do much better in time. *I.M. Ham & Mrs S.M. Francis — Weston & Banwell H. (Caroline Keevil).* 275 (CfMa).

CHOC .9-13.. 11 gr.g. Zambrano — Cisterce (Impecunious) 1. Angular brother to Zam Bam. Dam won PPOA novice riders (bad race, 25-1) and 2nd. P-t-P '00/3 r14 w2 (2 Members) p7 (5 2nds, remote of 3 once; and inc 3rd of 4); 6th twice, last and unseated 2. Sound jumping has enabled him to gain an annual success since '02, but generally easy to beat in competitive events, and presumably met with a setback following his Larkhill win in January. Works on the beach at Weston, but rather than being a mud-lover all of his wins have been gained on good or sound surfaces. *Mrs V. & E. Kenney-Herbert — Mendip F. (Venetia Kenney-Herbert).* 15 (R).

CHOICE CUT (IRE) ..8-6.. 12 b.g. Tirol — Lancette (Double Jump) 0p. Workmanlike half-brother to Desert Calm (IRE), and to several flat winners, including Darcy's Thatcher and Rasa Penang (both useful). NH FLAT '98 r4 p2 (3rds). NH '98/00 r10 w1 (3m110y Hdle) p3. HUNT CH '03 (for Mr M.J. Caldwell) r1 p0 (pulled up). Gained his only success in a Maiden Hurdle at Uttoxeter in '99, but clearly ailing when beaten a minimum of 36 lengths in just a handful of races since, and dropped dead in the box-park after pulling up at Hutton Rudby. *H.J. Pickersgill — Bilsdale.* 389 (Cf), 564 (L).

CHO POLU (IRE) ..9-13.. 8 ch.g. Un Desperado (FR) — Rainbow Alliance (IRE) (Golden Love) 2. Leggy compact. Dam won Maiden in Ireland. IR27,000 4yo. NH FLAT '02 r1 p0. NH '02/3 (for P.J. Hobbs) r5 p3 (2nds). Beaten between four lengths and six lengths in his three Hurdling seconds, but was disappointing, and wore blinkers on his final two attempts. Partnered by Julian Pritchard and sent off even money favourite in a Maiden on the second day of the season, but beaten by a 37-year old on his first winner, and failed to reappear. Can look a tricky ride, but as the third and fourth (15 lengths and 30 lengths behind respectively) went on to score there should certainly be a Maiden for him if he is fit. *M.J. Tuckey — Bicester with Whaddon (Tom Illsley).* 21 (OMa).

CHORAL DREAM (IRE) ..10-3.. 8 b.g. Yashgan — Daisy's Dream (Paddy's Stream) 641213. Well-made attractive. IRISH P-t-P '02/3 r5 w2 (6yo Maiden, and Open) p0; last, pulled up and carried out. Bought Doncaster, Aug 29,000. Made a bad start to the season and looked like proving an expensive flop, but got his act together when winning a Confined at Brafield-on-the-Green by 30 lengths, and followed a second behind Cantarinho in an Open with a rather scrambling defeat with a 12-year-old in similar company at Mollington. Surprisingly not partnered by the owner until his final start, but jumped as well for him as for anybody, and appeared to finish four lengths second over four miles at Dingley (the judge begged to differ). No world beater, but there should be other races for him at the right level. *R.S. Hunnisett — Pytchley (Caroline Bailey).* 34 (O), 125 (O), 466 (Cf), 650 (O), 1032 (O), 1216 (4m100yMO).

CHRISTY BEAMISH (IRE) ..10-9.. 8 br.g. Jolly Jake (NZ) — Ballinatona Bridge (Black Minstrel) 11. Smallish rather unfurnished. P-t-P '03 r2 w1 (Maiden) p0; and 4th of 5. Given a blatant school on his debut, but unbeaten in three appearances since, and clearly has Hunter Chase aspirations. Ridden for a turn of foot that has been readily produced to date, but like many of his trainers' charges has been very lightly raced, and has been kept to ground as close to perfect as possible. Has access to the leading riders, and as he has yet to come off the bridle could still be underrated by several pounds, and must continue to be followed. *M.T. Mann — N. Ledbury (Paul Jones).* 383 (R), 728 (I).

CHUNITO ..8-3.. 10 b.g. Beveled (USA) — Wasimah (Caerleon USA) 3p. Small half-brother to 2 flat winners, including Bedazzle. Dam won 2 5f races. FLAT '97/8 r10 p2 (3rds). NH '98/01 and '03 r15 p1 (2nd); pulled up 2. Blinkered once on the flat and unable to score even at Selling level over Hurdles, and his Pointing placing consisted of a 36 lengths third. Missed '02, and may have gone wrong again. *D.M. Lloyd — Llangeinor.* 203 (CfMa), 362 (CfMa).

CHURCHILL (U) ..3-13.. 9 br.g. unknown 7. P-t-P '02 r1 p0; 8th. Unlikely to ever give his rivals a two-fingered salute, but stepped up on his previous efforts in the Gunners' race, and improved his rating by no less than 27lb as a result (still did'nt reach the 4st range). *The King's Troop RHA — R.A. (Neil Cross).* 84 (2m4fC).

CIDER MAN ..10-8.. 10 b.g. Romany Rye — Champagne Peri (The Malster) 2. Tall home-bred half-brother to Alcofrolic and Champagne Thunder. Dam won 3 Points and 3rd. Grandam, Rockscope, was brought down in a Members. P-t-P '00 and '02/3 r10 w2 (2m4f Maiden and Restricted) p3 (2 2nds); pulled up 2, fell 2. Speedy and races with plenty of enthusiasm, but dogged by problems associated with sore shins, and averages fewer than three outings a year. Lost no caste in defeat on his only appearance in '04, but has also been heard to make a noise, and his physical troubles seem insurmountable. Suited by good or sound surfaces which exacerbate the problem. Wears a cross-noseband. *Mrs J. Hughes — Ledbury.* 255 (CCon).

CIMARRONE COVE (IRE) .10-8§.. 10 gr.g. Roselier (FR) — Sugarstown (Sassafras FR) 6fp6u2. Compact brother to Ossmoses (IRE) and to Chasing winner, Majors Legacy (IRE). Dam won 2m Hurdle in Ireland. NH FLAT '99 r1 p1 (2nd). NH '99/03 (for M. Pitman, and N.J. Henderson) r21 w3 (3m2f Hdle and 2 3m Chses) p5; pulled up 3, fell 2. Bought Doncaster, May 10,500. Won three races in the mud to December '00, but has always been unreliable, and his jumping gets him into trouble on occasions. Produced nothing worthwhile until his final two starts in '04, but then unseated three out at Hexham when in front and apparently still going well enough, and outbattled when three and a half lengths second over 3m7f at Huntingdon. Often wears headgear, including blinkers which fell over his eyes and caused him a great deal of consternation when he was running loose at Towcester. Still capable of ending his long losing sequence if he felt the urge. *The Grand National Racing Club Limited (D. Easterby) — Middleton (Mick Easterby).* 348 (3mH), 437 (3m1fH), 630 (2m4fH), 772 (4m1fO), 1179 (3m1fH), 1362 (3m6f110yH).

CIMMAROON (IRE) ..10-4.. 6 b.g. Synefos (USA) — Bayalika (FR) (Kashtan FR) 411p33131. Very small light half-brother to Un Jour A Vassy (FR), and to Chasing winner, Royale De Vassy (FR). An admirably tough little five-year-old who was in action from the first day of the season until the penultimate, and would have scored five times had he not fallen at the last at Bratton Down once (remounted). All his form is on good or firm surfaces, and looked to flounder in soft when disappointing once. Kept to the easiest opportunities so far, but some of his times suggest that he would be well up to Opens, and it would be no surprise to see him tried with success in staying Hurdles. A credit to connections. *B.A. Kilpatrick — Taunton V.H. (David Pipe).* 8 (2m4fOMa), 68 (OMa), 314 (R), 573 (I), 963 (Cf), 1129 (I), 1445 (M), 1508 (I), 1555 (I).

PLATE 30 963 Taunton Vale Intermediate: L to R, Cimmaroon (Ashley Farrant), 3rd, leads Gotha (Martin Sweetland), 6th, and Ellofamonkey (Richard Woollacott), 2nd PHOTO: Brian Armstrong

CITY GENT ..9-13.. 11 b.g. Primitive Rising (USA) — Classy Lassy (Class Distinction) p5u54. Strong compact home-bred. NH FLAT '98 r2 p0. NH '98/03 r32 w2 (2m-2m1f110y Chses) p6; pulled up 1. P-t-P/HUNT CH '99 and '03 (for Mr J. McGuinness) r6 p2 (2nds); last 2, unseated 1 and pulled up 1. Goes a good gallop, and usually makes the running, but a weak finisher, and has never looked likely to get home over three miles. Error prone and still in front when pitching the owner out of the saddle at the fifth-last in his Members, but the lengthening of his home track will be detrimental to his chances of a successful retrieval mission in '05. Has been tried in a tongue-strap and blinkers, and wore cheekpieces once last year. *Mrs E. Heaton — Cheshire Forest.* 228 (Cf), 712 (L), 748 (M), 1263 (L), 1342 (O).

CITY STANDARD (IRE) ..—§§.. 9 b.g. Rainbow Quest (USA) — City Fortress (Troy) 7. Lengthy unfurnished half-brother to flat and Hurdling winner, City Hall (IRE), and to several other winners here and abroad (some very useful) including Oriental Express (IRE) (English flat, subsequently won nearly £1,500,000 in Hong Kong). Dam won 2 10f races in France. FLAT '99/00 r8 p2 (3rds). NH '01/3 (for R. Williams, and M.F. Harris) r6 p0; pulled up 3. Has a star-studded pedigree, and was once sent to race at Cagnes-Sur-Mer, but has been on a long downward spiral, and followed three pulled ups over hurdles with a 90 lengths last in a Maiden (wore cheekpieces; previously visored once). Tends to hang violently as he did at Chaddesley. The owner has some depressingly bad animals, and needs a clearout. *Clock House Racing (A. Gould) — Bicester with Whaddon (Bradley Clarke).* 259 (CMa).

CIVIL GENT (IRE) ..10-4.. 6 ch.g. Flying Spur (AUS) — Calamity Kate (IRE) (Fairy King USA) 3312132. Compact. Dam placed 7th in Irish flat. 1000 3yo. NH '02/3 (for M.E. Sowersby) r4 p0; pulled up 1, fell 1. Beaten 66 lengths plus twice, pulled up and fell at odds of between 100-1 and 150-1 over Hurdles (was a moderate jumper), but much more adept in Points, and did not run a bad race all term. Lacks acceleration, but his two and a quarter lengths third in an Open is a good effort for a five-year old, and should maintain a similar level of success at six. *J. Payne — Blankney (Mary Sowersby).* 596 (2m5fOMa), 773 (2m4fCMa), 958 (OMa), 1162 (R), 1304 (CR), 1414 (O), 1500 (Cf).

CLAIRE'S NOMAD ..10-5.. 9 b.g. Nomadic Way (USA) — Clairet (Sagaro) p311p1. Small light brother to Three Way Split, and half-brother to Primitive Charles. Dam was 2nd in Hdle; and won 2 Points and 3rd. NH '02 r1 p0 (6th in Hdle). P-t-P '02/3 r13 w1 (Maiden) p2 (3rds, of 4 once); 4th twice, last 2, pulled up 3, ran out 2 and brought down. Most destructive in his debut season, and took a long while for the penny to drop, but has since forged a fine understanding with Rachel Clark. Forced to pull out all the stops in order to secure his Members, but would not have dreamt of co-operating on such a scale in previous years, and could win again if his current mood extends to '05. Makes the odd mistake, and appeared not to stay in the Grimthorpe, but is effective on all but extremes of going. Wears a cross-noseband and cheekpieces, and has been tried in a nosenet. *R.D. Jones — York & Ainsty S. (Liz Clark).* 109 (CR), 164 (R), 301 (R), 477 (Cnr), 772 (4m1fO), 1157 (M).

CLARE'S MEMORY ..—.. 7 br.m. Afzal — Forest Stone (Town And Country) fp. Small light. Dam won 10 Points (inc 4 Confineds, one on technicality) and placed 7 for the Francomes. P-t-P '03 r4 p0 (pulled up 4). Certainly appears to have inherited her dam's error prone nature, and after a vaguely promising debut has become bitterly disappointing, but stopped in the manner of a horse with a physical fault having been dropped right out at Ston Easton and has not been seen since. Wears a cross-noseband. *R.J. Francome — Beaufort (Sylvia Francome).* 53 (2m4fOMa), 600 (2m4fOMa).

CLARICE STARLING ..9-7.. 7 b.m. Saddlers' Hall (IRE) — Uncharted Waters (Celestial Storm USA) 3pp22. Lengthy half-sister to flat winners, Establishment and Land'n Stars. Dam won 2 flat, 10-11f. FLAT '01/3 (for C.A. Cyzer) r8 p0. Sold Ascot, Feb for 1238. No use on the flat (mostly on the all-weather), but managed to plug into three placings in West Wales Maidens (was behind Wiston Wizo once; and only five ran twice). Her jumping tended to be poor, and her current rating flatters her. Might run a bit faster if connections shouted that Hannibal Lector was after her. *L.J. Bridge — Llangeinor (Nikki Hughes).* 948 (OMa), 1239 (OMa), 1323 (CfMa), 1524 (OMam), 1550 (OMa).

CLARKY'S CHOICE (IRE) ..9-6.. 9 b.g. Supreme Leader — Galmoy Girl (Quayside) fppf2p. Compact. Dam, half-sister to Farnworth (*qv* '95 Annual) won 2 2m Hdles in Ireland. NH FLAT r2 p0. P-t-P '02 (for Mr J. Dwyer) r1 p0 (last). Generally let down by poor jumping in Welsh Maidens, and was destroyed when second-favourite to win one at Rhydygwern. C.H. Warner — Pembs (Beverley Thomas). 452 (R), 674 (R), 736 (CfMa), 1067 (OMa), 1193 (OMa), 1488 (OMa).

CLASSIC FABLE (IRE) ..9-0.. 13 b.m. Lafontaine (USA) — Rathmill Syke (True Song) 24p2p3. Small compact owner-bred. Dam, half-sister to Halfsharp (*qv* '99 Annual). NH FLAT '98 r1 p0. NH '00/2 r12 p0; pulled up 4, fell/unseated 2. An impetuous little mare who often front-runs and does her best to keep going, but woefully short of stamina, and has been unruly at the start and frequently had mishaps in the past (broke a blood vessel once). Has tried Selling Hurdles, and was a very distant last, pulled up thrice and unseated twice in Chases. Crept into the frame in four placings in Points, but was last in two of them and last but one once. Like the family stick, has been handed down for the Hanly's to chew on, and was ridden by father Pat on her debut in '98 and by son Andy in '04. *J.L. Needham — Ludlow.* 517 (CfMa), 834 (M), 1173 (2m110yH), 1340 (OMa), 1488 (OMa), 1553 (OMa).

CLASSIC MAID .—.. 6 b.m. Classic Cliche (IRE) — Maid To Match (Matching Pair) p. Dam, sister to Butlers Match (*qv* '03 Annual), won Irish Point and placed 4, and won 6 Points (inc 5 Ladies) and placed 2 for Helen Mobley. Her jumping was well below standard on her debut, but attractively bred, and may be able to do better when the penny drops. *Mrs H. Mobley — Grafton (Jeff Tredwell).* 1119 (CMam).

CLASS OF NINETYTWO (IRE) ..10-3.. 16 b.g. Lancastrian — Lothian Lassie (Precipice Wood) 3562322. Good-topped rangy half-brother to Precipice Run and Lothian Magic (IRE), and to Irish NH flat and Hurdles winner, Lothian Buckskin. IRISH NH FLAT '93 r5 p0. IRISH NH '93 r3 p0. IRISH P-t-P '95 r5 w3 (up to Winners of One) p1 (2nd); and fell 1. NH '95/9 r13 w5 (3m-3m3f Chses) p3 (inc 3rd in '96 4m NH Ch). P-t-P/HUNT CH '00/3 r23 w5 (3m110y Hunt Ch, Open and 3 Ladies) p11 (8 2nds, inc 2 Hunt Chses, last once; also disqualified from 2nd once; and inc 3rd in Hunt Ch); pulled up 3. Stays forever and retains plenty of ability for a veteran, but loses interest if unable to dominate, and has long since lost the ability to quicken. Rejuvenated by present connections, and owes them nothing, but it would have been nice if he had been able to resist Dancetillyoudrop's last gasp challenge at Tabley. Has been tried in headgear and spurs, and tongue-tied once in '01. *J.E. Stockton, A. Wynne, A. Mower, M. Williams & C. Oare — Sir W.W. Wynn's (Steve Wynne).* 230 (L), 407 (L), 712 (L), 987 (L), 1046 (L), 1203 (L), 1428 (L).

CLAUDE (IRE) ..—.. 7 b.g. Hamas (IRE) — Tigora (Ahonoora) pp. Tall half-brother to flat and Hurdles winner, Maradi (IRE). FLAT '02 r1 p0 (tailed off). NH FLAT '02 r1 p0 (tailed off). P-t-P '03 (for Mr B.V. Nuttall) r1 p0 (pulled up). Too slow under Rules, but has made mistakes and looked short of stamina in Points, and his future as a racehorse looks bleak. *The Lucky Ross Syndicate (B. Holt) — Belvoir (Antonia Bealby).* 112 (OMa), 303 (OMa).

CLAYWALLS .—.. 14 b.g. Meadowbrook — Lady Manello (Mandrake Major) p9p. Smallish lengthy half-brother to Miss Royello and Having A Party. Dam, half-sister to Bavington (*qv* '01 Annual), refused in 2 of 5 Points for Ann Hamilton, but was placed in 2 Hurdles for her. NH '98/9 r3 p0 (4th, 7th and last in Chses). P-t-P '96/7, '99/00 and '02 (for Mr S.H. & Mrs P.M. Shirley-Beavan) r23 w3 (Maiden, Restricted and Members) p8 (3 2nds, beaten neck once, and last once; and 4 3rds, last once); pulled up 1. A patent safety with an exemplary jumping record, but lightly raced and has managed to win only one race since '97, and appears to have suffered yet another setback. *The Maylam Family (A.C. Maylam) — E. Kent (Olivia Maylam).* 99 (I), 182 (CCon), 897 (Cfv&nr).

C L B JEMILLA ..9-0.. 12 ch.m. Lord Bud — Comarch (Ancient Monro) 65038. Very small sister to Elliott The Butler, and half-sister to Gudasmum and Honeyfantastic. Dam, half-sister to Comzan (*qv* '95 Annual), won 9 Points (inc 6 Opens) and placed 23 (inc 3 Hunt Chses) for Pam Wright, and grandam, Compro, won Maiden and placed 7 (inc 3rd in flat race and Sell Hdle) for her. NH FLAT '98 r1 p0 (remote 14th of 15). P-t-P '99/03 (for Mrs P.P. Wright) r24 w1 (Maiden) p6 (2 2nds); pulled up 1, fell/unseated 2. Won a poor Maiden at Hutton Rudby and finished third in a Ladies in '00, but regularly trounced in Restricteds since, and considering her lack of inches must find 11st9lb a real impost. Re-deployed as a schoolmistress in '04 and did an admirable job. *Miss G.T. Craggs — Tynedale.* 855 (R), 1040 (R), 1222 (R), 1310 (R), 1476 (R).

CLEAR AWAY (IRE) ..9-11.. 8 b.g. Clearly Bust — Twinkle Bright (USA) (Star De Naskra USA) p1. Small good-bodied. Dam won 7f race in Ireland. IR5200 3yo. IRISH P-t-P '02 r1 p1 (3rd). NH '02 (for P.G. Murphy) r1 p0. 52 lengths third in his Irish Point, and pulled up after 2m4f in a Welsh Restricted, but made no mistake when the money was down in a Bonvilston Maiden, in which he beat two other finishers by huge margins to land a punt from 5-1 to 5-4. It would be surprising if he could not follow up in better company. *A. & Mrs J. Lowrie — Glamorgan (Abbi Johns).* 1095 (R), 1324 (CfMa).

CLEAR BLUE WATER (IRE) ..—.. 12 b.g. Dancing Dissident (USA) — Fair Song (Pitskelly) p. Close-coupled half-brother to Irish flat winner, Alexander Confrance. IRISH FLAT '95, '97/8 and '00 r15 p2. IRISH NH '97/8 and '00/2 (for W.M. Roper) r18 w1 (2m Hdle) p0; fell 2, pulled up 1. Including long absences, his career has dragged on for ten years, and gained a sole success in a Ballinrobe Hurdle in September '97. Tongue-tied in Ireland. When he pulled up after two miles at Maisemore it stretched his unplaced sequence to 23. *W. John Day — Gelligaer F. (Lisa Day).* 727 (MO).

CLEOPATRA (U) .5-6.. 10 b.m. unknown u. P-t-P '01/2 r2 p1 (2nd); and 4th. Made the frame in two previous assaults on the Gunners' race, but partnered by a novice girl when second-favourite in the latest renewal, and she was bounced out of the plate at halfway. Possibly a tricky ride — like her namesake. *The King's Troop RHA — R.A. (Neil Cross).* 84 (2m4fC).

CLEVER DICKIE ..8-12.. 10 b.g. Rakaposhi King — Whew (Ginger Boy) 232. Plain good-topped. P-t-P '02/3 r5 p2 (2nds); pulled up and fell/unseated 2. Runner-up in four Maidens when beaten a maximum of six lengths, and theoretically good enough to go one better, but a weak finisher, and no more proficient at jumping than he was three years ago. Favourite in his last four attempts, and those who play the exchanges make fortunes on the likes of him. *G.C. Evans — Ludlow.* 840 (OMa), 1232 (OMa), 1395 (OMa).

PLATE 31 814 Bedale Open Maiden (Div 2): Clever Fella and Nick Tinkler are clear at the last
PHOTO: Roy Parker

CLEVER FELLA ..9-11.. 6 ch.g. Elmaamul (USA) — Festival Of Magic (USA) (Clever Trick USA) 31. Half-brother to Irish flat and Hurdles winner, Afrostar (IRE), and to flat winner, Ratified. Dam won 8f race on all-weather. NH FLAT '03 (for M. Dods) r1 p0. Eight lengths third over 2m4f at Hornby Castle in February, and appreciated the extra half mile when returning there in April, when he needed plenty of driving before justifying support from 7-2 to 11-8. Doubtless helped by the late withdrawal of Nought To Ninety because of rider injury, but probably has further improvement in him. *Mrs K. Walton — W. of Yore.* 342 (2m4fOMa), 814 (OMa).

CLIFFORD BAY (IRE) ..10-7.. 11 b.g. Phardante (FR) — Calfstown Night (Bargello) 2111. Tall half-brother to Gortroe Guy (IRE) (*qv*). NH '98/9 r3 p0. P-t-P '00 and '02/3 r8 w4 (Club Maiden, Restricted, Members and Intermediate) p3 (3 3rds, of 4 once, and last once). Lightly raced and soon dispensed with by two previous handlers, but has developed into a smart Pointer for Nicola Stirling despite not being the easiest to handle (and having to be roughed off with sore shins in '03). Tends to get wound up in the paddock where he has two handlers, and takes a keen hold, but can maintain a strong gallop for well over seven minutes and looks well worth trying in a Hunter Chase. Unlikely to be risked on firmish again, but virtually all his winning form is on easy surfaces in any case. Wears a cross-noseband. *Mrs P.C. Stirling — Lauderdale (Nicola Stirling).* 426 (Cf), 552 (Cf), 915 (Cf), 1308 (L).

CLOAK AND DAGGER ..—.. 12 b.g. Broadsword (USA) — Night Pry (Pry) ppp. Neat half-brother to Nearly Dark. Dam, half-sister to Kingfisher Blues (*qv* 2000 Annual), won 3 Points consecutively at Siddington and 2nd for Sheena Pilkington, and was previously placed in 4 Irish Points (also won one, but disqualified after failing a dope test). P-t-P '99/03 r12 w1 (Maiden) p1 (remote 2nd of 3); 6th, 9th, last pair 3, and pulled up 5. Won a weak Maiden at Garthorpe in his debut season, but beaten a minimum of 32 lengths since, and appears to register one setback after another. Went wrong again at Mollington and has surely reached the end of the road. *Miss S. Pilkington — Berks & Bucks.* 50 (I), 169 (R), 294 (R).

CLODAGH VALLEY (IRE) ..9-11.. 10 b.g. Doubletour (USA) — Raise A Princess (USA) (Raise A Native) pp1272. Compact attractive half-brother to 2 flat winners (one in Ireland). Dam dead-heated for 2nd in 5f race in Ireland, but was awarded dead-heat for first after disqualification. IRISH FLAT '99/00 r6 p0. IRISH NH FLAT '99/00 r5 p1 (3rd). IRISH NH '00 r5 p0. P-t-P/HUNT CH '02/3 r8 p1 (2nd); last, pulled up 5, and unseated 1. Pulled up in seven of his previous ten starts, and changes yards on a regular basis, but easily proved good enough to land a bad two-finisher Maiden at Whittington. Put up more meritorious performances in defeat subsequently, and now that he has a clean bill of health (was coughing in early '04) might be able to go one better in a Restricted. Appears to stay well and is suited by an easy surface. *R.J. Hewitt — Flint & Denbigh (Peter Morris).* 113 (OMa), 710 (Mah), 877 (OMa), 1048 (R), 1265 (R), 1345 (R).

CLOIGEANN RUA (IRE) ..—.. 12 ch.m. Glacial Storm (USA) — Cool Amanda (Prince Hansel) p. Half-sister to Captain Lowe, Earl Hansel, Auspiciousoccasion, Buck And Skip and Prince Amanda, and to NH flat and jumping winner, Guido (IRE). IR1650 4yo. IRISH P-t-P '98/9 r5 p1 (3rd); pulled up 1, fell 2. NH FLAT '99 r3 p0. NH '01 r5 p0 (pulled up 4, and unseated). Consistently terrible, at odds of up to 300-1. Can pull hard as she did at Whitwell (wore a cross-noseband and was sweating badly), but in nine attempts over fences she has completed only once (on the floor three times) and was pulled up and unseated in Hurdles. Tongue-tied once in the past. *Mrs K. Woodhead — Bilsdale (Eddie Caine).* 776 (CfMa).

CLONSHIRE PADDY (IRE) ..10-4§.. 9 gr.g. Roselier (FR) — Gusserane Princess (Paddy's Stream) 461p341p. Strong-topped brother to Mr Pickpocket, and to jumping winner, Ballystone (IRE), and half-brother to Overheard, and to Irish Pointing winner, Kyle Cailin. NH FLAT '00 r2 p0. NH '00/3 (for C. Grant) r14 p4 (inc 2 Chses up to 3m1f); fell/unseated 3. Combines boundless stamina with limited enthusiasm, and there is no telling which way he is going to run. Plugged past some feeble opposition to take a Novice Riders Restricted for Jacqueline Coward at Charm Park, but had tailed himself off after a mile next time. Followed a creditable third in the Grimthorpe with another downer but Thomas Greenall gave him a fine ride in the 4-mile Mixed Open at Dingley before he flopped over an even longer trip at Uttoxeter. Fell or unseated in three of six Chases to '03, but safe enough now. Visored once previously, and acquired blinkers on his three most recent outings. Sure to remain unpredictable. *Ryedale P-t-P Racing Club (Mrs E.M. Dunn) — Middleton.* 166 (OMa), 341 (R), 390 (Rnr), 593 (L), 772 (4m1fO), 956 (MO), 1216 (4m100yMO), 1376 (4m2fH).

CLOUDKICKER (IRE) ..—.. 12 b.g. Dry Dock — Last Sprite (Tug Of War) 4pf. Good-bodied. Dam won 2 NH Flat and 2m2f Hdle in Ireland. IR7400 4yo. NH FLAT '99 r2 p1 (3rd). NH '00/2 (for Miss V. Williams) r9 p1 (2nd); pulled up 2, fell/unseated 3. Bought Doncaster, May for 600. Used to have a little ability, but was a bad jumper who pulled up in two of four Hurdles and left the rider on the floor three times over fences. The pits in Points, and was about two fences behind and jiggered when taking a crashing fall at the last at Charm Park, after which the galloping potato sack Andrew Pennock insisted the saddle be kept on in the hope that his badly winded mount might miraculously arise so he could remount for the apparently much needed third prize money. This disgusting display cost him much ill-will amongst spectators, and a £200 fine. *Miss R.M. Trousdale — Staintondale (Andrew Pennock).* 58 (OMa), 113 (OMa), 388 (M).

CLOUDY BAY BOY ..9-12.. 7 gr.g. Petoski — Smoke (Rusticaro FR) 54f1. Lengthy well-made. Dam won 8f race in Ireland and 3 flat races (11-12f) in England. P-t-P '03 r2 w1 (Maiden) p0; and 4th. Has been weak and affected by a wind problem (may require a soft-palate operation) but appeared to appreciate the less testing conditions when making all at Clifton-on-Dunsmore, and might be capable of better still in his third season. Fitted with a cross-noseband for the first time at the Atherstone. *P. Poole & W. Roe — Pytchley (Caroline Bailey).* 37 (CR), 384 (R), 734 (2mH), 1123 (R).

CLOUDY CREEK (IRE) ..10-2.. 11 gr.g. Roselier (FR) — Jacob's Creek (IRE) (Buckskin FR) 3p232. Workmanlike. P-t-P '99/00 r3 w1 (2-finisher Maiden) p1 (3rd); and pulled up. NH '02/3 (for Miss H.C. Knight) r6 w1 (2m5f Hdle) p0 (4th, fell, last and pulled up in Chses). Got a leg after winning at Charing in '00, but defied a 750-day lay-off to score at 33-1 on his debut under Rules at Plumpton. Clearly still not easy to train, and returned from another long absence to make the frame on four occasions, and might have achieved even better results had he jumped more fluently. Acquired blinkers on his final start, and if his resolve is at fault it is hardly surprising. Risked only on easy surfaces. Wears a cross-noseband. *Prof. D.B.A. & Mrs H. Silk — Kent & Surrey Bloodhounds (Emma Leppard).* 239 (3m1fH), 541 (3mH), 607 (Cf), 640 (Cf), 1085 (Cv&nr).

COAL QUEEN ..7-5.. 6 b.m. Dajitus — Crown Royale (Some Hand) 2p. Dam, half-sister to Paddy For Paddy (*qv*), won 3 minor Points and placed 4. Unsurprisingly outclassed by a subsequent Open winner when 25 lengths last of two in a three-runner youngsters Maiden, but rather disappointing when backed from sixes to threes and pulled up after two miles next time. Out of a fair mare and in a good yard, so a successful retrieval mission is quite possible. *Mrs J.E. Tamplin — Gelligaer F. (Paul Hamer).* 1026 (OMa), 1240 (OMa).

COASTAL FLIGHT ..8-8.. 10 b.g. Chauve Souris — Lyme Bay II (Incredule) 4bp5. Strong-topped half-brother to Tudor Bay and French Invasion. Dam was 2nd of 3 in Cotley Members and pulled up thrice for Marilyn Burrough. P-t-P '02/3 r5 p0 (fell/unseated 2, and pulled up 3). Prominent when exiting twice inside the final mile in '02, but beaten about 25 lengths when completing, and keeping him sound seems to be a major problem. *Mrs M. Burrough — Seavington.* 580 (OMa), 865 (OMa), 1252 (OMa), 1353 (OMa).

COASTAL SAFARI ..8-9.. 10 ch.g. Green Adventure (USA) — Sea Sand (Sousa) 35p. Strong-topped home-bred half-brother to Rusty Blade, Sharp Sand, Triggerfish and Fiddler Crab. NH '01 r1 p0 (fell in 2m4f Hdle). P-t-P '01/3 r5 p1 (last of 3); 5th, last, and unseated 2. Impetuous and very lightly raced, and given no chance when strangled by a novice on his last two appearances. *Mrs A.F. Tullie — Berwicks.* 166 (OMa), 281 (M), 507 (I).

CODDINGTON GEORGE ..7-12.. 12 ch.g. Green Adventure (USA) — Emancipated (Mansingh USA) 0. Lengthy workmanlike home-bred brother to Coddington Girl (*qv*). A veteran debutant who was sent to Cottenham on the first day of the season, but despite the services of Julian Pritchard toiled home 70 lengths last. *Dr R. Ransford — N. Ledbury (Sue Ransford).* 6 (OMa).

CODDINGTON GIRL ..9-8.. 13 br.m. Green Adventure (USA) — Emancipated (Mansingh USA) 36. Plain sparely-made sister to Coddington George and Coddington Susie, and half-sister to Mansun and Coddington Star, and to jumping winner, Superior Finish. NH FLAT r1 p0 (tailed off). P-t-P/HUNT CH '99/03 r19 w3 (Maiden, Restricted and 2-finisher Members) p4 (3 2nds; and 3rd of 4); pulled up 3, brought down 1, and fell 3. Jumped with pinpoint accuracy when making all in her Members last year, and tried to follow suit in '04, but had to contend with much stiffer opposition, and her suspect stamina gave way before the home turn in both attempts. Ideally suited by an easy three miles on a sound surface, but has become very lightly raced, and whilst she looks the spit of Upton Adventure that is where the similarity ends. *E.T. Chapman — Croome & W. Warwicks (Heather Chapman).* 976 (M), 1391 (L).

CODDINGTON SUSIE .—.. 11 b.m. Green Adventure (USA) — Emancipated (Mansingh USA) p. Small compact homebred sister to Coddington Girl (*qv*). An elderly beginner who was tailed off by halfway before pulling up in a Mares Maiden. Like her brother two above is Coddington Codswallop. *Dr R. Ransford — N. Ledbury (Nicky Sheppard).* 978 (CMam).

CODYS CASTLE ..8-0.. 13 b.g. Ascendant — Hurricane Lizzie (Kalimnos) 58p. Tall narrow owner-bred brother to Tamars Cousin. IRISH P-t-P '03 r2 p0 (pulled up and fell). IRISH NH FLAT '99 r1 p0. IRISH NH '00 (for J.E. Collinson) r1 p0. Had his busiest season at 12, but has always been useless, and never finished within 57 lengths of a winner. Wore blinkers twice in '04. *Mrs E.M. Collinson — Cottesmore.* 378 (M), 444 (2mH), 561 (OMa).

COFFEE MORNING (IRE) ..8-12.. 7 b.g. Beneficial — Phar From Men (IRE) (Phardante FR) 4. Small compact. Bought Tattersalls Ireland, Aug '02 3972. Survived a couple of very bad late blunders when

29 lengths last in a Larkhill Maiden in January, but not seen again. Looks capable of better if his jumping improves, provided all is well with him. *D.H. Smyly — N. Cotswold (Giles Smyly).* 86 (OMa).

COLDABRI (IRE) ..10-0.. 9 b.m. Husyan (USA) — Goldens Monkey (Monksfield) 1. Stocky half-sister to Magnus Veritas (IRE). Dam won 2m6f Hdle in Ireland. IRISH P-t-P '01/2 r9 w1 (Nov Rdrs Adjacent Maiden) p2 (2nds); unseated/fell 2. IRISH NH FLAT '01 r1 p0. P-t-P '03 r3 w1 (Restricted) p0; 5th, and 6th. Presented with the race when Musical Tassel (now dead) lost her action near the finish and the jockey stopped riding at Garnons last year, but won entirely on merit at Howick, and despite her prolonged absence looks up to scoring again. Stays well and is suited by plenty of cut in the ground. *Mrs R. Evans — Croome & W. Warwicks (Charlotte Evans).* 698 (Inr).

COLLEGE SUPERMAN ..—.. 9 ch.g. Infantry — Deviji (Mansingh USA) pppp. Tall strong-topped good-looking brother to Inns Of Court. NH FLAT '01 r1 p0. NH '02 r1 p0. P-t-P '03 r2 p1 (2nd of 3); and pulled up. Beaten in excess of 30 lengths when completing over jumps, but invariably forced to pull up, and probably suffers with his legs and wind. *Mrs M.A. Conway — Atherstone (Roger Harvey).* 385 (OMa), 594 (OMa), 788 (CfMa), 946 (OMa).

COLLIER ..9-7.. 10 b.g. Miner's Lamp — Looking Swell (Simbir) 3221. Close-coupled half-brother to Friar Waddon (*qv*). NH FLAT '01 r1 p0. NH '01 r2 p0 (fell/unseated 2). P-t-P '03 r3 p2 (3rds); and fell. Failed to beat a rival in his bumper, and to get beyond the fourth over hurdles, but has settled into a much better rhythm in Points, and deserved to open his account when successful at Cotley Farm. On the negative side beat no future winners, and will need to improve further for Restricteds. Wears a cross-noseband. *T. Atkinson & N. Clarke — S. Dorset (Sarah Clarke).* 474 (OMa), 693 (OMa), 1009 (OMa), 1252 (OMa).

COLOMBE D'OR ..—.. 8 gr.g. Petong — Deep Divide (Nashwan USA) ppp. Compact half-brother to flat winner, Rich Gift. 17,000f, 19,000y. FLAT '99/02 r35 w2 (8f) p8 (in 3rd in Sell). NH '01/2 (for M.C. Chapman) r14 p2 (3rds). Bought Doncaster, Aug '02 for 1200. Completed a double on the all-weather in Feb/Mar '01 (a dreamy apprentice nearly waved away the victory once), but was beaten a little over 20 lengths in both Hurdling thirds, and unplaced in his final 11 attempts including Sellers under Rules. Has had a great deal of racing for his age and looks very much on the downgrade, and his stamina must be suspect even at 2m4f. Thrice blinkered in the past. *C.R. Leech — Warwicks (Mrs S.V.O. Leech).* 784 (Cf), 1299 (2m4f110yH), 1499 (2m4f110yH).

COLOMBIAN GREEN (IRE) ..9-13.. 11 b.g. Sadler's Wells (USA) — Sharaya (USA) (Youth USA) p34. Lengthy half-brother to 3 Irish flat winners, including Mempari. IRISH FLAT '97/8 r8 p6. NH '99/03 (for D.R. Gandolfo) r18 w1 (2m1f Hdle) p6 (inc 3rd in Ch); pulled up 1, fell 1. Gained his only success from 29 attempts in a Hereford Hurdle in soft in October '01, and his 13 placings are an indication of what a frustrating character he is. Can be a very poor jumper of fences, and often a weak finisher. Blinkered twice on the flat in Ireland, when he was runner-up at between one and five lengths on his final five appearances. Will not be mending his ways at 11. *T.J. Whitley — Cotley (Philip Greenwood).* 89 (O), 602 (MO), 747 (3m1f110yH).

COLONEL BLAZER ..9-7§.. 13 b.g. Jupiter Island — Glen Dancer (Furry Glen) p. Workmanlike brother to Red Jupiter, and half-brother to Hurdles winner, Talab. Dam won at 7f. NH FLAT '96 r3 w1 p1 (3rd). NH '96/01 r25 w6 (2 Hdles, 2m2f-2m4f, and 4 Chses, 2m-2m5f) p4; fell last with every chance once. P-t-P/HUNT CH '01/3 (for Miss S. Fenwick) r14 w3 (inc Ladies) p1 (3rd of 4); 4th twice, last pair 4 and pulled up 4. Quite a money-spinner over the years, and scored an annual success in three previous Pointing campaigns, but the rot had set in long before he broke down irreparably at Hereford. *Miss E. Bywater — Quorn.* 209 (3m1f110yH).

COLONEL CARATS ..9-10§.. 12 br.g. Golden Heights — Madam Carats (Mandrake Major) 5. Strong workmanlike half-brother to General Carats. Dam is an unraced sister to Carats Major, who won 8 Points and placed 12 for David Applewhite. P-t-P '99/00 and '02/3 r21 w2 (Maiden and Restricted) p7 (5 2nds, beaten head once; and remote 3rd once); pulled up 3, fell/unseated 3. Sported blinkers when successful twice on sound surfaces for Stuart Morris last year, but basically ungenuine, and needs everything to fall right. Never went a yard on his return, and it is not inconceivable that he suffered a setback as he failed to reappear. Wears a cross-noseband, and has been tried in cheekpieces. *Mrs L.N. Vergette — Cottesmore (Toby Saunders).* 41 (I).

COLONEL CONCA ..10-1.. 10 ch.g. Milieu — Lorna's Choice (Oats) p25p. Big strong brother to Tom's Man (*qv*). NH FLAT '99/00 r3 p0. NH '01 r3 p0; pulled up 1. P-t-P '02/3 (for The Rennington Racing Club) r7 w3 (Maiden, Restricted and Members, also disqualified from Restricted win for taking wrong course once) p0; 4th, 5th, and fell 1. Won four races on varying terrain in the previous yard, and looked likely to progress further, but flopped when well supported on the opening day of the season, and his campaign was over by the third week in February. Has always been prone to errors, but ran tongue-tied once in '02, and his lack-lustre performances this year tend to suggest his wind is the problem. Wears a cross-noseband. *A.G.C. Howland Jackson - Suffolk (Ruth Hayter).* 1 (C), 38 (Cf), 124 (CCon), 248 (Cf).

COLONEL LUDLOW (IRE) ..9-0.. 9 br.g. Jurado (USA) — Blue Suede Shoes (Bargello) 648. Workmanlike lengthy half-brother to Commercial Artist, to Irish NH flat and jumping winners, Mass Appeal, Andrea Cove (IRE) and Macallister (IRE). Dam won 14f NH flat and 2m3f Hurdle in Ireland. IRISH NH FLAT '01/2 r5 p0. IRISH NH '01/2 r7 p0. P-t-P '03 r7 w1 (Maiden) p2 (2nds, beaten ½l once); 4th twice, last and fell. Finally opened his account in a bad soft ground Maiden at Easingwold last year, but rendered largely incapable by a wind problem (had a soft palate operation in '03) and beaten a minimum of 20 lengths in Restricteds since. Wears a tongue-tie, and blinkered twice in '02. *C.J. Cundall — Holderness (Mary Sowersby).* 57 (R), 563 (R), 1162 (R).

COLONEL NORTH (IRE) ..9-12.. 9 b.g. Distinctly North (USA) — Tricky (Song) p2. Compact half-brother to 3 flat winners, Magic Orb, Witches Coven and Kay Two (in Ireland). IR9200y, 15000 2yo. FLAT '98/00 and '02 w2 (8f) p2 (2nds, beaten short-head once). NH '00 and '02/3 (for D. Pearson) r6 p0. Bought Doncaster, May for 2000. Completed a double on firmish ground on the flat in June '99 (thrice visored in that sphere), but has made few appearances over jumps, and beaten 49 lengths plus in all but one until he surprisingly got within a neck of the winner in an Open (a very sub-standard one) at Musselburgh. Will have a job to score in similar company. *W.M. Aitchinson, P. Mayland & Miss J. Martin — Border (Joanne Martin).* 282 (Cf), 509 (O).

PLATE 32 1331 Minehead Harriers & West Somerset Confined: Colquhoun and Ashley Farrant, 1st, leads S B S By Jove (Alex Charles-Jones), 2nd *PHOTO: Brian Armstrong*

COLQUHOUN ..10-8.. 11 b.g. Rakaposhi King — Red Rambler (Rymer) f4121112. Smallish attractive brother to Rambling Rajah, half-brother to Gingerbread Man, and to Hurdling winner, Red Nose Lady. Dam is an unraced half-sister to Certain Angle (*qv* '03 Annual). IRISH P-t-P '99 r1 w1 (5yo Maiden). IRISH NH FLAT '99 r1 p1 (2nd). NH '99/03 (for T.R. George) r15 w1 (2m4f Hdle) p7 (inc 6 Chses); pulled up 4, fell/unseated 2. Another Pipe inmate to have a busy and successful season (first day until penultimate), and was staging a revival as he had not previously scored since March '00. Extremely error-prone under Rules, but survived three mistakes in the Ladies Hunter Chase at Stratford, and able to reap the benefit when Lucy Bridges toppled off stablemate Polar Champ when four lengths ahead and in command at the last. Can still look idle and iffy, and blundered away an eight- length lead two out in a Mixed Open, and beaten at odds-on on his latest appearance. Superior training and riding have been major contributory factors in his favour. *B.A. Kilpatrick — Taunton V.H. (David Pipe).* 5 (L), 196 (O), 487 (O), 703 (MO), 1331 (Cf), 1369 (Cf), 1454 (3mH), 1556 (MO).

COLUMNA ..7-9.. 9 gr.m. Deploy — Copper Trader (Faustus USA) p4. Small light half-sister to flat winners, Established and Mary Culi. FLAT '98/01 r7 p0. NH '99/01 (for M.D.I. Usher) r5 p2 (3rds). Bought Ascot, Feb '01 for 700. Selling class under Rules and blinkered once on the flat, and a poor pointer who passed a walking rival to snatch 39 lengths fourth in an elders Maiden. *G. Lewis — Curre & Llangibby (Melvyn Lewis).* 1320 (Cf), 1395 (OMa).

COMBAT DRINKER (IRE) ..9-11.. 7 b.g. Mandalus — Auburn Park (Sonnen Gold) 1. Tall strong good-looking brother to Auburn Hall (IRE). Dam, half-sister to Deep Auburn (*qv* '88 Season Annual). Bought Doncaster, May '01 14,000. Survived a terrible mistake two out when striding to victory on his debut at Bishops Court, and looked a useful recruit despite the absence of talent among his eight rivals, but was not seen again. It was a novicey start, but potentially very interesting when he reappears. *R.P. Blackburn — Taunton V. (Richard Barber).* 326 (OMa).

COMBE FLOREY ..—.. 6 ch.m. Alflora (IRE) — Celtic Slave (Celtic Cone) p. Small neat sister to Hurdles winner, Alpine Slave, and half-sister to Keeps Going, to jumping winners, Celtino and Young Spartacus (smart, won Mildmay of Flete at Cheltenham Festival in '03), and to Irish Pointing winner, Wild Irish. Dam won 2m Hurdle and 4 Chases (3m-3m2f) raced for Bart Hellyer. Schooled for 2m2f at Brocklesby Park in March. Bred on the right lines, so might improve for the experience. *B.G. Hellyer & Mrs D. Hellyer — Cottesmore (Holly Campbell).* 476 (CfMa).

COME ON BOY .8-2.. 11 ch.g. Henbit (USA) — Miss Rewarde (Andy Rew) 58pp4ppp6u4f. Tall rangy workmanlike. Dam pulled up 3 and fell 2 in Points. Grandam, Maquisarde, won a Restricted, but pulled up 3 and unseated 3 in her other Points. P-t-P/HUNT CH '00 and '03 (for Mrs P. Mullen) r9 p1 (last of 3); 5th, last, pulled up 5 and brought down. Can bowl along for up to 2m4f but stops to nil almost immediately and only once better than last when partnered by Gareth Davies in '04. Makes mistakes and caused carnage when attempting to refuse at Bredwardine, and sure to remain a most unrewarding ride. Blinkered to no avail at Leicester, and running him in Hunter Chases is a joke. *T.G. Williams — Radnor & W. Herefords (Mark Doyle).* 259 (CMa), 405 (Inr), 443 (2m4f110yH), 621 (OMa), 667 (OMa), 734 (2mH), 840 (OMa), 1027 (OMa), 1226 (M), 1395 (OMa), 1486 (OMa), 1534 (OMa).

COMFORTABLY NUMB (FR) ..9-7.. 6 br.g. Charnwood Forest (IRE) — Regalante (Gairloch) 443. Rangy half-brother to jumping winner, Regal Exit (FR). His debut looked encouraging, but disappointing when 4-6 favourite over 2m4f next time, and then finished three-and-a-half lengths third after hanging and wandering in the closing stages over the full trip. Still seems very babyish, and an average Maiden should be within his scope. *J.S. Delahooke — Zetland (Jane Scott).* 216 (OMa), 343 (2m4fOMa), 710 (Mah).

COMMANCHE FOX (IRE) ..9-5.. 10 ch.g. Commanche Run — Shalom Joy (Kemal FR) 3. Rangy. Dam won NH flat, 2 flat (12-16f) and 2m Hdle in Ireland. IRISH FLAT '00 r1 p0 (well tailed off). IRISH P-t-P '00 r1 p0 (fell). IRISH NH '00 r3 p0; pulled up 2. NH '01 r9 p0; pulled up 6. P-t-P '02/3 r5 w1 (3-finisher Maiden) p1 (2nd); last, and pulled up 2. A persistent non-finisher prior to landing a bad three-finisher Maiden at Llanfrynach on his only start in '02, but normally runs himself into the ground, and only once better than last in a handful of appearances since. Can be a real handful before the race as well, and has been mounted on course and taken down early. Wears a cross-noseband. *The Bearwood Partnership (Miss C. Walker) — Radnor & W. Herefords (Caroline Walker).* 207 (R).

COMMANCHE LAW (IRE) ..10-7.. 12 b.g. Commanche Run — Laurenca (Laurence O) 54411. Small half-brother to Whats Your Problem, Ballilaurenka (IRE) and Tibs Eve (IRE), and to Irish Pointing winner, Glenabow. NH FLAT '98 r2 w1 p0. NH '00/2 r9 w1 (2m4f110y Hdle) p1 (3rd). P-t-P '03 r4 w1 (Ladies) p1 (½l 2nd); 4th and pulled up. Won his debut bumper, and subsequently sprang a 25-1 surprise over hurdles, but has always been something of an enigma, and has to be produced as late as possible. Timed his run to perfection in the Gerrard Final at Huntingdon, although in fairness the runner-up was probably in front too soon, and the fact that he was running back towards the boxes also helped. Does not stand many outings, and has looked ill at ease on sound surfaces, but his ability to quicken will always stand him in good stead. *J. Fenwick — Braes (Tim Reed).* 133 (L), 284 (L), 428 (3m5fL), 916 (L), 1360 (3mH).

COMMANCHE SPIRIT (IRE) ..7-7.. 11 b.g. Commanche Run — Emmett's Lass (Deep Run) p48p6. Lengthy. IRISH P-t-P '00 r3 p2 (3rds); and pulled up. NH '00/01 r3 p0 (pulled up 3). P-t-P/HUNT CH '02/3 r14 p5 (4 2nds, of 3 once); last pair 2, pulled up 6 and unseated. Racked up five consecutive placings in the latter half of '02, but despite being admirably safe is desperately slow, and has failed to beat a rival since. *Mrs S. Bell — Morpeth.* 137 (OMa), 215 (OMa), 341 (R), 542 (3m3fH), 658 (OMa).

COMMANCHE SUMMER ..9-9.. 11 b.m. Commanche Run — Royal Typhoon (Royal Fountain) p1. Compact plain half-sister to Royal Dadda, The Dangler (IRE) and Suets Him, and to Hurdles winner, Snowmore. NH '98/03 (for A. Whillans, A. Robson, and J.D. Frost) r27 p6; pulled up 2, unseated 1. Almost sprang a surprise on her penultimate appearance under Rules, but previously beaten in Sellers, and required 29 attempts to open her account. Forced up near the finish on firmish by the up-and-coming Andrew Glassonbury at Great Trethew, but finished lame, and will presumably be retired to the paddocks. *E.M. Treneer — Dartmoor (Nicky Frost).* 194 (CfMa), 312 (CfMa).

COMMANDER CONN ..—.. 10 b.g. Perpendicular — Bonny Bright Eyes (Rarity) p. Lengthy strong-topped half-brother to 2 flat winners (one in France). FLAT '98 r4 p0. NH '01 r6 p0; pulled up 1, unseated 1. P-t-P '02 r5 p4 (3 3rds, of 4 twice); and pulled up. Of no account under Rules, but showed up prominently in Points in '02, and would have won one had he been able to summon up an ounce more stamina. Twice a beaten favourite, but spent '03 on the sidelines, and forced into retirement after going wrong again on his comeback at Eaton Hall. *N. Lilley & B. Dowling — Brecon & Talybont (Richard Mathias).* 1143 (OMa).

COMMANDER CULLY (IRE) ..9-0.. 12 b.g. General Ironside — Leney Character (Reformed Character) Rp5p37p2. Small compact. Dam, half-sister to Mountain Master (*qv* '00). IRISH NH FLAT '99 r3 p0. IRISH CHARITY FLAT '00 r1 p0. IRISH HUNT CH '01 r1 p0 (pulled up). IRISH P-t-P '01/2 r6 w2 (7yo&up Maiden and Winners Of One) p2; pulled up 1. P-t-P '03 (for Mr A.C. Ward-Thomas) r4 p1 (last of 3); and pulled up 3. A dual winner in mud in Ireland, and scored going right-handed, but has hung and jumped violently to the left since, and not better than last in five English completions. Has worn a severe bit, and tried in a near-side pricker in his Members, but could not even finish when second prize was going begging, and must have something radically wrong with him. Wears a cross-noseband. *Mrs J.E. Brake — Taunton V.H. (Chris Brake).* 81 (I), 235 (O), 1003 (4mO), 1129 (I), 1195 (I), 1369 (Cf), 1445 (M), 1464 (I).

COMMASARRIS ..9-6.. 13 gr.g. Joli Wasfi (USA) — Lucy Aura (Free State) p3pp. Compact half-brother to Rough Aura. Dam, 2nd in Sell Hdle, pulled up in 2 Points ('lumbers along unimpressively'). P-t-P/HUNT CH '97/03 (for Mrs S. Wall) r35 w3 (2m4f Maiden, Restricted and Intermediate) p11 (7 2nds, last once, and inc Hunt Ch; and inc 3rd of 4 once); pulled up 12, fell/unseated 3. Won three races to '99, and ran to 10-7 when runner-up in a 2m5f Hunter Chase on his final start in '02, but nowhere near the level of that form since, and remains a weak finisher over the full trip. Carries too much condition, and has run tongue-tied.. *Mrs G. Drury — Mid Surrey F.* 781 (L), 805 (L), 1083 (Cf), 1442 (2m5fH).

CONQUISTADOR (IRE) ..9-11.. 9 b.g. Alphabatim (USA) — Reign Of Terror (IRE) (Orchestra) f312. Workmanlike lengthy. IR34,000 4yo. NH '01/2 r3 p0; pulled up 1. Pulled up in the last of his three Hurdles and soon fell when resuming in a Point two years later, but followed a ten lengths third with a four length success in a Horseheath Maiden, in which he was 25 lengths clear three out but blundered at the next and was tiring when he jumped the last slowly. Again running out of steam in the closing stages when caught on the run-in and beaten half a length in a Restricted (had been presented with an eight length lead three out), and clearly not the stoutest of stayers, so success in similar company is not a forgone conclusion. *Ms A.E. Embiricos — Thurlow.* 152 (OMa), 561 (OMa), 746 (OMa), 1152 (R).

CONTINGENCY..9-12§.. 12 b.g. Broadsword (USA) — Saucy Linda (Saucy Kit) 537. Tall good-topped brother to Sweet Scimitar. Dam won 2 Points (after remounting once) and placed 16, and is half-sister to smart NH flat and jumping winner, Brown Chamberlin. P-t-P/HUNT CH '99 and '01/3 r17 w3 (2m4f Maiden, Restricted and Intermediate) p7 (4 2nds, of 3 once; inc 3rd of 4 once); pulled up 2, fell 2. Gained an annual success on right-handed tracks in each of his first three campaigns (missed '00 due to a badly cut pastern) but ungenuine and worried out of another possible victory last year, and unimproved by the application of cheekpieces on his latest appearance. Seems likely to continue to slip down the ratings. Blinkered once in '02. *Miss C. Hill & Mrs J. Hill — Pytchley (Caroline Bailey).* 55 (Cf), 124 (CCon), 292 (MO).

CONTRA CHARGE ..9-3.. 11 gr.g. Arzanni — Winter Wonder (Sunyboy) 3. Tall angular. Dam, half-sister to Sustaining (*qv* '97 Annual), placed in a Maiden. NH FLAT '00 r3 w1 p0. NH '01 r3 p0. P-t-P '03 (for Mr R. Arthurs) r5 p1 (3rd of 4); 4th of 5, and pulled up 3. Did nothing over hurdles after landing a poor bumper at Ludlow on his debut, and beaten a minimum of 22 lengths in Points last year when apparently affected by a virus. Showed more than his fair share of temperament and finished lame on his first appearance for new connections. *Mrs M.S. Frampton & G.G.H. Tory — S. Dorset (Mary Tory).* 233 (M).

CONTRARY KING ..—§.. 9 b.g. Regal Embers (IRE) — Contrary Lady (Conwyn) ppppp. Small owner-bred half-brother to Bolshie Baron and Contradict. Dam, half-sister to Roman Sea (*qv* '92 Annual), won 4 Points consecutively (beaten a neck but awarded dead-heat once) and placed 7 (inc 2 Hunt Chses, one 4m). P-t-P '02 r3 p0 (last, and pulled up 2). Out of a decent mare and has shown speed for up to 2m4f but does not appear to stay any further. His real problem is controlling his volcanic temperament, and has made a real nuisance of himself in the paddock and at the start in the majority of his races. No better behaved in a visor on his penultimate start, and seems to have no wish to reform. Taken to post early latterly and has been mounted outside the paddock. *M.H. Weston — Worcs.* 731 (OMa), 760 (OMa), 1020 (OMa), 1258 (OMa), 1341 (OMa).

COOL ARCHIE .—.. 12 b.g. Roscoe Blake — Echo Lake (Tycoon II) ppp. Big rangy owner-bred. Dam was 2nd of 3 in a Point, but failed to finish in 6 other attempts. Grandam, Etoile Bleu, was placed in 2 Maidens (failed to finish in her 8 other Points). NH '01/2 r2 p0 (pulled up in Hdle, and last in Ch). NEWMARKET TOWN PLATE '01/2 p0 (15th and 5th). P-t-P '02/3 r8 p3 (2 2nds, of 3 once); pulled up 4 and fell 1. Has displayed plenty of stamina, and showed improved form when equipped with first-time blinkers at Alpraham last year, but no longer derives benefit, and stops to nothing as soon as he comes off the bridle. *R.A. Royle — Cheshire (Michelle Mullineaux).* 97 (CfMa), 709 (Mah), 877 (OMa).

COOLARNE LEADER (IRE) ..7-7§.. 11 b.g. Supreme Leader — West Run (Deep Run) Rppu4. Close-coupled brother to Irish NH flat and Hurdling winner, West Leader. IRISH NH FLAT '99/00 r4 p0. IRISH NH '99/00 and '02/3 (for M. O'Toole) r11 p0; ran out 1, pulled up 2. Provenly awful in Ireland where he ran out once and also veered badly twice, and wore blinkers twice and was pulled up in both his Chases. Predictably the inexperienced Rebecca Davies could not ride one side of him, but did manage to plod round for 20 lengths last after some poor jumping for a substitute at Lydstep. Has acquired a tongue-tie, and is totally unpromising. *Miss R.L. & M. Davies — Tivyside (Rebecca Davies).* 669 (M), 949 (L), 1095 (R), 1189 (L), 1525 (OMah).

COOLE CHIEF..9-2.. 12 ch.g. Weld — Beringa Bee (Sunley Builds) p4pp05. Lengthy good-looking half-brother to Bee-A-Scally and S And O P, and to Hurdles winner, Cap In Hand. Dam, sister to Builder Boy (*qv* '98 Annual). IRISH P-t-P '98/9 r8 p1 (3rd); pulled up 4. NH '01 r1 p0; pulled up. P-t-P/HUNT CH '01 and '03 (for Mr W.J. Warner & Mr R. Ford) r7 w1 (Maiden) p2 (2nd of 3, and last of 3); 5th, unseated 2 and pulled up. Sprang a 25-1 shock when successful at Eyton last year, but can be a very tricky ride, and was not ideal for a beginner in '04. Fared little better when partnered by a more experienced rider in the second half of the season, and looks a long shot to upgrade successfully. Wears a cross-noseband. *S.J. Gray & B.T. Twinn — E. Essex (Ron Green).* 155 (Cnr), 243 (M), 524 (R), 1217 (R), 1396 (C), 1503 (R).

COOLEEN STRONG (IRE) .9-11.. 9 b.g. Doubletour (USA) — Strong-Galeforce (IRE) (Strong Gale) 41p. Tall workmanlike. IRISH P-t-P '02/3 r5 p0 (last 2, brought down 1, pulled up 1, and unseated 1). A bad Irish Pointer who was beaten 44 lengths plus in both lasts, and added a similar display on his Welsh debut, but connections are past masters at transforming base metal, although in truth the opposition in his Ystradowen Members was so desperate that he hardly had to improve at all to score (the runner-up, beaten 30 lengths, was a stablemate whose jockey was having his first ride). The surprise was that the time was the fastest of the day by eight seconds, but he was never going well when favourite and pulled up next time. Has missed out on what would have been a gift in a Maiden, but may yet find compensation in a Restricted. *R.J. Rowsell — Ystrad Taf Fechan.* 362 (CfMa), 1021 (M), 1322 (R).

COOLEFIND (IRE) ..10-10.. 7 b.g. Phardante (FR) — Greavesfind (The Parson) 21111. Strong-topped half-brother to Hurdles winner, Bali Strong (IRE). Dam, half-sister to Drawn 'N' Quartered (*qv* '98 Annual). P-t-P '03 r2 w1 (Maiden) p0; and fell 1. A most progressive individual, and made a successful transition to Hunter Chases at the first attempt, but does not always find it easy to organise himself at the fences, and wins with less in hand than he should. Hails from a yard that knows how to prepare for the big races, and almost certainly still has more improvement in him, and if his jumping can be sorted could be heading towards a big prize in '05. Can quicken and gives the impression that a slog through mud is not ideal. *Mrs J. Wilson — Pytchley (Bill Warner).* 109 (CR), 384 (R), 783 (M), 1274 (Cf), 1361 (3mH).

COOLE GLEN (IRE) .10-1.. 9 b.g. Executive Perk — Cailin Liath (Peacock FR) 12d26. Rangy. Dam was placed 4 in Irish Points. P-t-P '02/3 r2 p2 (2nds). Very keen and pulled his way to the front after less than a mile when opening his account in sticky ground at Thorpe Lodge, but a weak finisher otherwise, and remains lightly raced. Should pick up a Restricted at least in '05, but does not look like being a patch on his stablemate above. *Mrs J. Wilson — Pytchley (Bill Warner).* 111 (OMa), 481 (R), 784 (Cf), 1359 (2m4f110yH).

COOLE'SABBOT (IRE) .9-11§.. 11 b/br.g. Glacial Storm (USA) — Galamear (Strong Gale) p18p. Sturdy compact. Dam won 2m Hdle in Ireland. IRISH P-t-P '99/00 r7 p1 (2nd); pulled up 6. NH '00/01 r3 p1 (3rd). P-t-P '02/3 r9 w3 (Maiden, Restricted and 3-finisher Intermediate) p3 (2 3rds, last once); and pulled up 3. The winner of four minor Points on good or easy surfaces, but never went about things with a passion, and was blinkered in the last two. Broke down at Ystradowen and has been retired. *P.J. Ponting — Curre & Llangibby (Robin Butterworth).* 117 (C), 356 (M), 612 (Cf), 1023 (Cf).

COOLE VENTURE (IRE) ..10-9§.. 11 b.g. Satco (FR) — Mandavard (IRE) (Mandalus) 211p24p. Tall workmanlike half-brother to Hurdles winner, Freeline Fontaine (IRE). Dam is half-sister to Coolflugh Hero (*qv* '01 Annual). IRISH P-t-P '00 r3 p2 (beaten 12-23*l*). IRISH NH FLAT '00 r2 p0. P-t-P/HUNT CH '02/3 r10 w6 (inc 3 Confineds, 5-timer '03) p3 (2 2nds, beaten neck in Hunt Ch once; and inc 3rd in Hunt Ch); and 4th. A useful Pointer and goes particularly well fresh, but unimpressive in both '04 wins on dead ground, and became progressively more jaded as the season wore on. Flopped when favourite for the Lady Dudley Cup, and despite seemingly ideal conditions was run down in the closing stages when blinkered for the first time at Bangor. A safe if unspectacular jumper, and perfectly capable of bouncing back to form in early '05, but needs treating with caution. *J.A. Griffiths & E.H. Crow — N. Salop (Sheila Crow).* 528 (O), 662 (O), 851 (O), 1016 (3m2fO), 1176 (3m110yH), 1375 (3m110yH), 1452 (3m4fH).

COOL GENERAL (IRE) ..—.. 10 gr.g. General View — Coolcroo Lady (Roselier FR) p. Lengthy. IRISH P-t-P '00 r3 w2 (4&5yo Maiden and Winners of One) p1 (3rd). IRISH NH FLAT '00 r1 p0. NH '00 r2 p0; pulled up 1. P-t-P '02 r2 p0 (last and pulled up). A dual winner on sound surfaces in Ireland, but quickly and cheaply disposed of by Paul Nicholls, and his view has been vindicated since. Blinkered once in '00. *T. Lucas — S. Pembs (Kirstie Lucas).* 671 (I).

COOL SHUIL (IRE) ..—§.. 9 b.m. Glacial Storm (USA) — Shuil Suas (Menelek) rp. Workmanlike good-bodied half-sister to Ballinacourty and Tomcappagh (IRE). Dam won an Irish NH flat. P-t-P '02/3 r4 p1 (remote last of 3); and pulled up 3. A fine specimen to behold, but looks as soft as they come, and not for the first time appeared to go wrong at Littlewindsor. *D.E.M. Young — Portman (Anne Young).* 237 (CfMa), 693 (OMa).

COOLTEEN HERO (IRE) .9-11.. 15 b.g. King Luthier — Running Stream (Paddy's Stream) 3f2234. Strong compact half-brother to Chasing winner (and stablemate), Beaurepaire (IRE). IRISH P-t-P '96 r3 p1 (2nd); fell 1. NH '96/03 (for R.H. Alner) r71 w11 (2-3m Chses) p29; fell/unseated 9, pulled up 2, and brought down 1. Yesterday's hero. Fell twice and pulled up on his final three attempts under Rules and had only one outing in '03, but had won at least once in each of seven previous years, on ground ranging from soft to firm. A frequent front-runner in the past who stayed better with age, and was very game at best, and apart from 11 wins he has garnered 34 placings, many of them good efforts in defeat. Too old and slow now, but can be retired with honours. *J.C. Browne, Mrs S. Woodhouse & Mrs F. Robertson — Portman (Sally Alner).* 261 (Cf), 351 (L), 577 (Cnr), 861 (M), 1101 (Cnr), 1367 (O).

COOL WAGER ..9-11.. 13 br.g. Arctic Lord — Gamblingway (Gambling Debt) 134p32. Lengthy owner-bred half-brother to Gilded Way. Dam, half-sister to The Nations Way, (*qv* '94 Annual), was heavily backed when winning a Restricted (her only Point). NH FLAT '98 r1 p0. NH '99 r4 p0. P-t-P '00 and '02/3 r15 w4 (inc Open) p8 (5 2nds, beaten ½*l* once, of 3 once, and last once; inc 3rd of 4 once); last, pulled up 1 and slipped up 1. Of no account under Rules, but has found his level in Points, and has scored an annual success in all four campaigns. Beat only one other finisher when easily picking up his Members in '04, but save for a flattering second to Vivid Imagination was otherwise well beaten, and the decision to lower his sights was spot on. Unsuited by easy surfaces. *R.C. & Mrs H. Pudd — W. Somerset (Tigger Pudd).* 273 (M), 319 (O), 471 (O), 964 (O), 1183 (Cf), 1384 (Cf).

COOMAKISTA ..10-3.. 8 b.m. Primitive Rising (USA) — Miss Eros (Royal Fountain) 121. Dam won Maiden and placed 5 for Ian Speke (*qv* '97 Annual). Connections waited a long time before she surfaced on the racecourse, but they had a very pleasant surprise when she beat vastly more experienced rivals in her Members at Corbridge (20-1). Squandered the chance of Maiden success, but after chasing home the potentially smart King Barry at Tranwell she had little difficulty collecting a Mosshouses Restricted in a good time. Bred from a modest mare, but looks substantially more progressive herself, and might be worth trying in a Maiden Hunter Chase at eight. *I.B. Speke — Tynedale (Tim Reed).* 425 (M), 918 (R), 1222 (R).

COOMBE QUEST ..9-8.. 9 b.g. Almoojid — Benen Ryal (King's Ride) 1pp4. Workmanlike owner-bred. Left to win considerably the slowest of the eight races at Buckfastleigh after Josanjamic had unseated at the last when holding him by three lengths (only two others got round, but both scored eventually), but foiled by a couple of terrible blunders next time, and has been disappointing since. Speedy enough, but tends to race too freely, and there are problems to address before he reappears. *S.C. Horn — Lamerton (Elaine Horn).* 195 (CfMa), 323 (R), 498 (R), 908 (Cf).

COOMBS SPINNEY ..9-0.. 8 b.g. Homo Sapien — Woodram Delight (Idiot's Delight) pu5u32. Good-bodied half-brother to Chasing winner, Bank Avenue. 5000 3yo. NH FLAT '02 r2 p0. NH '02 (for Mrs P.M. Sly) r1 p0. Moderate and tends to fade and make blunders, but connections hit on 2m4f for the first time on final start, and his two length second was the first time he had got within 25 lengths of a winner in nine outings. The trip is not an option in future, and will struggle to win. *Mrs J.E. Micklethwaite — Cottesmore (Holly Campbell).* 112 (OMa), 476 (CfMa), 887 (CfMa), 1061 (OMa), 1218 (OMa), 1402 (2m4fOMa).

COPPER GROVE (IRE) ..9-13.. 7 b.g. Presenting — Riseaway (Raise You Ten) 2. Workmanlike half-brother to Kamrise, to Irish Pointing winners, Yanbu Girl and Final Target, and to Hurdles winner, Guilt Of A Sinner (IRE). IRISH P-t-P '03 r1 p0 (6th of 7). Not seen until May and was 20-1 and apparently unfancied for a Chaddesley youngsters Maiden, but shaped with plenty of promise and left a fair second at the last. Attractively bred and in a good yard, and should soon be winning. *I. Anderson — Tanatside.* 1339 (OMa).

COPPICE LANE ..—.. 9 b.m. Sula Bula — Charossa (Ardross) R. Small plain half-sister to Hurdles winner, Phil Sanders. Immediately struggling to keep up in a February Maiden, and ran out at the fifth. *W. Hawkins — Albrighton.* 97 (CfMa).

COPYBOOK ..8-11.. 6 b.g. Danehill (USA) — Easy To Copy (USA) (Affirmed USA) p735*p*. Leggy narrow half-brother to 5 flat winners, including Two-Twenty-Two, Desert Ease (won in Ireland), Lord Dundee, and to successful Irish Hurdler, Easy Wonder. 40,000y. FLAT '02 r5 p0. NH '04 r1 p0 (pulled up in

2m110y Hdle: *hdwy 5, lost plce aft nxt, poor 6th when pu last*). Bought Tattersalls, Aug '02 for 4500. A curiosity for a stable who breed the vast majority of their runners, and they may not be tempted to seek out further Henry Cecil rejects after acquiring this disappointment. Had unseated and run loose to the post before his debut on the flat and later well tailed off thrice (beating one on those three occasions), but seemed to be something of a plot in the Haydon Maiden, in which he started favourite but typically jumped moderately before finishing 18 lengths last. A spin over Hurdles did not impress, and is still on the drawing board. *Messrs F.T. Walton — Border (Jimmy Walton).* 856 (2m4fOMa), 920 (2m4fOMa), 1081 (OMa), 1474 (2m4fOMa).

COQUET GOLD ..8-7.. 14 b.m. Rambling River — Carat Stick (Gold Rod) p5322. Small close-coupled home-bred half-sister to Be A Better Boy (*qv*). NH FLAT '95/6 r4 p0. NH '96/7 r9 p0; pulled up 3, slipped up 1. P-t-P '02 r1 p0 (last). Brought out of retirement to act as schoolmistress for Catherine Walton, and did a fine job, but beat only two rivals en route, and is flattered by three placings in which she was beaten an aggregate of 75 lengths. *J.B. & F.A. Walton — W. Percy (Jimmy Walton).* 69 (M), 286 (CfMa), 511 (OMam), 919 (CMa), 1042 (CMam).

CORAL BAY .—.. 7 ch.g. Afzal — Wenrisc (Boreen FR) pp. Workmanlike brother to NH flat winner, True Destiny. Dam, half-sister to Vineyard Special (*qv* '00 Annual). Well beaten when pulling up twice in February Maidens, and gave the impression that something was amiss in the latest. *Mrs C.R. Saunders — Pytchley (Caroline Bailey).* 111 (OMa), 290 (2m4fCfMa).

CORALINGA ..9-9.. 8 b.m. Terimon — Kintra (Sunyboy) 2. Compact half-sister to Hilarity (*qv*). NH FLAT '02 r1 p1 (2nd of 4). NH '02/3 (for Miss E.C. Lavelle) r3 p0; pulled up 2. Seven lengths second of four in a bumper (they don't come much worse), but 45 lengths seventh and pulled up twice over Hurdles. Wore cheekpieces for her Pointing debut at Black Forest Lodge in early February and showed some ability when five lengths second, but like the third and fourth failed to reappear, and the unforgiving ground on that scenic course may have claimed another victim. *P. & Mrs F. Shaw & Mrs N. Turner — Cattistock (Fiona Shaw).* 149 (OMa).

CORKY BROWNE ..10-0.. 9 b.g. Feelings (FR) — Shermago (Humdoleila) 621. Tall strong. Dam won 2 Sell Hdles (2m4f-3m) and 3m Ch. P-t-P '02 (for Mr A.R. & Mrs O.W. King) r1 p0 (4th). Created a favourable impression on his debut, but did not reappear for another 25 months, and has obviously had problems. Did not miss a meeting at Eyton in '04, and rounded off his campaign with a ready success in which the owner made more use of him than before. An imposing individual and looks likely to make an impact in Restricteds. *Miss J. Perry — S. Salop.* 530 (R), 934 (OMa), 1261 (OMa).

CORN GENERAL ..—.. 9 br.g. Governor General — Corncrop (Mycropolis) ppppp. Compact well-made half-brother to General Eddie, Good Gracious Me and No Battery Needed, and to Hurdles winner, The Mexicans Gone. P-t-P '03 r3 p0 (pulled up 3). Pulls up with monotonous regularity, and often for no apparent reason, but acquired a tongue-strap on his latest appearance and must be making a noise. Wears a cross-noseband. *Cribans Syndicate (P. Priday) — Radnor & W. Herefords (Billie Brown).* 517 (CfMa), 620 (OMa), 666 (OMa), 844 (R), 1027 (OMa).

CORNISH HOPE ..—§§.. 11 b.g. Henbit (USA) — Sleepers (Swing Easy USA) fpp. Small light-framed. Dam won 6 5f races, one at Cagnes, and including 4-timer at 6 (then Irish-trained, including 2 wins there). P-t-P '00 (for Mr K.F. Fisher) r3 p0 (ran out 2 and pulled up 1). NH '02 r1 p0 (pulled up — 200-1). Massacred on St Valentine's Day on his only outing under Rules, and went no more than two miles in each of his appearances in '04. Ungenuine, and stopped in a matter of strides on his most recent start. Has been taken to post early. Wears a cross-noseband. *D. Bryant & Miss S. Townrow — N. Cornwall (David Bryant).* 76 (M), 415 (R), 485 (OMa).

CORRIE MOR (IRE) ..9-13.. 10 ch.g. Moscow Society (USA) — Corrie Lough (IRE) (The Parson) 2p. Rangy. Dam never ran, but is sister to Butler John (*qv* '01 Annual), and half-sister to Moscow Express. NH FLAT '00 r1 p0. NH '00/01 r4 p0; pulled up 1. P-t-P '02/3 r12 w4 (Maiden, Restricted, Members and Club nov rdrs) p6 (4 2nds, short head last once, and of 3 once); last and fell. Prone to becoming very wound up in the preliminaries, but not as bad as he was, and has a fair record in minor Points. Travelled well out of his area to find fast ground in Hunter Chases in '04, but was no match for the winner at Catterick, and after failing to reappear may well have suffered a setback at Exeter. *Mrs S.E. Busby & G. Wright — Farmers Bloodhounds (Sue Busby).* 436 (3m1f110yH), 975 (2m7f110yH).

CORSTON JOKER ..9-11§§.. 15 b.g. Idiot's Delight — Corston Lass (Menelek) 35r2r1. Rangy good-topped brother to Corston Frisby, and half-brother to Corston Lad, Corston Springs and Corston Blaze, and to Hurdles winners, Corston Racer and Corston Rambo. NH '95/00 r28 w7 (2m3f-2m5f Chses) p5 (inc 2nd in Hdle; beaten neck once); refused to race 4. P-t-P/HUNT CH '01/3 (for Mr J.M. Turner) r21 w5 (4-timer '02, and inc 3m110y Hunt Ch and 2 Opens) p5 (3 3rds, last twice); 5th, last pair 4, refused 1, slipped up 1 and pulled up 4. Recorded the second four-timer of his career in '02, but has always been liable to be very unco-operative, and was applying the brakes all the way up the run-in when beating a former stablemate at Marks Tey. Provided Lisa Spence with her first taste of victory, but previously declined to jump off for the fifth time in his career at Horseheath, and had also refused to pass the box-park at Higham. Blinkered twice in '02. *Mrs E.M. Bousquet-Payne — E. Essex (Lisa Spence).* 222 (L), 249 (Cnr), 399 (L), 522 (L), 743 (L), 904 (L).

COSMIC FLIGHT (IRE) ..—.. 9 b.g. Torus — Palatine Lady (Pauper) pp. Compact sturdy half-brother to Quarter Marker (IRE), to Irish NH flat and Chasing winner, Bens Dilemma, and to Irish Pointing winner, Ashton Court. IR3800 3yo. NH FLAT '00/2 r4 p1 (3rd). NH '02/3 (for N.T. Chance, and N.M. Babbage) r3 p0; pulled up 1. Beaten 25 lengths plus in six of seven attempts which included a Selling Hurdle under Rules, and was too keen and faded very tamely in Points (favourite for the first of them, presumably because Gary Hanmer was riding). Lightly raced and unpromising. *M. Jones — N. Ledbury (Mike Daniell).* 621 (OMa), 981 (OMa).

COSMIC SKY ..9-11.. 8 ch.g. Charmer — Silver Cirrus (General Ironside) 2. Good-bodied half-brother to Silverspina and Arctic Cirrus. Dam was placed in 5 Points for Richard Wilson to '92 (was desperately unlucky on her debut — unseated at the last when in complete control). P-t-P '03 r2 p0 (pulled up 2). Stepped up on two uninspiring efforts in '03 to make the bulk of the running when ultimately no match for Rhythm King at Ampton, but spent the rest of the year on the sidelines, and presumably suffered a setback. *R.G. Abrey & Major R. Wilson — Suffolk (Robert Abrey).* 40 (OMa).

COTTAGE BOY (IRE) ..—.. 7 b.g. Camden Town — Duhallow Lady (IRE) (Torus) ppf. Compact good-bodied half-brother to Chasing winner, No Visibility (IRE). Took a fatal fall at the 13th at Ystradowen. P. Riddick — Gelligaer F. 362 (CfMa), 699 (CfMa), 735 (CfMa).

COTTEIR CHIEF (IRE) .—§§.. 14 b.g. Chief Singer — Hasty Key (USA) (Key To The Mint USA) 4ppp. Tall stocky half-brother to successful Hurdler, Cixi, and to several flat winners. Dam won at up to 9f in USA. FLAT '93/5, '97 and '99 r21 w6 (6-12f) p6. NH '97 and '99/00 r8 w4 (2m4f-2m5f Hdles) p3. P-t-P '03 (for Mr P. Riddick) r4 p2 (3rds); and pulled up 2. Contested Classics and Claimers in a varied and successful career under Rules, but spent three years on the sidelines after gaining his last win in '00, and has not enjoyed Pointing. Pulled himself up on his last three appearances and it would be a huge surprise were he to turn out again. Acquired blinkers at Llanfrynach. *L. Wood — Gelligaer F. (Jenny Williams).* 188 (O), 254 (O), 360 (O), 448 (O).

COTTON ON ..9-9.. 8 b.g. Henbit (USA) — Linen Leaf (Bold Owl) p1. Big strong. Dam is half-sister to Royle Burchlin (*qv* '01 Annual). P-t-P '02/3 r2 p1 (3rd); and pulled up. A typical Martin Wilesmith stamp of horse, and like most of the others has needed plenty of time, but came from a seemingly impossible position to lead close home at Upton. Whilst it may be doing Mark Wilesmith an injustice he gave the impression he was just out for a jolly which would have upset those who backed him down to favouritism, and the chances are that there is better still to come. Wears a cross-noseband. *M.S. Wilesmith — Ledbury.* 30 (CMah), 982 (2m5fOMa).

PLATE 33 1524 Carmarthenshire Open Maiden for Mares: Countess Kiri and Richard Burton, 1st, have a simple task *PHOTO: Brian Armstrong*

COUNTESS KIRI ..9-2.. 7 b.m. Opera Ghost — Ballagh Countess (King's Ride) ffp21p. Compact. Dam won 2m4f NH and 2m2f Chase in Ireland; and won 2m4f Chase in England. NH FLAT '03 r3 p1 (3rd). FLAT '03 (for P. Bowen) r1 p0. Showed some promise in bumpers (beaten 16 lengths when third), but fell at the second in her first Point, and her confidence seems to have been at a low ebb since. Fell very heavily next time and then pulled up, but finished eight lengths second at 25-1 (possibly her best display to date although flattered by the proximity), and survived an indifferent round when landing a feeble five-runner Mares Maiden at Lydstep. Jumped slowly and never went a yard next time, and does not look to be going in the right direction. *D.J. Evans — Pembs (Rhiannon Rees).* 619 (2m4fOMa), 677 (CfMa), 950 (2m4fOMa), 1091 (CMam), 1524 (OMam), 1548 (R).

COUNT KENI ..9-9.. 10 ch.g. Formidable (USA) — Flying Amy (Norwick USA) p3p. Tall rangy half-brother to Hurdles winner, Ede'iff. FLAT r3 p0. NH '98/03 r10 p1 (3rd). P-t-P/HUNT CH '01/3 r8 w3 (Maiden, Restricted and 3-finisher Members) p2 (2nds); 5th, and 6th twice. Won three minor races at Friars Haugh to '03, and also runner-up there once, but way below his best this year, and appears to have developed a wind infirmity. Tongue-tied after letting favourite backers down on his reappearance, and faces an uphill battle to recover his form. Often on his toes and sweating in the preliminaries, and has been taken to post early. *Mrs J.B. Roncoroni — Jedforest (Kate MacTaggart).* 73 (Cf), 1287 (I), 1307 (Cf).

COUNTRYSIDE COUNTS ..8-7.. 7 b.g. North Col — Country Art (Country Retreat) p69. Strong-topped owner-bred brother to Countryside March (*qv*). Beaten 38 lengths plus with just one behind him so far, and poor jumping has been a problem to date. *Mrs B. Russell — Silverton (Lucy Gardner).* 599 (2m4fOMa), 1133 (OMa), 1380 (OMa).

COUNTRYSIDE MARCH ..8-0.. 9 b.m. North Col — Country Art (Country Retreat) 4ff. Tall workmanlike sister to Countryside Counts, and half-sister to Baron Countryside. Dam, sister to Country Picture (*qv* '95 Annual), pulled up in Confined for Brenda Russell at 8. Grandam, Talking Picture, was last and pulled up 4 in Points for Mr Russell. Great-grandam, Lady Fortune, failed to finish in Points. P-t-P '02 (for Mrs B. Russell) r1 p0 (pulled up). Not wholly disgraced despite finishing 35 lengths last on her belated reappearance, and backed down to joint-favouritism at Cothelstone, but tipped up for the second time in the space of four days there, and once again it's back to the drawing board. Has two paddock handlers. *Mr & Mrs C. Brake — Silverton (Chris Brake).* 827 (CfMa), 1326 (OMa), 1370 (OMa).

COUNTY DERRY..11-0§.. 12 b.g. Derrylin — Colonial Princess (Roscoe Blake) 3213412. Workmanlike lengthy brother to Princess Derry, and to Hurdles winner, Brush A King. Dam, half-sister to Colonian King (*qv* '97 Annual), won 2 Points and 3rd 2. Grandam, Colonian Queen (always known erroneously as Colonial Queen) won 4 Hunt Chses and 17 Points and 3rd 3, and comes from a tremendous jumping family. P-t-P/HUNT CH '99/03 r32 w11 (inc 4 Hunt Chses, 3m-3m4f and 3 Opens) p5 (2 3rds, of 4 once, inc Hunt Ch; and 3 2nds, of 3 twice in Hunt Chses); pulled up 8, and unseated 1. Had three different owners before he won a race, but has developed into a very smart Hunter Chaser, and finally laid his Cheltenham hoodoo (beaten in seven previous visits) when landing the four-miler on his penultimate start. Largely consistent, but very moody, and does not always consent to get into top gear until the race is over, and whilst he has never fallen his jumping is often very hit and miss. Responded to the application of cheekpieces at Fontwell, but their effects are already negligible, and backing him at short odds brings a high risk factor. A credit to connections, and in particular to Neil Harris who has partnered him in all 13 successes, and sure to be a major force in stamina tests in '05. Tends to get on edge in the paddock where he has two handlers. *G.T. Lever — Devon & Somerset (Jeremy Scott).* 64 (O), 140 (MO), 280 (3m2f110yH), 543 (3m2f110yH), 991 (3m2f110yH), 1170 (4m1fH), 1376 (4m2fH).

COURAGE UNDER FIRE ..10-4.. 10 b.g. Risk Me (FR) — Dreamtime Quest (Blakeney) f252. Good-topped lengthy half-brother to Hurdles winner, Interdream. FLAT r16 w1 (12f, fibresand) p4 (short-headed once, beaten neck once). NH '98/00 r7 p0. P-t-P/HUNT CH '01 r3 w1 (3m110y Hunt Ch) p1 (3rd); and pulled up. NH '01/2 r16 w3 (2m6f110y-3m2f110y Chses) p8; pulled up 3. NH '04 r2 p1 (10l 2nd to Jimmy Tennis in 2m7f110y Ch: *chsd ldrs, ld app 2 out til hdd bef last, no ex flat*); and 5th in 3m Ch: *chsd ldrs, rdn 14, wknd 3 out*. Ultimately disappointing on the flat and over hurdles, but rarely out of the frame over fences, and did well for the yard until going wrong in the '02 Lincolnshire National. Missed '03 in it's entirety, and suffered the first fall of his career on his comeback, but showed there was still a race in him when chasing home Cantarinho at Fakenham. Suited by an easy surface. Visored once in '00, and wears blinkers now. *T.P. Radford — Belvoir (Chris Bealby).* 122 (3m1fH), 893 (3m110yH).

COURSEMAN (IRE) ..8-12.. 8 b.g. Mandalus — Linda's Course (IRE) (Crash Course) 3. Good-topped. IRISH P-t-P '02/3 r7 p1 (3rd); pulled up 3, ran out and fell 2. IRISH NH FLAT '03 r1 p0. IRISH NH '02/3 (for R.P. Rath) r2 p0. All he has to show at the end of three years of racing are a distant third, and 35 lengths third of four in a May Maiden, and is evidently very moderate. *Mrs M. Oliver & Mrs J. McErath — Worcester & W. Farmers (Martin Oliver).* 1393 (OMa).

COURT ADJOURN ..10-5.. 8 b.g. North Col — Tapalong (True Song) 21143. Sturdy brother to Ryans Star (*qv*). P-t-P '02 r1 p0 (fell). In command when left well clear at the last when successful at Chaddesley, and followed up in a very slowly-run three-runner Restricted, but ran his best race in defeat when third to Franco at Garthorpe in a time which equalled the course record. Jumped poorly in a strong Intermediate previously, and may require good or sound surfaces to be most effective, but looks to be on the upgrade and should certainly score again. *Sir Michael Connell — Grafton (Anne Connell).* 87 (OMa), 257 (CMa), 870 (R), 1092 (I), 1400 (CN).

COURT ALERT ..10-2.. 10 b.g. Petoski — Banbury Cake (Seaepic USA) 321. Sturdy owner-bred half-brother to Braod Steane, Larkross, Second Amendment and Goldsteane. Dam won 6 Points and placed 13. NH '01 r3 p0 (reluctant latterly when pulled up in 3 Hdles). P-t-P '00 and '02/3 r11 w4 (up to Confined) p3 (inc last of 3 twice); 5th, last, pulled up and unseated. Successful on five occasions on good or sound surfaces, but vulnerable on softer going, and has found some easy opportunities. Acquired blinkers in the latest, where the exit of the market leader at the fourth-last simplified his task, and did not look entirely keen when left in front. Benefits from the presence of Stuart Morris in the plate, but usually goes off at a false price as a result, and was beaten at 4-7 in his Members. *Sir Michael Connell — Grafton (Anne Connell).* 582 (M), 1199 (C), 1472 (I).

COUSIN GEORGE ..9-2§.. 8 ch.g. Henbit (USA) — Triggered (Gunner B) 431pp. Tall rangy owner-bred half-brother to Gunnerbe Posh, Pot Shot and Noble Action. Dam is half-sister to Cherry Gold (*qv*). P-t-P '02/3 r6 p1 (2nd); last, pulled up 3 and brought down. A talking horse and has let favourite backers down on three occasions, but finally managed to deliver when allowed to dominate proceedings at Garthorpe. Downed tools when pulled up next time, and is clearly tainted by ungenuine Henbit blood. Has been unruly at the start, and mounted on course and taken to post early in the past. *R.L. Burton — S. Salop (Pamela Sykes).* 7 (2m4fOMa), 97 (CfMa), 387 (OMa), 1018 (R), 1430 (I).

COWANSTOWN KING (IRE) ..—.. 7 b.g. Mandalus — Guernsey Girl (Deep Run) p. Dam, half-sister to Hangover (*qv* '00 Annual). Bought Doncaster, Nov for 3600. Not seen until mid-May, when tailed off and pulled up after two miles in a Maiden (lost his action after a bad mistake). *L. Wells — Chid, Lec & Cowdray.* 1405 (OMa).

COWANSTOWN PRINCE ..9-12.. 11 ch.g. Derrylin — Craftsmans Made (Jimsun) p2r. Smallish brother to NH flat and Hurdles winner, Winston Run, and half-brother to Orswell Lad and Crafty Gunner, and to Hurdles winner, Shannon Juliette (previously a successful Irish Pointer). IRISH NH '98/9 r7 p0. IRISH NH FLAT r8 p1 (2nd). NH '01 r2 p0. P-t-P '00/3 r12 w3 (up to Confined) p4 (3 3rds, last once; and short-head 2nd); 4th, last, pulled up 1, unseated 1 and refused 1. Ran to 10-5 when successful on three occasions for Nicky Sheppard, and staged something of a revival when runner-up in a weak Ladies at Howick, but has suffered with a fibrillating heart and stands few outings nowadays. Made mistakes before refusing at Cilwendeg and has never really gelled with the current rider. *Mrs C.A. Hughes — S. Pembs (Graham Hughes).* 206 (L), 361 (L), 670 (Cf).

COWSLIP LACE .—.. 9 b.m. Tulwar — Grecian Lace (Spartan General) pp. Small compact homebred half-sister to Grecian Star (*qv*). Tailed off and pulled up after two miles twice, and was all over the place when very green on her debut. Evidently not as precocious as connections hoped — these days they rarely let anything see a racecourse when it is as young as eight. *G.B. Tarry — Grafton (Rosie Goodwin).* 788 (CfMa), 1035 (OMa).

CRACKING DAY (U) ..—.. 11 gr.m. unknown p. Strong. Soon outpaced before pulling up after two miles in her Members. *Miss J. Paddock — N. Cotswold.* 921 (M).

CRACKRATTLE (IRE) ..9-10.. 11 ch.g. Montelimar (USA) — Gaye Le Moss (Le Moss) u37uR13. Compact brother to Montemoss (IRE), and half-brother to jumping winners, Galen (IRE) and Kingsmark (IRE). Dam, half-sister to The Capo Famiglia (*qv* '90 Annual) and from an excellent family, won NH flat. NH FLAT '99 r1 p0 (favourite). NH '03 r2 p0 (6th and 8th in Chses). P-t-P/HUNT CH '01/3 (for Mr, Mrs P. Polito, Mr S. Russell & Mr L. Stillwell) r10 w3 (Maiden, Restricted and Members) p4 (2 2nds, remote once); pulled up 3. Won three minor Points in a five-race spell to February '03, and landed a touch in the latest, but had trouble catching the new owner at first, and was 33-1 when successfully carrying four pounds of overweight at Clifton-on-Dunsmore. Probably lucky as the favourite broke down when looking sure to win, but has since suffered a similar fate himself. Never went a yard when tried in cheekpieces once last year. Runs tongue-tied. A.E. Brown — Fernie (Nicola Pollock). 4 (Cnr), 249 (Cnr), 379 (I), 784 (Cf), 942 (Cf), 1120 (Cf), 1429 (Cnr).

CRAIOVA COMET (IRE) ..9-5.. 11 b.g. Torus — Yankee View (Yankee Gold) 21p. Tall unfurnished. Dam won a 2m flat race in Ireland (finished 3rd in rough race, and promoted). P-t-P '03 r3 p0 (unseated 2 and pulled up 1). Very forward going and given an enterprising ride by Tom Weston when successful at Garnons, but was fast coming to the end of his tether on that occasion, and has failed to get home otherwise. Prone to blunder when fatigue sets in and is odds against to follow up. Has two paddock handlers. *M.H. Weston — Croome & W. Warwicks.* 259 (CMa), 621 (OMa), 976 (M).

CRAKE WAY ..—.. 6 b.g. Sabrehill (USA) — Miss Tealeaf (USA) (Lear Fan USA) pp. Half-brother to Have A Break, and to jumping winner, Mr Jake. Schooled on his debut, but sent off favourite next time, only to be pulled up and dismounted at the eighth (was quickly tailed off, and the rider was soon looking down as if fearing something was amiss). *Jumping For Fun Club (Mrs C.M. Mulhall) — Badsworth & Bramham Moor (Martina Mulhall).* 814 (OMa), 1417 (OMa).

CRAVEN HILL (IRE) .— §§.. 11 gr.g. Pursuit Of Love — Crodelle (IRE) (Formidable USA) ppp. Strong half-brother to flat winners, Ela Athena (won 736,283), Snow's Ride and Shifty. Dam 10f French flat winner. 10,000y. FLAT '96/7 r4 p0. NH '00/1 (for N.A. Twiston-Davies) r7 p0; pulled up 1, refsued to race 1. Swished his tail constantly on his racecourse debut, and has never been placed in 14 outings spread thinly over nine years (blinkered on four occasions in the past). Tried in Selling company, and thoroughly temperamental and usually reluctant to race (left once over Hurdles). Should have been called Craven coward. *P. Perryman & S. Lycett — N. Ledbury (Shaun Lycett).* 33 (L), 189 (L), 1341 (OMa).

CREAM SUPREME (IRE) ..—.. 15 gr.g. Supreme Leader — Grandpa's River (Over The River FR) p. Rangy half-brother to Irish winners, Beat The Second (IRE) (jumping), The King's Doctor (IRE) (NH flat) and The Cree River (IRE) (Hurdles). IRISH P-t-P '97 r4 w1 (Members) p0; pulled up 2. P-t-P/HUNT CH '98/01 and '03 r23 w8 (inc 2 Mixed Opens, Open, and 4 Confineds) p9 (4 2nds); last 2, fell 1, pulled up 1. A moody old soul who came out of retirement to record his first success since '00 last year, and made favourite to record a fifth victory at Bonvilston on his latest comeback, but pulled up lame on the run-in, and has surely been forced to call it a day this time. *Mrs J.M. Hegarty — Pentyrch (Cath Williams).* 1320 (Cf).

CREGG ROSE (IRE) ..—.. 15 br.m. Henbit (USA) — Buckscastle (Buckskin FR) p. Workmanlike. Dam of a '02 brown filly and '03 bay colt both by Salty Behaviour, who covers all the Caine mares. IRISH NH FLAT '95 r2 p0. IRISH NH '96 r5 p0. NH '98/00 r24 p2 (3rds); pulled up 10, fell/unseated 3, brought down 1. Her two placings consist of well tailed off lasts of three in Haydock Chases, including when behind a stablemate once. Often wears headgear and has always been useless. A non-finisher on 15 occasions for the present yard (on the floor in four of them). Resumed briefly after a long absence in '04, during which time she has bred two foals. *Mrs K. Woodhead — Bilsdale (Eddie Caine).* 1489 (3m3fH).

CRESSWELL GOLD ..9-2.. 8 b.m. Homo Sapien — Running For Gold (Rymer) p5. Compact half-sister to Saxon Gold (*qv*). NH FLAT '01/2 r2 p0. P-t-P '02 (for Mr B. McKay) r1 w1 (2-finisher Maiden). NH '02/3 r14 p0; last pair 3, and pulled up 5. Got off to the ideal start in Points, but never tried fences when switched under Rules where she was beaten in Sellers, and could muster only two fourths from 14 attempts. Made mistakes on her brief return to Pointing, and another change in codes would appear to be on the cards. Has been tried in cheekpieces and a tongue-tie. *D.A. Rees & P. Harris — Pembs (David Rees).* 1191 (R), 1237 (R).

CRESTED MANOR ..10-2.. 13 ch.g. Crested Lark — True Manor (True Song) p514. Robust attractive owner-bred brother to Fawsley Lake, and half-brother to Magical Manor, Fawsley Manor and Kilworth Manor. Dam, sister and half-sister to 3 Tarry Pointers including Sunshine Manor (*qv* '00 Annual), failed to stay in 6 Points for Bunny Tarry (failed to finish 4). P-t-P '03 r4 w1 (Maiden) p0; and pulled up 3. Typically unraced until he was approaching veteran status, but had been suffering from a virus prior to landing a 33-1 shock on his first completion at Dingley, and coped best with the testing conditions at Mollington (four fences were omitted owing to the state of the ground) this year. Seems game enough but may not have the speed to cope with another rise in class. *J.R. White & G.B., F.B. & G.J. Tarry — Grafton (Jimmy Tarry).* 383 (R), 582 (M), 1034 (R), 1214 (Cf).

CREVAMOY (IRE) ..10-12.. 8 ch.m. Shardari — Prudent View (IRE) (Supreme Leader) 1uu1251. Lengthy. IRISH P-t-P '02/3 r8 w1 (5yo&up Mares Maiden) p2 (3rds); pulled up 1, fell 1. A strong finisher by Pointing standards and has been unbeaten in two attempts when well handled by Andrew Richardson, but badly let down by the inexperienced 48-year old James Galbraith on their first four pairings (he had fallen off by the seventh twice), and would have won her Members given even minimal assistance. It all ended happily in a Corbridge Open and gave her partner his first winner when sprinting clear impressively in a fast time. A potentially decent Hunter Chaser, granted the right level of assistance. *J. Galbraith — Buccleuch (Bill Hughes).* 70 (R), 210 (Cf), 282 (Cf), 427 (I), 547 (M), 764 (O), 1038 (O).

CREWSKI ..—.. 10 br.g. Newski (USA) — Darlin' Again (Jolly Me) pp. Compact unfurnished owner-bred half-brother to Taffy. P-t-P/HUNT CH '00/3 (for Mr H.J. Manners) r17 w1 (Maiden) p2 (3rds, dead-heat once, and of 4 once); 5th, pulled up 11, and fell/unseated 2. Came from several fields behind to score in holding ground on his first completion at Kingston Blount in '02, but rarely fit enough to break into a gallop in the previous yard, and was a totally unsuitable ride for the owner to practice on in '04. *A.M. Gibbons — V.W.H., & Essex (Chris Lawson).* 610 (Cv&nr), 646 (M).

CROESY PENNANT .8-5.. 12 b.g. Nalchik (USA) — Courtney Pennant (Angus) pps. Lengthy unfurnished half-brother to Pyro Pennant, Rocket Radar and Stonemoss. NH FLAT '98/9 r2 p0. NH

'01 r2 p0 (pulled up 2). P-t-P '03 r8 p2 (3rds of 4); pulled up 4, ran out and fell. Often showed speed, but was too keen to get the trip in Points, and killed when slipping up at Ystradowen. P. Davies — Curre & Llangibby (Craig Davies). 362 (CfMa), 699 (CfMa), 736 (CfMa).

CROFT COURT ..9-12§.. 14 b.g. Crofthall — Queen Of Dara (Dara Monarch) p542p. Tall half-brother to jumping winner, Queens Brigade. NH '01 r2 w1 (3m2f Ch); and 4th. P-t-P/HUNT CH '96/7, '99, '01 and '03 r19 w1 (Maiden) p6 (2nds, promoted once); pulled up 6, and fell 1. A thorough stayer and connections showed enterprise when taking him to Flagg this year, but has never displayed much in the way of resolve, and failed to quicken having jumped the last upsides the winner. Otherwise beaten in excess of 25 lengths and usually takes little interest. Often blinkered though not when successful. *D.J. Renney — Heythrop (Nick Seal).* 175 (Cnr), 583 (Cf), 642 (O), 989 (Cnr), 1093 (4mMO).

CROMABOO COUNT .7-3§.. 7 b.g. Makbul — La Belle Epoque (Tachypous) pp2*p*. Workmanlike half-brother to Hurdles winner, Cromaboo Crown. NH '04 (for B.D. Leavy) r1 p0 (pulled up in 2m4f Ch: *a bhnd, mist 6, t.o when blun 4 out, pu nxt*). In a professional yard, but looked horribly unwilling when four lengths second at Brampton Bryan (a course which brings out the worst in a lot of contestants, as they have to pass the horse boxes before reaching the finish). Not to be trusted at present. *J. Wardle — N. Staffs.* 710 (Mah), 847 (M), 1116 (OMa).

CROSS RIVER ..10-8.. 10 b.g. Reprimand — River Maiden (USA) (Riverman USA) u1p1p1. Unfurnished half-brother to Irish flat and Hurdling winner, Zaidaan. Dam won at 6f in France. NH FLAT '99/00 r2 p0. NH '00 and '02 (for H.D. Daly, and Mrs S.J. Smith) r5 p0; pulled up 1. Tended to pull hard and jump badly when lightly raced in previous seasons, and can still be difficult, but much improved by his shrewd connections on balance in '04. Pulled up in his first two Hunter Chases, but from the way he scored in the Sticky Toffee Pudding Maiden at Cartmel it looked as if his whole season had been building up with this in mind (backed from 12s to nines; hopefully Harvey Smith did not insert his famed measuring stick into the prize named after the race and declare it too firm to be edible). Suited by distances in excess of three miles, and should continue to do well when wanted. Wears a cross-noseband and often tongue-tied. *Mrs S. Smith — Pendle Forest & Craven (Joss Saville).* 70 (R), 166 (OMa), 443 (2m4f110yH), 955 (R), 1177 (2m5fH), 1526 (3m2fH).

CROTTY (IRE) ..—.. 10 b.g. Shardari — My Grand Rose (IRE) (Executive Perk) pp. Sturdy half-brother to Hurdles winner, Ever Present (IRE). NH FLAT '00 r1 p0 (last). IRISH NH '00/1 (for Lord Tyrone) r5 p0; fell 1. Completely dismal, and has never finished within 30 lengths of a winner. More grotty than Crotty. *R.J. Francome — Beaufort (Sylvia Francome).* 258 (CMa), 731 (OMa).

CROWN AND CUSHION ..9-13.. 12 b.g. High Adventure — Soulieana (Manado) 5pp. Tall. FLAT '96 r4 p0 (inc Sell). NH '96/02 r21 w4 (3 2m1f-2m4f110y Hdles and 3m Ch) p3. P-t-P '03 r3 p1 (3rd); and pulled up 2. Won four races, including at 100-1 on his hurdling debut to March '00, and still retains plenty of enthusiasm, but never runs much, and was largely out of his depth in '04. Might be worth his while targeting his Members (which usually takes little winning) if he is fit to resume at 12. Pulled up when blinkered once in '97. *Mrs N.R. Matthews — Heythrop (Kim Sly).* 292 (MO), 490 (3m2fH), 784 (Cf).

CROWN RULE (IRE) ..9-0§§.. 10 ch.g. Be My Native (USA) — Super Deal (IRE) (Yashgan) 2. Lengthy workmanlike. Dam is half-sister to Pongo Waring (*qv*). NH FLAT '00 r1 p0. NH '00 r2 p1 (2nd). P-t-P '02/3 (for Mrs P. King) r14 p3 (2 2nds, of 3 once, and remote last once); 5th, 6th, and pulled up 9. Blinkered and a thorough rogue in the previous yard, and once put the wind up Andrew Sansome to such a degree that he pulled him up after two fences, but did little wrong when brushed aside in his Members in '04. Did not resurface and presumably used only as a hunter now. *J.M. Ratcliffe — Grove & Rufford (Henry Hill).* 590 (M).

CRUISING ALONG ..— §.. 7 gr.m. Thethingaboutitis (USA) — Cruising On (Cruise Missile) *r*009. Half-sister to Grey Snipe. Dam (*qv* '00 Annual) won 2m1f Ch and won Ladies and placed 4 for Carly Goodall. NH FLAT '04 r2 p0 (12th of 13 at Fakenham: *pulled hrd, a bhnd, t.o*; and last of 19 at Worcester: *a bhnd, t.o*). NH '04 (for P.T. Dalton) r1 p0 (last of 9 in 2m1f Hdle: *prom til wknd qckly app 5, t.o*). Refused at the second in a Maiden, and then performed terribly when beaten 79 lengths plus under Rules. A hard-puller and a waste of time. *Miss C.J. Goodall — Meynell & S. Staffs.* 597 (2m5fOMa).

CRYSTAL BROOK ..8-1.. 7 b.m. Alderbrook — Earles-Field (Wolverlife) 7pp54. Tall. P-t-P '03 (for Mr G.R. Davies) r2 p1 (3rd of 4); and pulled up. Quickly shown the door by the previous yard, and only once better than last since, and has tended to capitulate after showing speed for up to 2m4f. Wears a cross-noseband. *C. Staley — Golden V.* 410 (2m4fCfMa), 698 (Inr), 734 (2mH), 1231 (OMam), 1387 (M).

CRYSTAL SOLDIER ..9-2.. 7 ch.m. Infantry — Bottle Basher (Le Soleil) f32f. Small lengthy light-framed sister to Bottle Party and Glass Breaker. Dam, half-sister to Bottle Bank (*qv* '94 Annual). 580 3yo. FLAT '01/2 (for D. Burchell) r6 p0. Has a jumping pedigree and was useless on the flat (refused to race once, and 42 lengths last in her only Seller), but would have been placed at worst in three consecutive Maidens had she not fallen four out when leading in the latest (only three ran, but the winner rose successfully to

Open class later). Finished weakly when second, and it might be an idea to try 2m4f whilst she still can. *M. Arnold — Gelligaer F.* 454 (CfMa), 699 (CfMa), 735 (CfMa), 1026 (OMa).

CRYSTAL VEIN .—.. 7 gr.g. Miner's Lamp — Crystal Comet (Cosmo) uppp. Sturdy brother to Crystal Eclipse, and half-brother to Hurdles winner, Crystal Centauri. Dam won 2m2f Hdle. NH FLAT '02 r3 p0; unseated 1. NH '02/3 (for B.G. Powell) r3 p0; pulled up 3. Pulled up six times and unseated once over jumps, and makes many errors and gives the impression there is something wrong with him. In a competent yard, and it would not be surprising if they have said Buckett all. *Mrs D. Buckett — Hursley Hambledon.* 940 (OMa), 1067 (OMa), 1074 (OMa), 1322 (R).

CUMBERLAND YOUTH ..—§.. 14 b.g. Town And Country — Key Biscayne (Deep Run) pppr. Tall good-topped half-brother to Society Member and The Swangler. Dam won an Adjacent, and won 2 Hdles and 5 Chses, all 2m. NH FLAT '96 r1 p0. NH '96/8 r19 p1 (distant 3rd of 4); last, pulled up 7 and unseated in Chses; inc pulled up 4 in Hdles; in Sell. P-t-P/HUNT CH '00/3 (for Mr T. & Mrs P. George) r26 w1 (Maiden) p6 (5 3rds); pulled up 8, and refused 1. Ungenuine and shirked the issue in his first 33 attempts, but finally persuaded to keep his head in front in a 16-runner Maiden at Dingley in '02. A safe ride, but is only looking after number one, and far too cagey for the owner-rider to contend with. Acquired cheekpieces on his latest appearance, and has previously been tried in blinkers and a visor. *Mr P. Ikin — Pytchley.* 294 (R), 587 (R), 886 (Cf), 1217 (R).

CURROW KATE .8-1.. 8 br.m. Anshan — Dereks Daughter (Derek H) pp74R54. Unfurnished half-sister to Another Daughter. Dam won 2 Points and 2m4f Chse, and placed total of 12. P-t-P '03 r1 p0 (pulled up). Not without ability, and was poised to deliver a challenge when running out through the wing of the third-last once, but largely disappointing, and lack of stamina seems to be the problem. No longer eligible for short Maidens, and will probably continue to be expensive to follow. *H. Murphy — Atherstone (Roger Harvey).* 113 (OMa), 226 (CfMa), 387 (OMa), 686 (OMa), 850 (2m5fOMa), 1124 (OMa), 1403 (2m4fOMa).

CUT DOWN THE SOUND (IRE) ..—§.. 10 ch.g. Shiel Hill — Carolin Lass (IRE) (Carlingford Castle) ppp. Tall rangy. IRISH P-t-P '99/00 r5 p4 (2nds); and pulled up. NH '01 r1 p0 (pulled up in 3m110y Ch). P-t-P '01 and '03 (for Mr J.M. Bowen) r5 w1 (Maiden) p2 (2nds); and pulled up 2. Rated 9-5 after winning a Maiden at Lifton last year but looked thoroughly ungenuine when runner-up on six previous occasions, and clearly threw in the towel before halfway on his latest appearance. Has never appeared more than four times in a year, and his lack of resolve probably stems from a physical disability. Blinkered once in '01. *Miss L. Wonnacott — Spooners & W. Dartmoor.* 1002 (R), 1543 (R), 1561 (R).

PLATE 34 526 Tanatside Members: Cutina (David Barlow), 1st, leads Lord Of The West (Walter Puddifer), 2nd PHOTO: Brian Armstrong

CUTINA ..9-10.. 11 b.m. Tina's Pet — Cute Pam (Pamroy) 1241p7. Strong sister to Socute and Pampered Lad. Dam won 8 Points (inc an Open) and placed 8 ('quite a useful stayer on her day', *qv*

'92 Annual). NH FLAT '00 r1 p0. NH '00/2 (for S.A. Brookshaw) r12 p3; pulled up 3. Lightly raced and only once beaten less than 23 lengths under Rules, and pulled up in half the Chases she contested, but has found Pointing more to her liking, and scored twice in three-finisher events in soft. Took over eight minutes to land her Restricted, but ran poorly when well-fancied for the Radnor four-miler, and had also flopped when the money was down at Eyton previously. Only moderate and her enthusiasm remains questionable. *Mr W.R.J. Everall — Tanatside (Phil Jones).* 526 (M), 665 (R), 933 (CR), 1048 (R), 1228 (4mO), 1375 (3m110yH).

DAINTY MAN (IRE) ..9-10.. 13 b/br.g. Cardinal Flower — Web Of Gold (Bustineto) 38. Neat. IRISH P-t-P '98 r9 w1 (5yo&up Maiden) p4; pulled up 2, and fell 1. P-t-P/HUNT CH '99/00 and '02/3 r19 w1 (Restricted) p5 (2 2nds, remote once); pulled up 4. Avoids soft ground as best he can, and lightly raced after crossing the Irish Sea, but has proved impossible to place successfully since '99, and normally produces little off the bridle. Has been retired. *Miss M.A. De Quincey — Sir W.W. Wynn's (Anne Hewitt).* 228 (Cf), 379 (I).

DAISY DUKE .8-8.. 8 b.m. Rakaposhi King — Carlton Valley (Barolo) pp. Harvey-bred half-sister to Carlton Brae (*qv*). Lacked fluency and pulled up after less than 2m2f twice. *Miss J. Midgley & Mrs M. Harvey — Puckeridge (Joss Midgley).* 218 (OMa), 371 (OMa).

DAISY FAY ..10-2.. 10 b.m. Broadsword (USA) — Lily Of The West (True Song) 31. Tiny. Dam was 3rd in her only Point (subsequently 2nd in a Hdle), and grandam, Wanchai Lil won 3 Points and placed 4 (inc 3 flat). P-t-P '00 and '02/3 (for Mr P. McCanlis, Mr G. & Mrs K. Smyly) r10 w1 (2m4f Maiden) p0; 4th twice, fell/unseated 5, and pulled up 2. A tough little mare and scored on her only completion in '02, and was given away after breaking down last year, but subsequently returned. Well handled by Harry Dowty when springing a 20-1 shock at Didmarton, but presumably the firm ground took it's toll as she was not seen again. *P. McCanlis, Mrs G. Crofts & S. Evetts — N. Cotswold (Giles & Kim Smyly).* 294 (R), 369 (R).

DAISY LEIGH .—.. 11 b.m. Crested Lark — Mrs Pepperpot (Kinglet) pb. Small half-sister to To The Top. Dam (*qv* '90 Annual), won Ladies and 2nd twice, including Hdle. P-t-P '02 r5 w1 (Maiden) p0; and pulled up 4. NH '02/3 (from G.B. Balding's) r3 p0 (last and pulled up 2 in Chses). Won a weak Maiden at Bredwardine in '02 after pulling up in her first four attempts, but not better than last in a handful of appearances since. Bang in contention when brought down four out in a strong Restricted at Woodford, but whilst ability obviously still lurks within getting her to the track presents problems. *A.K. Leigh — Curre & Llangibby.* 844 (R), 1069 (R).

DAISY'S CHOICE ..8-0.. 10 b.m. Tigerwood — Official Lady (Official) 13pp3p4u. Very small light sister to Teigr Pren and Wiston Wizo. Dam, half-sister to Kerstin's Choice (*qv* '98 Annual), was last of 3 in a Maiden. P-t-P '00 and '02/3 r19 p4 (3 2nds, last once; and 3rd of 4); last pair 4, pulled up 5, and fell/unseated 6. Finally got off the mark at the 20th attempt, but the clear leader fell fatally at the last, and has continued to perpetuate her rounds with mistakes since. Beaten upwards of 40 lengths when making the frame in Restricteds (remounted once) and will need all the luck in the world to secure another success. *Mrs J. Llewellyn — Pembs (Brian Llewellyn).* 202 (CfMa), 358 (R), 674 (R), 740 (R), 953 (R), 1094 (R), 1238 (I), 1482 (R).

DAISYS RAINBOW ..— §.. 6 b.g. Dreams End — Daisy Miller (Daring March) ppp4. Sturdy. Dam, 2nd on flat, won 12 Points and placed 17 for Dilwyn Thomas. NH FLAT '04 (for Mrs D.A. Hamer) r1 p0 (4th over 2m1f at Hereford: *pulled hard, prom, ld over 6f out til hdd over 3f out, wknd 2f out*). Bred from a delightful mare who did connections proud, but hung so violently in all his Points that he became unrideable and had to be pulled up (and this with a jockey as fierce as Dai Jones). Probably has some ability, but is a real wild child at present. *D.R. Thomas — Llangeinor.* 1093 (4mMO), 1188 (Cf), 1322 (R).

DAKTARI (U) ..2-0.. 9 b.g. Duntroon — Piata (unknown) 6. Compact well-made. Hacked around to eventually finish three fences last in his Members. *R. Williams — Tiverton Stag.* 1554 (M).

DALE CREEK (IRE) ..8-13.. 10 b.g. Mandalus — Typhoon Signal (Aristocracy) p2r. Heavy topped half-brother to Cauld Signal (IRE). Dam 34-time maiden. IR5900 3yo. IRISH P-t-P '00 r2 w1 (5yo Maiden) p0. IRISH NH FLAT '00/1 r6 p1 (2nd). IRISH NH '99/02 r15 w1 (3m1f Ch) p0; pulled up 3, fell/unseated 4. IRISH HUNT CH '00 r1 p0. NH '02/3 (for R.H. Alner) r6 p1 (2nd); pulled up 1, unseated 1. Bought Ascot, Nov for 4285. A dual winner in Ireland, but has not scored since all out to land a Chase in August '01. Has regularly failed to finish and often looked badly troubled since, and after finishing over a fence behind his rival in a match for an Open he broke a blood vessel and refused two out when pursuing the only other still going in a three-horse Members. *Mr & Mrs J.F. Symes — Cotley (John Symes).* 703 (MO), 1010 (O), 1247 (M).

DAMIENS PRIDE (IRE) ..10-0§.. 15 b.g. Bulldozer — Riopoless (Royal And Regal USA) p421p1. Compact half-brother to Irish Hurdles winner, Arctic Clover (IRE). IRISH P-t-P '95 r3 p0 (pulled up 2 and refused). NH '01 r1 p0 (pulled up in 3m2f110y Ch). P-t-P/HUNT CH '97/03 r37 w4 (inc 2m3f110y Hunt Ch and Open) p18 (13 2nds, beaten neck once, of 3 once, and inc 2 Hunt Chses;

and inc 3rd twice in Hunt Chses); failed to finish 11 (fell 2, refused 2, ran out 2). Consistent in minor company, and has kept his form well for an old-timer, but does not always exert himself, and reserves his best effort for right-handed tracks (despite a tendency to jump left) and Lifton in particular. Has won in softish but his ability to handle fast ground gives him every chance of scoring again. Wears a cross-noseband. *Mrs S.J. Batchelor — Lamerton.* 200 (Cf), 412 (Cf), 566 (M), 823 (Cf), 1166 (2m5f110yH), 1349 (O).

DAMMITU ..7-7.. 9 ch.m. Elegant Monarch — Aunt Dicey (Never So Bold) p. Plain small. Dam failed to get beyond halfway in 3 Points for Carol Lawrence. P-t-P '02/3 r5 p0 (last 2, pulled up 3). Has never been able to stand a full season, and well tailed off last in both completions, and a potty gamble from 25s to tens on her latest foray at Cherrybrook. *Mrs C. Lawrence — Eggesford.* 795 (CfMa).

DAM THE BREEZE ..10-9.. 12 b.g. Ikdam — Cool Breeze (Windjammer USA) 26. Tall good-bodied half-brother to Cool Off. Dam pulled up in 4 Points. NH '99/03 r19 w6 (4 2m7f110y-3m1f110y Chses, and 2 3m110y-3m2f Hdles) p3 (inc 2 2nds); pulled up 3, and fell when looking probable winner once. P-t-P/HUNT CH '98/9 and '03 r12 w1 (Maiden) p2 (2nd of 3 once); 4th, 7th, last pair 2, pulled up, fell 2, and brought down 2. Learnt the ropes in Points, and now mixes Hunter Chases with a more successful career under Rules. Lacks a turn of foot and usually helps force the pace, and is difficult to peg back once he gets into a rhythm, but jumps away to the right and sometimes the victim of wholesale blunders. Conquered Aintree at the second attempt and despite advancing years should find another opportunity. Has won in softish, but more effective on a sound surface. Visored once in '00. *K. Glastonbury — Pentyrch (Evan Williams).* 346 (3m1f110yH), 732 (2m5f110yH).

DANCETILLYOUDROP (IRE) ..10-4.. 14 b.g. Clearly Bust — Keep Dancing (Lord Gayle USA) p7u431. Workmanlike brother to Keep Clear (IRE). IRISH NH FLAT '96 r1 w1. NH '96/02 r47 w8 (2m4f110y-3m2f110y Chses) p19 (11 2nds); pulled up 4, fell 5. HUNT CH '02/3 r5 w2 (3m2f-3m7f) p1 (2nd); pulled up 2. Formerly smart and rated a stone higher at his best, but has suffered with wind problems and broken blood vessels, and pulled up in both appearances last year. Never the most fluent of jumpers, but made an ideal schoolmaster for Turia Tellwright, and came with strong late burst to secure the spoils at Tabley. The rider made a shaky start but is certainly on the upgrade, and whilst connections have done a grand job in rejuvenating him they may feel the need to trade him in for a faster model. Has run tongue-tied, and acquired a cross-noseband in '04. *Hon Mrs C.F. Tellwright — Sir W.W. Wynn's.* 230 (L), 529 (L), 661 (Cnr), 931 (L), 1263 (L), 1428 (L).

DANCING DASI (IRE) ..9-3.. 6 b.m. Supreme Leader — Little Dasi (IRE) (Mandalus) 45f. Small. Bought Doncaster, May for 10,000. Had an adequate first season, and would have negotiated 53 fences successfully had she not fallen at the last when set to finish a modest fourth at Woodford. Should be capable of getting more seriously involved at six. *F.D.A. Snowden — Eggesford (Gillian Snowden).* 568 (CfMa), 701 (2m4f0Ma), 1075 (OMa).

DANCING FOSENBY ..10-6.. 9 b.g. Terimon — Wave Dancer (Dance In Time CAN) 341212r1. Good-topped half-brother to 2 winners abroad. Dam won 12f race and is well-related. NH '01/2 r10 p1 (3rd in Sell). P-t-P/HUNT CH '03 r7 w4 (Maiden, Club Restricted, Intermediate and Members; inc hat-trick) p1 (3rd); 4th and pulled up. Way below average under Rules, and gained his only placing in the lowest grade, but a revelation since joining the current yard, and has not stopped improving. Recorded his seventh success when landing a weak Hunter Chase at Folkestone, and should find further opportunities if sensibly placed. Jumps well and normally races with plenty of enthusiasm for Curly Holdsworth, but once thought that a tug on the reins was the notice to stop, and dumped the rider. Wears a cross-noseband. Blinkered thrice in '02. *The Mighty Friends (M. Holdforth) — Hursley Hambledon (Penny Lownds).* 168 (C), 422 (CCon), 623 (Cf), 642 (O), 938 (MO), 1185 (MO), 1355 (3m1fH), 1438 (3m2fH).

DANNICUS ..9-0.. 14 b.g. Derrylin — Kerris Melody (Furry Glen) 64p3R3. Workmanlike half-brother to Kerri-B, and to NH flat winner, Star Diva (IRE). NH '96/7 r6 p1 (19l 3rd); last and carried out in 2 Chses. P-t-P/HUNT CH '99/00 and '02 (for Mr D.A. Shone) r12 w4 (inc 2 Ladies) p4 (2nd of 3; and 3 3rds); pulled up 1, unseated 1. A fine jumper, and rated 10-8 after recording his fourth success at Littlewindsor in '02, but very injury-prone and has now developed stringhalt on his near hind. Usually takes a very keen hold, but employed as a part-time schoolmaster this year, and failed to beat a rival. Has a history of bleeding, and burst again at Dalston. Acquired cheekpieces on his latest start. *A.J. McElwee — Braes (Russell Ross).* 506 (Cnr), 564 (L), 763 (L), 1036 (M), 1289 (O), 1415 (L).

DANNY GALE (IRE) ..—.. 14 b.g. Strong Gale — Mary The Rake (On Your Mark) pp. Tall hobdayed. Dam won 3 2m Hdles in Ireland. NH FLAT '95 r1 p0. NH '95/7 and '01 r15 w1 (2m1f Hdle) p0; inc Sell; pulled up 3, brought down 1. P-t-P '99/00 and '02/3 r16 p3 (2 3rds; and last of 2); 4th of 5, pulled up 9, fell/unseated 2 and refused. Gained his only success at Bangor-on-Dee back in '96, but rendered totally useless by persistent wind problems since, and is a pathetic sight to behold now. Can hardly gallop, and jumps deliberately, and deserves to be humiliated no more. Wears a tongue-tie, and has been tubed, and blinkered once in '97 and visored once in '02. *P. Davies — Curre & Llangibby (Craig Davies).* 356 (M), 842 (O).

DANS BLARNEY (IRE) ..8-0§.. 8 b.g. Teenoso (USA) — Easby Mandrina (Mandalus) 82322r. Tall. Dam won NH FLAT and 3 Hurdles (2m-2m1f) and 2 Chases (2m-2m4f). IRISH P-t-P '03 r8 p0 (7th of 8, last, pulled up 5, and fell 1). Has contested 14 Points and only had five horses behind him, and grossly flattered by his form figures in '04 (beaten at least 25 lengths in three of the placings). Temperamental and can look difficult to steer, and is the antithesis of his game and competent mother. *B.R. Hughes - Llangeinor (Mair Hughes).* 119 (OMa), 202 (CfMa), 362 (CfMa), 617 (2m4fOMa), 950 (2m4fOMa), 1096 (OMa).

DANTE'S BANKER (IRE) ..9-7.. 9 ch.g. Phardante (FR) — Nancy Myles (The Parson) p15pp. Strong attractive. Dam won 3 NH flat, 3 flat (13-16f), 10 Hurdles (2m-2m4f) and 3 Chases (2m2f-3m) in Ireland. IRISH P-t-P '01/3 r8 w1 (Maiden) p2 (3rds). IRISH NH FLAT '01 r1 p0. NH '03 (for C.C. Bealby) r3 p1 (2nd of 3); fell 1. Bought Doncaster, May for 2500. Mother was sensationally successful in Ireland, where her boundless enthusiasm gained her 19 victories, but is nothing like her. Had won a Maiden in soft to show for three seasons of endeavour in his homeland, but was a distant second of three in one of two Hurdles and fell at the sixth in a Chase after arriving in England. Modest and looked reluctant when returned to racing between the flags and acquired cheekpieces on final start, but placed first by Blind 'Not A Clue' Pugh who judges at the South Notts after finishing half a length second (in a triumph of ineptitude, he got all the first four home in the wrong order, but in awarding the race to a horse who had omitted five fences he was completely correct, as it is the job of the Stewards to do the disqualifying!). Not better than last since, and getting very close to a squiggle. *Mrs J.A.C. Lundgren — Brocklesby.* 787 (CR), 944 (R), 1121 (O), 1216 (4m100yMO), 1397 (I).

DANTE'S PROMISE (IRE) .9-12§.. 9 b.g. Phardante (FR) — Let's Compromise (No Argument) 6. Tall half-brother to Rag Stream and Ora Pronobis, to jumping winners, Tarpromise and Strong Promise (IRE), and to Irish winners, Lets Promise (Chasing) and Gabrielle's Boy (bumpers). Dam, half-sister to Ratocchu (*qv* '91 Annual), won 2m Maiden Hurdle in Ireland. IRISH P-t-P '01 r2 p0 (pulled up and unseated). IRISH NH FLAT '01 r1 p0. P-t-P '02/3 r7 w2 (Maiden and Restricted) p3 (2nds); and pulled up 2. Displayed a ready turn of foot when successful on sound surfaces on his final appearances '02/3, but from a very quirky family, and has also inherited a temperamental streak. Disappeared after one early sighter in '04, and may have suffered a setback. Taken to post early, but only did so with the greatest reluctance at Tweseldown. *T. Bailey — Beaufort (Richard Smith).* 19 (CMod).

DANTIE BOY (IRE) ..10-6.. 9 br.g. Phardante (FR) — Ballybride Gale (IRE) (Strong Gale) 23. Workmanlike angular. NH '02/3 (for P.J. Hobbs) r17 w3 (2 2m4f-2m6f Hdles and 2m3f Ch) p8 (inc 7 2nds); fell 1. Won three times in '02 (had a wind operation after the first victory), and often travels well, but tends to get run out of races he looks like winning. That was never more evident than at Taunton, where he overtook the hanging Jabiru soon after the last only to be caught by a rocket-propelled Alska who was gaining a first English victory at the 40th attempt. Subsequently under two lengths third after finding very little at Exeter, where a blunder at the final fence cost him second. Needs a sound surface, but does not appear too easy to train now. *A.W. Congdon — Torrington F.* 993 (3mH), 1293 (2m7f110yH).

DANZANTE (IRE) .9-8§.. 13 b.g. Ajraas (USA) — Baliana (CAN) (Riverman USA) 56u. Big strong half-brother to 3 flat winners (one in France and one in Ireland), including Test The Water. NH FLAT '96 r1 w1. NH '96/01 r41 w2 (3m-3m2f Hdles) p12 (6 2nds); pulled up 13. P-t-P '02 r2 p0 (pulled up 2). Got off to the perfect start, but then took another four years to follow up, and wore headgear regularly under Rules. Has never won over fences, and beaten a minimum of 20 lengths in Points, but is safe and the dip on the bend out of the home straight was solely responsible for the severing of the partnership at Rhydygwern where the re-application of blinkers appeared to galvanise him. Normally shows little zest and can drop hold of the bridle at any stage. Has two paddock handlers. *R. & S. Moreton — Warwicks (Simon Moreton).* 1120 (Cf), 1214 (Cf), 1485 (Cnr).

DARAK (IRE) ..10-0.. 9 b.g. Doyoun — Dararita (IRE) (Halo USA) 2p2133. Good-topped attractive. Dam won 13f race in France and comes from a good family. FLAT '99 r2 p0. IRISH NH '00 r4 p0. NH '00/2 r14 w1 (2m1f110y Hdle) p0. P-t-P '03 r8 w1 (Open) p3 (3rd of 4 twice); and pulled up 4. NH '04 r1 p1 (dist 3rd of 4 in 2m1f110y Ch: *chsd ldrs, mist 1, wkng when blun 8, t.o when blun 3 out*). Changed hands for 26,000 in July '99, a month after Gary Stevens had partnered him in the last of two runs on the flat for Sir Michael Stoute, and recouped a small percentage of it 13 months later when successful on his first attempt in a Seller. Scoring for the first time since at Easingwold last year, and has shown rather more consistency for present connections, but needs to get clear in order to hang on, and is suited by an easy three miles. *N.D. Tutty — Hurworth (Karen Tutty).* 338 (Cf), 1161 (O), 1301 (Cf), 1413 (Cf), 1457 (O).

DARCEY MAE ..9-8.. 7 b.m. Afzal — Belhelvie (Mart Lane) up132. Lengthy half-sister to St Helier. Dam, half-sister to 3 Pointers, including Celtic Sport (*qv* '98 Annual), won Maiden and 2 Restricteds (desperately unlucky in another as the weightcloth fell off within spitting distance of the post) and placed 4 for Owen Stephens. Grandam, Bell-Amys, won 2m Sell Hdle, and won Hunt Ch and 5 Points (4 Ladies) and placed 6 (mostly for Mr Stephens). P-t-P '03 (for Mr O.J. Stephens) r1 p1 (3rd). Caught the eye last year, and possibly unlucky on her reappearance, but made amends in a three-finisher 2m4f Maiden on firmish at Larkhill. Has had plenty of use made of her over the standard trip to date, but not getting home, and may prove more effective when held up. Tends to get wound up in the preliminaries. Wears a cross-noseband. *Mrs H.M. Bridges — S. & W. Wilts.* 142 (OMa), 493 (OMa), 633 (2m4fCfMa), 864 (R), 1097 (M).

DARCY JONES .9-7.. 9 br.g. Mahrajan — Small Brook (Brianston Zipper) p. Sturdy compact. Dam is sister to Bert House (*qv* '98 Annual). Great-grandam, Spiritway, won 4 Points and placed 7. NH '00 and '02 r5 p0; pulled up 3. P-t-P '01 and '03 r9 p2; 5th of 6, pulled up 4, brought down and fell. Placed in two back-end Maidens last year, and might have prevailed had he winged the last once, but runs tubed, and only able to make one appearance in '04. Effective only when stamina is not at a premium. Wears blinkers. *E.A. Jones — Silverton.* 66 (OMa).

DARE ..10-3.. 10 b.g. Beveled (USA) — Run Amber Run (Run The Gantlet USA) 2311. Compact brother to flat winners Moon Over and Happy Hostage (also won Hurdling), and half-brother to 2 flat winners, including Quick Ransom. Dam won at up to 9f in USA. 9600y. FLAT '97/01 46 w7 (8-12f) p6. NH '98/03 (for P.D. Evans, and R. Lee) r28 w3 (2m-2m1f Hurdles) p8; fell 1, pulled up 1. A funny old customer who can be tricky, and gained the last of his ten wins under Rules (three on the all-weather) in November '01 (had been second in five consecutive Hurdles earlier that year). Most successful in Sept/Oct '99 when he completed a four-timer, and also won three in a row two years later, but was tailed off in four Chasing attempts (distant third of four, fourth, last and fell). Frequently pulls hard, but can be a weak finisher, and rather fortunate to unearth two modest Confineds in '04 (three got round once and only three set off once). Wears a tongue-tie, and equipped with headgear or cheekpieces on many occasions in the past. Connections did very well to rekindle a flame which had been reduced to a flicker. *J.E. Potter, J. Blurton & J. Lee — Tanatside (Jonathan Lee).* 251 (C), 660 (Cf), 932 (Cf), 1144 (Cf).

DARKARROW (IRE) .9-10§.. 10 b.g. Commanche Run — Darkdalus (Mandalus) ppRp13. Tall. Dam won 4&5yo Mares Maiden in Ireland. IRISH P-t-P '99/00 r3 w1 (Maiden) p0; fell 2. IRISH NH FLAT '00 r1 p0. IRISH NH '00/2 (for D. Queally) r12 p1 (2nd in Ch); pulled up 3. An ungenuine type who is usually easy to trounce, and was blinkered on five occasions in Ireland, but ended a run of seven consecutive non-completions (pulled up in six) when catching the idling Lah Di Dah Lad near the finish after looking well held at the final fence in a Kingston Blount Restricted (Jody Sole on one of his more enterprising days). Did not seem happy to have the owner aboard when 14 lengths third at Trecoed, and it does not take much for him to throw in the towel. *Mr T.D.B. Underwood — Worcs.* 720 (R), 1034 (R), 1208 (R), 1482 (R), 1517 (R), 1552 (I).

DARK CHALLENGER (IRE) ..10-0.. 13 b/br.g. Brush Aside (USA) — Great Aunt Emily (Traditionalist USA) p2p32p. Tall rangy brother to Market Poseur (IRE), and half-brother to Emily's Niece (dam of Call Me Again and Gunville *qv*), Raise A Smile, Kinon-Penny and Paradise Row (IRE). NH FLAT '96 r1 p0. NH '96/8 r6 p4 (2 Hdles, and 2nd of 4 and 3rd of 4 in Chses). P-t-P '00/3 r16 w3 (Maiden, Restricted and Intermediate) p9 (3 2nds, beaten neck once, and of 3 twice); 4th, last, and pulled up 2. Consistent and a patent safety, but never that keen to exert himself, and has found winning difficult. Had plenty of support in '04, and was made favourite for the Modbury four-miler on the back of a good second for Alex Charles-Jones over the course and distance, but flopped and simply has to have strong handling. Suited by some cut in the ground. Often blinkered in the past. *J.F. Weldhen — Four Burrow.* 484 (L), 570 (Cf), 707 (Cf), 911 (MO), 1003 (4mO), 1197 (4mL).

DARK COMEDY ..8-5.. 10 br.m. Lepanto (GER) — Happy Tino (Rugantino) 8R6. Lengthy half-sister to Happy Team (*qv*). P-t-P '02/3 r2 p0 (last and pulled up). Has shown some speed, but yet to display enough stamina, and not better than last in three completions. Busy by her standards in '04, but very lightly raced compared to others. *K.F. Fisher — N. Cornwall.* 824 (R), 913 (OMa), 1353 (OMa).

DARRELL BOY (IRE) ..9-4§§.. 10 b.g. Commanche Run — Free For Ever (Little Buskins) pp2pp. Tall angular half-brother to Wild Buck (IRE), and to Chasing winner, Abercromby Chief. IRISH NH FLAT '00/1 r2 p0. NH FLAT '01 r2 p0. NH '01/3 (for J.R. Norton) r10 w1 (3m3f110y Hdle) p3 (2 3rds); pulled up 3. All out when winning a long Selling Hurdle in soft, and his three placings have been moderate efforts (last of two in his Members in the latest). Wears headgear and is thoroughly ungenuine, and it would be a major surprise if anybody could be bothered to race him again. *D.W. Sharland — Ross H. (Christine Hardinge).* 49 (4mO), 229 (O), 402 (M), 612 (Cf), 841 (Cf).

DART VIEW LASS ..— §.. 8 ch.m. Riverwise (USA) — Cut Above The Rest (Indiaro) wppcp. Sister to Cats Cross (*qv*). Dam placed 4 in Points ('prone to bad blunders, and has little stamina'). Bought

Ascot, Aug for 1714. A troublesome mare who was withdrawn under orders on her debut after throwing the rider and galloping off in a false start (had been going bananas in the paddock), and could not be persuaded to the complete the course subsequently (including with cheekpieces on the three most recent attempts). Unpromising. *M.J. Tozer — Dart V.H. & S. Pool H. (Chloe Newman).* 13 (OMa), 702 (2m4fOMa), 826 (OMa), 1133 (OMa), 1248 (OMa).

DAT MY HORSE (IRE) ..10-10.. 11 b.g. All Haste (USA) — Toposki (FR) (Top Ville) u. Big workmanlike. IRISH P-t-P '99 r1 w1 (5yo Maiden). NH '00 and '02/3 r14 w3 (3m-3m2f Hdles) p3 (inc 3rd to subsequent Sun Alliance Chase winner One Knight); pulled up 2, fell 1. FLAT '02 r1 p0 (pulled up in Queen Alexandra Stakes at Royal Ascot). P-t-P/HUNT CH '01/2 r8 w2 (Open and Restricted) p1 (2nd); fell/unseated 4 and pulled up. Recorded a hat-trick over hurdles after winning two Points in '02, and runner-up to Iris's Gift at Cheltenham later the same year, but bitterly disappointing since, and remains compromised by his jumping technique (does not bend his back). Lost the rider at the first when favourite to regain some prowess at Llanfrynach, and has since returned to hurdling unsuccessfully. *A. & Mrs J. Lowrie — Glamorgan (Cath Williams).* 448 (O).

DAWN'S COGNAC (IRE) .—.. 12 b.g. Glacial Storm (USA) — Misty Venture (Foggy Bell) 8p11fpfp. Tall rangy half-brother to Aberaeron Girl (dam of Aaron's Venture, Annascan, Pudding And Pie and Prince Of Beal *qv*), Mysterious Run (IRE) and Knockaun Wood (IRE), to jumping winner, Super Rapier (IRE), and to Irish Hurdles winner, Regal Venture (IRE). NH '02 r1 p0; pulled up. P-t-P/HUNT CH '98/01 and '03 r29 w9 (inc 2 Opens and 3 Ladies, inc hat-trick '00) p5 (3 2nds, beaten head once); pulled up 4, and fell/unseated 7. A smart Pointer until going wrong in '02, and despite winning four races and taking his tally into double figures, has been unable to recapture his best form since. Won well at Erw Lon, where the odds-on favourite was given a shocking ride, but otherwise beat only one other finisher all year, and appears to lose heart if things don't go his way. Worth 10-4 at his best, but frequently let down by shoddy jumping, and now might be as good a time as any to call it quits. *D. Brace — Llangeinor.* 10 (L), 77 (O), 206 (L), 673 (L), 974 (3mH), 1093 (4mMO), 1367 (O), 1522 (L).

DAYDREAMER (USA) ..9-10.. 12 b.g. Alleged (USA) — Stardusk (USA) (Stage Door Johnny USA) 33. Strong-topped. Dam 5 races at up to 13f in USA, and is sister to champion turf horse, Johnny D. FLAT r1 p0. NH '97/8 r5 p2 (9-17l 3rds). P-t-P '00/2 r10 w2 (Maiden and Restricted) p5 (4 2nds; and 3rd of 4); unseated 2 and pulled up 1. Ridden from behind and produced late when successful twice to '02, but needs fast ground and an easy three miles to show his best, and has been very lightly raced indeed. Did not have conditions in his favour when failing to beat a rival in '04, but a difficult sort to catch right at the best of times, and has been a beaten favourite on five occasions. *A. & Mrs S. Hickman — E. Sussex & Romney Marsh (Sara Hickman).* 1050 (M), 1281 (Cf).

DEAN DEIFIR (IRE) ..9-8.. 13 b/br.g. Mandalus — Fiancee (Royal Match) p7. Tall strong half-brother to Knight Hunter (dam of Snowshill Shaker, *qv* '00 Annual), and Jan's Decision, and to 2 winners abroad. IRISH P-t-P '97/8 r7 p1 (25l 2nd); pulled up 4, and fell. IRISH NH '98 r1 p0. P-t-P '99/00 and '03 r19 w5 (inc Open) p4 (2 ¾l 2nds; inc last of 3 once); unseated 1, pulled up 2, and withdrawn under orders 1. Headstrong and has made the bulk of the running when successful in five minor events, but lucky in the latest, and only gets the trip when conditions aren't testing. Has worn bandages in front, and frequent exposure to fast ground may have induced a problem. Wears a cross-noseband, and has been tried in blinkers and cheekpieces. *Mrs K. Craggs — Morpeth (Alan Balmer).* 211 (C), 428 (3m5fL).

DEAR AS SAFFRON ..9-0.. 8 b.m. Almoojid — Saffron Lake (Shaab) p542f. Compact. Beaten by wide margins in her first two completions, and then flattered by being allowed to get within 25 lengths of Lady Misprint in a match for an Open (it could easily have been 25 lengths plus). An endearingly daft plunge from 14s to fours in an Intermediate, but fell after two miles, and collapsed walking back and given oxygen before collection in the horse ambulance. Has not yet shown she is good enough to win a Maiden, but it would at least make some sense to concentrate on them. *M. Biddick — N. Cornwall.* 488 (R), 571 (R), 1006 (CfMa), 1198 (O), 1544 (I).

DEAR LORD (IRE) .—.. 8 ch.g. Mister Lord (USA) — Carange (Known Fact USA) p. Strong half-brother to Miss Carange (IRE), Irish NH flat winner, Keltech Warrior, and to flat winners, Cheerful Groom (IRE) and Another Nightmare (IRE) (11 wins). NH '02/3 (for Mrs A.M. Thorpe) r4 p0; pulled up 2. Useless in Hurdles including Sellers (pulled up at the second with a slipped saddle once) and a Chase (pulled up), and started at 100-1 thrice. Resumed briefly in a Maiden, but weakened rapidly on the inordinately long run from two out and was tailed off and pulled up at the last (sent off at a ludicrously short 3-1). *Mrs V.R. Smart — Cleveland.* 272 (OMa).

DECENT BOND (IRE) ..10-5.. 8 b.g. Witness Box (USA) — Decent Skin (IRE) (Buckskin FR) 12u1u1123. Compact half-brother to Irish Pointing winner, Wing Back. Dam, half-sister to Commanche Rebel (*qv* '01 Annual). P-t-P '03 r4 p0 (4th, last, pulled up and fell). A progressive individual, and has hit the front in the final quarter-mile when successful on good or easy surfaces, but occasionally let down by his jumping, and stopped in his tracks by a blunder when contesting his first Open. Given far too much to do next time, but stays well and looks set to make amends in similar company. Well handled in the main by Roger Green. *V. Thompson — Percy.* 554 (CfMa), 657 (R), 797 (3m1fH), 854 (M), 1040 (R), 1077 (R), 1220 (C), 1309 (O), 1421 (O).

DE CHELLY ..10-3.. 10 b.m. Perpendicular — Spider Woman (Touching Wood USA) 1124. Sturdy. Dam, half-sister to Incy Wincy Spider (*qv*), won 2m Sell Hdle. NH FLAT '99 r1 w1. NH '99/00 r5 p3 (2 3rds). P-t-P '02/3 (for Mrs C. Owen & Mrs L. Meyrick) r10 w1 (Ladies) p6 (5 2nds); and pulled up 3. An expensive failure in the previous yard, but has not missed the frame when completing in Points, and boasts a defeat of Upton Adventure amongst her three successes. Very game on occasions but does not appear able to hold her form for very long and finished 32 lengths behind the mare when they next met. Safe but apt to jump deliberately, and should find further straightforward opportunities in West Wales. Acts on firmish and not inconvenienced by some cut in the ground. *Mrs C.E. Owen — S. Pembs.* 737 (L), 949 (L), 1189 (L), 1391 (L).

DECODED ..—.. 9 ch.g. Deploy — Golden Panda (Music Boy) ffu5pp. Strong-topped compact half-brother to 3 winners including Pandiculation (flat). Dam won 8f race. 16500y. FLAT '98/9 r8 p0. NH '99/03 (for G.M. Moore, and C. Grant) r17 w2 (2m4f Hdle and 3m1f Ch) p3; pulled up 1, fell 1. Used to have ability and won a four-runner Hurdle in soft and a staying Chase by a head on firmish (all out), but his jumping went completely to pot in the new yard, and was hopelessly tailed off last on the only occasion he struggled to completion. Meets very few fences in his stride now, and his confidence is shot to pieces. Often wears artificial aids, including cheekpieces on occasions in '04. *Mrs H.E. Aitkin — S. Durham (Sarah Dent).* 269 (O), 798 (3m1fH), 894 (3m3fH), 1068 (3m2f110yH), 1347 (2m6f110yH), 1444 (3m1fH).

DEEL QUAY (IRE) ..—.. 14 b.g. Tidaro (USA) — Quayside Charm (Quayside) ppp. Compact sturdy brother to Dancing Paws (IRE), and half-brother to Irish Pointing winner, Quayfield, and to Irish NH flat winner, Nicholl Lady (IRE). Dam won Irish NH flat. IRISH P-t-P '95 r1 p1 (2nd). NH FLAT '96 r1 p0. NH '96/9 r17 w1 (3m1f Ch) p5 (pulled up and continued for 3rd once); pulled up in 4 of final 6, inc Sell. P-t-P '00/3 r16 w1 (Members) p5 (3 3rds, of 4 twice); pulled up 1, carried out 1. Remarkably error prone under Rules, and went to pieces latterly, but much safer in Points, and unlucky not to retain his Members in '03. Has had a soft-palate operation, and often tongue-tied in the past, and never went a yard when pulled up after a maximum of 2m2f this season. Will surely be retired. Visored once in '99. *M.G. Chatterton — Belvoir.* 381 (O), 592 (O), 680 (M).

DEEP DALE .9-11.. 9 b.g. Pharly (FR) — L'Oraz (Ile De Bourbon USA) pp2p2. Good-topped half-brother to Magnus Maximus (*qv*). NH FLAT '00/1 r4 p0. FLAT '01/2 r10 p0. P-t-P '03 r2 w1 (2-finisher Maiden) p0; and pulled up. A very slow staying maiden on the flat, and never managed to finish within 14 lengths of the winner, but made all and finished a fence clear of the other finisher on his jumping debut, and similar tactics almost brought dividends on his latest appearance. Can take a strong hold, and jumps to the left, but has run tongue-tied, and ordinarily runs out of steam. *J. Milton — Ystrad Taf Fechan (Tony Jeffries).* 695 (R), 1021 (M), 1191 (R), 1388 (R), 1482 (R).

DEEP DESIGN (IRE) ..7-7.. 8 ch.g. Architect (USA) — Campyard (Deep Run) p478. Dam is sister to Royal Survivor, and half-sister to Leave It Be (*qv* '01 Annual). P-t-P '02/3 r2 p0 (4th and fell). Managed only one outing in each of the previous two years, and beaten a minimum of 34 lengths when able to keep on the go for three months in '04. Has shown speed for up to 2m4f but does not appear to get the trip, and short Maidens are no longer an option. Acquired blinkers on his latest appearance. *C. Dawson — S. Durham.* 75 (OMa), 596 (2m5fOMa), 768 (2m4fOMa), 1159 (OMa).

DEEP FRIED ..—.. 11 ch.g. Nader — Ten Deep (Deep Run) p. Owner-bred. P-t-P '03 r1 p0 (pulled up). Tongue-tied when making a belated debut at nine, and dropped dead on his return at Badbury Rings. *G.W. Giddings — S. & W. Wilts.* 264 (CfMa).

DEEP POCKETS (IRE) ..—.. 6 b.g. Fourstars Allstar (USA) — Pocket Price (IRE) (Moscow Society USA) fupp. Unfurnished. Fell and unseated at halfway in his first two attempts, having been supported from sixes to fours on his debut. Sent off favourite next time (not really a surprise, as his four rivals had all pulled up on their previous outing!), but was soon trailing and never looked like getting into contention. A case of empty pockets so far. *Mrs C. Keevil, P.M. Bryant & W. Bougourd — Mendip F. (Caroline Keevil).* 237 (CfMa), 368 (OMa), 826 (OMa), 1186 (OMa).

DEFENDTHEREALM ..9-12.. 14 br.g. Derring Rose — Armagnac Princess (Armagnac Monarch) 6p36p233R. Compact good-topped half-brother to Workamiracle (dam of Beyondtherealm and Itworked *qv*). NH FLAT '96 r2 p0. NH '96/03 r37 w5 (2 2m6f Hdles and 3 2m6f-3m2f110y Chses) p12; unseated 3, pulled up 3. P-t-P '03 (for Mr J.D. Frost) r7 w3 (inc Open) p1 (2nd of 3); 4th, and pulled up 2. A regular money spinner on the west country circuit, and did well to stage a resurgence in '03 when registering his first successes for three years. Has never fallen (though unseated his former owner thrice under Rules), and made a perfectly satisfactory schoolmaster for Alice Mills, but proved a shade recalcitrant on occasions, and never looked like winning. Blinkered once in '01. *Miss A. Mills — S. Devon.* 311 (L), 322 (L), 484 (L), 690 (L), 822 (L), 1004 (L), 1197 (4mL), 1350 (L), 1448 (L).

DEFINITE FLASH (IRE) ..8-2.. 7 b.m. Definite Article — Superflash (Superlative) u5. Workmanlike half-sister to Supergold (IRE), and to flat winner, Christmas Truce and 2 winners in Hungary. IR11,000y. FLAT '01/3 r9 p0. NH '03 (for M. Wellings) r2 p0; pulled up 1. Pathetic on the flat (visored final start) and over Hurdles (pulled up once; 100-1 and 200-1), and kept up the bad work in Points (unseated at the third, and 44 lengths fifth after mistakes). *Mrs L.A. Wellings — Albrighton Woodland.* 723 (OMa), 837 (OMa).

DELAWARE (FR) .9-9§.. 9 ch.g. Garde Royale — L'indienne (FR) (Le Nain Jaune FR) 3u4p44. Tall strong rangy half-brother to 3 winners in France (2 successful over jumps, including Johelle (FR) who also won flat). Dam won jump race in France. FRENCH FLAT r2 p0. FRENCH NH '99/00 r8 w1 (2m2f Ch) p1 (2nd Hdle); unseated 1. NH '00/3 (for M.C. Pipe) r17 w3 (2 2m6f Hdles and 2m4f Ch) p7; fell 2, brought down 1. Bought Doncaster, Oct for 4000. Beat Majed who has since had a chequered but sometimes useful career in England in a French Claiming Chase as a juvenile, but always untrustworthy, and having proved error-prone over fences his next connections switched him to Hurdling for his final ten attempts. Only proven at up to 2m6f, but it was convenient for him to pretend that he did not stay further in Points, and after finishing third first time out in '04 he did not beat another horse and dogged it every time. His normal headgear was discarded on his final two outings. Still makes mistakes, but clever enough not to hit the deck himself. *The Delaware Partnership (Mrs S. Martin) — Tiverton (Linda Blackford).* 880 (MO), 1128 (MO), 1183 (Cf), 1367 (O), 1542 (L), 1563 (L).

PLATE 35 442 Mallard Pawnbrokers HC, Leicester: Delgany Royal and Ben Pollock, 1st
PHOTO: Brian Armstrong

DELGANY ROYAL (IRE) ..11-0.. 13 b.g. Denel (FR) — Glen Of Erin (Furry Glen) 11pf. Tall good-bodied brother to NH flat and Hurdles winner, Erintante (IRE). IRISH P-t-P '98 r2 p1 (2nd); and pulled up. IRISH NH FLAT '98 r1 p0. IRISH NH '98/02 (for D.T. Hughes) r44 w5 (2m2f-3m1f Chses) p7; pulled up 7, fell/unseated 3. A bold galloping front-runner who was gaining his first success since December '01 when he romped home at High Easter, and quickly followed up by capturing a £6,864 prize with another dominant display at Leicester (far from the biggest bag of his career, as he earned £15,000 plus in his last Irish victory). Ideally needs some cut in the ground and was surprisingly able to find it at Marks Tey in May, but unfortunately fell three out when ten lengths clear and in command in a three-runner race. Signed off in Ireland with an appearance in cheekpieces, but they appeared to insult him. Should still have good prospects if resuming at 13. *C.M. Wilson — Woodland Pytchley (Nicola Pollock).* 221 (O), 442 (2m7f110yH), 991 (3m2f110yH), 1315 (O).

DELLONE ..9-6.. 13 b.g. Gunner B — Coire Vannich (Celtic Cone) 866. Strong half-brother to NH flat winner, Flower Of Pitcur. Dam won 2 Hdles, 2m-2m1f. NH '97 and '99/03 r27 w2 (2m1f Hdles) p5; fell/unseated 5. P-t-P '99/00 r5 p1 (2nd); 4th thrice and fell. NH '04 r1 p0 (6th in 2m Hdle: *chsd wnr to 2, lost plce aft 4, wl bhnd* 6). Not much better than a plater under Rules, but his enthusiasm could never be questioned, and ploughed through the mud to score twice over hurdles at Hereford to February '02. Always lacked fluency over the bigger obstacles, and has never shown anything like the stamina required to succeed in Points. Does not appear that sound nowadays. *M.C. Houghton — Cotswold (Carey Williams).* 5 (L), 94 (L).

DELTIC ARROW ..8-0.. 7 b.g. Deltic (USA) — Jolly Girl (Jolly Me) 23up. Lengthy half-brother to Colourful Boy, Bungle and Rickshaw. Dam, sister to Spambruco. Grandam, Colourful Girl, failed to finish in 3 Points. Ten lengths second on a February debut, but 43 lengths last next time, and continued to maintain a slump which ended with him pulling up when even money favourite. Needs to jump a lot better, but possibly capable of atoning if he does. *A. Simpson — S. Pembs (Beverley Thomas).* 120 (OMa), 676 (CfMa), 1096 (OMa), 1533 (OMa).

DENVALE (IRE) ..10-5.. 7 b.g. Denel (FR) — Brackenvale (IRE) (Strong Gale) 2211. Tall. Dam, half-sister to Amber Ruler (*qv* '97 Annual). P-t-P '03 r2 w1 (Maiden) p1 (3rd). On the upgrade and has ground out three minor successes, but not a flamboyant jumper, and will need to fence with more aggression as he rises in class. Stays well and has shown plenty of determination, and coped admirably in the fast deteriorating ground when scoring on an easy surface for the first time at Garthorpe. Sure to find further opportunities, and might be capable of aspiring to Open class in '05. *A. & Mrs P. Hurn — Pytchley (Caroline Bailey).* 19 (CMod), 169 (R), 787 (CR), 1059 (I).

DEPUTY LEADER (IRE) ..9-5.. 13 b.g. Florida Son — Larne (Giolla Mear) p74579. Tall brother to Irish jumping winner, Florida Star (IRE), and half-brother to Allen's Rock and Highlandman, and to Hurdles winner, Hunter Buoy. NH FLAT '97 r2 p1 (3rd). NH '98, '00 and '02 r8 p0; fell/unseated 3. P-t-P/HUNT CH '02/3 (for Mr K. Hunter) r18 w1 (Maiden) p2 (2nd of 3 once); pulled up 2, fell/unseated 2. NH '04 (from J.K. Hunter's) r1 p0 (9th in 2m1f110y Hdle: *a bhnd, t.o*). Managed only five appearances pre '02, but has since crammed in 28 more, and finally opened his account when dropped into a Maiden for the first time at Witton Castle. Over-ambitiously placed since, and only once better than last in '04. A safe jumper now but has always been hampered by a lack of stamina. *Miss A. Wilson — V. of Lune H.* 339 (L), 763 (L), 874 (L), 1290 (L), 1308 (L).

DERE STREET ..9-12.. 11 b.g. Derring Rose — Jed Again (Cagirama) 1332324. Plain short-backed half-brother to Mainhope (dam of Mozielaw, *qv*), Peelinick and Callawhope. Dam, half-sister to 4 Pointers including the dam of Fallalaw, was 3rd in a Maiden for Rhona Elliot. P-t-P/HUNT CH '00 and '02/3 r13 w5 (up to Confined) p3 (2 3rds, of 4 once); 4th twice, fell/unseated 2 and pulled up 1. Unbeaten in his first four completions, and has scored on his last two seasonal debuts, but largely frustrating since changing hands expensively in '02, and has never gone so well for Rose Davidson as he did for Morag Neill. An out-and-out stayer and suited by easy ground, but not one to take too short a price about. Might benefit from the application of headgear. *D. Davidson — W. Percy (Peter Elliot).* 69 (M), 133 (L), 213 (L), 550 (L), 763 (L), 1221 (L), 1307 (Cf).

DERRILADY ..—.. 13 b.m. Derrylin — Belsprit Lady (Belfalas) ppfp. Very small weedy half-sister to Toffee Lady (*qv*). NH '99 (for R.J. Price) r2 p0 (pulled up 2). Doesn't even look remotely like a racehorse (stablemate Lamerton Quest does, remotely, but isn't, either). *L.S. Rowe — Lamerton.* 824 (R), 1132 (R), 1268 (R), 1351 (Inr).

DERRYROSE .—§.. 12 br.g. Derrylin — Levantine Rose (Levanter) p7p. Small close-coupled half-brother to NH flat and Hurdles winner, Fragrant Rose. Dam, half-sister to Just Rose (*qv* '97 Annual), won 2 3m1f Hdles, inc a Sell. NH '99/01 r16 p3; pulled up 4, inc only Ch, unseated 1. P-t-P/HUNT CH '99 and '02/3 r12 w2 (inc 3m1f Hunt Ch) p3 (2 2nds; and 3rd in Hunt Ch); pulled up 4, and fell/unseated 2. A failure under Rules where he frequently looked ungenuine, but made a successful return to Hunt racing in '02, and landed a Hunter Chase at Kelso on his final appearance. Pulled up in five of six starts since, and makes little attempt to get involved. Blinkered twice in '02, and acquired cheekpieces this year. *R.J. Kyle — Jedforest.* 134 (O), 282 (Cf), 509 (O).

DERRYS CHOICE ..—.. 8 ch.m. Derrylin — Sister's Choice (Lepanto GER) u. Half-sister to Hurdles winner, Little Flora. Dam, half-sister to Bedtime Boys (*qv*). P-t-P '03 (for Mr N.M.L. Ewart) r1 p0 (fell). In touch until claimed by the fences after a maximum of two miles to date, and mucked about in the paddock before the latest. *Mrs S. Horner-Harker — Hurworth.* 215 (OMa).

DERRYS PREROGATIVE ..—.. 15 b.g. Nearly A Hand — Derrycreha Lass (Precipice Wood) pppp. Small good-bodied. Dam, half-sister to Boreen Owen (*qv* '99 Annual), won 2m2f Hdle in Ireland, and won 2 2m4f Hdles in England. NH FLAT '94 and '96 r2 p0. NH '96/7 r9 p1 (19/ 3rd in Ch); remote 5th of 6 and pulled up 3 in other Chses; inc Sell. P-t-P '99/00 and '02/3 r20 w1 (Maiden) p3 (3rds, of 4 twice); pulled up 6, ran out 1, fell/unseated 3. Left the lucky winner of a bad Maiden in softish at Chaddesley in '99, and rated 9-5 at best, but pulled up in his last six appearances, and sometimes leaves the impression that there is something amiss. Has been tried tongue-tied. *Miss N.J. Rudge & Miss R.K. Davies — N. Ledbury (Nicola Rudge).* 726 (R), 923 (L), 1069 (R), 1253 (M).

DESIGN X PRESS ..—.. 8 b.g. Henbit (USA) — Stubbs Daughter (Stubbs Gazette) p. Big half-brother to Monster Moss. Dam won NH Flat and 2m2f Hurdle in Ireland and 6 2m Chases in England. NH FLAT '02 r1 p0. P-t-P '03 (for Mr V.J. Hughes & Miss L. Llewellyn) r3 p0 (pulled up 2 and unseated 1). Beat one home in his bumper, but a very erratic jumper in Points, and went no more than a mile on his only appearance in '04. Clearly troubled, and probably ungenuine to boot. Wears a cross-noseband. *D.W. Drinkwater — N. Ledbury.* 982 (2m5fOMa).

DESTIN D'ESTRUVAL (FR) ..—.. 14 b.g. Port Etienne (FR) — Vocation (FR) (Toujours Pret USA) p5pp. Tall. FRENCH FLAT r3 w1 (10f) p1 (3rd). FRENCH NH '94/6 r13 w1 (2m2f Ch) p5 (2nds). NH '96/00 r23 w3 (2m4f-2m5f Chses, lucky once) p7 (inc 2 Hdles — caught near finish in both). P-t-P/HUNT CH '99/03 r18 w2 (2m4f110y-2m5f110y Hunt Chses) p5 (4 3rds; and 2nd in Hunt Ch); pulled up 5, fell/unseated 2. Formerly smart if somewhat unreliable, but has not scored since recording a Hunter Chase double in '99, and has never been able to get the trip in Points. Maintaining a downward curve and looks finished now. Blinkered once in '98. *C.J. Britton — Torrington F. (Ian Hambley).* 310 (O), 570 (Cf), 793 (Cf), 823 (Cf).

DETROIT DAVY (IRE) ..9-10.. 14 b.g. Detroit Sam (FR) — Pretty Damsel (Prince Hansel) 1u33. Tall strong half-brother to Idleigh's Comet and Golden Mac, to Irish Pointing winner, Western Breeze, and to successful Hurdler, Pretty Gayle. NH FLAT '96 r2 p0 (4ths). IRISH P-t-P '98 r5 p1 (3rd); last, pulled up 2, and fell 1. NH '96 and '01 r3 p1 (3rd); unseated 1. P-t-P/HUNT CH '99/00 and '02/3 r25 w5 (Maiden, Restricted, Intermediate and 2 Members) p6 (5 2nds, of 3 once, inc a Hunt Ch; and 3rd of 4); pulled up 3, brought down 1, and fell/unseated 3. Well placed to win six minor Points, and displayed plenty of determination in the latest, but hindered by joint problems latterly, and by jumping lapses throughout his career. Most effective with some cut in the ground. Tongue-tied once in '01. *Mrs J. Thomas — Pentyrch (Phil Williams).* 843 (L), 1089 (M), 1189 (L), 1536 (L).

DEVILS DOMINO .—.. 9 b.g. Faustus (USA) — Little Dot (Pony Express) uppp. Unfurnished owner-bred. Dam, (*qv* '94 Annual) 'knee high to a grasshopper', fell 2nd in a Point for Anne-Marie Rooney. Dumped the rider at the first on his debut, and pulled up after two miles when labouring in his next three attempts. Hanging left in the latest, and is surely useless. *Mrs A.M. Rooney — Quorn (Richard Walker).* 383 (R), 584 (I), 789 (CfMa), 1056 (M).

DEVIL'S PERK (IRE) ..10-0.. 7 b.g. Executive Perk — She Devil (Le Moss) Rs12. Leggy half-brother to stablemate and jumping winner, Devil's Run (IRE). NH '03 r1 p0 (last). Erratic in his first two Points and hung badly left and crashed through the wing and unseated at the last when two lengths clear at Duncombe Park before slipping up on the final turn at Charm Park where he was trying to rally on the inside of the probably useful Black Collar, but settled better at Whitwell-on-the-Hill, and beat two subsequent scorers over 2m4f. Unfortunately finished the season lame after a creditable second, just as he looked to be developing into a decent prospect. *J. Wade — S. Durham.* 272 (OMa), 393 (CfMa), 773 (2m4fCMa), 1288 (R).

DEVONSHIRE (IRE) ..9-10.. 12 b/br.g. King's Ride — Lispatrick Lass (Kambalda) u6. Compact narrow brother to Chasing winner, Tree Creeper (IRE), and half-brother to Gifted Man (IRE), and to Irish jumping winner, Expat (IRE). NH FLAT '98 r1 p1 (3rd). NH '98/00 r5 w1 (2m4f Hdle) p4 (3 2nds, beaten 16*l* in Ch once). P-t-P/HUNT CH '01/3 r8 p3 (2nds, inc Hunt Ch); 4th twice, 6th, and pulled up 2. Odds-on when partnered by Richard Dunwoody and successful at Market Rasen in '99 but has stood his racing badly and never able to fulfill his potential under Rules. Has to go right-handed, and made mistakes before unseating at Weston Park on his return, but tailed off subsequently, and it would be a shock if he discovered his old form at 12. *P.A. Bennett - Meynell & S. Staffs.* 229 (O), 381 (O).

DEXTER GORDON (IRE) ..10-0§.. 14 gr.g. Bar Dexter (USA) — Sabev (USA) (Saber Thrust CAN) p2. Tall lengthy half-brother to 3 flat winners (one in USA), and to Hurdles winner, Distinct Flyer (IRE). Dam won 6 flat races in USA. IRISH P-t-P '97/8 and '02 r18 w4 p5; pulled up 5. IRISH HUNT CH '98 and '02 r3 p2 (2nds). IRISH NH '98 r4 p1 (3rd). P-t-P '03 (for Mr P. & Mr A.J. Mahoney) r7 w1 (Open) p3 (2nds, last twice); and pulled up 3. Suited by mud when completing a four-timer in Ireland in '98, but unreliable and subsequently runner-up on eight occasions before ending a losing sequence of 24 when 20-1 at Trecoed last year. Into the veteran category now, and gives the impression that wear and tear is beginning to take its toll on him. Usually blinkered and tongue-tied, and has worn bandages. *M. Tucker — Gelligaer F. (Helen Pugsley).* 448 (O), 697 (L).

DEXTROUS ..—.. 8 gr.g. Machiavellian (USA) — Heavenly Cause (USA) (Grey Dawn II) pf. Small sturdy half-brother to 2 flat winners, including Pennys From Heaven, and to 2 winners in USA. Dam champion 2yo filly in USA in '80. FLAT '00/2 (for H.R.A. Cecil, and N. Tinkler) r17 p2 (3rds). Made an apparently promising debut on the flat at Newmarket, but was a morning glory, and virtually useless ever since. Followed that third over 5f (beaten five lengths) with a similar placing (but beaten

17 lengths), but has now been unplaced on 17 consecutive occasions, including with a tongue-tie in four. Jumped badly in Points, had also withdrawn at Charm Park after unseating twice and bolting on the latter occasion in the preliminaries, and as it seems painfully obvious that he cannot breath properly he should be retired. *O.R. Dukes — York & Ainsty S.* 60 (OMa), 596 (2m5fOMa).

DIAMOND DOT ..—.. 10 ch.m. Afzal — Diamond Bay (Buzzards Bay) p. Small close-coupled. P-t-P '02 (for Mr & Mrs B.M. Jackson) r3 p0 (pulled up 2 and fell). A consistently poor jumper and has never remotely looked like getting round. *D. Barber — Tivyside.* 669 (M).

DIAMOND ROAD (IRE) ..—.. 8 gr.g. Dolphin Street (FR) — Tiffany's Case (IRE) (Thatching) pp. Good-bodied half-brother to flat winners Golden Brief, Legal Set (both won 9 apiece) and Silken Brief. Dam won 3 8f races. FLAT '99/02 (for C.A. Horgan) r19 p3. Tailed off and pulled up in his Members (three ran) and a Maiden (jumped slowly). Was beaten head once in a four-runner race at Goodwood, where he gained all three placings (on his second until fourth outings), but tended to carry his head high, was blinkered twice and ungenuine, and even ended in that sphere with a pulled up. *Mrs A.M. Scrase — Chid, Lec & Cowdray.* 645 (M), 1285 (OMa).

DIAMOND STONE (IRE) ..9-4.. 7 b.g. Ajraas (USA) — Cloonacaunen (IRE) (Penistone) 1p. IRISH P-t-P '02 r1 p0 (fell). P-t-P '03 r2 p0 (pulled up 2). Overcame some sloppy jumping to outstay the placed runners when successful on his first completion at Charing, but subsequently off the course for 12 weeks, and was never going with any purpose in his first Restricted. Might be capable of better on easier terrain in his native area. *Mrs W.C. Boraman — Surrey U. (Phillip York).* 424 (CMa), 1517 (R).

DICK MCCARTHY (IRE) ..10-3.. 13 b.g. Lancastrian — Waltzing Shoon (Green Shoon) 23124112u. Sturdy brother to Mulkev Prince (IRE). IRISH NH FLAT '96/7 r3 p2 (2nds). IRISH NH '96/7 r4 p0. NH '98/03 (for R. Rowe) r34 w3 (2m1f-2m6f110y Chses) p18 (inc 11 2nds); pulled up 1. A veteran of the south-east scene since '98, and most adept at picking up prizes, but a real monkey and had avoided winning since March '00 until his enthusiasm was rekindled by Pointing. Odds-on in his first two wins, but showed an often unseen willingness to battle in the third, and as he rarely takes much out of himself could easily hold his rating at 13. Remains a patent safety, and has never fallen. Blinkered once in '03, and previously tried in cheekpieces. *J. & Mrs S. Ashby — Ashford V. (Sarah Ashby).* 184 (L), 421 (L), 536 (CfL), 641 (L), 781 (L), 807 (M), 1053 (L), 1283 (L), 1440 (3m1fH).

DIGITALIS ..—§§.. 12 ch.m. Henbit (USA) — Vulpine Lady (Green Shoon) 3p6pp. Long-backed half-sister to Portknockie, Frosty Lady, Wily Miss and Foxy Flora. Dam pulled up in 2 Points. P-t-P '99/00 and '02/3 (for Mr R.O. Oliver) r17 w2 (Maiden and Club Restricted) p0; 5th, 7th, pulled up 11, fell 1 and refused 1. Scored on her first completion, and reaped the benefit of a wind operation when following up three starts later, but subsequently sold cheaply, and has performed badly since. Not better than last in '04, and proved very reluctant to race on her Hunter Chase debut. Usually blinkered nowadays. *R.O. Oliver — Mrs L. Avery — S. Devon (Emma Oliver).* 411 (M), 794 (Inr), 823 (Cf), 1129 (I), 1363 (2m3f110yH).

DINAN (IRE) ..8-0§.. 13 gr.g. Step Together (USA) — Nobodys Lady (Nobody Knows) 5p333. Good-topped half-brother to Bobs Tornado (IRE). IRISH P-t-P '96/7 and '00 r6 p2; pulled up 1, fell 1. IRISH NH '96 and '99/00 r15 p0. P-t-P '02/3 r14 p1 (½l 2nd); 5th, last pair 5, pulled up 4, unseated 2, and refused 1. Usually makes the running, and proved he has the ability to win a race when a close third in his Members, but thoroughly untrustworthy, and otherwise beaten a minimum of 20 lengths in '04. Seems certain to remain unsuccessful if returning at 13. Wears a cross-noseband. *J. Binks — York & Ainsty N. (Joanne Brown).* 395 (CfMa), 502 (L), 1157 (M), 1292 (OMa), 1417 (OMa).

DINNYS DOUBLE ..—§§.. 7 b.m. Executive Perk — Olympic Rose (IRE) (Roselier FR) rRp. Tall rangy. Dam, half-sister to Olympic Class (*qv* '00 Annual). P-t-P '03 r1 p0 (ran out). A thoroughly nasty piece of work, and has dumped three different riders without leaving the ground (the latest was put through a hedge), but not without ability, and just the sort of challenge that Phillip York relishes. Tore off at a rate of knots on her latest appearance at Larkhill, and was 15 lengths clear until she threw in the towel going up the hill for the final time, but a ban looks inevitable unless she reforms quickly. Has been tried in a cross-noseband and a martingale. *Miss J. Oakey — Miss R. Murrell — Worcs (Michael Oliver).* 978 (CMam), 1337 (OMa), 1495 (OMa).

DINSEY FINNEGAN (IRE) ..10-3§.. 10 b.g. Fresh Breeze (USA) — Rose Of Solway (Derring Rose) 216p81f32. Lengthy good-topped brother to Skinsey Finnegan (IRE), and half-brother to Outside The Rain (IRE). IRISH P-t-P '99/01 r6 w1 (5&6yo Maiden) p0; pulled up 3. IRISH NH FLAT '00 r1 p0. IRISH NH '00 r1 p0. P-t-P/HUNT CH '02/3 r16 w3 (Members, Restricted and Intermediate) p5 (4 3rds, of 4 once and remote last once); pulled up 2, ran out 1. A consistent front-runner in minor company and occasionally buckles down when challenged, but normally declines to offer any resistance, and sure to remain unreliable. Usually jumps away to the right. Suited by good or sound surfaces. Wears headgear and bandages in front. *J.G. Phillips — V.W.H. (Simon Bloss).* 47 (Cf), 187 (Cf), 440 (2m7f110yH), 727 (MO), 758 (O), 937 (Cnr), 1168 (2m5fH), 1257 (O), 1514 (Cf).

DIPLODOCUS ..—.. 12 b.g. State Diplomacy (USA) — Welsh Slave (Vulgan Slave) p. Long-backed goose-rumped. Dam, half-sister to El Padre (*qv* '93 Annual). Quickly outplodocused by his two rivals in his Members. *Miss J.E. Tett — O. Berks, & Vine & Craven (Neil Thomas).* 968 (M).

DISTINCT (IRE) .9-6§.. 12 b.g. Distinctly North (USA) — Shy Jinks (Shy Groom USA) 36568. Small close-coupled. FLAT '95 r1 p0 (Sell). NH '98/00 r15 p2 (3rds); pulled up 4, fell 1. P-t-P/HUNT CH '02/3 r12 w1 (Maiden) p3 (2 2nds, of 3 once; also disqualified from 3rd once — took wrong course); 6th, ran out 1, refused 2, and pulled up 3. Stays well and landed a Maiden in soft at Friars Haugh in '02, despite Paul Robson dropping his whip four out, but requires strong handling and is quick to lose interest. Jumped safely for a novice in '04, but was only too pleased to be uncompetitive at the same time.Visored once in '99. *Mrs A.M. Tweedie — W. Percy (J. Ellwood).* 430 (R), 766 (R), 810 (R), 1077 (R), 1469 (R).

DISTRACTING ..9-12.. 8 b.m. Royal Fountain — Icelandic Poppy (Oats) p53511. Dam, sister to Cogitate (*qv* '97 Annual), and half-sister to Icelandic Spring (*qv*), won Maiden and 2nd twice for John Brockbank. P-t-P '03 r3 w1 (Maiden) p0; 6th and pulled up. Disappointing when beaten a minimum of 19 lengths in three completions after her initial success, but followed up on home territory, and then gained a far more meritorious victory when encountering a lively surface at Hexham. Stays well and fast ground may be key to future development. *J.E. Brockbank — Cumberland.* 431 (R), 766 (R), 876 (I), 1222 (R), 1306 (M), 1419 (R).

DIVINE MIST (IRE) ..9-1§§.. 8 gr.g. Roselier (FR) — Tate Divinity (IRE) (Tate Gallery USA) ufppfup4f2p. Compact unfurnished. 30,000 4yo. NH FLAT '01/2 r3 p1 (2nd). NH '03 (for J. O'Neill) r3 p0; fell 1, pulled up 1. This is the one the Turners have been waiting for months to read about, here goes. Showed plenty of waywardness over Hurdles (14th of 15 after nearly running out, pulled up and fell), and gained the new stable a unique honour by being the losing-most maiden of the season, with eight non-completions from ten attempts in that grade. Reluctant without fail and often jumps and hangs right, and almost eliminated himself at both of the final two fences when eventually staggering to 16 lengths fourth. On this occasion James Owen was fined £65 for improper use of the whip, but having fallen or unseated five times previously the horse (hardly a tender flower) probably never noticed a thing. Two outings later came the thrill of a second at Dingley, but the following Sunday doom and gloom returned when he gave possibly his worst display ever (and glory be, the punters sent him off favourite!). *J.M. Turner — Suffolk.* 151 (OMa), 219 (OMa), 245 (CfMa), 371 (OMa), 560 (OMa), 746 (OMa), 1000 (OMa), 1211 (OMa), 1404 (OMa), 1473 (OMa), 1518 (OMa).

DIXON VARNER (IRE) ..10-0.. 15 b.g. Sheer Grit — Raise The Bells (Belfalas) 251. Tall workmanlike rangy half-brother to Major League. Dam, half-sister to Treasure Again (*qv*), won Irish NH flat. IRISH P-t-P '95/7 and '99 r10 w9 (inc 7 Opens) p1 (2nd). IRISH NH '96/9 r9 w4 (3m-3m1f Hunter Chses) p1 (3rd); fell 3 and pulled up. P-t-P/HUNT CH '02/3 r12 w1 (Confined) p7 (5 2nds, beaten short head once, and inc Hunt Ch); last, pulled up 2 and unseated. The top-rated Pointer in Ireland in '97 but sidelined by leg trouble for three years to '02 and stands only light campaigns. An out-and-out stayer, and runner-up in the Detling 4-miler for the last three years, but gained a thoroughly deserved success when upholding the form in his Members. The ideal mount for a learner rider, and the Catsfield success would be the ideal way to end an honourable career. *Capt & Mrs F. Marshall — E. Sussex & Romney Marsh (Di Grissell).* 537 (4mMO), 744 (O), 1050 (M).

DJEDDAH (FR) .—.. 14 b.g. Shafoun (FR) — Union Jack III (FR) (Mister Jack FR) p. Tall brother to a French flat winner, and half-brother to Golden Jack (FR) and Extra Jack (FR), to French jumping winner, Hey Jack (FR), and to French flat winner, Jack Apel (FR). FRENCH FLAT r1 p0. FRENCH NH '96/03 (for F. Doumen) r62 w9 (3 2m5f Hdles and 6 2m Chses) p12 (inc 2nd in England). Proof that truth can indeed be stranger than fiction, because who could ever have guessed that a horse who earned £391,825 would end his life dropping dead in a Point-to-Point in Dorset. Part of his phenomenal earning success was due to the fact that he was campaigning in France where prizes are so much higher, but also scored twice at Ascot and once at Kempton (all worth more than £10,000 apiece). It also seems amazing that he was beaten on no fewer than 55 occasions, and being inconsistent and irresolute (wore blinkers) he never fulfilled his true potential. Refused twice including in the Velka Pardubice, and competed in four Grand Nationals, finishing 11th in '87, ninth in '00 and ditching the rider in both '01 and '02. Miss R. Heikkola — Cambridge Univ (James JJ Ryan). 263 (O).

DOC RYAN'S ..10-5§.. 11 b.g. Damister (USA) — Jolimo (Fortissimo) f2421. Small half-brother to Eddie Rombo, to flat and Hurdles winners, Joli's Great, Jolis Absent and Osric, and to NH flat winner, Forager. Dam won 7 flat, 12-18f. FLAT '96/00 and '02 r38 w7 (12-16f) p10. NH '99/00 and '02 r10 w1 (2m Nov Hdle) p3 (2 2nds); pulled up 2. P-t-P '02 r3 p1 (2nd); pulled up 1 and fell 1. A thinker and does not always do his level best, but can quicken when in the mood, and found conditions ideal when switched to a Ladies race for the first time at Trecoed. Run out of it on the flat six days earlier, though the rider tried hard to influence the Judge's decision with his usual salute, and ideally has to be produced as late as possible. Not a natural jumper, and suited by an easy three miles, but can handle fast ground and could find other opportunities now that his confidence has received a boost. Frequently blinkered to '04, and has been tried tongue-tied. *T.E. Vaughan & Miss A. Johns — Llangeinor (Abbi Johns).* 448 (O), 672 (O), 841 (Cf), 1537 (C), 1551 (L).

DOCTOR DUNKLIN (USA) .8-8§.. 16 gr.g. Family Doctor (USA) — Mis Jenifer's Idea (USA) (Capital Idea USA) 5. Small. NH FLAT '93 r3 p1 (head 2nd). NH '93/5 and '97/8 (visored once in '95) r21 w1 (2m6f Hdle) p3; last, and pulled up 4 in Chses. P-t-P/HUNT CH '99/00 and '02/3 r19 p5 (3 2nds, of 3 once, and last once; and remote last of 3 twice); pulled up 2, unseated 3. Recorded a 33-1 success at Sedgefield in '94, but defeated 43 times otherwise, and has spent his Pointing career solely educating beginner riders. Wears blinkers. *Mrs T.H. Hayward (The Cherry Tree Partnership) — N. Norfolk H. (Tina Hayward).* 1150 (M).

DO IT AGAIN (IRE) ..—§.. 11 b.g. Meneval (USA) — Just The Thing (Lucifer USA) upp4. Small fired half-brother to Crampscastle (IRE) and Irish Pointing winner, Johann Sebastian. IRISH P-t-P '99 and '02 r4 w1 (7yo&up Maiden) p1 (2nd); pulled up 1. IRISH NH FLAT '99 r2 p0. IRISH NH '00 r3 p0. IRISH HUNT CH '02 r2 w1 (3m Ch) p0. P-t-P '03 r6 w1 (2-runner Open) p1 (3rd); 4th, and pulled up 3. Reportedly under a cloud during his busiest ever campaign last year, but did much better than in '04, and was rated 10-1 after securing a match at Eaton Hall. Blinkered to no avail this term, and runs up the white flag without any provocation. Must still be ailing. *R. Edwards & F.D. Cornes — S. Salop (Pamela Sykes).* 229 (O), 465 (O), 711 (O), 930 (O).

DO IT ONCE (IRE) ..10-0.. 13 b.g. Strong Gale — Golden Privet (IRE) (Kemal FR) p51521. Dam is half-sister to Big Brown Bear (*qv* '88 Season Annual). IRISH NH FLAT '97 r1 p0. IRISH NH '97/9, r11 w1 (3m Hunt Ch) p1 (3rd in similar). IRISH P-t-P '99 r3 w1 (7yo&up Maiden) p1 (2nd); and pulled up 1. P-t-P '00 and '02/3 r13 w5 (inc 3 Ladies) p6 (4 3rds, of 4 once, and last once; and inc 2nd of 3); last and fell 1. Consistent and determined, and has been well placed to win five Ladies races, but easily brushed aside by better performers, and not as fluent as his record suggests. Suited by some cut in the ground. Wears a cross-noseband, and runs tongue-tied. *Mrs P. Tollit — Worcs.* 449 (L), 843 (L), 1137 (L), 1229 (L), 1343 (L), 1536 (L).

DOLITANLAD ..7-0.. 9 b.g. Endoli (USA) — Tanber Lass (New Member) pppfp84u45. Workmanlike sparely-made half-brother to Jolitan (*qv*). P-t-P '03 (for Mr & Mrs G. Wilson) r4 p1 (3rd); pulled up 2 and unseated 1. Made to look worse than he really is by the season's least successful rider (no wins from 90-odd attempts), and frequently coerced into making mistakes. Carries no condition at the best of times, but looked generally poor in the new yard, and badly tailed off last in all four completions. Must be crying out for another change of scenery. *P.J. Millington — Fernie.* 20 (OMa), 40 (OMa), 152 (OMa), 595 (OMa), 788 (CfMa), 887 (CfMa), 1061 (OMa), 1215 (CfMa), 1341 (OMa), 1505 (OMa).

DOLPHIN SQUARE (IRE) ..10-1.. 12 b.g. Phardante (FR) — Clarahill (Menelek) 731114. Compact brother to Albermarle (IRE), and half-brother to jumping winner, Cinnamon Run. P-t-P '99 and '01/2 r6 w1 (Maiden) p0; 6th, pulled up 3 and unseated 1. Has had to endure an incredibly stop-start career, but possesses boundless stamina, and completed a hat-trick after he had shaken off the rust that a 698-day break had deposited. Provided Harriet Bethell with her first success at Whittington, and looks the type to relish four miles, though his jumping does require attention. Suited by some cut in the ground. *W.A. Bethell — Holderness.* 268 (R), 341 (R), 499 (M), 771 (R), 876 (I), 1178 (3m1fH).

DOM PILIPPE (FR) ..—.. 8 b/br.g. Saint Cyrien (FR) — Moomaw (Akarad FR) p. Compact light-framed. Dam won flat race and 2 Hurdles in France. NH FLAT '01/2 r3 p0; last 2. NH '02 r1 p0 (pulled up). P-t-P '03 r1 p0 (unseated). Only once better than last in three bumpers and a Hurdle when in the care of Martin Pipe, and has jumped only seven fences successfully in Points. *Mrs C.L. Pople — Morpeth.* 767 (2m4fOMa).

DOM SHADEED ..—§§.. 10 b.g. Shadeed (USA) — Fair Dominion (Dominion) rr. Good-bodied compact half-brother to 2 winners in USA and flat winner, Mornings Minion. Dam won 2 flat (5-6f). 10,000y. FLAT '98/00 & '02/3 r20 w2 (8f) p1 (3rd in Sell). NH '99 and '02/3 (for R.J. Baker) r5 p0. Scored twice by narrow margins on the flat (including on the all-weather), and came with a very strong late run to spring a 33-1 shock once. Gained his third in a Seller, but unplaced in 24 other races, and his temperament has been increasing at an alarming rate. Left once over Hurdles and tried to refuse and unseated at the final flight next time (remounted), and had no intention of going anywhere in two Opens. Has twice been blinkered and once worn cheekpieces. Surely the last has been seen of him. *G. Brown — Taunton V.H. (Michael Sweetland).* 792 (MO), 964 (O).

DONALLACH MOR (IRE) ..9-8.. 13 b.g. Phardante (FR) — Panalee (Pitpan) 651p. Tall workmanlike half-brother to Irish NH flat winner, That's Gospel. NH '99/02 r7 w1 (2m6f Nov Ch) p2 (2nds); pulled up 3. P-t-P/HUNT CH '99 and '03 r5 w3 (inc 2 Hunt Chses 3m-3m4f) p0; 4th and pulled up 1. Won three races on the bounce when first produced by Venetia Williams, but subsequently let down by his jumping when raised in class, and has always stood his racing badly. Awarded a Confined at Corbridge on his Pointing debut, and won a Members race on ground that was previously unsuitable in '04, but also acquired blinkers and otherwise took little interest. *Mrs C. Sample — Morpeth (Val Jackson).* 425 (M), 655 (L), 914 (M), 1080 (Cf).

DONNEGALE (IRE) ..9-13§.. 13 b.g. Strong Gale — Marys Gift (Monksfield) 2p4pu223. Smallish workmanlike half-brother to NH flat and Hurdles winner, Dungarvans Choice (IRE). Dam won 2 Irish Hdles, 2m-2m3f. NH FLAT '97 r1 p0. NH '97/02 r24 w4 (3 3m1f110y-3m4f Hdles, and 3m3f Ch) p5; pulled up 4. P-t-P/HUNT CH '00 and '03 r12 w3 (3m1f110y Hunt Ch, and 2 Ladies) p2 (3rds, inc Hunt Ch); 4th, 6th, last pair 2, pulled up 2 and fell 1. A thorough stayer, but moody and inconsistent, and has been tried in all types of headgear. Retains enough ability to spring a surprise, but generally at his most unco-operative since scoring at Garthorpe last year, and is best ignored for betting purposes. Acts on any going. *The Mad Donnes (Miss J.E. Foster) — Pendle Forest & Craven (Jo Foster).* 213 (L), 339 (L), 712 (L), 772 (4m1fO), 1203 (L), 1302 (O), 1415 (L), 1459 (L).

DONNINI (IRE) ..—.. 8 ch.g. Kris — La Luna (USA) (Lyphard USA) fp4f. Angular brother to flat winner, Etoile, and half-brother to flat and Hurdling winner, Moon Shot, and to 3 winners abroad. Dam won 9f race in France. 22,000f, Ff450,000y. FLAT '00/1 r2 p0. NH '02/3 (for P.J. Hobbs, Miss K. Marks, and B.D. Leavy) r9 p2; fell 1, pulled up 2. Bought Doncaster, Aug for 1900. Placed in his first two Hurdles and fell at the last when holding a slight lead next time, but soon declined badly and was flopping in Sellers (tongue-tied once). Fell fatally at the seventh at Higham, and Millington put yet another blot on his already ink-splodged copybook by refusing to let him be destroyed until after the next race (with a fence omitted where he lay on the ground) had been concluded. P.J. Millington — Fernie. 7 (2m4fOMa), 21 (OMa), 105 (2m4fOMa), 153 (OMa).

DONRICO (IRE) .9-7.. 9 b.g. Lord Americo — Donegal Moss (Le Moss) 633253. Compact half-brother to Hurdles winners, French County (IRE) and Harrigale Moss (IRE). Dam, half-sister to Renard Quay (*qv* '97 Annual). IRISH P-t-P '02 r2 p1 (3rd); and unseated 1. IRISH NH FLAT '01 r2 p0. IRISH NH '02 r1 p1 (3rd). P-t-P '03 r5 w1 (Maiden) p3 (2 2nds, beaten head once); and 5th of 6. Ended his first English campaign with a ready success in a seven-minute Maiden at Bredwardine, but very expensive to follow otherwise, and consistently looks as slow as a boat. Benefits from the presence of leading riders, but prone to slovenliness and will need mud, a long track and a certain amount of luck to stage a follow up. *The After Dinner Partnership (Mrs S.E. Edwards) — S. Salop (Pamela Sykes).* 2 (R), 95 (R), 231 (CR), 530 (R), 715 (R), 853 (R).

DON RIO (IRE) ..9-3.. 8 b.g. Phardante (FR) — Test Drive (Crash Course) pp3f46634. Workmanlike half-brother to Irish Hurdling winner, Testify, and to Irish Chasing winner, Cluain Rua. IRISH P-t-P '02 r3 w1 (5&6yo Maiden) p0; pulled up, and fell. IRISH NH FLAT '02/3 r2 p0. IRISH PRIVATE SWEEPSTAKES '03 r1 p0. IRISH NH '02/3 (for M. Hourigan) r9 p0. Bought Doncaster, Oct for 2800. Normally a safe jumper and is able to make plenty of trips to the races, but very moderate even in Restricted company (was beaten 29 lengths plus in his final eight Irish Hurdles). Would perhaps like softer ground, but will have to meet some real plodders if he is to score. Tried tongue-tied once. *The Gatebridge Friends (P. Richmond) — W. of Yore (Peter Richmond).* 391 (MO), 501 (O), 684 (R), 771 (R), 955 (R), 1162 (R), 1288 (R), 1416 (R), 1456 (R).

DON ROYAL ..10-6.. 11 b.g. Rakaposhi King — Donna Farina (Little Buskins) 4354. Plain leggy hobdayed brother to Jobsagoodun, and to jumping winner, Mountain Path. Dam, half-sister to Farina Stream (*qv* '94 Annual), won Hdle and 5 Chses (4 consecutively), all at 2m. P-t-P/HUNT CH '00/3 r21 w4 (up to Confined) p5 (4 3rds, of 4 twice, and inc 2 Hunt Chses); 4th, and pulled up 11. Useless in two previous yards, but much improved in the current one, and has won four times on good or easy surfaces. Found the ground too lively on his first attempt in an Open, and absent for eight weeks between his last two outings, but has lacked the fluency required to make a serious impact over regulation fences. Has access to leading riders, but does not always find much off the bridle, and would appreciate a return to Points. Blinkered once in '00. *Mrs M.A. Hall, G.T. Lever & Mrs E.J. Scott — Devon & Somerset (Jeremy Scott).* 11 (O), 541 (3mH), 631 (2m6f110yH), 1452 (3m4fH).

DONS DELIGHT (IRE) ..10-1.. 13 br.g. Lord Americo — Irish Tara (Buckskin FR) p37. Sturdy compact. IRISH NH FLAT '97/8 r3 p1 (3rd). IRISH NH '97/8 and '00 r16 p5 (inc 2nd in Ch). P-t-P/HUNT CH '01/3 r9 w2 (Maiden and Restricted) p1 (2nd); fell/unseated 3, and pulled up 3. Had plenty of chances in Ireland, and finally scored at the 25th attempt, but struggles to get the trip ordinarily, and remains prone to blunders. Retains his rating virtue of a close third at Dunthrop, but becoming very lightly raced, and will do well to revive successfully at 13. Wears a cross-noseband. *G.R. Kerr — Pytchley (David Line).* 34 (O), 47 (Cf), 190 (C).

DON'TTELLTHETAXMAN (IRE) ..9-8.. 8 b.g. Executive Perk — Calfstown Night (Bargello) 6. Well-made attractive half-brother to Gortroe Guy (IRE) (*qv*). P-t-P '03 r1 w1 (2m4f Maiden). Had an '04 Hunter Chase winner in his wake when getting off to the perfect start at Dalston last year, but subsequently afflicted by sore shins, and failed to reappear after making a satisfactory debut in a Restricted. Young enough to atone once he has matured physically. *Mrs A. Stevenson — Tynedale (Tim Reed).* 268 (R).

DOOK'S DELIGHT (IRE) .9-4§.. 14 b.g. Satco (FR) — Mar Del Plata (Crowned Prince USA) 6upp. Tall workmanlike half-brother to 5 winners (one in France). Dam won 8f race and is half-sister Scorpio Sam (*qv* '97 Annual). IRISH NH FLAT '95 r4 w1 p0. IRISH NH '96/8 r29 w2 (2m4f Hdle and a 2m2f Ch) p5. NH '99/02 r23 w6 (2 3m3f-3m3f110y Hdles and 4 2m4f110y-3m3f Chses) p5 (3 3rds); pulled up 2, brought down 1. P-t-P '03 (for Miss C.P. Holliday) r4 w1 (3-finisher Ladies) p1 (3rd); 4th, and 5th. Won six races for Richard Fahey, including an 11-length defeat of Donnegale (*qv*) over 3m3f110y at Sedgefield, but was totally unpredictable and blinkered more often than not. Came with a typically strong late charge to collar the prematurely eased Spring Gale at Horseheath last year, but schooling a nervous beginner in '04, and was 25 lengths last in their only completion. *Mrs K. Horsfall — Quorn (Toby Saunders).* 373 (L), 585 (L), 785 (L), 1470 (L).

DORANS MAGIC .10-8.. 10 b.g. Gildoran — Mearlin (Giolla Mear) 4f21fu13. Big workmanlike half-brother to Hurdles winner, Country House. Dam won 3 (2m-2m5f) Hurdles and 3 (2m1f-3m1f) Chases. NH FLAT '00 r2 p0. NH '00/2 r12 w2 (2m6f Hdle and 2m4f110y Ch) p3 (2nds). P-t-P/HUNT CH '03 r7 w1 (3-runner Open) p1 (short head 2nd in Hunt Ch); 5th, last, unseated 2 and pulled up 1. A very thorough stayer and suited by mud, but prone to make clumsy mistakes, and but for such lapses would probably have scored at Corbridge and Heslaker in '04. Looked likely to come out second best when toppling at the last at Perth, but made amends at Wetherby, and lost no caste in defeat at Uttoxeter, where he overturned the Grimthorpe form with Sad Mad Bad. Finally gaining some continuity in the saddle, and can look forward to scoring on a more regular basis in future. *N.W.A. Bannister — Pendle Forest & Craven (Annabelle Armitage).* 214 (O), 429 (3m5fO), 772 (4m1fO), 875 (O), 1068 (3m2f110yH), 1204 (O), 1297 (3m1fH), 1376 (4m2fH).

DORSET FERN (IRE) ..9-0.. 9 b.m. Tirol — La Duse (Junius USA) 145. Small light-framed half-sister to 2 flat winners including Blushing Grenadier (11 wins). NH FLAT '00 r3 p0. NH '00/3 (for G.B. Balding, and J.K. Price) r22 p3 (Sells); unseated 1, pulled up 3. Sold Ascot, Jun for 2380. Bought Ascot, Oct for 1238. Part of an excellent season for Emma James, who apart from the triumph of Upton Adventure also won races with her own three cheapy mares. Only Selling company under Rules (beaten between two and 12 lengths when placed in that company), and was 35 lengths fourth and pulled up in Chases, and wore blinkers once. Found the ideal opportunity in an elders Maiden at Chaddesley Corbett, but it was a woeful contest and the four behind only managed one win from a total of 18 attempts. Had an interrupted season with two and a half months after her next outing (when she was even money favourite), and does not give the impression that there is a lot of scope for improvement. *Wild Prince Taylor Partnership (Miss E.E.L. James) — N. Ledbury (Emma James).* 258 (CMa), 452 (R), 1531 (R).

DOS DESPERADOS (IRE) ..7-10.. 9 b.g. Un Desperado (FR) — Ballycahan Girl (Bargello) 2. Good-topped half-brother to Step In Line (IRE) (*qv*). IR9500 4yo. IRISH P-t-P '01/2 r4 p0. NH '02 (for Miss E.C. Lavelle) r1 p0 (pulled up). Beat a total of four in his four Irish Points (stamina unproven), and looked unimpressive when 12 lengths last of two in his Members. Has managed only six appearances in four years, and probably has problems. *Miss J. Batho — Hursley Hambledon (David Phelan).* 260 (M).

DOUBLE BUBBLE (IRE) ..— §§.. 7 b/br.g. Mandalus — Double Talk (Dublin Taxi) fRr6p. Compact brother to Mandy Chat (IRE). IR10,000 3yo, 6000 4yo. NH FLAT '02/3 (for C.N. Kellett) r2 p0 (last 2). Hopelessly tailed off last in two bumpers, and was also withdrawn after going berserk in the preliminaries once. Andrew Glassonbury achieved a remarkable feat in getting him to complete the course despite many errors when 60 lengths sixth (mounted on the course and taken to post early), but a total lunatic otherwise and was pulled up after a mile after jumping wildly and hanging badly next time. Only negotiated a total of three fences in his first three Points, and putting an inexperienced girl on him twice was the height of stupidity. Should be warned off. *M. Stephens & L.E. Westcott — W. Somerset (Mark Stephens).* 962 (OMa), 1133 (OMa), 1326 (OMa), 1381 (OMa), 1511 (OMa).

DOUBLE RICH ..10-0.. 12 ch.g. Rich Charlie — Spartona (Cisto FR) 34p251. Big rangy. Dam was placed in 3 Hdles for Cherry Coward's father, Mick Easterby. Grandam, Dorothy May, would have been unbeaten in 4 stone wall Members '77/80 but for unseating when going strongly in '80. P-t-P/HUNT CH '98/9 and '02/3 r17 w3 (Maiden, Restricted and Members) p1 (3rd); pulled up 4, unseated 3. Has trouble with his wind, and went eventing after recording a double in '99, but returned to provide Tom Greenall with his initial win in '02, and gave younger brother Oliver his taste of success when sweeping through late at Chaddesley on his latest appearance. Just failed to make up ten lengths from the third-last on his reappearance at Garnons, but only had half that amount of ground to recover, and ultimately won going away. Lacks consistency due to his infirmity, and is suited by waiting tactics. Wears a cross-noseband, and has run tongue-tied. *Lord Daresbury — Sir W.W. Wynn's (Steve Wynne).* 405 (Inr), 708 (M), 989 (Cnr), 1264 (Cf), 1429 (Cnr), 1530 (I).

DOUBLET ..10-2.. 10 ch.g. Bustino — Pas De Deux (Nijinsky CAN) ppp1p. Lengthy half-brother to jumping winner, Insular, and to several flat winners, including, Starlet. Dam won 10f race. FLAT '98 and '01 r9 p2 (3rds). NH '99 and '01/2 r11 w3 (hat-trick 2m-2m1f Hdles) p5. P-t-P '03 r5 w1 (Club

Confined) p2; last and fell. Completed a hat-trick in modest Hurdles for Martin Pipe in '99, but left the yard after one more outing, and was gaining his first success since at Bratton Down last year. Returned to form when surviving an earth-moving blunder at the final ditch at Holnicote, but pulled up in four other attempts, and may require a hobdaying operation to rectify a breathing problem. Suited by top-of-the-ground conditions. Wears over-reach boots. *R.G. Rawle — Exmoor (Debbie Cole).* 64 (O), 470 (L), 822 (L), 1328 (MO), 1378 (M).

DOUBLE THATCH (IRE) ..9-8.. 9 b.g. Dobey Thatcher — Ballinturn (Hawaiian Return USA) 4. IRISH NH FLAT '01 r2 p1 (2nd). IRISH NH '02 r2 p0. IRISH P-t-P/HUNT CH '00 and '03 r3 w1 (4&5yo Maiden) p1 (2nd); and pulled up. P-t-P '03 (for Mr P.M. Mooney) r2 p1 (3rd); and pulled up 1. Scored as a four-year-old in Ireland, and beaten a length in his final Point there last year, but the subject of a misplaced gamble on his English debut, and rarely gets the opportunity to make amends. Limited evidence over jumps suggests he does not truly stay three miles, and his nomadic lifestyle that he is not easy to train. *K.R. Dance — N. Ledbury (Julian Pritchard).* 191 (R).

DOWN (FR) ..10-5.. 14 b.g. Le Nain Jaune (FR) — Izoba (FR) (Bamako III) 8121. Workmanlike brother to 2 French jumping winners, and half-brother to French/English Chasing winner, Elzoba (FR), and to 2 other winners in France. Dam won 4 races over jumps in France. FRENCH NH '95/9 r27 w5 (3 2m5f Chses and 2 Cross-Country races, 2m5f110y-2m6f110y) p4 (2 2nds); failed to finish 7 (fell/unseated 3). P-t-P/HUNT CH '01/3 r13 w5 (inc Nov Rdrs Mixed Open, Open and 2 4m Mixed Opens) p2; 4th, 9th twice, last pair 2 and pulled up 1. Apparently laid low by a virus in the early part of '04, but in fine fettle for his hat-trick attempt in the Pentyrch 4-miler, and duly justified favouritism. Earlier slowed down by the application of a cross-noseband when providing Jessica Waley-Cohen with her first race ride at Tweseldown, but otherwise has an outstanding record in minor Points, and with careful placing could score again at 14. Acts on all but extremes of going. *R.B. Waley-Cohen — Warwicks.* 175 (Cnr), 190 (C), 382 (O), 1093 (4mMO).

DRAGON LORD .9-13§.. 11 b.g. Warning — Cockatoo Island (High Top) u. Small sturdy brother to flat winner, Coachella, and half-brother to flat and jumping winner, Collier Bay (won '96 Champion Hurdle), and to flat winner, Treasure Island. Dam won 4 flat, 8-15f, inc walkover. NH FLAT '98 r4 w1 p2. NH '98/01 r6 p2; fell 1. P-t-P/HUNT CH '02/3 r8 p5 (4 2nds, beaten ½*l* once); 4th, and fell 2. Got off to the perfect start when beating 19 rivals in a Lingfield bumper in '98, but broke down the following year, and has never won over jumps. Looked sure to break the sequence at Kingston Blount last year, but surrendered tamely under pressure, and emphasised his lack of jumping acumen when unseating on his only appearance in '04. Lives outside to try to combat a problem with stomach ulcers, and who can blame him for being such a miserable sod. Wears a visor, and has been tried in cheekpieces. *S.P. Tindall & Mrs J. Gordon — Mid Surrey F. (Jenny Gordon).* 19 (CMod).

DR DEDUCTIBLE ..9-12.. 13 b.g. Derrylin — Tantrum (Leading Man) 772194. Compact attractive half-brother to Remove and Tantalum. Dam is an unraced sister to Thrip The Dye (*qv* '94 Annual). NH '99/00 r7 p1 (3rd in Ch); 5th, pulled up 3, and fell/unseated 2. P-t-P/HUNT CH '98/9 and '01/3 (for Mrs J.E. Brockbank) r23 w4 (inc 3m1f Hunt Ch and Open) p6 (3 2nds, inc Hunt Ch; and 3 3rds, of 4 once); pulled up 5, and fell 1. Most adept at course completion, and surpassed all previous form when galvanised by first-time blinkers in a Kelso Hunter Chase last year, but was most unimpressive in his execution, and reduced to acting as schoolmaster nowadays. Greatly flattered by his defeat of the owner-ridden Crevamoy in his Members, and finished 22 lengths behind that rival when they next met, but at least provided the newcomer Ronan Brown with his first success. Likes to dominate, and is suited by good or easy ground. Wore cheekpieces in '04. *Mrs H. Macfarlane & R.S. Brown — Buccleuch (Morag Neill).* 72 (O), 134 (O), 285 (O), 547 (M), 764 (O), 917 (O).

DREAMIE BATTLE ..9-8.. 7 br.m. Makbul — Highland Rossie (Pablond) 22. Leggy half-sister to 4 winners (one in Italy), including Diet (14 wins on flat) and The Overnight Man (Hurdling). Dam, sister to Plumbers Mate (*qv* '91 Annual), won 2 Sells on flat (7-10f). 3800y. FLAT '00/3 r22 p2. NH '02/3 (for R. Hollinshead) r9 p1 (3rd); unseated 1. Beaten between four lengths and 40 lengths when achieving three placings flat and Hurdling (at odds of 25-1 upwards), but was a regular in Sellers, and consistently outclassed. Surprisingly seems to have enough stamina for Points, and followed a 20-length second with a head defeat three months later (came within inches of giving Sue Sharratt a quick double at Kingston Blount). There should be a modest race with her name on. *Miss S. Sharratt — Albrighton.* 58 (OMa), 1108 (OMa).

DREAM OF MY LIFE (USA) ..10-0.. 12 gr.g. Danzatore (CAN) — Sureya (Sharpen Up) 1434356p. Lengthy workmanlike half-brother to 2 winners in USA. Dam won at 11f in France. FLAT r4 p0. NH '01 r1 p0 (tailed off last in 2m Nov Hdle). P-t-P '98/9 and '02/3 r24 w5 (up to Confined) p9 (7 2nds, beaten short-head once, of 3 once, and remote last once; and 3rd of 4, and last of 3); pulled up 3, and fell/unseated 3. Goes well fresh, and has scored on his seasonal debut on three occasions, but really only effective in minor events, and failed to beat a rival in his last four outings. Beaten at odds-on in '04, and can be safely ignored after his debut next year. Wears a cross-noseband and over-reach boots, and acquired a tongue-tie on his Hunter Chase debut. *Mrs L.C. Balmer — Morpeth (Alan Balmer).* 73 (Cf), 210 (Cf), 509 (O), 764 (O), 858 (Cf), 1220 (C), 1418 (Cf), 1499 (2m4f110yH).

DREAM ON THEN ..8-13.. 9 ch.m. Royal Vulcan — Dreamside (Quayside) 2. Lengthy unfurnished owner-bred. Dam, half-sister to Vital Issue (*qv*). NH '02 r1 p0. P-t-P '03 r1 p0 (fell). Whipped round at the start and always tailed off on her only appearance over hurdles, and fell at halfway on her Pointing debut, but backed from 14s to threes when runner-up at Cottenham, and had a subsequent winner behind. Raced keenly and did not appear to get home, but has access to good riders, and might find a race if connections continue to persevere. Has two paddock handlers. *S.J. Smith — Grafton.* 561 (OMa).

DRIMINAMORE (IRE) ..—.. 15 b.g. Buckskin (FR) — Miss Blue Jay (Blue Refrain) pp. Rangy. IRISH P-t-P '96 r2 p0 (last and pulled up). P-t-P/HUNT CH '97/00 and '02/3 r26 w2 (Maiden and Restricted) p8 (6 3rds, of 4 once, and last once); pulled up 3, and fell/unseated 4. Scored once apiece '98/9, and rated 9-12 at best, but blighted by a tendency to break blood vessels, and failed to reach the two-mile mark in '04. *Major General C.A. Ramsay — Berwicks.* 915 (Cf), 1220 (C).

DROM ISLAND ..9-6.. 11 b.m. Jupiter Island — Netherdrom (Netherkelly) p1p3p35. Sturdy half-sister to Another Drom, Sabre Drom, Dromalba and Doctor Spinney. Dam, sister to Dromakelly Lad (*qv* '92 Annual), won 2 Points and placed 3. P-t-P '99/03 r17 p3 (2nds, of 3 once, and last once); 4th, pulled up 11, and fell/unseated 2. Struggles to get the trip, and pulled up in 12 of 18 previous attempts, but finally found an opportunity when landing an elders Maiden on firmish at Laleston. Typically stopped to nil up the hill at Umberleigh, and the chances of her landing a Restricted are remote. Must have been affected by an unsightly open sore at the junction of her off-hind and belly in the second half of the season. *G. Richards — Tredegar F.* 1027 (OMa), 1193 (OMa), 1389 (R), 1481 (M), 1538 (R), 1548 (R), 1561 (R).

DROVERS ROAD ..8-10.. 9 b.g. Lapierre — Miss Trixie (Le Tricolore) 48. Tall attractive half-brother to Polynth and Stan. Appeared to shape with some promise on his debut, but never got remotely involved when last next time, and only lasted as long as February. Another Drovers Road was Hunter Chasing as recently as '92. *R. Dalton — Cleveland (Anne Dalton).* 167 (OMa), 271 (OMa).

DRUID PANDORA ..—.. 10 b.m. Lepanto (GER) — Kenton Belle (Hackness) ppp. Good-bodied owner-bred half-sister to Druid Merill and Druid Belle. Dam, half-sister to Gay Bergen (*qv* '88 Season Annual). Showed no ability when pulling up in Maidens, and went lame in the latest. *Miss E.J. Kessler — S. Devon (Emma Oliver).* 327 (OMa), 494 (OMa), 704 (CfMa).

DRUID'S BROOK ..9-0.. 16 b.g. Meadowbrook — Struide (Guide) 4p. Owner-bred half-brother to Royal Stream. NH '97/00 r17 w3 (2m6f-3m6f Chses) p4 (inc 3 2nds); 9th and fell in '98/9 Irish Grand Nationals, and unseated in '00 Grand National. P-t-P '96 and '02 (for E. Edmonstone & Major A. Everett) r10 w2 (Maiden and Restricted) p4 (3rds, of 4 twice, and last once); 4th, last pair 2 and ran out 1. An ex-eventer who won four of his first five races, but went to pieces latterly under Rules, and seems little more than a hunter now. Wears a cross-noseband, and has been tried in blinkers. *Mrs R.H. Reynolds — S. Dorset.* 233 (M), 690 (L).

DRUM BATTLE ..9-10.. 13 ch.g. Bold Arrangement — Cannon Boy (USA) (Canonero USA) 9405p4. Small lengthy brother to jumping winner, Maple Bay (also won 10 flat), and half-brother to Diamond Beach, and to 4 winners, including Donna Del Lago (10 jumping races). Dam won 9 at around 9f in USA, and a winner of 15 in USA. FLAT '95/6 (first 3 for R. Charlton) r4 p0. NH '96/03 r45 w5 (2 2m4f-2m5f110y Hdles and 3 2m3f110y-3m5f Chses) p14. P-t-P '03 (for Mr D. Chown) r1 w1 (Open). Returning from a brief spell on the sidelines when making an impressive Pointing debut at Barbury Castle last year, but has gone downhill rapidly since, and a persistent wind problem appears to have resurfaced. Unimproved by the re-application of a tongue-tie at Marks Tey, nor by cheekpieces and a visor on his last three starts, and has been retired. Wears a cross-noseband. *Mrs C. Gibbs — Pytchley (Caroline Bailey).* 34 (O), 110 (Cnr), 249 (Cnr), 381 (O), 943 (MO), 1274 (Cf).

DRUMDOWNEY LAD (IRE) ..9-6.. 6 b.g. Darnay — Alpencrocus (IRE) (Waajib) 3215p. Tall. 11,684 3yo. IRISH NH FLAT '03 (for M. Kinane) r2 p0 (beat one of 40 rivals). NH '04 r1 p0 (last of 5 in 2m110y Ch: *hld up & bhnd, hdwy app 7, wknd 4 out, t.o*). Won a bad race at Badbury in February (four of the five to finish behind him remain maidens), and was coming to the end of his tether, as he does not truly stay the trip. Even struggling to get home over 2m4f previously, and will not find Restricteds easy unless his stamina increases. Sub-standard under Rules on the evidence to date. *M. Power — Staff College (Ray York).* 8 (2m4fOMa), 104 (2m4fOMa), 264 (CfMa), 734 (2mH).

DRUMHORC (IRE) ..9-11.. 8 ch.g. Zaffaran (USA) — Dim Drums (Proverb) 43p1433. Small compact brother to Hurdles winner, Shelayly (IRE), and half-brother to NH flat winner, Did You know (IRE). IRISH P-t-P '02/3 r3 w1 (6yo&up Maiden) p1 (2nd); and pulled up 1. Did not cost much and has proved fair value, but very inconsistent, and tried in cheekpieces on his outing following the win at Charlton Horethorne. Beaten under two lengths in two of his thirds, and appeared to finish second in the first of them (was staying on well in the closing stages). Capable of scoring again, but not a dependable betting medium. *Miss L. Gardner — Silverton.* 79 (R), 197 (R), 324 (R), 354 (R), 705 (I), 823 (Cf), 1271 (I).

DRUMLIN (IRE) .9-10§.. 10 b.g. Glacial Storm (USA) — Shannon Lough (IRE) (Deep Run) 3. Strong workmanlike half-brother to Lough Dante (IRE). NH FLAT '99 r2 p0. NH '99/01 r7 w1 (2m Hdle) p2 (2nds); pulled up 1, ran out 1. P-t-P/HUNT CH '02/3 (for Mr J.M. Turner) r14 p2 (2nds, last once); last pair 5, and pulled up 7. Scored in soft at Plumpton and runner-up twice over hurdles to November '00, but immediately acquired blinkers, and has found nil off the bridle when in a challenging position since. Managed only one appearance for the new yard, and has always given the impression that an underlying physical problem was to blame. *Mrs A. Price — Teme V.* 448 (O).

DUBIOUS DEAL .—.. 8 ch.g. Seven Hearts — Heather Lane (Heres) frs. Workmanlike. P-t-P '03 (for Mr G.P. Hayes & Mr R.G. Andrews) r3 p0 (pulled up 2 and unseated 1). Very headstrong and has shown plenty of speed, but has yet to look like getting round in one piece. Ran in a kineton at Bratton Down, but appeared to do himself a mischief behind when slipping up after less than a mile. *R.G. Andrews & D. Millington — Mendip F. (Nikki Stephens).* 413 (2m4fOMa), 1098 (OMa), 1558 (R).

DUCHESS ACCOUNT ..9-2.. 8 b.m. Mesleh — Dutch Account VII (unknown) 317. Owner-bred half-sister to Ruff Account. Winning races with horses who have pedigrees which are far from blue-bloods has been a speciality of the Braders over the years (remember Magic Whip and Jeannie Brown? — tragically the former and her foal both died on the night connections were celebrating the victory of Duchess Account), and after a lull of some years they seem to have found another fair prospect. Followed a promising third on her debut with a game win in a youngsters Maiden at Easingwold, where she overcame some moderate early jumping to score in much the slowest time of the day, but never got into contention next time. Needs to improve a few pounds for Restricteds, but possibly capable of doing so. *R.G. Brader — Middleton (Charles Brader).* 776 (CfMa), 1159 (OMa), 1288 (R).

DUKESTOWN (IRE) ..7-0§.. 13 b.g. Duky — Small Iron (General Ironside) 44p. Compact well-made. Dam won 3m Hurdle in Ireland. IRISH P-t-P '96/7 r4 w1 (4&5yo Maiden) p0; pulled up 2. NH '97/8 and '00 (for G.B. Balding, and Miss L.V. Russell) r7 p1 (3rd); pulled up 1. Very unproductive since scoring in Ireland as a baby, and apart from a 20 lengths third over Hurdles was beaten 55 lengths plus on six occasions. Badly tailed off last in his two Ladies Opens completions, and is a difficult ride for the inexperienced owner, as he is prone to dwell, pull hard and hang. *Miss E.L. McWilliam — Fife.* 508 (L), 1078 (L), 1308 (L).

PLATE 36 212 College Valley & N. Northumberland Restricted: The last fence and it's it the bag for Dumadic and Nigel Tutty PHOTO: Alan Mitchell

DUMADIC ..10-4.. 8 b.g. Nomadic Way (USA) — Duright (Dubassoff USA) 13121. Small well-made. Dam, sister to Sea Script (*qv* '87 Season Annual), won 6 Points (inc 4m Grimthorpe) and Hunter Chase and placed 4 for Peter Sawney. NH FLAT '01/2 r3 p1 (3rd). NH '02 r2 p0; pulled up 1. P-t-P '03 r5 w1 (Maiden) p2 (2nds); and unseated 2. Can pull demonically and verging on the insane in '03, but beginning to adopt a calmer attitude on a more regular basis, and is progressing through the ranks as a result. Probably hit the front too soon and hung badly when beaten at Heslaker, but turned the tables on his vanquisher on a much easier track next time, and whilst he is never going to be sweetness and light should certainly score again. An improved jumper since Nigel Tutty accepted the ride. Wears a cross-noseband. *Miss J.A. Sawney & P. Willis — Cleveland (Sarah Dent).* 212 (R), 389 (Cf), 808 (CfCon), 1204 (O), 1414 (O).

DUN AENGUS ..— §§.. 9 b.g. Lighter — Bantel Bouquet (Red Regent) Rpppp. Small close-coupled half-brother to Bantel Baronet, Charlcot Storm and Lord Haashim. A highly reluctant donkey who was just as bad when blinkered once. The owner has some ancient-looking colours (probably those he used to wear when he was flopping around ineptly on another sub-equine called Oriel Candle countless moons ago). *C. Rutledge — N. Cotswold.* 370 (OMa), 588 (CfMa), 760 (OMa), 1488 (OMa), 1505 (OMa).

DUN DISTINCTLY (IRE) ..10-0.. 8 b.g. Distinctly North (USA) — Dunbally (Dunphy) 43. Small brother to Northern Castle (IRE), and half-brother to flat winner, Mr B Reasonable (IRE). FLAT '99/02 r18 w1 (12f) p2 (2nds, inc Sell). NH '00/2 r10 w1 (2m Hdle) p1 (3rd); pulled up 1. P-t-P '03 r6 p0 (4th, last pair 3, unseated and pulled up). Clobbered by the Handicapper after scoring narrowly over hurdles at Catterick in November '00, and forced to exploit a low mark on the flat for his next success, but has struggled to get the trip in Points. Beaten only a length when third to Balisteros at Hornby Castle, but did not get another chance to prove that was no fluke. Suited by good of sound surfaces. Visored once in '00. *Miss G.T. Lee — Hurworth.* 162 (L), 339 (L).

DUNMANUS BAY (IRE) ..—.. 8 gr.g. Mandalus — Baby Fane (IRE) (Buckskin FR) pp. Tall strong half-brother to Vics Fane (IRE), and to Irish jumping winner, Lord Fane. IR1750 3yo. IRISH P-t-P '01 r2 p2 (2nds). NH '02/3 (for B.G. Powell, R.H. Alner, and M.C. Pipe) r16 w2 (2m4f-3m3f Chses) p3; fell 2, pulled up 2. Bought Doncaster, Oct for 4000. Possesses plenty of stamina and a fair degree of ability, but makes countless mistakes and needs demonic driving, and gained the second of his Chasing wins under a sensational effort from McCoy, who never left him alone and bullied him home against his wishes. Normally wears headgear. He and his partners both need to be super-fit to have any chance, but Julie Read's charges are very well fed, so they are probably wasting their time with him. *Mrs P. King — Suffolk (Julie Read).* 239 (3m1fH), 893 (3m110yH).

DUNMANUS SOUND (IRE) ..8-9.. 8 ch.g. Alphabatim (USA) — Cainsbridge Queen (Crash Course) 22. Half-brother to Downtheground (IRE). Dam, half-sister to Onawing Andaprayer (*qv* '95 Annual), won Irish NH flat (also demoted to 2nd after winning similar), and won 2m6f Hurdle in England. IRISH P-t-P '02/3 r6 p1 (2nd) last, fell 2. Sold Doncaster, May for 5000. Resold Doncaster, Aug for 1600. His sharp drop in value at the sales over a three month period suggested there was something wrong with him, and beaten the length of the run-in in both Maidens (went lame in the latest). Could take some patching up. *R.J. Rowsell — Ystrad Taf Fechan.* 1324 (CfMa), 1487 (OMa).

DUNMANUS SUPREME (IRE) .8-6.. 8 b.g. Supreme Leader — Toghermore Lass (Pry) 3. Compact. Dam won Members Nomination Point and 2m5f Chase in Ireland. IRISH P-t-P '02/3 r4 p3. Does not get many opportunities, but has managed placings in four of five Points, and was ten lengths third in the latest. The race was run at a crawl (15 seconds slower than the other Maiden), and will need to do quite a lot better if he is to open his account. *Mrs L.P. Vaughan — Ross H. (Jane Evans).* 1139 (OMa).

DUNRIG (IRE) ..9-7§.. 10 b.g. King's Ride — Belon Brig (New Brig) p413343p. Small light half-brother to Eye Of The Storm (IRE). Dam won 3 Chses, 2m4f-3m. IRISH P-t-P '00/2 r10 w1 (7yo&up Maiden) p3 (2nds). IRISH HUNT CH '02 r1 p0 (pulled up). HUNT CH '03 (for Mr D. Coltman) r3 w1 (3m1f) p2 (2nds, beaten $^3/_4l$ once). Involved in three close finishes at Kelso last year, and came out on top in the latest, but regularly disappointed in Ireland previously, and gifted his only '04 success when The Red Boy downed tools after the last at Higham. Acquired blinkers on his next visit there, but only once beaten less than 17 lengths otherwise, and has gone from being very game to an outright pig in no time at all. Presumably wrong, and remains a very sketchy jumper. *J.M. Turner — Suffolk.* 42 (L), 221 (O), 397 (O), 650 (O), 830 (O), 1209 (O), 1243 (O), 1441 (3m7fH).

DUN ROSE .10-5.. 11 b/br.m. Roscoe Blake — Dun Gay Lass (Rolfe USA) 122. Small half-sister to Dun Victory. Dam, sister to Dun Rolfe (*qv* '92 Annual), won 6 Points and 3 Hunt Chses and 2nd 2 (beaten head in '91 Cheltenham Foxhunters or would have completed 10-timer — robbed after the stirrup leather wrenched free of saddle bar) for Mrs Chartres and Phyllis Claxton. NH FLAT '98 r2 p0. NH '99 r2 p0. P-t-P '00/3 r11 w5 (inc Open) p2 (2nds); 4th, pulled up 2 and fell 1. Out of an outstanding mare, and beaten only by subsequent Aintree Foxhunters hero Divet Hill in her first five

Points, but under a cloud in '02, and has never really recaptured her best. Returned the fastest time of the day when making a winning reappearance at Alnwick (where she was late to enter the paddock), but tends to get in a stew in the preliminaries, and had used up too much petrol when collared in the closing stages next time. Difficult to weigh up, but does not stand much racing, and risked only on good or easy surfaces. *Mrs P. Claxton — College V. & N. Northumberland.* 211 (C), 551 (O), 764 (O).

DUNSTON HEATH (IRE) .—.. 12 b.g. Durgam (USA) — Yola (IRE) (Last Tycoon) uuu. Small neat. NH FLAT '97 r1 p0. NH '97/03 (for B. Preece, and B.D. Leavy) r29 w2 (2m4f-2m5f Hdles) p3; pulled up 4. Gained the second of his two wins which include a Seller, in April '00, but was pulled up in two of his final four attempts under Rules (including his only Chase). Blinkered once in '97, and tongue-tied thrice. Appeared only once apiece in '01 and '03, and his new partner fell off at halfway each time. The nearby rides at Alton Towers are a safer option for her future thrills. *Miss A. Blake — N. Staffs.* 94 (L), 230 (L), 515 (L).

DUN VICTORY..10-2.. 10 b.g. Destroyer — Dun Gay Lass (Rolfe USA) 22p. Owner-bred half-brother to Dun Rose (*qv*). P-t-P '02/3 r7 w4 (up to Confined) p0; last, and pulled up 2. Recorded a four-timer on varying ground last year, but only scored by more than a length on one occasion, and tried to run out to the boxes when initiating the sequence. Lost no caste in defeat on his reappearance, but probably in front too soon at Friars Haugh, and pulled up with a reported breathing problem at Kelso. Clearly as much of a character as his sibling, and can win again if his wind can be rectified. *Mrs P. Claxton — College V. & N. Northumberland.* 210 (Cf), 552 (Cf), 797 (3m1fH).

DURSEY ISLAND (IRE) ..9-0.. 8 b.g. Commanche Run — Deverell's Lady (Sterling Bay SWE) 314p3. Lengthy unfurnished brother to NH flat and Hurdles winner, Sioux Raider (IRE), and half-brother to NH flat and Hurdles winner, Scarteen, to Irish Pointing winner, Penstall Lady, and to 3 flat winners (2 abroad, one also successful Hurdler). IRISH P-t-P '01/2 r6 p3 (2nds); pulled up 2. P-t-P '03 r2 p0 (5th and last). Landed a touch in a disaster-strewn Maiden at Milborne St Andrew, but not better than last since, and despite strenuous efforts to conserve energy has otherwise failed to get the trip. Will find it hard if not impossible to stage a follow up. *M.W. Cox & Mrs C. Williamson-Jones — Portman (Sarah Clarke).* 68 (OMa), 238 (CfMa), 415 (R), 689 (R), 1251 (R).

PLATE 37 5 Cambridgeshire Harriers Hunt Club Ladies Open: The ill-fated Dusk Duel (Jane Williams), 1st, leads Winter Gale (Laura Eddery), 2nd PHOTO: Tim Holt

DUSK DUEL (USA) ..11-0.. 10 b.g. Kris — Night Secret (Nijinsky CAN) 1p. Tall lengthy brother to Night City. Dam won 10f race. NH FLAT '99 r2 w1 p0. NH '99/01 and '03 (for N.J. Henderson) r11 w4 (2 2m Hdles and 2 2m-2m5f Chses) p4. Won five races in the soft to December '00, and although there were a maximum of five runners in the four jumping contests one of them gained him an £11,000 prize. Seen only once since '01 before bounding round Cottenham to take a Ladies in exuberant fashion, but sadly his old leg trouble flared up again two weeks later, and he had to be destroyed when on the verge of scrapping out the finish with Upton Adventure. A. Speelman — Wheatland (Juliet Minton). 5 (L), 33 (L).

DYNAMIC SEA ..—.. 8 b.g. Sea Raven (IRE) — Mildame (Milford) pp. Hobdayed (and had tie-back operation) half-brother to Chasing winners, Just Adam and Primitive Herb. Dam, half-sister to Well Matched (*qv* '04 Annual), ran badly in 2 Points and was 3rd of 4 in Hurdle. Sold Doncaster, Aug for 2700. Not seen until the Melton Maiden in mid-May, in which he and two other Millingtons had all been pulled up by the 11th. Acquired a tongue-tie next time, and did not actually do too badly for James Owen, but predictably looked awful, so it is hard to hold out much hope for him. Has been hobdayed and had a tie-back operation. You would not dream it in a million years looking at him now, but he was a former Lightweight Hunter and Supreme Champion at the North East Counties Show. The owner should quarter his string (22 in '04) and quadruple their rations. *P.J. Millington — Fernie.* 1403 (2m4fOMa), 1532 (OMa).

EARL OF BUCKINGHAM ..9-8.. 7 b.g. Alderbrook — Arctic Oats (Oats) 5723. Dam won 2 NH flat (1m6f-2m) and 2 Hurdles (2m4f-3m). 7680 3yo. Becoming disappointing. Only failed by a neck over 2m4f at Dingley (the trip may be inadequate for him), but could only manage eight lengths (officially a distance!) third when favourite next time. A steady jumper who can surely score eventually, and being by Alderbrook it is possible that he still needs time. *C.W. Booth — Grafton (Kim Gilmore).* 290 (2m4fCfMa), 589 (CfMa), 890 (2m4fOMa), 1125 (OMa).

PLATE 38 692 Cattistock Intermediate: Earl's Toy fails to shine despite the efforts of promising rider, Harry Fry *PHOTO: Brian Armstrong*

EARL'S TOY (IRE) ..9-7.. 10 b.g. Erdelistan (FR) — Grandolly (IRE) (The Parson) 126p4p. Small. Dam is sister to The Crazy Bishop (*qv* '01 Annual). NH FLAT '00 r2 p0. P-t-P '02/3 r7 w1 (Maiden) p0 (4th, 5th, 6th, ran out and pulled up 2). Successful on his last two seasonal debuts, and benefited from superior handling in the latest, but largely disappointing otherwise, and sometimes takes little interest. May not care for sound surfaces, but well worth a try in headgear. *R.A. & Dr C.E. Fry — Cattistock (Caroline Fry).* 65 (Rnr), 147 (I), 495 (I), 692 (I), 1329 (Cnr), 1382 (I).

EARL TOKEN ..8-10§.. 9 b.g. Primitive Rising (USA) — Lady Token f33p2. Small. Dam won 2m4f Hdle and 2 Chses, 3m-3m2f. Grandam, Princess Token, won 6 Points and placed 21 (inc Chses). NH '02/3 r2 p0 (pulled up 3). P-t-P '02/3 r8 p1 (2nd of 3); 8th, last, pulled up 3, and fell 2. Placed in four Maidens, and beaten less than a length in the latest, but otherwise beaten a minimum of 16 lengths, and has yet to display much in the way of determination. Twice a beaten favourite in '04, and his jumping remains consistently unreliable. *R.J. Armson — Atherstone.* 302 (OMa), 387 (OMa), 595 (OMa), 1124 (OMa), 1424 (OMa).

EARLY MORNING CALL (IRE) .9-7§.. 13 ch.g. Henbit (USA) — Golonig (Goldhill) u7p25ppu. Good-topped. Dam is half-sister to Golden Fame (*qv* '88 Season Annual). IRISH P-t-P '98 r4 p1 (2nd);

pulled up 2. NH '98, '00 and '03 r5 p4; and pulled up. P-t-P/HUNT CH '01/3 (for Mr C.D. Hazelwood (The It's My Job Partnership) r12 w2 (Maiden and Restricted) p5 (2 2nds, inc distant in Hunt Ch, and last once); 6th, and pulled up 4. Goes well fresh and scored on his previous two seasonal debuts, but lacks resolve, and well beaten when completing in the new yard. A reliable jumper but can be safely ignored in future. Wears a cross-noseband, and has been tried in cheekpieces and a tongue-tie. *The Definatley Blonde Partnership (J. Barnes) — Mendip F. (Clare Parfitt).* 147 (I), 193 (I), 321 (I), 598 (M), 881 (Inr), 1129 (I), 1369 (Cf), 1544 (I).

EARLY RIVERS ..—.. 6 b.m. Teenoso (USA) — Cherry Morello (Bargello) R*80*. Small compact homebred half-sister to American Black, Quick Quick Sloe, Mazzard, Acetylene, Second Bite and A Second Sloe. Dam won a Maiden and placed 3 for Simon Cave. NH FLAT '04 (for C.J. Down) r2 p0 (8th over 2m at Ludlow: *hld up & pulled hard, rdn & wknd 3f out*; and 10th over 2m1f at Newton Abbot: *a bhnd*). Nearly plum last when she crashed through the wing of the third and unseated at Bishops Court. The switch to bumpers suggests that she will need to calm down if she is ever to achieve anything. *Dr S.G.F. Cave — Eggesford (Penny Cave).* 325 (OMa).

EARTHMOVER (IRE) ..11-9.. 14 ch.g. Mister Lord (USA) — Clare's Crystal (Tekoah) 2131b. Tall rangy brother to Irish Pointing winner, Kilmurry Queen (IRE), and half-brother to Viking Buoy (IRE). Dam is half-sister to Killeshandra Lass (*qv* '97 Annual). NH '98/02 r26 w5 (3 3m-3m1f Chses, and 2 3m-3m2f Hdles) p8 (inc 5 Grade 2/3 events); fell/unseated 4, inc at 4th fence in '00/1 Grand Nationals, and pulled up 3. P-t-P/HUNT CH '96/8 and '03 r23 w18 (inc 11 Hunt Chses, 3m-3m4f, and 4 Ladies, inc 4-timer '03) p2 (2nds); 4th, pulled up 1, and fell 1. A remarkable old horse who followed Double Silk (who died in '04 aged 20) and Fantus into the record books as '90s Cheltenham Foxhunter winners who managed to regain their title. The fact that Earthmover took six years to achieve it is testimony to his durability and boundless enthusiasm, and in doing so became the first 13-year-old since the race was reduced in distance in 1978 to succeed. Looked an ideal candidate to go all the way under Rules, but injuries and ill health (spent much of '02 breaking blood vessels) put a stop to that, and the team at Ditcheat have worked wonders with him. Has always held a special affinity for Prestbury Park, and also successful five times at Chepstow, and has earned £122,833 in win prize money alone. Given a superb ride by Rilly Goschen at the Festival, and battled heroically up the hill for her, and confirmed the form with County Derry when landing the 4m2f Mount Argus for the second year running at Uttoxeter. Ideally suited by some cut in the ground (found conditions too fast between wins), and likes to gallop the opposition into submission, and jumps with more accuracy than was once the case. Hit the ground with a real thud at Stratford, but happily unscathed, and with retirement seemingly not an option at present (and with little real opposition on the horizon), it is eminently feasible that he can push back the boundaries even further in '05. A real star and deserves pride of place on the cover, the favourite horse of the trainer's daughter, and, for what it's worth, of the more elderly of the writers as well. *R.M. Penny — Blackmore & Sparkford V. (Paul Nicholls).* 280 (3m2f110yH), 543 (3m2f110yH), 991 (3m2f110yH), 1376 (4m2fH), 1453 (3m4fH).

EASBY BLUE ..—.. 13 b.g. Teenoso (USA) — Mellie (Impecunious) p8pppu. Compact half-brother to Chasing winner, Grazember, and to NH flat winner, Three Strong (IRE). Dam won 6 Hurdles, 2-3m1f. NH FLAT '97/8 r4 w1 p1 (3rd). NH '98/9 and '01/2 (for S.E. Kettlewell, and J.A. Pickering) r23 w1 (2m Hdle) p6 (inc 4 3rds in Chses); pulled up 2, fell 3. Won two races including a six-runner Hurdle to June '99, and often fooled those who did not know him into thinking that he was going well under Rules subsequently, as he can travel strongly, but finds absolutely nothing off the bridle. Descended to Sellers without success, and a total waste of time in '04, as he does not have an earthly of getting the trip and was over 100 lengths last on the only occasion he staggered to completion. Sometimes tongue-tied, and has broken blood vessels. Should not be racing. *R. Dobney — N. Staffs (Stephanie Reading).* 228 (Cf), 381 (O), 557 (O), 713 (Cf), 847 (M), 1354 (2m110yH).

EASE THE PRESSURE (IRE) ..10-5.. 8 b.g. Roselier (FR) — Height Of Pressure (Buckskin FR) 112. Compact well-made attractive half-brother to No Pressure (IRE), to Irish Pointing winners, Leader of Fashion and Supreme Fashion. Dam won Mares Maiden in Ireland but pulled up in 7 of 8 other attempts. IRISH P-t-P '02 r8 w1 (4&5yo Maiden, 3 ran — 2 finished) p2 (3rds). P-t-P '03 r4 w4 (4-timer, 2 Clubs, Restricted and Intermediate). Clearly an under-achiever in Ireland, and adjudged to have won his first six English Points (lucky twice as he was apparently beaten a head once, and held by Charlie Strong until that rival unseated at Milborne), but succumbed to a rejuvenated Hobbycyr at Buckfastleigh, and since reported dead. H.B. Geddes — Taunton V. (Richard Barber). 234 (L), 322 (L), 496 (MO).

EASTERN APPLE ..9-1§.. 8 ch.m. Afzal — Great Granny Smith (Fine Blue) u4p24pp. Close-coupled owner-bred half-sister to Bramley. Dam, half-sister to 9 Pointers including Royal Orchard (*qv* '02 Annual), won 7 Points (inc an Open) and placed 11 for the Marriotts. P-t-P '03 r3 p0 (pulled up 2 and unseated 1). On the verge of a minor success, and only beaten a length at Didmarton, but already looks decidedly moody, and remains a very sketchy jumper. Most of her family win sooner or later, and the chances are she will follow suit, but supporting her has a high risk factor. *C. & Mrs F.J. Marriott —*

Heythrop (Fran Marriott). 35 (CMam), 52 (OMa), 173 (OMa), 367 (OMa), 588 (CfMa), 1108 (OMa), 1275 (OMa).

PLATE 39 440 Sherwood Rangers Yeomanry Maiden HC, Leicester: Eastern Point wins her first Hunter Chase under Phillip York *PHOTO: Brian Armstrong*

EASTERN POINT ..10-7§.. 11 b.m. Buckskin (FR) — Deep Creek (Deep Run) u112131. Lengthy unfurnished half-sister to Wishy Washy (IRE) and Foxwood Polo. Dam is half-sister to Ashmead Rambler (*qv* '01 Annual). P-t-P/HUNT CH '02/3 (for Mr J. Hunt) r12 w3 (up to Confined) p2 (inc 3rd in Hunt Ch); last pair 2, refused 1, pulled up 3 and unseated 1. A talented madam, and has been the recipient of some barnstorming rides from Phillip York, but deserted by him at Folkestone, but for which she would probably have completed a four-timer. Amazingly scored on the bridle next time, but does not appreciate easy surfaces and usually gives her supporters heart failure. Well placed to have achieved what she has, and should continue to do well if her mood allows. Often forfeits ground at the start, and has been led in, and has been tried unsuccessfully in cheekpieces. *Mrs K.H. York — Staff College (Phillip York).* 124 (CCon), 223 (I), 332 (Cf), 345 (2m5fH), 440 (2m7f110yH), 642 (O), 970 (MO).

EASTERN ROYAL ..9-9.. 6 b.g. Royal Applause — Kentfield (Busted) up1pp2. Small light half-brother to Saleel (IRE), and to winning Hurdlers, Chief Cashier and Lord Rochester also to another winner. 18,500y. FLAT '01/3 (for K.A. Ryan, and Mrs L. Stubbs) r11 p0. Bad at up to nine furlongs including two Sellers on the flat (beaten 16 lengths plus in eight of 11 outings), but rather surprisingly showed some aptitude for Pointing, and apart from a win in a Market Rasen Maiden (a first success for Matthew Briggs) he was also only caught in the dying strides after being clear at the last in his Members. Has a very shaky relationship with Rachel Clark and never got round in four attempts for her (including at 4-5 once), so there was irony when it was she who got up to pip him on Claire's Nomad. Compensation should await. *Miss D. Hill — York & Ainsty S.* 59 (OMa), 166 (OMa), 304 (OMa), 390 (Rnr), 591 (CR), 1157 (M).

EASTLANDS RAIN ..—.. 7 b.m. Saxon Farm — Light O' Love (Lighter) p. Owner-bred sister to Eastlands Hi-Light and Eastlands Snowdrop. Dam, half-sister to Eastlands Monkey, won her Members (in '94) and placed 3 for Mr Staveley. Novicey when tailed off and pulled up after two miles at Dalston. Reported dead. J.G. Staveley — Liddesdale. 767 (2m4fOMa).

EBONY JACK (IRE) ..9-10.. 8 b.g. Phardante (FR) — Ebony Jane (Roselier FR) 341729. Tall workmanlike brother to Bolt Action (IRE) (won Hurdle impressively before breaking leg next time). Dam, half-sister to Rattle The Latch (*qv* '95 Annual), won Point and 7 Chses in Ireland 2m2f-3m5f, inc £55,200 Irish National in '93. P-t-P '03 r3 p2 (3rds); and unseated. Too big and backward to do himself justice at six, and still only just growing into his frame, but showed plenty of stamina when successful at Maisemore Park, and unlucky to meet Genereux on a going day when tackling four miles for the first time at Cold Harbour. Remains a disappointment on the whole, and two efforts in Restricteds have been particularly feeble, but worth another chance in '05. Likely to relish good or sound surfaces, but remains prone to make the occasional blunder. *K.W. & Mrs S.J. Biggins & Partners — Berkeley (Tracey Ide).* 308 (2m4fOMa), 493 (OMa), 725 (OMa), 977 (R), 1228 (4mO), 1469 (R).

ECCLESIASTES ..—.. 11 b.g. Almutanabbi — Fforest Mystery VII (unknown) pp. Big plain. It does not require the wisdom of Solomon to realise that he will not make a racehorse. *J.F. Douglas — Grove & Rufford (John Douglas).* 482 (OMa), 595 (OMa).

ECHO BLU (IRE) ..9-0.. 7 b.g. Sharifabad (IRE) — Muchsorrylady (IRE) (Boreen FR) 8. Tall workmanlike. IRISH P-t-P '03 r2 w1 (5yo Maiden) p0. Looks the type who might have been expensive, but showed no immediate promise when 34 lengths eighth on his English debut. Joint-second favourite in a field of 20, and is possibly capable of better. *P.J. Kennedy — Teme V. (Jo Priest).* 726 (R).

ECO WARRIOR (IRE) ..9-9.. 12 ch.g. Be My Native (USA) — Kerry Minstrel (Black Minstrel) 223u. Very tall half-brother to Turn It On (IRE). Dam is half-sister to Minstrels Joy (*qv* '97 Annual). NH '99/00 r7 p3 (2 2nds); pulled up 1. P-t-P/HUNT CH '02/3 r3 w1 (Maiden) p1 (2nd in Hunt Ch); and pulled up. Made a winning debut in Points, but only after Mullensgrove had fallen at the last with the race in safe keeping, and has always been difficult to keep sound. Given too much to do when third at Fakenham, but a difficult ride tactically as he tends to fade when ridden more aggressively, and is probably none too genuine. Wears a cross-noseband, and has run tongue-tied. *Mrs A. Bell — Belvoir (Nick Bell).* 680 (M), 990 (CR), 1152 (R), 1178 (3m1fH).

EDMOND (FR) ..9-12§.. 13 b.g. Video Rock (FR) — Galia III (FR) (Baraban) 324. Tall workmanlike half-brother to 6 flat winners in France (one also successful over jumps). Dam won 4 flat at middles distances up to 12f in France. NH FLAT '97 r1 p1 (2nd). NH '97/02 r24 w9 (3 3m110y-3m2f Hdles, and 5 2m6f-3m5110y Chses, inc 5-timer '98, and 4-timer '99) p7 (3 2nds); pulled up 1, fell 3. P-t-P '03 r3 w1 (Ladies) p1 (2nd); and pulled up 1. A specialist in testing conditions at Chepstow, and gained his last win under Rules in the Welsh Grand National there in '99, but moody and avoided scoring again until the first winner for Holly Campbell on his reappearance last year. Only once better than last in '04, and found conditions much too quick when giving a lifeless display at Clifton-on-Dunsmore, and must be staring retirement in the face. Often blinkered latterly to '02, and has always been prone to deliberate or sketchy jumping. *Lady Knutsford — Cottesmore (Holly Campbell).* 479 (L), 682 (L), 1122 (L).

EDSTONE (IRE) ..8-7§.. 13 b.g. Mandalus — Smashing Run (Deep Run) pppp. Lengthy good-bodied. Dam is half-sister to Half Free. NH '96/99 r25 p3 (2 3rds); pulled up 8. P-t-P '02/3 r6 p0 (last pair 3, and pulled up 3). Superbly bred, but trounced in the lowest grade, and broke down on the only occasion he showed the slightest interest in Points. Often blinkered latterly under Rules. *Mrs A. Morley & M. Hancock — Holderness (Mrs A. Morley).* 775 (CfMa), 959 (OMa), 1164 (OMa), 1417 (OMa).

EDWARD BEAR .—§.. 13 gr.g. Teenoso (USA) — Houston Belle (Milford) ppp4. Lengthy unfurnished half-brother to The Grey Texan and Piltdown Lady. Dam, half-sister to Twice Knightly (*qv* '98 Annual), won 3 2m Hdles. P-t-P '98/9 and '02/3 r14 w1 (Maiden) p0; 4th, pulled up 11 and unseated 1. Gained a hard fought success in holding ground at Eaton Hall in '99, but pulled up in 14 of 17 other attempts, and normally beats a hasty retreat after figuring prominently for two miles. Ridden in spurs in his last two outings, and completed the course for the first time in five years at Heslaker, but the script was the usual one, and it seems pointless running him again. Wears a cross-noseband, and has been tried in blinkers. *Mrs A.P. Glassford — Cheshire.* 715 (R), 752 (R), 933 (CR), 1205 (CR).

EFFESSBEE ..8-10.. 10 b.g. Tina's Pet — Burning Ryme (Rymer) u. Half-brother to Border Burn. Dam is half-sister to 5 Pointers, including Burning Scally (*qv* '00 Annual). P-t-P '02/3 r3 p0 (4th, last and pulled up 1). Shows some speed, but a racecourse appearance is a rarity, and only his inability to stay three miles is proven. *Mrs E.K. Gilruth — Sir W.W. Wynn's.* 1261 (OMa).

EIGHTY DAYS (IRE) ..10-5.. 6 b.g. Air Quest — Valley Hope (IRE) (Altountash) p112. Hobdayed. 5600y. Followed a gentle introduction at Alnwick with a head win over 2m4f at Hornby Castle after which his original owners promptly cashed in, but he remained progressive in the new yard, and (awful thought) perhaps they should have asked for a bit more. Went well for Rose Davidson when landing a Friars Haugh Restricted in which he showed abundant stamina in the soft, and then ran very well until unable to repel the late spurt of Commanche Law in a Tranwell Ladies. That winner promptly followed up in a Hunter Chase, and as the third horse Balisteros was on a roll having landed three of his previous four Ladies the form looks very solid. Game and consistent and should do well over the years to come, provided his wind is up to it (was hobdayed at a very early stage). *D. Davidson — W. of Yore (Morag Neill).* 212 (R), 342 (2m4fOMa), 548 (R), 916 (L).

PLATE 40 342 West of Yore Open Maiden 56&7yo (Div 1): Eighty Days (Ran Morgan, right), 1st, just leads Sweeping Storm (Chris Dawson), 2nd, at the last *PHOTO: Roy Parker*

ELA AGAPI MOU (USA) ..9-10§.. 12 b.g. Storm Bird (CAN) — Vaguar (USA) (Vaguely Noble) p76531. Small close-coupled half-brother to French flat winner. Dam won 10f race in France. FLAT '95/9 r14 w1 (15f) p2. NH '97/02 r49 w7 (2m110y-2m5f Hdles) p14. P-t-P '03 (for Miss H.M. Irving) r12 p3 (beaten ½l once, and of 4 once); 4th twice, last pair 6 and unseated 1. Quite a prolific winning Hurdler in his youth, and contested events at the '98/9 Cheltenham Festivals, but a real old monkey, and was scoring for the first time since '98 when finally choosing to display his turn of foot in a feeble Ladies in soft at Ashorne. Aided by the leaders going off too fast for the conditions, but sensibly handled by the part owner-trainer, and did a good job of tutoring her in her first season. Sure to shirk the issue when tasks are stiffer in the future but deserves some credit for ending his 51-race drought. Wears a blinkers, and visored once in '00. *I. Cumming & Miss D.A. Ball — Grafton (Dawn Ball).* 289 (CfL), 380 (L), 582 (M), 785 (L), 1033 (L), 1278 (Cnr).

ELEGANT APPLE .—.. 8 b.m. Elegant Monarch — Apple Charlotte VII (unknown) pprp. Stocky. Has shown temperament but no ability, and twice had the misfortune to be ridden by an elderly man putting up a stone or more overweight (refused at the third once). Tailed off and pulled up in a February Maiden. At least she has the right sort of pedigree for the job. *F.S.W. Daniels — Four Burrow.* 308 (2m4fOMa), 486 (OMa), 907 (M), 1545 (OMa).

ELEGANT LIGHT ..10-2.. 8 ch.m. Elegant Monarch — Light The Bay (Presidium) pp512p11. Compact. Dam won 2 Points (including a match for Intermediate on very firm) and placed 3 for E. Wonnacott to '99. P-t-P '03 r5 w1 (2m4f Maiden) p0; 6th of 7, pulled up 2 and unseated. On the upgrade, and already establishing a reputation for springing surprises, but top-of-the-ground and an easy three miles appear vital requirements, and only seems to perform for certain riders. An improved jumper, and unbeaten in both attempts under Sarah Gaisford, and well worth trying the combination in a Ladies. Has two paddock handlers. *E. Wonnacott — Spooners & W. Dartmoor (Diane Wilson).* 79 (R), 148 (R), 314 (R), 415 (R), 790 (M), 823 (Cf), 1195 (I), 1433 (Cf).

ELEGANT MAID ..—.. 10 b.m. Elegant Monarch — Man Maid (Mandamus) up. Small owner-bred sister to Elegant Man, and half-sister to Chocolate Buttons, Rum Customer and Little Hen. P-t-P '02/3 r6 p0 (fell/unseated 3, pulled up 2 and refused 1). Got a little further in each of her previous six appearances, and reached the 14th on her final start last year, but crocked the rider on her return, and a substitute called it a day after two miles next time. Error-proneand not worth bothering with again. Wears a tongue-strap. *J.R. Thomas — Exmoor (Hugh Thomas).* 274 (CfMa), 486 (OMa).

ELLEMFORD ..8-0§.. 10 b.m. Broadsword (USA) — Spandulay (USA) (Arts And Letters USA) pp4p. Small light half-sister to Dismissal (IRE) and Stormy Words. Dam won 5 Ladies and placed 6 (inc a Hunt Ch and a Hdle) to '94. NH '01 r1 p0 (pulled up). P-t-P '03 r2 p0 (unseated and refused).

Ominously not retained to race by the breeders, and has run and jumped badly in seven attempts. Thirty-seven lengths last on his only completion, and barely merits even a miniscule rating. *R. Douglas — Buccleuch.* 658 (OMa), 1041 (OMa), 1225 (OMa), 1475 (OMa).

ELLFIEDICK ..—.. 14 gr.m. Alfie Dickins — Tabellion (Tabbas) p. Owner-bred half-sister to Russian Lion, Marchellion and Andellion. P-t-P '97 (for Mrs F.M. Gray) r1 p0 (pulled up). Soon tailed off and pulled up after a maximum of two miles in Maidens seven years apart, and presumably busy doing other things in the interim. *H.L. Thompson — Cleveland (Tina Jackson).* 813 (OMa).

ELLIE BEE ..—.. 6 b.m. Primitive Rising (USA) — Hutcel Loch (Lochnager) p. Plain leggy. Dam won 2m Hurdle. Schooled in the rear for 2m4f at Duncombe Park, and has the pedigree to do better in time. *R.D.E. Woodhouse — Middleton.* 271 (OMa).

PLATE 41 1330 Minehead Harriers & West Somerset Intermediate: Ellofamonkey and Ashley Farrant are successful again *PHOTO: Brian Armstrong*

ELLOFAMONKEY ..10-3.. 11 b.m. Relief Pitcher — Chaise Longue (Full Of Hope) 31251. Strong-topped workmanlike half-sister to Sit Tight, and to Hurdles winner, Futona. Dam, half-sister to Matter Of Law (*qv* '93 Annual), won 2m Sell Hdle. NH '01 r2 p0. P-t-P '02/3 (for Mrs N. Hewitt & Mr A. Rogers) r6 w1 (mares Maiden) p0; 4th of 5, pulled up 2, fell 2. Largely let down by her jumping in the previous yard, but much improved in that department in '04, and recorded two wide margin successes. Clearly slow to mature, but quite impressive when clocking the fastest time of the day at Holnicote, and likely to find further opportunities on her preferred good or sound surfaces. *Mrs M.J. Dixon — Taunton V.* 279 (R), 473 (R), 963 (Cf), 1129 (I), 1330 (I).

EMALI ..9-10.. 8 b.g. Emarati (USA) — Princess Poquito (Hard Fought) pp1. Tall lengthy half-brother to Eurobox Boy, and to 3 flat winners (one abroad), including Magic Box (also a successful Hurdler). FLAT '99/01 r18 p5. NH '01/3 r5 p0 (last and pulled up 4). P-t-P '02 (for Mrs H.E. Rees) r3 w1 (Maiden) p0; and pulled up 2. Twice a beaten favourite in Claimers and basically of little account on the flat, and finished lame on his last appearance under Rules, but unbeaten when completing in Points, and there seemed no fluke about his Lifton success despite there being only two finishers. Sometimes visored on the flat, and has run tongue-tied, and future performances look certain to remain unpredictable, but does require an easy three miles. *The Roadwater Club (M. Edwards) — The Glasses Farm Partnership (W. White) — W. Somerset (late Chris White; Gordon Chambers).* 1131 (R), 1366 (R), 1543 (R).

EMERALD MIST (IRE) ..9-6.. 6 b.m. Sacrament — Jade's Gem (Sulaafah USA) 2p216. Small well-made. IR3600y. FLAT '01/3 r12 p0. NH '02/3 (for G.B. Balding) r8 p0; ran out 1. Outclassed in 20 races flat and Hurdling which included nine Sellers, and visored once on the level and beaten 23 lengths plus on her last 12 attempts, but did show some ability when running out at the last with every chance once. Given a blatant school on her Pointing debut (Polly Gundry should have been censured), but later showed the benefit, and won a Paxford youngsters Maiden by an all out half-length. Not always as confident a jumper as her form figures might suggest, and will need to progress further for Restricteds. *S.J. & Mrs S.J. Rawlins — R.A. (Sally Rawlins).* 238 (CfMa), 492 (OMa), 637 (CMam), 926 (OMa), 1184 (R).

EMMA'S DREAM ..—.. 6 ch.m. Karinga Bay — Some Dream (Vitiges FR) p*0*. Tall half-sister to Justabbi, and to flat winner, Some Dust. Dam, half-sister to Ballacashtal (*qv* '99 Annual), won 2 2m1f Hdles, and was subsequently placed in 2 Points. Bought Doncaster, May for 2000. NH FLAT '04 (for P.F. Nicholls) r1 p0 (10th over 2m1f at Newton Abbot: *a bhnd, t.o*). Immediately lost touch and kept swishing her tail in a Mares Maiden in January, and a subsequent tailed off effort in a bumper did not change the initial impression that she was one to ignore. *J.P. Blakeney — Cattistock (Richard Barber).* 35 (CMam).

EMPEROR ROSCOE ..10-5.. 10 b.g. Roscoe Blake — Royal Celt (Celtic Cone) 44p11. Good-topped. P-t-P/HUNT CH '00 and '02/3 r14 w2 (Maiden and Restricted) p3 (2nds, beaten neck once); 4th, pulled up 6 and fell 2. Thrice a winner on good or sound surfaces at Garthorpe, and recorded the fastest time of the day in the latest, but floundered badly after looking sure to win there on another occasion, and may not relish a struggle. An improved jumper, and granted more enterprising riding should enjoy further success. *A.A. Day — Atherstone.* 784 (Cf), 1059 (I), 1361 (3mH), 1397 (I), 1500 (Cf).

EMPEROR'S CASTLE .7-11.. 6 b.g. Emperor Jones (USA) — Riyoom (USA) (Vaguely Noble) u7. Half-brother to 2 flat winners (one prolific abroad) including Shining Desert. Dam won 8f race in Ireland. 9000y. FLAT '01/2 (for P.C. Haslam) r4 p0. Not better than ninth including three Sellers on the flat, and unseated in both Points (at the second in his Members, and going to the post in a Maiden, after which he was caught and remounted, but faded in the race to finish well beaten). Looks a hot ride. *R.P. Watts — Staintondale (Annabelle Armitage).* 954 (M), 1159 (OMa).

EMPEROR'S MAGIC (IRE) ..10-5.. 14 ch.g. Over The River (FR) — Sengirrefcha (Reformed Character) 24231uu22. Sturdy attractive half-brother to Monicasman (IRE) (*qv* '03 Annual). Dam won 2m4f Hurdle and 3m Chase in Ireland. NH FLAT '95 r1 p0. NH '95, '97, '99 and '01/3 (for N.B. Mason, and R.C. Guest) r34 w7 (2m4f-3m1f Ch) p14; fell/unseated 3. Overcame bad leg problems early in his career to win seven Chases in the mud, and a gallant veteran who despite being ridden in rather eccentric fashion by Sue Ward managed to give her plenty of fun in Points. Only once able to score, when 2-5 in his Members, but tried hard in defeat and was beaten three lengths or less in four of his placings. Usually tongue-tied and wears a visor or cheekpieces, but discarded all of them with no apparent ill-effects on his final two outings. Enjoys the Hexham Pointing track, and seven pound penalties were all that prevented him from completing a double there. *Miss S.M. Ward — Braes.* 211 (C), 391 (MO), 655 (L), 857 (4mMO), 1036 (M), 1221 (L), 1415 (L), 1418 (Cf), 1479 (Cf).

PLATE 42 1543 South Tetcott Restricted: Emali and William White are easy winners
PHOTO: Baths Photographic

EMPEROR'S SON .10-5.. 11 ch.g. Emperor Fountain — Miss Dicky (Lepanto GER) c14241. Neat. Dam won 6 flat in a 5-year career in Belgium. NH FLAT '98/9 r3 p0. NH '99/00 r8 p2 (distant last of 3; and 2³/₄*l* 3rd of 5 — jumped right and not fluent). P-t-P '01/3 r10 w2 (Maiden and Restricted) p4 (2 2nds); 4th, unseated 2 and slipped up 1. Not the easiest of rides, and is usually held up for a turn of foot, but becoming more predictable, and might have given the gambled on winner something to think about had he not been carried out at the third last on his return. Ejected the rider in his first two Points, but a nimble jumper now, and despite only averaging five outings in a normal year should score again. Acts on any going. Wears a cross-noseband. *Miss S. Brotherton — Sinnington.* 161 (I), 266 (M), 389 (Cf), 564 (L), 808 (CfCon), 1287 (I).

EM'SGEM ..—.. 11 b.m. Germont — Gaelic Empress (Regular Guy) pf. Half-sister to Em's Light. Dam, half-sister to Sumpt'n Smart (*qv* '99 Annual), won 4 Points (inc Ladies) and placed 9 for J.J. Paterson, previously placed 2 in Irish Points. Late to see the light and might as well have been kept in the dark. *J. John Paterson — Jedforest (Willie Hodge).* 658 (OMa), 877 (OMa).

ENDEAVOUR (FR) ..10-4.. 13 b/br.g. Video Rock (FR) — Ogigy (FR) (Quart De Vin FR) u21u121u. Sturdy compact half-brother to 2 flat winners in French Provinces. NH FLAT '96/7 r4 w1 p1 (3rd). NH '98 r3 p0; broke blood vessel in final. P-t-P '00/3 r17 w7 (inc 3 Confineds) p4 (3 2nds, beaten neck once, and ¹/₂*l* once); 5th, and fell/unseated 5. A decent performer when in the mood, and has been well placed to win 10 Points (half of them at Higham), but can be very difficult to sit on, and his temperamental streak has become more pronounced. Most effective when able to dominate in small fields, but backing him at short prices carries a high risk factor nowadays. Acts on extremes of going. *D.W. Clark — Essex & Suffolk (Cherie Cunningham).* 23 (Cf), 124 (CCon), 248 (Cf), 400 (C), 610 (Cv&nr), 778 (CCon), 828 (M), 1312 (M).

ENERGY MAN ..9-10§.. 12 b.g. Hadeer — Cataclysmic (Ela-Mana-Mou) 745p2. Compact half-brother to 3 flat winners (two in Holland), including Wannaplantatree. Dam won 2 12f races, and is half-sister to Hardihero (*qv* '97 Annual). FLAT (tried visored) r14 p0. NH '97/8 r3 p0 (tailed off in Sell final). P-t-P '00/3 (for Mr C.J.M. Cottingham) r8 w1 (Maiden) p0; pulled up 5, and unseated 2. Left clear at the last when landing a grief-stricken Maiden at Pentreclwydau on his Pointing debut, but unable to get round in three campaigns for the subsequent handler, and remains most unpredictable. Runner-up in the joint-fastest race of the day on his latest appearance, but a tail-swisher, and had not gone a yard in his previous outing, and must be treated with caution. Visored once in '97. *Lord Yarborough — Brocklesby (Mark Bennison).* 110 (Cnr), 301 (R), 477 (Cnr), 592 (O), 810 (R).

ENITSAG (FR) ..10-4.. 6 ch.g. Pistolet Bleu (IRE) — Rosala (FR) (Lashkari) f146f3. Small neat. Dam won at 8-12f in France. NH FLAT '02 r2 w2 (13f). NH '02 (for M.C. Pipe) r10 w3 (2m1f Hdles) p3. Made history when winning a 23-runner bumper at Newbury on his debut (it was the first such to be open to three-year-olds), and followed up in similar company and his first Hurdle, and although he added a further two successes including an appalling Seller he could look very doggy, and only McCoy was able to extract victories from him. Thrice beaten favourite including when odds-on twice, and wore headgear or cheekpieces on his final six outings. Asked to tackle fences at five and survived a string of errors for a very easy win in a Novices Hunter Chase at Fakenham (a good piece of placing), but invariably let down by his shoddy jumping otherwise, and is certainly not learning from all the blunders. Not asked to tackle three miles to date. Looks sweet enough now, but unfortunately his jumping remains a major drawback. *G. Byard — Radnor & W. Herefords (Steve Flook).* 316 (2m5fH), 544 (2m5f110yH), 892 (2m5f110yH), 1166 (2m5f110yH), 1359 (2m4f110yH), 1437 (2m5f110yH).

EPICURE (FR) ..10-3§.. 8 b/br.g. Northern Crystal — L'epicurienne (FR) (Rex Magna FR) 13. Tall half-brother to jumping winner, L'Epicurien (FR), and to another winner. NH FLAT '01/2 r2 p0. NH '02/3 (for M.C. Pipe) r16 w3 (2m1f-2m4f Hdles) p1 (2nd); pulled up 3. Unbeaten in his first three outings for Martin Pipe (soft twice and firmish), but beaten in his next 11 attempts including a Seller, and was thrice visored. On his best behaviour when resuming in a five-runner Ladies on firm at Kingston St Mary in mid-May, but usually gives up rapidly, and had already lost interest next time. Completely untrustworthy. *Mrs B. Harvey — Taunton V.H. (David Pipe).* 1448 (L), 1563 (L).

EPOP (IRE) ..—.. 8 b.g. Religiously (USA) — General Rain (General Ironside) p. Half-brother Irish NH flat winner, Deoch An Dorais. Dam won Mares Maiden in Ireland. 10,000 3yo. NH '02/3 (for J.H. Johnson) r5 p0; pulled up 2. 14th thrice and pulled up twice when beaten 58 lengths plus over Hurdles (beat two, and started at 66-1 or more on four occasions), and showed no signs of being any better at Pointing when pulling up in February. *R.G. Abrey — Suffolk.* 244 (CfMa).

EPSILO DE LA RONCE (FR) ..9-9§.. 13 b/br.g. Le Riverain (FR) — India Rosa (FR) (Carnaval) 230544. Rangy half-brother to French cross-country and Chasing winner, Famfoni (FR). Dam won over jumps in France. FRENCH FLAT '95 r1 p0. FRENCH NH '95/8 r21 w8 (2 1m7f Hdles, and 6 2m1f-2m3¹/₂f Chses) p3 (2nds in Chses). NH '98/9 r7 p1 (2nd in Ch); inc Hdles. P-t-P/HUNT CH '00/3 (for Mr S. Flook, Mr M. Quinlan, Mr G. Slade-Jones & Mr T. Jones) r33 w6 (2m3f110y-3m Hunt Chses) p10 (8

2nds, inc 6 Hunt Chses, and inc 3rd in Hunt Ch); pulled up 2, fell 2. Bought cheaply and rejuvenated by the previous trainer, and won six races and rated 10-13 at best, but often unwilling to exert himself fully, and appears to have lost interest totally. A very secure jumper, and has twice negotiated the big fences at Aintree without putting a foot wrong, but beaten a minimum of 17 lengths in Points since, and looks unlikely to co-operate again. Blinkered twice in '00. *W. Ramsay — Berwicks (Charles Ramsay).* 134 (O), 240 (3mH), 732 (2m5f110yH), 1299 (2m4f110yH), 1414 (O), 1477 (O).

ERCON (IRE) ..7-12.. 7 ch.g. Thatching — Certain Impression (USA) (Forli ARG) p5. Leggy half-brother to two flat winners (one in Italy) inc Impressive Flight. NH FLAT '02 r2 p0. NH '02/3 (for R. Hollinshead, and L. Waring) r3 p0; pulled up 3. Sold Ascot, Apr for 1238. Bought Ascot, Oct for 1428. Terrible at long odds under Rules, and also looked badly wanting in Points. After five opportunities over jumps he has been pulled up in four and finished 28 lengths last. *J.F. Weldhen — Four Burrow.* 796 (CfMa), 910 (2m4fOMa).

ERIN'S SURPRISE (IRE) ..—.. 9 b.g. Erin's Hope — Ballinlassa (IRE) (Mandalus) p. Small light half-brother to Southern Spirit (IRE). Dam is half-sister to Travel Bound (*qv* '00 Annual). P-t-P/HUNT CH '01/3 (for Mr P. Andrew) r18 p1 (3rd); last pair 2, pulled up 11, and fell/unseated 4. Made his way to a highly competent yard in '04, but what ability he may once have had was not tapped by two previous handlers, and promptly went lame at Horseheath. *E. Linehan — Cheshire (Gary Hanmer).* 130 (OMa).

ERNFORD SMOKINJOE .—.. 9 b.g. Terimon — Wicklewood (Ovac ITY) p. Owner-bred brother to Ernford Tommygun. Dam held a hunters certificate, but never ran. P-t-P '03 r1 p0 (fell). Remote when falling at the 15th on debut, and made erratic progress before pulling up after two miles on his only appearance in '04. Wore bandages in front and may have gone wrong, as he was hanging and jumping badly left from halfway. *Mrs M. McInnes Skinner — Dunston H.* 560 (OMa).

ERNI (FR) .—§.. 13 b.g. Un Numide (FR) — Quianoa (FR) (Beaugency FR) p0p. Leggy. NH '96/7 r5 p3. P-t-P/HUNT CH '99/00 and '02/3 (for Mr W.M. Burnell) r25 w3 (Club Maiden, Restricted and Intermediate) p6 (3 2nds, neck last once); pulled up 5, and fell/unseated 4. Successful in three seven-minute plus races to '02, but cursed with a vile temperament, and kept pulling himself up after a maximum of two miles in '04. No longer merits his former 10-2 rating, and looks finished. Wears headgear, but only a visor has worked the oracle. *A.A. Morris — Bilsdale.* 163 (O), 267 (Cf), 391 (MO).

PLATE 43 338 West of Yore Confined: Erzadjan (Lee Bates), 1st, flies the last to record his first (and last) win over jumps *PHOTO: Roy Parker*

ERZADJAN (IRE) ..9-12.. 15 b.g. Kahyasi — Ezana (Ela-Mana-Mou) u14734. Compact attractive half-brother to Irish flat winner, Ebaziya, and to successful Hurdles winner, Ezanak (IRE). Dam won at 12f in France. IRISH FLAT r4 w3 (12-13f, hat-trick under Johnny Murtagh) p0. FLAT r1 p0. NH '93/4 and '96/7 (occasionally blinkered, but never successfully) r20 w5 (2m1f-3m1f Hdles) p4 (beaten head once, and neck once). P-t-P/HUNT CH '01 and '03 r9 p4 (2 3rds, inc Hunt Ch); 5th, 6th, 13th, last and fell 1. Fractured a hock in a fall in '01, and has been patched up on numerous occasions, but has always retained ability, and scored for the first time since '96 when coming home typically jet-propelled at Hornby Castle. A real monkey, and normally mis-times his finishing burst with aplomb, but will no longer get the chance to frustrate as he has been retired. *J. Mackley — S. Durham (Sarah Dent).* 134 (O), 338 (Cf), 501 (O), 772 (4m1fO), 1202 (Cf), 1457 (O).

ESENDI ..10-0.. 10 b.g. Buckley — Cagaleena (Cagirama) 13pp. Tall half-brother to Abbeydore, Dore Bridge, Palm Lady and Celtic Abbey. Dam won 3 Chases (2m-3m1f). 12,500 3yo. NH FLAT '00 r1 p0. NH '01 and '03 (for G.M. McCourt, and Miss V. Williams) r7 p1 (3rd); pulled up 1, unseated 1. Bought Doncaster, Nov for 8000. Led from halfway to win a dreadful Higham Maiden very easily (no subsequent winners came out of the race), and a decent third next time, but then absent for over three months and pulled up twice when returning (favourite for the Restricted). Also let supporters down when market leader twice under Rules (including when unseating at the third in a Chase), and is essentially a disappointing individual who must have physical problems. *T.L. & Mrs A.E. Brooks — Grafton (Anna Brooks).* 26 (OMa), 50 (I), 1333 (R), 1497 (3mH).

ESKIMO GOLD ..9-1.. 12 b.m. Gold Dust — Eskimo Slave (New Member) pp4p54. Sparely-made sister to Mudslide, and half-sister to Eskimo Star, Shelly's Sam and Wilberforce. P-t-P '00 and '02/3 (for Mr A.J. Cottle) r13 w1 (Maiden) p2 (3rds, of 4 once); last, pulled up 7, and fell/unseated 2. Won a bad Maiden in softish at Mounsey Hill Gate in '02, but a short runner and only once better than last since, and beaten a minimum of 24 lengths in '04. Not a novice ride and tends to hang left and jump right. Wears a cross-noseband. *M. Pidsley — E. Devon (Michael Sweetland).* 15 (R), 62 (Cf), 318 (M), 572 (R), 966 (R), 1386 (R).

ESPRIT DE COTTE (FR) ..10-4§.. 13 b.g. Lute Antique (FR) — Rafale De Cotte (FR) (Italic FR) 90321. Compact attractive half-brother to Caprice De Cotte (FR). Dam won a flat race in France. FRENCH NH '96 and '98/9 r8 w3 (2m2f-2m6f Chses) p5. NH '99/01 r13 w1 (2m6f110y Hdle) p1 (2nd); pulled up 4, fell/unseated 3. P-t-P/HUNT CH '02/3 r13 w2 (inc Open) p7 (4 3rds, last thrice); last pair 2, and pulled up 1. Useful on well-watered ground in France, but largely disappointing since, and only Philip York has been able to motivate him successfully in Points. Beaten at odds-on in his Members, and last in two previous outings, but stopped the rot when scoring in much the fastest time of the day at Kingston Blount. Seems to prefer sound surfaces these days. Has been tried in blinkers, and certain to remain totally unreliable. *Mrs J.M. Newsome & Mrs A.A. Gurney — O. Surrey, Burstow & W. Kent (Richard Gurney).* 100 (O), 241 (2m4f110yH), 420 (O), 777 (M), 1105 (O).

ESSENCE OF TIME .—.. 6 b.g. Still Time Left — Tudor Ellie (Push On) up. Tall rangy angular. Soon tailed off and unseated after a mile at Bonvilston, and returned there to go an extra mile, but again without showing any speed. *Miss A.L. Williams - S. Pembs.* 1096 (OMa), 1324 (CfMa).

ESTERELLE (USA) ..9-10.. 10 ch.m. Trempolino (USA) — Duck Flighting (USA) (Far North CAN) p0445p*426*. Small half-sister to 3 winners in USA. FLAT '98/9 (from P.S. McEntee's) r5 p0. NH '98/01 r23 w1 (2m6f Hdle) p7. NH '04 (for H.J. Manners) r3 p1 (2nd in 3m3f Hdle: *bhnd til hdwy 3, lost plce 7, rallied 9, ld app 2 out, sn hdd, hung lft app last, one pce*); 4th in 2m4f Sell Hdle: *hld up, hdwy 7, rdn app 4 out, sn btn*; and 6th in 2m6f Hdle: *ld to 6, ld 3 out til app nxt, sn btn*. Won a Folkestone Selling Hurdle in heavy at 20-1 in January '00, but failed to get the trip in Points, and beaten more than 25 lengths if completing. Ran out once on the flat and can be a complicated ride, but might yet go well in a Seller with a low weight. Gets very warm in the preliminaries. *C.R. Cox — O. Berks (Charles Cox).* 47 (Cf), 175 (Cnr), 289 (CfL), 407 (L), 613 (L), 935 (M).

ET LIGHT (FR) ..10-4.. 13 gr.g. Dom Pasquini (FR) — Kalighte (FR) (Light Butterfly) 32. Strong compact half-brother to Hurdles winner, Jacklighte Bellevue (FR). FRENCH FLAT '95 r1 w1 (12f). FRENCH NH '96 and '99/01 r28 w2 (2m1f-2m3f Chses) p12. P-t-P '03 r4 w2 (Open and Club Conditional) p0; last and unseated 1. Jumps well and recorded a May double at Garthorpe last year, but only effective over an easy three miles, and unable to last home when odds-on in his Members on his latest appearance. Kept jumping away to the left on that occasion and may have suffered a setback. *A.M.E. Barlow — Bicester with Whaddon (Robert & Teresa Elwell).* 170 (O), 288 (M).

EURO ALERT (IRE) ..10-6.. 9 ch.g. Eurobus — Parsons Alert (IRE) (The Parson) p. Well-made good-looking. IRISH P-t-P '01 r2 w1 (Maiden) p1 (2nd). P-t-P '02 r3 w2 (Restricted and Intermediate) p1 (2nd). Thwarted by the gallant Copper Thistle when bidding to extend his winning sequence to four at Dingley in '02, and clearly suffered a setback as he subsequently vanished for 22 months. Wore bandages behind and looked just in need of the race when pulled up after running well for a long way on his reappearance at Thorpe Lodge, but unfortunately not out of the woods yet, and promptly returned to the sidelines. *Mrs J. Wilson — Pytchley (Bill Warner).* 106 (C).

EURO BOB (IRE) .10-4.. 8 ch.g. Bob's Return (IRE) — Aughclogeen Run (Deep Run) 3u3321. Lengthy half-brother to Buck Run (IRE) and Breezy Betsy (IRE), and to Irish Pointing winner, Hoolby Skint.

IRISH P-t-P '02/3 r5 w1 (6yo Maiden) p1 (2nd); brought down 1, fell 1. Does not know how to run a bad race and gave a string of good placed efforts, but found the rider a major encumbrance until managing to cart her home in front in a Cold Harbour Restricted. Would improve many pounds for a strong jockey, and his potential is not being realised whilst he is allowed to bumble along in the present fashion. *W. & Mrs A. Rucker — Worcs (Angela Rucker).* 94 (L), 191 (R), 529 (L), 726 (R), 1014 (M), 1230 (R).

EUROGAEDEL (IRE) ..9-9.. 6 b.g. Eurobus — Lisbawn (Pitpan) 1. Sold Tattersalls Ireland, Aug for 7729 (J. Smith). Backed from 16-1 to half those odds in a bad Ampton Maiden in March, and justified the support with a game win under a good ride from Rupert Stearn. The form did not work out, but he might be a horse with a future himself. *Miss J. Stevens — E. Anglian Bloodhounds (Cherie Cunningham).* 525 (OMa).

PLATE 44 771 Middleton Restricted: Euwiluwil staggers over and Ashley Farrant, 3rd, blows harder than ever *PHOTO: Brian Armstrong*

EUWILUWIL (IRE) .10-1.. 7 b.g. Eurobus — Market Romance (African Sky) 131. Tall rangy brother to jumping winner Caius (IRE), and half-brother to Final Beat (IRE). IRISH P-t-P '03 r2 p0 (pulled up 1, and unseated 1). Showed improved form when battling his way to victory in a Maiden and a Restricted on local tracks, but proved a disappointing favourite after the long haul to the Middleton in between. Did not look without hope when upgraded to a Hurdle but pulled up lame, so we could be deprived of his company for quite a while. *P.J. Finn — Middleton (David Pipe).* 494 (OMa), 771 (R), 1131 (R).

EVANLY MISS .9-0§.. 8 b.m. Michelozzo (USA) — Snitton (Rymer) 463p4. Leggy lengthy half-sister to Snitton Salvo (*qv*). P-t-P '03 r3 p0 (pulled up 2 and fell). Marginally improved in her second season, but remains error-proneand can take a strong hold, and beaten a minimum of 22 lengths to date. Acquired headgear on her last two starts, and looks to possess the temperament that afflicts most of her siblings. *L. Evans — Ludlow (Geoff Evans).* 410 (2m4fCfMa), 714 (CMam), 983 (2m5fOMa), 1266 (2m4fOMa), 1394 (OMa).

EVANS THE COAL .8-7§§.. 10 b.g. Southern Music — Young India (Indian King USA) upppfppupp4u. Small unfurnished. Dam, half-sister to Dromroe Duke (*qv* '94 Annual), won 2 flat (5-6f) and placed 4, and 3rd in two Selling Hdles, but pulled up in 4 Points ('very reluctant to break into a gallop'). P-t-P '03 r3 p0 (fell 2 and ran out 1). Probably the most unenviable ride of the last two campaigns, and has been partnered by most of the daredevil brigade, but amazingly only Ray Carey has been able to coax him to completion. Sometimes unstoppable and usually tries to take at least one fence home with him, but normally runs himself into the ground after a maximum of two miles, and is an utterly deranged pit pony. Can be unruly in the preliminaries, and sometimes mounted on course and taken to post early. It would be tempting fate to run him again. Has been tried in a cross-noseband and a tongue-tie. *R. Evans — Ystrad Taf Fechan.* 120 (OMa), 204 (CfMa), 363 (CfMa), 620 (OMa), 699 (CfMa), 736 (CfMa), 1021 (M), 1095 (R), 1324 (CfMa), 1395 (OMa), 1534 (OMa), 1553 (OMa).

EVOLUTION LAD (IRE) ..—.. 9 b.g. Sharp Charter — Neatly Does It (IRE) (Camden Town) u. Lengthy unfurnished. NH FLAT '01 r2 w1 p1 (3rd). NH '01/2 (for N.A. Twiston-Davies, and late D.J. Caro) r6 p0; pulled up 2. Made a winning start in a bumper on firmish, but beaten more than 20 lengths since, including when claiming third after being reluctant on the stable bend once. Ended up in a Seller under Rules, and resumed after a two-year absence only to unseat at the third in an Intermediate (the rider left in the air ambulance). Useless and very hard to train now. *M. Scudamore — Ross H.* 278 (Inr).

EXACT (FR) .9-7§.. 13 ch.g. Beyssac (FR) — Valse De Sienne (FR) (Petit Montmorency USA) p. Lengthy. Dam won 2 races in France. FRENCH FLAT r7 p3. FRENCH NH r15 w2 (2m3f-2m6f Chses) p1. NH '98/9 r8 w1 (3m Hdle) p1 (3rd); unseated 1. P-t-P/HUNT CH '02/3 r12 p5 (4 3rds, of 4 twice, and inc Hunt Ch); 4th, 5th twice, 6th, pulled up 2 and fell 1. Sometimes temperamental but signed off under Rules with a runaway success at Chepstow in '99, but spent the next three years on the sidelines, and went wrong again (with ultimately fatal consequences) on his reappearance at Friars Haugh. Wears a cross-noseband, and has been tried in blinkers and cheekpieces. Miss V.A. Russell — Jedforest (Morag Neill & Peter Elliot). 131 (M).

EXCLUSIVE AIR (USA) .—.. 6 ch.g. Affirmed (USA) — Lac Dessert (USA) (Lac Ouimet USA) pppppp. Small good-bodied. 9500y. Dam won 2 7f races, and later won 4 races in USA. FLAT '01/3 (for T.D. Barron) r26 w2 (8-12f) p3. Bought Doncaster, Aug for 4000. A dual winner on the Southwell all-weather, but trounced in Sellers on his last two attempts on the flat, and was tongue-tied and sometimes wore blinkers or cheekpieces. Tailed off and pulled up in all six Points (after just two miles in five of them), and looked utterly dejected. For some a day out at Southwell is a fate worse than death, but he would probably like to return to his days of happiness there. *P.J. Millington — Fernie.* 374 (O), 523 (O), 592 (O), 1214 (Cf), 1342 (O), 1471 (O).

EXCLUSIVELY ..—.. 10 gr.m. Absalom — Peters Pleasure (Jimsun) fp. Well-made attractive half-sister to Castle Jester and Soleil Express, and to flat winner, Steel Cavalier. FLAT r3 p0. NH '99 r2 p0 (last, and pulled up). P-t-P '01/3 (for Mrs R. Hodges & Mr D. Lancett) r7 w1 (mares Maiden) p1 (3rd); 5th, pulled up 3 and fell 1. Survived a few errors when winning a weak mares Maiden at Cold Harbour, and rated 9-3 as a result, but a non-finisher in five subsequent appearances. A lost cause and four different handlers have been unable to teach her to jump properly. Has run tongue-tied. *P., B. & Mrs R. Hodges — N. Ledbury (Caroline Chadney).* 614 (R), 726 (R).

EXCUSE ME SIR (IRE) ..—.. 12 b/br.g. Glacial Storm (USA) — Knockarctic (Quayside) p. Tall rangy half-brother to Vallingale (IRE), Sibmister (IRE) and dual Whitbread/Attheraces Gold Cup winner, Ad Hoc (IRE). Dam won 2m1f Hdle in Ireland. IRISH NH FLAT '97 r1 p1 (2nd). IRISH NH '97/01 r30 w3 (2m4f Hdle, and 2m4f-2m6f Chses) p6 (2nds). P-t-P '02/3 (for Mr D. Manning) r5 w1 (Members, 3 finished) p0; 5th, last, pulled up 1 and unseated 1. A triple winner in mud in Ireland to '99, and gained a first success since when triumphing at Eaton Hall in '02, but broke a blood vessel next time and not better than last in four subsequent starts. Unproven over three miles in a competitive event and his 9-12 rating is withdrawn. Blinkered once in '00. *Mrs C. Wynne — Sir W.W. Wynn's (Steve Wynne).* 713 (Cf).

EXECUTE (IRE) ..8-7.. 9 b/br.g. Executive Perk — McMufins Princess (Decent Fellow) 3p. Compact. IRISH NH '01 r6 p0. P-t-P '03 (for Mr B.J.C. Wright) r3 p0 (fell/unseated 2 and pulled up 1). Appears to have brushed up his jumping, but pulls too hard to be effective in Points, and does not seem able to stand much racing. Tongue-tied on four occasions in Ireland. *B.J.C. Wright — A. Green — W. Somerset V. (Arun Green).* 274 (CfMa), 1055 (OMa).

EXECUTIVE DAYS ..—.. 6 b.m. Executive Perk — Pharditu (IRE) (Phardante FR) p. Workmanlike. Dam, sister to Zaudante, and half-sister to Grimley Gale won 2 Irish Points and placed 10, but pulled up twice in English Points. Not asked to keep up with vastly more experienced rivals in her Members, and eventually pulled up after two miles. *Mr & Mrs R.M. Phillips — Ledbury (Sophie Oliver).* 722 (M).

EXMOOR EXPRESS ..—.. 6 b.g. Thowra (FR) — Old Roma (IRE) (Old Vic) p. Tailed off and pulled up after two miles on his debut, and had the misfortune to have Andrew Pennock thrashing around on his back. *S. Hamblett & J. Armsby — Dulverton W. (Andrew Pennock).* 958 (OMa).

EXTRA JACK (FR) ..10-7.. 13 b.g. Neustrien (FR) — Union Jack III (FR) (Mister Jack FR) 45312. Big rangy half-brother to Djeddah (FR) (*qv*) and Golden Jack (FR). FRENCH FLAT r1 p0. FRENCH NH '97/9 r26 w7 (2m5f Hdles and 6 2m2f-2m6f Chses) p4. NH '00/3 (for P.F. Nicholls) r18 w5 (2m7f Hdle and 4 Chses, 2m-2m6f) p2 (2nds); pulled up 1, fell 1. Bought Doncaster, May for 15,000. A paler version of the late lamented Djeddah (*qv*), and can also look less than keen, but nevertheless has a highly admirable record over the years. His career earnings stand at approx £145,763, including a £22,000 prize at Auteuil where his six victories in the heavily watered morass included

Claimers for the final three. Can be error-prone, and 2m6f or less was always ideal. Wears blinkers. Did not really get enough cut in the ground in Points, but still showed plenty of galloping power for a veteran, and made virtually all to land a Tranwell Open unchallenged. Charlie Shirley-Beavan has great horses and amazing facilities at his disposal, but his concentration being not always on the racing (and why not?) seems to have prevented him from becoming anything other than a very average jockey. *Mrs P.M. Shirley-Beavan — Jedforest.* 72 (O), 269 (O), 340 (O), 917 (O), 1161 (O).

EXTRA STOUT (IRE) ..9-10.. 13 ch.g. Buckskin (FR) — Bold Strike (FR) (Bold Lad USA) 53p42544. Strong half-brother to Mister Softie (IRE) and Mister Pepper (IRE), and to 10 other winners (6 abroad), inc a successful Hurdler. Dam won 3 races at around 8f in France. IRISH NH FLAT '96 r1 p0. IRISH NH '96 r4 p0 (Hdles). IRISH P-t-P '96 and '98 r4 w2 (6yo Maiden, and Winners of One) p1 (head 2nd). IRISH HUNT CH '98/9 r2 p0 (4th and fell 1). IRISH P-t-P '99 r2 w1 (Winners of 2) p1 (2nd). NH '99/00 r3 p0; pulled up 2. P-t-P/HUNT CH '99, and '01/3 r14 w5 (2 3m110y-3m1f Hunt Chses, and 3 Opens) p1 (2nd); pulled up 2, unseated 1. Won three of his first five races in England, and returned to form when scoring on three occasions in '02, but a weak finisher when generally well beaten this year, and another revival looks unlikely. Runs tongue-tied. *J.C. Clark — Lauderdale (Julia Furness).* 426 (Cf), 654 (Cf), 857 (4mMO), 1080 (Cf), 1223 (O), 1307 (Cf), 1418 (Cf), 1479 (Cf).

FABLE (U) ..—.. 14 b.m. Java Tiger — Folly 4. Small cobby hunter. Led for a while in her stone-wall Members, but took the even-more scenic route to the last. *Miss P. Winn — High Peak.* 984 (3m4fNCM).

FABLES GREEN ..8-12.. 12 b.g. Rolfe (USA) — Cuckmere Grange (Floriana) 544. Homebred half-brother to Mere Class and Grandmere. P-t-P '00 and '03 r4 p1 (3rd); last 2 and pulled up 1. Very slow and not as fluent as his record would suggest, but robbed of another minor placing by the Judge at Hackwood Park on his latest appearance. *Mrs J. Stuart Evans — Hampshire (Nick Evans).* 423 (CMa), 716 (M), 971 (OMa).

FAIRCATCHER ..8-0.. 10 b.g. Gildoran — Bampton Fair (Free Boy) fpp6ppp64. Lengthy brother to Gilt Air, and half-brother to jumping winner, Bay Fair. Grandam, Eyecatcher, was 3rd in Rag Trade's '76 National (Red Rum was 2nd). NH FLAT '00 r2 p0. P-t-P '02 (for Mr J.F. Long) r3 p0 (7th of 8, unseated 1 and pulled up 1). Ran passably when 25 lengths fourth on his latest appearance, but does not appear to have sufficient stamina, and has beaten only two rivals in 12 Points. Lacks fluency and has been tried in a tongue-tie. *Mrs E. Collier (Bintheredunit Club) — Woodland Pytchley (Ray Collier).* 129 (OMa), 295 (OMa), 589 (CfMa), 686 (OMa), 942 (Cf), 1061 (OMa), 1215 (CfMa), 1473 (OMa), 1505 (OMa).

FAIR CHARMEUR (IRE) ..9-12.. 11 ch.m. Buckskin (FR) — Beau Croft Lass (Beau Charmeur FR) u14p. Very small neat. Dam is sister to Knowe Head (*qv* '99 Annual). P-t-P '99/00 and '02/3 r17 w2 (Maiden and Restricted) p3 (2 3rds, of 4 once and last once); last, pulled up 7, and fell/unseated 4. Only able to complete in one of her first 12 outings, and still inclined to get very low at the fences, but has done remarkably well since, and displayed her usual resolve when gaining a second success at Cilwendeg. Averages only four races a year, and avoids ground any quicker than good now, and should be concentrating on Ladies races in west Wales. *R.R. Smedley — Tivyside.* 407 (L), 671 (I), 974 (3mH), 1229 (L).

FAIR EXCHANGE ..10-5.. 12 b.g. Bustino — Sharp Vixen (Laurence O) 2p2. Workmanlike half-brother to Shoot The Fox, and to Hurdles winner, Over The Burn. P-t-P/HUNT CH '98/03 r23 w12 (inc 3m1f Hunt Ch and 4 Opens, inc hat trick '02) p8 (5 3rds, last twice); last once, fell 1 and pulled up 1. A useful and thoroughly consistent Pointer, and up until the latest campaign had won half of the 22 Points he had contested, but has never been able to stand much racing. A win for him in '04 would have been particularly poignant, and it looked likely to happen at Marks Tey until overwhelmed near the finish by Lucky Master, but had been off the course since flopping at 1-2 on ground much quicker than ideal 12 weeks earlier. Stays and jumps well, but needs an outing to get fit, and is ideally suited by a stiff right-handed track. *Mrs M.G. Sheppard — J.M. Turner — Cambs with Enfield Chace.* 43 (O), 221 (O), 1314 (L).

FAIRFIELDS BOY ..—.. 9 b.g. High Kicker (USA) — Miss Poll Flinders (Swing Easy USA) p. Brother to Hurdles winner, Chilly Lad, and half-brother to four flat winners including Chill Lad (also successful Hurdler). Did not jump with fluency on his belated debut, and was tailed off when pulled up at halfway. *The Northern Racing College Club (S.J. Goodings) — York & Ainsty S. (Steven Goodings).* 594 (OMa).

FAIR GRAND ..—§.. 15 b.g. Primitive Rising (USA) — Grand Queen (Grand Conde FR) ppp. Small close-coupled brother to Hurdles winner, Harfdecent, and half-brother to Noreasonatall. Dam unseated in a Maiden as an 11-year-old in '93. P-t-P '95/7 (for Mrs J.M. Reynard & Mrs S. Wood) r16 p3 (2 3rds, 2 fences last once, and remote last once); failed to finish 10 (unseated 2). Placed on three occasions to '97, but beaten out of sight in two of them, and predictably tailed off and pulled up thrice on his return from a six-year absence in '04. Regained blinkers on his latest appearance. *B. Robinson — York & Ainsty N.* 1164 (OMa), 1292 (OMa), 1305 (OMa).

FAIR KIOWA (IRE) .9-12.. 10 ch.g. Commanche Run — Fair Gossip (IRE) (Le Bavard FR) 2fp22up4. Half-brother to Irish Pointing winners Leading Gossip and Gossip Column. Dam won Irish NH flat. IRISH P-t-P '00/3 r19 w2 (6yo&up Maiden, and Winner of Three) p5; pulled up 7 and fell 3. Took a long time to produce any winning form in Ireland, but finally managed to score twice in his fourth season, including a dead-heat. Consistently let down by his jumping in the new yard, and although generally not quite up to taking Ladies Opens the silly thing managed to blunder away his two best chances (fell three out when upsides Storm Castle in five-runner affair at High Easter, and sent the jockey spinning furiously into orbit when three lengths ahead and in command at Marks Tey, where his only rivals were a couple of ex-Turner dodge pots — started at 1-3). Seemed to lose heart afterwards, but all may not be lost if he can only manage that elusive error-free round. *Miss J. Stevens — E. Anglian Bloodhounds (Cherie Cunningham).* 25 (L), 222 (L), 246 (L), 649 (L), 781 (L), 904 (L), 1086 (L), 1314 (L).

FAIRMILE STAR ..—.. 9 gr.g. Weld — Damsong (Petong) fpp. Tall workmanlike brother to Spot On Millie. NH FLAT '00/1 r3 p1 (2nd). NH '01 (for J.M. Jefferson) r2 p0; pulled up 1. Five lengths second in a bumper on his debut, but seems to have had big training problems since. Resumed after missing only two years to fall at the last when holding every chance in a joke Maiden taking over eight minutes at Dalton Park, but tailed off and pulled up twice afterwards, and jumped terribly and to the right in the latest. Must be suffering. *Mrs J.M. Newitt — Middleton (Susan Balshaw).* 505 (CMa), 1291 (OMa), 1417 (OMa).

FAIR SIGNET ..—.. 7 br.g. King's Signet (USA) — Fair Sara (McIndoe) RRf. Small half-brother to Kingoftheswingers, to flat and Hurdling winner, Rather Gorgeous, NH flat and jumping winner, Fair Prospect, and to NH flat winners, Crowther Homes and Doctor Syntax. Dam won 8f Sell and 3 2m Hurdles. IRISH NH '03 (for M. Hourigan) r7 p0; pulled up 2, unseated 1. Bought Doncaster, Nov for 2200. Only once had more than one behind him in seven Irish Hurdles, and after running out at the fifth in his first two Points he took a fall at the tenth on his final attempt. A very hard puller and potentially lethal, and hopefully an absence since early March means that we have seen the last of him. *J. Cornforth — York & Ainsty N. (Philip Cornforth).* 166 (OMa), 271 (OMa), 392 (CfMa).

FAIR STORM (IRE) ..—§.. 11 b.g. Glacial Storm (USA) — Mary Gleason (Gleason USA) p. Medium-sized. NH FLAT '98 r1 p0 (pulled up). P-t-P '99/03 r18 p1 (2nd of 3); 11th, last pair 4, pulled up 11 and fell 1. Earned a prize for the only time in 20 attempts when 30 lengths second in his Members last year, but is remarkably ungenuine, and has never finished closer to the winner. Managed just one appearance for the third season out of the last five in '04. Has been tried in blinkers and a tongue-tie. *Mrs W. Ward & Mrs B. Martin — Granta H. (Martin Ward).* 220 (OMa).

FAIR WIND (IRE) ..10-11.. 13 b.g. Strong Gale — Corcomroe (Busted) 53112. Tall rangy half-brother to Ainlee Road. P-t-P/HUNT CH '99/03 r28 w7 (inc 2 2m7f110y-3m2f Hunt Chses, and Mixed Open) p9 (7 2nds, beaten short-head once, head once, and neck once; and 3rd in Hunt Ch); fell/unseated 4, refused 2, and pulled up 3. Under a cloud for much of last year, and began '04 in much the same vein, but immediately hit it off when teamed with Rilly Goschen and put up a marvellous performance to beat Aberfoyle Park at Larkhill. Proved his return to form to be no fluke when running away with a Hunter Chase at Towcester, and lost nothing in defeat at Exeter. Used to make the odd mistake, but jumped better than ever this year and it was good to see him running with his old zest. Acts on any going, but particularly suited to soft ground, and a right-handed circuit. Blinkered once in '03. *Mrs R.J.E. Bartlett — Wilton.* 63 (L), 140 (MO), 457 (MO), 891 (3m1fH), 1293 (2m7f110yH).

FAIRY BELL ..—§.. 12 b.m. Silly Prices — Queen Bell (King Sitric) p. Workmanlike sister to Barney Cross, and half-sister to Fourth Bell (dam of French Bell (*qv* '02 Annual) and Hetty Bell. Dam was 3rd of 4 and pulled up 2 in Points for Keith Waters. Grandam, Veronica Bell, won 7 Hunt Chses (inc dead-heat) and placed 9 (inc Hdle). Great-grandam, Viper Bell, won Points. P-t-P '99/03 r11 p1 (remote last of 3); (4th, last 2, refused 1, ran out 1 and pulled up 5). Ineptly handled with predictably dreadful results, and only once better than last in a drawn out career lasting just 12 races, and pulled up lame on her only appearance in '04. Has been tried in cheekpieces. *K. Waters — Braes.* 511 (OMam).

FALCON'S FLAME (USA) ..10-0.. 12 b/br.g. Hawkster (USA) — Staunch Flame (USA) (Bold Forbes USA) 1p1bp. Sturdy compact half-brother to 2 winners in USA. Dam won 9 races at up to 8f in USA. FLAT r15 w1 (9f) p2 (2nds, beaten head once). NH '96/9 r27 p12 (11 3rds, inc 9 Chses). P-t-P/HUNT CH '01/3 r11 p5 (3 2nds; and inc last of 3 once); 7th, last, pulled up 3 and fell 1. Previously unsuccessful in 38 attempts over jumps, and was roughed off early with a slight leg problem last year, but clung on to a diminishing advantage to spring a 20-1 shock on his reappearance and followed up in a much weaker affair a fortnight later. Often takes a keen hold and wears a cross-noseband, but not a very determined finisher and owes his wins to enterprising handling from Roger Green. Blinkered twice in '98. *V. Thompson — Percy.* 134 (O), 214 (O), 285 (O), 429 (3m5fO), 551 (O).

PLATE 45 285 Berwickshire Mens Open: Falcon's Flame (Roger Green), 1st, looks to have a simple task, but out of shot Dr Deductible is about to make a race of it PHOTO: Alan Mitchell

FAMI (FR) ..10-2.. 12 ch.g. Le Nain Jaune (FR) — Quimie II (FR) (Barbotan FR) pu2u2. Small brother to Gami (FR). Dam won 4 flat in France. FRENCH FLAT '97 r17 w2 (around 12f, provinces) p5. NH '98/02 r21 w3 (2m4f Hdle and 2 2m3f-3m2f110y Chses) p4; fell/unseated 7, pulled up 1. P-t-P '03 r5 w2 (Ladies and Members) p1 (3rd; also disqualified from 2nd once — not weigh-in); and last. Scoring for the first time since November '00 when scorching round Dingley on two occasions last year, but used to have terrible problems with his jumping which resurfaced to a lesser degree in '04. Likes to force the pace on good ground, but expensive to follow despite having ideal conditions this year, and found little or nothing at all for pressure. Bandaged in front, and on his near-hind on his latest appearance, and may well be feeling his legs now. *Mrs S. Hutchinson — Fernie (Patrick Hutchinson).* 682 (L), 987 (L), 1122 (L), 1399 (L), 1501 (L).

FAMOUS DEAL (IRE) ..—.. 12 b.g. Brush Aside (USA) — Dambydale (Deep Run) pp. Big workmanlike half-brother to Gypsy Race (IRE), and to Irish Hurdles winner, Husdale (IRE). Dam is sister to My Key Silca (*qv* '98 Annual). NH FLAT '98 r2 p0. P-t-P '02 r1 p0 (pulled up). Tailed off in bumpers, and pulled up after a maximum of two miles in Points, and gave the impression there was something badly awry when stopping to nothing in a few strides in the latest. Wears a cross-noseband. *M. Heuff — Taunton V.* 967 (OMa), 1200 (OMa).

FANCY A BUCK ..—.. 10 b.m. Buckley — Fortune's Fancy (Workboy) f. Small half-sister to a flat winner. Grandam, Polly Peachum, was smart sprinter. P-t-P '00/1 (for Miss H. Walsgrove) r2 p0 (pulled up and carried out). NH FLAT '01 r1 p0. NH '01/2 r6 p0 (last pair 4; inc Sellers; tongue-tied latterly). Has hinted at ability, and backed from 10's to fives on her short-lived return to Pointing, but yet to produce anything tangible, and appears to have a wind problem. *Mrs L. Pomfret & S. Davies — Cottesmore (Laura Pomfret).* 111 (OMa).

FANE COUNSEL (IRE) ..11-0.. 7 b.g. Leading Counsel (USA) — Fane Heights (First Consul) 11R3. Tall workmanlike half-brother to Fane's Treasure (IRE). Dam won 2m2f Hurdle in Ireland. IRISH P-t-P '02/3 r2 w1 (Adjacent Maiden) p0. About as impressive as it gets on his English Pointing debut at Horseheath, where he jumped well and made all in a clear lead, and despite never coming out of cruise control slaughtered the opposition by 25 lengths or more. Made the long journey to the track for an Intermediate a month later, and squashed Cantarinho who was destined to collect three Hunter Chases including the John Corbet subsequently (again adopted forcing tactics and registered a time which was even 12 seconds faster than the Ladies). Unsurprisingly sent off at 1-3 at Brampton Bryan, but cocked his jaw and ran out on the bend before the eighth, thus depriving spectators of what would have been a fascinating dual with Caught At Dawn (who in his turn easily registered the fastest time of the day). A slippery slope was then beckoning, and when switched to a left-hand track for the first time in '04 he kept jumping right and after being headed before three out he weakened from the last to record a second defeat (at 2-5). There is no doubt that his talent is immense, but starting to fox even Richard Burton, which is most worrying. At best he is wasting his time anyway in Points, and a decision should now be made to switch him to Novice Chases with a top professional on board (not an argument likely to go down well with the present trainer, but the owner should brook no opposition). *C.J. Hitchings — N. Salop (Sheila Crow).* 127 (R), 372 (I), 660 (Cf), 1342 (O).

FANION DE NOURRY (FR) ..9-9§.. 12 ch.g. Bad Conduct (USA) — Ottomane (FR) (Quart De Vin FR) p3r4p43. Tall rangy. FRENCH NH '97 r6 p0 (Hdle and 5 Chses; fell 3, pulled up 1). NH '98/9 and '01 r10 p0 (ran out 2, inc one of 2 Chses — the other was a Sell). P-t-P/HUNT CH '00/3 r22 w3 (inc 3m1f Hunt Ch) p7 (4 2nds, inc 2 Hunt Chses; inc 3rd of 4 once); pulled up 4, fell 1. NH '04 r1 p1 (34*l* 3rd to Gallion's Reach in 3m1f110y Sell Ch: *hld up, hdwy 11, rdn 13, wknd 3 out*). Rated almost a stone higher than his current mark when connections capitalised on his ability to stay extreme distances in '00, but reluctant to exert himself fully since, and only acquired headgear on his 44th and latest appearances. Otherwise beaten a minimum of 27 lengths in '04, and generally faced too stiff a task. Has become error prone, but still has the ability to spring a surprise if the right opportunity arose. *Miss H.M. Newell — Ledbury (Edmund Haddock).* 209 (3m1f110yH), 891 (3m1fH), 1017 (3m2fL), 1357 (3m1fH), 1512 (2m6f110yH), 1528 (Cf).

FANNY BY GASLIGHT ..—.. 7 b.m. Opera Ghost — Highly Inflammable (USA) (Wind And Wuthering USA) p. Small unfurnished. NH FLAT '03 r1 p0 (18th). P-t-P '03 (for Mr P. Fry & Mr B.S. Heath) r4 p0 (pulled up 3 and unseated 1). Error-proneand yet to finish in Points, and has broken a blood vessel on at least one occasion. *Miss S.A. & Mrs C. Derrick — Blackmore & Sparkford V. (Sherie-Anne Derrick).* 237 (CfMa).

FARFIELDS PRINCE .—.. 13 b.g. Weldnaas (USA) — Coca (Levmoss) 5ppp. Sparely-made half-brother to Tudor Fun and Rexy Boy, and to 5 flat winners (2 abroad, and one in Ireland), including Greenwich Papillon and Greenwich Bambi (also won Hurdling). 6200y. FLAT '94/5, '97, '99 and '01 r15 p3. NH '98/02 (for G.M. Moore, M.J. Wilkinson, and K.G. Wingrove) r27 w4 (2m-2m1f Ch) p6 (inc 2 2nds Hdles); fell/unseated 3, pulled up 1. Did his bit in the past with four Chasing wins and a total of nine placings, but last scored in September '01, and latterly descended to Selling Hurdles without success. Often wore headgear in previous seasons, including for one victory. Slumped into a woeful decline in the new yard, and tailed off last on his only completion. Deserves to return to retirement. *D.H. Preece — Wheatland (Emma Murray).* 593 (L), 664 (L), 931 (L), 1372 (2m4fH).

FAR FROM PERFECT (IRE) ..—.. 13 gr.m. Phardante (FR) — Kilistrano (Capistrano) uup. Lengthy half-sister to several winners, including in Ireland. Has a huge lump on her neck. Dam won 2 5f races at 2 in Ireland. P-t-P '00 and '02/3 r6 w1 (Maiden) p2 (2nds, beaten ½*l* once); pulled up 2 and unseated 1. Became a mum before she raced, and got her career off to a good start when successful at Maisemore Park in '00, but remains very lightly raced, and may have suffered yet another setback at Bitterley. Frequently stopped in her tracks by blunders, and her 9-11 rating has been withdrawn. *A.J. Williams — Curre & Llangibby (Sue Williams).* 450 (R), 726 (R), 839 (R).

FAR GLEN (IRE) .10-7.. 10 b.g. Phardante (FR) — Asigh Glen (Furry Glen) p. Very tall rangy brother to Irish Pointing and Chasing winner, Pharbeitfrome (IRE). NH '01/2 r12 p3; pulled up 3. P-t-P/HUNT CH '00/1 and '03 (for Mr R.D.E. Woodhouse) r6 w1 (Maiden) p1 (distant 2nd in Hunt Ch); pulled up 2, and fell 2. Very speedy and can trap along at high velocity, but impossible to place successfully in his first 17 races, and had to descend to a lowly Maiden at Easingwold in order to open his account. Previously split Earthmover and Sparky Gayle in an Ayr Hunter Chase, but raced only once since, and ran himself into the ground after two miles at Bangor. His rating is looking a trifle high, especially in non-sub-3m events. Sometimes treats obstacles with contempt, and the new yard have a job on their hands trying to find the right races for him. Has run tongue-tied. *W. Puddifer — Middleton (Peter Morris).* 435 (3m110yH).

FARLEY WATER ..—.. 8 br.g. Afzal — Lady Ector (USA) (King Pellinore USA) pp. Half-brother to Charter Member, Hurdles winner, Greenway Lady, and to winner in Italy. Tailed off and pulled up after 2m4f maximum when 25-1 in Restricteds. *D.J. & R. Branton — Devon & Somerset.* 791 (R), 1102 (R).

FARNANDO (IRE) .9-8.. 11 b.g. Zaffaran (USA) — Kasperova (He Loves Me) pf3. Brother to Night Fever (IRE), and half-brother to Irish Hurdling winner, Santa Ponsa Bay. Dam, half-sister to Giggiton (*qv* '92 Annual). IRISH P-t-P '98 r2 p1 (2nd). IRISH NH '98/01 (for M.F. Morris, and J.F. O'Shea) r19 w1 (2m4f Ch) p2 (2nds, Hdles); pulled up 4, fell/unseated 3. Won a Clonmel Chase in very soft in February '00, but also failed to finish seven times under Rules (on the floor in three), and was reviving after a three year absence in '04. Started at 100-1 when falling at Bechers in the Foxhunters, but the subject of some market interest in both Points, but performed as if he might not get the trip and could only labour home 33 lengths last of three in the better attempt. Blinkered once in '01. It will not be easy to find opportunities for him now. *D. Davies — Wheatland (Sean Parkyn).* 448 (O), 732 (2m5f110yH), 1138 (O).

FAR TOO CROWDED (IRE) ..10-2.. 8 b.m. Norwich — Mini Brennan (Pry) 21. Sturdy. P-t-P '03 r3 p0 (fell/unseated 3). Fell victim to jumping lapses in her debut season, but had shown some speed, and would have made a successful reappearance had she not blundered at the last. Made amends at Buckfastleigh, and the runner-up went on to frank the form, and should readily follow up in a Restricted provided her prolonged absence is not a bad sign. *T.J. Hawkins & P. Quinn — Taunton V. (Richard Barber).* 275 (CfMa), 493 (OMa).

FASSAN (IRE) ..9-0§.. 13 br.g. Contract Law (USA) — Persian Susan (USA) (Herbager) pp25445p. Big half-brother to 8 winners (5 in USA and one in Italy). Dam won 3 flat races (up to 9f) in USA. IRISH FLAT '95 r7 p1 (2nd). FLAT '96 and '02 r2 p0. NH '96/02 r46 w3 (2m Hdle and 2 2m Chses) p18. P-t-P/HUNT CH '03 (for Mr N.D. Tutty) r6 p1 (3rd); last 4 and pulled up 1. Gained both Chasing wins on Grade one tracks, but has always lacked enthusiasm, and beaten 33 times subsequently. Has not taken to Pointing, but not guaranteed to get three miles even if he had a change of heart. A very sketchy jumper but too clever to fall, and can be safely ignored in future. Frequently blinkered or visored in the past, and acquired cheekpieces in '04, and also a tongue-tie at Rhydygwern. *K. Richards — Llangeinor.* 447 (Cf), 670 (Cf), 738 (O), 841 (Cf), 1024 (O), 1188 (Cf), 1320 (Cf), 1485 (Cnr).

FASTER SWEEP (IRE) ..9-10.. 8 ch.g. Phardante (FR) — Sweeping Brush (IRE) (Brush Aside USA) 47. Lengthy strong-topped. Dam in half-sister to Young Dubliner (*qv* '96 Annual). P-t-P/HUNT CH '02/3 r6 p4 (2nds, of 3 once, and inc Hunt Ch); last and carried out 1. An accomplished jumper, and a natural front-runner, but a weak finisher, and has become very frustrating to follow. Reportedly laid low by a virus in '03, and could still be feeling its after effects, but has to be given a wide berth until he proves otherwise. *The Hot Chestnuts Club (P.R. Crawfurd) — Tynedale (Tim Reed).* 132 (CR), 269 (O).

FAST LANE HARRY (IRE) ..9-5.. 9 ch.g. Insan (USA) — Charleys Lane (IRE) (Remainder Man) 2f. Leggy attractive. Dam, sister to No More Nice Guy (*qv* '03 Annual). IRISH NH FLAT '02 r2 p0. IRISH NH '02 r1 p0. P-t-P '03 r4 p2 (2nds, beaten *½l* once); and last 2. Thrice runner-up in Maidens, and favourite to go one better at Charm Park, but broke his neck in a fall at the fifth last when in front and going strongly. P. Alderson & Mrs C. Spalding — Middleton (Chris Pimlott). 111 (OMa), 394 (CfMa).

FATALISTIC (IRE) .—.. 11 b.g. Good Thyne (USA) — Just Dont Know (Buckskin FR) pp. Tall workmanlike half-brother to Just Strong (IRE) (*qv*). IRISH P-t-P '00 r5 w2 (6yo Maiden, and Winners of 2) p2; and fell. IRISH NH FLAT '99 r2 p0. IRISH HUNT CH '00 r1 p0. IRISH NH '00/2 r14 w1 (2m4f Ch) p2 (2nds); pulled up 2, fell 1. P-t-P '03 r4 w1 (Confined) p0; 9th, and pulled up 2. Ran to 10-0 when landing a gamble in arduous conditions at Towcester on his final start last year, but needs deep mud to slow the rest down, and never went a yard when encountering fast ground in '04. Does not appear particularly healthy, and might not be sweetened successfully again. Runs tongue-tied. *P. Riddle, S. Tudor-Hughes & A. Clare — Grafton (Jenny Pidgeon).* 24 (O), 43 (O).

FATHER ANDY (IRE) ..10-3.. 12 ch.g. Executive Perk — Twinkle Sunset (Deep Run) 41f. Half-brother to NH flat and Hurdles winners, Glacial Sunset (IRE) and Deep Sunset (IRE) (latter also won Chasing). Dam is half-sister to Cracking Idea (IRE) (*qv* '01 Annual). IRISH P-t-P '98/9 r2 w2 (5yo Maiden and Winners of 2). IRISH NH FLAT '98/9 r5 p2 (just caught when *½l* 2nd once). IRISH NH '98/9 r5 p1 (27*l* 3rd in Hunt Ch). IRISH P-t-P '00 r1 p0. IRISH HUNT CH '00 r7 w2 p3 (2 2nds, beaten head once); fell 1. IRISH HUNT CH '01 r5 p3 (2nds). P-t-P/HUNT CH '00 and '02 r3 w1 (Open) p1 (2nd in Hunt Ch); and pulled up 1. A tough and consistent performer in Ireland, but struggled to win on a regular basis, and missed '03 after knocking himself the previous year. Did well to land a weak Open at Kingston Blount, but involved in the melee at Bechers next time, and has not been seen since. Wears a cross-noseband, and runs tongue-tied. *P. Newton — Berks & Bucks (Roger Wernham).* 34 (O), 188 (O), 732 (2m5f110yH).

FATHER JIM ..9-12§.. 10 b.g. Seymour Hicks (FR) — Deaconess (The Parson) Ru8p222r. Small half-brother to Goddess. Dam sister to Hurdles winner, Holy Joe, won Maiden and 2nd. IRISH NH FLAT '00 r2 p0. NH '00 r2 p0 (Hdles; well tailed off last, and pulled up). P-t-P '01/3 (for late L.G. & Mrs M.J. Tizzard) r13 w3 (Maiden, Restricted and Intermediate) p1 (3rd); 4th, last pair 4, pulled up 3 and slipped up 1. Won three of his first four Pointing completions, but afflicted by a virus last year, and most unconvincing now. Collapsed through the wing of the last fence on his return, and never looked likely to score in the races where he filled the runners-up spot subsequently, before finally making his feelings on firm ground very apparent at Mounsey Hill Gate. Has to go right-handed and blinkered to no avail at Bishops Court. *Mrs M.J. Tizzard — Quantock (Alan Tizzard).* 63 (L), 117 (C), 199 (L), 319 (O), 882 (C), 1011 (L), 1183 (Cf), 1462 (L).

FATHER MANSFIELD (IRE) ..10-6.. 11 b.g. Phardante (FR) — Lena's Reign (Quayside) 26221114. Good-bodied brother to Irish Hurdles winner, Phareign, and half-brother to Irish Pointing and Hurdles winner, Sleetmore Gale (IRE). Dam is half-sister to Saddler's Choice (*qv* '98 Annual). IRISH P-t-P '99 r6 w2 (inc Winners of One) p2; pulled up 1. NH '00 r1 p0. P-t-P '02/3 r8 p4 (2nds, of 3 twice); 4th, pulled up 1 and fell/unseated 2. Very frustrating and runner-up in seven of his first nine English completions, but then rattled off a hat-trick on good or sound surfaces, and would have made it a four-timer at Bratton Down had Caroline Prouse not been admiring the countryside until it was too late. Might have been inconvenienced by the tight left-handed bends, and well worth another chance now that connections appear to have worked him out. *Mrs S. Prouse — Eggesford.* 193 (I), 321 (I), 495 (I), 705 (I), 821 (M), 1129 (I), 1270 (Cf), 1383 (Cnr).

PLATE 46 1392 Golden Valley Welsh Border Counties Confined Championship: Father Tom (Julian Pritchard), 1st, at the last *PHOTO: John Mullen*

FATHER TOM (IRE) ..10-8.. 11 b.g. Mazaad — Pride's Imp (Imperius) ff1111. Close-coupled. IRISH P-t-P '03 r5 w2 (6yo Maiden, Confined) p0; unseated 1. IRISH NH FLAT '00 r1 p0. IRISH NH '00/2 r13 p0; pulled up 2. IRISH HUNT CH '03 (for G. Stewart) r1 p0 (pulled up). Poor when beaten 19 lengths plus in 15 races under Rules in Ireland (blinkered once, and well tailed off in three Chases — pulled up once), but did manage to pick up a couple of modest Points in '03 including a dead-heat in which he appeared to have finished a close second. Favourite but fell at around halfway in his first two Points for the new yard, but they quickly realised that he was being put into the race much too early, and now that he has settled in the rear he can thread his way through the field and find a turn of foot which easily puts Confined competitors in their place. Not a natural jumper, and there is little in front of the saddle to save the rider if he makes an error, so takes plenty of knowing. Old champion Julian Pritchard got very much overlooked during the epic Burton versus Farrant tussle of '04, but his lovely efforts on this horse were a reminder of what a fine horseman he is. *H.F. Sharpe & R. Liddington — Ledbury (Dick Baimbridge).* 516 (R), 726 (R), 839 (R), 1140 (Cf), 1227 (Cf), 1392 (C).

FAUGERE ..—.. 9 ch.g. Jupiter Island — Pinch (Ardross) pp. Strong-topped lengthy. P-t-P '02 r2 p1 (last of 3); and fell. NH '03 (for P.F. Nicholls) r2 p1 (½l2nd in 2m4f110y Hdle). Showed promise when sent off favourite on his debut, and even more so when runner-up over hurdles at Folkestone 11 months later, but clearly a nightmare to train, and on the verge of eruption in the paddock in both Pointing attempts in '04 (got loose at Tweseldown and galloped off into a car park). *J.J. Boulter & Miss F.J. Wilkins — Portman (John Boulter).* 172 (OMa), 604 (OMa).

FAWSLEY LAKE ..7-0.. 12 ch.m. Crested Lark — True Manor (True Song) ppp4. Owner-bred sister to Crested Manor (*qv*). Ushered in from the fields of Preston Capes to make her debut aged 11, and suffered the usual bemusement of the Tarry beginners, but did achieve a completion at the fourth attempt even though she was tailed off throughout the final two miles. Her brother won at 12 in '04, so there is no reason to give up on her yet. *G.B. Tarry — Grafton (Rosie Goodwin).* 587 (R), 789 (CfMa), 1035 (OMa), 1108 (OMa).

FAYALIE (IRE) ..9-0.. 10 b.m. Classic Memory — Much Obliged (Crash Course) 044. Close-coupled well-made sister to Holy Moses (IRE) (*qv*). IRISH NH FLAT '00 r3 p0. IRISH NH '01 r1 p0. IRISH P-t-P '02 r4 w1 (5yo Mares Maiden) p0; pulled up 2. P-t-P/HUNT CH '03 r5 p0 (pulled up 3, and fell/unseated 2). Displayed plenty of stamina when landing a 16-runner mares Maiden in Ireland in '02, but totally flummoxed by the fences last year, and only once better than last for a novice in '04. *J.H. Hewitt — York & Ainsty N. (Michael Brown).* 267 (Cf), 390 (Rnr), 503 (R).

FEARLESS BERTIE .—.. 14 b.g. Fearless Action (USA) — Rambert (Mandamus) pp. Small neat half-brother to a winner in Denmark. P-t-P '96/8, '00 and '02/3 (for Ms J. Johnston & Ms S. Miles) r13 w2 (2m4f Maiden and Open) p4 (3 2nds); failed to finish 4 (fell/unseated 2). Rated 10-0 after gaining his second success (five years after the first) in '02, but averages fewer than two outings per annum, and pulled up after a maximum of 2m3f at Mollington this year. Would have achieved more had he been problem free, but surely finished now. *Ms J. Johnston — Grafton.* 292 (MO), 586 (O).

FEDERAL CASE (FR) ..9-3.. 7 b.g. Nikos — Miss Normania (FR) (Iron Duke FR) p333p. IRISH P-t-P '03 r1 w1 (4&5yo Maiden). Bought Doncaster, Aug for 15,000. The owner has purchased some good horses over the years notably St Gregory, but this is not one of them, and made to look very expensive when capable only of finishing third at best (beaten between ten and 22 lengths) in Restricteds. The form of his Irish Pointing win (in soft) was probably meaningless, and consistently looks to have a struggle to get the trip. Never sent off at more than 4-1, and the local punters have far too much faith him in. *A.G.C. Howland Jackson — Suffolk (Ruth Hayter).* 250 (R), 524 (R), 648 (R), 902 (R), 1245 (R).

FEELING GRAND (IRE) .8-10.. 13 br.g. Naheez (USA) — Tourney's Girl (Yankee Gold) pf5p. Tall rangy brother to Irish Pointing winner, Quelle Femme, and half-brother to Nasayer (IRE) and James Isaac (IRE), to Irish Pointing winner, Davy Bustin, and to Irish NH Flat and Hurdling winner, Oak Court. IRISH NH FLAT '97 r1 p0. IRISH NH '97/02 r30 w6 (2m-2m3f Chses) p5 (inc 3 in Hdles). NH '03 r1 p0 (pulled up). P-t-P '03 r1 p0 (pulled up). A smart performer on sound surfaces at up to 2m3f in Ireland to '02, but has gone plummeting downhill since, and ran tubed when not better than last this year. Deserves to be humiliated no more. Wears a cross-noseband. *Mrs R. Arthur — Tynedale.* 163 (O), 425 (M), 654 (Cf), 764 (O).

FEELS LIKE RAIN ..9-3.. 9 b.g. Hatim (USA) — Gilzie's Touch (Feelings FR) p24. Good-bodied half-brother to Sunrise Sensation. Only modest in his delayed first season, but did have a total of six behind him when completing including one subsequent winner, so it may be worth persevering with him at nine. *The Foale Family (Mrs A. Foale) — Dart V.H. & S. Pool H. (Ian Foale).* 824 (R), 1006 (CfMa), 1381 (OMa).

FELIX RANDAL (IRE) ..9-7.. 9 ch.g. Be My Native (USA) — Odd Sox (FR) (Main Reef) 55. Workmanlike half-brother to Sock Hop (IRE). IR31,000 4yo. NH FLAT '01 r1 p0. NH '01/3 (for J. O'Neill) r10 w1 (2m5f Hdle) p3; pulled up 3. Bought Doncaster, May for 1200. An enigmatic character who gained his only win in a bad Hurdle, and two efforts in Chases resulted in a respectable second and a pulled up. A poor jumper who can stay on well if he feels like it, but sometimes looks reluctant, and lasted only until mid-March when achieving little in Points. Was tongue-tied and blinkered on his penultimate outing in the previous yard. *Miss T. Watkins — Radnor & W. Herefords.* 403 (Cf), 447 (Cf).

FELLOO (IRE) ..9-7.. 16 br.g. Decent Fellow — Cuckaloo (Master Buck) 85p2p. Workmanlike half-brother to Irish NH flat and jumping winner, Ballinarrid (IRE). NH '96/7 r10 p1 (short-headed in Ch). P-t-P/HUNT CH '98/9 and '01/3 r22 w4 (Maiden, Restricted, Members and Intermediate, inc hat-trick '03) p7 (4 2nds, inc Hunt Ch; inc 3rd of 4 once); pulled up 5, and fell 2. Well placed to find three races on sound surfaces as a 14-year-old, but only had a total of six finishers behind him, and gained his latest prize in a match. Genuine and less clumsy than he was, but never really had his ground in '04, and looks too old now. Blinkered once in '97. *Mrs R.E. Walker — Clifton-on-Teme.* 403 (Cf), 586 (O), 662 (O), 818 (MO), 1032 (O).

FENCETHEGAP (IRE) ..8-9.. 8 b.g. Archway (IRE) — Sally Gap (Sallust) 344u. Sturdy compact half-brother to Irish NH flat winner, Wally Wonder. IRISH P-t-P '01 r1 p0 (refused). IRISH FLAT '99/00 r3 p0. IRISH NH '00/2 (for T.J. Kidd, and R.P. Rath) r10 p0. Has contested 18 races, but beaten 17 lengths or more if completing in 14 of them. Made the frame on three occasions in '04, but only by default, and was about 40 lengths last twice. Gloomily, his rating has surely already peaked. Was tongue-tied in Ireland, and blinkered on his final appearance there. *N. Price — Golden V. (Jane Lloyd).* 982 (2m5fOMa), 1259 (OMa), 1393 (OMa), 1538 (R).

FENNY ROYAL .—.. 9 b.g. Platinum Royale — Zara Express (Pony Express) ppp. Strong half-brother to Fenny Prince. Dam, half-sister to Stainless Steel (*qv* '00 Annual), was about a fence 3rd in 2 Points for the Sweetlands (failed to finish in 10 of 15 attempts). Closely related to Silver Kracker (*qv*). Tailed off and pulled up after two miles maximum thrice, including when over two fences adrift once. Has been mounted on the course and taken to post early. One of the typically awful beasts that the luckless Mervyn Woodward ends up riding. *M.S. Sweetland — E. Devon.* 497 (Cf), 573 (I), 827 (CfMa).

FERGAL'S FIND (IRE) ..9-3.. 6 ch.g. Pierre — Nuan (IRE) (Teofane) 22. Compact attractive. IR2500, 3000 4yo. Beaten 12 lengths on his Bitterley debut, but lacked fluency at Ashorne next time, and having drawn five lengths clear and apparently going best three out he found himself overhauled near the finish. Not many five-year-old debutants need a tongue-tie, and evidently has wind problems to address, but certainly good enough to score if they are sorted out. *Mrs P. Duncan — Cotswold (Jelly Nolan).* 837 (OMa), 1273 (OMa).

FERNHILL BLAZE (IRE) ..—.. 12 b.g. High Estate — Bonnie Isle (Pitcairn) pp. Close-coupled half-brother to Island Forest (USA) (subsequent Chasing winner), to jumping winner, Tensile (IRE), and to flat winners in France and USA. Dam won 5 flat, 6-8f, and was 2nd in '79 Oaks. FLAT r1 p0 (last — started slowly and soon tailed off). P-t-P '98/00 and '02 r11 w1 (Maiden) p1 (3rd); last, pulled up 3, slipped up 1 and fell 4. Ridden in the paddock and taken to post early prior to landing a weak Maiden in softish at Rhydygwern in '02, but immediately went wrong, and appeared to suffer another setback at Howick. Never mastered the art of jumping at speed. *M.G. Jones — Gelligaer F.* 358 (R), 695 (R).

FERN LEADER (IRE) ..9-0.. 15 b.g. Supreme Leader — Mossbrook (Le Moss) 3u5up. Smallish compact half-brother to Cantenac Brown (IRE). NH FLAT '97 r1 p0. NH '97/8 and '01 r21 w2 (2m5f-3m Chses) p9 (inc 7 2nds); (fell/unseated 5). P-t-P/HUNT CH '95/6 and '00/2 r27 w3 (up to Confined) p6 (4 2nds, last twice, remote once); pulled up 4, and fell/unseated 4. Won five races to '98, but remarkably clumsy throughout his career, and only had to nudge a fence to dislodge the latest nervous rider to partner him. Still retains some ability, but forced to stop on the flat at Bratton Down, and will surely be pensioned off now. Visored twice in '00, and has been fitted with blinkers regularly. *R.C. Skinner — Eggesford (Linda Blackford).* 821 (M), 1005 (Cf), 1180 (M), 1365 (Cnr), 1383 (Cnr).

FERRYHILL (IRE) ..9-1.. 12 b.g. Over The River (FR) — Eden Valley (Kambalda) 66pu. Tall strong half-brother to Irish Pointing and Chasing winner, Tremble Valley. Dam won 2 Irish Chses, 2m4f-3m (wore blinkers). NH FLAT '98 r1 p1 (3rd). NH '98/02 r5 p0; brought down 1 and pulled up 1. P-t-P '00 r2 w1 (Maiden) p0; and 8th. Left clear at the last when the 10-length leader unseated at Larkhill in '00, but broke down at Hereford two years later, and only brought back into service to school novice riders in '04. Provided Lisa Britton with her first ride at Stafford Cross, but she fell off at the sixth. Wears a cross-noseband. *J.J. Boulter & Miss F.J. Wilkins — S. Dorset (John Boulter).* 31 (Cnr), 250 (R), 369 (R), 1132 (R).

PLATE 47 2 Cambridgeshire Harriers Hunt Club Restricted: Fertile Valley and Ladies Champion Polly Gundry leads Mens Champion Ashley Farrant on Oneminutetofive PHOTO: Tim Holt

FERTILE VALLEY (IRE) ..10-9.. 9 b.g. Sir Harry Lewis (USA) — Raisin Turf (IRE) (Phardante FR) 11. Tall. IRISH P-t-P '02/3 r5 w1 (7yo&up Maiden) p2; pulled up 1 and fell 1. IRISH NH FLAT '03 r1 p0. IRISH NH '03 (for K. Riordan) r2 p0. Won the fastest three mile race on the opening day at Cottenham, and repeated the dose at Chaddesley where he was again taken to post early before giving a determined display of galloping. Could be under-rated by a few pounds (worthy of the 11 stone range) as his Cottenham victim Oneminutetofive was not beaten in four subsequent Points including three Opens, but rather disappointingly approaches nine with only ten races behind him. The owner has previously had many horses who only merit the comment (hard cheese), but with this one and Balinova he has really raised the game. Will hopefully be fit in '05, and worthy of a place in a Hunter Chase if he is. *C.J. Bennett — Teme V. (Ben Tulloch).* 2 (R), 255 (CCon).

FESTIVAL TIME ..9-8.. 7 ch.g. Good Thyne (USA) — Kilty Hill (Kemal FR) p1. P-t-P '03 r1 p0 (refused). Got off to a most auspicious start, but got into the thick of the action briefly at Thorpe Lodge, and appreciated the drop back in trip when lucky to beat one other finisher at Garnons. Error-proneand has it all to prove in Restricteds now that he is forced to race over three miles again. *P. Milner — Cheshire (Gary Hanmer).* 111 (OMa), 617 (2m4fOMa).

FIDDLER CRAB ..—.. 7 br.g. Prince Daniel (USA) — Sea Sand (Sousa) pp. Homebred half-brother to Coastal Safari (*qv*). Horse and rider both looked very novicey before pulling up after less than two miles when tailed off in May Maidens. *Mrs A.F. Tullie — Berwicks.* 1292 (OMa), 1474 (2m4fOMa).

FIESTY FROSTY (IRE) ..9-0.. 7 b.m. Glacial Storm (USA) — Smashed Free (IRE) (Carlingford Castle) pp4pp. Dam, sister to Edstone (*qv*). P-t-P '03 r3 w1 (3-finisher Maiden) p0; and pulled up 2. Won a bad Maiden taking over seven minutes on her first completion, but badly let down by her jumping otherwise, and does not appear to possess much in the way of resolve. *Mrs E. Holt — Atherstone (John Holt).* 301 (R), 384 (R), 684 (R), 889 (CR), 1265 (R).

FILOU DU BOIS (FR) ..9-12.. 12 b.g. Shafoun (FR) — Jamaica (FR) (Tryptic) 4373143. Good-topped half-brother to Underway (FR), and to a French flat winner. Dam won flat race (at Seriches-sur-Loire) and Hurdle in France. FRENCH FLAT '97 r1 p1 (3rd). ITALIAN NH '97/8 p3 (Hdles). NH '98/00 r11 p2 (2nds); pulled up 1. NH '02 r1 p0 (pulled up in Ch). P-t-P '02/3 r4 w1 (Maiden) p3 (2nds). Busier than ever before as an 11-year-old, but predictably struggled to last home in better company, and only found a Restricted once the ground had dried out. Lacks acceleration but a steady jumper, and might be of value as a schoolmaster. Wears a cross-noseband. *Ms A.E. Embiricos — Cambridge Univ.* 44 (R), 127 (R), 250 (R), 649 (L), 745 (R), 1151 (Cf), 1397 (I).

FILSCOT ..10-0§.. 13 b.g. Scottish Reel — Fililode (Mossberry) 23553r2s5. Stocky compact half-brother to Ricky B. Dam won Maiden. NH FLAT '97 r3 w1 p1 (2nd). NH '98/02 r47 w5 (2 2m4f110y-2m5f Hdles and 3 2m4f-3m1f110y Chses) p17. HUNT CH '03 r3 p1 (neck 2nd); 4th and pulled up 1. A very frustrating individual, and can finish very strongly when he chooses, but has not won since '02, and is impossible to predict. Retains more than enough ability to win again but the chances are that he will continue to conceal just enough of it. Suited by an easy three miles on good or sound surfaces. Occasionally blinkered, visored once in '02, and acquired cheekpieces in '04. *Mr & Mrs P.J. Morgan — V. of Aylesbury with Garth & S. Berks (Sue Harbour).* 171 (L), 289 (CfL), 442 (2m7f110yH), 635 (L), 801 (3mH), 1168 (2m5fH), 1372 (2m4fH), 1497 (3mH), 1516 (L).

FINAL BELLE .—.. 6 ch.m. Alflora (IRE) — B Final (Gunner B) p. Lengthy unfurnished. Partnered by Richard Burton on her debut which was presumably why she started at a stingy 4-1, but was tailed off when pulled up at the 13th. *D.A. Malam — Cheshire (Donald McCain Jnr).* 714 (CMam).

FINAL CHORUS ..8-12.. 9 ch.m. High Lodge — Golden Chorus (Golden Mallard) p2p. Small with nothing in front of saddle owner-bred half-sister to Another Chant, Palm Gold, Pashby Wood and Brown's Beck. Dam, half-sister to Final Chant (*qv* '96 Annual), pulled up in 2 Points for David Brydon. P-t-P '02 r2 p0 (pulled up 2). Displayed her first signs of ability when five lengths second in her Members, but the following Restricted was run in a time 14 seconds faster, and has looked devoid of speed when pulled up in Maidens. *D.A.D. Brydon — Derwent.* 500 (CMam), 954 (M), 1165 (OMa).

FINAL ESCAPADE ..8-0.. 12 ch.g. St Columbus — Country Princess (Country Retreat) 4p9. Lengthy owner-bred brother to Easter Escapade. Dam is half-sister to Prince Fury (*qv* '90 Annual). Grandam, Roel Queen, won 2 Ladies and placed 9. NH '01 r1 p0 (pulled up). P-t-P/HUNT CH '02/3 r11 p1 (3rd); last pair 7, pulled up 2 and slipped up 1. A secure jumper, but plods badly from an early stage, and only once better than last in six attempts for Kay Garner. *Mrs E.M. Wharton — Warwicks (Kay Garner).* 1278 (Cnr), 1391 (L), 1516 (L).

FINAL MAGIC ..—.. 11 b.g. Cruise Missile — Magic Coin (unknown) pfup. Compact owner-bred brother to Magical Cruise, and half-brother to Double Magic and The Wizard. Pulls hard and can show early speed, but soon gallops himself into the ground, and never completes and seems to have little prospect of doing so. *Mrs R.W. Hall — Beaufort (Richard Smith).* 139 (R), 370 (OMa), 721 (OMa), 883 (OMa).

FINAL MICK ..—§§.. 9 b.g. Michelozzo (USA) — Final Flirtation (Clear Run) pRr. Small neat owner-bred half-brother to Final Rose, Final Quay, Final Dancer and Bold Flirtation. Dam, half-sister to 6 Pointers including Final Answer (dam of Final Cruise, (*qv* '00 Annual), won 4 Points and placed 8 for Mr E.D. Llewellyn. Grandam, Final Case, won 2 flat (5-13f), won on flat at Ostend, won 2 2m Hdles, and went lame when 2nd in an Adjacent. P-t-P '02/3 r3 p0 (pulled up 1, ran out 1 and unseated 1). A thick Mick with no brakes or steering, and causes chaos wherever he goes. Declined to set off at all at Bonvilston so at least it looks as though he has presented himself with his own red card before the authorities intervene. Wears a cross-noseband, and has run tongue-tied. *D.H. Llewellyn — S. Pembs.* 677 (CfMa), 952 (I), 1094 (R).

FINBAR (IRE) ..9-0.. 9 b.g. Good Thyne (USA) — Shuil Eile (Deep Run) p5. Workmanlike half-brother to Pure Grit (IRE), to Chasing winner, Lisdante (IRE), to 3 winners in Ireland, including Shuil Ar Aghaidh (NH flat and useful staying Hurdler) and Rawhide (very useful staying jumper). Dam, sister to Why Forget, and half-sister to Rhu Na Haven (*qv* '98 Annual), won NH flat and 2 Hdles (2m-2m4f) in Ireland. NH FLAT '02 r1 p0. P-t-P '03 r1 p0 (pulled up). Beat one home in an Ascot bumper, and pulled up lame on his jumping debut, but keeping on steadily at the finish when around 13 lengths fifth at Vauterhill, and might be capable of better if he stands regular racing. *Miss L. Gardner & R. Bostock-Smith — Silverton (Lucy Gardner).* 795 (CfMa), 1272 (OMa).

FINDER KEEPS (USA) ..10-0.. 10 b.g. Discover (USA) — Stark Home (USA) (Graustark) 231p2. Tall workmanlike half-brother to 3 winners in USA. Dam won 3 flat races at up to 10f in USA. NH FLAT '00 r1 p0. NH '00/1 r2 p0. P-t-P '02/3 r8 w2 (Maiden and Restricted) p1 (3rd); last 2, fell 2 and pulled up 1. Consistent and benefits from superior riding, but remains prone to jumping lapses, and usually has nothing in the tank when successful. Risked Only on good or easy surfaces, and therefore his campaigns are relatively short. *P. Dailey — O. Berks (Matt Hazell).* 92 (I), 379 (I), 584 (I), 756 (Cf), 1332 (Cf).

FIND ME ANOTHER (IRE) ..10-7.. 9 b.g. Shardari — Naujwan Too (Kafu) 22321421. Workmanlike. P-t-P '02/3 r11 w3 (Maiden, Intermediate and Club Moderate) p4 (2nds, of 3 once); last pair 3 and fell 1. Consistent and the winner of five races, and rounded off '04 in fine style at Huntingdon, but finds little off the bridle and needs everything to go his way. Won going left-handed for the first time when sporting new colours at Guilsborough, but a beaten favourite for the sixth time in his career when last of four at Garthorpe next time, and can never be supported with total confidence. Yet to encounter ground much softer than good. Blinkered once in '03. *C. Dixey — Mrs C. Stennett, Mrs C. Aldridge & Mrs E. King — Meynell & S. Staffs (Caroline Bailey).* 17 (O), 108 (L), 189 (L), 443 (2m4f110yH), 785 (L), 1058 (L), 1359 (2m4f110yH), 1497 (3mH).

FINE AND DANDY (IRE) .10-3.. 9 b.g. Roselier (FR) — Hawthorn Dandy (Deep Run) 22f1. Unfurnished half-brother to Althrey Dandy (*qv*). NH FLAT '01 r1 p0 (tailed off). NH '01 r3 p0 (4th, and pulled up 2). P-t-P/HUNT CH '03 r8 w3 (Maiden, Restricted and Confined, hat-trick) p4 (3 2nds, inc Hunt Ch); and fell 1. Of no account under Rules, but only once out of the first two in Points, and but for two falls at High Easter has done precious little wrong. No match for Star Glow or Hot Toddy in '04, but surprisingly became the first horse to win the Suffolk Members in the Turner colours since As You Were in 1989, and looks sure to win again when fast ground prevails. *J.M. Turner — Suffolk.* 28 (I), 41 (I), 223 (I), 520 (M).

FINEST OF MEN ..9-7.. 9 b.g. Tina's Pet — Merry Missus (Bargello) 0636. Homebred brother to Merry Tina, and half-brother to Gone Astray, Master Mischief and Merry Major, to Chasing winner, Merry Master, and to NH flat winner, Don't George. Dam won 2m Chse. NH FLAT '01/2 r3 p1 (3rd). NH '02 r1 p0. P-t-P/HUNT CH '02/3 r7 w3 (inc 2 Opens) p1 (2nd); 4th, and last pair 2. Improved in leaps and bounds last year and rounded the season off with a brace of Open wins, but bitterly disappointing in '04 when only able to beat two rivals. Never put in the race on his first two starts, but folded tamely at Aspatria, and had ground conditions go against him at Hexham. A thorough stayer, and young enough to atone, but not the first inmate from his yard whose fortunes fluctuate so wildly. *J.B. & F.A. Walton — Border (Jimmy Walton).* 764 (O), 917 (O), 1309 (O), 1421 (O).

FINE TIMES ..9-8.. 11 b.g. Timeless Times (USA) — Marfen (Lochnager) u4p4pp37p. Small sturdy brother to flat winner, Ramsey Hope. FLAT (usually visored) r24 p2 (2nd, 5-6f). NH '98 r2 p0 (last and pulled up, inc Sell). P-t-P/HUNT CH '99/03 r22 w7 (inc 3m1f Hunt Ch and 2 Opens) p3 (2 2nds, of 3 once); pulled up 5, and fell 3. Speedy and well placed to win seven races on good or sound surfaces, but totally lifeless in '04, and must have been wrong. Not a natural jumper, particularly of big fences, and tends to go away to the right, and it must be odds against him being rejuvenated next year. Wears a tongue-strap. *J.M. Robinson — Burton.* 54 (C), 156 (O), 478 (Cf), 557 (O), 997 (O), 1153 (O), 1302 (O), 1414 (O), 1500 (Cf).

FINEWOOD (IRE) ..—.. 11 b.g. Macmillion — Feodora (Songedor) p. Rangy half-brother to NH flat winner, Entertainment Park and Royal Entertainer. NH '98/9 and '01 (for J.M. Jefferson) r9 w3 (2m-2m4f Hdles) p2 (2nds); pulled up 1. A very competent Hurdler in the soft who would probably have made a useful Chaser had he had the chance, but has only made it to the racecourse twice since '99, and problems immediately resurfaced when he was brought out from under the dust covers to contest a match for an Open in which he pulled up and dismounted at the 12th when rapidly losing touch with Polar Champ. *The Finewood Friends (R.M. Woollacott) — Tiverton Stag (Emely Thompson).* 1541 (O).

FINLAYS FOLLY ..—.. 8 b.g. Fremont Boy — Twiglette (Aragon) ppp. Light-framed. FLAT '00 r2 p0. NH '00 (for P.R. Hedger) r2 p0. Sold Ascot, Oct '00 for 300. Dreadful on his rare appearances, and was visored in his second Hurdle. Invariably hopelessly tailed off, and gave a nasty display in the paddock once in Points. *P. Riddick — Gelligaer F.* 845 (CfMa), 1096 (OMa), 1240 (OMa).

FINNE GAOITHE (IRE) ..9-9.. 9 b.m. Witness Box (USA) — Graine Gale (Strong Gale) p. Dam won Mares Maiden in Ireland. IRISH P-t-P '00 and '02 r8 p1 (2nd); pulled up 3. P-t-P '03 r2 w1 (Mares Maiden) p1 (2nd). Won a weak mares Maiden despite approaching the end of her tether on her final appearance last year, but pulled up after 2m3f on her only outing in '04, and may have suffered a setback. Would need to improve further to take a hand in Restricteds in any case. *P., B. & Mrs R. Hodges — N. Ledbury (Caroline Chadney).* 665 (R).

FIOLINO (FR) ..6-0.. 12 b.g. Bayolidaan (FR) — Vellea (FR) (Cap Martin FR) 4pp86. Workmanlike half-brother to Irish NH flat and Hurdles winner, Jasmin d'Oudairies (FR), to NH flat and Hurdles winner, Icare d'Oudairies (FR), and to French flat and jumping winner, Elysea (FR). NH FLAT '98/9 r4 p0. NH '99/03 (for J.W. Curtis, and M.W. Easterby) r21 w1 (3m Ch) p5 (inc 3rd in Hdles); pulled up 6, fell 1. Bought Doncaster, Oct for 1900. Made errors when winning a five-runner Uttoxeter Chase in soft in December '01, and beaten a maximum of six-and-a-quarter lengths in four of five placings, but lost his form latterly, and pulled up on his final two appearances (blinkered once). Painfully slow (mostly for a novice) in Points, and after being beaten 47 lengths in his Members he was furlongs last in two other completions. Mother bred two other winners, but her son named Herpes performed as if he'd got it. *R.A. & Mrs C.R. Page — Cambridge Univ (Ruth Page).* 98 (M), 246 (L), 832 (Cf), 998 (L), 1313 (Cf).

FIRLE PHANTASY ..—§§.. 12 ch.g. Pharly (FR) — Shamasiya (FR) (Vayrann) puR*R08*. Small neat half-brother 2 flat wins inc Rock Symphony. Dam won 2 12f races in France. FLAT '95/6 r6 p1 (2nd). P-t-P '03 r3 p0 (refused, pulled up and fell). NH '04 (for G.F. Bridgwater) r3 p0 (ran out in 2m5f Sell Hdle: *hld up, hdwy 4, hung lft aft 8, bhnd when rn out nxt*; 10th in 2m Hdle: *2nd/3rd til wknd aft 4, t.o*; and 8th in 2m Sell Hdle: *went 2nd app 3 til hmpd 5, wknd aft nxt*). Flattered by finishing a neck second over a mile in '96, and has always shown a tendency to waywardness. Predictably made mincemeat of some feeble riding in '04, and is never going to get round in Points. Regained blinkers once in '04, and wore them again when misbehaving back under Rules. *P. Murtagh — Holderness (Julie Coulson).* 304 (OMa), 395 (CfMa), 595 (OMa).

FIRST AND FOURMOST (IRE) ..—§.. 8 b/br.g. Alphabatim (USA) — Molly Owen (IRE) (Kambalda) ppfp. Good-topped attractive. Dam won Mares Maiden in Ireland (div 3 — a meeting at which 8 out of 10 races were for Maidens!) NH '01 r3 p0. P-t-P '03 r4 p0 (pulled up 2, refused 1 and ran out 1). Had ability but far too ungenuine to reveal it all, and is now dead. D. Wales — W. Norfolk (William Wales). 244 (CfMa), 476 (CfMa), 652 (OMa), 1155 (OMa).

FISHERMAN JACK ..10-3.. 10 b.g. Carlingford Castle — Troublewithjack (Sulaafah USA) 34p1. Small compact owner-bred half-brother to Shipley Hill Lad, Jack Lynch and Jacks Helen. P-t-P '00 and '02/3 r9 w4 (inc Open) p2; 7th, pulled up 1 and fell 1. A thorough stayer and has recorded at least one success in each of his four campaigns, but most unimpressive in the latest in which he was never jumping with any zest. Pulled up when the rider thought he was wrong just 10 days earlier, and might just benefit from the application of headgear as he gets wiser. Revels in mud but needs an outing to get fit which leaves little opportunity to strike again as his appearances have been limited to a maximum of four in a year. *The Smith Burton Partnership (J. Burton) — S. Notts (John Burton).* 106 (C), 177 (3mH), 437 (3m1fH), 586 (O).

FIVE MINUTES ..8-12.. 9 b.m. Syrtos — Florence May (Grange Melody) p6p. Small half-sister to Homme De Fer (*qv*). NH FLAT '01 r1 p0. P-t-P '02/3 r7 p3 (2nds); unseated 2, and pulled up 2. Runner-up in three Maidens on good or easy ground, but downed tools when tried in a visor on her reappearance, and lamed by her exposure to fast ground (which she had shown a dislike for in '03) at Black Forest Lodge two starts later. *Mr & Mrs A.J.S. Knox — Silverton (Robert Chanin).* 149 (OMa), 275 (CfMa), 416 (CMam).

FLASH POINT (IRE) ..9-13.. 6 b/br.g. Executive Perk — Shine Your Light (Kemal FR) 1. Good-bodied half-brother to Irish NH flat and jumping winner, High-Spec, and to Irish Pointing and NH flat winner, Dantes Sun. Dam won 3 2m-2m6f Irish Hurdles. Bought Doncaster, Aug for 7000. Made the ideal start when winning a three-finisher Maiden at Wadebridge in mid-March and then put away. Gives the impression of being of above-average, and should be worth watching at six. *T. Hamlin, J.M. Dare & J.W. Snook - E. Devon (Ollie Bush).* 485 (OMa).

FLAT STANLEY ..10-2.. 6 b.g. Celtic Swing — Cool Grey (Absalom) 53312323. Compact. FLAT '01/3 r12 p1 (2nd). NH '03 (for R. Bastiman) r2 p0; pulled up 1. Only achieved one placing on the flat, when a length second on the all-weather (tried with cheekpieces once), and outclassed at long odds over Hurdles, but jumped really well for a five-year-old in Points and did not miss out on a prize in seven consecutive attempts after his debut. His sole victory was in a bad youngsters Maiden at Easingwold (seems to like the track, and should be worth noting there in future), but ended his campaign with a strong finishing six-and-a-quarter lengths third over 3m2f at Cartmel, having been given far too much to do (not the first time Jo Foster has cocked it up here). Beaten only a neck in a Restricted previously, and if he can be persuaded to be in the right place at the right time there is no reason why he cannot enjoy a good measure of success. *P. Grindrod & J.E. Endersby — Pendle Forest & Craven (Paul Grindrod).* 272 (OMa), 504 (CMa), 709 (Mah), 1158 (OMa), 1201 (M), 1304 (CR), 1469 (R), 1526 (3m2fH).

FLAT TOP ..10-0§.. 14 b.g. Blakeney — New Edition (Great Nephew) up4244. Small sturdy brother to Hurdles winner, Miss Pimpernell, half-brother to Hurdles winner, Caledonian Express, and to flat winner, Arabian King. Dam won 5f race. NH FLAT '95 r1 p0. NH '93/03 r65 w9 (2 3m-3m2f Hdles and 7 2m5f-3m1f Chses) p24; pulled up 9, fell/unseated 7. NH '04 r1 p0 (pulled up in 3m110y R.A. Gold Cup: *lost tch 11, sn t.o, rem 6th when pu last*). A stalwart of the Northern jumping scene and earned £71,899 in a long career which included nine wins on ground ranging from good to heavy. A triple scorer at Hexham, but has often thrown in blunders, and has broken blood vessels. Blinkered once way back in '96, partnered by Milo Manton on 17 occasions, but remarkably has never scored for him, and was given too much to do when 15 lengths third in a R.A. Gold Cup having been headed in the final stride in the same race the year before (lost it by being outjumped at the last). Looked unhappy and unenthusiastic in '04, and only completed for a substitute in his Members after running out and retracing. Looks sure to be pensioned off. *Lord Manton — Middleton (David Easterby).* 163 (O), 340 (O), 679 (3m1fH), 769 (M), 894 (3m3fH).

FLAXLEY ABBEY ..9-4.. 8 gr.m. Arzanni — Dunbrody Abbey (Proverb) 2. Dam, (*qv* '92 Annual), won 11 Points (the first in Ireland) and 2nd once and subsequently won 3m Chase. NH FLAT '02 r3 p0. NH '02/3 (for J.D. Frost) r3 p0; pulled up 1. Badly outclassed when beaten 28 lengths plus in six races for the previous yard, and did not achieve much when 15 lengths second in a youngsters Maiden with only a couple of rags behind her. Not seen since mid-February. *The Fun Club (A. Heseltine) — E. Essex (Paula Twinn).* 218 (OMa).

FLOCKMASTER (IRE) ..9-13.. 14 ch.g. Accordion — Only A Laugh (Torus) 537113. Robust. P-t-P/HUNT CH '97/00 and '02/3 r35 w4 (Maiden, Restricted, Intermediate and Members) p11 (5 2nds); pulled up 12, refused 1, and fell/unseated 3. Often a weak finisher, but has done well to score in five separate seasons, and rarely misses the frame when completing. Tends to jump sketchily on occasions, but made most to record a double for Charlotte Owen, and retired after failing to justify favouritism in a more competitive race at Rhydygwern. *M.G. Jones — Gelligaer F.* 361 (L), 843 (L), 1090 (Cf), 1235 (Cf), 1318 (M), 1485 (Cnr).

FLO KEEN ..9-4.. 6 ch.m. Alflora (IRE) — Sloe Hill (Le Moss) 2p. Workmanlike unfurnished. Dam won three Points (the first two in Ireland) and placed total of nine including three Chases and a Hurdle, and is half-sister to Dodgy Dealer (*qv* '97 Annual) and now a total of eight winners. Left a lucky second two out when 25 lengths second of three behind the impressive Combat Drinker at Bishops Court, but was tailed off and pulled up after 2m4f next time. Seemed to be given a steady start by competent connections, and may well take more of a hand in proceedings at six. *M.J. O'Connor — Mendip F. (Caroline Keevil).* 326 (OMa), 978 (CMam).

FLOODGATE ..8-9.. 8 b.g. Bin Ajwaad (IRE) — Miss Haversham (Salse USA) 3p. Tall unfurnished. FLAT '01 r1 p0 (tailed off). NH FLAT '01 r1 p0. P-t-P '02/3 r3 w1 (Maiden) p0; and pulled up 2. Left the lucky winner of a two-finisher Maiden at Bonvilston in '02, but only allowed to line up at Clifton-on-Dunsmore after being given the all clear by the vet last year, and appeared to suffer a setback at Larkhill. *G. Cheshire & D.L. Williams — Windsor & Chiltern (David Williams).* 819 (R), 1102 (R).

FLOOREX CARPETMAN ..8-10§.. 10 b.g. Damister (USA) — Charmed I'm Sure (Nicholas Bill) p64p6. Close-coupled. Dam won 2 2m2f Sell Hdles. NH FLAT '99 r2 p0. P-t-P '00 and '02/3 (for Mr P. Richardson) r16 p6 (5 3rds, of 3 once, last thrice; and dead-heat for 2nd); pulled up 3 and fell 2. Scrapes into the frame on a regular basis, but an ungenuine non-stayer, and only once better than last when novice ridden in '04. Has been tried in blinkers, and visored twice in '02. *Lady Lewinton — O. Berks (Lee Harfield).* 172 (OMa), 492 (OMa), 729 (OMa), 935 (M), 1193 (OMa).

FLORA MACDONALD ..9-9§.. 9 ch.m. Alflora (IRE) — Just A Tipple (IRE) (Roselier FR) u441. Neat. NH FLAT '00 r1 p0 (tailed off). P-t-P '01/3 r7 w1 (Members) p2 (3rds); 7th, pulled up 2 and fell 1. The winner of two minor races, but has always had to endure an interrupted campaign, and looked ill at ease on the fast ground when scoring under a chance ride from Ashley Farrant at Bratton Down. In command when Harry Wallace fell off her at the last on her reappearance, but never went a yard next time, and clearly has her own ideas. Goes well fresh, but will need to find improvement to upgrade successfully. *S.J. & Mrs S.J. Rawlins — R.A. (Sally Rawlins).* 85 (M), 324 (R), 1131 (R), 1385 (R).

FLUTED EDGE ..8-6.. 8 b.m. Piccolo — Serration (Kris) p74. Half-sister to flat winner, The Seer, and to Hurdles winner, Devon Peasant. Tailed off and pulled up after a mile on her debut, (clueless), and then plodded round for a couple of poor lasts. Will have to find plenty more if she is to get near the leaders. *R. Oliver — Four Burrow (Terance Oliver).* 150 (OMa), 701 (2m4fOMa), 907 (M).

FLY FOR PADDY ..9-6.. 7 b.g. Michelozzo (USA) — Tirley Pop Eye (Cruise Missile) 1b. Workmanlike. Dam, half-sister to Run For Paddy. NH FLAT '02 (for Mrs H. Dalton) r4 p1 (3rd). Showed a little ability in bumpers and was 25 lengths third on his debut, and proved good enough to win a 2m5f Maiden on dead ground at Sandon, but brought down at the fifth next time. Could possibly improve further, but missed '03 and is not standing much racing so far. *B.J. Perkins — N. Ledbury.* 850 (2m5fOMa), 1345 (R).

FLYING PAST .9-11.. 9 br.g. Past Glories — Eye Valley (Pamroy) 1up3. Tall lengthy. Dam (*qv* '94 Annual) won 11 Points (including a five-timer in Members) and placed 21 for Doreen Calder. Bred from a gallant mare who finished in 53 of her 56 starts, and made an immediate impact under Ran Morgan in a mid-February Maiden at Alnwick, where he came home 25 lengths plus ahead of three dismal rivals who have never won. The amazing Doreen (false teeth and bus pass?) had a go next time, and it was horrible to see this wonderful sport of many years standing plummet like a stone from the saddle (if this is the end of her racing career, then what a host of golden memories she has to look back on). Flying Past required a hobday and tie-back before he ever ran, and it looks as if wind problems are going to prevent him from achieving as much as he should (tongue-tied in the Confined, but faded to finish 28 lengths third). *A. Calder — Borders Bloodhounds (Doreen Calder).* 215 (OMa), 281 (M), 657 (R), 1080 (Cf).

FLYING PENNANT (IRE) .9-4.. 12 gr.g. Waajib — Flying Beckee (IRE) (Godswalk USA) up33u*0*. Small strong. Dam, half-sister to Spring Flight (*qv* '99 Annual). FLAT '95/01 r61 w3 (6-7f) p11. NH '99/01 r7 p2 (3rds). P-t-P '03 r5 w1 (3-finisher Confined) p1 (2 fences 3rd of 4); last, and fell/unseated 2. NH '04 (for I.R. Brown) r1 p0 (badly tailed off last in 2m3f Hdle: *drvn and t.o aft 5*). Ran only once as a two-year-old but on a further 60 occasions on the flat to '01, and enjoyed a degree of success but had not scored since July '00 until gifted a race at Cold Harbour last year. Only once better than last in four other Pointing completions and trounced like a non-stayer in '04. Regularly blinkered/visored latterly under Rules, and acquired cheekpieces when sent back over hurdles subsequently. *Miss S.J. Davies — Teme V.* 449 (L), 838 (L), 1064 (L), 1137 (L), 1263 (L).

FLYING RESPECT .—§.. 12 ch.m. Respect — Fortinas Flyer (Helluvafella) R. Lengthy. Dam, sister to Fort Alicia, and half-sister to Snapper (*qv* '01 Annual), was unplaced in 2 Hdles, and failed to finish in 2 Chases and 8 Points (pulled up 7) for Paul Reid to '98, 'has always been a complete waste of space'. NH '99 r4 p0; pulled up 1. P-t-P '03 r3 p0 (pulled up 2 and fell 1). A useless creature who has beaten only one rival in eight attempts, and hopefully vanquished for good after demolishing the wing of the sixth at Musselburgh. *P. Reid — Lauderdale.* 511 (OMam).

FOGGY HILL (IRE) ..8-11.. 8 ch.g. Un Desperado (FR) — McConnell Gold (Cidrax FR) 2. Small. Dam won 3m Hurdle in Ireland. IRISH P-t-P '02 r2 p0 (unseated 2). IRISH NH '02 r1 p0. P-t-P '03 r5 w1 (Maiden) p1 (2nd); last, and fell/unseated 2. Won a dire Maiden on firmish at Bonvilston last year, but badly let down by his jumping otherwise, and hardly looked the ideal candidate for Mark Whitehouse to debut on so it was a feather in his cap that he jumped round Ystradowen in one piece. Beaten 30 lengths however, and looks unlikely to upgrade successfully. *R.J. Rowsell — Ystrad Taf Fechan.* 1021 (M).

FOLLIDAY (FR) ..8-5§.. 12 b.g. Sharken (FR) — Oliday (FR) (Djarvis FR) f594f. Very tall half-brother to Lindsay (FR) (*qv*). IRISH NH FLAT '98/9 r3 p2. IRISH NH '98/9 and '01/3 (for A.L.T. Moore) r21 w3 (2m5f Hdle and 2 2m4f-2m6f Chses) p4; pulled up 3, fell/unseated 3. Bought Doncaster, Oct for 3000. Made virtually all when gaining three wins from four attempts in September/November '99 (all on easy surfaces), but fell when brought over to Aintree and was pulled up in three of five subsequent outings. Deplorable and reluctant and presumably suffering in Points, and wore cheekpieces or blinkers in the final three. Collapsed and died in the lorry park after falling in his Members. *The Go With The Flow Partnership (D. Ward) — Middleton (Chris Pimlott).* 107 (O), 298 (Cf), 389 (Cf), 478 (Cf), 769 (M).

FOLLY ROAD (IRE) .10-3§.. 15 b.g. Mister Lord (USA) — Lady Can (Cantab) u8. Tall rangy half-brother to Course-I-Can. IRISH P-t-P '96 r3 w1 (6yo Maiden) p2. IRISH NH FLAT '96 r1 p0. IRISH NH '96/7 r7 w2 (2m4f Hdle and 3m Ch) p0. NH '98/03 r41 w5 (3m-3m4110y Chses) p10 (5 2nds); pulled up 5, on floor 3. HUNT CH '03 r3 p1 (2nd); 8th, and last. NH '04 (for D.L. Williams) r1 p0 (last of 8 in 3m5f Ch: *ld til hdd & mist 16, sn wknd, t.o*). A dour stayer at best, and won eight races to March '02, but can be careless, and the owner broke her jaw when the partnership was severed at Larkhill. Needs mud and a long trip to be most effective, but only likely to deteriorate further if returning in '05.

Blinkered once in '00, and has been tried in a visor and cheekpieces since. *Miss L. Horner — Hurworth (Sarah Horner-Harker).* 9 (C).

FOR A PAGAN SONG ..8-3.. 7 b.g. Terimon — Rare Deal (Pitpan) p3. Half-brother to Ardeal (dam of Runningwiththemoon (*qv*), Mindbender and Pop Star. Dam, half-sister Slice Ofthe Action (*qv* '96 Annual). Tailed off and pulled up on his debut, but although 30 lengths behind the winner only missed second by half a length and will probably improve with experience. Like Runningwiththemoon is named after books by Jonny Bealby (motorbikes and heart aches), probably to be found in your local thrift shop for under a pound. *Mrs J. Bealby — Belvoir (Antonia Bealby).* 945 (OMa), 1403 (2m4fOMa).

FORCE TEN ..7-10.. 8 b.g. Regal Embers (IRE) — Whenthewindblows (Abwah) p6p5. Compact well-made trainer-bred half-brother to Wind On The Common (*qv*). P-t-P '03 r3 p1 (3rd); and pulled up 2. Very headstrong and unable to get the trip as a result to date, but it is worth bearing in mind that mum took 24 attempts to get off the mark, and his sibling 13. Apt to get in a muck sweat in the preliminaries and has two handlers, and needs to learn to relax, but the basic speed is there in abundance. *Mrs A. Beavan — N. Ledbury (Tim Stephenson).* 410 (2m4fCfMa), 725 (OMa), 837 (OMa), 983 (2m5fOMa).

FOREIGN FIELD (FR) ..7-12.. 6 b.g. Sleeping Car (FR) — Dame Laurel (FR) (Rose Laurel) 3p. Strong workmanlike. Bought Doncaster, May for 17,000. Faded badly in the closing stages when 32 lengths last of three on his debut, but tailed off and pulled up three out when tried over three furlongs shorter next time. Needs to prove he gets the trip. *K.W. & Mrs S.J. Biggins — Berkeley (Tracey Barfoot-Saunt).* 723 (OMa), 982 (2m5fOMa).

FOREST FORTRESS (IRE) .9-0.. 8 b.m. Air Display (USA) — Ferric Fortress (General Ironside) 4p1. Small neat. Dam, half-sister to Forest Moss (*qv* '01 Annual), won mares Maiden in Ireland. P-t-P '02/3 r10 p2 (2nds, of 3 once); 6th of 7, fell/unseated 4, ran out 1 and pulled up 2. Jumps and hangs right-handed, but benefited from the fitting of an off-side pricker when winning a weak mares Maiden on firmish at Black Forest Lodge where both horse and rider showed grim determination. Error-proneand lacks scope, and may have already reached the zenith of her powers. Wears a cross-noseband. *J.H. Young — New Forest.* 121 (OMa), 185 (CMam), 416 (CMam).

FOREST GUNNER ..11-7.. 11 ch.g. Gunner B — Gouly Duff (Party Mink) 315. Sturdy half-brother to Another Scally, Noble Question and Freddie Fox. Dam was 2nd in 4 Points (lame final). NH FLAT '99 r2 p0. NH '01/2 r12 w5 (3 2m4f-2m7f Hdles and 2 2m5f-2m6f Chses) p5. NH '04 r1 p0 (5th in 3m Ch: *prom, blun 10 & 13, wknd app 3 out*). A game front-runner and a good jumper who has never failed to finish, and put his sterling qualities to the maximum use when capturing the £19,430 Aintree Foxhunters under a fine ride from Carrie Ford (who having not long previously produced baby Hannah decided to hang up her boots soon after this fabulous career highlight; as long ago as 1991 she was being described as 'arguably the best girl rider in her area'). Had previously given a pleasing display when a modest third in a hot Hunter Chase at Fontwell, but Aintree had been the target for a very long time, and never looked like missing the bulls-eye as having taken up the running at the eighth he was always galloping too strongly for his rivals in a 25-runner contest. Prefers good or softish ground, and has always been an excellent mount for an amateur, but lacked his usual fluency for a professional in a valuable Perth Chase on final start. His training also deserves high praise, as he has only been seen 16 times in his life and missed '00 and '03. The last horse to complete the Aintree double was Spartan Missile in 1979, but Richard Ford rode Rolling Ball to victory in 1996, and he knows exactly what it takes, so perhaps Forest Gunner can emulate the late John Thorne's legend. *J. Gilsenan — Cheshire Forest (Richard Ford).* 280 (3m2f110yH), 732 (2m5f110yH).

FOREST JUMP (IRE) ..9-4.. 11 ch.g. Accordion — Mandy's Last (Krayyan) 4uup. Strong-topped brother to Irish NH flat and Hurdling winner, Wild Romance, and to jumping winner, Shepherds Rest (IRE), and to NH flat and Hurdles winner, Del Piero (IRE). NH FLAT '98/9 r3 p2 (3rds). NH '99/02 (for J.A.B. Old, and P.F. Nicholls) r13 w3 (2m4f Hdle and 2 2m6f -3m Chses) p5; pulled up 4. A triple winner in mud to January '01, but a sketchy jumper with a tendency to idle, and was badly out of sorts latterly under Rules (pulled up in his final three; wore blinkers on four occasions). Pulled up with a broken leg at Charlton Horethorne. The rider is less than competent and all too liable to topple off at present. Mr & Mrs P. Lee — Blackmore & Sparkford V. (Alan Tizzard). 31 (Cnr), 175 (Cnr), 319 (O), 352 (O).

FOREST RUN FOREST ..—§.. 13 b.g. Supreme Leader — Laurello (Bargello) pp. Compact half-brother to Ifallelsefails, to Irish NH flat and jumping winner, Chattering, to jumping winner, Easton Gale, to NH flat and Hurdles winners, My Baton and Valerio, and to the unraced dam of smart NH flat and Hurdles performer, Marello. IRISH P-t-P '99 r5 w1 (7yo&up Maiden) p0; pulled up 2, fell/unseated 2. IRISH NH FLAT '97 r2 p1 (3rd). IRISH NH '97/8 r8 p0. NH '99/02 r22 w3 (2m3f110y-2m4f110y Hdles) p5 (2 2nds); pulled up 1. P-t-P '03 r2 p0 (last and pulled up 1). A fair if somewhat inconsistent performer in mud over hurdles to '01, but never as good over fences, and has lost the plot completely since switching to Points. Wears blinkers. *Mrs S.A. Sansom — Mid Surrey F. (Ann Blaker).* 608 (L), 781 (L).

FORGLORI .8-10§§.. 10 b.g. Formidable (USA) — Glorietta (USA) (Shadeed USA) pp5p. Compact well-made brother to an Irish flat winner. FLAT '98/9 r6 p0. P-t-P '02 (for Mrs P. Strawbridge) r7 p1 (3rd of 4); pulled up 4, and refused 2. Set the pattern for the rest of his career when apt to dwell when racing from stalls, and is always looking for an opportunity to stop over fences. Beaten a minimum of 38 lengths but constantly diving violently left, and should be given the boot. *Mrs L.J. Herrod — Cotley (Gordon Herrod).* 494 (OMa), 580 (OMa), 884 (OMa), 1247 (M).

FORNAUGHT ALLIANCE (IRE) .9-7§§.. 12 br.g. Zaffaran (USA) — Carrick Shannon (Green Shoon) 4532. Workmanlike brother to Hurdles winner, Shannon Shoon (IRE), and to Irish Pointing winner, Swordlestown. Dam, half-sister to Renagown (*qv* '94 Annual). IRISH NH FLAT '98/9 r4 p1 (3rd). IRISH NH '98/00 r20 p10. IRISH NH '00/2 r16 w3 (3m3f110y Hdle and 2 2m5f-2m6f Chses) p4 (3 2nds); refused 1. P-t-P/HUNT CH '03 (for Mr P. Lancaster (Yarm Skip Alliance) r8 w1 (Open) p3 (2 3rds, inc Hunt Ch; and 2nd in Hunt Ch); 4th, 7th, and pulled up 2. A patent safety (brought down once, and refused at a fence on the cross country course at Cheltenham) and made an ideal schoolmaster, but very much looking after number one, and refuses to exert himself. Gained his last two wins at Sedgefield, but beaten a minimum of 15 lengths in '04, and can be safely ignored. Normally wears blinkers, visored twice in '01, and has been tried in cheekpieces. *J.S.E. Turner — Sir W.W. Wynn's.* 228 (Cf), 713 (Cf), 852 (Cf), 1144 (Cf).

FORT APACHE (IRE) ..7-13.. 10 b.g. Barry's Run (IRE) — Jonathan's Rose (IRE) (Law Society USA) f45p. IRISH FLAT '98/01 r26 p2 (2nds). IRISH NH '99/01 (for L. Comer) r14 p2 (3rds). Placed four times in Ireland (often blinkered there), and beaten between one and three lengths when second twice at up to two miles on the flat, but tailed off last once in his two Hurdling thirds. A three year absence has quashed even these faint glimmerings of ability, and was hopelessly tailed off with only Tiger Rag behind him when completing in Welsh Maidens. *P. Riddick — Gelligaer F.* 452 (R), 1239 (OMa), 1488 (OMa), 1534 (OMa).

FORT GLENDENNON ..—.. 6 b.g. Environment Friend — Northern Swinger (Northern State USA) pp. Workmanlike owner-bred. Given a blatant school on his debut (connections should have received a rap round the knuckles), and did not appear to be a great deal busier next time. Looks a fair type, and could be of interest once he receives the orders of anchors aweigh. *P.G. Harvey — Albrighton (Caroline Robinson).* 533 (2m4fCfMa), 754 (OMa).

FORTYKIX ..—.. 13 br.g. Arctic Lord — Bonne Fille (Bonne Noel) p. Lengthy workmanlike dipped brother to Captain George, and half-brother to Tattlejack (IRE). Tailed off by halfway and pulled up after two miles at Eaton Hall. Has evidently been spending his former life in other equine arenas. *D. Douglas — Cheshire.* 710 (Mah).

FORTY SHAKES (IRE) ..9-0.. 6 ch.g. Moonax (IRE) — Forty Quid (IRE) (Exhibitioner) 2pp. Half-brother to Irish Pointing winner, Lord Rockfield. IRISH P-t-P '03 r2 p0 (pulled up 1 and slipped up 1). Would have beaten the only other finisher at Whitwell-on-the-Hill had he not blundered at the final fence and come to a standstill when three lengths ahead (rallying after the last but could not get there), but unable to get round in his four other Points including when sent off at short odds in the two latest. It could only be an advantage to re-unite him with Lee Bates. *Miss M.D. Myco — S. Durham.* 775 (CfMa), 1291 (OMa), 1474 (2m4fOMa).

FORTYSIXALLOUT (IRE) .9-10.. 13 b.g. Salt Dome (USA) — Havana Moon (Ela-Mana-Mou) p4. Good-topped half-brother to Hurdles winner, Dispol Rock (IRE). Dam, half-sister to Duncan (*qv* '97 Annual), won 2 Irish flat, 7-8f. FLAT '94 r3 p0 (inc blinkered and pulled up in Sell). NH '98/9 r12 p1 (2nd); pulled up 1, fell 1. P-t-P '02/3 r8 w1 (Maiden) p3 (2nds, beaten ½*l* once); pulled up 2, and fell/unseated 2. Pretty hopeless under Rules, but gained a deserved success when well handled by Ollie Jackson at Buckfastleigh last year, and has not been disgraced in Restricteds since. Does best when held up, and has faded when ridden more aggressively, but his main problem is his inability to race regularly. Wears a cross-noseband. *Miss D. Green & Mrs O. Jackson — Devon & Somerset (Ollie Jackson).* 198 (R), 824 (R).

FOSSY BEAR ..10-3.. 13 br.m. Lir — Full Spirit (Bay Spirit) 13pp. Small neat. Dam, sister to Full Alirt (*qv* '02 Annual), only finished in one of 16 races (a Hurdle; competed in 14 Points) for the Youngs ('a useless pest, like mother'). P-t-P/HUNT CH '97/03 r31 w10 (inc Mixed Open and 2 Ladies) p4 (2nds, beaten head once, and neck once, and of 3 once); pulled up 7, and on floor 5. Adroitly placed to farm some weak races since '02, but wears bandages and frequent exposure to sound surfaces appears to be taking its toll now. Reported to be in season when favourite and pulled up at Great Trethew, and never going in a hot race when next appearing six weeks later. Stays well but often outpaced in steadily run races, and is ideally suited by a course with a stiff finish. Wears a Pelham. *B.R.J. Young, Miss S. Young & Mrs K. Rogers — E. Cornwall (Sue Young).* 305 (M), 569 (MO), 703 (MO), 1379 (MO).

FOSTON SECOND (IRE) ..9-8.. 8 ch.m. Lycius (USA) — Gentle Guest (IRE) (Be My Guest USA) 4331. Small compact half-sister to flat winners Freedom Chance (IRE) and Engstrum (IRE). FLAT '99/02 r11 p2 (beaten neck once). NH '01/2 r3 p1 (3rd). P-t-P '03 r3 p0 (pulled up 2 and fell 1). Often tailed off on the flat and over hurdles, but has appreciated the drop to Maidens, and won a match on firm at Mounsey Hill Gate after her rival missed a marker after a circuit. Not yet fluent, and hung badly on the run-in when third at Bratton Down, and needs to improve further for Restricteds. Tends to sweat freely. *M. & Mrs S. Beck — Devon & Somerset (Malcolm Beck).* 688 (2m4fOMa), 962 (OMa), 1380 (OMa), 1467 (OMa).

FOU DOUX (FR) ..9-8.. 9 b.g. Le Grillon II (FR) — Folie Douce (FR) (Fast FR) 6f6. Leggy compact half-brother to a French flat winner. FRENCH FLAT '00 r1 w1 (14f). FRENCH NH '99/00 r5 w1 (2m1f Hdle) p3 (2nds). FLAT '03 r1 p0. NH '02/3 (for D.G. Bridgwater, and P.W. Hiatt) r8 p1 (3rd); pulled up 4, unseated 1. Bought Ascot, Jul for 1190. A provinces horse in France and scored on the flat at Royan-la Palmyre and over Hurdles in soft at Pau, but last successful over hurdles in May '00 and has never scored since leaving his native land (where he was also short-headed twice). Never beaten less than 20 lengths in this country (including when third in a Selling Hurdle), and was pulled up twice and unseated in Chases. Tried with headgear, cheekpieces and a tongue-tie. Faced impossible tasks in hot Opens in '04, but there is nothing to suggest he would get the trip even in a much lower grade. *Miss S. Bond, P. Phillips & Mrs J. Moore — Axe V.H. (Paul Phillips).* 115 (MO), 196 (O), 1379 (MO).

FOUNTAIN STREET (IRE) .—§.. 12 b.g. Sharp Charter — Maylands (Windjammer USA) pppp. Good-topped. IRISH NH FLAT '98 r1 p0 (remote last). P-t-P '99/00 and '02/3 r21 w2 (Maiden and Restricted) p5 (3 2nds, last once); 4th of 5, pulled up 8, fell/unseated 3, ran out 1 and carried out 1. Suited by an easy three miles on a sound surface, and rated 10-1 after scoring twice with nothing in hand under Richard Burton to '02, but a regular non-finisher, and normally surrenders without a struggle. Sometimes unruly in the preliminaries, and has been mounted on course and taken down early. Wears a cross-noseband, and tried in cheekpieces twice in '03. *Mrs T.R. Kinsey — Cheshire Forest.* 377 (3m1fH), 630 (2m4fH), 749 (Cf), 1430 (I).

FOUR IN HAND ..9-7.. 7 b.m. Supreme Leader — Relkissimo (Relkino) p3uu. Tall half-sister to Tyke Gale (IRE). Bought Doncaster, Aug '02 for 3300. Backed from tens to 4-1 when three-and-a-half lengths third over 2m4f at Great Trethew, where she blundered badly at the last when trying to catch the winner but was demoted to third on the run-in after failing to recover, but got rid of Darren Edwards in her next two attempts (favourite once). If she ever works out how to jumps properly she can probably win races. *Mrs K.M. Sanderson — Tiverton.* 195 (CfMa), 307 (2m4fOMa), 883 (OMa), 1381 (OMa).

FOUR OF A KIND ..9-7.. 7 b.g. Most Welcome — Pegs (Mandrake Major) p2p. Strong compact. Dam, sister to Insiouxbordinate (*qv* '99 Annual). FLAT '02 r2 p0. NH FLAT '02 r3 p0. P-t-P '03 r4 p2 (2nds); and pulled up 2. Runner-up in three Maidens, including two over 2m4f, and would not be winning out of turn, but becoming expensive to follow, and may have suffered a setback at Kilworthy. Needs a race to get fit. *P.D. Rogers — Dartmoor (Tony & Pauline Geering).* 195 (CfMa), 327 (OMa), 568 (CfMa).

FOUR OPINIONS ..9-0.. 9 b.g. Cruise Missile — Stockton Slave (Bivouac) 6ffuf. Tall workmanlike brother to Yanto, and half-brother to Stockton Wolf and Slave's Adventure. Dam, sister or half-sister to 3 Pointers, including Cool Distinction (*qv* '93 Annual), won 8 Points (inc an Open) and placed 7 ('game and consistent ...'). P-t-P '03 r4 p0 (disqualified from 2nd once — not weigh-in); 8th, and unseated 2. A great big boat of an animal with room on his back for several jockeys, and could easily step over Pointing fences, but inordinately clumsy, and does not appear to learn from his mistakes. Has the ability to win a Maiden, and was a well-backed favourite and in command when toppling five-out at Brampton Bryan, but his kamikaze ways have floored three different pilots, and perhaps connections may wish to invest in a pair of spectacles for him. *Four Opinions Partnership (Ms C. Scott) — Radnor & W. Herefords (Clive Davies).* 668 (OMa), 981 (OMa), 1115 (OMa), 1232 (OMa), 1341 (OMa).

FOURS ARE WILD (IRE) ..10-0.. 12 ch.g. Montelimar (USA) — Lousion (Lucifer USA) 2fpu. Lengthy quite attractive. Dam won NH flat and 2m Chase in Ireland and is half-sister to Sir Lucky, *qv* '93 Annual). IRISH P-t-P '98/9 r4 w1 (6yo&up Maiden) p2; and brought down. IRISH NH FLAT '98 r1 p0. IRISH NH '99 r1 p0. NH '99/02 r12 w2 (2m4f110y Chses) p1 (2nd); pulled up 4, unseated 1. P-t-P '03 r3 p1 (3rd of 4); unseated and pulled up. Completed a double over fences in November '99, but lucky in the latter, and very lightly raced without success since. Often races keenly, but lacks any semblance of fluency, and has not been able to instill Jonathan Trevor-Roper with any confidence. Suited by a sound surface, but gives the impression that the trip might be beyond him in Points. *Mr & Mrs C. Dixey — Grafton (Andy Martin).* 582 (M), 924 (O), 1073 (O), 1447 (O).

FOURSPICE ALLSPICE (IRE) ..9-5.. 7 b.m. Fourstars Allstar (USA) — A'Dhahirah (Beldale Flutter USA) 441. Rangy light-bodied half-sister to Orswellthatenswell, to NH flat and flat winner, Row Ree, and to

2 winners in Sweden. IR30,000 3yo. NH FLAT '02 r3 p0. NH '02/3 (for J.W. Mullins, and B.R. Millman) r4 p0; pulled up 1, unseated 1. Beaten 22 lengths plus over Hurdles including a Seller, but performed adequately in her first two Maidens, and was left to win a youngsters Maiden at Charlton Horethorne (firm ground) after Lady Widd had unseated at the last when seemingly going better. Will probably have to progress further for Restricteds. *The J. Miller's Partnership (Mrs J.M. Miller) — Portman (Jessica Miller).* 142 (OMa), 264 (CfMa), 353 (OMa).

FOXY ROYALE ..9-0.. 9 b.g. Bold Fox — Celtic Royale (Celtic Cone) u4f. Workmanlike brother to Pendragon. Dam is half-sister to Tedstone Fox (*qv*), who is by Bold Fox. NH '01 r2 p0. P-t-P '02 r3 w1 (2m4f Maiden) p0; pulled up 1 and fell 1. Survived mistakes at the last two fences when successful in holding ground at Garnons on his Pointing debut, but not so lucky since, and not certain to have survived a bad spill at Hereford. *Mrs A. Price — Teme V.* 405 (Inr), 450 (R), 628 (2m3fH).

FRANCO (IRE) ..10-11.. 7 b.g. Rashar (USA) — Market Thyne (IRE) (Good Thyne USA) 11R21. Half-brother to Irish Chasing winner, Thyneforafryup. IRISH NH FLAT '02 r3 p0. IRISH NH '02/3 (for C.F. Swan) r5 p0; pulled up 1. Bought Doncaster, May for 5000. Only once showed any signs of ability for Charlie Swan in Ireland, when 13 lengths fourth of 30 in a Hurdle, but a useful and progressive Pointer in the new yard. Followed an impressive double in minor company with his only blip, when running out at the 14th in the lead at Dingley (1-2), but lost nothing in defeat when chasing home Nautical Lad in an Open. Ended his season on a high with a third victory at Garthorpe when he captured the Melton Novices without too much fuss and equalled the course record for three miles in the process, and will have to be seriously regarded if switched to Hunter Chases in '05. His stable created quite an impact in '04, and seem to be going places. *D. Brooks, A. Haley & A. Tharatt — Grafton (Anna Brooks).* 385 (OMa), 684 (R), 888 (O), 1057 (O), 1400 (CN).

FRANCO LADY (IRE) .9-2.. 12 ch.m. Lanfranco — Cpv Lady (Le Moss) p2f1. Small half-sister to Irish Pointing winner, Never Heard. IRISH P-t-P '98 r4 p0 (pulled up 3 and brought down 1). IRISH NH FLAT '98 r2 p0. IRISH NH '98 r2 p0. P-t-P '99 and '02/3 r8 p3 (2nds, of 3 once); last pair 2, pulled up 2 and refused 1. Finally gained a deserved success when justifying favouritism in much the slowest time of the day at Chaddesley, but victory came at a price on the firm ground, and with a previous history of leg problems seems most unlikely to reappear. *A.J. Godfrey — N. Hereford (Emma James).* 1020 (OMa), 1231 (OMam), 1395 (OMa), 1532 (OMa).

FRANK BYRNE ..9-12.. 13 b.g. Rakaposhi King — Polarita (Arctic Kanda) 6p2f2233231. Narrow unfurnished half-brother to Wind Spirit and Birchall Boy. Dam, half-sister to Amber Marsh (*qv* '94 Annual), won 2 2m2f-3m2f Hdles, inc a Sell. NH FLAT '97/8 r2 p1 (2nd). NH '98/01 r16 w1 (2m4f Ch) p5 (4 3rds); pulled up 3. P-t-P '02/3 r13 w6 (inc Ladies) p2 (3rd of 4 once); fell/unseated 3. A revelation since joining the current yard, and has been particularly effective with its' inexperienced riders, but sometimes the victim of bad mistakes, and largely frustrating in '04. Retired after making the most of a straightforward opportunity at Mounsey Hill Gate. *Mrs H.M. Goody — Blackmore & Sparkford V. (John Dufosee).* 32 (Cnr), 117 (C), 234 (L), 262 (L), 351 (L), 470 (L), 641 (L), 1004 (L), 1210 (L), 1368 (L), 1462 (L).

FRANKLY FEAR ..9-2.. 12 b.g. Lyphento (USA) — Frankly New (New Member) 22u76. Workmanlike lengthy half-brother to Sula Queen. Dam, half-sister to 5 Pointers, including Kings Bill (*qv* '93 Annual), failed to finish in 3 Points. Great-grandam, April Queen, won 6 Points and Liverpool Foxhunters. P-t-P/HUNT CH '99/00 and '02/3 (for Mrs G.M. Brake) r17 w1 (Maiden) p6 (5 3rds, of 4 once, and inc Hunt Ch; and 2nd of 3); pulled up 4, and fell/unseated 2. Took over seven minutes when scoring on his first completion at Great Trethew in '00, but surprisingly undone by a lack of stamina since, and went under by the narrowest of margins when he last made the frame at Black Forest Lodge. Makes the odd mistake, but a more reliable conveyance than what Nick Heath was used to in '03. Wears a cross-noseband and a tongue-strap. *Mr & Mrs N. Heath — Mrs S. Brigden — Blackmore & Sparkford V. (Nick Heath).* 14 (R), 65 (Rnr), 139 (R), 354 (R), 636 (Rnr).

FREDDIE MUCK ..10-1.. 15 b.g. Idiot's Delight — Muckertoo (Sagaro) p. Small compact half-brother to Frankie Muck, and to Hurdles winners, Madam Muck (also won Chasing) and Flora Muck. Dam, sister to Master Muck (*qv* '96 Annual), and half-sister to smart staying Hurdler Mrs Muck. NH FLAT '94 r3 p2. NH '94/01 r47 w9 (5 2m4f-3m Hdles, and 4 3m1f110y-3m2f Chses) p17 (10 2nds); pulled up 3, unseated 1. P-t-P '03 r3 w1 (Confined) p0; last and pulled up 1. Scoring for the first time since '00 when providing Ben Mounsey-Heysham with his first winner at Tranwell last year, but in semi-retirement then, and seems to have bought the villa in Spain now. His replacement Spring Double came from the same source, and did connections proud in '04. Blinkered latterly under Rules. *Mrs P.A. Mounsey-Heysham — Tynedale.* 211 (C).

FREE ..10-7.. 10 ch.g. Gone West (USA) — Bemissed (USA) (Nijinsky CAN) 321p1. Neat half-brother to 5 flat winners (2 in USA) inc Jet Ski Lady (Oaks), Kings of Europe and Dismissed. Dam very smart at 8½-9f in USA (won 5 and $353,907). FLAT '97/01 r24 w2 (14-16f) p6. NH '98/02 r25 w7 (3 2m-3m1f110y Hdles and 4 2m4f110y-3m2f Chses) p9 (4 2nds). P-t-P '03 r7 w2 (Ladies) p2

(2nds, of 3 once); unseated 2 and slipped up 1. Largely disappointing in the sphere that he was bred to excel in, but has made a highly successful jumper, and took his score over obstacles into double figures when typically making most at Garthorpe. Not enamoured by the underfoot conditions when pulled up at Huntingdon next time, but galloped the opposition into the ground at Kingston Blount, and looks sure to register further wins. A bold jumper on fast ground, and far more reliable than he used to be. Blinkered and visored on two occasions apiece, but wears cheekpieces now. *Mrs P.J. Hutchinson — Fernie (Patrick Hutchinson).* 558 (L), 785 (L), 1058 (L), 1360 (3mH), 1516 (L).

FREEDOM FIGHTER ..10-6.. 14 b.g. Fearless Action (USA) — Zuleika Hill (Yellow River) 4124114314. Strong workmanlike owner-bred. Dam ran badly in Points at 5 in '78. P-t-P/HUNT CH '98/03 r55 w6 (inc 3m Hunt Ch) p15 (8 3rds, last once; and inc 5 Hunt Chses); failed to finish 21 (carried out 1, fell/unseated 3). Previously thoroughly inconsistent, and failed to score at all in '03, but did nothing wrong when conditions were to his liking this year, and took his winning tally into double figures when ploughing through the mud at Towcester. Tends to sweat profusely and always has that straight out of the field look, but races with tremendous enthusiasm, and is suited by a stiff uphill finish. A credit to connections, and finally gained some fluency in '04, though Andy Martin's Mollington vendetta with James Owen was most unseemly and he was rightly done for improper riding. *Mrs R. Gasson — Farmers Bloodhounds.* 100 (O), 168 (C), 292 (MO), 437 (3m1fH), 583 (Cf), 758 (O), 997 (O), 1171 (3m2f110yH), 1357 (3m1fH), 1471 (O).

PLATE 48 634 Avon Vale Mens Open: Daryl Jacob gets a great leap from Free Gift, 1st, at the first ditch ahead of Porlock Hill (Neil Harris), 3rd, and Lord Of The Mist (Nick Williams), 2nd
PHOTO: Tim Holt

FREE GIFT .10-10.. 7 b.g. Presenting — Gladtogetit (Green Shoon) 1111111. Workmanlike half-brother to Black A Brook (*qv*). 18,000 4yo. NH FLAT '03 (for R.H. Alner) r2 p0. Pulled too hard when tailed off in bumpers, but took to Pointing like a duck to water, and after six decisive wins he was sent to Folkestone for a 2m5f Novices Hunter Chase and gave a very bold display of jumping to make virtually all the running in impressive fashion. Thoroughly genuine, a strong finisher, and goes extremely well for Daryl Jacob (who had not partnered a winner between the flags until their association began), but sound surfaces are certainly preferable for him although he has managed to score on dead ground. Generally faced quite easy tasks, but the way in which he disposed of Lord Of The Mist (five victories in '04) in an Open suggests that a 'switch' back to Robert Alner's yard would be all he needed to extend his sequence under Rules. Thoroughly likeable. *T. Chadney, D. Guyer, Miss M.V. Howard & Mrs P. Tozer — Portman (Sally Alner).* 12 (OMa), 139 (R), 458 (I), 634 (O), 862 (Cnr), 1213 (Cnr), 1439 (2m5fH).

FREESTYLER (IRE) ..—§§.. 13 b/br.g. Phardante (FR) — Financial Burden (Mandalus) r. Tall workmanlike brother to Will Hill (IRE). IRISH P-t-P '97 and '99 r13 w1 (7yo Maiden) p3; pulled up

5, unseated, ran out 2 and refused 1. IRISH NH FLAT '97/8 r4 p0. IRISH NH '98/9 r5 p0. NH '01 r2 p0; pulled up 1. P-t-P/HUNT CH '00 and '02/3 r14 w2 (Club Restricted and Confined) p3 (2 3rds; and 3 fences last of 2 after rejoining once); last 2, pulled up 3, refused 2, ran out 1 and unseated 1. Has won three minor races, and rated 10-4 at his best, but has always been decidedly quirky, and refused for the third consecutive time at Garnons. Has broken blood vessels in the past, but the time for excuses is long gone, and will surely not be seen in public again. Wears a tongue-strap, and has been tried in headgear. *A. Shaw — Cheshire (Gary Hanmer).* 615 (O).

FREEWAY .8-11.. 10 ch.g. Hubbly Bubbly (USA) — Fragrant Path (Warpath) 53. Tall strong-topped. Dam, half-sister to Fragrant Fellow (*qv* '97 Annual), pulled up in a Maiden. P-t-P '02/3 r6 p1 (3rd of 4); last pair 4, and pulled up 1. Can be relied upon to complete, but very much in his own time, and only once beaten less than 30 lengths. Wears over-reach boots. *Mrs V. Jackson — Morpeth.* 658 (OMa), 1082 (OMa).

FRENCH CEDAR ..10-3.. 9 b.g. Jupiter Island — Another Rumour (The Parson) 3f2R. Very tall half-brother to Irish jumping winner, Brown Paddy. Dam was twice placed in Irish Points but failed to finish five of six in similar in England. NH FLAT '01 r1 p0. NH '02 p0; pulled up 1. IRISH NH '02/3 (for Mrs J. Harrington) r11 w1 (2m4f Ch) p1 (3rd); pulled up 1. Won a Down Royal Chase in '03, and gave some fair displays in the new yard, but not an easy ride for Will Ramsay, and fell at the 15th when leading once and ran out at the penultimate when second and beaten once. Connections went home with the Berwickshire Members Trophy as usual in '04, and from the way French Cedar finished a good third half an hour later he would be a very worthy candidate for that contest if asked to do the honours. *Major General C.A. Ramsay — Berwicks.* 282 (Cf), 426 (Cf), 917 (O), 1079 (O).

FRENCH CHOCOLATE ..—§.. 8 ch.m. Chocolat De Meguro (USA) — Slim View (Slim Jim) ppp. Owner-bred half-sister to Rocky Fountain (*qv*). P-t-P '03 r3 p0 (pulled up 3). Displayed an instant dislike for Pointing in '03, and judging by her appalling efforts this year, has not had a change of mind. An erratic and reluctant jumper, and threw a tantrum in the paddock when blinkers were applied at Alnwick. *J.J. Dixon — Cumberland F. (Jackie Williamson).* 74 (OMa), 216 (OMa), 761 (M).

FRENCH GUEST ..—.. 6 ch.g. Most Welcome — Laleston (Junius USA) fp. Small sturdy half-brother to five 5f winners including Tony The Tap and First Footing. Dam won two 5f races. FLAT '01/2 r4 p1 (3rd). NH '03 (for P.J. Hobbs) r5 p0; pulled up 1, left 1. Bought Doncaster, May for 1800. A reluctant individual who raced chiefly in Sellers over Hurdles, and was left once, and there is so far no sign of him being any perkier in Points. His jumping is not good at present. *P.D. Rogers — Dartmoor (Tony & Pauline Geering).* 909 (2m4fOMa), 1353 (OMa).

FRENCH VENTURE ..9-5.. 8 b.g. Saddlers' Hall (IRE) — Tafila (Adonijah) u2. Brother to flat winner, Quitte La France, and half-brother to flat winners Include Me Out, Pleasant Dreams, and to French flat winner, Udina. Dam won 3 flat, 8-10f. Despite his pedigree was never sighted on the flat, and after unseating early in his debut Point he again jumped without fluency at Charm Park, where he led on the bridle after two out and looked in command at the last but could not withstand the whirling late finish of Nought To Ninety. Seems to need straightening out, but it would be no surprise to see him scoring with a more accurate round. *Mrs J. Dwyer — Middleton (Roger Marley).* 776 (CfMa), 960 (OMa).

FRERE DU CURE .—.. 7 ch.g. Nicholas Bill — Granny Pray On (Proverb) pp. Light-framed owner-bred half-brother to Le Cure (*qv*). Looked backward when making little show in Maidens, and gave the impression he needs more time. *P.G. Bevins — Avon V.* 87 (OMa), 493 (OMa).

FRIARS ISLAND (IRE) ..—.. 13 ch.g. Hozay (USA) — Singing Deer (Whistling Deer) pp1. Compact good-topped. IRISH P-t-P '97/00 r30 w5 (inc Winners of 2 on technicality, and 2 Opens) p13; pulled up 5 and fell 1. P-t-P '03 r1 p0 (pulled up). Won five races in mud in Ireland to '99 but disappeared for three years prior to '03, and appears to have broken blood vessels in all but his Barbury walkover since. Too fat to do himself justice in any case. *Major W.G. Crosbie-Dawson — Tedworth.* 138 (C), 972 (Cf), 1062 (M).

FRIAR WADDON ..10-6.. 12 b.g. Pablond — Looking Swell (Simbir) 23131141. Sturdy compact half-brother to Scott Elliott and Collier. NH '01 r2 p0 (6th in 2m6f Hdle, and pulled up in 3m2f110y Ch). P-t-P/HUNT CH '99/03 r25 w4 (inc Mixed Open) p8 (5 3rds, of 4 twice, and inc 2 Hunt Chses); pulled up 4, and fell/unseated 5. Scored an annual success in all previous campaigns barring F&M year, but never prolific and lost his confidence following two falls within the space of a month last year. Often lacks fluency, but jumped better than usual in '04, and registered his third course win when successful at Didmarton. Had to show plenty of courage in two of his three subsequent victories, which were hard-fought affairs. Has scored in soft but most effective on a lively surface over an easy three miles, and granted such conditions can move his tally into double figures. Wears a cross-noseband. *P.J. Clarke — Devon & Somerset (Keith Cumings).* 144 (Cf), 277 (O), 366 (MO), 576 (O), 863 (MO), 1180 (M), 1379 (MO), 1510 (O).

FRIENDLY GIRL (IRE) ..—.. 6 b.m. King's Ride — Royal Patrol (IRE) (Phardante FR) p. Lengthy. Sold Doncaster, May for 3500. Pulled up at halfway at Buckfastleigh. *N.J. Hawke — Seavington.* 494 (OMa).

FRILEUX ROYAL (FR) ..10-5§§.. 12 br.g. Sarpedon (FR) — La Frileuse (FR) (El Toro FR) 1rr. Compact well-made. FRENCH FLAT r1 p0. FRENCH NH '99 r12 w3 (2m6f-3m Chses) p1 (2nd). CZECH NH '01 r1 p0. NH '00/2 r19 w1 (3m2f110y Hdle) p3 (inc 2nd in Ch); pulled up 4, refused 4, and unseated 1. P-t-P '03 r4 w1 (Club) p2 (2nds); and pulled up 1. NH '03 r1 p0 (refused). Loves to bowl along at the head of affairs, and has not seen a rival in two wins at Dingley, but incredibly moody and will readily dig his toes in if unable to dominate. All of his best form is on right-handed tracks, but supporting him involves a high-risk strategy. Tried in headgear thrice in '01. *S.G.B. Morrison — Fernie (Nicola Pollock).* 885 (M), 1213 (Cnr), 1396 (C).

FROGHOLE FLYER ..—.. 6 ch.g. Presenting — Peptic Lady (IRE) (Royal Fountain) p. Big strong. Dam pulled up in Restricteds for David Silk. Unruly in the paddock and made several novicey jumps when settled well off the pace on his May debut, and gave the impression of being a character. *Prof. D.B.A. Silk, G.M. Addiscott & I.G. Burbridge — Kent & Surrey Bloodhounds (Emma Leppard).* 1273 (OMa).

FROGSMARSH ..—§.. 9 b.m. Mioko (FR) — Francolina (Balinger) rpp. Small neat owner-bred sister to Franko. Dam, half-sister to 3 Pointers, won 2m4f Maiden on her only completion from 4 attempts (approached the final fence in a remote 4th only to see the 3 leaders fall independently!) for the Williams'. Granddam, French Berry, won Open and 3m Nov Ch. P-t-P '02/3 r3 p0 (refused 1 and pulled up 2). Generally most unwilling, but led for almost two miles at Upper Sapey, however broke down so badly that she had to be removed by ambulance. Wears a cross-noseband, and acquired cheekpieces on her last two starts. *E.J. Williams — Ledbury (Andrew Graham).* 409 (CMam), 699 (CfMa), 1141 (OMa).

FROMRUSSIAWITHLOVE ..—.. 6 b.m. Moscow Society (USA) — Jack's The Girl (IRE) (Supreme Leader) pfpfp. Good-bodied half-sister to Jackson's Hole. Looked to have been given insufficient schooling preparation at home, and it was no surprise when she made plentiful errors and never looked like completing the course. The twelve pounds allowance means the rider sometimes have to put up over-weight. *J. Keel — Worcs (Penny Grainger).* 291 (2m4fCfMa), 617 (2m4fOMa), 714 (CMam), 929 (2m4fOMa), 1020 (OMa).

FROSTY FELLA .8-7.. 10 b.g. Gildoran — Snowy Autumn (Deep Run) p3b5. Compact half-brother to Sir Frosty (won 4 Chases since Pointing). Dam won 2m6f Hurdle. Finished 15 lengths third in an elders Maiden and nearly caught the runner-up, but subsequently acquired headgear and showed no enthusiasm and was tailed off last when favourite at Flagg Moor. Cannot be taken seriously as a racehorse. *A. & Mrs J. Bowen — Fernie (Nicola Pollock).* 129 (OMa), 482 (OMa), 651 (OMa), 985 (OMa).

FUERO REAL (FR) ..6-6.. 10 b.g. Highest Honor (FR) — Highest Pleasure (USA) (Foolish Pleasure USA) pp2pp. Strong-topped lengthy brother to French flat winner, Honor Kenmare. Dam won at 10f in France. ff340,000y. FRENCH FLAT '98 (for R. Litt) r3 w1 (12f) p0. FLAT '99/01 r13 w1 (12f) p3. NH '98/02 (for R.J. Hodges, and S.T. Lewis) r22 p1 (2nd); pulled up 10, unseated 2. Followed a French flat win at Toulouse with another success on the level in a Seller in May '00, but has been lucky to claim two poor seconds from 27 attempts over jumps. Duelled with another rival until he pulled up in a three-horse Ladies at Paxford, and left to chase home the sauntering Balinova in the slowest time of the day by far (in a Ladies!), but generally hopelessly tailed off, and has been pulled up in ten of his final 12 races including his only Chase. Blinkered once in '99. Surely suffering, and should be retired. *Miss H.L. James — N. Ledbury.* 515 (L), 664 (L), 923 (L), 1017 (3m2fL), 1391 (L).

FULL EGALITE .—§§.. 9 gr.g. Ezzoud (IRE) — Milva (Jellaby) r5rr6. Small workmanlike half-brother to Serious Time, and to five flat winners, including Galaxy Thunderbird, Mille End Quest, Miltiades (later successful flat/hurdling in Italy) and Milagro. Dam won at 6f. FLAT '98/03 r34 w2 (6-12f) p5. 19,000f, 27,000y. NH '02/3 r6 p0; pulled up 1, unseated 1. FLAT '04 r2 p0. NH '04 (for B.R. Johnson) r1 p0 (6th in 2m Hdle: *prom, ld 4-6, wknd 2 out*). Finished first past the post on three occasions on the flat including two on the all-weather, but made very heavy weather of it when taking a Seller by a short head (was not keen to overtake) and disqualified from an Amateurs contest after the rider had weighed-in 13 pounds light. A total no-hoper in Opens in which he was badly ridden, and only got round once, when almost two fences behind after crawling over the final obstacle with his partner stuck between his ears. Normally wears headgear, and has accrued 24 consecutive unplaced efforts. Most owners would find him a total embarrassment, but not this one. *K. Tork — Surrey U.* 188 (O), 420 (O), 609 (O), 643 (C).

FUN FOR GIRLS ..—.. 6 b.m. Alflora (IRE) — Inky (Impecunious) rp. Sturdy. Dam, half-sister to Niloufer (*qv*), won Maiden and pulled up five for Mrs Hart. Another dog in the Grainger manger, and she and Fromrussiawithlove are the girls who don't wanna have fun. *Mrs V. Hart — Ludlow (Penny Grainger).* 293 (CMam), 532 (OMa).

GABAKA DE THAIX (FR) ..9-0.. 11 ch.g. Quart De Vin (FR) — Masurka II (FR) (Brasero FR) 05p8554ppu. Medium-sized attractive brother to a French flat winner, and half-brother to a French Chasing winner. Dam won on flat in French provinces. NH FLAT '98 r1 p0. NH '00 r3 p0; pulled up 1. P-t-P '02 (for Mr P. Townsley) r7 w1 (Maiden) p3 (2 3rds, last once); last, refused 1 and pulled up 1. Won a bad Maiden on firm over a bare three miles at Godstone in '02, but not better than last since returning from a year on the sidelines, and well tailed off in the main. Made shoals of mistakes for the new novice rider but only managed to get shot of him once. *M.J. Caldwell — Cheshire Forest (Katie Caldwell).* 175 (Cnr), 301 (R), 530 (R), 715 (R), 748 (M), 933 (CR), 1147 (Cnr), 1265 (R), 1345 (R), 1426 (C).

GAETANO (IRE) ..8-5.. 10 ch.g. Executive Perk — Bright News (Buckskin FR) pppu05. Sturdy half-brother to Irish Pointing and English Hurdling winner, Bright Buck (IRE). IRISH P-t-P '01 r3 w1 (Maiden) p0; fell 1. IRISH NH FLAT '01 r1 p0. IRISH NH '02/3 (for T.J. Nagle) r6 p0. Grossly flattered by an Irish Maiden success, and fully exposed as a useless non-stayer over here. A poor last in both completions (blinkered in the latest), and should have been pulled up instead of being forced home when staggering on the previous attempt. *W.D. Edwards — N. Salop (Sheila Crow).* 231 (CR), 530 (R), 853 (R), 1114 (R), 1265 (R), 1345 (R).

GALAPIAT DU MESNIL (FR) ..11-0.. 11 b.g. Sarpedon (FR) — Polka De Montrin (FR) (Danoso) 2. Compact good-looking half-brother to French Chasing winner. Dam won jump race in France. NH '98/03 (for N.J. Henderson, one win, and P.F. Nicholls) r31 w9 (2m4f Hurdle 8 2m4f-3m1f Chases) p10; fell 1, pulled up 1. A smart performer at best and has gained nine victories on ground ranging from firmish to heavy, the last three of them being at Chepstow, and has been a nimble if one-paced contestant in 3m7f cross-country Chases at Cheltenham, gaining three seconds (beaten from half-a-length to six lengths — also a distant second in the La Touche at Punchestown). A game front-runner who has earned a magnificent £94,617, but must go left-handed (only once successful the other way round) and was totally unsuited by the track and barging into other rivals before finishing 11 lengths second at Folkestone in mid-February. Not seen since, and has clearly had a setback. *M. Fordham — Farmers Bloodhounds (Richard Phillips).* 239 (3m1fH).

GALAXY GIRL ..9-6.. 10 b.m. Jupiter Island — Thats Our Girl (Belfalas) 3R5. Good-bodied. Dam, sister to Cheshire Cove, and half-sister to Prideaux Prince (*qv* '99 Annual), was placed in 4 Irish Points, and subsequently ran very prominently in 4 Points for late Dennis Caro. NH FLAT '00 r2 p0. NH '00 r1 p0. P-t-P '03 r1 p1 (2nd). Still going well when squeezed out by the hanging eventual winner at the third last at Whitwick, but broke down when favourite to make amends next time. *late D.J. Caro — N. Ledbury.* 172 (OMa), 518 (CfMa), 978 (CMam).

GALAXY MINSTREL (IRE) ..9-10.. 10 b.g. Black Minstrel — Coppenagh Girl (Kambalda) u. Tall rangy half-brother to Mandalady (IRE). Dam won NH flat, 2 2m-2m2f Hdles and 2m2f Ch (only one of 3 to go clear) in Ireland. NH FLAT '00 r1 p0 (tailed off). P-t-P '01/3 r8 w2 (Maiden and Restricted) p1 (2nd); 4th, 5th, and pulled up 3. Had a soft-palate operation after winning readily at Badbury Rings in '02, but very lucky to follow up at Bredwardine last year (three in front of him all departed at the 14th) and clearly remains troubled (has also suffered with his back). Wears a cross-noseband, and a tongue-strap. *E.F.B. & Mrs J. Monck & A. Bull — Grafton (Jenny Pidgeon).* 28 (I).

GALEAWAY (IRE) ..9-9.. 11 b.g. Strong Gale — Geeaway (Gala Performance) bu19uu3p. Rangy brother to Bitofamixup (IRE) (*qv*). NH '00/3 r7 p1 (3rd in Ch); pulled up 3, fell 1. P-t-P/HUNT CH '00/1 and '03 (for Mr M.J. Roberts) r7 w2 (inc 3m Hunt Ch) p1 (3rd); 4th twice, 5th, and pulled up 1. NH '04 r1 p0 (unseated in 3m110y Grand Military Gold Cup: *chsd ldrs til blun bad 15, nt rec, poor 8th when ur last*). Won a Folkestone Hunter Chase on only his third appearance, but largely disappointing since, and only effective in weak events on sound surfaces now. Came with a strong late run to win in a finish of short heads at Charing, but otherwise not better than last in '04. His intrepid partner has obviously lost none of his style despite spending part of '03 swinging through the branches of the Sierra Leone jungle, and found himself desperately searching for a vine to cling onto on several occasions. Blinkered once in '02, and tongue-tied once the previous year. *Major J.R.D. Barnard — E. Sussex & Romney Marsh (Di Grissell).* 24 (O), 156 (O), 182 (CCon), 348 (3mH), 643 (C), 806 (C), 1054 (Cf).

GALE DAMAGE (IRE) ..8-10.. 11 ch.g. Mister Lord (USA) — Julie Mack (Strong Gale) pp3p. Light half-brother to Irish Pointing and English NH flat and jumping winner, Knock Leader (IRE). Dam is half-sister to Knox's Corner (*qv* '93 Annual). NH FLAT '00 r2 p1 (3rd); and 10th. P-t-P '02 r6 w1 (Maiden) p2 (3rds, of 4 once); pulled up 2, and fell 1. Won a 16-runner Maiden at Market Rasen convincingly in '02, but absent last year, and kept running out of steam after a maximum of 2m4f on his return. His trainer's string were all awry in '04, and it is possible that he could leave this form behind if he is given a clean bill of health next year. Wears a cross-noseband. *J.M. Robinson — Burton.* 57 (R), 503 (R), 944 (R), 1152 (R).

GALE ON THE LAKE (IRE) ..8-4.. 11 b.m. Strong Gale — By The Lake (Tyrant USA) ff33bpp. Small half-sister to Red Adhere, Red Tyrant, flat and Hurdling winner, Southend Scallyway, and to Chasing winner, Jokers Charm. Only two of dam's 8 runners have won. Bought Doncaster, September for 650. NH FLAT '99 r2 p0. NH '99 and '01 (for N.B. Mason) r3 p0; pulled up 1. Made a sticky start to Pointing with a couple of falls, but subsequently bagged two weak thirds (between ten and 25 lengths) in Maidens. Moderate in the extreme, but because of the Grissell connection was sent off an unworthy favourite twice. At least she cost next to nothing, and thrown in with her at the sales was her filly by Terimon who would be eligible to Point in 2007. *The Random Optimists (T.F.G. Marks) — Fitzwilliam (Di Grissell).* 423 (CMa), 539 (OMa), 782 (OMa), 996 (CMam), 1285 (OMa), 1405 (OMa), 1518 (OMa).

GALESHAN (IRE) .9-11.. 13 b.g. Strong Gale — Shan's Pal (Pals Passage) 6514f4. Strong-topped half-brother to Merrydale Farm, Vale River, and to flat winner, Leven Lass. Dam won 2m1f Maiden Hurdle in Ireland. NH FLAT '97 r1 p1 (3rd). NH '97/00 and '02 (for late G. & N.G. Richards, and Mrs H. Dalton) r14 w2 (2m4f-2m5f Chses) p3; pulled up 2, fell 1. Best at around 2m4f and does not truly get the trip in Points, but was left solo at the fifth in a match for a PPORA Novice Riders event at Andoversford, in which he provided Charles Huxley (16) with his first success. Has suffered tendon and wind problems (wears a tongue-tie) and has endured long absences before resuming in '04, when he fulfilled his role as a schoolmaster without achieving anything else. *Mr & Mrs P. Huxley — Albrighton (Andrew Dalton).* 477 (Cnr), 661 (Cnr), 817 (Cnr), 1140 (Cf), 1429 (Cnr), 1529 (MO).

GALEVANTER (IRE) ..9-0.. 11 b.g. Strong Gale — Cherry Crest (Pollerton) p. Enormously tall rangy half-brother to NH flat and jumping winner, Rowington. Dam, half-sister to Glen Cherry (*qv* '01 Annual), won 2m2f NH flat. NH FLAT '99 r1 p0 (7th). NH '01 r1 p0 (10th in Hdle). P-t-P '02/3 (for Mr C.S. Horton) r7 p1 (2nd of 3); 4th twice, last, and pulled up 3. Runner-up in a bad three-finisher Maiden at Maisemore Park in '02, but lightly raced and beaten a minimum of 20 lengths otherwise, and displayed a total lack of zest on his only appearance in '04. *T.P. Hitchman & Ms C. Hewson — Warwicks (Joanna Hitchman).* 588 (CfMa).

GALLANT GLEN (IRE) .10-10.. 12 b.g. Zaffaran (USA) — Furmore (Furry Glen) c11. Workmanlike brother to Chasing winner, Zaffamore (IRE) to NH flat and Hurdles winner, Retro's Lady (IRE), and to Irish Pointing/Hurdling winner, Sleetmore Gale, and half-brother to Father Mansfield. Dam failed to finish in 4 Irish Points. IRISH P-t-P '98/01 r11 w5 (inc 2 Opens) p2; pulled up 2, fell 1 and ran out 1. IRISH HUNT CH '00/1 r8 w2 (3m Chses) p2 (2nds). IRISH NH '01/2 r8 w1 (2m1f Ch) p0. P-t-P/HUNT CH '03 r5 w3 (2 Opens and Confined) p0; 4th of 5, and 6th. A speedy and useful Pointer who has won ten of his 13 completions in the sphere, and most impressive when clocking a fast time at Horseheath in the latest, but has met with setbacks in both English campaigns. Most effective in soft ground, and whilst he has scored on firmish it does not appear to suit him in the long run. Will hopefully be fit to resume in '05. Error-proneover big fences. *D.J. Harding-Jones — Puckeridge (Perry Harding-Jones).* 3 (O), 24 (O), 125 (O).

GALLION'S REACH (IRE) ..10-2.. 10 b.g. Good Thyne (USA) — Raise Our Hopes (IRE) (Salluceva) ppp2*1*. Strong workmanlike half-brother to Arise Adante (IRE). 30,000 4yo. NH FLAT '99/00 r3 p1 (3rd). NH '00/3 (for N.A. Twiston-Davies, and M.F. Harris) r28 w2 (2m Hdle and 3m Ch) p9; pulled up 6, fell/unseated 3. NH '04 (for I. Williams) r1 w1 (beat Alheri (*qv*) 10*l* in 3m1f110y Sell Ch: *made all, hit 5, clr 8, mist 12, unchall*). Moody and unpredictable and a poor jumper (pulled up six times and fell and unseated thrice in his campaign under Rules to '03), but capable of decent efforts on his day. Ended a bad run when a fair second in a Ladies, and then showed form on firmish for the first time (previously looked most effective in mud) when lifting a Hereford Selling Chase. Finished distressed and was quickly dismounted, and after a delayed auction there was no bid for him. Occasionally blinkered, and wind problems necessitate a tongue-tie. Sure to remain unpredictable if able to resume. *C.R. Leech — Warwicks (Mrs S.V.O. Leech).* 786 (O), 1170 (4m1fH), 1342 (O), 1470 (L).

GAME ENDEAVOUR (IRE) ..8-13.. 9 ch.g. Naheez (USA) — Jemma's Gold (IRE) (Buckskin FR) p. Compact well-made. Dam from family of Gaye Brief and Gaye Chance, is half-sister to Gaye Bard (*qv* '00 Annual). NH FLAT '01 r1 p0. P-t-P '03 r1 p1 (3rd of 4). A fair third on his jumping debut, and the only opposition to the odds-on favourite, and eventual winner, on his return at Black Forest Lodge, but pulled up and has since been reported dead. S. Stacey & Mrs J.C. Dawe — W. Somerset V. (Nick Dawe). 68 (OMa).

GAME GUNNER ..10-11.. 13 b.g. Gunner B — The Waiting Game (Cruise Missile) 1p. Giant-sized rangy. Dam is sister to Snaffles (*qv* '00 Annual). Grandam, Suntino, won a Maiden and placed 7 (appallingly ridden, or would have had a stack of wins). P-t-P/HUNT CH '00/1 and '03 r7 w2 (3m-3m1f110y Hunt Chses) p1 (3rd); 4th, 8th, pulled up 1 and fell 1. NH '01/2 r5 p1 (½*l* 2nd in 2m3f110y Ch); unseated 1, pulled up 1. A huge individual and has encountered most of the problems that come with his size, but a smart Hunter Chaser on his day, and galloped with great enthusiasm when making a successful reappearance at Ludlow. A chance ride for Charlotte Stucley on that occasion after Polly Gundry (who made no mention of his chances in a pre-race television interview) chose to partner the favourite, but gave him no ride at all in the Cheltenham Foxhunters and has not been seen since. Handles soft but most effective on faster ground, and considering he has nothing to work with at home Beverley Lewis does a good job in getting him fit first time out. *Miss B. Lewis — Worcs.* 176 (3mH), 543 (3m2f110yH).

GAMI (FR) ..—§.. 11 ch.g. Le Nain Jaune (FR) — Quimie II (FR) (Barbotan FR) ppp. Compact well-made brother to Fami (FR) (*qv*). FRENCH FLAT '98/9 r8 p0. NH '99/00 r4 p0. P-t-P '01/3 r15 w2 (Maiden and Members) p4 (3 3rds, of 4 once); 4th twice, pulled up 3, and fell/unseated 4. Rated 9-12 following wins at Larkhill and Stafford Cross in the previous two campaigns, but amazingly clumsy, and frequently takes no interest at all. Fancied to make a winning return, but not on a going day, and looks to have given up completely now. Wears a visor. *J.M. Salter — Axe V.H. (Philip Greenwood).* 15 (R), 689 (R), 864 (R).

GANGSTER ..9-4§.. 11 b.g. Gunner B — Moll (Rugantino) u93733. Tall good-topped half-brother to Seabrook Lad (*qv*). NH '01 r2 p1 (3rd in 3m2f Ch); and 7th. P-t-P '00/3 (for Sir Michael Connell) r14 w1 (Maiden) p7 (5 3rds, of 4 once); 4th twice, 6th, 7th, pulled up 1 and brought down 1. Made the ideal start when scoring easily at Southwell in '00, but a real let down since leaving Caroline Bailey, and has suffered 21 consecutive defeats. Ultimately made a safe conveyance for Susanne Tarry, but continues to find little off the bridle, and only once beaten less than 17 lengths. Blinkered twice in '03. *Miss S.J. Tarry — Pytchley.* 190 (C), 289 (CfL), 585 (L), 785 (L), 889 (CR), 1213 (Cnr).

GARDOR (FR) .8-7.. 7 b.g. Kendor (FR) — Garboesque (Priolo USA) u3. Compact. Dam won 12f race in France. Ff28,000, 5000y. FLAT '00/3 r14 p3. NH '01/3 (for late J.G. & T.J. Fitzgerald) r10 p2 (2nds); pulled up 1, fell 1. A young but experienced Maiden who has been placed six times, including when headed on the post once over Hurdles (fell at the last when lying second next time), but was resuming after a bout of lameness when he unseated at the first in a May Maiden. Faded rapidly in the final half mile when 33 lengths third subsequently, and found to have broken a blood vessel. Can hang left and tongue-tied on occasions, and his numerous health worries have debilitated him. *Yorkshire P-t-P Club (Miss J.E. Foster) — Pendle Forest & Craven (Jo Foster).* 1292 (OMa), 1305 (OMa).

GARETHSON (IRE) ..10-2.. 14 b.g. Cataldi — Tartan Sash (Crofter USA) u3. Tall strong brother to Ballymaloe Boy (IRE). IRISH P-t-P '95/6 r8 w2 (looked beaten both, but twice awarded a dead-heat!) p1 (3rd); pulled up 1, and fell 2. NH '96/9 r18 w2 (2m4f-2m6f Chses) p7 (short-headed once). P-t-P/HUNT CH '00/3 (for Mr A.R. & Mr O.W. King) r12 w2 (inc 2m3f110y Hunt Ch) p3 (3rds, Hunt Chses, inc distant of 4, and last); last, and pulled up 6. Recorded an early season double in '02 (his first wins since '98) and still retains plenty of speed, but has never been truly able to stay three miles, and stands very few outings. Could still find another opportunity if the right race presented itself. Suited by good or easy surfaces. *N. & Mrs S. Heath — Blackmore & Sparkford V. (Nick Heath).* 10 (L), 63 (L).

GAROLO (FR) ..10-5§.. 15 b.g. Garde Royale — Valgoya (FR) (Valdingran FR) 32415. Compact brother to a French flat winner, and half-brother to 2 winners there (one over jumps). Dam won 4 French flat, 9-10f. FRENCH FLAT '93/5 r16 w1 (12f) p1 (3rd). FRENCH NH '94/7 r7 w2 (2m110y-2m2f Hdles) p2 (2nds, beaten neck once); fell 1. NH '96/01 r23 w1 (2m Ch, 4 ran and 3 finished) p11 (beaten neck once). P-t-P/HUNT CH '01/3 r14 w7 (3m1f Hunt Ch and 6 Ladies) p2 (2nds); pulled up 2, brought down 1. A most enigmatic performer, and sometimes never takes hold of the bit, but capable of decent efforts when he encounters easy ground and a right-handed circuit, and Tory Tremlett proved an able deputy for the owner at Garthorpe. Sulked when a well-supported joint-favourite on a return visit and can never be relied on. Tongue-tied once in '01. Wears blinkers. *Miss S.L. Samworth — R.A. (Roger Wernham).* 5 (L), 48 (3m5f70yL), 146 (L), 380 (L), 682 (L).

GARRISON FRIENDLY (IRE) ..9-5§.. 12 b.g. Buckskin (FR) — Ikeathy (Be Friendly) 40p43. Smallish workmanlike half-brother to Another Garrison (IRE). Dam won at 5f in Ireland, and won 2m5f Hdle and 3 2m Chses there. IRISH P-t-P '97 r4 w2 p0; pulled up, and fell at last (might have completed hat-trick). NH '98/9 r11 w1 (3m Ch) p3 (2nds; 2 Hdles, and distant last in Ch). P-t-P/HUNT CH '00/3 r15 w1 (Club nov rdrs) p4 (2 3rds, of 4 once); 5th, last pair 5, pulled up 1, and unseated 1. Ended a run of 17 defeats dating back to '98 when successful in a three-finisher event on his reappearance last year, but normally lacks fluency and resolve, and having been subjected to a series of excessively hard rides looks irrevocably sour now. Normally blinkered, and tried in cheekpieces in the Detling 4-miler. *N. Wilson — E. Sussex & Romney Marsh (Sara Hickman).* 45 (Cnr), 249 (Cnr), 537 (4mMO), 607 (Cf), 898 (O).

GARRUTH (IRE) ..10-7§.. 11 gr.g. Good Thyne (USA) — Lady Sipash (Erin's Hope) 22d412. Workmanlike half-brother to Irish Hurdling winners Friend's Amigo and Phardana. IRISH P-t-P '00 r3 p2; fell 1. IRISH NH FLAT '98/00 r7 w1 (2m4f) p2 (3rds). IRISH NH '00 r2 p0. NH '00/3 (for T.D. Easterby, 5 wins, and P.F. Nicholls) r22 w7 (5 2m6f-3m1f Hdles and 2 3m2f-3m3f Chses) p7;

pulled up 2. Purchased for an astonishing 175,000gns by Paul Barber and what looked to be a potentially dodgy purchase was later summed up eloquently by Paul Nicholls when he said 'we must have left the keys to him in Yorkshire'. A high achiever in his prime and eight wins on ground ranging from firmish to heavy included a £29,000 Aintree Hurdle by a distance, a sum which bolstered to his fine total career earnings (although not as far as current connections are concerned!) of £89,971. Often a difficult ride who needs a great deal of persuading, and frequently blinkered and has been tongue-tied once (also operated on for his wind). Showed he can still do it when he chooses when coming home unchallenged in the weak Land Rover Final at Cheltenham, but made a couple of slow jumps and was unconvincing. Behaved like a prize pig next time when his habit of jumping right was exaggerated to the full, and although by no means an old stager it is difficult to see a way forward for him now. Physical problems must be at least partly to blame for his lack of generosity. *Axe Valley Racing Club (R. Barber) — Cattistock (Richard Barber).* 34 (O), 178 (3m1f110yH), 629 (3m1f110yH), 1171 (3m2f110yH), 1298 (3m1f110yH).

GATCHOU MANS (FR) ..10-3.. 11 gr.g. Royal Charter (FR) — Vindjica Mans (FR) (Quart De Vin FR) 33. Sparely-made. FRENCH FLAT '97 r2 p0. FRENCH NH '98/9 r17 w2 (2m4f Ch at Lyon D'Angers and 2m6f110y Cross Country at Durtal) p1 (3rd). P-t-P '00 and '02/3 r22 w4 (inc 2 Opens) p10 (7 2nds; and 3rd of 4 thrice); last, pulled up 3, and unseated 4. Quite useful on his day, and best when allowed to dominate inferiors, but much more adept at picking up place prize money, and has seen the back of several partners. Error-proneand strong handling is essential, but can handle all but extremes of going, and should win again providing his prolonged absence is not a bad omen. *A.G.C. Howland Jackson — Suffolk (Ruth Hayter).* 24 (O), 101 (L).

GATSBY (IRE) ..10-11.. 9 gr.g. Roselier (FR) — Burren Gale (IRE) (Strong Gale) 1. Tall rangy half-brother to NH flat and jumping winner, Russell Road (IRE). Dam, sister to Bervie House (*qv* '00 Annual). NH FLAT '01 r1 p0. NH '02 r2 p1 (3rd). P-t-P/HUNT CH '03 r3 p1 (2nd in Hunt Ch); 4th, and carried out 1. Took on some useful novices when Twiston-Davies-trained for the present owners under Rules, but looked an awkward ride on his Pointing debut, and well beaten when tried in cheekpieces next time. Appears to have been sorted out since, and readily beat 16 others in a soft ground Hunter Chase at Huntingdon despite racing very lazily on the elongated run-in, but his subsequent absence is worrying. *Mr & Mrs C. Powell — Wheatland (John Groucott).* 177 (3mH).

PLATE 49 506 Northern P-t-P Area Club Members (Nov Rdrs): Gaultier Gale and Alistair Findlay are clear at the last *PHOTO: Alan Mitchell*

GAULTIER GALE (IRE) ..9-12§.. 11 b.g. Ajraas (USA) — David's Pleasure (Welsh Saint) p4p6117pf. Compact attractive half-brother to a Irish Hurdling winner, and a flat winner in Italy. Dam won 13f race in Ireland and is half-sister to Supreme Norman (*qv* '00 Annual). IRISH FLAT '96/8 r15 w1 (7f) p7. IRISH NH '97/9 r16 w2 (2m Hdle and 2m2f Ch) p2. NH '00/2 r26 w3 (2m4f110y-2m5110y

Chses) p2. P-t-P '03 r11 w2 (Confined and Club nov rdrs) p3 (2 2nds, beaten head once, and last once); 5th twice, last, and pulled up 3. Pulls hard and does best when conditions are lively, but moody and inconsistent, and only able to string two wins together for the first time in '04. Lacks fluency over big fences, and his state of mind will hardly have been helped by the mother and father of all falls at Corbridge on his latest appearance. Had a tendency to rip his shoes off in the past. Occasionally blinkered under Rules, visored twice in '01, and tried in cheekpieces once last year. *Ms J.M. Findlay — Border.* 72 (O), 240 (3mH), 330 (3mH), 426 (Cf), 506 (Cnr), 656 (O), 764 (O), 917 (O), 1038 (O).

GAVROCHE COLLONGES (FR) ..5-0.. 11 b.g. Video Rock (FR) — Amazone Collonges (FR) (Olmeto) p4*p*. Big half-brother to French Chasing winner, Luteur Collonges. FRENCH NH '99/00 r14 w1 (2m3f Ch) p1 (3rd). NH '00/1 (for Mrs H. Dalton) r5 p0; pulled up 1. NH '04 (for Mrs J.A. Saunders) r1 p0 (pulled up in 2m5f Ch: *a bhnd, mist 8, t.o & pu 10*). Won a £10,000 Chase in heavy in France, but totally useless nowadays, and does not get many opportunities. Sometimes blinkered and tongue-tied, and is a keen sort who can lead early, and occasionally taken to post well in advance of his rivals. Must be suffering badly. *The Beaverfast Group (Mrs A.N. Jenkins) — Bicester with Whaddon (Toby Saunders).* 683 (O), 888 (O).

GAWNGADINN (IRE) .9-5§.. 13 b.g. Strong Gale — Castle-Lady (Little Buskins) 5p. Tall workmanlike half-brother to Vals Well (IRE), and to Irish Pointing winners, Lackagh Lad and Dutch Call (latter also successful English Hurdler). Dam is sister to Busk Fuzz (*qv* '88 Season Annual). IRISH P-t-P '97/00 r21 w2 (7yo&up Maiden and Winners of One) p5; pulled up 9, fell 3. P-t-P '02/3 r12 p2 (2nd of 3 once); 4th twice, 5th, pulled up 5, unseated 1 and refused 1. A thorough stayer, and won twice in Ireland in '99, but markedly reluctant to get involved now, and not worth bothering with again. Has been tried tongue-tied. *G.L. Lyster — Dunston H. (Nigel Bloom).* 521 (Cf), 647 (Cf).

GAY ABANDON ..—§§.. 10 ch.m. Risk Me (FR) — School Dinners (Sharpo) pfpuR*p*. Narrow compact. FLAT '97 r5 p0. P-t-P/HUNT CH '02/3 r11 p0 (pulled up 7, fell/unseated 3 and ran out). NH '04 (from D. Burchell's) r1 p0 (100/1 when pulled up in 2m1f Hdle: *hld up, jmpd lft 3, sn t.o, pu last, lame*). An utter disgrace, and should have been banned long ago, and has such a bad reputation in the changing rooms that no jockey will consent to partner her in Points any more. Amazingly allowed to run under Rules in May, but went lame at Hereford, and hopefully the poor mare will be found a kinder home. Reflects shamefully on connections who have not got a clue. *C.R. Johnson — Celtic Bloodhounds (Walter Burchell).* 203 (CfMa), 258 (CMa), 358 (R), 451 (R), 675 (CfMa).

GAY BARATINEUR (FR) .9-13.. 11 b.g. Gay Minstrel (FR) — Halucinee (FR) (Urf FR) 43p3. Unfurnished. FRENCH FLAT '99 r4 p1. FRENCH NH '99/00 r23 w1 (2m4f Ch) p11. P-t-P '03 r4 w2 (Club nov rdrs and Club) p0; and pulled up 2. Won twice under the guidance of his trainer on right-handed circuits last year, but a very weak finisher otherwise, and gives the impression he may be breaking blood vessels. Dispensed with cheekpieces and acquired a near-side pricker and Julian Pritchard when a well-supported favourite on his latest appearance, but stopped just as rapidly as before, and needs treating with the utmost caution. *Miss A.C. Clift & Mrs K. Baimbridge — Ledbury (Katie Baimbridge).* 664 (L), 816 (Cf), 1428 (L), 1502 (O).

GAYBLE ..8-13.. 7 b.g. Good Times (ITY) — High Kabour (Kabour) p4. Sturdy compact half-brother to Hurdles winner, Gaynor. NH FLAT '02 r1 p0. P-t-P '03 r2 p1 (3rd); and pulled up 1. Takes a keen hold and has shown good speed, but only seen in May on good or sound surfaces in Points, and finished lame at Bratton Down. Needs to brush up his jumping if he is able to reappear. *R.G. Gay — N. Cornwall (Mike Biddick).* 1543 (R), 1558 (R).

GAYNOR'S GAMBLE (IRE) ..9-9.. 8 ch.g. Alphabatim (USA) — Montrouge (IRE) (Executive Perk) 1. Small light. Dam, half-sister to Belmont King (*qv* '03 Annual). P-t-P '03 r2 p1 (3rd); and pulled up 1. Jarred up and spent three months on the sidelines between outings in '03, and disappeared back into the ether after scoring narrowly at Garnons. Very much at the end of her tether over an admittedly stiff 2m4f there, but has the make and shape of a Ladies horse if he is capable of getting the extra half mile. *Mr & Mrs M.E. Green — Cheshire (Gary Hanmer).* 619 (2m4fOMa).

GEAL FARRAIGE (IRE) ..9-6.. 6 b.m. Arc Bright (IRE) — Merry Shoon (IRE) (Brush Aside USA) 4pf. Compact. Sold Tattersalls Ireland, Aug for 927. Shows distinct signs of ability, but poor jumping has been a drawback, and gets tired very quickly in the closing stages. A possible winner if she gets the trip, and it would probably be a good idea to switch her to 2m4f for the present. *R.S. Racing (R.O. Addis) — Tredegar F. (Caroline Walker).* 837 (OMa), 1091 (CMam), 1394 (OMa).

GEE A TWO (IRE) ..7-6.. 8 gr.g. Roselier (FR) — Miss Doogles (Beau Charmeur FR) up5p. Compact half-brother to Doogles Son (IRE), Chasing winner, Narrow Water (previously successful Irish Pointer), and to Irish Pointing winners Coolkenno Girl and Lauren's Prince. IR£7500 4yo. NH FLAT '02/3 r2 p0. NH '03 (for F. Murphy) r1 p0. Bought Doncaster, May for 3500. Tailed off in those races in which he has managed to complete, and it would take a major optimist to wish to go to the bother of training him again. *M. & Mrs S. Thornton — Belvoir (Sally Thornton).* 92 (I), 304 (OMa), 387 (OMa), 686 (OMa).

GENERAL BEN .—§.. 9 ch.g. Romany Rye — Devna (General David) pp. Small sturdy. Dam (*qv* '96 Annual), half-sister to Implicitly Suzie, pulled up 4 and fell in Points spread over 5 years for Phil Dando. P-t-P '02/3 r6 p0 (pulled up 4, and ran out 2). Amazingly installed as favourite once, but has quickly usurped his dam as the most useless member of the family, and unimproved by blinkers twice. *P. Dando — Pentyrch.* 370 (OMa), 948 (OMa).

GENERAL CARATS .—§§.. 11 b.g. Cotation — Madam Carats (Mandrake Major) pp3pp. Compact workmanlike owner-bred half-brother to Colonel Carats (*qv*). P-t-P '02/3 r12 w1 (Maiden) p0; pulled up 8, ran out 2 and fell 1. Has shown his only form when allowed to dominate from the front, but will surrender without resistance as soon as something takes him on, and has an aversion to going round bends. Worth 9-7 on the rare occasions he is prepared to try, but blinkers have had little effect, and is best shunned. *D.W. Applewhite — Belvoir (Gill Walford).* 481 (R), 680 (M), 1205 (CR), 1397 (I), 1500 (Cf).

GENERAL CLAREMONT (IRE) ..10-8.. 12 gr.g. Strong Gale — Kasam (General Ironside) b21. Tall strong half-brother to NH flat winner, Oath Of Allegiance (IRE), and to and Irish Pointing winner. IR54,000 3yo. NH FLAT '98 r2 p1 (3rd). NH '98/03 r37 w5 (3m2f Hdle and 4 3m-3m3f Chses) p13; fell/unseated 5, pulled up 1. A dour stayer who relished the 3m7f trip when gaining a sixth career win in a Folkestone Hunter Chase, in which he was splendidly handled by Rilly Goschen on a probably unsuitable right-handed track, but did benefit from the gross error of judgement from Tom Malone on the runner-up. Can find some easy pickings and his two previous victories were in three-runner races, but very prone to blunder and throw away opportunities, and has left partners on the floor in seven to date. Tried in blinkers once. Keeps his form well, and there may be another decent prize in store for him yet. *K.G. Manley — Blackmore & Sparkford V. (Paul Nicholls).* 732 (2m5f110yH), 1170 (4m1fH), 1441 (3m7fH).

GENERAL CONFUSION (IRE) .—.. 11 gr.g. Invader General (IRE) — Where Am I (Kambalda) 3914uuupRp. Compact half-brother to Irish Pointing winner, Camden Confusion. IRISH P-t-P '99 & '02/3 r15 w1 (6yo&upward Maiden) p4; pulled up 2, fell 1. IRISH NH FLAT '99 r1 p0. IRISH NH '99 and '01 (for J.F. O'Shea) r6 p0; fell 1. Not too bad at his best if partnered by a competent jockey, and despite losing his whip on the flat Tim Lane managed to wave him home in front by a neck in a Members at Horseheath. After that the fun began, because Barbara Czepulkowski, of advancing years, who attended her first Point in the year 2003 and thought it looked jolly good fun, took to partnering him herself, and to her credit managed a respectable 12 lengths fourth on her debut. After that it all proved horribly predictable, because she fell off at the 15th, the 13th, and at the first when 2-5 (!!) and then with her nerve shattered, pulled up at the third, and ran out at the fourth. Finally acquired James Owen and made his fourth appearance in five days including his second of the afternoon, and was still in contention three out in a Restricted but faded and pulled up. It is not inconceivable that he could score in similar company if the owner can be somehow be weaned off him. Tried blinkered and tongue-tied in Ireland. Any similarity between him and George Cooper's local legend of the 70's is purely down to the name. *Miss B.H. Czepulkowski — Cambs with Enfield Chace (Simon Andrews).* 29 (R), 44 (R), 123 (M), 373 (L), 464 (L), 649 (L), 1241 (M), 1244 (L), 1314 (L), 1316 (R).

GENERAL CRAIG ..8-12§.. 9 b.g. Governor General — Craig Lass (Rasti FR) p. Tall strong half-brother to Craigson. Dam won Maiden and placed 4 for Mrs Hussey, and grandam, Craig Miss, won 4 Points (3 at Howick) and placed 12 for her. P-t-P '02/3 r8 p1 (3rd); 4th, slipped up 1, pulled up 3, and fell 2. Beaten 14 lengths in two completions, but anything but a pleasant ride, and tore off into a 30-length lead at Howick only to capitulate after two miles. Error-proneand ungenuine, and thankfully only manages short campaigns. *Mrs I.E.M. Hussey — Tredegar F. (Deborah Faulkner).* 204 (CfMa).

GENERAL GEM ..—.. 10 ch.g. Presidium — The Bean-Goose (King Sitric) pp. Powerful owner-bred half-brother to Blyth Brook (*qv*). P-t-P '02 r1 p0 (pulled up). A market springer and ran passably for two miles on debut, but absent throughout '03, and clearly does not remain problem free. *Mrs S.A. Sutton — Haydon (Tim Reed).* 268 (R), 762 (I).

GENERAL HOPKINS (IRE) ..—.. 10 b.g. Cataldi — Kewanee (Kafu) pp. Sturdy compact half-brother to Irish NH flat winner, Music Again. Dam won 2m2f Hurdle in Ireland. IRISH NH FLAT '00/1 r4 p0. IRISH NH '00/2 (for T.K. Geraghty) r6 p1 (3rd); pulled up 1. IRISH FLAT '02/3 r3 p0. Fifteen lengths third in an Irish Hurdle, but bad otherwise including when fifth in his only Chase there (blinkered once and wore cheekpieces once). Tailed off and pulled up in the closing stages of February Maidens, and looked hopeless. *N.J. Pewter — Suffolk.* 154 (OMa), 244 (CfMa).

GENERAL JAKE (IRE) .9-11.. 8 b.g. Jolly Jake (NZ) — Moscow Lady (IRE) (Moscow Society USA) 4123. Compact half-brother to Lord Ken (IRE). IRISH P-t-P '03/4 r3 p1 (3rd); last and pulled up 1.

NH '04 (for Miss S.E. Forster) r1 p1 (28l 3rd of 4 in 2m5f110y Ch: *chsd ldrs, ld 6 til hdd last, sn outpcd*). Has been improving and made the frame twice in contests won by Jimmy Walton horses, and led throughout the final two miles and stayed on well when scoring in a Maiden at Corbridge in between. His modest Chasing third earned him £695, and although he presently looks outclassed in that sphere a Restricted should be easy meat for him. *P.D. Innes — Buccleuch (Clive Storey).* 768 (2m4fOMa), 1041 (OMa), 1310 (R).

GENERAL SHORT ..—.. 9 b.g. General Surprise — Morpion (Scallywag) ppb. Small. Dam, sister to Time For Coffee (*qv* '92 Annual). Did not produce any rateable form in Maidens, although he was unfortunate not to pick up a second prize at least at Black Forest Lodge, where only three of the five starters were still going three out where the leader fell fatally and brought him down. *R.G. Westacott — Tiverton Stag (Emely Thompson).* 274 (CfMa), 328 (OMa), 417 (CfMah).

GENERAL WOLFE ..9-12.. 16 ch.g. Rolfe (USA) — Pillbox (Spartan General) 2. Tall good-topped stringhalt off-hind half-brother to Spartan Times and Ballot Box. Dam won a 3m Chase. NH FLAT '93 r1 p0 (6th). NH '93/99 and '01/2 r30 w8 (2m6f110y Hdle and 7 2m7f-3m Chses) p4 (2nds); pulled up 1, on floor 4. P-t-P/HUNT CH '02/3 r5 w1 (3m2f110y Hunt Ch) p4 (3 2nds, beaten head once, in Hunt Chses; and last of 3). A grand old warrior whose early career was marshalled by Captain Forster, and career highlights include back-to-back wins in the Peter Marsh Chase, and a second in the '96 Scottish Grand National. Spends his time in near retirement these days, but maintains a real enthusiasm for racing, and lost nothing in defeat to a rival less than half his age when wheeled back into action at Tabley. *M.D. Gichero — Llangeinor (Miss C. Gichero).* 1427 (O).

GENEREUX ..9-12§.. 12 ch.g. Generous (IRE) — Flo Russell (USA) (Round Table) p2325641p5. Neat smallish half-brother to 8 winners (6 abroad and one in Ireland, including Flow Back (flat) and Machikane Jindaiko (earned £500,000 in Japan). FLAT r1 p0. NH '97 and '01 r10 p5 (3rds); pulled up 2. P-t-P/HUNT CH '98, '00 and '02/3 r17 w2 (Maiden and Restricted) p3 (inc neck 2nd; and last of 3); 4th, 6th, last pair 4, pulled up 6. Unmasked as ungenuine from an early age, and would come off the bridle on the way to post if he were in the mood, but retains a deal of ability, and specialises in the unexpected. Recorded his first success since '98 when popping up at 33-1 in '02, and delivered punters another jaw-dropping experience when ending a losing sequence of 19 in the Radnor four-miler. Given a fine ride there by Rob Hodges, who usually comes in for more stick than praise in these pages, and was pestered back to the front after the last to win going away. Typically dogged it subsequently, and normally easy to omit from calculations. Makes plenty of errors but is far too cagey to get on the ground. Usually wears cheekpieces and a tongue-tie, and has been tried in a visor. *Mrs A. Price — Teme V.* 92 (I), 403 (Cf), 447 (Cf), 616 (C), 663 (I), 835 (Cf), 1117 (3m1f110yH), 1228 (4mO), 1358 (3m1f110yH), 1392 (C).

GENTLEMAN CHARLES (IRE) ..9-7.. 11 b.g. Jurado (USA) — Asinara (Julio Mariner) pp623. Tall workmanlike half-brother to flat and Hurdles winner, Prophits Pride (IRE). Dam won 2 Irish NH flat. NH FLAT '98/9 r2 p0. NH '99 r2 p0. P-t-P '00 and '02/3 r12 w1 (Maiden) p6 (5 2nds, of 3 once); 5th, last, pulled up 2 and brought down 1. A reliable jumper, and ended an encouraging debut season in Points with a win at Charm Park, but both lightly raced and a weak finisher, and collared on the line after looking home and hosed at Heslaker. Takes at least one outing to get fit. *Miss E.M. Hewitt — Middleton (Tony Walker).* 481 (R), 771 (R), 1060 (R), 1205 (CR), 1456 (R).

GENTLEMANS RELISH ..9-4.. 8 b.g. Sir Harry Lewis (USA) — Relishing (Relkino) 243. Lengthy brother to Patum Peperium. Dam, half-sister to Highlighter (*qv* '00 Annual), finished in 2 Maidens (broke down) for Bill Shand Kydd in '96. P-t-P '02/3 r6 p5 (4 3rds, of 4 once, and last once); and pulled up 1. Pretty sure-footed and has made the frame in all eight completions, but a woefully weak finisher, particularly over the full trip, and no longer has the option of 2m4f races. Deserves reward for his consistency, but punters will have long since deserted him. Blinkered once in '03. *Mrs W. Shand Kydd — Bicester with Whaddon (Fiona Kehoe).* 53 (2m4fOMa), 290 (2m4fCfMa), 890 (2m4fOMa).

GEORDIE MACGREGOR ..—.. 6 b.g. Presidium — Connie Leathart (El Conquistador) pp. Small plain. Dam, sister to NH flat and jumping winner, Quistaquay, and half-sister to Embley Buoy (*qv* '00 Annual) pulled up in a Point (subsequently bad under Rules). Sold Doncaster, Aug for 5200. Looks like a pit pony and had no idea what was required in the jumping stakes in late season Maidens. Limped round the paddock with a scabby staring coat at Dingley, and was an utter disgrace. *P.J. Millington — Fernie.* 1155 (OMa), 1218 (OMa).

GEORDIES EXPRESS ..10-7.. 13 b.g. Tina's Pet — Maestroes Beauty (Music Maestro) 144u2711u. Plain unfurnished. P-t-P/HUNT CH '98/03 r27 w5 (inc 2 3m1f Hunt Chses and 2 Opens, one a dead-heat) p8 (3 2nds, remote once; and 5 3rds; and inc 3 Hunt Chses); pulled up 2, fell/unseated 7. Inconsistent and prone to mistakes, but a useful performer on his day, and has won three Hunter Chases on good or sound surfaces at Kelso under different riders. Missed five weeks of the season through a poisoned leg, but the break appeared to freshen him up, and was joint-favourite to record the hat-trick when unseating yet another new pilot at Cartmel. Stays well in excess of three miles, and can also handle softish. Wears a cross-noseband. *G.T. Bewley — Jedforest.* 72 (O), 179 (2m6fH), 330 (3mH), 543 (3m2f110yH), 678 (3m1fH), 798 (3m1fH), 1309 (O), 1444 (3m1fH), 1490 (3m2fH).

PLATE 50 72 West Percy Mens Open: Geordies Express and Kevin Anderson, 1st
PHOTO: Alan Mitchell

GEORGES PLEASURE ..9-6.. 8 ch.m. Weldnaas (USA) — Poetic Fancy (Then Again) f15pp. Compact well-made. Dam, sister to Missmass (*qv* '01 Annual), won 2 2m1f Hdles, inc Sell. P-t-P '03 r4 p1 (3rd); last, unseated 1 and carried out 1. Got off to a very sticky start but improved by the application of blinkers latterly in '03, and did not need their aid when scoring in the fastest of four short Maidens on firmish at Great Trethew. Most disappointing since and headgear might be required once more. *S.J. Williams — Tetcott (Claire Williams).* 142 (OMa), 306 (2m4fOMa), 706 (R), 1131 (R), 1325 (R).

GERMANY PARK (IRE) ..9-8.. 7 ch.g. Germany (USA) — Lohunda Park (Malinowski USA) c14f6. Half-brother to Pats Minstrel and See You Always (IRE), to Irish Pointing and all-weather Hurdles winner, Ballylemon (IRE), and to Irish Pointing winner, Starlight Fountain. IRISH P-t-P '02/3 r13 p3; pulled up 3, fell 1, carried out 1. IRISH NH FLAT '03 (for E.M. O'Sullivan) r1 p0. Three Irish placings included a third behind Fane Counsel, and proved up to winning a bad three-finisher youngsters Maiden on firmish at Horseheath (the first Pointing success for Matthew Smith, reduced to the amateur ranks after one victory as a Conditional), but most disappointing when tailed off twice and a faller once since. A fizzy sort who has two paddock handlers and generally attempts to make all, but folds up quickly and does not seem to have much stamina. Immediately after his win, Fane Counsel obliged in the Intermediate. *C. Stewart — Worcs (William Stone).* 219 (OMa), 371 (OMa), 559 (R), 745 (R), 902 (R).

GERRY WATSON .—§.. 8 ch.g. Winter Words — Kingsfold Swift (Swing Easy USA) pp. Very tall rangy owner-bred half-brother to Ringsfold. Dam won a 7f race. P-t-P '03 r4 p0 (pulled up 2, fell 1 and brought down 1). Crammed four outings into the final weeks of last season, but proved to be a very difficult ride, and twice threw in the towel at around halfway in the space of a week in '04. *Mrs S.R. Jeffries — Bicester with Whaddon.* 1035 (OMa), 1125 (OMa).

GHALI (USA) ..—.. 10 b.g. Alleged (USA) — Kareema (USA) (Coastal USA) ppu. Compact half-brother to two winners in USA. Dam won 3 races at up to 10f USA. FLAT '97/8 r5 p1 (3 of 4). NH '98/02 (for J.F. Coupland) r24 p0; pulled up 6. Only once placed in 32 races, when a miserable nine lengths third of four on the flat. Has since tried Selling Hurdles, and jumped badly and pulled up at the seventh in his only Chase. Wears a tongue-tie, and previously blinkered once. His Pointing rider is very novicey, but would be useless for anybody. *Mrs J.M. Parr — Brocklesby.* 304 (OMa), 477 (Cnr), 1213 (Cnr).

GHUTAH ..9-11.. 11 ch.g. Lycius (USA) — Barada (USA) (Damascus USA) f65. Small neat half-brother to flat winners Barba Son (won 16), Pica and Amana River, and to Hurdles winner, Bartholomew Fair. FRENCH FLAT '96 r2 p1 (2nd). FLAT '97/8 r3 p0. FLAT '99/01 and '03 r11 p0. NH '99/03 (for M. Wane, G.A. Swinbank, and Mrs A.M. Thorpe) r42 w5 (2m-2m1f Hdle and 4 2m1f Chses) p5; pulled up 5, fell/unseated 5. Bought Ascot, Dec for 2190. Has qualified for the 'been there done that' tee shirt having started life with Andre Fabre as a two-year-old in Chantilly before decamping to the other training meccas of Dubai and Newmarket. An unpretentious sort who was much happier when he finally ended up in the back of beyond, and won four Selling Hurdles including a hat-trick between August and September '01 as well as a Chase when he was dispatched to North Yorkshire and Carmarthenshire. Would have finished a poor second of three had he not fallen two out in his first Ladies (jumped right), but well beaten although not wholly disgraced afterwards. Has fallen or unseated on six occasions, and essentially only a two miler. Occasionally wore headgear to '02. *Miss J. Owen — Albrighton (Paul Morris).* 253 (L), 1263 (L), 1391 (L).

GIGI BEACH (IRE) ..9-2§.. 14 ch.g. Roselier (FR) — Cranagh Lady (Le Bavard FR) Ruu55p. Unfurnished half-brother to Waterloo King, Cranagh Moss (IRE) and Gi Gi Brace (IRE). NH '97/02 r33 w4 (3m2f110y-3m6f Chses) p12 (inc 8 2nds); pulled up 4, and fell/unseated 3. P-t-P '96/7 and '03 (for Miss H. Steele) r12 w3 (Maiden, Restricted and Intermediate) p0; fell/unseated 5, and pulled up 1. Used to front run to good effect, and was a useful novice Pointer before graduating successfully to staying Chases, but last successful in '99, and has proved an unsuitable ride for inexperienced girls in recent times. Often blinkered latterly under Rules, and visored once in '01. *Mrs S.S. Reynoldson — Avon V. (Sarah Waugh).* 10 (L), 261 (Cf), 632 (M), 882 (C), 1329 (Cnr), 1365 (Cnr).

GILLIE'S NEPHEW ..9-12.. 7 b.g. Gildoran — Mistress Dasher (Relkino) 142. Sturdy. Dam, half-sister to Fresh Brew (*qv* '03 Annual), fell in Point for Colin Gee. Grandam, Bengal Lady, is half-sister to Teaplanter (*qv* '98 Annual) was placed in 5 Points. P-t-P '03 r2 p0 (pulled up 1 and fell 1). Gained some valuable experience last year, and put it to good use on his reappearance in a short Maiden at Dunthrop where he accounted for the frustrating Gentlemans Relish. Took on much more experienced campaigners next time, but only beaten two lengths in his first Restricted, and it will be a surprise if he cannot upgrade successfully in '05. Acts on firmish, and yet to encounter ground any softer than good. Wears a cross-noseband. *C.M. Gee — V. of Aylesbury with Garth & S. Berks (Lawney Hill).* 53 (2m4fOMa), 190 (C), 999 (R).

GILLONE ..10-1.. 13 b.g. Gildoran — Speakalone (Articulate) 313. Tall rangy brother to Doranslone, and half-brother to Brownslone, Hobnobber, Bucklelone, Bucks Law, Nelti, Chatabit and Ginger Moss. Dam won Maiden and last of 3, and grandam, All Alone II, won 16 Points, both for John Docker. P-t-P/HUNT CH '98/00 and '02/3 r18 w7 (inc 4 Confineds) p3 (2 2nds, remote once); 4th, last, pulled up 2, fell/unseated 3 and ran out 1. A smart Pointer on his day and won eight races for John Docker, but highly strung and would often boil over in the preliminaries, and then take a strong hold. Broke down when looking certain to record another success at Clifton-on-Dunsmore, and sadly could not be saved. Mr & Mrs J.H. Docker — Atherstone (John Docker). 381 (O), 943 (MO), 1120 (Cf).

GILLY WEET ..8-7.. 9 b.m. Almoojid — Sindos (Busted) 2p. Strong half-sister to two winners (one in Germany), inc flat and Hurdling winner, Hold Court. Dam won 2 flat 7-10f, and is half-sister to Supreme Warrior (*qv* '98 Annual). FLAT '98/9 r7 p0. NH '99 and '01 r9 p2 (2nds); pulled up 1. P-t-P '03 r1 p1 (fence 2nd of 3). Headstrong and an habitual front-runner, and runner-up in four assorted events, but beaten a minimum of 23 lengths in them, and does not stay in Points. *H.J. Barton — Llandeilo F.* 675 (CfMa), 948 (OMa).

GILZINE ..10-2.. 9 b.g. Gildoran — Sherzine (Gorytus USA) 13. Lengthy half-brother to Panto, and to Hurdles winner, Megazine. Dam won 12f race, and won 2m1f Hdle (both Sells). NH FLAT '00/1 r3 p1 (3rd). NH '02 r4 p0; unseated 1. P-t-P '03 (for Miss J. Reynolds & Mrs B. Bishop) r1 w1 (Maiden). Favourite for his second bumper, and beaten a minimum of 21 lengths over hurdles, but won his Maiden despite not looking fully wound up, and upgraded successfully in a similarly weak Restricted. Looked sure to be involved in the finish until all but falling two out next time, but typically sidelined since, and remains very difficult to train. Wears a cross-noseband. *E. Parry — Gelligaer F. (John Llewellyn).* 207 (R), 359 (Cf).

GINGER BISCUIT ..—.. 6 ch.g. Minster Son — Ingleby Flyer (Valiyar) b. Dam, sister to Solitary Reaper, and half-sister to Lord Of The Sky (*qv* '99 Annual; won two NH flat, two Hurdles and five Chases subsequently) was p3 points for Sue Frank (tended to run and jump badly). Brought down at the 14th in a January Maiden, and not seen again. His stable could be busy with several Maidens in '05 if all are fit. *Mrs S. Frank — Hurworth (Paul Frank).* 75 (OMa).

GINGER BUG ..9-5.. 11 ch.m. Vital Season — Loan Hill (Roselier FR) 04512p826. Strong-topped lengthy. Dam won mares Maiden and placed 5 in Ireland, and subsequently 3rd twice in English Points (after refusing once). P-t-P '02/3 r7 p0; 4th, 6th, last, pulled up 3 and fell 1. Beaten a minimum of 19 lengths, and last in her three previous outings prior to scoring unchallenged in her Members. Plodded into the runners-up berth in Restricteds twice subsequently, but bereft of speed and needs a long trip in mud to have any chance of scoring again. *A.G. Chinery — E. Essex (Paul Chinery).* 2 (R), 40 (OMa), 130 (OMa), 243 (M), 524 (R), 648 (R), 745 (R), 902 (R), 1085 (Cv&nr).

GINGER MISS (IRE) ..—.. 6 ch.m. Glacial Storm (USA) — Mum's Girl (Deep Run) p. Half-sister to Irish NH flat, Hurdling and Scottish Chasing winner, Cool Dante. Dam won 2m3f Hurdle. Struggling when pulled up after two miles in a 2m4f Maiden in February. Probably just a gentle intro. *Miss S. Collett — N. Cotswold (Fred Hutsby).* 290 (2m4fCfMa).

GINGER SPROUT (IRE) ..—.. 9 ch.m. Yashgan — Kates Well (IRE) (Rontino) uppp. Can set off enthusiastically and build up clear leads, but rapidly falls in a hole, and clearly devoid of ability. *R. Thomson — Ashford V.* 639 (R), 782 (OMa), 802 (R), 1285 (OMa).

GINMINI (IRE) ..8-4.. 9 ch.m. Husyan (USA) — Garryduff Lass (Green Shoon) pppp5p5u. Small lengthy half-sister to Virac Lad (IRE). Dam, sister to Hammer (*qv* '92 Annual), was awful Pointer in Ireland (failed to finish in 10 of 11 — last in the exception). IRISH P-t-P '01/3 r9 p0; pulled up 6. IRISH NH '02 (for P. Budds) r1 p0. Only able to achieve a completion in three of 17 Points, and even the misfortune of being partnered by Robert Ward-Dutton on occasions cannot excuse all her other bad displays. Unseated her overweight encumbrance at the first on final start, and then merrily galloped three circuits when loose. *B. Hawkins — M.J. Caldwell & R. Ward-Dutton — Worcs (Penny Grainger).* 532 (OMa), 714 (CMam), 753 (OMa), 989 (Cnr), 1211 (OMa), 1341 (OMa), 1424 (OMa), 1505 (OMa).

GIN N ICE (IRE) ..8-11§.. 12 gr.g. Glacial Storm (USA) — Theo's Gin (Teofane) 4. Good-topped. Dam, half-sister to Crown Hawk (*qv* '00 Annual). IRISH CHARITY FLAT '00 r1 p0. IRISH P-t-P '98 r1 w1 (5yo Maiden). IRISH NH '99/00 r12 w1 (2m3f Hdle) p1 (2nd). NH '00/2 r22 p3 (2 3rds); pulled up 6, fell/unseated 4. P-t-P '03 r6 p2 (remote 3rd once); last pair 2, and pulled up 2. Ungenuine and a regular non-finisher since gaining his last success in first-time blinkers at Kilbeggan in '99, and plodded into 45 lengths fourth on his only appearance in '04. Often blinkered under Rules, and visored twice in '01. *W.J. Turcan — Fernie.* 400 (C).

GIPSY CRICKETER .10-1.. 9 b.g. Anshan — Tinkers Fairy (Myjinski USA) u21p2*p*. Workmanlike brother to flat winner, College Princess. Dam is half-sister to Taramara (*qv* '94 Annual). NH FLAT '00 r1 p0. P-t-P/HUNT CH '02 (for Mr C. Coley (Yes, No, Wait & Sorries Partnership) r7 w2 (2m4f Maiden and Restricted) p2; 4th, 6th, and pulled up 1. NH '00/3 r19 w1 (2m Ch) p3; pulled up 4. NH '04 r1 p0 (pulled up in 2m3f Sell Ch: *ld til hdd 9, wknd nxt, t.o & pu aft 3 out*). Headstrong and goes a rattling good gallop in Points, but barely gets the trip, and is led to post early in a bid to expend as little energy as possible nowadays. A fine second to Upton Adventure on a track that hardly suited in '04, and as he proved at Kingston St Mary would be difficult to catch under different circumstances. Favourite when dropped back into a Seller for the first time since '01 subsequently but flopped, and ideally needs to race over the minimum trip under Rules. Suited by a sound surface. Wears a cross-noseband, and has run tongue-tied. *M. Scudamore Jnr — Ross H. (Michael Scudamore Snr).* 402 (M), 613 (L), 965 (L), 1168 (2m5fH), 1368 (L).

GIPSY GIRL ..10-7.. 10 b.m. Motivate — Young Gipsy (The Brianstan) 2111f. Small half-sister to Balinger Boy. Dam, half-sister to Willy Wagtail, won 2 Points and placed 3, Grandam, Grange Gipsy (half-sister to Witty Tom — won 8 Points and a Ch), won 2 Hdles (2m4f-3m1f) and 3m1f Ch. P-t-P '02 (for Mrs C.M. Marles) r3 p2 (2nds); and fell 1. NH '03 (from L.J. Williams's) r2 p0 (7th and pulled up in Hdles). Clocked decent times when recording a wide margin double at Howick, and much the fastest of the day when taking a strong Intermediate at Bonvilston, but robbed of a Hunter Chase success when tipping up at the second last when clear at Uttoxeter. Improving at a rate of knots, and providing the second fall of her career has not dented her confidence can look forward to another good year in '05. Sparingly raced to date, and has only once raced on ground faster than good. *O.J. Stephens — Curre & Llangibby (David Stephens).* 150 (OMa), 362 (CfMa), 695 (R), 1092 (I), 1377 (2m5fH).

GIPSY WOOD ..9-2.. 9 gr.m. Rakaposhi King — Silva Linda (Precipice Wood) p4. Tall strong half-sister to Atlas Mountain, to NH flat and Chasing winner, Linwood, and to Hurdles winner, Rosco. Dam, half-sister to Brollin (*qv* '87 Season Annual) won 3 Chases (2m-2m1f), and comes from family of Leading Optimist (*qv* '04 Annual). NH '03 (for P. Beaumont) r5 p0; pulled up 1. Beaten 42 lengths plus at odds of 20-1 or more over Hurdles, and pulled up in her first Point, but fared slightly better when eight lengths fourth next time. A hard puller who has acquired a nosenet, and still looks well short of winning standard. *Mrs S. Plowright — Rockwood H. (Stephen Wiles).* 960 (OMa), 1164 (OMa).

GIVE HIM A CHANCE (IRE) .9-4.. 10 b.g. Never Got A Chance — Shanabarr (Golden Love) 7p25pp. Tall. Dam is half-sister to Post House (*qv* '95 Annual). IRISH P-t-P '00 r5 p1 (46/ 3rd, promoted to 2nd); pulled up 1, and fell 1. P-t-P '01/2 r5 w1 (Maiden) p2; 5th, and pulled up 1. Adjudged to have gained a narrow success in a weak Maiden at Cottenham in '02, but finished lame next time, and spent last season on the sidelines. Fifteen lengths second in his Members in '04, but jumped poorly when well beaten in blinkers subsequently, and no longer looks to have the heart for a struggle. *B. Belchem — E. Essex (Robert Gardiner).* 2 (R), 102 (R), 243 (M), 524 (R), 648 (R), 829 (R).

GIVEN GRACE (IRE) .6-7.. 8 gr.m. Mr Confusion (IRE) — Italian Princess (IRE) (Strong Gale) p5p. Half-sister to Thorsgill. Dam, half-sister to Sherman Way (*qv* '91 Annual). P-t-P '03 r1 p0 (pulled up). Devoid of speed on the limited evidence to date, and badly tailed off last on her only completion. *Miss N. Clark — Zetland (John Davies).* 338 (Cf), 767 (2m4fOMa), 1286 (M).

GLACIAL BOY..9-7.. 11 b.g. Glacial Storm (USA) — Miss Posy (Pitskelly) 20p. Small compact Mathias-bred half-brother to Grampas' Girl (IRE), to jumping winners, Peaceman and Call Me Henry (in Ireland), and to NH flat winner, Ow Deadly. Dam, half-sister to Lichfield (*qv* '87 Season Annual), won 6f Sell at 2. IRISH NH FLAT '98/9 r9 p1 (3rd). IRISH NH '98/00 r9 p0. P-t-P '02/3 (for Mr R. Mathias, Mr S. & Mr G.R. Williams) r7 w1 (Maiden) p4 (2 2nds, ½*l* last once; and 3rd of 4, and last of 3); 4th of 5, and pulled up 1. Of no account in Ireland, but consistent in minor Points, and readily won a three-finisher Maiden at Erw Lon last year. Outjumped by the winner when turned over at 1-2 in his Members, but atypical of his sire's stock in that he looks pretty soft, and has been tried in headgear. *Miss S. Hyde & R.W. Williams — Brecon & Talybont (Richard Mathias).* 446 (M), 726 (R), 844 (R).

GLACIAL DANCER (IRE) ..9-9.. 12 b.g. Glacial Storm (USA) — Castleblagh (General Ironside) 3f3u535p. Lengthy brother to The Dasher Doyle (Irish Pointing and jumping), and half-brother to Native Daisy (IRE), to Iron Monty (Irish Pointing) and Pointing and Hurdling winner, Miracle Me. IRISH P-t-P '97/8 r5 w1 (Maiden) p1 (2nd); pulled up 1. NH '98/01 and '03 r14 w2 (3m-3m110y Hdles) p7 (3 2nds); pulled up 2. P-t-P '03 r6 p0; last, and pulled up 5. The lucky winner of a two-finisher Irish Maiden in '98, and all out to win over hurdles the following year, but out of luck since slogging through mud at Ayr in January '00, and is a very weak finisher now. Particularly disappointing when unable to mount a challenge in his Members, and there must be something wrong with him. *S.B. Clark — York & Ainsty S. (Liz Clark).* 55 (Cf), 163 (O), 316 (2m5fH), 679 (3m1fH), 1157 (M), 1301 (Cf), 1414 (O), 1489 (3m3fH).

GLACIAL PEARL (IRE) ..9-12.. 10 ch.g. Glacial Storm (USA) — Hopeful Dawn (Prince Hansel) 424. Neat good-topped half-brother to Northern Dawn, and to NH flat winner, Dark Phoenix (IRE). NH FLAT '00 r2 w1 (2m1f) p0. NH '01/2 r2 p0. P-t-P '03 r3 p1 (remote last of 3); and pulled up 2. Won a weak Sedgefield bumper by ten lengths on his debut in July '00, and returned to form on his last two starts, but flattered by his proximity to Bally Wirral, and faded badly from the second last at Woodford. Stands his racing badly, and has still to prove that he stays well enough to make his mark in Points. *Mrs J. Crew — V.W.H.* 728 (I), 972 (Cf), 1071 (I).

GLACIAL SYGNET (IRE) ..9-11.. 12 ch.g. Glacial Storm (USA) — Barnhill Rose (Lucifer USA) 435*p2*. Strong half-brother to to Celtic Buck, and to Irish NH flat and Hurdling winner, Strategic Intent. Dam won NH flat and 2m2f Hurdle in Ireland. IRISH FLAT '03 r1 p0. IRISH NH FLAT '98 r2 p1 (3rd). IRISH NH '99/03 (for J.J. Mangan) r44 w4 (2 3m Hdles and 2 2m4f-2m6f Chses) p8; pulled up 3, brought down 1. NH '04 r2 p1 (2nd in 2m5f Ch: *ld til rn wide bend app 2 out, rallied u.p flat*); and pulled up in 2m6f110y Ch: *nt jw, a bhnd, t.o & pu 12*. Won four races in Ireland including in fields of 16, 18 and 20, and his placings include second in a Chase worth £17,000 to the winner. Very inconsistent and moody, and has a tendency to run in snatches, but showed he retains ability when half-a- length second in a Handicap Chase which earned him £1,560, and could yet score in Open company at 12 if he decided. Would never be a reliable betting medium however. Normally tongue-tied, and wears blinkers or cheekpieces. Underrated by several pounds at his best. *J.L. Gledson — Ledbury.* 509 (O), 656 (O), 917 (O).

GLAD ALL OVER ..7-12.. 14 ch.m. Jupiter Island — Midsummer Gladness (Midsummer Night II) 758. Lengthy half-sister to Happy Blade. Dam, sister to Barmer Girl (*qv* '90 Annual), won 2m4f Hunt Ch and 8 Points and placed 9. P-t-P '99/03 r14 w2 (Maiden — 2 finished and Members — 3 ran — 2 finished) p2 (2nds, of 3 once); 4th, last pair 5, pulled up 1 and fell/unseated 3. A dual winner in two-finisher events on extremes of going at Marks Tey in '02, but tailed off last in four of seven completions since, and is remarkably slow now. *D. Hays — Essex F. & U. (David Hays).* 44 (R), 127 (R), 250 (R).

GLADIATORIAL (IRE) ..10-4.. 13 b.g. Mazaad — Arena (Sallust) 2pp2121p. Tall workmanlike half-brother to 4 flat winners, including in Ireland and in Scandinavia. IRISH NH FLAT '96 r4 w1 p2 (2nds). IRISH NH '96/7 r8 w1 (2m1f Hdle) p2. IRISH FLAT '97 r1 w1 (13f). FLAT '00 r1 p0 (last). NH '00 r18 r4; pulled up 4, fell/unseated 3. P-t-P '02/3 r21 w3 (inc Open) p5 (4 3rds, of 4 once); 4th, 5th, 6th, last pair 6, unseated 1 and pulled up 3. Badly impeded by the previous owner-rider, but rejuvenated by current connections, and recorded his first wins since '97 last year. Does best when stamina is not an issue, and followers were rewarded with a 25-1 success at Exeter where his five length advantage two out was being whittled away on the run-in, but has otherwise been let down by his jumping in Hunter Chases. Well handled by Tom Bishop. Visored twice in '00, and has run tongue-tied. Wears a cross-noseband. *Mrs F.D. Bishop — Blackmore & Sparkford V.* 471 (O), 602 (MO), 799 (2m3f110yH), 880 (MO), 1065 (O), 1130 (Cnr), 1293 (2m7f110yH), 1437 (2m5f110yH).

GLADYS .—.. 13 b.m. Gypsy Castle — Dizzy Dora (Rubor) pp. Lengthy light-framed plain half-sister to Bear Faced. Dam, sister to Barretts Hill (*qv* '87 Season Annual), won 2 Points and placed 4 (inc 2 poor 3rds in Chses) for Zoe Green. P-t-P '99/00 r9 p0 (last pair 2, and pulled up 7). Resurfaced after a four-year holiday to pull up after a maximum of two miles on consecutive weekends in March. Her record is as dreadful as she looks. Has run tongue-tied. *Miss Z.A. Green — Cumberland.* 511 (OMam), 553 (CfMa).

GLASTRIAN ..— §.. 7 b.g. Lancastrian — Glorious Day (Lepanto GER) ppp. Workmanlike brother to Laggan More. Shows no ability, but certainly possesses some temperament, and having been led to the start by his rider he was pulled up after trying to refuse at the 13th on his middle effort. *G. Perkins — Glamorgan.* 363 (CfMa), 1323 (CfMa), 1393 (OMa).

GLEMOT (IRE) ..8-5.. 17 br.g. Strong Gale — Lady Nethertown (Windjammer USA) pup7p. Tall sparely-made half-brother to Irish NH flat and jumping winner, Rash Decision, and to NH flat and Hurdles winner, Golden Rose (IRE). NH FLAT '92 r1 p0. NH '92/01 (for J. Hansen, J.H. Johnson, 3 wins, K.C. Bailey, 7 wins, and P.R. Webber, 5 wins) r71 w15 (2m1f Hdle and 14 2m-3m1f Chses) p23; pulled up 6, and fell/unseated 4. Capable of front-running to good effect when younger, and a sound jumper, but always inconsistent and unpredictable, and broke a blood vessel once in '96. Unseated in the '97 Grand National, but amassed 15 victories (with a maximum of five runners in nine) and prize money of £117,163 in a thoroughly honourable career which saw him score at least once annually '92/01. Revived in his dotage for Pointing, but apart from trundling round to finish well over a fence behind under the owner in his Members he was unable to complete. At least he looked healthy, and his partners were kind on him when his old legs began to turn to jelly. *J.E. Dillon — Fernie (John Dillon).* 3 (O), 156 (O), 786 (O), 885 (M), 1153 (O).

GLENAHARY ROSE (IRE) ..8-13.. 12 b.g. Roselier (FR) — Ara Go On (Sandalay) p7u6. Rangy workmanlike brother to Aralier Man (IRE). IRISH P-t-P '98/9 and '01/2 r17 w3 (inc 2 Opens) p9; fell 2. IRISH NH '99/00 r13 p1 (2nd). IRISH HUNT CH '01/2 r8 p2. P-t-P/HUNT CH '03 (for Mrs A.C. Martin & Mrs J. Keighley) r6 p0 (5th, 6th twice, last 2 and pulled up 1). Won three Irish Points in soft to '01, but beaten 27 times since, and has looked short on stamina in England. A first ride for Alison Tory at Bishops Court, and got her into the shake up for a long way on their final appearance. Blinkered once in '02. Wears a cross-noseband. *Miss A.E. Tory — Portman.* 322 (L), 603 (Cnr), 861 (M), 1383 (Cnr).

GLENALLA BRAES (IRE) ..8-11.. 12 b.g. Roi Guillaume (FR) — Willowho Pride (Arapaho) 1. Small workmanlike half-brother to Irish Pointing and NH flat winner, Glenalla Star. IRISH P-t-P '99/00 r11 p5; pulled up 4, fell 1. NH '01/3 (for M.J. Gingell) r8 p0; pulled up 3. A poor Irish maiden whose subsequent exploits under Rules in this country included 12th of 13 in a Selling Hurdle and badly tailed off last and pulled up in Chases (started at 50-1 or more in his final six attempts, when wearing a visor in the last three), but very luckily caught Rip Kirby on a big off day in his Members, and finally broke his duck to give Rosena Page a first victory on only her second ride (unsurprisingly she did not achieve it on one of her father's nags). Would be extremely fortunate to find a similar opportunity again. *R. Barr — Easton H. (April Gingell).* 217 (M).

GLEN AMBER (IRE) ..9-1.. 10 ch.g. Naheez (USA) — Karlinda (Karlinsky USA) 32. Dam, half-sister to Even-Ogan (*qv* '92 Annual). IRISH P-t-P '02 r6 p3 (3rds); pulled up 1. P-t-P '03 r2 p0 (last and pulled up 1). Very modest in Ireland, but no better for present connections, and gained his placings in the weakest races. Appears to lurch from one setback to another. *N.W. Padfield — Aldenham H.* 220 (OMa), 424 (CMa).

GLEN CANYON (IRE) ..—.. 8 b.g. Tidaro (USA) — Glenadore (Furry Glen) u. Half-brother to 6 losing jumpers. 2000 4yo. NH FLAT '02 (for T. Needham) r2 p0. Suffered a fatal injury when blundering badly and unseating in a Market Rasen Maiden. Lord Yarborough — Brocklesby (Mark Bennison). 58 (OMa).

GLENDAMAH (IRE) ..10-2.. 8 b.g. Mukaddamah (USA) — Sea Glen (IRE) (Glenstal USA) 8834225. Small compact. 24,000y. FLAT '99/02 r26 w1 (6f) p5. NH '02/3 (for J.R. Weymes) r12 w2 (2m1f Hdles) p2 (2nds). Won a firm ground sprint by a short-head (it took the judge over half an hour to come to a decision), and completed a double in Hexham Selling Hurdles in May '02 before finishing six lengths second in an Amateurs race when bidding for the hat-trick. A funny customer who holds several different positions during his races, and tactically a hard ride, but almost caught the leader napping when beaten a neck in an Easingwold Confined (would have been very flattered had he snatched the verdict). Jumps safely, and the owner was finally rewarded by her patience with Bankersdraft, so if prepared to sit it out she may get some overdue joy from this one. *Mrs S. Robinson — York & Ainsty N.* 267 (Cf), 389 (Cf), 683 (O), 812 (O), 1163 (Cf), 1289 (O), 1457 (O).

GLEN MIST (IRE) ..9-6.. 10 b.g. Maelstrom Lake — Zamana (Ya Zaman USA) ppu433ppp. Tall light-framed. NH FLAT '00 r1 p0. NH '01/2 r4 p0. P-t-P '03 r8 w2 (Maiden and Restricted) p3 (2 2nds, last once); last, pulled up 1 and fell 1. Recorded a double on sound surfaces last year, but in doing so benefited from superior riding, and had previously been unable to beat a remounter. Blinkered and only once better than last in '04, and often looks irresolute, but broke a blood vessel on his final appearance, and may have been doing so more regularly. *E. Donavan — Gelligaer F. (Lisa Day).* 116 (I), 359 (Cf), 447 (Cf), 698 (Inr), 739 (Inr), 841 (Cf), 1023 (Cf), 1092 (I), 1188 (Cf).

GLENMONT (IRE) ..9-7.. 13 b.g. Montelimar (USA) — Glenamara (Furry Glen) 4uppp2u157. Workmanlike half-brother to Irish NH flat and jumping winner, Dromineer (IRE). Dam, half-sister to Bonnie Boy (*qv* '90 Annual), won mares Maiden in Ireland. IRISH NH FLAT '97/8 r7 p0. IRISH NH '98/00 r13 p0 (pulled up only Hunt Ch). IRISH P-t-P '00 r4 w1 (7&8yo Maiden) p1 (2nd); pulled up 1. P-t-P '01/3 r15 w2 (Members and Restricted) p10 (6 2nds, remote last once, and of 3 once; and inc 3rd of 4 once); 6th, last and pulled up 1. Easily recorded his third success at Aldington when taking his Members, but ordinarily easy to beat, and seems to be steadily losing interest. Blinkered once in '99, and acquired cheekpieces in '04. *B. Neaves & Ms L. Stock — W. Street Tickham (Lisa Stock).* 41 (I), 182 (CCon), 422 (CCon), 607 (Cf), 778 (CCon), 896 (CCon), 1083 (Cf), 1280 (M), 1406 (I), 1516 (L).

GLENSAN (IRE) ..9-13.. 8 b.g. Insan (USA) — Strikes Glen (Le Moss) 12Rs1. Small sparely-made. 11,000 3yo. NH FLAT '01 r1 p0. NH '02 (for Mrs H. Dalton) r3 p0; pulled up 1. Bought Doncaster, May for 3000. Made nearly all when landing some good bets in a Market Rasen Maiden in which only two finished, and ended the season with a more meritorious success in a Dingley Restricted in which he jumped well and kept finding extra when pressed by the runner-up. Seems quite tough and may be able to find another race, but looking at him you would not think he would appreciate too much weight on his back. *M.E. Sowersby & C.N. Richardson — Holderness (Mary Sowersby).* 303 (OMa), 481 (R), 771 (R), 1163 (Cf), 1217 (R).

GLORY TRAIL (IRE) ..9-9.. 11 b.g. Supreme Leader — Death Or Glory (Hasdrubal) 32p3. Small well-made brother to Irish Pointing and jumping winner, Super Dealer (IRE), and half-brother to Final Option (IRE), and to Irish Pointing winner, Stormin To Glory. IRISH P-t-P '99/00 r7 w1 (Maiden) p1 (2nd); pulled up 3, and fell 3 out when looking likely winner. IRISH NH FLAT '00 r2 p0. NH '01 r1 p0 (6th in Hdle). P-t-P/HUNT CH '01/3 r6 w1 (Restricted) p1 (3rd); 4th, last, and fell/unseated 2. Made amends for an unlucky English debut when skating up at rain-soaked Charing in '02, but has been incredibly susceptible to setbacks since, and beaten a minimum of 20 lengths in '04. It seems he has been under a cloud too long to revive successfully. *Pinkies Partnership (R. Griffiths) — E. Sussex & Romney Marsh (Di Grissell).* 608 (L), 805 (L), 1083 (Cf), 1407 (L).

GLOVES OFF (IRE) ..—§.. 8 br.g. Naheez (USA) — River Dance View (IRE) (Orchestra) p55p. Leggy. IR4800 3yo. IRISH NH FLAT '01/2 r4 p0. IRISH NH '01/2 r5 p1 (3rd). NH '03 (for Mrs A.J. Hamilton-Fairley) r2 p0; pulled up 1. Left to claim 15 lengths third in a Chase after there had been several late defections, but has been in two stables since, and would not go a yard and resented every moment in the latest (hopelessly tailed off twice). Blinkered on his two most recent outings, and connections will have surely given up on him now. *Mrs K.F. Irving — Bicester with Whaddon (Heather Irving).* 20 (OMa), 51 (OMa), 192 (CfMa), 462 (OMa).

GO BOY..8-7.. 7 b.g. Sovereign Water (FR) — Tinkle (Petoski) 7p. Lengthy. NH FLAT '02 r2 p0. NH '02 r1 p0. P-t-P '03 r7 p3 (2 3rds, of 4 once and remote last once); last pair 2, and fell/unseated 2. Showed distinct signs of promise last year, and sent off favourite once, but lost his way during the season, and showed no aptitude at all in '04. Might be worth putting an experienced rider on board as the present one is certainly no asset. Wears a cross-noseband. *M. & Miss R. Holmes — Axe V.H. (Michael Holmes).* 119 (OMa), 693 (OMa).

GOD OF WAR ..8-5.. 7 ch.g. Primitive Rising (USA) — Sun Goddess (FR) (Deep Roots) ppu83. Rangy owner-bred brother to Primitive Rites (*qv*). Jumped badly and unfit and clueless in his early races, but after finishing well over two fences last he achieved a 43 lengths third for Steve Charlton (normally beginner ridden otherwise), and is probably just starting to get the hang of things. May be ready to take more of a hand in proceedings in his second season. *J. Hewitt — York & Ainsty N.* 393 (CfMa), 504 (CMa), 1158 (OMa), 1165 (OMa), 1300 (OMa).

GO GO GALLANT (IRE) .9-0.. 16 b.g. Over The River (FR) — Joyful Anna (Bluerullah) 766. Tall strong. Dam won 4&5yo Maiden in Ireland. IRISH P-t-P '94 and '01/2 r10 w4 (inc Ladies and 2 Opens) p2 (2nds); pulled up 1 and fell 1. IRISH NH '94/02 r31 w5 (2m6f-3m1f Chses) p5. IRISH HUNT CH

'95 r1 p0. P-t-P '03 r4 p1 (3rd); 5th, last and pulled up 1. A smart performer in mud in Ireland, and ran in seven Graded Chases to '00, but his loss of form coincided with his acquiring a tongue-strap, and had to return to Points to score again at 13. Has broken blood vessels in the past, and having been beaten a minimum of 25 lengths in '04 looks no more than a safe conveyance now. Blinkered once in '00. *Miss E.C. Wilesmith — Ledbury.* 403 (Cf), 979 (MOnr), 1392 (C).

GOING PRIMITIVE .—.. 14 b.g. Primitive Rising (USA) — Good Going Girl (Import) 9p. Compact stocky. Dam, sister or half-sister to 4 Pointers including Flying Lion, pulled up in 6 Points and a Hunt Ch (failed to stay, but was equally useless in shorter races). NH FLAT '97 r4 p3 (2nd once). NH '97 r1 p1 (2nd in Hdle). P-t-P/HUNT CH '98 and '02/3 r7 p0 (fell/unseated 4, and pulled up 3). Never missed the frame under Rules, but looked suspect on occasions and spent four years on the sidelines from '98, and reported dead after stopping to nil in a matter of strides for the umpteenth time at Cottenham. R.J. Lancaster — W. Street Tickham. 6 (OMa), 99 (I).

PLATE 51 770 Middleton Confined: Golden Chimes is the first leg of Grant Tuer's double
PHOTO: Brian Armstrong

GOLDEN CHIMES (USA) .10-7.. 10 ch.g. Woodman (USA) — Russian Ballet (USA) (Nijinsky CAN) 11. Good-topped attractive brother to 2 winners in Ireland inc Dr Johnson (2nd in Irish Derby), and half-brother to Hurdles winners, Lorenzino (IRE) and Domenico (IRE). IRISH FLAT '97/8 r4 w1 (10f) p0. FLAT '99/01 r15 w1 (14f) p2. NH '99/01 r10 w2 (2m5f110y Hdles) p3 (2nds). P-t-P/HUNT CH '03 r5 w2 (Open and Members) p2 (2nds); and 4th. A versatile performer who has won on the flat, and over hurdles and fences, but sometimes incapacitated by a breathing problem, and only stands light campaigns now. Retains a turn of foot, and surprisingly able to use it on ground previously thought to be unsuitable when clocking the fastest time of the day at Whitwell-on-the-Hill, and should win again. Has run tongue-tied. Blinkered twice in '99. *G. Tuer — Hurworth.* 436 (3m1f110yH), 770 (Cf).

GOLDEN DAWN ..8-7.. 8 gr.g. Gran Alba (USA) — Golden Curd (FR) (Nice Havrais USA) ppu5. Compact half-brother to Chasing winner, Red Emperor, and to NH flat and Hurdles winner, Silver Shred. Dam is French jumping winner. IR10,000 3yo. NH '01/2 (for G.M. Moore, and B.D. Leavy) r8 p0; pulled up 2. Has made 12 appearances, but never been beaten less than 19 lengths including in three Chases (pulled up once) and four Maidens. A model of mediocrity. *Miss J.L. Lundgren — Bilsdale.* 685 (OMa), 890 (2m4fOMa), 1339 (OMa), 1402 (2m4fOMa).

GOLDEN EMBERS .—§.. 7 b.g. Regal Embers (IRE) — Sallisses (Pamroy) pppp. Strong-topped lengthy owner-bred brother to Raymond James (*qv*), and half-brother to Rusty Fellow (*qv*). P-t-P '03 r2 p0 (last and pulled up 1). From a very quirky family that can take an awfully long time to mature, but already looking decidedly unwilling, and beaten two fences in his solitary completion. *Mrs G.M. Shail — Ledbury (Roy Shail).* 119 (OMa), 256 (CMa), 982 (2m5fOMa), 1233 (OMa).

GOLDEN HOST ..—§§.. 11 ch.g. Roman Warrior — Prominent Princess (Prominer) pps. Good-topped. Dam won Irish NH flat (ridden by Con Rutledge). NH FLAT '99/00 r3 p0. NH '00 r2 p0 (pulled up 2). P-t-P '02/3 r8 p0 (pulled up 7, and fell 1). One of the most ungenuine animals ever to look through a bridle, and decelerates with incredible rapidity as soon as push comes to shove. Has never recovered from an unnecessarily hard ride on his debut under Rules, and running him again would be pointless. Wears blinkers, when connections remember to put them on, and visored once in '03. *C. Rutledge — N. Cotswold.* 1395 (OMa), 1486 (OMa), 1532 (OMa).

PLATE 52 1492 14 Regiment Royal Artillery Confined: Golden Jack and David Dunsdon, 1st, take the ditch *PHOTO: Tim Holt*

GOLDEN JACK (FR) ..9-12.. 11 b.g. Matahawk — Union Jack III (FR) (Mister Jack FR) 472p651. Strong compact half-brother to Djeddah (FR) (*qv*). FRENCH NH '98/03 (for G. Chaignon when successful, and F. Doumen) r32 w1 (3m Ch) p7 (inc 5 cross-country races). Very much the poor relation of Djeddah and Extra Jack, but has his own slight merits, and employed as a safe schoolmaster in the new yard (best effort when four lengths second of four). Never looked like scoring until David Dunsdon took over in a Larkhill Confined on firm, and after being backed from fives to half those odds he disposed of three rivals without much fuss. Only aspires to around 9-4 when beginner ridden. *J.E.M. Morris — Portman (Ali Tory).* 626 (Cnr), 642 (O), 937 (Cnr), 1073 (O), 1329 (Cnr), 1383 (Cnr), 1492 (Cf).

GOLDEN PRIDE ..8-6.. 11 b.m. Blaze O'Gold (USA) — Percy's Pride (Rustingo) 7553. Rangy owner-bred sister to Blazing Pride (*qv*). Very slow, but safe, and left her brother trailing 30 lengths in her wake when finishing three lengths third in her Members (got badly outpaced with a mile to run in a joke contest, but was plugging on well at the death). *Mrs S.A. Haynes — Golden V.* 452 (R), 934 (OMa), 1232 (OMa), 1387 (M).

GOLDEN RIVET ..10-7.. 8 b.g. Weld — Golden Valley (Hotfoot) 11. Tall brother to Half Each and Another Half, and half-brother to Golden Lark, Only Me, Woolstonwood, See More Castles, Soso Gold and Ambersam. Dam pulled up in 3 Points. NH FLAT '02 r1 p0. P-t-P '02/3 r2 p2 (2nds). Failed the vet after going through the ring for 6,000 at Doncaster in '03, but potentially worth a lot more now following a double on good or sound surfaces this year. There are drawbacks with him though, and apart from the obvious brevity of his appearances has looked very cantankerous in the preliminaries. Has done nothing wrong on the course however, and looks an ideal candidate for a Novice Hunter Chase in '05. *A.T. Preston, Mrs G.B. Walford & Mrs R.W. Bromfield — Middleton (Gill Walford).* 59 (OMa), 389 (Cf).

GOLDEN SAVANNAH ..—.. 15 b.g. Presidium — Golden Pampas (Golden Fleece USA) pp. Strong hobdayed half-brother to 2 winners abroad (one useful in Spain). FLAT r3 p1 (3rd of 4). NH '93/6 and '98 (blinkered 2) r18 w1 (2m Hdle) p1 (last of 3); pulled up 4, unseated 1. P-t-P/HUNT CH '96, '98/

00 and '02 (for Mr C.J.W. Smyth) r33 w3 (inc 2 Opens) p11 (4 2nds, inc a Hunt Ch; and inc last of 3 once); pulled up 5, ran out 1, and on floor 4. Managed an annual success in three Pointing campaigns to '99, but went into a rapid decline in '02, and did not warrant a return as a schoolmaster. *Miss S. Morris — V.W.H.* 1332 (Cf), 1407 (L).

GOLDEN SHRED .9-6§.. 8 gr.m. Norton Challenger — Lady Seville (Orange Bay) 3333. Lengthy half-sister to Jaffa's Boy, Captain Marmalade and Marmalade Mountain, to NH flat winner, The Lady Captain, and to flat winner, Ballerina Bay. P-t-P '03 r2 p1 (3rd); and pulled up 1. Beaten upwards of 19 lengths when in third (promoted once) in five Maidens, and unimproved by blinkers in the last two. Has not lacked strength from the saddle, but appears to resent pressure, and may have been cast aside already. Wears a cross-noseband. *Mrs A. Villar & P. Beeton-Brown — Suffolk (Ruth Hayter).* 26 (OMa), 40 (OMa), 151 (OMa), 245 (CfMa).

GOLDEN SOVEREIGN ..—§ .. 10 b.g. Gold Dust — Dark Image (Bold As Brass) fuRp. Leggy angular owner-bred brother to Dark Venetian, and half-brother to Silver Image. Dam, half-sister to 3 Pointers, including Northern Sensation (*qv* '00 Annual), won 2 Points and placed 6 for Mr Down, and grandam, Dark Sensation, won Maiden and 2nd. Great-grandam, also Dark Venetian, won 8 Chses (3m-3m2f), and also won 2m Hdle, but disqualified on technical grounds. P-t-P '02/3 r4 p0 (unseated 1, ran out 1 and pulled up 2). A non-finisher in all eight starts spread over three years, and hardly warranted being supported from 14s to half those odds at Umberleigh, where regular partner Mark Dennis was no doubt only too pleased to be in the commentary box. *J. Down — Torrington F.* 494 (OMa), 1002 (R), 1507 (R), 1566 (OMa).

GOLDEN SPIRIT ..8-10.. 9 b.m. Goldsmiths' Hall — Game Reserve (Doeskin) 4. Good-bodied half-sister to Cardschool. Dam ran badly in 5 Points for Mr Smith, but grandam, Parkness, won 2 Points and was 2nd to The Dikler for him. Made considerable late progress to finish 12 lengths fourth in an elders Maiden in mid-April, but is an eight-year old who has not been spotted before or since. Looks to have a little ability if she has a chance to show it. *W.E. Smith — Taunton V. (Susan Honeyball).* 967 (OMa).

GOLDEN TANU ..—.. 12 b.g. Gold Dust — Gold Bid (Golden Mallard) pp. P-t-P '02/3 r2 p0 (pulled up 2). Lengthy attractive. Unraced until he was nine, and has done nothing but pull up so far, but has hinted at ability, and might be capable of a surprise if in a fit state in '05. *Mrs M. Gray — S. Devon (Nicky Frost).* 913 (OMa), 1272 (OMa).

GOLD KRIEK .10-2.. 8 b.g. High Kicker (USA) — Ship Of Gold (Glint Of Gold) p2*1*. Small compact brother to flat winners Freckles (subsequently won Hurdling in Belgium) and Gold Clipper. FLAT '99/01 r11 p0. NH '01 r8 p0; fell 1. P-t-P '03 r6 w3 (Maiden, Restricted and Intermediate) p2; and fell. NH '04 (for B.J. Llewellyn) r1 w1 (beat Sunshan 15*l* in 3m Ch: *a.p, mists 3 & 4, ld 6, blun 12, hdd nxt, ld 2 out, sn clr*). Slow on the level and fell on the only occasion he looked like making the frame over hurdles, but has finally cracked it now that he has been put over fences, and picked up £4,765 when scoring at Uttoxeter in June. Still lacks fluency but seems unlikely to revert to Pointing, at least in the near future. Handles softish but more effective on sound surfaces. *J. Parfitt — Llangeinor (Bernard Llewellyn).* 1090 (Cf), 1320 (Cf).

GOLF LAND (IRE) ..9-6.. 13 ch.g. Be My Native (USA) — Just Clara (Camden Town) 44. Compact attractive. NH FLAT '96 r4 p2. NH '96/7 r5 p1 (3rd in Hdle); tailed off last in Sell final. NH '98/9 r4 p0. P-t-P/HUNT CH '98, '00 and '02/3 r11 w3 (inc Open) p1 (2 fences last of 3); 4th, pulled up 3, ran out 1 and fell/unseated 2. Recorded the most praiseworthy success of his career in soft at Friars Haugh last year, but error-proneand unpredictable, and stands his racing badly. Most unlikely to achieve much in future. Wears a tongue-strap. *W.M. Aitchison — Border (Joanne Martin).* 134 (O), 1309 (O).

GOLLINGER ..9-6.. 9 b.g. St Ninian — Edith Rose (Cheval) p66452. Compact half-brother to Mr Boston. Dam won at 7f, and won 2m1f Hdle. NH FLAT '00 r1 p1 (2nd). HUNT CH '03 r3 p1 (3rd); 5th of 6, and pulled up. Second in a bumper and a Maiden four years apart, but otherwise only once better than last in '04, and struggles to get the trip in Points. Prone to bad mistakes, and needs to dominate and will capitulate if taken on, but can probably manage a small success on an easy track. Ran no sort of race in blinkers at Duncombe Park, but seems happier in cheekpieces since. *R.D.E. Woodhouse — Middleton.* 112 (OMa), 166 (OMa), 272 (OMa), 394 (CfMa), 504 (CMa), 1164 (OMa).

GONE ON (IRE) ..9-0.. 7 b.g. Charente River (IRE) — Kyle Aris (Energist) f41. Small close-coupled half-brother to Irish Hurdling and Pointing winner, Glencreen. IRISH P-t-P '03 r1 p0 (unseated). IRISH NH FLAT '03 (for F. Flood) r1 p0. Has suffered from jumping problems and was left winded after taking a heavy fall two out when holding every chance in a bad six-runner Maiden at Cothelstone, but finally got it right on his latest appearance, and took a similarly poor contest on firmish at Holnicote in May. Had a bit in hand, and should at least be capable of getting placed in Restricteds at seven. Can probably rate higher. *Mr & Mrs B. Watts — Worcs (Rose Vickery).* 475 (OMa), 884 (OMa), 1327 (OMa).

GO NOMADIC ..10-2.. 11 br.g. Nomadic Way (USA) — Dreamago (Sir Mago) 6123232. Compact brother to Nomadic Star and Nomadic Blaze, and half-brother to Ravensworth. Dam, half-sister to Sonydee (*qv* '92 Annual), won 2 Points and placed 5 for the Atkinsons. Grandam, Dreamadee, won 14 Points and placed 11 (inc a Hunt Ch). Great-grandam, Sams Dream, won 2m1f Hdle and was 3rd in Ladies. P-t-P/HUNT CH '99/03 r24 w6 (inc 2 3m1f-3m7f Hunt Chses, and 2 Opens) p12 (7 2nds, beaten head once, and of 3 once; and inc 7 Hunt Chses); 7th, last, and pulled up 4. A very determined stayer who normally makes the running, and is a reliable if unspectacular jumper, but very one-paced, and finds it difficult to win under normal conditions. May need to concentrate on Pointing stamina tests in future. Usually runs tongue-tied. *D.G. Atkinson — Bedale.* 269 (O), 429 (3m5fO), 542 (3m3fH), 678 (3m1fH), 894 (3m3fH), 1068 (3m2f110yH), 1296 (3m1fH).

GOOD BOY (FR) ..10-8.. 11 b.g. Cadoudal (FR) — Cazeres (FR) (Goodland FR) 4. Strong-topped. FRENCH NH '97/02 r74 w7 (4 2m1f-2m4f Hdles, and 3 2m1f-2m5f Chses) p17 (including in Switzerland). P-t-P/HUNT CH '03 r6 w3 (3m Hunt Ch, and 2 Opens) p1 (2nd); 4th, and 5th. Most adept at course completion, and took his winning tally into double figures when landing a Hunter Chase at Huntingdon last year, but presumably met with a setback after coming home exhausted at Tweseldown. A very precise jumper on sound surfaces, but does not stay too well otherwise, and might struggle to maintain his rating unless '05 is a dry year. Has been tried in blinkers. *M.H.D. Barlow — Bicester with Whaddon (Robert & Teresa Elwell).* 17 (O).

GOOD GRACIOUS .7-4.. 7 br.g. Good Times (ITY) — Protected (FR) (Blakeney) p45. Strong rangy owner-bred. Not jumping well enough so far, and beaten over 30 lengths in both completions. Still seems to be very green. *P.A. Tylor — Cury (Stephen Long).* 1432 (OMa), 1511 (OMa), 1559 (OMa).

GOOD HEART (IRE) ..9-12.. 10 ch.g. Be My Native (USA) — Johnstown Love (IRE) (Golden Love) 44314p. Tall rangy half-brother to Irish Pointing/English jumping winner, Richie's Delight (IRE). Dam, sister to Lover Bill (*qv* '95 Annual). NH FLAT '99 r1 w1. NH '99/01 and '03 r12 p1 (3rd); pulled up 1, fell 1. P-t-P '03 r2 p0; last, and fell 1. Had six subsequent jumping winners in his wake when landing a bumper at Haydock on his racecourse debut, but hugely disappointing himself, and was recording his first success since when enterprisingly sent to Peper Harow. Faltered and looked for a moment like throwing the race away but the runner-up proved equally weak-willed, and will undoubtedly find it hard to follow up. Suited by an easy surface. Visored once in '01, and wore cheekpieces and a tongue-strap once apiece last year. *M.J. Caldwell — Cheshire Forest (Katie Caldwell).* 420 (O), 663 (I), 750 (O), 1209 (O), 1372 (2m4fH), 1443 (2m5fH).

GOOD MORNING ..9-2.. 11 b.m. Current Edition (IRE) — Havenod (Tom Noddy) puu9441. Small half-sister to Nodalotte's Niece. Dam is sister to Nodalotte (*qv* '94 Annual). Grandam, Havelotte, a half-sister to Fitz, won 7 Points and placed 15. NH '01 r4 p0. P-t-P '02/3 (for Mrs G. & Miss J.J. England) r12 w1 (Maiden) p5 (2nds, of 3 four, remote once); last, pulled up 3, and fell/unseated 2. Required 14 races before she could be cajoled into winning, but already on her third Pointing owner, and beaten a minimum of 30 lengths in Restricteds prior to landing her Members which took 21 seconds longer than any other race on the card. Lacks fluency, and predictably had Ross Dickson in trouble at first, and has been tried in blinkers. *Mrs H. Dickson — N. Tyne.* 548 (R), 657 (R), 918 (R), 1222 (R), 1310 (R), 1419 (R), 1480 (M).

GOOD THYNE CHARLIE (IRE) ..—.. 6 b.g. Good Thyne (USA) — Glint And Shine (IRE) (Air Display USA) p. Pulled up and dismounted after a mile at Dalston. *R.A. Ross — Braes.* 768 (2m4fOMa).

GOOD THYNE MURPHY (IRE) ..8-11.. 9 b.g. Good Thyne (USA) — Early Pace (Black Minstrel) f5f. Brother to Northern Edition (IRE). Dam, half-sister to Lucky Helmet (*qv* '95 Annual), won Point and 2m2f Hdle in Ireland. NH FLAT '01 r1 p0. NH '01 r1 p0. P-t-P '02/3 r5 w1 (Maiden) p0 (last, pulled up 1, carried out 1 and unseated 1). Benefited from stronger handling when springing a 33-1 surprise on his final appearance last year, but let down by his jumping in '04, and was tailed off last on his only completion. Has been tried tongue-tied, and almost certainly defective. *Ms A. Counsell — Essex (Chris Lawson).* 124 (CCon), 400 (C), 606 (R).

GOOD TIME MELODY (IRE) ..10-9.. 12 b.g. Good Thyne (USA) — Raashideah (Dancer's Image USA) 301. Well-made half-brother to winner, Brassy Nell, to Irish NH flat and Hurdles winner, Ar Muin Na Muice (IRE), and to Irish NH flat winner, Aungier Gale. Dam won 6f race. NH FLAT '98 r1 p1 (2nd). NH '99/02 (for A. King, and J.W. Mullins, one run) r17 w3 (3m-3m2f Chses) p5 (2nds inc 2 Hdles); pulled up 2. A triple scorer in mud to May '01, but pulled up on his final attempt under Rules, and seemed rusty when returning two years later. Gave a gutsy display to end his latest season on a bright note, and although it was only a sub-standard Hunter Chase in which he beat Ronans Choice by two lengths at Fontwell his performance looked better in view of his past history, as he once suffered from a bad knee injury. Blinkered twice in previous campaigns, and needs a lot of driving. Perhaps he will be retiring on a high. *R.I. Webb-Bowen — R.A. (Sally Mullins).* 178 (3m1f110yH), 241 (2m4f110yH), 800 (3m2f110yH).

GO POSITIVE ..9-6.. 10 b.m. Profilic — Rather Gorgeous (Billion USA) 3. Lengthy good-topped half-sister to Posh Petong. Dam, half-sister to Kingoftheswingers (*qv* '97 Annual), won 14f race, and at 2m4f over Hdles. FLAT '98 r12 p4. NH '99 and '01 r6 p0. P-t-P '03 r3 p2 (remote 3rd of 4 once); and pulled up. Able and placed on seven occasions, but too headstrong to get the trip in Points, and very lightly raced since enduring a hectic campaign as a juvenile. *P.R. Silcock — Spooners & W. Dartmoor (Mrs H. Silcock).* 83 (OMa).

GORTROE GUY (IRE) .9-1§.. 13 b.g. Carlingford Castle — Calfstown Night (Bargello) p8u8497fpp. Close-coupled good-bodied brother to jumping winner, Ballygriffin Lad (IRE), and half-brother to Clifford Bay (IRE), Midnight Emperor (IRE) and Don'ttellthetaxman (IRE). Dam is half-sister to Reay Royal (*qv* '92 Annual). IRISH P-t-P '97/8 r11 w2 (inc Open) p4. IRISH HUNT CH '98 r1 p0. IRISH NH FLAT '98 r1 p0. IRISH NH '98/01 r18 p3. NH '01/2 r11 p0; pulled up 2, unseated 2. P-t-P '03 (for Mr A. Rodgers) r8 p2 (3rds, last once); 7th, last pair 3, pulled up 1, and fell 1. Beat Springford when initiating a double in Irish Points in '98, but turned over in 51 attempts since and only once better than last in '04. Error-proneand not the ideal mount for a learner, and sulked when regaining blinkers on his latest appearance. Wears a cross-noseband, and has run tongue-tied. *Mrs J. Marles & Miss K.J. Robinson — Warwicks (Julie Marles).* 108 (L), 190 (C), 289 (CfL), 380 (L), 464 (L), 785 (L), 869 (L), 1031 (Cf), 1276 (M), 1344 (C).

GOSH JOSH (IRE) ..—§.. 7 b.g. Blues Traveller (IRE) — Freedom's Flame (IRE) (Caerleon USA) upppp. Compact. NH FLAT '02 r1 p0 (well tailed off last). P-t-P '03 r2 p0 (refused 1 and pulled up 1). Displayed some brief speed when equipped with a tongue-tie for the first time at Eaton Hall, but the end result was the same, and has yet to reach the 12th without mishap. Not bred to jump or race over three miles, and is a waste of time in Points. *H. & D.E. Nicholls — N. Salop (Penny Grainger).* 96 (CfMa), 227 (CfMa), 531 (OMa), 710 (Mah), 1425 (OMa).

GOT ALOT ON (USA) ..8-5.. 7 b/br.g. Charnwood Forest (IRE) — Fleety Belle (GER) (Assert) p4. Tall workmanlike. 1000f, IR1500y, 7000 2yo. FLAT '00/1 r6 p0. NH '01/3 (for Miss M. Bragg) r8 p0; pulled up 2. A headstrong sort who has never got the trip in any of his 16 races, including Selling company and Maidens. Gets passed around like a hot potato, and was ending a sequence of three pulled ups when he finished 19 lengths last at Great Trethew in February, after which he vanished. *D. Heath — N. Cornwall.* 76 (M), 309 (2m4fOMa).

GOTHA (FR) ..9-11§.. 11 ch.g. Royal Charter (FR) — Royaute (FR) (Signani FR) 246. Tall. Dam won French flat race. IRISH NH FLAT '99 r3 p0. IRISH NH '99/00 r4 p1 (3rd); fell 1. NH '00/2 r17 w2 (2m6f110y Hdle and 2m3f Ch) p4; pulled up 2, fell 2. P-t-P '03 r9 w1 (Confined) p1 (remote last of 3); 4th, last pair 2, pulled up 2, and fell/unseated 2. Scoring over three miles for the first time when springing a 25-1 surprise in a slowly-run event at Holnicote last year, but error-proneand thoroughly inconsistent, and beaten a minimum of 23 lengths in '04. Has had a soft palate operation, and run tongue-tied, and seems unlikely to co-operate fully again. Blinkered once in '02, and previously visored. *C.J. Brake — Dulverton F.* 487 (O), 634 (O), 963 (Cf).

GOT NEWS FOR YOU ..10-7.. 11 gr.g. Positive Statement (USA) — Madame Ruby (FR) (Homing) 1. Tall. Dam won her first two Hurdles (2m1f). NH FLAT '98/9 r2 p0. NH '99/03 (for N.J. Hawke) r16 w2 (2m4f Hdle and 2m5f Ch) p2 (btn hd once); fell 2, pulled up 2. Bred from a mare who broke down in her third Hurdle having been unbeaten in the first two, and unfortunately inherited her legs. Twice scored under Rules including in soft once to October '01, but was a poor jumper of fences, inconsistent, and visored once. Made five lengths from the last when apparently failing by a head to catch Titus Bramble in a Tweseldown Open in early February (the Judge gave a dead-heat), whilst it was undoubtedly a game effort, but rarely manages to get to the racecourse now (one run apiece in '03 and '04) and having already been fired twice the portents looks poor. *Mrs R.J. Newman — Dart V.H. & S. Pool H. (Chloe Newman).* 170 (O).

GRAND AMBITION (USA) .9-5§.. 9 b.g. Lear Fan (USA) — Longing To Dance (USA) (Nureyev USA) pp338. Compact. Dam won flat race (sprint) in USA. IRISH FLAT '99 r5 p2 (2nds, beat Omni Cosmo Touch by short-head once, but disqualified). FLAT '00 r7 p0. IRISH NH '02 r7 p1 (3rd); fell 1. NH '00/1 and '03 r13 p2 (2nds); pulled up 3, fell 1. P-t-P/HUNT CH '03 (for Mr R.J. Marley (Thorney Racing Club) r5 w2 (inc 2m5f110y Hunt Ch) p1 (3rd); and 4th twice. Bought for peanuts and scored twice for previous connections, including a defeat of Cantarinho at Fakenham, but a beaten favourite in his next two starts under Rules, and quickly descended to Sellers. Required 29 attempts to break his duck, and has reverted back to a state of non-compliance. Tongue-tied once on the flat, and blinkered twice to '02, and acquired cheekpieces on his last two appearances. *Mrs P.M. Sly — Fitzwilliam.* 101 (L), 157 (L), 242 (2m5f110yH), 522 (L), 558 (L).

GRAND CANYON (IRE) .9-6§.. 12 b.g. Gallic Heir — Kay Kelly (Pitskelly) pp53p. Tall. IRISH NH FLAT '97 r1 p0. IRISH P-t-P '97/8 r4 w1 (5yo Maiden) p2. NH '98/00 r6 p1 (2nd); pulled up 2 in other Hdles, and last and pulled up 2 in Chses. P-t-P/HUNT CH '00/3 (for Mrs J. Shirley) r19 w3 (up to Confined) p8 (5 2nds, beaten head once, and last once; and inc 3rd of 4 twice); 4th 4, pulled up 3 and ran out 1. Likes to dominate, and thrice a winner on sound surfaces, but left solo in the latest, and in no mood to co-operate fully in '04. A sketchy and often deliberate jumper, but too clever to fall, and has been tried in headgear. *J. Duschere, P. Pariso & J. Rush — Bicester with Whaddon (Chris Loggin).* 16 (C), 168 (C), 187 (Cf), 466 (Cf), 868 (O).

GRAND GOUSIER (FR) .9-0.. 11 b.g. Perrault — Tartifume II (FR) (Mistigri) 6uppp. Compact well-made half-brother to jumping winner, Jakari (FR), and to NH flat winner, Halexy (FR). Approx 18,000 3yo. Dam won 2m4f Chase in France. NH '98/03 (for late Capt. T.A. Forster, and H.D. Daly) r21 w3 (3m4f-2m5f Chses) p7 (inc 3 2nds Hdles); pulled up 4. Won three races in the mud to January '01, but there were a maximum of five runners, and he was only seen once in '03. Has looked reluctant, and was pretty dreadful when returning, including with blinkers and a tongue-tie on his penultimate outing. Ended by pulling up in his Members, which will surely be his swan-song. *M.P. Wiggin — Ludlow (Geoff Evans).* 3 (O), 48 (3m5f70yL), 176 (3mH), 613 (L), 834 (M).

GRANDMERE .9-5.. 10 gr.m. Gran Alba (USA) — Cuckmere Grange (Floriana) p3. Small half-sister to Fables Green (*qv*). NH '03 (for P. Beaumont) r3 p0; pulled up 1. Lightly raced and has never shown anything worthwhile, and was tailed off a mile out before plugging into 24 lengths third in a Maiden. Very unlikely to be able to do better. *Miss F. Hartley & C. Brewer — Sinnington (Freya Hartley).* 266 (M), 395 (CfMa).

GRANNY DICK ..8-9§.. 10 ch.m. Broadsword (USA) — Penny's Colours (Hornet) fpp552ppp. Small rangy light-framed half-sister to Mr Match (*qv*). NH FLAT '00 r2 p1 (3rd). NH '00/2 r10 p1 (3rd); pulled up 2, fell 1. P-t-P '03 r4 p0 (4th, 5th twice, and pulled up 1). Made the frame in her first bumper and Hurdle, but beaten a distance in a Seller on her final start under Rules, and has proved equally modest in Points. Error-proneand not better than last in '04, and never went a yard when regaining blinkers on her latest start. *B. Dowling — Puckeridge.* 103 (OMa), 130 (OMa), 245 (CfMa), 375 (R), 561 (OMa), 741 (M), 1119 (CMam), 1246 (OMa), 1400 (CN).

PLATE 53 185 Mid Surrey Farmers Draghounds PPORA Club Members Mares: Granny Smith (Chris Gordon), 2nd, leads Forest Fortress (David I. Turner), pu PHOTO: Brian Armstrong

GRANNY SMITH (IRE) ..9-12.. 9 b.m. Mandalus — Green Apple (Green Shoon) 2131p. Sister to Chasing winner, Myblackthorn (IRE), and half-sister to Irish NH flat winner, Apple Crumble. IRISH P-t-P '02 r6 p2; pulled up 2, fell 1. Beaten 20 lengths and a distance in her Irish Pointing placings, but has improved for a change of scene. Won a Maiden at Godstone and a Restricted in which only two finished at Catsfield, but neither was competitive, and proved a disappointing favourite when upgraded to a Confined. May not find matters so easy in future now that the minor contests are under her belt. *S.P. Tindall — Southdown & Eridge (Jenny Gordon).* 185 (CMam), 611 (OMa), 639 (R), 1051 (R), 1083 (Cf).

GRANTIE BOY (IRE) ..7-0.. 6 b.g. Nashwan (USA) — Radiant (USA) (Foolish Pleasure USA) pp3p. Sturdy half-brother to Irish flat winners, Poolesta (previous winner in England) and Desert Fox (earned 150,000 between them). Dam won 6f race in USA. NH FLAT '03 (for W.M. Brisbourne) r2 p0. Very much one of the lesser lights in his stable as was obvious when it was Joe O'Brien who always rode him, and followed a distant last of four (promoted to third on a technicality) by pulling up lame when outsider of five for a Maiden. *M. Stewkesbury — N. Salop (Sheila Crow).* 533 (2m4fCfMa), 668 (OMa), 850 (2m5fOMa), 1143 (OMa).

GRAPHIC DESIGNER (IRE) ..8-3.. 16 b.g. Sheer Grit — Kates Princess (Pitpan) p55p2. Strong lengthy half-brother to Yeoman Cricketer and Princess Easy, to NH flat winner, Kate O'Kirkham, and to a winner in Belgium. Dam won 2m Hdle in Ireland. NH '95/6 r5 p1 (2nd); remote 7th of 8, pulled up 2 and fell in Chses. P-t-P/HUNT CH '99/03 r25 w5 (up to Confined) p7 (4 3rds, of 4 once, and last 3; and 2nd of 3 thrice); last pair 4, pulled up 8, and unseated 1. Has farmed some extremely bad races thanks to reliable jumping, but outclassed when employed as a schoolmaster in '04, and beaten a fence when last of two finishers in his Members. *J.J. Hazeltine — Surrey U.* 182 (CCon), 421 (L), 610 (Cv&nr), 781 (L), 1207 (M).

GRATOMI (IRE) ..9-9.. 15 b.g. Bustomi — Granny Grumble (Politico USA) 3p59p. Good-topped half-brother to Onesevenfour (IRE) and Burrells Wharf (IRE). Dam won Irish NH flat. IRISH P-t-P '95 r3 w1 (5yo&up Maiden) p0 (slipped up and fell — when 1/ 2nd at last). IRISH NH '95 r1 p0. NH '97/01 r44 w6 (2m4f Hdle and 5 2m-2m-2m4f Chses) p16 (9 2nds); pulled up 1, fell/unseated 4. P-t-P/HUNT CH '03 r6 p2 (3rds, of 4 once, inc Hunt Ch); 4th twice, and unseated 2. A game front-runner at his best, and retains enthusiasm, but frequently let down by his lack of fluency, and has never scored beyond 2m4f and only once since '99. Ran remarkably well on his favourite sound surface at Cottenham on his return, but unable to reproduce that effort again, and may have to rest on his laurels. Broke a blood vessel once in '99. *W.J. & Mrs A.E. Lee — Cambridge Univ (Ann Lee).* 997 (O), 1347 (2m6f110yH), 1396 (C), 1497 (3mH), 1502 (O).

GRAY KNIGHT (IRE) ..9-12.. 8 gr.g. Insan (USA) — Moohono (IRE) (Roselier FR) 161p1. Small neat attractive. Dam won 2 NH flat and 3m Hurdle in Ireland. NH FLAT '01 r1 p0. NH '01/3 (for Miss H.C. Knight) r6 p0; pulled up 1. Bought Ascot, Apr for 8571. Finished two-and-a-half lengths fourth in his debut Hurdle, but did not progress, and beaten 21 lengths subsequently. Only seen once in '03, but appreciated the drop in grade when returning, and made the most of easy opportunities in a 2m4f Maiden and a Restricted. Needs a sound surface and floundered in soft once, but ground and trip were ideal for him in a Maiden Hunter Chase at Folkestone, and the contest was not even of Intermediate standard. Connections are adept at placing him, and they will need to be even more so now he has to rise in class. *I.R. Mann & A. Hill — V. of Aylesbury with Garth & S. Berks (Lawney Hill).* 7 (2m4fOMa), 102 (R), 337 (R), 1332 (Cf), 1442 (2m5fH).

GREAT JUBILEE (IRE) ..10-2.. 7 ch.g. Beneficial — Red Donna (Don) 131. Strong-topped half-brother to Scarlet Emperor (IRE) (*qv*). P-t-P '03 (for Mr D.A. Johnson) r2 w1 (Maiden) p1 (2nd). NH '03 (from M.C. Pipe's) r1 p1 (3rd of 4 in 2m4f Hdle). A fair youngster who has done well to win half the races he has contested, but faced relatively simple tasks when successful in '04, and lacked strength in the saddle when going down narrowly in between. Clearly on the upgrade, but quite how far up the ladder he can go remains to be seen. *S.C. Robinson — Mid Surrey F. (Gina Weare).* 29 (R), 182 (CCon), 643 (C).

GRECIAN STAR ..10-2.. 13 b.g. Crested Lark — Grecian Lace (Spartan General) 42362. Strong deep-girthed Tarry-bred brother to Grecian Lark, and half-brother to Kingbrook, Fine Lace, Grecian Saint, Bobbin Lace and Cowslip Lace. Dam, sister to Spartan Lace, won Hunter Chase and 4 Points and placed 6 for Bunny Tarry. Grandam, French Lace, won 2 Irish Points at 4, and won 4 Ladies in England. P-t-P/HUNT CH '99/03 r24 w8 (inc 2 2m6f-3m6f110y Hunt Chses, and 2 Opens) p5 (3 2nds; inc last of 3 once; and inc 3 Hunt Chses); pulled up 3, and fell/unseated 5. A thorough stayer, and got to within half a length of registering a fifth course win at Mollington this year, but four times a beaten favourite too, and surprisingly did not see the trip out at Cheltenham. Often requires plenty of driving, and can make mistakes, and will need careful placing to win in '05. Acts on any going. *J.R. White & G.B., G.J. & Miss F.M. Tarry — Grafton (Jimmy Tarry).* 381 (O), 586 (O), 744 (O), 1170 (4m1fH), 1357 (3m1fH).

GREENHOPPER ..—.. 9 b.g. Greensmith — April's Crook (Crozier) f. Owner-bred half-brother to Avril Showers, Westwinds and April's Past (*qv*). Dam won 2 Points and placed 4 for June Atkinson. Grandam, April Flash, won 3 Points and placed 12 for her. Great-grandam, April Pennant, won 7 Points and a Novice Chase. Looked cumbersome on his belated debut, and was already struggling when he fell at halfway (tongue-tied). *R. Atkinson — Cattistock.* 475 (OMa).

GREEN ICE ..—.. 11 b.g. Good Times (ITY) — Rather Romantic (CAN) (Verbatim USA) p. Compact well-made half-brother to flat winner, Negative Equity. 3000 3yo. NH FLAT '98/9 r3 p1 (2nd). NH '00 (for J. Mackie) r6 p1 (3rd); pulled up 2. A four length second of 22 on his bumper debut looked encouraging, but very disappointing under Rules subsequently, and could manage nothing better than a 14 lengths third over hurdles. Visored once, and tried tongue-tied. Absent for four years until returning for an elders Maiden, but after proving headstrong and making a lot of the early running he pulled up after 2m3f when stopping to nil, and clearly has big problems. *Mrs D. Renney — Heythrop (Nick Seal).* 370 (OMa).

GREENKEYS (AUS) ..9-11.. 11 b.g. Bonhomie (USA) — Cindy Doll (AUS) (Cindy's Son USA) 61. Compact half-brother to six winners of 36 races in Australia. Dam won 3 races in Australia. NH FLAT '00 r2 p0. NH '00/1 and '03 (for A.W. Carroll, and R.C. Guest) r13 p0; fell/unseated 3. Bought Doncaster, Aug for 1000. Beaten 25 lengths or more in all but one of 15 races under Rules which included Selling Hurdles, and fell or unseated in three of six Chases (had to survive blunders in the other three). Discarded his normal cheekpieces in Points, and was backward first time out, but surprisingly got off the mark in a slowly-run Maiden on firmish at Dunthrop. His legs look dodgy, and although connections did very well to extract a success they may be very hard pressed to find another. *R.E. Dance — N. Ledbury (Tim Stephenson).* 6 (OMa), 52 (OMa).

GREEN LEADER (IRE) .—.. 13 b.m. Lapierre — Green Feathers (IRE) (Supreme Leader) ppu. Workmanlike. IRISH P-t-P '98 r6 p5; and pulled up. P-t-P '00/2 r6 p1 (2nd of 3); 4th, pulled up 3, and fell 1. Showed enough ability in Ireland to suggest a small success was within her compass, but rendered useless by various leg problems, and not worth bothering with again. *R. Andrews — Aldenham H. (Simon Andrews).* 652 (OMa), 996 (CMam), 1246 (OMa).

GREENSLEEVES ..9-7.. 7 gr.m. Environment Friend — Swashbuckle (Buckley) 4pf. Small neat. Dam, half-sister to Playing The Fool (*qv* '01 Annual), pulled up and fell in Points for Clive Bennett (lame after). Made a bad blunder three out and headed and unable to recover when 12 lengths fourth in a Mares Maiden, but floundered in ground with holding patches and never went a yard next time, and then the saddle slipped and she fell on the flat after two miles when giving a girl her first ride. Making too many mistakes and seems to have lost her confidence, but given a rest and some intensive schooling later she may return refreshed and ready to atone. *C.J. Bennett — Ledbury.* 978 (CMam), 1275 (OMa), 1394 (OMa).

GREET YOU WELL .10-0.. 8 gr.g. Neltino — Shamana (Broadsword USA) 12pfp. Lengthy workmanlike half-brother to Catley Cross, and to Hurdles winner, Cyanara. Dam, sister to Cottesmore (*qv* '01 Annual), won 2m Hdle and 7 2m Chses for Lady Northampton (all wins for Richard Dunwoody). P-t-P '03 r2 p1 (neck 2nd); and last. Too backward to do himself justice in '03, but showed immediate promise, and duly made most on his reappearance at Mollington. Just touched off in a torrential downpour at Brafield-on-the-Green next time, but pulled up with broken blood vessels twice since, and fell four out when holding every chance in between. A strong galloper, and potentially under-rated by several pounds if his affliction can be cured. A box walker. *The Marquess of Northampton — Pytchley (Caroline Bailey).* 296 (OMa), 467 (CR), 684 (R), 1069 (R), 1217 (R).

PLATE 54 182 Mid Surrey Farmers Draghounds S.E. Hunts Club Members Conditions: R to L, Perching (Mick Sheridan), 2nd, disputes with Great Jubilee (Stuart Robinson), 3rd, ahead of Acuteangle (Justin Morgan), pu PHOTO: Brian Armstrong

GREGORY PECKORY (IRE) ..—.. 7 b.g. Teamster — Vill Alba (IRE) (Cataldi) f. Workmanlike lengthy. NH FLAT '03 r2 p1 (2nd). NH '03 (for N.A. Twiston-Davies) r1 p0. Six lengths second in his first bumper (hung right and weakened), and has shown degrees of promise since, including when falling three out when weakening quickly in a holding ground Maiden (pulled too hard to have a chance of getting the trip). If he can be persuaded to settle better he is a potential winner (without resorting to jiggery pokery). *Mrs R. Mackness — Cotswold (Jelly Nolan).* 1275 (OMa).

GREYBROOK LAD (IRE) ..10-0.. 7 br.g. Norwich — Princess Project (IRE) (Project Manager) 1. Workmanlike lengthy. Made nearly all and was impressive beating nothing in a three-finisher Maiden at Higham in early February, but pulled up feelingly, and did not reappear. Would doubtless be good enough for Restricteds at the very least if he recovers. *S.C. Robinson — Southdown & Eridge (Gina Weare).* 153 (OMa).

GREY FANDANGO (IRE) ..9-8.. 8 gr.g. Roselier (FR) — Fancy Step (Step Together USA) p61. Lengthy brother to Silver Dancer (IRE), and half-brother to Irish NH flat winner, Yash Can Step (IRE). Dam won Irish NH flat. Very remote when pulled up (backward) and last in non-Maidens, but dropped to the correct grade over 2m4f at Dingley and made all and just retained a dwindling advantage at the last. Starting to go the right way and possibly has further scope, but gives the impression he would need less aggressive tactics to stay three miles. *M. Rimell — Croome & W. Warwicks.* 36 (CR), 584 (I), 890 (2m4fOMa).

GREY SNIPE .—.. 10 gr.g. Thethingaboutitis (USA) — Snipe Shooter (Le Coq D'Or) pp. Owner-bred half-brother to Cruising On (dam of Cruising Along *qv*, also by Thethingaboutitis (USA), Ashe Gorse, Kayak Point and Snipe Hill. Dam, 'useless and a tricky ride', pulled up 2 and ran out 1 in Points for Janette Goodall. Gave the impression of being every bit as bad as Cruising Along when pulled up in Maidens. *Mrs J.E. Goodall — Meynell & S. Staffs (Carly Goodall).* 594 (OMa), 848 (OMa).

GREY TARQUIN ..—.. 7 gr.m. Gran Alba (USA) — Monteviot (Scallywag) pp. Good-topped half-sister to Seviot and Border Fusion. Dam, placed in 4 Hurdles, pulled up and fell in Points. Jumped sketchily and often to the left when a false favourite on her debut, and again pulled up at unrealistically short odds next time. May be able to do a bit better eventually. *The Cindykit Partnership (D. Mills) — Cheshire (Gary Hanmer).* 714 (CMam), 848 (OMa).

GREY VALLEY .—.. 8 gr.g. Cornish Missile — Rising Mist (Sousa) p. Dam, sister to Come On Valley, and half-sister to Wesleys Choice (*qv* '01 Annual), won Points and placed 8 for Mrs Smith. Tailed off and pulled up after two miles in his Members, in which he raced erroneously as Cornish Mist. *Mrs M. Smith — E. Cornwall (Mark Ranger).* 305 (M).

GRIZZLY GOLFWEAR (IRE) ..10-4.. 11 b.g. Commanche Run — Dunwellan (Tekoah) 4p. Lengthy half-brother to Hurdles winner, Rosswellan (IRE). Dam won 2m2f mares NH flat in Ireland. IRISH P-t-P '99 r3 p0; pulled up and fell 2. NH '99/01 r10 p0; pulled up 3, fell 1. P-t-P/HUNT CH '02/3 r13 w2 (Geldings Maiden and Restricted) p8 (3 2nds; and inc 4 Hunt Chses); 4th, ran out 1 and fell 1. Very poor under Rules, but much improved by the current handler, and has shown plenty of stamina when successful in two and three-finisher events in softish. Set some stiff tasks since, and may have suffered a setback in the latest, but capable of scoring again when his sights are lowered, though he needs strong handling to keep him motivated. Wears a cross-noseband. *R.J. & Mrs S.E. Hughes — S. Pembs (Sarah Hughes).* 50 (I), 176 (3mH).

GROOVEJET..— §.. 6 b.g. Emperor Jones (USA) — Sir Hollow (USA) (Sir Ivor USA) Rfpfp. Leggy brother to flat and Hurdling winner, Moon Emperor (won about 85,000), and half-brother to two winners in France also to flat winner, Hollow Jo. Dam won at 8f in France. FLAT '01/2 r11 p3. NH '02/3 (for J.R. Jenkins) r2 p0; pulled up 2. Placed thrice consecutively from between 7-10f on the all-weather in '02, but was tailed off in his final three flat races and pulled up in both Hurdles (visored on a couple of occasions). A very nasty ride for Kelly Smith in Points, and after running out and falling twice from four attempts on him she has decided to hang up her boots. Pulled up with a substitute in his Members, and there is no point in persevering with this wayward juvenile. *M.S. Burman — Cambs with Enfield Chace.* 7 (2m4fOMa), 218 (OMa), 245 (CfMa), 401 (OMa), 1241 (M).

GUARD A DREAM (IRE) ..9-0.. 11 ch.g. Durgam (USA) — Adarenna (FR) (Mill Reef USA) 4p36p. Small light-framed flashy half-brother to a French flat winner, and to successful Irish/English Hurdles winner, Adaramann (IRE). FLAT r4 p1 (25/ 2nd of 4); inc Sells. P-t-P '00 and '02/3 r17 w2 (Maiden and Restricted) p2 (2nds, last once); 5th, 6th, last 3, pulled up 4, brought down 1 and fell/unseated 3. Won two weak races on sound surfaces to '02, and ran his best race for a long while when beaten less than three lengths on his reappearance, but not better than last since, and remains a very sketchy jumper. *Mrs S.W. Walker — Clifton-on-Teme.* 405 (Inr), 663 (I), 1135 (M), 1227 (Cf), 1484 (O).

GUDASMUM ..10-0.. 7 b.m. Primitive Rising (USA) — Comarch (Ancient Monro) uR3f2. Owner-bred half-sister to C L B Jemilla (*qv*). P-t-P '03 (for Mrs P.P. Wright) r2 w1 (Maiden) p0; and pulled up 1. Got off to the ideal start, but collapsed through dehydration next time, and has yet to gel completely with the new rider. Poised to score when crashing through the wing of the last at Dalston, and fell heavily two starts later, but had to be withdrawn from her next intended appearance after she was found to have broken a blood vessel in the paddock. Young enough to atone, and looks to have the basic speed for Ladies races eventually. *D. Davidson — Middleton (Morag Neill).* 657 (R), 765 (R), 918 (R), 1077 (R), 1476 (R).

GUEST ALLIANCE (IRE) ..8-7.. 13 ch.g. Zaffaran (USA) — Alhargah (Be My Guest USA) ppp8p. Close-coupled good-bodied half-brother to 3 flat winners (one in Italy). FLAT r37 w2 (16f on Lingfield all-weather) p9 (inc 2nd in Sell prior to wins). NH '97/8 r5 w1 (2m3f Hdle) p0. P-t-P '99/00 and '02/3 r8 p1 (last of 3); 4th, last, pulled up 4 and unseated 1. A thorough stayer on the level, and scored on his jumping debut in '97, but lightly raced and a weak finisher since, and carries too much condition. *T.E. Wardall — Atherstone.* 94 (L), 230 (L), 407 (L), 785 (L), 1470 (L).

GUIGNOL DU COCHET (FR) ..10-6.. 11 ch.g. Secret Of Success — Pasquita (FR) (Bourbon FR) 51522451161. Compact half-brother to two French jumping winners (one also successful on flat). FRENCH NH '98 r7 w1 (2m6f Ch) p0; pulled up 1. NH '99/03 (for Mrs L. Richards) r29 w2 (2m Chses) p11; pulled up 2, fell 1. Bought Ascot, Nov for 5714. Successful in a French Chase at Fontainebleau as a four-year old, and scored twice over the minimum trip for his next yard, but had not visited the winners enclosure since December '00 (was tongue-tied twice to '99, and often wore headgear in that period). The best example of Steve Flook's training skills in '04, and ridden by three different jockeys in his four victories. The much improved Glyn Slade-Jones was in the saddle twice and took the four-runner PPORA final at Stratford (but not after some heart-stopping moments in the closing stages when he eased prematurely to give victory salutes), and with Dave Mansell being unable to do the weight no chances were taken in the One and Only Handicap Hunter Chase at Newton Abbot, where Thomas Greenall was engaged and had little difficulty popping the £10,205 first prize in the bag. A great jumper who has completed in 36 of his last 37 attempts (fell in the exception), and effective at a bare three miles but usually concentrates on shorter trips. Extremely well placed, and Steve Flook has all the attributes of a professional and a rare eye for a bargain, but he would have to take care that if he switched to those ranks he said a very firm 'no' to the local owners who would doubtless send him their dross. *S. Flook & G. Slade-Jones — Radnor & W. Herefords (Steve Flook).* 32 (Cnr), 110 (Cnr), 179 (2m6fH), 317 (2m4fH), 441 (2m4f110yH), 545 (2m3f110yH), 630 (2m4fH), 801 (3mH), 1166 (2m5f110yH), 1372 (2m4fH), 1451 (3mH).

GUILSBOROUGH GORSE .10-4.. 10 b.g. Past Glories — Buckby Folly (Netherkelly) 1121*212*. Half-brother to Sharley Cop and Creaton Covert, and to Hurdles winner, Buckby Lane. Dam, bred by Sarah York, won 2m4f Hdle when trained for her by Maurice Camacho. P-t-P '00 (for Mrs E.C. York) r4 w1 (Maiden) p0; 4th, pulled up and fell. NH '00/3 r23 w2 (2m4f110y Chses) p11; pulled up 2, fell 1. NH '04 r4 w1 (beat Upham Lord 2*l* in 2m5f110y Ch: *a.p, ld app last, rdn out*) p3 (1*l* 2nd to Our Kev in 3m Ch: *a.p, ld 11 til hdd last, no ex*; 4*l* 2nd to Jaffa in 2m4f110y Ch: *hld up, went 2nd 7, ld on bit 2 out, rdn & hdd last, eased when btn nr fin*; and 2*l* 2nd to Catch The Perk in 2m4f110y Ch: *hld up, eff 10, ld last til hdd & no ex nr fin*). Took well over seven minutes to win his Maiden, but more of a 2m4f specialist under Rules, and only gets further when the opposition is weak. Landed a touch when confidently handled by Mark Walford at Cottenham, but already proving he can still hold his own in Handicaps, and seems unlikely to return to Points for the present. Suited by good or sound surfaces. Blinkered twice, and wore cheekpieces twice in '03. *P.L. Crafts — Middleton (Gill Walford).* 3 (O), 56 (C), 330 (3mH).

GUMLAYLOY ..9-0.. 6 ch.g. Indian Ridge — Candide (USA) (Miswaki USA) 2fup. Close-coupled well-made half-brother to winner in Hong Kong. Dam won 7f race in Ireland. IR55,000y. FLAT '01/2 (for Miss L.A. Perratt, and J.M. Bradley) r7 p0 (last 7). Bought Ascot, Nov '02 for 809. A highly-bred individual whose dam comes from the family of Bosra Sham and Hector Protector, but was beaten 30 lengths plus when last in all seven flat races at up to 9f (blinkered once). Looked a lot more promising when one-and-a-half lengths second in his first Point, but took a crashing fall three out when being joined for the lead next time, and then left in front momentarily at the penultimate only to emulate the leader and blunder and unseat (favourite). Weakened tamely on an apparent confidence restorer next time, and being so fizzy he is his own worst enemy at present, but if he will learn to jump and settle better he is plenty quick enough to win a Maiden. Potentially under-rated. *J. Priday — Radnor & W. Herefords (Steve Flook).* 453 (CfMa), 724 (OMa), 983 (2m5fOMa), 1393 (OMa).

GUNNABALLRIGHT .9-12.. 7 ch.g. Gunner B — Mistress Corrado (New Member) b1. Owner-bred half-brother to Master Jock (*qv*). Jumped stickily and was virtually tailed off when brought down at the eighth on his debut, but backed from 6-1 to 7-4 favourite at Kingston Blount, and slammed dire rivals with the minimum of fuss in a very slowly-run contest. Strictly speaking worth no more than 9-2, but is doubtless already considerably better than that, and may be able to achieve a similar measure of success to Master Jock in the coming years. *P.S. Burke — N. Ledbury (Paul Jones).* 1261 (OMa), 1337 (OMa).

GUNNERBE POSH ..9-3.. 11 ch.g. Rakaposhi King — Triggered (Gunner B) 33222. Workmanlike half-brother to Cousin George (*qv*). 3600 4yo. NH FLAT '99 r2 p2. NH '01/3 (for N.T. Chance, and B.G.

Powell) r11 p1 (2nd); pulled up 1. Placed in both his bumpers, but generally disappointing over Hurdles, and despite finishing all four Chases he was beaten 17 lengths once and tailed off thrice. Takes a strong hold and has to go to post early, and the owner has had a hard time on him and doubtless taken plenty of stick from his colleagues after getting beaten when favourite on his last four attempts. Came closest to breaking his duck when a head second at Hackwood, but broke down next time and his racing life looks over. Would certainly have won something (probably even a Hurdle) had he been dynamically handled. *Mrs S.J. & J. Maxse — Hampshire (Victoria Collins).* 120 (OMa), 264 (CfMa), 716 (M), 971 (OMa), 1211 (OMa).

GUNNER BE TRUE ..8-12§.. 9 ch.g. Gunner B — True Promise (Pragmatic) p4up4124. Strong rangy half-brother to Spanish Oath. Dam is half-sister to Kimswa (*qv* '95 Annual). P-t-P '02/3 r10 p3 (2 3rds, of 4 once); 4th, 5th, 7th, last pair 2, and pulled up 2. Slow and cumbersome, and hangs left, but only had to outbattle Carvilla in a race taking 27 seconds longer than any other on the card to land his Members on firmish at Cottenham. Andrew Corbett will almost certainly have to look elsewhere for his next winner. Has worn a near-side pricker, and tried in blinkers and cheekpieces in '04. *S.R. Andrews & Mrs J. Lewin — Aldenham H. (Simon Andrews).* 40 (OMa), 130 (OMa), 244 (CfMa), 463 (OMa), 525 (OMa), 995 (M), 1245 (R), 1316 (R).

GUNNER SID ..10-0.. 14 ch.g. Gunner B — At Long Last (John French) 332p. Strong-topped brother to NH flat and jumping winner, Gunnerblong, and half-brother to Oh To Be, and Irish Hurdling winner, Seminole Chief. Dam, half-sister to Baluchi (*qv* '93 Annual). NH FLAT '96 r4 p2. NH '98/00 and '02/3 (for B. Preece, W.M. Brisbourne, and W. Jenks) r28 w7 (2m-2m2f Hdles) p2; fell/unseated 3, pulled up 1, ran out 1. Gained his first win in a Seller and went on to add six more Hurdles until July '00, but they were nearly all soft options in Jersey, and was five times successful at Les Landes. Finished in all three Chases, but was beaten 33 lengths plus. Unreliable and sometimes blinkered, and ran out once way back in '98. Raced up with the pace and kept on steadily for three Pointing placings and beaten a maximum of eight lengths, but ended the season lame, which at 13 surely means curtains to his career. *A.G. Wadlow — Wheatland (Annabel Wadlow).* 190 (C), 528 (O), 713 (Cf), 932 (Cf).

GUNNERS MISTAKE .9-3§.. 8 ch.g. Gunner B — Malory's Mistake (Right Regent) 25231ppR. Sturdy homebred. Dam, half-sister to Bomba Charger (*qv*). P-t-P '03 r5 p2 (inc 2nd of 3); 4th, last and pulled up 1. Made the frame six times before finally opening his account in softish at Cherrybrook, but disappointing in Restricteds on faster ground since, and ran out when tried in cheekpieces at Trebudannon. Tends to jump left and looks rather a handful (taken to post early last year, and has two handlers). *Mrs R. Welch — Dartmoor.* 82 (OMa), 194 (CfMa), 307 (2m4fOMa), 485 (OMa), 796 (CfMa), 1002 (R), 1196 (R), 1435 (R).

GUN'N ROSES II (FR) ..11-2.. 11 gr.g. Royal Charter (FR) — Offenbach II (FR) (Ermitage FR) 13. Rangy half-brother to French Chasing winner, Indian Rock (awarded race after final 2). Dam won at 8f in France. FRENCH FLAT r4 w1 (12f) p1. FRENCH NH '97/8 r5 w2 (2m1f-2m2f Hdles) p2. NH '98/03 (for M.D. Hammond, one win, M.C. Pipe, 4 wins, and T.D. Easterby, one win) r21 w6 (2m Hdle 5 2m4f-2m6f Chses) p3; pulled up 6, fell 2. A renowned mudlark who had some decent form in France before being purchased by the current owner, and despite only averaging three outings per annum over the next seven years has kept his form well and amassed a total of £75,516. A game front-runner who found conditions ideal over 2m6f at Haydock (has never scored over further; did try the outer reaches in the '02 Grand National but fell at the seventh), and easily held Torduff Express despite idling, but can often be let down by his jumping and was not sufficiently fluent when 15 lengths third in the Aintree Foxhunters. Blinkered in his three most recent outings. Remains well above average on his day. *Lady Clarke — Avon V. (Paul Keane).* 179 (2m6fH), 732 (2m5f110yH).

GUNSMOKE ..—.. 7 gr.g. Thethingaboutitis (USA) — Fairy Princess (IRE) (Fairy King USA) f. Close-coupled. NH FLAT '03 r1 p0. NH '03 (for D. McCain) r1 p0 (pulled up). Pulled hard and made most for nearly 2m4f in a Chaddesley Maiden, but was 15 lengths third and tiring when he fell two out, and seems to have done himself a mischief. *D.H. Godfrey — Radnor & W. Herefords.* 256 (CMa).

GUNVILLE ..9-0.. 6 ch.g. Infantry — Emily's Niece (Balinger) fpf8. Workmanlike owner-bred half-brother to Call Me Again. Dam, half-sister to Dark Challenger (*qv* '04 Annual), won Maiden and Restricted and placed 3rd. Did not have a happy first season, but was assured of moderate seconds when he fell two out at Bishops Court and when he departed at the final fence at Barbury (would have been beaten about 25 lengths in both). Pulled up in between as the rider felt that he was amiss, and unsurprisingly given a quiet time when tailed off on final start. Needs a change of fortune, but is almost certainly capable of better. *Mrs J. Kelly — Cattistock (Fiona Shaw).* 326 (OMa), 599 (2m4fOMa), 1067 (OMa), 1380 (OMa).

GURU RINPOCHE .10-1.. 13 ch.g. Scallywag — Ishkhara (Hittite Glory) u21u261u. Well-made attractive half-brother to Mr Rory (*qv*). NH FLAT '98 r3 p1 (2nd). NH '98/02 r20 w2 (2m1f110y-3m110y Hdles) p3 (2 3rds); pulled up 4, fell 3. P-t-P '03 r9 p3 (2 2nds; and 3rd of 4); 4th, 6th, and last pair 4. Lost his way latterly under Rules, and had not scored since '00, but has generally enjoyed Pointing, and made all to win convincingly at Wadebridge. Followed up in a match at Bratton Down, but no match for the better Ladies horses, and tends to get too low at the obstacles. Wears bandages. *P.A. Tylor — Cury (Stephen Long).* 199 (L), 311 (L), 484 (L), 822 (L), 1197 (4mL), 1350 (L), 1509 (L), 1563 (L).

GUS BERRY (IRE) ..9-7.. 12 ch.g. Montelimar (USA) — Eurolink Sea Baby (Deep Run) p94. Strong-topped half-brother to Irish jumping winner, Royal Marine. Dam won flat race and Hurdle in Switzerland. NH FLAT '97 r1 w1. NH '98/02 r23 w3 (3m3f110y Hdle and 2 3m3f Chses) p3 (2nds); pulled up 6, on floor 2. P-t-P/HUNT CH '03 (for Mr P. England) r7 p2 (inc 3rd in Hunt Ch); 6th, last pair 3 and pulled up 1. An out-and-out stayer, but indolent and often blinkered under Rules, and has not scored since February '01. Gave a spirited display on his favourite course on his most recent appearance, but ideally wants it hock deep, and is reported to be a bad traveller. Has run tongue-tied. *J. Kilner — Badsworth & Bramham Moor (Alison Christmas).* 55 (Cf), 267 (Cf), 542 (3m3fH).

GUTSY DALTON (IRE) ..9-5.. 11 b.g. Good Thyne (USA) — No Not (Ovac ITY) p94. Workmanlike half-brother to Colonel No (IRE), and to Hurdles winner, Elmside (IRE). Dam, half-sister to After Kelly (*qv* '00 Annual). IRISH P-t-P '00/1 r4 w1 (7yo Maiden) p1 (last of 3); pulled up 2. IRISH HUNT CH '00 r1 p0 (tailed off). NH '01 r3 p0. P-t-P '03 r8 w1 (Restricted) p0; 5th twice, last pair 3, and pulled up 2. Won an Irish Maiden in soft, and put some modest efforts behind him when landing a Restricted on firm at Cothelstone last year, but broken winded and runs tubed, and not better than last in '04. Acquired blinkers on his last two starts. *R.H. Milton & Mrs V.J. Milton — W. Somerset V. (Laura Young).* 90 (I), 193 (I), 278 (Inr).

HACHLEY (FR) ..—.. 10 b/br.g. Grand Tresor (FR) — Tess Bowl (FR) (Rolling Bowl FR) pp. Lengthy. NH '01 r1 p0. P-t-P '02 r3 w1 (Maiden) p1 (2nd); and 6th of 7. Readily justified favouritism when quickening nicely to win at Pentreclwydau on his final start in '02, but clearly out of sorts since, missed '03 in its entirety, and had seven weeks off between outings this year. Looked like aspiring to the ten stone brigade, but that looks wishful thinking now. *W.F. Caudwell — O. Berks (Matt Hazell).* 572 (R), 1359 (2m4f110yH).

HADAWAY LAD ..9-9.. 13 ch.g. Meadowbrook — Little Swinburn (Apollo Eight) 32d2u7p. Strong compact half-brother to Brano Burn. Dam won 2 Points. NH FLAT '96 r1 p0. NH '96/7 r4 p0 (tailed off). P-t-P/HUNT CH '98/9 and '02/3 r22 w2 (Maiden and Restricted) p6 (3rds, last once); fell/unseated 4, pulled up 1, brought down 1, and refused 1. Recorded his first success since '98 last year, but generally a weak finisher, and has predictably been unable to bridge the gap to Intermediate company. Tends to make careless errors. Has been tried in blinkers. *K. Waters — Braes.* 507 (I), 762 (I), 1036 (M), 1287 (I), 1307 (Cf), 1479 (Cf).

HADEQA ..10-6§.. 9 ch.g. Hadeer — Heavenly Queen (Scottish Reel) pup21211. Small compact half-brother to flat winners Heavenly Abstone, Absinther and Abstone Queen. FLAT '98/01 r32 w4 (6-8f). NH '99/01 r12 w1 (2m1f110y Hdle) p1 (3rd); pulled up 2. P-t-P/HUNT CH '03 r8 p0 (4th, fell/unseated 4, pulled up 2 and ran out 1). Won three races in the summer of '99, but only once beaten less than 25 lengths in ten subsequent appearances over hurdles, and took an immediate dislike to Pointing last year. Appeared to have become very set in his ways when failing to complete for the 11th time in 12 starts when pulled up at Hutton Rudby, but had a sudden change of heart when reverting back to Ladies races. Ended a 32-race losing sequence at Easingwold, and scored twice more subsequently, though his nearest Heslaker victim, the odds-on favourite, finished lame. Retains a turn of foot, and is not averse to using it at present, but requires a sound surface, and good horses can still put him in his place. Often wore headgear under Rules, and has been tongue-tied. *M.J. Brown — York & Ainsty N.* 391 (MO), 501 (O), 565 (O), 811 (L), 1160 (L), 1290 (L), 1415 (L), 1459 (L).

HAILES GATE ..—.. 6 ch.g. Rakaposhi King — Nut Tree (King Of Spain) f. Bought Ascot, Jun for 2095. Dam won NH Flat and 2m4f Hurdle, both on all-weather, and is half-sister to Speedy Boy (*qv* '94 Annual). Made a mistake at the first and continued in last until falling at the fifth in a Higham Maiden in mid-January. *M. Power — Staff College (Phillip York).* 26 (OMa).

HAIL STONE (IRE) ..9-12§.. 10 b.g. Glacial Storm (USA) — Rockmount (IRE) (Cidrax FR) bpp22f312u22. Small well-made. Dam, half-sister to Adrian-John (*qv* '94 Annual). IRISH P-t-P '00 r4 w1 (4&5yo Maiden) p0; pulled up 2, and brought down. IRISH NH FLAT '00 r1 p0. IRISH NH '00/2 r7 p0; pulled up 1. P-t-P '03 r4 p2 (2nds, of 3 once); and pulled up 2. Sprang a 14-1 surprise when landing a Restricted at the 11th attempt, but frequently will not go a yard, and has failed to finish four times when tried in cheekpieces. Likely to remain a law unto himself, and best left alone for betting purposes. Blinkered once in '02. *Miss K.A. Williams — Gelligaer F.* 207 (R), 358 (R), 451 (R), 695 (R), 740 (R), 974 (3mH), 1094 (R), 1237 (R), 1318 (M), 1485 (Cnr), 1539 (I), 1552 (I).

HAILSTORM (IRE) .9-10.. 12 ch.g. Glacial Storm (USA) — Sindys Gale (Strong Gale) 5. Small lengthy. Dam won Maiden and NH flat in Ireland. IRISH NH FLAT '97 r4 p1 (2nd). NH '97/03 (for Miss L.V. Russell) r38 w3 (2m6f Hdle and 2 2m4f-2m6f Chses) p11 (inc 7 2nds); pulled up 5, and fell/ unseated 3. Fairly competent when winning three races to September '01, but has lost his form badly and been beaten in 21 attempts since (a non-finisher in eight). Error-prone, and once broke a blood vessel. Only tried one Point, and although not disgraced he failed to reappear, and could be struggling to get the trip in any case. *J. Alexander — Fife (Nick Alexander).* 210 (Cf).

HALF A STORY ..9-3.. 8 br.m. Henbit (USA) — Kelly's Story (Netherkelly) 62fp. Lengthy good-bodied half-sister to A Fine Story (*qv*). Finished 25 lengths behind the very easy winner at Higham, but the third did eventually find a race. Looks slow, but a long plod through the mud enabled A Fine Story to get off the mark aged eight in '04, so could be worth keeping going for another campaign. *Mr & Mrs H. Hill — Granta H. (Henry Hill).* 104 (2m4fOMa), 154 (OMa), 401 (OMa), 833 (OMa).

HALLBROOK .—.. 7 b.m. Alderbrook — Charlotte's Festival (Gala Performance) ppp. Half-sister to Thosewerethedays, to jumping winners, Charlotte's Flame and Stan's Your Man, and to successful Chaser, Ceilidh Boy. Attractively bred (her four siblings have won 29 NH races to date), but showed nothing herself prior to pulling up after two miles maximum in Maidens. The only hope is that she needs plenty of time. *J.R.B. Williams — Ystrad Taf Fechan (Myfanwy Miles).* 204 (CfMa), 362 (CfMa), 699 (CfMa).

HALLRULE (IRE) ..10-1.. 11 ch.g. Be My Native (USA) — Phantom Thistle (Deep Run) 121*114*. Sturdy half-brother to Copper Thistle (IRE), Leinthall Thistle (IRE), Crafty Phantom (IRE) and Supreme Craft (IRE), to Chasing winner, Indulge (IRE), and to Hurdles winner, Chilled (IRE). NH '99/ 00 and '03 r9 p0; fell 1, and pulled up 4. NH '04 r3 w2 (beat Bold Classic 3*l* in 3m1f Sell Ch: *a.p, rdn to ld app last, stayed on wl*; and Red Perk a hd in 3m2f Ch: *a.p, rmdrs 11, hit 4 out, ld nxt, hld on wl u.p*) p0 (4th in 3m1f Ch: *chsd ldrs, rdn 4 out, sn outpcd, rallied aft 2 out, kpt on flat*). Never seemed to be remotely fit in the previous yard and failed to finish in five of nine attempts over Hurdles and fences (tailed off and pulled up in the final three), but showed the benefits of joining a highly skilled outfit in '04, and did not give a bad display all year. Beat the only other finisher Miss Mattie Ross who immediately notched a hat-trick in Kelso Hunter Chases in an Alnwick Maiden, and followed an eight length second there by taking a Corbridge Restricted. Made the most of some unsurprisingly lenient handicapping in Chases, and completed a double which was initiated by a Seller. Has been sharpened by cheekpieces or a visor in his last four races, and there may yet be another decent prize for him under Rules. Could he have been another Copper Thistle had he followed the same paths? *Mr & Mrs R. Anderson Green — Border (David Parker).* 74 (OMa), 212 (R), 430 (R).

HAM LANE ..—.. 6 b.g. Paris Of Troy — Some Kathy (Some Hand) ff. Sturdy half-brother to Chequers Boy. Dam was useless, including 3 Points (last, pulled up 1 and fell 1). Shoddy jumping is costing him dear at present, and was in contention when he fell at the ninth and at the 11th, but may be able to do better if learning the error of his ways. *T.D. Goodman — Warwicks (Fred Hutsby).* 367 (OMa), 463 (OMa).

HANDLEY PARK ..—.. 13 ch.g. Ra Nova — True Divine (True Song) f. Stocky brother to Mullover (*qv*). P-t-P '98 and '02 r7 w1 (Maiden) p2 (½*l* 2nd, and last of 3); last, pulled up 2 and fell 1. Clung onto a diminishing advantage when successful on firmish at Dingley in '02, but presumably suffered another setback in the process, and his Mollington appearance this year was his first since. Almost fell at the 12th, and did so at the next, and promptly went back into hiding with his 9-8 rating withdrawn. *Mrs J. Pritchard — Warwicks (John Pritchard).* 1033 (L).

HANDSOME LAD (IRE) ..—.. 7 b.g. Inzar (USA) — Elite Exhibition (Exhibitioner) ppp. Small neat half-brother to flat winners Diesel Don (in Ireland) and Pardy Pet. IR11,000y. 10,500 2yo. FLAT '00 r2 p0 (last 2). NH '01/3 (for Miss V. Scott) r7 p0; last 2, and pulled up 3. A remote last in both flat races and well tailed off in all seven Hurdles (pulled up thrice), and although he led for a way in a couple of Points he was much too free-running to have any hope of getting the trip. Consistently fails to impress at all levels. *D.A. Smith — S. Salop (Willie Bryan).* 533 (2m4fCfMa), 754 (OMa), 1020 (OMa).

HANDSTAND ..9-11.. 8 ch.g. Nearly A Hand — Swaines Lane (Town And Country) 4. Sturdy owner-bred. P-t-P '03 r3 w1 (dead-heat Maiden) p1 (3rd of 4); and pulled up. Benefited from a gentle introduction when forcing a dead-heat with Butler Didit at Mounsey Hill Gate on his final start last year, but failed to reappear after finishing 17 lengths behind that rival in his first Restricted. Should be able to play a more prominent role if none the worse, but clearly unsuited by fast ground. *Mrs J.W. Snook — Cattistock (Nigel Legg).* 315 (R).

HANDY BOY ..9-11.. 10 b.g. Arzanni — Handymouse (Nearly A Hand) f. Workmanlike half-brother to NH flat and Hurdles winner, Fireaway. Dam, sister to 2 Pointers, including Hart Hill Lady (*qv* '94 Annual), won 2m1f Hdle and 2nd twice, and was placed in 2 Points. NH FLAT '01 r1 p0 (6th). P-t-P '00 and '02 (for Mr S. Badham) r5 w1 (3-finisher Maiden) p1 (last of 2); fell/unseated 2 and pulled up 1. Beat a subsequent winner when landing a long three-finisher Maiden at Maisemore Park on his final start in '02, but otherwise badly let down by his jumping, and has obviously proved very hard to train. *R.M. Phillips — N. Ledbury (Mark Jackson).* 177 (3mH).

HANDY HILL ..9-4.. 8 b.g. Nearly A Hand — Tytherington Hill (Nader) p. Lengthy owner-bred. Dam, half-sister to Drumbanes Pet (*qv* '03 Annual). P-t-P '03 r4 w1 (3-finisher Maiden) p0; pulled up 2 and unseated 1. Won a weak three-finisher Maiden on firmish at Barbury last year, but has looked a difficult ride otherwise, and appeared to suffer an immediate setback in '04. *G.W. & Mrs G.A. Giddings — S. & W. Wilts (Gordon Giddings).* 37 (CR).

HANISIA ..8-12.. 10 ch.m. Anshan — Ty High (IRE) (High Line) pp4p. Apart from an unimpressive 29 lengths last, was tailed off and pulled up each time. Surely incapable of any better. *S.P. Bradbury — York & Ainsty N. (David Atkinson).* 341 (R), 500 (CMam), 814 (OMa), 1157 (M).

HAPPISBURGH (U) ..—.. 12 b.g. unknown r. Named after a coastal village in Norfolk, pronounced 'Haisbro'. Negotiated one fence (after a fashion) before refusing. The trainer of the Gunner horses was obviously hai to ride him — wonder why. *The King's Troop RHA — R.A. (Neil Cross).* 84 (2m4fC).

HAPPY TEAM ..9-7.. 12 ch.m. Teamster — Happy Tino (Rugantino) 36pfp542su. Workmanlike half-sister to Mantinolas (dam of Countryside, *qv* '96 Annual), Happy News, Happy Padre, Parditino, My Happy Lord and Dark Comedy. Grandam, Happy Chat, won Maiden and 3 2-3m Chses (ridden by Ken Nicholas in 2). P-t-P '99/03 r27 w3 (up to Confined) p16 (12 2nds, beaten neck once, and last once; and inc 3rd of 4 once); last, pulled up 4, and on floor 3. Regularly in the frame but finds it difficult to keep her head in front, and has gone 23 races without a win. Not helped by frequent errors and only once beaten less than 12 lengths in '04, despite keeping the right company, and will continue to find a fourth success hard to come by. Wears a cross-noseband. *Happy Team Partnership (D. Branton) — Exmoor (Linda Blackford).* 81 (I), 193 (I), 321 (I), 472 (Cf), 792 (MO), 1004 (L), 1180 (M), 1378 (M), 1506 (C), 1557 (Cf).

HAPTHOR .9-9.. 6 ch.m. Zaffaran (USA) — My Goddess (Palm Track) fuf. Half-sister to Spectre Brown and Polly Peacock (*qv*). IRISH P-t-P '03 r4 p0; 4th, brought down 2 and slipped up. IRISH NH FLAT '03 (for H.P. Finegan) r1 p0 (tailed off). It was not her fault that she ended up on the floor in three of four Irish Points, but could not be excused some wild errors in '04. Six lengths clear when she fell four out at Overton, and made favourite next time, but only got as far as the third, whilst another spill was awaiting after two miles on final start (unruly in the paddock). Spectre Brown was a renowned nutcase, and she clearly has a temperamental streak herself. Being out of My Goddess it would have been more accurate to name her Hathor. *F. Jestin — Cumberland.* 659 (OMa), 767 (2m4fOMa), 915 (Cf).

HARDEN GLEN .10-2.. 14 b.g. Respect — Polly Peril (Politico USA) 231. Robust quite attractive wall-eyed half-brother to Breezy Sea, Roy's Little Peril, Lindean Peril and Noble Teviot, and to Irish Pointing winner, Ennis Seven Fifty. NH '98/00 r26 w1 (3m1f Ch) p7; pulled up 5. P-t-P/HUNT CH '96/8 and '02/3 r31 w4 (inc Open and Ladies) p13 (10 2nds, last twice, and inc Hunt Ch; and inc 3rd in Hunt Ch); pulled up 1, and fell/unseated 2. A fair Pointer at his best, and seemed as tough as old boots, but reported dead shortly after recording a hard-fought success in a weak three-finisher Ladies at Alnwick in February. Miss J.E. Riding — College V. & N. Northumberland (Clive Storey). 71 (L), 135 (Cfnr), 213 (L).

HARDING ..9-12.. 14 b.g. Dowsing (USA) — Orange Hill (High Top) f22. Well-made attractive owner-bred half-brother to Jackson Hill and Cadbury Castle, and to 2 flat winners (one in UAE) including Old Provence. Dam won 2 2m1f races, inc Cesarewitch. FLAT '93/6 r14 p5. NH '95/6 and '98/9 r16 w2 (2m5f Hdle and 2m Ch) p6 (4 3rds); fell/unseated 2. IRISH NH '99/00 r2 p0 (5th, and pulled up). P-t-P '02/3 r3 w2 (Open and Confined) p0; and pulled up 1. Very lightly raced since a brief and unsuccessful stint in Ireland, but showed his class when recording a soft ground double at Parham in '02. Suffers with joint problems and restricted to a solitary appearance last year, and jumps badly away to the left nowadays. Presumably retired after suffering a humiliating defeat at 1-3 in his Members. *S.P. Tindall — Kent & Surrey Bloodhounds (Jenny Gordon).* 239 (3m1fH), 608 (L), 645 (M).

HARDY MOUSE (IRE) ..—.. 10 b.m. Hollow Hand — Cornamucla (Lucky Guy) pp. Half-sister to The Major General, Sharp Thyne (IRE) and Tied For Time (IRE), and to Irish Hurdles winner, Ballinderry Glen. Dam won a NH flat race and a Point in Ireland. Bought Doncaster, Aug for 1900. Remote when pulling up after two miles maximum in May Maidens. *P.J. Cooper — W. Percy (Miss C.J. Arden).* 1224 (OMa), 1422 (OMa).

HARFDECENT ..—.. 14 b.g. Primitive Rising (USA) — Grand Queen (Grand Conde FR) upp4. Small close-coupled brother to Fair Grand (*qv*). NH FLAT '96 r3 p1 (3rd). NH '97/03 r36 w6 (2m5110y Hdle and 5 2m3f-3m Chses) p11 (5 2nds); pulled up 6, fell/unseated 4. P-t-P '03 (for Miss J. Tremain) r1 w1 (Confined). Scoring for the first time since recording a double in January '00 when making a winning debut in Points last year, but struggles to get the trip when conditions are testing, and his wind troubles appear to have resurfaced with a vengeance. Runs tongue-tied. *W.J. Day — Gelligaer F. (Lisa Day).* 205 (O), 359 (Cf), 448 (O), 672 (O).

HARJACH ..9-5.. 8 b.g. Sir Harry Lewis (USA) — Acolyn (Derrylin) u41p. Strong lengthy. Dam, half-sister to Acre Hill (*qv* '96 Annual). NH FLAT '01/2 r3 p0. NH '02 r1 p0. P-t-P '03 r5 p1 (3rd); 4th, fell/unseated 2 and pulled up 1. Headstrong and requires two paddock handlers, and made the bulk of the running when beating a subsequent winner in a three-finisher Maiden on firmish at Littlewindsor, but unfortunately broke down badly when a well supported favourite to follow up. Wears a cross-noseband. *P. Reed & P. & E. Phillips — Axe V.H. (Paul Phillips).* 327 (OMa), 469 (2m4fOMa), 1009 (OMa), 1251 (R).

PLATE 55 1561 Torrington Farmers Restricted: Harnage and Caroline Prouse, 1st, jump boldly in the lead from Askers Jack and Jamie Snowden, 2nd *PHOTO: Tim Holt*

HARNAGE (IRE) ..10-2.. 10 b.g. Mujadil (USA) — Wilderness (Martinmas) pb23111. Compact half-brother to several winners, including Scarlett Holly and Positive Attitude (both flat). Dam won 7f race. FLAT '97/00 r13 p1 (3rd). NH '00/1 r4 p0; fell 1. P-t-P '03 r5 p2 (3rds); fell/unseated 2 and pulled up 1. Set impossible tasks when placed at Lifton and Bratton Down, but speedy and much more effective when allowed to get into a rhythm, and well handled by Caroline Prouse (who skillfully managed to get a breather into him) in his last two Points. A tail swisher but seems genuine enough, and might be able to hold his own in Ladies when there is little emphasis on stamina. *R.T. Grant — Tiverton Stag.* 827 (CfMa), 1132 (R), 1353 (OMa), 1381 (OMa), 1466 (OMa), 1554 (M), 1561 (R).

HARPPY (FR) .8-11§§.. 10 b.g. Kedellic (FR) — Flute De Pan (FR) (Saint Estephe FR) pu24. Compact. FRENCH NH '99/00 r9 w1 (2m3f Chse) p1 (3rd). NH '00/1 r7 w1 (3m110y Hdle) p1 (2nd); pulled up 3, slipped up 1. P-t-P '02/3 (for Mrs C. Keen) r17 p1 (last of 2); last pair 3, pulled up 7, fell/unseated 3, ran out 2 and refused 1. Retains ability and quite happy to adopt an uncontested lead, but a conniving old fox, and has wriggled out of scoring since obliging on either side of the Channel in '00. Not always keen to jump off, and regained blinkers after a typically mulish display at Lydstep, but downed tools as soon as he was headed on his final start, and must be shunned. Wears a cross-noseband, and bandages behind, and has run tongue-tied. *G.B. Crees — Banwen Miners (S. Cashmore).* 1090 (Cf), 1235 (Cf), 1520 (O), 1549 (O).

HARRY HOTSPUR (IRE) ..5-0§§.. 12 gr.g. Celio Rufo — Midsummer Blends (IRE) (Duky) ppRp24p. Tall. IR26,000 4yo. NH FLAT '98 r1 p0. NH '99/00 and '02 (for I. Williams) r12 w1 (3m Ch) p3; pulled up 3. Rather surprisingly ended his career under Rules with a win, when taking a Huntingdon Chase on firmish, but like several of his stablemates is now a highly reluctant donkey, and is fences rather than lengths behind in last if he does consent to complete. Particularly enjoys taking the mickey out of the beginner owner-rider. *M.M.E.H. Dearden — Ludlow (Geoff Evans).* 49 (4mO), 346 (3m1f110yH), 835 (Cf), 979 (MOnr), 1145 (O), 1262 (O), 1427 (O).

HARRY JAY .6-12.. 8 ch.g. Bold Arrangement — Stanwick Monument (Grey Ghost) 4. Owner-bred half-brother to Stanwick Gypsy. Finished 78 lengths last in his Members, and deprived of third prize money after clambering over the last when very tired. *Miss S.L. Williamson — Zetland.* 1286 (M).

HARRY'S MARE (IRE) ..8-0.. 10 br.m. Mister Lord (USA) — Greenfield Glory (Pitpan) uppp3. Tall sparely-made half-sister to Elwill Glory (IRE) and Hugo Henry (IRE). Dam won mares Maiden in Ireland. IRISH NH FLAT '00 r1 p0. P-t-P '01/3 (for Countess S. Goess-Saurau & Mr A.T. West) r7 w1 (Maiden) p2 (2nds, of 3 once); last 2, and pulled up 2. Won at the sixth attempt, in her third season for previous connections, but never stood much racing, and proved to be a very weak finisher. A very indifferent jumper, and unimproved by new surroundings, and beaten 50 lengths when carrying Jill Hedley to her first completion at Hexham. Has acquired a cross-noseband. *The Hedley Family (Mrs K. Hedley) — Border (Margaret Hedley).* 283 (R), 431 (R), 765 (R), 1222 (R), 1423 (M).

HARVEST THE OAK ..—.. 8 b.g. Royal Fountain — Hope For The Best (Nearly A Hand) pp. Dam, half-sister to Beyond Hope (*qv* '04 Annual), won bad Maiden. Tailed off and pulled up after 2m4f in early season Maidens at Alnwick. *Miss C. Watson & Mrs M.A. Watson — Haydon (Mrs M.A. Watson).* 75 (OMa), 215 (OMa).

HAS SHE BUCKED YET ..9-4.. 7 b.m. North Col — True Sparkle (True Song) 6. Small light-framed. Dam, sister to True Hustler (*qv* '04 Annual) pulled up and fell in Points. Struggling throughout the final mile before finishing tailed off last in a mid-January Maiden won by Free Gift at Larkhill. *Mrs E. Keir — Grafton.* 12 (OMa).

HASTATE ..—.. 10 b.g. Persian Bold — Gisarne (USA) (Diesis) p. Good-topped compact half-brother to NH flat winner, Gismo. Dam, sister to Obelos (*qv* '01 Annual), won 2 10f races (inc Lupe Stakes). FLAT '97/9 r14 w1 (16f) p2. NH '99/00 r10 w1 (2m3f Hdle) p6 (3 2nds); unseated 1. P-t-P/HUNT CH '02/3 r5 p1 (3rd in Hunt Ch); last, unseated 2 and pulled up 1. Very capable on his day, and won over hurdles at Newbury in '00 and third to Tubber Roads and County Derry there two years later, but appears to lurch from one setback to another now, and looked fat when failing to complete '03/4. Lacks fluency and has never proved his effectiveness over three miles, and his 10-5 rating is withdrawn. Ran tongue-tied twice in '99. *The Red Lion Racing Club (N.M. Lampard) — Tedworth (Nick Lampard).* 348 (3mH).

HASTEN BAK ..10-3.. 12 ch.g. Shaab — Kirstins Pride (Silly Prices) 2632213. Small neat owner-bred half-brother to Bak To Bill and Bak On Board. Dam is half-sister to 4 Pointers, including Sergent Kay (*qv* '97 Annual). NH FLAT '99 r1 p0. NH '99/02 r29 w1 (2m1f110y Ch) p6; fell/unseated 5, pulled up 3. P-t-P '98/9 and '03 r13 w4 (Confineds) p5 (3 2nds, remote once; and last of 3 twice); 4th of 5, unseated 2 and refused 1. Scored four times during a hectic '03 campaign, but twice had the misfortune to run into Kestick this year, and is not always predictable. Beat Let's Fly convincingly at Trebudannon, but there was a 16-length turn around when they next met, and probably best when allowed to dominate. Suited by good or sound surfaces. Wears a cross-noseband and a dexter ringbit. Blinkered once in '03 and still liable to be mulish at the start. *R.T. & Mrs W.S. Cook — N. Cornwall (Mrs W.S. Cook).* 76 (M), 569 (MO), 703 (MO), 911 (MO), 1269 (MO), 1434 (MO), 1542 (L).

HASTE YE BACK (IRE) ..10-3.. 11 b.g. All Haste (USA) — Less Pressure (IRE) (Torus) 314. Compact well-made. IR10,000 3yo. IRISH P-t-P '99 r3 w1 (4&5yo Maiden) p0; pulled up 2. NH '99/03 (for N.A. Twiston-Davies when successful, and late D.J. Caro) r23 w1 (3m Ch) p4 (inc 3 Hdles); pulled up 5, fell/unseated 2. Suited by a long trip in mud, and gained his first success for 39 months in a Novice Riders event at Brampton Bryan, in which he held off a 13-year-old who did not score all season by a neck. Would have finished runner-up on his previous outing had the rider not dropped her hands close home, and was on better terms with himself in Points than he has often been under Rules (a sketchy jumper who has frequently looked reluctant). Mostly equipped with headgear, although not for the win. *M. Scudamore jnr — Ross H. (Michael Scudamore Snr).* 612 (Cf), 661 (Cnr), 1016 (3m2fO).

HATCH GATE ..10-0§§.. 12 gr.g. Lighter — Yankee Silver (Yankee Gold) r12pp. Compact well-made brother to Elmers Marsh and Iron Hill. P-t-P/HUNT CH '99/03 r19 w6 (inc 3m Hunt Ch, and inc hat-trick '02) p1 (2nd); pulled up 7, and unseated 1. Underwent a remarkable transformation when joining the current yard mid-way through '02, and has won seven races since, but only effective in weak events on sound surfaces, and made a noise when runner-up at Cottenham. Very reluctant to race in two subsequent outings and it would be a surprise if he was rejuvenated again. A sketchy jumper of big fences. Tongue-tied on his most recent appearance. *Mrs K.H. York — Staff College (Phillip York).* 24 (O), 331 (M), 997 (O), 1169 (3m2f110yH), 1515 (O).

HATTIE ..9-8.. 11 b.m. Sylvan Express — Hatsu-Girie (Ascertain USA) pp3143. Light-framed sister to Sola Topee, and half-sister to Buddy Girie. Dam, half-sister to Pepper Elder (*qv* '93 Annual), won 3 2m4f-3m3f Chses, for Robert Swiers. P-t-P '99/00 (for Mr R.W. Swiers) r5 p0 (6th, last 2, and pulled up 2). Spent three years on the sidelines prior to '04, but proved connections decision to bring her back into training correct when landing a bad two-finisher mares Maiden in a slow time at Corbridge.

Ordinarily pulls too hard, and fails to get the trip as a result, and looks likely to struggle in search of a follow up. Wears a cross-noseband. *J. Cornforth — York & Ainsty N. (Philip Cornforth).* 165 (OMa), 500 (CMam), 814 (OMa), 1042 (CMam), 1157 (M), 1398 (Cm).

HAVABASH .—.. 7 b.g. Shaab — Treloweth Julie (Flandre II) p. Lengthy light-framed homebred brother to County Bash. Jumped moderately and quickly lost touch when green on a May debut at Trebudannon. *Mrs R.T. Cook & Dr L.R. Olver — N. Cornwall (Sue Cook).* 1432 (OMa).

HAVE A CHAT ..9-7.. 7 b.g. Rakaposhi King — Royal Chitchat (Le Bavard FR) 3. Close-coupled half-brother to Country Captain. Dam, half-sister to Simply Joyful (*qv* '00 Annual). Scored in yielding in Ireland on the only occasion he beat another horse there, but could only manage 26 lengths third in a Garthorpe Restricted in which he was already getting reminders at halfway. Gives the impression of being one of the lesser lights in a powerful yard. *Mr & Mrs W.J. Warner — Pytchley (Bill Warner).* 1060 (R).

HAVETWOTAKETWO (IRE) ..—.. 11 b.g. Phardante (FR) — Arctic Tartan (Deep Run) upuf. Plain angular brother to Hurdles winners, My Man Dan (IRE) (in Ireland) and Townleyhall (IRE) (also won Irish NH flat). Dam won Irish NH flat. IRISH NH FLAT '00 r1 p0. IRISH NH '00 r2 p0. NH '01 r1 p0 (pulled up). P-t-P/HUNT CH '01/3 r12 w2 (Maiden and Confined) p3 (2 3rds); pulled up 3, and fell/unseated 4. Won two of his first three starts over fences, but expensive to follow subsequently, and has failed to complete in his last 11 appearances. Used to stay well, but prone to frequent jumping lapses, and running him in Hunter Chases is doing his confidence no good at all. *M. & Mrs S. Smith — Jedforest (Michael Smith).* 349 (3m1fH), 542 (3m3fH), 654 (Cf), 797 (3m1fH).

PLATE 56 1564 Torrington Farmers Intermediate: Hawkers Hill (Rilly Goschen), 1st, leads Menantol (Anna de Lisle Wells), 2nd, and Sherbourne Guest (Jan Kwiatkowski), 3rd
PHOTO: Baths Photographic

HAWKERS HILL ..9-9.. 10 b.g. Greensmith — Classy Miss (Homeboy) pp222fupp11. Sturdy brother to Arthur-K. NH FLAT '00 r2 p0. P-t-P '03 r4 w1 (Maiden) p1 (3rd); 4th of 5, and fell 1. Prone to sweat freely and race keenly, and has won three weak races on sound surfaces, but noticeably handled with kid gloves at times and looks likely to struggle now that the ante has been upped. Twice plunged on unsuccessfully in '04, but an unreliable jumper, and has clearly benefited from superior handling. *A.P. & Mrs M.L. Carter — Blackmore & Sparkford V. (John Dufosee).* 14 (R), 118 (R), 265 (R), 354 (R), 579 (R), 720 (R), 864 (R), 1063 (R), 1366 (R), 1491 (R), 1564 (I).

HAWTHORN ..—.. 9 ch.g. Primo Dominie — Starr Danias (USA) (Sensitive Prince USA) pff. Lengthy half-brother to 5 flat winners (one in Sweden) inc Out Of Sight and Chevin. NH FLAT '00 r3 p1 (3rd). NH '01/2 (from J.G. Fitzgerald's, and M.F. Harris's) r3 p0; pulled up 1. Sold Doncaster, May '02 for 3000. Six lengths third of 17 in a bumper on his debut, but never beaten less than 34 lengths since, and has now failed to finish on his four most recent attempts. Probably the worst in a stable which has some truly dismal inmates, and his jumping is verging on dangerous. *Clock House Racing — Bicester with Whaddon (Bradley Clarke).* 288 (M), 631 (2m6f110yH), 1341 (OMa).

HAY BLUFF LADY (IRE) ..—.. 6 b.m. Supreme Leader — Ballyeden (Beau Charmeur FR) p. Lengthy good-topped half-sister to Woolly Jumper (IRE). Dam won 2 3m-3m1f Hunt Chses and 8 Points (the first in Ireland, but all other wins for Philip Gough) and placed 11 (inc a Hdle) to '94. Tailed off and pulled up after two miles in a Restricted, in which she looked unfit and was novicey. Her pedigree suggests she should be able to do better in time. *Mrs J. Jones — Golden V. (Charlotte Fuller).* 357 (R).

HAY DANCE ..9-8.. 14 b.g. Shareef Dancer (USA) — Hay Reef (Mill Reef USA) pp27. Small neat half-brother to 6 flat winners (one in Belgium), and to successful Hurdler, Pharly Reef. Dam, half-sister to Wassi, won at 10f. FLAT '94/5 r8 p0. IRISH FLAT '96 r1 p0. IRISH NH '95/6 r5 w1 (2m Hdle) p1 (2nd). NH '96/9 r13 w4 (2-2m1f Hdles, 5 ran thrice) p4 (3 3rds); inc Sell, and fell 3. P-t-P/HUNT CH '00 and '02/3 r16 p5 (4 3rds, of 4 twice, last once, and inc Hunt Ch); 5th twice, last 2, pulled up 7. A competent hurdler on sound surfaces, and retains ability, but normally fails to get the trip in Points, and duly finished tamely when 33-1 and runner-up at Higham. A safe jumper but his Members looks his only hope in '05. *Mrs S.J. Ruddle — Waveney H. (John Ibbott).* 25 (L), 246 (L), 399 (L), 558 (L).

HAYDN JAMES (USA) ..10-5.. 11 ch.g. Danzig Connection (USA) — Royal Fi Fi (USA) (Conquistador Cielo USA) 2. Angular. Dam won her first 3 flat races, 5-6f. $45,000y. FLAT '96/9 r36 w3 (9-10f) p11. NH '00/2 (for P.J. Hobbs) r25 w8 (4 2m1f-2m6f Hdles and 4 2m2f-2m4f Chses) p3. A tough sort who has given plenty of fun in a long career, and the winner of 11 races (one on the all-weather and the rest on sound surfaces), plus a Charity flat race at a Point. Could have been even more successful had his jumping not let him down on occasions, but has still amassed prize money of about £50,000. Frequently wore headgear to '98, and occasionally since. Must have ground which is approaching firm, and from the way he performed in his only Open he could still be a force in similar company if turning up again in '05. *P. Browne, M. Scott, G. Brown & S. Stevens — Devon & Somerset (Stewart Stevens).* 1463 (O).

HAYLING STAR ..8-6§.. 11 ch.m. Out Of Hand — Lurex Girl (Camden Town) p34ppuu2263. Compact well-made roman-nosed half-sister to Winning Town (*qv*). NH FLAT '98 r1 p0. P-t-P '02/3 r16 p0 (last pair 5, pulled up 7, and fell/unseated 4). The epitome of uselessness with no redeeming features, and normally badly tailed off last when completing. Often makes appalling mistakes, and why Polly Gundry should agree to take the ride at Kingston St Mary is most perplexing. Has shown a tendency to misbehave in the preliminaries, and is mounted on course and taken to post early. Blinkered and tongue-tied at Bratton Down, but after showing her usual early speed jumped badly and was pulled up. Why bother? *R. Pike & Mrs M. Howard — Taunton V.H. (Michael Sweetland).* 82 (OMa), 326 (OMa), 416 (CMam), 493 (OMa), 967 (OMa), 1182 (CMam), 1326 (OMa), 1445 (M), 1466 (OMa), 1559 (OMa), 1565 (OMa).

HEAD GARDENER (IRE) ..9-3§.. 11 b.g. Be My Chief (USA) — Silk Petal (Petorius) p6p6p7346. Short-backed strong-topped half-brother to 4 winners, including Star Tulip (useful sprinter), Zeloso and Sweet Pea (both flat; former also a successful Hurdler). Dam, won 3 flat, 7-8f (one in Germany). FLAT '96/8 r31 w1 (11f) p9. NH '97/01 r25 w2 (2m4f110y Hdle and 3m1f110y Ch) p5 (inc 2 2nds); pulled up 1, and fell/unseated 3. P-t-P '02/3 r6 p1 (2nd); last pair 2, pulled up 1 and fell 1 (also disqualified from 4th once — not weigh-in). A dual winner in blinkers for Richard Lee to '00, but no longer prepared to co-operate, and beaten a minimum of 23 lengths in '04. A modest jumper and his losing sequence now stands at 29. *R.J. Williams — S. Herefords (Christine Hardinge).* 205 (O), 403 (Cf), 615 (O), 660 (Cf), 756 (Cf), 843 (L), 1025 (L), 1229 (L), 1343 (L).

HEADWRECKER (IRE) ..9-10.. 9 br.g. Good Thyne (USA) — Sallowglen Gale (IRE) (Strong Gale) 13p. Strong compact. Dam sister to Pongo Waring. NH FLAT '01/2 r2 p1 (2nd). NH '02 r3 p0. P-t-P '03 r1 p0 (unseated). Completing a double for the stable when a convincing winner in softish at Bishops Court, but absent with niggling problems including pulled muscles for much of last year, and twice a disappointing favourite subsequently. Clearly yet to exorcise his own demons. Wears a cross-noseband. *G.C. Maundrell — R.A. (Paul Thompson).* 325 (OMa), 720 (R), 879 (R).

HEARTLEYS QUEST (IRE) ..—.. 6 b.m. Broken Hearted — Jesse Twist (IRE) (Sandalay) r. Sold Tattersalls Ireland, Aug for 370. Bought Doncaster, Oct for 800. A remote last when taking a dislike to the third from home in a 2m4f Maiden, and stopped and threw the jockey off. *P. Phillips & D. Martin — Axe V.H. (Paul Phillips).* 1007 (2m4fOMa).

HEATHER LAD ..9-6.. 12 ch.g. Highlands — Ragged Rose (Scallywag) 7fpp. Close-coupled half-brother to Wild Briar and Garmondsway. Dam failed to finish in four Points for Mrs Taylor (looked a handful). P-t-P/HUNT CH '98/00 and '02/3 r30 w2 (Maiden and Restricted) p7 (6

2nds, inc beaten short head once, of 3 twice beaten head once; and inc 3rd of 4); pulled up 9, slipped up 1, fell/unseated 3. Landed 17 and 18-runner events to '02, but only effective when conditions aren't testing, and basically outclassed since. Best when persuaded to settle in behind, but prone to errors, and a regular non-finisher now. *C.B. Taylor — S. Durham.* 161 (I), 389 (Cf), 565 (O), 808 (CfCon).

HEATHYARDS ELEMENT ..9-1§.. 9 ch.g. Henbit (USA) — Moment's Pleasure (USA) (What A Pleasure USA) 423. Rangy half-brother to Moneystone, Pleasure Cruise, and to Hurdles winner, Twin Pleasures. 900 3yo. NH FLAT '00 r2 p1 (2nd of 17). NH '00/2 r17 p4 (inc 3 in Chses). A disappointing sort who has never produced much for pressure, and even tried Selling Hurdles without success (blinkered once). Did best when second of 17 on his debut in a bumper, but has flattered to deceive, and could not even justify support in some weak Maidens. Ended '02 lame, and the same fate befell him in '04. *D.A. Malam — Cheshire (Donald McCain Jnr).* 96 (CfMa), 710 (Mah), 1142 (OMa).

HEAVEN IS ABOVE (IRE) ..—.. 10 b.g. Hymns On High — Great Supper (Slippered) up. Compact attractive half-brother to Suppoze and Meadestown (IRE), and to Irish NH flat and Hurdles winner, Ballytigue Lad. IRISH NH '01/2 r7 p0. IRISH P-t-P '03 r3 w1 (6yo plus Maiden) p0; unseated 1. IRISH HUNT CH '03 (for Mrs P. Gore-Cogan) r1 w1 (3m). A dual Irish winner on firmish including a Cork Hunter Chase by 25 lengths, and must have cost present connections a pretty penny, but after the owner had fallen off at the eighth in a Ladies he pulled up in a Hunter Chase in early March and then vanished. Suspect at present, but if he recovered he might yet turn out to be useful with strong handling on the right surface. *Mrs D. Rowell — Mid Surrey F. (Sara Hickman).* 157 (L), 347 (3mH).

HEAVY WEATHER (IRE) .9-11.. 7 ch.g. Glacial Storm (USA) — Tinkers Lady (Sheer Grit) 1pfp. Small workmanlike half-brother to Hurdles winner, Ojays Alibi, and to Irish Chasing and Pointing winner, Gamblers Dream. IRISH P-t-P '03/4 r5 w1 (Confined Maiden) p1 (3rd); pulled up 1 and fell 1. Purchased after winning an Irish Maiden in January, and immediately came good for the new yard in a Restricted in holding at Eyton-on-Severn, but it was not a great contest and his jumping caused problems afterwards. Facing the wrong way when the starter let them go and did not take a fence on his most recent outing (to the total fury of the rider), and will need some intensive schooling lessons before he reappears. *P.J. Kennedy — Teme V. (Jo Priest).* 530 (R), 728 (I), 1227 (Cf), 1430 (I).

HEDZAMARLEY (IRE) ..9-9.. 12 gr.g. Ala Hounak — Marleygate (Monksfield) fpuuf. Neat. Dam, half-sister to The Green Fool (*qv*). IRISH P-t-P '98/01 r22 w1 (6yo&up Maiden) p4; pulled up 14, and fell 2. IRISH NH FLAT '99 r1 p0 (well tailed off). IRISH NH '99/00 r4 p0; pulled up 1, and fell/unseated 2. P-t-P '02/3 (for Mrs N.J.N. Bird) r13 w1 (Restricted) p2 (2nd of 3 once); last 4, unseated 2, and pulled up 4. Passed the post in front for the first time in 38 races when scoring on firmish at Paxford last year, but a wholly unsuitable mount for an inexperienced girl, and put Sian Davies on the floor in all three attempts in '04. Has run tongue-tied. *Miss S. Davies — Clifton-on-Teme.* 406 (Inr), 759 (I), 979 (MOnr), 1140 (Cf), 1472 (I).

HEIDI III (FR) ..10-7.. 10 b.g. Bayolidaan (FR) — Irlandaise (FR) (Or De Chine) 234*pp*. Close-coupled half-brother to two jumping winners in France. Dam won 11f race in France. FRENCH FLAT '98 r1 p0. FRENCH NH '99 r2 w1 (2m1f Ch) p0. NH '99/02 r18 w5 (3 2m1f-2m5f Hdles and 2 2m4f-3m Chses) p7. NH '04 r2 p1 (3rd in 2m4f110y Ch: *a.p, rmdrs aft 8, rdn app 3 out, one pce flat*); and pulled up in 3m1f Ch: *hld up, rdn app 7, lost plce 9, bhnd when pu 11*. Was in excellent heart when completing a hat-trick between April and June '00, and later bagged a major pot in the Great Yorkshire Chase (£31,850) at Doncaster which is the bulk of his total career earnings of £77,855. Has not scored since his big day in January '01, but was pipped by the minimum margin at Bangor three years later, and still capable of decent efforts although probably less game than he was in the old days. Can handle firmish, but particularly revels in mud. Adorned with cheekpieces or blinkers now. Future opportunities may be thin on the ground, so connections should try to place him to the very best advantage. *Turner Technology Ltd — Cheshire (Lisa Williamson).* 435 (3m110yH), 994 (3m110yH), 1512 (2m6f110yH).

HEIDI MOO (U) ..5-0.. 14 b.m. Lepanto (GER) — unknown 3. P-t-P '98 r1 p0 (unseated). Compact. The silly moo unseated in a Members in '98, when spelt Hiedi Moo and had another crack six years later and finished a fence behind in last (in a contest designed to confuse, Cornish Mist was actually Grey Valley). *Miss S.E. Rich & S. Rogers — E. Cornwall.* 305 (M).

HEISAMODEL (IRE) .9-12.. 7 b.g. Balla Cove — Liffeyside Lady (IRE) (Cataldi) fp21. Close-coupled. IRISH P-t-P '03 r4 w2 (5&6yo Maiden, and Winners of Two) p0. IRISH NH FLAT '03 (from J.P. Brennan's) r2 p0. Successful in 50% of his Irish Points, and although he halved that margin in '04 his season did end on a bright note when he was backed from 5-2 to 6-4 favourite at

Trebudannon. Seems to need firm ground and possibly also a short course, and can be less than accurate in his jumping, but it should not be difficult to find more opportunities for him when conditions are met. *J.J. Boulter & Miss F.J. Wilkins — Portman (John Boulter).* 321 (I), 692 (I), 1059 (I), 1431 (I).

HELIOTROPE (IRE) ..—.. 6 b.m. Hushang (IRE) — Jennie's First (Idiot's Delight) p. Small owner-bred sister to Henrietta, and half-sister to Hollyhock (*qv*). Related to a couple of corkers, but came to a devastating end in her very first race when she broke a leg at Bishops Court. B.A. Kilpatrick — Taunton V.H. (David Pipe). 329 (OMa).

HELLODOCK (IRE) ..10-0.. 10 b.g. Dry Dock — Hello October (Callernish) 2. IRISH P-t-P '01 r1 w1 (6yo&up Maiden). NH '02 r4 p1 (head 2nd to Highland Rose (*qv*); fell 2. P-t-P '03 (for Mr J. Milburn & Mr J. Watson) r1 p0 (pulled up). Heavily punted when winning in Ireland, and split two subsequent winners when runner-up at Whitwell-on-the-Hill, but roughed off with a leg and fired early last year, and it would appear that his legs have given way again. *Mrs N.C. Wilson & J. Milburn — Middleton (Nicki Wilson).* 771 (R).

HELLOFAJOB (IRE) ..—.. 6 ch.g. Pierre — Dameish (IRE) (Callernish) p. Very small half-brother to Irish NH Flat winner, Champaigne Ronnie. Sold Goffs Ireland, Jun for 3400. Tailed off and pulled up two out in a 2m4f Maiden at Ston Easton. Could certainly have done with being a bit bigger. *R. Barrow — Quantock (Julie Long).* 599 (2m4fOMa).

HELLO ROSCREA (IRE) ..10-0.. 12 b.g. Homo Sapien — Waterpark Lady (IRE) (Jamesmead) pf2211p. Small. IRISH P-t-P '98/9 and '01/3 r28 w1 (7yo&up Maiden) p7; pulled up 11 and fell 2. Achieved a remarkable feat for an Irish Pointer by making 28 appearances and only scoring the once (at the 19th attempt in '02), and was maintaining a similar level of mediocrity even when he beat two rivals in his Members at Badbury (one was 16 and one 15 although he acts much older). Unbelievably proved himself Lord of the Rings when returned there three weeks later, and in taking the Restricted by an easy 12 lengths he achieved the fastest time of the day, bettering two subsequent Hunter Chase winners and two subsequent Open winners! How that happened is one of life's mysteries, and on his only subsequent attempt he was tailed off and pulled up at Newton Abbot. Probably needs a sound surface, but words light and bushel seem most applicable. Normally worth around 9-7. *S. & Mrs S. Dixon — Wilton (Sharon Brown).* 169 (R), 262 (L), 337 (R), 459 (R), 574 (M), 864 (R), 1167 (3m2f110yH).

HENBURY DANCER ..9-0.. 9 br.m. Teamster — Record Flight (Record Token) 4561pp. Tall workmanlike. Dam won 4 Hdles (2m-2m5f) and a 2m Ch. FLAT '99 r2 p0. NH '01/2 r8 p0. P-t-P '03 r6 w1 (3-finisher Members) p0; 6th, last pair 2, and fell 2. Faced a simple task when retaining her Members title, and won on merit this time, but very susceptible to alarming blunders, and does not normally get the trip. Gets in a stew before her races and is often mounted on course and taken down early. *Mr & Mrs A. Watson — N. Staffs (Gary Hanmer).* 231 (CR), 614 (R), 715 (R), 847 (M), 1048 (R), 1265 (R).

HENDRIX ..9-0.. 9 b.g. Henbit (USA) — Florita (Lord Gayle USA) pp2f. Tall rangy half-brother to Highland Symphony, and to a winner in Jersey. Dam won 10f race. P-t-P '03 r2 p0 (4th, and unseated 1). An imposing individual, and well regarded at home, but an inept jumper at present, and yet to display much resolve when completing. Very close to a squiggle, and taken to post early when favourite on his most recent appearance. *T.H.J. & M. Bannister — Pendle Forest & Craven (Jo Foster).* 271 (OMa), 710 (Mah), 1143 (OMa), 1305 (OMa).

HENRY BRUCE ..9-10§.. 13 ch.g. Buckley — Booterstown (Master Owen) p36654. Good-topped half-brother to Master Enborne, Celtic Town, Bubble N Squeak and Ardstown. NH '98 and '01 r3 p0 (pulled up 3). P-t-P/HUNT CH '98/03 (for Mr B. Jackson & Mr P. Hicks) r36 w7 (inc 3m2f Hunt Ch, and inc 4-timer '99) p10 (5 2nds); pulled up 7, fell 2, and ran out 2. A very thorough stayer, and has won seven races on easy surfaces, but only once since '00, and largely unreceptive to all attempts to make him co-operate now. Typically ran in snatches when third at Garnons, but otherwise very doggy in '04, and the new rider did well in the circumstances. Has been tried in headgear, and ridden in spurs. *A.G. Brown — N. Hereford (David Drinkwater).* 31 (Cnr), 403 (Cf), 612 (Cf), 758 (O), 979 (MOnr), 1228 (4mO).

HENRY HENBIT ..9-0§.. 10 b/br.g. Henbit (USA) — Turn Mill (Latest Model) 5p5p. Lengthy. Dam, half-sister to Meadow Lad (*qv* '91 Annual), won 3 Points (including 2 Opens, including '90 Dudley Cup by short head at 20-1) and placed 5 (inc 2 Hunt Chses). Grandam, Ruby Sherry, won a Maiden. NH FLAT '00 r2 p0. P-t-P '00 and '02/3 r4 w1 (Maiden) p1 (2nd); last, and pulled up 1. Recorded the slowest time of the day when successful at Market Rasen in '02, but stands few outings, and fast becoming a typically unreliable Henbit. Makes mistakes and despite the presence of Stuart Morris in the saddle should be given a wide berth. *Mrs J. Wilson — Pytchley (Bill Warner).* 57 (R), 159 (R), 787 (CR), 1123 (R).

HENRY MURPHY .9-13.. 8 b.g. High Lodge — Scalby Mitre (Sir Mago) 1. Workmanlike brother to Mighty High (*qv*). Dam, sister to 3 Pointers including Smart Pilot (*qv* '94 Annual). P-t-P '03 r9 p1 (3rd of 4); 6th of 7, pulled up 5, and on floor 2. Hinted at ability when often stopped in his tracks by catastrophic errors in the previous yard, and romped a weak Maiden at Market Rasen on his return, but promptly vanished, and a first encounter with firm ground was clearly counter productive. Often tried tongue-tied in '03. *A.G. Dimmock — Middleton (Gill Walford).* 58 (OMa).

HENWYN ..9-3§.. 12 b.g. Henbit (USA) — Macusla (Lighter) up0p. Lengthy half-brother to Minusla, Ramnuggur and Hervey Bay, and to Hurdles winner, Akulite. Dam won NH flat, 2 Hdles (2m-2m4f) and 2m Ch. P-t-P '98/00 and '02/3 (for Mr M. Weir) r19 w1 (2m4f Maiden) p8 (7 2nds, beaten 1/2*l* once, of 3 once; and 3rd of 4); pulled up 8, and unseated 1. Won a short Maiden on firm at Eyton in '99, and much improved when Devon-based last year, but prone to breaking blood vessels in between, and stopped to nil on his last three appearances in '04. A Henbit, and needs little provocation to turn it in, and looks finished now. Has been tried in cheekpieces. *A.R. & Mrs S.J. Humphrey — Thurlow (Sarah Humphrey).* 155 (Cnr), 248 (Cf), 398 (R), 524 (R).

HERE COMES CHOOSEY (IRE) ..8-9.. 9 b/br.g. Good Thyne (USA) — Bridgetown Girl (Al Sirat) 2p. Small half-brother to Kustom Kit Grizzly (IRE) (*qv*). IRISH P-t-P '01 r2 p0 (pulled up and fell). IRISH NH '01/3 (for E.J. O'Grady) r6 p1 (3rd); pulled up 1. Third in his debut Hurdle in Ireland, but tailed off on his last three attempts there (pulled up once), and was blinkered twice. Finished a neck second on his English debut, but the form was badly devalued when the winner pulled up in three subsequent attempts and the third failed to reappear. Has never managed many outings, and judged on his next effort it would be a big surprise if he could win. *The Cherry Tree Partnership (Mrs T.H. Hayward) — N. Norfolk H. (Tina Hayward).* 129 (OMa), 482 (OMa).

HERE'S TO LUCY ..9-5.. 7 b.m. Anshan — Hilly Path (Brave Invader USA) 2. Light-framed half-sister to Hurdles winner, Bridal Path (IRE). Shaped encouragingly enough when ten lengths second in a youngsters Maiden at Stafford Cross, and it may be possible for her to go one better. *D. & Mrs J.S. Newton — E. Cornwall.* 1133 (OMa).

HERMANO (IRE) ..7-4.. 8 b/br.g. Malmsey (USA) — Ballyhornan VII (unknown) pp3d3. P-t-P '03 r1 p0 (fell). Headstrong and pulled his way to the front by the fifth at the latest in '04, but yet to look like lasting home, even over 2m4f, and sometimes pays scant regard to the fences. *Mrs M. Logan — Farmers Bloodhounds (Barry Logan).* 192 (CfMa), 386 (OMa), 850 (2m5fOMa), 1504 (2m4fOMa).

HERMES III (FR) ..10-12.. 10 b.g. Quart De Vin (FR) — Queenly (FR) (Pot D'Or FR) 2*b*1. Tall strong half-brother to a French Hurdling winner. Dam, half-sister to dam of Blanville, won on flat and over jumps in France. FRENCH FLAT '99 r1 p0. FRENCH NH '00 (for J-Y Artu) r1 w1 (2m2f Ch). NH '01/3 (for N. Henderson) r9 w3 (2 2m5f Hdles and 2m5f Ch) p3. NH '04 r1 p0 (brought down in 2m5f110y Topham Ch: *hld up, lost plce when bd 10*). Useful, and has a high strike rate considering how infrequently he appears, and was managing his fourth win (including a hat-trick in '02) from ten attempts in the United Kingdom when he won a 3m3f Perth Hunter Chase by a distance after Dorans Magic had fallen at the last with every chance but held. The runner-up Nisbit was unbeaten in two later attempts in the same grade, and there seems little doubt that Hermes could have achieved a great deal more had he had the chances. An easy surface looks essential. It could be worth trying to find a valuable Handicap for him in '05. *The Grand National Racing Club Limited — Middleton (Mick Easterby).* 241 (2m4f110yH), 1068 (3m2f110yH).

HERPEN ..—.. 8 b.m. Relief Pitcher — Pensun (Jimsun) ppppp. Strong compact attractive owner-bred half-sister to Penlet Too (*qv*). Tailed off and pulled up after two miles in four Maidens, and went an extra half mile in the other, but only after making several slow jumps. A hairy ride who can give trouble in the preliminaries, and has been mounted outside the paddock and taken to post early. Tends to stop rapidly, and may have a physical defect. *R.G. Weaving — Warwicks (John Pritchard).* 462 (OMa), 588 (CfMa), 789 (CfMa), 1119 (CMam), 1402 (2m4fOMa).

HERSWELL CASTLE .9-6.. 6 ch.g. Superlative — Anchor Express (Carlingford Castle) 22. Sturdy half-brother to Oscarsexpress. Dam, sister to Bruff Castle (*qv* '99 Annual), won 4 Irish Points and Hunter Chase and placed 13, and subsequently won Club race and failed to finish 3 in England. Bought Doncaster, Nov for 4500. Being placed in both Maidens (promoted from third to second once) was a competent start, and it will be disappointing if he cannot win a race or two before too much longer. *Mrs N. Gooder — Taunton V. (Mel Dixon).* 600 (2m4fOMa), 884 (OMa).

HERVEY BAY ..9-10.. 7 b.m. Primitive Rising (USA) — Macusla (Lighter) pp1p6553. Small neat half-sister to Henwyn (*qv*). P-t-P '03 r3 p0 (4th, and pulled up 2). Took over seven minutes to dispose of a rival who had run loose before the start at Friars Haugh, but gave his best display on firmish over 2m4f when tongue-tied, and has looked a non-stayer over the full trip otherwise. Wears a cross-noseband. *W. Goldie — Eglinton.* 132 (CR), 216 (OMa), 286 (CfMa), 548 (R), 1178 (3m1fH), 1373 (2m4f110yH), 1476 (R), 1499 (2m4f110yH).

HESSAC (FR) ..9-6§.. 10 b.g. Beyssac (FR) — Chic Lilie (FR) (Olmeto) 462633p4s. Very small neat half-brother to Kepi Royal (FR). P-t-P/HUNT CH '00 and '02/3 r12 w1 (Maiden — 3 finished) p3 (2 3rds, of 4 once); 4th, 5th, last 2, pulled up 1, and on floor 3. A soft ground winner at Kimble as a five-year-old, but largely disappointing since, and unable to score in 19 subsequent attempts. Looked like springing a surprise at Witton Castle but stopped in front, and his tendency to run in snatches suggests he is most ungenuine. The death of Ernie Fenwick during the season, robbed the sport of one of its most dedicated and c-c-olourful c-c-haracters. *late E. Fenwick — Mrs I. Fenwick — Mrs C. Orton — Zetland (Chris Dennis).* 2 (R), 70 (R), 162 (L), 428 (3m5fL), 564 (L), 766 (R), 955 (R), 1162 (R), 1304 (CR).

HEVER ROAD (IRE) ..9-7.. 6 ch.g. Anshan — The Little Bag (True Song) 42u. Owner-bred half-brother to Bacarese (*qv*). None too lucky so far, as he was caught close home and beaten a neck in a Parham Maiden, and then blundered and unseated two out when in front and looking likely to hold on at Garthorpe. Will only need to hold his current level of attainment to score, and with the advantage of Stuart Morris on his back it should not be long coming. May develop into a fair performer in time. *Prof. D.B.A. Silk & Mrs H. Silk — Kent & Surrey Bloodhounds (Emma Leppard).* 387 (OMa), 644 (OMa), 1061 (OMa).

HICKORY (IRE) ..—.. 10 b.g. Fayruz — La Mortola (Bold Lad IRE) u. Good-bodied half-brother to Irish flat winners Luttrellstown, More Risk and Orange Jasmine (all in Ireland), and to flat winners in Norway and Italy. Dam is half-sister to top-class miler, Katies. FLAT '97/9 r7 p0. NH '99 (for M.J. Haynes) r1 p0 (last). Bought Ascot, Apr '02 for 619. Badly tailed off last in a Hurdle in '99, and went into hiding for five years, and when he finally saw the light he unseated after two miles in his Members. Seems to have problems that even maestro Weir cannot solve. *M. Weir — Dartmoor.* 1001 (M).

HIDDEN EXIT ..—.. 9 b.m. Landyap (USA) — Queen Of The Nile (Hittite Glory) p. Neat half-sister to King Of Cairo, Mr Goonhilly and Thecabbageflinger, to Hurdles winner, Among Islands, and to flat winner, Burnditch Girl. NH FLAT '02 r4 p0. NH '02 (for Mrs L. Williamson) r9 p2; last 2. Bought Ascot, Oct for 1523. Managed a couple of weak placings over Hurdles, but was beaten over 40 lengths when he tried two Sellers. Tailed off and pulled up after 2m4f in a January Maiden, and seems to have gone wrong. *A. & Mrs J.W. Wheeler — N. Cotswold (Andrew Wheeler).* 21 (OMa).

HIDDEN PEARL (IRE) .8-13.. 9 b.g. Posen (USA) — Cockney Miss (Camden Town) p3553. Very tall brother to NH flat winner, Pearly Prince (IRE). Dam won 6f race in Ireland. NH '01/3 (for F. Murphy, and J.A. Supple) r13 p1 (3rd in 2m3f110y Sell Hdle); pulled up 3. Has achieved three thirds including in a Selling Hurdle from 18 attempts spread over four years, but was sixth of seven, last and pulled up in Chases. Capable of going a decent clip, but a woefully weak finisher, and although the two who finished directly behind him on his final start went on to score it may prove to be a false dawn. Has worn blinkers or cheekpieces on seven occasions. *C.J. Mooney — Zetland (Richard Mills).* 272 (OMa), 394 (CfMa), 436 (3m1f110yH), 595 (OMa), 1165 (OMa).

HIGHBRIDGE (IRE) .9-8§.. 12 b.g. Lafontaine (USA) — Lichen Lane (Le Moss) 4p51. Tall rangy. NH '99 r1 p0. P-t-P/HUNT CH '99/01 and '03 r11 w3 (up to Confined) p0; 8th, pulled up 5, refused 1 and ran out 1. The winner of four races on good or sound surfaces, but flat to the boards after making all in the latest, and does not stay in more competitive events. Stands few outings, but provided a first winner for Patrick Crozier. Wears a cross-noseband. *Mrs C. Crozier — Golden V. (Chris Crozier).* 513 (Cf), 662 (O), 1254 (Cf), 1387 (M).

HIGHCROFT BOY .9-6.. 10 gr.g. Silver Owl — Caroline Ranger (Pony Express) 3p2. Good-topped attractive. Dam won 2 Points at 33-1 at Larkhill (very lucky once) for Ann Weston, but otherwise only beat a 16yo in 11 other Points. Grandam Lady Ujiji won 7 Points. NH FLAT '01 r1 p1 (2nd). NH '02/3 (for P.J. Hobbs) r5 w1 (2m6f Hdle) p2 (2nds inc Ch); pulled up 2. Enjoys bowling along in front and made all to win a Wincanton Hurdle, but has always stood his racing badly, and was beaten 30 lengths in both placings in Points (blinkered in the latest). Has shown a tendency to make mistakes and jump right, and does not seem to have enough stamina for three miles. Needs firm ground, but it presumably pains his legs. *Mrs A. Weston — S. & W. Wilts (Guy Landau).* 332 (Cf), 455 (Cf), 717 (Cf).

HIGH FIELDS ..9-10.. 6 b.g. Sovereign Water (FR) — Once Bitten (Brave Invader USA) u2112p. Good-topped half-brother to Rubian Princess and Knickers (*qv*), and to Hurdles winner, Must Bite. NH FLAT '03 (for M.W. Easterby) r3 p1 (3rd). Jumped moderately in his first two Points, but reaped the benefit of first time blinkers when winning a 2m4f Maiden at Hornby Castle, and soon followed up in a stamina-sapping Restricted at Dalton Park. Has looked less than enthusiastic since, and beaten favourite for the third time when particularly disappointing on final start. Has the ability if he can be persuaded to use it, but must be regarded as untrustworthy for betting purposes. *Lord Daresbury — Middleton (David Easterby).* 167 (OMa), 304 (OMa), 344 (2m4fOMa), 503 (R), 769 (M), 1287 (I).

PLATE 57 769 Middleton Members: A contrast in family styles, High Fields (Thomas Greenall), 2nd, leads Scottish Roots (Oliver Greenall), 1st *PHOTO: Brian Armstrong*

HIGHFIELD'S CLOVER ..8-11.. 6 b.g. Petoski — Dipped In Clover (Golden Dipper) p2. Half-brother to Teenage Clover and Return To Clover. Dam, half-sister to Clover Coin (*qv* '00 Annual), won 3 minor Points at Heathfield (2, 3 & 4 finished) and placed 4. Grandam, Clover Doubloon, won 3 Points (hat-trick) and 2nd once. A Hunter Chase was much too big an ask on his debut, but found a Maiden more acceptable, and was a fair six lengths second at Penshurst. It was a bad and slowly-run contest taking 7min30s but he is probably going to be capable of scoring. *S.P. Tindall — Kent & Surrey Bloodhounds (Jenny Gordon).* 345 (2m5fH), 782 (OMa).

HIGHLAND BRIG ..9-9.. 9 b.g. Homo Sapien — Birniebrig (New Brig) 462255. Compact well-made half-brother to Big Mossy (*qv*). Dam and Grandam raced for William Hamilton. P-t-P '03 r5 w1 (Maiden) p0; 9th, last, pulled up 1 and fell 1. Easily won a bad Maiden at Aspatria last year, but expensive to follow in '04, and struggled to get home when aggressively ridden. Remains inclined to make mistakes, and no longer a good thing to follow up. *W. Hamilton, T. Butt & Miss D.J. Amos — Border (Tim Butt).* 70 (R), 164 (R), 430 (R), 548 (R), 797 (3m1fH), 1077 (R).

HIGHLAND DANCER (IRE) ..9-2.. 6 b.g. Barathea (IRE) — Dancer Tully (USA) (Seattle Dancer USA) 4p32. Dam won 4 flat in Italy, 9-11f. 10,000y. 1500 3yo. NH FLAT '02 r1 p0 (tailed off). NH '02/3 (for C.N. Kellett) r4 p0; pulled up 3 and last. Bought Doncaster, May for 950. Twenty-second of 23 in a bumper and hopelessly tailed off in Hurdles (last once and pulled up thrice), and acquired blinkers on his final start. Maidens have been a lot more appropriate and placed in his last two, and may be able to win one, particularly if his stamina increases from five to six. Does not seem suited by testing tracks at present. *Mrs J. Hunt — Grafton.* 219 (OMa), 385 (OMa), 651 (OMa), 1124 (OMa).

HIGHLAND ROSE (IRE) .10-6.. 9 b.m. Roselier (FR) — Carrick Grinder (Sheer Grit) p135113. Compact strong-topped sister to Irish Pointing winner, Carrick Rose. IR4000 3yo. 4600 4yo. NH FLAT '01 r1 p0. NH '02/3 (for Ms A.E. Embiricos) r9 w1 (2m1f Hurdle) p1 (2nd); pulled up 1 and fell 1. Started at 50-1 when winning a Huntingdon Hurdle in soft by a head, but was inconsistent under Rules, and maintained that trend in Points. Blitzed round Cottenham for her three victories which included an impressive double in very fast times in Ladies company, but beaten on every occasion she went left-handed, including at 4-7 on final start, when she made numerous mistakes or slow jumps. Races with plenty of enthusiasm at best, and worth trying in a Hunter Chase on a right-handed track (Huntingdon again would fit the bill). Worthy of a higher rating on occasions. *Mr & Mrs*

S.N.J. Embiricos — Thurlow (Tim Bryce). 23 (Cf), 98 (M), 158 (CCon), 246 (L), 558 (L), 998 (L), 1154 (L).

HIGHLANDS II (FR) ..—§.. 10 ch.g. Murmure (FR) — Oland (FR) (Saumon FR) ppf. Small light-framed half-brother to 2 winners, including useful jumper, Valfinet (FR). NH '01 r2 p0 (pulled up 2). P-t-P '02/3 r7 w1 (Maiden) p2 (2nd of 3; and 3rd of 4); last, and pulled up 3. Won a weak Maiden taking well over seven minutes at Sandon last year, but unable to get round in four attempts since, and acquired a visor on his most recent appearance. Runs tongue-tied and finds nothing off the bridle, and his 9-7 rating is withdrawn. *D. Manning — Sir W.W. Wynn's (Steve Wynne).* 95 (R), 715 (R), 752 (R).

HIGHLAND WONDER ..7-11.. 10 ch.g. Highlands — Friendly Wonder (Be Friendly) rp4. Compact brother to Highland Friend and Bobby Wonder. NH FLAT '01 r2 p0. NH '01 (for C. Grant) r1 p0 (pulled up). Never better than tailed off in his six races, and was completing the course for the first time over jumps when 53 lengths fourth in a Maiden. Has an unreliable temperament, and refused to race once. *Mrs L. Ward — Cleveland.* 814 (OMa), 960 (OMa), 1305 (OMa).

HIGH MOOD .9-11.. 15 b.g. Jalmood (USA) — Copt Hall Princess (Crowned Prince USA) up. Sturdy half-brother to Robero, and to 5 flat winners (2 in Italy), including, Privacy and Prince Merandi (also a successful Hurdler) and Dovedon Lady. Dam won at 7f. NH FLAT '94 r3 p0. NH '94/01 r32 w5 (2m-2m6f110y Chses) p7 (4 2nds); fell/unseated 5, pulled up 1. P-t-P/HUNT CH '03 (for Mrs D.M. Roberts & Mrs D.M. Bosworth) r6 w1 (Members) p2 (2nd of 3 once); pulled up 2 and unseated 1. Recording his first win since '00 when showing far more resolve than the runner-up in his Members last year, but pulled up lame for the second time in three years at Garnons on his latest outing, and another comeback looks unlikely. Has never looked a natural over obstacles. *D.B. Roberts — Ludlow (Jen Wall).* 1 (C), 403 (Cf).

HIGH PEAK ..10-5.. 8 b.g. Alflora (IRE) — High Heels (IRE) (Supreme Leader) f1111. Good-topped half-brother to Fashion House (Chasing winner since Pointing). Dam, half-sister to Ryton Guard (*qv* '98 Annual). NH FLAT '01 r3 p1 (3rd). NH '02/3 (for C. Grant) r10 p2. Showed some ability in bumpers and Hurdles, but became frustrating, and acquired a visor on his final three attempts. Fell at the first when favourite for his Pointing debut, but unbeaten afterwards, and was able to hold his own when quickly upgraded to Opens. Looked likely to finish second to Mademist Sam at Dalton Park until that rival fell two out, but beat him on his merits at Hornby Castle next time. Quite a determined finisher who stays extremely well, and probably worth trying again under Rules, although if the owner saw a tempting offer coming along he could doubtless be persuaded to part with him. *D.M. Easterby — Middleton.* 165 (OMa), 302 (OMa), 341 (R), 501 (O), 812 (O).

HIGHWAY OAK ..10-1.. 9 b.g. Sula Bula — Highway Light (Lighter) 1541. Plain rangy angular brother to Pebble Dasher, and half-brother to Highway Ten. Dam is half-sister to Highway Lad (*qv* '01 Annual), pulled up 4, fell 1 and refused in Points for Mr White. Grandam, Hilda's Way, won 2 Points and placed 3 for him. P-t-P '02/3 r11 w1 (2m4f Maiden) p5 (3 3rds, of 4 twice; inc 2nd of 3); last pair 3, pulled up 1 and unseated 1. Has been quite successful for a Sula Bula, but laid low by a virus in '03. A sound jumping front-runner when on song, and has battled his way to three minor wins. Only averages five outings a year, and in view of his size avoids ground any quicker than good, but gives the impression that he will struggle to upgrade successfully. *M. White — Cattistock (Ben White & Maya Horsey).* 37 (CR), 90 (I), 495 (I), 687 (M).

HIGHWAY TEN .—.. 8 b.m. Past Glories — Highway Light (Lighter) pp. Small homebred half-sister to Highway Oak (*qv*). P-t-P '03 r5 p0 (pulled up 3, unseated 1 and brought down 1). Got no further than the fourth on her first three attempts, and has been on confidence-boosting trips since, but still showing no improvement in her jumping, and connections may have given up already. *B. White & Miss M. Horsey — Portman.* 150 (OMa), 327 (OMa).

HIJACKED ..9-13.. 11 b.g. True Song — Scamper (Abwah) 1p1p45p3. Workmanlike unfurnished owner-bred half-brother to Sharp Alice. Dam won at 14f, and was unbeaten in 3 2-3m Hdles. P-t-P '99/00 and '02 r10 w1 (Maiden) p2 (2nds); 7th of 8, pulled up 5, and unseated 1. Does not lack stamina and has won three races on good or easy surfaces, but very lucky once, and seems to lose interest quickly. Pulled up at Whitwick when the rider omitted the wrong fence, but eight other non-completions have been down to him, and though he may revive when fresh it would not be wise to trust him for long. *A. Hollingsworth — Worcs.* 231 (CR), 513 (Cf), 616 (C), 728 (I), 1015 (Cf), 1071 (I), 1170 (4m1fH), 1357 (3m1fH).

HILARITY .8-12.. 10 b.m. Petoski — Kintra (Sunyboy) 64p. Good-topped half-sister to Coralinga. Dam, (*qv* '93 Annual) is half-sister to Glenisla, and was 2nd in her only Point for Mrs Turner. P-t-P '02 r1 p0 (last). Showed promise despite not looking fully wound up in three completions, but absent in '03, and broke down (again?) at Ston Easton. *Mrs J.R. Turner — Cattistock (Peter & Fiona Shaw).* 35 (CMam), 139 (R), 604 (OMa).

HILLCREST MANOR (IRE) ..8-0.. 11 b.g. Topanoora — Grassed (Busted) pp8. Small sturdy half-brother to Hurdles winner, Montel Girl (IRE). Dam won 2m1f Hurdle in Ireland. IRISH NH FLAT '98/9 r4 w1 p1 (3rd). IRISH NH '99/00 r5 p3. NH '00/1 (for Mrs D. Haine, and A.W. Carroll) r6 p1 (2nd); pulled up 3. Sold Ascot, Apr for 952. Won a Punchestown bumper with 20 runners by a short head in heavy, and beaten a maximum of six-and-a-half lengths in his five placings, but useless when returning from a long absence in '04, and was about two fences last on his only completion. Blinkered once and tongue-tied twice previously, and wore cheekpieces and seemed to take no interest for the new yard. *B. Jackson & P. Hicks — Teme V. (Sarah-Jayne Davies).* 513 (Cf), 663 (I), 835 (Cf).

HILL OF KILFEACLE (IRE) ..8-10.. 8 b.g. Detroit Sam (FR) — Cantabyrne (Majestic Maharaj) pp765359p. Compact brother to Sam Byrne (IRE) and Irish Chasing winner, Decanter (IRE), and half-brother to Commandeer (IRE). Dam is sister or half-sister to 5 Pointers, including the dam of Holland House (*qv* '99 Annual). IRISH P-t-P '02 r4 p2; pulled 2. IRISH NH '02 r4 p0. P-t-P '03 (for Mr P. Morris) r7 w1 (2m4f Maiden — 3 finished) p4 (2 2nds, of 3 once, and last once); and pulled up 2. Left clear at the last to finish solo at Alpraham last year, but a non-stayer over the full trip, and unimproved by the application of a tongue-strap in '04. *J.A. Ralphs — Sir W.W. Wynn's (Peter Morris).* 95 (R), 231 (CR), 530 (R), 708 (M), 752 (R), 933 (CR), 1148 (R), 1265 (R), 1456 (R).

HILL TOP FLYER (IRE) ..7-0.. 12 b.g. Orchestra — Idanna (Hays) 2. P-t-P '98 and '00 r8 p0 (pulled up 5, fell 2, and slipped up 1). Finally achieved a completion when a remote last of two in a war of attrition at Erw Lon, but absent in '99, and since '00 and immediately forced back onto the sidelines. Wears bandages behind, and obviously has Orchestra legs. *P. Riddick — Gelligaer F.* 204 (CfMa).

HILL TRAIL ..10-1.. 10 ch.g. Royal Match — Win Green Hill (National Trust) pp21f. Sturdy half-brother to Winnie Lorraine, Country Style and Derring Floss, and to top-class jumping winner, Earth Summit ('98 Grand National hero). Dam won 2m mares Nov Ch. Grandam, Bibbernette, was 3rd in 2 Points (last once, and disqualified once). NH FLAT '00 r1 p0. NH '00/1 r2 p0 (pulled up 1 and fell 1). P-t-P '02/3 r7 w1 (2-finisher Maiden) p2 (3rds); pulled up 3, and fell 1. Free-running and has made virtually all in two and three-finisher events on firmish, but hampered by wind problems and a tendency to break blood vessels, and appreciated a change of scenery prior to the latest. Speedy enough to win another weak event over an easy three miles provided his health remains intact. Has run tongue-tied, and wears a cross-noseband. *Mrs E.M. Wicheard, S.J. Clark & Mr & Mrs T.J. Bliss — Avon V. (Clare Parfitt).* 628 (2m3fH), 1063 (R), 1184 (R), 1325 (R), 1508 (I).

HILLVIEW HUT (IRE) ..—§.. 12 ch.g. Rising — Hillview Star (IRE) (Lord Ha Ha) ppp. Dam, half-sister to Any Other Business (*qv*), finished alone in 2m4f Maiden ('the funniest winner imaginable' from 3 out after three of her rivals had hit the deck). IRISH P-t-P '98 and '00/1 r11 w1 (Maiden) p3; pulled up 5. P-t-P '03 r2 p0 (pulled up 2). Scored on his penultimate appearance in Ireland, but exposed as modest in the extreme there, and has performed with marked reluctance since. Unimproved by blinkers on his last two appearances. *Miss J. Wilkinson — Hursley Hambledon (Lindsay Bower).* 1066 (CCon), 1101 (Cnr), 1409 (CR).

HIMALAYAN HEIGHTS ..8-7.. 10 ch.g. North Col — Chestertons Choice (Country Retreat) ppp5. Tall rangy owner-bred brother to Northern Prince (*qv*). P-t-P/HUNT CH '02/3 (for Mr J.P. Thorne) r8 p1 (2nd); 5th, 6th, last, fell 1 and pulled up 3. An encouraging six lengths second on his debut in mud, but a useless non-stayer over the full trip, and can be guaranteed to capitulate after a maximum of 2m4f. Tried in cheekpieces before a tongue-tie was employed on his last two starts. *G. Barber — N. Ledbury (Mandy Tatlow).* 621 (OMa), 760 (OMa), 927 (OMa), 1253 (M).

HI RUDOLF ..10-2.. 10 b.g. Ballet Royal (USA) — Hi Darlin' (Prince De Galles) up*34p14f*. Small neat owner-bred half-brother to Hizal, Darzal and Dicks Darlin'. Dam, half-sister to 3 Pointers including Knight Of Love, won 2 Points (promoted from 2nd once), a 2m6f Hdle, and a 2m4f Chse. Grandam, Hi Mia, was 3rd of 4 in Maiden, and remote last of 3 in Nov Ch. Sire was still running over jumps to '98, but then died. FLAT '97/8 r2 p0 (last twice). P-t-P/HUNT CH '02 r5 w1 (Maiden) p3 (3rd of 4 in Hunt Ch); 5th, fell/unseated 2 and pulled up. NH '98/9 and '01/3 r17 w1 (3-finisher 2m4f Ch) p3 (3rds); pulled up 6, fell 2. NH '04 r6 w1 (beat Palouse 3*l* in 2m4f Ch: *hld up, hdwy 7, ld 3 out, rdn out*) p1 (3rd in 3m Ch: *chsd ldrs, hit 10, ld 2 out til hdd & wknd last*); 4th in 2m2f-2m5f110y Chses: *hld up, lost plce 9, gd late hdwy*, and *chsd ldrs, ld 9-11, ev ch 2 out, wknd app last*; pulled up in 2m6f110y Hdle: *hld up, wknd app 3 out, bhnd when pu last*, and fell in 2m6f Ch: *bhnd til fell 8*. Won a long Maiden (!) at Larkhill on his Pointing debut, where Mrs Be and subsequent Chasing winner, Sir Cumference filled the places, but speedy and has done best at around 2m4f since. Remains inconsistent due to his frequent blunders, but has access to good amateurs, and sure to be placed to advantage again under Rules, though not shorter than 10-1 when successful. Suited by mud. *H.J. Manners — V.W.H.* 10 (L), 239 (3m1fH).

HI TECH MAN (IRE) ..9-7.. 7 ch.g. Presenting — Cherry Mist (IRE) (Aristocracy) p15pr. Lengthy. 8000 4yo. Unseated going to the start before being given an easy time on his debut, but looked more clued up at Horseheath, and won a youngsters Maiden at 14-1. Seems to have gone the wrong way since including when favourite and second favourite, and it was particularly disappointing that he should refuse on his final appearance. Will have to be regarded with suspicion until he looks like perking up. *E.J. Cantillon — E. Anglian Bloodhounds.* 39 (OMa), 128 (OMa), 398 (R), 524 (R), 591 (CR).

HI UP BRENKLEY..8-12.. 7 b.g. Dancing High — Shut Up (Kind Of Hush) p524. Dam won 2m2f Sell Hurdle for the Moscrops. Very unruly in the paddock and jumped poorly on his debut, and although he behaved better subsequently he was beaten about 25 lengths when making the frame twice (inherited second two out once). Would have to improve to figure in a finish. *G.R. Moscrop — Border.* 215 (OMa), 342 (2m4fOMa), 859 (CfMa), 920 (2m4fOMa).

HOBBYCYR (FR) ..10-6.. 10 b.g. Saint Cyrien (FR) — Sauteuse De Retz (FR) (Funny Hobby) 4133p. Compact lightly-made half-brother to Funny Genie (FR), and to a French flat and Chasing winner. Dam won 2 French flat. NH '99/00 r5 w1 (2m4f Hdle) p0; tailed off last only Ch. P-t-P/HUNT CH '01/3 r10 w3 (inc 3m Hunt Ch) p3 (2 3rds); 4th, and pulled up 3. Under the weather like the rest of his yard for much of '03, but the winner of five races on muddy surfaces, and a very rewarding 14-1 in the latest. Stays well and a most determined finisher, and seemed to get the four miles well enough at Cheltenham, but well below the level of that form subsequently. Sure to win again but may remain largely unpredictable. *R.G. Kelvin-Hughes — Spooners & W. Dartmoor.* 115 (MO), 496 (MO), 727 (MO), 1170 (4m1fH), 1376 (4m2fH).

HOBO ..7-12.. 7 b.g. Timeless Times (USA) — Skiddaw Bird (Bold Owl) 5. Unfurnished brother to Vals Whispa (*qv*). 8000y. FLAT '00 r4 p0. NH '01 (for D.W. Barker) r1 p0 (pulled up). His flat career came to an ignominious end when he was warned off for failing a stalls test, and has only managed two outings over jumps, pulling up in '01 and finishing an exhausted 47 lengths fifth in a Maiden in '04. Was still on the premises after three out but stopped to nil and did not get home in the conditions, but if fit he might just be interesting over 2m4f in similar company. The third Hobo to appear in these Annuals, but the memorable one won five Points for the still extant Joe Price in the 70s. *Miss A. Clift — N. Ledbury (Caroline Chadney).* 725 (OMa).

HOH TEL (IRE) .10-0§.. 11 ch.g. Montelimar (USA) — Party Dancer (Be My Guest USA) 672f52p. Lengthy half-brother to 5 winners including 2 abroad, including Irish Pointer, Finisk Dancer. NH FLAT '99 r2 p1 (2nd). NH '99 r12 p2; pulled up 1, and fell/unseated 3. P-t-P/HUNT CH '02/3 r15 w4 (up to Confined) p5 (3 3rds, of 4 once; 2 2nds, of 3 once, and inc Hunt Ch); 4th, 5th, 6th, and pulled up 3. A major under-achiever in the past, and has only scored for Chris Gillon (who packed up in '04) on right-handed tracks, but will not co-operate fully nowadays and earned Ran Morgan a fine when he returned marked on his latest appearance (brother Luke was also done on the winner). A thorough stayer, but error prone, particularly over big fences, and will need a great deal of sweetening if he is to stage a revival. Wears headgear. *The Rennington Racing Club (F.V. White) — W. Percy (George White).* 211 (C), 429 (3m5fO), 854 (M), 1178 (3m1fH), 1421 (O), 1477 (O), 1526 (3m2fH).

HOKEY WOKEY..8-10.. 7 b.g. Weld — Manley Girl (IRE) (Mandalus) 5p. Strong owner-bred. Dam was placed in 3 Irish Points; and was 20/ 2nd in Maiden for Mrs Edwards in '99 (pulled up in 3 of 4 other English Points). P-t-P '03 r3 p0 (last, and pulled up 2). Twenty-four lengths fifth of six at Weston Park represents his only form, and has looked wrong when pulled up on his final appearances in both campaigns. May have his own ideas, and looks a clone of mum. *Mrs S.E. Edwards & Mrs M. Williams - Tanatside (Russell Teague).* 97 (CfMa), 531 (OMa).

HOLDIMCLOSE ..9-12.. 15 b.g. Teamwork — Holdmetight (New Brig) 3. Short-backed half-brother to Hold And Fast, Hold And Fort and Hold Your Ranks. Dam failed to finish in 3 Points, but was later placed in 2 Hurdles and a Chase. NH FLAT '95 r1 p0. NH '95/00 r27 w5 (3 2m2f-2m6f Hdles, inc walk-over, and 2 2m3f-3m Chses) p9 (inc short-headed in Hdle). P-t-P/HUNT CH '01/3 r9 p5 (4 2nds, of 3 once); 7th, last, fell 1 and pulled up 1. Won four races in mud to '99, but unlucky to bump into some well above average performers in Points, and has had to call it a day after one appearance in each of the last two years. Deserves to find another race, but the odds are stacked against him even returning at 15. *Miss V.M. Tremlett — Berks & Bucks.* 31 (Cnr).

HOLDING THE FORT (IRE) ..10-3.. 11 b.g. Moscow Society (USA) — Lady Of Desmond (Menelek) pp1. Good-topped half-brother to Spurious. IRISH P-t-P '99 r3 p0 (last pair twice, and pulled up 1). NH '01 r1 p0 (8th in 2m3f110y Hdle). P-t-P/HUNT CH '00/2 r6 w1 (Maiden — promoted) p3 (2 2nds); pulled up 1 and fell 1. Scoring on merit for the first time when springing a 20-1 surprise in a 16-runner event at Dingley, but had previously pulled up when apparently losing his action at Eyton, and cannot handle easy ground. Fragile and missed '03, during which he was hobdayed, and three outings in a year is a hectic campaign for him, but a genuine front-runner and might be able to score again. Rather highly strung, and has two handlers. *I. Anderson — Tanatside.* 715 (R), 933 (CR), 1469 (R).

HOLD ON HARRY..10-1.. 9 ch.g. Endoli (USA) — Hold On Tight (Battlement) 12p2. Owner-bred. Dam is half-sister to Hold Your Ranks (*qv* '02 Annual). P-t-P '02/3 r8 p2; 4th, 5th, pulled up 2, unseated 1 and slipped up 1. Missed out on a Maiden success when accounting for a lame rival in a two-finisher

Restricted at Stafford Cross, but runner-up twice at Bratton Down since, and looks capable of going one better in an Intermediate. Seems more amenable to restraint than he was, but an easy three miles and top-of-the-ground are probably vital requirements. *S.J. Williams — Tetcott.* 1132 (R), 1382 (I), 1498 (3m2f110yH), 1555 (I).

HOLLYHOCK ..8-7.. 11 b.m. Rakaposhi King — Jennie's First (Idiot's Delight) 4up. Compact good-topped half-sister to Nortonthorpe-Rose, Horus (IRE) (useful Chasing winner since Pointing), Henrietta (IRE) and Heliotrope (IRE). NH '99/00 r7 p0; fell/unseated 2, pulled up 2. P-t-P '99 and '02 r5 w1 (Maiden) p2 (3rds); 5th, and fell. Romped a weak Maiden when Pipe-trained at Black Forest Lodge in '99, but flopped under Rules and ultimately went wrong, and gifted to present connections. Her latest comeback was ended after three runs when she suffered another setback in her Members. Tongue-tied once in '00. *Mrs G. D'Angibau — Essex & Suffolk.* 398 (R), 559 (R), 828 (M).

HOLLY PARK ..3-0.. 7 b.m. Syrtos — Mapleline (Shy Groom USA) Rp3pp. Small neat half-sister to Hopping Mad. Literally beaten a minute when last in an Ashorne Maiden, where the rider was cheered ecstatically by the crowd (in the true traditions of the Great British Loser). Not a racehorse, but might make a show jumper. *Mrs J. Breeden — Albrighton Woodland.* 1020 (OMa), 1125 (OMa), 1273 (OMa), 1424 (OMa), 1527 (M).

HOLY MOSES (IRE) ..9-9§.. 11 ch.g. Classic Memory — Much Obliged (Crash Course) 24. Small stocky brother to Fayalie (IRE), and half-brother to Irish Pointing winner, Tubber Streams and El Lute. P-t-P '99/00 and '02/3 r12 w1 (Maiden) p3 (2nds, beaten neck once, head once, and ½*l* once); 4th, last, unseated 1 and pulled up 5. Able but ungenuine, and was beating a rival for the first time when landing a bad three-finisher Maiden in mud at Ampton in '02, but very lightly raced since and his '04 campaign was over by the first weekend in February. Certainly not one to trust if he manages to return to action. *E.J. Cantillon — E. Anglian Bloodhounds.* 44 (R), 127 (R).

HOLYWELL GIRL ..—.. 8 b.m. Alhaatmi — Merry Maggie (Stanford) p. Unfurnished. Dam was placed 6 (2 NH flat, 2 Hurdles; and 2 Points for Messrs Morris & Tarratt). NH FLAT '02 r3 p0. NH '02 r1 p0 (pulled up). P-t-P '03 r4 w1 (2m5f Maiden) p1 (2nd); and pulled up 2. Showed her first signs of ability when runner-up at 33-1 in her Members last year, and promptly went one better in a short Maiden on firmish at Welbeck, but only got as far as the eighth fence before pulling up when a well backed favourite next time. Looked thoroughly disinterested when never going at any stage on her return, and her 9-8 rating has been withdrawn until she shows renewed vigor. *C Morris & T. Tarratt — Cottesmore (Tim Tarratt).* 378 (M).

HOME AGAIN (IRE) ..10-2.. 11 b.g. Homo Sapien — Texarkana (IRE) (Furry Glen) 23p21u. Small light. Dam won 2m3f Hurdle in Ireland and is half-sister to Dollard Lad (*qv* '92 Annual). IRISH P-t-P '99/02 r14 p1 (2nd); pulled up 6, fell/unseated 3. P-t-P '03 r9 w3 (Maiden, Restricted 3-finished and Members — finished alone) p2 (3rds, of 4 once, and last once); last, and pulled up 3. The winner of four races on good or sound surfaces, and has made most when successful, but struggles to get the trip when conditions are testing, and is inclined to make mistakes. Very much a Ladies horse to look at but paired with a beginner on his first venture into the sphere, and proved too error-pronefor her, but well worth trying with a competent girl up. *E.W. Morris — Pembs.* 205 (O), 434 (3m1f110yH), 628 (2m3fH), 671 (I), 952 (I), 1025 (L).

HOMELEIGH MEADOW ..8-0.. 7 ch.g. Meadowbrook — Puki Puki (Roselier FR) u5. Tall rangy half-brother to Sir Cumference (won 2 Chases since Pointing). Dam won mares Maiden in Ireland and 2m6f Hurdle on all-weather and placed total of 8 (inc 3rd in 3 Points) (had a squiggle). Got loose in the paddock before unseating at halfway on his debut, and then finished tailed off last at Ampton. Looks tricky at present, but is a big backward sort, and can possibly do a bit better. *Miss S. Wilson — Essex & Suffolk (Mrs Clover).* 128 (OMa), 525 (OMa).

HOME TOR ..9-0§§.. 8 b.g. Homo Sapien — Torus Queen (Torus) 18pu8p. Light-framed homebred half-brother to Tormoss Lady (*qv*) and Princess Tor. NH FLAT '02 r2 p0. P-t-P '03 r5 p1 (2nd); 4th of 5, unseated 1, refused 1 and pulled up 1. Looked a reformed character when clinging on by the skin of his teeth in a long Maiden at Weston Park on his reappearance, but pulled himself up in the closing stages next time, and galloped into a hedge and dumped the rider in his Members (subsequently remounted for a very distant last of three but the Judge had left his box). Downed tools quickly in his last two starts, and is a total bow-wow and must be avoided at all costs. Surprisingly yet to be tried in any form of headgear. *Miss H. Brookshaw — N. Salop.* 96 (CfMa), 530 (R), 665 (R), 928 (M), 1265 (R), 1429 (Cnr).

HOMME DE FER ..10-7.. 13 b.g. Arctic Lord — Florence May (Grange Melody) 14312. Compact half-brother to Five Minutes, and to Chasing winner, Flash Gordon. Dam, half-sister to Look At That (*qv* '91 Annual), won 2 Points and 3m Chase and placed a total of 3. IR4800 4yo. NH FLAT '97 r3 p0. NH '97/03 (for K.C. Bailey) r30 w8 (4 2m3f-2m5f Hdles and 4 2m5f-3m Chses) p10; pulled up 1. A great old battler who took his career total of wins into double figures when the first ride for George

Greenock in a three-runner Higham Open, in which the jockey showed his greenness by constantly looking round. Also placed on 12 occasions, and was twice caught close home when beaten three quarters of a length and a neck in Chases. Pulled up with a broken blood vessel once, but has never failed to complete otherwise, although he did take a nasty fall at the last before remounting in a Fakenham Hunter Chase (would have finished second). Has handled soft in the past, but is really better on sounder ground. Still tries hard and keeps his form quite well, and owes nobody anything. *Countess Cathcart — W. Norfolk (Nigel Bloom).* 156 (O), 242 (2m5f110yH), 442 (2m7f110yH), 830 (O), 1153 (O).

HONARY SECRETARY ..—.. 8 ch.g. Tuam — Stop The Clock (Grau Du Roi) r. Fat for a May Maiden, and climbed over the first before declining the third. Any secretary who thought that 'Honary' was a word would soon get the sack. *Miss A. Meakins — Carms.* 1239 (OMa).

HONEYFANTASTIC ..—.. 6 ch.m. Primitive Rising (USA) — Comarch (Ancient Monro) pp. Sister to Gudasmum (*qv*), and half-sister to C L B Jemilla (*qv*). Pulled up in the final half mile of April Maidens. Not as gudassis so far. *Mrs M. Fife - York & Ainsty S.* 960 (OMa), 1158 (OMa).

HONITON (U) .4-7.. 8 b.m. unknown 5. Bobbin' along in touch until the pace 'quickened'. No clot, but not the cream either. *The King's Troop RHA — R.A. (Neil Cross).* 84 (2m4fC).

HOODWINKER (IRE) .10-6.. 16 b.g. Supreme Leader — Merrybash (Pinzari) p. Compact well-made half-brother to The Camair Flyer (IRE), and to 3 other jumping winners, including, Bavard Ash. NH FLAT '94 r2 p0. NH '94/01 r40 w7 (4 2m4f-3m2f110y Hdles, and 3 2m7f110y-3m110y Chses) p10 (4 2nds); pulled up 4, fell 2, and refused 1. P-t-P '02/3 r15 w7 (Ladies) p3 (2 2nds, remote once; and 3rd of 4); 4th, last pair 3, and unseated 1. Wildly inconsistent and difficult to win with under Rules, but scored seven times in a 12-month period for present connections, and was the making of Jane Williams. Tragically broke a leg on his return at Higham. *Mrs A.D. Williams — Albrighton Woodland.* 157 (L).

HOORAY HENRY .9-5.. 6 b.g. Karinga Bay — Heathfield Gale (Strong Gale) pu23. Tall strong-topped owner-bred brother to Young Harry (*qv*). A much nicer person than Harry, and would have finished second in his last two Maidens had he not been demoted near the finish in the latest. Improving gradually, and his turn should come. *A.E. Ford — Taunton V.H.* 306 (2m4fOMa), 702 (2m4fOMa), 909 (2m4fOMa), 1133 (OMa).

HOPE VALUE ..8-7.. 10 b.g. Rock City — Folle Idee (USA) (Foolish Pleasure USA) *44*. Tall half-brother to Mhemeanles, and to winner in Yugoslavia. FLAT '97/8 r6 p1 (3rd). NH '98,00/1 and '03 r14 w1 (2m1f Hdle) p1 (2nd); pulled up 2, and unseated 1. NH '04 r1 p0 (dist last of 4 in 3m2f110y Ch: *hld up, lost tch 11, t.o*). Little better than Selling standard even at his best, and gained his sole win in a four-runner Hurdle in August '00. Blinkered twice, and has broken blood vessels on at least two occasions. Furlongs behind in both attempts for '04, and not worth racing if this is the best he can do. *G.F. Edwards — Dart V.H. & S. Pool H.* 276 (L).

HOPLITE ..9-8.. 8 ch.g. Infantry — Spartan Daisy (Spartan General) p. Big good-topped owner-bred half-brother to Horace, Tandem, Floral Reef and Cradle Mountain, and to NH flat and Hurdles winner, Give Me An Answer. Dam won 3m1f Nov Hdle and 3 Nov Chses (2m4f-3m2f), and is sister to General Rule (*qv* '93 Annual). Great-grandam, Bright Daisy, won 4 Points (inc a dead-heat) and placed 9. P-t-P '03 r3 w1 (Maiden) p0; and pulled up 2. Displayed the right qualities when successful at 12-1 in a Dingley Maiden last year, but pulled up in three other attempts, and suspiciously failed to reappear after just one outing in '04. Almost certainly too top-heavy for his Infantry legs. *Mrs A. Vaughan-Jones & G. Luck — W. Norfolk (Caroline Bailey).* 127 (R).

HORATIO (IRE) ..—.. 9 b.g. Warcraft (USA) — Coolruss Quay (Quayside) u. Workmanlike half-brother to All Monty (IRE), Irish Hurdling winner, Geodalus, and to Irish Pointing and English jumping winner, Ross Quay (IRE). IR15,000 3yo. Dam, half-sister to More Of It (*qv* '99 Annual). NH FLAT '00 and '02 r2 p0. NH '03 (for R.J. Hodges) r2 p0. Gets very few opportunities, and was tailed off in his final three races under Rules. Immediately side-lined after the rider had fallen off at the seventh in a February Maiden. *R.J. Hewitt — Flint & Denbigh.* 111 (OMa).

HORRIFIED ..9-2§.. 11 b.g. Deltic (USA) — Parlet (Kinglet) 4p4p3p4u. Tall strong. Dam was a useless Hurdler, and revived 6 years later by Janet Ackner to finish a fence 3rd in a Maiden (pulled up in 5 of 6 other Points). Great-grandam, Party Night, pulled up 4 and unseated in Points/Hunt Ch. P-t-P '01/2 r7 w1 (3-finisher Maiden) p2 (2nds, of 3 once); 4th of 5, and pulled up 3. Benefited from the wayward antics of the runner-up when springing a 16-1 surprise in a three-finisher Maiden at Black Forest Lodge in '02, but clearly suffered a setback on unsuitable fast ground and went missing last year. Allowed three rivals to overtake from the final fence when fourth at Vauterhill this year, but otherwise well beaten, and clearly has own ideas, as demonstrated by his unshipping of Darren Edwards at Bratton Down. Acquired blinkers in '04. *The Tufters (Mrs J.P. Ackner) — Devon & Somerset (Janet Ackner).* 14 (R), 118 (R), 314 (R), 541 (3mH), 706 (R), 966 (R), 1268 (R), 1385 (R).

HORS CONCOURS (NZ) .7-0.. 7 b.g. Starjo (NZ) — Lana (NZ) (Tristrams Heritage NZ) pf4. Compact. NH FLAT '03 (for R.C. Guest) r1 p0. Showed definite signs of promise before weakening and blundering at the 13th in a Barbury Open, but was again fading (in 12 lengths third) when he fell two out in a Maiden, and finally lost a lot of ground in the closing stages before finishing 40 lengths last. Seems to have stamina worries at present, but it might be unwise to right him off yet. *Ms C. Walker — Radnor & W. Herefords.* 93 (O), 666 (OMa), 1139 (OMa).

HORSEMANS GREEN .—§.. 9 ch.g. Weld — Saucy Eater (Saucy Kit) pppRfp. Tall lengthy roach-backed owner-bred brother to Hurdles winner, Mysie, and half-brother to Hannah Millie Nick, Long Melford, Favourite Song, Als Diner, Rule Out The Rest and One Boy. Dam won 7 2m-3m1f Hdles. P-t-P '02 (for Mr & Mrs R. Edwards) r2 p0 (ran out 1, and pulled up 1). Another Weld that has proved to be a nightmare ride, and looks far too excitable to make a Pointer. Got as far as the last at Umberleigh but not before rooting two fences, and connections seem uneasy about sending him to the races fully fit. Wears a cross-noseband, and cheekpieces. *C.T. & A. Samways — S. Dorset (Ken Nelmes).* 265 (R), 415 (R), 604 (OMa), 967 (OMa), 1370 (OMa), 1566 (OMa).

HORTON-CUM-PEEL (IRE) ..9-6.. 14 b.g. Swan's Rock — Lady Beecham (Laurence O) pp43up. Lengthy well-made half-brother to Staigue Fort (IRE), and to Irish Pointing winner, Aine's Antics. Dam completed hat-trick in Irish Points. NH '00 r1 p0 (fell in Ch). P-t-P/HUNT CH '98, '00 and '02/3 r23 w1 (Maiden) p7 (5 3rds, of 4 once, and inc Hunt Ch; and last of 2 twice); pulled up 2, fell/unseated 5. A thorough stayer, and landed a touch when making a winning debut in a long Maiden at Whittington in '98, but defeated 29 times since, and usually beaten out of sight when completing. Wears a cross-noseband. *Mrs T.R. Kinsey & Mrs G. Handley — Cheshire Forest (Julie Kinsey).* 341 (R), 715 (R), 748 (M), 989 (Cnr), 1205 (CR), 1426 (C).

HOSTETLER ..9-1.. 16 ch.g. Fit To Fight (USA) — Diana's Bow (Great Nephew) p. Smallish strong-topped half-brother to flat winner, Bespoken, and to Hurdles winner, So Keen. IRISH FLAT r3 p0. IRISH NH '92/3 r10 w1 (2m Hdle) p1 (3rd). NH '93/5 r19 p2 (Chses); inc Sell Hdles. P-t-P '96/00 and '02/3 r44 w2 (inc Confined) p7 (3 2nds, remote of 3 once; 4 3rds, remote once, and last once); pulled up 4, and fell/unseated 4. A safe conveyance, but antiquated and only able to shuffle along at low speeds, and left the impression something might have gone amiss on his only appearance in '04. Has not scored since '00, and wheeling him out again would be a waste of time. *Mrs J. Messenger — Pytchley.* 783 (M).

HOT BRANDY (IRE) ..—.. 6 br.g. Hubbly Bubbly (USA) — Risc Averse (Strong Gale) p. Tall well-made half-brother to 3 non-winning jumpers. Dam won Irish NH Flat. Expected to run well on his debut and Stuart Morris was engaged, but after being sent off joint-favourite his jumping let him down and he was tailed off when pulled up three out. Needs to have more confidence in himself. *C.B. Compton — Wheatland (Andrew Dalton).* 531 (OMa).

HOT BRICKS ..5-5.. 7 ch.g. Dancing High — Marejo (Creetown) p65. Good-topped owner-bred half-brother to Jupiter Jo (*qv*). Fat on his debut and was very nervous and was climbing the obstacles, and already nearly two fences behind when he pulled up after the seventh (!). Jimmy Walton has been bent on completing the course on him since, and finally achieved his goal before night fell, although he was about three fences adrift in both and almost fell at the last at Aspatria. Has swished his tail and might need blinkers or spurs, but if he reappears again it will certainly be because connections feel there is some ability to be exploited. *J.B. & F.A. Walton — Border (Jimmy Walton).* 286 (CfMa), 1311 (OMa), 1475 (OMa).

HOTELIERS' DREAM ..8-9§.. 7 b.m. Reprimand — Pride Of Britain (CAN) (Linkage USA) 6f4. Small sparely-made. Dam won 3 flat, 12-16f. FLAT '01/3 r11 p1 (3rd). NH '03 (for W.S. Kittow) r5 p0; last 1, pulled up 1 and fell 1. Finished nine lengths third of 20 over 12f when 66-1 on the flat once, but beaten 19 lengths plus on her ten other attempts including Sellers. Pulled up and fell in Novice Hurdles and then beaten more than 22 lengths in Sellers, and wore headgear on four occasions in those spheres and tongue-tied once. Very mulish in the preliminaries in her first two Points (reluctant to go to the start once), but did plug on steadily in the closing stages when three and a quarter lengths fourth on her latest attempt (40-1). It looks as if she could win a bad Maiden, but will have had to have got out of bed on the right side. *M.S. Sweetland — E. Devon.* 68 (OMa), 1126 (M), 1327 (OMa).

HOT PLUNGE ..10-4§.. 9 b.g. Bustino — Royal Seal (Privy Seal) p9346252. Small half-brother to Wardy Hill. NH FLAT '00/1 r3 w1 p1 (2nd); and 4th. NH '01 r1 p0 (4th). P-t-P '03 r6 w1 (2-runner Open) p1 (short-head 2nd); ran out 2, pulled up 1 and fell 1. Odds-on to win his debut bumper and duly obliged, but a fiery individual and his ability has only been harnessed once in 15 attempts over jumps. Looked tailor-made for sub-3m Hunter Chases and has made the frame more often than not, but beaten a minimum of nine lengths, and has not jumped well enough. Revealed his temperamental side at Huntingdon, and is best left alone for betting purposes in future. Has faulty steering as well as brakes, and normally kept to right-handed tracks. *Mrs J.P. Lomax & L. Nowell — Vine & Craven (Jane Lomax).* 89 (O), 241 (2m4f110yH), 317 (2m4fH), 444 (2mH), 799 (2m3f110yH), 1173 (2m110yH), 1359 (2m4f110yH), 1443 (2m5fH).

HOTTERS (IRE) ..9-12.. 10 b.g. Be My Native (USA) — Siul Currach (Deep Run) 35*upp*. Good-topped half-brother to Irish Hunter Chase winner, Manfred Mann. NH FLAT '01 r3 w1 p0. NH '01/3 (for M. Pitman) r12 p0; last 4, and fell/unseated 2. NH '04 (from J.R. Norton's) r4 p0 (5th in 2m5f Ch: *wl bhnd frm 5, t.o*; unseated in 3m1f Ch: *blun 1, hmpd 2, bhnd til hmpd & ur 10*; pulled up in 4m Ch: *a bhnd, lost tch & pu 13*; and pulled up in 2m5f110y Hdle: *a bhnd, rdn 5, t.o & pu 7*). Won a bumper on his second racecourse appearance, but a bitter disappointment since, and has been tried in headgear and cheekpieces. Finished six-and-a-half lengths third in a competitive Open on the first day of the season, but flattered to deceive, and is struggling to even complete the course in the bottom grade now. A sketchy jumper. There is probably something wrong with him. *Reddal Racing (I. McEwen) — N. Ledbury (Charlotte Jones).* 3 (O).

HOT TODDY (IRE) ..10-3.. 10 b.g. Glacial Storm (USA) — Technical Merit (Gala Performance) 111. Strong compact half-brother to Well Bank and Percy Pit. Dam won 2m6f Sell Hdle. P-t-P '00/1 and '03 r4 w2 (Maiden and Restricted) p0; last, and fell 1. Lightly raced and only beaten once when standing up, and benefits from quality handling, but largely unimpressive when disposing of second-class rivals in '04, and was risked on a sound surface for the first time at Ampton. Could still be underrated, but his winning times were on the slow side, and still has plenty to prove. *Miss H.J. Hinckley — Wheatland (Guy Landau).* 41 (I), 1015 (Cf), 1262 (O).

HOUGHAM GEORGE ..9-6.. 6 b.g. Mazaad — Pip (IRE) (Buckskin FR) p31. Sturdy. Pulled up on his debut and then finished 40 lengths third, but plugged through the rain-lashed ground at Garthorpe where the probable winner unseated two out and then hampered the horse who had been left in front. Veered left and stumbled near the finish and only just held on, but despite greenness has been showing the right attitude, and as he had not celebrated his fifth birthday when he scored there should be more to come (celebrations were not due until June 20th). *M. Barthorpe — S. Wold (Pat Barthorpe).* 476 (CfMa), 686 (OMa), 1061 (OMa).

HOUSE COLOURS ..8-13.. 9 b.g. Gildoran — Housemistress (New Member) pp6p5. Sturdy half-brother to Alleywell (*qv*). None too quick and beaten about 15 lengths in both completions, and not always the most fluent of jumpers. Would need a bad race to score. *W.A. Bethell — Holderness.* 6 (OMa), 74 (OMa), 271 (OMa), 504 (CMa), 1164 (OMa).

HOUSELOPE BECK .9-6§.. 15 ch.g. Meadowbrook — Hallo Cheeky (Flatbush) u5855uRR. Lengthy quite attractive brother to Houselope Brook, and half-brother to Sandedge and Houselope Spring. Dam won 9f Seller, and won 3 Sell Hdles, 2m-2m4f NH '98 r1 p0 (8th of 9). P-t-P/HUNT CH '95/03 (for Mr F.V. White) r40 w2 (Maiden and Ladies) p11 (6 3rds; and inc neck 2nd once); failed to finish 11 (fell/unseated 5, and ran out 1). Won two of his first four completions, and held his form well despite failing to add to his tally to '02, but has lost his enthusiasm since, and had to contend with an often out of control newcomer this year. Wears a cross-noseband, and has been tried in a tongue-strap. *F.V. White & Miss A.V. Wanless — Border (Angela Wanless).* 73 (Cf), 135 (Cfnr), 428 (3m5fL), 550 (L), 916 (L), 1039 (L), 1308 (L), 1423 (M).

HOW BURN ..9-9.. 12 b.g. Meadowbrook — Kinkell (Netherkelly) 5pf. Tall good-bodied owner-bred half-brother to Potsy's Lass (U). P-t-P '99/03 r14 w2 (Members and 3-finisher Restricted) p2 (3rds); 8th, last pair 5, brought down 1 and pulled up 3. His two wins were separated by three barren years, and has never been able to race on a regular basis, but normally a reliable jumper and his Balcormo Mains tumble was the first of his career. Has been sold. *Mrs V. Jackson — Morpeth.* 762 (I), 1028 (3mH), 1078 (L).

HOWGREENISMYVALLEY ..—.. 6 b.m. Executive Perk — Macklette (IRE) (Buckskin FR) p. Small. Tailed off and pulled up two out after being given a gentle introduction in a Mares Maiden in March. *Mrs R. Evans — Croome & W. Warwicks (Charlotte Evans).* 409 (CMam).

HOW TO RUN (IRE) ..9-8.. 12 b.g. Commanche Run — How Hostile (Tumble Wind) 4847. Tall half-brother to How Humble (IRE), and to useful jumping winner, Fighting Words (won '94 Kim Muir). NH FLAT '97 r1 p0. NH '98/01 r20 w1 (3m3f110y Hdle) p3 (3rds); pulled up 3, brought down 1, unseated 1. P-t-P '03 r2 w1 (Confined) p0; and pulled up 1. Scoring for the first time since '99 when landing a touch under Christian Williams in the fastest time of the day at Rhydygwern last year, but inconsistent and susceptible to leg trouble under Rules, and beaten a minimum of 22 lengths in '04. Blinkered once in '99. *Mrs J. Howells & L. Thomas — Llangeinor (William Howells).* 613 (L), 1090 (Cf), 1320 (Cf), 1391 (L).

HOWYA MATEY (IRE) ..9-6.. 8 ch.g. Treasure Hunter — Clonaslee Baby (Konigssee) 23. Good-topped brother to NH flat winner, Bradley My Boy (IRE), and half-brother to Undertheinfluence, Positive Influence and Court Thyne (IRE), to Irish NH flat winner, Lackey Hoey, to flat winner, Classical Influence, and to disqualified Hurdles winner, Classical Flame. IRISH P-t-P '02/3 r6 w1 (Geldings Maiden) p0; 4th, pulled up 3, fell 1. NH '03 (for M.C. Pipe) r3 p0; last 2. Fell at the last when in command in an Irish Maiden, but later able to make amends in similar company there. Bought expensively and proved a flop when beaten 25 lengths plus in Hurdles, and only able to muster a couple of modest placed efforts in Points (including 26 lengths third behind the Greenall boys in his Members). Possibly not a thorough stayer, and if he can collect a Restricted he will probably be doing well. *P.J. Finn — Middleton (David Pipe).* 689 (R), 769 (M).

HUBBLY BUBBLY .—§§.. 7 b.g. Gildoran — Spinayab (King Of Spain) rr. Dam, half-sister to Daisy's Pal (*qv* '98 Annual), was useless in 9 Points for John Mead (including last, pulled up 5 and fell 2). NH FLAT '02/3 r4 p0. P-t-P '03 (for Mr J.H. Mead) r1 p0 (unseated). Beaten a minimum of 27 lengths in bumpers, but yet to get beyond the fifth without mishap in Points, and badly in need of direction. *R. Oliver — The Niknak Club (S. Howe) — Four Burrow (Simon Howe).* 817 (Cnr), 936 (I).

HUGHIE ..—.. 10 ch.g. Super Sunrise — Clarilaw (White Speck) u. Hopelessly tailed off when losing the rider at the eighth at Ayr (made mistakes and looked clueless). *Mrs H. Fraser — College V. & N. Northumberland (Swanee Haldane).* 439 (2m5f110yH).

HUG THE BEND ..9-3.. 8 ch.g. Norton Challenger — Milross (Ardross) 1pp. Tall unfurnished. P-t-P '03 r2 p1 (2nd); and unseated 1. Trapped under a parked car briefly on his final appearance last year, but was clamped down on by the winner on his return in a long Maiden at Chipley Park, and got the race in the subsequent stewards enquiry. None of the placed horses have even finished since, and went no more than two miles in both Restricteds, but has presumably met with a setback. Wears a cross-noseband. *Mrs C. Handel & Mrs W. Jarrett — Taunton V. (Alison Handel).* 119 (OMa), 369 (R), 498 (R).

HUIC HOLLOA (IRE) ..—.. 9 b.g. Denel (FR) — Buckalgo (IRE) (Buckskin FR) pp. Strong lengthy. 12,000 4yo. NH FLAT '01 r4 p1 (3rd). NH '03 (for J.A.T. De Giles) r5 p0. Bought Ascot, Aug for 5238. A bad animal who has only once been beaten less than 23 lengths in 11 races, and there is probably something ailing him. *N.B. Jones — Llangeinor (Paul Haskins).* 21 (OMa), 121 (OMa).

HUNCA MUNCA (IRE) ..10-6.. 6 b.m. Presenting — Tulladante (IRE) (Phardante FR) f150. Robust. 7010 3yo. NH FLAT '04 (for N.J. Pomfret) r1 p0 (16th at Towcester: *prom 10f, t.o*). Well backed when falling after two miles on her debut, but atoned in rather holding ground in a youngsters Maiden at Brocklesby Park next time, and looked an above-average prospect. Has disappointed since most notably when favourite and fading tamely at Dingley, but may need to strengthen, and will be interesting if she returns to form. Does not appear on the laughably error-ridden list of unusual horses names with their meanings and pronunciations which is dispatched to commentators under Rules by the BHB, but phoning Mrs Tiggywinkle as your friend would soon reveal the identity of Hunca Munca. *J.R. Weatherby — Cottesmore (Laura Pomfret).* 293 (CMam), 476 (CfMa), 889 (CR).

HUNTER GATHERER ..—.. 7 b.g. Homo Sapien — Melissa Gold (Deep Run) pp. Half-brother to Lochnagold, Bitssa and Louis Le Moss. Dam finished in front of only 8 horses in 22 races, but beat one other completer (who was lame) in the United Members. Twice tailed off and pulled up after two miles at Kingston Blount, and has jumped slowly and not looked particularly keen. Connections will be in for a depressing time if he is as awful as Bitssa, who was last thrice and a non-finisher 11 times in Points. *S.M. Atkins — V. of Aylesbury with Garth & S. Berks (Karen Lawther).* 1337 (OMa), 1518 (OMa).

HUNTER GOLD (FR) ..9-11.. 10 br.g. Chamberlin (FR) — Une De Mai IV (FR) (Ice Light FR) 13f46f. Compact well-made hobdayed half-brother to winner in France. FRENCH NH '99/00 r4 w1 (2m3f Ch) p1 (2nd); pulled up 1. NH '00/3 (for T.R. George) r8 p4 (inc 2 Hdles); pulled up 2. Sold Ascot, Apr for 1333. Has been broken down and did not cost present connections much, but was able to gain the second victory of his career (the first was in a non-thoroughbreds Chase at Angers) when beating one other finisher in an Erw Lon Confined. Goes a merry gallop and likes to race right up with the pace, but a very weak finisher, and normally struggles to stay three miles. Tongue-tied on his final appearance in the previous yard, and only managed three outings '02/3. Prone to the occasional catastrophic error. *H.J. Barton — Llandeilo F.* 208 (Cf), 449 (L), 673 (L), 949 (L), 1090 (Cf), 1235 (Cf).

HUNTERSWAY (IRE) ..10-2.. 8 ch.g. Treasure Hunter — Dunmanway (Le Bavard FR) u334132. Compact stocky. Dam is sister to Royal Bav (*qv* '97 Annual). NH '02 r2 p0 (5th, and pulled up 1). P-t-P '02/3 r9 w1 (Maiden) p3 (2 2nds, of 3 once); 5th, last pair 2, unseated 1 and pulled up 1. Very one-paced and not as fluent as his record would suggest, but usually in the money, and found an ideal opportunity when beating one other finisher at Brampton Bryan. Tends to sweat excessively and does not always find much off the bridle, but can handle fast ground so the likelihood is that further gifts will present themselves. *Mrs A. Price — Teme V.* 406 (Inr), 516 (R), 661 (Cnr), 839 (R), 1114 (R), 1227 (Cf), 1392 (C).

HURDANTE (IRE) ..—.. 15 ch.g. Phardante (FR) — Hurry (Deep Run) 5p. Tall strong half-brother to Quay Run (IRE). Dam is half-sister to Friends Of Bernard (*qv* '01 Annual), who is by Phardante. IRISH NH FLAT '96 r3 w1 p1 (2nd). NH '96/7 and '00/1 r15 w2 (2m4f110y Hdle and 2m Ch) p3 (2 2nds); pulled up 3, unseated 1. P-t-P/HUNT CH '02/3 r12 w1 (Members) p4 (½*l* 2nd; 3 3rds, last once); 4th, 6th, 7th, pulled up 3 and carried out 1. Beaten less then three lengths in a Grade 2 Hurdle at Aintree in '97, and would have achieved more had he not been plagued by leg troubles, but went wrong for the umpteenth time at Cilwendeg and will surely have to call it quits. *D.W. Parker — Carms (Linda Parker).* 206 (L), 670 (Cf).

HURRICANE LAMP ..10-4.. 14 b.g. Derrylin — Lampstone (Ragstone) 467. Workmanlike half-brother to Cloud Cuckoo (who ended Jenny Litston's career), to NH flat and jumping winner, Martin's Lamp, and to Hurdles winner, Stoney Path. NH FLAT '96 r2 w1 p0. NH '96/03 r46 w11 (2 2m-2m1f Hdles and 9 2m-2m5f Chses) p15; fell/unseated 4, and pulled up 3. NH '04 r1 p0 (last of 7 in 3m Ch:

mists, chsd ldrs til wknd 3 out, t.o). Enjoyed a superb career with 12 victories and total prize money of £120,661, but never successful at beyond 2m5f, and sometimes made errors. Injured a tendon on his final outing of '03 and was to have retired, but brought back for a couple of modest efforts in Hunter Chases. Green fields surely beckon permanently now. *Mr & Mrs F. Welch & A. King — Cotswold (Alan King).* 178 (3m1f110yH), 346 (3m1f110yH).

HYDEMILLA ..8-12§.. 15 b.m. Idiot's Delight — Bellaloo (Privy Seal) 64. Small light half-sister to Threadbare and Bloowit. Dam is half-sister to Bumptious Boy (*qv* '99 Annual). NH FLAT '94 r1 p0. NH '94/9 r32 p6 (3rds); pulled up 1, unseated 1. P-t-P/HUNT CH '02/3 (for Mrs C.J.A. Suthern) r15 w1 (Maiden) p4 (2 2nds, of 3 once; 2 3rds, of 4 once and last once); last pair 6, pulled up 3 and brought down 1. A sound jumper, and suffered her first fall in 49 starts over jumps at Trecoed (remounted), but modest in the extreme, and rarely exhibits much in the way of resolve. Should have retired on a high back in '02. Has been tried in cheekpieces. *M. Wall — N. Hereford.* 1531 (R), 1548 (R).

HYLTERS CHANCE (IRE) ..10-0.. 14 ch.g. Zaffaran (USA) — Stickey Stream (Paddy's Stream) 2p23. Sturdy compact. NH FLAT '95 r1 p0. NH '96/8 r16 w2 (3m Hdle, and awarded 3m Chse as winner lost weight-cloth) p2 (2nds, short-headed once, and beaten neck once); pulled up 3, and fell 1. P-t-P '00 and '02/3 r21 w6 (inc Open and Mixed Open, hat-trick '03) p7 (4 2nds, beaten neck once, and last once; and last of 3 once); ran out 1, pulled up 3, and fell 1. The winner of six races under Colin Heard '02/3, but very moody and could not have it too firm, and retired after going wrong at Mounsey Hill Gate. The horse on which the aforementioned was found guilty of dangerous riding at Cothelstone, but he was rightly exonerated on appeal. *P.C. Browne, R.J. Hebditch & M.R. Scott — W. Somerset (Polly Curling).* 964 (O), 1185 (MO), 1367 (O), 1463 (O).

IADORA ..9-7.. 10 br.m. Gildoran — Combe Hill (Crozier) 63p24138. Light-framed half-sister to Beckford and Poppet. Dam won 2m6f Hdle and 3 2m4f Chses and placed 9 (inc 4 Hunt Chses). 5200 3yo. NH FLAT '01 r2 p1 (2nd). NH '01/3 (for J.A.B. Old) r8 p2 (3rds); pulled up 2, and unseated 1. Placed three times under Rules (but was 32 lengths fourth and pulled up twice in Chases), but slow and moderate in Points, and was lucky to come across a very bad Maiden at Flagg Moor, in which she took 7min36s to complete the course and no subsequent scorers finished behind her. Despite three placed efforts she was beaten 15 lengths or more and was last twice and last but one once. Unpromising material for Restricteds. *Mrs A. Greenwood — Cheshire (Pat Thompson).* 97 (CfMa), 226 (CfMa), 408 (CMam), 531 (OMa), 714 (CMam), 985 (OMa), 1048 (R), 1375 (3m110yH).

PLATE 58 1557 Tiverton Staghounds Confined: I Am Said I gives Ashley Farrant his record 54th and final winner of the season *PHOTO: Brian Armstrong*

I AM SAID I (IRE) ..10-5.. 7 b.g. Presenting — Moonlight Romance (Teenoso USA) 221p111. Tall lengthy half-brother to Chasing winner, Seven Mile Gale (IRE), and to 2 winners abroad (one French, one Belgian). IRISH P-t-P '03 r2 w1 (5yo Maiden) p0; and last of 4. Bought Doncaster, May for

40,000. A tough sort like so many of the David Pipe team, and although his jumping is not always faultless he is capable of maintaining a resolute gallop, and ran up an unbeaten sequence of four which culminated in a beginners Chase in which he only just scraped home by a head from a horse who was finishing second for the 14th time since his last victory. Not inconvenienced by yielding ground, but firm seems particularly suitable. Proved to be admirably consistent, and gave his only substandard display in the Grimthorpe Gold Cup on a day when Finn fun failed to materialise. After this great start he will have more to do in future, and could be made to look one-paced in competitive contests. *P.J. Finn — Taunton V.H. (David Pipe).* 36 (CR), 324 (R), 488 (R), 772 (4m1fO), 1181 (I), 1446 (Cf), 1557 (Cf).

IAN'S BOY..9-4.. 9 ch.g. Current Edition (IRE) — Lady Verdi (USA) (Monteverdi) ppp1u*p*. Good-topped owner-bred brother to Verdi Edition. Dam won at 12f. P-t-P '03 r2 p0 (pulled up 2). NH '04 (from W.K. Goldsworthy's) r1 p0 (pulled up in Hdle: *bhnd til pu aft mist* 7). Only once got beyond the tenth in five previous attempts, but came from well off the pace to spring a 20-1 surprise in a 15-runner Maiden on firmish at Lydstep. Having held an enquiry (!!) into his improved form the stewards accepted the explanation that he had recently changed yards, but was typically foiled by the first next time. Sure to remain unpredictable, but needs to improve radically for Restricteds. Has run tongue-tied. *F.H. Williams — C.J. Williams — Gelligaer F. (-; Lorna Williams).* 362 (CfMa), 452 (R), 699 (CfMa), 948 (OMa), 1320 (Cf).

ICAL (IRE) ..9-0.. 7 b.m. Broken Hearted — Royal Child (IRE) (Sandhurst Prince) uuupupu1. Compact. IRISH P-t-P '02/3 r3 w1 (4&5yo Mares Maiden) p0; last, pulled up 1. Galloped off loose in the preliminaries and withdrawn on her intended English debut, and then began a memorable partnership with complete beginner Christy Rogers who fell off at the first, at the fifth twice after being left 20 lengths at the start once, and at the 12th. Also failed to get round for three other jockeys, but Alex Merriam worked the oracle in a Northaw Members run in a quagmire, and she easily outplodded one other finisher (her stablemate, the 2-5 favourite, had an empty saddle after just one fence). The owner has now purchased a horse who contested the Irish Grand National in '04, and down at Lilley Bottom Farm they are already buying up all the Yuhu in Bedfordshire. *Miss C.A. Rogers — Cambs with Enfield Chace (Simon Andrews).* 101 (L), 123 (M), 249 (Cnr), 375 (R), 649 (L), 745 (R), 902 (R), 1241 (M).

ICENI QUEEN ..—.. 7 b.m. Formidable (USA) — Queen Warrior (Daring March) pu. Compact half-sister to flat winner, Malleus. Dam won 4 8f races. FLAT '01 r5 p0; last 2. NH '02 r2 p0 (pulled up 2). P-t-P '03 r3 p0 (pulled up 2, and unseated 1). Consistently hopeless in 12 assorted contests, and has yet to go clear over obstacles. Error-pronein Points, and out of her depth in '04. *C. Fowlie — Lamerton (Mark Ranger).* 63 (L), 118 (R).

ICONIC ..8-7.. 11 b.g. Reprimand — Miami Melody (Miami Springs) p4pp. Tall rangy half-brother to flat winner, April The Eighth. NH FLAT '98 r1 p0. NH '98/00 r8 p1 (2nd in Ch). P-t-P/HUNT CH '01/2 r4 p0 (4th, 5th, last, and pulled up 1). Runner-up in a weak race on his chasing debut, but a strong puller and does not stay in Points, and his weakness is exacerbated unless the ground rides fast. *D. Page & Miss S.R. Armstrong — Ashford V. (Trevor Crawford).* 345 (2m5fH), 423 (CMa), 539 (OMa), 782 (OMa).

IDIOT'S STAR ..9-7.. 13 b.g. Idiot's Delight — Trikkala Star (Tachypous) p. Small compact half-brother to River Gun, and to successful Hurdlers, Roker Joker and Star Blakeney. Dam won 2 2m4f-3m Hdles. IRISH P-t-P '00 r2 w1 (7&8yo Maiden) p0 (2nd once but disqualified — not weigh-in). IRISH NH FLAT '98 r1 p0. IRISH HUNT CH '00 r2 w1 (beat Father Andy by head) p0. IRISH NH '98/01 r13 p2 (2nds in Chses); pulled up 2, and fell/unseated 2. NH '02 r2 p0; pulled up 1. P-t-P '03 r2 p0 (last, and pulled up 1). Capable of decent efforts in mud in Ireland, but very lightly raced since his last success in '00, and pulled up lame at Corbridge. *S. Burley — Barlow (Jason Burley).* 429 (3m5fO).

IGAM OGAM ..5-0.. 8 ch.g. Henbit (USA) — Starch Brook (Starch Reduced) 4. Dam, half-sister to Cottage Kate. Completed on his debut at Dunthrop in January, but was hopelessly tailed off. *M.W. & Mrs A.N. Harris — Wheatland (John Groucott).* 51 (OMa).

IGLOUX ROYAL (FR) .8-5.. 9 b.g. Lights Out (FR) — Onde Royale (FR) (Danoso) fp36pppf. Compact half-brother to French Chasing winner, Ubloff Royal (FR). Dam won 12f race in France. NH FLAT '01 r1 p0 (well tailed off). Headstrong and often leads early, but stopped as if shot, and produced his only ratable form when 18 lengths third in an elders Maiden. Makes many mistakes, and the better the jockey the worse he jumps (fell with Stewart Morris, and jumped appallingly for Andy Martin). Putting him in a Hunter Chase was daft, and predictably fell when tailed off (80-1). *Mr & Mrs S.E. Bown — D.P. Smith — Pytchley (Toby Saunders).* 6 (OMa), 32 (Cnr), 130 (OMa), 295 (OMa), 385 (OMa), 927 (OMa), 1275 (OMa), 1377 (2m5fH).

ILE DISTINCT (IRE) ..8-3§.. 11 b.g. Dancing Dissident (USA) — Golden Sunlight (Ile De Bourbon USA) pf4. Compact half-brother to 5 flat winners (2 abroad), including Broctune Gold (12 wins), Posen Gold and Umbrian Gold. FLAT '96/00 r19 w2 (8-9f) p5 (short-headed once). NH '99/03 r17 p3; fell

2, and pulled up 2. P-t-P/HUNT CH '02/3 (for Mr K.R. Pearce) r2 p1 (2nd); and 5th of 6. A long-standing maiden over jumps, and typically failed to deliver when the subject of a gamble on his reappearance, and acquired a tongue-strap on his last two starts. Blinkered once in '00. *E.J. Ford — Carms (Bethan Williams).* 1235 (Cf), 1391 (L), 1536 (L).

IMAGO II (FR) .9-11.. 9 b.g. Chamberlin (FR) — Pensee D'amour (FR) (Porto Rafti FR) p2s. Compact half-brother to a French Chasing winner. Dam won 10f race in France, and is half-sister to Algan (*qv*). NH FLAT '01 r1 w1. NH '01/3 (for F. Murphy, and J. O'Neill) r7 p1 (3rd); pulled up 1. Looked on the brink of a useful career when he won a 19-runner Haydock bumper in soft, but a big disappointment over obstacles, and was pulled up in one of four Chases (prone to blunder). Showed he retains a smidgen of ability when eight lengths second of three in an Intermediate, but put up no resistance to the winner, and remains suspect. Blinkered on his final two outings under Rules. *B.R. Summers — Croome & W. Warwicks.* 728 (I), 867 (I), 1530 (I).

I'M DREAMING (IRE) .9-9.. 11 ch.g. White Christmas — Suffolk Bells (London Bells CAN) 7pp3p83. Tall lengthy hobdayed. Dam won 2m6f Hdle in Ireland, and is sister or half-sister to 3 Pointers, including Deep Bit (*qv* '99 Annual). IRISH NH FLAT '99 r1 p0. IRISH P-t-P '00 r4 w1 (Maiden) p1 (2nd). IRISH NH '00 r6 p1 (2nd in Hunt Ch — flattered by late departures); 4th, 7th and pulled up in other Hunt Chases. NH '01 r1 p0 (pulled up in 2m1f Ch). P-t-P/HUNT CH '01/3 r18 p8 (4 3rds, dead-heat of 4 once, last once, and inc Hunt Ch); pulled up 4, refused 1. Survived a bad mistake at the last when successful in Ireland, but a very weak finisher since, and his losing sequence stands at 29. Regressed further in '04 and looks finished now. *Mr & Mrs A.J. Martin — Heythrop (Andy Martin).* 383 (R), 541 (3mH), 726 (R), 759 (I), 1172 (3m1f110yH), 1359 (2m4f110yH), 1447 (O).

I'M NO FAIRY ..8-0.. 6 b.g. Efisio — Fairywings (Kris) 1u. Dam won 3 10f races at Beverley. In training with Lynda Ramsden with a view to running on the flat, but was too big and backward to make the course. Just about scraped a rating when getting up by a neck in arguably the worst Maiden of the year, which took over eight minutes at Dalton Park, and was certainly not advertised by the subsequent efforts of those behind. Virtually refused after two miles when already tailed off in his Members, and apart from the top of the Christmas tree (which he denies) it is difficult to think of a role he can usefully fill in future. *T.S. Sharpe & L. Barker — York & Ainsty S. (Tim Sharpe).* 505 (CMa), 1157 (M).

PLATE 59 702 East Cornwall Open Maiden 56&7yo (Div 2), 2m4f: Impatient Lady and Andrew Glassonbury, 1st *PHOTO: Baths Photographic*

IMPATIENT LADY ..10-1.. 8 b.m. Morpeth — Miss Firecracker (Relkino) 111. Bred by Jim Frost who thought she was batty, but certainly has the right temperament for racing, and after winning a 2m4f Maiden at Great Trethew she completed a double at Flete Park — beating the Frost representative

Lingering Fog in to second in both. Can produce some acceleration, and receives useful assistance from Andrew Glassonbury. Has done all the easy bits in good style, and there should be further chances for her in a higher grade. *G.W. & Ms L. Johnson — Dartmoor (Lucy Johnson).* 702 (2m4fOMa), 1001 (M), 1196 (R).

IMPERIAL LINE (IRE) ..9-9.. 11 ch.g. Mac's Imp (USA) — Ellaline (Corvaro USA) p0345. Lengthy good-bodied fired brother to Right To Reason (IRE), and half-brother to 2 flat winners (one in Germany, and the other, Mobile Miss (IRE), in Ireland). Dam won at 7f in Ireland. FLAT '97/8 r10 p0. NH '98 r2 p0. P-t-P/HUNT CH '99/00 and '02 r15 w1 (Ladies) p5 (4 2nds, inc Hunt Ch; and last of 3); fell/unseated 3, pulled up 1. Of no account under Rules, and struggled to see out the trip in Maidens, but sprang a 33-1 shock on his first venture in Ladies at Hexham in '02, and subsequently runner-up in a Cartmel Hunter Chase. Missed '03 and with it seemingly his last chance of success, as he was soundly beaten, though often in the face of stiff tasks, this year. Runs tongue-tied. Blinkered thrice in '97. *Mrs P.A. Cowey — Cleveland (Howard Thompson).* 679 (3m1fH), 732 (2m5f110yH), 1163 (Cf), 1420 (L), 1526 (3m2fH).

IMPERIAL PRINCE ..9-0.. 10 b.g. Prince Sabo — Joli's Girl (Mansingh USA) 8fp. Compact half-brother to Side Bar, and to flat winner, Joli's Princess. Dam won at 9f. FLAT r22 p8 (4 2nds). NH '99/00 r7 p2 (both Sell Hdles). P-t-P '02 (for Miss A. Clift) r5 w1 (3-finisher Maiden) p2 (2nds); and pulled up 2. Shirked a multitude of opportunities under Rules, and frequently wore headgear, but galvanised by the fitting of first-time cheekpieces when landing a three-finisher Maiden on firmish at Bitterley in '02. Immediately went to pot again, and after missing '03 showed no signs of retaining ability in three early season forays this year. *M.S. Burman — Cambs with Enfield Chace.* 2 (R), 102 (R), 127 (R).

IMPOSA .—.. 7 ch.g. Imp Society (USA) — Carmosa (USA) (Blushing John USA) R. Just about got over the second in a Corbridge Maiden, but ran out at the next. *P. Stonehouse — Braes (Bernard Stonehouse).* 433 (OMa).

IMPS WAY ..10-0.. 10 br.m. Nomadic Way (USA) — Dalton's Delight (Wonderful Surprise) 2311u135p. Small. Dam, sister to Implicity Suzie (*qv* '97 Annual), was qualified to run in '99 but failed to appear. NH '02 r3 p0; 100-1 when pulled up in 2 of 3 Chses. P-t-P '00 and '03 r9 w1 (Members) p5 (3 3rds, last once); 5th of 6, and pulled up 2. Took a while to come to hand, and only able to win one of her first 14 starts, but then recorded a Pointing hat-trick under different riders, though the last two were two-finisher affairs. Does not look cut out for Hunter Chases, where her jumping has been found wanting, but a return to Points should at least give her confidence a boost. Normally avoids ground any quicker than good. *Mrs T. Corrigan-Clark — Derwent.* 57 (R), 177 (3mH), 268 (R), 388 (M), 436 (3m1f110yH), 565 (O), 679 (3m1fH), 1178 (3m1fH), 1297 (3m1fH).

I'M THE MAN ..—.. 14 ro.g. Say Primula — Vinovia (Ribston) 0. Tall rangy brother to If You Say So, and half-brother to The Dabber (dam of Cracking Crumpet, *qv* '01 Annual) and What A Miss, and to Hurdles winner, Silver Howe. NH FLAT '96 r3 p0 (disqualified from 3rd once). NH '96/02 r49 w9 (3m Hdle and 8 2m4f110y-3m6f Chses) p13 (10 3rds); pulled up 5, fell/unseated 4. HUNT CH '03 r2 p2. A thorough stayer, and a very game front-runner on his day, but lacked consistency under Rules, and has stood very little racing since '01. Kept on heroically to finish third in the '03 Aintree Foxhunters (rated 10-10), but making his first appearance since when tailed off at Kelso, and looks to have come to the end of a long an honorable career. *Marco Syndicate (Col R.J. Martin) — Jedforest (Philippa Shirley-Beavan).* 798 (3m1fH).

IMUSTGETON ..9-5.. 11 b.m. North Col — Double Stitch (Wolver Hollow) p31. Neat half-sister to Short Encounter, and to 3 flat winners, including Purbeck Centenary and Chastleton. Dam won at 8f. NH FLAT '98 r2 p0. NH '00/1 r8 p1 (11/ 3rd of 4 in Sell); pulled up 2. P-t-P '01/2 r7 p1 (last of 2); last pair 4, and pulled up 2. A very poor performer, even in the lowest grade, and only once better than last when last seen in Points, but put her all into winning a bad three-finisher Maiden on firmish at Trecoed, and collapsed through dehydration having done so. Will find matters beyond her in Restricteds. Tends to get worked up in the preliminaries and has been mounted on course. Wears a cross-noseband, and has run tongue-tied. *E.H. Williams & T. Harries — Tivyside (Huw Williams).* 1027 (OMa), 1239 (OMa), 1553 (OMa).

I'M WILLIE'S GIRL ..9-0.. 9 br.m. Royal Fountain — Milton Lass (Scallywag) uuuu2. Small. Dam, half-sister to Celtic Connie (refused in 4 Points), carried out and unseated in Points. NH '02 (for F.P. Murtagh) r1 p0 (pulled up). A tricky little mare who managed to shed Jenny Riding in all their four attempts together, but was just in front when she did so two out once. Acquired Clive Storey in an elders Maiden at Balcormo, and he rode the storm, but she proved no match for the winner and was eventually beaten by an eased 25 lengths. Very moderate, and perhaps she has squandered her golden chance. *J. Threadgall — Lauderdale (Joanna Luton).* 215 (OMa), 287 (CfMa), 553 (CfMa), 859 (CfMa), 1082 (OMa).

PLATE 60 274 W. Somerset & Minehead Harriers Confined Maiden (Div 1): Inagh Road, who made nearly all, gives Alex Michael an anxious moment, behind is Bright Flash and David Luff, 4th
PHOTO: Tim Holt

INAGH ROAD (IRE) ..9-8.. 10 b.g. Broken Hearted — Fiodoir (Weavers' Hall) 1p. Sturdy brother to flat winner, Lindrick Lady (IRE), and half-brother to Chatergold (IRE) (won 3 Chses since Pointing), and to Irish flat and Hurdling winner, Motility, and to a flat winner in Italy. Dam won 4 12f races in Ireland. IRISH P-t-P '01/2 r4 p0; pulled up 2 and fell. NH FLAT '00 r3 p0. IRISH FLAT '02 r1 p0. IRISH NH '02 r1 p0. NH '03 (for B.N. Pollock) r6 p1 (3rd); last 2, unseated 1, and pulled up 1. Bought Ascot, Oct for 1904. Dramatically improved in first time cheekpieces when finishing five lengths third in a Hurdle in the previous yard, but that was not sustained, and has been trounced in Sellers. Has also worn blinkers, and tongue-tied once. A very hard puller who often front runs, and remarkably held the advantage to the finish in a Maiden at Holnicote in February, but it was a dreadful contest from which no subsequent scorers emerged, and faded rapidly and pulled up after two miles next time. Keeps plenty to himself, and highly unlikely to follow up. *K. Mantyk, A. Goddard & S. Walker — Taunton V. (Fiona Walker).* 274 (CfMa), 473 (R).

INCHING BROOK ..7-0.. 8 ch.g. Alflora (IRE) — Inch Ahead (IRE) (Over The River FR) 75pp. 2000 4yo. Beaten 45 lengths plus when completing twice (last in both), and then pulled up by halfway twice. Not an auspicious beginning. *Mrs M.G. Sheppard — Cambs with Enfield Chace.* 105 (2m4fOMa), 219 (OMa), 371 (OMa), 1246 (OMa).

INCROYABLE MAIS VRAI (FR) ..10-2§.. 9 b.g. Morespeed — Urtica V (FR) (Tourangeau FR) u. P-t-P '02/3 r9 w2 (Maiden and 2-runner Members) p3 (2 2nds); unseated 1, refused 1, and pulled up 2. Struck into when recording his second success last year, and subsequently underwent tie-back and hobday operations, but ran tongue-tied as usual on his reappearance, and held every chance when unseating three out in an above average Restricted at Tranwell. Quirky but a certainty to make amends if all is well in '05. Wears cheekpieces, and a cross-noseband. *J.H. Sordy & W. Telford — W. Percy (George White).* 918 (R).

IN DEMAND ..9-5.. 14 b.g. Nomination — Romantic Saga (Prince Tenderfoot USA) 44413643634. Compact rather unfurnished brother to flat winner, Lady Eclat. FLAT r5 p0. NH '99/01 r3 w1 (2m5f Nov Hdle) p0. P-t-P/HUNT CH '96/7, '99 and '02/3 r24 w4 (up to Confined) p5 (2 2nds; inc 3rd of 4 once); pulled up 2, on floor 3. Made full use of his fitness when landing a gamble to thwart Nesbit at Musselburgh, but typically lost his form in the second half of his busiest season to date. Did a fine job in schooling the newcomer Joanne Balmer, and has 22 consecutive completions to his credit, but often lacks fluency, and will do well to score again even when fresh. Acts on any going, but most successful on a sound surface. *A.J. Balmer — Morpeth.* 135 (Cfnr), 282 (Cf), 339 (L), 508 (L), 550 (L), 655 (L), 916 (L), 1221 (L), 1308 (L), 1420 (L), 1478 (L).

PLATE 61 508 Northern P-t-P Area Club Ladies Open: In Demand and Jean Balmer, 1st, are actually still 2nd at the last PHOTO: Alan Mitchell

INDIANA JOHN (FR) ..9-6.. 9 b.g. Gay Minstrel (FR) — Boule D'Or (FR) (Quart De Vin FR) 63323. Small neat half-brother to a French flat winner. P-t-P '01 and '03 r9 w1 Maiden) p2 (3rds of 4); and fell/unseated 6. Finally got off the mark at Kilworthy last year, but buried the rider on his last three appearances, and remains a trappy ride. Came closest to landing a Restricted at Trebudannon, but keen and often finds little off the bridle, and should not be trusted implicitly. *Mr & Mrs C. Cox — Lamerton (Charles Cox).* 706 (R), 912 (R), 1196 (R), 1435 (R), 1544 (I).

INDIAN RAIDER (IRE) .9-5.. 11 b.g. Commanche Run — Borecca (Boreen FR) p2p232. Plain half-brother to Mixies Jim and Phar Echo (IRE), and to Chasing winner, Noosa Sound (IRE), and to Irish Hurdles winner, Double Token. IRISH P-t-P '99/00 r7 w1 (6yo Maiden) p0; pulled up 2, fell 1, and refused 1. IRISH HUNT CH '00 r2 p0. P-t-P '02/3 r11 w1 (Members) p1 (3rd of 4); last pair 4, refused 1, and pulled up 4. Scoring for the first time on merit (his Irish win was gained on a technicality) when springing a 20-1 surprise in his Members last year, but normally a very weak finisher, and was caught in the dying strides at Vauterhill after looking all over the winner going to the last. Never went a yard when tried in cheekpieces at Newton Abbot previously, and probably not one to place much faith in. *R.G. Chapman — Four Burrow.* 498 (R), 907 (M), 1167 (3m2f110yH), 1268 (R), 1435 (R), 1543 (R).

INDIAN RENEGADE (IRE) ..8-8.. 7 b.m. Commanche Run — Tarary (Boreen FR) pppp4. Strong-topped half-sister to The Grandson (IRE) (*qv*). NH FLAT '02 (for J.S. Haldane) r1 p0 (last). Bought Doncaster, Aug '02 for 1000. Seventy-five lengths last in a bumper and pulled up in her first four Maidens, but finally revealed a little ability when 15 lengths fourth at Lifton. Looked very one-paced, and will still have to go a fair bit quicker if she is to score. *Mrs H.D. Power — N. Cornwall.* 309 (2m4fOMa), 486 (OMa), 567 (CfMa), 910 (2m4fOMa), 1353 (OMa).

INDIAN ROPE TRICK ..9-6.. 9 ch.g. Kris — Lassoo (Caerleon USA) 4. Sturdy brother to flat winner, Sioux, and half-brother to flat winner, Mustang. FLAT '99/00 r6 p0. NH '01/2 (for M.W. Easterby) r6 p1 (3rd); pulled up 1. Thirty-five lengths sixth and pulled up in Chases, but did conclude his career under Rules with a 13 length third. Looked to go wrong in the process, and clearly suffered an immediate relapse in a Point, as after making the bulk of the running he faded to finish 19 lengths fourth and was not seen again. Tongue-tied on his last three outings under Rules. *Yorkshire P-t-P Club (Miss J.E. Foster) — Pendle Forest & Craven (Jo Foster).* 165 (OMa).

INDIAN TRIX (IRE) ..7-8.. 7 b.m. Commanche Run — Ginger Trix (Le Moss) ppp44pp3. Small neat. Slouches round and often makes mistakes, and beaten a minimum of 15 lengths if completing (last once, and last barring a remounter once). Tried tongue-tied twice, and presumably suffering with a wind problem. *P.B. Miles — Ystrad Taf Fechan (Myfanwy Miles).* 202 (CfMa), 363 (CfMa), 454 (CfMa), 700 (CfMa), 735 (CfMa), 1239 (OMa), 1394 (OMa), 1486 (OMa).

INDIAN WINGS (IRE) .10-1.. 12 b.g. Commanche Run — Got To Fly (IRE) (Kemal FR) 2121. Rangy half-brother to Touching Down (IRE) (*qv*). IRISH P-t-P '98/00 r12 w3 (6yo&up Maiden, and 2 Ladies) p5 (4 2nds); pulled up 3. NH '01/2 (for A. Scott) r20 w2 (2m4f-2m7f Hdles) p5 (inc 2nd in Ch); pulled up 6. A decent Irish Pointer who made virtually all to complete a Hurdling double including in soft in November '01 but missed '03. Sent off favourite for all his Points in the new yard and made the very long journey to Charing for the first of them, but finished tired after a slow jump at the last, and then all out to score when on a retrieving mission at Tabley. Beaten at 8-11 at Eyton-on-Severn, and concluded his season with a seventh career victory in a three-runner Members there, but was unimpressive in landing odds of 1-4. A competent jumper, but not as good as his recent record might suggest, and unlikely to rate any higher at 12. *D.A. Smith — S. Salop.* 422 (CCon), 749 (Cf), 932 (Cf), 1260 (M).

INDIEN DU BOULAY (FR) ..10-1.. 9 ch.g. Chef De Clan II (FR) — Radesgirl (FR) (Radetzky Marsch USA) p1534f45. Compact well-made. FRENCH FLAT '00 r1 p0. FRENCH NH '00 r1 p0. NH '01/3 (for P. Monteith) r16 w4 (2 2m4f-2m4f110y Hdles and 2 2-3m Chses) p4; pulled up 3, and fell 2. Inconsistent and ungenuine, but competent on his day, and notched a hat-trick in '01. Pulled up on his final three outings in the previous yard (performed atrociously), and often wore headgear or cheekpieces, but seems to rather prefer an amateur bumping around in the saddle. Maintained the Ramsay stranglehold in the Berwickshire Members (the last time the Trotters got a look in was after Will had toppled off The Caffler at the last in '97, and Rupert suffered the indignity of being divided by the clan in '04). Deserved his place in Hunter Chases and beaten a maximum of ten lengths when making the frame thrice, and although he never looked like scoring he has proved a fun horse for connections. *Major General C.A. Ramsay — Berwicks.* 72 (O), 281 (M), 330 (3mH), 445 (3m110yH), 798 (3m1fH), 1174 (3m1fH), 1296 (3m1fH), 1490 (3m2fH).

INFAMELIA ..9-10§.. 9 b.m. Infantry — Incamelia (St Columbus) 2p3p33. Compact half-sister to Incbrush. Dam won 2m5f Hdle and 4 Chses (3m-3m2f) for the Hendersons. Grandam, Indamelia, won at 5f, and won 7 Hdles (2-3m; won another which was declared void) and 3 Chses (2m4f-2m6f) and 5 Hunt Chses (2m4f-3m2f) and 2 Points, and placed total of 21 for late John Thorne (Diana Henderson's father). Great-grandam, Barton's Sister, won 2m Ch for him. NH FLAT '01 r2 p0. NH '01/2 r4 p0; pulled up 1. P-t-P '02 (for Mrs D.A. Henderson) r2 w1 (Maiden) p0; and pulled up 1. Landed a gamble in first-time blinkers when partnered by Andrew Tinkler at Kingston Blount in '02, and easily good enough to register another minor success, but found nil in the closing stages when placed four times in '04, and has been unimproved by a visor. Wears a cross-noseband. *Miss T. Clark & Capt T.M. Bell — Sir W.W. Wynn's (Tessa Clark).* 161 (I), 541 (3mH), 715 (R), 853 (R), 1019 (Cm), 1430 (I).

INGLEMOTTE MISS ..8-6§.. 7 ch.m. Hatim (USA) — Phantom Singer (Relkino) pcfr. Sister to Benbeoch. Dam, half-sister to Vienna Woods (*qv '97 Annual*), won 11f race. FLAT '00/1 r3 p0; inc Sell. P-t-P '03 r5 p2 (last of 2 twice, beaten neck once); last, refused 1, and pulled up 1. NH '04 (for Ms L. Harrison) r1 p0 (refused in 2m1f Hdle: *sn t.o, ref 4*). Used to dwell on the flat and despite filling the runners-up berth twice last year has still to beat a rival over jumps. Set in her ways and a fall at Balcormo Mains has done nothing to boost her confidence. *The Corky & Kez Partnership (Mrs J. Williamson) — Cumberland (Margaret Harrison).* 768 (2m4fOMa), 856 (2m4fOMa), 1081 (OMa).

INIS CARA (IRE) ..9-11.. 13 b.g. Carlingford Castle — Good Sailing (Scorpio FR) 22p33p. Workmanlike half-brother to Noaff (IRE) (*qv*). IRISH FLAT '98 and '00 r2 p0. IRISH P-t-P '97 r1 w1 (5yo Maiden). IRISH NH FLAT '97 r2 w1 p0. IRISH NH '97/00 r36 w8 (4 2m4f-2m6f Hdles and 4 2m3f-3m Chses) p11. NH '01/2 r5 p0; fell in '01 Grand National, and pulled up in '02 Grand National. P-t-P/HUNT CH '03 r7 p2 (last of 3 once); 5th, last pair 3, and pulled up 1. A smart performer with Michael Hourigan in Ireland to '00, but very much a pale shadow of his former self, and has gone 28 races since his last win. Put up his best performance in ages when runner-up to Sohapara on his reappearance, but finds it hard to maintain his enthusiasm, and never went a yard at Bredwardine. Deserves to be humbled no more. *G.W. Thomas — Monmouths.* 359 (Cf), 612 (Cf), 974 (3mH), 1090 (Cf), 1320 (Cf), 1392 (C).

INIS EILE (IRE) ..9-2§.. 10 b.g. Peacock (FR) — Slippery Bell (No Argument) 2p. Small. Dam won Irish Maiden. IRISH P-t-P '00/1 r4 p1 (3rd); pulled up 3. IRISH NH FLAT '00 r1 p0. NH '01/2 r13 p3 (2 3rds); fell 1. P-t-P '03 (for Mr D.R. Churches) r8 p3 (2 2nds; and 3rd of 4); last, refused 1, pulled up 1, fell 1, and carried out 1. Often placed but still a maiden after 28 attempts and summed up the strength of some south-east Maidens when disputing favouritism on his return. Temperamental and went no more than two miles next time, and it would be no surprise to see him change hands yet again. Fell when blinkered once in '02. *P. Tipples — E. Sussex & Romney Marsh (Paul Hacking)*. 423 (CMa), 611 (OMa).

INNER STATE .8-2§.. 9 b/br.m. State Diplomacy (USA) — Bonnyhill Lass (Royal Fountain) pf35. Workmanlike trainer-bred half-sister to Little Vera and Nought To Ninety. Dam, is half-sister to Fell Mist (*qv* '99 Annual), was 2nd in a Maiden ('seems very moody'). P-t-P '03 (for Mrs D. Alderson) r2 p1 (remote 3rd of 4); and pulled up 1. Backed from 12s to sixes when a fair third in a slow mares Maiden at Holnicote, but still not an accomplished jumper, and ran like a hairy goat on a return visit. Clearly cast in the same mould as her dam. *Mrs P.M. Stevens — Bilsdale*. 637 (CMam), 967 (OMa), 1182 (CMam), 1327 (OMa).

INSPECTOR BLAKE ..9-6.. 11 ch.g. River God (USA) — Brenda Blake (Roscoe Blake) 3p. Sturdy. Dam won 2 Points (Maiden on disqualification, and Ladies) and placed 6. Grandam, Barton Princess, was placed in 3 Points. P-t-P '99 and '02 r3 w1 (Maiden) p1 (2nd of 3); and pulled up 1. Unlucky not to make a winning debut, and had to wait three years to rectify the situation, but obviously impossible to train, and jumped poorly when owner-ridden and pulled up Eyton. Has been tried in cheekpieces. *P. Morris — Albrighton*. 467 (CR), 933 (CR).

INTERCITY ..—.. 10 gr.g. Terimon — Whimbrel (Dara Monarch) p. Close-coupled half-brother to Hurdles winner, Golden Gravel (IRE). Dam, half-sister to Astwood Flier (*qv* '93 Annual), won 9f Sell. NH FLAT '99 r1 p0. NH '00 r3 p0 (9th, and pulled up 2). P-t-P '01/2 r7 p0 (last 2, pulled up 2, and unseated 3). Slow and has made frequent stops in Points, and appeared to come off the rails when dismounted on the run-in at Charing. *J.J. Hazeltine — Surrey U*. 186 (OMa).

INTER ROCK (FR) ..9-13.. 9 b.g. Video Rock (FR) — Aniste (FR) (Brezzo FR) 4. Compact. FRENCH FLAT '99 r3 w1 (12f) p1. NH '00/2 r12 w1 (2m7f110y Hdle) p1 (3rd); pulled up 3. P-t-P '03 (for Mr R.C. Harper) r5 w1 (Members) p1 (last of 2); 5th, and last pair 2. Lost his way badly under Rules, and was scoring for the first time since '00 when landing a three-runner Members on firm last year, but has never stood much racing, and disappeared after a promising debut for new connections. Not a natural jumper, and needs strong handling, but the odds against a successful comeback are large. Blinkered once in '01. *A.J. Cottle — Exmoor*. 823 (Cf).

INTERROGATOR ..9-3.. 9 gr.g. Terimon — Highgate Lady (Rubor) 143. Narrow unfurnished half-brother to Proper Charlie. Dam, half-sister to Highgate Amber (*qv* '92 Annual), won 21 Points (18 Ladies) and placed 10 (never missed the frame in her 36 completions; last 18 wins for Joey Newton). P-t-P '03 r3 p0 (pulled up 3). Unimpressive in his debut season, and allowed to start at an attractive price for the first time when landing a three-finisher Maiden at Garthorpe, but the subject of a stewards enquiry when an odds-on flop in his Members next time. The owners' explanation that the horse had failed to act on the course was accepted by the hierarchy, despite the fact he had won there just three weeks earlier! Beaten out of sight in his first Restricted, and has a long way to go to emulate his illustrious mother. *J.R. Newton — Belvoir (Emma Newton)*. 386 (OMa), 680 (M), 999 (R).

INTHAAR ..—.. 8 b.g. Nashwan (USA) — Twafeaj (USA) (Topsider USA) p0pup. Small half-brother to flat winner, Shanook. Dam won 3 6f races inc £20,000 prize at Deauville and £91,000 prize at The Curragh. Grandam Billy Sue's Rib won 13 flat at up to 9f in USA. 14,000 2yo. NH FLAT '01 r1 p0. FLAT '01/2 r27 w1 (12f) p5. NH '02 (for R. Brotherton) r2 p0. Won a Seller and placed five times on the all-weather, but deplorable on grass, and only two horses have finished behind him in seven attempts over jumps. Sometimes wears headgear, and jumped badly in blinkers in his last two Points. Alan Phillips must be wondering why he bothered to make a comeback to ride this sort of thing. *Miss J. Williams — N. Ledbury (Alan Phillips)*. 229 (O), 403 (Cf), 612 (Cf), 1110 (O), 1392 (C).

IN THE VAN ..9-0.. 13 b.g. Bedford (USA) — Sea Countess (Ercolano USA) p2bp8fp. Lengthy half-brother to Sober Island and Countess Rosie, and to Chasing winner, Count Oski. NH FLAT '97/8 r4 p2 (2nds). NH '98/9 r8 p0; last, pulled up and brought down in Chses (poor jumper). P-t-P '00 and '02/3 r17 w1 (Maiden) p8 (4 2nds, remote once); pulled up 1, unseated 2. Gained a deserved but fortunate success at Witton Castle last year, but generally on thoroughly bad terms with himself in '04, and not better than last. Dumped both Morleys before the start during the course of the year, and has been reported dead since. Mrs S.A. Morley — Derwent (Richard Morley). 268 (R), 388 (M), 503 (R), 563 (R), 955 (R), 1162 (R), 1304 (CR).

INVERDANTE (IRE) ..—.. 9 br.g. Phardante (FR) — Colleen Glen (Furry Glen) p. Half-brother to Hurdles winner, Fireside Girl (IRE). Dam won 2 Hurdles (2m1f-2m2f) and 4 Chases (2m-2m4f) in Ireland. IRISH P-t-P '02/3 r7 p2 (3rds); pulled up 4, and fell 1. Bought Doncaster, May for 5000. Tailed off and pulled up at Witton Castle in February when an all too rare ride these days for Adair Pickering, and seems to have gone wrong. Irish form suggests he could be quite moderate in any case. *G.J. Wilson — Brocklesby (Adair Pickering)*. 166 (OMa).

INVOLVED (IRE) ..10-3.. 9 b.g. Macmillion — Symphony Express (IRE) (Orchestra) p2p. Medium-sized. Dam, half-sister to Dantes Gold (*qv* '01 Annual). IRISH P-t-P '01 r2 p2. IRISH NH FLAT '01 r1 p0. IRISH NH '02 r1 p0. P-t-P '03 r6 w5 (5-timer, Maiden, Restricted, 2 Confineds and

Intermediate) p0; and pulled up 1. A progressive novice last year, and often well supported when justifying odds-on status on five occasions, but misbehaved before the start on his final appearance and was ultimately pulled up. Clearly out of sorts in '04, and was brushed aside by Gallant Glen at Horseheath before flopping in first-time blinkers at Weston Park. Reported to need soft ground, but will need watching wherever he reappears. *R.J. French — N. Salop (Sheila Crow).* 34 (O), 125 (O), 228 (Cf).

IORANA (FR) .8-6.. 9 ch.g. Marignan (USA) — Fareham (FR) (Fast Topaze USA) p7. Sparely-made brother to French flat winner, Le Bila (FR). Dam won at 10f in France. FLAT '00 r2 p2. FRENCH NH '99 r3 w1 (1m7f Hdle) p1 (3rd); and fell. NH '99/03 (all wins for M.C. Pipe, and Miss K. Marks) r30 w10 (8 2m-2m5f Hdles and 2 2m Chses) p7; unseated 1, and pulled up 2. One of Martin Pipe's better claims from France, and magnificently trained to win ten times including a four-timer in Autumn '02, and including three Sellers. Sometimes reluctant (tried to refuse and unseated once), and prone to errors over fences. Dismounted quickly after his final win and looked lame, but Nick Shutts rapidly snapped him up for 7,750gns, after which he made two appearances and was beaten over 40 lengths in both. Pulled up and a remote last in Points, and it is obvious that the bottom has been knocked right out of him now. *Miss L. Tasker — Albrighton (Paul Morris).* 465 (O), 661 (Cnr).

IRBEE ..10-7§.. 13 b.g. Gunner B — Cupids Bower (Owen Dudley) 56u43. Compact well-made brother to Beehawk, and half-brother to Wally's Dream and Karoo, and to Chasing winner, Kingsmoor. Dam won 2 2m-2m3f Hdles, but showed no form in 5 Points. NH '96 and '98/02 r27 w7 (2m110y Hdle, and 6 2m-2m5f Chses, inc a Grade 2 event) p10; fell 2. P-t-P/HUNT CH '97/8 and '03 r15 w7 (inc 2 2m5f110y-3m2f Hunt Chses, Mixed Open, and inc 4-timer '98) p5 (3 2nds, beaten head once, and of 3 once, inc 2 Hunt Chses; and 2 3rds in Hunt Chses, of 4 once); 4th twice, and fell 1. One of the top rated six-year-olds in '98, and went on to win four of his first five completions under Rules, but gained his last three wins in headgear, and had not scored since '00 until coaxed home by Charlotte Tizzard twice last year. Ran well for as long as stamina held in the Cheltenham Foxhunters, but foiled by Canal Turn at Aintree, and typically faded away when pressure was applied on his last two starts. Acts in soft ground and has done most of his winning in sub-3m trips, but will probably have to return to Points in order to score again. Wears blinkers. *Mrs B. Millard — Blackmore & Sparkford V. (Paul Nicholls).* 241 (2m4f110yH), 543 (3m2f110yH), 732 (2m5f110yH), 1168 (2m5fH), 1299 (2m4f110yH).

IRILUT (FR) ..9-10.. 9 br.g. Lute Antique (FR) — Patchourie (FR) (Taj Dewan) 2pp3. Compact. P-t-P '02/3 r7 w3 (Club Maiden, Club Restricted and Intermediate) p4 (2nds, beaten neck once). Successful on near extremes of going when recording a hat-trick last year, but in a virus hit yard in '04, and missed the first two in a Point for the first time when blinkered at Kingston Blount. Clearly not himself but had looked slightly suspect when surrendering tamely once last year, and nagging doubts about his resolve remain. Wears a cross-noseband. *R. Waley-Cohen — Warwicks.* 93 (O), 177 (3mH), 1172 (3m1f110yH), 1332 (Cf).

IRISH PADDY (IRE) .9-8.. 6 b.g. Idris (IRE) — Ceili Queen (IRE) (Shareef Dancer USA) 3p522f. Sturdy. Dam won 10f race, and won 3 Hurdles (2m-3m1f) and 2m6f Chase in Ireland. IR4200f, IR5000y, 9000 2yo. FLAT '01 r2 p0 (last 2). NH '02/3 r7 p0; pulled up 2. Blinkered and tailed off last in both flat races, and beaten a minimum of 29 lengths over Hurdles, including Sellers (pulled up on his final two attempts). Benefited from a drop to Maiden Points and was only overwhelmed in the closing stages by Flat Stanley at Easingwold, and seemed as if he was going to get off the mark eventually, but fell on a return visit and injured his shoulder, so likely to be on the sick list for a while. *W. Brown — Sinnington (Ian Brown).* 167 (OMa), 266 (M), 392 (CfMa), 959 (OMa), 1158 (OMa), 1300 (OMa).

IRISH SEA (USA) ..9-12.. 12 b.g. Zilzal (USA) — Dunkellin (USA) (Irish River FR) uup3. Small neat half-brother to 3 flat and Hurdles winners in USA, and to Hurdles winner, Green Card (USA). Dam won in USA. FLAT '96, '99 and '01 r17 w1 (15f) p4. NH '97/9, '01 and '03 r28 w4 (2m1f110y-2m3f110y Hdles) p5 (3 2nds); pulled up 5, on floor 3. P-t-P/HUNT CH '02/3 (for Mr G. Byard) r11 w1 (2m7f Hunt Ch, 3-finished) p3 (3rds in Hunt Ch); 4th twice, 6th, fell 2, and pulled up 2. Very busy in '99 but absent the following year, and has been lightly raced since, but a specialist over sub-3m trips, and has never looked like winning a Point. Can be clumsy and soon saw the back of Catherine Adam, but retains enough ability to register another success if connections can find the right race. Acts on any going. Blinkered twice to '97, and tried in cheekpieces last year. *Mrs S. Bowman & G. Adam — Southdown & Eridge.* 246 (L), 536 (CfL), 781 (L), 899 (L).

IRONBRIDGE ..8-13.. 10 gr.g. Scallywag — Bahama (Bali Dancer) 3. Enormous rangy tubed brother to Lydebrook (fell/unseated in 5 of 7 Points for John Wilson — rider was most insecure but horse had ability). Dam, half-sister to Rouse About (*qv* '93 Annual), fell in a Point in '91. NH FLAT '01 r1 p0. NH '01 and '03 (from M. Mullineaux's) r2 p0 (pulled up 2). P-t-P/HUNT CH '02/3 (for Mr J.R. Wilson) r5 p3 (3rds, of 4 once and inc last once); 4th, and fell 1. Takes a fierce hold and can bowl along merrily for up to 2m4f, but gone in the wind, and guaranteed to be running on vapor at the business end. A typically hyperactive Scallywag, and stands his racing incredibly badly. Has two paddock handlers, and is taken to post early. *Miss K. Wood & Mrs M. Moore — Cheshire (Kelda Wood).* 96 (CfMa).

IRON N GOLD .9-10.. 13 b.g. Heights Of Gold — Southern Dynasty (Gunner B) 60. Tall half-brother to Hurdles winner, Miss Michelle and flat winner, Snow Blizzard. Dam won 4 flat (10-12f). FLAT '94/6 r13 w2 (12-13f) p1 (2nd). NH '95/8 and '00/3 r28 w5 (2 2m1f Hdles and 3 2m4f-2m5f Chses) p11 (inc 7 2nds); pulled up 3. The winner of seven races including one on the all-weather, and it was planned to retire him after the most recent in May '03 (made all at Uttoxeter in the final three victories), but revived a year later to give Rachel Powell some fun. She seemed nervous and never put him in the race in Hunter Chases, but was much more positive in a Newton Abbot Amateurs Selling Hurdle, and the old boy stuck his neck out to defy a famous villain. A good jumper, but only appeared once apiece in '98, '00 and '02 and missed '99 altogether, and apart from having been broken down twice he has also suffered from bleeding. Tried in a visor once. Has been called some names in the past, but an heroic old soldier on his day, and the jockey must love him to bits. *Mrs R.A. Powell — Hursley Hambledon (Brendan Powell).* 1168 (2m5fH), 1497 (3mH).

IRON TROOPER (IRE) ..8-8.. 7 ch.g. Glacial Storm (USA) — Iron Star (General Ironside) 26ppuf4f4. Half-brother to The Hucklebuck, Julies Joy (IRE) and Berewolf, and to Chasing winner, Steel Moss (IRE). NH '03 r2 p0. Five lengths second at Witton Castle in his first Maiden, and looked quite promising at that stage, but has done little more than crash his way into trouble since, and the only piece of comparable form was when he fell at the last when still holding a chance at Mordon on his penultimate appearance. Unimproved by blinkers twice. There are ground for thinking he might score eventually, but unsympathetically handled, and seems to resent it. *J. Wade — S. Durham.* 167 (OMa), 216 (OMa), 344 (2m4fOMa), 776 (CfMa), 813 (OMa), 1158 (OMa), 1292 (OMa), 1417 (OMa), 1475 (OMa).

IRO ORIGNY (FR) ..—§§.. 9 b.g. Saint Cyrien (FR) — Coralline (FR) (Iron Duke FR) 4upf. Compact well-made half-brother to French Chasing winner, Must Origny. FRENCH FLAT r2 p0. FRENCH NH '00 r4 p1 (2nd in Ch); fell 1. NH '00/3 (from Miss V. Williams's) r14 p2 (3rds inc Ch); pulled up 1, and refused to race 2. A sour frog who was a bad claim, and refused to race twice in his English career under Rules, and pulled himself up at halfway once and dumped Alan Phillips twice as well as finishing 35 lengths fourth in Points. Previously tongue-tied and reported to have a breathing problem. See Inthaar. *A. & J. Morris — N. Ledbury.* 229 (O), 360 (O), 696 (O), 1227 (Cf).

ISEFOUL DE BELLEVUE (FR) ..8-7.. 9 b.g. Useful (FR) — Frika (FR) (Kashneb FR) p5635. Lengthy quite attractive. IRISH NH FLAT '00 r3 p0. IRISH NH '00/2 r11 p1 (2nd); fell 1. NH '03 (for R.M. Stronge) r5 p0; pulled up 2, and unseated 1. Bought Ascot, Jun for 2380. A very poor performer, and was tailed off last but one twice, pulled up and unseated in Chases (including a Seller) in the previous yard. Still struggling in Maidens, and beaten a minimum of 15 lengths in them. Blinkered once and tongue-tied thrice under Rules. A safe ride, but the chances of his scoring are slim. *C. Horton — V.W.H. (Betty Crew).* 760 (OMa), 971 (OMa), 1075 (OMa), 1337 (OMa), 1518 (OMa).

ISHMA (IRE) ..—§§.. 14 b.g. Kambalda — Scat-Cat (Furry Glen) rprrp. Close-coupled brother to NH flat and jumping winner, Bramblehill Duke (IRE). NH '96/7 r8 p0 (pulled up 8, inc Sell Hdle, and jumped badly in both Chses). P-t-P/HUNT CH '97/03 r55 w2 (Maiden and Members) p17 (9 2nds, last thrice; and inc last of 3 once); failed to finish 22 (on floor 4, refused 5, and ran out 1). The winner of three weak races on good or sound surfaces, but years of striving valiantly to contend with the owner-rider's inability to see a stride have taken their toll, and has become a serial stopper now. Should be retired before he is banned. Invariably blinkered. *D. Page, Ms S. Armstrong & M. Page — Ashford V. (Trevor Crawford).* 127 (R), 419 (CR), 606 (R), 648 (R), 807 (M).

IS WONDERFUL (USA) ..—.. 7 ch.g. Diesis — Falling In Love (IRE) (Sadler's Wells USA) ppp. Small hobdayed half-brother to 3 flat winners abroad (2 in USA and one in Japan). IR160,000y. FLAT '00/1 r9 w1 (14f) p3. NH '01 (for Mrs A.J. Perrett) r1 p1 (2nd). Bought Ascot, Jun for 1333. The very easy winner of a bad race at Yarmouth, but disappeared for three years after finishing second in his only Hurdle. Despite his having been tailed off and pulled up in his first two Opens connections went for a mammoth touch at Kingston Blount, but having been backed from 33-1 right down to 2-1 favourite he went lame when leading after two miles and had to be pulled up (the best laid plans of mice and men....). Wears a tongue-tie. Had he landed the coup, it really would have been rather outrageous. *J. Rudge — Croome & W. Warwicks (Jon Rudge).* 188 (O), 528 (O), 1515 (O).

ITALIAN CLOVER ..8-5.. 9 b.g. Michelozzo (USA) — National Clover (National Trust) pp455p. Workmanlike owner-bred half-brother to Four Leaf Clover, Welsh Clover, Mr Motivator and Scottish Clover, and to NH flat and top-class jumping winner, Go Ballistic, to NH flat winner, Mister Flint, and to Come On Clover (dam of Colonel Hook, *qv*). Dam, '84 Grand Marnier winner, won 27 Points, inc 24 Ladies and an Open, and placed 20. Grandam, Clover Bud, won Welsh Grand National and 6 other Chses (3-4m) and 9 Points. P-t-P '02/3 (for Mr M.H. Ings) r12 w2 (2m5f Maiden and Members p2 (neck last of 2 once); pulled up 5, and on floor 3. NH '03 (from Mrs H. Dalton's) r3 p0 (last, and pulled up 2). Asserted in the closing stages when recording a double last year, but runs tubed, and not better than last in nine subsequent attempts. Beaten 65 lengths in his Members, and not worth training again. Has been tried in blinkers, and acquired cheekpieces on his last two starts. *M.H. Ings — S. Flook — Radnor & W. Herefords (Andrew Dalton).* 530 (R), 740 (R), 819 (R), 1022 (R), 1226 (M), 1388 (R).

ITCHEN MILL ..9-10.. 8 b.m. Alflora (IRE) — Treble Chance (Balinger) 1fpu*p*. Sturdy. Dam, half-sister to Sun Of Chance (*qv* '01 Annual), won 8 Points and placed 24 (inc 11 NH). NH FLAT '03 r1 p0. NH '03 r3 p0. NH '04 (for R.H. Alner) r1 p0 (pulled up in 3m Hdle: *a bhnd, t.o when pu 4 out*). Produced her first worthwhile form when a well backed favourite in a Mares Maiden at Barbury, where Tom Dreaper (on his first British success, having had six previously in Ireland), had to survive a bad blunder at the eighth. Speedy (headstrong), but her tendency to make deplorable errors has prevented her from completing the course in four attempts since including a Hurdle in the latest. Wasted an ideal opportunity in a three-runner Restricted in which she unseated at the 11th and the winner finished alone, and is hardly inspiring confidence at present. *R. & Mrs V. Harrison — Portman (Sally Alner).* 35 (CMam), 232 (R), 498 (R), 939 (R).

ITS A HANDFULL .8-2§.. 12 b.g. Itsu (USA) — Star Part (West Partisan) p4dp4u2. Tiny brother to Start It Up. Dam, half-sister to Starember Lad and Newstarsky (*qv* '98 Annual), won 2-finisher Maiden and 3rd twice for Joe Price. P-t-P '98/00 and '02/3 r21 w2 (Maiden and 3-runner Members) p3 (3rds, of 4 once and last twice); failed to finish 14 (unseated 1, refused 1, and ran out 2). Lucky to have unearthed two shocking events, and regularly tailed off in the 15 Restricteds he has contested, but nearly stumbled across another simple opportunity at Lydstep which was markedly slower than both the concluding Maidens. Prone to make mistakes, and acquired a tongue-tie in '04. *J.J.E. Price — Curre & Llangibby.* 357 (R), 1022 (R), 1191 (R), 1322 (R), 1482 (R), 1523 (R).

IT'SALLINTHESTARS (IRE) ..—.. 6 b.g. Fourstars Allstar (USA) — Vita Veritas (Linacre) p. Compact half-brother to Heart Of Avondale (IRE), and to NH flat and jumping winner, Falmouth Bay (IRE). Dam, half-sister to Borleagh Pilot (*qv* '02 Annual), won NH flat and 4 Hdles (2m-2m2f) in Ireland. Schooled for two miles before pulling up in a May Restricted. Will probably do better in time. *Mrs S.R.W. Howlett & Ms S. Fryer — Dunston H. (Nigel Bloom).* 1217 (R).

ITSALLUPINTHEAIR ..9-9.. 9 b.g. Lion Cavern (USA) — Flora Wood (IRE) (Bob Back USA) pp3. Good-bodied. Dam is half-sister to Gabish (*qv* '96 Annual). P-t-P '02/3 r4 w2 (Maiden and Restricted) p1 (last of 3); and fell 1. Won weak races on good and sound surfaces last year, but then took a crashing fall next time, and has made no impression since. Possibly not right, but beaten out of sight when last of three in a weak Open at Lydstep, and failed to reappear. Has been taken to post early. Wears a cross-noseband. *Miss A. Meakins & L. Sloyan — Carms (Amanda Meakins).* 50 (I), 365 (I), 951 (O).

ITSDIGITALIS ..9-0.. 12 b.m. Itsu (USA) — Miss Foxglove (Tom Noddy) pp. Small. Dam, a very small half-sister to Itscinders (*qv* '03 Annual), was very remote 3rd in 2 Maidens (beat one horse). P-t-P '00 and '02/3 r9 p2 (2nd of 3 and 3rd of 4); 5th, and pulled up 6. Four lengths third in a bad Maiden at Ystradowen last year, but otherwise a very weak finisher, and appeared to suffer a setback there in '04. *C.W. Banwell — Ystrad Taf Fechan.* 699 (CfMa), 736 (CfMa).

ITSFORU ..9-0.. 13 b.g. Itsu (USA) — Game Trust (National Trust) uuf4. Strong compact half-brother to Bankit. Dam won 6 Points and 2 Hunt Chses (2m4f-2m6f) and placed 12 for late Colin Nash, and Itsforu is named in his memory. P-t-P/HUNT CH '98/02 r19 w2 (Maiden and Restricted) p6 (3 2nds, last once; and inc last of 3, and inc 3rd in Hunt Ch); pulled up 3, fell/unseated 5. Formerly a fair performer but dogged by ill luck and jumping lapses in equal measure, and has not scored since '99. Well supported on both visits to Kingston Blount in '04, but fell on the first circuit once, and faded tamely when tried in blinkers next time, and looks finished now. *Mrs S. Nash — O. Berks (Matt Hazell).* 381 (O), 717 (Cf), 1336 (I), 1514 (Cf).

IT'S MISSY IMP ..9-12.. 6 ch.m. Fearless Action (USA) — Swordella (Broadsword USA) 1432. Dam won Club Maiden and Restricted and placed 2 for Andy Martin. Gave a game display when passing three rivals from the third last to win over 2m4f at Cottenham on her debut, and has been running well since. Favourite for a Larkhill Restricted and should have scored easily, but jumped and hung badly left, and threw away far more lengths than the three she was eventually beaten. Ended with a commendable second at Woodford when going the other way round, and is likely to be back in the winners enclosure before long. *Mr & Mrs A.J. Martin — Heythrop (Andy Martin).* 104 (2m4fOMa), 294 (R), 459 (R), 1069 (R).

ITS MR BLOBBY ..—.. 9 b.g. Itsu (USA) — Lady Forrester (Official) pppp. Good-topped. Dam, half-sister to Itscinders (*qv* '03 Annual), was 3rd twice in Maidens for John Jones, and grandam, Ambley Wood, won 2 Points and placed 7 (including 2nd of 3 in Nov Hdle, and bad 3rd in Nov Ch). P-t-P '03 r2 p0 (pulled up 1, and fell 1). Well named, and has carried too much condition to date, but revved up by the application of cheekpieces at Rhydygwern, and was second-favourite for a bad race next time, but pulled up with the suspicion of a problem after two miles. Wears a cross-noseband. *J. Jones — Gelligaer F. (John Moore).* 620 (OMa), 1318 (M), 1488 (OMa), 1553 (OMa).

ITSMYTURNNOW (IRE) ..10-0.. 10 b.g. Glacial Storm (USA) — Snuggle (Music Boy) 037. Tall strong-topped. Dam, half-sister to Peanuts Pet (*qv* 2001 Annual), won at 5f, and won 4 Hdles on all-weather (2m-2m2f). NH '03 r2 p0. P-t-P/HUNT CH '01/3 r9 w3 (inc 3m2f Hunt Ch) p3 (2 2nds; and 3rd in Hunt Ch); 6th of 7, pulled up 1 and fell 1. NH '04 r1 p0 (7th in 2m5f110y Ch: *prom, ld 7-9 & 11-12, wknd app 2 out, t.o*). Firing on all cylinders when successful on three occasions last year, but three other campaigns have yielded a mere five appearances, and his tendency to jump badly away to the left remains. Ran well for a long way at Aintree, but seems unable to handle too much cut in the ground, and needs watching when he reappears. *M.J. Roberts — E. Sussex & Romney Marsh.* 732 (2m5f110yH), 1052 (O).

IT'S NORMAN ..—.. 9 b.g. Vantastic — Arrogant Daughter (Aragon) 4pppp. Small neat owner-bred. FLAT '99 r1 p0 (last). NH '99 (for T.R. Watson) r1 p0 (last). Last in a Seller on the flat and a Hurdle in '99, but did have one behind him in a Maiden. This personal triumph was not sustained, and pulled up in all four subsequent attempts (jumped left once, when 100-1 in a Hunter Chase) and ended up being collected by the horse ambulance at Thorpe. A waste of time. *R.P. Brett — Belvoir (Laura Pomfret).* 113 (OMa), 304 (OMa), 444 (2mH), 680 (M), 946 (OMa).

IT'SNOTSIMPLE (IRE) ..10-4.. 13 b.m. Homo Sapien — Perpetue (Proverb) 3533131. Sturdy compact half-sister to Irish NH flat and Chasing winner, Lucky Bust (IRE). IRISH NH FLAT '97 r2 p0. IRISH P-t-P '96/7 r3 w1 (2-finisher 5yo Maiden) p1 (2nd in match); and pulled up 1. NH '97/8 r7 p0 (last and pulled up 3 in Hdles, inc Sell; and 4th of 5, last, and pulled up in Chses). P-t-P/HUNT CH '99/03 r31 w6 (inc Open) p9 (7 2nds, dead-heated once); pulled up 11, slipped up 1. A safe jumper, and does well when conditions aren't testing, but easy to beat in competitive events, and has been seen to swish her tail. Recorded her third success at Lifton on her latest appearance, and has also scored thrice at Wadebridge, but will do well to run up to her present rating in '05. Wears a cross-noseband, and has been tried tongue-tied. *Mrs S.D. Messer-Bennetts — N. Cornwall (Becky Kennen).* 76 (M), 311 (L), 483 (Cf), 707 (Cf), 908 (Cf), 1130 (Cnr), 1350 (L).

ITS-ON-THE-CARDS (IRE) ..10-0.. 11 gr.g. House Of Cards — Summerello (Bargello) 3p. Good-bodied half-brother to Warm Relation (IRE). NH FLAT '98/9 r2 p0. NH '99/01 r18 p1 (2nd); pulled up 1, and fell/unseated 2. P-t-P '02 (for Mrs R. Atkinson) r12 w1 (Maiden) p5 (2 3rds, of 4 once, and 2 fncs last once); last 2, pulled up 2, and fell/unseated 2. His previous campaign ended in tragic circumstances when a fall at Dunstall Park resulted in the death of his owner-rider, and met his own demise at Market Rasen. A very sad tale indeed. P.M. Walker — S. Wold. 54 (C), 301 (R).

IT'S-THE-BIZ (IRE) .—.. 11 b.g. King's Ride — Deep Adventure (Deep Run) pp. Small narrow hobdayed half-brother to Tisanes Venture, to Irish Hurdles winner, Deep C Diva (IRE), and to Irish winners, My Sunny Glen and Windgap Hill (both NH flat and Hurdles), My Sunny Way (Hurdles) and Divided Opinion (NH flat). IRISH NH FLAT '99 r1 p1 (7*l* 2nd). IRISH NH '99 r2 p0 (pulled up in Chses). IRISH P-t-P '99/00 r2 w1 (5&6yo Maiden) p0; and pulled up 1. P-t-P '01/3 (for Mrs L.J. Young (The Chase Club) r8 p4 (2 3rds, of 4 once); pulled up 4. Made an impressive winning debut in Ireland, and rated 9-13 when returning to something like his best last year, but has a wind infirmity and finds nothing off the bridle, and very uninspiring under the new owner-rider in '04. Blinkered once in '02. Wears a cross-noseband. *D.P. Summersby — Lamerton (Emma Boone).* 200 (Cf), 324 (R).

ITSTHEBRASS ..7-7.. 9 b.m. Goldsmiths' Hall — Gold And Brass (IRE) (Lancastrian) pp5. NH FLAT '00/1 r3 p0. P-t-P '03 r4 p0 (fell/unseated 3, and brought down 1). Beaten more than a fence when finally coaxed into completing by Philip York at Detling, but eliminated by halfway in four previous ventures, and usually dumbfounded at the sight of a fence. Perhaps her clear round will have instilled some confidence at long last. *Mrs K. Crouch — E. Sussex & Romney Marsh (Alison Hickman).* 103 (OMa), 130 (OMa), 540 (CfMa).

ITWORKED ..10-1.. 10 b.g. Landyap (USA) — Workamiracle (Teamwork) ff. Strong topped half-brother to Beyondtherealm. Dam (*qv* '94 Annual), pulled up in a Hdle and failed to finish in 3 Points. Grandam, Armagnac Princess, won 3m3f Jeep/Christies Hunt Ch and 12 Points and 2nd 4 (inc 2 Hunt Chses), and subsequently won 5 Chses (3m1f-3m6f) and placed 6. NH FLAT '00 r1 p0. NH '01 r1 p0 (pulled up). P-t-P '03 r9 w2 (Maiden and 3-runner Intermediate) p3 (2 2nds, of 3 once); unseated 3, and pulled up 1. Made no appreciable errors when scoring twice on sound surfaces last year, but did manage to eject the rider thrice and both '04 ventures ended in crash landings. Not disgraced at Great Trethew, where he would have finished a distant last of three to Oneminutetofive but for the last fence, but lay winded for some time, and failed to reappear. *E.M. Treneer — Dartmoor.* 200 (Cf), 310 (O).

IVANS DREAM .9-5.. 11 gr.g. Silver Owl — Karaka (Good Times ITY) 2pp. Sturdy owner-bred brother to Treesmill Lad, and half-brother to Miltown Castle. P-t-P '00 and '02 r4 w1 (Maiden) p0; last, pulled up 1 and carried out 1. Benefited from a gentle introduction when landing a three-finisher Maiden at

Bratton Down under a strong ride from Leslie Jefford in '02, but promptly disappeared for 23 months, and another long spell of inactivity looks on the cards after suffering a setback at Lifton. *J.S. Papworth — Four Burrow.* 824 (R), 1132 (R), 1543 (R).

IVORY CROSS ..8-0.. 7 b.g. Muhtarram (USA) — Ivory Palm (USA) (Sir Ivor USA) fp6. Half-brother to flat winner, Tamara, and to Chasing winner, Tommy Carson. Dam won 2 flat (7-13f). Showed a first small glimmer of ability when 23 lengths sixth in a youngsters Maiden, and can possibly sneak close to the leaders in future. *T.R. Beadle — Bedale.* 342 (2m4fOMa), 768 (2m4fOMa), 1159 (OMa).

I WILL SURVIVE (IRE) ..9-6.. 10 ch.g. Good Thyne (USA) — Borgina (Boreen FR) p. Sturdy half-brother to Merry Shot (IRE) (*qv*). NH FLAT '99/00 r3 p0. NH '00/1 r2 p0; fell 1. P-t-P '03 r3 p1 (2nd); last, and pulled up 1. Only outpaced from the last when runner-up in an Ashorne Maiden last year, but has done nothing else to advertise his claims for success, and disappeared after the second Sunday in '04. *Mrs C.L. Goodinson — N. Hereford.* 15 (R).

IZZUTHEFOX (IRE) .8-13.. 8 b.g. Castle Keep — Tigrinium Splenden (Buckley) 34. Bought Doncaster, Nov for 2000. Ten lengths third over 2m4f on his debut, but seemed to do rather less well when 26 lengths last next time. A satisfactory jumper for a beginner, and may benefit from eligibility for elders Maidens in '05. *The Should Be Fun Group (C. Storey) — College V. & N. Northumberland (Clive Storey).* 856 (2m4fOMa), 1224 (OMa).

IZZYIZZENTY ..—.. 6 b.g. Myfontaine — More To Life (Northern Tempest USA) pp. Compact good-topped half-brother to flat winner, Will He Wish. Pulled up with half a mile left in Maidens, and wore an off-side pricker in the latest, but after being prominent at the 14th he stopped to nil. May be untrustworthy, but does not look anything like fit enough. *D.T. Todd — Burton (Louise Todd).* 890 (2m4fOMa), 1218 (OMa).

JABIRU (IRE) ..10-11§.. 12 b/br.g. Lafontaine (USA) — Country Glen (Furry Glen) 1p323261. Strong-topped rangy half-brother to Irish Hurdles winner, Sandra Louise. NH FLAT '97/8 r3 p1 (2nd). NH '98/9 r5 p2 (22-33*l* 3rds in Hdles). P-t-P/HUNT CH '00/3 r24 w11 (inc 5 2m7f110y-3m2f110y Hunt Chses, inc 4-timer in '02) p7 (5 2nds, inc 2 Hunt Chses); pulled up 1, and fell 2. The joint-fifth top-rated performer in '02, and began the season by farming his Members as usual, but much less convincing in victory than he used to be, and hangs and jumps markedly left-handed now. Needs to dominate and wears blinkers, but an unreliable betting proposition, and prone to making blunders though he rarely fails to complete. Has won in soft but at his best on sound surfaces, and despite his anti-clockwise inclinations has produced nine of his 13 wins on right-handed tracks. Enjoys racing at Newton Abbot, the scene of three of his other triumphs, and further trips there must be high on his agenda in '05. *Mrs K.M. Sanderson — Tiverton.* 114 (M), 178 (3m1f110yH), 347 (3mH), 631 (2m6f110yH), 993 (3mH), 1166 (2m5f110yH), 1453 (3m4fH), 1498 (3m2f110yH).

JACK HACKETT (IRE) ..9-9§§.. 13 b.g. Riberetto — View To Above (Lucifer USA) ppp1. Strong-topped compact. IRISH P-t-P '97/8 r4 p2 (20*l* last of 2, and 27*l* 3rd); fell 1. P-t-P '99 and '01/3 r10 w3 (Maiden — finished alone, Restricted and 3-finisher Members) p0; last pair 5, ran out 1 and pulled up 1. Galvanised by blinkers when recording a hat-trick on easy surfaces in '02, but a miserly and ungenuine old fecker, and only once better than last in his next seven starts. Stopped the rot in his Members, but hung badly left towards the runner-up on the flat and the third was done no favours as they converged, and was lucky that the stewards did not take a dim view of the manoeuvre. Apparently retired on the spot, and can spend the rest of his days chasing girls at the local Parochial House. *C.S. Hall, Mr & Mrs A.W. Cooper & Mrs P. Wilkins — Southdown & Eridge (Susanna Hall).* 19 (CMod), 41 (I), 124 (CCon), 605 (M).

JACKIE JARVIS (IRE) ..10-6§.. 8 b.m. Alphabatim (USA) — Miss Brantridge (Riboboy USA) 5251r212. Small sister to jumping winner, Agincourt (IRE). Dam won 3 2m-2m4f Sell Hdles. NH FLAT '01 r3 p0. P-t-P/HUNT CH '02/3 (for Miss E. Delaney) r11 w5 (inc 2m5f110y Hunt Ch and inc hat-trick '03) p4 (2nds, beaten ½*l* once); 5th of 6, and unseated 1. A decent mare when in the mood, and rapidly taking her winning tally towards double figures, but needs humouring and always liable to dig her toes in at the start. Took a liking to Eaton Hall (there's no accounting for taste) and scored twice there, but in a real strop at Leicester, and is largely unproven on easy surfaces. Likely to mop up in the North West providing no interlopers appear, but not one to take too short a price about. Wears a cross-noseband. *Mrs J.C.M. Wood — Cheshire (John Swindells).* 94 (L), 230 (L), 444 (2mH), 712 (L), 751 (L), 874 (L), 1146 (L), 1263 (L).

JACKOFALLTRADES (IRE) .8-3.. 7 b.g. Lord Americo — Wind Chimes (The Parson) u34up. Half-brother to Master Pangloss (IRE), and to an Irish Pointing winner. NH FLAT '03 r2 p0. NH '03 (for A.C. Whillans) r2 p0 (pulled up 2). Half-brother to three bad jumpers and out of a mare who pulled up in three of six Hurdles, and was tailed off in two bumpers and pulled up at 100-1 twice over Hurdles. Just about passable when making the frame in Maidens, but has declined again since, and there is very little to recommend him to date. *R. Robinson — Dumfries.* 137 (OMa), 215 (OMa), 342 (2m4fOMa), 767 (2m4fOMa), 1225 (OMa).

JACK OF KILCASH (IRE) ..9-0.. 11 br.g. Glacial Storm (USA) — Candora (Cantab) 5p45256p. Workmanlike compact half-brother to Oscail An Doras (IRE), to Irish Chasing winner, Doorslammer. Dam won Hunt race in Ireland. IRISH P-t-P '00/2 r12 p3 (pulled up 6, brought down 1, and unseated 1). P-t-P/HUNT CH '03 r7 w3 (Maiden, Restricted and Club nov rdrs, hat-trick) p1 (2nd); last pair 2, and unseated 1. Proved unsuited by mud in Ireland, and made all to complete a hat-trick on good or sound surfaces last year, but can be very clumsy and failed to cope with the rise in class in '04. The type to give up if he cannot dominate, and will find it hard to secure a fourth success. *N. Benstead — Kent & Surrey Bloodhounds.* 99 (I), 182 (CCon), 536 (CfL), 625 (L), 897 (Cfv&nr), 1212 (Cf), 1442 (2m5fH), 1516 (L).

JACKSON (FR) .10-6.. 8 b.g. Passing Sale (FR) — Tynia (FR) (Djarvis FR) 1u11u2. Compact well-made. NH FLAT '01/2 r3 p0. NH '03 r2 p0. A useful novice who was impressive when unbeaten in Points at up to Confined class (only faced by two rivals in that company at Sandon), but yet to translate his ability to Hunter Chases, and gave a very shoddy display of jumping before unseating in the first of them. His 28 lengths second at Chepstow is worthless, but there remains a chance that he can do better over the bigger obstacles eventually, and will again be difficult to beat between the flags. Often tongue-tied. *C.B. Brookes — Wheatland (Heather Dalton).* 256 (CMa), 377 (3m1fH), 665 (R), 852 (Cf), 1176 (3m110yH), 1294 (3mH).

JACKSON HILL ..9-8.. 12 b.g. Priolo (USA) — Orange Hill (High Top) 4p6p3. Good-bodied half-brother to Harding (*qv*). FLAT r5 w3 (7-10f) p0. P-t-P '00 and '02/3 r11 w2 (Mixed Open and Confined) p2 (2nds of 3); 4th twice, fell 2 and pulled up 3. A promising career on the flat was ended when he split a pastern at home, and spent four years in recuperation, but displayed plenty of speed when recording a double in the second half of the '02 season. Has never looked completely secure over fences, and occasionally finds nothing off the bridle, but only once better than last in '04, and will need to rediscover some enthusiasm to warrant an airing next year. Wears a cross-noseband, and has been tried tongue-tied. *T. Sprake — Blackmore & Sparkford V.* 234 (L), 322 (L), 350 (M), 602 (MO), 860 (Cf).

JACK'S THE BOY (IRE) ..7-13.. 7 b.g. Topanoora — Foxy Fairy (IRE) (Fairy King USA) 4f. Sturdy half-brother to flat winners, Sulu, Sunridge Fairy (IRE) (also won five Hurdles), and to a winner in Turkey. IRISH NH FLAT '03 (for T.E. Hyde) r2 p0. Bought Doncaster, May for 5000. Tried the shorter options in both attempts, but faded rapidly and became very tired after leading for a long way when 18 lengths fourth, and then fell when dropping right out of contention. Of very suspect stamina on the evidence to date. *G. Roberts & Mrs B. Smith — Albrighton (Graham Harris).* 618 (2m4fOMa), 850 (2m5fOMa).

JACK THE BEAR (IRE) ..9-7.. 11 b/br.g. Un Desperado (FR) — Vale Of Peace (Wolver Hollow) 755p. Very tall rangy half-brother to NH flat and Hurdles winner, Ben Cruachan (IRE), an Irish flat and Hurdling winner, and a French jumping winner. IRISH P-t-P '99 r1 w1 (4&5yo Maiden). NH '00/2 (for P.F. Nicholls) r10 w2 (3m2f-3m3f Chses) p6; fell 1. Beat The Bushkeeper and Ardmayle who both went on to enjoy a decent measure of success in England in a babies Maiden in Ireland, and then sold for a high price. Managed to win a couple of staying Chases in the mud and fell on the only occasion he missed the frame under Rules, but was disappointing on balance and very one-paced. Missed '03, and having proved slow in Points he ended the season with an apparent setback. Doubtless too big for his own comfort. *Miss C.L. Tuffin — Blackmore & Sparkford V.* 199 (L), 496 (MO), 603 (Cnr), 690 (L).

JACOB'S CHOICE ..9-8.. 6 b.g. Bonny Scot (IRE) — Clare's Choice (Pragmatic) 1pp2. Unfurnished half-brother to Hurdles winner, Nick's Choice and Lucky Pet. Bought Ascot, Jul for 1047. A cheap purchase who was smartly off the blocks when winning a feeble Maiden at Higham in January, but disappointing on his next two attempts. Probably under a cloud and was given a two month break, and returned with a better effort at Hackwood, where he only gave best on the run-in. A Restricted at least should be on the cards in '05, and may raise his rating further. *I. Cobbold — Staff College (Phillip York).* 27 (OMa), 44 (R), 159 (R), 973 (R).

JAG ..8-0.. 8 b.m. Lord David S (USA) — Berlinetta (Balinger) 6p. Half-sister to Landrover. A remote sixth on her debut, and tailed off and pulled up at halfway after jumping right next time. Seems to need her tracking adjusted. *R. Harraway — Beaufort.* 884 (OMa), 1074 (OMa).

JAKES PROGRESS (IRE) ..7-7.. 11 b.g. Jolly Jake (NZ) — Coteri Run (Deep Run) 3p. Tall good-bodied brother to Student Night (IRE), and Irish jumping winner, Runaway Jake. Dam won Irish NH flat. IR22,000 4yo. NH FLAT '00 r2 p0. NH '00/2 (for L. Lungo) r8 w1 (2m1f Hdle) p2 (short-headed once); pulled up 1. The fluke winner of a Selling Hurdle (was disputing sixth lengths third when left in front before the last), but also managed a short head second in a 20-runner affair. Fourth and pulled up in Chases before missing '03, and revived for a couple of insipid efforts in Confineds (last of three and over a fence behind after blundering at the final obstacle once). Barely stays two miles, so is in the wrong job. *G.G. & L. Lewis — Pentyrch.* 1023 (Cf), 1320 (Cf).

JALCANTO .10-0.. 15 ch.g. Jalmood (USA) — Bella Canto (Crooner) 15. Tall rangy half-brother to 5 flat winners (one in Belgium), including Tingle Bell (also a successful Hurdler). Dam won 4 flat, 8-10f. FLAT '92/6 r26 w2 (8-16f, inc Sell) p6. NH '94/8 r15 w4 (2m1f-2m6f Hdles, inc hat-trick '95) p5 (inc 2nd in Ch); pulled up 2, and unseated 1 in other Chses. P-t-P/HUNT CH '99/00 and '02/3 (for Mr T.M. Hayes) r15 w6 (inc 2 Opens and Mixed Open) p7 (5 2nds, beaten neck once; and inc 3rd in Hunt Ch); 4th and unseated. Never runs much and avoids easy surfaces, but retains plenty of ability, and despite being prone to clumsy mistakes has an exemplary record in Points. Has a never say die attitude, and battled on gamely from what seemed a hopeless position to pip Ashwell Boy in his Members, but never at the races at Cothelstone, and starting to lose his speed. Tends to sweat excessively. Wears a cross-noseband. *J. Rudge — Croome & W. Warwicks.* 976 (M), 1365 (Cnr).

JAMES DRUMMOND ..—.. 6 b.g. Shaddad (USA) — Miss Drummond (The Brianstan) uu. Half-brother to flat winner, Molly Drummond (later won in Denmark). Dam won 2 flat, 5-6f. FLAT '02/3 (for B. Mactaggart) r4 p0; last 3. Terrible on the flat (15th of 17 once and last thrice; started slowly twice), and completely tailed off when losing his partner at the 13th in a couple of Maidens. *R. MacDonald & T. White — Jedforest (Robert MacDonald).* 216 (OMa), 510 (OMa).

JAMES PINE (IRE) .—.. 6 b.g. Jamesmead — Princess Astrid (IRE) (Mandalus) pf. Bought Doncaster, Aug for 2500. Pulled up after a mile (looked awful) and fell at halfway when struggling (unseated and ran amok in the paddock) in May Maidens. Pining to be anywhere other than Market Harborough, probably. *P.J. Millington — Fernie.* 1403 (2m4fOMa), 1504 (2m4fOMa).

JAMES VICTOR (IRE) ..9-7.. 7 b.g. Be My Guest (USA) — Antakiya (IRE) (Ela-Mana-Mou) f. Light-framed half-brother to seven times French flat winner, Nippon Pillow Cool, and to a German flat winner. Dam won at 8f in France. NH '03 (for C.R. Egerton) r1 p0. Chased a lunatic until left clear at the tenth in a February Maiden, and was still just in front but tiring rapidly when he fell three out. Badly winded, and probably thoroughly shaken by the whole experience. *B.R. Burke — Quantock (Elsie Mitchell).* 238 (CfMa).

JAMIE BROWNE (IRE) ..8-13.. 8 ch.g. Sayaarr (USA) — Glowing Embers (Nebbiolo) f. Tall rangy. Dam, half-sister to Home Pool (*qv* '95 Annual), won 3 Irish flat, 7-10f (was useful). P-t-P/HUNT CH '02/3 r8 w1 (2m5f Maiden) p2; 4th, last, and pulled up 3. Won a two-finisher short Maiden on firm at Ayr last year, but hung like a gate when tailed off last on his Hunter Chase debut next time, and tipped up at halfway on home ground on his only appearance in '04. Gone in the wind, and is now tubed, and wears bandages in front. *W.G. Young — Lanarks & Renfrews.* 653 (M).

JAUNTY JANNER ..8-11.. 9 ch.g. Shaab — Strumpetus (Bold As Brass) 45p. Tall strong-topped brother to Hendra Chieftain. Dam won 3 Points and placed 10 for David Congdon (rated 9-0; only fell once in 8 seasons, and 'sometimes able to take advantage of incredibly bad opponents'). Grandam, Crumpetus, was a poor Pointer, but great-grandam, Muffin II, won 2 Points. P-t-P '03 r4 p0 (last 3, and pulled up). Ran passably when around ten lengths fourth on firmish at Great Trethew, but normally fades into obscurity, and needs to improve to make an impact in Maidens. *D.G. Congdon — Four Burrow (Stephen Long).* 312 (CfMa), 486 (OMa), 1272 (OMa).

JAY MAN (IRE) .—.. 15 ch.g. Remainder Man — Pas-de Jay (Pas De Seul) uu. Close-coupled flashy half-brother to Hurdles winner, Ma Petite Rouge (IRE) IRISH P-t-P '00 r1 p1 (2nd). IRISH FLAT '96 and '98 r5 p0. IRISH NH FLAT '96 r5 w1 p1 (3rd). IRISH NH '96/8 (for E.J. Kearns) r8 w1 (2m Hdle) p4; fell 1. Won a couple of races in Ireland in '96 but went very quiet after '98, and apart from finishing second in an Open in which he jumped well he had not been on the racecourse for six years until he surprisingly turned up in a couple of Hunter Chases at 14. Dumped the rider after blunders in both, and will surely be in permanent retirement now. *J. Saville — Pendle Forest & Craven.* 444 (2mH), 678 (3m1fH).

JAZZ NIGHT ..10-4.. 8 b.g. Alhijaz — Hen Night (Mummy's Game) Rp6216. Good-topped. 2600f, 2000y. FLAT '99/00 r4 p0. NH '01/2 (for N.A. Twiston-Davies) r4 p1 (2nd). Temperamental on the flat and refused to enter the stalls and withdrawn once as well as being blinkered twice, and again looked dodgy in his only Point, in which he crashed through the wing of the fifth with Julian Pritchard (favourite). Did not look a likely candidate for Hunter Chases, but twice went well for James Jenkins over the minimum trip, and after finishing one-and-a-half lengths second at Leicester (33-1) he scored in a very lowly contest at Hereford despite hanging left under pressure in the closing stages and taking the runner-up with him on the flat. There is no evidence that he stays any further, and connections must be congratulated on winning a £2,204 prize with him. *The Berryman Lycett Experience (P. Berryman) — N. Ledbury (Shaun Lycett).* 53 (2m4fOMa), 241 (2m4f110yH), 345 (2m5fH), 444 (2mH), 734 (2mH), 1173 (2m110yH).

JD TROUT ..8-5.. 6 ch.m. Keen — Rosa Trout (Goldhill) up5. Sturdy close-coupled half-sister to jumping winner, Rising Trout. Dam won 2m Hurdle and 7 Points (inc 5 Ladies) and placed 16. Bought Doncaster, Aug for 2600. Completed for the first time when 20 lengths last at Trebudannon, and may be able to advance in the right direction at six. *Lady Earle — Silverton.* 12 (OMa), 307 (2m4fOMa), 909 (2m4fOMa).

JELALI (IRE) ..9-1.. 12 b.g. Last Tycoon — Lautreamont (Auction Ring USA) 0. Lengthy half-brother to a winner in Japan. Dam won 2 French flat, 9-11f. FLAT r10 p1 (11/ 3rd). NH '96/9 r10 w1 (2m3f Hdle) p1 (3rd); remote 5th, pulled up, and fell in Chses; Sell Hdle final. P-t-P/HUNT CH '00 and '02/3 r5 p2 (3rd of 4 once); 4th, last, and pulled up 1. Won his hurdling debut back in '96, but hit an immediate snag, and was tongue-tied latterly under Rules. Boasts a couple of minor placings in Points, but unproven beyond 2m4f, and has become incredibly lightly raced. Blinkered once in '99. *Mrs T. Moore — Cheshire (Colin Moore).* 529 (L).

JEMANNETTE .9-2.. 8 ch.m. Almoojid — Auto Elegance (Brave Shot) 34p. Lengthy well-made owner-bred sister to Chopes Bridge, and half-sister to Jameswick, Country Gem and Russlers Rob. Dam won at 6f. P-t-P '03 r4 p0 (last 2, pulled up and fell). Not entirely disgraced when completing, but a weak finisher and not better than last, and appeared to suffer a setback at Buckfastleigh. *W.R. Britton — S. Tetcott.* 82 (OMa), 308 (2m4fOMa), 493 (OMa).

JEMARO (IRE) ..10-9.. 14 b.g. Tidaro (USA) — Jeremique (Sunny Way) p1521R21. Close-coupled half-brother to Paco's Boy. Dam, half-sister to Fixed Price (*qv* '90 Annual), won at 2m in Ireland. NH FLAT '96/7 r3 p0 (withdrawn under orders once — bolted). NH '97/01 r32 w6 (2m4f-3m Chses) p4 (3 3rds); pulled up 5, and fell/unseated 5. P-t-P/HUNT CH '02/3 r8 w3 (3m Hunt Ch and 2 Opens) p2 (3rds in Hunt Chses); pulled up 2, and fell 1. A bold-jumping front-runner, and difficult to peg back over an easy three miles, but vulnerable on courses with an uphill finish, and benefits from the presence of leading riders. Clocked an amazing time at Chaddesley, which suits him admirably, and is rated accordingly, but has always been liable to make mistakes over big fences, and does not appreciate being taken on for the lead. Very enthusiastic, and tends to boil over on occasions, but showing no signs of slowing, and despite having tweaked a tendon in '02 copes very well with firm ground. *J. Beasley & R. Mapp - Albrighton (Caroline Robinson).* 93 (O), 254 (O), 346 (3m1f110yH), 836 (O), 1145 (O), 1367 (O), 1471 (O), 1529 (MO).

JENKO (FR) ..9-6.. 8 b.g. Cadoubel (FR) — Maika D'Ores (FR) (Gaur) 33. Plain lengthy. FRENCH FLAT r1 w1 (12f). NH '00 and '02 (for M.C. Pipe, and M. Todhunter) r6 p0; pulled up 1. Won a Provinces race for non-thoroughbreds at Paray-Le-Monial but lightly raced since arriving in England and has only shown bits and bobs of minor form. Beaten 19 lengths plus in Points, and only one horse finished behind him. A hard puller who can make bad blunders, and has been tried tongue-tied. Probably has more ability than he is willing to show. *Mrs K. Cox — Taunton V. (Geoffrey Cox).* 961 (M), 1384 (Cf).

JENNY'S CHARMER ..9-6.. 12 ch.g. Charmer — Jenny Wyllie (Nishapour FR) 233f. Strong. FLAT '95/6 r9 p1 (3rd). NH '99/00 (for Mrs H. Mobley) r7 p1 (2nd). Blinkered once and last of three once on the flat, and finished second in a Hurdle, but has multiple gap years, and absent for a total of five before he took up Pointing aged 11. In front over the final fence at both Thorpe (beaten three-quarters-of-a-length) and Chaddesley (steadied at the obstacle and weakened to be beaten three lengths), but a poor last next time, and fell heavily three out when contesting the lead at Guilsborough. Deserves a little win, but his jumping has been rather a problem, and despite his lack of experience is now in the veteran stage. *D.E. Wilson — Bicester with Whaddon.* 113 (OMa), 258 (CMa), 370 (OMa), 788 (CfMa).

JENTAR EQUILIBRA (IRE) .9-13.. 13 b.m. Miner's Lamp — Cora Gold (Goldhill) p14. Good-topped half-sister to Hurdles winner, West Monkton, and to Irish Pointing winners, By Golly and Spancilhill Melody. Dam is half-sister to Andros Gale (*qv* '99). NH FLAT '98 r1 p0. NH '98 and '01 r6 w3 (2m110y-2m1f Hdles) p0. P-t-P '00 and '03 r4 w1 (Maiden) p2 (2nds); and pulled up. A dual winner on extremes of going at Bratton Down, and recorded a wide margin hat-trick over hurdles for Paul Nicholls in '01, but has always been very hard to keep sound, and unfortunately finished lame when a well backed favourite for her Members. Should make a cracking broodmare. *R.M. Woollacott — Tiverton Stag (Emely Thompson).* 117 (C), 1506 (C), 1554 (M).

JEROME JEROME .9-2§.. 13 b.g. Arctic Lord — Polaris Song (True Song) ppp4p36p. Small unfurnished. Dam is half-sister to Carrick Castle. Grandam, Polaris Royal (half-sister to Spartan Missile (*qv* '86 Annual) failed to finish four Points. Great-grandam, Polaris Missile, won 4m National Hunt Ch, a Hunt Ch and 2 Points. Great-great-grandam, Air Wedding, won 4 Points and a Ch. NH '98/00 r3 p1 (2nd); last 2. P-t-P/HUNT CH '97/8 and '01/3 (for Mr A.P. Gent since '01) r24 w1 (Maiden) p7 (5 2nds, remote once, and of 3 thrice; and inc last of 3); pulled up 8, ran out 2, unseated 1, and brought down 1. Thoroughly ungenuine and previous connections must have had a soft spot for him as they entertained him for three years without success. Does still retain some ability, but loses interest very quickly if unable to get his own way, and has never been a fluent jumper. Wears headgear. *M. & P. Smith — B. Dowling — Puckeridge (Mick Clark).* 127 (R), 223 (I), 375 (R), 466 (Cf), 648 (R), 786 (O), 1216 (4m100yMO), 1362 (3m6f110yH).

JERROBOAM (FR) ..9-2.. 8 b.g. Luchiroverte (IRE) — Banouda (FR) (Crin Noir II FR) 2. NH FLAT '02 r1 p0. NH '02 r2 p0; pulled up 1. Unfancied in just four races to date, including when 15 lengths second in a Howick Restricted. The form is worth almost nothing, and appears to be virtually impossible to train. *Hon Mrs S. Sherwood — Clifton-on-Teme.* 358 (R).

JE SUIS (IRE) ..8-3.. 9 b.m. Le Bavard (FR) — La Tortue (Lafontaine USA) pp2. Compact half-sister to Without The Agent (IRE), and to Irish Hurdles winner, The Tippler (IRE). Dam, half-sister to Rich Remorse (*qv* '88 Season Annual). Great-grandam, Kerolite, was placed in 2 Maidens. IR4000 4yo. NH FLAT '01/2 r3 p0. NH '02/3 (for B.J. Eckley) r2 p0; last pair 2. Only seen eight times in four years, and looked useless when pulled up in her first two Maidens, but at least achieved a placing when two-and-a-half lengths second of three at Flete Park (received plenty of reminders on the way round, and survived a bad blunder at the 16th). Certainly not the big I Am on form to date. *Miss R. Matheson & Mrs G. Windsor — N. Cornwall (Ian Hambley).* 704 (CfMa), 795 (CfMa), 1200 (OMa).

JETHRO TULL (IRE) ..9-6.. 6 b.g. Witness Box (USA) — Country Project (IRE) (Project Manager) p21p. Gave a couple of good displays for a first season five-year-old, when finishing second after holding every chance at the last at Hornby Castle, and when scoring at Welbeck, both over 2m4f. Had a lay off and did not seem at his peak when reviving for one Restricted, but can make amends in similar company. Almost certainly under-rated by several pounds. By the same sire Atticus Finch, a flighty Pointer at the beginning for these connections but sometimes useful in Handicap Chases since. *Mrs M.K. Stirk — W. of Yore.* 211 (C), 344 (2m4fOMa), 597 (2m5fOMa), 1310 (R).

JEUNE PREMIER (FR) ..9-10.. 8 ch.g. Jeune Homme (USA) — Misaine (FR) (Saint Cyrien FR) ff4f1f. Dam prolific winner at up to 12f in France (10 victories inc Listed race). Ff360,000y. FLAT '99/00 r10 p0; last 2. NH '00 (for D. Burchell) r3 p0; pulled up 1. Unplaced 13 times flat and Hurdling, including Sellers, and was tried in headgear on the level. Disappeared for four years, but proved quite speedy in Points, although alarming blunders let him down (literally) on four occasions. Bravely ridden by Gareth Perkins when taking a Howick Maiden, but it was back to normal when he crashed at Lydstep next time, and not seen since mid-April. Can take a strong hold, and wears restraining bridles. *Mr & Mrs W.T.D. Perkins — Llangeinor (Richard Evans).* 53 (2m4fOMa), 203 (CfMa), 295 (OMa), 413 (2m4fOMa), 699 (CfMa), 953 (R).

JEWEL SONG ..8-13.. 7 b.g. Faustus (USA) — Trustino (Relkino) 75. Compact well-made owner-bred. Dam, half-sister to Bankit (*qv*). Novicey when a remote last on his debut, but showed some improvement when ten lengths fifth over 2m4f next time. Would probably be better suited by the full trip, and can probably get involved in some finishes before long. *Mrs S. Nash — O. Berks (Matt Hazell).* 290 (2m4fCfMa), 599 (2m4fOMa).

PLATE 62 1506 Exmoor Countryside Alliance Club Members: Jentar Equilibra and Richard Woollacott, 1st *PHOTO: Brian Armstrong*

JIM DORE (IRE) ..—.. 10 b/br.g. Mac's Imp (USA) — Secret Assignment (Vitiges FR) f*pp86*. Small neat half-brother to 3 flat winners (two abroad) inc Secret Magic (in Ireland). Dam won 8f race. IR8000y. FLAT '97/8 r7 p0. IRISH FLAT '99/00 r3 p0. IRISH NH '00 r1 p0. NH '04 r4 p0 (pulled up in 2m-2m4f Hdles: *ld til wknd qckly 3, hit nxt, t.o when pu 5*, and *in tch til wknd qckly 5, pu nxt*; last of 8 in 2m1f Hdle: *prom til wknd app 5, t.o*; and 6th in 2m3f110y Hdle: *a bhnd, t.o 6*). Unruly in the paddock and fell at the second in his only Point in Wales, and has been dreadful in all his races in two other countries. Wears a tongue-tie. *R. Williams — Ystrad Taf Fechan.* 844 (R).

JIMMY BLUES .—.. 10 b.g. Durgam (USA) — Tibbi Blues (Cure The Blues USA) p. Owner-bred. Dam won at 8f in France. NH FLAT '99 r1 p0. NH '00/3 (for F. Murphy) r15 p1 (3rd in Ch); pulled up 2. Only once placed in 17 races, when 19 lengths third in a Chase, and did not impress when backward and sweating in his only Point. Tried in cheekpieces on his final appearance under Rules. *Miss B. Spittal — Eglinton.* 657 (R).

JIMMY CRICKET..10-4.. 8 ch.g. Primitive Rising (USA) — Norton Gale (IRE) (Le Bavard FR) f11. Small neat. Dam, half-sister to Stormy Fable (*qv* '02 Annual). Bought Ascot, April 2095. Went a purler at the second on his debut, and eschewed a Maiden when taking a Restricted at Weston Park in which he was backed from 14-1 to sixes. Hard driven before the last, but need not have been, as he came home 25 lengths in front, and gave another game display when again well supported in a Bitterley Confined in which he outbattled Petrouge. Quite talented and blessed with a fine attitude, and should continue to do well in better company. Connections might even be thinking about a Novices Hunter Chase for him in due course. *R S Racing (S.E. Addis) — Radnor & W. Herefords (Caroline Walker).* 37 (CR), 95 (R), 835 (Cf).

JIMMY JUMBO (IRE) ..9-12.. 12 ch.g. Dragon Palace (USA) — Sail On Lady (New Member) pffu25R. Small workmanlike half-brother to Bank On Lady. Dam, half-sister to Rightsaidfred (*qv* '03 Annual), was remote 2nd of 3 in Point (failed to finish in 9 of 11 other attempts — 'a flighty little minx, and it is hard to see why connections bother with her'). IRISH P-t-P '98/00 r8 w2 (5yo&up Maiden and Winner of Two) p0; pulled up 2, and fell 1. IRISH NH '99/00 r3 p0. NH '01 r1 p0 (pulled up). P-t-P/HUNT CH '02/3 (for Mr J.S. Swindells) r18 w3 (Intermediate and 2 Ladies) p5 (4 2nds, of 3 twice; also disqualified from 2nd once — not draw correct weight; and last of 3); 6th, 7th, last pair 2, pulled up 4, and unseated. A dual winner on the stayers' track at Whittington in the previous yard, but generally a weak finisher that lacks fluency, and proved to be a most unsuitable mount for the newcomer Ned Cecil (shed 22 pounds on the Atkins diet to ride in Points) who failed to get him round in '04. A fair second when regaining competent handling at Rhydygwern, but smashed the wing of the fourth fence to smithereens when reunited with the owner at Umberleigh, and he must be enjoying being back on the carbohydrates again. Only effective on sound surfaces. Acquired a tongue-strap this year. *R. Cecil — Cheshire (Nicky Sheppard).* 528 (O), 979 (MOnr), 1110 (O), 1390 (O), 1484 (O), 1529 (MO), 1562 (O).

JIMS BELIEF (IRE) ..9-8.. 8 b.g. Jurado (USA) — Jims Cousin (Jimsun) 3u133p. Big rangy brother to Secret Can't Say (IRE), and half-brother to Irish jumping and English Chasing winner, Rahanine Melody (IRE) (4-timer in '98 concluded by 3 visits to Scotland and Wales). IRISH P-t-P '02 r1 p1 (3rd). P-t-P '03 r3 w1 (Members, 3 ran — 2 finished) p0; 6th, and pulled up. Headstrong and runs from the front, and has won twice on good or sound surfaces at Marks Tey, but a weak finisher overall (has had a soft palate op) and tends to clobber fences as he tires. Totally unsuited by the mud when favourite on his latest appearance, and will need to find a similarly weak race on contrasting terrain to score again. Wears a cross-noseband. *Lady Green & T.L. Buxton — Essex F. & U. (Cherie Cunningham).* 2 (R), 159 (R), 250 (R), 607 (Cf), 742 (I), 1242 (Cf).

JIM'S GIFT (IRE) ..9-13.. 8 ch.m. Moscow Society (USA) — Another Dud (Le Bavard FR) f. Lengthy unfurnished half-sister to jumping winner, Bowles Patrol (IRE). Dam is half-sister to Cut 'n' Cured (*qv* '94 Annual). IRISH P-t-P '02 r1 w1 (Mares Maiden). P-t-P '03 r5 p3 (2 2nds); and last pair 2. Won a weak race in Ireland, and made the frame in all but one of five appearances last year, but lacked the resolve to score, and was tried in cheekpieces once. Good enough to win a Restricted if she put her mind to it, but presumably hurt by a crashing second-fence fall on her return at Barbury. *C.C. Shand Kydd — Bicester with Whaddon (Fiona Kehoe).* 36 (CR).

JINFUL DU GRAND VAL (FR) ..9-10.. 8 b.g. Useful (FR) — Marine (FR) (African Joy) uu221pp. IRISH P-t-P '02 r2 p1 (2nd); unseated. IRISH NH '03 (for A.L.T. Moore) r1 p0 (tailed off in 2m4f Ch). Effective whilst contesting Maidens, and having finished runner-up on three occasions he made all to beat two other finishers in a poor youngsters event taking nearly seven minutes at Balcormo. Much less convincing in better company, and has something of a habit of unseating the rider. Tried tongue-tied in Ireland. Can get on his toes and has two paddock handlers. Has faded dramatically in his last two attempts, and should be concentrating on Restricteds. *J.F. Alexander — Fife (Nick Alexander).* 216 (OMa), 349 (3m1fH), 659 (OMa), 768 (2m4fOMa), 1081 (OMa), 1220 (C), 1373 (2m4f110yH).

JOBEE JACK ..8-8.. 8 b.g. Perpendicular — Willow Path (Farm Walk) u6pf. Unfurnished half-brother to Wrenbury Farmer, to jumping winner, Back Before Dark, and to successful Hurdler, Back Before Dawn. P-t-P '03 r7 p0 (4th, pulled up 4, and fell/unseated 2). An unsafe conveyance who was teamed with the inexperienced owner on four occasions last year, and only got round once, and little better for another novice in '04. Slipped up and injured himself at Easingwold, and it will be no great shame if he does not reappear in public. Wears a cross-noseband. *Miss J. Burke — Cleveland (Lynne Ward).* 272 (OMa), 342 (2m4fOMa), 776 (CfMa), 1159 (OMa).

JOE LIVELY (IRE) .7-5.. 6 b.g. Flemensfirth (USA) — Forest Gale (Strong Gale) pp15. Small compact half-brother to Philtre (IRE) (*qv*). Bought Goffs Ireland, Jun for 7420. Pulled up in his first two Maidens, but then presented with a dreadful one at Brampton Bryan, where he was left second when Withybrook Lass fell at the last when in control, and soon overtook Cromaboo Count who was dogging it furiously. Even the bookies were not impressed, and he was sent off at 33-1 when finishing 45 lengths last in a subsequent Restricted. Three stone behind Philtre at present, but there may be some improvement to come in his second campaign (there will need to be). *Mrs A.M. Callow — Albrighton Woodland (Helen Needham).* 257 (CMa), 531 (OMa), 1116 (OMa), 1389 (R).

JOHN BUILDER ..—.. 9 b.g. Nader — My Molly (Averof) pp. Lengthy owner-bred half-brother to Chalvey Grove and Impenny. P-t-P '02/3 r5 p0 (last, pulled up 4). A useless non-stayer who hits a brick wall after a maximum of two miles, and totally out of his depth when tried in a sub- 3m Hunter Chase. *G. Ivall — N. Hereford (Jess Ivall).* 1067 (OMa), 1372 (2m4fH).

JOHN FOLEY (IRE) ..9-13.. 7 b.g. Petardia — Fast Bay (Bay Express) 3. Big half-brother to 3 winners abroad. FLAT '00/2 r19 p5 (5-8f, inc 2 Sells). NH '01/2 r5 p1 (3rd). P-t-P '03 r3 w1 (Maiden) p2 (2nds). Wore headgear latterly when handled by five different trainers on the flat, and entertained by a sixth when sent hurdling, but none were able to extract a success, and has only come to hand since switching to Points. Made all and jumped well to land a gamble on his final appearance last year, but not seen until May in '04, and ran as though just in need of the race. Definitely has a Restricted in him, but keeping him sound appears to be a hard task. *R.D.J. Swinburne — Albrighton (Paul Morris).* 1265 (R).

JOHNNY ROSS (IRE) ..8-4.. 7 ch.g. Phardante (FR) — Iacocca (Dunphy) 2. Half-brother to Our Friend Vinc (IRE). IRISH P-t-P '03 r6 p0 (pulled up 4 and fell 2). Unable to get round in six Irish Points, but made a bit of a race of it with Endeavour (who was unimpressive) until giving best from the last in his Members. It was a slowly run contest and the form is meaningless. *D.J. & Mrs W.E. Lay — Essex & Suffolk (David Lay).* 828 (M).

JOHNNYS GONE (IRE) .10-4§.. 10 b.g. Balinger — Therene (Levanter) 232f32u. Tall workmanlike half-brother to Buckleup (IRE), and to Irish Pointing winner, Downtopal. IRISH P-t-P '00/1 r4 w1 (6yo Maiden) p0 (pulled up 2, and ran out). IRISH NH FLAT '01 r2 p0. IRISH NH '01/2 r8 p0. P-t-P '03 (for Mr A. Simpson) r9 w2 (Restricted and Intermediate) p3 (2nds, inc of 3 once and last once); pulled up 2, ran out and fell. Goes a steady gallop, and has not missed the frame when completing in Points, but can be temperamental and has run out twice, and often let down by his jumping. Has found the racing more competitive since his move, but deserves another minor success. Tried in cheekpieces once in '03. *Mrs P.M. Shirley-Beavan — Jedforest.* 135 (Cfnr), 210 (Cf), 282 (Cf), 426 (Cf), 915 (Cf), 1080 (Cf), 1220 (C).

JOHNSAIR (IRE) .9-12.. 9 b.g. Un Desperado (FR) — Lady Bodmin (IRE) (Law Society USA) 21u. Brother to Top Commander (IRE), to an Italian flat winner, and to Irish Hurdles winner, Duggan Duff, and half-brother to flat winner, Illegal. IRISH P-t-P '02/3 r5 p1 (2nd); last, pulled up 2 and brought down 1. Lightly raced, but looked to have improved in the new yard, and might have scored at Dunthrop had Polly Gundry not been too strong on the winner (outridden and beaten half-a-length). Made all to win a highly suspect contest at Black Forest Lodge, where despite it being February the next three home failed to reappear, and vanished himself later that month after unseating at the seventh. Can go a reasonable gallop and might have a chance in Restricteds, but clearly none too hardy. *Mr & Mrs W.T.D. Perkins — Llangeinor (Richard Evans).* 51 (OMa), 149 (OMa), 294 (R).

JOHNS LEGACY ..10-11.. 10 gr.g. Almoojid — Flying Joker (Kalaglow) f2. Small. P-t-P '02/3 r2 w2 (Maiden and Restricted). Cut his teeth in hunter trials and events, but showed plenty of speed when able to win on his only appearances '02/3, and ran his best race yet in defeat at Newton Abbot. Had a Hunter Chase winner ten lengths in arrears, and can certainly go one better, particularly if he can race on a more regular basis. Yet to encounter an easy surface. *B. Robinson — Quantock (Sarah Robinson).* 975 (2m7f110yH), 1167 (3m2f110yH).

JOHNSTON'S VILLE (IRE) ..8-10.. 12 b.g. Commanche Run — Slavesville (Charlottesvilles Flyer) p31p. Workmanlike half-brother to Goner House, to Irish Hurdles winners, Oakland Buck and Herr Leutnant, and to an Irish NH flat winner. Dam is half-sister to Albero (*qv* '88 Season Annual). IRISH NH FLAT '97/8 r4 p1 (2nd). IRISH NH '98 r2 p0. NH '99 and '01 r7 p4 (2 2nds). P-t-P/HUNT CH '02/3 r4 p0 (last pair 2, pulled up 1 and fell 1). Lightly raced and ended '03 lame, but had always shown he had the ability to win, and landed a two-finisher Maiden at Ystradowen after a live danger had exited at the last. Looks up against it in Restricteds however. *J. Stephens — Llandeilo F. (Margaret Stephens).* 357 (R), 621 (OMa), 1027 (OMa), 1230 (R).

JOJO (IRE) ..—§.. 15 ch.g. Buckskin (FR) — Autumn Queen (Menelek) r. Workmanlike lengthy half-brother to Chasing winner, Murt's Man (IRE), to Hurdles winners, Snowy Autumn and Mickeen, and to Irish Hurdles winner, Ahead Of The Posse (IRE). NH '95/8 r12 w1 (2m4f Hdle) p2 (3rds, inc Ch). P-t-P/HUNT CH '99/03 r21 w3 (inc Confined) p5 (3 3rds, last once); 7th twice, pulled up 7, refused 1, and unseated 1. Formerly able when allowed to dictate, but a real villain and last consented to co-operate in '00, and for the second year running decided to draw stumps himself in his Members. Normally blinkered. *G. Barker & M.P. & Mrs D. Grissell — E. Sussex & Romney Marsh (Di Grissell).* 1050 (M).

J-OKAY (IRE) ..10-12.. 13 b.g. Buckskin (FR) — Moynalvey Lass (Tower Walk) R1. Neat half-brother to Chasing winner, Moon Devil (IRE), to Irish NH flat winner, Pristine Gale, and to Irish jumping winner, Mandy's Glen. IRISH NH FLAT '97/8 r5 p1 (3rd). IRISH NH '98/02 (for V.C. Ward) r26 w1 (2m3f Hdle) p6 (inc 2nd in Ch); only failed to finish 1 (brought down). Ran 31 times in Ireland but only managed the one victory, in a 25-runner Hurdle on firmish at Naas. Probably unlucky not to have found other opportunities, as four of his seven placings were in fields of between 21 and 26, and he only once failed to complete the course (brought down). Ran out early on his English debut, but then put up a useful display in an Open at Thorpe in which he easily bettered the times of Nautical Lad and Guignol Du Cochet. The next three home went on to win six between them and there was no fluke about his success, but having missed '03 he only lasted as long as February 1st in '04, which at rising 13 cannot be good news. *J-Okay Partnership (J. Williams) — Cheshire (Gary Hanmer).* 45 (Cnr), 107 (O).

JOLEJOKER .9-10.. 7 b.g. Alflora (IRE) — Jolejester (Relkino) 3. Well made half-brother to Oh So Droll. Dam, half-sister to Global Legend (*qv* '01 Annual), pulled up in a Point, but previously won a NH flat and 3rd 2 (inc a flat race). Made an encouraging start in a youngsters Maiden in Chaddesley Corbett in May, and kept on steadily to finish 11 lengths third. Oh So Droll was successful at up to Restricted grade for Pam Sykes, and should be able to emulate him. *D.E. Edwards — S. Salop (Pamela Sykes).* 1339 (OMa).

JOLI CHRISTMAS ..9-3.. 8 b.g. Joligeneration — Christmas Bash (Shaab) p43. Workmanlike. Dam won Maiden and Restricted for Gordon Chambers and placed 11 (inc 2 Hdles and 4 Chses) (*qv* '97 Annual). P-t-P '03 (for Mr G. Chambers) r2 p0 (5th of 6, and ran out 1). Very green to date, and has been difficult to steer on right-handed circuits, but having a patient policy employed for him at present, and should score eventually. *Mr & Mrs R. Rodrick — Modbury H. (Gordon Chambers).* 194 (CfMa), 306 (2m4fOMa), 469 (2m4fOMa).

JOLIE ROSLIN ..9-7.. 11 gr.m. Joli Wasfi (USA) — Robina (Royben) 2u3u3. Rangy homebred. Dam, half-sister to Rodden Brook, was placed in 2 Points and the Cattistock Buchanan (remember them?) for Hilary Tutte (the only horse she beat in 9 Points was a fatty carting 14 stone). P-t-P '00/2 r10 w2 (Maiden and Members) p2 (last of 2 twice); last 2, fell 1, and pulled up 3. A dual winner on right-handed tracks to '02, but lightly raced throughout her career, and has only beat two rivals in '04. Prone to errors and Fiona Vigar was a prime candidate to be ejected by them. *Mrs H. Tutte — Cattistock.* 498 (R), 687 (M), 1013 (R), 1196 (R), 1386 (R).

JOLITAN ..10-5§.. 10 b.g. Joligeneration — Tanber Lass (New Member) 1. Small neat half-brother to Dolitanlad. Dam, half-sister to 3 Pointers including, Good For Business (*qv* '97 Annual), won 5 Points (4 in '91) and placed 7. Grandam, Santan, won Maiden and 3rd twice. P-t-P/HUNT CH '00/3 r19 w4 (inc Ladies) p2; 4th, last, pulled up 7, ran out 2, and unseated 2. Most determined when only defeated once in his first four completions, but reported to have suffered with sore shins in the second half of '02, and has hung sharply left after the last on three occasions since. Almost (and according to some observers did) threw it away at Black Forest Lodge this year, and the resultant swerve caused Rilly Goschen to lose her irons, but presumably suffered a setback in the process, and has not been seen since. Suited by good or easy ground, but could not be trusted to co-operate if returning. Wears blinkers. *Mrs P.A. Wilkins & Mrs S. Evans — Taunton V. (Philip Greenwood).* 63 (L).

JOLLY JACK (IRE) ..—.. 14 b.g. Jolly Jake (NZ) — Hay Party (Party Mink) p. Smallish compact brother to Master Jay Jay (IRE), and half-brother to Full Of Chat (IRE). Dam won 2 2m-2m4f Irish Hdles. NH '01/2 r7 p0; pulled up 5. P-t-P/HUNT CH '99/00 and '03 (for Mr S.T. Lewis) r9 w1 (Intermediate) p1 (2nd of 3); unseated 2, refused 1, and pulled up 4. Rated 10-2 after scoring impressively at Maisemore in '99, but went wrong almost immediately, and has failed to finish in 12 of 14 subsequent attempts, including five over hurdles. Crippled and had no right to be on a racecourse in '04, and promptly pulled up lame at Weston Park. *The Foscombe Salers Cattle Partnership (Ms T. Warner) — Ledbury (Andrew Graham).* 93 (O).

JOLLY JAKE ..9-8§.. 11 br.g. Vital Season — Sols Joker (Comedy Star USA) 324621fp24. Workmanlike brother to Chasing winner, Nova Girl, and half-brother to Off Piste Sally. Dam is half-sister to 3 Pointers, including Nearly All Right (*qv* '01 Annual). P-t-P '02/3 r15 p6 (2nds, last once); 5th, 7th, last 2, and pulled up 5. Incredibly easy to beat, and required 21 attempts before he managed to hang on in a weak three-finisher Maiden at Upper Sapey. Even more amazing is the fact that punters have been falling over themselves to support him since, but typically frustrating and sure to remain that way. Often has two handlers and tends to sweat excessively. Wears a cross-noseband. *Miss E.J. Baker — N. Cotswold.* 6 (OMa), 52 (OMa), 258 (CMa), 443 (2m4f110yH), 820 (OMa), 1141 (OMa), 1366 (R), 1482 (R), 1531 (R), 1561 (R).

PLATE 63 1141 Clifton-on-Tem Open Maiden 8yo&up: Jolly Jake and Ed Walker, 1st, step over a tiny fence *PHOTO: Kathleen Mullen*

JOLLY MINSTER ..10-0.. 11 b.g. Minster Son — Dash Cascade (Absalom) fu4. Smallish compact half-brother to a winner in Turkey. NH FLAT '98 r2 p0. NH '98/9 r6 p2. P-t-P/HUNT CH '00/3 r12 w4 (inc 2 Hunt Chses, 2m5f-3m3f) p6 (4 2nds, inc Hunt Ch; and inc 3rd of 4 once); 6th, and fell 1. A very thorough stayer, and ultimately most progressive in the previous ownership, but never did any more than was necessary, and squandered by feeble riding since changing hands expensively in '02. Looked likely to take the winner's measure when unseating three out at Horseheath, but finished lame at Marks Tey next time, and had run tongue-tied on his only appearance in '03. Can handle deep mud, but once again a watching brief is advised if he reappears. *Mrs D. Rowell — Crawley & Horsham (Sara Hickman).* 42 (L), 126 (L), 246 (L).

JONA HOLLEY ..4-13§.. 12 b.g. Sharpo — Spurned (USA) (Robellino USA) u2pp. Workmanlike half-brother to 4 flat winners, including Hidden Meadow, Scorned and Kingsclere. Dam won 7f race. FLAT '95/01 r33 w3 (8-9f) p5. NH '98/01 r13 w1 (2m Hdle) p0; pulled up 1. P-t-P '03 r4 p1 (last of 3); pulled up 2, and fell. Had a succession of trainers under Rules, and was moderately successful, but unable to score since beating Jenny's Charmer (*qv*) at Uttoxeter in '99, and not better than two fences last when beginner-ridden in Points. Has been tried in headgear. *W. Barry — N. Staffs (Anna Blake).* 713 (Cf), 847 (M), 1045 (Cf), 1147 (Cnr).

JONNO ..8-2.. 7 b.g. Karinga Bay — Caoimhe (Pollerton) 4p. Enormous half-brother to Luggsy, and to NH flat and Hurdles winner, Sutherland Moss. Twenty-two lengths last over 2m4f on his debut, but tailed off and pulled up after two miles next time. By a successful sire of Points, but looks rather too jumboesque to be a racehorse. *M. Kehoe & T. Chorlton — Bicester with Whaddon (Fiona Kehoe).* 291 (2m4fCfMa), 871 (OMa).

JORODAMA KING ..9-11.. 11 b.g. Lighter — Princess Hecate (Autre Prince) 4. Good-topped half-brother to Kingsland Taverner. Dam, half-sister to Mesmerist (*qv* '90 Annual), won Maiden and placed twice, and subsequently won 7 Hdles (2m5f-3m1f) and placed 8. NH FLAT '99 r2 p1 (2nd). NH '99/03 (from R.J. Price's latterly) r26 w1 (3m2f Ch) p7 (5 3rds); pulled up 4, fell/unseated 4. HUNT CH '03 (for Mr P.J. Davis) r1 p0 (8th of 9). Won a bad three-finisher Chase at Plumpton when partnered by Tony McCoy in '02, but slow and a sketchy jumper, and beaten in 29 other attempts. Thirty-four lengths fourth of five on his Pointing debut, but immediately disappeared, and a successful comeback looks unlikely. Has been tried in blinkers. *Mrs G.M.S. Slater — Worcester & W. Farmers.* 351 (L).

PLATE 64 1565 Torrington Farmers Open Maiden (Div 1): It's Division I of the last race of the season and Josanjamic and Liam Heard eventually get it all right PHOTO: John Mullen

JOSANJAMIC ..9-9.. 8 b.m. King Luthier — Ndita (Be My Native USA) up3325u1. Workmanlike owner-bred half-sister to Gaelic Reign and Nditlir. Dam, half-sister to Maxine's Fountain (IRE) (*qv* '99 Annual), won 2 8f races and placed 2 (inc Sell), and was 2nd in Hdle, but last, pulled up 3 and unseated in Points for John Heard (looked a non-stayer). NH FLAT '01/2 r4 p3. NH '02/3 (for W.S. Kittow) r4 p1 (3rd). Had fabulous credentials for a Maiden on her best bumper form, as she finished one-and-a-quarter lengths second to Iris's Gift (11 wins and £291,193 to date), and six lengths second to Be Fair (who has won six), but had been less successful over Hurdles and was 37 lengths third of four in her only Chase. A plunge from tens to 3-1 at Buckfastleigh, and supporters must have been rubbing their hands in glee as she came to the last with a three-length advantage, but she clambered over and Liam Heard came adrift. Then endured a most frustrating sequence of defeats and was beaten first or second favourite in four, but finally broke her duck at the 16th attempt when easily beating a couple of donkeys at Umberleigh. Possibly temperamental but was not improved by a visor twice, and her jumping sometimes has her in trouble. At her best she might have a chance in Restricteds, but is not a safe betting medium. *K.C. & J.C. Heard — Eggesford (John Heard).* 195 (CfMa), 329 (OMa), 494 (OMa), 701 (2m4fOMa), 827 (CfMa), 1134 (OMa), 1545 (OMa), 1565 (OMa).

JOSH'S CHOICE (IRE) ..8-0§.. 10 ch.g. Tremblant — Normandy Lady (Normandy) r5u6p. Tall rangy half-brother to Irish Pointing winner, Gerrymander. P-t-P '00/2 r11 w1 (Maiden) p1 (last of 3); last pair 2, pulled up 5, and fell/unseated 2. Bitterly disappointing since opening his account at Horseheath in '02, and the subject of a misplaced gamble on his belated return to action at Higham. Error-proneand often blinkered now, and looks wrong. *C.H. Sporborg & H.D. Hill — Puckeridge (Christopher Sporborg).* 29 (R), 44 (R), 127 (R), 398 (R), 559 (R).

JOSHUA'S VISION (IRE) ..—.. 14 b.g. Vision (USA) — Perle's Fashion (Sallust) ppppp. Tall heavy-topped half-brother to Friendly House (IRE), and to 5 flat winners (one in Ireland and 2 abroad), including Cost Effective. Dam won 3 Irish flat, 9-12f. NH FLAT '95 r4 p3 (2 2nds). NH '95/6 and '99/01 r21 p5 (3 2nds); pulled up 3, and fell/unseated 3. P-t-P/HUNT CH '02/3 r13 w4 (Maiden, Intermediate, Confined and Club nov rdrs) p2 (3rd of 4 once); 4th twice, 5th twice, and pulled up 3. A very thorough stayer, and has won three races in mud, but basically slow, and now rendered useless having gone in the wind. Broke a blood vessel in '00, but unimproved by tubing having previously run tongue-tied, and retirement is his only option. Has been tried in cheekpieces and a visor. *Lady Susan Brooke — Teme V.* 616 (C), 838 (L), 994 (3m110yH), 1117 (3m1f110yH), 1229 (L).

JOURNEY ..10-3.. 12 ch.g. Tina's Pet — Lady Vynz (Whitstead) 311. Tall lengthy half-brother to jumping winner, Fred's In The Know. IRISH FLAT '97 r2 p0. IRISH NH FLAT '97 r1 p0. IRISH NH '98 r5 p0. NH '99 r1 p0 (8th in 2m Nov Ch). P-t-P/HUNT CH '99 and '02/3 r11 w1 (Maiden) p1 (2nd); 4th, 8th, 9th, last pair 2, pulled up 2, and fell/unseated 2. Emerged from a three-year spell of inactivity to land a Maiden at Stainton in '02, but much improved this year, and displayed hitherto unseen levels of stamina when romping home at Hutton Rudby. Speedy and likes to dominate, but Nigel Tutty was almost caught napping next time, and is definitely at his best on an easy track. Does not stand much racing now, but should win again if sensibly placed. *Mrs P. & Miss J.A. Sawney — Cleveland (Jackie Sawney).* 268 (R), 563 (R), 1163 (Cf).

JOVES SHADOW ..8-12.. 7 ch.g. Jupiter Island — Shades Of Oak (Pamroy) b5up. Sturdy half-brother to Shady Minx. Dam, half-sister to Front Cover and Proud Sun (*qv* '99 Annual), won Enfield Members twice and placed 3 for Nigel Macfarlane. P-t-P '03 r1 p0 (pulled up). Going well when brought down after two miles on his reappearance, and hit the front four out when apparently full of running next time, but disappointing on his final start, and has to prove that he gets the trip. *Mrs F. Macfarlane — Aldenham H. (Simon Andrews).* 154 (OMa), 244 (CfMa), 463 (OMa), 561 (OMa).

JOVIAN POND ..8-9.. 13 b.g. Jupiter Island — Water Ballet (Sir Gaylord) p4u33. Good-topped half-brother to a flat winner apiece in Ireland and Germany. Dam won 2 7f races at 2. NH FLAT '97/8 r4 p0. NH '98/00 r16 p1 (2nd); pulled up 3, and fell 3. P-t-P '02 r4 p0 (last pair 2, and pulled up 2). Fairly safe and frequently involved in Maidens, but does not get the trip well enough to succeed, and normally runs tongue-tied. *Mrs S. Sealey — Worcs (Robert Sealey).* 661 (Cnr), 840 (OMa), 1125 (OMa), 1395 (OMa), 1495 (OMa).

JOYCE BEL (FR) ..9-5.. 12 br.g. Rose Laurel — Jeanne De Laval (FR) (Gairloch) fp4p. Compact well-made. IRISH NH FLAT '00 r1 p0. IRISH NH '98/01 r30 w2 (2m2f-2m4f Chses) p4 (2nds, beaten short-head once); pulled up 2, fell/unseated 3. NH '02/3 r8 p1 (2nd); pulled up 1, fell/unseated 2. P-t-P '03 (for Mr A.N. Dalton) r1 w1 (Members). Thrice successful on sound surfaces in previous yards, but does not get the trip in competitive events, and needs strong handling. Floundered in the prevailing ground in '04, and made his usual jumping errors. Sometimes tongue-tied in Ireland. Blinkered once in '00, and tried in cheekpieces once last year. *Miss K.E. Crank — Cheshire (Reg Crank).* 230 (L), 529 (L), 751 (L), 1428 (L).

JOY FOR LIFE (IRE) ..10-0.. 14 b.m. Satco (FR) — Joy's Toy (Wolverlife) 743. Narrow unfurnished. Dam won 8f Sell. NH FLAT '96 r1 p0. P-t-P/HUNT CH '98/9 r8 w2 (inc 3m110y Hunt Ch) p4 (3 2nds; and inc 3 Hunt Chses); and last pair 2. NH '96/7 and '99/03 r28 w1 (3m110y Ch) p6 (inc 3 2nds); pulled up 8; fell/unseated 3. A real mudlark, and got Sam Stronge's career off on the right foot, but moody and inconsistent when returned to racing under Rules, and not better than last in five appearances after her shock 20-1 success at Southwell in March '02. Not disgraced since reverting to Points, but not the force she was, and only likely to deteriorate further at 14 unless she finds a morass. *Mrs B. Stronge — Ledbury (Sophie Brewer).* 107 (O), 612 (Cf), 722 (M).

PLATE 65 1432 South Cornwall Open Maiden: Joyful Jade gives Alex Charles-Jones his 100th winner (though Alex had tried to win it on the previous circuit) PHOTO: Baths Photographic

JOYFUL JADE (FR) ..8-10.. 8 b.m. Useful (FR) — Devon Orchid (Brianston Zipper) u1p. Workmanlike well-made. Won a farcical two-finisher youngsters Maiden by 25 lengths at Trebudannon, but only after Alex Charles-Jones on what turned out to be his 100th Pointing victory had mistaken the number of circuits and pulled up with one to go before realising his mistake and repassing the runner-up before two out (very fortunate that the opposition evaporated totally). Has failed to complete the course otherwise, and sending her hurdling after the season was far too ambitious a project. Pulled up when favourite for a Restricted, but will need to improve quite a lot to reach that standard. *R.E. White — Lamerton (Tony Boon).* 1134 (OMa), 1432 (OMa), 1543 (R).

JUBILEEMAN (IRE) ..9-13.. 9 b.g. Mandalus — Cherry Jubilee (Le Bavard FR) 4p2. Small neat half-brother to Sparkling Spring (IRE) (won Hurdling since Pointing), and to jumping winners, Sparkling Sunset (IRE) and Percolator (IRE). Dam, half-sister to Randolph Place (*qv* '95 Annual). IRISH P-t-P '01/2 r6 w1 (5yo Maiden) p2; pulled up 2 and fell 1. IRISH HUNT CH '02 r3 p1 (3rd). IRISH NH '02/3 (for Miss A. McMahon, and E. Sheehy) r5 p1 (3rd); pulled up 1. Bought Doncaster, May for 3000. Only once successful in his first 16 races, but ended a curtailed season in mid-February by keeping the subsequently much improved Claire's Nomad at full stretch in a Market Rasen Restricted. Could probably gain compensation in that grade if fit, but seems to have suffered a reverse. Blinkered twice in Ireland. *Miss H.L. Phizacklea — Atherstone.* 95 (R), 231 (CR), 301 (R).

JUDY'S LAD ..8-8§.. 6 ch.g. Master Willie — Flexwing (Electric) R3R0. Long-backed half-brother to Hurdling winner, Snipe. NH FLAT '04 (for Miss J. Southcombe) r1 p0 (12th over 2m1f at Hereford: *prom 7f, t.o*). Bought Ascot, Jun for 4000. Faded to finish 20 lengths last of three on the occasion he completed the course, but ran out twice otherwise, including when still just in front four from home at Cothelstone (jumped right and set a very slow pace). Currently a difficult ride, and needs putting in his place before he reappears. *Mrs J.C. Duffy — S. Dorset.* 962 (OMa), 1007 (2m4fOMa), 1371 (OMa).

JUICY LUCY ..—.. 8 b.m. Bonny Scot (IRE) — Bijou Georgie (Rhodomantade) p. Small light half-sister to Chasing winner, Nick The Jewel. Dam, half-sister to Georgie's Caper, won 2m3f Hunt Ch and 2 Points and p8. NH FLAT '03 r1 p0 (tailed off). NH '03 (from J.S. King's) r3 p0; pulled 2 and last. Bought Ascot, Oct for 2476. Tailed off in a bumper, 44 lengths last and pulled up twice in Hurdles, and remote when pulling up in her Members. Dismal. *Mrs J. Butler — Hursley Hambledon (Peter Butler).* 260 (M).

JUMP FOR PADDY .8-11.. 6 b.g. Michelozzo (USA) — Tudor Spartan (Spartan General) 332. Half-brother to Saxon Gale (*qv*). Placed in all three Maidens including one which took almost eight minutes, and came closest to success in the latest, when five lengths second of three to Lou Biarnes at Cold Harbour. Outjumped at the last and weakened, to the dismay of those who had supported him at 4-5. Still a baby, and granted some improvement from five to six he may be able to win. *B.J. Perkins — N. Ledbury.* 410 (2m4fCfMa), 754 (OMa), 1233 (OMa).

JUMPING JACK .9-3.. 9 b.g. Brooksway Oats (IRE) — Resolute Miss (Averof) 2p23. Tall rangy owner-bred. Ran well in all four races in his first season at eight, and had a hard luck story in a Guilsborough Confined Maiden, as he was carried off the course after the fourth fence and lost about 150 yards before rejoining, but although he managed to weave his way into contention he weakened quickly three out and pulled up at the next. Unable to justify favouritism twice since, but only beaten a neck once and six lengths once, and deserves a change of fortune. Tends to take a keen hold, and needs to learn to settle better. *Mrs C.E. Bell — Cottesmore (Toby Saunders).* 378 (M), 789 (CfMa), 1061 (OMa), 1473 (OMa).

JUMPING JEFFREY ..—.. 8 b.g. Winter Words — Biblical (Montekin) fpR. Tall strong. Dam won Maiden and 3rd twice (generally failed to stay). Seems to have been badly taught, and prone to do silly things. Can doubtless be ignored, at least if remaining in this stable. *Miss K. Thory — Fitzwilliam.* 128 (OMa), 219 (OMa), 371 (OMa).

JUPITER GEORGE ..9-6§.. 9 b.g. Jupiter Island — Celia's Halo (Mountain Call) 1p. Workmanlike owner-bred half-brother to Sam's Birthday, Stars, Celias Twink, Alfalfie, Shambob and Sassy's Circle. Dam won 10f Sell and 2m Sell Hdle and placed 7, inc remote 3rds in Points. NH FLAT '01 r1 p0. P-t-P '02/3 r9 p1 (3rd of 4); last pair 4, pulled up 3, and refused 1. Ungenuine and tried in blinkers in the previous yard, and looked to have bucked the trend when readily justifying favouritism on his reappearance at Tabley, but stopped to nil after 2m4f next time, and clearly not as reformed as first thought. *M. Beavan & N. Morgan — N. Salop (Sheila Crow).* 1425 (OMa), 1503 (R).

JUPITER JAY ..7-12.. 9 b.g. Jupiter Island — Liberty Jay (Broadsword USA) fp8. Small stocky. Dam, sister to Andrew's (*qv* '03 Annual), was 2 fences last of 3 in a Point (failed to finish 6 of 8 other attempts). P-t-P '03 (for Mrs A.J. McVay, Mrs J. Baxter & Mrs J.J. Cooper) r2 p0 (pulled up 1, and fell 1). Beaten more than the length of the run-in when finally registering a completion in first-time cheekpieces at Mollington, and let down by consistently inaccurate jumping, and like many by Jupiter

Island an inability to stay three miles. *Mrs C.E. Grayson & Mrs J. Cooper — Grafton (Dawn Ball).* 12 (OMa), 385 (OMa), 589 (CfMa).

JUPITER JO ..9-11.. 9 b.g. Jupiter Island — Marejo (Creetown) pf3. Smallish compact quite attractive half-brother to Marteeny, More Flair and Hot Bricks. Dam, half-sister to Sarona Smith (*qv* '00 Annual), won 8 Chses at around 2m for the Waltons (4 at Catterick). Grandam, Sarona, won 5 Hdles (2m-2m4f) and 10 Chses (2m-3m1f, inc a walkover). NH FLAT '01 r2 p0. NH '02 r2 p0 (4th and pulled up in Chses). P-t-P '02/3 r4 w1 (2m4f Maiden) p2 (neck last of 2 once); and pulled up 1. Readily landed a touch in a 16-runner Maiden at Dalston, but turned over by a tubed rival when odds-on in a match next time, and has still to prove his effectiveness over the full trip. Needs to brush up his jumping. *J.B & F.A Walton — Border (Jimmy Walton).* 765 (R), 1419 (R), 1476 (R).

JUPITER'S FANCY ..9-11.. 10 ch.m. Jupiter Island — Joe's Fancy (Apollo Eight) 5f7uf37. Tall lengthy half-sister to Imike, and to NH flat winner, Equiname's Fancy. Dam won 4 Hdles (2m4f-3m2f) and 3 Chses (2m6f-3m1f). NH FLAT '01/2 r3 p1 (3rd). NH '02 r2 p0; pulled up 1. P-t-P/HUNT CH '03 (for The Leak Fixers) r5 w1 (3-runner Maiden) p1 (3rd in Hunt Ch); 5th, and pulled up 2. Easily put two rivals to the sword on firm at Wetherby last year, and would have given the winner more to do but for falling two out at Corbridge and again at the last in the Heart, but disappointing in the main, and needs her confidence restoring. Flounders in soft ground, but should gain compensation in a Restricted in '05. *M.V. Coglan — S. Durham (Mark Coglan).* 316 (2m5fH), 430 (R), 563 (R), 1037 (I), 1178 (3m1fH), 1373 (2m4f110yH), 1499 (2m4f110yH).

JURIST ..9-6.. 11 b.g. Then Again — Forest Frolic (Celtic Cone) 3331. Tall half-brother to jumping winner, Foxtrot Romeo. Dam, half-sister to Dunnyside Up (*qv* '96 Annual), but not to Melnik, won 2m4f Hdle (should have won another Hdle, but refused at the last). NH FLAT '99 r1 p1 (2nd). P-t-P '01 (for Mr J.T. Brown) r1 p0 (fell). NH '01/3 (for B.S. Rothwell) r5 p0 (last, 7th, fell, and unseated in Chses). Very lightly raced, and equalled his previous record of four outings in a year, and provided Matthew Keen (who had picked up a spare which walked over in the Members earlier) with his first un-engineered success after many years trying at Kingston Blount. Proved more amenable to restraint there than usual, and held on well despite clouting two of the last three fences, but will find things difficult if not impossible in Restricteds. Wears a cross-noseband. *M. Keen — Berks & Bucks (Geoffrey Deacon).* 463 (OMa), 721 (OMa), 820 (OMa), 1518 (OMa).

JUSTADREAM ..9-10.. 8 b.g. Ski Dancer — The Manson Flyer (Green Shoon) 132. Tall half-brother to Pull On and Pull Off. Dam is half-sister to Parsoness (*qv* '93 Annual). P-t-P '02/3 r2 p0 (5th, and pulled up 1). Won a weak short Maiden very convincingly at Garnons, and has already performed well enough in Restricteds to suggest that there is one in '05 with his name on it. Certainly looks the part, but has been weak, and might improve his rating by several pounds if he were able to withstand a full campaign. *K. Young — N. Ledbury (Tim Stephenson).* 618 (2m4fOMa), 839 (R), 1256 (R).

JUST A LADY ..8-8.. 8 b.m. Primitive Rising (USA) — Pretty Tactfull (State Diplomacy USA) p4546. Small compact sister to Just A Man. Dam, half-sister to Just Coming (*qv*), pulled up in 2 Points for Richard Mason. Proved to be a competent jumper in her first season, but slow, and only two have finished behind her. Even found wanting in a Mares Maiden, so will struggle to find a race. *R.G.P. Mason — Middleton.* 272 (OMa), 395 (CfMa), 500 (CMam), 773 (2m4fCMa), 960 (OMa).

JUST A MAN ..6-11.. 7 b.g. Primitive Rising (USA) — Pretty Tactfull (State Diplomacy USA) p3ppp. Compact owner-bred brother to Just A Lady (*qv*). Made favourite for the Maiden which took over eight minutes at Dalton Park, but after leading before two out he was collared at the last and finished tamely. Maidens do not come any worse, and looks even more pedestrian than his sister. *R.G.P. Mason — Middleton.* 393 (CfMa), 505 (CMa), 775 (CfMa), 958 (OMa), 1292 (OMa).

JUST ARETHA .7-7§§.. 9 b.m. Weld — Just Something (Good Times ITY) 66p. Workmanlike unfurnished owner-bred half-sister to Batty's Island and Just Andy. P-t-P '03 (for Mr G.L. Edwards) r1 p0 (unseated). Another Weld tainted by madness, and has been withdrawn from three intended appearances (two under Rules) after going nuts in the preliminaries. Dumped Polly Gundry (she does agree to partner some rubbish in Maidens) en route to the start in the latest at Great Trethew, and should be dumped out of the sport as quickly as possible. Not better than last when completing. *Mrs S. Smith — Spooners & W. Dartmoor.* 121 (OMa), 486 (OMa), 704 (CfMa).

JUST BARNEY BOY .10-7.. 8 b.g. Past Glories — Pablena (Pablond) 21f1u42. Lengthy half-brother to Vital To Me, Elver Spring and Alston House, and to Hurdles winner, Granite Steps. NH '01/3 r12 p0; pulled up 4, fell/unseated 2. P-t-P/HUNT CH '03 (for Mr G.R.S. & Mrs S. Nixon) r7 w3 (Maiden, Restricted and Confined, hat-trick) p1 (2nd); unseated 1, pulled up 1, and carried out 1. Has failed to get round in half his starts under Rules, and not a patent safety in Points, but useful enough when he does jump round, and got 40-year-old Adam Waugh's riding career off to a dream start at Alnwick. Proved his ability to act in soft when successful at Friars Haugh, and possibly unlucky at both

Corbridge and Hexham. Stays well and further victories seem guaranteed. Tends to sweat excessively. *A. Waugh — Morpeth (Simon Waugh).* 72 (O), 214 (O), 429 (3m5fO), 551 (O), 917 (O), 1038 (O), 1421 (O).

PLATE 66 551 Duke of Buccleuch's Mens Open: L to R, Just Barney Boy (Adam Waugh), 1st, land a fraction ahead of Dun Rose (Tom Oates), 2nd, at the last PHOTO: Alan Mitchell

JUST BERT (IRE) .9-10.. 15 b.g. Kambalda — Cappagh Flier (Lock Diamond) 4346R. Small brother to Diamond Flier (IRE). P-t-P/HUNT CH '95/03 r42 w10 (inc 3m Hunt Ch, and 4 Ladies — one a match) p12 (6 2nds, of 3 once); fell/unseated 9, slipped up 1. A grand servant, and has been on the go for ten consecutive seasons, but lightly raced and without a win since '00, and must be approaching the end of his career. *Mrs J.S. Alford — N. Cornwall (Mike Biddick).* 311 (L), 351 (L), 487 (O), 793 (Cf), 911 (MO).

JUST CARAMEL ..8-2.. 9 b.m. Montelimar (USA) — Cream By Post (Torus) f42f4pp434. Lengthy half-sister to NH flat winner, Mister Wellard. Dam (*qv* '94 Annual), won 2m2f Hurdle and 7 Ladies and placed twice. NH FLAT '01 r3 p2 (2nds). NH '01/3 (for P.F. Nicholls, and A.G. Hobbs) r13 p4 (inc 3 2nds); pulled up 4. Favourite for the last Point of the year, and like Josanjamic who had won the previous division of the Maiden could boast a smart effort in a bumper, as she was beaten a head by Farmer Jack (seven wins and £85,589) with Duke Of Buckingham (won seven and £54,139 in third). Placed on five occasions under Rules subsequently, but latterly went to pieces and was last and pulled up on her final three attempts. Wears a tongue-tie and is a woefully weak finisher, and grossly flattered by making the frame six times. Often favourite or near the head of the market, and punters still have not grasped how bad she is. *E. Donavan — Gelligaer F. (Lisa Day).* 121 (OMa), 259 (CMa), 363 (CfMa), 699 (CfMa), 736 (CfMa), 1193 (OMa), 1324 (CfMa), 1488 (OMa), 1534 (OMa), 1566 (OMa).

JUST CHAMP..7-0.. 8 b.g. Gildoran — Double Handfull (Pas De Seul) Rf. Compact. Dam, placed twice on flat and 4 times over Hurdles, won 3 Points and placed 3 for the Clutterbucks ('a devilishly difficult ride'). Seems to have inherited his mother's temperament (but not her ability?), and after running out and unseating at the sixth on his debut he acquired blinkers and fell heavily at the final fence and winded when a remote last of four (should have pulled up). *Miss J.E. Clutterbuck — Berkeley (Alison Dare).* 600 (2m4fOMa), 1233 (OMa).

JUST CLIQUOT ..10-8.. 9 b.m. Gunner B — Formidable Lady (Formidable USA) 1111u. Workmanlike sister to Thatchers Longshot, and half-sister to Beau Bo's Return and Summer Court Lad. Dam, half-sister to Blushing Times (*qv* '95 Annual), won 2m Hdle. P-t-P '02/3 r8 w2 (Maiden and Restricted) p4 (2 2nds); refused 1, and fell 1. Has displayed signs of temperament, but supremely well handled by Gary Hanmer, and registered a Pointing four-timer before making a successful debut over regulation fences at Bangor. Might have remained unbeaten had she not unseated at Cartmel, and her turn of foot will always stand her in good stead. Normally dropped right out and brought through with a smooth run, and has shown herself to be effective on firmish and in soft, but ideally prefers the latter. *K.T. Hamer — Ludlow (Corinne Swarbrick).* 161 (I), 612 (Cf), 930 (O), 1176 (3m110yH), 1490 (3m2fH).

JUST COMING ..—.. 15 b.g. Primitive Rising (USA) — Fair Louise (Blakeney) pp. Lengthy light owner-bred half-brother to Pretty Tactfull, Les's Girl, Only Just and Gwillim Enterprise (won Hurdle on technicality). Dam won at 12f. P-t-P '95, '97, '99 and '01/3 r14 w2 (Maiden and Restricted) p2 (3rds); pulled up 6, fell/unseated 2, and refused 1. A dual winner at Charm Park to '99, and rated 10-3 at best, but has always been extremely elusive, and a non-finisher in seven of his last eight starts. Needs to make way for a younger model. *R.G.P. Mason — Middleton.* 269 (O), 389 (Cf).

JUSTENOUGH ..9-2.. 8 b.g. Alflora (IRE) — Mistress Ross (Impecunious) 53. Unfurnished. Dam won 3 Hdles 2m5f-3m2f, inc a Sell and is half-sister to Serphil (*qv* '96 Annual). NH FLAT '01 r1 p0. P-t-P '03 r2 p0 (fell 2). Booked for a place at worst when falling two out on his debut over 2m4f, but beaten when suffering a similar fate over the full trip next time, and appeared not to get home in '04. Wears bandages and has avoided sound surfaces since his debut. *R. Vickers — Cumberland F.* 432 (OMa), 659 (OMa).

JUST FABLE ..8-13.. 8 br.m. Just Zulu — Treleven (Town And Country) p. Compact well-made. Dam, half-sister to Trecometti (*qv* '98 Annual), won Maiden and placed 4 for Verity Nicholls (failed to stay in 16 of 18 attempts after her win). Grandam, Balitree, won 5 2m Hdles. P-t-P '02/3 r5 p0 (4th, last, fell and pulled up 2). Has shown some speed but precious little in the way of stamina, and her appearances dwindle with every passing season. *Miss V.J. Nicholls — Spooners & W. Dartmoor.* 701 (2m4fOMa).

JUST FLUSTER ..9-11.. 9 ch.g. Triune — Flamber (Hot Brandy) 22f. Tall rangy half-brother to Fledermaus. Dam, half-sister to Days Gorse (*qv* '88 Season Annual), was badly tailed off last in her only completion in 13 Points ('absolutely hates racing'). NH FLAT '02 r1 p0. NH '02 r3 p0; pulled up 1. P-t-P '03 r5 w1 (Maiden) p0; last, fell 2, and pulled up 1. Ended '03 by landing one of the worst races in the calendar, but has continued to go the right way, and is bordering on a Restricted success. Worried out of it at Witton Castle, and had no answer to High Peak next time, but was beaten when falling at the last at Hutton Rudby, and would not be one to take too short a price about. *Lady Susan Watson — Middleton.* 164 (R), 341 (R), 563 (R).

JUST FOR NOW (IRE) ..8-0.. 6 b.g. Flemensfirth (USA) — Sara's Pinkie (IRE) (Roselier FR) 5. Workmanlike short-backed. 9932 3yo. Schooling way off the pace until eventually finishing 64 lengths fifth at Bishops Court. Has the assistance of Polly Gundry, and might improve eventually. *Mrs J. Roberts — Berkeley (Sarah George).* 328 (OMa).

PLATE 67 161 Old Raby Hunt Club Intermediate: Just Cliquot and Gary Hanmer, 1st
PHOTO: Roy Parker

JUST HENRY ..—.. 8 gr.g. Arzanni — Silk Touch (Lochnager) fpp. Close-coupled. Dam, half-sister to The Birdie Song (*qv* '98 Annual), failed to finish in 3 Points for the Allsops. NH FLAT '02 r2 p0. NH '02 (for A. King) r1 p0 (last). Tailed off thrice under Rules, and a hard puller who jumped poorly in his first two Points. Acquired a tongue-tie in the latest, and stopped to nothing and pulled up at the 11th, suggesting that he has problems. *Mr & Mrs R. Allsop — N. Ledbury (Caroline Chadney).* 617 (2m4fOMa), 724 (OMa), 1259 (OMa).

JUSTIN MAC (IRE) ..10-0§.. 14 br.g. Satco (FR) — Quantas (Roan Rocket) 7u2324. Tall workmanlike half-brother to 4 flat winners (one in Norway), and to successful Irish Hurdler, Clover Hill Lad. Dam won at 6f. NH FLAT '97 r3 w2 p1 (2nd). NH '97/00 and '02/3 r21 w3 (2m-2m1f Hdles) p4 (inc 2nd in 2 Chses). HUNT CH '01/3 (for Mrs C. Shaw) r11 w3 (2m-2m5f110y) p0; 4th, 6th, 8th, refused 2, unseated 1, and pulled up 2. An enigmatic performer who used to be nigh on unbeatable on his seasonal debut, but has always been difficult to motivate otherwise, and has never won beyond 2m6f. Displayed renewed vigor in the new yard, but very much a veteran, and it's hard to envisage him winning again. Blinkered once over hurdles, and again in '01. *Miss K. Wood & Mrs K. Simpson — Cheshire (Kelda Wood).* 94 (L), 230 (L), 529 (L), 751 (L), 931 (L), 1072 (L).

JUST JAKE .—.. 12 b.g. Jendali (USA) — Dohty Baby (Hittite Glory) 7p. Small neat half-brother to Danbys Gorse and Miss Danbys. Dam won 6f Sell, and won 3 2m Sell Hdles. NH FLAT '97 r2 p0. NH '98/01 r31 w3 (2m Sell Hdle and 2 Chses, 2m110y-2m5f) p7 (3 2nds); pulled up 4, and fell/unseated 3. P-t-P/HUNT CH '02/3 r10 w4 (inc 2 Mixed Opens, and inc hat-trick) p2 (2nds); last pair 2, pulled up 2. Ended a long losing sequence when recording a hat-trick in '02, but lifeless in his last four appearances, and has reportedly been retired. Has been tried in blinkers and cheekpieces. *Mrs C.M. Tinkler — Middleton.* 270 (L), 339 (L).

JUSTJIM ..9-10.. 13 b.g. Derring Rose — Crystal Run VII (unknown) p556. Small sparely-made half-brother to Weekend Wonder and The Welder, and to Chasing winner, Eskleybrook (won 4 Chses consecutively in Spring '99; won 9 Chses and £67,543 for Vic Gethin). NH FLAT '96/7 r2 p0. NH '97/02 (for T. Keddy, N.A. Twiston-Davies, and Mrs H. Dalton) r32 w4 (2m-3m1f Chses) p5 (inc 4 2nds); pulled up 8, fell/brought down 2. Made the bulk of the running when notching four Chasing victories to August '00, but always unreliable, and failed to finish in ten of 17 subsequent attempts to '02 (pulled up in five of the final six). Beaten at least 20 lengths when resuming in Hunter Chases at 12, and has had no enthusiasm for the job for a very long time. Has occasionally been blinkered or tongue-tied, and presumably retired after jumping left in cheekpieces at Ludlow in early April. *E.T. Clarke — N. Hereford (Chris Gethin).* 209 (3m1f110yH), 317 (2m4fH), 435 (3m110yH), 801 (3mH).

JUST JOVE .9-13.. 7 b.g. Jupiter Island — Sunday School (Joshua) 3162. Very big owner-bred half-brother to Nelsun (*qv*). P-t-P '03 r1 p0 (fell). Made all to win the fastest of three Maidens at High Easter, but the form has still to be franked by the placed horses, and has struggled to get home since. Finished very tired after belting the last hard on a return visit the following month, and will need to find reserves of stamina to follow up. An imposing individual, and only risked on good or easy ground so far. *Mrs F. Macfarlane — Pytchley (Caroline Bailey).* 21 (OMa), 218 (OMa), 383 (R), 648 (R).

JUST LARK .9-6.. 11 b.g. Rubicund — Shelley's Lark (Sir Lark) p6313. Tall narrow. P-t-P '02/3 r6 w1 (2-finisher Maiden) p1 (2nd); pulled up 4. Breaking blood vessels when pulled up on his first four appearances, but largely unaffected since, and has managed to land two weak races on sound surfaces. A reliable jumper but will need to improve further to upgrade successfully. Wears a kineton. *Mrs V.K. Rickcord — R.K. Bliss — S. & W. Wilts.* 265 (R), 354 (R), 1022 (R), 1097 (M), 1442 (2m5fH).

JUST LUTE ..9-5.. 8 b.g. King Luthier — Mossfield (Le Moss) 3upp. Workmanlike lengthy half-brother to Sharplaw. Dam is an unraced sister to Tod Law (*qv* '98 Annual). P-t-P '03 r2 p0 (last pair 2). Twenty-three lengths last of three on his reappearance represented an improved showing, but never jumped with much fluency, and broke down irreparably at Horseheath. *Ms S. Hector & D. Hilton — Cranesfield Racing (Ms S. Hector) — Puckeridge (Sarah Hector).* 371 (OMa), 611 (OMa), 651 (OMa), 741 (M).

JUST SALLY ..10-0.. 7 b.m. Afzal — Hatherley (Deep Run) 2112. Sister to NH flat winner, Squire Shandy, and half-sister to Peasedown Tofana and Mrs Duf (Hurdles winner since Pointing). Dam is half-sister to Cool Bandit (*qv* '99 Annual). NH FLAT '02 r2 p0. P-t-P '03 r3 w1 (Maiden) p1 (3rd); and pulled up 1. A progressive mare, and has plundered Cornwall successfully on three occasions, but yet to beat a rival of note, and surprisingly outgunned by a 14-year-old at Lifton. An abundance of stamina should make up for her lack of toe, and now that her trainer can devote all his time to placing her correctly should certainly score again, but has been covered by Morpeth and will miss '05. Has won in softish and on firmish. Wears a cross-noseband. *Mrs G.A. Robarts — Dulverton F. (Ashley Farrant).* 79 (R), 315 (R), 489 (I), 823 (Cf).

JUST STRONG (IRE) .—.. 12 b/br.g. Strong Gale — Just Dont Know (Buckskin FR) f*8544*. Half-brother to Fatalistic (IRE), to Irish NH flat and Hurdles winner, Lady Of Grange, and to Irish Pointing and Chasing winner, Just Spring. Dam won NH flat race in Ireland. P-t-P '99 (for Mr P.K. Barber) r3 w1 (Maiden) p1 (3rd); and 5th of 6. NH '00/3 r24 w3 (2m4f-3m3f Chses; lucky once) p4; pulled up 5, fell 1. NH '04 r3 p0 (5th in 3m2f Ch: *hld up & bhnd, some hdwy when blun bad 5 out, sn btn*; and 4th in 2m5f-3m3f Chses: *a bhnd*; and *bhnd til hdwy app 3 out, nt rch ldrs*). A one-paced galloper, even in his prime, and has gained all his best results on good or sound surfaces, but lacks fluency over big fences and needs to return to Points if he is to score again. Has been hobdayed. *Miss J.M. Thompson — Zetland (Muriel Naughton).* 679 (3m1fH), 798 (3m1fH).

JUST THE JOB TOO (IRE) .10-4§.. 8 b/br.g. Prince Of Birds (USA) — Bold Encounter (IRE) (Persian Bold) 1. Good topped. Dam won 6f race and 2m Hurdle in Ireland. FLAT '99/02 r26 w5 (8-16f) p3 (3rds). NH '01/2 r3 p0. P-t-P '03 r3 w1 (Open, 3 ran 2 finished) p2. A fair performer on the all-weather, but often failed to deliver as much as expected, and was a beaten favourite three times in the same year he scored thrice. Gained several decent scalps when making a winning reappearance at Black Forest Lodge, but presumably met with a setback, and was not seen again. Has tended to find little off the bridle in Points, and three miles certainly stretches his stamina, but good enough to win again if he can be produced fit and well. Has been tried tongue-tied. *The Storm Trooper Partnership (T.A. Parker) — Dart V.H. & S. Pool H. (Liam & Sarah Corcoran).* 64 (O).

JUST WHISKEY (IRE) ..9-13.. 12 b.g. Satco (FR) — Illinois Belle (Le Bavard FR) 44p2. Tall brother to Irish Chasing winner, Nosalil. 7000 3yo. IRISH P-t-P '98/9 r4 p2; pulled up 2. IRISH NH FLAT '98 r1 p0. NH FLAT '99 r1 p1 (3rd). NH '99/03 (for N.A. Twiston-Davies) r9 w1 (3m2f Ch) p1 (2nd); pulled up 4. Won a staying Chase at Plumpton in the soft in October '01, but was a whiskey sour when pulling up in his three subsequent attempts under Rules. Broke his previous record of attendances when appearing four times in '04, and not disgraced in three of the Opens, but was very one-paced and easy to beat. Tongue-tied twice previously. Seems rather unlikely to continue at 12. *Mrs P.M. Shirley-Beavan — Jedforest.* 429 (3m5fO), 656 (O), 764 (O), 1079 (O).

J W (U) ..4-12.. 7 br.m. unknown — unknown 7. The first ride for her owner in a Members, and contested furlongs last with a thoroughbred on the final circuit until outwaddled by him for sixth near the finish. A plucky try. *Miss J. Mills-Hewitt — Cambridge Univ.* 98 (M).

KALAHARI FERRARI ..8-7.. 9 ch.g. Clantime — Royal Agnes (Royal Palace) p. Compact robust half-brother to Dancing Days, and to flat winners, She's Special and Antonia's Folly. Dam won at 14f. FLAT '98/01 r20 p7 (7-9f, inc Sell). NH '99/01 r6 p0; pulled up 1, unseated 1. P-t-P '03 (for Mr G. Hawker & Mr M. Stephenson) r2 w1 (2m4f Maiden) p0; and pulled up. Handed a freakish two-finisher 2m4f Maiden at Garnons on a plate last year, but barely got a mile on the flat, and pulled up lame on his only start in '04. Blinkered once in '99, and visored once two years later. *G. Hawker — N. Ledbury (Tim Stephenson).* 109 (CR).

KALYPSO DE LAUGERE (FR) ..9-5.. 7 b.g. Luchiroverte (IRE) — Diane De Laugere (FR) (El Badr) p25. Tall rangy. P-t-P '03 r1 p0 (pulled up). Looks the part and beat a subsequent winner when second at Tweseldown, but faded in the closing stages there, and again when around five lengths fifth at Mollington, and needs to prove he gets the trip. Better jumping would also help his cause. *Mrs E. Young & K. Smith — Grafton (Jenny Pidgeon).* 30 (CMah), 173 (OMa), 296 (OMa).

KANDY FOUR (NZ) ..9-5.. 10 ch.g. Zeditave (AUS) — Executive Suite (NZ) (Western Symphony USA) 2. Rangy. NZ FLAT w1 (9f). NZ NH '00 r3 p2 (3rds). NH '00/3 (for P.F. Nicholls) r20 w2 (2m4f-2m5f Chses) p11 (inc 2nd in Hdle); pulled up 1, fell 2. Finally got off the mark over fences in a meaningless contest at the 13th attempt (having been headed after a slow jump at the last on his previous effort), but immediately followed up, both in softish in July/August '02. Can be error-prone and too keen, and rapidly ran out of steam in the closing stages of a Ladies for which he was favourite at Mounsey Hill Gate. May not stay three miles, and looks difficult to place these days. *P. Nicholls — Blackmore & Sparkford V. (Chloe Roddick).* 1462 (L).

KANTURK STAR (IRE) ..9-0.. 9 b.g. Star Quest — Tonka Mary (Riot Helmet) p5p. Lengthy workmanlike. IRISH P-t-P '01 r3 p1 (3rd); pulled up 1. P-t-P '02/3 r6 p3 (3rds); pulled up 2, and unseated 1. Beaten between three and 28 lengths when placed in Points, but tubed unsuccessfully in '04, and retired after an equally abortive attempt in blinkers. *T.M. Gibson & M. Rastall — Tynedale (Theresa Gibson).* 859 (CfMa), 1041 (OMa), 1224 (OMa).

KARADIN (FR) ..10-1.. 11 b.g. Akarad (FR) — In River (FR) (In Fijar USA) 2421p. Good-topped half-brother to French flat winner, Rivermixa. FRENCH FLAT '96/7 and '99 r14 w2 (8f) p2. NH '99/03 (for R.H. Buckler) r21 w3 (2 2m Hdles and 2m6f Ch) p6; pulled up 1. Bought Doncaster, May for 7000. A Provinces horse on the flat in France and gained one of his two wins at Saint-Brieuc, and was blinkered twice there, and subsequently adapted well to jumping. Had only failed to finish once in his first 25 attempts, but then gave a lacklustre display when pulling up at Hereford. Beaten short-head in a Cherrybrook Confined, but quickly gained compensation six days later at Lifton, where he jumped well when taking the Ladies in a quick time. Should maintain a comparable level of form in '05, particularly if avoiding races in which he has to carry penalties (11 stone seems very suitable for him). *R. & Mrs M. Hand — Modbury H. (Mandy Hand).* 483 (Cf), 569 (MO), 793 (Cf), 822 (L), 1175 (3m1f110yH).

PLATE 68 822 Eggesford Ladies Open: Winners Karadin and Mandy Hand totally obscure the challenging Breteche and Bun Newman PHOTO: Baths Photographic

KARINGA LANE .9-7.. 8 b.g. Karinga Bay — Handy Lane (Nearly A Hand) 311626. Good-topped half-brother to Here Comes The Sun, Sulaafah Lane and Halsway Lane. Dam won 3 2m1f Hdles and 2 Chses (2m-2m4f). P-t-P '02/3 (for Mr G. Morley) r5 p0 (5th of 6, pulled up 2, and fell/unseated 2). Had two unproductive years in the previous yard, but much improved in '04, and won a short Maiden and a long Restricted on rain softened ground convincingly. Most disappointing, and not better than last since, and even turned over in a match for his Members which looked so one-sided that no bookmaker was prepared to bet on it. Despite having won a seven-minute race it seems likely that a stamina deficiency is his problem. Wears a cross-noseband. *O.I.F. Davies — Wheatland (Jo Priest).* 227 (CfMa), 533 (2m4fCfMa), 752 (R), 1015 (Cf), 1346 (M), 1426 (C).

KARINGA LEAP..9-11.. 8 ch.g. Karinga Bay — Church Leap (Pollerton) 413. Unfurnished half-brother to Hurdles winners, Vicar's Vase and Vicars Destiny. Dam, half-sister to Vintage Lad (*qv* '97), won 3m Hurdle. P-t-P '03 r2 p0 (4th, and pulled up 1). Benefited from the drop back to 2m4f when opening his account in soft at Whitwell-on-the-Hill, but clocked a much slower time than the first division (16 seconds to be precise), and has been less effective at the conventional trip. A steady jumper considering his inexperience, and should find a Restricted opening when stamina is not such an issue. *J. Cornforth — York & Ainsty N. (Philip Cornforth).* 504 (CMa), 774 (2m4fCMa), 1288 (R).

KARZHANG ..9-13.. 13 b.g. Rakaposhi King — Smokey Baby (Sagaro) ppp1p. Tall workmanlike half-brother to Jubilee Gunner, and to Hurdles winner, Smoking Gun. Dam is half-sister to Brown Baby (*qv* '00 Annual). NH FLAT '97 r2 p0. NH '98/00 r10 p2; pulled up 1. P-t-P/HUNT CH '02/3 r13 w2 (Club Maiden and Restricted) p3 (2 2nds); 6th, pulled up 5, fell 1, and brought down 1. Has stamped his authority on two weak races on easy surfaces, and walked over for another success in '04, but error-proneand apt to run out of steam very quickly. Wears a cross-noseband and a tongue-tie, and presumably forced to pull up so often because of a wind impediment. Dumped the rider and proved reluctant to go to post at Cothelstone, and clearly not happy with his lot at present. *J. Beasley — Albrighton (Caroline Robinson).* 157 (L), 751 (L), 838 (L), 1149 (I), 1365 (Cnr).

KASILIA (FR) ..10-1.. 7 b.g. Silver Rainbow — Basilia (FR) (Mont Basile FR) 2532. FRENCH NH '02/3 r19 p6 (Chses, all in provinces); fell 3, pulled up 3. Gave some competent displays in the new yard, making it look remarkable that he could not manage to win a Chase in the French Provinces (was frequently blinkered there). Showed he stays three miles when left a lucky second at the final fence in a Restricted, but 32 lengths fifth next time, and came into his own over shorter trips in Fakenham Novice Hunter Chases in which he was beaten about eight lengths in both. When he finished third to Enitsag there, all the first three home were bred in France — surely a first for the Pudding Norton venue. Mysteriously has never tried a Maiden, and should do so, as he would surely be a certainty to break his duck at long last. *T. Brown — Woodland Pytchley.* 231 (CR), 379 (I), 544 (2m5f110yH), 892 (2m5f110yH).

KATARINO (FR) ..—.. 10 b.g. Pistolet Bleu (IRE) — Katevana (FR) (Cadoudal FR) b. Unfurnished brother to French Hurdling winner, Karolina, and to a flat winner in Switzerland. FRENCH NH '98 r3 p1 (3rd); pulled up 1. NH '98/01 and '03 (for N.J. Henderson) r17 w6 (5 2m-2m1f Hdles and 2m4f Ch) p3; unseated at The Chair in '03 Grand National. Close up when brought down at two miles at Larkhill in mid-January, and not seen again. His past is littered with star performances, and was unbeaten in his first five English races including the £45,960 Triumph Hurdle. Made a very impressive Chasing debut, but unable to repeat his success in that sphere, made his final appearance under Rules when failing to complete the course for the first time, when he unseated at the 15th in the Grand National. Normally a fine jumper, and career earnings total £171,133 which includes a pot of nearly £40,000 at Punchestown and £32,293 for a second at Auteuil (given their levels of prize money, how much could he netted had he remained at home?!). Finished seventh in Istabraq's Champion Hurdle in '00. Unfortunately has a breathing problem, and watching him in a field in Wiltshire was the equivalent of seeing Gerard Depardieu in amateur dramatics at the Salisbury Playhouse. *R.B. Waley-Cohen — Warwicks.* 11 (O).

KATINKA ..10-2.. 12 b.m. Rymer — Millymeeta (New Brig) f1pp4f. Tall workmanlike lengthy half-sister to Macmurphy and Minibrig. Dam won 6 Ladies (to 3m5f) and placed 5. Grandam, Mee, won 5 Points (4 Ladies) and 2nd 2. Great-grandam, Lazy Jane, won 6 Points. NH '01/3 r7 p0; pulled up 2, and fell 1. P-t-P '03 r4 w2 (Restricted and Confined) p0; last, and fell 1. A decent performer in her grade, and only beaten once when completing in Points (a Maiden!), but prone to wholesale blunders, and wind related problems have restricted her appearances. Probably not up to Open standard, but could still find another race if her sights were lowered in '05. Wears a cross-noseband, and has run tongue-tied. *A.M. Thomson — Berwicks.* 134 (O), 282 (Cf), 764 (O), 858 (Cf), 1177 (2m5fH), 1373 (2m4f110yH).

KAYLEIGH (IRE) ..9-11.. 7 b.m. Kylian (USA) — Easter Baby (Derrylin) 3312. Small neat half-sister to flat winner, Kinkbury. Dam won 2m Hurdle. A competent juvenile who shows a willing attitude, and followed a couple of decent thirds with a win in a weak five-runner Mares Maiden on firmish at Charing in which she had to survive two or three erratic jumps. Beaten by a subsequent Confined winner (who defeated another York representative on that occasion) in a Restricted at Detling, and should have no difficulty going one better in similar company herself. Like others in her yard, she is a trier but lacks much physical scope. *R.M. Green — Staff College (Phillip York).* 35 (CMam), 87 (OMa), 185 (CMam), 538 (R).

KEEGAN BEARNAIS (FR) ..9-9.. 7 b.g. Tropular — Sofyland (FR) (Kashneb FR) u52185. Good-topped half-brother to French jumping winner, Elan Bearnais (FR), and to a French flat winner. Dam won 5 flat and 2m5f Chase in France. FRENCH NH '02 r4 p1 (3rd in Ch). NH '02/3 (for A.M. Hales) r4 p1 (3rd in Hurdle); pulled up 3. Bought Doncaster, May for 3500. Goes a fair gallop and outjumped and outstayed another French-bred when making virtually all in a Tweseldown Maiden, but tends to find little, and ended his career under Rules by pulling up in a Selling Hurdle (tongue-tied and wore cheekpieces, and was blinkered once previously). Has an average chance of Restricted success if prepared to work for it. *Mrs J.M. Mann — Warwicks.* 20 (OMa), 66 (OMa), 112 (OMa), 173 (OMa), 587 (R), 636 (Rnr).

KEEP THE DAY JOB ..8-5.. 6 b.m. Thowra (FR) — Mitsubishi Colour (Cut Above) 1. Robust half-sister to Hurdles winner, Enchanted Cottage. Made a mid-May debut in an extremely slowly-run Maiden on firmish at Cothelstone, and awarded a half-length verdict after Nadden Wilmington's triumphant salute had impressed the Judge (but not our man on the line, who thought she was beaten a head). May be able to progress. Her stablemates (Thunder Thighs, et al) must mock her for having such a drab and boring name. *N.M. Tory & B. Snape — Portman (Ali Tory).* 1371 (OMa).

KEITHO (IRE) .9-8.. 10 b.g. Niels — Swift Charmer (Beau Charmeur FR) 4. Big rangy. Dam, sister to Hazeleels Delight (*qv* '94 Annual). IRISH P-t-P '02 r3 p0; pulled up 2, and brought down. IRISH NH FLAT r2 p0. IRISH NH '02 r1 p0 (pulled up). NH '03 (for P.F. Nicholls) r3 p1 (3rd); pulled up 1. P-t-P '03 (for Mr J. Honeyball) r3 w3 (Maiden, Restricted and Intermediate). A change of yard brought staggering improvement last year, and galloped to an impressive hat-trick in Points, but a switch back to racing under Rules proved much less productive, and was tailed off in blinkers on his final start. Landed a gamble on his English debut, and punters got stuck into him again on his reappearance at Littlewindsor, but was really only schooling David Green and blew up at the second last. Capable of jumping very well, and should excel in his latest role if only he can be produced healthy. *M.G. Green — Taunton V. (Mary Tory).* 1012 (Cnr).

KEITH'S DREAM ..—.. 6 b.m. Gildoran — Musical Dream (Merrymount) pf. Compact half-sister to Dreamisle. Dam, sister to Mountville (*qv* '87 Season Annual), was 3rd in R.A. Members ('jumps wildly as often as not'). Bought Ascot, Jun for 3619. Showed some speed before fading and departing in early season Maidens, and needs to prove she gets the trip. Presumably owned by a man named Keith who has a dream. *K. Broomfield — O. Berks (Charles Cox).* 142 (OMa), 293 (CMam).

KELTIC LORD ..10-5.. 9 b.g. Arctic Lord — Scarlet Dymond (Rymer) 1ufpp3. Compact half-brother to Hurdles winner, Diamond Rose. Dam, half-sister to Aradia's Diamond (*qv* '01 Annual), won 3m Ch (suffered badly from dehydration). NH FLAT '00 r2 p0. NH '00/1 r3 p0. P-t-P '02/3 r6 w2 (Maiden and Restricted) p2 (2nds, beaten short-head once, and of 3 once); last, and fell 1. Speedy, and has won once in each of his three Pointing campaigns, but might not have prevailed in the latest had the runner-up kept straight, and has since had jumping problems. Heavily supported when effectively brought down in a melee at the second last at Badbury Rings, and although Hunter Chasing is not his game should retrieve losses if sensibly placed in '05. Suited by good or lively ground. *The Last To Leave Partnership (R.K. Crabb) — Avon V. (Sarah Waugh).* 141 (I), 263 (O), 541 (3mH), 799 (2m3f110yH), 993 (3mH), 1369 (Cf).

KENNY DAVIS (IRE) ..10-0.. 12 b.g. Mazaad — Very Seldom (Rarity) 2fuu331. Small light half-brother to 3 flat winners, including Euro Sceptic (IRE) and Jimmy The Skunk. FLAT r2 p0. P-t-P '98/03 r30 w3 (up to Confined) p8 (5 2nds, of 3 twice, fence last once; inc 3rd of 4, and last of 3 once); pulled up 3, on floor 8, and ran out 1. Four times a winner on good or sound surfaces, and retains ability, but generally easy to beat, and has a habit of losing the rider. Usually held up and produced late, but not one to take too short a price about, and gunned down himself when 4-7 in his Members. Sometimes taken to post early nowadays. *P. & Mrs L. Blagg — Coakham Bloodhounds (Paul Blagg).* 180 (M), 422 (CCon), 609 (O), 806 (C), 1054 (Cf), 1212 (Cf), 1410 (Cf).

KENO DU MOY (FR) ..—.. 7 b/br.g. Bright Dick (FR) — Allez Brecey (FR) (Pot D'Or FR) p. Sold Doncaster, Aug '02 for 3000, and sold again since. Those who participated in the plunge from tens to 4-1 at Mollington would probably have liked James Diment to have made a bit more effort, as he sat motionless when dropping out of contention from halfway before pulling up at the 14th. *S. Doody — Bicester with Whaddon (Fiona Kehoe).* 589 (CfMa).

KENTFORD BRACKEN ..8-11.. 7 b.m. El Conquistador — Busy Mittens (Nearly A Hand) 6. Workmanlike lengthy sister to jumping winner, Kentford Fern, and half-sister to Kentford Busy B. Dam (*qv* '93 Annual), half-sister to Nearly Buskins, won Restricted and 3m1f Hunter Chase and placed 7 (2nd in 2 NH flat and 2 Hdles; and placed in 3 Hunter Chses). P-t-P '03 r1 p0 (fell). Fell after a mile on debut, and not disgraced when around 14 lengths last in an above average short Maiden at Ston Easton, but seems a typically fragile El Conquistador. Might easily prove good enough to win if she could stand regular racing. *D.I. Bare — New Forest (James Young).* 599 (2m4fOMa).

KENTFORD BUSY B .9-12.. 11 b.m. Petoski — Busy Mittens (Nearly A Hand) 2u27. Small unfurnished half-sister to Kentford Bracken (*qv*). NH FLAT '98/9 r4 p2. NH '99/01 r11 w1 (2m6f110y Hdle) p2; pulled up 2. P-t-P/HUNT CH '02 (for Miss S.A. Loggin, Mrs K. Rolls, Mr D. Thompkins & Mr M. Blackford) r2 w1 (3-finisher Club Mares) p0; and last. Won a Hurdle at Exeter in '00, and followed up in a long race in mud at Mollington on her Pointing debut, but lightly raced in recent years, and prone to mood swings. Turned over at 4-5 on her first appearance in a Ladies, but sulked at Chaddesley, since when she has been sold out of the yard, and tragically killed in an accident at home. Mrs L. & Miss S. Loggin — Grafton (Sam Loggin). 583 (Cf), 891 (3m1fH), 1033 (L), 1343 (L).

KEPI ROYAL (FR) ..10-1.. 7 b.g. Royal Charter (FR) — Chic Lilie (FR) (Olmeto) p. Neat half-brother to Hessac (FR). P-t-P '03 r3 w1 (Maiden) p0; 4th of 5, and pulled up 1. Taken steadily at first, and created a very favourable impression when making virtually all the running to land a 16-runner Maiden at Garthorpe, but ultimately blown away by Fane Counsel at Horseheath and failed to reappear. Likely to make amends if he is unharmed. *S. Campbell & Miss H. Campbell — Cottesmore (Holly Campbell).* 127 (R).

KERRES NOIRES (FR) .10-0.. 7 b.g. Noir Et Or — Viagara (FR) (Mont Basile FR) pf6. Tall workmanlike. FRENCH FLAT '02 r3 w1 (14f) p0. FRENCH NH '02/3 r9 w3 (2 2m1f-2m2f Hdles and 2m6f Chse) p4. Has tasted the French exotica and sampled the delights of Royan-La-Palmyre, and La Teste de Buch and Toulouse in three of his four wins flat and jumping and despite being essentially a provinces performer amassed £32,271, including in non-thoroughbred contests. Was a close third and still going well when he fell four out at the top of the hill in a 2m5f Cheltenham Hunter Chase, but disappointed in his two other attempts in '04, and was tailed off at Warwick on his final start. Makes matters difficult for himself by fighting the rider, but may not have been in the best of health, and possibly capable of atoning if fully fit. *R. Waley-Cohen — Warwicks.* 528 (O), 1168 (2m5fH), 1299 (2m4f110yH).

KERRYGOLDSOVEREIGN ..—.. 9 ch.m. Blaze O'Gold (USA) — Kerry Blue Nun (Fine Blue) uuu. Very small owner-bred half-sister to Kerry Zulu Warrior. Dam, sister to Kerry Soldier Blue (*qv*). P-t-P '03 r3 p0 (fell/unseated 2, and pulled up 1). Got as far as the last when likely to make the frame at Garnons once, but basically too small to shrug aside her frequent mistakes, and has sent four different jockeys into orbit. Wears a cross-noseband, and bandages. *R.W.A. Price — Brecon & Talybont.* 204 (CfMa), 409 (CMam), 668 (OMa).

PLATE 69 1488 Tredegar Farmers Open Maiden (Div 3): Kerry Zulu Warrior and Tom Faulkner have spread-eagled the field *PHOTO: John Mullen*

KERRY ZULU WARRIOR ..9-11.. 8 ch.g. Aspect (USA) — Kerry Blue Nun (Fine Blue) up2u3pp1. Small neat owner-bred half-brother to Kerrygoldsovereign (*qv*). Has a demented streak and just wants to gallop flat out from the word go, but apart from a 15 lengths second of four at Brampton Bryan he did not beat another rival and exhausted himself in seven attempts for three different jockeys. Acquired Tom Faulkner for the first time at Rhydygwern, and after being taken to post early he soon spreadeagled the field and despite tiring from two out came home unchallenged at 20-1. Evidently likes firm ground, but seems sure to remain a major challenge. Not rated at more than 8-11 prior to his victory. *R.W.A. Price — Brecon & Talybont.* 68 (OMa), 453 (CfMa), 666 (OMa), 845 (CfMa), 1115 (OMa), 1233 (OMa), 1393 (OMa), 1488 (OMa).

KERSTINO TWO ..10-5.. 8 b.g. Cruise Missile — Cresswell (Push On) 12. Tall unfurnished brother to Cruisewell. Dam (*qv '94 Annual*), was not better than last in 4 Points. Grandam, Kick About, was 2nd in maiden. Great-grandam, Kerstin, won Cheltenham Gold Cup. P-t-P '03 r5 w1 (2-finisher Maiden) p3 (3rds, of 4 once, and last twice); and fell. Going very much the right way and probably still not fully strengthened, but connections may rue the day they ran him on ground as firm as that he encountered at Didmarton. Sauntered home at Larkhill previously, and though his jumping is still not foot perfect looks to have the engine that could propel him to success in Open races if able to resume in '05. *Mrs L. Suenson-Taylor — Mendip F. (Caroline Keevil).* 14 (R), 365 (I).

KESTICK ..10-10.. 10 b.g. Roscoe Blake — Hop The Twig (Full Of Hope) 13111. Compact. Dam won 2m Hdle on all-weather. P-t-P/HUNT CH '02/3 r12 w4 (inc 2 Mixed Opens) p7 (5 2nds, beaten neck once, and inc Hunt Ch; inc 3rd in Hunt Ch once); and fell 1. A smart Pointer in Cornwall, and limbered up for his most influential campaign yet by pot-hunting his Members, but proved his worth in the Hunter Chase arena by recording a double at Taunton. Usually dropped right out and produced in the final half mile, but could not match strides with Ask The Natives at Buckfastleigh, and Tabitha Cave was lucky to escape censure after dropping her hands and getting caught for second. Has won in soft but his best efforts have been on much better ground, and is ideally suited by an easy three miles.

Most consistent and looks sure to enjoy another good year in '05. *C.J. Rush — N. Cornwall (Mike Biddick).* 76 (M), 199 (L), 347 (3mH), 733 (3mH), 911 (MO).

PLATE 70 233 South Dorset Members: Kestle Mill wins for the now retired Nick Mitchell
PHOTO: Brian Armstrong

KESTLE MILL (IRE) ..9-10.. 9 ch.g. Be My Guest (USA) — Tatisha (Habitat) 1. Sturdy half-brother to flat winners inc. Shannon Express and Grove Daffodil. Dam won at 8f in France. IRISH NH FLAT '01 r2 p0. IRISH NH '01 r2 p0. NH '02 (for M.J. Coombe) r2 p0. Won his Members easily despite looking backward, but has not been sighted since mid-February, and having made just two appearances in '02 and missed '03 he is obviously extremely hard to train. Tailed off despite starting favourite for both Irish bumpers, and having gurgled on his debut he was subsequently operated on for a wind infirmity. Probably much better than he has ever been able to show. *D.A. & Mrs A. Gamble — S. Dorset (John Roberts).* 233 (M).

KHATANI (IRE) .10-8.. 10 b.g. Kahyasi — Khanata (USA) (Riverman USA) 42211221. Small sturdy half-brother to Irish flat winner, Khatara. Dam won 2 8f races in Ireland inc Listed race, and earned £138,000 (the great bulk of it from placings). IRISH FLAT '97/9 r7 w3 (10-16f) p1 (3rd). FLAT '00 r1 p0. NH '99/03 (for D.R. Gandolfo) r22 w7 (5-timer in 2m-2m4f Hdles and 2 2m3f-2m5f Chses) p6 (inc 5 3rds); pulled up 1. A useful animal on his day, and was in a rich vein of form between April and July '00 when he completed a five-timer, the last three wins being at Worcester. Performed poorly on his final four attempts in the previous yard, and was a wedding present from David Gandolfo to Robert Rowsell, and when he scored under Lee Stephens in an Open at Laleston it was his first success since the rider had partnered him to victory as a Conditional two years earlier. A resolute finisher who must have good ground or firmer, and later paired well with Lucy Rowsell, but the Stewards should have asked some questions when he was comprehensively beaten at 4-9 in a three-runner Ladies at Lydstep. Normally tongue-tied but not that day, and having had one tie-back operation he now needs another. Not previously tried over fences, but jumps small ones (at least) very fluently, and will again be noteworthy in late season in '05. *R.J. Rowsell — Ystrad Taf Fechan.* 842 (O), 1024 (O), 1089 (M), 1190 (O), 1483 (L), 1522 (L), 1549 (O), 1563 (L).

KHAYAL (USA) ..9-12.. 11 b.g. Green Dancer (USA) — Look Who's Dancing (USA) (Affirmed USA) 4pp31. Good-bodied. Dam won 3 races up to 9f in USA. FLAT r1 p0. NH '97/8 and '01/2 r12 p3 (2 3rds). P-t-P/HUNT CH '99/00 and '03 r13 w5 (inc 2 Mixed Opens, inc 4-timer '99) p4 (2nds, of 3 twice, inc Hunt Ch); 6th, last, pulled up 1 and unseated 1. The joint-second top-rated five-year-old in '99, but it has been generally all downhill for him since, and his Umberleigh match victory was his first for four years. Very moody in two previous outings this year, and downed tools when blinkers were applied at Bratton Down, but went sweetly enough for Rachael Green, despite jumping away to the right. Lightly raced throughout his career, but is only effective on good or sound surfaces. Visored once in '98. *Mr & Mrs D. Cossey — Dulverton F. (Linda Blackford).* 1384 (Cf), 1498 (3m2f110yH), 1510 (O), 1557 (Cf), 1560 (Cf).

KILCASKIN GOLD (IRE) ..9-12.. 10 ch.g. Ore — Maypole Gayle (Strong Gale) 386p. Angular half-brother to Maypole Fountain (IRE), and to Hurdles winner, Blackwater Bay (IRE). IRISH P-t-P '01/2 r10 w1 (5&6yo Maiden) p3. IRISH HUNT CH '02 r2 p0. IRISH NH '02 r1 p0. P-t-P/HUNT CH '03 r6 w2 (inc 3m1f Hunt Ch) p1 (2nd); 4th, and pulled up 2. Ended a long losing sequence when landing a two-finisher Members last year, but then proceeded to spring one of the shocks of the season when taking the Heart at Hexham at a resounding 25-1. Most uninspiring in '04, and Alastair Findlay could not motivate him at all, and if he does score again it will probably be at a similar price. Has been tried in blinkers. *The Pavillion Syndicate (R.A. Ross) — Braes (Russell Ross).* 214 (O), 269 (O), 429 (3m5fO), 542 (3m3fH).

PLATE 71 879 West Somerset Vale Restricted: Kildysart Lady (Ben Woodhouse), 1st, leads River Dante (Saul Kidston), 3rd *PHOTO: Brian Armstrong*

KILDYSART LADY (IRE) .9-10.. 9 br.m. King Of Shannon — Raj Kumari (Vitiges FR) p1524. Lengthy sister to Kates Ivy Hill (IRE), and half-sister to multiple flat winner, Queen Of Shannon (IRE). IRISH NH FLAT 00/1 r2 p0. IRISH NH '00/1 r12 p0. NH '01 r6 p0; pulled up 2, fell 1. P-t-P '03 r5 w1 (2m4f Maiden) p2 (3rds, of 4 once); 5th of 6, and pulled up 1. Useless under Rules, but has found Pointing more to her liking, and twice successful on good ground at Cothelstone. Given a very confident ride by Ben Woodhouse in the latest, but can go from full to empty in just a few strides, and basically finds three miles too taxing. Blinkered twice over hurdles. *Mrs C.M. Budd — Taunton V.* 473 (R), 879 (R), 1181 (I), 1369 (Cf), 1437 (2m5f110yH).

KILLARD POINT (IRE) ..10-3.. 6 b.g. Old Vic — Chic And Elite (Deep Run) b11. Compact. Dam won 2 2m1f Hurdles and 2 Chases (2m1f-2m4f). 13,600y. Brought down at halfway when favourite on his debut, but was the ready winner of a modest 2m4f Maiden at Mollington, and followed up in a Dingley Restricted before being put away for the season. A workmanlike performer who is sure to possess further scope, and looks set to make a name for himself in the years to come. *G.T.H. Bailey — Mrs S. Carsberg — Pytchley (Caroline Bailey).* 128 (OMa), 291 (2m4fCfMa), 889 (CR).

KILLERINE (FR) .10-4.. 10 b.g. Leading Counsel (USA) — Rose Petal (FR) (Pharly FR) 23131131. Compact well-made half-brother to a French maiden who earned E43,000!, French flat and Hurdles winner, Tite Fanny, and to French flat winners, Meleasta and Rougemont. FRENCH FLAT '97/8 and '02 r4 p2. FRENCH NH '98/9 and '02 r24 w2 (1m7f-2m4f Hdles) p10. NH '99/02 (for I.Williams) r17 w4 (2m3f-3m3f Chses) p3. Bought Doncaster, Aug for 20,000. A very thorough stayer who ideally prefers plenty of cut in the ground, and took his career total of wins into double figures when beating the favourite in a match at Kingston Blount, where he paid a high price by finishing lame (and evidently had problems in '03, having missed that season). Quite classy and can be determined, and earned £79,683 under Rules (two wins at Auteuil contributed over £25,000), but less than keen on occasions, and frequently blinkered (and tongue-tied to '02). Generally pleasing in Ladies Opens, and would probably achieve a similar level of success if able to return. Bet Ali Tory would like to get her hands on his half-sister, Tite Fanny (just for the name, of course!); and that Weatherbys' names guru, Nick Wilson, wouldn't have stood for such a thing. *A.C. Kemp & Miss H. Irving — Bicester with Whaddon (Heather Irving).* 18 (L), 48 (3m5f70yL), 189 (L), 246 (L), 464 (L), 585 (L), 785 (L), 1106 (L).

PLATE 72 181 Mid Surrey Farmers Draghounds Restricted: Killiney Bay (Phillip York), 1st, leads Rainbow Ranch (Chris Gordon), 2nd PHOTO: Brian Armstrong

KILLINEY BAY (IRE) .10-1.. 9 b.g. Mister Lord (USA) — Tatlock (Paico) 41. Brother to Irish Pointing winners, Kanturk Dinosaur and Warrior Princess, and half-brother to Hurdles winner, King's Country (IRE), and to successful Irish Pointer, Rare Vintage. IRISH P-t-P '02/3 r10 w1 (6yo and upwards Maiden) p1 (3rd); pulled up 6, fell 1. Usually failed to finish in Ireland, but looked to have improved in the new yard, and won a Charing Restricted on firmish in mid-February. Disappointingly not seen again, and there is a suspicion that his rating may be a little too high. *Mr & Mrs R. Gurney — O. Surrey, Burstow & W. Kent (Richard Gurney).* 102 (R), 181 (R).

KILLOUGH HILL (IRE) ..8-8.. 8 b.g. Fourstars Allstar (USA) — Bristol Fairy (Smartset) 3442. Compact half-brother to Irish NH Flat and Hurdles winner, Brave Thought. Dam won 2m Hurdle in Ireland, and is half-sister to Copper Fastener (*qv* '92 Annual). NH FLAT '02 r2 p0. P-t-P '03 r3 p0 (last, and unseated 2). Edgy and free-running, and went faster still when blinkered on his latest appearance, but would almost certainly have won had he not gone very lame on the run-in. Basically a non-stayer, and short Maidens will not be an option even if he is around in '05. Has been tried tongue-tied. *C.J. Bennett — Ledbury (Ben Tulloch).* 30 (CMah), 143 (OMa), 256 (CMa), 982 (2m5fOMa).

KILVOYDAN (IRE) .10-4§.. 10 ch.g. Montelimar (USA) — Vintage Harvest (Deep Run) p63up1212222. Half-brother to Riding Crop (IRE), Vintage Classic (IRE) and Dram Hurler (IRE). IRISH P-t-P '00 r4 p0 (pulled up, fell, refused and ran out). IRISH NH FLAT '00 r6 p1 (3rd). IRISH NH '00/2 r12 p2 (3rds); pulled up 1. P-t-P '03 r5 w1 (Maiden 2-finished) p1 (2nd); unseated 2, and pulled up 1. Capable and has won three races on good or easy surfaces, but thoroughly ungenuine and goes in snatches, and always liable to try to pull himself up. Has a turn of foot, and for that reason is always difficult to omit from calculations, but would rather finish second or preferably not at all, and Davy Phelan has done well with him. Wore cheekpieces on his '04 reappearance, and has been tried in blinkers and a tongue-tie. *A.C. Ward-Thomas — Hampshire (David Phelan).* 118 (R), 169 (R), 181 (R), 538 (R), 606 (R), 716 (M), 779 (R), 802 (R), 1083 (Cf), 1212 (Cf), 1365 (Cnr), 1438 (3m2fH).

KINCORA (IRE) ..10-2.. 14 b.g. King Persian — Miss Noora (Ahonoora) 12up3142. Smallish. Dam won 2 Irish flat, 8-10f. IRISH NH '96 r6 p0. IRISH P-t-P '96/8 r10 p4; pulled up 3. P-t-P/HUNT CH '99/03 r35 w8 (inc Confined Ladies and 5 Ladies, inc 4-timer '02) p12 (9 2nds, beaten head twice, and of 3 twice; inc 3rd in Hunt Ch); pulled up 1, unseated 3. Consistent and a reliable jumper, and does best when forcing tactics are employed, but had never scored first time out before, and was 20-1 when obliging at Ampton. A fine servant to Lisa Stock, and took his score into double figures when successful at Aldington, where he has won four times, and shows little sign of deteriorating with age. Handles softish but most effective on a sound surface. Wears a cross-noseband, and has run tongue-tied. *Ms L. Stock — E. Kent.* 42 (L), 421 (L), 608 (L), 1053 (L), 1086 (L), 1283 (L), 1438 (3m2fH), 1516 (L).

KINDLE A FLAME ..8-12.. 9 b.g. Nomadic Way (USA) — Tees Gazette Girl (Kalaglow) ff2u1. Lengthy half-brother to Hurdles winner, Time Marches On. Dam won 11f race. NH FLAT '00/1 r3 p0. NH '01 (for Mrs M. Reveley) r5 p2 (2nds). Bought Doncaster, Aug '02 for 4000. Runner-up behind Rebel Son in a couple of 2m6f Sedgefield Hurdles, and only beaten between two and three-and-a-half lengths, but has become very disappointing, and beaten favourite on four occasions before finally justifying his position at the head of the market when tongue-tied for the first time in a bad five-runner Maiden at Heslaker (the slowest time of the day by far). His jumping has caused big problems and presumably a typically awkward Nomadic Way, but if he has gained confidence he could probably be thereabouts in Restricteds. *M.E. Sowersby — Holderness (Mary Sowersby).* 167 (OMa), 215 (OMa), 482 (OMa), 686 (OMa), 1206 (OMa).

KING BARRY (FR) ..10-4.. 6 b.g. Cadoudal (FR) — Leonie Des Champs (FR) (Crystal Palace FR) 11. Brother to Irish jumping winner, Cadou Royal (FR), French Hurdling winner, Royal Auguin (FR), and French jumping winner, Royale Leonie, and half-brother to 2 French flat and one French Hurdles winners. Bought Doncaster, May '02 for 38,000. Unbeaten in a couple of modest races in softish at Corbridge (very slow time) and Tranwell, and achieved all that was asked of him in winning fashion. Probably a potential Rules horse, and will be interesting when he starts the proper job. *Mr & Mrs R. Anderson Green — Border (David Parker).* 432 (OMa), 918 (R).

KINGDOM OF SHADES (USA) ..—.. 15 ch.g. Risen Star (USA) — Dancers Countess (USA) (Northern Dancer) p. Tall good-topped half-brother to Alycount (USA), to flat and Hurdles winner, Akdam, and to several winners, including winner of a California Derby. Dam won 10 races at up to 9f in USA. FLAT '93/4 r5 p1 (2nd). NH '94/00 and '02 r25 w6 (2 2m110y Hdles and 4 2m5f-4m1f Chses) p10 (7 2nds, beaten short-head once); pulled up 3, and unseated 1. P-t-P '03 r1 p0 (6th). A very thorough stayer who used to revel in mud, but very prone to break blood vessels, and has been unable to score since '00. Restricted to a single appearance in each of the last two years, and looks a spent force now. *A. Phillips — N. Ledbury.* 115 (MO).

KINGFISHER STAR .8-7§.. 10 ch.g. Derrylin — Legata (IRE) (Orchestra) fu2u3p3. Tall workmanlike. IRISH P-t-P '00 r12 p4 (beaten 30*l* plus twice); pulled up 3. P-t-P/HUNT CH '01/3 (for Mr D. Morgan (White Stick Racing Club) r19 w3 (Maiden and 2 Members) p4 (2 2nds, of 3 once; and inc 3rd in Hunt Ch, and of 4 once); pulled up 5. Stays well and has won three minor races on good or sound surfaces, but very moody and an inconsistent jumper, and not surprisingly gave Jessie Lodge a hard time in her first season. Most unlikely to overexert himself in future, and can be safely ignored. Blinkered twice in '03. *Mr & Mrs R. Lodge — V. of Aylesbury with Garth & S. Berks (Philippa Lodge).* 191 (R), 622 (M), 866 (M), 1107 (R), 1278 (Cnr), 1409 (CR), 1517 (R).

KING FREDDY ..9-0.. 6 b.g. Rakaposhi King — The Clarsach (Nicholas Bill) 255. Grandam, half-sister to Combe Florey (*qv*), and Celtic Slave. Finished a length second in a youngsters Maiden at High Easter on his debut, but has not progressed, and followed a remote last with a 12½ lengths fifth behind three 33-1 shots when favourite on a return visit. Will have to do considerably better to score. At least his jumping is good for a novice. *G.T.H. Bailey — Pytchley (Caroline Bailey).* 219 (OMa), 385 (OMa), 651 (OMa).

KING MARLON ..—.. 13 ch.g. Brando — Quiet Queen (Richboy) pppf. Brother to Bewdley Boy and Little Queen. Dam was 2nd in Sell Hdle; and placed in 4 Points. P-t-P '99 (for Mr J. O'Mara) r1 p0 (unseated). Failed to go beyond two miles in all five attempts, and his resumption after a five-year break proved ill-timed as he met his maker at Howick. *J.E. Tuck — Berkeley.* 68 (OMa), 149 (OMa), 362 (CfMa), 699 (CfMa).

KING OF SWING (IRE) ..8-11.. 13 b.g. Lancastrian — Romantic Rhapsody (Ovac ITY) 322244. Compact half-brother to Lady Romance (IRE). NH FLAT '97 r3 p0. NH '97/00 r23 p2 (3rds); pulled up 2, unseated 1. P-t-P '02/3 r14 p2 (neck 2nd once); 5th, last pair 3, pulled up 4, and fell/unseated 4. The veteran of 46 outings but still searching for an elusive first success, and even failed to beat a rival that had spent the previous four years on the sidelines when 4-5 at Charlton Horethorne. Safer than ever before in '04, but just as feeble a finisher, and would have won by now if he was ever going to. Wears a cross-noseband. *Mrs F. Vigar — Cattistock (Elaine Webber).* 237 (CfMa), 355 (CfMa), 626 (Cnr), 883 (OMa), 1130 (Cnr), 1363 (2m3f110yH).

KING OF THE DAWN ..10-3.. 14 b/br.g. Rakaposhi King — Dawn Encounter (Rymer) upuu121. Workmanlike brother to Hurdles winner, Isis Dawn, and to NH flat winner, King Of The Light. Dam is an unraced half-sister to Rachael's Dawn (*qv* '99 Annual), who is by Rakaposhi King. IRISH NH FLAT '96 r2 w1 p0. IRISH NH '97 r1 w1 (2m Hdle). NH '97/8 r5 w1 (2m2f Hdle) p1 (2nd). P-t-P/HUNT CH '99 (for Mr J.J. Boulter) r7 w1 (Club nov rdrs) p1 (3rd in Hunt Ch); 4th, 7th, unseated 2, and brought down 1. NH '99/03 (for M. Campion, and P.R. Hedger) r23 w2 (2m4f110y-2m6f Chses) p9; pulled up 3, unseated 2. A mudlark who has now won eight races, and was the only one in a field of nine that revelled in the testing conditions when recording his latest success at Towcester. Does best at sub-3m trips, but generally lightly raced since '01 and connections did well to extract another two wins from him. Lost the sight of one eye in '03 which probably explains his frequent errors, though in truth has always been prone to make mistakes. *Mrs G. Worsley — O. Surrey, Burstow & W. Kent.* 43 (O), 156 (O), 581 (2m4fH), 631 (2m6f110yH), 777 (M), 1087 (O), 1354 (2m110yH).

KING OF THE SEA (IRE) ..6-5.. 8 b.g. Gone Fishin — Reign Of Swing (Star Appeal) pp2p. Lengthy unfurnished half-brother to winner in Italy. IR6200 4yo. NH FLAT '02 (for V.R.A. Dartnall) r2 p0 (tailed off). Bought Ascot, Aug for 1238. Fifteen lengths last of two behind a rival who had unseated five times and pulled up twice in her previous English Points, and has otherwise been hopelessly tailed off, including after jumping wildly in his latest attempt. Certainly not worth training again. *Miss S.L. Simmons — Cambs with Enfield Chace.* 104 (2m4fOMa), 123 (M), 1241 (M), 1396 (C).

KINGSBRIDGE (IRE) ..9-11§.. 11 b.g. Cataldi — Rockport Rosa (IRE) (Roselier FR) 1632R. Small light. NH FLAT '98 r1 p0. NH '01 r6 p1 (3rd); pulled up 1. P-t-P '00/3 r22 w6 (Maiden, 2 Members, Intermediate and 2 Club nov rdrs) p5 (3 3rds; and inc last of 2 once); 4th twice, last pair 6, ran out 1, and pulled up 2. A good ride for the yard's inexperienced jockeys, and kept up his fine record at Cothelstone (four wins) when making a successful reappearance there, but needs to dominate, and will surrender tamely when headed. Tried to rearrange the owner's girlfriend's good looks when in the process of running well at a big price at Umberleigh, and spookily enough had done exactly the same thing with a different partner 12 months earlier. Unsuited by soft ground. Has been tried in a near-side pricker. Wears a cross-noseband, and has been tried in headgear. *D.E. Pipe — Silverton.* 471 (O), 880 (MO), 1367 (O), 1494 (O), 1563 (L).

KINGS COMMAND ..9-2.. 8 b.g. Henbit (USA) — Country Festival (Town And Country) 3p. Lengthy unfurnished owner-bred half-brother to Rustic Revelry (*qv*). Dam's 2nd win for Janet Menzies. NH FLAT '03 r2 p0. NH '03 (for A. King) r2 p0; pulled up 1. Finished a tired 16 lengths third at Larkhill, where he led until approaching the omitted final fence, but disappointing when hauled to Great Trethew for a 2m4f event next time, and has been absent since February. Seems to have had a setback. *Miss J. Menzies — Mendip F. (Caroline Keevil).* 13 (OMa), 307 (2m4fOMa).

KING'S HERO (IRE) ..10-9.. 10 b.g. King's Ride — Dis Fiove (Le Bavard FR) 31f12. Tall strong half-brother Irish jumping winner, Outlook Good. Dam won NH flat, 4 Hurdles at up to 2m4f and 2m Chase in Ireland. IR25,000 3yo, IR26,000 4yo. IRISH P-t-P '00 r2 p1 (2nd); and pulled up 1. NH '01/2 (for late T. Casey, and A. Ennis) r7 p1 (2nd in Ch); pulled up 1. Only failed by a neck to win a Chase, and looked rather unlucky, but subsequently lost his confidence under Rules, and was given '03 off. Followed a ten lengths third in a Restricted with a win in a two-finisher Maiden at Garthorpe, where he led throughout and after being in total command in the final mile he was heavily eased on the flat, but fell four out when eight lengths clear and going strongly in a Confined. Set his customary fast pace at Dingley and galloped the opposition into the ground in a remarkable time which bettered that of Free Gift in the PPORA Novice Riders contest, and looked to have outstanding claims in a Hunter Chase, but had the misfortune to come up against the above-average Coolefind at Huntingdon, and after being headed before two out he ruined any chance by stumbling at the last and then hanging badly left. Loves to dominate, and if he has sufficient faith in himself he is definitely capable of winning Novice Chases from Chris Bealby's yard, if he does not remain the current side of the wall. *Mrs R. Price — Belvoir (Antonia Bealby).* 383 (R), 685 (OMa), 942 (Cf), 1214 (Cf), 1361 (3mH).

KINGSMILL CREEK .—.. 9 b.m. Le Moss — Kingsmill Imp (Noble Imp) Rp. Dam, sister to Kingsmill Quay, and half-sister to Ross Poldark (*qv*), won 3 Points (up to Restricted) and placed 8 for Jackie du Plessis. Grandam, La Jolie Fille, is half-sister to Transmitter (raced for David du Plessis until he was 19), won a Maiden and 2nd 2 for him. P-t-P '03 r2 p0 (pulled up 2). Pulled up twice in the space of a week in '03, and showed little sign of ability in two more appearances this year. *Miss J. du Plessis — E. Cornwall.* 494 (OMa), 913 (OMa).

KINGS MINSTRAL (IRE) ..9-11.. 15 ch.g. Andretti — Tara Minstral VII (unknown) 3335. Rangy brother to Irish NH flat Hurdles winner, Cloda's Minstral. NH '94/99 and '01/2 (for D.A. Lamb) r42 w3 (2m5f Hdle and 2 2m1f Chses) p7; pulled up 6, fell/unseated 3, left 1. A veteran who has not been sighted on the racecourse in nine of the past 11 years, and gained his final win in a Selling Chase. Inconsistent and prone to blunder over regulation fences, and refused to race once in '97. Beaten about ten lengths in each of his three Pointing thirds, and seemed to enjoy himself, but unsurprisingly proved very one-paced when it mattered. *Miss V. Angus — Miss V. Burrell-Corey — Percy (John Burke).* 854 (M), 1223 (O), 1418 (Cf), 1489 (3m3fH).

KING'S REPLY ..9-3.. 7 b.g. Rakaposhi King — Anamasi (Idiot's Delight) 44p1p. Workmanlike half-brother to Bittern, and to Hurdles winner, Navarone. Dam, half-sister to Bigsun (*qv* '94 Annual). A Richard Burton mount who let his supporters down when backed from 3-1 to evens at Eyton-on-Severn where he pulled up two out when well behind, but recouped losses in a Maiden at Cold Harbour, where he was two lengths clear at the last but weakened and only scrambled home by a head. His final display was a poor one, and will have to improve to reach Restricted standard. *P. Charter, Mrs P.G.D. Sykes & L.D.W. Chilton — S. Salop (Pamela Sykes).* 385 (OMa), 709 (Mah), 934 (OMa), 1232 (OMa), 1388 (R).

PLATE 73 236 Countryside Alliance Club Members (Nov Rdrs): Two useful mounts for Novice Riders (though it didn't turn out as they would have hoped) Kingston-Banker (Harry Wallace) leads Mouseski (Harry Fry) who fell in lead two out causing the former to unseat - was remounted for 2nd
PHOTO: Tim Holt

KINGSTON-BANKER ..10-12.. 9 b.g. Teamster — Happy Manda (Mandamus) 11211141. Tall well-made half-brother to Country Madam. Dam, half-sister to Happy Mannequin (*qv* '87 Season Annual), won 3m Hdle, but failed to finish in 5 of 6 Points (2nd in the exception). Grandam, Happy Chat, won Maiden. P-t-P '01 r1 p1 (2nd). NH FLAT '01 r1 p0 (6th). NH '01/3 (for R.H. Alner) r10 p5 (inc 3 2nds in Chses); pulled up 1, fell 1. Showed immediate promise in '01, and quickly shipped across to Robert Alner, but unlucky not to score under Rules. A top-of-the-ground performer, and quickly made his mark when returned to Points, and would have recorded a six-timer had Harry Wallace not fallen off at Milborne St Andrew. Only beaten once on merit, and forged a useful alliance with Tom Dreaper in Hunter Chases, but often lacks fluency and rarely wins with as much in hand as he should. Very genuine and with his top class connections should continue to make up for lost time when conditions dry up in '05. Wears a cross-noseband. *H. Wellstead & H.S. Butt — Portman (Sally Alner).* 36 (CR), 90 (I), 236 (Cnr), 541 (3mH), 747 (3m1f110yH), 975 (2m7f110yH), 1167 (3m2f110yH), 1440 (3m1fH).

KINGSTON VENTURE ..10-13.. 9 b.g. Interrex (CAN) — Tricata (Electric) p211. Close-coupled owner-bred half-brother to flat winner, Kingston Bill (and 6 losers), and to Emei Shan. FLAT '98/00 r11 w3 (7-10f) p1 (2nd). NH '99/00 and '02/3 (for W.G.M. Turner) r17 w2 (2m-2m1f Hdle) p7 (inc 3 2nds); pulled up 3. A quirky sort who resents the use of the whip, and wore headgear on five occasions in the previous yard, but won five races to June '00, after which he looked to lose interest and was 68 lengths fourth in his only Chase. Struck up a friendly association with Tigger Barnes in Mixed Opens, and relished the firmish ground to notch a double, and remarkably was the only horse to finish in front of Ballysicyos when he had a jamboree of five wins and a second in a six race sequence. Would be vulnerable in mud and is probably over-rated by several pounds, but it was still a good effort by connections to get him so sweet after a long spell of disappointments. *Miss C.J. Overton — Avon V. (Clare Parfitt).* 11 (O), 145 (O), 414 (MO), 1128 (MO).

PLATE 74 1128 Axe Vale Mixed Open: L to R, Kingston Venture (J. Barnes), 1st, disputes with Shobrooke Mill (N. Williams), fell *PHOTO: Tim Holt*

KING TUDOR ..—.. 12 br.g. Lir — Veronica Ann (Henbit USA) ppp. Compact good-topped owner-bred brother to Cath's Lass. Dam, temperamental, won at 12f. P-t-P '98/00 and '02 r20 p2 (2nds, of 3 once); last pair 3, pulled up 10, and fell/unseated 5. Runner-up to Elliewelliewoo at Wadebridge in '00, but failed to complete in his first nine attempts, and has followed suit in his last seven. Fell heavily twice last year, and is a complete waste of time now. *Mrs S.L. Bown — Lamerton (Catherine Bown).* 567 (CfMa), 795 (CfMa), 1353 (OMa).

KIRKFIELD (IRE) ..9-7.. 10 b.m. Commanche Run — Another Grange (Buckskin FR) 2. Sturdy attractive. Dam, half-sister to Grange Run (*qv* '93). IRISH NH FLAT '01 r1 p0. NH '02 r2 p0; pulled up 1. P-t-P '03 r3 p2; and pulled up. Placed thrice in Maidens, and favourite on her final two appearances last year, but a weak finisher to date, and stands her racing badly. Needs to improve further to open her account. *J.L. Needham — Ludlow.* 519 (CfMa).

KIRKHARLE (IRE) ..9-7.. 11 b.g. Commanche Run — Dardy Daughter (Side Track) p. Close-coupled. Dam is half-sister to Festival Light (*qv* '99 Annual). P-t-P/HUNT CH '99/02 (for Mr I. Hamilton) r12 w2 (Restricted and Members) p5 (3 2nds, of 3 once, and inc Hunt Ch); 4th, 5th twice, 7th, and pulled up 1. NH '01/3 (for K.F. Clutterbuck latterly) r7 p2 (3rds); pulled up 3. Displayed plenty of stamina when finally opening his account at the tenth attempt, and when following up immediately, but has been beaten a minimum of 23 lengths under Rules, and appears to have suffered a setback. Has been tried in cheekpieces. *Miss A.F.J. Bowles — Waveney H. (John Ibbott).* 41 (I).

KISSED BY MOONLITE ..8-3.. 9 gr.m. Petong — Rose Bouquet (General Assembly USA) f3p5. Compact half-sister to flat winner, Rising Spray. Dam won 6f race and is half-sister to George Dillingham (*qv* '03 Annual). FLAT '98/01 r16 p1 (2nd); including Sells. NH '02 r1 p0 (pulled up). P-t-P '03 r3 p0 (pulled up 3). Basically useless for a handful of trainers under Rules, and failed to finish in her first five attempts over obstacles, but though her jumping has improved a basic lack of stamina will always be a huge drawback in Points. *Mrs K.D. Day — Atherstone.* 226 (CfMa), 560 (OMa), 887 (CfMa), 996 (CMam).

KISS THIS ..—.. 7 b.m. Bedford (USA) — I'm Unforgettable (Dublin Taxi) r. Had no intention of letting her feet leave the ground at Llanfrynach, where her first fence refusal was accompanied by Rob's sobs. *P. Smith & Mrs S. Issac — Teme V. (Steve Isaac).* 454 (CfMa).

KNICKERS ..8-4.. 8 b.m. Afzal — Once Bitten (Brave Invader USA) p38. Small compact half-sister to Rubian Princess (*qv*). P-t-P '03 (for Miss L.H.D. Bridges) r2 p0 (last 2). Has never looked like coming down, but given a succession of negative rides by Jon Trice-Rolph, and only once better than last in four completions. *Mrs L. & Ms M. Redvers — Ledbury (Cynthia Clifford).* 408 (CMam), 725 (OMa), 978 (CMam).

KNIGHT CROSSING (IRE) ..—.. 7 b.g. Doyoun — Princess Sarara (USA) (Trempolino USA) up. Compact. IR5000y. FLAT '00/2 (from Mrs A. Duffield's) r13 p1 (3rd of 4). Hopeless on the flat and was third of four when gaining his only placing, and concentrated on six furlong races or less on his final four outings. Unseated at the first and tailed off and pulled up two out in Maidens, and surely does not have an earthly of getting the trip. *Miss C.L. Dennis — Hurworth.* 392 (CfMa), 596 (2m5fOMa).

KNIGHT OF KILCASH (IRE) ..9-5.. 10 ch.g. Buckskin (FR) — Lady Pauper (IRE) (Le Moss) pp. Light lengthy brother to Nattico (IRE), and half-brother to Nouvalari (IRE), and to Irish Pointing winner, Anne's Farewell. IRISH P-t-P '00 r1 p0 (fell). P-t-P/HUNT CH '02/3 r5 w1 (Maiden) p0; 5th, last, and pulled up 2. Made virtually all to justify favouritism in a weak Maiden at Lifton in '02, but incredibly fragile and has shown no other form in seven other starts. Blinkered once in '02. Wears a cross-noseband. *J. Jones — Ledbury (Mrs R.C. Jones).* 279 (R), 977 (R).

KNIGHT OF PASSION .10-3.. 13 b.g. Arctic Lord — Lovelek (Golden Love) 411. Small plain half-brother to Caribbean Dream. Dam, half-sister to Minstrels Joy (IRE) (*qv* '97 Annual), won 4 minor Points (maximum of 4 finishers) and placed 3 (inc an Irish Hdle). P-t-P/HUNT CH '97/00 and '03 r22 w8 (inc 3m1f Hunt Ch and Ladies; and inc hat-trick '99) p4 (2 3rds, inc Hunt Ch; and inc 2nd in Hunt Ch); pulled up 3, and fell 2. Successful in six of his last seven Points to '00, but went wrong when around 15 lengths eighth to Cavalero in that year's Cheltenham Foxhunters, and it was good to see him enjoying himself again when making all in two wins against vastly inferior rivals. Capable of jumping well, but also just as likely to make mistakes. Insulted by blinkers twice in '03. *R.K. Crabb — Cotley (Alan Tizzard).* 322 (L), 697 (L), 1247 (M).

KNIGHT OFTHE NORTH ..7-7.. 11 b.g. North Col — Midnight Mystic (Black Minstrel) 35p4. Lengthy owner-bred. NH FLAT '99 r1 p0. NH '01 (for Dr P. Pritchard) r1 p0 (brought down). A safe ride for a novice, but was hopelessly tailed off last in his three completions, and there is no way that he is going to make a proper racehorse. *Mrs T. Pritchard — Berkeley (Elizabeth Burrows).* 498 (R), 695 (R), 844 (R), 1070 (M).

KNIGHTON STAR ..9-7.. 9 b.m. Gildoran — Barrica (Main Reef) 2f3p. Lengthy rather unfurnished fired sister to Miss Gilda. Dam won 2m Hurdle, 2m3f Chase and placed 5; was subsequently placed in 2 Confineds. NH FLAT '01 r2 p0. NH '02 (for R.T. Phillips) r1 p1 (2nd). Bought Ascot, Oct for 3619. Runner-up in her only Hurdle and looked certain to win a Maiden after finishing one-and-a-quarter lengths second in a Mares event at Barbury (the third and fourth did manage to score), but beaten favourite in all three attempts since and has become bitterly disappointing. Fell at the eighth, finished weakly when four-and-three-quarter lengths last of three, and then only got as far as the 11th before pulling up. Surely has something troubling her, and should not be a serious betting proposition again unless she shows something far more positive. *Mrs P.J. Willis — Beaufort (Alison Dare).* 35 (CMam), 258 (CMa), 604 (OMa), 731 (OMa).

KNIGHT'S CREST (IRE) ..—.. 15 ch.g. The Parson — Sno-Cat (Arctic Slave) pp. Strong half-brother to smart jumping winner, Ten Plus, NH flat and jumping winner, The Milroy, and to jumping winner, Ten Below. IRISH P-t-P '96 r4 w1 (6yo and upward Maiden) p1 (3rd); pulled up 1, and fell 1. NH FLAT '96 r2 p0. NH '96/9 and '01/2 (for R. Dickin) r21 w2 (3m-3m2f) p6 (inc 5 2nds); pulled up 4, fell 1. Produced a storming late run for his first Chasing win, but only managed one other success (way back in December '98), and has been pulled up on his three most recent outings. Too old and gone at the game. *G. Hutsby — Warwicks (Rebecca Hutsby).* 979 (MOnr), 1213 (Cnr).

KNIVENIVEN (IRE) .8-0.. 12 b.g. Denel (FR) — Loughan-Na-Curry (No Argument) p4p3p6pu. Workmanlike lengthy brother to Bold Action (IRE) (*qv*). NH FLAT '98 r3 p0. NH '98/00 r3 p0 (pulled up 3). P-t-P '03 (for Mr R.D. Thomson) r7 w1 (2-finisher Maiden) p1 (3rd of 4); last, pulled up 2, and fell/unseated 2. Tailed off in bumpers and pulled up in all three starts over hurdles, but despite beating just two rivals in 15 Points has still managed to win one. Error-proneand normally grinds to a halt after a maximum of 2m4f, and must be ailing. *Miss C. Fenemore — Southdown & Eridge (Michael Furlong).* 419 (CR), 605 (M), 779 (R), 897 (Cfv&nr), 1051 (R), 1107 (R), 1208 (R), 1409 (CR).

KNOCKAUN WOOD (IRE) ..9-1.. 11 ch.g. Be My Native (USA) — Misty Venture (Foggy Bell) 4p5. Tall rangy half-brother to Dawn's Cognac (IRE) (*qv*). NH '99/00 and '02 r3 p0; pulled up 1. HUNT CH

'03 (for Mr C.A. Fuller) r1 p0 (pulled up). Virtually untrainable, and '04 was the first time he had managed more than one appearance in a year, but too fat to do himself justice, and finished lame at Holnicote. *C. Brake — Dulverton F.* 83 (OMa), 197 (R), 274 (CfMa).

KNOCKHOLT ..10-1.. 9 b.g. Be My Chief (USA) — Saffron Crocus (Shareef Dancer USA) 63434. Small compact well-made half-brother to 4 flat winners, (one in Norway) including Boule d'Or, Catoffle and Saffron Dancer (last pair in Ireland). Dam won 2 Irish flat, 12-13f. Grandam, Bright Crocus won May Hill Stakes. 22,000f, IR27,000y. FLAT '99/01 r19 w4 (12-16f) p3. NH '01/2 (from L. Lungo's) r5 p3 (2nds). Won four flat races on sound surfaces to July '00, and was short-headed once and promoted from fourth to third once, but inconsistent, and has never managed to score over jumps despite five placed efforts. Proved a safe ride for a learner in Ladies Opens, and not disgraced, but the likes of Balisteros and the Stirling horses were always going to prove too strong. Visored four times in the past. *J.A. Ogle & M. Hind — T. Reed & Mrs P. Pattinson — Tynedale (Tim Reed).* 270 (L), 425 (M), 763 (L), 1039 (L), 1308 (L).

KNOCK IT BACK (IRE) ..9-8.. 13 ch.g. Down The Hatch — Lady Hapsburg (Perhapsburg) pp6653. Tall good-looking brother to Kings Hatch, and half-brother to Irish Hurdles winner, Tom Kenny. IRISH P-t-P '97 r2 w1 (5yo&up Maiden) p1 (3rd). IRISH NH '97/8 r8 w1 (2m4f Hdle) p0; finished in all 3 Chses. P-t-P/HUNT CH '99/00 and '02 (for Mrs M.R. Lea) r9 w2 (Open and Club) p3 (3rds, last twice, distant after remounting once); last 2, pulled up 1 and fell 1. Did quite well in Ireland, but very lightly raced in the previous yard, and his '02 wins were his first for four years. An excitable sort, and retains some speed, but only once better than last in '04, and regularly ran into a brick wall after 2m4f. *P.C. & Mrs S.E. Handley — N. Salop (Peter Handley).* 93 (O), 228 (Cf), 528 (O), 662 (O), 749 (Cf), 1427 (O).

KNOCK STAR (IRE) ..9-11.. 14 gr.g. Celio Rufo — Star Of Monroe (Derring Rose) 21554. Sturdy compact. IRISH P-t-P '95 r2 p0; pulled up 1. NH '97/9 r23 p3 (inc 2nd of 20 and 3rd in Sells); remote 5th twice, pulled up 2 and fell in Chses. P-t-P/HUNT CH '00/3 r21 w2 (Maiden and Restricted) p8 (6 2nds, of 3 once, and last once); 4th, last pair 4, ran out 1, unseated 1, and pulled up 4. Consistent in minor Points and has won three races at or around Kilworthy, and 16-1 when gamely hanging on over the road in the latest, but turned over at 4-5 in his Members, and out of his depth in Hunter Chases where the red mist descends upon the rider. Often lacks fluency and struggles to get the trip, but might find another opportunity when his sights are lowered. *The Partridge Partnership (Miss E.A. Beaverstock) — S. Devon (Simon Partridge).* 411 (M), 793 (Cf), 1167 (3m2f110yH), 1437 (2m5f110yH), 1556 (MO).

KNOW THYNE (IRE) ..—.. 11 ch.g. Good Thyne (USA) — Bail Out (Quayside) p. Tall rangy half-brother to Bettys Rose (IRE). IRISH NH FLAT '01 r1 w1. NH '02/3 (for H.D. Daly, and P.T. Dalton) r6 p0; pulled up 4. Won a 19-runner Tipperary bumper on firmish when raced just the once in Ireland, but has been pulled up in five of seven ventures since being sold. Has a terrible bleeding problem, and jumped awfully in his only Point. *Mrs J. Williams — Glamorgan (Cath Williams).* 671 (I).

KOTORI (IRE) ..8-0.. 6 gr.g. Charnwood Forest (IRE) — La Kermesse (USA) (Storm Bird CAN) fppppp5. Good-bodied half-brother 2 French flat winners (one also since over jumps). Dam won 7f race. 12,000f; IR16,500y. FLAT '01/3 (for M.S. Saunders) r14 p1 (2nd in 5f Sell). Bought Ascot, Nov for 952. A familiar figure on the flat when he started slowly in nearly all of his 14 races (just one of them at beyond six furlongs), and gained his only placing when second in a five furlong Seller at Wolverhampton. Wore cheekpieces. Still has delusions of being a sprinter, and after six non-completions in Points he finally finished 30 lengths last when wearing a nose-net at Chaddesley Corbett. Surely connections will have got the message now. *Mrs C.J. Bibbey (The Kotori Partnership) — Radnor & W. Herefords (Clive Davies).* 619 (2m4fOMa), 723 (OMa), 983 (2m5fOMa), 1115 (OMa), 1266 (2m4fOMa), 1393 (OMa), 1532 (OMa).

KOVACH (IRE) ..10-0.. 12 b.g. Homo Sapien — Giolla's Bone (Pitpan) 1. Tall half-brother to Mutual Agreement, to Irish Hurdles and English Chasing winner, Mutual Trust, and to Irish Pointing winners, Lusmagh River and Sally Meadows. NH FLAT '98/9 r2 p0. NH '99/00 r9 w1 (2m5f Ch) p2 (3rds). P-t-P '02/3 (for Mr & Mrs C. Strang Steel) r9 p4 (2nds, of 3 once); 4th, last, unseated 1 and pulled up 2. Scored on only his second appearance over fences, but lightly raced since, and has found it difficult to see out the trip in Points. Sprang a huge surprise when enterprisingly ventured to Lydstep for a 3-runner Ladies, and three time '04 winner Khatani never looked like pegging him back. A reliable jumper and suited by a sound surface, but clearly stands his racing badly, and new connections did well to produce him fit and well. *F. Homer-Morris & D. Dobson — Albrighton (Graham Harris).* 1522 (L).

KRAC DE MIRANDE (FR) .9-3.. 7 b.g. Signe Divin (USA) — Dona Mirande (FR) (Pebble FR) 3. Workmanlike half-brother to French flat winner, and to a French jumping winner. FRENCH FLAT '01/2 r6 p3 (non-thoroughbred races). FRENCH NH '02 r5 p0. A very experienced French maiden of little distinction, and did not reappear after his 11 lengths third over 2m4f on the opening day. Was the only one of the first four not to score subsequently, but seems to be suspect and under a cloud. *R. Waley-Cohen — Warwicks.* 7 (2m4fOMa).

KRYSTAL TIP ..9-11.. 8 b.m. Super Sunrise — Niel's Crystal (Indiaro) 6. Small light half-sister to Sandyland (*qv*). P-t-P '03 (for Mr D.V. Gardner (Krystal Gazers) r6 w2 (Maiden and Restricted) p1 (3rd of 4); 4th, last, and unseated 1. Scored at the final two meetings in '03, and looked a progressive sort, but appeared to suffer an immediate setback this year. Genuine, but tends to wander when she tires, and a watching brief is advised when she reappears. Usually taken to post early. *Krystal Gazers Partnership (Miss L. Gardner) — Silverton (Lucy Gardner).* 116 (I).

KUPTO (FR) ..9-4.. 7 b.g. Luchiroverte (IRE) — Neva (FR) (Danoso) 3419. Compact well-made. Dam, winning cross-country Chaser at around 2m4f in France. NH '04 r1 p0 (9th in 2m4f Hdle: *prom, rdn 5, wknd nxt, t.o*). Sold Tattersalls Ireland, Aug '02 for 3504, and changed hands subsequently. Improving gradually, and after being beaten 20 lengths and ten lengths in his first two races he finally wore down a rival near the finish to open his account in a testing Ashorne Maiden (a powerful ride from Paul Cowley). Competing at a low level in Points so far, but has made no noticeable errors, and his rating may eventually prove to be very much on the mean side. *Mrs S. Busby & K.H. Hutsby — Farmers Bloodhounds (Sue Busby).* 291 (2m4fCfMa), 589 (CfMa), 1273 (OMa).

KUSTOM KIT GRIZZLY (IRE) ..9-13§.. 10 br.g. Be My Native (USA) — Bridgetown Girl (Al Sirat) 3165fp. Workmanlike half-brother to Here Comes Choosey (IRE), and to Irish Pointing and jumping winner, Rosetown Girl. Dam won 3m Chase, and is half-sister to Supreme Lad (*qv '00 Annual*). NH FLAT '00 r2 p1 (3rd). NH '00/1 r6 p0; pulled up 1. P-t-P '03 r6 w3 (Maiden, Club Restricted and Intermediate, hat-trick) p2 (3rd of 4 once); and pulled up 1. Quite useful in minor company, and is ideally suited by a sound surface, but has needed headgear in his last three wins, and has to go right-handed (has worn an off-side pricker). Loses his enthusiasm at the drop of a hat, and whilst he may revive when fresh it is best to leave him well alone as his requirements are so specific. Wears a cross-noseband. *The Crofters Club (M. Kehoe) — Bicester with Whaddon (Fiona Kehoe).* 16 (C), 47 (Cf), 168 (C), 440 (2m7f110yH), 938 (MO), 1105 (O).

KUWAIT FAITH (IRE) ..—§.. 9 b.g. Archway (IRE) — Jenny Dancer (Skyliner) upppp. Compact. P-t-P '03 (for Mr M. Stephenson) r1 p0 (pulled up). Yet to get round in six attempts, and whilst he may have been given time to begin with he acquired blinkers and a tongue-tie on his penultimate start, and looked far from keen. Needs to brush up his jumping. Wears a cross-noseband. *Miss S. Troughton — Ledbury (Mike Daniell).* 51 (OMa), 258 (CMa), 363 (CfMa), 730 (OMa), 1395 (OMa).

KUWAIT MILLENNIUM ..9-11.. 8 b.g. Salse (USA) — Lypharitissima (FR) (Lightning FR) 5. Compact half-brother to 5 flat winners (one in France) including One Dinar, Generals Diana, Desert Heat and Claradotnet. FLAT '00/1 r4 p0. NH '01/3 (for M.C. Pipe, late J. Neville, and Mrs A.M. Thorpe) r18 w2 (2m1f-2m7f Hdles) p8 (inc 6 2nds). Bought Doncaster, Oct for 3300. A dual Hurdling winner in soft, including a Seller, and has plenty of stamina, but generally proved to be a very frustrating dog when trained by Martin Pipe. Prior to '04 he often wore headgear or cheekpieces and was tongue-tied. Despite still being a youngster, he looks burnt out, and it would be most surprising if he enjoyed Pointing. *P. England — Badsworth & Bramham Moor.* 812 (O).

KYALAMI (FR) ..9-12.. 7 gr.g. Royal Charter (FR) — Reine Margot III (FR) (Trenel) 3f2f. Unfurnished half-brother to French/Italian jumping winner, Fier de L'Etre (FR). Dam won flat race in France. Bought Doncaster, May '02 for 12,000. Would have been placed in all three Maidens had he not fallen two out when left second at Bishops Court, but a weak finisher, and tried 2m5f at Uttoxeter where he had no chance (although left third) when he was hampered in a melee and fell two out. Remains eligible for the shorter Maidens, and can surely win one. *R. Kelvin-Hughes — Spooners & W. Dartmoor.* 142 (OMa), 329 (OMa), 567 (CfMa), 1377 (2m5fH).

LA COLINA (IRE) ..9-12.. 10 ch.g. Be My Native (USA) — Deep Stream (Deep Run) pf2p2. Tall workmanlike. IRISH NH FLAT '00 r6 p0. IRISH NH '00 r9 w1 (2m4f Hdle) p1 (3rd); fell 1. NH '01/3 (for C.J. Mann) r6 w1 (2m2f Ch) p0; fell 1. Bought Doncaster, Mar for 2100. Has only once finished first past the post, in an Irish Hurdle in '00, but later awarded an English Chase as the original winner had a banned substance in the sample. Enjoys front-running in Points and goes a decent clip, but previously looked best at up to 2m4f, and the closing stages of Points seem to tax his stamina to the hilt. Twice second at two lengths or less on home ground at Kingston Blount, and deserves to go one better there. Capable of jumping well, but has fallen in 25 per cent of his 12 attempts over fences. *A. Hill, M.P. Avery, K. Pearce & J. Dance — V. of Aylesbury with Garth & S. Berks (Lawney Hill).* 3 (O), 100 (O), 622 (M), 868 (O), 1104 (Cnr).

LADY ARCHENFIELD ..—§§.. 9 b.m. Blaze O'Gold (USA) — Swinging Molly (Swing Easy USA) frf. Plain narrow. P-t-P '03 r3 p0 (refused 2, and unseated 1). Truly shocking and has yet to get beyond the fifth in six attempts, and the kamikaze pilot of a rider clearly needs his head examining after remounting her on two occasions. Wore blinkers and ridden in spurs in the latest debacle, and needs to be banned pronto. *R. Staley — Golden V.* 408 (CMam), 447 (Cf), 934 (OMa).

PLATE 75 724 Ledbury Open Maiden 56&7yo (Div 1, Part 2): Andy Martin and Lady Baronette, 1st, are not quite right at the last *PHOTO: Tim Holt*

LADY BARONETTE .9-13.. 8 b.m. Baron Blakeney — Rueful Lady (Streetfighter) 3u21ru4. Lengthy workmanlike half-sister to jumping winner, Thistle Princess. Dam won 2m4f Hurdle. P-t-P '03 r5 p1 (2nd of 3); 4th, last 2, and pulled up 1. Poised to collect a mares Maiden at Mollington when the owner-rider leapt off at the last, but made amends two starts later when Andy Martin took over the reins in a three-finisher event at Maisemore. Out of her depth in Hunter Chases, though would have been a poor second to Lancastrian Jet at Hereford but for a last fence indiscretion, but her previous seven lengths second to Franco suggests that a Restricted is there for the taking in '05. Might not be entirely trustworthy. *I. Howe — Farmers Bloodhounds (Andy Martin).* 105 (2m4fOMa), 293 (CMam), 385 (OMa), 724 (OMa), 975 (2m7f110yH), 1175 (3m1f110yH), 1362 (3m6f110yH).

LADY BLACKTHORN ..5-7.. 7 br.m. Seymour Hicks (FR) — Myblackthorn (IRE) (Mandalus) 6p. Very small light owner-bred. Dam won 2 Irish NH flat, and 2m1f Handicap Chase in England. NH FLAT '03 r2 p0. NH '03 (for B.J.M. Ryall) r1 p0 (pulled up). Badly tailed off in all five races, and struggled round when beaten a couple of fences on her only completion over jumps. Attractively bred, but looks too weedy for racing. *J.A. Keighley — Cotley (Jane Western).* 328 (OMa), 1134 (OMa).

LADY DOT (IRE) ..9-4§.. 12 ch.m. Mister Lord (USA) — Anvil Chorus (Levanter) 1p4p. Lengthy sister to Kilfinny Cross (IRE), and half-sister to Act In Time (IRE), and to Chasing winner, Victory Anthem. P-t-P '99/03 r11 w1 (Maiden) p1 (3/4l 2nd); unseated 3, slipped up 1, and pulled up 5. Recording her first success since '99 when accounting for one other finisher in her Members, but probably lucky as the 2-5 favourite was homing in on her when taking a fatal fall at the third last. Normally obliged to pull up, and fenced even more erratically than usual when ridden by a girl and most irresolute on her latest appearance. Probably defective in some way. Wears a cross-noseband. *D.S. Dennis — Hursley Hambledon.* 260 (M), 579 (R), 1442 (2m5fH), 1517 (R).

LADYGAL (IRE) ..8-10.. 6 b.m. Accordion — Dozing Gal (IRE) (Bulldozer) pp432. Compact well-made. Bought Doncaster, May for 1000. Her form figures are deceptive as she did no more than plod round when making the frame three times, but is not helped by plentiful mistakes and arm-waving from the rider. Seems plucky enough, and if she did find a better rhythm it is conceivable that there might be a bad race for her. *J. Birt-Llewellin — Pembs (Rhiannon Rees).* 677 (CfMa), 948 (OMa), 1091 (CMam), 1394 (OMa), 1547 (M).

LADY MISPRINT ..10-11.. 9 ch.m. Classic — Miss Primrose (Primitive Rising USA) 111. Tall rangy. A gamble from 12s to fives in an elders Maiden at Great Trethew and did not disappoint, and then charged round in front from halfway in a Restricted at Trebudannon, where despite being eased she bettered the time of Kestick in the Mixed Open by eight seconds. Completed the hat-trick in an Open at Flete, but only two ran and her opponent was a maiden rated two stone inferior. Very slow to come to light, but looks a fascinating prospect, and given her connections it would be no surprise to see her under Rules. Can be fancied to score. *J. & Mrs D. Jordan — Mid Devon (Nikki Frost).* 704 (CfMa), 912 (R), 1198 (O).

LADY MORDAUNT (IRE) ..8-1.. 7 b.m. Mister Lord (USA) — Castle Flame (IRE) (Carlingford Castle) f3*fp*. Unfurnished sister to Irish Pointing and Chasing winner, Whatsgoingonbob, and half-sister to Irish Hunter Chasing and Pointing winner, Boss Murphy. NH '04 r1 p0 (pulled up in 2m5f110y Hdle: *hld up, wknd aft 5, t.o when pu aft nxt*). Bought Doncaster, Oct '02 for 2400. Yet to start at more than four to one in a Point, but has had jumping problems, and there was not much merit in her 14 lengths last of three when favourite at Godstone (unbelievably, Barbed Broach outstayed her!). Presumably being given a confidence booster over Hurdles, but will be back to square one when she resumes in Points. *R.H. York — Staff College.* 803 (2m4fOMa), 1404 (OMa), 1518 (OMa).

LADY OF JAZZ ..8-2.. 8 b.m. Alhijaz — Fairy Ballerina (Fairy King USA) f5. Small compact half-sister to flat and Hurdles winner, Aspirant Dancer (12 wins). Dam won 7f race in Ireland. NH FLAT '01 r2 p0. NH '01 (for N.J. Hawke) r3 p0; pulled up 2. Furlongs behind in a couple of bumpers and tailed off in three Hurdles (pulled up twice, with a broken blood vessel in the latest), and fell five out in a slight lead and 30 lengths fifth in Maidens. Very lightly raced and remains unimpressive. *G.C. Fox - Seavington (Chloe Newman).* 326 (OMa), 492 (OMa).

LADY PALAMON (IRE) ..9-3.. 11 b/br.m. Montelimar (USA) — Actress Mandy (IRE) (Mandalus) p31p2p. Well-made lengthy sister to Irish Pointing winner, Oh Me Oh Moigh. NH FLAT Jan '99 r1 p0. NH '99 r1 p0 (pulled up). P-t-P '00 (for Mr R. Perkins) r3 p1 (3rd of 4); last, and pulled up 1. Apparently used as nothing more than a riding horse since '00, but the decision to bring her back into training proved to be an inspired one, and clocked the fastest time of the three Maidens on the card at Cilwendeg. A weak finisher in her other races, and though her jumping is pretty assured looks odds against upgrading successfully. *G.W. Lewis — Carms.* 202 (CfMa), 357 (R), 676 (CfMa), 1022 (R), 1095 (R), 1322 (R).

LADY PAMROY ..—.. 11 ch.m. Joli Wasfi (USA) — Vowchurch Lady (Pamroy) f. Tall rangy. P-t-P '03 r4 p0 (pulled up 3, and ran out 1). A bad jumper, and has yet to get beyond the ninth in five attempts, and sent off at 100-1 in her Members. Wears a cross-noseband. *S. McCracken — Exmoor.* 1378 (M).

PLATE 76 912 Four Burrow Restricted: Lady Misprint and Derek McKenna make light work of it
PHOTO: Baths Photographic

LADY WIDD (IRE) ..9-7.. 7 ch.m. Commanche Run — Lady Geeno (IRE) (Cheval) 3u15. Lengthy sister to Hurdling winner, I D Technology. Dam, sister to Toureen Prince (*qv* '94 Annual). IR8000 3yo. NH FLAT '02 r3 p0. NH '02 (for S.J. Marshall) r4 p0; unseated 1, pulled up 1. Bought Doncaster, Nov for 4000. Looked erratic under Rules and was sent off at 100-1 or more on four occasions, and only completed in two of four Hurdles (unseated once), but did show a smidgen of ability. Favourite for her first Maiden but weakened to finish last of three, and then unseated at the final fence when apparently going just the best at Charlton Horethorne (Alex Michael left the course in an air ambulance). Finally came good at Cothelstone, but her first Restricted suggests she will need to find extra for that grade. *Friends of Eddy Hall (T. Harris) — Quantock (Sue Popham).* 121 (OMa), 353 (OMa), 884 (OMa), 1184 (R).

LAGAN LADY ..—.. 8 b.m. North Col — Gardenia Lady (Mummy's Game) pp. Close-coupled homebred sister to Colthorn, and half-sister to Gardenia's Song. Dam won 5f Seller. Tailed off and pulled up in two May Maidens, and made a lot of novicey mistakes. *Mrs I.J. Thorne — Warwicks (Robert Elwell).* 1273 (OMa), 1403 (2m4fOMa).

LAGANSIDE (IRE) ..9-13.. 12 b.g. Montelimar (USA) — Ruby Girl (Crash Course) 63p148p2. Lengthy half-brother to Chasing winner, Life Of A Lord (won 6 Points and 12 Chases in Ireland), to jumping winner, Letterfore, and to flat winner, Mrs Naughty. IRISH P-t-P '97/9 r8 w1 (5&6yo Maiden; also won Hunt but disqualified — prohibited substance) p0; pulled up 3, fell 1. IRISH NH '99 r2 p0. NH '99/02 r14 w3 (2m4f-3m Chses) p3 (2 3rds); pulled up 2. P-t-P/HUNT CH '03 r9 w2 (dead-heat Open and 3-runner, 2-finisher Members) p0; last pair 4, and pulled up 3. Often disappointing under Rules, and still lacks consistency, but has officially come out best on three occasions for James Muir, and gained his latest success in another close finish. Goes in snatches and frequently jumps to the right, and usually saddled with overweight. Suited by top-of-the-ground. Visored once in '01, and has run tongue-tied. *J.F.W. Muir — Lauderdale.* 134 (O), 285 (O), 426 (Cf), 509 (O), 678 (3m1fH), 764 (O), 1068 (3m2f110yH), 1219 (M).

LAGGAN MORE ..—.. 6 b.g. Lancastrian — Glorious Day (Lepanto GER) p. Workmanlike brother to Glastrian. Hinted at ability before fading and pulling up two out at Woodford. *Mr & Mrs F. Hutsby — Warwicks (Fred Hutsby).* 1074 (OMa).

LAH DI DAH LAD .9-12.. 11 b.g. Crested Lark — Classey (Dubassoff USA) 143p2. Very small compact owner-bred half-brother to Miss Hoity Toity (*qv*). P-t-P '02/3 r5 p1 (3rd); 4th, pulled up 2, and unseated 1. Typically unraced until he was eight, and has been sparingly competed since, but scored comfortably on his return at Mollington. Disappointed on a return visit, where the yard won the race with a lesser fancied runner, but should have won on his final outing, where the wily Tarry took things too leisurely on his idling partner. Should make amends in a Restricted in '05, but needs to smarten up his jumping. *J.R. White, & G.B., G.J. & Miss F.M. Tarry — Grafton (Jimmy Tarry).* 589 (CfMa), 787 (CR), 1034 (R), 1333 (R), 1517 (R).

LAKELAND PRINCE .8-5.. 6 b.g. Prince Daniel (USA) — Lakeland Edition (Respect) 6. Dam (*qv* '98 Annual) was last and pulled up in Points. Taken quietly when beaten 55 lengths on the first day of the season, and not sighted since. *H. Hobson - Puckeridge.* 7 (2m4fOMa).

LA MAESTRA (FR) ..9-3.. 7 b.m. Zayyani — Ginestra (USA) (L'Emigrant USA) p2pup. Small light. FRENCH NH '01 r5 p1 (2nd). NH '01/2 r8 w2 (2m-2m1f Hdles) p1 (3rd). P-t-P '03 r4 p0 (last 2, unseated 1, and pulled up 1). Runner-up at Auteuil before recording a double for Pipe and McCoy in '01, but immediately lost the plot in another yard, and ended the following year lame. Not better than last in Points, and gives every indication that she does not get the trip. Has been tried in cheekpieces. *W.J. Day — Gelligaer F. (Lisa Day).* 449 (L), 670 (Cf), 841 (Cf), 1235 (Cf), 1318 (M).

LAMBRINI KING (IRE) .8-10.. 11 b.g. Brush Aside (USA) — Windara (Double-U-Jay) 1upp736p. Tall rangy half-brother to Wolf Winter, Farney Glen and Act On Impulse (IRE), to Irish Pointing winner, Different Tune, and to Irish NH flat winner, The Bourda. Dam won 2m Hdle in Ireland. NH FLAT '99 r2 p0. NH '99/00 (for Mrs L. Williamson) r2 p0 (last, and fell 1). Bought Ascot, Jun '01 for 1800. Hopelessly tailed off at long odds in two bumpers and a Hurdle and fell at the first in a Chase to '00, but miraculously unearthed a contest desperate enough to give him a chance, and provided Lucinda Barrett-Nobbs with her first winner in a five-runner Members at Higham. Remote without fail since, and is an extremely weary trudger. *J.T. Ibbott — Waveney H.* 22 (M), 44 (R), 159 (R), 248 (Cf), 398 (R), 559 (R), 742 (I), 902 (R).

LAMBRINI MIST ..10-8.. 7 gr.g. Terimon — Miss Fern (Cruise Missile) 11. Dam won 5 2m4f-3m2f Chases, and is sister to Miss Shaw (*qv* '00 Annual). IR17,000 3yo. NH FLAT '02 r2 p1 (3rd of 4). NH '02 (for Mrs L. Williamson) r2 p0; pulled up 1. Third of four in a bumper, but badly tailed off thrice under Rules (including when ninth of ten and pulled up in Hurdles), and acquired cheekpieces on his final start. Bred from a competent mare, and improved out of all recognition in Tweseldown Points. Left to finish alone in the slowest time of the day in a Maiden when backed from 20-1 to half those odds (was already crossing the line as two surviving rivals declined the last), but the Restricted was the revelation as he galloped the opposition into the ground but this time in the fastest time of the day including that of Mister Benjamin in the Ladies. Unfortunately seems fragile, but would probably be Open class if healthy. *J. Halewood — Cheshire (Mark Williamson).* 20 (OMa), 169 (R).

LAMERTON QUEST ..5-0.. 9 br.g. Almoojid — Adjals Ace (London Glory) pppppp5p. Lengthy half-brother to Paddy's Glory. P-t-P '03 r1 p0 (fell). The subject of a gamble from eights to 4-1 on his reappearance, but could not complete in a race where there was only one finisher and that effort set the tone for the remainder of the season. Acquired blinkers and a tongue-strap on his penultimate start, and managed a first completion, but was 114 lengths last and dogging it under pressure throughout the final mile. Partnered by James Cole (he of the disintegrating breeches at Great Trethew in '03) at Umberleigh, but typically his tack fell apart after less than two miles, and was pulled up. A joke, and perhaps connections can get Jethro to sponsor them. *L.S. Rowe — Lamerton.* 417 (CfMah), 566 (M), 795 (CfMa), 913 (OMa), 1272 (OMa), 1543 (R), 1558 (R), 1565 (OMa).

LANCASTRIAN ISLAND ..7-11.. 7 b.m. Lancastrian — Kelly's Island (Jupiter Island) pp4u. Compact. Dam (*qv* '01 Annual) fell twice in Points for Mr Copley. NH FLAT '02 (for J.A. Harris) r1 p0. Beaten 24 lengths on her only completion, and has not impressed with her jumping or attitude (unseated when trying to refuse on final start). *G. Copley — Cottesmore (Tim Tarratt).* 152 (OMa), 304 (OMa), 597 (2m5fOMa), 945 (OMa).

LANCASTRIAN JET (IRE) ..10-12.. 14 b.g. Lancastrian — Kilmurray Jet (Le Bavard FR) 111u1. Tall half-brother to Beck And Call (IRE). NH FLAT r1 p0. P-t-P '97 (for late Capt. T.A. Forster) r1 w1 (Maiden). NH '97/03 r29 w6 (3m-4m Chses) p11 (inc 8 2nds); pulled up 3 (inc '00 Irish Grand National), unseated 1. Won his Maiden at Bitterley in '97 before embarking on a fine career under Rules during which he won the '00 Mildmay Cazalet at Sandown, and the 4-mile Devon Marathon at Exeter the following year. Beaten nine times in-between, and could get little relief from the handicapper subsequently so went Hunter Chasing in '04, and took his win prize money to in excess of £50,000 with four authoritative victories. Odds-on to make it five but was cannoned into by a riderless horse at Towcester. Likes to force the tempo, and right-handed tracks and soft ground are most ideal. Purists may not have been rubbing their hands with delight, but it was a pleasure to see him back on the winning trail. *Hon Mrs A.E. Heber-Percy — Ludlow (Henry Daly).* 209 (3m1f110yH), 437 (3m1fH), 679 (3m1fH), 891 (3m1fH), 1175 (3m1f110yH).

LANCE FEATHER (IRE) ..8-0.. 7 b.g. Petardia — Fantasticus (IRE) (Lycius USA) 7. Leggy light-framed. FLAT '00/1 r5 p0. P-t-P '03 (for Mrs C.M. Hussey) r2 p1 (last of 3); and pulled up 1. Useless on the flat, and on the limited evidence to hand does not look like being any better in Points in which he has yet to beat a rival. *W. Hawkins — Albrighton.* 7 (2m4fOMa).

LANDFORD LAD (IRE) ..9-5.. 9 ch.g. Mujtahid (USA) — Bold And Bright (FR) (Bold Lad USA) 33u2. Lengthy half-brother to several winners (inc in Italy) and jumping winner, Guest Performance. Dam won at 10f. FLAT '98/9 r5 p0. IRISH NH '00 r5 p1 (3rd). NH '00 r2 p1 (3rd). P-t-P '03 (for Mr T.R. Gretton) r2 p0 (5th of 6, and unseated 1). Resurfaced from a three-year absence last year and showed nothing, but gave Guy Armitage some good rides in '04, and might get him into the winner's enclosure if he can summon up some extra stamina. Would not be winning out of turn, and had two subsequent scorers behind when a fast-finishing second at Charm Park. *Mrs E.J. Crookenden — Sinnington.* 266 (M), 390 (Rnr), 482 (OMa), 958 (OMa).

LANSDOWNE PARK ..9-12.. 6 b.m. El Conquistador — Bickfield Approach (Dubassoff USA) u2. Workmanlike owner-bred half-sister to Miss Biddy (*qv*). Unseated at the 11th on a May dèbut, but did much better the following Saturday and chased home the impressive and probably useful Lord Oscar in a nine-finisher Maiden at Bratton Down. There was probably not much behind her, but the form should still give her strong claims in similar company. *A.G. Harris — Mendip F. (Ollie Bush).* 1327 (OMa), 1380 (OMa).

LATEEN ..4-7.. 10 b.m. Midyan (USA) — Sail Loft (Shirley Heights) 0. Small neat half-sister to four flat winners including Chandlery Colonia (won Norsk Derby). Dam, half-sister to Oaks winners, Scintillate and Juliette Marny, and to St Leger winner, Julio Mariner. 4000y. FLAT '98/9 r10 p0. NH '01 (for J.E. Collinson) r1 p0. Persistently bad on the flat including in a Seller, in a Hurdle, and in a Point when reappearing after three year absence (beaten over 100 lengths). *Mrs E.M. Collinson — Cottesmore.* 558 (L).

LATTERLY (USA) ..— §.. 10 b.g. Cryptoclearance (USA) — Latest Scandal (USA) (Two Davids USA) 4u6ppppp. Small neat. IRISH P-t-P '00 r3 p0 (pulled up 3). IRISH FLAT '97/9 r15 p1 (3rd). IRISH NH '99 r2 p0. FLAT '01 r3 p0. NH '00/1 (for F.T. Jordan) r10 p2 (3rds); pulled up 3, unseated 1. Third once on the flat and twice in Selling Hurdles, but has always been a difficult ride, and his record over fences is utterly deplorable (beaten about 70 lengths in two completions with a total one behind him, pulled up nine times and unseated twice). Blinkered on five occasions and wore cheekpieces on his latest outing, and was also tongue-tied latterly under Rules. A total waste of time. *I. Bostock — Oakley.* 103 (OMa), 187 (Cf), 259 (CMa), 461 (M), 652 (OMa), 927 (OMa), 1125 (OMa), 1443 (2m5fH).

LAURA LUGS (IRE) .. -.. 13 b.g. Strong Gale — Geeaway (Gala Performance) ppp. Workmanlike lengthy brother to Bitofamixup (IRE) (*qv*). IRISH P-t-P '98 r4 p1 (last of 3); last, pulled up 1 and fell 1. IRISH NH FLAT '98 r2 p0. IRISH NH '98 r2 p0 (Chses). NH '98/9 r4 p1 ($21^{1}/_{2}$*l* 3rd of 4 in Ch); and pulled up 3. P-t-P/HUNT CH '99 and '02/3 r8 w1 (Maiden) p3 (3rds, of 4 once, and last once); last pair 2, pulled up 1, and fell 1. Won a weak and slowly-run Maiden on firm at Corbridge in '02, but the rest of his form suggests he is lucky to have succeeded at all, and is hard to get fit, lightly raced and error prone. Has been tried in blinkers. *Mrs P.A. Mounsey-Heysham — Tynedale.* 132 (CR), 212 (R), 657 (R).

LAURELGIRL (IRE) ..8-3.. 8 b/br.m. Jurado (USA) — Klickitat (Seclude USA) 5pp. Compact. Dam won 2 flat (12-13f) and 2 Hurdles (2m-2m4f) in Ireland. IRISH P-t-P '02/3 r10 p1 (3rd of 4); pulled up 3, fell 2. A bad Pointer who has finished in the last pair in four of her six completions, and not improved by crossing the Irish Sea. Pulled up and dismounted after two miles on her latest attempt (was sweating badly). *R.A. Jones — Pentyrch.* 409 (CMam), 454 (CfMa), 1091 (CMam).

LAVA ..9-11.. 9 b.m. Tragic Role (USA) — Dishcloth (Fury Royal) 6. Small neat half-sister to Parahandy (IRE) (*qv*). NH FLAT '00/1 r2 p0. NH '01/2 r3 p0; pulled up 1. P-t-P '03 r3 w2 (3-finisher Maiden and Restricted) p0; and fell 1. Of no account under Rules, but found life much easier in Points last year and kicked for home with a half-mile to run when scoring twice. Only seen once in '04, and the unusually firm ground at Didmarton may well have caused problems. Takes a keen hold and wears a cross-noseband. *J. Dee & N. Hart — N. Cotswold (Claire Hart).* 365 (I).

LAZY LEMON .9-7.. 9 ch.m. Afzal — Spartan Lemon (Spartan Jester) p3p. Small compact. Dam, half-sister to Stormhill Warrior (*qv* '02 Annual), won 2 Points and placed 9 for Derek Llewellin. Grandam, Port'n Lemon, won 3m Ch; and won 3 Ladies and placed 4 (inc 2 Hunt Chses). P-t-P '02/3 r8 w1 (walkover Maiden) p1 (last of 2); last 2, and pulled up 4. A winner and in the frame four times in Points, but struggles to get the trip, and only once better than last, and needs to concentrate on the weakest Restricteds connections can unearth. Has been tried in a tongue-strap. Wears a cross-noseband. *D.G.L. Llewellin — E. Devon.* 198 (R), 318 (M), 472 (Cf).

LEACHBROOK LADY ..8-13.. 6 br.m. Alderbrook — Air Streak (Air Trooper) 1. Sturdy compact half-sister to Gwen's A Singer and Up Your Street. Dam, half-sister to Dawn Street (*qv* '91 Annual), won Maiden and placed 4 (inc 2nd in Hdle). Left to beat one other finisher in a Mares Maiden at Mollington in which she was held in third place until her two rivals departed independently at the last. It was easily the slowest race of the day, and will have to achieve something on her merits to be taken seriously. *J.G. Phillips — V.W.H. (Simon Bloss).* 293 (CMam).

LEADER DU TURF (FR) ..—.. 6 b.g. Panoramic — Rose Du Turf (FR) (Le Verglas) pp. Good-bodied. Sold Goffs France, Jul for 2164. Very prominent for two miles before dropping out rapidly and pulling up in Maidens. Backed from eights to fours in the latest, but there are certainly stamina doubts about him at present. *C.W.W. Dupont — Portman (Sally Alner).* 13 (OMa), 328 (OMa).

LEADING CASE ..9-10.. 9 b.g. Supreme Leader — The Little Bag (True Song) 32. Workmanlike compact homebred half-brother to Bacarese (*qv*). P-t-P '01/3 r7 w1 (Club Maiden) p3 (2 2nds); 5th, unseated (when 6*l* clear 2 out), and pulled up in void Maiden. Won his Maiden in softish at Charing in '02, and finished a fine third to a subsequent four-time Hunter Chase winner on his reappearance, but unable to cope with another potentially smart rival at Godstone, and typically failed to air again. Front runs, and a certainty for an average Restricted, but rather a weak finisher, and normally only ever risked on ground softer than good. *Prof D.B.A. Silk, R. Purkis & E. Warren — Kent & Surrey Bloodhounds (Emma Leppard).* 36 (CR), 606 (R).

LEAD STORY (IRE) ..10-5.. 12 br.g. Lead On Time (USA) — Mashmoon (USA) (Habitat) pp. Strong-topped compact half-brother to flat and Hurdles winner, Talathath (FR), and to Irish flat winner, Gold Braisim. Dam won 2 flat, 6-8f. FLAT r4 p0. NH '97/8 r5 p0; pulled up 2. P-t-P/HUNT CH '99/03 r29 w6 (inc 2 3m2f110y Hunt Chses and Open) p4 (2nds, beaten head of 3 once, and remote of 3 once); pulled up 6, fell 1. A dual Hunter Chase winner at Newton Abbot, and a useful Pointer when on song, but struggling to find any consistency in the last four years, and was laid low by a virus in '03. Blew up after two miles twice this year, and has been retired. *Mrs M. Trueman — Modbury H. (Gordon Chambers).* 196 (O), 310 (O).

LEASEBOURNE ..—.. 6 b.m. Puget (USA) — Truelyn (True Song) ppp. Good-bodied half-sister to Westington (*qv*). Showed speed for up to 2m4f in her last two Maidens, but is currently too headstrong to have any chance of getting the trip. *S. Hart — N. Cotswold (Claire Hart).* 589 (CfMa), 725 (OMa), 926 (OMa).

LEATHERBACK (IRE) ..9-10§.. 7 b.g. Turtle Island (IRE) — Phyllode (Pharly FR) p434143p2. Small close-coupled brother to Hurdles winner, Lewis Island (IRE), and half-brother to flat winner, College Dean. IR26,000f, IR95,000y. FLAT '00/3 r22 w4 (7-8f) p2. NH '01/2 (for N.A. Callaghan) r7 w1 (2m Hdle) p2 (3rds). Was useful in his prime on the flat and scored four times in the mud including in fields of 22 and 20, and notched a hat-trick in Oct/Nov '00, but became suspect latterly and was blinkered on his final two appearances. Touted by his former trainer as a potentially promising Hurdler, but only managed one victory. Decidedly ungenuine, but did manage to take a Higham Confined on firmish from two moderate rivals plus Algan who did not like the ground and was atrociously ridden. Took almost no interest otherwise, and although he made the frame on six occasions only two horses finished behind him and he was beaten 30 lengths plus in four. One to bet against. *J.M. Turner — Suffolk.* 100 (O), 158 (CCon), 376 (Cf), 556 (Cf), 832 (Cf), 1087 (O), 1242 (Cf), 1438 (3m2fH), 1515 (O).

LE CURE ..10-3.. 10 b.g. Sula Bula — Granny Pray On (Proverb) u3p611. Lengthy well-made owner-bred half-brother to Frere Du Cure. Dam, half-sister to Tavern Time (*qv* '95 Annual), won 2m4f Hdle and 2 in Ireland; won 3m2f Ch and placed 6 in England, and subsequently ran badly in 5 Points for Phil Bevins. P-t-P '02/3 r13 w3 (Members — finished alone, Intermediate and Club Restricted) p4 (3 3rds, of 4 once); 4th, last pair 2, pulled up 2, fell 1. Under a cloud after his first completion in '04, and subsequently missed five weeks of the season, but returned to win a weak race at Barbury, and claimed the scalp of Teme Willow when forcing tactics were ultimately re-used at Maisemore. Stays well and normally a good jumper, but sidelined Tigger Barnes briefly with a broken collar-bone after getting rid of him on his return. Suited by some cut in the ground. Wears a cross-noseband. *P.G. Bevins — Avon V.* 34 (O), 115 (MO), 196 (O), 496 (MO), 1066 (CCon), 1257 (O).

LEDGENDRY LINE ..10-2.. 12 b.g. Mtoto — Eider (Niniski USA) 4p. Small close-coupled brother to good flat and jumping winner, Foundry Lane, and half-brother to Eidolon (never finished in 5 Points) and Fred's Boy. Dam won at 9f. FLAT '96/02 r37 w2 (13-17f) p10. NH '97/02 r17 w5 (3 2m-2m4f Hdles, and 2 2m4f-3m1f Chses) p6 (4 2nds); fell 1. P-t-P '03 r6 w1 (Ladies) p4 (2 2nds); and last. Quite a useful performer under Rules, and won seven times to Nov '00, but does a great deal of thinking, and was recording his first success since when landing a Ladies at Witton Castle last year. Absent for ten weeks after a promising debut in '04, but ran a stinker at Whitwell-on-the-Hill and failed to reappear. A very careful jumper, but rarely exerts himself fully nowadays. *Miss S. Brotherton — Sinnington.* 71 (L), 770 (Cf).

LEGAL STORM (IRE) ..9-13.. 13 gr.g. Roselier (FR) — Stormy Waters (Typhoon II) 3u25f. Workmanlike lengthy half-brother to Irish Chasing winner, Johnny Setaside (IRE), to flat and Hurdles winner, Lady Netherton, to Hurdles winner, Jingle-Jangle, to Pointing and Hurdles winner, Croghan Will, and to a winner in West Indies. IRISH NH FLAT '97/8 r5 p2 (2nds). IRISH NH '97/01 r25 p5. IRISH P-t-P '00/1 r15 w5 p7; fell 2. P-t-P '02/3 (for Mr T.D.B. Underwood) r25 p12 (6 2nds, of 3 thrice, beaten short-head once; 6 3rds, of 4 thrice); pulled up 7, and brought down 1. Won the maximum number of four wins in Irish Points in '00, but failed to score in 25 appearances for the previous owner, and failed to survive a heavy fall at Leicester. *R.M. Green — Staff College (Phillip York).* 32 (Cnr), 45 (Cnr), 331 (M), 345 (2m5fH), 440 (2m7f110yH).

LEGENDA .—.. 6 b.g. Midnight Legend — Lasting Memory (Ardross) f. Dam won 4 2m1f-3m Hurdles. Tore into a clear lead at Witton Castle in early February, but fell at the eighth when 20 lengths ahead and presumably damaged himself. *J.M. Walker — Hurworth (Sarah Dent).* 160 (CMa).

LEGEND OF LIGHT (IRE) ..9-10.. 11 b.m. Electric — Khotso (Alcide) u142. Small compact half-sister to Sutton Court, Osoroyal, Brockton, Shesagud Girl, to Hurdles winner, Miss Me Not and Kilshannon Springs (in Ireland). NH '01 r1 p0. All that was known of her when she started Pointing at ten was that she had been pulled up in a Hurdle three years earlier (it later transpired that she had fallen down a precipice soon after being purchased as a three-year-old), and looked an unlikely prospect, but was most unlucky in an abysmal five-runner Maiden at probably the worst Whitwick ever, where she led at the last but stumbled badly on landing and unseated Steven Hughes 50 yards later. Found deserved compensation in an elders event at Maisemore where the runner-up was 12 and nothing behind her scored, but after a respectable six lengths fourth in a Restricted she did not stride out in the final mile of her Members and finished eight lengths second at 4-6. Another triumph for Steve Flook. Seems unlikely to reappear. *Mrs S.E. Vaughan — Teme V. (Steve Flook).* 518 (CfMa), 729 (OMa), 977 (R), 1109 (M).

LEGOLAS ..—.. 6 b.g. Primitive Rising (USA) — Teddy's Bow (IRE) (Archway IRE) pu. Small very light-framed. NH FLAT '03 r2 p0. Bought Doncaster, Aug for 3600. Beaten between 12 and 15 lengths when fourth in two bumpers, but despite looking ghastly and jumping erratically he was still plugging on in a fair sixth in his first Maiden when he almost unseated three out and was pulled up at the last. Parted with the owner-rider after a mile next time, and disappeared, so a tentative 9-0 rating is withdrawn. *P.J. Millington — Fernie.* 128 (OMa), 746 (OMa).

LEICAREE (IRE) ..—.. 10 b/br.g. Mandalus — Nicky's Dilemma (Kambalda) pp. Small brother to Irish Pointing and Hurdles winner, Joe Bosky (IRE), and half-brother to Ashgan (IRE) (*qv*). IRISH NH '00/1 r4 p0. IRISH P-t-P '01 r1 p0 (pulled up). P-t-P '02/3 r3 p2; and pulled up 1. Finished weakly when placed in both Maidens in '02, and roughed off after a single appearance last year, but not helped by the lengthening of the track at Tabley on his return, and appeared to suffer another setback next time. Would have won by now had he been eligible for 2m4f events, but his problems seem insurmountable. *Dr G. Poole — Cheshire (Gary Hanmer).* 753 (OMa), 1261 (OMa).

LE MILLENAIRE (FR) ..9-12.. 6 b/br.g. Ragmar (FR) — Ezaia (FR) (Iron Duke FR) 17. Small. 7000 3yo. NH FLAT '03 r1 p0. Sent off at 20-1 in a Duncombe Park Maiden after going ballistic in the preliminaries (unseated and bolted into the car park and was eventually led mounted to the start), but after approaching the final fence in six lengths third he was left second and produced a strong run up the hill to lead close home (the second, third and fifth all franked the form subsequently). Absent for over two months before reappearing in a Restricted, but after leading in the middle stages he appeared to blow up and was beaten 25 lengths. Looks speedy enough to score again. *S.H. Shirley-Beavan — Jedforest (Philippa Shirley-Beavan).* 272 (OMa), 1222 (R).

LEON GARCIA (IRE) ..10-0.. 12 b.m. Asir — Philosophical (Welsh Chanter) 31443142. Leggy sister to Jennie Bush (IRE), and to NH flat and Hurdles winner, John Bush (IRE). Dam won 4 Sells, 8-10f, and 2m Hdle. IRISH NH '98 r2 p0. IRISH P-t-P '97/9 r10 w1 (5&6yo mares Maiden) p6. IRISH NH '98 r2 p0. P-t-P '00/2 r12 w1 (Restricted) p6 (4 3rds); 4th four, and unseated 1. Consistent and has not missed the frame in 19 completions since leaving Ireland, but rather an enigmatic performer, and does not always appear to co-operate fully. Stays well and suited by some cut in the ground, but needs to come from behind, and does best going right-handed. The rider is much more polished than he was, and should partner plenty more winners. A box walker. *Mrs F. Bishop — Blackmore & Sparkford V.* 116 (I), 193 (I), 320 (Cf), 350 (M), 472 (Cf), 603 (Cnr), 963 (Cf), 1101 (Cnr).

LE PRINCE ..10-3.. 10 ch.g. Le Moss — Yuan Princess (Tender King) 5414. Small attractive. Dam won 14f Seller, 2m Selling Hurdle and Ladies, and placed 3 flat. NH FLAT '99 r2 p1 (3rd). NH '00/1 (for H.D. Daly) r5 w1 (2m5f Hdle) p2. Made precious few appearances during his first three years on the racecourse, but did manage to win a Ludlow Hurdle despite being off the bit at halfway. Missed '02 and '03 because of leg trouble, but showed he retains ability when returning, and well ridden by Emily Jones when beating four rivals in a Ladies at Tweseldown. Will pull hard and expend his energy too early if he gets the chance, and got tired in the final half mile when 21 lengths fourth in the Gerrard Final at Huntingdon. Would doubtless have achieved a lot more had his legs been less fragile. *Mrs M. Williams — N. Ledbury (Teresa Spearing).* 42 (L), 157 (L), 625 (L), 1360 (3mH).

LES THE LIZARD ..—.. 12 ch.g. Crested Lark — Florence Eliza (Floriana) urp. Small narrow homebred brother to Lottie The Lotus (*qv*). Unseated at the sixth and refused and dumped the rider at the second in his first two Maidens, and then pulled up after two miles having given an awkward display of jumping. The veteran beginners from his stable are often terrible (or tarryble) in their first season, but they can never be written off whilst they still have a working leg at each corner, as Sandy Lark was the latest to show at 12 in '04. *G.B. Tarry — Grafton (Jimmy Tarry).* 1035 (OMa), 1337 (OMa), 1473 (OMa).

LETHEM AIR ..9-10.. 7 ch.g. Aragon — Llanddona (Royal Palace) pu13pp. Compact half-brother to 3 flat winners abroad, and to a successful Hurdler. P-t-P '03 r3 p2; and pulled up 1. Presumably choked on his reappearance as he derived immediate benefit from the application of a tongue-tie when left clear two out at Corbridge, but ran unaided subsequently and failed to perform. His Restricted third at Overton strongly suggests he has a similar race in him, but clearly the ability to breath properly has to be addressed. *T. Butt & Miss D.J. Amos — Border (Tim Butt).* 74 (OMa), 165 (OMa), 433 (OMa), 657 (R), 1028 (3mH), 1373 (2m4f110yH).

LET'S FLY (FR) ..10-7.. 10 b.g. Rose Laurel — Harpyes (FR) (Quart De Vin FR) 5p33111221. Small neat half-brother to a French jumping winner. NH FLAT '00/1 r3 w2 p0. NH '01/2 r6 w2 (2m Hdles) p2. P-t-P '03 r4 p3 (2nds, beaten neck once, and of 3 once); and unseated 1. Won four races in soft ground under Rules, but could be incredibly mulish, and suffered defeats at 1-3 and 8-13. Has taken a while to get his act together in Points, but on his best behaviour when recording a hat-trick in minor events over a four-week period in mid season, and put another odds-on defeat behind him when successful at Bratton Down. Likes to dominate, and has grown to appreciate sound surfaces, and receives useful assistance from the improving William Biddick, but still not one to trust implicitly. *R. Oliver — Four Burrow (Terance Oliver).* 146 (L), 322 (L), 414 (MO), 570 (Cf), 707 (Cf), 907 (M), 1130 (Cnr), 1434 (MO), 1542 (L), 1556 (MO).

LETSGETON ..8-6.. 7 b.m. Jupiter Island — Fair Policy (Politico USA) pp7. Sturdy half-sister to Politina and Bel Affair. Dam, sister to Present Policy (*qv* '91 Annual), won a Maiden and placed 2nd. Got on badly in Maidens, pulling up after little more than two miles maximum in the first two and then finishing 34 lengths seventh in a Mares event. *Mrs S. Brazier & Mrs L.M. Rose — Bicester with Whaddon (Shirley Brazier).* 463 (OMa), 561 (OMa), 978 (CMam).

LET'S ROCK ..8-5.. 7 b.g. Rock City — Sizzling Sista (Sizzling Melody) 534d35. Small neat half-brother to winner in Italy. Bought Ascot, Jun '02 for 2000. Plugged round steadily to complete in all five races, but beaten a minimum of 23 lengths, and has not finished in front of a rival since he was fifth of sixth on his debut. Promoted from fourth to third once, but disqualified from fourth when the rider failed to weigh-in once. Generally tailed off, and would need a very bad race to have any hope of winning. *M.S.J. Green — S. & W. Wilts.* 12 (OMa), 238 (CfMa), 329 (OMa), 600 (2m4fOMa), 1074 (OMa).

LIBERTY LIVELIHOOD ..9-10.. 7 br.m. North Col — Portway (Pardigras) f. Big strong half-sister to Trueway Two. Dam, half-sister to 2 Pointers, including The Nations Way (*qv* '94 Annual), failed to finish in 6 of 8 Points for the Russells. P-t-P '03 r3 w1 (Maiden) p0; and unseated 2. Scored comfortably at Lifton last year, but only cleared one fence successfully in her first two attempts, and killed in a sixth-fence fall on her return at Black Forest Lodge. Mrs B. Russell — Silverton (Lucy Gardner). 148 (R).

LIBIDO .8-9.. 10 b.g. Good Thyne (USA) — Country Mistress (Town And Country) 4p564p406. Half-brother to Themanfromcarlisle, and to Irish Pointing/NH flat and Hurdles winner, Half An Hour. Dam, half-sister to High Sturt (*qv* '04 Annual), won bad 5-runner 2m1f Chase for Count Konrad Goess-Saurau. P-t-P '00 (for Countess S. Goess-Saurau) r1 w1 (3-runner Maiden). NH '00/3 (for H.D. Daly) r10 p3 (inc 2 2nds in Chses); pulled up 1, unseated 1. Won his Maiden easily on firm at Woodford in '00, and came close to a follow up in a 2m4f Novice Chase at Bangor the following year, but spent '02 on the sidelines, and apart from a fair effort at Flagg has performed abysmally since. *P. Andrew — Fernie (Nicola Pollock).* 223 (I), 383 (R), 559 (R), 684 (R), 989 (Cnr), 1101 (Cnr), 1213 (Cnr), 1396 (C), 1503 (R).

L'IDEFIX (IRE) .10-0.. 13 ch.g. Buckskin (FR) — Katty London (Camden Town) 2p3. Small. NH FLAT '97/8 r3 w1 p2. NH '98/02 (for T.R. George) r12 w2 (2m6f Hdle and 3m1f Ch) p2 (2nds); unseated 1. A triple winner in a bumper, a Hurdle and a Chase to Oct '00, but his career under Rules gradually stuttered to a halt, and after one run apiece in '01 and '02 he was absent in '03. Resumed with a highly creditable three lengths second in an Open (Well Ted was third), but was a lot less convincing afterwards and may have disliked the firmish ground on final start. It would be a surprise if he appeared again at 13. *Mrs E.W. Pegna — N. Cotswold (Dolly Maude).* 662 (O), 756 (Cf), 1140 (Cf).

LIFEBUOY (IRE) .—.. 14 b.g. Dry Dock — Shuil Na Gale (Strong Gale) ppp. Compact half-brother to NH flat and Hurdles winners, El Viejo (IRE) and Novi Sad (IRE), and to Irish Pointing and Chasing winner, Shuil Na Mhuire. Dam is half-sister to Shuil Alpha (*qv*). NH FLAT '96 r4 p0; fell 1. NH '96/9 r19 w2 (2m4f110y Hdle and 2m4f110y Ch) p3 (2nds); pulled up 3. P-t-P '02/3 r9 p3 (2 2nds, beaten neck once); disqualified from 4th once — not weigh-in, 5th, last, unseated, and pulled up 2. Last successful in November '97, but never got the trip in Points, and broke down and removed by ambulance in the latest. Blinkered once in '99. *T. Mastoras — Albrighton (Paul Morris).* 662 (O), 932 (Cf), 1426 (C).

LIFE OF A RIVER (IRE) ..9-10.. 12 b.g. Over The River (FR) — Myelife (Le Bavard FR) pp342u. Small compact well-made. Dam completed hat-trick in Irish Points and won 3m Chase there. IRISH P-t-P '98/9 r9 w1 (5&6yo Maiden) p3; pulled up 3. IRISH NH '99/01 r12 p2. P-t-P '02 (for Mr G. Hanmer) r5 w1 (Restricted) p0; 4th, and pulled up 3. Landed a punt from 14s to fives when successful at Dingley in '02, but clearly a problem horse, and usually takes too much out of himself to get the trip. A bold jumper, but does not look good enough for sub-3m races, and will be difficult to place successfully again. *Mrs D. Cope — Cheshire (Steve Wynne).* 92 (I), 529 (L), 664 (L), 849 (L), 1111 (L), 1372 (2m4fH).

LIFE'S WORK ..9-10§.. 13 b.g. Lyphento (USA) — Travail Girl (Forties Field FR) p55. Unfurnished lengthy. Dam won 2m5f Ch (also won 2m2f Sell Ch, but disqualified — prohibited substances). NH '97/00 r18 w3 (2 2m4f-2m6f Hdles, and 2m4f Ch) p6. P-t-P/HUNT CH '01/2 r9 w3 (inc 2 2m4f110y-3m2f Hunt Chses) p1 (2nd); pulled up 1, fell 2. Used to possess plenty of ability, but moody and error prone, and after suffering a setback in '02 failed to beat a rival on his return. An upturn in his fortunes would be surprising at 13, and is best ignored. *M.S. Gorman — Crawley & Horsham (Carolyn Gorman).* 17 (O), 170 (O), 640 (Cf).

LIFT THE LATCH (IRE) ..—.. 13 b.g. Strong Gale — Pallastown Run (Deep Run) ppfp. Big good-topped half-brother to Palladante (IRE). NH FLAT '97 r1 p0. NH '97 r1 p0. P-t-P '99/00 and '02/3 r12 w1 (Maiden) p1 (3rd of 4); last 2, pulled up 6, refused 1, and unseated 1. Only once better than last in 11 previous Points, and badly impeded by persistent wind problems, but landed a Maiden on firm at Brampton Bryan last year. Tubed and useless now, and remains prone to alarming errors. Acquired headgear on his last two starts. *Mrs J. Holloway — S. Herefords (Christine Hardinge).* 665 (R), 977 (R), 1114 (R), 1531 (R).

LIGHTNING FORK (IRE) ..9-5.. 8 gr.m. Common Grounds — Bahia Laura (FR) (Bellypha) fpu*3456*. Lightly-made sister to flat winners Amicable and Bali Breeze (in Ireland), and half-sister to 2 winners abroad (one in Italy). Dam won in France. NH '04 (for B.I. Case) r3 p0 (last of 4 in 2m4f Hdle: *hld up, hdwy 6, ev ch app 3 out, wkng when blun nxt*; 5th in 2m110y Sell Hdle: *hld up, hdwy 5, wkng when blun 3 out, t.o*; and last of 6 in 2m4f110y Hdle: *hld up & bhnd, hdwy 7, wknd 9, t.o*). Has made too many blunders including when an unworthy favourite once, and completed for the first time when ten-and-a-half lengths third in the desperate ground at Northaw (by this stage of the afternoon they were reduced to jumping ten fences; she hung right on the flat to lose second near the finish and the rider was given a £65 fine for excessive whip use). Not wholly disgraced including in a Seller when switched to Hurdles subsequently, and could perhaps go closer in a Maiden in '05. *Mrs J. Hulse - W. Norfolk (Charlie Ward).* 401 (OMa), 560 (OMa), 1155 (OMa), 1246 (OMa).

LIGHTNING REBEL ..6-7.. 11 b.g. Rambo Dancer (CAN) — Ozra (Red Alert) 6fpp. Small brother to flat winner, Mister Rambo, and half-brother to Wizzo (*qv* '00 Annual), and Jimlil (dam of Lilardo (*qv*). Dam won 3 flat, 6-7f (consecutively, inc 3 Sells). 4600y. FLAT '96/9 r16 p2. NH '98/9 (for P.W. Hiatt) r9 p0; fell/unseated 2, pulled up 2. A hard puller in his youth and has contested six Sellers, and was beaten 23 lengths plus over Hurdles (pulled up in the final two). Nearly three fences last on the only occasion he completed in a Point, and being bred for sprints it was a miracle he got round at all. Why bother? *J. Young — O. Surrey, Burstow & W. Kent (Clare Young).* 540 (CfMa), 611 (OMa), 777 (M), 833 (OMa).

LIGHT-O-DAY ..—.. 12 gr.g. Gods Solution — Brampton Lyn (Derrylin) pfpp. Close-coupled. Dam won 2m Hurdle for Don Lee. NH '02 (for C. Grant) r1 p0 (pulled up). A veteran no-hoper who was very slow to see the light-o-day on the racecourse, but at least took connections to some pretty venues in Durham, Yorkshire, Cheshire and Leicestershire. *D. Lee — Bilsdale (Denis Grattan).* 959 (OMa), 1292 (OMa), 1424 (OMa), 1473 (OMa).

LIGHTS ON ..9-9.. 9 b/br.g. Young Man (FR) — Lady Eccentric (IRE) (Magical Wonder USA) 134535. Half-brother to Sky Hook. NH '00 r1 p0. NH '01 r1 p0 (pulled up). P-t-P '02 r5 p3 (2 2nds); slipped up 1, and fell 1. NH '04 (for M.W. Easterby) r3 p1 (3rd in 2m7f Hdle: *hld up, hdwy 4 out, rdn & wknd app nxt, t.o*); 5th in 2m4f110y Hdle: *a bhnd, t.o*; and last of 5 in 2m110y Ch: *chsd ldrs til wknd 9, t.o.* Confidently ridden when gaining a deserved success in soft at Brocklesby Park, but beaten 17 lengths plus in Restricteds since, and has proved far too slow for racing under Rules. Needs to return to Points and seek out further opportunities when his proven stamina will come into play. *Lord Manton — Meynell & S. Staffs (David Easterby).* 482 (OMa), 591 (CR), 771 (R).

LIGHT THE RIVER (IRE) ..10-1.. 11 b/br.g. Over The River (FR) — Mysterious Light (Strong Gale) 1644. Workmanlike. IRISH P-t-P '99 r3 w1 (5yo Maiden) p2 (2nds). NH '99/02 r16 w1 (3m1f Ch) p2 (3rds); pulled up 5. P-t-P '03 r3 w1 (Ladies) p1 (3rd); and 4th. A thorough stayer, but bitterly disappointing when he first arrived in England, and has only won three races in blinkers since. Only seems able to maintain his interest for very short periods, and avoids ground any quicker than good. Quite capable of reviving successfully, but punters are advised to treat him with caution. Wears a tongue-tie and a cross-noseband. *Miss C. Metcalfe — Braes.* 71 (L), 122 (3m1fH), 270 (L), 428 (3m5fL).

LIGHT THE SKY ..9-10.. 12 b.g. Lighter — Saleander (Leander) 476. Half-brother to Chester Ben and Salvo, and to smart Irish jumping winner, Jeffell (also won Chasing in England). Dam won a Maiden and placed 3. NH '01 r1 p0 (9th in 2m4f110y Ch). P-t-P/HUNT CH '99/03 r32 w2 (3-finisher Maiden, and Restricted) p9 (5 2nds; inc 3rd of 4 once); pulled up 5, fell 1. A very reliable jumper, and has won two minor races, but normally a weak finisher, and easily brushed aside by decent animals. Needs to lower his sights, but probably only of value as a schoolmaster now. Has been tried in blinkers and a tongue-strap. *Mrs S. Norris — Pytchley.* 124 (CCon), 289 (CfL), 379 (I).

LIKE THE BUZZ (IRE) ..10-2.. 7 b.m. Lord Americo — Crash Course Katie (IRE) (Crash Course) 31p311. Very small strong. Dam, half-sister to Aortic (*qv* '93 Annual). P-t-P '03 r3 w1 (Maiden) p0; last, and pulled up 1. Prone to sketchy jumping, and not helped by her lack of inches in that respect, but reversed previous form with Rathgibbon at Lydstep, and confirmed her improvement when following up at Trecoed. Handles fast ground, but has yet to beat anything even half-decent, and might have to turn her attentions to Ladies races in future. *P. Williams — Mrs C., P. & R. Williams & Mr & Mrs Elliott — Pentyrch (Cath Williams).* 740 (R), 1022 (R), 1089 (M), 1188 (Cf), 1521 (Cnr), 1552 (I).

LILABET ..8-7.. 9 b.m. Bandmaster (USA) — Jubilee Leigh (Hubble Bubble) ppR. Quite attractive good-bodied owner-bred half-sister to Shobrooke Mill (*qv*). P-t-P '02/3 r4 p1 (3rd); and pulled up 3. Related to a decent performer, but has only been put into the race once in seven outings, and looks to be crying out for stronger handling. *Mrs S. Prouse — Eggesford.* 567 (CfMa), 827 (CfMa), 1131 (R).

LILARDO ..—.. 8 b/br.m. Son Pardo — Jimlil (Nicholas Bill) pppf. Compact half-sister to flat winner, Lilanita. Dam won 3 flat (6-8f), and is half-sister to Lightning Rebel (*qv*). FLAT '99 and '02/3 r14 w2 (12-16f) p0. NH '00/3 (for B. Palling) r10 p2 (3rds); pulled up 2. Her four prizes were all gained in Sellers including two all-weather wins on the flat, and faced tough tasks in Points and was nowhere near good enough (may have struggled to get the trip). Often tongue-tied. Not seen since falling in early March. *R.W.J. & Mrs S.M. Willcox — Llangeinor (Roger Willcox).* 64 (O), 115 (MO), 208 (Cf), 361 (L).

LILLY BEACH ..—.. 9 b.m. Milieu — Marlowvous (Relkino) fp. Dam won 2m4f Maiden when ridden by Nigel Tutty and placed 6 (inc 3rd in flat Sell). Fell two out when third but weakening on her belated debut, and tailed off and pulled up two out when favourite but stopping to nothing next time. On the admittedly scanty evidence, she is having a job to stay three miles. *N.D. Tutty — Hurworth (Karen Tutty).* 960 (OMa), 1164 (OMa).

LILY (U) .—.. 11 b.m. Wendika — Georgie Girl 3. Cobby hunter. Roamed the moor at Flagg to claim third in her stone wall Members despite the rider having no sense of direction. *Miss A. Farrell — High Peak.* 984 (3m4fNCM).

LILY BROWN ..9-2.. 10 br.m. Sula Bula — Lily Mab (FR) (Prince Mab FR) r545. Small compact sister to Bathwick Annie, and half-sister to NH flat and Hurdles winners, Tipping The Line and Barton Ward, and to NH flat winner, Barton Bill. Dam won at 12f, and won 2 2m Hdles. P-t-P '00/2 (for Mrs E. Harrington) r4 w1 (2m4f100y Maiden) p0; pulled up 1, refused 1, and fell 1. NH '02/3 (for D.P. Keane) r7 p0; fell 1, pulled up 3. Won a weak Maiden in testing ground at Cothelstone in '02, but only once better than last when attempting regulation fences subsequently, and subsequently well beaten in Restricteds. Has yet to prove her effectiveness over three miles. Wears a cross-noseband. *J.S. Swindells — Cheshire.* 95 (R), 530 (R), 1148 (R), 1265 (R).

LILY LANE ..8-6§.. 13 ch.g. Town And Country — My Pride (Petit Instant) pp7p. Rangy half-brother to Medway Boy, Sula Pride, Prides Delight and Charlie Smith. Dam failed to finish in 5 Points. P-t-P '97 and '00/3 r16 p1 (last of 3); pulled up 5, ran out 1, and fell/unseated 2. A long-standing maiden, and has been set some stiff tasks in the current yard, but predictably yet to rise to them, and continues to treat the fences with contempt. Sweats like a pig, which is not surprising as he carries too much condition. Wears a cross-noseband, and has run in a kineton. *Mrs H.J. Merriman — Blackmore & Sparkford V.* 235 (O), 319 (O), 350 (M), 604 (OMa).

LIMA BRAVO ..10-2.. 9 b.m. Aird Point — Archie's Niece (Sagaro) 21. Small light half-sister to Another Relation (dam of Swingingbridge, *qv*), and Meldrew. Dam is unraced half-sister to Baron's Heir (*qv* '98 Annual). NH '99/00 r6 p0; pulled up 1, unseated 1. P-t-P '02/3 r5 w2 (Maiden and Members) p0; pulled up 2, and fell 1. A gift-horse, and has only been beaten once when completing in Points, but only stands very light campaigns. Can quicken off a steady pace, and suited by good or sound surfaces, but often an unconvincing jumper, and tends to dive away to the left. The trainer continues to do well with the ammunition at his disposal. *Miss R. Cooper — Albrighton (Paul Morris).* 752 (R), 1388 (R).

LINDRON ..9-5.. 11 b.g. Gildoran — Artalinda (Indiaro) 2p. Workmanlike good-topped owner-bred brother to Happy Chappy, and half-brother to Linger Balinda, Timbo and Indiway. Dam was 3rd in Ladies from 10 Points/Hunter Chases. P-t-P '02/3 r6 p2 (2nds, last once); pulled up 2, fell 2. Runner-up in three Maidens, but easily brushed aside by the winner in the latest, and failed to reappear after pulling up at High Easter in February. Does not seem particularly hardy, and apparently needs a right-handed track, but deserves a small success. Has two handlers. *M.F. & Mrs S. Haydon — Mid Surrey F. (Cynthia Haydon).* 39 (OMa), 220 (OMa).

LINDSAY (FR) ..11-1.. 6 b.g. Chamberlin (FR) — Oliday (FR) (Djarvis FR) 2u. Sparely-made brother to French Chasing winner, Johnny's (FR) and French flat and jumping winner, Gladly II (FR), and half-brother to Folliday (FR). Dam won 5 flat races in France. FRENCH FLAT '03 r3 w1 (12f) p0. FRENCH NH '03 (for G. Macaire) r5 w3 (2m1f Hdle and 2 2m2f Chses) p2 (2nds). A competent Provinces horse in all spheres in France, and won on the flat at Montlucon-Neris, over Hurdles at Vichy, and twice in Chases at Compiegne (gained two of his victories in non-thoroughbred contests). Gave a bold display at Fakenham on his English debut where he was forced to give the winner Enitsag 15 pounds, but was tiring in the closing stages, and then unseated at the first in Huntingdon. It would be best to put him in a professional yard so that he could campaign over the shorter distances he needs. *J.R. Wilson — Cheshire (Gordy Edwards).* 544 (2m5f110yH), 1359 (2m4f110yH).

LINGERING FOG (IRE) ..9-13.. 11 br.g. Over The River (FR) — Mandasari (Mandalus) 6663342217. Compact. IRISH P-t-P '02 r8 p5; pulled up 3. IRISH NH FLAT '00/1 r2 p0. IRISH NH '00/2 r8 p0. NH '02 r1 p0. P-t-P '03 r8 w1 (3-finisher Maiden) p4 (2 3rds, of 4 once); and last pair thrice. An expert jumper who has never fallen in 28 races over fences, but has only managed to win two three-finisher events, and tends to plod badly in the final mile nowadays. Finished very lame at Bratton Down. Has been tried in cheekpieces. *D.R. & Miss M. McCarthy — Modbury H. (Nicky Frost).* 79 (R), 314 (R), 323 (R), 488 (R), 572 (R), 794 (Inr), 1001 (M), 1196 (R), 1351 (Inr), 1556 (MO).

LINGERING LAUGHTER (IRE) ..—§.. 14 ch.g. Balinger — Merry Mirth (Menelek) p. Compact brother to Neily Joe (IRE) and NH flat and jumping winner, Happy Hussar (IRE), and half-brother to Irish Chasing winner, Slaney Fayre (IRE), to Irish Hurdles winners, Cock Cockburn and General Norman, and to Irish NH flat winners, Arctic Red River (IRE) and Sheer Mirth. Dam won 2m2f Hdle in Ireland. NH FLAT '96 r1 p0. NH '00 r1 p0 (pulled up in 3m2f Nov Chse). P-t-P/HUNT CH '98, '00 and '02/3 (for Mr M.J. Lethbridge in '03) r9 w1 (Maiden) p0; pulled up 5, fell/unseated 3. Landed a three-finisher Maiden on firmish at Tweseldown in '98, but stands his racing very badly, and has failed to finish in ten subsequent appearances. A fence adrift when pulled up after two miles in his Members and can barely bring himself to break into a gallop these days. Fell when blinkered and ridden in spurs once in '03. *Miss A. Bucknall — Quantock.* 468 (M).

LINGHAM LADY ..9-10.. 12 b.m. Lord Bud — Old Mill Lady (Royal Goblin) 4p. Half-sister to Lingham Magic. Dam won 2 Sell Hdles and Nov Ch (all 2m); subsequently showed no form for Joe Swiers, inc Hunt Chses. P-t-P '99/00 and '02/3 r13 w1 (Maiden) p6 (4 3rds, of 4 once, last once); 4th, pulled up 3, and fell 2. Made the frame on six occasions before landing a 16-runner Maiden on firmish at Mordon with some authority in '02, but only seen thrice since, and looks troubled. Wears a cross-noseband. *Mrs D.W. Hill — Hurworth (Stephen Swiers).* 164 (R), 341 (R).

LINK COPPER ..8-10§.. 16 ch.g. Whistlefield — Letitica (Deep Run) 8pp. Compact good-bodied owner-bred half-brother to Lets Go Polly and Another Copper, and to jumping winner, Lets Be Frank. NH '92/4 r4 p0 (last, and pulled up 3, inc both Chses). P-t-P/HUNT CH '94/00 and '02/3 r52 w8 (inc 3 Confineds) p17 (11 2nds, beaten head once, of 3 once, and inc Hunt Ch; inc 3rd of 4 in Hunt Ch, and last of 3 once); also disqualified from 2nd after testing positive in Hunt Ch; pulled up 15, slipped up 1, and fell 3. Rated 10-5 after recording a four-timer in '98, but only able to score once in 30 subsequent outings (at 25-1 in '02) and has a long history of physical problems. Only effective on a sound surface, but lost interest after a couple of early mistakes on his latest appearance, and looks set for retirement. *Mrs E.J. Taplin — Devon & Somerset.* 963 (Cf), 1369 (Cf), 1446 (Cf).

LINLATHEN ..10-3.. 15 ch.g. Move Off — Loch Brandy (Harwell) 321. Compact good-bodied half-brother to Kingennie. Dam won 3m3f Hunt Ch and 4 Points and placed 14 (inc a Hdle). NH FLAT '94 r2 p0. NH '94/8 r22 w5 (4 2m-2m7f Hdles, inc hat-trick, and 3m Ch) p9 (5 2nds); fell/unseated 2. P-t-P/HUNT CH '99/03 r35 w6 (inc 5 Ladies) p13 (11 2nds; and inc 3 Hunt Chses; inc 3rd of 4 once); fell/unseated 6, pulled up 1, brought down 1. Cannot quicken much and needs to be in control almost throughout nowadays, but can still wing the fences, and recorded his sixth win for present connections when bravely hanging on at Kingston Blount. Has only missed the frame once in Points, and could enhance that record further at 15. Acts in soft, and on much sounder surfaces. Wears a cross-noseband. *Mrs S. Hutchinson — Fernie (Patrick Hutchinson).* 743 (L), 1106 (L), 1334 (L).

LION (U) ..—.. a ch.g. unknown p. Fat and refused at the second before continuing for less than two miles in his Members so not worthy of being lionized. *L. Metcalfe — V. of Lune H.* 872 (M).

LIPSTICK LASS ..—§.. 9 b.m. Goldsmiths' Hall — Farmer Dipstick (Right Flare) pp. Compact. Dam, failed to finish in 12 of 14 Points for Gordon Herrod ('utterly incapable of staying'). P-t-P '03 r3 p0 (pulled up 2, and refused 1). Pulled up in the four races in which she has consented to start, and has made mistakes in most. Bred to be useless, and certainly living up to the billing. Wears a cross-noseband. *G. Herrod — Cotley.* 325 (OMa), 967 (OMa).

LIRKIMALONG ..9-8.. 12 ch.g. Lir — Kimberley Ann (St Columbus) p4433. Good-bodied homebred brother to Belitlir (*qv*). NH '01/2 r2 p0; unseated 1. P-t-P '00 and '03 r8 w1 (2-finisher Maiden) p3 (2 2nds, of 3 once); 4th, and pulled up 3. Made the bulk of the running when landing a two-finisher Maiden at Trebudannon last year, but often given no chance of obtaining the best possible placing, and should have finished a distant second to Bengal Bullet at Newton Abbot. Clearly not easy to train, but still capable of springing a surprise if sensibly placed. Tends to get rather worked up and has two handlers. *Mrs J. Holden-White & B.R.J. Young — E. Cornwall (Jan Holden-White).* 572 (R), 706 (R), 1029 (3mH), 1363 (2m3f110yH), 1431 (I).

LIRSLEFTOVER ..10-0.. 13 ch.g. Lir — Full Tan (Dairialatan) 3541pp3. Small neat attractive Young-bred brother to Full Spirit (dam of Fossy Bear, *qv*), and Full Alirt. Dam, 'a useless pest', pulled up, and ran out in Points for Basil Young. NH '01/2 r6 p0. P-t-P/HUNT CH '98/01 and '03 r23 w4 (up to Confined) p5 (4 3rds, last once); pulled up 8, and unseated 1. Consistent in his grade, and primed for his latest success on an easy surface with a very quiet potter around Wadebridge, but ran no sort of race when second-favourite next time. Tends to hang left and has been pulled up and dismounted more than once, but will probably go in again when least expected, at least by the punters. *B.R.J. Young, Mrs K. Rogers & Miss S. Young — E. Cornwall (Sue Young).* 311 (L), 347 (3mH), 484 (L), 570 (Cf), 707 (Cf), 1437 (2m5f110yH), 1498 (3m2f110yH).

LISCOMBE ..8-0.. 9 b.m. Petoski — Take The Veil (Monksfield) 6. Workmanlike chasing-type half-sister to Sister Anna and Flying Veil. Dam, half-sister to Fisherman's Tale (*qv* '93 Annual), and to the dam of Party Politics, was useless including 3 Points. NH FLAT '01 r1 p0. NH '02 (for D.R. Stoddart) r1 p0 (pulled up). Hopelessly tailed off in a bumper (beat one) and pulled up in a Selling Hurdle, and making just her third appearance in four years when finishing a remote last in an elders Maiden (took a strong hold in the lead until headed at the 15th and weakened rapidly). *J.A. & Mrs V. Watson — Worcs (Valerie Watson).* 1340 (OMa).

LISTEN TO US (IRE) ..8-12.. 9 b.g. Mandalus — Lady Laburnum (Carlingford Castle) 3p. Good-topped. Dam, half-sister to Cherokee Red (*qv* '04 Annual). IR24,000 4yo. NH FLAT '01 (for N.J. Henderson) r1 p0. Making a first appearance for three years when 19 lengths third in his Members (in front four out but tiring and headed when making a mistake at the next), but in company with others went wrong at Black Forest Lodge next time. *Mrs B. Russell — Silverton (Lucy Gardner).* 61 (M), 150 (OMa).

LITTLE APPLE BAY ..8-6.. 8 b.m. Sula Bula — Sage Mountain (Spitsbergen) ppu33f. Small homebred half-sister to Wise Florizel. Dam is an unraced sister to Carrot Bay. Grandam, Gold Harp is half-sister to 5 Pointers who were all raced by Mrs Welch's father, won Maiden and placed 8 for him. Great-grandam, Bright Reply, was placed in 3 very bad Points for him. P-t-P '03 r1 p0 (pulled up). Gradually getting the hang of things, and beaten a maximum of 11 lengths when third in 2m4f Maidens once the ground had dried out, but needs to brush up her jumping. Tends to sweat excessively, and a more relaxed attitude would not go amiss. *Mrs R. Welch — Dartmoor.* 195 (CfMa), 329 (OMa), 491 (M), 702 (2m4fOMa), 910 (2m4fOMa), 1006 (CfMa).

LITTLE DISH ..9-7.. 12 b.m. Mutamarrid — Silver Thorn (Record Run) f2ff3. Small half-sister to Rodney Trotter and Hensil. Dam won 2m4f Sell Hdle. NH FLAT '97 r2 p0. NH '00 r3 p0; pulled up 1. P-t-P '03 (for Miss S. Rawcliffe) r6 p0 (6th, last 2, pulled up 2, and unseated 1). Speedy and often thereabouts, but consistently let down by her jumping, and her ability to get three miles. Deserves a small success on balance, and keeps the right company, but could never be supported with any confidence. Runs tongue-tied and has acquired a cross-noseband. *B. Eccles — N. Cotswold (Giles & Kim Smyly).* 258 (CMa), 588 (CfMa), 978 (CMam), 1119 (CMam), 1341 (OMa).

LITTLE FARMER ..10-5.. 11 b.g. Little Wolf — Sea Farmer (Cantab) 232145. Half-brother to Classic Bart, Pretty Boy George and Tubb Corner. Dam failed to finish in 3 races, inc 2 NH flat! NH '01 r3 p1 (3rd in 2m1f110y Hdle); 4th, and pulled up. P-t-P/HUNT CH '00/1 and '03 r6 w3 (hat-trick '03 inc 2m5f Hunt Ch) p1 (2nd); pulled up 1, and brought down 1. A habitual front-runner, and did not see a rival when completing a hat-trick in '03, but vulnerable on easy surfaces, and failed to see off Struggles Glory when 1-2 at Godstone. Murdered a well below par Splash And Dash at Catsfield, but disappointing at Folkestone where everything looked in his favour, and may have been feeling the effects of a hard race at Cheltenham. A sound jumper, and looks sure to pick up the winning thread when returned to Points. Highly-strung and has two handlers, and is often taken to post early. *C.S. Hall & A.W. Cooper — Southdown & Eridge (Di Grissell).* 100 (O), 348 (3mH), 609 (O), 1052 (O), 1171 (3m2f110yH), 1440 (3m1fH).

LITTLE HECK (IRE) ..—.. 8 b.g. Executive Perk — Princess Andromeda (Corvaro USA) ppfspp. Small light half-brother to About Midnight and Con's Nurse (IRE), to Hurdles winner, Court In The Act (IRE), and to successful Irish Pointer, Don't Tell Jo. Dam won 9f Sell. 8000 4yo. NH FLAT '03 (for T.D. Easterby) r1 p0 (well tailed off last). Bought Doncaster, Aug for 2100. Looked terrible in Maidens and the poor thing did not have the energy to get anywhere close to even completing the course. Tongue-tied on his last three appearances, and his jumping was as clueless at the end of the season as it had been at the beginning. *P.J. Millington — Fernie.* 128 (OMa), 476 (CfMa), 652 (OMa), 1339 (OMa), 1403 (2m4fOMa), 1532 (OMa).

LITTLE JOHN ..9-3§.. 9 b.g. Warrshan (USA) — Silver Venture (USA) (Silver Hawk USA) 21u5726. Strong-topped half-brother to flat winner in Scandinavia, and to English flat and Irish Hurdling winner, Exile. 14,000y. FLAT '98/03 r64 p27. NH '99/00 and '02 (for Miss L.A. Perratt) r4 p0. An infamous serial loser on the flat for six seasons, and although he could travel smoothly he could never deliver and was beaten a length or less in ten of 27 placings (one of which was in a Seller). Broke a blood vessel once, and occasionally wore headgear to '01. Unplaced in his final ten attempts for the previous yard, and looked as if he would be as frustrating as ever when second in his debut Point at Alnwick, but given a great ride by the very under-rated Andrew Richardson on a return visit, and was bullied clear after leading at the last. Back to normal afterwards and takes advantage if owner-ridden, but at least did it once even if it took 70 tries. *J. Galbraith — Buccleuch (Bill Hughes).* 75 (OMa), 216 (OMa), 431 (R), 548 (R), 766 (R), 1040 (R), 1222 (R).

LITTLE LORD LEWIS ..6-6.. 6 b.g. Sir Harry Lewis (USA) — Unspoken Prayer (Inca Chief USA) u5pu. Small sturdy. NH FLAT '03 (for Mrs H.O. Graham) r2 p0. Badly tailed off in two bumpers (beat one), and 18 lengths fifth on his only Pointing completion. Virtually useless, and does not seem to stay even 2m4f. *Mrs R. Fell & Mrs H. Graham — Jedforest (Rame Fell).* 486 (OMa), 702 (2m4fOMa), 1432 (OMa), 1545 (OMa).

LITTLE MICKEY ..9-2.. 7 ch.g. Rock Hopper — Sixslip (USA) (Diesis) 1. Compact sturdy half-brother to Slip The Ring (*qv*). IRISH P-t-P '02 r1 p0 (refused). NH FLAT '02 r2 p1 (3rd). NH '03 (for N.A. Twiston-Davies) r3 p1 (3rd); pulled up 1, and unseated 1. Two previous placings (beaten between eight and 16 lengths) certainly entitled him to favouritism in a Charing Maiden, but looked lucky to collect, as Lord Of The North was a length ahead and apparently going better when falling two out. Injured a leg and not seen again. Probably not one of the owner's big guns in any case. Was visored in his final two Hurdles. *S.P. Tindall — Southdown & Eridge (Jenny Gordon).* 186 (OMa).

LITTLE MISTER ..—§§.. 9 ch.g. Gran Alba (USA) — Chrissytino (Baron Blakeney) ppppuppp. Small good-bodied. Dam, (half-sister to dam of Rooster Booster), unseated 2nd only Point for N. Powell, and broke Nick Mitchell's collar-bone. NH FLAT '01 r1 p0. NH '01 and '03 (for N.R. Mitchell) r5 p0; pulled up 3, fell 1. A prize porker who was 93 lengths 12th of 13 in his first race over jumps, but (wait for this) he has actually fared even worse since, totting up 12 consecutive non-completions whilst loathing every moment. Normally wears cheekpieces or blinkers. In more enlightened countries they would eat horses like this. *N.J. Powell — S. Dorset (Elsie Mitchell).* 174 (OMa), 325 (OMa), 580 (OMa), 693 (OMa), 1132 (R), 1252 (OMa), 1327 (OMa), 1366 (R).

PLATE 77 790 Spooners & West Dartmoor Members: Little Native (Polly Gundry), 1st, leads Elegant Light (N. Harris), 2nd PHOTO: Tim Holt

LITTLE NATIVE (IRE) ..10-3.. 10 b/br.g. Be My Native (USA) — Royal Character (Reformed Character) 31315. Workmanlike brother to Irish Pointing winner, Nifty (IRE), and half-brother to Bit Of A Character, and to Hurdles winner, Establish (IRE), and to Irish Pointing winner, Erins Banker. P-t-P/ HUNT CH '00/1 and '03 r4 w1 (Maiden) p0; pulled up 1, and unseated 2. Restricted to a four appearances in his first three competitive seasons, and virus-afflicted in '03, but has won half his completions, and gained a notable scalp when rallying gamely to beat Rhythm King at Chipley Park. Much less convincing subsequently, and a 4-5 flop on his latest appearance, but may revive when there is an abundance of mud. Wears a cross-noseband. *R.G. Kelvin-Hughes — Spooners & W. Dartmoor.* 14 (R), 118 (R), 313 (I), 790 (M), 1005 (Cf).

LITTLE POPPY ..—.. 9 b.m. Afzal — Little Gift (Broadsword USA) pf. Small owner-bred. Dam sister to Dan De Lyon (*qv* '99 Annual). Soon struggling and out of the action before halfway in Maidens. *P.J.R. Gardner & F. Hutsby — N. Cotswold (Fred Hutsby).* 259 (CMa), 531 (OMa).

LITTLE ROSIE .7-10§§.. 10 b.m. Derring Rose — Haselbech (Spartan General) 2rp. Tiny half-sister to Sam Pepper, Jack Presto, Peter Presto, I'm A Bute and Ginger Duchess. Dam, ridden by Shan Farr, was 2nd in 2 Points. Grandam, Dark Parting, was 4th in big field for Oakley Maiden on only start. Great-grandam, Dark Rate, won 3 Points. P-t-P '02/3 (for Mrs S.M. Farr) r9 p0 (pulled up 5, refused 3, and unseated 1). Elevated to a miniscule rating when completing the course for the first time at Great Trethew, but was no match for the winner, and quickly returned to her evil ways. Blinkered twice in '03. *Mrs G. Stevenson & Miss P.D. Mitchell — E. Cornwall (Dawn Mitchell).* 305 (M), 485 (OMa), 704 (CfMa).

LITTLE SANTA (IRE) ..9-12.. 13 b.m. Little Bighorn — Santa's Gold (Tumble Gold) 5pu. Lengthy sister to One For Olly (IRE). IRISH P-t-P '97 r4 p0 (4th, pulled up 2, and brought down 1). P-t-P '98/00 and '02/3 r29 w3 (inc Ladies) p12 (10 2nds, beaten neck once, last once); unseated 3, pulled up 4, and ran out 1. Thrice a winner when stamina has not been a major issue, and her '04 campaign seemed geared to an assault on her Members, but had seemingly had her measure taken when unseating at the second last. Often edgy in the preliminaries, and has been led in at the start. Has run tongue-tied. *Mrs S. Davidson — W. Percy (Kirstie Hargreave).* 284 (L), 426 (Cf), 854 (M).

LITTLETON ZEUS (IRE) ..8-2.. 6 ch.g. Woodborough (USA) — La Fandango (IRE) (Taufan USA) pu4. Small half-brother to flat winner, Ashbourne Lady. IR8200f, 17,000y, 23,000 2yo. FLAT '01/3 r12 p0. NH '03 (for W.S. Cunningham) r4 p0; pulled up 1, unseated 1. Tried Sellers on the flat, beaten 30 lengths plus at 33-1 or more in Hurdles, and 49 lengths fourth of five in a youngsters Maiden on his only Pointing completion. Wore a visor once and cheekpieces four times to '03. Extremely bad at everything he turns his hand to. *P. Collins — Cleveland (Nick Smith).* 165 (OMa), 774 (2m4fCMa), 1300 (OMa).

LITTLE WORD ..8-9.. 6 b.m. Rakaposhi King — Preacher's Gem (The Parson) ppp33. Small neat half-sister to Rip Kirby (*qv*). Bought Ascot, Aug for 2476. Pulled up in her first three Maidens, and then claimed a couple of poor thirds (beaten 24 lengths once, but a fence behind when last of three). Bred to stay well, and as her placings were in above-average contests she can probably improve enough to score eventually. *Mrs D. Williams & N. Sais — Pentyrch (Phil Williams).* 53 (2m4fOMa), 119 (OMa), 599 (2m4fOMa), 700 (CfMa), 845 (CfMa).

LITTLE WORSALL (IRE) ..9-12.. 12 ch.g. Broadsword (USA) — In My View (King's Ride) 7u43p6. Tall. Dam is half-sister to Dingle Wood. NH FLAT '99 r2 p0. NH '99/01 r14 p4 (3 3rds); pulled up 5, and fell/unseated 2. P-t-P/HUNT CH '02/3 (for Mr N.D. Tutty) r14 w7 (inc 4 Opens) p0; 4th twice, 5th, 8th, pulled up, and fell/unseated 2. Won seven times in an 11-race spell from April '02 to May '03, mainly on good or sound surfaces, but keen and needs to be held up, and the new rider was largely ineffective. Might have won with stronger handling at Higham, and clearly retains ability, but only once better than last otherwise, and needs better organising at the obstacles. *Mr & Mrs F. Marshall — E. Sussex & Romney Marsh (Di Grissell).* 3 (O), 43 (O), 183 (O), 397 (O), 1052 (O), 1209 (O).

LIVELY DESSERT (IRE) .9-10§.. 12 b.g. Be My Native (USA) — Liffey Travel (Le Bavard FR) pfp15p63. Lengthy unfurnished half-brother to Hurdles winners, Tidal Force (IRE) (also won NH flat) and Orbicularis (IRE). Dam won 2m2f NN Flat in Ireland. IRISH NH FLAT '99 r1 p0. IRISH NH '98/00 r23 p3 (Hdles); pulled up 1, fell 1. NH '00/3 (for J. O'Neill, and F.P. Murtagh) r22 w4 (3m-3m1f Chses) p6; pulled up 6, fell 1. Won four Chases on good ground or in deep mud to April '01, and partnered to all the victories by A.P. McCoy, who was a great help to him. Often makes mistakes, and had run up a losing sequence of 18 (including pulled up ten and fell two) before he surprisingly decided to co-operate in a four-runner Confined at Alnwick. Rarely keen these days and beaten 20 lengths or much more subsequently, and lucky that everything fell right for him on the one day. Has been tried with a visor and cheekpieces, but they do not work. *Mrs M.E. James — W. Percy (George White).* 69 (M), 134 (O), 426 (Cf), 858 (Cf), 1038 (O), 1179 (3m1fH), 1307 (Cf), 1479 (Cf).

LIVELY LORD (IRE) ..10-3.. 11 ch.g. Mister Lord (USA) — Artic Squaw (IRE) (Buckskin FR) 3u1p1131. Lengthy brother to Hurdles winner, Brave Lord (IRE). Dam is half-sister to Do A Runner (*qv* '99 Annual). IRISH P-t-P '98 r1 p0 (fell). IRISH NH FLAT '98 and '00 r3 p0. IRISH NH '99/00 r7 p2; pulled up 1. P-t-P '02/3 r13 w7 (up to Confined, inc hat-trick '02) p2 (2nds, beaten neck once); 4th, pulled up 2, and fell. Disappointing in Ireland, and still prone to flop unexpectedly, but has done really well for an ex-crock, and took his winning tally into double figures in '04. Likes to bowl along in front, and is best served by sound surfaces, but owes his successes to excellent placing, and is vulnerable to decent performers. Wears a tongue-strap, and has been tried in all types of headgear. *S.P. Tindall — Southdown & Eridge (Jenny Gordon).* 175 (Cnr), 422 (CCon), 607 (Cf), 778 (CCon), 897 (Cfv&nr), 1085 (Cv&nr), 1209 (O), 1411 (M).

LIVE WIRE (IRE) ..9-10.. 14 b.g. Electric — Green Gale (Strong Gale) p257143. Sturdy half-brother to La Tormenta (IRE). P-t-P/HUNT CH '96/00 and '02/3 r31 w3 (Maiden, Club Confined and Club Conditional) p9 (4 2nds, of 3 once; 3 3rds, of 4 once, and last once); pulled up 5, and unseated 2. A safe if somewhat deliberate jumper, and has won four minor events spread over eight years, but tends to run in snatches, and gifted his latest win when the 1-3 favourite downed tools. Gives the impression of not being too genuine himself, and will be hard pressed to score again at 14. *Miss C. Benstead — Kent & Surrey Bloodhounds (Nigel Benstead).* 19 (CMod), 90 (I), 190 (C), 422 (CCon), 645 (M), 1054 (Cf), 1083 (Cf).

LOLLOPING LAD ..8-6.. 7 ch.g. Afzal — Missile Lady (Paddy's Stream) pp4. Rangy half-brother to Scalby Croft (*qv*). 2095 4yo. Did not jump well on his debut but kept up for two miles next time, and then finished 20 lengths fourth at Marks Tey after still being in contention three out. It looks as if he may have a hint of ability, and if produced in tip-top condition he might spring a surprise. *Miss K. Thory — Fitzwilliam.* 901 (OMa), 1155 (OMa), 1317 (CfMa).

LONDOLOZI LAD (IRE) ..9-13.. 6 b.g. Ali-Royal (IRE) — Ashdown (Pharly FR) pu5. Very small neat half-brother to flat winner, Standown, and to winner in Italy. 2500f, 8000y. FLAT '01/3 r14 w2 (8f) p0. NH '02 (for P.C. Haslam) r3 w1 (2m Hdle) p0; fell 1. A dual winner on the all-weather on the flat (also tried in Sellers, and with blinkers once), and successful in a Juvenile Hurdle, but as a result of these wins he faces very tough tasks in Opens particularly when burdened with a penalty. Retains ability, but given his diminutive stature he would surely be better in Ladies Opens with less weight on his back. *A. Jackson — Cleveland (Lynne Ward).* 391 (MO), 565 (O), 1161 (O).

LONE STAR (IRE) ..8-10§.. 13 b.g. Satco (FR) — Masterstown Lucy (Bargello) pp45pf. Tall half-brother to smart Chasing winner, Jodami (won 18 NH and about £500,000), and to Irish Pointing and Chasing winner, Crashtown Lucy. Dam, sister to Hurry Up Henry (*qv* '94 Annual). IRISH P-t-P '00 r4 w1 (6yo&up Maiden) p2 (2nds). IRISH HUNT CH '00 r1 p0. NH '98/02 r11 p2 (3rds); pulled up 4, fell/unseated 2. P-t-P/HUNT CH '03 r8 p3 (2nd of 3; 3rd of 4, and last of 3); last pair 2, and pulled up 3. Won a Maiden in soft in Ireland after it became apparent he wasn't going to make a breakthrough under Rules, but generally beaten out of sight since, and gave up in typically dramatic fashion after looking sure to be involved in the finish at Northaw on his penultimate start. A consistently inaccurate jumper. Wears blinkers, and has been tried in cheekpieces and a tongue-tie. *M. Ward & G. Wedd — Granta H. (Martin Ward).* 38 (Cf), 159 (R), 745 (R), 999 (R), 1245 (R), 1396 (C).

LONGDALE ..—.. 7 b.g. Primitive Rising (USA) — Gunnerdale (Gunner B) f. Owner-bred brother to Orton Scar. Dam, half-sister to Brooks (*qv* '03 Annual). Fell three out when a beaten third in a Maiden, and impossible to evaluate at present. *D. Curr — Hurworth (Chris Dennis).* 877 (OMa).

LONGSTONE BOY (IRE) ..10-4.. 13 br.g. Mazaad — Inger-Lea (Record Run) 113. Workmanlike half-brother to Cedar Father (IRE). Dam won 2m4f Sell Hdle. NH FLAT '97 r1 p0. NH '00 and '03 r4 p1 (2nd); pulled up 1. P-t-P/HUNT CH '98/00 and '02/3 r15 w5 (Maiden, Restricted, 2 Members and Intermediate) p7 (4 2nds, neck of 3 once, inc Hunt Ch; and 3rd in Hunt Ch); pulled up 1, and unseated 2. Consistent and has won more than half his completed starts in Points, but only manages light campaigns, and has shown his best form when there is some cut in the ground. Rewarded connections perseverance when scoring at the seventh time of asking over regulation fences at Leicester, though in truth the opposition was not of the highest calibre, and readily brushed aside next time. Holding his form well for a veteran and may be able to score again if sensibly placed in '05. *E.R. Clough & Mrs D.N. Harris — S. Pembs (Eric Clough).* 276 (L), 443 (2m4f110yH), 733 (3mH).

LONGSTONE LAD .10-0.. 13 b.g. Pittacus (USA) — Fatu Hiva (GER) (Marduk GER) p3. Tall rangy. Dam won 2 12f races, and won 2 Hdles, 2m4f-2m5f. NH FLAT '97 r2 p0. NH '99/00 r8 p3; ran out 1. P-t-P/HUNT CH '01/3 r21 w8 (inc Open) p6 (3 2nds, inc Hunt Ch; last of 3 once); 4th, ran out 1, pulled up 3, and unseated 2. Won seven of his first ten Pointing completions, and looked to be robbed by the Judge next time, but has always needed plenty of persuading, and spent much of '03 under a cloud. Beaten 35 lengths when third at Cherrybrook, and it will be difficult to make a case for him in future. Ideally suited by an easy surface. *R.G. Rawle — Exmoor.* 569 (MO), 792 (MO).

LONGSTONE LADY (IRE) ..9-6.. 8 b.m. Mister Lord (USA) — Monamandy (IRE) (Mandalus) p61. Sturdy. Dam won Mares Maiden in Ireland. IRISH P-t-P '02 r1 p0 (pulled up). NH FLAT '02 r1 p0. Has progressed steadily, and won a 2m4f Maiden at Trebudannon to initiate a double for Derek McKenna who enjoyed a good season. Beat nothing, but may be able to advance to Restricted standard herself. *J.D. Frost — Dartmoor (Nicky Frost).* 568 (CfMa), 701 (2m4fOMa), 909 (2m4fOMa).

LONGVILLE LAD ..10-6.. 9 b.g. Circus Light — Ditchling Beacon (High Line) 1112. Half-brother to King Neon, Herhorse, Cook's Flyer, Kickles Lass and Stonehill Prospect, and to jumping winner, Sandy's Beacon. P-t-P '03 r3 p1 (head 2nd); 8th of 9, and unseated 1. Related to a high class performer, and fast developing into a smart one himself, but can be very headstrong and always on the verge of eruption in the preliminaries. Quickly rattled off an impressive hat-trick by an aggregate of 57 lengths, and never saw a rival in so doing, but could not match Shanavogh's resolve at Garthorpe. Can jump with tremendous exuberance, and looks worthy of a crack at a Hunter Chase in '05, but has only been risked on ground close to good. Well handled by Paul Cowley. *G.F. & J. Cook, R.W. Fenemore, R.B. Clarke & J. Bodify — Grafton (Richard Webb).* 103 (OMa), 252 (CR), 681 (I), 1121 (O).

LOOKING DEADLY ..5-7§.. 11 b.m. Neltino — Princess Constanza (Relkino) p7. Tall rangy half-sister to Prince On The Ter. Dam, half-sister to Graham's Choice (*qv* '98 Annual), was 3rd in her only Point. 2800 4yo. NH FLAT '99 r1 p0. FLAT '02 r1 p0. NH '99/03 (for F.P. Murtagh) r22 p2 (2nds); pulled up 4, unseated 1. Second twice at long odds including in a Seller over Hurdles, but was nine lengths fourth, fifth, last thrice, pulled up twice and unseated in Chases. A bad and ungenuine maiden who was pulled up and hopelessly tailed off in '04, and not worth expending any more time on. *Mrs M.N. Nichol — Cumberland F. (Richard Nichol).* 74 (OMa), 167 (OMa).

LOOKING MAGIC (IRE) ..7-9.. 12 b/br.g. Strong Gale — My Lovely Rose (IRE) (Orchestra) pp3pf. Narrow angular. IRISH P-t-P '99 r3 p0; pulled up 2, and fell 1. NH '99/00 r8 p1 (2nd). P-t-P '02/3 (for Square Mile Racing) r6 p2 (2nd of 3; and remote 3rd); pulled up 4. Well beaten when plodding into the frame twice last year, and able to be competitive in a slowly-run Members in '04, but a regular non-finisher and killed in a fall at Garthorpe. C.J. Lawson — Essex. 244 (CfMa), 560 (OMa), 646 (M), 833 (OMa), 1505 (OMa).

LOOSE CANNON (IRE) .8-5.. 13 b.g. Executive Perk — Track Down (Take A Reef) 5. Lengthy half-brother to Conway Flyer, to Irish flat winner, Amazing Experience, and to a flat winner in Jersey. Dam won 3 flat (5-6f), inc Sell. IRISH NH FLAT '96 and '02 r3 w1 p0. NH '99 r4 p2 (2nds); fell 1. IRISH NH '02 r1 p0 (pulled up). P-t-P '03 (for Panama Bloodstock) r2 p0 (unseated 1, and pulled up 1). Carried the Magnier silks when beating 13 others at Leopardstown in November '96, but incredibly lightly raced since, and has spent more time on the ferry to and from Ireland than he has on a racecourse. Retains some ability, and looked dangerous briefly when 17 lengths fifth at Witton Castle, but immediately went back into hiding. *J. Saville — Pendle Forest & Craven.* 161 (I).

LORD ALPHA (IRE) ..9-8.. 7 b.g. Alphabatim (USA) — Distant Thoughts (General Ironside) 411. Half-brother to Assegai (IRE). IRISH P-t-P '03 r5 p2 (2nds); fell 1. Looked backward, but ran reasonably despite the burden of the owner-rider in the saddle on his English debut, but subsequently completed a double with David Phelan aboard, in a youngsters Maiden at Badbury and a four-runner Restricted at Aldington. Backed from fours to 2-1 favourite in the former, and is probably going to prove under-rated when he tackles Confineds. Should score again when strongly handled. *A. Ward-Thomas — Hursley Hambledon (David Phelan).* 419 (CR), 575 (OMa), 900 (R).

LORD ANNER (IRE) ..10-5.. 6 br.g. Mister Lord (USA) — Anner Lodge (IRE) (Capitano) 1p1. Big rangy. Bought Doncaster, May for 1000. A remarkably cheap purchase despite (or perhaps because of) his imposing stature, but created an immediately favourable impression on his debut at Bishops Court, where he was friendless in the market and started at 7-1 but stormed home unchallenged in easily the fastest of the five Maidens. Supported from fours to 7-4 in a Buckfastleigh Restricted but never got to grips with Vivid Imagination and was 15 lengths second and struggling when pulling up five out, but despite jumping left he returned to winning ways at Woodford. Can still be green and novicey in his jumping, but has plenty of galloping power, and perhaps he will be worthy to take his place in Hunter Chases eventually. *Axe Valley Racing Club (R.J. Barber) — Cattistock (Richard Barber).* 328 (OMa), 498 (R), 1069 (R).

LORD ATTERBURY (IRE) ..11-6.. 9 ch.g. Mister Lord (USA) — Tammyiris (Arapahos FR) 1p34. Small sturdy. Dam won 4 Irish Points (inc an Open on a disqualification). Grandam, Oxfam VI, won 6 Irish Points. IRISH P-t-P '01/2 r6 w1 (5&6yo Maiden) p2 (last of 3 once). P-t-P/HUNT CH '03 (for Miss J. Holmes) r7 w5 (inc 3 2m7f110y-4m1f Hunt Chses) p1 (2nd); and ran out 1. NH '04 r1 p1 (5/ 3rd to Amberleigh House in 4m4f Grand National: *mists, a.p, 3rd ½way, ev ch flat, no ex*). Reminiscent of the '04 Cheltenham Foxhunters hero, Earthmover (also by Mister Lord) in that he too strolled through his seven-year-old campaign only to stumble slightly in the next. Scored in workmanlike fashion on his reappearance, and was quickly installed ante-post favourite for the big race at Prestbury Park, but the subsequent bulletins eminating from Pond House were never too upbeat, and was badly let down by his jumping in the race. Surprisingly took his place in the Grand National next time, but ran an amazing race despite making plentiful mistakes, and only gave way in the last hundred yards of the run-in. Found the ground much too lively when on a retrieving mission in the Intrum Justitia Cup, but looks the sort that the maestro can win plenty more races with, and Aintree must be high on his agenda in '05. *D.A. Johnson & P.J. Finn — Taunton V.H. (Martin Pipe).* 34 (O), 543 (3m2f110yH), 1453 (3m4fH).

LORD BEAU (IRE) .8-13.. 9 b.g. Beau Sher — Bonny Joe (Derring Rose) 1. Brother to Patagonian Passion (IRE), and half-brother to Who Am I (IRE), to flat and jumping winner, October Mist (IRE) (9 wins total, and broke his duck on flat aged 10 in '04), and to Irish Pointing winner, Chateau Martin. Dam, half-sister to Lord Dorcet (*qv*). IRISH P-t-P '03 r3 p0 (4th, pulled up 1, and slipped up 1). Showed nothing in Irish Points, but it would have been hard for him not to win a Maiden at Badbury where his seven opponents included some of the worst in this or any other county (Queens House, Port Valenska, Forglori and Little Mister). At least the runner-up scored (but pulled up in five other attempts), but his own continued lack of outings looks a worry. *P.R. Bateman — Devon & Somerset (Aaron Bateman).* 580 (OMa).

LORDBERNIEBOUFFANT (IRE) .10-4.. 12 b.g. Denel (FR) — Noon Hunting (Green Shoon) 24211. Tall good-topped half-brother to Brymar Lass (IRE), to Chasing winner, Major Kinsman, to NH flat & Hurdles winner, Mid Day Chaser (IRE), to Hurdles winner, Tulach Ard (IRE), and to Irish Pointing winner, Hidden Agenda. NH FLAT '98 r2 p1 (3rd). NH '99/02 (for J.T. Gifford) r24 w4 (2m5f Hdle and 3 3-3m4f Chses) p8; fell 2. Scored an annual victory '99/02 when trained in Sussex, and two big prizes of £13,000 plus took his career earnings under Rules to £60,433. Only failed to complete the course twice, including when in a slight lead two out in a Chase once. Gained a big pot at Fontwell and was hauled there again for a Hunter Chase, but lacked fluency and was always looking lacklustre, and it must have seemed a very long way home (favourite). Got outbattled in the closing stages in his first two Points, but was sharpened by the acquisition of cheekpieces and made virtually all for a Hexham double. His Members was particularly noteworthy, as it was the 150th pointing victory for the marvellous Pauline Robson, and it also ensured that all David Parker's charges won a race in '04. A very thorough stayer, but should probably have achieved more than he did in the previous stable.

Reportedly retired. *The Marvellous Partnership (R. Anderson Green) — Border (David Parker).* 428 (3m5fL), 800 (3m2f110yH), 1220 (C), 1423 (M), 1479 (Cf).

LORD CASTLE (IRE) ..9-12.. 9 ch.g. Mister Lord (USA) — Amandas Castle (IRE) (Carlingford Castle) pu1pp55. Tall workmanlike. Dam, half-sister to Prince Amanda (*qv* '97 Annual). IRISH P-t-P '01/2 r5 p0; pulled up 4. IRISH NH '02 r1 p0. P-t-P/HUNT CH '03 r7 p2 (2nds); pulled up 4, and unseated 1. A frequent non-finisher, and gives the impression of being ungenuine, but capable of fair efforts, and picked up a bad Ladies on firm at Whiwick for which he was sent off favourite! An enterprising move it may have been, but not a fluent jumper and future prospects are limited. Visored once in '03, and unseated at the first when tried in cheekpieces this year. *M. Wennington — Heythrop (Claire Herrington).* 95 (R), 303 (OMa), 515 (L), 727 (MO), 994 (3m110yH), 1073 (O), 1390 (O).

LORD DORCET (IRE) ..9-10.. 15 b.g. Remainder Man — Lady Dorcet (Condorcet FR) f7. Compact dipped half-brother to Go Universal (IRE), and to Irish NH flat winner, Bridge Hotel (IRE). Dam won at 9f in Ireland. NH FLAT '94 r3 p1 (2nd). IRISH NH '96/8 r3 p2. NH '94/00 r38 w9 (4 2m-2m1f Hdles, and 5 2m-2m110y Chses) p11 (7 2nds); pulled up 3, and fell/unseated 2. P-t-P '02 r2 w2 (Confined and Ladies). A former top-class two-mile Chaser whose achievements were well documented in the '03 Annual, and surprisingly came out of retirement to contest races on consecutive Sundays in '04. Suffered only the second fall of his career at Hornby Castle, and hopefully will not be called into service again, as it would be a great shame to lose him. Blinkered on four occasions in '99. *J. Hogg — N. Tyne (John Burke).* 339 (L), 426 (Cf).

LORD EDWARDS ARMY (IRE) ..10-4.. 10 b.g. Warcraft (USA) — Celtic Bombshell (Celtic Cone) u64f215u. Tall strong half-brother to NH flat winner, Light The Fuse (IRE). IRISH NH FLAT '99/01 r9 w2 (2m1f-2m3f) p1. IRISH FLAT '01 r1 p0. IRISH NH '00/3 (for P. Mullins) r26 w1 (2m4f Ch) p4 (2nd in 3 Hdles, and 3rd in Ch); pulled up 1. Bought Doncaster, Aug for 6200. A triple scorer at up to 2m4f on good or firmish ground in Ireland in '01, but ended there with a dismal losing sequence of 22. Much improved by the new trainer but let down by the inexperienced veteran owner-rider who does not meet the fences in rhythm and causes his mount to fumble, but gave vastly better displays for Ran Morgan when two lengths second at 50-1 at Kelso where he made nearly all until caught at the last, and then kept on stoutly when gaining a first success for three years over 3m4f at Ayr where the odds-on favourite sulked. The return of the owner sealed his fate next time, and then unseated Ran Morgan in the Intrum Justitia at Stratford. Suited by very long trips, but future prospects will depend upon who is in the saddle. *G. Willoughby — Tynedale (Tim Reed).* 135 (Cfnr), 316 (2m5fH), 349 (3m1fH), 439 (2m5f110yH), 798 (3m1fH), 992 (3m3f110yH), 1179 (3m1fH), 1453 (3m4fH).

LORD ESKER (IRE) ..9-2.. 13 b.g. Glacial Storm (USA) — April Rhapsody (Main Reef) up2p. Tall lengthy workmanlike. Dam is half-sister to Soleil Dancer (*qv* '99 Annual). IRISH NH FLAT '97 r1 p0. IRISH NH '97 r7 w1 (2m Hdle) p2. NH '98/01 r28 w7 (2m-2m4f Chses) p6 (3 2nds); pulled up 5. P-t-P '02 r2 w1 (Mixed Open) p0; and pulled up 1. A decent top-of-the-ground performer in his prime, but always a bit of a softie, and clearly suffered a setback after winning at Hackwood Park in '02, which necessitated a year on the sidelines. Put up a string of dismal efforts on his return and beaten 40 lengths in his only completion, but broke a blood vessel in the latest, and may well have done so previously. Looks finished now. *T.D.B. Underwood — V. of Aylesbury with Garth & S. Berks.* 263 (O), 332 (Cf), 455 (Cf), 623 (Cf).

LORD EURO (IRE) ..9-11.. 8 b.g. Lord Americo — Orchards Beauty (IRE) (Miner's Lamp) 1f242p. Tiny. IRISH P-t-P '02/3 r6 w1 (5&6yo Maiden) p2; pulled up 1. A winner in heavy in Ireland and scored first time out for the new yard in a PPORA Confined Moderate at High Easter, where he jumped right several times but found the two other finishers nothing of a pest. Has galloped well on occasions since and was a creditable second to Algan at Cottenham, but runner-up at 4-5 at Marks Tey where he again jumped right and lost all chance after trying to demolish the 17th. Such a tiddler that it must be a massive effort for him to clear the fences, and his quirks will always make him a difficult ride. *A.W.K. Merriam — Dunston H. (Nigel Bloom).* 224 (CMod), 376 (Cf), 556 (Cf), 742 (I), 905 (Cf), 1151 (Cf).

LORD GEORGE ..9-3.. 13 ch.g. Lord Bud — Mini Gazette (London Gazette) p. Small sparely-made half-brother to St Amour and Rough Edge. P-t-P/HUNT CH '97/00 and '02/3 r37 w3 (inc Open) p9 (6 2nds, beaten ½*l* once, and of 3 once); pulled up 9, and fell 3. Thrice successful on sound surfaces at Easingwold to '02, and runner-up in a weak Ladies for the previous handler last year, but only gets the trip on easy tracks, and running him in holding at Penshurst (where the rider was fined £65 for excessive use of the whip) was a pointless exercise. Sported cheekpieces on that occasion, and has been tried in blinkers. *N. Morgan — N. Salop (Sheila Crow).* 780 (O).

LORD JURADO (IRE) ..6-13.. 9 b.g. Jurado (USA) — Via Del Tabacco (Ballymoss) up3p. Good-topped half-brother to Italian Man (IRE), to Irish NH flat and smart English Hurdles winner, Vicario Di Bray

(ITY), and to 3 winners in Italy. Dam won 2 races in Italy. IRISH NH FLAT '01 r1 p0. IRISH NH '01 r2 p0. NH '02 r2 p0. P-t-P '03 r1 p0 (last). Doubled his previous best tally of outings in a season, but only confirmed his lack of stamina, and has beaten just three rivals in nine starts over jumps. Tongue-tied from day one and stops as if shot after two miles. *R.A. Maletroit & Dr C. Mahmoud — Brocklesby (Robin Maletroit).* 59 (OMa), 112 (OMa), 302 (OMa), 482 (OMa).

LORD KEN (IRE) ..10-3§.. 7 b.g. Lord Americo — Moscow Lady (IRE) (Moscow Society USA) r1r21. Very small neat half-brother to General Jake (IRE). IRISH P-t-P '03 r7 p2 (2nds); pulled up 1. A natural front-runner with a fair amount of ability, but frequently jumps slowly or crookedly, and any opportunity to stop is gratefully received. Won a youngsters Maiden at Maisemore after the runner-up had blundered and almost unseated at the last, and scored again there in a Restricted in which he looked like downing tools after a mile but was persuaded to get going again and eventually seized the initiative near the finish. Also a length second once, and refused and unseated two out twice, including when looking poised to beat the only other of the three starters who was still continuing in a Lockinge Restricted. Visored since his English debut. A typically queer fish by Lord Americo (like Lord Euro, *qv*), but certainly has the ability to score again if the mood takes him. Has been visored since his English debut. *J.G. Phillips — V.W.H. (Simon Bloss).* 87 (OMa), 723 (OMa), 939 (R), 1063 (R), 1256 (R).

LORD KILPATRICK (IRE) ..10-5.. 11 ch.g. Mister Lord (USA) — Running Frau (Deep Run) 12. Strong-topped. Dam, half-sister to Sapega (IRE) (*qv*), won Maiden in Ireland, and won 2 Club races and placed 4 in England. IRISH P-t-P '99/00 and '02 r20 w2 (Maiden and Winners Of 1) p8 (inc 4 2nds); left 1, ran out 1, unseated 1. NH '03 (for Mrs L.J. Young) r2 p1 (2nd); and pulled up. P-t-P/HUNT CH '03 r3 p0; 4th, 5th, and unseated 1. No great shakes and somewhat unreliable in Ireland, but runner-up in last year's R.A. Gold Cup, and landed a gamble on his reappearance at Barbury. No match for Martha's Boy next time, and failed to reappear, but has prospects of another win if sound in '05. *T.W.C. Edwards — Albrighton Woodland (Diana Williams).* 31 (Cnr), 158 (CCon).

LORD LANE ..9-7.. 12 bl.g. Lord Bud — Gala Lane (Gala Performance) 3f1. Small neat homebred half-brother to Liffey Lane, Kings Lane, and to jumping winner, Coqui Lane. NH '00/1 r11 p0; pulled up 5. Very poor when last seen under Rules to '01 and was pulled up in five of 11 races including his only Chase (mistakes) and both Selling Hurdles, but proved much more efficient in Maidens, and followed a staying on one-and-a-quarter lengths third with an unlucky defeat at Alnwick where he fell two out in a two length lead. Got his just desserts in an elders contest at Balcormo, where he slammed four bad rivals in a bad time. Has left it late, but would merit consideration in a modest Restricted if returning at 12. *J.M. Dun — Lauderdale.* 553 (CfMa), 859 (CfMa), 1082 (OMa).

LORD MONTAGU (IRE) ..9-1.. 10 b.g. Castle Keep — Dorals Last (Bulldozer) pp25. Huge hobdayed (and had tie-back op). Dam won 6yo&up Maiden and 2m4f Chase in Ireland. IRISH P-t-P '03 r4 w1 (7yo&up Maiden) p1 (3rd); fell 1. IRISH NH FLAT '99 r2 p0. IRISH NH '00 r2 p0. IRISH HUNT CH '03 (for C.A. McBratney) r2 p0 (pulled up 2). Bought Doncaster, Nov for 1500. Found a suitably poor Maiden when scoring in Ireland, but is extremely moderate, and could only manage 12 lengths second of four when equipped with cheekpieces for the first time in his Members. Subsequently 21 lengths fifth in a Restricted, and looks sure to prove too slow even for that company. *Miss A. Page — Fitzwilliam (Katie Thory).* 223 (I), 375 (R), 555 (M), 902 (R).

LORD NICK ..9-8.. 15 b.g. Silly Prices — Cheeky Pigeon (Brave Invader USA) 4p. Small neat owner-bred half-brother to Catch The Pigeon and Penny Peppermint. Dam, half-sister to Lion Hill (*qv* '88 Season Annual), was entered for Points as a 15-year-old in '97, but failed to appear. NH FLAT '96 r2 p0. NH '96 r1 p0. P-t-P '98, '00 and '03 r9 w1 (Maiden) p3 (2 2nds; and 3rd of 4); 5th, 7th, pulled up 2, and fell 1. Won his Maiden on firm at Mordon in '98, but has always stood his racing incredibly badly, and pulled up lame Witton Castle. *Mrs C. Barr — Cleveland.* 810 (R), 1288 (R).

LORD OF HEAVEN (USA) ..9-1.. 7 ch.g. St Jovite (USA) — Fire And Shade (USA) (Shadeed USA) p44pp2. Compact well-made half-brother to flat winners Freedom Flame, Miss Shema (USA), Shadowland and Guerre Et Paix (in France). Dam won 6f race. FRENCH FLAT '02 (for Mme C. Head-Maarek) r1 p1 (3rd). Last of four in his first two completions, and would again have failed to beat a rival had he not been waved round the final fence when exhausted at Barbury (as there was only one other still going, albeit 25 lengths ahead, the rider was unsurprisingly keen to keep going). Finally beat another horse when second of three at Larkhill, but finished lame in the process. Always gave the impression that he would have done better with stronger handling. *J.T. Brown — Berks & Bucks (Albertine Blanchard).* 337 (R), 459 (R), 627 (OMa), 760 (OMa), 1067 (OMa), 1098 (OMa).

LORD OF LOVE ..— §§.. 10 b.g. Noble Patriarch — Gymcrak Lovebird (Taufan USA) urr. Compact half-brother to flat winner, Dominelle, and to winner in Sweden. Dam won 5 flat, 5-10f the first 2 Sells. 6000y. FLAT '97/8&'01/2 r19 p2 (3rds). NH '98/02 (for T.D. Easterby, D.L. Williams, and D. Burchell) r50 w4 (2m3f-3m3f Hdles) p15; fell/unseated 3, pulled up 1. Kept hectically busy in his youth and won four Hurdles on ground ranging from firmish to heavy to May '00, but ominously fell in his only Chase (after trying to refuse). Had top jockeys in Points but loathed competing, and none of them could get him further than the 11th. Has no intention of behaving decently again. *Mouse Racing (R. Williams) — Glamorgan (Robert Williams).* 360 (O), 404 (O), 672 (O).

LORD OF THE BRIDE (IRE) .— §§.. 8 ch.g. Mister Lord (USA) — Carrigan Springs (IRE) (Tale Quale) ppup98. Good-bodied. IRISH P-t-P '02/3 r5 w1 (6&7yo Maiden) p2 (3rds); fell. IRISH NH '02 r2 p0. NH '03 r3 p1 (2nd); pulled up 1. NH '04 (for M.C. Pipe) r2 p0 (9th in 3m Hdle: *bhnd frm 8, t.o*; and 8th in 2m6f Hdle: *a bhnd*). Bought Doncaster, May for 15,000. Consented to win an Irish Maiden and later sold for far too much money, and has gained his only placing for the present owner when five lengths second in a Chase in which he was headed on the run-in after being left clear three out (terrible race). Tried tongue-tied once, and with headgear. A prize pig in '04, and even the champion could not get him round in their four outings together. *D.E. Pipe — M.C. Pipe — Silverton.* 37 (CR), 139 (R), 572 (R), 1366 (R).

LORD OF THE CHASE (IRE) ..8-0.. 12 ch.g. Le Bavard (FR) — Katy Quick (Saucy Kit) pup0. Lengthy attractive. IRISH NH FLAT '97/8 r7 p4. IRISH NH '97/00 and '02 r23 w2 (2m2f -2m4f Chses) p6; pulled up 6. P-t-P '03 r1 p0 (pulled up). Won twice in Ireland for Charlie Swan to October '00, but tongue-tied on his final appearance in that year, and subsequently disappeared for 18 months. Tailed off in all eight attempts since, and a non-finisher in six and not worth bothering with again. *The Garley Family (Mrs E. Garley) — Pytchley (Betty Garley).* 382 (O), 466 (Cf), 784 (Cf), 1120 (Cf).

LORD OF THE FLIES (IRE) ..9-3§.. 12 b/br.g. Lord Americo — Beau's Trout (Beau Charmeur FR) 3p5f42. Compact half-brother to Sierra Bay (IRE). NH FLAT '98 r3 w1 p0. NH '98/01 (for Miss H.C. Knight) r20 w3 (2m2f Hdle and 2 2m Chses) p6 (inc 5 2nds); fell 3. Sold Ascot, Jun '01 for 10,000, resold Ascot, Feb '02 for 5000. Another oddball by Lord Americo (see Lord Ken) and is totally unpredictable with a mind of his own. Won three races at up to 2m2f to November '99 (blinkered once that year), but has been beaten 16 lengths or more in his 12 most recent outings, and only had five horses behind him in Points, in which he either cannot or will not get the trip. *Mrs B.M. Ansell — W. Street Tickham (Jane Goddard).* 534 (M), 607 (Cf), 650 (O), 806 (C), 896 (CCon), 1280 (M).

LORD OF THE MIST (IRE) ..10-9.. 11 b.g. Mister Lord (USA) — Brogeen View (Kambalda) 2112111f2. Lengthy hobdayed workmanlike half-brother to Irish Hurdles winner, Boston Melody. NH FLAT '00 r1 p0. NH '00 r1 p0. P-t-P '03 r7 w1 (Maiden) p2 (3rds); pulled up 2, and fell/unseated 2. Lightly raced and disappointing at first, but transformed by a wind operation in '04, and benefited from his association with Nick Williams. Impressive when clocking the fastest time of the day at Buckfastleigh, and only Free Gift stopped him from landing a six-timer. Normally takes a keen hold under restraint, but can quicken, and though he is still inclined to root the odd fence has become a good jumper in Points. Less convincing in Hunter Chases, but certain to be placed to advantage again in '05. Handles softish, but the majority of his form is on sound surfaces. *P. Maltby — Seavington (Richard Barber).* 232 (R), 279 (R), 495 (I), 634 (O), 963 (Cf), 1127 (Cf), 1250 (C), 1437 (2m5f110yH), 1454 (3mH).

LORD OF THE NORTH (IRE) ..9-10.. 8 br.g. Arctic Lord — Ballyfin Maid (IRE) (Boreen FR) 4uf1223p. Small neat half-brother to Ballyoso (IRE). IR6000 3yo, 2000 4yo. NH FLAT '01 r1 p0. NH '02/3 (for M.R. Hoad) r6 p1 (3rd); pulled up 1. Could only manage an 18 lengths third in a five-runner Selling Hurdle for the previous yard, but had shown some ability, and was a fun ride in Points who looked like scoring at Charing until he fell in the lead two out. Gained compensation there over 2m4f when faced with just four opponents, but unfortunately ended his campaign with a broken fetlock at Kingston Blount, and had to be destroyed. N. Benstead — J.T.B. Hunt & G. Sanders — Kent & Surrey Bloodhounds (Nigel Benstead). 21 (OMa), 87 (OMa), 186 (OMa), 803 (2m4fOMa), 1051 (R), 1208 (R), 1409 (CR), 1517 (R).

LORD OF THE RIVER (IRE) ..—.. 13 br.g. Lord Americo — Well Over (Over The River FR) *72110*. Tall brother to NH flat and Hurdles winner, Ruby Gale (IRE), and half-brother to Miners Melody (IRE), and to Hurdles winner, Welcome Call (IRE). Dam won 3 Irish Points. IR80,000 4yo. (then a record for a Store horse). NH FLAT '97 r1 p0. NH '97/9 & '02/3 (for O. Sherwood, and N.J. Henderson) r16 w6 (3 2m4f-2m5f Hdles and 3 2m3f-3m1f Chses) p3 (2nds); fell/unseated 2. NH '04 r4 w2 (beat Tremallt 7*l* in 3m110y Ch: *2nd til ld aft 9, mist nxt, clr app 2 out, r.o wl*; and Midland Flame 7*l* in 3m1f Ch: *a.p, lft in ld aft 9, mist 15, clr app last, comf*) p1 (2nd in 3m Ch: *chsd ldrs, went 2nd 11, ev ch when mist last, no ex*); and 12th in 3m1f Ch at Punchestown: *prom, ld 4 out to nxt, wknd app 2 out*. Barely qualifies for this Annual as he could only finish 64 lengths seventh at Wetherby which meant that plans to qualify for the '04 Cheltenham Foxhunters went awry. In the light of subsequent achievements, that hardly mattered, and has now taken career earnings to £127,531. Until '04 he had not visited the winners enclosure since February '99, having gone lame when second in the Sun Alliance Chase at the Festival where he was beaten a distance by Looks Like Trouble after Nick Dundee had fallen when cantering three out. To get him back to his best was a superb training feat, and shows yet again why Nicky Henderson is head and shoulders above all the other Lambourn trainers. *J. Palmer-Brown & B.T. Stewart-Brown — Vine & Craven (Nicky Henderson).* 122 (3m1fH).

LORD OF THE ROAD ..9-9.. 6 b.g. Gildoran — Ethels Course (Crash Course) 1. Lengthy strong-topped homebred brother to Mr Splodge (*qv*). Stuart Morris was wisely chosen for his debut at Woodford (there is nobody better on a Maiden), and after attracting support from tens to 7-1 he led three out and was soon in command. Beat nothing, but his manner was emphatic, and surely has plenty of scope for improvement (his new purchaser will certainly be hoping so!). *R.B.G. Fairbarns — V.W.H. (James Richardson).* 1074 (OMa).

LORD OF THE WEST (IRE) ..9-9.. 16 b.g. Mister Lord (USA) — Caroline's Girl (Roman Warrior) pu24pr. Big. NH '95/01 r39 w9 (2m6f110y Hdle, and 8 2m7f110y-3m2f Chses) p8; pulled up 7, and fell/unseated 5. P-t-P/HUNT CH '94/5 and '03 r14 w5 (3-runner 2-finisher Open and 2-runner Open) p4 (3 2nds, of 3 once); 4th, last pair 2, and pulled up 2. Only beaten once in his first four Points, but ultimately failed to fulfill his potential under Rules, and went to pieces latterly. Successfully revived for the first time since '98 last year, but looked jaded by the end of the season, and has gone to pot once again. Refused and collapsed onto the belly of the last fence at Eaton Hall, and will surely be humiliated no more. Has been tried in blinkers. *P.H. Morris & S. James — Tanatside (Peter Morris).* 228 (Cf), 292 (MO), 526 (M), 711 (O), 875 (O), 1145 (O).

PLATE 78 1380 Dulverton West Open Maiden (Div 1): Foston Second (Martin Sweetland), 3rd, still just leads Lord Oscar (Ashley Farrant), 1st, and The Nelson Touch (David I. Turner), 6th
PHOTO: Brian Armstrong

LORD OSCAR (IRE) ..10-4.. 6 b.g. Oscar (IRE) — Americo Rose (IRE) (Lord Americo) 1. Lengthy unfurnished. A little novicey when favourite for his mid-May debut in a Maiden at Bratton Down, but showed plenty of speed to dart clear three out and register an impressive success. He could do no more than beat modest opponents in style, and will be one to watch with great interest as he rises in grade. *D.E. Pipe — E. Devon.* 1380 (OMa).

LORD SAXBURY .—.. 6 b.g. Overbury (IRE) — Saxon Gift (Saxon Farm) ppp. Compact half-brother to Monsieur Mossiman and Saxon Moss. Dam, half-sister to Dear Do (*qv* '01 Annual). Grandam, Earlsgift, won 5 Points and placed 5. 15,000 4yo. Did not jump especially well when showed no worthwhile speed before pulling up in Maidens. *R. Kent — Ludlow (Penny Grainger).* 410 (2m4fCfMa), 709 (Mah), 850 (2m5fOMa).

LORD SCROOP (IRE) ..9-0§.. 11 br.g. Supreme Leader — Henry Woman (IRE) (Mandalus) upupp. Compact brother to Nunnety (IRE). NH FLAT '99 r2 p0. NH '99/02 r20 p5 (inc 2 Chses). P-t-P '03 r6 w1 (Maiden) p3 (2 2nds; and 3rd of 4); and pulled up 2. Finally opened his account at the 28th attempt in soft at Mordon last year, but previously a regular non-finisher under Rules, and has reverted to type. Never went a yard at Hornby Castle, and was taken to post early next time, and can be safely dismissed. Has been tried in blinkers and a tongue-tie. *E.A.W. Hardwick & R. Morley — Derwent (Richard Morley).* 164 (R), 341 (R), 503 (R), 810 (R), 1469 (R).

LORDSTON (IRE) ..—.. 9 b.g. Mister Lord (USA) — Dawstown (Golden Love) pp. Big rangy good-looking half-brother to Irish Hurdles winner, Dawdante (IRE). Dam, sister to Snowy Pearl, and half-sister to Majority Major (*qv*), won 4&5yo Mares Maiden in Ireland. NH FLAT '01 r2 p0. NH '01 r1 p0. P-t-P '02 r3 w1 (Maiden) p1 (½l 2nd); and pulled up 1. Rated 9-11 after winning a Maiden in soft at Charing in '02, but pulled up in his last three appearances (4-6 once) and stopped as if shot at Folkestone. Clearly has major problems, and his wind is the most likely culprit. *late J. Plackett — Crawley & Horsham (Brendan Powell).* 239 (3m1fH), 975 (2m7f110yH).

LORD STROLLER .7-10.. 9 b.g. Petong — Breakfast Boogie (Sizzling Melody) p. Small unfurnished brother to a flat winner in Turkey. Dam won 5f race. FLAT '98/9 r10 p0. P-t-P '03 r5 p1 (2nd of 3); last, pulled up 1, fell 1, and brought down 1. Made favourite for his racecourse debut over 5f at Bath, but missed the break and only beat four home, and has performed with equal ineptitude since. Totally unsuitable for Pointing and it would be a major surprise if anyone was to bother with him again. Has been tried in blinkers, and a tongue-tie. *Miss B. Summers — Cambs with Enfield Chace.* 462 (OMa).

LORD VALNIC (IRE) ..10-8.. 9 b.g. Mister Lord (USA) — Any Wonder (Hardboy) Rf. Very big rangy. P-t-P '02 r2 w2 (3-finisher Maiden and Restricted). Made the ideal start when recording a double in mud at Marks Tey in '02, but has obviously had his problems, and clearly not out of the woods yet. Upsides the eventual winner when ducking out at the fourth last on his belated return to action, but fell heavily at the first at Huntingdon, and has not been seen since. *Ms A.E. Embiricos & C.J. Hays — Cambridge Univ (Alex Embiricos).* 38 (Cf), 177 (3mH).

LORD WOODYARD .8-13§.. 9 ch.g. Primitive Rising (USA) — Bebe Hattie (Gracious Melody) 2pp. Lengthy unfurnished brother to Shirostran. P-t-P '03 r3 p0 (pulled up 3). Had three subsequent winners behind when runner-up at Garnons, but pulled up in five other attempts, and looked anything but keen when blinkered in the latest. In a successful yard, but they have their work cut out in trying to get to the bottom of him. Wears a cross-noseband. *J.S. & Mrs J.A. Scott — Worcs (Nicky Sheppard).* 621 (OMa), 840 (OMa), 1020 (OMa).

LOTHIAN EMERALD .—§.. 8 ch.m. Greensmith — Lothian Rose (Roscoe Blake) pu. Sturdy. Dam, sister Lothian Admiral (*qv* '95 Annual). NH FLAT '02 r1 p0. NH '02 r1 p0 (pulled up). P-t-P '03 (for Mr B. Andrews & Miss N.M. Stephens) r5 p0 (pulled up 3, and fell/unseated 2). Badly tailed off last in her bumper, and despite showing some speed has failed to complete in eight starts over jumps. Went missing for 17 weeks between outings in '04, and looked amazed to be confronted by a fence at Bratton Down. Has been tried in cheekpieces, and a tongue-tie. *R. Andrews & D. Millington — Mendip F. (Nikki Stephens).* 143 (OMa), 1559 (OMa).

LOTHIAN RISING ..9-7.. 7 ch.g. Primitive Rising (USA) — Lothian Lightning (Lighter) f4. Owner-bred half-brother to Lothian Pilot, Lothian Lily, Lothian Commodore and Officer Lothian, and to Chasing winner, Lothian Commander. Fell after two miles on his debut, but showed promise when 27 lengths fourth against far more experienced rivals in his Members. The fifth and six went on to score, and should be worth noting for Maiden success. *Mrs S.M. Wood — Tynedale (Chris Dennis).* 160 (CMa), 425 (M).

LOTTERY LIL ..9-10.. 10 ch.m. Petoski — Quarry Machine (Laurence O) p. Tall good-topped half-sister to Red Hot Robbie. Dam won 3 NH flat (2m-2m2f) in Ireland and 3 Hurdles (2-3m; the first in Ireland). NH FLAT '99 r1 p0. P-t-P/HUNT CH '02 r5 p3 (2 2nds, of 3 once); pulled up 1, and fell 1. Ran some fair races in defeat in '02, but has hit upon hard times since, and was still lying a poor second when forced to call it a day at the second last in her Members. Lack of stamina and a weak constitution look like conspiring against her. Wears a cross-noseband. *I. Hudson — Oakley.* 461 (M).

LOTTIE THE LOTUS ..9-10.. 16 ch.m. Crested Lark — Florence Eliza (Floriana) 4d11444. Strong homebred sister to Sporting Lark, Lily The Lark, Lennie The Lord and Les The Lizard, and half-sister to Larry The Lamb. Grandam, Estoile, was placed in 4 Hunt Chses and 3 Points. P-t-P '97/03 (for Mr G.B. Tarry & Mr S. Watts) r26 w4 (inc 2 Confineds) p15 (11 2nds, beaten short-head once, of 3 once); 4th, pulled up 1, and fell/unseated 5. Fabulously consistent and has never missed the frame when completing, but always far more liable to be placed than win, and usually manages to get into full flight too late. Made the most of simple tasks at Hackwood Park in '04, but error-proneand easily outpaced by decent animals, and may not be so lucky in future. *Miss R. Goodwin — Grafton.* 189 (L), 719 (Cnr), 969 (Cnr), 1104 (Cnr), 1334 (L), 1501 (L).

LOTTIE (U) ..7-7.. 11 b.m. Lorton Footprint — North Tyne Flyer VII (unknown) 3. Owner-bred half-sister to Reeker Pike. Tottered round when third but a fence behind the leaders throughout the final mile in her Members. *R.H. Walton — Haydon.* 1480 (M).

LOU BIARNES (FR) ..8-12.. 9 b.g. Start Fast (FR) — Lita (FR) (Big John FR) 531p. Very tall heavy half-brother to Hurdles winner, Almire Du Lia (FR). P-t-P '02 r5 p0 (pulled up 5). A huge hulking boat and rarely went more than two miles in his debut season, and missed '03, but easily proved good enough to land a three-finisher Maiden in softish at Cold Harbour. Has tended to jump markedly left-handed, and pulled up when favourite for a Restricted next time, and will probably flounder further in similar company. Has been tried in a near-side pricker. *M.H. Ings — Teme V. (Billie Brown).* 668 (OMa), 840 (OMa), 1233 (OMa), 1538 (R).

LOUGH ERIN SHORE .—.. 7 b.m. Alhaatmi — Ocara (USA) (Danzig Connection USA) p8. Dam won 8f race. P-t-P '03 r1 p0 (pulled up). Clueless on her debut, but ran well to a point on her reappearance only to pull up again next time. The chances are she has insufficient stamina to make her mark in Points. *P.E. Rodgers — Rockwood H.* 500 (CMam), 890 (2m4fOMa).

LOVE AT DAWN ..10-0.. 11 b.g. Dawn Johnny (USA) — Grafton Maisey (Jimsun) 221136. Small half-brother to Shy Lizzie, Percy Medlicott and Masitat. Dam won Hunt Chse and 2 Points and 2m6f Hdle and placed total of 5 for Alex Mason. P-t-P '02/3 r9 w1 (Maiden) p1 (3rd); 5th, 6th, last, pulled up 1, fell 1, and ran out 2. Unraced until he was eight, and won a poor Maiden on firm at Woodford in '02, but disappointing last year, and earned himself a squiggle after running out twice. Strongly handled by the improving Peter Mason when completing a double in the space of three weeks in '04, and defeated Camden Carrig in the latest, but still makes far too many mistakes for his own good. Visored twice in '03. *A.J. Mason — V.W.H.* 15 (R), 406 (Inr), 614 (R), 759 (I), 979 (MOnr), 1390 (O).

LOVE POTION ..—.. 10 br.m. Neltino — Celtic Honey (Celtic Cone) f. Small compact. Dam, half-sister to My Glendalough (*qv* '03 Annual), won 2m Hurdle in Ireland. NH FLAT '00 r3 p2. NH '00 and '02 (for E.L. James) r6 p1 (3rd); pulled up 1. Finished two lengths second in a bumper on her debut, but much worse since, and a distant third in a Selling Hurdle when gaining her other prize. Turned a somersault at the first at Barbury, and killed herself. R.J. Smith — Beaufort. 35 (CMam).

LOXLEY-LAD .—.. 13 gr.g. Zambrano — Loxley Air (Romany Air) p. Lengthy half-brother to Gipsy Rew. Dam won Maiden and placed 4 for Mr Cox. NH '01 r6 p0 (pulled up 3). P-t-P '99/03 r19 w1 (Maiden) p2 (3rds, last once); last, pulled up 13, and unseated 2. Sprang a 33-1 surprise on his first Pointing completion at Holnicote in '00, but soundly beaten in the vast majority of his 18 subsequent appearances, and appeared to go wrong again in '04. Wears a cross-noseband, and has been tried in a visor and a tongue-strap. *I.N. Jones — Taunton V.H.* 1325 (R).

LUCKENBURN ..—.. 10 b.g. Super Sunrise — Sky Missile (Cruise Missile) p. Dam, *qv* '99 Annual), won Maiden by over a fence, but was very unsound. Tailed off and pulled up after two miles in an Alnwick Maiden. *R.W. Telford — W. Percy (Ailsa Tweedie).* 859 (CfMa).

LUCK IN RUN'IN ..8-9.. 12 b.g. Lapierre — Lady Run (Deep Run) 23u. Workmanlike owner-bred half-brother to Moss Deeping. NH FLAT '98 r3 p0. NH '99 and '01/2 r5 p0. P-t-P '03 r1 p0 (pulled up). Very lightly raced and showed no signs of ability in his first nine starts, but crept into the prizes twice in '04, and was only beaten two lengths in a very weak Maiden at Tabley. Needs to play to his strengths to stand any chance of success, and running in Hunter Chases is using up miles he does not have up his sleeve. *Miss B. Dutton & R.J. Bevis — R.J. Bevis — Sir W.W. Wynn's (Geoff Dutton).* 1206 (OMa), 1424 (OMa), 1526 (3m2fH).

LUCKY BRUSH (IRE) ..10-0§.. 11 b.g. Brush Aside (USA) — Luck Daughter (Lucky Brief) 342. Workmanlike half-brother to Hurdles winner, Miners Luck. Dam won 3 Irish Points for half-breds (won another, but disqualified for carrying wrong weight), and won 3 Chses (3m-3m1f) there including the prestigious Thyestes Chase. IRISH P-t-P '00 r4 w1 (Confined Maiden) p3. P-t-P/HUNT CH '01/3 r13 p7 (4 3rds, inc last, inc 2 Hunt Chses); 4th, 5th, last pair 3, and brought down 1. Hardly ever misses the frame, and has been knocking at the door in Restricteds for three years, but consistently manages to mistime any challenge, and has to be treated with extreme suspicion. Wears bandages in front, and avoids ground any quicker than good now. *J.F. Alexander — Fife (Nick Alexander).* 765 (R), 1077 (R), 1222 (R).

LUCKY MASTER (IRE) ..10-0.. 13 b.g. Roselier (FR) — Golden Chestnut (Green Shoon) 44352134. Sturdy brother to Hurdles winner, Belle Rose (IRE), and half-brother to Fair Crossing and Free To Conker (IRE), and to Irish Pointing winners, Gathering Moss and Official Portrait (IRE) (also won Hurdling there). NH FLAT '98 r2 p0. NH '98/02 r28 w2 (2m6f Hdle and 3m Ch) p11; pulled up 2. Won a Hurdle and a Chase to November '99, but error-prone over the bigger obstacles, and his career petered out under Rules with 15 consecutive defeats. Normally too slow to keep up in Ladies Opens (and probably can't be bothered to try), but ultra-safe and stays really well, and kept plugging on to catch Fair Exchange in the final 100 yards at Marks Tey, where he appreciated the seven minute trip and the soft ground. A first success for 37-year-old Gina Swan. *J.R. Upson — Miss G. Swan — Grafton (Gina Swan).* 108 (L), 230 (L), 613 (L), 869 (L), 1017 (3m2fL), 1314 (L), 1391 (L), 1470 (L).

LUCKY WYN ..9-13.. 7 ch.g. Triune — Sweet Wyn (Sweet Monday) 541. Good-topped. Dam, half-sister to Our Wyn-Ston (*qv* '98 Annual), was pulled up in 3 Points for Bruce Heywood. A modest last in his first two Points (made mistakes on his debut), but beat three newcomers and a joke in a youngsters Maiden in softish at Chaddesley Corbett. Gradually getting the hang of things, and may improve sufficiently for Restricteds. *B. Heywood — Devon & Somerset.* 618 (2m4fOMa), 962 (OMa), 1339 (OMa).

LUGS BRANNIGAN (IRE) ..10-1.. 16 b.g. Supreme Leader — Maria Tudor (Sassafras FR) 5. Compact angular. NH FLAT '95 r1 p0. NH '95/9 r20 w1 (2m6f Hdle) p2 (3rds); pulled up 2, and fell 4. P-t-P '02 r3 w1 (3m5f70y Ladies) p0; 4th, and 6th. Twice successful for female riders, and gained his last success six years after the first, but very lightly raced since '98, and beaten 30 lengths in his bid to regain the Lyon Trophy at the Heythrop. Very spirited for a veteran, but must be on the verge of permanent retirement. Blinkered once in '99. *Mrs A. Jefferis — Bicester with Whaddon.* 48 (3m5f70yL).

LUTTEUR BLEU (FR) ..9-11.. 6 b.g. Franc Bleu Argent (USA) — Sirene Du Lac (FR) (Missolonghi USA) 3312. Small close-coupled half-brother to French flat winner, It's Magic Lac (FR). Bought Goffs France, Jul for 9894. Seemed to appreciate the drop to 2m4f when winning a five-runner three-finisher race on firmish at Littlewindsor in which he made virtually all, but left in front two out until after the last and unable to quicken in a Bratton Down Restricted next time. Consistent, but may need to stick to the shorter tracks for the time being, and has only experienced sound surfaces so far. *J.J. Boulter & Miss F.J. Wilkins — Portman (John Boulter).* 174 (OMa), 367 (OMa), 1007 (2m4fOMa), 1386 (R).

LYDFORD CASTLE .9-7§.. 11 b.g. Thornberry (USA) — Our Generator (Starch Reduced) 3pp. Compact well-made half-brother to Our Brook. Dam was 3rd in 2 Points as a 13-year-old. NH '98 r1 p0 (tailed off). P-t-P '99/00 and '02/3 r21 w2 (Maiden and Restricted) p10 (4 2nds, of 3 once; and inc 3rd of 4 once); last 4, pulled up 4, and fell 1. Won his Maiden in heavy at Lemalla in '00, and galvanised by first-time blinkers at Flete Park last year, but has failed to co-operate since, and can be safely ignored. *R. & E. Jarman & Mrs B.J. Fuller — Lamerton (Belinda Fuller).* 566 (M), 733 (3mH), 1003 (4mO).

LYDIA'S ECHO .8-4.. 9 b.m. Backchat (USA) — Lydia's Well (Current Magic) 2. Small neat. NH FLAT '02 r2 p0. NH '02 r2 p0; pulled up 1. P-t-P '03 (for Mr A. & Mrs D. Burgess) r1 p0 (pulled up). Looked to have unearthed the ideal opportunity when 15 lengths clear on the run to the fifth last in a three-runner Maiden on good to frosty at Larkhill, but not for the first time in her career stopped to nil in the closing stages, and was collared near the finish. Only appears very rarely, and if she was ever going to succeed that was the race. *W. Lusted, S. Kington, H. Pearson-Gregory & P. Miller — Tedworth (Tony Gorman).* 334 (OMa).

LYNWOOD LEGEND ..7-0.. 7 ch.g. Gold Dust — Beths Wish (Rustingo) p3pp. Tall lengthy. Dam, sister to Lyningo, and half-sister to Beths Gift (*qv* '03 Annual). NH FLAT '03 (for B.J. Llewellyn) r2 p0. Dropped out very tamely in Points, and was one-and-a-half fences last in his Members in his only completion. Evidently hopeless. *C.M. Price — Brecon & Talybont.* 363 (CfMa), 446 (M), 845 (CfMa), 1240 (OMa).

LYPHARD'S FABLE (USA) ..9-2§.. 14 b.g. Al Nasr (FR) — Affirmative Fable (USA) (Affirmed USA) 89u265637. Small compact well-made brother to flat winner, Majorne, and half-brother to a winner in USA. Dam won 8f in USA. FLAT r12 w1 (9f, fibresand) p3 (2nds). NH '94/01 r40 w1 (2m3f Sell Hdle) p12 (inc 4 Chses); finished in all 9 Chses, but fell 5 over Hdles. P-t-P/HUNT CH '01/3 (for Miss L. Langdale) r17 p5 (4 3rds, of 4 thrice); unseated 1, pulled up 2. Used to treat hurdles with contempt, but a very safe conveyance over fences, and has made the ideal schoolmaster. Won a Seller at Chepstow in '97, but beaten in 65 other appearances over jumps, and after only finishing once better than last in '04 has been retired. Occasionally wears blinkers. *J.C. England — Cotswold (Marcella Bayliss).* 32 (Cnr), 292 (MO), 437 (3m1fH), 514 (O), 727 (MO), 758 (O), 1228 (4mO), 1335 (O), 1390 (O).

LYRICAL SEAL ..9-2.. 15 b.m. Dubassoff (USA) — Sea-Rosemary (Seaepic USA) 554. Very small neat homebred. NH FLAT r3 p0. NH '95/6 r10 p2 (30 lengths 3rd, and distant last of 3 in Chses); last once, and pulled up 2 in other Chses; 6th, last, and pulled up 3 in Hdles. P-t-P/HUNT CH '97/03 (for Mr A. MacLaren) r22 w2 (inc 3m1f110y Hunt Ch) p6 (5 3rds, of 4 thrice, and last once); 5th twice, 7th, last pair 8, and unseated 2. A good jumper, but wears blinkers and always found it difficult to win, and lightly raced since gaining her last success in '00. Has been retired. *late Mrs J. Dening — S. & W. Wilts (Sarah Waugh).* 626 (Cnr), 969 (Cnr), 1097 (M).

LYRINGO .—.. 11 b.m. Rustingo — Lyricist (Averof) up. Small close-coupled sister to Rusty Music and Project's Mate, and half-sister to Hurdles winners, Donna's Token and Drakestone. NH FLAT '99/00 r4 p0. FLAT '00 and '03 r2 p0. NH '00/3 (for R.L. Brown, and B.J. Llewellyn) r9 w1 (2m1f Hdle) p0; pulled up 3. Beat April Treasure (*qv*) in a Stratford Selling Hurdle in soft in Oct '00, but never placed otherwise, and blinkered once and wore cheekpieces once under Rules. Unseated at the first and tailed off and pulled up at halfway when outclassed in early season Opens, and looks a back number. *A. MacLaren — Llangeinor (Hannah Roberts).* 64 (O), 205 (O).

MACARONI BEACH ..9-11.. 11 ch.m. Jupiter Island — Real Princess (Aragon) 3p4522. Unfurnished. Dam won 7f race. Grandam, Mange Tout was very quick. FLAT '96 r3 p0. P-t-P '02/3 r8 w1 (3-runner 2-finisher Maiden) p2 (last of 3 once); last, and pulled up 4. Speedy and normally sets off in front, but only able to maintain her advantage once, and consistently let down by a lack of stamina.

As usual will be difficult to place in future. Blinkered once in '96. Wears a cross-noseband. *T.J. Brady — Portman (Ali Tory).* 262 (L), 369 (R), 864 (R), 1131 (R), 1363 (2m3f110yH), 1493 (L).

MACFIN (IRE) ..10-2.. 12 b.g. Brevet — Lough Sholin (Kemal FR) p112133. Good-topped. Dam won 2m2f Irish NH flat. IRISH P-t-P '98 r4 w1 (5&6yo Maiden) p0; pulled up 2. P-t-P/HUNT CH '99/03 r24 w2 (Restricted and Members) p6 (2 2nds, of 3 once; inc 3rd of 4 once); unseated 2, and pulled up 5. Unsuccessful in his first 19 English starts (subsequently awarded his Members on a technicality reducing the sequence to 15) and began '04 with a typically moody display, but sprang a 20-1 surprise when cheekpieces were re-applied next time, and proceeded to mop up Ladies races at Horseheath. Likes to dominate on good or sound surfaces, but decent performers have nothing to fear, and only seems prepared to battle on his favourite track. Reported to suffer from a pollen allergy. *T.M. Fowler — Cottesmore (Louise Allan).* 55 (Cf), 126 (L), 373 (L), 593 (L), 743 (L), 987 (L), 1399 (L).

MACGEORGE (IRE) ..11-3.. 15 b.g. Mandalus — Colleen Donn (Le Moss) 611232. Big rangy brother to Hurdles winner, Macnance (IRE) and Irish Chasing winner, No Upside. NH FLAT '95 r3 p1 (3rd). NH '95/02 r37 w10 (2m6f Hdle and 9 2m4f110y-3m2f Chses, inc 4-timer '98) p8 (5 2nds); pulled up 2, fell/unseated 5. HUNT CH '03 r7 w3 (3m1f110y-3m2f) p1 (2nd); pulled up 2, and unseated 1. One of the most genuine performers to have graced the scene in a long while, and has gained a third of his 15 wins, amassing £96,580, since becoming a teenager. Never forgiven by the handicapper for landing the '99 Martell Cup at Aintree, but every bit as good as he was 12 months ago, and loves to bowl along in front. Suited by distances in excess of three miles, and can jump splendidly, but still inclined to make the occasional mistake. Acts in mud but can also handle much faster conditions. Bought by the Watsons as an unbroken three-year-old, and has done them, and his trainer Richard Lee proud ever since, and will remain in training in '05. Half of his last eight wins have been gained at Warwick. *J.H. & Mrs H.E. Watson — Cheshire (Richard Lee).* 179 (2m6fH), 490 (3m2fH), 629 (3m1f110yH), 991 (3m2f110yH), 1169 (3m2f110yH), 1512 (2m6f110yH).

MACGYVER (NZ) ..10-1.. 9 b.g. Jahafil — Corazon (NZ) (Pag-Asa AUS) pp6p*21*. Compact light-made. NZ FLAT r7 w1 (2nd). NZ NH '02 r4 w1 (1m6f Hdle) p1 (2nd). NH '02/3 (for Mrs L.C. Taylor) r9 p3; pulled up 1. NH '04 (for D.L. Williams) r2 w1 (beat River Mere 5*l* in 2m Ch: *prom til lost plce app 7, rallied 3 out, ld 2 out, clr when hit last, r.o wl*) p1 (½*l* 2nd in 2m2f Sell Ch: *a.p, ld 9, rdn 2 out, hdd & pckd last, kpt on wl flat*). A winner at Te Awamutu and Wanganui in his native land, but unable to score for his first two English yards. A mighty headstrong front-runner who regularly failed to get the trip, and although he managed three placings in two mile Chases (beaten between one-and-a-half lengths and two lengths twice) he was really in the doldrums in the start of '04, when he consistently burned himself out in an Open and Hunter Chases. Transformed when joining the shrewd Dai Williams who is a past master at coping with problem horses, and a complete change of regime has worked wonders. In sparkling form between late May and July and scored twice for Lucy Horner (with whom he has developed a useful rapport). Seems very relaxed now, so it is quite possible that he may be able to stay further. A training triumph. *M. Blackford — Farmers Bloodhounds (Mervyn Loggin).* 89 (O), 177 (3mH), 444 (2mH), 628 (2m3fH).

MACHALINI ..10-8.. 12 b.g. Machiavellian (USA) — Trescalini (IRE) (Sadler's Wells USA) 1u61u. Strong compact half-brother to flat winners, Fantazia and Commisar. Dam won 10f race in Ireland. IRISH FLAT '95/7 r15 w2 (7-8f) p4 (inc hd and nk 2nds). FLAT '00 r2 p0. NH '97/01 (for T.R. George) r37 w5 (2m2f-3m Chses) p14 (inc 6 2nds); pulled up 3, fell 1. Sold Doncaster, Nov '01 for 8000. Useful on his day and a great galloper, and seven wins under Rules included a hat-trick in Apr/May '99. A bit of a character who has worn headgear on five occasions under Rules and was tongue-tied twice in '00, but showed he retains plenty of ability when romping round Cothelstone in the fastest time of the day in a Novice Riders event. Also made light of an easy task in his Members, and should have won a Mixed Open at Maisemore, but Andrew Morley lost an iron after two out and fell off coming to the last. Also ended up riderless at Chaddesley, and his partner does well on occasions and is a liability on others. Still looks as if he would be speedy enough for success in a Hunter Chase, and Ludlow would suit, as he has already enjoyed three victories there in the past. *A.J. Morley — Beaufort (Alison Dare).* 364 (M), 727 (MO), 980 (Cf), 1365 (Cnr), 1529 (MO).

MACKOY (IRE) .9-6.. 12 b.g. Riverhead (USA) — Urdite (FR) (Concertino FR) 54. Compact good-topped half-brother to Thunderpoint (IRE) and Mighty Mack (IRE), and to a French flat and jumping winner. IRISH P-t-P '98/9 r10 w1 (Maiden) p0; pulled up 7. P-t-P '00/3 r16 p4 (3 3rds, dead-heated once, of 4 twice); pulled up 6, unseated 2. Scored on his penultimate appearance in Ireland, but found wanting in the stamina department since crossing the water, and beaten 24 lengths plus in his last 12 starts. A safe jumper, and beginner-ridden of late, but does not stand much racing. *Mrs D.M. Hall — Cambridge Univ (April Gingell).* 157 (L), 558 (L).

MACROBERT'S REPLY (IRE) ..7-10.. 9 ch.g. Phardante (FR) — Koshear (Hardgreen USA) 2. Tall angular. Dam won 2 flat (12-16f) and 2 Hurdles (2m-2m6f) in Ireland. IRISH NH FLAT '01 r1 p0. NH '02 r1 p0. P-t-P '03 r1 p0 (7th of 8). Well tailed off once apiece for Arthur Moore and Paul Nicholls, and duly had an annual airing in the five-runner elders Maiden at Fakenham in '04, where he and a stablemate were left to fill the first two places. Typically the guv'nor picked the wrong one, and having been left in front at the third last folded tamely under some wild riding, and was ultimately beaten 20 lengths. It goes without saying that neither were selected for the best-turned-out award. *P.J. Millington — Fernie.* 1156 (OMa).

MACY (IRE) ..8-7§.. 12 ch.g. Sharp Charter — Lumax (Maximilian) p43pp. Workmanlike Half-brother to Pontoon Bridge, and to Irish NH flat and Hurdles winner, Ring Four. Dam won Norwegian Oaks, and won a Hurdle there. IRISH NH FLAT '97 r1 p0. NH FLAT '97 r3 w1 (2m2f) p0. NH '97/01 r27 w1 (2m3f Hurdle) p5 (4 3rds); pulled up 3, fell 3. P-t-P/HUNT CH '02/3 r8 w2 (Confined and 3-finisher Members) p2 (3rd of 4 once); last pair 3, and pulled up 1. Scoring beyond 2m3f and since '97 for the first time when springing a 20-1 surprise at Andoversford last year, and managed to follow up when odds-on in his Members, but tailed off without fail since. Particularly feeble when evens favourite, and last of three in his local, and folds tamely as soon as pressure is applied. Reported to have broken a blood vessel once in the past. Visored twice in '00, and wears cheekpieces. *Mrs J. & Mrs M. Jones — Cotswold V.F. (Martin Jones).* 727 (MO), 757 (L), 815 (M), 1172 (3m1f110yH), 1254 (Cf).

MADAAR (USA) ..—§§.. 6 b.g. Spinning World (USA) — Mur Taasha (USA) (Riverman USA) r5r. Well-made half-brother to flat winners, Iftitah, Mahroos (USA) (also won in Dubai) and Darting. Dam won 3 flat (7-8f). FLAT '02/3 (for Sir M. Stoute, and P.D. Evans) r17 p2 (3rds). Beaten about six lengths after dwelling in two Sellers at 8-9f (long odds in both), but slow starting has frequently been a problem with him. Regularly visored on the flat, and wore a tongue-tie in his latest Point. Thoroughly unpleasant now, and declined to set off once and stopped at the last once from three attempts in Maidens. *Flying Donnes Partnership (Miss J.E. Foster) — Pendle Forest & Craven (Jo Foster).* 814 (OMa), 1159 (OMa), 1291 (OMa).

MADAM ATTORNEY ..8-3.. 9 ch.m. Baron Blakeney — Madam Advocate (Avocat) 54. Dam (*qv* '00 Annual) won 7 Points (inc 3 Ladies) and placed 12. Beaten 24 lengths plus twice in Maidens, and although she was close up for 2m4f in both she tired rapidly and appeared not to stay. *P.J. Lutman — W. Street Tickham (Kay Lutman).* 424 (CMa), 1088 (OMa).

MADAME CHOLET ..7-8.. 8 ch.m. Be My Native (USA) — Sonlaru (Deep Run) up54. Very small light sister to Border Laird (IRE), and half-sister to Carriglawn and Fellow Countryman (subsequent Chasing winner). Shows early dash, but completely runs out of momentum, and a poor last in both completions. Wears a tongue-tie and goes to post early. Unpromising. *Ms S.A. Greenaway — S. Devon.* 796 (CfMa), 1006 (CfMa), 1182 (CMam), 1370 (OMa).

MADEMIST SAM ..10-3§.. 13 b.g. Lord Bud — Mademist Susie (French Vine) p4f2p2p. Strong compact owner-bred brother to Mademist Jaz, and half-brother to Mademist Sparky. Dam, half-sister to 5 Pointers including Royal Pocket (*qv* '02 Annual), won 8 Points, and 2 Hunter Chses and placed 8 (inc 5 Hunt Chses) for Mr Hill before breaking down. Grandam, Ginger Fury, pulled up and unseated in Points. NH FLAT '97 r3 p0. NH '97/00 and '02 (for P. Beaumont) r24 w2 (2m5f Chses) p8; fell 1, pulled up 1. Gained one of his two wins in 2m5f Chases when beating his odds-on stablemate in a four-runner affair, but is ungenuine and totally unreliable, as he again showed in '04. Looked like winning an Open at Dalton Park until he fell when leading two out, but was 25 lengths last of two at 4-7 six days later. Beaten four lengths or less when making the frame twice, but is just as likely to decide to pull up. Scored in first time blinkers in '00, but they do little for him now. *M.J. Hill — Hurworth.* 163 (O), 269 (O), 501 (O), 565 (O), 679 (3m1fH), 812 (O), 1297 (3m1fH).

MADEMIST SPARKY .9-0.. 10 b.m. Minster Son — Mademist Susie (French Vine) 544. Lengthy half-sister to Mademist Sam (*qv*). P-t-P '03 r1 p0 (pulled up). Unraced until she was eight, but beaten 17 lengths plus in Maidens, and needs to find some extra stamina if she is to get any closer. *M.J. Hill — Hurworth.* 167 (OMa), 272 (OMa), 500 (CMam).

MAD JACK ..9-5.. 10 b.g. Mazaad — Glazepta Final (Final Straw) pu5. Good-bodied half-brother to Hurdles winner, Cobb Gate. Dam, half-sister to Supreme Charter (*qv* '91 Annual). NH FLAT '99/00 r2 p0. NH '01 r1 p0 (pulled up). P-t-P '02 (for Mr E. Retter) r2 p2 (2nd of 3 once). Can travel well for 2m4f, but missed '03 and returned with a tongue-tie, and does not appear to have enough wind in his sails to get home. Wears a cross-noseband. *P. Picton-Warlow — Exmoor.* 571 (R), 883 (OMa), 1075 (OMa).

MADMARIEA (IRE) ..—.. 10 b.m. Be My Native (USA) — Miss Good Night (Buckskin FR) uu. Half-sister to jumping winner, Lord 'n' Master (IRE), and to Irish Pointing winner, Gaora Bridge. IRISH P-t-P '02/3 r4 w1 (5yo&up Adjacent Maiden) p2. IRISH NH FLAT '00 r2 p0. IRISH NH '00 and '03 r6 p0. IRISH HUNT CH '03 (for D.P. Murphy) r4 p2. Seemed a better horse in Ireland than her successful English stablemate Darkarrow but blundered and unseated at the 13th and at the eighth in Restricteds, so the theory remained unproved. Blinkered once in '03. *T.D.B. Underwood — V. of Aylesbury with Garth & S. Berks.* 191 (R), 419 (CR).

MADMIDGE .10-5.. 10 b/br.g. Jendali (USA) — No Rejection (Mummy's Pet) R111p1. Small compact lop-eared half-brother to flat and Hurdles winner, Wadada. NH FLAT '01 r2 p0. P-t-P '02/3 (for Mr P. England) r13 p5 (3 2nds, of 3 once); 4th, last 2, fell/unseated 3, and pulled up 2. Moderate and looked a non-stayer for previous connections, but his new yard was firing on all cylinders in '04, and finally produced some worthwhile form. Unbeaten when completing, and two wins in softish at Marks Tey bordered on taking seven minutes, but only defeated modest opposition, and was trounced on his Hunter Chase debut. Unlikely to be as prolific next year, and his syndicates' name is very much tongue in cheek. *Next Stop Cheltenham Syndicate (D.J. Kemp) — Suffolk (David Kemp).* 151 (OMa), 244 (CfMa), 398 (R), 742 (I), 892 (2m5f110yH), 1313 (Cf).

MAGGIES BROTHER ..10-7.. 12 b.g. Brotherly (USA) — Sallisses (Pamroy) 44554343. Workmanlike owner-bred half-brother to Raymond James (*qv*). P-t-P/HUNT CH '98/03 r37 w7 (inc 3 3m-4m2f Hunt Chses) p9 (4 2nds, of 3 once, inc 3 Hunt Chses; 4 3rds, promoted once); pulled up 10, and fell/unseated 4. A very thorough stayer, and has already shown the ability to gallop successfully through mud for ten (!) minutes, but incredibly moody and runs in snatches and sometimes tails himself off from flag-fall. Reserves his best efforts for the closing months of the season, but has scored only once in his last 20 starts, and needs to travel far and wide in search of four-milers in '05. Acts on any going. *Mrs G.M. Shail — Ledbury (Roy Shail).* 117 (C), 209 (3m1f110yH), 437 (3m1fH), 629 (3m1f110yH), 979 (MOnr), 1172 (3m1f110yH), 1376 (4m2fH), 1497 (3mH).

MAGICAL APPROACH (IRE) .9-9.. 15 ch.g. Callernish — Farm Approach (Tug Of War) 766. Rangy half-brother to useful Irish jumping winner, Feathered Gale. IRISH P-t-P '96/7 r3 w2 (inc Winners of One) p1 (2nd). IRISH NH '97/03 r26 w3 (2m4f-2m6f Chses) p10. P-t-P/HUNT CH '02/3 (for Major B.D.A. Ridge) r5 p1 (2nd); disqualified from 4th once, pulled up 2, and ran out 1. The winner of five races in Ireland, all of them in mud, and one of them at Punchestown in '99 netted almost £10,000, but a light of days gone by now, and no more than a lightly-raced schoolmaster now. Wears a cross-noseband. *T. Phillips — Warwicks.* 31 (Cnr), 292 (MO), 404 (O).

MAGICAL FUN (IRE) ..9-8.. 13 b.g. Magical Strike (USA) — Roundstone Lass (Montekin) 5223. Small. Dam won 6f race in Ireland. IRISH FLAT '94/7 and '02 r18 w2 (8f) p4. IRISH NH '96/02 (for W.P. Mullins, and E. Sheehy) r47 w2 (2m Hdle and 2m Ch) p12 (inc 9 2nds); fell 1. Gained the last of his four Irish wins (on ground ranging from firm to heavy) in Oct '01, having not scored for four years before that. Blinkered on four occasions and tongue-tied once there. Has amassed a losing sequence of 19, but tried pluckily for a girl novice rider in his final three Points until he ran out of stamina at the business end. *Mr & Mrs F. & Miss T. Hayes — Tiverton Stag (Jenny Hayes).* 1127 (Cf), 1329 (Cnr), 1506 (C), 1554 (M).

MAGICIEN (FR) .9-13.. 9 b.g. Muroto — French Look (FR) (Green River FR) rp45p1u53. Tall brother to Irish Hurdles winner, Murolook (FR). Dam won 6 races in France. FRENCH FLAT '99 r1 p1 (3rd). NH '99/02 r5 p0; pulled up 2. P-t-P '02/3 r8 w1 (Maiden) p3 (2 2nds; and last of 3); last, and pulled up 4. The only one in a field of six to go clear at Upper Sapey in '02, but pulled up in five of his next nine starts, and not surprisingly 25-1 when prevailing in a finish of heads and short-heads at Chaddesley. Normally a weak finisher and jacks it in when male-ridden, but was not done with when unseating a female first-timer next time, and clearly appreciates less draconian measures. Will struggle to score now that he has got out of Restricteds. *Mrs B.L. Gibbons — Teme V. (Steve Isaac).* 231 (CR), 252 (CR), 406 (Inr), 450 (R), 628 (2m3fH), 1018 (R), 1109 (M), 1227 (Cf), 1392 (C).

MAGIC LODGE ..10-1.. 6 b.g. Grand Lodge (USA) — Samsung Spirit (Statoblest) u1fpp1. Small close-coupled half-brother to flat winners, Mystical Land (2nd in '04 Norfolk Stakes) and Spiritual Air. Dam won 2 6f races. 32,000y. FLAT '01/2 (for M.R. Channon, and J.R. Weymes) r10 p0. Bought Doncaster, Aug '02 for 1400. Flat racing was not his cup of tea and acquired blinkers on his final three attempts, but able to produce fair form on occasions in Points, and won a six-runner PPORA Restricted at Godstone. Finished 20 lengths second in a Marks Tey Maiden in February, but awarded the race as the winner had lost his weight cloth. Often let down by his jumping, but still a baby, so it might improve, which could give him prospects in Confineds. *G.I. Cooper — Essex F. & U. (Cherie Cunningham).* 219 (OMa), 245 (CfMa), 559 (R), 779 (R), 999 (R), 1409 (CR).

MAGIC PERFORMER .9-13.. 9 b.g. Tragic Role (USA) — Hot Performer (Hotfoot) 1p. Compact home-bred half-brother to Mon Performer (*qv*). FLAT '98 r2 p0 (beaten 20l plus in Sells). P-t-P '02/3 r4 p3 (2 2nds; and last of 3); and fell 1. Gained a deserved success when given a confident ride by Nicky Tinkler at Witton Castle, though was possibly lucky as the 15-length leader was bowled over by a loose horse approaching the fourth last, but stood his racing badly and broke down irreparably next time. M.J. Harland — Hurworth (Chris Dennis). 160 (CMa), 430 (R).

MAGIC ROUTE (IRE) ..9-5.. 8 b.g. Mr Confusion (IRE) — Another Chapter (Respect) 23. Tall. NH FLAT '01 r1 p0. NH '01/3 (for J.H. Johnson) r7 p1 (2nd); pulled up 4. Bought Doncaster, Nov for 5000. Second in a five-runner Hurdle but also pulled up four times including his final two attempts in the previous yard, and was 32 lengths fifth of six in a Chase. Did not look keen, and wore cheekpieces once. Found Maidens more acceptable and beaten between five and nine lengths when placed, and could probably win a modest race if he stayed on a bit better. *H.L. Thompson — Cleveland (Tina Jackson).* 774 (2m4fCMa), 1158 (OMa).

MAGNATISM ..8-0.. 8 b.g. Charmer — Bright-One (Electric) pfp. Tall workmanlike half-brother to Star General English flat, to Hurdling winner, Mill-Dot, to Scottish Hurdling, Irish flat and Chasing winner, Albrighton. Dam won 2 2m Hurdles and is half-sister to High Learie (*qv* '04 Annual). NH FLAT '02 (for C.W. Thornton) r3 p0. Bought Doncaster, Oct for 3600. Shows no ability, and did not get any further than the ninth at most on his last two attempts. Performs as if there is something wrong with him. *Mrs S. Morgan — Meynell & S. Staffs (Tim Eley).* 227 (CfMa), 387 (OMa), 533 (2m4fCfMa).

MAGNEMITE (IRE) ..9-10§.. 9 b.g. Dromod Hill — Rostoonstown Lass (IRE) (Decent Fellow) pup. Narrow light. IRISH P-t-P '02 r7 p1 (2nd); pulled up 1, fell/unseated 4. P-t-P '03 r4 w1 (Maiden) p3 (2 2nds, beaten neck once, and of 3 once; and 3rd of 4). Made the most of a simple opportunity on lively ground at Stafford Cross last year, but had previously looked a decidedly feeble finisher on stiffer tracks, and proved very expensive to follow in '04. Backed from fives to 7-4 when acquiring blinkers at Black Forest Lodge, but was a beaten third and stopping quickly when unseating two out, and his first sub-3m attempt ended when pulled up after 1m2f. Probably not in love with the job, and will struggle to make amends. *C.A. White — W. Somerset V. (Nick Dawe).* 14 (R), 65 (Rnr), 628 (2m3fH).

MAGNUS MAXIMUS ..9-5.. 13 b.g. Takachiho — L'Oraz (Ile De Bourbon USA) 34pp. Tall half-brother to Deep Dale. Grandam, Oraza, won German 1000 Guineas and Oaks. NH FLAT '97 r3 p0. NH '98 r1 p0 (tailed off last in Sell). P-t-P '00/3 r7 w1 (Maiden) p1 (remote last of 3); 4th twice, and pulled up 3. Running on vapour by the time he crossed the line when successful on firmish at Garthorpe in '02, and has usually conked out well short otherwise. Stands few outings, but does not appear to handle easy surfaces. Has two handlers. Wears a cross-noseband. *S. & Mrs L. Lamyman — Blankney (Lynda Lamyman).* 745 (R), 1060 (R), 1359 (2m4f110yH), 1503 (R).

MAGNUS VERITAS (IRE) ..10-3.. 7 br.g. Jolly Jake (NZ) — Goldens Monkey (Monksfield) 01. Compact well-made half-brother to Coldabri (IRE) (*qv*). IRISH P-t-P '03 r4 w1 (5yo Maiden) p1 (3rd); fell 1. Jarred up after finishing tailed off at Cottenham on the opening day, but reappeared nearly two months later at Parham to win a three-finisher Restricted in most decisive fashion. Had Out The Black (*qv*) behind him in his Irish win, and looks a potentially useful stayer, but will probably always need give in the ground. *S.C. Robinson — Mid Surrey F. (Gina Weare).* 2 (R), 639 (R).

MAHARAJAH (IRE) ..9-8.. 11 b.g. Be My Native (USA) — Fayafi (Top Ville) 8. Workmanlike half-brother to Cool Summer (IRE). Dam, half-sister to Southern Cross (*qv*), won at 14f in Ireland, and won 2 2m Hurdles there. NH FLAT '99 r1 p0. NH '01 r3 p0; pulled up 1. P-t-P '02 r4 w1 (2-finisher Maiden) p1 (2nd); and last pair 2. Beat one other finisher in a long Maiden in soft at Wetherby in '02, but missed '00 and '03, and disappeared back into the ether after being taken very gingerly round Ampton on his latest comeback. *J.R. Weatherby — Cottesmore (Ashley Bealby).* 44 (R).

MAI CURE .—.. 6 b.m. Terimon — Quilpee Mai (Pee Mai) p. Small homebred half-sister to Mai Point (*qv*). Given a jolly before pulling up at Marks Tey in mid-April. Will probably improve, and can hopefully go some way towards compensating connections for the sad loss of Mai Point. *D.L. Claydon & Mrs P. Twinn — E. Essex (Paula Twinn).* 901 (OMa).

MAIDSTONE MONUMENT (IRE) ..10-11.. 10 b.g. Jurado (USA) — Loreto Lady (Brave Invader USA) p20p*037*. Lengthy workmanlike half-brother to Furry Loch, Kilminfoyle, and to Irish Hurdling winner, Josie Murphy. NH FLAT '00 r1 p0. NH '00/3 r43 w6 (2 2m-3m2f Hdles and 4 3m-3m3f Chses) p11; pulled up 11, unseated 1. NH '04 r3 p1 (3rd in 3m1f Ch: *chsd ldrs, jmpd slow 13, outpcd aft 15, stayed on flat*); last of 11 in 3m3f Hdle: *prom to 9, t.o*, and last of 7 in 3m2f110y Ch: *ld to 10, ld 13-14, wknd 16, t.o.* A front-runner who possesses abundant stamina, and can battle on his day, but sometimes gives up pretty tamely. Needs firmish ground and a left-handed track (has never scored when going in the other direction), and a very sound jumper who has unseated once but never fallen (nevertheless, he did not have the bottle for the Aintree Foxhunters). Blinkered once in '01. Left a remote second at the last before being beaten 20 lengths by Macgeorge at Warwick, but showed no other comparable Hunter Chase form, and is better off in Handicaps. *D. Jenkins — Gogerddan (Alison Thorpe).* 280 (3m2f110yH), 490 (3m2fH), 732 (2m5f110yH), 991 (3m2f110yH).

MAINLIER ..9-4.. 12 gr.g. Roselier (FR) — Maintown (Remainder Man) 4. Close-coupled half-brother to Main Missile. Dam won 2m1f Sell Hurdle and 2 2m Chases when trained for Gerald Spencer by Martin Pipe. NH FLAT '98 r1 p0. NH '99 r2 p1 (2nd). P-t-P '00/3 r11 p6 (4 3rds, of 4 once, and last once; 2 2nds, of 3 once); pulled up 4, and fell. Has threatened to win on several occasions, but a combination of sketchy jumping and weak finishing has conspired against him, and has never managed more than four outings in a year. Downed tools after five out when 40 lengths last at Maisemore and looks destined never to lose his maiden status. Has been tried in blinkers and cheekpieces. *G.M. Spencer — N. Ledbury.* 730 (OMa).

MAI POINT ..9-12.. 12 b.m. Blakeney — Quilpee Mai (Pee Mai) p532. Small neat half-sister to Just Patrimony, Kelly's Eye, Just Maisy (dam of Just Mai-Bee, *qv* '01 Annual), Bengers Moor (subsequent Chasing winner), Newick Park, Mai Knight and Mai Cure. Dam won at $11^{1}/_{2}$f, and was placed 8, including 2 Points for David Claydon. P-t-P/HUNT CH '99/03 r22 w6 (inc 2 Ladies) p4 (3 3rds, of 4 twice); pulled up 3, fell/unseated 3. A speedy mare who enjoyed a purple patch in '02, but largely under a cloud since falling at the first on her Hunter Chase debut, and had only scored in one of ten subsequent outings. Tragically dropped dead after finishing second at Higham in what was her final start before retiring to the paddocks. Mrs P. Twinn & D.L. Claydon — E. Essex (Paula Twinn). 38 (Cf), 156 (O), 399 (L), 831 (L).

MAITRE DE MUSIQUE (FR) ..10-1.. 14 ch.g. Quai Voltaire (USA) — Mativa (FR) (Satingo) 21324. Tall rangy half-brother to jumping winner, Voyage Sans Retour (previously a French flat winner), and to another French flat winner. NH FLAT '95 r2 w1 p0. NH '95/00 r26 w2 (2m4f-2m5f Chses) p8 (inc 3 Hdles, and 3rd in '99 John Hughes; inc neck 2nd); pulled up 3. P-t-P/HUNT CH '01/3 r20 w3 (inc 2 Confineds) p10 (5 3rds, of 4 once, and inc 5 Hunt Chses); 4th, 6th twice, last pair 3, and pulled up 1. As sure-footed as a five-legged mountain goat, and has never lost a rider in 51 starts over jumps, and has recorded an annual success in four campaigns for Michael Tate, but also let down by the good doctor's inability to ride a finish on several occasion in that period. Outstayed the runner-up to land his Members in a howling gale (the meeting was abandoned after three more races), but should have won at Heslaker, and would have, had the riders been transposed. Suited by an easy surface, providing it is not sticky. Has had a breathing problem, and run tongue-tied in previous seasons. *Dr M.P. Tate — Hurworth (Richard Tate).* 389 (Cf), 562 (M), 957 (Cf), 1202 (Cf), 1489 (3m3fH).

MAJADOU (FR) ..—.. 11 b.g. Cadoudal (FR) — Majathen (FR) (Carmarthen FR) p. Tall workmanlike half-brother to a French jumping winner. FRENCH NH '98 r6 w1 (2m1f Hdle) p4. NH '99/02 r16 w5 (2m-2m5f Chses, inc 4-timer '99) p2 (3rds); pulled up 2. P-t-P '03 r1 p0 (last). Once very smart, and completed a four-timer in '99 when running away with the Mildmay of Flete at Cheltenham, but last of five to Macgeorge in the Martell Cup next time, and only managed to win one of 11 subsequent starts under Rules. Very lightly raced since '01, and confirmed his career had gone down the pan completely when pulled up at Penshurst, but after winning connections almost £100,000 he owes them nothing. *C.M. Batterham & Mrs H. Silk — Kent & Surrey Bloodhounds (Emma Leppard).* 780 (O).

MAJESTIC APPROACH (IRE) ..9-12.. 11 br.g. Mandalus — Approach The Dawn (IRE) (Orchestra) 66. Tall rangy half-brother to Irish NH flat winner, Bewleys Berry, and to Irish Hurdling winner, Logical Approach. IRISH P-t-P '00 r2 p0 (pulled up 2). NH '01/2 (for P.R. Webber) r6 w1 (2m5f Ch) p0; pulled up 3. Made a winning English debut in a five-runner Chase on firmish in which he made all, but a very weak finisher under Rules since, and pulled up in three of his final five attempts. Clearly had a big problem, and although he was not discredited when plugging home for sixth in two Points there is no definite evidence that he is out of the woods. *K. Smith-Bingham — Cottesmore.* 1120 (Cf), 1396 (C).

MAJOR ADAMS ..10-0.. 10 b.g. Roscoe Blake — Celtic View (Celtic Cone) 2f23. Tall strong brother to Wee Kelpie, and half-brother to a jumping winner. NH FLAT '01 r3 p2 (3rds). NH '01/2 r4 p0. P-t-P '03 r3 w2 (Club Maiden and 3-finisher Intermediate) p0; and pulled up 1. A good galloper, and made much of the running to win his first two Points, but made to look very onepaced since, and questions have to be raised about his willingness to battle. Does not stand many outings but will be receiving a squiggle if he does not convert another opportunity soon. Has shown a tendency to sweat freely. *Mrs D. Williams — Sir W.W. Wynn's (Anne Hewitt).* 708 (M), 932 (Cf), 1229 (L), 1426 (C).

MAJOR BELLE (FR) ..—.. 6 ch.m. Cyborg (FR) — Mistine Major (FR) (Major Petingo FR) pp*6f1*. Compact half-sister to French Chasing winner, Miss Major (FR), and half-sister to French jumping winner, Miss Marsonniere (FR) (both successful at Pau). FRENCH NH '02/3 r4 w1 (2m Hdle and 2m2f Ch) p1 (2nd); unseated 1. NH '04 (for M.C. Pipe) r3 w1 (beat Sir Walter 5*l* in 2m3f110y Sell Hdle: *hld up, ld 3 out, clr last, r.o wl*) p0; last of 6 in 2m3f Hdle: *hld up, went 2nd aft 6 til blun 3 out, eased when btn flat*, and fell in 2m1f Claiming Hdle: *hld up & bhnd, mist 2, hdwy aft 3 out, 2nd & clsng when fell last*. Bought Goffs France, Jul for 11,131. Won a Fillies Hurdle at Pau and a half-breds Chase at Toulouse, both in the mud, but did not seem to get the trip in Points and was quickly demoted to a Selling Hurdle with good effect (scored on firmish). Had been two lengths second and staying on when she fell at the last in a Claimer on her previous attempt, and is competent at the bottom level, but connections had no qualms about letting her go and she immediately slumped in the latest yard. *J.J. Boulter & Miss F.J. Wilkins — Portman (John Boulter).* 196 (O), 322 (L).

MAJOR RENO (IRE) ..9-2.. 8 b.g. Little Bighorn — Make Me An Island (Creative Plan USA) pp6f41. Strong-topped. Dam won 2m Hurdle and 2 Chases (2m-2m4f) in Ireland. IRISH NH FLAT r1 p0. IRISH NH '02/3 (for Ms F.M. Crowley) r6 p0; unseated 2. Unimpressive when beaten a minimum of 38 lengths in his first 11 races (blinkered once), but did a little better when 13 lengths fourth, and sustained the improvement to win a very bad 2m4f Maiden at Garthorpe. Suspect over the full trip, and connections have doubtless done very well to extract a win from him. *T.G. Williams — R.C. Harper — Ystrad Taf Fechan.* 584 (I), 701 (2m4fOMa), 890 (2m4fOMa), 1266 (2m4fOMa), 1402 (2m4fOMa), 1504 (2m4fOMa).

MAKE IT PLAIN ..—.. 6 b.m. Alflora (IRE) — Gemmabel (True Song) r0p. Compact owner-bred. Dam sister to Emmabella (*qv* '97 Annual). NH FLAT '04 r2 p0 (13th over 2m1f at Hereford: *hmpd start, a bhnd, t.o*; and pulled up over 2m1f at Southwell: *pu aft 2f*). Made it plain that she was not going to try in a Woodford Maiden and stopped and threw Gary Hanmer off at the first, and subsequently 80 lengths 13th of 14, and pulled up after two furlongs when the jockey thought she was lame in bumpers. *A. Hollingsworth — Worcs (Alan Hollingsworth).* 1074 (OMa).

MAKE UP YOUR MIND (IRE) ..—.. 13 b.g. Little Bighorn — Our Decision (Hawaiian Return USA) pu. Dam is sister to Hawaiian Prince (*qv* '98 Annual). IRISH P-t-P '97/8 r8 p1 (2nd); last, pulled up 5, and fell 1. IRISH NH FLAT '98 r3 p0. IRISH NH '99 r1 p0. P-t-P '00 and '02/3 r4 w1 (Maiden) p1 (2nd); last, and pulled up 1. Rated 9-4 after scraping home on firmish at Cold Harbour in '02, but very lightly raced since leaving Ireland, and has failed to finish in just three outings since. The subject of a stewards enquiry on his reappearance where the rider stated he thought the horse had lost his action, but typically ran out of steam after two miles next time. *R. Hancox & M. Filby — N. Ledbury (Ron Hancox).* 1069 (R), 1253 (M).

MAKHPIYA PATAHN (IRE) .9-4§.. 13 gr.g. Nestor — Our Mare Mick (Choral Society) p87214345p. Tall rangy half-brother to Hurdles winner, Gangsters R Us (IRE). Dam is half-sister to Sanballat (*qv* '94 Annual). NH '98/00 r11 p1 (2nd in Ch); pulled up 2. P-t-P/HUNT CH '01/3 r20 w2 (Maiden and walk-over Restricted) p9 (6 2nds); 4th, 5th, last pair 2, pulled up 4, and fell 1. Inordinately clumsy and thoroughly ungenuine, and usually comes off the bridle on the way to post. Gained his first competitive success in 20 starts when winning a two-finisher Confined at Larkhill in most unimpressive fashion after which he was only once better than last. David Turner must wear out whips quicker than any other jockey, and his has been seen to glow after dismounting from this most reluctant beast. Must be shunned at all costs. Has been tried unsuccessfully in cheekpieces, and visored in his walk-over. Wears a cross-noseband. *J.H. Young — New Forest.* 19 (CMod), 116 (I), 182 (CCon), 261 (Cf), 455 (Cf), 576 (O), 972 (Cf), 1100 (O), 1367 (O), 1496 (I).

MALONEY (IRE) ..8-12.. 8 b/br.g. Borovoe — Juggling Act (IRE) (Be My Native USA) pu8upp2442. Good-bodied. IRISH P-t-P '02 r3 p0 (5th of 6, pulled up 1, and fell 1). A bad maiden who has already had 13 chances and only beat one horse in his first nine attempts (failed to finish in seven), but at least keeps plugging to completion now and came closest to success when five lengths second on the only occasion Lee Stephens partnered him. Always soundly beaten with Christine Evans including when 20 lengths second in the last race of the year, but to her credit she is improving her competency after being very wobbly in early season, and perhaps the pair will get lucky one day. *R.J. Rowsell — Ystrad Taf Fechan.* 363 (CfMa), 453 (CfMa), 700 (CfMa), 735 (CfMa), 845 (CfMa), 1096 (OMa), 1486 (OMa), 1533 (OMa), 1550 (OMa), 1566 (OMa).

MALTBY SON ..9-8.. 13 b.g. Infantry — Top Soprano (High Top) 4pu64. Compact brother to Soldier's Song, and half-brother to Jack Ramsey, Big Country and Fortunes Wood, to flat and jumping winner, Setter Country, to NH flat and useful jumping winner, Linton Rocks, and to successful Hurdler, Sovereigns Sound. Dam won at 5f. P-t-P/HUNT CH '97/00 and '03 (for Mrs J. Shirley & Mrs M. Brown) r21 w4 (inc Open and Ladies) p6 (2nds); last pair 2, pulled up 5, unseated 2 and brought down 1. A secure jumper and recorded an annual success to '00, but only once beaten less than 37 lengths when novice-ridden this year, and has always been lightly raced. Formerly quite a weak finisher, but an all round plodder these days. Has been tried in a tongue-tie. *S.J. Smith — Grafton.* 47 (Cf), 289 (CfL), 466 (Cf), 558 (L), 785 (L).

MALVIC (IRE) ..—.. 6 b.g. Old Vic — Buck Maid (Buckskin FR) sfpp. Compact half-brother to Irish jumping, Czech Hurdling and English Chasing winner, Merchants Friend (IRE) (just caught in '04 Kim Muir). Has an abysmal record so far, and only negotiated a total of eight fences in his four outings. Dwells at the start and looks a horrible ride, and Dai Jones dismounted at the second on final start. *M.G. Jones — Gelligaer F.* 454 (CfMa), 699 (CfMa), 1323 (CfMa), 1488 (OMa).

MAMBO (U) ..—.. 11 b.m. unknown u. The 31 pounds overweight rider thudded off at the sixth in a Members, when already tailed off, but remounted to complete another mile before giving up. *D. Campbell — Southdown & Eridge.* 605 (M).

MAN AT THE TOP.9-0§.. 9 b.g. Northern Park (USA) — Kotsina (Top Ville) 34u21. Tall half-brother to a winner abroad. Dam is half-sister to Backsheesh (*qv*). NH '02 r1 p0 (pulled up). P-t-P '03 r4 p0 (pulled up 2, and fell/unseated 2). A non-finisher in his first five starts, and missed '03 with a broken knee, but good enough to land a shocking Maiden on firmish at Heslaker which was run 25 seconds slower than any other race on the card. Outbattled the runner-up on the run-in, but had looked a most awkward cuss himself when tried in blinkers at Fakenham, and a follow up does not look on the cards. *Lord Yarborough — Brocklesby (Mark Bennison).* 594 (OMa), 813 (OMa), 1156 (OMa), 1305 (OMa), 1458 (OMa).

MANAVITE (IRE) ..—.. 10 ch.g. Invited (USA) — Rosie Dear (Mon Capitaine) fp. Tall half-brother to Ring Of Freedom (IRE). Dam, half-sister to Krakus (*qv* '91 Annual), won Point and 2m Chase in Ireland. IRISH NH FLAT '00 r3 p1 (3rd). IRISH NH '99/00 r5 p1 (3rd). IRISH P-t-P '02 r5 w2 (Maiden and Open) p1 (3rd); unseated 1. P-t-P '03 r1 p0 (unseated). Accounted for Always On The Line (*qv*) — 21 lengths behind — when recording the second of two wins in Ireland, but their career paths have taken very different routes since, and his is very much on a downward curve. Took on vaunted opposition in '04, and was close behind Lord Atterbury when falling after two miles on his return, but exhausted when pulled up at Horseheath on the first weekend in February and failed to reappear. Probably better than he has been able to show in England, but needs to jump much more fluently, and clearly has physical issues to deal with. *C.C. Shand Kydd — Bicester with Whaddon (Fiona Kehoe).* 34 (O), 125 (O).

MANDAGUS (IRE) ..8-6.. 7 ch.g. Try My Saldy (ITY) — Forestnightengale (Sallust) p55. Compact attractive. IRISH P-t-P '02/3 r3 p0 (last, pulled up 1, and fell 1). Yet to beat another horse in six Points, and it appeared he had no stamina when stopping to nil on his English debut. Backed down from fives to 5-2 favourite on his latest attempt over 2m4f, but was beaten 26 lengths, and is not impressing at present. *S.D. Jones & Mrs J. Pepworth — Cheshire (Peter Morris).* 619 (2m4fOMa), 929 (2m4fOMa), 1049 (2m4fOMa).

MANDATE MAN (IRE) .9-7.. 11 b.g. Mandalus — Atalaya Park (King Of Spain) 24p39. IRISH P-t-P '99 and '01 r2 w1 (4&5yo Maiden) p0; and pulled up. IRISH NH FLAT '00 r2 p0. IRISH NH '00/1 r5 p0. P-t-P/HUNT CH '02 r3 p1 (2nd); 4th, and 7th. Won his only start in '99, and filled the runners-up berth on his last two seasonal reappearances, but has been consistently lightly raced and '04 was his busiest campaign to date. A safe enough jumper, but acquired cheekpieces on his last two starts, and only looks an outside bet to achieve a Restricted success. *D. Johnson — Sinnington (John Cranage).* 390 (Rnr), 591 (CR), 772 (4m1fO), 955 (R), 1288 (R).

MANHATTAN RAINBOW (IRE) ..—.. 14 b.g. Mandalus — Clara Girl (Fine Blade USA) pp. Unfurnished half-brother to Pantara Prince (IRE). Dam won a bumper in Ireland. IRISH NH FLAT '97 r1 p0. IRISH NH '98 r1 p0 (pulled up in Hunt Ch). IRISH P-t-P '98 r5 p1 (3rd); pulled up 2, and fell. NH '98/9 r11 p5 (Chses, beaten 7-33*l*). P-t-P/HUNT CH '00/1 and '03 (for Mrs C.J. Kerr) r12 w4 (inc 3 3m1f Hunt Chses) p2 (2nds in Hunt Chses); pulled up 2. Rated 10-10 when unbeaten in three trips to Kelso in '00, but lightly raced and beaten 22 lengths plus since, and made a lot of mistakes when pulled up in both starts this year. Does not look to be enjoying himself any more, and will surely be retired. Visored twice in '99. *Mrs J.M. & Miss J. Hollands — Lauderdale (Joan Hollands).* 213 (L), 678 (3m1fH).

MANHATTON STORM (IRE) ..9-2.. 9 b/br.g. Denel (FR) — Bring It With You (Callernish) 8f3p232. Light-framed. Dam, half-sister to Rare Manor (*qv* '93 Annual), won 3 Points (inc Mares Open) in Ireland. IRISH NH FLAT '01 r1 p0. IRISH P-t-P '02 r5 p0 (7th and pulled up 4). P-t-P '03 r4 p2; and pulled up 2. Placed on six occasions, and deserves his moment of glory, but a consistently weak finisher, and lacks the scope to shrug aside his frequent blunders. Takes little getting fit and often bounces round the paddock taking the eye, but only once beaten less than 12 lengths, and will always struggle to carry the weight in Maidens. *A. Winchester — E. Anglian Bloodhounds (Sam Hodge).* 6 (OMa), 40 (OMa), 152 (OMa), 525 (OMa), 651 (OMa), 833 (OMa), 1317 (CfMa).

MAQUILLEUX ..10-2.. 12 ch.g. Gildoran — Marque De Soleil (Sunyboy) fp. Tall rangy half-brother to Marquis Of Bedford. Dam is half-sister to Miss Martlet (*qv* '95 Annual). Grandam, Foot Mark, pulled up in 2 Points. P-t-P '00 and '02 r7 w2 (3-finisher Maiden and Restricted) p3 (2nds); and pulled up 2. A thorough stayer, and gained both '02 successes in seven-minute events, but can appear rather clumsy, and has not stood his racing well. Blew up after helping force the pace for nearly 2m4f in the fastest race of the day at Maisemore Park, and his problems clearly restrict the amount of work connections can do with him at home. *The Stanton Racing Club (Mrs K. Smyly) — N. Cotswold (Giles & Kim Smyly).* 107 (O), 728 (I).

MARBANK LAD (IRE) ..—.. 9 b.g. Marju (IRE) — Hollybank Lady (USA) (Sir Ivor USA) ppp. Small well-made long-backed. P-t-P '02/3 (for Mrs T. Holditch) r6 p2 (3rds, remote of 4 once); pulled up 3, and unseated 1. Error-prone and beaten 20 lengths plus in both completions, and does not seem to stay much beyond two miles. Acquired cheekpieces on his last two starts. *Miss T. Coulson — Fitzwilliam.* 746 (OMa), 1061 (OMa), 1108 (OMa).

MARCIANO .9-3§.. 9 b.g. Rock Hopper — Raintree Venture (Good Times ITY) 4332p5. Small neat half-brother to a winner in Italy. Dam is half-sister to Faraday (*qv* '00 Annual). FLAT '98/00 r7 p0. NH '99/01 r11 p2; pulled up 1. P-t-P '02/3 r4 p1 (3rd); last pair 2, and pulled up 1. A difficult ride and was tried in headgear under Rules, but remains a maiden despite 28 starts under all codes. Entrusted with favouritism in his Members, but was never going at any stage, and whilst he has the ability to win a small race cannot be relied on to put his best foot forward. Unimproved by cheekpieces in '04. Wears a cross-noseband. *F. Allan & Mrs B Vergette — Fitzwilliam (Louise Allan).* 151 (OMa), 386 (OMa), 555 (M), 746 (OMa), 1061 (OMa), 1439 (2m5fH).

MARCUS WILLIAM (IRE) ..9-13.. 8 ch.g. Roselier (FR) — River Swell (IRE) (Over The River FR) 5. Compact. NH FLAT '02 r3 p0; unseated 1. NH '02/3 (for B.G. Powell) r5 w1 (2m3f Hdle) p2 (3rds). Got up in the final stride to spring a 66-1 shock in a Fontwell Hurdle in heavy, and would probably have the ability to be a competent Pointer if at his best, but seemed to go wrong immediately having finished ten lengths fifth in the first Open of the year. *P.H. Betts — Suffolk (Simon Stearn).* 3 (O).

MARGERY COPSE ..—.. 10 b.m. Baron Blakeney — Truelyn (True Song) pb. Very small owner-bred half-sister to Westington (*qv*). Brought down at the fourth and fatally injured at Bredwardine. Mr & Mrs R. Bartlett — N. Cotswold (Claire Hart). 927 (OMa), 1395 (OMa).

MARGERY'S OPERA ..9-5.. 8 ch.m. Opera Ghost — Bay Blossom (El Conquistador) fu3. Lengthy attractive. Let down by her jumping to date, but beaten just under three lengths at Cothelstone on her first completion, and had a subsequent winner 20 lengths in arrears. Should win a Maiden with a little more practice. *Miss K. Tripp — Weston & Banwell H.* 469 (2m4fOMa), 633 (2m4fCfMa), 884 (OMa).

MARKET POSEUR (IRE) ..—.. 11 br.g. Brush Aside (USA) — Great Aunt Emily (Traditionalist USA) p. Brother to Dark Challenger (IRE) (*qv*). P-t-P '00 and '02 r2 p0 (pulled up 2). Runs once biennially and always pulls up, and having broken down in '02 his appearances look numbered. *Mrs J.D. Dillon — Rockwood H. (Stephen Wiles).* 958 (OMa).

MARKET SPRINGER (IRE) ..9-10.. 14 gr.g. Roselier (FR) — An Carthanach (Good Thyne USA) 4pp. Tall. NH FLAT '97 r2 p0. NH '98 r6 p1 (distant 2nd in Ch, only 2 went clear — the pair who had been clear both fell, and one remounted); pulled up 1, and fell 2 in other Chses. P-t-P '99/00 and '02/3 (for Mrs M.L. Williams & Mrs C.M. Marles) r13 w4 (Maiden and 3 Ladies) p3 (neck 2nd of 3; and 2 3rds); 7th, pulled up 1, and unseated 4. Recorded a hat-trick at Erw Lon when successful on his '03 reappearance, but only risked on easy surfaces, and never going with any purpose when pulled up in three of his last four starts. Can be clumsy, and it would be surprising to see him revive in '05. Wears a cross-noseband. *Miss B. Williams — Curre & Llangibby (Bethan Williams).* 63 (L), 206 (L), 449 (L).

MARKET VALUE (IRE) .8-5§§.. 9 b.g. Montelimar (USA) — Derring Lass (Derring Rose) 5p. Lengthy brother to Jack Robbo (IRE) and Court Award (IRE), and to NH flat winner, Valiant Memory (IRE). IRISH P-t-P '01 r3 p0 (pulled up 2, and unseated). IRISH NH FLAT '01 r1 p0 (tailed off). P-t-P '02/3 (for Mr W.J. Evans) r8 p2 (last of 3 once); pulled up 5, and slipped up 1. An outright rogue, and unimproved by his third yard in as many years, and predictably having only once finished better than last in 13 Points the fun of taking him to the races has worn thin. Has been tried in blinkers and a tongue-strap. *R.W.J. Willcox — Llangeinor.* 948 (OMa), 1027 (OMa).

MARLMONT LAD (IRE) .7-11.. 14 b/br.g. Homo Sapien — Patricias Choice (Laurence O) 3pp. Tall half-brother to Scrabo View (IRE), and to Irish Hurdles winner, Sharri Dee. IRISH NH FLAT '95 r1 p0. IRISH NH '96 and '99 r3 p0 (inc 9th in Hunt Ch). IRISH P-t-P '98/9 r7 w1 (7yo&up Maiden for novice riders) p1 (3rd); pulled up 1, brought down 1, unseated 1. P-t-P '01 and '03 (for Miss E. Lloyd) r2 p0 (pulled up 2). Landed a touch in mud in Ireland, but was never prolific over there, and has been a very rare sight in three English campaigns for different sets of connections. Trundled round Dunthrop when last of three in his Members, which was only slightly faster than the Ladies run over five furlongs further, but has been tried in a tongue-strap, and stopped to nil when pulled up on his latest appearance. *A. Campbell — Heythrop.* 46 (M), 756 (Cf), 925 (R).

MARQUIS MAX ..9-9.. 8 ch.g. Elegant Monarch — Thing O'Beauty (Sir Lark) p. P-t-P '03 r8 w2 (Maiden and Restricted 3 finished in both) p2 (2nds, remote of 3, and last); 4th, pulled up 2, and ran out. Completed a double in modest events at Lifton in a busy debut season, but jumps persistently left-handed, and may have suffered a reverse when the subject of a market move on his first venture into Open class. Did not look a straightforward ride last year, and will need watching even if he is able to resume quickly. Quite excitable and has two handlers. *Mrs V.A.J. Dunne — Lamerton.* 64 (O).

MARSDEN ..8-4.. 11 b.g. Lochearnhead (USA) — Fishing Smack (Bustiki) 2p4upp. Dam won 2 2m Sell Hdles and placed 13 (inc 6 Chses) for late Barry Byford, and subsequently won a Confined and placed 2 for him before breaking down. P-t-P '99/00 (for Mrs R. Byford) r2 p0 (pulled up 2). Only lasted two outings before suffering a similar fate to his dam, and despite showing speed for two miles on occasions was beaten a minimum of 20 lengths on his resumption after a four-year lay-off. *Mr & Mrs B. Andrews & Mrs P. Twinn — Mr & Mrs R. Hanley & Mr & Mrs A. McCrory — E. Anglian Bloodhounds (Paula Twinn).* 217 (M), 525 (OMa), 652 (OMa), 1156 (OMa), 1317 (CfMa), 1405 (OMa).

MARSTON MOSES ..10-5.. 11 ch.g. Le Moss — Wild Sap (Sapsford) 210. Rangy half-brother to Marston Miriam. Dam, half-sister to 4 Pointers, including Rushing Wild, was placed in 6 Hurdles;

subsequently won 2 Points and placed 3 for Billy Foulkes. P-t-P '02/3 r7 w2 (Maiden and Club Restricted) p3 (2 3rds); and last 2. Thrice a winner of stamina tests on easy surfaces, and ran Nautical Lad to half-a-length on his reappearance, but totally ineffective once the ground dries out, and for the second year running his season was over by the first weekend in March. Well worth keeping on the right side of if he encounters mud and a long track, and it is a pity he is so one dimensional. *C.W. Foulkes — Quorn.* 106 (C), 228 (Cf), 379 (I).

MARTBY .9-9.. 9 gr.g. Past Glories — Baroness Spider (Baron Blakeney) 15ppp. Tall rangy. Dam, half-sister to 7 Pointers, including Conkerdor (*qv* '03 Annual), won 3 Points and placed 7 ('a lovely mare ... should have achieved far more than she has'). Grandam, Lolly Spider, half-sister to Crane Fly and cousin to Romany Biscuit, was 3rd twice in Points. Great-grandam, Brown Spider, won 8 Points and a Cheltenham Hunter Chase and placed 8, and great-great-grandam, Miss Muffet IV, won 3 Points. P-t-P '03 r4 p2; last, and pulled up 1. Displayed ability in his first season, and duly won a long Maiden in soft at Chipley Park in which the placed horses were all subsequently successful, but let down by woefully weak handling when a well supported favourite next time, and only went two miles when encountering a sound surface on his latest outing. Very much a family concern but likely to under-achieve unless a stronger pilot is sought. *The Atkinson Family (R. Atkinson) — Cattistock (Nicky Atkinson).* 121 (OMa), 197 (R), 323 (R), 687 (M), 966 (R).

MARTEENY ..9-11§.. 10 b.m. Teenoso (USA) — Marejo (Creetown) 6. Smallish owner-bred half-sister to Jupiter Jo (*qv*). NH FLAT '99/00 r3 p0. NH '00/1 and '03 r10 p0. P-t-P '03 r6 w2 (Maiden and Restricted) p1 (2nd); last, pulled up 1, and fell 1. A very poor performer under Rules, and displayed as much temperament as ability when recording a double in May last year, but only tried twice since, and has either suffered a setback or been covered. Needs to improve substantially to take a hand in Ladies if she returns to action. *J.B. & F.A. Walton — Border (Jimmy Walton).* 71 (L).

MARTHA JANE ..8-9.. 8 b.m. Syrtos — Just Hannah (Macmillion) 65fu5p. Tall workmanlike homebred half-sister to Mid Point Park, and to jumping winner, Banjo Hill. Dam, half-sister to Bold Charade (*qv* '02 Annual). Her 26 lengths last of five at Welbeck was not too bad and earned her a lowly rating, but running her in the Dudley Cup was bizarre (fell at the third), and her jumping can be most erratic. Sometimes partnered by a novice girl and finished one-and-a-half fences last with her on the latest completion. Could possibly spring a surprise if acquiring a better jockey than she has had so far. *Mrs J. Breeden — Albrighton Woodland.* 387 (OMa), 597 (2m5fOMa), 1016 (3m2fO), 1124 (OMa), 1339 (OMa), 1425 (OMa).

MARTHA'S BOY (IRE) ..10-8.. 14 b.g. Supreme Leader — Madame Martha (Carlingford Castle) 1p. Angular workmanlike brother to Martha Leader (IRE), and half-brother to Irish Pointing winner, Minstrel Madame. IRISH P-t-P '96 r2 p0 (pulled up, and fell). NH '01/2 r3 p0; pulled up 3. P-t-P/HUNT CH '97/8, '00 and '03 r11 w6 (inc 3 Hunt Chses, 3m-3m1f) p0; pulled up 1, and fell/unseated 4. A very rare gem, and remains unbeaten in seven completions, but sadly never able to scale the heights that once seemed attainable, and suffered another setback when splitting a shoe at Fontwell (the fifth race in succession in which he has been pulled up over regulation fences). Toyed with the opposition when successful at Higham, and retains stacks of ability, and has been confidently handled by David Dunsdon in recent times. *Mrs M. Robinson — Mid Surrey F.* 158 (CCon), 800 (3m2f110yH).

MARTIN OSSIE .9-9.. 8 b.g. Bonny Scot (IRE) — So We Know (Daring March) f. Tall workmanlike owner-bred. NH FLAT '02/3 r3 p0. NH '03 (for Dr P. Pritchard) r3 p0. Beaten 28 lengths plus at 50-1 plus in six attempts under Rules, but led from four out until headed and falling at the last in a Harkaway youngsters Maiden, and broke Julian Pritchard's collar-bone. The form of the race worked out well with the first three home all scoring at least once subsequently, and if Dick Baimbridge can get him back on the course he must be a certainty for a Maiden at least. *D. Smith — Berkeley (Dick Baimbridge).* 257 (CMa).

MARTY'S LAMP..7-11.. 10 b.m. Miner's Lamp — Marty's Round (Martinmas) 5p. Minscule half-sister to Lufah Wood and Albamart Wood (*qv*). Bought Ascot, Oct for 1142. Finished 42 lengths last on her belated debut, and showed some pace next time, but although she would probably like to be a racehorse her pony size is obviously going to stop her. *C. & Mrs R. Ivory — V.W.H. (Robyn Ivory).* 731 (OMa), 1074 (OMa).

MARZIBITS ..—.. 8 b.m. Alflora (IRE) — Trigony Hill VII (unknown) R. Big strong. Registered as half-bred (dam believed to be by Bronze Hill). Ducked out at the third in her Members. *M.S. & Miss A.P. Lee — V. of Lune H. (Carrie Ford).* 872 (M).

MASALARIAN (IRE) ..10-10.. 10 b.g. Doyoun — Masamiyda (Lyphard USA) 2p1213. Small. FRENCH FLAT '98/9 r4 w1 (12f) p3 (2nds). IRISH FLAT '01 r1 p0. IRISH NH '99/03 (for A.L.T. Moore) r24 w4 (3 2m-2m2fHdles and 2m Ch) p9. Classy enough to win a £15,070 Listed race at Chantilly, and beaten two lengths or less in three flat placings in France before moving on to Ireland where four wins to October '01 included a £41,935 prize in a Hurdle at Fairyhouse. Plenty of very good placed efforts include a four length second to Moscow Flyer at Punchestown in '01, and those who punted him from 16-1 to 9-2 in a Novice Riders event at Tweseldown were (in the light of what followed) rather unlucky not to collect, as he went ten lengths clear after two out but got tired and was headed on the run-in. Subsequently collected a four-runner Badbury Confined, and followed this welcome return to the winners enclosure with a victory over 2m5f at Folkestone two outings later (12-1). Not particularly consistent, and ended his season with 20 lengths third at Uttoxeter. Blinkered once in the past. A strong finisher at best and has earned over £92,000, and is thoroughly likeable. His partner Lucy Bridges is one of the most improved jockeys around. *Mrs H.M. & Miss L.H.D. Bridges - S. & W. Wilts.* 175 (Cnr), 348 (3mH), 860 (Cf), 1099 (L), 1443 (2m5fH), 1512 (2m6f110yH).

MASHWE (IRE) ..10-6.. 11 b.m. Samhoi (USA) — Glittering Steel (Golden Love) 2. Tall light-framed half-sister to Oflaherty's Babe (IRE) and Kinsale Florale (IRE) (lost 27 English Points between them). Dam won Irish Point. IRISH P-t-P '00 r6 w1 (5&6yo mares Maiden) p1 (2nd); pulled up 3, and unseated. P-t-P '02 (for Mr F. Crawford) r12 w4 (up to Confined, inc hat-trick) p3 (2 3rds); pulled up 3, and fell 2. Much improved in the second half of the '02 season, and came very close to notching a 5-timer, but has never appeared in consecutive years, and only managed one outing in '04. Showed she retains all her ability when a head second at Welbeck, and hopefully will be able to resume for a full campaign next year. Acts on fast ground. *H. & S. Thorp — Brocklesby (Harry Thorpe).* 592 (O).

MASITAT ..9-2.. 9 b.m. Gabitat — Grafton Maisey (Jimsun) pf. Small neat owner-bred half-sister to Shy Lizzie (*qv*). Novicey when tailed off and pulled after two miles on her debut, and fell three out when second but weakening next time. Possibly worth persevering with, as Love At Dawn was a late maturer, but there is some worry that having a sprinting sire will leave her short of stamina. *A.J. Mason — V.W.H.* 370 (OMa), 637 (CMam).

MASTER ADAM (IRE) .8-9.. 14 b.g. Noalto — Slaney Maid (Furry Glen) 4p32. Compact half-brother to Brook Cottage (IRE), and to Irish flat winner, Island Breeze. Dam, smart, half-sister to Slaney Prince (*qv* '94 Annual), won 7 flat, 7-8f, 6 in Ireland and one at Ascot. IRISH FLAT '95 r1 p0. IRISH NH FLAT '95 r1 p0. IRISH NH '95 and '98 r3 p0. IRISH P-t-P '99/00 r9 w3 (inc Adjacent) p3; pulled up 3. P-t-P '02/3 r10 w1 (Members) p0; last, pulled up 4, slipped up 1, fell 2, and brought down 1. Can jump boldly and bowl along in front provided the company is weak, but a consistently feeble finisher in England, and has only one win from 14 attempts to shout about. No match for the winner when attempting to retain his Members title in '04, and otherwise beaten a minimum of 30 lengths. *C.N. Edminson — Zetland (Kate Edminson).* 299 (L), 479 (L), 593 (L), 1286 (M).

MASTER CHIEF (IRE) ..8-7§.. 11 b/br.g. Euphemism — Shan's Lass (Mandalus) p3436p. Big rangy. Dam is half-sister to Merrydale Farm (*qv* '94 Annual). IRISH P-t-P '99/00 r11 p1 (11/ 3rd); pulled up 9, and fell. P-t-P '02 (for Mr T.R. Beadle) r5 p0 (last pair 2, and pulled up 3). NH '03 (for A. Turnell) r2 p1 (last of 3); and last. Only once better than last in his first 19 attempts, and collapsed after the race when tongue-tied and 104 lengths last of three on his final appearance under Rules, but has no stamina to speak of, and races too keenly to be of any use in Points. Wears a cross-noseband. *D.F. Donegan — Mid Surrey F. (Victoria Park).* 186 (OMa), 423 (CMa), 540 (CfMa), 802 (R), 1211 (OMa), 1442 (2m5fH).

MASTER CLUB ROYAL ..9-7§.. 10 b.g. Teenoso (USA) — Miss Club Royal (Avocat) 1312244. Tall workmanlike lengthy half-brother to Hurdles winners,, Club Royal and Another Club Royal, and to Chasing winner, Mister Club Royal. Dam won 2m3f Hurdle and 5 Chases (3m-3m3f). NH FLAT '00 r1 p0. NH '00/3 (for D. McCain) r24 p10 (Chses); pulled up 3, fell 1. Finished first in a 3m3f Amateur Chase at Sedgefield in November '02 on his 21st appearance, but was disqualified for having a banned substance in his sample. Definitely has ability as he showed when winning a Weston Park Maiden in which he tried to down tools after three out, and followed a reluctant six-and-a-quarter lengths third (favourite) by beating the dreaded Snitton West in a Restricted at Eaton Hall in which he made strenuous efforts to follow a loose horse out at the seventh. Showed his true colours afterwards and was second of three when 4-5 in an Intermediate and beaten 20 lengths when 2-5 in a match for his Members in which he was without his usual headgear. A severe challenge to his jockeys and they will be doing very well if they can cajole him home in front in future. At least he has no intention of ever falling. *D.A. Malam — Cheshire (Donald McCain Jnr).* 97 (CfMa), 530 (R), 715 (R), 876 (I), 1043 (M), 1202 (Cf), 1429 (Cnr).

MASTER CRUISE ..8-7.. 9 b.g. Zambrano — Miss Cruise (Cruise Missile) 45. Strong compact brother to Country Cruise. Dam, sister to Miss Shaw (*qv* '00 Annual), was a bad and blinkered Pointer for Mr Bowkett (failed to finish in 4 of 6 Points). NH '03 (for N.M. Babbage) r1 p0 (pulled up). Had the assistance of Julian Pritchard in both elders Maidens, but was well beaten with only one horse behind him, and would have to do better to score. *C. Bowkett — Ledbury (Nigel Ridout).* 1258 (OMa), 1395 (OMa).

MASTER GRASS ..9-8.. 10 b.g. Newski (USA) — Woody Isle (Precipice Wood) p5. Sturdy half-brother to Wood Buzzard (*qv*). Dam raced for Alex Mason. P-t-P '02/3 r10 w1 (Maiden) p4 (3rds, of 4 twice);

4th, pulled up 2, and fell 2. Successful at Dunthrop on his first completion last year, but beaten a minimum of 12 lengths in Restricteds, and presumably stumped up by the prevailing firm ground when not disgraced at Didmarton. Tends to jump indifferently. *A.J. Mason — V.W.H.* 169 (R), 369 (R).

MASTER JAY JAY (IRE) ..—.. 9 b.g. Jolly Jake (NZ) — Hay Party (Party Mink) ppp. Rangy brother to Jolly Jack (IRE) (*qv*). Pulled up after a maximum of two miles thrice, and jumped badly and immediately struggling when only going a mile on his latest attempt. Useless. *Mrs C.M. Righton — Farmers Bloodhounds.* 295 (OMa), 370 (OMa), 731 (OMa).

MASTER JOCK ..10-4.. 11 ch.g. Scottish Reel — Mistress Corrado (New Member) u4105p. Strong-topped attractive half-brother to Master Will, Gunnabeallright and Mistress Return. Dam, sister to Members Rights, pulled up in 2 Points for Peter Burke. Grandam, Mistress Rights, was bad 3rd and fell twice in Points. Great-grandam, Flaming Fiddler, was a poor Pointer. P-t-P/HUNT CH '99/00 and '02/3 r10 w5 (inc 3m Hunt Ch) p3 (2nds, of 3 once); and 4th twice. Successful in five of seven Points, and added a Stratford Hunter Chase last year, but nowhere near his best in '04, and gained his only win in a bad Novice Riders event on patchy ground at Tweseldown. Beaten around 50 lengths in the Aintree Foxhunters where he would have found the trip much too sharp, but never went a yard on unsuitably fast ground on his latest appearance, and hopefully not going to be tarnished for good. Goes well fresh and could return to 10-10 if of a mind to in '05, but has never been particularly easy to train. *P.S. Burke — N. Ledbury (Paul Jones).* 209 (3m1f110yH), 435 (3m110yH), 626 (Cnr), 732 (2m5f110yH), 1172 (3m1f110yH), 1512 (2m6f110yH).

MASTER LORD (IRE) .—.. 9 b.g. Mister Lord (USA) — Abandon Rose (Crozier) p. Tall lengthy. P-t-P '03 r2 p0 (pulled up 2). Yet to display much in the way of ability, and enters his third campaign with precious little experience under his belt. Needs to eradicate jumping errors if he is ever to get competitive. *Miss A.M. Jepson — S. Notts (Holly Campbell).* 226 (CfMa).

MASTER OF FASHION ..—.. 9 ch.g. Triune — Fashion Princess (Van Der Linden FR) pppp. Lengthy half-brother to Von Trapp. Dam, half-sister to Parte Prima (*qv*), won 2 2m1f-2m3f Sell Hdles (both on hard). NH FLAT '01 (for S.G. Knight) r2 p0. Well tailed off in two bumpers in '01 (beat one), and surely physically defective from the appalling way he performed in Points (blinkered in latest three). *S.J. Williams — Tetcott.* 194 (CfMa), 312 (CfMa), 474 (OMa), 568 (CfMa).

MASTER WOOD ..10-4.. 14 b.g. Wonderful Surprise — Miss Wood (Precipice Wood) 275p. Compact good-topped. Dam won Members, and subsequently won 2m Hurdle and 3 Chases (2m-2m4f), and is half-sister to Brabiner Rambler (*qv* '94 Annual). NH '97/00, '02 and '03 r34 w8 (2m4f-3m1f Chses, inc hat-trick '98) p3 (2 3rds); pulled up 9, fell 2. HUNT CH '03 r5 w2 (2m6f-3m1f) p2 (2nds, of 3 once); and unseated 1. A grand campaigner, and ended a losing run spanning 26 months (though did not run at all in '01) when beating Torduff Express at Haydock last year, but deteriorated markedly in '04, and clearly coming to the end of a long career that has seen him score seven times at Wetherby. Has earned nearly £65,000 and owes connections nothing. *C. Grant — S. Durham.* 122 (3m1fH), 179 (2m6fH), 992 (3m3f110yH), 1296 (3m1fH).

MATRIX (AUS) ..—.. 8 b.g. Centaine (AUS) — Iced Lass (NZ) (Half Iced USA) u. Good-topped compact. NH FLAT '02 r2 p0. NH '02/3 (for K.C. Bailey) r4 p0. Beaten 26 lengths plus since his debut in a bumper, but was backed from 5s to 3s in a youngsters Maiden at Maisemore only to crash into a faller and unseat three out when attempting to get into contention (from the way the race panned out would surely have done so). Seems to have a little ability, but gets very few chances. Having failed in his quest to find a dominatrix, the owner settled for Matrix. *Lord Leigh & Partners — Heythrop (Nigel Ridout).* 724 (OMa).

MAYBE A DOUBLE .9-5.. 7 b.m. El Conquistador — Givusashot (Gunner B) 51245. Small owner-bred. P-t-P '03 r3 p1 (3rd); refused, and pulled up. Left clear when a potential danger fell fatally two out at Bishops Court, but has struggled to get home since, and needs to find some extra stamina for Restricteds. Has two handlers. Wears a cross-noseband. *The Havashotts Partnership (Miss M. Taylor) — Portman (Ali Tory).* 120 (OMa), 329 (OMa), 473 (R), 879 (R), 1069 (R).

MAYDAY GIRL .8-9§.. 7 gr.m. Weld — May Day Belle (Scallywag) puf. Very small. Dam, sister to Lovely Rascal, and half-sister to Owenweld (*qv* '03 Annual). P-t-P '03 r3 p0 (last, and pulled up 2). A headstrong midget, and twice misbehaved at the start prior to breaking her off-hind in a fall at Tabley. D. Raynor — Pendle Forest & Craven (Paul Grindrod). 532 (OMa), 714 (CMam), 754 (OMa).

MAZURY (USA) ..9-7.. 6 b.g. Langfuhr (CAN) — Assurgent (USA) (Damascus USA) u4. Lengthy good-topped half-brother to eight winners in USA. 40,000y. Dam won at 7f in USA. FLAT '01/2 r12 w1 (8f) p3. NH '03 r7 p0; pulled up 1. Gained four prizes on the flat consecutively from his second outing onwards, and scored on the all-weather as well as finishing a neck second to Londolozi Lad (*qv*), but beaten 25 lengths plus over Hurdles including in a Seller. Does not help himself by pulling hard, but after unseating three out when still second in his Members he finished over a fence behind in last in a Ladies at Ystradowen where he was totally unsuited by the twisty switch-back track. Does not look an ideal Pointer, and might do better to have another go at Selling Hurdles. *Miss J.P.S. Davis — Beaufort.* 364 (M), 737 (L).

MCGINTY ALL STARS (IRE) ..—.. 7 b.m. Fourstars Allstar (USA) — Dowdstown Miss (Wolver Hollow) fpu*06*. Small narrow sister to Irish Hurdling winner, Dowdstown Star, half-sister to Legal Artist (IRE), and to Bitofabuzz (IRE), and to 3 winners in USA. Dam, half-sister to Strong Gale, won twice at up to 12f in USA. NH FLAT '02 r1 p0. NH FLAT '04 r1 p0 (14th over 2m at Worcester: *hld up & bhnd, hdwy 7f out, rdn & wknd over 3f out*). NH '04 (for R.J. Price) r1 p0 (6th in 2m3f110y Hdle: *a bhnd, t.o*). Fell or unseated in two of her three Maidens including when backed from 6s-3s in the first of them, and almost did so on the other occasion but the jockey somehow wrestled her back from the ground. An unpleasant ride who seems to be devoid of ability. *A. McCubbing — Ross H.* 409 (CMam), 619 (2m4fOMa), 725 (OMa).

MEADOWS BOY .—§§.. 13 gr.g. Derrylin — What A Coup (Malicious) rprp. Strong half-brother to Coup De Catherine, Whats Money and In The Spirit. Dam won 2m4f Hdle and 6 3m Chses. NH FLAT '98 r3 p0. NH '99/03 (for B. Palling, and R. Lee) r29 w2 (2m4f-2m5f Hdles) p3 (inc 3rd in Ch); refused to race 5, fell/unseated 4, pulled up 1. FLAT '03 r4 p0. Famously intractable at the start and did not consent to win a race until he was ten, but also fell at the last when five lengths clear once and was 30 lengths ahead when unseating at the same obstacle once. Made four appearances in Chases and was 17 lengths third to Ad Hoc, but last, unseated and left in the other ventures and made his final 21 appearances under Rules over Hurdles. Tried tongue-tied twice, blinkered thrice, and with a hood and cheekpieces once. Every effort was made to try and sweeten him and even given four spins on the flat in '03, but dwelt in three of them. Refused to race on five occasions, and probably withdrawn by the starter on others. Wholly predictable in Points and would not set off at all twice, whilst he was also very slowly away twice and having reached the final fence and inherited a remote second at Eaton Hall Alastair Beedles wisely pulled him up as he was exhausted. If he has not already been banned then he should be. *E.W. Tuffin — United (Rachel Williams).* 254 (O), 528 (O), 1113 (Cf), 1145 (O).

MEADOWS PRINCE (IRE) ..8-0§§.. 6 b.g. Alzao (USA) — Anita Via (IRE) (Anita's Prince) Rf44p. Compact. NH FLAT '03 (for B. Palling) r1 p0. Immediately displayed a thoroughly unpleasant temperament, and ran out and unseated at the fifth and fell at the second (unruly in the paddock) on his first two starts. Has worn cheekpieces or blinkers since and continued to show a high degree of reluctance (beaten 15 lengths at least with one horse behind him), and should be given a very wide berth. *R.W.J. & Mrs S.M. Willcox — Llangeinor (Roger Willcox).* 66 (OMa), 119 (OMa), 453 (CfMa), 619 (2m4fOMa), 700 (CfMa).

PLATE 79 426 Tynedale Confined: L to R, Meander (Jeremy Mactaggart), 1st, and French Cedar (Will Ramsay), fell, ahead of hidden Clifford Bay (Nicola Stirling), 2nd, Red Gauntlet (Kevin Anderson), 3rd, and Piper's Rock (Vicky Russell), ur, Trivial (Luke Morgan), 4th, is behind PHOTO: Alan Mitchell

MEANDER (IRE) ..10-3.. 10 br.g. Mandalus — Lady Rerico (Pamroy) 5613. Big strong brother to Paddy For Paddy (IRE) (*qv*). IR40,000y. NH FLAT '00 r2 p0. NH '00/3 (for Miss H.C. Knight) r9 w1 (3m1f Ch) p2 (2nds). Won a three-finisher Southwell Chase by a distance in December '01 after the six-length leader had fallen two out, and also second twice at two-and-a-half lengths maximum, but was trounced on his final four attempts under Rules and broke a blood vessel at least once. Has never failed to complete the course and benefited from first time cheekpieces when winning a Confined at Corbridge, and then a reasonable third in an Open, but four outings in a year is about all he can manage, and not seen since March. Connections did well to get him back to form following his lean spell. *Mrs I.J.B. Sole — Jedforest (Kate MacTaggart).* 72 (O), 133 (L), 426 (Cf), 551 (O).

MECCA PRINCE (IRE) ..9-12§.. 10 ch.g. Shalford (IRE) — Fashion Parade (Mount Hagen FR) p4p343. Close-coupled half-brother to 3 flat winners (one in Ireland, and one in Holland). NH '98/9 r5 p0; pulled up 2. P-t-P/HUNT CH '00 and '02/3 r19 w4 (up to Confined) p7 (6 2nds, short-head last once, of 3 thrice; 3rd of 4 once); 4th twice, 5th, pulled up 4, and fell 1. A weak finisher, and is unsuited by easy surfaces, but failed to score for the first time in four Pointing campaigns in '04. Blinkered once in '98, and put more effort into his last outing when tried in cheekpieces than before, but needs to seek out the easiest opportunities in order to win again. *J.W. Tudor — Llangeinor.* 208 (Cf), 359 (Cf), 447 (Cf), 671 (I), 952 (I), 1484 (O).

MEENTAGH LOCH ..9-7.. 8 ch.g. Never So Bold — Miss Pisces (Salmon Leap USA) 1. Lengthy half-brother to Blue Marlin, Young Saffy and Berties Landing, and to NH flat winner, Suffolk Girl. Dam won at 7f. Made a winning start in a Geldings Maiden at Eaton Hall, and the form of the race received several boosts when four who finished behind him went on to score. Not seen again, but would certainly look to have potential for Restricteds when fit. A first success in the saddle for Jonathan Jarrett. *Miss H. Brookshaw — N. Salop.* 709 (Mah).

MEL IN BLUE (FR) ..10-10.. 7 b.g. Pistolet Bleu (IRE) — Calligraphie (FR) (R B Chesne) 1. Medium-sized attractive half-brother to Opal'lou (FR) (*qv*). NH FLAT '02 (for N.J. Henderson) r1 w1. Won a 23-runner Newbury bumper in which ten lengths covered the first ten home, and reappeared two years later in an Intermediate at Weston Park. Backed from 6-1 to 5-2 and caught the eye in the paddock, and led throughout the final two miles and kept galloping to record a time very similar to Bay Island in the Open and Ask The Natives in the Ladies. His stable were under a cloud in the following weeks and unfortunately failed to reappear, but gives the impression that he would be an achiever under Rules if his health permitted. *R. Waley-Cohen — Warwicks.* 92 (I).

MELITMA .—.. 10 gr.g. Gods Solution — Melsil (Silly Prices) u*pp5p*. NH '04 r4 (to Jun '04 p0 (pulled up in Hdle: *nt jw, a bhnd, t.o & pu 2 out*; 5th in 2m5f110y Hdle: *a bhnd, blun 2 out, t.o*; pulled up in Hdle: *in tch til wknd 7, t.o & pu 4 out*; and pulled up in Hdle: *in tch til wknd 6, t.o & pu 3 out*). Unseated at the second in a Maiden, and subsequently 60 lengths fifth and pulled up three times when sent off at very long odds in Hurdles. No use for racing purposes. *G.R.S. Nixon — Buccleuch.* 165 (OMa).

MEMSAHIB KI BEHAN ..8-6.. 9 b.m. Catch The Thatch — Occatillo (Maris Piper) 4p4. Workmanlike lengthy owner-bred half-sister to Hurdles winners, Holkham Bay and Memsahib Ofesteem (latter also won NH flat). Dam pulled up 2, and fell 2 in Points. NH FLAT '01 r1 p0. NH '01 r1 p0 (pulled up). P-t-P '02/3 r4 p0 (last, pulled up 1, ran out 1, and unseated 1). Has shown some speed, but beaten a minimum of 31 lengths when completing, and does not appear to possess sufficient stamina. *Mrs F.P.J. Coole — Granta H. (Martin Ward).* 561 (OMa), 833 (OMa), 996 (CMam).

MENANTOL ..9-8.. 10 br.g. Landyap (USA) — Menabilly (Sit In The Corner USA) p1p122. Workmanlike lengthy. Dam is half-sister to Menadarva (*qv* '92 Annual). Grandam, won 3 Points and 3rd twice. Great-grandam, Fort Lodge, won 3 Chses, 2 Hunter Chases and 15 Points and placed 10. P-t-P '02/3 r9 p1 (3rd); last pair 3, pulled up 4, and fell 1. Previously very moderate and beaten a minimum of 20 lengths over the full trip, but readily outbattled the infamous Northsprite to spring a 25-1 surprise at Kimble, and followed up in a bad three-runner Restrcited at Lifton. Has hardly had to improve by much, and will find matters altogether more taxing in competitive events, but connections have done well to unearth what they already have. *Mrs L.J.C. Tylor - Cury.* 82 (OMa), 871 (OMa), 1102 (R), 1352 (R), 1544 (I), 1564 (I).

MENSCH (IRE) ..10-6.. 9 ch.g. Husyan (USA) — Floating Dollar (Master Owen) 12pp1*8215*. Small angular half-brother to 3 winners over jumps. IR8800 3yo. IRISH P-t-P '00 r1 p0 (fell). NH '01/2 r5 p0; unseated 1. NH '03 r1 p0 (pulled up). P-t-P/HUNT CH '03 r4 w2 (Maiden and Restricted) p1 (2nd in Hunt Ch); and 4th. NH '04 (for E. Williams) r4 w1 (beat Ah Yeah $1^1/_2$*l* in 3m1f110y Ch: *blun 3, mist 6, bhnd til hdwy 10, went 2nd 14, ld app 3 out, drvn out*) p1 (2*l* 2nd to Sunshan in 3m Ch: *hld up, hdwy 11, ld 4 out til pckd nxt, one pce*); last of 8 in 3m2f Hdle: *prom, ld til hdd u.p app 3 out, sn wknd, t.o*; and last of 5 in 3m1f110y Ch: *hld up & bhnd, mist 15, sn btn*. Has a good record in minor Points, and will battle gamely on his day, but can handle fast ground and is already carving out a niche for himself under Rules with his most recent Pointing pilot. Has only fallen once, but liable to make blunders over big fences, and always has the hurdling option to fall back on if he needs to now. Blinkered once in '02, and has often worn cheekpieces since. *P. Morgan — Llangeinor (Richard Williams).* 19 (CMod), 116 (I), 177 (3mH), 360 (O), 447 (Cf).

MERLIN CIDER ..—.. 7 b.m. Un Desperado (FR) — Millers Venture (Sunyboy) p. Dam, half-sister to Dawn's Cognac (*qv*). Bought Doncaster, Aug '02 for 1300. Clueless in an early February Maiden, in which she promptly lost touch and pulled up at halfway. *R. Oliver — Four Burrow (Terance Oliver).* 149 (OMa).

MERLIN MEG ..8-12.. 6 b.m. Executive Perk — Icy Gunner (Gunner B) u2. Compact. Dam, half-sister to Chill Factor (*qv* '03 Annual). Bought Doncaster, Aug for 3100. A close second when a terrible mistake at the 11th shot the rider from the saddle on her debut, and again showed ability when one-and-a-half lengths second next time in early March, but like the winner and three of the other six contestants failed to reappear. Should be able to take a Mares Maiden if sound, and hopefully has not paid the high price of racing on firmish at Black Forest Lodge where the ground is worryingly unforgiving unless topped up by masses of recent rain. *R. Oliver — Four Burrow (Terance Oliver).* 309 (2m4fOMa), 416 (CMam).

MERLINS BAY (IRE) ..9-0.. 11 b.g. Nearly A Nose (USA) — Kabarda (Relkino) 34. Lengthy workmanlike half-brother to NH flat winner, Dunnet Head and Irish Hurdling winner, Delgany Toulon. NH FLAT '98 /02 (for J.T. Gifford, and J.F. Panvert) r12 p0; pulled up 5, fell/unseated 2. Showed next to nothing under Rules and only beat two in 11 of his 12 races over jumps including Selling Hurdles, and Chases (26 lengths fourth of five and pulled up). A hard puller who raced prominently in Maidens, but weakened tamely in the closing stages of both. Has only made seven appearances since '99, and like the two horses above seemed to be stumped up after a visit to Black Forest Lodge (in his case only lasted until early February). *R. Heard — Modbury H.* 66 (OMa), 149 (OMa).

MERLOTS MYSTERY (IRE) ..—.. 7 ch.g. Presenting — Lovely Run (Deep Run) p. Dam won NH flat and 2m2f Hurdle in Ireland. Tailed off and pulled up after 2m4f at Parham in late March. Has the right sort of pedigree, and potentially interesting. *S.C. Robinson — Mid Surrey F. (Gina Weare).* 644 (OMa).

MERRY CHRISTMAS ..9-9.. 12 ch.m. Handsome Sailor — Merry Jane (Rymer) 5. Narrow half-sister to Merry Scorpion and Merry Noelle. Dam won 6 2m-2m6f Hurdles. NH FLAT '97 r1 p0. NH '98/01 r11 p1 (3rd); pulled up 5, fell 1. P-t-P '02 r3 w2 (Members 3 ran, 2 finished and 3-runner Club Mares) p0; and pulled up 1. Made virtually all to record a double in holding ground at Eaton Hall in '02, but clearly suffered a setback when favourite next time, and missed the following year altogether. Reappearing for the first time in almost exactly 24 months when blowing up in the final half-mile of her Members and promptly went back into hiding. *Mrs J. Owen — Flint & Denbigh.* 708 (M).

MERRY MAJOR .—§.. 12 br.g. K-Battery — Merry Missus (Bargello) 6pp. Workmanlike owner-bred half-brother to Finest Of Men (*qv*). NH FLAT '97 r1 p0. NH '99/00 r3 p0; fell in both Chases. P-t-P/HUNT CH '98/9 and '01/2 (for Mr J.B. Walton) r13 w1 (Maiden) p7 (6 2nds, of 3 once; and 3rd of 4); last pair 2, pulled up 2, and fell. Finally delivered the goods at the 15th attempt when cruising home at Hexham in '02, and does not lack stamina, but has been troubled with a fibrillating heart in the past and will not entertain a struggle. Refused to exert himself in the new yard, and his 9-10 rating has been withdrawn. Wears a cross-noseband. *Mrs P. Tollit — Worcs.* 614 (R), 1014 (M), 1389 (R).

MERRY MELODY ..9-3.. 10 b.m. Almoojid — Merry Marigold (Sonnen Gold) 632p. Good-bodied. Dam won 3 flat, 6-12f. FLAT '98/9 r5 p0. NH '99 (for R.J. Hodges) r1 p0 (pulled up). Tailed off in a Seller in her final flat race and pulled up in one Hurdle, and disappeared for five years. Mysteriously started favourite for her first Maiden but could only finish last, and again failed to beat another horse when a fence behind in her Members, but did better when eight lengths second in a Mares Maiden. Might have had a chance of collecting a similar contest, but pulled up and dismounted after a mile at Cothelstone and had to be removed by the horse ambulance. *P. Browne, J. Apps, P. Norman, N. Canes, & R. Harroway — W. Somerset V. (Sarah Robinson).* 274 (CfMa), 878 (M), 1182 (CMam), 1371 (OMa).

MERRY MINSTREL (IRE) .9-0.. 12 b.g. Black Minstrel — Merry Lesa (Dalesa) ffp3p70p. Tall lengthy brother to Irish Pointing winner, Not Too Dusty, and half-brother to top class Chasing winner, Merry Gale (IRE) (won 18 races and £305,509) (also won 2 Points there), and to Irish Hurdling winner, Laughing Lesa. Dam won 2m Hurdle and Open in Ireland. IRISH P-t-P '99/01 r5 w1 (7yo&up Maiden) p2. IRISH HUNT CH '00 r3 p0. IRISH NH '00/1 (for Miss L. Wood) r9 w2 (2m-2m2f Ch) p2; fell/unseated 2. NH '02/3 (for C.J. Mann) r6 w1 (2m1f Ch) p3; pulled up 2, and fell 1. Was in good heart when winning four races on ground ranging from soft to firm until '01, but fell or unseated thrice and was let down by bad mistakes on other occasions. Never ran over further than 2m5f since

'00, and predictably failed to stay in Points, in which he usually has two paddock handlers, and has been taken to post early. Truly dismal these days, and apart from when finishing 30 lengths third of four he has never bettered last in his ten most recent attempts. Deserves retirement. *J.T.B. Hunt — Pytchley (Carol Elderton).* 1 (C), 158 (CCon), 381 (O), 556 (Cf), 783 (M), 997 (O), 1168 (2m5fH), 1468 (C).

MERRY SHOT (IRE) ..9-6.. 13 b.g. Cataldi — Borgina (Boreen FR) r2pp34. Strong half-brother to I Will Survive (IRE). NH FLAT '97 r2 w1 p0. NH '98/9 r10 p3 (2nds in Chses); pulled up 5. P-t-P/HUNT CH '00 and '02/3 r16 w1 (Intermediate) p3 (2 2nds, of 3 once; and 3rd of 4); last 3, pulled up 9. Got off the mark over jumps at the 24th attempt when springing a 20-1 surprise at Woodford last year, but has only beaten two rivals since, and was not produced anywhere near fit enough in '04. Only effective on sound surfaces. Blinkered latterly in the previous yard. *C.A. Green — S. & W. Wilts.* 263 (O), 460 (C), 576 (O), 863 (MO), 1097 (M), 1451 (3mH).

MERVSINTROUBLE .9-1§.. 8 b.g. Primitive Rising (USA) — Bodfari (Lighter) sp3R2p. Small well-made. Dam, half-sister to Lixwm (*qv* '99 Annual), won 7 Points (inc 3 Opens) and placed 8 for Mr Morris, (a diabolical jumper in Hunter Chases, and became most irresolute latterly). NH FLAT '01 r1 p0 (last). P-t-P '02/3 r9 p2 (2 fences 2nd of 3; and remote last of 3); disqualified from Maiden win for taking a lead from a mounted steward once; last, pulled up 4, and fell 1. Plodded reluctantly into ten lengths second at Eyton, but all his form is over 2m4f, and is utterly useless when racing over further. Liable to dart off the track without warning, but went lame at Chaddesley, and connections may not have to worry about where to place him in future. Wears cheekpieces, and was visored twice in '02. *P.H. Morris & M. Tomlinson — Tanatside (Peter Morris).* 97 (CfMa), 533 (2m4fCfMa), 929 (2m4fOMa), 1049 (2m4fOMa), 1266 (2m4fOMa), 1339 (OMa).

MERV'S MAGIC ..—§§.. 10 gr.g. Daily Sport Soon — Judy's Dowry (Dragonara Palace USA) pfR. Heavy-topped half-brother to flat winner, Gay Breeze. Dam won 3 flat, 5-8f (2 Sells) and 3 2m Hurdles (2 Sells). 3000 4yo. NH FLAT '01 r1 p0. NH '02 (for R.J. Baker) r1 p0 (unseated). Broke a blood vessel in both a bumper and a Hurdle (in which he unseated at the fifth after some bad jumping; 100-1), and pulled up at the second, fell at the first and ran out at the third (after dwelling and clambering over the first two; retraced but refused at the same fence) in Points. A total barmpot and connections deserve a severe rap over the knuckles for taking him to the racecourse in such a state. *Mrs S. Rowe — Tiverton Stag (Michael Sweetland).* 1326 (OMa), 1380 (OMa), 1510 (O).

MIAHEYYUN ..8-11.. 9 b.g. Bonny Scot (IRE) — Daunt Not (Kalaglow) 48. Compact. NH FLAT '00 r2 p1 (3rd). NH '00/1 (for B.J. Llewellyn) r5 p0. NH '04 (to June '04; for C. Roberts) r1 p0 (8th in 2m110y Sell Hdle: *hld up, hdwy 5, wknd nxt, t.o*). Completed a miserable day for the Welsh contingent at Clifton-on-Dunsmore, where stablemate Charlestown Lass crashed into the wing of the last when poised to land a monster coup, whilst he was supported from 7s-3s but never looked like recouping the losses and finished 26 lengths fourth in a Maiden. Apart from an 11 lengths third has never been placed, and usually wears a tongue-tie and has been blinkered or worn cheekpieces on three occasions. Unimproved by a switch to Selling Hurdles in the summer, and was tailed off each time, being pulled up in the final two. Has only sent out negative vibes. *Mrs T. O'Toole — Banwen Miners (John Moore).* 1124 (OMa).

MICKTHECUTAWAY (IRE) ..10-0.. 13 b.g. Rontino — Le-Mu-Co (Varano) 1f4u3p. Tall lengthy half-brother to Irish Genius (IRE). IRISH P-t-P '97/8 r9 w2 (Hunt, and Winners of 2) p1 (3rd); pulled up 2, and fell/unseated 3 (at last with every chance once). IRISH NH '97/8 r5 p2 (Hunt Chses). P-t-P/HUNT CH '99/00 (for Mr & Mrs A.J. Brazier) r13 w5 (inc 2m7f110y Hunt Ch and 2 Opens) p7 (5 2nds, of 3 once; 2 3rds, inc Hunt Ch); and ran out 1. NH '00/3 (for Mrs H. Dalton) r15 w5 (2m4f110y-3m1f Chses) p3 (2nds); fell/unseated 3, pulled up 1. A strong galloper in mud, and made a very successful transition to racing under Rules in England, and had gone up by 35lb in the ratings after recording his fifth and final Handicap success over a 14-month period to March '02. Returned to Points in a triumphant manner at Barbury, where he got up in the last strides to provide Dan Skelton with a winner on his first ride, but has always had his quirks, and the combination did not gel again. Fell at the last with victory assured at Weston Park, but never went a yard next time, and bolted going to the first and unseated at Towcester before suffering a career-ending injury at Cheltenham. Always at his very best when fresh. *D. Skelton — Worcs.* 32 (Cnr), 229 (O), 465 (O), 891 (3m1fH), 1029 (3mH), 1170 (4m1fH).

MICKY MANSIONS (IRE) ..9-12.. 11 gr.g. Phardante (FR) — Reneagh (Prince Regent FR) 2. Well-made attractive half-brother to Irish NH flat winner, Rendari (IRE). Dam, half-sister to Vicosa (*qv*), won at 5f in Ireland, and won 2 2m Hdles there. IRISH P-t-P '00 r2 p0 (unseated 1, and brought down 1). P-t-P/HUNT CH '01/3 r7 w1 (Maiden) p2 (3rds, of 4 once); pulled up 3, fell 2. A catalogue of disasters in his first five attempts, but had always shown ability, and bolted up on the first occasion he encountered a sound surface. Headstrong and does not stay when conditions are testing, but only able to run once apiece '03/4, and exposure to fast ground is clearly having an adverse effect. *W.M. Aitchison — Border (Joanne Martin).* 507 (I).

PLATE 80 1463 Dulverton Farmers Mens Open: Midnight Coup and recent Martin Pipe stable amateur, Guy Weatherley *PHOTO: Nick Jay*

MIDNIGHT COUP.9-11§.. 9 br.g. First Trump — Anhaar (Ela-Mana-Mou) 12d45312234. Small strong-topped half-brother to Son Of Anshan (*qv*), to flat winner, Half Inch, to flat and Hurdles winner, Ellamine, to Irish Hurdling winner, Four Aces, and to a German jumping winner. IRISH FLAT '98/9 r9 w2 (14-16f) p2 (3rds). IRISH NH '99/01 (for G.T. Hourigan) r8 p0; pulled up 1. FLAT '01/3 r18 w2 (14-15f) p1 (3rd). NH '02/3 (for B.G. Powell) r12 w1 (2m Hdle) p2 (inc 2nd at Les Landes). Bought Ascot, Jul for 2857. Won two Irish flat races to June '99, but his only subsequent wins until the current campaign were gained on the cliff tops at Les Landes in Jersey where he appreciated the firm ground and could toy with modest rivals. Tried English Sellers without success, and was tongue-tied twice, and regularly equipped with blinkers or cheekpieces latterly (again wore headgear in Points). A ultra-safe jumper who would hate to fall and has completed in all 13 attempts over fences, and was up to winning his Members (four ran) and a Flete Park Confined (six ran), but dogs it far more often than not and defeats included when second of three and when sent off at 8-11 in a match. Handles firm surfaces, but must always be regarded as highly unreliable for betting purposes. *D. Williams — Silverton (David Pipe).* 61 (M), 144 (Cf), 200 (Cf), 320 (Cf), 412 (Cf), 1005 (Cf), 1194 (Cf), 1349 (O), 1434 (MO), 1463 (O).

MIDNIGHT COWBOY..9-3.. 12 ch.g. Gunner B — Expletive (Shiny Tenth) 331p. Lengthy half-brother to Out Of The Blue and Derry Blue. Dam won 8 flat, 5-12f (the first a Sell; won 3 at Leicester aged 7). NH '00 r3 p0. P-t-P '03 r4 p0 (5th, last, and pulled up 2). Completely tailed off over hurdles, but resumed last year after a three-year break, and followed two fair thirds (where he was in front between the last two fences in both) with a narrow but game success at Dingley. Predictably burnt off by Franco next time, and will find it difficult to upgrade successfully, but considering he has had foot problems, and was bought for next to nothing in '01, the owner deserves great credit in turning round what looked a hopeless case. *Mrs A.E. Lee — Cambridge Univ.* 887 (CfMa), 1061 (OMa), 1218 (OMa), 1400 (CN).

MIDNIGHT ECLIPSE (IRE) ..—.. 6 b.g. Midnight Legend — Bridge Delight (Idiot's Delight) p. Dam, sister to Skip 'N' Time (won 5 Points and 2 Hunter Chases for Messrs Rose & Miller). Bought Ascot, Jun for 3809. Given an easy time before pulling up after two miles on a mid-March debut. *M.S. Rose — Portman (Richard Miller).* 469 (2m4fOMa).

MIDNIGHT EMPEROR (IRE) ..—.. 10 b.g. Supreme Leader — Calfstown Night (Bargello) p. Well-made half-brother to Gortroe Guy (IRE) (*qv*). NH FLAT '99 and '01 r3 p1 (2nd). NH '01 (for R.J. Hodges) r10 p3; fell 2, pulled up 1. A frustrating maiden who was second of 20 in a bumper and beaten between five and nine lengths in three placings over Hurdles, but a poor jumper of fences when fifth of six, last, pulled up and falling twice. Disappeared for three years, and broke a knee at Bishops Court and destroyed on his comeback run. H.S. Channon & Messrs Hughes, Elford, Sleep & Bower — Lamerton (Yvonne Watson & Jo Channon). 325 (OMa).

MIDNIGHT LORD (IRE) ..9-8.. 8 b.g. Mister Lord (USA) — Friary Town (IRE) (Barbarolli USA) u212. Dam won 2m Hurdle in Ireland. IRISH P-t-P '02/3 r7 p3 (3rds); pulled up 3, and ran out 1. Placed four times in his first nine Points including a creditable three lengths second at Tweseldown, and provided Jay Pemberton with a memorable first ride over fences when he won a 15-runner Maiden at Penshurst in holding ground. It was a slowly-run contest taking 7min30s (considerably the slowest time of the day), and none of those who finished behind managed to score. A disappointing favourite when ten lengths last of two on the same course next time. Probably going to prove to be very one-paced, although a long race at somewhere like Parham in mud might suit. *N. Benstead — Kent & Surrey Bloodhounds.* 424 (CMa), 627 (OMa), 782 (OMa), 1084 (R).

MIDNIGHT MOON ..9-0.. 10 b.g. Jupiter Island — Nunswalk (The Parson) 577f. Compact attractive half-brother to North Pass, Mariner's Walk, Nuns Cone, Nunson, Nuns Toy Boy and Nuns Best Friend, and to Hurdles winners, Nuns Royal and Nuns Jewel. Dam won Sell Hdle and Ch, both 2m. IRISH P-t-P '00 r1 p0 (pulled up). IRISH NH '00 r3 p0 (tailed off). NH '00 and '02 r4 p0. P-t-P '03 r3 p0 (last, fell 1, and brought down 1). Useless in a variety of races for four different trainers, and broke his neck in a third-fence fall at Corbridge. Mrs E.M. Horn & T. Penrose — Rockwood H. (Jason Burley). 112 (OMa), 166 (OMa), 271 (OMa), 430 (R).

MIDNIGHT REIVER ..7-2.. 7 b.m. Mutamarrid — Reprieve (Riberetto) u6p. Strong owner-bred. Tailed off on her only completion, and stopped to nil after errors and pulled up at the 13th on her latest attempt. Always wears a tongue-tie, and looks troubled. *Mrs E. Fletcher — Lauderdale (Joan Hollands).* 215 (OMa), 920 (2m4fOMa), 1042 (CMam).

MID SUMMER LARK (IRE) .10-7.. 9 b.g. Tremblant — Tuney Blade (Fine Blade USA) p7pR21. Big plain half-brother to Wild Blade (IRE) (*qv*). IRISH P-t-P '02 r3 p1 (2nd); pulled up 1. P-t-P '03 (for Mrs A.R. Thompson) r3 p0 (4th, and 5th twice). Five lengths second on the west coast of Ireland once in '02, but beaten a minimum of 17 lengths in his first seven starts since crossing the water, and had got Lynsey Kendall into all sorts of bother. Finally ironed out by Miles Seston and the application of a visor, and made all to secure the spoils in the Heart at Hexham on his latest appearance. Hung right on the run-in, but had run second at Carlisle a fortnight earlier and there seemed no fluke to his success, and whilst clearly never going to be an easy ride should enjoy further success if the partnership can be maintained. *Mrs A.J. McMath — Cumberland (Ian McMath).* 341 (R), 432 (OMa), 766 (R), 919 (CMa), 1028 (3mH), 1178 (3m1fH).

MIDY'S RISK (FR) ..9-0.. 8 gr.g. Take Risks (FR) — Martine Midy (FR) (Lashkari) p6p5p. Small neat half-brother to French flat winners, Sierra Negra (FR) (also successful over jumps) and Deauvillais (FR). Dam won 2 11f races in France. FRENCH FLAT '00 r2 p1 (2nd). FRENCH NH '00 r1 p0. FLAT '01/3 r5 p3. NH '01/3 (for Mrs N. Smith) r13 w1 (2m Hdle) p4 (inc 2nd in Ch). Bought Ascot, Jun for 5523. Has only won one of 26 races, a Plumpton Hurdle in heavy, in which the probable winner fell three out when six lengths clear and going well. Blinkered once and wore cheekpieces once to '03, and concluded his flat campaign in a Seller. Always finished over jumps before joining the present yard, but was badly over-faced in Hunter Chases, and tailed off in both completions in Ladies Opens. No longer seems to have any confidence in himself. *J.D.N. Siviter — N. Hereford (Sarah-Jayne Davies).* 94 (L), 230 (L), 628 (2m3fH), 757 (L), 1354 (2m110yH).

MIGHTY MACK (IRE) ..8-5.. 6 br.g. Carroll House — Urdite (FR) (Concertino FR) 4p7. Sturdy half-brother to Mackoy (IRE) (*qv*). A poor jumper so far, and was tailed off from a long way out before finishing last twice. Still has a lot to learn. *Miss K. Earle — Silverton.* 796 (CfMa), 1007 (2m4fOMa), 1133 (OMa).

MIGHTY WILLING ..10-5.. 8 br.g. Bollin William — Wild Ling (Mufrij) 24522. Tall rangy. P-t-P '03 r5 w2 (Maiden and Club Restricted) p0; pulled up 2, and brought down 1. Unbeaten when completing in '03, and displayed abundant stamina, but lacked the pace to succeed in Hunter Chases this year, and looks difficult to hold together when he comes off the bridle at present (certainly so at Cartmel where the girth broke embarking on the final circuit). Appeared not to stay in the Grimthorpe, but still only a youngster and could easily atone in '05 when he should be the finished article. *P.W. Clifton — Holderness (Mary Sowersby).* 177 (3mH), 541 (3mH), 772 (4m1fO), 1297 (3m1fH), 1526 (3m2fH).

MIKES ACRE ..— .. 9 ch.m. Cigar — Indian Stream (Royal Boxer) pup. Stocky compact half-sister to Hurdles winner, Milling Brook. Dam won 2m Hurdle on all-weather, and won 2 2m4f-3m1f Chases.

P-t-P '02/3 r6 w1 (Maiden) p1 (neck 2nd of 3); and pulled up 4. A typical chestnut mare, and belied odds of 33-1 to score at Llanvapley in '02, but turned over at 1-2 in her Members last year, and has failed to finish since. Worth 9-6 at best, but seems to possess a mind of her own, and acquired a tongue-tie and a cross-noseband on her last two outings. *P.A. Summers — Curre & Llangibby (Victoria Parnell).* 694 (M), 844 (R), 1388 (R).

MILAMOSS ..8-8.. 10 ch.g. Le Moss — Hilly's Daughter (Hillandale) sufp7p51p. Strong-topped half-brother to flat and Hurdles winner, Ruth's Gamble. IRISH P-t-P '01/2 r4 p1 (3rd); fell 1. Tends to make mistakes and only had two horses behind him (both in Ireland) in his first 11 races, but by huge good fortune stumbled on a desperate Maiden at Brampton Bryan, and beat a virtual hunter whose rider was a passenger and a tearaway lunatic in a six-runner three-finisher contest (the likely winner fell when in front at the 15th). Soon floundering in a Restricted next time, and surely has no hope in that grade. *L. Wood — Gelligaer F. (Jenny Williams).* 20 (OMa), 191 (R), 258 (CMa), 363 (CfMa), 450 (R), 731 (OMa), 736 (CfMa), 1115 (OMa), 1388 (R).

MILBRIG ..8-11.. 9 b.m. Milieu — Meadow Brig (Meadowbrook) fp3. Compact owner-bred. NH '03 (for A.C. Whillans) r5 p0; pulled up 3. Beaten 57 lengths plus twice and pulled up thrice over Hurdles, and fell early, pulled up and 24 lengths last of three in Points. Led for two miles in the final two, but finished very weakly, and does not look to have any prospects. *Mrs A. Taylor — Dumfries (Diana Carter).* 765 (R), 859 (CfMa), 1291 (OMa).

MILITAIRE (FR) ..10-5.. 7 ch.g. Bering — Moon Review (USA) (Irish River FR) p3133p. Compact well-made brother to French flat winner, Monacita (FR), and half-brother to 4 French flat winners, including Mazalunna (FR) (also successful over jumps), Mahora (FR), Moly (FR), and to a French jumping winner. FRENCH FLAT '01 (for F. Head) r8 w1 (9f) p3. FRENCH NH '01/2 r4 p2. NH '02/3 (for M.D. Hammond) r6 w1 (2m Hdle) p1 (2nd); pulled up 2. FLAT '03 r2 p0. Bought Doncaster, Aug for 15,000. A French flat winner at Compiegne and later successful in a Wetherby Hurdle, but has often disappointed, and was tongue-tied twice and finished 48 lengths fifth in his only Chase. Broke a blood vessel once in an English flat race. Mostly disappointing in the new yard and can look reluctant, but did manage to collect an Open at Cottenham which was run in a slower time than the Restricted, and also went well when third to Cantarinho in a Fakenham Hunter Chase in which he only lost second close home and also finished clear of his useful stablemate Celtic Duke. Always capable of producing if he feels like it, but not one to have great faith in, and might derive benefit from blinkers. *J.M. Turner — Suffolk.* 156 (O), 374 (O), 557 (O), 893 (3m110yH), 1153 (O), 1408 (O).

MILLA'S MAN (IRE) ..10-0.. 13 b.g. Satco (FR) — Rullahola (Bluerullah) pu52p. Tall rangy. IRISH NH '96/8 r6 p2 (2nds, of 28 once). NH '99 and '02 r3 p1 (2nd in 2m5f110y Ch) p0; and fell 2. P-t-P '99 and '03 r8 w2 (Maiden and Members) p2 (3rds); last pair 2, pulled up 1, and unseated 1. Won a long Maiden in soft at Great Trethew in '99, and runner-up over fences at Newton Abbot later that same year, but has stood his racing badly throughout his career, and still remains eligible for Restricteds at 13. Struggles to get the trip ordinarily, and judged by his size one would hazard a guess that his wind is the problem. *W.W. Dennis — S. Tetcott.* 791 (R), 824 (R), 912 (R), 1351 (Inr), 1437 (2m5f110yH).

MILLCROFT REGATTA (IRE) ..—.. 13 br.g. Miner's Lamp — Stradbally Bay (Shackleton) pp. Strong-topped half-brother Drumdoney (IRE), and to Irish Hurdles winner, Goodnight Irene. NH '96/9 r12 p4 (Chses); pulled up 4. P-t-P/HUNT CH '00/3 r15 w2 (Maiden and Restricted) p3 (2 2nds; and inc 3rd in Hunt Ch); 8th, last, pulled up 4, unseated 3, and refused 1. Bitterly disappointing as a youngster, and took 21 starts to open his account, but slipped a tendon off a hock two outings after doubling his winning tally in '02, and has failed to get round in five appearances since. Suited by a sound surface and an easy three miles, but has always been lightly raced and looks finished now. Has been tried in blinkers. Wears a cross-noseband. *Mrs R.E. Gatland — Portman (Ali Tory).* 261 (Cf), 365 (I).

MILLDALUS (IRE) ..9-6.. 10 b/br.g. Mandalus — Chancery Vision (Pauper) 4p. Tall brother to Allthewayfromtuam (IRE). Dam, sister to Chancery Buck, and half-sister to Henceyem (*qv* '98 Annual). IRISH P-t-P '02 r2 w1 (6yo Maiden) p0. Bought Ascot, Nov for 5714. Won an Irish Maiden in soft in '01 and finished 15 and a quarter lengths fourth on his English debut three years later (was last), but although he probably retains ability he has only been able to make four appearances in his life and ominously pulled up in the latest. *G. Wilson — Devon & Somerset (Linda Blackford).* 473 (R), 912 (R).

MILLENIUM RUN (IRE) ..9-1§.. 10 b/br.g. Commanche Run — Pollys Grind (Crash Course) pf42p222. Strong rangy half-brother to At It Again (IRE). IRISH P-t-P '01/3 r10 p3; pulled up 4, unseated 1. IRISH NH FLAT '99 r1 p0. IRISH NH '99/00 (for C.F. Swan, and E.J. O'Grady) r5 p0. Bought Doncaster, May for 1100. Placed on seven occasions, and it would have been eight had he not fallen heavily at the last when holding every chance at Ystradowen, where he lay winded for several minutes. A tentative jumper and bone idle, and unimproved by cheekpieces once. Could easily have won a Maiden had he put his mind to it, but now retired to the rest home of a kindly auntie and will probably be lying on the settee with a gin and tonic as we write. *M. Mochrie, C. Williams & R. Western — Glamorgan (Cath Williams).* 948 (OMa), 1027 (OMa), 1193 (OMa), 1240 (OMa), 1324 (CfMa), 1525 (OMah), 1534 (OMa), 1553 (OMa).

MILLENIUM WAY (IRE) ..10-2§.. 11 ch.g. Ikdam — Fine Drapes (Le Bavard FR) p42p22p2. Tall well-made half-brother to NH flat and jumping winner, The Khoinoa (IRE). Dam is half-sister to Fenton Bridge (*qv* '99 Annual). IRISH P-t-P '99 r1 p1 (2nd). NH '99/01 r14 p9 (3 2nds); pulled up 3. P-t-P/HUNT CH '02/3 r12 w3 (up to Confined) p6 (4 2nds, beaten ½*l* once, and inc Hunt Ch); 4th, and last pair 2. Stays well and suited by good or sound surfaces, but no longer retains the same enthusiasm as in previous years, and showed no inclination to battle when regaining blinkers on his last four appearances. Has become a very sketchy jumper, and James Owen does well to overcome his blunders, but will be difficult to sweeten successfully again. *J.M. Turner — Suffolk.* 125 (O), 247 (O), 523 (O), 744 (O), 1151 (Cf), 1295 (3m110yH), 1361 (3mH), 1472 (I).

MILLENNIUM GOLD ..9-11.. 10 ch.g. Be My Chief (USA) — Forbearance (Bairn USA) 45pp2. Compact. Dam won at 8f, and won 2m Hdle. IRISH NH FLAT '00 r3 p0. IRISH NH '00/1 r7 p1 (3rd). P-t-P/HUNT CH '02/3 (for Go With The Flow Partnership) r13 w2 (Members and Restricted) p3 (3rds, of 4 once, and inc Hunt Ch); 4th, pulled up 4, unseated 2, and brought down 1. Can go a good gallop, and took Earthmover along for two miles at Uttoxeter, but nowhere near good enough to bridge the class divide that faced him in '04, and needs to concentrate on weak Ladies Opens in Wales, in which he has been beaten a maximum of six lengths. Blinkered once in '00, and acquired a visor on his last two starts. Has been tried in a tongue-tie. Wears a cross-noseband. *Glyn Tarrel Stud — Brecon & Talybont (Mark Frieze).* 843 (L), 1029 (3mH), 1092 (I), 1376 (4m2fH), 1536 (L).

MILLINERS GUIDE ..8-11.. 7 b.m. Hatim (USA) — Hiltie Skiltie (Liberated) fupp5. Sturdy. Dam, half-sister to Moscow Mule (*qv* '97 Annual) was 2nd in 2 Points and won Lauderdale cross-country race. Bought Doncaster, Aug for 2000. Gave the owner (in his 33rd season — he seems determined to go on for even longer than his famed mentor Sir Guy Cunard) a horrible fall at the second at Charm Park, and partnered by other riders since, but managed only one completion, when 32 lengths fifth. Pulls hard and looks an awkward customer, but there is possibly a little ability lurking deep. *C.J. Cundall — Holderness (Mary Sowersby).* 392 (CfMa), 500 (CMam), 685 (OMa), 776 (CfMa), 1158 (OMa).

MILL LORD (IRE) .9-9.. 12 b.g. Aristocracy — Millflower (Millfontaine) 1p2. Lengthy. IRISH NH '98 r3 p0. IRISH NH FLAT '99 r1 p0. FLAT '01 r1 p0. NH '00/3 (for C.J. Drewe) r27 p4 (3rds in Chses inc 2nd in Sells); pulled up 8, fell 1. A long-standing maiden whose four placings at between 16 and 24 lengths included two Selling Chases, but finally got off the mark at the 33rd attempt when jumping steadily and making all in a clear lead in a Cottenham Maiden. Can take a keen hold and again raced prominently in his next two attempts, but got tired in both, although he gamely kept going for a 12 lengths second over 2m5f at Folkestone. Frequently wore headgear in the previous yard, and failed to finish five times consecutively to May '01. Gave the new connections some fun, but will not find matters easy as a doubtful stayer at 12. *C.J. Lawson — Essex.* 1000 (OMa), 1396 (C), 1442 (2m5fH).

MILLYHENRY .9-10.. 14 b.g. White Prince (USA) — Milly's Chance (Mljet) p6u353p42. Workmanlike lengthy half-brother to Final Chance. Dam, sister or half-sister to 4 Tizzard Pointers, including Venn Boy (*qv* '00 Annual), was 3rd in 2 Points for them, Grandam, Ace Chance, a disappointing tail-swisher, was placed in 7 Points and a Chase for them. NH '00/2 r18 w2 (3m-3m2f Chses) p8; pulled up 2. P-t-P/HUNT CH '97/00 and '03 (for The Tizzard Family) r35 w13 (inc 3 Mixed Opens, inc 7-timer '00) p8 (6 3rds, last twice; 2 2nds, of 3 once); fell/unseated 4 (looked unlucky once), and pulled up 6. Won 11 of his 15 Points '99/00, and scored twice in mud when switched under Rules to April '02, but a shadow of his former self these days, and has been allowed to run up a losing sequence of 19 races. Served basically as a schoolmaster in '04, but never summoned up much enthusiasm, and having failed to peg back a lame rival at Bratton Down deserves to be humiliated no more. Pulled up when blinkers were applied once in '01. *The Tizzard Family — Mr & Mrs P. Lee — A. & Miss C. Tizzard — Eggesford (Alan Tizzard).* 200 (Cf), 603 (Cnr), 691 (O), 1012 (Cnr), 1101 (Cnr), 1250 (C), 1362 (3m6f110yH), 1540 (Cf), 1557 (Cf).

MILLYS FILLY ..8-1§.. 7 b.m. Polish Precedent (USA) — Lemon's Mill (USA) (Roberto USA) 7p3r. Compact half-sister to winner in Italy. Dam won 12f race, 4 2m-2m4f Hurdles, and 4 3m-3m3f Chases. FLAT '01 r2 p0; unseated 1. NH '03 (for O. Sherwood, and Miss K. Marks) r9 p1 (3rd); pulled up 3. Bought Doncaster, Oct for 2000. Bred from a useful mare who won nine races, but has too much temperament herself, and placings consist of a 23 lengths third in a Hurdle run at a farcical pace and 50 lengths third of four in a Maiden in which she was tailed off throughout the final mile.

Has tried Sellers. Jinked right and reared and unseated on her racecourse debut, and refused and threw the rider off on her latest appearance. *P. & R.N. Thomas, G. Nelson, A. Brown & M. Williams — Glamorgan (Paul Thomas).* 53 (2m4fOMa), 173 (OMa), 363 (CfMa), 1096 (OMa).

MILNSTORM (IRE) ..9-8.. 9 b.g. Glacial Storm (USA) — Miss Performance (IRE) (Lancastrian) 32. Tall. NH FLAT '01 r1 p0. NH '01/2 r4 p1 (3rd). P-t-P '03 (for Mr A.G. Fear) r2 p2 (3rds, remote of 4 once, and last once). A reliable jumper and has made the frame in all four Points, but only moderate, and although an average Maiden should be within his range a further step up in class looks a bridge too far. Only risked on ground easier than good. *C.T. Moate — W. Somerset V. (Marie McGuiness).* 139 (R), 604 (OMa).

MINDEROO .—.. 7 b.g. Efisio — Mindomica (Dominion) pp. Good-topped brother to flat winner, Molotov, and half-brother to Minstrel Hall (also successful Hurdler). Dam won 2 7f races. FLAT '01/3 (for B.W. Hills, J.M. Bradley, and J. Poulton) r28 w2 (6f) p1 (2nd). Bought Ascot, Aug for 3809. A tail-swisher who scored twice over 6f including in an all-weather Seller, and wore blinkers or cheekpieces and was tongue-tied twice. As is virtually inevitable with ex-sprinters he was barking up the wrong tree in Points, and despite attracting market support in both Opens he had to be pulled up when well behind. It seems as if connections have already given up the unequal struggle. *R.E. White & T.W. Boon — Lamerton (Tony Boon).* 115 (MO), 310 (O).

MIND THE GATE ..10-1.. 12 b.g. Ardross — Mulloch Brae (Sunyboy) 8p2. Compact brother to Hurdles winner, Mini Moo Min. Dam, half-sister to Bigsun (*qv* '94 Annual), won 2m3f Hdle, and 4 Chses (2m4f-3m1f) consecutively. NH FLAT '98 r2 p0. NH '00 r1 p0 (pulled up). P-t-P '02 r4 w1 (Maiden) p1 (last of 3); last, and pulled up 1. Won his Maiden convincingly in mud at Siddington, but never going well when favourite on patchy ground next time, and clearly suffered a setback which necessitated a year on the sidelines. Blinkered over hurdles and regained them on his latest start when he made much of the running to finish second at Dingley. Requires strong handling, but even at 12 should still have the ability to take a soft ground Restricted, provided his behaviour at the start does not get any worse. *P. Oram — Croome & W. Warwicks (Anne Dudley).* 31 (Cnr), 587 (R), 889 (CR).

MINELLA HOTEL (IRE) ..10-0.. 13 b.g. Be My Native (USA) — Due Consideration (Sir Herbert) 4p4. Tall good-looking half-brother to Duty Officer, to Chasing winner, Leinthall Princess, and to Irish Hurdler, Carron Hill. Dam won 4 Hurdles (2-3m) and 2m4f Nov Chse in Ireland. IRISH NH FLAT '97/9 r6 w2 p1 (3rd). IRISH FLAT '00 r2 p1 (3rd). IRISH NH '99/02 r16 w2 (2m Hdles) p6. P-t-P '03 r5 w2 (3 ran 2 finished Members and Confined) p2 (remote 3rd once); and pulled up. Quite useful on his day, and ended a three-year drought when recording a double for Joe Docker last year, but looked out of sorts after a promising reappearance in '04, and clearly did not appreciate the underfoot conditions at Market Rasen. Disappointed when tried in cheekpieces and the subject of market support next time, and it may be that three miles puts too much emphasis on his stamina, though he has broken blood vessels in the past. Could not be supported with any confidence in future. *Mrs M. Sharland — Atherstone (John Holt).* 106 (C), 298 (Cf), 683 (O).

MINELLA LEADER (IRE) ..—.. 8 b.g. Supreme Leader — Tivoli Run (Deep Run) pp. Big strong. No signs of early promise when pulled up in Maidens. *Mrs M. Sharland — Atherstone (John Holt).* 596 (2m5fOMa), 788 (CfMa).

MINELLA SILVER (IRE) ..10-10.. 12 gr.g. Roselier (FR) — Mrs Minella (Deep Run) 11. Lengthy unfurnished half-brother to Irish Hurdles winner, Minella Leisure (IRE). IRISH NH '98 r1 p0. IRISH P-t-P '98/9 r5 w2 (5&6yo Maiden, and poor Open — 4 ran and 2 finished) p1 (last of 3). P-t-P/HUNT CH '00/2 r7 w5 (inc 2 3m110y Hunt Chses and dead-heat Open, 4-timer '01) p0; pulled up 1, and fell 1. NH '02/3 (for Mrs H. Dalton) r3 p1 (last of 3); and 4th twice, inc last once. A smart stayer and is unbeaten in his last nine hunt racing completions, but normally only ever risked on easy surfaces, and averages fewer than three outings per annum since leaving Ireland in '99. Made surprisingly hard work of scoring at Flagg where only Richard Burton's strength got him home, but he deserted him in favour of Fane Counsel at Chaddesley, and Adrian Wintle proved more than an able deputy. Front runs with tremendous zest, and is very difficult to pass once he gets the bit between his teeth, and hopefully will be able to grace the scene with his presence in '05. *Miss H.J. Hinckley — Wheatland (Guy Landau).* 986 (Cf), 1342 (O).

MINELLA STORM (IRE) ..10-3.. 13 b.g. Strong Gale — Maul-More (Deep Run) p2115u. Tall lengthy hobdayed half-brother to NH flat and Hurdles winner, The Phair Crier (IRE). Dam won 2m Hurdle in Ireland. IRISH NH FLAT '97 r2 w1 p1 (2nd). IRISH NH '97/8 r9 w1 (2m2f Hdle) p2 (2nds); fell 1. NH '99/03 (for D.J. Wintle) r19 w1 (3m Ch) p6 (inc 5 2nds). Bought Doncaster, May for 4200. Three wins in Ireland included a 27-runner Hurdle and a four-runner three-finisher Chase in '01, which was his first victory for over three years. Also placed on nine occasions and fourth nine times there, but generally disappointing and was blinkered once. Surprisingly showed renewed enthusiasm at 12, and followed a 16 lengths second to Lancastrian Jet at Hereford with a victory in a poor five-horse contest there before completing a double in an Open at Cilwendeg. His season ended on a low with a distant last at Chepstow (favourite) and in an unseat at Bredwardine, where he returned lame, and will probably struggle to return to the track. A welcome boost to the riding career of Paul Sheldrake, who has worked his way into prominence amongst the better riders in Wales after being in the background for so long. *C.J. Williams — S. Pembs (Lorna Wilkins).* 34 (O), 209 (3m1f110yH), 434 (3m1f110yH), 672 (O), 974 (3mH), 1390 (O).

PLATE 81 1342 Wheatland Mens Open: Minella Silver (Adrian Wintle), 1st leads Fane Counsel (Richard Burton), 3rd, and The Campdonian (Ed Walker), 2nd, at the last PHOTO: David Jones

MINI CRUISE ..9-8.. 15 ch.g. Cruise Missile — Mini Pie (Dike USA) 57. Good-bodied lengthy half-brother to Hurdles winner, Mac's Gift. Dam dead-heated for 8f race. NH '95/6 r5 p0; pulled up 1. P-t-P/HUNT CH '97/00 and '02/3 r31 w5 (inc Open) p11 (5 3rds, of 4 once, and last once); pulled up 8. Won five Points, the last four under an enterprising Luke Morgan, but generally eclipsed in Hunter Chases, and has been reported dead. Miss J. Fisher — Lauderdale. 240 (3mH), 330 (3mH).

MININO (IRE) ..10-2§.. 12 ch.g. Glacial Storm (USA) — Haughty-Ha (Lord Ha Ha) 1r23p1. Tall rangy. Dam won 2 Points in Ireland, and grandam, Hovering, won 4 Points there. IRISH P-t-P '98 r5 p3; fell 1. IRISH NH '98/9 and '01/2 r11 w1 (2m6f Ch) p1; pulled up 2, ran out 1. IRISH NH FLAT '99 r1 p0. P-t-P '00 and '03 r11 w2 (Maiden and Club Confined) p5 (3 3rds, of 4 once); last 2, and fell 2. A bold-jumping front-runner, and has a good record in minor Points, but has always possessed a recalcitrant streak, and his behaviour at the start has become progressively worse. Declined to jump off at all at Horseheath, and blinkers were reapplied next time, but can be notably game when he wants, and seems to do best when fresh. Wears a cross-noseband. *B.J. Kennedy — Essex F. & U. (Wilf Tolhurst).* 38 (Cf), 125 (O), 221 (O), 247 (O), 523 (O), 903 (O).

MINISTERIAL (IRE) ..9-13.. 8 b.g. Spanish Place (USA) — Parsonage (The Parson) u1422. Dipped. IRISH P-t-P '03 r7 p2 (3rds); pulled up 3, fell 1. Quite speedy in minor company, but cannot seem to get the hang of jumping properly, and a fall at the last in an Aldington Restricted proved costly as he was clear of the only one of three rivals who was still continuing at the time (remounted). Survived a blunder three out to win a Maiden at Parham by a neck under a forceful ride from Chris Gordon, but never fluent enough in a four-horse race when even money favourite next time and finished 33 lengths last, and ended his season with a head second after errors had again proved costly. Compensation surely awaits in a Restricted, but would make it so much easier for himself if he could find a smooth jumping rhythm. *N. Benstead — Kent & Surrey Bloodhounds.* 627 (OMa), 644 (OMa), 900 (R), 1282 (R), 1333 (R).

MINSTER BELLE ..9-3.. 10 ch.m. Minster Son — Palmahalm (Mandrake Major) 2ppp. Small sparely-made. Dam, 3rd in flat race, won Hunt Ch and 11 Points (inc 5 Opens) and placed 9, 'virtually invincible in second class races'. NH FLAT '00 r3 p0 (refused to race final outing). P-t-P '02/3 r11 w1 (Maiden) p3 (2 2nds); last, pulled up 5 and unseated 1. Justified favouritism in a bad Maiden on firm at Trecoed at the 13th attempt, and a shade unlucky not to follow up immediately, but prone to costly mistakes and only gets the trip when conditions aren't testing. Will be hard pressed to register another success. *D.W. Barber & D.A. Rees — Tivyside (David Barber).* 669 (M), 974 (3mH), 1095 (R), 1389 (R).

MINSTER ECHO ..8-11§.. 10 ch.m. Minster Son — Fair Echo (Quality Fair) 8pp1p5. Compact half-sister to Bold Echo, and to Hurdles winner, Thegift. P-t-P '00 and '02/3 r16 w2 (Maiden and Members) p0; 4th, 6th twice, pulled up 6, fell 2, carried out 1, and ran out 2. The winner of three weak races at Charm Park, and has made the bulk of the running in the last two, but sometimes of a mind to be utterly mulish, and aside from retaining her Members failed to beat a rival in '04. Sure to be trained with her local in mind next year. Has been tried unsuccessfully in blinkers. *J.A. Featherstone — Staintondale (Mary Sowersby).* 164 (R), 268 (R), 390 (Rnr), 954 (M), 1288 (R), 1416 (R).

MINSTER SUNSHINE ..10-0.. 11 ch.g. Minster Son — Own Free Will (Nicholas Bill) 1. Tall rangy half-brother to Posh As You Like, Hurdles winner, Duke Of Perth, and to flat winner, Codicil. Dam won 5 flat (7-11f), the first a Sell. 16,000 4yo. NH FLAT '99/00 r2 p1 (3rd). NH '00/3 (for K.C. Bailey) r9 p3 (Chses); pulled up 2. Bought Doncaster, Aug for 3200. Placed in a bumper and three Chases and beaten a maximum of two-and-a-quarter lengths on three occasions, but arrived at Cottenham on the opening day as an exceptionally lightly-raced 10-year-old maiden. Finally gained a richly deserved success, but paid a high price, as he finished lame, which surely must bring a career in which he was seen all too infrequently to a close. *P.A. Hill-Walker — Zetland (Chris Dennis).* 6 (OMa).

MINSTREL'S QUAY (IRE) ..—§.. 14 ch.g. Black Minstrel — Quayside Lady (Quayside) p. Workmanlike. IRISH P-t-P '96/7 r16 w1 (Maiden) p2; failed to finish 8 (fell/unseated 4 and ran out 1). IRISH NH '97 r1 p0 (pulled up in Ch). NH '99 r2 p0; pulled up 1. P-t-P '98/00 and '02/3 (for Mr R.J. Brown) r16 w1 (Restricted) p1 (2nd of 3); fell/unseated 4, and pulled up 7. Clumsy and a regular non-finisher, but survived two mistakes, including a bad one at the last where two challenging rivals departed when successful at Eyton in '99. Lightly raced since leaving Ireland, but went to pot completely in '03 and looks finished now. Has been tried in blinkers. *P.D. Thomas — Carms.* 208 (Cf).

MIORBHAIL ..9-11.. 14 br.g. Wonderful Surprise — Florrie Palmer (Deadly Nightshade) pu61u9. Compact half-brother to Another Formula and Florries Daughter, and to jumping winner, Florries Son. Dam, half-sister to H And K Wager (*qv* '91 Annual), was 3rd in Chase, and won 3 Points and placed 2 for Mrs Gray. P-t-P '98, '00 and '02/3 r15 w1 (Maiden) p5 (3 3rds, of 4 once, and last twice, remote once); 6th, last pair 5, pulled up 1, fell 1, and brought down 1. Has had myriad problems, and forced onto the sidelines in '99, and '01, but can still take a strong hold, and appreciated the drop in class when registering his first success since '98 at Easingwold. Struggles to get the trip at the best of times, and another change to his qualifying pack might be required unless the Bilsdale run a Members race in '05. *Mrs F.M. Gray — Bilsdale (Carole Dennis).* 564 (L), 811 (L), 1160 (L), 1301 (Cf), 1459 (L), 1499 (2m4f110yH).

MISS BARTON RIDGE .—.. 8 b.m. Broadsword (USA) — Yamrah (Milford) p. Sister to Hurdles winner, Capricorn Princess, and half-sister to Mr Modplan and Barton Bandit. Dam won 3 flat races (8-12f), the first a Sell. NH FLAT '03 (for J.M. Bradley) r1 p0. Sold Ascot, Feb for 2952. Bought Ascot, Jul for 2666. Badly tailed off in a bumper and in a mid-February Maiden where she pulled up at the final fence. *W.D. Lewis — Pembs (Mark Lewis).* 202 (CfMa).

MISS BIDDY ..9-3.. 10 ch.m. Sula Bula — Bickfield Approach (Dubassoff USA) p315. Small light. Sister to Bettie Blue, and half-sister to Lansdowne Park. Dam, half-sister to Express Free Gift (*qv* '93 Annual), won Maiden and placed 6 for Tony Harris ('must be one of the weakest finishers in the business'). NH '03 r1 p0 (4th in 2m6f Hdle). P-t-P '02/3 (for Mr A.G. Harris) r10 p3 (2nds); 4th, 5th, pulled up 3, refused 1, and ran out 1. Headstrong and unable to score despite making the frame on five occasions in the previous yard, but managed to settle off a suicidal pace when providing Olivia Maylam with her first winner at High Easter. Backed down to second-favourite for a 12-runner Restricted at Fakenham next time, but jumped stickily and quickly became tailed off, and a follow up seems unlikely. *The Maylam Family (A. Maylam) — E. Kent (Olivia Maylam).* 152 (OMa), 185 (CMam), 652 (OMa), 1152 (R).

MISS CHARLOTTE ..—.. 9 b.m. Cruise Missile — Charlotte Lane (Mart Lane) pu. Small. Dam, half-sister to Charlotte's Rose (*qv* '01 Annual), won 5 Points (including 2 Ladies) and placed 9 (including a

Hdle) for Shan Farr. P-t-P '03 (for Mrs S.M. Farr & Mrs P. Brace) r3 p0 (fell 2, and pulled up 1). A gormless jumper and has yet to get beyond the 12th without mishap, but amazingly sent off joint-second-favourite for a 13-runner elders Maiden at Ystradowen on her latest appearance. Typically the confidence proved misguided, and Ryan Bliss was ejected at the tenth. *The F & B Partnership (Mrs S.M. Farr) — Ystrad Taf Fechan (Shan Farr).* 736 (CfMa), 1027 (OMa).

MISS CHLOE (IRE) ..8-3.. 10 b.m. King's Ride — Audley Lady (Deep Run) up424pp. Good-topped half-sister to Audley Lass (IRE). NH FLAT '99/00 r2 p0. NH '00/1 r2 p0 (pulled up 2). P-t-P '03 r2 p0 (pulled up 2). Possesses a modicum of ability, and finished 15 lengths in front of a future winner when runner-up at Cothelstone, but often looks far from keen, and would be a surprise scorer herself. At her very busiest in '04 having appeared to go wrong three years previously. *Staverton Owners Group (M. Blake) — Avon V. (Michael Blake).* 35 (CMam), 119 (OMa), 327 (OMa), 474 (OMa), 883 (OMa), 1091 (CMam), 1404 (OMa).

MISS DANBYS ..8-0§.. 10 b.m. Charmer — Dohty Baby (Hittite Glory) 4fpp*Rp*. Workmanlike owner-bred half-sister to Danbys Gorse and Just Jake. Dam won 6f Sell, and won 3 2m Sell Hdles. NH FLAT '99 r3 p0. NH '99 r3 p0 (hung badly right and ran out once). P-t-P '01/3 r8 p1 (3rd); last, and pulled up 6. NH '04 (for J.M. Jefferson) r2 p0 (ran out in 2m Hdle: *pulled hrd, sn prom, ld 3 til hung lft & rn out aft 3 out*; and pulled up in 2m110y Sell Hdle: *prom, ev ch app 2 out, wknd qckly & pu last*). FLAT '04 r1 p0. A very difficult and unrewarding ride, and does not stay the trip in Points, and looks too dangerous to be unleashed under Rules again. *D.T. Todd — Burton (Louise Todd).* 60 (OMa), 297 (M), 500 (CMam), 595 (OMa).

PLATE 82 469 Quantock Staghounds Open Maiden 56&7yo: Miss Flinders and Ryan Bliss have a marginal lead at the last, but Virgos Bambino and Alex Charles-Jones are about to sweep past
PHOTO: Baths Photographic

MISS FLINDERS ..9-6.. 8 b.m. Sula Bula — Pollys Owen (Master Owen) 21. Owner-bred half-sister to Wadswick Lady and Bill Owen (Chasing winner since Pointing), and to Hurdles winners, Relkowen and Country Store (also won Chasing). Dam won 2 Hdles and Chse (all 2m) for the Bartons. NH FLAT '01 r1 p0. NH '01 (for J.W. Mullins) r1 p0. Missed '02 and '03 after being outclassed under Rules twice as a juvenile, but returned for a respectable second in a 2m5f Maiden and then scored unchallenged in Mares company on firmish at Holnicote. It was the slowest time of the day, but she still looked as if she could be made fitter, and as she seems enthusiastic about the job she may be able to score again. *Mrs M.I. Barton — Avon V. (Ryan Bliss).* 469 (2m4fOMa), 1182 (CMam).

MISS FOLEY ..9-8.. 12 b.m. Thethingaboutitis (USA) — Rue De Remarque (The Noble Player USA) u. Sturdy compact. NH FLAT '97 r3 p0. NH '99 and '01 r16 p4 (3 3rds); pulled up 5. P-t-P '03 (for Herbert Foley Group) r7 w1 (Members) p2; last pair 2, and pulled up 2. Got off the mark at the 21st attempt when able to outbattle a 14-year-old in her Members at Eyton last year, but has often spent long periods on the sidelines, and disappeared after incapacitating Anita Gibbons at Howick in '04. Visored once in '01, and previously tried in blinkers. *Miss A.C. Gibbons — N. Ledbury.* 698 (Inr).

MISS HOITY TOITY .10-0§.. 13 b.m. St Columbus — Classey (Dubassoff USA) 2434226. Small neat light owner-bred sister to Bit Of A Snob (successful Hurdler since Pointing), and half-sister to Lah Di Dah Lad and Sir Lancelot. P-t-P '00 and '02/3 r14 w2 (mares Maiden and Restricted) p2 (3rds, last once); 4th, last, pulled up 2, and fell/unseated 6. Headstrong and error-prone, but won a third of her completions to '03, and looked set for more success after chasing home Nautical Lad on her reappearance, but has found winning difficult since, and not helped by her often mulish temperament. Good enough to find another race if she chose to co-operate, but now might be as good a time as any to pack her off to the paddocks. *R.W. Morris & G.B. Tarry — Pytchley (Jimmy Tarry).* 379 (I), 584 (I), 886 (Cf), 1120 (Cf), 1336 (I), 1468 (C), 1516 (L).

MISSILEBROOK LASS ..7-0§.. 9 ch.m. Cruise Missile — Netherbrook Lass (Netherkelly) pu. Tall rangy owner-bred half-sister to Netherbrook Lad and Broadbrook Lass. Dam is an unraced homebred half-sister to 5 Pointers, including Dunsbrook Lad (*qv* '96 Annual). Grandam, Dunsbrook Lass, won 8 Points (inc 4m and 4m4f Opens) and 2nd 4. Great-grandam, Dunsmore Lass, won 4 Points for the Ings family. P-t-P '02/3 r5 p1 (last of 3); 5th of 6, and pulled up 3. A tail-swishing camel, and has been tailed off last in both completions, but mysteriously halved in price before running like a hairy dog in her Members. It would be amazing if anyone could be bothered to race her again. *M.H. Ings — Radnor & W. Herefords (Andrew Dalton).* 667 (OMa), 1226 (M).

MISS ILLUSTRIOUS ..9-9.. 12 ch.m. Gunner B — Battle Fleet (Alias Smith USA) 5. Compact. Dam, distant last of 3 in flat race, won 3 Points (inc ladies) and placed 5. NH FLAT '99 r1 p0. NH '00 r4 p0 (pulled up 2, and fell/unseated 2). P-t-P '02/3 r9 w1 (2-finisher mares Maiden) p0; last 2, pulled up 2, unseated 1, brought down 1, and refused 2. Blinkered latterly under Rules, and failed to get round in her first eight attempts over jumps, but managed to keep going well enough to account for one other finisher in the slowest time of the day at Holnicote last year. Not better than last since but posted a good effort at 100-1 under a substitute partner on her only appearance in '04, and could still spring another surprise at 12. *H.R. & Mrs B. Thomas - Exmoor (Hugh Thomas).* 279 (R).

MISS KARINGAROO .9-4§§.. 9 ch.m. Karinga Bay — Little Romany (Day Is Done) p4r1p. Small neat sister to Up To The Minute and The Squab. Dam, grandam never ran, but great-great-grandam, Another Minute, won 12 Points. P-t-P '03 (for Mr D. Ridge & Mr A.B. Pope) r4 p0 (pulled up 2, and fell/unseated 2). Has been pretty unruly in the preliminaries to date, but slowly getting the hang of things on course, and responded to William White's urgings to spring a surprise when outsider of three in her Members. Needs to progress further for Restricteds, and her hot-headed temperament must improve as a whole. *A.B. Pope — W. Somerset V.* 326 (OMa), 474 (OMa), 604 (OMa), 878 (M), 1184 (R).

MISS MAN ..9-2.. 11 ch.m. Man Among Men (IRE) — Rustys Special (Rustingo) p34R3. Tall narrow half-sister to Miss Motivate. Dam, half-sister to 2 Pointers, including Auburn Tint (*qv* '94 Annual). NH FLAT '99 r2 p0. NH '00/1 (for R.L. Brown) r3 p0; pulled up 2. Pulled up in two of three Hurdles and broke a blood vessel at least once, and very nervously ridden in her first four Points (tailed off and crawling over the obstacles throughout the final mile when two fences last of three in her Members, and also ran out once), but produced a better effort when Joe Price took over at Laleston, and was 20 lengths third after fading quickly in the closing stages. Still looks very moderate, but possibly worth another try with the stronger handling. *E.C. King — Curre & Llangibby (Ron Harris).* 191 (R), 356 (M), 699 (CfMa), 841 (Cf), 1193 (OMa).

MISS MATTIE ROSS ..10-10.. 9 b.m. Milieu — Mother Machree (Bing II) 2*u*111f2. Lengthy plain owner-bred half-sister to Trooper Thorn and Donovans Reef. Dam is sister to La Boeuf, and half-sister to Davy Blake (*qv* '99 Annual). P-t-P '01 r1 p0 (pulled up). NH '02/3 r8 p0; pulled up 3. NH '04 r1 p0 (unseated in 3m1f Ch: *in tch til blun & ur 4*). Selling class and beaten a minimum of 13 lengths over hurdles, but a revelation since switching to the larger obstacles, and recorded a Kelso Hunter Chase hat-trick in the space of four weeks under Michael McAlister. Assumed command after the last fence in all three, and clearly enjoys coming up the long run-in, but had her run at the Roxburghshire venue interrupted by Boulta (whom she had beaten when initiating the sequence) on her latest appearance, and needs to brush up her jumping if she is to tackle bigger and better things in '05. Tough and genuine, and is suited by some cut in the ground. *S.J. Marshall — Percy.* 74 (OMa), 349 (3m1fH), 678 (3m1fH), 798 (3m1fH), 1068 (3m2f110yH), 1174 (3m1fH).

MISS MOSS .9-12.. 8 b.m. Le Moss — Strong Tempo (IRE) (Strong Gale) 15p2p. Rangy light-framed. Dam is half-sister to Wot About Me (*qv*). P-t-P '02/3 r5 w2 (Maiden and Restricted) p0; ran out 2, and pulled up. Completed a hat-trick in minor Points on good or sound surfaces when accounting for a single rival in her Members on her reappearance, but largely disappointing subsequently, and her penchant for jumping right-handed has not been cured. Presumably her quirks are caused by a physical problem and can only be watched when she returns, though her Tabley second gives her strong claims in similar company. *A.J., Mrs S.M. & Miss E.J. Simcock — N. Hereford (James Simcock).* 512 (M), 728 (I), 1019 (Cm), 1430 (I), 1530 (I).

MISS O'GRADY (IRE) .10-6.. 13 ch.m. Over The River (FR) — Polar Mistress (IRE) (Strong Gale) 114341. Lengthy sister to Mabel's Memory (IRE). NH '01 r1 p0 (pulled up in 2m4f Ch). P-t-P/HUNT CH '98/03 r32 w12 (inc 2 2m4f-2m5f Hunt Chses, 3 Mixed Opens and 2 Opens, inc 5-timer '99) p10 (7 2nds, inc 3 Hunt Chses); 4th, fell/unseated 3, and pulled up 6. A smart mare with a turn of foot whose career tally of 15 wins could have been even greater but for a tendency to break blood vessels. Speedy enough to score in two sub-3m events, but less predictable over regulation fences, and sometimes found less than seemed likely off the bridle. A great credit to the Alners and retired to the paddocks on a winning note at Badbury Rings where a date with Karinga Bay was the immediate plan. *Mrs J.M. Miller — Portman (Sally Alner).* 115 (MO), 235 (O), 347 (3mH), 545 (2m3f110yH), 733 (3mH), 861 (M).

PLATE 83 74 West Percy Open Maiden (Div 1): Miss Mattie Ross and Roger Green, 2nd
PHOTO: Alan Mitchell

MISS PORTCELLO .9-12.. 12 b.m. Bybicello — Port Mallaig (Royal Fountain) pp453. Small narrow. P-t-P/HUNT CH '98/03 r28 w4 (inc 3m Hunt Ch) p12 (4 2nds, beaten ½*l* once, inc Hunt Ch; 8 3rds, of 4 twice, and inc 4 Hunt Chses); unseated 4, and pulled up 5. A dour stayer, but usually undone by her lack of acceleration, and ideally requires mud and a stiff track to slow the opposition down. Has never found winning opportunities easy to find as a result, but beaten a minimum of 15 lengths in '04, and seems to be in decline. Remains a safe jumper, and has never fallen. *W.F. Jeffrey — Lauderdale (Joan Hollands).* 133 (L), 284 (L), 550 (L), 763 (L), 1078 (L).

MISS ROYELLO ..10-1.. 8 b.m. Royal Fountain — Lady Manello (Mandrake Major) 3143123. Small light half-sister to Claywalls (*qv*). Dam raced for Ann Hamilton. P-t-P '02 r2 p0 (4th, and last). An out-and-out stayer, and landed two of three Points she contested in '04, but has tended to get done for toe in Hunter Chases, and beaten between seven and 32 lengths in them to date. A reliable jumper, and has not failed to get round in nine attempts, and though she has done nothing wrong for Dale Jewett her stature suggests it may pay to contest Ladies races with an experienced partner in

'05. Yet to encounter ground faster than good. *I. Hamilton — Tynedale (Ann Hamilton).* 75 (OMa), 167 (OMa), 316 (2m5fH), 349 (3m1fH), 657 (R), 797 (3m1fH), 1028 (3mH).

PLATE 84 657 Lanarkshire & Renfrewshire and Eglinton Restricted: Miss Royello (Dale Jewett), 1st, parts the birch but lands ahead of Decent Bond (Roger Green), 2nd PHOTO: Alan Mitchell

MISSUSLARGE ..—.. 7 b.m. Contract Law (USA) — Scorpotina (Scorpio FR) ppu. Tiny. Dam, half-sister to Albert Blake (*qv* '03 Annual), was placed in two Maidens for the Kinseys. Tried valiantly to cope with the obstacles, but being a tiddler unsurprisingly found it all too much. Named with irony, and connections would never have raced something so bizarre had they not bred it themselves. *Mrs T.R. Kinsey — Cheshire Forest.* 754 (OMa), 1049 (2m4fOMa), 1231 (OMam).

MISSY MOSCOW (IRE) ..—.. 7 b.m. Moscow Society (USA) — Bright Shares (IRE) (Mandalus) p. Dam won 4&5yo Mares Maiden in Ireland. IRISH P-t-P '02/3 r5 w2 (5&6yo Mares Maiden and Winner of One) p1 (2nd); last and fell 1. IRISH NH FLAT '03 (for D. Hassett) r1 p1 (2nd). Bought Doncaster, May for 22,000. Came from Ireland with a tall reputation and earned a big price tag, but only managed one disappointing January outing and clearly not right since. Potentially capable of much better if fit, and Monica Dickinson would be a welcome sight in any winners enclosure. *Mrs M. Dickinson — Badsworth & Bramham Moor (Richard Tate).* 72 (O).

MISS ZARNNI .9-12§.. 11 ch.m. Arzanni — Miss Lawn (FR) (Lashkari) 43p21p. Lengthy half-sister to Alice Parker Jones. Dam won 2 2m4f Hdles at Southwell, inc a Sell. NH FLAT '99 r2 p0. P-t-P '02/3 r7 w1 (Maiden) p2 (2nds, of 3 once); 6th, last, and pulled up 2. The winner of two weak races on good or sound surfaces, but seems moody and unpredictable, and regularly peppers her rounds with errors. Might be worth a try in headgear but does not seem likely to bridge the gap to Ladies Opens. *The Orton Racing Group (Roger Harvey) — Atherstone (Roger Harvey).* 57 (R), 191 (R), 383 (R), 853 (R), 1107 (R), 1343 (L).

MISS ZIGGERSON ..9-8.. 8 b.m. Sula Bula — Tregale (Chukaroo) p4u2. Small light-framed. Dam won 2 Points and placed 10 for Jackie Du Plessis (*qv* '96 Annual). Grandam, Cornish Gale, won a Maiden and placed 4. P-t-P '02/3 r5 p0 (pulled up 4, and fell 1). Very slow to learn from her mistakes, but has often attracted market support, and got to within a neck of making her first clear round a successful one at Great Trethew. Has the basic speed to be able to win an average Cornish Maiden in '05, though her stamina over the full trip is untested. Normally has two paddock handlers. *Miss J. du Plessis & N. Edmonds — E. Cornwall (Jackie Du Plessis).* 195 (CfMa), 492 (OMa), 568 (CfMa), 701 (2m4fOMa).

MISTER AUDI (IRE) ..9-6§.. 13 br.g. Good Thyne (USA) — Symphony Orchestra (Orchestra) 505446246. Close-coupled half-brother to Butlers Cross (IRE), and to Irish Pointing and Hurdles winner, The Boylerman. IRISH NH FLAT '96/7 r4 p0. IRISH NH '97/8 r7 p0 (finished in both Hunt Chses). IRISH P-t-P '98 r3 w1 (Adjacent Maiden) p1 (3rd). NH '99 r1 p0 (6th in Ch). P-t-P/HUNT

CH '00/2 r16 w1 (Restricted) p9 (6 2nds, beaten head once, of 3 once; and inc 3rd in Hunt Ch); 4th, 6th, and pulled up 4. Very rarely fails to complete, and is far too clever to fall, but plods reluctantly nowadays, and only beat a total of five rivals in '04. Regained blinkers on his last four outings but their effects are negligible, and his decline irreversible. Wears a cross-noseband. *M. Ward & J. Bowles — Granta H. (Martin Ward).* 126 (L), 249 (Cnr), 373 (L), 522 (L), 649 (L), 743 (L), 904 (L), 1154 (L), 1362 (3m6f110yH).

MISTER BENJAMIN (IRE) ..11-2.. 10 b.g. Polish Patriot (USA) — Frau Ahuyentante (ARG) (Frari ARG) 11. Tall heavy-topped fired half-brother to Irish flat and Hurdles winner, Miss Roberto (IRE) (subsequently successful English Hurdler), and to several winners abroad. FLAT '97/9 r19 w4 (7-10f) p6 (5 2nds, beaten head once). NH '99/02 r16 w4 (2 2m3f110y Hdles and 2 2m3f-2m3f110y Chses) p6 (3 2nds); pulled up 1, fell 1. P-t-P '03 r6 w5 (5-timer inc Mixed Open and 3 Ladies) p0; and unseated 1. Won half of his first eight starts on the flat, and equally successful when joining Paul Nicholls, but only ran once in '02, and looked to be on the downgrade until totally rejuvenated by the switch to Points last year. Would doubtless have remained undefeated had he not unseated on his debut, but pulled muscles behind when completing his 5-timer, and has also had to recover from a fractured pelvis since. At his most destructive when produced for a turn of foot, but both '04 wins were typical cakewalks, and deserves to be allowed to have a cut at the top prizes if his health permits next year. Handles firmish but ideally suited by some cut in the ground. Insulted by a visor once in '99, and finished tailed off. *P.F. Nicholls — Blackmore & Sparkford V. (Chloe Roddick).* 171 (L), 311 (L).

PLATE 85 1040 Braes of Derwent Restricted: Mister Bromley and Serena Brotherton, 1st, are clear at the last *PHOTO: Alan Mitchell*

MISTER BROMLEY..9-7.. 8 ch.g. Minster Son — Little Bromley (Riberetto) 131. Small attractive. Dam, half-sister to Millstone Hill, won 3 2m Hdles. Grandam, Bromley Rose, is closely related to 6 Pointers, including Springwood (*qv* '91 Annual). NH FLAT '02 r2 p0. P-t-P '03 r5 p3 (2 2nds, beaten neck once); last, and pulled up 1. Took longer than anticipated to lose his maiden tag, but was very lucky when he did, and subsequently took advantage of Decent Bond's exit at Corbridge, where the following Maiden was run seven seconds faster. Has yet to impress with his general attitude, but might be the type that will appreciate a stone less weight on his back in future. Wears a cross-noseband, and has run tongue-tied. *Mrs D.R. Brotherton — Middleton (Serena Brotherton).* 395 (CfMa), 563 (R), 1040 (R).

MISTER BRUCE (IRE) .—.. 9 ch.g. Over The River (FR) — Lady Bye-Bye (Montekin) ppp. Strong compact. Dam won 7f race, 2m Hurdle and 2m2f Chase in Ireland. IRISH P-t-P '01/2 r4 w1 (6yo Maiden) p0; fell 1. An Irish winner in '02, but missed '03, and looked a bad animal in three early season pulled ups in the new yard. Performed as if there was something seriously wrong with him. *Mrs S. Collett — N. Cotswold (Fred Hutsby).* 37 (CR), 109 (CR), 294 (R).

MISTER CONE ..9-9.. 11 b.g. Long Leave — Miss Cone (Celtic Cone) ppp3. Compact brother to Morris Piper (*qv*). NH FLAT '00 r1 p0. NH '00 r5 p0 (last trio 3 and fell 2 in Hdles). P-t-P '99 and '02 r13 w1 (3-finisher Maiden) p2 (2nds, beaten ½*l* once, and of 3 once); pulled up 6, carried out 1, fell 2, and brought down 1. Won a three-finisher Maiden on firm at Great Trethew in '02, and also attracted the attentions of the stewards on two occasions, but has long been fairly intractable, and prone to making mistakes. Preserved his rating when a fair third in a first-time tongue-tie on a course that suits on his latest appearance, but pulls up as often as not, and sure to remain impossible to predict. *The Ansell Partnership (W.D.H. Ansell) — N. Cornwall (Ian Hambley).* 76 (M), 314 (R), 488 (R), 824 (R).

MISTER FALCON (FR) .9-8§.. 8 b.g. Passing Sale (FR) — Falcon Crest (FR) (Cadoudal FR) ppb51p19p. Small compact brother flat and jumping winner, Seven (FR), and to Hurdles winner, Falcon Sale (FR). Dam won 2 flat and jumping races in France. FRENCH FLAT '00 r11 w1 (13f) p2. FLAT '01 r1 p0. NH '01/2 (for M.C. Pipe) r15 w3 (2m5f-2m7f Hdles) p5; pulled up 2. Bought Ascot, Aug '02 for 1904. Won a 20-runner flat race at Maisons-Laffitte and subsequently successful in three Hurdles between May and July '01, but could also be very reluctant, and wore headgear (it was only tried once in '04). Generally in an un-cooperative mood in Hunter Chases and Points and tailed of last twice and failed to finish on five occasions, but connections (who like their French breds) left no stone unturned in their attempt to find something he would enjoy, and were rewarded when he took both Opens at Ystradowen, a course as quirky as himself. Three ran at the Glamorgan and the close-up comments make interesting reading, and it was a truly dire contest, but giving Khatani seven pounds and a four length beating at the Ystrad Taf Fechan showed what he can do when he wants. Suited by a sound surface, but keeping him sweet is always going to be a major challenge. *M. Quinlan — Radnor & W. Herefords (Steve Flook).* 229 (O), 447 (Cf), 544 (2m5f110yH), 628 (2m3fH), 738 (O), 892 (2m5f110yH), 1024 (O), 1176 (3m110yH), 1437 (2m5f110yH).

MISTER JULIUS ..—.. 8 b.g. Mister Lord (USA) — Princess Pool (Push On) pp. Compact rather unfurnished. Dam, sister to Nat Gold (*qv* '03 Annual) (Hurdling winner since Pointing), finished alone in 3 starter Maiden on hard and 3rd for the Harries (was a terrible jumper, and only one finished behind her in 9 Points). Looked a character and was very novicey when pulling up in mid-season Maidens (went no more than two miles). *Mrs B.D. Harries — Pembs (Marc Barber).* 675 (CfMa), 948 (OMa).

MISTER MOSS (IRE) ..9-13.. 12 b.g. Don Tristan (USA) — Lindas Statement (IRE) (Strong Statement USA) p2p. Good-topped brother to Irish Pointing winner, Thison. IRISH P-t-P '98 r4 p0 (last twice, pulled up, and fell). P-t-P/HUNT CH '99/00 and '02/3 r12 w3 (up to Confined) p4 (3 3rds, last once, inc 2 Hunt Chses); 4th, and pulled up 4. Very speedy but breaks blood vessels with monotonous regularity, and is very unlucky not to have won many more races than the three that have come his way. Not helped by being so headstrong but dropping him back in trip has had little effect, and unless a cure can be found placing him successfully in future could prove to be a real headache. *D.A. Malam — Cheshire (Gary Hanmer).* 92 (I), 749 (Cf), 1427 (O).

MISTER PARTY .—§§.. 10 b.g. Henbit (USA) — Sally's Dove (Celtic Cone) fp. Tall brother to Hurdles winner, Dove From Above. Dam won 3 2m Hurdles, inc a Sell. Great-grandam is Red Dove. NH FLAT '00 r2 p0. NH '01 r2 p0 (pulled up, and fell). P-t-P/HUNT CH '03 (for Mr & Mrs A.J. Martin) r8 w1 (3-finisher Maiden) p0; last pair 2, and pulled up 5. Rated 9-1 after making all to record a narrow success in a three-finisher Maiden at Mollington last year, but normally works himself into a real state in the preliminaries, and has otherwise only beaten one rival in 11 starts over jumps. Tore off like a scalded cat when punted from 14-1 to half those odds on his reappearance but stopped to nil after the 12th, and was barely crawling in the rear when falling heavily at the next (Tim Eades was lucky to escape censure). Went less than two miles when paired with a more experienced rider next time, and it looks as if connections have already cut their losses. *D. Williams — Silverton (David Pipe).* 65 (Rnr), 148 (R).

MISTER PEPPER (IRE) ..10-3§.. 9 br.g. Leading Counsel (USA) — Bold Strike (FR) (Bold Lad USA) pp3132124331. Compact half-brother to Extra Stout (IRE) (*qv*). IRISH FLAT '98/9 r4 p0. IRISH CHARITY '00 r1 p0. IRISH NH '99 and '02 r3 p0 (6th in Hdle, and 4th and pulled up in Chses). IRISH P-t-P/HUNT CH '00/3 r13 w1 (4&5yo Maiden, 2 finished) p6 (4 2nds, beaten neck once, and beaten ½*l* once; and inc 3rd in Hunt Ch); and pulled up 2. P-t-P '03 r7 w2 (2 runner Restricted and Intermediate) p3 (2nds); last, and pulled up 1. Tough and consistent, and suited by exaggerated waiting tactics, but not the most resolute and only too pleased to settle for a place if the owner cocks up. Can handle very firm ground, and for that reason alone looks certain to add to his tally, but an unsafe betting medium, and thrice a beaten favourite in '04 (including at 4-11 once). Often blinkered in Ireland. *T.D.B. Underwood — V. of Aylesbury with Garth & S. Berks.* 138 (C), 187 (Cf), 422

(CCon), 622 (M), 717 (Cf), 1031 (Cf), 1212 (Cf), 1338 (M), 1410 (Cf), 1492 (Cf), 1514 (Cf), 1549 (O).

PLATE 86 1464 Dulverton Farmers Intermediate: Mister RF's second victory is a first for Ricky Isgar
PHOTO: Baths Photographic

MISTER RF (IRE) ..9-2.. 12 b.g. Dry Dock — Poor Elsie (Crash Course) up18p. Tall strong half-brother to Camden Loch (IRE) (*qv*). P-t-P '99 and '02/3 r12 w3 (Restricted and 2 Members) p1 (2nd); 4th, 5th, last pair 3, and pulled up 3. A reliable jumper and much improved when scoring twice last year, but normally fails to get the trip and only effective on sound surfaces. Provided the raw novice Rikki Isgar with a first success on his second ride at Mounsey Hill Gate, but only had one rival (who was giving away lengths at each fence) to beat, and was hopelessly tailed off last next time. Sweats excessively, and always needs an outing to get fit, but no more than a schoolmaster now. *Miss K. Tripp — Weston & Banwell H.* 365 (I), 1364 (M), 1464 (I), 1556 (MO), 1562 (O).

MISTER RINGA .10-0.. 8 b.g. Karinga Bay — Panda Pops (Cornuto) u1p11p. Tall rangy half-brother to Badger Beer (*qv*). P-t-P '02 r1 p0 (pulled up). Pulled up in a three-runner Maiden on debut, and presumably met with a setback as he spent the next 21 months on the sidelines, but ideally-bred and making up for lost time since. Won his Maiden and Restricted comprehensively enough, but otherwise badly let down by his jumping, and only has experience of good or sound surfaces. As good a rider as Andrew Braithwaite is looks the type that could blossom with professional guidance, but extensive re-schooling could also pay dividends. Has worn over-reach boots. *Mrs C.H. Sporborg — Puckeridge (Christopher Sporborg).* 8 (2m4fOMa), 219 (OMa), 375 (R), 524 (R), 741 (M), 1151 (Cf).

MISTER ROSE (IRE) ..8-7.. 10 b.g. Mister Lord (USA) — Toohami (Nicholas Bill) 2rpp. Compact. Dam won 7f race in England and subsequently won 2m1f Hurdle in Ireland. NH FLAT '00 r2 p0. P-t-P '02/3 r10 p4 (3 3rds, of 4 once, and last once); last pair 2, pulled up 3, and fell 1. Placed on five occasions but stops in the manner of a horse that cannot breathe properly, and has been tried tongue-tied. His yard was under a cloud all year, and it is not inconceivable that a revival is possible, but has been tried in blinkers and cheekpieces, and beginning to look thoroughly jaded. *J.M. Robinson — Burton.* 297 (M), 594 (OMa), 946 (OMa), 1417 (OMa).

MISTER SOOTY ..—.. 7 b.g. Dilum (USA) — Spring Flyer (IRE) (Waajib) f. Good-bodied half-brother to Hurdles winners, Miss Tango and Roveretto (also won Chasing). Dam won 3 flat (7-9f). NH FLAT '03 r1 p0. NH '03 (for M.C. Pipe) r1 p0 (pulled up). Bought Ascot, Dec for 4285. Took a fatal fall at the fourth at Mollington. P.J. & Mrs K. Morgan — Eggesford (Sue Harbour). 295 (OMa).

MISTER SWALLOW ..10-3§.. 8 b.g. Homo Sapien — Ninfa (IRE) (The Parson) 32p2r. Stocky. Dam won 6 2m5f-3m1f Chses. P-t-P '02/3 r6 w2 (Maidens, awarded the first after season ended) p0; pulled up 3, and refused 1. Very able, and came from out of the clouds to clinch a three-finisher Maiden at

Larkhill last year, but has developed into a thoroughly ungenuine pig, and proved very expensive to follow in '04. A certainty for a Restricted if he reproduced his Kingston St Mary running, but always wary of where the boxes are, and is usually reluctant to pass them. Sometimes very keen in the early stages, and connections have resisted the temptation to apply headgear, but it may be their only resort. *R.N. Miller — Portman.* 118 (R), 198 (R), 369 (R), 966 (R), 1366 (R).

MISTRESS RETURN ..—.. 6 ch.m. Bob's Return (IRE) — Mistress Corrado (New Member) p. Owner-bred half-sister to Master Jock (*qv*). Favourite for an early May Maiden over 2m4f, but seemed to lose her confidence after a mistake at the first and was never going well after. May well prove capable of better when she is more clued up. *P.S. Burke — N. Ledbury (Paul Jones).* 1266 (2m4fOMa).

MISTRIO ..8-7.. 8 gr.g. Linamix (FR) — Mistreat (Gay Mecene USA) f2. P-t-P '03 r2 p0 (pulled up 1, and fell 1). NH '04 (for K.C. Bailey) r1 p1 ($3^1/_2$*l* 2nd to Musical Stage in 2m110y Hdle: *2nd til ld app 3 out, sn clr, hdd & jmpd lft last, no ex*). Pulls much too hard to get the trip in Points, and tipped up two out when totally exhausted at Higham in January, but a subsequent appearance over hurdles, when a 66-1 chance, gave hope that he could achieve something over the minimum trip in that sphere. *D.J. Harding-Jones — Puckeridge (Perry Harding-Jones).* 26 (OMa).

MISTY HILLS ..—.. 6 gr.g. Accondy (IRE) — Nuala (Grundy) p. Did not seem to have much idea on his debut, and jumped slowly in the rear until the jockey gave up the unequal struggle after five fences. *Mrs G.F. White — W. Percy (George White).* 433 (OMa).

MISTY RAMBLE (IRE) ..10-0.. 10 b.g. Roselier (FR) — Ramble Bramble (Random Shot) u1uuf3fR. Small compact half-brother to Tommy Hotspur (IRE) (*qv*). IR45,000 3yo. NH FLAT '00 r2 p0. NH '00/3 (for F. Murphy) r15 p8 (inc 2nd in Hdle and 4 Chses); unseated 1. Bought Doncaster, May for 11,000. A difficult ride under Rules because of his reluctance to overtake, and proved deeply frustrating, as he achieved eight placings (beaten under ten lengths in six) at up to 3m3f. Was tongue-tied for the final five attempts, and added blinkers in the latest. Finally got off the mark when giving Graeme McPherson his first winner in a Maiden at Thorpe (the partnership was almost severed at the eighth, but held a clear lead from that point), but a chapter of disasters otherwise and was 26 lengths third in his Members on the only other occasion he got round. Regained blinkers in his most recent Point, and ran out when a poor last in a three-starter Bar bore. Had a Restricted at Weston Park wrapped up when he made a bad mistake at the last and sent his partner into orbit, but the problem is that he never gets any useful assistance including with an uninspired substitute once (fell). The trainer is surely itching to get Julian Pritchard onto his back. *G.P. & Mrs S. McPherson — Cotswold (Jill Carenza).* 51 (OMa), 112 (OMa), 231 (CR), 369 (R), 587 (R), 755 (M), 925 (R), 1199 (C).

MODESTY FORBIDS ..8-12.. 9 b.m. Formidable (USA) — Ming Blue (Primo Dominie) 23. Well-made. FLAT '98/9 r7 p1 (3rd). NH '99 r1 p0. P-t-P '03 r2 p2 (2nd of 3, and 3rd of 4). Resurfaced after four years in the wilderness in '03, and has run passably when making the frame in all four Points, but beaten a minimum of 28 lengths this year, and looks too slow to succeed. *Mrs M. Wall — Monmouths (Liz Morgan).* 846 (M), 1091 (CMam).

MOLLYCARRS GAMBUL ..9-8.. 6 b.m. General Gambul — Emma's Vision (IRE) (Vision USA) 4. Unfurnished. Dam, pulled up twice and ran out in Points for Jeanette Carr-Evans 'thoroughly unpleasant, and an equal waste of time over two miles'. NH '02 (for W.G.M. Turner) r3 p0; pulled up 1. Error-prone when tailed off in Hurdles including a Seller in the latest (pulled up), and 22 lengths fourth in a Saddle Club event in mid-January. Suffers long absences, but might be of interest if fit enough to contest a Maiden. *Mrs J. Carr-Evans — Quantock (Sarah Robinson).* 9 (C).

MONARCH RULER ..9-13.. 6 ch.g. Be My Chief (USA) — Busters Sister (Hasty Word) 61. Dam, half-sister to Shameless Lady (*qv* '01 Annual) won 2 Points at Horseheath and 2nd twice from 5 starts for George Cooper. Bred from a decent mare who would probably have achieved more had she had the chance, and followed an encouraging debut at Marks Tey by beating two subsequent scorers in a three-finisher Maiden there. Looks a bright prospect, and might become a regular East Anglian winner in the years to come. *G.I. Cooper — Essex F. & U. (Cherie Cunningham).* 244 (CfMa), 901 (OMa).

MONEY MAGIC .9-5.. 9 ch.m. Weld — Susie's Money (Seymour Hicks FR) 3. Tiny light-framed half-sister to Manly Money, and to NH flat and jumping winner, The Sawdust Kid. Dam, half-sister to Seymore Money (*qv* '97 Annual). P-t-P/HUNT CH '02/3 (for Miss S.E. Broadhurst & Mr J.R. Parrott) r9 p3 (2 3rds; and 2nd of 3); pulled up 4, unseated 2. Speedy and often leads for a fair percentage of the journey, but yet to look like getting home, and seems to have missed the boat now that 2m4f Maidens are no longer an option. *D. Lomax — Holcombe.* 1261 (OMa).

MONKS ERROR (IRE) ..11-1.. 12 b.g. Eve's Error — Miss Outlaw (IRE) (Lancastrian) 31. Close-coupled. IRISH NH FLAT '97 r2 p0. IRISH NH '98/03 (for F. Berry, and M. Halford) r35 w2 (2m3f Hdle and 2m Ch) p10; fell/unseated 3, pulled up 1. Not much of an achiever in Ireland where he was only twice successful in 37 races, but showed he had ability when gaining a £9,750 prize in December '01 in the second of his wins. Acquired blinkers or cheekpieces on his final three attempts, but was much more positive and consistent in the new yard, and followed a splendid run over 3m7f (which seemed a bit far) with a notable defeat of Macgeorge and Masalarian over a mile less at

Uttoxeter. Continued in good heart with seconds in Handicap Chases in the summer (given a very negative ride once, and occasionally jumped right when only beaten one-and-three-quarter lengths next time), and could find another good prize if fairly weighted. *J. Parfitt — Ystrad Taf Fechan.* 1441 (3m7fH), 1512 (2m6f110yH).

MONNAIE FORTE (IRE) ..10-3.. 15 b.g. Strong Gale — Money Run (Deep Run) 4. Tall half-brother to Billy Buckskin, and to Hurdles winner, Silk Trader. Dam, half-sister to Jake The Rake (*qv* '94 Annual), won 2 Hurdles and Chase, all 2m in Ireland. NH '95/02 (for A. Turnell, one win, and J.R. Adam) r45 w10 (5 2m1f-2m2f Hdles and 5 2m3f-2m4f Chses) p14; pulled up 7, fell 4 (inc 3 consecutively). Made a surprise reappearance in an Ayr Hunter Chase, and did his best, but eventually faded to finish 25 lengths fourth. A former admirable performer who has earned £96,901, but his great exuberance gave him early problems over fences (fell in three consecutive Chases) and tried to run out in one of them, but then won three Hurdles in a row in March/April '97. Lucky in one Chasing victory (was eight lengths third when left clear at the last) but after taking his haul into double figures he was unable to score after April '98. Has shown a tendency to hang left, was tongue-tied once in '99, and reported to have breathing difficulties in '01. To cap it all, he ended '02 by pulling up lame. Will hopefully enjoy a richly deserved retirement. *J.R. Adam — College V. & N. Northumberland (Clive Storey).* 439 (2m5f110yH).

MON PERFORMER .8-7.. 11 ch.g. Mon Tresor — Hot Performer (Hotfoot) 27. Small light-framed brother to Magic Performer. Dam won 4 flat (7-12f), the first 2 Sells. FLAT r4 p0. NH '97 r3 p0 (inc 2 4ths, beaten 12-20l). P-t-P '99 r2 p1 (2nd); and slipped up. FLAT '02 r2 p0. NH '02/3 (for D.W. Barker) r6 p1 (3rd in Sell Hdle); pulled up 2. Plunged on from eights to 7-4 favourite on his Pointing debut in '99, but slipped up on a bend, and proved moody when unable to dominate under Rules subsequently. Frail and does not get the trip well enough in Points, and was getting the worst of the argument when all but falling at the last on his latest appearance. Blinkered twice in '97. *M.J. Harland — Hurworth (Chris Dennis).* 877 (OMa), 1165 (OMa).

MONSTER MOSS ..—.. 10 ch.g. Le Moss — Stubbs Daughter (Stubbs Gazette) p. Tall plain half-brother to Design X Press (*qv*). Jumped very erratically and soon well tailed off on his belated debut at Maisemore, and the rider sensibly pulled up after only four fences whilst still alive. *Miss J. Williams — Gelligaer F.* 729 (OMa).

MONSUKH (IRE) ..7-11§.. 10 b.m. Magical Wonder (USA) — Still River (Kings Lake USA) pp3. Workmanlike half-brother to 4 winners (3 flat, including 2 abroad, and one Irish NH flat). Dam placed 3 times in France. IRISH NH FLAT '99/00 r4 p0. IRISH NH '02 r1 p0 (pulled up). IRISH P-t-P '02 r4 w1 (5-7yo Mares Maiden) p3. P-t-P '03 r5 p1 (last of 2); and pulled up 4. Won a bad Maiden in Ireland, but useless in eight attempts for present connections, and has only finished in front of a remounted rival. Acquired blinkers in '04, and certainly not worth racing again. *Miss C. Eagle — E. Essex (Paula Twinn).* 45 (Cnr), 124 (CCon), 243 (M).

MONTENEGRO .9-12.. 7 gr.g. Terimon — Spartan Sprite (Country Retreat) 41. Tall rangy. Dam, half-sister to Sparkling Spirit (*qv* '01 Annual), won 3m2f Hunt Chase and 9 Points (5 Opens) and placed 7 for the Somerleytons (10-8 and capable of winning very impressively in her heyday, but became very sour). NH FLAT '03 (for F. Murphy) r1 p0. The fourth generation of his family to race for the Somerleytons, and followed a promising fourth at Marks Tey with a gutsy win in a youngsters Maiden at Fakenham in which he pipped On The Day (who had previously finished 12 lengths ahead of him) in the dying strides. Probably some way short of his peak, and it would be exciting to think that he could emulate his mother. One to keep an eye on. *Lord Somerleyton — Dunston H. (Nigel Bloom).* 244 (CfMa), 1155 (OMa).

MONTY'S LASS (IRE) ..10-8.. 9 b.m. Montelimar (USA) — Smash N Lass (Crash Course) 25. Compact well-made. Dam, half-sister to Botany Blade (*qv* '93 Annual), won 2m4f Chase in Ireland. P-t-P/HUNT CH '02/3 r9 w4 (inc 3m2f110y Hunt Ch, inc hat-trick '03) p4 (2nds); and 4th. A thorough stayer, and completed a hat-trick in '03, but taken off her feet when a strong-finishing second to the ill-fated Right To Reply on her return, and given no assistance from the saddle when joint-favourite for a race that looked tailor-made at Kilworthy next time (finished 14 lengths behind the runner-up and the rider was fined £125 by the local stewards for failing to ride the horse to achieve the best possible placing). Not seen since but will surely be able to atone with strong guidance in '05. Has won on firmish, but beat nothing in the process, and is far more effective in mud. *Mrs S. Prouse — Eggesford.* 196 (O), 569 (MO).

MOONLITE MAGIC (IRE) .—§.. 11 br.g. Phardante (FR) — Lucey Allen (Strong Gale) 6pp. Small. NH FLAT '00 r1 p1 (3rd). NH '00/3 (for F. Murphy, and Miss Z.C. Davison, one run) r18 w1 (3m4f Hdle) p2 (2nds); fell/unseated 3. Won a pathetic long-distance Selling Hurdle in soft at Sedgefield in November '01, but was beaten 18 lengths plus in five Chases (unseated once) and made mistakes and was not keen. Only sighted once in '03, and was a waste of time in Ladies Opens, finishing a furlong last on his only completion. Wears headgear or cheekpieces. *Miss J. Wickens — Kent & Surrey Bloodhounds.* 189 (L), 246 (L), 1086 (L).

MOON TIGER ..10-5.. 12 b.g. Tigerwood — Moon Haven (Brave Simon) 4p. Small. Dam, sister to Cefn Andy (*qv* '90 Annual), pulled up 4 in '94. Grandam, Cefn Inver, pulled up 7 and fell/unseated 2, and great-grandam, Exinver, was placed 9; all Pointed for Dilwyn Thomas. NH FLAT '97 r1 p0 (16th of 17). NH '97 r1 p0 (pulled up). P-t-P '98/00 and '03 r32 w8 (inc 3 Opens, inc 4-timer '03) p11 (6 2nds; 4 3rds, of 4 once); pulled up 6, fell 1. Hails from a long line of equine bag ladies, but all heart himself, and made hay when sun shone in '03, and recorded a four-timer on sound surfaces in which there were a maximum of three finishers. Sometimes gives the impression that three miles is a shade too far, and cannot handle mud, but unfortunately appeared to go wrong at Llanfrynach, and time is no longer on his side. *D.R. Thomas — Llangeinor.* 360 (O), 448 (O).

MOOREPARK JOY (IRE) ..7-6.. 8 br.g. Jolly Jake (NZ) — Dark Friend (IRE) (Mandalus) 6. IRISH P-t-P '03 r6 p0 (6th of 7, and pulled up 5). Has only beaten one horse in seven Points, and was 38 lengths last in the latest. Unpromising. *Mrs D. Buckett — Hursley Hambledon.* 52 (OMa).

MOORFOOT BLAZE .8-10.. 8 b.g. Blaze O'Gold (USA) — Auntie Mo (Bronze Hill) 3. Owner-bred. Dam, half-sister to Lucy's Brig (*qv* '93 Annual). Twelve lengths third in a weak Mosshouses Maiden on his debut, and it may be worth trying him in a similar grade again. *Miss H. Brown — Lauderdale (Joan Hollands).* 1225 (OMa).

MOORLAND ROSE .9-6.. 10 br.m. Lir — Moorland Heath VII (unknown) 343p. Small stocky sister to Moorland Abbot, and half-sister to Moorland Highflyer. P-t-P/HUNT CH '00 and '02/3 r18 w3 (Maiden, Restricted and Members) p3 (3rd of 4 twice, and last once); last pair 7, pulled up 4, and refused 1. Came with a wet sail to score twice for Sue Young in '02, but totally ineffective without an easy surface and strong handling, and was always labouring reluctantly to catch up on unsuitable ground this year. Likely to slow up even further next year, and in danger of being lapped on some of the shorter West Country tracks. *Miss P.D. Mitchell — E. Cornwall.* 908 (Cf), 1197 (4mL), 1348 (Cf), 1433 (Cf).

MOORLANDS AGAIN ..—.. 10 b.g. Then Again — Sandford Springs (USA) (Robellino USA) R. Tall brother to Irish Pointing and English Chasing winner, Moorlands Spring, and half-brother to NH flat winner, Moorlands Return. Dam won 12f race. NH FLAT '99 r2 p0. FLAT '00/1 r15 p1 (3rd). NH '01 and '03 (for J.M. Bradley, and C.L. Tizzard) r6 w1 (3m3f Ch) p2 (2nds inc Hdle); fell 1. Won a three-finisher staying Chase in soft at Fontwell in which he made all and came home nearly two fences clear, and was beaten under two lengths in both seconds including a Hurdle. Finished half-a-length third of 20 in a flat race, and fell at the last when a close second but looking held in a Chase. Blinkered once on the level. Led until running out at halfway in a Ladies on the second day of the season, and failed to resurface. Inconsistent and seems to have gone wrong (missed '02), but his best form would give him claims in Points. *W.J. Odell — N. Cotswold (Shauna Odell).* 10 (L).

MORAIRA (IRE) ..8-13.. 6 ch.g. Flemensfirth (USA) — Rossmill Lady (IRE) (Be My Native USA) p4. Shaped pleasingly when five lengths fourth in a Conditions Maiden on his second appearance, and should have a better than average chance of winning at six. *Mrs C.M. Tinkler — Middleton.* 773 (2m4fCMa), 960 (OMa).

MORATTI (IRE) .—.. 7 b.g. Farhaan — Marble World (IRE) (Top Of The World) p. Workmanlike. 16,000 4yo. Made mistakes and pulled up after only five fences when already tailed off on an inauspicious debut on the first day of the season. *G.C. Maundrell — Berks & Bucks (Paul Thompson).* 8 (2m4fOMa).

MORE FLAIR ..10-3.. 8 ch.m. Alflora (IRE) — Marejo (Creetown) 531211. Owner-bred half-sister to Jupiter Jo (*qv*). NH FLAT '02 r2 p0. P-t-P '03 r4 p2; and pulled up 2. Novicey and taken very steadily at first but repaid that kindness in full in '04, and only Decent Bond denied her a four-timer. A well-backed favourite for all three successes in softish and on firmish, and jumped well enough to suggest that she might be worth trying again under Rules in the near future. Wore a tongue-tie and a cross-noseband when successful at Tranwell. *J.B. & F.A. Walton — Border (Jimmy Walton).* 433 (OMa), 767 (2m4fOMa), 919 (CMa), 1077 (R), 1310 (R), 1418 (Cf).

MORPH ..9-11.. 11 gr.g. Baron Blakeney — Amber Marsh (Arctic Kanda) 2f1p2. Tall owner-bred brother to Noah and Amber Life. Dam ran in just 8 races to 13, including 2 Points for Ray York. NH FLAT '98/9 r2 p0 (tailed off — pulled up debut). NH '01 r2 p0 (tailed off in Hdles). P-t-P '00 and '02 r4 p1 (½*l* 2nd); and fell 3. NH '02 r2 p1 (2nd); and pulled up. Has been incredibly unlucky, and finally gained a thoroughly deserved success when trouncing modest opposition at Higham, but still inclined to fall over, and had not recovered fully from being struck into on his previous start when hanging left on the run-in when second at Cottenham. Frail like most of his relatives, but should find a Restricted if ready to resume in '05. *R.H. York — Staff College.* 6 (OMa), 40 (OMa), 154 (OMa), 294 (R), 559 (R).

MORRIS PIPER ..10-0§.. 12 b.g. Long Leave — Miss Cone (Celtic Cone) 11p2p. Small unfurnished half-brother to Mister Cone. Dam, half-sister to Still In Business (*qv*), won 2 Points and placed 3rd. Grandam, Mill Miss, won Ladies (beat rejoiner in freak contest) and 3rd. P-t-P/HUNT CH '98/01 and '03 (for Mr I. Farleigh) r29 w3 (up to Confined) p8 (4 2nds; and inc last of 3, and 3rd in Hunt Ch); 4th, 5th, last pair 7, pulled up 6, refused 2, and fell 1. Scored twice in '00, and was recording a third successive win when completing a double at Black Forest Lodge this year, but has never been straightforward, and back problems (which cause him to jump right-handed) and a tendency to act the goat at the start have meant he lacks consistency. Ideally suited by an easy three miles, but strong handling and a sound surface are essential. Has been tried in a tongue-strap. *D. Partridge — Tiverton (Rose Partidge).* 147 (I), 412 (Cf), 799 (2m3f110yH), 1127 (Cf), 1269 (MO).

MORRISTHEMILK .—.. 7 b.g. Arms And The Man — Ginny (Push On) p. Strong-topped. P-t-P '03 (for Mr E.W. Morris) r2 p0 (pulled up 2). Tailed off and pulled up by the 13th at the latest in three Welsh Maidens, and has only shown speed for a mile in one of them. Wears a cross-noseband. *I. Lewis — Pembs (Wynne Morris).* 204 (CfMa).

MOSCOW'S RETURN (IRE) ..9-3§.. 8 ch.g. Moscow Society (USA) — Arkinfield (IRE) (Ovac ITY) p74p23. Very tall. Dam, half-sister Layham Low (*qv* '03 Annual). IRISH P-t-P '02 r6 w1 (5&6yo Maiden) p0; pulled up 2, refused 1. P-t-P '03 r5 p0 (pulled up 5). The only one of 16 starters to complete the course when successful in mud in Ireland, but pulled up in his first six English outings, and exposed as a real villain since. Looked dangerous approaching the last when six lengths fourth at Didmarton, but put his head in the air and refused to go through with his effort, and hung left on the run-in after joining the winner at the last at Kimble, and must be shunned at every opportunity. *J. Trice-Rolph — Heythrop.* 36 (CR), 294 (R), 369 (R), 587 (R), 870 (R), 1123 (R).

MOSCOW TRADITION (IRE) .9-11.. 7 b.g. Moscow Society (USA) — Bucks Grove (IRE) (Buckskin FR) p3p2up. Strong-topped brother to NH flat and Hurdling winner, Society Buck (IRE). IR12,000 3yo. IRISH P-t-P '02 r1 w1 (4yo Maiden). NH '02/3 (for J. O'Neill) r6 p2; unseated 1. Won an Irish four-year old Maiden in heavy and subsequently pipped on the post when short-headed in one of two placings over Hurdles, but certainly not straightforward, and jumped poorly and was never going well before unseating in his only Chase (favourite). Has shown a tendency to hang left, and managed another unseat when 4-5 in his Members, but frustratingly appeared to win a Restricted at Thorpe by half-a-length only for the Judge (who had less idea of what was going on than even the most casual spectator) to place him two lengths second. Deserves compensation, but matters are made worse by his habit of breaking blood vessels, and is never a reliable betting medium. *Mrs J.H. Docker — Atherstone (John Docker).* 383 (R), 481 (R), 787 (CR), 944 (R), 1118 (M), 1217 (R).

MO'S GREY ..—.. 7 gr.m. Baron Blakeney — Lizzie Boon (Le Moss) p. Compact. Dam, half-sister to 7 Pointers, including Gunner Boon (*qv* '02 Annual), pulled up once and fell twice in Points for David Brace. Grandam, Miss Boon, was unbeaten in 2 flat (12f), and won 5 Hdles at around 2m and 3 Chses (2m-2m4f) and placed 8. P-t-P '03 r1 p0 (pulled up). Reported to be suffering with sore shins after pulling up after two miles on her debut, and presumably similarly afflicted when forced to call it a day after a mile on her return (led to post early and jumped poorly). *D. Brace — Llangeinor.* 453 (CfMa).

MO'S O FRIENDLY..8-12.. 9 ch.h. Lir — Miss Kernow (Cruise Missile) 5pp46f2. Small neat. Dam, half-sister to Stoke Hand (*qv* '97 Annual), was 3rd in Maiden (only beat one horse in 8 races — a bad jumper, and failed to finish 6). P-t-P '02/3 r6 p0 (4th, last 2, and pulled up 3). A Pointing rarity in that he remains an entire, but exposed as modest in the extreme (only beaten five rivals in seven completions), and has never finished within 15 lengths of the winner. Considering his delicate undercarriage one would imagine he would pick his feet up at the fences, but remains prone to parting the birch (brings tears to the eyes). Has worn a cross-noseband, and been tried in a tongue-tie. *C. Fowlie — Lamerton (Mark Ranger).* 68 (OMa), 148 (R), 567 (CfMa), 795 (CfMa), 1272 (OMa), 1353 (OMa), 1436 (OMa).

MOSSCROFT JACK ..9-4.. 8 b.g. Le Moss — Doris Blake (Roscoe Blake) p5p8p1. Workmanlike home-bred half-brother to China Lal (*qv*). Did not beat another horse in his first five races and took a long time to get the hang of jumping (was clueless on his debut), but partnered by Tessa Clarke for the first time in a 2m4f Maiden in soft at Alpraham and kept plugging on to score. Has worn a tongue-tie on his last three appearances. Can possibly be thereabouts in Restricteds if maintaining the progress and providing his wind does not worsen. *Miss E. Tomkinson — Cheshire (John Swindells).* 4 (Cnr), 96 (CfMa), 226 (CfMa), 709 (Mah), 985 (OMa), 1049 (2m4fOMa).

MOSTYN .—§.. 14 ch.g. Astral Master — Temple Rock (Melody Rock) 2p3r. Good-topped compact home-bred. Dam was a useless Pointer (pulled up in 5 of 7 Points). P-t-P/HUNT CH '96/03 r40 w7 (inc 2m3f110y Hunt Ch, Open and 2 Ladies) p9 (5 2nds, of 3 once; and inc last of 3 twice); pulled up 10, fell/unseated 2, and refused 1. A bold-jumping front-runner in his prime, and lowered the track record at Larkhill in '02, but has always mixed good efforts with bad ones, and nearly declined to set off for the second time in his career prior to refusing at halfway on his latest appearance. Seems to have lost all enthusiasm and it would be no surprise if connections drew stumps. *R.J. Weaver — Berkeley (John Tuck).* 816 (Cf), 1099 (L), 1321 (MO), 1493 (L).

MOTHER'S RUIN ..9-1.. 12 b.g. Oedipus Complex — Pretty Penny (Naucetra) 2. Small neat owner-bred. P-t-P '03 r2 p1 (3rd of 4); and 4th of 5. Makes the odd mistake, though seems safe enough, but readily outpaced come the business end, and beaten upwards of 11 lengths to date. Does not appear to take the sport too seriously, and has only the faintest chance of winning at 12. *H. & S. Thorpe — Brocklesby (Harry Thorpe).* 302 (OMa).

MOUNTAIN LILY ..9-0.. 8 b.m. Southern Music — Delight's Daughter (Amboise) pp2513p. Small. Dam, half-sister to Pay-U-Cash (*qv* '99 Annual), was placed in 4 Points for the Prichards. Grandam, Abbots Delight, won 3 Points and placed 7 for them. P-t-P '02/3 r8 p3 (2 2nds, last once); 4th, pulled up 3, and carried out 1. Twice a beaten favourite and runner-up thrice before she eventually scored at the 14th attempt, but had absolutely nothing left in the tank at Cilwendeg, and it is not certain she would have succeeded had Black Hope not made her exit at the last. Lacks fluency and almost certainly too weak a finisher to add a Restricted. Has run tongue-tied. *I. Prichard — Pentyrch.* 35 (CMam), 204 (CfMa), 362 (CfMa), 453 (CfMa), 675 (CfMa), 1089 (M), 1388 (R).

MOUNTAIN TROOPER ..9-8.. 6 b.g. Infantry — Mountain Glen (Lochnager) p22. Compact well-made half-brother to Glendoran. Dam won 2 Points and 2nd twice, including a 2nd for Andrew Mobley, and is half-sister to 6 Pointers, including Honourable Man. Grandam, Woodland Maiden, won 4 Ladies (inc Middleton 4-miler) and placed 8. Traces back to some stars of the 80s (Honourable Man should have won the Cheltenham Foxhunters in 1982) and followed a schooling run when backward on his debut by finishing runner-up in two Maidens at Mollington. Beaten five lengths by Killard Point, who looks to be going places, over 2m4f, and then beaten slightly less by Lah Di Dah Lad over the full trip. Could do with jumping a little better, but is surely a winner in waiting, and might turn out to be pretty decent. *A. Mobley — Bicester with Whaddon.* 127 (R), 291 (2m4fCfMa), 589 (CfMa).

MOUNT ALPHA (IRE) .—.. 9 ch.g. Alphabatim (USA) — Youthful Capitana (Hardboy) p. Strong half-brother to 4 unplaced jumpers. Dam, half-sister to Captive (*qv*). IR4500 4yo. NH FLAT '02 r1 p0. NH '02 (for D. McCain) r2 p0 (pulled up 2). Bought Ascot, Jun for 2095. Very lightly raced, and was pulling up for the third time in succession over jumps (including a Chase) at Brocklesby Park. Very suspect. *Miss J.L. Lundgren — Brocklesby.* 482 (OMa).

PLATE 87 1493 14 Regiment Royal Artillery Ladies Open: Defying his years Mounthenry Star wins for Charlotte Tizzard *PHOTO: Brian Armstrong*

MOUNTHENRY STAR (IRE) ..10-2.. 17 b.g. Kambalda — Rathoe Princess (Never Slip) 1. Workmanlike half-brother to Hollow Wood (IRE) and Tom Brown (IRE). Dam is an unraced half-sister to Barton Bank. IRISH NH FLAT '92/3 r4 w1 (2m4f) p1 (2nd). IRISH NH '92/7 r41 w3 (2 2m4f Hdles and 2m1f Ch) p7. IRISH P-t-P '97 r3 p1 (2nd); pulled up 1. NH '98 r6 p2 (2nds in 2m4f-3m Chses); unseated 1. P-t-P/HUNT CH '98/9 and '02/3 r22 w10 (inc 4 Opens and Mixed Open, 4-timer '98, hat-trick '02) p5 (2 3rds, inc Hunt Ch); pulled up 1, fell/unseated 2. Despite rapidly advancing years remains a phenomenally quick Pointer, and illustrated that his enthusiasm remains undiminished when blitzing round Larkhill in just under six minutes on his only appearance in '04. Sometimes let down by his tendency to hurdle the fences, and is only effective over a bare three miles on sound surfaces. Apparently not the type to accept honourable retirement, and will probably die with his boots on. *Mrs V. Ramm — Cotswold (Jelly Nolan).* 1493 (L).

MOUNTSORREL (IRE) ..9-10.. 6 b.g. Charnwood Forest (IRE) — Play The Queen (IRE) (King Of Clubs) p214. Small well-made half-brother to flat winners, Salty Jack, Franco Mina, Oh Never Again and Terraquin. Dam won 7f race in Ireland. 6000f, 32,000y. FLAT '02/3 r12 p2 (2nds). NH '02/3 (for T. Wall) r3 p0. Placed in two Sellers at around 12f on sound surfaces, but was beaten 54 lengths plus including in the bottom grade over Hurdles. Wore blinkers or cheekpieces on four occasions, and tongue-tied once. More effective in Points, and followed a second with a win over 2m4f at Eyton-on-Severn, where he was backed from 6s to 5-2 and was already in command by three out. Twenty lengths fourth in a Restricted next time and not disgraced, but may have to prove he gets the trip in that grade. *D. Pugh — N. Salop (Gordy Edwards).* 227 (CfMa), 533 (2m4fCfMa), 929 (2m4fOMa), 1265 (R).

MOUSE BIRD (IRE) .9-12§§.. 15 b.g. Glow (USA) — Irish Bird (USA) (Sea Bird II) p. Compact half-brother to 5 flat winners, including Assert (smart), Bikala (Prix du Jockey-Club), and to Almoojid (never won, but sire of Tomoojid, *qv*). Dam won at 11f in France and is half-sister to Irish Ball (won Irish Derby). IRISH FLAT '93 r4 p4 (beaten head once). NH '93/02 r47 w7 (2 2m1f Hdles and 5 2m-2m4f110y Chses) p20 (13 2nds); pulled up 6, fell 1. P-t-P '03 r2 p0 (last pair twice). Always possessed too much sense to be as good as he was bred to be, but put his acceleration to good use on seven occasions, and enjoyed a career highlight when landing the Greenalls Chase at Haydock in '99. Refused to do a tap subsequently, and found Pointing no less demeaning, and sadly broke down irreparably at Barbury. C. Smyth — V.W.H. 32 (Cnr).

MOUSESKI ..11-1.. 11 b.g. Petoski — Worth Matravers (National Trust) pf21111f. Small half-brother to Worthahand, and to Irish Chasing winner, Forget The Past. Dam won 2 Points (also disqualified from Ladies for missing a fence) and placed 8 for Michael Dare. P-t-P '99 r1 p0 (pulled up). NH FLAT '99/00 r4 p1 (2nd). NH '01/2 (for R.J. Hodges) r7 w1 (2m1f Hdle) p2 (3rds); pulled up 1, fell 1. Averaged three outings per annum to April '02, and spent the next 21 months on the sidelines, but scored on his second appearance over hurdles, and needed time to get his act together over fences. Ran up a four-timer in the second half of the season, and has blossomed since being switched to sub-3m events. Ideally switched off and brought through as late as possible, and found himself going for home plenty soon enough at Exeter, but revelled in conditions previously thought to be unsuitable at Cheltenham, and looks sure to be hard to beat in '05. *M.H. Dare — Blackmore & Sparkford V. (Richard Barber).* 89 (O), 236 (Cnr), 319 (O), 578 (L), 799 (2m3f110yH), 1173 (2m110yH), 1372 (2m4fH), 1454 (3mH).

PLATE 88 131 Jedforest Members: L to R, Mozielaw (Morag Neill), 1st, has the measure of Native Alibi (Charlie Shirley-Beavan), 2nd PHOTO: Alan Mitchell

MOZIELAW ..9-4.. 10 b.m. Le Moss — Mainhope (Cruise Missile) 1655p. Small lengthy. Dam (*qv* '95 Annual), sister to Callawhope, and half-sister to Dere Street (*qv*), won Maiden and third thrice for the Elliots. Grandam, Jed Again, was 3rd in Maiden for Rhona Elliot. P-t-P '02/3 r14 w2 (Maiden and

Restricted) p3 (3rds, of 4 twice); 5th, 7th, pulled up 5, and fell/unseated 2. A thorough stayer, and unlucky not to have scored on all three seasonal debuts, but moody and inconsistent, and a waste of time unless the going is on the easy side. Will struggle to make any sort of impression in competitive events. *The Cheviots (Mrs R.L. Elliot) — Jedforest (Morag Neill).* 131 (M), 210 (Cf), 427 (I), 857 (4mMO), 1080 (Cf).

MR BALDWIN (IRE) ..7-8.. 7 ch.g. Roselier (FR) — Charming Mo (IRE) (Callernish) 8p5. Well-made half-brother to NH flat winner, Northern Native (IRE). IRISH P-t-P '03 r4 p0 (6th, pulled up 2, and unseated 1). Equally unimpressive in Ireland and England, and had one horse behind him when a very remote finisher twice in '04. Nicknamed Mike or Stanley at home. *W.J. Turcan — Fernie.* 885 (M), 1215 (CfMa), 1403 (2m4fOMa).

MR BALOO ..8-12§§.. 11 b.g. Petoski — Miss Bunce (Mummy's Game) pr2. Good-bodied owner-bred. Dam is sister to Torenaga's Triumph (*qv* '94 Annual). P-t-P '00/3 r10 p1 (3rd); last, pulled up 4, refused 3 and fell 1. A prize thief, and has stopped once in four out of five campaigns, and only once better than last in 13 appearances. Has ability but needs to dominate, and was allowed to lead until the winner breezed past at the last at Holnicote, but prone to making blunders, and is best shunned. Wears blinkers. *Womans Logic Racing Partnership (Mrs J.M. Prendergast) — S. & W. Wilts (Sarah Waugh).* 325 (OMa), 884 (OMa), 1326 (OMa).

PLATE 89 1012 Seavington PPORA Club Members (Nov Rdrs): Blackwater Brave gives George Fry his first winner at the expense of Mr Ben Gunn and Vicky Heal *PHOTO: Brian Armstrong*

MR BEN GUNN ..9-12.. 13 ch.g. Newski (USA) — Long John Silvia (Celtic Cone) 644332152R. Smallish. Dam failed to finish in 3 Points, but grandam, Hidden Treasure, won 2m4f Ch and 5 Points and placed total of 10. P-t-P '99/00 (for Mr M.A. Tylor) r10 w1 (Maiden) p3 (2 3rds; also disqualified from 2nd once — not weigh-in); 5th, 8th, fell 1, and ran out 2. NH '01/3 (for J.D. Frost) r17 w1 (3-finisher 2m4f Ch) p4 (3rds); fell 1, pulled up 3. Won his Maiden in '99, and followed up in a 4-runner Market Rasen Chase 18 starts later, and whilst he has never looked the easiest of rides did well for newcomer Victoria Heal, and gained a third success when backed from sixes to half those odds at Larkhill. Normally easy to beat and the rider allowed David Dunsdon to steal a march on a return visit to Salisbury Plain, and will struggle to find suitable opportunities in future. All his form is on right-handed tracks and remains liable to duck out if racing in the other direction. Wears a cross-noseband. *W.F. & Miss V. Heal — Blackmore & Sparkford V. (Vicky Heal).* 63 (L), 140 (MO), 262 (L), 350 (M), 603 (Cnr), 1012 (Cnr), 1101 (Cnr), 1369 (Cf), 1492 (Cf), 1556 (MO).

MR BUCKLE (IRE) ..8-12.. 6 ch.g. Broken Hearted — Annesley Lady (IRE) (Over The River FR) R33. Dam won 4&5yo Mares Maiden in Ireland. Bought Doncaster, May for 2000. Ran out and unseated at the fifth on his debut, and then beaten over 20 lengths in both Maiden thirds. Only lost second in the closing stages once, but will have to improve a few pounds to score. *Mrs J. Mackie — Meynell & S. Staffs (William Mackie).* 303 (OMa), 985 (OMa), 1124 (OMa).

MR BUSBY ..—.. 12 b.g. La Grange Music — Top-Anna (IRE) (Ela-Mana-Mou) pp3pppp5. Tall lengthy dipped half-brother to flat winner, Vincent (10 wins on all-weather to date). Dam won 5 flat, 12-16f. NH FLAT '98 r4 w1 p1 (2nd). FLAT '01 r1 p0. NH '98/02 (for Mrs M. Reveley, both wins, and J.L. & J.A. Harris) r26 w2 (2m-2m2f Hdles) p8 (inc 3rd in Sell); fell 1, pulled up 2. Bought Doncaster, Nov for 1000. Won a 25-runner bumper at 50-1 and later successful twice over Hurdles to February '99 (all successes on easy surfaces), but showed his only form in six Chases when falling at the last in two lengths second, and reverted to the smaller obstacles for his final ten attempts. Did surprisingly well to finish five-and-three-quarter lengths third to Bohemian Spirit over 2m6f at Ayr (50-1 again), but otherwise appalling in the new yard and was last once and pulled up six times. Stable-companion of Havetwotaketwo and The Met Man — what an awful trio. *M. & Mrs S. Smith — Jedforest (Michael Smith).* 72 (O), 163 (O), 439 (2m5f110yH), 798 (3m1fH), 994 (3m110yH), 1179 (3m1fH), 1373 (2m4f110yH), 1477 (O).

MR COONEY (IRE) ..—§.. 11 b.g. Van Der Linden (FR) — Green Orchid (Green Shoon) ppp. Strong-topped half-brother to Ballyday Snow (IRE), and to Irish Pointing winner, Ballyday Dawn. P-t-P '01/2 (for Mr J. Clements) r4 w1 (Maiden) p1 (3rd of 4); 4th, and last. IRISH P-t-P '04 (for J. Clements) r2 p0 (pulled up 2; in Winners of One at The Pigeons: *bhnd til pu 8*; and in 4m Open at Limavady: *prom til wknd aft 15, t.o when pu aft 3 out*). Rated 9-10 after winning a weak Maiden taking over seven minutes at Brocklesby Park in '02, but a big disappointment in his other starts, and performed as though something was gravely amiss when pulled up before halfway on his reappearance from a new yard. Fared little better in Ireland subsequently where he qualified with a Newry certificate. Wore blinkers at Wetherby. *D. Mossop — Eglinton (John Parkes).* 122 (3m1fH).

MR EVANS .—.. 10 ch.g. Current Edition (IRE) — Manor Park Crumpet (True Song) pp. Strong-topped. Dam, sister to two Pointers, and half-sister to Just Like Madge (*qv* '03 Annual) was a pygmy who fell, unseated and refused in Points for John Jones. NH FLAT '01 r3 w1 p0. NH '02 (for Miss E.C. Lavelle) r3 p1 (2nd in Ch); pulled up 1 and unseated 1. Pulled up after two miles in two races in which he did not have the faintest hope. *J. Jones — Gelligaer F.* 147 (I), 447 (Cf).

MR FEARLESS ..—.. 10 gr.g. Fearless Action (USA) — Pentino (Rugantino) 4. Strong-topped homebred brother to Penaction. Dam, sister to Rugy, and half-sister to 2 more Pointers, won 2 Points and placed 15 (inc 8 Hunt Chses); failed to score for Robin Rainbow latterly. P-t-P '03 r3 p0 (pulled up 3). Twenty-five lengths last of two in the heavyweight section of his Members, but fences behind the principals, and clearly not built for speed. Wears a cross-noseband. *G. Lockwood & R. Rainbow — N. Cotswold (Florence Lockwood).* 921 (M).

MR HAWKEYE (USA) ..10-8.. 6 ch.g. Royal Academy (USA) — Port Plaisance (USA) (Woodman USA) 1. Tall. Dam won 4 races at up to 12f in France and USA. FLAT '02/3 (for W.J. Haggas, and Ms A.E. Embiricos) r6 p1 (3rd). NH '03 r1 p0 (pulled up). Bought Newmarket, Aut '02 for 2500. A disappointment on the flat when the best he could manage was ten lengths third (visored once, and beaten 36 lengths plus on his final three attempts), but reported to have been used to lead William Haggas's Group horses at home. Pulled up in his only Hurdle, but was a very impressive winner in a Maiden at Higham in which he soon spreadeagled the field and came home 35 lengths clear despite being eased on the run-in, and registered the second fastest time of the day (even beating Spring Gale in the Ladies). His apparent touch of class may now come in useful, and sold with a career under Rules in mind, and a hawkeye should be kept on him. *Ms A.E. Embiricos — Thurlow.* 833 (OMa).

MR KAAR ..—.. 8 b.g. Royal Fountain — City Lighter (Lighter) ppp. Workmanlike well-made owner-bred. NH '04 (for R. Johnson) r1 p0 (pulled up in 2m4f110y Hdle: *a bhnd, t.o & pu 2 out*). Struggling when pulled up after two miles in late season Hexham Maidens, and looked no more interested when sent under Rules (was equipped with cheekpieces once). *J.L. Gledson — Border.* 1422 (OMa), 1474 (2m4fOMa).

MR KENT ..—.. 10 b.g. Teenoso (USA) — Emily Kent (Royal Palace) p. Workmanlike lengthy half-brother to Loddon Lad and Little Nipper, to jumping winner, Emily's Star, and to Hurdles winner, Buzzi Boy. NH FLAT '00 r1 p0. NH '00 (for R.J. Smith) r2 p1 (dist last of 3 in 2m5f Ch); and pulled up 1. Hopelessly tailed off when 15th of 16 in a bumper, and a remote third after jumping slowly in a Chase as well as pulling up in a Hurdle in which he did not look keen. Dredged up from the depths four years later only to pull up after two miles in a Maiden. *Miss K. Millership — Warwicks (Cynthia Clifford).* 760 (OMa).

MR KERMIT ..9-11.. 14 b.g. Rolfe (USA) — Sea Dart (Air Trooper) 353. Small compact brother to NH flat and Hurdles winners, Trooper Tom and Needwood Muppet, and half-brother to flat and Hurdles winner, Needwood Sprite and Hurdles winner, Silver Charmer. Dam won 11f Sell. NH FLAT '95 r2 p0. NH '95/7 and '99/00 r13 w1 (3m110y Hdle) p3. P-t-P/HUNT CH '03 r6 w1 (Club) p3 (2 2nds);

4th, and pulled up 1. Very lightly raced under Rules, and resumed after a three-year absence to record his first success since '96 at Chaddesley last year, but unable to reproduce that form since. Ideally requires a severe test of stamina, but clearly needs much nursing and probably reserves a bit for himself these days. Blinkered once in '00. *D.G. Blagden — Albrighton (Jane Froggatt).* 91 (M), 529 (L), 713 (Cf).

MR KNOW WHAT (IRE) ..9-3.. 8 b.g. Bonnie Prince — Sangschaw (USA) (Mac Diarmida USA) fp23p1p. Compact well-made. Dam won 12f race in Ireland. IRISH P-t-P '02 r1 p0 (pulled up). IRISH NH '02/3 (for D.J. Barry, and D.T. Hughes) r6 p0; pulled up 3, fell 1. A bad horse in Ireland when hopelessly tailed off in two Hurdles and a non-finisher in five attempts over fences (never got further than five out in the Chases, in which he was pulled up three times and fell once), but did better in English Points, and eventually won a Godstone Maiden from two other finishers to give Claire Bartlett her first success. The rider showed a great deal of greenness in her debut season and he was lucky to survive a crashing fall when tailed off and exhausted first time out, and twice given far too much to do in placed efforts, but she stuck to her task for a happy ending. Unless galvanically handled it looks as if he may be too slow for Restricteds. *Mrs J.E. Shaw — Cambs with Enfield Chace.* 123 (M), 561 (OMa), 652 (OMa), 1155 (OMa), 1246 (OMa), 1405 (OMa), 1503 (R).

MR LOWRY ..—.. 13 b.g. Rambo Dancer (CAN) — Be Royal (Royal Palm) f. Small light-framed half-brother to flat winner, Native Oak. Dam won 5f race. 5200y. FLAT '94/5 and '97 r11 p1 (3rd) inc Sell. NH '95/7 and '99 (for L.J. Barratt) r12 w1 (2m1f Hdle) p2; pulled up 2, fell 1. Won a Bangor Hurdle in May '97 to give his then trainer a first success for three-and-a-half years, but missed '96 and '98 and went in to what should have been permanent retirement. A surprise resumption at Cottenham left him with a broken neck. Mrs J.A. Wall — Ludlow. 4 (Cnr).

MR MACKENZIE (IRE) .9-12.. 7 b.g. Torus — Northern Push (Push On) f. Workmanlike half-brother to Le Vienna (IRE), Northern Yarn (IRE) and Bavard Push (IRE), to jumping winner, Cokenny Boy, and to successful Hurdler, West Bay. P-t-P '03 (for Mr J.L. Lewis) r1 p0 (fell). Called by his illustrious namesake when venturing to Higham on his debut, but the eponymous one was in far-flung Devon as the equine version met his tragic end when looking sure to score at Erw Lon. The joy of the news which soon spread round Wales 'Mr Mackenzie is dead' was severely tempered by the discovery that the victim was the horse. His sadly abbreviated career contrasts sharply with that of Selby (*qv* '87 Season Annual). Ms C.P. Richards — Banwen Miners (John Moore). 202 (CfMa).

MR MAGGET (IRE) ..9-0.. 13 gr.g. Salluceva — Linda Dudley (Owen Dudley) 3. Close-coupled well-made. IRISH NH FLAT '96/7 r4 p0. IRISH NH '96/9 r12 p2 (2nd in Hdle and Ch). NH '01 r3 p0 (7th, and fell 2 in Chses). P-t-P/HUNT CH '00/3 r20 w3 (Maiden, Restricted and Intermediate — hat-trick) p4 (3 2nds; and 3rd in Hunt Ch); 4th, 9th, last pair 3, pulled up 6, and fell/unseated 2. NH '03 (for D.P. Keane) r2 p0; pulled up 1. Recorded a hat-trick in weak races in '00, but has lacked sufficient motivation and defeated 21 times since, and seems to have been semi-retired now. Has been tried in blinkers and cheekpieces. Wears a cross-noseband. *R. & B.A. Hawker — Beaufort (Richard Hawker).* 364 (M).

MR MAHDLO ..10-7§.. 11 b.g. Rakaposhi King — Fedelm (Celtic Cone) p113p. Compact well-made half-brother to Fed On Oats. NH FLAT '98 r3 p0. NH '98/03 r38 w4 (2m1f Hdle 3 3m1f-3m3f Chses) p12 (inc 7 2nds); pulled up 17, fell 1. An extraordinary character who has pulled up on no fewer than 19 occasions including when petrified by the fences in the Aintree Foxhunters on final start, but a dour stayer who can produce good efforts on left-handed tracks on good ground or in mud. Kept going stoutly to complete a double in Opens at Duncombe Park (33-1) and Charm Park, and is unbeaten Pointing, but much more suspect over the bigger obstacles and produced nothing better than a 15 lengths third in a Hunter Chase. Has been tried in headgear, cheekpieces and a tongue-tie (but none of them in '04), and far too cunning to fall, but not at all adverse to bringing himself to a grinding halt. *R.D.E. Woodhouse — Middleton.* 122 (3m1fH), 269 (O), 391 (MO), 546 (3mH), 732 (2m5f110yH).

MR MATCH ..—.. 12 b.g. Lighter — Penny's Colours (Hornet) ppp. Short-backed half-brother to Granny Dick. Dam won 2m1f Sell Hdle. NH '01 r5 p0; pulled up 4. P-t-P '98 and '03 r4 p0 (5th, last, and pulled up 2). A safe jumper for the owner who is often forced to put up overweight, but slower than a hearse, and has been pulled up in nine of 12 appearances. *D.W. Hockridge — Pytchley.* 887 (CfMa), 1218 (OMa), 1396 (C).

MR MAX (IRE) ..9-13.. 12 b.g. Parliament — Aria (Saintly Song) f45. Compact half-brother to flat winner, African Opera, and to successful Irish Hurdler, Same As That. Dam won 2 Irish flat, 10-12f. NH FLAT '98 r2 p0. P-t-P/HUNT CH '99/03 r15 w4 (up to Confined) p2; 5th, last pair 3, and pulled up 5. Unbeaten in three completions in '02, and returned to something like his best when 20 lengths fourth at Maisemore Park, but broke a cannon bone in '98, and has stood little racing since. Ploughs through mud effectively, but needs to lower his sights for a fifth success to be on the horizon. *N.D. Edden — V.W.H. (Sally Caton).* 292 (MO), 727 (MO), 891 (3m1fH).

MR MCDUCK (IRE) ..10-0§.. 13 ch.g. Denel (FR) — Coldwater Morning (Laurence O) pp4b2265. Lengthy brother to Irish NH flat and jumping winner, The Noble Rouge (IRE), and half-brother to Irish Chasing winner, Close At Hand. NH FLAT '97 r1 p0. NH '98/00 r9 p0; pulled up 2, and fell 1. P-t-P/HUNT CH '02/3 r17 w4 (inc 2m6f110y Hunt Ch) p4 (3 3rds, of 4 once, and inc Hunt Ch); 4th, last pair 4, unseated 1, slipped up 1, and pulled up 2. NH '04 (for C. Grant) r1 p0 (last of 5 in 2m6f110y Ch: *sn wl bhnd, mist 2, t.o 4*). Previously a very poor performer, but had a sudden and radical change of heart last year, and recorded convincing doubles in April and May. Has quickly reverted to his ungenuine ways of old, and posted a particularly feeble effort when beaten at 1-2 in his Members. Most effective over a bare three miles on sound surfaces, but it would be folly to trust him again. Has been tried in blinkers. *J.A.V. Duell — S. Durham (Sarah Duell).* 391 (MO), 770 (Cf), 1161 (O), 1177 (2m5fH), 1347 (2m6f110yH), 1412 (M), 1499 (2m4f110yH).

MR MCDUFF (IRE) ..9-1.. 9 b.g. Mandalus — Le Glen (Le Bavard FR) 8f6. Close-coupled half-brother to Ruby Glen (IRE). Dam, sister to Loughbrickland (*qv* '97 Annual). NH FLAT '00 r1 p0. NH '01/3 (for R.H. Alner, and M.J. Gingell) r25 w1 (2m Hdle) p7 (inc 5 3rds in Chses with max 8 runners); fell/unseated 3, pulled up 1. Bought Doncaster, Nov for 4500. The winner of a Worcester Hurdle, and seven placings include five thirds in Chases with a maximum of eight runners, but lacks confidence, and has been beaten 30 lengths or much more on his eight most recent starts. Blinkered once under Rules. It did not look as if he got the trip in Points. *Mrs F. Ross, R. Scott & Mrs J. Hollands — Mrs F. Ross, R. Scott & L. Aitken-Walker — Lauderdale (Joan Hollands).* 282 (Cf), 655 (L), 763 (L).

MR MILLER (IRE) .—.. 13 b.g. The Bart (USA) — Celtic Connection (Martinmas) pp. Smallish compact. Dam is sister to Celtic Promise (*qv* '87 Annual). IRISH P-t-P '98 r3 w2 (5&6yo Maiden, and Winners of One) p1 (2nd). NH '99/00 r13 p3; pulled up 4, brought down 1. P-t-P/HUNT CH '01/2 (for Mr P. Flaherty) r5 w3 (Ladies, 3 ran 2 finished once, and 2 ran once) p0; 4th, and pulled up. NH '02/3 (for O. Sherwood) r7 p0; fell/unseated 2, pulled up 2. Scoring for the first time since '98 when recording a hat-trick in Points in '02 (the sequence was interrupted by a fruitless assault on the Cheltenham Foxhunters) but has always been fairly fragile, and has returned to the disappointing ways that perpetuated his career under Rules where he was often blinkered. Looks unlikely to revive successfully at 13. *Mrs H. Silk — Kent & Surrey Bloodhounds (Emma Leppard).* 126 (L), 641 (L).

MR MOONBEAM (IRE) ..—§.. 13 b.g. Satco (FR) — Rosy Moon (FR) (Sheshoon) ppsppuu. Gigantic half-brother to French Chasing and Irish jumping winner, Royal Rosy, and to flat winners, Rouyan (also successful jumper), Rasmara and Roushayd. Dam won at 11f in France. IRISH NH '99 r4 p0. P-t-P/HUNT CH '02/3 (for Mr C. Stockton & Mr M. Vaughan) r10 w1 (Maiden) p3 (2 3rds; and 2nd of 3); last, and pulled up 5. Won a three-finisher Maiden taking nearly eight minutes at Eaton Hall in '02, but a non-finisher in 11 of his last 12 starts, and ran rings round Mark Buchan in '04. A complete waste of time these days. Visored once in '03, and acquired cheekpieces on his last two starts. *M.J. Buchan — E. Essex.* 155 (Cnr), 375 (R), 524 (R), 648 (R), 745 (R), 906 (Cnr), 1316 (R).

MR MORGAN ..—.. 8 ch.g. Current Edition (IRE) — Its Queenie (Itsu USA) pp. Owner-bred. Dam, sister to Prince Itsu (*qv* '01 Annual). Pulled up in two Maidens without showing any ability. A race involving himself and stablemates Mr Evans, Its Mr Blobby and Mr Tobias would certainly tax the patience of the Judge, because the climax (if ever it came) would be an extremely long time coming. *J. Jones — Gelligaer F.* 204 (CfMa), 453 (CfMa).

MR NABORRO (IRE) ..9-5§.. 8 b.g. Hollow Hand — Grow Up (Kambalda) p3pppp5. Sturdy half-sister to Ardmore (IRE). P-t-P '02/3 r13 w2 (Club Maiden and Restricted) p4 (2 2nds, of 3 once); 4th, last pair 3, and pulled up 3. A very secure jumper and won two races largely unchallenged last year, but has steadfastly failed to co-operate since, and thoroughly deserves his squiggle. Presumably made a noise when pulled up and dismounted at Paxford as he ran tongue-tied on his latest appearance, and his reluctance is obviously brought on by his disability. Wears cheekpieces, and has been tried in blinkers. *J.D. Callow — Albrighton Woodland (Helen Needham).* 19 (CMod), 56 (C), 158 (CCon), 255 (CCon), 663 (I), 922 (I), 1113 (Cf).

MR PENDLEBERRY..10-1.. 11 ch.g. Symbolic — Antonoua (Anton Lad) 21123414. Tall. NH '99 and '01/2 r11 w1 (2m4f110y Hdle) p1 (2nd); pulled up 2. P-t-P '03 r4 p3 (2nds, of 3 once); and 4th. Quirky and difficult to train under Rules, but has enjoyed his spell between the flags, and has not missed the frame in 12 starts. Recorded his first success since '99 when forced up close home at Witton Castle, and proceeded to oblige in first-time blinkers (at Duncombe Park) and first-time cheekpieces (at Charm Park, though appeared to be beaten a head), but a visor did not have the desired effect, and without the strong handling of Nicky Tinkler would have little to show for his endeavours. Headgear already seems to be ineffectual and he looks one to lay rather than support, particularly at cramped odds, in future. Suited by good or easy ground. *Mrs C.M. Tinkler — Middleton.* 107 (O), 163 (O), 267 (Cf), 391 (MO), 501 (O), 772 (4m1fO), 956 (MO), 1289 (O).

PLATE 90 267 Sinnington Confined: Mr Pendleberry (Nick Tinkler), 1st, leads Bohemian Spirit (Steve Charlton), 5th PHOTO: Roy Parker

MR RORY ..—.. 11 br.g. Landyap (USA) — Ishkhara (Hittite Glory) pRu. Tall rangy half-brother to Guru Rinpoche. Dam, half-sister to Gay Galant (*qv*), won at 16f, and won 5 2m4f-2m6f Hdles. P-t-P '02/3 (for Mr P.A. Tylor) r6 p0 (pulled up 4, unseated 2). Dreadful. Tubed and unable to complete in the previous yard, and proved a totally unsuitable mount for the novice owner in '04. Highly excitable and once dropped the rider on the way to post, and went down early on his latest debacle. Should not be on a racecourse. *Miss P. Moorhouse — Four Burrow.* 486 (OMa), 1353 (OMa), 1436 (OMa).

MRS BE (IRE) ..10-11§.. 9 ch.m. Be My Native (USA) — Kilbrack (Perspex) 22233. Compact half-sister to Quick Opinion. NH FLAT '01 r1 p0 (4th). P-t-P '02/3 r9 w5 (inc Open, and inc 4-timer '03) p3 (2 2nds; and last of 3); and pulled up 1. Most progressive when unbeaten in '03, but had displayed the odd streak of temperament, and would not race on an even keel throughout in any of her '04 starts. A very accomplished jumper, but beaten at 8-11 and 1-3, and even set herself an impossible task when tried over 3m4f at Stratford, and has to be avoided until showing signs that her mood has changed. Never encountered ground softer than good this year, and might revive in mud. *J.H. Burbidge — Taunton V. (Ollie Bush).* 10 (L), 176 (3mH), 1064 (L), 1167 (3m2f110yH), 1452 (3m4fH).

MRS FIDGET .—.. 8 b.m. Mistertopogigo (IRE) — Feeling Rosey (Uncle Pokey) pppp. Half-sister to Roseys Son. Dam (*qv* '95 Annual) won 3 Hdles (2m-3m3f) and placed 8 (inc 2 NH flat, and 2nd in Mixed Open) for David Todd. Grandam, Rose's Code, won 2m6f Hunt Ch and 5 Points, and placed 11 for him. Great-grandam, Antique Rose, finished alone in South Wold Members and 3rd for him. P-t-P '03 r2 p0 (pulled up 2). Useless, and tailed off and pulled up in all six starts, and does not seem to want to try. *D.T. Todd — Burton (Louise Todd).* 58 (OMa), 386 (OMa), 597 (2m5fOMa), 890 (2m4fOMa).

MRS GOLDFARB ..9-2.. 6 b.m. Alderbrook — Chacewater (Electric) p24. Leggy half-sister to flat winner, Whitewater Bay, and to a winner abroad. Thirty lengths second of three over 2m4f at Larkhill, and again made the frame when 15 lengths fourth over the full trip at Stafford Cross, where she tired going to the last. Had a perfectly satisfactory debut season, and may be ready to score at six. *J. Williams — Blackmore & Sparkford V. (Rose Vickery).* 494 (OMa), 633 (2m4fCfMa), 1133 (OMa).

MR SMUDGE .10-1.. 13 ch.g. Fearless Action (USA) — Amerian County (Amerian USA) 2463. Compact owner-bred brother to Fraction, and half-brother to Sumerian Lad and Ski Country. P-t-P/HUNT CH '98 and '00/3 r32 w6 (inc 3m1f110y Hunt Ch and 3 Opens) p11 (7 2nds, of 3 once, and last twice, inc Hunt Ch; and inc 3rd in Hunt Ch); pulled up 9, and fell 2. Sprang a shock at Cheltenham in '01, but recorded half his career successes last year, and has been largely difficult to win with. A thorough stayer, and suited by an uphill finish, but indolent and needs plenty of driving, and could not quite time his finish at either Dunthrop or Mollington this year. Usually needs an outing to get fit. *C. & Mrs F.J. Marriott — Heythrop (Fran Marriott).* 49 (4m0), 170 (O), 445 (3m110yH), 586 (O).

MR SNOWMAN ..10-0.. 13 b.g. Lightning Dealer — Eventime (Hot Brandy) 1213. Tall strong half-brother to My Best Man and Arble March. Dam won 3 Points (inc 4m Ladies) and placed 3. Grandam, Hunting Eve, won 3 Chases (2-3m) and 4 Points and placed 11 in total. P-t-P/HUNT CH '98/02 r16 w7 (inc 3 2m4f110y-3m2f Hunt Chses) p5 (4 2nds, beaten head once, inc 2 Hunt Chses, short-headed once); 4th, 7th, pulled up 1, and unseated 1. A smart Hunter Chaser in his prime and rated 11-1 in '01, but has always had restricted opportunities, and having raced just once the following year had to abstain from competition in '03 with a fractured hock. Not the force of old any more, but made the most of a simple task in his Members, and added a Towcester Hunter Chase run in desperate ground, but faded tamely on both trips to Kingston Blount. Appears to handle almost all types of going. *S.N. Wilshire & Mrs T. Hill — V. of Aylesbury with Garth & S. Berks (Lawney Hill).* 866 (M), 1105 (O), 1355 (3m1fH), 1515 (O).

MR SONSHINE ..—.. 9 b.g. Minster Son — Colishine (Coliseum) ppf. Sturdy compact owner-bred half-brother to Ingleby Metro, Ingleby Imp, Ingleby Frankie, Ingleby Wot, Ingleby Nip Nip, Yogi's Mistress, Ingleby Dennis and Castletina. Dam, half-sister to Not Quite A Lady (*qv* '93 Annual). P-t-P '02/3 r5 w1 (Maiden) p2 (2nds, of 3 once); and pulled up 2. Followed two seconds with a win in a long Maiden at Wetherby where two subsequent scorers followed him home, but pulled up in his next three starts, including when apparently going well with four to jump at Witton Castle, and subsequently absent for 12 weeks. Clearly amiss at present and his 10-0 rating has been withdrawn. *Mr & Mrs S. Frank — Hurworth (Paul Frank).* 70 (R), 164 (R), 1288 (R).

MRS PEGGOTY ..9-0§.. 10 ch.m. Rakaposhi King — Pegleg (New Member) 9p422ppupu34214. Unfurnished half-sister to Crock D'Or. Dam was hopeless in 6 Points. P-t-P '01/3 r12 w1 (mares Maiden) p5 (3 3rds, last thrice); 6th twice, pulled up 2, unseated 1 and brought down 1. Averaged just four outings per annum to '04, but incredibly busy by her standards in the latest campaign, and added a bad three-runner Restricted at Bratton Down in which she was the only one to go clear to her Maiden success gained last year. Normally blinkered, and for good reason, as she often runs in snatches or declines to pick up the bridle at all, and barring another act of God will not be able to upgrade successfully. *Mrs J.C. Dawe & S. Stacey — W. Somerset V. (Nick Dawe).* 65 (Rnr), 118 (R), 148 (R), 197 (R), 279 (R), 415 (R), 498 (R), 572 (R), 966 (R), 1184 (R), 1325 (R), 1366 (R), 1465 (R), 1507 (R), 1555 (I).

MR SPLODGE ..10-5.. 11 b.g. Gildoran — Ethels Course (Crash Course) 144u11. Lengthy plain brother to Lord Of The Road, and half-brother to Shoplatch. Dam, half-sister to Buck's Delight (*qv* '99 Annual), won 2m4f Hdle. NH FLAT '99 r2 p0. NH '00/1 r6 p2; pulled up 1. P-t-P '02/3 r8 w1 (Maiden) p1 (3rd); last, pulled up 2, unseated 2, and ran out 1. Much more relaxed in his approach in '04, and reaped the benefits, and is fast becoming a specialist at Kingston Blount where he has gained all four wins (and was very unlucky once in '03). Normally switched off at the back and produced with a turn of foot in mind, and is ideally suited by good or sound surfaces, but prone to silly mistakes and has yet to beat anything worth shouting about. Wears a cross-noseband. *A. Hill — V. of Aylesbury with Garth & S. Berks (Lawney Hill).* 191 (R), 345 (2m5fH), 443 (2m4f110yH), 867 (I), 1103 (C), 1514 (Cf).

MRS SHERMAN ..9-2.. 10 b.m. Derrylin — Temporary Affair (Mandalus) p5. Small half-sister to Royal Fling and Seemore Sunshine. Dam won Tanatside Maiden and 2nd 2. P-t-P '00 and '03 (for Mr C.E.R. Greenway) r9 w1 (Maiden) p2 (3rd of 4 once); 4th, last 2, unseated 2, and brought down 1. Had Tanager 14 lengths in arrears when opening her account at Dunthrop on her reappearance last year, but consistently let down by her jumping since, and remains a weak finisher. Will continue to struggle to follow up. *Miss C. Pennycook & P. McNaughton — Lauderdale (Caroline Pennycook).* 765 (R), 855 (R).

MR TOBIAS ..—.. 8 b.g. Current Edition (IRE) — Matching Green (Green Ruby USA) r. Small owner-bred. Dam won 3 flat (10-15f), but later refused to race thrice. Already well tailed off when clambering over the fourth at Garnons, and stopped at the next. It would have been a much bigger surprise if he had got to the finish (see Mr Morgan). *J. Jones — Gelligaer F.* 617 (2m4f0Ma).

MUCKY MAN (IRE) ..9-10.. 12 b/br.g. Exodal (USA) — The Tidy One (Hildenley) 512432116. Small lengthy. IRISH P-t-P '97/03 r50 w11 p23; pulled up 7, unseated 1. IRISH HUNT CH '00 and '02/3 r6 p2. IRISH P-t-P '04 r8 w3 (beat Storm Ten and Treaty Rebel 2*l* and 15*l* at Kildorrey: *hld up, hdwy 8, 2nd & rdn aft 4 out, ld 3 out, stayed on wl*; Super Franky and Telecom Affair ½*l* and 12*l* at Askeaton: *a.p, 3rd when mist 11, ld 4 out, all out*; and Foxey Dove and Briar's Mist 1*l* and neck at

Dromahane: *ld 4, clr 8, stayed on wl*) p3 (5*l* 2nd to Mr Shush at Crecora: *a.p, ld 9, mist 4 out, hdd 2 out, one pce*; 19½*l* 3rd to Lord Alphieross at Ballynoe: *hld up, went 2nd 6 til app 3 out, sn btn*; and 4*l* 2nd to Super Franky at Inch: *a.p, 2nd when mist 11, rdn & no imp when mist last*); also 42*l* 5th at Kilfeacle: *prom til wknd 11, t.o*; and 11½*l* 4th at Tuam: *prom, went 2nd 6-11, sn outpcd*. Wins the gold medal for gallantry in Ireland where he has competed for eight consecutive seasons for Agnes Hurley, winning 14 races including eight Opens and three Ladies as well as being placed on 26 occasions between the flags. Last failed to complete the course on his seasonal debut in '00, but has never managed to score in Hunter Chases, and his jumping let him down when brought over for the John Corbet where blunders twice had the rider perched between his ears. Wears a tongue-tie. Acts on extremes of going. Must be a joy to own. *Mrs A. Hurley — Coolnakilla (Martin Hurley, in Ireland).* 1452 (3m4fH).

MULLARTS LAD (IRE) ..9-9.. 6 b.g. Needle Gun (IRE) — Ibelieveinyou (IRE) (Montekin) 31fp. Small compact. IRISH NH FLAT '03 (for F. Ennis) r1 p0 (tailed off last). One-and-a-quarter lengths third in a Maiden taking 8min15s (!) at Alpraham, but this gruelling contest had no immediate ill-effects and he won a five-runner three-finisher Maiden taking two minutes less at Eaton Hall the following Sunday. Went to the well twice too often subsequently, but his first two efforts were admirable, and will hopefully be able to return to winning ways at six. *Miss J.P. Froggatt — W.M. Wanless — Meynell & S. Staffs (Jane Froggatt).* 1044 (OMa), 1143 (OMa), 1345 (R), 1430 (I).

MULLENSGROVE ..10-11.. 11 b.g. Derrylin — Wedding Song (True Song) p34191f5122317. Sturdy owner-bred brother to Tommy Flanders, and half-brother to Weavers Choice. Dam, half-sister to Sidewinder (*qv* '95 Annual), won 4 Points and placed 9. Grandam, Woodland Wedding, dead-heated for Air Wedding Hunter Chase, named after her dam, who won 4 Points. NH FLAT '99 r1 p0. NH '99 and '01 r3 p0; pulled up 2. P-t-P/HUNT CH '01/3 r19 w6 (inc 3m110y Hunt Ch, inc 5-timer '02) p7 (4 2nds, last once, inc 2 Hunt Chses; and 3rd of 4 twice); last 3, unseated 2, and pulled up 1. As moody as they come, and never runs two races alike these days, but appears to thrive on racing, and is quite useful at best. Likes to get his own way, and gets every assistance from Sarah Phizacklea, but lacks fluency over big fences, and his Aintree spill was only a matter of time coming. Sure to remain wholly unpredictable, but his best results have come at Garthorpe, Ludlow and Bangor. Has won in soft but appreciates much faster ground, and an easy three miles is most suitable. *D.J. Lowe & M.D.R. Williams — Atherstone (David Lowe).* 108 (L), 176 (3mH), 280 (3m2f110yH), 346 (3m1f110yH), 543 (3m2f110yH), 630 (2m4fH), 732 (2m5f110yH), 801 (3mH), 994 (3m110yH), 1117 (3m1f110yH), 1169 (3m2f110yH), 1347 (2m6f110yH), 1399 (L), 1453 (3m4fH).

MULLOVER .8-7.. 14 ch.g. Ra Nova — True Divine (True Song) p0. Brother to Handley Park, and half-brother to Samsword and Sams Sister. Dam, half-sister to Foolish Hero (*qv* '98 Annual), pulled up in 2 Points. Grandam, Indian Diva, won 3 Hunt Chses (2m4f-3m2f) and 5 Points and placed 8 (inc 2 Hunt Chses and HCap). IRISH NH FLAT '96 r2 p0. IRISH NH '96/7 and '99 (for Mrs J. Harrington) r11 w1 (2m Hdle) p2 (2nds); pulled up 2. A delve into the history books shows that he won a Clonmel Hurdle in November '96, and was also second in tiny fields twice (beaten head once), but missed '98, appeared just twice in '99, and resurrected five years later when he seemed excited to be back only to find his pensioners' legs could not carry him fast enough. Suffers leg problems and retired. *Mrs S.M. Lane — Woodland Pytchley (Derek Lane).* 885 (M), 1120 (Cf).

MULTI FRANCHISE ..9-8.. 12 ch.g. Gabitat — Gabibti (IRE) (Dara Monarch) p56. Small attractive brother to 4 flat losers. Dam won 3 flat (5-6f). FLAT '95/00 r50 w4 (7-10f) p5. NH '98/01 (for R.M. Flower, 1 win, Mrs L.C. Jewell, R.M. Stronge, 1 win, and D.L. Williams, 1 win) r50 w3 (2 2m2f Hdles and 3m2f Ch) p8; pulled up 3, fell/unseated 4. Raced no fewer than 100 times in seven years to '01, and seven victories included three on the all-weather and two in Sellers (one of them a Hurdle). Additionally, was placed on 13 occasions and fourth on 19. Occasionally blinkered or visored. Remarkably for a sprint-bred animal he was sufficiently switched off to collect a 3m2f Chase, but has declined substantially and only beaten one horse in his seven most recent attempts (about 25 lengths adrift in both Pointing completions). *Miss R.L. Byas — Middleton (Rachel Byas).* 769 (M), 956 (MO), 1290 (L).

MUQADARS DELIGHT ..—.. 6 b.g. Muqadar (USA) — Idiot's Run (Idiot's Delight) pf. Half-brother to Rolfes Delight. His jumping is not yet up to scratch, and tailed off in both 2m4f Maidens (pulled up two out, and fell at the tenth). *G.L. Edwards — Tanatside.* 1049 (2m4fOMa), 1266 (2m4fOMa).

MURPHYMEBOY (IRE) ..—.. 7 b.g. Good Thyne (USA) — Batease (Quiet Fling USA) ppp. Tall good-looking half-brother to Specialarrangement (IRE), Spalease, Jack's Nephew and Pipistrella. Dam, half-sister to Sheer Jest, was 3rd in a Hdle, and won 2 Points and 2nd for Judy Wilson and Bill Warner. An attractive sort who started at 5-1 in all his Maidens, and looks capable of better on his debut, but never got warmed up and was very disappointing when only getting as far as halfway next time, and again lacklustre over 2m4f on his final start. Has a lot to prove at present. *Mrs J. Wilson & Mrs C.A. Warner — Pytchley (Bill Warner).* 789 (CfMa), 1124 (OMa), 1504 (2m4fOMa).

MURPHY'S MAGIC (IRE) ..9-11.. 7 br.g. Hubbly Bubbly (USA) — Wishing Trout (Three Wishes) 133. Half-brother to Lucky Trout, Smooth Escort and Joyful Poppy (IRE). P-t-P '03 r1 p0 (last). Joint-favourite for his debut, but sustained a hairline crack in a foot, but completed a double for the yard when landing a Maiden at Kingston Blount on his reappearance. Subsequently off the track for another eight weeks, and disappointed on his return, but held every chance at the last on his final appearance, and should be able to land an average Restricted in '05. Avoids ground any quicker than good. *Mr & Mrs C. Harris — V. of Aylesbury with Garth & S. Berks (Lawney Hill).* 192 (CfMa), 870 (R), 1333 (R).

MUSCADIN ..8-6.. 7 br.g. Shaamit (IRE) — As Mustard (Keen) 8. Good-topped. NH FLAT '02 r2 p1 (2nd); and pulled up. NH '03 (for A.C. Whillans, and M.J. Gingell) r5 p0; fell 1, pulled up 1. Sold Doncaster, Aug for 2700. Bought Doncaster, Nov for 1000. Lost his action and pulled up when favourite for a bumper on his debut, but 14 lengths second next time. Showed regressive form over Hurdles and ended up by falling when tailed off in a Seller, and failed to impress in his first Maiden. Gives the impression of having something wrong with him. *Mrs M. Armstrong — Tynedale (Kevin Robson).* 768 (2m4fOMa).

MUSICAL HIT ..8-13§.. 14 ch.g. True Song — Rapagain (Deep Run) 5p. Good-bodied lengthy home-bred brother to Deep Song, and half-brother to Bangagin and Rapaboy. NH FLAT '95/6 r4 p1 (3rd). NH '96/7 r11 p1 (3rd of 4 in Ch — beaten one and a half fences after many mistakes); pulled up 7, inc 3 Hdles. P-t-P '98 and '00/3 (for Mrs M. Ibbott) r26 w2 (Maiden and Confined) p6 (2 2nds, of 3 once, and inc 3rd of 4, and last of 3 twice); last pair 7, pulled up 7. A reliable jumper, and the winner of two bad races on sound surfaces, but never aspired to anything higher than a 9-3 rating, and dropped dead at Ampton. J. Bevan — Waveney H. (John Ibbott). 22 (M), 521 (Cf).

PLATE 91 453 Brecon & Talybont Confined Maiden 56&7yo (Div 1): Musical Sleuth, 1st, would have given Joe Price an even nastier shock had the last fence been properly packed, they lead the riderless Maloney and Gumlayloy (Steve Hughes), 2nd PHOTO: John Mullen

MUSICAL SLEUTH ..9-4.. 6 ch.g. Piccolo — My Dear Watson (Chilibang) 4p13f. Tall narrow half-brother to 3 flat losers. 14,500y, 20,000y. FLAT '02/3 (for G.C. Bravery) r14 p3. Bought Ascot, Jul for 857. Placed on three occasions from between five to six furlongs on the flat (only tried once beyond 7f), but his last run was when blinkered and tailed off in a Seller. Can pull hard and make mistakes in Points, and normally fails to stay, but found a bad youngsters Maiden at Llanfrynach and kept going steadily to score (the next three home have not won). Tailed off last in his other completions, and jumped right when the best part of two fences behind in his Members. It is starting to look increasingly surprising that he unearthed an opportunity. *Mrs S. Anstey & Mrs C.E. Breese — Curre & Llangibby (Sarah Kent).* 202 (CfMa), 362 (CfMa), 453 (CfMa), 694 (M), 1095 (R).

MUSICAL SOCKS ..9-2.. 10 b.m. Rambo Dancer (CAN) — Musical Princess (Cavo Doro) 2. Compact half-sister to Musical Danny, to 3 winners, including Drummer Hicks and Oh Danny Boy (both flat). Dam won 4 flat races at 5 (12-16f). NH FLAT '00 r1 p0. NH '00 r3 p0; pulled up 1. P-t-P '02/3 r10 w1 (Maiden) p2 (2nd of 3, and 3rd of 4); 5th of 6, and pulled up 6. Won a weak Maiden on firm at Corbridge in '02, but pulled up in her next five starts, and beaten 30 lengths when second of three finishers on her only appearance in '04. Wore blinkers and a tongue-strap once in '00. *S.J. Leadbetter — College V. & N. Northumberland.* 283 (R).

MUSSEL BUOY (IRE) ..10-6.. 9 b.g. Phardante (FR) — Windy Run (Deep Run) 1. Workmanlike half-brother to Storm Valley (IRE), and to NH flat winner, Carry The Card (IRE). Dam, half-sister to Mr-Paw (*qv* '96 Annual). IRISH P-t-P '01/2 r5 w1 (5&6yo Maiden) p2 (3rds). IRISH HUNT CH '02 r2 p0. P-t-P '03 r1 p0 (fell). Landed a gamble when losing his maiden status in holding ground in Ireland in '02, but tweaked a tendon last year, and once again restricted to a solitary outing this year. Made it count however, and clocked a good time when beating 16 others at Mollington. Gives the impression that he could cope with another rise in class, and it is a pity that his opportunities are so sparse. Wears a cross-noseband. *M.J. Tuckey — Bicester with Whaddon (Tom Illsley).* 294 (R).

MUSTANG MOLLY ..9-0.. 13 br.m. Soldier Rose — Little 'n' Game (Convolvulus) p9pp. Small. Dam, half-sister to Tom The Light (*qv* '93 Annual), pulled up in a Point at 13 for Andy Martin. NH '02 r4 p2 (2nds). P-t-P/HUNT CH '98/03 r24 w2 (Maiden and Restricted) p6 (3 2nds, inc Hunt Ch; and 2 3rds, last once, inc Hunt Ch); pulled up 11, fell 1. The winner of two weak events on sound surfaces, but headstrong and normally fails to get the trip, and has pulled up in half her races. Wears a cross-noseband. *Mr & Mrs A.J. Martin — Heythrop (Andy Martin).* 11 (O), 379 (I), 544 (2m5f110yH), 922 (I).

MY BEST BUDDY ..10-5.. 9 b.g. Vital Season — Trade Only (Andrea Mantegna) f423123. Stocky compact shin-fired brother to Soleil D'Ete. P-t-P '02/3 r8 w2 (Maiden and Restricted) p3 (2 3rds, of 4 once); 4th, and fell 2. A thorough stayer, and consistently improving his rating, but persistently let down by his jumping, and has proved largely one-paced. Expensive to follow, and five times a beaten favourite, but unable to find ground that was soft enough in '04, and might be a different proposition when encountering mud. *Mrs C.R. Saunders — Pytchley (Caroline Bailey).* 289 (CfL), 379 (I), 783 (M), 1031 (Cf), 1071 (I), 1396 (C), 1500 (Cf).

MY BROTHER JACK ..9-5.. 11 b.g. Faustus (USA) — Lola Black (FR) (Relkino) u5334. Rangy brother to Lucky Jim, and half-brother to Hurdles winners, Thornton Gate (useful; also successful on flat) and Royal Crest. Dam won at 10f in France. P-t-P '02 r2 p0 (last, and fell). Looks rather a plodder, and beaten between six and 28 lengths when placed in Maidens, but becoming a reliable jumper, and a small success appears well within his range. *Miss K. Lovelace — S. Dorset (Jane Lovelace).* 233 (M), 264 (CfMa), 967 (OMa), 1252 (OMa), 1380 (OMa).

MYDANTE (IRE) .9-5.. 10 b.m. Phardante (FR) — Carminda (Proverb) 46. Small neat sister to Irish Pointing winners, Pharminda and Miracle Escape, and half-sister to Gaelic (IRE). Dam won 4 Points (inc an Open). IR3400 3yo. NH FLAT '99 r3 p1 (3rd). NH '99/02 (for J.S. Moore) r30 w5 (2m2f-3m2f Hdles) p12. Bought Ascot, Nov for 5714. Quite a money-spinner in the previous yard, and five Hurdling wins on ground ranging from firmish to soft included a victory at Navan worth £13,259. Thirteen placings included a half length second, and would have won had she not blundered at the last when five lengths clear. Tried visored on four occasions. Missed '03 and proved a rare failure for Steve Flook in Hunter Chases, and having made the late switch to fences at the age of nine she found them rather a mystery and finished tired when favourite for a weak Novices event at Catterick. Tailed off next time, and has clearly become difficult to train. *S. Flook — Radnor & W. Herefords.* 436 (3m1f110yH), 630 (2m4fH).

MY JESS ..9-5.. 11 b.m. Jester — Miss Levantine (Levanter) ppp33f. Lengthy half-sister to Forty Winks. Dam won 2 Members and placed 3, and is half-sister to 6 Pointers, including Eagle Tavern (*qv* '93 Annual). P-t-P '99/00 and '02/3 r15 w1 (Maiden) p1 (2nd); 6th, pulled up 7, fell/unseated 4, and refused 1. Completing for the first time when making all in a three-finisher Maiden at Lifton in '02, but normally tears off in front and fails to get home, and is liable to jump badly. Often mounted on course and taken to post early. Wears a cross-noseband. *Mr & Mrs A.J. Cottle — Exmoor (Alan Cottle).* 279 (R), 323 (R), 824 (R), 1268 (R), 1378 (M), 1506 (C).

MY LITTLE LADY ..9-1.. 7 b.m. Afzal — Friendly Lady (New Member) p2u. Small. Dam won 3m4f Hunt Chase (John Corbet) and 8 Points and placed 6 (inc a Chase) for Grant Cann. Bred from a delightful mare and almost scored second time out in a youngsters Maiden at Lifton, but after being left with a share of the lead at the last she was outridden and beaten half-a-length close home. Unseated next time, but is probably capable of scoring, although it is a pity she is not a sturdier type of individual. *Mrs O. Bush — E. Devon.* 575 (OMa), 826 (OMa), 1182 (CMam).

MY MOONDANCER (FR) ..9-6.. 6 b.g. Muhtarram (USA) — Key Role (Be My Guest USA) 3. Compact half-brother to French flat winner, Effluve (FR), to Hurdles winner, Krabloonik (FR) and three winners abroad. Never really got into contention when joint-favourite but 20 lengths third in a Black Forest Lodge Maiden, and like other visitors to the track seemed to go home with a problem. *R. Kelvin-Hughes — Spooners & W. Dartmoor.* 149 (OMa).

MY NAD KNOWS ..—.. 12 b.g. Derrylin — Early Run (Deep Run) p. Strong-topped lengthy half-brother to Ship The Builder and Early Dawn. NH '97/8 r4 p0 (8th, last, pulled up 1, and fell 1; Sell final). P-t-P '99/00 and '02 (for Mrs B. Baimbridge) r10 w1 (Maiden) p0; last 2, refused 2, and pulled up 5. Kept going steadily to win a long Maiden at Maisemore Park in '99, but not better than last since, and dropped dead at Cothelstone. The Nosey Parkers Partnership (Mrs D. Green) — W. Somerset (Kate Gliddon). 473 (R).

MY NATIVE KNIGHT (IRE) .10-2.. 11 b.g. Be My Native (USA) — Ask The Madam (Strong Gale) p2241. Unfurnished half-brother to Calleva Star (IRE) (*qv*). IRISH NH FLAT '98/9 r3 p0. IRISH NH '99/00 r4 p0. P-t-P '02/3 r10 w1 (Maiden) p6 (4 2nds; and inc 3rd of 4 once); 5th, and pulled up 2. Gained reward for his consistency when scoring on firmish at Bonvilston last year, and brought with his usual late flurry to upset the odds-on jolly at Tabley on his latest appearance. Needed to recoup losses, as a previous jaunt to Wales went awry when he whipped round at the start, and another minor success on fast ground looks a distinct possibility. Has choked and pulled up twice in Points, and runs tongue-tied now. Wears a cross-noseband. *S.R. Wadlow — Wheatland (Annabel Wadlow).* 95 (R), 252 (CR), 450 (R), 1191 (R), 1426 (C).

MY NATIVE LAND (IRE) .8-11.. 10 b.g. Be My Native (USA) — Papukeena (Simbir) 7. Neat angular half-brother to Irish flat and English jumping winner, Papajoto, and to Irish NH flat and hurdling winner, Lively Buck. Dam won 13f race in Ireland. IRISH NH FLAT '01 r3 p0. IRISH NH '01 r7 p3. NH '02 r8 p0; pulled up 2. Showed definite ability at best over Hurdles and was beaten under nine lengths when making the frame four times at up to 2m6f (his best English display was when four lengths fourth in a 23-runner event), but has lacked fluency when disappointing on his seven most recent outings. Missed '02, and like several others who turned up at Cottenham with high hopes on the opening day of the season failed to get back on the track (the firmish ground on the 4th of January taking its toll). *Miss T.M. Ide — Berkeley.* 6 (OMa).

MY ROCK ..—.. 9 b.g. Rock Hopper — My Desire (Grey Desire) pp. Leggy owner-bred. Dam won 7 flat (12-17f), and won 3m3f Hurdle. P-t-P '03 r1 p0 (pulled up). Has made very erratic progress in three Maidens, but yet to get beyond the 13th, and looks to have no chance of staying three miles. *Miss J. Spensley — Zetland (Chris Dennis).* 165 (OMa), 272 (OMa).

MY SHENANDOAH (IRE) ..—.. 14 br.g. Derrylin — Edwina's Dawn (Space King) p. Sturdy compact half-brother to Gymcrack Dawn and Rachael's Dawn, and to Hurdles winner, Big Max. NH FLAT '96 r1 p0. NH '96/03 (for H. Oliver, and J.H. Johnson, all wins) r36 w7 (2m4f-2m6f Hdles) p7; fell/unseated 3, ran out 1. A useful Hurdler on his day and capable of travelling very strongly, but gained all wins going right-handed (four of them at Musselburgh), and had a tendency to hang right (and once to the left). Seven placings include short-head and neck defeats in which he threw away better prizes by failing to keep a straight course, but has been a useful gambling medium most notably when gaining his first win for three years in '01. Blinkered once in '99. Only appeared once in '03, and it was sad to see him breakdown in a Point in '04. *J.A.V. Duell — S. Durham (Sarah Duell).* 1289 (O).

MYSTICAL SPOT .8-4.. 8 b.m. Lancastrian — Mystic Music (Hansel's Nephew) pp. Half-sister to Three Spires (*qv*). P-t-P '03 r1 p0 (7th). Beaten more than 40 lengths in her only completion, and stopped quickly in both subsequent attempts, but her sibling showed nothing until he was nine so perhaps she should not be written off just yet. *K. Anderson — Cumberland.* 658 (OMa), 767 (2m4fOMa).

MYSTIC ISLE (IRE) .10-4.. 15 b.g. Callernish — Sleemana (Prince Hansel) 33. Rangy half-brother to NH flat and Hurdles winner, Supreme Toss (IRE). Dam won NH flat, 4 Hdles (2m2f-2m6f), and 2m4f Ch in Ireland, and subsequently won 2m flat there. NH FLAT '95 r2 p1 (2nd). NH '95/00 r27 w5 (2m7f Hdle, and 4 3m2f Chses) p7; fell last with every chance in Hdle once. P-t-P '01 (for T.R. George) r1 p0 (last). NH '02 r1 p0 (pulled up). Effective in small fields on soft ground, but very lightly raced since gaining his last success in March '00, and ran surprisingly well for a veteran on his resumption following a two-year absence. Often blinkered under Rules. *C.R. Millington — Fernie (Nicola Pollock).* 885 (M), 1214 (Cf).

MYSTIC WARRIOR (USA) ..10-0.. 10 b.g. Majestic Light (USA) — Phoenix Sunshine (USA) (Encino USA) 2113. Good-topped half-brother to a winner in USA. Dam won 9 races and $226,889 in USA. NH FLAT '99 r1 p0. P-t-P '00 and 02/3 r14 w1 (2m4f Maiden) p3 (3rds, 3rd of 4 once, and last once); 4th, last 2, pulled up 5, and fell/unseated 2. Won a 2m4f Maiden at Black Forest Lodge in '02, and the placed horses have followed suit, but has needed time to get over a virus, and hit back with a vengeance this year. Suited by top of the ground, but often lacks fluency and does not stand much racing, and will find it tougher to score now that he is out of Intermediates. Has been tried in cheekpieces. *N. & Mrs J. Elliott — Modbury H. (Gordon Chambers).* 791 (R), 1002 (R), 1271 (I), 1433 (Cf).

MYTIMIE (IRE) ..10-3§ .. 10 b.g. Be My Native (USA) — Snoqualmie (Warpath) 1134. Compact well-made half-brother to NH flat and jumping winner, Kings Measure (IRE), and to Irish jumping winner, Coq Hardi Diamond. NH FLAT '99/00 r3 w1 p1 (3rd). NH '00/3 (for J.M. Jefferson) r16 w2 (2m2f Hdle and 2m Ch) p9; pulled up 3. Able and has won five races including a double in Ladies Opens in February, but always lacks fluency, and was never looking keen when proving too duck-hearted for Hunter Chases. Appreciates plenty of give in the ground and has been effective from two to three miles, but his attitude and jumping problems mean that he achieves a good deal less than he should. Tried in cheekpieces once under Rules. Unbeaten between the flags, but did not derive enough confidence from them when the big prizes were at stake. *Mr & Mrs R. Anderson Green — Border (David Parker).* 133 (L), 284 (L), 798 (3m1fH), 1068 (3m2f110yH).

MY WHISPER (IRE) ..9-10.. 6 b.m. Zaffaran (USA) — Floreamus (Quayside) 21. Half-sister to Puzzleman (*qv*). NH FLAT '03 (for A. King) r2 p0. Followed a five length second at Great Trethew with a win in a Maiden at Lifton, and the time was reasonable and the second and third went on to score. Should be able to score again. *The G & P Partnership (Mrs V.M. Graham) — S. Devon (Valerie Graham).* 702 (2m4fOMa), 827 (CfMa).

NAHTHEN LAD (IRE) ..—.. 16 b.g. Good Thyne (USA) — Current Call (Electrify) fp. Robust half-brother to 2 Irish NH flat winners, including Santa Maria (also successful Pointer there). Dam is half-sister to Charter Party and Avinchey (*qv* '90 Annual). NH FLAT '94 r1 p0. NH '94/9 r33 w8 (4 2m-2m5f110y Hdles, and 4 2m4f-3m1f Chases) p9 (4 2nds); pulled up 6, fell 1. P-t-P/HUNT CH '02/3 r11 w1 (Ladies) p4 (2 2nds, of 3 once, and inc Hunt Ch, and 3rd of 4 twice, inc Hunt Ch; also disqualified from 3rd once — not weigh-in); 12th, last, and pulled up 3. The hero of the '96 Sun Alliance Chase, and made four further appearances at the Festival, but has broken down in the past, and now looks to have come to the end of a long and honourable career during which he earned £122,505. Normally blinkered or visored since '98. *J.A. Danahar — Worcester & W. Farmers.* 490 (3m2fH), 757 (L).**NAILED ON ..9-8..** 6 ch.g. Factual (USA) — Highlights (Phountzi USA) 23. Rangy. Dam won 8f race. Tried a couple of 2m4f Maidens, and after being beaten eight lengths on his debut he reduced that deficit by half despite making at least three errors next time. Can do with brushing up his jumping, but his name looks appropriate where chances of a success are concerned. Gives the impression that he will be able to stay the full distance at six. *Mr & Mrs A.J. Martin — Heythrop (Andy Martin).* 105 (2m4fOMa), 290 (2m4fCfMa).

NAMCHE BAZAAR (IRE) ..—.. 8 ch.g. Glacial Storm (USA) — Carrow Way (IRE) (Buckskin FR) pp. Hobdayed. IRISH P-t-P '01 and '03 r4 p1 (3rd of 3); pulled up 2, and fell 1. Sold Doncaster, Mar for 3100. Bought Ascot, Jul for 857. Has only once completed the course, when 65 lengths last of three, and his latest display was a personal worst as he stopped rapidly after four fences and had to be pulled up before the next. *Miss K. Thory — Fitzwilliam.* 525 (OMa), 1246 (OMa).

NAMRON (IRE) ..9-12.. 12 br.g. Strong Gale — Rigton Angle (Sit In The Corner USA) p. Unfurnished. IRISH NH '98/9 r8 p0 (inc 5 Chses — 6th, last 2, and pulled up 2). P-t-P/HUNT CH '00 and '02/3 r14 w1 (Maiden) p4 (3 2nds, of 3 once, and last once); last pair 3, and pulled up 6. Won a Maiden in the slowest time of the day at Holnicote in '00, but has had to contend with terrible wind problems for years, and runs tubed. His appearances have dwindled to next to nothing and the writing looks on the wall now. Blinkered once in '02. *Miss P. Wood & Mrs A. Beney — Coakham Bloodhounds (Paul Hacking).* 181 (R).

NAOMH PADRAIG (IRE) ..9-5§.. 9 b.g. Be My Native (USA) — Shirley's Dream (IRE) (Mister Majestic) p. Workmanlike. IRISH NH FLAT '00/1 r4 w1 p0. IRISH NH '01/2 r9 w1 (2m4f Ch) p3 (inc 2 Hdles). NH '02 r1 p0 (pulled up). P-t-P '03 (for Mr R.S. Hunnisett) r6 p0 (4th, 6th, last pair 3, and pulled up 1). Changed hands for an exorbitant sum after the second of his two wins at Down Royal, but proved a major flop for previous connections, and already giving new connections cause for concern. Blinkered once in '01. *Mr & Mrs J.M.B. Cookson — Morpeth (James Cookson).* 211 (C).

NARIAR (U) ..—.. 10 b.g. unknown f. Heavy-topped lengthy. Already losing touch with two thoroughbreds when he fell heavily at the fifth in his Members (landing on the frosted ground must have been a nasty experience for his 12 pounds overweight partner). *Miss S. Mountain — Staff College.* 331 (M).

NASHVILLE STAR (USA) ..9-0§.. 14 ch.g. Star De Naskra (USA) — Mary Davies (Tyrnavos) p72p7. Lengthy well-made half-brother to a winner in USA. Dam won 7-10f. FLAT '94 (visored 3) r9 w3 (10-12f) p3. IRISH NH '95 r1 p0. NH '94/02 r47 w5 (4 2m110y-2m1f Hdles, and 2m Ch) p10 (3 2nds); pulled up 4. HUNT CH '02 r2 p0 (pulled up 2). A busy campaigner under Rules, and was successful in a low grade, but temperamental with it and has not scored since December '97. Does not get the trip in Points, and his distant Hunter Chase second at Fontwell was a desperate affair in which the rider was more animated than he was on the run-in. Wears a visor, and a cross-noseband. *R.K. Mathew — Heythrop (Claire Herrington).* 94 (L), 441 (2m4f110yH), 581 (2m4fH), 785 (L), 1299 (2m4f110yH).

NATIAIN ..—.. 6 ch.g. Danzig Connection (USA) — Fen Princess (IRE) (Trojan Fen) p*p*. Big strong half-brother to flat winners, Prince Namid, Fiori (also won jumping — total 11 wins), Prince Ashleigh, Ceasar and Ben's Ridge (later successful in USA). Dam won 2 15f races. 10,000y. FLAT '01/2 (for P.C. Haslam) r4 p0. NH '04 (for W.S. Coltherd) r1 p0 (pulled up in 2m4f Hdle: *ld til wknd 6, t.o & pu 2 out*). Sold Doncaster, Nov '02 for 2000. Even money favourite for his Members (punters were obviously pinning their hopes on the jockey, as the first and second home had far superior credentials but were partnered by novices), but fell at halfway and having remounted a fence behind he pulled up after two out only to be mistakenly placed fourth by the Judge. Not less than 50-1 in four of five other attempts, which is far more realistic, and has looked an awkward ride to date. *Mrs J. Brown — Buccleuch.* 547 (M).

NATIONAL DEBT ..7-12.. 10 b.g. Be My Native (USA) — Jim's Darleen (Jimsun) pp2d. Workmanlike half-brother to Vital Hesitation. Dam, extremely moderate, won Maiden and placed 9 (inc a Ch). P-t-P '02/3 r3 p0 (pulled up 2, and unseated). Plugged into 12 lengths second on his first completion at Bratton Down, but disqualified after losing his weight-cloth on the run-in, and has appeared very fragile otherwise. Pulled up apparently lame there the previous month, and had stopped as if shot at Vauterhill on his reappearance. Would need to find a weak race in order to get off the mark. *Miss S.J. Cutcliffe — Devon & Somerset (Emely Thompson).* 1272 (OMa), 1380 (OMa), 1559 (OMa).

NATIVE ALIBI (IRE) ..9-10.. 8 b.g. Be My Native (USA) — Perfect Excuse (Certingo) 1223. Half-brother to Chasing winner, Salmon Cellar (IRE). Dam won an Irish NH flat race. P-t-P '02 r2 p1 (short-head 2nd); and pulled up 1. NH '02/3 r3 p0; unseated 1. Beaten a minimum of 22 lengths in Novice Chases, but was wrong in his blood last year, and appreciated the return to Points when landing a three-finisher Maiden in softish at Alnwick. Turned over at 4-5 in his Members, and has finished weakly otherwise, including at Kelso where the runner-up turned the Alnwick form round to the tune of 24 lengths. Might be worth campaigning in sub-3m events in '05. Wears a cross-noseband. *Mrs P.M. Shirley-Beavan — Jedforest.* 75 (OMa), 131 (M), 431 (R), 797 (3m1fH).

NATIVE CHRISTY (IRE) ..9-2§§.. 12 ch.g. Be My Native (USA) — Christys Best (IRE) (The Parson) pp. Sturdy. Dam is half-sister to Luke The Duke (*qv* '01 Annual). NH FLAT '99 r2 p0. P-t-P '02/3 r10 p2 (3rd of 4 once); last 2, pulled up 3, and fell/unseated 3. Has created a bad impression from day one, and threw away a winning opportunity when swerving across the track at Lifton last year, and proceeded to do a virtual u-turn at Trebudannon when 4-5 (!) next time. It would appear that connections have finally lost patience with him. Fell when blinkered once in '03. *R.G. Chapman — Four Burrow.* 486 (OMa), 913 (OMa).

NATIVE DAISY (IRE) ..9-13.. 10 b.m. Be My Native (USA) — Castleblagh (General Ironside) 6. Tall half-sister to Glacial Dancer (IRE) (*qv*). NH FLAT '00 r3 p0. IRISH P-t-P '02 r8 w1 (6yo&up Maiden) p2 (3rds); fell/unseated 2. IRISH HUNT CH '03 r2 p0. IRISH P-t-P '03 r6 w1 (Winners of 3) p4. HUNT CH '03 (for Mr E. O'Brien) r1 p0 (unseated). Had a Stena season ticket when trained in Ireland, but badly tailed off last on her latest voyage to Cheltenham, and has plenty to prove in the new yard. *K. Burke — Modbury H. (Nicky Frost).* 1169 (3m2f110yH).

NATIVE DRUM (IRE) .—.. 10 b.g. Be My Native (USA) — Lantern Lass (Monksfield) ppppppp. Lengthy half-brother to Party Lad (IRE). Dam, half-sister to Monk's Mistake (*qv* '97 Annual). won 2m flat, 2 2m1f Hdles and 2m Ch in Ireland. IRISH NH FLAT '00 r2 p0. IRISH NH '01 r2 p0. P-t-P '02 (for Mr I. Bray) r8 w3 (Maiden, Restricted and Confined) p1 (3rd of 4); last, unseated 1, ran out 1, and brought down 1. NH '02/3 (for M.W. Easterby) r3 p0; pulled up 2. Won three races in '02 after changing hands for a reported £30,000, but also possessed a wayward streak and could be a very difficult ride. Failed under Rules, and pulled up without fail on his return to Points, and stopped in a matter of strides on his first and last appearances. Ran tongue-tied in Ireland, and must be wrong in his wind. Blinkered twice in '03. *J.F. Weldhen — Four Burrow.* 193 (I), 495 (I), 573 (I), 794 (Inr), 907 (M), 1129 (I), 1433 (Cf).

NATIVE ISLE (IRE) ..9-0.. 13 ch.g. Be My Native (USA) — Shuil Ard (Quayside) 73pp. Small half-brother to Shuil Americo (IRE) and Lord Lard (IRE), to Hurdles winner, Knayton Prospect, and to NH flat and jumping winner, Irish Hussar (IRE). NH '00/2 r8 p0; pulled up 6. P-t-P '97, '99/00 and '03 (for Mr T.A. & Miss J. Fowler & Mrs J. Caro) r7 w1 (2m4f Maiden) p2; 4th, last pair 2, and pulled up 1. Won a three-finisher Maiden in soft at Garnons in '99, and arguably unlucky in a Restricted the following year, but dreadful when his attentions were switched under Rules, and has consistently given the impression that the full trip is beyond him. Only stands light campaigns, and remains prone to making mistakes. *Mrs J. Caro — Cotswold V.F. (Denis Caro).* 726 (R), 1230 (R), 1322 (R), 1389 (R).

NATIVE KING (IRE) ..10-4§.. 13 b.g. Be My Native (USA) — Outdoor Ivy (Deep Run) p2d2. Well-made brother to NH flat winner, Native Ivy (IRE), and half-brother to Hurdles winner, Bracey Run (IRE). Dam, half-sister to Tartan Torchlight (*qv* '91). NH FLAT '98 r1 p1 (3rd). NH '98/02 r19 w3 (2m110y Hdle and 2 2m4f-2m4f110y Chses) p6 (4 2nds); pulled up 2. P-t-P '03 r2 p0 (4th, and ran out 1).

Began his career with three wins from his first six starts, but quickly developed a tendency to hang, and has failed to score since January '00. Runner-up on six occasions since, and still retains plenty of ability, but downed tools when blinkers were reapplied on his latest appearance, and only ran on again when it was too late. Visored and tongue-tied once in '02. *Newhouse Farm Partners (J. Hatherell) — Beaufort (Richard Smith).* 145 (O), 364 (M), 1344 (C).

NATIVE MAN (IRE) .10-3.. 11 b.g. Be My Native (USA) — Try Your Case (Proverb) f342. Workmanlike brother to Irish Hurdles winner, Be My Case, and to Irish NH flat and English Chasing winner, Drom Wood (IRE). Dam, half-sister to dam of One Man, won Mares Maiden in Ireland. IRISH FLAT '99 r1 p1 (3rd) IRISH NH FLAT '98/9 r2 p1 (3rd). IRISH NH '99/00 r12 w2 (2m-2m4f Hurdles) p4. NH '00/3 (for J. O'Neill) r17 w4 (2m5f-3m Ch) p2 (2nds); unseated 1, pulled up 5. A former strong finisher at his best and has seven wins to his credit, principally on easy surfaces, but can lack fluency and has appeared to be plagued by physical problems at times. Tried in a tongue-tie under Rules (makes a noise; has also broken a blood vessel), and was hopelessly tailed off in his final five appearances (pulled up thrice), but seemed to find Ladies Opens less stressful and ran fairly well when making the frame in all three. Can lack fluency, and has become very onepaced, but could not be begrudged another success if tried again. *J. Malam, Mrs M. Barlow & Mrs J. Francis — Cheshire (Charlie Barlow).* 254 (O), 380 (L), 529 (L), 712 (L).

NATIVE SPIN (IRE) ..9-5§.. 12 bl.g. Be My Native (USA) — Distant Lady (Buckskin FR) p2p3r. Tall workmanlike half-brother to Chief Gale (IRE) (*qv*). P-t-P '02/3 r8 w1 (Maiden) p1 (3rd); last, pulled up 3, refused 1, and ran out 1. Only once better than last until dominating a long Maiden at Parham last year, but decidedly uncooperative since, and his '04 placings were gained in weak three and four-finisher events at Hackwood Park. Inherited a clear lead at the second last on his latest start but put the brakes on when he saw Ministerial and Phillip York on the other side, and has to be given short shrift. Often jumps badly away to the right now. *D.S. Dennis — Hursley Hambledon.* 419 (CR), 720 (R), 779 (R), 973 (R), 1282 (R).

NATIVE THUNDER (IRE) ..9-11.. 10 b.g. Be My Native (USA) — Huntstown Gale (IRE) (Strong Gale) 31. Big strong brother to Native Hunter (IRE). Dam is half-sister to Samson Bill (*qv* '95 Annual). NH FLAT '00 r1 p0. NH '02 r3 p0. P-t-P/HUNT CH '03 r2 p1 (2nd); and pulled up 1. Lightly raced and very keen, but benefited from there being only 11 obstacles (mainly due to low sun) when scoring unchallenged by a wide margin at Mollington. Typically disappeared into the ether, but would stand a chance in Restricteds on an easier track. Wears a cross-noseband. *Mrs S.A. Roe — Berks & Bucks (Geoffrey Deacon).* 462 (OMa), 588 (CfMa).

NAUGHTY DANDY (IRE) ..9-9.. 12 gr.g. Celio Rufo — Annie Will Run (Deep Run) 24. Workmanlike. IRISH P-t-P '99 r2 w1 (6yo&up Maiden) p0; and pulled up 1. NH '99/02 r14 p0; pulled up 2, fell 1. P-t-P '03 r6 p2 (3rds); 4th, 7th, and pulled up 2. Won an Irish Maiden as a six-year-old, but had to descend to Sellers to finish within 20 lengths of the winner in a drawn out career under Rules, and has been beaten between seven and 20 lengths when placed in Restricteds since. Generally a weak finisher and ran tongue-tied once in '03. Wears a cross-noseband. *Mrs C. Andrews — Ashford V. (Liz Howes).* 155 (Cnr), 181 (R).

NAUGHTY NOAH .8-5.. 7 b.g. Rakaposhi King — Rockmount Rose (Proverb) Rp4pf3. Owner-bred. Dam won Mares Maiden (previously disqualified from similar for missing marker) and placed 7 in Ireland, but no form in 5 Hunt Chases in England subsequently. P-t-P '03 r2 p0 (pulled up 2). Error-prone and beaten a minimum of 20 lengths in two completions over 2m4f, but does not stay even that distance, and future prospects do not look rosy. *A.J.S. Palmer — O. Surrey, Burstow & W. Kent (Steven Saltmarsh).* 104 (2m4fOMa), 250 (R), 418 (2m4fCMa), 611 (OMa), 782 (OMa), 803 (2m4fOMa).

NAUTICAL LAD ..10-8.. 10 b.g. Crested Lark — Spanish Mermaid (Julio Mariner) 11111p2. Tall strong. Dam is half-sister to Second Attempt (*qv* '95 Annual). P-t-P '00/3 r10 w3 (up to Confined) p2 (neck 2nd once); 5th, pulled up 3, and fell 1. Restricted to a maximum of three appearances in his previous campaigns, and always looked as though something was amiss, but finally able to fire on all cylinders for a full season in '04, and quickly registered a five-timer. Likes good ground, and has struggled to cope with holding, but still needs to be firmly handled, and was idling and hanging on the run-in when inflicting the only defeat upon Franco at Garthorpe. Fell at the first on debut, but has learnt his lesson, and despite his Cheltenham drubbing is well worth trying in Hunter Chases next year. *N.J. Hubbard, A. West & R. Brandrick — Atherstone (John Docker).* 106 (C), 379 (I), 480 (O), 786 (O), 1057 (O), 1171 (3m2f110yH), 1401 (O).

NDITLIR ..8-7.. 6 ch.m. Lir — Ndita (Be My Native USA) 3p342. Close-coupled homebred half-sister to Josanjamic (*qv*). Takes a keen hold and has soon become a concerted front-runner, but does not leave herself with sufficient reserves for the closing stages, and is invariably tiring at the end. Came closest to success in a five-runner youngsters event at Lifton where she was still just in front but being hard pressed by two rivals when she fell at the last (remounted for third), but ended the season with an exhausted 25 lengths last of two. Should score eventually, but it is surprising that she does not concentrate on 2m4f events for the time being. *K.C. & J.C. Heard — Eggesford (John Heard).* 306 (2m4fOMa), 567 (CfMa), 826 (OMa), 1272 (OMa), 1432 (OMa).

NEALIE MAC (IRE) ..9-2.. 9 b.g. Safety Catch (USA) — Fortune Favours (Tanfirion) pp1p. Tall workmanlike. Dam won 2m Hurdle in Ireland, and is half-sister to Kanjo Olda (*qv* '01 Annual. IRISH P-t-P '02 r4 p0; pulled up 3. P-t-P '03 r5 p1 (3rd of 4); last, pulled up 2, and refused 1. Has only beaten three rivals in 13 Points, and pulled up in eight of them, but put his jumping ability to good use when beating a single rival in his Members in which no betting took place as the match looked so one-sided. Fails to stay when attempting to sustain racing pace and a follow up looks an impossibility. Has two handlers. *D.H. Preece — Wheatland (Emma Murray).* 668 (OMa), 840 (OMa), 1346 (M), 1388 (R).

NEAR AND PHAR (IRE) ..9-10.. 10 b.m. Phardante (FR) — Forty Watts (Sparkler) 2f1Rpu. Small and light half-sister to Ardross Gem (IRE) (*qv*). A first winner for Sarah Buckley when taking a Mares Maiden at Dalton Park where she showed plentiful stamina in a modest contest, but ran out when leading at the 14th in a Thorpe Restricted and continued missing the fences until jumping the last to create the illusion that she had won! Another pathetic riding display followed at Dingley where she was immediately steadied 30 lengths behind the rest and continued hopelessly tailed off until finally pulled up at the last, but when Kevin Green was given a chance at Garthorpe a bad blunder unseated him at halfway. Insubstantial and can find the fences troublesome, but would have claims in Club and Members races at Market Rasen if strongly handled. Her partner ended the season £200 poorer after fines of £75 and £125 had been imposed, and the owner was dealt a similar blow on the second occasion. *Mrs S. Mollett — Burton.* 54 (C), 297 (M), 500 (CMam), 944 (R), 1217 (R), 1398 (Cm).

NEARLY A MILDRED ..9-4.. 8 ch.m. Nearly A Hand — Scallytex (Scallywag) 3ppp. Compact well-made. Dam, half-sister to Madame Derry (*qv* '99 Annual). P-t-P '03 r1 p0 (5th). Has shown promise on both seasonal debuts, but disappointing when sent off at 7-1 or shorter since, and needs to prove she stays three miles for starters. Wears a cross-noseband. *B. Long & Miss R. Lewis — S. & W. Wilts (Sarah Waugh).* 325 (OMa), 599 (2m4fOMa), 883 (OMa), 1259 (OMa).

NEARLY DARK ..7-4.. 8 b.m. Neltino — Night Pry (Pry) p3. Very small owner-bred half-sister to Cloak And Dagger (*qv*). Pulled up at halfway having unseated before the race on her debut, and then gave a poor display of jumping when 32 lengths last in a shocking three-runner Maiden at Larkhill. Looks to lack any scope. *Miss S. Pilkington & W.E. Knight-Gray — Berks & Bucks (Sheena Pilkington).* 53 (2m4fOMa), 334 (OMa).

NEARLY GOLD ..9-3.. 11 ch.g. Nearly A Hand — Golden Medina (Cornuto) p26p5454. Lengthy unfurnished brother to Nearly Easter. NH FLAT '98 r1 p0. NH '99/00 r8 w1 (2m4f Mdn Ch) p2; unseated and pulled up 2. P-t-P '99 and '01/3 r22 w3 (2 Opens and walkover Ladies) p11 (5 2nds, dead-heated once; 6 3rds, of 4 once, and last once); 4th, 5th twice, fell/unseated 3, and pulled up 2. Formerly consistent and a reliable jumper, but usually fails to deliver as much as seems likely, and beat a total of three rivals in his last two successes. Appeared lame behind on his return, and subsequently beaten 30 lengths plus, and looks to have totally lost interest. Has been tried in blinkers and cheekpieces. *Nearly Gold Partnership (Mrs T. Dufosee) — Blackmore & Sparkford V. (John Dufosee).* 33 (L), 77 (O), 196 (O), 471 (O), 642 (O), 1003 (4mO), 1209 (O), 1328 (MO).

NEARLY NOBLE (IRE) ..10-0.. 12 b.g. The Bart (USA) — Crofter's Law (Furry Glen) pp. Tall unfurnished. Dam is half-sister to Depoweromoney (*qv* '03 Annual). IRISH NH FLAT '99/00 r4 p0. IRISH NH '99 and '01 r3 p0. NH '02 r1 p0 (4th in 3m Ch — 150-1). P-t-P '02/3 r11 w4 (inc Mixed Open) p3 (2 2nds); 4th, 6th, and pulled up 2. A reliable jumper, and landed a monster gamble when trained in Wales, but previous connections failed to extract as much as present ones, and proceeded to farm three weak races on sound surfaces last year. Disappointing when joint-favourite and pulled up at Cothelstone on his latest outing, but has never proved himself in a truly competitive event, and may well have suffered a setback. Wears a cross-noseband. *B. Dixon — Taunton V. (Mel Dixon).* 277 (O), 471 (O).

NEEDSMORETIME (IRE) ..7-11§.. 13 b.g. Strong Gale — Sue's A Lady (Le Moss) 9pppr. Tall rangy brother to useful jumping winner, Audacter (IRE), and half-brother to jumping winner, Sir Rembrandt (IRE). Dam won Irish NH flat. IRISH P-t-P '97/8 r9 w2 (5&6yo Maiden and Winners of 2) p0; pulled up 4, brought down 1 and fell 1. IRISH NH '98/00 r23 p3 (2 Hdles, and 2nd in Ch). P-t-P/HUNT CH '01/2 r5 p2 (distant 3rd of 4 in Hunt Ch once); pulled up 1, refused 1, and fell 1. Quite decent in Ireland, but eventually required blinkers there, and his English efforts have quickly deteriorated into predictable non-completions. Briefly perked up when tried in cheekpieces at Hornby Castle, but another sight of regulation fences soon extinguished all fire. *S.J. Robinson — Zetland.* 161 (I), 269 (O), 429 (3m5fO), 808 (CfCon), 1178 (3m1fH).

NEEDWOOD NEPTUNE ..7-0§.. 15 b.g. Rolfe (USA) — Needwood Nymph (Bold Owl) 4R5p608p4. Small sturdy brother to Hurdles winner, Needwood Spirit. Dam won 3 flat, 12-13f. NH '94 r2 p0 (4th and pulled up in Sells). P-t-P '96/00 and '03 r34 w3 (inc Open) p7 (4 3rds; and neck 2nd twice, and last of 2); 6th, 7th, last pair 13, pulled up 5, and on floor 4. Slothful and only goaded into positive action in Points by Andrew Sansome, but partnered exclusively by the owner in '04, and only once better than last. Embarrassing to watch and the poor old thing should have been pensioned off long ago. Has been tried in a visor, and ridden in spurs. *P.A. Bennett — Meynell & S. Staffs.* 225 (M), 477 (Cnr), 683 (O), 786 (O), 989 (Cnr), 1120 (Cf), 1213 (Cnr), 1471 (O), 1502 (O).

NEELEY .—.. 6 b.g. Darnay — French Project (IRE) (Project Manager) Rppp. Workmanlike. Dam won 7f race and 2m Hurdle in Ireland. Sold Doncaster, May for 3000. Bought Tattersalls Ireland, Aug for 4328. Horse and rider made a decidedly unimpressive pairing in Maidens, and the latter lost his irons at some stage in each of their first three attempts together. Ended a dire season by blundering at the tenth at Garnons and pulling up with an injured hind leg. *N. Shutts — Ludlow (Penny Grainger).* 256 (CMa), 410 (2m4fCfMa), 533 (2m4fCfMa), 619 (2m4fOMa).

NELSUN ..9-11.. 11 gr.g. Neltino — Sunday School (Joshua) uu4. Tall good-topped half-brother to Just Jove. Dam won 11 Points (inc 6 Opens) and placed 16 (inc 2 Hunt Chses), but was disastrous for Mrs Macfarlane after being purchased for 12,000 (failed to finish in 3 of 4 attempts, and broke down on final start). P-t-P '00 and '03 r8 w1 (Maiden) p3 (2nds, of 3 once); last, and pulled up 3. Scraped home in front in the slowest time of the day at Cottenham last year, but a very weak finisher and was always very susceptible to injury, and reported dead after fading into 25 lengths fourth at Tweseldown. Mrs F. Macfarlane — Aldenham H. (Fred Hutsby). 31 (Cnr), 110 (Cnr), 175 (Cnr).

NEMINOS (IRE) ..9-9.. 6 b.g. Lake Coniston (IRE) — Bandit Girl (Robellino USA) 3R1. Tall. Dam won 2 flat, 7-8f. IRISH FLAT '01/3 (for Joanna Morgan) r13 p0. An unimpressive flat performer who made two visits to England from his Irish base (including for a Seller), and wore blinkers or cheekpieces in the last two outings. Looks much more of a jumping type, and although sluggish in the early stages of a youngsters Maiden at Bredwardine he became more assured as the race progressed and scored readily despite running green in the closing stages. In a shrewd yard, and (with the probable proviso that he stays with them) should have further scope. Normally tongue-tied. *G. Williams & J. Apperley — Brecon & Talybont (Richard Mathias).* 1049 (2m4fOMa), 1240 (OMa), 1393 (OMa).

NERONIAN (IRE) ..— §.. 11 ch.g. Mujtahid (USA) — Nimieza (USA) (Nijinsky CAN) up. Small half-brother to French flat winner, Waleema (FR). FLAT '97 and '99/01 (for B.W. Hills, 1 win, K.R. Burke, Miss D.A. McHale, 1 win, and J.A. Gilbert) r40 w2 (7f-1m110y) p6. NH '97/9 (for J.H. Johnson) r8 p1 (3rd); pulled up 2. An old rogue who has done the rounds in Lambourn and Newmarket amongst other venues, but did manage to pick up a couple of flat races on sound surfaces including an Amateurs event to June '00 (the previous triumph had come three years earlier). Occasionally wore headgear to '99. The Edwards lurch caused the saddle to slip and decant her at the first in a Members before pulling up at halfway when tailed off (seven pounds overweight). *Major M.S. & Mrs H. Edwards — Suffolk (Helen Edwards).* 520 (M), 647 (Cf).

NESSARC (IRE) ..8-9.. 6 ch.g. Anshan — Showphar (IRE) (Phardante FR) f2p. Small light half-brother to Thyne Man (IRE) (*qv*). Only came close to success once, when partnered by Phil York in a youngsters Maiden at Upper Sapey in which he finished three lengths second after being headed on the run-in. Hung left at halfway on that occasion, and also looked a difficult ride and had jumping problems in his other two outings. Not without hope, but may take a bit of sorting out. *Miss V. Champken — Worcs (Martin Oliver).* 926 (OMa), 1139 (OMa), 1394 (OMa).

NEVER COMPROMISE (IRE) ..11-8.. 10 br.g. Glacial Storm (USA) — Banderole (IRE) (Roselier FR) 112*f*. Strong. IRISH P-t-P '03 r3 w2 (7yo&up Maiden, Winner of Two) p1 (2nd). IRISH NH FLAT '02 r2 p1 (2nd). IRISH NH '00/3 r17 p5 (inc 4 Chses). IRISH HUNT CH '03 r2 w2. IRISH P-t-P '04 r1 w1 (beat Bewleys Hotels 5*l* in Ballon Ladies Open: *a.p, ld 8, easily*). IRISH HUNT CH '04 r1 w1 (beat Spot Thedifference 1*l* at Leopardstown: *made virt all, rdn clr aft 2 out, edged lft last, stayed on u.p*). IRISH NH '04 r1 p0 (fell in 3m5f Irish Grand National: *fell 1*). Remarkably failed to score in 19 races under Rules in Ireland (placed six times; blinkered twice) but has shown remarkable improvement since switching to Points and Hunter Chases, and now the top-rated horse in Ireland. The trainer avowed his intention to go for some big pots in '04, and his charge gave an excellent display when four lengths second to Earthmover in the Cheltenham Foxhunters where he jumped the last with the winner, but could not quicken up the hill (had a host of well known performers 12 lengths or much more behind him), but only got as far as the first fence in the Irish Grand National. Has been improving hand over fist and had completed a six-timer on the run up to Cheltenham, and will be strongly fancied with plenty of justification if he makes another foray to the Festival in '05. *D.F. Desmond — S. Co. Dublin H. (Ted Walsh, in Ireland).* 543 (3m2f110yH).

NEVER IN DEBT .9-0§.. 13 ch.g. Nicholas Bill — Deep In Debt (Deep Run) 2r. Tall rangy owner-bred half-brother to Forever In Debt, and to Hurdles winner, Keep Out Of Debt. Dam won 2m Hurdle. NH FLAT '96/7 r4 w1 p2. NH '97/02 r20 w2 (2m4f Hdles) p3 (2nds, beaten head once); pulled up 1, fell only Ch. P-t-P/HUNT CH '01/3 r8 w2 (Confined and Open) p1 (2nd of 3); last, and pulled up 4.

Scored for the first time in four years when unbeaten in Points in '02, but unreliable and a difficult ride, and only once better than last since. Downed tools once headed in his Members, and his intentions have been made perfectly clear. Wears cheekpieces, and was visored once in '99. *E.R. Clough — S. Pembs.* 208 (Cf), 947 (M).

NEVER SAYAARR (IRE) ..6-13.. 9 b.m. Sayaarr (USA) — Fariha (Mummy's Pet) upu. Small light half-sister to Hurdles winner, Bold Stroke. P-t-P '03 (for Mrs M. Sullivan & Mrs J. Barber) r1 p1 (last of 3). Beaten more than a fence when last of three on debut, but failed to get pass the third twice in '04, and looks most unpromising. *Miss K. Yates — Pembs.* 673 (L), 948 (OMa), 1193 (OMa).

NEWBY END (IRE) ..9-8§.. 11 br.g. Over The River (FR) — Comeallye (Kambalda) upp642p2pp2p. Lengthy well-made brother to Kenmare River (IRE), and half-brother to Sandy King (IRE). NH FLAT '98 r3 p1 (2nd). NH '98/9 and '01 r10 p3. P-t-P/HUNT CH '00/2 (for Mr J.D. Brownrigg) r16 w2 (inc Open) p3 (3 2nds, inc Hunt Ch); 5th, last, pulled up 6, and fell/unseated 3. NH '02/3 (for M. Madgwick) r6 p2; pulled up 2. Badly awry when pulled up on all six Points in '02, but regained some respectability when runner-up in a Chase at Fontwell later in the year, and retains a similar level of ability to that when he was last successful in '00. Wholly unreliable in running and jumping however, and has been ridden in spurs, and only a supreme optimist would trust him to deliver. Blinkered once in '99, and runs visored now. *D.S. Dennis — Hursley Hambledon.* 32 (Cnr), 421 (L), 536 (CfL), 626 (Cnr), 641 (L), 719 (Cnr), 781 (L), 969 (Cnr), 1281 (Cf), 1294 (3mH), 1356 (2m6fH), 1452 (3m4fH).

NEWGATE WELLS (IRE) ..9-6§.. 11 b.g. Accordion — Newgate Fairy (Flair Path) 1p. Lengthy brother to flat, NH flat and top-class Hurdles winner, Dato Star (IRE), and to NH flat and jumping winner, Hoh Invader (IRE). Dam is half-sister to Hellcatmudwrestler (*qv* '97 Annual). NH FLAT '00 r1 p1 (2nd). NH '01/2 r8 p3 (2nds). P-t-P '03 r2 p1 (2nd); and fell 1. Lightly raced and largely disappointing, but finally managed to open his account in the nick of time at Market Rasen before typically letting favourite backers down in his death throes next time. *C.J.M. Cottingham — Brocklesby (Nick Kent).* 60 (OMa), 301 (R).

NEWHOUSE LIRA ..—.. 7 b.m. Lir — Ella Street (King Of Spain) ppp. Sturdy. Dam pulled up 7 and fell in Points for the Cooks 'appalling and should not be racing'. Tailed off and pulled up after a maximum of two miles thrice, and clearly as untalented as mother. Wore a tongue-tie in her last two races. *Mr & Mrs A. Cook — Dart V.H. & S. Pool H. (Melissa Darke).* 195 (CfMa), 1006 (CfMa), 1200 (OMa).

NEW LODGE EXPRESS (IRE) ..9-11.. 7 ch.g. Grand Lodge (USA) — Wakt (Akarad FR) R21333. Strong compact. Dam won 12f race, 2 Selling Hurdles (2m6f-3m2f) and 3 Chases (3m2f-3m3f). IRISH FLAT '01/2 r4 p0. IRISH NH '01 (for J.F. O'Shea) r3 p0. Beaten 49 lengths plus in seven races in Ireland, but proved successful at a modest level in Points, and won a five-runner three-finisher Maiden on firm at Whitwick (a desperate affair). Plugged round steadily for a place in four other contests, but is easy to outpace in the closing stages. Jumping reliability should enable him to score again eventually. *B. Hawkins & R.G. Wright — N. Ledbury (Tim Stephenson).* 111 (OMa), 256 (CMa), 519 (CfMa), 665 (R), 925 (R), 1389 (R).

NEWMARKET MAGIC (IRE) ..8-5.. 9 b.g. Vasco (USA) — Prodical Daughter (Faraway Son USA) p11. Half-brother to 4 losers of 32 races (no placings). Dam won 12f race in Ireland. IRISH P-t-P '00 and '02/3 r8 p2; pulled up 2. NEWMARKET TOWN PLATE '04 r1 p0 (v distant 10th of 12 finishers; ridden at a stone overweight by Craig Jarvis). Finished in the last pair in all six Irish completions, but was only just caught when a head second of three to Canterbury Jack (*qv*), and sent off even money favourite for his Welsh debut, but pulled up three out when weakening rapidly. Subsequently found two dreadful opportunities, a two-finisher Maiden at Bonvilston which he would not have won had the six-lengths leader not fallen two out, and a four-runner Restricted at Lydstep in which the odds-on favourite ran off the course at an early stage. His rating is a strict interpretation of the form, but comes from a good yard, and it is possible that he deserves a few pounds more. *K.R. Pearce — Carms.* 1027 (OMa), 1323 (CfMa), 1523 (R).

NEW ROSS (IRE) .9-10§.. 13 gr.g. Roselier (FR) — Miss Lucille (Fine Blade USA) 1u7p1p5. Lengthy unfurnished half-brother to Bang And Blame (IRE). NH FLAT '97 r1 p0. NH '97/9 r6 p1 (18/ 3rd in 3m2f Sell Hdle); last and unseated 2 in Chses. P-t-P/HUNT CH '98 and '01/3 (for Mrs M. Merriam) r23 w5 (Maiden, Restricted, Members, Intermediate and Club nov rdrs) p4 (3 2nds, of 3 once; and 3rd of 4); 4th, 5th, last pair 3, pulled up 7, and fell/unseated 2. Moody and inconsistent, and only reveals his real ability fleetingly, but the recipient of a simple task on his reappearance when left to finish solo in the Staff College four-miler. Most effective on fast ground, and provided newcomer Annabel Turner (who does not ride in Ladies Opens as she would not do the weight) with her first success, but virtually dug his toes in completely in his Members, and is not a safe betting medium. Wears blinkers, and was visored thrice in '02. *J.S.E. Turner — Sir W.W. Wynn's.* 333 (4mMO), 477 (Cnr), 708 (M), 749 (Cf), 1147 (Cnr), 1429 (Cnr), 1485 (Cnr).

NEWS FLASH (IRE) ..10-10.. 13 b.g. Strong Gale — Gale Flash (News Item) 3c29142. Tall strong brother to Hurdles winner, Iggins (IRE). Dam is half-sister to Roadster (*qv* '90 Annual). 20,000 4yo. NH '97, '00 and '02/03 (for A. Turnell, and E.R. Clough) r11 p0; fell/unseated 3, pulled up 1. Incredibly lightly raced in previous years and missed '98/9 and '01 altogether, and managed only one outing apiece '00 and '03. Beaten a minimum of 28 lengths under Rules, but did show some ability when departing three out in two Chases (fell when holding a slight lead in a Seller, and a poor third when unseating once). Only seen in two Points, but eventually followed a staying-on 12 lengths third with a win in an elders Maiden at Chaddesley Corbett, in which he made all and romped home unchallenged. Never disgraced in Hunter Chases and was 29 lengths second at Stratford, but the revelation was when he finished three lengths second to Cantarinho when 66-1 in the 3m4f John Corbet there. Tends to sweat and get on his toes and has had two paddock handlers, and often headstrong, but keeps going with a good degree of resolution, and it is remarkable that it took him so very long to ever achieve anything worthwhile. With so few miles on the clock he may be able to hold his form at 13. *Lady Susan Brooke — S. Pembs.* 668 (OMa), 801 (3mH), 1029 (3mH), 1168 (2m5fH), 1341 (OMa), 1358 (3m1f110yH), 1452 (3m4fH).

NEW WORLD COMET ..8-7.. 8 ch.g. North Col — New World (St Columbus) pp. Tall rangy owner-bred half-brother to Sydney Hobart (*qv*). P-t-P '03 r1 w1 (2-finisher Maiden). Out for a jolly when ultimately left in front to collect a two-finisher Maiden on debut, and given a similarly easy time on his reappearance, but not seen since pulling up again at Maisemore in March, and is obviously difficult to train. What he will achieve when the brakes are lifted remains a mystery. *J.P. Thorne — N. Ledbury (Tim Stephenson).* 450 (R), 726 (R).

NICE APPROACH (IRE) .8-12§.. 12 ch.g. Over The River (FR) — Gayles Approach (Strong Gale) 85344u36. Well-made brother to Harwell Lad (IRE), and half-brother to Willy Waffles (IRE) and Dramatic Approach (IRE). IRISH P-t-P '97 r2 p1 (2nd); and pulled up 1. NH FLAT '97 r1 p1 (2nd). NH '97/00 r20 p3 (Chses; beaten head once, but last pair twice); pulled up only Sell Hdle. P-t-P/HUNT CH '01/3 (for Miss L.E. Wilson Fitzgerald) r28 w1 (Maiden) p7 (6 2nds, of 3 twice, and inc Hunt Ch; and remote last of 3); 5th, last pair 6, pulled up 11, and unseated 2. Got off the mark at the 38th attempt on firm at Badbury Rings in '02, but has since accrued a further 21 defeats, and apart from being a safe ride has little else going for him. Has been tried in blinkers. *Miss V.S. Murphy — Blackmore & Sparkford V. (John Dufosee).* 65 (Rnr), 354 (R), 719 (Cnr), 969 (Cnr), 1063 (R), 1365 (Cnr), 1558 (R), 1561 (R).

NICHOLLS CROSS (IRE) ..9-11.. 13 b.g. Mandalus — Milan Pride (Northern Guest USA) pf33. Angular brother to Hersilia (IRE), Oh So Cosy (IRE) and Fearless Mel (IRE), and to Irish NH flat and jumping winner, Finchpalm (IRE). Dam, half-sister to Pontentino (*qv* '94 Annual), won an Irish NH flat. IRISH P-t-P '97 r2 w1 (5&6yo Maiden) p0. IRISH NH FLAT '97 r2 p0. IRISH NH '97/02 r49 w5 (2m1f Hdle and 4 2m-3m1f Chses) p16; fell/unseated 6, brought down 1. HUNT CH '03 r1 p0 (last). Regularly amongst the prizes in Ireland, but also frequently on the floor, and gives the impression that three miles is too far. Will only settle if he gets a strong pace, but suffered another crashing fall at Ludlow, and connections appear stuck between a rock and a hard place. *D.A. Malam — Cheshire (Donald McCain Jnr).* 93 (O), 317 (2m4fH), 875 (O), 1144 (Cf).

NICKIT (IRE) ..9-8§.. 9 gr.g. Roselier (FR) — Run Trix (Deep Run) 43221257. Small. 23,000 4yo. NH '01/3 (for M.J. Wilkinson, and Miss V. Williams) r10 p3; fell 2. Beaten between three and 14 lengths when placed three times at around three miles in a Hurdle and two Chases (also fell in two of three other attempts over fences), and looked to have extremely strong claims in a Maiden, but that was not taking into account the fact that he is a little dog, and when he finally scored at Guilsborough at the 15th attempt he was all out and unimpressive. Wore first-time cheekpieces on that occasion, and previously tried blinkered once and with a near-side pricker once. Makes frequent mistakes, and simply will not have a cut at his fences. Beaten favourite or joint-favourite on seven occasions, but the lesson never seems to sink in with his faithful (and bereft) supporters. *J. Nicholls — Pytchley (Toby Saunders).* 37 (CR), 112 (OMa), 296 (OMa), 462 (OMa), 788 (CfMa), 1060 (R), 1400 (CN), 1469 (R).

NICKY THE KIP (IRE) ..8-7.. 12 br.g. Dromod Hill — Burning Decree (USA) (Noble Decree USA) 46. IRISH NH FLAT '98 r1 p0. IRISH NH '98/9 and '01 r21 p5. IRISH P-t-P '99 r8 w2 (inc Open) p2 (3rds); pulled up 2. P-t-P '02/3 r3 p1 (3rd); last, and ran out 1. Twice successful in Ireland in '99, but very lightly raced since, and receives minimal assistance from the owner-rider. Acts on a sound surface. Runs tongue-tied. Blinkered twice in '01. *W. Puddifer — Cheshire Forest (Gary Hanmer).* 713 (Cf), 1213 (Cnr).

NICODEMUS ..9-0.. 11 br.g. St Ninian — Qurrat Al Ain (Wolver Hollow) 3. Compact half-brother to Simply Dashing (IRE). Dam, half-sister to Antinous (*qv* '95 Annual), won 4 2m Hdles. NH FLAT '98 r2 p0. NH '99 r4 p0. P-t-P '02 (for Mrs J.C. Cooper) r4 w1 (Club Maiden) p0; 4th, and pulled up 2. NH '02 (for K.F. Clutterbuck) r2 p0 (pulled up 2). Won a Maiden taking over eight minutes at Dalton Park in '02, but jumped poorly on his debut over regulation fences later in the year, and has proved too slow to cope under normal conditions. Fifty-five lengths last of three in his Members, and seems to live in semi-retirement these days. *Miss H. Williams — Middleton.* 807 (M).

NIGEL'S BOY ..—.. 13 b.g. Bold Fort — Furnace Lass VII (unknown) fp. Lengthy well-made half-brother to Sleepy Boy and Romany General. NH FLAT '96 r2 p0. NH '99/00 r7 w1 (3m1f Sell Hdle) p0. P-t-P/HUNT CH '98/9 and '01/3 r14 w3 (Maiden, Restricted and Ladies) p4 (2 2nds, inc beaten ½*l* in Hunt Ch); refused 1, unseated 1 and pulled up 5. Capable of decent form in his prime, and has won three Points on sound surfaces, and chased home Look In The Mirror in an Exeter Hunter Chase in '02, but always very lightly raced, and has been susceptible to breaking blood vessels on a regular basis. Backed down to second favourite on his reappearance, but fell in the lead at halfway, and has now failed to finish in his last six starts, and looks ready for retirement. *Miss V.J. Scott — Pentyrch.* 361 (L), 737 (L).

NILOUFER ..9-4.. 14 br.m. Nader — Latanett (Dairialatan) 38. Workmanlike half-sister to Some Action, Stephleys Girl, Oil Be Damned and Inky (dam of Fun For Girls *qv*). P-t-P/HUNT CH '00/2 r8 w1 (Maiden) p5 (3 3rds, last once); 4th, and pulled up 1. Won on her debut as a nine-year-old, and has made the frame in seven out of eight subsequent completions, but beaten upwards of 33 lengths in '04, and despite her surefootedness looks too slow to stage a successful revival at 14. *D. & Mrs C. Hobbs — S. & W. Wilts (Caroline Hobbs).* 695 (R), 977 (R).

NIMBUS STRATUS .9-0§.. 12 br.g. Welsh Captain — Touching Clouds (Touching Wood USA) 2u5p. Compact. NH FLAT '99 r1 p0. NH '99/02 r10 p2 (3rds). P-t-P '98/9 and '02/3 (for Miss M.A. McCarthy) r23 w3 (Maiden, Members and Club) p6 (3 2nds, beaten neck of 3 once); last pair 6, pulled up 6, slipped up 1, and unseated 1. Ended a losing sequence of 22 when farming two two-finisher events at Flete Park last year, but very moody and easy to beat in competitive races, and would not do a tap on his latest appearance. Had debutante Jenny Sims in all sorts of trouble at Larkhill, but her joy at completing at Littlewindsor was self-evident. Alternates between cheekpieces and blinkers, but neither have any effect. *A. Ross & Miss J. Sims — S. Dorset (Andrew Ross).* 233 (M), 455 (Cf), 1012 (Cnr), 1330 (I).

NIP ON ..10-0.. 11 b.g. Dunbeath (USA) — Popping On (Sonnen Gold) 5f2f5. Sturdy hobdayed half-brother to NH flat and Hurdles winner, Just Nip. Dam won 2m4f Hurdle. NH FLAT '98 r1 p0. NH '99/00 and '02/3 r25 w2 (2m5f-3m4f Hdles) p7; pulled up 4, fell 1. NH '04 r1 p0 (last of 5 in 3m2f Hdle: *hld up, rdn 9, wknd aft 2 out*). Sold Doncaster, Nov for 2800 (to vendor). Possesses abundant stamina as he showed when gaining one of his two Hurdling wins over 3m4f, but was not convincing in Chases, and finished 36 lengths eighth of nine and pulled up twice (made mistakes). Only beaten half-a-length by Winter Gale in a Charm Park Confined, but was also on the deck twice (beaten in both) and generally only capable of very modest efforts these days. Occasionally wears blinkers or cheekpieces, and has been tongue-tied. *M.E. Sowersby — Holderness (Mary Sowersby).* 389 (Cf), 501 (O), 957 (Cf), 1161 (O).

NISBET .10-8.. 11 b.g. Lithgie-Brig — Drummond Lass (Peacock FR) 21211. Small sturdy brother to Harry Hooly, and half-brother to Bold Navigator and Moorflash. Dam won 4 Points (including an Open) and placed 7 (including 2nd in a Hunt Ch). P-t-P '99/02 r15 w2 (Maiden and Intermediate) p3 (2 2nds); last pair 2, fell/unseated 3, and pulled up 5. NH '02/3 (for Miss L.V. Russell) r16 p5; pulled up 3. Lightly raced until he was eight, and had a very poor strike-rate with two wins from his first 32 starts, but much improved since joining Maxine Bremner, and earned £7,734 from his three Hunter Chase wins in Scotland. An improved jumper, and notably game, and best when allowed to stride along in front but has tended to get bogged down in soft ground. Should continue to do well if placed as sensibly as in '04. Wears a cross-noseband. *Mrs A. Rutherford & Countess of Lanesborough — Lauderdale (Maxine Bremner).* 508 (L), 797 (3m1fH), 1068 (3m2f110yH), 1296 (3m1fH), 1373 (2m4f110yH).

NITEATTHEWORKHOUSE (IRE) .—.. 10 ch.g. Capitano — Princess Peppy (Pitskelly) uf. Half-brother to Natures Gentleman (IRE), and to Irish flat and Hurdles winner, Uncle Baby (won 4 races in his fifth season). IRISH P-t-P '00 and '02 r8 p0 (5th, pulled up 4, and fell 3). IRISH NH '00 (for N.F. Glynn) r1 p0. Looked dismally bad in Ireland, and only got as far as the fifth fence twice before shedding his rider in England. As depressing as his name. *R.D. Thomson — Ashford V.* 103 (OMa), 186 (OMa).

NOAFF (IRE) ..10-2.. 11 b.g. Mandalus — Good Sailing (Scorpio FR) 232. Attractive half-brother to Inis Cara (IRE). Dam won 2 7f races. IRISH P-t-P '99/00 and '02 r5 w1 (7yo&up Maiden) p1 (2nd); pulled up 1. IRISH NH '99 and '01/2 r9 p0; pulled up 1. P-t-P/HUNT CH '03 r6 w3 (Restricted, Members and Intermediate) p3 (2 2nds, inc Hunt Ch). Of little account in Ireland, but much more of a potent force in Wales, and landed a punt on his debut there before recording two further wins in '03. Takes a keen hold and is suited by an easy three miles, and got outstayed on his reappearance at Llanfrynach, and only managed a further two outings. Wears a cross-noseband, and acquired a tongue-tie in '04. Might be worth trying in sub-3m Hunter Chases. *I. Thomas - Banwen Miners (John Moore).* 447 (Cf), 974 (3mH), 1090 (Cf).

NOBLE ACTION ..10-6.. 6 ch.g. Mister Lord (USA) — Triggered (Gunner B) p22112R. Compact half-brother to Cousin George (*qv*). Bought Doncaster, May for 8500. A five-year old of above-average competence, and after taking a 2m4f Maiden at Littlewindsor with the minimum of fuss he followed up in a Kingston St Mary Restricted in which he needed some vigorous driving to hold on by three-quarters-of-a-length. Not the stoutest of finishers at present, and subsequently beaten a head after landing three lengths clear at the last, but was unlucky at Bratton Down on final start, as he looked poised to score until the saddle slipped and he ran out before the last (4-6). Earlier finished three lengths second in soft when he got very tired in the closing stages of a Maiden (had looked like scoring), but can certainly be placed to advantage again, and might even have prospects in shorter races under Rules. *D. Chown — Cattistock (Richard Barber).* 86 (OMa), 142 (OMa), 494 (OMa), 688 (2m4fOMa), 966 (R), 1129 (I), 1382 (I).

NOBLE AFFAIR ..10-0.. 10 b.m. Lancastrian — Abinovian (Ra Nova) 12f445. Compact sister to Highfield Lady, and half-sister to Araminta. Dam is an unraced half-sister to Mercedes Boy and Lark Of The Valley. P-t-P '02/3 r8 w1 (Maiden) p2 (2nds); 4th, 5th, and pulled up 3. Previously thought to stay well and gained her initial success in mud, but coped admirably with much faster conditions on her reappearance, and would have recorded a third success had she not been claimed by the third last when 2-5 in her Members. Generally below par subsequently, and acquired a tongue-tie on her latest start, but certainly seems to get home better when stamina is not such an issue nowadays. Both her wins have been gained at Market Rasen, and also second there once. *J. & Mrs L. Noble — Cottesmore (Laura Pomfret).* 57 (R), 298 (Cf), 378 (M), 544 (2m5f110yH), 886 (Cf), 1214 (Cf).

NOBLE COLOURS ..8-10.. 12 b.g. Distinctly North (USA) — Kentucky Tears (USA) (Cougar CHI) pp5p5p6p. Compact half-brother to flat winners, En-Cee-Tee, Kentrucky Dreams and Dance Little Lady. 22,000y. FLAT '95/6 r5 p0. NH '96/9 and '01 (for S.G. Griffiths, when successful, and R. Wilman) r35 w4 (2m1f-2m5f Hdles) p9; fell 4, brought down 1. The winner of four Hurdles with a maximum of seven runners on good or firmish ground, and was at his peak in '97 with three victories, but last scored in June '99 and missed '00 and only seen twice in '01. Also fell when holding a winning chance twice, and did well when trained in the depths of Wales having previously only been Selling class on the flat (and was also left once and unruly at the start once). Untried over fences until he was 11, and proved a very sorry spectacle in the new yard, having only one horse behind him and beaten a minimum of 30 lengths in eight outings. Wears a tongue-tie. Does not stay three miles, and hopefully retired. *The Star & Garter Partnership (Mrs P.J. Ikin) — Fernie (Carol Ikin).* 1 (C), 106 (C), 229 (O), 444 (2mH), 544 (2m5f110yH), 892 (2m5f110yH), 1104 (Cnr), 1213 (Cnr).

NOBLE HYMN ..10-0.. 12 br.g. Arctic Lord — Soraway (Choral Society) 35. Rangy. Dam, half-sister to Carpenters Gloss (*qv* '88 Season Annual), won 2 Points (including 2-finisher Maiden on hard) and 3rd 3, and grandam, Skyros Lady, won 2 Irish Points and placed 3. NH FLAT '98 r2 p1 (3rd). NH '99 r4 p0; pulled up 1. P-t-P/HUNT CH '00/3 r15 w3 (Maiden, Restricted and Intermediate) p4 (3 2nds, inc 2 Hunt Chses; and 3rd in Hunt Ch); 4th, 5th, 6th, pulled up 3, and fell 2. Only suffered one defeat in his first four Points, but a consistently weak finisher since, and has gone 13 (which for him is three seasons worth) races without a win. Can pull hard and is usually dropped right out the back, and came from an impossible position to finish nine lengths third at Alnwick, but tailed off last over an extended trip next time, and set to frustrate even more if he resumes in '05. Has run tongue-tied. *Mrs C.M. Mulhall — Badsworth & Bramham Moor.* 211 (C), 542 (3m3fH).

NOBODY'S HEROINE ..—.. 10 ch.m. Minster Son — Go Gipsy (Move Off) cpRp. Small light half-sister to Romany Move (*qv*). A late starter who proved useless in Maidens, and her non-completions included when she ran out on a bend before three out at Kingston St Mary and dumped Dominic Alers-Hankey in a ditch and disappeared over a hedge. *Miss A. Durie — Cotley (Jane Western).* 329 (OMa), 492 (OMa), 967 (OMa), 1252 (OMa).

NOCANDO (IRE) ..—.. 7 b.m. Mister Lord (USA) — Lady Bellaghy (IRE) (Salt Dome USA) p. 10,752 3yo. An unworthy favourite for a 2m5f Maiden at Sandon, but lacked fluency in last and was pulled up after 1m4f. *Mrs J. Thornton — Wheatland (Guy Landau).* 850 (2m5fOMa).

NOCASH (IRE) ..9-8.. 8 b.g. Ajraas (USA) — Grangeclare Fancy (Le Bavard FR) 422. IRISH P-t-P '03 r3 p2 (3rds). Beaten between half-a-length and three-and-a-half lengths in two Irish placings (last once), and came closest to success in England when headed close home in a Maiden at Hackwood. Favourite for his last two attempts and is becoming disappointing and clearly not the stoutest of stayers, but Tim Underwood has won races with much worse horses than this, and can surely be placed to advantage eventually. *T.D.B. Underwood — V. of Aylesbury with Garth & S. Berks.* 424 (CMa), 721 (OMa), 940 (OMa).

NODFORM RETURNS ..9-0.. 7 ch.m. Minster Son — Gale Storm (Midland Gayle) p142. Compact. Dam, half-sister to Cairndhu Misty, won 3 Points and placed 10 (2 in Ireland). NH FLAT '03 r3 p0. NH '03 (for D. Eddy) r1 p0 (pulled up). Outclassed at long odds in bumpers and a Hurdle, but managed to win a 2m4f Maiden at Alnwick in decisive enough fashion. Faded when beaten 20 lengths next time, and ended her campaign with a shocker in a Members in which she was opposed by three virtual hunters and started at 1-3 but could not capitalise on a contest run at a crawl. Will have no hope in Restricteds if this is the best that she can do. *D. Carr — Haydon (Ted Stanners).* 659 (OMa), 856 (2m4fOMa), 1040 (R), 1480 (M).

NO DRAMAS (IRE) ..9-10.. 12 br.g. Be My Native (USA) — Madam Owen (Master Owen) p. Good bodied half-brother to Cool Bandit (IRE), and to Irish NH flat winner, Merry Taggle. NH '99 and '01 r7 p3 (3rds); pulled up 2. P-t-P '03 r4 w2 (3-finisher Maiden and Restricted) p0; last, and pulled up 1. Usually feebly handled under Rules, and made the most of two simple opportunities on sound surfaces last year, but presumably suffered a setback after an easy run on his '04 reappearance. No great shakes, and not particularly fluent over big fences, but worth keeping an eye on if the opposition is weak, and the present handler is prepared to persevere. Wears a tongue-tie. *The Crisp Partnership (Mrs A. Blaker) — O. Surrey, Burstow & W. Kent (Ann Blaker).* 223 (I).

NOEL'S PRIDE ..9-13.. 9 b.g. Good Thyne (USA) — Kavali (Blakeney) 2R47. Small well-made half-brother to Belarus (IRE) (*qv*). IR10,500 3yo. NH FLAT '00/1 r4 p3. NH '01/3 (for J.M. Jefferson) r22 w7 (2m-3m2f Hdles) p9 (inc 3rd in Ch); pulled up 1. Bought Doncaster, Aug for 27,000. A game hurdler with no stamina worries at best, and won three times from a four race spell between June and August '01 (just caught when beaten a head in the exception) and later notched a hat-trick in Aug/Sept '02. Most effective on a sound surface, but inclined to jump big and slowly when tried over fences (third and seventh in this sphere) and reverted to Hurdling for his final nine outings. Tried in cheekpieces once, and was pulled up at the fifth on his only run of '03, but nevertheless sold later for a massive sum. Hugely disappointing in the new yard and came closest to success when 12 lengths fourth at Hexham (was badly hampered by a loose horse at halfway), and inherited a 15 length second at the final fence in a Mixed Open, but also ran past the seventh when out of control, and unadventurously ridden as usual in a Hunter Chase. Would be ideal material for Points if he returned to his best (might be more suspect in Hunter Chases), and is the sort of horse who might go very well for somebody like Gemma Hutchinson. *Mrs A. Bell — Belvoir (Nick Bell).* 943 (MO), 1153 (O), 1179 (3m1fH), 1497 (3mH).

NO FIDDLING (IRE) ..10-1§.. 14 br.g. Glenstal (USA) — Gradille (Home Guard USA) 225. Rangy half-brother to 3 Irish flat winners, including Canadian Patriot, and to another in Belgium. Dam, half-sister to Gravity Force (*qv* '93 Annual), won 2 flat, 6-7f. IRISH FLAT p1 (2nd). NH '95/9 and '01 r19 w3 (2m7f Hdle, and 2 2m5f-3m Chses) p4; pulled up 3, and fell 1. P-t-P/HUNT CH '00/3 r21 w2 (3m Hunt Ch, and Open) p8 (4 2nds, of 3 twice; 4 3rds, remote of 4 once, and inc Hunt Ch); last pair 5, pulled up 6. Produced after the last to win three races under Rules, and aspired to a rating of 11-1 when landing a Hunter Chase at Chepstow in '00, but largely uncooperative since and has suffered 21 consecutive defeats. Only just worried out of it in a match for his Members, but was 8-11, and threw in the towel much sooner next time. Normally wears cheekpieces, and has been blinkered, but ran without artificial aids in '04. *Miss R.S. Reynolds — N. Hereford.* 206 (L), 512 (M), 612 (Cf).

NOGGLER ..8-7.. 6 b.g. Primitive Rising (USA) — Sun Goddess (FR) (Deep Roots) up35. Big owner-bred brother to Primitive Rites (*qv*). Looked extremely green in early season, but his 12 lengths third of four (albeit in an extremely poor contest) was a step in the right direction. Probably having an easy introduction, and may do better when he strengthens. *M.J. Brown — York & Ainsty N.* 1157 (M), 1417 (OMa), 1458 (OMa), 1504 (2m4fOMa).

NO INFO (IRE) ..8-8.. 7 ch.m. Shardari — Barnmeen Lass (IRE) (Floriferous) p2p. Half-sister to Hunters Wood (IRE). IRISH P-t-P '03 r7 p1 (3rd); last 4, brought down and pulled up. Bought Doncaster, May for 1400. Finished ten lengths second at Hornby Castle, but none of her other efforts deserve any praise, and has been last or a non-finisher in eight of ten Points. Will have a job to win. *Miss A. Dalton — Cleveland.* 160 (CMa), 813 (OMa), 1158 (OMa).

NO KEEP (IRE) ..9-2.. 7 b.g. Castle Keep — No Debt (Oats) p3f5. Compact half-brother to Irish Hurdles and Scottish Chasing winner, Just In Debt, and to Irish Hurdles winner, Flower Hunter. IRISH NH FLAT '03 (for P. Hughes) r1 p0. Soundly beaten in both completions including when 37 lengths third in a youngsters Maiden, but bred along the right lines, and it is conceivable that he might be able to produce something a bit better in his second Pointing season. Tongue-tied first time out in '04. *M. & D. Vaughan — Sir W.W. Wynn's (Peter Morris).* 96 (CfMa), 256 (CMa), 618 (2m4fOMa), 710 (Mah).

NOKIMOVER ..10-10.. 11 ch.g. Scallywag — Town Blues (Charlottown) R221p1. Strong brother to jumping winner, Mega Blue (10 wins over jumps), and to Hurdling winner, Major Blue. NH FLAT '98/00 r4 w1 p0. NH '00/3 (for J.G.M. O'Shea) r18 w3 (2m4f-3m2f Hdle and 2 2m7f Chses) p3 (3rds); fell/unseated 3, pulled up 1. Bought Doncaster, Aug for 10,000. A very volatile character (was named with feeling), and failed to finish in four of eight Chases (fell/unseated thrice), but likes to race from the front and can sustain a brisk gallop if he feels like it. Unpredictable, and although he won a Ladies at Welbeck and an 18-runner Club Members at Garthorpe he also managed to get beaten at 2-5 in his

Members. Occasionally wears cheekpieces. Lacks charm, and the jockey does well on him. His rating represents the peak of his achievement, and certainly should not be taken for granted. *Mrs S. Hutchinson — Fernie (Patrick Hutchinson).* 108 (L), 246 (L), 479 (L), 593 (L), 885 (M), 1396 (C).

NOMADIC BLAZE ..9-10.. 8 b.g. Nomadic Way (USA) — Dreamago (Sir Mago) b22. Small light owner-bred brother to Go Nomadic (*qv*). P-t-P '03 r4 p2; 8th of 9, and pulled up 1. Incredibly unlucky on his reappearance at Witton Castle when bowled over by a loose horse approaching the fourth last when still 15 lengths clear and full of running, but has been unable to make amends, and missed eight weeks of the season after an odds-on defeat at Corbridge. Likely to prove as one-paced as his siblings (who incidentally have both run tongue-tied) but it will be a travesty if he does not open his account soon. *D.G. Atkinson — Bedale.* 160 (CMa), 433 (OMa), 1291 (OMa).

NOMADIC STAR ..10-0.. 10 br.g. Nomadic Way (USA) — Dreamago (Sir Mago) 12u642. Tall owner-bred brother to Go Nomadic (*qv*). P-t-P/HUNT CH '01/3 (for Mr D.G. Atkinson) r12 w2 (3-finisher Maiden and Restricted) p5 (3 2nds; and 3rd of 4 twice); 5th twice, 6th twice, and pulled up 1. A determined stayer, and looked to have no chance on his reappearance until the runners met the rising ground, and ultimately won going away, but Zoe Lilly was totally outridden by Philip York next time, and then fell off him when likely to be involved in the finish over four miles at Detling. Once again not helped by the rider's inexperience at Godstone, but an honest sort and should find further opportunities in his grade. Has run tongue-tied. *M. Lilly & A. Vivier — The Lucy Lu Group (Miss F. Brown) — O. Berks (Fiona Browne).* 175 (Cnr), 332 (Cf), 537 (4mMO), 629 (3m1f110yH), 759 (I), 1406 (I).

NOMIRET (IRE) ..—.. 8 b.g. Terimon — Country Carnival (Town And Country) pp. Close-coupled attractive half-brother to Primrose Hill, and to Hurdles winner, Primitive Heart. Dam won 2 8f races including Sell, and won 2m Hurdle. NH FLAT '01 r1 p0. NH '02 (for J.H. Johnson) r3 p0. Bought Doncaster, May '02 for 1000. Awful in all six races including a Selling Hurdle, and pulled hard and made mistakes before pulling up after two miles in both Maidens. May have the excuse of a defect. *Mrs S. Horner-Harker — Hurworth.* 394 (CfMa), 814 (OMa).

NO MOUR FOOLING ..—.. 9 b.g. Aydimour — Funny Sarah (Cawston's Clown) p. Pulled up with some difficulty at the 12th in a February Maiden and not seen again. *Miss J. Kerr — Sinnington.* 111 (OMa).

NO NAY NEVER (IRE) .8-7.. 10 b.g. Tremblant — Monread (Le Tricolore) 3f355. Unfurnished half-brother to Carrigeen Lad. IR5200 4yo. NH FLAT '99/00 r3 p1 (3rd). NH '00/3 (for J.W. Mullins) r8 p0; brought down 1. Fourth thrice under Rules including when tailed off last in a Chase, but also tried Selling Hurdles without any success. Very much a plodder in Points, and was beaten 12 lengths in a Members and 16 lengths in a Maiden when claiming modest thirds. It would be a very bad race if he won. *The Good Craic Club — Waveney H. (John Whyte).* 22 (M), 398 (R), 525 (OMa), 652 (OMa), 833 (OMa).

NONPLUSSED .8-7§.. 10 b.m. Gildoran — Personality Plus (Master Owen) pppp656p. Workmanlike half-sister to La Gazelle Noir. Dam won 5 3m-3m2f Chses. P-t-P '02/3 r8 w1 (Maiden) p2 (3rds, of 4 once); last pair 3, and pulled up 2. Scored in a 7min 12s Maiden in holding at Bishops Court in '02 for previous connections, but predictably useless since changing hands, and normally lagging badly from an early stage. Unimproved by the application of headgear on her last four starts, and beaten furlongs when completing. Her name must have summed up her mood when she found out where she was heading in '03. *P. Andrew — Fernie (Claire Andrew).* 127 (R), 250 (R), 467 (CR), 591 (CR), 787 (CR), 885 (M), 1152 (R), 1216 (4m100yMO).

NO PENALTY ..9-12.. 8 b.g. Neltino — Penny Catcher (Barolo) f1d1. Compact half-brother to Insulate and Fixed Penalty. Dam, bad-legged, failed to finish in 4 of 5 Points for Stephen March, Grandam, Forepenny Lass, failed to finish in 5 Points. Great-grandam, Fair Clyde, was distant 2nd in Maiden after pulling up. P-t-P '02 r1 p0 (pulled up). Absent in '03 and fell after two miles on her belated return, but bolted up by 20 lengths at Marks Tey only to discover that the weight cloth had fallen off with a mile to cover. Swiftly made amends when making all at Higham, and clearly has a very decent engine, but if the wheels turn out to match those of his mother it will be a real shame. Has two handlers. *S. March — E. Essex.* 154 (OMa), 245 (CfMa), 401 (OMa).

NO PRESSURE (IRE) ..9-5.. 7 b.g. Florida Son — Height Of Pressure (Buckskin FR) p2up. Strong half-brother to Ease The Pressure (IRE) (*qv*). P-t-P '03 r1 p0 (pulled up). Taken very quietly in his early starts, and Alex Charles-Jones did a very good impersonation of a statue when steering him into second at Larkhill, but Dominic Harvey fell off him next time and appeared to suffer a reverse at Brafield-on-the-Green. Had a subsequent winner behind him at Larkhill and looks an interesting prospect if he stays sound. *Miss S. Pilkington — Berks & Bucks.* 30 (CMah), 143 (OMa), 291 (2m4fCfMa), 463 (OMa).

NORBERT (IRE) ..7-13.. 7 ch.g. Imperial Frontier (USA) — Glowing Reeds (Kalaglow) f6u4fp. Small light. NH FLAT '03 r2 p0. NH '03 (for M.F. Harris) r1 p0 (last). Made his debut over jumps in a

Selling Hurdle, and the best he has achieved in a Point was when a tired 29 lengths fourth of five over 2m5f (a remote last but one in his other completion). Whipped round at the start and reluctant to set off on his latest appearance, and jumped wildly, and his high incidence of crashes make him a dangerous ride. Jockeys beware. *Mrs S.D. Booker — Bicester with Whaddon (Bradley Clarke).* 53 (2m4fOMa), 174 (OMa), 469 (2m4fOMa), 982 (2m5fOMa), 1266 (2m4fOMa), 1403 (2m4fOMa).

NORDIC CREST (IRE) ..10-8.. 11 b.g. Danehill (USA) — Feather Glen (Glenstal USA) 3211. Compact well-made attractive half-brother to a winner in Germany. FLAT '96/7 r8 p3. NH '98 and '00/2 r14 w2 (2m Hdle and 2m110y Ch) p5 (beaten head once); pulled up 2. P-t-P/HUNT CH '03 r9 w3 (inc Open) p3 (2nds, beaten neck once); last, pulled up, and fell. Enjoyed his busiest and most successful year to date in '03, but began the latest campaign in ignominious style when turned over at 4-6 in his Members, and looked set to return to the disappointing ways that ultimately cut short his career under Rules. However, bounced right back to form, and but for the Judge at Charm Park (where he appeared to pip Mr Pendleberry on the line) would have completed a hat-trick. Needs to be ridden like a non-trier, and not put in the race until the last moment and Mark Walford has carried out instructions to the letter. Suited by an easy three miles, and Easingwold fits the bill perfectly, and should comfortably have the speed to be a big threat in a sub-3m Hunter Chase. Runs tongue-tied. Visored once in '02. *T.D. Rose & Miss K.P. Barron — Middleton (Cherry Coward).* 499 (M), 956 (MO), 1161 (O), 1302 (O).

NORDIC SPREE (IRE) ..9-1§.. 13 b.g. Nordico (USA) — Moonsilk (Solinus) 324. Compact well-made half-brother to Moon River, and to 4 flat winners, (one in Italy, and one Night Spell, in Ireland), including Moonax (IRE) ('94 St Leger, and £425,779). IRISH FLAT r4 p0. IRISH NH '95 r3 p0. FLAT r1 p0. NH '96/9 r28 w1 (2m5f Hdle) p9 (inc 5 Chses). P-t-P/HUNT CH '00/2 r9 p6 (2 2nds, inc Hunt Ch; and 4 3rds, remote of 4 once, last once, inc Hunt Ch); and pulled up 3. Often looked ungenuine under Rules, and only succumbed to success once (when brilliantly handled by A.P. McCoy) but only going through the motions in Points, and beaten upwards of 25 lengths in '04. Visored when successful, and has been tried in blinkers and cheekpieces since, and will not go a yard without artificial aid. Has also run tongue-tied. *Mrs L. Gibbon — Dunston H. (Nigel Bloom).* 521 (Cf), 903 (O), 1313 (Cf).

NO REMORSE ..9-8.. 7 b.g. Alflora (IRE) — G'Ime A Buzz (Electric) 1pp. Workmanlike compact owner-bred half-brother to flat winner, Cosmic Buzz. Dam won NH flat and two Hurdles, 2m-2m2f. Made a winning start at Weston Park in mid-February after Gary Hanmer had been at his cheekiest when securing a neck verdict, but his hapless victim is still without a win, and was most disappointing himself when pulling up twice (4-5 once). Had a gap of about six weeks between outings, and may not have been too healthy, so it is possible that he may be able to return to some better form in due course. *G.E. Leech — Cheshire (Gary Hanmer).* 226 (CfMa), 752 (R), 1469 (R).

NO REWARD (IRE) ..9-8.. 9 b.g. Persian Mews — Tara's Dream (Polar Jinks) 2p3f14. Small neat. IRISH P-t-P '01 and '03 r3 p0 (pulled up 3). Essentially modest, but managed to win a three-finisher Aldington Maiden in rain-soaked ground (the time was the slowest of the day by far). Performed reasonably when making the frame thrice, but does not seem to stay too well, and when he tried 2m5f at Folkestone he got tired in the straight and hung left on the run-in. A Bank Holiday Restricted might be his best future chance. *N.A.E. & Mrs A. Jones — E. Sussex & Romney Marsh (Sara Hickman).* 103 (OMa), 250 (R), 540 (CfMa), 833 (OMa), 1285 (OMa), 1439 (2m5fH).

NORLANDIC (NZ) ..10-0.. 13 ch.g. First Norman (USA) — April Snow (NZ) (Icelandic) 2p3. Sturdy brother to winner in Malaysia. NH FLAT '97 r1 p0. NH '97/03 (for P.J. Hobbs) r27 w6 (3m2f Hdle and 5 3m-3m2f Chses) p10; pulled up 2, fell/unseated 2. Ended his career under Rules with a win in May '03 (his first for two-and-a-half years), but finished lame, and although he showed he retains some ability at 12 his races were picked with insufficient care, and did not have the faintest hope of beating the pot-hunting Vivid Imagination in his Members or of getting anywhere near the dead-heaters Springford and Oneminutetofive in a three-runner Open. Prone to blunder over the bigger fences. Has done his bit, and must be on the verge of retirement. *Mrs S.M. Trump — E. Devon (Leslie Jefford).* 318 (M), 629 (3m1f110yH), 825 (O).

NORMANIA (NZ) ..9-10.. 13 b.g. First Norman (USA) — Brigania (NZ) (Brigand USA) 54p12. Strong compact brother to a flat winner, and half-brother to another. Dam, like her flat progeny raced in New Zealand, and won at 8f there. NH FLAT '97 r3 p1 (2nd). NH '97/00 r15 w1 (2m5f Hdle) p5 (inc 3 3rds in Chses); pulled up 2 and fell 4 in other Chses. P-t-P/HUNT CH '01/3 r9 p4 (2 2nds, remote of 3 once, inc Hunt Ch; inc last of 3 once); 4th, last pair 2, pulled up, and fell. Struggles to stay even a bare three miles, and had not scored since '98, but jumped well and maintained a clear lead throughout the last two miles when gaining a deserved first Pointing success in his Members. Turned over in a match next time, and needs to target the same race in '05. Suited by a sound surface. Wears a cross-noseband, and has been tried in a tongue-strap. *C.D.J. West — Weston & Banwell H. (Sarah West).* 541 (3mH), 631 (2m6f110yH), 892 (2m5f110yH), 1364 (M), 1509 (L).

NORMAN WAY ..9-2§.. 10 b.g. Nomadic Way (USA) — Skycap Lady (Derek H) p. Close-coupled half-brother to Captain Primitive and Blazing Times. Dam, sister or half-sister to 3 Pointers, was placed in 3 Points for John Cornforth (unlucky not to have won). Grandam, Skyvan, won 5 Irish Points. P-t-P '00/3 r20 w1 (Maiden) p2 (3rd of 4 once); pulled up 9, refused 2, ran out 1, fell 1, and carried out 1. Did little wrong when winning a bad three-finisher Maiden at Witton Castle in '02 on his 13th career start, but a catastrophe waiting to happen previously, and has been soundly beaten since. Looked far from keen on his only appearance in '04, and can be safely dismissed if returning. Wore cheekpieces once in '03, and has been regularly tongue-tied. *J. Cornforth — York & Ainsty N. (Philip Cornforth).* 268 (R).

NORSE ..8-1.. 12 ch.g. Risk Me (FR) — Absent Lover (Nearly A Hand) 4pp3. Spare-made half-brother to Stone Chatt. Dam won 3 flat, 8-11f (also won another 11f race, but disqualified). NH '02 (for S.E.H. Sherwood) r3 p0 (last 2, and pulled up). A remote finisher in four completions from seven attempts, and looked to have a breathing problem in Chases in which he was twice tongue-tied. The only horse ever to have finished behind him is The Last Shout, and has probably had his own last shout after going lame in his Members. *S.K. Isaac Racing Partnership (Mrs S. Issac) — Teme V. (Steve Isaac).* 358 (R), 517 (CfMa), 731 (OMa), 1109 (M).

NORSKI LAD ..10-6.. 10 b.g. Niniski (USA) — Lady Norcliffe (USA) (Norcliffe CAN) 2121p. Workmanlike half-brother to 5 flat winners, including Kriscliffe (also successful Hurdler), Last Haven and Lady St Lawrence. Dam won 6 races (up to 11f and about $300,000) in USA. FLAT '97/8 r12 w4 (12-17f) p4. NH '99/02 r18 w7 (4 2m110y-2m4f110y Hdles and 3 2m3f110y-3m Chses) p3 (2 3rds); pulled up 3, unseated 1. P-t-P '03 r2 w1 (Club) p0; and pulled up. Quite a high achiever and won more than a third of his races under Rules, and picked up £48,110 in win prize money alone, but did cost the previous owner 62,000 off the flat, and required a wind operation in '00. Successful on three occasions in blinkers and a tongue-tie in Points, but yet to beat anything of real note, and ran like a stuffed pig when asked to race in an anti-clockwise direction at Woodford. Has to go right-handed but should never be considered invincible, and certainly not one to take too short a price about. *H.B. Geddes — Taunton V. (Richard Barber).* 9 (C), 138 (C), 603 (Cnr), 690 (L), 1072 (L).

NORTHALL LAD ..8-5.. 8 b.g. Ra Nova — Northall Lady (Chief Singer) pfu3. His first season was marred by errors, and had no chance when unseating at the last when an unworthy favourite once. Finally managed a completion when a tired 44 lengths third, but will need to do much better still to get a sniff of the winners enclosure. *Willoughby Racing Partnership — Grafton (Richard Webb).* 105 (2m4fOMa), 371 (OMa), 588 (CfMa), 746 (OMa).

NORTH CROFT ..—.. 9 b.g. North Street — Sock Jinks (New Member) pp. Tall rangy half-brother to Handy Jinks. Dam, a useless Hurdler, fell at third in a Point. NH FLAT '01/2 r3 p0. NH '02/3 (for C.J. Gray) r6 p0; pulled up 3. A large cumbersome animal who has been tailed off in all 11 races (including three Selling Hurdles — pulled up each time), and never sent off at less than 20-1. Wore cheekpieces once under Rules. It is surely time to bring the curtain down on his inglorious career. *Mrs W. Doyne-Ditmas — E. Cornwall (Derek Doyne-Ditmas).* 149 (OMa), 485 (OMa).

NORTHERN BLUFF ..—.. 15 b.g. Precocious — Mainmast (Bustino) pppu. Workmanlike half-brother to flat winners, Instantaneous and Progression (won '94 Czech Derby). FLAT r8 p2 (3rds). NH '94/5 r3 p0. P-t-P/HUNT CH '96/00 (for Mr J. Deutsch (Bluffers Partnership) r29 w6 (5-timer inc 2m5f Hunt Ch '96) p8 (6 2nds, inc Hunt Ch; remote 3rd of 4 once); pulled up 6, and fell/unseated 3 (at last with every chance once). A useful six-year-old, and rounded off his five-timer with a win over 2m5f at Uttoxeter, but only successful once in 26 subsequent outings, and the decision to bring him out of retirement was the wrong one. Stopped to nil after two miles thrice, and made David Turner look a right 'nana in the Staff College 4-miler, and his wind has been up the creek for eons. Has run tongue-tied. Visored latterly on the flat, and blinkered once in '95. *E.W. Smith — Beaufort (Richard Bryan).* 10 (L), 47 (Cf), 140 (MO), 333 (4mMO).

NORTHERN BREEZE ..8-9.. 7 ch.m. Lancastrian — The Mount (Le Moss) fu2pp. Small light half-sister to Kilgal (Hurdles winner since Pointing). NH FLAT '03 r1 p0. NH '03 (for N.J. Pomfret) r1 p0 (pulled up). Fell or unseated in her first two Points, but was only headed on the flat (by an animal who was finally scoring at the 16th attempt) when a neck second in a Mares Maiden at Cottenham (sweating badly, and took up the running two out). Very disappointing since despite trying the 2m4f trip which looked as if it might have suited her. Still not a confident jumper, and does not look the sort who appreciates shouldering 12 stone. *R. Tranter — Cottesmore (Laura Pomfret).* 58 (OMa), 386 (OMa), 996 (CMam), 1403 (2m4fOMa), 1504 (2m4fOMa).

NORTHERN CASTLE (IRE) ..8-10.. 7 b.g. Distinctly North (USA) — Dunbally (Dunphy) p5. Tall brother to Dun Distinctly (IRE) (*qv*). IR3800f, IR3400y and IR5000y. FLAT '00 r4 p0. NH '01/2 (for P.C. Haslam) r4 p0. Badly outclassed flat and Hurdling, and was fading in the closing stages when he finished 17 lengths fifth in a 2m4f Maiden. Hopeless on the evidence to date. *J. Watson — Cleveland (Joe Lytollis).* 160 (CMa), 344 (2m4fOMa).

NORTHERN FLEET .—.. 12 b.g. Slip Anchor — Kamkova (USA) (Northern Dancer) 8f. Compact good-bodied brother to Irish NH Flat and flat winner, Alongise, and half-brother to French and USA flat winner, Kirkwall. FLAT '95/7 and '99/02 (for G. Harwood, one win, and Mrs A.J. Perrett) r24 w2 (14-16f) p3. NH '96/7 and '99/02 (for Mrs A.J. Perrett, when successful, M. Campion, and P.R. Hedger) r28 w1 (2m5f Hdle) p8 (inc 2 Sell Hdles); pulled up 4. Won three races including a four-runner Hurdle by a distance at 1-5 to July '99, but ended under Rules with 28 consecutive defeats and was beaten 22 lengths plus in eight Chases (pulled up in the final three). Blinkered on six occasions, and tried with an off-side pricker on the flat, and was a difficult ride in general. Ended his life in a Military Riders Members at Larkhill, in which only two ran, but after crawling over two out he was forced to jump the last when exhausted and took a crashing fall which broke his back (a shocking piece of riding by Jody Sole, who was exceptionally lucky to escape censure). *Mrs G. Worsley — O. Surrey, Burstow & W. Kent.* 100 (O), 336 (C).

NORTHERN LYNE ..—.. 7 gr.m. Gran Alba (USA) — My Muszka (Viking USA) p. Half-sister to Glenbower. Dam won at 10f. P-t-P '03 r3 p1 (3rd); and pulled up 2. Finished well when 13 lengths third on her debut, but tongue-tied in all her '03 appearances, and has pulled up in all three subsequent ventures. Disappeared after one start in February this year, and her wind is clearly not what it could be. *Mrs A. Waddell — Lauderdale (Joan Hollands).* 136 (OMam).

NORTHERN MOTTO ..—§.. 12 b.g. Mtoto — Soulful (FR) (Zino) p. Small compact. Dam won 3 races ($7^1/_2$-12f) in France. FLAT '95/02 r69 w8 (12-16f) p12. NH '96/02 r25 p7 (5 3rds); pulled up 1, fell/unseated 3. P-t-P/HUNT CH '03 (for Mr T. Jewitt) r6 w1 (Nov Rdrs Mixed Open) p0; 6th of 7, pulled up 3, and unseated. The veteran of 101 races, and gained his first success over jumps when springing a 20-1 surprise at Upton-on-Severn last year, but has tended not to take much interest recently, and pulled up lame after leading for the second mile at Rhydygwern on his first appearance for a yard that specialises in running has-beens very infrequently. Broke a blood vessel once in '02. Often tried in headgear in the past. *D.C. Stewart — Tredegar F.* 1481 (M).

NORTHERN PRINCE ..9-3.. 12 br.g. North Col — Chestertons Choice (Country Retreat) f1. Lengthy brother to Himalayan Heights, and half-brother to Chesterton Song and True Choice. Dam is half-sister to Motor Bike Man (*qv* '93 Annual). P-t-P '00/1 and '03 r6 p0 (4th, 7th, pulled up 3, and refused 1). Only averages two outings per annum, and beaten upwards of 30 lengths in two previous completions, but had always showed he had the basic speed, and despite finishing very tired picked off the reluctant leader in the final 50 yards of a bad elders Maiden at Garnons. Would not have the stamina to make much of an impression in Restricteds even if he got the chance. *The Allen Family (C. Allen) — Berkeley (Claire Allen).* 296 (OMa), 620 (OMa).

NORTHERN THATCH ..8-10.. 6 b.m. Distinctly North (USA) — Tomard (Thatching) p3. Sister to Regardez-Moi, and half-sister to flat winners, Towardot, Forest (both in Ireland), Tophard, and to two winners in Belgium. Dam won 5f race in Ireland, and is half-sister to Jovian Pond (*qv*). Bought Ascot, Jun '02 for 952. Pulled up after two miles on her debut, and then finished nine-and-a-half lengths third over 2m4f at Trebudannon. Earned a modest rating, but it is not encouraging that a tongue-tie has been employed so early in her career. *K.R. Redwood — Lamerton (Kirsty Mathews).* 701 (2m4fOMa), 909 (2m4fOMa).

NORTH PASS ..7-12§.. 7 b.g. North Col — Nunswalk (The Parson) f5p4. Sturdy half-brother to Midnight Moon (*qv*). P-t-P '03 r2 p0 (pulled up 1, and brought down 1). Crashes through fences at will, and beaten upwards of 35 lengths, but already looks thoroughly ungenuine, and was under constant pressure from flag-fall when blinkered on his latest appearance. *B. Eccles — N. Cotswold (Giles & Kim Smyly).* 52 (OMa), 295 (OMa), 589 (CfMa), 926 (OMa).

NORTH PEAK ..—.. 6 b.g. North Col — Tapalong (True Song) pp. Small neat brother to Ryans Star (*qv*). Tried valiantly to keep up with the leaders after a mistake at the tenth in his Members, but was labouring when he pulled up at the 13th. Yet to go more than two miles. *Mrs P.M. Pile — Warwicks (Simon Pile).* 887 (CfMa), 1276 (M).

NORTHSPRITE ..9-10§ .. 11 b.g. North Col — Misprite (Master Stephen) f3322221. Big strong owner-bred half-brother to Billsley and Mismetallic. Dam won 2 Points and placed 10. Grandam, Lily Pond II, was close 3rd in 2 Adjacents. P-t-P '00/3 r14 p8 (3rds, of 4 twice, last once); 4th, and fell/unseated 5. Came back rider-less five times in a six-race spell once, and remains error-prone, but finally opened his account after 14 placed efforts when landing a three-finisher Maiden in soft at Ashorne at the 22nd attempt. Often ridden with little purpose and will go in snatches if he feels like it, and will always be worth fielding against in Restricteds. Has two handlers. Wears a cross-noseband and cheekpieces, and has been tried in blinkers. *Mrs A.P. Bird — Warwicks (Julie Marles).* 51 (OMa), 113 (OMa), 296 (OMa), 463 (OMa), 731 (OMa), 871 (OMa), 1125 (OMa), 1275 (OMa).

NORTON WOOD (IRE) ..7-0.. 9 ch.g. Shardari — Colligan Forest (Strong Gale) pp754b. Tall rangy. Dam won 6yo&up Maiden in Ireland, and is sister to Strong Medicine (*qv*). NH '02 r2 p0; fell 1. P-t-P '03 r1 p0 (ran out). Atypical of his yard and has shown a modicum of ability, but cumbersome and error-prone, and beaten in excess of 29 lengths to date. Gives the strong impression that he is physically impaired. Wears a cross-noseband and a tongue-tie. *Mrs A. Price — Teme V.* 517 (CfMa), 621 (OMa), 668 (OMa), 840 (OMa), 1116 (OMa), 1395 (OMa).

NOTABLE EXCEPTION ..9-2.. 16 b.g. Top Ville — Shorthouse (Habitat) p78. Good-topped half-brother to flat winners, Ever Genial (smart filly) and Lowawatha (also successful Chaser). Dam won 2 7f races. 29,000y. FLAT '91/3 r14 p3. NH '92/6, '98/00 and '02 (for Mrs M. Reveley, all wins, and R. Dickin) r60 w12 (9 2m-2m6f Hdles and 3 2m5f-3m1f Chses) p15 (btn 1/2*l* or less in 3 2nds); pulled up 5, fell/unseated 4. A multiple winner to October '96 and had a golden spell when he scored in five of six attempts (fell in the exception) from May to November '94, but was essentially only Selling class, and gained seven of his victories in that grade. Wore headgear twice, and was unplaced on his final 15 attempts. Has only made four appearances since '00, and did no more than jump the fences without incident in his dotage. *Miss K. Henry — Warwicks.* 1276 (M), 1485 (Cnr), 1516 (L).

NOTATION (IRE) ..—.. 11 b.g. Arazi (USA) — Grace Note (FR) (Top Ville) fpppppp. Compact attractive half-brother to 7 flat winners (one in France), including Belmez (won £427,226 including King George VI and Queen Elizabeth Stakes), Dowland, Opera Cornique (both in Ireland), Shimaal, Gracilis (also successful Hurdler) and Dvorak. Dam won 10f race. FRENCH FLAT '97 r2 p0. FLAT '97/02 (for D.W. Chapman) r74 w4 (12-14f) p6. Won two flat races in '97 and another brace three years later, and they included two on the all-weather. Was sent off at 50-1 once, and snatched victory from the jaws of defeat when producing an amazing late rattle which saw him pass eight rivals and make 30 lengths in the straight once. Subsequently ran up a sequence of 28 defeats including in Sellers, and wore blinkers quite regularly (but not when successful) and tongue-tied on his final attempt. Sent jumping for the first time with embarrassing results at the age of ten, and his lack of stamina meant that he was never able to complete the course. Hopefully the lesson has sunk in and he will be allowed to retire in one piece. *Miss A.L. Knowlson — Sinnington.* 267 (Cf), 389 (Cf), 565 (O), 772 (4m1fO), 1161 (O), 1289 (O).

NOT FOR PARROT (IRE) .9-5.. 13 ch.g. Be My Native (USA) — Sugar Quay (Quayside) u4p. Lengthy. IRISH NH FLAT '96 r1 p0. IRISH P-t-P '96/7 r3 p1 (3rd); fell/unseated 2. NH '97/01 r21 w1 (2m Hdle) p5 (3 2nds); pulled up 2. P-t-P/HUNT CH '02/3 (for Mr G. Martin, Mr E. Kearney & Mr J. Whitaker) r7 p0 (last pair 2, pulled up 4, and fell 1). Scored over the minimum trip at Wincanton in '98, but was flat out to repel the runner-up by half-a-length, and has been unable to follow up in 26 subsequent attempts. Can pull hard, and has no chance of getting the trip in Points, and additionally prone to frequent mistakes. Blinkered twice in '01. *G. Martin — Cotswold.* 755 (M), 816 (Cf), 1073 (O).

NOTHING BETTER (IRE) ..—.. 6 b.m. Flemensfirth (USA) — Slave Gale (IRE) (Strong Gale) u2bfu. Small well-made. Dam won NH flat and 2m2f Hurdle in Ireland. 6143 2yo. Her three lengths second over 2m4f at Garnons was acceptable, and she was buckling down well to her work at the finish, but a gormless jumper otherwise, and has left the rider on the deck in all her other four attempts. Her confidence seems to be in shreds at present so a rating of 9-9 is withdrawn. May atone if she can get her act together. *J.R. Weston — Worcs (Penny Grainger).* 256 (CMa), 410 (2m4fCfMa), 619 (2m4fOMa), 723 (OMa), 929 (2m4fOMa).

NOTSOTINY ..9-0.. 9 b.g. Southern Music — Goodbye Roscoe (Roscoe Blake) p. Half-brother to Tiny and Oh So Brave. Dam won 2 Points and placed 7 (inc a Ch). P-t-P '02/3 (for Mrs J.M. Hegarty) r5 w1 (Maiden) p0 (pulled up 2, and fell 2). NH '03 (for E. Williams) r4 p0; fell 1. Overcame several mistakes when making all to land a four-runner Maiden at Cilwendeg last year, but not so lucky when 4-5 next time, and beaten 40 lengths plus when switched to Selling Hurdles subsequently. Visored on his latest outing under Rules, and appeared to throw in the towel after a circuit on his only start for new connections in '04. *P.D. & Mrs D. Mortimer — Pentyrch (Deborah Mortimer).* 1517 (R).

NOT YET DECENT (IRE) ..9-5.. 12 gr.g. Decent Fellow — Yet (Last Fandango) 40u. Light-framed. Dam won at 10f. P-t-P/HUNT CH '00 and '02/3 (for Mr T.J.C. Seegar) r15 w1 (Maiden) p3 (2 2nds); 4th twice, 5th, last, pulled up 6, and unseated 1. Scored at Ston Easton on his first completion, despite hanging left on the run-in, and ran well when runner-up at Larkhill twice in '03, but not better than last when owner ridden this year, and took full advantage of some feeble handling. Favourite on his reappearance (despite the fact that Alex Puddy had not race-ridden for seven years, and even then only had one ride) but not since, and after a comedic episode at Garnons the combination were seen no more. *A. Puddy — N. Cotswold (Giles & Kim Smyly).* 15 (R), 252 (CR), 406 (Inr).

NOUGHT TO NINETY ..9-12.. 7 b.g. Mazaad — Bonnyhill Lass (Royal Fountain) p11. Compact owner-bred half-brother to Inner State (*qv*). NH FLAT '02 r1 p0. NH '03 (for C. Grant) r1 p0 (last). Tailed off in his first three races, but showed a surprising turn of foot to make 15 lengths from two out when winning the Maiden at Charm Park which is confined to horses who have never finished in the first three, and showed the same remarkable acceleration in an Easingwold Restricted in which he had appeared to be in a hopeless position after two miles. Looks a real character (verging on mad), but whilst he continues to produce his late bursts he will be irresistible in Points even as he rises in class. *Miss C.C. Raw — S. Durham.* 776 (CfMa), 960 (OMa), 1162 (R).

NOUSAYRI (IRE) ..9-11.. 10 b.g. Slip Anchor — Noufiyla (Top Ville) f2p545. Compact half-brother to flat winners, Noufari (won 19), Narwala (smart) and Noukari (IRE) (won 13; also won 5 Hurdles). NH FLAT '99 r4 w1 p2. NH '00/2 r15 p6 (4 2nds, inc Ch). P-t-P/HUNT CH '03 (for Mr & Mrs A.R. Humphrey) r6 p1 (remote last of 3); 5th, last, pulled up 2, and fell 1. Bred in the purple, and beat subsequent '02 Peter Marsh Chase winner, Red Striker in mud at Perth in '99, but an abject failure over jumps himself, and has not managed to follow up in 29 subsequent attempts. Can pull hard and makes mistakes, and fell twice on his reappearance, but only just failed to get up at Kingston Blount, and might have done so had he been ridden with an ounce more aggression. Ran passably at Ludlow, and probably better off seeking place money in sub-3m events than he is in Points. Wears a cross-noseband. *J.W. & Mrs N.A. Hedges — Warwicks (Julie Marles).* 34 (O), 187 (Cf), 365 (I), 584 (I), 1276 (M), 1372 (2m4fH).

NOWORNEVER (IRE) ..9-10.. 12 b.g. Tidaro (USA) — China Blake (Private Walk) 3365714. Workmanlike well-made. IRISH NH FLAT '99 r1 p0. IRISH P-t-P '99/00 r5 w1 (7yo&up Maiden) p1 (3rd); pulled up, and fell 2. P-t-P/HUNT CH '01/3 r10 p2; last pair 2, pulled up 4, refused 1, and unseated 1. Ran up a sequence of 16 defeats after scoring in Ireland in '00, and was long odds on to prolong it when jumping the third last eight lengths behind the leader at Fakenham, but he capitulated in the closing stages and David Kemp was able to galavanise his mount to the front in the final 50 yards. Favourite on the back of his yard's good season on two occasions in '04, but a most indifferent jumper, and tends to run in snatches, and will struggle to upgrade successfully again. *M.A. Kemp, Mr & Mrs J. Ridge & J. & Mrs P. Hamilton — Thurlow (David Kemp).* 123 (M), 248 (Cf), 524 (R), 745 (R), 999 (R), 1152 (R), 1406 (I).

NOW YOUNG MAN (IRE) ..8-10.. 16 br.g. Callernish — Claddagh Pride (Bargello) 3up87. Workmanlike half-brother to Win Electric. Dam won NH flat and dead-heated for Maiden in Ireland. NH FLAT r3 p0. NH '94/5, '97/9 and '01 r28 w4 (3 2m7f Hdles and 3m2f Ch) p7 (4 2nds). P-t-P/HUNT CH '97 and '02 r3 w1 (3m1f Hunt Ch) p1 (2nd); and 4th. A thorough stayer and suited by sound surfaces, but has spent long periods on the sidelines, and has not scored since recording his fourth success at Kelso in '97. Not better than last this year, and nothing more than a slow old schoolmaster now. Has been tried in blinkers. *Miss P. Moore — Tiverton.* 114 (M), 577 (Cnr), 1130 (Cnr), 1250 (C), 1329 (Cnr).

NUBRO (IRE) ..9-12§.. 11 ch.g. Abednego — Miss Magello (Bargello) pp2. Small brother to Irish Hurdle/Chasing/Pointing winner, Nuaffe (useful — also won Greenall Whitley at Haydock), and half-brother to Bit Of Order and Count Surveyor, and to Irish Pointing winners, Mullabawn and Satin Sheen. IRISH P-t-P '01 r1 p1 (3rd). P-t-P '02/3 r8 w2 (Maiden and Restricted) p2 ($^{1}/_{2}$*l* 2nd once); and pulled up 4. A dual winner on good or sound surfaces in '02, but ungenuine and inconsistent, and has pulled up in more than half his English Points. Stays long trips, but error-prone and never went a yard on his reappearance, and outbattled from the last by Brackenheath when tried in blinkers at Aldington. Can probably be ignored. *M.R. Smith — E. Sussex & Romney Marsh (Sara Hickman).* 537 (4mMO), 778 (CCon), 1281 (Cf).

OAKLANDS BILLY ..7-7.. 16 b.g. Silly Prices — Fishermans Lass (Articulate) 5. Sturdy close-coupled half-brother to Carole's Delight and Mamica (Chasing winner since Pointing), and to Hurdles winner, Royal Invader. Dam failed to finish in 10 Points (fell/unseated 3). NH '97 r2 p0 (5th of 6, and pulled up in Chses). P-t-P/HUNT CH '98/00 and '02 r12 p3 (2 3rds, of 4 once; and last of 2); pulled up 6, fell 2, and brought down 1. Placed three times and has often made the running, but normally decelerates rapidly after a maximum of 2m4f, and beaten a minimum of 14 lengths. Stands very little racing, and made a surprise return in '04, but predictably well tailed off at Easingwold. *R.G. Russ — Cleveland.* 1305 (OMa).

OAKLANDS LUIS ..9-8.. 6 b.g. Primitive Rising (USA) — Bally Small (Sunyboy) 331. Sturdy brother to Chasing winner, Ocean Dancer, and half-brother to Plowshare Tortoise and Arctic Ridge. Gradually improving, and followed a $16^{1}/_{2}$ lengths third with a creditable eight lengths third at Duncombe Park, and gained the reward of consistency when beating one other finisher at Whitwell-on-the-Hill (looked held until the rival blundered at the last and came to a standstill). A red-letter day for the ever-enthusiastic vet Graham Russ, who has now had two winners in 30 years of owning Pointers. Game and a steady jumper, and may progress sufficiently for Restricteds. *R.G. Russ — Cleveland.* 165 (OMa), 271 (OMa), 775 (CfMa).

OAKLANDS TED ..8-4.. 7 b.g. Royal Fountain — Brig's Gazelle (Lord Nelson FR) pp64. Dam won 3 3m1f-3m2f Chases. P-t-P '03 r1 p0 (5th of 6). Starting to show some improvement, but faded badly from the last when 21 lengths fourth at Whitwell-on-the-Hill, and may have suffered a setback. *R.G. Russ — Cleveland.* 160 (CMa), 211 (C), 563 (R), 774 (2m4fCMa).

OCKI ..9-6.. 12 gr.g. Octogenarian — Royalty Miss (Royalty) 21p. Small. Dam, half-sister to Fort Diana (*qv* '98 Annual), won 2 2m-2m6f Hdles, (the first a Sell). NH '99 r2 p0; pulled up 1. P-t-P/HUNT CH '02/3 r3 p0 (5th of 6, pulled up 1, and fell 1). Very lightly raced and overtaxed in his first five starts, but scored as soon as he was dropped into Maiden company, and was a resounding 33-1. Outstayed some weak opponents, but predictably trounced in a Hunter Chase next time, where his jumping was typically not up to scratch. Wears a cross-noseband. *R.S. & M.R. Eagleton — W. Street Tickham (Mary Eagleton).* 534 (M), 651 (OMa), 1438 (3m2fH).

OCTAGONAL (IRE) ..9-2.. 8 b.g. Woods Of Windsor (USA) — Strawberry Belle (IRE) (Vision USA) 2996*u*. Compact well-made. IRISH FLAT '99/00 r7 p0. IRISH NH '00/2 (for Ms F.M. Crowley) r14 w2 (2m4f Hdles) p2 (3rds); fell 1, pulled up 1. NH '03 r1 p0 (pulled up). NH '04 r3 p0 (9th in 2m4f110y Sell Hdle: *hld up, rdn & wknd 8, t.o*; 6th in 2m3f110y Sell Hdle: *in tch til rdn & wknd 6*; and unseated in 2m7f110y Ch: *hld up, stdy hdwy when jmpd rt 11 & 12, wkng when blun & ur 3 out*). Ended his Irish career by completing a double within three days in 2m4f Hurdles (one on firm, blinkered in both), but has declined alarmingly since being bought expensively by present connections, and only inherited 15 lengths last of two in a Ladies after two departures in the final mile. Headgear has no beneficial effects now. Gone beyond recall, at least in this yard. *N. Shutts — Ludlow (Karen Marks).* 253 (L), 407 (L).

OCTANE BOOSTER (IRE) ..8-5.. 8 b/br.g. Architect (USA) — Furry Dream (Furry Glen) upp34u. Brother to Buddy Bear (IRE), and half-brother to Irish Pointing winner, Seagrass. IRISH P-t-P '03 r6 p2; last, pulled up 1, unseated 1 and refused 1. IRISH NH FLAT '02 r2 p0. IRISH NH '02 (for M.F. Morris) r1 p0. Sold Ascot, Nov for 3047 (H. Flaherty). Tailed off thrice under Rules, and in four Pointing completions from 11 attempts, only two horses have finished behind him, and beaten 40 lengths plus on three occasions. Can be hard to sit on, and there is no evidence to suggest he stays three miles. *The Mighty Friends (M. Holdforth) — Hursley Hambledon (Penny Lownds).* 173 (OMa), 264 (CfMa), 424 (CMa), 627 (OMa), 721 (OMa), 1186 (OMa).

O'ECH ..10-0.. 11 gr.m. Baron Blakeney — Hand Maid (Some Hand) 23321. Smallish unfurnished half-sister to Mariners Hand and Some Boy. Dam won 2m Sell Hdle. P-t-P '99 and '02/3 r5 p1 (last of 2); 5th, pulled up 2 and fell 1. Very lightly raced and let down by her jumping in previous years, but managed to keep on the go from January to mid-May in '04, and followed four consecutive placings in which she was only once beaten more than five lengths with a convincing success on firmish at Bratton Down. Had Harnage 12 lengths in arrears, and there stands a good chance that her much more reliable jumping will stand her in good stead in Restricteds. *Mrs C. Lawrence — Eggesford.* 83 (OMa), 312 (CfMa), 568 (CfMa), 704 (CfMa), 1381 (OMa).

OFCOURSEHEKHAN (IRE) .9-10.. 7 b.g. Phardante (FR) — King's Gift (IRE) (King's Ride) p312. Brother to Irish Pointing winner, Let Them Have It. IRISH P-t-P '03 r5 p0 (pulled up 4 and refused 1). Bought Doncaster, Aug for 2800. Bought cheaply after bad efforts in Irish Points, but has improved for a change of scenery, and followed a one-and-a-half lengths third with a win in a Mosshouses Maiden, which he took easily despite almost veering off the course on the run-in. Had twice proved unsteerable previously, but speedy, and if able to be cured of this unpleasant foible there is certainly a Restricted at least for him (despite running green, has already finished two-and-a-half lengths second in this grade). His talented rider Nicola Stirling does particularly well with this type of horse (e.g. Clifford Bay), so signs are promising. *Miss N.C. Stirling — Lauderdale.* 767 (2m4fOMa), 920 (2m4fOMa), 1224 (OMa), 1419 (R).

OFFICE HOURS ..9-6.. 13 b.g. Danehill (USA) — Charmina (FR) (Nonoalco USA) 5pbp. Compact brother to flat winner, Great Child, and half-brother to 4 flat winners (3 abroad). Dam won at 8f in France. FLAT '94/9 r24 p5. NH '96/9 r14 p1 (2½l 3rd in Sell); pulled up 4, fell 4. P-t-P '00 and '02/3 r8 w1 (Maiden) p4 (3 2nds, of 3 once); 5th, last, and pulled up 1. Won a bad three-finisher Maiden at Thorpe Lodge last year, and often flatters to deceive, but consistently let down by his inability to stay three miles. Sometimes takes diabolical liberties with the fences. Has run tongue-tied and blinkered. *Miss B.M. Neal — Burton (Tony Walker).* 1162 (R), 1304 (CR), 1416 (R), 1469 (R).

OFFICER CADET (IRE) ..9-7.. 6 b.g. Warcraft (USA) — Flinging (Good Times ITY) p. Good-topped half-brother to Our Man Flin (IRE). Dam, half-sister to 3 Pointers, including Brimstone Hill (*qv* '96 Annual). Bought Doncaster, May for 21,000. Considered by connections to be potentially the best of the trio of newcomers they introduced at Bishops Court, and after Combat Drinker and Lord Anner had done the business confidence was sky-high, but after being backed from 4s to 5-4 Officer Cadet let the side down badly. Whilst heavily restrained mixed several mistakes with the odd good jump, and having been given a lot to do by Nicky Williams ('he thought he was on a motor bike' in the words of one jaundiced spectator) he was still only seventh and ridden four out and with no response forthcoming was pulled up. Not seen again (like Combat Drinker), but more positive efforts should be forthcoming when fit. *K. Biggins & P. Nicholls — Taunton V. (Richard Barber).* 329 (OMa).

OFF PISTE ..9-1.. 8 b.g. Petoski — Coquette (Gildoran) p. Small light owner-bred. P-t-P '02 r3 p2 (dead-heat 2nd once); and last. Twice a beaten favourite when making the frame in all three attempts in his debut season, but absent in '03, and collapsed in the box-park before pulling up after two miles on his belated return and was not seen again. Clearly has major problems to overcome. *P.A. Deal — Taunton V.H. (David Pipe).* 30 (CMah).

OFFSHORE (IRE) ..9-9.. 12 b.g. Over The River (FR) — Parson's Princess (The Parson) 3pp. Lengthy unfurnished half-brother to Irish NH flat winner, Indalo. NH FLAT '98 r3 p1 (3rd); and 4th twice. P-t-P/HUNT CH '00 and '02 (for Mr F.R. Jackson) r7 w1 (Club) p0 (4th, and pulled up 5). NH '02/3 (for T.D. McCarthy) r4 p 1 (dist 2nd of 3 in 3m2f110y Ch); pulled up 3. Revelled in the ever worsening conditions when beating 15 rivals in well over seven minutes at Barbury in '02, but pulled up in ten of 13 other starts over fences, and beaten 20 lengths plus in the remainder. Blinkered once in '03 and his enthusiasm has looked suspect, but his problems probably stem from a physical fault, and appeared to suffer a setback at Towcester. *Puttenden Partnership (Miss S. Palmer) — O. Surrey, Burstow & W. Kent (Steven Saltmarsh).* 99 (I), 239 (3m1fH), 437 (3m1fH).

OFFSPRINGER .9-3.. 8 b.g. Royal Fountain — Charons Daughter (Another River) pup. Workmanlike lengthy homebred half-brother to Raging Torrent (*qv*). P-t-P '03 r1 w1 (2-finisher 2m4f Maiden). Beat the only other finisher by a neck in a five-runner 2m4f Maiden on firm at Alnwick on his only appearance in '03, but let down by his jumping when second-favourite at Friars Haugh this year, and seems to possess a volatile temperament. Unruly in the paddock on his debut, and at the start on his most recent outing, and has been mounted on course and taken to post early. Needs sorting out before he reappears. *A. Waugh — Morpeth (Simon Waugh).* 212 (R), 283 (R), 430 (R).

OFF THE HOOK (IRE) ..9-5.. 9 b.g. Montelimar (USA) — Hook's Close (Kemal FR) 33ubp. Small close-coupled half-brother to Chasing winner, Tailored (IRE). Dam, sister to One For The Moon, and half-sister to Playlord (*qv* '03 Annual). NH FLAT '00 r3 p1 (3rd). NH '01 r6 p0; pulled up 1. P-t-P '03 r2 p0 (4th, and pulled up). Not disgraced when beaten between eight and 15 lengths in Maidens, but tends to expend a bit of nervous energy in the preliminaries, and will need to relax more in order to open his account. Missed '02 and appeared to suffer a setback last year, and five outings in a season is his record. Has two handlers. *P., W. & D. Ansell & Ms M. Carden — N. Cornwall (Ian Hambley).* 327 (OMa), 486 (OMa), 568 (CfMa), 1006 (CfMa), 1167 (3m2f110yH).

O'FLAHERTY'S (IRE) ..8-0.. 13 ch.g. Balinger — Deise Lady (Le Bavard FR) 67f7p. Small. Dam won Irish Point. IRISH P-t-P '98 r4 p2 (2nds); fell 2 (when 2nd at last once). IRISH HUNT CH '98 r1 p0. P-t-P/HUNT CH '99/03 r18 w1 (Maiden) p3 (2 2nds, beaten ½*l* once, and of 3 once; and 3rd of 4 in Hunt Ch); 8th, last pair 6, pulled up 2, slipped up 1, and fell/unseated 4. Booted out of a leading yard after winning a typically weak Maiden in the slowest time of the day at Upper Sapey in '00, and predictably trounced since, and only once better than last in his 12 most recent appearances. Sometimes takes a keen hold but always stops quickly after a maximum of 2m4f in Points, and is obviously breaking blood vessels on a regular basis. Acquired blinkers on his last three starts. *G.D. Blagbrough — Avon V.* 90 (I), 345 (2m5fH), 443 (2m4f110yH), 636 (Rnr), 1166 (2m5f110yH).

OH HIGHLY LIKELY (IRE) ..10-0.. 8 ch.g. Glacial Storm (USA) — Suir Venture (Roselier FR) 1. Half brother to Irish NH Flat and Hurdling winner, Pateley. Dam won NH flat and two Hurdles (2m4f-3m) in Ireland. IRISH NH '01/3 (for A.L.T. Moore) r19 w1 (2m6f) p1 (2nd); refused to race 1, pulled up 3. Bought Doncaster, Oct for 9500. Beaten 28 lengths plus in his first 13 Irish races, but improved latterly, and won a Chase in Northern Ireland at Downpatrick. Refused to race once there, and wore blinkers on his final two appearances. Promptly off the mark for the new yard in a Market Rasen Open, where he was helped by the 4-9 shot Red Rebel having an off day, but not seen again. Provided all is well with him he should give connections fun in '05. *R.J. Jackson — S. Notts.* 300 (O).

O J SELYM (IRE) .9-3.. 11 b.g. Be My Native (USA) — Myle Avenue (Push On) 63735. Tall rangy half-brother to Amandas Fancy (IRE) (*qv*). IRISH P-t-P '98/00 r6 w2 (4&5yo Maiden, Winners of One) p2; pulled up 2. IRISH NH FLAT '99 r2 p0. NH '00/2 (for H.D. Daly) r12 w1 (2m1fCh) p2 (3rds); pulled up 2. The winner of three races on easy surfaces including a three-finisher Towcester Chase over little more than the minimum trip by a distance, but error-prone, and having pulled up on his final start of '02 missed '03. Broke a blood vessel once under Rules. Safe enough for Guy Opperman in Points, but he is not fit enough and gets more tired than the horse, and the closest he came to a winner was when 15 lengths third in a Mixed Open at Didmarton. Would possibly be struggling to get the trip in any case. *M. Opperman — Ludlow.* 254 (O), 366 (MO), 586 (O), 834 (M), 1015 (Cf).

OLE GUNNAR (IRE) ..9-9§.. 13 b.g. Le Bavard (FR) — Rareitess (Rarity) 5rp. IRISH P-t-P '98 r1 p1 (2nd). NH '01/2 r2 p1 (3rd in Hdle); and pulled up 1. P-t-P '99/00 and '02/3 r18 w2 (Maiden and Restricted) p5 (4 2nds; and 3rd of 4); 4th twice, pulled up 5, refused 1, brought down 1 and fell 2. Very much a law unto himself, and has proved disappointing since scoring in unsuitably tacky ground at Rhydygwern in '02, and threw away certain victory when refusing at the final open ditch in his Members last year. Capable of finishing very strongly when inclined but has to come as late as possible, and was in front much too soon when tried in cheekpieces for the first time at Brampton Bryan (fast back-pedaling when refusing and unseating two out). Sometimes awkward at the start and never went a yard next time, and seems most unlikely to reform at 13. Wears a cross-noseband. *Miss E.C. Wilesmith — Ledbury.* 513 (Cf), 663 (I), 922 (I).

OLLY MAY ..9-4.. 10 b.m. Silver Owl — Chevitino (Rugantino) 13. Workmanlike half-sister to Braw Lad. Dam is half-sister to Siwel (*qv* '90 Annual). NH FLAT '99 r2 p0. FLAT '00 r4 p0 (tailed off 3, inc a Sell). NH '99/00 r5 p0; pulled up 2, unseated 1. P-t-P '02/3 (for Mr J.B. Shears) r7 p0 (last pair 3, and pulled up 4). Consistently hopeless in all spheres in previous yards, and had only beaten one rival in her first seven Points, but came in for sustained market support on her reappearance, and got up in the last strides under a strong ride from Richard Woollacott. Clocked the slowest time of the day, and failed to reappear after being beaten 31 lengths in her first Restricted. Blinkered once in '00. *B. Taylor & P. Wedlake — S. Devon (Barry Taylor).* 66 (OMa), 415 (R).

OLYMPIC STORM (IRE) .—§§.. 7 b.g. Glacial Storm (USA) — Philly Athletic (Sit In The Corner USA) prr*R*7. Tall well-made. Dam won 2 Hurdles, 2m1f-2m4f. IRISH P-t-P '03 r4 w1 (5&6yo Maiden) p0; unseated 1. NH FLAT '04 r2 p0 (ran out over 2m at Ayr: *in tch 8f, wl bhnd when rn out 5f out*; and 7th over 2m110y at Perth: *a bhnd, rdn 8f out, t.o*). Scored in heavy in Ireland, and doubtless has some ability, but revealed a wicked streak in the new yard, and refused to race twice consecutively having been most unruly and unseated in the preliminaries in both. Ran off the course in his debut bumper, but was at least coaxed round for 49 lengths seventh next time. Probably might represent a welcome challenge to a Dick Baimbridge or a Harvey Smith, but Jamie Alexander will surely be full of trepidation about any future encounters. *J.F. Alexander — Fife (Nick Alexander).* 552 (Cf), 654 (Cf), 766 (R).

OMNI COSMO TOUCH (USA) ..10-11.. 9 b.g. Trempolino (USA) — Wooden Pudden (USA) (Top Ville) 11du12. Neat well-made brother to a French flat winner. IRISH FLAT '99/00 r5 w1 (8f) p1 (3rd). IRISH NH '00 r1 p1 (2nd). NH '00/2 r16 w4 (2m-2m4f Hdles) p4 (2nds, inc Ch); refused to race four. P-t-P '03 (for Mr F. Jackson & Mrs S. Smith) r1 w1 (Open). Most recalcitrant latterly under Rules, but has been sweetened to great effect in the present yard, and only beaten by Mullensgrove (on one of his real going days) in his last five completions. Has made all in the past, but best when coming from behind and has to do everything on the bridle, but still retains an awkwardness at the start, and punters should always bear that in mind. Used to like the going like the road, but handles much softer ground nowadays. Disqualified from his win at Sedgefield in February after a banned substance was found in a post-race sample. Blinkered in '01 but refused to jump off, and the experiment has not been repeated. *Mrs S. Smith — M.H. Potts — Pendle Forest & Craven (Joss Saville).* 100 (O), 316 (2m5fH), 543 (3m2f110yH), 683 (O), 994 (3m110yH).

ON A FULL WAGER ..8-3.. 8 b.g. Homo Sapien — Ntombi (Trasi's Son) p54ppp. Lengthy unfurnished half-brother to NH flat winner, Tirikumba. Dam won 2m4f Hurdle. NH FLAT '02 r2 p0. NH '02/3 (for P. Bowen) r4 p0; pulled up 1. Prone to blunders and only beat one horse in his final seven races (blinkered in the two latest), and ended his dismal career by pulling up for the fourth consecutive time and having to be destroyed as he was lame. R. Owen & P. Fullagar — V. of Aylesbury with Garth & S. Berks (Karen Lawther). 20 (OMa), 52 (OMa), 173 (OMa), 443 (2m4f110yH), 627 (OMa), 871 (OMa).

ONEANTHREEQUARTERS (IRE) .8-11.. 13 ch.g. King Luthier — Khaki Kate (Brigadier Gerard) 5u54226. Tall. Dam won 5 flat (11-13f) as 4yo and is half-sister to Caspian Flyer (*qv* '95 Annual). IRISH P-t-P '98 r4 w2 (6yo&up Maiden and Winners Of One) p0; fell 1. NH '98/01 r28 w3 (2m5f-3m1f110y Chses) p9 (4 2nds, inc 2 Sell Chses); pulled up 5, fell 1. P-t-P '03 r5 p2 (2nds, of 3 once); last, and unseated 2. Won five races to April '00, and unlucky not to capture another 12 months later, but has had all sorts of problems over the years, and his losing sequence now stands at 25. Runner-up in both assaults on his Members, and in two other Points, but his novice partner has vacated the saddle without much provocation twice, and might proffer more assistance if he dropped his leathers a couple of holes. Plods rather badly now and only really of use as a schoolmaster. Occasionally blinkered under Rules. *R.W.S. Jagger — S. Salop (Russell Teague).* 93 (O), 251 (C), 528 (O), 661 (Cnr), 930 (O), 1260 (M), 1375 (3m110yH).

ONE FOR OLLY (IRE) ..8-10.. 7 b.g. Little Bighorn — Santa's Gold (Tumble Gold) 5u6u. Small compact brother to Little Santa (IRE). 8447 3yo. A poor jumper thus far, and was 32 lengths sixth of seven over 2m4f on the only occasion he finished in front of another horse. Not entirely unpromising, but needs to find some confidence. *C.O. King — O. Berks.* 8 (2m4fOMa), 30 (CMah), 290 (2m4fCfMa), 368 (OMa).

ONEFORTHEFROG (IRE) ..9-7§.. 12 ch.g. Good Thyne (USA) — Deep Black (Deep Run) p16. Big rangy. NH FLAT '98 r1 p0. NH '99 r2 p0 (pulled up 2). P-t-P '00 and '03 r7 p0 (4th, pulled up 4, slipped up 1, and refused 1). Beaten 48 lengths on his only previous completion over jumps, and has had myriad problems, but sprang a surprise under the promising Gerry Tumelty when landing a long

Maiden in softish at Maisemore Park. Had pulled up at the sixth and the ninth in his two most recent outings, and firmly put in his place in a subsequent Restricted. *M.A. & Mrs A.J. Sproule & L.J. Daniels — Taunton V. (Angela Sproule).* 370 (OMa), 730 (OMa), 977 (R).

ONE MINUTE MAN (IRE) ..—.. 7 gr.g. Presenting — Par-Bar (IRE) (The Parson) p. Lengthy. Dam, half-sister to High Park Lady (*qv* '01 Annual) won Mares Maiden in Ireland but failed to finish in 5 of 7 English Points ('thoroughly ungenuine and bitterly disappointing'). Struggling until he pulled up at the eighth on a May debut at Bredwardine. *Miss J. Oakey — Worcs (Martin Oliver).* 1393 (OMa).

PLATE 92 319 East Devon Mens Open: Oneminutetofive is a very easy but probably lucky winner for Ashley Farrant PHOTO: Baths Photographic

ONEMINUTETOFIVE .11-1.. 8 b.g. Neltino — Island Beat (Jupiter Island) 211141. Small neat. Dam, sister or half-sister to 5 Pointers, including Opal Ridge (*qv* '03 Annual), was 32*l* last of 3 in Maiden (failed to finish in 3 of 4 other Points). P-t-P '03 r1 w1 (Maiden). Defeated only once in Points, when apparently wrong in his blood, but considered beaten by rider and trainer when left well clear by Right To Reply's exit at Bishops Court, and appeared to have succumbed to Springford when adjudged to have dead-heated at Lifton. Emerged from the Cheltenham Foxhunters with immense credit, particularly because of his inexperience, and looked to be travelling best of all coming down the hill, and looks the sort that his part-owner could easily develop into a smart Handicapper in no time at all. Still has a few ragged edges, and lack of fluency is one, but providing he remains free from injury a long and successful career should lie ahead. Wears a cross-noseband. *D.E. Pipe — B.A. Kilpatrick - Taunton V.H. (David Pipe).* 2 (R), 198 (R), 310 (O), 319 (O), 543 (3m2f110yH), 825 (O).

ONE OF THE NATIVES (IRE) ..9-0.. 11 b.g. Be My Native (USA) — Take Me Home (Amoristic USA) 75p74. Compact half-brother to Golden Bar (IRE) and Calling Home (IRE), to Irish Pointing winner, Stealing Home, and to NH flat winners, Festive Teak (IRE) and Home James (IRE) (latter also winning Hurdler). Dam, half-sister to The Honest Poacher (*qv* '01 Annual), won NH flat, 2m4f Hdle and 2m Ch in Ireland. NH FLAT '99 r2 p0. NH '02 r3 p1 (3rd in Ch); 7th and pulled up. P-t-P/HUNT CH '00/3 r15 w4 (inc Mixed Open) p3 (2 2nds, last once; and 3rd of 4); 4th, 7th, last 2, pulled up 3, and fell 1. Won four Points in a five-race spell to February '01, and rated 10-8 at the time, but bitterly disappointing since leaving Seaborough, and normally retreats with a whimper after sometimes making the early running. Tailed off without exception in '04, and had to contend with much arm-waving from the owner-rider, though she may just have been acknowledging the crowd as she is the most famous National Hunt performer's lass. Wears a cross-noseband, and acquired a visor on his last three starts. *Miss J.H. Jenner — Berks & Bucks.* 16 (C), 31 (Cnr), 187 (Cf), 631 (2m6f110yH), 937 (Cnr).

ON HIS TOES ..10-0.. 9 b.g. Joligeneration — On Her Toes (Hotfoot) u221. Compact owner-bred half-brother to Hurdles winner, On My Toes. Dam (only tiny) won a 2m1f Sell Hdle. P-t-P '02/3 r2 p1 ($^{1}/_{2}$*l*

2nd of 3); and unseated 1. Twisted a front fetlock when distracted by a loose dog on his only appearance last year, but has always been held in high regard by the owner, and finally able to get off the mark when trouncing weak opposition at Holnicote. A nervy individual and tends to get worked up in the preliminaries, and dropped the rider on the way to post at Buckfastleigh, but the win should have boosted his confidence no end, and can succeed on a regular basis when he learns to relax more. *G. Chambers — Silverton.* 319 (O), 493 (OMa), 795 (CfMa), 1186 (OMa).

ON THE DAY (IRE) .9-11§.. 8 ch.g. Roselier (FR) — Solar Jet (Mandalus) p33422412. Well-made attractive half-brother to Spring Double (IRE) (*qv*). 58,000 3yo. NH '02/3 (for L. Lungo) r5 p4; and pulled up 1. Finally got his head in front when beating a perennial maiden by 12 lengths at Marks Tey, in a contest taking 7min25s, but generally loves to get beaten, and favourite or joint-favourite in similar grade on four previous occasions. Nine placings include when short-headed in a 3m4f Hurdle, and was beaten a head in a youngsters event at Fakenham in which he went over a length ahead on the run-in. Getting him in the right place at the right time was a constant challenge for James Owen in '04, and the problem may be exacerbated in Restricteds. By the same sire as renowned stablemate Divine Mist, and because the pair take such care of themselves they are at least durable and able to go to the sports most weekends. *J.M. Turner — Suffolk.* 128 (OMa), 244 (CfMa), 401 (OMa), 651 (OMa), 833 (OMa), 1155 (OMa), 1246 (OMa), 1317 (CfMa), 1409 (CR).

ON THE DECK ..—§.. 7 b.g. Teenoso (USA) — Frost In Summer (Busted) ppp. Light. P-t-P '03 (for Mr D.J. Dickson) r1 p0 (last). Got his name because of his habit of ejecting riders from the saddle in the previous yard who promptly got shot after one run, and vindicated their decision in '04, though the presence of the season's least successful rider hardly helped his cause. Threw in the towel when visored at Dingley, and looks a total waste of time. *P.J. Millington — Fernie.* 30 (CMah), 219 (OMa), 1215 (CfMa).

ON THE MEND (IRE) ..9-10.. 12 ch.g. Broken Hearted — Mugs Away (Mugatpura) pp6p441. Strong attractive half-brother to NH Flat and jumping winners, Glebe Lad (won Irish Grand National), Stashedaway, Ontheroadagain, Bennie's Pride, to NH Flat and Hurdling winner, Away Home and also Hurdles winner, Born To Win (all 6 in Ireland; total 25 wins). IRISH NH FLAT '97 and '99/00 r8 p1 (3rd). IRISH NH '99/03 (for M.J.P. O'Brien) r28 w5 (3 2m4f-2m6f Hdles and 2 2m2f Chses) p9 (inc 4 2nds); pulled up 2, fell/unseated 4. Bought Doncaster, Aug for 5000. Had a profitable career in Ireland where he won five races in the mud to 2m6f (including 18, 19 and 20-runner races), and earned £50,189, but also fell and unseated on four occasions there, and could be sticky in England. Was not getting the trip under the bigger weights in early season, but a switch to Ladies Opens eventually paid off when he won a three-runner event at Easingwold, where he made all and despite Freya Hartley dropping her whip at the ditch took advantage of the reluctance of the 1-5 favourite Ridgeway to overtake. Will again struggle in competitive races if returning at 12. *Mrs J.M. Newitt — Middleton (Susan Balshaw).* 269 (O), 391 (MO), 441 (2m4f110yH), 630 (2m4fH), 811 (L), 1160 (L), 1303 (L).

ON THE RUN (IRE) ..—.. 11 ch.m. Don't Forget Me — Chepstow House (USA) (Northern Baby CAN) ppp*44*. Small half-sister to Roscolvin (IRE), and to jumping winner in USA. IRISH FLAT '97/8 r3 p0. IRISH NH '97/9 r11 p2 (hdd 1). NH '00/3 r23 w1 (2m Hdle) p9 (inc 2 in Ch); pulled up 1, fell/unseated 2. NH '04 (for D.J. Wintle) r2 p0 (4th in 2m3f110y Sell Hdle: *hld up & bhnd, hdwy 7, wknd aft 3 out*; and 4th in 2m Hdle: *hld up, hdwy 7, rdn 2 out, one pce*). Has been in action for seven years, but gained his sole win in a Southwell Selling Hurdle in August '01. Sometimes makes bad blunders, and can pull very hard. Wears a tongue-tie. Did not take to Pointing and pulled up each time, and then returned to continue extending her long losing sequence under Rules. *L.W. & M.D. Jones — Gelligaer F. (Lisa Day).* 404 (O), 727 (MO), 1017 (3m2fL).

ONWARD BOUND ..9-4§§.. 9 br.g. Mister Lord (USA) — Miss Cannon (Black Minstrel) f44p. Tall workmanlike. Dam, sister to Mister Tuftie (*qv* '96 Annual), was 3rd in 2 Irish Points, but tailed off in 3 English Points, (pulled up 2). P-t-P '03 r7 w1 (3-finisher Maiden) p0; last 2, pulled up 3, and refused 1. Displayed a tendency to hang when landing a three-finisher Maiden at Cilwendeg last year, but has only finished in front of Wiston Wizo in nine subsequent attempts, and is a complete dog that will stop to nil as soon as pressure is applied. *W.D. Lewis — Tivyside (Mark Lewis).* 207 (R), 357 (R), 669 (M), 953 (R).

OPAL'LOU (FR) ..10-1.. 9 b.m. Garde Royale — Calligraphie (FR) (R B Chesne) 1p441. Tall rangy half-sister to Mel In Blue (FR). FRENCH FLAT '00 r1 p0. FRENCH NH '00/1 r11 p5; fell 1. NH '01/3 (for P.F. Nicholls) r9 p5 (Chses; inc 2 2nds); pulled up 1. Most disappointing when failing to score in the French Provinces and in English Chases, but rather unlucky in the latter as she was short-headed once and beaten a head once and only just caught in both. Sometimes finds little, and was tongue-tied and pulled up on her final start in the previous yard. A good jumper who enjoyed her Pointing, and began and ended her season with a victory at Holnicote, where she employed forcing tactics both times to beat modest opposition. Vulnerable in competitive events, and as he spends his weekdays in London, Richard Pyman is sometimes not fit enough to do her full justice. An ideal mount for a novice nonetheless, and is turned out to a high standard by Jane Western. *R. Pyman — Cattistock (Jane Western).* 278 (lnr), 496 (MO), 603 (Cnr), 1101 (Cnr), 1329 (Cnr).

PLATE 93 1329 Minehead Harriers & West Somerset Countryside Alliance Club Members (Nov Rdrs): L to R, Opal'lou (Richard Pyman), 1st, and Gigi Beach (Susannah Reynoldson), 5th
PHOTO: Brian Armstrong

OPTIMISTIC THINKER ..— §§.. 11 ch.g. Beveled (USA) — Racemosa (Town Crier) u5p7ffp. Heavy-topped half-brother to 2 winners abroad. Dam won 2 12f races at Leicester. NH FLAT '98 r2 w1 (1m6f) p0. NH '98/03 (for T.R. George) r31 w4 (2m1f Hdle and 3 2m-2m1f Chses) p8; unseated 1, pulled up 10. NH '04 r1 p0 (7th in 3m110y R.A. Gold Cup: *lost tch 8, t.o 11*). The winner of five races principally in the mud but at up to just 2m1f, but has always been very quirky and often reluctant, and frequently wears blinkers or cheekpieces. Has had a soft-palate operation, and was tongue-tied twice in '99. Appalling in his last 14 outings including a Selling Hurdle, and only one horse has finished behind him, when he was seventh of eight and fences adrift in the R.A. Gold Cup. Deplorably handled by the incompetent owner (at a stone or more overweight) twice and decked when furlongs behind in both. Once an optimistic thinker, he is now a pessimistic stinker. *Mrs S. Cartridge & Miss T. McCurrich — A.J. & E. Shaw — Worcs (Theresa McCurrich).* 33 (L), 45 (Cnr), 158 (CCon), 661 (Cnr), 1014 (M), 1528 (Cf).

ORANBAY (IRE) ..9-8.. 13 b.g. Lancastrian — Brandy Supreme (Derring Rose) 24. Half-brother to Here We Go Barney (IRE), and to Irish Pointing/Hunter Chase winner, Killowenly Boy (IRE). Dam is half-sister to Cudor (*qv* '91 Annual). IRISH NH '97/01 (for P.J. Flynn, and V.T. O'Brien, all wins) r55 w3 (2m4f-3m Hdles) p13 (inc 6 Chses); pulled up 4, fell/unseated 5. Had plenty of good efforts to his name as a youngster in Ireland, but last scored in August '99, and then accumulated 36 consecutive defeats and was unplaced in the final 11 (fell or unseated five times over there). Revived after an absence to act as a schoolmaster, and showed willing with a 12 lengths second of three and a 17 lengths last (two pounds overweight in both), and could still have pretensions in the Puckeridge Members at 13 (although the Sporborgs will always be able to find one better). *G.M. Freeney — Puckeridge.* 1242 (Cf), 1408 (O).

ORCHESTRA'S BOY (IRE) .9-12.. 10 b.g. Homo Sapien — Ballycurnane Lady (Orchestra) 3221. Very tall rangy half-brother to Irish Pointing and Chasing winner, Rare Harvest. IR19,000 3yo, 3800 6yo. NH FLAT '01 r3 p1 (2nd). NH '01/2 (for Mrs A.M. Thorpe) r3 p2 (2nds). Sold Doncaster, Nov '02 for 6000. Finished four lengths second of 18 in a bumper, but lightly raced and became disappointing in the previous yard, and there were a maximum of four runners when he gained his two Hurdling seconds. Took his number of placings to seven from nine attempts when he finished two lengths second in an Intermediate at Garthorpe, and readily justified odds of 4-7 when gaining his richly-deserved reward in an elders Maiden there. It was a bad race and the runner-up a 12-year old having only his fourth outing, and the time was very slow. Should at least keep plugging into the frame in Restricteds, but is always going to be very one-paced. *The Absent Friends Group (M. Goddard) — Brocklesby (Ron Green).* 304 (OMa), 946 (OMa), 1397 (I), 1505 (OMa).

ORIENT EXPRESS (IRE) ..—.. 8 b.g. Blues Traveller (IRE) — Oriental Splendour (Runnett) f. Good-topped half-brother to flat winners, Miss Opulence, Really Chuffed (in Ireland — also won Hurdling there), Raisin Splendour and Sizzling. Dam won 5 flat, 7-8f, the first a Seller. 13,000y. FLAT '00 r9 p2 (3rds). NH '02 (for J.T. Gifford, and Mrs L. Richards) r7 p3 (inc 2 Chses); pulled up 2. Placed a total of five times on the flat and over Hurdles and fences, but pulled up in his last two Chases having been reluctant to set off in both. A hard puller who never did himself any favours, and paid the ultimate price when falling fatally at Lydstep. *J. Tudor — Llangeinor.* 950 (2m4fOMa).

ORINOCO'S FLIGHT (IRE) .9-8.. 7 ch.g. Spectrum (IRE) — Silk Route (USA) (Shahrastani USA) 53up221. Workmanlike brother, and half-brother to winners in Turkey. 5000f, IR6000y, 12,000 2yo. FLAT '01 r2 p0. NH '02 (for J. O'Neill) r2 p0; pulled up 1. Sold Doncaster, Mar '02 for 5000. Bought Ascot, Dec for 761. Outclassed flat and Hurdling and did not beat another horse whilst his novice rider got a feel of him in his first four Points, but showed improved form in a couple of seconds (behind Barber and Pipe representatives), and gave Michael Holmes a first success in a three-runner two-finisher Members at Stafford Cross in which he pulled hard (as he often does) and jumped right (which he normally doesn't). Has lost out on a Maiden, and will have more to do in Restricteds. *M. Holmes — Axe V.H.* 149 (OMa), 195 (CfMa), 325 (OMa), 492 (OMa), 688 (2m4fOMa), 962 (OMa), 1126 (M).

ORLEANS (IRE) ..9-13§§.. 10 b.g. Scenic — Guest House (What A Guest) 72336. Tall strong half-brother to Hurdles winner, Silent Guest (IRE), and to a winner in Scandinavia. Dam won 2 12f races in Ireland. FLAT '97/8 and '01 r10 p1 (3rd). NH '98/9 and '01 r6 p2; ran out 1. P-t-P/HUNT CH '03 r8 w1 (Maiden) p0; 4th twice, 7th, refused 2, pulled up 1, and fell 1. Showed a trace of ability under Rules, and was prepared to reveal all of it when winning a Maiden at Hutton Rudby (in which Bohemian Spirit finished third) last year, but highly temperamental, and usually goes from hard on the steel to labouring badly in a few strides. Certainly has the wherewithal to upgrade successfully but cannot be trusted to put his best foot forward. Visored once in '01, and wears blinkers exclusively now. *S.J. Robinson — Zetland.* 316 (2m5fH), 563 (R), 810 (R), 1177 (2m5fH), 1476 (R).

ORPHAN SPA (IRE) ..8-4.. 14 ch.g. Phardante (FR) — Knockdrumagh (Harwell) 33pp. Tall rangy half-brother to Irish Pointing and Chasing winner, Ogan Spa. Dam won 2 Points and 3 Hunt Chses in Ireland, and won 2 2m4f Chses there. IRISH P-t-P '97 r3 p1 (3rd); pulled up 1, unseated 1. IRISH NH FLAT '97 r1 p0. NH '97/9 r16 w1 (2m5f HCap Ch) p3 (2 2nds); pulled up 2, on floor 3. P-t-P '02/3 r5 p0 (pulled up 3, ran out 1, and unseated 1). Won over fences in mud at Folkestone in '99, but a moderate jumper and beaten upwards of 55 lengths in Points, and gives the impression of being defective in some way. *S.P. & Mrs S.L. Rooney — Ystrad Taf Fechan (Steve Rooney).* 1021 (M), 1190 (O), 1320 (Cf), 1484 (O).

ORTON HOUSE ..—§.. 18 b.g. Silly Prices — Who's Free (Sit In The Corner USA) p. Sparely-made brother to Who's Silly Now. Dam, pony-sized, won 4 Hdles, 2-3m, and 3m Ch and placed 18 (inc 3 flat), but was unplaced in 7 Points and a Hunt Ch at 5. NH '91/5 r10 p1 (3rd); 7th only Ch — mistakes. P-t-P/HUNT CH '96/00 and '02 r41 w4 (inc Open) p8 (4 2nds, of 3 once, last once; 4 3rds, inc of 4 twice, and last); pulled up 7, refused 1, and fell/unseated 2. A safe ride and won four races to '99, but has only once looked even remotely interested in ten starts since, and pulled up after two miles when fat and 100-1 in his Members in '04. Blinkered once in '98, and has run tongue-tied. *Mrs A.P. Kelly — Flint & Denbigh (Stephen Kelly).* 708 (M).

ORTON PLAYBOY ..—.. 7 b.g. Tulwar — Orton Lady (Oats) ppu. Lengthy. Dam, half-sister to Moonlight Story (*qv* '02 Annual) won Maiden and Members and pulled up 2 for Roger Harvey. Failed to get any sight of the winning post in May Maidens, and has jumped sketchily and looked novicey to date. *R. Harvey — Atherstone.* 1275 (OMa), 1402 (2m4fOMa), 1504 (2m4fOMa).

OSCAR WILDE ..9-11.. 13 b.g. Arctic Lord — Topsy Bee (Be Friendly) 5285337. Tall workmanlike half-brother to The Grey Baron, and to jumping winner, Gottabe. NH FLAT '98 r2 p0. NH '98/00 and '02 r12 w1 (2m5f Ch) p2 (2nds). P-t-P '03 r8 w5 (3 Club nov rdrs, Mixed Open and Confined, inc hat-trick) p2 (2nds); and pulled up 1. Ultimately disappointing and lightly raced under Rules, but took to Pointing with a vengeance last year, and provided the newcomer Dan Drake with a season to remember. Unable to handle the soft patches at Charlton Horethorne once, and took an eternity to find his rhythm at a wet Bratton Down on his final start, but otherwise won his races convincingly. Never displayed the same zest in '04, and it is hard to see his career enjoying another peak at 13. *R.H. Alner — Portman (Sally Alner).* 11 (O), 235 (O), 348 (3mH), 576 (O), 938 (MO), 1100 (O), 1443 (2m5fH).

O SO BOSSY ..9-11.. 15 ch.g. Sousa — Bubbling Spirit (Hubble Bubble) p1f42. Tall plain owner-bred half-brother to Horwood Drummer. Dam, half-sister to 4 Pointers, including Lucky Friday, won 5

Points (one on a disqualification) and placed 4 for Andrew Congdon. Grandam, Kelpie Spirit, won a Maiden and placed 3. P-t-P/HUNT CH '97/00 and '02/3 r31 w7 (inc 5 Confineds) p9 (6 2nds, of 3 thrice, and last once; and inc 3rd of 4, and inc Hunt Ch); pulled up 3, fell/unseated 7. Can be a most indifferent jumper, but has an excellent record in minor Points once he has run himself fit, and showed far too much resolve for the runner-up when 6-1 outsider of three at Black Forest Lodge. Only stands light campaigns now and no match for a rejuvenated Rice Point when 4-6 in his Members, but still has the ability to spring another surprise, even at 15. Acts on any going. *A.W. Congdon — Torrington F.* 62 (Cf), 144 (Cf), 347 (3mH), 793 (Cf), 1267 (M).

OSWALD ..6-2.. 9 b.g. Distant Relative — River Dove (USA) (Riverman USA) 4. Well-made half-brother to flat winners, Square Deal and Mungo Park. Dam won 6f race. 28,000y. FLAT '99/00 (for C.W. Thornton) r4 p0. Sold Doncaster, Jan '00 for 4000 (M.W. Easterby). Three of his four flat races to '00 were 5f scurries, so it must have been a culture shock when faced by fences and three miles in his Members, but although he responded gallantly to the challenge it was significant that the horse who finished one place ahead of him was beaten 88 lengths next time. *Mr & Mrs S.R. Hardy — Staintondale Goathland (Sally Hardy).* 954 (M).

OUR FRIEND VINC (IRE) .—.. 9 ch.g. Rock Chanteur — Iacocca (Dunphy) p. Tall half-brother to Johnny Ross (IRE). P-t-P '02/3 (for Mrs A.L. Gardiner) r5 p0 (pulled up 4, and unseated 1). Tailed off and pulled up on five occasions, and typically made mistakes when running for a new yard in '04. *D. Tyler & C. Chadney — N. Ledbury (Caroline Chadney).* 667 (OMa).

OUR GIRL FLEUR ..—.. 6 b.m. Karinga Bay — Bingham's Nanny (IRE) (Strong Gale) p. Dam, half-sister to Ourman (*qv* '04 Annual). Wore a tongue-tie on a Woodford debut, and pulled up after a mistake three out when struggling. Charlotte Bingham's (was she Fleur?) Nanny must be knocking on now, bless her. *T. Brady — Portman (Ali Tory).* 1074 (OMa).

OUR WEDDINGPRESENT (USA) .8-13.. 6 ch.g. Known Fact (USA) — All A Lark (General Assembly USA) 2pf. Neat half-brother to flat winners, Pierre Damiani (USA), Karoo Lark (USA), and to winners in USA. Dam won 3 Irish flat, 8-9f. 23,000f, 13,000y, 28,000y. FLAT '01/2 (for M.C. Pipe) r6 p0. Did not miss a meeting at Black Forest Lodge and was short-headed by a previously awful performer on his debut there (three lengths clear and looked the winner at the last, but faded and just caught), but did not jump well when trounced at 4-5 next time, and then regained the visor he wore once on the flat and took a crashing fall at the fourth. Reported to have died in the lorry going home. D.E. Pipe — Taunton V.H. 66 (OMa), 150 (OMa), 413 (2m4fOMa).

PLATE 94 321 East Devon Intermediate: One of the season's best novices, Out The Black and Jamie Snowden are impressive winners again *PHOTO: Tim Holt*

OUT THE BLACK (IRE) ..10-10.. 7 b/br.g. Presenting — Executive Wonder (IRE) (Executive Perk) 1u111u2. Small. IRISH P-t-P '03 r7 p2 (2nds); pulled up 1, ran out 1. An indifferent performer in

Ireland and came closest to success when a head second of three, but improved out of all recognition by the new yard, and had a sparkling season which was only marred by errors on occasions (does not have the substance to recover easily from mistakes, but had the excuse of a slipped saddle when eventually unseating three out when a 4-7 shot once). Faced his stiffest challenge by far in the Dudley Cup and emerged with honours, chasing home the smart Caught At Dawn, although again let down by his jumping including notable blunders at the 12th and again when beaten at the last. Very game and regularly returns fast times, and would have outstanding claims in Hunter Chases if he can cope with the fences. Still very much in the baby stage, and is a credit to connections. *J.R. Drummond — Mendip F. (Caroline Keevil).* 30 (CMah), 139 (R), 232 (R), 321 (I), 576 (O), 758 (O), 1016 (3m2fO).

OVER THE BECK (IRE) ..9-13.. 12 b.g. Over The River (FR) — Echo Creek (IRE) (Strong Gale) p. Strong-topped. NH FLAT '97 r3 w1 p0. NH '97/01 r18 w3 (2m4f-3m Hdles) p4 (3rds); pulled up 3, unseated 1. P-t-P '02/3 r7 w1 (Ladies) p1 (2nd); 4th, 7th, last, and refused 2. Won a bumper and three of his first four starts over hurdles on good or sound surfaces to February '98, but scoring for the first time since when clinging onto a rapidly diminishing advantage in mud at Witton Castle last year. Tongue-tied latterly under Rules, and pulled up at halfway when attempting to follow up at the Old Raby, and wind trouble has clearly resurfaced with a vengeance. *J.L. Marks & Mrs H.D. Marks — S. Durham (Heather Marks).* 162 (L).

OVER THE COUNTRY ..—.. 13 b.g. Over The River (FR) — Country Seat (Paddy's Stream) p. Half-brother to Royal Estate. Dam is half-sister to 6 winners, including Legal Emperor (*qv* '92 Annual). IRISH P-t-P '97 and '00 r4 w1 (4&5yo Maiden) p1 (3rd); pulled up 1. IRISH NH '00 r1 p0. IRISH HUNT CH '00 r3 w1 p0. P-t-P '02 r2 p0 (pulled up 2). A dual winner in Ireland and clearly possessed plenty of ability, but also amazingly fragile and missed '98, '99, '01 and '03 after breaking down the previous year. Tailed off and pulled up after two miles at Marks Tey, and his latest comeback will surely be his swansong. *Mrs E. Ashby — Ashford V. (Sarah Ashby).* 246 (L).

OVER THE MASTER (IRE) ..10-0.. 13 ch.g. Over The River (FR) — Covette (Master Owen) 122. Tall rangy half-brother to Who-Have-I, and to Irish Hurdles winner, Eskimo Jack (IRE). NH '97/8 r4 p0 (fell 2, inc only Ch). P-t-P '99/00 and '02/3 r19 w2 (Maiden and Confined; also disqualified once — tested positive) p4 (3rds, of 4 once); 4th twice, pulled up 6, and fell/unseated 4. Bought for peanuts after falling in half his races under Rules, and won three Points in '99, but the then owner was fined twice as much as he paid for him after failing a dope test. Raced nine times that season, but only managed four appearances in the next three, and was recording his first success for five years when providing Toby Coles with his first winner in his Members. Has proved too one-paced in better company since, but with more careful placing would have scored at Thorpe Lodge, where he was only denied by a stablemate. Suited by some cut in the ground. *Miss M. Samworth — Cottesmore.* 378 (M), 681 (I), 942 (Cf).

OVER THE RHEE (IRE) ..9-1.. 9 ch.g. Over The River (FR) — Park Belle (IRE) (Strong Gale) 3. Tall strong half-brother to Uncle Ada (IRE) (*qv*). P-t-P '02/3 r2 p0 (last, and pulled up 1). Seems impossible to get fit, and got his annual appearance out of the way typically early, and was tucked up in his cotton wool wrappings by the first weekend in February. *Mrs M.G. Sheppard — Cambs with Enfield Chace.* 129 (OMa).

OVER THE WELD ..—.. 9 ch.m. Weld — Over The Shannon (IRE) (Over The River FR) p. Dam, sister to Pennine Pride, and half-sister Coach And Four (*qv* '95 Annual). Jumped left and tailed off before halfway before pulling up at the 12th in a May Maiden. *G. Brown — Silverton (Lucy Gardner).* 1200 (OMa).

OWENABUE VALLEY (IRE) ..9-7.. 9 b.g. Yashgan — Lek-Lady (IRE) (Royal Fountain) 3452ppp. Tall lengthy. Dam, half-sister to Minstrels Toy (*qv* '97 Annual). IRISH P-t-P '01/2 r6 p1 (2nd); pulled up 2, fell 1. IRISH NH FLAT '02 r1 p0 (brought down). IRISH NH '01/2 r4 p0. P-t-P '03 r9 w3 (Maiden, Restricted, and Confined; hat-trick) p2 (3rds); pulled up 2. Ran mistakenly as Sendonthecheque in '03 following an after Sales cock up, and won three minor races by coming from off the pace, but only beat one rival in each of his next four starts, and ended the season by pulling up in a Welsh Intermediate at 33-1. Beaten little more than three lengths at Twesledown this year, but otherwise trounced by 20 lengths or more, and never passed a rival on his final three appearances. *T.D.B. Underwood — V. of Aylesbury with Garth & S. Berks.* 90 (I), 168 (C), 261 (Cf), 458 (I), 936 (I), 1242 (Cf), 1406 (I).

OWENS INVADER ..—.. 9 b.g. Muqadar (USA) — Jyponica (Wabash) p. Home bred half-brother to Quango King and Gold Talisman (*qv* '01 Annual). Dam won 2 Points and placed 11. There have been some extremely slow Pointers by Muqadar, and it looks as if he may be another of them. *Miss C.A. Owen — N. Salop (Sheila Crow).* 848 (OMa).

OWEN'S PET (IRE) ..10-1.. 11 b.g. Alphabatim (USA) — Ballinlovane (Le Moss) 3p3. Small good-bodied. Dam won 3 Irish Points. IRISH P-t-P '99/00 r13 w3 (inc Open) p4; pulled up 2, brought down 1, fell 1. NH '01/2 (for R.T. Phillips) r7 p3 (inc 2 Chses); pulled up 1. Bought Doncaster, Jan for 1200. Signed off in Ireland with a hat-trick on easy surfaces, but has only managed ten outings and been disappointing since. His first effort of '04 looked decent, but was too keen next time, and not interested at all when a distant third at Fontwell in early April. Seems to have suffered another of his setbacks. When Tash McKim purchased him she was credited in the papers as N. Nickim! *Miss S.A. Loggin, Miss N.A. McKim & J. Blencowe — Grafton (Sam Loggin).* 125 (O), 679 (3m1fH), 800 (3m2f110yH).

OWL VULGAN (IRE) ..9-8.. 10 b.g. Persian Mews — Gracious View (Sir Herbert) pfp. Half-brother to Banker's Gossip, to jumping winner, Ivy House (IRE), and to NH flat and jumping winners, The Gooser (in Ireland) and Mick O' Dwyer. Dam won 2m4f Hdle in Ireland. IRISH NH FLAT '00 r2 p0. IRISH NH '00 r2 p0. NH FLAT '00 r1 p0. NH '00 r2 p0. P-t-P '02/3 r4 w2 (Maiden and Restricted) p0; pulled up 2. Successful in both Pointing completions on sound surfaces, but unimpressive in the latest, and did not have ground conditions to suit when the reins were handed to a girl in '04. Probably has stamina limitations, but has looked moody if unable to get his own way, and even his handler might have to admit defeat. Tends to sweat up, and does not stand his racing well. *Dr P.P. Brown — Berkeley (Dick Baimbridge).* 407 (L), 757 (L), 1255 (L).

OXENDALE .9-10§.. 12 ch.g. Primitive Rising (USA) — Saucy Moon (Saucy Kit) 454624126. Small lightly-made brother to Moon Rising, and half-brother to Sun N Moon (dam of Astro Moods *qv* '04 Annual) and Moonlight Cruise. Dam won 2 2m Chses. P-t-P/HUNT CH '98/03 (for Mrs S.P. Dench) r27 w4 (up to Confined) p13 (6 2nds, beaten head once, and last once; 7 3rds, of 4 twice, and last once); fell/unseated 5, and pulled up 2. The winner of five races on ground ranging from firmish to softish, but has only once beaten more than three finishers, and lucky in the latest where the runner-up fluffed his lines at the final fence. Regularly blinkered in the second half of the season nowadays, but needs plenty of driving, and is generally easy to brush aside. Ridden in spurs on his penultimate outing. *Mrs D. Broad — Ashford V. (Stephen Spice).* 99 (I), 182 (CCon), 535 (CfO), 642 (O), 807 (M), 1053 (L), 1083 (Cf), 1284 (O), 1438 (3m2fH).

PACON (GER) ..9-13.. 12 b/br.g. Polar Falcon (USA) — Padang (GER) (Ile De Bourbon USA) u121p5p. Strong lengthy. GERMAN FLAT w4 (up to 12f, inc. Listed race). IRISH FLAT '99 r1 p0. IRISH NH '98/02 (for Mrs S.A. Bramall) r23 w2 (2m1f-2m3f Hdles) p4 (inc last of 3); fell 1. Has led an interesting life and was useful on the flat in Germany, and has been all over the place since including France on his final start under Rules. Won a couple of Ladies Opens with five and six runners (the former a gift, but the latter more competitive), but below par on his last three outings and wore a tongue-tie once. Blinkered on four occasions to '02. Was gaining his first victories for three years in the new yard, and they did well to get a tune out of him after apparent physical problems had intervened. *Mrs T.R. Kinsey, Mrs D. Halstead & Miss G. Handley — Cheshire Forest (Julie Kinsey).* 1 (C), 253 (L), 751 (L), 931 (L), 1263 (L), 1343 (L), 1470 (L).

PADDIES BOY (IRE) ..9-10.. 10 ch.g. Astronef — Bushfield Lady (Le Bavard FR) u38p67p43. Good-topped. Dam, half-sister to Keep It Zipped (*qv* '99 Annual). IRISH FLAT '98 r5 p0. IRISH P-t-P '00/2 r13 w3 (6yo Maiden, and Confined Hunt) p6; pulled up 1, unseated 1. IRISH NH '99/00 and '02/3 r15 p1 (3rd); pulled up 1. IRISH HUNT CH '02/3 r7 w2 p2. HUNT CH '03 (for Mr H. Muldoon) r1 p0. Relatively successful over fences in Ireland, but less so on his occasional forays to England in the previous yard, and has always lacked consistency. Mainly employed as a schoolmaster in '04, and displayed minimum enthusiasm when beaten upwards of 18 lengths in five of six completions, but gave the impression that stronger handling would have seen him successful at Mollington when beaten less than three lengths in the exception. Acquired cheekpieces latterly. Acts on any going. *S.K. Young — Heythrop (Jon Trice-Rolph).* 34 (O), 188 (O), 292 (MO), 404 (O), 586 (O), 758 (O), 979 (MOnr), 1032 (O), 1105 (O).

PADDY BETTALOT ..9-9.. 10 b.g. Derrylin — Gunna Be Precious (Gunner B) pp2372. Good-topped half-brother to Gunna Be King (*qv*). NH FLAT '00 r1 p0. NH '00 r2 p0; pulled up 1. P-t-P '02/3 r11 w1 (Maiden) p6 (4 2nds, beaten neck once, and of 3 twice); 4th, fell/unseated 2, and pulled up 1. Scored convincingly at Whitwick last year, and has made the frame in six of seven subsequent completions, but can be error-prone and a weak finisher, and contrived to go under by a head to a 25-1 chance on his most recent appearance. Has already had ten chances to land a Restricted, and the odds against him finding one are lengthening. Blinkered once in '00. *Miss P. Morris — Croome & W. Warwicks.* 109 (CR), 231 (CR), 516 (R), 614 (R), 839 (R), 1018 (R).

PADDY FOR PADDY (IRE) ..10-12.. 11 b.g. Mandalus — Lady Rerico (Pamroy) 41pp1. Big strong brother to Meander (IRE), and Irish jumping winner, Tyndarius (IRE), and half-brother to Crown Royale (dam of Coal Queen *qv*). Dam, half-sister to Good For A Laugh (*qv* '01 Annual), won Restricted and 3rd. P-t-P/HUNT CH '99/01 and '03 r10 w4 (inc 3m1f Hunt Ch) p4 (2nds, inc beaten short-head in Hunt Ch); 4th, and pulled up 1. A very thorough stayer and found the extended 3m6f journey at Huntingdon tailor-made on his latest appearance, but made to look slow over conventional trips, and beaten at 4-6 and 4-5 in '04. Jumps securely and should be concentrating his efforts on four-milers in future, but only averages three outings per season, and ideally requires mud. *Mrs J. Thornton — Wheatland (Guy Landau).* 43 (O), 292 (MO), 629 (3m1f110yH), 1110 (O), 1362 (3m6f110yH).

PADDY'S DREAM (IRE) ..9-13.. 10 b.g. Cataldi — Kerries Magic (Strong Gale) 2pu. Tall good-looking. IRISH P-t-P '01 r3 p1 (2nd); pulled up, and fell. P-t-P '02/3 r9 w1 (Maiden) p3 (2 3rds, of 4 once); 4th, pulled up 3, and unseated 1. Won his Maiden when tried in a first-time tongue-tie at Higham, and has been placed in three Restricteds subsequently, but does not get the trip ordinarily, and absent since being cannoned into by a loose horse on the first weekend in March. Might yet get lucky on a short course if able to resume in '05. *B. Belchem — E. Essex (Robert Gardiner).* 29 (R), 250 (R), 398 (R).

PADDY'S GLORY .—.. 10 b.g. Thornberry (USA) — Adjals Ace (London Glory) pp. Half-brother to Lamerton Quest. Unimpressive in Maidens in his belated first season, and was backward and not fluent on his debut. *S.C. Horn — Lamerton (Elaine Horn).* 312 (CfMa), 827 (CfMa).

PAGERMAR (IRE) ..9-13.. 11 b/br.g. Camden Town — Another Coup (Le Patron) p62423. Big workmanlike half-brother to Dustys Trail (IRE), and to Irish NH flat, Pointing and jumping winner, Smooth Coup. IRISH P-t-P '99/01 r8 w1 (Maiden) p2; pulled up 2. IRISH NH '01 r3 p0. P-t-P/HUNT CH '02/3 r7 w2 (2-finisher Restricted and Intermediate) p1 (last of 2); last pair 3, and pulled up 1. A good jumper and has won three minor races (two in deep mud), but has developed a wind problem since his last success in '02, and beaten 30 lengths plus in two of his placings this term. A well backed even money favourite at Alpraham, but plodded badly throughout the final mile, and unless his breathing can be sorted looks sure to prove expensive to follow in future. Wears a cross-noseband, and has been tried tongue-tied. *Mrs P. Sykes & Mrs R. Cambray — S. Salop (Pamela Sykes).* 93 (O), 228 (Cf), 381 (O), 586 (O), 852 (Cf), 1045 (Cf).

PALISANDER (IRE) ..10-9.. 11 ch.g. Conquering Hero (USA) — Classic Choice (Patch) 1124. Compact attractive half-brother to Mytton's Choice (IRE), to a winner in Italy, and 3 other winners (one abroad). IR6200y, 31,000y. FLAT '96/8 r19 w2 (10-13f) p1. NH '98/02 r26 w5 (2m-2m1f Hdle) p11; pulled up 1, fell 1. NH '04 (for R. Ford) r2 p1 (2l 2nd to Weaver George in 3m2f Ch: *hld up, hdwy 9, ld 11-15, ld 4 out til hdd & no ex flat*); and 4th in 2m4f110y Ch: *ld, qcknd 10, hdd aft 2 out, one pce*. Won seven races including four Sellers to June '00, and gained both flat successes on the all-weather (wore an eye-shield four times on the level), but lost his way, and needed a tongue-tie. Backed from 14-1 to sixes when making virtually all in a Ladies at Tabley, and then blitzed round Heslaker for an impressive victory in a very fast time (again sent to post early, and was sweating). Has continued in good heart since being switched to Chases, and rather unlucky to be pounced on by a strong finisher after first prize had looked in the bag once. Deserves to register a success over the bigger obstacles. Caroline Hurley is shaping well, and is now trying her hand as a Conditional. *D. Teasdale & K. Hesketh — V. of Lune H. (Carrie Ford).* 751 (L), 1203 (L).

PALMAND ..—.. 12 ch.m. Palm Track — Maid Mandarin (Prince Mandarin) p. Small light owner-bred. Dam, half-sister to Sand Track (by Palm Track; *qv*), pulled up and fell in Points. Grandam, Weather Maid, a maiden after 8 seasons, was 2nd in 3 Points (failed to finish 16). P-t-P '03 r3 p0 (pulled up 3). A late starter and completed a quartet of pulled ups when appearing for the only time in her Members in '04. *Mrs S. Morley — Staintondale.* 954 (M).

PAMPERED GALE (IRE) ..10-0§.. 11 b.g. Strong Gale — Pampered Russian (Deep Run) p3u31R. Workmanlike half-brother to Russian Castle (IRE) and Rockford (IRE), and to Chasing winner, Castle Red (IRE). NH FLAT '98 r2 p1 (3rd). NH '99/01 r10 p2; pulled up 1. P-t-P/HUNT CH '02/3 (for Mr J.M. Turner) r17 w4 (up to Confined) p9 (5 3rds, of 4 thrice, last once; 4 2nds, beaten head once, of 3 once); 5th, 6th, ran out 1, and pulled up 1. Successfully sweetened in the previous yard, and to a lesser degree in the current one, and outstayed 15 rivals in a Novice Riders event at Marks Tey, but has twice ducked out at the same fence at Ampton, and remains totally unreliable. Suited by ground close to good. Broke a blood vessel on his final appearance last year. *The Marriage Family (Mrs J.K. Marriage) — Essex (Simon Marriage).* 4 (Cnr), 23 (Cf), 45 (Cnr), 155 (Cnr), 249 (Cnr), 522 (L).

PAMPERED LAD ..—.. 6 b.g. Tina's Pet — Cute Pam (Pamroy) upp. Brother to Socute and Cutina (*qv*). Bought Ascot, Dec for 3809. Tailed off in Maidens, and did not look keen in the latest (unsurprisingly, considering the bumping that was going on in the saddle). If his breeders thought he was the slightest bit of use they would doubtless have kept him. *J. Flint — Tanatside (Andrew Pennock).* 960 (OMa), 1300 (OMa), 1474 (2m4fOMa).

PAMS OAK .9-4§.. 7 b.g. Afzal — Kins Token (Relkino) p1p6Rp. Tall half-brother to Kingussie Flower and Queens Token. Dam, half-sister to dam of Celtic Token (*qv*). P-t-P '03 r5 p1 (2nd); fell/unseated 3, and pulled up. Won a weakly contested three-finisher youngsters Maiden over 2m4f on firmish at Lydstep, having finished three lengths second over course and distance in '03, but a difficult ride otherwise, and is unproven over the full trip. Has twice tried to run out at Bonvilston, and succeeded once, and proved totally intractable when 4-5 on his latest appearance. Desperately needs anchoring if he is to achieve anything else worthwhile. Has two handlers. *P.S. Payne & Mrs P. Davies — Pentyrch (Phil Williams).* 362 (CfMa), 950 (2m4fOMa), 1094 (R), 1237 (R), 1318 (M), 1523 (R).

PANDELI ..8-9§.. 7 b.g. Alhijaz — Bercheba (Bellypha) ppp2p1p. Good-bodied half-brother to Kedge, and to flat winner, Shirl. An odd character who normally pulls up, but gave a better display when three lengths second at Badbury (with some complete rubbish behind him), and a couple of outings later got home in front after a very forceful ride from David Phelan in a three-finisher Aldington Maiden. Never looked keen in a four-runner Restricted when returned there next time, and is thoroughly unreliable with a mind of his own. Seems likely to disappoint in future. *Miss E.K. Jellin, C. Richards & D. Phelan — Hursley Hambledon (David Phelan).* 120 (OMa), 172 (OMa), 540 (CfMa), 580 (OMa), 782 (OMa), 895 (OMa), 1282 (R).

PANHANDLE ..9-13.. 11 b.m. Riverwise (USA) — Pallanda (Pablond) u1. Leggy workmanlike sister to Chasing winner, Tullons Lane. Dam won Maiden for Elsie Mitchell. Grandam, Landshire Loper, is half-sister to 4 Pointers and 2 jumping winners, was distant 3rd in Restricted. Great-grandam, Landshire Lane, won Open and 2 2m4f-3m1f Chses. NH FLAT '00 r3 p0. NH '01/2 r11 p2; pulled up 4. P-t-P '03 r4 p2 (head 2nd; and last of 3); and pulled up 2. Showed a little ability under Rules, and unlucky not to get a Bratton Down Maiden in the stewards room last year, but gained compensation when left clear two out to beat one other finisher in much the slowest time of the day at Cothelstone. Tends to jump to the left and stands very few outings, but might have prospects in Restricteds if fit to resume in '05. *Mrs E. Mitchell — S. Dorset.* 329 (OMa), 475 (OMa).

PANOORAS LORD (IRE) ..9-6.. 11 b.g. Topanoora — Ladyship (Windjammer USA) pf5. Small neat half-brother to Irish NH flat and Hurdling winner, Lewisham, and to 2 winners abroad. Dam won 8f race. FLAT '96, '98 and '00/1 r16 p1 (2nd). NH '97/03 (for J.S. Wainwright) r29 w2 (2m-2m1f Hdle) p3; pulled up 3, fell/unseated 2. Won a couple of short-distance Selling Hurdles to June '00, but basically a prolific loser, and has now run up a sequence of 27 consecutive defeats. Visored once in '98, and was a distant last in a Chase on his only appearance in '03. Sent off at long odds in '04, and the best he could manage was 26 lengths last. Almost certainly struggles to stay three miles. *Ms J. French — Middleton (Martyn Hill).* 55 (Cf), 377 (3m1fH), 1163 (Cf).

PANTO ..8-6.. 8 b.g. Lepanto (GER) — Sherzine (Gorytus USA) p3pp3. Workmanlike lengthy half-brother to Gilzine (*qv*). NH FLAT '02 (for breeder M.E. Hill) r1 p0. Often shows some early pace, but invariably fades, and has only had one horse behind him when beaten 15 lengths plus in two completions. Clearly extremely moderate. *Miss K. Lovelace — S. Dorset.* 367 (OMa), 575 (OMa), 865 (OMa), 1074 (OMa), 1248 (OMa).

PANTO PIXIE .9-7.. 9 br.m. Lepanto (GER) — Perspex Way (Perspex) 534p. Small neat half-sister to Regent's Way, Arctic Way and Nick's Way. Dam, half-sister to Pitway (*qv* '87 Season Annual), won 8 Points (the first in Ireland) and placed 8. P-t-P '03 r7 w1 (Maiden) p2 (3rds); 5th, pulled up 2, and fell 1. Comfortably landed a division of a Trebudannon Maiden last year, but clocked a remarkably slow time, and beaten 35 lengths and upwards in Restricteds this year. *C.J. Rush — N. Cornwall (Becky Kennen).* 79 (R), 314 (R), 488 (R), 912 (R).

PA PIERRE (IRE) ..10-4.. 7 b.g. Pierre — Shoon River (IRE) (Over The River FR) 2. Light-framed. Dam, half-sister to Ardscud (*qv* '01 Annual). IRISH P-t-P '03 r2 w1 (5yo&up Maiden) p0. Bought Doncaster, May for 4000. Ran a cracker on his English debut in a Restricted at Cottenham, and after being backed from fives to 3-1 he took up the running after the last only to be touched off by Step And Run. The only one of the six finishers who did not go on to score (the third horse Banana Ridge took a Hunter Chase next time, and Gray Knight who was last home also scored in similar grade), and when he gets another chance he will surely rectify the situation. Potentially very promising if problem-free. *Mrs N. Ford — Crawley & Horsham (Louise Brewer).* 102 (R).

PARADE RACER ..10-0§.. 14 b.g. Derring Rose — Dusky Damsel (Sahib USA) 31r596p. Lengthy half-brother to Dark Comic, Duskey Comic, Country Damsel and Panto Lady. Dam won at 6f, and completed a hat-trick in 2m1f Newton Abbot Nov Hdles. NH FLAT '95/6 r2 p0. NH '96/9 r17 w1 (2m5f Hdle) p3 (inc 39/ 3rd in Ch). P-t-P/HUNT CH '00 and '02/3 r19 w8 (inc 3 Hunt Chses, 2m4f110y-3m1f and 2 Opens, and inc hat-trick of Confineds '00; also disqualified from Confined — carried wrong penalty) p6 (2 2nds, inc Hunt Ch ; and 4 3rds inc 3 Hunt Chses); last pair 2, and pulled up 2. A very resolute stayer on his day, and worried the odds-on Lordberniebouffant out of a 3m5f Ladies at Corbridge this year, but has had to endure a long-standing breathing disorder, and was additionally laid low by a virus in '04. Ran to 10-9 on that occasion, but refused to race next time, and lost 30 lengths at the start the time after, and has performed dismally since. Will find it difficult to bounce back to form at 14. *T. Butt — Border.* 72 (O), 428 (3m5fL), 546 (3mH), 656 (O), 798 (3m1fH), 812 (O), 1068 (3m2f110yH).

PARADISIO (FR) ..10-4.. 9 b.g. Albert Du Berlais (FR) — Pretty Lady (FR) (Le Gregol FR) 3. Strong. FRENCH FLAT '99 r5 w1 (10f) p2. FRENCH NH '00 r10 w2 (2m Hdle and 2m1f Ch) p6. P-t-P/HUNT CH '03 r4 p2 (3rds, last once); 5th of 6, and pulled up 1. A good jumper and goes a brisk gallop, and tried hard to match strides with Placid Man at Higham, but does not get the trip in Points, and lameness prevented him from turning out again. *W.J. Tolhurst — Essex & Suffolk.* 157 (L).

PARAHANDY (IRE) ..10-5.. 15 b.g. Lancastrian — Dishcloth (Fury Royal) 33121. Workmanlike unfurnished half-brother to Woody's Mop, Lava and M'Lord. Dam, half-sister to Venturi (*qv* '90 Annual), won 3 Points and placed 3 (inc a Hunt Ch), and won 5 2m Hdles and 4 Chses (2m-2m4f) and placed 17 in an exceptionally busy career. IRISH P-t-P '95/6 r8 w2 (inc Winners of 2) p2; pulled up 3. NH '96/01 r22 w3 (3m1f110y-3m2f110y Chses) p8 (6 2nds); pulled up 1, fell/unseated 2. P-t-P/HUNT CH '02/3 r13 w3 (hat-trick of 2 Opens and Club nov rdrs) p5 (3 2nds, inc Hunt Ch; 2 3rds, beaten head and neck once); 4th, 5th twice, 7th, and pulled up 1. A grand old boy and took his winning tally into double figures when faced with a straightforward task at Andoversford, but one-paced and needs plenty of stoking up, and only risked on good or easy surfaces. Expert at course completion and gets every assistance from Harry Dowty. Looked set for retirement at the end of '03 but has taken on another new lease of life and a winning return at 15 cannot be dismissed lightly. Blinkered once in '99. *G.E. & H. Dowty — Cotswold (Giles & Kim Smyly).* 107 (O), 122 (3m1fH), 404 (O), 755 (M), 816 (Cf).

PARSIFAL ..9-11.. 6 b.g. Sadler's Wells (USA) — Moss (USA) (Woodman USA) f665412. Well-made brother to flat winner, Elrehaan, and half-brother to flat winners, Rousing Thunder and Wahsheeq. 170,000f IR160,000y. FLAT '01/2 r7 p0. NH '03 (for J.H. Johnson) r6 p2 (short-head 2nd final start); pulled up 1. Bought Doncaster, Oct for 7000. A hard puller who does not usually settle well enough to get the trips in Points, but kept going better than usual when winning a weak Maiden at Witton Castle. Gave another creditable display when six lengths second five days later, and if he can find a little more stamina there could be a Restricted for him. Has shown temperament in the past, but behaves reasonably now. *M.D. Abrahams — W. of Yore (Pat Tate).* 160 (CMa), 344 (2m4fOMa), 392 (CfMa), 959 (OMa), 1159 (OMa), 1292 (OMa), 1304 (CR).

PARTE PRIMA ..10-5.. 9 b.g. Perpendicular — Pendle's Secret (Le Johnstan) 2u136p3. Close-coupled half-brother to Alchemistress (dam of Grey Lodge (*qv* '01 Annual), to 5 winners, including Pride Of Pendle and Respect A Secret (both flat), and to successful Hurdles winners, River Secret (also successful on flat), Paul's Secret and Fashion Princess. Dam won at 10f. FLAT '99/00 r11 p4 (3rds); inc Sell. NH '99 r2 p0; unseated 1. P-t-P '02/3 r9 w3 (hat-trick '03 inc 2m4f Maiden, Restricted and Intermediate) p2 (2nds); 7th of 8, fell 2, and pulled up 1. Previously a long-standing disappointment, but finally managed to overcome severe jumping frailties, and showed plenty of determination in completing a hat-trick on good or sound surfaces last year. Predictably less successful in a much higher grade in '04, but overcame mistakes at the last two fences to score over 2m5f at Folkestone where Richard Woollacott was the difference between winning and losing. Still inclined to make errors but should remain profitably employed in sub-3m Hunter Chases. Has been tried in headgear. Wears a cross-noseband. *A. & Mrs J. Walter — Taunton V.H. (Alan Walter).* 78 (L), 316 (2m5fH), 345 (2m5fH), 444 (2mH), 734 (2mH), 1166 (2m5f110yH), 1358 (3m1f110yH).

PASSING DANGER (FR) ..10-4.. 10 b.g. Passing Sale (FR) — Destination Danger (FR) (Bois Mineau FR) 12311231. Small neat. FRENCH FLAT w1 (12f) in provinces. IRISH FLAT '99 r1 p0. IRISH NH '98/00 r12 w1 (2m Hdle) p3. NH '00/1 r8 p2; pulled up 1. P-t-P '02/3 r7 w1 (Confined) p3 (2 2nds); 4th, and last pair 2. Enigmatic and wildly unpredictable and blinkered in previous yards, but a model of consistency in his last two campaigns, and more than doubled his previous winning tally in '04. Stays really well and made up almost ten lengths from the last over 3m5f at Corbridge, and found the four-mile trip ideal at Alnwick before responding positively to the application of first-time cheekpieces at Hexham. A good jumper and ridden with plenty of flair by Rose Davidson, and will again be hard to beat in seven-minute plus races in '05. Reported lame in '01 and avoids sound surfaces now. *D. Davidson — Jedforest (Peter Elliot).* 135 (Cfnr), 284 (L), 428 (3m5fL), 655 (L), 857 (4mMO), 1078 (L), 1308 (L), 1478 (L).

PAST FORTE ..7-9.. 9 b.m. Past Glories — My Music (Sole Mio USA) p4fp. Well-made owner-bred half-sister to Jackson Blue, Great Gusto, Marsh's Law, Reel Rascal, Steel My Song and My Gracie. Only got round once, when last and over a fence behind at Guilsborough (despite it being her second outing, she still looked backward). Shows a hint of ability, but seems to have a breathing problem, and acquired a tongue-tie on her latest appearance. *Miss D.B. Stanhope & G.T. Alder — Woodland Pytchley (Diana Stanhope).* 685 (OMa), 788 (CfMa), 1119 (CMam), 1505 (OMa).

PATS CROSS (IRE) ..—.. 16 b.g. Abednego — No Hunting (No Time) p. Workmanlike half-brother to Eagles Run, to Chasing winner, Complete Optimist, and to Irish winners, Roebuck Lass (NH flat and Chasing) and Pothill (Pointing). IRISH NH FLAT '94/5 r6 p2. IRISH P-t-P '94 and '96 r7 w1 (7yo&up Maiden) p2; fell/unseated 3. IRISH NH '95/6 r6 p1 (2nd); one run at Perth. NH '97/00 r13 w3 (2m5f-3m2f Chses) p5; pulled up 3, and unseated 1. P-t-P/HUNT CH '97/9 and '01 (for Mr J. Byrne) r15 w3 (inc 3m1f Hunt Ch) p3 (2 2nds; and 3rd in Hunt Ch); pulled up 1, fell/unseated 3, and ran out 2. NH '01 (for A. Crook) r3 p0; pulled up 2. An habitual front-runner, and rated 10-9 in his prime, but has only been able to appear four times since falling in the lead at Bechers in the '01 Foxhunters, and looked to suffer an immediate setback at Market Rasen. Presumably spends his time teaching would-be jockeys at the Northern Racing College, and it would be a pity if he is no longer able to do so. *S.J. Goodings — York & Ainsty S.* 1347 (2m6f110yH).

PATUM PEPERIUM ..—.. 6 ch.g. Sir Harry Lewis (USA) — Relishing (Relkino) pp. Lengthy homebred brother to Gentlemans Relish (*qv*). Showed nothing in Mollington Maidens, and jumped sketchily on his debut. As Patum Peperium and Gentlemans Relish are one and the same thing the Shand Kydds were running out of original names, but the death of the mare after the birth of the former at least precludes our seeing 'Idon'tlikemustard'. *Mr & Mrs W. & Mr & Mrs C.C. Shand Kydd — Bicester with Whaddon (Fiona Kehoe).* 296 (OMa), 588 (CfMa).

PAULS LEGACY ..7-12.. 9 ch.g. Nicholas Bill — Extremity (Quayside) fp1p. Small sturdy. Dam placed twice in Irish Points, won Maiden taking nearly eight minutes in heavy at Lemalla. NH '03 (for J.D. Frost) r1 p0 (last). Has a one in front of his name rather than a winner by dint of being the only runner to complete the course in a five-starter Geldings Maiden at Black Forest Lodge (the probable winner fell fatally three out). Has done absolutely nothing to suggest that he was a worthy recipient of the largesse. *J.D. Frost — Modbury H. (Nicky Frost).* 82 (OMa), 328 (OMa), 417 (CfMah), 572 (R).

PAVILLION PRIDE ..—.. 6 b.m. Tower Of Magic (AUS) — Almost America (Hillandale) Rpu. Owner-bred. Dam, half-sister to Sovereigns Match (*qv* '03 Annual). Soon struggling when failing to complete thrice, but the owner-rider is too shaky to be an asset on a young novice. *M.J. Hayes — Weston & Banwell H. (Thomasia Rowe).* 881 (Inr), 1075 (OMa), 1364 (M).

PEACEFUL BOW (IRE) .9-3.. 8 b/br.g. Beau Sher — Peaceful Kyle (IRE) (Tanfirion) 31. IRISH P-t-P '02/3 r9 p0; pulled up 7. Woeful in Ireland and did not look any better when well over a fence last on his Welsh debut, but unearthed a dreadful Geldings Maiden at Lystep and with the help of a tongue-tie was able to score. The form is worth absolutely nothing, and Restricteds will be a totally different matter. *K.R. Pearce — Carms.* 1324 (CfMa), 1525 (OMah).

PEARL DANTE (IRE) ..—.. 15 ch.g. Phardante (FR) — Bassett Girl (Brigadier Gerard) pp. Lengthy attractive. IRISH NH FLAT '95 and '97 r2 p0. IRISH P-t-P '96/7 r12 w2 (inc Winners of 2) p1 (2nd); pulled up 2, and unseated 1. NH '99/00 r4 p0 (pulled up 3). P-t-P/HUNT CH '98/9 and '03 r8 p0 (6th twice, fell/unseated 3, pulled up 2 and refused 1). Won two races on sound surfaces in Ireland to '97, but subsequently wrecked by inept riding after changing hands for 10,000gns, and has only managed two very brief campaigns for present connections in which he has failed to get round (under a novice in '04). Wears a cross-noseband. *T.J. Hampton — Wilton (Anne Hampton).* 236 (Cnr), 261 (Cf).

PEAR TREE PERCY .—§.. 12 ch.g. Broadsword (USA) — Howanever (Buckskin FR) p. Workmanlike brother to Nervous Times, and half-brother to Stick Or Bust. Dam, 'little more than a pony', was 5th and fell in Points; previously won 2-finisher mares Maiden and 2nd 2 (inc NH flat) in Ireland. P-t-P '99/00 and '02/3 r19 w3 (Maiden, Restricted and Intermediate) p2 (3rds, of 4 once); 5th, last, fell/unseated 5, and pulled up 7. Rated 10-2 after winning two of his last three races in '02, but his transformation ended there, and has pulled up in four of his five subsequent attempts. Did not look to be enjoying himself at Garnons in the latest, and presumably connections have taken the hint. *M.J. Roberts — N. Ledbury (Mandy Tatlow).* 612 (Cf).

PEATS RIDGE (IRE) ..8-9.. 7 b.g. Salluceva — Bibi's Girl (Boreen FR) p43. Strong lengthy. Dam, half-sister to Drummond Warrior (*qv* '01 Annual). IRISH P-t-P '03 r3 p1 (2nd); last and pulled up. Bought Doncaster, May for 10,000. His head second in Ireland entitled him to start favourite for his English debut, but he never looked like obliging, and has since been well beaten when making the frame twice. Evidently a plodder, but has been carrying plenty of condition, and might be able to go closer if produced fully fit. *Mr & Mrs S.J. Stearn — Suffolk (Penny Stearn).* 901 (OMa), 1155 (OMa), 1317 (CfMa).

PEBBLE DASHER ..—.. 10 b.m. Sula Bula — Highway Light (Lighter) fpp. Small sister to Highway Oak (*qv*). Fell at halfway on her belated debut, and then appeared to pull up lame twice (having jumped just one fence at Umberleigh). *A.J.S. Knox & T. Chanin — Silverton (Robert Chanin).* 827 (CfMa), 1370 (OMa), 1565 (OMa).

PEGGYS GOLD ..—.. 9 br.m. Blaze O'Gold (USA) — Lady Bronwen (Scorpio FR) Rfp. Plain compact. Dam, half-sister to Billy-Gwyn (*qv* '00 Annual). Ran out at the ninth, fell at the seventh, and tailed off and pulled up at the 15th after sticky jumping — exactly what one would expect from something with the misfortune to be ridden by Steven Graham. *C. Staley — Golden V.* 1115 (OMa), 1233 (OMa), 1395 (OMa).

PEKAN POLLY ..8-6.. 10 ch.m. Henbit (USA) — Pollys Toi (Pollerton) pp5pp. Stocky sister to Bit Of A Chick, and half-sister to Alstoe, Roppongi Crossing and Bishop Castle. Dam won 2 Irish Points and placed 3; and was subsequently 2nd in an English Ladies. P-t-P '02/3 r4 p0 (pulled up 4). Has shown a trace of ability, and completed for the only time to date when 24 lengths fifth at Eaton Hall, but normally runs out of steam after a maximum of 2m4f, and looks a most unlikely winner. *Mrs G.A. Spencer — Albrighton.* 93 (O), 227 (CfMa), 714 (CMam), 848 (OMa), 1340 (OMa).

PELE MELE (FR) ..—.. 10 b.g. Tel Quel (FR) — Star System (FR) (Northern Treat USA) pppu. Small neat brother to French flat winner, Kerrygold (FR), and half-brother to 4 French flat winners, and successful French Chaser, Bon Tresor (FR). FRENCH FLAT '98/00 r13 w2 (8-11f) p3. NH '02 (for Miss V. Williams) r5 p0; unseated 1. A dual winner in the mud on Paris tracks, and collected a £15,070 prize at Saint Cloud but useless when changing countries and codes and was beaten 24 lengths plus over Hurdles (broke a blood vessel when tongue-tied). Looked similarly distressed in Points, and after pulling up when tailed off in three Ladies Opens he unseated at the 14th when leading but probably not destined to stay there in a Novice Riders event. *Miss S. Firmin — Bicester with Whaddon.* 126 (L), 373 (L), 757 (L), 1278 (Cnr).

PENDILS CHARM ..9-1§.. 14 b.m. Scorpio (FR) — Pendella (Pendragon) pu. Strong-topped compact sister to Reuter and Pendil's Delight, and to Chasing winner, Stephen's Brae, and half-sister to Pendleton, Pendle Princess (dam of 6 Pointers including Silver Castle, *qv*), Pendil's Niece (dam of Handsome Henry, *qv* '04 Annual), Pendil's Pride, Pendil's Joy and Pendil's Nephew. Dam is sister to '70s jumping superstar, Pendil. P-t-P '02/3 r8 p2 (3rds of 4); 4th, 5th, and pulled up 4. A very late starter and has plodded into the frame on three occasions, but has required plenty of driving, and looked thoroughly reluctant before unseating after 1m2f on her most recent appearance in February. From a long line of successful Pointers, but will surely not be attempting a fourth season at 14. *A.C. Lee-Smith — Dunston H.* 39 (OMa), 153 (OMa).

PENDLE HILL .10-4.. 10 gr.g. Roscoe Blake — Pendle Princess (Broxted) 31522. Strong compact brother to Silver Castle (*qv*), and half-brother to Pendil's Pleasure, Regal Shadow, Regal Bay and Zodiac Prince. Dam, half-sister to Pendil's Joy, won a Maiden (also last, pulled up 2, and fell/unseated 3 — was tubed latterly). 13,000 4yo. NH FLAT '00 r4 p1 (3rd). NH '00/3 (for P. Beaumont) r16 w1 (2m4f Hdle) p3 (2nds inc. 2 Chses). Quite an aggravating character as he probably has considerably more ability than he is normally prepared to show, but did win a Hurdle at 25-1 in the heavy, and also successful at 10-1 in an Open at Ampton, where he beat Fair Exchange fair and square. Beaten favourite twice since, and made mistakes in the Hunter Chase, and found little in an Open at Aldington in which he looked to have the measure of Real Value until headed close home (4-7). Was runner-up to prolific scorers Man Murphy and The Bajan Bandit in Chases, and beaten four lengths maximum, but nothing like as good as that since. *Mrs K. Digweed — E. Sussex & Romney Marsh (Sara Hickman).* 1 (C), 43 (O), 177 (3mH), 535 (CfO), 898 (O).

PENDRAGON ..9-13.. 13 b.g. Bold Fox — Celtic Royale (Celtic Cone) 2pp4p. Tall rangy brother to Foxy Royale (*qv*). P-t-P/HUNT CH '98 and '00/2 r17 w2 (Maiden and Restricted) p4 (2nds, inc Hunt Ch); 5th twice, last pair 4, fell 3, and pulled up 2. Does best fresh and only stands light campaigns, but would have registered a third success had he kept straight on the run-in when collared close home on his reappearance at Larkhill. Seemed to take the defeat personally and ran lifelessly in all four subsequent attempts, and acquired blinkers at Uttoxeter. Lacks fluency and needs to return to Points if he is to atone at 13. Visored once in '00. *Mr & Mrs N. Faulks — Dulverton F. (Sarah Faulks).* 141 (I), 321 (I), 629 (3m1f110yH), 1294 (3mH), 1376 (4m2fH).

PENLET TOO ..8-7.. 10 b.g. Kinglet — Pensun (Jimsun) 44p6p3p. Workmanlike owner-bred brother to Penlet, and half-brother to Penly, Tinsun, Rolpen, Penaword and Herpen. Dam is half-sister to 4 Pointers, including Rugy. P-t-P '02 r6 p1 (3rd of 4); last, pulled up 3, and unseated 1. Has made the frame in four Maidens, but normally pulls too hard to get home, and beaten between five and 55 lengths when doing so. Raced even more keenly when equipped with blinkers, and was returned at 100-1 when they were dispensed with on his sub-3m Hunter Chase debut. An improved jumper, but still a long shot to emulate big brother. Wears a cross-noseband. *R.G. Weaving — Warwicks (John Pritchard).* 129 (OMa), 296 (OMa), 463 (OMa), 589 (CfMa), 746 (OMa), 1275 (OMa), 1359 (2m4f110yH).

PENNYAGO (IRE) .—.. 8 b.g. Good Thyne (USA) — Boro Penny (Normandy) p. Half-brother to jumping winners, Boro Sovereign (IRE) (also won NH flat) and Sir Leonard (IRE), and to Chasing winner, Monks Jay (IRE). IR£50,000 4yo. NH FLAT '03 (for Mrs H. Dalton) r1 p0. Bought Doncaster, May for 4500. Attractively bred, but depreciated by about £45,000 in two years which was highly suspect, and pulled up after only a mile in a Maiden. Presumably has a big problem. *D.J. Renney — Heythrop (Nick Seal).* 386 (OMa).

PENNYAHEI ..10-9.. 14 b.m. Malaspina — Pennyazena (Pamroy) 482f1. Small half-sister to NH flat and jumping winner, Stewarts Pride. Dam won Hunt Chase and 11 Points (inc 10 Ladies) and p5 for Zena Brookshaw to '89 (signed off with 5-timer; 'it would be hard to find a braver mare'). Grandam, Pennyalina, won 4 Points consecutively, but retired after smashing a fetlock. NH '97/01 r38 w1 (3m2f Ch) p8 (6 2nds); pulled up 5, fell/unseated 3, refused 1. P-t-P/HUNT CH '03 r8 w3 (hat-trick of Ladies, 2 finished twice) p3 (2 2nds, inc beaten neck in Hunt Ch); 5th of 6, and pulled up 1. Something of an enigma, and her career has endured many peaks and troughs, but still capable of smart form despite her advancing years, and came with a wet sail to collar previous dual course winner, Mullensgrove at Ludlow. Did not seem to be fit enough or sparking earlier in the year, and it may be that she does not come to herself until late April as her '03 hat-trick was gained in April/May. A thorough stayer, and always gets excellent assistance from Sam Beddoes, and could yet find another race before she heads to the paddocks. *Miss H. Brookshaw — N. Salop.* 94 (L), 529 (L), 664 (L), 931 (L), 1117 (3m1f110yH).

PENNY BLUE ..8-11.. 6 br.m. Sovereign Water (FR) — Suzy Blue (Relkino) 3u1. Homebred. Fifteen lengths third when green and given an easy time on her debut, and then unseated at the first, but was able to justify favouritism in a weak youngsters Maiden at Upper Sapey despite the saddle having slipped and the rider losing an iron three out (was beaten a head, but Geoff Barfoot-Saunt gave a bravura riding performance to regain the initiative). The form amounts to nothing, but is in a leading yard, so it would be no surprise if she could improve by a good few pounds at six. *Mr & Mrs F. Leighton — Ledbury (Nicky Sheppard).* 667 (OMa), 1020 (OMa), 1139 (OMa).

PENNY NATIVE (IRE) ..10-4.. 13 ch.g. Be My Native (USA) — Penny Maes (Welsh Saint) 2203*0*. Half-brother to Hurdling winners, Kingstanding (in Ireland) and Fenian Court (IRE), and to Irish NH flat and Hurdling winner, Penny Holder. IRISH FLAT '98 r3 p1 (3rd). IRISH NH '96/9 and '01/2 (for A.L.T. Moore) r28 w3 (2m Hdle and 2m Ch) p10 (inc 9 2nds); pulled up 1. NH '04 (for Miss S.E. Forster) r1 p0 (13th in 2m Ch: *in tch til wknd 6*). Collected what is now a notable scalp when beating Amberleigh House at Leopardstown in '97, but has been unable to score since October '01, although commendable placed efforts have been plentiful (11 seconds include a head defeat, and in fields of 28 and 30). Made bold bids on three occasions in '04 when beaten a maximum of five lengths, but was never able to keep enough back for the final flourish, although he looked very game. It would be good to see him return at 13 to pinch a prize, but at his age it might be rather optimistic. *W.F. Kerr — Dumfries (Julia Furness).* 330 (3mH), 439 (2m5f110yH), 798 (3m1fH), 1220 (C).

PENNY POOR (IRE) .9-2.. 6 b.g. Idris (IRE) — Rachel Pringle (IRE) (Doulab USA) ps. Half-brother to flat winner, Cobourg Lodge, Castanetta, Flamingo Bay (all 3 in Ireland), and to Denise Margaret. IRISH FLAT '01/2 r9 p0. IRISH NH '03 (for J.T. Gorman) r1 p0. Showed nothing on the flat (thrice blinkered) or in a Hurdle (a very remote 18th of 19) in Ireland, and pulled up on his Welsh debut, but was nevertheless evens favourite for a youngsters Maiden at Laleston, but was already weakening when he slipped and fell heavily before two out. Coming a week after the Charlestown Lass and Miaheyyun disasters, if it was stable money that made him such a short price they really will be pounds poor. *C. Campbell — Banwen Miners (John Moore).* 203 (CfMa), 1192 (OMa).

PEPPERNICK .10-0.. 9 br.g. Alflora (IRE) — Nicolini (Nicholas Bill) 1. Half-brother to Nick Ross and Sunnycliff. Dam, bred by Bobby Brewis, won 3 flat (10-12f) for him. P-t-P '02 r2 w1 (2m4f Maiden) p1 (3rd of 4). Adjudged to have recorded his second success at Alnwick when dead-heating with Rainha, but looked to have been beaten a neck, and did not get another chance to perform. Clearly well above average but missed '03, and must be nigh on impossible to train. *R. Brewis — Percy (Rhona Brewis).* 855 (R).

PERCHANCER (IRE) ..10-6.. 9 ch.g. Perugino (USA) — Irish Hope (Nishapour FR) p31. Compact half-brother to Irish Double (IRE), and to a flat winner in Italy. Dam won at 8-12f in Italy. 10,500y, 22,000 2yo. FLAT '98/03 r58 w7 (7-11f) p14. NH '01/3 (for P.C. Haslam) r8 w1 (2m5f Hdle) p3 (inc 2nd in Ch); fell/unseated 3. A real old friend to Annabelle Armitage (she could talk about him for days), and there can be few girls who have won a flat race (in January '00) and a Hunter Chase on the same horse. Also second over Hurdles for her, and in their seven pairings together they have made the first three on five occasions including a Hurdle. Has tried a lot including the all-weather (three victories) and a Seller, has fallen two out when clear in a Hurdle once, and amazingly has scored for five different apprentices. Wore headgear thrice in '99. Unreliable and frequently starts slowly, and is a hard puller, but can finish strongly at best, and took advantage of Rupert Abraham's leap from the saddle when 18 lengths clear (they time it with the stopwatch now) at Market Rasen. Has raced 69 times and maybe suffering from some wear and tear, but what a fabulous character. *Mrs E.J. Crookenden — Rydale P-t-P Racing Club (Miss A. Armitage) — Sinnington (Annabelle Armitage).* 957 (Cf), 1160 (L), 1347 (2m6f110yH).

PERCHING (IRE) ..9-12.. 11 b.g. Strong Gale — Fiona's Blue (Crash Course) p25. Tall workmanlike half-brother to Hurdles winners, Nupdown Boy (IRE) and Native Emperor (won £132,849 to date, and won 4m NH Chase at Festival in '04), and to NH flat winner, Spirit of New York (won his only race to date, '04). NH '99/00 and '02/3 (for J.T. Gifford, when successful, and P. Butler) r13 w1 (3m Ch) p2 (2nds); fell/unseated 2, pulled up 2. A bad jumper under Rules but did manage to win a Lingfield Chase when putting in his best round, although the very probable winner fell two out. Wore cheekpieces on his final two appearances. Two fences behind before pulling up on his Pointing debut, but much more positive at Charing next time, and only surrendered to the late flourish of Galeaway by a head after taking the lead at the final fence. Beaten 18 lengths in a similar Conditions race on a return visit, and not seen since early March. Never stands much racing, and physical problems have doubtless prevented him from achieving more. *late J.G. Plackett — Crawley & Horsham (Rachel Deakin).* 89 (O), 182 (CCon), 422 (CCon).

PERFECT BEAR .8-5.. 11 b.g. Wing Park — Sarah Bear (Mansingh USA) p. Tall rangy half-brother to flat winner, North Bear, and to a winner in Belgium. Dam won 4 flat in Belgium. FLAT '96/7 r4 p0 (Sell final). NH '99/00 r7 p0; inc Sells. P-t-P '03 r3 p0 (4th of 5, and pulled up 2). Beaten 20 lengths plus under Rules, and 41 lengths in his solitary Pointing completion, but rarely gets a chance to prove himself, and only went two miles in '04. *The Forestburn Partnership (D. Milburn) — Morpeth (Vicki Knox).* 74 (OMa).

PERFECT FINISHER ..9-5.. 14 b.g. Captain Maverick (USA) — Miss Eutopia (Dunphy) pu6u6puuu4. Strong. NH '94 r1 p0 (tailed off). P-t-P '98/01 (for Mr M.A. Hawkins & Miss C. Smy) r22 w2 (Maiden and Club Restricted) p3 (2 3rds, last once; and head 2nd); fell/unseated 2, and pulled up 11. Gifted to previous connection after breaking down in '94, and won them two minor races, but never looked a particularly easy ride, and was prone to errors. Resurfaced after a three-year absence to school the newcomer Rheanna Lobley, but broke a blood vessel on his reappearance, and she then proceeded to fall off in five of their six subsequent pairings. Still retains plenty of enthusiasm but it will be a miracle if the same can be said for the turf-munching owner. *Miss R.J. Lobley — Grafton (Jackie Hunt).* 18 (L), 32 (Cnr), 110 (Cnr), 189 (L), 289 (CfL), 443 (2m4f110yH), 582 (M), 785 (L), 867 (I), 1105 (O).

PERFECT PICTURE .—.. 6 b.g. Octagonal (NZ) — Greenvera (USA) (Riverman USA) u. Lengthy half-brother to Royal Rebel (won 7 flat and £447,753 to date) won Ascot Gold Cup '01/2 and to Yoshua (won 3 of 4 flat to date '03/4). FLAT '02/3 (for M. Johnston) r7 p1 (2nd). Half-brother to two useful performers for Mark Johnston, and was a very expensive yearling, but the best he could manage for that yard on the flat was a seven lengths second over 9f on firm, and was well tailed off in four of six other attempts including when tongue-tied twice. Must have problems, and is a very unlikely candidate for Pointing (unseated the owner at the first in his only attempt to date). *O.R. Dukes — York & Ainsty S.* 959 (OMa).

PERKYS PRIDE (IRE) ..10-7.. 9 b.g. Executive Perk — Josie Mac (Pitpan) 42. Lengthy half-brother to four losing jumpers. IRISH NH FLAT '00/1 r5 w1 p4. IRISH FLAT '02 r1 p0. IRISH NH '01/2 (for M. Cunningham) r7 w2 (2m2f-2m5f Hdles) p2 (3rds). NH '02/3 (for M.C. Pipe) r7 p0; pulled up 2. Made all when winning three races on easy surfaces in Ireland (27 ran in one of the Hurdles), and six placings included a second of 26. Most disappointing after joining Martin Pipe, and weakened quickly and pulled up when visored on his final attempt. Seventeen lengths fourth in his first Open, but then showed a return to something like his best when two lengths second to Kingston Venture at Black Forest Lodge where he made virtually all until outjumped at the last, but clearly had a setback on the unsuitably firmish ground and was not seen again. Sadly it looks as if he may have returned to the doldrums. *D. Pipe — Eggesford.* 64 (O), 414 (MO).

PERKY'S WISH (IRE) ..7-10.. 7 b.g. Executive Perk — Mikes Wish (IRE) (Modern Dancer) pppfp5. Small sturdy. P-t-P '03 (for Mr C. Dawson) r4 p0 (pulled up 3, and unseated 1). Usually on the premises to halfway, but always decelerates rapidly and tails right off, and beaten 69 lengths when finally managing to stagger to completion. Must have a chronic defect. Wears a cross-noseband. *S.J. Robinson — Zetland.* 160 (CMa), 343 (2m4fOMa), 768 (2m4fOMa), 920 (2m4fOMa), 1291 (OMa), 1300 (OMa).

PERNICKETY KING ..7-2.. 6 b.g. Rakaposhi King — Fussy Lady (Idiot's Delight) ppppp4. Small angular. Dam won 2 Hurdles, 2m-2m6f, including a match, and is half-sister to Royal Sunshine (*qv* '92 Annual). NH FLAT '03 (for P.J. Hobbs) r2 p0. Trudged wearily into 34 lengths fourth of five over 2m4f on final start, but otherwise conforms to the predictable Millington script — looks like a scarecrow, makes plentiful errors, and keeps pulling up. *P.J. Millington — Fernie.* 39 (OMa), 1155 (OMa), 1246 (OMa), 1339 (OMa), 1402 (2m4fOMa), 1504 (2m4fOMa).

PERRYMAN (IRE) ..9-10.. 14 ch.g. Good Thyne (USA) — Poetic Lady (Rymer) 3. Well-made attractive. Dam is half-sister to High Park Lad (*qv*). IRISH P-t-P '96 r4 w1 (4&5yo Maiden) p1 (3rd). NH FLAT '97 r1 p0. NH '97/00 r14 w4 (3m110y-3m2f110y Chses; inc hat-trick '99) p3 (2nds); pulled up 2, fell/unseated 2, refused 1. P-t-P '02/3 r10 w3 (Open, Mixed Open and Club) p3 (2 2nds, of 3 once; and 3rd of 4); 4th twice, last, and unseated 1. Ended his career under Rules with a hat-trick in '99, and revived to splendid effect in '02 after being gifted to present connections, but lives life at a much more genteel pace these days, and beaten 25 lengths on his only appearance in '04. Has been tried in headgear, and best when allowed to dominate, and it would be a surprise if he turned out at 14. *Countess S. Goess-Saurau — V.W.H.* 1066 (CCon).

PERRY OF TROY ..— §.. 6 b.m. Paris Of Troy — Perryline (Capricorn Line) pp. Small short-backed well-made. Dam, half-sister to Perryland (*qv* '03 Annual), won 2m4f Maiden and Restricted and 3rd thrice for Reg Fellows (hardly got the full trip). Already looks most unwilling, and was tailed off by the fourth after sticky and reluctant jumping on her latest attempt. One to avoid. *Miss J. Fellows — Clifton-on-Teme.* 403 (Cf), 983 (2m5fOMa).

PERSIAN BANDIT (IRE) ..— §.. 7 b.g. Idris (IRE) — Ce Soir (Northern Baby CAN) pp. Close-coupled half-brtoher to flat winners, Lover's Moon, Greek Night Out, and to another winner. Dam won 11f race in Ireland. IR5000f & y (twice as yearling). IRISH FLAT '00 r7 p3. FLAT '00/3 r7 p1 (3rd in Sell).

SPANISH FLAT '01/2 r13 w2 (6f) p4. NH '02 (for J.R. Jenkins) r2 p0; pulled up 1. A dual sprinting winner on the all-weather at Mijas and should have stayed in the sun, because he is a complete waste of time for jumping purposes. Has worn headgear on six occasions, and often looks reluctant and carries his head in the air. Tailed off and pulled up after two miles in both Points, and gave a very erratic display of jumping on his debut. *Mrs T. Holditch — Fitzwilliam.* 158 (CCon), 376 (Cf).

PERSIAN DAWN ..7-0.. 12 br.m. Anshan — Visible Form (Formidable USA) p84pppp. Close-coupled attractive half-sister to Russian Vision, to 4 flat winners (one in Germany), including Azeb and Living Image, to successful Hurdler, Spofforth, and to Irish flat and Hurdles winner, Gift Token. Dam won 2 flat, 6-10f. FLAT r11 p1 (8/ 3rd). NH '96/9 r13 p2; mostly Sells. P-t-P '00 and '03 r7 w1 (Maiden) p1 (2nd); last, pulled up 3, and fell 1. Broke down one race after winning a youngsters Maiden at Stafford Cross in '00, and spent '01 and '02 on the sidelines, and clearly retains very little in the way of ability now. Made mistakes and failed to beat a rival in '04 and still looked backward when making an appearance at the penultimate meeting of the season. Blinkered once in '97. *R. John — Eggesford.* 197 (R), 323 (R), 821 (M), 1268 (R), 1384 (Cf), 1543 (R), 1557 (Cf).

PERSIAN HERO (IRE) .10-2.. 9 ch.g. Persian Mews — Garrenroe (Le Moss) 6223r1. Compact strong-topped half-brother to Irish Pointing winner, Knocktoran Lady. Dam is half-sister to Eliogarty and Boycott (*qv* '97 Annual). P-t-P '02/3 r9 w2 (Maiden and Restricted) p1 (3rd); pulled up 3, fell 2. Has ended all three campaigns with a win, but is not one to trust implicitly, and without James Owen to drive him along and intimidate the opposition would not have scored at Godstone. Slowly away on that occasion, and had declined to jump off at all on his previous start, and never makes life easy for himself. Has the ability to end '05 with a bang, but does not look reliable enough to score in Open class. *J.M. Turner — Suffolk.* 99 (I), 521 (Cf), 742 (I), 1151 (Cf), 1313 (Cf), 1406 (I).

PERSONA PRIDE ..9-7§.. 11 gr.g. St Enodoc — Le Jour Fortune (Twilight Alley) pp52321p43. Lengthy brother to Petite Fortune. Dam, 3rd in Hdle, won 9 Points (inc 4 Ladies) and placed 6 (inc 2 3rds in Hunt Chses) for Percy Priday. NH '03 r1 p0 (pulled up). P-t-P/HUNT CH '00/3 r22 w3 (up to Confined) p7 (4 3rds, of 4 twice; inc 2nd of 3 once); unseated 1, pulled up 6. Needs to dictate but can only do so in minor events, and has only been fully effective in May/June when partnered by Julian Pritchard. Capable of jumping well but just as likely to make mistakes, and is totally unreliable in all respects and sure to remain so. Acts in softish and on firm. *P. Priday — Radnor & W. Herefords (Billie Brown).* 176 (3mH), 514 (O), 660 (Cf), 842 (O), 1024 (O), 1110 (O), 1226 (M), 1358 (3m1f110yH), 1392 (C), 1539 (I).

PETER PARKGATE ..—.. 6 gr.g. Kuwait Beach (USA) — Nellie's Joy VII (unknown) uppup. Lightly-made half-brother to Smetherds Tom. Utterly dreadful in both running and jumping, and comes very near the top of the 'why bother?' category. *Mrs R.O. Hutchings — S. Dorset (Elsie Mitchell).* 264 (CfMa), 475 (OMa), 575 (OMa), 1134 (OMa), 1370 (OMa).

PETE THE PAINTER (IRE) ..9-12.. 8 b.g. Detroit Sam (FR) — Rambling Moss (Le Moss) 2211R2. Sturdy brother to Rambling Mick (IRE). P-t-P '02/3 r5 w1 (Maiden) p1 (2nd); unseated 1, and pulled up 2. NH '04 r1 p1 (9/ 2nd to Gallik Dawn in 2m6f110y Ch: *jmpd rt, ld app 4, mist 10, hdd aft 3 out, wknd app last*). Doing well in minor Points, but has only beaten dross on good or sound surfaces, and his tendency to race lazily and hang prompted connection to apply blinkers in his last three Points. Only went a mile before he ran out through the wing on a right-handed track on his final outing, but already producing better results with professional guidance, and it makes sense to exploit his ability to handle fast ground under Rules, at least for the time being. *J.W. Tudor — Llangeinor.* 357 (R), 674 (R), 953 (R), 1187 (M), 1390 (O).

PETRIE ..8-7.. 8 ch.g. Fraam — Canadian Capers (Ballacashtal CAN) p. Compact. Dam won 2 flat (5-7f). FLAT '99/02 r28 p6. NH '01 r2 p0 (pulled up 2). P-t-P '03 r5 p0 (6th, last, pulled up 2, and fell 1). Gained his best results on the flat at up to seven furlongs, but has proved predictably useless as a Pointer, and makes mistakes and stops to nil after a maximum of two miles. It appears connections have already given up the unequal struggle. Visored once in '01. Wears a cross-noseband. *Mrs S. Isaac — Teme V. (Steve Isaac).* 1339 (OMa).

PETROUGE .9-11§.. 9 b.g. Petoski — Red Spider (Red God) ppp221u3. Good-topped half-brother to Blushing Spy, Mr Dick, Gordon and Incy Wincy Spider, to the winners, Spider Woman (Hurdles, and dam of De Chelly *qv*), Volcanoes Spark (flat), Golden Fox and Vanart (both Hurdling), Abu Kadra (flat and jumping, and Little Red Spider (NH flat). Dam, half-sister to Patchouli's Pet (*qv* '94 Annual), won at 8f in Ireland. NH FLAT '01 r3 p0. NH '02 r4 p1 (3rd). P-t-P '03 r5 w2 (Club Maiden and Club Restricted) p1 (2nd); 4th, and carried out 1. Comes from a family of talented oddballs, and is very easily distracted, and despite the presence of leading riders is apt to down tools without warning. Proved he can do it when landing a weak Confined at Brampton Bryan, but also beaten when entrusted with favouritism twice in '04, and the safest policy is to exclude him from all betting activity. Has scored in soft and on firmish. Normally wears cheekpieces but has been tried in a visor. *J.G. Beasley — Albrighton (Caroline Robinson).* 92 (I), 255 (CCon), 443 (2m4f110yH), 663 (I), 835 (Cf), 1113 (Cf), 1392 (C), 1530 (I).

PHANTHOM WALKER ..—.. 8 b.g. Opera Ghost — Midnight Walker (Exodal USA) pppp. Small. Tailed off and pulled up in four Maidens, and was blinkered in the latest. Devoid of talent, and the mis-spelling of his name would probably irritate Andrew Lloyd-Webber. *R.L. Black & S.R. Alford — Tiverton (Richard Black).* 275 (CfMa), 328 (OMa), 1186 (OMa), 1272 (OMa).

PHAR AFIELD (IRE) ..9-0.. 11 b.g. Phardante (FR) — Kemita (IRE) (Kemal FR) pp1pp3. Strong lengthy. Dam is half-sister to Muddle Head (*qv* '98 Annual). NH FLAT '99 r1 p0. NH '00 r3 p0; pulled up 2. P-t-P '02/3 (for Mr M. Weir) r3 w1 (Maiden) p2 (2nds). Won an elders Maiden in the slowest time of the day at Great Trethew last year, but previously useless under Rules, and has yet to upgrade successfully. Shared favouritism with a stablemate in his Members, and scored under a substitute rider, but had the form reversed when they renewed rivalry in May. *Mrs B.M. Ansell — W. Street Tickham.* 19 (CMod), 127 (R), 534 (M), 779 (R), 1084 (R), 1280 (M).

PHARAILDE .9-13.. 7 ch.m. Phardante (FR) — Canal Street (Oats) 511pfp. Sturdy sister to Dante's Porridge (IRE) (*qv* '04 Annual). Dam, half-sister to Club Caribbean (*qv* '00), was 3rd in NH flat and placed in 2 Hdles. NH FLAT '02/3 r2 p0. NH '03 (for M.J. Roberts) r2 p1 (last of 3). Finished 37 lengths last of three in a Hurdle, but showed first signs of ability when dropped to a Maiden, and then won a youngsters event with plenty to spare at Ystradowen. Surprisingly proved good enough to follow up in an Open at Llanvapley a week later, but it was only a poor five-runner affair, and has since failed to finish in three more competitive events. Missing out on a Restricted was not very wise, and she will have to jump better and have her races picked carefully if she is to achieve much in future. Not without hope if these criteria are met. *L. Alder — Curre & Llangibby (Sarah Stentiford).* 700 (CfMa), 735 (CfMa), 842 (O), 1093 (4mMO), 1190 (O), 1390 (O).

PHAR AND AWAY ..—.. 11 br.m. Phardante (FR) — Lady Rosanna (Kind Of Hush) pRfp. Small. Dam won 4 flat (13-16f) and 2 2m-2m1f Hurdles. NH FLAT '98 r3 p0. NH '99 (for Countess Goess-Saurau) r3 p0; pulled up 1, unseated 1. Goes bombing along in the lead for about 1m4f, but stops in a matter of strides, and was beaten 72 lengths in a Hurdle on the only occasion she has completed the course from seven attempts over jumps. Prone to make alarming blunders, and it was lunacy to allow Holly Bevan to partner her twice. *A.R. & Mrs C. Bevan — Cotswold V.F. (Chris Bevan).* 370 (OMa), 729 (OMa), 756 (Cf), 816 (Cf).

PHAR FROM CHANCE ..10-2.. 10 ch.g. Phardante (FR) — Chancer's Last (Foggy Bell) p14143. Big strong half-brother to Tricky Trevor (IRE) (*qv*). P-t-P '00/1 r4 w3 (2m4f Maiden, Restricted and Intermediate) p1 (head 2nd). NH '01/2 (for P.F. Nicholls) r10 w1 (3m2f110y Ch) p2 (3rds); fell/unseated 3, pulled up 1. Only beaten once in his first two seasons Pointing and deserved a chance to prove himself under Rules, but let down by a combination of poor jumping and a tendency to break blood vessels, and only managed to land a weak race at Newton Abbot off a low rating, and was a beaten favourite four times. Put a shocking effort on his reappearance behind him when springing a 14-1 surprise at Ston Easton, but hung left in the closing stages and hung fire after the last when scoring by the narrowest of margins at Woodford subsequently. Retains more ability than he cares to reveal these days, and his consistency is non-existent, but the chances are that he will be coaxed home successfully again. Has scored in softish but livelier terrain is more suitable. Wears a cross-noseband. *A. West, Countess Susie Goess-Saurau, G. MacEchern, S. Day & E.L. Goodhind — V.W.H. (James Richardson).* 464 (L), 602 (MO), 758 (O), 1072 (L), 1298 (3m1f110yH), 1551 (L).

PHARLINDO (IRE) .9-7§.. 14 b.g. Phardante (FR) — Linda Martin (Furry Glen) u3p47u. Compact half-brother to Linda's Prince (IRE). Dam won Irish NH flat. IRISH NH '95/6 r9 p0. P-t-P '97/03 r33 w6 (inc Ladies) p7 (4 2nds); failed to finish 18 (ran out 3, and fell/unseated 8). Held his form really well for seven seasons, and only failed to score in '98 and F&M year, but has always proved a difficult ride, and has to go right-handed. Looked frail in '04 when beaten upwards of 15 lengths and it would be a surprise if he turned out again. Wears a cross-noseband, and has been tried in an off-side pricker. Blinkered once in '96. *Mrs J.W. Furness — Hurworth.* 162 (L), 270 (L), 502 (L), 593 (L), 1290 (L), 1399 (L).

PHAR LORD (IRE) ..—.. 11 br.g. Phardante (FR) — Buckskin Lady (Buckskin FR) u. Tall half-brother to Chasing winner, Grundon (IRE). P-t-P '00 and '02 (for Mr D.C.J. Skinner) r3 w1 (Maiden) p0; 5th of 6, and pulled up 1. Made a winning start in a weak Maiden at Black Forest Lodge in '00, but seemed to go wrong almost immediately, and missed '01 and '03. Had already made two noteworthy errors before he parted company with the rider at the tenth on his latest comeback, but was apparently put off by a camera flash next to the fence. Failed to see the light of day again, and his 9-6 rating has been withdrawn. *Ms M. Hopkins & Mrs J. Lawrence — Ledbury (Margaret Hopkins).* 867 (I).

PHARMISTICE (IRE) ..10-2.. 14 b.g. Phardante (FR) — Lucylet (Kinglet) 23p1p11123. Tall attractive half-brother to Luciman (IRE) and Garryspillane (IRE), and to jumping winner, Supreme Fortune (IRE). Dam won NH flat and 3 Hdles (2m-2m2f). NH FLAT '96 r3 p0. NH '96/8 r6 w2 (2m7f Hdles) p1 (2nd); 4th and 8th in Chses. P-t-P/HUNT CH '99/03 r27 w10 (inc 3m1f Hunt Ch and 8 Ladies) p8 (5 2nds, of 3 once; inc 3rd of 4 once); pulled up 1, unseated 3. An amazingly consistent Ladies horse, and has recorded 11 of his 16 wins in the past three years. Used to possess a turn of foot that was best utilised in small fields on sound surfaces, but can also handle soft/holding. Thrice successful at Kelso and Corbridge, but needs to get clear of the opposition nowadays, and only likely to slow further at 14. Wears a cross-noseband. *Mrs P.C. Stirling — Lauderdale (Nicola Stirling).* 133 (L), 284 (L), 428 (3m5fL), 550 (L), 798 (3m1fH), 1039 (L), 1078 (L), 1221 (L), 1420 (L), 1478 (L).

PHARSHU (IRE) .9-4.. 8 gr.m. Phardante (FR) — Bruna Rosa (Roselier FR) 4. Small. Dam, half-sister to Mr Invader (*qv* '00 Annual). P-t-P '03 r3 p1 (2nd); and fell 2. Fell at halfway in her first two attempts, and beaten 20 lengths when second in a weak Maiden at Bratton Down subsequently, but appeared to suffer a setback when last on firmish at Great Trethew on her only appearance in '04. *I.R. Snowden — Taunton V. (Philip Greenwood).* 307 (2m4fOMa).

PHAR TO COMFY (IRE) ..9-2.. 10 b.m. Phardante (FR) — Roseowen (Derring Rose) p. Very small neat half-sister to Mr Dow Jones (IRE). P-t-P/HUNT CH '03 (for Greenacre Racing Partnership) r7 p3 (2 2nds, of 3 once); fell/unseated 3, and pulled up 1. On the verge of a small success when beaten a minimum of six lengths in three placings in Wales last year, but often let down by her erratic jumping, and lamed at infamous Black Forest Lodge when a well-backed favourite on her return. *Ms K.N. Evans & T. Evans — Llangeinor (John Moore).* 416 (CMam).

PHASE THREE (IRE) ..9-11.. 8 ch.g. Torus — Winning Fare (Le Bavard FR) 313pu2. Brother to Hurdles winner, Mead Court (IRE). IRISH P-t-P '02/3 r10 p5. IRISH NH FLAT '03 r1 p0. IRISH P-t-P '04 r4 w1 (beat Supreme Tadgh in 7yo&up Maiden at Aghabullogue: *made all, stayed on wl*) p2 (3rd at Dromahane: *ld, mists 3 & 5, hdd app 2 out, sn wknd*; and last of 3 at Killeagh: *ld, blun 7, mist 13, hdd aft mist 3 out, sn wknd*); and pulled up 1. His length second in a 19-runner four-finisher Restricted at Llanvapley was a decent effort, but may be one of the Torus's who do not care so much for winning, and compared to eight placings he has managed to register one success in a weak Irish Maiden in soft in his third season. Impetuous and likes to employ forcing tactics, and could be more interesting if Jane Williams takes over in the saddle. *Mrs A.D. Williams — Albrighton Woodland.* 695 (R), 844 (R).

PHATIC (IRE) ..—.. 9 b.g. Alphabatim (USA) — Pharisee (IRE) (Phardante FR) p. Good-topped half-brother to Caught At Dawn (IRE) (*qv*). Made a distressing start at Marks Tey where he set a fast pace for 2m4f but faded quickly and collapsed twice after pulling up two out, and lay on the course for so long that the next race was delayed for 20 minutes. Recovered sufficiently to contest Chases for a different owner in the Autumn, and although pulled up was not wholly disgraced, and it might just be worth returning him to Maidens. *N.W. Padfield — Worcs.* 901 (OMa).

PLATE 95 178 Stewart Tory Mem Trophy HC, Wincanton: John Storey's pride and glory, the eventual winner Philson Run parades before the race PHOTO: Linda Charles

PHILSON RUN (IRE) ..11-0.. 9 b.g. Un Desperado (FR) — Isis (Deep Run) 1. Hobdayed. IRISH P-t-P '03 r2 w1 (7&8yo Maiden) p1 (3rd). Bought Doncaster, May for 6500. Gave a competent display of jumping on only his third racecourse appearance when winning a Wincanton Hunter Chase quite impressively from Garruth (who was subsequently disqualified) (was 25-1) but unfortunately had an immediate setback and unable to reappear. Clearly of well above average competence, but it is most worrying that he has already fallen prey to wind and leg problems at such an early stage in his career. *Gale Force One (J.G. Storey) — Dulverton F. (Nick Williams).* 178 (3m1f110yH).

PHILTRE (IRE) ..10-6.. 11 b.g. Phardante (FR) — Forest Gale (Strong Gale) 23423252. Smallish unfurnished half-brother to Sir Galeforce (IRE), Forest Fountain (IRE), Wishing William (IRE), Snowtre (IRE) and Joe Lively (IRE). NH '01/2 r3 w2 (2m7f110y-3m Chses). P-t-P/HUNT CH '99/03 r22 w7 (inc 2m5f Hunt Ch, 2 Opens and Mixed Open) p6 (2 3rds, inc Hunt Ch; and 4 2nds, short head of 3 once); pulled up 3, and fell/unseated 4. NH '03 r1 p0 (5th in 2m7f110y Ch). Jumps well and likes to force the pace, and decidedly useful when conditions are right, but although unbeaten when completing in '03 did not look the force he was, and could not keep his head in front at all this year. Stopped as though something was amiss when 4-6 and 24 lengths third at the Harkaway, but finished weakly in the vast majority of his starts, and may not have been firing on all cylinders. Punters will need tremendous faith to support him in future. *J.D. Callow — Worcs (Helen Needham).* 156 (O), 251 (C), 662 (O), 924 (O), 1117 (3m1f110yH), 1390 (O), 1453 (3m4fH), 1529 (MO).

PHOENIX PHLYER .10-3.. 11 b.g. Ardross — Brown Coast (Oats) 231u2545. Compact half-brother to Polly Come Back. Dam is half-sister to Sausolito Boy. Grandam, Brown Sauce, won 2 Points and placed 8. NH FLAT '98/9 r2 p0. NH '99/01 r17 w1 (2m3f110y Ch) p6 (inc 4 Chses, beaten 7-25l). P-t-P/HUNT CH '01/3 r17 w8 (inc 7 Ladies, 4-timer '03) p5 (3 2nds, of 3 twice, beaten head once; and inc last of 3); last pair 2. Speedy and is hard to catch if allowed to dominate, and galloped away at the head of affairs when springing a 14-1 surprise at Ludlow, but has to go right-handed and is vulnerable on easy surfaces. Makes the odd mistake but is very adept at course completion, and only unseated at Taunton as he was hampered. Wears a cross-noseband and a near-side pricker, but his visors have been traded in for cheekpieces. *Miss C.C., Sir Hugh & Lady Stucley — Eggesford (David Pipe).* 63 (L), 146 (L), 317 (2m4fH), 347 (3mH), 630 (2m4fH), 799 (2m3f110yH), 1166 (2m5f110yH), 1350 (L).

PHYLLIS ..9-11.. 10 b.m. Primitive Rising (USA) — Lindy Two VII (unknown) p4p. Workmanlike. P-t-P '02/3 (for Mr R. Tate) r16 w3 (Maiden, Restricted and Intermediate) p1 (last of 3); 4th, last 2, pulled up 2, and fell/unseated 7. Remarkably clumsy at first, and parted company with the rider in seven of her first 13 starts, but had always looked able, and scored on her first three completed starts. Remains error-prone and not better than 26 lengths last in the new yard, and broke down at Brocklesby Park. *R. Greenway — Cheshire (Mark Williamson).* 93 (O), 251 (C), 477 (Cnr).

PICKET PIECE .9-11.. 14 br.g. Shareef Dancer (USA) — Jouvencelle (Rusticaro FR) 532r3225fp. Workmanlike lengthy half-brother to Valiant Warrior, to flat and smart jumping winner, Land Afar, to Hurdles winners, Hatta Breeze, Full Minty and Damoiselle, to NH flat winner, Joyeuse, and to flat winner, Granite Boy. FLAT '94 r4 p0. NH '95 and '98/02 (for D. Nicholson, 4 wins, R.T. Phillips, 2 wins, and N.A. Twiston-Davies) r33 w6 (4 2m-2m3f and 2 3m-3m1f Chses) p10; fell 1, pulled up 1, brought down 1. Became very jarred up on the flat and later needed three years off, but repaid the patience with six wins on easy surfaces under Rules including a £20,832 Hurdle at Newbury in '99 and a hat-trick in Jan/Feb that year (his total career earnings were £62,319). Managed five placed efforts in Points (it would probably have been six had he not fallen four out in a four miler once) and came closest to success when a rallying neck second in a Novice Riders contest, but has not managed to reach the winner's enclosure since March '01. Has always been unreliable, and wears blinkers and often makes mistakes or jumps left nowadays. *Mrs R. Mackness — Cotswold (Jelly Nolan).* 17 (O), 110 (Cnr), 229 (O), 404 (O), 465 (O), 661 (Cnr), 758 (O), 1016 (3m2fO), 1093 (4mMO), 1429 (Cnr).

PILLAGER ..9-6.. 8 b.g. Reprimand — Emerald Ring (Auction Ring USA) 2. Half-brother to Don Rubini, and to 2 flat winners, (one in Italy), including Warring. Dam won 6f race. FLAT '99/02 r14 p1 (2nd). NH '02 r1 p0. P-t-P '03 r1 p1 (2nd). Gained his placing on the flat over a mile, but has since finished runner-up in his Members twice, and had he not let the winner slip clear might have scored in '04. Seems a reliable enough jumper, and well worth a spin in a Maiden or two. *Miss E. Freeman — O. Berks.* 935 (M).

PILOT'S HARBOUR ..9-0.. 9 b.g. Distant Relative — Lillemor (Connaught) 2u. Lengthy good-topped brother to flat winners, Pelleman and Lilleman, and half-brother to 3 flat winners (one in Germany), including Caleman. FLAT '98/01 r17 w2 (7-8f) p2. NH '00/1 and '03 (for F.P. Murtagh) r23 w2

(2m2f-3mHdles) p5 (hd 2nd once); pulled up 4, fell 1. Successful twice apiece on the flat and over Hurdles to May '01 from a total of 40 outings, but has also tried Sellers without success, and was 48 lengths fourth of five, pulled up and fell in Chases. Often looks ungenuine, and was blinkered twice to '00. Pulled up lame in '01 and absent for nearly two years, and his 12 lengths last of two in a Members from just two attempts in '04 does not suggest that his future is rosy. *M. Hughes — Cumberland.* 1306 (M), 1444 (3m1fH).

PINK MOSAIC ..—.. 9 b.m. Safawan — Stoneydale (Tickled Pink) p. Sturdy half-sister to flat winners, Esatto, Halbert, Runs In The Family and Delrob (all won between 4-6 races — none beyond 6f). Dam won 5 5f races, and is out of winning sprinter, and half-sister to prolific sprint winner, Balatina. 6000y. FLAT '99/00 (for J.G. Smyth-Osbourne) r6 p0. The black ewe in a family of highly successful sprinters none of whom were successful at beyond 6f, and did not try further during her unsuccessful forays on the flat. Unbelievably started at 2-1 in a Mares Maiden at Cottenham (it must have been a con), and unsurprisingly ground to a halt three out. Needs another career. *Miss L.M. Wain — Grafton.* 996 (CMam).

PINMOOR HILL .9-11.. 9 b.g. Saddlers' Hall (IRE) — Pennine Pink (IRE) (Pennine Walk) pp23f. Small compact good-bodied. Dam won 4 flat at 3, 8-10f. FLAT '98 and '00 r6 p0 (beaten 20*l* plus in 5). P-t-P '02 (for Mr J.E. Swiers) r2 w1 (Maiden) p0; and 5th. Looked set for better things when landing a seven-minute Maiden in softish at Hornby Castle in March '02, but that was his final appearance of that campaign, and spent '03 on the sidelines. Took a while to run himself fit this year, but showed signs of a return to form at Kilworthy, and with sensible placing should find another opening. *E. Wonnacott — Spooners & W. Dartmoor (Diane Wilson).* 324 (R), 488 (R), 571 (R), 1294 (3mH), 1437 (2m5f110yH).

PIPERS BOY ..—.. 9 b.g. Buckley — Pipers Reel (Palace Music USA) r9. Lengthy owner-bred. Dam won 8f race. P-t-P '03 r1 p0 (unseated). NH '04 (for D. Burchell) r1 p0 (9th in 2m1f Hdle: *a bhnd, t.o*). A first ride for the sartorially challenged veteran rider when making his own debut on the final day of the '03 season, but unseated after two miles, and declined the first on his reappearance at Andoversford. Looks a typically unmotivated Buckley, and was 50-1 when tailed off on his subsequent hurdling debut. *G. Davies — Brecon & Talybont (Melvin Davies).* 760 (OMa).

PIPER'S ROCK (IRE) ..10-1.. 14 ch.g. Zaffaran (USA) — Misclaire (Steeple Aston) pu36p52. Compact well-made half-brother to Irish NH flat and useful English jumping winner, Thumbs Up. NH FLAT '96 r2 p0. NH '97/01 r32 w6 (2 2m-2m5f110y Hdles, and 4 2m110y-2m5f Chses) p6 4 2nds); pulled up 6, and fell 2. P-t-P '02/3 r14 w1 (Ladies) p2 (2nd of 3 once); 4th twice, 5th twice, last pair 3, fell/unseated 3, and pulled up 1. Won six races at up to 2m6f under Rules, and ended a two-year long drought when scoring at Hutton Rudby in '02, but always prone to jump and hang left, and has been generally well beaten since. Had been retired after putting up his best display for some time at Hexham, but will race on for a novice girl in Scotland in '05. Has been tried in a visor and a near-side pricker. Wears a cross-noseband. *Miss V.A. Russell — Jedforest (Morag Neill).* 133 (L), 426 (Cf), 552 (Cf), 678 (3m1fH), 1039 (L), 1308 (L), 1478 (L).

PISTOL KNIGHT ..9-4.. 11 b.g. Jupiter Island — Porchester Run (Deep Run) 324up. Workmanlike. Dam (*qv* '91 Annual), sister to Oh To Be (not the recent Pointer), won Maiden and 2nd twice for Nick Bowman. P-t-P '02/3 r7 p2 (2nds, of 3 once); unseated, and pulled up 4. Thrice runner-up in Maidens at Godstone, but tends to plod badly, and beaten a fence in the latest. Ran to 10-2 when around 21 lengths third at Folkestone, and would be a Maiden certainty if he could reproduce it, but does not appear to stay that well, and connections targeted another sub-3m event unsuccessfully subsequently. *N.J. Bowman — Southdown & Eridge (Sarah Bowman).* 345 (2m5fH), 611 (OMa), 746 (OMa), 1055 (OMa), 1439 (2m5fH).

PITCHFORK PETE ..9-9.. 6 b.g. Petoski — Sugar Mommy (Relkino) f. Workmanlike attractive. Bought Doncaster, Aug for 8000. Coming with a strong late run to challenge when he took a crashing fall two out in the last of the 12 races at Bishops Court, and tragically died in the dark. R.G. Tizzard — Blackmore & Sparkford V. (Alan Tizzard). 329 (OMa).

PLACE ABOVE (IRE) ..9-12§.. 9 b.g. Alphabatim (USA) — Lucky Pit (Pitpan) 1ur. Compact well-made. IRISH P-t-P '01/2 r6 w1 (5&6yo Maiden) p1 (2nd); pulled up 1, fell 1. NH '03 r4 p0. Sold expensively after winning an Irish youngsters Maiden in the soft, but was beaten 58 lengths plus at 40-1 or more in four Hurdles subsequently. Revived to take a Witton Castle Restricted narrowly under a forceful ride from Lee Bates, but a disaster in Hunter Chases afterwards, and unseated at the second, and refused to race. Reported to have had numerous problems, and has to be regarded as suspect for the time being. *E.A. Elliott — S. Durham.* 164 (R), 541 (3mH), 546 (3mH).

PLATE 96 164 Old Raby Hunt Club Restricted: Place Above (Lee Bates), 1st, leads Just Fluster (Richard Wakeham), 2nd, at the last *PHOTO: Roy Parker*

PLACID MAN (IRE) ..11-5.. 11 br.g. Un Desperado (FR) — Sparkling Gale (Strong Gale) 11u11u. Strong rangy half-brother Irish Pointing winner, Quincy What. IRISH P-t-P '99 r1 w1 (4&5yo Maiden). IRISH NH FLAT '00 r1 p1 (2nd). NH '01/3 (for N.J. Henderson) r3 w1 (2m4f Ch) p1 (3rd in Hdle); and pulled up 1. Bought Doncaster, May for 5600 (to vendor). Remarkably (and frustratingly) was only able to appear once per annum '99/03, but did manage two victories including a Fontwell Chase in heavy. Made the most of his long-awaited chance in his sixth year, and enjoyed an excellent season. Completed an impressive double in Ladies Opens at Higham and made virtually all and kept quickening in both (blundered and nearly unseated at the first at the Waveney), but after unseating at the second in his hat-trick bid there (1-4) he was left virtually solo at the final fence in a 2m4f Fontwell Hunter Chase which should have gone to Silence Reigns. Was very exuberant and Alex Embiricos found him a real handful on this occasion, and Nick Moore was aboard when he upset the odds-on Sikander A Azam at Warwick. Tried a mile further in the Interim Justitia, but unseated two out when three lengths fourth and still going well enough. Goes a cracking gallop and is a smart animal, but far from placid, and although capable of very bold jumping he can be inclined to put down at the last moment. Particularly effective at 2m4f, but clearly stays a good bit further. Some of his past problems were caused by a broken pelvis. *T. Jones & Partners — Cambridge Univ (Tim Bryce).* 25 (L), 157 (L), 399 (L), 581 (2m4fH), 1299 (2m4f110yH), 1453 (3m4fH).

PLAIN CHANT .9-7.. 8 b.g. Doyoun — Sing Softly (Luthier) 3p*432*. Small narrow half-brother to jumping winner, Dominent Serenade, flat winners, Eliza Acton and Supreme Sand (£321,921 inc in USA), and to flat and Hurdles winner, Top Cees (£278,986). Dam won 3 flat (6-12f), inc Pretty Polly Stakes and Lancashire Oaks. FLAT '00/1 r6 p1 (3rd). NH '01/2 r5 p0; pulled up 2. P-t-P '03 r2 w1 (3-finisher Maiden) p1 (3rd of 4). NH '04 r3 p2 (1½*l* 2nd to Yassar in 2m4f110y Ch: *hld up, hdwy aft 11, stayed on u.p flat*; and 26*l* 3rd to Saby in 2m110y Ch: *chsd wnr 5 til wknd app last*); and 4th in 2m Ch: *a bhnd, blun bad 3 out, t.o*. Has yet to come up to expectations under Rules, but a drop into Maiden company brought immediate dividends last year when taking full advantage of the leader's third last fence fall at Cold Harbour. Made the odd mistake and appeared not to get home when 12 lengths third in his first Restricted, but has since picked up £2,427 in place prize money in Chases. Has acquired cheekpieces. *S. Harrison — Tredegar F. (Craig Roberts).* 452 (R), 695 (R).

PLAIN POLLY (IRE) ..—.. 7 b.m. Supreme Leader — Mountain Beauty (IRE) (Executive Perk) upup. Small half-sister to Mountain Native (IRE). Dam, half-sister to Comeragh Gale (*qv* '00 Annual). Bought Doncaster, Aug for 2100. Another dull and dismal Millington maiden who can't get round, and only negotiated a total of three jumps in a couple of her outings. A waste of time. *P.J. Millington — Fernie.* 746 (OMa), 887 (CfMa), 1061 (OMa), 1215 (CfMa).

PLANET IRELAND (IRE) ..9-2.. 13 b.g. Mandalus — Seapatrick (The Parson) 4. Strong half-brother to Irish Pointing and NH flat winner, Genial Gent (IRE). NH '98/00 r10 p0; pulled up 3 and fell/unseated 2. P-t-P/HUNT CH '98 and '01/3 (for Mrs J.M. Hollands) r17 p5 (3 2nds, of 3 once, last once; inc 2 fences last of 3 once); pulled up 2, unseated 1, and slipped up 1. A long-standing maiden, and has been foiled by a lack of stamina and jumping prowess, and appears to be rapidly winding up his racing operations. Has been tried tongue-tied. Fell when blinkered once in '00. *A.J. Wight — Berwicks (Jacqui Wight).* 281 (M).

PLAY ALONE (IRE) ..9-3.. 10 b.m. Mandalus — Solo Player (Blue Refrain) 35541p. Neat attractive sister to Soloman (IRE), and half-sister to a flat and jumping winner in Switzerland. P-t-P '00/3 r11 p3 (2 2nds, of 3 once); 5th twice, pulled up 5, and fell 1. Failed to get round in six of her first eight starts spread over three seasons, and beaten a minimum of 15 lengths in her first nine completions, but finally rewarded connections perseverance when scraping home from another non-stayer under a galvanic ride from Nibby Bloom on firmish at Cottenham. Will be extremely lucky to find a similarly weak Restricted. *S. Wood & D. Wales — W. Norfolk (David Wales).* 154 (OMa), 245 (CfMa), 746 (OMa), 833 (OMa), 996 (CMam), 1152 (R).

PLAYAWAY (IRE) ..—.. 11 b.g. Black Minstrel — Actually Stell (Deep Run) pp. Good-topped hobdayed half-brother to Irish NH flat winner, Oh June. Dam won 2 2m Hurdles and 2 Chases (2m3f-2m4f) in Ireland. NH FLAT '00 r2 p0. NH '01/2 r3 p0; pulled up 1. P-t-P '03 r2 p0 (pulled up 2). Beaten upwards of 22 lengths over hurdles, and pulled up in all five appearances since June '02. *Mrs J. Conway — Cranwell Bloodhounds.* 685 (OMa), 1000 (OMa).

PLENTY INN HAND ..7-7§.. 9 b.g. Alflora (IRE) — Shean Deas (Le Moss) pp3ppp. Workmanlike. Dam won 4-y-o Maiden in Ireland; and won 5 Points (inc 3 Confineds) and placed 3. P-t-P '02 (for Mr P.R. Burling) r4 p0 (refused 2, and pulled up 2). NH '02/3 (for H.D. Daly, and M.F. Harris) r9 p2 (3rds over Hdles); pulled up 3, fell/unseated 2. A proven dog, and slowed rapidly after making the running for two miles when beaten the length of the run-in on his only Pointing completion. Amazingly yet to be tried in headgear, and that will surely be his only hope of salvation. *Clock House Racing (A. Gould) — Bicester with Whaddon (Bradley Clarke).* 52 (OMa), 172 (OMa), 788 (CfMa), 981 (OMa), 1261 (OMa), 1532 (OMa).

PLYNLIMON .—.. 8 b.g. King Luthier — Pennal (Oats) fp. Sturdy compact. Dam, sister to No Work (*qv* '98 Annual), failed to finish in 18 of 19 Points (refused 4) ('an absolute disgrace'). Showed no immediate ability in May Maidens, and fell after a mile on his debut. Could hardly be bred from a worse mare. *A.D. Taylor — Pentyrch.* 1192 (OMa), 1394 (OMa).

POACHER'S PRIDE ..6-8.. 7 b.m. Librate — Inglifield (Whistlefield) pp. Close-coupled sister to Sandville Lad. Dam, 'an utterly useless non-stayer of pint-sized proportions', failed to finish in all 9 Points. P-t-P '03 r2 p0 (4th of 5, and refused 1). Still in contention when pulled up after two miles on her reappearance, and further fuelled the fears that she had a problem when capitulating at Pentreclwydau. Wears a cross-noseband. *N. Poacher — Llangeinor.* 676 (CfMa), 1240 (OMa).

POLAR BRIGHT (IRE) .9-5.. 10 b.g. Glacial Storm (USA) — Rock Solid (Hardboy) p3up2. Workmanlike dipped brother to Tudor Lodge (IRE), and half-brother to Supreme Dream (IRE), and to Hurdles winner, Envopakleada (IRE). P-t-P '03 r2 p0 (last, and pulled up 1). Got the trip better than usual when four lengths second on firmish at Vauterhill, and looks a possible winner if maintaining improvement, but nagging doubts about his stamina remain. Wears a cross-noseband. *The Just One More Club (Miss A.V. Handel) — W. Somerset (Alison Handel).* 370 (OMa), 493 (OMa), 693 (OMa), 967 (OMa), 1272 (OMa).

POLAR CHAMP..10-10.. 12 b.g. Polar Falcon (USA) — Ceramic (USA) (Raja Baba USA) 1110212u1. Small well-made brother to Hurdles winner, Polo Venture, and half-brother to 3 flat winners (one in Sweden). FLAT '95/8 r34 w5 (10-12f) p11. NH '98/03 (for N.A. Gaselee, 2 wins, and M.C. Pipe) r39 w14 (10 2m1f-3m3f Hdles and 4 3m-3m3f Chses) p6; pulled up 3, unseated 1. A marvellous campaigner for ten years, and his exploits under Rules earned £95,000 and the Channel 4 trophy in '01 for having collected the most televised races. Successful on the all-weather once and has been effective from 10f to 3m3f, and completed a seven-timer between May and October '00, having gained his initial win in his sole Seller after which Martin Pipe bought him for 9,600. Also notched a hat-trick in June/July '02, and frequently wins very easily, but can jump poorly, and unseated at the eighth in the '03 Grand National. Wears headgear. Kept pumping up his career total of victories in '04, and should have taken his tally to a remarkable 25, but lost Lucy Bridges at the final fence in the Ladies Hunter Chase at Stratford (at least his departure paved the way for a stablemate). There were a maximum of six runners in his five Pointing wins, and generally unchallenged, but entitled to throw in the odd stinker and certainly did so at 1-4 in a match at Barbury where he never wanted to keep up with Gladiatorial. It is safe to say that he would never have achieved anything like so much had

Martin Pipe not taken a shine to him, and there seems no reason to suppose that this fabulously tough old character cannot enjoy a similar level of achievement at 12. *Mrs A. Malde — Silverton (David Pipe).* 77 (O), 145 (O), 277 (O), 543 (3m2f110yH), 1065 (O), 1183 (Cf), 1379 (MO), 1454 (3mH), 1541 (O).

PLATE 97 1183 Devon & Somerset Staghounds Confined: The winner Polar Champ with Ashley Farrant in typical pose *PHOTO: Baths Photographic*

POLAR FLIGHT ..10-8.. 11 br.g. Polar Falcon (USA) — Fine Honey (USA) (Drone USA) p3113. Tall attractive half-brother to Royal Crimson, and to several flat winners. Dam won a 5f race. FLAT '96/7 r11 w2 (8f) p3 (beaten head once). NH '98/00 r9 w3 (2m4f Nov Hdles) p4 (3 2nds); 4th, and 8th. P-t-P '02/3 r10 w4 (Opens, inc 2 Mixed) p1 (3rd); fell/unseated 4, and pulled up 1. Capsized and succeeded in equal measures in '02, and is a speedy Pointer whose jumping has marginally improved, but tends to sweat excessively and not find much off the bridle, and looked sure to be consumed by Machalini at Maisemore until his rider fell off approaching the last. Will need careful placing if he is to maintain his excellent wins-to-runs ratio in future. Acts in heavy and can handle firmish. Wears a cross-noseband. *The Lads & Lasses Syndicate (Mrs R.A. Vickery) — Blackmore & Sparkford V. (Rose Vickery).* 5 (L), 196 (O), 472 (Cf), 727 (MO), 1379 (MO).

POLAR KING (IRE) ..10-0§.. 12 b.g. Glacial Storm (USA) — Our Little Lamb (Prince Regent FR) 6f2p5. Compact good-looking half-brother to Chasing winner, The Bushkeeper (IRE). NH FLAT '97 r3 p1 (2nd). NH '97/9 r10 p4 (¾l 2nd, caught 50yds out in 3m2f Hdle once). P-t-P '00/3 r13 w3 (up to Confined) p1 (2nd); 4th twice, last pair 2, pulled up 3, and fell/unseated 2. Won his first three completed Points in '00, but had looked unreliable under Rules previously, and although still able the regular rider has been unable to motivate him sufficiently. Backed from 16s to 7-1 when travelled out of his area to Mollington but typically flattered only to deceive, and remains liable to make mistakes. Blinkered once in '02 but messed around at the start, and the experiment was not repeated. *P.L. Southcombe — Cattistock.* 199 (L), 311 (L), 585 (L), 1100 (O), 1379 (MO).

POLAR PROSPECT ..—.. 12 b.g. Polar Falcon (USA) — Littlemisstrouble (USA) (My Gallant USA) p7p. Tall strong. FLAT '96/8 and '00 r17 w2 (7-9f) p5. NH '97/02 r33 w6 (4 2m-2m1f Hdles, and 2 2m110y-2m3f110y Chses) p17 (10 2nds, beaten head once); fell 1. HUNT CH '03 (for Mrs J. King) r1 p0 (pulled up). A useful money-spinner under Rules, and only failed to complete once in his first 33 starts over jumps, but a non-finisher in three of the last four from two different yards, and looks troubled now. Only once successful beyond the minimum trip and it would be a surprise if he saw the light of day again. *M. Woodman & D. Nibblet — Berkeley (Sarah George).* 347 (3mH), 630 (2m4fH), 1372 (2m4fH).

POLITICAL CRUISE ..—.. 7 b.g. Royal Fountain — Political Mill (Politico USA) f*009033*. Small neat homebred half-brother to Hurdles winner and stablemate, Political Sox. NH FLAT '02/3 r3 p0. NH

'04 r6 p2 (3rd in 2m4f110y Hdles: *blun 1, sn wl bhnd, nvr nrr*; and *wl bhnd frm 5*); last of 10 in 2m4f Hdle: *nt jw, a bhnd, t.o*, 10th in 2m4f Hdle: *hld up, rdn 5, sn wknd, t.o*, 9th in 2m6f110y Hdle: *bhnd frm 7, t.o*, and 12th in 2m110y Hdle: *a bhnd*. Fell at the first in a February Maiden, but subsequently achieved a couple of distant thirds in 2m4f110y Perth Hurdles. 50-1 plus in eight of nine races to date under Rules and beaten 33 lengths plus in all nine (blinkered once), but might be able to find a little Point if returned to them. *G.R.S. Nixon & Mrs S. Nixon — Buccleuch (Rayson Nixon).* 167 (OMa).

POLKA ..10-2.. 10 b.g. Slip Anchor — Peace Dance (Bikala) 22412. Compact good-bodied. FLAT r4 p0 (tailed off). NH '01/2 r8 p0; pulled up 2. P-t-P '00 and '03 r8 w2 (Maiden and Restricted) p2; 5th, last, and unseated 2. Had a tie-back operation in his youth, and was next to useless under Rules, but a competent Pointer in his grade, and ran his best race yet in defeat on a course where he has won twice on his latest appearance. Does best when stamina is not at a premium. *V.G. Greenway — Devon & Somerset.* 117 (C), 278 (Inr), 472 (Cf), 881 (Inr), 1180 (M).

POLLERTON RUN (IRE) ..—.. 7 b.g. Executive Perk — Whitebarn Run (Pollerton) Rp. Big rangy brother to Whitebarn Vixen (IRE), and half-brother to Irish Pointing winner, Whitebarn Grit. Dam won 2 Irish Points. Has looked none too co-operative since joining the present yard, and another similar effort will be earning him a squiggle. *T.G. Williams — Ystrad Taf Fechan.* 982 (2m5fOMa), 1021 (M).

POLLY COME BACK ..8-13.. 6 br.m. Bob's Return (IRE) — Brown Coast (Oats) 5p. Light-framed half-sister to Phoenix Phlyer (*qv*). Ran reasonably when 16 lengths fifth on her debut, but not seen after a modest effort the following month. Her half-brother is a multiple winner for the yard, which at least makes her of some interest. *D. Underhill — Dulverton F. (David Pipe).* 275 (CfMa), 492 (OMa).

POLLY DUST ..—.. 9 b.m. Gold Dust — Windfall Penny (Blast) pppp. Small neat half-sister to Penny's Prince and Pennys Boy. Dam won 4 Points and placed 12 (inc a Sell Hdle). P-t-P '03 (for Mr J. Sprake) r3 p0 (ran out 1, pulled up 1, and fell 1). Twice a market springer, and has figured prominently for two miles, but still seeking that elusive first completion, and not worthy of further support until she does. *Thinking Twice Partnership — J. Chaffey, G. Brown & J. Holmes — Axe V.H. (Michael Sweetland).* 328 (OMa), 494 (OMa), 693 (OMa), 967 (OMa).

POLLY FLINDERS ..9-8.. 7 b.m. Polar Falcon (USA) — So True (So Blessed) f2. Lengthy unfurnished sister to useful flat winner, Bomb Alaska (won £105,449), and half-sister to Pukka Sahib (Pointed for Sylvia Edmunds), and to flat winners, Phonetic and Keep Your Word. Dam won 2 flat (5-8f), including Esher Cup. FLAT '01/2 (for G.B. Balding) r8 p0. Gave her best display on the flat when a length fourth, but was tailed off in her final two attempts and broke a blood vessel in the latest. Momentarily left in the lead at the last in a Mares Maiden at Mollington, but fell heavily and was badly winded, but again showed promise when ten lengths second to Caipiroska at Garthorpe a month later, when there were two subsequent scorers a very long way behind her. Would obviously have strong claims in similar company if she returns, but also looks to have value in an alternative career as a brood mare. *Mrs S.K. Edmunds & J.H. Busby — Grafton (Sylvia Edmunds).* 293 (CMam), 686 (OMa).

POLLY PEACOCK ..—.. 10 b.m. Peacock (FR) — My Goddess (Palm Track) f. Owner-bred half-sister to Spectre Brown and Hapthor (*qv*). Dam won a Restricted and 3rd 4 (inc Sell Hurdle) for Fergus Jestin. A remote last of three and tired when she broke down and took a crashing fall four out in her Members. *F. Jestin — Cumberland.* 1306 (M).

POLLY TINO .—§§.. 9 b.m. Neltino — Flying Mistress (Lear Jet) p. Small neat sister to Flying Maria, and to jumping winner, Flying Instructor. Dam won 5 2m-3m2f Chses. NH FLAT '01 r2 p0. NH '01/2 r5 p0. P-t-P '03 (for Mr P.J. & Mrs C. Ikin) r3 p0 (refused 2, and pulled up 1). Well-bred, but useless and unpleasant to date, and failed to reach the first in a bungled start on her only appearance in '04. Has run tongue-tied. Wears a cross-noseband. *E. Spain — Fernie (Carol Ikin).* 113 (OMa).

POLO PONY (IRE) ..9-11§.. 13 b.g. The Noble Player (USA) — Mangan Lane (Le Moss) 7u8u4f. Small. Dam is half-sister to Daybrook's Gift (*qv* '98 Annual). NH '96/00 r30 w3 (2 2m5f-3m4f Sell Hdles, and 3m3f Ch) p5. P-t-P '01/2 (for Mrs K.D. Horan) r7 p4 (3 2nds; and 3rd of 4); 4th twice, and 6th. Stays extreme distances, but a difficult ride and does not often consent to give generously, and his jumping of regulation fences remains incredibly haphazard. Hospitalised Tracey Habgood at Towcester, and then fell with James Diment at Guilsborough, and the application of cheekpieces has done nothing to remedy the problem. Has not scored since '98 and his decline looks certain to continue. Occasionally blinkered under Rules. Tracey Habgood runs Harley Racing, a thriving racing equipment business, which generously sponsored the National Novice Riders Race Championship in '04, and her amazing recovery from potentially life-threatening injuries was one of the high points of the season. *Mrs K.D. Horan — Grafton.* 10 (L), 48 (3m5f70yL), 289 (CfL), 437 (3m1fH), 582 (M), 784 (Cf).

POLO RIDGE (IRE) ..10-0§.. 13 gr.g. Phardante (FR) — Fane Bridge (Random Shot) 5576361. Smallish lengthy fired. Dam won 2m4f Irish NH flat. NH FLAT '97 r2 p0. NH '97/00 r10 w1 (2m6f Nov Hdle) p5; pulled up 1, fell 1. P-t-P '02/3 (for Mrs M.E. Barton) r9 w1 (Ladies) p1 (3rd of 4); fell

4, and pulled up 3. Scoring for the first time since '97 when successful under enterprising handling at Lydstep last year, but all too often on the floor in the previous yard, and has suffered persistent leg trouble. Did not jump as fluently as his record might suggest in '04, and was last on four occasions, but again benefited from a positive ride when landing a three-finisher Confined in mud at Northaw. Regained blinkers on his last four starts. *M. Ward & J. Glenister — Granta H. (Martin Ward).* 221 (O), 397 (O), 557 (O), 650 (O), 832 (Cf), 997 (O), 1242 (Cf).

POOL OF LYPHE .—.. 7 gr.m. Lyphento (USA) — Platinum Springs (Miami Springs) p. Dam, half-sister to Glevum (*qv* '01 Annual), was last of 3 and pulled up in Points for Mr Baker. Did not jump too well until pulling up after two miles in a Restricted. *J. Baker — R.A. (Ned Cummins).* 864 (R).

POPPERS ..8-7.. 12 ch.g. Germont — Night Profit (Carnival Night) 3. Strong owner-bred half-brother to Gold Profit (dam of Overton Girl, *qv* '01 Annual), Poppers Lad, Poppers Girl, Watchknowe Lad, Night Time Girl, Sound Profit, Good Profit and Normans Profit. Dam, pulled up in 3 of 4 races for Billy Young (inc 3 Points). NH '00 r3 p0 (9th, last and pulled up 1). P-t-P '00/3 r20 w1 (Maiden) p2 (last of 3 twice, beaten 2 fences once); 4th, last 2, pulled up 10, on floor 4. Only once better than last in his first 13 starts, and was the chief beneficiary of the unassailable leader's third last fence fall at Corbridge in '02, but inclined to make mistakes and beaten a minimum of 50 lengths since. Often tongue-tied. *W.G. Young — Lanarks & Renfrews.* 653 (M).

POPPET ..10-1.. 9 gr.m. Terimon — Combe Hill (Crozier) 5f. Small light-framed half-sister to Iadora (*qv*). NH '03 (for N.J. Henderson) r2 w1 (2m1f Hdle) p0. Left to collect a Hereford Hurdle after the probable winner had fallen at the last when a length ahead, and ran perfectly respectably when 35 lengths fifth to Lord Atterbury in an Open at Barbury, but fell three out when struggling next time, and has not been seen since early February. Not lacking in ability, but her outings are severely restricted. *The Mushroom Syndicate (N. Patton) — Vine & Craven (Mary Gordon-Watson).* 34 (O), 170 (O).

POPPY MAROON ..10-5.. 7 b.m. Supreme Leader — Maries Party (The Parson) 5. Light-framed half-sister to Pushy Parson, and to Irish Pointing and Hurdles winner, Maries Polly. P-t-P '03 r2 w1 (2m4f Maiden) p1 (2nd). Looked a useful prospect when trouncing three subsequent winners by 15 lengths and more over 2m4f at Littlewindsor on only her second start, but presumably suffered a setback when beaten 25 lengths in her first Restricted. Needs to jump more accurately when she embarks on her comeback. *Mrs M.R. Dangerfield — S. Dorset (Richard Miller).* 169 (R).

PORLOCK HILL ..10-1.. 11 b.g. Petoski — Gay Ticket (New Member) f33321. Unfurnished half-brother to Winsford Hill, and to NH flat and Hurdles winner, Mounsey Castle. Dam is half-sister to Withycombe Hill (*qv* '00 Annual). NH '99 and '01 r7 p0; pulled up 3, fell 2, and refused 1. P-t-P/HUNT CH '02/3 r19 w7 (inc 3 Opens) p2 (remote last of 3 once); 4th, last pair 3, pulled up 3, refused 1, and unseated 2. Inconsistent in running and jumping, and thrice a beaten favourite in '04 (including at 1-2), but always seems to find a way to bounce back, and sought salvation in a match on firm at Larkhill. Needs an easy three miles, but punters always place too much faith in him, and it is always worth finding one to beat him. Wears a cross-noseband. *G.T. Lever — Dart V.H. & S. Pool H. (Jeremy Scott).* 62 (Cf), 471 (O), 634 (O), 1269 (MO), 1328 (MO), 1494 (O).

PORTO (IRE) ..10-0.. 10 b/br.g. Torus — Fare Twist (IRE) (Phardante FR) pRu8p1. Tall workmanlike. Dam, half-sister to Phase Three (*qv*). IRISH P-t-P '02/3 r5 w1 (7&8yo Maiden) p1 (2nd); pulled up 2, and fell 1. IRISH NH '03 (for A. Slattery) r1 p0 (fell). Bought Doncaster, Aug for 3500. Has failed to finish in eight of 12 races, and did not really appear to have the credentials to justify support from 10s to 9-2 in a Bratton Down Restricted, but having looked well beaten two out Neil Harris galvanised him to effect and he caught River Dante (who was dogging it furiously) in the final 50 yards. Takes a strong hold and normally makes plenty of the early running, but has a wind problem and stops to nil unless a tongue-tie is applied. Connections did very well to extract another success from him. *N. & Mrs J. Elliott — Modbury H. (Gordon Chambers).* 148 (R), 279 (R), 415 (R), 912 (R), 1268 (R), 1558 (R).

PORT VALENSKA (IRE) ..6-10§.. 12 b.g. Roi Danzig (USA) — Silvera (Ribero) p5ppp35. Small half-brother to several winners. Dam won at 8f. NH FLAT '97 r1 p0. NH '97 and '01 r15 p1 (3rd in Sell). P-t-P/HUNT CH '00 and '02/3 r22 p1 (2nd of 3); 4th 4, 7th, last pair 7, unseated 2, refused 1, and pulled up 6. A desperately bad performer, and soured irrevocably by constant racing despite being physically disabled (runs tubed), and beaten out of sight when staggering to completion in '04. In no fit state to be on a racecourse. Runs tongue-tied, and has been tried in blinkers and cheekpieces. *M.E. Vick — Taunton V.* 485 (OMa), 580 (OMa), 760 (OMa), 865 (OMa), 1327 (OMa), 1450 (OMa), 1495 (OMa).

PORTWAY SADIE .—§.. 9 gr.m. Beveled (USA) — Portway Anna (Hot Brandy) pppppp. Small sturdy half-sister to Portway Sorrel (*qv*). P-t-P '03 r2 p0 (pulled up 2). Has shown marked reluctance to jump off on several occasions, and stops to nil after a maximum of 2m4f if she does get a flier, and clearly has major problems to contend with. *M.R. Rollett — N. Cotswold.* 588 (CfMa), 730 (OMa), 927 (OMa), 978 (CMam), 1495 (OMa), 1553 (OMa).

PORTWAY SORREL ..—.. 10 ch.m. Interrex (CAN) — Portway Anna (Hot Brandy) p. Workmanlike good-topped half-sister to Annastate, Cashaban and Portway Sadie (*qv*). Dam, sister to 4 Pointers, including Portway Grey (*qv* '93 Annual), unseated in a Point. Sorrel and Sadie were 25-1 shots in the Mares Maiden at Upton-on-Severn, and tubby Sorrel went slightly less far, being pulled up two out when tailed off. *Miss E.J. Lloyd — Ross H.* 978 (CMam).

POSH STICK ..9-10.. 8 b.m. Rakaposhi King — Carat Stick (Gold Rod) p41427. Small homebred half-sister to Be A Better Boy (*qv*). NH FLAT '02 r4 p0. NH '02/3 r10 p1 (2nd); pulled up 2. NH '04 r1 p0 (7th in 2m110y Hdle: *hld up, rdn 4 out, sn btn*). Was slow to reveal any form, but it always looked as if she might have some ability, and finally achieved a second over Hurdles at the eighth attempt. Needed 17 attempts to open her account, but finally did so with some ease in a 2m4f Maiden at Dalston. Has continued to give the odd fair display, and ten lengths second to Lordberniebouffant in her Members was no disgrace. Should be able to find another prize or two before she eventually goes to stud to perpetuate the family line. *J.B. & F.A. Walton — Border (Jimmy Walton).* 215 (OMa), 549 (CMam), 768 (2m4fOMa), 1222 (R), 1423 (M).

POT SHOT ..10-3.. 7 b.g. Alflora (IRE) — Triggered (Gunner B) 21f. Rangy owner-bred half-brother to Cousin George (*qv*). P-t-P '03 (for Mr R.L. Burton & Mrs P. Sykes) r2 w1 (2m4f Maiden) p1 (2nd). Talented and won his Maiden and Restricted at the second attempt, but took a long time to assert his superiority in the latter, and seems rather highly-strung. Had he not fallen at the first at Brampton Bryan (6-4 fav) we would have found out a lot more about him as the race went to Sapega, but he certainly looks to have further scope, and is sure to be a warm order wherever he reappears. *R.L. Burton & L.R. Griffiths — S. Salop (Pamela Sykes).* 37 (CR), 467 (CR), 663 (I).

POTTER'S WHEEL .—.. 6 b.g. Elmaamul (USA) — Bewitch (Idiot's Delight) ppRf. Unfurnished. Achieved four-non completions for four different riders, and not seen since the latest unpromising display, when he took a crashing fall two out at Eyton-on-Severn and was winded (would have finished third, but only because two finished). *D.B. Roberts — B.T. & G.R. Roberts — Ludlow (Jen Wall).* 8 (2m4fOMa), 53 (2m4fOMa), 410 (2m4fCfMa), 533 (2m4fCfMa).

POUR CHI PAS .—.. 10 ch.m. Oedipus Complex — Martell Lady (Petit Pretendre) r. Sister to Trial And Error. Dam won her Members and placed 5 (inc a Hurdle). Would not jump the first in a Market Rasen Maiden, and threw the rider off. *A.J. Le Pennec & R.A. Maletroit — Brocklesby (Robin Maletroit).* 304 (OMa).

PRAH SANDS ..8-7§.. 12 b.g. Henbit (USA) — Minor Furlong (Native Bazaar) p982. Big rangy half-brother to Mini Furlong, Abitbizarre and Countrywide Lad, and to Chasing winner, The Carrot Man. Dam, a twin, is an unraced half-sister to Miss Furlong (dam of Pillow Spin, (*qv* '97 Annual). P-t-P/HUNT CH '99/00 (for Mrs G.M. Brake) r13 w1 (3-finisher Maiden) p7 (6 2nds, of 3 once, and last once); last, pulled up 3, and fell 1. NH '00/2 (for C.L. Tizzard) r15 p5 (inc 4 2nds); pulled up 5. Took a while to get the hang of things, and won his Maiden at Cothelstone at the tenth attempt, but could hardly have found more difficult tasks as a Novice Chaser (fourth to Best Mate, won £964,665, with Bindaree, won £477,366, and Shooting Light, won £215,701, filling the places at Exeter in '00; and runner-up to Mister Benjamin once) and wore headgear latterly. Provided the owner with her first ride for eight years on his re-introduction to Points, but typically ran up the white flag after 2m3f, and failed to beat a rival before finishing lame at Stafford Cross. Wears a cross-noseband. *Mrs L.J. Young — Eggesford.* 88 (L), 199 (L), 879 (R), 1132 (R).

PRATE BOX (IRE) .10-4.. 15 b.g. Ela-Mana-Mou — Prattle On (Ballymore) 5411. Tall. IRISH FLAT '92 and '94/6 r7 p1 (3rd). IRISH NH FLAT '94 r4 p0. IRISH NH '94/7 r21 w5 (2 2m Hdles and 3 2m-2m4f Chses) p5. NH '97/8 and '00/1 r8 w1 (2m3f110y Ch) p2 (2nds); pulled up 3, and fell 2. P-t-P/HUNT CH '02/3 r8 w2 (Members and Confined) p3 (2nds, beaten neck once, of 3 once, and inc a Hunt Ch); 5th, pulled up 1, and fell 1. Had a good record in Ireland, and present connections have done well to rejuvenate his flagging career, but has benefited from good placing, and the below par effort of the 4-9 favourite at Umberleigh. Tends to make mistakes, but still shows plenty of resolve, and can handle most types of going. *Mrs P. Corbett — Warwicks (Fred Hutsby).* 168 (C), 434 (3m1f110yH), 1276 (M), 1562 (O).

PREACHER BOY ..9-12.. 6 b.g. Classic Cliche (IRE) — Gospel (IRE) (Le Bavard FR) 21f26. Rangy. Dam won 3 Hurdles (2-3m) and 2m Chase. Bought Tattersalls Ireland, Jun '02 for 2135. A mixed bag in his first season, when his galloping was a lot better than his jumping, and won a youngsters Maiden at Larkhill (clambered over the final fence) when odds-on, having previously finished an equal 25 lengths second to Free Gift there. Fell at the third in his third race, just failed to catch Winners Enclosure in the gales in a Restricted at Ston Easton, but badly lacked fluency when last at Woodford. Problems with the fences are holding him back at present, but may prove to be a decent performer if they can be rectified. *J.A. Keighley — Blackmore & Sparkford V. (John Dufosee).* 12 (OMa), 143 (OMa), 498 (R), 601 (R), 1069 (R).

PREFERRED (IRE) ..9-4.. 7 b.g. Distant Relative — Fruhlingserwachen (USA) (Irish River FR) ppfp32. Compact half-brother to winner in Germany, and to German/English flat winner, Fruhlingssturm. Dam won 8f race in France. IR£9000f, 18,000y. FLAT '00/2 r14 w2 (5-6f) p4 (3rds). NH '02 (for O. Sherwood) r6 p3 (3rds). Won sprints on his second and third outings on the flat, and subsequently accumulated seven 3rds including a Selling Hurdle, but unsurprisingly failed to get the trip in Points, and when he finally managed to complete he was 21 lengths third of four and 12 lengths second of three in his Members behind a 14-year old who was tasting glory for the first time for seven years. Wore headgear thrice to '02. Has no scope to rate higher. *Mrs A. James & J. Arthers — Atherstone (Malcolm Arthers).* 106 (C), 251 (C), 382 (O), 683 (O), 942 (Cf), 1118 (M).

PREMPTED ..—.. 11 ch.g. Crested Lark — Prevada (Soldier Rose) p. Sturdy attractive half-brother to Flycatcher. Dam won 2m5f Maiden from only 2 starts for Jim Mahon, and grandam, Trovada, pulled up in all 3 Points as a 5-y-o for him (ultimately lame). P-t-P '00 and '02 r4 p1 (2nd); pulled up 3. Races very keenly and has shown enough ability to win a Maiden, but hails from a long line of crocks, and has still to prove he has sufficient stamina. Wears a cross-noseband. *Mrs B. Graham & J.G. Mahon — Croome & W. Warwicks (Gabe Mahon).* 976 (M).

PRESENT MOMENT (IRE) ..9-9.. 7 b.g. Presenting — Springphar (IRE) (Phardante FR) 23. Workmanlike half-brother to Irish Hurdling winner, Etak. Dam is half-sister to Spring Gale (*qv*). NH FLAT '02 r2 p0. P-t-P '03 r3 w1 (Maiden) p0; last, and pulled up 1. Left clear at the last when successful on firmish at Fakenham last year, and most unlucky to meet Fane Counsel in his first Restricted, but beaten 55 lengths in another. Has looked suspect once push becomes shove, and appeared to take no interest whatsoever on his latest start, and looks a prime candidate for headgear. Wears a cross-noseband. *A.G.C. Howland Jackson — Suffolk (Ruth Hayter).* 127 (R), 375 (R).

PRESTON BROOK ..9-5.. 8 b.g. Perpendicular — Tommys Dream (Le Bavard FR) f546. Workmanlike half-brother to Who's The Man. Dam, half-sister to Paddy's Glen (*qv* '87 Season Annual), won Irish NH flat and 4 English Hurdles (2m-3m1f). NH FLAT '01 r4 p3. NH '01/2 r6 w1 (2m5f Hdle) p2 (2nds). NH '04 r2 p0 (4th in 2m Hdle: *trckd ldrs, jmpd slow 2, rdn & no ex 2 out*; and 6th in 2m6f Hdle: *chsd ldrs, rdn 3 out, sn btn*). A Hurdling winner in heavy and has been placed on five occasions, but pulled up on his final appearance of '02 and missed '03. Looked to need the run and was twice hampered before halfway when eventually falling in a tired and beaten fourth two out on his comeback at Huntingdon, but could not recover from a blunder at the last when still lying handy at Kelso next time. Retains some ability, but a descent to Points would give him more chance of scoring. Would probably prove to be under-rated in them. *Lord Daresbury — Middleton (Mick Easterby).* 177 (3mH), 349 (3m1fH).

PRETORIA DANCER ..10-2§.. 13 b.g. Dancing Brave (USA) — Pretoria (Habitat) 4223. Small good-bodied brother to French Chasing/English jumping winner, Aardwolf, and half-brother to jumping winner, Pontevedra (IRE), to NH flat and jumping winner, Waterberg (IRE), and to flat winner, Nassma (IRE). Dam won 2 flat (7-10f), including Listed race in Rome. FLAT '95 r7 w1 (14f) p0. NH '96 r5 p2 (21-25l 3rds, to 3m3f). P-t-P '97/8, '00 and '02/3 r30 w4 (inc Mixed Open and Open) p10 (6 2nds, of 3 once, and last once; and inc last of 3 once); pulled up 2, unseated 1. Ungenuine and needs to get his own way, and fooled favourite backers into thinking he would reproduce his second to Caught At Dawn on his last two starts, but a patent safety and to his credit has completed in 36 of 39 starts over jumps. Has gained all his jumping wins going right-handed, and has scored in soft and on firmish, but it would be a brave man to predict a sixth victory. Wears blinkers. *Mrs C. Mackness — Cotswold (Jelly Nolan).* 755 (M), 979 (MOnr), 1138 (O), 1428 (L).

PRICKLY GREEN ..—.. 8 b.g. Liberated — Liberty Delight VII (unknown) p. Lengthy workmanlike. Jumped deliberately and was tailed off when pulled up after two miles in his Members. *P.B. Williams — Brecon & Talybont.* 446 (M).

PRIDE OF KASHMIR ..10-0.. 12 gr.g. Petong — Proper Madam (Mummy's Pet) 322342. Neat brother to 5f winner, Osomental, and half-brother to Flashman, and several other winners (mainly sprinters). Dam won 6 flat (5-6f). FLAT r18 p3 (beaten a head once). NH '97/9 r20 w5 (4 2m1f-2m5f Hdles, inc hat-trick '97, and 2m5f Ch) p3. P-t-P '00 and '03 r8 p4 (2 2nds, of 3 once); 4th thrice, and unseated. A very difficult ride who has been worried out of several close finishes since gaining the last of his five wins under Rules in September '98, but the trainer is on record as saying she would give up if she could not extract another success, and still has not lost faith. Has never won beyond 2m5f, and finds it difficult to get the trip in Points, and twice beaten a neck at Kingston Blount in '04, but there would be few more deserving winners in '05 (even if it means we have to put up with Jenny for another 30 years). Tried in headgear latterly under Rules. *E.F.B. & Mrs J.M. Monck, P. Clayton & A. Bull — Grafton (Jenny Pidgeon).* 25 (L), 189 (L), 407 (L), 625 (L), 938 (MO), 1334 (L).

PRIDE OF PENNKER (IRE) ..—.. 12 b.m. Glacial Storm (USA) — Quitrentina (Green Shoon) ppf. Lengthy. NH FLAT '97 r1 p0. NH '98/03 (for A.G. Newcombe, when successful, and G.A. Ham) r32 w1 (2m4f Hdle) p4 (2nd in Hdle and 3 3rds in Chses); pulled up 10, fell/unseated 3. Won a Taunton

Hurdle on firm in October '98, but a notoriously weak finisher, and has suffered 29 consecutive defeats since. Pulled up on 12 occasions including in two of three Sellers, and has also fallen or unseated four times. Predictably useless at 33-1 or more in Points. *M. Flynn — Monmouths.* 1023 (Cf), 1090 (Cf), 1227 (Cf).

PRIESTTHORN (IRE) ..9-11.. 10 b.g. Denel (FR) — Pollys Flake (Will Somers) puu4p. Compact half-brother to Searcher, Classsical Pop and Chasing winner, Smith's Band (IRE), and to Irish Hurdles winner, Bells Bridge. Dam won 2m2f flat and 3 Hdles (2m-2m2f) in Ireland. NH '00/1 r9 w2 (2m3f-2m7f Hdles) p0; fell/unseated in 2 of 3 Chses. P-t-P '00 and '03 r8 w2 (2m4f Maiden and Ladies) p1 (3rd of 4); 4th, last 2, pulled up 1, and unseated 1. Won three of his first five races, including a Hurdle at Lingfield at 20-1, but seemed to lose his bottle when tried over regulation fences, and has never looked the same horse since. Remains a very sketchy jumper and gives the rider no confidence, and beaten 29 lengths in his only completion in '04. Has been tried in cheekpieces. *P.L. Southcombe — Cattistock.* 33 (L), 171 (L), 234 (L), 635 (L), 822 (L).

PRIMATICCIO (IRE) ..—.. 10 b.g. Priolo (USA) — Martinova (Martinmas) p. Lengthy half-brother to 6 winners, including in Ireland and abroad, including Malafemmera (English-trained winner in Italy) and Export Price (smart French sprinter). Dam, half-sister to useful flat winner and sire, Lucky Wednesday, won 3 Irish flat (5-7f), and was 3rd when favourite for 1000 Guineas there. FLAT '97/00 r9 w2 (14-17f, inc Amat on fibresand) p1 (2nd). IRISH NH '99 r2 p0. P-t-P/HUNT CH '01/2 (for Mr V.J. Hughes & Miss L. Llewellyn) r8 w4 (4-timer in 2m5f-3m4f Hunt Chses) p2 (2nds, of 3 once, and inc Hunt Ch); pulled up 2. Transformed into an 11-10 rated Hunter Chaser in '02, and ended that campaign with a runaway success in the Intrum Justitia Cup, but picked up a tendon strain and missed '03, and remains very much on the suspect list after pulling up at Ludlow in March when favourite on his comeback. Suited by a sound surface. Regained blinkers on his return, and has been tried in a visor and cheekpieces. *I. Williams — Worcs.* 346 (3m1f110yH).

PRIME COURSE (IRE) ..10-2.. 16 b.g. Crash Course — Prime Mistress (Skymaster) upu5443. Big strong brother to Irish NH flat and Hurdles winner, Beglawella, and half-brother to Irish NH flat winner, Osmo, and Irish NH flat and Chasing winner, Kings Hill. NH FLAT r2 p0 (tailed off 2). NH '95, '97 and '00/1 r5 p0; pulled up 2, unseated 1. P-t-P/HUNT CH '96/03 r40 w10 (inc 5 Opens) p14 (8 2nds, dead heat once, of 3 twice, and last once; and 6 3rds, of 4 once, and remote last once, and inc Hunt Ch); last 2, pulled up 10, and fell/unseated 3. Failed to score for only the second time in nine Pointing campaigns in '04, and got Chris Gordon into hot water on the only occasion he showed anything like his best form at Folkestone. Stays well and is suited by a sound surface, but needs plenty of cajoling, and remains as clumsy as ever. Will need to be in a thoroughly co-operative mood to score again at 16. Has been tried in a visor. *E.J. Farrant — E. Sussex & Romney Marsh (Anne Farrant).* 537 (4mMO), 897 (Cfv&nr), 1053 (L), 1085 (Cv&nr), 1283 (L), 1407 (L), 1438 (3m2fH).

PRIMERO (IRE) ..9-0.. 11 b.g. Lycius (USA) — Pipitina (Bustino) 7p3p. Tall rangy hobdayed half-brother to Hurdles winner, Barcelona, and a German flat winner. Dam won 2 flat, 15-16f. FLAT r5 p0 (beat one). NH '97/9 and '01/2 r17 w2 (2m5f110y-3m2f110y Chses; awarded race once) p3 (3rds); pulled up 4, and fell/unseated 4. P-t-P '99/01 and '03 r19 w3 (Maiden, Restricted and Confined) p6 (inc 3 2nds); 4th thrice, last pair 2, pulled up 3, and fell 2. The winner of five races on sound surfaces, and often supported as though he still retains plenty of ability, but hampered by breathing difficulties from an early age, and remains a sketchy jumper. Soundly beaten in '04 and does not look likely to end a losing sequence dating back to '01. Wears a cross-noseband and a tongue-tie. Blinkered twice over hurdles, and once on the flat. *M.J. Gallagher & A.J. Hill — Tiverton (Jonathan Apps).* 963 (Cf), 1100 (O), 1331 (Cf), 1446 (Cf).

PRIMITIVE CHOICE ..—.. 7 b.m. Primitive Rising (USA) — Robins Choice (Scallywag) pfp. Dam, sister to Another Hooligan (*qv* '00 Annual), won Hunter Chase and 2 Points and placed 6 for Robin Tate (also failed to finish 16). Has looked none too knowledgeable in her races to date, and the jury is still out on the matter of her possessing any latent ability. *R. Tate — Hurworth (Pat Tate).* 773 (2m4fCMa), 958 (OMa), 1159 (OMa).

PRIMITIVE DELIGHT .—.. 7 b.m. Primitive Rising (USA) — Minty Muncher (Idiot's Delight) pp. Compact sturdy half-sister to Rakaposhi Raid, and to Chasing winner, Red Minster. Dam, half-sister to Gale On The Lake (*qv*). Bought Doncaster, May for 3800. Has pulled up when struggling badly in two attempts to date, and jumped poorly on her debut. *D.R. Mead — Weston & Banwell H. (Rose Vickery).* 326 (OMa), 474 (OMa).

PRIMITIVE RITES ..9-10.. 8 b.g. Primitive Rising (USA) — Sun Goddess (FR) (Deep Roots) p5. Small brother to God Of War and Noggler, and half-brother to Oban, and Personal Guarantee. Dam won 2 French flat. P-t-P '02/3 r5 w1 (Maiden) p1 (2nd); 4th, fell 1, and carried out 1. Won a slowly-run Maiden convincingly in softish at Charm Park last year, and beat a subsequent dual Chasing winner in the process, but restricted to three appearances since, and clearly proving difficult to train. Ultimately found things happening too quickly at Duncombe Park in '04, but one to keep on the right side of when another stamina test presents itself. Wears a cross-noseband. *M.J. Brown — York & Ainsty N.* 122 (3m1fH), 268 (R).

PRIMITIVE SATIN .10-1.. 10 ch.g. Primitive Rising (USA) — Satinanda (Leander) f33pp. Half-brother to Target Taken, With Respect and Satin Flash. Dam, half-sister to Washakie (*qv* '99 Annual), won at 5f, and was placed in 7 Points/Hunt Chses ('probably ungenuine and not worth trusting, and still a maiden over jumps despite 35 chances'). NH '01 r2 p0 (pulled up and unseated in Chses). P-t-P/HUNT CH '00/2 r10 w2 (inc 3m1f Hunt Ch) p4 (3 2nds, inc Hunt Ch); 4th, last pair 2, and pulled up 1. Stays well, and won strictly on merit when landing a Hexham Hunter Chase five starts after breaking his duck in '02, but not one to trust implicitly, and done no favours by having to spend '03 on the sidelines. Far from disgraced when making the frame twice this year, but ended his campaign on a low when appearing to go wrong at Kelso. Wears blinkers. *R. Tate — Hurworth (Pat Tate).* 679 (3m1fH), 956 (MO), 1179 (3m1fH), 1297 (3m1fH), 1444 (3m1fH).

PRIMITIVE SON ..9-8.. 8 b.g. Primitive Rising (USA) — Bramcote Centenary (Alleging USA) 2515p41. Compact half-brother to The Bedouin. NH FLAT '02 r1 p0. NH '02/3 (for N. Wilson) r4 p0. Bought Doncaster, Aug for 5500. Outclassed under Rules, but has found Pointing more appropriate, and inherited second at the last on his first attempt in that sphere. 6-4 favourite for a youngsters Maiden next time, but steadied by Paul Morris at the start and was always tailed off. Unsurprisingly he was not invited to ride again after this dreadful display, but Emma James took over with success, and steered him to victory in a Maiden at Brampton Bryan and his Members at Chaddesley Corbett. Can go a steady gallop, but recorded the second slowest time of the day in both wins, and has been found wanting in competitive contests. Good jumping and reliability may enable him to pick up a Restricted. *Ms W. Bayliss & Mrs S. Jordan — Albrighton Woodland (Wendy Bayliss).* 257 (CMa), 368 (OMa), 666 (OMa), 977 (R), 1256 (R), 1389 (R), 1527 (M).

PRIMITIVE WAY ..10-3.. 13 b.g. Primitive Rising (USA) — Potterway (Velvet Prince) 32562. Close-coupled owner-bred brother to The Dust Buster and Fell Gill, and half-brother to Keep A Secret. Dam, sister to 3 Pointers, won 3m3f Hunt Ch and 6 Points and placed 8 for the Atkinsons. NH '01/2 r14 w1 (3m1f Ch) p5. P-t-P/HUNT CH '97/8, '00/1 and '03 r20 w3 (Maiden, Restricted and Members) p2 (short head 2nd once); 4th, 5th twice, last pair 7, pulled up 2, and fell/unseated 3. Has scored just once in 30 starts since recording a hat-trick in minor races in '98, and very much in the doldrums last year, but ran some good races in defeat in '04, and earned £1,542. Is something of a professional loser now, and often compounds matters by making mistakes, and has been tried in all types of headgear now that a visor was introduced at Kelso. *Hon G. Maitland-Carew — College V. & N. Northumberland (Sandy Forster).* 330 (3mH), 546 (3mH), 798 (3m1fH), 992 (3m3f110yH), 1444 (3m1fH).

PRINCE DUNDEE (FR) .10-5§ .. 10 ch.g. Ecossais (FR) — Princesse Normande (FR) (Belgio FR) 123. Rangy. NH FLAT '99 r1 p1 (2nd). NH '99/02 (for late J. Neville) r26 w1 (2m2f Hdle) p7 (head 2nd once); pulled up 3, fell/unseated 3. Won a Folkestone Hurdle in heavy in December '00, despite not looking resolute under pressure, but beaten in his next 18 races including Selling Hurdles latterly, and was nine lengths fourth, pulled up, fell and unseated at the first twice in Chases. Regularly wore headgear and tongue-tied once, and had become very sour, so new connections did well to get him motivated for a Pointing win first time out in an Open at Garthorpe. His interest was probably already waning when he finished one-and-a-half lengths second in a Ladies in which he was level with the winner at the last (evens favourite), and then had no hope of beating Mouseski when 28½ lengths third over 2m at Cheltenham. Able, but will continue to be a major challenge if he returns. *Prince Dundee Partnership — M. Keighley — N. Cotswold (Martin Keighley).* 382 (O), 757 (L), 1173 (2m110yH).

PRINCE MOUSE ..8-6.. 8 ch.g. Carlingford Castle — Pushie Mouse (Push On) uf7f4. Dam, sister to Katy Country Mouse (*qv* '97 Annual). Left a novice on the floor after a mile in his first two attempts, but has since been ridden by Nick Kent, and finally produced a rateable effort when nine lengths fourth at Tabley. It was a bad late season Maiden, and would need to do substantially better still to score. *B.L. Watson — Grove & Rufford (Richard Phillips).* 58 (OMa), 106 (C), 890 (2m4fOMa), 1124 (OMa), 1424 (OMa).

PRINCE OF BEAL ..9-4.. 7 b.g. Le Moss — Aberaeron Girl (Neltino) 6. Compact half-brother to Pudding And Pie (*qv*). P-t-P '03 r4 p1 (2nd); pulled up 2, and fell 1. Had an '04 winner behind him when 20 lengths second at Ashorne on his only completion as a five-year-old, but beaten six lengths further on his reappearance, and got no further experience to improve upon matters. *J.L. & S.M. Atkins — V. of Aylesbury with Garth & S. Berks (Karen Lawther).* 53 (2m4fOMa).

PRINCESS DERRY ..9-7.. 11 b.m. Derrylin — Colonial Princess (Roscoe Blake) 8349p5p3. Smallish sister to County Derry (*qv*). NH FLAT '99 r1 p0. NH '99/00 r10 p2; 4th, last twice, pulled up and unseated in Chses — beaten 25l minimum. P-t-P '01/3 r15 w2 (Maiden and Club Mares) p7 (5 2nds, beaten short-head once, and fence once; inc 3rd of 4 once); 5th, 6th, last 2, and pulled up 2. A dual winner in '02, but a one-paced tail-swisher under normal conditions, and soundly beaten, including when acquiring headgear this year. Jumps securely but her 16-race drought only looks likely to be extended in future. *C.J. Cundall — Holderness (Mary Sowersby).* 161 (I), 372 (I), 592 (O), 772 (4m1fO), 1163 (Cf), 1216 (4m100yMO), 1397 (I), 1460 (I).

PRINCESS HATIE .8-0.. 6 b.m. Petoski — Culm Country (Town And Country) u6. Dam, sister to Fleet Mill (*qv* '03 Annual). NH FLAT '03 (for P.R. Hedger) r1 p0. Badly tailed off in a bumper and unseated at the fifth on her Pointing debut, but shaped with a faint degree of promise before a fading 31 lengths last. One of four in the race who failed to reappear, suggesting that the January ground at Black Forest Lodge had claimed another batch of victims. *B. Broomfield — E. Devon (Michael Sweetland).* 12 (OMa), 66 (OMa).

PRIORITISATION (IRE) ..9-0.. 6 b.g. Shernazar — No One Knows (IRE) (Kemal FR) 2p3. Good-bodied. Dam won 2 Points in Ireland (weak races, including a Farmers). 20,000 4yo. One-and-a-half lengths second of three behind a horse who failed to reappear when Ashley Farrant put up four pounds overweight in a Wadebridge Maiden (kept his rival up to his work), but tailed off and pulled up when 4-6 next time (part of the repelled raid on the Middleton) and ended with a last of three at 4-7. His enthusiasm is looking highly questionable at present, and hardly a bargain. *P.J. Finn — Middleton (David Pipe).* 485 (OMa), 775 (CfMa), 1009 (OMa).

PLATE 98 527 Tanatside Intermediate: Pristeen Spy (Richard Burton), 2nd, leads Step And Run (Jane Williams), 1st, and Rhythm King (Godfrey Maundrell), fell PHOTO: Brian Armstrong

PRISTEEN SPY ..10-3.. 8 b.g. Teenoso (USA) — Sikera Spy (Harvest Spirit) 121112. Lengthy attractive. Dam, half-sister to Seymour's Double (*qv* '01 Annual), won 2 2m Hdles and 10 Chses (2m4f-3m6f) for David Heys (who bred her); scored at least once in all of her 7 seasons. NH '03 r3 p0 (4th, 7th, and pulled up). P-t-P '02/3 r5 w1 (Maiden) p0; last, and pulled up 3. A headstrong front-runner, and has made the most of some simple opportunities in Points, but twice turned over at odds-on in '04, and found little off the bridle on both occasions. A fluent jumper, and suited by good or fast ground, but may need things his own way, and will find things harder if he has to step up in class again. Wears a cross-noseband. *D.W. Heys — N. Salop (Sheila Crow).* 375 (R), 527 (I), 713 (Cf), 928 (M), 1264 (Cf), 1426 (C).

PRIVATE PERCIVAL ..8-7.. 12 b.g. Arrasas (USA) — Romacina (Roman Warrior) fp4pp31. Tall half-brother to Romabit Tom. Dam, a non-stayer, only completed in 3 of 10 attempts over fences — was 2nd in a Maiden. FLAT '96 and '98 r8 p0. NH '96 r1 p0 (tailed off last). P-t-P '98 (for Mr J. Poulton) r2 p0 (6th of 7, and pulled up 1). NH '01/2 (for J. Poulton) r8 p1 (3rd in 2m1f Ch); pulled up 1. Goes missing on a regular basis, and absent in '97, '99/00, and '03, but has always shown plenty of speed, and although he had never finished within 12 lengths of the winner in any of his previous 25 starts had too much in the tank for two other finishers at Godstone. Had nothing in reserve, and

Barbed Broach was finishing to greater effect (!), and will need another miracle to follow up. *P. & Mrs L. Blagg & P. Hollis — Coakham Bloodhounds (Paul Blagg).* 103 (OMa), 423 (CMa), 611 (OMa), 644 (OMa), 1055 (OMa), 1211 (OMa), 1404 (OMa).

PRIVATE PETE .9-12.. 12 ch.g. Gunner B — Vedra (IRE) (Carlingford Castle) p4. Sturdy compact brother to Gunner Welburn, and half-brother to Wild Dream. IRISH P-t-P '00 r4 w2 (7yo&up Maiden, and Winners of One) p0; pulled up 2. P-t-P/HUNT CH '01/3 r10 w5 (inc 2m7f110y Hunt Ch, Mixed Open and Open) p3 (3rds, of 4 once); 7th, and pulled up 1. A useful performer on easy surfaces, and up to '04 had only been beaten once in Points, but only averages three outings per annum, and never had his ground this season. Never travelling on firmish at Tweseldown, and disappeared after finishing 22 lengths fourth at Garthorpe, and has it all to do should he resume at 12. Tends to get away with a lot of sketchy jumps. *Sir Michael Connell — Grafton (Anne Connell).* 170 (O), 382 (O).

PROBY LADY (IRE) ..9-10.. 10 br.m. Insan (USA) — Katie Dick (IRE) (Roselier FR) 3166. Compact. IRISH NH FLAT '99/01 r8 p1 (2nd). IRISH NH '00/1 r4 p0. P-t-P '03 r8 w1 (3-finisher Maiden) p3 (2 2nds, of 3 once; and 3rd of 4); 4th, last, ran out 1, and fell 1. A safe ride for the owner, and has won twice on good or sound surfaces, but the first was a three-finisher affair, and was fortunate that the favourite forfeited more ground than she was beaten in the Restricted. Already exposed as far too pedestrian for Ladies races, and future options will need to be chosen carefully if she is to score again. *Hon Miss D. Harding & Miss A. Findlay — Portman (Sally Alner).* 232 (R), 459 (R), 635 (L), 822 (L).

PROCEDURE (USA) .— §§.. 9 br.g. Strolling Along (USA) — Bold Courtesan (USA) (Bold Bidder) pppp. Workmanlike half-brother to 4 flat winners, including Diesan (subsequent success in Germany), Crown Court and a winner in USA. 40,000f. FLAT '98/9 and '01 r10 w2 (10-12f) p2 (3rds). NH '01/3 (for J.A.B. Old) r8 p2 (inc 3rd in Ch); pulled up 2. Completed a double on firmish on the flat in May/June '99 when trained by Sir Michael Stoute, but has always been a bitter disappointment over jumps, and two Chasing efforts resulted in a 42 lengths third and a pulled up. Looked very reluctant on his Pointing debut and continued in similar vein including when a loony punt from 12s to sixes and when again 6-1 after 33s had been available very early. One to shun. *G. Kivell — Eggesford (Keith Cumings).* 196 (O), 310 (O), 497 (Cf), 1540 (Cf).

PROCOL'S BOY ..9-8.. 10 b.g. Meadowbrook — Brown Bee III (Marcus Superbus) 4p72p. Workmanlike brother to Brook Bee (*qv*). P-t-P '00 and '02/3 r9 w1 (Members) p1 (3rd); 5th, last pair 2, and pulled up 4. Won a joke race in which the entire field took the wrong course at Dalton Park last year, but surrendered an eight-length lead over the third last when beaten half-a-length at Mordon in '04, and otherwise beaten a minimum of 19 lengths. Modest in the extreme, and looks too slow to follow up under normal conditions. *P.M. Hodges — Holderness (Tony Walker).* 499 (M), 591 (CR), 955 (R), 1416 (R), 1456 (R).

PROLOGUE (IRE) ..9-5.. 14 b.g. Mandalus — Advance Notice (Le Bavard FR) p35f. Tall brother to Auchendolly (IRE), and half-brother to Irish Hurdles winner, Anvil Lord (IRE). IRISH P-t-P '96 r1 p0 (pulled up). IRISH NH FLAT '96 r1 p0. IRISH NH '96/7 r4 p0. NH '02 r2 p1 (3rd); and 5th. NEWMARKET TOWN PLATE '02 r1 p0 (7th of 18). P-t-P '98/00 and '02 (for Mr R. Greenway) r21 w2 (Maiden and Club) p9 (4 2nds, of 3 twice; and 5 3rds, last once); pulled up 2, fell 3, ran out 1. A big slow boat and pounds along laboriously, and not better than last over jumps in the new yard. Ended his and the owner's season when crashing at the first at Horseheath. Visored once in '99. *C. Jarvis — Suffolk (Caroline Fryer).* 38 (Cf), 224 (CMod), 248 (Cf), 372 (I).

PROMINENT ..9-13§.. 11 b.g. Primo Dominie — Mary Bankes (USA) (Northern Baby CAN) p13p. Good-topped lengthy half-brother to flat winner, Mild Rebuke. FLAT r10 p1 (3rd). NH '00/2 r10 p2 (3rds); pulled up 2, and fell 1. P-t-P/HUNT CH '99/00 and '03 (for Lord Daresbury) r15 w6 (inc 2 Mixed Opens, inc 4m1f, and Open, inc hat-trick '00) p2 (3rd in Hunt Ch once); last 2, pulled up 3, refused 1, and unseated 1. Rated 10-12 when unbeaten in Points as a six-year-old, and numbered the Grimthorpe amongst his successes, but a grave disappointment under Rules, and was recording his first success since when making all at Tabley. Stays remarkably well considering his pedigree, but can be very moody, and apt to act the goat at the start, and subsequently twice a beaten favourite. Capable of running 8lb above his current mark but cannot be trusted. Blinkered once in '03. Wears a cross-noseband. *G.W. Briscoe & Mr & Mrs R.J. Hankey — Cheshire (Gary Hanmer).* 616 (C), 750 (O), 988 (O), 1427 (O).

PROPER PRIMITIVE ..9-10.. 12 gr.m. Primitive Rising (USA) — Nidd Bridges (Grey Ghost) 53p. Small well-made. Dam is half-sister to Divet Hill (*qv* '04 Annual). NH FLAT '97 r2 p0. NH '97/02 r36 w4 (2m1f-2m4f Chses) p5. P-t-P '03 r4 w1 (Ladies) p2; and pulled up 1. Made the most of a simple task when scoring at 4-7 in a weak Ladies on firmish at Upper Sapey last year, but struggles to get the trip in more competitive races, and does not stand her racing well any more. Wears bandages in front. *Miss W.M. Bayliss — Albrighton Woodland.* 1019 (Cm), 1229 (L), 1372 (2m4fH).

PROVINCE ..10-1.. 12 b.g. Dominion — Shih Ching (USA) (Secreto USA) 321128. Strong topped half-brother to Hurdles winner, Katie Oliver, and to a German flat winner. FLAT r2 w1 (8f) p1 (3rd). NH '96/01 r30 w4 (2m1f-2m5f Hdles) p10 (inc 2nd in Ch); last in other Ch, and ran in 10 Hdles since. P-t-P '01/3 r10 w1 (Open) p8 (3 2nds, beaten ½l once, of 3 once; and 5 3rds, of 4 twice, and last thrice); and pulled up. Game and consistent and displayed plenty of stamina in his first two Pointing wins at Great Trethew, and found the four-mile trip no barrier to success at Flete Park. Handles mud and firmish, but only effective in minor company, and benefits from the presence of Leslie Jefford in the saddle. Has done well to return from a fractured sesamoid in '03. Often wore headgear in previous yards. *Mr & Mrs T. Winzer — Silverton (Gordon Chambers).* 200 (Cf), 497 (Cf), 703 (MO), 1003 (4mO), 1175 (3m1f110yH), 1293 (2m7f110yH).

PUDDING AND PIE ..8-10.. 10 b.m. Henbit (USA) — Aberaeron Girl (Neltino) pp2. Good-topped lengthy half-sister to Aaron's Venture, Annascanan and Prince Of Beal (*qv*). Dam, half-sister to Knockaun Wood (IRE) (*qv*). A competent jumper, and left to claim 20 lengths second in a Mares Maiden at Clifton-on-Dunsmore after two who had been well ahead of her departed in the home straight. About as quick as her name suggests she would be. *R. Chandler — Belvoir (Tim Tarratt).* 788 (CfMa), 946 (OMa), 1119 (CMam).

PULHAM DOWNE .9-12.. 10 ch.g. Baron Blakeney — Dame Nellie (Dominion) p13p24p. Compact good-topped brother to Baron's Belle (IRE), and half-brother to Hurdles winners, Con Tricks and St John's Hill, and to Jersey Hdles winner, Anotherone To Note. Dam won at 7f. P-t-P '00/3 r14 w1 (Maiden) p3 (2 3rds, remote last once; also disqualified from 2nd once — not weigh-in); 7th, last, pulled up 5, fell/unseated 2. Much improved when beating 15 others in softish at Cothelstone in '02, and added a three-finisher Restricted on firm at Badbury Rings this year, but generally a weak finisher, and will prove difficult to place in future. Certainly wasting his time in sub-3m Hunter Chases. Wears a cross-noseband. *Stan The Man's Gang (N. Freak) — Portman (Ali Tory).* 118 (R), 265 (R), 365 (I), 799 (2m3f110yH), 936 (I), 1129 (I), 1437 (2m5f110yH).

PURE STEEL (IRE) ..10-1.. 11 b.g. Miner's Lamp — Mary Deen (Avocat) 24pp222. Compact tubed half-brother to Daddy Long Leggs, and to Chasing winner, Twinnings Grove (IRE). NH FLAT '99 r1 p0 (hampered and fell). NH '01 r2 p0 (4th, and pulled up Hdles). P-t-P '01 r2 p1 (3rd); and 6th of 7. NH '01/2 (for J.I.A. Charlton) r6 p3; fell/unseated 2. An unlucky individual who proved too clumsy under Rules, and has now gone in the wind, but came back into form when the ground dried up and made valiant attempts to make all at Hexham on his last three starts. Only failed by the minimum margin to hang on once, and thoroughly deserves a small success, and should achieve one on a less demanding track. Wore cheekpieces on his four May appearances. *M.H. Walton — College V. & N. Northumberland (Clive Storey).* 215 (OMa), 431 (R), 659 (OMa), 1178 (3m1fH), 1422 (OMa), 1475 (OMa), 1499 (2m4f110yH).

PUREVALUE (IRE) ..9-5.. 14 b/br.g. Kefaah (USA) — Blaze Of Light (Blakeney) 54p. Strong. NH FLAT '95 r2 p1 (3rd). NH '95/01 r36 w9 (4 2m-3m Hdles, and 5 2m110y-3m Chses) p9 (5 2nds); pulled up 6, unseated 3. P-t-P '02/3 (for Lord Daresbury) r5 p3 (2 2nds, beaten head once); and 6th twice. Suited by plenty of cut, but moody and inconsistent under Rules, and has stood few outings and proved far too cagey to score in Points. Jumped badly on ground that was patently too fast for him at Hornby Castle, and it would be surprising to see him in public again. Wears blinkers, and has been tried tongue-tied. *Mrs C.A. Coward — Middleton.* 338 (Cf), 477 (Cnr), 811 (L).

PURPLE JEAN ..10-0.. 10 gr.m. Perpendicular — Ask Jean (Ascertain USA) p72132. Rangy half-sister to Joe Smoke. Dam, sister or half-sister to 5 Pointers (including the dam of Dear Jean, (*qv* '99 Annual), won 5 Points and placed 7 (inc 2nd in Hunt Ch) for Mary Sowersby's late father, and grandam, Fort Jean, ran in 3 Points for him. NH FLAT '00 r1 p0 (tailed off). NH '01/2 r4 p0; pulled up 2. P-t-P '01 and '03 (for Mr M.E. Sowersby) r7 w1 (Maiden) p2 (2nds); 4th, 6th, and unseated 2. A thorough stayer and does best when able to help force the pace, but hampered by her lack of acceleration, and gave the impression that something may have gone amiss when turned over at 4-6 at Heslaker. Does not appear to have much scope for improvement. Ran tongue-tied once in '02. Wears a cross-noseband. *T.J. Stubbins — Holderness (Mary Sowersby).* 57 (R), 212 (R), 503 (R), 810 (R), 1204 (O), 1460 (I).

PURSLET ..9-0.. 14 b.m. Kinglet — Persue (Perhapsburg) 45. Small neat sister to Perking, and half-sister to Sunymanor, Perboy and Perjoy. Dam won Maiden and placed 8. Grandam, Astwood Susie, failed to finish in 8 Points, but great-grandam, Davy's Sweetheart, won 10 Points. P-t-P '98/00 and '02/3 r21 p8 (7 3rds, of 4 thrice, and last once); 7th, last pair 3, pulled up 8, and fell 1. A long-standing maiden whose history of leg trouble has restricted her activities, and carried too much condition when beaten upwards of 35 lengths in '04. Normally a weak finisher and prone to mistakes, and seems certain to retire to the paddocks unsuccessful. Can be a handful in the preliminaries, and is mounted outside the paddock and taken to post early. Wears a cross-noseband. *Miss N.J. Stallard — Cotswold V.F.* 68 (OMa), 174 (OMa).

PUSEY SANCE ..8-0.. 7 br.g. Puissance — Pusey Street (Native Bazaar) 5f. Compact half-brother to flat winners, Pusey Street Girl, Pusey Street Boy (also won Hurdle) and Windrush Girl, and to NH flat and jumping winner, Regal Holly. Dam won 8 flat, 5-6f. FLAT '01 r4 p0. NH '02 (for B.L. Lay) r2 p0 (pulled up 1, and unseated 1). Trounced on the flat and pulled up at the sixth and unseated at the second in Selling Hurdles, and having finished a remote and tired fifth in a 2m4f Maiden he fell at the eighth in late February and was not seen again. The prospect of his staying three miles seems negligible. *Miss S. Firmin — Bicester with Whaddon (Richard Webb).* 104 (2m4fOMa), 256 (CMa).

PUZZLEMAN ..10-1.. 12 ch.g. Henbit (USA) — Floreamus (Quayside) 232. Rangy well-made hobdayed half-brother to Run On Flo (IRE) and My Whisper (IRE). NH FLAT '98/9 r2 p0. NH '00/2 r12 p1 (2nd — 100-1). P-t-P '03 r4 w2 (Intermediate nov rdrs and Club 2 ran — finished alone) p0; 5th, and unseated 1. Disappointing under Rules, but made the most of two relatively straightforward opportunities last year, and achieved a higher rating though ultimately unsuccessful in '04. Goes a fair gallop but has little in the way of acceleration, and it is uncertain if he would have been able to overhaul Badger Beer had he not fallen two out (subsequently remounted) on his latest appearance. Blinkered once in '01. *S.C.T. Wheeler — Blackmore & Sparkford V.* 9 (C), 138 (C), 263 (O).

QUANGO ..10-0.. 13 b.g. Charmer — Quaranta (Hotfoot) 7. Workmanlike brother to Quarterstaff, and half-brother to 8 winners (2 abroad), including Quinlan Terry (Cambridgeshire), Quantity Surveyor and Quinzii Martin (all flat), to Irish flat and jumping winner, Quinze. Dam won at 5f. FLAT '95/6 r8 w2 (8-10f) p1 (2nd). NH '97/9 r26 w3 (2 2m1f Hdles and 2m110y Ch) p9 (5 2nds); pulled up 3. IRISH NH '99 r3 p0. P-t-P/HUNT CH '02/3 r12 w3 (inc Ladies) p4 (2 2nds, beaten head once); 4th, 5th twice, 6th, and unseated. Won five races to '98 for the late Jimmy Fitzgerald, and revived successfully in Points four years later, but has always had two ways of running, and is unpredictable. Struck into himself on his return at Duncombe Park, and will find it hard to resume successfully at 13. Suited by an easy three miles, but can handle all but extremes of going. Occasionally blinkered in the past, and wore cheekpieces in '04. *Yorkshire P-t-P Club (Miss J.E. Foster) — Middleton (Jo Foster).* 267 (Cf).

QUANTOCK'S RETURN ..—.. 7 ch.m. Zambrano — Quantock Superbrat (Owen Anthony) r. Strong compact owner-bred half-sister to Brenni's Firstbrat. Fat for a mid-May debut, and had evidently never seen a fence before, because she was barely able to scrape over the first three before wisely declining the fourth. Embarrassing to watch. *Mrs J.R. Langley — W. Somerset (Georgina Langley).* 1371 (OMa).

QUEENIES GIRL .8-11§.. 9 b.m. Primitive Rising (USA) — Riverboat Queen (Rapid River) pu22. Dam, half-sister to Lula Pattie (*qv* '96 Annual), won Hunter Chase and 4 Points (including a Ladies on disqualification) and placed 9. A poor and exhausted third when she clambered over two out and was immediately pulled up on her debut, and unseated after a mile next time, but went better when acquiring Phillip Kinsella at Mordon and was only headed by Bankersdraft near the line in a three-finisher Maiden. Favourite for a similarly bad contest next time, but after holding every chance at the last she was hanging and irresolute on the flat. It looks as if it will be hard to persuade her to score. *Mr & Mrs A.G. Frank — Hurworth (Paul Frank).* 775 (CfMa), 1291 (OMa), 1417 (OMa), 1458 (OMa).

QUEEN OF ARAGHTY .9-2.. 8 ch.m. Phardante (FR) — Queen's Darling (Le Moss) 2. Unfurnished sister to Hurdles winner, Amber Moss. Dam won NH Flat. NH FLAT '02 r3 p1 (3rd). NH '02 r2 p0. P-t-P '03 r3 p1 (last of 2); ran out, and pulled up. Shaped with promise when third in her middle bumper but a beaten favourite next time, and tailed off in both outings over hurdles. Runner-up in both completed Points, and achieved more in the latest when beaten 12 lengths at Musselburgh, but seems particularly fragile, and needs to improve further to open her account. *W. & Mrs P. Hodge — Jedforest (Willie Hodge).* 511 (OMam).

QUEENS HOUSE ..7-10.. 10 b.m. Arctic Lord — Courtlands Girl (Crimson Beau) upff3fpp4243p. Small unfurnished sister to Ball In The Net (*qv*). Dam won 3 Hdles at around 2m. NH FLAT '01 r1 p0 (16th). NH '01 r3 p0 (11th, and pulled up 2). P-t-P '01 r2 p0 (pulled up 2). Probably ran in more Maidens than any other horse in the land, and exposed herself to be inept at jumping, and only managed poor placings in the direst of contests. The amazing thing about her is that she was sent off joint-favourite once. *S. Lee — New Forest (Elsie Mitchell).* 237 (CfMa), 264 (CfMa), 354 (R), 474 (OMa), 580 (OMa), 865 (OMa), 1098 (OMa), 1251 (R), 1371 (OMa), 1450 (OMa), 1495 (OMa), 1559 (OMa), 1566 (OMa).

QUEEN'S SHILLING ..—.. 7 ch.m. Past Glories — Hasty Salvo (Hasty Word) ppp. Owner-bred sister to Battle Honours (*qv*). A cumbersome jumper who has only got as far as the 11th each time. She and her siblings contested ten Points in '04, and amidst nine non-completions Battle Honours miraculously found a winning opportunity. Future glories for the trio look highly improbable. *G.F. Wheeler — E. Sussex & Romney Marsh (Di Grissell).* 105 (2m4fOMa), 418 (2m4fCMa), 1211 (OMa).

QUEL REGAL (FR) ..9-0.. 7 b.g. Comte Du Bourg (FR) — Rigala (FR) (Roi Dagobert) fpbp3. Close-coupled. Dam won 11f race in France. NH '01/3 (for A.R. Dickin) r6 p1 (3rd); pulled up 2. Bought

Doncaster, Aug for 850. Has managed a couple of thirds, but only five ran in the Hurdle and there were three in the Ladies in which he sported first time cheekpieces and was beaten 27 lengths. The latter at least ended a run of six consecutive non-completions comprised of two Selling Hurdles and four Maidens, and has so far made too many blunders over fences. Does not look the sort who wants to be carrying 12 stone. *Mr & Mrs P.E. Clark — York & Ainsty S. (Liz Clark).* 303 (OMa), 393 (CfMa), 774 (2m4fCMa), 1159 (OMa), 1303 (L).

QUESTIONAIRE ..10-1.. 12 b.m. Northern State (USA) — Broken Melody (Busted) pf1411. Small sturdy half-sister to 3 flat winners (one in Denmark), including Bold Melody (also a successful Hurdler) and Fanfold. FLAT r2 p0. P-t-P/HUNT CH '98/00 and '02/3 (for late C.C. Morgan) r22 w4 (inc 3m Hunt Ch) p6 (3 2nds, of 3 once; inc 3rd of 4 once); 4th twice, 5th, last pair 3, fell/unseated 2, and pulled up 4. Only stands light campaigns and has never aspired to a rating higher than her current one, but well placed to win seven races on predominantly good or sound surfaces, and might have done better still but for a tendency to root the fences from time to time. Only worthy of consideration at the worst of the Welsh gaffes these days. Unseated and fell when tried a visor on two occasions. *D.O. Stephens — Curre & Llangibby.* 145 (O), 356 (M), 694 (M), 882 (C), 1023 (Cf), 1188 (Cf).

QUESTIONIT ..9-3.. 6 b.m. Sovereign Water (FR) — Query Line (High Line) p4u1. Half-sister to Quizzal (*qv*). Bought Doncaster, May for 2000. Won a youngsters Maiden which was considerably slowest of the nine races at Stafford Cross, and has been improving gradually with experience. If able to maintain the trend she could have a chance in Restricteds. *Miss L. Gardner — Silverton.* 600 (2m4fOMa), 702 (2m4fOMa), 796 (CfMa), 1134 (OMa).

QUETAL (IRE) .10-5.. 12 ch.g. Buckskin (FR) — Cantafleur (Cantab) pf32. Rangy half-brother to The Go Ahead (IRE), Copius Notes (IRE) and Atlantic Drift (IRE), and to Irish Pointing and jumping winner, Trench Hill Lass. IRISH P-t-P '98 r2 w1 (4&5yo Maiden) p0; and fell. NH '98/00 r7 p1 (2nd); pulled up 1, fell 2. P-t-P/HUNT CH '02/3 r7 w4 (inc 3 Hunt Chses, 3m-3m2f, inc hat-trick '02) p0; 13th, last, and pulled up 1. Bought cheaply by present connections after failing under Rules, but unbeaten and rated 11-4 in '02, and looked worthy of a crack at either Foxhunters the following year. Began '03 with a ready success but tailed off at Cheltenham, and moved like a cripple when pulled up on his final appearance. Lifeless again on his latest reappearance, and though he staged something of a revival when 10 lengths second to Sohapara his next entry was at Ascot Sales. *Miss K.J. Kitching — Eggesford (Laura Young).* 543 (3m2f110yH), 891 (3m1fH), 1175 (3m1f110yH), 1358 (3m1f110yH).

QUICK RESPONSE (IRE) ..9-12.. 12 gr.g. Roselier (FR) — Deceptive Response (Furry Glen) 52p5. Small sparely-made brother to Irish Pointing winner, Parabellum. IRISH P-t-P '99 r4 p0 (pulled up 4). P-t-P/HUNT CH '00/1 (for Mr M. Harris) r12 w2 (inc 2m5f Hunt Ch) p1 (2nd); pulled up 5, fell/unseated 3, and brought down 1. NH '01/2 (for M.W. Easterby, one run, and M.F. Harris) r7 p1 (2nd); pulled up 4. A consistently poor jumper in the previous yard, and suffered one disaster after another, but speedy enough to win a 2m5f Hunter Chase at Folkestone before embarking on a short and unsuccessful spell under Rules. Only beaten two lengths on his Pointing return, but can be very keen and went too fast in the early stages to get home next time, and disappointed subsequently. Suited by some cut in the ground, and a bare three miles. Wears a cross-noseband. *M.J. Roberts — E. Sussex & Romney Marsh.* 16 (C), 45 (Cnr), 607 (Cf), 998 (L).

QUICKSWOOD (IRE) ..10-4.. 12 b.g. Yashgan — Up To Trix (Over The River FR) 13221. Well-made half-brother to Irish Pointing and English Chasing winner, Justforgastrix (IRE), and to Chasing winner, Hill Trix. NH FLAT '97/8 r3 p0. NH '98/02 r37 w4 (2m5f-3m2f Hdles) p7 (4 2nds); pulled up 5, fell/unseated 2. P-t-P '03 (for The Double XXs Group) r7 w2 (Open and Confined) p4 (2nds, beaten ¾*l* once); and unseated 1. Unpredictable and frequently visored under Rules, and failed to get round in three starts over fences, but has become a very consistent Pointer, though punters have come to rely on him too often. Keeps the right company and might yet reach double figures. Suited by good or easy ground, and avoids anything faster. Blinkered once in '03. *G.C. Maundrell — Avon V. (Paul Thompson).* 16 (C), 117 (C), 190 (C), 360 (O), 718 (MO).

QUIZZAL ..9-8.. 7 b.m. Afzal — Query Line (High Line) p12. Compact half-sister to Questionit. Dam, half-sister to Broad Statement (*qv* '02 Annual). Grandam, Spartiquick, is half-sister to Hunter Chase and Pointing winner, Optomism, won Maiden and 2m4f Chase and placed total of 3, and great-grandam, Quick Answer, won Hunt Ch and 5 Opens. P-t-P '03 (for Lady Earle) r4 p3 (2nds; of 3 once, and last once); and unseated 1. Gained reward for her previous consistency when landing a seven-minute Maiden at Guilsborough, but the proximity of the placed horses, and the fact that another division was run in a time 14 seconds faster rather lets the form down. Runner-up in a three-finisher Restricted three weeks later, and had every chance at the last, but not for the first time finished tamely, and may prove just as frustrating to follow in future. *Miss E. Inman — Cottesmore (Tim Tarratt).* 476 (CfMa), 789 (CfMa), 1123 (R).

QUINN (U) .—.. 8 gr.g. unknown 2. It was all up in the air at the penultimate wall at Flagg where the leading pair landed level, but whilst the rider of the winner took the direct route to the last the befogged partner of Quinn went the long way with costly consequences (even more so if there had been any prize money on offer). *N.J. Fogg — High Peak.* 984 (3m4fNCM).

RACONTEUR (IRE) ..9-13.. 11 b.g. Top Of The World — Blackrath Gem (Bargello) pup244. Workmanlike half-brother to The Jeweller, and to NH flat and jumping winner, Connor Macleod (IRE). IRISH P-t-P '99 r3 w1 (Confined Maiden) p0; pulled up 1 and fell 1. IRISH NH FLAT '99 r1 p0. IRISH NH '99/01 r25 w1 (2m1f Maiden) p4. P-t-P/HUNT CH '03 (for Mrs Musgrave) r3 p2 (3rds, of 4 once); and pulled up. Of little account when owner-ridden (he just sits there until he falls off and then throws a tantrum) but David Greenway got a fair tune out of him twice, including at Eyton where he was backed from 12s to 5-1 and finished in front of a subsequent hat-trick scorer under Rules in a slowly-run Open. A non-winner since June '00, and does not seem to get the trip well enough in Points. Blinkered once in '00. *W. Puddifer Jnr — Cheshire Forest (Peter Morris).* 93 (O), 749 (Cf), 932 (Cf), 1262 (O), 1344 (C), 1426 (C).

RADBROOK HALL ..9-4.. 6 b.g. Teenoso (USA) — Sarah's Venture (Averof) 316. Workmanlike half-brother to Who Dares Wins (*qv*). NH FLAT '01 (for M.W. Easterby) r1 p0. Won a three-finisher youngsters Maiden at Didmarton to give the stylish Paul Callaghan his first Pointing success (he has also scored over Hurdles), but weakened rapidly in the final half-mile when beaten around 20 lengths in both other completions. Not a bad youngster, but broke a blood vessel when he scored, and it looks as if he may be doing so on a regular basis. *T.R. George — Cotswold.* 86 (OMa), 367 (OMa), 726 (R).

RAFFLES ROOSTER ..9-7§.. 13 ch.g. Galetto (FR) — Singapore Girl (FR) (Lyphard USA) p5u. Close-coupled half-brother to smart French flat winner, Gunboat Diplomacy (FR) (won £148,013) and several other winners in France. Dam won 3 French flat, 8-14f (was useful). Ff26,000y. FRENCH FLAT '95 r10 p5. FLAT '95/8 r21 w4 (11-12f) p9. NH '96/03 (for A.G. Newcombe, and Miss V. Williams, all wins) r30 w6 (2m3f-3m3f Chses) p13 (inc 4 Hdles); fell/unseated 2. Started life on the flat in France (blinkered once there) and has been on the go for ten years since, winning ten races including three on the all-weather and accumulating total prize money of £91,630 (the biggest individual prize was £10,845 in a Lady Amateurs event on the flat). Suited by plenty of give in the ground, and placed on 27 occasions, but error-prone and needs to do it all on the bridle, and has not deigned to score since December '01. Seen just once in '03, and did not take any interest in Hunter Chasing on his return. Amongst the numerous frustrations there have been plenty of good days, and deserves to be allowed to rest on his laurels. *M.A. Leatham — Middleton (Louise Revell).* 122 (3m1fH), 445 (3m110yH), 679 (3m1fH).

RAGGY JUMPER ..—.. 7 b.g. Primitive Rising (USA) — Chummy's Last (Palm Track) upbp. Strong. Dam, half-sister to dam of Primitive Choice (*qv*), was 3rd in 3 Maidens for Robin Tate (a hooligan who needed 9 attempts to even get round). Officially named after the famous raggy jumper which accompanied Robin Tate and Fiona Needham in so many races and which was at its most moth-eaten when it passed the post first in the Cheltenham Foxhunters, but from the way he has jumped so far the double meaning has been appropriate. Might get the knack eventually, but connections could be in for a very long wait. *R. Tate — Hurworth (Pat Tate).* 392 (CfMa), 774 (2m4fCMa), 960 (OMa), 1158 (OMa).

RAGING TORRENT ..9-13.. 10 b.g. Meadowbrook — Charons Daughter (Another River) 392235. Lengthy owner-bred half-brother to Morwick Mill and Offspringer. Dam, half-sister to Black Spur (*qv* '98 Annual), won 2m Mdn Ch and last of 3; and won Ladies and 2nd twice for the Howies ('very impetuous, but barely stays 3m'). P-t-P/HUNT CH '02/3 r13 w2 (Maiden and Restricted) p4 (2 2nds, of 3 once); 4th, pulled up 3, ran out 2, and fell 2. Competent in minor company and not as wayward as he once was, but needs plenty of driving, and never looked like increasing his winning tally in '04. Appears to handle all but very soft ground. Wears a cross-noseband. *S. Waugh & Mrs A. Howie — Morpeth (Simon Waugh).* 73 (Cf), 316 (2m5fH), 915 (Cf), 1178 (3m1fH), 1374 (3m1fH), 1499 (2m4f110yH).

RAG WEEK (IRE) ..10-3.. 8 b.g. Roselier (FR) — Lady Rag (Ragapan) 12f11. Small sturdy half-brother to Mill O'the Rags (IRE), and to jumping winner, Lord Strickland. IRISH NH FLAT '03 r1 p0. IRISH NH '03 (for A.J. Kennedy) r2 p0. Badly tailed off thrice in Ireland, but has progressed rapidly in the new yard, and gained three Pointing wins by an aggregate of 53 lengths (the one major surprise was that Bill Haze was able to beat him once, although his jumping was poor on that occasion). Suited by forcing tactics, and has proved very gutsy since being sent under Rules. Should continue to pay his way. The trainer's husband is making a name for himself in a remarkably short time as a professional. *Mrs C. Williams & Ms H. Oakes — Glamorgan (Cath Williams).* 845 (CfMa), 1094 (R), 1237 (R), 1322 (R), 1539 (I).

RAINBOW FRONTIER (IRE) ..—.. 11 b.g. Law Society (USA) — Tatchers Mate (Thatching) pp. Small compact. IRISH FLAT '96/7 r15 w3 (11-14f) p6 (hd 2nd once). IRISH NH '97 r5 w5 (2m Hdles).

FLAT '98/00 r4 p2 (2nds). NH '98/01 (for M.C. Pipe) r17 w2 (2m-2m1f Hdles) p4; fell 2. Formerly highly successful on good ground or in mud, and had a fantastic year in '97 when he won eight races. His career earnings stand at £124,440, 20% of which was accrued in the Swinton Hurdle at Haydock, and a similar amount shared between the Ascot Stakes (29 ran) and the Northumberland Plate (20 ran) even though he was only runner-up in both. Last scored in January '00, and tried in headgear twice including his only Chase in which he started at 1-4 but finished a distant last of two after being very wary of the fences and breaking a blood vessel. Beaten in 19 of his 20 most recent attempts, and only revived to give a girl beginner a couple of jaunts in Points (tailed off and pulled up in both, and tongue-tied in the latest). It was astonishing that he had achieved so much by the age of six, but paid the high price of burn out factor afterwards. *Miss J.M. Janes — Blackmore & Sparkford V.* 603 (Cnr), 882 (C).

RAINBOW RANCH (IRE) ..9-12.. 10 b.g. Mister Lord (USA) — Arianrhod (L'Homme Arme) 212p. Workmanlike rangy brother to What The Heck (IRE), and to Hurdles winners, Ariadler (IRE) and Lord Pat (IRE). P-t-P '01/2 r4 w1 (2m4f Maiden) p2 (2nd of 3 once); and pulled up. Got off to the best possible start and has not missed the frame in five completions since, but restricted in opportunities by leg and wind trouble, and has not made the anticipated progress. Thrice a beaten favourite in '02 but punters seem to have got his number now, and only market leader when recording his second success at Charing this year. Avoids ground any softer than good and might find another minor event if connections keep him on the payroll. *S.P. Tindall — Kent & Surrey Bloodhounds (Jenny Gordon).* 181 (R), 419 (CR), 806 (C), 1410 (Cf).

RAINBOW STAR (FR) ..—§§.. 11 b/br.g. Saumarez — In The Star (FR) (In Fijar USA) prp. Compact half-brother to several winners in France. Dam won 10f race in France. FRENCH FLAT '97 r4 p1 (3rd). FRENCH NH '97 r4 p2 (Hdle and Ch). FLAT '00 and '02 r2 p0. NH '98/02 r25 w5 (2m110y-2m3f110y Hdles) p4. P-t-P '03 (for Mr K.R. Ford) r4 p0 (pulled up 3, and refused). Persuaded to win five Hurdle races by Martin Pipe, but an abject disaster since, and will not consent to co-operate at all now. Failed to complete for the eighth time in succession at Llanfrynach, and as usual gave the field a huge head-start, and it would be a miracle were anyone to bother to race him again. Has been tried in all types of headgear. *P.B. Miles — Ystrad Taf Fechan (Myfanwy Miles).* 208 (Cf), 317 (2m4fH), 447 (Cf).

RAIN DELAY ..10-0.. 10 b.g. Henbit (USA) — Miss Nero (Crozier) 5312. Compact half-brother to NH flat winner, Latin Mistress. Dam won 2 Irish NH flat; and won 8 Hdles (2m1f-3m1f) and placed twice in Waterford Crystal Stayers Hdle at Cheltenham. IRISH NH '00 r3 p0. P-t-P '01/3 r9 w2 (Maiden and Restricted) p4 (3 2nds; and remote last of 3); 6th, last, and pulled up. Takes a keen hold and races prominently, and has delivered the goods thrice in three-finisher events, and finished a highly respectable second to Father Tom at Cold Harbour, but does not stand many races, and never looks entirely straightforward. Should find another opportunity in '05. Has two paddock handlers. *K.B. Rogers — N. Hereford (Ray Rogers).* 365 (I), 663 (I), 867 (I), 1227 (Cf).

RAINHA .10-1.. 8 b.m. Alflora (IRE) — Political Prospect (Politico USA) 11. Owner-bred half-sister to Polly Cinders and Sunset Flash. NH FLAT '02 r2 p1 (3rd). P-t-P '03 r4 p2; 10th of 11, and fell. Thrice a beaten favourite in '03, but did not let backers down on her reappearance, and won in a common canter after the clear leader had fallen four out. Appeared to have won outright on her first start in Restricteds at Alnwick, but the Judge could not split her and Peppernick in a head-bobbing finish. Clearly going the right way now, but has suffered a setback and will miss '05. *J.D. Goodfellow — Border (David Parker).* 659 (OMa), 855 (R).

RAINTON ..9-13.. 9 gr.g. Kasakov — Strathleven (My Swanee) 444. Tall half-brother to Jasleven. Dam is half-sister 4 Pointers, including Holborn Head (*qv* '88 Season Annual), was placed in 5 Points (Tynedale qualified latterly; 'exceptionally unwilling to go about her business'). NH FLAT '00 r1 p0. NH '00/1 r10 p1 (3rd); pulled up 2, unseated 1. P-t-P/HUNT CH '02/3 r8 w2 (2m4f Maiden and Restricted) p3 (3rds, of 4 once); 4th, 7th, and unseated. A highly volatile character, and is taken to post early, and normally charges off in front at high speed, but has been unable to get away with such headstrong behaviour since recording a double in '02. A family concern and Nicola Stirling is top class on others in the yard, but it might pay to persuade a strong male rider to try to anchor him. Wears a cross-noseband. *Mrs P.C. Stirling — Lauderdale (Nicola Stirling).* 427 (I), 655 (L), 1037 (I).

RAISEAPEARL ..9-11.. 10 b/br.g. Pocketed (USA) — Little Anthem (True Song) fp63631145. Tall rangy brother to Pocket Oscar. Dam 'can be a proper madam' (half-sister to 3 Pointers, including General Rule, *qv* '93 Annual), won 2 appalling Points for Christine Forber and placed 10 (including 2 NH flat races and a Hdle). Grandam, Bright Daisy, won 4 Points (inc dead-heat) and placed 7. Sire comes from a very good family, but his 3 wins in 2m Hdles for John Jenkins included a Seller. P-t-P '02 (for Mrs C.T. Forber) r1 p0 (ran out). Bought at Beeston Market for next to nothing, and a hard-pulling lunatic in his early ventures, but eventually learnt to relax under Ian Clyde, and got the trip better than usual when providing him with his first winner over jumps at Sandon (had partnered an Arab winner at Bangor in '03). Promptly turned over the 2-5 favourite in a match for his Members taking over eight minutes, but was outclassed, though not disgraced in Hunter Chases. Inclined to make the odd mistake, but looks a certainty for an average Restricted next year. *A. Williams — Cheshire (Patrick Thompson).* 96 (CfMa), 227 (CfMa), 405 (Inr), 532 (OMa), 709 (Mah), 749 (Cf), 848 (OMa), 1043 (M), 1176 (3m110yH), 1375 (3m110yH).

RAKAPOSHI RAID ..9-5.. 9 b.m. Rakaposhi King — Minty Muncher (Idiot's Delight) p2. Small unfurnished half-sister to Primitive Delight and Chasing winner, Red Minster. Dam, half-sister to Gale On The Lake (*qv*). NH '01/2 (for N.B. Mason) r12 p2. Sold Doncaster, Sept '02 for 1200. Beaten around six lengths when placed twice in Selling Hurdles at around 2m4f, but subsequently ran in six better races under Rules and could make little impact including when 38 lengths last in a Chase. Blinkered once and tongue-tied on her final outing to '02. Finished three lengths second to a matron in an elders Maiden at Welbeck, but not seen again, and it looks as if wonky legs have been causing her problems for a long time. *Mr & Mrs S.W. Gray — Atherstone (Paul Newton).* 466 (Cf), 594 (OMa).

RAMIREZ (IRE) ..10-3.. 7 ch.g. Royal Abjar (USA) — Flooding (USA) (Irish River FR) 1213. Strong-topped half-brother to flat winners, Lough Swilly and Water Baby, and to 4 winners abroad (including in Spain). 5200 3yo. NH FLAT '03 (for M. Pitman) r3 p1 (2nd). Bought Doncaster, Oct for 9500. Beaten a neck on his bumper debut before becoming disappointing, but showed a revival of interest when winning a Club Members at Market Rasen (very easily) and a modest Open at Welbeck (just held on by a head) as well as finishing three-quarters-of-a-length second in a Confined. Remains unpredictable as he showed when favourite and 23 lengths last of three on his latest outing, when he was not fluent and never looked happy. Not one to lump on at short prices, but has proved good value at 7-1 and 6-1, and could again be of interest at those sort of odds. *C.J.M. Cottingham — Brocklesby (Nick Kent).* 54 (C), 478 (Cf), 592 (O), 943 (MO).

RAMON ALLONES (IRE) ..8-9.. 7 br.g. Good Thyne (USA) — Cuban Vacation (Ovac ITY) fup94p4. 3762 3yo. NH '03 (for Mrs R.L. Elliot) r1 p0 (last). An ex-eventer who has managed two fourths, when beaten between ten lengths and 25 lengths in 2m4f Maidens. Jumping better after a disastrous start, but goes to post early now, and looks rather a hot ride. Still has some way to go if he is to reach winning standard. *D. Davidson — W. Percy (Morag Neill & Peter Elliot).* 69 (M), 137 (OMa), 215 (OMa), 768 (2m4fOMa), 856 (2m4fOMa), 1081 (OMa), 1474 (2m4fOMa).

RANDOM TRIX ..8-0.. 7 b.m. Past Glories — Random Miss (Random Shot) 52p7. Small unfurnished. Dam, half-sister to Dromin Leader (*qv* '00 Annual) was placed 3 in Points. P-t-P '03 r3 p1 (5 fences last of 3); last, and pulled up. Only once better than last in seven attempts, and often makes tortured progress towards a completion, and usually makes errors along the way. Finally given the go ahead to get competitive at Cothelstone, but had shot her bolt by halfway, and looks uesless. *B. Robinson - Quantock (Sarah Robinson).* 121 (OMa), 475 (OMa), 693 (OMa), 884 (OMa).

RAREGEM ..9-12.. 7 b.g. Syrtos — Ruby's Vision (Balinger) 112. Good-topped brother to small sturdy Brockbuster (*qv*). Made the perfect start when completing a double in a Maiden in soft at Kilworthy (drew clear from the last) and a Restricted on the adjacent course at Cherrybrook (again had plenty in hand), but suffered a shock defeat when 2-9 in a four-runner Intermediate in which he lacked fluency early and produced nothing when asked to challenge before two out. Was shaping up nicely, and provided this was only a temporary lapse he could be in for a decent season in '05. Possibly needs give in the ground to be seen at his best. *J. & Mrs S. Alford — N. Cornwall (Mike Biddick).* 568 (CfMa), 791 (R), 1195 (I).

RASH MOMENT (FR) .8-7.. 6 b.g. Rudimentary (USA) — Ashura (FR) (No Pass No Sale) f465. Small attractive half-brother to flat winner, Maranta (in France), and successful Hurdler Lady Amanda (in France). Capable of showing reasonable speed, but was 14 lengths fourth and tired over 2m4f and a remote last when tried over the full distance twice, and simply does not get the trip. Will have to concentrate on the shorter options if he is to have any chance, if connections decide to persevere in the hope that his stamina increases. *W.J. Tolhurst — Essex & Suffolk.* 7 (2m4fOMa), 104 (2m4fOMa), 652 (OMa), 1155 (OMa).

RATHBARRY LAD (IRE) ..9-10.. 8 b.g. Phardante (FR) — Doolin Lake (IRE) (Salluceva) p473. Compact well-made. Dam is half-sister to Granville Grill (*qv*). P-t-P '02 r4 w1 (Maiden) p1 (3rd); pulled up, and fell. Ran out a 20-length winner at Guilsborough on only his second appearance, but has obviously had problems since, and missed '03. Remains prone to wholesale blunders, but heavily supported on his last two appearances, and finished strongly under a powerful drive from Stuart Morris in the latest after taking an age to get into top gear. Might be more effective with some give in the ground. *Mrs J. Wilson — Pytchley (Bill Warner).* 383 (R), 889 (CR), 1396 (C), 1503 (R).

RATHBAWN PRINCE (IRE) ..10-11.. 13 ch.g. All Haste (USA) — Ellis Town (Camden Town) 22. Tall strong half-brother to Optimism Reigns (IRE). IRISH NH FLAT '96/8 r8 w3 p0. IRISH FLAT '98/02 r19 w2 (16f) p8 (hd 2nd twice). IRISH NH '98/03 (for D.T. Hughes) r37 w5 (2 2m-2m2f and 3 2m2f-2m6f Chses) p9 (inc 3rd in '03 Kim Muir 2nd in '01 Irish Grand National); pulled up 5, fell/

unseated 4. Formerly a smart performer in Ireland and gained ten wins on good or easy surfaces to November '00, and ran at four Cheltenham Festivals finishing fourth in the '00 Arkle (a year in which he won four races) and third in the '03 Kim Muir. His career earnings total £112,814, and the biggest contribution was actually from a second placing, when beaten by Davids Lad in the '01 Irish Grand National (earning £20,332). Blinkered once and wore cheekpieces on his final appearance of '03, and tended to look less keen than in his hey-day, but gave good displays in both Hunter Chases and was promoted to second behind Philson Run at Wincanton where his jumping was a little sketchy, and then had no answer to the storming turn of foot of Right To Reply at Newbury. A fine servant to previous connections, but looks to be getting near the end of the line now. *Miss S.L. Samworth — R.A. (Henrietta Knight).* 178 (3m1f110yH), 348 (3mH).

RATHGIBBON (IRE) ..9-9§.. 14 b.g. Phardante (FR) — Harp Song (Auction Ring USA) pppp2225. Strong half-brother to a flat winner, and to Irish NH flat winner, Rathure (IRE). Dam won 5f Sell at 2. IRISH NH FLAT '95/6 r5 w1 p0. IRISH NH '96/9 r43 w5 (3 2m4f Hdles and 2 Chses, 2m-2m3f) p9. CELEBRITY FLAT '99 r1 p0. NH '99/01 r21 w2 (2m4f Chases) p7 (4 2nds); pulled up 1, unseated 1. P-t-P/HUNT CH '02/3 r16 p3 (2 3rds, remote of 3, and last); 4th, last pair 3, pulled up 8, and fell. Scored four times in Ireland to '96, and twice at Plumpton since, but without a win for three years, and only beat three rivals when staging a mini renaissance in '04. Prone to slovenly jumping though rarely fails to complete because of it, but his enthusiasm has long since been compromised, and has regularly worn headgear. Has run tongue-tied. *Mrs M.B. Stephens — Llandeilo F.* 208 (Cf), 360 (O), 447 (Cf), 672 (O), 1023 (Cf), 1188 (Cf), 1521 (Cnr), 1549 (O).

RATHNALLY PARK ..9-13.. 8 b.g. Henbit (USA) — Pollerton's Pride (Pollerton) 3p. Rangy. Dam won 2 Hurdles, 2m-2m7f. IRISH P-t-P '02 r3 p1 (2nd); pulled up 2. IRISH NH '03 (for A.J. Martin) r3 w1 (2m Hdle) p0. A strong puller who finished three-and-a-half lengths third when carrying a penalty in a Dunston Confined, but tired rapidly in the closing stages and was tailed off when pulled up at the last in an Open in early February. Had a setback, and not seen again. It may be significant that the best display of his career was over the minimum trip, when he won a Wexford Hurdle on firmish. *Mrs G. Clements & D.J. Harding-Jones — Puckeridge (Perry Harding-Jones).* 38 (Cf), 156 (O).

RAVENSCAR ..9-10.. 7 b.g. Thethingaboutitis (USA) — Outcrop (Oats) 2333p31. Small compact. Dam won youngsters Maiden (looked lucky — left clear at last), but jumped diabolically and fell/unseated 4 times consecutively in her final season ('it would be an outrage if connections ran her again'). Grandam, Night Out III, half-sister to 7 Pointers, was 3rd in Hdle, but was on the floor in 3 of 4 Points. P-t-P '03 r4 p0 (pulled up 3, and ran out). Would have won an unplaced Maiden at Charm Park last year had he not galloped straight on when six lengths clear on the home turn, but has taken an awful long time to atone, and a beaten favourite twice before he landed a three-finisher event at Witton Castle. Can finish strongly but does nothing very quickly, and looks to need a long trip in soft ground. Has been sold out of the yard. *Mrs P.A. Russell — Middleton.* 165 (OMa), 272 (OMa), 393 (CfMa), 476 (CfMa), 775 (CfMa), 958 (OMa), 1291 (OMa).

RAVENSWORTH ..9-6.. 9 b.g. Sea Raven (IRE) — Dreamago (Sir Mago) p4. Robust half-brother to Go Nomadic (*qv*). P-t-P '02/3 (for Mr P.J. Millington) r13 w1 (Maiden) p5 (4 2nds; and 3rd of 4); 4th, 6th, last 2, pulled up, and fell 2. Followed a string of placed efforts with a deserved success on firmish at High Easter last year, but has quickly developed serious wind problems, and ran tubed when eventually placed fourth at Thorpe Lodge. Forced to pull up when tongue-tied previously so the op has worked to some degree, but he looks a long shot to upgrade successfully. *Miss M. Samworth — Cottesmore.* 481 (R), 944 (R).

RAYMOND JAMES .9-8§§.. 8 b.g. Regal Embers (IRE) — Sallisses (Pamroy) pp3p34. Compact well-made owner-bred brother to Golden Embers, and half-brother to Rusty Fellow, Maggies Brother and Sallioko. Dam won a Point and a 3m1f Hunt Ch and placed total of 7 for late Ray Shail. P-t-P '02/3 r8 w1 (Maiden) p1 (2nd of 3); last 2, pulled up 3, and brought down. Stereotypical of his family's traits, and won his Maiden once he had worked things out for himself, but will not do a tap without much bullying now, and is thoroughly inconsistent. Would waltz a Restricted on either of his thirds at Woodford and Bredwardine, but never went a yard when cheekpieces were applied once, and in his current mood has to be shunned. *Mrs G.M. Shail — Ledbury (Roy Shail).* 726 (R), 977 (R), 1069 (R), 1230 (R), 1388 (R), 1531 (R).

REAL VALUE (IRE) ..9-12.. 14 b.g. Matching Pair — Silent Verb (Proverb) fp3213. Sparely-made. Dam won 56&7yo mares Maiden in Ireland. IRISH P-t-P '97 r2 p0 (pulled up 2). NH '00/1 r6 w1 (3m110y Ch) p1 (3rd); fell 1. P-t-P/HUNT CH '98/00 and '02/3 r30 w13 (inc 2 Hunt Chses 2m7f110y-3m and 3 Opens, and inc hat-trick '00) p6 (5 2nds, inc 4 Hunt Chses; and inc 3rd of 4 in Hunt Ch); 9th, last, fell 6, and pulled up 3. Top class in his hey-day, and unbeaten in his first 11 completions, and only the ill-fated Cavalero took his measure in '00, but has been on a steady downward spiral since and will surely not be asked to trudge round the likes of Detling and Aldington at 14. *Cockerell Cowing Racing (A. Cowing) — E. Sussex & Romney Marsh (Di Grissell).* 3 (O), 239 (3m1fH), 535 (CfO), 780 (O), 898 (O), 1284 (O).

REBEL YELL (IRE) .—.. 14 b.m. Noalto — Domestic Goddess (Roselier FR) pp. Very small compact. P-t-P/HUNT CH '96/9 and '01/2 (for Mr N. Jones & Mr A.J. Morris) r27 w1 (Members 3 ran — finished alone) p2 (2nds, remote once); pulled up 19. Left to come home alone in her Members in '02, but the height of ineptitude in most of her other 28 starts, and has pulled up no fewer than 21 times. Missed '03 and quickly remote before calling it a day soon after halfway in '04. Blinkered once in '02. *Miss A.J. Morris — Ystrad Taf Fechan.* 357 (R), 695 (R).

RECTORY GARDEN (IRE) ..9-10.. 16 b.g. The Parson — Peace Run (Deep Run) 4f. Rangy half-brother to Brave Edwin (IRE), and to Hurdles winner, Highland Way (IRE). NH FLAT '93 r1 p0. NH '94/9 r29 w8 (2m Hdle, and 7 2m5f-3m2f Chses) p15. P-t-P/HUNT CH '00/3 (for Mr T.W. Biddlecombe) r20 w8 (inc 4 Opens, and 3 Mixed Opens, inc hat-trick) p8 (6 2nds, beaten neck once, last once, and inc Hunt Ch); last, 11th, and unseated 1. A splendid servant who has proved equally as successful in Points as he was under Rules, but has been winding his operation down in recent years, and looks to have bowed out following the first fall of his career. *Miss G. Emtage — N. Cotswold (Robert Biddlecombe).* 583 (Cf), 727 (MO).

RED BROOK LAD ..10-10.. 10 ch.g. Nomadic Way (USA) — Silently Yours (USA) (Silent Screen USA) 241p7p. Compact half-brother to flat winner, Tommy Tempest. Dam won 5f Sell. FLAT r9 w1 (16f, equitrack) p0. NH '98/9 r7 p1 (3rd). P-t-P/HUNT CH '01/3 r14 w7 (2 2m5f-3m1f110y Hunt Chses, 2 Opens, Mixed Open and 2 Ladies) p4 (2 2nds, remote of 3 once, and inc Hunt Ch; and 2 3rds); and fell/unseated 3. A very poor performer under Rules, and fractured an ulna on only his second start over fences, but has since recorded eight wins, including three Hunter Chases, and is particularly effective at trips short of three miles. Overcame his customary jumping errors when storming clear up the hill at Sandown, and is ideally dropped out in the rear and ridden for a turn of foot, but appears to have left his engine behind at Cheltenham for the time being. Should be able to atone after a break, and an 11st performer at his peak. Suited by ground close to good. Blinkered twice over hurdles. *C. St V. Fox — Cattistock.* 11 (O), 89 (O), 241 (2m4f110yH), 543 (3m2f110yH), 799 (2m3f110yH), 1166 (2m5f110yH).

RED CHANNEL (IRE) ..7-13.. 15 b.g. Import — Winscarlet North (Garland Knight) ppRp6. Smallish unfurnished half-brother to Irish Chasing winner, Lotto Lolly, to Hurdles winner, Gypsy (IRE), and to a jumping winner in Belgium. FLAT r2 p0. NH '95/6 r8 p0 (inc pulled up 3 in Hdles; 4th, and 6th in Chses, not jump well once, and inc Sell). P-t-P/HUNT CH '97/03 (for Mr A. Hickman, Miss S. Parker & Mr D. Peile) r23 w3 (2m4f Maiden, Restricted and Intermediate) p4 (3 3rds, last twice); 4th, last pair 2, pulled up 11, and fell/unseated 2. Made most to win three poor races on sound surfaces to '98, but very lightly raced since and despite his tendency to pull hard and gallop with his head between his knees has been employed as a schoolmaster most recently. Retirement has been shelved once, but hardly ever completes the course now, and it will be a huge surprise if he remains in service in '05. *A. & Mrs S.J. Hickman — E. Sussex & Romney Marsh (Sara Hickman).* 4 (Cnr), 781 (L), 899 (L), 1283 (L), 1407 (L).

RED GAUNTLET ..10-8.. 12 b.g. Wonderful Surprise — Border Minstrel (Menelek) 2311*p*. Well-made half-brother to Christiemouse. Dam won 2-finisher Maiden (16 started) and placed 15 for Mary Bowie (could be doggy). P-t-P/HUNT CH '01/3 r9 w4 (inc 3m5f Open) p1 (2nd); 7th, pulled up and fell/unseated 2. NH '04 r1 p0 (pulled up in 3m110y Hdle: *ld til wknd 4 out, t.o & pu 2 out*). Unraced until he was eight, and has only averaged three outings per annum since, but has quickly developed into a useful front-running Pointer, and is effective on all types of going. Makes the odd mistake and tends to sweat freely, and has been taken to post early, but it will be a surprise if these factors conspire to prevent him scoring again. Well handled by Kevin Anderson. *Mrs M.A. Bowie — Buccleuch (Alison Hamilton).* 214 (O), 426 (Cf), 764 (O), 1421 (O).

RED HARE (NZ) ..—.. 11 ch.g. Famous Star — Mutual Belle (NZ) (Western Bay NZ) p. Compact attractive brother to winner in New Zealand. Dam won 6 races in New Zealand. NZ FLAT '97/9 r18 w2 ($6^1/_2$-7f) p5. NH '00/2 r16 w3 (2 2m4f-3m110y Hdles and 3m Ch) p3 (2 2nds); pulled up 1, fell 2. NH '03 r3 p1 (2nd); and pulled up 2. HUNT CH '03 r2 p0 (pulled up 2). Used to possess ability, and won his final race for the previous yard at Taunton in October '02, but has always been thoroughly inconsistent, and pulled up in five of six starts for present connections. In no state to be on a racecourse in '04, and only went 1m4f reluctantly at Eyton. Blinkered once in '01, and wore cheekpieces once last year. *Mrs C. Shutts — Ludlow.* 528 (O).

REDHOUSE CHEVALIER ..9-8.. 6 b.g. Pursuit Of Love — Trampolo (USA) (Trempolino USA) 352. Lengthy good-topped. NH FLAT '03 r2 p0. NH '03 (for J.R. Adam) r1 p0 (pulled up). Tailed off in three races under Rules, but able to make a reasonable showing in Maidens, and came closest to success when five lengths second of three in a youngsters event at Balcormo on final start. Has the assistance of Clive Storey, and should have a fair chance of scoring at six. *J.R. Adam — College V. & N. Northumberland (Clive Storey).* 554 (CfMa), 768 (2m4fOMa), 1081 (OMa).

RED JUPITER ..9-2.. 8 b.g. Jupiter Island — Glen Dancer (Furry Glen) p54pu434. Strong compact brother to Colonel Blazer (*qv*), and half-brother to flat winner, Dance Star. 3000 4yo. NH FLAT '02 r1 p0. NH '02/3 (for N.B. Mason, and R.C. Guest) r7 p0; pulled up 2. Bought Doncaster, May for 1500. Gets decent marks for his jumping, but slow and exceedingly moderate, and the best he has achieved in 16 races is a six lengths third in a slowly-run Maiden (23 lengths is the second closest he has come to a winner). Blinkered once in a Hurdle and pulled up in cheekpieces in his only Chase. It would be a dreadful race if he ever managed to score. *W.M. Aitchson, Miss J. Martin & P. Mayland — Border (Joanne Martin).* 74 (OMa), 287 (CfMa), 433 (OMa), 554 (CfMa), 856 (2m4fOMa), 1041 (OMa), 1311 (OMa), 1423 (M).

RED LAKE (IRE) ..—.. 7 ch.g. Long Pond — Naida (IRE) (Cardinal Flower) ppppp. Tall angular. Bought Doncaster, Aug for 2000. Yet another sorry spectacle for Millington who was devoid of energy and jumped poorly and never got round the course. *P.J. Millington — Fernie.* 247 (O), 387 (OMa), 652 (OMa), 789 (CfMa), 890 (2m4fOMa).

RED NATIVE (IRE) ..10-5.. 9 b.g. Be My Native (USA) — Larry's Peach (Laurence O) 32f121u. Workmanlike compact brother to Hurdles winner, Native Peach (IRE), and half-brother to Irish NH flat winner, Sweep The Peach (IRE). Dam won Point, 3 Hdles (2m4f-3m) and 2m4f Ch in Ireland. NH FLAT '00 r1 p0. NH '00 r1 p0. P-t-P '02/3 r9 w4 (4-timer '03, inc Open) p3 (2 3rds, of 4 once); pulled up, and fell. A good galloper and difficult to peg back on sound surfaces, but stopped to nil after the last at Ston Easton and is only effective over an easy three miles. Failed to get round when blinkered twice in '04, but not his fault once and is generally an accurate jumper. Made to look better than he really is by superior handling, but sure to unearth further straightforward tasks. *P. Maltby — Seavington (Richard Barber).* 496 (MO), 602 (MO), 747 (3m1f110yH), 1010 (O), 1249 (MO), 1463 (O), 1563 (L).

RED NECK .10-2.. 14 ch.g. Nishapour (FR) — Roda Haxan (Huntercombe) 35113p113. Angular half-brother to a flat winner. FLAT r7 p0 (inc Sell). NH '97 r6 w1 (2m4f Hdle) p2. P-t-P/HUNT CH '97 and '00/3 r19 w6 (4 Confineds and 2 Members) p5 (3 2nds, inc Hunt Ch; and inc 3rd in Hunt Ch); 4th, 5th twice, fell and pulled up 4. A fine servant to connections and withstood his busiest campaign to date for the second year running in '04, and shows no signs of deteriorating with age, but only beat a total of six finishers when successful and was odds-on each time. Appeared to hate the sticky ground when pulled up at Bonvilston, and readily outspeeded by better animals, and will be lucky to find a similar number of easy tasks in '05, though his Members looks ripe for the taking for a fourth-year in succession. Wears a cross-noseband and bandages, and runs tongue-tied. *Mrs C.E. Goldsworthy — Tredegar F. (John Moore).* 206 (L), 449 (L), 670 (Cf), 951 (O), 1093 (4mMO), 1321 (MO), 1481 (M), 1520 (O), 1549 (O).

RED REBEL ..9-12§.. 13 gr.g. Scallywag — Little Red Flower (Blakeney) 2313fpp. Compact. P-t-P/HUNT CH '97/03 r39 w14 (inc 3 2m-3m2f Hunt Chses, inc 4-timer '02, Mixed Open and Open) p9 (5 2nds); 4th, last pair 2, ran out, pulled up 2, refused 2, slipped up, and fell/unseated 7. Reported to be a handful in the hunting field and plans to retire him were shelved in '04, and recorded a 15th career win at Brafield-on-the-Green, but very moody and needs to dominate, and looks to have spat the dummy out completely now. Unless connections change their minds again we have seen the last of him in public. Visored once in '04. *Mrs M.E. Moody — Pytchley (Caroline Bailey).* 56 (C), 300 (O), 465 (O), 592 (O), 943 (MO), 1121 (O), 1277 (MO).

RED RINGA ..8-10.. 7 ch.g. Karinga Bay — Ankerdine Belle (Paddy Boy) u2. Small owner-bred half-brother to Majic Belle and Green Anker. Dam won 2m Hdle. P-t-P '03 r3 p0 (refused, ran out and pulled up). Eliminated by the 13th in his first four attempts, and only just managed to stagger home a fence second of three in a long Maiden at Maisemore where he stopped to nil after the third last and proved virtually unsteerable on the home turn. Deeply unimpressive like his siblings. *D.J.B. Denny — Berks & Bucks (Cheryl Weller).* 290 (2m4fCfMa), 724 (OMa).

RED RISK ..— §.. 10 ch.g. Risk Me (FR) — Red Sails (Town And Country) pfpf. Sparely-made brother to flat winner, Enchanting Eve. 8000y. FLAT '97/9 r17 p1 (3rd). NH '98/9 (for S.G. Knight) r3 p0 (pulled up 2 and refused). Finished seven lengths third in a 7f race on the all-weather in '98, but has always been a total waste of time over jumps and a non-finisher in all seven attempts. Does not even have the merit of being a remotely pleasant ride. *J.F. Jones — Axe V.H. (Michael Sweetland).* 492 (OMa), 571 (R), 791 (R), 1132 (R).

RED ROOKIE ..—.. 7 ch.g. Lancastrian — Energance (IRE) (Salmon Leap USA) pf. Robust compact brother to Red Salmon Dancer, and half-brother to Hurdling winner, Beau Coup. Dam, half-sister to Nordic Flash (*qv* '98 Annual), won NH Flat and 2m Hurdle in Ireland. P-t-P '03 r2 p0 (pulled up 2). A deplorable jumper to date. Tailed off and pulled up in his first three attempts, and was chasing the leader when falling after less than a circuit next time, but has not been seen since, and may have sustained an injury. *Mrs L. Pomfret — Cottesmore.* 112 (OMa), 686 (OMa).

RED ROSE DIXIE ..7-10.. 7 b.m. Lancastrian — Monette (Nomination) 43p. P-t-P '03 r1 p0 (fell). Largely unimpressive to date, and beaten upwards of 12 lengths when completing, and has not got home over the full trip, but relatively unexposed and might yet be capable of better. *Mrs G. Sunter — Cleveland (George Sunter).* 344 (2m4fOMa), 432 (OMa), 814 (OMa).

RED SALMON DANCER ..9-0.. 6 ch.g. Lancastrian — Energance (IRE) (Salmon Leap USA) pfp. Compact brother to Red Rookie (*qv*). Would have gone close had he not fallen three out when a close second in a 2m4f Maiden at Garnons, but it was a bad race, and his next effort was modest. May be able to achieve something more positive at six. *R.W.J. & Mrs S.M. Willcox — Llangeinor (R.W.J. Willcox).* 454 (CfMa), 617 (2m4fOMa), 845 (CfMa).

REDSANDS (IRE) ..—.. 10 ch.g. Alphabatim (USA) — Sandyela (Sandy Creek) ppp6. Big rangy half-brother to Hurdles winners, Sandante (IRE), Sandy's Native (in Ireland — also won NH flat there) and Sew It Seams (in Ireland — also won Chasing there). Dam won 2 Irish Hurdles (2m-2m1f). IRISH NH FLAT '00 r2 p0. P-t-P '02/3 r6 w1 (Maiden) p1 (3rd); pulled up 3, and fell. Overtook four rivals from the third last when successful in a youngsters Maiden on firmish at Stainton in '02, but pulled up in five of eight subsequent attempts, and does not appear to have rid himself of the effects of a virus that blighted his yard last year. Stopped to nil after two miles on his last two starts, and his lowly rating is withdrawn until he shows signs of a clean bill of health. *Miss E.M. Hewitt — Middleton (Tony Walker).* 503 (R), 810 (R), 1162 (R), 1304 (CR).

RED SEPTEMBER ..9-6.. 8 b.g. Presidium — Tangalooma (Hotfoot) 4. Small neat brother to flat winner, Tupgi U Tango, and half-brother to flat winners, Time Temptress, Time Out and Time To Tango, and to a winner in Italy. Dam won 2m Hurdle. FLAT '99/01 r12 p1 (3rd). NH '00/1 r6 p2. P-t-P '03 r5 p2 (3rd of 4 once); 4th, 6th, and refused. Has made the frame in nine assorted events, but does not appear to do anything with a great deal of enthusiasm, and 15 lengths last of four on his only appearance in '04. Blinkered twice in '00, and wore cheekpieces thrice last year. *Mrs S. Horner-Harker — Hurworth.* 160 (CMa).

RED SEVEN (U) .—.. 6 b.g. Moscow Society (USA) — Mandalesa (IRE) (Mandalus) p. Dam, half-sister to Merry Minstrel (*qv*). Sold Doncaster, Nov for 3800. Tailed off and pulled up after two miles in his Members. *M. Allison — Zetland (Sally Williamson).* 1286 (M).

RED SPARK .9-0.. 13 ch.g. Electric — Sarah Carter (Reesh) 2Rp533p. Small neat. Dam won at 5f. P-t-P '99/00 and '02/3 r15 p3 (2 2nds, of 3 once; and last of 3); 5th, last pair 4, refused, pulled up 5, and fell. A steady enough jumper and has made the frame on eight occasions, but a very weak finisher and failed to improve on his three-quarters-of-a-length second on his reappearance at Maisemore. Running out of time and has already spurned some easy opportunities. Wears a cross-noseband. *Mrs A.D. Hope & Mrs S.W. Walker — N. Cotswold (Sally Walker).* 729 (OMa), 1020 (OMa), 1075 (OMa), 1340 (OMa), 1488 (OMa), 1532 (OMa), 1565 (OMa).

RED SQUARE KNIGHT (IRE) .8-10.. 10 b.g. Roselier (FR) — Suny Salome (Sunyboy) 2. Brother to Music Therapy (IRE), and to Irish Pointer and top-class jumping winner, Suny Bay (IRE) (earned £361,608), and half-brother to Howaryasun (IRE). NH FLAT '00 r2 p0. NH '00 r1 p0. Raced three times in November/December '00 and showed signs of ability, but did not resurface until '04, when he was 12 lengths second in a Brampton Bryan Maiden. Connections have had abundant patience with a horse who seems permanently plagued by problems, but unfortunately for them he is clearly as frail as ever. *Mrs L. Williamson — Cheshire.* 667 (OMa).

RED SQUARE PRINCE (IRE) ..9-5.. 9 b.g. Alphabatim (USA) — Dawn Rising (Le Moss) pp3pp. Small. Dam, half-sister to Selskar Abbey (*qv* '00 Annual). NH FLAT '01 r2 p0. P-t-P/HUNT CH '03 r4 w1 (2-finisher Maiden) p1 (2nd); and pulled up 2. Landed a touch in a two-finisher Maiden in softish at Parham which the local stewards neglected to investigate last year, but pulled up in six of eight other Points, and unimproved by the application of a visor once in '04. Prone to make bad mistakes and clearly harbours a fault. *Mr P. Hickman — E. Sussex & Romney Marsh (Alison Hickman).* 44 (R), 127 (R), 538 (R), 639 (R), 1084 (R).

RED STRANGER (FR) .—§§.. 8 b.g. Le Balafre (FR) — Abeille Royale (USA) (Turn To Mars USA) pp. Small narrow half-brother to jumping winner, Dark Stranger (FR) (won Hurdle and 6 Chases and £138,323 when trained by Martin Pipe), and to a French Chasing winner. NH FLAT '01 r3 p1 (3rd). NH '01/2 (for M.C. Pipe) r8 p1 (2nd); pulled up 3. Beaten favourite in his first two bumpers and showed he has ability when one-and-three-quarter lengths third in that grade, but has always been horribly reluctant, including when visored on four occasions and tongue-tied twice under Rules. Has now been pulled up five times consecutively including in Maidens in which he wore cheekpieces or blinkers, and never went a yard when supported from 4s to 7-4 favourite in the first of them. Connections must be sick of the sight of him by now. *D. Pipe — Silverton (Ashley Farrant).* 67 (OMa), 120 (OMa).

RED TYRANT ..7-4.. 7 b.g. Minster Son — By The Lake (Tyrant USA) pu8p. Small light-framed half-brother to Gale On The Lake (IRE) (*qv*). NH FLAT '02/3 r4 p0. NH '03 (for R.C. Guest) r7 p2 (3rds); ran out 1. Bought Doncaster, Aug for 3200. A long-standing maiden like his Pointing half-sister, and despite attracting excitement in the ring twice in Points he never looked like coming up with the goods. Ran out once over Hurdles, and unseated at the first once in '04, while he was a remote last on his only completion. Has worn cheekpieces on three occasions including when pulling up lame on final start. *Mrs M. Smales — Braes (Russell Ross).* 75 (OMa), 165 (OMa), 216 (OMa), 510 (OMa).

REEFER DANCER ..—§§.. 10 ch.g. Keen — Silent Dancer (Quiet Fling USA) ppp. Good-topped half-brother to Master Dancer, and to Hurdles winner, Silent Princess. Dam won 2 13f races. NH FLAT '99 r2 p0. NH '00/1 r11 p1 (3rd); pulled up 3. P-t-P '02/3 r10 w2 (Maiden and Restricted) p4 (2 3rds, of 4 once); last, pulled up 2, and fell. Too short of talent to make an impression under Rules, but scored twice in minor Points in April '02, and possesses enough ability to warrant the kind of support that was vested in him on his return, but a total dog and has set his stall out for all to see now. Worth 9-10 if he could be persuaded to co-operate but Dave Mansell was relieved of £65 when trying to do just that at Upper Sapey, and headgear had no lasting effect. *A.P. Gent — S. Herefords (Christine Hardinge).* 447 (Cf), 759 (I), 1138 (O).

REEKER PIKE .8-0.. 9 ch.m. Green Adventure (USA) — North Tyne Flyer VII (unknown) pR5pup. Tiny light-framed owner-bred half-sister to Lottie (U). Only got round once, when furlongs last, and finds it difficult to manoeuvre her way over the fences. Would look more at home in pony races with a kiddy aboard. *R.H. Walton — N. Tyne.* 215 (OMa), 433 (OMa), 549 (CMam), 658 (OMa), 1042 (CMam), 1291 (OMa).

REFLECTED GLORY (IRE) ..10-2.. 6 b.g. Flemensfirth (USA) — Clashdermot Lass (Cardinal Flower) 21. Strong half-brother to Irish NH flat and jumping/Pointing winner, Aglish Pride, to Irish Chasing winner, Bracing Breeze, and to Irish NH flat and Hurdling winner, Slieve Bernagh. Sold Doncaster, May for 6000 (Heather Dalton). Closely related to some competent performers under Rules in Ireland, and followed an encouraging 12 lengths second with a ten lengths win, both in 2m4f Maidens at Eyton-on-Severn. Was in command when he jumped right three out and even more violently so at the next where he nearly ran off the course in the latter, but once straightened he soon regained command to put bad rivals in their place. Strictly worth 9-5, but it will be disappointing if he cannot aspire to something much higher in future. A bit of a bull in a china shop at present, but luckily has Richard Burton to correct his meanderings. *Mrs P. Beasley — Albrighton (Caroline Robinson).* 929 (2m4fOMa), 1266 (2m4fOMa).

REGAL BRIDE ..9-4.. 11 b.m. Alhaatmi — Regal Ranee (Indian Ruler) p. Workmanlike lengthy owner-bred half-sister to Singh Song and Regal Role. Dam won Maiden and placed 4. NH '01/2 r4 p1 (3rd); pulled up 2. P-t-P '00/1 and '03 r6 w1 (Maiden) p0; pulled up 3, and fell 2. Takes a keen hold and failed to finish in her first five Points, but displayed a little ability over hurdles in '02, and landed a bad Maiden on firmish at Garthorpe last year. Soon tailed off and pulled up after two miles on her return, and has surely met with a setback. *R. Chandler — Belvoir (Tim Tarratt).* 159 (R).

REGAL RUMOUR ..—.. 8 b.g. Regal Embers (IRE) — Murroa (Imperial Crown) pp. Good-topped. Dam placed in Point. Grandam, Marvellous, was 2nd in Maiden. Tailed off and pulled up after two miles twice in February. *R. Coombes & Mrs L. Talbot — N. Cotswold.* 191 (R), 256 (CMa).

REGARDEZ-MOI ..— §§.. 8 b.m. Distinctly North (USA) — Tomard (Thatching) ppu. Small light sister to Northern Thatch (*qv*). 7000y. FLAT '99/01 r30 p4 (3rds). NH '02/3 (for Miss M. Bragg) r9 p0; brought down 1. Third four times from between five and eight furlongs including two Sellers, but her appalling displays in Points took her unplaced sequence to 27. Blinkered twice in '00, and having been very reluctant in her penultimate Point she acquired cheekpieces next time, but Jo Buck (Miss Wobble) managed to fall off going round a corner. A total waste of time. *R. Francis — W. Somerset V.* 599 (2m4fOMa), 1366 (R), 1462 (L).

REGENCY RAKE ..—.. 13 b.g. Ti King (FR) — Midnight Owl (FR) (Ardross) pf. Compact good-bodied half-brother to flat winners, Floot (subsequently successful in Italy) and Feathertime. IRISH FLAT '97/8 and '01 r8 w2 (12-14f) p3. IRISH NH FLAT '96 r1 p0. IRISH NH '96/02 (for A.L.T. Moore) r50 w4 (3 2m-2m2f Hdles and 3 2m1f Chses) p20; pulled up 1. Sold Doncaster, May '02 for 14,500. Won a weak renewal of the '99 Imperial Cup at Sandown by a short head to collect a prize of £21,475, but apart from a Charity Sweepstake has been unable to score since October of that year. Six victories and 23 placings earned him £65,504, but having been sold for a remarkably large sum for a near-veteran in '02 he returned for a couple of uninspired displays in Points in which he did not get the trip (two miles was his ideal distance). Blinkered once in '00. *E. James — Worcs.* 1274 (Cf), 1365 (Cnr).

RESCINDO (IRE) ..9-8§.. 6 b.g. Revoque (IRE) — Mystic Dispute (IRE) (Magical Strike USA) 2fs21. Compact brother to flat winner, Mabel Riley, and half-brother to flat winner, Specific Sorcerer. 55,000y. FLAT '01 r3 p0. NH '03 (for M.C. Pipe) r9 p5. Bought Doncaster, Aug for 3400. Made the frame nine times over Hurdles and beaten nine lengths or less, but has long been expensive to follow, and beaten favourite on eight occasions including all of his first four Points (odds-on twice, and would probably have scored at Cilwendeg had he not fallen when leading three out). Also half-a-length second to Rostock, and finally came good at the 17th attempt in a bad five-runner youngsters Maiden at Trecoed, where he found little in front but his rivals were too weak to capitalise. Frequently wears a visor, and is quick to throw in the towel if he thinks hard work beckons. Must never be trusted, although this is a lesson punters seem very loath to accept. *W.D. Oakes — Llangeinor.* 454 (CfMa), 676 (CfMa), 1096 (OMa), 1393 (OMa), 1550 (OMa).

RETORRICK ROSE ..8-8.. 7 b.m. Lancastrian — Sexton's Service (The Parson) 3p. Small sister to Parson's Rose. Dam won 2m4f Hurdle in Ireland, and is half-sister to Rattle The Latch (*qv* '95 Annual). Grandam won 8 Irish Points, and bred Ebony Jane (dam of Ebony Jack (*qv*). Bought Doncaster, Aug '02 for 2000. Made mistakes before finishing an adequate 13 lengths third over 2m4f on her debut, but pulled up in the rear two out in early March and seems to have been yet another victim of 'see Black Forest Lodge and say goodbye' syndrome. *R. Oliver — Four Burrow (Terance Oliver).* 309 (2m4fOMa), 416 (CMam).

RETRIBUTION ..—.. 10 b.g. Henbit (USA) — Snippet (Ragstone) pp. Compact half-brother to Snappit, Ring Me Back, Snippetoff and Stretchit, and to jumping winner, The Eens. NH FLAT '00 r2 p0. NH '01 r5 p0; pulled up 3. P-t-P '03 (for Mr D., Miss T. McCurrich & Mr M. Rollett) r2 p0 (unseated, and pulled up). Error-prone and not better than last in nine starts over jumps, but can take a very strong hold, and was still 20 lengths clear when pulling up apparently lame at the 14th in an elders Maiden on his latest appearance. May not get the chance to prove that the intervention was of a divine nature. *T. & D. McCurrich, M. Rollett & C. Morris — Miss T. Watkins & K. Parry — Clifton-on-Teme (Theresa McCurrich; Tracey Watkins).* 112 (OMa), 840 (OMa).

RETURN THE CALL (IRE) .9-9.. 8 b.g. Bob Back (USA) — Ring Four (IRE) (Supreme Leader) pp43. Workmanlike. Dam, half-sister to Macy (*qv*), won 2 NH Flat (2m1f-2m4f) and 2m2f Hdle in Ireland. NH FLAT '01 r1 p0. NH '02 r1 p0 (tailed off). P-t-P '03 (for Mr H.S. Smith & Mr H. Winton) r5 w1 (Maiden) p1 (last of 3); 6th of 7, and pulled up 2. Previous connections persevered with him long enough to land a weak Maiden at Garthorpe last year, but found disappointingly little off the bridle, and flopped when favourite on a return visit. Jumped moderately and beaten upwards of 14 lengths in the new yard, and needs to find more for Restricteds. Wears a cross-noseband. *The Staverton Owners Group (M. Blake) — Avon V. (Michael Blake).* 65 (Rnr), 232 (R), 354 (R), 636 (Rnr).

PLATE 99 882 W. Somerset Vale PPORA Club Members: Rhythm King and leading owner/rider Godfrey Maundrell, 1st, leads Timpani (Richard Woollacott), 3rd *PHOTO: Tim Holt*

RHYTHM KING ..10-3.. 10 b.g. Rakaposhi King — Minim (Rymer) u1241f1R11. Big strong brother to Hurdles winner, Just A Touch, and half-brother to Just A Minute, and to jumping winner, Red Ark. Dam, half-sister to Rizzio (*qv* '90 Annual), won 2m mares Chase. NH FLAT '01 r2 p0. NH '01/3 (for J.A.B. Old) r9 p0; fell/unseated 4. A difficult ride under Rules, and still not entirely straightforward, but finally able to show his true ability in Points, and had excuses in all of his defeats. Tends to hang left and proved unsteerable in the closing stages when successful at Cothelstone once, but a strong galloper who can jump really well, and has shown form on all types of going. A revelation in the new yard and should have little difficulty graduating to Open class in '05. *G.C. Maundrell — Avon V. (Paul Thompson).* 21 (OMa), 40 (OMa), 118 (R), 279 (R), 324 (R), 527 (I), 632 (M), 778 (CCon), 882 (C), 1238 (I).

RIAN BO PADRAIG (IRE) ..9-5.. 11 b/br.g. Mazaad — Miami Queen (Miami Springs) p. Close-coupled good-topped half-brother to a winner in Denmark. IRISH P-t-P '00/1 r3 p1 (2nd); and 4th twice. IRISH NH '01 r1 p0. P-t-P '02/3 (for Mr D. Davies) r6 w1 (Maiden) p1 (2nd); 4th, and pulled up 3. Showed a little ability in Ireland, and scored in a bad five-runner Maiden on firm at Cold Harbour in '02, but pulled up in all bar one of his five subsequent attempts, and ambled round miles behind until calling it a day at the last on his only appearance in '04. Wears a cross-noseband. *Ms J. Barton — Bicester with Whaddon.* 50 (I).

RIBBLE ASSEMBLY ..9-6.. 10 ch.g. Presidium — Spring Sparkle (Lord Gayle USA) p2. Sturdy half-brother to winner in Yugoslavia. 3800y. FLAT '97/00 r27 w2 (8f) p4 (inc 2 2nds Sells, his first 2 outings). NH '99/01 r13 w1 (2m1f Hdle) p3; fell 1, pulled up 1. IRISH FLAT '02 r1 p0. IRISH NH '02 (for P. McCreery) r15 p1 (3rd); fell 2. Won three races at up to 2m1f to September '00, but has also been beaten in Sellers, and took his losing sequence to 24 when he finished 15 lengths second of three in his Members. Sometimes equipped with headgear, but only once since '99. Busy in his youth, but missed '03 and only appeared twice in '04, and evidently hard to train now. *Miss F. Goldsworthy & M.J. Spuffard — S. Pembs (Edith Goldsworthy).* 208 (Cf), 947 (M).

RICE POINT ..9-11.. 12 b.g. Gold Dust — My Kizzy (The Ditton) 11. Rangy well-made owner-bred brother to Kandles-Korner, and half-brother to Tarka Country, Tarka Trail and Joesofine. Dam walked over for Stevenstone Members and was placed in 3 Points for John Squire (distant last of 3 after unseating once — would have won), Grandam, Top Of The Pops II (dam of Pop Song), won 2-finisher Stevenstone Members and placed 7 for him. P-t-P/HUNT CH '98/00 and '02 r13 w2 (Maiden and Restricted) p2; 4th, last, pulled up 6, and fell. Speedy and returned from a year out of action to double his previous haul when landing two three-finisher Members races. Turned over an odds-on shot in both, and showed no signs of stopping as he had previously, but an easy three miles and fast ground are essential ingredients for him. *J. Squire — Stevenstone.* 1267 (M), 1378 (M).

RICHES TO RAGS (IRE) ..—§.. 15 ch.g. Castle Keep — Merry Buskins (Little Buskins) pppu. Very narrow angular. Dam, half-sister to Valley So Deep (*qv* '92 Annual), won 2m4f Ch in Ireland. NH FLAT '96 r2 p0. NH '97/9 and '02 r14 p3 (2 2nds, beaten head once, and distant 3rd); inc Sell; pulled up 1, fell 1. P-t-P '00 and '03 r6 p2; last, pulled up 2 and fell. Twice runner-up over hurdles in '98 but shirked the issue when partnered by A.P. McCoy on the first occasion and a beaten favourite when they teamed up in a Seller subsequently. Ungenuine and predictably poor in Points, and looked in no state to be racing when only once getting beyond halfway in '04. Has been tried in headgear. *J. Nicholas & W.J. Day — Gelligaer F. (Jo Nicholas).* 731 (OMa), 844 (R), 1240 (OMa), 1324 (CfMa).

RICH RETURN (IRE) ..—§§.. 9 ch.g. Good Thyne (USA) — Queen's Parson (IRE) (The Parson) r. Rangy hobdayed. Dam is half-sister to Hurricane Linda (*qv* '00 Annual). IRISH P-t-P '02 r2 p0 (6th and pulled up). P-t-P '03 (for Mr D. Heath) r7 w1 (Maiden) p0; pulled up 5, and ran out. Sprang a 50-1 surprise when ridden in spurs to land a weak Maiden at Lifton last year, but incredibly indolent and a non-finisher in eight other Points, and refused to break into a gallop prior to refusing after a mile on a May return. His tentative 9-4 rating has been eradicated. *C.D. Faulkner — Atherstone.* 1265 (R).

RICH SONG (IRE) ..8-13.. 7 b.g. Treasure Hunter — Sonnet Lady (Down The Hatch) 2. Bought Tattersalls Ireland, Aug for 1360. Chased home a hitherto very frustrating performer who had been placed in eight of his previous nine attempts when four lengths second in a Mosshouses Maiden, and may be able to improve on this satisfactory debut. *S. Waugh — Morpeth.* 1225 (OMa).

RICKY B ..10-0.. 9 b.g. Rakaposhi King — Fililode (Mossberry) pu4u1R. Small well-made lop-eared half-brother to Filscot (*qv*). NH FLAT '01 r2 p0. NH '01/2 r8 p0; pulled up 2. P-t-P '03 r3 w1 (Club Maiden) p1 (2nd); and pulled up. A very poor performer under Rules but out of a winning Pointer, and scored on just his second appearance over fences at Dalton Park last year. Wilful and likes to get on with things, and Will Kinsey has not mastered him yet, but made fewer mistakes than usual when Richard Burton took over the reins at Heslaker, and landed a touch in the process. The former was in the plate when crashing out through the wing of the last when upsides the leader on his final appearance, and compensation awaits as soon as stronger handling is regained. Wears a cross-noseband. *R.J. Hewitt — Flint & Denbigh.* 109 (CR), 231 (CR), 530 (R), 708 (M), 1456 (R), 1530 (I).

RIDGE MANOR (IRE) ..—.. 6 b.g. Charnwood Forest (IRE) — Tony's Ridge (Indian Ridge) p. Compact good-bodied. FLAT '01/2 (for P.W. Harris, and B.G. Powell) r3 p0. A bad flat performer who eventually pulled up when about two fences behind on a clueless Pointing debut (tailed off and reluctant after a mile). *Miss P. Herbert — Pembs.* 677 (CfMa).

RIDGEWAY (IRE) .10-3§.. 10 b.g. Indian Ridge — Regal Promise (Pitskelly) 1232u. Lengthy brother to a flat winner in Hong Kong, and half-brother to several other winners. Dam won 11f race in Ireland. FLAT '97/9 and '01/2 r17 w2 (8f) p2 (beaten head once). NH '00/2 r6 p2. HUNT CH '03 (for Miss J.E. Foster & Mr B. Hardy) r5 w1 (3m1f110y) p3 (2nds); and fell 1. A dual winner on the flat, but an expensive failure over jumps under Rules, and has gained both subsequent wins first time out in the current yard. Given a positive ride by the trainer in the latest, but quirky and turned over at 4-5 next time, and then set another impossible task by Jo Foster at Ludlow. Broke a blood vessel in '02, and clearly refused any invitation to overtake when 1-5 on his return to Points, and has to be ignored following his seasonal reappearance in '05. Wears cheekpieces, and has been tried in blinkers. *S.B. Hardy — Middleton (Jo Foster).* 55 (Cf), 299 (L), 346 (3m1f110yH), 1303 (L), 1490 (3m2fH).

RIDWARE BOY ..—.. 7 b.g. State Diplomacy (USA) — Sailors Pride (Tycoon II) pp. Compact owner-bred half-brother to Ridware Pride (*qv*). P-t-P '03 r4 p0 (pulled up 3, and unseated). A hairy ride, and tends to pull hard and make mistakes, and no closer to achieving a first completion. *R.J. Froggatt — Meynell & S. Staffs (Jane Froggatt).* 97 (CfMa), 225 (M).

RIDWARE GEORGE .9-5.. 9 b.g. Sizzling Melody — Sailors Pride (Tycoon II) 4p23416. Lengthy good-topped half-brother to Ridware Pride (*qv*). P-t-P '02/3 r7 p1 (2nd); pulled up 4, unseated and refused. The Ridware standard bearer, and followed three placings with a deserved success in a slowly-run Maiden in soft at Alpraham where first-time blinkers were a decisive factor. Ran visored when 26 lengths sixth in his first Restricted, but it was a well above average race of its type, and might stand a chance of following up if unearthing an easier version. *R.J. & Mrs S.M. Froggatt — Meynell & S. Staffs (Richard Froggatt).* 226 (CfMa), 531 (OMa), 595 (OMa), 848 (OMa), 934 (OMa), 1044 (OMa), 1265 (R).

RIDWARE PRIDE ..9-7.. 11 b.g. Rolfe (USA) — Sailors Pride (Tycoon II) 3f1spu4. Small half-brother to Ridware Rose, Ridware George and Ridware Boy. Dam, half-sister to Navy Lark (pulled up 1 and fell 1 in Points for Richard Froggatt), was placed in 4 Hdles for him. Grandam, Royal Sailor ran out in a Point for him. P-t-P '02/3 r7 p1 (3rd); 5th, and pulled up 5. Produced carrying too much condition previously, but a slimmed down version outstayed a modest crew in a long Maiden in softish at Tabley, and was unlucky not to follow up at Flagg, where Richard Burton inadvertently steered the winner across his path and caused him to fall approaching the last. Not better than last subsequently, and may not get many easier opportunities. *R.J. Froggatt — Meynell & S. Staffs.* 225 (M), 709 (Mah), 753 (OMa), 990 (CR), 1048 (R), 1345 (R), 1430 (I).

RIDWARE ROSE ..9-0.. 10 b.m. Tromeros — Sailors Pride (Tycoon II) pfpp32u56. Well-made attractive owner-bred half-sister to Ridware Pride (*qv*). P-t-P '02/3 r9 p1 (3rd); pulled up 7, and fell. A consistently poor jumper, and only able to get round once in her first 13 starts, but like most of her siblings possesses a trace of ability, and has made the frame on three occasions. Tends to run in snatches, and beaten a minimum of 13 lengths in '04, and needs to find further improvement to open her account. *R.J. & Mrs A.W. Froggatt — Meynell & S. Staffs (Richard Froggatt).* 96 (CfMa), 227 (CfMa), 409 (CMam), 532 (OMa), 714 (CMam), 985 (OMa), 1119 (CMam), 1261 (OMa), 1424 (OMa).

RIFTON BRAMBLE ..5-10.. 8 ch.m. Out Of Hand — Just Rose (Legal Eagle) R43. Robust. Dam was placed in 4 Points for Mr Palfrey (*qv* '97 Annual), and previously won 2m5f Hurdle and placed two. Ran off the course approaching the first on her debut and then finished furlongs last of four with even Port Valenska (*qv*) ahead of her and 35 lengths third of four in a Maiden which took nearly a minute longer than the Open (again showed veering tendencies when running wide on the bend after the second). Looks a dosser and is quick to take advantage of any opportunity to crab-wise, but it might just be worth trying a top rider on her. *B.J. Palfrey — Tiverton Stag.* 1327 (OMa), 1450 (OMa), 1511 (OMa).

RIGADOON (IRE) ..9-13.. 9 b.g. Be My Chief (USA) — Loucoum (FR) (Iron Duke FR) 2. Compact well-made half-brother to Ajdar, and to flat winners, Iktasab (also successful Hurdler), Always Baileys, Brilliantrio and Our Glenard. Dam won 7 at up to 9f in USA. FLAT '98/03 r31 w3 (16-17f) p7. NH '99/03 (for M.W. Easterby) r20 w2 (2m Hdle and 3m Ch) p5; fell 1, pulled up 4. His big year was '99 was when he won four races, but only able to score once since, and was lucky in the Chasing victory as he looked third best until the leading pair collided at the final fence. Pulled up in three of his final four attempts over the bigger obstacles, and has always saved plenty for himself. Wore blinkers previously, and cheekpieces in an Open in which he finished a creditable three-quarters-of-a-length second after getting outbattled on the run-in. Ran 51 times in six years, but may now be difficult to train. *Mrs J.L. Haley — Zetland.* 300 (O).

RIGHT TO REASON (IRE) ..—.. 9 b.m. Mac's Imp (USA) — Ellaline (Corvaro USA) p. Sister to Imperial Line (IRE) (*qv*). Gave trouble in the preliminaries and then dwelt before pulling up after a blunder at the fifth on an inauspicious debut in an elders Maiden at Laleston. *A.D. Taylor — Pentyrch.* 1193 (OMa).

PLATE 100 196 South Pool Harriers Mens Open: The impressive Right To Reply and Neil Harris, 1st
PHOTO: Baths Photographic

RIGHT TO REPLY (IRE) ..11-6.. 11 b/br.g. Executive Perk — Sesheta (Tumble Wind) u1u13pf. Well-made. Dam won 14f race in Ireland. NH FLAT '99/00 r4 w1 (2m2f) p1 (2nd). NH '01 (for N.T. Chance) r3 w2 (2m4f Hdle and 2m5f Ch) p1 (2nd). Won thrice and placed twice from just seven attempts in three years to '01, but was prone to make mistakes and suffered from leg problems. Had been absent for three years before he resurfaced in a Larkhill Open and was a plunge from 20s to threes, but unseated three out when holding every chance of beating Aberfoyle Park. He was then an impressive winner at Buckfastleigh, equalling the time of Ask The Natives (carrying a stone less) in the Ladies, but pecked and unseated four out when looking to have the measure of Oneminutetofive and Mouseski at Bishops Court. Upgraded to a Hunter Chase at Newbury he was ridden with supreme confidence in the rear before overtaking rivals as if they were trees inside the final three-quarters of a mile, and storming clear from the last. He was none too fluent on that occasion, and it was the same story next time when a disappointing favourite and 36 lengths third to Macgeorge at Exeter, after travelling smoothly he seemed to flounder in the softish ground. An even more disappointing favourite when returned there and pulling up, he was back to his speedy best in the Interim Justitia, and was with the winner from three out until falling at the last and bringing down Earthmover. Although he got up and ran down the course briefly, he collapsed dead — a dreadful end for his connections. Commiserations to them, but they can console themselves a little with the memory of his phenomenal victory at Newbury, arguably the most impressive display of any horse in '04. Mrs M. Cook — Devon & Somerset (Jeremy Scott). 89 (O), 196 (O), 319 (O), 348 (3mH), 629 (3m1f110yH), 799 (2m3f110yH), 1453 (3m4fH).

RIGHTUN ..9-6.. 9 b.g. Neltino — Bright Bonnet (Spartan General) 1u5. Tall rangy owner-bred half-brother to Rolcap. P-t-P '03 r4 p0 (pulled up 4). Tired rapidly after a maximum of two miles when pulled up without fail in '03, but pulled hard and made the bulk of the running when successful at 33-1 in a slow time at Mollington on his return. Stopped as if shot after the 13th on a return visit, and obviously still has problems to overcome. Wears a cross-noseband. *R.G. Weaving — Warwicks (John Pritchard).* 295 (OMa), 467 (CR), 1034 (R).

RIMPTON BOY ..10-3.. 10 gr.g. Interrex (CAN) — Ardelle Grey (Ardross) 1R43. Lengthy well-made home-bred. Dam won 7f Sell at 2, and was later successful in Switzerland. NH '01 r2 p0 (4th and 7th in Hdles). P-t-P/HUNT CH '00/3 r19 w9 (inc 2m5f Hunt Ch, Mixed Open and 4 Ladies) p5 (3 2nds, last once); 4th, 6th, fell/unseated 2, and ran out. A smart Pointer on good or easy surfaces, and took his score into double figures when fending off the late charge of Mrs Be on her return at Larkhill, but intimidated and ran out through the wing of the second last at Holnicote, and stopped to nil in the closing stages of both subsequent attempts when tried in blinkers. Clearly awry at present, but his 8lb drop in the ratings could be only temporary if the key to his problems can be found. *Axe Valley Racing (R.J. Barber) — Cattistock (Richard Barber).* 10 (L), 276 (L), 496 (MO), 635 (L).

RING OFF ..—.. 7 b.g. Karinga Bay — Phar Better Off (IRE) (Phardante FR) pp. Tall owner-bred. Pulled up at the ninth in both attempts, having made a bad mistake at the fifth in the latest. *Mrs J.M. Bailey — R.A.* 633 (2m4fCfMa), 962 (OMa).

RINGSIDE VIEW (IRE) ..9-5.. 8 b.g. Keen — Ringawoody (Auction Ring USA) 5. Small close-coupled brother to German flat and French and German jumping winner, Reveillon (GER) (also won English Chase), and half-brother to 2 Irish flat winners (one later successful in 3 continental countries), to jumping winner, Rich Life (IRE), and to Irish NH flat and Hurdling winner, Cloghans Bay (IRE). Dam won 3 Irish flat, 5-7f. IRISH FLAT '99 r3 p0. NH '00/1 (for F. Murphy, when successful, and C.J. Mann) r10 w1 (2m Hdle) p3. Bought Ascot, Nov '01 for 3000. Comes from a prolific winner-producing family and did have his own brief moment of glory when winning his only Seller, a 24-runner affair at Worcester despite cocking his jaw. Making a first appearance for three years when he finished 43 lengths last in a May Open, and we only see bouts of inactivity looming. *Lady D. Powell — O. Berks (Emma Pring).* 1328 (MO).

RINGS OF POWER (IRE) ..9-12.. 8 ch.g. Mister Lord (USA) — Rainbow Gurriers (IRE) (Buckskin FR) f1. Tall rangy. IRISH P-t-P '03/4 r8 p1 (3rd); pulled up 5, fell 1. Pulled up five times and fell twice in his first nine attempts, but was possibly unlucky on his English debut at Cotley Farm, as he was closing on the winner when he fell three out in a five-runner affair. Soon gained compensation at Lifton where he beat Harnage who ended his own season with a hat-trick, and looks to have a fair bit of ability, but quirky and not straightforward, and connections may need to handle him with kid gloves. *Mrs G. Touzel — S. Dorset (Elsie Mitchell).* 1248 (OMa), 1353 (OMa).

RIO POPS ..9-5.. 7 b.m. Broadsword (USA) — Hops And Pops (Lighter) 53. Compact well-made. Dam, half-sister to 6 Pointers, including Badger Beer (*qv*) was incredibly impressive when completing unbeaten 4-timer in Points to '93, and subsequently won 6 Hurdles (2m-2m5f) and 3 Chses (2m-2m3f). P-t-P '03 r1 p0 (pulled up). Being brought along very steadily, and stayed on in pleasing style on her return, but tired in the lifeless ground when 18 lengths third at Bishops Court, and has not been seen since. Out of an outstanding mare, and looks a ready-made Maiden winner in '05, but her lack of outings is rather worrying. *Mrs R.H. Woodhouse — Portman (John Dufosee).* 35 (CMam), 329 (OMa).

RIO'S LORD (IRE) ..10-7.. 12 b.g. Good Thyne (USA) — Rio Dulce (Rio Carmelo FR) p. Plain heavy-topped half-brother to NH flat and jumping winner, Rio's King (IRE), and to successful Irish Pointer, Dulcast. Dam, half-sister to My Man On Dundrum (*qv* '99 Annual), won at 9f in Ireland, and won 2 Hdles (2m-2m4f) there. IRISH P-t-P '99/00 r8 w1 (6yo&up Maiden) p1 (2nd); pulled up 3, fell/unseated 2, and ran out. P-t-P/HUNT CH '01/3 r23 w4 (up to Confined) p2 (3rds, of 4 once); 9th, last pair 3, pulled up 11, ran out and unseated. Uninspiring and successful in just one of his first 19 starts in England, but underwent an amazing transformation in the second half of '03, and won three races, including one in the fastest time of the day at Garthorpe. Suited by good ground and an easy three miles, but pulled up lame on the prevailing firm surface when blinkered on his reappearance at Market Rasen. Visored in all his English wins, and runs tongue-tied. *Miss M. Samworth — Cottesmore.* 298 (Cf).

RIP KIRBY ..9-10§.. 10 b.g. Derrylin — Preacher's Gem (The Parson) p391f141. Small half-brother to Ballee Betty (IRE) and Little Word, to jumping winner, Joliver, and to winning Hurdler, Kind Cleric. Dam, half-sister to Mountain Crash (*qv* '94 Annual) and Rolls Rambler, won 2m4f Hdle. IRISH NH FLAT '00/1 r4 p0. IRISH NH '00 r5 p1 (3rd). IRISH P-t-P '01 r2 w1 (5&6yo Maiden) p1 (3rd). P-t-P '02/3 r13 p4 (3 3rds; and last of 2); 4th 4, last, unseated 3, and pulled up. Has ability, and provided newcomers Rob Cundy and Matt Cobbald with their initial wins in '04, but ungenuine and the latter's win was achieved only after two stable companions had got tangled up in the first half-mile at Marks Tey — he too was baulked at the third but continued solo propelled by his tail. Beaten at 4-6 in another Members after which blinkers were dispensed with, and can never be taken at face value. Tongue-tied once in '01. *G.I. Cooper — E. Anglian Bloodhounds, & Essex (Cherie Cunningham).* 127 (R), 217 (M), 249 (Cnr), 646 (M), 745 (R), 902 (R), 1085 (Cv&nr), 1312 (M).

RISING TALISKER ..9-2§.. 12 ch.m. Primitive Rising (USA) — Dialect (Connaught) 64p3p2r. Smallish lengthy owner-bred. Dam is half-sister to Shutafut (*qv* '96 Annual). NH '98/00 r9 p1 (3rd); 7th, fell, and unseated in Chses. NH '01 r2 p0 (pulled up 2). P-t-P '01/2 (for Miss D. Hill) r9 p2 (last of 3 once); last pair 3, pulled up 3, and unseated. Often shows prominently for a long way, and beaten between two and 100 lengths in four Pointing placings, but both error-prone and ungenuine, and normally wears headgear. Rachel Clark has worked the oracle on another errant beast in the shape of Claire's Nomad, but this one looks beyond redemption. *O.R. Dukes — York & Ainsty S.* 161 (I), 271 (OMa), 338 (Cf), 500 (CMam), 679 (3m1fH), 776 (CfMa), 1347 (2m6f110yH).

RISK ADVISORY (IRE) ..8-2.. 11 b.g. Camden Town — Quick Romance (Lucky Brief) 33. Good-topped brother to David Bruce (IRE), and half-brother to Caddlestown, to NH flat and jumping winner, Scoring Pedigree (IRE), to Hurdles winner, Referral Fee, to 2 Irish NH flat and Hurdles winners, and to successful Irish Pointer, Those Brown Eyes. Dam won 2m Hdle (3 ran) in Ireland. NH FLAT '99 r2 p0. NH '99 and '01/2 (for J.W. Mullins, and Mrs S.M. Johnson) r10 p1 (3rd); pulled up 1, brought down 1. Gained his only placing under Rules when a distant and exhausted third in a Selling Hurdle in heavy, but beaten 28 lengths plus in his final nine attempts, and was brought down in his only Chase. Beaten about 40 lengths when last of three in two Points, and after leading for a way in both he was floundering badly in the closing stages. Wears cheekpieces now, and often tongue-tied. Clearly has defects, and only raced three times in three years. *Miss C. Manning — Golden V. (Steve Lloyd).* 451 (R), 620 (OMa).

RIVER ALDER .10-4.. 7 b.m. Alderbrook — River Pearl (Oats) 21*1*. Hobdayed half-sister to NH flat and Hurdles winner, Silken Pearls. Dam won 3 Hurdles (2m4f-2m6f) and 4 Chases (2m1f-2m5f). Dam, half-sister to Buckley's Pearl (*qv* '00 Annual). NH '04 (for Miss S.E. Forster) r1 w1 (beat Monolith 4*l* in 2m4f Hdle: *a.p, ld 6, r.o wl*). Bought Doncaster, Aug for 2600. Very progressive, and followed a five lengths second to the potentially smart King Barry at Corbridge with a ready win in a Mares Maiden in soft at Friars Haugh. Quickly followed up in a Carlisle Hurdle, and was due to have a subsequent outing at Perth, but pulled out at the last moment and put away for the season. Comes from a delightful line on the distaff side, and apart from mother having won seven races over jumps her grandmother won a Hurdle and four Chases. Presumably so cheap because she had been hobdayed, but if she can stay clear of wind problems she should have a future over fences. *J.M. Dun — Lauderdale (Clive Storey).* 432 (OMa), 549 (CMam).

RIVER BAILIFF (IRE) ..10-0§.. 9 ch.g. Over The River (FR) — Rath Caola (Neltino) 58p1622. Narrow lightly-made half-brother to NH flat and Hurdles winner, Pure Fun (IRE). Dam, half-sister to Lothian Jem (*qv* '99 Annual), won mares Maiden in Ireland. IRISH P-t-P '00/1 r6 w1 (5yo Maiden) p1 (2nd); pulled up 1. P-t-P/HUNT CH '02 r5 p3 (2 3rds; and 2nd of 3); 4th, and pulled up. NH '03 (for J.H. Johnson) r5 p0. Largely disappointing since winning his Maiden in Ireland, and usually finds zero at the business end whatever the trip, but the combination of first-time cheekpieces, hold up tactics, and the presence of Phillip York worked the oracle in a two-finisher Restricted in holding at Penshurst. Almost surrendered a clear advantage that day, but did so without much of a struggle next time, and went back to his usual ways subsequently. Cannot be trusted in future. *S. Garrott — O. Surrey, Burstow & W. Kent (Richard Gurney).* 102 (R), 241 (2m4f110yH), 421 (L), 779 (R), 1054 (Cf), 1209 (O), 1408 (O).

RIVER BANDIT .—.. 8 b.g. Locksman (USA) — Berata (New Member) f. Half-brother to Alex In Action (*qv*). Handy when falling at the tenth in a 2m4f Alnwick Maiden on Easter Saturday, and did not reappear. *C. Hall — Braes (Carolyn Hall).* 856 (2m4fOMa).

RIVER DANTE (IRE) ..9-12§.. 8 ch.g. Phardante (FR) — Astral River (Over The River FR) Rffp334322. Tall rangy hobdayed half-brother to Chasing winner, Fear Siuil (IRE). Dam, half-sister to Dromin Leader (*qv* '00 Annual), won 2 Points, a 2m Hdle and 5 Chses (2m4f-3m) in Ireland. P-t-P '02/3 r7 w1 (Maiden) p4 (3 2nds, of 3 once); 4th, and ran out. Had two operations to combat a breathing problem before he even made it to the track, but has knocked the wind out of favourite backer's sails on five occasions, and will not produce anything off the bridle. Makes mistakes, but pulls hard and travels with menace only to fade tamely in the closing stages, and having surrendered a 20 lengths lead from the third last when visored at Bratton Down should be left well alone for betting purposes. Wears a cross-noseband. *18 Red Lions Partnership — Devon & Somerset (Linda Blackford).* 279 (R), 324 (R), 443 (2m4f110yH), 706 (R), 879 (R), 1102 (R), 1184 (R), 1366 (R), 1491 (R), 1558 (R).

RIVER DEED .—.. 6 ch.g. Wesaam (USA) — House Deed (Presidium) ppp. Half-brother to Hurdling winner, Mondeed. A hard puller who showed some speed before pulling up in Maidens, but was destroyed at Garthorpe. Miss J.E.A. Harbison — Grafton (Richard Webb). 746 (OMa), 1124 (OMa), 1504 (2m4fOMa).

RIVER LOSSIE ..10-3.. 16 b.g. Bustino — Forres (Thatch USA) u. Compact half-brother to Findhorn Bay, and to 3 winners, including Cromarty (flat and Hurdles), and to flat winner, Lossiewells. NH FLAT r2 p2. NH '93/4, '96 and '98/9 r15 w7 (3 2m-2m2f Hdles, and 4 2m4f-3m Chses) p3 (inc $^3/_4$*l* 2nd to Large Action on debut); one run at Punchestown. P-t-P/HUNT CH '01/3 r8 w2 (inc 4m Mixed Open) p3 (2nds, beaten $^1/_2$*l* once); last, and fell/unseated 2. A smart front-runner in blinkers on easy surfaces to '99, and staged a revival in Points three years later, but very lightly raced throughout his career, and lost the newcomer Lee Sloyan at the seventh on his debut when 1-2 in a match for his Members on his only appearance in '04. A loose school round Erw Lon looks likely to be his swansong. *late Mr Chris Brasher — Carms (Amanda Meakins).* 201 (M).

RIVER NESS ..10-6.. 9 br.m. Buckskin (FR) — Stubbin Moor (Kinglet) 2u411. Spare-made half-sister to Pennywise, to jumping winner, Edgemoor Prince, and to Chasing winner, Captain Stockford. Grandam, Pennyless, won 8 Points (7 Adjacents) and placed 8, and won 2 Hdles and a Chase (all 2m). NH '01/3 (for N.G. Richards) r15 w2 (2m6f-3m1f Hdles) p5 (2nds); pulled up 2. Completed a Hurdling double in March/April '02 and was also runner-up on five occasions, but 31 lengths fourth in her only Chase (8-15 but never going well). A thorough stayer who came back to form in Points, and went well for the novice Vicky Thirlby, who sometimes had very little connection with the saddle but still managed to register her first success at Garthorpe before following up a couple of weeks later at Flagg. Subsequently put in foal to Terimon. *T. Thirlby & Miss K.L. Smith — Atherstone (John Holt).* 110 (Cnr), 299 (L), 380 (L), 682 (L), 987 (L).

RIVER TREASURE (IRE) ..9-7.. 8 b.m. Over The River (FR) — Erins Treasure (Brave Invader USA) 2. Compact half-sister to Green Goddess, and to jumping winner, Irish Option (IRE). IRISH P-t-P '02/3 r10 p2 (2nds); pulled up 3, fell 2. IRISH NH '03 (for J.A. Berry) r1 p0 (pulled up). Second of three in two Irish Points (beaten between four and 20 lengths), and also fell two out when looking the likely winner once. Still knocking at the door in a mares Maiden at Upton-on-Severn, where she was in front from approaching two out until after the last, but could not quicken. Will be eligible for elders Maidens in '05, and if fit it will be disappointing if she cannot win one. *R. Mathias — Brecon & Talybont.* 978 (CMam).

ROBBIE'S ADVENTURE ..10-0.. 11 ch.g. Le Coq D'Or — Mendick Adventure (Mandrake Major) p5p1555. Neat. Dam, half-sister to Manhattan Beach (*qv* '94 Annual), won 2 flat (5-6f). P-t-P '99 (for Mr D.L. Williams) r2 p0 (pulled up, and fell). NH '99/03 (for D.L. Williams) r31 w2 (2m1f110y Sell Hdle and 3m Ch) p7 (inc 6 3rds); pulled up 7, fell 2. A dual winner in mud for Dai Williams in January '01, but visored or tried in cheekpieces latterly, and failed to finish in half of his last ten starts under Rules. Regularly prone to shoddy jumping, but stamina has never been a problem, and plugged on gamely to spring a 20-1 surprise in the Detling 4-miler. Beaten 32 lengths plus otherwise, and will need to be placed with greater care if he is to achieve much in future. *The Adventure Partnership (Miss E. Wettern) — Southdown & Eridge (Emma Wettern).* 18 (L), 88 (L), 280 (3m2f110yH), 537 (4mMO), 800 (3m2f110yH), 1170 (4m1fH), 1441 (3m7fH).

ROBERTS RETURN .—§§.. 9 b.g. Michelozzo (USA) — Bittleys Hand (Nearly A Hand) RRp. Small compact half-brother to Tilleys Orchid. Dam, half-sister to Tom Furze (*qv* '01 Annual), was last (bar a rejoiner once) or a non-finisher in 25 of 26 Points for the Cooksleys ('the rider suffers from perpetual inertia'). Great-grandam, Orchid Moor, won 14 Ladies (also disqualified once) and 2nd thrice, but broke down when completing a 10-timer. P-t-P '02 r2 p0 (pulled up, and fell). Mishandled from day one, and has no right to be on a racecourse. Kept napping to the box-park whilst walking round the paddock at Kingston St Mary, and for the second time strangled under an iron grip to stop him running out and soon fences behind. Liable to kill someone if connections continue with him. *A. Cooksley — Weston & Banwell H.* 1272 (OMa), 1331 (Cf), 1446 (Cf).

ROBERT THE RASCAL ..10-0§.. 12 ch.g. Scottish Reel — Midnight Mary (Celtic Cone) up64up16p. Compact. Dam won 2m Sell Hdle when ridden by John Carden. P-t-P/HUNT CH '99/00 and '02/3 r11 p1 (2nd); 7th twice, last pair 2, refused, and pulled up 5. Temperamental and lightly raced in previous years, and remains a fiery individual, particularly in the preliminaries, but finally grasped the nettle at the 18th attempt, and scored in the slowest time of the day on firmish at Eaton Hall. Looked flattered by his proximity to the principals at Bangor next time, and was tailed off subsequently, but would stand a chance in an average Restricted if he co-operated fully. Qualifies with some obscure packs (on his own?), and has never had the chance to contest a Members race. *C. James — N.E. Cheshire (Charmaine James).* 95 (R), 435 (3m110yH), 710 (Mah), 753 (OMa), 985 (OMa), 1044 (OMa), 1142 (OMa), 1176 (3m110yH), 1512 (2m6f110yH).

ROBINS PRIDE (IRE) ..9-8.. 15 b.g. Treasure Hunter — Barney's Sister (Abednego) ppp2p. Unfurnished. NH FLAT '94 r2 p1 (3rd). NH '94/03 (for N. Tinkler, and C.L. Popham, all wins) r76 w7 (2 2m-2m2f and 5 2m1f-3m Chses) p21; pulled up 7, fell/unseated 7. Won seven races principally in the mud to January '01, and 22 placings included three Sellers. Too long in the tooth now, and apart from when finishing 15 lengths last of two in his Members he was a regular puller up in Points and a Hunter Chase. Wears blinkers and has been unreliable, and still soldiering on in his 11th season, but not enjoying himself and it is time to draw stumps. *Mrs S. Popham — Quantock (Chris Popham).* 34 (O), 115 (MO), 317 (2m4fH), 468 (M), 965 (L).

ROBOASTAR (USA) ..9-2§§.. 8 b/br.g. Green Dancer (USA) — Sweet Alabastar (USA) (Gulch USA) 3213. Compact. FLAT '99/02 r10 p2 (3rds). NH '01/2 r7 p0; refused 2. P-t-P '03 r5 p1 (distant last of 3); 4th, pulled up, fell, and brought down. Prone to roguish behaviour, and his '03 campaign ended when sustaining a bad cut at Bredwardine, but has plenty of ability, and finally prepared to reveal most of it when scoring totally unchallenged in a two-finisher youngsters Maiden at Bonvilston. Gave the rider no cause for ecstasy when downing tools on a return visit, and it would be unwise to trust him again. Wears blinkers, and has been tried in a visor. *T.E. Vaughan & Miss A. Johns — Llangeinor (Abbi Johns).* 450 (R), 845 (CfMa), 1096 (OMa), 1322 (R).

ROBSAND (IRE) ..—.. 16 b.g. Sandalay — Remindful (Bargello) ppp. Compact brother to The Big Fella (IRE) and Royal Arctic (IRE), and half-brother to The Caumrue (IRE). IRISH P-t-P '94 r3 w1 (5 plus Maiden) p0; pulled up 2. NH '94/8 r19 p6 (beaten 20l> *plus in 4, inc 4m NH Ch). P-t-P/HUNT CH '00 and '02 r10 p0 (last pair 4, pulled up 4, ran out, and fell). Scored in bottomless ground in Ireland, but broke blood vessels and proved an expensive failure under Rules, and only turns out bi-annually now. Lumbered along for two miles or less thrice, but resembled a tub of lard, and needs to be pensioned off. A.L. Shaw — N. Cotswold.* 662 (O), 836 (O), 1123 (R).

ROCASTLE LAD (IRE) ..9-10.. 9 gr.g. Roselier (FR) — Ivory Queen (Teenoso USA) Rpf. Strong-topped. 4800 5yo. NH FLAT '01/2 r2 p0. NH '02 (for N.J. Hawke) r2 p0 (pulled up 2). Pulled up in both Hurdles including a Seller, and failed to finish in his three Points in which he could show a decidedly temperamental streak, but despite a very slow start was in the process of giving a much improved display when he fell heavily at the final fence at Cothelstone and had to be destroyed. Mrs L. Fielding-Johnson & R. Mitford-Slade — Taunton V. (Clare Wyatt). 275 (CfMa), 325 (OMa), 474 (OMa).

ROCK DANCER ..—.. 7 b.g. Rock Hopper — Polish Dancer (USA) (Malinowski USA) pp. Well-made owner-bred half-brother to flat winner, Presto. Pulled up in a couple of Points, and appeared to go wrong when dismounting at the fourth at Bratton Down. *Mr & Mrs A.J. Cottle — Exmoor (Alan Cottle).* 306 (2m4fOMa), 1384 (Cf).

ROCKFIELD LANE (IRE) ..7-12.. 9 b/br.g. Sharifabad (IRE) — Suir Surprise (Rusticaro FR) 2. Good-bodied Compact. Dam won 8f race in Ireland. IR3200 3yo. IRISH P-t-P '00 and '02 r4 p1 (2nd); pulled up 2. IRISH NH FLAT '02 r3 p0. IRISH NH '00 and '02 r3 p0. NH '02/3 (for G.F. Bridgwater) r8 p1 (3rd); pulled up 1. Bought Ascot, Aug for 1904. Has three placed efforts to his name including when two distances last of three at 50-1 in his only Chase, but has also tried Selling Hurdles, and beaten 36 lengths plus in his final seven races under Rules. Visored once, and has looked very reluctant. Second in a Members which took 53 seconds longer than the following Confined, and can safely be ignored. *The Blinkered Partnership (J. Trice-Rolph) — Heythrop (Jon Trice-Rolph).* 46 (M).

ROCKFORD (IRE) ..8-12.. 9 b.g. King's Ride — Pampered Russian (Deep Run) 4su22. Tall half-brother to Pampered Gale (IRE) (*qv*). 15,000 4yo. NH FLAT '01 r2 p1 (3rd). NH '02/3 (for A. King) r5 p0; pulled up 1. Essentially very slow and can be a difficult ride, but did manage a couple of seconds in Maidens at Kingston Blount, and was beaten between four lengths and 12 lengths. Does not really deserve to win on what he has achieved so far. *A. Bosley — Bicester with Whaddon.* 871 (OMa), 1035 (OMa), 1273 (OMa), 1337 (OMa), 1518 (OMa).

ROCK ROSE ..10-2.. 12 b.m. Arctic Lord — Ovington Court (Prefairy) 66up. Workmanlike half-sister to Diwan-I-Khas, Jeremy Fisher and Spot The Business. Dam was 4th of 5, pulled up 2, and unseated in Points. P-t-P '99 r2 p1 (2nd); and pulled up. NH FLAT '99 r1 p0 (5th). NH '99/03 (for N.R. Mitchell, C.L. Tizzard, when successful, and B.J.M. Ryall) r20 w1 (3m Ch) p4 (inc head 2nd in 2m5f Hdle); pulled up 2, unseated 2, brought down 1, ran out 1. Won in mud at Taunton in '02, but has never stood her racing particularly well, and has done best going right-handed. Clearly retains plenty of ability, but injured her near hind at Badbury Rings, and had to be removed by ambulance. Wears a cross-noseband. *Mrs A. Davis — S. Dorset (Graham Davis).* 10 (L), 241 (2m4f110yH), 347 (3mH), 578 (L).

ROCKY BALBOA ..—§.. 13 b.g. Buckley — Midnight Pansy (Deadly Nightshade) pp. Workmanlike half-brother to Sister Jim, and to several winners, including Jimsintime, Jimbalou and Taxi Lad (all successful Hurdlers). NH FLAT '97 r1 p0. NH '01 r1 p0 (11th in 2m3f Hdle). P-t-P/HUNT CH '98/9 and '01/2 r11 w1 (Maiden) p0; 4th of 5, pulled up 7, and ran out 2. NH '02 r3 p0 (pulled up 3). Won a bad Maiden in soft at Maisemore in '98, but temperamental and very lightly raced since, and jumped poorly on his return from his latest enforced absence. Pulled up in five of his last six appearances, and is a waste of time now. *B. Davies — Worcester & W. Farmers.* 1256 (R), 1356 (2m6fH).

ROCKY FOUNTAIN ..9-6.. 9 b.g. Royal Fountain — Slim View (Slim Jim) p. Owner-bred half-brother to Moore View, Chestnut View and French Chocolate. Dam is an unraced sister to Pennine View (*qv* '02 Annual). P-t-P '02/3 r4 p1 (3rd of 4); unseated, and pulled up 2. Showed some ability when third in his Members last year, but never looked an easy ride, and broke a leg at Witton Castle. *J.J. Dixon — Cumberland F. (Jackie Williamson).* 165 (OMa).

RODNEY TROTTER ..10-7.. 11 b.g. True Song — Silver Thorn (Record Run) 1p. Sturdy attractive half-brother to Little Dish (*qv*). P-t-P '00 and '02/3 (for Mr G.A. Cure & Mr N. Sutton) r10 w2 (Maiden and Restricted) p2; 4th, 5th 2, last pair 2, and pulled up 1. Has gained all three wins either first or second time out, and put up his best performance when beating a subsequent Hunter Chase winner on firmish at Dunthrop, but sadly ruptured a tendon when favourite to follow up at Garnons. Wears cheekpieces. *D.J. Keyte — Worcs (Giles & Kim Smyly).* 50 (I), 403 (Cf).

RODY (IRE) ..9-9§.. 8 b/br.g. Foxhound (USA) — Capable Kate (IRE) (Alzao USA) RRR2R2R1. Small compact half-brother to flat winners, Obe Bold, Golden Biff and Eyes To The Right. IRISH FLAT '99/00 r6 p0. NH '01/2 (for F.T. Jordan, and I.R. Brown) r13 p0; pulled up 6, fell 1. Bought Ascot, Jul for 1523. Useless on the flat, and over Hurdles including Sellers in which he was beaten 22 lengths plus (normally far more) at very long odds, and pulled up six times (with a broken blood vessel once) and fell once. Totally intractable for his first two Pointing jockeys and also ducked out with Dave Mansell twice, but he was also able to wrestle him into submission on three occasions, and following two seconds (one at only half-a-length after he had led until the last) he came home unchallenged at Cothelstone after dictating from the front at a very slow pace (his rider celebrated the triumph with a flying dismount). Gained blinkers and Mansell at the same time and both have been very beneficial, and also wears a cross-noseband and tried with a pelham and an off-side pricker. Connections had received a warning letter from the Jockey Club as to his future conduct (after five run outs the official body were remarkably forbearing!), so their victory really was one to savour. Likely to find Restricteds hard work. *Mrs E. England — Berkeley.* 149 (OMa), 368 (OMa), 700 (CfMa), 760 (OMa), 1020 (OMa), 1075 (OMa), 1339 (OMa), 1370 (OMa).

ROEBUCKS WAY ..8-2.. 7 b.g. Shaamit (IRE) — Alwal (Pharly FR) 3. Tall unfurnished half-brother to Hurdles winner, Quedex, and to a winner in Italy. Dam won Dutch Oaks, and 3 other flat in Holland. NH FLAT '02 (for D. Shaw) r1 p0. Nine lengths third in his Members and almost caught the runner-up napping, but the form is probably meaningless and only had an unregistered hunter behind him. *D.J.W. Edmunds & Swan Racing — Grove & Rufford (David Edmunds).* 590 (M).

ROLLING MAUL (IRE) ..9-7.. 10 b.g. Simply Great (FR) — Soyez Sage (FR) (Grundy) p54. Good-topped half-brother to Count Balios (IRE), and to 2 German flat winners, including Saltinbocca (IRE). Dam won 2 flat races in France. IRISH P-t-P '00 r2 p1 (2nd); and pulled up. IRISH NH FLAT '99/00 r6 p1 (3rd). IRISH FLAT '99 r2 p0. IRISH NH '99/01 (for M. Cunningham) r19 w1 (2m4f Hdle) p3 (inc 2 Chses); fell 1. NH '01/3 (for Miss C.J.E. Caroe) r11 p4 (3rds); pulled up 2. Bought Ascot, Jun for 3619. Won a Hurdle at Ballinrobe in July '00, and also crept into eight placings which include six Chases — beaten 23 lengths plus (with a total of two behind in the four English ventures), but essentially a prolific loser. Often wore headgear under Rules. Outclassed in Opens, and did not perform as if he got the trip. *C.S. Horton — V.W.H. (Betty Crew).* 170 (O), 254 (O), 366 (MO).

ROLL WITH IT (IRE) ..—.. 12 b.g. Royal Fountain — Deirdre Elizabeth (Salluceva) p. Workmanlike half-brother to Lordinthesky (IRE) and Banteer Bet (IRE). IRISH P-t-P '97/9 r7 w1 (5yo Maiden) p2 (2nds, inc dead-heat); fell 2. IRISH NH FLAT '98/9 r7 p1 (2nd). IRISH NH '98/9 r8 p2 (2 3rds in Hdles, inc dead-heat). NH '00 r2 p1 (2nd in 3m Nov Hdle). P-t-P/HUNT CH '00 and '02/3 r12 w2 (Restricted and Intermediate) p5 (3 3rds, inc 2 Hunt Chses); 4th, 5th, pulled up 2, and fell. The winner of three Points on easy surfaces, and rated 10-7 as recently as '02, but only stands very light campaigns, and has performed as though badly out of synch when pulled up in his last three attempts. *I. Anderson — Tanatside.* 228 (Cf).

ROMABIT TOM .7-0.. 10 ch.g. Henbit (USA) — Romacina (Roman Warrior) 84466. Tall rangy half-brother to Private Percival (*qv*). P-t-P '02/3 r4 p1 (2 fences last of 3); last pair 2, and pulled up. Nearly always plods to completion, but shows limited enthusiasm and only once better than last in '04. Has two handlers. *K.B. & R.J. Rogers — N. Hereford (Ray Rogers).* 668 (OMa), 981 (OMa), 1075 (OMa), 1232 (OMa), 1395 (OMa).

ROMANYBAAN ..8-10.. 9 ch.g. Romany Rye — Nellybaan (Ayyabaan) ppu6f3p. Tall rangy. Dam, 'a nutty jumper and evidently useless', was very remote in her only completion in 8 Points. P-t-P '02/3 (for Mr K. Needham) r9 w1 (Maiden, 3 ran — 2 finished) p0; pulled up 4, and fell/unseated 4. Won a shocking Maiden on very firm ground at Ystradowen in his first season, but has changed hands twice since, and is akin to an equine bulldozer. Has two handlers and can take a strong hold, but only once better than last in '04, and the latest rider is asking for trouble. Wears a cross-noseband. *Miss V. Burn — Fernie.* 383 (R), 587 (R), 784 (Cf), 885 (M), 1123 (R), 1279 (R), 1396 (C).

ROMANY MOVE ..9-10.. 11 b.g. Silly Prices — Go Gipsy (Move Off) pu513p2up115. Compact brother to Lucky Tanner, and half-brother to Nobody's Heroine. NH '00/2 r8 p0. P-t-P/HUNT CH '03 (for Miss M.D. Myco) r6 p5 (3 3rds, remote last once); and fell 1. Basically slow and gets into trouble as soon as the pace lifts, but incredibly lucky, and gifted two races and fortunate in another in '04. Got off the mark at the 18th attempt at Cothelstone when left clear by the fatal fall of the probable winner at the last, and would have finished a poor third at Bratton Down had the two leaders not fallen separately at the last. There was more merit in his Restricted success, but the favourite was not stopping in front when making his exit at the second last, and will clearly find matters altogether more taxing in future. Only effective on sound surfaces to date. *Mrs J.C. Reed & Mrs S. Cobden — Seavington (Sally Godfrey).* 78 (L), 238 (CfMa), 325 (OMa), 474 (OMa), 689 (R), 879 (R), 1013 (R), 1325 (R), 1366 (R), 1386 (R), 1508 (I), 1556 (MO).

ROMANY PEARL ..9-12.. 13 ch.g. St Columbus — Lucky Diamond (Eborneezer) 51132. Plain lengthy brother to Miss Solitaire, Dromain and Lady Emerald. Dam was placed thrice in 11 Points. Grandam, Lady Barbara II, failed to finish in 3 Points. P-t-P '02/3 r11 w1 (3-finisher Maiden) p4 (2nds, beaten ½*l* once, and ¾*l* once); last pair 3, pulled up 2, and fell. A typically late-starting Tarry-bred, but cottoned onto what was required much quicker than most, and has made the first two in half his races. Faced a straightforward task when equipped with first-time cheekpieces in his Members, and recorded an overdue Restricted success in a three-finisher event at Hackwood Park before shaking up the favourite on his Open debut. Liable to perform several pounds below his rating if owner ridden, and has been motivated best by James Owen. Has two handlers. *Miss R. Goodwin — Oakley.* 191 (R), 461 (M), 720 (R), 867 (I), 1032 (O).

ROMANYS CHANCE ..7-2.. 9 b.m. Supreme Chance — Christines Lady (Roman Warrior) 3. Sturdy half-sister to Castle Warrior, and to Hurdles winner, Lloyds Dream. Dam, half-sister to Burbridge King St (*qv* '94 Annual), pulled up and refused in Points. P-t-P '03 (for Mr D. & Mrs C. Hobbs) r2 p0 (refused, and pulled up). Emulated mum in her debut season, and then surpassed her pathetic efforts when around 41 lengths last of three in her Members, but does not get the trip well enough to make a successful Pointer. *Sir Nicholas Powell — O. Berks (Emma Pring).* 935 (M).

ROMMEL ..9-7.. 8 ch.g. Baron Blakeney — Sizzling Sun (Sunyboy) u6373. Sturdy trainer-bred half-brother to Bold Baby. Dam pointed to '98 and won Club Maiden for Lynn Redman; was also 3rd in Hdle. NH FLAT '01 r2 p0. NH '01/2 r2 p0. P-t-P '03 r6 w1 (Maiden) p2 (head 2nd once); last, pulled up, and fell. Won a bad Maiden emphatically at Kingston Blount last year, and came within a head of following up at the next fixture, but very expensive to follow in '04, and fell victim to Jon Trice-Rolph's unenterprising riding. Ran out of gas quickly when ridden more prominently on his final appearance and possibly under the weather all year, but can only be watched when reappearing. Continues to lack fluency. *D.J. Jeffrey, R.B. Felmingham, Mrs L. Redman, C. Witherspoon & M. Thomas — V. of Aylesbury with Garth & S. Berks (Lynne Redman).* 191 (R), 294 (R), 369 (R), 587 (R), 1107 (R).

PLATE 101 320 East Devon Confined: Ronans Choice and Richard Darke, 1st, at the last
PHOTO: Baths Photographic

RONANS CHOICE (IRE) .10-6.. 12 b.g. Yashgan — Petite Port (IRE) (Decent Fellow) 112s6. Big strong half-brother to Irish NH flat winner, Oldtown Court, and to Super Gasper (won 13 flat and 3 jumping races in Italy). IRISH P-t-P '00 r1 w1 (7yo&up Maiden). NH '00/2 (for G.M. McCourt) r10 w1 (3m3f Ch) p1 (2nd); pulled up 5. Bought Doncaster, Aug '02 for 4500. A thorough stayer who always sets off in front, and was able to maintain a bold gallop when completing a double in Confineds at Buckfastleigh (supported from 25-1 to 14-1) and Bishops Court. Tried hard to complete the hat-trick when upgraded to a Hunter Chase at Fontwell, but was wobbling in the closing stages and had to give best by two lengths, and then slipped up when leading after two miles at Taunton, and finished about 20 lengths sixth. Can lack fluency over the bigger obstacles, and is not particularly predictable, but game on his day despite his customary blinkers. Tongue-tied once under Rules. Seems to go well fresh, and it might pay to try him in a Hunter Chase first time out in '05. *R.O. Oliver — S. Devon (Emma Oliver).* 200 (Cf), 320 (Cf), 800 (3m2f110yH), 993 (3mH), 1293 (2m7f110yH).

RON MIEL (IRE) .8-12.. 11 b.g. Brush Aside (USA) — Try Le Reste (IRE) (Le Moss) 43p332. Strong-topped lengthy half-brother to Hurdles winner, Secret Drinker (IRE). Dam is half-sister to Ryton Guard (*qv* '98 Annual). IRISH P-t-P '99 r5 p0 (last, pulled up 3 and unseated). P-t-P/HUNT CH '00 and '02/3 r14 p3 (2 3rds, of 4 once); 7th, last 4, pulled up 5, and fell. A very modest performer by anyone's standards, and beaten between three-quarters-of-a-length and 45 lengths when making the frame in Maidens, but looked home and hosed on his latest appearance, and might have held on had he winged the last. Will get fewer easier opportunities. Suited by a sound surface. *Miss J.C. Meredith — N. Ledbury (Paul Senter).* 731 (OMa), 760 (OMa), 981 (OMa), 1020 (OMa), 1425 (OMa), 1495 (OMa).

ROONEYRAN ..—.. 9 br.g. Arctic Lord — Moy Ran Lady (Black Minstrel) pp8. Compact good-topped brother to Chasing winner, Sir Norman, and half-brother to Palladium Lady and Lady Anglesby. Dam, half-sister to Clove Bud (*qv* '93 Annual) and several Irish winners, dead-heated for mares Maiden in Ireland; and was subsequently 3rd in a Point. IRISH P-t-P '02 r2 p0 (last, and unseated). P-t-P '03 (for The Hunting Farmers Group) r3 w1 (2m4f Maiden) p0; unseated, and pulled up. Scored on his English debut over 2m4f at Eyton, but also underwent two operations for his wind in '03 that were obviously unsuccessful as he ran tubed latterly this year. Worth 9-9 at best, but cannot handle soft ground, and connections may decide that they have wasted enough time and money on him already. *F.D. Cornes, T.C. Gittins, E.W. Tuffin & L.A. Humphries — S. Salop (Pamela Sykes).* 95 (R), 252 (CR), 665 (R).

ROOSTER ..10-1.. 10 b.g. Roi Danzig (USA) — Jussoli (Don) f645. Tall strong half-brother to Hurdles winner, Miss Ellie, and to flat winner, So Amazing. Dam won 4 Irish flat (7-10f). FLAT '98/9 and '01 r8 p1 (2nd). NH '98/01 r8 w1 (2m110y Hdle) p2. HUNT CH '03 r4 p2; 4th, and pulled up. Made all to score over hurdles at Doncaster in '00, but fell at the second on his Chasing debut 14 months and just four starts later, and missed '02 entirely. Has made the frame in four sub-3m Hunter Chases for the present handler, but will continue to struggle to find a winning opportunity unless he is produced fit enough to do himself justice. *Mrs P. King — Suffolk (Julie Read).* 544 (2m5f110yH), 892 (2m5f110yH), 1359 (2m4f110yH), 1443 (2m5fH).

ROSALEE ROYALE .9-9.. 13 ch.m. Out Of Hand — Miss Ark Royal (Broadsword USA) 2p. Lengthy. Dam won 2m2f Sell Hdle. FLAT r6 p0 (inc last 4, and unseated; inc Sells). NH FLAT '96 r2 p0. NH '96/7 r2 p0 (6th, and last in Sells). P-t-P/HUNT CH '98/00 and '02/3 r23 w1 (mares Maiden) p8 (3 2nds, of 3 once; and 5 3rds, of 4 thrice, remote once, and last once); fell/unseated 4, and pulled up 5. Useless under Rules, but finally got off the mark at the 30th attempt when scoring completely unchallenged at Holnicote last year, and gave a good account of herself when totally outclassed behind the pot-hunting Jabiru in her Members. Usually displays a distinct lack of stamina, and gave the impression something was amiss next time and failed to reappear. Tailed off last when blinkered once on the flat in '97. *Mrs S. Kittow — Tiverton.* 114 (M), 279 (R).

ROSCOE BURN ..10-1.. 13 ch.g. Meadowbrook — Rosecko (White Speck) 51p44p. Tall owner-bred brother to Royalecko. P-t-P '98/03 r25 w1 (Maiden) p4 (3 3rds, of 4 once); pulled up 6, and fell/unseated 3. Goes a good gallop and scored on firmish at Musselburgh four years after losing his maiden status, but normally fails to get the trip, and was over-faced subsequently. Missed out on a Restricted and with no Members available to him will continue to struggle. Blinkered once in '02. *Mrs E. Johnstone — Borders Bloodhounds (Katie Massie).* 212 (R), 507 (I), 1028 (3mH), 1220 (C), 1421 (O), 1489 (3m3fH).

ROSEACRE (IRE) .8-3§.. 8 b.g. Roselier (FR) — Brown Forest (Brave Invader USA) 24954p3r5. Small short-backed half-brother to Knockanoran (IRE) and Forest Musk (IRE), and to Irish Pointing winner, Cookoo Charlie (IRE). P-t-P '03 (for Mr J.A. Keighley) r2 p0 (pulled up 2). Receiving reminders from an early stage when plodding into ten lengths second on his reappearance at Larkhill, but has shown minimal enthusiasm when beating just three rivals since, and blinkered to no avail on four of his last five starts. Does not lack strength in the saddle, but error-prone and probably wrong in some way. *The Forde Grange Friends (G. Allen) — Cotley (Jane Western).* 13 (OMa), 87 (OMa), 314 (R), 327 (OMa), 494 (OMa), 962 (OMa), 1098 (OMa), 1326 (OMa), 1381 (OMa).

ROSEGROVE ROOSTER ..9-2§.. 8 b.g. Henbit (USA) — Cornbelt (Oats) pp2p2. Lengthy well-made owner-bred. NH FLAT '02 r2 p0. NH '03 (for late D.J. Caro) r2 p0 (pulled up 2). Pulled up in his first five races over jumps and can be very temperamental including in the preliminaries (has been mounted on the course and taken to post early), but showed he has some ability when three-quarters-of-a-length second of four over 2m4f and ten lengths second of three in Maidens (very unwilling when adding another pulled up in between). Evidently has the ability to win a bad race, but there is no guarantee that he will be prepared to try. *J. Roper — N. Ledbury (Tim Stephenson).* 252 (CR), 452 (R), 619 (2m4fOMa), 982 (2m5fOMa), 1020 (OMa).

ROSEHILL DOORBELL ..9-2.. 8 b.m. Miner's Lamp — Boherash (Boreen FR) p. Unfurnished half-sister to RBF Arianne and Nearly A Score. Dam won NH flat and 2m3f Hdle in Ireland and placed 9 inc 2 Points there; and was 3rd in 2 English Hdles before running atrociously in 4 Points. NH FLAT '01 r1 p0. NH '01 r1 p0. P-t-P '02/3 r8 p2 (3rd of 4 once); last pair 2, pulled up 4. Showed improvement on previous efforts when placed twice in Maidens last year, and was sent off favourite in the latest, but has great difficulty getting the trip, and lamed on her reappearance at Holnicote. Wears a cross-noseband. *The Just One More Club (S.H. Jarrett) — W. Somerset (Alison Handel).* 274 (CfMa).

ROSEMEAD TYE ..9-5.. 9 b.m. Kasakov — Nouvelle Cuisine (Yawa) pfpu21p. Tiny half-sister to Hurdles winner, Feanor. Dam, half-sister to Rallegio (*qv* '02 Annual), won 2 flat (12-16f) and 2 Hdles at around 2m. P-t-P '02 (for Mr R. Howe) r5 p0 (pulled up 2, fell/unseated 3). NH FLAT '02 r1 p0. NH '02/3 (for J.A. Moore, and D.W. Thompson) r10 p1 (dist last of 3 in 2m1f110y Ch); pulled up 2. Beaten 24 length plus over hurdles, including Sellers, and has had severe problems negotiating the bigger obstacles, but cannot be accused of not having heart and won a bad Maiden in softish at Chaddesley at the 22nd attempt. Was a deserving winner having twice exited in the lead with half-a-mile to run previously, but normally races too keenly to get home, and will have to toil long and hard to follow up. *T. Jewitt — Cotswold V.F.* 613 (L), 731 (OMa), 981 (OMa), 1141 (OMa), 1255 (L), 1340 (OMa), 1388 (R).

ROSE OF THE HILL (IRE) ..9-12.. 6 gr.g. Roselier (FR) — Golden Leaf (Croghan Hill) 11. Brother to Irish NH flat winner, The Well. 12,986 4yo. Created a good impression for a five-year old when unbeaten in two visits to Littlewindsor, but the times were slow and there were only three runners in the Restricted. Should cope with a modest rise in class at least, and may turn out to be quite useful. *D.E. Pipe — Silverton.* 693 (OMa), 1013 (R).

PLATE 102 507 Northern P-t-P Area Club Intermediate: Roscoe Burn and the enthusiastic Michael McAlister, 1st, are clear at the last *PHOTO: Alan Mitchell*

ROSETA (IRE) .9-10.. 13 ch.g. Roselier (FR) — Urrin Valley VII (unknown) f. Angular. IRISH NH FLAT '97 r1 p0. IRISH NH '99 r2 p0. NH '99/01 r13 w2 (2m4f110y-2m6f110y Chses) p2 (3rds); pulled up 2, and fell/unseated 2. P-t-P '02 r2 p1 (head 2nd); and pulled up. A competent performer on his day, but incredibly lightly raced throughout his career, and both he and Vanessa Shaw had their season curtailed by a heavy fall at Great Trethew. Errors have been an unwelcome feature of his races over fences, and it would be no surprise if the latest spill was career-threatening. Blinkered once, and tongue-tied twice in '01. *Mrs P.J. Shaw — Dartmoor.* 311 (L).

ROSETTA ..9-6.. 8 b.m. Fraam — Starawak (Star Appeal) p172. Compact attractive half-sister to Brand New Dance, and to several other winners, including, Fame Again and Army of Stars. Dam won 12 race. FLAT '99/02 r21 p1 (3rd). NH '01 r2 p0; unseated 1. P-t-P '03 r1 p0 (brought down). Useless on the flat, and not better than last in four previous attempts over jumps, but sprang a 50-1 surprise when coming with a strong late run to secure the spoils on firmish at Holnicote. Both the runner-up and the third went on to score, but only beat one rival herself subsequently, and gave the impression that a lack of stamina was the problem. Wears a cross-noseband. *Ms S.J. Gordon — Weston & Banwell H.* 87 (OMa), 275 (CfMa), 879 (R), 1364 (M).

ROSEY BOY (IRE) ..—§.. 12 gr.g. Roselier (FR) — Rossian (Silent Spring) pfpp. Angular brother to Touring-Turtle (IRE) (*qv*). NH '98/9 and '02/3 (for M. Pitman, one win, and H. Morrison, one win) r14 w2 (3m2f-3m2f) p2; pulled up 2, fell/unseated 2. Sold Doncaster, May for 3000. Bought Doncaster Aug for 3000. Used to stay long trips and have ability, but has always been a very difficult ride, and hung off the course and pulled up once over Hurdles and hung badly left and unrideable when pulling up in one Chase and unseated after some erratic jumping in the other. Failed to finish when blinkered twice. Useless in Opens, and a reappearance looks highly unlikely. *A.J. Brook & R. Anderson — Hurworth (Karen Tutty).* 107 (O), 214 (O), 501 (O), 770 (Cf).

ROSIE STROUD (IRE) .9-2§.. 10 br.m. Mandalus — Galway Grey (Gala Performance) 522p3. Good topped sister to Dreamin George (IRE). Dam is half-sister to Pride Of Down (*qv* '87 Season Annual). IRISH P-t-P '99 r1 p0 (pulled up). P-t-P '02/3 (for Mr K.R. Dance) r5 p1 (2nd of 3); last pair 3, and pulled up 1. Makes the frame on a regular basis, but a desperately weak finisher, and hung violently towards the paddock exit and threw away an ideal opportunity at Garnons. Pulled up in blinkers once in '02, and seems intent on clinging to her maiden status by every manner or means. *Mrs G.M. Pritchard & Mrs J. Rawlings — N. Ledbury (Julian Pritchard).* 111 (OMa), 409 (CMam), 620 (OMa), 730 (OMa), 1141 (OMa).

ROSS POLDARK ..9-10.. 12 b.g. Arctic Lord — La Jolie Fille (Go Blue) pp. Owner-bred half-brother to Kingsmill Imp (dam of Kingsmill Creek, *qv*), Easter Again (dam of Tamar Lily, *qv* '01 Annual), Tamar Lass, Kingsmill Quay and Pillmere Lad. Dam, half-sister to Transmitter (*qv* '87 Season Annual, raced for David Du Plessis until he was 19), won a Maiden and 2nd for him. P-t-P '02/3 r4 w1 (Maiden) p1 (2nd of 3); pulled up 1, and unseated 1. Normally a free-running individual, and gave an exuberant display when successful at Kilworthy in '02, but reportedly very cold-backed and planted in the paddock and was reluctant to go to post on his reappearance. Only runs twice a year, and needs to concentrate on Restricteds if able to reappear. *Miss J. du Plessis — E. Cornwall.* 573 (I), 705 (I).

ROSTOCK (IRE) ..10-6.. 8 br.g. Roselier (FR) — Royal Greenwood (IRE) (Radical) w11211p. Rangy Dam won 5yo Maiden and 2m4f NH flat in Ireland. IRISH P-t-P '02/3 r8 p0 (last, pulled up 5, fell and ran out). Useless in Ireland and tried tongue-tied, and showed early signs of temperament which immediately resurfaced on his debut for the new yard when he had to be withdrawn at the start after taking off in the wrong direction. Has had two paddock handlers since and was still behaving in a loopy fashion at Cartmel on his most recent appearance (where he was pulled up after losing his action), but is useful when his speed can be effectively harnessed, and ran up a sequence of four wins and a second in Wales. Beat Pete The Painter who has subsequently won a £4,000 first prize in a Worcester Beginners Chase, so would have clear claims under Rules, but it has to be said that connections have a pretty disappointing record in this sphere. *D. Brace — Llangeinor.* 13 (OMa), 454 (CfMa), 674 (R), 952 (I), 1090 (Cf), 1321 (MO), 1526 (3m2fH).

ROUGE LADY ..—.. 7 b.m. Rakaposhi King — Castle Rouge (Carlingford Castle) R4. Lengthy homebred. NH '04 (for D. McCain) r1 p0 (4th in 2m Sell Hdle: *ld til hdd & jmpd slow 5, sn wknd, t.o*). Ran out at the tenth in a Maiden before finishing 81 lengths fourth of five in a Selling Hurdle, and looks a crab. *D. McCain Jnr — Cheshire.* 1266 (2m4fOMa).

ROUGH TIGER (IRE) ..8-11§.. 12 ch.g. Glacial Storm (USA) — Mourne Trix (Golden Love) u57. Tall rangy stringhalt near-hind half-brother to Good Thyne Guy (IRE) and Letterfrack Lad (IRE). P-t-P/HUNT CH '99 and '01/3 (for Mrs V. McKie) r13 w5 (up to Confined) p3 (2 3rds, inc Hunt Ch); 4th, 6th, fell, and pulled up 2. Able and won five races to '03, but needs plenty of driving along and has appeared to down tools when not in the mood. Provided Ben Tuckey with his first rides in '04, but he proved totally ineffective, and tailed off last in both completions. Only stands light campaigns, and looks finished in competitive events now. Has been tried in a visor. *Mrs I. McKie — M. Tuckey — Bicester with Whaddon (-; Tom Illsley).* 583 (Cf), 868 (O), 1104 (Cnr).

ROUND THE BEND ..10-0.. 13 b.g. Revolutionary (USA) — No Love (Bustiki) p. Close-coupled brother to Give It A Whirl. P-t-P/HUNT CH '00/3 r20 w3 (Maiden, Restricted and Members) p7 (5 2nds, beaten head once, of 3 once, and last, inc Hunt Ch; and inc last of 3); 4th, 5th, last pair 3, unseated and pulled up 4. An over-enthusiastic galloper, and has tended to boil over in the preliminaries, but ended a long losing run when making all to record a double in minor events last year. Jumps for fun but appeared to suffer a setback on his return at Fakenham. Wears a cross-noseband. *F. Allan & P. Phazey — Fitzwilliam (Louise Allan).* 544 (2m5f110yH).

ROUND THE ISLES .8-12.. 7 b.g. Jupiter Island — Beenaround (IRE) (King's Ride) 234. Strong lengthy owner-bred. Dam, half-sister to top class Irish NH flat and jumping winner, Native Upmanship. Followed what looked to be a promising 20 lengths second on his debut with an 11 lengths third when favourite at High Easter, but was most disappointing when 50 lengths fourth at Dingley where he never looked keen in the final mile. Capable of winning a Maiden if he wishes, but would not be far off a squiggle after his latest display. Possibly had excuses so it is withheld. *P. Rackham — Pytchley (Caroline Bailey).* 371 (OMa), 652 (OMa), 1218 (OMa).

ROUTE ONE (IRE) ..10-5.. 12 b.g. Welsh Term — Skylin (Skyliner) 601435. Lengthy workmanlike brother to Route Two (IRE). Dam won 5f race at 2. FLAT '00 r5 p0. NH FLAT '97 r1 w1 (1m5f110y). NH '98/00 r10 w2 (2m-2m1f Hdles) p2 (2nds); fell 1. P-t-P/HUNT CH '02/3 r14 w2 (2m3f110y-2m4f110y Hunt Chses) p6 (3 2nds, inc 3 Hunt Chses; and inc 3rd twice in Hunt Chses); 5th, 8th, pulled up 2, and fell 2. Does not get the trip in Points, and only uses them to limber up nowadays, but capable of smart form in sub-3m Hunter Chases, and is particularly well suited by going right-handed. Jumped with much more conviction than he had at Sandown previously when successful over the minimum trip at Leicester, and not disgraced subsequently, but his needs are specific, and good or fast ground is another essential. May be able to find another opening when conditions are right in '05. Blinkered once in '99. *D.S. Frankland — Grafton.* 100 (O), 241 (2m4f110yH), 444 (2mH), 630 (2m4fH), 1372 (2m4fH), 1497 (3mH).

ROUTE TWO (IRE) .9-3.. 11 b.g. Welsh Term — Skylin (Skyliner) 75. Workmanlike brother to Route One (IRE) (*qv*). NH FLAT '98/9 r3 w1 p1 (3rd). NH '99/01 r5 p3 (3rds). P-t-P '03 r6 p0 (5th of 6, fell 2, slipped up, ran out, and pulled up). Made a winning debut at Ludlow in '98, but incredibly lightly raced and unable to score over jumps, and beaten a minimum of 23 lengths in Points. At least that was an improvement on his dire performances of '03, but still gives the impression that he has problems. *N. Thomas & Mrs P. Greenwood — V.W.H. (Paul Greenwood).* 187 (Cf), 405 (Inr).

ROWLEYRASCAL ..—.. 10 gr.g. No Evil — Mother Meldrum (Sergeant Drummer USA) ppp. Rangy light. Pulled up after 2-2m4f in all three attempts, and has created an immediately unfavourable impression. *H. Bray — Exmoor (Debbie Cole).* 275 (CfMa), 329 (OMa), 573 (I).

ROXTONS ..8-12.. 8 b.g. Sula Bula — Tango Country (Town And Country) f. Workmanlike owner-bred. Dam, half-sister to Vivaque (*qv* '92 Annual). P-t-P '03 r2 p0 (last, and fell). Showed a little ability on his debut, but fell twice after a mile subsequently, and broke a hind leg on his return. *J. Baker — R.A. (Ned Cummins).* 13 (OMa).

ROYAL ACTION .10-0.. 12 b.g. Royal Academy (USA) — Ivor's Honey (Sir Ivor USA) 2112212413. Compact half-brother to Tolmin, to flat winners, Honeybird, Artaius Mead and Stiffelio (IRE), and to a winner in France. Dam won at 10f in Ireland. FLAT r15 w4 (8-10f, all on all-weather) p3 (beaten head once). NH '96/8 r7 w1 (2m3f Hdle, 3 ran) p4. P-t-P '00 and '02/3 r26 w2 (inc Open) p10 (6 3rds, of 4 twice; inc 2nd of 3 once); 4th twice, 7th, last pair 4, fell/unseated 3, and pulled up 4. Won five races in the 12 months to November '97, culminating in a three-runner Hurdle at Warwick, but had a lot of problems with breaking blood vessels latterly, and proved easy to beat in his first three seasons Pointing. Regained some motivation in '04, and won four minor events on good or sound surfaces at stayers' tracks, but ended the year on a depressing note when breaking down at Penshurst. Blinkered once in '96. *A.G. Chinery — E. Essex (Paul Chinery).* 23 (Cf), 45 (Cnr), 155 (Cnr), 249 (Cnr), 400 (C), 523 (O), 610 (Cv&nr), 744 (O), 906 (Cnr), 1087 (O).

ROYAL ARCTIC (IRE) ..8-9§§.. 15 ch.g. Sandalay — Remindful (Bargello) 4. Rangy brother to Robsand (IRE) (*qv*). IRISH P-t-P '96/7 r8 w2 (7yo plus Maiden, and Winners of Two) p3; pulled up, fell and unseated. NH '97/9 and '00 r24 w2 (2m5f Hdles) p5 (inc 3 2nds); pulled up 1. P-t-P/HUNT CH '00 and '02 (for Mr J. Worth) r10 p1 (2nd); pulled up 1, fell 1. Won two races on Grade One tracks in '98, but immediately embarked on a losing run that now stretches to 28, and delights in taking zero interest nowadays. Tailed off throughout the final mile when last in his Members, and is not worth bothering with again. Has been tried in headgear, and ridden in spurs. *M.S. Burman — Cambs with Enfield Chace.* 123 (M).

ROYAL BARGE ..10-3.. 15 b.g. Nearly A Hand — April Airs (Grey Mirage) 7201. Small neat owner-bred half-brother to Handsome Harvey, Princess Pool (dam of Mister Julius *qv*), and Nat Gold. Dam is an unraced half-sister to Jack Sound (*qv* '96 Annual). P-t-P '96 (for Mr E.L. Harries) r3 p0 (refused, ran out and pulled up). NH '97/9 and '01/2 (for P. Bowen) r23 w6 (2 2m6f-3m110y Hdles, and 4 2m7f110y-3m3f Chses) p10; pulled up 2, unseated 1. A total miscreant when he first emerged, but moulded into a very successful summer jumper by Peter Bowen, and recorded a four-timer in '98. Absent through lameness in '00, and has been lightly raced since, but resurfaced after another absence looking in tremendous nick in '04, and it was good to see him back in the winners enclosure, albeit following a simple task in his Members. Has always shown a tendency to jump away to his right, and forfeited many lengths in so doing at Aintree, but has never fallen. *D. Quinn — Pembs (Marc Barber).* 115 (MO), 448 (O), 732 (2m5f110yH), 1547 (M).

ROYAL CENTURY (IRE) .—.. 7 b.g. Royal Academy (USA) — Royal Lorna (USA) (Val De L'Orne FR) u Half-brother to Hurdles winners, Darzee and Rothari. IRISH FLAT '02/3 (for D. McDonogh) r7 p (3rd). IRISH NH FLAT '02 (for W.P. Mullins) r1 p0. Found little when one-and-three-quarter length third in a 2m Irish flat race, which was his only form (tongue-tied four times there). Unseated at th ninth in an Erw Lon Maiden, and fatally injured after crashing through ropes when loose. P. Riddick — Gelligaer F. 202 (CfMa).

ROYAL CRIMSON ..10-1§.. 14 b.g. Danehill (USA) — Fine Honey (USA) (Drone USA) 44p14692 Well-made half-brother to Polar Flight (*qv*). IRISH FLAT '93/5 r21 w3 (6-8f) p3 (3rds). IRISH N '94/5 r2 p1 (3rd). NH '95/00 r25 w5 (2m Hdle and 4 2m110y-2m4f Chses) p4; pulled up 4, fell 1 P-t-P/HUNT CH '02/3 r10 w1 (Members) p3 (3rds, inc Hunt Ch); 6th, last pair 3, and pulled up 2 The veteran of 66 races, and for all his foibles has a good winning record, and took his tally int double figures when retaining his Members title at Hornby Castle where he finished solo at 1-2. Sti retains ability and not disgraced despite finishing last of two on his most recent outing, but likes to ge his own way, and will not tolerate bullying. Broke a blood vessel once last year. Has been tried i headgear. *Major R.R. Alers-Hankey — Bedale (Annabelle Armitage).* 267 (Cf), 445 (3m110yH) 770 (Cf), 809 (M), 1163 (Cf), 1202 (Cf), 1396 (C), 1457 (O).

ROYAL CRUISE (IRE) ..8-13.. 8 b.g. Wakashan — Polly Preacher (Decent Fellow) 23p21. IRISH P-t '03 r2 p0 (pulled up and fell). A weak finisher who tends to disappoint and was beaten 14 length and upwards in three placings, and last in two of them including with cheekpieces in the latest Normally partnered by Phil York, and his assistance seemed invaluable when he finally lasted hom in a Maiden taking 7min15sec at Peper Harow. Not impressing as a Restricted prospect so far, an later withdrawn from a Folkestone Hunter Chase won by Free Gift because of a passport irregularit *S. Garrott — O. Surrey, Burstow & W. Kent (Richard Gurney).* 418 (2m4fCMa), 539 (OMa), 78 (OMa), 1055 (OMa), 1211 (OMa).

ROYAL CZARINA ..9-11.. 8 ch.m. Czaravich (USA) — Sabrata (IRE) (Zino) 3334133. Sturdy compac half-sister to flat winners, Receivedwiththanx and Head Scratcher. Dam won at 5f in France. 1400 FLAT '99/00 r5 p0. NH '00/2 (for M. Salaman) r10 p2; unseated 2. Bought Ascot, Jun for 1904 Beaten between eight and 18 lengths in two placings over Hurdles, but was little more than Sellin class, as she was on the flat. Only of average competence in all her first four Maidens but havin made the frame in all four she deserved her success at Hackwood, where she was all out to hol Gunnerbe Posh by a head. Fell at the last and remounted for third next time, and then raised he rating by about seven pounds with a ten lengths third over 2m5f at Folkestone, where Free Gift coul have trebled the margin had his rider desired. Consistent and a steady jumper, but always strugglin to get the trip. May find another easy opportunity. *J. Myerscough-Walker — Blackmore & Sparkfor V. (John Dufosee).* 67 (OMa), 173 (OMa), 413 (2m4fOMa), 599 (2m4fOMa), 971 (OMa), 120 (R), 1439 (2m5fH).

ROYAL DEW (IRE) ..8-12§.. 12 b/br.g. Royal Fountain — Ardglass Mist (Black Minstrel) p3 Workmanlike compact. NH '98 r2 p0. P-t-P '99/03 r23 w2 (Maiden and Restricted) p5 (3 2nds, of once, and last once; and inc last of 3 once); pulled up 8, unseated 1. Won a bad Maiden in '00, an walked-over at Hackwood Park two years later, but normally most irresolute, and beaten a fence whe third of four in a Members on his latest appearance. Has been tried unsuccessfully in headgear. *D.B Evatt — Southdown & Eridge (Heather Cobb).* 605 (M), 638 (M).

ROYALECKO ..10-5.. 9 b.g. Royal Fountain — Rosecko (White Speck) pu1312. Workmanlike owner bred half-brother to Roscoe Burn. P-t-P '02/3 r6 w1 (3-finisher Maiden) p0; pulled up 4, and fel Unbeaten in his first two completion, and has finally strung together a decent sequence of results, bu rather an excitable sort, and may need things his own way. Capable of jumping boldly and well, an likes to front run, and looks speedy enough to continue to make an impression in Ladies races. Yet t encounter mud, but unlikely to appreciate it. *Mrs E. Johnstone — Borders Bloodhounds (Joa Hollands).* 212 (R), 657 (R), 766 (R), 1037 (I), 1080 (Cf), 1308 (L).

ROYAL PLUM ..—§§.. 9 ch.g. Inchinor — Miss Plum (Ardross) rOrppurp. Good-topped. Dam won 3 fla (12-19f), and 2 Hurdles (2m7f-3m1f). NH FLAT '00 r4 w1 p1 (2nd). FLAT '00/1 r8 p0. NH '01/ (for Mrs M. Reveley) r8 w1 (3mHdle) p1 (2nd). Bought Doncaster, May for 2300. Won a bumper an a stayers Hurdle from 20 attempts under Rules, but was ungenuine even in those days and foun little, often after travelling well. Forced on although totally exhausted on his Pointing debut, and ha hated the rider for the experience and not taken a willing step since. Regularly wears blinkers o cheekpieces. Hopefully pity will have been taken on him at last, because he should not be on racecourse in this state. *S.J. Robinson — Zetland.* 214 (O), 267 (Cf), 542 (3m3fH), 764 (O), 81 (O), 1301 (Cf), 1421 (O), 1477 (O).

ROYAL SNOOPY (IRE) ..10-8.. 12 b/br.g. Royal Fountain — Lovely Snoopy (IRE) (Phardante FR) 1u4. Lengthy brother to Irish NH Flat and Hurdles winner, Royal Signature. Dam is half-sister to Pronounced (*qv* '95 Annual). IRISH NH FLAT '98 r4 w1 p2 (3rds). IRISH NH '98/9 r6 p1 (3rd). NH '99/02 r23 w5 (4 2m5110y-2m6f Hdles and 3m Ch) p9. P-t-P/HUNT CH '03 r4 p3 (2 3rds, of 4 once; and 2nd in Hunt Ch); and 4th of 5. Contested the Cheltenham Festival bumper as a five-year-old, and bucked up his ideas when blinkered over hurdles, but never a natural jumper of fences, and only won one of 12 Chases before leaving Charlie Mann. Scoring for the first time since May '01 when making all and bolting up in the fastest time of the day at Witton Castle, but old jumping frailties resurfaced with victory assured next time, and could never get to the front on his latest start. Likes to be left to do his own thing, and more than capable of holding his own in similar company, even at 12. *M.D. Abrahams — W. of Yore (Robin Tate).* 1289 (O), 1347 (2m6f110yH), 1497 (3mH).

ROYAL SQUEEZE (IRE) ..8-11.. 9 b.m. King's Ride — Ballykilleen (The Parson) 7. Tall rangy. Dam is sister to Blue Is The Colour (*qv* '04 Annual). P-t-P '02 r2 p1 (3rd of 4); and last. A steady jumper and well connected, but beaten between 14 and 35 lengths to date, and does not appear to have sufficient stamina. Missed '03 and restricted to a single appearance this year, and obviously almost impossible to train. *A. West & Countess Goess-Saurau — V.W.H. (James Richardson).* 35 (CMam).

ROYALTINO (IRE) ..10-6.. 13 b.g. Neltino — Royal Well (Royal Vulcan) pp. Good-bodied. Dam, sister to Royal Ryde (*qv* '96 Annual), and half-sister to Teeton Mill (*qv* '99 Annual). NH FLAT '96 r1 w1. FRENCH NH '96/9 r18 w5 (4 2m2f-2m5f Hdles and 2m3f Ch) p6 (beaten short-head once). NH '97 and '99 r3 w1 (2m5f Hdle) p0. HUNT CH '03 r2 p1 (2nd); and pulled up. A very smart performer in mud in his youth, and returned from a four-year absence to finish a praiseworthy second at Bangor last year, but sadly broke down irreparably at Haydock. *Mrs S. Cartridge & Miss T. McCurrich — Worcs (Theresa McCurrich).* 107 (O), 179 (2m6fH).

ROYAL TRADITION (IRE) ..—.. 12 br.g. Royal Fountain — Just For Today (Proverb) ufp. Plain leggy. Dam, half-sister Killarney Man (*qv* '99 Annual). NH FLAT '99 r3 p1 (2nd). NH '00/1 (for R. Rowe, and Mrs L.C. Jewell) r4 p0; pulled up 2. Second in a bumper, but beaten 42 lengths plus twice and pulled up twice over Hurdles, and looked to have a problem even in those days. Returned after three years to unseat at the sixth and fall at the second, and then with his confidence in tatters he managed to clamber over two fences and was promptly pulled up. A very sorry spectacle, even by the expected Maggie Stephens standards. *J. Stephens — Llandeilo F. (Margaret Stephens).* 204 (CfMa), 948 (OMa), 1193 (OMa).

ROY MY BOY .—.. 6 b.g. Riverwise (USA) — Pretty Pantoes (Lepanto GER) uf. Half-brother to Dido's Dream (*qv* '03 Annual). Great-grandam, Joyful Tears, failed to finish in 4 of 5 Points, but bred Run To Me (*qv* '90 Annual). Bought Ascot, Aug for 1428. Unseated at the sixth and fell at the 14th in Maidens at Black Forest Lodge, and the rider did not seem to be much of an asset. *J. Cole — Lamerton (Amanda Cole).* 149 (OMa), 417 (CfMah).

ROYRACE ..9-0§.. 13 b.g. Wace (USA) — Royal Tycoon (Tycoon II) 2f35. Tall owner-bred half-brother to Tycoon Ted and Drunkards Corner, and to flat winner, Tycoon Tina. Dam won 2 2m Hdles, inc a Sell for the Brisbournes. FLAT '94/9 r14 p0. NH '96/02 r32 p4 (3 3rds); pulled up 12, and fell/unseated 2. P-t-P '02/3 r5 p2 (3rds); 6th, last, and slipped up. The loser of 55 races, and typically let supporters down when backed from 5-2 to 5-4 in a dreadful Maiden at Chaddesley in '04, but clearly a beloved pet, and connections continue to show great faith. Has been tried in headgear. *A. Evans & Mrs M. Brisbourne — Tanatside (Anthony Brisbourne).* 1148 (R), 1261 (OMa), 1340 (OMa), 1473 (OMa).

RUBIAN PRINCESS .9-3.. 10 b.m. Kinglet — Once Bitten (Brave Invader USA) p7p. Small compact half-sister to Carrick Lanes, Miss Vagabond (dam of Catalan Girl, *qv*), Cautious Leader, Knickers and High Fields, and to NH flat winner, Celtic Park. Dam won 2m1f Sell Hdle. P-t-P '00/3 r12 w2 (Maiden and Restricted) p1 (3rd of 4); last pair 6, fell and pulled up 2. The winner of two weak races on good or sound surfaces at Howick last year, but tailed off after two miles in each of her three appearances in '04, and does not appear to be particularly hardy. *M.W. Lasper — Ystrad Taf Fechan.* 116 (I), 359 (Cf), 447 (Cf).

RUBISSIMO (IRE) ..— §.. 12 b.g. Phardante (FR) — Rubydora (Buckskin FR) pp0. Tall narrow half-brother to Foxydora (IRE) and My Dora (IRE). Dam won NH flat and 2m4f Hurdle on all-weather, and is half-sister to Niffy Nora (*qv* '93 Annual). FRENCH FLAT r1 p0. FRENCH NH '98/01 (for F. Doumen) r30 w3 (Hdle and 2 2m6f Chses, including Prix des Drags) p8; pulled up 5, fell 1. Was in excellent heart in the spring of '99, but generally a huge disappointment since, and can look reluctant. Won £129,523 for Francois Doumen, principally in very soft ground at Auteuil, and picked up pots of £53,821 and £32,293. English visits were a total disaster, as he pulled up in a Hurdle and pulled up four times and fell in Chases, and maintained that level of awfulness in the new yard including when a gamble from 10s to 3-1 once. Normally wears blinkers. Was on a comeback mission after three years, and it would be surprising to see him tried again. *Mrs S. Cartridge & Miss T. McCurrich — Worcs (Theresa McCurrich).* 1015 (Cf), 1344 (C), 1497 (3mH).

RUBON PRINCE (IRE) .8-7.. 14 ch.g. Kambalda — Oh Clare (Laurence O) pp554p. Compact half-brother to River Clare and Fate A Compli (IRE). NH FLAT '97 r2 p0. NH '97/02 r32 p10 (inc 8 Chses); pulled up 3, unseated 4. P-t-P '00 (for Mr N.B. Mason) r2 w1 (Restricted) p0; and 5th of 6. Won Pointing at the first opportunity, but missed out on a Maiden, and was a prolific loser with a tendency to make mistakes under Rules. Only ran once in '02,and missed the following year, and only once better than last when resuming. Slow and ancient but must feel like turning round and biting Trevor Glass, who is too liberal with his use of the whip. Acquired cheekpieces once in '04, and regained blinkers on two occasions. *Manor Farm P-t-P Club (J.A. Lytollis) — Bedale (Joe Lytollis).* 772 (4m1fO), 1161 (O), 1202 (Cf), 1301 (Cf), 1460 (I), 1526 (3m2fH).

RUBY DANTE (IRE) ..9-8.. 7 b.m. Ajraas (USA) — Phar Glen (IRE) (Phardante FR) f2u12p. Light-framed half-sister to Pharout (IRE). Dam is sister to Jabiru (*qv*). P-t-P '03 r1 p0 (unseated). NH FLAT '03 (for P. Bowen) r3 p1 (3rd). Showed a little ability in bumpers, and her galloping ability is not in question, but badly let down by her jumping until surviving a shoal of mistakes at Bonvilston, and is fast becoming a license for bookmakers to print money. Tends to boil over in the preliminaries, but capable of upgrading successfully as soon as she jumps a clear round. *M.G. Jones — Gelligaer F.* 363 (CfMa), 700 (CfMa), 845 (CfMa), 1091 (CMam), 1237 (R), 1482 (R).

RUDGE HILL .—.. 9 b.g. Almushmmir — Time After Time (High Award) fp. Tall workmanlike. Dam won Restricted and placed 2nd. NH FLAT '02 r2 p0. NH '02/3 (for G.A. Ham, and S.C. Burrough) r5 p0; pulled up 3. A non-finisher in five of seven attempts over jumps including when pulled up in his only Chase (soon tailed off and jumped moderately), and has not looked remotely like completing in Points. Good luck to Heather Merriman who seems to have a lot of enthusiasm for Pointing, but she is beating her head against a brick wall with the likes of this one, Boy Band, Sixth Sense and Lily Lane (one completion in '04 between the lot of them). *Mrs H.J. Merriman — Blackmore & Sparkford V. (Heather Merriman).* 495 (I), 604 (OMa).

RULING THE ROAST ..9-0.. 10 b.g. Supreme Leader — Culinary (Tower Walk) p6. Tall heavy-topped brother to Irish NH flat and Hurdles winners, Kings Banquet (also won Chasing) and Hang'em High, and half-brother to Mr Tees Components. Dam, half-sister to St Helens Boy (*qv* '97 Annual), won 2m Sell Hdle. NH FLAT '00 r2 p0. P-t-P '02 r2 p2 (2nds). Beat two subsequent scorers when runner-up twice in '02, but missed the following season, and looked in need of the runs when not better than last in two spins this February. Looks to retain some ability, but has always looked too top heavy. *C.R. Cox — O. Berks.* 139 (R), 296 (OMa).

RUMOUR HAS IT (IRE) .9-0.. 8 b.g. Corrouge (USA) — Greyford River (Over The River FR) p2p. Workmanlike half-brother to 3 losing jumpers. A six lengths second at Detling was acceptable, but has jumped far too erratically otherwise, including when favourite on final start. Might be able to atone if intensive schooling can do the trick. *N.A.E. Jones & Dr C. Hargreaves — E. Sussex & Romney Marsh (Di Grissell).* 153 (OMa), 540 (CfMa), 895 (OMa).

RUNAWAY RALPH ..—§§.. 11 ch.g. Rolfe (USA) — Swift Messenger (Giolla Mear) ppbp. Well-made attractive half-brother to Hermes Harvest, Swift Pokey, Welsh Harvest and Reliance Leader. Dam won 2m1f Hdle in Ireland, and won 3 Chses at around 3m from Dai Williams' yard. NH FLAT '99 r1 p0. NH '00 and '02 r5 p0; pulled up 1, unseated 1. P-t-P '03 (for Mr C. Richards & Mr D.C. Faulkner) r5 w1 (Maiden) p1 (3rd); last, ran out, and fell. Finally persuaded to co-operate to a degree when landing a Maiden under the talented James Diment at Pentreclwydau last year, but has missed his presence since, and hung and jumped left throughout '04 and appeared to go wrong at Rhydygwern. Has two handlers and sweats excessively, and his 9-5 rating has been revoked. *Mrs D.C. Faulkner — Tredegar F.* 357 (R), 674 (R), 844 (R), 1484 (O).

RUNDETTO (IRE) ..8-5.. 8 b.g. Warcraft (USA) — Deep Link (Deep Run) pppp7p. Tall rangy half-brother to Dublin Hill (IRE) and Bohola Pete (IRE). Dam was placed 10 times in Ireland, including 2 Points. P-t-P '03 (for Mr H. Lonsdale & Mr P. Grindrod) r2 p0 (unseated, and ran out). A bad jumper whose inadequacies are exaggerated by the rider, and has capitulated after two miles in those races in which he has got that far, and beaten 36 lengths in his only completion. Wears a cross-noseband. *S. Moreton — Warwicks.* 112 (OMa), 368 (OMa), 531 (OMa), 600 (2m4fOMa), 887 (CfMa), 1125 (OMa).

RUN FOR HANNAH ..8-6.. 10 b.g. Henbit (USA) — Normazoo (Rhodomantade) p. Small half-brother to NH flat and Chasing winner, Scobie Girl (IRE), and to Irish NH flat and jumping winner, Scobie Boy (IRE). Dam, half-sister to Coral Eddy (*qv* '98 Annual), won NH flat. NH FLAT '99 r2 p0. NH '00 r3 p0 (pulled up 3). P-t-P '02/3 (for Mrs S. Rowe) r13 p3 (3rds, of 4 twice, last once); last, pulled up 6, unseated, and ran out 2. Speedy and has tended to whizz past rather than over the fences at times, but gone in the wind (has run tubed) and now one of the wheels has dropped off (went lame at Tweseldown). Only beat one rival in each of the two previous yards and it would be a waste of time trying to nurse him back. Wears a cross-noseband. *The JTR Racing Club (J. Trice-Rolph) — Heythrop (Jon Trice-Rolph).* 20 (OMa).

RUN FOUR ..—.. 6 b.g. Runnett — Four M's (Majestic Maharaj) f8. Workmanlike homebred half-brother to Banny Hill Lad and Lady Buckland. Dam, half-sister to 3 Pointers, won 2 2-finisher Points and 2nd. NH '04 (for C.P. Morlock) r1 p0 (8th of 10 over 2m1f110y at Market Rasen: *a bhnd, rdn 6f out, t.o*). Fell at the first at Ston Easton, and then tailed off in a bumper. *C.M. Bosley — O. Berks (Matt Hazell).* 600 (2m4fOMa).

RUN MONTY (IRE) ..9-9.. 10 ch.g. Montelimar (USA) — Bridevalley (Deep Run) p63pp. Robust attractive half-brother to Thats Dedication (IRE). Dam is half-sister to Dan Raise (*qv* '92 Annual). IRISH NH FLAT '99 r2 p0. IRISH NH '99/00 r4 p1 (3rd). IRISH P-t-P '00 r3 p0 (pulled up, fell, and ran out). P-t-P '02/3 r7 w1 (Maiden) p4 (3 2nds, beaten ½*l* once, and of 3 once); 4th, and fell. Has looked a difficult ride, but beat a subsequent Hunter Chase winner when successful at Marks Tey last year, and came within half-a-length of following up in a Restricted three starts later. Ran passably when third in '04, but otherwise badly let down by his jumping, and looked faulty when pulled up twice subsequently. Wears a cross-noseband. *D.J. & Mrs W.E. Lay — Essex & Suffolk (David Lay).* 2 (R), 29 (R), 250 (R), 375 (R), 902 (R).

RUNNING EARTH (IRE) ..—.. 6 gr.g. Roselier (FR) — Drumdeels Star (IRE) (Le Bavard FR) cp. Half-brother to Chasing winner, Guid Willie Waught (IRE). Dam won NH flat and 2m4f Hurdle in Ireland and is half-sister to Bradbury Star (won 18 jumping races). Bought Doncaster, May for 31,000. Carried out by a loose horse after a mile on his debut, so effectively having a first outing when favourite for a youngsters Maiden at Stafford Cross, but ran green and was not sufficiently fluent and eventually pulled up two out. Given his breeding and connections it would be no surprise if time proved him to be capable of much better. *R.M. Penny — Cattistock (Richard Barber).* 600 (2m4fOMa), 1133 (OMa).

RUNNING HOT ..9-12§.. 7 b.g. Sunley Builds — Running Cool (Record Run) 1. Owner-bred half-brother to Georgie Porgie. Dam won her Members for Mr Newman, and returned 5 years later to pull up once in '95 (was eventing in the interim). P-t-P '03 r1 p0 (last). Talented, and made all and survived one serious blunder when scoring completely unchallenged at Tweseldown, but totally neurotic to boot, and refused to come into line when withdrawn at Ston Easton on his next intended outing. The answer as to whether Jekyll or Hyde assumes control of his personality is eagerly awaited. *C.G. Newman — Seavington (Chloe Newman).* 174 (OMa).

RUNNING ON RED ..8-7.. 12 b.g. Vouchsafe — Miss Oates (Sunyboy) 69f2. Workmanlike. Dam was placed in a Ladies. P-t-P '02/3 r8 w1 (Members — 3 ran) p1 (3rd); pulled up 4, and fell 2. Unraced until he was nine, and found an ideal opportunity when beating two rivals in his Members, but has been susceptible to blunders otherwise, and failed to collar the fading leader in the same race in '04. Very unlikely to upgrade successfully at 12. *E.D. Perry — Golden V. (Nick Perry).* 450 (R), 665 (R), 1114 (R), 1387 (M).

RUNNING TIMES (USA) ..10-0.. 8 b.g. Brocco (USA) — Concert Peace (USA) (Hold Your Peace USA) pp4. Strong lengthy half-brother to a winner in USA. FLAT '99/01 r14 p4. NH '01/3 r15 w3 (2m3f110y-2m5f110y Hdles) p2 (2nds); pulled up 2. P-t-P '03 r4 p0; last, pulled up, and fell 2. A fair Hurdler at best, but previous connections must have laughed all the way to the bank after offloading him in a Seller in May '02, since when he has failed to finish in half of his 14 appearances. Ran surprisingly well when 13 lengths last of four in the Heythrop 4-miler, but has not been seen since, and the form has to be treated with extreme caution. Blinkered once in '00, and has been tried in eye-shields and visors most recently. *H.J. Manners — V.W.H.* 11 (O), 34 (O), 49 (4mO).

RUNNINGWITHTHEMOON ..9-10.. 9 b.g. Homo Sapien — Ardeal (Ardross) p314. Tall rangy. Dam, half-sister to Pop Star (*qv* '03 Annual), won Points and placed 2 for the Bealbys. NH FLAT '02 r1 p0. NH '02/3 (for C.C. Bealby) r5 p1 (3rd). NH '04 r1 p0 (4th in 3m2f Ch: *chsd ldrs, mist 6, blun 12, rdn & wknd app 3 out*). Thirty-two lengths third in a Hurdle, but pulled up in his only Chase before transferring his attentions to Pointing, with fair results. An experiment with cheekpieces in a Maiden was not repeated after they seemed to have detrimental effects, but ran surprisingly well when five-and-a-half lengths third in his Members, and then beat a subsequent scorer in a three-finisher race at Thorpe. Lacked fluency when tried again in a Chase, but his 16 lengths fourth should give him strong credentials in a Restricted on good ground or firmer. Hopefully Jonny Bealby is keeping up to speed with his scribbling (see For A Pagan Song) or his relatives will be running out of names. Runningwiththemoon will be racing for an East Anglian legend in '05, and great excitement is expected. *Mrs S.M.V. Bealby — Belvoir (Antonia Bealby).* 302 (OMa), 680 (M), 946 (OMa).

RUN RIVER RUN .—§.. 11 b.m. River God (USA) — Run Lady Run (General Ironside) pffp. Very small neat half sister to an Irish Pointing winner. NH FLAT '99/00 r2 p0. NH '00/1 r3 p0. P-t-P '03 (for Mr M. Ward & Mr J. Glenister) r5 p0 (pulled up 3, refused 1 and fell 1). Considered to be a non-trier by the Stewards on her racecourse debut, but her attitude is one of total apathy, and not helped by connections who run her in an appalling state. Jumps atrociously and can barely break out of a canter, and will struggle to get round over fences as long as she has a leg at each corner. Has been tried in blinkers and a tongue-tie. *M.A. Hill — Albrighton.* 35 (CMam), 91 (M), 241 (2m4f110yH), 490 (3m2fH).

RUSHING AGAIN ..10-5.. 10 br.g. Rushmere — Saunders Grove (IRE) (Sunnyboy) 4p1p234. Big workmanlike. Dam pulled up in a Point in '98. Grandam, Beeches View, was 3rd in 4 Points, and is half-sister to 4 Pointers, including Rushing Wild (*qv* '93 Annual). P-t-P '00/1 (for Mr J.A. Keighley) r3 w1 (Maiden) p0; pulled up 2. NH '02/3 (for P.F. Nicholls, and Dr P. Pritchard) r19 p3 (inc 2 2nds of 4); pulled up 7, unseated 1. Landed a gamble at Larkhill in '00, but quickly sent packing by Paul Nicholls, and failed to finish in nearly half his subsequent outings under Rules. Not the first to be improved following a spell with Dr Pritchard, and beat some well renowned fainthearted performers at Garnons, but seems to have an intermittent fault, and lacks any semblance of consistency. May be unsuited by easy ground. Blinkered once in '03. *M. Harper — Berkeley (Sarah George).* 252 (CR), 323 (R), 403 (Cf), 727 (MO), 756 (Cf), 980 (Cf), 1172 (3m1f110yH).

RUSH JOB ..8-0.. 7 ch.g. Devil's Jump — Some Value (Some Hand) fR5. Lengthy half-brother to Thornbird and Derriton Miller. Dam, half-sister to Merrington and Holsworthy. Fell at the eighth on his debut and at the second next time (remounted and continued to jump all the fences barring the 13th which he whizzed around (!), and then finished a bad last in an Intermediate in which he was novicey and given a school. Masqueraded as Typical Women (U) in his Members, perhaps not so surprising given the appearance of the occasional moustacheod lady rider in Cornwall. *C.J. Rush — N. Cornwall (Mike Biddick).* 76 (M), 1545 (OMa), 1555 (I).

RUSNETTO (IRE) ..9-10.. 15 b.g. Torus — Moynetto (Bustineto) u. Workmanlike brother to Irish NH flat and Hurdles winner, Blazing Arrow (IRE). IRISH P-t-P '96 and '99 r8 w1 (6yo&up Maiden) p2 (3rds), pulled up 3. NH '98 and '01 r5 w1 (3m Ch) p2; pulled up 1. P-t-P/HUNT CH '00/1 and '03 r16 w3 (up to Confined) p4 (2 2nds, beaten head once; and inc 3rd in Hunt Ch); 4th twice, 7th, last pair 3, unseated and pulled up 2. Won three minor Points in '00, and got up close home to win a Chase at Ludlow the following year, but often unreliable, and looks finished after the wobbly Rebecca Davies fell off for the second time in succession on his return. Wears a visor. *Ms R.L. & M. Davies — Carms (Rebecca Davies).* 673 (L).

RUSSIAN CONNECTION (IRE) ..9-1.. 11 ch.g. Moscow Society (USA) — Glenastar VII (unknown) ppp332p8f. Lengthy well-made half-brother to King Of The Naul (IRE). Dam won NH Flat and 2 Hurdles (2m-2m5f) in Ireland; p4. IRISH P-t-P '99/00 and '02 r15 w2 (7yo&up Maiden and Winners of One) p1 (3rd); pulled up 4, fell/unseated 2. P-t-P '03 r4 p1 (last of 3); last pair 2, and pulled up. Won twice in Ireland in '02, but appeared to be lucky on both occasions, and has not been so fortunate in 13 English attempts. Retains a little ability, but the owner-rider has none, and the combination ended the season with a crashing fall at Peper Harow. *A.C. Ward-Thomas — Hampshire (David Phelan).* 116 (I), 168 (C), 537 (4mMO), 610 (Cv&nr), 716 (M), 804 (O), 897 (Cfv&nr), 1085 (Cv&nr), 1212 (Cf).

RUSSIAN FRIEND .10-1.. 8 b.g. Petoski — Courtlands Girl (Crimson Beau) R1f. Small half-brother to Ball In The Net (*qv*). NH FLAT '02 r3 p1 (3rd). P-t-P '03 r2 p2 (3rds, of 4 once). Acquired blinkers in '04, and ran out through the wing of the fifth first time, but jumped boldly in a clear lead virtually throughout when landing a three-finisher Maiden at Thorpe, and looked sure to follow up when falling three out at Fakenham. Sure to gain compensation in a similar event and might have prospects as a Ladies horse in time, though his frailties are all too apparent. His current partner, Richard Collinson looks well above average. Wears a cross-noseband. *Miss M. Samworth — Cottesmore.* 385 (OMa), 945 (OMa), 1152 (R).

RUSTIC REVELRY ..—§.. 12 b.g. Afzal — Country Festival (Town And Country) p3upup. Lengthy unfurnished Half-brother to Kings Command. Dam, half-sister to Gemini Mist (*qv* '02 Annual), won 2 Points and 3rd (ran to '96). Grandam, Festive Season, won 5 Points and 2nd 2. NH FLAT '98 r3 p0. NH '98 and '01/2 r10 p1 (3rd). P-t-P/HUNT CH '99/03 (for Mr R.H. York) r37 w10 (inc 2 Hunt Chses, 2m5f-3m) p14 (11 2nds, of 3 twice, and inc 3 Hunt Chses; and 2 3rds in Hunt Chses); ran out 1, brought down 1, fell 2. Largely consistent in the previous yard, where he won ten races and was rated 10-6, but often lacked fluency and found little off the bridle, and did not appeal as a novice ride as Charlie Whittaker found to his cost in '04. Ran out and retraced when completing for the only time at Milborne St Andrew, and regained blinkers latterly, but needs to regain strong handling if he is not to fall further into rack and ruin. Wears a cross-noseband. *The Yeoman Family (C.R. Whittaker) — Avon V. (Sarah Waugh).* 89 (O), 236 (Cnr), 352 (O), 603 (Cnr), 1329 (Cnr), 1365 (Cnr).

RUSTY BUCK ..—.. 13 b.g. Buckley — Rusty To Reign (General Ironside) p. Compact quite attractive brother to Iron Buck, and half-brother to Scraptastic and Rusty King. Dam was 2nd in 2 Points. P-t-P '98/00 (for Mr & Mrs C.M. Burleigh) r17 w4 (Maiden, Restricted and 2 Members) p2 (last of 3 once) 4th, 5th, last 2, fell/unseated 2, and pulled up 5. Rated 10-1 after recording doubles '99/00, but could be incredibly moody, and stopped to nil after two miles on a surprise return to action a

Brampton Bryan. Seems unlikely to turn out again. *The Bottle Bank Club (M. Ewing) — Ledbury (Debbie Ewing).* 663 (I).

RUSTY FELLOW ..9-9§.. 15 b.g. Rustingo — Sallisses (Pamroy) 2f546567. Plain lengthy half-brother to Raymond James (*qv*). P-t-P/HUNT CH '95/03 r58 w7 (inc 2 3m6f110y Hunt Chses and Open) p18 (11 2nds, distant once, bad last once; and inc distant 3rd twice, of 4 once; and inc 3 Hunt Chses); failed to finish 17 (ran out 1, refused 3, and on floor 7). An out-and-out stayer whose past crimes and misdemeanours are well chronicled but has not scored in his last 14 attempts, and his rating fluctuated wildly in '04. Can take forever to reach top gear, and came from miles behind to claim a fair second at Chaddesley, but seemed unnerved by an early fall next time, and declined to co-operate fully subsequently. A real character but must be fast approaching the end of his career. Has been ridden in spurs. *Mrs G.M. Shail — Ledbury (Roy Shail).* 254 (O), 366 (MO), 722 (M), 980 (Cf), 1073 (O), 1362 (3m6f110yH), 1485 (Cnr), 1528 (Cf).

RUTHERFORD ..9-10.. 11 b.g. Nomadic Way (USA) — Kilglass (Fidel) 322221. Lengthy unfurnished half-brother to Kildante (IRE), and to Hurdles winner, Just Lizzie. Dam won 4&5yo mares Maiden in Ireland. Grandam bred Oscail An Doras (*qv* '03 Annual). NH FLAT '00 r1 p0 (tailed off last). P-t-P '03 r9 p4 (2 3rds, of 4 once); 6th, last, pulled up 2, and fell. A most reliable jumper, and accrued nine placings from between one-and-a-half and 25 lengths before finally opening his account when odds-on at Mosshouses, but often found little in the closing stages and required cheekpieces to get the job done. May have to toil for just as long to find another opportunity. *A.J. Balmer — Morpeth.* 137 (OMa), 286 (CfMa), 554 (CfMa), 658 (OMa), 914 (M), 1225 (OMa).

RUTH'S BOY (IRE) ..9-13.. 16 br.g. Lord Ha Ha — Club Belle (Al Sirat) u. Leggy unfurnished. NH FLAT r1 p0. NH '94/5 and '97/01 r25 w2 (2m5f-3m1f Plumpton Chses) p8 (inc 6 2nds); pulled up 2, fell 1. P-t-P/HUNT CH '96/7 and '00/3 r23 w2 (Maiden and Restricted) p10 (7 2nds, inc Hunt Ch; and inc 3rd of 4 twice); pulled up 1, fell 2. A fair performer under Rules, but lightly raced and unsuccessful since '98, and looks to have been pensioned off after carrying first-timer Natalie McGoldrick as far as the fourth last at Cottenham before she fell off. Blinkered once in '97. *Ms A.E. Embiricos — Cambridge Univ.* 558 (L).

RYANS STAR ..9-13.. 12 ch.g. North Col — Tapalong (True Song) 123313. Brother to Court Adjourn and North Peak. Dam, sister to Thornton Flyer (*qv* '00 Annual), won Maiden and placed 2 for Henry Hutsby (suffered badly with her legs). Sire, by Head For Heights, won 3 French flat (9-15f). P-t-P/HUNT CH '98/9 and '02/3 (for Mr H. Hutsby) r10 w3 (Maiden, Restricted and Intermediate) p2; pulled up 5. Broke down on his only appearance in '99, and resumed successfully following a three-year absence, and did so again in '04 having raced just once the previous season. Scored in two weak three-finisher events, but showed he was no back-number when placed in better events, though has become a relatively weak finisher. *Mrs W. Bamford & Mrs J.C. Parris — Heythrop (Fred Hutsby).* 46 (M), 289 (CfL), 464 (L), 869 (L), 1033 (L), 1334 (L).

RYDERS HILL ..8-10.. 6 b.m. Zaffaran (USA) — Deirfiur (IRE) (Buckley) 1. Dam, half-sister to Hardy Mouse (*qv*). Bought Doncaster, Aug for 2000. Made mistakes in a 2m4f Maiden at Trebudannon, but kept galloping regardless, and eventually beat some bad rivals. Was one of four of the seven contestants who failed to reappear, which looks rather ominous. *M. Weir — Dartmoor.* 910 (2m4fOMa).

RYDON BROOK ..—.. 7 ch.m. Meadowbrook — Lady Magenta (Rolfe USA) fR. Good-bodied homebred half-sister to Travelling Jack (*qv*). P-t-P '03 r2 p0 (pulled up 2). Learning things the hard way at present, and not seen since crashing through the wing of the first fence at Buckfastleigh in March. *Mrs F.J. Walker & Mrs G. Durman — Taunton V. (Fiona Walker).* 238 (CfMa), 492 (OMa).

SABENA CANYON ..9-13.. 9 b.g. Nalchik (USA) — Gay Saucy (Gay Meadow) f52p1R. Small light-framed. NH FLAT '00 r2 p0. NH '01 r3 p0. P-t-P '03 r5 w1 (Maiden) p2 (5 fences last of 3 once); last, and unseated 1. An excitable hard-pulling sort, and makes mistakes and rarely settles into a good rhythm, but has twice won weak races on sound surfaces for Richard Burton. Also a beaten favourite twice when partnered by him, and will need maintain improvement now that he is out of Restricteds. *D.P. Constable — Ludlow (Jen Wall).* 665 (R), 834 (M), 1265 (R), 1469 (R), 1531 (R), 1552 (I).

SADLER'S REALM .10-5.. 12 b.g. Sadler's Wells (USA) — Rensaler (USA) (Stop The Music USA) pu53133. Compact brother to flat winner, Opera Lover, and half-brother to Silence Reigns, and to six flat winners, including Damsel, Rendition, In The Money (12 wins) and Tour De Force (also successful Irish Hurdler). Dam 8f winner in USA. 110,000y. FLAT '95/6 and '99 r7 w1 (14f) p2. NH '97/03 (for P.J. Hobbs) r31 w7 (5 2m-2m5f Hdles and 2 2m4f-2m5f Chses) p11; pulled up 2, and fell 1. Has produced some praiseworthy efforts in a career which has spanned some nine years, and took advantage of a very favourable rating when scoring on the flat at six (around five stone lower than his Hurdling mark!) but injured a leg on his only subsequent outing on the level. Gained his eighth win over jumps (all on good or muddy surfaces) in a 2m3f Hunter Chase at Hereford, and beat very weak rivals by big margins, but the trip was the key, because although he can give prominent displays he does not stay three miles in Points. Regularly prone to blunders in the past, but was error-free in '04, although Jo Buck fell off some way after the first on the only occasion she partnered him. Still a tryer, but it is difficult to find the right races for him now. Once finished second in the Imperial Cup at Sandown, but was last twice, pulled up and fell on his final four appearances under Rules, so the new trainer did well to sweeten him. *J.F. Tucker — Weston & Banwell H. (Sarah Gordon).* 33 (L), 88 (L), 322 (L), 470 (L), 628 (2m3fH), 799 (2m3f110yH), 1128 (MO).

SADLER'S VIC ..—§§.. 7 b.g. Old Vic — Lorna-Gail (Callernish) RO. Strong compact. Dam, half-sister to Marico (*qv* '03 Annual), won 3 Irish Hurdles (2-3m). P-t-P '03 r3 p0 (refused 1, ran out 1 and pulled up 1). NH FLAT '04 (for A.J. Chamberlain) r1 p0 (16th over 2m110y at Huntingdon: *pulled hrd, w ldrs til wknd 6f out, t.o*). An uncontrollable raving maniac, and has yet to get beyond the fifth without managing to do something deranged in Points. Took a demonic hold when switched to a bumper, and needs to be inside a hound rather than running behind one. *D.W. Parker — Carms (Linda Parker).* 204 (CfMa).

SAD MAD BAD (USA) .10-7§.. 11 b.g. Sunny's Halo (CAN) — Quite Attractive (USA) (Well Decorated USA) 311225. Small compact half-brother to flat winner in USA. Dam multiple winner in USA. 97,000y. FLAT '96/9 and '01/2 r20 w2 (8-14f) p5. NH '97/03 (for Mrs M. Reveley) r43 w11 (3 2m-2m2f Hdles and 8 2m4f-3m5f Chses) p10; pulled up 5, fell/unseated 2. Won at least one race per annum in the seven years to '02, and although he failed to maintain that record in '03 he revived for a double in the new yard, taking his career earnings to over £105,000 (the biggest individual contribution was a £23,200 Chase). Fifteen victories (two of them in headgear) is a tremendous achievement, and was blessed with a turn of foot which he still retains, but can be totally exasperating and was in one of his strops when he finished a length-and-a-half lengths second to Lord Edwards Army at Ayr, where he gave a modest display of jumping and would not concentrate on the job in hand until it was too late (4-6). Appreciates an extreme distance and cut in the ground, and after a promising Pointing debut he passed four rivals from three out to score easily over 3m3f at Sedgefield and then landed a Pointing classic in the Grimthorpe Gold Cup at Whitwell-on-the-Hill, where everything went to his liking. Very sulky since, but given his great record produced at regular intervals he can be forgiven — and at least he is not dangerous to know. *G.F. Tuer — Hurworth.* 269 (O), 542 (3m3fH), 772 (4m1fO), 992 (3m3f110yH), 1179 (3m1fH), 1376 (4m2fH).

SAFAWI ..9-3.. 6 b.m. Safawan — Pejawi (Strong Gale) 3p. Very small neat half-sister to Charango Star (*qv*). Bought Doncaster, Oct for 1500. Twenty-seven lengths last of three on her debut, but jumped very big and appeared to hate the firm ground until pulling up when second in a three-runner Maiden. Her 20 lengths second in a bumper on an easy surface was a much better effort, although it looked a bad affair barring the winner. Not unpromising, but could have done with being a hand bigger. *J.G. Cann — E. Devon (Ollie Bush).* 1186 (OMa), 1466 (OMa).

SAFFRON HILL (IRE) .9-4.. 6 br.g. Presenting — Milltown Lady (Deep Run) p23uR. Good-topped compact half-brother to Indian Miller, and to Irish Pointing winners, Deel Time (subsequent successful English Chaser) and Winston Murphy. IRISH P-t-P '03 r1 p0 (last). His neck second at Didmarton (only caught close home) and third over 2m4f at Ston Easton marked him down as a very probably future winner, but was eliminated after about a mile when favourite on his last two attempts, including after the saddle slipped and he had run out when backed from 5-2 to 4-5. Possibly prefers the shorter trips at present, but it will be disappointing and surprising if he does not find an opportunity before much longer. *Miss A.M. Reed — Hursley Hambledon (Kate Buckett).* 87 (OMa), 368 (OMa), 599 (2m4fOMa), 871 (OMa), 1098 (OMa).

SAFFRON MOSS .9-6.. 15 ch.g. Le Moss — Saffron's Daughter (Prince Hansel) 4u. Compact rather light brother to Hurdles winner, Tartan Moss (IRE), and half-brother to Sister Gale and Wolfie's Daughter, and to Hurdles winner, So Pink (IRE) (in Ireland, also won NH flat there). Dam won 3m1f Ch. NH FLAT r2 p0 (40 ran — beat one). P-t-P/HUNT CH '95/03 (for Mouse Racing Partnership) r62 w5 (inc 3m Hunt Ch, 4m Mixed Open and 2 Opens) p14 (9 2nds, last once; and last of 3 twice; inc Hunt Ch); failed to finish 23 (inc fell/unseated 9, and ran out 1). A thorough stayer at his best, and has won five races, but not since '00, and is frequently let down by his jumping. Never passed a rival in '04, and looks finished now. Has been tried unsuccessfully in blinkers. *Mrs S.M. Farr — Ystrad Taf Fechan.* 1021 (M), 1090 (Cf).

SAILORS FOLLY (IRE) .10-2.. 10 gr.g. Roselier (FR) — Ankud (IRE) (Dominion) 4d1fp4. Small. Dam won 2m1f Sell Hdle. NH FLAT '99 r2 p0. NH '00 r3 p0. P-t-P '01/3 r8 w4 (inc 2 Ladies) p0; 4th twice, pulled up 1 and unseated 1. Unbeaten when completing in his first four Points, and recorded his fourth success at Black Forest Lodge in '04, but not at his best since succumbing to a virus last year, and only really effective on good or easy surfaces. Suited by small fences, and well worth bearing in mind at his favourite venue providing the opposition is not too hot. Wears a cross-noseband. *R.G. Kelvin-Hughes — Spooners & W. Dartmoor.* 33 (L), 146 (L), 253 (L), 322 (L), 1004 (L).

SAINT-DECLAN (IRE) .9-13.. 12 b.g. Polykratis — Welsh Symphony (Welsh Saint) 51. Half-brother to Kilmakee and Another Machine, and to Irish Chasing winner, Machinery Man. Dam won 2 2m Hurdles in Ireland. IRISH P-t-P '99/00 r5 p1 (3rd); pulled up 3. IRISH FLAT '01 r1 p0. IRISH NH FLAT '97 and '02 r4 p0; slipped up 1. IRISH NH '00/2 (for J.A. Codd) r14 p3 (Chses); fell 1, pulled up 1. Often front-runs and is a very good jumper, but had not shown any form in Ireland since the last of his three Chasing places in November '01. Was tongue-tied there, and was also tried blinkered twice. Faded to finish 19 lengths fifth in a 2m Hunter Chase, but made all at a brisk pace in a Maiden at Clifton-on-Dunsmore and although tiring from two out and clambering over the last Stuart Morris always had matters in control. Getting off the mark at an advanced age, and would be far from certain to get the trip in competitive Restricteds. *Mrs H. Bubb & R. Mathias — Brecon & Talybont (Richard Mathias).* 734 (2mH), 1125 (OMa).

SALER SAL ..—.. 8 ch.m. Primitive Rising (USA) — Portonia (Ascertain USA) 1. Lengthy. Dam, half-sister to Youaskhim (*qv*), won 3 Hdles (3m1f-3m3f) and 9 Chases (3m-3m4f); previously won a Maiden in '91. P-t-P '02 (for Mr C.D. Carr) r2 p0 (pulled up 1, and fell 1). NH '02 (for J. O'Neill, and P.D. Niven) r3 p0 (pulled up 3). Has an attractive pedigree, but a non-finisher in all five attempts over jumps, and gained her success in a walk-over for her Members. *Mrs M.R. Bennett — Badsworth & Bramham Moor (Ian Bennett).* 1455 (M).

SALES DODGER (IRE) ..9-6§.. 12 gr.g. Celio Rufo — Lynn Grange (Northern Guest USA) uRf541rp. Strong compact half-brother to Basil Grainger (IRE). Dam is half-sister to Ponentino (*qv* '94 Annual). IRISH NH '98/9 r9 p0; pulled up 2, brought down 1. IRISH NH FLAT '99 r1 p0. P-t-P '00 (for Mrs J.P. Spencer) r5 p0 (last pair 2, and pulled up 3). Blinkered latterly in Ireland, and ran badly in his first English campaign, but resurfaced after a four-year absence with Steve Flook at the helm, and typically managed to find him an opening after an inauspicious start. Collared a notoriously weak finisher close home to land a three-finisher Maiden in softish at Andoversford, but ran a shocker on much faster terrain next time, and looks certain to struggle to follow up. Acquired cheekpieces on his last five starts. *S. Flook — Teme V.* 51 (OMa), 113 (OMa), 258 (CMa), 621 (OMa), 668 (OMa), 820 (OMa), 1136 (R), 1389 (R).

SALLY SCALLY ..10-0.. 13 ch.m. Scallywag — Petite Cone (Celtic Cone) 3p226. Small neat. Dam is half-sister to Young Mariner (*qv* '02 Annual). NH FLAT '97 r3 p1 (3rd). NH '97/9 r14 p1; pulled up all 3 Chses. P-t-P/HUNT CH '00/3 r20 w4 (inc 2 Ladies) p5 (4 2nds, beaten head once, of 3 once and inc Hunt Ch; and 3rd in Hunt Ch); 4th, 5th, 6th, last pair 3, pulled up 2 and fell/unseated 3. Recorded her first successes for three years in '03, and is most agreeable to restraint these days, but remains difficult to win with, and failed by half-a-length to spring a 20-1 surprise at Cartmel having come from well off the pace. Blinkered once in '99. Wears a cross-noseband. *H.L. Thompson — Cleveland (Tina Jackson).* 502 (L), 564 (L), 1160 (L), 1490 (3m2fH), 1526 (3m2fH).

SAMS DAY (IRE) .—.. 11 b.g. Samhoi (USA) — Daras Day (Arapahos FR) p. Compact. Dam won Irish Maiden. IRISH P-t-P '99 r5 p1 (3rd); pulled up 2. P-t-P '00 and '02/3 r6 w2 (Maiden and Club Restricted) p2 (3rds, last once); 4th, and last. Won his first two English Points on easy surfaces, and rated 10-2 after running third in first-time blinkers on his only start last year, but clearly very difficult to keep sound, and went wrong immediately in '04. *G. Samuel — N. Salop (Sheila Crow).* 1112 (C).

SAMS SISTER ..8-8.. 9 ch.m. Broadsword (USA) — True Divine (True Song) pRp44. Strong plain half-sister to Mullover (*qv*). P-t-P '03 r1 p0 (pulled up). The subject of a market move when completing for the first time at Clifton-on-Dunsmore, and qualified for a small rating when finishing 32 lengths last, but has not shown anywhere near enough stamina to warrant another tilt at the ring. *Mrs J.M. Gurney & L.J. Owen — Grafton (Kim Gilmore).* 584 (I), 789 (CfMa), 940 (OMa), 1119 (CMam), 1340 (OMa).

SAMS WAY ..9-7.. 8 b.g. Nomadic Way (USA) — Samonia (Rolfe USA) f17. Tall owner-bred half-brother to Son Of Sam (*qv*). P-t-P '03 r4 p2 (3rd of 4 once); last, and unseated 1. Fell two out when unassailable on his return, and maintained his steady improvement when gaining compensation in soft at Whitwell-on-the-Hill next time, but taken off his feet in his first Restricted, and needs to seek out much greater tests of stamina in future. *J.W. Barker — Hurworth (Sandra Barker).* 395 (CfMa), 776 (CfMa), 1162 (R).

SAN ANTONIO (U) ..5-0.. 14 b.g. Le Chevreuil — Yaige De Lias 4. Hunter. Went round at hunting pace to finish two and a half fences last in his Members on the first ride for the owner. *S. Clement — Grove & Rufford.* 590 (M).

SANDY DUFF ..10-8.. 11 ch.g. Scottish Reel — Not Enough (Balinger) 572121111. Tall strong half-brother to Filthy Reesh, Newton Mo, and to NH flat and Chasing winner, The Parsons Dingle and Chasing winner, Cash 'N' Credit. 7800 4yo. NH FLAT '99 r2 w1 p0. NH '99/03 (for P.R. Webber, all wins, and J.D. Frost) r18 w4 (2 2m1f-2m2f Hdles and 2 2m-2m2f Chses) p6; pulled up 2, fell 1. Won five races at up to 2m2f to October '01, but having been successful on three of his first five appearances he became very disappointing and was beaten into second at 30-100 once (jumped very poorly), wore headgear twice, and lacked fluency in three attempts over trips beyond those at which he had been successful. Unconvincing in his first three Points and did not get the trip on dead ground once, but the drier conditions later really played into his hands, and an additional improvement was that the feisty Mary McCarthy became much more forceful on him, with splendid results. Would have completed a six-timer but for the intervention of Let's Fly at Great Trethew where his rival had too much stamina, but with a maximum of four opponents in his last three outings he was able to complete the season on a high. Thoroughly enjoying himself now, and given similar conditions he should be equally successful in '05. Would be worth trying in a Hunter Chase as he has already beaten Bengal Bullet. *Miss M. McCarthy — Modbury H. (Nicky Frost).* 199 (L), 311 (L), 412 (Cf), 497 (Cf), 707 (Cf), 792 (MO), 1004 (L), 1199 (C), 1542 (L).

PLATE 103 497 Dart Vale & Haldon Harriers Confined: Sandy possibly, but certainly not duff; Mary McCarthy and Sandy Duff win the first of five races together PHOTO: Baths Photographic

SANDYLAND ..—.. 10 b.g. Silly Prices — Niel's Crystal (Indiaro) ppp. Strong-topped half-brother to Primulas Daughter and Krystal Tip. Dam won 8min 20s Members on her debut at 5, and was 3rd on her only subsequent venture. Grandam, half-sister to Matchboard, won 3 Points (disqualified from another) and placed 7. P-t-P '03 (for late V.T. Bradshaw) r5 p0 (7th of 8, pulled up 3, and fell). Attained a miniscule rating when creeping to completion once in '03, but shows no stamina, and looks a waste of time. *Mrs S. Brazier & Mrs L.M. Rose — Bicester with Whaddon (Shirley Brazier).* 129 (OMa), 462 (OMa), 560 (OMa).

SANDY LARK ..9-13.. 13 b.g. Crested Lark — Lucky Sandy (St Columbus) p331pf. Tall plain owner-bred brother to Tarry Awhile, Lucky Crest, Dolly Bloom, Tarry No More and Dennis. Grandam, Ebony Girl, was 5th, last twice, pulled up 7, and fell in Points. P-t-P '03 r5 p0 (pulled up 5). Typically unraced until he stood still long enough in the Tarry fields to allow himself to be caught, and pulled up in his first six races, but landed a little touch when receiving the strong handling of James Owen for the first time at Dingley. Looked none too keen on occasions, and was back-pedalling when a fall at the fourth last at Kingston Blount left him with a broken shoulder. G.B. Tarry — Pytchley (Rosie Goodwin). 462 (OMa), 871 (OMa), 1108 (OMa), 1215 (CfMa), 1469 (R), 1517 (R).

SANDY'S WAY ..—.. 6 gr.m. Silver Owl — Marasol (Siberian Express USA) ppp. Dam won 2 flat (8-9f). Has been pulled up after a maximum of 2m3f in her races to date. *Mrs J. Goudge — Four Burrow (Alan Goudge).* 306 (2m4fOMa), 492 (OMa), 907 (M).

SAN FRANCISCO ..10-4.. 11 b.g. Aragon — Sirene Bleu Marine (USA) (Secreto USA) 22p2. Compact well-made half-brother to flat winner. FLAT '97 r3 p0. NH '97/03 (for A.C. Whillans) r44 w4 (2m Hdle and 3 2m-2m6f110y Chses) p15 (inc 5 2nds); pulled up 3, unseated 1. HUNT CH '02 (for Mr C. Bird) r3 p0 (6th, last, and fell 1). At his best over the minimum trip in mud, and has not scored since recording a double at Ayr in March '02, but ran some valiant races in defeat this year, and almost managed to hang on for what would have been a most deserved success at Witton Castle. Has struggled with his wind, and regularly tongue-tied in the past. *Miss F. Hartley — Sinnington.* 163 (O), 269 (O), 391 (MO), 480 (O).

SAN MALO (IRE) ..—.. 8 b.g. Toulon — Laurel Escort (Mandalus) ppp. Tall strong-topped. IRISH P-t-P '03 r2 p0 (pulled up 2). Has been depressingly bad to date, having pulled up in all his five races. Performs as if there is something wrong with him. *M.J. Roberts — E. Sussex & Romney Marsh.* 8 (2m4fOMa), 20 (OMa), 218 (OMa).

SANTI (FR) ..—.. 7 b.g. Brief Truce (USA) — Sun River (IRE) (Last Tycoon) pppp. Compact half-brother to French flat and Hurdling winner, Starting Line (FR) (won £30,000 prize at Auteuil in '04). FRENCH FLAT '03 r1 p0. FRENCH NH '01/3 r5 w2 (2m1f-2m2f Ch) p0. A precocious talent in the French Provinces when winning over Hurdles and fences at Pau and Compiegne, both in mud at up to 2m2f (blinkered for one victory), but has laboured badly at a wide range of trips in the new yard, and wore a tongue-tie to no avail when 100-1, and pulled up yet again on his latest attempt. Surely suffering from a major defect. *S.N. Wilshire — Grafton (Kim Gilmore).* 158 (CCon), 628 (2m3fH), 1354 (2m110yH), 1497 (3mH).

SAPEGA (IRE) ..10-10.. 10 b.g. Homo Sapien — Suzi Hegi (Mon Capitaine) 111. Small unfurnished half-brother to Running Free (dam of Lord Kilpatrick IRE, *qv*), and Short Circuit (IRE), and to Irish Pointing winner, Smokey Lonesome. Dam won 2 Irish Points. IRISH P-t-P '00 and '02 r7 w1 (Maiden) p1 (2nd); unseated 1. P-t-P '03 r2 w1 (Restricted) p0; and 4th. Only defeated on his debut for present connections, and clocked the fastest time of the day when successful at Upton, but tends to boil over in the preliminaries and does not stand much racing. Has brushed aside modest rivals with the minimum of fuss, and jumps well enough to be considered a good thing for a Hunter Chase, and gets excellent assistance from the polished Jane Williams. Handles firmish, and has also scored in softish. *Mrs A.D. Williams — Albrighton Woodland.* 663 (I), 980 (Cf), 1229 (L).

SARONICA'S BOY ..—.. 10 b/br.g. Motivate — Saronica-R (Rolfe USA) ppp. Dam won Members from 22 starts for L. Remnant (inc pulled up 12, and fell/unseated 4) ran to '00. A poor jumper who barely raises a gallop, and has no hope of making a racehorse even at the worst level. *L.J. Remnant — Curre & Llangibby.* 700 (CfMa), 844 (R), 1027 (OMa).

SASSY'S CIRCLE ..— §.. 6 b.m. Lancastrian — Celia's Halo (Mountain Call) ppp. Compact owner-bred half-sister to Jupiter George (*qv*). Pulled up in all three Maidens, and it was most discouraging to see her stop as if shot when equipped with a first-time visor on final start. Has made mistakes, and it does not look as if she is going to take any interest in racing. *C.R. Millington — Fernie (Nicola Pollock).* 386 (OMa), 788 (CfMa), 1119 (CMam).

SATANAS (FR) ..5-9.. 7 b.g. Dress Parade — Oiseau Noir (FR) (Rex Magna FR) ppf4d6ppp. Tall strong half-brother to French Hurdling winner, Lenor (FR). Dam won French flat race. NH FLAT '02 r2 p0. NH '02/3 (for O. Sherwood) r5 p0; pulled up 2. Bought Doncaster, May for 3100. Pulled up in two of five Hurdles, and only able to manage to exceptionally remote lasts (disqualified from the fourth when the rider failed to draw the weight) from eight attempts in Points. If he does get into contention he fades rapidly, and was dismounted after yet another dire display on his latest appearance. There would be no sense in racing him again, even if he was sound. *The Blackhorse Four — Belvoir (Sally Thornton).* 95 (R), 302 (OMa), 385 (OMa), 463 (OMa), 680 (M), 890 (2m4fOMa), 1061 (OMa), 1125 (OMa).

SATANASS (IRE) ..—.. 6 ch.g. Barathea (IRE) — Berhala (IRE) (Doyoun) p. Workmanlike half-brother to Irish flat winner, Moy Toy and two winners in Japan. Bought Doncaster, May for 2700. An ex-Luca Cumani inmate, but saw the light of day on a racecourse for the first time at Buckfastleigh, and having jumped two fences appallingly Nick Mitchell wisely aborted the kamikaze mission before the third. *J.B. Shears — Mid Devon (Mark Shears).* 195 (CfMa).

SATCHMO (IRE) ..11-1.. 13 b.g. Satco (FR) — Taradale (Torus) 143. Big rangy. IRISH P-t-P '98/9 r9 w2 (6yo Maiden, and Open) p2 (2nds); pulled up 1, fell 2. IRISH NH '00 r1 p1 (2nd in 3m1f Hunt Ch). P-t-P/HUNT CH '00 r4 w2 (inc 2m4f110y Hunt Ch) p1 (2nd in Hunt Ch); and unseated 1. NH '00/1 (for D.M. Grissell) r10 w2 (2m4f110y Chses) p1 (2nd to Struggles Glory); fell 2, pulled up 1. IRISH NH '03 (for E.J. O'Grady) r4 p1 (3rd). A smart performer at around 2m4f, and has made frequent trips to and from Ireland, but never reached the heights that looked feasible because of a tendency to make mistakes. Scoring for the first time since he beat Foly Pleasant at Huntingdon in '01 when gaining revenge over Struggles Glory on his return to Pointing at Charing where a gamble from sevens (!) to fours was landed. Would have finished much closer at Aintree but for almost falling at the last ditch, but typically let down by his joint-owner at Folkestone where he finished full of running after receiving minimal guidance. Missed '02 and lightly raced since, but would still have more than enough class to run up a sequence in sub-3m Hunter Chases if the right pilot was found. Wears a cross-noseband. *G.J.D. Wragg & R. Perkins — E. Sussex & Romney Marsh (Di Grissell).* 420 (O), 732 (2m5f110yH), 1443 (2m5fH).

SATCO PRINCE (IRE) ..8-11.. 12 bl.g. Satco (FR) — Persian Caprice (Persian Bold) ppp3. Tall workmanlike. Dam won 14f race in Ireland. IRISH P-t-P '97/8 and '00/2 r17 w1 (Confined Hunt Lightweight) p2; pulled up 8 and fell 2. It seems miraculous that he won a Point in Ireland (in soft in '00), because before he finished eight lengths last of three at Rhydygwern (not a bad effort, at least by his standards) he had been pulled up nine times consecutively. His normal problem is a failure to get the trip, and becomes very tired as his stamina evaporates. It would be too much to hope that he could score at 12. *P. & A.J. Mahoney — Gelligaer F. (P. Mahoney).* 844 (R), 1094 (R), 1322 (R), 1482 (R).

SATCOTINO (IRE) ..9-8§.. 14 b.m. Satco (FR) — Autumn Bounty (Plano FR) u62u. Workmanlike half-sister to Irish Pointing and English Hurdles winner, Garrynisk (IRE). IRISH P-t-P '96 r2 p1 (2nd); and fell. NH '96/00 r19 w3 (3m3f Hdle, awarded race; and 2 2m5f-3m Chses, inc Sell) p4. P-t-P/HUNT CH '01/3 r12 w2 (2 Club Members Mares) p3 (3rds, of 4 once, and last once); last 2, pulled up 3, and unseated 2. Unbeaten in English Points to the start of '03, but indolent and has always needed plenty of persuading, and only once beaten less than 21 lengths since. A first ride for the appropriately named Clare Pointing at Parham, but typically lost interest after leading for a mile, and was a poor third when unseating four out. Blinkered once in '00. *I. & Mrs H.J. Cobb — Crawley & Horsham (Ian Cobb).* 182 (CCon), 422 (CCon), 623 (Cf), 638 (M).

SAUCY ARETHUSA ..10-0.. 10 ch.m. Scallywag — Sailor's Shanty (Dubassoff USA) 122. Good-bodied owner-bred sister to Sea Urchin, and half-sister to Bobby Shaftoe. Dam, home-bred half-sister to Davy's Lad (*qv* '98 Annual), was placed in 5 Points for Mr Philips. Grandam, Colisfare, won 3 Points at the Lanark and Renfrews and placed 12. Great-grandam, Fanfare III, won a Point and placed 4. P-t-P '02 r3 p1 (2nd); 4th of 5, and fell 1. Overcame blunders at the last two fences when returning successfully from a lay-off in a three-finisher mares Maiden on firmish at Larkhill, but unlucky when getting tangled up with the eventual third there next time, and finished lame at Garthorpe. A typically hot ride by Scallywag but certainly had the ability to increase her tally. Wears a cross-noseband. *J.H. Philips — W. Somerset (Jeremy Scott).* 637 (CMam), 1102 (R), 1398 (Cm).

SAWBRIDGE ..8-11.. 9 b.g. Infantry — Dane Hole (Past Petition) pup3. Small good-topped owner-bred half-brother to Thursby (subsequent Chasing winner), Jack's Barn, Trafford Bridge, Boddington Hill, Gawcott Wood and Half Moon Spinney. P-t-P '02 (for Mrs A. Cockburn) r3 p0 (pulled up 3). Presumably bought because of his kinship to Half Moon Spinney, who Ann Blaker trained to win twice in the late 90's, but jumps nowhere near well enough to emulate him at present, and was seven lengths last of three when completing. At least he looks to be on the upgrade, but the fact that he runs tongue-tied now is a big negative. *Mrs M. Platt — O. Surrey, Burstow & W. Kent (Ann Blaker).* 782 (OMa), 1055 (OMa), 1088 (OMa), 1405 (OMa).

SAXON GALE ..—.. 10 b.m. Tirley Gale — Tudor Spartan (Spartan General) p. Strong-topped half-sister to Jump For Paddy. Dam, half-sister to Celtic Tudor (*qv* '87 Season Annual). Grandam, Tudor Rambler, half-sister to Pointing winner and smart Chaser, Clear Cut, won 4 Points (inc Cotswold VF Members thrice) and 2m3f Hunt Ch and placed 3 (inc 3rd in Hunt Ch). P-t-P '03 r1 p0 (fell). Has shown some speed, but a handful and on the point of erupting before her reappearance, and did not look totally tractable when underway. Carries condition and looks too top-heavy to make a racehorse. *T. & Mrs J. Brine — S. & W. Wilts (Sally Brine).* 66 (OMa).

SAXON GOLD ..10-0.. 10 ch.g. Saxon Farm — Running For Gold (Rymer) p3p2. Strong half-brother to Only Harry, Cresswell Gold and Melchior. Dam is sister to Certain Angle (*qv*, also by Saxon Farm). NH FLAT '99 r2 p0. NH '99/00 r2 p0 (pulled up 2). P-t-P '02 (for Mr R.J. Marley & Mrs L. Bainbridge) r4 w2 (Maiden and Restricted) p0; and fell/unseated 2. Completed a double at Charm Park in '02, and looked sure to upgrade successfully, but absent the years either side, and four starts per annum remains his record. Still lying second when forced to pull up through fatigue at Guilsborough, and proved he retains ability when well-backed and forcing Minella Silver to pull out all the stops at Flagg subsequently. Could have done with jumping more fluently that day, but another small success looks on the cards if connections can keep him fit. Only risked on good or easy ground nowadays. *R. Prince — Meynell & S. Staffs.* 379 (I), 681 (I), 786 (O), 986 (Cf).

SAXON VICTORY (USA) .9-11§.. 10 b.g. Nicholas (USA) — Saxon Shore (USA) (Halo USA) p46. Workmanlike brother to Irish flat winner, MacNicholas. FLAT '97/8 r11 p3. NH '98/01 r36 p12 (6 2nds); fell/unseated 2. P-t-P/HUNT CH '02/3 r10 w3 (up to Confined) p1 (remote 3rd); 4th, 5th twice, last pair 3. Highly unreliable under Rules, and defeated 47 times, but responded to forcing tactics in three of his first eight Points, and showed a liking for good or sound surfaces. Appears to have regressed to his habits of old, and it would be unwise to expect another change of heart. Usually wears headgear. *D.E. Jones — Belvoir (Tim Tarratt).* 177 (3mH), 298 (Cf), 592 (O).

S B S BY JOVE ..9-12§.. 12 ch.g. Jupiter Island — Mill Shine (Milan) pp02. Tall strong-topped half-brother to Luvly Bubbly, Easy Breezy, Easy Perks and Old King Cole, and to NH flat and Hurdles winners, Konvekta Control and Oh So Bright. Dam won NH flat and 2 Hdles (2m-2m4f), in Ireland. P-t-P '99/03 r12 w4 (up to Confined) p2 (2nd of 3; and 3rd of 4); 4th, fell/unseated 3, and pulled up 2. A reformed lunatic, and has not missed the frame in eight Pointing completions, but stands his racing badly and has not been able to score since '02. Suited by an easy three miles on top of the ground, and needs to concentrate on the easiest options available. *Mrs S. Child & D. Cocks — Silverton (Linda Blackford).* 793 (Cf), 975 (2m7f110yH), 1168 (2m5fH), 1331 (Cf).

SCALBY CROFT ..8-0.. 9 b.m. Jupiter Island — Missile Lady (Paddy's Stream) p55p. Sturdy half-sister to Lolloping Lad. Dam, half-sister to Spartan Missile, Cruise Missile and La Coupee (*qv* '02 Annual), won 2m4f Maiden ('lurched home exhausted' and pipped The Rum Mariner). P-t-P '02/3 (for Mr A. Pennock) r13 p3 (2nd of 3; and 2 3rds, of 4 once, and last once); last pair 2, pulled up 7, and unseated 1. A very moderate non-stayer, and has missed the target in 17 attempts, and yet to finish within 16 lengths of a winner. Usually taken to post early. *R. Saych — Essex (Simon Marriage).* 996 (CMam), 1088 (OMa), 1317 (CfMa), 1404 (OMa).

SCALLYBUCK (IRE) ..9-10.. 13 br.g. Scallywag — Miss McNight (Master Buck) p25. Workmanlike. Dam won 2m Amateur Hurdle in Ireland. IRISH P-t-P '97/99 r4 w2 (inc Open) p1 (3rd); and pulled up 1. IRISH NH FLAT '97/8 r3 p0. IRISH HUNT CH '98/9 r7 p1 (3rd); fell 1. IRISH NH '97/02 (for M. Hourigan) r50 w4 (2m3f-3m1f Chses) p15 (inc 3 Hdles); pulled up 2, fell/unseated 3. NH '02/3 (for R.H. Buckler) r6 p1 (3rd); pulled up 1. Bought Ascot, Jul for 1428. Won four Irish Chases to July '00, and 16 placings there include four defeats of half a length or less, including a neck second after being eased near the finish (!). Blinkered there on three occasions, but derived no benefit. Has declined badly with advancing years, and after finishing a hopelessly tailed off last of two in a Members he again whipped the field in at Rhydygwern, where he wore a hackamore and finished lame. *T.D.B. Underwood — V. of Aylesbury with Garth & S. Berks.* 938 (MO), 1103 (C), 1484 (O).

SCALLY'S GEORGE ..—.. 7 b.g. Deltic (USA) — Scally's Daughter (Scallywag) p. Small neat. Dam, sister to Cedor's Gem, and half-sister to Cedor Hicks (*qv* '01), won 13 Points (inc 4 Ladies and 6 Opens) and placed 9 for Jean Thomas. Bred from a smart mare, but his debut told us nothing, as he pulled hard and was novicey in the rear and eventually pulled up at the 11th after the reins had broken. *Mrs J. Thomas — Pentyrch (Phil Williams).* 1393 (OMa).

SCALLYWELD .8-7.. 7 ch.g. Weld — Scally Jenks (Scallywag) fp. Brother to Master Welder, and half-brother to The Pedlar, Scally Hicks and Scallywace. Grandam, Acuity, won Hunt Ch (left lucky 2nd, and later awarded race on technical disqualification) and Maiden and placed 6 for Ken Edwards. P-t-P '03 r1 p0 (last). Has made limited and erratic progress to date, but attracted market support on his reappearance, and would do better if he calmed down and learnt how to jump properly. *K.C.G. Edwards — Ludlow (Geoff Evans).* 666 (OMa), 1233 (OMa).

SCARLET BOY ..8-11.. 6 gr.g. Arzanni — Scarlet Berry (Zambrano) 3. Attractive. Dam won 4 Points (inc 2 Intermediates) and placed 5 (last 3 wins for P. Sanderson; raced in '01) and also distant last of 3 in Hurdle. Finished 45 lengths third in his Members having raced towards the rear throughout, but did plug on steadily in the closing stages, and it is possible that there might be better to come. *P.J. Sanderson — Radnor & W. Herefords.* 1226 (M).

SCARLET EMPEROR (IRE) ..—.. 11 b.g. Supreme Leader — Red Donna (Don) pfp. Well-made brother to Irish jumping winner, Donna's Princess (IRE), and half-brother to Great Jubilee (IRE) and Irish Pointing and Hurdles winner, Oh Donna. NH FLAT '98/9 r5 w2 p0. NH '99/01 r4 w2 (2m4f110y-2m6f Hdles) p0; unseated 1. P-t-P '02/3 (for Mrs F. Bishop) r6 p2 (2nd of 3 once); 4th, fell/unseated 2, and pulled up 1. Won four races for the Pitmans, and provided Jenny with her final success at Huntingdon in '99, but has never looked safe or happy in Points, and his former handler would go ballistic if she had seen him in '04. A bad jumper of fences, and gets no assistance from the rider, and both should be retired. *G.R. Rochester — Pentyrch.* 208 (Cf), 359 (Cf), 1485 (Cnr).

SCARLET GLORY ..9-9.. 8 b.m. Past Glories — Majestic Spider (Majestic Maharaj) 41p1fp. Tall workmanlike owner-bred half-sister to Simply Sam (*qv*). P-t-P '03 r3 p1 (3rd of 4); and pulled up 2. A dual winner when favourite on right-handed tracks, but leaves the money in the bookmakers' satchels on a regular basis, and jumped with no confidence at all on her latest start having crashed and broken the rider's collar-bone at Badbury Rings the time before. Has two handlers. Wears a cross-noseband. *R.A. & Dr C.E. Fry — Cattistock (Caroline Fry).* 35 (CMam), 120 (OMa), 498 (R), 689 (R), 860 (Cf), 1351 (Inr).

SCARROTS ..— §.. 11 b.g. Mazilier (USA) — Bath (Runnett) pppp. Sturdy close-coupled half-brother to flat winner, Thai Morning. Dam won 5 flat (7-8f). 6500y. FLAT '96/8 r18 w3 (7-12f) p2. NH '97/9 r13 p5; pulled up 2. IRISH NH '01 (for Lord Tyrone) r6 p2 (2nds in Chses); refused 1 and unseated 1. IRISH P-t-P Jan /Feb '04 r2 p0 (pulled up 2:*rr, prog to 6th 9; mist 11; mod 6th when pu aft 3 out*; and *chsd ldrs, 5th 9, sn lost plce, t.o & pu 11*). Won three races on good or firm ground on the flat to June '97 (made virtually all twice; was successful in his only Seller), but a Maiden over obstacles, and although placed on seven occasions he has also shown temperament, including when refusing once. A quirky sort who pulled himself up in a four-runner Ladies and a Hunter Chase, but showed he still has some well-concealed ability when finishing with a flourish in a Selling Hurdle on his latest attempt in the Summer. Wore cheekpieces on that occasion, and equipped with headgear four times in '98. *J.R. Tuck — Beaufort.* 1255 (L), 1512 (2m6f110yH).

SCENIC STORM (IRE) ..9-7.. 10 b.g. Scenic — Sit Elnaas (USA) (Sir Ivor USA) u1p. Compact half-brother to Hurdling winner, Sujud. Dam, sister to French Hurdling, and half-sister to Deano's Beano, won 3 flat (14-17f). 40,000 4yo. NH FLAT '00 r1 p0. NH '01/2 (for F. Murphy) r9 p0; pulled up 3. Pulled up in three of six Chases including his final two, but able to show ability for the first time when switched to Points after missing '03, and beat some very disappointing sorts in a Maiden at Easingwold. Pulled up lame at Witton Castle next time, and his legs are clearly very fragile. *M.E. Broad — Bedale.* 809 (M), 1164 (OMa), 1288 (R).

SCHOLAR GREEN .—§§.. 13 b.g. Green Adventure (USA) — Quelle Chemise (Night Shift USA) pppp. Good-bodied lengthy. Dam is half-sister to Quarterstaff (*qv*). NH FLAT '96 r3 p0. NH '97 and '99 r4 p0; pulled up 3. P-t-P '00 and '03 r8 p0 (last pair 2, and pulled up 6). Error-prone and highly ungenuine, and pulled up in 13 of 16 attempts over jumps. Blinkered once in '99, and occasionally ridden in spurs since. *Miss M.A. Lloyd — Irfon & Towy.* 406 (Inr), 451 (R), 844 (R), 1141 (OMa).

SCHOOLHOUSE WALK ..10-5.. 7 b.g. Mistertopogigo (IRE) — Restandbejoyful (Takachiho) 322*1*. Stocky. Dam, sister to Restanbeplayful (*qv* '00 Annual). NH FLAT '02 r4 p0. P-t-P '03 r4 w1 (2m4f mares Maiden) p1 (2nd); last, and fell. NH '03 r3 p1 (3rd); pulled up 1. NH '04 (for M.E. Sowersby) r1 w1 (beat Prayerful 8*l* in 2m3f110y Hdle: *a.p, ld aft 3 out, clr nxt, unchall*). Speedy and enterprisingly ridden when scoring over 2m4f at Whitwell-on-the-Hill last year, but let down by his jumping in the closing stages over the full trip since, and looks sure to remain under Rules where opportunities for him are more plentiful. *Lord Manton & M.E.R. Sowersby — Holderness (Mary Sowersby).* 301 (R), 499 (M), 591 (CR).

SCOOBY DOO (U) ..—.. 8 b.g. Lafontaine (USA) — Harry's Diamond Lass p. Immediately struggling in his Members, and eventually pulled up after three out when tailed off. *L. Kerr — Eglinton (Jackie Williamson).* 653 (M).

SCOTCH BOB (IRE) .9-0.. 10 b/br.g. Mandalus — Flashey Thyne (IRE) (Good Thyne USA) 8p53. Half-brother to Irish Pointing winner, Kilgarvanspride (IRE). IRISH P-t-P '00 r6 p1 (3rd); pulled up 3, fell, and ran out. P-t-P '01/3 r15 w2 (Maiden and Restricted) p4 (3rds, remote of 4 twice, and last of 3 once); 4th, 5th, last, and pulled up 6. A front-runner and made all to win a bad Maiden at Charing and upgraded successfully in a match at Catsfield, but eclipsed in more competitive events, and only once better than last in '04. Has been tried in blinkers and cheekpieces. *P. Hughes — E. Sussex & Romney Marsh (Alison Hickman).* 182 (CCon), 421 (L), 805 (L), 1210 (L).

SCOTSBROOK LASS ..8-7.. 9 ch.m. Buckley — Two Shares (The Parson) 5. Workmanlike half-sister to Panacea, and to Irish Hurdles winner, Knockaulin. Dam won 2 2m2f Hdles at Downpatrick. P-t-P '03 r3 p0 (unseated 3). Ejected three different riders by the sixth fence at the latest in '03, but the promising Rhys Hughes showed them how it should be done at Maisemore and skilfully sat all she could throw at him. Amazingly was still in front at the fourth last, but weakened to finish 26 lengths last, and was not seen again. *A.E. Price — Ross H. (Alastair McCubbing).* 729 (OMa).

SCOTTISH ROOTS ..10-9.. 10 b.g. Roscoe Blake — Lothian Queen (Scorpio FR) 2p1311. Small neat. Dam, half-sister to Lothian Admiral (by Roscoe Blake, *qv* '95 Annual). NH FLAT '01 r2 p1 (3rd). NH '02 r3 p0. P-t-P '03 r5 w3 (up to Confined) p0; 7th, and pulled up 1. A major failure under Rules, but much more successful since joining David Easterby, and although sometimes moody has progressed into a decent sub-3m Hunter Chaser. Returned at 7-1 when providing Oliver Greenall with his first success in his Members, from his stablemate favourite with big brother on board, and was lucky to justify favouritism at Uttoxeter, but looked to be gaining in confidence when bouncing off the quick ground at Hexham, and could maintain his improvement into '05. Appears to handle all types of going. *Mrs C.N. Weatherby & Lady Daresbury — Middleton (David Easterby).* 316 (2m5fH), 377 (3m1fH), 769 (M), 1178 (3m1fH), 1377 (2m5fH), 1499 (2m4f110yH).

SCOUNDREL ..—.. 14 gr.g. Scallywag — Nicholcone (Celtic Cone) ppp. Strong-topped. Dam, half-sister to Motivator (*qv* '96 Annual). NH FLAT '96 r4 w2 p2 (behind Marello in both). NH '97, '99 and '01 r8 w1 (2m4f Hdle) p1 (3rd in Sell). P-t-P '03 r1 p0 (pulled up). A useful bumper horse but until '04 had only been able to appear biennially over jumps and a pale spectre of what he was now. Started at between 50-1 and 100-1 in '04, and was immediately lagging and ultimately well tailed off and pulled up thrice. Ended '03 lame and lucky not to finish up the same way this year as he was enormously overweight. *F.L. Matthews — Wheatland.* 490 (3m2fH), 630 (2m4fH), 994 (3m110yH).

SCOWLIN BRIG ..9-9.. 9 ch.g. Minster Son — Gideonscleuch (Beverley Boy) f5. Close-coupled. NH FLAT '01 r2 p0. NH '01/3 (for F.P. Murtagh) r13 p3 (3rds); pulled up 4. Placed in a Hurdle and two Chases, all at Sedgefield from between 2m5f to 3m3f, but also unplaced in a Selling Hurdle once and pulled up on four occasions including in blinkers once. Gave a good display in a Maiden at Alnwick until he fell two out when holding every chance, and although only Hallrule and Miss Mattie Ross completed they later won six races including two Chases and three Hunter Chases between them. Nailed-on for a Maiden if he could repeat that form, but clearly went wrong on his disappointing next attempt, as he has been asbsent since early February. Has now contested 17 races, but only once beaten less than 27 lengths. *A.J. Brown — Buccleuch.* 74 (OMa), 166 (OMa).

SCUTTLEBROOK (IRE) ..—.. 6 b.m. Glacial Storm (USA) — Arabian Sprite (IRE) (The Parson) p. Small. Dam won Irish NH flat. Sold Goffs Ireland, June 4638. Given a gentle introduction before pulling up two out at Paxford. *Miss S. Collett — N. Cotswold (Fred Hutsby).* 926 (OMa).

SEABROOK LAD ..10-2§.. 14 b.g. Derrylin — Moll (Rugantino) 37pf3. Big workmanlike half-brother to Rymolbreese, Kelly's Court, Sharpside and Gangster with stringhalt both hind legs. Dam won 2m5f Nov Hdle at 50-1. NH FLAT '96 r2 p0. NH '96/9 and '01 r26 w3 (2m5f110y Hdle and 2 2m4f-3m Chses) p6 (4 2nds); pulled up 3, and fell/unseated 3. P-t-P/HUNT CH '02/3 r13 w1 (Open) p10 (5 2nds, beaten head once, of 3 once, and inc a Hunt Ch, and inc 2 3rds in Hunt Chses); 4th, and brought down 1. A Ludlow specialist and has won only once going left-handed, but hugely frustrating on the whole, and usually settles for place money instead. Largely unimproved by the application of cheekpieces on his last three starts, and fell heavily once, and looks unlikely to improve his strike-rate at 14. Suited by a sound surface. *Seabrook Partners — Bicester with Whaddon (Fiona Kehoe).* 49 (4mO), 175 (Cnr), 490 (3m2fH), 868 (O), 1396 (C).

SEABURN ..—.. 15 b.g. State Trooper — Star Display (Sparkler) u. Sturdy half-brother to flat winner, Gloss and jumping winner, Avonmouthsecretary. NH FLAT '94 r1 p0. NH '94 and '98/9 (for N.B. Mason) r10 p0; pulled up 5, fell 1. Useless and a very poor jumper, and has never been beaten less than 27 lengths. Tongue-tied and blinkered once under Rules. A non-finisher in seven of 11 attempts over jumps, and it was no surprise when the insecure owner fell out the front door in his Members. Gets excellent holidays with his job, and was away for four years after '94 and for five after '99. *N.B. Mason & W. Barron — Braes.* 1036 (M).

SEA GRIT ..—.. 6 b.g. Bold Fox — Diddums-Do (Oats) p. Small neat. Bought Ascot, Nov for 1428. Lost 20 lengths at the start and continued shakily until pulling up after a mile at Bredwardine in mid-May. *I.R. Smith — Albrighton (Paul Morris).* 1394 (OMa).

SEA HAITCH EM ..—.. 10 ch.g. Norton Challenger — One Way Circuit (Windjammer USA) ppp. Tall lengthy lightly-made brother to The Doc. NH FLAT '00 r1 p0. NH '00/1 r6 p0. P-t-P/HUNT CH '03 r4 w3 (inc 2m5f Hunt Ch) p1 (2nd in Hunt Ch). Transformed from a poor Selling Hurdler into a strong-galloping winning Hunter Chaser, and only beaten once when rated 10-10 in '03, but stopped to nothing on his first two starts this season, and sadly broke down irreparably at Taunton. *Miss L. Llewellyn & V.J. Hughes — Llangeinor (Vivian Hughes).* 348 (3mH), 630 (2m4fH), 733 (3mH).

SEAN'S MINSTREL (IRE) ..9-8§.. 12 gr.g. Black Minstrel — Gala Star (Gail Star) up. Workmanlike. IRISH P-t-P '99/00 r7 w3 (hat-trick to Winners of Two) p1 (3rd); fell/unseated 2. IRISH HUNT CH '00 r1 p0 (fell). NH '01 r1 p0 (tailed off and pulled up in 2m6f Ch). P-t-P/HUNT CH '01/3 (for Random Optimists) r9 w1 (Confined) p2 (3rds; remote of 4 once, and last once); 4th, 6th, 7th, and pulled up 3. Recorded a hat-trick in Ireland in '00, and landed a touch when scoring narrowly at Parham last year, but often performs as though defective, and showed no trace of ability in the new yard. Found nothing off the bridle when tried in cheekpieces once last year, and his loss of form seems permanent this time. *A.S. Nelson — N. Tyne (Tina Hammond).* 542 (3m3fH), 764 (O).

SEA PRINCESS ..—.. 8 b.m. Sea Raven (IRE) — Mighty Miss (Doc Marten) pfpp. Compact well-made half-sister to Mighty Rising (*qv*). Dam, half-sister to First Trick (*qv* '94 Annual), won 2 Points and placed 4 to '94. NH FLAT '02 (for M.E. Sowersby) r2 p0; pulled up 1. Tailed off in her first bumper and pulled up at halfway next time, and ignored by the punters when failing to complete in Maidens. Has made some bad blunders (fell at the first once) and given no indication of being able to get the trip. *N.D. Tutty — Hurworth (Karen Tutty).* 775 (CfMa), 1159 (OMa), 1291 (OMa), 1417 (OMa).

SEARCH PARTY (FR) ..9-5.. 6 b.g. Efisio — Hunt The Thimble (FR) (Relkino) up215. Small half-brother to jumping winner, Roi De La Chasse, to Irish Chasing winner, Green Finger, and to French Hurdling winner, Look Sharp. Ff90,000y. FLAT '01/2 (for T.D. Easterby) r7 p0. Too slow for the flat and was tailed off in four of seven attempts including a Seller, but better suited by Pointing, and followed an eight-lengths second over 2m4f with a win over the full trip at Charm Park. Has had three subsequent scorers behind him, and given average improvement from five to six he should be able to figure prominently in Restricteds, particularly now that he has started to get the hang of the jumping. *Mrs P.A. Russell — Middleton.* 167 (OMa), 271 (OMa), 773 (2m4fCMa), 959 (OMa), 1288 (R).

SEASMITH .9-4.. 10 ch/gr.g. Greensmith — Sea Spice (Precipice Wood) fp3. Tall good-topped brother to NH flat winner, Sargasso Sea, and half-brother to Country Spice. Dam, half-sister to Keep Watch (*qv* '90 Annual), won 2 NH flat and 3 Hdles (2m4f-2m5f), all wins in her debut season and subsequently let down by jumping over fences. NH FLAT '01 r1 p0. NH '01/3 (for L. Lungo) r8 p0; fell 1. Bought Doncaster, May for 3700. Has only run 12 times in four years, and was beaten 31 lengths plus under Rules. Races prominently for up to 2m4f in Points, but does not get the trip, and although he was five-lengths third on the short course at Easingwold it will be difficult for him to win. *Mrs P.M. Shirley-Beavan — Jedforest.* 215 (OMa), 766 (R), 1164 (OMa).

SEA SNIPE ..9-11.. 8 b.m. King Luthier — Seal Marine (Harwell) 1313. Attractive good-bodied half-sister to Sweet Manatte, My Main Man, Merlin's Lad, Penguin, No Trouble and Sister Swing. Dam, half-sister to South Sunrise (*qv* '96 Annual), won 3m2f Hunter Chse and 6 Points and placed 2nd twice. P-t-P '02/3 r3 p1 (3rd); 4th, and last. Has had her opportunities restricted because of foot problems, but a sound jumper, and has won two races convincingly on easy surfaces. Faded tamely when a well-backed 22 lengths third in her first Intermediate, but losses may be only lent, and could up her rating into the ten stone range in '05. *H. Messer-Bennetts — N. Cornwall (Becky Kennen).* 82 (OMa), 198 (R), 323 (R), 573 (I).

SEA TARTH .9-8.. 14 gr.m. Nicholas Bill — Seajan (Mandamus) 54p5p. Half-sister to Seachest, Sea Arrow and Sea Sky (dam of Call The Duke, *qv* '03 Annual). Dam won at 14f, and won 3 3m Hdles. NH FLAT '97 r4 w1 (33-1 at Bangor) p2 (2nds). NH '97/02 r26 w3 (2 3m-3m2f Hdles and 2m7f110y Ch) p5. P-t-P '96 and '02/3 r16 w2 (Ladies) p9 (5 2nds, beaten head twice; 4 3rds, of 4 once, and remote last once); 4th, fell 2, refused 1 and brought down 1. Scoring for the first time since '99 when completing a double last year, but normally exposed by her lack of acceleration, and plodded badly in cheekpieces in '04. A safe if somewhat deliberate jumper, and stays really well, but only of use as a schoolmistress or broodmare now. Broke a blood vessel when tongue-tied once in '98. Wears a cross-noseband. *Mrs T.R. & Mrs T.W. Kinsey — Cheshire Forest (Julie Kinsey).* 5 (L), 42 (L), 712 (L), 987 (L), 1229 (L).

SEA VICTOR ..—.. 13 b.g. Slip Anchor — Victoriana (USA) (Storm Bird CAN) 4pup. Strong attractive half-brother to flat winners, Victorian Order (in France) Vicereine, Victorian Style, Voracious, and to Hurdles winner, Victory Star. Dam won 5f race in France and is from a top-class family. FLAT '94/7, '01 and '03 (for J.H.M. Gosden, J.L. & J.A. Harris) r46 w6 (10-19f) p12 (btn ½*l* or less in 5). NH '96/7 (for J.L. Harris) r7 w2 (2m1f-2m5f Hdles) p1 (3rd). Was a very gutsy stayer at best in his prime and battled home to four of his victories by a neck or less, and after gaining one success in an all-weather Claimer he later took the infamous Top Cees race at Chester in '96. His career earnings totalled £64,375, and was beaten half a length or less in five of his placings. Occasionally wore a visor to '97, but only made two appearances after that year before he fell on extremely hard times when joining the latest yard for Pointing, and had to be destroyed after injuring himself at Fakenham. The Grange Family (M. Grange) — Fitzwilliam (Michael Grange). 555 (M), 784 (Cf), 1031 (Cf), 1151 (Cf).

SECRETE CONTRACT ..9-12.. 7 b.g. Contract Law (USA) — Secret Account (Blakeney) 2. Compact. FLAT '00/1 r4 p0. NH '02 r5 p0; pulled up 2. P-t-P '03 (for The Secrete Society Partnership) r2 w1 (Maiden) p0; and brought down 1. Won a bad Maiden on firmish at Aldington easily, and did enough in his first Restricted to suggest he would soon go one better, but does not seem very easy to train. Wore blinkers and a tongue-tie when a bad performer under Rules, and it is a pity that now he is showing some ability he has become so fragile. *Mrs A.E. Dawes — Coakham Bloodhounds (Paul Hacking).* 250 (R).

SECRET STREAMS (IRE) ..—.. 11 br.g. Over The River (FR) — Brigette's Secret (Good Thyne USA) p. Small compact. P-t-P/HUNT CH '99/01 (for Sir Chips Keswick & Mr C.H. Sporborg) r11 w3 (inc 2m4f110y Hunt Ch) p5 (2nds, inc Hunt Ch); last, pulled up 1, and fell 1. Speedy though not the easiest of rides when rated 10-5 at best to '01, but his previous campaign was curtailed when found to be suffering from ulcers, and missed two full seasons prior to an abortive comeback in '04. *C.H. Sporborg — Puckeridge, & Cambridge Univ.* 400 (C).

SEE MORE FUN ..8-11.. 7 ch.g. Seymour Hicks (FR) — Arctic Madam (Town And Country) fpp1. Workmanlike. Dam, half-sister to Derring Knight (*qv* '98 Annual), won Maiden and Members and 2nd for the Barbers. P-t-P '03 (for Mr C.L. & Mrs E.J. Barber) r1 p0 (last). Fell at the first on his return but seemed to benefit from an eight-week break after two confidence boosters, and narrowly landed a punt from sevens to 7-2 in a three-finisher Maiden at Cotley Farm. The form means nothing, and the time was slow, but in a good yard and there is a strong chance he is capable of much better. *Mr & Mrs R.H.H. Targett — Blackmore & Sparkford V. (Rose Vickery).* 30 (CMah), 142 (OMa), 353 (OMa), 1248 (OMa).

SEEMORE SUNSHINE ..—.. 8 br.g. Seymour Hicks (FR) — Temporary Affair (Mandalus) p7*p*75. Workmanlike half-brother to Mrs Sherman (*qv*). NH '04 (for R. Johnson) r4 p0 (last of 7 in 2m6f110y Hdle: *hld up & pulled hrd, hdwy 5, wknd aft nxt, t.o*; pulled up in 3m Hdle: *a bhnd, lost tch 7, t.o & pu last*; 7th in 2m110y Hdle: *a bhnd*; and 5th in 2m5f Ch: *hld up & pulled hard, hdwy 10, wknd qckly aft 3 out, t.o*). Bought Doncaster, Nov '02 for 1200. Unruly in the paddock before pulling up when tailed off in Maiden, and a hard-puller who looked very awkward under Rules subsequently, and was a distant fifth in his only Chase and beaten 29 lengths plus in Hurdles. Unpromising. *M. & Mrs S. Smith — Jedforest (Michael Smith).* 215 (OMa).

SEE RED BILLDAN (IRE) .—§§.. 9 br.g. Riverhead (USA) — Sweet Mayo (IRE) (Sexton Blake) ppRpR*p*. Tall angular goose-rumped. IRISH P-t-P '03 r5 p0 (pulled up 5). NH '04 (for T.P. McGovern) r1 p0 (pulled up in 3m Hdle: *in tch til wknd aft 9, t.o & pu 2 out*). Capable of racing prominently, but a truly horrid character who has never got round in 11 races, and normally tries to run off the course (has succeeded in two of his last three attempts in Points). *R.J. Lancaster — W. Street Tickham.* 103 (OMa), 345 (2m5fH), 539 (OMa), 651 (OMa), 1405 (OMa).

SEFTON CLOVER ..8-8.. 8 gr.m. Baron Blakeney — Come On Clover (Oats) u6uu. Small sturdy half-sister to Buckaroo, Colonel Hook, Gone Ballistic, Lady Clifford and Legbourne. Dam, half-sister to Italian Clover (*qv*). Managed to complete for 32 lengths sixth once, but has otherwise developed a cunning knack of unseating riders, and will have to jump much better to achieve anything. *Mrs J. Baldwin — Golden V. (Jane Lloyd).* 453 (CfMa), 978 (CMam), 1387 (M), 1533 (OMa).

SELECTRIC (IRE) ..4-0.. 14 b.g. Electric — Sweet Annabelle (Deep Run) pp3. Unfurnished half-brother to Mr Kats. NH FLAT '96 r2 p0. NH '96/7 (for J. Wade) r2 p0 (pulled up 2). Pulled up in his first four attempts over jumps with a seven-year gap before he embraced Pointing, and ended with a 75 lengths third in his Members (was already tailed off when he made a bad mistake at the 14th). Predictable at least. *P.F. Gibbon & Miss E. Cox — Zetland (Stuart Gibbon).* 813 (OMa), 1164 (OMa), 1286 (M).

SELECT STAR (IRE) ..—§.. 11 b.g. Arcane (USA) — Chevrefeuille (Ile De Bourbon USA) pppf. Small compact half-brother to Esthal (IRE). Dam, 15,500y, won at 12f, and is out of smart flat winner, Vielle. FLAT '96/8 r19 p5. NH '98/00 r23 w4 (2m3f110y-3m110y Hdles) p7 (4 3rds). P-t-P '03 r10 p0 (4th twice, 5th, last 2, fell/unseated 3, and pulled up 2). Did all his winning from Jun '99-Mar '00, but Martin Pipe extracted all his ability and resolve, and has shown absolutely no inclination to put his best foot forward over fences. Fell and broke Jenny Congdon's collarbone at Lifton, and should have been left well and truly in retirement. Wears a tongue-tie and headgear. *Horwood Hopefuls Group (Miss J. Congdon) — Torrington F. (Andrew Congdon).* 322 (L), 414 (MO), 792 (MO), 823 (Cf).

SELFCERTIFIED ..—.. 6 b.g. Lancastrian — Class Mate (Decent Fellow) pp. Homebred. Given an easy time in a couple of April Maidens, and showed a trace of ability at Catsfield, so may be capable of better in time. *Mr & Mrs P. Bull — E. Sussex & Romney Marsh (Peter Bull).* 782 (OMa), 1055 (OMa).

PLATE 104 1248 Cotley Open Maiden 56&7yo: See More Fun (Nick Williams), 1st, leads Panto (Kate Lovelace), 3rd *PHOTO: Tim Holt*

SENIOR MOMENT ..8-0.. 7 b.g. Faustus (USA) — Supreme Wings (IRE) (Supreme Leader) 54p. Workmanlike owner-bred. Dam, half-sister to Odysseus (*qv* '97 Annual). Finished over 35 lengths last in two completions, and then pulled up when exhausted on a disappointing finale. A steady jumper, but has certainly not proved that he gets the trip. Perhaps a switch to 2m4f Maidens would help. *Mrs K. Birchenhough — Blackmore & Sparkford V. (John Dufosee).* 142 (OMa), 575 (OMa), 1067 (OMa).

SENOR CID .9-2.. 6 b.g. El Conquistador — Leatan (Leander) f2. Lengthy half-brother to Ashor Ted (*qv*). Fell at the last when tailed off on his debut, but a five-length second of three over 2m4f at Littlewindsor was better (mounted on the course and led to the start early). May prove good enough to win a race. *J.H. Cobden — Seavington (Jane Reed).* 600 (2m4fOMa), 1007 (2m4fOMa).

SEPTEMBER HARVEST (USA) ..9-10.. 9 ch.g. Mujtahid (USA) — Shawgatny (USA) (Danzig Connection USA) p054. Lengthy half-brother to flat winner, Mister Saif. Dam won 9f race in Ireland. IR30,500y. FLAT '98/02 r51 w2 (8f) p7. NH '99/02 (for Mrs S. Lamyman) r17 p0; fell 1, pulled up 1. Bought Ascot, Nov '02 for 857. A dual winner on the flat to January '01, and gave an amazing performance on the all-weather once, as he was last three furlongs out but managed to overtake 15 rivals (!). Never placed over Hurdles, and fell at the second in his only Chase. Occasionally wears headgear and has participated in Sellers, and is a monkey who has only once been placed in his 26 most recent outings. Made some late progress for 17 lengths fourth at Rhydgwern, but it would never be possible to have any faith in him, and certainly not worth the rating in his other Points. *R. Shute — Berkeley (R. Champion).* 277 (O), 403 (Cf), 1024 (O), 1485 (Cnr).

SERGWYN ..—.. 9 ch.g. Gwynfi Ni — Serenweno (Deep Lake) ppuR. A difficult and unco-operative ride who has gone less than 2m4f to date, and may well be incapable of better. *J.W. Miles — Gelligaer F.* 203 (CfMa), 363 (CfMa), 451 (R), 1324 (CfMa).

SERVES YOU RIGHT ..8-2.. 6 ch.g. Alderbrook — Balancing Act (Balinger) 8p. Homebred half-brother to Tickle The Tiller (IRE), and to Hurdles winners, The Laird's Entry (IRE) and Door To Door (IRE) (latter also won Chasing). Dam is an unraced half-sister to Granville Again and Morley Street, and is out of Matchboard, a fine Pointer/Chaser for Bill Shand-Kydd. Tailed off after a mile when last on his debut, and resumed two months later to pull up when struggling. If he has any ability he will probably need time before being able to produce it. *W. Shand-Kydd & Lady Kleinwort — V. of Aylesbury with Garth & S. Berks (Karen Lawther).* 53 (2m4fOMa), 644 (OMa).

SETT ASIDE ..8-12.. 7 b.g. Set Adrift — Fields Of Fortune (Anfield) ur1. Sturdy. Awkward at the start and unseated before the first on his debut, and refused after a mile after some very nervous jumping and becoming tailed off early next time, but given a marvellous Julian Pritchard ride over 2m5f at Upton-on-Severn, and after being taken steadily and still only in seventh place throughout he kept going and was able to profit from the departures of the leading pair two out. A very lucky winner, but should have derived confidence and may continue to progress. *Mrs A. Brewer — Ledbury (Sophie Brewer).* 619 (2m4fOMa), 723 (OMa), 983 (2m5fOMa).

SEVENSIDER (IRE) ..9-7.. 7 b/br.g. Satco (FR) — Pretty Beau (IRE) (Beau Charmeur FR) 21p23. Good-topped. NH FLAT '02 r2 p0. NH '02/3 (for M.W. Easterby) r5 p0; pulled up 1. Beaten 20 lengths or considerably more at 20-1 plus in seven attempts under Rules (pulled up in blinkers on final start), but more effective in Points, and having been overwhelmed close home by the late burst of Le Millenaire at Duncome Park he scored by 40 lengths in a 5&6yo Maiden at Charm Park and later lost nothing in defeat when runner-up to Cross River, again at Charm Park. One-paced and looked to flounder in the soft once, but should be capable of winning an average Restricted on good ground. *Mrs S.E. Mason — Middleton (Ian Mason).* 272 (OMa), 392 (CfMa), 771 (R), 955 (R), 1162 (R).

SEVERN MAGIC ..10-0.. 12 b.m. Buckley — La Margarite (Bonne Noel) u. Workmanlike half-sister to Pamela's Lad. Dam won 2m6f Hdle in '88. P-t-P/HUNT CH '99/02 r13 w2 (inc Open) p4 (3 3rds, of 4 twice; and last of 2); pulled up 1 and fell/unseated 3. Returned to form and enjoyed her busiest season to date when joining the present yard last year, but only effective in a low grade, and only cleared one fence successfully in '04. Stays well and is suited by soft ground, but her current rating must be considered suspect if she returns. *R. Packer — Monmouths (David Thomas).* 347 (3mH).

SEX KITTEN ..8-5.. 7 ch.m. Riverwise (USA) — Cut Above The Rest (Indiaro) 42. Light-framed sister to Cats Cross (*qv*). Gave encouragement on her debut, and appeared to snatch the verdict on the line by a head in a Cothelstone Maiden, but the judge thought otherwise, and awarded a half-length verdict to Keep The Day Job (cat calls from connections would have been justified). It was an extremely slowly-run contest and may have been her golden opportunity, but can hopefully find compensation. *The Storm Trooper Partnership (E.J. McClafferty) — Ystrad Taf Fechan (Liam Corcoran).* 910 (2m4fOMa), 1371 (OMa).

SEYMOUR OF ME ..7-10.. 10 ch.g. Riverwise (USA) — Seymour Lady (Malicious) ppu3. Dam won 4 2m-2m2f Selling Hurdles. NH FLAT '00 r2 p0. NH '00/1 (for N.R. Mitchell) r5 p0; pulled up 1. Bought Ascot, July '01 for 600. Beaten 40 lengths plus in seven races under Rules including four Selling Hurdles to '01, and failed to complete in his first three Points, but managed a three lengths last in a Maiden at Aldington behind a winner who also pulled up on five occasions in '04. Had every chance at the last, but always runs out of stamina, and did so yet again. We would rather seymour of the Sex Kitten above. *S.D. Briggs — Ashford V. (Lisa Stock).* 539 (OMa), 611 (OMa), 782 (OMa), 895 (OMa).

SEYMOUR ROSES ..—§§.. 9 b.m. Seymour Hicks (FR) — Rose Rambler (Scallywag) r. Small light half-sister to The Snow Burn. Dam is half-sister to My Dawn (*qv* '01 Annual). P-t-P '02 (for Mr R. Edwards) r4 p0 (ran out 2, refused 1 and pulled up 1). Highly unpleasant and a nightmare ride, and did all she could to delay the inevitable on her return, and needs to be banned immediately. *P.C. & Mrs S.E. Handley — N. Salop (Peter Handley).* 668 (OMa).

SHADAR (IRE) ..9-2.. 6 b.g. Gabitat — Hi Eden VII (unknown) pu2. Pulled up after the rider had lost an iron at the fifth in his Members and unseated a different jockey in the Maiden on the same card, but acquiring a competent pilot in Dai Jones was a wise move, and finished two lengths second in a youngsters Maiden at Bonvilston (all his appearances have been there). By a sprinter, but he can get stayers, and looks a possibility to score at six. *P. Riddick — Gelligaer F.* 1318 (M), 1324 (CfMa), 1533 (OMa).

SHADY AFFAIR (IRE) ..9-1.. 14 b.g. Black Minstrel — Golden Ice (Golden Love) p5. Lengthy. Dam won Irish Maiden (beating the memorably named Aimless Armadillo); earlier won in similar company, but took the wrong course and disqualified. P-t-P '98 (for Mr P. Hill) r2 p0 (pulled up 1 and fell 1). NH '00/3 (for R.N. Bevis) r14 w1 (2m1f110y Ch) p1 (2nd); pulled up 5 and unseated 1. Came from another parish to register a 25-1 success over fences at Bangor in '01, but often a sketchy jumper and frequently took no interest, and wore cheekpieces when descending to a Seller on his final start under Rules. Very lightly raced since his moment of triumph under Gary Lyons, and looked typically unenthusiastic in Points. *R.J. Bevis, B. Bevis & K. Shore — Cheshire (Robert Bevis).* 1263 (L), 1426 (C).

SHADY MINX .—.. 6 ch.m. Gildoran — Shades Of Oak (Pamroy) f. Owner-bred half-sister to Joves Shadow (*qv*). Close up when falling at the 12th in a March Maiden, and may be able to produce better efforts if she has not harmed herself. *Mrs F. Macfarlane — Bicester with Whaddon (Fred Hutsby).* 462 (OMa).

SHAFI (IRE) ..—§.. 14 b.g. Reference Point — Azyaa (Kris) ffp. Small neat half-brother to flat winners, Hadith, Yarob, Mukhatab and Ihtiraz, and to winning Hurdler, Samsaam (IRE). Dam won at 8f. FLAT r8 w1 (11f) p3. DUBAI FLAT '95 and '97 w4 (10-12f). NH '98 and '01 r4 p0 (4th, last, and pulled up 2). P-t-P/HUNT CH '99/02 r15 w3 (2m110y Hunt Ch and 2 Opens) p8 (6 2nds, and 3rd of 4 once, all Hunt Chses) pulled up 2, unseated 1. Quickened impressively to win his first two Points, and had more than enough speed to despatch 21 rivals in a 2m Hunter Chase at Cheltenham, but often makes mistakes, and looks to have regressed for good. Suited by a sound surface. *G. Byard — Radnor & W. Herefords (Mark Doyle).* 1024 (O), 1173 (2m110yH), 1372 (2m4fH).

SHAFTS CHANCE (IRE) ..9-5.. 8 br.m. Over The River (FR) — Lunar Approach (IRE) (Mandalus) 1f54R. Small compact. IRISH P-t-P '02/3 r4 p1 (2nd); last, pulled up and fell. IRISH NH FLAT '03 r2 p0. IRISH NH '03 r1 p0. NH '03 (for C.R. Egerton) r4 p1 (3rd); fell 2. Second in an Irish Point and 11 lengths third of four in an English Chase, but also well tailed off last once and fell twice in the latter, and was blinkered on her final attempt. Capable of alarming blunders, but was able to give Stuart Ross his first winner in a typically bad Mares Maiden at Garnons before some modest subsequent efforts, although she was a staying on 14 lengths fourth after an insipid ride from her owner once. Ended the season by running out when tailed off, and is no better than very moderate. *Miss K.M. Wood — Cheshire.* 408 (CMam), 614 (R), 853 (R), 1069 (R), 1265 (R).

SHAKING CHIEF (IRE) ..9-8.. 7 br.g. Executive Perk — Trembling Lass (IRE) (Tremblant) R413. Compact. P-t-P '03 r1 p0 (pulled up). Backed from sixes to 5-2 on his first completion, but ideally wants to go right-handed, and comfortably landed a weak Maiden on dead ground at Brampton Bryan. Came out worst in a three-way photo at Chaddesley Corbett on his Restricted debut, and looks to have the scope to win in that grade soon. *J.D. Callow — Albrighton Woodland (Helen Needham).* 30 (CMah), 97 (CfMa), 667 (OMa), 1018 (R).

SHALABIBUBBLY ..9-6.. 10 ch.g. Hubbly Bubbly (USA) — Shalabia (Fast Topaze USA) ppfu. Rangy. Dam won 2 flat (6-7f). P-t-P '03 r2 p1 (2nd); and pulled up 1. Tried hard when a length second in a weak elders Maiden on firmish on his debut, but consistently let down by his jumping since, and in grave danger of losing his tentative rating. *R.H. Lee — Rockwood H. (Nick Kent).* 595 (OMa), 685 (OMa), 946 (OMa), 1125 (OMa).

SHALLEE TERM (IRE) ..8-6.. 7 b.g. Welsh Term — Mrs Mustard (IRE) (Le Johnstan) p44. Narrow angular. IRISH NH FLAT '02 r1 p0. IRISH NH '02/3 (for E.J. O'Grady) r7 p0. Bought Doncaster, Aug for 2600. Soundly beaten under Rules in Ireland, and blinkered on his last two attempts there, but managed to scrape round in a couple of fourths in Maidens in '04 (beaten about 25 lengths in both, and his jumping and paddock appearance did not impress). A veritable star by Millington standards, but absent since mid-February so has presumably gone wrong. *P.J. Millington — Fernie.* 8 (2m4fOMa), 39 (OMa), 218 (OMa).

SHALLOW RIVER (IRE) ..9-2.. 14 b.g. Over The River (FR) — Rule The Waves (Deep Run) 3p76. Workmanlike. Dam won Irish NH flat (previously won similar but demoted to 2nd). NH FLAT '95 r1 p0. NH '95/6 and '97 r11 w1 (2m6f Hdle) p3 (inc distant 3rd of 4 in Ch). P-t-P/HUNT CH '98/9 and '01/3 r21 w2 (Ladies, inc 3m2f) p8 (6 2nds, inc Hunt Ch); pulled up 1 and fell/unseated 3. A thorough stayer and rarely puts a foot wrong, but becoming increasingly one-paced, and only stands light campaigns. Has never found winning easy, and only beat one rival in '04. *R.W. Phizacklea — Atherstone (Hannah Phizacklea).* 1118 (M), 1214 (Cf), 1428 (L), 1500 (Cf).

SHAMBOB ..8-3.. 7 b.g. Shambo — Celia's Halo (Mountain Call) 6p6. Tall workmanlike owner-bred half-brother to Jupiter George (*qv*). Yet to show any flair, and was beaten about 30 lengths in both completions (last once). Wore an off-side pricker on his debut, indicating that he has shown a tendency to hang at home. *C.R. Millington — Fernie (John Dillon).* 887 (CfMa), 1215 (CfMa), 1402 (2m4fOMa).

SHAMEL .—.. 9 b.g. Unfuwain (USA) — Narjis (USA) (Blushing Groom FR) pppf. Neat brother to Mamlakah (won May Hill Stakes) and Shamikh (won Chesham Stakes), and half-brother to flat winner, Elakik (later successful in USA), and to French flat winner, Thakeyyah. Dam won 5f race. FLAT '98/00 r9 w1 (14f) p3. NH '03 (for C.J. & A.E. Price) r2 p0 (last and pulled up 1). Beautifully bred for the flat, but managed to win only a desperate contest at Yarmouth. Seventy-one lengths last and pulled up in Hurdles (66-1 plus), and after labouring badly in his first two Points and a Hunter Chase he fell two out when fading in a dire four-runner Open in mid-March. A wind defect has scuppered him, and tying his tongue down has not worked, so does not look to have any future prospects. *G. Byard — Radnor & W. Herefords (Steve Flook).* 33 (L), 229 (O), 444 (2mH), 514 (O).

SHANAVOGH .10-8.. 14 b.g. Idiot's Delight — Honeybuzzard (FR) (Sea Hawk II) f31211f. Workmanlike angular half-brother to 5 winners (including abroad), including Jopanini (Hurdles). Dam won at 10f in Ireland. IRISH P-t-P '95 r2 p1 (last of 3); and pulled up 1. NH FLAT '95 r1 p0. NH '95/9 r18 w4 (3 2m4f-2m5f Hdles, and 2m5f Ch) p9 (fell and remounted once); fell 2 out or would probably have won 2m Ch once. P-t-P/HUNT CH '00/3 r18 w7 (Opens) p7 (6 2nds, beaten 1/2l twice); 4th twice, ran out 1 and pulled up 1. A bold jumping front-runner, and suited the owner-rider down to the ground, and never missed the first three in 19 Pointing completions. Difficult to beat over a sharp three miles on a sound surface, but never subjected to arduous campaigns, and his demise at Garthorpe was tragic. R.S. Hunnisett — Pytchley (Caroline Bailey). 24 (O), 156 (O), 381 (O), 683 (O), 888 (O), 1121 (O), 1401 (O).

SHANAVOHER (IRE) ..9-7.. 13 ch.g. Phardante (FR) — Lane Baloo (Lucky Brief) 5f3p. Lengthy brother to Irish Hurdles winner, Ash Baloo, and half-brother to 4 winners in Ireland, including, Lucky Baloo (flat and jumping). IRISH NH FLAT '97/8 r2 w1 p0. IRISH NH '98/00 r30 p5 (4 Chses, beaten short-head once). P-t-P/HUNT CH '03 (for Mr A.C. Ward-Thomas) r3 p0 (6th, pulled up 1, and fell 1). NH '03 (for B.G. Powell) r1 p0 (pulled up). Won a bumper at Roscommon in '98, and thrice beaten half-a-length or less over jumps but remained a maiden in that sphere and dropped dead at Cothelstone. M. Wyatt & A. Hill — Devon & Somerset (M. Wyatt). 880 (MO), 1128 (MO), 1249 (MO), 1367 (O).

SHANKLY ..10-4.. 10 b.g. King's Ride — Brandy Run (Deep Run) 25. Compact good-topped. Dam is half-sister to Cowage Brook (*qv* '97 Annual). NH '99/01 r6 p0; pulled up 4. P-t-P/HUNT CH '02/3 r12 w3 (up to Confined; also disqualified from Maiden win — not weigh-in) p3 (2nd of 3; and 3rd of 4 twice); 4th, unseated 2, and pulled up 2. Very average until he was eight, but finally became more amenable to restraint last year, and forged a highly successful alliance with Mark Walford. Too exuberant on his return, and found nil when collared at the last, but had a warning light flash on once last year, and failed to reappear after going lame at Charm Park in March. *A.C. Barker — Sinnington (Christopher Barker).* 266 (M), 391 (MO).

SHANROD VIEW (IRE) ..—.. 10 b.g. Roi Guillaume (FR) — Golden Hearted (Corvaro USA) uppp. Half-brother to Hurdles winner, Kilcourt Lad (IRE). IRISH P-t-P '01 r3 w1 (6yo plus Maiden) p1 (2nd). Sold Tattersalls Ireland, Jan '02 for 7302. Won a Maiden in soft in the last of his three Irish Pointing attempts, but unable to get round when revived three years later, and consistently looks as if he is defective. *Mrs B. Ansell & Miss J. Goddard — Ashford V. (Trevor Crawford).* 181 (R), 250 (R), 648 (R), 807 (M).

SHARLOM (IRE) ..9-12.. 8 br.g. Shardari — Sarahs Music (IRE) (Orchestra) 2u6313. Workmanlike. Dam, half-sister to Daring Native (*qv* '03 Annual). NH FLAT '01 r1 p0. NH '01/2 r12 p1 (3rd); pulled up 4 and fell/unseated 2. P-t-P '03 (for Mr M.W. Harris) r3 w2 (Maiden and Restricted) p0; and unseated 1. Error-prone, and has failed to build on last year's performances, and benefited from accidents to more fancied rivals when scoring at Tabley. Largely consistent, but tends not to find a great deal off the bridle, and might be difficult to place successfully in future. Blinkered once in '02.

Has two handlers. *M. Kemp & S. Hammond — Albrighton (Paul Jones).* 91 (M), 255 (CCon), 663 (I), 932 (Cf), 1430 (I), 1528 (Cf).

PLATE 105 1223 Lauderdale Mens Open: Sharpaman (Charlie Shirley-Beavan), 4th, takes the permanent open ditch (an increasingly rare beastie) PHOTO: Alan Mitchell

SHARPAMAN ..9-10§.. 10 b.g. Mandalus — Sharp Glance (IRE) (Deep Run) p86p1245r. Lengthy half-brother to Hurdles winner, Digup St Edmunds. NH '02 r1 p0 (fell in Ch). P-t-P '00 and '02/3 r16 w2 (Maiden and Restricted) p2 (2nds, head last once); last pair 2, pulled up 6, and on floor 4. Improved by the application of blinkers and strong handling last year, and recorded his third win at a rewarding price when making most at Dalston in '04, but thoroughly unreliable, and will throw in the towel at a moment's notice. Found to be lame after refusing on his Hunter Chase debut. *S.H. Shirley-Beavan — Jedforest (Philippa Shirley-Beavan).* 161 (I), 211 (C), 282 (Cf), 427 (I), 762 (I), 858 (Cf), 1223 (O), 1418 (Cf), 1526 (3m2fH).

SHARP EMBRACE ..9-0.. 12 ch.g. Broadsword (USA) — Running Kiss (Deep Run) 95u4. Small light-framed brother to Ickford Okey. NH FLAT '97 r1 p0. NH '97/8 r11 p2 (3rd in Hdle, and 2nd in Ch); pulled up and fell other Chses; inc Sells. P-t-P/HUNT CH '99/00 and '02/3 r17 p4 (3 3rds of 4, inc Hunt Ch); last pair 7, pulled up 2, and unseated 4. A long-standing maiden, and looked irresolute when tried in headgear under Rules, and although beaten less than three lengths when Jason Burley took over the reins at Alpraham in '04 the race took well over eight minutes. Easily brushed aside at normal racing pace, and the owner-rider is always liable to fall off. *Miss S.M. Rodman — High Peak H.* 270 (L), 594 (OMa), 751 (L), 1044 (OMa).

SHARP FOUNTAIN ..9-2.. 8 b.m. Royal Fountain — Mount St Mary's (Lochnager) 1p. Half-sister to Monynut, Blue Chequer, Blaweary and Red Bob. Dam, half-sister to Price Of Peace (*qv* '90 Annual), won 2m Ch. P-t-P '03 r6 p0 (4th of 5, pulled up 3, ran out 1, and carried out 1). Attracted market support on several occasions last year, and finally rewarded the faithful when successful in a long three-finisher Maiden at Friars Haugh on her return, but went awol for 13 weeks, and was done with after two miles when backed from tens to threes at Aspatria. Still has plenty to prove, both to us and her legion of loyal owners. *The Sharp Thyne Society Partners (K. Hush) — Border (Clive Storey).* 136 (OMam), 1310 (R).

SHARP SARAH ..8-4.. 10 ch.m. Sabrehill (USA) — Sarah's Love (Caerleon USA) p557p. Good-bodied attractive half-sister to flat winner, Indifferent Guy (later successful in Norway), and to a winner in Spain. 26,000y. FLAT '98 (for B.W. Hills, and D. Nicholls) r7 p2. Sold Newmarket, Dec '98 for 800. Beaten between eight and 18 lengths in two flat placings (six and five ran), but also hung badly left throughout once, and disappeared for six years. Beaten at least 25 lengths when completing in Points, but although she can show early speed she does not get the trip, and frequently dives badly left-handed at the fences (worst at Ampton). *K.M. Skilton — E. Essex (Paul Chinery).* 27 (OMa), 39 (OMa), 151 (OMa), 244 (CfMa), 525 (OMa).

SHARP SEAL .10-5.. 11 b.g. Broadsword (USA) — Little Beaver (Privy Seal) 13. Small close-coupled half-brother to B For Business and Going Solo. Dam, half-sister to Dan De Lyon (*qv* '99 Annual), was 3rd in a Point, but subsequently won 2m Chse, and was placed in 2 Hdles and 5 Chses. P-t-P '00/2 (for Mr J.D. Brownrigg) r9 p0 (4th twice, 8th, pulled up 4, and fell 2). NH '01/3 r10 p5; pulled up 2, and fell/unseated 2. Very ordinary and beaten a minimum of 22 lengths in his first 13 starts but provided 37-year-old Frank Buckett with a win at his first attempt on his reappearance at Tweseldown. Came from too far behind to get into a much more competitive race next time, and promptly disappeared, but would have a solid chance in similar company if able to resume in '05. *M. Madgwick — Hursley Hambledon.* 21 (OMa), 169 (R).

SHEILA MCKENZIE ..9-12.. 8 b.m. Aragon — Lady Quachita (USA) (Sovereign Dancer USA) u4142u2p3. Short-backed plain half-sister to Hurdles winner, Oulton Broad. P-t-P/HUNT CH '02/3 r12 w2 (2m4f Maiden and Restricted) p3 (2 2nds, of 3 once); 4th, last, pulled up 2, unseated 1, ran out 1 and brought down 1. Recorded a determined double on easy surfaces in '02, and collared the stalling The Red Boy at Cottenham this year, but also beaten a length or less on four occasions. Error-prone, and has jumped badly in Hunter Chases, but seems to have difficulty getting the trip in Points, and will surely continue to frustrate. *C.O. King — O. Berks.* 3 (O), 19 (CMod), 99 (I), 292 (MO), 465 (O), 734 (2mH), 938 (MO), 1172 (3m1f110yH), 1408 (O).

SHEKELS (IRE) .8-12.. 14 ch.g. Orchestra — Rare Currency (Rarity) pp6. Strong lengthy good-looking half-brother to Christy Jnr (IRE), and to Hurdles winner, Tosheroon (IRE). NH FLAT '96 r3 p1 (3rd), NH '97/9 r16 w4 (2m Hdle, and 3 2m4f-2m5f Chses) p3; pulled up 4, and fell/unseated 2. P-t-P/HUNT CH '00 and '02/3 r10 w2 (inc 2m5f110y Hunt Ch) p4 (3 3rds, of 4 once); 6th, last pair 2 and pulled up. Made all when successful four times under Rules, and landed a 16-runner 2m6f Hunter Chase at Stratford in '00 but has had a soft-palate operation and normally capitulates after two miles now. Blinkered twice in '99. Wears a cross-noseband. *W.P. Gretton — N. Cotswold (Andrew Wheeler).* 661 (Cnr), 921 (M), 1454 (3mH).

SHEMARDI ..10-0.. 8 b.g. Jumbo Hirt (USA) — Masirah (Dunphy) 31264222. Lengthy attractive half-brother to flat winner, Rosa Bonheur, and to Hurdles winner, Ibn Masirah and a winner in Greece. NH FLAT '01 r2 p0. NH '01/3 (for M. Madgwick) r16 p1 (2nd); fell/unseated 2. Bought Ascot, April for 4380. Only placed once under Rules, when two lengths second in a Hurdle on his final attempt (started at 40-1; the first seven home were covered by nine lengths), but well tailed off fourth, fell and unseated in Chases, and was often visored. Improved in Points and gave some consistently good displays, but his only win was over 2m4f at Garnons, where Rob Hodges (not a bad rider now after umpteen years of practice) fell off after the finish. Also in the lead three out or later on four occasions, but can produce little in the closing stages, although he was beaten only about two lengths in three of his seconds. A very sound jumper, and can probably gain a deserved victory in a Restricted. *Mrs B.L. Gibbons, C. Gibbons & M. Gibbons — Teme V. (Steve Isaac).* 257 (CMa), 410 (2m4fCfMa), 452 (R), 665 (R), 1018 (R), 1113 (Cf), 1230 (R), 1388 (R).

SHERBOURNE GUEST (IRE) ..9-4.. 10 b/br.g. Tauchsport (EG) — Jemima Yorke (Be My Guest USA) 56344533. Workmanlike half-brother to 4 flat winners abroad (3 in Germany; 1 in Italy). IRISH FLAT '01 r1 p0. IRISH P-t-P '01/2 r4 w1 (Maiden) p1 (2nd) fell 2. IRISH NH FLAT '00/1 r4 p0. IRISH NH '01 r4 p0. P-t-P '03 (for Mr J.L. Woolford) r4 w1 (Restricted) p1 (3rd); 5th, and unseated 1. A dual winner in mud, and quite impressive when landing a Restricted at Bishops Court last year, but had to contend with inept handling in '04, and only once beaten less than 23 lengths (and was last five times). Could still win races if a decent pilot was engaged. Blinkered twice in '01. *A. Kwiatkowski — Blackmore & Sparkford V. (John Dufosee).* 321 (I), 472 (Cf), 577 (Cnr), 881 (Inr), 1066 (CCon), 1382 (I), 1555 (I), 1564 (I).

SHERFIELD LASS ..—.. 7 b.m. Tina's Pet — Mindyerownbusiness (IRE) (Roselier FR) p. Dam won 5yo&up Mares Maiden in Ireland. NH FLAT '03 r1 p0 (last). NH '03 (for Mrs H. Dalton) r1 p0. Bought Doncaster, May for 2500. Has been remote in a bumper, a Hurdle and a Maiden (never recovered from a bad blunder at the fifth) to date. *P. Clifton — Holderness (Mary Sowersby).* 58 (OMa).

SHERIFF'S FRIEND (IRE) ..10-12.. 10 b/br.g. Supreme Leader — Arctic Scale (IRE) (Strong Gale) 1fp111. Dam is sister to Dusky Day, and half-sister to Parson's Corner (*qv* '00 Annual). IRISH P-t-P '00 r2 p1 (2nd); and pulled up. NH '00/1 r5 p1 (2nd); pulled up 2. P-t-P/HUNT CH '02/3 r9 w9 (5-timer '02, and 4-timer '03, inc 3m4f Hunt Ch, Mixed Open and 2 Opens). Quite a character, and would not co-operate when raced exclusively in mud under Rules, but unbeaten in 13 completions in the present yard, and looks sure to run up further sequences. Takes a keen hold, but never does any more than he has to and rarely wins impressively, and had his limitation exposed at Cheltenham. Has nothing to prove in Points, especially in his Area, and it would be good for his local rivals if he concentrated solely on Hunter Chases in future. Five times a winner at Charing, and also fell four out there when upsides Satchmo in '04. Handles all but extremes of going. Has been tried in a near-side pricker, and wears a cross-noseband. *S.P. Tindall — Mid Surrey F. (Jenny Gordon).* 183 (O), 420 (O), 543 (3m2f110yH), 781 (L), 899 (L), 1087 (O).

SHE'S A TERROR .—.. 6 gr.m. Terimon — Shedid (St Columbus) ppp. Half-sister to He's A Lad. Dam, ('a very game wee mare') half-sister to 7 Pointers, including Hehas (*qv* '03 Annual), won 3m2f Hunt Chase and 13 Points (7 Ladies) and placed 25 for Pat Rowe. Bred from a grand mare who was a prolific winner, but has so far only pulled up when remote in Maidens, although she did show some early speed in the two latest. *Clavering Connections (Mrs P. Rowe) — Suffolk (Tory Hayter).* 244 (CfMa), 561 (OMa), 833 (OMa).

SHESKINQUEEN (IRE) ..10-0.. 10 b.m. Black Monday — Our Lady Sofie (Ile De Bourbon USA) p6up2. Small light. NH FLAT '01 r2 p0. NH '01/3 (for M.G. Quinlan, when successful, and R. Wilman) r8 w1 (2m Hdle) p1 (2nd). A winning Hurdler in soft, but her final five efforts were poor, and wore a tongue-tie twice. Normally outclassed in Ladies Opens, and although she ran well above her normal standard when dividing Keltic Duke and Highland Rose at Fakenham she was doubtless flattered, as the third certainly did not give her true running. Has accumulated a losing sequence of 12. *Miss A. Wells — Fernie.* 299 (L), 380 (L), 558 (L), 785 (L), 1154 (L).

SHE'S NO LADY ..—.. 6 b.m. Charmer — Statfold Solva (Oats) pp. Dam, half-sister to Grey Warrior (*qv* '04 Annual), pulled up 6 and refused in Points (final 5 for Jim Marks; behaved appallingly). Pulled up with a slipped saddle on her debut, but was hanging and not looking keen when she tried to run out next time, and is one to have reservations about at the moment, as she could be aptly named. *Mr & Mrs J.L. Marks — S. Durham (Heather Marks).* 1292 (OMa), 1474 (2m4fOMa).

SHILLELAH LAW ..9-5§.. 9 ch.g. Weld — Compasita (Old Jocus) R4. Tall half-brother to I'm A Lady. Dam, half-sister to Vivaque (*qv* '92 Annual). IRISH P-t-P '02/3 r5 w1 (5yo&up Maiden) p0; pulled up 2, and ran out 1. NH '03 (for M.C. Pipe) r4 p1 (3rd); pulled up 1. An Irish Maiden winner who has since finished six lengths third over Hurdles, but has twice ran out, and like I'm A Lady is definitely not in love with the game. *Mrs M.J. Mein & Ms J. Tucker — Avon V. (Sarah Waugh).* 579 (R), 1102 (R).

SHINING LIGHT (IRE) ..8-13.. 16 b.g. Crash Course — Arumah (Arapaho) pfrp8. Tall rangy half-brother to NH flat winner, Brave King (IRE). NH FLAT '93/4 r2 p0. NH '94/9 r33 w8 (2 2m-2m2f Hdles, and 6 2m4f-2m5f Chses) p8. P-t-P/HUNT CH '01/3 r14 w2 (Opens) p2 (2nd of 3; and last of 3); 4th, 5th, 9th, last pair 6, and pulled up. Won eight races on right-handed tracks under Rules to '99, and ended a long barren period when successful at 33-1 in '02, but achieved little when taking a three-finisher Open last year, and looks to have gone at the game completely now. It will be a huge surprise, and very disappointing for the old horse, if he turns out again. *S.J. Robinson — Zetland.* 162 (L), 340 (O), 917 (O), 1289 (O), 1414 (O).

PLATE 106 528 Tanatside Mens Open: Shiny Bay (Nick Pearce), 1st PHOTO: Brian Armstrong

SHINY BAY (IRE) ..10-5.. 12 ch.g. Glacial Storm (USA) — Raby (Pongee) ppu11p1p. Small brother to Irish NH and flat winner, Frezerium, and half-brother to Carlingford Lad (IRE), and to Irish Pointing winner, Megamunch (IRE). Dam, half-sister to 4 Pointers, won 2 Sell Hurdles (2m2f-3m) on consecutive days. IRISH NH FLAT '98 r4 p0. IRISH FLAT '00 r1 p0. IRISH NH '98/01 (for W.J. Lanigan, and T.M. Walsh, all wins) r35 w4 (2m-2m4f Hdle and 3 2m2f Chses) p10; pulled up 2, and fell 3. Won four races to 2m4f in soft or heavy in Ireland to February '01 (there were a minimum of 15 runners), but had been missing for three years until he returned in '04. A very thorough stayer who produced some dour efforts when registering an unseat and three wins for Nick Pearce in Points, but much less convincing in Hunter Chases (pulled up in both). Regularly makes mistakes, and his lack of substance makes him costly over the bigger obstacles. Seems best if able to take the lead about half a mile from home and then battles on gamely to the finish. Looked rather an unlikely prospect in early season, and connections have done very well to rekindle his interest. *Mrs D. Lowther & G. Smith — Pytchley (Jenny Garley).* 3 (O), 170 (O), 404 (O), 528 (O), 784 (Cf), 994 (3m110yH), 1110 (O), 1361 (3mH).

SHIROSTRAN ..8-10.. 7 ch.g. Primitive Rising (USA) — Bebe Hattie (Gracious Melody) 232. Brother to Lord Woodyard. P-t-P '03 (for Mr K. Needham) r3 p0 (last, unseated, and pulled up). Backed from 14-1 to sixes on his debut in the new yard, and led everywhere but the line, but has been unable to recover losses, and hung right and was collared again in the closing stages at Easingwold last time. Thankfully remains eligible for 2m4f Maidens, and ought to find an opportunity in that sphere, but it will be very hard graft thereafter. *R. Hopkins — Bilsdale (Paul Williamson).* 343 (2m4fOMa), 774 (2m4fCMa), 1159 (OMa).

SHOBROOKE MILL ..10-2.. 12 ch.g. Shaab — Jubilee Leigh (Hubble Bubble) 2244f2u2. Gigantic rangy half-brother to Creedy Valley and Lilabet. Grandam, Hanago Leigh, was distant last of 3 in Eggesford Members for Sarah Prouse. P-t-P/HUNT CH '99/03 r25 w4 (inc Open) p8 (5 2nds, inc Hunt Ch; and 3 3rds, of 4 once and inc Hunt Ch); pulled up 2, fell/unseated 6, and brought down 1. Previously gained an annual success in all but F&M year, and remains a decent Pointer on his day, but surrendered tamely when 4-6 and beaten eight lengths at Kilworthy in '04, and often let down by his clumsiness subsequently. Will require careful placing in future. Acts on any going. Wears a cross-noseband, and acquired cheekpieces on his last three starts. *Mrs S. Prouse — Eggesford.* 310 (O), 366 (MO), 570 (Cf), 975 (2m7f110yH), 1128 (MO), 1348 (Cf), 1463 (O), 1540 (Cf).

SHOCK'S PRIDE (IRE) ..9-6§.. 13 b.g. Glacial Storm (USA) — Ewood Park (Wishing Star) f254p. Robust half-brother to Hurdles winner, Mr Musicmaker (IRE) and Irish NH flat and Hurdles winner, Blackburn. Dam, half-sister to Fiery Glen (*qv* '88 Season Annual), won 2 NH flat and 3 Hdles (2m1f-2m4f) in Ireland. IRISH NH '98 r1 p0 (pulled up). IRISH P-t-P '99/00 r12 w1 (7yo&up Maiden) p3; pulled up 3, and brought down 1. P-t-P/HUNT CH '02/3 r10 w2 (Restricted and Intermediate) p4 (2nd of 3; and 3 3rds, last once); 4th, pulled up 1 and refused 2. A dual winner for Alex Charles-Jones, and was still very much in the shake-up when falling two out on his return at Badbury Rings, but moody and took minimal interest subsequently, and never went a yard for a girl last time. Might be worth a try in headgear, but has always seemed a bit of a softie. *C.H. Sclater — Cattistock (Sarah Clark).* 263 (O), 691 (O), 963 (Cf), 1250 (C), 1368 (L).

SHOEMAKER (IRE) ..—.. 11 b.g. Good Thyne (USA) — Kalanshoe (Random Shot) p8. Tall half-brother to Prince Ronan (IRE), and to successful jumper, Strong Paladin (IRE). Dam won 2m2f NH flat in Ireland. P-t-P/HUNT CH '00/1 r5 w3 (inc 3m Hunt Ch) p0; pulled up, and brought down. Rated 10-8 and unbeaten in three previous completions, and looked a horse to follow, but clearly badly ailing and absent '02/3, and on the recent evidence connections are unlikely to persevere with him. *Mrs J. Wilson — Pytchley (Bill Warner).* 886 (Cf), 1120 (Cf).

SHORTCUT SHORTY ..9-10.. 13 b.g. Winter Words — My Hostess (Gabitat) 132556. Good-topped lengthy. P-t-P '00 and '02/3 r11 w2 (Maiden and Members) p1 (2nd); 4th twice, 7th, last 2, and pulled up 3. Slow and lightly raced and only effective in Members races, but a very reliable jumper and showed plenty of determination when successful for the second time at Mollington. Not helped by the farcical pace when 4-7 on a return visit, but his one pace looks unlikely to be quick enough for Restricteds. *S.T & Mrs L.S. Shepherd — Bicester with Whaddon (Lucy Shepherd).* 288 (M), 587 (R), 1030 (M), 1107 (R), 1333 (R), 1469 (R).

SHOT OF JOLLOP (IRE) ..8-9§.. 6 b.g. Top Of The World — Larrys Commanche (IRE) (Commanche Run) p32f5. Dam, half-sister to The Happy Monarch (*qv* '04 Annual). Bought Doncaster, May '02 for 1500. A slow and erratic jumper with a tendency to hang, and after finishing 26 lengths third and 15 lengths second of three (was going badly left before the last and would not run on) he acquired blinkers and fell at halfway and finished 26 lengths fifth. Has shown waywardness at a very early stage, and looking a real disappointment at present. *P. Rackham — Dunston H. (Nigel Bloom).* 104 (2m4fOMa), 219 (OMa), 386 (OMa), 651 (OMa), 890 (2m4fOMa).

SHRADEN EDITION ..10-7.. 8 b.g. Tina's Pet — Star Edition (Leading Man) 2p1p. Tall strong. Dam is sister to Shraden Leader, and half-sister to Beeworthy (*qv* '03 Annual), was 5th in a Maiden. P-t-P '02/3 (for Mr R. & Mrs B. Everall) r2 w1 (Maiden) p0; and pulled up 1. A very likeable individual, and made Kingston-Banker work very hard on his reappearance at Stratford, and well supported when landing an 18-runner Restricted at Eyton, but has looked to flounder in soft ground and clearly not of a build that will take much racing on faster surfaces. Should easily win more Points, but his races will have to be picked with the utmost care. *The Shraden Partnership (P.A. Jones) — Tanatside (Phil Jones).* 541 (3mH), 994 (3m110yH), 1265 (R), 1374 (3m1fH).

SHU GAA (IRE) ..10-4.. 12 ch.g. Salse (USA) — River Reem (USA) (Irish River FR) 8. Heavy-topped half-brother to flat and Hurdles winner, Shoofk, to NH flat and Hurdles winner, Sahara Reem (IRE), and to a winner in Belgium. FLAT '95/6 r8 w1 (8f) p1 (3rd). NH '96/01 r26 w4 (3 2m-2m110y Hdles, and 2m4f110y Ch) p4 (3rds); pulled up 2, and fell 3. P-t-P/HUNT CH '02/3 r3 w1 (dead-heat for 2m5f Hunt Ch) p1 (3rd); and pulled up. Very much a sub-3m specialist, but has done the rounds, and was scoring for the first time since '00 when forcing a dead-heat at Folkestone last year. Stands no racing at all these days, and was tailed off last after being badly hampered at the second on his solitary appearance in '04, and his rating has to be treated with extreme caution. Visored latterly under Rules, and has been tried in blinkers. *C.P. Goulding — Farmers Bloodhounds.* 631 (2m6f110yH).

SHY LIZZIE ..9-10.. 13 ch.m. Buzzards Bay — Grafton Maisey (Jimsun) 83221423. Half-sister to Love At Dawn (*qv*). P-t-P '98 and '03 r7 p0 (4th, last pair 3, pulled up 2 and fell). Finally vindicated the '99 Annual which suggested that 'she may win a Maiden' when outstaying the opposition at Garnons, but tends to hit a flat spot in all her races, and will need an extreme test of stamina in order to follow up. Ended '03 lame after returning from a five-year absence, but enjoyed her busiest season to date in '04. *A.J. Mason — V.W.H.* 35 (CMam), 52 (OMa), 174 (OMa), 192 (CfMa), 409 (CMam), 616 (C), 636 (Rnr), 1063 (R).

SHYLOCK (IRE) .8-13.. 11 b.g. Buckskin (FR) — Sly Maid (Rapid River) 7ppp8. Workmanlike. Dam won 5f Seller, and subsequently won 4 flat in Italy. IRISH NH '99 r4 p0. P-t-P/HUNT CH '01/3 (for Mr T.H. Caldwell) r9 w1 (Maiden) p1 (3rd); 6th, last pair 2, unseated 3 and pulled up. Returned from an 11-week absence to land a poor Maiden on rough ground at Weston Park in '02, but ditched the rider in three of his next four starts, and beaten 37 lengths or more since. Tried in blinkers at Tranwell, but consistently looks wrong. *Mrs M. Armstrong — Tynedale (Kevin Robson).* 430 (R), 548 (R), 766 (R), 918 (R), 1222 (R).

SHY PADDY (IRE) ..9-10.. 13 b.g. Shy Groom (USA) — Griqualand (Connaught) f4. Unfurnished. Dam, half-sister to Marsh Lane (*qv* '91 Annual). FLAT '94/7 and '00 r18 w1 (1m1f79y) p3. NH '95/6 and '01 r5 p1 (3rd); pulled up 1. P-t-P '03 r4 p1 (2nd); and fell/unseated 3. Gained his only success on New Years Eve '94 amongst the revellers at Dunstall Park, but very lightly raced over jumps since, and ended up rider-less in 66% of his Points. Retired after finishing 16 lengths fourth at Badbury Rings. *Mrs S. Osmond & M. Whatley — Wilton (Sharon Brown).* 171 (L), 261 (Cf).

SIGN OF THE TIGER .—.. 8 b.g. Beveled (USA) — Me Spede (Valiyar) pp. Brother to flat winner, Gablesea, and half-brother to flat winner, Reeds Rains. FLAT '99/01 (for P.C. Haslam) r18 w3 (7-8f) p3. A triple winner in the first five months of '00 including two successes on the all-weather (there were 20 runners in his final victory) but declined afterwards including in a Seller, and was tailed off in three of his final four attempts. Thrown in at the deep end in Points and pulled up at the 11th in both, having made a couple of bad jumps in the Open. Very unpromising in the new role. *J. Watson — Cleveland (Joe Lytollis).* 501 (O), 770 (Cf).

SIJUJAMA (IRE) ..8-9.. 10 b.g. Torus — Knights Bounty (IRE) (Henbit USA) 5353. Workmanlike. IR7500 3yo. IRISH NH FLAT '99 r1 p0. IRISH NH '99 r4 p0. NH '00/3 (for Miss L.V. Russell) r15 p4; pulled up 6, and fell 1. Has been placed in four Chases from between 2m-3m1f and in two Maidens including when last of three, but remains without a win after 24 opportunities, and gives up quickly when pressured. Tongue-tied on his final appearance under Rules and beat only one horse in his final six attempts (pulled up in four; also pulled up twice and fell once previously), but although well beaten he did have the merit of being a very safe ride for an inexperienced girl in '04. *Mr & Mrs R.F. Patterson — Jedforest (Philippa Shirley-Beavan).* 216 (OMa), 286 (CfMa), 430 (R), 859 (CfMa).

SIKANDER A AZAM .11-3.. 12 b.g. Arctic Lord — Shanlaragh (Gaberdine) 122. Small compact attractive half-brother to House Member and Lara's Princess. Dam won Maiden and 2nd. NH FLAT '97/8 r5 w1 p2. NH '98/02 r19 w5 (2 2m110y Hdles and 3 2m-2m110y Chses) p4 (3 3rds); fell 1. P-t-P '03 (for Lord Daresbury) r2 w2 (Confineds). A very spirited little horse, and was gaining his first victory under Rules since '00 when readily accounting for a decent field at Ascot, but probably found the ground plenty quick enough for him when an excellent second in the Aintree Foxhunters, and subsequently found Placid Man too speedy at Warwick. Stays three miles if the company is weak, but much better at shorter distances, though his appearances are strictly rationed and gives firmish ground a wide berth. Well handled by Tom Greenall, and looks certain to take his winning tally into double figures in '05. Fell once over hurdles at Perth in '98, but otherwise has a blemish-free completion record. *The Grand National Racing Club Limited — Middleton (David Easterby).* 545 (2m3f110yH), 732 (2m5f110yH), 1299 (2m4f110yH).

SILENCE REIGNS .10-12.. 11 b.g. Saddlers' Hall (IRE) — Rensaler (USA) (Stop The Music USA) u1b5u. Sturdy compact brother to Tour de Force (flat and subsequent Irish Hurdling winner), and half-brother to Sadler's Realm (*qv*). 75,000y. FLAT '97/8 (for Sir M. Stoute) r11 w2 (10f) p4 (2nds). NH '98/03 r15 w4 (2 2m-2m1f Hdles and 2 2m2f-2m2f Chses) p2; pulled up 1, and fell/unseated 2. A useful middle-distance horse on the flat who proved equally successful over jumps until registering his last win in December '01, but lost his form badly latterly and with his confidence gone was 46 lengths sixth (in a Hurdle) and pulled up, fell and unseated in Chases on his final four outings. Prior to that had been beaten a head for a £24,000 prize, and was also a good second twice in £10,000 to £20,000 events on the level. Began his new season with an unlucky unseat at the final fence at Fontwell where he would have beaten Placid Man, but found compensation at Newbury when wearing first time blinkers, and slammed Jabiru by 16 lengths. Has always been unreliable jumper and has begun to disappoint his supporters again, including when losing Chloe Roddick at the third when wearing a tongue-tie at Stratford. Should stay three miles, and might be capable of another smart effort at 11 if his jumping does not let him down. *The Madness Prevails Partnership — Blackmore & Sparkford V. (Paul Nicholls).* 581 (2m4fH), 631 (2m6f110yH), 732 (2m5f110yH), 1166 (2m5f110yH), 1454 (3mH).

SILENT ACTION (USA) ..9-0.. 13 b/br.g. Greinton — Heather Bee (USA) (Drone USA) p383. Compact half-brother to flat winner, Air Display. Dam won 4f in USA. IRISH NH FLAT '96 r2 p1 (2nd). NH FLAT '97/8 r2 p0. NH '98 and '00/3 r31 p6 (3rds); pulled up 3, and fell 1. P-t-P/HUNT CH '03 (for Mr V. Hollier) r7 w2 (Maiden and Restricted) p1 (neck 2nd); 4th, last pair 2, and fell. Got off the mark at the 37th attempt when scoring by the narrowest of margins at Maisemore Park last year, and incredibly followed up next time, but only finished in front of one rival in four feeble displays in the new yard, and was beaten a minimum of 37 lengths. Suited by fast ground. Runs tongue-tied. *D.P. Smith — N. Ledbury (Sarah Kellard-Smith).* 759 (I), 922 (I), 1101 (Cnr), 1351 (Inr).

SILENT KEYS (SWE) ..8-0.. 13 br.g. Eighty Eight Keys (USA) — Habilage (Horage) 7p6. Small narrow. Dam won 2 Irish flat (6-10f). NH '96/01 and '03 r59 w8 (2m4f Hdle and 7 2m2f-2m5f Chses) p21. An excellent money-spinner who was principally raced in Scandinavia, and earned about £75,000 there, with five jumping wins coming at Taby, two at Stromsholm and one at Ovrevoll. The hero of the Svenskt Grand National in '00 and '03, and was ridden by David Dunsdon (who partnered him twice in '04) in his final three wins. Only successful at up to 2m5f and his local standard was probably no better than at an average mid week meeting over here. Ran deplorably and did not look keen in England, and was tongue-tied twice and blinkered once. Too bad to be true, and must have something wrong with him. Pining for the Fjords? *Capt T. Oscarsson — E. Sussex & Romney Marsh (Alison Hickman).* 317 (2m4fH), 347 (3mH), 800 (3m2f110yH).

SILENT VOICE (IRE) ..—.. 8 ch.g. Unfuwain (USA) — Symeterie (USA) (Seattle Song USA) p. Strong compact half-brother to 2 flat winners in Italy (at San Siro) (one also successful in France), and to Hurdling winner there. ITALIAN FLAT '00 (for J.L. Dunlop) r2 w1 (12f) p0. FLAT '00 r1 p0. NH '02 r2 p0; pulled up 1. An Italian flat winner at San Siro in '00, but has never shown a shred of ability over here, and has been 83 lengths 11th of 12 and pulled up in Hurdles and pulled up after two miles in an Open (fat). Has clearly been virtually impossible to train. *Sir John & Lady Barlow — Cheshire (John Barlow).* 1471 (O).

SILK ST BRIDGET ..9-3.. 8 b.m. Rock Hopper — Silk St James (Pas De Seul) pru. Compact well-made sister to Silken Lady, and to flat winner, Lady Rockstar (won 9 including 8-timer in just 4 weeks in '98), and half-sister to 5 flat winners, including Kingchip Boy (won 25), Silk St John (won 10), Prima Silk (won 9) and Misty Silks (won 7). FLAT '99/00 and '02/3 r20 p1 (2nd of 3). NH '02 (for W.M. Brisbourne) r1 p0 (pulled up). Bought Ascot, Oct for 1095. Gained her only flat placing when eight lengths second of three behind a 1-40 shot (the other contestant virtually refused to race), but was tailed off on several occasions, tried a Seller, and was blinkered thrice. A tricky ride who has not got round in four attempts over jumps, and although still just in front when blundering and unseating two out in a 2m5f Maiden she was coming to the end of her tether. Showed speed for 2m4f despite hanging right and wanting to run out at one stage in her debut Point, but refused to set off next time, and apart from stamina doubts is totally untrustworthy. *P.H. King — Taunton V.* 367 (OMa), 724 (OMa), 983 (2m5fOMa).

SILK VESTMENTS .9-10§.. 13 b/br.m. Rakaposhi King — Preachers Popsy (The Parson) u589u5u4R. Small neat half-sister to NH flat winner, Scarlet Poppy. Dam is half-sister to Kilruddery (*qv* '92 Annual). NH FLAT '98 r3 p2. NH '98/9 r10 w1 (2m5f Hdle) p6 (3 2nds). P-t-P '00 and '02/3 (for Mr P. & Mrs L. Bryan-Brown) r18 p3 (3rds, 2 fences last once); failed to finish 11 (unseated 6, and ran out 1). Exasperating before she finally opened her account in '99, but had luck on her side on that occasion, and has since suffered 33 defeats. Tiny to have tackled regulation fences, and two girls have found it almost impossible to stick with her in Points, but no longer appears to have much of an appetite for racing, and is best left well alone. Has run tongue-tied. *Mrs M.R. Dunning — High Peak H. (Jason Burley).* 108 (L), 162 (L), 270 (L), 428 (3m5fL), 749 (Cf), 986 (Cf), 1203 (L), 1428 (L), 1459 (L).

SILLY BOY ..9-0.. 10 ch.g. Crested Lark — Sutton Lass (Politico USA) p9156. Lengthy. Dam, sister or half-sister to 4 Pointers including Just Bruce (*qv*), won Maiden and 2nd 2 over 5 seasons (inc '97) for Mr Harper ('does not truly get the trip'). P-t-P '00 and '02 (for Mr H.C. Harper) r11 w1 (2m4f Maiden) p0; 5th of 6, pulled up 8 and unseated. NH '02/3 (for R.C. Harper) r3 p0 (pulled 2 and fell). Does not get the trip ordinarily, but the owner-rider managed to slip the field successfully in his Members, and in doing so partnered his first winner. Not better than last in Restricteds, and his case there looks hopeless. *A. Foster — O. Berks (Lee Harfield).* 498 (R), 726 (R), 935 (M), 1191 (R), 1333 (R).

PLATE 107 1300 Bilsdale Open Maiden 56&7yo: Silogue and Nigel Tutty have been left well clear PHOTO: Roy Parker

SILOGUE (IRE) ..9-10.. 8 b/br.g. Distinctly North (USA) — African Bloom (African Sky) 411. Small compact half-brother to flat winners, African Spur, Falcons Dawn, and Hogons Hero, and to Irish Pointing and NH flat and Hurdling winner, African Dante. Dam won two 7f races. FLAT '00/2 r11 p2 (2nds). NH '02/3 (for O. Brennan) r11 p3 (3rds). Bought Doncaster, Nov for 1500. Gained all his previous prizes in Sellers, with two seconds on the flat, and three thirds at between five and 11 lengths over Hurdles, and wore a visor on his final two outings. Clearly had some potential for Pointing, and won a youngsters Maiden at Easingwold by a distance after Irish Paddy had fallen four out when level and apparently going the better, and then forced ahead near the finish in a Restricted at Mordon in which he had to recover from a couple of serious blunders. Was slow to reach the winners enclosure, but may have a little more to offer now that he has got there. *N.D. Tutty — Hurworth (Karen Tutty).* 958 (OMa), 1300 (OMa), 1416 (R).

SILVER BARON ..8-11.. 9 gr.g. Baron Blakeney — Truelyn (True Song) r. Small unfurnished half-brother to Westington (*qv*). P-t-P '03 r1 p0 (6th). Not wholly disgraced in either outing, and would have been a distant last of two had a loose horse not crossed his path at the last fence at Tweseldown, but incredibly short on experience for a nine-year-old, and needs to improve further to be considered a future winner. *R. Coombes & Mrs L. Talbot — N. Cotswold (Andrew Wheeler).* 20 (OMa).

SILVER BUZZARD (USA) ..10-2.. 6 b/br.g. Silver Hawk (USA) — Stellarina (USA) (Pleasant Colony USA) f4f. Close-coupled. Dam won at up to 15f in USA. FLAT '01/2 r2 p0. NH '02/3 (for J. O'Neill) r9 w1 (2m Hdle) p2 (2nds). A Hurdling winner who was also beaten a maximum of four lengths despite mistakes in two seconds, but has been rather too keen for his own good in Points. Acquired cheekpieces in a Mixed Open at Thorpe and after racing prominently he fell at the last when still holding every chance of beating Gillone, and was winded. There are problems to address with him, and his jumping certainly needs to improve, but has the speed to become a decent Pointer if connections can get him sorted out. Will miss '05. *Mrs S. Hutchinson — Fernie (Patrick Hutchinson).* 478 (Cf), 682 (L), 943 (MO).

SILVER CASTLE ..10-3.. 9 gr.g. Roscoe Blake — Pendle Princess (Broxted) 1s2. Lengthy brother to Pendle Hill (*qv*). IRISH P-t-P '01/Nov '02 r9 p2 (last of 2, and 3rd of 4); pulled up 3, ran out 1. IRISH P-t-P/HUNT CH '03 r5 p1 (short-headed); 4th twice and ran out 2. P-t-P '03 (for Mr R. Rowsell) r2 w2 (Maiden and Restricted). Disappointing and sometimes wayward in Ireland, but completed a hat-trick in Welsh Points when landing a three-finisher Intermediate at Bonvilston. Faded rather tamely at Trecoed, where the ground would have been plenty fast enough for him, and as in '03 may have met with a minor setback, but should not find it too difficult to make amends. *P. Roberts — Ystrad Taf Fechan (Robert Rowsell).* 1319 (I), 1536 (L), 1551 (L).

SILVERDALESURESHOT ..10-5.. 13 b.g. Wace (USA) — Upshot (Marcus Superbus) 4. Compact. Dam, 'a horror' who 'frequently proves uncontrollable' beat one horse when placed in 3 Points (last of 2 after falling once) for Mrs Evans. P-t-P/HUNT CH '98/01 r21 w8 (4 Hunt Chses, 3m110y-3m1f110y; inc 4-timer '99) p7 (5 2nds, inc 3 Hunt Chses; and 2 3rds in Hunt Chses); unseated 2, pulled up 1. Indicated that he had problems when registering his last success in '01, and promptly broke down next time, and was off the course for 969 days. Displayed much of his old ability when 12 lengths fourth at Barbury, but clearly suffered a flare-up, and it would be most surprising if he made another comeback at 13. *Mrs P. Evans — Cheshire Forest (Julie Kinsey).* 32 (Cnr).

SILVER GROOM (IRE) ..10-4.. 15 gr.g. Shy Groom (USA) — Rustic Lawn (Rusticaro FR) 1u22. Close-coupled well-made half-brother to Hurdles winner, Tiger Grass (IRE). FLAT (visored once in '98) r54 w3 (8-10f, inc £35,300 William Hill Cup at Goodwood) p11 (inc 6 defeats at 1/2*l* or less; earned £10,800 in William Hill Cup; demoted 2nd after winning £6240 8f race once). NH '94/8 and '01 r21 w3 (2m1f Hdles; would have won 2 more in '94 but for late blunders) p5 (beaten a head once); pulled up 1. P-t-P/HUNT CH '01/3 r17 w9 (inc 8 Ladies, 4-timers '02 and '03; would have been 5-timer in '02 but disqualified — not draw correct weight) p3 (2 2nds; and 3rd in Hunt Ch); 6th, unseated 2, and carried out. Very nearly top class under Rules, and handled superbly by Jo Foster in eight of his Pointing successes, but the much less experienced Jacqueline Coward has rather overdone the waiting tactics on a horse whose speed is not what it was, and was lucky that the leaders stopped when they did on his reappearance. Outstayed by Balisteros at Hornby Castle, but set a monumental task next time, and may well have gone into well deserved retirement, as the ground he appreciates was freely available subsequently. *Miss K.P. Barron & T.D. Rose — Holderness (David Easterby).* 162 (L), 299 (L), 339 (L), 502 (L).

SILVER IMAGE .7-10.. 8 gr.g. Silver Owl — Dark Image (Bold As Brass) up. Good-bodied quite attractive owner-bred half-brother to Golden Sovereign (*qv*). P-t-P '02/3 r4 p1 (last of 3); pulled up 2, and fell 1. Twenty-nine lengths last of three at Lifton last year, but hardly ever runs and never looks fit, and may have suffered a setback when trying to refuse at Bratton Down. Has two handlers. *J. Down — Torrington F.* 1380 (OMa), 1559 (OMa).

SILVER KRACKER ..— §§.. 10 b.g. Naskracker (USA) — Silver Zip (Padro) pppp. Small good-topped. Dam won Torrington Maiden and placed 3 for the Sweetlands, and is half-sister to Stainless Steel (*qv* '00 Annual). A late beginner who wishes he had never started at all, and pulls himself up after great displays of tail-swishing. Connections evidently harboured a wild dream that he might emulate mother in the last race of the year, but in their hearts they would have known it was never on the cards. *M.S. Sweetland — E. Devon.* 83 (OMa), 194 (CfMa), 318 (M), 1566 (OMa).

SILVER LAKE (IRE) ..9-10.. 11 gr.g. Roselier (FR) — Over The Pond (IRE) (Over The River FR) 48ppp32p. Good-topped fired brother to Rosglinn (IRE) and Carrick Troop (IRE) (won 7 Chases since Pointing). IRISH P-t-P '98/00 r11 w6 (inc 3 Opens) p2 (3rds). NH '00 (for N.T. Chance) r3 w2 (2m-2m5f Hdles) p1 (3rd of 4). A top-class Irish Pointer as a novice, notably in the heavy, and again showed an appreciation of mud after joining Noel Chance, for whom he won two Hurdles by a head and was finally a distant third of four in a competitive Chase. His legs gave way in '00, and is virtually a family pet now, but ran quite well in two of the three occasions he made the frame, and has proved safe for an inexperienced girl. Wore cheekpieces on his last two outings. Never failed to complete prior to his latest campaign after the four-year absence, and could have reached for the stars, but as with so many brave animals injuries got in the way. If connections aimed him at the lowest level instead of wasting time in Hunter Chases (pulled up in all three) they might get a sweet reward. *F.R. Jackson — O. Surrey, Burstow & W. Kent (Stephen Breen).* 3 (O), 48 (3m5f70yL), 170 (O), 239 (3m1fH), 348 (3mH), 777 (M), 899 (L), 1170 (4m1fH).

SILVER MAN ..9-6.. 11 gr.g. Silver Owl — What An Experiance (Chance Meeting) up3344. Compact half-brother to Susies Prince, Prince Warrior and Fabbl Approved. Dam, half-sister to Spambruco (*qv* '96 Annual), a non-stayer was 3rd in a Maiden (failed to finish in 8 of 12 other attempts) for Dennis Turner. Grandam, Colourful Girl, failed to finish in 3 Points. P-t-P '99/00 and '02/3 r16 w2 (Maiden and Restricted) p3 (2 2nds, beaten neck once; and 3rd of 4); failed to finish 6 (unseated 1). Won a two-finisher Maiden at Lemalla in '99, and was scoring for the first time since when responding to first-time cheekpieces at Lifton last year, but a confirmed non-stayer in competitive events, and failed to bring home the each-way money when well supported in tow of his last three starts. *Mrs M.E. Turner — Modbury H. (Dennis Turner).* 193 (I), 705 (I), 1005 (Cf), 1194 (Cf), 1431 (I), 1544 (I).

SILVER ORCHID ..9-3.. 6 gr.g. Fourstars Allstar (USA) — Minster Scally (Scallywag) 42. Crow-bred half-brother to O K Flo Jo. Dam, 'a smart performer who sustains a relentless gallop from the front', won 5 Points (including 3 Opens) and a Hunter Chase (broke down at Bangor) and 2nd twice (only ran 10 times). Shaped with promise when 27 lengths fourth on his debut, and then only failed by a head after making a mistake at the last in a Maiden at Cold Harbour. It was a weak affair, but would have won had the jockeys been reversed and sure to gain compensation. His pedigree alone makes him look of above-average interest. *S. Haworth & G.W. Roberts — N. Salop (Sheila Crow).* 929 (2m4fOMa), 1232 (OMa).

SILVER POT BLACK .9-6§.. 10 gr.g. Ron's Victory (USA) — Haunting (Lord Gayle USA) 7354218213. Lengthy unfurnished brother to Italian jumping winner, and half-brother to Biloxi Blues, to Irish Hurdles winner, Invisible Armour, and to 9 winners including abroad, and over jumps, including Amigo Sucio (useful), Mrs Gray and Valley Mills. NH FLAT '00 r1 p0. NH '00/1 r8 p2; fell 1. P-t-P/HUNT CH '02/3 r10 w2 (3-finisher Maiden and Restricted) p1 (last of 3); 5th, pulled up 4, and fell/unseated 2. Won two of his first three Points, but none of his next 12, and only ended the sequence in a three-runner Intermediate for novice riders where he was sent off at 1-3. The only one of 11 entries to declare for the so called West Wales Grand National at Pentreclwydau, but would surely have been beaten had anything else run as he was 50 lengths last of three in his Members next time. Error-prone and moody, and can be safely ignored. *W.J. Day — Gelligaer F. (Lisa Day).* 116 (I), 147 (I), 359 (Cf), 447 (Cf), 698 (Inr), 739 (Inr), 843 (L), 1025 (L), 1236 (4mMO), 1318 (M).

SILVER SIROCCO (IRE) ..—.. 13 gr.g. Razzo Forte — Oronocco Gift (Camden Town) p. Good-topped half-brother to Irish Pointing and Chasing winner, Prince Of Pleasure (IRE). Dam is half-sister to Campello's Love (*qv* '91 Annual). IRISH P-t-P '96 r1 w1 (4yo Maiden). NH FLAT '97/8 r3 p2 (3rds). NH '98/01 r14 p2; pulled up 3, and unseated 2. P-t-P/HUNT CH '02 r6 p1 (2nd); 5th, and pulled up 4. Won an Irish Maiden as a four-year-old, but very lightly raced and unable to score in 24 other appearances, and resurfaced from a year on the sidelines only to pull up after 2m3f at Eaton Hall. Blinkered twice in '01. *Mrs A.P. Kelly — Flint & Denbigh (Stephen Kelly).* 715 (R).

SILVER SOVEREIGN ..—.. 8 gr.g. Thethingaboutitis (USA) — Sovereign Love (He Loves Me) ppp. Half-brother to flat winners, Kerb Crawler and Paradise Forum. Dam 8f winner in France. Went a little further on each appearance, and showed speed until the 14th on his latest attempt, but still to enter the final half-mile before pulling up, and needs to dispel doubts about his stamina. *J.L. & Mrs H.D. Marks — S. Durham (Heather Marks).* 431 (R), 591 (CR), 813 (OMa).

SILVER STYX ..9-0.. 6 gr.g. Terimon — Sconie's Poppet (Alias Smith USA) pfp3. Tall rangy. Dam, half-sister to Uncle Den (*qv*). Has been green and error-prone, but gave a considerably improved display when two and a half lengths third over 2m4f at Garthorpe, where he had to survive a blunder two out. The fourth has scored since, and should have little difficulty opening his own account when he begins to jump with fluency. *R. Swinburne — Atherstone (John Holt).* 385 (OMa), 561 (OMa), 1125 (OMa), 1402 (2m4fOMa).

SILVER TRAY (IRE) ..8-5.. 6 gr.m. Supreme Leader — Virginia Ironside (General Ironside) pp4. Sister to Irish Pointing and Hurdling winner, Emmet. 2102 3yo. Tends to make blunders and has jumped right, but completed for the first time when 23 lengths fourth at Holnicote. Was weakening in the closing stages, and as it was an extremely poor Mares Maiden run in a very slow time plenty more will be required if she is to get seriously involved. *Mrs S. Rowe — Devon & Somerset (Linda Blackford).* 702 (2m4fOMa), 883 (OMa), 1182 (CMam).

SIMBER HILL (IRE) ..9-12§.. 11 ch.g. Phardante (FR) — Princess Wager (Pollerton) 5454. Good-topped half-brother to jumping winner, Bone Setter (IRE). IR13,500 3yo. NH FLAT '98/9 r3 w1 p0. NH '99/03 r27 w4 (3m1f Hdle and 3 3m Chses) p14; fell 2, and pulled up 1. NH '04 r2 p0 (5th in 3m110y Grand Military Gold Cup: *sn prom, went 3rd 12-19, wknd aft 3 out*; and 4th in 3m1f110y Ch: *hld up & bhnd, hdwy 11, rdn app 4 out, wknd 2 out*). Able, and the winner of five races principally on firmish surfaces, but frequently blinkered and can need much driving, and is error-prone and has a fairly high incidence of off days. Struggled under 11st12lb in his final victory and his attentions were briefly turned to Hunter Chases, but did not impress. Has had a lot of jostling rides from Richard Johnson and is the type of character who might now prefer to be left alone by a novice in Points. *C. de P. Berry, C. Moore & P. Rowe — Stevenstone (Philip Hobbs).* 801 (3mH), 993 (3mH).

SIMONS CASTLE (IRE) .—§.. 12 b.g. Scenic — Miss Toot (Ardross) p. Workmanlike half-brother to Hurdles winner, Dr Charlie, and to flat winners, Kool Kat Katie and Kalypso Katie. Dam won 2 flat,

10-15f (her only starts; debut in Sell). IRISH NH FLAT '97 r1 w1. NH FLAT '97 r2 p2 (beaten short-head once). NH '97/02 r22 w2 (2m-2m110y Hdles) p9 (4 2nds, inc 2 Chses, inc Sell); pulled up 1, and unseated 1. P-t-P '03 r1 p0 (last). Gained both his jumping successes in softish over hurdles in '98, but very lightly raced and most unreliable since and appeared to suffer another setback at Ston Easton. Blinkered once in '00. *B. & Mrs G.A. Robarts — Dulverton F. (Ashley Farrant).* 602 (MO).

SIMONY SAM (IRE) ..—.. 13 b.g. Satco (FR) — Well Carted (Never Slip) pppu. Compact well-made half-brother to Irish Pointing winner, Benalf. Dam is half-sister to Namestaken (*qv* '97 Annual). IRISH NH FLAT '98 and '00 r3 p0. IRISH NH '98 and '01 r5 p0. IRISH P-t-P '99/00 r8 p0; pulled up 3, and unseated 1. P-t-P '02/3 r9 w1 (2-finisher Members) p2 (3rds, of 4 once); 5th of 6, 6th, and pulled up 4. Very lucky when opening his account at the 21st attempt at Penshurst in '02, but beaten in excess of 20 lengths in 28 other starts, and never looked likely to get round in '04, despite being the subject of a madcap gamble at Hackwood Park once. Wears a cross-noseband. *Mrs H.L. Sarchet — O. Surrey, Burstow & W. Kent.* 181 (R), 538 (R), 610 (Cv&nr), 719 (Cnr).

SIMPLY A STAR (IRE) ..8-2§.. 15 ch.g. Simply Great (FR) — Burren Star (Hardgreen USA) u97. Light-framed. FLAT r3 p0. DUTCH FLAT w1 (9f). BELGIAN FLAT r3 w1 (9f). NH '96 and '00 r2 p0. P-t-P '96/02 (for Mr R. Kelton) r21 w2 (Confined and Members) p5 (4 3rds); pulled up 7, and fell/unseated 4. Recorded his first win for five years when successful on his only appearance in '01, but only employed as a schoolmaster in recent times, and returned from another spell of inactivity to tutor a shaky beginner this year. Often blinkered in the past. *Mrs J. Steward — Woodland Pytchley.* 885 (M), 1120 (Cf), 1214 (Cf).

SIMPLY BRUNO ..8-11.. 7 b.g. Relief Pitcher — Majestic Spider (Majestic Maharaj) 24. Big workmanlike half-brother to Simply Sam (*qv*). Left second at the last when beaten eight lengths over 2m4f on his debut, but acquired a hood next time, and seemed to go considerably worse when 42 lengths last of four. His half-brother has reached Intermediate standard, and may have ability himself, but one to have reservations about for the time being. *T.F. Thorne — Torrington F. (Emely Thompson).* 309 (2m4fOMa), 567 (CfMa).

SIMPLY SAM ..10-2.. 10 ch.g. Nearly A Hand — Majestic Spider (Majestic Maharaj) 17114p. Good-topped owner-bred half-brother to Scarlet Glory and Simply Bruno. Dam, half-sister to 7 Pointers, including Spiderdore (*qv* '03 Annual), won 2 Points and placed 7 (both wins at Clyst St Mary, but a regular short-runner otherwise). P-t-P '02/3 r12 w1 (Maiden) p3 (2 2nds, remote last once); 4th, pulled up 5, ran out 1, and unseated 1. An improved jumper and handles soft ground, and recorded a praiseworthy success when the subject of a market move on his reappearance at Wadebridge, but did not have to be at his best to follow up in two Novice Riders events subsequently, and appeared to hate the firmish ground on his latest appearance. Benefits from having such a good youngster in the plate and will be much more difficult to place in future. Wears a cross-noseband. *R.A. & Dr C.E. Fry — Cattistock (Caroline Fry).* 79 (R), 321 (I), 577 (Cnr), 794 (Inr), 1249 (MO), 1383 (Cnr).

SIMPLY SILVER LADY ..—.. 10 ch.m. Push On — Pentwd Mundy (Vital Season) upp. Lengthy. NH FLAT '01 r1 p0. NH '02 r2 p0 (pulled up 2). P-t-P/HUNT CH '03 (for Mr R.D. Graham) r5 p0 (4th, and pulled up 4). Not better than last in any of her 11 races, and appears to be rendered useless by a breathing problem. Has run tongue-tied. *Mrs S. Corbett — Border (William Corbett).* 215 (OMa), 287 (CfMa), 430 (R).

SIMPLY THE ONE (IRE) ..10-3.. 8 ch.g. Simply Great (FR) — Lady Mearlane (Giolla Mear) 211. Lengthy half-brother to Irish NH flat and Hurdling winner, Myheartisbroken. Dam won 8 Irish Chases (2-3m). NH '01/3 (for Mrs H. Dalton) r8 p1 (2nd of 3 in Ch); fell 1, pulled up 2. A bad animal under Rules and was a distant second of three in a Chase prior to pulling up twice and falling on his final three attempts (blinkered twice). Much improved by a drop in class and the training of Jenny Pidgeon, and followed a decent second in a Maiden with a ready success in diabolical conditions at Mollington. Went about his work in most determined fashion when following up in a Brewardine Restricted, and is going from strength to strength at present. Perhaps he could be worth trying in a Novices Hunter Chase in '05. *G. Lloyd — Grafton (Jenny Pidgeon).* 172 (OMa), 1035 (OMa), 1389 (R).

SING HIGH ..9-7.. 9 b.m. Golden Heights — Ranee's Song (True Song) 3p2. Small sturdy owner-bred half-sister to Romany Chat. Dam was useless in Hurdles and a Point (pulled up) for Roger Gasson. Grandam, Indian Ranee, won 4 Points and placed 5 (inc 3rd in Hunt Ch). P-t-P '02/3 r15 w1 (Maiden) p5 (2nd of 3; and 4 3rds, of 4 thrice); 4th twice, last, and pulled up 6. Made the frame six times consecutively before she was rewarded with a three-finisher Maiden at Paxford, and almost sprang a 33-1 shock on her return, but normally races too keenly to get home. If she does find a

Restricted she will find it impossible to climb any further up the ladder. Wears a cross-noseband. *Mrs R. Gasson — Farmers Bloodhounds.* 584 (I), 756 (Cf), 1449 (R).

SINGLE MAN (IRE) ..8-12.. 12 b.g. Mansooj — Sniggy (Belfort FR) 4pp5f. Tall rangy half-brother to Just A Single (IRE). NH '97/00 r3 p0 (last, and pulled up 2, inc Sell). P-t-P '02/3 r4 p0 (last, pulled up 2, and unseated). Six lengths third in the previous running of the High Peak Cross Country Members in '00, and sent off a well-backed favourite in the race after Flagg's very welcomed return in '04, but though Sue Rodman is Secretary of the meeting she clearly does not know her way round and she got lost twice (much to the chagrin of the plonkers who had steamed in at evens) en route. Useless in proper races where Jason Burley does the steering without recourse to a map. *Miss S.M. Rodman — High Peak H.* 227 (CfMa), 595 (OMa), 753 (OMa), 984 (3m4fNCM), 1261 (OMa).

SIOBHANS QUINNER (IRE) ..9-0.. 8 b.m. Erins Isle — Upsail (Top Ville) p31f. Dam won 2m1f Hurdle in Ireland. IRISH P-t-P '02 r6 p2 (3rds); pulled up 4. P-t-P '03 r2 p0 (5th, and unseated). Recorded a wide margin success from one other finisher in softish at Catsfield, where despite there being two fewer fences the race was run in the slowest time of the day by 11sec. Not very quick, and needs to improve further to be taken seriously in Restricteds, but seems rather fragile, and was pulled up when the rider thought she had gone wrong on her reappearance (though she cantered back sound). *Miss S.H. Widdicombe — Southdown & Eridge.* 293 (CMam), 418 (2m4fCMa), 1055 (OMa), 1084 (R).

SIP OF BRANDY (IRE) ..9-12.. 12 ch.g. Sharp Charter — Manhattan Brandy (Frankincense) u267f. Narrow half-brother to April's Baby (won bad Chase after Pointing), to Irish Hurdles winner, Jimmy's Brandy, and to prolific Irish winner, Captain Brandy (NH flat, jumping and Pointing). IRISH P-t-P '97/8 r11 w1 (5yo&up unplaced Maiden) p1 (3rd); pulled up 2, and fell 2. P-t-P/HUNT CH '99/00 and '02/3 (for Greenacre Racing Partnership) r31 w3 (inc 3m Hunt Ch and Open) p9 (4 2nds, of 3 once; 5 3rds, of 4 once); last pair 5, pulled up 6, and fell/unseated 5. Sprang a 33-1 shock at Ludlow last year, but unreliable in running and particularly in jumping, and desperately needs to return to the relative safety of Points, where the rider will also be less of a liability. Stays well but only able to manage short campaigns nowadays. Has been tried in blinkers. *Miss J. Hughes — S. Pembs.* 209 (3m1f110yH), 434 (3m1f110yH), 631 (2m6f110yH), 801 (3mH), 1117 (3m1f110yH).

SIR ALF ..9-12.. 9 ch.g. Alflora (IRE) — D'Egliere (FR) (Port Etienne FR) 21p. Good-topped. Dam, half-sister to Algan (*qv*). NH FLAT '01 r1 p0 (pulled up). NH '01/2 (for M. Pitman) r3 p0; pulled up 2. Bought Doncaster, May for 3500. Pulled up in a bumper and in two of three Hurdles (tongue-tied once), but found Pointing much more appropriate, and after a praiseworthy three lengths second to Cross River in early February he returned to beat the incredibly frustrating Mr McDuck in his three-runner Members in mid-May. Lost all chance with a bad blunder four out the following weekend, but is probably good enough to take a Restricted at best. His outings to date have been strictly rationed. *Miss M. D. Myco — S. Durham.* 166 (OMa), 1412 (M), 1476 (R).

SIR DANTE (IRE) ..10-3.. 14 ch.g. Phardante (FR) — Tumvella (Tumble Wind) 1p2413. Big strong half-brother to Elegant Stranger, to jumping winners, Native Charm (IRE) and Sir Valentine (IRE), and to 2 Irish Hurdles winners, including Swingsville (also successful on flat there). NH FLAT '95/6 r4 w1 p0. NH '96/02 r29 w8 (hat-trick of 2m110y-2m4f Hdles, and 5 2m4f110y-2m5f Chses) p4 (3 2nds); pulled up 1, fell 2. P-t-P '03 r4 w1 (Mixed Open) p2 (3rds, of 4 once); and 4th. A gift horse to present connections following a career under Rules that netted over £70,000 in win and place money, and his '03 campaign culminated in his first win for over three years. Made uncharacteristic mistakes on his successful return, and subsequently found to have a poisoned foot after being pulled up at Ston Easton, but came back to form at Ashorne in ground that he used to have no use for. Genuine and consistent but not as fluent as he once was, and seems to be slowly losing his speed, and with it his necessity for good or firmish ground. Has suffered leg and wind trouble, and tongue-tied on his final appearance under Rules. Wears a cross-noseband. *S.J. Claisse — N. Cotswold (Lucy Brack).* 360 (O), 602 (MO), 868 (O), 1073 (O), 1277 (MO), 1390 (O).

SIR D'ORTON (FR) .10-5.. 9 ch.g. Beyssac (FR) — Prime Target (FR) (Ti King FR) 4131243. Small brother to two jumping winners in France. 30,000 3yo. NH FLAT '00 r3 p3. NH '00/3 (for O. Sherwood, and P.F. Nicholls, when successful) r17 w2 (2m4f Chses) p10 (inc 8 Hdles); pulled up 3. Tended to jump right when completing a Plumpton double in October/November '01, both on easy surfaces and including a match, but was pulled up in two of his final three attempts under Rules. Can sometimes look jaded, and wore headgear on three occasions in the past, but generally in a co-operative frame of mind in '04, although he probably only passed the post in front once in Ladies Opens, when landing a modest three-finisher affair at Cothelstone. Also adjudged to have scored at Larkhill, where he looked to be headed near the finish. The good efforts petered out latterly, and found nothing when very disappointing at 4-5 and only finishing fourth, and was then 15 lengths third in the Gerrard Ladies Hunter Chase. May revive when fresh. Welcome respite for Alan Tizzard, who had the misfortune to lose three of his horses in '04. *Mr & Mrs R. Richards — Blackmore & Sparkford V. (Alan Tizzard).* 10 (L), 88 (L), 320 (Cf), 470 (L), 635 (L), 1099 (L), 1360 (3mH).

PLATE 108 88 Royal Artillery Ladies Open: L to R, Sir D'Orton (Charlotte Tizzard), 1st, and Tales Of Bounty (Rachael Green), 2nd *PHOTO: Tim Holt*

SIR HARRY HENBIT .—§.. 8 ch.g. Henbit (USA) — Debbigene (Royal Vulcan) pp. Lengthy. Dam, half-sister to Pollygloss (*qv* '94 Annual), won Maiden and 3rd for the Clarkes. Grandam, Wicken Folly, a non-stayer, was placed in 2 bad Points for Mr Clarke (also pulled up 1, and on floor 5). NH FLAT '02 r1 p0 (last of 15). P-t-P '03 r6 p0 (5th of 6, pulled up 3, and fell/unseated 2). Dreadful and only once better than last in nine starts, and has no intention of revealing the true extent of his abilities. Has been tried in blinkers. *M.R. Clarke — Grafton (Di Clarke).* 890 (2m4fOMa), 1275 (OMa).

SIR HENRIK (IRE) .—.. 7 b.g. Tidaro (USA) — Let'shaveaparty (IRE) (Bowling Pin) pRp. Close-coupled. 2920 4yo. Unpleasant so far, and after pulling up and then running out after two miles in Maidens he consistently jumped left and only went a circuit at Folkestone. Not the sort of horse Christine McCarthy would have entertained lightly in her glory days of the '80s. *G. Keast — Mrs D.H. McCarthy — Mid Surrey F. (Christine McCarthy; -).* 1088 (OMa), 1404 (OMa), 1442 (2m5fH).

SIR LANCELOT ..10-0.. 10 gr.g. Crested Lark — Classey (Dubassoff USA) 2124. Compact Tarry-bred brother to Lah Di Dah Lad, and half-brother to Miss Hoity Toity (*qv*). P-t-P '03 r3 p0 (pulled up 3). Taking things leisurely in '03, but much more positive this year, and won his Maiden convincingly in softish at Dingley. Beaten a maximum of six lengths in two subsequent visits, and looks a good thing to land an average Restricted in '05. *G.B. Tarry & Mrs S. Watts — Pytchley (Jimmy Tarry).* 789 (CfMa), 887 (CfMa), 1217 (R), 1469 (R).

SIR WILLIAM ..10-6.. 11 ch.g. Karlinsky (USA) — Charmezzo (Remezzo) 12p1f12. Robust brother to Charminsky (*qv*). NH '01 r2 p0 (pulled up 1). P-t-P '00/3 r21 w4 (inc 2-finisher Open) p7 (2nd of 3 twice; 5 3rds, beaten short head and neck once, and last once); last pair 3, pulled up 3, ran out 1, and fell/unseated 3. Only successful once in his first 14 starts, and his back still cause him problems from time to time, but much more prolific in the last two seasons, and a change of scenery appears to have done him good. Can quicken, but sometimes lacks fluency, and would have recorded a hat-trick in '04 but for falling at the final ditch in his Members. Did not appear particularly enamoured with the very firm ground on his final appearance, and does not want it muddy either, but looks sure to prove difficult to beat when the right criteria are met in '05. Runs tongue-tied, and wears a cross-noseband. *R.G. Westacott — Devon & Somerset (Emely Thompson).* 62 (Cf), 276 (L), 414 (MO), 880 (MO), 1180 (M), 1367 (O), 1447 (O).

SIR WILLIAMWALLACE (IRE) .9-6§.. 12 br.g. Strong Gale — Kemchee (Kemal FR) 4p. Tall rangy brother to Strong Tartan (IRE), and half-brother to jumping winner, Indian Scout (IRE) and NH flat winner, Riothamus (IRE). Dam won NH Flat and 2 2m Hurdles in Ireland, and is half-sister to

Durnford Bay (*qv* '03 Annual). IRISH NH FLAT '98 r1 p0. IRISH NH '98/00 r21 w2 (2m-2m2f Chses) p5. NH '01/2 r18 p3; pulled up 7. P-t-P/HUNT CH '03 r4 w1 (Confined) p0; last pair 2, and pulled up. Scoring for the first time since May '00 when landing a gamble on firm at Marks Tey last year, but plagued by myriad problems, and sometimes looks most ungenuine. Well tailed off last on his reappearance, and looked thoroughly jaded when pulled up at Fakenham, and can be safely ignored if returning. Blinkered once, and broke a blood vessel at least once in '02, and has often run visored and tongue-tied. *Mr & Mrs D. Claydon — E. Essex (David Claydon).* 905 (Cf), 1151 (Cf).

SISSINGHURST STAR (IRE) .9-9§.. 10 b.g. Moscow Society (USA) — Raplist (Arapaho) 633f464. Unfurnished. NH FLAT '00 r1 p0. NH '00/2 r14 p2 (3rds); pulled up 3. P-t-P '03 r9 w1 (3-finisher Maiden) p3 (2 2nds; and 3rd of 4); failed to finish 3 (unseated 1, and ran out 1). Ultimately disappointing and wore headgear latterly under Rules, but persuaded to make most in a three-finisher Maiden at Thorpe Lodge last year. Usually novice-ridden since, and has not co-operated fully, but stays well and there is still a slim chance that he could score again. Wears a cross-noseband. *Mrs J.M.E. Mann — Warwicks.* 16 (C), 65 (Rnr), 109 (CR), 191 (R), 467 (CR), 587 (R), 726 (R).

SISTER ALI (IRE) ..8-0.. 13 br.m. Altountash — Golden Eily (Golden Love) 4b4. Compact half-sister to Riot Lady (IRE). IRISH P-t-P '98 r4 p1 (2nd); pulled up 3. NH '98/00 r8 p0 (pulled up in one of 2 Hdles; pulled up 4 and fell 2 in Chses, inc Sell). P-t-P '01/3 r17 p4 (last of 2 twice; 3rd of 4, and last of 3); last pair 4, fell/unseated 5, and pulled up 4. Can show speed, but a regular non-finisher over jumps, and not better than tailed off last in '04. Has never been beaten less than 30 lengths in Points, and is a waste of time. Blinkered once in '99. *J.R. Young — O. Surrey, Burstow & W. Kent (Clare Young).* 26 (OMa), 103 (OMa), 152 (OMa).

SIX CLERKS (IRE) ..9-5§.. 12 b.g. Shadeed (USA) — Skidmore Girl (USA) (Vaguely Noble) 6f8. Small compact well-made half-brother to a winner in Italy. FLAT r15 p5. NH '96/9 r23 w1 (2m Hdle) p9 (inc 2 Chses); inc Sell Hdles final 6. P-t-P/HUNT CH '00/3 r22 p5 (3 3rds in Hunt Chses; and inc 2nd in Hunt Ch); fell 3, pulled up 4. A frustrating individual, and only successful in one of his 62 races, and invariably fails to stay in Points, and was close to pulling up in both '04 completions. Has been tried in headgear. *W.J. Odell — N. Cotswold (Shauna Odell).* 48 (3m5f70yL), 541 (3mH), 869 (L).

SIXES AND SEVENS (IRE) ..—.. 9 ch.m. Aristocracy — Eyrefield Rose (Monksfield) pfpp9fpp8. Strong attractive. IRISH P-t-P '02 r4 p0; pulled up 2. IRISH NH FLAT '01 (for E.J. O'Grady) r1 p0. NH '04 (for B.N. Pollock) r1 p0 (8th in 2m110y Sell Hdle: *hld up & bhnd, some hdwy app 5, sn wknd, t.o*). Bred from a mare who could not win from 22 attempts under Rules in Ireland, and is utterly deplorable herself, having walked in after crawling over the last when about two fences adrift on her only completion from nine attempts in '04. Does not even have the saving grace of being a pleasant ride, as she frequently makes mistakes and is prone to fall heavily. *G.R. Kerr — Pytchley (David Line).* 35 (CMam), 51 (OMa), 172 (OMa), 386 (OMa), 589 (CfMa), 783 (M), 887 (CfMa), 1119 (CMam).

SIX OF TOTHER .—.. 7 ch.g. Elegant Monarch — Minnie Madam (Tudor Diver) pp. Tall angular. Dam, minute, was fence last and failed to finish in 8 Points for Mrs Carter, 'connections are trying to get blood out of a stone', and is half-sister to Mr Sponge (*qv* '95 Annual). Twice the size of mother but looked just as useless when pulling after a maximum of two miles twice, and is making plenty of bad jumps. *Mrs A. Carter — Devon & Somerset (Linda Blackford).* 1327 (OMa), 1559 (OMa).

SIXTH SENSE (IRE) ..—.. 11 b.g. Be My Native (USA) — Fallen Glass (Shack USA) fpp. Angular half-brother to Irish NH flat and Hurdles winner, Portobello Lady (IRE). IRISH P-t-P '99 r3 p0 (last, pulled up and fell). NH '00 r2 p0 (pulled up 2 in Chses - not jump well). P-t-P '00 and '02/3 r11 p4 (2 2nd, of 3 once); 4th of 5, unseated 3, and pulled up 3. Placed in four Maidens over a four-year period, and seemed on the verge of a small win at one stage, but does not stand much racing, and there was no merit in any of his '04 performances. *Mrs H.J. Merriman — Blackmore & Sparkford V.* 232 (R), 320 (Cf), 689 (R).

SIXTIES MELODY ..9-0.. 11 b.g. Merdon Melody — Balidilemma (Balidar) 4p. Workmanlike lengthy half-brother to Strong Point, and to flat winner, Abel Mabel. Dam, half-sister to Joshua, won 2 8f races, inc a Sell. FLAT '96/7 r7 p2 (short-headed once). IRISH CHARITY FLAT r1 p0. IRISH NH '00 r1 p0 (last). P-t-P/HUNT CH '02/3 r5 p2 (3rds); 4th, pulled up, and fell. Beaten a maximum of 18 lengths when making the frame in Points, but gets precious few chances, and his '04 campaign lasted a fortnight in May. Gave the impression that all was not well when pulled up after an early mistake in the Hunter Chase. Wears a cross-noseband. *Mrs D.H. Clyde — Border (Kathryn Bewley).* 1422 (OMa), 1499 (2m4f110yH).

SIZER (IRE) ..9-12.. 8 ch.g. Eurobus — Costenetta (IRE) (Runnett) R1p3. Half-brother to Poppycock (IRE). Dam, half-sister to Against The Agent (*qv*). Bought Doncaster, May '01 for 4500. A keen sort who ran out at the fourth when leading on his debut, but then beat two subsequent winners without coming off the bridle in a 2m5f Maiden at Welbeck (was steadied way off the pace in the early stages). Soon pulled up with a slipped saddle next time out, and then finished 14 lengths third in a

Confined won by a 14-year-old. Scored on the only occasion that he was not sent off favourite, and is excitable and a difficult ride, but gives the impression that he might be a great deal better than his rating suggests, and it will be interesting to see what shrewd connections can achieve in '05. *A. & M.H. Potts — Pendle Forest & Craven (Joss Saville).* 167 (OMa), 596 (2m5fOMa), 684 (R), 873 (Cf).

SIZZLING RIVER ..—.. 14 b.g. Sizzling Melody — Bustellina (Busted) fp. Half-brother to Dawn Mission and Step Lively, to jumping winner, Salford, to 3 flat winners (one in Hong Kong), including Cumbrian Rhapsody (also a successful Hurdler) and Emmer Green. Dam won at 8f. P-t-P '02 r2 p0 (pulled up 2). Unraced until he was 11, but looked problematical in '02, and failed to get beyond the 11th when resuming after a year off. *H.T. Tindall — Staintondale.* 954 (M), 1305 (OMa).

SKI COUNTRY ..—.. 7 b.m. Petoski — Amerian County (Amerian USA) psfu. Small homebred half-sister to Mr Smudge (*qv*). An unimpressive-looking little mare, but showed ability despite sticky jumping before fading and pulling up three out on her debut. Has had continued misfortune since, and the normal rider is no help, but was partnered by Andy Martin once, and might be able to do substantially better with his regular assistance. *C. & Mrs F. Marriott — Heythrop (Fran Marriott).* 725 (OMa), 1035 (OMa), 1273 (OMa), 1337 (OMa).

SKI PASS ..9-8.. 10 b.g. Petoski — Cover Your Money (Precipice Wood) 5f1ff. Lengthy owner-bred half-brother to jumping winners, Sticky Money, Red Marauder (won '01 Grand National), Red Striker (won £26,000 Peter Marsh Chase in '01) and Anna Karnali (latter also won NH flat), and to NH flat winner, Irish Banker. Dam, half-sister to Provincials Best (*qv* '87 Season Annual), won 3 Hurdles (2m1f-2m4f). Grandam, Lira, won 2m Hurdle and 4 3m Chses and placed 18. Great-grandam, Tiberina, is sister to Tiberetta — dam of Spanish Steps et al. NH FLAT '00 r2 p0. NH '01/2 r6 p1 (2nd); pulled up 1. P-t-P '03 (for Mr D. Jenks) r3 p0 (4th, slipped up, and fell). Has a pedigree steeped in Grand National history, but a very risky jumper himself and fell twice before and twice after he had finally opened his account. Made no noticeable errors when successful at Paxford, but had every chance when exiting four out in his first Restricted, and would have made the frame in the latest. Theoretically a good thing to atone but already four times a beaten favourite in Points, and his confidence must be at a low ebb. *A.W. Argent & B. Hawkins — R.G. Wright & B. Hawkins — Albrighton Woodland (Tim Stephenson).* 6 (OMa), 667 (OMa), 927 (OMa), 1230 (R), 1388 (R).

SKIP 'N' TUNE (IRE) ..10-6.. 8 b.m. Mandalus — Molten (Ore) p11226. Workmanlike quite attractive half-sister to winning Hurdler, Richter Scale (IRE). P-t-P '02/3 r8 w2 (Maiden and Restricted) p2; last pair 2, pulled up 2. A secure jumper, and has won four races exclusively on sound surfaces, and clocked fast times in both '04 victories, but disappointing on her Hunter Chase debut, and may have found the 3m2f trip too far. Unlucky when 1-2 and going for a third win at Badbury Rings, and having chased home subsequent Chasing winner Out The Black on her Open debut looks set to score in that sphere herself in '05. *The Skippers (M.S. Rose) — Portman (Richard Miller).* 116 (I), 261 (Cf), 365 (I), 576 (O), 860 (Cf), 1167 (3m2f110yH).

SKIPPERS CANYON ..—.. 11 b.m. Milieu — Starry Brig (New Brig) pppp. Small neat sister to Gee Mac, and half-sister to Tweed Brig. Dam won 5 Points (4 Ladies, inc hat-trick) and placed 10. P-t-P '02/3 r6 p0 (pulled up 4, and fell 2). Depressingly bad and now gone in the wind having run tubed at Sandon, but has no known excuses for her often inaccurate fencing. It would be a pointless exercise running her again. *Mrs G.A. Spencer — Albrighton.* 91 (M), 226 (CfMa), 714 (CMam), 848 (OMa).

SKIRMISHING ..—.. 12 b.g. Infantry — Miss Barle (Prince Barle) p. Half-brother to Miss Simitar. Dam won 3 Points and placed 2 for Dudley Moore, and grandam, Miss Queensway, won a Point and placed 16 various (last 4 for Dudley Moore). P-t-P '00 and '02 r6 w1 (3-finisher Maiden) p1 (2nd); 4th of 5, pulled up 2 and unseated. Rated 9-5 when flat out to win a bad three-finisher Maiden on firm at Marks Tey in '02, but absent in '01 and '03, and her latest comeback lasted one race. *T.W. Moore — Essex F. & U. (Ruth Hayter).* 224 (CMod).

SKY SORCERER ..—.. 6 b.g. Comme L'Etoile — Welsh Witch (No Evil) Rp. Tall workmanlike. Has been at the back when running out after a mile and pulling up after two miles so far. *Mrs N. Vaughan — Pembs (Julian Vaughan).* 677 (CfMa), 950 (2m4fOMa).

SLANEY LASS .10-4.. 11 b.m. Arctic Lord — Deep Cut (Deep Run) p1u. Small sister to The Croppy and The Croppy Boy, and half-sister to Son Of A Gunner. NH FLAT '00 r2 p0. NH '00/1 r9 p1 (2nd); pulled up 1, ran out 1, fell 1. P-t-P '03 (for Mr M.J. Jackson) r3 w1 (Maiden) p1 (2nd); and fell. A speedy little mare, and has blitzed round Cothelstone for both Pointing successes on sound surfaces, but hung violently left-handed when taken to Dingley and 11-10 to win a six-runner Restricted, and nearly ran off the course before ditching Richard Burton at the fourth last when still holding a narrow advantage. An ideal type for summer jumping, and has gone back into training with Richard Lee. Tongue-tied once in '01. *R.M. & Mrs M. Phillips — N. Ledbury (Mark Jackson).* 516 (R), 1366 (R), 1472 (I).

SLANEY NATIVE (IRE) .9-7.. 12 b.g. Be My Native (USA) — Mean To Me (Homing) 9f6. Light half-brother to Irish NH flat and Hurdling winner, Slaney Fox. IR10,500 3yo. IRISH NH FLAT '97/8 r4 w1 (p2) 2nds). IRISH NH '98/01 and '03 (for Mrs J. Harrington) r30 w7 (3 2m-2m4f Hdles and 4 2m-2m4f Chses) p13; pulled up 2, and refused 1. The smart winner of eight races all in mud to February '01 in Ireland, and scored three times apiece at Thurles and Gowran Park and twice at Punchestown, and amassed earnings of £91,857. Only failed to finish on three occasions (but refused at the first in a Chase once in '00), and made two visits to Cheltenham including when seventh in the Arkle. Only just caught in three of his 15 placings including a £29,000 Hurdle, but missed '02 and has been a pathetic in just five outings since. Plodded along unenthusiastically when humbled in Ladies Opens, and hopefully this former lovely campaigner will not be degraded again. *Miss M. Mullineaux — Cheshire.* 94 (L), 230 (L), 529 (L).

SLAVE'S ADVENTURE .9-7.. 11 b.m. Green Adventure (USA) — Stockton Slave (Bivouac) up. Small neat half-sister to Four Opinions (*qv*). Dam raced for the Edwards. NH FLAT '99 r1 p0. P-t-P '02/3 r9 w1 (Maiden) p3 (3rd of 4 twice); 4th of 5, fell 3, and pulled up. Regularly stopped in her tracks by catastrophic blunders, and survived several errors when winning a bad Maiden at Upper Sapey (is there any other variety there?) but has only got round once since, and her chances of a follow up are not bright. *R.G. Edwards — Clifton-on-Teme (Steve Isaac).* 660 (Cf), 726 (R).

SLEDMERE (IRE) ..8-7§§.. 10 ch.g. Shalford (IRE) — Jazirah (Main Reef) 47pp. Strong-topped compact half-brother to flat winner, Finsbury Flyer (IRE). Dam is half-sister to The Engineer (*qv* '99 Annual). FLAT r3 p0 (inc Sell). NH '00 r5 p0; pulled up 2. P-t-P/HUNT CH '00 and '02/3 r18 w1 (Members) p1 (remote 2nd); failed to finish 11 (fell/unseated 5, and refused 3). Opened his account at the 18th attempt, and proved he still retains ability when coming from another parish to finish 15 lengths fourth to Just Cliquot on his reappearance, but a complete dog and pulls himself up at the drop of a hat. Has run tongue-tied, in a visor and with cheekpieces. *G.R. Moscrop — Border.* 161 (I), 341 (R), 377 (3m1fH), 1423 (M).

SLEEPING MUSIC (FR) ..—.. 8 b.g. Sleeping Car (FR) — Music Sobre (FR) (Crowned Music USA) pp. Close-coupled good-bodied half-brother to a jumping winner in France. FRENCH NH '00/1 r6 p2 (Chses); pulled up 1. NH '01/2 (for J.R. Best) r7 p0; pulled up 2. Placed in two Chases in France and was short-headed at Dax, but useless since crossing the Channel, and has been 13 lengths fourth and pulled up four times consecutively over fences. A poor jumper, and normally blinkered under Rules. Surely has something wrong with him. *E.C. Brooke — E. Sussex & Romney Marsh (Sara Hickman).* 644 (OMa), 895 (OMa).

PLATE 109 1366 Weston & Banwell Restricted: Cothelstone specialist, Slaney Lass keeps up Richard Burton's title bid *PHOTO: Brian Armstrong*

SLEEPING PANTHER ..—.. 8 ch.g. Tigani — School Dance (Scottish Reel) pppp. Plain rangy. P-t-P '03 r3 p0 (pulled up 2, and fell). Typically unimpressive in the paddock, but stands out in his races as the one that parts more birch than the rest put together and fenced no better when tried in a visor on his latest start. Crouching Tiger, Hidden Dragon — Sleeping Panther, Useless Camel. *P.J. Millington — Fernie.* 40 (OMa), 371 (OMa), 476 (CfMa), 890 (2m4fOMa).

SLIABH FOY (IRE) ..9-13.. 12 b.g. Electric — Lily Gale (IRE) (Strong Gale) 313. Compact half-brother to Lynnes Daniella (IRE). IRISH P-t-P '98/9 r7 p1 (16/ 3rd); pulled up, fell 2, and ran out (impeded). IRISH NH '99 r4 p0. P-t-P '00 (for Mr & Mrs F. Marshall) r8 w1 (Maiden) p0; 4th, last, unseated 4, and pulled up. Broke down after winning a dire Maiden in soft at Aldington in '01, and has been afflicted by a back problem since, but has shown great fortitude, and nursed back to form to land a two-finisher Restricted at Penshurst. Runs from the front, and beaten just over three lengths when 6-4 favourite in an Intermediate next time, but time itself is against him now. Ran tongue-tied in Ireland. *Random Optimists — E. Sussex & Romney Marsh (Di Grissell).* 900 (R), 1084 (R), 1406 (I).

PLATE 110 1133 Axe Vale Open Maiden 56&7yo (Div 1): Sliema (Naddan Wilmington), 1st, leads Hooray Henry (Tim Dennis), 3rd, obscuring Boy Band (Joe Tickle), pu, and Chasing Buttercups (Rilly Goschen), 5th PHOTO: Brian Armstrong

SLIEMA (IRE) ..9-9.. 7 b.g. Desert Style (IRE) — Ascoli (Skyliner) 22d1. Unfurnished half-brother to 2 flat winners (one in Turkey). Dam won 2 flat (10-12f) and 2m Hurdle in Ireland. NH FLAT '02 r2 p0. NH '02 r1 p0. P-t-P '03 r3 p0 (pulled up 3). Pulled too hard for his own good when a non-finisher in '03, but rather more settled this year, and backed from 14-1 to less than half those odds when runner-up over 2m4f at Ston Easton, but was disqualified after missing a marker through the chicane before the home straight. Easily made amends in a youngsters Maiden at Stafford Cross, and has the scope to improve further, but will always require an easy three miles. *Mrs F. Shaw & Lady Acland — Cattistock (Fiona Shaw).* 121 (OMa), 600 (2m4fOMa), 1133 (OMa).

SLINGSBY LADY ..8-5.. 6 b.m. Tragic Role (USA) — Hilltop Lady (Puissance) ppp4. Small long-backed light. Bought Doncaster, Aug for 1200. Has a scabby staring coat, looks in abject despair, and tends to jump alarmingly, but at least the little dear has a heart, and finished 18 lengths fourth at Chaddesley Corbett when visored for the first time. Will probably have that heart broken. *P.J. Millington — Fernie.* 1218 (OMa), 1402 (2m4fOMa), 1473 (OMa), 1532 (OMa).

SLIP THE RING ..10-4.. 11 ch.g. Belmez (USA) — Sixslip (USA) (Diesis) 24. Angular half-brother to Little Mickey, and to NH flat winner, Point. Dam won 2 flat races (10-14f). NH '00/1 r9 p2 (2nds); slipped up 1. P-t-P '02 (for Mr N. Shutts) r4 w1 (Maiden) p2 (2nds); and pulled up 1. NH '03 (for Miss K. Marks) r3 p0; fell 1, and pulled up 1. An expensive purchase when in the previous yard, and only had one win in a long Maiden at Nottingham to show for his 20,000 guineas price tag from 12 starts. Presumably cost current connections rather less, but ran well when chasing home Free Gift at

Larkhill, and it was a pity he did not get another chance to prove himself in Points. A one-paced stayer, but theoretically plenty good enough to waltz an average Restricted if granted a clean bill of health in '05. *M.E. Senter & L. Burford — P. Senter — N. Ledbury.* 139 (R), 490 (3m2fH).

SLOE COACH ..—.. 8 b.g. Carlton (GER) — Petalouda (Avgerinos) uup. Owner-bred. Lost a wobbly Gareth Wiggley before halfway twice, and then tailed off and pulled up at the 11th for Brea Donnelly. In thy name thy destiny? *M.R. Codd — Southdown & Eridge (Mickey Furlong).* 186 (OMa), 418 (2m4fCMa), 611 (OMa).

SLYTHERIN FALLS ..9-2.. 8 br.g. Milieu — Linn Falls (Royal Fountain) u431. Dam, half-sister to Pitcruivie (*qv* '87 Season Annual) was placed NH Flat and 3 Hurdles, and won 2 Ladies and placed 7 when Fife-qualified. P-t-P '03 r1 p0 (pulled up). Possibly unlucky when parting company with the rider at the third last on her reappearance in a race where only one went clear, but made amends on her latest start when ideally suited by the drop back in trip at Hexham. Very headstrong and prone to errors, and has still to prove herself over the full trip, but her enthusiasm can't be knocked. Wears bandages, and a cross-noseband. *S.N. Clark — Fife.* 510 (OMa), 659 (OMa), 1076 (M), 1474 (2m4fOMa).

SMALL-LIR ..8-10.. 11 ch.m. Lir — Kimberley Ann (St Columbus) p43. Small compact home-bred sister to Belitlir (*qv*). P-t-P '02/3 r4 p0 (5th, pulled up 2, and fell). Has hinted at ability and finished quite strongly when 17 lengths last of three at Trebudannon, but knowing where and when she will be unleashed in earnest will be a mystery until it actually happens. *Mrs J. Holden-White & B.R.J. Young — E. Cornwall (Jan Holden-White).* 312 (CfMa), 704 (CfMa), 1436 (OMa).

SMART CAVALIER ..9-7.. 6 b.g. Terimon — Smart Topsy (Oats) 1p. Lightly-made. Dam, sister to Smart Casanova (*qv* '00 Annual), was poor last of 3 in Maiden (failed to finish in 5 of 7 Points, and failed to stay). Bought Doncaster, Aug for 28,000. Made a decisive move after three out when winning a 2m4f Maiden at Ston Easton in which he was flagging on the run-in but lasted home by three-quarters of a length, but not always fluent when 4-6 in a Restricted, and after holding a prominent pitch before two out he weakened rapidly and was pulled up at the last. It looks as if he may have inherited his dam's lack of stamina, and if so connections may feel tempted to try him over shorter trips under Rules. *J.M. Dare — Cattistock (Richard Barber).* 599 (2m4fOMa), 1131 (R).

SMARTIES SURPRISE (IRE) ..—.. 8 ch.g. Commanche Run — Handy Lady (Nearly A Hand) p. Dam, half-sister to Baron's Heir (*qv* '98 Annual). IRISH P-t-P '01/2 r5 p1 (3rd); pulled up 3 and fell. Has only completed the course once in four years, when 26 lengths third in Ireland, and seems to be devoid of ability. *G.D. Hanmer — Cheshire.* 1266 (2m4fOMa).

SMARTY (IRE) ..10-6.. 12 b/br.g. Royal Fountain — Cahernane Girl (Bargello) 4765. Workmanlike compact half-brother to Sacrosanct, and 5 jumping winners, including Chasing winners, Over The Deel (11 Chases) and Grate Deel (IRE) (latter also won Hurdling and 9 Chases), to Irish Pointing/ Hunter Chase winner, Aiguille (IRE), and to NH flat winner, Inca (IRE). Dam won 2m flat, 3 Hurdles (2m-2m2f), and 2m Chase, all in Ireland. IR16,500 3yo. NH FLAT '97 r1 p0. NH '97/02 r26 w6 (2m5f Hdle and 3 3m-3m2f Chses) p6; pulled up 5, and fell 1. NH '04 r3 p0 (7th in 3m Ch: *a bhnd*; 39*l* 6th in 4m4f Grand National: *hld up, 10th ½way, no hdwy 20*; and dist 5th in 4m1f Scottish Grand National: *hld up & bhnd, eff u.p 19, sn wknd, t.o*). Won five staying Chases on good ground or in mud and then collected a bad Hurdle to November '01, and his golden days were when he scored five times in a six-race spell from December '98 to December '00. Distant last of two in the infamous '01 Grand National, in which he jumped very well but finished exhausted in the gruelling conditions behind Red Marrauder, and was also a splendid second to Amberleigh House in the '01 Becher Chase. Badly hampered at the first and pulled up at the eighth in the '02 National, and given a warm up in a Newbury Hunter Chase in which he finished 22 lengths fourth before a 39 length sixth at 100-1 at Aintree and a remote fifth at 66-1 at Ayr in further Nationals. Frequently wears headgear or cheekpieces. Has earned £181,594, but only £37,167 came via first prizes! Opportunities for him at 12 will be virtually non-existent, so must be on the brink of retirement. *Mrs T. Brown — Cotswold V.F. (Mark Pitman).* 348 (3mH).

SMILE PLEEZE (IRE) ..10-0§.. 13 b.g. Naheez (USA) — Harkin Park (Pollerton) pp32543. Workmanlike compact. Dam is half-sister to 7 winners, including Fame The Spur (*qv* '93 Annual). NH FLAT '97 r1 p0. NH '97 r4 p0. P-t-P/HUNT CH '98/03 r34 w7 (inc 4 Opens) p8 (4 3rds, last once); pulled up 6, and fell/unseated 2. A most enigmatic Pointer, and often takes no interest and sulks round in the rear, but capable of producing a barn-storming finish if in the right frame of mind, and has exploited a low handicap mark since transferring to Matt Sheppard's in the summer. Suited by a test of stamina on a sound surface. Blinkered thrice in '99. *Miss S. Troughton — Ledbury (Mike Daniell).* 34 (O), 93 (O), 360 (O), 722 (M), 980 (Cf), 1121 (O), 1262 (O).

SMOKEY JOE (IRE) ..9-8.. 13 br.g. Lord Americo — Badsworth Madam (Over The River FR) 331. Compact well-made half-brother to Badworth Gale (IRE). NH FLAT '98 r2 p0. P-t-P '99 and '02/3 r10 p4 (3 2nds, beaten neck once, of 3 once, and last once; and 3rd of 4); 4th, last, and pulled up 4.

Fragile, and has only once managed more than three outings in a year, but has always indicated he had ability, and got off the mark when walking over in his Members. Given a school of epic proportions on his reappearance, and stayed on to be 22 lengths third behind Lord Anner at Bishops Court next time, but it would take a real optimist to suggest he could land a Restricted. *A.J. & Mrs A.E. Heywood — Tetcott (Chris Heywood).* 150 (OMa), 328 (OMa), 1546 (M).

SMOKEY ROBOT (IRE) ..7-13.. 12 b.g. Riberetto — Smokey Queen (Proverb) p84pp. Well-made brother to Irish Pointing winner, Convent Lane, and half-brother to Irish Pointing winner, Kinvarra. NH FLAT '97 r1 p0. NH '98/01 r11 p4; pulled up 1, unseated 1. P-t-P '03 r1 p0 (pulled up). NH '04 r1 p0 (dist last of 8 in 3m110y R.A. Gold Cup: *nt jw, sn wl t.o*). His best form under Rules would have given his strong claims in a Maiden, but beaten 45 lengths on his only completion in that sphere, and has looked very suspect on several occasions. A very moderate jumper, and was soon fences behind when sent to Sandown for the Royal Artillery Gold Cup. Often tongue-tied under Rules. *D.S. Dennis — Hursley Hambledon.* 120 (OMa), 644 (OMa), 971 (OMa), 1337 (OMa).

SNEEDHAM'S GREEN ..—§.. 9 gr.g. Newski (USA) — Dark Acre (Peacock FR) ppppup. Compact owner-bred brother to Piccadilly Wood and Matson Girl. Dam won 3 minor Points and placed 8 for Jason Warner (previously 3rd once in Ireland). P-t-P '03 r3 p0 (pulled up 3). An abject disaster, and has never looked like getting round in Points, and often gets into a stew beforehand. Incredibly backed from 14s to sevens in his Members, but stopped dead after 1m4f despite running tubed, and it would be irresponsible to run him again. *J.S. Warner — Cotswold V.F.* 172 (OMa), 259 (CMa), 519 (CfMa), 815 (M), 1193 (OMa), 1341 (OMa).

SNEEZE ..—.. 10 ch.m. Cotation — Gardella (Garnered) fpp. Half-sister to Splodge. Compact well-made owner-bred half-sister to Slodge. Dam, sister to Medway Gauntlet (*qv* '90 Annual), was quickly tailed off twice in Brocklesby Members (3rd once). NH FLAT '01 (for J.F. Coupland) r1 p0 (last). Still in contention when she fell four out in her first Maiden, but has run badly and pulled up twice on firmish ground since. Sarah Judge does not have much luck with her Sneezes and Splodges. *Miss S.L. Judge — Brocklesby.* 130 (OMa), 303 (OMa), 746 (OMa).

SNITTON SALVO ..9-3§§.. 10 b.g. Cruise Missile — Snitton (Rymer) f5242. Big strong brother to Snitton South, and half-brother to Jo Jos Best Friend, Snitton West and Evanly Miss. Dam, temperamental half-sister to Snitton Stream (*qv* '98 Annual), was placed in 2 Points. P-t-P '00 and '02/3 (for Mr & Mrs J. Barker & Mr & Mrs A. Davies) r18 p3 (3rds, of 4 twice, remote once); 5th, last 2, refused 2, pulled up 6, ran out, and fell/unseated 3. A thoroughly temperamental dog, and has failed to finish more than half his races, but frustratingly has the ability to win, and only failed by half-a-length to overhaul Robert The Rascal at Eaton Hall. Has never been actively involved in the finish otherwise, and gives the impression that a physical defect is at the root of his problems. Wears blinkers. *Mr J. Barker — Ludlow (Geoff Evans).* 517 (CfMa), 709 (Mah), 1142 (OMa), 1261 (OMa), 1425 (OMa).

SNITTON WEST .9-2§.. 9 b.g. Derrylin — Snitton (Rymer) 1263pf. Strong good-looking owner-bred half-brother to Snitton Salvo (*qv*). P-t-P/HUNT CH '02/3 (for Capt. J.M.G. Lumsden) r16 p5 (4 3rds, of 4 thrice; and last of 2); 4th twice, last pair 5, pulled up 3, and ran out. The only way he would ever win was if it was handed to him on a silver salver, and was luckily left virtually solo at the last when taking a two-finisher Maiden on firm at Whitwick on his reappearance. Was not caught off guard again, and declined to overtake Master Club Royal in a battle of weak wills at Eaton Hall after which his interest waned completely. Visored when successful, and has been tried in blinkers and a near-side pricker. *L. & Miss J. Evans — Ludlow (Geoff Evans).* 518 (CfMa), 715 (R), 839 (R), 1148 (R), 1265 (R), 1531 (R).

SNIZORT (USA) ..9-8.. 7 b.g. Bahri (USA) — Ava Singstheblues (USA) (Dixieland Band USA) u212662. Workmanlike half-brother to flat winner in USA. Dam won 2 races at up to 8f in USA. FLAT '00/2 r10 p1 (3rd). NH '02 (for M.E. Sowersby) r3 p0; pulled up 1. A flop on the flat (six lengths third once) and over Hurdles including Sellers, and was last twice and pulled up once in the latter. Ploughed home in front in a Maiden at Dalton Park which took 7min40s, and outstayed the opposition, but his seconds have not been impressive, and beaten 30 lengths plus twice, and two lengths after travelling well but finding little. Blinkered on three occasions, including his latest Point. Not the most enthusiastic, but young enough to have a chance in a long Restricted if connections keep persevering. *P. Watson — York & Ainsty S. (Mary Sowersby).* 303 (OMa), 393 (CfMa), 504 (CMa), 684 (R), 955 (R), 1157 (M), 1456 (R).

SNOOTY ESKIMO (IRE) .10-0§.. 13 ch.g. Aristocracy — Over The Arctic (Over The River FR) 1623538. Tall lengthy half-brother to NH flat and jumping winner, Itsonlyme (IRE), and to Irish NH flat winner, It's Only Him (IRE). Dam, half-sister to Speriamo (*qv* '88 Season Annual), won 2 Irish Points. NH FLAT '96/7 r4 p0. NH '97/9 and '01 r15 p1 (27*l* 2nd); pulled up 5; inc in one of 3 Chses. P-t-P/HUNT CH '00/3 (for Mr J.S. Haldane) r12 p1 (3rd); pulled up 5. Frequently overfaced but gained a long overdue success at the 32nd attempt when outstaying a better fancied stablemate in the fastest

12st time of the day at Friars Haugh. Displayed his inconsistencies when 11-8 favourite and last of three in his Members, but was beaten a minimum of 17 lengths in Hunter Chases, and needs to concentrate on the easiest options available. *T.R.P.S. Norton — Morpeth (Tim Reed).* 132 (CR), 349 (3m1fH), 762 (I), 914 (M), 1173 (2m110yH), 1359 (2m4f110yH), 1499 (2m4f110yH).

PLATE 111 132 Jedforest Restricted: L to R, Wild Edgar (Andrew Richardson), 2nd, and Snooty Eskimo (Henry Norton), 1st, are locked together at the last PHOTO: Alan Mitchell

SNOW NYMPH ..8-9.. 10 b.m. Buckley — Forest Nymph (NZ) (Oak Ridge FR) 56. Small half-sister to Forest Maze, and to Hurdles winners, Toby Brown and Christopher (latter also won NH flat). Dam won at 8f in New Zealand. P-t-P '03 r4 p1 (2nd); and pulled up 3. A reliable jumper, but does not get enough chances to become fighting fit, and beaten upwards of 25 lengths in both attempts in '04. *Mrs S.J. Gospel — Farndale.* 813 (OMa), 1165 (OMa).

SNOWTRE (IRE) ..10-3§.. 8 b.g. Glacial Storm (USA) — Forest Gale (Strong Gale) 323pb5p2111. Small half-brother to Philtre (IRE) (*qv*). NH FLAT '02 r1 p0. P-t-P '02/3 r13 w1 (Maiden) p5 (2 2nds, beaten ¾*l* once; inc last of 3 once); 5th, pulled up 4, and fell/unseated 2. Not very brave, and liable to run a stinker, but ran Cantarinho to a neck in first-time cheekpieces at Higham, and came into his own on short courses with fast ground in the closing weeks of the season after Adrian Wintle had given up the ride to the title-chasing Richard Burton. Beat two finishers in the first two, but the Chaddesley success represented a step up in class, and provided his confidence levels are still high should be placed to advantage again. Wears a cross-noseband. *J.D. Callow — Albrighton Woodland (Helen Needham).* 57 (R), 159 (R), 252 (CR), 369 (R), 614 (R), 665 (R), 1063 (R), 1136 (R), 1449 (R), 1496 (I), 1528 (Cf).

SOCIETY SCANDAL (IRE) ..8-7.. 10 ch.g. Moscow Society (USA) — Turbulent Wind (Strong Gale) pppp3413p7. Leggy light-framed. Dam, half-sister to Sambucka Boy (*qv* '93 Annual), won 4 Irish Chases, 2m3f-2m6f. IRISH NH FLAT '01 r2 p0. IRISH NH '01 r4 p0. P-t-P '02 r4 p1 (2nd); 6th of 7, and pulled up 2. The only bright spot in an otherwise barren year for the owner, and it was typical that he should chose to ride the wrong one at Fakenham. Apart from his win has never beaten another rival which emphasises just how lucky he was to find such a ghastly race. Blinkered once in Ireland, and usually tongue-tied now. *P.J. Millington — Fernie.* 6 (OMa), 103 (OMa), 220 (OMa), 651 (OMa), 946 (OMa), 1000 (OMa), 1156 (OMa), 1245 (R), 1400 (CN), 1503 (R).

SOCUTE ..9-10.. 10 b.m. Tina's Pet — Cute Pam (Pamroy) p5. Small sister to Cutina (*qv*). NH '02 r1 p0. P-t-P '02/3 (for Not So Blonde Partnership) r8 w1 (Maiden) p1 (2nd); ran out 2, and pulled up 4. Only got beyond the seventh fence once in her debut season, but sprang a 33-1 surprise on firm at Ston Easton last year, and backed it up with a fair second next time. Restricted to an even more truncated campaign than usual in the new yard, and did not really get a chance to prove herself in Restricteds on ground that was probably softer than ideal. Wears a cross-noseband. *Miss J. Reynolds & Mrs B. Bishop — Weston & Banwell H. (Clare Parfitt).* 148 (R), 323 (R).

SOHAPARA ..10-6.. 10 ch.m. Arapahos (FR) — Mistress Boreen (Boreen FR) 1122113. Small close-coupled sister to Forest Feather (IRE), and half-sister to The Sky Is Blue. FLAT '00 r1 p0 (tailed off). NH FLAT '99 r1 p0. NH '00 r1 p0. P-t-P '02/3 r15 w3 (Maiden, Intermediate and Club mares) p8 (6 2nds, of 3 once; and last of 3 twice); fell/unseated 3, and pulled up. Game and consistent, and suited by good or sound surfaces, and easily took apart a Hunter Chase field that had four previous winners in it at Hereford, but also gifted two wins in '04. Looked sure to score at Bonvilston but slipped up on the final bend and injured herself in the process, and will miss '05 as she has paid a visit to Sir Harry Lewis instead. Wears a cross-noseband. *Mrs S.E. Mathias — Llangeinor (Jane Mathias).* 359 (Cf), 696 (O), 974 (3mH), 1190 (O), 1358 (3m1f110yH), 1535 (O), 1537 (C).

SOL MUSIC ..10-6.. 13 ch.g. Southern Music — Tyqueen (Tycoon II) p4343343. Small compact brother to Hurdles winner, Elvis. Dam was 3rd in a Maiden. NH FLAT '96 r3 p0. NH '97/01 r23 w4 (2m1f Hdle, and 3 2m-2m1f Chses) p6. P-t-P/HUNT CH '01/3 r13 w7 (inc 5 2m-2m4f110y Hunt Chses) p1 (2nd in Hunt Ch); 7th, last pair 2, and pulled up 2. NH '04 r2 p1 (16/ 3rd to Chevalier Bayard in 2m3f Ch: *prom til wknd 3 out*); and 4th in 2m110y Ch: *chsd ldr 3 til blun 8, sn wknd*. Very speedy, and almost invincible in sub-3m events in the past, and confined to Hunter Chases in '04 after his usual prep at Black Forest Lodge, but proved bitterly disappointing, and was beaten 10 lengths minimum. Ran well off a big weight in the Handicap race at Newton Abbot, but let down by his jumping more often than not, and typically found out by the testing conditions when sent off at 4-6 at Towcester subsequently. Owes connections nothing, but a return to Handicaps has failed to arrest his decline, and is not getting any younger. *The G. & P. Partnership (P. Thomas) — S. Devon (Leslie Cottrell).* 77 (O), 317 (2m4fH), 441 (2m4f110yH), 799 (2m3f110yH), 1166 (2m5f110yH), 1354 (2m110yH).

SOLO GENT ..9-5§.. 16 br.g. Le Bavard (FR) — Go-It-Alone (Linacre) 904436536. Tall rangy. Dam won at 5f, and is half-sister to Royal Irish (*qv* '00 Annual). NH FLAT '93 r2 p0. NH '93/9 and '00/1 r58 w9 (2m6f Hdle, and 8 2m5f-3m7f Chses) p13. P-t-P/HUNT CH '00 and '03 (for Mr M. Jones & Mrs M. Radbourne) r20 w2 (3m Hunt Chses) p6 (3 2nds, of 3 once; and inc 2 Hunt Chses); last pair 7, fell 1, and pulled up 1. A Huntingdon specialist under Rules, and has fulfilled his role as schoolmaster admirably since resurfacing in '03, but carried plenty of condition throughout '04, and was beaten a minimum of 20 lengths. Never known for his consistency, and trundles along at slow speeds in competitive events now. Has a very sparse tail, going bald in his old age? Has been taken to post early (sometimes by as much as 15 minutes), and tried in headgear and a tongue-tie. *The Jones Family (M.E. Jones) — Avon V. (Kayley Jones).* 5 (L), 175 (Cnr), 414 (MO), 610 (Cv&nr), 632 (M), 757 (L), 1407 (L), 1493 (L), 1551 (L).

SOLOMAN (IRE) ..—.. 12 br.g. Mandalus — Solo Player (Blue Refrain) p. Tall brother to Play Alone (IRE) (*qv*). NH '97/02 r22 w3 (2m Hdle and 2 2m4f110y-3m2f Chses) p11 (5 2nds); pulled up 1. P-t-P '03 r2 p0 (pulled up 2). Formerly useful under Rules, where he was well served by a stiff track with an uphill finish, but stricken by broken blood vessels and very lightly raced since '00, and has pulled up in his last three attempts. The mind is willing but the body not, and looks to have descended into retirement. *H.T. Pelham — S. & W. Wilts (Jane Galpin).* 178 (3m1f110yH).

SOLSGIRTH .9-9§.. 14 br.g. Ardross — Lillies Brig (New Brig) 2. Tall half-brother to Kinglassie and Moon Mist. Dam, half-sister to Kinneston (*qv* '95 Annual), won a Hunt Ch (on a disqualification) and 2 Points and placed 9 (inc 3 Chses). Grandam, Dysie Mary, was 3rd in Maiden. NH '96/02 r45 w6 (2m Hdle and 5 2m-2m4f Chses) p12 (8 3rds); pulled up 9, and fell/unseated 4. P-t-P/HUNT CH '03 r7 w1 (3-runner 2-finisher Members) p0; 4th twice, pulled up 3, and refused. A useful mudlark in Scotland to '00, and turned back the clock to register a seventh success in his Members last year, but basically retired nowadays, and could not justify being 11-10 on his only appearance in '04. Tongue-tied once in '03. *M. Alexander — Fife (Nick Alexander).* 1076 (M).

SOLVANG (IRE) ..9-13.. 13 b.g. Carlingford Castle — Bramble Bird (Pitpan) 4pp. Close-coupled half-sister to Supreme Bramble (IRE). Dam, half-sister to Pat Alaska (*qv* '98 Annual). IRISH FLAT '97/8 r2 p1 (2nd). IRISH P-t-P '96/7 r3 w1 (5&6yo Maiden) p0; unseated and ran out. IRISH NH FLAT '97 r2 w1 (2m1f) p0. IRISH NH '97/8 r15 w4 (2m1f-3m Chses) p4. NH '98/02 r18 w2 (3m1f Hdle and 2m4f Ch) p5 (3 2nds); pulled up 3, fell 1. P-t-P '03 (for Mrs J. Marles & Mrs N.A. Hedges) r3 p1 (3rd); last, and pulled up. A useful performer on good or sound surfaces, but went into a steady decline after his last success at Aintree in November '99, and was tongue-tied latterly under Rules. Lightly raced and a shadow of his former self since, and another who must be staring retirement in the face. *Mrs N.A. Hedges — Warwicks (Julie Marles).* 441 (2m4f110yH), 630 (2m4fH), 799 (2m3f110yH).

SOLWAY SAFFY .—.. 10 b.m. Safawan — Out On A Flyer (Comedy Star USA) pp. Small light sister to No Problem Jac. Dam won at 6f, and subsequently won 2 Sell Hdles (2m-2m1f; 3 and 5 ran) on hard for David Harrison. P-t-P '00/1 r6 p3 (2 3rds, of 4, and last); and pulled up 3. NH FLAT '00 r3 p1 (3rd). NH '01/2 r5 p0 (last, and pulled up 4). Had ability and was only beaten a length in her first bumper, but rendered useless by a breathing problem, and pulled up in her last six starts. Only went two miles in '04, and it is a shame she has her infirmities, but the real tragedy was the death of Liz Harrison in a car crash in October. *Mrs E.J. Harrison — Cumberland (Jackie Williamson).* 136 (OMam), 765 (R).

SOME GO WEST (IRE) ..9-6.. 11 b.g. Un Desperado (FR) — Costly Lady (Bold Lad IRE) p623p. Strong-topped compact half-brother to Hurdles winner, Middle Marker (IRE). NH '99/01 r13 w1 (2m4f Ch) p2 (2nds). P-t-P/HUNT CH '01/2 r8 w1 (Open) p3 (Hunt Chses, neck 2nd once); pulled up 3, and unseated. Scored at Doncaster in '02 and revived successfully in a weak Open at Parham two years later, but hampered by wind problems for a long time, and only able to show a fraction of his old ability in '04. Three miles has never been his trip, but stopped dead after two when visored on his latest appearance, and looks finished. Has run tongue-tied. Blinkered once in '00. *S. Bullimore — Thurlow (Caroline Bailey).* 170 (O), 382 (O), 786 (O), 1057 (O), 1372 (2m4fH).

SOME TOOL ..8-2.. 8 b.g. Jupiter Island — Melodys Daughter (Sizzling Melody) p4cp. Strong-topped. Dam won 5f race. FLAT '02 r1 p0. NH '02 (for J.A. Harris) r2 p0. Bought Ascot, Oct for 1238. Beaten 45 lengths plus in a flat race and two Hurdles (including a Seller), and was 18 lengths fourth on his only completion in a Point. Gets very few opportunities and does not look much good. *M. Blagg — Stevenstone (Verity Nicholls).* 701 (2m4fOMa), 909 (2m4fOMa), 1133 (OMa), 1267 (M).

SOME TOURIST (IRE) ..8-0.. 17 b.g. Torus — Noellespir (Bargello) 2. Strong-topped half-brother to Teninarow (IRE), and to jumping winner, Ambleside (IRE). Dam won mares Maiden in Ireland. IRISH P-t-P '94/6 r16 w1 (Maiden) p3 (3rds); pulled up 6. P-t-P/HUNT CH '97/02 (for Mr N. Benstead) r27 w7 (Restricted, 3 Members, Club Moderate and 2 Club Novice Riders) p4 (2 3rds, of 4 once); ran out 1, and pulled up 3. Remarkably safe and a thorough stayer, but flattered by seven successes, three of which have been gained by beating a total of two finishers. Lives in virtual retirement now but resurfaced to give a game display in his Members. Has been ridden in spurs. *J.M. Gordon-Watson — Kent & Surrey Bloodhounds.* 574 (M).

SONGINO (IRE) ..9-3.. 9 ch.g. Perugino (USA) — Sonbere (Electric) pp3. Neat half-brother to Irish flat winner, Thunder Alley. Dam won 8f race. IR3500f. FLAT '98 r4 p0. IRISH P-t-P '01/3 r7 p0; pulled up 2, fell 2. IRISH FLAT '00/1 and '03 r7 p0. IRISH NH '99/02 (for J. Clements) r12 p1 (3rd). FLAT '03 (for J. Parkes) r2 p0. Has totted up 35 defeats over the years, including Selling Hurdles when sent from Ireland to the U.K. on three occasions, and two measly placings consist of a third over Hurdles in August '01 and a seven lengths third at Charm Park, where remarkably the two behind him went on to score. It hardly seems credible that he has improved, and could be rated many pounds too high (had only beaten two horses in nine previous Points). Occasionally wore blinkers or cheekpieces to '03. *P.N. & Mrs R.A. Robinson — Sinnington (Rowena Robinson).* 165 (OMa), 504 (CMa), 959 (OMa).

SONNANT (FR) ..9-11.. 6 ch.g. Cyborg (FR) — Schwarzente (IRE) (Entitled) 41. Tall light-framed half-brother to French flat winner, Schlawiner and French Hurdling winner, River Charm (won £38,000 prize in '04). FRENCH NH '03 r4 p0. Backed from tens to fives but came up against Free Gift and faded after leading for 2m4f when beaten 40 lengths on his English debut, but switched to the shorter trip and justified favouritism next time at Cottenham, where he was never headed. Absent since the 1st February, and although he looks progressive that would be with the proviso that he can stay three miles. *S.N. Wilshire — Grafton (Kim Gilmore).* 12 (OMa), 105 (2m4fOMa).

SONNET SUPREME (IRE) ..—.. 6 b.m. Supreme Leader — Sakonnet (IRE) (Mandalus) f. Rangy unfurnished. Fell at halfway at Bratton Down in mid-May. *A. Murphy — Taunton V. (Caroline Keevil).* 1380 (OMa).

SON OF ANSHAN ..10-9§.. 12 b.g. Anshan — Anhaar (Ela-Mana-Mou) 2361332. Good-topped attractive half-brother to flat and Hurdles winner, Ellamine, and Midnight Coup, and to Irish Hurdles winner, Four Aces, including a German jumping winner. Dam is half-sister to Itchy Feet (*qv* '99 Annual). FLAT r1 p0; refused to enter stalls intended debut. NH '96/00 r23 w4 (3 2m-2m2f Hdles, and 3m Ch) p9. P-t-P/HUNT CH '01/3 r13 w5 (inc 3 3m3f Hunt Chses and Open) p4 (2 3rds, last once, inc Hunt Ch; and inc distant 2nd of 3 in Hunt Ch once); 4th, 5th, pulled up, and fell. Disappointing and became ungenuine under Rules, and was recording his first success for four years in '02, but still inclined to run well below expectations. Took his winning tally for the Tuers to six at Sedgefield where he has scored four times over 3m3f, but never wanted to overtake Ben From Ketton on a return visit, and having been turned over on another three occasions when favourite in '04 punters are advised to look for alternatives. Runs tongue-tied. Blinkered twice in '00. *G.F. Tuer — Hurworth.* 240 (3mH), 429 (3m5fO), 798 (3m1fH), 894 (3m3fH), 1038 (O), 1362 (3m6f110yH), 1489 (3m3fH).

SON OF SAM ..9-10.. 11 b.g. Minster Son — Samonia (Rolfe USA) p8f8s4. Leggy light-framed brother to My Sam, and half-brother to Political Sam, Priceless Sam and Sams Way. Dam fell in only Point, but won 3 Hdles (2m-2m4f), inc a Sell for Mr Barker. NH FLAT '98 r2 p0. NH '01 r1 p0 (fell). P-t-P/HUNT CH '00/1 r3 w1 (Maiden) p0; fell 2. Romped the quickest of the three youngsters Maidens at Hornby Castle on his jumping debut, but on the floor in five of nine subsequent attempts, and shows no signs of improving his technique. Fenced appallingly but looked the likely winner of a Mordon Restricted when slipping up on the bend before four out, and good fortune is clearly never going to smile on him again. *J.W. Barker — Hurworth (Sarah Dent).* 341 (R), 563 (R), 810 (R), 1288 (R), 1416 (R), 1476 (R).

SOOTSIR ..8-11.. 9 b.g. Baron Blakeney — Furry Bear (Rymer) u417p63p. Compact good-bodied half-brother to Charliebob. Dam, 'a very slow old lady', contested 2 Points at 12 for Sarah Hawker. Grandam, Blueberry Pie, sister or half-sister to 8 Pointers, was 2nd in a Maiden. P-t-P '02/3 r9 w1 (3-finisher Maiden) p2 (last of 2 once); 4th, last pair 4, and fell. Seems rather fortunate to have unearthed two winning opportunities, and two lengths covered all five finishers in the latest, and otherwise beaten between 24 and 38 lengths when completing in '04. Looked as slow as a boat and pulled up when two fences behind at halfway on his latest appearance and it will be amazing if he manages to eek out another win. Often makes mistakes, and needs to go right-handed. Wears a cross-noseband. *R. & Mrs S. Hawker — Beaufort (Richard Hawker).* 44 (R), 118 (R), 197 (R), 495 (I), 629 (3m1f110yH), 1071 (I), 1181 (I), 1539 (I).

SO PEACEFUL .10-1.. 11 b.m. Prince Of Peace — Indian Election (Sula Bula) 11. Small good-looking owner-bred half-sister to Black Oak and Goldoak. Dam is half-sister to Indian Knight (*qv* '03 Annual). NH '01 r1 p0. P-t-P '00 and '02/3 r11 p4 (3 2nds, of 3 once, last once); 4th twice, 6th of 7, fell/unseated 3, and pulled up. Error-prone and a non-stayer in previous seasons, but displayed no such deficiencies when landing a weak Maiden at Cothelstone, and finished strongly to land a touch at Holnicote after a blunder at the 13th had seemingly put her out of contention. Does not stand her racing well, but clearly much improved, and would warrant consideration in other minor races next year. Suited by good or sound surfaces. *Mrs S.M. Jones & I. Stephens — Minehead H. (Belinda Powell).* 883 (OMa), 1184 (R).

SOUDEN LYRIC .—.. 12 b.g. Tumble Gold — Palmy (USA) (Buckfinder USA) b. Home-bred. Dam is half-sister to 4 Pointers, including, Midfielder (*qv* '98 Annual). P-t-P '00 r2 p0 (pulled up, and fell). On the heels of the leaders when brought down five out on his belated comeback at Alnwick, but did not get another chance to prove himself. *G.T. Bewley — Jedforest (Emma Anderson).* 75 (OMa).

SOUL KING (IRE) ..10-2.. 10 b.g. King's Ride — Soul Lucy (Lucifer USA) p543p42. Tall unfurnished half-brother to Irish Pointing and English NH flat and jumping winner, Sister Stephanie (IRE) (won Irish Grand National), Irish jumping winner, Galky Gale, and to Irish NH flat and jumping winner, The Carrig Rua (IRE). Dam won NH flat, 2m Hdle and 2 Chses (2m4f-2m6f) in Ireland. NH '00/2 r8 p0. P-t-P '02/3 r7 w2 (Maiden and Restricted) p3 (2 2nds); last, and pulled up. Competent at a low level, and ran way above his station when two lengths third at 100-1 at Towcester, but otherwise let down by his jumping in '04 and has little or no acceleration. Cannot be guaranteed to run up to his current rating, and is a borderline squiggle. Has run tongue-tied. *Staverton Owners Group (M. Blake) — Avon V. (Michael Blake).* 33 (L), 116 (I), 321 (I), 437 (3m1fH), 629 (3m1f110yH), 891 (3m1fH), 1181 (I).

SOUND SENSE ..9-7.. 7 br.g. So Factual (USA) — Sight'n Sound (Chief Singer) 52p221f. Unfurnished half-brother to flat winner, Magic Mistress. Dam won 13f race. FLAT '01 r3 p0. P-t-P '03 (for Mr A. Hodge) r6 p0 (pulled up 3, and fell/unseated 3). Looked potentially lethal in the previous yard, and made more than his fair share of mistakes in '04, but connections did well to get a race out of him. Mrs J. Perry — Torrington F. (Laura Young). 119 (OMa), 308 (2m4fOMa), 347 (3mH), 568 (CfMa), 796 (CfMa), 1272 (OMa), 1386 (R).

SOUNDS PROMISING ..—.. 10 b.g. Profilic — Blakeney Sound (Blakeney) p. Good-topped half-brother to Cashew Chaos, to NH flat and jumping winner, Sounds Like Fun, to winning Hurdler, Master Rastus, and to 2 flat winners (one on Sweden), including Glen Miller. Dam is half-sister to Mend (*qv* '97 Annual). NH '02 r1 p0 (pulled up). P-t-P '02/3 r10 w1 (Maiden) p2 (neck 2nd; and 3rd of 4); fell 3, and pulled up 4. Pulls like stink, and had his exuberance channelled in the right direction for once when scoring unchallenged on firmish at Higham last year, but has gone out like a light in both subsequent attempts, and his 9-8 rating is withdrawn. Tends to jump to the right, and might be trying to save a leg. *J. Burton — Atherstone.* 57 (R).

SOUNDTRACK (IRE) .10-7.. 12 b.g. Orchestra — Misty Boosh (Tarboosh USA) 12p3. Tall half-brother to Sheepcote Hill (IRE), and to Irish Pointing winner, Kilara. Dam won Maiden and NH flat in Ireland. P-t-P '98/9 (for Mr J.M. Kinnear) r10 p1 (2nd); failed to finish 5 (ran out 2, fell 1, and carried out 1). NH FLAT '99 r3 w1 p2 (2nds). NH '99/03 (for Miss V. Williams) r18 w6 (3 2m3f110y-2m6f110y Hdles, and 3 3m-3m2f Chses) p2; fell 1, pulled up 2. Made most in recording seven wins under Rules (a four-timer, and a hat-trick) to March '01, and also fell at the last when 12 lengths clear once, but not the same horse since falling at Aintree the following month, and missed most of '02. Found the ideal race in which to make a triumphant return to Pointing, and duly won unchallenged, but could not cope with an on-song Coole Venture in a match at Sandon, and went off much too fast for the prevailing conditions at Cheltenham. Turned the tables with Coole Venture at Bangor, but still finished 23 lengths off the winner, and will probably have to return to Opens to score at 12. Has lost little of his basic speed, and can still jump well, though inclined to be over-bold on occasions. *J.N. Eaton — Cheshire (Gary Hanmer).* 711 (O), 851 (O), 1171 (3m2f110yH), 1375 (3m110yH).

SOUTHERN CROSS .9-12§.. 13 ch.g. Buckley — Muznah (Royal And Regal USA) 473fp. Tall strong half-brother to 5 Hurdling winners, including Anzum (smart), Jazilah (FR) (useful; also successful on flat) and Nahar (useful); the other pair including Formal Affair, both also won on flat, and to NH flat winner, Roscom (in Ireland) and Sh Boom (also won Hurdling). Dam won 2 flat, 7-8f. NH FLAT '96 r4 w1 p1 (3rd). IRISH NH '98/9 r3 p0. NH '97/8 and '01 r13 p4; fell 1. P-t-P '00 and '02/3 r8 p4 (2 2nds, last once); last pair 2, unseated, and pulled up. Won a bumper on his first completion, but overwhelmed by his temperament and dropped the rider at the start on debut, and has contrived to remain a maiden over jumps despite 29 starts. Retains ability, but often makes mistakes, and managed to get left at the start when a well-backed favourite for his Members. Must be shunned. Has been tried in blinkers. *M. Stephenson — N. Ledbury (Tim Stephenson).* 403 (Cf), 612 (Cf), 836 (O), 1016 (3m2fO), 1253 (M).

SOUTHERN HA'I ..8-12.. 7 ch.m. Southern Music — Miss Bali Ha'i (Balinger) pf. Half-sister to Swan Song (*qv*). P-t-P '03 r2 p0 (unseated, and pulled up). Speedy and takes a strong hold, but had just been headed when falling at the last in a 2m4f Maiden at Mollington, and failed to reappear. Had also been in front when foiled by the fourth last once last year, and clearly has the ability to win over the shortened trip if she can eradicate her errors. Wears a cross-noseband. *T. Ellis — Warwicks.* 58 (OMa), 291 (2m4fCfMa).

SOVEREIGN DOVE ..9-5.. 6 b/br.m. Sovereign Water (FR) — Emerald Dove (Green Adventure USA) 22. Small. Second of three beaten four lengths and 20 lengths in Maidens, and gave encouragement in both and was not punished, and would probably appreciate less horrible conditions under foot. Seems sure to win in similar company before long. *W. & Mrs S. May — Worcs (Fred Hutsby).* 1035 (OMa), 1275 (OMa).

SOVEREIGN GALE (IRE) ..10-1.. 11 b.m. Strong Gale — Sovereign Sox (Don) 23111. Small half-sister to Terrano Star (IRE) and Nissan Star (IRE). IRISH P-t-P '99/00 r5 p1 (3rd); pulled up 2, and fell 1. NH '01 r4 p0; fell 1. P-t-P '01/2 r2 p0 (pulled up, and unseated). Injured by a loose horse when cannoned into on her only appearance in '02, and spent last year on the sidelines, but a speedy little thing, and completed a hat-trick in mares races on her return. Clocked a respectable time when scoring at Chaddesley, and possibly a shade fortunate at Garthorpe where the runner-up finished lame, but displays an attacking attitude and might be able to make an impression in Ladies races. Suited by good or fast ground. *Miss T. & L.H. McCurrich & J.E Doolittle — Clifton-on-Teme (Theresa McCurrich).* 151 (OMa), 259 (CMa), 714 (CMam), 1019 (Cm), 1398 (Cm).

PLATE 112 12 Army 567&8yo Open Maiden (Div 1): Spanish Dolphin and Nick Williams get away with a blunder at the fifth but later fell at 14th *PHOTO: Tim Holt*

SPANISH DOLPHIN (IRE) ..10-0.. 6 b.g. Dolphin Street (FR) — Alhambra Palace (IRE) (Cyrano De Bergerac) f1*0*. Tall workmanlike. NH FLAT '04 (for P.F. Nicholls) r1 p0 (11th over 2m110y at

Chepstow: *hld up & bhnd, hdwy 8f out, wknd 5f out, t.o*). Bought Doncaster, May for 7500. Fell at the 14th when in contention in a Larkhill Maiden, and then beat two subsequent scorers there despite pulling hard and lacking fluency. Missed the next three months and was badly tailed off in a bumper in May, but evidently rated good enough to warrant the transfer to Paul Nicholls, and may do better when switched to Hurdling. *C.W.W. Dupont — Cattistock (Richard Barber).* 12 (OMa), 86 (OMa).

SPARKLE (U) ..8-7.. 13 b.g. unknown u6. Compact. Contested a couple of Members races, and unseated at the sixth on the jockey's first ride before plugging round to finish 50 lengths last (a gallant effort for an unregistered 12-year-old). *M. Stevens — W. Somerset, & Devon & Somerset.* 273 (M), 1180 (M).

SPARKLING CASCADE (IRE) ..9-9.. 13 b.m. Royal Fountain — Yukon Law (Goldhill) u4. Small plain unfurnished half-sister to Molly Smith (IRE). P-t-P '99/00 (for Mr M.G. Tootell) r8 w1 (Maiden) p1 (2nd); 6th, and pulled up 5. NH '00/3 (for A.G. Newcombe) r13 p5 (inc 4 2nds in Chses); pulled up 3. Won a long Maiden at Flete Park in '00, and subsequently placed five times over fences without ever looking likely to score to August '02, but does not stand many outings, and flounders in mud. A first ride for Alex Lindner in her Members, and typically took a long time to warm to her task, but came with a storming run from the fourth last and was upsides the winner when the rider toppled off at the last. Far from disgraced when a never nearer two lengths last of four at Maisemore, and would be a most deserving winner in '05. *M.K.F. Seymour — N. Cotswold (Alexandra Lindner).* 921 (M), 1256 (R).

SPARKLING MISSILE ..8-12.. 12 ch.m. Cruise Missile — Sparkling Tarqua (Never Die Dancing) p1p. Rangy sister to Early Morning, and half-sister to Emilys Trust and Muckle Jack. Dam won 7 2m-3m2f110y Chses (inc 4-timer), and was 2nd in Grand Annual Ch for Mr James. P-t-P '99 r1 p0 (pulled up). Absent doing nothing since pulling up at long defunct Stallenge Thorne in '99, but surprisingly resurfaced this year, and stayed on to catch the odds-on favourite close home in a two-finisher Maiden on firm at Charlton Horethorne. Found wanting in competitive events and looks sure to have to rest on her laurels. *Dhobiwallah Racing (W.N. James) — Quantock (Sarah Robinson).* 322 (L), 355 (CfMa), 468 (M).

SPECIAL FRIEND (IRE) ..9-9.. 8 b/br.g. Be My Native (USA) — Lady Denys (Saint Denys) 1p. Well-made half-brother to Big Brazil (IRE), and to Irish NH flat winner, Gold-Buck. P-t-P '02/3 r2 p1 (2nd); and pulled up. Oozed quality when romping to victory in a slow Maiden on firmish on his reappearance at Higham, but has encountered all manner of niggling problems in his three-year career, and was not seen again for 15 weeks. Backed form 9-4 to 6-4 at Chaddesley, and went second behind the clear leader with a mile to run, but stopped in a matter of strides before pulling up three out. May have been inconvenienced by the cut in the ground, but although he is potentially underrated can only be watched when he returns. Wears a cross-noseband. *Mrs J. Thornton — Wheatland (Guy Landau).* 39 (OMa), 1345 (R).

SPEED BOARD (IRE) ..10-2.. 13 b.g. Waajib — Pitty Pal (USA) (Caracolero USA) p12p. Lengthy well-made half-brother to successful Hurdler, Bo Dancer (IRE), and to a flat winner. Dam a winning sprinter at 2 in USA. IRISH FLAT '94/5 r6 p1 (3rd). IRISH NH '95/02 r62 w7 (3 2m4f-3m1f Hdles and 4 2m4f-3m Chses) p9; ran out 1. P-t-P/HUNT CH '03 r2 p1 (½*l* 2nd); and unseated. Won his share in Ireland, and still retains ability, but there was more merit in his staying-on second of three finishers over four miles at Bonvilston than there was in his latest victory in a bad two-finisher Open on firm at Whitwick. Unfortunately went lame after a mile on his latest appearance. Often wears blinkers. *D. Pugh — Gelligaer F.* 209 (3m1f110yH), 514 (O), 1093 (4mMO), 1321 (MO).

SPENCIVE ..7-0.. 8 b.g. El Conquistador — Wood Heath (Heres) p3p. Plain strocky half-brother to jumping winner, Trying Again (9 wins), and to NH flat and Hurdles winner, Sprig Muslin. Dam fell and seventh in Points (*qv* '90 Annual). Pulled up at the fifth on arguably the worse debut of the year (looked appalling, almost refused at the first three fences, and was completely tailed off from the start; Quantock's Return is another live candidate), and then finished 60 lengths last of three after getting very tired and scrambling over the final three fences, and was pulled up after two miles (after early blunders). Seems to have come from the ragged school, and needs many more lessons. Spencive by John Manners' standards is usually dirt cheap compared to everybody else's. *H.J. Manners — V.W.H.* 368 (OMa), 633 (2m4fCfMa), 1067 (OMa).

SPICEY CASE ..8-7.. 6 b.m. Overbury (IRE) — National Case (Push On) ppp5. Small unfurnished. Dam, half-sister to Carbury's Case (*qv* '01 Annual), won Maiden for Nigel Lilley (*qv* '00 Annual). Toddled along before pulling up after 2m4f maximum in her first three Maidens, and then achieved a completion when 50 lengths last. Will have to improve a great deal if she is to get seriously competitive, but at least in the right yard if she does have any potential. *N. Lilley — Pentyrch (Cath Williams).* 676 (CfMa), 1192 (OMa), 1533 (OMa), 1550 (OMa).

SPIERS PEACE (IRE) ..8-12.. 6 b.g. Shernazar — Burling Moss (Le Moss) 1p. Well-made. Dam ran in 2 Points. Bought Doncaster, May for 5400. Won a Maiden at the first Larkhill meeting, but it was an awful contest, and the other three who got round have never managed to score. The elimination of Rostock (before the race) and Wild Chimes (who fell three out) was a huge help, and he was always lagging badly in a Restricted next time. Will have to improve to make a mark in that company. *P.S. & Mrs P.J. Awdry — Blackmore & Sparkford V. (John Dufosee).* 13 (OMa), 169 (R).

SPIKEY PASSAGE ..6-4.. 11 ch.g. North Col — Tuftess (Spartan General) 3. Half-brother to Southern Target. Dam is half-sister to 5 Pointers, including True Dowry (*qv* '94 Annual). P-t-P '01 r1 p0 (pulled up). Very much a part-time racehorse, and beaten 38 lengths when providing a newcomer with safe passage in his Members. *Mrs J.K. Buckle — Essex & Suffolk.* 828 (M).

SPILAW (FR) ..—.. 9 b.g. Sky Lawyer (FR) — Spinage (FR) (Village Star FR) fp. Lengthy. Dam won 2m Hurdle in France. FRENCH FLAT r2 p0. FRENCH NH '99/01 r10 w2 (1m7f Hdle and 2m2f Ch) p2 (2nds). NH '01/3 r21 w1 (2m Ch) p4; fell/unseated 3, pulled up 2. Effective in thick mud when winning a Hurdle at Toulouse and a Claiming Chase at Enghien, but has declined and generally shown little interest since, and although he did win a 2m Chase in November '01 has also been beaten in Selling Hurdles. Seemed to lose his confidence after falling on his Hunter Chase debut, and jumped like a clot and made numerous mistakes next time. May struggle to stay three miles and beyond. *J.S. Allen — Worcs.* 176 (3mH), 490 (3m2fH).

PLATE 113 1559 Tiverton Staghounds Open Maiden: Spinning Silver (Merv Woodward) wins a modest event PHOTO: Brian Armstrong

SPINNING SILVER ..8-2.. 10 b.g. Nearly A Hand — Paid Elation (Pia Fort) fu21. Lengthy. Tall strong-topped. Dam 'badly bred and virtually useless' (*qv* '97 Annual) was placed twice in Points (2nd of 3 and 3rd of 3). NH FLAT '00 r2 p0. NH '01/2 (for P.R. Rodford, and D.J. Minty) r6 p0; fell 2, pulled up 2. Awful under Rules at very long prices, and pulled up (soon tailed off) and fell at the first in Chases and was eighth, last, pulled up and fell in Hurdles including a Seller. Fell three out with Darren Edwards on his Pointing debut, and Merv Woodward so often associated with the most dreadful of horses (e.g. Roberts Return and Merv's Magic) then took over for an unseat at the first and a two fences last of two in a match after missing a marker and having to retrace. But it was good see him get the reward for perseverance in the direst of Maidens at Bratton Down on firm. Having struck once, lightning cannot be expected to do so again. *R.T. Grant — Tiverton Stag.* 1370 (OMa), 1450 (OMa), 1467 (OMa), 1559 (OMa).

SPINOSA ..7-12.. 7 br.m. Afzal — Rose Water (Waterfall) 3up. Small compact. NH FLAT '03 r1 p0. NH '03 (for Mrs P. Sly) r1 p0 (last). Has never given a good display, and was 48 lengths last of three in her only placing. Unable to complete since, and shows no sign of having any ability. *T.M. Fowler — Cottesmore (Louise Allan).* 945 (OMa), 1119 (CMam), 1402 (2m4fOMa).

SPIZZICHINO .9-6.. 9 b.g. Lancastrian — Garjun (IRE) (Orchestra) p73. Good-bodied lengthy owner-bred. NH FLAT '02 r1 p0. P-t-P '03 r5 w1 (3-finisher Maiden) p0; last, refused, pulled up, and fell.

Wayward in his early races, and left clear approaching the second last when landing a three-finisher Maiden at Hexham last year, but showed improved form when 17 lengths third in a Tabley Restricted on his latest appearance. Seemed to take exception to the open ditch, and took it at right angles both times, and needs to find extra to score in that grade. Wears a cross-noseband. *S. & Mrs G. Currie — V. of Lune H. (Stuart Currie).* 95 (R), 715 (R), 752 (R).

SPLASH AND DASH (IRE) .10-5.. 10 ch.g. Arcane (USA) — Quilty Rose (Buckskin FR) 561f21. Tall rangy half-brother to Irish Pointing and Chasing winner, Take The Lot (IRE). Dam won 14f amateur flat, and a NH flat race in Ireland. IRISH P-t-P '99/01 r6 w1 (6yo Maiden) p2; fell 1. P-t-P/HUNT CH '02/3 r6 w4 (inc 3m Hunt Ch and Open) p1 (2nd); and fell. Very lightly raced in the past, and hailed as a potential star performer after scoring on his Hunter Chase debut at Stratford last year, but bitterly disappointing in '04, and gained both wins in sub-standard Opens. Very lucky in the latter and clearly not right all year, and connections will have to re-think their strategy. Avoids ground any quicker than good. Has been bought by the Hickmans for syndication. *M.R. Smith — E. Sussex & Romney Marsh (Sara Hickman).* 100 (O), 280 (3m2f110yH), 642 (O), 800 (3m2f110yH), 1052 (O), 1315 (O).

SPORTING CHANCE ..10-7.. 13 ch.g. Ikdam — Tumbling Ego (Abednego) pp6p4u1. Sparely-made. Dam is half-sister to Parsons Brig (*qv* '99 Annual). NH FLAT '97 r1 p0. NH '97/8 and '02 r7 p0. P-t-P/HUNT CH '99/03 r14 w2 (Maiden and Restricted) p2 (inc 3rd in Hunt Ch); 4th, 5th, last pair 2, and pulled up 6. Landed a touch in a weak Maiden at Lifton in '99, but does not get the trip well enough in Points, and has specialised in springing surprises since. Scored at 25-1 last year, and sent off at the same price when allowed to bowl along instead of being held up on his final appearance at Newton Abbot. Clearly appreciated the change of tactics which had a beneficial effect on his jumping, but the sub-3m trip was also very much to his liking, and needs to concentrate on that sphere solely in future. Resented being tongue-tied once last year. *H.S. Channon — Lamerton (Yvonne Watson & Jo Channon).* 116 (I), 321 (I), 347 (3mH), 799 (2m3f110yH), 993 (3mH), 1166 (2m5f110yH), 1437 (2m5f110yH).

SPORTY SPICE (IRE) ..9-6.. 10 b.m. Indian Ridge — Intrinsic (Troy) 3p1. Leggy half-sister to Worthy Memories, to Irish flat and Hurdling winner, Bizana, and to a winner in Czech Republic. FLAT '97/9 r16 p1 (2nd). NH '99/00 r4 p0; pulled up 2. P-t-P '03 r5 p1 (2nd); pulled up 3, and carried out. Beaten in the lowest grade flat and Hurdling, but finally opened her account at the 28th attempt when landing a touch in a weak mares Maiden on firm at Musselburgh. Pulls hard, and has looked a non-stayer otherwise, and will have improve a good deal further for Restricteds. Blinkered once in '98. *R. Watt — Jedforest.* 131 (M), 287 (CfMa), 511 (OMam).

SPOT THE BUSINESS ..9-9.. 7 ch.g. Alderbrook — Ovington Court (Prefairy) 1. Half-brother to Rock Rose (*qv*). P-t-P '03 r1 p0 (fell). Typically favourite in both his starts, and looked rather a handful in '04, but led from halfway and battled on well enough to suggest he could achieve better things in the years ahead. Needs to prove he is not permanently fragile first. *R.G. Williams — Taunton V. (Richard Barber).* 307 (2m4fOMa).

SPOT THEDIFFERENCE (IRE) ..10-11.. 12 b.g. Lafontaine (USA) — Spotted Choice (Callernish) 22551. Tall. Dam is half-sister to Double Tricks (*qv* '95 Annual). IRISH P-t-P '98 and '03 r5 w2 (inc Open) p1. IRISH HUNT CH '01/2 r8 w2 p4 (3 2nds). IRISH NH '98/9 and '01/3 r12 w2 (3m100y-3m1f Chses). NH '99, '02 and '03 r3 p2 (2nds; in 4m NH Chse, and 4m110y Summer National); and unseated in '02 Grand National. HUNT CH '00 and '03 r3 p0 (6th, 8th and unseated 1). IRISH P-t-P '04 r1 p1 (4*l* 2nd to Arctic Times in Nenagh Open: *hld up, hdwy 9, ev ch 2 out, one pce*). IRISH HUNT CH '04 r1 p1 (1½*l* 2nd to Never Compromise at Leopardstown: *a.p, went 2nd aft 4 out, outpcd 2 out, rallied & nt much room flat, stayed on*). NH '04 r1 p0 (35*l* 5th in Grand National: *sn bhnd, mists 5 & 7, 20th ½way, stayed on wl frm 3 out, nvr nrr*). IRISH NH '04 r1 w1 (beat Shady Lad 14*l* in 4m2f La Touche Cup: *a.p, went 3rd 17 & 2nd 3 out, rdn to ld aft 2 out, clr last, comf*). A cracking horse who has contested many of the best staying Chases on both sides of the water, and proved to be as good as ever when stamina was at a premium in '04, but often takes an eternity to get into full flight, and remains a sketchy jumper. Recorded the biggest win of his career when romping home in the £11,500 La Touche at Punchestown, and plans are afoot to return to Cheltenham in March when a Cross Country Chase will be run for the first time at the Festival. Has been tried in blinkers and cheekpieces. *J.P. McManus — Limerick (Enda Bolger, in Ireland).* 543 (3m2f110yH).

SPOT THE NATIVE (IRE) ..9-1.. 9 ch.g. Be My Native (USA) — Shannon Foam (Le Bavard FR) R2u4. Tall half-brother to Chasing winner, Bunratty Castle (IRE). IR95,000 4yo. NH FLAT '01 r1 p0. NH '01/3 (for Miss H.C. Knight, and Mrs S.J. Smith) r12 p3 (2nd in Chse, 2 3rds in Hdles); unseated 2, and pulled up 1. Ten lengths second in a Chase and beaten between 14 lengths and 27 lengths when third in two Hurdles, but was tailed off last, pulled up and unseated at the first twice in Chases on his final four attempts under Rules. Can be very clumsy and has hung right, and soon left the course with a jockey having his first ride at Eyton-on-Severn, but was only beaten a neck in a Geldings Maiden at Eaton Hall where four subsequent winners finished behind him. Did not repeat that effort and was second and beaten when unseating two out in his Members (4-5), and ended the season with an 11 lengths fourth. Certainly has the ability to win a modest contest, but continually squanders opportunities, and is a long-standing disappointment. *F. Livesey — Holcombe (Michael Meagher).* 532 (OMa), 709 (Mah), 872 (M), 1142 (OMa).

SPRINGBOK NOODLES .—.. 6 b.g. Primitive Rising (USA) — Rivering (Rapid River) r. Half-brother to Dottie McQuirk. Dam was 3rd in her Members, and grandam, Star Slipper, was useless including in 2 Points. Reluctant to start in a Maiden, and having eventually decided to get going she would not jump the first fence. *G. & Mrs S. Frank — Hurworth (Paul Frank).* 774 (2m4fCMa).

SPRING CABBAGE (IRE) ..—.. 13 b.g. Mister Lord (USA) — Angie's Delight (London Gazette) pp. Strong workmanlike. Dam won mares Maiden in Ireland. IRISH P-t-P '98/9 r7 w1 (6yo&up Maiden) p2 (2nds); fell 2. IRISH NH FLAT '97 and '99 r4 p0. IRISH NH '99 r1 p0. P-t-P '02/3 r7 p1 (2nd); 4th, last pair 2, and pulled up 3. Got a flyer and made all in a long lead when scoring in heavy in Ireland in '99, but a rare failure in the current yard, and has frequently capitulated after giving prominent displays. Prone to clumsy mistakes, and unimproved by a tongue-tie once in '03. Clearly has insurmountable problems. *Dr P.P. Brown — Berkeley (Dick Baimbridge).* 759 (I), 1256 (R).

SPRING DOUBLE (IRE) ..10-3.. 14 br.g. Seclude (USA) — Solar Jet (Mandalus) 5122124. Close-coupled half-brother to On The Day (IRE), and to Irish Hurdling winners, Air Force One and Solar Quest (also won Chasing there). NH FLAT '96 r4 w1 p1 (3rd). NH '96/03 (for N.A. Twiston-Davies) r35 w4 (3 2m4f-3m1f Hdles and 3m Chse) p13; pulled up 5. A thorough stayer who won five races on good ground or in mud to November '01, and also placed on 14 occasions, but frequently wore headgear and was prone to slow jumps, and showed no zest on his final eight attempts under Rules. Found his way to the Mounsey-Heyshams from Uncle Nigel Twiston-Davies, and surprisingly showed renewed vigor at 13 and was able to supply both of the boys with a victory. Clearly likes the smaller fences and to his credit kept making the frame, but is one-paced, and at his most effective in moderate Confineds. *Mrs P.A. Mounsey-Heysham — Tynedale.* 134 (O), 210 (Cf), 340 (O), 425 (M), 654 (Cf), 857 (4mMO), 915 (Cf).

SPRINGFORD (IRE) ..11-8.. 13 b.g. King's Ride — Tickenor Wood (Le Bavard FR) 121112. Tall rangy hobdayed half-brother to Bolton Forest (IRE). Dam is sister to Carrickway (*qv* '88 Season Annual). IRISH P-t-P '96/8 r9 w1 (5&6yo Maiden) p3 (inc last of 3 twice); pulled up 1, fell 1. NH FLAT '98 r2 p0. NH '98/01 r12 w1 (2m6f Ch) p4 (3 2nds); pulled up 2. P-t-P/HUNT CH '02/3 r9 w3 (2 Opens and Mixed Open) p2 (2nds, beaten neck once); 5th of 6, fell/unseated 2, and pulled up. Ultimately disappointing under Rules, and scored just once from 14 attempts, but the current yard have certainly found the key to him, and has scored in seven of his last 10 starts. At his very best when going right-handed, but gained his current rating when runner-up in the Intrum Justitia Cup where he was really fourth best on merit. Normally a very fluent jumper, and most effective on good or fast ground, and looks sure to win more races when conditions are in his favour. A great advert for the skills of Caroline Keevil, and also gets excellent assistance from Dominic Alers-Hankey. Wears a cross-noseband. *M.J. O'Connor — Mendip F. (Caroline Keevil).* 598 (M), 733 (3mH), 825 (O), 1100 (O), 1298 (3m1f110yH), 1453 (3m4fH).

SPRING FROLIC ..—.. 7 b.g. Safawan — Springlark (IRE) (Lafontaine USA) uupu. Dam was placed in 4 of 6 Points. Unseated after a mile or less in three of four attempts, and twice got rid of a jockey having his initial rides at the very first fence. Had acquired blinkers by his third outing, and has been no fun thus far. *G.I. Cooper — Essex F. & U. (Cherie Cunningham).* 217 (M), 746 (OMa), 833 (OMa), 1312 (M).

SPRING GALE (IRE) .10-6§.. 14 b.g. Strong Gale — Orospring (Tesoro Mio) 32211113. Workmanlike lengthy brother to Hurdles winner, Cootehill Boy (IRE). NH FLAT '96 r2 p1 (3rd). NH '96/9 r23 w5 (3 2m4f-2m7f Hdles, and 2 2m4f-2m6f Chses) p12. P-t-P/HUNT CH '00/3 r32 w12 (2 3m110y Hunt Chses, and 10 Ladies, inc 4-timer) p15 (11 2nds, beaten head thrice, and inc 2 Hunt Chses; inc 2 3rds in Hunt Chses); refused 1, and fell/unseated 2. A model of consistency and a wonderful servant since joining the Turners in '00, and although he has been worried out of several close finishes in recent years still proves too good for his South Eastern counterparts on a regular basis. A very clever jumper, and acts on any going, but becoming increasingly mulish in the preliminaries, and is usually mounted on course and taken down early. Further strategic placing should enable him to score again. Often blinkered latterly under Rules. *J.M. Turner — Suffolk.* 126 (L), 373 (L), 558 (L), 831 (L), 1086 (L), 1244 (L), 1407 (L), 1516 (L).

SPRINGLEA TOWER ..9-8.. 12 b.g. Meadowbrook — Tringa (GER) (Kaiseradler) 4316285. Tall workmanlike half-brother to Hurdles winner, Turkish Tower, and to a jumping winner abroad. Dam won in Germany. Has stringhalt on off-hind. NH '97/01 r40 w1 (3m2f Chase) p7 (3 2nds); pulled up 7, and fell/unseated 5. P-t-P '02/3 r12 w1 (Confined) p8 (5 3rds, of 4 once; 3 2nds, beaten ½l once); and last pair 3. A very safe conveyance now, and has completed all 19 Pointing starts, but incredibly one-paced and needs plenty of driving along to stop him losing interest. Plugged on well from an unpromising position to score at Brocklesby Park, but his Members did not provide a stiff enough stamina test, and will be hard pressed to score again. Blinkered twice in '99. *R.S. Hunnisett — Quorn (Caroline Bailey).* 55 (Cf), 298 (Cf), 478 (Cf), 784 (Cf), 1056 (M), 1396 (C), 1500 (Cf).

SPRING MARATHON (USA) ..9-2§.. 15 b.g. Topsider (USA) — April Run (Run The Gantlet USA) 64. Tall good-bodied half-brother to 2 Irish Flat winners. Dam (trained in France by Francois Boutin) won 8 flat (10½-13½f), including Prix Vermeille, Turf Classic (twice), and Washington D.C. International, and made the frame in the Japan Cup and 2 Arcs. IRISH FLAT r1 p0. FLAT r3 p0. NH '93/5 and '97/9 r29 w5 (4 2m1f-3m2f Hdles and 3m2f Ch) p6; taken to Ireland once. P-t-P '97 and '00/3 (for Miss E.C. Tory) r26 w4 (inc Mixed Open and 2 Opens) p9 (5 2nds, beaten ½*l* once, and last once; inc 3rd of 4, and last of 3 once); pulled up 5, and unseated 1. A fair staying Hurdler, but never as convincing over fences, and his last two Pointing wins were very straightforward affairs. Provided David Green with his first rides, and led for a long way in his Members, but contributed to an annus horibilis for his trainer when sadly breaking down in the closing stages. *M.G. Green — S. Dorset (Mary Tory).* 11 (O), 233 (M).

SPRING PROMISE ..—§§.. 11 b.g. Petoski — Flippit (Dairialatan) r. Compact half-brother to Freddy Freckles, Samuelson, Dubit, Keep On Trying, Raymond's Lad and Just In Business. Dam won 2 Hunt Chses (3m-3m2f) and 8 Ladies and placed 15 (inc ½*l* 2nd in '80 John Corbet Cup). Grandam, Maiden Flight, won 2 Points and placed 9. P-t-P '03 r6 p1 (3rd); refused 2, pulled up 2, and unseated. Ominously blinkered on his debut, and set the tone for the rest of his career when refusing at the second. Beaten 38 lengths in his only completion, and tried visored when making the long journey to Cottenham on the opening day of the season, but threw in the towel yet again. Probably left behind on purpose as he has not been sighted since. *E.W. Dauncey — Blackmore & Sparkford V. (Rose Vickery).* 6 (OMa).

SPRING ROCK ..—.. 8 b.g. Rock Hopper — Shaft Of Sunlight (Sparkler) ppp. Lengthy well-made. NH FLAT '02 r2 p0. P-t-P '03 (for Mr R.M. Whitaker) r3 p1 (last of 3); and pulled up 2. Has had the assistance of five different riders in Points, all of whom are perfectly capable, but only one has managed to coax a completion out of him, and has jumped poorly for them all. Visored once in '02. *W.M. Aitchison — Border (Joanne Martin).* 137 (OMa), 433 (OMa), 1041 (OMa).

SPRINGWOOD HILL ..—.. 7 br.g. Totem (USA) — TV Pitch (FR) (Fast Topaze USA) p. Small close-coupled. Dam won 2m Hurdle at 50-1 for Don Lee. Very green and always last in a five-runner Maiden, and eventually pulled up after 2m3f. *D. Lee — Bilsdale.* 1206 (OMa).

SPRINGWOOD WHITE ..9-13.. 11 gr.g. Sharkskin Suit (USA) — Kale Brig (New Brig) p5p222p23. Tall half-brother to Hungry Jack. Dam, half-sister to Douglas Brig (*qv* '92 Annual), won a Restricted. NH '02/3 r5 p1 (3rd); unseated 1. P-t-P/HUNT CH '02/3 (for Mr J.L. Gledson) r12 w1 (Restricted) p2 (3rd in Hunt Ch once); pulled up 4. Missed out on a Maiden success when holding on to dead-heat for a soft ground Restricted at Alnwick last year, and beaten just under three lengths in a Hexham Chase on his only decent effort under Rules, but of greater value as a schoolmaster in the latest yard, and provided the newcomer Tim Park with a succession of good rides. Came closest to winning in a three-runner Open at Flagg, but has never been a strong finisher, and looks set to frustrate more often than not in '05. Has been tried in cheekpieces. *The Park Family (T. Park) — Cheshire Forest (Vicki Park).* 92 (I), 228 (Cf), 527 (I), 711 (O), 748 (M), 988 (O), 1171 (3m2f110yH), 1429 (Cnr), 1454 (3mH).

SPRUCE GOOSE (IRE) .8-2.. 9 b.g. Phardante (FR) — Whakapohane (Kampala) p3Rupp. Tall rangy hobdayed brother to jumping winner, Sublime Fellow (IRE), and half-brother to Irish Pointing and Hunter Chase winner, Thornbury Lady, to Irish NH Flat and English Hurdles winner, Lord Native (IRE). IRISH P-t-P '02 r6 p2 (2nds); pulled up 4. P-t-P '03 (for Mr N. Wilson) r2 p0 (pulled up 2). A poor performer. Beaten upwards of 15 lengths in three placings, but rendered next to useless by severe breathing problems, and unimproved by the application of a tongue-tie in '04. Wears a cross-noseband. *J. Hart — E. Sussex & Romney Marsh (Sara Hickman).* 539 (OMa), 611 (OMa), 895 (OMa), 1055 (OMa), 1395 (OMa), 1534 (OMa).

SPY BOY (IRE) ..9-4.. 9 b.g. Balla Cove — Spy Girl (Tanfirion) p3pp2p. Close-coupled half-brother to 3 flat winners, including Pearl Dawn, Witney-De-Bergerac, and to Irish Pointing winner, Dearmister-shatter. NH FLAT '00 r4 p1 (3rd); fell 1. IRISH NH FLAT '00/1 r3 p0. NH '00/3 (for J.S. Moore, when successful, and S.T. Lewis) r26 w1 (2m4f Hdle) p3 (3rds); ran out 1, unseated 2, and pulled up 4. Bought Ascot, Apr for 571. Won an awful Novices Claiming Hurdle run at Fontwell in driving rain when tried in a first-time visor (has also been blinkered since) but tried Sellers, and had been beaten 23 lengths plus in 21 consecutive races before he finished four lengths second in his Members on penultimate start. Normally deplorable, and Hunter Chasing him is a joke, although he did earn a little prize money after eventually walking in four furlongs last of three at Fontwell. *A. Green — Southdown & Eridge.* 422 (CCon), 581 (2m4fH), 800 (3m2f110yH), 1054 (Cf), 1411 (M), 1443 (2m5fH).

SQUADDIE .9-12.. 13 ch.g. Infantry — Mendelita (King's Company) 3p2212. Small lengthy brother to Company Commander. Dam won 3 Hdles and 3 Chses, all 2m. NH FLAT '97 r4 p3 (2 3rds). NH '98 r9 p1 (3rd). P-t-P/HUNT CH '00/3 r28 w4 (inc Mixed Open and 2 Opens, inc walkover and hat-trick '02) p6 (3 2nds; and inc 3rd of 4 twice, inc Hunt Ch); pulled up 6, and fell/unseated 4. Takes a keen hold, and completed a hat-trick in weakly contested events in '02, but does not get the trip particularly well, and looked doomed after finishing last year lame. Recovered sufficiently to make the frame five times in '04, and scored for the second time at Lifton, but turned over at 1-4 in a match at Umberleigh, and will surely struggle to find another opportunity at 13. *Mrs C. & Miss K.E. Lawrence — Eggesford (Carol Lawrence).* 80 (Cf), 320 (Cf), 821 (M), 1270 (Cf), 1540 (Cf), 1560 (Cf).

STABLE GIRL ..—.. 11 b.m. Baron Blakeney — Blazing Manor (True Song) p. Small unfurnished owner-bred half-sister to Manor's Maid, Tanborough and My Megan. Dam, sister, and half-sister to 3 Pointers, including Fury Manor, was 2nd in a Maiden for Mark Keith (broke down when poised to score on final appearance). P-t-P '00 and '03 r9 p1 (3rd of 4); (last, pulled up 6, and refused). Gave a fairly respectable display when nine lengths third of four in a slowly-run maiden on firmish at Mollington once, but the rest of her form is deplorable, and only went two miles in '04. Tends to jump slowly or make mistakes, and is probably not enjoying herself. *M.R. Keith — Pytchley.* 293 (CMam).

STAG PARTY (IRE) ..10-5.. 12 b.g. Buckskin (FR) — Men's Fun (Menelek) 24. Sturdy compact half-brother to De Profundis, to Irish NH flat and Chasing winner, Blazing Dawn (subsequently successful in England), and to Irish Pointing winner, The Vicarette. Dam won 2m2f Hurdle and 2m Chase in Ireland. IRISH NH '98/03 (trained for Edward Galvin by J.R.H. Fowler, when successful, himself, and A.J. Martin) r21 w1 (2m4f Ch) p4; fell 2, and pulled up 5. Won a Navan Chase in heavy in March '99, but normally disappointed in Ireland, and was pulled up on five occasions and fell twice, and tried in blinkers once. Has only made five appearances in the last three years, and having managed an apparently encouraging length second in a Confined he set himself too much to do when favourite for an Open and could only plug into 11 lengths fourth. Has never had the winning habit, and unlikely to acquire it at 12. *E. Galvin — N. Cotswold (Katie Baimbridge).* 980 (Cf), 1390 (O).

STALBRIDGE ROSE ..9-10.. 7 b.m. El Conquistador — Abridged (Nearly A Hand) 24f611. Small compact homebred sister to Stalbridge Bill, and half-sister to Stalbridge Return and Stalbridge Gold. P-t-P '03 r4 p0 (4th, last, and pulled up 2). Recorded narrow successes at both Hackwood Park meetings but proved reluctant to line up in the latest and hung left after she had hit the front. Strong handling seems vital, but needs to improve further if she is to cope with another step up in class. *Mrs T. Dufosee — Blackmore & Sparkford V. (John Dufosee).* 68 (OMa), 172 (OMa), 306 (2m4fOMa), 325 (OMa), 721 (OMa), 973 (R).

STAND ON ..9-4.. 7 b.g. Stani (USA) — Pennulli (Sir Nulli) pp1. Narrow compact owner-bred half-brother to Bright Beacon (*qv*). Sire, by Shahrastani, won 3 flat races (7-8f) for Ben Hanbury. Ran green and made mistakes in his first two races, but showed improvement to win a youngsters Maiden at Bonvilston, which looked an uncompetitive affair. The late lamented Bright Beacon will be a hard act to follow, but it is quite possible that he still has further improvement to come. *Mrs P. Tollit — Pentyrch (Cath Williams).* 676 (CfMa), 1096 (OMa), 1533 (OMa).

STANLEY ISLAND ..4-2.. 8 b.g. Stani (USA) — Teminny (Grey Love) 5fp. Leggy narrow half-brother to Elephants Child. Dam won 2-runner 2m Hurdle (her sole outing over jumps). Grandam, Scottish Colleen, won Maiden and placed 7. NH '02 (for M. Sheppard) r2 p0 (pulled up 2). About one and a half fences last on his only completion from five attempts, and after Jo Buck had nearly fallen off at the third he was tailed off from halfway. Would be useless even if competently handled. *Mrs C. Regan — Worcester & W. Farmers (James Danahar).* 982 (2m5fOMa), 1074 (OMa), 1532 (OMa).

STANTONS CHURCH ..8-11.. 8 b.g. Homo Sapien — Valkyrie Reef (Miramar Reef) p6p2u43. Compact. Dam won 2m2f Novice Selling Hurdle. NH '02/3 (for H.D. Daly) r6 p0; pulled up 1.A bad Hurdler who was tailed off when wearing cheekpieces in a Seller on his final attempt, and is inconsistent and probably ungenuine in Points, but did manage a couple of placings in Maidens. Two and a half lengths second over 2m5f after being present with the lead when the front pair departed two out, but found nil when collared at the last, and seven lengths third over the full trip. Would need an extremely weak race to score. *M.W. Jones — N. Hereford (Mark Doyle).* 256 (CMa), 410 (2m4fCfMa), 443 (2m4f110yH), 983 (2m5fOMa), 1393 (OMa), 1487 (OMa), 1533 (OMa).

STANWICK GYPSY ..9-5.. 7 b.m. Nomadic Way (USA) — Stanwick Monument (Grey Ghost) f3f241. Small neat half-sister to Harry Jay. Dam won 2 Points at Witton Castle (very lucky once) and 2 3rds. Her jumping is not the best, but had a fair first season when completing, and ended with a win at Alnwick where she was probably not going to catch Lord Lane until presented with the advantage two out. Had earlier chased home his useful stablemate River Alder, but normally starts at short prices, and not as good as the punters think. Will probably have to improve further for Restricteds. *I. Stark — Buccleuch.* 136 (OMam), 287 (CfMa), 433 (OMa), 549 (CMam), 767 (2m4fOMa), 859 (CfMa).

STAPLE SOUND ..8-0.. 8 b.g. Alflora (IRE) — Loch Scavaig (IRE) (The Parson) pp2p4. Workmanlike. Dam won NH flat and 5 Hurdles (2m3f-3m3f). NH FLAT '01 r3 p0. NH '02/3 (for W. McKeown, and J. Moffatt) r5 p0; pulled up 2. Normally looks very slow and cumbersome, and has worn a visor or cheekpieces, including in a Selling Hurdle. Plodded into the frame twice in '04 including when beaten a neck by I'm No Fairy in the most desperate of Maidens at Dalton Park (which took eight minutes), but probably too reluctant to have more than the tiniest hope of ever winning. *W. Burnell & R. Dobson — Badsworth & Bramham Moor (Wayne Burnell).* 271 (OMa), 394 (CfMa), 505 (CMa), 775 (CfMa), 985 (OMa).

STARBUCK ..10-1.. 11 b.g. Brush Aside (USA) — Clonmello (Le Bavard FR) p8p622311314. Good-topped half-brother to jumping winner, Rockcliffe Gossip, and to smart NH flat and Hurdles winner, Marello (11 wins unbeaten first 9 races). Dam, half-sister to Forest Run Forest (*qv*). NH FLAT '99 r1 p0. NH '00/1 r6 p1 (2nd). P-t-P '03 r11 w3 (Maiden, Restricted and Confined) p3 (2 2nds); 4th twice, and pulled up 2; also disqualified from 4th once — took wrong course. Appears to take a lot of getting fit, and has failed to score until eighth time out in both Pointing campaigns, and has done all his winning in the last week of April and May. A proven stayer, but one-paced, and finds some relatively straightforward tasks, and was beaten 19 lengths on his Hunter Chase debut when cheekpieces were re-applied. Thrice successful at Hexham. *Miss J. Fisher — Lauderdale.* 72 (O), 134 (O), 210 (Cf), 330 (3mH), 506 (Cnr), 656 (O), 917 (O), 1079 (O), 1219 (M), 1296 (3m1fH), 1477 (O), 1526 (3m2fH).

PLATE 114 405 Ross Harriers Intermediate (Nov Rdrs) (Div 1): L to R, Star Changes (Natalie Lloyd), 1st, and Stride To Glory (Matt Hooper), 2nd *PHOTO: David Jones*

STAR CHANGES ..10-0.. 12 b.g. Derrylin — Sweet Linda (Saucy Kit) 1131. Smallish compact half-brother to Troubadour Boy and Spirit Of Success. Dam won Members and placed 7. NH FLAT '98 r1 p0. NH '01 r1 p0 (6th). P-t-P/HUNT CH '98/03 (for Mr A. Hollingsworth) r32 w4 (up to Confined) p10 (short-headed once; and 5 3rds, of 4 twice; also disqualified from 3rd once — not weigh-in); pulled up 6. Won his share in the previous yard, but never raised his rating above 10-2 in six campaigns, and rarely strung two decent runs together. The sight of newcomer Natalie Lloyd in a tight-fitting Mohair sweater has clearly done him a power of good (as well), and the combination recorded three hard fought successes in minor contests together, but typically trounced in a more competitive race at Sandon. Led to post early in '04. Makes the odd mistake but has never fallen. Blinkered once in '99. *Miss N. Lloyd — Sir W.W. Wynn's (S.H. Lloyd).* 405 (Inr), 708 (M), 849 (L), 989 (Cnr).

STAR GLOW ..10-6.. 11 b.g. Dunbeath (USA) — Betrothed (Aglojo) 1. Small angular half-brother to Cartoft Dancer and Engaged, to Hurdles winner, Peep O Day, and to Irish NH flat winner, The Paddiad (IRE). Dam won 2 2m Hdles, inc Sell. NH FLAT '99/00 r4 p0. NH '00/1 r6 p2; pulled up 1. P-t-P

'02/3 r8 w4 (up to Confined) p2 (2nds, last once); fell and pulled up. A most progressive individual in '03, and had notched a four-timer by March 9th, and kept up the good work when successful at Higham for the third time on his reappearance, but injured in an accident involving a horse-walker subsequently and has not been seen since. Gives the impression he would score in Open class if he has come to no lasting harm. Acts in softish and on firmish. *R.H. York - Staff College.* 28 (I).

STARLIGHT STRIKER ..—.. 7 b.g. El Conquistador — Bunyan Striker (Baron Blakeney) p. Big strong. Dam (*qv* '97 Annual) won Maiden and placed 4 for Pattie Dod (famed as the lady pole-axed by the flag at Larkhill). Pulled up after two miles in a mid-March Maiden. *Mrs P. Dod — Blackmore & Sparkford V.* 493 (OMa).

STAR OF KILCASH (IRE) ..9-4.. 12 b.g. Nearly A Nose (USA) — Attagirl (Kemal FR) p5. Dam, half-sister to Butterfly Lilly (*qv* '87 Season). IRISH P-t-P '99 and '02 r9 w1 (Maiden) p0. P-t-P '03 r1 p0 (7th). Won his only start of '99, but missed the next two years, and has performed as though something is amiss in a mere three outings for present connections. *A.E.S. Nuttall, Mrs V.M. Graham, S. & Mrs G. Cooke — S. Devon (Valerie Graham).* 706 (R), 824 (R).

STAR OF RAVEN ..10-8.. 8 b.m. Sea Raven (IRE) — Lucy At The Minute (Silly Prices) p122p. Small light. Dam was a very moderate Pointer (rated 9-0) for Nick Saville. IRISH NH FLAT '01/2 r3 p0. P-t-P/HUNT CH '03 (for Panama Bloodstock) r4 w2 (Maiden and Restricted) p1 (2nd); and unseated. Game and a thorough stayer, and suited by mud, and showed the benefit of a pipe-opener at Alnwick when springing a 16-1 surprise at Wetherby, where course specialist Master Wood chased her home. Never got conditions to suit subsequently, and was particularly disappointing in the John Corbet, but in a shrewd yard, and looks certain to atone in '05. *J. Saville — Pendle Forest & Craven.* 72 (O), 122 (3m1fH), 442 (2m7f110yH), 1374 (3m1fH), 1452 (3m4fH).

STAR OF WILLIAM (IRE) ..8-11.. 6 ch.g. Idris (IRE) — Fais Vite (USA) (Sharpen Up) p3f. Small light-framed half-brother to Maximus (IRE), to jumping winner, Druid's Glen (IRE), and to 2 flat winners (one on France), including Bo Knows Nigel. Related to fair winners, but a weedly specimen himself, and the best that he has managed is a 15 lengths third of four. Led for over two miles on that occasion and looks rather headstrong, but has not shown he gets the trip so far. *W. McKeown — B. Gill — Celtic Bloodhounds.* 1495 (OMa), 1525 (OMah), 1565 (OMa).

STARPATH (NZ) ..9-12.. 13 ch.g. Starjo (NZ) — Centa Belle (NZ) (Centurius) 46p*p*. Big rangy. NZ FLAT '97 r3 w1 (10f). NZ NH '97/9 r12 w1 (2m4f Ch) p3 (3rds). P-t-P/HUNT CH '00/3 r18 w4 (inc 3m7f Hunt Ch and 4m Ladies) p4 (2nds, of 3 once and inc Hunt Ch); 4th thrice, 5th, last pair 3, pulled up and fell/unseated 2. IRISH P-t-P '04 r1 p0 (pulled up at Tattersalls Farm: *bhnd til pu 12*). IRISH NH '04 (for A.J. Martin) r1 p0 (pulled up in 4m2f La Touch at Punchestown: *a bhnd, t.o & pu 6 out*). A dour stayer on his day, and rated 10-9 at his best, but seemingly under a cloud '02/3, and only averages four outings per annum nowadays. A sound jumper, and suited by mud, and ran his best race for some time when 15 lengths fourth over 3m5f at Dunthrop, but easy to outpace over standard trips, and probably only of use as a schoolmaster now. Qualified with a Tara certificate in Ireland, but both outings there in April proved fruitless. Wears a cross-noseband. *J.J. Boulter & Miss F.J. Wilkins - S. Dorset (John Boulter).* 48 (3m5f70yL), 175 (Cnr).

START IT UP..7-0.. 9 b.g. Itsu (USA) — Star Part (West Partisan) 4b2p3p. Very small light owner-bred brother to Its A Handfull (*qv*). P-t-P '02/3 r7 p1 (3rd of 4); last, pulled up 3, ran out, and carried out. Makes the frame whenever he completes, but a weak finisher and beaten 12 lengths plus to date, and will need to be extraordinarily lucky to stumble across a winning opportunity. Wears a cross-noseband. *J.J.E. Price — Curre & Llangibby.* 363 (CfMa), 699 (CfMa), 1027 (OMa), 1324 (CfMa), 1487 (OMa), 1525 (OMah).

STATE AFFAIRS (IRE) .—.. 9 ch.g. Political Merger (USA) — Bridewell Belle (Saulingo) fp. Tall strong half-brother to Tumbled Bride, to Hurdles winner, Fandango Kiss, and to Irish NH flat winner, Fair Gayle and an Italian flat winner. Dam won at 8f in Ireland. NH FLAT '00 r2 p0. NH '03 (for R. Hollinshead) r3 p0 (pulled up 3). His five outings over jumps have yielded four pulled-ups and a fall, and looked useless in a couple of early season Maidens. *Mr & Mrs R.H. Kerswell — Dart V.H. & S. Pool H. (Liam Corcoran).* 67 (OMa), 326 (OMa).

STATELY BIV .—.. 10 b.g. State Diplomacy (USA) — Another Biv (Bivouac) u. Compact. Dam failed to finish in 5 Points for Mary Wilkin ('as useless as her dam'). Grandam Another Tudor pulled up 3, and fell in Points for her. Jumped hesitantly and was already toiling when he blundered and unseated at the fourth in an early March Maiden. Bred to never complete the course, and it would beggar belief if he did so. *Miss M. Wilkin — Middleton (Cherry Coward).* 395 (CfMa).

STATELY PROGRESS (IRE) ..7-10.. 7 b.g. Nashwan (USA) — Khamsin (USA) (Mr Prospector USA) 8p. Half-brother to 4 flat winners (one in France), including Khalkissa, Subeen and Springtime Romance. Bought Doncaster, Nov for 3000. With Ed Dunlop for the flat but never ran, and tailed off in both Points including when hopelessly tailed off last once. Seems troubled. *Mrs S. Corbett — Border (William Corbett).* 920 (2m4fOMa), 1224 (OMa).

PLATE 115 1461 Dulverton Farmers Members: State Medlar (Richard Woollacott), 1st, leads Chapners Cross (Tigger Barnes), pu *PHOTO: Brian Armstrong*

STATE MEDLAR ..9-11.. 14 ro.g. Pragmatic — Lizzie The Twig (Precipice Wood) 31u2211. Strong-topped half-brother to Raise A Loan, to Chasing winners, Our Ghillie and Miss Wizadora, and to Hurdles winner, Crazy Crusader. Dam, half-sister to the dam of Reptile Princess (*qv* '00 Annual), was 2nd in an Adjacent. P-t-P '97, '00 and '02/3 (for Mrs N.P. Horton) r9 w1 (Maiden) p0; 5th, last pair 2, pulled up 3, carried out 1 and ran out 1. Another to benefit from a move to the current yard, and raced almost as often in '04 as he had in four previous campaigns, and landed a touch in a soft ground Restricted at Kilworthy. As in the past proved to be less effective on firmish, but connections can reflect on a job well done, even if he does not manage to boost his winning tally next year. Jumps well and the only time he has lost a partner was at the first when novice ridden. *D. Underhill — Dulverton F. (Emely Thompson).* 323 (R), 571 (R), 794 (Inr), 1271 (I), 1431 (I), 1461 (M), 1544 (I).

STAY LUCKY (NZ) ..9-5§.. 16 b.g. Sir Sydney (NZ) — Against The Odds (NZ) (Harbor Prince USA) p. Workmanlike brother to a winner in New Zealand, and half-brother to another. NZ FLAT w4. NZ NH w1 (Ch). NH '96/9 r9 p4 (2nd in Hdle, and 3 Chses); one run Punchestown. P-t-P/HUNT CH '00/3 r21 w2 (Confined and Club Novice Riders) p7 (6 3rds, of 4 twice); pulled up 2. Occasionally blinkered under Rules. Scoring for the first time since leaving his homeland when tried in first-time cheekpieces at Dunthrop in '02, and was awarded his next race on a technicality, but tends to make mistakes and run in snatches, and has not co-operated since. Most unlikely to make an appearance at 16. *J.G. Phillips — V.W.H. (Simon Bloss).* 756 (Cf).

ST BEE ..9-4.. 10 br.g. St Ninian — Regal Bee (Royal Fountain) 9854p4322317. Big strong owner-bred half-brother to Stinging Bee. Dam, half-sister to Zam Bee (*qv* '00 Annual), won 2m4f Hdle. Grandam, Brown Bee III, won 2m Hdle and placed 2, and won an Open. NH '00 r2 p0 (last and pulled up). P-t-P '02 r6 p1 (3rd of 4); 4th, 6th, last pair 2, and pulled up 1. NH '02/3 r13 p0; fell/unseated 4, and pulled up 3. Adept at course completion in Points, and finally graduated at the 32nd attempt when getting up in the shadows of the post to catch an equally frustrating character at Hexham. A thorough stayer, but beaten a minimum of 25 lengths over regulation fences, and looks like proving difficult to pace successfully again. Very fat in early season '04. Wears blinkers, and has been tried in cheekpieces. *W.G. Reed — Tynedale.* 212 (R), 330 (3mH), 425 (M), 553 (CfMa), 766 (R), 857 (4mMO), 1041 (OMa), 1224 (OMa), 1311 (OMa), 1422 (OMa), 1475 (OMa), 1526 (3m2fH).

STEADY LASS (IRE) ..6-0§.. 7 b.m. Glacial Storm (USA) — Adare Moss (IRE) (Le Moss) 36up. Unfurnished. Dam sister to There Tis For Ya (*qv* '99 Annual). P-t-P '03 r2 p0 (pulled up 2). Barely qualified for a miniscule rating when one-and-a-half fences last of three at Friars Haugh, and has looked far from keen since. *Mrs J.D. Bulman — Cumberland F. (Sue Murtagh).* 136 (OMam), 286 (CfMa), 761 (M), 859 (CfMa).

STEEL GEM (IRE) ..9-0.. 16 b.g. Flash Of Steel — Ferjima's Gem (USA) (Wajima USA) 224p. Long-backed half-brother to a star performer in Venezuela. IRISH FLAT r11 p2. IRISH NH '93/5 r10 p5. NH '95/7 r7 p2. P-t-P/HUNT CH '99/01 and '03 r13 w1 (Maiden) p3 (remote 2nd; and 2 3rds, last once, and inc Hunt Ch); 5th, and pulled up 8. Won a long Maiden at Sandon in '99, and placed five times subsequently, but never lived a charmed life, and dropped dead after pulling up at Llanvapley. Mrs C.E. Breese — Curre & Llangibby (Sarah Kent). 356 (M), 451 (R), 740 (R), 844 (R).

STEEL RIGG (IRE) ..8-4.. 13 ch.g. Lancastrian — Cute Play (Salluceva) pOpu. Compact half-brother to Cheater (IRE), and to jumping winners, Gysart (IRE) and Tribal Dancer (IRE) (latter also won NH flat), to Irish Hurdles winner, Risetotheoccasion (IRE), and to Irish Pointing winner, Crooked Answer. Dam is half-sister to high-class Irish Hurdler/useful Chaser, Straight Row. NH FLAT '98 r3 p1 (2nd); 4th, and 9th. NH '98/02 r8 w1 (2m4f Nov Hdle) p2 (2nd in Ch; and distant 3rd). P-t-P/HUNT CH '98 and '00/3 r24 w1 (Open) p6 (3 2nds, beaten ½*l* once; 3 3rds, inc Hunt Ch); pulled up 7, and fell/unseated 4. A dual scorer at Hexham to '00, but a consistently dreadful jumper, and has slumped into an irreversible decline. Has been tried in blinkers and a tongue-strap. *O.R. & H. Dukes — York & Ainsty S.* 163 (O), 267 (Cf), 338 (Cf), 389 (Cf).

STENNIKOV (IRE) ..10-1.. 9 b.g. Good Thyne (USA) — Belle Bavard (Le Bavard FR) 3u23134. Tall lengthy half-brother to Better By Half (IRE), to Chasing winner, Couldn't Be Better (won '96 Hennessy Cognac Gold Cup, and a £16,125 Chase at Gowran in '97), to NH flat and Hurdles winner, Queenford Belle, and to Irish Chasing winner, Mr Moylan. Dam won 2m Hurdle. IR75,000 4yo. NH FLAT '01 r3 w1 p0. NH '02/3 (for P.F. Nicholls) r5 p2. A bumper winner in soft, and was beaten between three and 29 lengths when placed in a couple of 2m4f Hurdles. Only seen once in '03, but returned for a decent season in Points, and won his Members at Paxford after the only danger had unseated at the last. Also second in a finish of short heads at Mollington, and failed to complete the course for the only time over jumps when the saddle slipped and he unseated on the bend at Bishops Court. Consistent, and may be able to find another opportunity. *Mrs B.A. Marshall — N. Cotswold (Emma Baker).* 141 (I), 321 (I), 584 (I), 728 (I), 921 (M), 1071 (I), 1254 (Cf).

PLATE 116 527 Tanatside Intermediate: Step And Run initiates a double for Jane Williams at the meeting *PHOTO: Brian Armstrong*

STEP AND RUN (IRE) ..10-5.. 9 ch.g. Step Together (USA) — Judy Run Home (IRE) (Deep Run) 1113. Compact well-made half-brother to Irish NH flat and Hurdling winner, Judy's Home Valley. IRISH P-t-P '01/3 r12 w1 (6yo&up Maiden) p2 (3rds); pulled up 6, and slipped up 1. Had a modest record in Ireland, but Jane Williams has got a much better tune out of him, and completed a hat-trick before being let down by his jumping when odds-on to beat Upton Adventure at Chaddesley Corbett (was already struggling four out, and eventually lost second in the final strides). Errors are never far away with him, and can look a difficult ride tactically, as he tends to lose his place after two miles only to rally gamely in the important stages. Left it until the last moment in a Cottenham Restricted, but much more emphatic in the next two wins, and is a thorough stayer who will be difficult to beat in Ladies Opens when avoiding the local heroine. *Mrs A.D. Williams — Albrighton Woodland.* 102 (R), 527 (I), 664 (L), 1017 (3m2fL).

STEPASIDEBOY ..10-2.. 15 b.g. Idiot's Delight — Waterside (Shackleton) f22. Tall strong brother to Red Rory, and half-brother to Chasing winner, Countess Blakeney. P-t-P '95/6 (for Mr E.H. Crow) r4 w2 (Club Maiden and Restricted) p0; ran out 2. NH '98/01 (for R. Curtis, when successful, and Miss D. Cole) r12 w2 (2m4f Hdle, and 3m Ch) p1 (2nd); pulled up 5. Speedy, and won both his completed Points in '96, and over hurdles and fences in '98, but subsequently pulled up four times in succession '99/00, and was found to be breaking blood vessels. Racing for the first time since October '01 when falling at Bratton Down, but was not disgraced, and was unlucky to come up against Harnage in his Members which was run in the fastest time of the day there next time. Wore bandages behind and jumped stickily when last of two on the mechanically lifted ground at Umberleigh, but it was good to see him enjoying himself again after so much time off. *I.J. Webber — Tiverton Stag.* 1510 (O), 1554 (M), 1562 (O).

STEP IN LINE (IRE) ..9-3.. 13 gr.g. Step Together (USA) — Ballycahan Girl (Bargello) ppp4p. Small half-brother to Dos Desperados (IRE). IRISH NH '96 r2 p0. IRISH P-t-P '97 r2 w1 (4&5yo Maiden) p0. NH '97/01 r40 w3 (2m110y-2m5f110y Chses) p14; inc Sells. P-t-P/HUNT CH '98 and '02/3 (for Fernhurst Racing Club) r17 w2 (inc Ladies) p11 (5 2nds, and inc 3rd in Hunt Ch); last pair 3, and pulled up 1. A patent safety, and won three of his first five Points, and subsequently on three of his 20 visits to Newton Abbot when in the care of Jimmy Frost, but woefully one-paced now, and out of luck in his last 23 starts. Has run tongue-tied, and gurgled on his reappearance, and his wind seems so bad now that it will be surprising if he reappears. Wears a cross-noseband. *Mrs S.A. Hodge — E. Anglian Bloodhounds.* 5 (L), 157 (L), 522 (L), 650 (O), 1154 (L).

STEP ON EYRE (IRE) ..10-0§.. 15 b.g. Step Together (USA) — Jane Eyre (Master Buck) 1p123. Tall rangy brother to American Eyre, and half-brother to 3 Irish winners, including Noble Eyre (NH flat — subsequently won English jumping). Dam won an Irish Point. IRISH NH FLAT '95/6 r5 w2 (2m-2m4f) p0. IRISH FLAT '96 r1 p0. IRISH NH '96/7 r5 w2 (2m Hdles) p2 (2nds). NH '97/02 r26 w6 (2m4f110y-4m1f Chses) p8. P-t-P/HUNT CH '03 r5 w1 (Open) p1 (3rd of 4 in Hunt Ch); 4th twice, and pulled up 1. A very thorough stayer and suited by mud, and having gurgled in '03 underwent a soft-palate operation, and reaped the benefits when adding another two firsts to his portfolio this year. Lucky at Weston Park, where Mickthecutaway was in command when falling at the last, but scored on merit under a strong drive from Richard Burton at Flagg before suffering a surprise defeat at 1-3 in an eight-minute race at Alpraham. Might have given the winner more to do had he not rooted the last over four miles at Cold Harbour, but becoming very much a plodder now, and will be difficult to place if returning at 15. Blinkered once in '00. *J.E. & C. Stockton, A. Wynne, R. Hewitt & G. Moir — Sir W.W. Wynn's (Steve Wynne).* 229 (O), 435 (3m110yH), 988 (O), 1047 (O), 1228 (4mO).

STEPONTHEBANDIT .8-0.. 9 b.m. Safawan — Anagmor's Daughter (Funny Man) ppp. Lengthy. Dam won 2 Hurdles (2m4f-2m6f) and 2 3m-3m2f Chses; and pulled up when ridden by Jimmy Frost once, and is half-sister to Annaghmor's Son (*qv* '94 Annual). Pulled up in the closing stages on each of her three outings, but was favourite for the middle run, and still held every chance when she ran very wide on the bend after three out and failed to recover. Well beaten next time, but it might be too soon to right her off just yet. *J.D. Frost — Dartmoor.* 1001 (M), 1200 (OMa), 1371 (OMa).

STEVE FORD ..8-9.. 16 gr.g. Another Realm — Sky Miss (Skymaster) 33f554p. Compact brother to Alsemero, and half-brother to 3 flat winners. NH FLAT '93 r3 p0. NH '94/5 '97/9 and '01 r32 w4 (2 2m-2m5f Hdles, and 2 2m5f Chses) p10 (inc 2 Sell Hdles to '95, but never run in them since). P-t-P/ HUNT CH '01/3 r9 p2 (remote last of 3 once); 5th, last pair 3, pulled up 2, and fell 1. Won four races on sound surfaces at up to 2m5f to '98, but never remotely involved at the finish in Points, and it was sad to see him pull up lame when 150-1 at Umberleigh. *I.F. & Miss E. Harbour — V. of Aylesbury with Garth & S. Berks (Sue Harbour).* 622 (M), 866 (M), 1029 (3mH), 1104 (Cnr), 1399 (L), 1492 (Cf), 1563 (L).

STEVIE DEE .9-6.. 11 ch.g. Emperor Fountain — Babe In The Wood (Athens Wood) u6pu. Sturdy half-brother to 5 flat winners (2 abroad). Dam is half-sister to Tangier Star (*qv* '93 Annual). IRISH NH FLAT '99 r3 p1 (3rd). IRISH NH '99/00 r12 p2. NH '00/1 r5 p1 (3rd); pulled up 3. P-t-P '02 (for Mrs P. Clowe-Jowsey & Mrs S. Nicholls) r5 w1 (Maiden) p3 (2nds); and 5th. Landed a long Maiden in soft at Wetherby in '02, but formerly disappointing under Rules, and forced onto the sidelines last year. Error-prone and not better than last in the new yard, and gives the impression of being wrong. Visored once in '01. *R.A. Maletroit & Dr C. Mahmoud — Brocklesby (Robin Maletroit).* 54 (C), 106 (C), 377 (3m1fH), 481 (R).

STICK OR BUST ..9-3.. 10 b.g. Bustino — Howanever (Buckskin FR) p144u3. Light-framed half-brother to Pear Tree Percy (*qv*). P-t-P '00/3 r12 w1 (Maiden, 3 ran — 2 finished) p3 (2 2nds; and 3rd of 4); 4th of 5, 5th, unseated 1, and pulled up 5. Won a two-finisher Maiden on firmish at Horseheath in '02, and benefited from the application of cheekpieces when successful in a four-runner Members this year, but has had an operation to try to correct a sinus problem, and has been beaten a minimum of 15 lengths in Restricteds. Upsides the leader when unseating three out at a Bank Holiday meeting once, but will struggle to score when the opposition is stronger. *R.D. & Mrs S. Green — Fitzwilliam (Katie Thory).* 223 (I), 555 (M), 902 (R), 1152 (R), 1245 (R), 1316 (R).

STICKWIYADAD ..—.. 9 b.g. Perpendicular — Sister Racine (Dom Racine FR) ppp. Tall rangy. A lumbering hulk who has jumped poorly, and seems to be exceptionally slow. *T. Wood — Cleveland (Lynne Ward).* 167 (OMa), 394 (CfMa), 1165 (OMa).

STINGO .—.. 8 b.m. Scorpio (FR) — Mary's Double (Majetta) pp. Small sister to Can't Smile, and half-sister to Onawing Andaprayer and Ad Lib, and to Irish NH flat and English Hurdles winner, Cainsbridge Queen. Dam won 2m5f Hurdle in Ireland. Went less than a mile before the saddle slipped on her debut, and was then very tired and tailed off when pulling up in a 2m5f Maiden. *R. Haddow — Cottesmore.* 476 (CfMa), 596 (2m5fOMa).

STOCKTON WOLF ..9-2.. 12 b.g. Little Wolf — Stockton Slave (Bivouac) 203p. Stocky compact owner-bred half-brother to Four Opinions (*qv*). P-t-P '02/3 r7 p2 (2nds, remote once); last, pulled up 2, and fell/unseated 2. Unraced until he was nine, and thrice runner-up in Maidens, and beaten half-a-length in the latest, but inclined to make mistakes, and does not stand his racing well. Looks like losing his race against time. *R.G. Edwards — Clifton-on-Teme (Sally Isaac).* 258 (CMa), 403 (Cf), 519 (CfMa), 1020 (OMa).

STONESBY (IRE) ..9-13.. 13 b.g. The Bart (USA) — Maid In The Mist (Pry) 314. Compact half-brother to Bruce's Castle. NH FLAT '97 r2 p1 (3rd). NH '97/00 r14 w2 (2m3f Hdle and 2m Ch) p4 (3 3rds); pulled up 1, and fell 1. P-t-P/HUNT CH '02/3 r5 w1 (2-runner Members) p2 (3rds); and pulled up 2. Won once apiece over hurdles and fences to '99, and has beaten one rival when recording back-to-back wins in the Berks & Bucks Members, but tends to hang and jump right, and does not truly get the trip in Points. A first success after 11 years trying for Matthew Keen (who clearly did not want to rely solely on his own Jurist in the concluding Maiden) at Kingston Blount. *Mrs J.M. Duckett — Warwicks, & Berks & Bucks (Geoffrey Deacon).* 1276 (M), 1513 (M), 1516 (L).

STONE VALLEY ..9-12.. 8 ch.g. Triune — Elmley Brook (Paddy's Stream) u11f4. Compact sturdy half-brother to Brook A Light. Dam fell, ran out 2 (continued for last of 3 once) and refused 3 in Points. Trying to refuse when he blundered badly and unseated at the sixth on a novicey debut, but then showed versatility when completing a double in a 2m4f Maiden on firmish at Great Trethew and a long Restricted taking nearly seven minutes in soft at Kilworthy. Fell at the second after getting a bad start next time, and then 16 lengths last when beaten favourite, but may be able to put these disappointments behind him and return to the winners enclosure in '05. *A.J.S. Knox & J. Chanin — Silverton (Robert Chanin).* 61 (M), 309 (2m4fOMa), 572 (R), 823 (Cf), 1271 (I).

STONEY RIVER (IRE) .9-12§.. 11 b.g. Riverhead (USA) — Another Space (Brave Invader USA) 55353. Workmanlike half-brother to Paddy Burke (IRE) and Another Ace. IRISH P-t-P '99 r2 p0 (pulled up 2). NH '01 r3 p2 (3rds in 2m7f110y-3m2f110y Chses). P-t-P/HUNT CH '00/3 r18 w5 (up to Confined, inc hat-trick '00) p5 (4 2nds, beaten head once, and neck of 3 once); 4th thrice, 5th, pulled up 3 and unseated 1. Made an impressive start to his career in England, but made a noise when thwarted in his bid for a four-timer, and left the previous yard under a cloud. Still retains ability but will not entertain revealing it to the full, and merely looks after number one these days. One of Simon Walker's better mounts in '04 — what a waste. *P. England — Badsworth & Bramham Moor.* 340 (O), 592 (O), 808 (CfCon), 1459 (L), 1501 (L).

STORM AHEAD (IRE) ..9-0.. 11 b.g. Glacial Storm (USA) — Little Slip (Super Slip) 52f. Good-topped brother to Normins Hussar (IRE). IR12,000 4yo. IRISH NH FLAT '99/00 r5 p2. IRISH NH '00/1 r5 p0; fell 1. NH '01/3 (for N.G. Richards, and A. Parker) r12 p1 (2nd); pulled up 3, and unseated 1. Should have the ability to win a Maiden, but a weak finisher, and was outridden when three lengths second on his best attempt of '04. Often tongue-tied and wore cheekpieces once under Rules, and was a poor jumper in Chases in which he finished 35 lengths fourth, pulled up twice and unseated. Already beaten 26 times, and is a bit of an old bore. *Mrs S.H. Shirley-Beavan & Col R.J. Martin — Jedforest (Philippa Shirley-Beavan).* 137 (OMa), 287 (CfMa), 1224 (OMa).

STORMALONG (IRE) ..9-5.. 9 b.g. Little Bighorn — Mamie's Fun (Lord Gayle USA) 54p. Compact brother to Irish Hurdles winner, Timmy's Holly (IRE). NH FLAT '01 r1 p0. P-t-P '02 r3 p1 (2nd of 3); last pair 2. Finished lame when 12 lengths second over 2m4f at Hexham in '02, and forced onto the sidelines last year, but returned tongue-tied, and only lasted two more races before breaking down again. *Mrs A.D. Wauchope — College V. & N. Northumberland (Clive Storey).* 211 (C), 658 (OMa), 859 (CfMa).

STORM CASTLE (IRE) .10-4.. 13 b.g. Carlingford Castle — Strong Rum (Strong Gale) 414321u74. Close-coupled good-quartered. IRISH P-t-P '98 r5 w1 (6yo&up Maiden) p1 (2nd); fell 2. NH '98/00 r12 w1 (3m1f Hdle) p4 (inc 3rd in Ch); 4th in other Ch, after falling at last (kept jumping left). P-t-P/HUNT CH '01/3 r17 w7 (3m1f110y Hunt Ch and 6 Ladies) p7 (4 2nds, inc 2 Hunt Chses; and inc last of 3 once); 6th, last, and unseated 1. Disappointing under Rules, and did not take to regulation fences, but races with tremendous enthusiasm in Points, and fast approaching his tenth success for present connections. Showed too much resolve for Mrs Be in his latest win on ground that was plenty quick enough, but typically let down by his jumping in Hunter Chases since. Only deteriorating slowly, and should be up to scoring at 13 with little difficulty, providing he is sensibly placed. Thrice a winner at Charing. *N. Cronin — Kent & Surrey Bloodhounds (Julie Wickens).* 88 (L), 222 (L), 421 (L), 781 (L), 869 (L), 1064 (L), 1117 (3m1f110yH), 1293 (2m7f110yH), 1440 (3m1fH).

STORM FORECAST (IRE) .9-4.. 13 b.g. Strong Gale — Cooleogan (Proverb) 389. Small well-made brother to Irish NH flat and Hurdles winner, Kilcash Castle (IRE), and half-brother to jumping winner, Tullymurry Toff (IRE). Dam won mares Maiden, 2m5f NH flat, and 4 Hdles (2m-2m4f) in Ireland. NH FLAT '97 r1 p1 (neck 2nd). NH '97/00 r15 w2 (2m7f Hdle and 2m3f Ch) p3. P-t-P '01/3 r11 w2 (2 Club Nov Rdrs) p3 (2 3rds; and 2nd of 3); 4th twice, pulled up 2 and unseated 2. A dual winner at Milborne St Andrew in the previous yard, but the current owner-rider has been unable to do him justice, and not better than tailed off last in '04. Has never stood much racing and looks finished now. Blinkered latterly under Rules, and tried in cheekpieces once last year. *P. Andrew — Fernie (Claire Andrew).* 4 (Cnr), 382 (O), 592 (O).

STORM VALLEY (IRE) .—.. 13 b.g. Strong Gale — Windy Run (Deep Run) p. Leggy half-brother to Mussel Buoy (IRE), and to NH Flat winner, Carry The Card. IRISH NH FLAT '97 r1 p0. IRISH/UK NH '98/00 (for Mrs S.A. Bramall) r12 p0; pulled up 3, and unseated 1. NH '00/3 (for P. Mitchell, one win, J.R. Cornwall, one win, and T. Wall) r11 w2 (2m4f-3m1f Ch) p2 (3rds); pulled up 4, and unseated 1. Bought Doncaster, May for 700. Won two Chases to October '01, but has failed to finish in six of seven attempts since, and was well tailed off last in the only completion. A bad jumper who has tried Sellers, and often tongue-tied. His golden days are very much a distant memory. *R. Wilding — United.* 660 (Cf).

STORMY PASS ..10-1.. 8 b.g. Dolphin Street (FR) — Noble Choice (Dahar USA) p62322. Tall strong. Dam won 3 flat (8-11f) and 3 2m Hurdles in Ireland. NH FLAT '01 r2 p0. NH '01/2 r3 p0; pulled up 1. P-t-P '03 r4 w1 (3-finisher Maiden) p2; and fell 1. Of no account under Rules, but scored on his Pointing debut in a three-finisher Maiden at Larkhill, and unlucky not to follow up in a Restricted. Beaten between one-and-three-quarter lengths and 14 lengths in four placings in them, but is devoid of any late acceleration, and probably does not get the trip that well. Deserves to find compensation. Visored and tongue-tied once in '01. *Mrs R.C. Hayward — Warwicks.* 169 (R), 191 (R), 294 (R), 787 (CR), 925 (R), 1276 (M).

STORMY SESSION ..9-8.. 15 b.g. Celestial Storm (USA) — No Jazz (Jaazeiro USA) p33. Workmanlike half-brother to A Suitable Girl, and to Hurdles winner, Marx Mistress. NH FLAT '94 r2 p0. NH '94, '97 and '99 r18 w1 (2m6f Ch) p6 (inc 2nd in Hdle). P-t-P/HUNT CH '00/1 (for Mr M. Harris) r10 w1 (Open) p0; unseated 2, slipped up 1, and refused 1. NH '01 and '03 (for M.F. Harris) r2 p0; pulled up 1. A weak-finishing front-runner under Rules, and suffered leg trouble and gained his only success in '99, but sprang a 25-1 surprise on the opening day of the '01 season, and still retains some zip. Not better than last under a newcomer in '04, but though he never looked a suitable novice ride did the job securely. Has been tried in headgear. *J. Benfield — Heythrop.* 727 (MO), 924 (O), 1401 (O).

STORMY SUNRISE (IRE) ..9-6.. 9 b.g. Glacial Storm (USA) — Commanche Maid (Commanche Run) 2R2715p. Good-topped compact brother to Irish Hurdling winner, Lightning Storm. IRISH NH FLAT '01 r1 p0. IRISH NH '01/3 (for J. Larkin, and E. Bolger) r14 p0; pulled up 1, and slipped up 1. A major failure in Ireland where he was never even placed in 19 races, and wore a tongue-tie in the bumper and was beaten 26 lengths plus over jumps including five Chases (pulled up once, and slipped up once in the non-completions). Ran out once in '02 and did so again with a novice putting up a stone overweight in '04, but proved consistent in Maidens when trainer-ridden, and followed two seconds (lucky once) with a win in a weak contest at Easingwold. Has been badly outclassed in Hunter Chases and a Ladies, and has clear limitations, so would do best to concentrate on Restricteds in future. Tends to pull hard, and is not an easy ride. *P. & Mrs J.M. Hodgson — Bedale (Annabelle Armitage).* 160 (CMa), 300 (O), 395 (CfMa), 444 (2mH), 1165 (OMa), 1177 (2m5fH), 1470 (L).

ST PALAIS ..8-12.. 6 b.m. Timeless Times (USA) — Crambella (IRE) (Red Sunset) 336p. Small. IRISH P-t-P '02 r4 p0 (last, pulled up 2, and ran out). FLAT '01/2 r4 p0. NH '02/3 (for D.L. Williams) r12 p1 (2nd); pulled up 1, and ran out 1. Beat a total of four horses in four flat races, and came closest to a winner over Hurdles when 20 lengths second at 66-1. Ran out on a bend once, tried in Sellers, and often wore a visor or cheekpieces as well as being tried with a hackamor. Appeared to have given an improved display when third at Llanfrynach, but that has not been sustained, and does not seem to be much of a trier and could also have stamina limitations. *T. Faulkner — Tredegar F. (Deborah Faulkner).* 202 (CfMa), 453 (CfMa), 700 (CfMa), 845 (CfMa).

STRAIGHT BARON ..8-4§.. 12 gr.g. Baron Blakeney — Straight Gin (Ginger Boy) 432p13. Half-brother to Straight Touch. Dam, sister to Cool Ginger, and half-sister to Kaloore (*qv* '98 Annual), won 2m2f Hdle and 2m4f Ch for Mr Taylor. P-t-P '99/01 and '03 r10 w1 (Members) p1 (3rd); last pair 2, ran out 1, and pulled up 4, and void race. Gifted two weak races, and was booked for a poor third until the leaders made late exits in the latest, but unlucky in a Members at Godstone previously, as he was very badly impeded by the front pair on the run-in when beaten only three-quarters-of-a-length. Normally a weak finisher, and will require similar good fortune to score at 12. *A.J. Taylor — Southdown & Eridge.* 538 (R), 605 (M), 900 (R), 1051 (R), 1282 (R), 1411 (M).

STRAND ONTHE GREEN (IRE) ..—.. 7 b.g. Ela-Mana-Mou — Fleuretta (USA) (The Minstrel CAN) fpp. Tiny. Dam won 6f race in Ireland. FLAT '01/2 r5 p0. P-t-P '03 r8 p2 (2nds); 5th of 6, pulled up 3, and fell/unseated 2. Improved by cheekpieces and rated 9-4 after two respectable seconds in '03, but miniscule and thrice claimed by the first fence, and went lame when backed down to second favouritism at Bishops Court. Wears a cross-noseband. *G.B. Foot — Seavington.* 121 (OMa), 237 (CfMa), 327 (OMa).

STRAW EXCHANGE ..—.. 6 ch.m. Bahamian Bounty — Mrs Musgrove (Jalmood USA) ppp. Half-sister to flat winners, Dom One and Al Jinn, and to a winner in Australia. Looked useless when tailed off and pulled up in Maidens, and showed signs of reluctance on her debut. The man who took the straw will be laughing all the way to the bank. *A.G. Chinery — E. Essex (Paul Chinery).* 401 (OMa), 560 (OMa), 833 (OMa).

STREET PARADE .—.. 6 b.m. Regal Embers (IRE) — Winter Gem (Hasty Word) p. Very small. Dam fell in first mile in 2 Points. Produced looking horrible on a deeply unimpressive debut, and scrambled over the fences in alarmed fashion until being pulled up after a mile. *A. Wright — Teme V. (Billie Brown).* 837 (OMa).

STREET SMART (IRE) .9-3.. 9 gr.g. Roselier (FR) — College Street (IRE) (Strong Gale) u6216. Big strong. IR25,000 4yo. IRISH NH FLAT '01 r1 p0. IRISH NH '01/2 r2 p0; pulled up 1. NH '02/3 (for C.J. Mann) r4 p0; pulled up 2. Outclassed under Rules and was pulled up in his only Chase and in two of four Hurdles, but finally gained a first placing at the tenth attempt when runner-up at High Easter, and then scored at Detling to give Brea Donnelly her first English winner having previously partnered three in Ireland. Likely to be a thorough stayer, but one-paced, and more will be needed for Restricteds. *M.J. Roberts — E. Sussex & Romney Marsh.* 6 (OMa), 44 (R), 220 (OMa), 540 (CfMa), 745 (R).

PLATE 117 529 Tanatside Ladies Open: Stretching wins for Jane Williams in borrowed colours
PHOTO: Brian Armstrong

STRETCHING (IRE) ..10-7.. 12 br.g. Contract Law (USA) — Mrs Mutton (Dancer's Image USA) 1312. Compact attractive half-brother to several winners, including in Ireland. FLAT r7 p1 (2nd). NH '96 and '98/00 r28 w1 (2m1f Sell Hdle) p6 (inc 31/ 3rd in Ch). P-t-P/HUNT CH '01/2 r6 w2 (Ladies) p2 (2nds of 3, beaten head once); 5th, and pulled up 1. Consistent, and successful in half his completed Points, and returned from a year off to record two convincing wins under Jane Williams at Eyton in which he was well supported. Also turned over at 4-7 there when the ground was not as soft as he desires, and brushed aside by Upton Adventure at Bredwardine, but a good jumper and should be placed to advantage again. Tried in headgear in a largely depressing career under Rules. *M.A. Lloyd & A. Goodwin — Teme V. (Jo Priest).* 529 (L), 931 (L), 1263 (L), 1391 (L).

STRIDE TO GLORY (IRE) ..9-3§.. 14 b.g. Superpower — Damira (FR) (Pharly FR) 2p7p2. Small stocky half-brother to 3 flat winners abroad. P-t-P/HUNT CH '96/03 r37 w5 (up to Confined) p9 (6 3rds, of 4 twice, remote last once; and 3 2nds, inc Hunt Ch, and remote last); fell/unseated 6, and pulled up 4. The winner of five races on an irregular basis, and looked to have unearthed another opportunity when leading after the last on his reappearance at Garnons, but could not resist the winner's late burst. Failed to co-operate fully again, and acquired a visor at Bredwardine before regaining blinkers on his latest appearance. His rating fluctuates between 9-12 and the current one, but his mood is mostly one of non-compliance nowadays, and is best left alone. Suited by good or fast ground. *N.L. Hooper & R. Heath — N. Ledbury (Matt Hooper).* 405 (Inr), 661 (Cnr), 979 (MOnr), 1390 (O), 1496 (I).

STRONG CHAIRMAN (IRE) ..9-0.. 14 br.g. Strong Gale — The Furnituremaker (Mandalus) p7uuuf. Tall roman-nosed brother to Chasing winner, Strong Cabinet (IRE), and half-brother to jumping winner, Dene View (IRE). NH '97/9 r8 w1 (3m Nov Chse) p2 (2nds). P-t-P/HUNT CH '96/7 and '00/3 (for Mr R. Waley-Cohen) r29 w9 (inc 3 Opens and Mixed Open, inc undefeated 5-timer '97) p9 (5 3rds, of 4 twice, and inc Hunt Ch; 4 2nds, of 3 once); 6th twice, last pair 3, pulled up 4, and unseated 2. A smart six-year-old when unbeaten in Points, and revived successfully in the previous yard after a disappointing time under Rules, but the new owner-rider had great difficulty locating the saddle in '04, and was well tailed off on his only completion. Acquired cheekpieces, and latterly blinkers in '03, and looks gone at the game now. *K.G. O'Brien — Atherstone (John Holt).* 300 (O), 381 (O), 683 (O), 989 (Cnr), 1118 (M), 1263 (L).

STRONG FINISH ..8-11.. 10 ch.g. Montelimar (USA) — Atlantic View (Crash Course) 4R. Lengthy well-made hobdayed half-brother to NH flat winner, Mincarlo. NH FLAT '00 r2 p0. NH '01/2 r14 p2 (Chses). P-t-P '03 (for Mr P.J. Ponting) r8 p3 (3rds, of 4 once, and last once); 7th, last, and pulled up 3. A long-standing maiden who has been placed on five occasions, but severely impaired by a serious wind problem, and has only once been beaten less than 20 lengths. Has run tubed and tongue-tied, and it would appear that connections have admitted defeat. *R. Butterworth — Curre & Llangibby.* 119 (OMa), 258 (CMa).

STRONG KING (IRE) ..9-4.. 11 b/br.g. Strong Gale — Mrs Simpson (Kinglet) p58. Tall rangy brother to Chasing winner, Kings Mistral (IRE). Dam is sister to Brown Windsor (*qv* '97 Annual). Grandam, Cauldron, won 2 3m-3m3f Hunt Chses (at 5 and 6 years). NH '01/2 r5 p0; pulled up 2. P-t-P '02 (for Mr D.W. Watson) r7 p4 (2nds, of 3 thrice); fell/unseated 3. Flattered to deceive on numerous occasions in the previous yard, and acquired headgear latterly, and typically finished weakly when around four lengths fifth in an eight-minute Maiden at Alpraham in '04. Tailed off in both races run at a true pace otherwise, and let supporters down when backed at long odds on his belated return. *Mrs J. Cardwell — Cheshire Forest (Ralph Hirons).* 748 (M), 1044 (OMa), 1176 (3m110yH).

STRONG TARTAN (IRE) ..10-6.. 11 br.g. Strong Gale — Kemchee (Kemal FR) p4. Robust brother to Sir Williamwallace (IRE) (*qv*). IR30,000 4yo. NH FLAT '99/00 r2 w1 p0. NH '00/3 r16 w3 (2m5f-3m Ch) p7 (inc 3 3rds Hdles); fell 3, and pulled up 1. The winner of a bumper and three Chases on ground ranging from soft to firmish, but has his problems these days, and reported to have lost his action when favourite but pulling up in an Ayr Hunter Chase (never recovered from a bad blunder at the 12th). Acquired a tongue-tie to go with his regular cheekpieces when about five lengths fourth and not disgraced there next time, but gives the impression of labouring under his physical handicaps these days. *Mr & Mrs R. Anderson Green — Border (Andrew Parker).* 439 (2m5f110yH), 992 (3m3f110yH).

STRONG TEA (IRE) ..10-3.. 14 b.g. Electric — Cutty Sark (Strong Gale) 15227. Stocky dipped half-brother to Irish NH flat and Hurdles winner, Sarcastic (IRE), and to Irish Chasing winner, Newtown Native (IRE). P-t-P '98/9 and '01/3 (for Mrs J. Tucker & Mrs M.J. Mein) r25 w4 (up to Confined) p11 (7 3rds, of 4 once); fell/unseated 4, and pulled up 2. Retains ability well, and four times successful at Larkhill, but gave favourite backers an uneasy time on his reappearance, as he typically looked to have switched off and lost interest after two miles. Needs strong handling to galvanise him, and can finish very strongly, but becoming moodier and needs treating with caution. Mounted on course and taken down early. *M.R. Lilley — Avon V. (Sarah Waugh).* 9 (C), 138 (C), 632 (M), 891 (3m1fH), 1172 (3m1f110yH).

STRONG WELD ..8-7.. 8 br.g. Weld — Shoreham Lady (Strong Gale) fp3. Workmanlike homebred. Dam, half-sister to Ruby Davies (*qv* '95 Annual). Has shown no merit so far and finished 13 lengths last of three behind an unimpressive penalised winner in his Members. *R. Teague & Mrs S. Gowling — S. Salop (Russell Teague).* 532 (OMa), 668 (OMa), 1260 (M).

STRUGGLES GLORY (IRE) ..10-8.. 14 b.g. Kamehameha (USA) — Another Struggle (Cheval) 22131. Workmanlike half-brother to Always Good (IRE), and to Irish Pointing winner, All A Struggle (IRE). IRISH P-t-P '96 r2 p2. NH '00/2 r9 w3 (2m4f110y-3m1f110y Chses) p0; brought down at first in 2002 Grand National. P-t-P/HUNT CH '97, '99/00 and '03 r19 w12 (inc 3 3m-3m2f Hunt Chses, Mixed Open and 4 Opens, inc 5-timer '99) p3 (2 2nds in Hunt Chses; and 3rd of 4); 4th, pulled up 1 and fell/unseated 2. Only defeated by Earthmover in '97, and won his first two races under Rules once Ben Hitchcott was let loose on him, but never won the big prize that his talent deserved, and reduced to trouncing inferiors when successful in '04. Lost his unbeaten record at Charing when succumbing to Sheriff's Friend on his reappearance, and to another old adversary in the shape of Satchmo, but recorded his seventh success there in April after an odds-on defeat, and that looks a good note to bow out on. *D.C. Robinson — Mid Surrey F.* 183 (O), 420 (O), 609 (O), 780 (O), 804 (O).

STUDENT NIGHT (IRE) ..—.. 6 b.g. Jolly Jake (NZ) — Coteri Run (Deep Run) R. Lengthy brother to Jakes Progress (IRE) (*qv*). 15,460 4yo. Odds-on favourite for the farcical youngsters Maiden at Trebudannon which was eventually won by Joyful Jade, but bubbled over and performed erratically until running out when leading at halfway. *D.E. Pipe — Taunton V.H.* 1432 (OMa).

STYLINO (USA) ..—§.. 8 ch.g. Trempolino (USA) — Smartly Styled (USA) (Cox's Ridge USA) ppp. Compact good-topped half-brother to French flat winner, Smartly Tax. FRENCH FLAT '99 and '01 r5 p1 (2nd). FRENCH NH '00/1 r12 p3 (2nds Chses). NH '02 (for C.C. Bealby) r3 p0 (last, and pulled up 2). Used to have ability and was second in a flat race and three Chases in France (beaten a head once), but has proved expensive rubbish in the present ownership, and consistently looks reluctant and has only got round once in six attempts. Sometimes blinkered to '02, and tried tongue-tied once. Shows marked reluctance, and it must be significant that Richard Hunnisett never rides him and Caroline Bailey does not train him. *R.S. Hunnisett — Quorn (Sarah Botterill).* 945 (OMa), 1056 (M), 1215 (CfMa).

STYLISH DAVE (NZ) ..9-4.. 11 bl.g. Stylish Century (AUS) — Calcutta (NZ) (My Friend Paul USA) 43p3. Successful in New Zealand, but has only showed a modicum of ability over here, and tends to jump stickily and to the right. Has not improved on a 16 lengths fourth at Cottenham, but it is possible that a competent jockey could still get something out of him. *Mrs D. Rowell — Mid Surrey F. (Sara Hickman).* 101 (L), 536 (CfL), 608 (L), 896 (CCon).

SUGAR TOI ..8-6.. 9 b.m. Supreme Leader — Strong Toi (Strong Gale) 4. Dam, closely related to 4 Pointers, was highly alarming in 2 Points for the Silks (did not reach halfway). P-t-P '01 r1 p0 (pulled up). Has hinted at ability in two Maidens three years apart, and 18 lengths last after holding every chance three out in '04, but clearly nigh-on impossible to train. *Prof D.B.A. Silk, W. Bellamy & D. Tickner — Kent & Surrey Bloodhounds (Emma Leppard).* 782 (OMa).

SULA HILL ..—.. 9 ch.m. Sula Bula — Miss Rughill (New Member) 5p. Plain angular. Dam won Ladies (bad race on hard at Stibb Cross) and placed 5. Great-grandam, Pride And Joy, won 2 Points. P-t-P '02/3 r5 p0 (6th of 7, pulled up 3, and unseated 1). Has shown a trace of ability, but beaten a minimum of 57 lengths in two completions, and looked too much of a handful for an inexperienced girl this year. Wore a cross-noseband, and taken to post early in '04. *Mrs P.J.M. Smith — Tiverton Stag (Dean Richards).* 474 (OMa), 883 (OMa).

SULALAH SUNRISE ..7-12.. 6 b.m. Shambo — Levantesetcubantes (Levanter) 4. Small stocky. Looked very backward and given a school on a mid-April debut, but did at least keep plugging away to eventually finish 48 lengths fourth. Can possibly speed up when fitter. *M.B. Bent — N. Cotswold (Giles Smyly).* 983 (2m5fOMa).

SULA QUEEN ..8-6.. 10 b.m. Sula Bula — Frankly New (New Member) u1u. Small sturdy owner-bred half-sister to Frankly Fear (*qv*). P-t-P '02/3 r4 p0 (4th of 5, pulled up 2, and unseated 1). Very lightly raced, and escaped off Badbury Rings after unseating on her return, but her loose two-mile jaunt up the B3082 clearly put her Spot-on for her next engagement, and duly landed a shocking three-runner Maiden on good to frosty at Larkhill. David Turner had to survive a blunder on that occasion, but has not been so lucky otherwise, and had stopped to nil by the time the partnership was severed at Ston Easton. Needs to go right-handed, and has worn an off-side pricker. *Mrs J.M. Fear — Avon V. (Robert Fear).* 264 (CfMa), 334 (OMa), 601 (R).

SUMERIAN LAD ..9-9.. 9 b.g. Sulaafah (USA) — Amerian County (Amerian USA) u73R12. Small well-made half-brother to Mr Smudge (*qv*). P-t-P '02/3 r4 p1 (3rd); pulled up 2 and unseated 1. One of only two dangers to the 20-length winner when unseating three out on his return, but displayed some waywardness and further slapdash jumping before recording a wide margin success over a lame rival on firm at Rhydygwern. Made a host of errors in his first Restricted, and will need to jump a whole lot better if he is to go one better in them. *S. Jones — Llangeinor.* 363 (CfMa), 700 (CfMa), 927 (OMa), 1395 (OMa), 1487 (OMa), 1548 (R).

SUMMER SNOW ..8-12.. 11 gr.g. Arctic Lord — Allyfair (Scallywag) f. Compact unfurnished. NH FLAT '99 r2 p0. NH '00 r2 p0. P-t-P '02/3 r7 p0 (6th twice, pulled up 1, fell/unseated 2 and slipped up 1, and disqualified from win once — missed marker). Won unchallenged in a bad four-runner Maiden at Holnicote last year, but had missed a marker and was disqualified, and otherwise a total disaster in Points. Careers off at high speed but usually runs out of steam, and prone to blunder or fall in the closing stages. Wears a cross-noseband and cheekpieces. At least his partner Owyn Nelmes is making a name for himself in a much bigger pond. *Mrs H.R.J. Nelmes — S. Dorset (Ken Nelmes).* 67 (OMa).

SUNBURNT ..10-4.. 11 b.g. Henbit (USA) — Sunshine Gal (Alto Volante) 2. Sturdy compact half-brother to Weather Wise. Dam won 3 flat, 10-16f (the first a Sell), and 5 2m1f-2m5f Hdles. NH FLAT '99 r2 p0. NH '99/02 r18 w1 (2m Ch) p3 (inc 2 3rds in Hdles). P-t-P/HUNT CH '03 r7 w2 (inc Ladies) p1 (3rd in Hunt Ch); 4th, last twice, and pulled up 1. Scoring for the first time in nearly three years when recording a double on good or sound surfaces in '03, and ended the year with a good third to Balisteros in a Stratford Hunter Chase, but taken to Black Forest Lodge for his reappearance, and failed to see the light of day again. Often a weak finisher, and has run tongue-tied in the past. *G. Salter — Berkeley (Julie Houldey).* 146 (L).

SUNCZECH (IRE) ..9-6.. 15 b.m. Sunyboy — Miss Prague (Mon Capitaine) 44p6p. Light-framed half-sister to Uncle's Emma and Velka. Dam won an Irish Point, and an English Restricted. IRISH P-t-P '95/7 r10 p5; pulled up 4. P-t-P/HUNT CH '98/03 r25 w3 (Maiden, Restricted and Intermediate) p6 (4 2nds, of 3 twice); failed to finish 10 (fell/unseated 3). Viewing the winners enclosure for the first time since '99 when making most in a firm ground double at Kimble last year, but disappointing after reappearance in '04, and appeared to go wrong at Kingston Blount. Wears a cross-noseband. *S.C. Clark & D. Thomas — V. of Aylesbury with Garth & S. Berks (Sue Harbour).* 187 (Cf), 440 (2m7f110yH), 869 (L), 938 (MO), 1103 (C).

SUNLEYS QUEST .8-7.. 7 b.m. Sunley Builds — Dinkies Quest (Sergeant Drummer USA) ppfu. Compact half-sister to NH flat winner, Bula's Quest. Dam, sister to Soeur Marie (*qv* '01 Annual), won Maiden and placed 2. Not getting a lot of luck so far, and efforts include having to be pulled up with a slipped saddle, and a fall two out when eight lengths third but weakening (in a race in which only two completed). Managed to avoid completion yet again when unseating after a mile, but has had four different jockeys, and it would be a good idea to settle on just one who can get the hang of her. Possibly has some concealed ability. *B. Andrews — Mendip F. (Nikki Stephens).* 598 (M), 1098 (OMa), 1326 (OMa), 1495 (OMa).

SUNSHINE LEADER (IRE) ..—.. 10 b.m. Supreme Leader — Cherry Run (Deep Run) up. Small half-sister to Cherry Glen (IRE), and to Irish Pointing winners, Executive Marshall and Cherry In A Hurry. IR4100 3yo. IRISH P-t-P '00 r1 p1 (2nd). IRISH NH FLAT '00 r1 w1. NH FLAT '00 r1 p1 (2nd). NH '01/2 (for E.L. James) r11 w1 (2m5f Hdle) p8 (inc 2 Chses). Two wins and nine placings from just 13 attempts under Rules are commendable, but became disappointing latterly and was prone to slow jumps over fences. Tried blinkered once. Missed '03, and jumped in a most ungainly fashion in Points, and no longer has any aptitude for the job. *Mrs D.C. Samworth — Cottesmore.* 33 (L), 380 (L).

SUNY HENRY ..8-10.. 8 ch.g. Henbit (USA) — Suny Zeta (Sunyboy) pp6. Lengthy. Dam won a Maiden and placed 3 for the Goldies. P-t-P '02 r1 p0 (fell). Beaten 34 lengths when managing to jump round in a 2m4f Maiden at Dalston, but error-prone and unruly previously, and does not have much to recommend him. Wears a cross-noseband. *R.H. Goldie — Cumberland F.* 432 (OMa), 554 (CfMa), 768 (2m4fOMa).

SUPERCHARMER ..10-4.. 11 ch.g. Charmer — Surpassing (Superlative) 07321f24. Close-coupled well-made brother to a winner in Italy. Dam won at 7f. FLAT r18 p2 (3rds). NH '97 r2 p0 (beat one, inc Sell). P-t-P/HUNT CH '99/03 r29 w7 (inc 2 Opens and 2 Ladies) p2 (3rd of 4 once); failed to finish 17 (fell/unseated 6, and carried out 1). A former sprinter on the flat, and can still be impossible to restrain and has to go right-handed, but difficult to beat granted a clear round and an easy three miles, and along with Texas Ranger the only horse to beat Hadeqa in Ladies races in '04. Can jump boldly but also prone to wholesale blunders, and appeared to show the effects of some hard races when making the long haul to Trecoed on his latest appearance. Likely to win again when conditions are right. Blinkered once in '97, and wears a cross-noseband. *M.A. Humphreys — Farndale.* 270 (L), 443 (2m4f110yH), 682 (L), 763 (L), 1290 (L), 1360 (3mH), 1497 (3mH), 1551 (L).

SUPER DOLPHIN ..9-2.. 6 ch.g. Dolphin Street (FR) — Supergreen (Superlative) bu1pp*0*. Well-made attractive brother or half-brother to six flat losers. FLAT '01/3 r9 p1 (2nd); refused to race 1. NH '02/3 r5 p0. NH '04 (for T.P. Tate) r1 p0 (13th in 2m Hdle: *chsd ldrs til wknd 5, t.o*). Beaten a head in a

7f race on firm once, but also refused to start once on the flat, and was finally scoring at the 17th time of asking when he got up on the line to win a bad six-runner 2m4f Maiden at Hornby Castle which has produced no subsequent winners. Barely lasts that distance, and unable to complete under his ungainly rider over the full trip. Selling Hurdles might be his only future hope. *R.T.A. Tate — Badsworth & Bramham Moor.* 75 (OMa), 272 (OMa), 343 (2m4fOMa), 481 (R), 955 (R).

SUPERIOR FOOTWORK ..7-7.. 8 ch.g. Thethingaboutitis (USA) — Havrin Princess (Scallywag) ppup7. Strong half-brother to Dunston Slick and Princess Scully. Dam was 3rd in Sell Hurdle and Adjacent (failed to finish in 5 of 8 other Points). P-t-P '03 r1 p0 (pulled up). Pulls hard and makes mistakes, and appeared not to get the trip when 43 lengths last on his first completion at Chaddesley Corbett. Still has much to learn. *Mrs S. Davies — Albrighton (Paul Morris).* 96 (CfMa), 385 (OMa), 929 (2m4fOMa), 1020 (OMa), 1532 (OMa).

SUPERIOR RISK (IRE) ..—.. 16 b.g. Mandalus — Hal's Pauper (Official) p. Big rangy fired half-brother to Hal's Prince and Shildon (IRE). IRISH P-t-P '95 r5 w2 (6&7yo Maiden and Winners of One) p1 (2nd); pulled up 2. IRISH NH FLAT '95 r1 w1 (2m4f). NH '95/6 and '99/02 (for M.C. Pipe, 2 wins, and T.R. George) r18 w6 (3 2m4f-3m1f Hdles and 3 2m1f-2m4f Chses) p6; fell/unseated 2, and pulled up 2. The winner of seven races principally in mud, but has not gained a success since he took a Claiming Hurdle in December '01. Has normally made all if successful, but error-prone on occasions, and unseated when visored once. Broke down in '96 and vanished for three years, and absent again in '03 before a brief and unpromising revival at 15. *The Cherry Tree Partnership (Mrs T.H. Hayward) — N. Norfolk H. (Tina Hayward).* 110 (Cnr).

SUPERIOR WEAPON (IRE) ..10-1.. 11 b.g. Riverhead (USA) — Ballytrustan Maid (IRE) (Orchestra) *25128p*. Strong close-coupled. P-t-P/HUNT CH '99/01 r6 w2 (2m4f Maiden and Restricted) p1 (2nd); last, pulled up 1 and ran out 1. NH '01/2 (for F.P. Murtagh) r10 w1 (2m1f Ch) p3; pulled up 2. NH '04 r5 w1 (beat Winter Garden 3½*l* in 2m Ch: *ld, blun 2, hdd 9, rallied & ld app last, stayed on game*) p1 (½*l* 2nd in 2m110y Ch: *ld, rdn when lft clr 4 out, wknd flat, hdd nr fin*); 5th in 2m4f Ch: *ld to 8, ev ch 2 out, wknd flat*; last of 8 in 2m1f Ch: *prom til wknd app 2 out, t.o*; and pulled up in 2m1f Hdle: *ld til mist 3, wknd aft 5, wl bhnd when pu last*. Has a high cruising speed and best when allowed to bowl along in front, but much more profitably employed in races over the minimum trip under Rules than in Points, and picked up a £4,200 Chase at Ayr in March. Has a breathing problem and runs tongue-tied. Acts on any going. *I. Hamilton — Tynedale (Ann Hamilton).* 73 (Cf).

SUPERSTAR EXPRESS (IRE) ..9-9.. 8 br.g. Jurado (USA) — Easter Bee (IRE) (Phardante FR) p14f2ppu. Tall. Dam, half-sister to Simply Dashing (*qv* '02 Annual). IR1250 3yo. NH FLAT '02 r4 p0. NH '03 (for J.I.A. Charlton) r3 p0. Won a Friars Haugh Maiden with something to spare and was not disgraced when eight lengths second in a Dalston Restricted, but sometimes victim of very bad errors, and it is disappointing that he has got round only once in his last five attempts. Often wears a tongue-tie, and tends to run out of steam in the closing stages. Does not seem to have much scope for improvement. *Ms J.M. Findlay — Border.* 74 (OMa), 287 (CfMa), 548 (R), 657 (R), 766 (R), 918 (R), 1178 (3m1fH), 1423 (M).

SUP OF TEA (IRE) ..8-7.. 8 b.g. Commanche Run — Ballyrock Lady (Decent Fellow) ppp72u. Lengthy. Dam won 5yo&up Maiden in Ireland. IRISH P-t-P '02/3 r7 p1 (2nd); pulled up 3, fell 2, and ran out 1. Has had plenty of opportunities in the lowest grade, and remains a Maiden after 13 chances. Has failed to finish on ten occasions, and looked very doggy when blinkered on his English debut (has not worn them since). Has finished second twice, but a distant last in Ireland, and beaten five lengths in an awful contest which took almost a minute longer than the Open on firm at Bratton Down (only five ran). Does not deserve to score. *P. Musgrave & K. Hooper — Eggesford (Laura Young).* 195 (CfMa), 962 (OMa), 1134 (OMa), 1380 (OMa), 1511 (OMa), 1559 (OMa).

SUPREME CITIZEN (IRE) ..10-10.. 13 b.g. Supreme Leader — Kelenem (Menelek) 111u. Tall rangy half-brother to Lovely Citizen, Call Me Citizen and Citizen Moss, and to Irish Pointing winners, Golden Citizen, Clare Citizen and Korean Citizen. Dam, half-sister to Drive Easy (*qv* '90 Annual). IRISH P-t-P '97/8 and '01/2 r22 w4 (inc 2 Opens) p9; pulled up 2, and fell/unseated 3. IRISH NH FLAT '98 and '02 r2 p0. IRISH NH '99 r1 p0. IRISH HUNT CH '01/2 r2 p0 (fell/unseated 2). P-t-P '03 r6 w3 (Ladies) p2 (2nds, short-headed once); and unseated 1. A useful Open performer on both sides of the Irish Sea, and took his winning tally into double figures with a typically powerful display of galloping at Brocklesby Park, but not wholly convincing otherwise in '04, and was being caught by the modest Certain Surprise when attempting to duck out and unseating at the last at Brampton Bryan. Stays well, and prefers plenty of cut in the ground, but ran in snatches when defeated once in '03, and probably not one to support at cramped odds in future. Blinkered once in '01. *Mrs A.D. Williams — Albrighton Woodland.* 101 (L), 230 (L), 479 (L), 1111 (L).

SUPREME ROBBER (IRE) .—.. 7 b.g. Supreme Leader — Filch (Precocious) pp. Tubed. Looked useless when pulled up after less than two miles twice, and it was a very bad sign that he needed tubing before he even ran. *I. Thomas — Banwen Miners (John Moore).* 950 (2m4fOMa), 1239 (OMa).

SUPREME SILENCE (IRE) ..10-2.. 8 b.g. Bluebird (USA) — Why So Silent (Mill Reef USA) 5p12pp438132. Good-topped half-brother to six flat winners (4 by Danehill, including useful trio Leporello, Poppy Carew, Calypso Grant and Juno Marlowe), Oh Hebe and Rose Peel. FLAT '00/3 r22 w2 (16f) p1 (3rd). NH '01/3 (for J. O'Keeffe) r13 w1 (2m5f Hdle) p1 (3rd in Ch); pulled up 6. Bought Doncaster, May for 1150. A dual winner on the all-weather and also successful once over Hurdles, but has had a soft palate operation, and his latest connections were able to purchase him very cheaply. Proved as tough as old boots in '04 and able to make 12 appearances, and although totally unpredictable his best efforts were fine. Scored at 33-1 in a Market Rasen Ladies and at 6-1 in a Tabley Open, and was also staying on when it was too late in a couple of Hunter Chase placings. Often wore headgear or cheekpieces and had a tongue-tie to '03, but no such aids has been required since. Stays extremely well, and turned out to be quite a bargain. *R.H. Lee — Rockwood H. (Nick Kent).* 56 (C), 122 (3m1fH), 299 (L), 377 (3m1fH), 544 (2m5f110yH), 679 (3m1fH), 987 (L), 1058 (L), 1372 (2m4fH), 1427 (O), 1489 (3m3fH), 1502 (O).

SUPREME STORM (IRE) ..9-12.. 10 b.g. Supreme Leader — Angolass (Al Sirat) u302. Tall workmanlike half-brother to Irish Pointing and English jumping winner, Hannigan's Lodger, and to Chasing winner, Scrahan Cross. NH FLAT '99 and '01 r3 p0. NH '02 (for B.G. Powell) r6 w1 (2m5f) p1 (3rd in Hdle); pulled up 1. Good enough to win a Chase in '02, but has suffered with his legs, and pulled up lame when 4-5 on his final appearance under Rules. Resumed again in '04 and placed in two Opens, but was beaten 40 lengths when third and ten lengths when runner-up to a 1-4 shot in a three-horse affair. Difficult to place, because he probably needs races that are shy of three miles. *Mrs D. Buckett — Hursley Hambledon.* 603 (Cnr), 868 (O), 1168 (2m5fH), 1335 (O).

SUPREME VINTAGE (IRE) ..—.. 8 b.g. Supreme Leader — Slaney Wine (IRE) (Remainder Man) puuupu. Workmanlike. Dam won NH flat and 2m2f Hurdle in Ireland. IRISH NH FLAT '02 r2 p0. IRISH NH '03 (for J.A. White, and R. O'Leary) r10 p0; fell 1, and pulled up 1. Beaten 20 lengths plus (often far more) and blinkered once in 12 Irish races, and consistently unseated or pulled up in Points, in which he invariably failed to get the trip having been in contention after 2m4f on occasions. Ex-professional jockey Chris Pimlott had the misfortune to train some awful horses (eg Billymax and Folliday). Surely his first Pointing jockey cannot be as old as he looks (although he does claim to have learned his trade at Neville Crump's which must have been aeons ago). *Go With The Flow (D. Ward) — Middleton (Chris Pimlott).* 112 (OMa), 344 (2m4fOMa), 394 (CfMa), 773 (2m4fCMa), 960 (OMa), 1158 (OMa).

SURE HOW BAD (IRE) ..9-0.. 10 b.g. Great Eastern — Gorazhire (Pauper) u3pp. Workmanlike compact. IRISH P-t-P '00 r4 p0 (last, and pulled up 3). P-t-P '02/3 r11 p2 (remote last of 2, and last of 3); pulled up 4. Ran his best race to date when eight lengths third in softish at Buckfastleigh, but could not back it up, and pulled up twice on much faster ground subsequently. Safe enough but not a stout stayer, and will be very lucky to find an opening. *Mrs S.A. Brown & Miss J. Curtis — Cotley (Gordon Herrod).* 329 (OMa), 492 (OMa), 693 (OMa), 1252 (OMa).

SUSIES MELODY (IRE) ..10-0.. 14 ch.g. Carlingford Castle — Stardust Melody (Pas De Seul) pf. Plain angular lengthy. P-t-P '96, '98/00 and '02/3 (for Miss A.M. Reed) r26 w6 (up to Confined) p9 (6 2nds); pulled up 1 and fell/unseated 3. A fast ground specialist and thrice a winner at Badbury Rings, and looked sure to record a fourth in his Members until turning a double somersault and breaking his back at the third last. Mrs D. Buckett — Hursley Hambledon. 89 (O), 260 (M).

SUTTON COURTENAY (IRE) ..10-0.. 8 b.g. Executive Perk — Cuilin Bui (IRE) (Kemal FR) 32231. Good-bodied half-brother to Hurdles winners, King Harald (IRE) and Prince Madoc (IRE) (latter also won NH flat). Dam, half-sister to Forest Thyne, won 4 Hdles (2m5f-3m) and 2m6f Ch in Ireland. P-t-P '03 r5 w1 (2m4f Maiden) p0; pulled up 3, and fell 1. Won a 2m4f Maiden on his only completion last year, and backed from 12s to eights when supplementing gains in a soft ground Restricted at Kingston Blount under a very determined ride form Jim Jenkins, but not a convincing stayer otherwise. Absent for six weeks between his last two starts, and may not have been right previously, and might still be capable of improvement. *W.F. Caudwell — O. Berks (Matt Hazell).* 37 (CR), 95 (R), 323 (R), 571 (R), 1333 (R).

SUTTON LIGHTER .8-7.. 15 b.g. Lighter — Happy Returns (Saucy Kit) p6. Leggy quite attractive owner-bred half-brother to Dancing Returns (dam of Tiger Ted *qv*), and Rascaletto. Dam, half-sister to Rousing Fortune, won '79 BMW Final Hunt Ch and 8 Ladies. P-t-P '96, '00 and '02 r13 p2 (3rds); pulled up 9, unseated 1 and ran out 1. An elderly lunatic and regularly tears along in front, but normally runs himself into the ground after two miles, and is a regular non-finisher. Goes missing for long periods and is evidently difficult to train. Usually taken to post early. Has been tried in cheekpieces and a tongue-tie. *E. Turner — Ludlow (Mark Trott).* 294 (R), 452 (R).

SWANBANK ..—.. 9 b.g. Ypsilantis — Janets Foss (Idiot's Delight) ppp. Owner-bred. Dam, half-sister to Bright Beacon (*qv*). Safe enough, but shows very little speed, and looks hopeless. *Mrs L. Edge — Thurlow (Gib Edge).* 245 (CfMa), 746 (OMa), 1317 (CfMa).

SWAN SONG .—.. 10 ch.m. True Song — Miss Bali Ha'i (Balinger) upp. Robust half-sister to Master Banker and Southern Ha'i. Dam was 6th and pulled up 3 in Points. Grandam, General Outlook, won 2 Points (one on a disqualification) and placed 4. Great-grandam, Steal-A-Look, won a Maiden. Great-great-grandam, Icy Steel, won 11 Points. Did not jump well and immediately lost touch before unseating before two miles on her debut, and then pulled up after a similar distance when tailed off twice. Does not look like a racehorse. *Mrs R.H. Reynolds — S. Dorset.* 233 (M), 693 (OMa), 865 (OMa).

SWEEPING STORM (IRE) .10-0.. 8 ch.g. Glacial Storm (USA) — Sweeping Gold (Quayside) 23114. Angular. Dam, half-sister to Tartan Trademark (*qv* '96 Annual), won Mares Maiden in Ireland. NH '02 r1 p1 (3rd). P-t-P '03 (for Miss M.D. Myco) r5 p1 (2nd); last, ran out 2, and pulled up 1. A most unenviable ride in the previous yard, and earned a double squiggle after throwing several winning opportunities away through wayward behaviour, and worried out of a close finish on his return, but scored convincingly over 2m4f at Dalston and followed up over the full trip next time. Probably still not entirely straightforward, and may need to hit the front as late as possible, but seems to get on much better with Chris Dawson than he did with the previous pilot, and he may able to put his turn of foot to good use again. *Mrs E. Smith — S. Durham.* 342 (2m4fOMa), 433 (OMa), 767 (2m4fOMa), 1288 (R), 1499 (2m4f110yH).

SWEET CHESTNUT ..8-13.. 9 b.g. Norton Challenger — Harvest Fair (Oats) p34. Dam, elephantine, pulled up 3 and fell in Points (was tubed latterly). His best effort by far was when 11 lengths third at Alnwick in mid-February, but obviously flattered, as none of the eight finishers have won since. A 27 length last next time was in a Dalston Restricted (ineligible for the easier option), and would be better off seeking out elders Maidens. *Mrs A.J. McMath — Cumberland (Ian McMath).* 166 (OMa), 216 (OMa), 765 (R).

SWEET KARI (IRE) ..9-3.. 10 b.g. Lashkari — Sucre Fan (IRE) (Lear Fan USA) p82p47. Compact. IRISH P-t-P '99 r3 w1 (4yo Maiden) p1 (2nd); and pulled up. NH '00/1 r5 p0 (pulled up 5). P-t-P '02/3 r2 p0 (last pair 2). Won the last of three starts in Ireland, but pulled up in his first five English starts after changing hands for 33,000 gns, and has looked consistently faulty since. Beaten 25 lengths when runner-up at Black Forest Lodge, but has tended to weaken alarmingly, and his problems remain deep-seated. Blinkered once in '00. *G. Weatherley — Tiverton Stag (Frankie Sotheran).* 139 (R), 314 (R), 415 (R), 791 (R), 966 (R), 1196 (R).

SWEET REWARD ..9-4.. 10 ch.g. Beveled (USA) — Sweet Revival (Claude Monet USA) p. Strong-topped lengthy half-brother to Classic Revival. Dam won 10f race. FLAT '97/02 r43 w3 (5-10f) p13. NH '00/1 r4 p0; pulled up 1. P-t-P '03 r2 p0 (4th, and pulled up 1). Barely stayed ten furlongs on the flat, and gained the last of his three wins after embarking on a jumping career in '01, but of no account over timber, and has no winning potential in Points. Very lightly raced since '02. *J. Tredwell — Grafton.* 168 (C).

SWEET SOLITAIRE (U) ..—.. 13 ch.m. Moor House — Sundown III (unknown) p. A fence behind his two rivals when pulled up after two miles in his Members (made some slow jumps). *J.C.P. Elwood — Bedale.* 809 (M).

SWIFT WOOD ..—.. 6 b.g. Shambo — Swift Reward (Kinglet) u. Tall good-topped. Dam, half-sister to Stormwift (*qv* '00 Annual), won 2m4f Maiden and placed 3rd thrice. Grandam was another Swift Wood (*qv* '98 Annual). Bought Doncaster, May for 5000. Unseated after two miles on a mid-May introduction. Has some interesting forbears, but naming after his gran did not show much imagination. *Mrs M.J. Felton — Blackmore & Sparkford V. (Keith Cumings).* 1381 (OMa).

SWINGINGBRIDGE ..8-4.. 9 ch.m. Gildoran — Another Relation (Relkino) up. Tiny light-framed half-sister to Flowing Again and Dragon's Dream. Dam, half-sister to Meldrew (*qv* '00 Annual), fell in a Point. P-t-P '03 r4 p0 (6th of 7, pulled up 2, and unseated 1). Has shown speed, and would have been placed had she not demolished the last and unseated once last year, but blunders are common place for her, and has shown a tendency to hang. *R.H.P. Williams — Glamorgan.* 676 (CfMa), 1091 (CMam).

SWITCHBACK (IRE) ..9-7.. 7 b.g. Doubletour (USA) — Two-Shoes (Prince Sabo) fsp. Dam won 5f Sell at 2, and subsequently won race in Switzerland. Grandam won two 6f races at three. Bought Doncaster, Aug for 3000. Fell at the last when three lengths second and beaten on his debut, and then baulked and slipped up on a bend next time, and his bad luck got even worse when he broke down in the lead two out at Charm Park (evens favourite). *Mrs S. Smith — Pendle Forest & Craven (Joss Saville).* 75 (OMa), 503 (R), 960 (OMa).

SWORDFACE (IRE) ..—.. 8 b.g. Moscow Society (USA) — Parson's Dream (The Parson) pu. Brother to Hurdles winner, The Red Rector (IRE), and half-brother to Run For Brownie (IRE) and Christian Era (IRE). His jumping has not been good enough in just two outings to date. *F. Crawford & Mrs N. Morrison — Zetland (Chris Dennis).* 344 (2m4fOMa), 505 (CMa).

SWORD FIGHTER ..8-10§.. 10 ch.g. Broadsword (USA) — Salford Raphaella (Deep Run) 23u2. Tall lengthy owner-bred. P-t-P '02 r2 p2 (last of 2 once). Placed in all five completions, and would have filled a minor berth when unseating, but a dog. Got Phillip York into trouble with his liberal use of the whip once, and unimproved by a visor on his latest appearance. Thrice beaten in excess of 20 lengths, and does not deserve to score. *Miss J.P. Hawkins — Crawley & Horsham (Ian Cobb).* 295 (OMa), 644 (OMa), 1055 (OMa), 1285 (OMa).

SYDNEY HOBART ..9-3.. 10 b.g. True Song — New World (St Columbus) p55. Workmanlike lengthy brother to Smart Song, and half-brother to Grain Hill and New World Comet. Dam, half-sister to 3 Pointers, won 2 Points and placed 3. Grandam, Bright Daisy, won 4 Points (including a dead-heat) and placed 7. P-t-P '02/3 r12 w1 (Maiden) p6 (4 2nds, beaten head of 3 once; and inc 3rd of 4 twice); 4th, last, and fell/unseated 3. Won a 16-runner Maiden at Dingley last year, but previously a beaten favourite on six occasions, and ridden with a complete lack of urgency by Alex Vaughan-Jones since he fell off him at the last once. Performed reasonably when 20 lengths fifth at Marks Tey but seems to need plenty of time off, and a squiggle still hangs over him. *Mrs A. Vaughan-Jones & G. Luck — W. Norfolk (Caroline Bailey).* 31 (Cnr), 159 (R), 250 (R).

SYLCANNY.9-0.. 11 ch.m. Sylvan Express — Candery (Derek H) pp. Medium-sized quite attractive half-sister to Canny's Fountain. Dam, half-sister to Sylcan Abbey (*qv*), failed to finish in 2 Points for the Gibbons, as did grandam, Canny's Tudor, who was subsequently 2nd in a Ch. P-t-P '00 and '02 (for Miss R. Cooper) r8 w1 (Maiden) p4 (3rds, last twice); 7th, pulled up 1, and fell 1. Gained compensation for a previously unlucky penultimate fence fall when successful at Hornby Castle in '02, but went missing last year, and showed no signs of retaining her ability in a campaign lasting three weeks in '04. *P.F. Gibbon — Zetland (Stuart Gibbon).* 563 (R), 765 (R).

SYLVIAS DREAM ..7-8.. 10 gr.m. Thethingaboutitis (USA) — Koritsaki (Strong Gale) fpR4p. Small half-sister to Ben Buckley (*qv*). NH FLAT '01 r1 p0. NH '02 (for B.P.J. Baugh) r2 p0; pulled up 1. Faded when 33 lengths fourth on her only completion in Points, and was eliminated before the end of the first mile in two of four other attempts. Seems little better than useless. *Miss R. Cooper — Albrighton (Paul Morris).* 729 (OMa), 753 (OMa), 840 (OMa), 1231 (OMam), 1424 (OMa).

TABERNACLE ..9-5.. 10 ch.g. Selkirk (USA) — Tabyan (USA) (Topsider USA) pp6p. Good-bodied half-brother to flat winner, Cap Juluca. Dam won 6f race. FLAT '98 r2 p0. NH '98/01 r11 p0. P-t-P '03 r4 w1 (Maiden) p2 (3rd of 4, and remote last of 3); and pulled up 1. Enterprisingly handled by Andrew Glassonbury when springing a 20-1 surprise at Bratton Down last year, and ran well on much firmer ground at Umberleigh next time, but seems to take a long time to hit form, never stands many outings, and appeared to go wrong at Flete Park. *E.M. Treneer — Dartmoor.* 495 (I), 706 (R), 791 (R), 1002 (R).

TABLE FOR FOUR ..9-7§.. 9 b.g. Sunley Builds — Prying Nell (Pry) pp34u41. Workmanlike brother to Table For Five. NH FLAT '01 r1 p0. NH '02 r3 p2 (3rds). P-t-P '03 r6 w1 (Maiden) p0; 6th, last, fell/unseated 2, and pulled up 1. Made all to land a three-finisher Maiden at Garthorpe last year, and put a string of modest efforts behind him when justifying favouritism in a poor Restricted in soft at Marks Tey on his latest appearance, but looks decidedly ungenuine at times, and reduced to wearing headgear. Does not respond to the owner, and has failed to complete in four starts under him, but whoever partners him in future will struggle to lift him home. Wears a cross-noseband. *P. Andrew — Fernie (Nicola Pollock).* 57 (R), 155 (Cnr), 384 (R), 648 (R), 990 (CR), 1107 (R), 1316 (R).

TAKE THE BRUSH (IRE) ..9-0.. 11 b.m. Brush Aside (USA) — Ballywilliam Girl (Royal Match) 6. Workmanlike. IRISH P-t-P '98 r2 p2 (2nds). NH '99 and '02 r2 p0 (well tailed off 7th of 8, and fell 1). P-t-P/HUNT CH '00 and '02/3 r12 w2 (2m4f Maiden and Members) p0; last pair 3, pulled up 6, and unseated 1. Won a bad 2m4f Maiden in '00, and finished alone in her Members last year, but does not stay the full trip, and stands very little racing nowadays. Only once better than last in her last 10 starts, and needs another miracle to score again. *F. & Mrs J. Hayes — Tiverton Stag (Jenny Hayes).* 1268 (R).

TAKE THE GAMBLE .—.. 9 b.m. Afzal — Martina's Magic (Martinmas) fp. Small unfurnished owner-bred half-sister to Annie's Magic. Dam is half-sister to Another Lucas (*qv* '95 Annual). P-t-P '03 r2 p0 (unseated 1, and pulled up 1). A very poor jumper and has yet to go more than two miles without mishap, and fell at the third when cheekpieces were applied on her reappearance. Already looks to have been consigned to the rubbish tip. Wears a cross-noseband. *Mrs S.A. & Miss A. Meakins — Carms (Amanda Meakins).* 204 (CfMa), 675 (CfMa).

TALEBAN ..9-7.. 10 b.g. Alleged (USA) — Triode (USA) (Sharpen Up) 3. Smallish angular. Dam won 2 flat (8-10f). ITALIAN FLAT '97 (for L.M. Cumani) r1 w1 (8f). FLAT '98 r3 p0. NH '99/01 and '03 (for C.J. Mann, and J. Wade) r14 p4 (inc 2 2nds in Chses). An Italian flat winner as a two-year-old, but never successful over jumps, although he has been placed on five occasions and was second at between two and 18 lengths in Chases, and 20 lengths third in his only Hunter Chase. Blinkered once under Rules, and wore cheekpieces on his final two attempts. Missed '02, and appeared to have an immediate setback in '04. *J. Wade — S. Durham.* 436 (3m1f110yH).

TALE BRIDGE (IRE) ..9-8§.. 12 b.g. Tale Quale — Loobagh Bridge (River Beauty) 757564453. Compact brother to Tell Tale (IRE) (*qv*). NH FLAT '98 r1 p0. NH '98 r3 p0. P-t-P/HUNT CH '99/00 and '02/3 (for Mr J.G. Cann) r24 w2 (Maiden and Intermediate) p9 (6 3rds, inc Hunt Ch); 4th twice, 5th thrice, 6th, last 2, and pulled up 5. A very steady jumper and has won two weak stamina tests readily, but indolent and needs strong handling, and John Russell, in his first season, could not galvanise him early enough in any of his races. Tried in cheekpieces and visors, and increasingly reluctant as the season wore on, and can be safely ignored. *R.G. Russell — Pytchley (Caroline Bailey).* 32 (Cnr), 175 (Cnr), 249 (Cnr), 466 (Cf), 583 (Cf), 783 (M), 1031 (Cf), 1213 (Cnr), 1468 (C).

TALES OF BOUNTY (IRE) ..10-8.. 10 b.g. Ela-Mana-Mou — Tales Of Wisdom (Rousillon USA) 2121p5. Tall rangy half-brother to flat winner, Mystic Quest. Dam, half-sister to Moving Out (*qv* '00 Annual), won at 12f. FLAT r13 p2 (3rds). NH '98/01 r11 w2 (2m1f-2m6f Hdles) p5. P-t-P '01 r2 p0 (fell/unseated 2). NH '02/3 r6 w2 (3m110y Hdle, and 3m Ch) p1 (2nd). Thrice a winner over hurdles, and required three attempts before he got the hang of jumping fences, but switched back to the smaller obstacles for his last two starts under Rules, and acquired blinkers in the latest. Appeared to be done an injustice by the Judge on his return to Points at Larkhill, but held on to a dwindling advantage there next time, and regained headgear when winning a race for Military personnel at Sandown in which Jamie Snowden was easily the best rider. Not a natural jumper, and will not entertain being in front for too long (*viz* the Coronation Cup) and will probably have to return to Richard Barber in order to score again. Has done all his winning on right-handed tracks. *H.B. Geddes — Taunton V. (Paul Nicholls).* 88 (L), 140 (MO), 277 (O), 445 (3m110yH), 994 (3m110yH), 1169 (3m2f110yH).

TALLABURN ..9-1.. 9 br.m. Mutamarrid — Make The Grade (Last Fandango) 24pr3p3. Short-backed light-framed owner-bred. Dam is half-sister to Haneesha (*qv* '91 Annual). NH FLAT '01 r2 p0. P-t-P '02/3 r8 p1 (2nd of 3); 6th, last pair 2, and fell/unseated 4. Placed in four races but a non-stayer and has never been involved in any finishes, and remains prone to errors. Has run tongue-tied. Wears a cross-noseband. *I. Thomson — Border (Jane Findlay).* 136 (OMam), 286 (CfMa), 549 (CMam), 919 (CMa), 1224 (OMa), 1422 (OMa), 1475 (OMa).

TALL HAT (IRE) ..9-4.. 10 b.g. Jimmys Pixie (IRE) — Fast And Straight (IRE) (Shirley Heights) 5. Tall. Dam won 12f race in Ireland. IRISH P-t-P '00/2 r11 p2 (2nds); pulled up 6, fell 1. P-t-P '03 r4 p3 (3rds, of 4 once, and last twice); and pulled up 1. Often showed good speed, and achieved five placings, but did not get the trip well enough to score, and broke down irreparably on his reappearance. *A. & Mrs J. Bowen — Fernie (Nicola Pollock).* 21 (OMa).

TANAGER ..10-8§.. 10 ch.g. Carlingford Castle — Tangara (Town Crier) 4523141uu71. Tall rangy half-brother to Reedfinch, and to Hurdles winner, Bell Bird. NH FLAT '00 r1 p0. P-t-P '02/3 r12 w4 (Maiden, Restricted and 2 Members) p4 (3 3rds, of 4 once); 5th, and pulled up 3. Hit a rich vein of form in the second half of last season, but an enigmatic character, and acquired blinkers in '04, and should have won more frequently. His association with Ben King began with three straight wins, but then things went awry, and he fell off him when going best in the Land Rover Final at Cheltenham, and when a length up at Towcester, and Joe Docker was reinstated at Stratford where his jumping lacked confidence. King regained the ride on his final appearance, and always travelling sweetly, romped home at a very backable 9-4 at Kingston Blount. Likes firmish but can handle mud when in the mood, and whilst his performances can never be predicted he looks sure to find further opportunities, and deserves compensation in a Hunter Chase. *P.G. Fullagar, J.A. Nash, R. Owen & P. Jacomine — V. of Aylesbury with Garth & S. Berks (Karen Lawther).* 16 (C), 50 (I), 168 (C), 440 (2m7f110yH), 624 (O), 640 (Cf), 868 (O), 1171 (3m2f110yH), 1356 (2m6fH), 1452 (3m4fH), 1515 (O).

TAP DANCE .9-5§.. 7 ch.g. Dancing Spree (USA) — Trachelium (Formidable USA) 22dp. Compact well-made half-brother to Hurdles winners, Uniform (also won flat), Innes, and to flat winner, Turn Back. NH '01/3 (for Miss S.E. Hall, and M.E. Sowersby) r14 p4 (2nds); pulled up 4. Sold Doncaster Nov '02 for 3000. Second in four Hurdles at between three and 16 lengths, but also unplaced in three Sellers, and pulled up on four occasions. Tongue-tied twice and wore headgear on his final two appearances to '03, and has consistently been very disappointing and ungenuine. Only beaten a head on his Pointing debut, but a poor second next time and was not keen (disqualified after the rider had failed to weigh-in), and after having changed hands he immediately went lame for the latest yard. One to beware of even if he manages to reappear. *R.W. Fife, C.R. Piercy & Mrs M. Fife — A.G. Brown — York & Ainsty S. (Marjorie Fife).* 60 (OMa), 392 (CfMa), 1259 (OMa).

TARPON TALE (IRE) ..9-0§.. 8 b.g. Mujadil (USA) — Lady Of The Mist (IRE) (Digamist USA) 5u5u53. Small close-coupled. 8800y. FLAT '99 r3 p0. IRISH FLAT '00 r1 p0. IRISH NH '01 and '03 (for J.J.

Murphy) r14 p0; pulled up 3. NH '03 (for M.C. Pipe) r5 p0; last 2, pulled up 1, ran out 1. Has managed to evade winning any of his 29 races, and after pulling up in his final three attempts over jumps in Ireland he performed badly five times for Martin Pipe including when a poor last twice, pulling up and running out in Chases. Tried a Seller on the flat, and often wears a visor or cheekpieces. Unseated a girl novice in two of their three attempts together, and although he finished 12 lengths third in his latest Maiden his lack of enthusiasm makes him permanently untrustworthy. *Mrs A.L. Colledge — S. Devon.* 469 (2m4fOMa), 567 (CfMa), 721 (OMa), 962 (OMa), 1006 (CfMa), 1353 (OMa).

TARTAN RISING ..5-0.. 6 b.g. Primitive Rising (USA) — Tartan Buck (IRE) (Buckskin FR) pp7. Dam, sister to Injectabuck, and half-sister to Ask The Doctor was 3rd in 2m4f Maiden for Chris Dawson (her only start). Has had no idea of what is required so far, and finally crept home about three fences adrift when last in a youngsters Maiden in which he had led for almost two miles. *C. Dawson — Zetland.* 762 (I), 919 (CMa), 1158 (OMa).

TARTAR SABRE .9-8.. 8 b.g. Broadsword (USA) — Tartar Holly VII (unknown) 3u212f. Workmanlike lengthy owner-bred half-brother to Harry Tartar and Henry Tartar. P-t-P '03 (for Mr J.D. Parker) r1 p0 (pulled up). Backward and finding his feet, and beaten a minimum of 25 lengths in his first four starts, but managed to outbattle Tooley Park in a three-finisher Maiden at Cottenham next time. Backed from 14s to 5-1 in his first Restricted, and finished a respectable 15 lengths second, but already off the bridle when falling at half way subsequently. Needs to jump with more fluency but there should be an average East Anglian Restricted with his name on it in '05. *The Sporting Endeavour Partnership (I. Adam) — Waveney H. (John Ibbott).* 28 (I), 153 (OMa), 401 (OMa), 560 (OMa), 745 (R), 1152 (R).

TEA BOX (IRE) ..10-3.. 14 b.g. Meneval (USA) — Elteetee (Paddy's Stream) p. Small neat half-brother to jumping winner, The Granby (IRE). IRISH P-t-P '96/7 r3 p3. IRISH NH FLAT '97 r2 p0. IRISH NH '96/7 r5 p0 (9th, and unseated in Hunt Chses; and inc Hdle). P-t-P/HUNT CH '98, '00 and '02 r19 w10 (inc 3 2m4f-3m1f110y Hunt Chses, and hat-trick inc Ladies '98, 4-timer '02) p4 (2 2nds, of 3 once; and 2 3rds in Hunt Chses); 5th, 7th, pulled up 2 and fell 1. Completing a five-timer, and his tenth success in all when scoring readily in a Fakenham Hunter Chase in '02, but was already showing signs of fragility, and broke down on his return from a year on the sidelines at Higham. One of the few disappointments for the yard in '04. *Mr & Mrs M.A. Kemp — Suffolk (David Kemp).* 158 (CCon).

TEACH ALTRA (IRE) ..9-13.. 8 b.g. Warcraft (USA) — Miss Pushover (Push On) 91524d. Well-made lengthy half-brother to Heavenly Citizen (IRE) and Irish Pointing winner, Push Gently. IRISH P-t-P '02/3 r10 w1 (5yo&up Maiden) p4; fell 1. IRISH NH FLAT (for W.J. Burke) r1 p0. A consistently reliable jumper who has done very well to complete in 14 of 15 Points (fell on his debut), and was gaining his second win in a three-race spell when he took a Restricted at Ampton after being backed from 10s to 7-1. Not finding it easy to get into contention since, and was beaten 30 lengths when second at Detling. May be able to unearth another opportunity. *M.J. Roberts — E. Sussex & Romney Marsh.* 2 (R), 44 (R), 239 (3m1fH), 536 (CfL), 743 (L).

TEASDALE HOUSE (IRE) ..—.. 6 br.g. Carroll House — Mrs Teasdale (Idiot's Delight) f. Dam, sister to two Pointers including Queen Of Sparta (*qv* '95 Annual), and half-sister to Shameless Lady (*qv* '01 Annual) unseated in a Point and subsequently withdrawn NH flat (bolted in both) 'clearly one sandwich short of a picnic'. Bought Goffs Ireland, Dec '02 for 1577. Did not impress in the paddock on a Dalston debut, and having been led to the start where he unseated the rider he ended his day with a fall at the eighth. *S. Waugh — Morpeth (John Charlton).* 767 (2m4fOMa).

TEA TIME (IRE) .7-13.. 10 b.g. Glacial Storm (USA) — Blaze Of Hope (IRE) (Le Moss) 3p. Tall. Dam, sister to Young Gun (*qv* '97 Annual). NH '02 r2 p0 (pulled up 2). P-t-P '03 r2 p0 (pulled up 1, and fell 1). Completing for the first time in five attempts when 40 lengths third of four at Cottenham, where he ran well considering his lack of peak fitness and jumping errors, but broke a blood vessel at Marks Tey in February, and has not been seen since. Probably retired. *C. Pocock — Cambs with Enfield Chace (Simon Andrews).* 103 (OMa), 245 (CfMa).

TEETON DIAMOND ..9-7.. 7 br.m. Broadsword (USA) — Teeton Frolic (Sunley Builds) p5p33. Strong workmanlike owner-bred sister to Teeton Priceless (*qv*). P-t-P '03 r3 p1 (3/4l 2nd); and fell 2. Marked down as a future winner when three-quarters-of-a-length second over 2m4f at Dingley in '03, but disappointingly failed to see out the full trip this year, and only once better than last. Could be made fitter but her size suggests that she will not appreciate sound surfaces which she avoided in '04. *Mrs J.M. Tice — Pytchley.* 386 (OMa), 588 (CfMa), 788 (CfMa), 1035 (OMa), 1215 (CfMa).

TEETON FIZZ ..9-13.. 9 ch.m. Sunley Builds — Sunday Champers (True Song) 5pp22224. Strong workmanlike sister to Teeton Builds and Teeton Toast. Dam won 3 Points and placed 4 (inc a Hunt Ch) for Joan Tice. Grandam, Poppywee, won 3 Points (2 Opens) and 3rd 2. Great-grandam, Carnival Candy, won a Maiden and 3rd. P-t-P '02/3 r9 w1 (Maiden) p3 (2nds, last once); 5th, and pulled up

4. Runner-up in five Restricteds, and got to within half-a-length of causing a 25-1 shock at Mollington once, but also beaten 15 and 25 lengths in them, and when 4-5 once. Sometimes makes mistakes, and gives the strong impression that she does not place all her cards on the table. *Mrs J.M. Tice — Pytchley (Jenny Garley).* 2 (R), 44 (R), 169 (R), 375 (R), 587 (R), 787 (CR), 1034 (R), 1217 (R).

TEETON GLAIVE ..9-1.. 10 b.m. Broadsword (USA) — Tamara Bay (Furry Glen) ffp1u. Small unfurnished. Dam, half-sister to San Fernando (*qv* '00 Annual). P-t-P '03 r5 w1 (Maiden) p1 (2nd); 4th, 5th, and pulled up 1. Given a peach of a ride by Stuart Morris when successful at Garthorpe in '03, and left solo when successful in a three-runner Restricted at Lockinge this year, but frequently let down by jumping deficiencies. As experienced as Heather Irving is she is just not gelling with her, and a change of rider might produce better results. Wears a cross-noseband. *Mrs S.K. Edmunds & J. Busby — Grafton (Sylvia Edmunds).* 169 (R), 294 (R), 384 (R), 939 (R), 1120 (Cf).

TEETON PRICELESS ..10-3.. 10 b.m. Broadsword (USA) — Teeton Frolic (Sunley Builds) p231211. Workmanlike sister to Teeton Diamond, and half-sister to Teeton Mirage, Teeton Bubbley, Teeton Belle and Teeton Prince. Grandam, Sunday Champers (dam of Teeton Builds, *qv* '01 Annual), won 3 Points and placed 4 (inc a Hunt Ch), but was overwhelmed by temperament latterly. Great-grandam, Poppywee, won 3 Points (2 Opens) and 3rd 2. Great-great-grandam, Carnival Candy, won a Maiden and 3rd. P-t-P/HUNT CH '01/3 r13 w3 (Maiden, Restricted and Intermediate) p2 (3rd of 4 once); 4th, 5th twice, pulled up 2 and fell/unseated 3. Very much the Teeton flag-bearer in '04, but even she did not click into gear until her fourth start, and had luck on her side when successful in a muddy three-finisher Hunter Chase at Towcester. A secure jumper now, and scored on merit when instigating a stable double at Dingley, but seems best when going right-handed. Acts on any going. *Mrs J.M. Tice — Pytchley.* 124 (CCon), 374 (O), 783 (M), 1031 (Cf), 1213 (Cnr), 1356 (2m6fH), 1468 (C).

TEETON PRINCE ..9-7.. 6 b.g. Shambo — Teeton Frolic (Sunley Builds) 41. Strong owner-bred half-brother to Teeton Priceless (*qv*). Did not look fully wound up in his first season, but followed a 19 lengths fourth in May with a ready defeat of some frustrating rivals at Dingley later in the month. Possesses further scope, and it is encouraging that his half-sister (four years older) successfully reached Hunter Chase standard in '04. *Mrs J. Tice — Pytchley.* 1339 (OMa), 1473 (OMa).

TEETON TOAST ..6-12.. 7 ch.g. Sunley Builds — Sunday Champers (True Song) 3p. Owner-bred brother to Teeton Fizz (*qv*). Novicey when 19 lengths third in an appalling five-runner Maiden at Brampton Bryan (the proximity of the horse-boxes seemed to be commanding the attention of most of his opponents), and pulled up after 2m4f next time. Should be able to do better with experience. *Mrs J.M. Tice — Pytchley.* 1116 (OMa), 1339 (OMa).

TEG ..—.. 7 b.m. Petong — Felinwen (White Mill) p. Lengthy half-sister to 2 flat winners (one in Italy), including Brynkir. FLAT '01/3 (for S.C. Williams, and I.A. Wood) r7 p0. Beat ten horses from a total of 97 runners when 16 lengths or more adrift in seven flat races (visored on final start), and had an unhappy passage before pulling up when tailed off after 2m4f in a Restricted (hampered twice in the very early stages, and made a mistake at the 12th). Does not look to have encouraging credentials. *R.A. Linfoot — Tivyside.* 452 (R).

TEJAQUE ..9-3§.. 10 b.m. Lord Of Arabia — Devil's Gold (Goldfella) p. Compact. NH '02 r1 p0 (pulled up). P-t-P '00 and '02/3 r7 p0 (4th, last pair 2, pulled up 2, brought down 1, and refused 1). Showed her first signs of ability when making the frame and beaten 13 and 15 lengths in '03, but normally displays great reluctance, and hardly ever looks fit. *Mrs S.Y. Farthing — Worcester & W. Farmers (Brian Farthing).* 1232 (OMa).

TELLAPORKY ..9-0.. 16 b.g. Bold Fort — Ab Dabh (Spanish Gold) 3p. Smallish. NH '96/9 and '02 r16 p5 (inc Sellers, and 2 Chses); visored penultimate start. P-t-P/HUNT CH '97 and '00/3 r27 w1 (Maiden) p6 (3 3rds, inc in Hunt Ch); 4th five, 5th, last pair 5, pulled up 5, and fell/unseated 4. A triumph for persevering connections when scoring at the 38th attempt last year, and provided the trainer's father with his first Point-to-Point ride 27-years after hanging up his boots under Rules, but would have travelled faster if wife Jenny had given him a piggy-back, and was outpaced as soon as son James pressed the button on the eventual winner. Wears a cross-noseband, and has worn cheekpieces. *Mrs J. & Miss E.L. Owen — Bicester with Whaddon (Emma Owen).* 1030 (M), 1245 (R).

TELLER OF TALES ..10-4.. 9 ch.g. Arazi (USA) — Water Splash (USA) (Little Current USA) 213p. Small compact half-brother to French flat/English Hurdling winner, Water Sports, to flat winner and useful jumper, Stately Home (IRE), to Irish flat winner Blue Judge (also 2nd in Derby), and to flat winner, Bint Alsarab (in Ireland). Dam won 12f race for The Queen. FRENCH FLAT '00 (for A. Fabre) w3 (12-14f) p1. NH '01 (for C.J. Mann) r4 w2 (2 2m5f Hdles) p0; fell 1. Sold Ascot, Aug '01 for 3000. Won three flat races in France including at Vichy and was unbeaten when blinkered in his final two Hurdles, but was returning in Points after breaking down. Immediately showed he retained ability when four lengths second in a military race at Larkhill, and finished alone in a match in similar company there next time, but was unfortunately to meet his own end two outings later when his legs gave way again at Hackwood Park. Mrs R. Fuller — Vine & Craven (Charlotte Fuller). 138 (C), 336 (C), 457 (MO), 717 (Cf).

TELLITASITIS ..—.. 9 ch.g. Thethingaboutitis (USA) — Stellify (Maris Piper) 1. Won the (allegedly) 3m4f stone wall Members race at Flagg Moor (easily the fastest time of the day!), and the rider triumphed by making a beeline for the final obstacle whilst her main rivals were fannying about in the countryside with no sense of direction. A silly contest, but what a joy to have this marvellous meeting back again. *Miss N. Brady — High Peak.* 984 (3m4fNCM).

TELL TALE (IRE) ..10-7.. 13 b.g. Tale Quale — Loobagh Bridge (River Beauty) *p2622321*. Small compact brother to Tale Bridge (IRE), and half-brother to Irish winners, Break Away Bridge (NH flat) and Must Stay (Pointing). P-t-P/HUNT CH '97/03 (for Mrs P. Pengelly & Mrs H. Stoneman) r25 w4 (inc Open) p6 (2 2nds; 4 3rds, of 4 twice); pulled up 7, fell 2. NH '04 (for J.G. Cann) r3 w1 (beat River Shamrock 6*l* in 3m6f Ch: *chsd ldrs, ld 4 out, clr aft last, easily*) p1 (3rd in 3m2f Ch: *hld up & bhnd, rdn & lost tch 14, stayed on frm 2 out, nt rch ldrs*); and pulled up in 2m7f110y Ch: *a bhnd, rdn 7, t.o & pu 10*. An out-and-out stayer, and suited by mud, but has never stood an awful lot of racing, and been extremely difficult to win with. Has learned to handle fast ground, but set a hopeless task by the normally very competent Tom Malone at Folkestone, and appreciated the easier underfoot conditions when the pair teamed up to land the £8,225 Veterans Grand National at Cartmel in May. Deserved his win, as did connections whose policy to concentrate on extreme stamina tests should be continued. *Mrs P. Pengelly — E. Devon (Ollie Bush).* 347 (3mH), 490 (3m2fH), 747 (3m1f110yH), 975 (2m7f110yH), 1441 (3m7fH).

TELL THE NIPPER (IRE) .10-0.. 14 b.g. Riberetto — Divine Dibs (Raise You Ten) 2414253. Workmanlike half-brother to Irish Chasing and NH flat winner, Love And Porter, and to NH flat winner, Paddy The Piper (IRE). IRISH FLAT '00 r2 p0. IRISH P-t-P '95 and '00 r7 w3 p4 (unlucky once). NH and IRISH NH '95/00 r39 w4 (2m3f Hdle, and 3 Chses, 2m4f-3m1f) p9 (inc 2nd in Kim Muir). P-t-P/HUNT CH '01/3 r16 w1 (3m2f Hunt Ch) p5 (2 2nds, last once; 3 3rds, of 4 once, inc distant last in Hunt Ch); 5th, 8th, last pair 5, unseated 2, and pulled up 1. A high earner under Rules, principally in Ireland, but needs to be held up and finds little off the bridle, and has only won twice since '97. Normally suited by easy surfaces, and scoring on fast ground for the first time at Charing, but thrice beaten two lengths or less in '04, and typically seems intent on proving most frustrating. Frequently blinkered in the past. *Mrs C.M. Gorman — Crawley & Horsham.* 16 (C), 182 (CCon), 422 (CCon), 537 (4mMO), 638 (M), 1054 (Cf), 1410 (Cf).

TEME WILLOW (IRE) ..10-3.. 14 ch.g. Henbit (USA) — Nevada Lady (Trimmingham) 331213. Strong-topped half-brother to Maltese Cross (IRE) and Lady Nevada (IRE). P-t-P '98/00 and '02/3 (for Mr R.T. Baimbridge & Mr T.S. Warner) r21 w7 (inc Mixed Open, Open and 2 Ladies, inc 4-timer '02) p4 (2 2nds, last once; and inc last of 3 once); 5th, last pair 2, unseated 2 and pulled up 5. Has had many different pilots in Points, but only Alison Dare and Julian Pritchard have truly mastered his eccentricities, and he remains a challenging ride. Plundered Upper Sapey and Bredwardine for the second time each in '04, but consistently gives away lengths by jumping right-handed, and a bad blunder at the second last at Andoversford probably cost him yet another race. Gave the impression he did not relish a struggle in softish when 4-11 at Maisemore, and taken off his feet on firm at Chaddesley on his latest start, but fast approaching a score in double figures, and should achieve it if he remains in training at 14. *T.S. Warner — Berkeley (Dick Baimbridge).* 254 (O), 758 (O), 1138 (O), 1257 (O), 1390 (O), 1529 (MO).

TEMPLEBREEDY (IRE) .10-0§.. 11 br.g. Torenaga — Points Review (Major Point) 1p43p. Smallish unfurnished half-brother to Haven Light, and to Irish Pointing winner, Knocknagore (IRE). Dam is half-sister to Charlie Chalk (*qv* '03 Annual). IRISH P-t-P '00 r5 p2; 5th, pulled up 1, and fell 1. P-t-P '02/3 r9 w3 (Maiden, Restricted and Intermediate) p3 (2 2nds, last once); 4th, pulled up 1, and refused 1. A nervy individual, and struggles to get home when conditions are testing, but scoring for the fourth time in five completed starts when resolutely making all on firmish at Horseheath on his reappearance. Usually sets off at a very brisk gallop, and helped Highland Rose get home in under six minutes at Cottenham subsequently, but otherwise disappointing, and continues to find nil under pressure whatever the underfoot conditions. *R.J. French — N. Salop (Sheila Crow).* 374 (O), 630 (2m4fH), 750 (O), 998 (L), 1502 (O).

TEMPLE GLEN ..8-13.. 6 gr.g. Accondy (IRE) — Wish Me Well (Asir) p43. Has looked green, but starting to show a little promise, and followed a 12 lengths fourth with a four lengths third over a probably inadequate 2m4f. Should be capable of winning a Maiden. *J. Pate — Lauderdale (Joan Hollands).* 1081 (OMa), 1311 (OMa), 1474 (2m4fOMa).

TEMPLENOE HARE (IRE) ..9-5.. 12 b.g. Lafontaine (USA) — Bellalma (Belfalas) 0u42pfp. Workmanlike compact half-brother to jumping winner, Jacdor (IRE), and to NH flat winner, Greywell (IRE). IRISH NH FLAT '97 and '99 r3 p0. IRISH NH '97 and '99 r5 p0; pulled up 1. IRISH P-t-P '00 r6 w1 (Maiden) p0; pulled up 2, fell 2. NH '01 r1 p0 (11th in 2m4f110y Hdle). P-t-P/HUNT CH '01/

3 r7 p1 (last of 3); 4th twice, 5th, last pair 2, and pulled up 1. A winner in heavy in Ireland, but a weak finisher in four seasons in the present yard, and apparently under the weather in '03 when a virus caused him to break blood vessels. Prone to bad mistakes, and still gives the impression there is something wrong with him. *Mrs M. Cambray — S. Salop (Pamela Sykes).* 2 (R), 95 (R), 587 (R), 933 (CR), 1048 (R), 1265 (R), 1389 (R).

TENACIOUS MELODY ..9-13.. 9 b.g. Tina's Pet — High Run (HOL) (Runnymede) p312. Tall strong brother to She's Not A Lady, and half-brother to 3 flat winners (2 abroad), including Hever Golf Lady. Dam won twice in Holland, and was runner-up in Oaks and 1000 Guineas there. FLAT '00 r3 p0. NH '01/2 (for Mrs L. Williamson) r2 p0; pulled up 1. No good in rare spins on the flat (troublesome at the start in the first two) and over Hurdles (a remote tenth of 11, and pulled up), but more effective in Points. Can take a fierce hold and make mistakes, and was 30 lengths last of three at Bonvilston, but led after a mile and was in full command a mile later in a Maiden at Pentreclwydau, and ended his season with a creditable second to Simply The One at Bredwardine. Like Fair Charmeur is another 'takes no prisoners' ride for the fearless Isabel Thompsett, and should be able to charge round in front for the odd success in future (provided his legs take the strain). *J.L. Brown — Pembs (Graham Lavis).* 948 (OMa), 1095 (R), 1239 (OMa), 1389 (R).

TEN BOB (IRE) ..10-3.. 7 b.g. Jurado (USA) — Rush For Gold (Mugatpura) 11p. Tall good-topped half-brother to Ten Poundsworth (IRE). Dam won Point, 2 NH flat (2m-2m2f), 2m Hdle, and 2m2f Chase in Ireland. Bought Doncaster, May '02 for 4000. Toyed with his rivals after leading on the bit at the 15th in a Witton Castle Maiden, and again stayed on stoutly in a Brocklesby Park Restricted but a disappointing favourite at Whitwell-on-the-Hill where he lost his place quickly from four out and certainly did not give his true running. Can pull hard and look awkward, but has given the impression of having sufficient speed and stamina for a Novices Hunter Chase success when he recovers his form. Quickly able to assume the identity of a Mark Tompkins flat winner who broke his leg as recently as '98. *Mrs S. Smith — Pendle Forest & Craven (Joss Saville).* 165 (OMa), 481 (R), 770 (Cf).

TENDER TANGLE ..9-12.. 10 ch.g. Crested Lark — Red Tango (Legal Tender) 1. Tall owner-bred. Dam, half-sister to Mister Kelly (*qv* '95 Annual), pulled up 4 and fell/unseated 2 in Points for Pauline Pugh. NH '02 r5 p0; pulled up 2, fell/unseated 2. P-t-P '03 r1 p0 (5th). Useless under Rules, but backed from 12s to 7-1 on his only appearance last year, and scored unchallenged in much the fastest of four Maidens on the card on firmish at Chaddesley in '04. Would have obvious prospects in a Restricted, but is clearly very difficult to keep sound. *Mrs P.M. Pugh — Farmers Bloodhounds (Sam Loggin).* 259 (CMa).

TENINAROW (IRE) ..10-1.. 11 b.g. Camden Town — Noellespir (Bargello) 23122. Tall workmanlike half-brother to Some Tourist (IRE) (*qv*). NH FLAT '99 r2 p0. NH '00 r6 p0; pulled up 2, fell 1. P-t-P '03 r3 w2 (Maiden and Restricted) p0; and fell 1. Resurfaced after a long absence to record a double at Trebudannon in '03, and beat subsequent hat-trick scorer Father Mansfield in a Great Trethew Intermediate this year, but surprisingly turned over at 8-11 next time, and suffered another narrow defeat at Trebudannon subsequently. Seems inconvenienced by fast ground, and his jumping suffers as a result, but very determined and deserves to have his consistency rewarded again. *M. Weir — Dartmoor.* 313 (I), 495 (I), 705 (I), 908 (Cf), 1433 (Cf).

TENSING ..—.. 10 b.g. North Col — Thetford Chase (Relkino) ppup. Strong home-bred brother to Colbert and Aiming High, and half-brother to Highland Chase and Autumn Blunder. P-t-P '02 r2 p1 (2nd); and pulled up 1. Peaked when a promising two-and-a-half lengths second over 2m4f at Ston Easton in his debut season, and has gone downhill since returning from a lay-off. Showed speed to halfway thrice in '04, but kept hanging right at Maisemore Park, and is clearly troubled. Wears a cross-noseband. *C.F.C. Jackson & J.P. Thorne — N. Ledbury (Sarah Jackson).* 620 (OMa), 731 (OMa), 927 (OMa), 1232 (OMa).

TERIMON'S DREAM .9-10.. 8 gr.g. Terimon — I Have A Dream (SWE) (Mango Express) pp41. Strong. FLAT '00 and '02/3 r6 p0. NH '02 (for A.W. Carroll) r1 p0. Bought Ascot, Apr for 1619. Bad on the flat including in a Seller, and in a Hurdle (18th of 19), but better in Points, despite looking a hot ride who has had two paddock handlers and been sent to post early on his last two attempts (went very fast to the start in the latest). Wants to go flat out from the word go, and Dave Mansell did a very good job of keeping him in check sufficiently to have some reserves for the closing stages (in which he wandered when winning a youngsters Maiden at Bredwardine). Could be more suspect in Restricteds, unless some way can be found to calm him down. *R.E. Dance - N. Ledbury (Martin Jones).* 8 (2m4fOMa), 410 (2m4fCfMa), 1253 (M), 1394 (OMa).

TERINO .9-4.. 9 b.g. Terimon — Ashmo (Ashmore FR) 4331. Compact good-topped half-brother to Young Manny (*qv*). NH FLAT '01/2 r3 p0. NH '02/3 (for breeder A.E. Jessop) r8 p0; fell 1. Bought Ascot, Oct for 1238. A complete failure in his first three years and was beaten 43 lengths plus in seven of eight Hurdles including Sellers, but Maidens have been much more his level, and after making the frame in his first three (beaten under six lengths twice) he scored by a very easy 20 lengths when partnered by the champion for the first time at Lifton (his usual jockey had the misfortune to be aboard the runner-up). A sensible jumper who gets the trip well, and may not be too far away in Restricteds. *A.W.G. Geering, A.C. Cowlishaw & Miss J. Barkwill - Lamerton (Tony & Pauline Geering).* 194 (CfMa), 827 (CfMa), 1272 (OMa), 1545 (OMa).

PLATE 118 564 Hurworth Ladies Open: Texas Ranger and Jo Foster are the easy winners
PHOTO: Roy Parker

TEXAS RANGER ..10-8.. 7 b.g. Mtoto — Favorable Exchange (USA) (Exceller USA) u3111f12. Small close-coupled half-brother 6 flat winners (one abroad), including Shonara's Way (also successful Hurdler), Unchanged, Sterling Fellow and Total Love. Dam won three French flat (10-12f). 6000f and IR20,000y. FLAT '01 r8 p4 (3rds). NH '02/3 (for C.J. Mann) r11 w4 (2m-2m4f Hdles) p2. Bought Doncaster, May for 15,000. Showed ability on the flat, and was in glittering form when completing a four-timer over Hurdles in May/June in '02, principally on firmish ground but once in softish. Still a colt in those days, but equally effective since losing his tackle, and gave Jo Foster plenty of thrills when winning four Ladies Opens, generally after making the bulk of the running. Speedy and resolute and probably finds 11 stone ideal, but did suffer a couple of shock defeats when odds-on, and although there were no excuses for defeat at 2-5 when he fell at the last, he had a hard luck story when 4-6 at Heslaker, as he unfortunately spoiled a fine season by finishing lame. Had the makings of a prolific winner, but the future now looks rather less rosy. *R. Chew — Middleton (Jo Foster).* 162 (L), 391 (MO), 502 (L), 564 (L), 811 (L), 1160 (L), 1420 (L), 1459 (L).

THANKS JIM (IRE) ..10-5.. 6 b.g. Jolly Jake (NZ) — Summing Oak (IRE) (Summing USA) 2f. Sturdy compact half-brother to a winner in USA. Bought Doncaster, Aug for 7000. Looked to show plenty of promise when a good second with the rest well beaten on his debut, but was struggling to justify odds of 4-7 when he fell at Charm Park, and tragically broke his neck. D.J. Dickson — Middleton (Gill Walford). 476 (CfMa), 959 (OMa).

THAT'S CASH (IRE) .—§.. 7 b.g. Tornabuoni — Gina O'Flynn (Golden Love) pr. Tall. Dam won Mares Maiden in Ireland. IRISH NH '03 (for M. Hourigan) r2 p0; fell 1. Bought Doncaster, Nov for 1400. Eighty-eight lengths tenth of 11 and fell in Irish Hurdles, and pulled up when tiring after two miles and refused to race when equally unpromising in Cornish Maidens. *R.G. Chapman — Four Burrow.* 909 (2m4fOMa), 1432 (OMa).

THATSFOREEL ..10-0.. 12 b.g. Scottish Reel — That Space (Space King) pf7. Lengthy good-bodied home-bred brother to Hurdles winner, Cuillin Caper, and half-brother to Wrekin Lad, Piu Moto, Space Voyager, Freight King, Spacious Sovereign, Miswiskers and Safeasthat. NH '01/2 r7 p3 (inc 2 2nds); pulled up 3. P-t-P/HUNT CH '98/00 and '03 r12 w4 (inc 3m Hunt Ch) p5 (4 2nds); 4th, 8th, and pulled up 1. Sold to the current owner for 35,000gns after scoring twice as a five-year-old, but disappointing under Rules, and has only managed to win one of ten subsequent Points. Blew up completely in his first two starts in '04, including when backed from 11-2 to fours once, and not seen since finishing 16 lengths seventh of eight at Upton. Consistently gives the impression that there is something amiss. Blinkered twice '01/2. *C.J. Hitchings — N. Ledbury.* 448 (O), 615 (O), 980 (Cf).

THAT'S MY BOY (IRE) ..9-8.. 7 gr.g. Roselier (FR) — Narcone (Kambalda) 2f. Very small neat half-brother to Leaping Lady (IRE), and to Irish Pointing and Chasing winner, Native Ray. Dam, half-sister to Balda Boy (*qv* '96 Annual), won Mares Maiden in Ireland and 2m4f Chase in England. P-t-P '03 (for Mr J.G. Cann) r1 p1 (½l 2nd of 3). Beaten half-a-length when favourite in his first two starts, and odds-on to atone at Maisemore Park, but had just joined the winner when falling at the fourth last. Will surely get his just reward, and might make a useful Ladies horse in time. *Mrs P. Pengelly — E. Devon (Ollie Bush).* 486 (OMa), 723 (OMa).

THATS THE CRACK (IRE) ..—.. 11 b.g. King's Ride — Mighty Crack (Deep Run) p. Workmanlike brother to Irish Pointing and Hurdles winner, Wicked Crack, and half-brother to Whats The Crack, and to Irish Pointing winner, Blazing Crack. Dam, half-sister to Three Parsons (*qv* '92 Annual). IRISH P-t-P '99 r3 w1 (4&5yo Maiden) p1 (2nd); and pulled up 1. NH '99/01 r6 w1 (2m4f110y Ch) p1 (2nd); pulled up 2. P-t-P/HUNT CH '03 r2 p0 (unseated, and pulled up). Won in Ireland as a four-year-old, and returned from injury to beat Iron N Gold (*qv*) on firmish at Lingfield in '01, but virtually impossible to train since, and stopped very quickly after four out on his only appearance in '04. Clearly retains some ability but his problems appear insurmountable. *A.J. Brown — Buccleuch.* 73 (Cf).

THE ARCHDEACON (IRE) ..9-6.. 12 b.g. Mandalus — Best Of Kin (Pry) p7253f. Lengthy half-brother to The Rural Dean (IRE), to NH flat and Hurdles winner, Exterior Profiles (IRE), and to Irish Pointing and English Chasing winner, The Reverend Bert (IRE). Dam won a Maiden in Ireland. IRISH P-t-P '98 r6 p0 (pulled up 2, fell/unseated 2, brought down 1, and ran out 1). NH '99 r2 p0. P-t-P '99/00 and '02/3 r15 w3 (Maiden, Restricted and Intermediate) p2 (3rds, of 4 once); 4th, 7th, last pair 2, pulled up 3 and fell 3. Completing a Pointing hat-trick when successful at Maisemore Park in '00, but out of luck when sparsely campaigned in three seasons since, and beaten a minimum of 19 lengths in '04. A weak finisher nowadays and appears unsuited by easy surfaces. *Miss P. Morris — Croome & W. Warwicks.* 229 (O), 404 (O), 513 (Cf), 662 (O), 1015 (Cf), 1254 (Cf).

THEATRELAND (USA) .9-4§.. 8 b.g. Dynaformer (USA) — Mime (Cure The Blues USA) p4pp5. Close-coupled good-topped half-brother to winner in Japan. Dam won at up to 9f in USA. 90,000y. FLAT '99/00 r5 p0. NH '00/2 (for P.J. Hobbs, when successful, and S.E.H. Sherwood) r10 w1 (2m Hdle) p4; pulled up 1, unseated 1. Made a successful jumping debut in a Worcester three-year-old Hurdle despite twice jinking badly at flights, and was beaten a maximum of three-and-a-half lengths in three of four placings, but ended his career under Rules by unseating in his only Chase. Occasionally wore headgear to '01, and was blinkered for his win. Very safe in Points and able to get Hugh Phipps round the course (albeit a fence behind) in his first race ride for 15 years, but is temperamental and not interested in exerting himself, and safely ignored. *H. & Mrs P. Phipps — Croome & W. Warwicks (Hugh Phipps).* 254 (O), 976 (M), 1073 (O), 1390 (O), 1528 (Cf).

THE BABBLER ..—.. 7 b.m. Charmer — Rose Albertine (Record Token) p. Homebred half-sister to Tinafoil, Running Mute and Black Beatle. Tailed off and pulled up after 2m4f in a Mosshouses Maiden. Certainly not named after his rider, who is more of a lovable chatterbox. *J.E.M. Vestey — Jedforest (Philippa Shirley-Beavan).* 1225 (OMa).

THE BOMBERS MOON .—§.. 12 br.g. Lord Bud — Oakington (Henry The Seventh) pp. Tall strong half-brother to Hurricane Gilbert. NH FLAT '97 r2 p0 (tailed off). NH '98 r2 p0 (pulled up 2). P-t-P/HUNT CH '98, '00 and '03 r13 w1 (3-finisher Maiden) p3 (2nd of 3 once; and 2 3rds); 5th, last pair 3, pulled up 2, ran out 1, fell 1, and brought down 1. Won unchallenged in a three-finisher Maiden at Dingley last year, but often hangs left and finds nothing off the bridle after racing keenly, and has had his 9-8 rating withdrawn after two lifeless efforts in '04. *Mrs C.H. Covell — Belvoir.* 481 (R), 680 (M).

THE BOUNDER .9-8.. 15 b.g. Uncle Pokey — Young Romance (King's Troop) 5454. Smallish lengthy brother to NH flat and smart jumping winner, Young Pokey, and to a flat and Hurdles winner, and half-brother to 4 winners. NH FLAT r3 w1 p0; severed a tendon, and absent for 18 months after. NH '95/6 and '99/01 r17 w2 (2m Hdle and 2m Ch) p7; pulled up 4. P-t-P/HUNT CH '97/8 and '03 r8 w6 (3m1f110y Hunt Ch, and 5 Opens) p1 (3rd); and fell 1. One of the best pointers ever, and rattled off an arrogant six-timer and rated 11-10 '97/8, but went wrong after the last of those wins, and has spent much time on the sidelines since. Beat two rivals in '04 and hopefully connections have had the good sense not to humiliate him any more. Insulted by blinkers once in '96. *Mrs M.J. Tizzard — Blackmore & Sparkford V. (Alan Tizzard).* 33 (L), 171 (L), 472 (Cf), 792 (MO).

THE BROKEN MAN ..9-10.. 12 b.g. Rakaposhi King — School Run (Deep Run) p36433. Lengthy unfurnished half-brother to Open The Box. Dam is half-sister to Ozier Hill (*qv* '02 Annual). IRISH P-t-P '98/01 r16 w1 (6yo&up Maiden) p7; pulled up 4. IRISH HUNT CH '01 r1 p0. P-t-P/HUNT CH '02/3 (for Mr D. Davidson) r16 p2; 4th twice, 5th, 6th, 9th, last pair 4, pulled up 3, unseated 2. A sound jumper, and has never fallen, and beat Garruth (*qv*) in Ireland in '00, but unable to score in 29 subsequent attempts, and only once beaten less than 16 lengths in '04. Does a good job of tutoring Kelly Bryson, but has been tried in blinkers and cheekpieces, and keeps a fair bit up his sleeve. *Mrs P.M. Shirley-Beavan — Jedforest.* 212 (R), 283 (R), 430 (R), 855 (R), 1040 (R), 1077 (R).

THE BROOKLET ..9-11.. 7 br.g. Alderbrook — The Howlet (New Brig) cpp1. Workmanlike owner-bred half-brother to Greg's Profiles and Perdix, and to NH flat and Hurdles winner, Nevermind Hey. Dam won 3 Chases at around 2m. Carried out by Sett Aside before the first at Garnons and was exceptionally green and made countless mistakes (including by jumping right) in his next two attempts, but transformed in a youngsters Maiden at Maisemore and scored readily at 10-1 having made just one noticeable blunder two out. Evidently stays very well, and should maintain his upward rise. It seemed highly implausible at the time, but wily old Julian Pritchard was eventually going to coax victory from both the Garnons protagonists. *C.J. Hitchings — N. Ledbury.* 619 (2m4fOMa), 725 (OMa), 837 (OMa), 1259 (OMa).

THE BUTTERWICK KID ..10-7.. 12 ch.g. Interrex (CAN) — Ville Air (Town Crier) 31733. Tall heavy-topped half-brother to flat winner, Bonne Ville. Dam won 6f (only run), and is half-sister to Cornish Air (*qv* '93 Annual). FLAT '95/02 r48 w9 (5-14f) p13. NH '96/02 r27 w6 (2 Hdles, 2m-2m7f, and 4 Chses, 2m4f-3m1f) p8 (4 2nds); pulled up 1, unseated 1 and refused 1. P-t-P/HUNT CH '03 r5 w2 (3m1f Hunt Ch, and Mixed Open) p1 (2nd); 4th of 5, and unseated 1. The veteran of 85 races, and not a year has gone by since '95 when he has not registered at least one victory, and gained the latest when ploughing through thick mud (a favourite commodity) at Newcastle. Has never fallen and jumped round Aintree without touching a twig, but generally easy to beat in '04, and likely to deteriorate further at 12. Refused to race when tongue-tied once in '99, but a tougher individual is difficult to imagine, and will hopefully be able to register a 20th success in the near future. Wears blinkers, and often visored in the past. *R.T.A. Tate — Badsworth & Bramham Moor (Richard Tate).* 179 (2m6fH), 546 (3mH), 732 (2m5f110yH), 994 (3m110yH), 1297 (3m1fH).

THE CAMPDONIAN (IRE) ..10-6.. 14 ch.g. Clearly Bust — Not At All (Royal Highway) 12232222u2. Tall strong half-brother to Always Grumbling, and to Chasing winners, Rein De Tout and Macamore Gale (in Ireland). Dam won 4 flat (14-16f) and 2 2m Hurdles and 2m2f Chase in Ireland. NH FLAT '95/6 r4 p0. NH '96, '99/00 and '02 (for H. Oliver, and O. O'Neill, when successful) r22 w2 (2m6f-3m Chses) p5; pulled up 5, fell 1. Won two bad Chases including in soft to July '00, but has had long absences from the track, and missed '97/8, '01 and '03. Often tongue-tied, although not in '04, when he had a remarkable season. Began with a 20-1 win in a Club Members at Chaddesley Corbett, but then connections had to endure no fewer than eight placings, including seven seconds, six of them defeats of five lengths or less. A good jumper who keeps up a steady gallop, but his lack of acceleration unfortunately lets him down time and time again. Lightly raced for a veteran, and was able to hold his form very well at 13. Could certainly not be grudged another success. *Mrs L. King & J.L. Robbins — N. Cotswold (Emma King).* 251 (C), 404 (O), 727 (MO), 756 (Cf), 1015 (Cf), 1073 (O), 1254 (Cf), 1342 (O), 1454 (3mH), 1528 (Cf).

THE CINCINNATI KID .9-9.. 11 gr.g. Kahyasi — Pepper Star (IRE) (Salt Dome USA) 1p36. Lengthy. IRISH NH FLAT '99 r3 p1 (2nd). IRISH NH '99 r4 p0. P-t-P '02/3 r4 p0 (last pair 2, and pulled up 2). Fired and has undergone a wind operation since joining the present yard, and finally rewarded their patience with a convincing success in softish at Overton where he was in front throughout the final mile. Not disgraced in his first Restricted but needs to improve further to win one. Wears a cross-noseband, and has been tried in blinkers and a tongue-tie. *V. Thompson — Percy.* 658 (OMa), 762 (I), 855 (R), 1037 (I).

THE COOLING AGENT .8-12.. 7 b.g. Regal Embers (IRE) — Arctic Quest (Abednego) u2p2. Lengthy. Dam, sister to Pointer, and half-sister to Artic Ground (*qv* '04 Annual), won Maiden and 3rd. Bought Doncaster, Aug for 4100. Shows ability, but has been very green, and looks a difficult ride tactically. Staying on in the closing stages of both seconds, and catching the winner close home when beaten one-and-a-half lengths at Holnicote, where he got badly outpaced three from home before rallying. Possibly needs a left-handed course. It would be surprising if he did not win a Maiden at least in '05. *T. Hamlin — E. Devon (Ollie Bush).* 575 (OMa), 725 (OMa), 1133 (OMa), 1327 (OMa).

THE CROPPY .—.. 9 b.g. Arctic Lord — Deep Cut (Deep Run) p. Lengthy brother to Slaney Lass (*qv*). NH FLAT '00 r1 p0. NH '01/2 r2 p0. P-t-P '03 r1 p0 (pulled up). Maintained the trend of an annual appearance since '00 at Woodford, and ran well until pulling up lame just after the fourth last. Wears a cross-noseband and a tongue-tie. *A.J. Williams — Curre & Llangibby (Sue Williams).* 1075 (OMa).

THE DOC ..—.. 9 gr.g. Norton Challenger — One Way Circuit (Windjammer USA) pb. Small brother to Sea Haitch Em. P-t-P '03 r5 p0 (pulled up 5). Often shows speed to halfway, but still looking for a first completion, and appears to have no stamina. Tongue-tied once in '03. *Mrs S.J. Storer — Cranwell Bloodhounds (Jillian Conway).* 304 (OMa), 946 (OMa).

THE EARTH MOVED (IRE) ..9-8.. 11 b.g. Brush Aside (USA) — S T Blue (Bluerullah) 41. Lengthy half-brother to Fundy (IRE). Dam won 2m mares Hdle in Ireland. P-t-P '99/00 and '02 (for Mr R.M. Penny) r8 w2 (Maiden and Restricted) p3 (2 2nds, beaten ¾*l* once); fell 1 and pulled up 2. Quite impressive when winning twice to '00, but has had jumping and physical (broke a blood vessel in '02) problems to contend with, and only just managed to outpace a family rival (the 1-2 favourite) in his Members which was run at a crawl for 2m4f in '04. *Mrs S. Godfrey — Seavington.* 573 (I), 1008 (M).

THE FLYING DRAGON ..8-7.. 11 b.m. Cruise Missile — Dragon Lass (Cheval) u42u. Small close-coupled sister to Woodram Lass and Stede Quarter, and half-sister to jumping winner, Bonnie Dundee. Dam, 3rd in Hdle, fell in her only Point. P-t-P '00/3 (for Mr R.T. Dench) r12 p2; fell/unseated 5 and pulled up 5. Beaten between two and 13 lengths when placed in Maidens, but exposed as very moderate, and will be lucky to win one. Plods badly and runs tongue-tied, and has never lost her propensity to make mistakes. *S. Spice — Ashford V.* 103 (OMa), 185 (CMam), 539 (OMa), 644 (OMa).

THE FOOTSY .7-11.. 9 br.g. The Footman — Lucky Story (Lucky Sovereign) pf62. Small neat half-brother to Lucky Christopher, Copredy Lad and Larks Tail. P-t-P '03 (for Mr D. Williams & Mr A.B. Shaw) r2 p0 (pulled up 2). In a successful yard that has access to good riders, but an error-prone weak-finisher to date, and gained his 15 lengths Bratton Down second on a disqualification. Lacks scope. Wears a cross-noseband. *R. Bunn — Ledbury (Janet Hughes).* 981 (OMa), 1232 (OMa), 1532 (OMa), 1559 (OMa).

THE GAMBLING LADY..9-0.. 9 b/br.m. General Gambul — Coach Rd Express (Pony Express) upf. Leggy Lengthy half-sister to Season Express. Dam, (*qv* '93 Annual) is sister to Military Express, and half-sister to Coachroadstarboy ('the Miss Havisham of Points', also by Vital Season; (*qv* '97 Annual), was placed in 11 Points. Grandam, failed to finish in 4 Points. Great-grandam, Starless II, was last of 3 in 2 Points. NH '02/3 (for C.L. Tizzard) r3 p0 (fell and pulled up 2). Pulled up twice and fell (when tongue-tied in a Seller) over Hurdles, and still cannot get round the course in Points, although she was still in a close third when she fell four out on final start. It seems she may have a smidgen of ability, but poor jumping has so far been a constant drawback. *Mrs H.A. Heal — Quantock (Sarah Robinson).* 967 (OMa), 1131 (R), 1186 (OMa).

THE GILLY SMITH ..—.. 7 b.g. Gildoran — Sally Smith (Alias Smith USA) p. Dam, sister to Grey Smoke (*qv* '01 Annual), failed to finish in 3 of 6 Points and placed in Hurdle). IRISH P-t-P '03 r2 p1 (3rd); and pulled up 1. IRISH NH FLAT '03 (for E.M. O'Sullivan) r2 p0 (beat one). Second favourite in a field of 14 at Cothelstone in mid-April, but blundered at the 12th when weakening and was promptly pulled up. Has hinted at promise, but tongue-tied in his second Irish Hurdle, and has had a very quiet time so far in the new yard. *E.W. Dauncey — Worcs (Rose Vickery).* 883 (OMa).

THE GLEN ROAD (IRE) ..9-6.. 8 ch.g. Star Quest — Claret Mist (Furry Glen) 2p44. Good-bodied. Dam, half-sister to My Tobias (*qv* '96 Annual). IRISH P-t-P '02 r5 p1 (3rd). P-t-P '03 r8 w2 (Maiden and Restricted) p2 (head 2nd of 3, and 3rd of 4); 4th, pulled up 2, and ran out 1. Won two weak races on sound surfaces in '03, but had previously displayed wayward traits, and the Stewards found his rider Andrew Sansome guilty of such on his reappearance when he struck Claire Bartlett (having her first ride) with his whip at Horseheath. Went down by a neck on that occasion, but trounced in better company since, and looks to have lost all zest. *N.W. Padfield — Cambs with Enfield Chace.* 123 (M), 376 (Cf), 521 (Cf), 647 (Cf).

THE GRADUATE .10-4.. 11 ch.g. Indian Ridge — Queen's Eyot (Grundy) 3p224. Tall rangy half-brother to flat winners, Island Blade and Persuasive (also winning Hurdler), to Hurdles winner, Rocky Island, and to NH flat winner, Ardarroch Prince. Dam won 2 10f races. FLAT '98 r4 p0. NH '00/1 r2 p0. P-t-P '02/3 r3 w2 (Restricted and Members); and pulled up 1. Used to lead Group 3 winner Duck Row in his work when with James Toller, and recorded a soft-ground double in Points in '02, but laid low by a virus last year, and has been unable to recapture his sparkle. Can still go a strong gallop, and beaten two lengths maximum in three Pointing completions in '04, but clearly difficult to get and remain fit. Deserves to find another opportunity. Wears a cross-noseband. *Mrs C. Robertson — Holderness (Tony Walker).* 478 (Cf), 770 (Cf), 1059 (I), 1287 (I), 1361 (3mH).

THE GRANBY (IRE) ..10-3.. 11 b.g. Insan (USA) — Elteetee (Paddy's Stream) 31221u7f3. Compact good-sized half-brother to Tea Box (IRE) and Irish Pointing winner, Nash Na Habhainn. NH FLAT '98 r2 p0. NH '99/03 (for Mrs M. Reveley) r18 w7 (5 2m-2m4f Hdles and 2 3m Chses) p5; fell/unseated 2. Bought Doncaster, Oct for 12,000. Was in his prime when completing a five-timer to April '00 (had fallen at the last in a length lead on his previous outing), but cannot finish as strongly as he once did now, and most of his better efforts have been on good or firmish ground. Had a fair season in '04 and won two Ladies races, but his efforts in Hunter Chases got steadily worse after a one-and-three-quarter lengths second to Lancastrian Jet at Towcester (could not quicken under wild urgings on the flat), and following a 27 lengths second at Exeter he put the rider on the floor three out twice including when still holding every chance at Huntingdon. Ended the season with a bitterly disappointing return to a Point at Dingley, where he started at 4-7 but never looked keen from halfway and gave up completely from two out. May have lost his nerve, but a decent break might erase the memories, and can possibly return to a reasonable level of form. *Miss H.M. Irving & A.C. Kemp — Bicester with Whaddon (Heather Irving).* 171 (L), 289 (CfL), 437 (3m1fH), 629 (3m1f110yH), 869 (L), 1029 (3mH), 1168 (2m5fH), 1361 (3mH), 1470 (L).

THE GRANDSON (IRE) ..8-12.. 10 b.g. Husyan (USA) — Tarary (Boreen FR) 3p. Tall strong-topped half-brother to Indian Renegade (IRE). Dam, sister to One Hard Man (*qv* '03 Annual). NH '02 r5 p0 (last, and pulled up 4). P-t-P '03 r1 p0 (pulled up). Only once better than last in eight attempts (pulled up in six) but wears bandages and hobbled along like a great-grandad until pulled up lame after two miles at Maisemore Park. *S.T. Lewis — Ystrad Taf Fechan.* 730 (OMa), 1258 (OMa).

THE GREEN GOBLIN (NZ) ..9-6.. 9 b.g. Noble Jewel (NZ) — Fairy Row (NZ) (Long Row) 4. Sparely-made. P-t-P '03 (for Mrs R. Mackness) r1 p0 (pulled up). In a good yard, and ridden by a former champion, but stands his racing incredibly badly, and 25 lengths fourth of five after tiring in the closing stages on his only appearance in '04. Might be worthy of consideration if connections (who had a year to forget) persevere with him. Wears a cross-noseband. *W. O'Brien — Cotswold (Jelly Nolan).* 112 (OMa).

THE GREY BARON .9-2.. 8 gr.g. Baron Blakeney — Topsy Bee (Be Friendly) p12pp7. Tall rangy half-brother to Oscar Wilde (*qv*). NH '03 (for A. Ennis) r2 p0 (pulled up 2). Wears a tongue-tie and tends to fade rapidly, but backed from 6s to 3-1 and managed to upset the 4-7 favourite Kenny Davis in his Members (the other two contestants were virtual hunters). Missing out on a Maiden has been costly, and after a 15 lengths second in a Restricted he has merely pulled up twice and finished last but one. Will be lucky to find another opportunity. *A. Coveney & Miss F. Field — O. Surrey, Burstow & W. Kent (Andrew Coveney).* 102 (R), 180 (M), 419 (CR), 777 (M), 1051 (R), 1085 (Cv&nr).

THE GREY SHADOW .9-0.. 13 gr.g. Zambrano — Kara Star (Whistlewood) 36. Tall rangy plain half-brother to Don't Argue. Dam was placed in 2 Points. P-t-P '00 and '03 r6 w1 (Maiden) p0; 4th, 5th, last, pulled up 1, and unseated 1. Won a slowly-run three-finisher Maiden at Bratton Down last year, but has always been very lightly raced, and looks certain to prove too slow for Restricteds. *M. Edwards — W. Somerset (Chris White).* 278 (Inr), 879 (R).

THE HARE (IRE) ..—§.. 8 br.g. Allegoric (USA) — Broken Mirror (Push On) p. Small short-backed half-brother to Learner Driver, Mount Glass (IRE) and Brother Joseph (IRE), and to Hurdles winner, Lumaca (IRE). P-t-P '02/3 r5 p0 (last 2, and pulled up 3). Used to send the bookies running for cover, but has never beaten a rival in six attempts, and is a doggy short-runner. *Miss V. Champken — Worcs (Martin Oliver).* 667 (OMa).

THE HEARTY JOKER (IRE) ..10-0.. 10 b.g. Broken Hearted — Furryway (Furry Glen) 7p38*12713*. Rangy. IR7000 4yo. IRISH P-t-P '00 r1 p0 (fell). NH '00/3 r26 w1 (2m6f Ch) p10; pulled up 4, fell 1. NH '04 r6 w2 (beat Killy Beach 7*l* in 2m3f110y Ch: *a.p, ld 3 out, clr last, drvn out*; and Pangeran 25*l* in 2m3f110y Ch: *chsd ldr, hit 10, ld 3 out, clr last, easily*) p2 (2nd in 2m3f Hdle: *hld up, hdwy 3 out, ld app 2 out, mist last, hdd & nt qckn flat*; and 3rd in 3m Ch: *hld up, mist 9, rdn 3 out, wknd nxt*); pulled up in 3m1f Ch: *ld to 14, wkng when mist 3 out, sn pu*; and 7th in 2m3f Hdle: *prom til rdn & wknd 3 out*. A front-running fast ground type who is best at around 2m4f, and tried those trips in Hunter Chases, but the best he could manage was a 49 lengths third. Often wears headgear. Better off looking for bad handicaps, and one of his summer victories was in the direst of contests. Pretty moderate, and lucky to be in a yard who are skilful at placing their charges to best advantage. *Mrs M. O'Kelly — Hampshire (Brendan Powell).* 241 (2m4f110yH), 628 (2m3fH), 799 (2m3f110yH).

THE JAM SAHEB ..—.. 8 b.g. Petong — Reem El Fala (FR) (Fabulous Dancer USA) pfp. Close-coupled brother to a French Hurdles winner, and half-brother to Classic Dame (FR). Dam won 2 French flat (8-11f). 10,000f, 9600y. FLAT '99/00 r6 p0. NH '01 (for J. Poulton, and N.J. Hawke; claimed for 4,000) r7 p0; pulled up 2, unseated 1. A bad animal who has absolutely no aptitude for jumping. Tongue-tied four times on the flat, and beaten 25 lengths plus over Hurdles including three Sellers, and has failed to finish in six of his seven most recent attempts. Tried with blinkers and cheekpieces in '04, and was all over the place when going a maximum of two miles thrice. *Mrs H. Margetts — Taunton V. (Philip Greenwood).* 87 (OMa), 325 (OMa), 469 (2m4fOMa).

THE KINGS FLING ..10-2.. 9 b.g. Rakaposhi King — Poetic Light (Ardross) 2142pp. Workmanlike well-made home-bred half-brother to NH flat winner, Popgoestheweasel. Dam is half-sister to Perfect Light (*qv*). P-t-P '02/3 r10 w4 (up to Confined) p5 (4 2nds, beaten ½*l* once; and 3rd of 4); and pulled up 1. Only once out of the first two in 12 completed Points, and recorded a fifth success when beating subsequent Chasing winner Mensch at Chipley Park, but jumped poorly on his Hunter Chase debut, and maintained the trend in Ladies Opens. Probably not himself latterly, and only went two miles at Cothelstone, and might be able to bounce back to form when fresh. Wears a cross-noseband. *A. West*

& *Countess Goess-Saurau — V.W.H. (James Richardson).* 1 (C), 116 (I), 239 (3m1fH), 743 (L), 1016 (3m2fO), 1368 (L).

THE LAST SHOUT (IRE) ..—.. 12 b.g. Yashgan — Apia Sunshine (Simbir) 0p5pp2. Tall strong. Dam won 3 Irish flat (12-16f). IRISH NH '98 r1 p0. IRISH P-t-P '98/9 r9 p3; pulled up 5. P-t-P/HUNT CH '00 and '02/3 r16 w1 (Maiden) p1 (2nd); 4th, last 2, and pulled up 11. Kept going in a determined manner to beat 15 others in an elders Maiden at Bonvilston in '02, but pulled up on his only appearance last year, and beaten fences when primarily used as a schoolmaster and not better than last in '04. Acquired blinkers and cheekpieces on his last two starts. *B.R. Hughes — Llangeinor (Mair Hughes).* 65 (Rnr), 207 (R), 358 (R), 614 (R), 953 (R), 1187 (M).

THE LEAZES .— §.. 6 b.g. Shaamit (IRE) — Air Of Elegance (Elegant Air) pp. Compact well-made. NH FLAT '03 (for A. Dickman) r4 p0; pulled up 2. Bought Doncaster, Aug for 3500. Pulled up in his first two bumpers (after hanging badly right on his debut) and then tongue-tied when beaten 25 lengths plus twice. Again looked a hard ride in Maidens and gave poor displays of jumping before pulling up at the 13th twice. Had to be taken to the boxes to be mounted on his latest appearance. *Mrs G. & Miss J.A. England — Tredegar F. (Glynis England).* 700 (CfMa), 1096 (OMa).

THE LORD ROBERTS (IRE) ..9-8.. 12 b.g. Strong Gale — Thousand Flowers (Take A Reef) pp1p. Tall. Dam, half-sister to Mr Tittle Tattle (*qv* '00 Annual), won 2 flat (12-13f), a 2m Hdle and 2 2m2f-2m4f Chses in Ireland. NH FLAT '98/9 r4 p2 (3rds). NH '99 r1 p0. P-t-P '02/3 r10 w1 (Maiden) p2 (short-head 2nd; and remote last of 3); 8th of 9, pulled up 5, and brought down 1. Suited by good or sound surfaces, and has won two feeble races, but a regular non-finisher, and is not an easy ride. Tends to sweat excessively. Acquired a tongue-tie on his latest start. Wears a cross-noseband. *Miss M.A. De Quincey — Sir W.W. Wynn's (Anne Hewitt).* 384 (R), 1018 (R), 1148 (R), 1530 (I).

THE LORDS CROSS (IRE) ..8-5.. 8 b.g. Jolly Jake (NZ) — Deep Chestnut (IRE) (Black Minstrel) 4p32. Workmanlike. IRISH P-t-P '01/3 r6 p0 (last, and pulled up 5). Did not beat another horse in Ireland, and only once did so in U.K. Points, when 24 lengths fourth. Goes to post early nowadays, and has been mounted outside the paddock. Beaten 20 lengths plus in both placings, and it would be a bad race if he ever scraped a win. *R.J. & Mrs S.E. Hughes — S. Pembs (Sarah Hughes).* 53 (2m4fOMa), 142 (OMa), 950 (2m4fOMa), 1096 (OMa).

THE LUDDITE ..8-7.. 7 br.g. Primitive Rising (USA) — Gilston Lass (Majestic Streak) 54p43. Small neat. Dam, half-sister to Robinrock (*qv*) won 4 2m6f-3m1f Chses. P-t-P '03 r4 p1 (3/4l 3rd); and pulled up 3. Looked a certain future winner when beaten a length on his debut at Garthorpe, but exposed as a short-runner since, and normally stops to nil after running prominently for as much as 2m4f. Unimproved by blinkers once, and by the application of a tongue-tie on his last two starts. *J. & A. Bullock, Mrs J. Alvis & M. & W. Rollett — N. Cotswold (Giles Smyly).* 87 (OMa), 257 (CMa), 368 (OMa), 725 (OMa), 926 (OMa).

THEMASTER'S CHOICE (IRE) ..8-12.. 11 br.g. Good Thyne (USA) — Lisfuncheon Adage (Proverb) pp453. Enormous rangy half-brother to Trimage (IRE), to Irish Pointing/Chasing winner, Prime Target (IRE), and to Irish Pointing/Hurdles winner, Buck's Adage. NH FLAT '99 r3 p1 (3rd). NH '00 r4 p0; pulled up 2. P-t-P '02 (for Mr R.H. Buckler) r4 w2 (Maiden and Restricted) p0; and unseated 2. Well-backed when completing a double in softish in '02, but previously too slow to keep up under Rules, and a similar scenario has been achieved in Points after returning from a two-year absence. One of the biggest horses in training, and wears over-reach boots. *T.E. Willes & P.R. Davies — N. Ledbury (C.R. Willes).* 141 (I), 728 (I), 922 (I), 1092 (I), 1319 (I).

THE MAVERICK ..—.. 8 br.g. Sula Bula — Panto's Pride (Lepanto GER) p. Tall workmanlike. Dam placed in 3 Points for Sarah George in '99. P-t-P '03 r2 p0 (4th of 5, and pulled up 1). Inordinately slow and pulled up twice, and beaten two fences on the only occasion he has crossed the finish line. A carthorse, not a racehorse. *Miss S. George — Berkeley.* 410 (2m4fCfMa).

THE MELTING POT (IRE) .8-9§.. 11 b.g. Top Of The World — O Ana (Laurence O) pu. Small neat half-brother to Polar Ana (IRE). IRISH NH FLAT '99/01 r6 p1 (2nd). IRISH NH '00/1 r3 p0. P-t-P '03 r6 p1 (3rd); 4th, 5th of 6, fell 2, and pulled up 1. Finished five lengths in front of Kilvoydan (*qv*) when runner-up in a bumper at Bellewstown in '00, but the rest of his career has been an anti-climax, and is most unenthusiastic nowadays. Entrusted with favouritism twice last year, but largely unfancied in '04, and should continue to be kept at arms-length. Acquired blinkers at Charm Park after sporting cheekpieces on four occasions. *Miss M.D. Myco — S. Durham.* 160 (CMa), 395 (CfMa).

THE MET MAN (IRE) ..—§.. 9 b.g. Executive Perk — Supplicate (Furry Glen) up. Workmanlike. Dam won 2m Hurdle in Ireland and is half-sister to Sea Search (*qv* '01 Annual). IRISH P-t-P '02 r3 w1 (6yo&up Maiden) p0; pulled up 1 and fell 1. IRISH NH FLAT '02 r1 p0. P-t-P '03 r2 p0 (unseated 2). Beat the real Owenabue Valley into second place in Ireland, and unseated after the fourth last when unassailable once last year, but lost the rider for the third race in succession at Perth, and looked anything but a straightforward ride subsequently. Very headstrong and error-prone, and at present his waywardness masks whatever ability he retains. Wears a cross-noseband. *M. & Mrs S. Smith — Jedforest (Michael Smith).* 1068 (3m2f110yH), 1419 (R).

THE MIDNITE GROCER .—.. 13 ch.g. Town And Country — Nearly A Lady (Nearly A Hand) puf. Tall good-topped brother to Country Lord, and half-brother to Keep On Dreaming (dam of Spuddler's Dream and Another Offer) and Linroyale King. Dam, half-sister to Baron's Heir (*qv* '98 Annual). NH '99/00 r8 p0; pulled up 1, fell 1. P-t-P '03 (for Mr G.V. & Mr R.V. Westwood) r1 p0 (pulled up). A clumsy fat oaf and resurrecting his career following a three-year break in '03 has proved to be a big mistake. Not better than last over fences, and seems to be the grocer eating all the pies. Wears a cross-noseband. *Mrs S. Gillespie — Lanarks & Renfrews (Janette Kerr).* 553 (CfMa), 653 (M), 1082 (OMa).

THE MILECASTLE (IRE) ..8-5.. 6 b.g. Oscar (IRE) — Kiladante (IRE) (Phardante FR) p5. Dam won three NH flat and 10f flat in Ireland. Bought Doncaster, May for 1000. Not always fluent on a novicey debut, but shaped a little better before being eased to finish 37 lengths fifth next time, and can probably get more seriously involved in his second season. *M. Hind & J.A. Ogle — Haydon (Tim Reed).* 920 (2m4fOMa), 1311 (OMa).

THE MINISTER (IRE) ..10-2.. 16 br.g. Black Minstrel — Miss Hi-Land (Tyrant USA) 3. Lengthy brother to Hurdles winner, Burgundy Boy, and half-brother to Irish NH flat winner, Derrishal Lord (IRE). Dam won at 8f in Ireland. IRISH P-t-P '93 r3 p0 (4th, pulled up 1, and unseated 1). NH '93/8 and '02 r13 w2 (2m-2m5f Chses) p0; pulled up 5. P-t-P/HUNT CH '99/00 and '02 r16 w4 (Ladies) p5 (2nds, of 3 once); 4th, 5th, 6th, fell/unseated 2, and pulled up 3. A decent performer on sound surfaces, and has won four races for Tina Jackson since '99, but never able to run much, and seems to be winding down completely. Not disgraced behind two of the better Ladies horses in Yorkshire at Hornby Castle on his only appearance this year, but has always been prone to make mistakes, and has been remarkably clumsy over big fences. *H.L. Thompson — Cleveland (Tina Jackson).* 811 (L).

THE MURPHY MEISTER (IRE) ..9-3§.. 9 b/br.g. Cardinal Flower — Kilbrien Star (Goldhill) 13. Workmanlike half-brother to Irish NH flat and jumping winner, Mohera King (IRE). Dam, half-sister to Cleaning Up (*qv* '94 Annual), won mares Maiden in Ireland. NH FLAT '01 r1 p0 (well tailed off). P-t-P '02/3 r7 p2 (3rds); last pair 2, and pulled up 3. Benefited from a soft-palate operation before the season when romping a slow Maiden on firmish at Hornby Castle, but finished exhausted when stamina was more of a issue next time, and is clearly still suspect. *G.F. Tuer — Hurworth.* 813 (OMa), 1419 (R).

THE NELSON TOUCH ..9-0.. 8 b.g. Past Glories — Kellys Special (Netherkelly) pR2p226. Tall rangy plain one-eyed half-brother to Kellys Conquest (Chasing winner since Pointing), and to NH flat winner, Special Conquest. NH FLAT '01 r1 p0. NH '02/3 (for J.W. Mullins) r9 p1 (dist 3rd in 2m7f110y Ch); pulled up 5. Outclassed under Rules, and was pulled up in four of seven Hurdles and a distant third and pulled up in Chases. More effective in Maidens and achieved three seconds, but is extremely moderate and easy to beat. Does not seem to have his eye on victory. *F.G. Matthews — Blackmore & Sparkford V.* 265 (R), 492 (OMa), 575 (OMa), 688 (2m4fOMa), 865 (OMa), 1248 (OMa), 1380 (OMa).

THE NOBLEMAN (USA) .9-6§.. 9 b.g. Quiet American (USA) — Furajet (USA) (The Minstrel CAN) 137p7. Workmanlike. FLAT '98 and '00/1 r10 p2 (3rds). NH '00/1 r12 w1 (2m4f110y Hdle) p0; pulled up 1. P-t-P/HUNT CH '03 r8 w1 (walkover Members) p3 (short-head 2nd of 3 once); 4th, 5th, and pulled up 2. Capable of fair form on firm ground, and sprang a 20-1 surprise when recording his first competitive success since May '01 at Market Rasen, but a bad value joint-favourite in holding next time, and typically lost interest subsequently. Has to be treated with extreme caution. Blinkered once in '01, and has run tongue-tied. *Mrs J.E. Todd — Blankney (Margaret Morris).* 298 (Cf), 477 (Cnr), 592 (O), 942 (Cf), 1500 (Cf).

THE NOBLE ROMAN ..8-11.. 7 ch.g. Sir Harry Lewis (USA) — Antica Roma (IRE) (Denel FR) f2p3. Workmanlike. Dam placed in two Irish Points; and won three Points and placed twice for Anne Cockburn. Finished weakly when beaten about 15 lengths in two placings, and also fell at the fifth, and pulled up at halfway having being left 100 yards and continued tailed off. Clearly has quirks, but there may be some ability to be exploited if he will co-operate. Made an enemy for life at Eyton-on-Severn where he lashed out in the paddock and smashed his hoof into a face of a spectator who had the misfortune to be leaning on the rails, and who left a large pool of blood as he was escorted away. *Mrs E. Cockburn & Mrs B. Seales — Warwicks (Anne Cockburn).* 256 (CMa), 532 (OMa), 709 (Mah), 837 (OMa).

THE ONLY OPTION (IRE) ..10-1.. 10 b.m. Phardante (FR) — Sirrah Madam (Tug Of War) u1. Workmanlike half-sister to Sirrah Aris (IRE) (chasing winner since Pointing). Dam is half-sister to Dear Course (*qv* '94 Annual). NH '01/2 r4 p0; pulled up 2. P-t-P '02/3 (for Mr R. Tate) r8 w1 (Maiden) p0; 6th of 7, pulled up 3, fell/unseated 4. Displayed much improved form when landing a 12-runner Restricted on good ground at Great Trethew (16-1) but did not get another chance to prove herself, and typically lost the rider, for the fifth time over fences on her reappearance. Gained her previous win in mud, but might be able to be more effective in Intermediates on better ground if she can go clear. *J.F. Weldhen — Four Burrow.* 488 (R), 706 (R).

THE PANJSHIR ..8-2.. 9 b.g. Lighter — Molinello (Balinger) pppfp. Tall. Dam, half-sister to The Proud Pound (*qv*). P-t-P '03 r7 p0 (last pair 2, pulled up 3, and unseated 2). Useless when owner-ridden, and has looked temperamental, but in the process of running a personal best when falling four out with Luke Morgan at Overton, and might be capable of springing a surprise if strongly handled. Has been tried tongue-tied. *G. Willoughby — Tynedale (Tim Reed).* 137 (OMa), 271 (OMa), 429 (3m5fO), 658 (OMa), 1311 (OMa).

THE PICKLED DUKE (IRE) ..8-11.. 13 gr.g. Duky — Silk Empress (Young Emperor) 5pp. Tall rangy half-brother to Desert Emperor and Kalalee, and to Chasing winner, Quassimi. NH FLAT '97/8 r2 p2 (2nds). NH '98/02 r21 w6 (3 2m4f-3m1f Hdles and 3 2m4f-3m110y Chses) p2 (2nds); pulled up 5, unseated 2, refused 1. P-t-P '03 r1 p0 (last). A useful front-runner in mud in his prime, but has not looked convincing over fences for a long while, and not better than last in his final six appearances dating back to February '02. May have gone wrong at Stafford Cross, and retirement seems the only option. *C.H. Sclater — Cattistock (Sarah Clarke).* 64 (O), 602 (MO), 1128 (MO).

THE PREACHER MAN (IRE) ..9-12.. 10 b.g. Be My Native (USA) — Frankford Run (Deep Run) 8. Strong half-brother to Tartan Tornado and Charley Lambert (IRE), and to smart Irish NH flat/jumping winner, Sound Man (IRE) (won 15 and £288,783 inc in England). Dam is half-sister to Heir Of Gold (*qv*). IRISH NH FLAT '00/1 r2 p1 (2nd). IRISH NH '00/1 r4 p0. P-t-P/HUNT CH '02/3 r10 w1 (Maiden) p6 (5 2nds, beaten short-headed once, of 3 once; and 3rd of 4); 4th, 5th, and unseated 1. Seven times a beaten favourite, and gained a long overdue success in a long Maiden in soft at Wetherby last year, but seems to lose heart quickly, and unable to reappear after finishing tailed off at Sedgefield in February. A reliable jumper in Points, and still has claims to a Restricted if he can be restored to full health. Wears a cross-noseband. *V. Thompson — Percy.* 316 (2m5fH).

THE PROUD POUND ..—.. 14 b.g. Kinglet — Cut And Thrust (Pardal) u. Neat half-brother to Matchplay, Goldtopper and Cut A Niche, to flat winner, Abielle, and to a winner in Holland. Dam won at 8½f. NH FLAT '97 r1 p0. NH '98/00 r9 p1 (distant last of 2); 5th of 6, and pulled up 4 and fell/unseated 3. P-t-P '99 and '02/3 r18 w2 (3-finisher Maiden and Ladies- 3 ran, finished alone) p5 (3 2nds, of 3 once; and inc 3rd of 4 once); 4th, pulled up 6, and unseated 4. Often blinkered in the past, and has had multiple homes, and recorded two lucky wins, but has never gone clear for present connections, and the latest pilot baled out after only four fences in '04. *M.J. Caldwell — Cheshire Forest (Katie Caldwell).* 94 (L).

PLATE 119 706 East Cornwall Restricted: The Only Option gives Joe Tickle his first winner
PHOTO: Baths Photographic

THEREALBAT (IRE) ..9-12.. 11 ch.g. Rashar (USA) — Callmemeala (Callernish) 1u2u2. Strong rangy brother to Irish Pointing winner, Cauhar. IRISH P-t-P '99 r1 p1 (3rd). IRISH NH FLAT '99/02 r5 p0. IRISH NH '99/03 (for E. Sheehy, M. Cullen, Miss A.M. Doran, and E. Doyle) r21 p6 (inc 3rd in Ch); unseated 1. Peaked in Ireland in his first two placings in May/June '00, when he finished half-a-length second twice (just failed once), but was only 21 lengths third in a Chase, and tried tongue-tied on his final start. Made a winning debut for a new yard when beating a 15-year-old in a three-finisher Restricted at Llanfrynach, and has made some bold attempts since, but headed at the last or on the run-in in both seconds, and also unseated after bad blunders twice. Enjoys front-running, and might be able to score again if he can nab a sufficiently clear advantage to see him home. Wears a cross-noseband, and blinkered on his latest appearance. *D. Davies, Mrs B. & R. Beavan — Wheatland (Sean Parkyn).* 451 (R), 922 (I), 1140 (Cf), 1430 (I), 1530 (I).

THE REAL MURPHY (IRE) ..8-9.. 10 ch.g. Hamas (IRE) — Rocket Alert (Red Alert) p73. Gigantic rangy half-brother to Launch Pad, and to several winners, including flat winners, Ardlui and Rejoice. Dam won 5 flat (5-7f), and subsequently won 3 in USA (total value about £65,000). NH FLAT '00/1 (for R.H. Buckler) r2 p1 (3rd; originally 5th but promoted). Eleven lengths third at 25-1 in a bumper, but then went missing for three years. Labours in Points and was 28 lengths last of three in a Restricted, and his huge bulk always seemed bound to cause problems (broken winded?). *W.S. Rogers & Miss S.E. Rich — E. Cornwall (Sarah Rich).* 604 (OMa), 824 (R), 1352 (R).

PLATE 120 1 Cambridgeshire Harriers Hunt Club Members: Is Andrew Braithwaite stifling a yawn as The Red Boy takes the second last? *PHOTO: Tim Holt*

THE RED BOY (IRE) .—§§.. 11 ch.g. Boyne Valley — River Regent (Over The River FR) 1122355. Workmanlike. P-t-P '00/1 and '03 r10 w3 (2m4f Maiden, Restricted and Members) p4 (3 2nds, of 3 once; and 3rd of 4); 4th twice, and unseated 1. A useful Pointer on sharp and easy tracks, and his first four wins were gained at Cottenham, but his tendency to idle in front has manifested into all out belligerence, and threw away certain victory twice in '04. Acquired cheekpieces on his final start, but dogged it furiously after the last, and was reduced to a walk crossing the line, and the fine imposed on Andrew Braithwaite at Cottenham was made to look even more unfair. Could easily return to around 10-6 when fresh, but few will be willing to trust him further. *C.H. Sporborg — Puckeridge.* 1 (C), 23 (Cf), 99 (I), 397 (O), 557 (O), 892 (2m5f110yH), 1153 (O).

THERIDAMAS (IRE) ..9-5.. 7 ch.g. Persian Bold — Lovat Spring (USA) (Storm Bird CAN) 3. IRISH NH FLAT '02/3 r3 p0; refused to race 1. Refused to race on his Irish bumper debut and finished miles behind twice when ridden by his current partner, and was a lucky 25 lengths third in his Members (made nearly all until the 14th but soon weakened). Does not impress as a likely stayer. *Mr & Mrs E.M. Collinson — Cottesmore (Ellen Collinson).* 378 (M).

THE SEA CLUB (IRE) ..9-3.. 10 b.g. Be My Native (USA) — Furry Slipper (Furry Glen) u341pup. Dam, half-sister to Shoemaker (*qv*). 10,200 4yo. NH FLAT '01 r1 p0. NH '01 (for H. Alexander) r6 p0; pulled up 2. NH '04 (for J.S. Wainwright) r1 p0 (pulled up in 3m Hdle: *prom til lost pl 6, t.o & pu 9*). Sold Doncaster, Mar '02 for 800. Won a bad Maiden at Easingwold to give Laura Robson (who looked stylish) a first success at the fourth attempt, but inconsistent, and beaten favourite in two of three other attempts for her. Can make blunders, and needs to be looking for the easiest opportunities (has never been beaten less than 20 lengths under Rules). *A. Nicholls — Middleton.* 679 (3m1fH), 960 (OMa), 1165 (OMa), 1305 (OMa), 1456 (R), 1499 (2m4f110yH).

THE SINGING NUN (IRE) ..9-8.. 8 b.m. Religiously (USA) — Dark Horizon (IRE) (Strong Gale) 4. IRISH P-t-P '02/3 r12 w1 (5&6yo Mares Maiden) p6; pulled up 3. Signed off in Ireland with a win for baby Mares Maiden in soft, and was a creditable 11 lengths fourth in a Restricted at Hornby Castle in late February, but faded in the closing stages and has not been seen since. Jumped safely, but took a long time to open her account, suggesting she is on the moderate side. *The Blue Bell Partnership (D. Kinsella) — Bilsdale (Sarah Dent).* 341 (R).

THE SKY IS BLUE ..9-4.. 9 ch.g. Alflora (IRE) — Mistress Boreen (Boreen FR) u1pf6p4. Compact good-bodied half-brother to Sohapara (*qv*). NH FLAT '00 r1 p1 (3rd). NH '00/3 (for S.E.H. Sherwood, and Mrs P. Townsley) r8 p0; pulled up 5, fell 1. Eight lengths third in a bumper, but fourth of five, pulled up thrice and fell in Chases, and pulled up in two of three Hurdles. Had a most peculiarly plotted campaign in '04 as he alternated appearances in the North West with visits to the South East, but the very long trip to Charing proved worthwhile when he easily won a bad early March Maiden which threw up no subsequent scorers from the five finishers. It was highly significant that Phil York partnered him on that occasion, because he has a very unimpressive record when owner-ridden, and poor presentation at the fences gets him into trouble. Not certain to have prospects in Restricteds, but stronger handling would certainly help. *M.J. Caldwell — Cheshire Forest (Katie Caldwell).* 97 (CfMa), 423 (CMa), 1048 (R), 1208 (R), 1429 (Cnr), 1439 (2m5fH), 1503 (R).

THE SQUAB .—.. 7 ch.g. Karinga Bay — Little Romany (Day Is Done) f. Brother to Miss Karingaroo (*qv*). Departed at the second at Woodford. Fat, clumsy, plump and squashy, thick and heavy, squat, and as a verb intransitive, to fall heavily. Some of the dictionary definitions of his name — take your pick. *T. & Mrs G. Greenwood — Cotley (Philip Greenwood).* 1074 (OMa).

THE SYCOPHANT (IRE) ..9-2.. 8 ch.g. Gone Fishin — Mitsubishi Art (Cure The Blues USA) 223fu3. Well-made quite attractive half-brother to Hurdles winner, Ready To Draw (IRE), and to 3 winners abroad. IRISH P-t-P '02 r5 p0 (pulled up 4, and fell 1). IRISH NH FLAT '01 r1 p0. IRISH NH '03 (for J.A. Berry) r7 p0. Has improved on woeful Irish efforts, and finished one-and-a-half lengths second at Milborne St Andrew, but beaten ten lengths or much more in three other placings (remounted for third after unseating at the last when exhausted once), and is an unreliable jumper who consistently struggles to get the trip. Tongue-tied on his final start of '03. Does not merit our servile flattery. *Mr & Mrs S. Dixon — Wilton (Sharon Brown).* 67 (OMa), 237 (CfMa), 353 (OMa), 575 (OMa), 633 (2m4fCfMa), 865 (OMa).

THE TIMBERMAN ..—.. 13 gr.g. Grey Desire — Heldigvis (Hot Grove) pp. Compact hobdayed brother to flat and Chasing winner, Grouse-N-Heather, and to Hurdles winner, Hotdiggity, and half-brother to flat winner, Lucky Owl, and to jumping winner, Fast Thoughts. Dam won 2 flat (7-8f), inc Sell. NH '00 r5 p1 (3rd); pulled up 1. P-t-P/HUNT CH '98/9 and '02/3 (for Mr T. Butt) r18 w2 (Maiden and Restricted) p1 (2nd of 3); last 2, refused 1, pulled up 6, and fell/unseated 6. Outspeeded a single rival on firm at Ayr last year to register his second success, but has to contend with appalling breathing difficulties, and has pulled up in all three subsequent attempts. Looks finished now, and his 9-7 rating has been withdrawn. Has run tubed, and in a tongue-tie. *B. Storey & Miss J. Hutchinson — Cumberland (Brian Storey).* 1418 (Cf), 1479 (Cf).

THE UNAMED MAN .—§.. 9 ch.g. Weld — Orange Spice (Orange Bay) pppp. Workmanlike half-brother to Arctium. Dam is half-sister to Roman Jack (*qv* '88 Season Annual). P-t-P '02/3 r11 w2 (Maiden and Restricted) p2; 4th, 5th, pulled up 4, and unseated. Rated 10-1 after recording a double in May for Richard Burton in '03, but his work ethic has altered radically since, and would not do a tap for three different partners this year. A very sketchy jumper, and has no need for easy ground, and has become almost as shifty as his sibling was. Has been tried in cheekpieces. *M.J. Rowley — N. Salop (Pamela Sykes).* 527 (I), 663 (I), 1228 (4mO), 1430 (I).

THE VINTAGE DANCER (IRE) .10-1.. 9 b.g. Riberetto — Strong Swimmer (IRE) (Black Minstrel) 54333. Small compact. IRISH P-t-P '01/2 r6 w1 (5yo Maiden) p2; ran out 1. P-t-P '03 r6 w1 (Club Restricted) p1 (2nd); 6th, fell/unseated 2, and pulled up 1. Won the last of his six starts in Ireland, and stayed on to catch the faltering leader close home at Dingley in '03, but has lacked the speed to get seriously involved in sub-3m events, and did better when returned to the full trip at Bangor. An improved jumper and deserves to have his consistency rewarded again. *G.R. Kerr — Fernie (Nicola Pollock).* 19 (CMod), 138 (C), 443 (2m4f110yH), 892 (2m5f110yH), 1176 (3m110yH).

THE WEE GENERAL (IRE) ..9-0.. 11 b.g. General Sprite Bow VII — Too Do (Manado) p6. Half-brother to Tigers Pet, and to Irish NH flat winner, Will This Do. IRISH P-t-P '00 r3 p0; last, and pulled up 2. NH '00 r3 p0; pulled up 1. P-t-P '02/3 (for Mrs H. Robinson, Mrs B. Tarr & Mr M. Reeves) r11 w1 (Maiden) p6 (4 2nds, of 3 once; and inc 3rd of 4); 5th twice, last, and unseated 1. A reliable jumper and made the frame seven times before gaining a deserved success on firmish at Godstone last year, but normally fails to get the trip, and reverted back to his old lightly-raced self in '04. Wears a cross-noseband, and a tongue-tie. *M.C.W. Reeves — Hursley Hambledon (Simon Cobden).* 169 (R), 181 (R).

THE WELL LAD (IRE) .8-6.. 6 ch.g. Moonax (IRE) — Caribbean Rose (IRE) (Regular Guy) p4u. Good-bodied. IRISH P-t-P '03 r3 p0 (pulled up 3). Has only completed the course once from six attempts, when 28 lengths last. Pulled up and unseated after two miles in his other outings of '04, including when favourite for the latest. Will need to improve if he is to take a hand in any finishes. *M. Hammond — Worcs.* 1020 (OMa), 1425 (OMa), 1525 (OMah).

THE WILEY KALMUCK (IRE) ..10-4.. 11 b.g. Be My Native (USA) — Beecom Silk (English Prince) 4241154131. Workmanlike half-brother to three winners, including one abroad. Dam won 12f race, and 2m Hdle in Ireland. IRISH P-t-P '98 r2 w1 (4&5yo Maiden) p0; and pulled up 1. IRISH NH FLAT '98/9 r4 p0. IRISH NH '98/00 r21 w1 (3m Hdle) p3. NH '00/2 r13 w1 (3m Hdle) p1 (2nd); pulled up 1. P-t-P/HUNT CH '03 r12 w5 (Ladies) p3 (2 2nds); 4th, and pulled up 3. Won impressively as a four-year-old in Ireland, but rather lost the plot under Rules, and became unreliable, and had not scored since '00 until finding some easy pickings in Points last year. Typically took a while to hit form in '04, but took his winning tally into double figures at Ampton, and found two further opportunities. Likes to dominate, and can sulk if he doesn't, but can handle sound surfaces and usually avoids decent performers, and seems sure to win again. Tried in headgear in previous yards. *J.M. Turner — Suffolk.* 25 (L), 101 (L), 222 (L), 399 (L), 522 (L), 743 (L), 998 (L), 1210 (L), 1314 (L), 1470 (L).

THE WRITER (IRE) ..10-1.. 12 b.g. Royal Fountain — Novelist (Quayside) p5313. Tall half-brother to Borrisimo (IRE) (*qv*). IRISH P-t-P '98 r3 p2; and fell. NH '98/00 r8 w2 (3m110y Hdle, and 3m Ch) p2 (3rds). P-t-P '03 r1 w1 (Members). Suited by top-of-the-ground, and has a decent record, but never easy to train, and pulled up and dismounted when still well in contention on his reappearance. Failed to cope with Upton Adventure when backed from tens to 5-2 at Bitterley, but won his three-runner Members, and with more careful placing should score again. Inclined to make the odd mistake. Wears a cross-noseband. Blinkered once in '99. *Rosemary Viscountess Boyne & Hon. Mrs L. Sherwood — Clifton-on-Teme (Lucy Sherwood).* 360 (O), 490 (3m2fH), 838 (L), 1135 (M), 1254 (Cf).

THEYDON STAR (NZ) ..—.. 8 b.g. Classic Fame (USA) — Hilarity (NZ) (St Hilarion USA) pp. Tall half-brother to a NZ flat/Australian jumping winner. NH FLAT '01 r1 p0. NH '01/2 (for Mrs N. Smith) r3 p0; unseated 1. Bought Ascot, Jul '02 for 2857. Has been extremely lightly raced, and unseated at the third and beaten 52 lengths plus twice over Hurdles. Wore blinkers when tailed off and pulled up in both 2m4f Maidens, and looks useless and has to contend with a very ungainly rider. *R.C. Skinner — Eggesford (Linda Blackford).* 469 (2m4fOMa), 702 (2m4fOMa).

THINK COMMERCIAL (IRE) ..9-10.. 6 b.g. Mister Lord (USA) — Dingle Gal (IRE) (Phardante FR) 2p13. Lightly-made. His jumping has been very sketchy, and beaten between ten and 25 lengths when placed (last once), but the champion managed to get him home in front in a youngsters Maiden at Kingston St Mary, and all the three behind him have scored since. Not an easy ride, and has hung left, and been tried with a near-side pricker. Greater accuracy will be required for Restricteds, but still a baby, so can possibly progress. *D.A. Johnson — E. Devon (David Pipe).* 195 (CfMa), 326 (OMa), 962 (OMa), 1491 (R).

THIS ONE IS A BOY (IRE) ..9-3.. 9 b.g. Executive Perk — Belinda Vard (Le Bavard FR) u1*p*. Tall workmanlike half-brother to NH flat winners, Best Of The Girls (IRE) (in England) and Believe You Me (IRE) (in Ireland). Dam is sister to Carrickavolley (*qv* '88 Season Annual). NH FLAT '01 r1 p0. NH '01 r3 p0; pulled up 2. P-t-P '02 r2 p1 (2nd); and last. NH '04 r1 p0 (pulled up in 3m110y Hdle: *a bhnd, t.o & pu 11*). A typical Wilesmith-type, and lightly raced to boot, but returned from a year on the sidelines to thwart a gamble on the runner-up in an elders Maiden at Bitterley. Pulled up in three attempts over hurdles, the latest in May, but has an aversion to easy surfaces and might have the scope for Restricteds. Wears a cross-noseband. *M.S. Wilesmith — Ledbury.* 729 (OMa), 840 (OMa).

THIXENDALE ..8-5§.. 8 b.m. Reprimand — Havenwood Lady (Fair Season) pp2p52p4. Half-sister to Mirror Image, Brackenhill and Dalby Carr. Dam is half-sister to Havenwood (*qv*.'90 Annual). P-t-P '03 r2 p0 (pulled up 2). NH FLAT '03 (for M.W. Easterby) r2 p0. Completing for the first time over jumps when ten lengths second to the subsequently unbeaten Sovereign Gale at Eaton Hall, but bitterly disappointing otherwise, and cheekpieces have no effect on her performance. Pitched into Hunter Chases too soon, and presumably thought to be lacking in stamina. *Miss J.E. Foster & R. Chew — Pendle Forest & Craven (Jo Foster).* 316 (2m5fH), 500 (CMam), 714 (CMam), 776 (CfMa), 958 (OMa), 1300 (OMa), 1417 (OMa), 1458 (OMa).

TH'MOONS A BALLOON (IRE) ..—.. 11 b.g. Euphemism — Gerti's Quay (Quayside) 4pppp9uR. Workmanlike lengthy. IRISH P-t-P '99 r1 p0 (unseated). P-t-P/HUNT CH '01/3 r10 w2 (Maiden and Restricted) p3 (2 3rds); 4th, last and pulled up 3. Sprang a 25-1 surprise in '02, and held on gamely to a dwindling advantage at Lifton last year, but has been stopped in his tracks by broken blood vessels, and now a breathing problem appears to have raised its' head. Tongue-tied on his last four starts, and blinkered at Bratton Down where his hasty approach caused him to miss a marker and the rider failed to retrace costing him a £75 fine. Worth 10-0 if his troubles can be cured. *Miss E.A. Baverstock & S.G. Partridge — S. Devon (Simon Partridge).* 193 (I), 321 (I), 495 (I), 570 (Cf), 1129 (I), 1293 (2m7f110yH), 1363 (2m3f110yH), 1555 (I).

THORSGILL ..9-0.. 7 ch.g. Denel (FR) — Italian Princess (IRE) (Strong Gale) bp. Sturdy half-brother to Given Grace (IRE). Dam half-sister to Sherman Way (*qv* '91 Annual). P-t-P '03 r1 p1 (3rd of 4). Gave the impression he could improve on a six lengths third of five on an adequate debut, but brought down at the 14th when a well-backed favourite on his return, and appeared to hate the firm ground when attempting to recover losses at Musselburgh. Has presumably done himself a mischief. *T.W. Ellwood — Zetland (Chris Dennis).* 75 (OMa), 510 (OMa).

THREE OF CLUBS (IRE) ..8-12.. 16 b.g. Roselier (FR) — Calyx Pit (Pitpan) 4p. Tall good-looking half-brother to Hurdles winner, Henry Vill (IRE), and to Irish Pointing winner, The Moderator. NH FLAT '93 r1 p0. NH '94/5 r7 p3 (2nd in Hdle, and 3rd in Chses). P-t-P/HUNT CH '99/03 r18 w1 (Maiden) p4 (3 2nds, of 3 once; and remote last of 3 once); last pair 5, pulled up 6, and fell 2. Won his Maiden at Ampton in '99, but lightly raced and has broken blood vessels since, and only once better than last in his last seven attempts. His calling card is jumping constantly left-handed. Occasionally blinkered. Wears a cross-noseband. *D.F. Donegan — Mid Surrey F. (Victoria Park).* 180 (M), 421 (L).

THREE SAINTS (IRE) .9-0.. 16 b.g. Rising — Oh Dora (Even Money) 633p4. Rangy half-brother to an Irish NH flat winner. Dam won 2m Hdle in Ireland. IRISH NH FLAT '95 r2 p1. NH '95/9 r12 w1 (2m5f Ch) p2 (inc 3rd in Hdle). P-t-P/HUNT CH '00 and '02/3 r13 w2 (2 Members, 2 ran finished alone once) p8 (6 2nds, of 3 once; and inc 3rd in Hunt Ch); last, and fell/unseated 2. Used to rely on his ability to gallop all day, but has always been very lightly raced, and appears to be slowing appreciably with age. Sometimes not too certain at the fences and it will be surprising if he returns at 16. Unsuccessful when blinkered '98/9. *V. Dutton — Sir W.W. Wynn's (Geoff Dutton).* 449 (L), 708 (M), 986 (Cf), 1045 (Cf), 1203 (L).

PLATE 121 1037 Braes of Derwent Intermediate: L to R, Three Spires (Andrew Richardson), 1st, jumps past Royalecko (Jane Hollands), 3rd, at the last, Trooper Collins, 2nd, is lurking out of shot PHOTO: Alan Mitchell

THREE SPIRES ..10-2.. 10 ch.g. Minster Son — Mystic Music (Hansel's Nephew) 211313. Strong compact half-brother to Mystical Music and Mystical Spot. Dam, half-sister to 3 Pointers including

Mystic Major (*qv* '00 Annual), won 13 2m4f-3m2f Chases, inc 2 Horse and Hound Cups, and 7 points inc 4 Opens, and placed 9 (inc 6 2nds in Hunt Chses) Grandam, Mystic Mintet, won 3 Points and placed 3. NH FLAT '99 r1 p0. NH '99/00 r4 p0. P-t-P '01/3 (for Miss K.L. Thory) r11 p2 (3rds); last 2, pulled up 4, ran out 1 and fell 2. Useless in previous yards and blinkered once, and bought by present connections as a schoolmaster, but Tim Reed succeeded where others had failed, and Alice Pattinson never got to partner him in public. Won thrice going right-handed, and did little wrong, but his habit of getting worked up pre-race means he has two handlers. A triumph for competent handling, and Andrew Richardson also enters that category, and the combination should continue to do well. *Mrs P. Pattinson — Haydon (Tim Reed).* 137 (OMa), 271 (OMa), 431 (R), 764 (O), 1037 (I), 1307 (Cf).

THREE WAY SPLIT .—§.. 8 ch.g. Nomadic Way (USA) — Clairet (Sagaro) pppp. Strong-topped owner-bred brother to Claire's Nomad (*qv*). P-t-P '03 r1 p0 (pulled up). Completed a nap-hand of pulled ups in '04, and is as unpleasant to ride as his sibling was, but went lame at Easingwold and unlike him may not get the chance to be reformed by cheekpieces. *Mr & Mrs P.E. Clark — York & Ainsty S. (Liz Clark).* 167 (OMa), 272 (OMa), 773 (2m4fCMa), 1300 (OMa).

THROWAPARTY ..9-6.. 6 b.g. Thowra (FR) — Basic Fun (Teenoso USA) 3. Compact half-brother to Hurdles winner, Ndr's Cash For Fun. Dam won 4 2m Hurdles (one on all-weather), inc a Sell and 2 Claimers. Jumped round in competent fashion without ever really threatening in a Woodford Maiden (beaten seven-and-a-half lengths), and has the right sort of pedigree, so should be able to win in due course. *N.M. Tory & B. Snape — Portman (Ali Tory).* 1075 (OMa).

THUNDERPOINT (IRE) ..7-11.. 13 b.g. Glacial Storm (USA) — Urdite (FR) (Concertino FR) 8. Neat half-brother to Mackoy (IRE) (*qv*). NH FLAT '97 r4 p2. NH '97/03 (for T.D. Easterby, 3 wins, and R.J. Pricè, 4 wins) r61 w7 (4 2m-2m4f Hdles and 3 2m3f-3m Chses) p14; pulled up 6, refused 2, fell/unseated 6. The winner of seven races on good or firmish ground including a Selling Hurdle, and enjoyed three victories in '03, but has been dodgy in other campaigns, and was blinkered in five of his victories (also tried visored). Refused once in '99. Entered his eighth campaign in '04 but performed very badly at Leicester and was hopelessly tailed off after a mile before finishing last. Normally a summer type, but on the go for eight years, and looks to have suffered a reverse. To be commended on some expert jumping. *E.J. Whilding — N. Hereford (Richard Price).* 441 (2m4f110yH).

THUNDER THIGHS ..10-0§.. 10 gr.m. Baron Blakeney — Capalice (Derek H) p5f132R. Small compact half-sister to Proper Job. Dam, sister or half-sister to 4 Pointers, won a Maiden and placed 7 (inc 2 Sell Hdles). Grandam, Skyvan, won 5 Irish Points. P-t-P '02/3 r9 w1 (Maiden) p1 (3rd); 4th, 5th of 6, fell 4, and pulled up 1. Speedy and invariably makes the running, but consistently gets her wires crossed at the fences, and only really effective when the emphasis is not on stamina. Willful and cocked her jaw and ran out at Bratton Down, and will need to be on her best behaviour to stand any chance of upgrading successfully. Wore cheekpieces once in '04. Thankfully the days of Naddan Wilmington suffering from Tourette's syndrome appear to have passed. Has been unruly in the preliminaries, and is mounted on course and taken down early. Wears a cross-noseband. *N.R. Freak, Mrs S. Wadey & C. Kendall — Portman (Ali Tory).* 116 (I), 232 (R), 324 (R), 579 (R), 861 (M), 1071 (I), 1382 (I).

THURLES PICKPOCKET (IRE) ..8-12.. 14 b.g. Hollow Hand — Sugar Lady (Dalsaan) p55247. Tall rangy half-brother to Irish NH flat winner, Monksaan (IRE). P-t-P '96/03 (for Miss J.S. Stevens) r32 w6 (inc 3 Ladies) p13 (8 2nds, last twice; inc last of 3 once); 6th, last 3, pulled up 6, and fell/unseated 3. Consistently in the money in the previous yard, and was particularly effective going right-handed, but a wily customer and requires enterprising handling and has not scored since '02. Beaten a minimum of 35 lengths for the new owner-rider, and is only going through the motions now. Blinkered once in '03, and equipped with a visor at Garthorpe in March. *B.A. Elson — Belvoir (Tim Tarratt).* 155 (Cnr), 300 (O), 680 (M), 888 (O), 1057 (O), 1213 (Cnr).

THYNE EXPRESS (IRE) ..8-6.. 9 ch.g. Good Thyne (USA) — Annie's Alkali (Strong Gale) 3. Half-brother to Irish Hurdles winner, Croi Bhriste. IRISH P-t-P '01/2 r7 w1 (4&5yo Maiden) p1 (3rd); pulled up 5. IRISH HUNT CH '02 r1 p0 (pulled up). Must have won a bad babies Maiden in Ireland, because his other efforts have been really poor, and finished exhausted when well over a fence third of four in a Marks Tey Confined. Missed '03, and looks troubled. *Miss C. Scott — Thurlow (William Stone).* 905 (Cf).

THYNE MAN (IRE) ..10-7.. 7 br.g. Good Thyne (USA) — Showphar (IRE) (Phardante FR) 1123. Lengthy half-brother to Nessarc (IRE), and to Irish Pointing and Hurdling winner, Harry Husyan. IRISH P-t-P '03 r4 p3; and fell 1. IRISH NH FLAT '02 (for P. Cody) r2 p0. Surprisingly failed to score in Ireland, but did finish five lengths second behind the facile winner Fundamentalist (now smart in England) on his final start. Opened his account on his seventh attempt in a weak Maiden at

Tweseldown (the slowest time of the day), but looked a top novice when surging clear for an impressive 25 lengths win in a Restricted at Eyton-on-Severn (beat nothing, but his manner was very decisive). Ran well when four lengths second at Bangor on his Hunter Chase debut (the rest were very soundly beaten), but although one-and-a-half lengths third at Stratford it was still a hugely disappointing effort at 4-6, as he was always reluctant to extend himself on the firmish ground and his lack of fluency cost him dear. Worth trying again over the bigger obstacles when underfoot conditions are more suitable. *M.J. Parr — Albrighton (Paul Jones).* 627 (OMa), 933 (CR), 1375 (3m110yH), 1451 (3mH).

THYNY GLEN (IRE) .8-0.. 10 b.g. Good Thyne (USA) — Shuil Alanna (Furry Glen) 42. Small. Dam, half-sister to La Emni (*qv* '01 Annual), won 2m Hdle in Ireland. P-t-P '02/3 (for Mr P.J. Millington) r13 p3 (2 3rds, last once); last pair 3, fell/unseated 2, and pulled up 5. Taught bad habits in the previous ownership, and jumped with his usual lack of accuracy on his reappearance, and to the right when beaten the length of the run-in in his Members. His lack of resolve seems too ingrained to produce anything worthwhile in future. Has been tried in blinkers and a visor. *P.J. Houldey — G. Salter — Berkeley (Julie Houldey).* 666 (OMa), 1070 (M).

PLATE 122 4 Cambridgeshire Harriers Countryside Alliance Club Members (Nov Rdrs): Tictac, 1st, starts Tim Eades season with a bang PHOTO: Brian Armstrong

TICTAC (FR) ..10-4.. 9 ch.g. Beyssac (FR) — Native D'acres (FR) (Native Guile USA) 1p1p. Small close-coupled. FRENCH NH '00 (for T. Civel) r5 w2 (2m2f Chses) p1 (3rd in Hdle). A dual French Chasing winner in mud in '00, but after claiming him for £16,811 connections had to wait four years before they were able to get him back onto the track. Rewarded the immense patience shown when taking a Cottenham Novice Riders Point of the first day of the season (only three finished), but sold at Exeter market after pulling up at the final fence when tailed off in similar company (even money favourite after some 8-1 had been snapped up early), and then bought very cheaply by the latest owner. Promptly picked up a sub-standard Open at Llanfrynach (again, only three got round), but pulled up quickly at Ludlow next time, and appeared to go wrong. Capable of sustaining a strong gallop, and would probably have achieved a great deal had he not been so remarkably fragile. *D.E. Pipe — G. Fynn & I. Johnson — Taunton V.H. (-; Ian Johnson).* 4 (Cnr), 32 (Cnr), 448 (O), 1117 (3m1f110yH).

TIDAL BEACH ..9-0.. 6 b.g. Lugana Beach — Efficacy (Efisio) 5. Smallish. Dam won 3 6f races on Wolverhampton all-weather. 5000y. FLAT '01/2 (for C.W. Thornton) r13 p1 (3rd). Sold Doncaster, Oct '02 for 500. Once finished third over 6f on the flat, but tried unsuccessfully in Sellers and wore blinkers, and not asked to tackle trips beyond 10f. Twelve lengths fifth on his Pointing debut, but it was a very slowly run race, and he began to struggle from two out. Sprint-bred, and would be far from certain to get the trip. *Miss C.C. Jones — N. Ledbury.* 1142 (OMa).

TIDAL RACE (IRE) ..—.. 13 b.g. Homo Sapien — Flowing Tide (Main Reef) pp. Workmanlike half-brother to Keep Flowing (IRE), and to jumping winner, Bindaree (IRE). NH FLAT '96/7 r3 p0. NH '97/8 (for J.S. Haldane) r2 p0 (pulled up 2). Miles behind in bumpers, and pulled up in two Hurdles and then (after a six year absence) after about two miles in early February Maidens. Can show some early speed, but his end results are always appalling. *J.K. Buckle — Essex & Suffolk.* 103 (OMa), 129 (OMa).

TIDAL REEF (IRE) ..7-0§.. 13 br.g. Tidaro (USA) — Windsor Reef (Take A Reef) pp4. Small neat attractive half-brother to Crobeg. Dam won 2 Irish NH flat. NH '01/2 r11 p0; pulled up 5. P-t-P/HUNT CH '97/01 and '03 r26 w4 (inc 2m5f Hunt Ch, hat-trick '00) p0; failed to finish 16 (refused 1, and fell/unseated 2). Capped a fine season by landing a 2m5f Hunter Chase at Folkestone in '00, but subsequently unsuccessful under Rules, and generally tailed off. Won a match at Parham last year but has deteriorated badly, and otherwise not better than last since October '01. Blinkered on three occasions to '02. *R. Fielder — Southdown & Eridge.* 605 (M), 1054 (Cf), 1411 (M).

TIGER RAG ..7-7.. 12 b.m. Tigerwood — Sian Melody VII (unknown) p644. Small light-framed owner-bred half-sister to Sing Cherry Ripe and Black Dan. P-t-P '02/3 r3 p0 (last, and pulled up 2). Races keenly and wears a cross-noseband, and has eventually plotted her way to completion on four occasions, but not better than last, and beaten a minimum of 90 lengths in '04. Mounted on course and taken down early now. *Mrs A. James — Pembs (Wynne Morris).* 676 (CfMa), 1488 (OMa), 1524 (OMam), 1547 (M).

TIGERSUN ..—.. 11 b.g. Tigerwood — Sunfly (Sunyboy) ppp. Leggy light brother to Tiger Moth. Dam, sister or half-sister to 3 Pointers, including Tumbril (*qv* '97 Annual), won Maiden and Restricted and placed 5 for Dilwyn Thomas. P-t-P '00 and '02 r10 w1 (Maiden) p2 (3rds); and pulled up 7. Won a poor Maiden on firm at Erw Lon in '00, but ended his next campaign lame, and showed no signs of retaining ability in '04. Takes a keen hold and is inclined to make mistakes. Wears a cross-noseband. *D.R. Thomas — Llangeinor.* 358 (R), 674 (R), 740 (R).

TIGER TALK .9-9§.. 9 ch.g. Sabrehill (USA) — Tebre (USA) (Sir Ivor USA) p55. Small neat half-brother to winner in Czech Republic. Dam won 12f race in Ireland. FLAT '98/02 r20 w2 (7-8f) p2 (2nds). NH '00/3 (for M.E. Sowersby) r40 w2 (2m1f Hdles) p9 (inc 2nd of 2 in Ch); pulled up 6, unseated 1. Bought Doncaster, Aug for 4200. Has had his moments on the flat and over Hurdles, but never impressive over fences, and was a distant last of two when gaining his only placing in a Chase. Jaded these days and if he does decide to run on he always leaves it too late, and after disappointing in Points (the trip was probably too far) he has reverted to modest Hurdles including Sellers without showing any verve. Normally wears headgear or cheekpieces. Had he not failed the vet as a three-year-old, he would now be residing in the more exotic climes of Macau. *D. Pipe — Silverton.* 62 (Cf), 484 (L), 822 (L).

TIGER TED ..8-10.. 8 ch.g. Le Moss — Dancing Returns (Bali Dancer) f9. Small neat owner-bred brother to Freddie Moss. Dam, pulled up 2, ran out in Points and pulled up in 2 Chses (looked decidedly scatty) for Mr Turner. Grandam, Happy Returns, won '79 BMW final Hunter Chase and 8 Ladies, and is the dam of Sutton Lighter (*qv*). P-t-P '03 r1 p0 (pulled up). Displayed a little ability though ultimately 53 lengths last in a Restricted at Upton, but needs to be made fitter, and to pay more respect to the fences before he can be considered winning material. *E. Turner — Ludlow (Mark Trott).* 668 (OMa), 977 (R).

TIGHT FISTED BENNY (IRE) ..9-5.. 7 b.g. Beneficial — Meaney (Delamain USA) p2. 9216 3yo. Showed speed for two miles but faded and pulled up at the last on his debut (backed from 12s to 7-1, but ran green), and then gave a tidy display when five lengths second over 2m4f at Dalston, where two subsequent scorers finished behind him. Led until the last, and looks sure to go one better before long. Promising. *Mrs A. Stevenson — Haydon (Tim Reed).* 433 (OMa), 767 (2m4fOMa).

TIGRE BOIS ..—.. 8 b.g. Mon Tresor — Gentle Star (Comedy Star USA) fpp. Good-topped half-brother to Chasing winners, Lodestone Lad (IRE) and Polish Spirit (also won flat), and flat winner, Tell Me This. Dam, won 3 6f races, half-sister to Dante's Delight (*qv* '95 Annual). FLAT '99 and '01 r10 p0. NH '01 r2 p0. P-t-P '03 r1 p0 (ran out). Charges off uncontrollably, but does not stay even two miles, and has no hope of completing in Points. Decked by an idiotic piece of riding at Brampton Bryan, but at least Ray Carey learnt his lesson, and has pulled him up when he gets knackered since. *J.W.E. Weaver — Clifton-on-Teme.* 667 (OMa), 820 (OMa), 1139 (OMa).

TILLY TIME ..—.. 7 b.m. Then Again — Baybellina (IRE) (Robellino USA) pp. Sturdy. Pulled up in May Maidens when ridden by Heards on consecutive Saturdays, and the old man should have had a warning for schooling in public in the latest. *S.J. Williams — Tetcott.* 1186 (OMa), 1326 (OMa).

TIMBERLEY .10-2.. 11 ch.g. Dancing High — Kimberley Rose (Monksfield) 333fpp351. Good-topped compact owner-bred half-brother to Kimothy. Dam won W. Percy Members and placed 6 for Rhona Brewis (was incredibly indolent, but did complete in all but the last of her 20 Points). P-t-P '02/3 r9 w1 (Maiden) p2 (2nd of 3 once); last pair 3, pulled up 2, and unseated 1. Made all to score with some authority on his eighth attempt, and looked likely to pick up a Restricted rather quicker, but lost his confidence following a fall at Corbridge in '04, and only did so at the ninth time of asking. Both his wins have been gained at Hexham, and another stamina test there looks his best chance of a follow up. Has made a noise, and runs tongue-tied. *R., Miss R. & Mrs G.E. Brewis — Percy (Rhona Brewis).* 69 (M), 132 (CR), 212 (R), 431 (R), 548 (R), 918 (R), 1222 (R), 1419 (R), 1476 (R).

TIMBER TOP (IRE) .—§§.. 12 b.g. Supreme Leader — Modelligo Wood (IRE) (Ragapan) prr. Workmanlike. P-t-P '99/00 and '02/3 r11 w1 (Maiden) p3 (2 3rds, of 4 once); last 2, and pulled up 5. Rated 9-9 after winning a Maiden in softish in the slowest time of the day at Black Forest Lodge in '02, but has never managed more than four outings in a season, and performs with increasing reluctance in the current yard. Mounted on course and taken down early in '04. *Mrs C.P. Swarbrick — S. Dorset (Kathy Thomas).* 198 (R), 473 (R), 601 (R).

TIME CAN TELL .9-5§.. 11 ch.g. Sylvan Express — Stellaris (Star Appeal) p2f45754. Lengthy half-brother to Ashdren, Crimson Brocade, Rapid Liner and Royal Velvet, and to flat winners, Celestine and Blue Radiance. 4000f, 5500y, 2500 2yo. FLAT '96/03 r77 w4 (8-16f) p22; unseated 1. NH '98, '00 and '02 (for A.G. Juckes) r6 p1 (3rd); pulled up 1. Bought Ascot, Oct for 761. Regularly in the money over eight seasons when hectically campaigned on the flat, and having gained his first victory in a Seller he then progressed to better company. Unusually, is a winner on each of the three all-weather tracks, but always far more likely to collect a place only. Most of his Hurdling campaign was in Sellers, and only had four horses behind him in his eight outings of '04, and beaten 14 seconds when inheriting second at the last in an Open at Garnons. Often wears headgear or cheekpieces, and tailed off in all three Hunter Chases. Can make numerous blunders, and his enthusiasm is at a very low ebb. Another nine outings and he will have clocked a century. *G. Band & E.A. Thomas — N. Hereford (Eric Thomas).* 404 (O), 615 (O), 727 (MO), 836 (O), 1140 (Cf), 1372 (2m4fH), 1454 (3mH), 1512 (2m6f110yH).

TIMES TWO ..9-5.. 9 ch.g. Weld — Sheppie's Double (Scallywag) p43p. Small owner-bred. Dam (*qv* '90 Annual), failed to finish in 5 Points and a Hurdle. Grandam, Quadrille II, ran and jumped badly in Points. Great-grandam, Windsor Toi, won a Ch. P-t-P '02/3 r4 p1 (3rd of 4); pulled up 2, and fell 1. Headstrong and usually leads at some stage in his races, but a beaten favourite twice, and never has any response once headed. Failed to stay any better when held up at Chaddesley Corbett, and will need a bad race to score. Wears a cross-noseband. *Mrs J. Smith — Sir W.W. Wynn's (Steve Wynne).* 531 (OMa), 710 (Mah), 753 (OMa), 1341 (OMa).

TIMPANI (IRE) .9-11§.. 9 b.g. Broken Hearted — Queen Kam (IRE) (Kambalda) p3p2p. Small neat. NH FLAT '01 r2 p0. NH '01/2 r6 p1 (3rd); pulled up 2. P-t-P '02/3 (for Mrs S. Maude, Mrs H. Sparrow & Mr A. Burton) r6 w2 (Maiden and Restricted) p1 (2nd of 3); last 2, and pulled up 1. A dual winner on contrasting surfaces in '02, but not an easy ride, and even A.P. McCoy could not get a positive response in three subsequent appearances together over hurdles. A weak finisher in general, and though his often erratic jumping has improved it looks odds against him co-operating enough to score again in Points. Wears a cross-noseband, and has been tried in headgear and a tongue-tie. *Mrs S. Maude — Dulverton F.* 635 (L), 882 (C), 1071 (I), 1508 (I), 1555 (I).

TINARANA LORD (IRE) ..9-7§.. 8 br.g. Teamster — Tinerana League (IRE) (Gallic League) R8443. Workmanlike. IRISH P-t-P '03 r5 w1 (5&6yo Maiden) p1 (3rd); pulled up 1. IRISH NH '03 (for J.A. Codd) r1 p0 (fell). Won an Irish Point on his debut but who fell when blinkered in his only Hurdle, but never looked very enthusiastic in the new yard, and although he made the frame on three occasions he was never beaten less than 19 lengths. Can be in contention after 2m4f, but seems to give up quickly, and is a disappointment. *The Crazy Gang (G. Hanmer) — Cheshire (Gary Hanmer).* 164 (R), 383 (R), 614 (R), 853 (R), 1217 (R).

TINDER-BOX ..9-8.. 8 br.g. Miner's Lamp — Sovereign's Oak (Precipice Wood) 16p. Small close-coupled. Dam, (*qv* '92 Annual), sister to Dog Wood, was placed in 5 Points for the Caves. Grandam, Daddy's Sauce, failed to finish in 9 of 11 Points for Dr Cave. P-t-P '02/3 r7 w1 (Maiden) p2 (3rds, of 4 once); 4th, ran out 1, unseated 1 and pulled up 1. Twice a beaten favourite after winning his Maiden at Cothelstone, but enterprisingly travelled to Wales to win his Restricted, and did so with great ease. Disappointing in better company on faster ground since, and was never going at any stage on his latest appearance. Presumably has an intermittent fault that clearly has a detrimental effect on his jumping. Wears a cross-noseband. *Dr S.G.F. Cave — Blackmore & Sparkford V. (Penny Cave).* 740 (R), 1129 (I), 1330 (I).

TIRALDO (FR) ..9-11.. 12 b.g. Royal Charter (FR) — Tamilda (FR) (Rose Laurel) p884. Lengthy brother to Chasing winner, Tacolino (FR), and to a French jumping winner, and half-brother to four winners in France (including 3 over jumps). FRENCH NH '97 r14 w1 (2m2f Hdle) p9. NH '98/02 r25 w4 (2m4f110y-3m1f Chses) p7; pulled up 4, and fell 3. HUNT CH '03 (for Dr D. Woodhouse & Mr J. Woodhouse) r1 p0 (last). Showed signs of a revival in the new yard, but only once better than last, when dropping out of contention very quickly in the last half-mile at Chaddesley, and his season was ended in February. Prone to make errors over big fences. Has been tried in blinkers and cheekpieces. *Mrs S.E. Vaughan, P. Hicks, T. Jones & J. Hawkes — Teme V. (Steve Flook).* 33 (L), 122 (3m1fH), 209 (3m1f110yH), 254 (O).

TIRLEY GALE ..9-6.. 13 b.g. Strong Gale — Mascara VII (unknown) 96130. NH FLAT '97 r2 p0. NH '98/01 r19 w1 (2m7f110y Ch) p2 (3rds); pulled up 4, fell 2 and refused 1. NH '03 r1 p0 (10th in Ch). P-t-P/HUNT CH '97 and '02/3 r12 w2 (Members and Club nov rdrs) p3 (2 2nds, of 3 once; and distant 3rd in Hunt Ch); 4th twice, last, pulled up 2, unseated 1, and refused 1. Quirky and unpredictable, and normally folds tamely under pressure, but has managed to score in all but his initial Pointing campaign. Looks to be deteriorating fast and his Members looks his only hope in '05. Has run tongue-tied. Wears a cross-noseband. Usually mounted on course and taken down early, but only does so reluctantly nowadays. *D. Smith — Cotswold V.F. (Nicky Smith).* 403 (Cf), 661 (Cnr), 815 (M), 1295 (3m110yH), 1497 (3mH).

TISALLOVER (IRE) ..9-5.. 7 b.g. Germany (USA) — Gars Delight (IRE) (Al Hareb USA) 53p. IRISH P-t-P '03 r3 p1 (last of 2); last, and fell 1. A confirmed front-runner who has been placed twice including when ten-and-a-half lengths third at Woodford. Looked to have found a golden opportunity at Rhydygwern and was sent off at 1-2, but pulled up lame on the firm ground when leading after two miles. His name looks all too prophetic. *The Bridgwater Partnership (M. Hammond) — Worcs (Michael Hammond).* 848 (OMa), 1074 (OMa), 1487 (OMa).

TITUS BRAMBLE ..10-6.. 8 b.g. Puissance — Norska (Northfields USA) 115f2. Well-made half-brother to at least five flat winners (two in Italy), including Eponine (also won jumping). FLAT '99/01 r15 w2 (10-11f) p0. NH '00/2 r21 w1 (2m1f Hdle) p5 (2 2nds, inc Ch); pulled up 3, and fell/unseated 2. P-t-P '03 (for Mrs L. Smith) r4 w1 (Confined) p2; and pulled up. No better than a plater under Rules, but completed a Pointing hat-trick when appearing to win outright at Tweseldown in February, and returned to form following two defeats as market leader (every chance when fell once) when beaten the minimum margin at Woodford. Likes to dominate, and suited by good or fast ground, but not always prepared to battle, and his style of hurdling the fences often gets him into trouble. All four jumping wins have been achieved going right-handed, and looks set to win again when conditions are right. Wears blinkers and a tongue-tie, and has often run visored in the past. *Mrs L. Garrett — Berkeley (Dick Baimbridge).* 17 (O), 170 (O), 727 (MO), 836 (O), 1072 (L).

T'NIGHTSTHENIGHT ..9-12.. 11 b.g. Scallywag — Misty Sky (Hot Brandy) Rpf. Big strong brother to Cloud Cover, and half-brother to Beinn Mohr. Dam won 3 Points and placed 4 (inc Nov Hdle). P-t-P '99/00 and '02/3 (for Mr C.J.B. Barlow, Mr & Mrs J. Malem) r12 p4 (neck 2nd; and 3 3rds, of 4 twice, and last once); 4th, last 2, pulled up 1, refused 2 and fell 2. Beaten a neck at Eyton last year, and was still hard on the steel when missing a marker with three to jump on his first start for new connections, but a very weak finisher in general, and typically stopped to nil next time. In view of his size presumably hampered by a breathing difficulty, and if so will need to have this and his tendency to make mistakes rectified if he is to open his account. *L. Slattery — Cumberland F. (Liz Slattery).* 161 (I), 287 (CfMa), 439 (2m5f110yH).

TOD'S BROTHER .10-3.. 11 b.g. Gildoran — Versina (Leander) 2p115. Big rangy owner-bred half-brother to Coppinger's Cave, Trewornan Bridge and Tom's Influence. Dam won 2 Points and placed 2. Grandam, Verosina, won 2 Hunt Chses (2m4f-3m) and 4 Points and placed 7. P-t-P '00 and '02 r8 w2 (Maiden and Club Restricted) p1 (last of 3); and pulled up 5. Highly strung and sweats freely, and only able to appear every other year, but put his proven stamina to good use in '04, and completed an April double. Lucky on the first occasion, but scored entirely on merit at Catsfield, and can increase his winning tally, probably in '06. Let down by his jumping, particularly in Hunter Chases, and needs to concentrate on Points. Suited by plenty of cut in the ground. *A.W.K. & Mrs J. Merriam — E. Sussex & Romney Marsh (Di Grissell).* 247 (O), 541 (3mH), 778 (CCon), 1054 (Cf), 1438 (3m2fH).

TOFFEE LADY ..9-2.. 8 b.m. Respect — Belsprit Lady (Belfalas) 3fuu4. Strong owner-bred sister to Imatoff, and half-sister to Hill Sprite and Derrilady. Dam won NH flat. P-t-P '03 r2 p0 (last, and pulled up). A staying-on six lengths third in a weak mares Maiden at Garnons, but fell at the third last when just in front there next time, and lucky not to lose the rider thrice more subsequently. Has the ability to win a small race if her jumping ever becomes proficient. Wears a cross-noseband. *Miss P.E. Porter — N. Hereford.* 408 (CMam), 617 (2m4fOMa), 666 (OMa), 926 (OMa), 1074 (OMa).

TOM BROWN (IRE) ..10-0.. 7 ch.g. Grand Plaisir (IRE) — Rathoe Princess (Never Slip) p. Tall narrow half-brother to Mounthenry Star (IRE) (*qv*). P-t-P '03 r2 w1 (2m4f Maiden) p0; and pulled up 1. Made a fine start when winning a 2m4f Maiden on dead ground at Eyton, but absent for two months before reappearing in '03, and pulled up lame when risked on firmish at Chaddesley this year. Looked a bright prospect in embryo. *P.A. Jones — Tanatside.* 252 (CR).

TOMCAPPAGH (IRE) ..8-2.. 14 br.g. Riberetto — Shuil Suas (Menelek) 6pp6u4p. Big half-brother to Cool Shuil (IRE). P-t-P/HUNT CH '96/00 r19 w2 (inc 2m5f Hunt Ch) p6 (4 3rds, of 4 twice; and 2 2nds; inc 4 Hunt Chses); pulled up 6, and fell 2. NH '00/3 r31 w1 (3m2f Ch) p8; pulled up 11, carried out 1, unseated 2. Often made the running when in the money despite his tendency to make mistakes under Rules, and won at Plumpton in December '01, but lost his form completely, and was pulled up in six of his last eight appearances. Plodded badly under a novice and only once better than last in '04, and his fall into disrepair seems complete. *Mrs S. Wall — E. Sussex & Romney Marsh.* 155 (Cnr), 249 (Cnr), 537 (4mMO), 610 (Cv&nr), 640 (Cf), 897 (Cfv&nr), 1410 (Cf).

TOM COBBLER (IRE) ..10-5.. 11 ch.g. Zaffaran (USA) — Po Bo Pu (Pollerton) 1211336. Workmanlike compact half-brother to Irish Hurdles winner, Bradley's Corner. Dam is half-sister to The Bodhran (*qv* '99 Annual). NH FLAT '99 r4 w1 p2. NH '99/01 r17 w3 (2 2m-2m6f110y Hdles, and 2m7f110y Ch) p3 (2 3rds); unseated 1. P-t-P/HUNT CH '02/3 r8 w1 (Ladies) p5 (3 3rds, of 4 twice, inc Hunt Ch); and 4th twice. A thorough stayer, and does best when fresh, and enjoyed his most productive year ever in '04. Turned sour under Rules, and did not appear to relish the sight of regulation fences at Folkestone, and sometimes a slovenly jumper in Points, but another break seems certain to do him good. Seems happiest going right-handed, and is suited by good or easy ground. Blinkered thrice in '01. *C.S. Hall, Mr & Mrs A. Cooper & Mrs P. Wilkins — Southdown & Eridge (Susanna Hall).* 18 (L), 126 (L), 608 (L), 641 (L), 1053 (L), 1283 (L), 1441 (3m7fH).

TOM DE SAVOIE (IRE) ..10-2§.. 12 br.g. War Hero — Black Pilot (Linacre) 3212. Tall workmanlike half-brother to Barton Bulldozer (IRE), and to Irish Hunter Chase winner, Digacre (IRE). P-t-P/HUNT CH '98/00 and '02/3 (for Mr W.G.N. Barber) r27 w9 (inc 3m110y Hunt Ch and 2 Opens) p12 (6 2nds, inc 2 Hunt Chses; 6 3rds, of 4 once, inc Hunt Ch); 5th of 6, pulled up 1, and fell 4. A smart Pointer '99/02, but became thoroughly untrustworthy last year, and only took his score into double figures when 4-7 in a feeble Members in which he looked irresolute when coming off the bridle. Still retains plenty of ability, and would win regularly were he genuine, but has to be avoided at all costs. Suited by good ground. *The Wishful Thinking Partnership (J. Fryer) - W. Norfolk (Nigel Bloom).* 647 (Cf), 886 (Cf), 1150 (M), 1313 (Cf).

TOM DOVE ..—.. 10 gr.g. St Enodoc — Another Dove (Grey Love) ppp. Small half-brother to Low Homes, Another Cruise and Eaton Dove. Dam won 6 Hdles at around 2m. Grandam, Red Dove, won 16 Hdles, and bred the winners of 38 races, including Shadey Dove, the dam of Champion Hurdler, Flakey Dove. Great-grandam, Cottage Lass II, was placed twice in Points in the late 40's and later changed hands for £25 at Ludlow market. NH '00 r1 p0 (unseated). P-t-P '02/3 r7 p0 (5th of 6, and pulled up 6). A non-finisher in ten of 11 starts over jumps, and surely has something very badly wrong with him. Wears a cross-noseband, and has run tongue-tied. *H.S. Channon — Lamerton (Yvonne Watson & Jo Channon).* 83 (OMa), 194 (CfMa), 913 (OMa).

TOMMY FLANDERS .—§.. 9 ch.g. Derrylin — Wedding Song (True Song) pp. Tall compact owner-bred brother to Mullensgrove (*qv*). P-t-P '02/3 r6 p0 (pulled up 6). As moody and as error-prone as his sibling, but nowhere near as talented and it would be a surprise if connections could be bothered to race him again. Wears a cross-noseband. *D.J. Lowe — Atherstone.* 60 (OMa), 385 (OMa).

TOMMY HOTSPUR (IRE) .9-6§.. 12 b.g. Royal Fountain — Ramble Bramble (Random Shot) 42. Good-topped half-brother to Misty Ramble (IRE), to smart jumping winner, Seven Towers (IRE), to Hurdles winner, Pharrambling (IRE), and to Irish Pointing winners, Tone Bramble and Hansbury. Dam, from splendid jumping family, is half-sister to The Humble Tiller (*qv* '98 Annual). NH FLAT '98 r1 p0. NH '99/01 r6 p0. P-t-P '03 r9 p6 (4 2nds, of 3 twice; and inc head and head 3rd once); 5th, and pulled up 2. Tried in blinkers for the first time, and sent off favourite for the third time when eight lengths last of two finishers at Market Rasen, but over-reached badly in the process, and was not able to run again. Placed on seven occasions now, and consistently looks to be on the verge of winning, but tends to run in snatches, and seems intent on clinging to his maiden status. *Mrs J.H. Docker & Mrs S. Buckler — Atherstone (John Docker).* 111 (OMa), 303 (OMa).

TOM PUTT .9-10§.. 9 b.g. Sulaafah (USA) — Miss Crabapple (Sunyboy) 815234. Workmanlike. Dam, half-sister to 9 Pointers (8 of them winners), including Royal Orchard (*qv* '02 Annual), was 2nd in Point, but failed to finish in 6 of 10 other attempts ('crabby Miss Crabapple looks the black sheep'). Grandam, Windfall VI, won 2 Points and placed 8 (inc a Hunt Ch) for Fran Marriott. P-t-P '02/3 r12 w1 (Maiden) p2 (2nds); 4th (also disqualified from 4th twice — nt weigh-in both times), 5th, 7th, unseated 3, and pulled up 1. Stayed on under heavy pressure to open his account at the 12th time of asking in a 17-runner Maiden at Andoversford, and wasted little time in landing a three-finisher Restricted on firm at Whitwick Manor, but becoming increasingly indolent, and requires much driving. Lacked fluency when tried in cheekpieces at Paxford, and the experiment was not repeated. *Mr & Mrs H.C. Pauling, R. Weeks & S. O'Sullivan — Heythrop (Howard Pauling).* 294 (R), 516 (R), 759 (I), 922 (I), 1274 (Cf), 1397 (I).

TOM'S GOLD ..—.. 7 br.g. Gildoran — Tom's Star (Comedy Star USA) ppp. Robust owner-bred brother to Gilded Star. Dam half-sister to Tom's Little Will (*qv* '95 Annual). P-t-P '03 r1 p0 (pulled up). Error-prone when loitering in the ruck in Maidens, and needs to be ridden with much more enterprise if he is ever to achieve anything worthwhile. *Mrs S. Towler — Heythrop (Jon Trice-Rolph).* 291 (2m4fCfMa), 588 (CfMa), 926 (OMa).

TOM'S MAN .9-9.. 11 ch.g. Milieu — Lorna's Choice (Oats) pp. Close-coupled brother to Colonel Conca, and half-brother to Delwood and Annie-jo. Dam was 3rd in Percy Members, and 3rd in dire Hurdles on hard. NH FLAT '98 r2 p0. NH '98 and '01 r7 p0; pulled up 3. P-t-P/HUNT CH '00/3 r15 w1 (Club Maiden) p5 (4 2nds, beaten neck once, and of 3 once; and 3rd in Hunt Ch); 4th twice, pulled up 6, and fell. Finally got off the mark at the 22nd attempt on firm at Tranwell last year, but ordinarily fails to get the trip in Points, and is very accident-prone. A non-finisher in his last four starts, and will be difficult to place successfully again. Wears a cross-noseband, and a tongue-tie. *The Rennington Racing Club (F.V. White) — W. Percy (George White).* 240 (3mH), 1177 (2m5fH).

TOM'S RIVER (IRE) ..—.. 13 ch.g. Over The River (FR) — Nesford (Walshford) p. Lengthy half-brother to Malvernian, Tom Snout (IRE) and Ballyea Boy (IRE), to Irish Pointing winners, Summer Blade, Freewheeling Bob, Winters Hill (also jumping winner there), and to all-weather Hurdles winner, Proverbs Girl. Dam won 2m Hurdle in Ireland. NH FLAT '97 r2 w1 p1 (2nd). NH '97/03 (for Mrs M. Reveley, all wins, and R.J. Hodges) r36 w4 (3m1f Chses) p8 (inc 2 Hdles, and 3rd in Selling Ch); pulled up 5, fell/unseated 4. Bought Ascot, Dec for 1523. The winner of four 3m1f Chases at Catterick, all on good or easy surfaces, and was capable of staying on strongly from off the pace on his favourite sharp track, but has only once been successful since December '99. Very much on the downgrade, and presumably retired after pulling up at Hereford in February. *C. Nenadich & N. Nenadich — N. Hereford (Chris Nenadich).* 209 (3m1f110yH).

TOM TOBACCO .9-12.. 8 b.g. Afzal — Monsoon (Royal Palace) 24411. Workmanlike unfurnished half-brother to The Early Bird, and to jumping winner, Willy Willy. Dam won 2m6f Hdle. P-t-P '02/3 r7 p0 (last of 6, pulled up 5, and fell 1). Disappointing and not better than last in his first two seasons, but helped by much improved jumping managed to struggle home in front when backed from threes to 7-4 in a 2m4f Maiden on firmish at Garthorpe. Followed up when 12-1 at the next meeting, but once again was all out, and his apparent shortage of stamina may prevent further success. *Mrs C.R. Saunders — Pytchley (Caroline Bailey).* 597 (2m5fOMa), 890 (2m4fOMa), 1125 (OMa), 1402 (2m4fOMa), 1503 (R).

TONRIN ..9-5§§.. 13 b.g. General Wade — Hot Tramp (Country Retreat) 75upp. Smallish. Dam won 4 Hdles at around 2m (the first a Sell), and revived for 4 outings aged 14 after missing the 6 previous seasons. NH FLAT '97 r1 p0 (pulled himself up). NH '97 r2 p0 (pulled up in Hdles). P-t-P '99/03 r24 w1 (Maiden) p8 (5 2nds, beaten neck once, and last once); pulled up 6, refused 1 and fell/unseated 3; also refused to race in void Maiden. A prize thief who was conned into scoring at the 23rd attempt by Phillip York at Detling last year, but ground to a halt after being left 20 lengths clear approaching the last next time, and not better than last in '04. It seems pointless racing him again. *D. Walker — Staff College.* 181 (R), 419 (CR), 538 (R), 639 (R), 802 (R).

TONY ..—.. 7 b.g. Marju (IRE) — Present Imperfect (Cadeaux Genereux) pp. Sturdy. FLAT '00/1 r9 p0. P-t-P '03 (for Mr M.J. Brown & Mr N. Duxbury) r3 p0 (pulled up 3). Often started slowly and looked a difficult ride on the flat, and little has changed since switching codes, and appeared to suffer a reverse when tried tongue-tied at Dalton Park. Wears a cross-noseband. *M.J. Brown — York & Ainsty N.* 342 (2m4fOMa), 505 (CMa).

TOOLEY PARK .9-5§.. 8 b.g. Homo Sapien — Aintree Oats (Oats) 23p221. Strong-topped. Dam, half-sister to Stab In The Dark (*qv* '97 Annual), won 4 modest Points and placed 6. Grandam, Lucy Parker, won 4 2m-3m2f Chses, and placed 15 (inc English/Irish Points). P-t-P '02/3 r5 p0 (4th, and pulled up 4). Rather cumbersome, and twice a beaten favourite in '04, but left with an unassailable lead at the third last when well supported at Garthorpe, and came home by 30 lengths despite looking to pull himself up in the straight. Gives the impression that the full trip will present problems in a higher grade. Has worn over-reach boots. *J.T.B. Hunt — Pytchley (Carol Elderton).* 7 (2m4fOMa), 60 (OMa), 218 (OMa), 560 (OMa), 1000 (OMa), 1403 (2m4fOMa).

TOON SOCIETY (IRE) ..9-3.. 7 b.g. Moscow Society (USA) — Sweet Defeet (Deep Run) 3321. Small light. NH FLAT '03 r2 p0. NH '03 (for J. O'Neill) r1 p0 (dist 4th in 2m5f Sell Hdle). Clearly held in very low regard by a powerful stable previously, and was a distant fourth of five in a Seller in his only Hurdle for them (blinkered on last two appearances), but proved consistent in Maidens, and followed a couple of thirds in which he was beaten about nine lengths with a rather unlucky three-quarters of a length second over 2m4f (not left with much room on the run-in). Finally gained his reward for consistency in a two-finisher event at Holnicote where he was set a facile task, and may be able to progress sufficiently for Restricteds. *The Exmoor Partners (J. Atkins) — Devon & Somerset (Jeremy Scott).* 143 (OMa), 275 (CfMa), 413 (2m4fOMa), 1326 (OMa).

TOO PHAR TO TOUCH ..7-0.. 10 br.m. Wace (USA) — Carew Mill (Hubble Bubble) pp. Small strong compact. Dam, half-sister to Phar Too Touchy (*qv* '98 Annual), was last of 2 and 3rd of 4 (fence behind in both) in Maidens for the Spuffards. P-t-P/HUNT CH '00 and '02/3 (for Mr M.J. Spuffard &

Mr F. Goldsworthy) r12 p3 (2 2nds; and 3rd of 4); 4th, pulled up 7 and refused 1. A regular non-finisher, and only once beaten less than 20 lengths, and does not stay three miles. Has run tongue-tied. *Miss F. Goldsworthy — S. Pembs (Edith Goldsworthy).* 948 (OMa), 1524 (OMam).

TOORAK (USA) ..9-11.. 8 b.g. Irish River (FR) — Just Juliet (USA) (What A Pleasure USA) 42. Compact half-brother to several winners (mostly abroad), including Julietta Mia (flat). Dam 2yo sprint winner in USA. 44,000y. FLAT '99/00 and '02 r5 p0. NH '01/3 (for C.J. Mann, and Mrs T.J. McInnes Skinner) r8 p1 (3rd); pulled up 1. A very modest contestant under Rules, and was beaten a minimum of 42 lengths on his final six attempts. A little more effective in Points and might just about be good enough to take a Maiden at best, but it does not look encouraging that he was only able to manage a couple of outings in February (both at Friars Haugh). *A.R. Trotter — Berwicks.* 137 (OMa), 281 (M).

TOP BOOTS (IRE) .7-7.. 6 b.g. Executive Perk — Lancastrian Height (IRE) (Lancastrian) 2r. Brother to Irish Pointing winner, Sarogini, and half-brother to Irish NH flat winner, Atlantic Run, and to Irish Pointing winner, Deise Rose. Bought Doncaster, May for 6000. Favourite for his Members but lost ground with some very novicey jumping early on, and although he recovered to have every chance at the last he was outpaced by a rival with a jockey putting up almost a stone overweight. Never went a yard next time, and finally refused and unseated at the final fence when an exhausted fourth and furlongs behind. Needs the return of Andrew Braithwaite to the saddle at present. *The Marriage Family (Mrs J.K. Marriage) — Essex (Simon Marriage).* 646 (M), 901 (OMa).

TOP COMMANDER (IRE) ..—.. 8 ch.g. Un Desperado (FR) — Lady Bodmin (IRE) (Law Society USA) p. Brother to Johnsair (IRE) (*qv*). 1996 4yo. Did not make it to the racecourse until May, and was pulled up after 2m4f when struggling. *H.W. Lavis — Pembs.* 1240 (OMa).

TOPICAL TIP (IRE) ..9-9.. 16 b.g. Tip Moss (FR) — Sami (FR) (Sukawa FR) 29453. Lengthy half-brother to Chasing winner, Philatelic (IRE). Dam, sister to Prince Wo (winner of Prix La Barka), won 3 flat and 2 Hdles in France. IRISH P-t-P '93 r1 w1 (4yo Maiden). IRISH NH '94/6 and '98 r25 w2 (2m3f-2m5f Chses) p7 (inc 3rd at Cheltenham in '95). P-t-P '00 and '02/3 (for Miss E. Boone) r20 w1 (Members) p12 (7 2nds, dead-heat once, and of 3 twice, beaten head once); 5th, 6th twice, pulled up 1 and unseated 3. Won three races in Ireland to '96, and staged a successful revival in '00, but out of luck since, and all of his brave efforts for Emma Chugg have been in vain. Jumps and stays well, and it is a pity his Members is not run on a more testing track. Has been tried in blinkers. *Mrs E. Chugg — Quorn.* 31 (Cnr), 175 (Cnr), 249 (Cnr), 784 (Cf), 1056 (M).

PLATE 123 1326 Minehead Harriers & West Someset Open Maiden (Div 1): Toon Society (Neil Harris), 1st, asserts at the last from sole remaining rival Mr Baloo (Alex Charles-Jones), 2nd
PHOTO: Nick Jay

TOP LIGHT ..9-3.. 9 b.g. Miner's Lamp — Myrtilla (Beldale Flutter USA) pu22p. Rangy half-brother to Bishop's Blade (*qv*). NH FLAT '00/1 r3 p1 (3rd). NH '02/3 (for R.H. Buckler) r9 p0 (last pair 3, pulled up 3, and fell 3). Third in a bumper, but only in front of one horse in five Hurdles (beaten 63 lengths plus twice, and pulled up thrice) and a desperate jumper in Chases (distant fourth of five, and fell thrice). Also prone to blunders in Points and made a bad one two out when five lengths second in a Badbury Maiden, but looked to have been given the chance of a lifetime in a match at Larkhill and was sent off at 1-4, but after being given an uninspired ride he was trounced by his rival who finished lame. Letting an inexperienced girl partner him once was daft (unsurprisingly she got unseated), and is a bad mover who may have gone wrong on his final start. *R. & Mrs A.J. Long & Mrs K. Blackman — R.A. (Kathy Blackman).* 37 (CR), 139 (R), 264 (CfMa), 456 (OMa), 721 (OMa).

TOP OF THE CHARTS ..9-3§.. 9 b.g. Salse (USA) — Celebrity (Troy) p3246. Workmanlike half-brother to Hurdles winners, Stompin (also won flat) and Entertainment, and to a winner in Italy. Dam won 10f race. FLAT '98/01 r16 w1 (16f) p0. NH '00/1 r15 p2. P-t-P/HUNT CH '03 r6 p3 (inc 3rd of 4 twice); 5th, ran out 1, and pulled up 1. Often wore headgear when meeting limited success on the flat, but remains a maiden despite 26 starts over jumps, and has failed to get the trip in Points. Has been ridden in spurs, and is normally quick to concede defeat after making the running. *Miss T. McCurrich — Clifton-on-Teme.* 616 (C), 937 (Cnr), 1135 (M), 1400 (CN), 1528 (Cf).

TOP WELD ..9-0.. 10 ch.g. Weld — Moya's Girl (Prince Titian) pfpf23. Very small. Dam is half-sister to 4 Pointers including River Moy (*qv*). P-t-P '03 r2 p1 (last of 3); and fell 1. A weedy individual and was on the deck in three of his first six attempts, and though only beaten a neck at Alpraham the race took 8min 15sec, and was beaten 32 lengths by the rival who finished immediately behind him next time. Has two handlers, and wears a cross-noseband. *Mr & Mrs K.R. Owen — Flint & Denbigh (Robert Owen).* 95 (R), 531 (OMa), 710 (Mah), 985 (OMa), 1044 (OMa), 1143 (OMa).

PLATE 124 46th Intrum Justitia Cup Champion Hunter Chase, Stratford: The winner, Torduff Express (Nick Williams), disputes with Right To Reply (Neil Harris) *PHOTO: Tim Holt*

TORDUFF EXPRESS (IRE) ..11-10.. 14 b.g. Kambalda — Marhabtain (Touching Wood USA) 28511. Smallish well-made brother to Irish Pointing winner, Lady Sylvie. IRISH P-t-P '96/7 r10 w4 p1 (3rd); pulled up 3, and fell 1. NH '97/01 and '03 r20 w6 (2m6f110y Hdle and 5 3m110y-3m2f110y Chses) p7 (4 2nds); pulled up 1, fell/unseated 2 (at 13th and 27th in '00 and '03 Grand Nationals). HUNT CH '02/3 r7 w3 (2m5f110y-3m2f110y) p3 (2 2nds, last once); and 4th of 5. A terrific money-spinner to date (£103,799 in wins alone) and rated the leading Hunter Chaser in '02, and returned from five successive defeats to run his rivals ragged when stamina was the order of the day at Cheltenham in April. Proved himself to be every bit as good as he was (though officially 20lb inferior now) when landing the Intrum Justitia Cup, where the exit of his two nearest pursuers at the last eased his passage, and once again finds himself on top of the ratings. The likelihood is that he will return with his exalted stablemate for another crack at the leading prizes in '05, and only needs the Cheltenham Foxhunters to complete Hunter Chasings' Triple Crown. Suited by some cut in the ground, but proved at Stratford that a much faster surface holds no terrors, at least over an extreme distance. Wears blinkers. *Two Plus Two — Taunton V. (Paul Nicholls).* 179 (2m6fH), 543 (3m2f110yH), 732 (2m5f110yH), 1169 (3m2f110yH), 1453 (3m4fH).

TOR HEAD ..10-5.. 9 b.g. Then Again — Free Form (Glenstal USA) 1f2*p*. Close-coupled well-made half-brother to flat winner in Denmark. Dam won 2m Selling Hurdle. IRISH P-t-P '01 and '03 r5 w1 (7&8yo Maiden) p0; pulled up 4. NH '04 r2 p1 (5*l* 2nd to The Nomad in 2m110y Ch: *a.p, outpcd 3 out, stayed on wl flat*); and pulled up in 2m5f Ch: *prom til pu lame aft 8*. Followed four pulled ups in Ireland with a win on his final start there, but looked much improved in '04, and although very flattered by getting within nine lengths of Omni Cosmo Touch (subsequently disqualified) at Sedgefield it was a good run nonetheless. Hampered and fell at the first when favourite next time and then five lengths second in a Chase, but was not a lucky horse, and had to be destroyed after pulling up lame (favourite again). J. Howard Johnson — Braes. 316 (2m5fH), 349 (3m1fH).

TORMOSS LADY ..—§§.. 9 ch.m. Le Moss — Torus Queen (Torus) uf. Lengthy half-sister to Princess Tor and Home Tor. NH FLAT '01 r2 p0. P-t-P '03 (for Mr P. & Mr C. Davies) r5 p0 (pulled up 4, and refused 1). A useless and reluctant cow, and should be banned before she kills someone. Visored once in '03. *Mrs B.C. Richards — Curre & Llangibby (Melvyn Lewis).* 452 (R), 700 (CfMa).

TORN SILK ..10-3.. 11 b.g. Top Ville — Cut Velvet (USA) (Northern Dancer) p121. Strong good-looking half-brother to 4 winners abroad. Dam won twice on flat in USA. IRISH FLAT '97 r4 w1 (13f) p3 (2nds). NH '97/02 r34 w7 (2m1f110y Hdle, and 6 2m-3m Chses) p7; fell/unseated 5. HUNT CH '03 r3 p0 (4th, last, and pulled up 1). A useful stayer on the flat, and proved himself a decent if somewhat unreliable performer over jumps, but never fit enough to do himself justice in '03, and his May double at Heslaker this year were his first wins since June '02. Lightly raced in recent years, and has broken blood vessels in the past, and the key to him is to produce him as late as possible. Connections did well to nurse him back to form. Acts in soft and on firmish. Frequently blinkered since '99 but not in '04. *P. England — Badsworth & Bramham Moor.* 163 (O), 1204 (O), 1414 (O), 1457 (O).

TORTUGAS (FR) ..9-4.. 8 b.g. Subotica (FR) — Northern Whisper (FR) (Vacarme USA) p6. Small. Dam won seven French flat races (8-9f). NH '00/3 (for M.C. Pipe, when successful, G.M. McCourt, and Mrs H. Dalton; all for Julia Oakey) r17 w1 (2m1f Hdle) p2; pulled up 2, fell 3. Won a bad three-year-old Novices Selling Hurdle, but two placings included a second at 1-2, and fairly lethal over regulation fences (about 20 lengths fourth twice, and fell after a mile or less thrice). Visored once. Pulled up at the 11th after one of his alarming blunders in his first Confined, and it looked as if he did not get the trip next time. Unpromising. *Miss J. Oakey — Worcs (Martin Oliver).* 980 (Cf), 1140 (Cf).

TOSCANINI (GER) .8-12§.. 9 b.g. Goofalik (USA) — Tosca Stella (GER) (Surumu GER) 634p. Compact. Dam won £17,000 2m race at Baden-Baden. GERMAN FLAT '00 r9 w5 (10-13f) p2 (2nds). NH '01/2 (for D.R. Gandolfo) r9 w1 (2m3f Hdle) p2 (3rds); pulled up 1. A flat winner at Hanover and a Hurdles scorer in a four-runner event at Exeter (both in soft), but a bit of a thinker who normally disappoints, and apart from a four-and-a-half lengths third in a Novice Riders Members (in which a 12-year-old Maiden was runner-up) his Pointing efforts were feeble. Never going well on his latest attempt, and pulled up after two miles. *P.E. Legge — I. of W.* 17 (O), 626 (Cnr), 780 (O), 969 (Cnr).

TO THE TOP..9-6.. 7 b.g. Petoski — Mrs Pepperpot (Kinglet) 32c3r. Leggy half-brother to Daisy Leigh (*qv*). P-t-P '03 r3 p0 (pulled up 2, and fell 1). Beaten between two and 11 lengths when placed in Maidens, and looked sure to score jumping the second last at Mollington once, but a combination of poor jumping and insufficient stamina have conspired against him, and has been very expensive to follow. Remains eligible for 2m4f Maidens in '05, and his competent trainer will surely unearth an opportunity for him eventually. *P.C. Froud — V. of Aylesbury with Garth & S. Berks (Lawney Hill).* 104 (2m4fOMa), 290 (2m4fCfMa), 627 (OMa), 789 (CfMa), 1108 (OMa).

TOUCHEZ DU BOIS (IRE) ..9-2.. 10 ch.g. Cadeaux Genereux — Fire Flash (Bustino) p41f. Strong-topped brother to flat winner, Million Lights, and half-brother to six more, including in Austria (two), and Ireland. FLAT '98 r5 w1 (11f) p0. P-t-P '01/3 r8 p0 (last 2, pulled up 4, and fell 2). A three-year-old winner in heavy at Hamilton Park, and finally broke his duck over jumps at the 11th attempt when sporting first-time cheekpieces and beating one other finisher in his Members. Will continue to struggle in more competitive events. Has run tongue-tied. *D.S. & Mrs M.J. Byers — Cumberland F. (Hector Barnfather).* 163 (O), 654 (Cf), 761 (M), 873 (Cf).

TOUCHING DOWN (IRE) ..9-3.. 13 ch.g. Buckskin (FR) — Got To Fly (IRE) (Kemal FR) 2. Tall rangy stringhalt near hind half-brother to Indian Wings (IRE), and to NH flat winner, Control Man (IRE). IRISH NH FLAT '97 r1 p0. IRISH P-t-P '97/8 r5 w2 (inc Winners of 1) p1 (3rd); pulled up 2. NH '98/9 r7 p1 (2nd); pulled up 4. NH '02 r1 p0 (12th in Grand Military Gold Cup). P-t-P '02/3 r13 w1 (3-runner Club) p3 (last of 3 thrice); 4th, last pair 5, and unseated 3. An expensive import from Ireland in '98, but only able to score once since, and only once better than last in his last eight appearances.

No more than a safe conveyance now. *The Biddick Family (M. Biddick) — N. Cornwall (Mike Biddick).* 489 (I).

PLATE 125 308 East Cornwall Open Maiden 56&7yo (Div 3): Touch Of Flame gives Michael Miller his 100th winner *PHOTO: Baths Photographic*

TOUCH OF FLAME .9-9.. 6 b.g. Terimon — Flame O'Frensi (Tudor Flame) 1f. Good-bodied. Dam won 22 Points and 2 2m5f Hunter Chases and placed 18 for Mr Clarke. Mother was wonderfully tough and courageous, and got his own career off to a perfect start in a 2m4f Maiden at Great Trethew in February, but did not reappear for three months, and then fell at the first. Multiple winners such as mother are really thin on the ground these days, but there seems every hope that he can enjoy a decent career himself in the years to come. *P.J. Clarke — Devon & Somerset (Keith Cumings).* 308 (2m4fOMa), 1385 (R).

TOUGH TERMS (IRE) .10-0.. 13 b.g. Welsh Term — Glenardina (Furry Glen) f. Tall rangy half-brother to Exhibition Prince (IRE), and to 3 flat winners (2 in Ireland; one also a successful jumper), including Noel (IRE). Dam won 7f in Ireland (also won at 8f there, but demoted to 2nd). IRISH NH FLAT '97 r3 p1 (2nd). NH '98 and '00/1 r5 p1 (3rd); pulled up 2, and unseated 1. P-t-P/HUNT CH '02/3 r9 w3 (hat-trick inc 2m5f Hunt Ch) p2; pulled up 3 and fell 1. Much improved when completing a hat-trick in effortless style in '02, but badly let down by his jumping since, and fell with fatal consequences at Charing. *D.F. Donegan — Mid Surrey F. (Victoria Park).* 183 (O).

TOUJOURS (IRE) ..9-12.. 8 ch.g. Toulon — Kept In The Dark (Kemal FR) 111. Half-brother to Annaghmore Gale (IRE), and to Irish Hurdles winners, River Rhyme and Pure N Simple. Dam sister to Outside Edge, and half-sister to South Sunrise (*qv* '95 Annual). Grandam, Smooth Lady, is half-sister to '84 Grand National winner, Hallo Dandy. IRISH P-t-P '02 (for Simon Tindall) r2 p1 (2nd); and pulled up 1. Joined Nigel Twiston-Davies after finishing second in an Irish Point, but broke down, and a proposed career under Rules was put on ice when he settled for Pointing in '04. Romped to an effortless hat-trick, but faced by a total of 13 opponents, and could hardly have had simpler tasks. A keen galloper who can finish strongly in lowly company at least, and if his legs are up to it a Novices Hunter Chase would be an achievable target in '05. Potentially under-rated by several pounds. *S.P. Tindall — Southdown & Eridge (Jenny Gordon).* 418 (2m4fCMa), 606 (R), 896 (CCon).

TOURING-TURTLE (IRE) ..9-4.. 13 gr.g. Roselier (FR) — Rossian (Silent Spring) p6762. Small sparely-made brother to Thinkaboutthat (IRE) and Rosey Boy (IRE), and half-brother to Golden Croft. IRISH P-t-P '96/8 r17 w1 (2m6f Hdle) p5. NH '98/9 r4 p0 (pulled up 4). P-t-P '00 (for Mrs H.M. Goody) r4 p1 (6th, and last pair 3). NH '00/2 (for C.L. Tizzard) r12 w1 (2m3f Ch) p5 (inc 4 3rds); pulled up 3. A winner on firmish in Ireland in '97, and four years later in softish at Taunton, but lightly raced since leaving his homeland, and a onepaced schoolmaster these days. Not a secure jumper of big fences.

Blinkered once in '02. Wears a cross-noseband. *W.D. Procter — Blackmore & Sparkford V.* 89 (O), 320 (Cf), 1250 (C), 1365 (Cnr), 1446 (Cf).

PLATE 126 1368 Weston & Banwell Ladies Open: Veteran correspondent Granville Taylor and Gail Hill's Traditional is successful for Rachael Green *PHOTO: Brian Armstrong*

TRADITIONAL (IRE) ..10-0§.. 9 ch.g. Erins Isle — Noorajo (IRE) (Ahonoora) p4ppp413. Sturdy compact brother to Irish NH flat winner, Breaking Ball. IRISH FLAT '99/00 r12 w3 (12-16f) p0. IRISH NH '00 and '02 (for P.J. Rothwell) r10 w2 (2m5f-2m6f Hdles) p1 (2nd). NH '03 (for N.J. Hawke) r9 p0; pulled up 2. Had a 20 per cent strike rate of victories when competent in Ireland, but occasionally blinkered there (although not for his successes) and was tongue-tied once in '99. Has lost his zest since and cheekpieces brought no response thrice in '04, and resents bullying, but after his cause had looked forlorn with four pulled-ups from five attempts he brightened up for Rachael Green and ended a losing sequence of 15 when outstaying Gipsy Cricketer from the last in a Ladies at Cothelstone. Error-prone and had a more typical fit of the sulks when favourite next time, but at least he consented to do it once. *G.D. Taylor & Ms G. Hill — Seavington (Chloe Newman).* 442 (2m7f110yH), 628 (2m3fH), 799 (2m3f110yH), 993 (3mH), 1166 (2m5f110yH), 1350 (L), 1368 (L), 1448 (L).

TRAGIC BELLE ..—.. 8 b.m. Tragic Role (USA) — Pokey's Belle (Uncle Pokey) ppf. Small narrow sister to Belle's Last, and half-sister to Derrybelle, Minibelle and Rolfe's Belle. Dam is half-sister to Beau Signeur. Grandam, Belle Of Sark, won at 9f in Ireland. NH FLAT '01 r1 p0. P-t-P '03 r1 p0 (pulled up). Showed some speed but a consistently poor jumper, and broke a leg at Bonvilston. *D.C. Gibbs — Ystrad Taf Fechan.* 67 (OMa), 362 (CfMa), 1091 (CMam).

TRAVELLING JACK ..10-0§.. 10 ch.g. Lyphento (USA) — Lady Magenta (Rolfe USA) 3p6333. Tall lengthy half-brother to Summer Pudding and Rydon Brook. P-t-P/HUNT CH '00/3 r12 w3 (Maiden, Restricted and Intermediate) p3 (2nds, beaten short-head once, inc of 3 once); last, fell 2 and pulled up 3. Unbeaten in his first three completions on right-handed circuits, but beat nothing of note, and has never stood his racing well. Often gives the impression something is seriously amiss, and appeared to down tools when blinkers were first applied at Holnicote, but still retains ability and only beaten a length there next time. Inclined to make bad mistakes, and must be treated with caution. Has two handlers. *M. Rowe — Eggesford (Laura Young).* 17 (O), 89 (O), 200 (Cf), 497 (Cf), 1185 (MO), 1328 (MO).

TREASULIER (IRE) ..9-2.. 8 gr.g. Roselier (FR) — Flashy Treasure (Crash Course) p4p31. Small neat. IRISH P-t-P '02/3 r6 p1 (2nd); fell 2, ran out 1. IRISH NH FLAT '03 (for E.J. O'Grady) r1 p0. Slow to achieve a success and only had one horse behind him in his first four English Points (beaten a long way when making the frame twice), but made all to beat four dire rivals in a Maiden on firm at Rhydygwern. Will presumably be sent down the road, and it will be a miracle if he can follow up on the evidence to date. *Mrs J.M. Woodward — Worcs (Martin Oliver).* 531 (OMa), 754 (OMa), 983 (2m5fOMa), 1259 (OMa), 1486 (OMa).

TREASURE DOME (IRE) ..9-0§.. 11 b.g. Treasure Kay — Royal Saint (USA) (Crimson Satan) 25r. Strong compact half-brother to 4 flat winners (2 in France), including Ceili Queen (IRE) (in Ireland — also won jumping there). Dam won 5 flat in USA. IRISH FLAT r11 p0. FLAT r2 p0 (inc Sell). IRISH NH '97/8 r8 w1 (2m1f Hdle) p1 (2nd). NH '98/9 r4 p1 (2nd). P-t-P/HUNT CH '01/3 r11 w1 (3-finisher Members) p2 (2nds, of 3 once); 4th, last, pulled up 5, and unseated 1. Ended a long losing run dating back to '98 when successful in his Members at the third attempt last year, but failed to land a punt in this year's renewal, and normally displays minimal interest. Has been tried in blinkers. *The Good Craic Club (P.J.G. Aldous) — Waveney H. (John Whyte).* 22 (M), 155 (Cnr), 224 (CMod).

TREBLE TROUBLE .8-5.. 9 b.g. Minster Son — Ferneyhill Lady (Menelek) ppp4ppf. Small. Dam, sister to Shamrock Master (*qv* '92 Annual), won Fife Members in '98 and placed 3, ('generally jumps very poor and predictably struggled to follow up'). NH FLAT '00 r1 p0 (last). P-t-P/HUNT CH '02 (for Mr R.J. Marley) r3 w1 (Maiden) p0; last, and fell 1. NH '02/3 (for C.C. Bealby) r7 p1 (3rd of 4 in 2m5f110y Ch); pulled up 4, fell 1. Vastly improved when winning in holding at Duncombe Park in '02, but virtually useless in 16 other attempts over jumps, and has otherwise only beaten two rivals. Ran and jumped as well as he looked in '04, and his win is nothing short of miraculous on reflection. *P.J. Millington — Cottesmore.* 36 (CR), 127 (R), 250 (R), 378 (M), 524 (R), 591 (CR), 889 (CR).

TREBLE VISION (IRE) ..—.. 11 ch.g. Down The Hatch — General Vision (General Ironside) pp. Compact. IRISH P-t-P '00 r3 p2. P-t-P '02/3 r4 w1 (Maiden) p1 (3rd); pulled up 1, and fell 1. Won readily from 16 rivals in a Maiden on firmish at Kingston Blount in '02, but has performed as though crippled since and unimproved by blinkers in '04. In no state to be on a racecourse. *W.G. Young — Lanarks & Renfrews.* 283 (R), 431 (R).

TREVVEETHAN (IRE) .8-10.. 16 ch.g. On Your Mark — Carrick Slaney (Red God) 4. Good-bodied fired half-brother to an Italian flat winner, and to an Irish Hurdles winner. FLAT r4 p0 (inc Sell). NH '92/6 r19 p6 (inc 2 Sells). P-t-P/HUNT CH '97/00 (for Mr N. Sutton & Mrs R. Lane) r17 w4 (Maiden, 2 Members and PPORA) p4 (2 3rds, last once); 4th, last pair 3, pulled up 2, and on floor 3. Gained an annual success in three Pointing campaigns to '99, but broke a blood vessel in that year, and has stood his racing badly since. Brought out of retirement to give a beginner a ride at Cold Harbour, and beat three others in finishing around 45 lengths fourth. Fell when visored once in '96. *P. Rogers — Radnor & W. Herefords (T.P. Rogers).* 1226 (M).

TRIAL TRIP..9-6.. 10 ch.m. Le Moss — Model Lawyer (Latest Model) 134f. Small half-sister to Nesbitt. Dam (*qv* '95 Annual) is half-sister to Itswillie (*qv*), was unplaced in 15 Points (did not earn a penny in a 6 year career). Grandam, Pensham's Lawyer is an unraced half-sister to Pensham's Son. Great-grandam, Pensham, won 44 Points and a Maiden Hunt Ch and placed 26. P-t-P '02/3 r9 p3 (2nds, beaten head once); 4th of 5, and pulled up 5. Runner-up in her three previous completions, and finally opened her account in a two-finisher Maiden at Erw Lon despite rooting the second last, but a weak finisher otherwise, and will require plenty of luck to follow up. Wears a cross-noseband. *Mrs C. Banks — Pentyrch (Cath Williams).* 204 (CfMa), 674 (R), 844 (R), 1191 (R).

TRICKY TREVOR (IRE) ..10-5.. 12 b/br.g. Arctic Lord — Chancer's Last (Foggy Bell) 5f11213. Lengthy good-bodied half-brother to Chancy Oats, Spaceage Gold, Splint, Hurricane Harry, Phar From Chance and Solar King, and to Irish NH flat winner, Winter Wishes (IRE). NH FLAT '98 r3 p2. NH '98/9 r7 p1 (2nd in Hdle); 5th and fell in Chses. P-t-P/HUNT CH '00/3 r22 w7 (inc 4 Opens, inc hat-trick '02) p10 (7 2nds, beaten ½*l* twice, and last once, inc Hunt Ch; and inc last of 3); unseated 1, ran out 1, and pulled up 3. Quirky and a difficult ride but brought into line by Nicky Tinkler in the previous yard, and Phillip York has continued the good work since he was sold relatively cheaply in May '02. Stays well and is suited by some cut in the ground, but needs to be kept up to his work at all times, and is not one to take too short a price about, particularly in Hunter Chases where his jumping lacks fluency. Blinkered twice in '99. *I. & Mrs H.J. Cobb — Crawley & Horsham (Ian Cobb).* 183 (O), 345 (2m5fH), 535 (CfO), 638 (M), 1054 (Cf), 1284 (O), 1361 (3mH).

TRIGGER AGAIN ..9-10.. 10 ch.g. Then Again — Festive Season (Silly Season) p1p. Tall rangy half-brother to Arctic Revel, Country Festival (dam of Rustic Revelry and Kings Command, *qv*), Phaedair, Polar Party and Gemini Mist. Dam won 5 Points and 2nd twice. NH FLAT '99 r1 p0. NH '00 r2 p0 (remote 10th of 11, and pulled up 1). P-t-P '01/2 (for Mrs J. Bugg, Mr D. Coombes & Mr G. Woods) r4 p3 (2 2nds); and unseated 1. Broke down in '02, and did well to score in a three-finisher Maiden at Ston Easton after just one pipe-opener, but trailed the field until pulling up at the 11th next time, and has presumably suffered another setback. Wears a cross-noseband. *D.M. Coombes — S. Dorset (Mary Tory).* 139 (R), 604 (OMa), 966 (R).

TRIGGER CASTLE ..7-10§.. 10 b.m. Henbit (USA) — Jane's Daughter (Pitpan) p4s. Sister to Solo Trip, and half-sister to Tulane, Mister Muddypaws, River Don (Chasing winner since Pointing), Grindalythe and Willoughby Flyer. P-t-P '00 and '02 r5 p1 (3rd); 6th of 7, pulled up 2, and fell 1. NH '03 (for J.S.

Wainwright, and P.T. Midgley) r3 p0 (pulled up 3). Hinted at ability in her debut season, but stands her racing incredibly badly, and displays more temperament than talent these days. *S. Birkinshaw — Middleton (Tony Walker).* 1165 (OMa), 1206 (OMa), 1305 (OMa).

TRINITY BUOY (IRE) ..9-8.. 10 b.g. Phardante (FR) — Vinegar Hill (Pauper) 52. Tall workmanlike brother to smart French jumping winner, Bog Frog (IRE) (won £90,000 Grande Course de Haies D'Auteuil), and half-brother to Rebel Priest (IRE). Dam is half-sister to Shilgrove Place (*qv* '98 Annual). NH FLAT '99/00 r3 p0. NH '00/1 r15 p4; pulled up 2, fell 1. P-t-P '02/3 r6 w1 (Maiden) p2; 4th, pulled up 1, and unseated 1. Tried blinkered and tongue-tied when an abject disaster under Rules, but appreciated the combination of weak opposition, firm ground and cheekpieces when bolting up in a Maiden at Northaw on his final appearance last year. A disappointing even money favourite in his second Restricted, and may have suffered a setback. *D.J. Harding-Jones — Puckeridge (Perry Harding-Jones).* 648 (R), 829 (R).

TRIVIAL (IRE) ..10-4.. 13 b.m. Rakaposhi King — Miss Rubbish (Rubor) 42u1231. Small close-coupled attractive owner-bred half-sister to Little Idiot. Dam was 2nd in 2 Maidens for Tim Brockbank, and subsequently won 4 Chses (2m4f-3m) and placed 4 (inc 3rd in a Hdle, and Scottish Grand National) for him. P-t-P '98/01 r17 w4 (2m4f Maiden, Intermediate and 2 Members) p3 (2nds, inc beaten head once; and neck 2nd of 3 once); 6th, pulled up 3, refused 1, and fell/unseated 3. NH '01/3 r15 w1 (2m4f110y Hdle) p4; pulled up 2, refused 1, unseated 1. A difficult ride and can look reluctant, but does well on balance, and appreciates good or sound surfaces. Benefited from the exits of more fancied rivals when scoring at 14-1 at Cartmel, and the chances are that she will be placed to advantage again. *J.T. Brockbank — Cumberland (John Brockbank).* 426 (Cf), 654 (Cf), 1179 (3m1fH), 1223 (O), 1307 (Cf), 1444 (3m1fH), 1490 (3m2fH).

TROEDRHIWDALAR ..9-9.. 8 b.m. Gunner B — Delladear (Sonnen Gold) f1*u*. Tall workmanlike. NH FLAT '02 r2 p0. NH '02/3 r6 p2 (3rds); pulled up 1. NH '04 (for Mrs D.A. Hamer) r1 p0 (unseated in 2m4f110y Ch: *prom til lost plce 4, blun & ur nxt*). His two thirds over Hurdles were of little merit (beaten a distance once and promoted from 32 lengths fourth once), but they nevertheless gave him prospects in a Maiden, and duly obliged when dropped to that grade for the first time in a youngsters event at Laleston, in which he was going clear approaching two out when left virtually solo to beat one other finisher. Can look temperamental and has worn a visor or cheekpieces, and his jumping is not reliable, but would probably be thereabouts if returned to a Restricted. *Mrs L.G. Foster — Irfon & Towy (Paul Hamer).* 740 (R), 1192 (OMa).

TROJAN LOVE (IRE) .—.. 12 b.m. Cyrano De Bergerac — Love Of Paris (Trojan Fen) ppp. Small sturdy. NH FLAT '97 r1 p0 (remote last). P-t-P '00 r2 p0 (pulled up 1, and fell 1). Took off like a scalded cat on her belated reappearance with the rider sawing at her mouth, and was still in front when pulled up exhausted after nearly two miles, but went no further when anchored subsequently, and is a total waste of time. *Mr & Mrs T.M. Bagley — Essex (Terry Bagley).* 646 (M), 832 (Cf), 996 (CMam).

TROOPER COLLINS (IRE) ..10-2§.. 7 b.g. Dolphin Street (FR) — Born To Fly (IRE) (Last Tycoon) 222. Well-made attractive half-brother to flat winner, Blue Flyer (IRE). Dam, half-sister to Itchy Feet (*qv* '99 Annual). FLAT '01/2 r7 p0. NH '01/2 r8 p2 (3rds). P-t-P '03 r7 w2 (3-finisher Maiden and Restricted) p2 (2nds); 4th twice, and pulled up 1. Had no difficulty in landing a double in weak Points last year, but previously a most frustrating Hurdler, and managed to get worried out of the finish on each appearance in '04. Doubtless good enough to win again if he will co-operate fully. Often blinkered in the previous yard, and runs tongue-tied. *G.F. Tuer — Hurworth.* 427 (I), 808 (CfCon), 1037 (I).

TROUBLEINALLENWOOD (IRE) ..—.. 6 b.g. Big Sink Hope (USA) — Gometra (Lomond USA) *r0*. Small plain. NH FLAT '04 (for B.D. Leavy) r1 p0 (12th of 14 over 2m110y at Chepstow: *a bhnd, t.o*). Bought Ascot, Oct for 952. Turned out looking dreadful for a Weston Park Maiden, and it was absolutely no surprise when he refused at the first (continued to jump three fences before giving up). He and stablemate Run River Run are disgraces. *M.A. Hill — Albrighton.* 96 (CfMa).

TROUBLE LOVES ME (IRE) ..8-5.. 7 b.g. Yashgan — Crash Street (Crash Course) 6p. Good-topped half-brother to Major Tom (IRE). P-t-P '03 r3 p0 (pulled up 2, and slipped up 1). A typically excitable Yashgan, and has shown early speed, but 58 lengths sixth of seven on his only completed start, and looks useless. *P. Richardson — Grafton.* 105 (2m4fOMa), 721 (OMa).

TROUBLESHOOTER .9-0§.. 7 b.g. Ezzoud (IRE) — Oublier L'Ennui (FR) (Bellman FR) 22514p44p. Small neat half-brother to flat winners, Shudder, and Arctic High. Dam won 3 2m-2m3f Hdles, and 2m4f Chase. FLAT '00/2 r18 p4 (all at 2). NH '02 r2 p1 (3rd). P-t-P '03 r5 p0; 6th, pulled up 2, fell 1, and disqualified after winning 3-runner Maiden. Ultimately disqualified from his three-runner Maiden triumph at Brocklesby Park last year, and his owner fined £2,300 (a record for an indiscretion in Points) but recouped £100 when making all to justify favouritism at Cottenham in '04. Beaten 32 lengths plus in Restricteds since, and often looks decidedly unwilling once taken on for the lead. Has been tried in blinkers, cheekpieces, and a tongue-tie. *J.M. Robinson — Burton.* 59 (OMa), 152 (OMa), 476 (CfMa), 561 (OMa), 999 (R), 1152 (R), 1304 (CR), 1416 (R), 1503 (R).

TROUVAILLE (IRE) ..9-4§.. 14 b.g. King's Ride — Dream Run (Deep Run) 4. Lengthy half-brother to NH flat and Hurdles winner, Celtic Vision (IRE). Dam is half-sister to Be The Dream (*qv* '03 Annual). NH '95/9 r27 w3 (2m Hdle, and 2 2m5f-3m Chses) p12. P-t-P '03 r7 w1 (Members) p0; last, pulled up 4, and unseated 1. Won three races on firmish under Rules, and returned from a three-and-a-half year absence to score in fortuitous circumstances last year, but has always been a sketchy jumper, and beaten 33 lengths on his only appearance in '04. Has been tried in a visor. *W.J. Moore — Belvoir.* 300 (O).

TRUE CHIMES ..9-8.. 14 ch.g. True Song — Ballytina (Rugantino) 33p12. Very tall strong half-brother to Ballyaction and Ballyalbert. Dam, sister or half-sister to 4 Pointers, including Ashford Ditton, was 3rd in a Maiden for Ena Cardew. NH FLAT r2 p0 (tailed off 2). NH '96 r1 p0. P-t-P/HUNT CH '97/03 r31 w3 (2m4f Maiden, Restricted and Intermediate) p7 (2 2nds, beaten ½*l* once; and 5 3rds, of 4 twice, and inc Hunt Ch); pulled up 6, and fell/unseated 4. Usually takes a keen hold and gives a prominent display, but does not truly get the trip, and his last two wins have been gained in farcical circumstances. Took well over eight minutes to dispatch two rivals in a Members in '04 (five minutes had elapsed before the field reached halfway!) but also frequently let down by his jumping, and is generally easy to beat now. Acquired blinkers on his last two starts, and has previously worn cheekpieces. Wears a cross-noseband. *Mrs E.V. Cardew — Bicester with Whaddon (Jenny Owen).* 288 (M), 460 (C), 583 (Cf), 1030 (M), 1243 (O).

TRUICEAR ..9-1.. 8 b.g. Petoski — Fit For A King (Royalty) fup32. Compact half-brother to Caracol, to jumping winner, King's Bounty, and to Hurdles winner, Revolt. Dam won 2 2m Hurdles. NH FLAT '02 r1 p0. NH '02 (for A. Ennis) r1 p0 (last). Badly tailed off in a bumper and a Hurdle (last) in '02, and had many jumping problems when resuming two years later, but ten lengths last of three despite some slow leaps was a bit better, and then ran much his best yet, when three lengths second after holding every chance at the final fence in a Stafford Cross Maiden. Needs his tongue-tie, and if able to maintain the improvement he might manage to score. *A.T.P. Racing Partnership (L. Corcoran) — Dart V.H. & S. Pool H. (Liam Corcoran).* 195 (CfMa), 328 (OMa), 733 (3mH), 913 (OMa), 1134 (OMa).

TRUMPER ..9-13.. 9 b.g. First Trump — Sayida-Shahira (Record Run) 21221. Compact half-brother to Hurdles winners, Fisio Sands and Proceed. NH FLAT '00 r2 p0. NH '00/3 (for J.T. Gifford) r20 p3 (inc 3rd in Ch); pulled up 3. Showed a very low level of achievement in 22 attempts under Rules, when his best effort was a neck second in a 3m2f Hurdle, but all too prone to blunders, and wore blinkers or cheekpieces on his final six attempts. Can still lack fluency in Points, but gets the trip well, and strong riders have helped him to win an elders Maiden at High Easter and a Restricted at Larkhill. Will probably be made to look very one-paced in competitive events in future. *Mrs D. & A. Lawes — Chid, Lec & Cowdray (Andrew Lawes).* 86 (OMa), 220 (OMa), 639 (R), 802 (R), 1102 (R).

TRUST FUND (IRE) ..10-0.. 7 ch.g. Rashar (USA) — Tuney Blade (Fine Blade USA) 21. Rangy half-brother to Wild Blade (IRE) (*qv*). 17,527 4yo. Immediately showed promise when three-quarters-of-a-length second over 2m4f at Ston Easton, and was impressive beating nothing by wide margins in a Badbury Maiden on firmish. Gets in rather a stew in the preliminaries and has been mounted on the course, but in a top yard and potentially well above average, and should be worth following. *T. Collins — Portman (Sally Alner).* 599 (2m4fOMa), 865 (OMa).

TRUST GER ..— §§.. 9 b.g. Royal Vulcan — Sams Queen (Another Sam) ppupup. Small. Dam, half-sister to Royal Mountbrowne (*qv* '03 Annual), who is by Royal Vulcan. Gave a string of deplorable displays, and did not even get beyond halfway on four occasions. Prone to make very slow jumps, and has absolutely no intention of exerting himself. *F.K. Baxter & Mrs I. Pollard — Grafton (Iris Pollard).* 258 (CMa), 594 (OMa), 1035 (OMa), 1125 (OMa), 1473 (OMa), 1505 (OMa).

TRY A BLUFF (IRE) ..9-11.. 13 b.g. Hollow Hand — Happy Hereford (Bonne Noel) 461p. Rangy half-brother to Scotchie (IRE). IRISH P-t-P '97/9 r7 w2 (4&5yo Maiden) p1 (3rd); pulled up 2. IRISH NH '97 r1 p0. IRISH HUNT CH '99 r1 p1 (3rd). NH '99/01 (for Miss L.V. Russell) r13 w1 (3m1f Ch) p3; pulled up 4. His long career has been beset by physical problems, and has broken a blood vessel, whilst his fragile legs kept him off the course in '98 and '02/3. Quite moderate and has required the patience of Job, but two Irish Points (one in '97 and the other in '99), a lucky Kelso Chase, and his '04 win (a first success for Emma McWilliam in a three-runner Members) have made the long waits worthwhile. Visored twice in the past. *Miss E.L. McWilliam — Fife.* 506 (Cnr), 550 (L), 1076 (M), 1418 (Cf).

TRY ME AND SEE ..9-6.. 11 ch.g. Rock City — Al Raja (Kings Lake USA) 234uu6. Tall half-brother to flat winner, Arran Pilot and NH flat and Hurdling winner, Tealby. Dam won 10f race. NH FLAT '98 r3 p1 (2nd). NH '02 r4 p0. NH '04 r1 p0 (6th in 2m5f Ch: *hld up, hdwy 6, ld 13 til app 3 out, wkng when mist nxt*). Half-a-length second in a bumper on his debut, but went missing for exactly four years after his next outing, and then stood four runs including a Selling Hurdle in '02 (tongue-tied once). Managed his busiest year by far at ten, and made the frame in three Points for a beginner (beaten five lengths once and about 20 lengths twice, and asked to do far too much in the lead), and it was totally predictable that his rider would be unseated twice when foolishly upgraded to Hunter Chases long before his partner was ready for them (went a mile or less). Still has the ability to win a Maiden, but is never going to do so if he is sent a fence clear as he was in the latest. *A.M. Crow — Jedforest.* 216 (OMa), 431 (R), 554 (CfMa), 678 (3m1fH), 797 (3m1fH).

TUBBER ROADS (IRE) ..9-10§.. 12 b.g. Un Desperado (FR) — Node (Deep Run) 7p2pp2pp. Close-coupled. IRISH P-t-P '98 r1 p1 (2nd). IRISH NH FLAT '98 r2 p1 (3rd in race for Pointers). P-t-P/HUNT CH '00/3 r20 w5 (inc 4 2m5f110y-3m Hunt Chses) p5 (3rds, of 4 once, inc 3 Hunt Chses); pulled up 3, unseated 1. A useful Hunter Chaser at around 2m6f, and recorded a hat-trick in '02, but damaged a foot when jumping round Aintree next time, and subsequently pulled up lame at Cheltenham. Revived to a large degree when blinkered and runner-up at Kingston Blount, but their effects have already worn off, and may have suffered another reverse last time. Will surely be pensioned off. *W.F. Caudwell — O. Berks (Matt Hazell).* 34 (O), 93 (O), 188 (O), 319 (O), 465 (O), 1066 (CCon), 1172 (3m1f110yH), 1515 (O).

TUCK TIN ..9-4.. 13 b.g. Neltino — Kentucky Lady (Roman Warrior) 3. Twelve lengths third in his Members was a valiant effort, but it was not a serious contest. *S.C. Robinson — Mid Surrey F. (Gina Weare).* 180 (M).

TUDOR LUCKY BOY ..—.. 7 b.g. Platinum Royale — Tudor Lucky Charm (Ascendant) p. Lengthy homebred. P-t-P '03 r2 p0 (pulled up 2). Showed a little ability in one start last year, and led the field at a crawl to halfway on his return, but went wrong and was pulled up at the 15th. *Mrs J. McCullough & J.M. Salter — Axe V.H. (Philip Greenwood).* 86 (OMa).

TUFTEX KING ..7-0.. 8 b.g. Syrtos — More Laughter (Oats) 5p. Tall strong. Dam, half-sister to Our Laughter (*qv* '00 Annual). NH FLAT '02 r1 p0. NH '02/3 (for I. Williams, and Mrs S. Gardner, one run) r9 p0; ran out 1. Sold Doncaster, May for 1000. Bought Ascot, Aug for 2380. Beaten 29 lengths plus in eight of ten races under Rules, and ran out once, and looked a dog when blinkered in a Seller once. Tackled fences for the first time in '04 and was about one-and-a-half fences behind when last on his debut, and would doubtless have been forced to another very remote completion had the memory of the £200 fine from the Cloudkicker incident earlier in the day not being fresh in the jockey's mind. *S. Hamblett & J. Armsby — Staintondale (Andrew Pennock).* 304 (OMa), 394 (CfMa).

TULLINEASKEY KITTY (IRE) ..6-7.. 7 b.m. Kasmayo — Roll Of Faith (Bishop Of Orange) 6p. Workmanlike lengthy. 1656 4yo. Tailed off on consecutive weekends in April, and was last after showing early speed once, and pulled up after jumping left next time. *C. Dawson — S. Durham.* 813 (OMa), 1042 (CMam).

TUPELOV (IRE) .9-0.. 10 b.g. Moscow Society (USA) — Ballela Maid (Boreen FR) 43p. Brother to Irish flat winner, Moscow Maid, and to successful Hurdler Super Lucky (previously Irish Pointing winner). IRISH P-t-P '03 r7 p2 (2nds); pulled up 3, brought down 1. IRISH NH FLAT '00 r1 p0. IRISH NH '99/02 (for E.M. O'Sullivan) r14 p2 (3rds); fell/unseated 2, pulled up 2. A very long-standing maiden who once endured a sequence of seven consecutive non-completions, and despite starting favourite or co-favourite twice in England the best that he has managed was a nine lengths third in a poor Maiden. One of his Irish placings was an eight lengths third in a farcical Chase, in which the probable winner fell twice, ultimately with fatal consequences. Does not look to have the stamina to get the trip in Points. *D.S. Dennis — Hursley Hambledon.* 174 (OMa), 424 (CMa), 721 (OMa).

TURN IT ON (IRE) .—.. 10 ch.g. Black Monday — Kerry Minstrel (Black Minstrel) pp. Strong lengthy half-brother to Eco Warrior (IRE) (*qv*). IRISH P-t-P '00 r1 p0 (fell). A nine-year-old who has managed just three outings in his life, and failed to complete in all of them. Showed speed for over two miles in both English Points, but pulled up behind the rhubarb sheds at Paxford, and the horse ambulance had to be dispatched to collect him. The name of his sire proved horribly accurate on Easter Monday. *Miss L. Price & Mrs S. Collett — N. Cotswold (Harry Wheeler).* 604 (OMa), 927 (OMa).

TURSAL (IRE) ..9-9.. 16 b.g. Fine Blade (USA) — Turlough Pet (Retieme) 2p4. Big strong. NH FLAT '95 r2 p0. NH '95/7 r7 p1 (3rd); ran out in Sell; also pulled up 1, and fell 2. P-t-P/HUNT CH '99/00 and '02/3 r24 w5 (inc Open) p6 (4 2nds, of 3 once; inc last of 3 once); pulled up 2, refused 1 and fell/unseated 3. Failed to score for the first time in five Pointing campaigns in '04, but did well to finish at all in his Members, where a beginner did her best to leap out of the saddle at many of the fences. Failed to stay four miles next time, and tailed off last at Balcormo Mains, and his winning days are surely over. Often makes mistakes. *A.R. Campbell — Lanarks & Renfrews (C. Campbell).* 653 (M), 857 (4mMO), 1079 (O).

TWILIGHT DANCER (IRE) ..10-1.. 7 b.m. Sri Pekan (USA) — Manhattan Sunset (USA) (El Gran Senor USA) p1. Unfurnished half-sister to two flat winners (one in Turkey), including Tramonto (IRE). Dam won 7f race. FLAT '00/2 r14 p0. P-t-P '03 r3 w1 (2m4f Maiden) p1 (2nd); and pulled up 1. A hard puller, and has made virtually all in both Pointing wins, and clocked a very respectable time at Howick, but does not stand her racing well any more. Would have prospects in a higher grade if she were problem free in '05. Blinkered once in '02. *Miss H.E. Roberts — Llangeinor.* 14 (R), 357 (R).

TWINKLE TOE TITCH (IRE) .7-3.. 6 ch.m. Hubbly Bubbly (USA) — Hill Ranger (Love Tale) R36. Bought Goffs Ireland, Jul for 741. Soon ran out on her debut, and then went gallumphing round in a Members (17 lengths third of four) and a Maiden (88 lengths last). This Twinkle Toe's ain't got no rhythm. *J. McGuinness — Staintondale (Andrew Pennock).* 302 (OMa), 954 (M), 1305 (OMa).

TWO BY FOUR ..—§.. 12 ch.g. Sunley Builds — Zenaida (Lear Jet) ppp. Small compact owner-bred half-brother to Wergild and Drakeford. Dam, half-sister to 5 Pointers, won 3m2f Hunt Ch and 8 Points (won another, but judge erred) and placed 9 for Mrs Lundgren. Grandam, Zena, won a Maiden and placed 9 (inc 5 Chses) for her. NH '01 r1 p0 (pulled up). P-t-P '02 r2 p0 (pulled up 1, and fell 1). A typically highly-strung Sunley Builds, and has made many mistakes and not looked like getting round in any of his six starts. *Mrs J.A.C. Lundgren — Pytchley (Caroline Bailey).* 111 (OMa), 220 (OMa), 482 (OMa).

TWO HOOTS ..9-6.. 7 b.m. Dancing High — Farm Track (Saxon Farm) 1. Half-sister to Hanoi Hanna. Dam, half-sister to Dear-Do (*qv* '01 Annual), was 5 fences last of 3 in Maiden. Grandam, Earlsgift, won 5 Points and placed 5. Won a modest 2m4f Maiden at Tranwell in competent fashion on her debut, and then galloped off to the sales to make a bizarrely high price. Given her humble pedigree (Hanoi Hanna was a joke) we wouldn't give two hoots for her prospects under Rules. *C. Dawson — S. Durham.* 920 (2m4fOMa).

TWO OCEANS (IRE) ..—.. 7 gr.g. Mandalus — Sister Of Peace (Warpath) ppp. Brother to Peacetown (IRE). Dam, sister to Copgrove (*qv* '93 Annual). Bought Doncaster, May '02 for 14,000. Showed speed for two miles in his last two outings, but rapidly dropped out of contention, and either cannot or will not sustain the gallop. Particularly disappointing when visored on his latest appearance, and it would not be surprising if the stable had had enough of him. *G.T.H. Bailey — Pytchley (Caroline Bailey).* 20 (OMa), 192 (CfMa), 1124 (OMa).

TWO OF DIAMONDS ..7-9§§.. 11 b.g. Mr Fluorocarbon — Shelleys Rocky Gem (Kemal FR) pppp7r. Plain good-topped. P-t-P/HUNT CH '00/3 r10 p1 (fence 2nd); last 2, pulled up 5, unseated 1 and refused 1. Useless and a total waste of time in Hunter Chases, and little better in Points, and has only once finished better than last in 16 starts, when a fence second in '03. Showing his true colours now, and has begun to be troublesome at the start. *Miss R. Williams — Surrey U.* 802 (R), 1055 (OMa), 1207 (M), 1354 (2m110yH), 1442 (2m5fH), 1518 (OMa).

TYCOON TED ..9-6.. 12 b.g. Starch Reduced — Royal Tycoon (Tycoon II) f73. Good-bodied half-brother to Royrace (*qv*). FLAT r2 p0 (beat one). NH '97/8 r6 p0 (32*l* 4th, and pulled up 5, inc Sells). P-t-P '99 and '02 r5 w1 (Maiden) p1 (2nd); last, and pulled up 2. Much improved when landing a Maiden at 20-1 on firm at Holnicote in '99, but has only made six appearances since, and prospects look grim after finishing lame at Bratton Down, where he ran an honest race to be seven lengths third of four. *D.M. Partridge — Tiverton (Rose Partridge).* 324 (R), 791 (R), 1385 (R).

UMBOPA (USA) ..—§§.. 7 b.g. Gilded Time (USA) — How Fortunate (CAN) (What Luck USA) pp. Lengthy half-brother to flat winners, Tin Fa (USA) and Moments of Fortune (USA), and to 4 other winners. 57,000y. FLAT '00/2 (for K.R. Burke) r16 w1 (12f) p6. NH '02 (for P. Bowen) r2 p0 (last and pulled up). An all-weather winner in November '01, but has been 59 lengths last (in a Selling Hurdle) and pulled up three times over jumps, and is a complete dog these days. Blinkered in Points, and has also been visored. *J. Harris, G. Skone & K. Phelan — S. Pembs (Dawn Harries).* 670 (Cf), 947 (M).

UNCLE ADA (IRE) ..9-11§.. 10 ch.g. Phardante (FR) — Park Belle (IRE) (Strong Gale) 211p. Lengthy half-brother to Over The Rhee (IRE). Dam is half-sister to Pits Delight (*qv* '96 Annual). P-t-P '00/3 r13 p4 (2nds, beaten neck once, last once); pulled up 3, ran out and fell/unseated 5. Finally persuaded to put his best foot forward after several near misses when clinging onto a slender lead at Brafield-on-the-Green, but a notoriously hard ride, and hung into the path of the probable winner and caused him to fall on the approach to the last when following up in a three-finisher Restricted at Flagg. Prone to blunders, and one at the fifth last sealed his fate on his Open debut, and has to be left alone as far as betting activities are concerned despite the continued presence of Richard Burton. Wears blinkers, and has been tried in cheekpieces. *Mrs C. Robinson — Albrighton.* 227 (CfMa), 463 (OMa), 990 (CR), 1204 (O).

UNCLE DEN ..8-2.. 15 b.g. Uncle Pokey — Meggies Dene (Apollo Eight) 2. Robust half-brother to Little Greyside, Ramstar and Charlie Dene, and to NH flat and Hurdles winner, Gastornis. Dam won 2m1f Hdle and 3 Chses, 2-3m. P-t-P/HUNT CH '98/00 and '02 r19 p3 (2 2nds, beaten fence once; also disqualified from 3rd once — not weigh-in); 4th, last, pulled up 7, fell/unseated 6. A regular non-finisher in the past, and only wheeled out to provide a beginner with a spin in his Members in '04, but plodded on steadily to claim 30 lengths second from the second-favourite. *I. Hudson — Oakley.* 461 (M).

UNCLE NEIL (IRE) ..9-13.. 8 gr.g. Roselier (FR) — Bobs My Uncle (Deep Run) p222. Tall half-brother to Irish jumping winner, Putsometnby. Bought Doncaster, May '01 for 40,000. Ran a spectacular race considering he was only making his second appearance when five lengths second in a 3m5f Open at Corbridge, where Son Of Anshan and Blank Cheque were amongst those behind, but then short-headed by Briery Hill in a Dalston Restricted (evens favourite) and even more disappointing when 4-6 and beaten seven lengths in a Maiden at Corbridge. The worry was that he never looked very keen on his latest outing, and may need a long trip in mud and possibly also blinkers if he is to stage a revival of fortunes. Seems to have plenty of ability if only it can be wheedled out of him. The 40,000gns he cost as a four-year-old looks money ill-spent. *Mrs A. Stevenson — Tynedale (Tim Reed).* 272 (OMa), 429 (3m5fO), 765 (R), 1041 (OMa).

UNDER MILK WOOD ..9-2.. 13 b.g. Still Time Left — Springaliance (Reliance II) p. Very small. Dam won 2m Sell Hdle. P-t-P '98/00 and '02/3 r21 w1 (Maiden) p2 (2nds, of 3 once and last once); 4th, last pair 5, pulled up 6, and fell/unseated 6. Left to finish solo in bizarre ground at St Hilary in '99, but a total crock, and usually hobbles away from the races looking very much the worse for wear, and a trip to Howick in '04 was no different. Error-prone. Wears a cross-noseband. *C.J. & Mrs G. Pritchard — Ystrad Taf Fechan (Gillian Pritchard).* 358 (R).

PLATE 127 1249 Cotley Mixed Open: Unlimited Free (Dido Harding), 1st
PHOTO: Brian Armstrong

UNLIMITED FREE (IRE) ..10-8.. 11 ch.g. Ile De Chypre — Merry Madness (Raise You Ten) 113915. Tall workmanlike half-brother to Irish jumping winner, Merry People (IRE) (won 16 including a Point), to Irish NH flat and Hurdles winner, Over The Bar (IRE), and to NH flat and Hurdles winner, Merry Masquerade (IRE) (won nine). Dam, won Mares Maiden in Ireland, and is half-sister to Merry Chieftain (*qv* '03 Annual). NH FLAT '00 r1 p0. NH '00/2 r13 w1 (2m7f110y Ch) p5. P-t-P/HUNT CH '03 r5 p2; 5th twice, and 6th. Had more ability than he cared to reveal under Rules, and became most disappointing, but clearly on good terms with himself in '04, and seemed to appreciate being left to do things his way. Jumped particularly well in a February soft ground double on right-handed tracks, and subsequently showed more resolve than Red Native at Cotley Farm, but most disappointing in the Gerrard Final, and may need to be fresh. Wears a cross-noseband. *Hon. Miss D. Harding — Portman (Sally Alner).* 117 (C), 239 (3m1fH), 490 (3m2fH), 732 (2m5f110yH), 1249 (MO), 1360 (3mH).

UPHAM LORD (IRE) ..10-10.. 12 b.g. Lord Americo — Top O The Mall (Don) 13f5fu2. Rangy well-made. Dam won 2 2m Hdles in Ireland. IR 12,000 4yo. NH FLAT '98 r1 p1 (3rd). NH '98/00 r14 w3 (2 2m4f-2m5f Hdles, and 2-finisher 3m Ch) p3; fell in 2 other Chses, with every chance 2 out once. NH '01 r2 p1 (3rd in 3m110y Ch), and 4th. P-t-P '01/3 r22 w20 (Ladies, inc 11-timer '02 and 8-timer '03) p0; and fell/unseated 2. NH '04 r1 p1 (2nd to Guilsborough Gorse in 2m5f110y Ch: *ld to 3 & 6 to 7, ld 12 til rdn & hdd app last, one pce*). The perfect Ladies Pointer, and ran up 20 consecutive wins, but many of them were bloodless affairs, and normally long odds-on in them. Finally returned to Peter Beaumont to contest Hunter Chases, and immediately romped to an unchallenged success at Fakenham, but had previously had problems with regulation fences, and old jumping frailties returned for much of the rest of his campaign. Tried blinkered latterly under Rules, and found little off the bridle when third at Bangor, but far happier in Points, and a decision to return to his old stomping grounds in '05 looks sure to be made. *Mrs E.W. Wilson — Middleton (Peter Beaumont).* 242 (2m5f110yH), 435 (3m110yH), 543 (3m2f110yH), 994 (3m110yH), 1168 (2m5fH), 1295 (3m110yH).

UP THE PUB (IRE) .10-2.. 7 ch.g. Carroll House — Brave Ruby (Proverb) 2. Tall strong half-brother to Handsome Is (IRE). Dam won mares Maiden in Ireland. P-t-P '03 (for Mr R.H. Alner) r1 p0 (pulled up). Favourite for both races for obvious reasons, and stepped up on his debut effort when dead-heating for second 25 lengths behind stablemate Free Gift at Larkhill, but already looking decidedly fragile. A surefire winner when he can be produced in tip-top condition. Wears a cross-noseband. *G. Keirle — Portman (Sally Alner).* 12 (OMa).

PLATE 128 1017 Worcestershire Ladies Open: Horse & Hound Leading Horse of 2004 Upton Adventure and Emma James, 1st, have taken the lead from Fanion De Nourry and Sue Sharratt, ref, PHOTO: David Jones

UPTON ADVENTURE ..10-11.. 12 br.m. Green Adventure (USA) — Country Rise (Country Retreat) 1311121111. Sparely-made. Dam, half-sister to Little Rise (*qv* '95 Annual), failed to finish in 9 of 10 Points for Peter Corbett, but grandam, Dido's Hill, won Maiden and 3rd 4 for him. P-t-P '99/03 r29 w13 (inc 6 Ladies, 3m-3m2f, inc hat-trick '03) p10 (8 2nds, of 3 once); 4th, and on floor 5. One of the best Ladies horses in recent memory, and even on her rare off days makes the frame, and took her winning tally to 21 when becoming the winning-most Pointer in '04. Usually needs a run, and was probably lucky when making a successful return for the first time ever at Barbury, but brushes most rivals aside with disdain, and Emma James has an impressive turn of foot at her disposal. Thoroughly game and consistent, and rarely touches a twig nowadays, and though she avoids ground firmer than good can handle all types of going. Has little to prove in her sphere, but the owner will resist the temptation to run her under Rules, and another sequence of wins looks very achievable next year. A credit to all concerned. *P.J. Corbett — Ledbury (Nicky Sheppard).* 33 (L), 108 (L), 407 (L), 449 (L), 613 (L), 737 (L), 838 (L), 1017 (3m2fL), 1255 (L), 1391 (L).

UPTON CRUSADER ..—.. 8 ch.g. Cruise Missile — Spartan City (Dubassoff USA) pp. Lengthy. Dam (*qv* '96 Annual) was 3rd in Selling Hurdle; and won 10 Points (inc 8 Ladies) and placed 17 for Peter Corbett. Mother was a delightful mare, but father has bred plenty of goats in his time, and unfortunately it already looks as if this might be another of them. *P.J. Corbett — Ledbury (Nicky Sheppard).* 87 (OMa), 410 (2m4fCfMa).

UP TO THE MINUTE .9-4.. 8 ch.g. Karinga Bay — Little Romany (Day Is Done) 4. Well-made brother to Miss Karingaroo (*qv*). P-t-P '03 r5 p2 (2nds, last once); last, unseated, and pulled up. Beaten a maximum of three lengths when runner-up twice in '03, and looks a likely winner, but only able to appear once this year, and has presumably met with a setback. *Miss R. Fear — Taunton V. (Philip Greenwood).* 328 (OMa).

URBAN HUNTER (IRE) ..9-9.. 12 ch.g. Salt Dome (USA) — Muligatawny (Malacate USA) p. Big strong half-brother to Irish NH flat and English jumping winner, Maestro Paul, and to Irish jumping winners, Collon Diamonds and Caitriona's Choice (IRE). P-t-P '02/3 (for Mrs D. Lewes, Mr D. Little, Mr D. Chelton, Mr M. White, Mr S. Lindley & Miss A. Bucknall) r7 w2 (Maiden and 3-runner Members) p1 (2nd); pulled up 2, fell/unseated 2. Only defeated once when completing in Points, and would have achieved more had he started earlier and been less clumsy, but a racecourse visit is a rarity, and never looked happy on his only appearance in '04. *Miss A. Bucknall — W. Somerset V.* 1066 (CCon).

USEDTOBEASWEETBOY ..—.. 6 b.g. Sylvan Express — Royal Justice (Royal Vulcan) puf. Half-brother to Dancing Dingo. Dam, half-sister to Just Max (*qv* '94 Annual). Has run and jumped badly so far, and also showed signs of temperament in his second outing, when he was reluctant to race and finally set off 25 lengths behind. Named with feeling? *P. Richardson — Grafton.* 1124 (OMa), 1402 (2m4fOMa), 1504 (2m4fOMa).

VAIGLY NORTH ..—.. 7 b.m. Minshaanshu Amad (USA) — Straight Gold (Vaigly Great) pp. Small light. Dam won 5f race, 2 Hurdles, 2m-2m4f, pulled up (total of 7; was subsequently fifth in Ladies and is half-sister to Northern Village (*qv* '98). NH FLAT '02 (for A.G. Newcombe) r4 p1 (3rd). NH '03 (for J.A. Moore) r2 p0; pulled up 1. Finished 32 lengths third in a bumper, but has been unplaced once (beaten 62 lengths) and pulled up thrice over jumps. Gave the impression of lacking stamina in two Maidens two months apart. *Mrs Z. Hammond — Worcs (Michael Hammond).* 256 (CMa), 1020 (OMa).

VAIN MINSTREL (IRE) ..—.. 13 b/br.g. Royal Fountain — Minstrel Top (Black Minstrel) pp. Half-brother to Mister Black (IRE) and Chasing winner, Kerry Lads (IRE). Dam is half-sister to Cabbery Rose (*qv* 2001 Annual). IRISH P-t-P '97/8 r9 w3 (up to Winners of 2) p2 (2nds); pulled up 2, slipped up, and fell. IRISH NH '98/00 r21 w3 (2m-2m4f Chses, inc £8652 prize) p3 (2nds, beaten head once). P-t-P/HUNT CH '01 and '03 (for Mr M.J. Parr) r5 w2 (Open and Ladies) p0; ran out, and fell/unseated 2. A smart Pointer who invariably establishes his superiority from an early stage, and rated 10-7 when on song, but lacks fluency and has stood his racing badly in recent years, and ran as though something was very much amiss in '04. Only risked on easy surfaces. *M.T. Mann — N. Ledbury (Paul Jones).* 100 (O), 465 (O).

VALENTINES VISION ..—.. 8 b.g. Distinctly North (USA) — Sharp Anne (Belfort FR) f. Good-bodied half-brother to 5f flat winners, Its All Relative, and Sharp Monty. Dam won 7 flat (5-6f) races. FLAT '99/02 r19 w1 (7f) p2. NH '01 r1 p0. P-t-P '03 r2 p0 (fell/unseated 2). In his pomp at up to a mile on sand, but dangerous in Points, and would not settle under an iron grip until crashing after a mile on his only start in '04. It would be irresponsible to run him again over jumps. Blinkered once in '02. *A.J. Le Pennec & R.A. Maletroit — Brocklesby (Robin Maletroit).* 298 (Cf).

VALJEAN (IRE) ..9-6.. 9 b.g. Alzao (USA) — Escape Path (Wolver Hollow) p2. Tall compact half-brother to Irish flat and jumping winner, Sea Fisher (IRE). IRISH FLAT '98/00 r9 p0. NH '01/2 r4 p0. P-t-P/HUNT CH '03 r11 w2 (3-finisher Maiden and finished alone Members) p2 (2nd of 3 once); 4th twice, last pair 3, refused 1, and fell 1. Lightly raced in previous years, but crammed 11 starts into '03, and was rewarded with two easy wins in weak races. Not a thorough stayer, and did not get home when ten lengths second of three at Erw Lon, but two runs in four days was his lot. Runs tongue-tied. Blinkered once in '00. *P.B. Miles — Ystrad Taf Fechan (Myfanwy Miles).* 176 (3mH), 207 (R).

VALLEY ERNE (IRE) ..9-13.. 14 b.g. King's Ride — Erne Gold VII (unknown) 556p4. Neat. IRISH P-t-P '96 r2 w1 (5yo Maiden) p0; and pulled up. IRISH NH FLAT '96 r4 w1 (p2 (2nds). IRISH FLAT '97 and '99 r3 w1 (14f) p1 (3rd). IRISH NH '96/7 and '99/03 (for M. Cunningham) r43 w5 (3 2m-2m4f Hdle and 2 2m3f Chses) p10; fell 4, and pulled up 1. Won eight races in Ireland on good or easy surfaces to April '00, including four victories at Punchestown (22 ran once, and 20 ran once) and earned a £10,400 prize in his final victory there. Frequently let down by his jumping, and fell on four occasions, and was going strongly in three of them. A veteran whose glory days are long gone, but did give one respectable display in '04, when seven lengths fourth in a Cartmel Hunter Chase. Too slow for Hurdling now, including Sellers, and insulted by cheekpieces on his latest start. *N. Sanderson — Lanarks & Renfrews.* 282 (Cf), 439 (2m5f110yH), 656 (O), 894 (3m3fH), 1490 (3m2fH).

VALLEY GARDEN ..8-11.. 15 b.g. Valiyar — April (Silly Season) 2pp. Neat sturdy half-brother to Wordsworth, Focus On Foster and Aprils Hope, and to Successful Hurdlers, Dolly Wardance and Fantastical. Dam won 4 10f races. NH FLAT '94 r3 w2 p0. NH '94/7, and '00 r16 w1 (2m5f110y Hdle) p3; pulled up 6. P-t-P '03 r2 w1 (Members) p0; and pulled up 1. Resurfaced after a three-year absence to record his first success since '96 last year, but turned over at 4-6 in the latest renewal of his Members, and far too slow and portly to keep up in more competitive races. *Mrs B. Butterworth — Cumberland F.* 761 (M), 1220 (C), 1307 (Cf).

VALMAN (IRE) ..—.. 9 b/br.g. Valville (FR) — Omania (Runnett) ppppp. Compact. NH '01 and '03 (for C.J. Down) r6 p1 (last of 3); pulled up 3, unseated 1. P-t-P/HUNT CH '02/3 (for Mrs L.M. Edwards & Mr P. Warren) r11 w2 (Maiden and Restricted) p2 (3rds); 8th, pulled up 5, and fell 1. A dual winner in the previous yard, and landed a gamble and claimed the scalp of Kestick in the latest, but not better than last since, and has jumped from the frying pan into the fire. A sketchy jumper at the best of times, and had Patrick Millington wrapping the reins around himself on several occasions in '04. Has been tried in blinkers and a visor. *P.J. Millington — Quorn.* 158 (CCon), 372 (I), 650 (O), 742 (I), 942 (Cf).

VALS WHISPA ..—.. 8 ch.g. Timeless Times (USA) — Skiddaw Bird (Bold Owl) u. Compact brother to Hobo, and to flat winner, Foreman. 6500y. FLAT '99 (for S.E. Kettlewell) r10 p1 (3rd). Finished third in a 7f Seller as a two-year-old and was visored once that season, but tailed off when unseating at the 11th in a Maiden five years later. Unpromising. *M.A. Humphreys — Farndale.* 395 (CfMa).

VANSELL ..9-12.. 14 b.m. Rambo Dancer (CAN) — Firmiter (Royal Palace) p23. Leggy light. NH FLAT '96 r1 p0. NH '96 r1 p0. P-t-P '98/00 and '03 r24 w3 (Maiden, Members and Restricted) p5 (4 3rds); 4th, 5th, 7th, pulled up 6, and on floor 4. Won three races on sound surfaces to '99, but ended the following season lame, and has been lightly raced sinc e returning. Retains ability, and regularly makes the frame, but prone to errors, and typically faded up the hill when third at 40-1 on her latest appearance at Bratton Down. Tends to sweat excessively, and has two handlers. *Mrs J. McCullough — Axe V.H. (Philip Greenwood).* 692 (I), 1126 (M), 1382 (I).

VELVET DOVE ..9-10.. 6 b.m. Rakaposhi King — Careful Dove (So Careful) 32. Small close-coupled. Dam, half-sister to Etta Dove (*qv* '00 Annual). Grandam is Red Dove. Bought Ascot, Aug for 3047. Six-and-a-half lengths third on a promising debut in a Mollington Maiden (the two directly behind her went on to score), and unlucky at Guilsborough, where she finished two lengths second after being badly hampered three out and then making a very slow jump at the next. Has the right attitude and promises to be a thorough stayer and should atone soon. *Mrs P. Adams — Pytchley.* 589 (CfMa), 788 (CfMa).

VELVET VICTORY (IRE) ..8-1.. 6 b.m. Old Vic — Cooks Lawn (The Parson) pf3. Rangy workmanlike half-sister to NH flat and Hurdles winner, Dix Bay. Had jumping problems and got no further than the tenth on her first two attempts, but a 12 lengths third at Cothelstone was better, although it was an extremely slowly-run Maiden and the form only entitles her to a tiny rating. May be able to progress in her second season. *The DT9 Partnership (R. Willis) — Portman (Richard Miller).* 688 (2m4fOMa), 1134 (OMa), 1371 (OMa).

VERCHENY ..9-7§.. 10 b.m. Petoski — Ekaytee (Levanter) p3pppp. Compact. Dam, half-sister to Ryming Cuplet (*qv* '01 Annual), won 6 Points (5 Ladies) and placed 21 (including 6 Hdles) for Gerald Tanner (who bred her). P-t-P '00 and '02/3 (for Mr G. Tanner) r15 w2 (Maiden and Restricted) p2 (2nds, beaten head once, and of 3 once); last pair 2, pulled up 5, and fell/unseated 4. Unbeaten when completing in '02, and ran well when 15 lengths third at Buckfastleigh, but a regular non-finisher, and is anything but a straightforward ride. Has been seen to swish her tail, and twice pulled up in a distressed state, and her jumping can be very variable. Wears a cross-noseband. *D. Heath — E. Devon (Monique Pike).* 50 (I), 193 (I), 365 (I), 705 (I), 822 (L), 1195 (I).

VEREDARIUS (FR) ..6-0.. 14 b.g. Le Nain Jaune (FR) — Villa Verde (FR) (Top Ville) p4p9p. Big heavy-topped half-brother to 2 French flat winners, and to a jumping winner there. Dam won 2 flat and 6 jump races in France. IRISH NH FLAT '96 r1 p0. IRISH NH '96/9 r26 w3 (2m Hdle, and 2 2m4f-2m5f Chses) p1 (2nd). NH '00 r7 p0 (Sell final). P-t-P/HUNT CH '01/3 r17 p3 (3rds, remote once, of 4 once and last once); last pair 4, pulled up 9, and unseated 1. Won three races in mud in Ireland to '97, but has plodded badly for a long time now, and is one of the slowest thing on four legs imaginable. Has been tried in headgear. *Mrs S.E. Tyler — Fernie.* 380 (L), 585 (L), 743 (L), 885 (M), 1516 (L).

VERO BEACH ..—.. 9 ch.g. Nicholas Bill — My Moody Girl (IRE) (Alzao USA) uppp. Strong-topped. NH FLAT '01 r1 p0. NH '03 (for Mrs S.D. Williams) r2 p0; pulled up 1. Bought Ascot, Aug for 2572. Has failed to finish in five of his last six outings, and got no further than the fourth on two occasions in Points. Acquired a visor on his last three starts and was an uninspired gamble from 8s to 4-1 once, but continually looks hopeless. *Mrs E.M. Worth & T.D.H. Hughes — Lamerton (Tony & Pauline Geering).* 195 (CfMa), 312 (CfMa), 567 (CfMa), 704 (CfMa).

VEXFORD LUCY .—.. 12 b.m. Latest Model — Suchong (No Mercy) fu. Half-sister to Jims Joy and Vexford Deltic. Dam, 2nd of 3 in Nov Chase, was a non-stayer in Points (3rd twice, pulled up 10, and fell) for Gerald Greenway. NH FLAT '97 r1 p0 (pulled up). NH '00 r1 p0 (pulled up). Pulled up in a bumper (at halfway) in '97 and a Selling Hurdle in '00, fell at the first in a Maiden on the 1st of February, and unseated at the eighth after looking a horrible ride in similar company on the 1st of May. If you ever hear that she has achieved anything it will be the 1st of April. *V.G. Greenway — Devon & Somerset.* 119 (OMa), 1182 (CMam).

VICARS CHALET (IRE) ..9-12.. 11 b.g. Actinium (FR) — Edna Cottage (The Parson) 161p. Small light half-brother to Brave The Waves (IRE), to Irish Pointing winner, Brid-Og, and to Irish NH flat winner, Strand Road Rocket (IRE). IRISH P-t-P '00/2 r7 w1 (6yo&up Maiden) p1 (2nd); pulled up 1, unseated 1. IRISH NH FLAT '99 and '01 r2 p0; pulled up 1. P-t-P '03 (for Lt T. Edwards) r2 p0 (4th, and pulled up 1). Won his only Point in '01, and has never stood much racing, but still retains ability, and sprang a 20-1 surprise on his debut for the new yard on his reappearance at Llanfrynach. Appeared to finish unsound next time, but able to beat one rival in his Members, and another small success could still present itself if he remains healthy. *Mrs D. Tranter — Monmouths (Lisa Day).* 452 (R), 613 (L), 846 (M), 1092 (I).

VIC'S BRUSH (IRE) ..9-5.. 13 b.g. Brush Aside (USA) — Fair Vic (Fair Turn) 44. Compact half-brother to Eternal Credit, to Hurdles winner, Bishops Tipple, to Irish Chasing winner, Ollatrim Lady, and to winning Irish Pointer, Tullaghfin. Dam won 2m Hdle in Ireland. IRISH P-t-P '98 and '01 r3 p0; pulled up 3. IRISH NH FLAT '00 r1 p0. IRISH NH '00 r4 p0. P-t-P/HUNT CH '03 r5 w2 (3-finisher Maiden and 3-runner Intermediate nov rdrs) p0; 5th of 6, unseated 1, and pulled up 1. Much improved when successful in two three-finisher events on sound surfaces last year, but fractured a splint bone (which was subsequently removed) in his hat-trick bid, and suffered an interrupted campaign in '04. Connections have already worked miracles with him, but gives the impression he will find it difficult to score again. *R.A.B. Brassey — Modbury H. (Gordon Chambers).* 277 (O), 1005 (Cf).

VICS FANE (IRE) ..8-11.. 7 ch.g. Old Vic — Baby Fane (IRE) (Buckskin FR) 3. Workmanlike half-brother to Dunmanus Bay (IRE), and to Irish jumping winner, Lord Fane. 4089 4yo. Novicey when a remote third on a Charm Park debut, but would have been a bit closer had he not made a terrible mistake three out (subsequently promoted from fourth to third). Gave the impression that he would do better next time, but did not get the opportunity, and evidently had a setback. *R.J. Marley — Middleton.* 392 (CfMa).

VICTIM (IRE) ..8-12.. 8 ch.g. Alphabatim (USA) — Castlemartin (IRE) (Carlingford Castle) 4. Small half-brother to Hurdles winner, Mandy's Native (IRE). Finished about seven lengths fourth in a youngsters Maiden at Didmarton, but the form did not work out, and the three ahead of him were all disappointing subsequently. Would presumably be racing under Rules if connections thought him capable, and perhaps more attention should be paid to his jockey David England who gives the impression that he is a lot more talented than his mounts (e.g. Lyphard's Fable). *N.A. Twiston-Davies — Cotswold.* 368 (OMa).

VICTORIA'S BOY (IRE) ..10-6.. 12 b.g. Denel (FR) — Cloghroe Lady (Hardboy) 12223. Tall lengthy. IRISH P-t-P '97 r3 p2 (2nds, last once); and fell. IRISH NH FLAT '97 r1 p0. IRISH NH '98 r2 p0 (last in Hdle and Hunt Ch). NH '00/2 r15 p3 (inc 2 2nds); pulled up 2. P-t-P/HUNT.CH '99/00 and '03 r18 w7 (inc 2 Hunt Chses, 3m1f-3m2f) p6 (4 2nds, of 3 once; and 2 3rds, last once); 4th, 9th, last pair 2, and pulled up 1. Lacked the necessary speed to win under Rules, but admirably consistent in Points, and scored on his reappearance for the first time when successful on his favoured fast ground at Hornby Castle. A sound jumper and likes to make the running, but his lack of acceleration often makes life difficult for him nowadays. Blinkered twice in '01. *J.J. Coates — Pendle Forest & Craven (Wendy Wild).* 340 (O), 750 (O), 875 (O), 1171 (3m2f110yH), 1490 (3m2fH).

VICTORY MARCH ..—.. 7 b.g. Infantry — Ludoviciana (Oats) p. Dam, half-sister to Craftsman (*qv* '98 Annual) won Maiden and placed three times for George Paul (a cracking galloper but almost impossible to keep sound). Never near the leaders before pulling up three out when barely galloping in a Higham Maiden. Has some interesting relatives, but mother was renowned for her leg problems and father has bred a very high incidence of unsound animals, so it hardly looks like a match made in heaven. *G.W. Paul — Essex & Suffolk.* 401 (OMa).

VICTORY SALUTE ..—§.. 8 ch.m. Past Glories — Hasty Salvo (Hasty Word) pp. Rangy owner-bred sister to Battle Honours (*qv*). P-t-P '02/3 r4 p0 (pulled up 2, refused 1, and fell 1). A dreadful jumper who has yet to go more than two miles, and stands her racing badly. *G.F. Wheeler — E. Sussex & Romney Marsh (Di Grissell).* 27 (OMa), 611 (OMa).

VIEW HOLLO .9-0.. 7 b.g. Liberated — Brief Glance (Official) 1. Tall unfurnished. Crept round Larkhill to beat the 1-4 favourite in a match for a Maiden, but finished lame, which looks particularly ominous as his legs have never had the strain of any previous racing. *Mrs M.J. Arnold — N. Cotswold (Emma Baker).* 456 (OMa).

VIKING LILY (IRE) ..9-11.. 11 ch.m. Yashgan — Powis Lass (Buckskin FR) p. Deep-girthed lengthy. IRISH P-t-P '99 r1 w1 (5yo mares Maiden). P-t-P '00/3 r8 w2 (Restricted and Members) p3 (3rds, last once); 4th, and pulled up 2. A dual winner in '02 but laid low by a virus in '03, and for the second year running was restricted to a single appearance in '04. Stays well and is suited by an easy surface. *Mrs D. Rowell — Crawley & Horsham (Sara Hickman).* 41 (I).

VILLAGE COPPER .9-10.. 13 b.g. Town And Country — Culm Valley (Port Corsair) 6f42p2237. Sturdy half-brother to Valley's Choice, Copper Valley and Atoski, and to NH flat and Hurdles winner, Majority Verdict. Dam, sister, and half-sister to 3 Pointers, won a 2m1f Hdle, 2 Chses (3m1f-3m2f) and 6 Points and placed total of 7. P-t-P/HUNT CH '97/03 r32 w8 (inc Ladies) p14 (9 2nds, beaten head once; inc 3rd of 4 once); last pair 6, pulled up 1. His eight wins have been equally divided between Ampton and Cottenham, but suffered the first fall of his career at the former venue in '04, and blinkered for a two-race spell two starts later. Often a weak finisher in Points now, and will find it very hard to push his winning tally into double figures. Wears a cross-noseband. *A.G.C. Howland Jackson — Suffolk (Ruth Hayter).* 5 (L), 42 (L), 155 (Cnr), 520 (M), 557 (O), 906 (Cnr), 998 (L), 1244 (L), 1359 (2m4f110yH).

PLATE 129 572 Lamerton Restricted (Div 2): Village Queen stoops to avoid the low-flying Dominic Harvey *PHOTO: Baths Photographic*

VILLAGE QUEEN (IRE) .8-12.. 8 b.m. Good Thyne (USA) — Lady Henbit (IRE) (Henbit USA) f535. Rangy. IR2200 3yo. NH '02 (for P.J. Hobbs) r2 p0. Finished eight lengths third in a youngsters Maiden at Stafford Cross, and usually shows a degree of speed, but beaten a minimum of 25 lengths otherwise, and has so far given the impression of being unable to stay the trip. Never tried 2m4f, and now it is no longer an option. *Mrs J. Edwards-Heathcote & R. White — Devon & Somerset (Tessa White).* 572 (R), 791 (R), 1134 (OMa), 1380 (OMa).

VINNIE BOY (IRE) .10-4.. 8 b/br.g. Detroit Sam (FR) — Castle Ita (Midland Gayle) 111. Workmanlike brother to Bannagh Express (IRE) and Bannagh Mor, and half-brother to Ita's Fellow (IRE) and Bannagh Beg (IRE). P-t-P '02 r1 p1 (last of 3). Missed '03 when a suspicion of leg trouble emerged, but unbeaten in minor company this year, and despite lacking fluency at times has shown himself to be a strong finisher. Hung right on the run-in at Bratton Down, and it is hoped that he was not feeling the firmish ground as he looks destined for another successful year in '05. *J.H. Burbidge — Taunton V. (Ollie Bush).* 87 (OMa), 1063 (R), 1382 (I).

VINTAGE CHOICE (IRE) ..—.. 13 b.g. Brush Aside (USA) — Shady Jumbo (Callernish) pp. Tall rangy. IRISH P-t-P '97 r3 p3 (promoted from 4th to 3rd once). P-t-P/HUNT CH '98 and '00 (for Mr F.S. Jackson) r7 w1 (Maiden) p2 (distant 3rd of 4 in Hunt Ch, and 2 fences last of 3); and pulled up 4. Won on firmish at Market Rasen in '98, but absent in '99 and since '00, and his latest comeback was typically fruitless. *B. Robinson — York & Ainsty N.* 810 (R), 1162 (R).

VINTAGE ROCK ..—.. 8 b.g. Rock City — Classical Vintage (Stradavinsky) pp. Small light-framed half-brother to flat winners, Simply Sooty (dam of smart flat winner Umistim), Abos, and to another winner. Dam won 5f race. NH FLAT '01 r1 p0. FLAT '01 (for R. Hannon) r1 p0. Furlongs last in a bumper and 37 lengths ninth of ten in a flat race, and tailed off and pulled up after two miles in both Maidens (almost refused in the latest). A ridiculous choice for Pointing as he has absolutely no hope of getting the trip. *N. Sarson — Warwicks (Nigel Ridout).* 128 (OMa), 618 (2m4fOMa).

VIRGOS BAMBINO (IRE) ..9-11.. 8 ch.m. Perugino (USA) — Deep In September (IRE) (Common Grounds) 7212213. Close-coupled. FLAT '99 and '01 r5 p0. P-t-P '03 r3 p1 (2 fences last of 3); last, and fell 1. Too slow for the flat, and not better than last in her first four Points, but appreciated the drop back to 2m4f when successful at Cothelstone, and gamely hung on to make all in a weak Restricted subsequently. Headstrong and likely to find her stamina deficiency exploited too often in more competitive events over the full trip now. Wears a kineton. *Mrs M. Nicholls — Spooners & W. Dartmoor (Verity Nicholls).* 194 (CfMa), 329 (OMa), 469 (2m4fOMa), 706 (R), 912 (R), 1435 (R), 1540 (Cf).

VIRTUOSO .9-12.. 11 ch.g. Suave Dancer (USA) — Creake (Derring-Do) 4f44144. Well-made attractive half-brother to 4 flat winners, including Creon (subsequent jumping winner, including in Ireland — most recent success in '04 Pertemps Final at Cheltenham Festival), to Affaire De Coeur (also won Hurdling), and to Hurdling winner, Chocolate Ice. IRISH FLAT '97 r3 p2. FLAT '03 r1 p0. NH '97/03 (for C.J. Mann, all wins, and B.G. Powell) r39 w6 (2 2m Hdles and 4 2m-2m6f Chses) p7; fell 1. Formerly capable of producing praiseworthy efforts in the mud to December '01, but none of his six victories came at beyond 2m3f, and normally struggles to get the trip in Points. Has been beaten 30 lengths plus in 11 of his 13 most recent outings, so in the circumstances it was amazing that he should be able to produce a virtuoso effort in a five-runner Ladies on firmish at Larkhill which contained both Masalarian and Sir D'Orton (outsider of the quintet, and a first success for Sarah Corcoran). Blinkered once in '99. Fell at the first once in '98 and two out when tiring in '04, but otherwise can boast an excellent 44 completions over jumps. *If Not Why Not Partnership (Sarah Corcoran) — Dart V.H. & S. Pool H. (Liam Corcoran).* 62 (Cf), 484 (L), 690 (L), 822 (L), 1099 (L), 1368 (L), 1448 (L).

VISCOUNT BANKES ..9-13.. 7 ch.g. Clantime — Bee Dee Dancer (Ballacashtal CAN) 14522p44p. Small half-brother to flat winner, Breakin Even, and to a winner in Italy. FLAT '00 and '02 r6 p0. NH '02/3 r3 p0; pulled up 1. P-t-P '03 (for Mrs K. While) r2 p1 (3rd); and 4th of 5. Pulls hard and galloped away with a youngsters 2m4f Maiden on the opening day of the season, but the race only took 4min 36sec, and not surprisingly finds it impossible to get the full trip. Profitably employed in sub-3m events, but regulation fences put a greater strain on his suspect jumping, and has not encountered the right conditions in them so far. Visored once in '02 and acquired cheekpieces on his last three starts. Typically scruffy and sweaty in the paddock, and has two handlers. Wears a cross-noseband. *Mrs R. Gasson — Farmers Bloodhounds.* 8 (2m4fOMa), 169 (R), 294 (R), 628 (2m3fH), 734 (2mH), 999 (R), 1173 (2m110yH), 1354 (2m110yH), 1437 (2m5f110yH).

VITAL ISSUE (IRE) .8-6§.. 13 b/br.g. Electric — Dreamello (Bargello) 6RpO. Compact half-brother to Irish Pointing winners, Tidal Moon and Toberella, and to 2 Irish NH flat winners (one also a successful Hurdler there, the other also a successful Pointer there). Dam is half-sister to Bright Dream (*qv* '90 Annual). IRISH P-t-P '97 r1 w1 (5yo Maiden). IRISH NH FLAT '97 r1 w1. NH FLAT '97 r1 p0. NH '98 r3 w1 (3m1f Hdle) p1 (2nd); and 4th. P-t-P/HUNT CH '00/3 r15 w2 (3m-4m2f Hunt Chses) p3 (2nds, inc Hunt Ch); 5th, last, pulled up 3, and fell/unseated 5. Sprang surprises in two Hunter Chases in the previous yard, but has always proved difficult to keep sound, and had decent riders at his disposal. Owner-ridden in the last two campaigns, and has regressed badly as a result and only once better than last under his lack of guidance. Wears a cross-noseband. *P.S. Johnson — Cambridge Univ (Tim Bryce).* 557 (O), 832 (Cf), 997 (O), 1396 (C).

VITINSEL ..9-3.. 9 ch.m. Vital Season — Tinsel Rose (Porto Bello) f1. Very small sister to Prickly Paws. Dam, half-sister to Love On The Rocks (*qv* '97 Annual), won 2m Sell Hdle. P-t-P '02/3 (for Mr P. Williams) r7 p1 (3rd); 4th, 5th, last 2, pulled up 1, and unseated 1. Only a diddy and did well to score in the final race of the season, but the other division of the Maiden was run 16 seconds faster, and her prospects in better company appear remote. Tongue-tied in '04. *P.E. Froud — Blackmore & Sparkford V.* 637 (CMam), 1566 (OMa).

PLATE 130 1566 Torrington Farmers Open Maiden (Div 2): Vitinsel (Jamie Snowden), 1st, leads Maloney (Christine Evans), 2nd, and Beehive Lad (Jody Sole), 3rd, Golden Sovereign (Alex Charles-Jones) is partly visible behind PHOTO: Brian Armstrong

VIVA BINGO (IRE) .—§§.. 9 ch.g. Phardante (FR) — Kitty Frisk (Prince Tenderfoot USA) pf*p*. Strong compact brother to Irish NH flat and English Hurdling winner, Kimanicky (IRE), and half-brother to Sirocco Sprite, and to flat winner, Sinclair Lad. IRISH NH FLAT '01/2 r5 p2. NH '02/3 (for M.J. Gingell) r7 p0; last 3, pulled up 2, and refused 1. NH '04 (for C.L. Popham) r1 p0 (pulled up in 2m4f Sell Hdle: *pulled hrd, prom, mists 2 & 3, wknd 6, blun nxt, pu aft 3 out*). Bought Ascot, Jul for 857. Once finished three-quarters-of-a-length second in an Irish bumper despite getting no assistance from a girl rider, and also third in similar company, but hates jumping, and refused at the fifth in his only Chase. Behaved appallingly and only got as far as the third in both Points, and equally revolting under Rules subsequently including when pulled up in a Selling Hurdle. Often blinkered nowadays. Should be banned. *P. Williams — Quantock.* 275 (CfMa), 468 (M).

VIVALDI ROSE (IRE) ..8-12.. 10 b.m. Cataldi — Peaceful Rose (Roselier FR) 22u. Neat half-sister to Hurdles winners, Caribbean Cove (IRE) and Desert Captain (IRE) (latter also won NH flat). IR2000 4yo. IRISH P-t-P '00 r1 p0 (fell).NH FLAT '01 r1 p0. NH '01/3 (for L. Lungo) r10 p1 (3rd); pulled up 2. Always well beaten under Rules including a Selling Hurdle, and was 33 lengths fourth and pulled up in Chases. Wore a visor or cheekpieces in her final two attempts. Flattered by two placings in Maidens as she was 30 lengths second of three and 15 lengths last of two, and stopped to nothing and got very tired in the final half mile when novice-ridden in both. Willing to try, but simply cannot get the trip, and would need all the opposition to evaporate if she was to score. *J.M. Ratcliffe — Grove & Rufford.* 153 (OMa), 293 (CMam), 525 (OMa).

VIVID IMAGINATION (IRE) ..10-13.. 6 b.g. Moonax (IRE) — Sezu (IRE) (Mister Lord USA) 1111u11. Small very light-framed. IRISH P-t-P '03 r1 p1 (3rd). NH '03 (for M.C. Pipe) r1 p0. Finished six lengths third of four in his only Irish Point, and the winner Raven's Last subsequently won an English bumper. Given one spin in a Hurdle, and then turned his attentions to Pointing with huge success, winning six times (often impressively and always with plenty in hand) and suffered his only defeat when unseating at the 14th in an Open at Woodford (4-9; it should have been a very revealing contest, as his toughest opponent of '04, Camden Carrig, subsequently landed a Hunter Chase). Possesses a great deal of speed and can go buzzing clear as soon as Ashley Farrant wishes, and can surely put this excellent pace to good use under Rules in '05. Only small and lacking in substance, but the Pipes excel with this type of animal, and no other trainers remotely approach their achievements with tiddlers. *D.A. Johnson - E. Devon (David Pipe).* 194 (CfMa), 318 (M), 498 (R), 692 (I), 1073 (O), 1269 (MO), 1384 (Cf).

WADDON HILL ..7-10.. 8 gr.g. Le Moss — Parslin (The Parson) 2. Tall quite attractive half-brother to Hurdles winner, Loch Nevis. P-t-P '03 (for Mrs L. Borradaile) r1 p0 (pulled up). Nibbled at in the market when 20 lengths second of four in a very slowly-run Maiden at Lifton, but will need to speed up and jump a great deal better if he is to achieve something more tangible. *M. Weir — Dartmoor.* 1545 (OMa).

WADERS (IRE) ..10-0.. 11 b.g. Good Thyne (USA) — Lochda (Crash Course) fp13p. Big lengthy. Dam, half-sister to Takemethere (*qv* '95 Annual), won 2 Hdles (2m-2m1f) in Ireland. NH FLAT '99 r2 p0. NH '00/2 r11 w1 (3m2f Ch) p1 (3rd); pulled up 4, refused 1, and fell/unseated 2. P-t-P/HUNT CH '03 r7 w2 (Open and 3-runner 2-finisher Members) p1 (2nd); 5th twice, unseated, and pulled up. A regular non-finisher under Rules, but has a better record in Points, and unearthed another straightforward opportunity when landing his Members for a second time. Made all in first-time blinkers, but did not look particularly keen, and acquired a tongue-tie on his latest appearance. Remains very prone to jumping errors, and cost James Tudor his front teeth when falling at the second on his return. *Miss G. Evans — Tivyside.* 34 (O), 205 (O), 669 (M), 842 (O), 1093 (4mMO).

WAG THE BRUSH ..10-0.. 13 br.g. Scallywag — Foxy Fort (Ampney Prince) p4. Tall strong half-brother to Hurdles winners, Fort Rank and Miss Foxy. Dam, half-sister to 3 Pointers, only finished once in 4 Points for Paul Tylor (when last). Grandam, Fort Lodge, won 3 Chses (3m-3m2f), 2 Hunt Chses and 15 Points and placed 10 for him. NH '99/01 r16 w1 (2m Hdle) p4; fell 3. P-t-P '98 and '03 (for Miss L.J.C. Sweeting) r6 w1 (Ladies) p2 (*3/4l* 2nd once); last, pulled up, and fell. Capable but has always been very difficult to win with, and has never been able to eradicate jumping errors from his make up. Becoming increasingly lightly raced, and the lack of a home meeting will make it difficult for him to score in future. *Mrs L.J.C. Tylor — Cury.* 78 (L), 869 (L).

WAKY LADY (IRE) ..—.. 8 b.m. Wakashan — Lady Of Sonas (IRE) (Lancastrian) pff. Compact. Jumped deliberately in the rear until pulling up on her debut, and although she led for a while in both subsequent attempts she was still very unconvincing at the fences and ended up on the deck twice (was a fence behind and idiotically not pulled up when enduring the latest crash). *M. Hammond — Worcs.* 1014 (M), 1139 (OMa), 1192 (OMa).

WANDERING LIGHT (IRE) ..10-0.. 16 b.g. Royal Fountain — Pleaseme (Javelot) 31142. Workmanlike rangy fired half-brother to 2 flat winners, and to successful Hurdler, Sloane Street. Dam won 4 flat (5-6f). IRISH P-t-P '94/5 r7 w3 (inc Open) p2 (2nds); unseated 1. NH '95/9 and '01/2 r12 w4 (3-4m Chses, inc £21,135 NH Chase at Cheltenham) p1 (3rd). P-t-P/HUNT CH '01 and '03 r8 w2 (inc Open) p4 (2 2nds, inc Hunt Ch); and pulled up 2. A useful but very lightly raced performer under Rules, and won at the Cheltenham Festival on his only appearance in '98, and gifted to present connections in '02. Suited by mud, and still retains plenty of enthusiasm, and took his winning tally into double figures when landing a four-runner event at Sandon. Confirmed his superiority over Cascum Lad in ideal conditions at Alpraham, but never able to go the pace at Eyton, and beaten by a rival who has also seen better days at Towcester. Would have been a leading stayer but for his fragile legs, but may be heading towards the twilight home now. *R.B. Francis — Sir W.W. Wynn's.* 712 (L), 849 (L), 1046 (L), 1263 (L), 1355 (3m1fH).

WANDERING WILD ..9-0.. 10 ch.m. Nomadic Way (USA) — Wild Child (Grey Ghost) 35uf45. Small neat sparely-made sister to Wilfie Wild, and half-sister to Winnie Wild. Dam, sister or half-sister to 3 Pointers, including Bugley (*qv* '98 Annual), won 2m4f Hunt Ch on technicality and 6 Points (inc an Open) and placed 9 (inc a Hunt Ch) for Stuart Fletcher, and grandam, Girl Sunday, won 2 Points and placed 2 for him. NH '01 r4 p0. P-t-P '00/3 (for Mr H.S. Fletcher, Mrs E M Jackson & Mrs V Cunningham) r15 w1 (Maiden) p2; 4th twice, 6th twice, last pair 3, pulled up 2, and on floor 3. Won a bad race as a five-year-old, but has struggled badly in the main since, particularly with the bigger weights, and failed to jump round both times when cheekpieces were applied in '04. Wears a cross-noseband, and has run tongue-tied. *Mrs E.M. Jackson — Lianus Friends (Mrs L. Ward) — Cleveland (Lynne Ward).* 162 (L), 270 (L), 564 (L), 771 (R), 1288 (R), 1304 (CR).

WANNA BE BAY ..7-12.. 10 ch.m. Jupiter Island — Moonlight Bay (Palm Track) pf6. Neat sister to Hurdles winner, Moonlight Venture. Dam, half-sister to Moonlight Shadow (*qv* '88 Season Annual), won 8f Sell and 2m Hdle. P-t-P '02/3 (for Mr J.D. Sole) r6 p0 (5th, pulled up 2, and fell/unseated 3). Has shown some speed, but a consistently poor jumper, and despite the best efforts of Phillip York seems likely to be consigned to the scrap heap. *Mrs S. Walker — Staff College (David Walker).* 293 (CMam), 539 (OMa), 996 (CMam).

WANNABE GANGSTER ..—.. 9 b.g. Homo Sapien — Rare Luck (Rare One) p. Brother to jumping winner, Muck Savage, and half-brother to Chasing winner, Four Mile Clump. Dam won 2m6f Hurdle, and 3 3m1f Chases at Plumpton. Has some competent relatives, but always last and tailed off by halfway before pulling up on a January debut as an eight-year-old, and seems to have problems. *M. Trott — Ludlow.* 51 (OMa).

WAR BRIDE ..9-3.. 7 ch.m. Deploy — Dom One (Dominion) 3p. Strong-topped half-sister to flat and Hurdling winner, One Domino. Dam won 3 flat races (5-7f). NH '02 (for Miss K.M. George) r1 p0. Urged into 28 lengths third in the closing stages of her Members, but broke down next time, and reportedly destroyed. *P. & J. Lowe — Tivyside (Peter Lowe).* 669 (M), 948 (OMa).

WARKSWOODMAN ..6-0.. 17 gr.g. Zambrano — Amberama (Sweet Ration) 4. Tall plain rangy. Dam pulled up in 3 of 5 Points. P-t-P '96/9 r16 p4 (3rds, of 4 twice, and last once); pulled up 4. A very safe jumper, and has excelled in other jumping disciplines, but a long-standing Maiden in Points, and it was a surprise to see him on a racecourse for the first time in five years when hunting round for a very remote last of four in his Members. *Mrs H. Dickson — N. Tyne, & Border.* 1480 (M).

WARNER FOR PLAYERS (IRE) ..9-8.. 14 b.g. Good Thyne (USA) — Bramble Hatch (Pry) 43p. Workmanlike half-brother to Ran Wild (IRE), and to jumping winner, Major Summit (IRE). Dam, half-sister to Cheadle Green (*qv* '94 Annual). NH FLAT '96 r3 w1 p2 (3rds). NH '96/8 and '00/2 r17 w3 (2m7f Hdle, and 2 2m4f-3m1f110y Chses) p5. P-t-P/HUNT CH '03 r6 w1 (3-runner Open) p2 (2nds, of 3 in Hunt Ch once); 5th, last, and unseated. Very lightly raced under Rules, and was scoring for the first time in nearly two years when making all to land a three-runner Open at Sandon in '03, but typically gave up quickly when pressure was applied this year. It would appear that the leg problems that have plagued him throughout his career resurfaced at Alpraham. Wore cheekpieces in his previous four starts. *D. Manning — Sir W.W. Wynn's (Steve Wynne).* 404 (O), 711 (O), 1045 (Cf).

WARREN HILL ..9-12.. 10 ch.g. Triune — The Warreness (Gargoor) 4fpf. Strong compact. NH '02 r1 p0 (tailed off). P-t-P '03 (for Mr T. Needham) r2 p1 (3rd); and pulled up. Beaten between five and 28 lengths when completing in Points, but veered left on the run-in in the latest, and let down by his jumping since. Clearly good enough to win a Maiden, and would have been placed but for both falls, and stronger handling should do the trick. *N.J. & Mrs M.A. Tory — S. Dorset (Monica Tory).* 120 (OMa), 233 (M), 328 (OMa), 636 (Rnr).

WATCHYOURBACK (NZ) ..10-4§.. 11 ch.g. Watchman (NZ) — English Lass (NZ) (English Harbour) u3313. Compact quite attractive. NH '00 r6 w1 (2m4f110y Hdle) p2. P-t-P/HUNT CH '00 and '02/3 r14 w1 (Open — promoted) p4 (2nd of 3 in Hunt Ch; 3 3rds, of 4 twice); last, pulled up 5 and fell/unseated 3. A moderate jumper of fences, and scoring for the first time on merit since '00 when successful at Bitterley, where the two market leaders cut each other's throats, and allowed him to land a touch from tens to 6-1. Ran well for a long way when 25 lengths third in the Lady Dudley Cup, but runs tongue-tied, and normally finishes weakly. Wears a visor, and has been tried in blinkers and cheekpieces. *Miss S. Bold — Ludlow (Mark Trott).* 48 (3m5f70yL), 292 (MO), 377 (3m1fH), 836 (O), 1016 (3m2fO).

WATERGATE BOY (IRE) ..—.. 9 ch.g. Fast Frigate — Princess Heronia (Down The Hatch) upupp. Rangy half-brother to Puntingbud (IRE), and to Irish NH flat and Hurdles winner, Stoneleigh Turbo (IRE). Dam is half-sister to Nero Wolf (*qv* '91 Annual). IRISH NH '01 r3 p0. P-t-P '02/3 r12 w1 (Maiden) p3 (3rds, of 4 twice); last pair 2, ran out 2, pulled up 3, and unseated. Backed down to joint-favourite when successful in a poor Maiden at Cold Harbour in '02, but headstrong and only able to get round in one of his last nine starts, and twice foiled by the first fence in '04. Only jockeys desperate to prove themselves are willing to partner him now. Wears a cross-noseband. *P.J. Tannant — Tanatside (Phillip Mills).* 665 (R), 1018 (R), 1114 (R), 1230 (R), 1389 (R).

WATERLINER .8-12.. 6 b.m. Merdon Melody — Double Touch (FR) (Nonoalco USA) 4p. Small sister to flat winner in Sweden, and half-sister to four flat winners. 950y. FLAT '01 r7 p0. NH '03 (for P.S. McEntee) r4 p1 (3rd). Not good enough for the flat (mostly Sellers, and wore headgear twice) or Hurdling (beaten 19 lengths plus, and was a distant third once), and it looks like being the same story in Points, as all she has achieved so far is a 35 lengths last of four. Absent since March. *Miss S.L. Simmons — Cambs with Enfield Chace.* 154 (OMa), 561 (OMa).

WATERLOO LEADER (IRE) ..9-10.. 10 b.g. Supreme Leader — Victor's Valley (Deep Run) pp51p1. Rangy unfurnished brother to Irish NH flat winner, Proud Leader (IRE), and half-brother to Mountainous Valley (IRE) to Irish Pointing winner, Aughnabrogha, and to an Irish NH Flat winner. Dam, half-sister to Valley So Deep (*qv* '92 Annual), won 2m4f Hdle in Ireland. IRISH NH '00 r3 p0. P-t-P '02/3 r6 w1 (Maiden) p1 (2nd); 4th of 5, unseated 2, and pulled up. Failed to finish in five consecutive races after winning his Maiden, but seemed to glean some confidence from a clear round at Mollington, and justified odds-on (!) favouritism in a weak four-runner Restricted at Andoversford. Put another bad jumping round behind him when successful in a three-finisher Intermediate, but will find life much more exacting in future. Suited by an easy surface. *D.P. Smith — Heythrop (Sarah Kellard-Smith).* 109 (CR), 467 (CR), 587 (R), 819 (R), 1059 (I), 1336 (I).

WAYWARD SPREE ..9-10.. 11 b.m. Teenoso (USA) — Garvenish (Balinger) 1u. Small compact. Dam is half-sister to Phil's Dream (*qv* '97 Annual). P-t-P '00 and '02/3 r3 p1 (3rd); and pulled up 2. Has suffered a cracked pelvis, and a check ligament injury, and restricted to a single appearance in each of her three previous campaigns, but rewarded connections patience when making all on her reappearance in softish at Bishops Court. Next seen seven weeks later, and pulled hard in the lead until unseating at the fourth at Woodford, and probably needs to adopt a calmer approach to succeed in Restricteds. *Mrs G. Greenwood — Cotley (Philip Greenwood).* 327 (OMa), 1069 (R).

WEALLWAYSWILLBEONE (IRE) ..9-4§.. 8 ch.g. Commanche Run — Fernhill (IRE) (Good Thyne USA) pp4pp. Good-topped. Dam won Mares Maiden in Ireland. IRISH NH '01 r2 p0; unseated 1. IRISH P-t-P '02 r6 p0; pulled up 4, unseated 1. P-t-P '03 r4 w1 (Maiden) p2; and pulled up. Improved steadily throughout '03 and ended that campaign with a comfortable success in a bad Maiden at Cold Harbour, but disappointing this year, and appeared to suffer a setback when around 12 lengths fourth at Brampton Bryan. Effectively refused to race next time, and flopped when backed from fives to 7-4 at Upper Sapey, where the fast ground was probably unsuitable, but can't possibly be right at present. *Miss V. Champken — Worcs (Martin Oliver).* 294 (R), 530 (R), 665 (R), 925 (R), 1136 (R).

WEAVERS CHOICE .9-7§.. 12 ch.g. Sunley Builds — Wedding Song (True Song) 5ppf52. Tall rangy attractive half-brother to Mullensgrove (*qv*). P-t-P/HUNT CH '99 and '01/3 r17 w3 (Maiden, Restricted and Club Conditional) p5 (3 2nds, of 3 once; and inc 3rd of 4 once); 4th, 5th, 6th, and pulled up 6. Has made much of the running in three minor successes, and goes well fresh, but has proved largely ineffective in Open class, and sulks if he cannot dominate. Unimproved by blinkers at Brampton Bryan, and best left alone in future or until his current mood changes. Does not appreciate sound surfaces. *Mrs J.M. Tice — Pytchley.* 106 (C), 177 (3mH), 374 (O), 650 (O), 886 (Cf), 1112 (C).

WELBURN BOY ..9-8.. 13 b.g. Kalaglow — Teevano (Blakeney) pp4642248. Lengthy unfurnished half-brother to an Italian flat winner. Dam won at 18f. NH FLAT '96 r3 p1 (3rd). NH '96/7 r3 p0; pulled up 1. P-t-P '98 (for Mr N.J.B. & Mr H.C. Duxbury) r9 w1 (Maiden) p3 (2 2nds; and last of 3); 4th, pulled up 2, and fell/unseated 2. NH '98/03 (for M. Sheppard) r32 w2 (3m2f Hdle, and 3m Ch) p5 (inc 4 3rds); pulled up 7, fell/unseated 3. A thorough stayer though little better than a plater under Rules, and pulled up in four of his last seven starts in that sphere, but a fairly reliable jumper, and proved ideal for the new owner to cut her teeth on. Gave his Members rivals a good run for their money, where Lucy Allfrey was at her most enterprising, but otherwise well beaten, and has now failed to score 24 times consecutively. Wears blinkers and a tongue-tie. *Miss L.C. Allfrey — N. Ledbury (Nicky Sheppard).* 110 (Cnr), 613 (L), 697 (L), 843 (L), 1017 (3m2fL), 1137 (L), 1253 (M), 1343 (L), 1391 (L).

WELCOME NEWS ..10-1.. 7 ch.m. Bob Back (USA) — Rosie O'Keeffe (IRE) (Royal Fountain) 21. Workmanlike half-sister to General O'Keeffe. NH FLAT '03 (for Mrs H. Dalton) r2 p0. Short-headed in a Weston Park Maiden by a subsequently bitterly disappointing Home Tor, and should have won, but got out-ridden after the last. Made amends when returning there two weeks later, and showed too much resolution for the reluctant Uncle Ada. Has shown ability to jump and stay, and looks a good thing for a Restricted, but had a curtailed season, so all may not be well with her. *Mrs C. Shaw — Albrighton (Andrew Dalton).* 96 (CfMa), 227 (CfMa).

WELLFIELD LAD ..—.. 7 b.g. Syrtos — Zarbo (Orange Bay) p. Workmanlike angular. Dam, half-sister to Titchwell Molly (*qv* '00 Annual), was placed in three Points for the Owens ('an antiquated maiden'). Tailed off and pulled up three out on a May debut. Not bred to go very fast. *Mr & Mrs J. Owen — Grafton (Jeff Tredwell).* 1275 (OMa).

WELLHESEEMEDSOLOW (IRE) .10-0.. 9 b/br.g. Good Thyne (USA) — Infanta Helena (Pollerton) 11. Workmanlike lengthy half-brother to Hurdling winner, Moorside River (in Ireland), and to all-weather Hurdling winner, Lafanta (IRE). IRISH P-t-P '01 r5 p0 (last, pulled up, fell, ran out, and refused). A bad and temperamental Irish Pointer in '01, and went missing for three years, but proved to be another triumph for the Rowsells. Did not start until the 31st of May, but quickly made up for lost time, and notched a double in an elders Maiden at Bonvilston (after a premature announcement that the vet had withdrawn him at the start proved to be incorrect) and a five-runner Restricted at Trecoed five days later. Has been beating poor rivals with plenty to spare, and may be able to justify his rather high rating when he rises in class. *P. Roberts — Ystrad Taf Fechan (Robert Rowsell).* 1534 (OMa), 1548 (R).

WELL SAID SAM .9-8.. 9 b.g. Weld — Auto Sam (Even Say) pp22f. Half-brother to Ring Sam and Autoscally. Dam won 2m Nov Hurdle. Badly placed and is certainly rushing things in Hunter Chases, but showed some ability when two-and-a-half lengths second at Tabley in one of just two Maiden opportunities, and may be rewarded if campaigned more realistically. Was also 30 lengths last of two behind Pristeen Spy (won four in '04) in his Members, and had no hope of beating that rival, but could surely have been superior to Whatamonkey had he tried the Maiden on the card instead. *P.C. & Mrs S.E. Handley — N. Salop (Peter Handley).* 226 (CfMa), 679 (3m1fH), 753 (OMa), 928 (M), 1375 (3m110yH).

WELL TED (IRE) ..10-8.. 13 ch.g. Carlingford Castle — Pollyfane (Pollerton) 3131. Good-topped. IRISH P-t-P '97 r3 w1 (4&5yo Maiden, looked lucky) p1 (head 2nd); and fell at 1st. IRISH NH FLAT '97 r4 p0. IRISH NH '97 r2 p0. NH '01 r1 p1 (3rd in Hdle). P-t-P '99/03 r20 w8 (inc 4 Opens; also disqualified from further win — not weigh-in) p5 (2 3rds, of 4 once); last, pulled up, and unseated 4. A useful Pointer, and makes the most of his limited opportunities, and took his winning tally into double figures in '04, but remains prone to terrible blunders but for which he would have achieved the feat even quicker. Benefits from expert handling, and is ridden from behind and produced for a turn of foot, and Julian Pritchard has been seen at his best on him. Holds his form well for a veteran, and has his maestro trainer to thank for that, and still likely to be a potent force in '05. Has won in soft but finds sounder surfaces more preferable now. *G.J. Fisher & M. Seabourne — Berkeley (Dick Baimbridge).* 662 (O), 924 (O), 1073 (O), 1471 (O).

WELSH MARCH (IRE) ..9-13.. 13 b.g. Over The River (FR) — Welsh Tan (Welsh Saint) 33p2pb5. Robust half-brother to Welsh Rupert (IRE), to Hurdles winner, Lurpak Legend (IRE), and to a French Hurdles winner. Dam wom 2m1f Hurdle in Ireland. IRISH P-t-P '97 r4 w1 (5&6yo Maiden) p2; and pulled up. NH '97/03 (for G.M. Moore) r34 w5 (2m-2m5f Chses) p14; pulled up 3, fell 2. Won an Irish Point and five U.K. Chases with a maximum of eight runners in the mud to January '01 (three of them at Ayr), but only seen once under Rules after December '02. Normally a sound jumper and used to be a frequent front-runner, but has always been difficult to settle and had some trouble getting the trip in consequence (once fell at the last in a Chase when eight lengths clear but tired). A veteran who extended his losing sequence to 19 after some drab efforts in Points, and after starting the season with a couple of thirds beaten about eight lengths he declined and was an exhausted five lengths second of three in the gales in his Members in which he looked in command until weakening at the last. Acquired cheekpieces on his latest attempt. Looks booked for retirement. *N.D. Tutty — Hurworth (Karen Tutty).* 134 (O), 267 (Cf), 391 (MO), 562 (M), 772 (4m1fO), 1163 (Cf), 1289 (O).

WELSH WARRIOR ..9-4.. 12 b.g. Librate — Mayo Melody (Highland Melody) up. Tall lengthy half-brother to Fathers Footprints, and to Chasing winner, Stardust Roc. FLAT '98 r4 p0 (inc 2 Sells). NH '98 r1 p0 (pulled up 1). P-t-P '00 and '02/3 r35 w3 (Maiden, Restricted and Intermediate) p11 (7 2nds, of 3 thrice, last once; and inc 3rd of 4, and last of 3 once); 4th, 5th, last pair 4, pulled up 6, fell/unseated 8, and carried out. Thrice successful on good or sound surfaces to '02, but subjected to 29 races in a two-year period to the beginning of this year, and it is hardly surprising that the wheels appear to have dropped off now. Error-prone at the best of times, but coerced into numerous mistakes per round by a rider who shows no signs of improving, and will find it difficult to stage a revival at 12. *K. Richards — Llangeinor.* 64 (O), 208 (Cf).

PLATE 131 1485 Tredegar Farmers PPORA Club Members (Nov Rdrs): Wend's Day (Matt Hooper), 1st, is successful on Sunday *PHOTO: John Mullen*

WEND'S DAY (IRE) ..10-6.. 10 br.g. Brief Truce (USA) — Iswara (USA) (Alleged USA) 13. Good-topped half-brother to 2 French flat winners. IR15,000f, IR22,000y. FLAT '98/00 and '02/3 r8 p1 (3rd). NH '99/00 and '02 (for S.E.H. Sherwood, one win, and A.M. Hales, one win) r6 w2 (2m-2m1f Hdles) p1 (2nd). Bought Doncaster, May for 2500. A dual winner over Hurdles including a Claimer, but has only averaged about two outings per annum over the last seven years, and connections were able to purchase him quite cheaply. Made light of a penalty and doubtless landed some worthwhile bets when taking a Novice Riders event on firm at Rhydygwern under a tidy ride from Matt Hooper, but never got into contention when 21 lengths third in a far more competitive contest next time. Wears a tongue-tie. Has probably done the job he was bought for, so the future may be immaterial. *J. Rudge — M.L. Hooper — Croome & W. Warwicks (Jonathan Rudge).* 1485 (Cnr), 1556 (MO).

WENDYS DYNAMO ..—.. 8 b.g. Opera Ghost — Good Appeal (Star Appeal) ppp. Small neat owner-bred half-brother to Kimber Hill Lad. Dam, half-sister to For A Lark (*qv* '95 Annual), won a Maiden in '96 (also placed 5). P-t-P '03 r2 p0 (pulled up 2). Tailed off and pulled up in all five starts, and has no scope for improvement. Wears a cross-noseband. *Mrs W. Murphy — Lamerton (Yvonne Watson & Jo Channon).* 307 (2m4fOMa), 328 (OMa), 486 (OMa).

WENSLEY BLUE (IRE) ..9-5.. 6 b.g. Blues Traveller (IRE) — Almasa (Faustus USA) p506. Strong-topped half-brother to flat winners, Mac's Express and Viva La Diva (in Ireland). Dam won 2 6f races. 5200 2yo. FLAT '01/2 r12 p1 (3rd). NH '02/3 (for P.C. Haslam) r3 w1 (2m5f Hdle) p0. Has only won one of 19 races, a 2m5f Hexham Novices Selling Hurdle by a neck after being given a very aggressive ride by A.P. McCoy. Normally disappointing, and wore blinkers or cheekpieces on three occasions prior to '04. Last in all three Pointing completions and beaten a minimum of 37 lengths, and does not seem to have much interest in the job. *W.M. Aitchison — Border (Joanne Martin).* 210 (Cf), 509 (O), 764 (O), 1038 (O).

WESTAR LAD (IRE) ..8-1.. 9 ch.g. Pips Pride — Mummys Best (Bustino) 2fp. Sturdy brother to Irish flat winner, Rush Brook, and half-brother to flat winner, Tiviski and successful Irish Hurdler Take Your Mark. Dam won 10f race in Ireland. IRISH FLAT '00/2 r12 p0. IRISH NH '00/1 (for P. McCreery) r4 p0; pulled up 1. Never better than sixth in 16 races in Ireland (blinkered once on the flat) and beaten 49 lengths plus in four Hurdles, and although he led for a way in all of his Points he pulled much too hard and never had any hope of getting the trip. Twenty lengths second of three (the third was Wiston Wizo), weakened and took a crashing fall at the 12th and on the ground for several minutes, and again faded when pulled up at the 14th. Subsequently sold in the summer for far more than he is worth (he is actually little better than worthless) and immediately ran a shocker for new connections when 68 lengths seventh in a Hurdle. *H.J. Barton — Pembs (John Moore).* 677 (CfMa), 1027 (OMa), 1193 (OMa).

WESTCOAST ..9-12.. 14 b.g. Handsome Sailor — Pichon (Formidable USA) 24fp. Small neat. Dam half-sister to Quite Right (*qv* '87 Season Annual). FLAT '93, '95 and '01 r11 p2 (3rds). NH '95 and '97/02 r37 w3 (2m5f110y-3m Hdles) p5. P-t-P/HUNT CH '03 r8 p2; last 2, pulled up 2, and fell/unseated 2. Thrice successful over hurdles in blinkers to March '00, but has avoided winning over fences and indeed his last 21 starts over jumps. Error-prone, and wears bandages in Points, and only seems likely to extend the sequence if returned at 14. *O.I.F. Davies — Wheatland (Jo Priest).* 228 (Cf), 660 (Cf), 1228 (4mO), 1344 (C).

WESTER LAD ..—.. 16 b.g. Germont — Lawsuitlaw (Cagirama) ppp. Compact good-bodied brother to Gemma Law and Lethem Laird. P-t-P '95, '97 and '99/03 r10 p0 (4th thrice, pulled up 3, and fell/unseated 4). A sprightly veteran with very few miles on the clock, but races too keenly to get the trip in Points, and has not completed the course since '00. *T. Butt — Border.* 1221 (L), 1311 (OMa), 1423 (M).

WESTERN CHIEF (IRE) ..—.. 11 b.h. Caerleon (USA) — Go Honey Go (General Assembly USA) p*p*. Small neat half-brother to flat winners, Sweet Supposin (won 13 on all-weather), Royal Partnership (won 3 on all-weather), Tasbok and Theatregoer (in Ireland). Dam won at 8f in France and 9f in USA. IR 80,000y. IRISH FLAT '97 (for D.K. Weld) r11 w2 (12f) p2 (short head last of 2 once). FLAT '99 r8 p1 (3rd). NH '98/99 and '01/2 r26 w4 (2 2m Hdles and 2 2m4f-2m5f Chses) p8; pulled up 1, unseated 1. FRENCH NH '04 r1 p0 (pulled up in 2m4f110y Hdle: *prom til wknd aft 6, pu aft 9*). Has had a long and varied career and was four lengths third of 29 in the 29-runner Ascot Stakes during his only English flat campaign, but peaked with four consecutive wins in 16 days in May '99 (three of them were on firmish; a Selling Hurdle was then followed by three Chases at around 2m4f). Has never scored since, and after missing '03 he was pulled up twice in '04, once in a Hurdle at Pau and once in Ladies Open at Larkhill. Often wore headgear to '98 but never since, and is frequently tongue-tied. Still comparatively young, but gives the impression of being a spent force. *D.L. Williams — Windsor & Chiltern Bloodhounds.* 10 (L).

WESTERN FRONTIER (IRE) ..9-10.. 6 ch.g. Shernazar — Bucks Slave (Buckskin FR) 4u15p. Tall lengthy half-brother to Chasing winner, Toulouse-Lautrec (IRE). Dam won Mares Maiden in Ireland.

Sold Doncaster, May 11,000 (M. Bosley). Had a reasonable season for a five-year-old newcomer, and won a youngsters Maiden on firm at Didmarton by a neck after Jamie Snowden had driven him past three rivals from approaching the omitted last, but the form did not work out, and his jumping can still be rather hit and miss. May be more prominent in Restricteds at six. *M.J. O'Connor — Mendip F. (Caroline Keevil).* 66 (OMa), 329 (OMa), 368 (OMa), 601 (R), 966 (R).

WESTERTON (IRE) ..10-6.. 12 b.g. Glacial Storm (USA) — Killiney Rose (Buckskin FR) 5p. Good-bodied short-backed. Dam won Irish NH flat, and is half-sister to Chief Ironside (*qv* '95 Annual). NH FLAT '98 r3 w1 p1 (2nd). NH '98/01 r9 w1 (2m4f110y Hdle) p2. HUNT CH '03 r4 w2 (3m1f) p1 (last of 3); and pulled up. Never runs much, but a game battler on his day, and made the enterprising journey to Kelso pay off in the second of two Hunter Chase victories in '03. Not seen since appearing twice in February this year, and his well being can never be taken for granted. Prone to making mistakes. Suited by easy surfaces. *Mr & Mrs F.A. Hutsby & Mrs P. Corbett — Warwicks (Fred Hutsby).* 107 (O), 241 (2m4f110yH).

WESTFIELD JOHN ..10-2.. 10 ch.g. Little Wolf — Moonbreaker (Twilight Alley) pp411p. Tall rangy half-brother to Tycoon Moon (dam of The Commentator, *qv* '03 Annual), Linlithgow Palace, Rawyards Brig and Whiskey Galore. NH FLAT '00/1 r3 p0. NH '01/2 r4 p1 (3rd); ran out 1. P-t-P/HUNT CH '03 r9 w3 (3-finisher Maiden, Restricted and dead-heat Confined) p5 (2 2nds, inc a Hunt Ch); and pulled up. An expensive failure in the previous yard, but has found his level in Points, and returned to form when blinkers were applied and backed from nines to 6-1 when scoring unchallenged in the fastest time of the day at Higham. Again benefited from the strong handling of James Owen next time, but was often wayward under Rules, and it may not pay to trust him too far in future. Suited by top of the ground. *J.M. Turner — Suffolk.* 38 (Cf), 124 (CCon), 248 (Cf), 400 (C), 647 (Cf), 892 (2m5f110yH).

PLATE 132 653 Lanarkshire & Renfrewshire and Eglinton Members: Westie and Luke Morgan, 1st, who led all the way take the first fence in the first ever race at Overton from The Midnite Grocer (R. Westwood), ur, and Tursal (Miss J. Campbell), 2nd PHOTO: Alan Mitchell

WESTIE .9-9.. 9 b.m. Primitive Rising (USA) — Easterly Gael (Tudor Music) pp14fp. Small workmanlike home-bred sister to Si Celia, and half-sister to Mummy's Toy Boy and The Coventry Flyer, and to Chasing winner, Timanfaya. Dam won 11f Sell, and 6 2m-2m4f Hdles, inc 3 Sells (fell 2 out when leading in her only other Hdle). P-t-P '02/3 r8 w2 (Maiden and Members) p3 (2 2nds of 3, beaten head once); and pulled up 3. Successful in two of the last three runnings of her Members, but had much the best rider in the '04 renewal, and never looked in danger despite hitting several fences. Has generally struggled in a higher grade, but was in the process of running well when falling two out at Balcormo Mains, but may have suffered a setback next time. *Miss F. Deans — Eglinton (Jackie Williamson).* 133 (L), 212 (R), 653 (M), 766 (R), 1077 (R), 1419 (R).

WESTINGTON ..9-0.. 12 b.g. Relief Pitcher — Truelyn (True Song) f5pp. Workmanlike lengthy brother to Exmoor Forest, and half-brother to Margery Copse, Silver Baron and Leasebourne. Dam pulled up in 2 Points. P-t-P '00/3 r13 p0 (4th, 5th, last pair 4, pulled up 2 and fell/unseated 5). Has displayed ability, but highly perilous over fences, and has returned with an empty saddle on six occasions. Not better than last in '04, and looks too long in the tooth to open his account. Wears a cross-noseband. *Miss C.V. Hart — N. Cotswold.* 52 (OMa), 258 (CMa), 668 (OMa), 1340 (OMa).

WEST PAL (IRE) ..9-7§.. 11 ch.g. Lancastrian — Buck And Roll (Buckskin FR) 64fpp. Big rangy plain. Dam half-sister to Mossiman (*qv* '98 Annual). IRISH P-t-P '00/1 r5 p1 (2nd); last, and fell/unseated 3. IRISH NH FLAT '01 r2 p0. IRISH NH '01 r4 p0; pulled up 1, fell 2. P-t-P '03 (for Mr T.D.B. Underwood) r2 w1 (Maiden) p0; and fell. Error-prone and untalented in Ireland, and began his English career with a fall when the subject of a market move, but did little wrong when successfully paired with Phillip York at Kingston Blount next time. Way out of his depth and not better than last in Hunter Chases in which his jumping was once again put under tremendous strain, and desperately needs to return to Points. Acquired blinkers after his latest fall, and effectively refused to race at Huntingdon. *Mrs S.J. Humphrey — Worcs.* 437 (3m1fH), 679 (3m1fH), 1029 (3mH), 1441 (3m7fH), 1497 (3mH).

WESTWOOD LIR ..—.. 8 b.m. Lir — Brandy Season (High Season) p. Dam, 'moody and untrustworthy', was placed in 2 of 19 Points for Mr Sluggett. Bred from a bad mare, and was tongue-tied when tailed off and pulled up on her debut. It was a costly day for the owner, who copped a £50 fine for having an 'illegal' bridle. *Wide Valley Racing (J. Sluggett) — S. Devon (Amanda Barnett).* 701 (2m4fOMa).

WEXFORD (IRE) ..—.. 11 ch.g. Be My Native (USA) — Mizuna (Ballymore) p6p. Hobdayed half-brother to Lord Earth (IRE), to Irish Pointing winner, Laura Croft, to Irish NH flat winner, Crosschild, and to Irish jumping winner, Halfpenny Bridge. Dam, half-sister to Generous Scot (*qv* '97 Annual), won 14f race in Ireland. IRISH NH FLAT '99 r1 p0. IRISH NH '99/02 r18 p4; pulled up 2, fell 1. P-t-P/HUNT CH '03 r5 p0 (pulled up 5). Placed thrice in succession in Ireland in '00, but blinkered in the latest, and had already been tried tongue-tied, and only placed once in more in 19 subsequent starts. A complete waste of time now. *Miss S.K. Lamb — Percy.* 854 (M), 916 (L), 1225 (OMa).

WHAT A CHARMER (IRE) .—.. 9 b.g. Be My Native (USA) — Deadly Charm (USA) (Bates Motel USA) ppp. Good-topped. Dam won 4 2m Hurdles and 4 Chases, 2m-2m5f. IRISH P-t-P '03 r1 w1 (7yo Maiden). IRISH HUNT CH '03 (for E.J. O'Grady) r1 p0 (unseated). Made a winning debut in what was probably a very poor contest, and has never been able to get round the course since. Gave the impression that there was something wrong with him in '04, and reported to have lost both his front shoes (to the embarrassment of his trainer) on his first outing. *J.E. Dillon & Miss K. Talbot — Fernie (John Dillon).* 127 (R), 252 (CR), 375 (R).

WHATAFELLOW (IRE) .9-10§.. 15 ch.g. Arapahos (FR) — Dara's March (March Parade) p3. Good-bodied brother to Ourownfellow (IRE), to Irish Pointing winner, Ardmore Princess, and half-brother to Bishop Town Boy. Dam won 3 Irish Points and placed 7. IRISH P-t-P '94/5 r7 w1 (4yo Maiden on disqualification) p2 (3rds); pulled up 2. P-t-P/HUNT CH '96/00 and '02/3 (for Mr G.M. Samuel) r47 w19 (inc 3m2f Hunt Ch and 9 Opens, inc 5-timer '99) p18 (10 2nds, last once); pulled up 1, fell 4 (would have won once). Took his winning tally to 20 when defeating subsequent Chasing winner Step Quick at Dunstall Park in '02, but most unpredictable at times, and hung right and found nil when his customary blinkers were left off on his latest appearance. Did not seem the sort that Sarah Edwards would gel with, and has presumably slinked off into retirement. *Mrs S.L. Edwards — Tanatside (Gordy Edwards).* 228 (Cf), 526 (M).

WHAT A FUSS ..—.. 12 b.g. Great Commotion (USA) — Hafwah (Gorytus USA) pp. Stocky half-brother to flat winners, Courageous Dancer and Rupan. FLAT '96/7 and '99/00 (for B. Hanbury when successful) r16 w2 (7-11f) p4. NH '97/01 (for Miss H.C. Knight, one win, M.W. Easterby, 2 wins, and P.J. Hobbs, one win) r26 w4 (2m-2m6f Hdle and 3 2m2f Chses) p4; pulled up 4, fell 1. The winner of six races to '01, including one on the all-weather (also short-headed on that surface), but has had wind problems and suffered from a fibrillating heart, and was reappearing after a three year absence when he pulled up twice in Points. Looks certain to slink back into retirement. *Mrs C.A. Coward — Middleton.* 479 (L), 770 (Cf).

WHATAMONKEY ..9-9.. 12 gr.g. Thethingaboutitis (USA) — Shrood Biddy (Sharrood USA) p1p. Half-brother to Wizadora. Dam is half-sister to Sunlight Express (*qv* '94 Annual). P-t-P '00 and '02/3 r8 p3 (2 2nds, beaten head of 3 once); 4th, last, and pulled up 3. Averages fewer than three outings a year, and had previously been the victim of several injudicious rides, but the owner timed his challenge just right at Eyton, and the form was boosted when the runner-up scored at the next meeting. Will not find it easy to upgrade successfully. Wears cheekpieces. *P. Morris — Albrighton.* 463 (OMa), 934 (OMa), 1358 (3m1f110yH).

WHAT A MOVER ..10-12.. 9 b.m. Jupiter Island — Si-Gaoith (Strong Gale) 1131. Compact. Dam is half-sister to Quick Quay (*qv* '95 Annual). Grandam, Ruby Rossa, won an Irish Point. P-t-P '02/3 r7 w3 (Maiden, Restricted and Intermediate) p2 (last of 3 once); pulled up 2. A smart performer on top of the ground and predictably proved suited to the lighter weights in Ladies races, and only beaten once in her last seven starts. Stays well, and found things happening too quickly on the short Lifton circuit, but stuck to her guns well at Bratton Down subsequently despite Polly Gundry having dropped her whip a mile out. Not a fluent jumper, and probably never will be, and Hunter Chasing does not seem an option, but sure to remain hard to beat when the right conditions prevail in '05. Four miles at Flete Park would be ideal. *T. Hamlin, J.M. Dare & J. Snook — E. Devon (Ollie Bush).* 48 (3m5f70yL), 635 (L), 822 (L), 1379 (MO).

WHAT A NIGHT ..8-4.. 6 gr.g. Environment Friend — Misty Night (Grey Desire) p5. Dam won 6 Points including 3 Ladies (one 3m5f) and placed 6 (inc 2 flat and Hurdle); and Pointed for Bowie family. Started at 3-1 or less in both Maidens, but was 35 lengths last when achieving a completion. Bred from a useful mare and is in a knowledgeable yard, and it would be no surprise at all if he could do better. *J.P.G. & Mrs A.C. Hamilton & J. Bowie — Buccleuch (Alison Hamilton).* 659 (OMa), 856 (2m4fOMa).

WHAT NEXT (IRE) ..8-7.. 8 b.g. Beau Sher — Sandywish (Sandalay) 2u4p. Small neat. IRISH P-t-P '02/3 r9 p2 (2nds); pulled up 3, fell 1. Beaten two lengths and three lengths in his Irish seconds, but was 30 lengths adrift of the very easy winner, Esendi, on his debut for the new stable, and has faired even worse since, notably when reappearing from a ten-week absence at Catsfield where he jumped badly left at times and never got out of last place. Despite having made the frame on seven occasions '03/4, he still has a great deal to prove. *N.A.E & Mrs A. Jones — E. Sussex & Romney Marsh (Sara Hickman).* 26 (OMa), 39 (OMa), 128 (OMa), 1055 (OMa).

WHATS THE FUSS (IRE) ..—.. 7 b.m. Montelimar (USA) — Camden Beg (IRE) (Camden Town) p. Tall workmanlike. IRISH P-t-P '03 r2 p1 (3rd). Bought Doncaster, May for 7000. Last in both Irish Points beaten between 15 and 23 lengths, and showed nothing before pulling up after two miles in her back garden in March. *Lord Yarborough — Brocklesby (Mark Bennison).* 476 (CfMa).

WHAT'S THE PROBLEM (IRE) ..—.. 12 b.g. Yashgan — Woodcliffe (Harwell) p. Tall strong half-brother to Mont Mirail and Miss Huntcliffe, and to Irish Pointing and English Chasing winner, Deep Cliff. IRISH P-t-P '99/00 r5 w1 (7yo&up Maiden) p2; pulled up 2. NH '00/1 r2 p0 (pulled up 2). P-t-P '02/3 (for Mr M.J. Tozer) r7 p1 (3rd of 4); 4th, last 3, and pulled up 2. A typically excitable Yashgan, and has been to as many sales rings as racecourses, and only went two miles once in '04. Finishes last or pulls up as often as not, and his 9-9 rating has been withdrawn. *K. & Mrs T. Dilworth — W. Street Tickham (Keith Dilworth).* 102 (R).

WHATS UP JAKE ..8-9§.. 9 ch.g. Gunner B — Head Lass (Funny Man) p464p. Stocky half-brother to Moorside Lad. Dam pulled up and fell in Points. P-t-P '03 (for Mr S. Wynne) r5 p0 (4th, pulled up 3, and unseated). Bred to stay well and be suited by mud, but afflicted by sore shins in '03, and does not appear to have much in the way of ability. Wore cheekpieces thrice in '03. Wears a cross-noseband. *D. Manning — Sir W.W. Wynn's (Steve Wynne).* 532 (OMa), 848 (OMa), 1044 (OMa), 1232 (OMa), 1425 (OMa).

WHATS UP MAID ..8-8.. 8 b.m. Emperor Fountain — Roman Maid (Roman Warrior) ppp32. Small compact. Dam won 3 Points (including match for Open) and placed 4, but also failed to finish 23, and ran out all 3 attempts in final season. NH FLAT '01 r1 p0. P-t-P '03 r2 p0 (pulled up 2). Pulled up in her first five Points, and 30 lengths third of four, and three lengths second over 2m4f since. Short Maidens are no longer on the menu and does not appear to have the stamina for the full trip. Wears a cross-noseband. *H.S. & N.F. Channon — Lamerton (Yvonne Watson & Jo Channon).* 82 (OMa), 308 (2m4fOMa), 485 (OMa), 796 (CfMa), 910 (2m4fOMa).

WHAT WILL BE (IRE) ..9-0.. 11 ch.g. Denel (FR) — Catree Cottage (Cantab) 5p. Good-topped. NH '99 r2 p0 (last and pulled up). P-t-P '99 and '01/3 r8 w1 (3-finisher Maiden) p1 (3rd); 4th, 5th and pulled up 4. Landed a gamble from sevens to 7-2 when successful in a three-finisher soft ground Maiden taking eight minutes at Towcester in '03, but stands his racing badly, and has proved too slow for more conventional events. *Mrs C.L. Goodinson — N. Hereford.* 95 (R), 231 (CR).

WHERESBOB ..—§§.. 11 ch.g. Jumbo Hirt (USA) — Cathys Clown (Moray Mink) pfp. Strong compact. P-t-P '00 (for Mrs M. Robinson) r4 p0 (ran out 2, and pulled up 2). Had not been inflicted on the jockey population for four years, but did his best to rearrange Lynsey Kendall's looks at Friars Haugh, and will hopefully not be allowed to return to wreak havoc again. Acquired headgear in '04. *Mrs A.J. McMath — Cumberland (Ian McMath).* 71 (L), 286 (CfMa), 431 (R).

PLATE 133 286 Berwickshire Confined Maiden (Div 1): Wheresbob (Lynsey Kendall), fell, leads round the first bend PHOTO: Alan Mitchell

WHETHER THE STORM (IRE) ..10-7.. 9 b.g. Glacial Storm (USA) — Minimum Choice (IRE) (Miner's Lamp) 14138. Strong brother to Chasing winner, Tallow Bay, and half-brother to All-Inclusive (IRE). Dam, half-sister to Buckland Filleigh (*qv* '97 Annual). NH FLAT '00 r2 p1 (3rd). NH '00 and '02/3 (for Miss H.C. Knight) r6 w1 (2m3f Hdle) p0; pulled up 1. Won a Hurdle in soft in December '00, but beaten 40 lengths plus in just four subsequent attempts under Rules after vanishing for 13 months. Showed he retains substantial ability when doing well for the new yard, and won a highly competitive Ladies at Thorpe from Find Me Another and Upton Adventure, and also urged ahead in the final stride for a short head victory at Bangor, but got much too far behind when beaten at 4-7 in between. Lacks consistency, but exceptionally lightly raced in the past and said to have had bleeding problems, and could doubtless have achieved a great deal had he always been healthy. *Miss I.E.L. Craig — R.A.* 108 (L), 206 (L), 435 (3m110yH), 747 (3m1f110yH), 1168 (2m5fH).

WHICH MOSCOW (IRE) .—.. 8 ch.g. Moscow Society (USA) — Beguiled (IRE) (Be My Guest USA) pp. Tall strong half-brother to Irish flat winners, Trickery, Life Closs and Ten Tricks. IRISH P-t-P '02/3 r2 p1 (2nd); and pulled up. Finished three lengths second in an Irish Point in Autumn '02, but a major disappointment when pulled up in a mere three attempts since. Looks the part and was backed from 6s to 5-2 favourite on his latest attempt, but was struggling after two miles, and seems to have some physical disability at present. *The Just One More Club (Miss A.V. Handel) — W. Somerset (Alison Handel).* 275 (CfMa), 962 (OMa).

WHICH POCKET (IRE) ..9-4.. 7 br.g. Norwich — Toran Pocket (Proverb) 51. Good-topped. Dam won Mares Maiden in Ireland. Bought Goffs Ireland, Jun '02 for 5550. Made an encouraging start at Dunthrop in January, and confirmed the promise with a win in a youngsters Maiden at Bitterley in mid-April (backed from 4-1 to half that price). The five behind him have disappointingly failed to score since, but some of them looked as if they would do better in '05, and he should have further scope himself. *A.D. Peachey — N. Cotswold.* 53 (2m4fOMa), 837 (OMa).

WHITEBARN VIXEN (IRE) ..8-0.. 8 b.m. Executive Perk — Whitebarn Run (Pollerton) 3. Sister to Pollerton Run (IRE) (*qv*). IRISH P-t-P '02/3 r3 p1 (3rd; pulled up 1. IRISH NH '02 (for S. Aherne) r2 p0. Finished one-and-a-half fences last of three at Llanfrynach, where she started proceedings by throwing herself down in the paddock. Not a gay day for Chris Penycate who was unceremoniously dumped at the first fence by Gay Abandon on his only other mount. *R.J. Rowsell — Ystrad Taf Fechan.* 454 (CfMa).

WHITEGATES WILLIE ..9-13.. 13 b.g. Buckskin (FR) — Whitegates Lady (Le Coq D'Or) p541pp. Compact half-brother to Hurdles winners, Whitegate's Son and Whitegatesprincess (IRE). Dam, sister to Ardesee (*qv* '98 Annual), won 2 2m4f Hdles. NH FLAT '96 r3 p0. NH '96/8 r13 p4 (Chses, to 2m5f). P-t-P/HUNT CH '99/00 and '02 r11 w3 (inc Open) p0 (5th, pulled up 6, and fell). Unbeaten in three Pointing completions '00/2, and given a good ride by David Greenway to score at Heslaker in '04, but frequently affected by broken blood vessels, and is a very risky betting medium. Stays well and is suited by easy ground, but often pulls too hard for his own good, and is thoroughly exposed in Hunter Chases. *W. Puddifer Jnr — Cheshire Forest (Peter Morris).* 251 (C), 750 (O), 1045 (Cf), 1202 (Cf), 1375 (3m110yH), 1457 (O).

WHITLEYGRANGE GIRL ..7-6.. 8 b.m. Rudimentary (USA) — Choir's Image (Lochnager) 5pp. Dam is half-sister to Murphys Way (*qv* '01 Annual). FLAT '00/1 r7 p0. NH '01 r1 p0 (pulled up). P-t-P '03 r1 p0 (pulled up). Useless on the flat, and 18 lengths last in a short Maiden, but pulled up in four other attempts over jumps, and looked decidedly mulish when planting herself in the paddock at Dalton Park once. *Miss G.T. Lee — Hurworth.* 343 (2m4fOMa), 505 (CMa), 1162 (R).

WHIZZIE LITE ..—.. 8 b.m. Opera Ghost — Paddy's Apple (Paddy's Stream) R. Workmanlike. Dam, half-sister to Bay Blossom (*qv* '97 Annual), failed to finish in 8 of 9 Points. P-t-P '03 r2 p0 (unseated, and pulled up). Proved impossible to steer on the bend leaving the back straight at Holnicote, and whilst she may have some ability is slowly making her way towards mother's unenviable record. *J.W. Haydon & Miss E.C. White — W. Somerset (Chris White).* 275 (CfMa).

WHO DARES WINS ..10-5.. 12 b.g. Kala Shikari — Sarah's Venture (Averof) 64273831p. Workmanlike half-brother to Molly's Adventure and Radbrook Hall. Dam won 7 12f races, and won 2 2m Hurdles. NH FLAT '98 r3 p3. NH '98/03 (for T.R. George, both wins, and C. Grant) r27 w2 (3m2f Chses) p16; unseated 1, pulled up 1. Won two 3m2f Chases in heavy in '00, but barely able to creep home in the Uttoxeter mire (three finished) in the latest. Also placed on 19 occasions, but lost his form latterly, and took a while to regain it in '04. Showed what he can do when he puts his mind to it when beating Sad Mad Bad by five lengths in a Hexham Hunter Chase, but had previously finished 11 lengths third to that rival over 3m3f at Sedgefield. Ended the season by pulling up when a fence adrift in a three-runner Confined in which he started at 4-6, and the rider felt he had gone lame, although he appeared to recover afterwards. Blinkered twice in '99, and wore cheekpieces once in '03. Unreliable and unpredictable, but can boast an excellent completion record of 33 from 36 attempts over jumps (unseated once and pulled up twice in the exceptions). *J.A.V. Duell — S.*

Durham (Sarah Duell). 72 (O), 122 (3m1fH), 267 (Cf), 389 (Cf), 542 (3m3fH), 772 (4m1fO), 894 (3m3fH), 1179 (3m1fH), 1413 (Cf).

WHO LET THE DOGOUT ..—§.. 9 ch.g. Romany Rye — Dark Spinster (Captain Drake) uff. Tall rangy. Dam, (*qv* '92 Annual), failed to finish in 4 Points for R. Jones. Grandam, Beckon, won 2 Adjacents and placed 3 for him (her 3 Pointing foals managed 2 lasts and 22 non-completions!). P-t-P '02/3 r4 w1 (Maiden) p0; pulled up 2 and unseated. Won a three-finisher Maiden at Rhydygwern on only his second attempt, but a non-finisher in six other starts, and for the second year running went no more than two miles in '04. Reports of his death have been greatly exaggerated. *R. Williams-Jones — Llangeinor.* 50 (I), 207 (R), 1538 (R).

WHO'S EDDIE (IRE) ..9-9.. 8 b.g. Jolly Jake (NZ) — Rare Choice (IRE) (Rare One) 14343. Strong. Dam, half-sister to Smokey Thunder (*qv* '98 Annual). IRISH P-t-P '02 r5 p3 (2nds); unseated 1. P-t-P '03 r3 p2 (2nds); and 4th. Finally broke his duck, after an array of placings, when all out to repel Noble Action at Larkhill, but typically weak at finishing since, and failed to slip the field sufficiently on his latest appearance. A reliable jumper but may have to toil long and hard to be rewarded in a Restricted. Wears a cross-noseband. *Mrs K.M. Price — N. Cotswold (Harry Wheeler).* 142 (OMa), 383 (R), 601 (R), 925 (R), 1256 (R).

WIBBLEY WOBBLEY .10-0.. 13 b.g. Arctic Lord — Burrow Star (Four Burrow) 4u2p21. Workmanlike lengthy owner-bred. Dam won 5 minor Points (3 as a 12-year-old) and 2nd. P-t-P/HUNT CH '98/03 r29 w7 (inc Open) p8 (4 2nds, short-headed once; inc 3rd of 4 once); pulled up 2, refused 1, ran out 2, and fell/unseated 4. In top form when winning four races by an aggregate of 95 lengths in '00, and has managed an annual success since, but although often error-prone has a good record with novice riders, and provided Laura Ellis with her first winner at Kingston Blount. Worth campaigning more regularly in novice riders races as they often take little winning. Acts on firmish, and in softish, but needs to go left-handed. *T. Ellis — Warwicks.* 56 (C), 253 (L), 466 (Cf), 650 (O), 838 (L), 1104 (Cnr).

WICKED IMP ..9-2.. 13 ch.g. Scallywag — Naughty Niece (Bribe) p724p. Half-brother to Best Boy. Dam won 3m1f Hunt Ch and 8 Opens and placed 8. Grandam, Aunty Angel, failed to finish in 3 Points. NH FLAT '98 r2 p1 (2nd). NH '98/01 r11 p1 (2nd). P-t-P '97 and '03 r4 w2 (Maiden and Members) p0; last, and pulled up. Won a Maiden in '97, and runner-up in two of his first three starts under Rules, but failed to live up to expectations, and only successful in one of his next 21 starts. Beaten 30 lengths when runner-up at Cotley Farm, and a Restricted looks well beyond his capabilities now. *E. Wonnacott — Spooners & W. Dartmoor (Diane Wilson).* 323 (R), 912 (R), 1251 (R), 1435 (R), 1558 (R).

WILD BLADE (IRE) .8-9§§.. 12 ch.g. Meneval (USA) — Tuney Blade (Fine Blade USA) p6p345u8. Tall good-topped brother to Whatasucker (IRE), and half-brother to Mid Summer Lark (IRE) and Trust Fund (IRE). Dam is half-sister to Staigue Fort (*qv* '00 Annual). NH FLAT '98 r2 w1 (finished 2nd, awarded race) p0. NH '98/02 r14 w1 (2m4f Hdle) p1 (3rd). P-t-P '03 r6 p2; last pair 2, refused, and pulled up. Gained his only won on merit over hurdles in '99, and has displayed minimal enthusiasm in Points in which he does not get the trip. Only effective on firm ground, but makes lots of sketchy or slow jumps, and is easy to omit from calculations. Wears cheekpieces and a cross-noseband, and acquired a tongue-tie on his last two starts. *R.G. Jenkins — Ledbury (Nicky Sheppard).* 19 (CMod), 190 (C), 359 (Cf), 513 (Cf), 722 (M), 1344 (C), 1392 (C), 1528 (Cf).

WILD CHIMES (IRE) ..9-12.. 6 b.g. Oscar (IRE) — Jingle Bells (FR) (In The Mood FR) fu213. Workmanlike half-brother to 4 winners in France (3 of them over jumps). Dam won jump race in France. NH FLAT '04 (for P.F. Nicholls) r1 p1 (3rd over 2m2f at Plumpton: *hld up & bhnd, hdwy u.p 6f out, ev ch 2f out, one pce*). Bought Doncaster, May for 9500. Beaten favourite in his first three races, and fell three out when two lengths second and closing, unseated at the fourth when proving difficult to settle, and three lengths second at 4-5 after being virtually tailed off at the eighth and then making mistakes at three of the final four obstacles when attempting to get on terms. Finally got it right when 4-5 in a Buckfastleigh Maiden, but supporters must have had their hearts in their mouths when he pitched onto his nose briefly three out. Joined Paul Nicholls for a bumper and finished three-and-a-quarter lengths third after holding every chance, and this promising run over an inadequate trip marks him down as a probable scorer over Hurdles. At his normal cramped odds it will be hard to get rich from backing him. *D. Chown — Cattistock (Richard Barber).* 13 (OMa), 87 (OMa), 325 (OMa), 492 (OMa).

WILD EDGAR (IRE) ..10-5.. 8 ch.g. Invited (USA) — Ou La La (IRE) (Be My Native USA) 21p2f. Sturdy. IRISH P-t-P '02 r4 w1 (5yo Maiden) p1 (3rd); fell 1. P-t-P '03 r1 p0 (pulled up). Won in yielding in Ireland, and was clearly under the weather in '03, but almost scored at Friars Haugh on his reappearance, and made no mistake when coming home totally unchallenged at the next meeting there. Subsequently missing for seven weeks, and ran as though in need of the race when returning, but back to form when splitting Crevamoy and Son Of Anshan at Corbridge, and would probably have been placed but for tripping up approaching the last on his Hunter Chase debut. Gets terribly worked up in the preliminaries, and tends to race too freely, but certainly looks speedy enough to tackle sub-3m races again. Possibly inconvenienced by mud. *A.R. Trotter — Haydon (Tim Reed).* 132 (CR), 283 (R), 915 (Cf), 1038 (O), 1177 (2m5fH).

WILD EDRIC ..9-7§.. 13 b.g. Weld — Paper Lady (Document) p34f5157. Dam won 2 Points and placed 8 for Lucy McFarlane; was previously 2nd in an Irish Hdle, and in an English Maiden. P-t-P '97/8, '00 and '02/3 r23 w5 (Maiden, Restricted, Intermediate and 2 Members) p11 (7 3rds; of 4 thrice, last once); 5th, 8th, last, refused and pulled up 3. Recorded his fourth success at Brampton Bryan when landing his Members for a third time in '04, but most unimpressive in his execution, and would probably have been worried out of it had a rival not unseated when upsides two out. Otherwise beaten 17 lengths plus, and proved most reluctant on occasions, and looks to have been soured for good. Wears blinkers, and has been tried in cheekpieces. *Mrs R.M. McFarlane - United (Lucy McFarlane).* 93 (O), 229 (O), 528 (O), 660 (Cf), 835 (Cf), 1109 (M), 1228 (4mO), 1392 (C).

WILD IMAGINATION ..—.. 7 b.g. Royal Fountain — Bright Polly (Politico USA) p. Mother was useless in 15 races over jumps, and looked as if he might become a straggler himself after eventually pulling up when a fence behind in a Musselburgh Maiden. *The Should Be Fun Group (C. Storey) — College V. & N. Northumberland (Clive Storey).* 510 (OMa).

WILFIE WILD .9-6.. 9 b.g. Nomadic Way (USA) — Wild Child (Grey Ghost) 2263p. Sturdy brother to Wandering Wild (*qv*). P-t-P/HUNT CH '02/3 r10 w1 (Maiden) p2; 4th twice, 5th, 6th, 7th, and pulled up 2. Sprang a 20-1 surprise when landing a three-finisher Maiden taking 7min 42sec in soft at Wetherby on his racecourse debut, but out of luck in 14 subsequent outings, and despite his rider's wild urgings could not peg back Crevamoy on his most noteworthy appearance in '04. Stays well and has no jumping deficiencies, but it is possible that he has been bottomed already. *A. Jackson — Cleveland (Lynne Ward).* 70 (R), 268 (R), 389 (Cf), 503 (R), 810 (R).

WILLIAM LIONHEART ..10-7.. 11 b.g. Henbit (USA) — Come To Tea (IRE) (Be My Guest USA) f211. Tall workmanlike. Dam won 7f race in Ireland. NH FLAT '99 r2 p0. NH '00 r4 p0. P-t-P '02 (for Mr G.P. Galpin & Mrs J. Dowson) r5 w2 (3-finisher Maiden and Restricted) p2; and ran out. NH '02/3 (for Mrs J. Galpin) r7 p0; pulled up 1, unseated 1. Of no account in two spells under Rules, but has recorded Pointing doubles in '02 and '04, and typically improved since joining the current set up. Looked assured of victory until falling two out on his reappearance, but lost no caste in defeat to Christy Beamish, and made all at a punishing gallop to score at Paxford and Woodford. Shows none of the usual Henbit traits, and further success should be a formality, though never likely to be sent off at a realistic price. *N.E.J. Cook — Berkeley (Dick Baimbridge).* 251 (C), 728 (I), 922 (I), 1070 (M).

WILLIE THE KID ..9-1.. 6 b.g. Overbury (IRE) — The Dizzy Mole (IRE) (Salluceva) pfu. Homebred half-brother to Migsy Malone. Pulled up at the 11th and fell at the third in his first two Maidens, but seemed to be in the process of giving a better display when he unseated four out in five lengths third at Cold Harbour. Obviously has jumping problems to address, but can possibly do better if becoming more proficient. *R.N. Jukes — V. of Clettwr (Beverley Thomas).* 202 (CfMa), 1067 (OMa), 1232 (OMa).

WILLOUGHBY FLYER .9-9.. 7 b.g. Homo Sapien — Jane's Daughter (Pitpan) p3222. Good-topped half-brother to Trigger Castle (*qv*). IR2300 3yo. NH '02/3 (for J.R. Upson) r4 p0; pulled up 2. Hopelessly tailed off at odds of 50-1 or more in Hurdles (seventh, last and pulled up twice), but much more effective in Maidens, and placed in four consecutively (favourite for the final three). Has a habit of getting outpaced with about half-a-mile to run, but can rally and stay on steadily, and might have finally broken his duck at Bredwardine had he not been out-ridden in the vital stages. Becoming rather irritating, but is a good jumper with no stamina worries, and connections will surely be rewarded eventually. *P. Ponting — Curre & Llangibby (Robin Butterworth).* 121 (OMa), 368 (OMa), 699 (CfMa), 1074 (OMa), 1394 (OMa).

WILLOW RYDE (IRE) .9-2.. 7 b.g. Presenting — Willowmere (IRE) (King's Ride) 362p2. Compact well-made. Dam, half-sister to Whistling Eddy (*qv* '99 Annual). Sold Doncaster May '02 14,000 (H Daly). Has become frustrating since finishing 12 lengths third on his debut, and did not show much resolution in his next three attempts including when left a very remote last of two at Garthorpe. Acquired cheekpieces on his latest attempt and led at a very slow pace in a Dingley Maiden, but was collared close home and beaten a neck. Looks low on battling qualities, but has the ability to score if he feels so inclined. *Mrs A. Vaughan-Jones — W. Norfolk (Caroline Bailey).* 128 (OMa), 245 (CfMa), 685 (OMa), 945 (OMa), 1218 (OMa).

WILL SHAKESPEARE ..9-3.. 8 b.g. Minster Son — Sudberry Lady (IRE) (Commanche Run) p4uu. Sturdy compact. Dam third twice in Irish NH flat races. P-t-P '03 r2 p1 (3rd); and last. Coming along steadily, and would surely have been involved in the finish at Maisemore Park, but still inclined to make errors, and not seen since the end of March. A trouble-free round should ensure he opens his account in '05. Wears a cross-noseband. *G.D. Taylor & Ms G. Hill — Seavington (Chloe Newman).* 172 (OMa), 325 (OMa), 493 (OMa), 724 (OMa).

WILL YOU COME ON (IRE) ..7-12.. 7 br.m. Carroll House — Tengello (Bargello) 6p. Very small neat half-sister to Cumberland Blues (IRE), to Irish Pointing and English Hurdles winner, Galway Gal, to Irish Pointing and Chasing winner, Bobbie Magee (IRE), to Hurdles winner, Border Star (IRE), and to Irish flat and NH flat winner, Grangemills. Dam won 2m Hurdle in Ireland. Bought Tattersalls Ireland, Aug '02 for 2453. Tailed off in both attempts including when last on her debut (made errors), and although she comes from a super family her pony-sized stature seems likely to consign her to the also-rans. *J.A. Danahar — Worcester & W. Farmers.* 408 (CMam), 982 (2m5fOMa).

WILTON BRIDGE (IRE) ..9-12.. 11 b.g. Clearly Bust — Pai-Collect (Paico) 41. Sturdy compact half-brother to Irish Hurdling winners, Moydrum Castle and Vienna Shop. IRISH NH FLAT '98 r2 p0. IRISH NH '99/03 (for E.J. Creighton, and A.J. Martin, all wins) r25 w4 (2m5f Hdle and 3 2m2f-3m Chses) p5; fell/unseated 4. Bought Doncaster, May for 6500. Won four races when trained in Ireland including a successful foray to Carlisle once (also survived several errors once) but not the most reliable of jumpers (fell or unseated in four of his Chases) and had not scored since December '01 (tongue-tied on that occasions). Already remote when almost unseating two out on his Pointing debut and then disappeared for nearly three months, but romped home a fence ahead of his nearest rival in a four-runner Confined at Marks Tey. A game sort who may yet score again, but may need mollycoddling these days and unlikely to appear very often. *R. Burroughs & A.H.B. Hodge — E. Anglian Bloodhounds (Sam Hodge).* 38 (Cf), 905 (Cf).

WINCY SPIDER ..10-0.. 11 b.g. Wace (USA) — Sound 'n' Rhythm (Tudor Rhythm) 11. Neat half-brother to Chasing winner, En El Em Flyer. Dam (*qv* '94 Annual) was last and pulled up in 7 Points ('useless, a poor jumper, looks unwilling'). 3000 5yo. NH FLAT '00 r4 p0. NH '00 (for R.J. Smith) r2 p1 (2nd); and pulled up. Sold Ascot, Aug '01 800; reported bought by current connections subsequently for 600. Well beaten in bumpers before pulling up in his first Hurdle, but then finished three-and-a-half lengths second over 2m7f at 100-1 (discarded the blinkers he had been wearing previously). Had been off the course since '00 before he won a slowly-run elders Maiden at Horseheath by a ready three lengths, and then impressive in a Cottenham Restricted which took only a second longer than the Open. Potentially very volatile but has been kept in check by James Diment, and another tribute to the training of Anna Brooks. It is a pity that we cannot see a lot more of him. *T.L. & Mrs A.E. Brooks — Grafton (Anna Brooks).* 130 (OMa), 999 (R).

WIND ON THE COMMON ..10-0.. 9 br.g. Green Ruby (USA) — Whenthewindblows (Abwah) 4311. Compact well-made half-brother to Force Ten. Dam, half-sister to Prince Zeus (*qv* '98 Annual), won Maiden and placed 12 for Mike Stephenson ('cunningly contrives to mistime any challenge'). NH FLAT '00 r1 p0. P-t-P '02/3 r9 p4 (3 3rds, of 4 once); 4th of 5, and fell/unseated 4. Almost as frustrating as mum, but improved jumping brought its rewards, and scored at the 12th time of asking on firmish at Upton. Wasted no time in finding a Restricted in softish, and now that his confidence is at an all-time high he could find further opportunities if sensibly placed. *M. Stephenson — N. Ledbury (Tim Stephenson).* 621 (OMa), 731 (OMa), 981 (OMa), 1345 (R).

WINK AND WHISPER ..10-2.. 10 b.m. Gunner B — Lady Hannah (Daring March) p324u. Workmanlike unfurnished owner-bred half-sister to Jimannie. Dam is half-sister to Progressive (*qv* '95 Annual). P-t-P '00/1 r5 p3 (2nd of 3; 3rd of 4, and last of 3); and unseated 2. NH '01/2 (for A. King) r7 w1 (2m3f Ch) p3. A well-backed favourite when dumping the rider twice to '01, but a spell of Hurdling sorted out her problems, and scored on her first appearance over regulation fences in soft at Taunton the following year. Missed '03, and returned to home base in '04, but looked ring-rusty and could not find another opportunity, and particularly disappointing when encountering a sound surface at Kingston St Mary. Clearly retains ability but will need to find some mud to extract it to the full. *R.J. & Mrs V.A. Tory — S. Dorset (Mary Tory).* 33 (L), 234 (L), 322 (L), 965 (L), 1298 (3m1f110yH).

WINLEAH ..—.. 9 gr.g. Petong — Tower Glades (Tower Walk) pppp. Sturdy attractive half-brother to 2 flat winners (one in France). Dam, half-sister to Black Magic (*qv*), won at 5f. FLAT '98/00 r8 p0 (beaten 11l plus); inc Sells. P-t-P '02 r3 p0 (fell/unseated 2, and pulled up). Bred along totally the wrong lines for Pointing, and it is hardly surprising that he has been an unmitigated disaster in the sphere. *The Clark Family (S.C. Clark) — V. of Aylesbury with Garth & S. Berks (Sue Harbour).* 463 (OMa), 627 (OMa), 760 (OMa), 940 (OMa).

WINNERS ENCLOSURE (IRE) ..10-0.. 9 b.g. Step Together (USA) — Willabelle (Will Somers) u135. Compact attractive half-brother to Ronans Glen and Via De La Valle (IRE), to flat winner, Justella (subsequently successful in France), and to Irish Pointing winner, Mellon Point. IRISH P-t-P '01 r1 p1 (2nd). P-t-P '02 r1 p0 (pulled up). Ruptured a tendon in his first English start and missed '03, but came through with a steady run to lead at the last at Ston Easton, and had the fortitude to fend off the rallying runner-up and cope with the near gale force winds that resided. Got in a muck sweat and pulled like a train when novice ridden next time, and landed Michael Miller in hot water at Chepstow, but should be competitive in '05 provided his legs are up to it. *J.J. Boulter & Miss F.J. Wilkins — Portman (John Boulter).* 197 (R), 601 (R), 881 (Inr), 1294 (3mH).

WINNICK (IRE) ..8-12.. 11 b/br.g. Fools Holme (USA) — Injection (On Your Mark) fp2. Small neat half-brother to 3 flat winners (2 abroad). Dam, half-sister to Night Nurse, won 8f race. NH FLAT '99 r1 p0. NH '99/01 r14 p4. P-t-P '02 r1 p1 (3rd). A non-finisher for the first time in 17 starts when falling at the seventh on his reappearance, and broke a blood vessel next time, but very nearly gained a deserved and long overdue success when just outpointed in the closing stages at Chaddesley. The winner finished lame and the third is also a perennial maiden, and his chances of unearthing an opportunity have diminished further. *Miss A. Maller & G.W. Meredith — Cotswold (Amanda Maller).* 940 (OMa), 1258 (OMa), 1532 (OMa).

WINNIE THE POOH ..9-3.. 11 br.g. Landyap (USA) — Moorland Nell (Neltino) p3231b. Small lengthy half-brother to Pooh Stick, and to Hurdles winner and stablemate, Baloo. Dam is half-sister to the monstrous pair, Regent Son and Mrs Somebody ('Fred and Rosie'). NH '00 r2 p1 (2nd). NH '00/3 r13 p1 (2nd); pulled up 4, fell 1. Second in a bumper and a Hurdle, but pulled up in two of three Chases and wore cheekpieces in the latest. Found a drop to Maidens most acceptable, and finally became Winnie the winner at the 20th attempt in a five-runner three-finisher elders event at Trebudannon. Could hardly have found a worse contest, but consistent in similar grade previously, and deserved the success. Restricteds will be harder. *J.D. Frost — S. Devon (Nicky Frost).* 494 (OMa), 704 (CfMa), 913 (OMa), 1006 (CfMa), 1436 (OMa), 1543 (R).

WINNING LEADER (IRE) ..9-7.. 9 b.g. Supreme Leader — Cromogue Lady (Golden Love) up7*p*4332. Tall workmanlike brother to NH flat and Hurdles winner, Little Fencote (IRE) to Irish Hurdling winner, Happiest Days, and to Irish Pointing winner, Cromogue Minstrel. Dam won 6yo&up Maiden in Ireland on disqualification. IRISH P-t-P '02/3 r5 w1 (7&8yo Maiden) p0; last 2, fell and carried out. NH '04 r1 p0 (pulled up in 3m110y Grand Military Gold Cup: *prom til lost plce 8, t.o 11, blun 14, pu nxt*). His Irish form had caveat emptor stamped all over it, as apart from a win in a Maiden in which only seven and eight-year-olds were allowed to compete he had not beaten another horse. Forced into errors whilst the owner was lumbering around on him on his first four attempts after being purchased for a disastrously expensive 20,000gns, but even when competent riders took over he proved to be woefully one-paced, and only once came within 15 lengths of success, when runner-up in a Bratton Down Restricted (a three lengths lead at the last had evaporated to become a two-and-a-half length deficit at the line). Thoroughly exposed, so there is no reason to think that he can do any better in '05. *R.C. Skinner — Devon & Somerset (Linda Blackford).* 79 (R), 278 (Inr), 323 (R), 791 (R), 1002 (R), 1180 (M), 1385 (R).

WINNING TOWN ..9-4§.. 12 ch.g. Jester — Lurex Girl (Camden Town) 964532. Very small quite attractive half-brother to Hayling Star. Dam won 2 2m races. NH FLAT '97 r2 p0. NH '98 r3 p0. P-t-P/HUNT CH '99/00 and '02/3 r22 w2 (2m4f Maiden and Members) p10 (8 2nds); 6th, last pair 6, pulled up and unseated 2. A safe ride, and the winner of two weak races in which he has assumed control at a late stage, but has a habit of running in snatches, and can be guaranteed to be going backwards at the finish nowadays. Has been tried in cheekpieces. *Miss S.H. Talbot — Albrighton Woodland.* 252 (CR), 407 (L), 715 (R), 1018 (R), 1191 (R), 1527 (M).

WINSLEY SPIRIT ..8-7§.. 11 b.m. Triune — Seasonal Spirit (High Season) ppp. Small light-framed. Dam won 2-finisher Exmoor Members and placed 5 for Jane Jeyes. NH FLAT '99 r2 p0. P-t-P '03 r8 w1 (Maiden) p0; last, pulled up 4, and fell/unseated 2. Recorded a narrow success at Bratton Down on her first completion in Points, but the company was particularly feeble, and has failed to get round in four of five subsequent attempts. Went little more than two miles reluctantly thrice in '04, and has reportedly been retired. *C. & Mrs J. Jeyes — Exmoor (Sue Maude).* 689 (R), 1251 (R), 1378 (M).

WINTER GALE (IRE) ..10-3.. 13 b/br.g. Strong Gale — Winter Fox (Martinmas) 2221u421. Workmanlike half-brother to Pharstar (IRE), to the winners, Belstone Fox (jumping), Back To Ben Alder (IRE) (NH flat), Leinthall Fox (NH flat) and Sylvia Fox (Irish flat and Hurdles). IRISH FLAT r1 p1 (3rd). IRISH NH FLAT '98 r3 p1 (3rd). IRISH NH '98 r1 p1 (3rd in Hdle). NH '00/2 r16 w3 (hat-trick in 2m-3m1f Chses) p4; pulled up 2, fell 1. P-t-P/HUNT CH '99 and '03 r12 w3 (hat-trick — Maiden, Restricted and PPORA) p6 (4 2nds; and inc remote 3rd of 4 once); 5th, and pulled up 2. A decent performer on sound surfaces, and recorded a hat-trick in Points in '99, and under Rules the following year, but very hard to win with since, and went another 21 races before he got his head in front again. Gained reward for his consistency at Charm Park, and ended his campaign with a game success at Garthorpe. One-paced and needs forcing tactics to succeed nowadays but a very reliable jumper, and could easily find further opportunities at 13. *Mrs J.E. Eddery — Middleton (Gill Walford).* 5 (L), 55 (Cf), 477 (Cnr), 957 (Cf), 1290 (L), 1347 (2m6f110yH), 1451 (3mH), 1501 (L).

WIN THE TOSS ..9-13.. 13 b.g. Idiot's Delight — Mayfield (USA) (Alleged USA) 2pu26. Small light. NH FLAT '96/8 r4 p2 (2nds). NH '98/01 r18 w1 (2m4f110y Hdle) p2 (2nds); pulled up 2, unseated 1.

P-t-P/HUNT CH '02/3 (for Mr R.M. Green) r18 w3 (up to Confined) p2 (3rds, remote of 3 once); 6th, last pair 7, pulled up 2, and unseated 3. Thrice a narrow winner of bad races on sound surfaces at Hackwood Park, but does not usually get the trip in Points, and his jumping frailties are easily exposed in sub-3m Hunter Chases, particularly if Richard Green is aboard. Blinkered once in '98, and has been tried tongue-tied. *Mrs L. Lim — Staff College (Phillip York).* 24 (O), 241 (2m4f110yH), 1173 (2m110yH), 1354 (2m110yH), 1443 (2m5fH).

WINWARD ..8-0§.. 13 b.g. Lafontaine (USA) — Crackingham (Trimmingham) 4p4p. Very tall half-brother to Cracked Ice, and to Irish Hurdles winner, Romanoski. P-t-P/HUNT CH '98/00 and '02 r20 p0 (6th, last pair 5, pulled up 12, and fell/unseated 2). Slow as a boat, and beaten fences when eventually bumbling to completion, which is not very often. Has been tried in blinkers and a tongue-tie. *R.F. Wright — W. Street Tickham (Miss S. Frazer).* 534 (M), 802 (R), 1280 (M), 1405 (OMa).

WISE ADVICE (IRE) ..8-4.. 15 b.g. Duky — Down The Aisle (Godswalk USA) 2p4. Lengthy half-brother to Hurdles winner, Maryjo (IRE). NH FLAT '94 r2 p1 (2nd). NH '95/9 r41 w7 (2m110y Hdle and 6 2m1f110y-2m4f110y Chses) p16; pulled up 3, and fell 3. P-t-P/HUNT CH '02/3 (for Mr & Mrs M.A. Kemp) r14 w1 (dead-heat Confined) p5 (3 3rds, inc Hunt Ch); 4th thrice, 8th, last pair 2, and pulled up 2. Scoring for the first time in excess of 2m4f, and since May '98 when forcing a dead-heat last year, but normally easy to beat in Points, and looks a spent force now. Visored and blinkered once apiece in '96. *Mrs W. Ward & Mrs J.O.P. Morrison — Granta H. (Martin Ward).* 396 (M), 649 (L), 831 (L).

WISHFUL THINKER ..9-3.. 8 b.g. Prince Sabo — Estonia (Kings Lake USA) 6u53uu. Neat brother to flat winner, The Groveller, and half-brother to flat and Hurdling winner, Cry Baby. Dam won 11f Irish flat and 2m English Selling Hurdle. FLAT '99/01 r16 w1 (11f) p4. NH '00/1 (for N. Tinkler) r4 p2. Sold Doncaster, March '01 1000. Won a Maiden Seller at Redcar in July '00, in which the eight contestants had made 57 previous appearances between them and garnered a mere seven placings. Some of his other efforts were creditable, including a second of 22 on the flat and second in a 19-runner Selling Hurdle (inherited that position at the final flight), but was taken out of training in '01 and did not return for three years. Poor in Points and beaten at least 20 lengths, and a girl beginner partnered him in five races and fell off in three. Tongue-tied on his last three outings. Not worth persevering with. *M.J. Norman & Mrs S. Scott — Buccleuch (Sylvia Scott).* 162 (L), 426 (Cf), 506 (Cnr), 547 (M), 654 (Cf), 1080 (Cf).

WISTON WIZO ..8-3§.. 9 b.g. Tigerwood — Official Lady (Official) 45u332p3up3. Small plain brother to Daisy's Choice (*qv*). P-t-P '03 r10 p1 (2nd); last 2, pulled up 3, ran out 2, unseated, and slipped up. Plumbs the depths of the very worst Welsh Maidens, and has six placings to his name, but willful and has a very wonky steering column, and has already passed up some very easy opportunities. Blinkered on his last seven starts. Wears a cross-noseband. *Mrs J. Llewellyn — Pembs (Brian Llewellyn).* 203 (CfMa), 357 (R), 452 (R), 677 (CfMa), 736 (CfMa), 948 (OMa), 1092 (I), 1240 (OMa), 1487 (OMa), 1525 (OMah), 1547 (M).

WITHYBROOK LASS ..9-1.. 7 b.m. Teenoso (USA) — Broadbrook Lass (Broadsword USA) pf1. Strong lengthy. Dam, half-sister to Missilebrook Lass (*qv*), won 2 Points and placed second (all her starts), and subsequently won 2 Chases (2m4f-2m5f) and placed second to '03 for Michael Ings. P-t-P '03 r1 p0 (ran out). Failed to get round on her first three attempts, but had shown more than enough ability to win a Maiden, and took advantage of a simple opportunity in softish at Cold Harbour. Has looked quite a character, and thought twice about passing the box-park at Brampton Bryan once, but has access to leading riders and the scope for further improvement. *M.H. Ings — Radnor & W. Herefords (Andrew Dalton).* 668 (OMa), 1116 (OMa), 1231 (OMam).

WITHYCOMBE ..9-8.. 9 b.g. Greensmith — Cindercombe (Ra Nova) p63. Compact. Dam, (*qv* '00 Annual), won Maiden and placed 8 (inc 3rd in Hdle) for the Snowdens ('a very competent jumper, but rather pedestrian in Restricteds'). P-t-P '02 r4 w1 (Maiden-finished alone) p0; and pulled up 3. Responded to a first-time visor when successful on his first completion at Stafford Cross in '02, but missed '03 and dropped dead after finishing a distant third at Bishops Court. I.R. Snowden — Cotley (Philip Greenwood). 14 (R), 139 (R), 324 (R).

WONDERFUL REMARK ..9-3.. 9 b.m. Golden Heights — Queen Of Dreams (Ti King FR) u5211. Small neat. Dam placed 4 all-weather races for Joanne Wood and subsequently ran badly in 3 Points for her. NH FLAT '00 and '02 r3 p0. NH '02/3 (for J.A. Pickering, and P.T. Dalton) r9 p0; pulled up 5. Useless under Rules and pulled up in four of eight Hurdles including Sellers and pulled up in her only Chase (wore blinkers or cheekpieces on three occasions), and started off unpromisingly in Points, but showed improvement when two lengths second in a Sandon Maiden, and then won a Mares event at Clifton-On-Dunsmore in exceptionally fortuitous circumstances as she was only a remote third coming to two out but inherited the prize after late defections. Followed up in a three-runner Restricted at Ashorne, and was starting to enjoy herself, but sadly for connections she died of colic in the summer.

Mrs J. Woods — Cranwell Bloodhounds (Rob Woods). 595 (OMa), 686 (OMa), 848 (OMa), 1119 (CMam), 1279 (R).

WOOD BUZZARD .—.. 13 b.g. Buzzards Bay — Woody Isle (Precipice Wood) ppp. Good-bodied brother to Bay Hobnob, and half-brother to Master Grass. Dam won 2 Points and placed 4. NH '00 r1 p0. P-t-P/HUNT CH '00/3 r15 w1 (Maiden) p4 (3 2nds, beaten neck once, and last once); 4th of 5, fell/unseated 2, refused, and pulled up 6. Successful in the slowest time of the day at Pentreclwydau in '02, but a weak finisher otherwise, and has pulled up in six of seven subsequent attempts. Runs tongue-tied. *Miss S.H. Widdicombe — Southdown & Eridge.* 294 (R), 577 (Cnr), 639 (R).

WOODLANDS BEAU (IRE) ..9-12§.. 13 b.g. Beau Sher — Never Intended (Sayyaf) 343f32276. Stocky lengthy. NH '98/02 r41 w3 (3m1f-3m1f110y Chses) p15 (inc 11 2nds); unseated 6, and pulled up 3. P-t-P/HUNT CH '97/8 and '03 r20 w7 (inc 3 Mixed Opens, 3m-4m) p10 (7 2nds, of 3 twice, beaten head once, last once; and inc 3rd of 4 once); 4th, refused, and fell. Took his winning tally into double figures when recording his third success in '03, but a very crafty individual who could have scored even more often had he chose, and needs strong handling. Nowhere approaching his best form in '04, and was last in half his completions, and it will take a lot of skill to revitalise him at 13. A very clumsy jumper, and hits fences at will, but normally clever enough to remain upright, and has only ever fallen twice. Has been tried in headgear. *Club Ten (R. Jenks) — Portman (Sally Alner).* 89 (O), 235 (O), 352 (O), 543 (3m2f110yH), 863 (MO), 1100 (O), 1250 (C), 1441 (3m7fH), 1556 (MO).

WOODLAND WARRIOR ..—.. 8 b.g. Lyphento (USA) — Dutch Majesty (Homing) fff0. Compact half-brother to Barton Nic, and to Hurdles winner, Lets Go Dutch. Dam won 2m2f Hurdle on AW. NH FLAT '01 r1 p0. NH '01/2 (for A. Ennis) r6 p0; pulled up 1, slipped up 1. NH '04 (for C. Roberts) r1 p0 (12th in 3m110y Sell Hdle: *a bhnd, t.o*). Bad over Hurdles including in Sellers and broke a blood vessel once and visored twice, but that was nothing compared to his Pointing exploits, as he crashed at the first, at the seventh, and at the sixth when a crazy punt from sixes to 3-1. Promptly reverted to the smaller obstacles, but it looks as though there is no job he can fulfill competently. *W.J. Day — Gelligaer F. (Lisa Day).* 202 (CfMa), 362 (CfMa), 454 (CfMa).

WOODWARD STREET (AUS) ..—.. 10 b.g. Coronation Day (AUS) — Super Unicorn (AUS) (Ksar) pp. Compact workmanlike. NZ FLAT r13 w3 (7-8f). NH '00/2 (for N.J. Henderson) r7 w1 (2m Hdle) p0; pulled up 3. A triple winner in testing ground on the flat in New Zealand, and made a successful English debut in a Haydock Hurdle in heavy, but went to pieces afterwards, and has been last once and pulled up on five occasions from eight subsequent attempts. Can take a strong hold, but not a good jumper, and three miles seems much too far for him. *B.P. Sillis — Essex (Chris Lawson).* 43 (O), 397 (O).

WOODYOUEVER (IRE) ..8-3.. 10 br.g. Good Thyne (USA) — Lady Sirat (Al Sirat) 7. Dam won 4 Points and NH flat in Ireland. IRISH P-t-P '99/02 r11 w1 (7yo Maiden) p3; pulled up 3, ran out 2. IRISH HUNT CH '02 r1 p0 (brought down). IRISH NH '02 (for J. Quinn) r5 p0. Did manage to win an Irish Point (beat Lingering Fog and Jack Of Kilcash, both subsequently successful English Pointers) in '02 but beaten in 17 other attempts, and was struggling after a mile before plugging home in a Restricted in early February. Absent since, and would not be of interest if he did reappear. *S.A. Todd & R. Foster — S. Durham (Steven Todd).* 164 (R).

WOOKEY WOODS (IRE) ..—.. 8 b.g. Muharib (USA) — Best Served Cherry (IRE) (Sheer Grit) Rp. Dam, Grandam, Great-Grandam and Great, great-Grandam never ran! 5000 4yo. Ran through the wing of the seventh and unseated on his debut, and then struck into himself with fatal consequences at Howick. L. Wood — Gelligaer F. (Jenny Williams). 256 (CMa), 362 (CfMa).

WORCESTER WAY (IRE) .—.. 11 br.g. Roselier (FR) — Seagate (IRE) (Decent Fellow) p. 15,500 4yo. NH FLAT '00 (for N.A. Twiston-Davies) r1 p0. A twice-raced oldster who pulled up after 2m4f at Erw Lon in February. *J.L. Brown — Pembs (Graham Lavis).* 202 (CfMa).

WORTH A SHOT (IRE) .8-2.. 8 b.g. Sharp Charter — Lucky Woe (IRE) (Insan USA) ppp23p. 2687 4yo. Capable of showing some speed, but his placings consist of 15 lengths second of four over 2m4f and 31 lengths last of three. Does not even seem to stay the shorter trip (no longer an option), and is prone to make mistakes. The best that can be said about him is that David Phelan won a Maiden in '04 on Pandeli, who had pulled up on four occasions earlier in the season. *Miss V. Kemp — Hursley Hambledon (David Phelan).* 186 (OMa), 424 (CMa), 611 (OMa), 803 (2m4fOMa), 1285 (OMa), 1404 (OMa).

WORTHY MAN ..—.. 8 b.g. Homo Sapien — Marnworth (Funny Man) pfp7fppp*6p*. Leggy compact half-brother to Hurdling winner, Ragu. Dam, sister to Riverside Boy and another Pointer, and half-sister to Choir Boy (*qv* '03 Annual) won 2 Points (extremely lucky once) and 3rd. 18,000 3yo. NH FLAT '02/3 r2 p0. NH '03 (for T.R. George) r2 p0. NH '04 r3 p0 (pulled up in 2m2f110y Sell

Hdle: *ld, clr when hit 2, hdd & wknd rap aft 6, t.o & pu 2 out*; last of 6 in 2m Hdle: *pulled hrd, 2nd til wknd aft 5*; and pulled up in 2m110y Hdle: *a bhnd, t.o & pu 2 out*). A pathetic creature who only got round once in Points/Hunter Chases, when walking in two fences adrift of the winner. Wears a tongue-tie and stops to nothing as if he is being garroted internally. Subsequently returned to Hurdling including a Seller, and acquired blinkers on his latest attempt. Often makes blunders, and is embarrassing to watch. *Mrs W.H. Walter & Lady Talbot — S.T. Lewis — Taunton V.H. (Simon Lewis; -)*. 13 (OMa), 67 (OMa), 150 (OMa), 725 (OMa), 983 (2m5fOMa), 1173 (2m110yH), 1363 (2m3f110yH).

WRAPAROUND YOU (IRE) ..8-3.. 8 b.g. Shernazar — Wraparound Sue (Touch Paper) pp4. Close-coupled half-brother to It's A Wrap (IRE), and to Hurdles winners, Supreme Music (IRE) and Spoof (IRE). Dam, half-sister to Coolegale (*qv* '96 Annual). IRISH P-t-P '03 r2 w1 (6yo Maiden) p0; and pulled up. IRISH NH '01/2 r5 p0; refused to race 1. IRISH NH '02 (for T.M. Walsh) r1 p0. Bought Doncaster, Aug for 4800. Just scraped home in an Irish Maiden on his final start there, which was perfect for the sales, where he changed hands for far more than he is worth. Quite headstrong and races prominently for 2m4f, but does not stay a yard further, and compounds rapidly including when last and well over a fence behind on his latest outing. Whipped round at the start before finishing 64 lengths adrift in an Irish bumper (tongue-tied) and refused to race in the other. *F. Homer-Morris & Mrs B. Smith — Albrighton (Graham Harris)*. 91 (M), 752 (R), 1230 (R).

WYCHNOR KING (IRE) ..9-6.. 11 b.g. Torus — Eva's Fancy (Distinctly USA) upu32. Enormous rangy half-brother to Irish flat and Hurdling winner, Monty's Fancy, and to Irish NH flat winner, Fancy Thynes. Dam won 3 Irish Hurdles, 2m2f-2m4f. NH FLAT '99/00 r2 p0. NH '01/2 (for A. Streeter, and M. Mullineaux) r4 p0; pulled up 1. Soundly beaten in just six outings under Rules, and was last (after unseating and remounting) and pulled up in Chases. Very moderate and a sketchy jumper in Points, but plugged into 28 lengths third of four in a Ladies, and then gave the owner an exciting ride when only beaten a length in a five-runner Novice Riders event at Eaton Hall. Had easily his busiest season in '04 (being akin to an elephant must create problems) and it would be a little surprising if he unearthed a winning opportunity at 11. *Mrs D. Caine — Cheshire (Michelle Mullineaux)*. 94 (L), 529 (L), 710 (Mah), 874 (L), 1147 (Cnr).

WYNFORD EAGLE ..9-4.. 6 b.g. Sula Bula — Tawny Silk (Little Buskins) p1. Compact light-framed half-brother to Rossaleen. Dam won mares Maiden in Ireland (also disqualified from similar after omitting a fence). Given a Polly Gundry school on his debut, and then urged home in front of a lame rival by Alex Merriam in a three-finisher Maiden on firmish at Larkhill. It was easily the slowest race of the day and the form means nothing, and will have to keep up the good work to have a chance in Restricteds. *Mrs J. Turner — Cattistock (Peter Shaw)*. 791 (R), 1098 (OMa).

WYNYARD DANCER ..9-9§.. 11 b.m. Minster Son — The White Lion (Flying Tyke) uup. Light-framed sister to Jarode, and half-sister to NH flat and jumping winners, Wynyard Knight and Wynyard Lady, and to NH flat and successful Hurdler, Wynyard Damsel. Dam, half-sister to Flying Lion (*qv* '00 Annual), won 6 flat (7-9f), inc a Sell. NH FLAT '98/9 r3 p2 (3rds). NH '99/00 r5 p1 (2nd). P-t-P/HUNT CH '01/3 r13 w1 (2m4f110y Hunt Ch) p8 (7 2nds, beaten head once, and ½*l* once, and last once); 4th, pulled up and fell 2. Impossible to place successfully in Points, and gained his solitary win over 2m4f at Hexham in '02, but typically let down by his jumping in a truncated season, and never went a yard when cheekpieces were removed at Heslaker. Sure to frustrate further if returning. *A. Jackson — Cleveland (Tina Jackson)*. 956 (MO), 1177 (2m5fH), 1459 (L).

XRAYSAUCE ..—.. 7 ch.m. Elegant Monarch — City Passenger (Sit In The Corner USA) pp. Workmanlike plain. Tailed off and pulled up after two miles twice, including with David Stephens putting up 16lb overweight once. Not a raysauce. Ironically the horse named Ray Source is an ex-racehorse, having dropped dead at Bangor. *F.S.W. Daniels — Four Burrow*. 198 (R), 485 (OMa).

YER 'UMBLE (IRE) .9-0.. 14 b.g. Lafontaine (USA) — Miners Girl (Miner's Lamp) p7u. Small. NH '94/7, '99/00 and '02/3 r36 w2 (2m7f Hdle and 3m Ch) p4; pulled up 6, fell 1. Won a Hurdle and a Chase, both around three miles at Stratford, and at odds of 20-1 and 50-1, and also fell when eight lengths clear two out in a Hurdle once. A quirky little horse who has not scored since July '00, and often wore headgear to '97. Jumped poorly and showed no zest in Points including when badly tailed off last once, and subsequently pulled up in a Selling Hurdle. Rather a bolshie servant to connections for the past 11 years, and is ready to go shuffling off into the twilight home. *J.K.S. & E.M. Cresswell — Staffordshire Moorland (J.K.S. Cresswell)*. 229 (O), 712 (L), 987 (L).

YORKSHIRE EDITION (IRE) ..9-12.. 12 br.g. Strong Gale — Rent A Card (Raise You Ten) p531454. Tall brother to Jacques The Lad (IRE), and half-brother to Reydon and Garrison Commander (IRE), to Irish NH flat and Chasing winner, Shanes Hero (IRE), and to Irish Hurdles winner, Pair Of Queens. Dam, half-sister to Monkscombe (*qv* '94 Annual). NH FLAT '98 r1 p0. NH '98/02 (for P.F. Nicholls) r17 w5 (2 2m6f Hdles and 3 3m2f Chses) p1 (3rd); pulled up 4, fell/unseated 2. Proved an ideal mount for the beginner Wendy Gibson in Points and the pair completed in all six attempts together, including a win in a four-runner Ladies at Whittington. Although this was the sixth victory of his career it was his first away from Wincanton. Formerly quite useful, but had a habit of idling, and tends to give up quite tamely if the going gets tough nowadays. When asked what Sir Robert Ogden would think of the Whittington triumph Chris Dennis came up with the great line 'he probably doesn't know that he's running!'. *Sir Robert Ogden — Hurworth (Chris Dennis).* 72 (O), 339 (L), 508 (L), 874 (L), 957 (Cf), 1160 (L), 1290 (L).

YOU CAN CALL ME AL ..9-1.. 8 b.g. Almoojid — Coraletta (Buckley) 3. Small. Dam is half-sister to Coraco (*qv* '00 Annual). NH FLAT '02 r2 p0. P-t-P '02/3 r2 p1 (3rd of 4); and pulled up. Beaten 15 and 18 lengths when third in Maidens, but a decidedly iffy jumper, and gets precious little racecourse experience. Wore cheekpieces in '03. *J.A. Danahar — Worcester & W. Farmers.* 618 (2m4fOMa).

YOUNG GENERAL ..9-5§.. 11 ch.g. Scottish Reel — Make A Signal (Royal Gunner) p. Compact hobdayed brother to NH flat and Hurdles winner, General Chase, and half-brother to 4 winners (2 abroad), including Surefoot Sillars (Hurdles) and Make A Stand (flat and Hurdles — Champion Hurdler in '97). NH FLAT '98 r3 w1 p1 (3rd, beaten head and short head — just caught). P-t-P '00 and '02/3 r18 w2 (Intermediate and Members) p5 (fence last of 2; and 4 3rds, of 4 thrice, remote once); 4th, 5th, pulled up 8, and refused. Related to a champion, and had plenty of ability himself, but a very awkward customer from day one, and is thoroughly unreliable. Walked over in his Members last year, and is normally pulled up. Has been tried in blinkers. *Mrs S.A. Berwick — S. Devon (John Berwick).* 310 (O).

YOUNG HARRY ..—§§.. 7 b.g. Karinga Bay — Heathfield Gale (Strong Gale) prpr*06p*. Well-made brother to Hooray Henry. Dam won NH flat and 2m5f Hurdle for Mr Ford. NH FLAT '04 r2 p0 (12th over 2m1f at Exeter: *hld up, hdwy 4f out, wknd qckly wl over 1f out*; and 6th over 2m1f at Newton Abbot: *chsd ldr til wknd over 2f out*). NH '04 (for M.C. Pipe) r1 p0 (pulled up in 2m5f Hdle: *pulled hrd, prom til wknd aft 7, bhnd when pu 2 out*). A total villain who pulled himself up after two miles or far less in all four Points. Subsequently joined Martin Pipe, but was not worth the training bills. Normally blinkered or visored. Scant reward for the owner-breeder after six years of cosseting him. *A.E. Ford — Taunton V.H. (Alan Walter).* 83 (OMa), 197 (R), 309 (2m4fOMa), 571 (R).

YOUNG LIRRUP..—.. 7 ch.g. Lir — Blue-Bird Express (Pony Express) f. Strong. Dam (*qv* '97 Annual) sister to Kiwizz, and half-sister to Danribo and Kandsy, won Maiden and Restricted and placed 4 for the Kittows. NH FLAT '02/3 (for W.S. Kittow) r4 p0. Looked a mad cap in the first of his bumpers in which he virtually ran off the course on the home bend, and tore off at a maniacal pace in a Maiden at Milborne St Andrew, but broke a leg taking off at the tenth and literally crashed headlong into the fence. W.G. Kittow — Taunton V.H. 238 (CfMa).

YOUNG MANNY .9-4§.. 14 ch.g. Executive Man — Ashmo (Ashmore FR) 433up. Small lengthy half-brother to Flemings Fleur and Terino, and to Irish NH flat winner, Flemings Footman. Dam was a useless Pointer. NH FLAT '95/7 r3 p0. P-t-P '98/00 and '02/3 r38 w6 (inc Open and Ladies) p13 (8 2nds, of 3 twice, last once; and inc 3rd of 4 thrice); last pair 7, fell/unseated 5, ran out, and pulled up 6. A good servant to connections, but lucky in two of his six wins, and too long in the tooth to return from what appeared to be a sideline inducing setback at Ystradowen. *H.J. Barton — Pembs.* 361 (L), 697 (L), 737 (L), 843 (L), 1025 (L).

YOUNG TOMO (IRE) ..9-10§.. 13 b.g. Lafontaine (USA) — Siege Queen (Tarqogan) R2p842p. Rangy half-brother to Forest Moss (IRE), and to Irish Pointing winners, Mossy Fortress (IRE) and Ferric Fortress (IRE). Dam, half-sister to Kilnockin (*qv* '94 Annual). NH FLAT '97 r1 p1 (2nd). NH '97/02 r26 w5 (2 2m4f-2m5f110y Hdles, and 3 3m-3m3f Chses) p7; pulled up 3, and fell 3. P-t-P '03 (for Mr F. Lloyd) r1 p0 (5th of 6). Thrice a winner at Sedgefield and also twice successful at Musselburgh, and revived to a certain degree in '04, but could not be persuaded to score for the first time since November '01. Backed from 33s to 14-1 when a length second at Clifton-on-Dunsmore, and looked to have cracked it when produced to lead at the last, but typically rolled over when challenged on the flat, and seems determined to frustrate in future. Has been tried in blinkers and cheekpieces. *Mrs J.E. Goodall — Meynell & S. Staffs (Carly Goodall).* 107 (O), 225 (M), 437 (3m1fH), 592 (O), 986 (Cf), 1120 (Cf), 1489 (3m3fH).

YOUR TURN ROSIE ..—.. 10 b.m. Relief Pitcher — Bremhill Rosie (Celtic Cone) p. Short-backed well-made half-sister to 5 times Hurdling winner, Honeybed Wood (3rd of 4, last, pulled up, fell and unseated in Points for the Browns prior to leaving them for success under Rules) Dam won 2m Hurdle on debut, but pulled up three times in all subsequent ventures. NH FLAT '01 r1 p0. NH '02 r1 p0. Hopelessly tailed off in a bumper in '01, 53 lengths ninth in a Hurdle in '02, and tailed off and pulled up three out in a Maiden in '04 (badly hampered at the second, and nearly fell at the fifth). Enough said. *I.R. Brown — Teme V.* 1395 (OMa).

YOUWOUDHAVETHAT (IRE) .8-9.. 7 b.m. Gone Fishin — Snatchingly (Thatch USA) 5pp32. Workmanlike half-sister to Hurdles winner, Job Rage (IRE). Dam won 6f race in Ireland. IRISH P-t-P '03 r4 p0 (last, and pulled up 3). Makes plentiful errors and did not beat another horse in her first seven Points, but has since finished 27 lengths third and 20 lengths second (blundered at the 14th, and jumped poorly and seemed to be hanging left after). Marginally improved, but still looks a very long way from a win. *D.P. Constable — Ludlow (Michael Hammond).* 257 (CMa), 666 (OMa), 929 (2m4fOMa), 1231 (OMam), 1370 (OMa).

ZABADI (IRE) .8-7§.. 13 b.g. Shahrastani (USA) — Zerzaya (Beldale Flutter USA) pup4. Small sturdy half-brother to flat winners, Zafzala, Zabargar (also won Hurdle) and Zerpow (1st pair in Ireland). Dam won 4 10f races consecutively. IRISH FLAT '95 r3 w2 (7f) p1 (2nd). FLAT '96 r1 p0. NH '95/8 and '00/3 (for D. Nicholson, 4 wins, and Miss V. Williams) r57 w9 (4 2m-2m2f Hdles and 5 2m1f-2m6f Chses) p23; fell 2, pulled up 6. A classy little horse at his best and won 11 races and placed 24 times to earn a total of £111,285 (the main contribution being £28,424 from a victory in an Aintree Hurdle in which he showed a great turn of foot), and scored four times between October and December '01 and also successful in a Charity flat race during that sequence. Has never visited the winner's enclosure since, and now has an unplaced total of 14 behind him. Thrice blinkered to '93, and contested the '97 Champion Hurdle and finished 11th. Has had a habit of cantering along merrily until it is time to make an effort, and promptly giving up, as he graphically demonstrated when finishing runner-up eight times in a nine race spell (won the exception). Very careful not to fall so made a safe ride for the beginner Rosie Napier in Points, and just held off a stablemate when 46 lengths fourth in his Members. *D. Napier — N. Norfolk H. (Tina Hayward).* 479 (L), 556 (Cf), 906 (Cnr), 1150 (M).

ZAFAN (IRE) ..9-3.. 10 ch.g. Zafonic (USA) — Anjuli (Northfields USA) u45p4. Big rangy half-brother to 3 flat winners, including the splendid Kooyonga (won Coronation Cup and 2nd in 1000 Guineas in '91). P-t-P '00/1 and '03 r9 w1 (Maiden) p0; last pair 2, fell and pulled up 5. Looked a decent prospect with plenty of scope when winning at Dingley in '00, but nothing but troubled since, and looked fat when beaten a minimum of 23 lengths in '04. Has been tried in cheekpieces. *Mrs P. King — Suffolk (Julie Read).* 2 (R), 29 (R), 181 (R), 559 (R), 829 (R).

ZAKLEY ..9-12.. 9 b.g. Sula Bula — Summer Bride (Harvest Sun) 213p. Tall rangy half-brother to Derri Bride. Dam is half-sister to Trevenning Lad (*qv* '88 Season Annual). Grandam, Bartered Bride, won 6 Points and placed 9. P-t-P '02/3 r3 p2 (head 2nd, and 2nd of 3); and pulled up. Backed from 14s to 6-4 favourite on his reappearance, but had the misfortune to meet the potentially smart Lord Anner in a 17-runner Maiden at Bishops Court, but recovered losses in soft at Kilworthy. Connections went to the expense of having him operated on for his wind after '03, but all the good work was undone when they risked him on firmish at Vauterhill, and he pulled up lame. Wears a cross-noseband. *Mrs C. Lawrence — Eggesford.* 328 (OMa), 567 (CfMa), 966 (R), 1268 (R).

ZAMHAREER (USA) .9-12.. 14 b.g. Lear Fan (USA) — Awenita (Rarity) 853635. Small neat brother to flat winner, Fly Away Soon, and half-brother to 2 winners in USA. FLAT '93/8 r29 w2 (16f) p4. NH '94/02 r42 w6 (4 2m110y-3m3f110y Hdles, and 2 3m3f-3m4f110y Chses) p12; fell/unseated 4. P-t-P '03 r6 w1 (Ladies) p2 (3rds, last once); last pair 2, and unseated. A cracking old horse who enjoyed his schoolmaster status last year, but takes an inordinately long time to get into top gear nowadays, and ideally needs five miles plus. Regained a visor on his latest appearance, and it would be no surprise if connections took the view that he is no longer in love with the game any more. Tongue-tied once in '00. *D.E. Harrison — Cheshire Forest (Carrie Ford).* 94 (L), 230 (L), 407 (L), 987 (L), 1203 (L), 1428 (L).

ZEBS LAD ..—.. 7 b.g. Abdullah (USA) — Arden Grove (Magnolia Lad) ppppp. Tall plain. Tailed off and pulled up in all five Maidens, and not even his dearest admirer would consider him to be a racehorse. *R. Walker — West of Yore.* 272 (OMa), 344 (2m4fOMa), 392 (CfMa), 1159 (OMa), 1292 (OMa).

ZINGIBAR ..7-12§§.. 13 b.g. Caerleon (USA) — Duende (High Top) 883. Half-brother to flat winners, Mr Bombastique (IRE) (also a successful Hurdler) and The Deep. Dam won at 6f. FLAT r10 w1 (7f) p1 (3rd). NH '95/9 r45 w6 (4 2m-2m7f Hdles, and 2 2m7f-3m2f Chses) p13 (inc 3rd in Sell in '96; short-headed once, and beaten head once). P-t-P '00/3 r14 p5 (3 2nds; and 3rd of 4 twice); 10th, last pair 5, refused, pulled up, and slipped up. Hugely reluctant and has not consented to score since '98, but still retains some ability, and finished strongly, though ultimately too late for those each-way backers who had invested at 12-1, when third in his Members. Wears a visor, and is ridden in spurs, and has been tried blinkered. *Miss J. Houldey — Berkeley.* 603 (Cnr), 979 (MOnr), 1070 (M).

ZOLA (IRE) .9-11§.. 9 ch.g. Indian Ridge — Fluella (Welsh Pageant) 1p5224. Tall strong-topped half-brother to 4 winners, (one in Italy), including Pre-Eminent (useful Irish flat — won 12), and to good hurdler, Jubail. Dam won 10f race. FLAT '98/00 (blinkered 1) r28 w2 (16f) p3. NH '99/00 r4 p0;

pulled up 1. P-t-P '02 r4 w1 (Members) p0; last pair 2, and pulled up. Missed '01 and returned from another long spell of inactivity to land his Members for a second time, but there was little merit to the win as his sole rival, the 1-2 favourite, sent a beginner into orbit before halfway. Typically looked reluctant to co-operate fully subsequently, and ended yet another campaign on three legs at Rhydygwern. Visored once in '99, and blinkered once two years later. *Mrs J. Sidebottom — V. of Clettwr.* 201 (M), 836 (O), 1090 (Cf), 1235 (Cf), 1321 (MO), 1484 (O).

The Point-to-Point Associations

Point-to-Point Owners & Riders Association

Chairman: Simon Claisse, Upper Coscombe Barns, Temple Guiting, Glos GL54 5XU (Tel: 01386 584082; Fax: 01386 584720; Mob: 07785 293966; email: simon.claisse@rht.net)

President: Percy Tory, Crab Farm, Shapwick, Blandford, Dorset DT11 9JL (Tel: 01258 857206; Fax: 01258 857513)

Secretary: Jeanette Dawson, The Coach House, 7 Mill Road, Sturry, Canterbury, Kent CT2 0AJ (Tel: 01227 713080; Fax: 01227 713088; email: jeanette_dawson@hotmail.com)

Area Representatives

SOUTH EAST: Anthony Alcock, The Willows, Brook, Ashford, Kent TN25 5PD (Tel/Fax: 01233 812613)

SANDHURST: Jackie Porter, Two Hoots, St Georges Terrace, Lambourn, Hungerford, Berks RG17 8PW (Tel: 01488 73381; Fax: 01488 73513)

WESSEX: Jeremy Barber, Peckmore Farm, Henley, Crewkerne, Somerset TA18 8PQ (Tel: 01460 74943)

Leonard Vickery, Knowle End, South Barrow, Yeovil, Somerset BA22 7LN (Tel: 01963 440043)

DEVON & CORNWALL: Keith Cumings, Eastwood, Bishops Nympton, South Molton, N. Devon EX36 4PB (Tel: 01769 550528)

WEST WALES: Cynthia Higgon, Humble Croft, Much Marcle, Ledbury, Herefordshire HR8 2ND (Mob: 07774 835224)

SOUTH WALES: Joan Williams, Oakdene, Tyr Winch Road, St. Mellons, Cardiff CF3 9UX (Tel: 02920 790218)

WELSH BORDERS: Graham Saveker, 26 Cotswold Drive, Kings Acre, Hereford HR4 0TG (Tel/Fax: 01432 343655)

WEST MIDLANDS: Katharine Smith-Maxwell, Phepson Manor, Himbleton, Droitwich, Worcs WR9 7JZ (Tel: 01905 391206)

SOUTH MIDLANDS: Chris Loggin, Gaydons, Hinton-in-the-Hedges, Northants NN13 5NF (Tel: 01869 810594)

EAST ANGLIA: Pat Rowe, Curles Manor, Clavering, Saffron Walden, Essex CB11 4PW (Tel: 01799 550283; Fax: 01799 550052)

MIDLANDS: John Docker, Rookery Farm, Northbrook Road, Coundon, nr Coventry, Warwicks CV6 2AJ (Tel: 02476 332036)

NORTH WEST: Tim Garton, White Barn Farm, Slade Lane, Over Alderley, nr Macclesfield, Cheshire SK10 4SF
(Tel: 01625 584543; Mob: 07739 948873)

YORKSHIRE: Tom Bannister, Coniston Hall, Coniston Cold, Skipton, N. Yorks BD23 4EB (Tel: 01756 748136; Home: 01729 749551)

NORTHERN: Gus Minto, Gilson, Spylaw Park, Kelso, Borders TD5 8DS (Tel: 01573 223162)

Jockeys Representatives

NORTHERN: Stephen Swiers, The Old Manor House, Norton-Le-Clay, Helperby, York YO6 2RS (Tel: 01423 324155; Mob: 07768 661308)

EASTERN: John Sharp, PO Box 110, Newmarket, Suffolk CB8 9UW (Tel: 01638 508836, Fax: 01638 508008; Mob: 07802 236277)

WESTERN: David Barlow, Kingston Grove, Kingston Blount, Chinnor, Oxon OX39 4SQ (Tel: 01844 351344)

SOUTHERN: Grant Cann, Newlands, Cullompton, Devon EX15 1QQ (Tel: 01884 32284)

Point-to-Point Secretaries Association

Chairman: John Wilson
The Riddings, Tushingham, Whitchurch, Shropshire, SY13 4QL
Tel: 01948 664997 (home);
Fax: 01948 664997 (home);
Tel: 0151 432 7271 (work);
Fax: 0151 432 7942 (work);
Mob: 07831 262321;
email: jwilson@gdcooking.co.uk;
theriddings1btopenworld.com

Vice-Chairman: Robert Killen
Littlemead, Tortworth, Wotton under Edge, Gloucestershire, GL12 8HJ
Tel: 01454 261764 (home);
Mob: 07778 895803; Fax: 01454 261764;
email: robertkillen@littlemead.freeserve.co.uk

Secretary: Miss Lucy Brack
Upper Coscombe Barns, Temple Guiting, Cheltenham, Gloucestershire, GL54 5SB
Tel: 01386 584082 (home);
Fax: 01386 584720; Mob: 07771 528258;
email: lucyb@care4free.net;
lbrack@thejockeyclub.co.uk

DEVON & CORNWALL

Chairman: Peter Kivell
Longstone House, Alverdiscott, Bideford, Devon, EX39 4PW
Tel: 01237 472853 (home); Mob: 07730 648970; email: peter.kivell@btinternet.com

Vice Chairman/Secretary: Frank Yeo
Moortown Farm, Tavistock, Devon, PL19 9JZ
Tel: 01822 614491 (home);
Fax: 01822 616605; Mob: 07071 880201;
email: fyeo@marketing.eclipse.co.uk

New Secretary: Gordon Chambers
Higher Wallaford Farm, Buckfastleigh, Devon, TQ11 0HG
Tel: 01364 642755 (home);
Tel: 01364 652304 (work);
Mob: 07957 737019; Fax: 01364 652762;
email: djr@sawdyeandharris.co.uk

EAST ANGLIA

Chairman; Simon Marriage
Bedfords Farm, Good Easter, Chelmsford, Essex, CM1 4SQ
Tel: 01245 231353 (home);
Fax: 01245 231175; Mob: 07770 881575

Secretary: Mrs Jackie Hodge
Orchard Grove, Bustards Green, Forncett St. Peter, Norwich, Norfolk, NR16 1JE
Tel: 01508 530 869 (home);
Mob: 07739 518 731; email:
jackiehodge@freebie.net

MIDLANDS

Chairman: Joey Newton
Hall Farm, Stonesby, Melton Mowbray, Leicestershire, LE14 4PY
Tel: 01664 464259; Fax: 01476 861367;
Mob: 07785 291915

Secretary: Mrs Karen Pickering
Hill Garth Farm, Ulceby, North Lincolnshire, DN39 6TT
Tel: 01469 588192 (home); Fax: 01469 588980; Mob: 07989 442981;
email: adair1@btinternet.com

NORTHERN

Chairman: Peter Elliot Esq
The Yett, Hownam, Kelso, Roxburghshire
Tel: 01573 440268 (home);
Fax: 01573 440268

Secretary: Tony Hogarth Esq
Mosshouses, Galashields, Selkirkshire, TD1 2PG
Tel: 01896 860242 (home);
Fax: 01896 860366; Mob: 07836 600243;
email: mosshouses@mosshouses.plus.com

NORTH WESTERN

Chairman: Roger Everall
Shawardine Castle, Shawardine, Shewsbury, SY4 1AJ
Tel: 01743 850253

Secretary: John Wilson, The Riddings, Tushingham, Whitchurch, Shropshire, SY13 4QL
Tel: 01948 664997 (home);
Fax: 01948 664997 (home);
Tel: 0151 432 7271 (work);
Fax: 0151 432 7942 (work); Mob: 07831 262321;
email: jwilson@gdcooking.co.uk;
theriddings1btopenworld.com

SANDHURST

Chairman: Philip Scouller, Bottom House, Bix, Oxon, RG9 6DF
Tel: 01491 574776 (home)

Secretary: Steven Astaire
40 Queen Street, London, EC4R 1HN
Tel: 0207 332 2680 (work);
Fax: 0207 332 2650; Mob: 07785 112620;
email: steven@astaire.co.uk

SOUTH EAST

Chairman: Colin Squance, 31 Roseacre Gardens, Chilworth, Guildford, Surrey, GU4 8RQ
Tel: 01483 561597; Fax: 01483 561597;
c.squance@btinternet.com

Secretary: Mrs Nicky Featherstone
28 Exeter Close, Tonbridge, Kent, TN10 4NT
Tel: 01732 353518 (home); email:
nicky_featherstone@hotmail.com

SOUTH MIDLANDS

Chairman: Christopher Marriott, Hull Farm, Chipping Norton, Oxon, OX7 5QF
Tel: 01608 642616 (home);
01367 242422 (work); Fax: 01608 642616;
Mob: 07970 749658;
email: Christopher.Marriott@marriotts.co.uk

Secretary: Miss Sara Moule
45 Weybourne Street, London, SW18 4HG
Tel: 0208 879 0271 (home);
Mob: 07931 286695; 07769 643390 (work);
email: sara_moule@yahoo.co.uk

SOUTH WALES & MONMOUTHSHIRE

Chairman: Jim Thomas
Court Cottage, Barry, Vale of Glamorgan, CF62 4QJ
Tel: 01446 750291 (home)

Secretary: Colin Cross
67 Van Road, Caerphilly, CF83 1LA
Tel: 02920 866453 (home);
Mob: 07811 812206; email:
cross.da@tiscali.co.uk

WELSH BORDER COUNTIES

Chairman: Frank Morgan
Easter Court, Leominster, Herefordshire, HR6 0DE
Tel: 01568 611166 (work); Fax: 01568 619779;
email: f.morgan@brightwells.com

Secretary: Dick Pike
The Priory, Kilpeck, Herefordshire, HR2 9DN
Tel: 01981 570366 (home);
Mob: 07803 135086; Fax: 01981 570778;
email: pike@thepriory.fsnet.co.uk

WESSEX

Chairman: Neil Rainsford
Silver Birches, Blackpool Corner, Axminster, Devon, EX13 5UH
Tel: 01297 678285 (home);
Fax: 01297 678285; Mob: 07977 446992;
email: jeanneil.ransford@tiscali.co.uk

Secretary: Tom Killen
The Cake House, Upper Lodge Farm, Ston Easton, Bath, BA3 4DH
Tel: 01761 241127 (home); Fax: 01761 241117;
Mob: 07971 686285; email: tomkillen@aol.com

WEST MIDLANDS

Chairman: Mrs Katherine Smith-Maxwell
Phepson Manor, Himbleton, Droitwhich, Worcestershire, WR9 7JZ
Tel: 01905 391206 (home)

Secretary: Robert Killen
Littlemead, Tortworth, Wotton under Edge, Gloucestershire, GL12 8HJ
Tel: 01454 261764 (home);
Fax: 01454 261764; Mob: 07778 895803;
email: robertkillen@littlemead.freeserve.co.uk

WEST WALES

Chairman: Dennis Reed
Trevayne Farm, Saundersfoot, Pembrokeshire, SA69 9DL Tel: 01834 813402

Secretary: Mrs Cynthia Higgon
Newton Hall, Crundale, Haverfordwest, Pembs, SA62 4EB
Mob: 07774 835224

YORKSHIRE

Chairman: John Furness
Mustardfield House, Burneston, North Yorkshire, DL8 2JD
Tel: 01845 537321

Secretary: Mrs Sarah Stebbing
Mustard Field House, Burneston, North Yorkshire, DL8 2JD
Tel: 01677 424424 (home); Fax: 01677 425508;
email: stebbing@mustardfield.freeserve.co.uk

Point-to-Point Secretaries 2005

Entries Secretaries (where differing from the Meeting Secretary) or Secretaries of all the Point-to-Points scheduled in 2005 with their contact details where race entries may be made

ALBRIGHTON — Entries Secretary: Mrs Lorna Wickens, Torridon, Bridgnorth Road, Norton, nr Shifnal, Shropshire TF11 9DY Tel: 01952 730651; Fax: 01952 730261

ALBRIGHTON WOODLAND — Secretary: Mrs Jen Hancox, Farley Farm, Farley Lane, Romsley, Halesowen, West Midlands B62 0LN Tel/Fax: 01562 710087

ALDENHAM HARRIERS — Receiver of Entries: Weatherbys Chase by telephone to: 01933 304840 (9am-5pm Mon-Fri) with credit/debit card payment, or by post: to David Ingle, Weatherbys Chase, Weatherbys, Sanders Road, Wellingborough, Northants NN8 4BX enclosing payment

ARMY — Entries Secretary: Mrs Babs Mitcheson, Kings Hill Cottage, Netheravon, Wilts SP4 9PL Tel/Fax: 01980 670285; Mob: 07799 175029; email: babsmitcheson@aol.com

ASHFORD VALLEY — Receiver of Entries: Mrs Sarah Day, Gate House Farm, Marden, Tonbridge, Kent TN12 9SG Tel: 01892 730236 Fax: 01892 730237

ATHERSTONE — Secretary: Mrs S. Garland, Jubilee House Farm, Appleby Magna, Swadlincote, Derby DE12 7AJ Tel: 01530 270252; Fax: 01530 273879

AVON VALE — Secretaries: Philip & Annie Bevins, West End Stables, Foxham, Chippenham, Wiltshire SN15 4NB Tel/Fax: 01249 740441

AXE VALE — Entries Secretary: Jennie Salter, 1 Pinhay Cottages, Rousdon, Lyme Regis, Dorset DT7 3RG Tel/Fax: 01297 444348

BADSWORTH & BRAMHAM MOOR — Entries Secretary: Mrs J. Burnell, Millfield Farm, Tockwith, York YO26 7PA Tel/Fax: 01423 359175

BANWEN MINERS — Secretary: Mr Lode De Smet DVM, MRCVS, Waun Hir Farm, Ammanford, Carmarthen SA18 2PW Tel: 01269 595873; Mob: 07866 753384

BEDALE — Entries Secretary: Mrs P.M. Hodgson, Richmond Equestrian Centre, Brough Park, Tunstall, N. Yorks DL10 7PL Tel: 01748 811629 or 811295; Fax: 01748 818019

BELVOIR — Entries Secretary: Mrs Sally Hudson, The Old Inn, Waltham-on-the-Wolds, Leics LE14 4AH Tel/Fax: 01664 464312; email: sally@hudson-waltham.fsnet.co.uk

BERKELEY — Secretary: Mr Tim King, The Bungalow, Pedington Elm Farm, Berkeley, Glos GL13 9LQ Tel: 01666 826411; Mob: 07813 802949; email: p2p@courtconsulting.co.uk

BERKS & BUCKS DRAGHOUNDS — Entries Secretary: Mrs A. Pitcher, Kilnwood, Dorney Wood Road, Burnham, Berks SL1 8PZ Tel: 01628 666655

BERWICKSHIRE — Entries Secretary: Mrs Ailie Tullie, Whitemire, Duns, Berwickshire TD11 3PY Tel: 01890 818743; Fax: 01890 818791

BICESTER WITH WHADDON CHASE (April)— Entries Secretary: Mrs F. Kehoe, The Croft, Wing Road, Stewkley, Leighton Buzzard, Beds LU7 0JB Tel/Fax: 01525 240749

BICESTER WITH WHADDON CHASE (February)— Entries Secretary: Miss L. Gosling, Manor Farm, Stratton Audley, Bicester, Oxon OX27 9BJ Tel: 01869 277251

BILSDALE — Entries Secretary: David Kinsella, Bluebell Inn, Ingleby Arncliffe, Northallerton, North Yorks Tel: 01609 882272

BLANKNEY — Entries Secretary: Mrs M. Morris MFH, The Old Hall, Brant Broughton, Lincoln LN5 0RZ Tel: 01400 273931 Fax: 01400 273753

BORDER — Entries Secretary: Mrs Helen Gledson, Buteland, Bellingham, Northumberland NE48 2EX Tel/Fax: 01434 220218

BRAES OF DERWENT — Entries Secretary: Mrs Angela Minto, Low Meadows Cottage, Lanchester, Co. Durham DH7 0RE Tel: 01207 528285; Mob: 07779 318087

BRECON & TALYBONT — Receiver of Entries: Mrs S. Price, Cwmgwengad, Aberyscir, Brecon LD3 9NR Tel: 01874 622815

BROCKLESBY — Secretary: Miss J. Burt, Grange Cottage, Riby, nr Grimsby DN37 8NT Tel/Fax: 01469 560266; email: burt@farming.me.uk

BURTON — Secretary: Miss B.M. Neal, Sandbeck, Wressle, Brigg, North Lincs DN20 0BN Tel: 01652 654168 (home) or 01652 653107 (office); Fax: 01652 650502

CAMBRIDGESHIRE HARRIERS HUNT CLUB — Receiver of Entries: Weatherbys Chase, by telephone to: 01933 304840 (9am-5pm Mon-Fri) with credit/debit card payment, or by post: to David Ingle, Weatherbys Chase, Weatherbys, Sanders Road, Wellingborough, Northants NN8 4BX enclosing payment

CAMBRIDGESHIRE WITH ENFIELD CHACE (Horseheath)— Secretary: Mrs N.A. Ward, Rockery Farm, Bourn, Cambs CB3 7TA Tel: 01954 718111 Fax: 01954 718924 email: wendyward@lineone.net

CAMBRIDGESHIRE WITH ENFIELD CHACE (Northaw) — Joint Secretary & Entries Secretary: J.M. Pirie, 12 The Dart, Hemel Hempstead, Herts HP2 6EW Tel/Fax: 01442 248439; Mob: 07811 371684; email: john@jpirieherts.fsnet.co.uk

CAMBRIDGE UNIVERSITY DRAGHOUNDS — Receiver of Entries: Weatherbys Chase by telephone to: 01933 304840 (9am-5pm Mon-Fri) with credit/debit card payment, or by post: to David Ingle, Weatherbys Chase, Weatherbys, Sanders Road, Wellingborough, Northants NN8 4BX enclosing payment

CARMARTHENSHIRE — Secretaries: Mrs Vicky Teal, Bannister Farm, Laugharne, Carms SA33 4RS Tel: 01994 427582; Mrs P. John, Wood House, New Mill, Llanddowror SA33 4HS Tel: 01994 453275

CATTISTOCK — Entries Secretary: Mrs Nicky Atkinson, Holway Farm, Cattistock, Dorchester, Dorset DT2 0HH Tel: 01300 320246 or 01300 320683; Fax: 01300 321522

CHESHIRE — Entries Secretary: Mrs R. Swindells, Higher Barn Farm, Willington, Tarporley, Cheshire CW6 0LY Tel/Fax: 01829 751297

CHESHIRE FOREST — Entries Secretary: P. Heaton Esq, Whitehall Farm, Little Budworth, Tarporley, Cheshire CW6 9EL Tel: 01829 760767

CHIDDINGFOLD, LECONFIELD & COWDRAY — Receiver of Entries: Mr Andrew Lawes, Westcroft Farm, Vann Road, Fernhurst, Haslemere, Surrey GU27 3NI Tel: 01428 652863

CLEVELAND — Entries Secretary: Miss A. Sunter, 16 Salvin Terrace, Fishburn, Stockton-on-Tees TS21 4AG Tel: 07843 431593 (after 6pm)

CLIFTON-ON-TEME — Secretary: Mrs Emma Carpenter, Kiln Cottage, Upper Sapey, Worcs WR6 6EU Tel/Fax: 01886 853255

COLLEGE VALLEY & NORTH NORTHUMBERLAND — Entries Secretary: Miss Veronica Peet, Sunilaws Farm, Cornhill-on-Tweed TD12 4RD Tel/Fax: 01890 882475

COTLEY — Entries Secretary: Mrs M. Handel, Rose Cottage, Furley, Axminster, Devon EX13 7TU Tel: 01404 881699; Fax: 01404 881852

COTSWOLD — Entries Secretary: Miss Susanna Charrington, Glenbrook Farm, Gretton Fields, Cheltenham, Glos GL54 4HH Tel/Fax: 01242 620682

COTSWOLD VALE FARMERS — Secretary: Jason Warner Esq, Ongers Farm, Brookthorpe, Glos GL4 0UT Tel: 01452 813344; Mob: 07976 549373

COTTESMORE — Secretary: Miss E. Inman, Grange Cottage, Tickencote, Stamford, Lincs PE9 4AE Tel/Fax: 01780 753770

COUNTRYSIDE ALLIANCE CLUB (WALES) — Secretary: Miss Beverley Thomas, Puntingbud Farm, Boulston, Haverfordwest, Pembrokeshire SA62 4AH Tel: 01437 767919

CRAWLEY & HORSHAM — Entries Secretary: Mrs J. Gibson, 9 Heath Close, Mannings Heath, Horsham, West Sussex RH13 6EE Tel: 01403 263454; Fax: 01403 267167

CROOME & WEST WARWICKSHIRE — Entries Secretary: Mrs Julia Hopkins, Fern Cottage, Russell Street, Great Comberton, Pershore, Worcs WR10 3DT Tel: 01386 710224

CUMBERLAND — Entries Secretary: Mrs Elizabeth Jestin, Hill Top Farm, Brocklebank, Wigton, Cumbria CA7 8DL Tel/Fax: 01697 478439

CUMBERLAND FARMERS — Entries Secretary: Miss Charlotte Gash, Round Hill, Welton, Carlisle, Cumbria CA5 7HH Tel: 01697 476337; Fax: 01697 476005

CURRE & LLANGIBBY (February)— Secretary: Miss Sarah Kent, 4 Somerset Cottages, St Ann's Street, Chepstow NP16 5HE Tel: 01291 628249

CURRE & LLANGIBBY (March)— Receiver of Entries: Miss Melanie Ward, Lower Ton-y-Felin Farm, Croespenmaen, Crumlin, Newport NP11 3BE Tel: 01495 243016; Mob: 07815 491361

DART VALE & HALDON HARRIERS — Entries Secretary: Mrs D.J. Treneer, Thynacombes, South Brent, Devon TQ10 9EB Tel: 01364 72327 (evenings only)

DARTMOOR — Entries Secretary: Mrs S. Reynard, Yeo Cott, Yealmpton, Plymouth, Devon PL8 2LW Tel: 01752 880405

DERWENT — Entries Secretary: C.J. Cundall Esq, The Cottage, Sherburn Lodge, Sherburn, Malton YO17 8EW Tel/Fax: 01944 710676

DEVON & SOMERSET STAGHOUNDS — Joint Secretaries: Mrs T. White, Benshayes, Bampton, Tiverton, Devon EX16 9LA Tel: 01398 331441; Hugh Ticehurst, The Old Forge, Morebath, Bampton, Devon EX16 Tel: 01398 332053

DUKE OF BEAUFORT'S — Secretary: Mrs Carol Y. Clift, Ebbdown Farm, North Wraxall, Chippenham, Wilts, SN14 7AT Tel: 01225 891293 or 07974 396764

DUKE OF BUCCLEUCH'S — Secretary: Mrs Virginia Scott-Watson, Easter Softlaw, Kelso, Roxburghshire TD5 8BJ Tel: 01573 224641; Fax: 01573 224681

DULVERTON FARMERS — Entries Secretary: Mrs J. Ackner, Hunt Stables, Exford, Somerset TA24 7PX Tel: 01643 831287

DULVERTON WEST — Entries Secretary: Mrs K. Cumings, Eastwood, Bishops Nympton, South Molton, Devon EX36 4PB Tel: 01769 550528; Fax: 01769 550941

DUMFRIESSHIRE — Entries Secretary: Mrs Margaret Robinson, Distillery Farm, Annan DG12 5LL Tel/Fax: 01461 202852

DUNSTON HARRIERS — Joint Secretaries: Mrs J. Howlett, Kirk Hall, Rocklands, Attleborough, Norfolk NR17 1XN Tel/Fax: 01953 483154; B.R. King, Woods Farm, Fersfield, Diss, Norfolk IP22 2BL Tel: 01379 687302

EAST CORNWALL (both meetings)— Secretary: Elizabeth Martin, Hawkmoor Farm, Newbridge, Gunnislake, Cornwall PL18 9LH Tel: 01822 832750; Fax: 01822 832750

EAST DEVON — Entries Secretary: Mrs L. Parker, Oaklee, Harp Lane, Aylesbeare, Exeter, Devon EX5 2JL Tel: 01395 233332; Fax: 01395 232216

EAST ESSEX — Secretaries: Mr & Mrs Stephen March, Vinesse Farm, Little Horkesley, Colchester, Essex CO6 4DT Tel: 01206 271405 Fax: 01206 271231; email: eastessexpt2pt@btopenworld.com

EAST KENT — Receiver of Entries: Mrs N. Featherstone, 28 Exeter Close, Tonbridge, Kent TN10 4NT Tel: 01732 353518, Fax: 01732 506182

EASTON HARRIERS — Secretary: Mrs Jean Merriam, Oak Lawn House, Eye, Suffolk IP23 7NN Tel: 01379 870362; Fax: 01379 873468; email: merriam999@aol.com

EAST SUSSEX & ROMNEY MARSH — Entries Secretary: Mrs Ana West, Tower Hill Farm, Battle, East Sussex TN33 0HW Fax: 01424 773191

EGGESFORD — Entries Secretary: Mrs V. Quick, Birch Farm, East Leigh, Coldridge, Crediton, Devon EX17 6BG Tel/Fax: 01363 83216; Mob: 07976 012135

EGLINTON AND LANARKSHIRE & RENFREWSHIRE — Secretary: Sheila Tannock, c/o Stewart Gilmour & Co, 24 Beresford Terrace, Ayr KA7 2EG Tel: 01292 266768 (day); Fax: 01292 611295; email: langholm@globalnet.co.uk

ESSEX — Secretary: Mrs J. Marriage, Bedfords Farm, Good Easter, Chelmsford, Essex CM1 4SQ Tel: 01245 231353; Fax: 01245 231175

ESSEX & SUFFOLK — Secretary: Mrs L. Greenlees, High Pale, Bures, Suffolk CO8 5JP Tel: 01787 228575 Fax: 01787 228586

ESSEX FARMERS & UNION (Easter)— Secretary: Dudley Moore, Park Gate Farm, Layer Marney, Colchester, Essex CO5 9UH Tel: 01621 815470; Fax: 01621 819613

ESSEX FARMERS & UNION (May)— Secretary: M. Taylor, Hawkins Farm, Hackmans Lane, Cock Clarks, Chelmsford, Essex CM3 6RE Tel: 01621 829595; Fax: 01621 829795; Mob: 07734 140846

EXMOOR — Secretary: Mrs B. Thomas, Higher Westland, Kentisbury, Barnstaple, Devon EX31 4SH Tel/Fax: 01598 763502

FARMERS BLOODHOUNDS — Secretary: Mrs S.E. Busby, Thornton Manor, Ettington, Stratford-upon-Avon, Warwicks CV37 7PN Tel/Fax: 01789 740210; Mob: 07831 603328

FERNIE — Entries Secretary: Susie Harris, Eyebrook Lodge, East Norton, Leics LE7 9XD Tel: 0116 259 8350; Fax: 0116 259 8360

FIFE — Secretary: Mr John Gilmour, Balcormo Mains, Leven, Fife KY8 5QF Tel: 01333 360229 Fax: 01333 360540

FITZWILLIAM (MILTON) — Receiver of Entries: Weatherbys Chase by telephone to: 01933 304840 (9am-5pm Mon-Fri) with credit/debit card payment, or by post: to David Ingle, Weatherbys Chase, Weatherbys, Sanders Road, Wellingborough, Northants NN8 4BX enclosing payment

FLINT & DENBIGH — Entries Secretary: Mrs Rebecca Hewitt, 3 Lower Hall Mews, Holywell Lane, Clutton, Tattenhall, Cheshire CH3 9ET Tel: 01829 782266

FOUR BURROW (both meetings)— Secretary: Mr D.G. Congdon, Higher Hendra, Wendron, Helston, Cornwall TR13 0NR Tel/Fax: 01326 340368

14 REGIMENT ROYAL ARTILLERY — Entries Secretary: Mrs Sally Rawlins, Ablington Farm, Figheldean, Salisbury, Wiltshire SP4 8JX Tel: 01980 670336

GELLIGAER FARMERS — Secretary: Mrs S.A. Turner, Pant-y-Gwreiddyn Farm, Hollybush, Blackwood NP12 0SD Tel: 01495 224925

GLAMORGAN — Receiver of Entries: Mrs Olive Thomas, Court Cottage, Flemingston, Barry CF62 4QJ Tel: 01446 750291

GOLDEN VALLEY — Entries Secretary: Mr Will Holland, New Barn Cottage, Clyro, via Hereford HR3 5SG Tel: 01497 820710; Fax: 01497 821710

GRAFTON — Entries Secretary: Mrs J. Tredwell, Fields Barn Farm, Westbury, Brackley, Northants NN13 5JQ Tel/Fax: 01280 704889

GRANTA HARRIERS — Secretary: Simon Martin, 8 Winders Lane, Histon, Cambs CB4 4EZ Tel: 01223 237112; Fax: 01223 234025; email: entries@point2point.info

GROVE & RUFFORD — Entries Secretary: Mrs Jane Bowen, Bracken Lane Farm Bungalow, Bracken Lane, Retford, Notts DN22 0PL Tel/Fax: 01777 711850; Mob: 07788 523917

HAMPSHIRE — Receiver of Entries: Weatherbys Chase by telephone to: 01933 304840 (9am-5pm Mon-Fri) with credit/debit card payment, or by post: to David Ingle, Weatherbys Chase, Weatherbys, Sanders Road, Wellingborough, Northants NN8 4BX enclosing payment

HARBOROUGH RACE CLUB — Entries Secretary: Mrs K.E. Reynolds, Cowthick Cottage, Weldon, Northants NN17 3JF Tel: 01536 264779; Fax: 01536 269604

HARKAWAY CLUB — Secretary: Mrs Jen Hancox, Farley Farm, Farley Lane, Romsley, Halesowen, West Midlands B62 0LN Tel/Fax: 01562 710087

HAYDON — Entries Secretary: Helen Carr, Highwood Farm, Hexham, Northumberland NE46 3RR Tel: 01434 603783; Fax: 01434 603783

HEYTHROP — Entries Secretary: P.J.H. Wills, Kirkham Farm, Lower Slaughter, Cheltenham, Glos GL54 2JS Tel: 01451 830552; Fax: 01451 830900

HIGH PEAK — Entries Secretary: Mrs E. Pearson, Lower Fold Farm, Rowarth, High Peak, Derbyshire SK22 1ED Tel: 01663 745116

HOLCOMBE — Entries Secretary: Mrs Angela Beardsworth, 67 Stopes Brow, Lower Darwen, Darwen, Lancs BB3 0QP Tel: 01254 260901

HOLDERNESS — Entries Secretary: Mrs B. Hart, Touchwood, Main Street, Burstwick, Hull HU12 9EA Tel: 01964 624016

HURSLEY HAMBLEDON — Secretaries: Mr & Mrs A. Barnden, Forest Farm, Newtown, Fareham, Hampshire PO17 6LL Tel/Fax: 01329 833374

HURWORTH — Secretary: Miss G. Lee, 36 Coronation Crescent, Yarm, Cleveland, TS15 9EA Tel: 01642 897748 Fax: 01642 887190

JEDFOREST — Secretary: Mrs Hilary Mactaggart, Greendale, Hawick, Roxburghshire TD9 7LH Tel/Fax: 01450 372086

LAMERTON — Entries Secretary: Mrs Louise Cox, 33 The Village, Milton Abbot, Tavistock, Devon PL19 0PB Tel/Fax: 01822 870534; email: louisecox@miltonabbot.freeserve.co.uk

LAUDERDALE — Entries Secretary: Mr Tony Hogarth, Mosshouses, Galashiels TD1 2PG Tel: 01896 860242; Fax: 01896 860366

LEDBURY — Entries Secretary: Mrs V. Grundy, Hill Farm, Clenchers Mill Lane, Eastnor, Ledbury, Herefordshire HR8 1RR Tel/Fax: 01531 650646 Mob/Ansaphone: 07761 461611

LINCOLNSHIRE UNITED HUNTS CLUB — Secretary: Miss Emma Forman, The Orchard, 19 East End, Kirmington, North Lincs, DN39 6YS Tel: 01652 688799; Mob: 07766 200538; Fax: 01652 680863

LLANDEILO FARMERS — Entries Secretary: Mr & Mrs A. Lewis, Tyssul Stud, Cwmduad, Carmarthen SA33 6AT Tel: 01559 371282

LLANGEINOR — Secretary: Mrs J.S. Tudor, Ty Wrth Y Coed, Merthyr Mawr, Bridgend CF32 0NU Tel: 01656 650001

LUDLOW — Receiver of Entries: Weatherbys Chase by telephone to: 01933 304840 (9am-5pm Mon-Fri) with credit/debit card payment, or by post: to David Ingle, Weatherbys Chase, Weatherbys, Sanders Road, Wellingborough, Northants NN8 4BX enclosing payment

MELTON HUNT CLUB — Secretary: Mrs Sally Hudson, The Old Inn, Waltham-on-the-Wolds, Melton Mowbray, Leics LE14 4AH Tel/Fax: 01664 464312; email: sally@hudson-waltham.fsnet.co.uk

MENDIP FARMERS — Secretary: Charles E. Green Esq, The Gallery, Kingshill, Chewton Mendip, nr Radstock, Somerset BA3 4PD Mob: 07717 151333

MEYNELL & SOUTH STAFFORDSHIRE — Entries Secretary: Mr D. Westwood, Wales End Farm, Barton-under-Needwood, Burton-on-Trent, Staffs DE13 8JN Tel: 01283 713769

MID DEVON — Entries Secretary: Miss A. Boyden, Denshams Cottage, Chagford, Newton Abbot, Devon TQ13 8HH Tel: 01647 433264

MID SURREY FARMERS DRAGHOUNDS — Secretary & Receiver of Entries: Mrs J. Donegan, Chart Stud Farm, Heverham Road, Kemsing, Sevenoaks, Kent TN15 6NE Tel: 01732 761451; Fax: 01732 760485

MIDDLETON — Entries Secretary: Mrs S. Mason, Thirkleby Warren, Kirby Grindalythe, Malton, YO17 8DG Tel/Fax: 01944 738631

MIDLANDS AREA CLUB — Entries Secretary: Mrs Sally Hudson, The Old Inn, Waltham-on-the-Wolds, Melton Mowbray, Leics LE14 4AH Tel/Fax: 01664 464312; email: sally@hudson-waltham.fsnet.co.uk

MINEHEAD HARRIERS AND WEST SOMERSET — Secretary: Mrs S. Doggrell, Toomer Farm, Henstridge, Templecombe, Somerset BA8 0PH Tel/Fax: 01963 250237

MODBURY HARRIERS — Entries Secretary: Miss E. Pinsent, Warren Cottage, Higher Ludbrook, Ermington, Ivybridge, Devon PL21 0LL Tel: 01548 830698

MONMOUTHSHIRE — Receiver of Entries: Mrs E. Egerton, The Stables, Treveddw Farm, Pandy, Abergavenny, Monmouthshire NP7 7PE Tel: 01873 890448

MORPETH — Entries Secretary: Mrs Vicki Dungait, Lough House Farm, Stannington, Morpeth, Northumberland NE61 6EB Tel: 01670 789447

NEW FOREST — Secretary: M.D. Rabbetts Esq, Ibsley Grange, Ringwood, Hampshire BH24 3PR Tel: 01425 472092; Fax: 01425 461937; email: michael@ibsley.com

NORTH CORNWALL — Joint Secretaries: Mr & Mrs W. Cook, Little Downderry, Coombe, St Austell, Cornwall PL26 7LT Tel/Fax: 01726 882247

NORTH COTSWOLD — Entries Secretary: Mrs R.E. Walker, 1 Yew Tree Cottage, Laverlon, nr Broadway, Worcs WR12 7NA Tel: 01386 584327

NORTH HEREFORD — Secretary: F.J.A. Morgan, Easters Court, Leominster HR6 0DE Tel: 01568 611166 (day) or 01568 708248 (evenings)

NORTH LEDBURY — Entries Secretary: Miss Jane Allfrey, Wild Goose Hill Farm, Storridge, nr Malvern, Worcs WR13 5EL Tel: 01886 880224

NORTH NORFOLK HARRIERS — Secretary: Mrs Tina Hayward, Heydon, Norwich NR11 6RE (this is full address) Tel: 07778 755168; Fax: 01263 587805; email: mail@tinahayward.com; or on Closing Day only Tel/Fax: 01603 872116

NORTH SHROPSHIRE — Receiver of Entries: Weatherbys Chase by telephone to: 01933 304840 (9am-5pm Mon-Fri) with credit/debit card payment, or by post: to David Ingle, Weatherbys Chase, Weatherbys, Sanders Road, Wellingborough, Northants NN8 4BX enclosing payment

NORTH STAFFORDSHIRE — Entries Secretary: Miss Diane Cope, Marsh Farm, Offley Marsh, Eccleshall, Staffs ST21 6HE Tel: 01785 280758; Fax: 01785 280412; email: chris.mellard@btopenworld.com

NORTH WEST POINT-TO-POINT CLUB — Entries Secretary: Mr N. Bostock, Owls Nest, Bearstone Road, Norton-in-Hales, Market Drayton, Shropshire TF9 4AP Tel: 01630 656461

OAKLEY — Secretary: Mrs Liz Mitchinson, 227 Bedford Road, Rushden, Northants NN10 0SQ Tel/Fax: 01933 418195; Mob: 07793 988850; email: lmitchinso@aol.com

OLD BERKSHIRE — Entries Secretary: Miss Tessa Good, Lower Farm Cottage, West Ginge, Wantage, Oxfordshire OX12 8QR Tel: 01235 833952; Fax: 01235 770675

OLD RABY HUNT CLUB — Secretary: Miss S. Town, Woodlands, Station Road, Scorton, Richmond, N. Yorks, DL10 6DF Tel: 01748 810545; Fax: 01748 818031

OLD SURREY, BURSTOW & WEST KENT (both meetings) — Receiver of Entries: Mrs N. Featherstone, 28 Exeter Close, Tonbridge, Kent TN10 4NT Tel: 01732 353518; Fax: 01732 506182

OXFORD UNIVERSITY HUNT CLUB — Entries Secretary: Mrs A. Pitcher, Kilnwood, Dorney Wood Road, Burnham, Berks SL1 8PZ Tel: 01628 666655

PEMBROKESHIRE — Secretaries: Mr & Mrs D. Roach, 19 St Brides View, Roch, Haverfordwest, Pembrokeshire SA62 6AZ Tel/Fax: 01437 710643; Mob: 07980 789244

PENDLE FOREST & CRAVEN — Entries Secretary: N. Bostock Esq, Owl's Nest, Bearstone Road, Norton-in-Hales, Market Drayton, Shropshire TF9 4AP Tel: 01630 656461

PENTYRCH — Secretary: Mr Phillip Williams, The Annexe, Village House, Marcross, Llanwit Major, Vale of Glamorgan CF61 1ZG Tel: 01656 890660; Mob: 07799 155463; email: philsquire@btopenworld.com

PERCY — Secretary: Mr George White, 6 Market Street, Alnwick, Northumberland NE66 1TL Tel: Office 01665 603231 Fax: 01665 510872 Home: 01665 577430

POINT-TO-POINT OWNERS & RIDERS CLUB (both days) — Entries Secretary: Mrs J. Tredwell, Fields Barn Farm, Westbury, Brackley, Northants NN13 5JQ Tel: 01280 704889

PORTMAN — Entries Secretary: Mrs N.C. Turner, Sunnyside Farm, Winterborne Whitechurch, Blandford Forum, Dorset DT11 9AP Tel/Fax: 01929 471750

PUCKERIDGE — Secretary: Mrs R. Sporborg, Park Cottage, Gardners End, Ardeley, Herts SG2 7AR Tel: 01438 861567; Mob: 07792 748197; Fax: 01438 86177; email: thesporborgs@hotmail.com

PYTCHLEY — Entries Secretary: Mrs C. Bailey, Holdenby North Lodge, Spratton, Northampton NN6 8LG Tel: 01604 770234 or 883729; Fax: 01604 770423

QUANTOCK STAGHOUNDS — Secretary: B.L. Bartlett Esq, Adscombe Farm, Over Stowey, nr Bridgwater, Somerset TA5 1HN Tel/Fax: 01278 732260

QUORN — Secretary: Mrs J. Murfitt, Manor Cottage, West Leake, Loughborough, Leics LE12 5RF Tel/Fax: 01509 853792 (home); Tel: 01509 267721 (office - not Fax)

RADNOR & WEST HEREFORD — Secretary: Mrs A. Rogers, Cornhill Cop, Leominster HR6 9DA Tel: 01568 612324

ROSS HARRIERS — Secretary: Mrs Verity Look, Chantry Farm, Perrystone, Ross-on-Wye, Herefords HR9 7QU Tel: 01989 780255; Mob: 07816 478213; email: veritylook@aol.com

ROYAL ARTILLERY — Entries Secretary: P. Hodson Esq, Amphora, Allington, Salisbury, Wiltshire SP4 0BW Tel/Fax: 01980 610764; Mob: 07790 660071

SEAVINGTON — Secretary: G. Rendell Esq, 2 Myrtle Close, Beaminster, Dorset DT8 3BW Tel: 01308 863779

SILVERTON — Secretary: Mr G.T. Chambers, Higher Wallaford Farm, Buckfastleigh, Devon TQ11 0HG Tel: 01364 642755

SINNINGTON — Entries Secretary: Miss W. Bennett, Thorpe Grange, Ampleforth, York, YO62 4EG Tel/Fax: 01439 788286

SIR W.W. WYNN'S — Entries Secretary: Nicci Hugo, 1 Brassey Contract Road, Edge, Malpas, Cheshire SY14 8LB Tel: 01948 820649; Mob: 07736 360550

SOUTH & WEST WILTS — Secretary: Mrs P. Bristol, Little Pound, Motcombe, Shaftesbury, Dorset SP7 9HX Tel/Fax: 01747 853965

SOUTH DEVON — Joint Secretaries: Mr & Mrs J. Greatrex, Higher Lydgate Farm, Postbridge, Devon PL20 6TJ Tel: 01822 880274; Fax: 01822 880319

SOUTH DORSET — Entries Secretary: Mrs J. Lovelace, Honeypuddle, Piddlehinton, Dorchester, Dorset DT2 7TE Tel: 01300 348393

SOUTHDOWN & ERIDGE (both meetings)— Receiver of Entries: Mrs A. Peate, Spring Farm, Spring Lane, Five Ashes, Mayfield, Sussex TN20 6LD Tel/Fax: 01825 830626

SOUTH DURHAM — Secretary & Entries Secretary: Mrs S. Dent, Field House Farm, Kirklevington, Yarm, Cleveland TS15 9PZ Tel/Fax: 01642 782928

SOUTH EAST HUNTS CLUB — Receiver of Entries: Mrs J. Gibson, 9 Heath Close, Mannings Heath, Horsham, W. Sussex RH13 6EE Tel: 01403 263454; Fax: 01403 267167

SOUTH HEREFORDSHIRE — Secretary: Liz Morgans, Stockmans House, Netherton, Harewood End, Hereford HR2 8LA Tel: 01989 730418; Mob: 07812 852992; email: stockmans@waitrose.com

SOUTH MIDLANDS AREA CLUB — Entries Secretary: Mike & Fiona Kehoe, The Croft, Wing Road, Stewkley, Leighton Buzzard, Beds LU7 0JB Tel/Fax: 01525 240749; Mob: 07930 314002

SOUTH NOTTS — Secretary: Miss A. Jepson, Lansic Cottages, Post Office Yard, Hoveringham, Notts NG14 7JR Tel: 01159 664188 Fax: 01159 555800

SOUTH PEMBROKESHIRE — Secretary: Mrs Jan Mathias, Shipping Hill Farm, Manorbier, Tenby, Pembrokeshire SA70 8LE Tel: 01834 871667

SOUTH POOL HARRIERS — Entries Secretary: Mrs A. Foale, Higher Kellaton Farm, Kellaton, Kingsbridge, S. Devon TQ7 2ES Tel/Fax: 01548 511514

SOUTH SHROPSHIRE — Receiver of Entries: Weatherbys Chase by telephone to: 01933 304840 (9am-5pm Mon-Fri) with credit/debit card payment, or by post: to David Ingle, Weatherbys Chase, Weatherbys, Sanders Road, Wellingborough, Northants NN8 4BX enclosing payment

SOUTH TETCOTT — Secretary: Mr M.B. Clark, Garlands Farm, Highampton, Devon EX21 5JR Tel/Fax: 01409 231106

SOUTH WOLD — Secretary: D.E. Ingle Esq, The Old Vicarage, Skendleby, Spilsby, Lincolnshire PE23 4QA Tel/Fax: 01754 890648; Mob: 07720 441739

SPOONERS & WEST DARTMOOR — Entries Secretary: Mrs J. Petch, Sunset Cottage, Harrowbeer Lane, Yelverton, Devon PL20 6EA Tel: 01822 853533; Mob: 07790 874954

STAFF COLLEGE & R.M.A. SANDHURST DRAGHOUNDS — Entries Secretary: Miss Chris Elliott, The Croft, Paice Lane, Medstead, Alton, Hants GU34 5PT Tel/Fax: 01420 562268; Mob: 07770 941493

STAINTONDALE — Secretary & Entries Secretary: Mrs W.P. Osborne, Hunt Cottage, Staintondale, Scarborough YO13 0EL Tel/Fax: 01723 871017; Mob: 07929 185294

STEVENSTONE — Secretary: Mrs J.M. Wickett, Hill Farm, Shebbear, Beaworthy, Devon EX21 5ST Tel/Fax: 01409 281370

SUFFOLK — Secretary: B.R. King, Woods Farm, Fersfield, Diss IP22 2BL Tel: 01379 687302; Fax: 01379 688017

SURREY UNION — Receiver of Entries: Mrs N. Featherstone, 28 Exeter Close, Tonbridge, Kent TN10 4NT Tel: 01732 353518; Fax: 01732 506182

TANATSIDE — Entries Secretary: Jean Balmer, Ty Canol, Guilsfield, Welshpool, Powys SY21 9PS Tel: 01938 590509; Fax: 01938 590545

TAUNTON VALE — Secretary: Mrs F. Walker, Greenway Farm, North Newton, Bridgwater, Somerset TA7 0DS Tel/Fax: 01278 663801

TAUNTON VALE HARRIERS — Entries Secretary: Miss M. Alford, Straightash Farm, Culmstock, Devon EX15 3JX Tel: 01823 680283; Fax: 01823 681003

TEDWORTH — Secretaries: Richard & Jane Denny, Charldown, East End, Newbury, Berks RG20 0AH Tel/Fax: 01635 250588; email: point2point@charldown.com

TEME VALLEY — Secretary: Miss Pauline Duggan, Little Folly, Eardisland, Leominster, Hereford HR6 9BS Tel: 01544 388258; Fax: 01544 388559

TETCOTT — Secretary: Clare Heywood, East Milford Farm, Hartland, Bideford, Devon EX39 6EA Tel: 01237 441268; Mob: 07900 982708; Fax: 01237 441197; email: clarehey@uk2.net

THURLOW — Entries Secretary: Mr R.A. Fenwick, Lark Hall, Six Mile Bottom, Newmarket, Suffolk CB8 0UT Tel: 01638 570206; Fax: 01638 570333

TIVERTON — Entries Secretary: S. Sampson Esq, Frys Farm, Culmstock, Cullompton, Devon EX15 3JT Tel: 01823 680308

TIVERTON STAGHOUNDS — Entries Secretary: Mrs A. Palfrey, Higher Rifton, Stoodleigh, Tiverton, Devon EX16 9RT Tel: 01884 881413

TIVYSIDE — Secretaries: Mr & Mrs W.D. Lewis, Pantycaws Stud, Efailwen, Clynderwen SA66 7XD Tel: 01994 419272

TORRINGTON FARMERS — Entries Secretary: Miss Lorna Symons, 67 Stafford Way, Dolton, Winkleigh, Devon EX19 8PY Tel/Fax: 01805 804844; Mob: 07968 061780

TREDEGAR FARMERS — Secretary: Colin Cross, 67 Van Road, Caerphilly CF83 1LA Tel: 02920 866453

TWESELDOWN RACING CLUB — Entries Secretary: Miss Sarah Dawson, 43 Elm Park, Cranleigh, Surrey GU6 8UG Tel/Fax: 01483 271262; email: entries2005@aol.com; website: http://jump.to/tweseldownracing

TYNEDALE — Entries Secretary: Mrs Lesley Walby, East House Farm, Dalton, Ponteland, Newcastle-upon-Tyne NE18 0AE Tel: 01661 822272 Fax: 01661 822183

UNITED PACK — Entries Secretary: Miss L.R. McFarlane, Coates Bungalow, Ratlinghope, Shrewsbury, Shropshire SY5 0SS Tel/Fax: 01588 650412; email: lucy_mc@lineone.net

UNITED SERVICES — Entries Secretary: Flt Lt T. Burgess DFC, Woodlands, Woodborough, Pewsey, Wilts SN9 5PG Tel/Fax: 01672 851682; Mob: 07813 837918

VALE OF AYLESBURY WITH GARTH & SOUTH BERKS (Kimble)— Entries Secretary: Mrs C. Sutcliffe, Sandford End, Aston Sandford, Aylesbury, Bucks HP17 8LP Tel: 01844 291125; Fax: 01844 292787

VALE OF AYLESBURY WITH GARTH & SOUTH BERKS (Kingston Blount, April)— Receiver of Entries: Weatherbys Chase by telephone to: 01933 304840 (9am-5pm Mon-Fri) with credit/debit card payment, or by post: to David Ingle, Weatherbys Chase, Weatherbys, Sanders Road, Wellingborough, Northants NN8 4BX enclosing payment

VALE OF AYLESBURY WITH GARTH & SOUTH BERKS (Kingston Blount, May)— Secretary: Mrs Helen Jackson, Hanger Farm, Fingest, nr Henley, Oxon RG9 6QB Tel: 01494 881321 (before 9pm); Fax: 01494 882514

VALE OF CLETTWR — Secretary: Mr & Mrs A. Lewis, Tyssul Stud, Cwmduad, Carmarthen SA33 6AT

VALE OF LUNE — Entries Secretary: Mrs S. Askew, 29 Russell Drive, Torrisholme, Morecambe, Lancs LA4 6NK Tel: 01524 421416

V.W.H. — Entries Secretary: Miss Lucy Brack, Upper Coscombe Barns, Temple Guiting, Cheltenham, Glos GL54 5SB Tel: 01386 584082; Fax: 01386 584720

VINE & CRAVEN — Entries Secretary: Mrs J. Porter, Two Hoots, St George's Terrace, Lambourn, Hungerford, Berks RG17 8PW Tel/Fax: 01488 73381; Mob: 07775 814166

WARWICKSHIRE — Entries Secretary: Mrs S.E. Busby, Thornton Manor, Ettington, Stratford-upon-Avon, Warwicks CV37 7PN Tel/Fax: 01789 740210; Mob: 07831 603328

WAVENEY HARRIERS — Secretary: J.W. Whyte, Becks Green Farm, Ilketshall St Andrews, Beccles NR34 8NB Tel: 01986 781221; Fax: 01986 781406

WESTERN — Joint Secretaries: Mrs S. Baker & Mrs C. Britten, Treen Farm, Gurnards Head, Zennor, St Ives, Cornwall TR26 3DE Tel: 01736 330229 (daytime) or 01736 797080 (evening); Fax: 01736 365307; email: sarah@legalcost.co.uk

WEST NORFOLK — Secretary: Mrs Suzy Lyles, Muckelton Farm, Burnham Market, Kings Lynn, Norfolk PE31 8JT Tel: 01485 518318; Fax: 01485 518015

WEST OF YORE — Entries Secretary: R. Wells Esq, 14 East Witton, Leyburn, North Yorkshire DL8 4SH Tel/Fax: 01969 623211

WESTON & BANWELL HARRIERS — Secretary: J. Fear Esq, Manor Farm, Southwick, Mark, Highbridge, Somerset TA9 4LH Tel/Fax: 01278 783261

WEST PERCY — Entries Secretary: George White, 6 Market Street, Alnwick NE66 1TL Tel: 01665 603231 (office)

WEST SOMERSET AND MINEHEAD HARRIERS — Secretary: Mrs S. Doggrell, Toomer Farm, Henstridge, Templecombe, Somerset BA8 0PH Tel/Fax: 01963 250237

WEST SOMERSET VALE — Secretary: Miss Katherine Cooke, Brook Farm, Bath Road, Upper Langford, Bristol BS40 5DN Tel: 01934 853330

WEST STREET TICKHAM — Receiver of Entries: Mrs J. Gibson, 9 Heath Close, Mannings Heath, Horsham, W. Sussex RH13 6EE Tel: 01403 263454, Fax: 01403 267167

WEST STREET TICKHAM — Receiver of Entries: Mrs A. Blaker, Dovecote Farm, Nutley, Sussex TN22 3HE Tel/Fax: 01825 712197

WHEATLAND — Entries Secretary: Mrs V. Chesters, Lower Duddlewick House, Stottesdon, Worcs DY14 8TH Tel: 01746 718502; email: eurogrid@bt.com

WILTON — Secretaries: Mr & Mrs M. Elgar, Slate Cottage, Homington, Salisbury, Wiltshire SP5 4NQ Tel: 01722 718368; Fax: 01722 718219

WOODLAND PYTCHLEY — Secretary: Mrs K.E. Reynolds, Cowthick Cottage, Weldon, Northants NN17 3JF Tel: 01536 264779 Fax: 01536 269604

WORCESTERSHIRE — Entries Secretary: Mrs Christine Banks, Shell Manor, Himbleton, Droitwich, Worcs WR9 7LA Tel: 01905 391640; Fax: 01905 391206

YORK AND AINSTY — Entries Secretary: Mrs E, Clark, Low Towthorpe Farm, Farlington, York YO61 1NP Tel/Fax: 01347 878463; Mob: 07710 267109

YSTRAD TAF FECHAN — Secretary: Mrs E. Popham, Tyn-y-Plancau Farm, Hensol, Pontyclun CF72 8JX Tel: 01443 225273; Mob: 07966 681029; email: eilpopham@aol.com

ZETLAND — Secretary & Entries Secretary: Miss S. Town, Woodlands, Station Road, Scorton, Richmond, N.Yorks DL10 6DF Tel: 01748 810545; Fax: 01748 818031

Important Races - Hunter Chases

CHRISTIES FOXHUNTERS' CHALLENGE CUP

Cheltenham

Foxhunter Challenge Cup, 4m

1946	Mrs H. Freeman-Jackson's	ILOILO	(Owner)	H. Freeman-Jackson	16
1947	Mr S.C. Bank's	LUCKY PURCHASE	(Owner)	J. Nichols	26
1948	Lt Col H. Llewellyn's	STATE CONTROL	(Owner)	Owner	38
1949	abandoned because of frost				
1950	Mr J. Stuart Evans'	GREENWOOD	(Owner)	Owner	25
1951	Capt R.B. Smalley's	HALLOWEEN	(W. Wightman)	Owner	26
1952	Mr A. Walton's	PARASOL II	(Owner)	I. Kerwood	19
1953	Miss P. Bruce's	DUNBOY II	(Owner)	C. Scott	22
	Mr J.U. Baillie's	MERRY	(A. Kerr)	G. Kindersley	
1954	Mr A. Moralee's	HAPPYMINT	(J. Wight)	Owner	21
1955	abandoned because of snow				
1956	Mr C.D. Scott's	THE CALLANT	(J. Wight)	J. Scott-Aiton	17
1957	Mr C.D. Scott's	THE CALLANT	(J. Wight)	J. Scott-Aiton	9
1958	Mr R. Brewis'	WHINSTONE HILL	(Owner)	Owner	16
1959	Mr T.D. Rootes'	SOME BABY	(Owner)	M.J. Thorne	15
1960	Mr R. Brewis'	WHINSTONE HILL	(Owner)	Owner	15
1961	Mr L.R. Morgan's	COLLEDGE MASTER	(Owner)	Owner	17
1962	Mr L.R. Morgan's	COLLEDGE MASTER	(Owner)	Owner	17
1963	Mr G. Shepheard's	GRAND MORN II	(Owner)	R. Bloomfield	20
1964	Mr R.R. Tweedie's	FREDDIE	(Owner)	A. Mactaggart	10
1965	Mr R.H. Woodhouse's	WOODSIDE TERRACE	(Owner)	Owner	19
1966	Mr W.J.A. Shepherd's	STRAIGHT LADY	(Owner)	R. Shepherd	21
1967	Mr I.H. Patullo's	MULBARTON	(Owner)	N. Gaselee	13
1968	Mr G.R. Dun's	BRIGHT BEACH	(Owner)	C. Macmillan	12
1969	Mr W. Wade's	QUEEN'S GUIDE	(Owner)	G. Wade	10
1970	Mr R.H. Woodhouse's	HIGHWORTH	(Owner)	Owner	13

Sun Alliance & London Foxhunter Challenge Cup, 4m

1971	Mr D. Windel's	HOPE AGAIN	(Owner)	R. Smith	18
1972	Mr C.D. Collins'	CREDIT CALL	(W.A. Stephenson)	Owner	9
1973	Mrs E. Barker's	BULLOCKS HORN	(R. Turnell)	Lord Oaksey	20

Foxhunter Challenge Cup, 4m

1974	Mrs G. Fairbairn's	CORRIE BURN	(Owner)	I. Williams	16
1975	Mrs B.L. Surman's	REAL RASCAL	(Owner)	G. Hyatt	16
1976	Mr A.E. Cowan's	FALSE NOTE	(J. Horton)	B. Smart	16
1977	Mr R.J. Shepherd's	LONG LANE	(Owner)	Owner	16

Foxhunter Challenge Cup, 3m2f

1978	Mr R.J. Shepherd's	MOUNTOLIVE	(Owner)	Owner	16

Christies Foxhunter Challenge Cup, 3m2f

1979	Mr M.J. Thorne's	SPARTAN MISSILE	(Owner)	Owner	10

Foxhunter Challenge Cup, 3m2f

1980	Mr B. Brazier's	ROLLS RAMBLER	(F. Winter)	O. Sherwood	7
1981	Mr F.H. Gilman's	GRITTAR	(Owner)	C.R. Saunders	17
1982	Mr B. Munro-Wilson's	THE DRUNKEN DUCK	(A. Smith)	Owner	19
1983	Miss C. Beasley's	ELIOGARTY	(B. Kelly, Ire)	Owner	16
1984	Mr N.E.C. Sherwood's	VENTURE TO COGNAC	(F. Winter)	O. Sherwood	21

Christies Foxhunter Challenge Cup, 3m2f

1985	Mr W. Mawle's	ELMBOY	(Owner)	A. Hill	17
1986	Mrs J. Magnier's	ATTITUDE ADJUSTER	(M. Morris, Ire)	T.M. Walsh	14
1987	R.E.A. Bott (Wigmore St) Ltd.'s	OBSERVE	(F. Winter)	C. Brooks	14
1988	Mrs J. Campbell's	CERTAIN LIGHT	(Owner)	P. Hacking	9
1989	Miss K. Rimell's	THREE COUNTIES	(Mrs M. Rimell)	Owner	16

1990	Mr J. Clements'	CALL COLLECT	(J. Parkes)	R. Martin	15
1991	Mr E.J. O'Sullivan's	LOVELY CITIZEN	(E.M. O'Sullivan)	W. O'Sullivan	18
1992	Mr J.A. Keighley's	RUSHING WILD	(R. Barber)	J. Farthing	24
1993	Mr R.C. Wilkins'	DOUBLE SILK	(Owner)	R. Treloggen	18
1994	Mr R.C. Wilkins'	DOUBLE SILK	(Owner)	R. Treloggen	5
1995	Mr J.A. Keighley's	FANTUS	(R. Barber)	Miss P. Curling	13
1996	Mr J.P. McManus'	ELEGANT LORD	(E. Bolger, Ire)	E. Bolger	17
1997	Mr J.A. Keighley's	FANTUS	(R. Barber)	T. Mitchell	18
1998	Mr R.M. Penny's	EARTHMOVER (IRE)	(R. Barber)	J. Tizzard	11
1999	Mr C. Dixey's	CASTLE MANE (IRE)	(Caroline Bailey)	B. Pollock	24
2000	Mr H.J. Manners'	CAVELERO	(Owner)	A. Charles-Jones	24
2001	abandoned due to foot-and-mouth restrictions				
2002	Mr R. Tate's	LAST OPTION	(Owner)	Mrs F. Needham	
2003	Mr A. Sendell's	KINGSCLIFF	(Mrs S. Alner)	R. Young	
2004	Mr R.M. Penny's	EARTHMOVER (IRE)	(P. Nicholls)	Miss A. Godchen	24

MARTELL FOXHUNTERS' CHASE

Liverpool

Foxhunters Chase, 4m856yds

1947	Mr S.C. Banks'	LUCKY PURCHASE	(OWNER)	J. Nichols	6
1948	Mr H.W. Metcalfe's	SAN MICHELE	(Maj G. Cunard)	Maj G. Cunard	
1949	Mrs J. Makin's	BALLYHARTFIELD	(Owner)	J. Straker	5

Foxhunters Chase, 2m7f110yds

1950	Mr L.H. Dalton's	HILLMERE	(Owner)	P. Brookshaw	14
1951	Mr R. Brewis'	CANDY II	(Owner)	Owner	17
1952	Col H.T. Alexander's	PAMPEENE II	(Owner)	Owner	11
1953	Mr M.J. Brewis'	SOLO CALL	(Owner)	Owner	7
1954	Mr L.A. Colville's	DARK STRANGER	(Owner)	J. Bosley	14
1955	Mr A. Moralee's	HAPPYMINT	(J. Wight)	Owner	13
1956	Mr J.A. Keith's	MR SHANKS	(Owner)	J. Everitt	8
1957	Mr L.R. Morgan's	COLLEDGE MASTER	(Owner)	Owner	6
1958	Mrs S. Richard's	SURPRISE PACKET	(Owner)	T. Johnson	13
1959	Miss W.H.S. Wallace's	MERRYMAN II	(N. Crump)	C. Scott	10
1960	Mr M. Fear's	APRIL QUEEN	(Owner)	J. Daniell	8
1961	Mr L.R. Morgan's	COLLEDGE MASTER	(Owner)	Owner	13
1962	Mr K.J. Beeston's	DOMINION	(Owner)	C. Foulkes	12
1963	Mr F.D. Nicholson's	SEA KNIGHT	(W.A. Stephenson)	P. Nicholson	15
1964	Mr M. Fear's	AERIAL III	(R. Armytage)	J. Daniell	8
1965	Mr F.D. Nicholson's	SEA KNIGHT	(W.A. Stephenson)	P. Nicholson	14
1966	Mr C.J.T. Alexander's	SUBALTERN	(Owner)	J. Lawrence	14
1967	Miss B. Johnson's	MINTO BURN	(Owner)	J. Lawrence	14
1968	Mr P.H.J. Will's	JUAN	(Owner)	Owner	8
1969	Mr V. Hunter Rowe's	BITTER LEMON	(Owner)	Owner	15
1970	Mr P.C.R. Wate's	LISMATEIGE	(Owner)	A. Wates	5
1971	Mr G.A.C. Cure's	BRIGHT WILLOW	(Owner)	R. Chugg	15
1972	Mr C.D. Collins'	CREDIT CALL	(W.A. Stephenson)	Owner	8
1973	Mrs E. Barker's	BULLOCKS HORN	(R. Turnell)	Lord Oaksey	14
1974	Mrs J. Brutton's	LORD FORTUNE	(Owner)	D. Edmunds	10
1975	Hon Mrs R.L. Newton's	CREDIT CALL	(W.A. Stephenson)	J. Newton	10

Greenall Whitley Foxhunter Chase, 2m6f

1976	Hon Mrs R.L. Newton's	CREDIT CALL	(Owner)	J. Newton	9
1977	Mr N.J. Henderson's	HAPPY WARRIOR	(F. Winter)	Owner	20

Whisky Haig Hunters Chase, 2m6f

1978	Mr M.J. Thorne's	SPARTAN MISSILE	(Owner)	Owner	19

Haig Whisky Hunters Chase, 2m6f

1979	Mr M.J. Thorne's	SPARTAN MISILE	(Owner)	Owner	15
1980	Mr B. Barker's	ROLLS RAMBLER	(F. Winter)	O. Sherwood	24

Haig Fox Hunters Chase, 2m6f

1981	Mr F.H. Gilman's	GRITTAR	(Owner)	C.R. Saunders	25
1982	Mr J. Docker's	LONE SOLDIER	(Owner)	P. Greenall	12
1983	Mrs D. Hehir's	ATHA CLIATH	P. Mullins, Ire)	W. Mullins	8
1984	Mr J.G. Dudgeon's	GAYLE WARNING	(Owner)	A. Dudgeon	17

R.E.A. Bott Fox Hunters Chase, 2m6f

1985	Mrs J. Mann's	CITY BOY	(Mrs A. Underwood)	T. Thomsom Jones	18
1986	Miss C. Beasley's	ELIOGARTY	(D.J.G. Murray-Smith)	Owner	20
1987	Mr J.S. Delahooke's	BORDER BURG	(G. Cook)	A. Hill	25

Seagram Fox Hunters Chase, 2m6f

1988	Mr M.A. Johnson's	NEWNHAM	(Owner)	S.R. Andrews	23
1989	Mr J.Clements'	CALL COLLECT	(J. Parkes)	R. Martin	16
1990	Mrs W. Tulloch's	LEAN AR AGHAIDH	(S. Mellor)	D. Gray	25
1991	Mr D.J. Harding-Jones's	DOUBLE TURN	(J.R. Jenkins)	P. Harding-Jones	27

Martell Fox Hunters Chase, 2m6f

1992	Mr G.A. Hubbard's	GEE-A	(F. Murphy)	Paul Murphy	29
1993	Mr R.C. Wilkins'	DOUBLE SILK	(Owner)	R. Treloggen	27
1994	Mr H.J. Manners'	KILLESHIN	(Owner)	G. Brown	28
1995	Mrs J. Wilson's	SHEER JEST	(Bill Warner)	A. Hill	26
1996	Mrs H.J. Clarke's	ROLLING BALL (FR)	(S. Brookshaw)	R. Ford	26
1997	Mrs B. Graham & Mr J. Mahon's	BLUE CHEEK	(J. Mahon)	R. Thornton	14
1998	Mr H.J. Manners'	CAVALERO	(Owner)	A. Charles-Jones	30
1999	Mr J.P. McManus'	ELEGANT LORD	(E. Bolger, Ire)	P. Fenton	23
2000	Mr R. Gibbs'	BELLS LIFE (IRE)	(P. Hobbs)	D. O'Meara	26
2001	Mr W.A. Ritson & Mr D. Hall's	GUNNER WELBURN	(Mrs C. Bailey)	Julian Pritchard	27
2002	Mr T. Hubbard, Mr A. Heard, Mr J. George & Mr R. Metherell's	TORDUFF EXPRESS (IRE)	(P. Nicholls)	Miss P. Gundry	30
2003	Mr I. Hamilton's	DIVET HILL	(Mrs A. Hamilton)	D. Jewett	
2004	Mr J. Gilsenan's	FOREST GUNNER	(R. Ford)	Mrs C. Ford	25

INTRUM JUSTITIA (HORSE & HOUND CUP)

Horse and Hound Cup, Stratford, 3m4f

1959	Mr V.R. Bishop's	SPEYLOVE	(Owner)	J. Jackson	15
1960	Mr H.W. Dufosee's	BANTRY BAY	(Owner)	M. Tory	17
1961	Mr H.W. Dufosee's	BANTRY BAY	(Owner)	M. Tory	8
1962	Mr J. Reade's	BAULKING GREEN	(Owner)	R. Willis	16
1963	Mr J. Reade's	BAULKING GREEN	(T. Forster)	A. Frank	17
1964	Miss M. Arden's	ROYAL PHOEBE	(R. Whiston)	M. Gifford	13
1965	Mr J. Reade's	BAULKING GREEN	(T. Forster)	G. Small	8
1966	Mr C.D. Collins'	SANTA GRAND	(W.A. Stephenson)	Owner	10
1967	Mrs C. Radcliffe's	CHAM	(F. Cundell)	J. Lawrence	16
1968	Mr A.M. Darlington's	GREEN PLOVER	(J. Ford)	A. Maxwell	8
1969	Mr G. Darlington's	TOUCH OF TAMMY	(Owner)	R. Guilding	14
1970	Mr H.S. Poole's	SOME MAN	(Owner)	R. Knipe	15
1971	Mr C.D. Collins'	CREDIT CALL	(W.A. Stephenson)	G. Macmillan	10
1972	Mr C.D. Collins'	CREDIT CALL	(W.A. Stephenson)	Owner	11
1973	Mr C.D. Collins'	CREDIT CALL	(W.A. Stephenson)	Owner	5
1974	Mr H. Counsell's	STANHOPE STREET	(Owner)	B. Venn	12
1975	Hon Mrs R.L. Newton's	CREDIT CALL	(W.A. Stephenson)	J. Newton	12
1976	Mr O.J. Carter's	OTTER WAY	(Owner)	G. Cann	10
1977	Mr M.W. Bishop's	DEVIL'S WALK	(Owner)	T. Rooney	16
1978	Mr B. Brazier's	ROLLS RAMBLER	(F. Winter)	N. Henderson	9
1979	Mr M.J. Thorne's	SPARTAN MISSILE	(Owner)	Owner	8
1980	Mr B. Brazier's	ROLLS RAMBLER	(F. Winter)	O. Sherwood	16
1981	Mr O.J. Carter's	OTTERY NEWS	(Owner)	A.J. Wilson	17
1982	Mrs L. Clay's	LOYAL PARTNER	(T. Clay)	T. Clay	10
1983	Mr O.J. Carter's	OTTER WAY	(Owner)	A.J. Wilson	17
1984	Mr T.D. Easterby's	PROMINENT KING	(M.H. Easterby)	Owner	20
1985	Mr A. Calder's	FLYING ACE	(Owner)	Miss D. Calder	10

1986	Mr M.J. Langton's	THE PAIN BARRIER	(O. Sherwood)	Miss A. Langton	10
1987	Mrs M. Rimell's	THREE COUNTIES	(Owner)	Miss K. Rimell	11
1988	Miss K. Rimell's	THREE COUNTIES	(Mrs M. Rimell)	Owner	14
1989	Miss H. Wilson's	MYSTIC MUSIC	(Mrs K. Anderson)	K. Anderson	16
1990	Miss H. Wilson's	MYSTIC MUSIC	(Mrs K. Anderson)	K. Anderson	9
1991	Mr P. Bonner's	FEDERAL TROOPER	(Mrs C. McCarthy)	T. McCarthy	16
1992	abandoned because of waterlogged course				
1993	Mr P. Craggs'	GENERALS BOY	(Owner)	P. Craggs	6
1994	Mr M.E. Pinto's	MIGHTY FROLIC	(Miss S. Edwards)	T. Hills	12
1995	Miss B.W. Palmer's	HERMES HARVEST	(Owner)	A. Balding	16
1996	Mr S. Pike's	PROUD SUN	(Owner)	J. Culloty	14

Horse & Hound Cup, Stratford, 3m4f

1997	Mr G.J. Powell's	CELTIC ABBEY	(Miss V. Williams)	D. Jones	11
1998	Winning Line Racing Ltd's	TEETON MILL	(Miss V. Williams)	Miss S. Vickery	9
1999	Mr & Mrs R.M. Phillips'	GRIMLEY GALE (IRE)	(M. Jackson)	Julian Pritchard	7

Intrum Justitia (Horse & Hound Cup) Champion HC, Stratford, 3m4f

2000	Mr C. Dixey's	CASTLE MANE (IRE)	(Mrs C. Bailey)	B. Pollock	7
2001	Mr C. Hammett's	LOOK IN THE MIRROR	(F. O'Brien)	Miss A. Nolan	14
2002	Mr V.J. Hughes & Miss L. Llewellyn's	PRIMATICCIO (IRE)	(D. Williams)	C. Williams	16
2003	Mr M.J. Roberts'	BITOFAMIXUP (IRE)	(Owner)	Mrs J. Gordon	
2004	Two Plus Two's	TORDUFF EXPRESS (IRE)	(P. Nicholls)	N. Williams	11

WEATHERBY'S CHASE JOHN CORBET CHAMPION NOVICES HUNTER CHASE

John Corbet Cup, Stratford, 3m

1965	Miss J. Hilditch's	TELADO	(A.W. Jones)	W. Foulkes	18
1966	Mr T.G. Cambidge's	HANDSEL	(Owner)	W. Foulkes	10

John Corbet Cup, Stratford, 3m2f

1967	Mr C.D. Collins'	TITUS OATES	(W.A. Stephenson)	Owner	23
1968	Mr W.J.A. Shepherd's	POULAKERRY	(Owner)	R. Shepherd	10
1969	Mr F. Sutton's	BLUE DEAN	(Owner)	R. Simpson	16
1970	Mr C.D. Collins'	CREDIT CALL	(W.A. Stephenson)	Owner	16
1971	Mr G.H. Yardley's	DEBLIN'S GREEN	(Owner)	D. Edmunds	17
1972	Mrs K. Poppe's	POSEIDON PRINCE	(C. Miller)	J. Bishop	19
1973	Mr R. Hutchinson's	JOLLY'S CLUMP	(N. Pegge)	J. Docker	15
1974	Mr C.D. Collins'	CORNWALLIS	(W.A. Stephenson)	Owner	18
1975	Mr O.J. Carter's	OTTER WAY	(Owner)	G. Cann	15
1976	Mr G.W. Renilson's	KING CON	(Owner)	P. Craggs	18
1977	Mr P. Greenall's	TIMMIE'S BATTLE	(W.A. Stephenson)	Owner	11
1978	Mr M. Fear's	ROYAL AIR	(Owner)	R. Fear	11
1979	Miss G. Harrison's	TRENTISHOE	(Owner)	J. Frost	11
1980	Mr D.A. Wales'	SWIFT WOOD	(Owner)	W. Wales	20
1981	Mrs J.A. Baimbridge's	PRECIPITOUS	(Owner)	Miss A. Dare	18
1982	Mr A. Sanderson's	LADY BUTTONS	(Miss J. Sanderson)	N. Tutty	10
1983	Mr J.F. Thompson's	CASA KNIPE	(Owner)	K. Reveley	16
1984	Mr R.G. Reynold's	BRIGADIER MOUSE	(Owner)	B. Thomas	11

Land Rover Final Champion (John Corbet Cup), Stratford, 3m2f

1985	Mrs J. Mann's	CITY BOY	(Mrs A. Underwood)	T. Thomson-Jones	10

Coopers Champion Novices (John Corbet Cup), Stratford, 3m2f

1986	Mr J.S. Delahooke's	I GOT STUNG	(G. Cook)	A. Hill	9

Red Bank Champion Novices (John Corbet Cup), Stratford, 3m2f

1987	Mr G.F. Cook's	KING NEON	(Owner)	Miss L. Johnson	14

Coopers Champion Novices (John Corbet Cup), Stratford, 3m2f

1988	Mrs M. Rimell's	DEEP PROSPECT	(Owner)	M. Sheppard	12

Autocar Transporter Champion Novices (John Corbet Cup), Stratford, 3m2f

1989	Mr R.P. Sandys-Clarke's	JELUPE	(Owner)	Owner	7
1990	Mr J.A. Riddell's	BLUE RAVINE	(R. Lamb)	S. Bell	10

John Corbet Champion Novices Cup, Stratford, 3m2f

1991	Mr H. Taylor's	SPARTAN CHIEF	(Mrs G. Jones)	N. Jones	13
1992	Mrs J. Wilson's	SHEER JEST	(W. Warner)	A. Hill	16

John Corbet Champion Novices Cup, Stratford, 3m4f

1993	Mr J.G. Cann's	FRIENDLY LADY	(Owner)	Miss P. Curling	16
1994	Mr G.J. Powell's	CELTIC ABBEY	(Mrs C. Hardinge)	D. Jones	8
1995	Mr S.L. Pike's	PROUD SUN	(Owner)	M. Felton	11

Horse and Hound John Corbet Champion Novices Cup, Stratford, 3m4f

1996	Mr & Mrs E.L. Harries'	HANDSOME HARVEY	(B. Lavis)	J. Jukes	16
1997	Mr R.M. Penny's	EARTHMOVER (IRE)	(R. Barber)	Miss P. Gundry	9

Weatherbys John Corbet Champion Novices Cup, Stratford, 3m4f

1998	Mr R. Tate's	LAST OPTION	(Owner)	Mrs F. Needham	11
1999	Mrs C. Sample's	DONALLACH MOR (IRE)	(Miss V. Williams)	Miss S. Vickery	14
2000	Mr M.J. Parr's	LORD HARRY (IRE)	(Mrs S. Crow)	A. Crow	16
2001	Mr J.D. & Mrs A.M. Callow's	PHILTRE (IRE)	(Mrs H. Needham)	A. Wintle	11
2002	Mr R. Andrews'	MONTYS TAG (IRE)	(S.R. Andrews)	J. Diment	15

Weatherbys Chase John Corbet Champion Novices, Stratford, 3m4f

2003	Mr S.P. Tindall's	SHERIFF'S FRIEND (IRE)	(Mrs J. Gordon)	C. Gordon	15
2004	Mrs M. Harrison & Mr D. Kemp's	CANTARINHO	(D. Kemp)	D. Kemp	12

LAND ROVER GENTLEMEN'S POINT-TO-POINT CHAMPIONSHIP

Players Gold Leaf Trophy, Newbury, 3m2f

1968	Miss L. Jones'	BARTLEMY BOY	(Owner)	J.Daniell	17

Haydock Park, 3m4f

1969	Mr R.A. Bethell's	FORTY LIGHT	(Owner)	J. Walker	14

Newbury, 3m2f

1970	Mrs J. Brutton's	LORD FORTUNE	(Owner)	G. Hyatt	16

Haydock Park, 3m4f

1971	Mr G.A.C. Cure's	MIGHTY RED	(Owner)	J. Chugg	8

Newbury, 3m2f

1972	Mrs A.D. Wiseman's	DOCTOR ZHIVAGO	(Owner)	J. Docker	10
1973	Mr J.H. Jewell's	GRAVEL PITS	(Owner)	B. Venn	12

Hereford, 3m3f

1974	Mr H.V. Counsell's	STANHOPE STREET	(Owner)	B. Venn	11

BMW Championship, Chepstow, 3m3f

1975	Mr W.G. Barker's	JAUNTY JANE	(Owner)	J. Ormston	20
1976	Mr M. Churches'	PANMURE	(Owner)	R. Treloggen	13
1977	Mr R.J. Shepherd's	MOUNTOLIVE	(Owner)	Owner	12
1978	Mr L. Worner's	MASTERSHIP	(Owner)	B Stevens	12
1979	Mr G.R. Dun's	CARNDONAGH	(Owner)	J. Dun	16

Jeep/Christies' Championship, Chepstow, 3m3f

1980	Mr A. Sanderson's	WHIGGIE GEO	(Owner)	N. Tutty	11
1981	Mr R.G. Frost's	ARMAGNAC PRINCESS	(Owner)	J. Frost	12

Christies'/TKM Championship, Chepstow, 3m3f

1982	Mr A. Sanderson's	LADY BUTTONS	(Owner)	N. Tutty	11

Webster's Yorkshire Bitter Championship, Chepstow, 3m3f

1983	Mrs G. Spratt's	LITTLE BILSHAM	(W. Bryan)	W. Bryan	13

Diners Club Championship, Chepstow, 3m3f

1984	Mr M.W. Easterby's	URSER	(Owner)	T. Thomson Jones	9
1985	Mr M.W. Easterby's	URSER	(Owner)	T. Thomson Jones	11

Land Rover Championship, Chepstow, 3m3f

1986	Mr G. Richards'	FIXED PRICE	(Owner)	J. Llewellyn	18
1987	Mr K.W. Dunn's	CAL MAL	(Owner)	P. Scholfield	12
1988	Mr D.J. Kellow's	ARIZONA BELLE	(R. Buckler)	R. Buckler	8

Land Rover Championship, Towcester, 3m190y

1989	Mr D. Jeffries'	CASTLE ANDREA	(Owner)	T. Illsley	9
1990	Mr J.A. Riddell's	BLUE RAVINE	(R. Lamb)	S. Bell	13
1991	Mr D.M. Forster's	GRANNY'S PRAYER	(Owner)	R. Lawther	10
1992	Mr J.D. Jemmeson's	GLEN LOCHAN	(Owner)	N. Tutty	12
1993	Mrs F.T. Walton's	MIGHTY MARK	(Owner)	P. Johnson	11
1994	Mr R.G. Russell's	AVOSTAR	(Miss C. Saunders)	Owner	9
1995	Mr G.W. Lewis's	WELSH LEGION	(Owner)	J. Jukes	14

Land Rover Championship, Cheltenham, 3m1f110y

1996	Mr G. Tanner's	RYMING CUPLET	(M. Trickey)	R. White	13

Land Rover Championship, Towcester, 3m1f

1997	Mrs D.B. Lunt's	MAGNOLIA MAN	(Miss D. Cole)	N. Harris	6
1998	Mr H.J. Manners'	CAVALERO	(Owner)	A. Charles-Jones	6
1999	Mr R.K. Crabb's	KNIGHT OF PASSION	(Mrs P. Tizzard)	M. Miller	6
2000	Mr R.S. Hunnisett's	COPPER THISTLE	(Mrs C. Bailey)	Owner	9
2001	abandoned due to foot-and-mouth restrictions				
2002	Mr G.T. Lever's	COUNTY DERRY	(J. Scott)	N. Harris	
2003	Mr G.T. Lever's	COUNTY DERRY	(J. Scott)	N. Harris	

Land Rover Championship, Cheltenham, 3m2f110y

2004	Axe Valley Racing Club's	GARRUTH (IRE)	(R. Barber)	N. Williams	9

GERRARD LADIES POINT-TO-POINT CHAMPIONSHIP

BMW Championship, Chepstow, 3m3f

1977	Mr D.F.T. White's	HOROSCOPE	(Owner)	Mrs R. White	7
1978	Mr V.H. Welton's	ZANETTA	(Owner)	Mrs F. Belcher	8
1979	Miss P. Kerby's	HAPPY RETURNS	(Owner)	Owner	8

Jeep/Christies' Championship, Chepstow, 3m3f

1980	Mrs D.M. Watkins'	STARNELLO	(Owner)	Mrs R. White	4
1981	Mr J.F. Weldhen's	MOONSTEP	(Owner)	Miss K. Halswell	14

Christies'/TKM Championship, Chepstow, 3m3f

1982	Mr A. Hornblower's	PASTRY BRUSH	(Owner)	Miss M. Kimnell	16
1983	Mr A. Bray's	BAULKING BYWAY	(Miss R. Harper)	Miss R. Harper	14
1984	Mr B.B. Isaac's	COBLEY EXPRESS	(Owner)	Mrs J. Mills	18
1985	Mr A. Calder's	FLYING ACE	(Owner)	Miss D. Calder	10
1986	Mrs M. Rimell's	THREE COUNTIES	(Owner)	Miss G. Armytage	14
1987	Mr C.D. Dawson's	SWEET DIANA	(Owner)	Miss J. Grinyer	10
1988	Mr J. Parfitt's	TARVILLE	(Owner)	Miss H. McCaull	10

RMC Group Championship, Warwick, 3m1f

1989	Mr R. Fear's	AIR STRIKE	(Owner)	Miss J. Southcombe	7
1990	Mr J.M. Turner's	AS YOU WERE	(Owner)	Miss N. Bothway	8
1991	Mr C. Davies's	PADDY'S POND	(N. Reece)	Miss C. Thomas	7
1992	Mr J.M. Turner's	SKYGRANGE	(Owner)	Miss Z. Turner	14

Champagne Taittinger Championship, Huntingdon, 3m

1993	Mrs A. Leat's	QANNAAS	(W. Smith)	Mrs P. Nash	8
1994	no corresponding race				
1995	no corresponding race				
1996	no corresponding race				

Greig Middleton Championship, Chepstow, 3m

1997	Mr R.M. Penny's	EARTHMOVER (IRE)	(R. Barber)	Miss P. Gundry	7
1998	Miss V. Roberts'	BOXING MATCH	(Owner)	Miss V. Roberts	8

Greig Middleton Championship, Warwick, 3m2f

1999	Miss T. McCurrich's	MASTER OF TROY	(Owner)	Miss T. McCurrich	12

Greig Middleton Championship, Uttoxeter, 3m2f

2000	Mrs B.K. Thomson's	BALISTEROS (FR)	(Owner)	Miss J. Wormall	7

Gerrard Championship, Exeter, 3m1f110y

2001	abandoned due to foot-and-mouth restrictions				
2002	Mr N. Cronin's	STORM CASTLE (IRE)	(Miss J Wickens)	Miss J Wickens	11

Gerrard Championship, Wetherby, 3m1f

2003	Mr N.W.A. Bannister's	JR-KAY (IRE)	(Miss A. Armitage)	Miss A. Armitage	

Gerrard Championship, Huntingdon, 3m

2004	Mr J. Fenwick's	COMMANCHE LAW (IRE)	(T. Reed)	Mrs A. Hamilton	9

Important Races - Point-to-Point

LORD ASHTON OF HYDE'S CUP

Heythrop Open Fox Farm, Stow-on-the-Wold, 4m

1953	Mr L.A. Colville's	DARK STRANGER	I. Kerwood	18
1954	Mr S.C. Turner's	NYLON	G. Morgan	11
1955	Mr H. Phillips'	CHANDIE IV	J. Jackson	15
1956	Mr H.M. Ballard's	CASH ACCOUNT	W. Foulkes	13
1957	Mr S.L. Maundrell's	STARBAR	Owner	14
1958	Mr S.L. Maundrell's	KOLPHAM	P. Dibble	11
1959	Mr R.J. Horton's	ANDY PANDY	D.J. Horton	19
1960	Mr R.I. Johnson's	MASCOT III	R. Woolley	9
1961	Maj H.P. Rushton's	HOLYSTONE OAK	A. Biddlecombe	18
1962	Mr W.H. Firkins'	EVERYTHING'S ROSY	D. Tatlow	19
1963	Mr C.D. Collins'	WILD LEGEND	Owner	10
1964	Mr W.J.A. Shepherd's	STRAIGHT LADY	R.J. Shepherd	19
1965	Mrs J. Brutton's	SNOWDRA QUEEN	H. Oliver	15
1966	Miss V. Diment's	BOB SAWYER	G. Dartnell	14
1967	Mr J. Jordan's	BARLEY BREE	D. Tatlow	14
1968	Maj P. Ormrod's	WINTER WILLOW	D. Williams-Wynn	9
1969	Miss L. Jones'	BARTLEMY BOY	J. Daniell	21
1970	Mrs J. Brutton's	LORD FORTUNE	G. Hyatt	16
1971	Mrs J.S. Townsend's	CREME BRULE	R. Knipe	16
1972	Mr M.H. Ings'	DUNSBROOK LASS	Owner	17
1973	Maj M.R. Dangerfield's	ALL A MYTH	R.N. Miller	27
1974	Mr A.E. Cowan's	FALSE NOTE	Owner	29
1975	(i) Mr J.W. Brown's	TAKE COVER	Owner	11
	(ii) Mr M.R. Churches'	RICH ROSE	R.N. Miller	9
1976	Mrs J. Brutton's	LORD FORTUNE	D. Edmunds	10
1977	Mrs J. Brutton's	LORD FORTUNE	D. Edmunds	13
1978	Mrs P. Morris'	SPARKFORD	J.R. Bryan	8
1979	Mr E.J. Bufton's	HEADMASTER	A. James	14
1980	Mr H. Wellon's	SPARTAN SCOT	T. Houlbrooke	16
1981	Mr J.B. Sumner's	NOSTRADAMUS	I. McKie	13
1982	Mr H. Wellon's	SPARTAN SCOT	T. Houlbrooke	13

Dunthrop Farm, Heythrop, c 4m

1983	Mr J.B. Sumner's	NOSTRADAMUS	I. McKie	14
1984	Mrs E. Dowling's	LAY-THE-TRUMP	B. Dowling	17
1985	Mr J.B. Sumner's	NOSTRADAMUS	I. McKie	7
1986	Mr T. Perry & Mr J. Deutsch's	PADDY'S PERIL	J. Deutsch	16
1987	Mr P. Hemelik's	POLITICAL WHIP	D. Naylor-Leyland	8
1988	Mr T. Perry & Mr J. Deutsch's	PADDY'S PERIL	J. Deutsch	7
1989	Mr C. Main's	LOLLYS PATCH	Owner	13
1990	Mr J. Cullen's	POLAR GLEN	M. Felton	7
1991	Mr J. Deutsch's	DROMIN JOKER	J. Deutsch	8
1992	Mrs M.E. Terry's	SPEEDY BOY	T. McCarthy	10
1993	Mrs P.A. White's	UNCLE RAGGY	R. Lawther	14
1994	Mr E.C. Knight's	HOLLAND HOUSE	C. Vigors	6

1995	Mr G. Nock's	SEVENS OUT	E. James	3
1996	Mrs M.R. Daniell's	KETTLES	A. Phillips	10
1997	Mrs M.R. Daniell's	KETTLES	A. Phillips	7
1998	Mr C.J. Hitchings'	BETTER FUTURE (IRE)	T. Stephenson	9
1999	Mr G. Nock's	CAMP BANK	Julian Pritchard	7
2000	Mr I.K. Johnson's	RUSTY BRIDGE	R. Burton	16
2001	abandoned due to foot-and-mouth restrictions			
2002	Mr J.N. Dalton's	BELMONT KING (IRE)	Julian Pritchard	2
2003	Mr J.H. Burbidge's	BRIGHT APPROACH (IRE)	Julian Pritchard	9
2004	Mr J.H. Burbidge's	BRIGHT APPROACH (IRE)	Julian Pritchard	7

LADY DUDLEY CUP

Worcestershire Open

Chaddesley Corbett (different course), 3m

1946	Mr E. Holland-Martin's	HEFTY	T. Holland-Martin	6
1947	Mr A.W. Garfield's	AROD	Dr K. McCarthy	7
1948	Mr P. Kerby's	VINTY	P.J. Kerby	13
1949	Mr G. Hutsby's	SIR ISUMBRAS	Owner	11
1950	Mr P.T. Cartridge's	MAYBE II	Owner	12

Upton-upon-Severn, 3m4f

1951	Mr A.H. Thomlinson's	PAUL PRY	W.A. Stephenson	15
1952	Mr G.R. Maundrell's	RIGHT AGAIN	D. Maundrell	15

Upton-upon-Severn, 3m2f

1953	(i) Mr G.R. Maundrell's	COTTAGE LACE	D. Maundrell	13
	(ii) Mr H. Sumner's	FLINT JACK	J. Fowler	16
1954	(i) Mr C.S. Ireland's	BLENALAD	C. Hart	7
	(ii) Mr H. Sumner's	FLINT JACK	J. Fowler	7
1955	(i) Mr H.M. Ballard's	CASH ACCOUNT	M. Tate	7
	(ii) Mr C. Nixon's	CREEOLA II	C. Harty	8
1956	(i) Mr H.M. Ballard's	CASH ACCOUNT	W. Foulkes	13
	(ii) Mr G.A. Miles'	GALLOPING GOLD	C. Nesfield	13
1957	(i) Mr H.M. Ballard's	CASH ACCOUNT	W.H. Wynn	19
	(ii) Mr J.R. Hindley's	PROSPERO	P. Brookshaw	21
1958	(i) Mr C. Davies'	MASTER COPPER	Owner	19
	(ii) Mr J.R. French's	DOMABELLE	Owner	12
	(iii) Mr T.D. Roote's	SOME BABY	M.J. Thorne	15
1959	(i) Mr G. Llewellin's	CLOVER BUD	D. Llewellin	14
	(ii) Miss L. Jones'	FLIPPANT LAD	J. Daniell	13
1960	(i) Mr K. Small's	PRECIOUS GEM	G. Small	13
	(ii) Miss L. Jones'	CULLEEN PARK	J. Daniell	14
1961	(i) Miss L. Jones'	FLIPPANT LAD	J. Daniell	15
	(ii) Miss L. Jones'	CORN STAR	J. Daniell	15
1962	(i) Mr T.D. Holland-Martin's	MIDNIGHT COUP	Owner	8
	(ii) Maj J.L. Davenport's	POMME DE GUERRE	P. Davenport	9
1963	(i) Mr R.P. Cooper's	FOROUGHONA	Owner	13
	(ii) Mr W. Shand Kydd's	NO REWARD	Owner	14
1964	Mr W.J.A. Shepherd's	STRAIGHT LADY	R. Willis	17
1965	Mrs J. Brutton's	SNOWDRA QUEEN	H. Oliver	18
1966	Mr T.G. Cambidge's	HANDSEL	Owner	13
1967	Mrs D.L. Freer's	TAILORMAN	P. Hobbs	10
1968	Mr G.A. Cure's	BRIGHT WILLOW	R. Chugg	13
1969	abandoned because of waterlogged course			

Chaddesley Corbett, 3m500yds

1970	Mrs E.C. Gaze's	FROZEN DAWN	H. Oliver	14

Chaddesley Corbett, 3m600yds

1971	Mr D.T. Surman's	REAL RASCAL	G. Hyatt	5
1972	Mr G.A.C. Cure's	MIGHTY RED	J. Chugg	11
1973	Mr G.A.C. Cure's	MIGHTY RED	R. Woolley	10

Chaddesley Corbett, 3m520yds

1974	Mr P.A. Rackham's	LAKE DISTRICT	M. Bloom	5
1975	Mr P.T. Brookshaw's	MICKLEY SEABRIGHT	Owner	16
1976	Mrs P. Morris'	JIM LAD	J.R. Bryan	6
1977	Mr R. Wynn's	LITTLE FLEUR	J.R. Bryan	8
1978	Miss J. Hey's	SPORTING LUCK	T. Smith	9
1979	Miss P. Morris'	SPARKFORD	J.R. Bryan	8
1980	Mr W.R.J. Everall's	MAJOR STAR	S. Brookshaw	5
1981	Mr W. Price's	PETITE MANDY	N. Oliver	8
1982	Mr D.L. Reed's	NORMAN CASE	P. Mathias	8
1983	Mrs P.M. Jones'	CLEAR PRIDE	D. Trow	12
1984	Mr M.F. Howard's	DARLINGATE	T. Jackson	11
1985	Mr R.A. Phillips'	RIDGEMAN (NZ)	I.K. Johnson	8
1986	Mr P. Greenall's	HIGHLAND BLAZE	Owner	10
1987	Mr J. Harris & Mr A. Leighton's	PRIDE OF TULLOW	T. Bowen	7
1988	Mr J. Palmer's	NORTH KEY	A. Ulyet	9
1989	Mr P.A. Deal's	BORDER SUN	S. Sweeting	12
1990	Mrs S. Potter's	TURN MILL	M. Hammond	9
1991	Mr & Mrs P.R. Haley's	THE RED ONE	S. Swiers	11
1992	Mr R.J. Mansell's	BRUNICO	R. Treloggen	6
1993	Mr R.J. Mansell's	BRUNICO	R. Treloggen	11
1994	Mr R.F. Jones'	YAHOO	M. Rimell	13
1995	Mr P.K. Barber's	BOND JNR (IRE)	T. Mitchell	9
1996	Mrs J. Yeomans'	SHARINSKI	M. Jackson	15
1997	Mr R.C. Wilkins'	DOUBLE THRILLER	J. Tizzard	7
1998	Mr V.Y. Gethin & Miss F. Shone's	PERFECT LIGHT	M. Jackson	5
1999	Mrs S.L. Barber's	SOLBA (USA)	A. Dalton	8
2000	Mrs D.J. Jackson's	DISTINCTIVE (IRE)	A. Wintle	4
2001	abandoned due to foot-and-mouth restrictions			
2002	Mrs J.K. Powell & Mrs M. Scudamore's	GREENWICH	R. Biddlecombe	11
2003	Mr A. Auer, J. Eddis & C.R.R. Sweeting's	PAYMASTER (NZ)	Julian Pritchard	3
2004	Mr M.H. Weston's	CAUGHT AT DAWN (IRE)	T. Weston	11

CORONATION CUP

United Services Mixed Open
Larkhill, 3m

1950	(i) Mr J. Tudor-Evans'	GREENWOOD	J. Evans	31
	(ii) Mr R. Winslade's	TAI FORD	Owner	25
1951	(i) Mr L.G. Cottrell's	ROYAL SUN	F. Ryall	25
	(ii) Mr L.A. Coville's	LUCIFER VI	Capt Wright	21
1952	(i) Lt Col J.R. Hanbury's	GREEN FROG	R. Black	38
	(ii) Mr J.H. Jones'	MYTHICAL RAY	T. Rogers	26

Coronation Cup

1953	(i) Mr P. Dufosee's	LUCRATIVE	Owners	25
	(ii) Mr J.H. Edgar's	PAUL PRY	Owner	18
1954	(i) Mr L.A. Coville's	RIVER HEAD	I. Kerwood	17
	(ii) Miss H.C. Cross'	FAIR EPINARD	R.E. Hunt	15
1955	abandoned because of snow			
1956	Miss H.C. Cross'	FAIR EPINARD	D. Windel	7
1957	(i) Mr T.D. Rootes'	SOME BABY	J. Barnett	22
	(ii) Mrs E.D. Benson's	SURPRISE PACKET II	Brig V. Street	24
1958	(i) Mr W.H.G. Sprott's	VAIN WAX	Owner	22
	(ii) Mr M. Fear's	APRIL QUEEN	G. Small	18
1959	(i) Mr H.W. Dufosee's	BANTRY BAY	A. Dufosee	17
	(ii) Mr J.D. Watney's	STAFFORDSHIRE BLUE	M.L.C. Meredith	15
1960	(i) Hon D. Rhys'	STAR PIONEER	Capt R. Smalley	24
	(ii) J.W. Davey's	OXFORD HILL	H. Davey	20
	(iii) H. Handel's	SPINNING COIN II	I. Balding	19

1961	(i) H. Handel's	SPINNING COIN II	R. Banks	13
	(ii) A. Dufosee's	LANDSHIRE LANE	M. Tory	16
	(iii) Hon D. Rhys'	STAR PIONEER	D. Moore	18
1962	(i) Mrs G. Gale's	ROKOS	D. Moore	11
	(ii) Mr T.J.S. Nicholson's	BIJOU	Owner	15
	(iii) Mr G. Harwood's	SPINSTER'S FOLLY	Owner	17
1963	abandoned because of frost and snow			
1964	(i) Mr W.W. Hobbs'	PAY OUT	Capt B. Fanshawe	21
	(ii) Mr M. Atkinson's	PETER PIPER II	Owner	21
	(iii) Mr S. Parker's	ERIN'S LEGEND	A. Welton	17
1965	(i) Mr P.J.H. Wills'	JUAN	Owner	15
	(ii) Mr F.J. Bugg's	CHEMIN DE FER	P.J. Bugg	14
	(iii) Mr J.H. Manners'	OAKLEIGH WAY	G. Dartnall	12
1966	(i) Mrs D. Maundrell's	HUCKLEBERRY HOUND	D. Maundrell	22
	(ii) Mrs J. Brutton's	SNOWDRA QUEEN	H. Oliver	21
	(iii) Mr W.L. Pilkington's	CENTRE CIRCLE	D. Tatlow	23
1967	(i) Mrs D. Maundrell's	LIZZY THE LIZARD	D. Maundrell	19
	(ii) Mrs J. Brutton's	SNOWDRA QUEEN	H. Oliver	20
	(iii) Mr G. Guilding's	MASTER TAMMY	R. Guilding	22
1968	(i) Miss S. Abbott's	HURSTBERRY	R. Alner	25
	(ii) Mr P. Cave's	BRONZE MILLER	Owner	24
	(iii) Mr G. Guilding's	TOUCH OF TAMMY	R. Guilding	19
	(iv) Mrs C. St V. Fox's	MOON RIVER	C. Fox	23
1969	abandoned because of frost			
1970	(i) Mr G. Guilding's	TOUCH OF TAMMY	R. Guilding	25
	(ii) Mr E.W. Bomford's	SALLY FURLONG	T.D. Holland-Martin	22
	(iii) Mr G. Guilding's	MASTER TAMMY	R. Guilding	19
	(iv) Mrs M.M. Brinkworth's	LORD UPHAM	V. Dartnall	24
1971	(i) Mr A.M. Darlington's	GREEN PLOVER	T.D. Holland-Martin	16
	(ii) Cdr G. Latham's	PROPHET IV	Capt M.A. Villiers	14
1972	(i) Mrs J. Brutton's	LORD FORTUNE	D. Edmunds	18
	(ii) Mrs A.M. MacEwan's	FOREMAN	P. Frost	19
1973	(i) Mr P. Hawksfield's	MOONVIEW	J.P. Hawksfield	2
	(ii) Mr W. Bush's	INNISFOIL	N. Bush	14
1974	(i) Mrs S.P. Pattemore's	ORIENT WAR	M. Reeves	15
	(ii) Mrs J. Brutton's	LORD FORTUNE	D. Edmunds	18
	(iii) Mrs E.W. Bomford's	LADYBANK	T.D. Holland-Martin	19
1975	(i) Dr W. Fullerton's	ALEXANGLE	C. Down	15
	(ii) Mr R.J. Shepherd's	SIR KAY	Owner	19
	(iii) Mr R.W. Draper's	DEBONAIR BOY	R.N. Miller	13
1976	(i) Mrs J. Brutton's	LORD FORTUNE	D. Edmunds	25
	(ii) Mr M. Stephen's	EARL MOUSE	Mrs S. Horton	19
	(iii) Mr G.C. Maundrell's	LAFITTE	Owner	19
1977	(i) Mr M.J. Thorne's	POPPYWEE	Owner	23
	(ii) Mr L.G. Tizzard's	BOOKIE'S OPINION	A. Tizzard	24
	(iii) Mrs J. Brutton's	LORD FORTUNE	D. Edmunds	19
	(iv) Mr C.R. Rendell's	MARSHALSLAND	Miss F. Geddes	16
1978	abandoned because of frost and snow			
1979	abandoned because of frost and snow			
1980	(i) Mrs I.R. McKie's	MAN OF EUROPE	I. McKie	14
	(ii) Mrs J. Gill's	GYPSY INN	J. Delahooke	16
	(iii) Mr H.S. Butt's	WOODHAY	R. Alner	19
1981	(i) Mr B. Pike's	BALLYTARTAR	J. Dufosee	21
	(ii) Mr M. Low's	ROYAL ARCHER	Owner	21
	(iii) Hon D. Sieff's	KIANI	Miss D. Yeomans	16
	(iv) Mr M.S. Tory's	MORNING HEATHER	M. Felton	23
1982	(i) Mr J. Sumner's	NOSTRADAMUS	I. McKie	16
	(ii) Mr R. West's	LOCHUS	I. McKie	15
	(iii) Mr H.S. Butt's	WOODHAY	R. Alner	17
1983	abandoned because of snow			

1984	(i) Mr J.W. Dufosee's	BALLYTARTAR	Miss V. Mitchell	22
	(ii) Mr R.J. Cake's	TAWNY MYTH	R. Cake	18
	(iii) Mr T.D. Holland-Martin's	BALBEG	Owner	18
1985	abandoned because of frost and snow			
1986	abandoned because of frost			
1987	(i) Mrs J. Cooper & Mr R. Willis'	DAWN STREET	Miss A. Dare	12
	(ii) Lord Vestey's	GOLDSPUN	M. Felton	11
	(iii) Mr T. Perry & Mr J. Deutsch's	PADDY'S PERIL	J. Deutsch	13
1988	(i) Mrs S.N. Embiricos'	KING BA BA	Miss A. Embiricos	17
	(ii) Mr T.D. Holland-Martin's	HOT FEVER	Owner	17
	(iii) Mrs J. Cooper's	DAWN STREET	Mrs J. Litston	13
	(iv) Mr D. Naylor-Leyland's	CURAHEEN BOY	Owner	16
1989	(i) Mr J.S. Delahooke's	BORDER BURG	A. Hill	10
	(ii) Mr R.J. Hill's	NEARLY HANDY	Miss M. Hill	17
	(iii) Mrs J. Cooper's	DAWN STREET	Mrs J. Litston	8
1990	(i) Mr M. Chamberlayne's	WHITSUNDAY	M. Chamberlayne	20
	(ii) Mr W. Gooden's	MY MELLOW MAN	Mrs J. Litston	22
	(iii) Mr R. Waley-Cohen's	DROMORE CASTLE	N. Ridout	18
1991	abandoned because of frost			
1992	(i) Mr J.R. Vail's	WELLINGTON BROWN	M. Batters	10
	(ii) Miss C. Gordon's	BEECH GROVE	M. Felton	9
1993	(i) Mr G. Harwood's	HURRY UP HENRY	Miss A. Harwood	11
	(ii) Mr A. Boucher & Mr G.L. Barker's	MR DIPLOMATIC	J. Farthing	14
1994	(i) Mr N.R. Freak's	BARON BOB	M. Miller	11
	(ii) Mr E.C. Knight's	HOLLAND HOUSE	C. Vigors	10
1995	Mr J.A. Keighley's	FANTUS	Miss P. Curling	10
1996	Mrs L.J. Roberts'	WHAT A HAND	Miss P. Curling	9
1997	Mrs S. Humphreys'	BRACKENFIELD	Miss P. Curling	6
1998	Mr H.J. Manners'	CAVALERO	A. Charles-Jones	9
1999	Mr M.S. Rose's	SKIP'N'TIME	M. Miller	10
2000	Mr H.D. Hill & Mr C.H. Sporborg's	RUPERTS CHOICE (IRE)	S. Sporborg	10
2001	Miss J. Pimblett's	ONE OF THE NATIVES (IRE)	A. Farrant	12
2002	Mrs H.E. Rees'	SUPREMISM	L. Jefford	14
2003	Mr C. St V. Fox's	RED BROOK LAD	N. Mitchell	13
2004	Mr H.B. Geddes'	TALES OF BOUNTY (IRE)	N. Williams	7

GRIMTHORPE GOLD CUP

Middleton Open
Lord Grimthorpe Gold Cup
Whitwell-on-the-Hill, 3m4f

1946	Mr H W Metcalfe's	SAN MICHELE	G B Metcalfe	9
1947	Mr H W Metcalfe's	SAN MICHELE	C Metcalfe	18
1948	Mrs H W Gilpin's	ROLLING RIVER	Capt C MacAndrew	13
1949	(I)Mr C Chapman's	FINOLLY	Major G Cunard	9
	(II)Mr A Simpson's	THE JOKER VII	W R Simpson	11
1950	Mr W A Stephenson's	GENERAL RIPPLE	Owner	20
1951	Mr A Tomlinson's	PAUL PRY	W A Stephenson	14

Whitwell-on-the-Hill, 4m

1952	Mr G F Fawcett's	TRUSTY	H M Elliott	19
1953	Miss V Porter-Hargreaves'	TURKISH PRINCE	A Dickinson	15

Whitwell-on-the-Hill, 4m4f

1954	Mrs J Makin's	KITTY BROOK	C Smith	15
1955	Mr W A Stephenson's	MR GAY	Owner	23
1956	Mr S Webster's	MORE HONOUR	Owner	13
1957	Mr H M Ballard's	CASH ACCOUNT	W Wynn	15
1958	Mr R W Ratcliffe's	BROWN SUGAR	P Fox	11
1959	Mr S Webster's	MORE HONOUR	Owner	14
1960	Mr J H Thompson's	GAY WILLIAM	M Thompson	8

1961	Mr J Peckitt's	GLANN	T Wilkin	17
1962	Mr R Heaton's	BRASS TACKS	P Brookshaw	19

Ralph Grimthorpe Gold Cup

1963	Mr F T Gibbon's	HARROW HALL	R Moody	17
1964	Major G Cunard's	FERNCLIFFE	Owner	12
1965	Mr R A H Perkins'	FARUNO	Owner	10
1966	Mrs R G Hutchinson-Bradburne's	BANJOE	J Hutchinson-Bradburne	8
1967	Maj G Cunard's	PUDDLE JUMPER	Owner	13
1968	Mrs A E Dickinson's	SHANDOVER	M Dickinson	14
1969	Mr C B Harper's	MY NIGHT	J Leadbeater	10
1970	Mr D E Willson's	YOUNG HIGHLANDER	D G J Gibson	13
1971	Capt. R M Micklethwait's	KANGAROO JIM	A H Berry	12
1972	Mr J W Walton's	OLD MAN TROUBLE	Owner	15
1973	Mr F D Nicholson's	MOYLEEN	A Nicholson	16
1974	Mr P Rackham's	WATCH NIGHT	M Bloom	12
1975	Mrs J Gilmour's	FALLING LEAVES	J Gilmour	17
1976	Mr L H Barker's	VILLA COURT	Owner	17
1977	Mr J B Walker's	ESCAMIST	J Barton	20
1978	Mr J Scott-Aiton's	SEA PETREL	I Scott-Aiton	17
1979	Mr T M Wilson's	RAKAMAR	T Smith	12
1980	Mr A W Johnson's	SCALBY CRESTA	G Halder	8
1981	Mr J A Cooper's	MOUNTAIN LAD	J Peckitt	9

Whitwell-on-the-Hill, 4m4f

1982	Mr J M Evetts'	BORDER MARK	Owner	7
1983	Mr A Sanderson's	LADY BUTTONS	N Tutty	16
1984	abandoned because of firm ground			
1985	Mr J D Jemmeson's	SALKELD	D Kinsella	13
1986	Mrs M F Strawson's	FREDDIE TEAL		20
1987	abandoned because of waterlogging			
1988	Mrs S Frank's	INGLEBY STAR	N Tutty	10
1989	Mr T Bell's	OLD NICK	S Whitaker	12
1990	Mr R G Watson's	CERTAIN RHYTHM	M Sowersby	4
1991	abandoned because of snow			

Middleton Mixed Open

1992	Mr B. Heywood's	OCEAN DAY	Mrs A Farrell	8
1993	Mr B. Heywood's	OCEAN DAY	H Brown	9
1994	Mrs S. Brotherton's	ACROSS THE LAKE	Miss S Brotherton	11
1995	Mr P. Sawney's	DURIGHT	N Tutty	14
1996	Mr H. Bell's	HIGHLAND FRIEND	P Atkinson	19
1997	Mr J.R. Burns's	ASK ANTONY (IRE)	N Wilson	21
1998	abandoned because of waterlogging			
1999	Mr J. Wade's	OVERFLOWING RIVER (IRE)	T Glass	10
2000	Mr M.J. Brown's	PROMINENT	D Easterby	13
2001	abandoned because of foot-and-mouth disease			
2002	Miss F. Hartley's	TEMPLE GARTH	Miss F Hartley	11
2003	Mr G.F. Tuer's	SON OF ANSHAN	G Tuer	16
2004	Mr G.F. Tuer's	SAD MAD BAD (USA)	G Tuer	17

PLATE 134
1384 Dulverton West Confined: Vivid Imagination gives National Champion Ashley Farrant his record-breaking 44th win of the season
PHOTO: Brian Armstrong

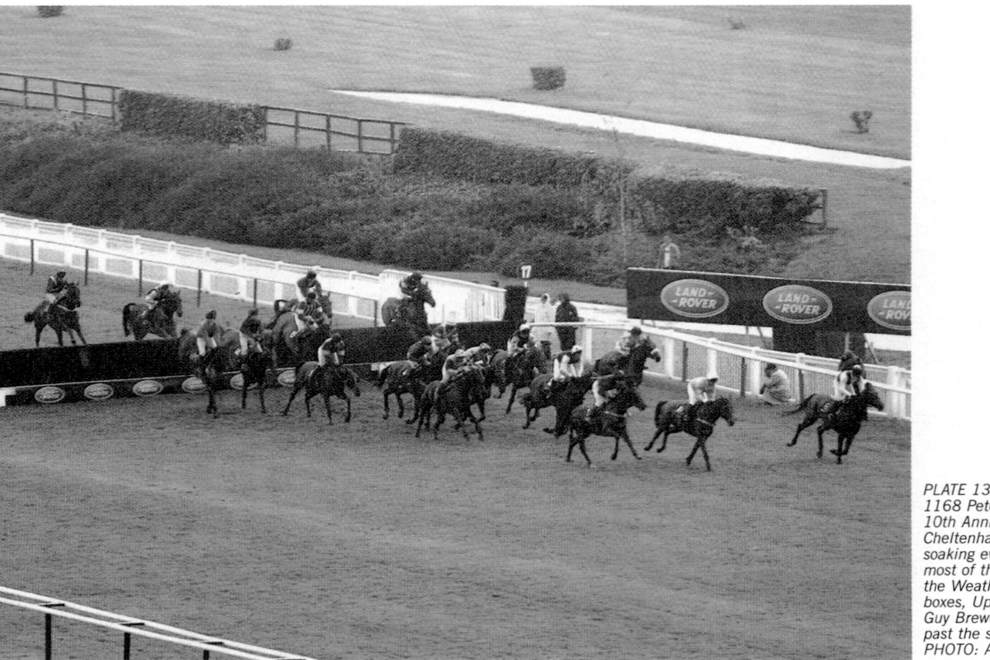

PLATE 135
1168 Peter Davies Media 10th Anniversary HC, Cheltenham: On a soaking evening when most of the crowd filled the Weatherbys Chase boxes, Upham Lord and Guy Brewer lead the field past the stands
PHOTO: Adrian Long

PLATE 136
1560 Torrington Farmers Confined: Khayal (Rachael Green), 1st, kicks up his heels and the dust at the third last
PHOTO: Tim Holt

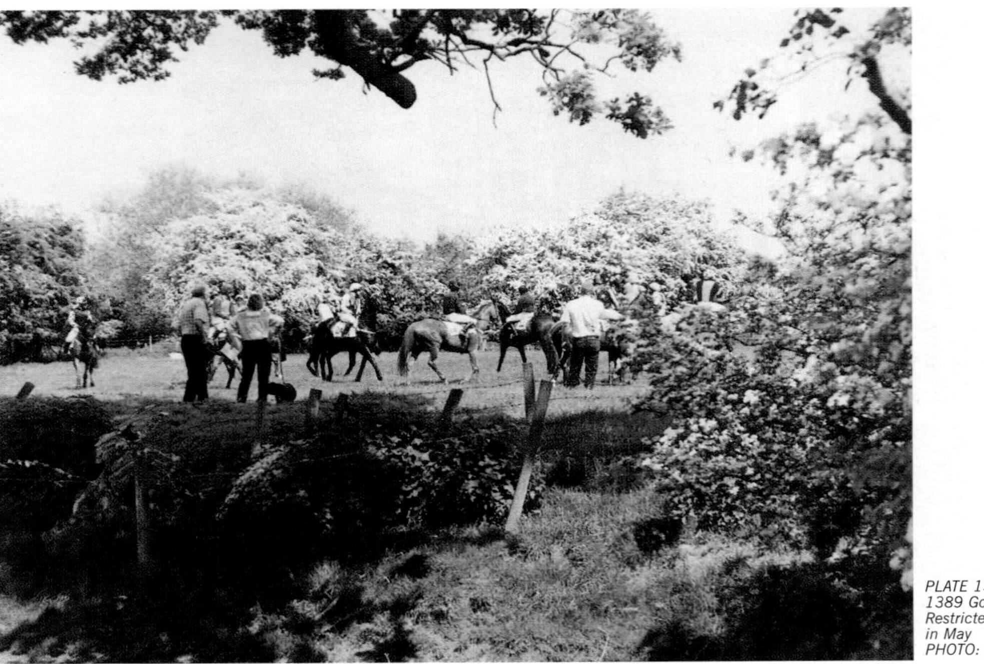

PLATE 137
1389 Golden Valley
Restricted: At the start
in May
PHOTO: Kathleen Mullen

PLATE 138
10 Army Ladies Open: And pretty maids all in a row : L to R Emily Jones (Hi Rudolf), Rilly Goschen (Caldamus), Charlotte Tizzard (Sir D'Orton), Georgina Harvey (Polo Pony), Sophie Heath (Garethson), Belinda Keighley (Bosuns Mate, stars) and Fiona Wilson (Dawn's Cognac) at the fourth fence
PHOTO: Tim Holt

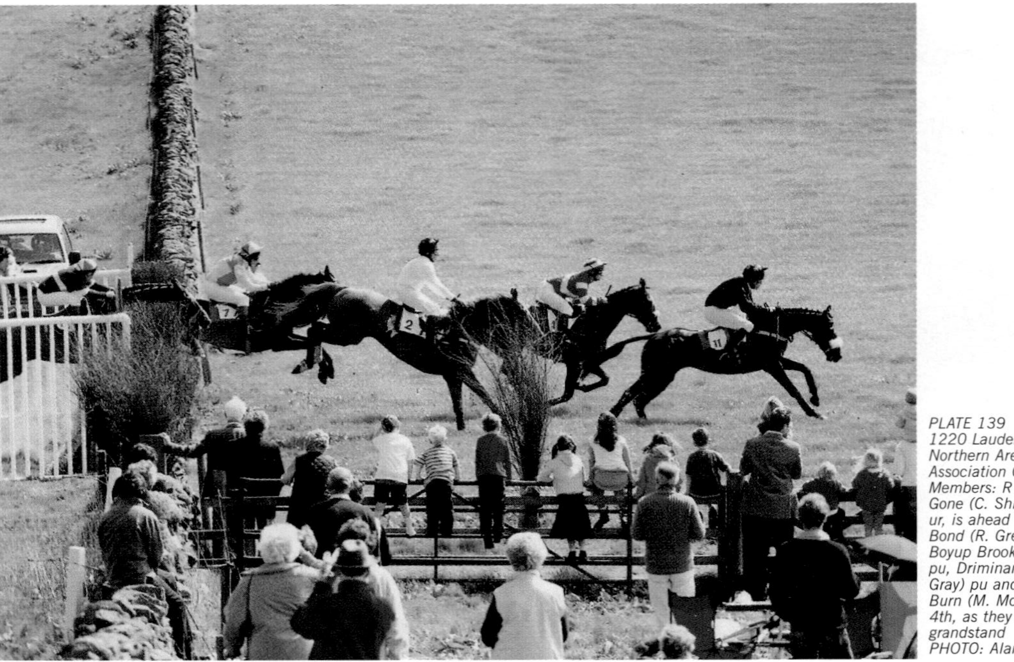

PLATE 139
1220 Lauderdale Northern Area P-t-P Association Club Members: R to L, Johnnys Gone (C. Shirley-Beavan), ur, is ahead of Decent Bond (R. Green), 1st, Boyup Brook (T. Morrison) pu, Driminamore (Miss H. Gray) pu and Roscoe Burn (M. McAlister), 4th, as they pass the grandstand
PHOTO: Alan Mitchell

PLATE 140
1197 Modbury Harriers Ladies Open: Ardross Gem and Rachael Green pose on the hill before winning the race
PHOTO: Nick Jay

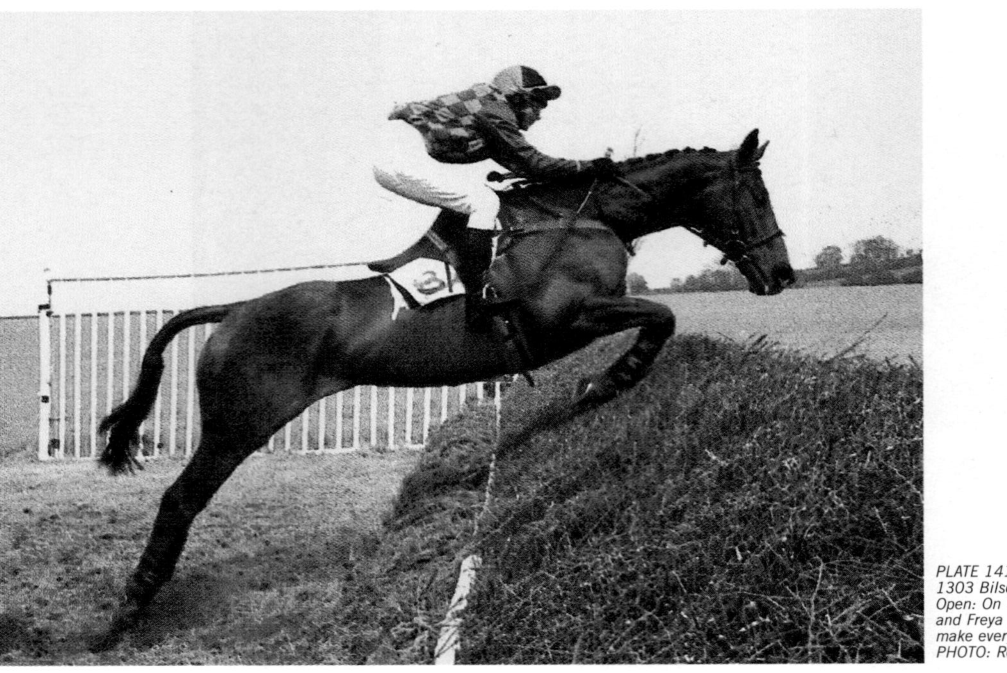

*PLATE 141
1303 Bilsdale Ladies Open: On The Mend and Freya Hartley make every yard
PHOTO: Roy Parker*

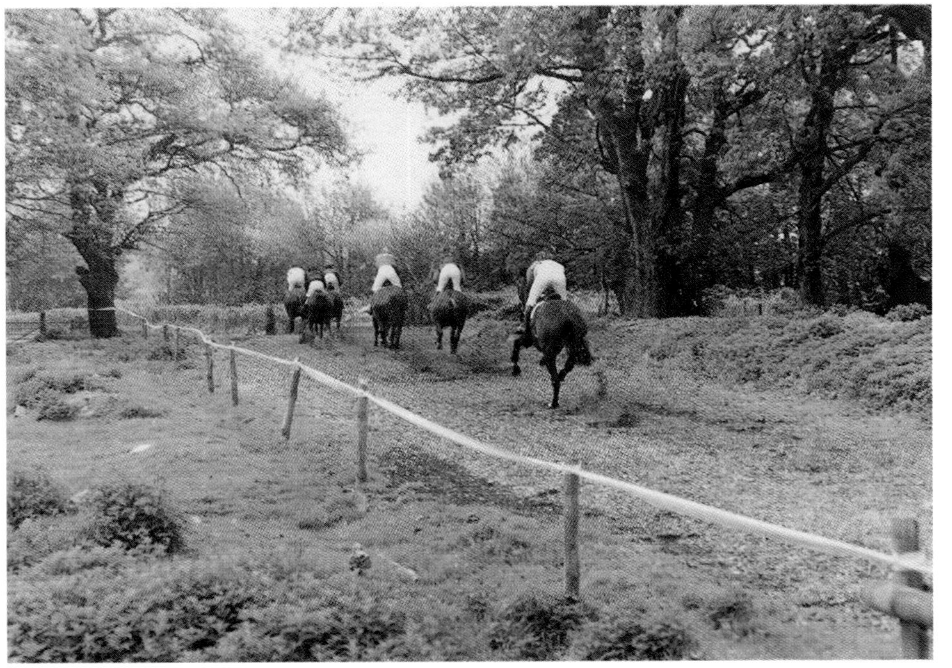

PLATE 142
1191 Llangeinor
Restricted: All For Jake leads the field through the woods
PHOTO: Kathleen Mullen

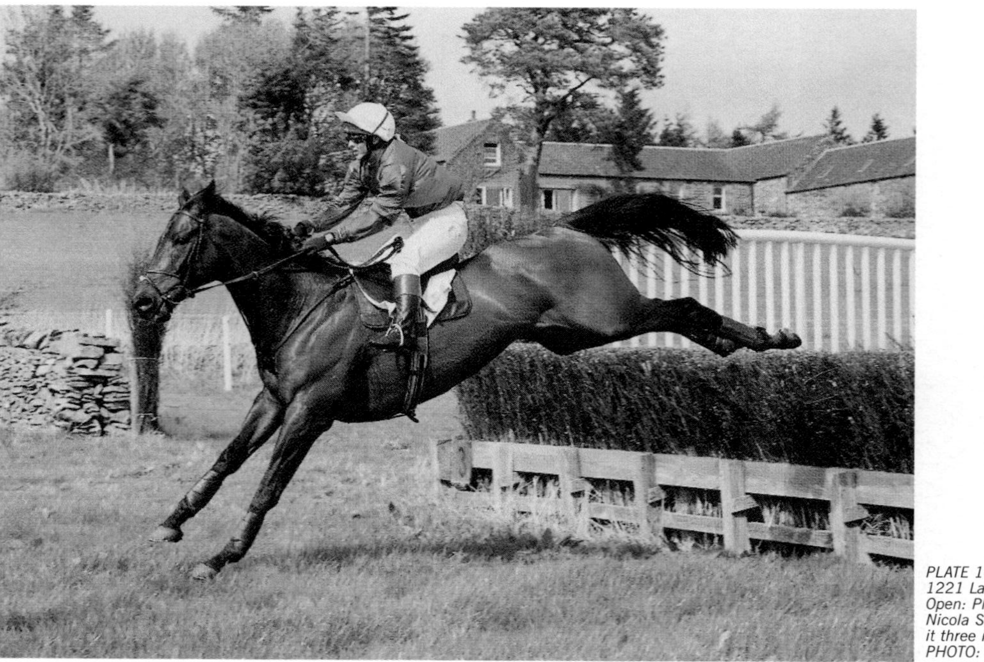

PLATE 143
1221 Lauderdale Ladies Open: Pharmistice and Nicola Stirling, 1st, make it three in a row
PHOTO: Alan Mitchell

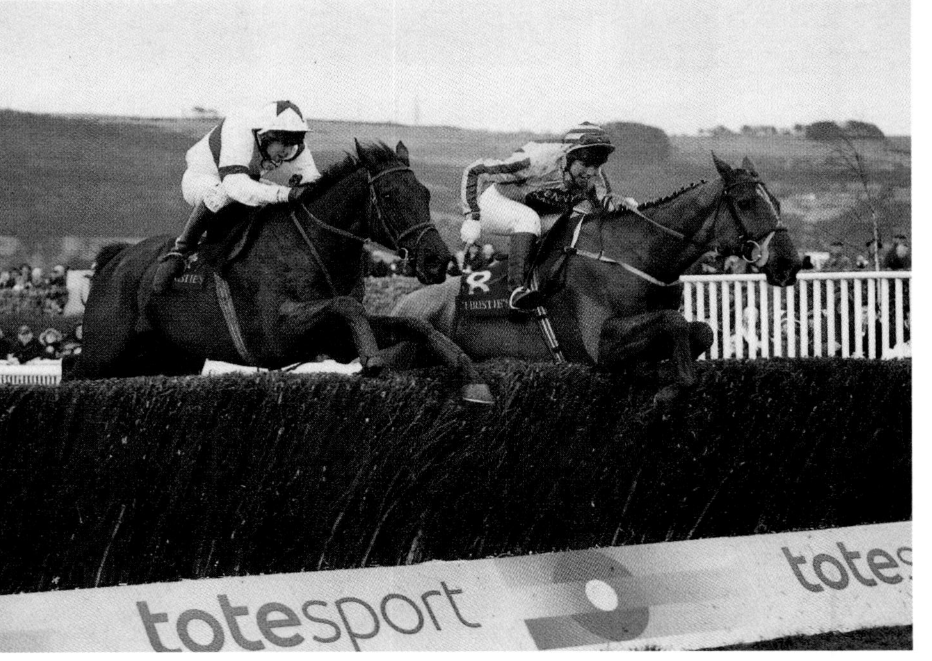

PLATE 144
543 Christie's Foxhunter HC, Cheltenham: At the last with all to play for L to R, Never Compromise (Alan Crowe), 2nd, and Earthmover (Rilly Goschen), 1st
PHOTO: Tim Holt

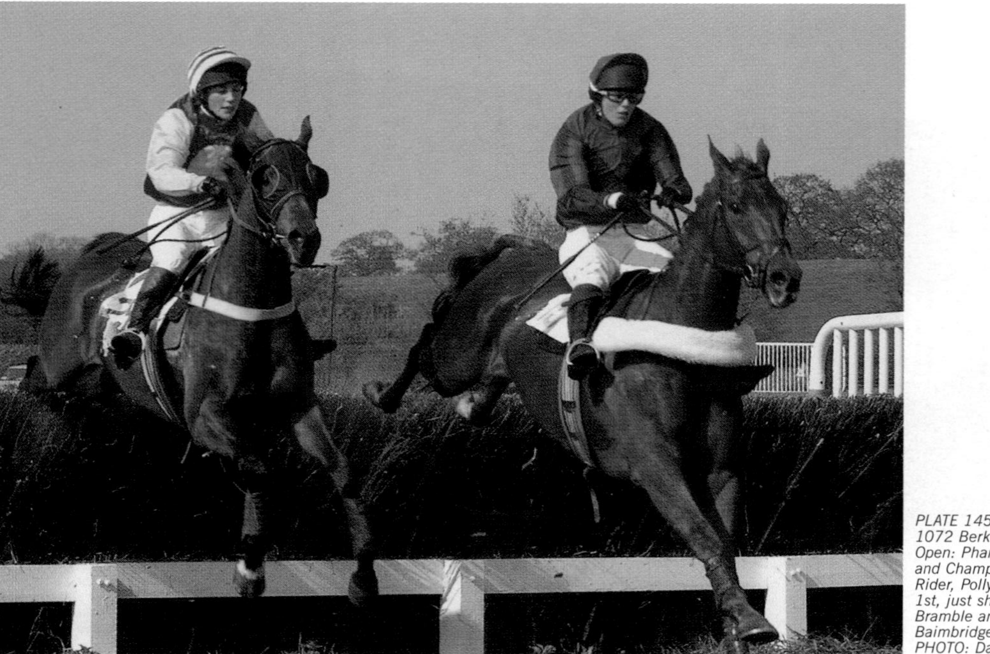

PLATE 145
1072 Berkeley Ladies Open: Phar From Chance and Champion Lady Rider, Polly Gundry, 1st, just shades Titus Bramble and Katie Baimbridge,2nd
PHOTO: David Jones

PLATE 146
358 Curre & Llangibby Restricted: The fence staff watch Ballyalbert and Anna de Lisle Wells leading the field downhill to the 4th fence
PHOTO: John Mullen

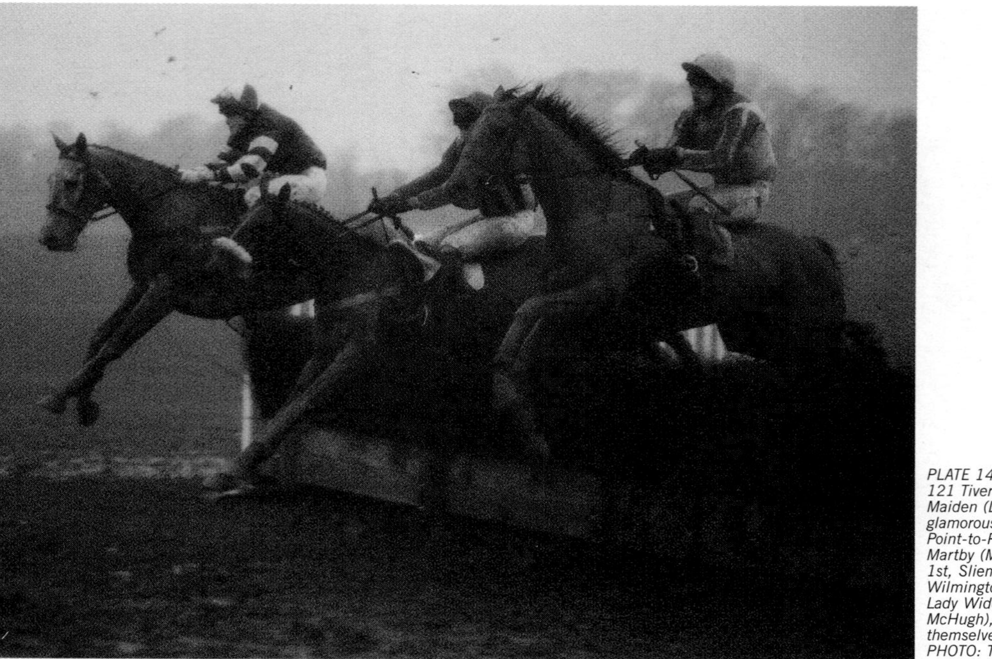

PLATE 147
121 Tiverton Open Maiden (Div 3): The glamorous world of Point-to-Pointing: L to R, Martby (Martin Atkinson), 1st, Sliema (Naddan Wilmington), 2nd, and Lady Widd (Saul McHugh), 3rd, enjoying themselves
PHOTO: Tim Holt

PLATE 148
772 Middleton Mixed Open (Grimthorpe Gold Cup): Sad Mad Bad and Grant Tuer take the last to win the Grimthorpe
PHOTO: Brian Armstrong

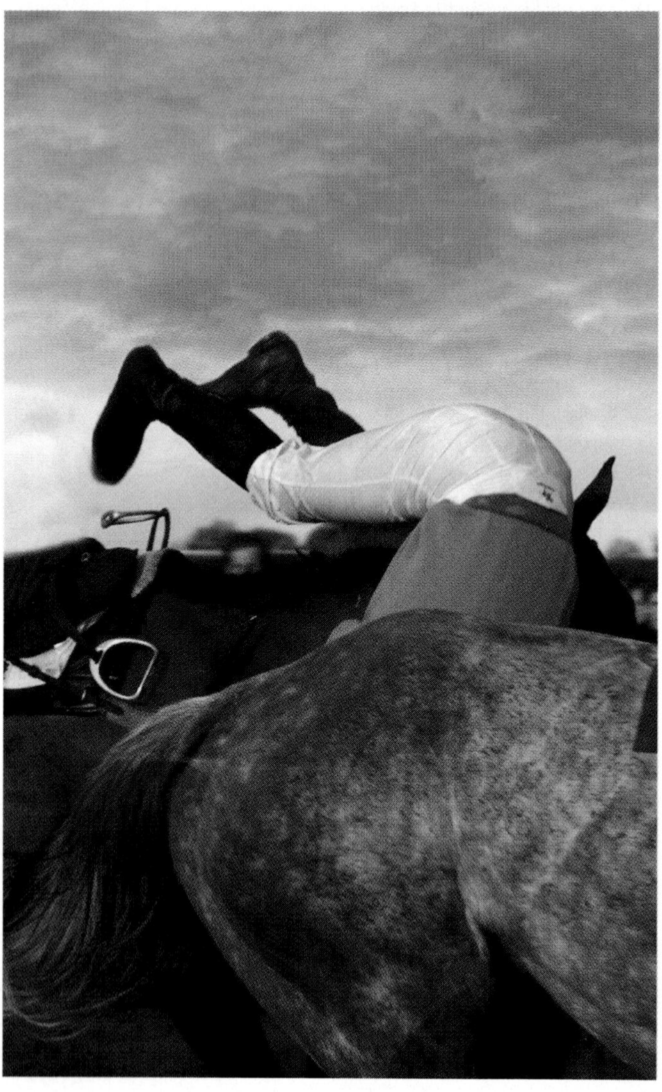

PLATE 149 467 Oakley PPORA Club Members Restricted: Tom Ellis (recently aboard Rightun alongside grey, Greet You Well) fails his audition for the Spanish Riding School PHOTO: Christopher Beasley

Point-to-Point Courses

All Point-to-Point races are supposed to be run over a minimum of three miles. Actual distances are not given for each course unless they are known to be well in excess of the minimum.

SF: 2004 Safety Factor*
LH or RH: Left or Right-handed
circs: Circuits of course per race
F: Fences on course
Riders: Leading Riders in the last five years
J: Jumps in race
T: Approx average race time**
od: open ditches
wj: water jumps
(1947): Year opened***

* Lower Safety Factors are normally for Maidens and the other for other races; when more than two Safety Factors are given the middle figures generally refer to Restricteds; special instances are listed; figures in brackets are for 2m4f Maidens. SAFETY FACTORS QUOTED RELATE TO 2004 AND DO NOT INCLUDE THE RECENT JOCKEY CLUB REVISONS.

** The average of the race times of the five most recent years (excluding two-runner contests and any in which fences were omitted).

*** Pre-war dates shown are the earliest found (unfortunately early returns are vague and incomplete).

We would welcome any further information or personal reminiscences of early courses.

Changes notified for the coming season are incorporated, but these descriptions are of the courses as last used and may, therefore, include some that are now defunct.

ALDINGTON, Kent. (1950)
South of A20 and M20, 6m SE of Ashford (Exit 10 or 11, M20).
Meetings: East Kent; West Street Tickham (May).
SF: 16-20. LH 2 circs. 9F; 19J; 2od (6/15). T: 6min 50.2s.
Slightly undulating galloping course; downhill bend after 1st can be slippery when wet; quick-draining clay and chalk soil, can be hard in dry years, and heavy along bottom of track when wet; 9(18)th is a drop fence. Watering has been successful in past seasons. Plentiful car parking, but one exit (uphill) can cause problems. Good viewing from hillside car parks and centre of course.
Riders: *Ms L. Stock 7, P. Bull 4, A. Hickman 4, P. York 3, D. Phelan 3, P. Hall 2, N. Benstead 2, Mrs J. Gordon 2, F. Marshall 2, D. Parker 2, C. Gordon 2.*

ALNWICK, Northumberland. (1949)
3m NE of Alnwick (signposted from A1).
Meetings: West Percy; College Valley & North Northumberland; Percy (4m Mixed Open).
SF: 18-22 (18). LH 2 circs. 9F. (2m4f): 15J; 1od (9). T: 5min 34.7s. (3m): 18J; 2od (3/12). T: 6min 41.8s. (4m): 24J; 2od (9/18). T: 9min 07.9s.
Gently undulating course; fairly sharp; usually true ground with good going on old turf; mixture of permanent and portable fences. Permanent wooden changing room, weighing room, etc. Access to car parks good, but exit can be difficult if wet; on steep hill so check handbrake and engage reverse; excellent viewing from there, but come prepared for the bitter winds which can blow from visible North Sea. Ideal for early season meetings as this pocket of land rarely gets frosty. Wonderful setting.
Riders: *Miss P. Robson 12, C. Storey 8, A. Richardson 7, K. Anderson 6, T. Oates 5, Miss M. Neill 4, A. Robson 4.*

ALPRAHAM, Cheshire. (1959*)
3m SE of Tarporley, nr A51.
Meeting: Cheshire.
SF: 18-22 (18). RH 2¼ circs. 8F. (3m): 18J; 2od (3/11). T: 7min 47.6s. (2m4f): 14J; 1od (7). T: 5min 33.6s.
A slightly undulating rectangular stayers' course — races are approx 3m4f; can become holding when wet especially in dip between last two fences. Drop fence 4(12) causes problems — course narrow at that point; sharp bend after 8(16)th; permanent fences well built. Good car parking, but exit is often slow. All fences in view from centre of course — binoculars hardly necessary, but the dip before last fence and huge crowd on inside of run-in mar closing stages. Facilities very compact. Big fields a rarity as track

is so testing. A proper old-fashioned Point-to-Point, and turnout winner was announced as 'the best dressed horse'.
Riders: *Miss S. Sharratt 5, D. Barlow 4, Julian Pritchard 3, C. Barlow 3, Mrs M. Barlow 2, Miss T. Clark 2.*
**** A course at Alpraham existed pre-WWII***

AMPTON, Suffolk. (1971)
4m N of Bury St Edmunds, nr A134.
Meetings: Dunston Harriers; Suffolk.
SF: 15 (Nov Rdrs)-19. RH 2¾ circs. 7F; 20J; 2od (7/14). T: 6min 50.0s.
Compact and undulating course, not for those of doubtful stamina particularly if muddy; two quite acute bends, but fairly easy to negotiate and three uphill fences including the open ditch; ground cuts up on bends. Good car parking, only 100 yards off main road and wide gate avoids congestion, but parking inside course hampers view; start is nigh on invisible from any reasonable vantage point; resiting of the paddock, and the provision of a separate and well-fenced unsaddling enclosure, has greatly improved crowd safety. The Tote tent, which is tucked away at end of refreshment tent, is worthy of more support particularly given the extreme stinginess of local bookies; the Suffolk announcer should consider alternative employment. This course has greatly improved in recent years and received good support from owners in latest season & all credit to the efforts of the Clerk of the Course and his team.
Riders: *A. Sansome 8, C. Ward-Thomas 7, S. Morris 3, D. Kemp 3, R. Burton 2, P. Taiano 2, P. Chinery 2, N. Bloom 2, Mrs S. Hodge 2, J. Owen 2, A. Bealby 2, A. Ayers 2.*

ANDOVERSFORD, Glos. (1960)
6m SE Cheltenham, nr junc of A40 and A436. (Exit 11A, M5).
Meetings: Cotswold; Cotswold Vale Farmers.
SF: 18-20 (Membs)-23. RH 2 circs. 9F; 19J; 2od (4/13). T: 6min 26.1s.
Undulating course with uphill finish; downhill fences in back straight can cause problems; going can be firm and short runners can score; fences are well-built; facilities compact. Good car parking both inside and outside course, but exit often slow. Viewing reasonable, but it is impossible to see all the course from one place. Track kept in very good order. Strong betting market.
Riders: *Julian Pritchard 3, A. Martin 3, T. Scudamore 2, G. Barfoot-Saunt 2.*

ASHORNE, Warwicks. (1985)
4m S of Warwick between B4087 and B4100. (Exit 13 M40).
Meeting: Warwickshire.
SF: 18-20 (Nov Rdrs, Rest)-25. RH 2¼ circs. 8F; 18J; 2od (4/12). T: 6min 34.0s.
Course rectangular, slightly undulating, uphill finish; dip between 3rd (11th) and 4(12)th; sharp bend after straight; small portable fences. Car parking good with one wide entry/exit. A good course for spectators, plenty of trees, but viewing fair from top end, though the hedge in front of the fence after the winning post needs trimming regularly before meeting; number board poorly sited.
Riders: *F. Hutsby 6, S. Morris 3, Julian Pritchard 3, M. Wall 2, J. Trice-Rolph 2, A. Martin 2.*

ASPATRIA, Cumbria. (1991)
At Heathfield, nr A596, 1½ miles NE of Aspatria, between Carlisle and Maryport.
Meeting: Cumberland.
SF: 18-21. LH 2¼ circs. 8F; 19J; 2od (5/13). T: 6min 22.2s.
Well-built fences; fairly stiff uphill run after 3rd; viewing from main spectator area hampered by hedges, crops and undulations. Best viewing involves a long walk to top of hill in main car park. Long home straight. Very attractive setting with Solway Firth in background and overlooked by Skiddaw in distance, yet another jewel in the crown of the Northern Area.
Riders: *R. Morgan 6, L. Morgan 4, T. Scott 2, Miss N. Stirling 2, C. Storey 2.*

BADBURY RINGS, Dorset. (1949)
4m NW of Wimborne on B3082 (local beauty spot owned by National Trust).
Meetings: Hursley Hambledon; Wilton; Portman.
SF: 16-18. LH 1¾ circs. 10F; 19J; 2od (3/13). T: 6min 21.9s.
Course is rectangular and undulating with three sharp bends round the edge of one large (100 acre) enclosure; uphill to last bend and sharply downhill from last; good turf covering on quick drying chalk gives perfect going in early season, can get very firm later; well-built portable fences can be tricky on run from back straight; used to suit short-runners, but less markedly after changes of recent years; plastic running rails on all bends. Car parking handy to paddock etc, and there is a cheaper park handy to the course, but only one exit. Viewing is superb from the hillside, but start is out of sight from rails. Watering is no longer out of the question, but the number board — set up on an old trailer — is often unintelligible

and badly needs upgrading.
Riders: *M. Miller 8, N. Mitchell 5, A. Charles-Jones 5, R. Bliss 3, Miss P. Gundry 3, Miss A. Goschen 3, G. Weatherley 3, A. Honeyball 3.*

PLATE 150 Balcormo Mains: How Burn (Val Jackson) leads the field past the crowds in Race 1078 Fife Ladies Open PHOTO: Alan Mitchell

BALCORMO MAINS, Fife. (1907)
3m N of Leven between A915 and A916.
Meeting: Fife.
SF: 18-20. RH 2¼ circs. 8F; 18J; 2od (8/16). T: 7min 08.6s.
Superb wide oval galloping course; home and back straights level, but ground falls and rises in between; fences portable; ideal for good jumping stayers'. Permanent shed used for weighing room, changing, etc. Car parks adjacent to course with good access. Viewing is excellent from many locations — best on inside of course; crowds cheer every time the horses come past; most of the student population of St Andrews turn up and behave amusingly (or outrageously according to your viewpoint). A grand spot for racing — a visit is thoroughly recommended.
Riders: *L. Morgan 4, R. Morgan 3, Miss N. Stirling 3, J. Alexander 3, Miss P. Robson 2, Miss J. Hollands 2, C. Storey 2.*

BARBURY CASTLE, Wilts. (1992*)
3m NW of Marlborough. Main entrance off Marlborough to Broad Hinton road. (10m from Exits 15 & 16, M4).
Meetings: Point-to-Point Owners & Riders Club; Tedworth.
SF: 18 (Nov Rdrs)-20. LH 2¼ circs. 8F; 18J; 2od (6/14). T: 6min 42.7s.
Set well off the road in natural amphitheatre; a gently undulating oblong course; superb downland grass, uphill from before two out; fences well-built; on chalk so gives perfect going in early season. Viewing is superb with the whole course visible from selected spots. Car parking satisfactory with access/exit via long hard track (but it still costs £5 to walk in). The lack of toilets in the riders changing rooms and the size of the ladies changing area are two negative points that need addressing. Paddock is superb. An outstanding venue; the PPORC meeting is a must, and is to be held over two days in 2005; weather can be diabolical so come prepared!
Riders: *G. Maundrell 5, N. Mitchell 4, Miss P. Gundry 3, A. Charles-Jones 3, T. Bishop 2, R. Biddlecombe 2, P. York 2, N. Harris 2, Mrs B. Keighley 2, Miss G. Young 2, Miss C. Tizzard 2, M. Rimell 2, J. Jenkins 2, J. Barnes 2, F. de Giles 2, C. Studd 2.*
**** Was used as a Point-to-Point course from 1953-62***

PLATE 151 Bishops Court: The runners parade for the Race 322 East Devon Ladies Open; the only thing missing is Oliver Carter in his white coat *PHOTO: Tim Holt*

BISHOPS COURT, Devon. (1979)
½m SW of Ottery St Mary, off B3174, S of A30 (Exit 29, M5).
Meeting: East Devon.
SF: 17-18-20. LH 2⅔ circs. 7F; 19J; 2od (7/14). T: 6min 50.1s.
Flat and rather sharp Linley course, drainage not good and going can be very testing particularly by the open ditch; portable fences with big bellies; compact facilities; a very popular course and had by far the most runners in 2004. Excellent viewing, and binoculars not essential. Entrance and exits to car parks good; alternative hard exit when wet; has the worst Starter in the country — there is no perceptible movement of his flag at any time and riders themselves seem to decide when they will go — race times are guesswork, and the poor commentator invariably ends up apoplectic. A charming venue otherwise, kept afloat by the autocratic Oliver Carter who deserves credit (nearly as much as those who have to deal with him) for his eccentricity and tenacity, but he has squandered much goodwill by his arrogant and boorish bullying of officialdom in recent seasons trying to obtain an Easter date (why go then when he has the stage almost to himself now?).
Riders: *A. Farrant 7, T. Mitchell 3, N. Williams 3, Miss R. Green 2, Miss P. Gundry 2, Miss O. Green 2, L. Jefford 2, J. Snowden 2, G. Maundrell 2.*

BITTERLEY, Salop. (1969)
4m NE of Ludlow, nr A4117.
Meeting: Ludlow.
SF: 18 (Ladies)-20. LH 2¼ circs. 8F; 18J; 2od (7/15). T: 6min 19.7s.
Short but galloping, basically flat course with gradual uphill finish from 3 out; fences very small but hard, and not to be hurdled; last fence very narrow. Access good to car parks and alternative exit along old railway if wet. Viewing excellent from large bank near finish — all fences visible. Delightful setting. Watering of the course has been particularly successful in the past.
Riders: *R. Burton 8, R. Cooper 4, A. Wintle 3, S. Lloyd 2, Miss E. James 2, M. Wilesmith 2, Julian Pritchard 2, G. Barfoot-Saunt 2, B. Shaw 2.*

BLACK FOREST LODGE, Devon. (1997)
5m S of Exeter, nr B3381 between A380 and Starcross. Only 6m off end of M5.
Meetings: Silverton; Mid Devon; South Devon.
SF: 16-18 (15). RH 2¼ circs. 8F; (3m) 19J; 2od (6/14). T: 6min 21.1s. (2m4f) 17J; 2od (4/12); T: 5min 40.5s.
Course is oval and undulating, all grass with some tight bends including into home straight. Open ditch

permanent, all other fences portable. Car parking satisfactory. Viewing very good from hill overlooking final fence but long way from finish. Ground firms up remarkably quickly.
Riders: *A. Farrant 12, R. Woollacott 9, N. Harris 9, T. Scudamore 7, Miss P. Gundry 7, D. Alers-Hankey 6.*

PLATE 152 Black Forest Lodge: Two fences behind the last finisher in Race 65 Restricted (Nov Rdrs) The Last Shout (Amanda Hughes) heads slowly for the line past the paddock and tents
PHOTO: Brian Armstrong

BONVILSTON, Glam. (1997)
4m W of Cardiff, nr A48 (5m from Exit 33, M4).
Meetings: Pentyrch; Gelligaer Farmers; Countryside Alliance Club (Wales).
SF: 16-18. RH 2½ circs (3m). 7F; 18J; 2od (5/12). T: 6min 14.2s. (4m): 24J; 3od (4/11/18). T: 8min 21.5s.
Very undulating course — good covering of grass; steady uphill climb from 4 out to finish; long downhill run from 5(12)th to 7(14)th followed by sharp bend (mind the pylons), the bends after 6/13 have proved trappy. Finish is on a separate chute. Small fences well-built, but easily jumped. Viewing good; all fences clearly visible if you choose your spot carefully, but finish posts still impossible to pick up from best viewing spot (since organisers have chosen not to turn the markers to face the crowd, perhaps they might consider using taller posts). Entrance on a hard track past farm buildings. Might become testing in a wet year.
Riders: *E. Williams 15, T. Vaughan 12, D. Jones 8, S. Waley-Cohen 4, N. Williams 4, L. Stephens 4.*

BRAFIELD-ON-THE-GREEN, Northants. (2004)
1m S of village, adjacent to Horton road on A428, 6m SE of Northampton.
Meeting: Oakley.
SF: 18-20. LH 2¼ circs. 8F; 18J; 2od (5/13). T: 6min 58.0s.
Gently undulating, rectangular course with two portable fences on each side; sweeping bends; 200 yd run-in; mainly old turf on former aerodrome. Likely to be a stayers' course, even in a dry season (which its opening year was not). Superb permanent paddock area, but facilities crammed between road and finishing straight led to much congestion for spectators and the course crossings could be better sited. Viewing poor in debut season, but a raised viewing area has been installed for 2005. Car parking on inside and outside of course is well organised but hindered view of home straight; only one entrance/exit. A positive and welcome improvement on Towcester, but will never rival Newton Bromswold.
Riders: *R. Cope 3, R. Burton 2, Miss R. Goodwin 1, Miss H. Irving 1.*

BRAMPTON BRYAN, Hereford. (1929)
11m W of Ludlow, nr A4113.
Meetings: Teme Valley; United.
SF: 18 (Nov Rdrs)-20. RH 2¼ circs. 8F; 18J; 2od (6/14). T: 7min 06.7s.
Virtually flat galloping course of 3m1f, with sharp and sometimes slippery bends at end of straights; course extended in direction of River Teme; can be watered when necessary. Good access and exits to car parks. Viewing very fair, and vastly improved from the old days when the only good perch was on a cattle trough. Picturesque setting and charming old-fashioned atmosphere. Frequently attracts plenty of runners. A long way from anywhere.
Riders: *R. Burton 7, Miss E. James 5, Miss C. Thomas 4, W. Hill 3, T. Stephenson 3, M. Wall 3, A. Wintle 3, A. Beedles 3.*

BRATTON DOWN, Devon. (1955*)
Alongside A399. 11m N of South Molton 3m S of Blackmoor Gate.
Meetings: Dulverton West; Exmoor; Tiverton Staghounds.
SF: 16 (Rest)-18. LH 2⅓ circs. 8F; 19J; 2od (8/16). T: 6min 27.1s.
Undulating course on side of hill; sharp turns into and out of home straight can be very slippery; long uphill finish and results of many races change after last fence; going usually good (despite late season dates) on old moorland turf; fences now more substantial and well built. Plenty of parking space, but only one entrance/exit. Facilities include a large paddock and a permanent if rustic changing room for male jockeys. Number board now resited near main tented area. Viewing, which had improved, has been ruined by a new bank with bushes on top planted through the very middle of the course, and the last fence and run-in are usually obscured by the crowd. Over 1000 feet above sea level with grand view of Exmoor, but grazed by sheep with resulting hazards for unsuspecting racegoers and falling riders.
Riders: *Miss P. Gundry 7, L. Jefford 6, D. Edwards 6, A. Farrant 6, R. Woollacott 5, N. Harris 4, M. Sweetland 4.*
**** A course existed at Bratton Down before WWII***

BREDWARDINE, Hereford (1947)
7m E of Hay-on-Wye, on B4352, 2m off A438.
Meeting: Golden Valley.
SF: 18 (Ladies)-20-22. RH 2½ circs. 8F; 18J; 2od (5/12). T: 6min 53.9s.
Flat oval galloping riverside track, with one rather sharp bend; start is in chute and first fence jumped once only. Car parking on hillside, and access and exit reasonable. Viewing quite good with all except first fence in view from hill by open ditch, though finish is then head on. Since moving to May generally very good ground has been produced, thanks in no small measure to the watering system. All the Safety Factors seem too high given the sharpness of the bends (that of the Maiden, in particular, should be reduced). Beautiful setting, and a very popular meeting, but rather a victim of its own success, and has trouble coping with the volume of horses and racegoers.
Riders: *Julian Pritchard 6, S. Lloyd 3, R. Burton 3, Miss A. Dare 2, M. Wall 2, E. Williams 2, D. Stephens (Wales) 2, D. Mansell 2, A. Dalton 2.*

BROCKLESBY PARK, Lincs. (1958*)
Nr A18 10m W of Grimsby (5m E of Exit 5, M180).
Meetings: Brocklesby, South Wold.
SF: 18 (Ladies, Hunt Members and Nov Rdrs)-20 (Conf)-22. LH 2¼ circs. 8F; 18J; 2od (6/14). T: 6min 42.7s.
Mainly flat course, uphill from 100 yards before 2nd (10/18th) to finish; long run (about ⅓m) between 7(15)th and 8(16)th; fences are all permanent and a work of art, well-built and irregularly spaced; rail on landing side of 2nd (10/16)th to deflect loose horses has been extended to give additional protection. Judge's stand is well back from line and paddock resited to far side of changing tents is much more convenient. Viewing good from inside of course and bank near paddock. Hard road access and well-sited car parks. Bookies very fair. A fair test and form usually reliable. The approach through a triumphal arch sets the stage for what is a proper old-fashioned Point-to-Point. Well worth a visit.
Riders: *S. Charlton 5, J. Docker 4, S. Morris 3, G. Brewer 3, R. Cope 2, R. Burton 2, O. Williams 2, N. Bell 2, Mrs J. Dawson 2, Mrs F. Needham 2, M. Tate 2.*
**** An earlier course was sited on the other side of the A18.***

BUCKFASTLEIGH, Devon. (1998*)
1m W of town, alongside A38, use junction for Lower Dean (returning eastbound traffic must travel through outskirts and use the A384 junction east of the town).
Meetings: South Pool Harriers; Dart Vale & Haldon Harriers.
SF: 16-18. RH 2⅓ circs. 7F; 19J; 2od (7/14). T: 6min 26.9s.

Roughly triangular undulating sharp course on sloping ground alongside A38; Fences, four in line adjacent to main road and three in home straight, are well presented. Attracts good-sized fields. Excellent viewing and access no problem. Judge's wagon has been moved about, but is always much too close to finishing post and disputed results are commonplace. Old grandstand not in use, but may be restored in the future (not a straightforward task).
Riders: *L. Jefford 12, A. Farrant 6, T. Dennis 4, Miss P. Gundry 4, C. Heard 4, Richard Darke 3, R. Walford 3, N. Williams 3, Miss T. Cave 3.*
**** There was a NH course here from 1883 until 1960; used as Point-to-Point venue from 1963 to 1977.***

PLATE 153 Buckfastleigh: The paddock and last fence from the top of the hill PHOTO: Tim Holt

CATSFIELD, E. Sussex. (1986)
At Buckholt Farm, Sidley, just off A269, N of Bexhill.
Meeting: East Sussex & Romney Marsh.
SF: 16-20. RH $2^1/_3$ circs. 8F; 18J; 2od (6/14). T: 6min 43.9s.
Course (formerly known as Bexhill) is an undulating long narrow oval, with bends at both ends on higher ground, fences inviting, but soft; very testing track — times indicate over 3 miles; Car parking fair but slow exit as all vehicles leave along single track lane. Viewing excellent from top car park.
Riders: *A. Hickman 3, P. York 2, Miss H. Grissell 2, C. Gordon 2.*

CHADDESLEY CORBETT, Worcs. (1925*)
Next to A448 midway between Bromsgove and Kidderminster (Exit 4 or 5, M5, Exit 1, M42).
Meetings: Harkaway Club, Worcestershire, Wheatland, Albrighton Woodland.
SF: 18-23 (Intermediate)-25. LH $2^1/_4$ circs. (Worcs) 8F; 20J; 2od (6/14). T: 6min 54.4s. (Others) 8F; 18J; 2od (4/12). T: 6min 16.9s.
Fairly flat track; easy 3 miles with one sharp bend, extended for Open races at Worcestershire meeting; winners usually well there by 3 out; run in of 125 yards; fences all portable (fences 1, 2 and 3 being metal-framed) are well-packed except for open ditch. Good access to car parks, and downhill exits which can be slow (but it is wise to use them when very wet, as many who have tried vainly to depart uphill will testify). Viewing is good from all parts of course, but foliage at later meetings is a nuisance. Big fields and crowds. Strong betting market. Excellent number board.
Riders: *R. Burton 13, Julian Pritchard 8, M. Harris 7, Miss E. James 5, T. Stephenson 4, R. Biddlecombe 4, D. Mansell 4, A. Wintle 4.*
**** Prior to 1951 the course was sited on the far side of the road***

CHARING, Kent. (1964*)
12m E of Maidstone. Nr A20 and M20. (Junction 8 and join A20)
Meetings: Mid Surrey Farmers Draghounds; South East Hunts Club; Ashford Valley.
SF: 18-23 (18). LH 2$^1/_3$ circs. 8F. (3m): 19J; 2od (4/12). T: 6min 40.1s. (2m4f): 15J; 1od (8). T: 5min 16.1s.
Course is undulating and suits stayers'; quick-draining chalk based pasture land is seldom heavy, an excellent venue for early season meetings and regularly attracts horses from neighbouring areas but conversely becomes very firm later in the season; fences firm and well-built mixture of portable and permanent; downhill fences sometimes taken too fast. Car parking is good with well-made access/exit tracks. Viewing is good especially from inside the course. Minimal walking to all facilities.
Riders: *C. Gordon 18, P. York 15, D. Dunsdon 5, D. Robinson 4, A. Hickman 4, Miss J. Wickens 3, B. Hitchcott 3.*
***** There was a previous course at Charing from 1929 to 1963 which was at Newlands Farm about a mile to the south of the existing course.***

CHARLTON HORETHORNE, Somerset. (1995)
Off B3145, 3m NE of Sherborne.
Meeting: Blackmore & Sparkford Vale.
SF: 18 (Rest)-20. LH 2$^1/_4$ circs. 8F; 18J; 2od (5/13). T: 6min 53.8s.
Fairly flat oval stayers' course on top of downs (reverted to left-handed in '03) with a slight dog-leg after 6(14)th fence; very long home straight (all plastic-railed — a massive undertaking); going can vary; fences all portable and well built. Car parking good with easy access and exit. Facilities now more compact, with reasonable viewing from centre of course. Usually attracts good fields and quality horses, but the latest running was marred by firmish going. A superbly well-organised and efficiently run meeting. .
Riders: *M. Miller 4, Miss E. Tory 2, Miss A. Goschen 2, J. Barnes 2.*

CHARM PARK, N. Yorks. (1949)
Nr Wykeham, off A170, 6m SW of Scarborough.
Meetings: Derwent; Staintondale Goathland.
SF: 18-20 (Nov Rdrs)-24. LH 2$^1/_8$ circs. 9F; 19J; 2od (5/14). T: 6min 50.8s.
Course is flat and races are 3m1f; mostly well drained, but can be sticky near 3rd (12th) fence; fences are small and softish, but rather upright, the open ditch may the smallest in the country; going usually good for March meeting, but sometimes firm for second meeting; popular with owners of inexperienced horses; races often won from behind. An exposed spot so wrap up well. Satisfactory access and exits to car parks and handy to facilities. Viewing superb for the agile from top of old railway embankment, but binoculars necessary to see fences at far end of course, and low sun can also be a problem (including for horses).
Riders: *G. Brewer 6, M. Walford 5, N. Tinkler 4, Mrs F. Needham 4, W. Burnell 3, S. Charlton 3, Miss S. Brotherton 3, M. Morley 3, C. Mulhall 3.*

CHERRYBROOK, Devon. (1986)
2m N of Tavistock nr A386.
Meeting: Spooners & West Dartmoor.
SF: 15-18. LH 2$^1/_2$ circs. 7F; 18J; 2od (5/12). T: 6min 16.0s.
Course is undulating with sharp descent after winning post and slight incline from final bend to winning post; sharp bend after 5(12)th and 7(14)th; mixture of portable and narrow permanent fences, most well-constructed, but open ditch is upright and above regulation height. Separate entrance and exit to car parks. Viewing reasonable, best near winning post. Judge's stand right on line. Commentator head on to finish. Bookies fair. Adjacent to Kilworthy (*qv*), and shares two fences with it — 2 and 7 here being 6 and 7 next door.
Riders: *Miss S. Young 4, L. Jefford 4, Miss L. Gardner 3, C. Heard 3, R. Woollacott 2, Miss T. Cave 2, Miss P. Gundry 2.*

CHIPLEY PARK, Somerset. (2000)
3m NE of Wellington, on B3187 (Junc 26 M5)
Meeting: Tiverton.
SF: 16-20. RH 2$^1/_2$ circs. 7F; 18J; 2od (7/14). T: 6min 40.7s.
Undulating very open oval course on side of slope; first fence (8/15th) followed by long sweeping bend into home straight; slight dog leg after 3rd (10/17th); inner favoured after two out; 120yd uphill run in. Quick draining, but mud can be on to course after home bend — and sometimes very boggy with standing water. Large permanent building used by officials and riders. Car park is handy to tarred entrance from nearby main road (no problems getting in or out). Very good viewing and a popular meeting

in early February which regularly attracts horses from Wales and West Midlands.
Riders: *R. Woollacott 5, Miss P. Gundry 3, D. Edwards 3, N. Williams 2, Miss P. Jones 2, M. Miller 2, J. Jukes 2, G. Maundrell 2, C. Williams 2.*

CILWENDEG, Dyfed. (2002)
$^1/_2$m E of Boncath on B4332 to Newcastle Emlyn.
Meeting: Tivyside.
SF: 15-18. RH 3$^1/_4$ circs. 7F; 19J; 3od (4/10/16). T: 6min 57.7s.
Fairly flat pear-shaped course with the paddock and car park near the larger end; sharp bend after the finish with adverse camber carries the horses wide; start is in chute in the middle of the course and 1st fence only jumped once only. Fences are big. Site is bisected by road leading to a retirement home, and paddock has been resited to same side as the course but bookies are on the other side. Viewing good, best from inside of course, but horses go out of view behind a small copse. Good car parking, but local roads will be congested should the meeting ever clash with Mothers Day!
Riders: *M. Lewis 3, E. Williams 3, Miss I. Tompsett 2, Miss F. Wilson 2, M. Barber 2.*

CLIFTON-ON-DUNSMORE, Warwicks. (1953)
Next to A5, 3m NW of M1 junc 18, 2m E of Rugby.
Meeting: Atherstone.
SF: 18-20. LH 2$^1/_4$ circs. 8F; 19J; 2od (7/15). T: 6min 11.2s.
Old Rugby racecourse; gently undulating with start and finish on uphill part of the course; going usually good even when very dry; bend after 4(12)th sometimes slippery when wet or after watering; fences very small, but hard; 7(15)th causes problems; not a course for a novice jumper. Easy access and exit for vehicles. Activities of private car park on adjoining land have led to entry charge for spectators rather than cars. Viewing is fair from inside of course, but can be obstructed by cars; good general view from outside at top end of course. Attracts large crowds, usually plenty of runners and often competitive racing.
Riders: *S. Morris 6, R. Hunnisett 2, R. Armson 2, N. Kent 2, L. Hicks 2, J. Docker 2.*

PLATE 154 Cold Harbour: The runners for Race 1227 Radnor & West Herefordshire Confined are already mounted in the paddock; spot the number board under the tree — it is bright red
PHOTO: Kathleen Mullen

COLD HARBOUR, Herefordshire. (2002)
Near Monkland (3m W of Leominster) Close to junction of A44/A4110.
Meeting: Radnor and West Hereford.
SF: 18-20. RH 2$^1/_4$ circs. 8F. (3m) 18J; 2od (5/13). T: 6min 24.3s. (4m) 24J; 3od (3/11/19). T: 8min 29.2s.

Flat galloping oval course with three fences in home straight, a cross fence and four fences including ditch in back straight. Excellent viewing from natural grandstand adjacent to paddock. One entrance/exit for cars (separate entrance for horseboxes) but no problems encountered. A very attractive spot with views right across to Clee Hill.
Riders: *Julian Pritchard 6, T. Stephenson 4, S. Blackwell 3, R. Burton 3, Miss J. Williams 2, M. Munrowd 2, M. Keel 2, G. Barfoot-Saunt 2, A. Wintle 2.*

CORBRIDGE, Northumberland. (1920)
3m N of town, off A68 on B6318.
Meetings: Tynedale (3m5f Mens & Ladies Opens); Braes of Derwent.
SF: 17-18-20. RH 2 circs. 9F. (3m): 18J; 2od (3/12). T: 6min 29.6s. (3m5f): 21J; 2od (6/15). T: 7min 58.6s.
Undulating stayers' course with three fairly sharp bends; last two fences and finish uphill; old turf on clay gives good galloping surface; the start of the 3m5f races has been moved forward by one fence, to give 21 jumps in these races; fences well made. Viewing is best on inside of track near commentator's tower. Access to car parks is over ridge and furrow field; hardcore exit road. Permanent facilities. Has a variety of SF's for both meetings.
Riders: *Miss P. Robson 10, A. Richardson 6, J. Walton 5, T. Scott 4, Miss N. Stirling 4, T. Oates 3, C. Storey 3, C. Gillon 3.*

COTHELSTONE, Somerset. (1996)
2m NE of Bishops Lydeard off A358. (Exit 25, M5).
Meetings: Quantock Staghounds; West Somerset Vale; Weston & Banwell Harriers.
SF: 16 (Nov Rdrs)-18 (14). LH 2½ circs. 7F; (3m) 19J; 3od (3/10/17) T: 6min 22.8s. (2m4f) 16J; 2od (7/14) T: 5min 22.8s
A very picturesque almost flat very sharp triangular Linley course set under the Quantock Hills; slightly uphill from 3rd(10/17)th to 4(11/18)th; very gently downhill from next; fences portable and quite well built; compacted sub-soil can make it difficult to provide decent going. Best viewing from centre of course, but this usually planted with crops and spectators are warned off; finishing post is lined up with the only tree in the home straight (and should be moved). Facilities compact. Car parking satisfactory. A well-supported course and the mid-week May evening fixture has a good friendly atmosphere.
Riders: *R. Woollacott 4, Miss T. Cave 4, Miss C. Tizzard 4, D. Alers-Hankey 4, T. Eades 3, R. Stephens 3, M. Woodward 3, L. Jefford 3, J. Young 3, C. Heard 3, A. Charles-Jones 3.*

COTLEY FARM, Somerset. (1953)
2m SW of Chard, 1½ miles off A30 — signposted from western end of Chard.
Meeting: Cotley.
SF: 17-20. LH 1¾ circs. 9F; 18J; 2od (4/13). T: 6min 39.1s.
Undulating galloping stayers' course with precipitous dip after 9 which can be very heavy in wet, with steep climb and sharp turn before next which can prove slippery; downhill from 5(14)th with rising ground coming to last; all fences are portable and well-built and regulation height; masses of chestnut paling around the finish/paddock. Plenty of room in car parks, but access/exit can be slow through long winding lanes. Tolerable viewing though 5(14)th and approach to last difficult to see. Four painted milk churns decorate the centre of the paddock — a nice touch.
Riders: *N. Williams 4, L. Jefford 3, R. Young 2, N. Mitchell 2, Miss T. Cave 2, Miss C. Tizzard 2, J. Barnes 2.*

COTTENHAM, Cambs. (1931)
4m N of Cambridge nr B1049. (Exit 14, M11).
Meetings: Cambridgeshire Harriers Hunt Club; Cambridge University Draghounds; Fitzwilliam; Aldenham Harriers.
SF: 18-23-25 (16) RH 2¼ circs. 9F; (3m) 19J; 2od (4/13). T: 6min 23.1s. (2m4f) 15J; 1od (9). T: 4min 59.6s.
Totally flat oval course; fences well-built and maintained throughout season; three fairly sharp bends suits front runners; open ditch can cause problems when fields are large; old NH course — small grandstand (half of which is supposed to be reserved) still in use. The resited Judge's box seems have alleviated the problems in the past. Car parking very good though large crowds can lead to queues. A variety of SF's used to appy for each meeting (likely to change). Excellent viewing from grandstand and banks by paddock and last fence. Very popular meetings, superbly organised and the trial of taking entries by telephone in 2004 proved very successful. Watering facilities available.
Riders: *N. Bloom 9, S. Morris 7, R. Burton 5, N. King 5, Miss J. Williams 4, A. Braithwaite 4.*

PLATE 155 Cottenham: The field in Race 3 Cambridgeshire Harriers Hunt Club Mens Open pass the stands after the first fence PHOTO: Tim Holt

DALSTON, Cumbria. (1927 — at least)
4m SW of Carlisle on B5299. (Exit 42, M6).
Meeting: Cumberland Farmers.
SF: 21-23 (18). RH 2¼ circs. 8F; (2m4f) 15J; 2od (3/11). T: 5min 24.9s. (3m) 18J; 2od (6/14). T: 6min 19.3s.

Flat course; one of the easiest of northern tracks although galloping nature means horses are unable to get breather; fences (all portable) are very small and flimsy and well below standard. Good viewing from hillside car park and from centre of course. Single access road gets more rutted each year and is a tight squeeze for horseboxes, and exit through narrow gateway from hillside car park needs improving. Big fields and races are invariably divided. Judge's trailer is too near the line. The very narrow gateway after the third fence could make for potential danger on a course with a high safety factor.
Riders: *Miss P. Robson 3, T. Oates 2, T. Morrison 2, R. Morgan 2, Miss J. Hollands 2, J. Walton 2, C. Storey 2.*

DALTON PARK, Yorks. (1954)
5m NW of Beverley nr B1248. (Exit 38, M62).
Meeting: Holderness.
SF: 18-20-22. RH 2½ circs. 8F; 20J; 2od (6/14). T: 7min 34.9s.

Course slightly undulating; races are 3m1f; going usually soft and sometimes heavy; fences (portable except open ditch) tend to be small and soft. Horses must be well there and on inside by 2 out to have a chance on short run-in; stamina essential. Satisfactory car parking and exit downhill. Good viewing if prepared to keep on the move — best in centre toward start. Judge's stand is right against line. Superb parkland setting.
Riders: *T. Greenall 2, S. Walker 2, S. Swiers 2, G. Brewer 2.*

DETLING, Kent. (1973)
2m E of Maidstone nr A249, 1m N of village (Exit 7, M20, Exit 5, M2).
Meeting: West Street-Tickham (March).
SF: 18-24. LH 2¼ circs. 9F. (3m): 21J; 2od (7/16). T: 6min 25.5s. (4m): 28J; 3od (7/16/25). T: 8min 35.1s.

Fairly flat oval course with easy bends; four fences in back straight; long and slightly uphill run-in suits fast finishing stayers'; can be holding despite underlying chalk, but gets hard in dry spells; fences large and firm, but inviting. Fences 1 and 9 are omitted on final circuit of grandiosely titled 4m Kent Grand National. Good access, but exit is down one road and very slow. Viewing best from centre of course, and

it is possible to get close to the action, but crowds ruin sight of finish which rather defeats the object. Vigilant stewards. The Hunt committee try very hard to put on a good meeting (unlike most of the others in the Area).
Riders: *P. York 3, Mrs J. Gordon 3, C. Gordon 3, S.R. Andrews 2, P. Bull 2, A. Hickman 2.*

DIDMARTON, Glos. (1956)
Nr A433, 6m SW of Tetbury (8m NE of Exit 18, M4).
Meeting: Duke of Beaufort's.
SF: 18-25. LH 1¾ circs. 10F; 18J; 3od (3/9/13). T: 6min 22.8s.
Undulating course on hillside; downhill from 3rd (13th), uphill from 9; sweeping bends; fences are well made; well drained; a deservedly popular well-organised meeting and bookies generous; very large number of trade stands. The downhill 8th (last) fence can cause problems. Good car parking, but be early to avoid queue. Excellent viewing from most parts though back straight difficult in bad weather.
Riders: *F. Hutsby 4, Julian Pritchard 3, Miss P. Gundry 2, D. Edwards 2, A. Wintle 2.*

DINGLEY, Northants. (1931*)
3m E of Market Harborough, nr A427.
Meetings: Woodland Pytchley; Fernie; Harborough Race Club.
SF: 16-18-20-22 (16). RH 2¼ circs. 8F. (3m): 18J; 2od (7/15). T: 6min 36.9s. (2m4f); 16J; 2od (5/13). T: 5min 41.7s. (4m); 24J; 3od (5/13/21). T: 8min 38.0s.
Slightly undulating and in places very narrow course with a run in of 155 yards in valley bottom; fences smaller and softer than previously since '95 and water jump removed. Fence 6(14)th and 8(16)th portable, bend by start can be tricky when wet. Has a variety of SFs for each meeting. Some permanent buildings; parking on steep hillside; good access, but exit difficult in wet weather. Excellent viewing from natural grandstand, and minimal walking to see everything. Water course altered and a drainage system was installed in 2002 — ideal for May/June racing.
Riders: *R. Cope 9, A. Sansome 4, S. Morris 3, R. Hunnisett 3, R. Armson 3, G. Hanmer 3.*
**** Used to be a bona-fide venue***

DUNCOMBE PARK, Yorks. (1975)
½m SW of Helmsley off A170 12m E of Thirsk.
Meeting: Sinnington.
SF: 18-22-25. RH 2 circs. 9F; 18J; 2od (4/13). T: 6min 39.1s.
Course is set on hillside with sharp bend before stiff 350 yard uphill run to last; completely revamped in '99, when all the downhill fences on the back straight were removed; the fifth last became two out, and produced an incredibly long run to the last; much safer, and better appreciated by the riders. Fences portable and well-built; going often good despite early date. Single access/exit — some queues. Viewing good, but finish head on from main spectator area; try centre of course. Crossing gap manned by security staff is far too narrow and a dreadful scrum often ensues.
Riders: *D. Easterby 4, Miss P. Robson 3, N. Tinkler 2, L. McGrath 2, L. Bates 2.*

DUNTHROP, Oxon. (1983)
2m NE Chipping Norton at junc of A3400 & A361.
Meetings: Heythrop; Farmers Bloodhounds.
SF: 18-20 (Farmers Rest)-22 (Heythrop)-25 (Farmers) (18). RH 2 circs. 9F. (3m2f); 18J; 2od (4/13). T: 7min 02.6s. (3m5f) 21J; 2od (7/16). T: 7min 54.2s. (4m); 23J; 2od (9/18). T: 8min 36.9s. (2m4f): 14J; 1od (9). T: 5min 08.9s.
Well-drained 3m2f mostly flat course, but uphill from start until after 2nd fence and quite steeply downhill to last, suiting front runners; the six island fences are portable; run-in 300 yards. Car parking good. Viewing satisfactory if you can select your spot. Bookies numerous and odds fair. The Heythrop's move to a January date continues to be most successful even though the ground has been on the firmish side at both runnings to date.
Riders: *Julian Pritchard 6, A. Martin 6, F. Hutsby 4, J. Jenkins 3, T. Stephenson 2, R. Lawther 2, Miss P. Gundry 2, J. Trice-Rolph 2, J. Diment 2, H. Dowty 2.*

EASINGWOLD, Yorks. (1965*)
14m NW of York, nr A19.
Meetings: York & Ainsty; Bilsdale.
SF: 16-18-23. LH 2¼ circs. 8F; 18J; 2od (3/11). T: 6min 06.1s.
Slightly undulating course with sharp bends, particularly that before the penultimate; uphill finish; fences variable; suits non-stayers (the fastest course in the country); can be slippery on turns; produced some of the best going in the area in latest season and rewarded with 98 runners in late April. Car parking satisfactory in very long grass; downhill exit. Viewing good, although far side near river partially out of

sight — best from top of hill above car park.
Riders: *N. Tutty 7, Miss J. Foster 5, M. Walford 3, L. Bates 3, S. Charlton 2, P. Cornforth 2, P. Atkinson 2, Miss F. Hartley 2, M. Mackley 2, K. Needham 2, B. Woodhouse 2.*
**** Racing took place on a course at Easingwold before WWII***

EATON HALL, Cheshire. (1963)
4m S of Chester, nr A483 and A55.
Meetings: Flint & Denbigh; Sir W. W. Wynn's.
SF: 18-22. RH 2$^1/_3$circs. 8F; 18J; 2od (7/14). T: 6min 16.7s (new layout)
Until 1999 was a very long galloping oval course, but then modified to almost three circuits with two fences less and the start and first fence in a chute; '04 had a similar layout but with all eight fences back in use with shorter straights (this will probably now be the permanent set up); run in 145yds. Fences big and well-made; ground usually very soft in early season, so stamina essential; very firm later on — only 38 runners in eight races at second meeting in 2004. Cars park on hard surface — old airfield runways. Viewing best from small bank between paddock and finishing straight unless crowd is large, then try inside course between last two fences. Rather a dull course, but partially redeemed by the view of a beautiful red sandstone church which is where they bury the Grosvenors, and breed Classic winners.
Riders: *G. Hanmer 13, R. Burton 7, Mrs C. Ford 4, A. Crow 4, R. Owen 2, Mrs K. Diggle 2, M. Worthington 2, G. Thomas 2.*

ERW LON, Carms. (1979)
13m N of Carmarthen on B4336.
Meeting: Vale of Clettwr.
SF: 16-18. LH 2$^1/_3$ circs. 8F; 18J; 2od (6/14). T: 6min 30.1s.
Triangular mainly flat galloping course on mountain grazing land with easy bends; start in chute; downhill from 1st (9/17th); rarely becomes deep, but can be sticky; fences well-made and well-sited. Easy access and separate exit. Poor viewing — be prepared to move around; best in centre of course, 4(12)th fence obscured by horse boxes and last fence also difficult to see; might be better if the finish was moved. A move to the top of the hill would give a view of the final stages of the race unfolding for racegoers and the commentator. Forget winter woollies at peril, very exposed and weather can be diabolical. Sets Welsh season in motion in early February.
Riders: *T. Vaughan 11, E. Williams 9, M. Lewis 7, P. Sheldrake 6, D. Jones 6, Miss P. Jones 4, J. Jukes 4, C. Williams 4.*

EYTON-ON-SEVERN, Salop. (1923)
7m SE of Shrewsbury, nr B4380 via A5 and M54 (Exit 7).
Meetings: Tanatside; North Shropshire; South Shropshire.
SF: 18-21 (18). LH 1$^1/_3$ circs. 13F. (3m): 18J; 2od (6/12). T: 6min 37.9s. (2m4f): 14J; 2od (2/8). T: 5min 32.0s.
Very flat galloping course; fences fairly soft with final 3 close together; well drained alongside river. Access to car parks satisfactory, but exit always slow. Excellent view from hill, but horses very distant at far end of course. Shares with Larkhill the distinction of having most individual fences, but fences 1, 2, 9 and 10 now metal-framed (fence 7 appeared to have been substantially rebuilt in wood); open ditch (6) absent in 2004 due to drainage problems. Lovely rural spot with views to The Wrekin and the Long Mynd. Not easy to find for first-time visitors and suggestion is that racegoers should turn off at the Wroxeter Roman Site and follow a windy lane to the course entrance beside a farm. A superb old course, and hopefully will continue to flourish despite recent problems.
Riders: *R. Burton 20, Miss S. Beddoes 5, D. Barlow 5, A. Crow 5, Miss J. Williams 4, G. Hanmer 4.*

FAKENHAM, Norfolk. (1978)
2m SW of town.
Meeting: West Norfolk.
SF: 15-18. LH 3 circs. 6F; 18J; 3od (4/10/16), 3 wj (2/8/14). T: 6min 31.1s.
Undulating one mile circuit on outside of NH steeplechase course with horses always on the turn, but good sweeping bends never cause problems; winners usually well there at least a mile out. Portable fences. Watering system available if required, and going regularly close to perfect. Race course car parks; excellent viewing, horses never far away. Unlike other NH tracks has a fair pointing atmosphere. Chiropterologists will be glad to know that there is a resident bat in the commentator's box (and we don't mean Mackenzie!).
Riders: *N. Bloom 8, D. Kemp 5, Miss Z. Turner 2, A. Ayers 2.*

FLAGG MOOR, Derbys. (1892)
On A515, 6m SE Buxton, 15m NW Ashbourne.
Meeting: High Peak.
SF: 18 (Ladies)-20. LH 2 circs. 9F. (3m4f): 18J; 2od (3/12). T: 7min 52.2s.
Very testing well-drained course of 3m4f encircling two farms and crossing four roads; start and finish in same place; long (half a mile) uphill pull from end of back straight; fences big, but not hard; fence 4(13) is a drop fence. Members Race run over stone walls starts down in Flagg village whence contestants make their way by various routes before joining course proper for the equivalent of one circuit. Judge's stand is still right against ropes; permanent facilities for male jockeys, but ladies reduced to an adjacent tent; the tragic loss of the toilet in the unsaddling enclosure causes extreme queues for the portaloos. Satisfactory car parking, but some delay entering due to large crowd. Splendid old-fashioned and clear announcer. Viewing good from bank, but back straight partly obscured and fence 6(15) invisible behind farm; very exposed and open to elements — wrap up well. At last returned to action in 2004 after a number of different problems and held a most successful meeting. A dramatic and unique place, and the highest course in the country at over 1100ft — an exhilarating spot to go racing; long may it continue to flourish.
Riders: *R. Burton 3, S. Prior 2, N. Fogg 1, Mrs V. Thirlby 1, Miss T. Clark 1, Miss N. Lloyd 1, Miss N. Brady 1, Miss J. Froggatt 1, Miss H. Irving 1, B. Foster 1.*

FLETE PARK, Devon. (1980)
Off A379 10m E of Plymouth, leave A38 at Ivybridge via A3121.
Meetings: Dartmoor (4m Mens Open); Modbury Harriers (4m Ladies)
SF: 16-18. RH 2¼ circs. 8F. (3m): 20J; 2od (7/15). T: 6min 51.0s. (4m): 25J; 3od (4/12/20). T: 8min 09.7s.
Hilly demanding course with a sharp bend and long downhill run to 3rd (11/19th) fence; dog-leg onto 140 yard run-in and sharp bend out of finishing straight and uphill through start; very short run-in. Steep downhill entrance to car parks, but separate firm and level exits. Facilities compact though a fair step to changing rooms in cricket pavilion! (course goes round the pitch which is smaller than most bowling greens). Reasonable viewing from high ground overlooking run-in, but one or two fences obscured by trees. Very pleasant setting, once home of top amateur rider the late Lord Mildmay of Flete. A well maintained track — organisers usually try to provide decent ground.
Riders: *L. Jefford 9, Miss M. McCarthy 5, Miss T. Cave 3, G. Welch 3, D. McKenna 3, Richard Darke 2, Miss S. Young 2, Miss S. Gaisford 2, Miss L. Gardner 2, Miss A. Barnett 2, L. Heard 2, A. Glassonbury 2, A. Farrant 2.*

FRIARS HAUGH, Borders. (1953)
Just W of Kelso, nr A699.
Meetings: Jedforest; Berwickshire; Duke of Buccleuch's.
SF: 16 (Nov Rdrs)-20-23. LH 2⅓ circs. 8F; 18J; 2od (5/12). T: 7min 03.1s.
Course is 3m2f mostly flat with one uphill climb; inviting island fences all well constructed; ground drains well and going usually good even in February; races are run at fast pace; fence 18 and finish in separate central chute; one fence was moved in 2003 from the riverside to form a new 2nd last. Car parking good with easy access. Most of action visible from centre of course, and finish can now be viewed satisfactorily from best vantage point. Meetings very well organised. Loose horses sometimes go for a dip in the River Tweed.
Riders: *C. Storey 16, Miss P. Robson 8, A. Richardson 8, Miss J. Hollands 4, W. Ramsay 3, T. Oates 3, R. Morgan 3, R. Green 3, Miss R. Davidson 3, Miss N. Stirling 3, Miss M. Neill 3.*

GARNONS, Hereford. (1984 — RH in 1st year).
8m W of Hereford, just off A438 (Exit 4, M50).
Meetings: South Herefordshire; Ross Harriers.
SF: 16 (Intermed Nov Rdrs)-18 (Ladies)-20 (16). LH 2½ circs. 7F. (3m): 18J: 2od (7/14). T: 6min 50.5s. (2m4f): 15J; 2od (4/11). T: 5min 51.4s.
Very undulating and very sharp; portable fences stiff. Separate entrance and exit to car parks. Viewing used to be good (best from inside of course below finishing post), and could be again if the judicious use of a chainsaw was employed, but management seem to have a cynical attitude towards their public. Access on steep grass slope can be very slippery when wet, and narrow gateway very hazardous then, but owner's private driveway may be used. Exit often slow. Picturesque, but it palls unless you like trees, trees and more trees.
Riders: *T. Stephenson 6, A. Wintle 6, Miss E. James 5, Miss L. Brooke 3, G. Hanmer 3, T. Weston 2, S. Thomas 2, S. Blackwell 2, R. Hodges 2, R. Burton 2, P. Mason 2, M. Keel 2, E. Williams 2.*

GARTHORPE, Leics. (1955)
6m E of Melton Mowbray on B676, 7m W of A1.
Meetings: Cottesmore, Belvoir, Quorn, Melton Hunt Club, Blankney.
SF: 18 (Ladies except Melton)-20 (Melton Ladies)-24 (18). RH $2\frac{1}{4}$ circs. 8F; (3m): 18J; 2od (3/11). T: 6min 25.1s. (2m4f): 15J; 1od (8). 5min 19.3s.
Rectangular well-drained course, the undulations having been levelled and downhill stretches have been drained; run-in of 190 yds slopes to outside; fences big and well constructed; 3 new fences for 2004 included the pen fences 5(13) and 6(14); the inside of fences 1-4 and 18 are usually dolled off and kept for the Melton meeting. Superbly maintained, watering system available and decent ground available throughout dry spells. Good access and exit to car parks. Good view from car park on outside of straight. Extra toilets and viewing area for disabled. Permanent facilities for jockeys, officials etc. Number board should have painted boards rather than badly chalked ones. Strong betting market.
Riders: *S. Morris 13, J. Docker 9, Mrs J. Dawson 8, R. Armson 7, M. Mackley 7, Miss L. Coney 5.*

GODSTONE, Surrey. (2002)
W of Town, less than a mile from Junction 6 of M25.
Meetings: Southdown & Eridge (March and May).
SF: 16-18. RH $2\frac{1}{3}$ circs. 6F; 18J; 3od (3/9/15). T: 6min 25.7s
Undulating course set in parkland with sharp gradient changes — could be a problem on extremes of going; lengthened since inaugural season and is now 3 miles; fences small but firm and well presented. Viewing best from centre of course with action never far away, but start is now at foot of the hill and invisible from best vantage point. Compact facilities. Both meetings continue to attract large crowds but fields have become disappointing. Announcer very clear.
Riders: *C. Gordon 10, P. Hall 4, Mrs J. Gordon 4, A. Hickman 3, P. Blagg 2.*

GREAT TRETHEW, Cornwall. (1986)
1m S of A38; 3m SE of Liskeard.
Meetings: East Cornwall (February and March).
SF: 16-18 (14). RH $2\frac{1}{2}$ circs. 7F; (3m) 19J; 2od (7/14). T: 6min 44.3s. (2m4f) 16J; 2od (4/11) T: 5min 38.0s
Course is a very hilly elongated oval with long straights and two sharp bends; long galloping run from 6(13)th downhill through start; a deep cleft bisects the course; uphill finish. Run-in very short — less than 100 yards. Fences (all portable) are in straights, and well-built. Car park in centre of course can be slippery; separate box park. Viewing good from finishing area though run back to start out of sight.
Riders: *Miss S. Young 6, L. Jefford 6, A. Farrant 5, Miss T. Cave 4, Miss P. Gundry 4, R. Woollacott 3, Miss L. Gardner 3, A. Glassonbury 3.*

GUILSBOROUGH, Northants. (1951)
Nr A5199, 10m NW of Northampton (Exit 18 M1, or via A5199 from A14).
Meeting: Pytchley.
SF: 18 (Rest)-20. LH $2\frac{1}{2}$ circs. 8F; 19J; 2od (7/15). T: 6min 35.9s.
Flat course with two long straights and two sharp bends; can be slippery when wet; long run to first, short run-in; finishing line set at an angle, favouring horses on inside; fences very well built and inviting — 5(13)th portable. Watering possible. Exemplary number board retrieved from late Newton Bromswold course. Good access to and exit from car parks (on steep hill), hard road laid down in one car park to alleviate climb back to road when wet. The cutting down of trees and hedges has greatly improved viewing in back straight, although fence 8(16) is still hard to see. Rural and pleasant. Usually masses of runners and huge crowd for good reason.
Riders: *S. Morris 5, R. Cope 4, R. Lawther 2, R. Hunnisett 2, Miss A. Stennett 2, J. Docker 2, J. Diment 2.*

HACKWOOD PARK, Hants. (1952)
2m SE Basingstoke, signposted from A339 Alton road (Exit 6, M3).
Meetings: Hampshire; Vine & Craven.
SF: 16-18-20. LH $2\frac{3}{4}$ circs. 7F; 18J; 2od (5/12). T: 6min 27.3s.
Course on a slope with downhill back straight and uphill finish; very sharp, but by no means easy; fences permanent, attractively presented, but now rather soft; a much improved venue since management changed, but limitations of site sadly always apparent and the lack of watering facilities does often produce very small fields. Viewing will always be a problem as facilities and crowd are crammed together in the middle of the course; the commentator stands in a high scaffolding tower, which is essential to see all the action. Car entry satisfactory, but exit very slow particularly at very popular Bank Holiday meeting.

£3 racecard at Hampshire meeting in 2004.
Riders: *P. York 8, G. Maundrell 6, Miss A. Goschen 3, D. Dennis 3, R. Green 2, Miss R. Goodwin 2, Miss C. Cowe 2, J. Owen 2, J. Barnes 2.*

HESLAKER, Yorkshire (2002)
1m SW of Skipton, close to and signposted from A59.
Meetings: Pendle Forest & Craven; Badsworth and Bramham Moor.
SF: 16-18. LH 3 circs. 6F; 19J; 3od (3/9/15). T: 7min 32.4s.
Undulating course with very long downhill stretch between fences 6(12/18) and 7(13/19) and uphill from ditch; run in of 80 yards; winners usually well up on inner from two out; first fence jumped four times; times indicate a distance of 3m4f-3m5f. Carpet laid in jockeys changing tent in '04. Limited viewing from main car park, best from centre of course and some moving about is essential to see all of the fences. Pendle meeting is a very friendly affair with a two-course hot lunch being laid on for the local farming fraternity. Picturesque setting also used for horse trials — worth walking the course for magnificent views of Skipton.
Riders: *G. Brewer 4, W. Burnell 2, R. Burton 2, N. Kent 2, N. Bannister 2, Miss J. Foster 2, D. Coates 2.*

HEXHAM, Northumberland. (1995)
1m SW of town between B6305 & B6306 on NH racecourse.
Meetings: Border; Haydon.
SF: 17 (Border maiden)-18 (Rest)-20 (15). LH 2¼ circs. 8F; (3m): 19J; 2od (5/13). T: 7min 00.8s. (2m4f): 14J; 1od (8). T: 5min 39.3s.
Gently undulating course on inside of racecourse; All fences completely rebuilt. Last fence resited and run in extended to 200yds. Good viewing in fine setting, but finish distant and atmosphere inevitably lacking. No number board so a blackboard is used (sited adjacent to the parade ring). Wonderful for NH racing — a useless venue for Pointing. Doubts still remain about the going, which is never going to be ideal and has suffered from extremes in history of course.
Riders: *Miss P. Robson 5, J. Walton 5, K. Anderson 3, T. Oates 2, R. Morgan 2, Miss N. Stirling 2, Miss J. Foster 2, L. Morgan 2, A. Richardson 2.*

HIGHAM, Suffolk. (1958)
8m NE of Colchester via A12 and B1068.
Meetings: Waveney Harriers; North Norfolk Harriers; Granta Harriers; Essex & Suffolk.
SF: 15-18. LH 2½ circs. 8F; 19J; 2od (6/14). T: 6min 16.3s.
Flat very tight circuit suits front runners; sandy soil usually gives good going even in early season which ensures regular raiders from outside local area are attracted; fences are easier than they used to be. Watering possible. Bookies poor. Flat car parking and no problems, but arrive early to avoid some delay at entrance. Best viewing from centre of course, though finish difficult from there. Gents toilets greatly improved. Well-supported, although attendance at the relatively new Granta Harriers meeting is often lower than the others.
Riders: *P. York 9, A. Hickman 7, N. King 5, N. Bloom 5, J. Owen 5, G. Cooper 5, D. Kemp 5, D. Dunsdon 5, A. Sansome 5.*

HIGH EASTER, Essex. (1992*)
8m NW of Chelmsford nr A1060 (Exit 8, M11).
Meetings: Easton Harriers; Essex.
SF: 15-20-22. LH 2 circs. 9F; 19J; 2od (4/13). T: 6min 43.1s.
Undulating roughly kidney-shaped course with fairly stiff climb to two out, back straight on ancient water meadows so has softer going than higher ground in finishing straight; turn into back straight has been eased; downhill stretch and slight drop on fence 4(13). Well-built inviting portable fences, those in back straight moved to outside of track and taken in form of gentle arc. Viewing greatly improved by construction of mound on outside of course and new tower features stewards' hut and commentator's box, but not for those with vertigo. All jumps now visible though finish is head-on. Watering possible. Compact facilities; positions of paddock and bookies/tote transposed to good effect, and the historic number board has been used in the past at a number of defunct courses in Essex. Fun fair for children at both meetings. Weak betting market. Entrance/exit rather slow as course is in the middle of a maze of country lanes. Pleasant rural setting.
Riders: *N. Bloom 5, Miss Z. Turner 5, W. Wales 2, S. Sporborg 2, S. Salmon 2, P. York 2, P. Millington 2, Miss N. Barnes 2, Miss J. Wickens 2, G. Cooper 2, D. Kemp 2, A. Sansome 2, A. Merriam 2, A. Coe 2, A. Ayers 2.*
**** Essex held a meeting at Great Hassels in 1886, within view of present site***

HOLNICOTE, Som. (1997*)
Near A39, 3m W of Minehead, 2m E of Porlock.
Meetings: West Somerset & Minehead Harriers; Devon & Somerset Staghounds; Minehead Harriers and West Somerset.
SF: 15 (Nov Rdrs)-17. RH 2½ circs. 7F; 19J; 3od (3/10/17). T: 6min 38.6s.
Slightly undulating, all grass, tear drop shaped course a few hundred yards from original course. Course is downhill into back straight and slightly uphill from approaching 3rd (10/17th) through finish. Fences (portable) firm and up to height, but 2nd (9/16th) very narrow. Compacted sub-soil. Viewing adequate (good if right spot picked), but hindered by tents and trees. Car parking satisfactory. Facilities compact, but Judge's box right against ropes. Very scenic, under Dunkery Beacon on slopes of Exmoor National Park with good view of Selworthy church.
Riders: *C. Heard 7, A. Farrant 6, A. Charles-Jones 5, D. Edwards 4, T. Scudamore 3, W. White 2, R. Pyman 2, N. Mitchell 2, N. Harris 2, Miss T. Cave 2, Miss S. Robinson 2, Miss P. Gundry 2, Miss O. Green 2, Miss J. Cumings 2, Miss C. Tizzard 2, M. Miller 2, J. Barnes 2, H. Thomas 2, D. Alers-Hankey 2, C. White 2, A. Honeyball 2.*
*** The original Holnicote course, opened in 1948, was a few hundred yards away***

HORNBY CASTLE, Yorks. (1947)
3m W of A1, S of Catterick.
Meetings: West of Yore; Bedale.
SF: 18-20-25 (16). LH 2¼ circs. 8F; (3m) 18J; 2od (3/11). T: 6min 46.2s. (2m4f) 13J; 1od (6) T: 5min 09.6s.
Undulating stayers' course; ridge and furrow now removed; fences well-built. Car parking flat, plenty of room. All fences visible from centre of course, but run to 6th fence out of sight, and finish rather distant. PA system not clear at better vantage points. Very weak betting market (needs fresh blood urgently), West of Yore meeting choose their own bookmakers and their officials are mostly professionals who give their services free. In '04 West of Yore dropped their Members race — more Hunts should take note of this move. Scenic setting with the cute castle perched on a hill.
Riders: *G. Tuer 5, R. Clark 3, R. Abrahams 3, N. Tutty 3, Miss J. Foster 3, L. Bates 3, G. Brewer 3.*

HORSEHEATH, Cambs. (1972)
4m W of Haverhill on A1307. (Exits 9 or 10, M11).
Meetings: Cambridgeshire with Enfield Chace; Thurlow; Puckeridge.
SF: 18-25. RH 1¾ circs. 10F; 18J; 2od (3/12). T: 6min 39.5s.
Undulating galloping course of over three miles; start in chute; uphill finish; fences well built; 1st and 10th jumped only once, 6th (taken downhill) causes most problems; chalk subsoil drains well, but gets very holding in back straight. Plenty of room for parking, but crowds large so arrive early to avoid queue. Viewing very good, but pick vantage point for best sight of finish. Dries out fast and a pathetic track in a dry year — definitely should be exploited in early season. Has a little fun fair for the children, but may need resiting as the helter-skelter obscured the commentator's view in 2004.
Riders: *P. Taiano 7, A. Braithwaite 7, D. Kemp 6, Miss Z. Turner 5, A. Sansome 5, R. Cope 4, R. Burton 4, J. Owen 4.*

HOWICK, Gwent. (1952)
2m W of Chepstow on B4293. (Exit 2, M48).
Meetings: Curre & Llangibby (February and March).
SF: 16-18 (Ladies)-20. LH 1¾ circs. 9F; 18J; 2od (3/12). T: 6min 33.3s.
Undulating almost triangular course with one sharp and two sweeping bends; the course layout has been changed regularly in recent seasons; most fences are permanent and quite stiff; fence 2(11) is on the crest of a hill and is quite small; fences 4(13) and 5(14) at far end of course fall away to the inside and vary in height by nearly two feet from one side to the other. Spacious, but unorganised car parking, and exit can be slow through the farm. Viewing fair from the hill, but finish in a chute could not be worse sited. Signposting poor from M48. Unpretentious and very friendly atmosphere.
Riders: *E. Williams 13, A. Price 8, D. Jones 5, R. Stephens 4, S. Blackwell 3, Miss F. Wilson 3.*

HUTTON RUDBY, Yorks. (1997*)
4m W of Stokesley between A19 and A172.
Meeting: Hurworth.
SF: 18-20-23. LH 2¾ circs. 8F; 20J; 2od (8/15). T: 6min 41.6s.
Sharp, undulating kidney-shaped course of almost three circuits; start is in a chute with first fence jumped once. Good turf and deservedly approved by owners. Some fences are skimpy. Viewing is good from many points, including near the start. A very attractive setting, more like a Hunter Trial course.

Meeting had to be abandoned after four races in 2004 due to continuing high winds.
Riders: *G. Tuer 3, T. Glass 2, N. Tutty 2, L. Bates 2, D. Easterby 2.*
Hurworth raced on a course also in Skutterskelfe Park, Hutton Rudby from 1957-1984

KILWORTHY, Devon. (1925)
1m N of Tavistock, 1m W of A386.
Meeting: Lamerton.
SF: 16-20-21. LH 2½ circs. 8F; 18J; 2od (3/11). T: 6min 31.5s.
Flat rectangular galloping stayers' course with mostly sweeping bends and 4 fences along each side; very stiff uphill finish up chute. Fences well-built (*qv* Cherrybrook). Excellent old turf. Essential to maintain correct racing line over last four fences. Judge's stand is badly positioned right on the line. Hard track access to car parks, but single entrance/exit causes delays. Viewing improved since spectators have been allowed to use natural grandstand, though fence 7(15) is still difficult to see.
Riders: *A. Charles-Jones 5, L. Jefford 4, T. Dennis 3, R. Woollacott 3, S. Partridge 2, Richard Darke 2, Miss S. Young 2, Miss L. Gardner 2, A. Farrant 2.*

KIMBLE, Bucks. (1912)
5m S of Aylesbury on B4009. 6m from A41.
Meeting: Vale of Aylesbury with Garth and South Berks (Easter).
SF: 18-22. LH 2¼ circs. 9F; 19J; 2od (7/16) 2wj (6/15). T: 6min 44.1s.
Flat stayers' course of '3m1f and about 38yds'; portable island fences of average size and build. Car parks have downhill exits; huge crowd at Easter meeting so allow plenty of time. Good viewing, but restricted by parked cars. Strong betting market. Judge's stand very near line.
Riders: *B. King 5, Miss H. Irving 3, B. Pollock 3, R. Morgan 2, Miss L. Ingram 2, M. Baldock 2, James Tudor 2, F. Hutsby 2, A. Barlow 2.*

KINGSTON BLOUNT, Oxon. (1971)
8m NW of High Wycombe off B4009 (Exits 5 or 6, M40).
Meetings: Oxford University Hunt Club; Thames Valley Combined Hunts Club; Vale of Aylesbury with Garth and South Berks (May); Berks & Bucks Draghounds.
SF: 16-18-20-22-24. LH 2¼ circs. 8F; 18J; 2od (5/13). T: 6min 33.3s.
Undulating course; steep climb after 5(13)th and downhill again before 6(14)th; can be firm due to chalk soil, but sticky in wet weather — water drains off chalk ridge above course; watering system available and can be a boon in May. Variety of SFs apply. Very spacious paddock more conveniently sited than in the past. Car parking good with downhill exit, but can be slippery in wet weather; cheaper off course parking available (ideal in wet though still costs more than many others do on-course!). Good viewing from slope above finish, but is a long walk. Wagon kindly provided for press, though its position away from the finishing line means few (mostly non-press) make use of it (why not move it along a bit?). Ornithologists can usually spot a red kite or two if the afternoon gets tedious.
Riders: *P. York 10, R. Lawther 7, J. Tarry 5, A. Martin 5, Miss G.emma Hutchinson 4, B. King 4.*

KINGSTON ST MARY, Som. (1987)
3m N of Taunton, off A361. (Exit 25, M5).
Meetings: Taunton Vale; Taunton Vale Harriers.
SF: 16-17-18. RH 2¼ circs. 8F; 19J; 2od (6/14). T: 6min 29.7s.
Very undulating course; steep climb after 5(13)th and downhill from 8(16)th; all portable fences. Car parking exits and entrances good but signposting to course could be improved. Good grass covering. Viewing only adequate; hedge bisecting course should be cut down, and start is out of sight (official times are guesswork and action disappears from view at most interesting stage two out). Bookies sparse and poor value. The Taunton Vale Harriers inaugural meeting held on firm ground on a mid-week evening in May had a good atmosphere (moves to Easter for '05).
Riders: *A. Farrant 5, N. Williams 2, Mrs O. Jackson 2, Miss P. Gundry 2, Miss C. Stucley 2.*

LALESTON, Mid-Glam. (1998)
Nr A48 2½m W of Bridgend, 3m from Exit 37, M4.
Meeting: Llangeinor.
SF: 15-18. LH 3 circs. 6F; 18J; 3od (4/10/16). T: 6min 32.2s.
Small tight oval course; with section of wood chips through small wood; bends can be slippery; paddock on opposite side of a busy road and many drivers are unhappy at being kept waiting for the streams of spectators crossing to the course; situation is made worse by car drivers trying to enter through the pedestrian gate, but a separate exit/entrance has been made for horses to cross the road — all very dangerous. Viewing is adequate from the paddock side of the road, but most spectators cross and watch

from the centre. Car parking was well manned by numerous attendants in fluorescent jackets.
Riders: *E. Williams 4, D. Jones 4, James Tudor 3, T. Vaughan 2, Mrs L. Rowsell 2, Miss F. Wilson 2, M. Barber 2, J. Jukes 2.*

PLATE 156 Laleston: ... the field cross the Llangewydd road onto the racecourse proper ...
PHOTO: Kathleen Mullen

LARKHILL, Wilts. (1947)
5m NW of Amesbury, 10m N of Salisbury, nr A303, A345 and A360.
Meetings: Army, Royal Artillery, United Services, Staff College & RMA Draghounds, New Forest, Avon Vale, South & West Wilts, 14th Regiment Royal Artillery.
SF: 16 (Nov Rdrs only)-18 (4m Open)-25 (18). RH $1^1/_3$ circs. 13F (3m): 18J; 3od (3/16 & 11). T: 6min 22.8s. (4m): 22J; 4od (2/15 & 7/20). T: 8min 22.1s. (2m4f): 15J; 2od (8/13). T: 6min 19.6s
Roughly triangular undulating galloping course; stiff climb to the 13th can catch out the non-stayer; all portable fences; chalk soil gives good going even in the wettest weather, but can be firm in late season; bookies plentiful. Car parking extensive and excellent (virtually go where you like); entrance and exit by long gravel track round Camp avoiding armed guards, but can be pot-holey. Excellent viewing from most parts though horses get rather distant and disappear behind bushes between 8 and 9, and after 12, but the view of the last mile is second to none. The feature Coronation Cup has been reduced to one division only since '95, but is still very competitive, and form here always works out well. Despite pretenders in other Areas this is the sport's premier course and considerable recent investment has been made to keep it in the forefront; extensive new plastic fencing (with useful gaps by winning post and winner's enclosure for racegoers of certain age and size — known as 'Selby gaps'); permanent two-storey changing/weighing room and hospitality complex well received, but presentations have more atmosphere when held near the winners enclosure as before. A new raised Judge's box sited further back than before will be in place for the new season. Has several early meetings, and you need to wrap up well — no wind-break between here and Marlborough Downs almost 20 miles away.
Riders: *Miss P. Gundry 19, A. Charles-Jones 10, O. Ellwood 8, Miss A. Goschen 8, D. Alers-Hankey 8, A. Farrant 8.*

LIFTON, Devon (1993)
3m E of Launceston, N of A30.
Meetings: Eggesford; Tetcott; South Tetcott.
SF: 15-17. RH: $2^2/_3$ circs. 7F; 19J; 2od (7/14). T: 6min 11.5s.
Virtually flat roughly triangular course, but with slight rise coming back towards the spectators. Facilities compact. Good viewing, except for run to two out, best on inside of course near finish. Going patchy, and

prone to waterlogging; the revised siting of the fences caused problems in the past, but this has been sorted out. Very pleasant setting in the shadow of Launceston Castle, and deservedly popular with owners and spectators. Due to very narrow bridge near the course all horseboxes coming from the east must continue through Launceston and take the Holsworthy road (A388), from which the course is signposted (cars can cut through from A30 near Liftondown) .
Riders: *A. Farrant 5, Richard Darke 4, Mrs M. Hand 4, Miss L. Gardner 4, L. Jefford 4, R. Woollacott 3, N. Mitchell 3, Miss M. McCarthy 3, C. Heard 3, A. Charles-Jones 3.*

LITTLEWINDSOR, Dorset (1993)
3m S of Crewkerne nr A3066. (16m from Exit 25, M5).
Meetings: Cattistock; Seavington.
SF: 16 (Nov Rdrs)-18 (16). RH: 2½ circs. 7F; (3m): 19J; 3od (3/10/17). T: 6min 35.6s. (2m4f): 16J; 2od (7/14). T: 5min 32.2s.
Roughly rectangular undulating Linley course; stiff climb from 2nd (9/16); downhill from 6(13)th. All portable fences, well made and all bar one recently renewed; uphill climb to the finish is taken three times; very testing when soft, but surprisingly easy at other times. Both meetings feature a 2m4f Maiden. Fields tend to be on the small side. Facilities compact. Number board sets a standard which other courses in the area should follow. Car parking, entrances and exits very good; no problems even when very wet. Viewing fine — best from inside course near finish, or from natural bank overlooking course. Beautiful views.
Riders: *N. Mitchell 9, A. Farrant 7, Miss P. Gundry 5, R. Young 4, L. Jefford 4, Mrs M. Roberts 2, Miss R. Green 2, M. Miller 2, H. Fry 2.*

LLANFRYNACH, Brecon. (1963)
3m SE of Brecon off B4558, 2m off A40.
Meeting: Brecon and Talybont.
SF: 15-18 (Membs and Ladies)-20. RH 2¾ circs. 8F; 18J; 2od (6/13). T: 6min 37.7s.
Course is flat and twisty — each race involves 10 bends (2 sharp); start is in fairly long separate chute and first fence jumped only once; can withstand torrential rain although going is usually soft/heavy; early season meeting finds out the unfit horses — many non-finishers; normally huge fields and nine or more races since '86. Appalling number board and announcer was equally poor. Awful fences — very flimsy. Viewing reasonable from natural bank. Car parking good with a separate downhill exit, so no problems despite it often being muddy. Beautiful setting.
Riders: *T. Vaughan 3, S. Lloyd 3, J. Price 3, D. Jones 3, A. Price 3, S. Blackwell 2, P. Sheldrake 2, N. Oliver 2, Miss P. Jones 2, Miss F. Wilson 2, Miss E. James 2, E. Williams 2, A. Hanly 2.*

LLANVAPLEY, Gwent. (1953)
4m E of Abergavenny, nr B4233. 4m from A40.
Meeting: Monmouthshire.
SF: 16-18 (Ladies)-20. LH 2½ circs. 7F; 18J; 2od (6/13). T: 6min 41.2s.
Course is mainly flat and twisty though two bends long and sweeping; short downhill stretch to 2nd (9/16th) and run-in; scenic setting if you ignore the massive pylons. All fences are permanent except 7(14)th. Car parking satisfactory; two entrances/exits. Viewing very good from hillside, but copse between 1st (8/15th) and 2nd (9/16th) obscures part of course. The latest meeting had a stretch of plough which seems a regular feature of this course. Safety Factor for Restricted is too high.
Riders: *T. Vaughan 3, E. Williams 3, C. Williams 3, S. Blackwell 2, James Tudor 2, J. Cook 2, D. Jones 2.*

LOCKINGE, Oxon. (1953)
2m SE of Wantage on B4494 (8m NW Exit 13, M4).
Meeting: Old Berkshire.
SF: 18 (Nov Rdrs)-25. LH 2 circs. 9F; 18J; 2od (7/16). T: 6min 29.4s.
Undulating galloping oval course; old downland turf on chalk can get firm, but usually gives good going for the Easter Monday fixture; fences of average height and build; long run-in since course altered by passing fence near winning post. Many spectators walk the course beforehand with dogs (and drinks!). Car parking good on steep slope (engage handbrake and reverse); always a very large crowd so long queues on access and exit; follow signs if coming from south. Viewing excellent from hillside with superb view of start and finish. Excellent betting market. A well organised meeting.
Riders: *J. Jenkins 4, R. Young 3, S. Waley-Cohen 2, F. Hutsby 2.*

LYDSTEP, Dyfed. (1948)
3m SW of Tenby, nr A4139 on E edge of Lydstep village.
Meetings: South Pembrokeshire; Carmarthenshire.
SF: 16-18 (16). LH 2^1/3 circs. 8F; (3m): 19J; 2od (6/14). T: 6min 24.1s. (2m4f) 16J; 2od (3/11). T: 5min 14.2s.
Course is slightly undulating and almost square; two particularly tight bends; does not suit big long-striding horses; two fences are downhill and can cause errors; all fences which are metal-framed except 3(11/19) which is permanent are small, very soft and unkempt; sandy soil drains well. Car parking ample; access/exit takes two lanes of traffic. Racecards need improvement — South Pembs had no numbers and the Carmarthenshire's was littered with typographical errors. Excellent viewing if the right spot is chosen but racegoers are prevented from standing in the centre of the course. Glorious views to spectacular Pembrokeshire cliffs and Caldey Island opposite the course. Carmarthenshire are off again in 2005, to Pentreclwydau.
Riders: *D. Jones 5, C. Williams 5, T. Vaughan 4, M. Barber 3, Mrs B. Lewis 2, Miss P. Jones 2, Miss F. Wilson 2, M. Lewis 2, J. Keen 2, H. Evans 2, E. Williams 2.*

MAISEMORE PARK, Glos. (1982)
Nr A417, 3m NW of Gloucester (Exit 11, M5).
Meetings: Ledbury; North Ledbury.
SF: 16-20 (Nov Rdrs)-23. LH 2^1/2 circs. 7F. 18J; 2od (7/14). T: 6min 52.9s.
Totally flat, oval course bounded on two sides by River Severn; six metal fences, last two re-sited in 2000 to produce a slightly longer run-in. Fences are well-built, and course was in particular good order for '04 with an excellent Ledbury meeting producing the second highest number of runners for the season. Car park access is difficult in wet, and bumpy when hard. Viewing from natural grandstand much improved by pruning, but also excellent from middle of the course (when you are allowed to go there).
Riders: *Julian Pritchard 11, A. Wintle 9, T. Stephenson 4, R. Spate 3, R. Burton 3, Miss P. Gundry 3, D. Mansell 3, A. Martin 3.*

MARKET RASEN, Lincs. (1992)
1m E of town on S side of A631 (P-t-P entrance is off Legsby road).
Meetings: Lincolnshire United Hunts Club, Burton.
SF: 16 (Rest)-18-20 (Opens & Clubs). LH 2^1/2 circs. 7F; 18J; 2od (5/12). T: 6min 43.7s.
Mainly flat left-handed course inside right-hand NH circuit. Situation makes for tight bends — uphill bend at far end of course is unavoidably narrow; tight last bend after penultimate makes it desirable to be in contention on inside. All portable fences, the second last has been moved out of the dip. Grass coverage getting better, except at the top of hill, and the ground can get poached approaching the last. Viewing excellent from NH stands and facilities first class. Watering possible and every effort is made to provide the best going and viewing on the day. Number board is still poor. Lacks atmosphere (like so many Point-to-Points run on National Hunt courses).
Riders: *M. Mackley 7, S. Charlton 5, Mrs J. Dawson 4, M. Walford 4, T. Greenall 3, S. Morris 3, R. Hunnisett 3, R. Cope 3, N. Tinkler 3, N. Kent 3, Miss R.achel Clark 3, J. Docker 3, G. Brewer 3, C. Mulhall 3.*

MARKS TEY, Essex. (1952)
5m W of Colchester, at junc of A12 & A120.
Meetings: East Essex; Essex Farmers & Union (April & May).
SF: 18 (Nov Rdrs)-25. LH 1^3/4 circs. 10F. 20J; 2od (3/13) T: 7min 01.1s.
Galloping slightly undulating course with uphill finish; one sharp bend; under all conditions it is a true stayers' course and when wet becomes holding and a severe test of stamina; soon becomes hard in a dry spell; fences fair and inviting and good for maidens. Car parking excellent with plenty of room. Viewing best from bank near paddock (but not really big enough despite usual paucity of crowd) and much improved by thinning and trimming of hedges and trees, but 5(15)th still hidden. New smaller paddock though apparently not to everyone's taste. Bookies (hopeless) and trade stands resited which gives a clearer view of start, but is a morass when wet. Unattractive setting, and probably the Area's least popular course with the public (Easter apart), but the going has been much improved in recent years and it is much favoured by owners.
Riders: *G. Cooper 8, Miss Z. Turner 6, P. Chinery 4, N. Bloom 4, D. Kemp 4, A. Ayers 4.*

MILBORNE ST ANDREW, Dorset. (1991)
Off A354, ^{1}/2m SE of village, midway between Blandford and Dorchester.
Meeting: South Dorset.
SF: 18 (Nov Rdrs)-20. LH 2^1/2 circs. 8F; 19J; 2od (7/15). T: 6min 27.4s.
Undulating roughly triangular Linley course, all grass on chalk downland; downhill from start to after

2nd, then uphill to last and through finish, downhill again from 6th to 7th (open ditch). All fences portable and very well-built and provide a proper test of jumping. Viewing generally poor — best from inside course near winning post or from slope near bookies; some thinning out of the copse has been made but much more is needed to allow a proper view of the three fences after the open ditch. Car parking satisfactory, now two entrances but only one exit.
Riders: *N. Mitchell 5, T. Mitchell 2, R. Young 2, Miss R. Green 2, Miss P. Gundry 2, Miss E. Tory 2, Miss D. Harding 2, M. Miller 2, M. Goess-Saurau 2, D. Alers-Hankey 2.*

MOLLINGTON, Oxon. (1972)
On A423, 5m N of Banbury. Nr M40.
Meetings: Bicester with Whaddon Chase (February and April); Grafton.
SF: 18-20-22 (15). RH: 2¼ circs. 8F; (3m) 18J; 2od (7/15). T: 6min 42.1s. (2m4f) 15J; 2od (4/12). T: 5min 33.6s
Wide undulating galloping track with four long sweeping bends and stiff uphill finish; portable fences very small; fields tend to be large and of good quality. Car parking good; uphill exits, but no problems. Viewing above average, whole of circuit in view until the runners disappear behind the house between the last two fences. Compact facilities. A model course and has regained its reputation after the problems of 2002. Crowds are often huge at Sunday meetings making moving around freely rather difficult.
Riders: *S. Morris 5, R. Burton 5, R. Cope 4, J. Tarry 4, E. Walker 4, P. Cowley 3, Miss C. Spearing 3, Julian Pritchard 3, J. Owen 3, J. Jenkins 3, F. Hutsby 3, C. Wadland 3, A. Martin 3.*

MORDON, Durham. (1990)
Nr A1 (M), 4 miles S. of Sedgefield, 1 mile N of Great Stainton.
Meeting: South Durham.
SF: 18-22. LH: 2½ circs. 8F; 20J; 2od (6/14). T: 6min 13.7s.
Undulating roughly rectangular course with a run-in of 140 yards — uphill from 8(16)th to 9(17)th and very long downhill run from 2nd(10/18)th to 4(12/20)th. All fences portable. Facilities compact and near finish. Viewing reasonable from that area, but start out of sight. Barn used for declarations and changing rooms. Good, prompt announcements. Hard road entrance. Poor betting market. Lacks charm, very exposed and windswept so wrap up well even in May. Successfully experimented in '04 with free entry for racegoers and a £3 racecard.
Riders: *N. Tutty 5, Miss J. Foster 4, T. Glass 3, S. Swiers 2, M. Morley 2, L. Bates 2.*

MOSSHOUSES, Borders. (1948)
4m NE of Galashiels between A7 and A68.
Meeting: Lauderdale.
SF: 18-20-22. LH 2¼ circs. 8F; 19J; 2od (5/13). T: 6min 19.7s.
Hilly course with very steep climb after fence 5(13) and sharp bend after 8(16). Suits good jumping stayers'; fences big and well-built; one drop fence jumped twice. Good access and exits. Perfect viewing from large natural grandstand and finish still obscured by trailer! Well attended and popular meeting with added bonus that if weather is inclement racing can be watched from the car park. Entrance charge of £5 per person.
Riders: *C. Storey 7, L. Morgan 4, Miss N. Stirling 3, R. Morgan 2, J. Walton 2.*

MOUNSEY HILL GATE, Som. (1984)
4m N. of Dulverton nr B3223 (Exit 27, M5 via A361 and A396).
Meeting: Dulverton Farmers.
SF: 16-18. RH 2¾ circs. 7F; 20J; 3od (2/9/16). T: 7min 03.8s.
Oval slightly undulating course with sharp bends; all portable fences which are soft and unkempt. Maximum of five fences visible from one or two spots, but impossible to see all fences without somehow getting off the ground — two banks running transversely across course offer some assistance. Cars and horse boxes park on outside of course, handy to paddock etc. Layout changed frequently, but will never be any good for spectators, and two commentators are necessary to give any idea of the pattern of the races (not that the second commentator has much idea). A beautiful spot with views over the Exmoor countryside, but there is nowhere to hide if weather is bad.
Riders: *D. Barlow 4, M. Sweetland 3, L. Jefford 3, J. Barnes 2.*

MUSSELBURGH, East Lothian. (2002)
At Musselburgh Racecourse E of Edinburgh, M8 and City by-pass for A1 and A198 from E and A7/A68 and A702 from the S.
Meeting: Northern P-t-P Area Club.
SF: 16-18. RH 2¼ circs. 8F; 18J; 2od (8/16) T: 6min 07.9s.
Oval almost flat course with sharp turns set out between the NH hurdles and chase courses; run-in of

190 yards; small and soft portables allow sloppy jumpers get away with mistakes. Viewing excellent from racecourse facilities, which are all available. Like other meetings run at NH tracks it lacks the atmosphere of a true Point-to-Point. Will not be used in 2005.
Riders: *K. Anderson 4, Miss P. Robson 3, L. Morgan 2, A. Findlay 2.*

NORTHAW, Herts. (1968*)
2m NE of Potters Bar off A1000 (Exit 24, M25).
Meeting: Cambridgeshire with Enfield Chace (May).
SF: 15 (Membs)-18 (Mdn)-20. LH 2½ circs. 7F; 18J; 2od (7/14). T: 6min 29.8s.
Oval undulating course; horses start with their backs to the open ditch;
first two fences are close together followed by a long run to next on the home turn (2nd last) with only one fence (4/11/18th) in the straight; horses need to be on the inside after three out. Fences, all portable (four metal-framed ones include the ditch), are generally small and soft. Viewing best from far side, difficult to hear the commentator on inside of the course. Paddock too small for bank holiday crowd; number board poor — no blinkers, overweights, etc and they are not announced. Officials transported to start in a smart horse-drawn carriage. Car parking satisfactory, but large crowd can cause delays. Very poor racecard. Remarkably rural setting considering proximity to Central London. Most patrons are not remotely interested in the racing (more in the contents of the picnic hamper), but are happy to cheer any horse they see on the course, including those which have long since pulled up! Might be even more successful as a mid-week evening fixture.
Riders: *A. Sansome 4, Miss Z. Turner 2, M. Baldock 2, A. Williams 2, A. Ayers 2.*
**** various Hunts raced on a course at Northaw before World War 1 and between Wars.***

OVERTON, S. Lanarkshire. (2004)
Off A72, 3m SW of Carluke, accessible from J8 M74.
Meeting: Lanarkshire & Renfrewshire and Eglinton.
SF: 18-20. LH 2½ circs. 8F; 19J; 2od (7/15). T: 6min 23.1s.
Flat roughly oval twisting course close to River Clyde with a dog-leg between fences 7(15) and 8(16); will suit front-runners; fences all portable. Facilities compact with the paddock close to finish encouraging the crowd to gather, adding to the atmosphere. Viewing acceptable in inaugural year, but could do with a stand. Car parking good. Well supported, and easy to find. When the few small teething problems (with the PA system and number board) are overcome the course can be a major addition to the Scottish scene. All credit to Willie Young's example and enthusiasm in setting it up. Also the site of a large and well-known car boot sale so quite capable of coping with large crowds.
Riders: *Miss R. Davidson 1, A. Findlay 1, R. Green 1, D. Jewett 1, L. Morgan 1, B. Mounsey-Heysham 1, Miss P. Robson 1.*

PARHAM, Sussex. (1953)
Nr A283, 4m SE of Pulborough, 1m W of Storrington.
Meetings: Chiddingfold, Leconfield & Cowdray; Crawley & Horsham.
SF: 16-24. RH 2¼ circs. 8F; 18J; 2od (4/12). T: 6min 55.9s.
Slightly undulating oval stayers' course of 3m2f; slight rise before post; 3 permanent fences with remainder being well-built portables. Can be taxing in early season. Car access and exits good. Viewing good, most of course can be seen from hill above finish. Bookies very competitive. Chalked names on number board are barely intelligible. The course adjoins a gliding school and warnings about low flying aircraft before racing should be heeded at your peril!
Riders: *P. Hall 5, P. York 4, C. Gordon 4, P. Bull 3, D. Dunsdon 3, Stuart Robinson 2, Mrs P. Hall 2, Miss H. Irving 2, Miss C. Benstead 2, J. Hawksfield 2, A. Hickman 2.*

PAXFORD, Glos. (1997) (LH prior to 2002)
2m E of Chipping Campden between B4035 and B4479.
Meeting: North Cotswold.
SF: 18-20-22. RH 2 circs. 8F; 18J; 2od (7/15). T: 6min 32.0s.
Flat basically oval course, completely revised and reversed in '02; runners now start with back to the brook and jump fence 1(9/17) before home straight; downhill run to fence 4(12) and short but gradual climb between 8(16)th and 9(17)th; short run-in so inside vital on final turn. Viewing is excellent from bank alongside finishing straight. Facilities compact with paddock adjacent to course. Permanent building now provides accommodation for changing rooms, declarations office, sponsor's reception area, etc, all under one roof. Has some old rhubarb sheds after fence 6(14) — where Pete Mansell obtains his race comments! Wide downhill entrance and no problems despite usual large Easter crowd.
Riders: *Julian Pritchard 6, Miss P. Gundry 3, T. Stephenson 2, T. Gretton 2, Miss A. Dare 2, E. Walker 2, A. Wintle 2.*

PENSHURST, Kent. (1977)
3m SW of Penshurst, W of B2188, well sign-posted. (12m Exit 5, M25).
Meetings: Old Surrey Burstow & West Kent (both meetings)
SF: 18-20. LH 2½ circs. 7F; 18J; 2od (6/13). T: 7min 00.9s.
Undulating roughly rectangular course with testing uphill finish; two sharp bends into and out of bottom straight (can be slippery); course changed since 2001 and horses no longer disappear into dip; has slight dog leg between 2(9/16) and 3(10/17); portable fences small and soft; only one sited in finishing straight; drains well except on lower stretches which can be heavy. No car parking problems. Viewing tricky but best from inside of course for overall view but nowhere is ideal.
Riders: *C. Gordon 8, P. York 3, R. Ross 2, P. Bull 2, P. Blagg 2, N. Benstead 2, Miss Z. Turner 2, Miss J. Grant 2, D. Robinson 2, D. Dunsdon 2, D. Dennis 2.*

PLATE 157 Pentreclwydau: The jockeys are up for Race 1239 Banwen Miners Open Maiden (Div 1); No 14 is Indian Trix ridden by Marc Barber *PHOTO: John Mullen*

PENTRECLWYDAU, West Glamorgan. (1999)
Nr A465, midway between Neath and Merthyr Tydfil.
Meeting: Banwen Miners.
SF: 16-19-20 (4m Open). LH 2 circs. 7F; (3m) 18J; 2od (7/14). T: 6min 25.2s. (4m) 24J; 3od (6/13/20). T: 8min 32.5s
Flat galloping course which meets with approval from most owners and trainers, though the facilities for spectators are not ideal. Viewing is reasonable although not helped by hedges and trees. The course has a boggy patch between 2 out and the final fence. Normally has plenty of runners. Parking now more central. Tends to be a party atmosphere where some racegoers drink excessively and then proceed to disrobe — much to the amusement/annoyance of everybody else!
Riders: *T. Vaughan 3, E. Williams 3, L. Stephens 2, J. Keen 2.*

PEPER HAROW, Surrey. (1950)
Nr A3, 3m W of Godalming, 6m SW of Guildford. (15m from Exit 10, M25).
Meeting: Surrey Union.
SF: 14-16 (Members)-18. LH 2½ circs. 8F; 18J; 2od (8/14). T: 6min 55.1s.
Flat very sharp course; horses always on turn; start and finish up centre of course; sharp bend into home straight now pushed out with the benefit of a running rail; course very narrow after fence 4(10/16) where marked through natural bog with small hurdles; fences well-made; going can vary greatly across course. Commentator has hydraulic hoist, but still cannot see fence 6(12) and stewards make do with a bus. Viewing worse than ever, obstructed by a funfair inside course, and fences 5 and 6(11/12) invisible. Numberboard fenced off to eliminate risk of injury if it falls over (it happened once). Ample car parking;

access very good, exit very slow as no longer directly on to A3. Attracts huge crowd of people-watchers to whom racing is totally inconsequential (and often they're about right) and an enormous number of stalls to keep them amused.
Riders: *C. Gordon 4, Miss J. Grant 3, P. York 2, P. Bull 2, Miss Z. Turner 2, D. Dunsdon 2.*

RHYDYGWERN, Gwent. (2002*)
4m W of Newport on A468 at Lower Machen. (Exit 28, M4)
Meeting: Tredegar Farmers.
SF: 16 (Nov Rdrs)-18. LH 2½ circs. 7F; 18J; 2od (7/14). T: 6min 36.6s.
Oval undulating course with sharp turn after finish; short run to 1st(8/15th) fence then a climb from 2nd(9/16th) to 3rd(10/17th); fences all metal portables except 6(13)th and generally flimsy. Ample car parking. Viewing, now improved by moving the third last and resiting the horseboxes, is best from the outside of course above finish. Easy access from main road and move to a Sunday avoids clash with football finals at Cardiff, no problems getting away. Facilities compact, under wood on hillside. An attractive setting and a visit is recommended.
Riders: *T. Vaughan 6, T. Faulkner 2, Mrs L. Rowsell 2, M. Barber 2, E. Williams 2, C. Williams 2.*
**** Course was previously used until 1979 by Gelligaer Farmers when known as Lower Machen.***

SANDON, Staffs. (1982)
4m SE of Stone, nr A51. (Exit 14, M6).
Meeting: North Staffordshire.
SF: 18-20 (Ladies)-22 (16). RH 2¼ circs. 7F; (3m) 19J; 2od (6/13). T: 7min 09.8s. (2m4f) 14J: 2od (1/8). T: 5min 36.0s
Oval slightly undulating course; one sharp bend; portable fences of average size and build; attracts good fields. Course was turned round to right-handed in 1998 though the start and finish remain in their old positions; the uphill finish has done away with the old tricky downhill last fence. Run-in 135 yds. Car parking good, but queues on exit. Viewing excellent from embankment along side of course, apart from some foliage.
Riders: *G. Hanmer 6, R. Burton 5, Miss S. Sharratt 4, L. Hicks 3, Mrs M. Barlow 2, A. Crow 2.*

SIDDINGTON, Wilts. (1934*)
2m S of Cirencester, nr A419. (20m from Exit 13, M5 & Exit 15, M4).
Meeting: Vale of White Horse.
SF: 18-25. LH 2 circs. 10F; 18J; 2od (3/13). T: 6min 18.5s.
Tough almost flat course; several drop fences; last in back straight (after 14th) causes most problems whilst final fences catches out tired horses; going often soft. Often a huge crowd. Car parking good; entry/exit no problem. Viewing is good from most parts of course, but finish some way away from best area. One of the most historic courses still in use and well worth maintaining properly.
Riders: *Julian Pritchard 3, S. Bush 2.*
* ***The Royal Agricultural College raced on a course at Siddington before World War 1***

STAFFORD CROSS, Devon. (1966*)
3m W of Seaton, nr A3052. (Exit 30, M5).
Meeting: Axe Vale Harriers.
SF: 15 (Nov Rdrs)-17. RH 2⅓ circs. 8F; 18J; 2od (3/11). T: 6min 06.1s.
Flat and sharp, but easy course favouring speed merchants (races often run flat out all the way); fences now stiffer and up to height. Good level car parks; easy access and exit. Viewing moderate (much better if you can get off the ground!), best from slightly higher ground near 4/12th, but start and run to penultimate out of sight from there, as is top bend behind tents. Close to the coast and sea fret can cause visibility to become very poor.
Riders: *N. Williams 3, R. Woollacott 2, L. Jefford 2, J. Snowden 2, A. Charles-Jones 2.*
****Earlier course (opened 1947) was on seaward side of main road***

STAINTON, Cleveland. (1995)
4m SW of Middlesborough at junction of A19 and A174, entrance off A174.
Meeting: Cleveland.
SF: 18 (Members)-20. RH. 2¾ circs. 7F; 20J; 2od (7/14). T: 6min 20.3s.
Gently undulating sharp course on patchy ground. Portable fences. Facilities including paddock inside the course, and fairly good viewing from opposite finish. Judge's stand too near line making his job more difficult. Although course is visible from A19 it can be poorly signposted and there have been problems in the past with the signs being stolen!!
Riders: *N. Tutty 3, C. Storey 2, C. Mulhall 2.*

STON EASTON, Somerset. (1999)
8m N of Shepton Mallet, alongside A37.
Meeting: Mendip Farmers.
SF: 16 (Nov Rdrs)-18 (14). RH 2½ circs. 7F; (3m) 18J; 2od (5/12). T: 6min 29.3s. (2m4f) 15J; 2od (2/9). T: 5min 21.0s.
Fairly sharp undulating course with reverse bend between fences 2(9/16) and 3(10/17), uphill through finish and downhill through starting area and back straight. Fences portable and considerably improved. Open ditch is now fence after finish. Car parking satisfactory, but viewing is not good — a little reminiscent of the old Nedge course, it being impossible to see the last two fences and run-in once more than three people arrive (a great pity as atmosphere very friendly and attracts big crowd, top horses and good fields) — crowd is forced to use the stone walls despite requests not to. The ancestral home of the Killen family, who run the sport for hundreds of miles around, and Robert of that ilk introduced another sibling, his lovely sister, Charlotte, at the National Point-to-Point Dinner — Tom had better watch his back!
Riders: *Miss P. Gundry 8, R. Young 3, R. Biddlecombe 2, E. Kenney-Herbert 2, C. Studd 2, A. Honeyball 2.*

TABLEY, Cheshire. (1997)
1½m W of Knutsford between A556 and M6 (use Exit 19).
Meetings: Cheshire Forest; North West P-t-P Club.
SF: 18-22. RH 2¾ circs. 7F; 20J; 2od (7/14). T: 6min 56.5s (new course).
Flat, sharpish rectangular course about ½m from former course at Sudlow Farm; all portable fences, course lengthened by moving the start back before the first fence in the back straight; following fences are close together until long run between 4th and 5th; run-in is 170yds. Access/exit OK. Viewing poor (too flat) — best in centre. Very large crowd, but bookies and paddock area improved and movement no problem now. Lovely setting in parkland in front of Tabley Hall, the Palladian mansion which was the seat of the Leicester family for 700 years. Great for plane spotters as course is directly under flight path to Manchester Airport.
Riders: *R. Burton 10, G. Hanmer 9, Miss S. Sharratt 2, J.R. Barlow 2.*

THORPE LODGE, Notts. (1976)
4m SW of Newark-on-Trent, nr A46. 5m from A1.
Meetings: Midlands Area Club; South Notts.
SF: 16 (Nov Rdrs)-18 (Ladies)-20. LH 2½ circs. 7F; 19J; 2od (6/13). T: 6min 53.1s.
Flat almost square course providing a fair test; long run between 17th and 18th, but positioning of latter can vary by 100 yards; first bend is sharp and horses often slip, but remedial work has been done to correct adverse camber on bend after penultimate; winners usually in contention 3 out. Judge at South Notts meeting in 2004 had an aberration in the Restricted Race and incorrectly placed the first four horses home — an urgent replacement should be sought. All portable fences, firm and consistent. Car parking good, one entrance/exit, but traffic flows well. Viewing excellent from slope overlooking finishing straight, though hedges are getting out of control. Good betting market even on Bank Holiday.
Riders: *J. Docker 7, M. Mackley 6, S. Morris 3, Julian Pritchard 3, T. Lane 2, S. Walker 2, R. Cope 2, R. Barrett 2, R. Armson 2, N. Kent 2, Mrs J. Dawson 2, G. Hanmer 2.*

TRANWELL, Northumberland. (1967)
3m SW of Morpeth, nr B6524. Handy to A1.
Meeting; Morpeth.
SF: 18-22 (18). LH 2 circs. 9F; (3m) 18J; 2od (7/16). T: 6min 30.4s. (2m4f) 15J; 2od (4/13). T: 5min 47.3s.
Mainly flat galloping course with slight uphill finish; 180 yard run-in; Judge's stand right against the line. Good covering of grass. Excellent car parking on runways of old airfield; good access and exits. Good viewing from bank in centre of course, but finish cannot be judged from there.
Riders: *Mrs V. Jackson 4, Miss N. Stirling 4, J. Walton 4, Miss P. Robson 3, L. Morgan 2, C. Storey 2.*

TREBUDANNON, Cornwall. (2000)
5m E of Newquay, nr A39 close to St Columb Major.
Meetings: Four Burrow; South Cornwall.
SF: 14-16 (14). LH 2¾ circs. 7F; (3m) 20J; 3od (4/11/18). T: 6min 10.6s. (2m4f) 16J; 2od (7/14). T: 5min 21.5s
Fairly flat course with slight rise towards final bend; all portable fences. Compact layout. Excellent viewing from hillside overlooking home straight. Originally designed to have eight fences and 19 jumps, but to date the meetings held have used the layout shown above. An excellent job of watering was done for the South Cornwall meeting in 2004. The most westerly course in England and very scenically attractive.
Riders: *Miss L. Gardner 7, Miss T. Cave 6, R. Woollacott 4, Miss S. Young 4, Miss S. Gaisford 4, D. McKenna 3.*

TRECOED, Pembrokeshire. (2002)
Off A40 at Letterston, 5m S of Fishguard.
Meeting: Pembrokeshire.
SF 15-18. RH 2¼ circs. 7F; 18J; 2od (7/14). T: 6min 16.6s.
Oval course with an uphill stretch from fence 3(11) through finish to the back straight and downhill from fence 8(16); fences very soft. Facilities compact. A good job of watering was done in 2004. Viewing excellent from bank adjacent to paddock and on inside of run-in. Closes the Welsh season, and has an end-of-term party atmosphere. Long distance travellers should beware of Anglophobe radar-toting Welsh policemen lurking on the M4.
Riders: *M. Barber 4, T. Vaughan 2, Julian Pritchard 2.*

TWESELDOWN, Hants. (1949*)
3m W of Aldershot, 6m from M3 (Exit 4 or 5).
Meetings: Tweseldown Racing Club; South Midlands Area Club; Vale of Aylesbury with Garth and South Berks (March).
SF: 18-22 (Clubs and Vet & Nov Rdrs)-24. RH 2 circs. 9F; 19J; 2od (7/16) 2wj (5/14). T: 6min 27.6s.
Gently undulating triangular course; uphill bend to last tests stamina when soft, but short-runners often win on good or firm; fences exemplary; sandy soil drains well, but can be wet at bottom near water jump; some old racecourse facilities including stables still available- at final meeting in 2004 paddock and trade stands were resited together with some additional hard footing. Best viewing from central hill via unique subway (often flooded) and is now much improved, all fences are now in view with less galloping round the hill! Number board in front of grandstand no longer exists and one in the paddock needs some improvement. Car parking excellent, access and exits good but could do with some better signposting to the course. Looked to have a very bleak future in '02, but now back under new (and enthusiastic) management, and its future seems secure. One of the plusses of '04 with this historic course holding three meetings again and long may it continue to thrive. Its renaissance owes much to the enthusiasm of Steven Astaire.
Riders: *R. Biddlecombe 3, Julian Pritchard 3, S. Sporborg 2, R. Burton 2, P. Scouller 2, M. Holdforth 2, D. Dunsdon 2, A. Charles-Jones 2.*
Tweseldown was a NH course from 1884 until 1932 and then the venue of several bona fide military meetings until they were absorbed into Point-to-Pointing in 1949

PLATE 158 Umberleigh: Agrivation at the last fence at Umberleigh *PHOTO: Kathleen Mullen*

UMBERLEIGH, Devon. (1971)
Off the A377 at Chapelton Barton, 5m SE Barnstaple.
Meeting: Torrington Farmers.
SF: 16-18. LH 2¾ circs. 6F; 18J; 3od (4/10/16). T: 6min 23.8s.

Sharp course mostly on side of hill; first 4 fences close together on valley floor; 3rd is appreciably higher on landing side; stiff uphill climb after ditch to 5(11/17)th; long downhill run through finish and back to start takes it toll when ground is fast. Judge's stand right on line. Facilities compact. Single entrance/exit from narrow lane; most cars parked on inside of course. Viewing just about adequate from central hill, but necessary to move from one side to the other to see all action; panoramic view of last and run-in. Stages the season's finale and has a party atmosphere encouraged by the canned music played over the loudspeaker, and much alcohol.
Riders: *Miss J. Congdon 2, Miss A. Goschen 2, L. Jefford 2, J. Snowden 2.*

PLATE 159 Upper Sapey: Spot the run-in between the two ranks of Portaloos (the popular water feature is a part of the Horse Trials course) PHOTO: Kathleen Mullen

UPPER SAPEY, Worcs. (1984)
At Wolferlow, 6m N of Bromyard nr B4203 (15m W of Exits 5 & 6, M5).
Meeting: Clifton-on-Teme.
SF: 18-20-22. RH 2¼ circs. 8F; 18J; 2od (4/12). T: 6min 27.0s.
Very hilly course; long uphill climb from 3rd (11th) to 6(14)th and then sharp descent to 9(17)th; followed by sharp turn into home straight. Car parking and viewing satisfactory. Compact facilities. Racing is regularly of a low standard. Lacks atmosphere.
Riders: *Julian Pritchard 7, R. Hodges 3, E. Walker 2, D. Duggan 2, A. Dalton 2.*

UPTON-ON-SEVERN, Worcs. (1909)
Nr the A38, 8m S of Worcester, handy to M5 & M50 (Exit 1).
Meeting: Croome and W. Warwicks.
SF: 18-22 (Nov Rdrs)-25 (18). RH 1¾ circs. 10F. (3m) 18J; 2od (6/16). T: 6min 37.3s. (2m5f) 15J; 2od (3/13). T: 5min 22.8s.
Flat testing galloping riverside track; suits stayers'; has a couple of sharp bends and vital to take a good line; firm, but well-sloped fences can catch out poor jumpers; two metal fences — a travesty on such a historic course; sometimes soft patches even when rest is good to firm; improved almost beyond recognition in recent years with much work having been done to improve viewing and drainage. Loudspeakers badly placed and totally ineffectual for announcements, but commentary audible from hill overlooking finish where viewing is best (also fine from centre of course). Parking is plentiful and easy; good entry and exits with proper roads on course. Strong betting market.
Riders: *Julian Pritchard 4, S. Blackwell 2, R. Burton 2, M. Wilesmith 2, M. Rodda 2, M. Keel 2.*

VAUTERHILL, Devon (1995)
2m SW of Umberleigh, 10m S of Barnstaple, nr B3217.
Meeting: Stevenstone.
SF: 16-18. RH 2½ circs. 7F; 19J; 3od (3/10/17). T: 6min 23.5s.
Mainly flat, kidney-shaped course; on the turn much of the way with left hand deviation immediately after start; slightly uphill run-in of only 135 yards. Portable fences. Laid out within two separate fields, so the going can be variable and run-throughs can become boggy. Facilities compact. Good viewing from a number of vantage points. Single entrance/exit, signposted locally, but be prepared for a few miles of country lane. Very scenic views of North Devon countryside.
Riders: *Richard Darke 2, Miss S. Young 2, C. Heard 2.*

WADEBRIDGE, Cornwall. (1986)
At Royal Cornwall Showground, 1m W of town nr A39.
Meetings: North Cornwall; Western.
SF: 14-16. LH 2½ circs. 8F; 18J; 2od (5/12). T: 6min 30.9s.
Dumbell-shaped very well drained course set on slope at edge of showground; first fence jumped once only from starting chute (adjacent to cemetery!); first six fences all on uphill gradient; long downhill run between fences 7 and 8; last 2 and run-in are uphill with a section of sand. Fences portable and quite soft. Access, exit and car parking excellent. Viewing reasonable. Showground facilities; the bookies are in large barn which has also served as paddock in poor weather.
Riders: *A. Farrant 12, L. Jefford 9, Miss L. Gardner 7, Miss P. Gundry 6, C. Heard 4, Miss T. Cave 3, Miss O. Green 3, Julian Pritchard 3.*

WELBECK, Nottinghamshire. (2003)
Off B6034, 4m SW of Worksop on the Ollerton road (use Exit 30, M1).
Meeting : Grove and Rufford.
SF: 16-18 (16). RH circs. 8F: (3m) 19J; 2od (5/13). T: 6min 27.5s. (2m4f) 17J; 2od (3/11). T: 5min 53.0s.
Undulating course with uphill run to 3 out, but not too testing; turf on sand-based soil has been untouched for centuries except when ploughed in World War 2. Can be watered if necessary. Viewing good from area near the winning post. Superb parkland setting not usually accessable to the public with views of Welbeck Abbey, lake and the magnificent ancestral home of the Dukes of Portland (one of whom invented the horsebox and used it in great secrecy to take St Simon to land a coup in the Derby!). Official car entrance through long ornamental drive. Ample parking with good viewing on sloping ground above the course. A valuable addition to the Midlands courses and well worth a visit.
Riders: *G. Brewer 3, R. Armson 2.*

WESTON PARK, Shropshire. (1983)
4m NE of Shifnal, nr A5 and A41. (Exit 12, M6, or Exit 3, M54).
Meetings: Albrighton; Meynell & South Staffordshire.
SF: 18-22. LH 2¼ circs. 7F; 18J; 2od (5/12). T: 6min 55.6s.
Course is basically flat on old parkland; uphill climb after ditch and gentle descent to back straight; three permanent and four portable fences; short run-in and races usually decided by time last fence is reached. Entrance and exit to car parks on hard road so no problems even in the worst weather. Best viewing from inside of track opposite winning post. Albrighton moved from May to January in '04 and were well rewarded with big fields, improved racing and a large crowd.
Riders: *R. Burton 7, G. Hanmer 6, W. Hill 4, S. Morris 3, J. Downes 3, A. Crow 3.*

WHITTINGTON, Lancs. (1936)
2m SW of Kirkby Lonsdale on B6254, 8m from M6 (Exits 35 and 36).
Meetings: Holcombe ; Vale of Lune.
SF: 18-23. LH 2¼ circs. 8F; 18J; 2od (8/16). T: 6min 57.2s.
Flat very testing 3m2f course on water meadows; 5(13)th fence has higher ground on landing side and causes problems, but very well-built fences; sharp bend after last on 300 yard run-in; going often good; attracts novice horses and riders though experienced jockeys have advantage. Car parking good; hard road access, downhill exit. Beautiful setting. Viewing excellent from steep bank above run-in though horses do go rather far away.
Riders: *D. Coates 4, R. Morgan 3, Mrs S. Johnson 3, L. Morgan 3, N. Saville 2, Mrs K. Diggle 2, Miss P. Robson 2, Miss C. Hurley 2, Miss A. Thompson 2, J.R. Barlow 2, D. Jewett 2, C. Barlow 2.*

PLATE 160 Whitwell-on-the-Hill: The panoramic view from the hill PHOTO: Brian Armstrong

WHITWELL-ON-THE-HILL, Yorks. (1927)
Alongside A64, 6m SW of Malton, 10m NE of York.
Meeting: Middleton.
SF: 18-23-25 (18). RH 2 circs. 9F. (3m): 18J; 2od (2/11). T: 6min 42.4s. (2m4f): 15J; 1od (8). T: 5min 42.0s. (4m): 24J; 2od (8/17). T: 9min 10.5s.
Good galloping 3m1f out-and-out stayers' course, mainly flat, but uphill to last fence; two sharp bends, one before last; the clay soil can become very heavy although much work has been done recently to improve drainage. Car parking good, exit downhill, but over rough ground. Viewing is excellent from adjacent slopes. The Grimthorpe Gold Cup is now a Mixed Open. Safety Factor high considering the tight bend before last.
Riders: *G. Brewer 5, G. Tuer 3, T. Greenall 2, T. Glass 2, N. Tutty 2, Miss F. Hartley 2, G. Carenza 2, C. Mulhall 2.*

WHITWICK MANOR, Herefordshire. (1951)
At Newtown, 8m NE of Hereford nr junc of A417 and A4103. (Exit 2, M50).
Meeting: North Herefordshire.
SF: 18-24. LH 2 circs. 8F; 18J; 2od (7/15). T: 6min 51.4s.
Undulating stayers' course with a run in of 110 yards; early season and always popular meeting; going can be heavy; fences easy; huge fields. Only one access/exit so long queues. Good viewing from hill overlooking paddock although trees obscure the action from four out until approaching two out. Wellies vital, paddock and bookies area can become a morass. Usually the most popular course in the country (certainly with owners) and regularly tops the chart with its number of runners, but not in '04 when the meeting had to be postponed. Very well-organised.
Riders: *Julian Pritchard 4, T. Stephenson 3, A. Wintle 3, M. Jackson 2, G. Hanmer 2, D. Barlow 2, A. Dalton 2.*

WITTON CASTLE, Co. Durham. (1984)
5m W of Bishop Auckland nr A68, 12 miles from A1 (M).
Meetings: Old Raby Hunt Club; Zetland.
SF: 18-20-25. RH 2½ circs. 7F; 19J; 2od (6/13). T: 6min 37.1s.
Course is level, all grass, set in grounds of Witton Castle, runs around the lakes; good galloping course. Fences small which cause horses to take liberties and produces more fallers than expected. Car parking satisfactory; viewing excellent from bank below paddock. Going is often near to good in May, and the atmosphere is friendly and informal.
Riders: *L. Bates 5, Mrs F. Needham 4, Miss J. Foster 4, C. Mulhall 4, N. Tutty 3, N. Tinkler 3, Miss S. Brotherton 3, T. Glass 2, S. Swiers 2, R. Abrahams 2, N. Saville 2, F. Crawford 2, D. Raw 2.*

WOODFORD, Glos. (1946)
Nr A38, 15m N of Bristol (3m from exit 14, M5).
Meeting: Berkeley.
SF: 18-20-22. LH 2 circs. 10F; 19J; 2od (5/14). T: 6min 31.8s.
Course is flat, in water meadows; has one right-hand bend after 5th; seldom harder than good to firm for late April/early May meeting so usually plenty of runners; and good quality; start in a chute and fence 1 only jumped once; sharp bend after 10th can be a problem; run-throughs at fences are narrow. Strong betting market. Panoramic viewing from hill though horses disappear after 5(14)th and the next fence is out of sight; finish is head-on which rather defeats the object. Hedges have been allowed to grow as part of Countryside Stewardship Scheme and this has not improved matters, and generally does not look as good as it did. Why not move the tents, bookies, etc to the sloping ground across the stream to the left of the finish? It must be done!
Riders: *Miss P. Gundry 3, Miss A. Dare 3, T. Stephenson 2, N. Williams 2, M. Miller 2, G. Barfoot-Saunt 2, A. Wintle 2.*

YSTRADOWEN, Glam. (2002)
On A4222 between Cowbridge and Pontyclun, M4 Juncs 34 or 35.
Meetings: Glamorgan; Ystrad Taf Fechan.
SF: 14-16. LH 2½ circs. 7F; 18J; 2od (6/13). T: 6min 50.6s
Very undulating course with a sharp drop from fence 5(12) followed by a right hand bend; has been altered to make the plunge less steep; short run-in followed by sharp bend. Viewing reasonable although horses disappear on long run between fence 7(14) and 8(15); finish is head on from enclosures. Facilities very compact. Would lend itself to a figure-of-eight course if it was allowed. Very picturesque, and a fitting finale to the Courses Section!
Riders: *E. Williams 7, T. Vaughan 4, Miss E. Jones 3, M. Barber 3, R. Hughes 2, L. Stephens 2, James Tudor 2, A. Hanly 2.*

So you still think you know about Point-to-Pointing?

This year's Quiz is, as usual, in two sections, with a first prize for each.

The first section, with 10 questions and a **first prize of £50 and a free 2006 Annual**, is again for the Enthusiasts who do not want to spend hours poring over the record books.

And for the Scholars who enjoy researching the answers to more difficult questions, there are the usual further 20 questions. **A year's free subscription to the Loose-Leaf Results service awaits the Scholar who achieves the highest score to all 30 questions**.

This year the questions have been kindly set for the first time by Peter Stevens (always a very successful participant in the past).

Enthusiast's Quiz

Ten questions for a £50 prize and a free 2005 Annual.

In 2004:

1. Which Point-to-Point course staged eight meetings?
2. Which rider finished runner-up in the Jockeys Championship with 50 winners?
3. Who were the two women riders who won the Cheltenham and Aintree Fox Hunters'?
4. Which horse was unbeaten in six Point-to-Points and one Hunter Chase?
5. Who rode his 100th winner, and also won the leading Owner/Rider award?
6. Which horse was retired as a 15-y-o after winning 29 Point-to-Points and 4 Hunter Chases in his career?
7. Who rode nine Hunter Chase winners?
8. Which 16-y-o horse won on his only outing at Larkhill?
9. Which horse equalled the Garthorpe course record?
10. Which Point-to-Point meeting attracted the most runners with 146 in 12 races?

Scholarship Questions

A further 20 questions to win a 2004 Loose-Leaf Subscription (worth £210). All questions relate to the post World War II period.

11. Which horse won a Point-to-Point on the same day he had run in a Hunter Chase?
12. Name the horse who ran at two different Point-to-Point courses on the same day?
13. Which rider's Point-to-Point career spanned from 1948 to 1994?
14. Which horse made his racecourse debut in a Point-to-Point as a 21-year-old?
15. Which horse described as 'not good enough to make a racehorse on current evidence' in the Annual, won seven Point-to-Points the following year?
16. Which winner of a major staying chase had drawn the Annual comment 'May turn out like his half-brother - speedy, a bad jumper, and only able to last a bare 3m', a few years previously?
17. Which winner of four Point-to-Points was sired by a horse who had won ten Point-to-Points?
18. Who rode their first winner and then completed an extra circuit of the course, jumping all the fences?!
19. Which mare, who won 17 Point-to-Points, was reputed to have been bought for £3 at Newport cattle market?
20. Which two winning Point-to-Pointers have exclamation marks in their names.
21. Which horse died after finishing fourth, and was then posthumously disqualified?
22. Who was the first horse to be disqualified from a Point-to-Point after a positive dope test?
23. Which Point-to-Point race had 39 runners?
24. Which horse ran with an amount of money inscribed on his blinkers?
25. Which Point-to-Point winner subsequently won a Market Rasen Handicap Chase by a short-head and a short-head?
26. Which Point-to-Point winner subsequently finished alone in a Cheltenham steeplechase?
27. Who was the last horse to run in English Point-to-Points at three and four years of age.
28. Which meeting did four of the five winners also win three days earlier at the same Point-to-Point?

29. Name three racehorse trainers holding full licences in 2004 who rode in Point-to-Points in the 1940s.

30. Which winner of three Point-to-Points later became the first recorded horse to win a flat race on a Sunday in Great Britain?

Send your answers (including your name and address) to:
Hunter Chasers & Point-to-Pointers Quiz
Weatherbys Chase, Stour House, 68 Grove Road, Wimborne, Dorset, BH21 1BW
to arrive by Saturday 29th January 2005

All entrants names (from both parts of the Quiz) will go into the hat and the first four drawn will each receive a complimentary copy of the 2005 Annual.

The winners will be announced, and the answers given, in the Loose-Leaf Results and the Weekly and Fortnightly Supplements, and will appear in next year's Annual.

Results of Last Year's Quizzes

As usual the 2004 Quiz proved to be a very tight affair at the top, but was won by **Stewart Nash** of Walton-on-Thames who commendably got them all right. The top scorers were: Stewart Nash 30, David Potter 29½, Peter Stevens 29 and Henry Franklin 26.

Darryl Smith from Ashford, Kent receives £50 as the winner of the Enthusiasts Quiz. Free copies of *Mackenzie, Selby & Harris's Hunter Chasers & Point-to-Pointers 2005* were won by **Jane Armson** of Melbourne in Derbyshire, **Mrs J.M. Holmes** of Howden, Goole, **Denise Reynolds** of Bridport, Dorset, **Jordan Spain** of Balsall Common and **Carolyn Tanner** of *Horse & Hound* (who, for the record, did manage to answer Question 11 correctly).

Answers to the Enthusiast Questions

1. **Mister Benjamin** won five races for Chloe Roddick.
2. **Upham Lord**, with eight wins, was the leading Point-to-Point horse for the second successive season.
3. **Bright Approach** was second in the Cheltenham Christies Foxhunter Chase and the Intrum Justitia Cup
4. Julian Pritchard rode four winners at the **Clifton-on-Teme** at **Upper Sapey on 27th April.**

5. **Oscar Wilde** won five races for Dan Drake.
6. **Nick Mitchell** rode his 100th Point-to-Point winner when Askers Jack won Division Two of the Open Maiden at the West Somerset Vale at Cothelstone on 13th April.
7. **Braes Of Mar** finished second for H.M. The Queen in the V.W.H Hunt Members race at Siddington on 22nd March.
8. Ray Geddes's **Ease The Pressure** won four races at Larkhill.
9. **County Derry** won the Land Rover Championship for the second year running.
10. **Ashley Farrant**, **Harry Fowler** and **Tom Greenall** won on Lord Atterbury.

Answers to the Scholarship Questions

11. **Kula**, named after a town in Turkey, won nine Point-to-Points for Horse & Hound correspondent Carolyn Tanner between 1983 and 1989.
12. Happymint - winner of the 1954 Cheltenham Foxhunters and the 1955 Liverpool Foxhunters for owner-rider Danny Moralee - finished unplaced behind Silver Buck (not the 1982 Cheltenham Gold Cup winner!) in the **Haydon Adjacent Hunts Maiden** at **Limestone Bank** on **7th April 1951**.
13. 19-year-old **Royal And Ancient** finished second in the West Street Hunt race at Aldington on 11th May 1968.
14. At the reported age of 55, **Robin Tate** rode a four-timer at the York & Ainsty at Easingwold on 24th April 1993. **Major Guy Cunard** achieved the same feat when he rode a four-timer at the Middleton & Middleton East on 13th May 1967.
15. 63-year-old **Tom Tilbrook** rode his first winner when Corramacorra won the South & West Wilts Adjacent Hunts Novice Riders race at Larkhill on 21st April 1984.
16. Jumbo (Major Robertson) was unplaced in the Farmers' and Puppy Walkers' Challenge Cup (fourth race) while another Jumbo (Bob McCreery) was unplaced in the Adjacent Hunts Maiden race (fifth race) at the **Wilton** at Well House Farm, Salisbury on **6th April 1949**.
17. **Nigel Bloom** rode five winners at the Essex at High Easter on 26th March 1994 while **Tim Jones** rode four winners at the Curre at Howick.
18. **The ill-fated Salmon River**, bred by John Thorne won the 1965 Melton Novices Championship for Major Eldred Wilson. His namesake won two Hunter Chases in 1957 for owner/trainer/rider John Thorne.
19. **Black Diamond** won three 1967 Cottenham Point-to-Points and ran in the 1964 Champion Hurdle for the Wales family.

20. **Rosie's Cousin,** winner of nine Point-to-Points and 16 Hunter Chases for Major Harold Rushton, had won the County Limerick Foxhounds Open Maiden race at Ballywilliam on Tuesday 10th March 1959 under Alan Lillingston (rider of 1963 Champion Hurdler, Winning Fair)

21. **Sixteen-year-old Another Flash** (D.J. Moorhead) won the first Sunday Irish Point-to-Point at the Kildare Hunt and Naas Harriers at Punchestown on 22nd February 1970. Ten years previously, Another Flash had won the Champion Hurdle under Bobby Beasley.

22. **Peter Craggs** retired after winning the Morpeth Members on Dein Deifer on 13th April 2003, 31 years after riding his first winner on Charge Straight in the equivalent race on 21st April 1972.

23. Detling was disqualified for taking the wrong course after winning the **Eridge Ladies Open** at **Heathfield** on **19th April 1976**. Barbury Castle won the **Mendip Farmers Adjacent Hunts Maiden** at **Nedge** on **22nd February 1975**.

24. **Bill Shand-Kydd** (18 winners) was runner-up to Michael Bloom (19) in the 1969 Mens championship after Star Of Arum was disqualified from his 19th April Whaddon Chase win on the technicality that the horse was 'subject of a lease'.

25. **Four By Two** was awarded a handicap mark of 5-1 in the 1987 Annual, with the proviso that he was 'probably over-rated'

26. Captain Donald Swan won the **Weston Harriers Hunt Members** at Nedge on **27th March 1965** on Camay II after all four runners had come to grief.

27. Justin Farthing rode four winners at the Cattistock at Toller Down Gate on 30th March 1991.

28. Richard Barber trained the first three home in both the 1996 Coronation Cup and Division 2 of the 2003 East Devon Open Maiden.

29. Miss S.A. Bailie, Mrs J. Barons, Mrs E. Borthwick, Miss U. Brander-Dunbar, Miss J. Brock, Mrs R. Henson, Miss C. Jones, Miss S. Rimell, Miss F.E. Robarts, Mrs M.S. Thomas and Miss G. Walker **all rode five winners in the 1963 season**. Miss S Rimell appears in the Champion Riders table with the footnote that she had the most seconds.

30. **Big Muddy** is the Horse and Hound Cup runner (1980) who shares the same name as the ranch sold by Julie Maragon (Jean Simmons) to Jim McKay (Gregory Peck) in The Big Country. It may have helped that the BBC broadcast the film just days after the Annual was published in November.

The Leading Young Horses of 2004

The Leading Five-Year-Olds

Lindsay (FR) *(b.g.) Chamberlin (FR) - Oliday (FR) (Djarvis FR)* 11-1
Vivid Imagination (IRE) *(b.g.) Moonax (IRE) - Sezu (IRE) (Mister Lord USA)* 10-13
Black Collar *(br.m.) Bob's Return (IRE) - Rosemoss (Le Moss)* 10-8
Mr Hawkeye (USA) *(ch.g.) Royal Academy (USA) - Port Plaisance (USA) (Woodman USA)* 10-8
Hunca Munca (IRE) *(b.m.) Presenting - Tulladante (IRE) (Phardante FR)* 10-6
Noble Action *(ch.g.) Mister Lord (USA) - Triggered (Gunner B)* 10-6
Eighty Days (IRE) *(b.g.) Air Quest - Valley Hope (IRE) (Altountash)* 10-5
Lord Anner (IRE) *(br.g.) Mister Lord (USA) - Anner Lodge (IRE) (Capitano)* 10-5
Thanks Jim (IRE) *(b.g.) Jolly Jake (NZ) - Summing Oak (IRE) (Summing USA)* 10-5
Cimmaroon (IRE) *(b.g.) Synefos (USA) - Bayalika (FR) (Kashtan FR)* 10-4
Civil Gent (IRE) *(ch.g.) Flying Spur (AUS) - Calamity Kate (IRE) (Fairy King USA)* 10-4
Enitsag (FR) *(ch.g.) Pistolet Bleu (IRE) - Rosala (FR) (Lashkari)* 10-4
King Barry (FR) *(b.g.) Cadoudal (FR) - Leonie Des Champs (FR) (Crystal Palace FR)* 10-4
Lord Oscar (IRE) *(b.g.) Oscar (IRE) - Americo Rose (IRE) (Lord Americo)* 10-4
Killard Point (IRE) *(b.g.) Old Vic - Chic And Elite (Deep Run)* 10-3
Flat Stanley *(b.g.) Celtic Swing - Cool Grey (Absalom)* 10-2
Reflected Glory (IRE) *(b.g.) Flemensfirth (USA) - Clashdermot Lass (Cardinal Flower)* 10-2
Silver Buzzard (USA) *(b/br.g.) Silver Hawk (USA) - Stellarina (USA) (Pleasant Colony USA)* 10-2
Caipiroska *(b.g.) Petoski - Caipirinha (IRE) (Strong Gale)* 10-1
Magic Lodge *(b.g.) Grand Lodge (USA) - Samsung Spirit (Statoblest)* 10-1
Spanish Dolphin (IRE) *(b.g.) Dolphin Street (FR) - Alhambra Palace (IRE) (Cyrano De Bergerac)* 10-0
Blackanblue *(b.g.) Alflora (IRE) - Emmabella (True Song)* 9-13
Brer Bear *(b.g.) Perpendicular - Nessfield (Tumble Wind)* 9-13
Flash Point (IRE) *(b/br.g.) Executive Perk - Shine Your Light (Kemal FR)* 9-13
Londolozi Lad (IRE) *(b.g.) Ali-Royal (IRE) - Ashdown (Pharly FR)* 9-13
Monarch Ruler *(ch.g.) Be My Chief (USA) - Busters Sister (Hasty Word)* 9-13
Bilingual *(b.g.) Prince Daniel (USA) - Gymcrak Cyrano (IRE) (Cyrano De Bergerac)* 9-12
Border Fusion *(b.g.) Weld - Monteviot (Scallywag)* 9-12
It's Missy Imp *(ch.m.) Fearless Action (USA) - Swordella (Broadsword USA)* 9-12
Lansdowne Park *(b.m.) El Conquistador - Bickfield Approach (Dubassoff USA)* 9-12
Le Millenaire (FR) *(b/br.g.) Ragmar (FR) - Ezaia (FR) (Iron Duke FR)* 9-12
Preacher Boy *(b.g.) Classic Cliche (IRE) - Gospel (IRE) (Le Bavard FR)* 9-12
Rose Of The Hill (IRE) *(gr.g.) Roselier (FR) - Golden Leaf (Croghan Hill)* 9-12
Wild Chimes (IRE) *(b.g.) Oscar (IRE) - Jingle Bells (FR) (In The Mood FR)* 9-12
Beehawk *(b.g.) Gunner B - Cupids Bower (Owen Dudley)* 9-11
Best Accolade *(b.g.) Oscar (IRE) - Made Of Talent (Supreme Leader)* 9-11
Clever Fella *(ch.g.) Elmaamul (USA) - Festival Of Magic (USA) (Clever Trick USA)* 9-11
Lutteur Bleu (FR) *(b.g.) Franc Bleu Argent (USA) - Sirene Du Lac (FR) (Missolonghi USA)* 9-11
Parsifal *(b.g.) Sadler's Wells (USA) - Moss (USA) (Woodman USA)* 9-11
Sonnant (FR) *(ch.g.) Cyborg (FR) - Schwarzente (IRE) (Entitled)* 9-11
Black Leopard (IRE) *(b/br.g.) Presenting - Glen Laura (Kambalda)* 9-10
High Fields *(b.g.) Sovereign Water (FR) - Once Bitten (Brave Invader USA)* 9-10
Mountsorrel (IRE) *(b.g.) Charnwood Forest (IRE) - Play The Queen (IRE) (King Of Clubs)* 9-10
My Whisper (IRE) *(b.m.) Zaffaran (USA) - Floreamus (Quayside)* 9-10
Think Commercial (IRE) *(b.g.) Mister Lord (USA) - Dingle Gal (IRE) (Phardante FR)* 9-10
Velvet Dove *(b.m.) Rakaposhi King - Careful Dove (So Careful)* 9-10
Western Frontier (IRE) *(ch.g.) Shernazar - Bucks Slave (Buckskin FR)* 9-10

The Leading Six-Year-Olds

Fane Counsel (IRE) *(b.g.) Leading Counsel (USA) - Fane Heights (First Consul)* 11-0
Cantarinho *(b.g.) Alderbrook - Hot Hostess (Silly Season)* 10-12
Bohemian Spirit (IRE) *(b.g.) Eagle Eyed (USA) - Tuesday Morning (Sadler's Wells USA)* 10-11
Franco (IRE) *(b.g.) Rashar (USA) - Market Thyne (IRE) (Good Thyne USA)* 10-11
Coolefind (IRE) *(b.g.) Phardante (FR) - Greavesfind (The Parson)* .10-10
Free Gift *(b.g.) Presenting - Gladtogetit (Green Shoon)* 10-10
Mel In Blue (FR) *(b.g.) Pistolet Bleu (IRE) - Calligraphie (FR) (R B Chesne)* 10-10
Out The Black (IRE) *(b/br.g.) Presenting - Executive Wonder (IRE) (Executive Perk)* 10-10
Born To Dream (IRE) *(b.m.) Supreme Leader - Ethel's Dream (Relkino)* 10-9
Lambrini Mist *(gr.g.) Terimon - Miss Fern (Cruise Missile)* 10-8
Texas Ranger *(b.g.) Mtoto - Favorable Exchange (USA) (Exceller USA)* 10-8
Thyne Man (IRE) *(br.g.) Good Thyne (USA) - Showphar (IRE) (Phardante FR)* 10-7
Bunratty's Sole (IRE) *(br.g.) Phardante (FR) - Bucks Gift (IRE) (Buckley)* 10-5
Denvale (IRE) *(b.g.) Denel (FR) - Brackenvale (IRE) (Strong Gale)* 10-5
I Am Said I (IRE) *(b.g.) Presenting - Moonlight Romance (Teenoso USA)* 10-5
Militaire (FR) *(ch.g.) Bering - Moon Review (USA) (Irish River FR)* 10-5
Poppy Maroon *(b.m.) Supreme Leader - Maries Party (The Parson)* 10-5
Schoolhouse Walk *(b.g.) Mistertopogigo (IRE) - Restandbejoyful (Takachiho)* 10-5
Pa Pierre (IRE) *(b.g.) Pierre - Shoon River (IRE) (Over The River FR)* 10-4
River Alder *(b.m.) Alderbrook - River Pearl (Oats)* 10-4
Beet De Bob (IRE) *(b/br.g.) Bob Back (USA) - Beet Statement (IRE) (Strong Statement USA)* . . 10-3
Lord Ken (IRE) *(b.g.) Lord Americo - Moscow Lady (IRE) (Moscow Society USA)* . . . . .10-3§
Magnus Veritas (IRE) *(br.g.) Jolly Jake (NZ) - Goldens Monkey (Monksfield)* 10-3
Pot Shot *(b.g.) Alflora (IRE) - Triggered (Gunner B)* 10-3
Ramirez (IRE) *(ch.g.) Royal Abjar (USA) - Flooding (USA) (Irish River FR)* 10-3
Ten Bob (IRE) *(b.g.) Jurado (USA) - Rush For Gold (Mugatpura)* 10-3
Great Jubilee (IRE) *(ch.g.) Beneficial - Red Donna (Don)* 10-2
Like The Buzz (IRE) *(b.m.) Lord Americo - Crash Course Katie (IRE) (Crash Course)* 10-2
Trooper Collins (IRE) *(b.g.) Dolphin Street (FR) - Born To Fly (IRE) (Last Tycoon)* . . . . .10-2§
Up The Pub (IRE) *(ch.g.) Carroll House - Brave Ruby (Proverb)* 10-2
Cannon Bridge (IRE) *(ch.g.) Definite Article - Hit For Six (Tap On Wood)* 10-1
Euwiluwil (IRE) *(b.g.) Eurobus - Market Romance (African Sky)* 10-1
Kasilia (FR) *(b.g.) Silver Rainbow - Basilia (FR) (Mont Basile FR)* 10-1
Kepi Royal (FR) *(b.g.) Royal Charter (FR) - Chic Lilie (FR) (Olmeto)* .10-1
Twilight Dancer (IRE) *(b.m.) Sri Pekan (USA) - Manhattan Sunset (USA) (El Gran Senor USA)* . 10-1
Welcome News *(ch.m.) Bob Back (USA) - Rosie O'Keeffe (IRE) (Royal Fountain)* 10-1
Boddidley (IRE) *(b.g.) Be My Native (USA) - Boardwalker (IRE) (Waajib)* 10-0
Carat *(b.g.) Alflora (IRE) - Diamond Wind (USA) (Wind And Wuthering USA)* 10-0
Charango Star *(b.g.) Petoski - Pejawi (Strong Gale)* 10-0
Devil's Perk (IRE) *(b.g.) Executive Perk - She Devil (Le Moss)* 10-0
Greybrook Lad (IRE) *(br.g.) Norwich - Princess Project (IRE) (Project Manager)* 10-0
Gudasmum *(b.m.) Primitive Rising (USA) - Comarch (Ancient Monro)* .10-0
Just Sally *(b.m.) Afzal - Hatherley (Deep Run)* 10-0
Kerres Noires (FR) *(b.g.) Noir Et Or - Viagara (FR) (Mont Basile FR)* .10-0
Tom Brown (IRE) *(ch.g.) Grand Plaisir (IRE) - Rathoe Princess (Never Slip)* 10-0
Trust Fund (IRE) *(ch.g.) Rashar (USA) - Tuney Blade (Fine Blade USA)* 10-0
Banana Ridge *(ch.m.) Primitive Rising (USA) - Madison Girl (Last Fandango)* 9-13
Charlie's Angel *(gr.m.) Rakaposhi King - Dunnohalm (Kalaglow)* 9-13
Copper Grove (IRE) *(b.g.) Presenting - Riseaway (Raise You Ten)* 9-13
John Foley (IRE) *(b.g.) Petardia - Fast Bay (Bay Express)* 9-13

The Leading Seven-Year-Olds

Balinova (IRE) *(b.g.) Lord Americo - Shuil Comeragh (Laurence O)* 11-1
Oneminutetofive *(b.g.) Neltino - Island Beat (Jupiter Island)* 11-1
Bengal Bullet *(b.g.) Infantry - Indian Cruise (Cruise Missile)* 10-13
Crevamoy (IRE) *(ch.m.) Shardari - Prudent View (IRE) (Supreme Leader)* 10-12
Bishop's Blade *(b.g.) Sure Blade (USA) - Myrtilla (Beldale Flutter USA)* 10-9
Black Smoke (IRE) *(gr.g.) Ala Hounak - Korean Citizen (IRE) (Mister Lord USA)* 10-9
Christy Beamish (IRE) *(b.g.) Jolly Jake (NZ) - Ballinatona Bridge (Black Minstrel)* 10-9
Star Of Raven *(b.m.) Sea Raven (IRE) - Lucy At The Minute (Silly Prices)* 10-8
Agua Ardente *(ch.g.) Afzal - Armagnac Messenger (Pony Express)* 10-7
Golden Rivet *(b.g.) Weld - Golden Valley (Hotfoot)* 10-7
Just Barney Boy *(b.g.) Past Glories - Pablena (Pablond)* 10-7
Shraden Edition *(b.g.) Tina's Pet - Star Edition (Leading Man)* 10-7
Asthefellowsaid (IRE) *(ch.g.) Glacial Storm (USA) - Celias Fancy (IRE) (Mandalus)* 10-6
Carthago (IRE) *(b.g.) Roselier (FR) - Hi Cousin (Condorcet FR)* 10-6
Chancy Guy *(b.g.) Tragic Role (USA) - Malacanang (Riboboy USA)* 10-6
Jackie Jarvis (IRE) *(b.m.) Alphabatim (USA) - Miss Brantridge (Riboboy USA)* . . . . . 10-6§
Jackson (FR) *(b.g.) Passing Sale (FR) - Tynia (FR) (Djarvis FR)* 10-6
Rostock (IRE) *(br.g.) Roselier (FR) - Royal Greenwood (IRE) (Radical)* 10-6
Skip 'n' Tune (IRE) *(b.m.) Mandalus - Molten (Ore)* 10-6
Titus Bramble *(b.g.) Puissance - Norska (Northfields USA)* 10-6
Beauchamp Oracle *(gr.g.) Mystiko (USA) - Beauchamp Cactus (Niniski USA)* 10-5
Court Adjourn *(b.g.) North Col - Tapalong (True Song)* 10-5
Decent Bond (IRE) *(b.g.) Witness Box (USA) - Decent Skin (IRE) (Buckskin FR)* 10-5
Ease The Pressure (IRE) *(b.g.) Roselier (FR) - Height Of Pressure (Buckskin FR)* 10-5
High Peak *(b.g.) Alflora (IRE) - High Heels (IRE) (Supreme Leader)* 10-5
Kerstino Two *(b.g.) Cruise Missile - Cresswell (Push On)* 10-5
Mighty Willing *(br.g.) Bollin William - Wild Ling (Mufrij)* 10-5
Wild Edgar (IRE) *(ch.g.) Invited (USA) - Ou La La (IRE) (Be My Native USA)* 10-5
Alittlebitopower *(ch.g.) Alflora (IRE) - What A Moppet (IRE) (Torus)* 10-4
Ashgreen *(b.g.) Afzal - Space Kate (Space King)* 10-4
Dumadic *(b.g.) Nomadic Way (USA) - Duright (Dubassoff USA)* 10-4
Euro Bob (IRE) *(ch.g.) Bob's Return (IRE) - Aughclogeen Run (Deep Run)* 10-4
Jazz Night *(b.g.) Alhijaz - Hen Night (Mummy's Game)* 10-4
Jimmy Cricket *(ch.g.) Primitive Rising (USA) - Norton Gale (IRE) (Le Bavard FR)* 10-4
Just The Job Too (IRE) *(b/br.g.) Prince Of Birds (USA) - Bold Encounter (IRE) (Persian Bold)* . . . 10-4§
Vinnie Boy (IRE) *(b/br.g.) Detroit Sam (FR) - Castle Ita (Midland Gayle)* 10-4
Beadnell Bay *(b.g.) Past Glories - Sherry Season (Vital Season)* 10-3
Bedtime Boys *(gr.g.) Gran Alba (USA) - Path's Sister (Warpath)* 10-3
Cedar Chief *(b.g.) Saddlers' Hall (IRE) - Dame Ashfield (Grundy)* 10-3
Choral Dream (IRE) *(b.g.) Yashgan - Daisy's Dream (Paddy's Stream)* 10-3
Coomakista *(b.m.) Primitive Rising (USA) - Miss Eros (Royal Fountain)* 10-3
Epicure (FR) *(b/br.g.) Northern Crystal - L'epicurienne (FR) (Rex Magna FR)* . . . . . 10-3§
Mister Swallow *(b.g.) Homo Sapien - Ninfa (IRE) (The Parson)* . . . . . 10-3§
More Flair *(ch.m.) Alflora (IRE) - Marejo (Creetown)* 10-3
Pristeen Spy *(b.g.) Teenoso (USA) - Sikera Spy (Harvest Spirit)* 10-3
Rag Week (IRE) *(b.g.) Roselier (FR) - Lady Rag (Ragapan)* 10-3
Simply The One (IRE) *(ch.g.) Simply Great (FR) - Lady Mearlane (Giolla Mear)* 10-3
Snowtre (IRE) *(b.g.) Glacial Storm (USA) - Forest Gale (Strong Gale)* . . . . . 10-3§
Braceys Girl (IRE) *(b/br.m.) Be My Native (USA) - Minigirls Niece (IRE) (Strong Gale)* 10-2
Elegant Light *(ch.m.) Elegant Monarch - Light The Bay (Presidium)* 10-2

Champion Sires

** includes a deadheat*

Point-to-Points and Hunter Chases

Year	Sire	Wins
1960	Trappeur II	18
1961	Domaha	23
1962	Whiteway	26
1963	Whiteway	20
1964	Whiteway*	25
1965	Whiteway	31
1966	Whiteway	34
1967	Vulgan	21
1968	Exodus	22
1969	Exodus	20
	Vulgan	20
1970	Spiritus	24
1971	Spiritus	27
1972	Fortina	20
1973	Rose Knight	21
	Vulgan	21
1974	Fortina	21
	Romany Air	21
1975	Even Money	25
1976	Indian Ruler	19
1977	Spartan General	39
1978	Spartan General	43
1979	Spartan General	68
1980	Spartan General	34
1981	Spartan General	39
1982	Spartan General	29
1983	Spartan General	43
1984	Spartan General	30
1985	Spartan General	28
1986	Spartan General	32
1987	Menelek	24
1988	Deep Run	27
1989	New Member	28
1990	New Member	23
1991	Pony Express	30
1992	New Member	25
1993	Sunyboy	32
1994	Celtic Cone	34
1995	Strong Gale	32
1996	Strong Gale	33

Point-to-Points only

Year	Sire	Wins
1997	Strong Gale	58
1998	Strong Gale	35
1999	Strong Gale	60
2000	Phardante (FR)*	38
2001	Roselier (FR)	11
2002	Strong Gale	50
2003	Be My Native (USA)	45
2004	Phardante (FR)	37

Leading Point-to-Point Sires 2004

1 PHARDANTE (FR) **37**

b. 1982 (Pharly FR - Pallante) - died in 1998

Horse	Wins
Pharmistice (IRE)	4
Clifford Bay (IRE)	3
Coolefind (IRE)	3
Dolphin Square (IRE)	3
Father Mansfield (IRE)	3
Bunratty's Sole (IRE)	2
Phar From Chance	2
Pharailde	2
Sir Dante (IRE)	2
Uncle Ada (IRE)	2
Briery Fox (IRE)	1
Cashew Cache (IRE)	1
Dante's Banker (IRE)	1
Donallach Mor (IRE)	1
Ebony Jack (IRE)	1
Mussel Buoy (IRE)	1
Near And Phar (IRE)	1
Ofcoursehekhan (IRE)	1
Phar Afield (IRE)	1
Polo Ridge (IRE)	1
The Only Option (IRE)	1

2 ROSELIER (FR)....................33
gr. 1973 (Misti IV - Peace Rose) - died in 1998
Rostock (IRE)........................4
Highland Rose (IRE)..................3
Rag Week (IRE).......................3
Clonshire Paddy (IRE)................2
Ease The Pressure (IRE)..............2
Minella Silver (IRE).................2
New Ross (IRE).......................2
Rose Of The Hill (IRE)...............2
Bally Blue...........................1
Black Optimist (IRE).................1
Bright Approach (IRE)................1
Carthago (IRE).......................1
Fine And Dandy (IRE).................1
Grey Fandango (IRE)..................1
Lucky Master (IRE)...................1
Misty Ramble (IRE)...................1
Nickit (IRE).........................1
On The Day (IRE).....................1
Sailors Folly (IRE)..................1
Street Smart (IRE)...................1
Treasulier (IRE).....................1

3 BE MY NATIVE (USA)...............26
b/br. 1979 (Our Native USA - Witchy Woman USA) - died in 1997
The Wiley Kalmuck (IRE)..............4
Ask The Natives (IRE)................2
Hallrule (IRE).......................2
Little Native (IRE)..................2
Mytimie (IRE)........................2
Red Native (IRE).....................2
Alexander Nevsky.....................1
Be My Dream (IRE)....................1
Boddidley (IRE)......................1
Braceys Girl (IRE)...................1
Good Heart (IRE).....................1
Kustom Kit Grizzly (IRE).............1
Lively Dessert (IRE).................1
My Native Knight (IRE)...............1
Native Alibi (IRE)...................1
Native Thunder (IRE).................1
Special Friend (IRE).................1
The Sea Club (IRE)...................1

4 GLACIAL STORM (USA)..............25
b. 1985 (Arctic Tern USA - Hortensia FR) - stands at The Beeches, Tallow, Co Waterford, Ireland.
Asthefellowsaid (IRE)................3
Hot Toddy (IRE)......................3
Shiny Bay (IRE)......................3
Snowtre (IRE)........................3
Dawn's Cognac (IRE)..................2
Minino (IRE).........................2
Sweeping Storm (IRE).................2
Aunt Gladys (IRE)....................1
Coole'sabbot (IRE)...................1
Hail Stone (IRE).....................1
Heavy Weather (IRE)..................1
Oh Highly Likely (IRE)...............1
Stormy Sunrise (IRE).................1
Whether The Storm (IRE)..............1

4 STRONG GALE......................25
br. 1975 (Lord Gayle USA á Sterntau) - died in 1994
Spring Gale (IRE)....................4
Celtic Duke..........................3
Sovereign Gale (IRE).................3
Belvento (IRE).......................2
Do It Once (IRE).....................2
Winter Gale (IRE)....................2
Fair Wind (IRE)......................1
Galeaway (IRE).......................1
Galeshan (IRE).......................1
Minella Storm (IRE)..................1
News Flash (IRE).....................1
Pampered Gale (IRE)..................1
The Lord Roberts (IRE)...............1
Tirley Gale..........................1
Yorkshire Edition (IRE)..............1

6 RAKAPOSHI KING 24
b. 1982 (Bustino - Supper Time) - stands at Shade Oak Stud, Bagley, Ellesmere, Shropshire. SY12 9BY
Rhythm King 5
Colquhoun 3
Mr Mahdlo 2
Ask Again 1
Bessie Bunter 1
Buckland Bobby 1
Buckland Boy 1
Charlie's Angel 1
Frank Byrne 1
Karzhang 1
King's Reply 1
King Of The Dawn 1
Mrs Peggoty 1
Posh Stick 1
Ricky B. 1
The Kings Fling. 1
Trivial (IRE). 1

7 MISTER LORD (USA) 23
b. 1979 (Sir Ivor - Forest Friend) - left stud in 2004
Lord Of The Mist (IRE) 5
Lively Lord (IRE). 4
Lord Anner (IRE). 2
Noble Action. 2
Killiney Bay (IRE) 1
Lady Dot (IRE) 1
Longstone Lady (IRE) 1
Lord Atterbury (IRE) 1
Lord Castle (IRE) 1
Lord Kilpatrick (IRE). 1
Midnight Lord (IRE) 1
Rainbow Ranch (IRE). 1
Rings Of Power (IRE) 1
Think Commercial (IRE) 1

8 SUPREME LEADER 19
b. 1982 (Bustino - Princess Zena) - died in 2002
Caught At Dawn (IRE) 5
Sheriff's Friend (IRE) 4
Supreme Citizen (IRE). 3
Canterbury Jack (IRE). 2
Waterloo Leader (IRE). 2
Autcaesar Autnihil (IRE) 1
Born To Dream (IRE) 1
Martha's Boy (IRE) 1

9 ALFLORA (IRE) 18
b. 1989 (Niniski USA - Adrana) - stands at Shade Oak Stud, Bagley, Ellesmere, Shropshire SY12 9BY (Tel: 01939 270235)
High Peak. 4
More Flair. 3
Rainha 2
Blackanblue 1
Carat 1
Flora Macdonald. 1
Itchen Mill 1
No Remorse 1
Peppernick 1
Pot Shot 1
Sir Alf. 1
The Sky Is Blue 1

10 PRESENTING 17
br. 1992 (Mtoto - D'Azy) - at stud in Ireland
Free Gift 6
I Am Said I (IRE) 4
Out The Black (IRE) 4
Anniejo 1
Hi Tech Man (IRE) 1
Hunca Munca (IRE) 1

11 NOMADIC WAY (USA) 15
b. 1985 (Assert - Kittyhawk) - stands at Louella Stud, Bardon Grange, Hugglescote, Leics LE6 2ST (Tel:01530 813357)
Claire's Nomad 3
Dumadic. 3
Imps Way 3
Go Nomadic 1
Kindle A Flame. 1
Nomadic Star 1
Rutherford 1
Sams Way 1
Stanwick Gypsy 1

12 ARCTIC LORD. 14
b/br. 1980 (Lord Gayle USA - Arctic Chimes) - died 2003
Tricky Trevor (IRE) 3
Homme De Fer. 2
Knight Of Passion 2
B B Boy 1
Brown Seal 1
Cool Wager 1
Keltic Lord 1
Lord Of The North (IRE) 1
Slaney Lass 1
Wibbley Wobbley 1

13 CRESTED LARK 13
ch. 1976 (Crowned Prince - Bird Of Dawning) - to stud 1984
Nautical Lad 5
Lottie The Lotus 2
Crested Manor 1
Lah Di Dah Lad 1
Sandy Lark 1
Silly Boy 1
Sir Lancelot 1
Tender Tangle 1

13 GILDORAN 13
b. 1980 (Rheingold - Durtal) - died in 2003
Mr Splodge 3
Tod's Brother 2
Bengal Boy 1
Chasing The Bride 1
Dorans Magic 1
Gillie's Nephew 1
Gillone 1
Gilzine 1
Iadora 1
Lord Of The Road 1

13 GOOD THYNE (USA) 13
b. 1977 (Herbager - Foreseer USA) - died in 2001
Althrey Dandy (IRE) 2
Thyne Man (IRE) 2
Wellheseemedsolow (IRE) 2
Better Future (IRE) 1
Black A Brook (IRE) 1
Festival Time 1
Headwrecker (IRE) 1
Oneforthefrog (IRE) 1
Stennikov (IRE) 1
Waders (IRE) 1

13 HENBIT (USA) 13
b. 1977 (Hawaii - Chateaucreek USA) - died in 1997
Campden Kitty 3
Call Me Sonic 2
Teme Willow (IRE) 2
William Lionheart 2
Another Bit 1
Cotton On 1
Cousin George 1
Rain Delay 1

13 HOMO SAPIEN 13
b. 1982 (Lord Gayle - Bold Caress) - died in 1997
Sapega (IRE) 3
Hello Roscrea (IRE) 2
It'snotsimple (IRE) 2
Home Again (IRE) 1
Home Tor 1
Kovach (IRE) 1
Orchestra's Boy (IRE) 1
Runningwiththemoon 1
Tooley Park 1

13 PETOSKI 13
b. 1982 (Niniski - Shushila) - stands at Conduit Farm Stud, Churchill, Oxon (Tel: 01608 658274)
Caipiroska 2
Charango Star 2
Alleywell 1
Babs Wheal 1
Cloudy Bay Boy 1
Court Alert 1
Mouseski 1
Petrouge 1
Porlock Hill 1
Russian Friend 1
Ski Pass 1

Sires of Point-to-Point Sires of Point-to-Point Winners in 2004

** includes a deadheat*

Sire	Winners
Absalom	2
Accordion	3
Actinium (FR)	3
Afzal	10
Air Display (USA)	1
Air Quest	2
Aird Point	1
Ajraas (USA)	4
Akarad (FR)	1
Alderbrook	6
Alflora (IRE)*	18
Alhijaz	1
All Haste (USA)	1
Almoojid	1
Alphabatim (USA)	8
Anshan	2
Aragon	2
Arapahos (FR)	4
Arazi (USA)	1
Arcane (USA)	2
Architect (USA)	1
Arctic Lord	14
Ardross	1
Aristocracy	2
Arrasas (USA)	1
Arzanni	1
Asir	2
Aspect (USA)	1
Bad Conduct (USA)	3
Bahri (USA)	1
Balla Cove	1
Baron Blakeney	12
Be My Chief (USA)	2
Be My Guest (USA)	1
Be My Native (USA)	26
Beau Sher	2
Beneficial	2
Bering	2
Beveled (USA)	3
Beyssac (FR)	4
Bluebird (USA)	2
Bob's Return (IRE)	3
Bob Back (USA)	1
Bonhomie (USA)	1
Bonnie Prince	1
Bonny Scot (IRE)	1
Boyne Valley	3
Brevet	3
Brief Truce (USA)	1
Broadsword (USA)	6
Broken Hearted	3
Brush Aside (USA)	5
Buckley	3
Buckskin (FR)	8
Bulldozer	2
Bustino	2
Buzzards Bay	1
Cadeaux Genereux	1
Cadoudal (FR)	3
Camden Town	6
Cardinal Flower	2
Carlingford Castle	11
Castle Keep	1
Cataldi	2
Celio Rufo	2
Celtic Swing	1
Chamberlin (FR)	1
Charente River (IRE)	1
Charmer	1
Charnwood Forest (IRE)	1
Chef De Clan II (FR)	1
Chief's Crown (USA)	1
Circus Light	3
Clantime	1
Classic	3
Classic Cliche (IRE)	1
Clearly Bust	4
Commanche Run	12
Conquering Hero (USA)	2
Contract Law (USA)	2
Crested Lark	13
Cruise Missile	4
Current Edition (IRE)	2
Cyborg (FR)	1
Czaravich (USA)	1
Damister (USA)	1
Dancing High	2
Danehill (USA)	3
Danzatore (CAN)	1
Darnay	1
Dauphin Du Bourg (FR)	1
Dawn Johnny (USA)	2
Definite Article	3
Denel (FR)	6
Derring Rose	3
Derrylin	9
Desert Style (IRE)	1
Detroit Sam (FR)	6
Discover (USA)	1
Distinctly North (USA)	2
Dolphin Street (FR)	2
Dominion	2
Doubletour (USA)	2
Doyoun	2
Dry Dock	2
Dunbeath (USA)	1
Ecossais (FR)	1
Efisio	2
El Conquistador	4
Ela-Mana-Mou	3
Electric	4
Elegant Monarch	3
Elmaamul (USA)	1
Emarati (USA)	1
Emperor Fountain	2
Endoli (USA)	1
Erdelistan (FR)	1
Erins Isle	2
Eurobus	5
Executive Perk	8
Ezzoud (IRE)	1
Fearless Action (USA)	4
Feelings (FR)	1
Fijar Tango (FR)	2
First Norman (USA)	1
First Trump	5
Flemensfirth (USA)	2
Flying Spur (AUS)	2
Fourstars Allstar (USA)	1
Foxhound (USA)	1
Fraam	1
Franc Bleu Argent (USA)	1

Fresh Breeze (USA). 2
Garde Royale 3
Generous (IRE) 1
Germany (USA). 1
Gildoran 13
Glacial Storm (USA) 25
Gold Dust 3
Golden Heights 2
Gone West (USA) 2
Good Thyne (USA) 13
Gran Alba (USA) 3
Grand Lodge (USA). 3
Grand Plaisir (IRE) 1
Green Adventure (USA). . . . 8
Green Dancer (USA) 2
Green Ruby (USA) 2
Greensmith 2
Grey Desire. 1
Gunner B 8
Hadeer 3
Hatim (USA). 1
Hawkster (USA) 2
Henbit (USA) 13
High Lodge. 1
Hollow Hand 1
Homo Sapien 13
Hozay (USA). 1
Hubbly Bubbly (USA) 1
Husyan (USA). 3
Idiot's Delight 6
Ile De Chypre 2
Imperial Frontier (USA). . . . 1
Indian Ridge. 3
Infantry. 1
Insan (USA) 7
Interrex (CAN). 3
Invader General (IRE) 1
Invited (USA) 1
Jalmood (USA) 1
Jendali (USA) 5
Jeune Homme (USA) 1
Joligeneration 2
Jolly Jake (NZ) 5
Jumbo Hirt (USA). 1
Jupiter Island 7
Jurado (USA) 6
Kahyasi. 5
Kambalda. 3
Kamehameha (USA) 2
Karinga Bay 7
Karlinsky (USA) 4
Kasakov 1
King's Ride* 6
King Luthier 3
King Of Shannon. 1
King Persian 2
Kris. 1
Kuwait Beach (USA). 1
Kylian (USA). 1
Lafontaine (USA) 2
Lake Coniston (IRE) 1
Lancastrian. 6
Landyap (USA) 3
Lanfranco 1
Le Bavard (FR) 2
Le Coq D'Or 1
Le Moss 11
Le Nain Jaune (FR). 2
Le Pontet (FR) 2
Leading Counsel (USA). . . . 9
Liberated 1
Lighter 3
Lightning Dealer 1
Lir. 2
Little Bighorn 1
Little Wolf. 3
Long Leave 2
Lord Americo 9
Lord Bud 1
Luchiroverte (IRE). 1
Lute Antique (FR) 1
Lycius (USA). 1
Machiavellian (USA) 2
Majestic Light (USA). 2
Mandalus 9
Matahawk. 1
Matching Pair 1
Mazaad. 11
Meadowbrook 3
Meneval (USA) 1
Mesleh 1
Michelozzo (USA) 1
Milieu 1
Miner's Lamp 3
Minster Son 9
Mirror Boy 1
Missed Flight 2
Mister Lord (USA). 23
Montelimar (USA). 6
Moonax (IRE) 6
Morpeth 3
Moscow Society (USA) 4
Motivate 3
Move Off. 1
Mtoto 4
Mujadil (USA). 3
Muroto 1
Mystiko (USA). 3
Nalchik (USA). 1
Nearly A Hand 5
Needle Gun (IRE) 1
Neltino* 8
Nestor. 1
Neustrien (FR) 1
Never So Bold 1
Newski (USA). 1
Nicholas Bill. 1
Nikos 5
Niniski (USA) 2
Nishapour (FR). 4
Nomadic Way (USA). 15
Nomination. 1
North Col 7
Northern Crystal 1
Northern Park (USA). 1
Northern State (USA) 3
Norton Challenger. 1
Norwich 3
Octogenarian. 1
Old Vic 2
Opera Ghost 1
Orange Reef 5
Orchestra 2
Oscar (IRE). 4
Over The River (FR) 9
Pablond 5
Passing Sale (FR) 9
Past Glories 10
Perpendicular 4
Persian Mews 2
Perugino (USA). 2
Petoski 13
Phardante (FR). 37
Piccolo 1
Pistolet Bleu (IRE) 1
Pocketed (USA). 2
Polar Falcon (USA) 9
Polish Patriot (USA) 2
Polykratis 1
Positive Statement (USA)* . 1
Pragmatic 3
Presenting*. 17
Primitive Rising (USA) . . . 12

Sire	Count
Primo Dominie	1
Prince Daniel (USA)	1
Prince Of Birds (USA)	1
Prince Of Peace	2
Puget (USA)	1
Puissance*	2
Quai Voltaire (USA)	1
Quiet American (USA)	1
Ra Nova	1
Ragmar (FR)	1
Rainbow Quest (USA)	1
Rakaposhi King	24
Rashar (USA)	5
Relief Pitcher	2
Reprimand	2
Respect	1
Revoque (IRE)	1
Riberetto	2
Rich Charlie	1
Riverhead (USA)	1
Riverwise (USA)	1
Rock Hopper	1
Roi Guillaume (FR)	1
Rolfe (USA)	1
Romany Rye	1
Ron's Victory (USA)	2
Rontino	1
Roscoe Blake	8
Rose Laurel	4
Roselier (FR)	33
Royal Abjar (USA)	2
Royal Academy (USA)	5
Royal Applause	1
Royal Fountain	12
Royal Match	1
Royal Vulcan	1
Rubicund	1
Rushmere	1
Rymer	1
Sacrament	1
Saddlers' Hall (IRE)	4
Sadler's Wells (USA)	1
Safety Catch (USA)	1
Saint Cyrien (FR)	1
Salluceva	3
Salse (USA)	1
Sarpedon (FR)	1
Satco (FR)	4
Scallywag	7
Scenic	1
Scottish Reel	7
Sea Raven (IRE)	1
Seclude (USA)	2
Secret Of Success	1
Set Adrift	1
Seymour Hicks (FR)	1
Shaab	1
Shafoun (FR)	1
Shambo	1
Shardari	8
Sheer Grit	1
Shernazar	4
Shy Groom (USA)	1
Silly Prices	3
Silver Owl	1
Simply Great (FR)	2
Sir Harry Lewis (USA)	3
Sirsan (IRE)	1
Sizzling Melody	1
Ski Dancer	1
Slip Anchor	1
So Factual (USA)	1
Sousa	1
Southern Music	1
Sovereign Water (FR)	4
Spanish Place (USA)	1
Spectrum (IRE)	1
Sri Pekan (USA)	1
St Columbus	2
St Enodoc	1
St Hilarion (USA)	1
St Ninian	1
Stani (USA)	2
Start Fast (FR)	1
Step Together (USA)	6
Storm Bird (CAN)	1
Strong Gale	25
Suave Dancer (USA)	1
Sula Bula	11
Sulaafah (USA)	2
Sumayr	1
Sunley Builds	2
Sunny's Halo (CAN)	1
Supreme Leader	19
Sure Blade (USA)*	2
Sylvan Express	1
Symbolic	3
Synefos (USA)	5
Syrtos	2
Teamster	3
Teenoso (USA)	10
Terimon	11
The Bart (USA)	1
Then Again	2
Thethingaboutitis (USA)	3
Thowra (FR)	1
Tidaro (USA)	4
Tigerwood	2
Tina's Pet	8
Tirol	1
Top Ville	2
Torenaga	1
Torus	4
Toulon	3
Town And Country	1
Tragic Role (USA)	4
Treasure Hunter	2
Trempolino (USA)	2
Triune	3
Tropular	1
True Song	4
Turtle Island (IRE)	1
Un Desperado (FR)	3
Unblest	3
unknown	1
Useful (FR)	2
Valville (FR)	1
Vaquillo (USA)	1
Vasco (USA)	2
Video Rock (FR)	3
Vital Season	4
Waajib	1
Wace (USA)	2
Wakashan	1
War Hero	1
Warcraft (USA)	1
Warrshan (USA)	1
Watchman (NZ)	1
Weld	4
Weldnaas (USA)	1
Winter Words	1
Witness Box (USA)	5
Wonderful Surprise	3
Woodman (USA)	1
Yashgan	8
Young Man (FR)	1
Zaffaran (USA)	8
Zambrano	1

Most Prolific Winners 2004

** also winning Hunter Chaser in 2004*
*** also winning Point-to-Pointer in 2004*

POINT-TO-POINTS

Upton Adventure	8
Free Gift	6*
Vivid Imagination (IRE)	6
Ballysicyos (FR)	5
Bard Of Drumcoo (IRE)	5
Caught At Dawn (IRE)	5*
Lord Of The Mist (IRE)	5
Nautical Lad	5
Polar Champ	5
Rhythm King	5
Sandy Duff	5
Cedar Chief	4
Cimmaroon (IRE)	4
Decent Bond (IRE)	4
Father Tom (IRE)	4
Friar Waddon	4
High Peak	4
I Am Said I (IRE)	4
Killerine (FR)	4
Let's Fly (FR)	4
Lively Lord (IRE)	4
Madmidge	4
Oneminutetofive	4
Out The Black (IRE)	4
Passing Danger (FR)	4
Pharmistice (IRE)	4
Pristeen Spy	4
Red Neck	4
Rostock (IRE)	4
Royal Action	4
Sheriff's Friend (IRE)	4
Spring Gale (IRE)	4
Texas Ranger	4
The Wiley Kalmuck (IRE)	4
Agua Ardente	3
Aljoash (IRE)	3
Asthefellowsaid (IRE)	3
Balisteros (FR)	3
Ballad (IRE)	3
Bally Wirral (IRE)	3
Beauchamp Oracle	3
Bill Me Up (IRE)	3
Campden Kitty	3
Cannon Bridge (IRE)	3
Celtic Duke	3*
Chancy Guy	3
Claire's Nomad	3
Clifford Bay (IRE)	3
Colquhoun	3*
Coolefind (IRE)	3*
Crevamoy (IRE)	3
Dick McCarthy (IRE)	3
Dolphin Square (IRE)	3
Dumadic	3
Eastern Point	3*
Elegant Light	3
Endeavour (FR)	3
Father Mansfield (IRE)	3
Franco (IRE)	3
Freedom Fighter	3*
Gipsy Girl	3
Hadeqa	3
Harnage (IRE)	3
Highland Rose (IRE)	3
Hot Toddy (IRE)	3
Impatient Lady	3
Imps Way	3
Jackson (FR)	3
Jemaro (IRE)	3
Just Cliquot	3*
Khatani (IRE)	3
Lady Misprint	3
Like The Buzz (IRE)	3
Longville Lad	3
Macfin (IRE)	3
Miss O'Grady (IRE)	3
Mister Pepper (IRE)	3
Mister Ringa	3
More Flair	3
Mr Pendleberry	3
Mr Splodge	3
Questionaire	3
Rag Week (IRE)	3
Rip Kirby	3
Romany Move	3
Sapega (IRE)	3
Shanavogh	3
Shiny Bay (IRE)	3
Simply Sam	3
Sir William	3
Snowtre (IRE)	3
Sohapara	3*
Sovereign Gale (IRE)	3
Springford (IRE)	3*
Star Changes	3
Starbuck	3
State Medlar	3
Step And Run (IRE)	3
Supreme Citizen (IRE)	3
Tanager	3
Three Spires	3
Tom Cobbler (IRE)	3
Toujours (IRE)	3
Tricky Trevor (IRE)	3
Vinnie Boy (IRE)	3
What A Mover	3

HUNTER CHASES

Bohemian Spirit (IRE)	4
Kingston-Banker	4**
Lancastrian Jet (IRE)	4
Cantarinho	3**
Guignol Du Cochet (FR)	3**
Miss Mattie Ross	3
Mouseski	3**
Mullensgrove	3**
Nisbet	3
Bengal Bullet	2
Chasing The Bride	2**
County Derry	2
Earthmover (IRE)	2
Kestick	2**
Macgeorge (IRE)	2
Placid Man (IRE)	2**
Scottish Roots	2**
Torduff Express (IRE)	2

Leading Post-War Point-to-Point Riders

Leading riders since the war in order of total winning rides.(Accuracy is limited by the inadequacy of past records and wishful thinking)

D. Turner 345
Julian Pritchard* 326
Miss A. Dare 287
J. Llewellyn 270
Maj. G. Cunard 268
M. Felton 225
Miss P. Curling 220
F. Ryall 218
G. Cann 217
R. Alner 211
Miss P. Jones 201
J. Tarry* 198
E. Williams* 196
A. Crow* 194
T. Mitchell 185
J. Jukes 184
R. Burton* 179
R. Miller 178
P. Scholfield 178
J. Daniell 175
Mrs J. Sheppard 173
N. Bloom* 171
Mrs P. Tollit 171
R. Hacking 170
S.R. Andrews* 169
L. Jefford* 168
J. Sharp 167
P. Greenall 160
D. Jones* 159
R. Treloggen 157
A. Farrant 156
Miss P. Robson* 151
Miss P. Gundry* 149
S. Brookshaw 148
P. Hacking* 148
Mrs J. Dawson* 146
A. Sansome* 146
M. Bloom 145
Mrs S. Horton 145
T. Rooney 144
P. Hamer* 142
G. Hanmer* 137
A.E. Hill 136
R. Guilding 135
D. Tatlow 133
N. Tutty* 133
T. Stephenson* 131
P. Craggs* 130
A. Dalton 130
T. Jones 129
Miss S. Vickery 129
Mrs M. Hand* 128
Miss J. Pidgeon 126
G. Cooper* 125
J. Farthing 124
M. Williams (Wales) 124
Mrs S. French 119
Mrs J. Davies* 117
C. Gordon* 117
C. Down 116
P. Scouller 116
J. Bryan 115
K. Anderson 113
Mrs L. Gibbon 113
R. Greenway 113
W. Jones 113
I. McKie 112
C. Storey* 112
D. Wales 110
N. Harris* 109
T. Wilkin 109
M. Miller* 107
J. Newton 107
Col C. Spencer 107
S. Swiers* 107
R. Tate . . . . .107+
G. Maundrell* 106
N. Mitchell 106
M. Williams (Devon) 103
A. Charles-Jones* 101
C. Macmillan 101
D. Stephens (Wales) 101
P. York* 101
R. Edwards 100
R. Woolley 99
G. Barber 97
S. Crank 97
R. Davies 97
R. Hunt 97
T. Moore 97
Miss L. Blackford 96
T.S. Jeanes 95
Miss T. Cave* 94
A. Hill 94
J. Trice-Rolph* 93
W. Wales* 92
D. Gibson 91
F. Mathias 91
N. Bush 90
H. Wheeler 90
T. Holland-Martin 89
D. Duggan* 88
S. Morris 87
P. Taiano* 87
A. Wintle* 85
D. Barlow* 84
R. Chugg 84
W.G. Macmillan 83
W. Elliott 82
Miss P. Fisher 82
J. Price* 82
R. Shepherd 82
J. Walton* 82
A. Ulyet 81
A. Charlton 80
Mrs D. Chown 80
B. Pollock* 80
J. Dufosee 79
J. Hickman 79
Mrs F. Needham 79
A. Parker* 79
N. Wilson* 79
M. Arthers 78
A. Berry 78
R. Bloomfield 78
A. Hickman* 78
H. Cowell 77
T. McCarthy* 77
S. Sporborg 77
J. Frost 76
J. Docker 75
T. Greed* 75
M. Sowersby 75
W. Bryan 74
R. Cowell 74
Mrs M. Crouch 74
D. Kinsella 74
T. Philby 74
G. Turner 74
J. Tudor 73
Miss D. Calder* 72
Miss S. Morgan 72
P. Mathias 71
W. Shand-Kydd 71
P. Warren 71
W. Foulkes 70
R. Nuttall 70
H. Rowe 70
I. Widdicombe 70

Champion Point-to-Point Riders

GENTLEMEN

1946	A. Grantham	6
	H. May	6
	T. Southern	6
	R. Turner	6
1947	W. How	14
1948	Maj P. Rawlings	11
1949	Maj G. Cunard	20
1950	A. Hill	19
1951	Maj G. Cunard	12
1952	Maj G. Cunard	15
1953	Maj G. Cunard	13
1954	F. Ryall	13
	J. Trevisick	13
1955	J. Everitt	15
1956	E. Greenway	12
	F. Mathias	12
1957	Maj R. Ingall	14
1958	R. Edwards	12
	N. Williams	12
1959	D. Wales	16
1960	R. Edwards	14
	F. Ryall	14
1961	J. Daniell	16
1962	A.E. Hill	12
1963	Maj G. Cunard	15
1964	Maj G. Cunard	22
1965	D. Tatlow	18
1966	D. Tatlow	25
1967	D. Tatlow	24
1968	D. Tatlow	18
1969	M. Bloom	19
1970	D. Turner	19
1971	R. Davies	29
1972	R. Miller	21
1973	R. Miller	23
1974	D. Turner	26
1975	D. Turner	24
1976	D. Turner	22
1977	D. Turner	29
1978	J. Bryan	32
1979	D. Turner	17
1980	I. McKie	20
	D. Turner	20
1981	I. McKie	18
1982	P. Greenall	24
1983	J. Llewellyn	19
1984	D. Turner*	20
	P. Greenall	19
1985	P. Greenall	23
1986	P. Greenall	28
1987	M. Felton	26
1988	P. Scholfield	37
1989	M. Felton	26
1990	M. Felton	27
1991	J. Farthing	26
1992	R. Alner	31
1993	A. Crow	22
1994	N. Bloom	22
1995	A. Crow	30
1996	J. Jukes	34
1997	Julian Pritchard	37
1998	A. Dalton	33
	Julian Pritchard	33
1999	Julian Pritchard	43
2000	L. Jefford	42
2001	D. Dunsdon	5
	C. Gordon	5
	L. Jefford	5
2002	E. Williams**	38
	Julian Pritchard	37
2003	R. Burton	37
2004	A. Farrant	54

LADIES

1946	Miss I. Croxon	4
	Miss K. Tatham-Warter	4
1947	Miss A. Covell	5
	Miss M. Coke	5
1948	Miss K. Tatham-Warter	4
	Miss J. Brutton	4
1949	Miss K. Tatham-Warter	7
1950	Miss D. Brooke	8
1951	Miss P. Rushton	9
1952	Miss G. Moore	8
1953	Miss G. Moore	9
1954	Miss J. Renfree	7
1955	Miss J. Renfree	13
1956	Miss J. Renfree	11
1957	Mrs S. French	8
	Miss J. Renfree	8
1958	Miss D. Guilding	8
	Miss J. Renfree	8
1959	Mrs D. Coaker (nee Brooke)	12
1960	Mrs P. Tollit (nee Rushton)	9
1961	Miss F. Robarts	10
1962	Mrs P. Tollit (nee Rushton)	9
1963	Miss S. Rimell***	5
1964	Mrs P. Tollit (nee Rushton)	10
1965	Mrs P. Tollit (nee Rushton)	15
1966	Miss U. Brander-Dunbar	10
1967	Mrs P. Hinch	11
1968	Miss S. Aston	15
1969	Miss J. Turner	14
1970	Miss S. Aston	14
1971	Miss S. Aston	14
1972	Miss S. Aston	15
	Mrs P. Tollit (nee Rushton)	15
1973	Mrs M. Forrest	17
1974	Mrs J. Bothway (nee Turner)	20
1975	Mrs J. Bothway (nee Turner)	17
1976	Mrs J. Bothway (nee Turner)	17
1977	Mrs J. Shepherd (nee Turner)	17
1978	Mrs R. White	11
1979	Miss P. Fisher	10
1980	Miss L. King	14
1981	Miss L. King	14
1982	Miss J. Pidgeon	18
1983	Miss J. Pidgeon	18
1984	Miss M. Lingard	13
	Miss J. Pidgeon	13
1985	Miss J. Pidgeon	18
1986	Miss A. Dare	19
1987	Miss A. Dare	17
1988	Mrs J. Litston	16
1989	Miss L. Crow	15
1990	Miss A. Dare	20
1991	Miss A. Dare	26
1992	Miss A. Dare	21
1993	Miss P. Curling	25
1994	Miss P. Curling	35
1995	Miss P. Curling	40
1996	Miss A. Dare	31
1997	Miss S. Vickery	30
1998	Miss P. Jones	30
1999	Miss P. Jones	25
2000	Miss P. Gundry	30
2001	Miss P. Gundry	6
2002	Miss P. Gundry	20
2003	Miss P. Gundry	25
2004	Miss P. Gundry	26

** included 2 walk-overs (one contrived)*

*** included 3 walk-overs (one contrived)*

**** 11 Ladies each had 5 winners - Miss Rimell had the most 2nds*

Leading Riders 2004
Point-to-Point
Gentlemen

**winning Hunter Chase Rider 2004*

Jockey	1st	2nd	3rd	Career Wins
R. Burton*	50	15	8	179
P. York*	26	27	11	101
S. Morris*	19	9	18	87
R. Cope	18	22	8	56
Julian Pritchard	18	8	11	326
D. Jones*	16	14	11	159
G. Hanmer*	16	6	14	137
N. Williams*	15	16	1	38
C. Gordon	14	10	7	117
J. Owen	13	20	14	40
A. Charles-Jones	13	19	7	101
R. Woollacott*	13	16	11	55
M. Miller	13	7	6	107
D. Kemp*	13	4	3	27
G. Maundrell	12	4	2	106
G. Brewer*	11	16	6	41
T. Vaughan	11	13	8	69
James Tudor*	11	10	10	25
L. Stephens	11	10	2	24
J. Docker	11	8	7	57
D. Jacob*	10	5	1	10
R. Morgan*	9	11	6	56
N. Pearce*	9	9	9	16
M. Walford*	9	4	1	16
P. Cowley	9	2	10	23
N. Saville*	9	1	1	14
T. Stephenson	8	12	8	131
N. Tutty	8	12	7	133
A. Richardson	8	9	5	26
A. Merriam	8	6	3	15
A. Martin*	8	5	8	55
D. Alers-Hankey*	8	5	3	53
R. Green	8	3	4	29
N. Kent	8	2	5	24
C. Heard	7	9	8	66
J. Snowden*	7	8	8	22
N. Bloom	7	7	5	171
P. Hall	7	6	9	26
A. Hickman	7	5	4	78
J. Diment	7	3	1	20
H. Fry	7	3	1	9
T. Weston*	7	2	0	9
G. Barfoot-Saunt	6	10	5	57
M. Barber*	6	8	3	21
J. Cook	6	6	6	17
D. Phelan	6	6	3	9
P. Chinery	6	6	2	9
N. Harris*	6	5	6	109
L. Jefford	6	5	5	168
R. Stephens	6	5	3	9
M. Mackley	6	5	2	40
D. Barlow	6	4	2	84
G. Cooper	6	3	5	125
K. Anderson	6	3	3	119
E. Williams*	6	3	0	196
N. Tinkler	6	2	3	18
T. Greenall*	6	2	2	14
D. McKenna	6	0	3	11
A. Wintle	5	11	6	85
A. Wadlow	5	10	8	9
C. Storey	5	10	4	112
D. Edwards*	5	9	9	22
L. Heard	5	7	6	11
F. Hutsby	5	7	4	48
N. Mitchell*	5	6	4	106
Richard Darke	5	6	3	57
N. Wilmington	5	6	2	7
A. Braithwaite	5	5	3	18
L. Bates*	5	4	3	24
L. Morgan*	5	4	2	39
R. Hughes	5	3	2	5
Stuart Robinson	5	3	2	24
N. Oliver	5	2	3	14
J. Barnes	5	3	1	32
T. Lane	5	2	8	40
H. Dowty	5	2	4	9

Ladies

Jockey	1st	2nd	3rd	Career Wins
Miss P. Gundry	26	17	15	149
Miss A. Goschen*	15	13	11	68
Miss J. Williams	14	3	2	26
Miss E. James	13	2	2	38
Miss P. Robson	12	4	4	151
Miss Z. Turner*	11	4	3	55
Miss L. Gardner*	9	5	11	39
Miss T. Cave*	9	4	6	94
Miss R. Green	9	4	5	15
Miss N. Stirling	9	4	4	29
Miss F. Wilson	9	3	8	23
Miss M. McCarthy	8	4	2	11
Miss H. Irving	8	1	5	53
Miss S. Brotherton*	7	3	2	32
Miss C. Tizzard	6	11	4	22
Miss J. Foster	6	10	7	34
Miss R. Davidson	6	7	6	7
Miss C. Prouse	6	4	1	9
Ms A. Embiricos*	6	0	6	44
Miss Gemma Hutchinson	5	6	2	13
Miss C. Roddick	5	1	0	10
Miss T. Clark	5	5	9	16
Mrs C. Owen	5	3	2	8
Miss S. Sharratt	4	9	6	29
Miss C. Stucley*	4	6	3	19
Mrs J. Gordon	4	5	3	40
Miss S. Gaisford	4	4	7	18
Ms L. Stock	4	3	1	14
Miss H. Lewis	4	2	1	13
Miss Rachel Clark	4	0	3	5
Mrs M. Hand	3	5	2	128
Miss A. de Lisle Wells	3	5	1	9
Miss I. Tompsett	3	4	3	5
Mrs S. Ashby	3	3	1	28
Miss J. Riding*	3	3	1	4
Miss S. Young	3	2	6	62
Mrs A. Rucker	3	2	3	33
Mrs J. Reed	3	2	1	7
Miss L. Allen	3	1	5	14
Mrs P. Hall	3	1	4	7
Mrs S. Godfrey	3	1	1	11
Miss E. Jones	3	0	2	22
Miss R. Goodwin	3	0	1	5
Miss D. Harding*	3	0	1	16
Miss N. Lloyd	3	0	1	3
Miss C. Hurley	3	0	0	4

Hunter Chase Riders

*** winning Point-to-Point Rider 2004*

Jockey	1st	2nd	3rd	Career Wins
N. Williams**	9	3	0	11
Miss A. Goschen**	6	3	1	15
M. Barber**	6	2	2	6
T. Greenall**	5	7	2	8
T. Dreaper**	5	0	1	5
N. Harris**	4	1	5	18
Miss T. Cave**	4	0	0	6
S. Charlton**	4	0	0	4
G. Tuer**	3	4	1	15
N. Saville**	3	3	2	3
Miss S. Phizacklea**	3	2	2	4
M. McAlister**	3	1	0	4
D. Kemp**	3	0	0	4
Miss C. Stucley**	2	2	0	2
J. Jenkins**	2	1	2	2
M. Seston	2	1	1	2
R. Morgan**	2	1	0	6
Miss J. Riding**	2	1	0	2
S. Morris**	2	0	3	10
D. Mansell**	2	0	1	9
C. Mulhall**	2	0	0	10
James Tudor**	2	0	0	3

Winning & Placed Point-to-Point Riders 2004

** Winning Hunter Chase Rider 2004*

Rider	No Rides	No Wins	Winning and Placed Rides
R. Abrahams	9	**2**	F, (1289), (1292), 1304^2.
D. Alers-Hankey *	33	**8**	(9), 13^3, (14), (30), 145^3, (232), (576), (598), (825), 878^2, 961^2, 1016^2, (1100), 1183^3, 1252^2, 1384^2.
R. Alers-Hankey	7	**1**	(809), 1457^2.
J. Alexander	12	**1**	659^2, 765^3, 768^2, (1081), 1222^2.
M. Alexander	1	**0**	1076^2.
Miss L. Allan	16	**3**	(126), (373), 522^3, 555^3, 593^2, (743), 987^3, 1058^3, 1399^3.
T. Allanson	3	**1**	(1200).
Miss C. Allen	2	**1**	(620).
Miss L. Allfrey	9	**0**	1137^2, 1253^2.
K. Anderson	32	**6**	(72), 214^2, 283^2, 426^3, (510), 548^2, 657^3, (764), (858), (1421), (1422), 1479^3.
P. Andrew	21	**0**	4^3.
Mrs C. Andrews	4	**0**	155^2, 807^2.
G. Armitage	4	**0**	266^3, 390^3, 958^2.
Miss A. Armitage *	18	**1**	160^2, 270^3, 395^2, 682^3, 772^2, 1160^3, (1165), 1459^3.
R. Armson	55	**4**	370^2, 384^2, 387^3, 560^3, 595^3, (789), 942^3, (944), 985^3, (1056), 1118^2, 1119^2, 1123^2, 1402^3, 1424^2, (1500), 1503^2, 1505^3.
F. Arthur	8	**1**	(553).
Mrs S. Ashby	9	**3**	184^2, 421^3, (536), 641^2, (807), (1053), 1283^2.
Miss R. Athay	2	**0**	739^3.
M. Atkinson	11	**2**	(121), (236).
Miss C. Atkinson	7	**0**	276^3, 862^2, 1446^3.
P. Atkinson	9	**1**	(429), 433^2, 1291^2.
T. Atkinson	4	**1**	474^3, 693^2, 1009^2, (1252).
Mrs K. Baimbridge	18	**2**	726^2, 756^2, 816^3, (977), 1072^2, (1340).
Miss D. Ball	6	**1**	1033^3, (1278).
Miss J. Balmer	12	**1**	(508), 550^3, 914^2, 1221^3, 1420^3.
R. Bandey	15	**0**	868^3, 1335^2.
M. Barber *	60	**6**	147^3, 203^2, 208^2, 448^2, (669), 670^2, 676^2, 842^3, (947), (1023), (1092), 1095^2, 1096^2, (1188), 1486^3, 1488^2, (1547).
Mrs R. Barclay	3	**0**	687^3, 1383^2.
G. Barfoot-Saunt	62	**6**	35^2, 308^3, 409^2, (451), 618^2, 667^3, 723^3, (725), 728^2, 758^3, (760), 816^2, (818), (1070), 1138^3, (1139), 1140^2, 1484^2, 1530^2, 1532^2, 1559^2.
A. Barlow	7	**1**	16^3, (47), 170^3, 288^2.
C. Barlow	10	**0**	256^3.
D. Barlow	27	**6**	251^2, (526), 660^3, 665^2, (932), (1048), 1049^2, (1144), (1265), 1266^3, 1339^2, (1469).
J.R. Barlow	10	**1**	(1142), 1261^3.
J. Barnard	6	**1**	(182), 806^3.
J. Barnes	43	**5**	145^2, (414), 598^2, 1007^3, (1066), (1128), 1184^2, (1257), (1325).
Miss N. Barnes	14	**1**	23^3, 155^3, (249).
Miss L. Barrett-Nobbs	18	**2**	(22), 28^3, 399^2, 401^2, 559^3, (560), 745^2.
Miss C. Bartlett	7	**1**	652^2, 1155^3, (1405).
L. Bates *	43	**5**	(164), 267^2, (338), (565), 775^2, 813^3, 956^3, (960), (1162), 1202^3, 1412^2, 1474^2.
A. Bealby	4	**1**	106^2, (228).
Miss S. Beddoes *	14	**1**	(96), 664^2, 998^3.
A. Beedles	15	**1**	95^3, 229^3, 231^3, (1109).
Miss E. Bell	4	**0**	1241^2.
N. Bell	6	**0**	680^2, 943^2, 990^2, 1152^3.
J. Benfield	3	**0**	924^3, 1401^3.

Rider	Rides	Wins	Races
I. Bennett	1	**1**	(1455).
M. Bennison	13	**1**	594^{3}, 810^{2}, 1305^{2}, (1458).
Miss C. Benstead	8	**1**	(645), 1083^{3}.
N. Benstead	8	**0**	897^{2}, 1208^{2}.
Miss H. Bethell	1	**1**	(876).
Miss J. Bevin	7	**0**	885^{2}.
W. Biddick	25	**2**	414^{3}, 416^{2}, 489^{2}, (1130), 1198^{2}, (1556).
T. Bishop *	14	**3**	116^{3}, (193), 471^{2}, 472^{3}, (603), 880^{2}, (1065), 1101^{2}, 1130^{2}.
S. Blackwell	10	**0**	403^{2}, 452^{3}.
P. Blagg	14	**2**	180^{2}, 1054^{3}, 1211^{3}, 1212^{3}, (1404), (1410).
Miss A. Blake	5	**0**	847^{2}.
R. Bliss	45	**3**	15^{3}, (329), 337^{3}, 469^{2}, 473^{3}, 474^{2}, 695^{3}, 1022^{3}, (1097), 1181^{2}, (1182).
N. Bloom	40	**7**	(38), 129^{2}, 152^{3}, 154^{3}, (156), 219^{3}, 224^{2}, 245^{2}, 248^{2}, 386^{2}, 521^{3}, 647^{3}, (648), 886^{2}, (996), (1150), (1151), (1155), 1313^{2}.
Miss R. Booth	3	**1**	(351), 690^{3}.
Miss A. Bowles	15	**0**	22^{3}, 525^{3}, 904^{2}.
Miss N. Brady	1	**1**	(984).
A. Braithwaite	41	**5**	(1), (23), 27^{2}, 38^{2}, 40^{3}, 99^{2}, 397^{2}, (401), (524), 557^{3}, 646^{2}, 648^{3}, (741).
G. Brewer *	73	**11**	163^{2}, 269^{2}, (303), (340), 344^{2}, 393^{2}, 395^{3}, 480^{2}, 481^{2}, 482^{2}, 500^{2}, 503^{2}, (504), 591^{2}, (594), 596^{3}, (597), 684^{2}, 773^{3}, (810), (954), 957^{2}, (958), 990^{3}, 1162^{2}, 1204^{3}, (1206), (1217), (1304), 1414^{3}, 1456^{2}, 1460^{2}, 1500^{2}.
Miss L. Bridges *	15	**2**	175^{2}, 234^{3}, (633), (860), 864^{3}, 1097^{2}, 1099^{2}.
M. Briggs	14	**2**	130^{3}, (304), 680^{3}, (946), 1157^{2}.
D. Brightling	11	**0**	534^{3}.
S. Brodie	1	**0**	1199^{2}.
Miss L. Brooke	16	**1**	515^{2}, 668^{3}, (1341).
Miss S. Brotherton *	20	**7**	(266), (395), 563^{3}, 564^{2}, 811^{2}, (1040), (1160), (1287), 1290^{2}, (1415), 1458^{3}, (1459).
A. Brown	13	**1**	249^{3}, 403^{3}, (1120), 1429^{3}.
Mrs J. Brown	5	**0**	1157^{3}, 1292^{3}, 1417^{3}.
R. Brown	6	**1**	285^{2}, (547).
Miss K. Bryson	7	**0**	283^{3}, 1040^{3}, 1077^{3}.
Miss J. Buck	21	**1**	(881), 1352^{2}, 1449^{3}, 1561^{3}.
F. Buckett	1	**0**	169^{3}.
F. Buckettt	1	**1**	(21).
Miss S. Buckley	7	**1**	54^{2}, (500), 1058^{2}, 1399^{2}.
P. Bull	38	**4**	39^{2}, (180), 419^{2}, 423^{3}, (539), 605^{3}, 606^{2}, 607^{2}, 802^{3}, 898^{2}, 900^{2}, (1083), 1085^{2}, 1281^{2}, (1282), 1284^{2}, 1411^{3}.
W. Burnell	16	**0**	505^{2}.
Miss E. Burrows	4	**0**	498^{3}.
R. Burton *	139	**50**	(20), 37^{2}, (39), (41), (91), 97^{3}, 125^{2}, (127), (169), 227^{2}, (254), (256), 259^{3}, (292), (372), (374), (375), 381^{2}, (382), (383), (387), 462^{2}, (463), (467), 527^{2}, 528^{2}, (662), (665), 667^{2}, 710^{2}, (713), (749), (752), (754), (851), (852), (928), 929^{2}, 932^{2}, (986), (988), (990), (1015), 1045^{3}, 1047^{2}, (1113), (1145), (1149), (1205), 1228^{3}, (1231), (1232), (1260), (1262), (1264), (1266), 1339^{3}, 1342^{3}, (1366), 1395^{2}, (1424), (1425), 1426^{2}, (1449), (1456), 1471^{2}, (1496), (1524), (1528), (1529), 1530^{3}, (1531), 1550^{3}.
Miss A. Bush	8	**0**	826^{2}, 1186^{3}, 1380^{2}.
Mrs D. Caine	5	**0**	874^{3}, 1147^{2}.
P. Callaghan	12	**1**	86^{3}, (367), 662^{2}, 1427^{2}.
Miss H. Campbell	5	**0**	479^{3}, 682^{2}.
Miss J. Campbell	1	**0**	653^{2}.
Miss A. Cavanagh	4	**0**	356^{3}.

Rider	Rides	Wins	Races
Miss T. Cave *	43	**9**	(76), (82), 198^3, 199^3, 276^2, 314^3, 315^2, (323), 351^3, 353^2, (568), 573^3, (740), (791), (911), (1002), 1195^2, (1271), 1433^3.
I. Chanin	3	**1**	1005^2, (1383).
Mrs J. Chapman	5	**0**	757^3, 815^2, 1344^3, 1483^2.
A. Charles-Jones	97	**13**	8^2, (141), 143^2, (170), (174), 196^2, 306^2, (309), 310^2, 321^2, 329^2, 366^2, 423^2, (469), (472), 497^3, (572), 573^2, 604^3, 632^2, (727), 792^2, 912^2, 1003^2, (1006), 1066^2, (1272), 1326^2, (1327), 1331^2, 1369^3, 1379^3, 1381^2, 1384^3, (1432), (1435), 1511^2, 1540^3, 1565^3.
S. Charlton *	23	**1**	(297), 302^2, 592^2, 1161^3, 1300^3.
P. Chinery	32	**6**	23^2, (45), (155), (243), 249^2, 400^2, (523), 524^2, 610^2, 901^3, 902^2, (906), 1087^3, (1088).
Mrs E. Chugg	5	**0**	31^2, 1056^3.
Miss Rachel Clark	31	**4**	164^3, (299), (301), (477), 500^3, (1157), 1303^3.
Miss T. Clark	34	**5**	161^2, 226^3, 228^3, 380^3, 531^2, 708^2, 712^2, 715^3, (849), (985), 1019^3, (1046), 1048^3, (1049), (1148), 1229^2, 1343^3, 1426^3, 1430^3.
R. Clark	31	**0**	55^3, 161^3, 167^3, 776^2, 959^2, 1158^2, 1301^3.
S. Clark	4	**1**	1076^3, (1474).
Miss A. Clifford	2	**1**	(967).
I. Clyde	10	**2**	532^3, 749^3, (848), (1043).
D. Coates	9	**2**	163^3, 501^2, 750^2, (873), 875^2, (1201).
M. Cobbald	1	**1**	(1312).
T. Coles	7	**1**	(378), 681^2, 942^2, 1218^3, 1402^2.
N. Collier	1	**0**	84^2.
P. Collins	4	**1**	(394).
R. Collinson	16	**1**	378^3, 745^3, (945).
Miss L. Coney	7	**0**	299^3, 380^2, 1122^3, 1216^2.
Miss J. Congdon	7	**1**	(144).
D. Cook	5	**0**	1116^2.
J. Cook	39	**6**	362^2, (514), 674^3, (675), (845), 947^2, 1021^3, (1022), 1089^3, 1093^2, 1188^3, 1190^3, 1524^3, 1525^2, 1534^2, (1539), (1552), 1553^2.
G. Cooper	23	**6**	2^3, 27^3, 124^2, 217^3, (248), (250), 607^3, (610), 742^3, 778^2, (828), (901), (902), 1246^2.
R. Cope	86	**18**	17^2, 19^2, 21^3, 30^2, 56^2, 124^3, 169^2, (172), (218), 219^2, (291), (294), (296), 371^2, 374^2, 386^3, (462), (465), (466), 467^2, 592^3, 597^2, 648^2, 650^2, 652^3, 685^2, 686^2, 783^2, 786^2, (787), 885^3, (886), 887^2, (889), 1057^3, (1059), 1060^2, 1061^2, (1071), (1123), 1214^2, 1215^2, (1338), 1396^2, (1402), (1473), 1500^3, (1503).
A. Corbett	6	**1**	(995), 1245^2.
Mrs S. Corcoran	6	**1**	(1099).
P. Cornforth	16	**2**	(774), 814^3, (1042), 1288^3, 1398^3.
Miss J. Coward	14	**2**	(162), 339^2, (390), 502^2.
Miss C. Cowe	18	**0**	719^2, 969^2, 971^3, 1404^2.
P. Cowley	60	**9**	99^3, (103), (105), 187^3, (252), 255^3, (288), 291^3, (385), (582), 583^3, (681), 746^3, 783^3, 784^3, 890^2, (1031), 1032^3, 1121^2, 1125^3, (1273).
Miss G. Craggs	5	**0**	1310^3.
A. Crow	3	**1**	93^3, (531).
G. Crow	3	**0**	216^2, 431^3.
P. Crozier	1	**1**	(1387).
C. Cundall	9	**0**	372^3, 1460^3.
R. Cundy	3	**1**	(646).
Miss K. Cuthbertson	7	**0**	1098^2.
C. Dailly	7	**0**	636^3, 1070^3.
Miss J. Dallow	1	**0**	461^2.
Richard Darke	37	**5**	(200), 313^2, 315^3, (320), 327^2, (491), (705), 827^3, 908^2, (910), 1002^2, 1272^3, 1433^2, 1545^2.

Rider		Wins	Races
Miss R. Davidson	30	**6**	(69), 133^{3}, (135), 213^{3}, 284^{2}, 428^{3}, (548), 550^{2}, (655), 763^{3}, 854^{2}, (857), 916^{2}, 918^{3}, 1078^{2}, 1221^{2}, 1308^{3}, 1476^{2}, (1478).
D. Davies	12	**1**	1239^{3}, 1394^{3}, 1547^{2}, (1553).
Miss A. Davies	1	**0**	1187^{2}.
Miss S. Davies	14	**0**	1064^{3}, 1137^{3}.
J. Davis	10	**0**	394^{3}, 877^{2}, 1165^{3}.
C. Dawson	38	**3**	342^{2}, 343^{3}, 432^{3}, 433^{3}, 597^{3}, (767), (920), (1288).
D. Dennis	23	**3**	(260), 424^{3}, 720^{2}, (968), 973^{3}, (1349).
M. Dennis	9	**0**	1351^{2}.
T. Dennis	43	**3**	82^{3}, (195), 566^{2}, 791^{3}, (823), 909^{2}, 912^{3}, 1133^{3}, 1196^{3}, 1267^{3}, (1378), 1435^{2}.
R. Dickson	8	**1**	(1480).
Mrs K. Diggle	11	**2**	230^{2}, (712), 874^{2}, (1146), 1263^{2}.
J. Diment	26	**7**	(26), 95^{2}, (130), (684), 938^{2}, (940), (999), 1057^{2}, 1151^{3}, (1400), (1403).
G. Disney	9	**1**	32^{2}, 191^{2}, 383^{2}, (636), 1400^{2}.
J. Docker	60	**11**	(106), 128^{2}, 168^{2}, 223^{3}, 300^{3}, (379), 381^{3}, (386), 387^{2}, (480), 481^{3}, 596^{2}, (686), 746^{2}, (786), (942), (943), 944^{2}, 945^{2}, 999^{3}, (1057), (1060), 1120^{3}, (1124), 1401^{2}, 1469^{3}.
N. Docker	29	**2**	(298), 303^{2}, 383^{3}, 477^{3}, 1104^{2}, (1397).
Miss B. Donnelly	20	**1**	45^{2}, 220^{2}, 536^{2}, (540), 897^{3}.
H. Dowty	35	**5**	(50), 107^{3}, (369), (404), 666^{3}, (723), 755^{2}, (816), 981^{2}, 1258^{3}, 1341^{3}.
D. Drake	20	**0**	235^{2}, 580^{3}, 938^{3}, 1100^{3}.
T. Dreaper *	20	**1**	11^{3}, 12^{2}, (35), 89^{3}, 233^{3}, 261^{3}, 352^{3}, 1100^{2}.
Miss S. Duckett	6	**1**	462^{3}, (588), 637^{3}, 1276^{3}.
D. Dunsdon	12	**2**	102^{2}, (158), 250^{2}, 538^{3}, (1492).
T. Eades	5	**2**	(4), (471).
Miss L. Eddery	6	**2**	5^{2}, 55^{2}, 477^{2}, (957), (1501).
Miss K. Edminson	4	**0**	593^{3}, 1286^{2}.
D. Edwards *	68	**5**	(114), 117^{2}, (119), 148^{3}, 197^{2}, (273), 279^{2}, 307^{3}, 319^{3}, 493^{3}, 633^{2}, 706^{3}, (884), 1132^{2}, 1180^{2}, 1182^{3}, 1185^{3}, 1186^{2}, 1269^{3}, 1272^{2}, 1328^{3}, (1511), 1540^{2}.
T. Edwards	9	**2**	(31), 158^{2}, (755), 844^{2}.
Miss L. Ellis	3	**1**	(1104).
T. Ellis	40	**1**	294^{2}, (295), 466^{2}, 532^{2}, 651^{3}, 787^{3}, 837^{3}, 925^{2}, 1124^{2}, 1275^{3}, 1276^{2}.
B. Elson	6	**0**	888^{2}.
Ms A Embiricos *	19	**6**	(25), (98), 101^{3}, 127^{3}, (157), 158^{3}, (558), 649^{3}, (745), (998), 1154^{3}, 1397^{3}.
D. England	12	**0**	514^{2}, 1335^{3}.
H. Evans	8	**1**	(948), 950^{3}.
Miss C. Evans	9	**0**	1566^{2}.
S. Evans	2	**1**	(698).
D. Evatt	2	**0**	638^{3}.
A. Farrant	130	**54**	2^{2}, (34), 36^{2}, (61), 66^{2}, (68), (77), 79^{2}, 119^{3}, (145), (148), (194), 195^{2}, (198), (277), (310), (313), (314), (315), (318), (319), 324^{2}, 328^{2}, 412^{3}, 414^{2}, 485^{2}, (486), (487), (488), (489), (494), 495^{3}, 496^{3}, (498), (567), (569), 689^{2}, (691), (692), (693), 770^{2}, 771^{3}, 823^{2}, (824), (825), (962), 963^{3}, (964), 966^{3}, 1009^{3}, (1010), (1013), 1065^{2}, (1069), 1128^{2}, 1129^{3}, (1131), (1181), (1183), (1185), (1269), 1270^{2}, 1328^{2}, (1330), (1331), 1348^{2}, 1349^{2}, 1367^{3}, (1369), 1379^{2}, (1380), (1381), (1384), (1385), (1445), (1446), (1447), (1463), 1494^{2}, 1508^{3}, 1510^{2}, (1540), (1541), (1545), (1555), 1556^{2}, (1557), 1560^{2}, .
T. Faulkner	43	**3**	202^{3}, 447^{3}, 453^{3}, 672^{3}, 841^{2}, 844^{3}, (1095), 1139^{3}, 1238^{3}, 1481^{2}, 1482^{3}, (1488), (1537).
Miss L. Fear	8	**1**	(1156).

Rider	Rides	Wins	Placings
A. Findlay	39	**4**	136^2, 214^3, (287), (506), 507^3, (656), 766^2, (856), 915^2, 1224^3, 1225^2, 1475^3, 1480^2.
Miss V. Flood	6	**1**	138^2, (336), 457^3, 819^3.
N. Fogg	1	**0**	984^2.
A. Foster	9	**1**	(935).
Miss J. Foster	44	**6**	(55), 213^2, 270^2, 299^2, 338^3, 391^3, (502), 504^3, (564), 709^3, 714^2, (811), (1158), 1201^2, 1206^3, 1290^3, 1300^2, 1303^2, 1304^3, 1415^2, (1420), 1459^2, 1469^2.
H. Fowler *	43	**3**	22^2, 172^2, 173^2, 396^3, 557^2, 587^2, 744^2, 832^3, 980^2, (1035), (1242), (1389).
Miss E. Freeman	1	**0**	935^2.
G. Freeney	2	**0**	1242^2.
Miss A. Frieze	5	**0**	1536^2.
G. Fry	4	**1**	862^3, (1012).
H. Fry	25	**7**	(65), (79), (120), 147^2, (460), (577), 603^2, 687^2, (689), (794), 1386^3.
Miss S. Gaisford	31	**4**	(83), 314^2, 411^3, (488), 491^2, 570^2, 702^3, 704^3, 705^3, 910^3, 911^3, 913^2, 1006^3, (1195), (1433).
J. Galbraith	9	**1**	547^2, (1038), 1040^2.
B. Gallagher	6	**0**	976^2.
G. Gallagher	14	**0**	803^3, 1088^3.
Miss L. Gardner *	70	**9**	61^3, 62^3, 76^2, 197^3, (275), 311^2, 321^3, (354), (484), (573), 703^3, 793^3, 823^3, (826), 907^3, 911^2, 1128^3, (1134), (1194), 1197^2, 1269^2, 1271^3, (1434), (1509), 1542^3.
Mrs C. Gardner	1	**0**	872^2.
Miss G. Garton	5	**0**	748^3, 1045^2, 1147^3.
S. Gibbon	5	**0**	1286^3.
Miss W. Gibson	11	**1**	162^2, 508^3, 564^3, 766^3, (874).
F de Giles	7	**1**	(1067).
T. Glass	31	**3**	165^3, 166^2, 167^2, 271^3, (773), (775), 1159^3, 1288^2, (1412).
A. Glassonbury	36	**4**	309^3, (312), (702), 907^2, (1001), (1196), 1200^3, 1268^2, 1370^3, 1435^3, 1543^2.
Miss S. Gledson	6	**0**	548^3.
Mrs S. Godfrey	13	**3**	(474), 689^3, (1008), 1013^2, (1508).
W. Goldie	20	**1**	(286), 506^2, 511^2, 653^3, 917^3.
M. Goldstein	20	**0**	110^3, 229^2, 406^3, 465^3, 661^2, 758^2, 837^2, 979^2, 1138^2, 1140^3, 1273^2, 1319^3.
Miss C. Goodall	1	**0**	225^2.
Miss R. Goodwin	8	**3**	(461), (719), 867^3, (969).
S. Gordon-Watson	10	**0**	574^2.
C. Gordon	51	**14**	38^3, (44), 181^2, (183), 185^2, (186), 332^3, (418), (419), 424^2, 605^2, (606), (607), (611), (644), 645^2, 717^2, 782^2, (803), 806^2, 895^2, (896), (1051), 1052^3, (1087), 1209^3, (1335), 1405^3, 1409^3, 1518^3, 1565^2, .
Mrs J. Gordon	26	**4**	18^3, (537), 608^2, 639^3, (781), 805^3, (899), 1053^2, 1086^2, 1207^2, 1407^2, (1411).
M. Gorman *	12	**1**	3^2, 16^2, 100^3, (422), 638^2, 1410^3.
Miss A. Goschen *	68	**15**	(13), 33^2, (63), 68^2, (184), 234^2, 237^2, 322^3, 325^3, 329^3, 335^2, 337^2, (350), 351^2, 353^3, 354^2, (413), (457), 459^2, (574), 625^2, 641^3, 718^2, (721), (757), 860^3, 863^2, (864), 865^3, (973), 1004^3, 1098^3, 1099^3, (1102), 1210^2, 1368^3, (1462), (1491), (1564).
S. Graham	17	**0**	615^2.
J. Grantham	1	**1**	(84).
Miss H. Gray	2	**0**	506^3.
Miss T. Gray	5	**1**	(1301).
S. Gray	23	**1**	292^3, 358^2, (836), 1226^3.
K. Green	8	**1**	304^3, 946^2, 1397^2, (1505).
M. Green	5	**0**	238^3, 600^3.

Rider	Rides	Wins	Races
Miss R. Green	33	**9**	(10), 88^2, (234), (322), (353), 470^2, (578), 635^3, (690), 864^2, 961^3, (1197), (1368), 1448^3, 1450^2, 1557^3, 1559^3, (1560).
R. Green	27	**8**	74^2, (134), (285), (554), 657^2, (658), (854), 855^3, (1077), (1220), 1222^3, 1309^2, 1418^3, 1421^3, (1476).
Richard Green	4	**0**	24^2, 32^3, 331^2.
O. Greenall	8	**2**	405^3, (769), 1264^2, (1530).
T. Greenall *	17	**6**	(302), 304^2, (341), (344), 499^3, (501), (503), 769^2, 772^3, (1216).
G. Greenock	2	**1**	(830), 1153^2.
D. Greenway	32	**1**	929^3, 933^3, (1202), 1262^2, 1266^2.
Miss H. Grissell	11	**0**	608^3, 805^2, 998^2, 1050^2, 1244^3, 1407^3.
Miss P. Gundry	104	**26**	1^2, (2), 10^2, 12^2, 13^2, 14^3, 30^3, (48), (51), (86), (87), (116), (118), 139^3, 140^3, 142^3, (143), (146), 149^3, 193^3, 199^2, 238^2, (255), (307), 313^3, (403), (485), 486^2, (496), 601^2, (602), 604^2, (635), 637^2, (722), 725^2, 727^3, (728), 743^2, (790), 795^3, 822^3, (923), (925), (926), 980^3, 982^2, (1063), 1064^2, 1066^3, (1072), 1254^2, 1327^2, (1379), (1382), 1445^2, 1472^3, 1551^3.
G. Haines	1	**0**	98^3.
J. Haley	4	**0**	300^2.
Mrs P. Hall	10	**3**	(18), 126^2, (608), (641), 899^3, 1053^3, 1210^3, 1283^3.
P. Hall	43	**7**	44^3, 100^2, (129), 186^3, (420), 535^3, 537^3, 540^2, (605), 609^2, 780^2, 782^3, (898), 900^3, 996^3, (1052), 1055^2, (1084), (1281), 1284^3, 1406^3, 1410^2.
I. Hambley	21	**0**	327^3, 486^3, 824^3, 909^3, 1200^2.
Mrs A. Hamilton *	6	**1**	(916), 1078^3.
M. Hammond	13	**0**	850^2, 1074^3.
Mrs M. Hand	20	**3**	483^2, 567^2, 570^3, (707), 793^2, (822), (907), 1194^3, 1434^2, 1542^2.
J. Handley	12	**0**	753^2, 928^2, 1427^3.
A. Hanly	35	**0**	207^2, 517^2, 519^2, 619^3, 788^3, 1233^3, 1340^2, 1553^3.
G. Hanmer *	80	**16**	(97), (161), (226), 467^3, 530^3, 531^3, (612), (617), (619), 663^2, 708^3, (710), (711), (715), (748), 749^2, (750), 851^2, (930), 932^3, (933), 986^3, 988^3, 1043^2, (1045), 1073^3, (1075), 1142^3, 1144^3, 1148^2, 1206^2, 1217^3, 1340^3, 1424^3, (1430), 1528^3.
Miss E. Harbour	12	**0**	171^2, 289^3, 622^3, 866^3.
Miss D. Harding *	6	**3**	(117), 232^3, (459), (1249).
J. Harris	4	**0**	1523^2.
M. Harris	33	**4**	43^3, (142), 151^2, 601^3, 660^2, 867^2, 977^2, (1014), (1019), 1135^2, 1274^2, 1279^2, (1398), 1450^3.
N. Harris *	24	**6**	64^3, 140^2, 143^3, (196), 275^3, 413^2, (415), 471^3, 576^3, 634^3, (637), 790^2, 1102^2, (1326), 1398^2, (1494), (1558).
Miss T. Harrison	6	**0**	407^3, 1203^3.
Miss F. Hartley	7	**1**	(1303), 1501^3.
D. Harvey	15	**0**	334^3, 1134^3.
R. Hawker	8	**1**	(197), 364^3, 1181^3.
Miss L. Hawkings	9	**0**	78^2, 794^3.
Miss C. Haydon	5	**0**	45^3.
Miss T. Hayes	5	**0**	1329^2, 1506^2, 1554^3.
P. Haynes	6	**0**	1115^2.
T. Haynes	4	**0**	1387^3.
Miss V. Heal	10	**1**	350^3, 603^3, 1012^2, (1101), 1492^2.
C. Heard	55	**7**	(80), 82^2, 83^2, 144^2, 200^2, 277^3, 306^3, 307^2, 312^3, (366), (483), 485^3, 568^3, 569^2, 704^2, (796), 821^2, 826^3, (1184), (1268), 1367^2, 1434^3, 1463^3, (1510).
L. Heard	50	**5**	80^3, 83^3, 114^2, (306), 494^3, 566^3, 701^3, 827^2, 1006^2, (1132), (1267), (1348), 1382^2, 1432^2, 1463^2, 1544^3, 1555^2, (1565).
Mrs S. Heath	2	**0**	63^3.

Rider	Rides	Wins	Races
N. Heath	6	**0**	14^2, 65^2.
Mrs J. Hedley	3	**0**	1423^3.
P. Hemmings	4	**0**	709^2.
M. Heuff	4	**0**	114^3.
C. Heywood	2	**0**	150^3, 328^3.
Miss N. Hickling	5	**0**	1273^3.
A. Hickman	26	**7**	1^3, 26^2, 103^2, (152), (247), 535^2, (538), 540^3, (640), (642), 830^2, 1050^3, 1052^2, 1281^3, (1285), (1315).
L. Hicks *	42	**3**	191^3, 556^3, (595), 681^3, (853), (1118), 1120^2.
W. Hill	31	**4**	3^3, 91^2, 225^3, 227^3, 228^2, 422^2, (530), (532), (533), (627).
Miss L. Hislop	14	**1**	131^3, (511), 549^3, 1291^3.
Mrs S. Hodge	17	**1**	25^2, 42^3, 399^3, 649^2, 781^2, 831^2, (905).
R. Hodges	52	**4**	257^3, 258^2, (410), 448^3, 451^3, 452^2, 516^3, 519^3, 616^2, 620^3, 1016^3, 1109^3, 1110^2, 1113^2, (1114), (1135), (1228), 1230^2, 1254^3, 1259^3, 1388^2.
M. Holdforth *	12	**2**	168^3, (623), 627^3, 642^2, (938), 1185^2.
Miss J. Hollands *	22	**2**	(766), 1037^3, (1080), 1225^3, 1308^2, 1474^3.
M. Holmes	9	**1**	195^3, 688^2, 962^2, (1126).
Miss S. Holmes	7	**0**	94^2, 464^2, 849^2, 1046^2.
M. Hooper	28	**1**	139^2, 359^2, 405^2, 612^2, 760^3, 846^2, 982^3, 1090^3, 1320^3, (1485), 1496^2, 1556^3.
Miss L. Horner	9	**0**	339^3, 562^3.
J. Horton	8	**0**	1337^3.
Miss J. Houldey	5	**0**	146^2, 1070^2.
J. Howard	5	**0**	590^3.
Mrs L. Howard	1	**1**	(590).
I. Howe	4	**0**	46^3, 105^3, 385^2.
S. Huggan	26	**0**	659^3, 1477^3.
Miss A. Hughes	5	**0**	698^3, 739^2.
Miss J. Hughes	10	**2**	(276), 361^2, 1025^3, (1522).
R. Hughes	33	**5**	661^3, (726), (738), (820), (1024), (1115), 1227^3, 1387^2, 1392^2, 1485^2.
S. Hughes	24	**3**	53^3, 453^2, (517), (676), 1109^2, (1254).
R. Hunnisett	15	**4**	156^3, 298^3, (381), (478), 683^2, (888), 1056^2, (1121), 1216^3.
Miss C. Hurley	7	**3**	(751), (872), (1203).
Miss Gemma Hutchinson	22	**5**	246^2, 479^2, 558^3, (593), 743^3, 785^2, (1058), 1106^2, 1122^2, (1334), (1396), 1501^2, (1516).
F. Hutsby	40	**5**	113^2, 258^3, 368^2, 369^2, 370^3, 599^3, 868^2, 1019^2, 1035^2, (1136), 1275^2, (1276), (1277), 1390^3, (1502), (1562).
Miss R. Hutsby	7	**1**	(1122), 1278^2, 1483^3.
C. Huxley	6	**1**	(817).
P. Ikin	10	**0**	1279^3.
J. Innes	3	**1**	(1041), 1310^2.
Miss H. Irving	24	**8**	18^2, 48^3, 171^3, (189), 246^3, (289), (464), (585), 785^3, (869), (870), (939), (1106), 1470^3.
R. Isgar	4	**1**	(1464).
M. Jackson	29	**1**	(518), 715^2, 840^2, 983^3, 1142^2, 1145^2, 1148^3, 1232^3, 1425^2.
Miss T. Jackson	11	**0**	502^3, 774^2, 811^3, 1158^3, 1160^2, 1163^3, 1165^2.
Mrs O. Jackson *	28	**1**	78^3, 703^2, 1002^3, 1126^2, 1382^3, 1385^2, (1448), 1563^3.
Mrs V. Jackson	13	**1**	(914), 1082^3.
D. Jacob *	21	**10**	(12), (36), (89), (90), (139), 457^2, (458), 492^2, 577^2, 599^2, (634), 861^2, (862), (865), 1101^3, (1213).
R. Jagger	6	**0**	930^2, 1260^2.
Miss E. James	32	**13**	(33), 108^3, (258), (407), (449), (613), (666), 737^2, (838), (1017), (1111), 1229^3, 1231^2, (1255), (1391), (1527), (1532).
Miss H. James	5	**0**	923^2.
J. Jarrett	10	**2**	(709), 1044^2, (1108), 1143^3.

Rider	Rides	Wins	Races
C. Jarvis	4	**0**	224^{3}.
L. Jefford	49	**6**	51^{3}, 79^{3}, 81^{3}, 194^{3}, 318^{2}, (566), 572^{2}, (701), 702^{2}, (703), 791^{2}, (795), 824^{2}, 825^{3}, (827), (1003).
J. Jenkins *	26	**1**	37^{3}, 92^{2}, 323^{2}, 379^{3}, 571^{3}, 633^{3}, 940^{3}, 1332^{2}, (1333), 1364^{2}.
R. Jenkins	8	**0**	513^{3}.
D. Jewett *	23	**3**	72^{3}, 73^{2}, 75^{3}, (167), (433), (657).
Mrs S. Johnson	5	**0**	1146^{3}.
D. Jones *	87	**16**	34^{3}, 202^{2}, (203), (359), 362^{3}, (363), (446), (450), 616^{3}, 617^{2}, (696), 699^{3}, 700^{2}, 735^{2}, 842^{2}, 947^{3}, 950^{2}, 951^{3}, 952^{3}, 1024^{3}, (1089), (1091), (1094), 1190^{2}, (1191), (1192), 1237^{2}, 1319^{2}, 1320^{2}, (1323), 1324^{3}, 1520^{2}, (1523), 1524^{2}, (1525), 1533^{2}, (1535), 1537^{3}, (1538), 1539^{3}, 1550^{2}.
J. Jones	12	**1**	(815).
Miss E. Jones	12	**3**	(108), 206^{3}, (421), (625), 949^{3}.
Miss K. Jones	10	**0**	632^{3}, 1493^{3}.
Mrs E. Jones	5	**1**	673^{2}, (1519).
S. Joynes	24	**0**	730^{2}, 1253^{3}, 1258^{2}.
W. Kavanagh *	7	**1**	(1495), 1496^{3}.
Miss S. Keay	1	**0**	828^{3}.
M. Keel	33	**1**	(834), 1113^{3}, 1123^{3}.
M. Keen	6	**2**	463^{3}, 721^{3}, 820^{3}, (1513), (1518).
Mrs B. Keighley	3	**0**	10^{3}, 33^{3}, 757^{2}.
D. Kemp *	31	**13**	123^{3}, (124), (159), (244), 248^{3}, 372^{2}, 376^{2}, (398), (521), 647^{2}, (650), (742), (744), 828^{2}, (829), 1150^{3}, (1152), (1153), (1313), (1408).
Miss L. Kendall	15	**0**	216^{3}.
E. Kenney-Herbert	5	**1**	(15), 884^{3}.
N. Kent	31	**8**	(54), (60), (300), 478^{2}, (592), 887^{3}, (941), 943^{3}, 945^{3}, 997^{3}, 1061^{3}, (1204), (1218), (1427), 1502^{2}.
G. Kerr	14	**0**	47^{3}.
S. Kidston	25	**0**	61^{2}, 879^{3}, 880^{3}, 1102^{3}, 1180^{3}, 1270^{3}, 1366^{3}, 1491^{2}, 1558^{2}.
B. King	15	**2**	49^{2}, (868), (1515).
J. King	7	**0**	1504^{3}.
W. King	8	**0**	969^{3}, 1329^{3}, 1383^{3}.
P. Kinsella	41	**2**	60^{2}, 343^{2}, 774^{3}, (776), 1159^{2}, (1164), 1417^{2}, 1458^{2}.
Miss H. Kinsey	24	**2**	(253), 664^{3}, 751^{2}, (931), 1111^{2}.
W. Kinsey	29	**2**	(626), (877), 989^{3}, 1048^{2}, 1345^{2}.
J. Kwiatkowski	8	**0**	577^{3}, 1555^{3}, 1564^{3}.
C. Lambert	2	**0**	85^{2}.
T. Lane	57	**5**	49^{3}, 53^{2}, (99), 103^{3}, (123), (128), 218^{3}, 250^{3}, 465^{2}, 466^{3}, 890^{3}, (1061), (1332), 1408^{3}, 1471^{3}.
C. Lawson	2	**0**	646^{3}.
R. Lee	8	**0**	1012^{3}.
M. Legge	13	**0**	623^{3}, 626^{3}.
M. Lewis	22	**3**	205^{2}, (208), 675^{2}, (677), (952), 1322^{2}.
Miss H. Lewis	18	**4**	(515), 698^{2}, (739), (846), 1025^{2}, (1236), 1318^{3}.
Miss S. Lewis	4	**0**	148^{2}, 694^{2}.
Mrs B. Lewis	13	**0**	449^{3}, 697^{3}, 737^{3}.
Miss Z. Lilly	5	**1**	(175), 332^{2}, 1406^{2}.
E. Linehan	12	**1**	(847).
Miss C. Llewellin	2	**0**	318^{3}.
J.L. Llewellyn	14	**1**	(207), 359^{3}, 446^{3}, 1318^{2}.
Miss N. Lloyd	5	**3**	(405), (708), 849^{3}, (989).
Miss J. Lodge	7	**0**	866^{2}, 1278^{3}, 1517^{3}.
Miss K. Lovelace	10	**0**	575^{3}, 967^{3}, 1248^{3}, 1252^{3}.
M. Mackley	76	**6**	(24), (57), 59^{2}, 106^{3}, (125), 152^{2}, 298^{2}, (561), 829^{2}, 996^{2}, (1000), 1246^{3}, (1316).
J. Mactaggart	4	**1**	(426), 551^{3}.
J. Mahot	11	**0**	172^{3}, 815^{3}, 1230^{3}.
P. Mann	8	**0**	65^{3}, 109^{3}, 174^{2}.

Rider	Rides	Wins	Races
T. Mann	6	**1**	112^{2}, (173).
D. Mansell *	60	**4**	254^{2}, 402^{2}, 618^{3}, 724^{3}, (729), 730^{3}, 760^{2}, (976), 978^{3}, 1069^{3}, 1075^{2}, (1370), 1388^{3}, (1394).
M. Manton	8	**2**	(225), 301^{3}, (482), 499^{2}, 591^{3}.
Miss L. Marriott	17	**0**	98^{2}, 373^{3}, 396^{2}, 1244^{2}.
F. Marshall	9	**1**	397^{3}, 537^{2}, (1050).
A. Martin *	42	**8**	(8), (104), 105^{2}, (168), 290^{3}, 292^{2}, (360), 459^{3}, (583), 584^{3}, 586^{3}, 588^{3}, (724), (758), 759^{3}, 1000^{3}, 1069^{2}, 1341^{2}, 1447^{3}, 1449^{2}, (1450).
P. Mason	29	**3**	15^{2}, 52^{3}, 192^{2}, 406^{2}, (409), (614), 636^{2}, (759), 972^{2}, 979^{3}, 1063^{3}.
G. Maundrell	30	**12**	(16), (40), 77^{2}, 117^{3}, 118^{2}, 190^{2}, (324), (325), (356), 360^{2}, (632), (717), (718), 720^{3}, (882), (972), (1112), (1238).
J. Maxse	5	**0**	120^{3}, 264^{3}, 716^{2}, 971^{2}, 1211^{2}.
Miss O. Maylam	7	**1**	185^{3}, (652).
M. McAlister *	14	**1**	(507), 875^{3}, 876^{2}.
Miss M. McCarthy	22	**8**	412^{2}, 488^{3}, (497), 572^{3}, 707^{2}, (792), 1001^{2}, (1004), 1196^{2}, (1199), (1351), (1436), (1542), (1546).
R. McCarthy	26	**1**	(64), 119^{2}, 278^{2}, 913^{3}, 1134^{2}, 1249^{3}, 1371^{2}.
N. McDiarmid	23	**0**	881^{3}.
A. McElwee	3	**0**	1036^{3}.
S. McHugh	4	**0**	121^{3}.
D. McKenna	29	**6**	77^{3}, (411), (417), 487^{3}, (704), (909), (912), 1005^{3}, (1198).
Miss D. McKenna	1	**0**	984^{3}.
G. McPherson	7	**1**	(112), 755^{3}.
Miss E. McWilliam	6	**1**	(1076).
A. Merriam	36	**8**	(11), 89^{2}, (219), (224), 247^{2}, 524^{3}, 556^{2}, 651^{2}, (778), 833^{3}, 902^{3}, (903), 905^{2}, (1054), (1098), (1241), 1317^{2}.
J. Merry	20	**2**	621^{3}, (780), 895^{3}, 1023^{2}, (1027).
T. Messenger	20	**0**	741^{2}, 1213^{2}.
Miss C. Metcalfe	16	**1**	(71), 1036^{2}, 1415^{3}.
A. Michael	9	**2**	174^{3}, (274), 334^{2}, (335).
M. Miller	62	**13**	(67), 68^{3}, (115), 118^{3}, 198^{2}, (235), (238), (261), (308), (365), 367^{3}, 576^{2}, (601), 691^{2}, 860^{2}, (861), (863), 966^{2}, (1007), 1059^{2}, (1180), 1184^{3}, 1251^{3}, 1371^{3}, 1386^{2}, (1431).
P. Millington	75	**0**	946^{3}, 1156^{2}, 1245^{3}.
Miss A. Mills	9	**0**	484^{3}, 1004^{2}, 1197^{3}, 1350^{3}.
Miss D. Mitchell	4	**0**	305^{2}, 908^{3}.
N. Mitchell *	53	**5**	11^{2}, (37), 141^{2}, (233), 235^{3}, (263), 265^{2}, 352^{2}, 579^{2}, 602^{3}, (687), 688^{3}, 863^{3}, 1250^{2}, (1353).
G. Moloney	5	**2**	848^{2}, (1119), (1279).
N. Moore *	38	**2**	29^{2}, 39^{3}, 41^{3}, 127^{2}, 217^{2}, 218^{2}, 243^{2}, 245^{3}, 375^{3}, 525^{2}, 561^{3}, (746), (833), 1152^{2}.
J. Morgan	10	**0**	1411^{2}.
L. Morgan *	39	**5**	73^{3}, 530^{2}, (653), 654^{2}, 656^{2}, (1079), (1219), 1220^{3}, (1223), 1307^{2}, (1477).
R. Morgan *	55	**9**	(73), 137^{3}, (215), 286^{2}, (342), 344^{3}, (425), 429^{2}, 430^{2}, 509^{3}, 658^{2}, 764^{2}, 765^{2}, 767^{2}, 856^{2}, 858^{3}, 918^{2}, 1041^{2}, 1080^{3}, (1222), 1223^{3}, (1225), (1306), (1311), (1419), 1477^{2}.
A. Morley	5	**2**	(364), (1365).
J. Morley	6	**0**	388^{2}.
M. Morley	39	**2**	57^{2}, (388), 394^{2}, 683^{3}, 684^{3}, 1163^{2}, 1289^{2}, 1416^{3}, (1417).
C. Morris	6	**0**	937^{2}.
P. Morris	23	**2**	257^{2}, 382^{3}, 752^{2}, (934), 1265^{3}, (1388).

Rider	Rides	Wins	Placings
S. Morris *	92	**19**	26^3, 29^3, 36^3, 58^3, 87^2, 109^2, (111), 112^3, 125^3, 130^2, 151^3, (188), 192^3, (229), (231), (257), (259), 296^2, (370), 378^2, (384), 385^3, (559), 582^3, (586), 640^3, 644^2, (685), 686^3, (783), 784^2, (788), 1000^2, 1060^3, (1074), 1121^3, (1125), (1214), (1274), 1277^2, 1400^3, (1401), 1403^3, (1472), 1473^3, 1503^3.
G. Morrison	3	**1**	(885).
T. Morrison	13	**3**	(761), (765), (1307).
B. Mounsey-Heysham	4	**1**	(654), 857^2.
T. Mounsey-Heysham	6	**1**	(210), 340^2, 425^2.
J. Muir	10	**1**	285^3, (509), 1079^3, 1219^2.
C. Mulhall *	20	**2**	102^3, 211^3, (268), 1414^2, (1457).
M. Munrowd *	40	**1**	571^2, 796^3, 910^2, 981^3, (1258), 1436^2.
Miss V. Murphy	9	**0**	719^3, 1558^3.
P. Needham	10	**0**	1014^3, 1114^2, 1527^3.
Miss M. Neill	12	**2**	(131), 425^3, 430^3, 768^3, (859), 920^2.
J. Newbold	16	**1**	561^2, 888^3, (1504).
Miss T. Newman	12	**2**	(262), 484^2, 578^2, 822^2, 965^2, 1072^3, (1189), 1350^2.
P. Newton	16	**0**	594^2, 1119^3.
R. Nichol	12	**0**	136^3, 761^2.
H. Norton	4	**1**	(132), 762^2, 914^3.
J. O'Brien	8	**0**	850^3, 1232^2.
J. O'Rourke	9	**1**	(85).
H. Oakes	5	**0**	738^3.
W. Oakes	16	**2**	454^2, (841), 948^3, 1393^2, (1550).
T. Oates	24	**1**	69^3, 72^2, 132^3, 210^2, (211), 212^3, 215^3, 341^3, 551^2, 552^2, 554^2.
N. Oliver	39	**5**	(95), 204^2, 207^3, (668), (731), 750^3, (835), 839^2, (1209), 1345^3.
G. Opperman	5	**0**	366^3, 834^3.
H. Owen	1	**0**	1030^3.
J. Owen	100	**13**	28^2, 41^2, (43), 159^3, 188^2, 244^3, 288^3, 291^2, 294^3, 374^3, 376^3, (397), 398^2, (400), 401^3, 458^3, 460^3, (520), 521^2, 523^2, (557), (584), 588^2, 589^2, (647), 650^3, (720), 742^2, 830^3, (832), 833^2, (1030), 1032^2, 1088^2, 1151^2, 1153^3, 1155^2, (1215), 1242^3, 1243^3, (1317), (1406), 1409^2, 1472^2, 1473^2, 1505^2, 1515^2.
Mrs C. Owen	14	**5**	697^2, (737), 843^3, (949), 1189^2, (1235), (1318), 1485^3, 1521^2, (1551).
D. Page (Kent)	12	**1**	534^2, (651), 1280^2.
Miss R. Page	15	**1**	(217), 400^3, 829^3, 1316^2.
D. Painter	1	**0**	1393^3.
T. Park	4	**0**	711^2, 748^2, 988^2, 1429^2.
Mrs J. Parris	6	**2**	(46), 289^2, 464^3, 869^3, (1033), 1334^3.
S. Partridge	9	**1**	411^2, (793).
Miss N. Patterson	4	**0**	286^3, 859^3.
Miss A. Pattinson	3	**0**	1039^3.
B. Pauling	11	**1**	367^2, (516), 922^2, 1274^3.
L. Payter	5	**0**	50^3.
N. Pearce *	71	**9**	128^3, 375^2, (476), (528), 560^2, 583^2, (587), 589^3, (680), (784), 787^2, 788^2, 1031^3, (1032), 1034^2, 1035^3, (1110), 1112^2, 1116^3, 1214^3, 1215^3, 1218^2, 1262^3, (1337), 1396^3, 1403^2, (1468).
K. Pearson	18	**0**	752^3, 873^2, 876^3.
Miss K. Pegram	2	**0**	777^3, 899^2.
J. Pemberton	3	**1**	(782), 1084^2.
A. Pennock	13	**0**	954^3.
C. Penycate	11	**0**	454^3.
G. Perkins	13	**2**	51^2, (149), (699).
Miss J. Perry	3	**1**	934^2, (1261).
D. Phelan	31	**6**	181^3, 260^2, 418^3, (575), 580^2, (716), 779^2, (802), 803^2, (895), (900), (1055), 1083^2, 1212^2, 1285^3.
G. Phillips	8	**3**	47^2, (187), (293), (937), 1514^2.

Rider	Rides	Wins	Races
Miss K. Phillips	2	**1**	(1253).
N. Phillips *	12	**3**	50^2, 223^2, 759^2, (936), 1063^2, (1073), (1256), 1257^3.
Miss H. Phizacklea	12	**0**	301^2, 1118^3.
Miss S. Phizacklea *	20	**1**	25^3, 189^2, 407^2, 625^3, 1033^2, (1399).
B. Pollock *	11	**1**	(221), 384^3, 482^3.
J. Price	43	**4**	356^2, 451^2, (453), 694^3, (735), 736^2, (842), 951^2, 1027^2, 1193^3, 1239^2, (1395), 1487^3, 1538^2.
James Price	34	**1**	1323^2, (1521).
Miss V. Price	4	**1**	612^3, (661).
Miss E. Pring	1	**0**	935^3.
Julian Pritchard	83	**18**	(17), 21^2, (49), 80^2, (81), (109), (170), (192), 254^3, 255^2, 620^2, 621^2, 662^3, 668^2, 722^3, 835^3, (839), (922), (924), 926^3, (983), 1092^3, 1136^3, (1138), (1140), 1141^3, (1226), (1227), 1228^2, 1257^2, (1259), 1333^3, (1390), (1392), (1471), 1502^3, 1529^3.
W. Procter	5	**0**	1446^2.
Miss C. Prouse	18	**6**	193^2, 495^2, 705^2, (821), (1129), (1270), 1353^2, 1381^3, (1466), (1554), (1561).
W. Puddifer	13	**0**	526^2, 1047^3.
R. Pyman	5	**2**	(278), (1329).
C. Ramsay	3	**0**	281^3.
W. Ramsay	11	**1**	134^2, (281), 282^3, 917^2.
Mrs J. Reed	9	**3**	(237), 354^3, 1007^2, 1008^2, (1251), (1386).
D. Renney	6	**0**	989^2.
Miss R. Reynolds	34	**1**	206^2, 253^2, 512^2, 983^2, (1018), 1020^3, 1392^3, 1425^3, 1495^2, 1533^3.
A. Richardson	46	**8**	(70), 75^2, 132^2, 137^2, 166^3, (216), (271), (283), (427), (431), 507^2, 509^2, 764^3, 859^2, (1037), 1038^2, 1041^3, 1224^2, 1307^3, 1311^2, 1422^3, (1475).
Miss J. Riding *	15	**3**	71^2, 135^3, (213), (428), 508^2, 763^2, (1290).
M. Rimell	6	**1**	889^2, (890), 1256^3.
D. Robinson	2	**1**	780^3, (804).
Miss S. Robinson	19	**1**	(355), 475^2, 878^3, 1182^2, 1251^2.
P. Robinson	10	**0**	959^3.
S.J. Robinson	30	**2**	427^3, 563^2, 762^3, 810^3, (1286), 1413^2, (1460).
Stuart Robinson	14	**5**	(29), (153), 180^3, 182^3, 183^2, 420^2, (609), 611^2, (639), (643).
Miss L. Robson	5	**1**	960^3, (1305).
Miss P. Robson	21	**12**	71^3, (74), (133), 212^2, (270), (284), (339), 428^2, (430), (432), 655^3, (659), (855), 916^3, (918), 1039^2, 1220^2, 1287^3, (1423), (1479).
Miss C. Roddick	8	**5**	(94), (171), (199), (311), (600), 1462^2.
R. Rogers	33	**2**	404^3, 408^3, (512), 614^2, 663^3, (867), 977^3, 1227^2, 1430^2.
S. Rogers	4	**0**	305^3, 1352^3.
R. Ross	12	**0**	1378^2.
S. Ross	22	**4**	96^3, (408), 930^3, 1044^3, (1047), (1143), (1429).
L. Rowe	14	**0**	1545^3.
Mrs T. Rowe	4	**0**	1321^3.
Mrs D. Rowell	9	**0**	536^3, 896^3.
Mrs L. Rowsell	7	**2**	1481^3, (1483), 1487^2, 1522^2, 1551^2, (1563).
Mrs A. Rucker	12	**3**	94^3, 529^3, 726^3, 1014^2, (1137), (1230), 1343^2, (1536).
Miss G. Russell-Holmes	1	**0**	574^3.
J. Russell	9	**0**	1468^3.
Miss V. Russell	7	**0**	552^3, 1478^2.
J. Ryan	3	**0**	1085^3, 1313^3.
Miss S. Samworth *	5	**0**	5^3.
C. Sands	6	**0**	921^3.
A. Sansome	72	**4**	7^2, 54^3, 60^3, 123^2, 186^2, 220^3, 379^2, (683), 786^3, 789^2, 886^3, (887), 903^2, 995^2, (1034), 1217^2, 1243^2, (1245), 1336^2, 1468^2.

Rider	Wins	Races
N. Saville * 26	**9**	(100), (165), (166), (481), (499), (596), (771), 873^{3}, (875), (955), 1143^{2}.
Miss K. Scott 5	**0**	547^{3}.
T. Scott 8	**1**	(1309), 1311^{3}.
R. Sealey 5	**0**	1395^{3}, 1495^{3}.
Miss S. Sharratt 52	**4**	58^{2}, 91^{3}, 230^{3}, 595^{2}, 713^{3}, 714^{3}, (753), 848^{3}, 853^{2}, 985^{2}, 986^{2}, 987^{2}, (1020), (1044), 1046^{3}, (1107), 1108^{2}, 1124^{3}, 1203^{2}, 1428^{2}.
B. Shaw 24	**3**	96^{2}, 97^{2}, (227), 526^{3}, 533^{2}, 754^{2}, 840^{3}, (929), 934^{3}, (1233), 1261^{2}.
Miss V. Shaw 3	**1**	(150).
P. Sheldrake * 42	**4**	(201), (202), 358^{3}, (448), 669^{2}, 671^{2}, (672), 677^{3}, 735^{3}, 736^{3}, 948^{2}, 953^{3}, 1091^{2}, 1192^{2}, 1235^{2}, 1240^{3}, 1321^{2}.
M. Sheridan 12	**1**	182^{2}, 183^{3}, (997).
D. Sherlock 7	**1**	1260^{3}, (1344).
C. Shirley-Beavan 36	**4**	(75), 131^{2}, 135^{2}, 210^{3}, (272), 282^{2}, 287^{2}, 340^{3}, 431^{2}, 549^{2}, (762), 858^{2}, 915^{3}, (917), 1079^{2}, 1080^{2}, 1161^{2}, 1164^{3}.
Miss V. Simpson 2	**0**	231^{2}.
D. Skelton 3	**1**	(32).
R. Skinner 8	**0**	821^{3}.
G. Slade-Jones * 3	**1**	(110).
D. Smith 11	**2**	(819), 922^{3}, (1336), 1351^{3}.
M. Smith 26	**2**	(371), (555), 905^{3}, 1316^{3}.
N. Smith 11	**0**	1302^{2}, 1305^{3}.
J. Snowden * 52	**7**	9^{2}, 67^{3}, (138), 173^{3}, 274^{2}, (321), 324^{3}, 326^{2}, (327), 365^{2}, (368), 413^{3}, 416^{3}, 460^{2}, (468), 598^{3}, (971), 1097^{3}, 1131^{2}, 1208^{3}, 1507^{2}, 1561^{2}, (1566).
J. Sole * 32	**4**	264^{2}, 456^{2}, (534), (777), 927^{3}, 1087^{2}, (1487), (1517), 1548^{2}, 1566^{3}.
Miss W. Southcombe * . . . 14	**0**	88^{3}, 585^{2}, 965^{3}.
Mrs L. Spence 8	**1**	222^{3}, 243^{3}, 522^{2}, (904).
S. Spice 6	**0**	539^{2}, 1280^{3}.
R. Stearn 36	**3**	4^{2}, 40^{2}, (245), (525), 906^{2}, 1150^{2}, 1317^{3}, (1409).
Miss A. Stennett * 20	**1**	42^{2}, 108^{2}, 157^{3}, 189^{3}, 222^{2}, (785), 831^{3}, 1334^{2}.
L. Stephens 47	**11**	695^{2}, 740^{2}, 841^{3}, (1021), 1024^{2}, (1026), 1089^{2}, 1094^{3}, (1190), 1193^{2}, (1237), (1240), (1319), (1320), (1321), 1324^{2}, (1484), 1486^{2}, (1534), 1539^{2}, (1548), 1549^{2}, 1552^{2}.
Mrs M. Stephens 2	**0**	1519^{2}.
R. Stephens 26	**6**	150^{2}, 357^{3}, 360^{3}, (362), 363^{2}, 472^{2}, (475), (580), (694), (695), 700^{3}, 879^{2}, (883), 964^{2}.
T. Stephenson 66	**8**	(52), (107), 256^{2}, 513^{2}, 516^{2}, 518^{2}, (519), 614^{3}, (616), (618), 619^{2}, 665^{3}, 722^{2}, 723^{2}, 731^{3}, 834^{2}, 836^{3}, 839^{3}, 925^{3}, (927), (981), 1015^{3}, 1018^{2}, 1020^{2}, 1141^{2}, 1256^{2}, (1345), 1389^{3}.
Miss N. Stirling 23	**9**	133^{2}, 284^{3}, 426^{2}, (550), (552), 553^{3}, (915), 920^{3}, (1039), (1078), (1082), (1221), (1224), (1308), 1419^{2}, 1420^{2}, 1478^{3}.
Ms L Stock 18	**4**	(42), 421^{2}, (805), 896^{2}, 1086^{3}, (1280), (1283), 1516^{2}.
C. Storey 46	**5**	70^{2}, (136), (137), 215^{2}, (282), 287^{3}, 432^{2}, (549), 553^{2}, 554^{3}, 654^{3}, (855), 856^{3}, 1081^{2}, 1082^{2}, 1223^{2}, 1306^{2}, 1422^{2}, 1475^{2}.
Miss C. Stucley * 15	**4**	63^{2}, (78), 81^{2}, 146^{3}, 262^{2}, 470^{3}, 613^{2}, 690^{2}, 838^{3}, (961), (965), (1011), 1368^{2}.
Miss G. Swan 8	**1**	613^{3}, 1017^{2}, (1314), 1391^{3}.
M. Sweetland 62	**1**	326^{3}, 487^{2}, 962^{3}, 1195^{3}, 1268^{3}, 1378^{3}, 1380^{3}, 1464^{2}, 1466^{2}, (1467), 1511^{3}.
P. Taiano 13	**0**	43^{2}, 129^{3}, 244^{2}.
Miss S. Talbot 13	**0**	1191^{3}, 1527^{2}.
J. Tarry 9	**1**	586^{2}, (589), 744^{3}, 1034^{3}, 1517^{2}.
Miss S. Tarry 6	**0**	585^{3}, 889^{3}, 1213^{3}.

Rider	Rides	Wins	Races
J. Tate	7	**0**	658^3.
M. Tate	3	**1**	(562), 957^3, 1202^2.
Richard Tate *	5	**1**	(343), 389^2.
G. Tawell	6	**0**	461^3, 871^3, 1108^3.
J. Taylor	2	**1**	(402).
Miss T. Tellwright	6	**1**	1263^3, (1428).
H. Tett	9	**0**	666^2, 1115^3.
Mrs V. Thirlby	6	**2**	110^2, (682), (987).
D. Thomas	13	**1**	390^2, (505), 770^3, 955^3, 1289^3.
J. Thompson	10	**0**	656^3.
L. Tibbatts	12	**0**	492^3.
J. Tickle	12	**1**	(706).
N. Tinkler	28	**6**	(6), 107^2, (160), (163), (267), 342^3, 391^2, 501^3, 710^3, (814), (956).
Miss C. Tizzard	49	**6**	62^2, (88), 115^2, 320^3, 350^2, 468^2, (470), 579^3, 635^2, (697), 882^2, 1011^2, 1183^2, (1247), 1250^3, 1325^3, 1448^2, 1465^2, (1493), (1507), 1557^2.
Miss I. Tompsett	21	**3**	(361), 449^2, 669^3, (671), 843^2, 949^2, 1095^3, (1239), 1389^2, 1547^3.
Miss E. Tory	16	**1**	67^2, 322^2, 365^3, (604).
Miss V. Tremlett	5	**1**	31^3, 48^2, (380).
J. Trevor-Roper	2	**0**	582^2.
J. Trice-Rolph	43	**1**	46^2, 111^3, 113^3, 187^2, 188^3, 226^2, 295^3, 296^3, 369^3, 463^2, 725^3, 729^3, 731^2, 870^2, 871^2, 927^2, 1107^3, 1125^2, (1275).
B. Trickey	3	**0**	483^3, 707^3, 1130^3.
Mrs T. Trickey	4	**2**	76^3, (908), (1350).
R. Trotter	2	**0**	281^2.
James Tudor *	59	**11**	(7), (53), 104^3, (191), 290^2, (337), 357^2, 398^3, 622^2, (624), 671^3, 674^2, 675^3, 738^2, 740^3, 789^3, (866), 870^3, (953), 999^2, (1103), 1105^2, 1107^2, (1187), 1188^2, 1240^2, 1484^3, (1514), 1515^3, (1533), 1534^3, .
G. Tuer *	11	**3**	269^3, 427^2, 429^3, (770), (772), 808^2, 812^3, (813), 1037^2, 1038^3, 1419^3.
G. Tumelty	14	**1**	(730), 937^3.
Miss B. Tunley	1	**0**	84^3.
D.I. Turner	34	**3**	261^2, (334), (416), (455), 575^2, 865^2, 972^3, 1248^2.
Miss A. Turner	11	**2**	(333), 852^3, 1144^2, (1147).
Miss Z. Turner *	21	**11**	101^2, 126^3, 157^2, (246), 373^2, (399), (522), 558^2, (649), (831), (1086), (1154), (1210), (1244), 1314^3, (1407), (1470), 1516^3.
N. Tutty	59	**8**	134^3, 160^3, (212), 267^3, 268^3, 271^2, 338^2, 389^3, 504^2, 562^2, (563), 565^2, (808), 812^2, 813^2, 814^2, (1163), 1204^2, 1292^2, (1300), 1301^2, 1412^3, (1413), (1414), (1416), 1457^3, 1504^2.
D. Underwood	9	**0**	1523^3.
T. Underwood	31	**3**	90^3, 422^3, 455^2, 458^2, (622), 717^3, 1031^2, 1103^2, (1212), 1338^2, 1492^3, 1514^3, (1549), 1552^3.
T. Vaughan	80	**11**	19^3, 120^2, 447^2, 450^3, (670), 672^2, 676^3, 677^2, 696^2, (700), (736), (844), 845^2, (951), 953^2, 1022^2, 1026^2, 1090^2, 1092^2, 1093^3, (1096), (1234), 1237^3, 1238^2, 1322^3, (1324), (1481), (1482), (1520), 1525^3, 1537^2, 1549^3.
Mrs F. Vigar	9	**0**	237^3, 355^2, 498^2, 626^2, 883^2, 1013^3.
C. Wadland	21	**0**	587^3, 940^2, 1030^2, 1337^2, 1518^2.
A. Wadlow	50	**5**	(93), 190^3, 252^2, 408^2, 410^3, 450^2, 528^3, 711^3, 713^2, (714), 753^3, 754^3, (850), 852^2, 853^3, 933^2, 978^2, 1049^3, 1226^2, 1233^2, 1346^2, (1393), (1426).
N. Wain	5	**0**	1104^3.
R. Wakeham	33	**3**	111^2, 164^2, 272^2, 341^2, (392), 776^3, (812), 954^2, 955^2, (1159), 1162^3.
S. Waley-Cohen	13	**3**	7^3, (92), 93^2, (190), 382^2, 724^2, (1093), 1332^3.

Rider		Wins	Races
M. Walford *	23	**9**	(3), (56), (58), (59), 266^2, (389), 392^2, (393), 476^2, (591), 956^2, (1161), 1205^3, (1302).
E. Walker	51	**4**	6^3, 52^2, 141^3, (251), 404^2, (456), 584^2, 727^2, 728^3, 729^2, 756^3, 818^2, 819^2, 820^2, (921), 1015^2, 1071^3, 1073^2, 1135^3, (1141), 1342^2, 1488^3, 1528^2, 1531^2, 1532^3.
N. Walker	3	**0**	153^2, 293^2, 555^2.
S. Walker	39	**2**	165^2, 272^3, 393^3, 476^3, 478^3, 773^2, 808^3, 958^3, (959), 1059^2, 1205^2, 1287^2, (1291), 1416^2, 1456^3.
M. Wall	42	**3**	(113), (837), 1231^3, 1265^2, (1346), 1531^3.
H. Wallace	8	**1**	236^2, (1062).
M. Walters	19	**1**	368^3, 699^2, 1074^2, (1339), 1344^2, 1394^2.
J. Walton	28	**4**	69^2, 767^3, (768), 854^3, (919), 1077^2, 1081^3, 1309^3, (1310), (1418), 1423^2, 1476^3.
Miss C. Walton	7	**0**	511^3, 919^2, 1042^2.
R. Walton	1	**0**	1480^3.
A. Ward-Thomas	11	**0**	610^3, 716^3, 804^2, 1365^2.
C. Ward-Thomas	19	**0**	24^3, 153^3, 221^2, 247^3, 520^2.
Miss S. Ward	9	**1**	211^2, 655^2, 857^3, (1036), 1418^2, 1479^2.
Mrs L. Ward	14	**0**	70^2, 162^3, 268^2, 503^3.
Miss H. Watson	13	**0**	361^3, 838^2, 1470^2.
A. Waugh	6	**2**	(214), (551), 1421^2.
G. Weatherley	24	**1**	415^2, 1003^3, (1005), 1194^2, 1331^3, 1353^3, 1491^3, 1554^2, 1562^2.
Miss A. Wells	7	**0**	1154^2.
Miss A de Lisle Wells	19	**3**	(358), (871), 921^2, 1255^2, 1330^2, (1352), 1428^3, 1544^2, 1564^2.
Miss S. West	10	**2**	262^3, 712^3, 1127^3, 1325^2, (1364), 1366^2, (1465), 1493^2, 1509^2.
T. Weston *	22	**7**	259^2, (406), 410^2, (513), (621), (660), (756), (979), (1016).
F. Wheeler	6	**1**	(1207).
S. Wheeler	4	**0**	9^2, 138^3, 263^2.
W. White	28	**3**	66^3, 273^2, 278^3, 692^2, 794^2, 795^2, (878), 881^2, (1186), 1365^3, (1543).
M. Whitehouse	3	**0**	1021^2.
C. Whittaker	6	**0**	236^3.
Miss J. Wickens	10	**2**	(222), 781^3, 869^2, (1064), 1314^2.
G. Wigley	19	**2**	44^2, 175^3, 371^3, 807^3, (897), (1085).
M. Wilesmith	16	**2**	(840), 976^3, (982).
A. Williams	23	**3**	154^2, 221^3, (396), 523^3, 590^2, 832^2, 901^2, (1243), (1246), 1315^2.
E. Williams *	20	**6**	(19), 116^2, (204), (205), 446^2, (447), (615), 1094^2, (1322).
Miss J. Williams	26	**14**	(5), (101), (102), (230), (479), (527), (529), (663), (664), (763), 931^3, (980), 1017^3, 1146^2, (1229), (1263), (1343), 1391^2, 1563^2.
N. Williams *	64	**15**	34^2, 64^2, (140), 142^2, 232^2, 275^2, 277^2, (279), 319^2, 320^2, 325^2, (326), (328), 409^3, (492), (493), 494^2, (495), 496^2, (599), 602^2, 634^2, (688), (963), (966), (1090), (1127), 1129^2, (1248), 1249^2, (1250), 1370^2.
O. Williams	25	**0**	297^2, 302^3, 944^3, 1302^3.
N. Wilmington	39	**5**	121^2, 149^2, 233^2, (265), 473^2, (579), 861^3, 936^2, (1009), 1071^2, 1075^3, (1133), (1371).
N. Wilson (South)	9	**0**	611^3, 898^3.
Miss F. Wilson	48	**9**	203^3, (206), (357), 363^3, (454), (673), (674), (843), 845^3, (950), 952^2, 1023^3, (1025), 1091^3, 1189^3, 1191^2, (1193), 1482^2, 1536^3, 1548^3.
A. Wintle	58	**5**	56^3, 57^3, 92^3, 156^2, 159^2, 251^3, 252^3, 364^2, (452), (667), 835^2, 836^2, 924^2, 926^2, (978), 1018^3, (1116), 1136^2, 1259^2, (1342), 1390^2, 1529^2.
Miss K. Wood	14	**0**	529^2, 751^3, 931^2.

B. Woodhouse	31	3	(269), (391), 392^3, 505^3, 769^3, 771^2, (879), 960^2, 1164^2, 1369^2.
M. Woodward	25	1	1467^2, (1559).
R. Woollacott *	94	13	(62), (66), 115^3, (147), 200^3, 279^3, 309^2, 312^2, 323^3, (352), (412), 415^3, 469^3, (473), 493^2, 497^2, (571), 600^2, 706^2, 792^3, (880), 882^3, 884^2, 963^2, 964^3, 967^2, 1010^2, 1127^2, 1133^2, 1271^2, 1327^3, (1328), (1367), 1385^3, 1431^2, 1447^2, (1461), (1506), 1508^2, (1544).
P. York *	97	26	6^2, 8^3, (27), (28), 35^3, 86^2, 87^3, 90^2, 104^2, (151), (154), (181), (185), (220), (223), (264), 265^3, (290), 295^2, (331), (332), (376), 418^2, 419^3, 420^3, (423), (424), (535), 538^2, 539^3, (556), 559^2, 623^2, 627^2, (638), 639^2, 640^2, 642^3, 643^2, 644^3, 721^2, 777^2, (779), 802^2, (806), (970), 973^2, 997^2, 1051^2, 1054^2, (1105), 1139^2, (1208), 1209^2, (1211), 1282^2, (1284), 1285^2, 1333^2, 1336^3, 1404^3, 1405^2, 1408^2, (1486).
J. Young	25	0	17^3, 194^2, 196^3, 274^3, 308^2, 567^3, 568^2, 796^2, 883^3.
Jack Young	6	0	1105^3.
Miss S. Young	29	3	(305), 311^3, 569^3, (570), 701^2, (913), 1131^3, 1267^2, 1348^3, 1431^3, 1436^3.

Winning & Placed Hunter Chase Riders 2004

** Winning Point-to-Point Rider 2004*

Rider	No Rides	No Wins	Winning and Placed Rides
D. Alers-Hankey *	3	1	733^2, (1298), 1453^2.
Miss L. Allan *	3	0	242^3, 377^2.
Miss A. Armitage *	5	1	(1347), 1497^2.
P. Atkinson *	5	0	542^2, 678^3, 894^2, 1068^3, 1296^2.
R. Bandey	7	0	628^3, 1298^3.
M. Barber *	21	6	(209), 434^3, (437), (490), (629), (679), 991^2, 1169^3, (1175), 1512^2.
D. Barlow *	9	0	541^2, 1172^3, 1497^3.
L. Bates *	13	1	542^3, (1179), 1347^2.
Miss S. Beddoes *	1	1	(1117).
T. Bishop *	3	1	(1293).
R. Bliss *	6	0	437^3, 1363^2, 1442^3.
N. Bloom *	4	0	442^3.
G. Brewer *	12	1	177^2, (242), 435^3, 1171^2, 1297^2, 1490^3, 1526^2.
Miss L. Bridges *	4	1	(1443), 1512^3.
Miss L. Brooke *	7	0	1029^2, 1452^2.
Miss S. Brotherton *	2	1	(892).
R. Burton *	16	1	239^2, 435^2, 544^2, 1173^3, 1176^2, 1294^2, (1362).
P. Callaghan *	2	0	1373^3.
Miss T. Cave *	6	4	(347), (733), (1167), (1363).
A. Charles-Jones *	9	0	891^2.
S. Charlton *	9	4	(377), (439), (1168), (1374).
Miss T. Clark *	5	0	1355^2, 1454^3.
R. Clark	2	0	316^3.
R. Cope *	3	0	443^2.
P. Cornforth *	2	0	1177^2.
P. Cowley *	14	0	436^2, 1375^2.
A. Crowe	1	0	543^2.
Richard Darke *	3	0	800^2.

Rider	Rides	Wins	Races
D. Dennis *	5	**0**	1356^{2}.
J. Diment *	15	**0**	438^{3}, 631^{3}, 801^{3}, 1372^{2}, 1441^{3}.
J. Docker *	7	**0**	440^{3}, 1357^{2}.
H. Dowty *	1	**0**	122^{3}.
T. Dreaper *	10	**5**	(541), 545^{3}, (747), (800), (975), (1440).
Miss L. Eddery *	2	**0**	1451^{2}.
D. Edwards *	12	**1**	347^{3}, 631^{2}, 733^{3}, 993^{3}, 1166^{2}, 1293^{3}, 1358^{2}, (1498).
T. Edwards *	2	**0**	445^{2}, 801^{2}.
Ms A Embiricos *	5	**1**	242^{2}, (581).
T. Faulkner *	3	**0**	1355^{3}.
Mrs C. Ford	1	**1**	(732).
Miss J. Foster *	6	**0**	346^{3}, 1526^{3}.
H. Fowler *	8	**1**	(177), 1440^{3}.
Miss L. Gardner *	3	**1**	(628), 799^{3}.
F de Giles *	2	**0**	1439^{2}.
T. Glass *	2	**0**	436^{3}.
W. Goldie *	5	**0**	1296^{3}, 1499^{3}.
C. Gordon *	10	**0**	1438^{3}.
M. Gorman *	6	**1**	(441), 1168^{2}.
Miss A. Goschen *	18	**6**	280^{2}, (438), (543), (891), 991^{3}, (1029), 1170^{2}, 1293^{2}, (1376), (1441).
S. Gray *	2	**0**	377^{3}.
T. Greenall *	29	**5**	122^{2}, 241^{2}, 316^{2}, (545), 679^{3}, 732^{2}, (1068), (1166), 1178^{3}, 1299^{2}, 1361^{2}, 1362^{2}, (1377), (1499).
Miss P. Gundry *	18	**0**	176^{2}, 1167^{3}, 1168^{3}, 1170^{3}, 1172^{2}, 1452^{3}, 1454^{2}.
P. Hall *	7	**0**	348^{3}.
Mrs A. Hamilton *	1	**1**	(1360).
T. Hampton	1	**0**	581^{3}.
G. Hanmer *	14	**1**	(1176), 1357^{3}, 1375^{3}, 1451^{3}.
Miss D. Harding *	4	**1**	(239), 490^{3}.
N. Harris *	16	**4**	(178), (280), (348), 541^{3}, 543^{3}, 629^{3}, (1170), 1175^{3}, 1294^{3}, 1376^{2}.
Miss F. Hartley *	2	**0**	1490^{2}.
L. Heard *	5	**0**	799^{2}, 1299^{3}, 1437^{2}, 1498^{2}.
L. Hicks *	4	**1**	(1375).
M. Holdforth *	3	**1**	(1438).
Miss J. Hollands *	3	**1**	797^{3}, (1373).
Miss J. Hughes *	5	**0**	434^{2}.
S. Hughes *	11	**0**	280^{3}, 317^{2}, 441^{2}, 1377^{2}.
Miss H. Irving *	5	**0**	437^{2}, 629^{2}.
Mrs O. Jackson *	2	**1**	(1454).
D. Jacob *	2	**1**	(1439).
L. Jefford *	9	**0**	441^{3}, 1166^{3}, 1175^{2}, 1354^{3}.
J. Jenkins *	11	**2**	(179), 444^{2}, 732^{3}, (734), 1356^{3}.
D. Jewett *	12	**1**	349^{3}, 440^{2}, 797^{2}, (1028).
D. Jones *	2	**1**	974^{2}, (1358).
J. Jones *	2	**0**	1295^{3}.
Miss E. Jones *	5	**0**	1440^{2}.
W. Kavanagh *	8	**1**	678^{2}, (1444).
M. Keel *	4	**0**	545^{2}.
Mrs B. Keighley	4	**0**	241^{3}.
D. Kemp *	7	**3**	(893), (1359), (1452).
N. Kent *	6	**0**	1489^{3}.
G. Kerr	5	**0**	443^{3}, 892^{3}, 1176^{3}.
P. Kinsella *	5	**0**	992^{3}.
M. Mackley *	7	**0**	1442^{2}.
P. Maitland-Carew	5	**0**	330^{3}, 546^{2}, 1444^{2}.
T. Malone	14	**1**	178^{3}, 347^{2}, 747^{2}, 975^{2}, (991), 1441^{2}, 1453^{3}.
D. Mansell *	17	**2**	(544), (801), 1437^{3}.
M. Manton *	3	**0**	679^{2}.
A. Martin *	15	**1**	628^{2}, 734^{2}, 1171^{3}, (1357).
M. McAlister *	14	**3**	(349), (678), (798), 1174^{2}.
R. McCarthy *	5	**0**	581^{2}.

Rider	Rides	Wins	Races
A. Merriam *	5	**0**	975[3].
N. Mitchell *	10	**1**	(241).
N. Moore *	3	**1**	(1299).
L. Morgan *	7	**1**	439[2], 1178[2], 1374[3], (1490).
R. Morgan *	11	**2**	(240), 798[2], (992).
M. Morley *	2	**0**	177[3].
P. Morris *	7	**0**	630[3], 734[3].
S. Morris *	13	**2**	239[3], (444), 800[3], (1361), 1372[3].
C. Mulhall *	9	**2**	(316), (1177).
M. Munrowd *	5	**1**	(1437).
O. Nelmes	9	**0**	893[2].
H. Norton *	5	**0**	1359[3].
T. Oates *	2	**0**	349[2].
J. Owen *	14	**0**	317[3], 893[3], 1173[2], 1295[2], 1443[2].
N. Pearce *	5	**1**	(1356).
D. Phelan *	1	**0**	1438[2].
N. Phillips *	2	**1**	(1294).
Miss S. Phizacklea *	13	**3**	176[3], (346), (630), (994), 1117[2], 1169[2], 1347[3].
B. Pollock *	1	**1**	(442).
W. Ramsay *	8	**0**	240[3], 445[3].
Miss J. Riding *	4	**2**	(797), 1068[2], (1296).
Miss S. Robinson *	1	**0**	1167[2].
S.J. Robinson	5	**1**	1177[3], (1489).
Stuart Robinson *	1	**0**	345[3].
Miss P. Robson *	6	**0**	798[3], 1028[3], 1444[3].
Miss S. Samworth	4	**1**	178[2], 348[2], (435), 747[3].
N. Saville *	20	**3**	(122), 442[2], 994[2], 1179[3], (1297), 1374[2], 1376[3], (1526).
M. Seston	18	**2**	439[3], 1028[2], (1174), (1178).
Miss S. Sharratt *	4	**0**	891[3].
P. Sheldrake *	5	**1**	209[2], (434).
D Da Silva	2	**0**	894[3].
Miss V. Simpson	2	**0**	544[3], 892[2].
D. Skelton *	3	**0**	1029[3].
G. Slade-Jones *	3	**1**	(1451).
J. Snowden *	4	**1**	(445), 1439[3].
J. Sole *	6	**1**	345[2], (1354).
Miss W. Southcombe	3	**1**	438[2], (993).
Miss A. Stennett *	5	**1**	1359[2], (1497).
R. Stephens *	6	**0**	209[3], 490[2].
C. Storey *	9	**0**	330[2], 1174[3], 1373[2], 1499[2].
Miss C. Stucley *	12	**2**	(176), (317), 630[2], 1360[2].
J. Tate	1	**0**	1297[3].
Richard Tate *	3	**1**	179[3], (546), 994[3].
Miss C. Tizzard *	8	**0**	1360[3].
James Tudor *	5	**2**	(1355), (1442).
G. Tuer *	10	**3**	240[2], (436), (542), (894), 992[2], 1179[2], 1362[3], 1489[2].
Miss Z. Turner *	3	**1**	(1295).
T. Vaughan *	1	**0**	974[3].
M. Walford *	1	**1**	(330).
T. Weston *	1	**1**	(1172).
E. Williams *	6	**1**	(974).
N. Williams *	30	**9**	179[2], 346[2], (443), (631), (799), (1169), (1171), (1173), 1298[2], (1372), (1453), (1512).
A. Wintle *	5	**0**	1117[3].
B. Woodhouse *	7	**0**	546[3].
R. Woollacott *	7	**1**	(345), 444[3], 1358[3].
G. Wragg	1	**0**	1443[3].
P. York *	11	**1**	(440), 1354[2], 1361[3].
Miss S. Young *	6	**0**	993[2], 1363[3], 1498[3].

The Busiest Riders in 2004

	Point-to-Points				Overall	Hunter Chases			
Total	1st	2nd	3rd	Rider	Total	1st	2nd	3rd	Total
139	50	15	8	R. Burton	155	1	5	1	16
130	54	23	11	A. Farrant	134	0	0	0	4
104	26	17	15	Miss P. Gundry	122	0	3	4	18
100	13	20	14	J. Owen	114	0	3	2	14
97	26	27	11	P. York	108	1	1	1	11
97	13	19	7	A. Charles-Jones	106	0	1	0	9
92	19	9	18	S. Morris	105	2	0	3	13
94	13	16	11	R. Woollacott	101	1	0	2	7
80	16	6	14	G. Hanmer	94	1	0	3	14
64	15	16	1	N. Williams	94	9	3	0	30
86	18	22	8	R. Cope	89	0	1	0	3
87	16	14	11	D. Jones	89	1	1	0	2
83	18	8	11	Julian Pritchard	88	0	0	0	5
68	15	13	11	Miss A. Goschen	86	6	3	1	18
73	11	16	6	G. Brewer	85	1	4	2	12
76	6	5	2	M. Mackley	83	0	1	0	7
60	6	8	3	M. Barber	81	6	2	2	21
80	11	13	8	T. Vaughan	81	0	0	1	1
68	5	9	9	D. Edwards	80	1	3	4	12
60	4	4	6	D. Mansell	77	2	0	1	17
71	9	9	9	N. Pearce	76	1	0	0	5
75	0	1	2	P. Millington	75	0	0	0	0
72	4	11	5	A. Sansome	75	0	0	0	3
60	9	2	10	P. Cowley	74	0	2	0	14
70	9	5	11	Miss L. Gardner	73	1	0	1	3
60	11	8	7	J. Docker	67	0	1	1	7
62	13	7	6	M. Miller	67	0	0	0	5
55	9	11	6	R. Morgan	66	2	1	0	11
66	8	12	8	T. Stephenson	66	0	0	0	0
62	6	10	5	G. Barfoot-Saunt	65	0	0	0	3
59	11	10	10	James Tudor	64	2	0	0	5
53	5	6	4	N. Mitchell	63	1	0	0	10
59	8	12	7	N. Tutty	63	0	0	0	4
58	5	11	6	A. Wintle	63	0	0	1	5
62	1	3	7	M. Sweetland	62	0	0	0	0
51	14	10	7	C. Gordon	61	0	0	1	10
57	5	2	8	T. Lane	61	0	0	0	4
55	4	7	7	R. Armson	59	0	0	0	4
55	7	9	8	C. Heard	58	0	0	0	3
52	4	7	10	R. Hodges	58	0	0	0	6
49	6	5	5	L. Jefford	58	0	1	3	9
42	8	5	8	A. Martin	57	1	2	1	15
49	6	11	4	Miss C. Tizzard	57	0	0	1	8
43	5	4	3	L. Bates	56	1	1	1	13
52	4	9	7	Miss S. Sharratt	56	0	0	1	4
52	7	8	8	J. Snowden	56	1	0	1	4
50	5	7	6	L. Heard	55	0	3	1	5
46	5	10	4	C. Storey	55	0	3	1	9
51	4	13	8	E. Walker	53	0	0	0	2
46	8	9	5	A. Richardson	52	0	0	0	6
50	5	10	8	A. Wadlow	52	0	0	0	2
45	3	3	5	R. Bliss	51	0	1	2	6
43	3	7	2	H. Fowler	51	1	0	1	8

Leading Point-to-Point Owners 2004

1. **Mr J.M. TURNER** 19
   Spring Gale (IRE) 4
   The Wiley Kalmuck (IRE) 4
   Celtic Duke 3
   Westfield John 2
   Dunrig (IRE) 1
   Fine And Dandy (IRE) 1
   Leatherback (IRE) 1
   Militaire (FR) 1
   On The Day (IRE) 1
   Persian Hero (IRE) 1

2. **Mr S.P. TINDALL** 15
   Lively Lord (IRE) 4
   Sheriff's Friend (IRE) 4
   Toujours (IRE) 3
   Granny Smith (IRE) 2
   Little Mickey 1
   Rainbow Ranch (IRE) 1

3. **Mr G.C. MAUNDRELL** 11
   Rhythm King 5
   Bally Wirral (IRE) 3
   Quickswood (IRE) 2
   Headwrecker (IRE) 1

3. **Mr B.A. KILPATRICK** 11
   Cimmaroon (IRE) 4
   Oneminutetofive* 4
   Colquhoun 3
   ** owned jointly with Mr M.C. Pipe*

5. **Mrs A.D. WILLIAMS** 9
   Sapega (IRE) 3
   Step And Run (IRE) 3
   Supreme Citizen (IRE) 3

5. **Mr P.J. FINN** 9
   I Am Said I (IRE) 4
   Canterbury Jack (IRE) 2
   Euwiluwil (IRE) 2
   Auntie Kathleen 1
   Lord Atterbury (IRE)* 1
   ** owned jointly with Mr D.A. Johnson*

7. **Mr P.J. CORBETT** 8
   Upton Adventure 8

7. **Mr R.A. & Dr C.E. FRY** 8
   Blackwater Brave (IRE) 2
   Scarlet Glory 2
   Earl's Toy (IRE) 1

7. **Mr D.A. JOHNSON** 8
   Vivid Imagination (IRE) 6
   Think Commercial (IRE) 1
   Lord Atterbury (IRE)* 1
   ** owned jointly with Mr P.J. Finn*

10. **Mr D. BRACE** 7
   Rostock (IRE) 4
   Dawn's Cognac (IRE) 2
   Braceys Girl (IRE) 1

10. **Mr D. DAVIDSON** 7
   Passing Danger (FR) 4
   Eighty Days (IRE) 2
   Dere Street 1

10. **Mr J.G. PHILLIPS** 7
   Camden Carrig (IRE) 2
   Dinsey Finnegan (IRE) 2
   Lord Ken (IRE) 2
   Leachbrook Lady 1

10. **Mrs P.C. STIRLING** 7
   Pharmistice (IRE) 4
   Clifford Bay (IRE) 3

10. **Mr P. MALTBY** 7
   Lord Of The Mist (IRE) 5
   Red Native (IRE) 2

10. **Mr V. Thompson** 7
   Decent Bond (IRE) 4
   Falcon's Flame (USA) 2
   The Cincinnati Kid 1

Horse & Hound Leading Horse

Grand Marnier National Owners Championship

1970	Barty	Mr A. Gordon-Watson	10 Wins
1971	Golden Batman	Mr C.M.C. Hancock	8 Wins
1972	Pensham	Mrs H.P. Rushton	11 Wins
1973	Master Vesuvius	Mr J.M. Turner	11Wins
1974	Boy Bumble	Mr J.M. Turner	12Wins
1975	Even Harmony	Mr J.M. Turner	11 Wins
1976	Hardcastle	Mr J.M. Turner	9 Wins
1977	Hardcastle	Mr J.M. Turner	11 Wins
1978	Little Fleur	Mr R. Wynn	12Wins
1979	Hargan	Mr P. Tylor	10 Wins
1980	Florida King	Mr T. Hunnable	8 Wins
1981	Nostradamus	Mr J. Sumner	9 Wins
1982	MacKelly	Mr R. Bulgin	8 Wins
1983	Seine Bay	Mrs B. Perry	8 Wins
1984	National Clover	Mr D.G.L. Llewellin	9 Wins
1985	Brigadier Mouse	Mrs C. Foote-Forster	9 Wins
1986	Sweet Diana	Mr C.D. Dawson	9 Wins
1987	Mantinolas	Mrs K.R.J. Nicholas	8 Wins
1988	Stanwick Lad	Mr T.F.G. Marks	10 Wins
1989	For A Lark	Mr J.F. Weldhen	10 Wins

Daily Telegraph Leading Horse

1990	Timber Tool	W.J. Evans	11 Wins
1991	Fort Hall	Mrs L. Wadham	10 Wins
1992	Brunico	Mrs R.J. Mansell	12 Wins
1993	Melton Park	Mr A.J. Papworth	12 Wins

Grand Marnier National Owners Championship

1994	Melton Park	Mr A.J. Papworth	7 Wins
1995	Handsome Harvey	Mr & Mrs E.L. Harries	10 Wins
1996	Phar Too Touchy	Miss R.A. Francis	10 Wins
1997	Butler John (IRE)	Mr N. Viney	10 Wins
1998	St Gregory	Mr & Mrs A. Howland Jackson	9 Wins

Horse & Hound Leading Horse

1999	Copper Thistle	Mr R. Hunnisett	10 Wins
2000	Balisteros (FR)	Mrs B. Thomson	10 Wins
2001	not awarded because of foot-and-mouth epidemic		
2002	Upham Lord (IRE)	Mrs E.W. Wilson	11 Wins
2003	Upham Lord (IRE)	Mrs E.W. Wilson	8 Wins
2004	Upton Adventure (IRE)	Mr P.J. Corbett	8 Wins

Top of the Handicap

1959	Whinstone Hill	**12-7**	*R. Brewis*	Percy
1960	Whinstone Hill	**12-7**	*R. Brewis*	Percy
1961	Pride Of Ivanhoe	**12-10**	*S.T. Hewitt*	Atherstone
1962	Pride Of Ivanhoe	**12-10**	*S.T. Hewitt*	Atherstone
1963	Freddie	**12-7**	*R. Tweedie*	Duke of Buccleugh's
1964	Freddie	**12-8**	*R. Tweedie*	Duke of Buccleugh's
1965	Baulking Green	**12-2**	*J. Reade*	Old Berkshire
1966	Baulking Green	**12-0**	*J. Reade*	Old Berkshire
1967	Baulking Green	**12-0**	*J. Reade*	Old Berkshire
	Cham	**12-0**	*Mrs C. Radclyffe*	Old Berkshire
1968	Titus Oates	**12-7**	*C.D. Collins*	Zetland
1969	What A Myth	**12-8**	*Lady Weir*	Quorn
1970	Battle Royal II	**11-13**	*Lord Mostyn*	Flint & Denbigh
1971	Grey Sombrero	**12-1**	*W.F. Caudwell*	Old Berkshire
1972	Credit Call	**12-2**	*C.D. Collins*	Quorn
1973	Hilbirio	**12-0**	*C.D. Collins*	Quorn
1974	Hilbirio	**12-0**	*C.D. Collins*	Quorn
1975	Forest Rock	**11-12**	*P.C.R. Wates*	Chiddingfold, Lec & Cowdray
1976	Otter Way	**12-8**	*O.J. Carter*	East Devon
1977	Long Lane	**11-8**	*R.J. Shepherd*	Cotswold
	Remigio	**11-8**	*Mrs G.M. Paterson*	Old Surrey & Burstow
1978	Spartan Missile	**12-0**	*M.J. Thorne*	Warwickshire
1979	Spartan Missile	**13-0**	*M.J. Thorne*	Warwickshire
1980	Spartan Missile	**13-0**	*M.J. Thorne*	Warwickshire
1981	Spartan Missile	**12-7**	*M.J. Thorne*	Warwickshire
1982	Grittar	**12-0**	*F.H. Gilman*	Cottesmore
1983	Eliogarty	**11-10**	*Miss C. Beasley*	Meath
1984	Venture to Cognac	**11-10**	*N.E.C. Sherwood*	East Essex
1985	Further Thought	**11-9**	*Mrs V. Vanden Bergh*	East Sussex & R. Marsh
	Royal Judgement	**11-9**	*Lady Rootes*	East Sussex & R. Marsh
1986	Border Burg	**11-12**	*J.S. Delahooke*	Whaddon Chase
1987	Border Burg	**11-8**	*J.S. Delahooke*	Bicester with Whaddon Chase
1988	Certain Light	**11-11**	*Mrs J. Campbell*	Tickham
1989	Call Collect	**12-0**	*J. Clements*	Sinnington
1990	Call Collect	**12-0**	*J. Clements*	Sinnington
1991	Mystic Music	**11-12**	*Mrs H. Forster*	Dumfriesshire
1992	Rushing Wild	**11-7**	*J.A. Keighley*	Blackmore & Sparkford Vale
	Teaplanter	**11-7**	*R.G. Russell*	Pytchley
1993	Double Silk	**12-0**	*R.C. Wilkins*	Mendip Farmers
1994	Double Silk	**12-0**	*R.C. Wilkins*	Mendip Farmers
1995	Fantus	**11-8**	*J.A. Keighley*	Blackmore & Sparkford Vale
1996	Elegant Lord (IRE)	**12-1**	*J.P. McManus*	Scarteen
1997	Fantus	**11-12**	*J.A. Keighley*	Blackmore & Sparkford Vale
1998	Earthmover (IRE)	**12-7**	*R.M. Penny*	Cattistock
1999	Castle Mane (IRE)	**12-4**	*C.R Dixey*	Meynell & S. Staffs
2000	Castle Mane (IRE)	**12-2**	*C.R Dixey*	Meynell & S. Staffs
2001	Blanville (FR)	**12-0**	*P.A.D. Scouller*	Garth & S. Berks
2002	Torduff Express (IRE)	**12-0**	*T. Hubbard, A. Heard, J. George & R. Metherell*	Torrington Farmers
2003	Kingscliff (IRE)	**12-2**	*A.J. Sendell*	Weston & Banwell Harriers
2004	Torduff Express (IRE)	**11-10**	*Two Plus Two*	Taunton Vale

Performance of the Handicap in the 2004 Hunter Chases

126 Hunter Chases were run in 2004. Of these 123 were won by rated horses (the remainder were won by horses — mostly ex-NH performers — prior to publication of their ratings). 69 of the 123 winners (56%) came from the top two of the Handicap (67% of them being top-rated).

The best priced top-rated winners (Tote dividends in brackets) were:

1490	Trivial (IRE)	14-1	(£11.90)	241	Red Brook Lad	11-2	(£6.00)jt
1453	Torduff Express (IRE)	11-1	(£13.60)	1172	Caught At Dawn (IRE)	5-1	(£6.10)
1360	Commanche Law (IRE)	9-1	(£15.70)jt	1361	Coolefind (IRE)	7-2	(£5.50)jt
1438	Dancing Fosenby	6-1	(£8.80)	1376	Earthmover (IRE)	3-1	(£3.60)

The best second top-rated winners were:

122	Star Of Raven	16-1	(£26.90)jt	734	Jazz Night	5-1	(£7.00)jt
346	Mullensgrove	12-1	(£21.00)jt	1452	Cantarinho	6-1	(£7.00)
891	Fair Wind (IRE)	8-1	(£7.20)	1169	Torduff Express (IRE)	9-2	(£5.80)jt
1354	King Of The Dawn	15-2	(£10.20)	377	Ababou (FR)	9-2	(£4.90)jt

Backing the two top-rated (inc joints) in either order on the Tote Exacta produced the following:

122	Star Of Raven & Master Wood	£188.20
1169	Torduff Express (IRE) & Mullensgrove	£47.70
734	Jazz Night & Viscount Bankes	£42.50
629	Macgeorge (IRE) & The Granby (IRE)	£39.60
377	Ababou (FR) & Supreme Silence (IRE)	£22.70

Backing the two top-rated (inc joints) in either order as a Computer Straight Forecast reversed produced:

122	Star Of Raven & Master Wood	£57.91
734	Jazz Night & Viscount Bankes	£53.21
629	Macgeorge (IRE) & The Granby (IRE)	£41.50
377	Ababou (FR) & Supreme Silence (IRE)	£31.91
1169	Torduff Express (IRE) & Mullensgrove	£29.87

Leading Sales Prices in 2004

Horses that Point-to-Pointed and were sold at Auction in 2004

Caipiroska	65,000 gns	Simon Christian	Doncaster, May
Lord Of The Road	50,000 gns	Highflyer Bloodstock	Doncaster, May
Black Collar	41,000 gns	Kim Bailey	Doncaster, May
Reflected Glory (IRE)	33,000 gns	Highflyer Bloodstock	Doncaster, May
I Am Said I (IRE)	24,000 gns	C.J. Barnett	Doncaster, Aug
Ask Again	23,000 gns	Lavender Hill Stud	Doncaster, May
Grey Fandango (IRE)	22,000 gns	H. Hogarth	Doncaster, May
Uncle Neil (IRE)	20,000 gns	H. Crow	Doncaster, May
Mr Hawkeye (USA)	17,000 gns	Ian Hamilton (private sale)	Doncaster, May
Mytimie (IRE)	14,000 gns	D.E. Harrison	Doncaster, May
Parsifal	12,500 gns	Peter Wegmann	Doncaster, Oct
Strong Tartan (IRE)	10,000 gns	Mrs J. Joules	Doncaster, May
Redhouse Chevalier	9000 gns	Robin O'Ryan	Doncaster, May
Master Club Royal	€7800	Neil King	Ascot, Jun
Keitho (IRE)	€7500	Mr & Mrs M. Green	Ascot, Feb
Raging Torrent	7000 gns	Mrs H. Cobb	Doncaster, Oct
Rip Kirby	7000 gns	Hoscote Estate	Doncaster, Aug
Lady Widd (IRE)	€7000	Crohane Stud	Ascot, Jun
Traditional (IRE)	€7000	A. Tizzard	Ascot, Jul
Epsilo De La Ronce (FR)	6000 gns	Matt Gingell	Doncaster, Aug
Soundtrack (IRE)	6000 gns	Nick Sarson	Doncaster, Aug
Yorkshire Edition (IRE)	5500 gns	Mrs E. Inman	Doncaster, Oct
Kayleigh (IRE)	€5200	Cash	Ascot, Jun
Native Daisy (IRE)	€5000	W.R. Baddiley	Ascot, Jun
Cross River	5000 gns	David Heys	Doncaster, Oct
Fair Kiowa (IRE)	5000 gns	David Smyly Bloodstock	Doncaster, Aug
Golden Rivet	5000 gns	T. Abbott	Doncaster, Aug

Horses Sold at Auction in 2004

All For Jake (IRE)	£2500	William Fife	Ascot, Jun
Alvero (FR)	4400 gns	Matt Gingell	Doncaster, Aug
Alvero (FR)	500 gns	Suzy Crossman	Doncaster, Oct
Arctic Snip	2000 gns	Stephen Place	Doncaster, May
Ashgan (IRE)	3000 gns	Dr Philip Pritchard	Doncaster, May
Ask Again	23,000 gns	Lavender Hill Stud	Doncaster, May
Athenian Law	£1500	Cash	Ascot, Jun
B B Boy	£4200	Mrs P. Lucy	Ascot, Aug
Barry Lydon (IRE)	£2500	Chris Popham	Ascot, Jun
Beauty Star (IRE)	800 gns	C. Thomas	Doncaster, Aug
Black Collar	41,000 gns	Kim Bailey	Doncaster, May
Bloowit	£2700	Susan Fenton	Ascot, Aug
Caipiroska	65,000 gns	Simon Christian	Doncaster, May
Calinash (IRE)	£1250	Richard Barber	Ascot, Jul
Callitwatulike	£3500	Patrick Picton-Warlow	Ascot, Jul
Captive (IRE)	£1900	Miss V. Burn	Ascot, Jun
Carvilla (IRE)	£3300	B. Ansell	Ascot, Oct
Castlediva	£1300	Mrs M. Stephens	Ascot, Jul
Catalan Girl	£4500	Murray Farms Ltd	Ascot, Jun
Cedar Grove	900 gns	Vicky Pincombe	Doncaster, May
Chief Mouse	£3100	Jim Price	Ascot, Feb
Chief Seattle (IRE)	2200 gns	Redbridge	Doncaster, Aug
Contrary King	£900	M. Furlong	Ascot, Jun
Coombe Quest	£1100	Cash	Ascot, Oct
Coral Bay	£1400	J. Weldhen	Ascot, Oct
Cosmic Flight (IRE)	£550	Tony Boon	Ascot, Oct
Cotteir Chief (IRE)	£1000	Cash	Ascot, Apr
Crewski	£2300	A. Gibbon	Ascot, Feb
Cross River	5000 gns	David Heys	Doncaster, Oct
Crystal Vein	£1550	M. Roe	Ascot, Feb

Deep Design (IRE)	£800	H. Sharpe	Ascot, Oct
Design X Press	£2100	Chris Lawson	Ascot, Jul
Do It Again (IRE)	1200 gns	Anne Robson	Doncaster, May
Dolitanlad	£1400	N. Page	Ascot, Aug
Donrico (IRE)	1250 gns	Magnolia Bloodstock	Doncaster, May
Drumhorc (IRE)	£4600	P.J. Morgan	Ascot, Jun
Epsilo De La Ronce (FR)	6000 gns	Matt Gingell	Doncaster, Aug
Execute (IRE)	£2100	Arun Green	Ascot, Apr
Exmoor Express	3300 gns	Hannah Barnard	Doncaster, Jan
Fair Kiowa (IRE)	5000 gns	David Smyly Bloodstock	Doncaster, Aug
Final Belle	£2700	Cash	Ascot, Jun
Fine And Dandy (IRE)	£3000	Nigel Hooper	Ascot, Jun
Fluted Edge	£1000	Paul Thomas	Ascot, Jul
Frosty Fella	1600 gns	S. Rodman	Doncaster, May
Gayble	800 gns	D. Smith	Doncaster, Oct
General Craig	£1050	Louise Gibbons	Ascot, Jul
Genereux	£3700	Mrs Rising	Ascot, Jun
Glacial Boy	£2900	R. Harraway	Ascot, Aug
Glacial Sygnet (IRE)	2500 gns	J.L. Gledson	Doncaster, Jan
Glen Mist (IRE)	1500 gns	Miss L. Harfield	Ascot, Jun
Golden Rivet	5000 gns	T. Abbott	Doncaster, Aug
Good Thyne Charlie (IRE)	2750 gns	Ruth Wollerton (private sale)	Doncaster, May
Got Alot On (USA)	£1800	F.E. Sutherland	Ascot, Apr
Grand Ambition (USA)	3000 gns	Sarah Edwards	Doncaster, Aug
Grey Fandango (IRE)	22,000 gns	H. Hogarth	Doncaster, May
Gunner Be True	£3000	Cash	Ascot, Jul
Hail Stone (IRE)	£2700	R. Page	Ascot, Oct
Heathyards Element	£1000	W.R. Baddiley	Ascot, Jun
Hendrix	£1500	M. Furlong	Ascot, Jun
Hi Up Brenkley	2400 gns	Mr & Mrs B.K. Holt	Doncaster, Aug
Holywell Girl	2000 gns	Home Farm Racing	Doncaster, May
Honeyfantastic	£2700	B. Andrews	Ascot, Oct
Howya Matey (IRE)	1000 gns	R. O'Sheen Bloodstock	Doncaster, May
Howya Matey (IRE)	£3000	Mr Hooper	Ascot, Jul
Hubbly Bubbly	£650	M. Roe	Ascot, Feb
I Am Said I (IRE)	24,000 gns	C.J. Barnett	Doncaster, Aug
Ile Distinct (IRE)	£1800	Deborah Smith	Ascot, Jul
Imposa	1200 gns	Ruth Wollerton	Doncaster, Aug
Inner State	£4000	Mrs P.M. Stevens	Ascot, Feb
Inner State	£1500	Jill Carenza	Ascot, Aug
Italian Clover	£1050	C. Nenaditch	Ascot, Jul
Izzuthefox (IRE)	2500 gns	Nick Sarson	Doncaster, Aug
Kayleigh (IRE)	£5200	Cash	Ascot, Jun
Keitho (IRE)	£7500	Mr & Mrs M. Green	Ascot, Feb
La Colina (IRE)	£1500	Cash	Ascot, Jul
Lady Widd (IRE)	£7000	Crohane Stud	Ascot, Jun
Lazy Lemon	£1800	Cash	Ascot, Jul
Let's Rock	£3200	Ann Price	Ascot, Jun
Littleton Zeus (IRE)	1200 gns	Ruth Wollerton	Doncaster, Aug
Lord Of The Road	50,000 gns	Highflyer Bloodstock	Doncaster, May
Major Reno (IRE)	£2100	Cash	Ascot, Feb
Master Club Royal	£7800	Neil King	Ascot, Jun
Meadows Prince (IRE)	£1800	G. Bryan	Ascot, Apr
Merry Major	£850	Julie Mathias	Ascot, Jun
Midnight Coup	£1400	E. Tyler	Ascot, Oct
Millennium Gold	£3000	Cash	Ascot, Oct
Mistrio	£4800	P.A. Tetley	Ascot, Oct
Moonlite Magic (IRE)	£1700	T. Hitchman & Mrs C. Hewson	Ascot, Aug
Morph	£1500	Wyn Morris	Ascot, Oct
Mr Hawkeye (USA)	17,000 gns	Ian Hamilton (private sale)	Doncaster, May
Mytimie (IRE)	14,000 gns	D.E. Harrison	Doncaster, May
Native Daisy (IRE)	£5000	W.R. Baddiley	Ascot, Jun
Native King (IRE)	£1500	W.J. Day	Ascot, Jul

New Ross (IRE)	4000 gns	R.J. Symonds	Doncaster, Aug
Newmarket Magic (IRE)	£3400	Neil King	Ascot, Jul
Nip On	1000 gns	Mike Sowersby	Doncaster, Jan
Noaff (IRE)	1300 gns	E. Williams	Doncaster, Aug
On The Deck	£800	R.D. Thomson	Ascot, Aug
Onward Bound	£3000	Mr Wakeham	Ascot, Jun
Owenabue Valley (IRE)	£3000	T. Vadasz	Ascot, Oct
Parsifal	12,500 gns	Peter Wegmann	Doncaster, Oct
Peaceful Bow (IRE)	£2800	Jill Carenza	Ascot, Aug
Plain Polly (IRE)	£1500	Linda Court	Ascot, Jun
Pure Steel (IRE)	1000 gns	A. Jacobs	Doncaster, Aug
Raging Torrent	7000 gns	Mrs H. Cobb	Doncaster, Oct
Rainbow Star (FR)	£900	M. Sweetland	Ascot, Oct
Ravenscar	3800 gns	C. Pogson	Doncaster, Aug
Red Tyrant	500 gns	Miss S.K. Richards	Doncaster, Aug
Redhouse Chevalier	9000 gns	Robin O'Ryan	Doncaster, May
Reflected Glory (IRE)	33,000 gns	Highflyer Bloodstock	Doncaster, May
Regency Rake	£2300	Edward James	Ascot, Feb
Rip Kirby	7000 gns	Hoscote Estate	Doncaster, Aug
Rosegrove Rooster	2000 gns	C. Wanless	Doncaster, Oct
Rouge Lady	£2200	Nick Sarson	Ascot, Jun
Rundetto (IRE)	£1700	R. Bainbridge	Ascot, Jul
Russian Connection (IRE)	£2100	G. Edwards	Ascot, Oct
Rutherford	1000 gns	Benjamin Walker	Doncaster, May
Sadler's Vic	£3200	F.J. Brennan	Ascot, Feb
Sadler's Vic	1800 gns	T.L. Brooks	Doncaster, May
Sales Dodger (IRE)	£1200	G. Adam	Ascot, Oct
Scallybuck (IRE)	£900	Gavin Adam	Ascot, Oct
Shame I	£1600	Vendor	Ascot, Jul
Silver Pot Black	£3400	Cash	Ascot, Jun
Siobhans Quinner (IRE)	£1850	Pamela Cook	Ascot, Aug
Sixes And Sevens (IRE)	1200 gns	Lucy Bell	Doncaster, Aug
Soundtrack (IRE)	6000 gns	Nick Sarson	Doncaster, Aug
Spot The Business	3000 gns	Graeme McPherson	Doncaster, May
Strong Tartan (IRE)	10,000 gns	Mrs J. Joules	Doncaster, May
Super Dolphin	4200 gns	Forge Bloodstock	Doncaster, Aug
Tap Dance	£4500	Adrian Brown	Ascot, Apr
Terino	£4100	A. Tizzard	Ascot, Jul
The Glen Road (IRE)	£4200	Tony Carroll	Ascot, Jul
The Grandson (IRE)	£450	S. Morton	Ascot, Jun
The Green Goblin (NZ)	£1600	Ruth Wollerton	Ascot, Jun
Think Commercial (IRE)	4000 gns	Churston Family	Doncaster, May
Thixendale	£3100	S. Durant	Ascot, Jul
Thunderpoint (IRE)	£1500	Nick Sarson	Ascot, Aug
Tiger Talk	2000 gns	Richard Guest	Doncaster, May
Tiraldo (FR)	£1050	Mrs H. May	Ascot, Jul
Traditional (IRE)	£7000	A. Tizzard	Ascot, Jul
Travelling Jack	£3600	T. Garton	Ascot, Jun
Treasulier (IRE)	£3500	Les Trott	Ascot, Oct
Truicear	£1200	T.E. Wardell	Ascot, Jun
Uncle Ada (IRE)	3000 gns	D.J. Minty	Doncaster, May
Uncle Neil (IRE)	20,000 gns	H. Crow	Doncaster, May
Viva Bingo (IRE)	£500	R.D. Thomson	Ascot, Jun
War Bride	£1400	P. Lowe	Ascot, Feb
Warren Hill	£2100	J.H. Young	Ascot, Oct
West Pal (IRE)	£1800	Cash	Ascot, Jul
Whats Up Jake	£550	Mrs C. Thomas	Ascot, Jul
Woodland Warrior	£1000	R.D. Thomson	Ascot, Jun
Worthy Man	£1900	S.T. Lewis	Ascot, Feb
Worthy Man	£1900	B. England	Ascot, Jul
Yorkshire Edition (IRE)	5500 gns	Mrs E. Inman	Doncaster, Oct

Point-to-Point Statistics 2004

Type of Races	Weight	No Races	No Runners	AVERAGE
Club Members	*12st5lb*	6	51	8.50
Club Members	*12st*	25	176	7.24
Club Members (Nov Rdrs)	*12st5lb*	4	46	11.5
Club Members (Nov Rdrs)	*12st*	31	249	8.03
Club Members (Vet & Nov Rdrs)	*12st5lb*	1	9	9.00
Club Members (Vet & Nov Rdrs)	*12st*	1	9	9.00
Club Members Conditions	*12st5lb*	1	12	12.0
Club Members Conditions	*12st*	7	65	9.29
Club Members Confined Moderate	*12st5lb*	1	6	6.00
Club Members Mares	*12st*	2	11	5.50
Club Members Moderate	*12st*	1	15	15.0
Club Members Novices	*12st5lb*	1	9	9.00
Club Members, 2m4f	*12st*	1	10	10.0
Club Members Sub-Total*		82	668	8.15
Confined	*12st5lb*	11	65	5.91
Confined (Nov Rdrs)	*12st*	1	6	6.00
Confined (Vet & Nov Rdrs)	*12st*	1	7	7.00
Confined Conditions	*12st*	1	6	6.00
Confined	*12st*	117	907	7.75
Mens Confined	*12st*	1	4	4.00
Ladies Confined	*11st*	2	21	10.5
Confineds Sub-Total		134	1016	7.58
Hunt Members	*12st5lb*	78	363	4.65
Hunt Members	*12st*	79	365	4.62
Hunt Members (stone walls), 3m4f	*12st*	1	6	6.00
Hunt Members Sub-Total		158	734	4.65
Intermediate (Nov Rdrs)	*12st*	8	54	6.75
Intermediate	*12st*	70	503	7.19
Intermediates Sub-Total		78	557	7.14
Ladies Open	*11st*	156	1058	6.78
Ladies Open, 3m2f-4m	*11st*	4	35	8.75
Ladies Sub-Total		160	1093	6.83
Mens Open	*12st5lb*	49	387	7.90
Mens Open	*12st*	108	706	6.54
Mens Open, 3m2f-4m	*12st5lb*	2	18	9.00
Mens Open, 3m5f-4m	*12st*	3	28	9.33
Mens Open Sub-Total		162	1139	7.03
Mixed Open	*12st*	33	219	6.64
Mixed Open, 4m-4m1f	*12st*	7	61	8.71
Mixed Open (Nov Rdrs)	*12st*	1	13	13.0
Mixed Opens Sub-Total		41	293	7.15
Club Members Maiden	*12st5lb*	3	29	9.67
Club Members Maiden	*12st*	7	70	10.0
Club Members Mares Maiden	*12st*	16	167	10.4
Club Members Horses & Geldings Maiden 6&7yo	*12st*	1	12	12.0
Club Members Maiden Sub-Total		27	278	10.3

Confined Maiden	*12st5lb*	6	66	11.0
Confined Maiden	*12st*	57	602	10.6
Confined Horses & Geldings Maiden	*12st*	1	5	5.00
Confined Maidens Sub-Total		64	673	10.5
Open Maiden	*12st5lb*	39	372	9.54
Open Maiden	*12st*	228	2291	10.1
Open Maiden Mares	*12st*	4	28	7.00
Open Horses & Geldings Maiden	*12st*	3	35	11.7
Open Maidens Sub-Total		274	2726	9.95
Confined Maiden 56&7yo, 2m4f	*12st*	5	49	9.80
Open Maiden 56&7yo, 2m4f	*12st*	40	405	10.1
Club Members Maiden 56&7yo, 2m4f88y	*12st*	3	27	9.00
Open Maiden 56&7yo, 2m5f	*12st*	4	42	10.5
2m4f Sub-Total		52	523	10.1
All Maidens Sub-Total		417	4200	10.1
Restricted	*12st5lb*	23	236	10.3
Restricted	*12st*	166	1568	9.45
Restricted (Nov Rdrs)	*12st*	1	7	7.00
Restricted (Nov Rdrs)	*12st*	2	22	11.0
Club Members Restricted	*12st5lb*	3	28	9.33
Club Members Restricted	*12st*	13	119	9.15
Restricteds Sub-Total		208	1980	9.52
Total		1440	11680	8.11

* *for members of the Army Saddle Club, Cambridgeshire Harriers Hunt Club, Countryside Alliance, Harborough Hunts Club, Harkaway Club, Lincolnshire United Hunts Club, Melton Hunt Club, Midlands Area Hunt Club, Northern Area P-t-P Association, Old Raby Hunt Club, Oxford University Hunt Club, Pegasus Club, Point-to-Point Owners & Riders Association, South East Hunts Club, South Midlands Area Club, Thames Valley Club, Tweseldown Racing Club, United Services and Welsh Border Counties Area Club*

Most Popular Meetings

Nine meetings more than 100 runners, they were:

Ledbury	*Maisemore Park*	144 runners
East Devon	*Bishops Court*	146 runners
Ledbury	*Maisemore Park*	118 runners
Golden Valley	*Bredwardine*	117 runners
Point-to-Point Owners & Riders Club	*Barbury Racecourse*	111 runners
Teme Valley	*Brampton Bryan*	110 runners
Cottesmore	*Garthorpe*	108 runners
Old Raby Hunt Club	*Witton Castle*	106 runners
Brecon & Talybont	*Llanfrynach*	102 runners
Ross Harriers	*Garnons*	102 runners

Not-Quite So Popular Meetings

New Forest	*Larkhill*	20 runners
Cotswold Vale Farmers	*Andoversford*	21 runners
Dulverton Farmers	*Mounsey Hill Gate*	21 runners
Staff College & R.M.A. Sandhurst Draghounds	*Larkhill*	21 runners
Exmoor	*Bratton Down*	23 runners
Seavington	*Littlewindsor*	24 runners
Vine & Craven	*Hackwood Park*	25 runners
Carmarthenshire	*Lydstep*	26 runners
West Street Tickham	*Aldington*	27 runners
14 Regiment Royal Artillery	*Larkhill*	28 runners
Taunton Vale Harriers	*Kingston St Mary*	29 runners
Vale of Aylesbury with Garth & S. Berks	*Tweseldown*	29 runners
Vale of Lune	*Whittington*	29 runners

Most Races

East Devon	*Bishops Court*	12 races
East Cornwall	*Great Trethew*	11 races
Cottesmore	*Garthorpe*	10 races
Ledbury	*Maisemore Park*	10 races
South Herefordshire	*Garnons*	9 races
Bicester with Whaddon Chase	*Mollington*	9 races
Brecon & Talybont	*Llanfrynach*	9 races
Dulverton West	*Bratton Down*	9 races
Golden Valley	*Bredwardine*	9 races
Harkaway Club	*Chaddesley Corbett*	9 races
North Norfolk Harriers	*Higham*	9 races
Ross Harriers	*Garnons*	9 races
Teme Valley	*Brampton Bryan*	9 races
Tivyside	*Cilwendeg*	9 races
Tynedale	*Corbridge*	9 races
York & Ainsty (North and South)	*Easingwold*	9 races

Least Races

Hurworth	*Hutton Rudby*	4 races

Meeting abandoned early because of high winds

The Biggest Cavalry Charges

Ledbury Restricted	*Maisemore Park*	20 runners
Point-to-Point Owners & Riders Club Mens Open	*Barbury Racecourse*	20 runners
Albrighton Mens Open	*Weston Park*	19 runners
Monmouthshire	*Restricted Llanvapley*	19 runners
Brecon & Talybont Confined	*Llanfrynach*	18 runners
Cambridgeshire with Enfield Chace Restricted	*Horseheath*	18 runners
Melton Hunt Club Members Conditions	*Garthorpe*	18 runners
Point-to-Point Owners & Riders Club Ladies Open	*Barbury Racecourse*	18 runners
South Shropshire Restricted	*Eyton-on-Severn*	18 runners
Teme Valley Open Maiden (Div 2)	*Brampton Bryan*	18 runners

Walkovers

Badsworth & Bramham Moor Hunt Members	*Heslaker*
Banwen Miners Hunt Members	*Pentreclwydau*
Banwen Miners Mixed Open (West Wales Grand National), 4m	*Pentreclwydau*
Berks & Bucks Draghounds Hunt Members	*Kingston Blount*
Countryside Alliance Club (Wales) Mens Open	*Bonvilston*
Sir W.W. Wynn's Intermediate	*Eaton Hall*
South Notts Hunt Members	*Thorpe Lodge*
South Tetcott Hunts Members (with Tetcott)	*Lifton*
Tedworth Hunt Members	*Barbury Racecourse*
Vale of Aylesbury with Garth & S. Berks Mens Open	*Tweseldown*
Vine & Craven Mixed Open	*Hackwood Park*

Analysis of Runners

3896 Hunters Certificates were registered in 2004 (excluding any second Certificates lodged and any that were subsequently revoked). 28 unregistered horses were among the 3395 horses that actually ran in Point-to-Points. A breakdown shows that 2682 (79.0%) were geldings, 709 (20.9%) were mares and 4 (0.12%) were entire; these figures seldom fluctuate by more than a single per cent.

Entries

The total number of entries at Point-to-Point meetings in 2004 was 28,493 including abandoned meeetings, The six abandoned meetings accounted for a further 862 entries.

Most Entries in an Undivided Race

Entries were made for 1454 races in 2004 (including 41 at abandoned meetings). The most entries in races not divided at close of entries were:

V.W.H. Open Maiden	*Siddington*	56 entries
Worcestershire Open Maiden	*Chaddesley Corbett*	55 entries
Duke of Beaufort's Open Maiden 8yo&up	*Didmarton*	53 entries
Wheatland Open Maiden 8yo&up	*Chaddesley Corbett*	52 entries
Wheatland Restricted	*Chaddesley Corbett*	51 entries
Weston & Banwell Harriers Open Maiden	*Cothelstone*	51 entries
Ledbury Restricted	*Maisemore Park*	50 entries
Wheatland Mens Open	*Chaddesley Corbett*	50 entries
Melton Hunt Club Members Conditions	*Garthorpe*	50 entries
Tanatside Restricted	*Eyton-on-Severn*	48 entries
Tredegar Farmers PPORA Club Members (Nov Rdrs)	*Rhydygwern*	48 entries
Ledbury Mixed Open	*Maisemore Park*	47 entries
Croome & West Warwickshire Open Maiden 56&7yo, 2m5f	*Upton-on-Severn*	47 entries

The Least Entries were for:

South Tetcott Hunts Members (with Tetcott)	*Lifton*	2 entries
Vale of Clettwr Hunt Members	*Erw Lon*	3 entries
Farmers Bloodhounds Hunt Members	*Dunthrop*	3 entries
Monmouthshire Hunt Members	*Llanvapley*	3 entries
High Peak Hunt Members (stone walls), 3m4f	*Flagg Moor*	3 entries
Aldenham Harriers Hunt Members	*Cottenham*	3 entries
Berks & Bucks Draghounds Hunt Members	*Kingston Blount*	3 entries
Badsworth & Bramham Moor Hunt Members	*Heslaker*	4 entries

The average was 20.2 entries per race.

Most Entries for a Meeting

Entries were made for 209 meetings (including all those abandoned, even if later re-arranged). The following received the most entries:

Ledbury	*(Maisemore Park)*	289 entries
East Devon	*(Bishops Court)*	277 entries
Wheatland	*(Chaddesley Corbett)*	273 entries
Harkaway Club	*(Chaddesley Corbett)*	272 entries
Teme Valley	*(Brampton Bryan)*	247 entries
Golden Valley	*(Bredwardine)*	238 entries
Duke of Beaufort's	*(Didmarton)*	237 entries
Cottesmore	*(Garthorpe)*	237 entries
Brecon & Talybont	*(Llanfrynach)*	236 entries

The Fewest Entries for a Meeting were:

Ashford Valley	*(Charing)*	62 entries
Hampshire	*(Hackwood Park)*	62 entries
Essex & Suffolk	*(Higham)*	66 entries
Surrey Union	*(Peper Harow)*	68 entries
Badsworth & Bramham Moor	*(Heslaker)*	74 entries
Vale of Aylesbury with Garth & S. Berks	*(Tweseldown)*	74 entries
Cotswold Vale Farmers	*(Andoversford)*	79 entries
Fife	*(Balcormo Mains)*	80 entries
West Street Tickham	*(Aldington)*	80 entries

The average was 140.5 entries per meeting

Entries by Horse

3677 individual horses were entered in Point-to-Point races (including abandoned meetings). The most entered horse was entered 41 times, whilst 327 horses were entered only once,the complete breakdown is:

Times Entered	No of Horses	Percentage
1-4	2091	32.9%
5-9	1244	33.8%
10-14	732	19.9%
15-19	339	9.22%
20-24	108	2.94%
25-29	27	0.73%
30-34	10	0.27%
35-39	6	0.16%
40-49	2	0.05%

The average was 7.98 entries per horse.

Most Entered Horse

Mr A West & Countess Goess-Saurau's	The Kings Fling	44
Mr W & Mrs A Rucker's	Euro Bob (IRE)	41
Mrs M Williams's	Le Prince	39
Miss V S Murphy's	Nice Approach (IRE)	38
Nice Approach Partnership's (Miss T Leahy)	Nearly Gold	37
Mrs K M Price's	Ballyalbert	36
Mr M A Lloyd & Mr A Goodwin's	Stretching (IRE)	36
Mr B A Kilpatrick's	Colquhoun	35
Miss R Heikkola's	Algan (FR)	34
Mr R G Kelvin-Hughes's	Hobbycyr (FR)	34
Mr D Brace's	Dawn's Cognac (IRE)	33
Mr M J Caldwell's	The Sky Is Blue	33
Mrs P A Deal's	Ballysicyos (FR)	32
Mr D S Dennis's	Newby End (IRE)	32
Mr J T B Hunt's	Merry Minstrel (IRE)	30
Mr R Pyman's	Opal'lou (FR)	30
Mr H & Mrs P Phipps's	Theatreland (USA)	30
Mr T Hamlin, Mr J M Dare & Mr J Snook's	What A Mover	30

Most Entered Horse which Never Ran

Mr D J Lee's	Aqua Star (IRE)	13
Mrs R Mackness's	Party Lad (IRE)	13
Mrs E Scott's	Derosa	11
Mr A Hollingsworth's	Mildan Grace	10
Mr & Mrs C Underwood's	Kitley Creek	9
Mr T S Ide's	Twenty To Eight	9
The Gare Hill Club's	Gare Hill (IRE)	8
Mr C B Taylor's	Garmondsway	8
Mr J Jones's	Itsfreddie	8
Mr H W Lavis's	Derring Dove	7
Mr J Milton's	Gregale	7
Mr S R Hanney's	Maori Chief (IRE)	7
Miss S Brotherton's	Willynilly	7
Mr M K Titchner's	Alotofbull (IRE)	6
Mr S J Leadbetter's	Desert Music	6
Miss W D M Mills's	Doubblue Teenso	6
Mr J M Ratcliffe's	Lilac Lady	6

Point-to-Point Runners Analysis 2004

Fate	Total	Percentage
1st	1444	12.4%
1st disq	1	0.01%
2nd	1414	12.1%
2nd disq	7	0.06%
3rd	1271	10.9%
3rd disq	3	0.03%
4th	988	8.46%
4th disq	8	0.07%
5th	643	5.50%
6th	369	3.16%
7th	199	1.70%
8th	116	0.99%
9th	52	0.45%
10th	41	0.35%
Finishers sub-Total	**6556**	**56.1%**
Pulled-ups	3474	29.7%
Fell	610	5.22%
Unseated	692	5.92%
Ran Out	151	1.29%
Refused	112	0.96%
Slipped Up	29	0.25%
Brought down	40	0.34%
Carried out	14	0.12%
Other	2	0.02%
Non-Finishers sub-Total	**5124**	**43.9%**
TOTAL	**11,680**	

Index to Advertisers

Baileys . . . . . cover
Brightwells . . . . . IFC
David Trundley 8-9
National Point-to-Point Archive 64
Point-to-Point Owners & Riders Association 1065
Race Reader 1173
Racing Post . . . . . 6 & 15
Talking Point 4
Tattersalls 10
TTI Video 28
UK Racing 30
Westcountry Videos 21
www.pointopoint.co.uk 25
Weatherbys Insurance 12

Annual Statistics

* *All cross-country races excluded*

Year	Point-to-Points				Hunter Chases			Overall		
	Pt-to-Pt Meetings	Races	Total Runners	Average per Race	Hunter Chases	Total Runners	Average per Race	Horses Competing	Total Runners	Average per Race
1961	196	1040	8157	7.84	95	934	9.83	2296	9091	8.01
1962	197	1046	7876	7.53	87	847	9.73	2141	8722	7.70
1963	175	925	7614	8.23	76	777	10.24	2115	8391	8.38
1964	197	1037	8107	7.82	91	780	8.57	2111	8887	7.87
1965	194	1024	7624	7.44	89	772	8.67	2153	8396	7.54
1966	185	995	8528	8.57	80	739	9.23	2262	9267	8.62
1967	192	1028	9002	8.75	81	724	8.93	2353	9726	8.77
1968	183	1004	8546	8.48	97	910	9.38	2344	9456	8.58
1969	180	986	8635	8.75	84	761	9.05	2450	9396	8.78
1970	190	1049	9804	9.34	88	873	9.69	2536	10,677	9.39
1971	182	1008	8994	8.92	101	953	9.43	2463	9947	8.96
1972	182	1022	9706	9.50	100	1049	10.49	2556	10,755	9.58
1973	184	1044	8825	8.45	125	1226	9.81	2528	10,051	8.60
1974	178	1036	9545	9.21	116	1169	10.08	2720	10,714	9.30
1975	166	1010	10,932	10.82	115	1242	10.80	2860	12,174	10.82
1976	183	1067	9186	8.61	129	1294	10.03	2824	10,480	8.76
1977	179	1086	10,709	9.86	126	1370	10.87	2923	12,079	9.97
1978	169	1062	11,514	10.84	118	1382	11.71	3086	12,896	10.93
1979	168	1058	11,021	10.45	111	1208	10.88	2933	12,229	10.46
1980	177	1110	10,647	9.59	128	1415	11.05	3218	12,062	9.74
1981	179	1180	12,487	10.58	122	1428	11.70	3264	13,915	10.69
*1982	184	1182	12,148	10.28	144	1576	10.94	3395	13,724	10.35
*1983	172	1150	12,553	10.92	120	1428	11.90	3352	13,981	11.09
*1984	188	1237	11,791	9.53	138	1504	10.90	3398	13,295	9.67
*1985	175	1164	12,301	10.57	121	1375	11.36	3454	13,676	10.64
*1986	176	1191	12,304	10.33	98	1200	12.24	3341	13,504	10.48
*1987	190	1237	11,708	9.46	122	1176	9.64	3333	12,884	9.48
*1988	193	1269	12,427	9.79	124	1252	10.10	3399	13,679	9.82
*1989	189	1282	12,429	9.69	135	1289	9.54	3508	13,718	9.68
*1990	196	1279	10,546	8.24	124	1098	8.85	3446	11,644	8.30
*1991	195	1293	11,613	8.98	127	1343	10.57	3499	12,956	9.12
*1992	202	1401	12,659	9.04	133	1396	10.50	3577	14,055	9.16
*1993	199	1425	13,086	9.18	143	1336	9.34	3765	14,422	9.20
*1994	202	1485	14,117	9.51	133	1268	9.53	3869	15,385	9.51
*1995	203	1492	12,815	8.57	137	1311	9.57	3790	14,126	8.67
*1996	207	1520	13,430	8.86	130	1271	9.77	3818	14,701	8.91
1997	205	1473	11,706	7.95	141	1256	8.91	3680	12,970	8.04
1998	193	1451	12,464	8.59	135	1229	9.10	3758	13,693	8.63
1999	198	1538	14,007	9.11	129	1352	10.48	4005	15,353	9.21
2000	201	1537	13,978	9.09	139	1422	10.23	4027	15,400	9.19
2001	50	218	2,270	10.41	87	1257	14.45	1906	3,527	11.56
2002	205	1543	13,513	8.76	131	1344	10.26	3656	14,856	8.88
2003	201	1463	11,957	8.17	124	1213	9.78	3563	13,170	8.30
2004	203	1440	11,680	8.11	126	1270	10.1	3493	12,950	8.27

Point-to-Point Horses, Runners and Winners in 2004 by Age and Sex

AGE	5	6	7	8	9	10	11	12	13	14	15	16	17	18	19	20	aged	TOTAL
GELDINGS																		
How many Raced	200	289	358	370	339	318	291	259	130	70	47	9	1	0	0	0	0	**2681**
How often they Won	80	117	184	147	202	167	125	93	62	22	6	3	0	0	0	0	0	**1208**
How often they Ran	545	855	1258	1301	1302	1181	1056	986	533	215	142	24	1	0	0	0	0	**9399**
Percentage Wins/Runs	14.7%	13.7%	14.6%	11.3%	15.5%	14.1%	11.8%	9.43%	11.6%	10.2%	4.22%	12.5%	0.00%	0.00%	0.00%	0.00%	0.00%	**12.9%**
MARES																		
How many Raced	85	123	119	119	113	69	35	26	16	3	1	0	0	0	0	0	0	**709**
How often they Won	13	28	54	38	40	34	17	10	0	0	2	0	0	0	0	0	0	**236**
How often they Ran	200	360	392	373	408	250	127	98	41	9	6	0	0	0	0	0	0	**2264**
Percentage Wins/Runs	6.50%	7.78%	13.8%	10.25	9.80%	13.6%	13.4%	10.2%	0.00%	0.00%	33.3%	0.00%	0.00%	0.00%	0.00%	0.00%	0.00%	**10.4%**
ENTIRES																		
How many Raced	0	1	0	1	0	1	1	0	0	0	0	0	0	0	0	0	0	**4**
How often they Won	0	0	0	0	0	0	0	0	0	0	0	0	0	0	0	0	0	**0**
How often they Ran	0	4	0	7	0	1	4	0	0	0	0	0	0	0	0	0	0	**16**
Percentage Wins/Runs	0.00%	0.00%	0.00%	0.00%	0.00%	0.00%	0.00%	0.00%	0.00%	0.00%	0.00%	0.00%	0.00%	0.00%	0.00%	0.00%	0.00%	**0.00%**
TOTAL																		
How many Raced	285	413	477	490	452	388	327	285	146	73	48	9	1	0	0	0	0	**3394**
How often they Won	93	145	238	185	242	201	142	103	62	22	8	3	0	0	0	0	0	**1444**
How often they Ran	745	1219	1650	1681	1710	1432	1187	1084	574	224	148	24	1	0	0	0	0	**11679**
Percentage Wins/Runs	12.5%	11.9%	14.4%	11.0%	14.2%	14.0%	12.0%	9.50%	10.8%	9.82%	5.40%	12.5%	0.00%	0.00%	0.00%	0.00%	0.00%	**12.4%**

Index to Point-to-Point Fixtures in 2005

Albrighton *(Weston Park)* . . . 12
Albrighton Woodland *(Chaddesley Corbett)* 203
Aldenham Harriers *(Cottenham)* . . . 135
Army *(Larkhill)* . . . 2
Ashford Valley *(Charing)* . . . 84
Atherstone *(Clifton-on-Dunsmore)* . . . 142
Avon Vale *(Larkhill)* . . . 112
Axe Vale *(Stafford Cross)* . . . 182
Badsworth & Bramham Moor *(Mordon)* . . . 85
Banwen Miners *(Pentreclwydau)* . . . 167
Bedale *(Hornby Castle)* . . . 126
Belvoir *(Garthorpe)* . . . 113
Berkeley *(Woodford)* . . . 148
Berks & Bucks Draghounds *(Kingston Blount)* . . . 202
Berwickshire *(Friars Haugh)* . . . 127
Bicester with Whaddon Chase *(Mollington)* . . . 44, 143
Bilsdale *(Easingwold)* . . . 175
Blackmore & Sparkford Vale *(Charlton Horethorne)* . . . 67
Blankney *(Garthorpe)* . . . 200
Border *(Hexham Racecourse)* . . . 196
Braes of Derwent *(Corbridge)* . . . 136
Brecon & Talybont *(Llanfrynach)* . . . 61
Brocklesby *(Brocklesby Park)* . . . 39
Burton *(Market Rasen Racecourse)* . . . 33
Cambridgeshire Harriers Hunt Club *(Cottenham)* . . . 1
Cambridgeshire with Enfield Chace *(Horseheath)* . . . 15
Cambridgeshire with Enfield Chace *(Northaw)* . . . 168
Cambridge University Draghounds *(Cottenham)* . . . 7
Carmarthenshire *(Pentreclwydau)* . . . 189
Cattistock *(Littlewindsor)* . . . 116
Cheshire *(Alpraham)* . . . 144
Cheshire Forest *(Tabley)* . . . 128
Chiddingfold, Leconfield & Cowdray *(Parham)* . . . 40
Cleveland *(Stainton Vale)* . . . 145
Clifton-on-Teme *(Upper Sapey)* . . . 194
College Valley & North Northumberland *(Alnwick)* . . . 34
Cotley *(Cotley)* . . . 169
Cotswold *(Andoversford)* . . . 68
Cotswold Vale Farmers *(Maisemore Park)* . 129
Cottesmore *(Garthorpe)* . . . 69
Countryside Alliance Club (Wales) *(Bonvilston)* . . . 204
Crawley & Horsham *(Parham)* . . . 72
Croome & West Warwickshire *(Upton-upon-Severn)* . . . 110
Cumberland *(Aspatria)* . . . 176
Cumberland Farmers *(Dalston)* . . . 117
Curre & Llangibby *(Howick)* . . . 45, 73
Dartmoor *(Flete Park)* . . . 149
Dart Vale & Haldon Harriers *(Buckfastleigh Racecourse)* . . . 79
Derwent *(Charm Park)* . . . 54
Devon & Somerset Staghounds *(Holnicote)* . 177
Duke of Beaufort's *(Didmarton)* . . . 50
Duke of Buccleuch's *(Friars Haugh)* . . . 62
Dulverton Farmers *(Mounsey Hill Gate)* . . 201
Dulverton West *(Bratton Down)* . . . 195
Dumfriesshire *(Netherby)* . . . 46
Dunston Harriers *(Ampton)* . . . 6
East Cornwall *(Great Trethew)* . . . 47, 118
East Devon *(Bishops Court)* . . . 51
East Essex *(Marks Tey)* . . . 35
East Kent *(Aldington)* . . . 97
Easton Harriers *(High Easter)* . . . 28
East Sussex & Romney Marsh *(Catsfield)* . 130
Eggesford *(Lifton)* . . . 137
Eglinton and Lanarkshire & Renfrewshire *(Overton Farm)* . . . 74
Essex *(High Easter)* . . . 114
Essex & Suffolk *(Higham)* . . . 123
Essex Farmers & Union *(Marks Tey)* . . 98, 178
Exmoor *(Bratton Down)* . . . 206
Farmers Bloodhounds *(Dunthrop)* . . . 36
Fernie *(Dingley)* . . . 163
Fife *(Balcormo Mains)* . . . 150
Fitzwilliam (Milton) *(Cottenham)* . . . 75
Flint & Denbigh *(Eaton Hall)* . . . 119
Four Burrow *(Trebudannon)* . . . 99, 159
14 Regiment Royal Artillery *(Larkhill)* . . . 199
Gelligaer Farmers *(Bonvilston)* . . . 179
Glamorgan *(Ystradowen)* . . . 86
Golden Valley *(Bredwardine)* . . . 184
Grafton *(Mollington)* . . . 80
Granta Harriers *(Higham)* . . . 55
Grove & Rufford *(Welbeck)* . . . 56
Hampshire *(Hackwood Park)* . . . 146
Harborough Race Club *(Dingley)* . . . 197
Harkaway Club *(Chaddesley Corbett)* . . . 23
Haydon *(Hexham)* . . . 190
Heythrop *(Dunthrop)* . . . 8
High Peak *(Flagg Moor)* . . . 111
Holcombe *(Whittington)* . . . 63
Holderness *(Dalton Park)* . . . 70
Hursley Hambledon *(Badbury Rings)* . . . 41
Hurworth *(Hutton Rudby)* . . . 76
Jedforest *(Friars Haugh)* . . . 16
Lamerton *(Kilworthy)* . . . 87
Lauderdale *(Mosshouses)* . . . 164
Ledbury *(Maisemore Park)* . . . 120
Lincolnshire United Hunts Club *(Market Rasen Racecourse)* . . . 13

Llandeilo Farmers *(Cilwendeg)* 115
Llangeinor *(Laleston)* 160
Ludlow *(Bitterley)* 131
Melton Hunt Club *(Garthorpe)* 185
Mendip Farmers *(Ston Easton)* 88
Meynell & South Staffordshire *(Weston Park)* .. 37
Mid Devon *(Black Forest Lodge)* 24
Middleton *(Whitwell-on-the-Hill)* 121
Midlands Area Club *(Thorpe Lodge)* 18
Mid Surrey Farmers Draghounds *(Charing)* 138
Minehead Harriers and West Somerset
(Holnicote) 188
Modbury Harriers *((Flete Park)* 180
Monmouthshire *(Llanvapley)* 124
Morpeth *(Tranwell)* 100
New Forest *(Larkhill)* 81
North Cornwall *(Wadebridge)* 17
North Cotswold *(Paxford)* 101
North Hereford *(Whitwick Manor)* 29
North Ledbury *(Maisemore Park)* 170
North Norfolk Harriers *(Higham)* 3
North Shropshire *(Eyton-on-Severn)* 171
North Staffordshire *(Sandon)* 89
North West Point-to-Point Club *(Tabley)* .. 191
Oakley *(Brafield-on-the-Green)* 64
Old Berkshire *(Lockinge)* 102
Old Raby Hunt Club *(Witton Castle)* 19
Old Surrey, Burstow & West Kent
(Penshurst) 122, 151
Oxford University Hunt Club
(Kingston Blount) 25
Pembrokeshire *(Trecoed)* 207
Pendle Forest & Craven *(Heslaker)* 161
Pentyrch *(Bonvilston)* 152
Percy *(Alnwick)* 96
Point-to-Point Owners & Riders Club
(Barbury Racecourse) 5
Portman *(Badbury Rings)* 139
Puckeridge *(Horseheath)* 90
Pytchley *(Guilsborough)* 132
Quantock Staghounds *(Cothelstone)* 77
Quorn *(Garthorpe)* 155
Radnor & West Hereford *(Cold Harbour)* .. 165
Ross Harriers *(Garnons)* 82
Royal Artillery *(Larkhill)* 11
Seavington *(Littlewindsor)* 156
Silverton *(Black Forest Lodge)* 9
Sinnington *(Duncombe Park)* 30
Sir W.W. Wynn's *(Eaton Hall)* 57
South & West Wilts *(Larkhill)* 162
South Devon *(Black Forest Lodge)* 103
South Dorset *(Milborne St Andrew)* 38
Southdown & Eridge *(Godstone)* 20, 52
South Durham *(Mordon)* 186
South East Hunts Club *(Charing)* 31
South Herefordshire *(Garnons)* 58
South Midlands Area Club
(Tweseldown Racecourse) 21
South Notts *(Thorpe Lodge)* 104
South Pembrokeshire *(Lydstep)* 105
South Pool Harriers
(Buckfastleigh Racecourse) 32
South Shropshire *(Eyton-on-Severn)* 106
South Tetcott *(Lifton)* 205
South Wold *(Brocklesby Park)* 83
Spooners & West Dartmoor *(Cherrybrook)* . 133
Staff College & R.M.A. Sandhurst Draghounds
(Larkhill) 59
Staintondale *(Charm Park)* 107
Stevenstone *(Vauterhill)* 172
Suffolk *(Ampton)* 71
Surrey Union *(Peper Harow)* 181
Tanatside *(Eyton-on-Severn)* 48
Taunton Vale *(Kingston St Mary)* 134
Taunton Vale Harriers
(Kingston St Mary) 108
Tedworth *(Barbury Racecourse)* 125
Teme Valley *(Brampton Bryan)* 153
Tetcott *(Lifton)* 192
Thurlow *(Horseheath)* 43
Tiverton *(Chipley Park)* 22
Tiverton Staghounds *(Bratton Down)* 208
Tivyside *(Cilwendeg)* 53
Torrington Farmers *(Umberleigh)* 209
Tredegar Farmers *(Rhydygwern)* 198
Tweseldown Racing Club
(Tweseldown Racecourse) 4
Tynedale *(Corbridge)* 60
United Pack *(Brampton Bryan)* 91
United Services *(Larkhill)* 26
Vale of Aylesbury with Garth & South Berks
(Kimble) 92
Vale of Aylesbury with Garth & South Berks
(Kingston Blount) 154, 187
Vale of Clettwr *(Erw Lon)* 27
Vale of Lune *(Whittington)* 93
V.W.H. *(Siddington)* 78
Vine & Craven *(Hackwood Park)* 109
Warwickshire *(Ashorne)* 173
Waveney Harriers *(Higham)* 14
Western *(Wadebridg)* 65
West Norfolk *(Fakenham)* 157
West of Yore *(Hornby Castle)* 49
Weston & Banwell Harriers *(Cothelstone)* . 193
West Percy *(Alnwick)* 10
West Somerset and Minehead Harriers
(Holnicote) 42
West Somerset Vale *(Cothelstone)* 147
West Street Tickham *(Aldington)* 66, 174
Wheatland *(Chaddesley Corbett)* 183
Wilton *(Badbury Rings)* 94
Woodland Pytchley *(Dingley)* 95
Worcestershire *(Chaddesley Corbett)* 140
York & Ainsty *(Easingwold)* 158
Ystrad Taf Fechan *(Ystradowen)* 141
Zetland *(Witton Castle)* 166

Point-to-Point Fixtures in 2005

(by arrangement with the British Horseracing Board)

[D] Dodson & Horrell PPORA Club Members Series qualifier
[G] Gerrard Ladies Open Championship qualifier
[H] Hiscox Intermediate Championship qualifier
[N] Novice Riders Championship qualifier
[P] Panacur/TBA PPORA Club Mares Maiden Series qualifier

No.	Qualifier	Fixture	Venue
		MONDAY 3rd JANUARY	
1	[N]	**Cambridgeshire Harriers Hunt Club**	*Cottenham*
		SUNDAY 9th JANUARY	
2		**Army**	*Larkhill*
3	[D] [N]	**North Norfolk Harriers**	*Higham*
4	[N]	**Tweseldown Racing Club**	*Tweseldown Racecourse*
		SATURDAY 15th JANUARY	
5	[D] [H]	**Point-to-Point Owners & Riders Club (Day 1)**	*Barbury Racecourse*
		SUNDAY 16th JANUARY	
6	[N]	**Dunston Harriers**	*Ampton*
	[P] [N]	**Point-to-Point Owners & Riders Club (Day 2)**	*Barbury Racecourse*
		SUNDAY 23rd JANUARY	
7		**Cambridge University Draghounds**	*Cottenham*
8		**Heythrop**	*Dunthrop*
9	[G] [N]	**Silverton**	*Black Forest Lodge*
10		**West Percy**	*Alnwick*
		SATURDAY 29th JANUARY	
11		**Royal Artillery**	*Larkhill*
		SUNDAY 30th JANUARY	
12		**Albrighton**	*Weston Park*
13	[D]	**Lincolnshire United Hunts Club**	*Market Rasen Racecourse*
14	[H]	**Waveney Harriers**	*Higham*
		SATURDAY 5th FEBRUARY	
15	[D]	**Cambridgeshire with Enfield Chace**	*Horseheath*
16	[D]	**Jedforest**	*Friars Haugh*
17		**North Cornwall**	*Wadebridge*
		SUNDAY 6th FEBRUARY	
18	[D] [N]	**Midlands Area Club**	*Thorpe Lodge*
19		**Old Raby Hunt Club**	*Witton Castle*
20	[P]	**Southdown & Eridge**	*Godstone*
21	[N]	**South Midlands Area Club**	*Tweseldown Racecourse*
22	[D]	**Tiverton**	*Chipley Park*
		SATURDAY 12th FEBRUARY	
23		**Harkaway Club**	*Chaddesley Corbett*
24		**Mid Devon**	*Black Forest Lodge*
25		**Oxford University Hunt Club**	*Kingston Blount*
26		**United Services**	*Larkhill*
27		**Vale of Clettwr**	*Erw Lon*
		SUNDAY 13th FEBRUARY	
28	[D]	**Easton Harriers**	*High Easter*
		SATURDAY 19th FEBRUARY	
29		**North Hereford**	*Whitwick Manor*
30		**Sinnington**	*Duncombe Park*

No.	Code	Fixture	Venue
31		**South East Hunts Club**	*Charing*
32	[P]	**South Pool Harriers**	*Buckfastleigh Racecourse*
		SUNDAY 20th FEBRUARY	
33		**Burton**	*Market Rasen Racecourse*
34	[D]	**College Valley & North Northumberland**	*Alnwick*
35	[N]	**East Essex**	*Marks Tey*
36		**Farmers Bloodhounds**	*Dunthrop*
37	[D]	**Meynell & South Staffordshire**	*Weston Park*
38	[N]	**South Dorset**	*Milborne St Andrew*
		SATURDAY 26th FEBRUARY	
39	[P]	**Brocklesby**	*Brocklesby Park*
40		**Chiddingfold, Leconfield & Cowdray**	*Parham*
41		**Hursley Hambledon**	*Badbury Rings*
42	[N]	**West Somerset and Minehead Harriers**	*Holnicote*
43	[G]	**Thurlow**	*Horseheath*
		SUNDAY 27th FEBRUARY	
44	[P]	**Bicester with Whaddon Chase**	*Mollington*
45		**Curre & Llangibby**	*Howick*
46		**Dumfriesshire**	*Netherby*
47		**East Cornwall**	*Great Trethew*
48		**Tanatside**	*Eyton-on-Severn*
49		**West of Yore**	*Hornby Castle*
		SATURDAY 5th MARCH	
50	[H]	**Duke of Beaufort's**	*Didmarton*
51		**East Devon**	*Bishops Court*
52	[D] [N]	**Southdown & Eridge**	*Godstone*
53		**Tivyside**	*Cilwendeg*
		SUNDAY 6th MARCH	
54		**Derwent**	*Charm Park*
55		**Granta Harriers**	*Higham*
56	[D]	**Grove & Rufford**	*Welbeck*
57	[G] [H] [N]	**Sir W.W. Wynn's**	*Eaton Hall*
58	[D]	**South Herefordshire**	*Garnons*
59	[N]	**Staff College & R.M.A. Sandhurst Draghounds**	*Larkhill*
60		**Tynedale**	*Corbridge*
		SATURDAY 12th MARCH	
61		**Brecon & Talybont**	*Llanfrynach*
62	[H] [P]	**Duke of Buccleuch's**	*Friars Haugh*
63		**Holcombe**	*Whittington*
64	[D]	**Oakley**	*Brafield-on-the-Green*
65		**Western**	*Wadebridg*
66		**West Street Tickham**	*Detling*
		SUNDAY 13th MARCH	
67	[H]	**Blackmore & Sparkford Vale**	*Charlton Horethorne*
68		**Cotswold**	*Andoversford*
69		**Cottesmore**	*Garthorpe*
70	[P]	**Holderness**	*Dalton Park*
71		**Suffolk**	*Ampton*
		SATURDAY 19th MARCH	
72		**Crawley & Horsham**	*Parham*
73		**Curre & Llangibby**	*Howick*
74		**Eglinton and Lanarkshire & Renfrewshire**	*Overton Farm*
75		**Fitzwilliam (Milton)**	*Cottenham*
76		**Hurworth**	*Hutton Rudby*
77		**Quantock Staghounds**	*Cothelstone*
78	[N]	**V.W.H.**	*Siddington*

SUNDAY 20th MARCH

79 **Dart Vale & Haldon Harriers** .... *Buckfastleigh Racecourse*
80 **Grafton** .... *Mollington*
81 **New Forest** .... *Larkhill*
82 [N] [P] **Ross Harriers** .... *Garnons*
83 [N] **South Wold** .... *Brocklesby Park*

EASTER SATURDAY 26th MARCH

84 **Ashford Valley** .... *Charing*
85 **Badsworth & Bramham Moor** .... *Mordon*
86 [N] **Glamorgan** .... *Ystradowen*
87 **Lamerton** .... *Kilworthy*
88 [N] **Mendip Farmers** .... *Ston Easton*
89 **North Staffordshire** .... *Sandon*
90 **Puckeridge** .... *Horseheath*
91 **United Pack** .... *Brampton Bryan*
92 [H] **Vale of Aylesbury with Garth & South Berks** .... *Kimble*
93 **Vale of Lune** .... *Whittington*
94 [N] **Wilton** .... *Badbury Rings*
95 [D] **Woodland Pytchley** .... *Dingley*

EASTER SUNDAY 27th MARCH

96 **Percy** .... *Alnwick*

EASTER MONDAY 28th MARCH

97 [N] **East Kent** .... *Aldington*
98 [H] [N] **Essex Farmers & Union** .... *Marks Tey*
99 **Four Burrow** .... *Trebudannon*
100 [D] **Morpeth** .... *Tranwell*
101 **North Cotswold** .... *Paxford*
102 [N] **Old Berkshire** .... *Lockinge*
103 [N] **South Devon** .... *Black Forest Lodge*
104 **South Notts** .... *Thorpe Lodge*
105 **South Pembrokeshire** .... *Lydstep*
106 **South Shropshire** .... *Eyton-on-Severn*
107 **Staintondale** .... *Charm Park*
108 **Taunton Vale Harriers** .... *Kingston St Mary*
109 [N] **Vine & Craven** .... *Hackwood Park*

EASTER TUESDAY 29th MARCH

110 [N] [P] **Croome & West Warwickshire** .... *Upton-upon-Severn*
111 [N] **High Peak** .... *Flagg Moor*

SATURDAY 2nd APRIL

112 [N] [P] **Avon Vale** .... *Larkhill*
113 [H] **Belvoir** .... *Garthorpe*
114 **Essex** .... *High Easter*
115 **Llandeilo Farmers** .... *Cilwendeg*

SUNDAY 3rd APRIL

116 **Cattistock** .... *Littlewindsor*
117 **Cumberland Farmers** .... *Dalston*
118 **East Cornwall** .... *Great Trethew*
119 [P] **Flint & Denbigh** .... *Eaton Hall*
120 **Ledbury** .... *Maisemore Park*
121 **Middleton** .... *Whitwell-on-the-Hill*
122 **Old Surrey, Burstow & West Kent** .... *Penshurst*

SATURDAY 9th APRIL

123 [G] **Essex & Suffolk** .... *Higham*
124 **Monmouthshire** .... *Llanvapley*
125 **Tedworth** .... *Barbury Racecourse*

		SUNDAY 10th APRIL	
126	[G]	**Bedale**	*Hornby Castle*
127	[N]	**Berwickshire**	*Friars Haugh*
128		**Cheshire Forest**	*Tabley*
129	[N]	**Cotswold Vale Farmers**	*Maisemore Park*
130		**East Sussex & Romney Marsh**	*Catsfield*
131		**Ludlow**	*Bitterley*
132	[D]	**Pytchley**	*Guilsborough*
133	[N]	**Spooners & West Dartmoor**	*Cherrybrook*
134		**Taunton Vale**	*Kingston St Mary*
		SATURDAY 16th APRIL	
135	[P]	**Aldenham Harriers**	*Cottenham*
136	[P]	**Braes of Derwent**	*Corbridge*
137		**Eggesford**	*Lifton*
138	[G]	**Mid Surrey Farmers Draghounds**	*Charing*
139	[H] [N]	**Portman**	*Badbury Rings*
140		**Worcestershire**	*Chaddesley Corbett*
141		**Ystrad Taf Fechan**	*Ystradowen*
		SUNDAY 17th APRIL	
142	[P]	**Atherstone**	*Clifton-on-Dunsmore*
143		**Bicester with Whaddon Chase**	*Mollington*
144		**Cheshire**	*Alpraham*
145		**Cleveland**	*Stainton Vale*
146	[H] [N]	**Hampshire**	*Hackwood Park*
147	[D] [N]	**West Somerset Vale**	*Cothelstone*
		SATURDAY 23rd APRIL	
148		**Berkeley**	*Woodford*
149	[G]	**Dartmoor**	*Flete Park*
150		**Fife**	*Balcormo Mains*
151	[H] [N]	**Old Surrey, Burstow & West Kent**	*Penshurst*
152	[P]	**Pentyrch**	*Bonvilston*
153		**Teme Valley**	*Brampton Bryan*
154	[N]	**Vale of Aylesbury with Garth & South Berks**	*Kingston Blount*
		SUNDAY 24th APRIL	
155	[G]	**Quorn**	*Garthorpe*
156	[D] [N]	**Seavington**	*Littlewindsor*
157	[H]	**West Norfolk**	*Fakenham*
158	[G]	**York & Ainsty**	*Easingwold*
		SATURDAY 30th APRIL	
159		**Four Burrow**	*Trebudannon*
160		**Llangeinor**	*Laleston*
161	[H]	**Pendle Forest & Craven**	*Heslaker*
162	[N]	**South & West Wilts**	*Larkhill*
		SUNDAY 1st MAY	
163	[N]	**Fernie**	*Dingley*
164		**Lauderdale**	*Mosshouses*
165		**Radnor & West Hereford**	*Cold Harbour*
166		**Zetland**	*Witton Castle*
		MONDAY 2nd MAY	
167		**Banwen Miners**	*Pentreclwydau*
168		**Cambridgeshire with Enfield Chace**	*Northaw*
169		**Cotley**	*Cotley*
170	[N]	**North Ledbury**	*Maisemore Park*
171		**North Shropshire**	*Eyton-on-Severn*
172		**Stevenstone**	*Vauterhill*
173	[N]	**Warwickshire**	*Ashorne*
174	[N]	**West Street Tickham**	*Aldington*

SATURDAY 7th MAY
175 [D] **Bilsdale** .... *Easingwold*
176 **Cumberland** .... *Aspatria*
177 [P] **Devon & Somerset Staghounds** .... *Holnicote*
178 **Essex Farmers & Union** .... *Marks Tey*
179 **Gelligaer Farmers** .... *Bonvilston*
180 **Modbury Harriers** .... *Flete Park*
181 [G] **Surrey Union** .... *Peper Harow*

SUNDAY 8th MAY
182 [N] **Axe Vale** .... *Stafford Cross*
183 **Wheatland** .... *Chaddesley Corbett*

SATURDAY 14th MAY
184 **Golden Valley** .... *Bredwardine*
185 **Melton Hunt Club** .... *Garthorpe*
186 **South Durham** .... *Mordon*
187 **Vale of Aylesbury with Garth & South Berks** .... *Kingston Blount*
188 [N] **Minehead Harriers and West Somerset** .... *Holnicote*

SUNDAY 15th MAY
189 [N] **Carmarthenshire** .... *Pentreclwydau*
190 **Haydon** .... *Hexham*
191 [N] **North West Point-to-Point Club** .... *Tabley*
192 [N] **Tetcott** .... *Lifton*

WEDNESDAY 18th MAY
193 [N] **Weston & Banwell Harriers** .... *Cothelstone*

SATURDAY 21st MAY
194 [N] **Clifton-on-Teme** .... *Upper Sapey*
195 [N] **Dulverton West** .... *Bratton Down*

SUNDAY 22nd MAY
196 **Border** .... *Hexham Racecourse*
197 **Harborough Race Club** .... *Dingley*
198 [N] **Tredegar Farmers** .... *Rhydygwern*

WEDNESDAY 25th MAY
199 **14 Regiment Royal Artillery** .... *Larkhill*

SATURDAY 28th MAY
200 **Blankney** .... *Garthorpe*
201 **Dulverton Farmers** .... *Mounsey Hill Gate*

SUNDAY 29th MAY
202 **Berks & Bucks Draghounds** .... *Kingston Blount*

MONDAY 30th MAY
203 **Albrighton Woodland** .... *Chaddesley Corbett*
204 **Countryside Alliance Club (Wales)** .... *Bonvilston*
205 **South Tetcott** .... *Lifton*

SATURDAY 4th JUNE
206 **Exmoor** .... *Bratton Down*
207 **Pembrokeshire** .... *Trecoed*

SUNDAY 12th JUNE
208 **Tiverton Staghounds** .... *Bratton Down*

SATURDAY 18th JUNE
209 **Torrington Farmers** .... *Umberleigh*

Jockey Club Enquiries in 2004

Race 28 Dunston Harriers Restricted Race 2003

The Disciplinary Panel of the Jockey Club held an enquiry on 16th September 2004 into the analysis of the urine ordered to be taken from EARLY MORNING CALL (IRE), owned by Mr C.D. Hazelwood, by the Stewards at the Dunston Harriers Point-to-Point held at Ampton after the gelding had finished first in the Restricted Race on 19th January 2003.

The urine of the horse was found to contain morphine, which is a prohibited substance. After considering the evidence, including statements from Mr Hazlewood and others, the Panel was satisfied that the source of the substance was a batch of Connolly's Red Mills 14% Racehorse Cubes which were being used in the yard at the material time.

The Panel accepted an admission from Mr Hazelwood that he was in breach of Regulation 45. It was however satisfied that the prohibited substance was not administered intentionally and that the trainer had taken all reasonable precautions to avoid a breach of Regulation 45 and accordingly waived the fine under that Rule. Under Regulation 150 (ii), the Panel disqualified EARLY MORNING CALL (IRE) from the race, placing GANGSTER first, SOUND GOSSIN (IRE) second, and MERD OF DRUMCOO (IRE) third.

Race 192 Easton Harriers Open Maiden 56&7yo Race 2003

The Disciplinary Panel of the Jockey Club held an enquiry on 16th September 2004 into the analysis of the urine ordered to be taken from ALL IN THE STARS (IRE), owned by Mr D.P. Keane, by the Stewards at the Easton Harriers Point-to-Point after the gelding had finished first in the Open Maiden Race on 16th February 2003.

The urine of the horse was found to contain morphine, which is a prohibited substance. After considering the evidence, including statements from Mr Keane and others, the Panel was satisfied that the source of the substance was a batch of Connolly's Red Mills 14% Racehorse Cubes which were being used in the yard at the material time.

The Panel accepted an admission from Mr Keane that he was in breach of Regulation 45. It was however satisfied that the prohibited substance was not administered intentionally and that the trainer had taken all reasonable precautions to avoid a breach of Regulation 45 and accordingly waived the fine under that Rule. Under Regulation 150 (ii), the Panel disqualified ALL IN THE STARS (IRE) from the race, placing RAVENSWORTH first, THE GLEN ROAD (IRE) second, and PARDON ME SON third.

Race 1105 Berkeley Hunt Members Race 2003

Miss L. Kerr

The Disciplinary Panel of the Jockey Club held an enquiry on 15th January 2004 to consider whether or not Miss L Kerr had committed a possible breach of Regulation 50(ii) of the Jockey Club Regulations for Point to Point Steeple Chases, in respect of her riding in The Thomas Silvey Berkeley Hunt Race at the Berkeley Hunt Point-to-Point on 26th April 2003 whilst not holding the required Riders Qualification Certificate.

Having considered the evidence, including a written statement from Miss Kerr, the Panel accepted an admission from her that she was in breach of Regulation 50(ii) and imposed a fine of £150 upon her.

Miss V. Champkin & Mr T.D.B. Underwood

The Disciplinary Panel of the Jockey Club held an enquiry on 6th May 2004 to consider whether or not Mr T.D.B. Underwood, the owner of SENDONTHECHEQUE (IRE) had committed a breach of Regulation 35(i)(c) of the Jockey Club Regulations for Point to Point Steeple Chases, in the light of paragraph 2A to Appendix B, headed 'Passport Instructions', concerning his failure to check the identity of SENDONTHECHEQUE (IRE) from the markings shown in the gelding's passport as soon as the passport was received. The failure to check SENDONTHECHEQUE (IRE)'s identity had resulted in the incorrect horse, later identified as OWENABUE VALLEY (IRE), running on 9 occasions during the 2003 Point-to-Point season and a subsequent 'Correction of Performance' having to be issued

Having considered the evidence, including a written statement from Mr Underwood, the Panel accepted an admission from him that he was in breach of Regulation 35(i)(c), in that he had only checked the gelding's vaccinations when he received the passport rather than the gelding's identity and vaccinations as required. The Panel imposed a fine of £150 upon him

Race 144 Mid Devon Confined Race

The Disciplinary Panel of the Jockey Club held an enquiry on 24th June 2004 to consider an objection to MIDNIGHT COUP, owned by Mr D. Williams, placed second in the Confined Hunts Race at the Mid-Devon Point-to-Point on 8th February 2004, on the grounds that the gelding having won a Hurdle race in Jersey on 21st April 2003 incorrectly carried 12st, rather than 12st7lb, as required by the conditions of the race.

The Panel also considered Mr Williams' possible breaches of Regulation 114 (iii) of the Jockey Club Regulations for Point-to-point Steeple Chases, in respect of his failure, as the owner of MIDNIGHT COUP, to ensure the gelding carried the correct weight, in accordance with the conditions of the race, at both the Mid-Devon Foxhounds Point-to-Point and in its previous race, the Hunt Race at the Silverton Foxhounds Point-to-Point on 25th January 2004.

Having considered the evidence, including written statements from Mr D. Pipe and Mr A. Farrant, the respective trainer and rider of the gelding, the Panel found Mr Williams to be in breach of Regulation 114 (iii) in that MIDNIGHT COUP had not carried the required 7lb penalty at either the Mid-Devon Foxhounds or the Silverton Foxhounds Point-to-Points. It therefore imposed a fine of £200 upon him.

Under Regulation 131 (iv) the Panel disqualified MIDNIGHT COUP from the Mid-Devon Foxhounds Point-to-Point, placing FRIAR WADDON second

Race 316 John Smith's Extra Smooth Novices HC, Sedgefield

The Disciplinary Panel of the Jockey Club held an enquiry on September 30th, 2004 into the analysis of the urine ordered to be taken from OMNI COSMO TOUCH (USA), owned by Mrs Sue Smith, by the Stewards at Sedgefield after the gelding had finished first in the John Smith's Extra Smooth Novices Hunters Steeple Chase on February 24th, 2004.

The urine of the horse was found to contain felbinac, which is a prohibited substance. After considering the evidence, including statements from Mrs Smith and others, the Panel was unable to establish the source of the substance, and could not therefore be satisfied that the administration of the substance was accidental and that the trainer had taken all reasonable care.

The Panel accepted an admission from Mrs Smith that she was in breach of Rule 53 and imposed a fine of £600 upon her. Under Rule 180 (ii), the Panel disqualified OMNI COSMO TOUCH (USA) from the race, placing TOR HEAD first, SCOTTISH ROOTS second, GLACIAL DANCER (IRE) third and MISS ROYELLO fourth.

Race 569 Lamerton Mixed Open Race

The Disciplinary Panel of the Jockey Club held an enquiry on 3rd June 2004 to consider an appeal by Miss C Prouse, the rider of MONTY'S LASS (IRE), against the decision of the Stewards at the Lamerton Foxhounds Point-to-Point on 20th March 2004, following the running of the Mixed Open Race, to find her in breach of Regulation 128 of the Jockey Club Regulations for Point to Point Steeple Chases, and fine her £125.

Having considered the evidence, including written submissions from Miss Prouse and the Stewards, and having viewed the video recording of the race, the Panel was not satisfied that Miss Prouse had made sufficient effort on MONTY'S LASS (IRE) to comply with the requirements of Regulation 128. It therefore dismissed the appeal, confirmed the fine of £125 and ordered Miss Prouse's deposit to be returned.

Race 928 North Shropshire Hunt Members Race

The Disciplinary Panel of the Jockey Club held an enquiry on 6th May 2004 to consider an objection to HOME TOR, owned by Miss H Brookshaw, placed third in the Hunt Members Race at the North Shropshire Hunt Point-to-Point on 12th April 2004, on the grounds that the Judge had left the Judge's Stand before the gelding passed the winning post and should not therefore, under Regulation 25(i) of the Jockey Club Regulations for Point to Point Steeple Chases, have been placed by the Stewards.

Having considered the evidence, including a written statement from Miss Brookshaw, the Panel found the Judge to have understandably left his stand, after the first two horses had finished and HOME TOR had run off the course. The Panel therefore disqualified HOME TOR from the race.

Index to Photographs

At least a part of these horses is visible in the Plates indicted

(Plates are numbered sequentially through the book: Plates 1-7 in the Review of 2004, 8-15 in the Results, 16-133 in the Horses Section, 134-149 make up the Colour Section and 150-160 in the Courses)

Horse	Plate No
Acuteangle	54
Alice Reigns	16
Alittlebitopower	17
All For Jake	18, 142
Alska	19
Ardross Gem	140
Askers Jack	55
Ask The Natives	20
Balinova	20
Balisteros	21
Ballet Red	13
Ballyalbert	146
Ballysicyos	22
Bally Wirral	2
Bay Of Dreams	23
Beehive Lad	130
Ben From Ketton	24
Blackwater Brave	89
Bohemian Spirit	90
Bosuns Mate	138
Boy Band	110
Boyup Brook	139
Breteche	68
Bright Flash	60
Buadhach	9
Burley Don Carlos	25
Caldamus	26, 138
Cantarinho	27
Cape Stormer	28
Captain's Log	11
Chapners Cross	115
Chasing Buttercups	110
Chasing The Bride	29
Cimmaroon	30
Clever Fella	31
Clifford Bay	79
Coal Queen	13
Colonel Conca	8
Colquhoun	32
Countess Kiri	33
Cutina	34
Darak	24
Dawn's Cognac	138
Decent Bond	84, 139
Delgany Royal	35
Dream Of My Life	12
Driminamore	139
Dumadic	36
Dun Rose	66
Dusk Duel	37
Earl's Toy	38
Earthmover	144
Eastern Point	39
Eighty Days	40
Elegant Light	77
Ellofamonkey	30, 41
Emali	42
Erzadjan	43
Euwiluwil	44
Falcon's Flame	45
Fane Counsel	81
Fanion De Nourry	128
Father Tom	11, 46
Ferryhill	9
Fertile Valley	47
Forest Fortress	53
Forest Jump	9
Foston Second	78
Free Gift	48
French Cedar	79
Galeshan	11
Garethson	138
Gaultier Gale	49
Geordies Express	50
Gigi Beach	93
Golden Chimes	51
Golden Jack	52
Golden Sovereign	130
Gotha	30
Granny Smith	53
Great Jubilee	54
Guignol Du Cochet	28
Gumlayloy	91
Harnage	55
Hawkers Hill	56
Headwrecker	2
Hedzamarley	11
High Fields	57
High Mood	8
Hi Rudolf	138
Hooray Henry	110
How Burn	150
I Am Said I	58
Impatient Lady	59
Inagh Road	60
In Demand	61
Indian Trix	157
Inner State	14
Jentar Equilibra	62
Johnnys Gone	139
Jolly Jake	63
Josanjamic	64
Joyful Jade	65
Just Barney Boy	66
Just Cliquot	67
Just Fluster	96
Karadin	68
Kerry Zulu Warrior	69
Kestle Mill	70
Khatana	6
Khayal	136
Kildysart Lady	71
Killiney Bay	72
Kingston-Banker	73

Horse	Plate No
Kingston Venture	74
Lady Baronette	75
Lady Misprint	76
Lady Widd	147
L'Idefix	11
Little Native	77
Lord Castle	15
Lord Of The Mist	48
Lord Of The West	34
Lord Oscar	78
Lynwood Legend	13
Maloney	91, 130
Martby	147
Meander	79
Menantol	56
Merry Minstrel	8
Midnight Coup	80
Millenium Run	13
Mind The Gate	9
Minella Silver	81
Minella Storm	15
Miss Flinders	82
Miss Mattie Ross	83
Miss Royello	84
Mister Bromley	85
Mister RF	86
Mounthenry Star	87
Mouseski	73
Mozielaw	88
Mr Baloo	123
Mr Ben Gunn	89
Mr Pendleberry	90
Musical Sleuth	91
Native Alibi	88
Nelsun	9
Never Compromise	144
Oneminutetofive	47, 92
On The Mend	141
Opal'lou	93
Out The Black	94
Panto	104
Pendle Hill	8
Perching	54
Pharailde	15
Phar From Chance	145
Pharmistice	143
Philson Run	95
Piper's Rock	79
Place Above	96
Poacher's Pride	13
Polar Champ	97
Polo Pony	138
Porlock Hill	48
Port Valenska	14
Prince Dundee	26
Pristeen Spy	98
Quickswood	2
Rainbow Ranch	72
Red Gauntlet	79
Rhythm King	2, 98, 99
Right To Reply	100, 124
Rightun	149
River Dante	71
Ronans Choice	101
Roscoe Burn	17, 102, 139
Royalecko	121
Sad Mad Bad	148
Sandy Duff	20, 103
S B S By Jove	32
Scottish Roots	57
See More Fun	104
Sharpaman	105
Sherbourne Guest	56
Shiny Bay	106
Shobrooke Mill	74
Silogue	107
Sir Dante	15
Sir D'Orton	108, 138
Six of Tother	14
Slaney Lass	109
Sliema	110, 147
Snooty Eskimo	111
Spanish Dolphin	112
Spinning Silver	113
Star Changes	114
State Medlar	115
Step And Run	98, 116
Stretching	117
Stride To Glory	114
Sweeping Storm	40
Sydney Hobart	9
Tales Of Bounty	108
Teme Willow Philtre	15
Texas Ranger	118
The Campdonian	81
The Cooling Agent	14
The Kings Fling	8
The Last Shout	153
The Midnite Grocer	132
The Nelson Touch	78
The Only Option	119
The Real Bat	11
The Red Boy	120
Three Spires	121
Tictac	122
Timberley	17
Time Can Tell	11
Timpani	99
Titus Bramble	145
Toon Society	123
Top Commander	13
Torduff Express	124
Tortugas	11
Touch Of Flame	125
Traditional	126
Trivial	79
Trooper Collins	121
Tursal	132
Unlimited Free	127
Upham Lord	135
Upton Adventure	128
Vicky Heal	89
Village Queen	129
Virgos Bambino	82
Vitinsel	130
Vivid Imagination	134
Wend's Day	131
Westie	132
Wheresbob	133
Wild Edgar	111
Winter Gale	37
Wiston Wizo	13